IDENTIFICATION GUIDE TO NORTH AMERICAN BIRDS

PART II

Identification Guide to North American Birds

Part II
Anatidae to Alcidae

by Peter Pyle

with the collaboration of
Steve N.G. Howell
Siobhan Ruck
David F. DeSante

A compendium of information on identifying, ageing, and sexing waterbirds, diurnal raptors, and gallinaceous birds in the hand.

Illustrations by Siobhan Ruck and Steve N.G. Howell

Slate Creek Press
Point Reyes Station, California
2008

ISBN: 9780961894047
Library of Congress Control Number: 97069065

Cover illustated by Siobhan Rusk, and designed by Peter Pyle and David DeSante.

Printed in the United States of America by Sheridan Books, Inc., Ann Arbor, Michigan.

Special thanks to Priscilla Yocom, and to Kathy Brown of Sheridan Books, Inc.

Designed and produced by Peter Pyle, Priscilla Yocom, Siobhan Ruck, Steve N.G. Howell, and David F. DeSante for Slate Creek Press, P.O. Box 1064, Point Reyes Station, California, 94956.

Cover: Replacement patterns among remiges following complete sequential molts in shorebirds (above) and falcons (below); denser stippling equals fresher feathers.

See www.SlateCreekPress.com for ordering information and updates

A product of:

The Institute for Bird Populations
P.O. Box 1346
Point Reyes Station, CA 94956

In recognition of

Rollo Beck

who collected roughly half the specimens used to gather information for this guide

and

Larry B. Spear

a recent counterpart to Rollo Beck

Table of Contents

Acknowledgements

It has been a long haul, but a rewarding one. I had planned to take at most 1-2 years off between completing Part I and embarking on Part II, but, sifting through my troves of back-up files, I find that I did not enter my first word of Part II until late December 2001, over four and a half years after writing the preface to Part I. The sheer magnitude of the task at hand promoted substantial procrastination on my part. But now, 433,000 words, 848 pages, 556 figures, 71 tables, 289 bar graphs, 93 museum-collection visits, and 6.5 years later, I am writing the preface to Part II. In so doing I am attempting to end this project at the right time, having caught as many typographical errors and other miscues as possible, while avoiding the endless fiddling that can obscure focus and result in information becoming out-dated before it reaches final print. Despite months of proofing I am resigned to the fact that there will be typographical (and probably some more serious) errors and inconsistencies among these 848 pages, but I must *hele* on. Thus, this effort is perhaps best viewed as a first draft, for us all to work on to improve. To help facilitate this we will be establishing a website, SlateCreekPress.com, where I hope we can construct an erratum, share information, and continue to develop our knowledge of the subjects covered within these pages. I thank, in advance, all those who participate.

I give foremost acknowledgment to the three collaborators, listed on the title page, for countless hours of time and devotion to the completion of this book. Steve N.G. Howell developed initial drafts for the sections on gulls, terns, skuas, and jaegers, prepared illustrations for 62 figures in those sections, and provided astute comments on almost all text; factual errors within the sections noted above are my responsibility and likely result from my alterations of Steve's original text. Without Steve's contributions to our understanding of molts and plumages in birds (see pp. 12-18 and Literature Cited), along with innumerable discussions we have had over the years, this series would be a mere skeleton of what it has become. I sincerely thank Siobhan Ruck for the 2-3 years of life I stole from her, as we stumbled along preparing the remaining 494 figures. Without her rasty sense of humor and perseverance through the long and less-rewarding sections, we may not have made it. I also thank Siobhan for insights on molts and plumages of diurnal raptors, gleaned through her work with the Golden Gate Raptor Observatory. Finally, I owe a tremendous amount to Dave DeSante, not only for publishing this series through Slate Creek Press, but for employment through The Institute for Bird Populations which included some wiggle-room to work on this guide as time and funding allowed. Dave's eye to detail and stamina for correctness provide an exemplary influence which I hope is reflected, at least for the most part, in this work.

My sincere and deep gratitude goes to Priscilla Yocom for tireless and efficient typesetting and layout, from cover to cover, and for extensive advice with software questions.

I examined 20-25,000 museum skins to gather important information included here. I am greatly indebted to the curators who allowed me to visit their collections and assisted me while there: Maureen Flannery, Douglas J. Long, Jack Dumbacher, and Kathleen Burke at the California Academy of Sciences, San Francisco, California; Carla Cicero at the Museum of Vertebrate Zoology, Berkeley, California; James Dean, Storrs Olson, Helen James, and Roger Clapp at the National Museum of Natural History, Washington, D.C.; Philip Unitt at the San Diego Natural History Museum, San Diego, California; Carla Kishinami at the Bernice Pauahi Bishop Museum, Honolulu, Hawaii; Kimball L. Garrett at the Los Angeles County Natural History Museum, Los Angeles, California; Linnea S. Hall at the Western Foundation of Vertebrate Zoology, Camarillo, California; and Hannah Nevins at the Moss Landing Marine Laboratory, Moss Landing, California. Steve Howell was further assisted by Paul Sweet at the American Museum of Natural History, New York; Mark Adams and Robert Prŷs-Jones at the

British Museum of Natural History, Tring, U.K.; and Rebecca Desjardins, John A. Gerwin, and H. Douglas Pratt at the North Carolina State Museum, Raleigh, North Carolina; Renée Cormier and Kristen Lindquist provided additional assistance to Steve Howell while measuring specimens. I would also like to acknowledge the Slater Museum of Natural History, Tacoma, Washington, for establishing their Wing Image Collection (www.ups.edu/x5662.xml), a very useful resource for information on molt and for the preparation of illustrations in this guide.

I have received tremendous feedback and support from both the USGS Bird Banding Laboratory (BBL) and the Canadian Wildlife Service (CWS). I especially thank Monica Tomosy, Leslie-Anne Howes, Danny Bystrak, and Mary Gustafson for assistance with unpublished information, positive feedback, and reviews of text, band-sizes, and alpha codes. Banders who contributed unpublished information to the BBL and CWS files, incorporated here, include Andy Ammann, Keith A. Arnold, Myrtle Bateman, Bruce D.J. Batt, Eric J. Bienvenu, Robert J. Blohm, H. Boyd, William Burnham, Samuel M. Carney, William S. Clark, Salvatore Cozzolino, Richard D. Crawford, Randall Dibblee, J. Dinsmore, Margaret Donnald, William R. Eddleman, Thomas C. Erdman, A.J. Erskine, Irma J. Fisk, Richard Fogarty, Anthony J. Gaston, Francis Hamerstrom, Arthur S. Hawkins, Geoff Hogan, Richard M. Hopper, M. Alan Jenkins, Joe Johnson, R.W. Johnson, Warren A. Lamb, William J. Mader, Robert E. Mangold, Fant Martin, Joanne Mason, Jerry D. McGowan, R.I.G. Morrison, Helmut C. Mueller, Burkett S. Neely, Gary L. Nuechterlein, J.W. Parker, Austin Reed, John P. Ryder, Ralph W. Schreiber, Jay M. Sheppard, William E. Shoemaker, Helen Snyder, Arie L. Spaans, Howard E. Spencer Jr., Joseph G. Stauch Jr., Stanley A. Temple, Charles H. Trost, Leslie M. Tuck, Charles Vaughn, and LeRoy Wilcox.

Numerous individuals have assisted me directly by sharing unpublished information, providing images to evaluate, hosting me in the field, and asking intelligent questions. These include Josh Adams, David Ainley, George Armistead, Jim W. Arterburn, Paul Ashley, Richard C. Banks, Jessie Barry, Richard Barth, Sandy Bartle, Gina Barton, Jim Barton, Ben Becker, Chris Benesh, Michel Bertrand, Louis Bevier, Mark Billings, Alex Bond, Matt Brady, Ned Brinkley, Charles R. Brower, Ralph Browning Jr., Joe Buchanan, Paul Buckley, Ken Burton, Adam M. Byrne, Harry Carter, Bob Chandler, Alan Chartier, Bill Clark, Luke Cole, Charles T. Collins, Alan Contreras, Chris Corben, Pierre-André Crochet, Gabriel David, Reggie David, Jeff Davis, Kate Davis, Bob Day, Dave DeSante, Bruce Deuel, Tony Diamond, Nate Dias, Donna Dittman, Peter Doherty, Peter Donaldson, Don Doolittle, Jon Dunn, Ann Edwards, Knut Eisermann, Martin T. Elliott (to Steve Howell), Chris Elphick, Andy Engilis, Richard A. Erickson, Sarah Faegre, Doug Faulkner, Clayton Ferrell, Catherine Flick, Marty Folk, Mike Force, Dan Froehlich, Peter Gaede, Aaron Gallagher, Kimball Garrett, River Gates, Dan Gibson, Bob Gill, Greg Gillson, Sean Graesser, Cheri Gratto-Trevor, Andrea Green, Darrell Gulin, Mary Gustafson, Buzz Hall, Robb Hamilton, Philip Hansbro, Keith Hansen, Al Harmata, Hiroshi Hasegawa, Floyd Hayes, Rick Heil, Matt Heindel, Laird Henkel, Anthony Hertzel, Nancy Hoffman, Alan Hopkins, Rachel Hopper, Steve Howell, Lisa Hug, Marshall Illif, David Irons, Al Jaramillo, Joseph Jehl Jr., Ian Jones, Kenn Kaufman, David Krementz, David Lank, Rosario Lara, Keith Larson, Paul Lehman, Nick Lethaby, Ron LeValley, Tony Leukering, Julio Lobato, Casey Lott, David Lukas, Bruce Mactavish, Jeff Marks, Eduardo Martinez, Amy McAndrews, Alan McBride, Guy McCaskie, Todd McGrath, Ian McLaren, Bert Tristan McKee, Andy Mears, Rigoberto Mendoza, Peter Milburn, Steve Mlodinov, David Monticelli, Alison Moody, Stan Moore, Joseph Morlan, Killian Mullarney, Kristie Nelson, Steve Nesbitt, Hannah Nevins, Richard Newell, Michael O'Brien, Glenn Olsen, Gary Page, Tony Palliser, Brainard Palmer-Ball, Michael Patten, Mike Patterson, Ian Paulsen, Dennis Paulson, Bruce Peterjohn, Jim Pike, Ron Pittaway, Alan Poole, Doug Pratt, Eric Preston, Caleb Putnam, Michael Reed, Martin Reid, Dan Reinking, Van Remsen, Robert Ridgely, Don Roberson, David Roemer, Danny Rogers, Sievert Rohwer, Siobhan Ruck, Douglas E. Runde, Will Russell, Matt Sadowsky, Brett Sandercock, Mike San Miguel, Paul Scofield, Tom Schulenberg, Spencer

Sealy, Hadoram Shirihai, David Sibley, Dan Singer, Dan Small, James P. Smith, Cyndi Smith, Marjorie Sorensen, Larry Spear, Paul Springer, Jean-Claude Stahl, Rich Stallcup, Bob Steele, Susan Steele, Karen Steenhof, John Sterling, Brian Sullivan, Hanna Suthers, Jack Sutton, Phil Swanson, Ryan Terrill, Scott Terrill, Julie Thayer, Chris Thompson, Jim Tietz, Norman van Swelm, Chuck Vaughn, Daniel Lopez Velasco, Philip Unitt, Terry Wahl, Paul Walbridge, Noel Warner, Nils Warnock, Sophie Webb, Kerrie Wilcox, Claudia P. Wilds, Angus Wilson, Rik Winters (to Steve Howell), Chad Witko, Jared Wolfe, Alan Wormington, and Brenda Zaun. Less directly, I have benefited greatly from discussion on the NBHC ID-Frontiers, Frontiers of Field Identification website (http://listserv.arizona.edu/archives/birdwg01.html) and acknowledge Will Russell for establishing the forum and all of those who have contributed.

Special thanks to the staff of the California Academy of Sciences Library, Anne Malley, Leslie Segedy, Susan Campinelli, and Larry Currie, for extensive assistance with references. Jim DeStaebler also provided much help obtaining papers during the early part of the project. I would also like to single out Debi Shearwater (Shearwater Journeys) for the many pelagic trips on which I learned a lot about seabird molt, Sam Droege for hosting us during trips to the National Museum of Natural History, Chris Swarth for the invaluable color guides by Ridgway (1886a) and Keeler (1893), passed down from his estimable grandfather Harry (see Literature Cited), and Rowena, Rio and Zephyr Forest for patience and assistance with this seemingly endless project.

My office mates at The Institute for Bird Populations helped me in various ways throughout the duration of this project, especially with respect to computer issues. My thanks to Mary Chambers, Dave DeSante, Amy Finfera, Kelly Gordon, Danielle Kaschube, Nicole Michel, Teryk Morris, Phil Nott, Jim Saracco, Victor Sepulveda, Rodney Siegel, Ron Taylor, Kerry Wilcox, and Bob Wilkerson. This is Contribution # 344 of The Institute for Bird Populations.

Although well over half the work on this guide was on my own time, it would not have been completed without moderate funding from various sources, administered by The Institute for Bird Populations and with the indispensable support of Dave DeSante. My thanks to Monica Tomosy and Mary Gustafson for providing a grant from the Bird Banding Laboratory to produce the Bar Graphs (pp. 44-45) and, by extension, some of the work to develop them. The Neotropical Migratory Bird Conservation Act, administered by the U.S. Fish and Wildlife Service, supplied funding (Grant #2601) to develop ageing techniques as related to Neotropical species. Critical matching funds for this grant were supplied by Charles Osgood and by sales of Dan Froehlich's (2003) *Ageing North American Landbirds by Molt Limits and Plumage Criteria*; I sincerely thank Dan for writing the guide, Barbara Ralston and the Bureau of Reclamation, Boulder City, Nevada, for printing it, and Slate Creek Press for publishing it. I also thank C.J. Ralph, Stephanie Jones, Alan Poole, Paul Radley, and The Institute for Bird Populations for other grants and funding that included my visits to museum collections to study molts and plumages. Finally, my parents, Robert and Leilani Pyle, have provided support for me in many ways throughout this project. My father passed away in July 2007 knowing that I had finished the text and was well on the way toward production. *Lele ka hoaka*.

Peter Pyle
13 July 2008
Honolulu

Introduction

In contrast to previous compilations in this series (Pyle et al. 1987, Pyle 1997), the information presented here on molt, ageing, and sexing of North American waterbirds, gallinaceous birds, and diurnal raptors, has relied much more heavily on field work and specimen examination than on published information. Not only has much less been published on molts and plumages by age in these taxa than in landbirds, but information currently found in the literature is often inadequate if not completely erroneous. Thus, there is much new information presented here for the first time. This has an advantage of providing fresh new material for consideration, but a disadvantage in that its accuracy will require further field-testing, preferably on known-age individuals. In addition, many species treated here had inadequate specimen material available to fully document predefinitive molts, plumages, and plumage aspects, and it is fully expected that users will encounter errors, as well as information in need of minor or major refinement. Nevertheless, by reflecting our current knowledge on molt patterns, subspecies, age, and sex in waterbirds, gallinaceous birds, and raptors, it provides a baseline for the further development of our understanding of these topics. As with the previous identification guides, a primary objective here is to call attention to unsolved problems.

An important goal of the present guide is to summarize our current understanding of molt strategies within a broader evolutionary context, as initially advanced by Humphrey & Parkes (1959, 1963) in their landmark papers. S.N.G. Howell et al. (2003, 2004) added important revisions to Humphrey-Parkes (H-P) nomenclature, stressing the importance of molt cycles, and redefining the first cycle as beginning with the complete prejuvenal molt that results in juvenal plumage. The terminology, cycle-based reasoning, and four molt strategies (see Fig. 10, pp. 13-16) proposed by Howell et al. (2003) are thus stressed in this guide. We have found that the use of this revised terminology has greatly enhanced understanding of molt in birds, and users are encouraged to fully learn the molt and plumage nomenclature presented here, to use it to classify both individual feathers and plumages (here defined as one or a composite of feather generations; see pp. 12-13), and to apply it to age determination in their study species (see pp. 12-30 for details). Applying a consistent approach to molt strategies and terminology in a wide diversity of bird families and species is an important contribution of this guide.

In addition to changes in molt, plumage, and plumage-aspect terminology, users of Part 1 will find several smaller differences in format and presentation herein. Many of these changes respond to feedback of Part-1 users, with the goal of simplifying, as much as possible, the substantial complexities inherent in the subject matter. Characteristics for separation of species, subspecies, ages, and sexes are now listed in order of diagnostic strength, rather than by topography, which will enable users to more easily stress certain features over others when considering multiple criteria (see p. 4). An attempt was made to standardize subspecies recognition, resulting in the presentation of alternative treatments (generally conservative; see pp. 37-38) for several species. Measurement ranges are given in tables combining several related species (*vs* within the text of each species) for greater ease of comparison between species, subspecies, sexes, and (occasionally) age groups, and tables and figures are cross-referenced to page numbers if not found on the immediate two-page spread. Other small changes include the addition of information on molt cycles and plumage designations (pp. 41-43) to the standard calendar-based age categories used in Part 1, the listing of literature citations in alphabetical rather than chronological order, and the splitting of these citations among several sections. For the most part, however, the format of Part 1 has been preserved (see pp. 38-46). As a result, those who have learned the system presented there should have no trouble using this guide, and hopefully will find it easier to use as a result of the abovementioned changes.

As with the first edition, the author strongly encourages users to publish contradicting, additional, or supporting information, or to contact him so that it may be incorporated into future editions. Numerous questions and areas in need of further study are pointed out, with hopes of inspiring investigation and publication of further information. Although this guide is designed primarily for live or dead birds in the hand, the advent of crisp digital imagery, easily shared via the internet, allows field-ornithologists and birders to study individual feather characters of wild birds, and to contribute substantially to a further understanding of molts and plumages. The website www.SlateCreekPress.com will facilitate corrections, updates, and feedback to this guide.

SCOPE

Totals of 310 species and 276 subspecies of waterbirds, gallinaceous birds, and diurnal raptors and are treated in this guide. This compares with 392 species and 856 subspecies of landbirds treated in Part 1. All or most species which regularly breed or have bred at least once, respectively, in North America (north of Mexico) are included, as well as visitors (primarily marine) that breed elsewhere but occur in North America annually in numbers. Three introduced species and no extinct species are included. The information presented in the accounts of migratory species is applicable on breeding (often "summer"), non-breeding (often "winter"), and molting grounds; information from tropical and/or pelagic non-breeding and molting grounds is often fragmentary and in need of further study. Species taxonomy and order follow the American Ornithologists' Union (AOU) check-list (AOU 1998), as modified by AOU supplements through Banks et al. (2007) and, for gulls, as anticipated in future supplements (see p. 629). The recent decision by the AOU to revise species order in annual supplements (rather than with each new Check-list) has resulted in difficulty for users to find species in guides such as this; it is anticipated that taxonomic order will soon change further, perhaps before final printing of this volume. See **Geographic variation** (pp. 37-38) for strategies used in treating subspecies.

BIRD TOPOGRAPHY

In order to understand molts and plumages and to focus on generations of individual feathers within a plumage, it is imperative that feather nomenclature and flight-feather numbering be consistent. The names of feather groups used in this guide follow the approach of Sibley (2000, 2001, 2002), which reflect terms widely and commonly used in the current ornithological literature (Figs. 1-2). Primaries (**pp** or **p**) are numbered **distally** or **outward** (innermost to outermost; p1 to p10 or p11), secondaries (**ss** or **s**) **proximally** or **inward** (outermost to innermost; s1 to s13 or more, including tertials), and rectrices (**rects**) distally on each side of the tail, as in Figure 1. "Functional primaries" refer to the visible feathers of the wing, excluding the outermost (usually 11th) vestigial feather, sometimes considered a primary but also considered a "remical" or modified covert (*cf.* Miller 1915, Stresemann 1963a). Tertials (**terts**) represent the modified innermost secondaries, often three in number but up to seven, attached to the skin surrounding the end of the ulna (*cf.* Berger & Lunk 1954), reflecting common recent usage; the term "tertiaries" (also know as "tertials" in the older literature) for feathers among the humerals (*cf.* Hickman in press), is not used here. Rectrices (**rects**) refer to the tail feathers.

Primary coverts (**p covs**) refer to the upperwing greater primary coverts, and lesser coverts (**les covs**), median coverts (**med covs**), and greater coverts (**gr covs**) to upperwing "secondary coverts" (**s covs**) collectively (Fig. 1). Marginal coverts are a subset of the lesser coverts and refer to smaller feathers along the leading edge of the wing. Primary and greater coverts are numbered to reflect the corresponding primary or secondary that they cover; e.g., greater covert 5 represents the covert corresponding to s5, the fifth secondary from the innermost primary (p1; *cf.* Fig. 1). Tertial coverts (**tert covs**) cover the bases of tertials and are important feathers for ageing and sexing some ducks. Unmodified reference to wing coverts in text indicates those found on the upperwing surface. Corresponding feathers on the underwing are prefaced; e.g., "underwing greater coverts".

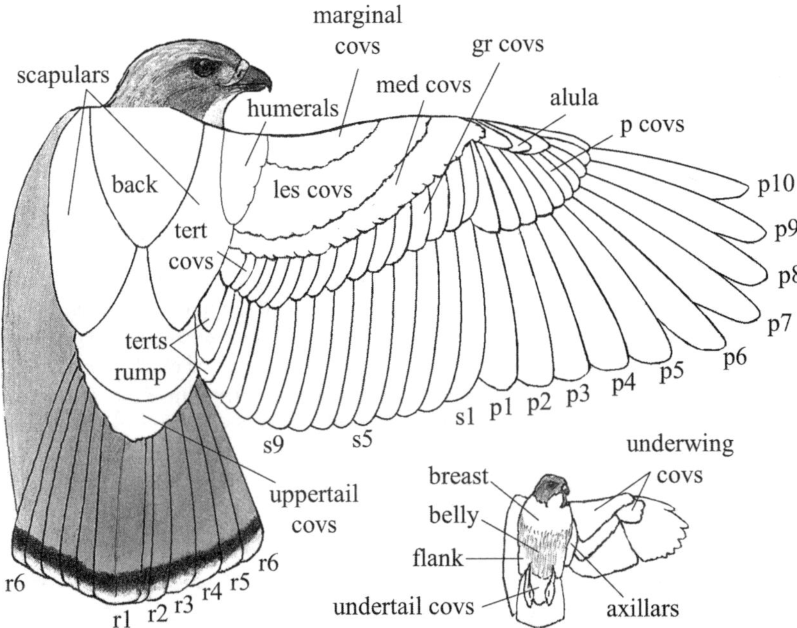

FIGURE 1. Abbreviations used in this guide to represent bird topography; see text for further information and for a few definitions of more specific feathers or regions. Primary coverts (p covs) here refer to the greater primary coverts; the lesser primary coverts (not shown) are referred to occasionally. "Secondary coverts" (s covs) refer to the lesser (including marginal), median, and greater coverts collectively. Unmodified reference to primary and secondary coverts pertains to the upper surface of the wing; the under surface has similar covert tracts, referred to with the modifier "underwing". Primaries (pp) are numbered distally and secondaries (ss) are numbered proximally, including the tertials. Primary coverts and greater coverts are numbered according to corresponding primaries and secondaries, respectively. Humerals are often more fully developed; e.g., in Procellariiformes (*cf.* Fig. 182, p. 240). See Figure 2 for topography of the head.

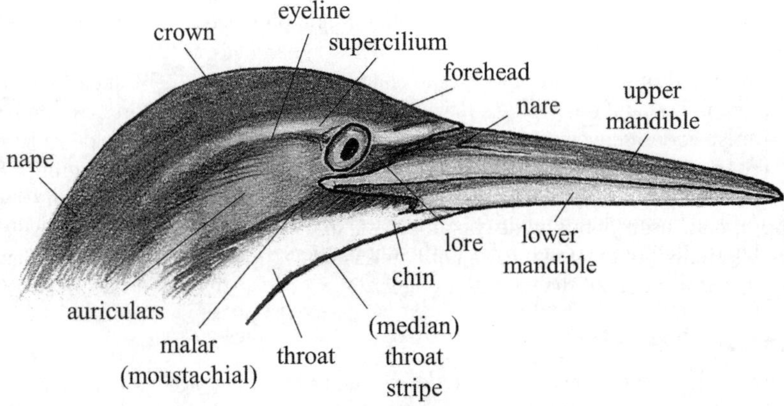

FIGURE 2. Topography of the head region; see text for further information and for a few definitions of more specific feathers or regions. Terms follow those used for feather groups by Sibley (2000, 2001, 2002). The malar region pertains to the feather group surrounding the posterior end of the gape and extending back to the neck; when it is darker, as in this Figure, it can be referred to as the moustachial stripe (as in falcons, p. 457). Stripes ventral to the malar region, often referred to as "malar stripes", are termed lateral throat stripes here.

Other feather groups and areas used occasionally in this guide, and not specifically pointed out in Figures 1-2, include lesser primary coverts (the row of feathers above the greater primary coverts), carpal covert (the small covert distal to the outermost greater covert), lower back (between the upper back and rump), and femoral group (feathers of the femur or "thigh"). "Upperparts" refer collectively to the crown, nape, scapulars, back, and rump. "Underparts" refer collectively to the chin, throat, breast, belly, flanks, and vent. See also Figure 342 (p. 455) for additional terms of the legs and feet.

IDENTIFICATION, AGEING, AND SEXING TECHNIQUES

The accurate identification, ageing, and sexing of North American birds is complicated by a high degree of variation in size, molt patterns, and plumage aspects found within each species, subspecies, and age/sex class. In this series, a format which summarizes the distinguishing features of each group, with **comparative phrases**, has been chosen over a dichotomous-key approach, because it better represents this variability and the complexity of the subject. Comparative phrases, listed in order of diagnostic strength, are matched by corresponding comparative phrases under each section describing species, subspecies, and age/sex groups (see pp. 39-43 for more details). This method emphasizes two important aspects leading to accurate identification, ageing, and sexing that should always be kept in mind by users of the accounts:

1) **Determinations should be based on a synthesis or combination of all available characters, any or all of which may or may not coincide with descriptors of one particular species, subspecies, or age/sex class.**

2) **Intermediate individuals and exceptions will occur which are not reliably placed in a particular species, subspecies, or age/sex class by in-hand criteria alone.**

An understanding and acceptance of these concepts is critical for the accurate identification, ageing, and sexing of birds in the hand or the field. Given normal distributions (consistent variation around means), degree of variation within populations and overlap between populations can be represented statistically by 95% confidence intervals (Pyle 1997). These intervals exclude aberrant individuals within populations ("outliers"), which will occasionally be encountered and potentially mis-classified. However, statisticians and certain ornithological groups (*e.g.*, the Canadian Wildlife Service [CWS] and Bird Banding Laboratory [BBL] when assessing the age and sex codes assigned by banders) are typically satisfied with 95% accuracy.

Throughout this series, ranges in measurements and plumage aspect are presented based on the concept of 95% confidence intervals. Thus, 5% of individuals will be expected to fall outside of given ranges in timing, measurements, and character descriptions, 2.5% at each end of a range. Measurement ranges and descriptions may overlap; thus, a variable proportion of individuals will fall into overlap zones between groups and will not be reliably aged, sexed, and/or identified with any one criterion or, potentially, with all of the criteria given for a particular group. By understanding these concepts, combining all criteria with in-hand experience, and being conservative when appropriate, users of this guide should be able to make determinations with well above 95% accuracy. References to the combination of criteria and to the potential for intermediates in specific cases occur throughout the species accounts.

MEASUREMENTS

Mensural data should always be considered when identifying, ageing, or sexing a bird in the hand. Although size overlap between populations often occurs, good mensural data can allow reliable determinations of population subsets. Mated pairs also may be reliably sexed by mensural characters that may not be as diagnostic at the population level (*cf.* Fletcher & Hamer 2003). Measurement ranges given in this guide have been derived based on 95% confidence intervals (see above); thus, means can be assumed to be midpoints of given ranges, and a quarter of each range represents approximately one standard deviation. This strategy has been utilized to facilitate ease of presentation.

Ranges of wing chord (**wg chord**), tail length (**tl**), exposed culmen (**exp culmen**) or some other bill-length metric, bill depth, and tarsus length (**tarsus**) in millimeters (**mm**) are given in tabular format as an indicator of taxonomic identification, sex, and occasionally age. Other physical measures given occasionally in text include bill width (*cf.* Fig. 100, p. 147), bill nail size (*cf.* Fig. 43, p. 73), head width (*cf.* Fig. 183, p. 242), and footpad, toe, and/or claw length, including that of the hallux (*cf.* Fig. 342, p. 455). In gulls, the distance from the back of the head to the tip of the bill (**head-bill length**; Fig. 453, p. 630) is useful for sexing, and this metric should be considered within other taxa (e.g., Green 1980a, Mallory & Forbes 2005, Rogers 1995, Thalmann et al. 2007), especially terns (*cf.* Craik 1999). For many species, published discriminant function analyses (**DFAs**; *cf.* Brennan et al. 1991, Green & Theobald 1988, Shealer & Cleary 2007) or other formulae, which model size criteria to distinguish subspecies or sexes of a given population, are referenced. Because of geographic variation in size within most species, however, the use of these analyses may be limited in potential geographic scope (Evans et al. 1993, Leafloor & Rusch 1997, McGowan & Zonfrillo 1995), and may be reliable only when using metrics obtained from study populations.

In several bird families or groups (e.g., boobies, frigatebirds, hawks, falcons, jaegers, and many shorebirds) females (♀♀) average larger than males (♂♂); in other groups (e.g., waterfowl, gamebirds, pelicans, cormorants, herons, gulls, and some shorebirds) males average larger than females; and in some groups (e.g., most Procellariiformes, tropicbirds, vultures, terns, plovers, and alcids) sexual dimorphism in size is generally slight or variable. The extent to which the sexes overlap in size depends both on the species and the measurement being considered. Wing chord is generally the quickest and easiest measurement to take, and often serves as a useful representative of the size of an individual within a taxonomic group. Measurements of bill length, bill depth, and tarsus can also be of value to indicate species and sex in waterbirds, whereas tail lengths tend to be less sex specific. Considering a suite of available measurements and combining these with other criteria often enables the most accurate determinations possible under field conditions.

Certain measurements in birds vary with age, but to a lesser extent than with sex. In many species (e.g., waterfowl, gulls), juvenal primaries tend to be slightly (5-10%) shorter than definitive basic primaries, whereas in others (e.g., diurnal raptors) juvenal primaries can be longer than basic primaries. In long-billed species, it may take up to six months or even a year or more for the bills of first-year individuals to become fully developed (see below). Measurements are seldom reliable for ageing, but the tendency for values of first-cycle individuals to average shorter or longer than those of adults can help to sex known-age individuals and age known-sex individuals. For example, individuals with juvenal primaries often exhibit wing-chord lengths in the bottom portions of ranges by sex, whereas those with basic primaries will average longer wing lengths, often falling in the upper portions of the ranges.

When using metrics for identifying, ageing, or sexing individuals, it is critical that measurement techniques be standardized. Published measurements have often been derived using different techniques (or in many cases techniques are not adequately described), resulting in substantially different values for the same reported metric. It should also be noted that inexperience of an observer in taking measurements can introduce bias (*cf.* Rasmussen et al. 2001). Measurement techniques used to derive values presented in this guide are detailed on pp. 6-12. Published values incorporated into tables were confirmed by checking specimens (generally with at least ten individuals of each sex per species or subspecies), and adjusted if measuring technique differed or appeared to. If available, samples of at least 20-30 values for each sex of each listed taxon were included from the literature (listed among **References**) and specimens; bill depth and occasionally tail length values sometimes were based on fewer samples, as indicated in footnotes to the tables. Samples of "100" indicate that at least 100 individuals were included. Ranges of measurements exclude subspecies occurring entirely outside of North America (north of Mexico), as indicated in footnotes.

Wing Length

In this guide, measurements of the wing refer predominantly to the wing chord (**wg chord**; Fig. 3**A**), as this is the length most frequently used by North American ornithologists and most widely published for North American birds. In a few accounts the **flat wing length** (Fig. 3**B**) is used because published studies have used this method. A third metric, the "maximum flat" (or "flattened and straightened") wing length, obtained when the wing is both flattened and the primaries are straightened, is used more often in Europe and is not referenced here. In larger birds these three methods can result in substantially different results (*cf.* Palmer 1976a:3-4, Svensson 1992, Baker 1993), but when performed properly and in a standardized way, all three methods produce consistent and reproducible results. Wing chord, however, is an easier method to use with larger birds (Baker 1993).

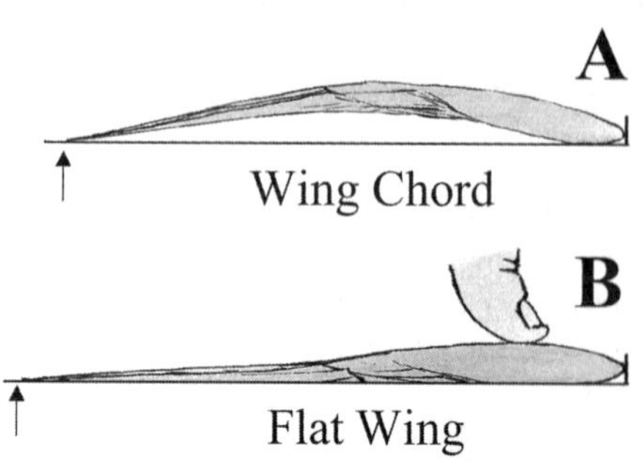

FIGURE 3. Examples of wing measurements used in this guide. Wing chord (**A**), representing the chord of the wing in its natural curved position, is the predominant wing measure referred to here. Flat wing length (**B**), obtained by eliminating the curvature of the wing by pressing it flat against a ruler, is used in only a few cases here but is the predominant wing measure used in Eurasia and Australasia. A third method, "maximum flattened wing length", where the wing is both flattened and straightened, is not used in this guide.

To measure wing chord it is best to have a ruler with a perpendicular stop at zero (Fig. 3). Alternatively, one's thumb or hand can, with care, serve as a stop. The ruler should be inserted under the wing, and the bend of the wing (carpal joint) should be pressed snugly against the stops, with no more pressure than the wing itself applies when the ruler is moved in a posterior direction (Yunick 1986). Once the wing is in place (carpal joint to wing tip parallel with the ruler), lower the wing tip and read the wing chord length while the wing maintains its natural curvature (Fig. 3**A**). To achieve a flat wing length, press the wing flat against the ruler (Fig. 3**B**). Specimen work on species treated in this guide indicates that flattened wing length varies from 6 to 15% longer than wing chord, depending on the species and the extent of curvature to the wing.

When measuring the wing make sure that the longest primary is not missing, broken, or growing. Older and more worn outer primaries, often in spring and summer for species treated here, result in slightly shorter measurements (by 1-5%) than freshly grown outer primaries in fall and winter (Rogers 1990). In addition, dampened wings will be slightly flatter, resulting in slightly longer chords, than dry wings (Evans 1964, Svensson 1992), and museum specimens will exhibit a slightly shorter wing length (up to 3%) due to shrinking during drying (Barth 1967, Engelmoer & Roselaar 1998, Green 1980b, Greenwood 1979). These effects should be taken into consideration when measuring damp or wet birds, or when comparing data from live individuals with those from specimens.

Wing Morphology

Wing morphology (or "formula") reflects the shape of the wing and is represented by measures between the tips of primaries and secondaries. Wing morphology varies with migration distance and can differ among otherwise similar species or subspecies (and even among age/sex groups within species).

In this guide, wing morphology is most often indicated by the distance from the tips of longer primaries (usually among p6-p10) to those of other primaries or the longest tertial (Fig. 4**A**), or sometimes to the longest primary covert. When determining the distance between primary tips, it is often easiest to measure each against the longest primary and take the difference between these lengths. A good method to obtain these measurements is to place a transparent ruler against the wing in its naturally closed position (see Fig. 10 in Pyle 1997). Ensure that the primaries are not broken, missing, or growing. If an incoming feather is still in its sheath it may not be fully

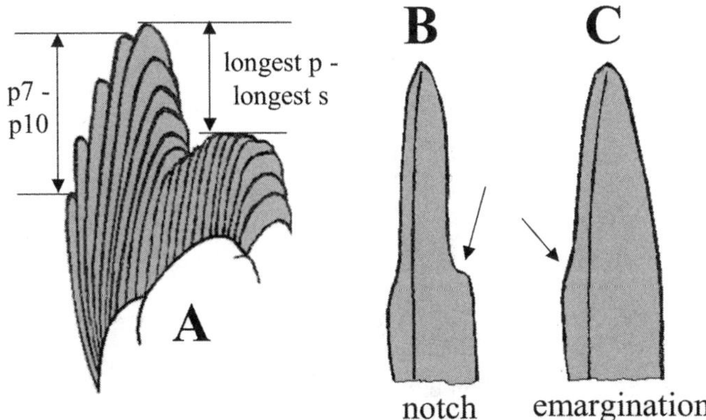

FIGURE 4. Wing morphology (**A**) and examples of primary notching (**B**) and emargination (**C**) for identification of birds. Note that, for clarification, the wing (**A**; depicting a Sharp-shinned Hawk, p. 415) is shown slightly open; more accurate measures are obtained on a closed wing (see Fig. 10 in Pyle 1997 for techniques). In this guide, positive values represent distances from longer to shorter feathers; e.g., p7 – p10 and longest p – longest s in **A**. Negative values are sometimes used, indicating that the first feather of the formula is shorter than the second. In this guide, notches and emargination are referred to primarily to distinguish diurnal raptors (pp. 391-473); their use in identifying species of other groups should be further investigated.

grown and should not be used in analyses of wing morphology. The measurement between the tips of two primaries, *e.g.*, the 8th and the 10th, is abbreviated as "p8 – p10", as separated from the format "p8-p10" indicating primaries 8, 9, and 10.

Wing morphology can also be indicated by the relative lengths of each primary in format, e.g., "p9 ≥ p5" (p9 is longer than or equal in length to p5) or in format e.g., "usually p8≈p9>p7>p10>p6>p5," indicating that p8 and p9 are roughly equal in length, and that the positions of the tips of the other primaries usually follow in the indicated order. Note that in some species the order can exhibit variation in where the tips of one or more similar-length primaries fall relative to the others. Specimen work by the author indicates that primary and primary-covert morphology tends to remain intact between live birds and specimens, but that relative distances between and among tertials and secondaries, and between these feathers and primaries, can be affected by specimen preparation. Caution should thus be used when using primary-to-secondary or secondary-to-secondary measures derived from specimens.

Related to wing morphology, and often useful in identifying species (and sometimes ages; *cf.* Fig. 95, p. 140), is whether or not a given primary is **notched** (Fig. 4**B**), **emarginated** (Fig. 4**C**), or both (see also Fig. 287, p. 392). Some primaries of a given species may exhibit "slight" or variably slight to no emargination or notching.

Tail Length

Unless otherwise noted, tail length (**tl**) is defined as the distance between the tip of the longest rectrix and the point of insertion of the two central rectrices (Fig. 5**A**, p. 8). In certain species that have elongated ornamental rectrices, the distance to the tip of r2 or r1 (Fig. 5**B-C**) is given here, to better reflect variation between groups. Tail length is often measured with dividers, especially on museum specimens, but dividers can be difficult to use with larger and/or live birds, and accurate and reproducible measurements can be achieved with a ruler (see Fig. 5). As with the wing, it is important to ensure that pertinent rectrices are not missing, broken, or in molt, and to realize that older and more-worn feathers will result in reduced values (by up to 15% or more on very worn tails). Note also that if the longest rectrix is not the innermost (and particularly if it is the outermost), an attempt should be made to reduce bias caused by the slight angle between the insertion of the central rectrix and the tip of the tail.

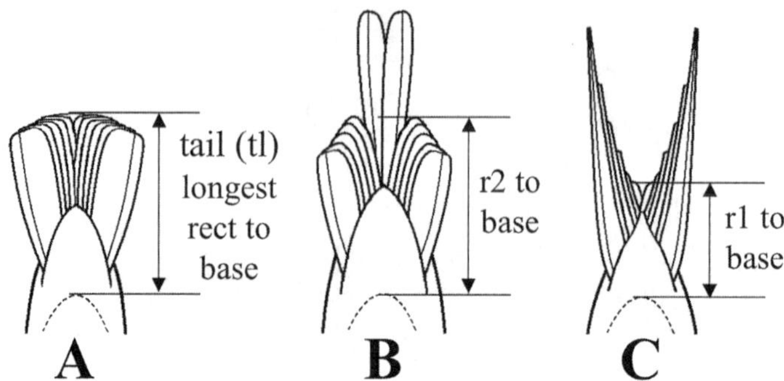

FIGURE 5. Measures of tail length (tl) in birds. Examples shown are Red-tailed Hawk (p. 444; **A**), Pomarine Jaeger (p. 735; **B**), and Arctic Tern (p. 716; **C**). Tail length (tl) is defined as the distance between the insertion of the two central rectrices and the tip of the longest rectrix along a perpendicular axis (**A**). In certain species that have elongated ornamental central (e.g., tropicbirds, jaegers), or outer (e.g., terns) rectrices, the distance to the tip of r2 (**B**) or r1 (**C**), respectively, better reflects variation between species or age groups, as the length of ornamental rectrices exhibit considerable individual and seasonal variation. To measure the tail it is important to use as thin a ruler as possible, with the end of the ruler coinciding with zero. The ruler can either be held perpendicular to the tail and inserted between the two central rects (*cf.* Fig. 6 in Pyle 1997), or held parallel to the tail and inserted between the rectrices and undertail coverts. Studies by the author and others have indicated that these two measures produce comparable values, with error introduced by different observers and/or through variation in ruler pressure swamping those found between the methods themselves. In each case, the zero end of the ruler should be pushed firmly against the end of the caudal muscle.

Tail Morphology

As with wing morphology, tail morphology (or "formula") reflects the shape of the tail and is represented by measures between tips of rectrices (Fig. 6). Tail morphology can also differ among otherwise similar species and be useful for separating these species in the hand.

The most common measure of tail morphology is the distance between the outer rectrix (often r6) and inner rectrix (r1) to indicate the degree of tail fork or notch (Fig. 6**A**). Such distances can be represented as r6 – r1; for wedge-shaped tails, in which r1 > r6, this distance can be negative or represented by r1 – r6 and with a positive value (Fig. 6**B**). Occasionally other rectrices are involved in tail morphology calculations, for example, r6 – r5 (by age) in Swallow-tailed Kite (**C**), values involving r3 and r4 in species exhibiting "double-rounded" tails, and r1 – r2 for ageing or identifying certain species with elongated central rectrices (*cf.* Fig. 4**B**). As with tail length, check that feathers are not missing or broken when obtaining tail morphology values, and measure along the axis of the tail rather than at the slight angle that occurs when these feathers are spread or in their natural position.

Bill Length

As with wing length, several measures of bill length have been employed, depending on the point at the base of the bill from which measurements are taken (Fig. 7). Exposed culmen (**exp culmen**) is most frequently used for bill length, and indicates the distance between the tip of the forehead feathering at the base of the bill along the ridge of the culmen, and the tip of the bill (Fig. 7**A**). For strongly decurved bills the exposed culmen represents a straight-line chord (Fig. 7**B-C**). In hawks and vultures, bill length is commonly taken from the tip of the cere to the tip of the bill (Fig. 7**B**) and in some species (see Fig. 8, p. 10) there is a band of bare skin across the forehead at the base of the bill, in which case the measure is taken from the interface between bill and skin (*cf.* Fig. 8**B**). In some juvenile waterfowl (*cf.* Table 4; Fig. 44**F**, pp. 75-76), shorebirds, and other species this band can be downy, and is generally included in the exposed culmen measurement (Engelmoer & Roselaar 1998), although beware that the down can slough off in older

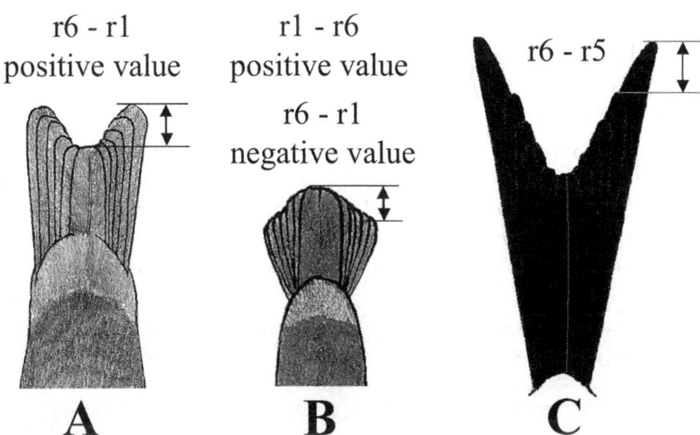

FIGURE 6. Examples of tail morphology measures in Leach's Storm-Petrel (p. 280; **A**), Least Storm-Petrel (p. 288; **B**), and Swallow-tailed Kite (p. 398; **C**). Distances between rects are usually represented as the longest to the shortest in format, e.g. r6 – r1 (**A**), r1 – r6 (**B**), or r6 – r5 (**C**). Negative values (for difference from shorter to longer tip) can also be used when comparing species or individuals in which the first tip position can be either shorter or longer than the second position. A clear plastic ruler placed flush with the closed tail is the best way of achieving this measurement.

individuals or specimens, affecting the point at which the forehead feathers terminate (*cf.* Abbott et al. 2001). Exposed culmen measures also tend to shrink very slightly in specimens as compared to the live birds before collection (Engelmoer & Roselaar 1998, Summers 1976).

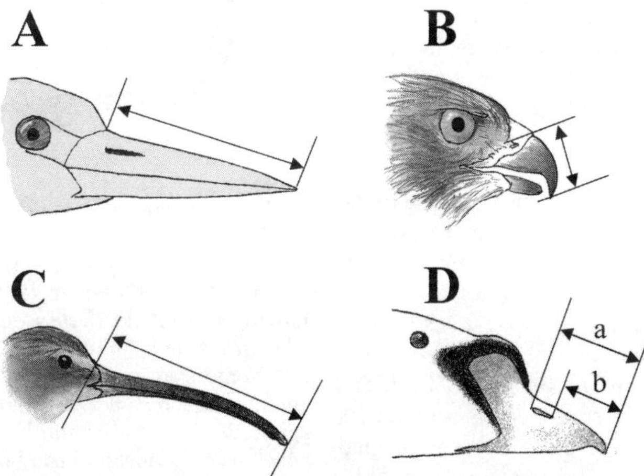

FIGURE 7. Examples of bill lengths in Black-crowned Night-Heron (p. 363; **A**), Broad-winged Hawk (p. 430; **B**), Long-billed Curlew (p. 564; **C**), and King Eider (p. 123: **D**) showing different types of measures. In most species treated in this guide, exposed culmen values are given and represent a straight-line distance between the distal end of the forehead feathers and the tip of the bill (**A**). It is actually a chord, as emphasized more when culmens are strongly decurved (**B-C**) or recurved (*cf.* Fig. 403, p. 540). In vultures and hawks, the proximal point is commonly from the tip of the cere rather than the tip of the forehead feathers (**B**), and in other species with featherless areas across the forehead, the measure is best taken from the proximal end of the bill where it meets the skin (*cf.* Fig. 8**B**, p. 10. Distance from the proximal (**D**a) or distal (**D**b) ends of the nares are also referred to, especially in species where the extent of forehead feathers may vary with ornamentation or for other reasons (e.g., see Fig. 44**F-G**, p. 76). Calipers or dividers may be preferred to measure bill length; however, with care, an accurate measurement can also be achieved with a ruler.

In several species treated in this guide, the exposed culmen can be difficult to obtain in a standardized manner due to variable extension of forehead feathers (*cf.* Figs. 80, p. 123, & 132, p. 182) or the presence of ornamental swelling or appendages (*cf.* Figs. 83, p. 125, & 94, p. 139), and it may be preferable to take the measure from the **distal or proximal end of the nares** (Fig. 7**D**). Another measure, the "total culmen" or length between the bill tip and the notch at the base of the upper mandible where it enters the base of the skull (see Svensson 1992, Baker 1993), is often used in skeletal studies but is difficult to obtain from live birds or specimens in a standardized manner, and has not been referred to in this guide.

The exposed culmen and other bill-length measurements are taken along the central ridge (culmen) of the bill, not from the tips of the nostril feathers or those on the sides of the upper mandible; beware some measures of "culmen" in the waterfowl literature are from the lateral extensions of malar feathers (*cf.* Fig. 80. p. 123) and can be shorter or longer. Ensure that the bill tip is not broken or deformed when taking bill-length measures. Age-related variation can occur in species with longer culmens (e.g. ibis, storks, and certain shorebirds), first-year individuals taking up to six months or more to achieve lengths similar to those of adults (*cf.* Figs. 273, p. 378, & 422, p. 565).

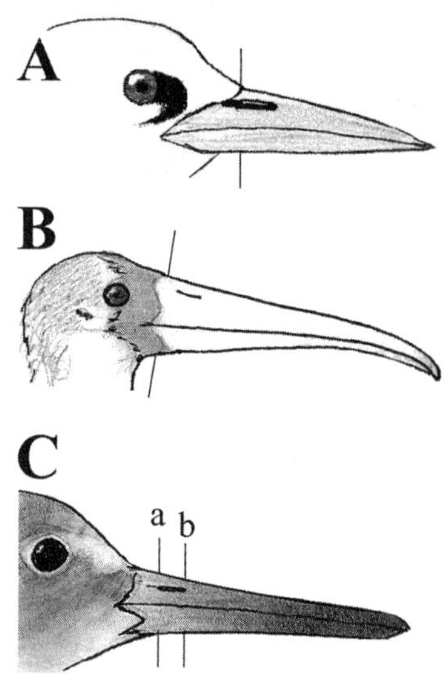

FIGURE 8. Points of bill-depth measures in White-tailed Tropicbird (p. 291; **A**), juvenile Wood Stork (p. 377; **B**), and Willet (p. 554; **C**), showing different locations for this measure. In most species bill depth measures refer to those taken from the tip of the forehead head feathers (**A**). Some species (e.g. many Pelecaniformes, egrets, ibis, and storks) have a band of bare skin across the forehead at the base of the bill, in which case the measure can be taken from the interface between bill and skin (**B**); exposed culmen is also typically taken from this point on these species (*cf.* Fig. 7, p. 9). Other bill-depth measures sometimes taken include those from the proximal or distal ends of the nares (**C**). Bill width measures (*cf.* Fig. 100, p. 147) can be taken from these same locations. Calipers should be used to obtain bill-depth and bill-width measures, although a rough approximation can sometimes be achieved with a ruler. When measuring bill depth and width, be certain that calipers are oriented at a 90° angle to the axis of the bill.

Bill Depth and Other Metrics

Bill depth in this guide refers primarily to measurements taken at the distal end of the forehead feathers (Fig. 8**A**), where the proximal point of the exposed culmen measure is taken (Fig. 7**A**, p. 9). Other locations for bill depth measures include the interface between skin and bill for certain species (Fig. 8**B**) and the proximal or distal ends of the nares (Fig. 8**C**; *cf.* Fig. 7**D**). Certain groups of species have other locations for bill measures; e.g., the point just distal to the tubenares in Procellariiformes (Figs. 195, p. 256, & 198, p. 261) or at the gonydeal angle in gulls and terns (Fig. 453, p. 630).

Bill depth measures on specimens is often affected by preparation that has left the bill partially open at the base (*cf.* Fjeldså 1980). It can also be difficult to measure specimens of species with gular pouches, as these can harden and extend beyond the base of the lower mandible, inflating this measure (in these cases it is often possible to obtain a bill depth measure from the side of the bill). As with exposed culmen, certain species with ornamental appendages at the base of the bill will require special considerations when measuring the depth of the bill (*cf.* Figs. 42, p. 71; 83, p. 125; 94, p. 139; & 553, p. 782. Other bill metrics that can be useful for separation of species or sex include bill width (*cf.* Fig. 100, p. 147) and nail width, length, and depth (*cf.* Figs. 43, p. 73, & 198, p. 261).

Tarsus

Tarsus length is given for all species and can be an important variable for identification and sex determination. Two different tarsal measurements have been described, which result in substantially different values. Indication of method frequently does not accompany published tarsal metrics, so caution is advised when comparing values from the field with those of the literature.

All tarsus values presented here refer to the more traditional distance (*cf.* Pyle 1997) from the notch at the end of the lateral condyle of the tibiotarsus, on the back side of the leg, to the last tarsal scute on the front of the leg, at the base of the foot (Fig. 9**A**). This is also known as the "outside tarsus" or "diagonal tarsus" measure. Note that, because it is taken from the bottom rear to the top front of the tarsus, the measure is not parallel to the axis of the tarsus but at a slight angle (Fig. 9**A**-**B**). Waterfowl lack scales so tarsus can be measured to the tarso-metatarsal joint when the foot is held at a perpendicular angle (Fig. 9**B**). A longer tarsal measurement, most frequently performed on waterfowl (*cf.* Byers & Cary 1991), is from the end of the medial condyle of the tibiotarsus on the front of the leg to the tarso-metatarsal joint (Fig. 9**B**) or last tarsal scute. This distance is also known as the "inside tarsus", "straight tarsus", or "total tarsus" measure, and is taken parallel to the axis of the leg (Fig. 9**B**). Tarsal width and depth measures are also referred to occasionally here; width is from side to side and depth is from front to back. Other measures involving the feet include footpad length and length of toes and/or claws, including the hallux (*cf.* Fig. 342, p. 455).

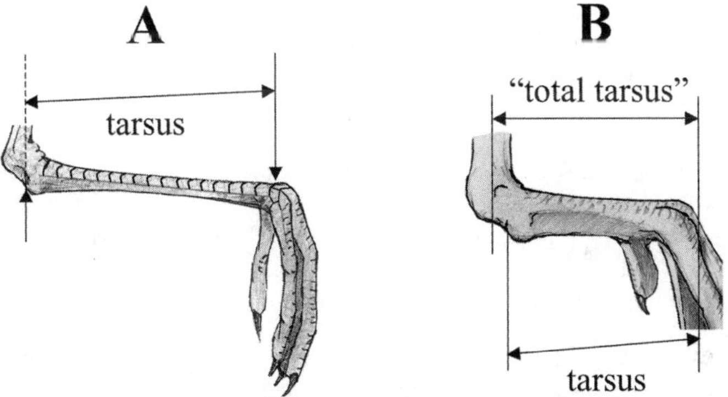

FIGURE 9. Measures of the tarsus in birds. The most widely taken measure refers to the distance between the notch at the end of the lateral condyle of the tibiotarsus, on the back side of the leg, to the last undivided tarsal scute on the front of the leg, taken at a slight angle to that of the tarsus (**A**-**B**). Waterfowl lack tarsal scutes so the measure is taken to the tarso-metatarsal joint when the foot is held at a perpendicular angle to the tarsus (**B**). Another measure, "total tarsus", sometimes taken in waterfowl, is from the medial condyle of the tibiotarsus to the tarso-metatarsal joint, taken parallel to the tarsus (**B**). Total tarsus is not referred to further in this guide. Tarsal length can be taken either with calipers, dividers, or simply with a ruler placed along the side of the leg (comparable results can be achieved with each of these methods), whereas tarsal depth (front to back) and width (side to side) should be taken with calipers.

Weight

Bird weight (representing mass at the earth's surface) can vary substantially with geography, condition of the individual, stomach contents, and season or period within the life cycle of each particular species; thus, this measurement is not as useful for categorizing birds as are linear measurements. In a few instances, however, weight values in grams (g) are provided as a useful metric for sexing or subspecific identification, or are referred to as part of discriminant function or other multiple-variable analyses (p. 5). Important considerations when weighing birds are the amount fat present (see Rogers 1991), and whether or not females have an egg in the oviduct, both of which can increase a bird's baseline weight. "Lean weight" refers to the weight of the bird adjusted downward in consideration of the amount of subcutaneous fat present (cf. Gibson & Kessel 1989). Dunning (1993) provides sample weights for most North American birds and should be referred to when considering bird weights.

MOLT

An understanding of timing, sequence, and extent of molts is essential for ageing and sexing birds in the hand. It is also critical for studies of stable isotopes within feathers, attempting to resolve questions of connectivity and diet (*cf.* Hobson 1999, 2002). Note that stable isotopes can provide information on locations of molts (Pérez & Hobson 2006) which, in many species, are poorly known (see also p. 40). Good summaries of bird molt include those of Dwight (1902, 1907), Ginn & Melville (1983), Jenni & Winkler (1994), Palmer (1972), Payne (1972), Voitkevich (1966), and Watson (1963a). Readers should consult these treatments for an overall understanding of the physiological mechanisms and processes of bird molt. Here molt is summarized and discussed as it pertains to ageing and sexing waterbirds, diurnal raptors, and gallinaceous birds in the hand.

Molt and Plumage Terminology

Molt and plumage terminology in birds has been a complex and, at times, controversial topic (Howell & Corben 2000a; S.N.G. Howell et al. 2003, 2004; Humphrey & Parkes 1959, 1963; Jenni & Winkler 1994, 2004; Parkes 1995; Piersma 2004; Pittaway 2000; Pyle 1997; Rohwer et al. 1992; Stresemann 1963b; Thompson 2004; Thompson & Leu 1994; Wilds 1989; Willoughby 1992, 2004, 2007). Much confusion over molt terminology has stemmed from the complicated and variable nature of molts (Figs. 10-11, pp. 13-16). In this guide the terminology of Humphrey & Parkes (1959, 1963) as modified by Howell et al. (2003, 2004) is followed. This nomenclature standardizes terminology based on homologous molts and plumages among species, rather than relative to breeding seasons or time of year, thus promoting an understanding of the evolutions of molts in a context independent from other annual events. The primary basis for the naming of molts under the Humphrey-Parkes (H-P) system is the evolutionary pathways of these molts from ancestral to present-day taxa. Here it is emphasized that molts appear to have evolved initially in response to constraints on feather wear and bleaching, followed by adaptation of plumage-aspect coloration. Thus, coloration of ensuing plumage aspect, which can also vary between and within individuals relative to molt timing (see below), relates little to the initial evolution of molts (*cf.* Howell et al. 2004, Pyle 2005a).

For most birds, our ability to determine molt homologies is still in its infancy (Jenni & Winkler 1994, 2004). It is hoped that the adoption of the H-P system of molt and plumage terminology in this guide and elsewhere will motivate researchers to consider the evolutionary histories of molts, to predict molt homologies (*cf.* Jukema & Piersma 2000, Pyle 2007), and to further refine H-P terminology, both generally and on a species-specific basis. See Howell (2000, 2003a, 2003b) for user-friendly summaries on the use of H-P terminology in birds.

Molt Cycles and Plumages

Critical aspects of the H-P system, emphasized and reorganized by Howell et al. (2003), are the concepts of molt cycles and inserted molts. All birds have regular molts termed **prebasic molts**, which define **basic molt cycles** (hereafter simply "molt cycles"), the period from the beginning of one prebasic molt to the beginning of the following prebasic molt (Fig. 10, p. 14). Prebasic molts are typically **complete** (all feathers) or **incomplete** (most to all body feathers but not all flight feathers) and produce **basic plumages**. A **plumage** is here defined as the single or composite generation of feathering following a particular molt, as opposed to a **plumage aspect**, which describes the outward appearance of the plumage in question (Humphey & Parkes 1959). Thus, it is technically the plumage aspect rather than the plumage that can be bright or dull, fresh or worn, etc. This definition of plumage combines the terms "plumage" and "feather coat" of Humphrey & Parkes (1959), the former not practically applicable and the latter never gaining wide use. Here, a molt (e.g., prealternate) produces a plumage (alternate) consisting of all feathers, no matter how many feathers were replaced during the molt. The traditional H-P definition of "plumage" (referring to a single feather generation) is here replaced with the term "feathers" or "feathering".

The first coat of pennaceous feathers is considered the **juvenal (juv) plumage**, acquired by a prejuvenal molt. It is now (Howell et al. 2003) considered synonymous with the **first basic plumage** (**B1**) and is acquired by the **first prebasic molt** (**PB1**). **Note that in this guide "first basic" plumage or feathers are hereafter referred to as "juvenal" (juv), plumage or feathers, such that the term "basic" strictly indicates subsequent (non-juvenal) basic plumages or feathers.** Ensuing molt cycles begin with the second prebasic molt (**PB2**) producing second basic plumage (**B2**), the third prebasic molt (**PB3**) producing third basic plumage (**B3**), the fourth prebasic molt (**PB4**) producing fourth basic plumage (**B4**), and so on. Birds with delayed plumage-aspect maturation, such as certain albatrosses, condors, and large gulls, can be identified by plumage aspect in their third, fourth, or later basic plumages, whereas many other species attain a mature or definitive plumage aspect in their first or second basic plumages. **Definitive basic plumage** (**DB**), has been defined as that for which plumage aspect does not markedly change further with age (Humphrey & Parkes 1959), although subtle age-specific changes may still take place. Here it is considered the "definitive basic aspect" (see below).

A molt cycle is here defined as beginning and ending when the initial primary is dropped during prebasic molts. In birds, this is often the innermost primary (p1) but can be other primaries in larger species that exhibit various sequences of primary replacement (Fig. 12, p. 19). Although replacement of body or other feathers during a prebasic molt may precede replacement of primaries in some cases, the first loss of a primary is a more precise and identifiable event with which to signify the completion and start of a molt cycle. The **first molt cycle** begins with initiation of the first prebasic molt, when juvenal plumage is developed in nestlings or chicks, and completes with the dropping of the first primary during the second prebasic molt, which occurs at six months to a year of age in most species; the **second molt cycle** initiates at this point and continues until the beginning of the third prebasic molt; and so on. **Definitive molt cycles** have generally been defined as those occurring between definitive prebasic molts, which produce definitive basic aspect (see above). In this guide, however, definitive molt cycles and definitive prebasic molts are defined based on molt regimes initially reaching stasis in terms of timing and extent, irrespective of the plumage aspect (Howell et al. 2003). In some albatrosses and California Condor (p. 388), the definitive molt cycle becomes established well before definitive plumage aspect is acquired, whereas in other species (e.g., among shearwaters and storm-petrels), juvenal plumage aspect equates to definitive plumage aspect, even though 2nd prebasic molts can be defined based on differences in timing or other factors. In the majority of cases, however, the definitive molt cycle coincides with attainment of definitive plumage aspect.

In North American and other temperate species, molt and plumage cycles typically coincide with annual cycles that also include breeding and migration, and thus extend for approximately one year, but in certain species a molt cycle may be shorter or longer in duration (Humphrey & Parks 1959). Some species or individuals with two-year breeding cycles (e.g. among albatross, *cf.* Edwards 2008; and frigatebirds, *cf.* Valle et al. 2006) may have two-year molt cycles, but further study is needed to determine if this is the case.

Inserted Molts and Plumages

All North American bird species undergo complete or near-complete prebasic molts and have well-defined molt cycles (Figs. 10-11). Inserted molts are additional molts, typically less than complete, that have been added to a molt cycle through evolution, and produce inserted plumages. An inserted molt is defined as a regular, hormonally induced replacement of at least some feathers in at least some individuals of a species. The ensuing plumage is defined by the molt, even though only a proportion of feathers have usually been replaced. Up to three inserted molts can occur within the first cycle and up to two within definitive cycles; the number of inserted molts and plumages per cycle

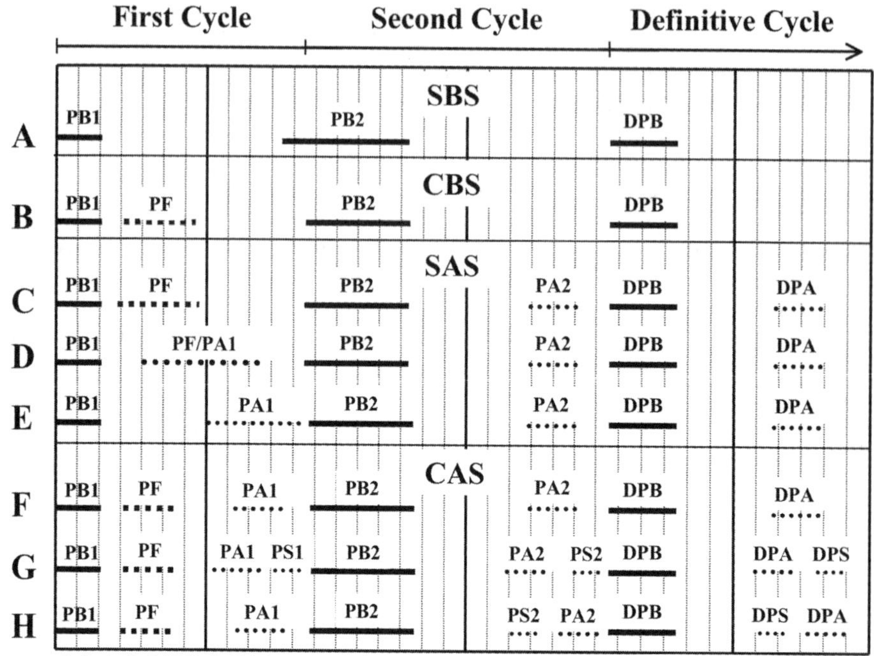

FIGURE 10. Examples of timing and extent of molts in North American birds exhibiting the four molt strategies defined by Howell et al. (2003): Simple Basic Strategy (**SBS**; **A**; see also Fig. 11**C**), Complex Basic Strategy (**CBS**; **B**), Simple Alternate Strategy (**SAS**; **C-E**; see also Fig. 11**F**), and Complex Alternate Strategy (**CAS**; **F-H**; see also Fig. 11**A-B**, **D-E**, & **G**). Molts are abbreviated as follows: **PB1**, **PB2**, and **DPB** = first (prejuvenal; see p. 13), second, and definitive prebasic molts; **PF** = preformative (post-juvenal; see below); **PA1**, **PA2**, and **DPA** = first, second, and definitive prealternate molts; and **PS1**, **PS2**, and **DPS** = first, second, and definitive presupplemental molts. "**PF/PA1**" indicates a molt that may have been derived from a merging of the PF and PA1 in SAS species (see p. 16). Extent of molts are indicated by bar style and width. Note that the DPS and DPA can occur in either order within the definitive cycle (**G-H**), and perhaps even between sexes among ptarmigan (p. 182; Pyle 2007). See Figure 11 (p. 17) for examples of species exhibiting further variation in molt strategies.

can be no more than the number of times the most-frequently molted feather has been replaced between prebasic molts (Humphrey & Parkes 1959). Inserted molts sometimes can be suspended and/or protracted (Fig. 11, p. 17), but unless follicles have been activated twice, only one inserted molt has occurred. Due to nutritional stressors or other factors, some individuals may skip an inserted molt that is present at the species level, and these individuals do not acquire that inserted plumage.

There are three types of inserted molts. **Preformative molts** (**PFs**) occur in most species of birds, are only found in the first cycle (Figs. 10-11), and produce **formative plumages** (**F1**). The preformative molt (along with a few other molts) was referred to as the "first prebasic molt" by Humphrey and Parkes (1959; *cf.* Pyle 1997), but S.N.G. Howell et al. (2003) demonstrated that it should be considered a unique inserted molt within the first cycle, and that the first cycle should begin with the "first prebasic" or prejuvenal molt (see above). Wild Turkey (p. 198), possibly some ducks (*cf.* Fig. 11**A**), and some passerines may replace some feathers twice during the preformative molting period. Here this second replacement is termed an **auxiliary preformative molt** (**PFa**) following Howell et al. (2003); elsewhere it has been referred to as a presupplemental molt (e.g., Thompson & Leu 1994). This molt can occur either before (as proposed for ducks) or after (as proposed for Wild Turkey) the preformative molt, depending on which molt is homologous with preformative molts of related or ancestral species. The auxiliary preformative molt produces **auxiliary formative plumage (F1a)**.

Preformative molts serve primarily to replace weaker juvenal plumage with more-durable feathering that will remain functional through the first cycle. At the species level, preformative molts vary in extent from **absent** (e.g., loons, some Procellariiformes, boobies, vultures, and large gulls) to complete (Plain Chachalaca, p. 162; some shorebirds; Limpkin, p. 491; Sabine's Gull, p. 637; most terns; possibly some storm-petrels; and some passerines) but are most often **limited** (only some body feathers replaced) to **partial** (most to all body feathers, sometimes some secondary coverts, and occasionally tertials and/or central rectrices replaced). Within species, the preformative molt can also vary among individuals, in some cases (eg. some Procellariiformes; some cormorants; Wood Stork, p. 377; and many hawks and falcons) being absent in a proportion of individuals of the species, which thus remain in juvenal (first basic) plumage until the second prebasic molt, but limited in other individuals of the species, which thus acquire a formative plumage.

Definitive prealternate molts (DPAs) are inserted molts within definitive cycles, that produce **definitive alternate (DA) plumages** and plumage aspects. They occur within certain taxonomic groups treated here (including ducks, loons, grebes, pelicans, cormorants, ibis, and most Charadriiformes) but are absent in other taxa (including geese, swans, Procellariiformes, tropicbirds, boobies, herons, vultures, diurnal raptors, and rails). Most species that exhibit definitive prealternate molts also have, within the first cycle, a first prealternate molt (**PA1**), producing first alternate plumage (**A1**; Fig. 11**D-H**, p. 17), but a few species (e.g., among scoters, pelicans, cormorants, shorebirds, and alcids) lack prealternate molts until the second cycle (Fig. 11**C**). Ensuing prealternate molts include the second prealternate molt (**PA2**) producing second alternate plumage (**A2**), the third prealternate molt (**PA3**) producing third alternate plumage (**A3**), and so on. The definitive prealternate molt sometimes can reach a definitive state (in terms of timing and extent) before the definitive prebasic molt (*cf.* Fig. 11**B**), even though it is not yet part of the definitive basic cycle.

Prealternate molts serve primarily to replace worn feathers in species exposed to harsher environmental elements. In many species the alternate plumage aspect has also evolved to become brighter than the basic plumage aspect for purposes of display, whereas in ducks and some gamebirds it has evolved to become more cryptic, helping to camouflage individuals undergoing wing molt. Prealternate molts are usually limited to body feathers but sometimes can include wing coverts, tertials, and/or rectrices. Franklin's Gull (p. 648) and many terns (Fig. 492, p. 693), along with some passerine species, can also replace some to all primaries and secondaries during prealternate molts.

In several taxa treated in this guide, protracted and/or suspended prebasic molts have long been misclassified as prealternate molts (*cf.* Pyle & Howell 2004, Pyle unpublished ms.). This appears especially true concerning specialized ornamental plumes, which require substantial energy to produce (*cf.* Veit & Jones 2003) and thus cannot be replaced more than once per cycle (Pyle & Howell 2004). In other cases, such as cormorants (Nelson 2005) and perhaps some alcids (Pyle unpublished ms.), ornamental plumes are represented by filoplumes (see also Chandler 1916, Imber 1971, James 1986), which may develop from specialized follicles only activated once per year and thus are not part of a prealternate molt. Further study is needed on the development of specialized ornamental plumes and their relationships with molt terminology.

A few bird species also can have a second molt inserted within the definitive cycle, termed the **presupplemental molt (PS)**. This molt can sometimes occur within the first cycle (Fig. 10**G**), as well, but is usually restricted to second and definitive cycles (Figs. 10**H** & 11**G**). Presupplemental molts can be difficult to distinguish from protracted and/or suspended prealternate molts and are thus frequently reported for species (e.g., Long-tailed Duck, p. 140, and perhaps pelicans) in which they may do not exist. Presupplemental molts are often limited to body feathers, as in ptarmigan and some shorebirds, but can include primaries during the unique molts of terns (Figs. 11**G** & 492). Within a definitive cycle, presupplemental molts can either precede (Fig. 10**H**) or follow (Fig. 10**G**) prealternate molts, depending on the evolution of the presupplemental molt from ancestral species that had lacked it. It has also been proposed that order of presupplemental and prealternate molts may vary by sex within species (Pyle 2007).

Four Molt Strategies in Birds

Based on the number of molts (and plumages) in the first and definitive cycles, S.N.G. Howell et al. (2003) defined four underlying molt strategies of increasing complexity that incorporate all known patterns of plumage succession (Figs. 10-11). The strategy undertaken by a species reflects both life-history traits and phylogenetic relationships, and can be used to help understand the evolution of molts (see Howell et al. 2003 for details). These four strategies are as follow:

Simple Basic Strategy (**SBS**): No inserted molts in the first or definitive cycles (Fig. 10**A**).

Complex Basic Strategy (**CBS**): One inserted molt in the first cycle and no inserted molts in definitive cycles (Fig. 10**B**).

Simple Alternate Strategy (**SAS**): One inserted molt in the first cycle and one inserted (prealternate) molt in definitive cycles (Fig. 10**C-E**).

Complex Alternate Strategy (**CAS**): Two (rarely three) inserted molts in the first cycle and one (occasionally two) inserted molts in definitive cycles (Fig. 10**F-H**).

The SBS thus includes the basic molt strategy found in all birds, and the ensuing three strategies build upon the SBS by adding, through evolution, varying numbers of inserted molts within the first and definitive cycles (Fig. 10). Thus, species exhibiting the CBS have evolved an inserted preformative molt within the first cycle, and species exhibiting the CAS have evolved inserted preformative and prealternate molts within the first cycle and prealternate molts within definitive cycles. Species exhibiting the SAS may have acquired this strategy through one or more of four evolutionary pathways: 1) an ancestral SBS species may have evolved an inserted molt into both first and definitive cycles; 2) an ancestral CBS species may have evolved a prealternate molt in the definitive cycle that did not evolve in the first cycle; 3) an ancestral CAS species may have lost either the preformative or the first prealternate molt in the first cycle; and/or 4) the preformative and first prealternate molts of an ancestral CAS species may have merged over time. Thus, within the first cycle, SAS species may exhibit a preformative molt, a prealternate molt, or a molt representing a merging of these two molts (termed "**PF/PA1**" here). In the species accounts a proposed strategy is given for all species, with recognition that some of the strategies may need revision as more data on molt become available. Definitions of first-cycle molts (i.e., PF, PA1, or PF/PA1) for SAS species have also been proposed, based on consideration of molt strategies in related or ancestral taxa. Further study may indicate that some of these species may actually undergo other strategies or that new strategies may need defining. Note that these four strategies are defined at the species level: individuals skipping a molt do not exhibit a different molt strategy than their conspecifics.

Timing, Location, and Sequence of Molts

The H-P system provides a sound structure for the definitions of molts and plumages within an adaptive framework (Fig. 10). However, molts can be quite variable in timing, location, and sequence (Figs. 10 & 11). They can also suspend for phases of breeding, migration, or periods of reduced resources, typically during winter (e.g. Figs. 11**B-G**; see also Figs. 15, p. 23, & 289, p. 393) or, for Pacific coastal seabirds, during food shortages associated with, e.g., El Niño-Southern Oscillation events. All or part of an inserted molt, furthermore, can overlap with another ongoing molt in timing (e.g., Figs. 11**A-C** & **F-G**). It thus can be difficult to define certain molts and plumages, and some of the conclusions on terminology reached in this guide may need to be reassessed.

Most species treated in this guide undergo the definitive prebasic molt (DPB) following breeding, in the boreal fall for north-temperate species (Fig. 10), when feathers tend to be worn and in need of replacement. In some species, particularly those that migrate to tropical or southern latitudes, the DPB can be protracted throughout the boreal winter, completing in spring (e.g., Fig. 11**D** & **G**). In species with wide latitudinal non-breeding distributions, the DPB may either be compacted and occur in the fall, or protracted and occur over the winter (*cf.* Table 45, pp. 501-505). Preformative molts (PFs) often occur or begin during the first few months of life whereas first prealternate molts (PA1s) often begin or occur in the fall in SAS species and in the spring in CAS species (Fig. 10). But these molts can also exhibit considerable variation in timing (Fig. 11**D-G**). Definitive prealternate molts (DPAs) typically occur during the latter halves of cycles, when basic feathers are most in need of replacement (Fig. 10) but again there can be exceptions (Fig. 11**F**). The timing of molts is often dependent on the breeding status of the individual, with PBs (e.g. the PB2 and sometimes subsequent PBs) typically occurring earlier and PAs (e.g. the PA1 and sometimes subsequent PAs) later in non-breeding individuals relative to breeding adults.

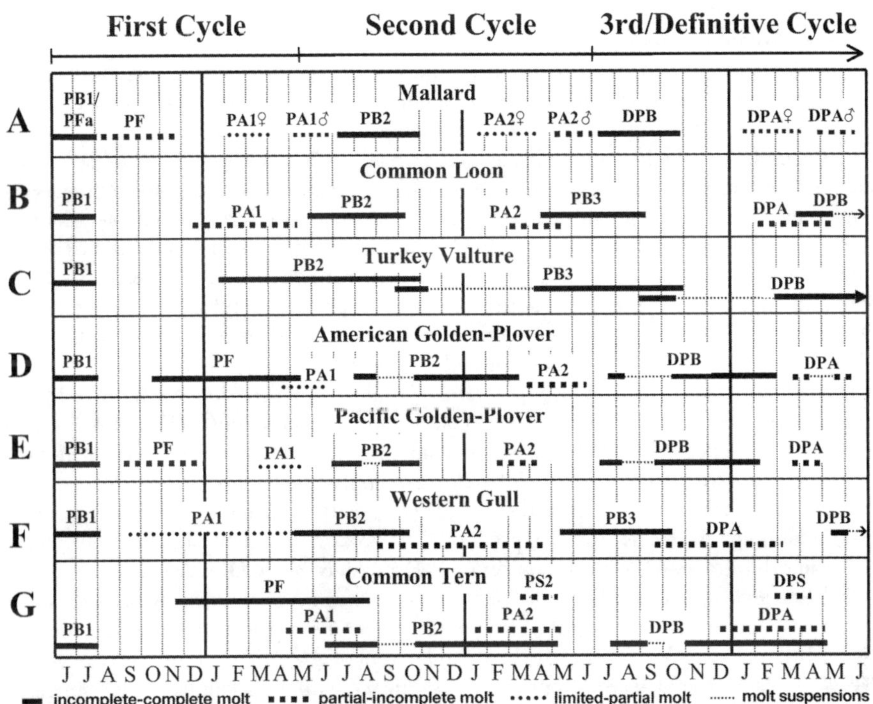

FIGURE 11. Molt patterns in selected species to illustrate varying molt strategies found in North American birds. See Figure 10 for abbreviations and symbols. Dabbling ducks (**A**; pp. 78-116), Wild Turkeys (p. 198), and some passerines may have an extra molt preceding the PF, termed an "auxiliary preformative molt" (**PFa**; pp. 14-15). Ducks also exhibit highly sex-specific patterns to the PAs, unusual in birds. In larger loons (**B**; see p. 219) and Tufted Puffin (see p. 784) the DPB can be suspended for breeding, wing feathers being replaced during spring (overlapping a DPA of body feathers), and the remainder of the molt occurring in fall (Howell & Pyle 2005). North American vultures (**C**; see p. 386) exhibit a similar suspension of the DPB for breeding, 1-3 inner pp typically replaced in fall and usually overlapping with the previous DPB, followed by suspension for winter and continuation of primary replacement with the remainder of the molt in the following spring-summer (Chandler et al. unpublished ms.; see also Fig. 281, p. 387). In shorebirds and other taxa exhibiting extensive latitudinal distribution to the winter grounds, species or individuals with different migration strategies and wintering latitudes can exhibit different molt strategies. For example, American Golden-Plover (p. 512; **D**) exhibits a **Southern Hemisphere Strategy**, typified by more-extensive PFs, protracted DPBs, and prolonged and often suspended DPAs, whereas Pacific Golden-Plover (p. 515; **E**; see also Fig. 10**F**) exhibits a **Northern Hemisphere Strategy**, typified by less-extensive PFs and more-rapid DPBs (in fall) and DPAs (Table 15, pp. 501 505). Large gulls (pp. 650 600; **E**) exhibit an unusual simple alternate strategy (Fig. 10**E**) whereby the DPA can begin in fall, suspend or protract through the winter, and complete in spring (Howell & Corben 2000b). Terns are unusual in that the inner primries can be replaced up to four times in first-cycle HY/SYs (in Least Tern; p. 704) and three times in definitive-cycle AHY/ASYs (**E**); here these inserted replacements of primaries are considered part of PFs, PAs, and PS's (Fig. 492, p. 693).

In migratory bird populations, the location of molts can also vary, both between species and among individuals of a species. DPBs can occur on or near the breeding grounds (e.g., Fig. 11**C** & **F**), at defined stopover sites or "molting grounds" (Fig. 11**A**), or primarily or entirely on the non-breeding grounds (Fig. 11**D-E**). In many species the DPB can begin on the breeding grounds and complete on the non-breeding grounds (Fig. 11**D-E** & **G**). Other strategies include commencement of the DPB on the non-breeding grounds before breeding and completion on the summer grounds after breeding (Fig. 11**B**), or commencement on the breeding grounds one year and completion on the breeding grounds the following year (Fig. 11**C**). Predefinitive PBs (e.g., PB2s and PB3s in some species) may occur more often on the non-breeding grounds, particularly in species that **over-summer** on wintering grounds for their first year or two of life (Fig. 11**B** & **F-G**). PFs also can occur on either breeding grounds (Fig. 11**A**) or non-breeding grounds (Fig. 11**D-E** & **G**), whereas PAs more regularly occur on non-breeding grounds (Fig. 11**B** & **E-G**), but can sometimes suspend for migration or occur at stopover sites (Fig. 11**D**).

During complete molts in birds, replacement of feathers follow certain general sequences. Body-feather molt often begins with the head and back, proceeds to the breast, and completes with rump, flanks, and ventral tracts. Flight-feather molt typically spans the period of body-feather molt, although in some species or individuals some or all flight feathers may be replaced at times or locations either before (e.g., large loons) or after (e.g., some shorebirds) body molts occur. Secondary coverts are often but not always replaced at the same time as primaries and secondaries; the median secondary covert tract can often be replaced early, during initial stages of body molt. In species treated here, primary coverts are typically replaced with corresponding primaries.

Flight feathers show various replacement strategies and sequences dependent upon life-history patterns (Pyle 2006a). Primaries can be replaced either synchronously (Fig. 12**A**), sequentially in "typical sequence" (Fig, 12**B**), or sequentially in atypical sequences involving multiple molt series (Fig. 12**C**; see also Fig. 182, p. 240). Replacement of secondaries often proceeds proximally from s1 and s5 and distally from the tertials (Fig. 12**B**). Incomplete prebasic molts can exhibit **staffelmauser patterns** (Fig. 16, pp. 23-24) whereas incomplete preformative molts of shorebirds can exhibit **eccentric patterns** (Figs. 13**F**, p. 20, & 376**A-D**, p. 504). Molt of rectrices usually begins with the central pair of feathers (r1) and can proceed distally on each side of the tail (r1 to r6), although perhaps just as frequently, r6 can be replaced before other rectrices, resulting in feathers among r2-r5 being the last feathers replaced (*cf.* Figs. 17, p. 25; 26, p. 48; 288, p. 392; & 379, p. 507). Flight-feather replacement sequence within taxonomic groups appears to be relatively stable, although the endochrinological signals dictating sequential replacement of flight feathers are unknown and in need of further study. Replacement of wing feathers usually occurs symmetrically, the same feathers being replaced on both wings at the same time, although small and occasionally large discrepancies can occur (see Fig. 16).

Understanding timing, location, and sequences of molts in migratory species can be important when sampling feathers for stable isotope or other analyses. When molts are suspended for migrations (*cf.* Figs. 11**B-E** & **G**, p. 17, & Fig. 15, p. 22) feather replacement before and after suspension can occur at widely different locations. Close examination can reveal suspension limits within wings (Fig. 15), among rectrices (*cf.* Fig. 17, p. 25), and even among body feathers, which can be used to sample feathers developed at more than one location from a single individual. In order to identify suspension limits and sample feathers from different locations of feather development, however, it is important to consider sequence of molt, age, and life-history tactics of a study species.

MOLT LIMITS AND WING-FEATHER CONTRASTS

"**Molt limits**" are boundaries between replaced and retained feathers following partial or incomplete molts (Froehlich 2003, Pyle 1997). The most-useful molt limits for age determination can be found among feathers of the wing (Figs. 13-16). These molt limits are best utilized in combination with relative shapes and conditions of primaries, secondaries, and wing coverts (Fig. 19**A-L**, p. 28). Following partial or incomplete preformative and/or first prealternate molts, molt limits designate birds in their first cycle (Fig. 13). By comparison, older individuals in their

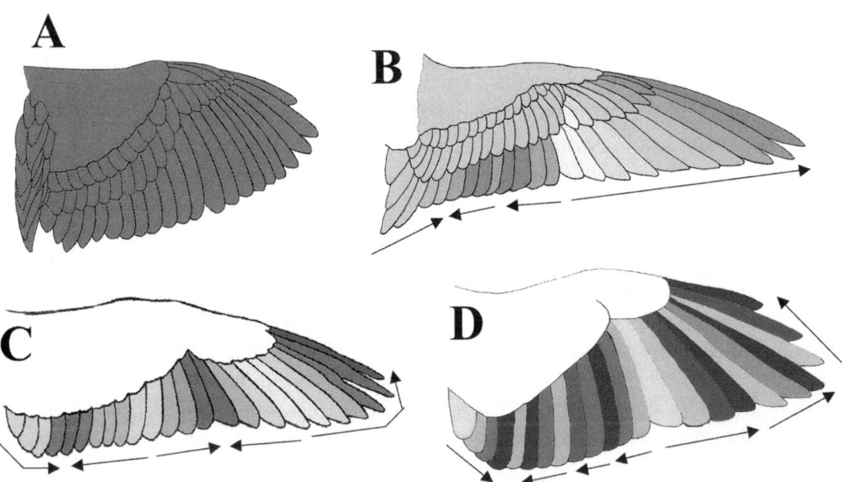

FIGURE 12. Examples of replacement sequences during definitive prebasic molts among North American waterbirds and diurnal raptors, here showing a rail (**A**; Fig. 357, p. 474), a shorebird (**B**; Fig. 375, p. 503), a falcon (**C**; Fig. 344, p. 457), and a larger bird exhibiting "staffelmauser" (**D**; Fig. 16, p. 24). Tails of arrows represent molt initiation centers, or locations after incomplete molts, and arrows indicate sequences of molt; fresher feathers are shaded darker. See Figure 1 (p. 3) for flight-feather numbering. Several species groups, including waterfowl, loons, grebes, anhingas, rails, and some alcids, molt wing feathers synchronously during DPBs, resulting in uniform pp and ss after the molt (**A**). Although feathers are replaced rapidly, typical sequences may be maintained in these species (more study is needed). In most birds with complete molts, pp (along with corresponding primary coverts) are replaced distally (from p1 to p10) and ss are replaced proximally from s1 and s5 and distally from the tertials (**B**). S1 is usually not replaced until the inner 3-7 pp have been replaced (*cf.* Dwight 1900b), resulting in an "s1-p1 contrast" (Fig. 14**B**, p. 21). The center at s5 is likely related to dyastataxy or evolutionary loss of this feather by many but not all species of birds (Miller 1915, Sibley & Alquist 1990, Bostwick & Brady 2002); those species not exhibiting dyastataxy (Galliformes; American Woodcock, p. 621; and at least two *Aethia* alcids, pp. 774-778 among species treated here) probably exhibit other sequences; e.g., many Galliformes replace ss proximally and distally from s3 (*cf.* Fig. 140, p. 191). Some species undergo replacement of pp in atypical sequence, involving "multiple-series waves" that can proceed in opposite directions. In falcons for example, both pp and ss are replaced both proximally and distally from s4/s5 and p4/p5 (**C**; Miller 1941). Albatrosses (Fig. 182, p. 240) and other Procellariiformes (Fig. 188, p. 240) also can exhibit multiple-series waves inopposite directions among pp. During staffelmauser (see Fig. 16, pp. 23-24 for details) typical replacement sequences are maintained but molts are incomplete, resulting in multiple waves and sets of feathers after several DPBs have occurred.

definitive cycles typically exhibit uniformly basic feathers (or nearly so) following complete or incomplete prebasic molts (Fig. 14, p. 21). In larger species, molt can often be protracted and/or suspended (*cf.* Fig. 15, p. 22), which can complicate the use of molt limits for age determination. For birds in active molt, it is most useful to look for molt limits among the older feathers, i.e., those not being replaced during the ongoing molt. "**Pseudolimits**", or color changes across or within feather tracts that may simulate a molt limit in passerines (Pyle 1997), are found only occasionally in species treated in this guide and thus do not pose much of a problem in identifying true molt limits.

Molt Limits among Wing Feathers

During partial PFs and/or PA1s, a variable number of lesser, median, and greater coverts can be replaced, usually in a fairly predictable sequence, beginning with median coverts and inner feathers, and ending with greater coverts and outer feathers (Fig. 13**B-D**). When most or all of these coverts have been replaced, one or more tertials can be replaced, often beginning with the second feather out (Fig. 13**C**-**D**). Depending on length of breeding season, extent of geographic range, and other factors, the amount of intraspecific variation in the replacement of these feathers can be limited or quite extensive.

Incomplete PFs and/or PA1s (involving at least some but not all primaries or secondaries other than the tertials) are not common among species treated in this guide, being found only among Galliformes, many shorebirds, a few gulls, and terns. In shorebirds and Heermann's Gull (p. 650), incomplete molts usually occur in **eccentric sequence**, whereby outer primaries and inner secondaries are replaced, leaving a block of juvenal feathers in the center of the wing (Fig. 13**F**). In Galliformes (Figs. 115, p. 154, & 154, p. 202), and some shorebirds (Fig. 376**D**, p. 504) and gulls, incomplete PFs or PA1s can result from an arresting of the typical molt sequence (Fig. 14**B**, p. 21), resulting in outer primaries and/or medial secondaries being retained (Figs. 14**C** & 16**B**, p. 24). All of these molt-limit patterns indicate HY/SYs (see pp. 41-42 for age terminology) in their first cycle. Only a few species treated in this guide can undertake a complete PF and/or PA1, after which molt limits cannot be used to determine first-cycle HY/SYs.

In species that can have a partial PF and/or PA1, any bird exhibiting symmetrical and sequen-

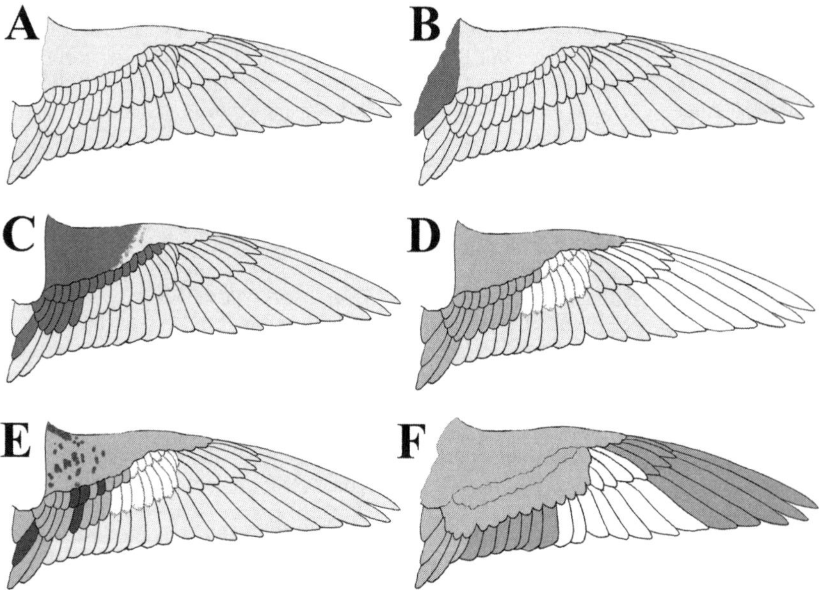

FIGURE 13. Molt limits among wing feathers after partial or incomplete preformative (PF) and/or first prealternate (PA1) molts, indicating HY/SY birds in their first cycle. Darker shading indicates fresher feathers. The illustrations depict the wings of many first-cycle (HY/SY) shorebirds (see also Figs. 375-376, pp. 503-504); similar patterns of molt limits can be found among first-cycle (HY/SY) waterfowl (Fig. 26, p. 48), loons, grebes, tropicbirds, anhingas, herons, egrets, rails (Fig. 357, p. 474), and other Charadriiformes, whereas HY/SY Galliformes (Figs. 115, p. 165, & 154, p. 202), Limpkins (Fig. 368, p. 492), some shorebirds (Fig. 376**D**), and terns (Fig. 492, p. 693) show first-cycle molt limits in other patterns.

Juveniles (Juvs) of all species have uniformly juvenal (juv) wing feathers (**A**). Following the PF, variable numbers of wing feathers can be replaced, resulting in varying molt-limit patterns with which to identify first-cycle (HY/SY) individuals. Molt limits can occur between wing feathers and humerals or scapulars (**B**) and/or among secondary coverts, in fall just after a partial molt (**C**) or in spring when juv feathers are more worn (**D**). A few species (notably smaller shorebirds) with both PFs and more extensive PA1s can also display a few replaced first-alternate coverts in spring, but this does not obscure original molt limits between formative and juv feathers (**E**). Finally, some shorebirds (along with passerines and occasionally gulls or other species) can exhibit **eccentric** patterns, involving replacement of outer pp and inner ss during the PF (**F**).

tial primary or medial secondary molt can be reliably assumed to be in its second (SY/TY) or later (ASY/ATY) cycle. In addition, the timing of molt also can vary substantially in later cycles (see below); e.g., the second or later prebasic molts of non-breeding individuals often begin earlier than those of breeding individuals, due to the lack of constraints from breeding. In marked cases, such as those of Procellariiformes (Table 24, p. 249), diurnal raptors, large gulls, terns, and jaegers, timing of molts can be used to help infer age or breeding-status groups; this could be useful in other taxa as well.

Birds in their second or subsequent cycles, having undergone the second or definitive prebasic molts, can exhibit various patterns of replacement that differ from first-cycle individuals (Figs. 14-16, pp. 22-24). These include synchronous replacement patterns, uninterrupted molt clines, suspended molt, retained feathers, and staffelmauser (*cf.* Pyle 2005c and 2006a for details). Many species exhibit synchronous replacement of wing feathers beginning with the PB2 (Fig. 14**A**) and

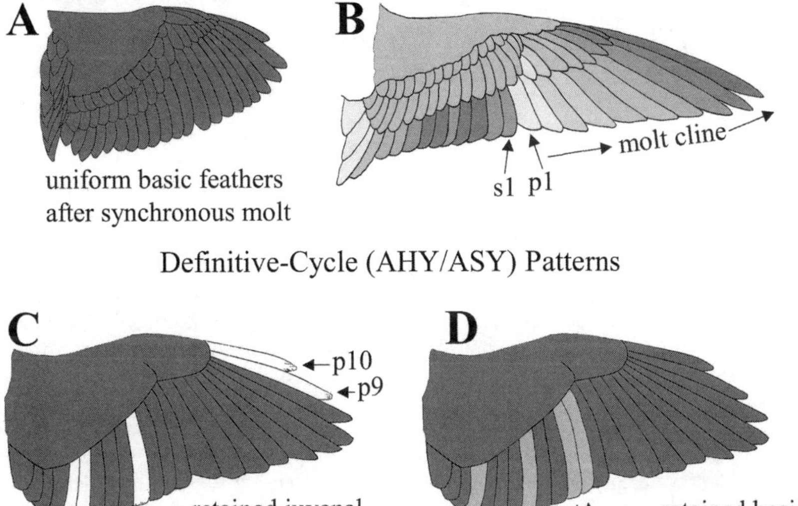

FIGURE 14. Patterns among wing feathers after complete or incomplete prebasic (PB) molts, indicating birds in at least their second (AHY/ASY) or third (ASY/ATY) cycle. Darker shading indicates fresher feathers. Many avian groups treated in this guide (see Fig. 12, p. 19) molt wing feathers synchronously during definitive prebasic molts (DPBs), resulting in uniform pp and ss after the molt (**A**); first-cycle HY/SYs of these groups show either uniformly juvenal wing feathers or molt limits within the wing (Fig. 13, p. 20). Following complete PBs in typical sequence (**B**; see also Fig. 12**B**), a distal **molt cline** through the pp can often be detected, as well as an **s1-p1 contrast** which results from s1 dropping at approximately the same time that p4-p7 are molted and up to a few weeks or more after p1 has been replaced. Molt clines and s1-p1 contrasts result from the fact that subsequently replaced feathers appear sequentially fresher due to lags in time between feather replacement, and are most evident in birds that have protracted molts; e.g., shorebirds and other species or individuals that migrate to tropical latitudes or opposite hemispheres during non-breeding seasons. Larger species can exhibit incomplete 2nd (**C**) or definitive (**D**) PBs. Retention of juvenal feathers during the PB2 allows identification of second-cycle SY/TYs; these are usually the last feathers replaced during a typical molt and can include the outer pp, ss among s3-s4, and ss between s5 and the tertials, e.g., among s7-s9 in species with 13-15 ss (**C**). Species exhibiting staffelmauser also exhibit incomplete PB2s in these patterns (Fig. 16**B**, p. 24), whereas some species or individuals can retain ss but not outer pp (**C-D**). Retention of basic ss during the DPB allows identification of ASY/ATYs in at least their third cycle (**D**); placements of retained ss sometimes match those typically found in 2nd-cycle SY/TYs (**C**) but often will involve other ss (**D**), perhaps indicating at least two previous incomplete molts and ATY/A4Y; more study needed.

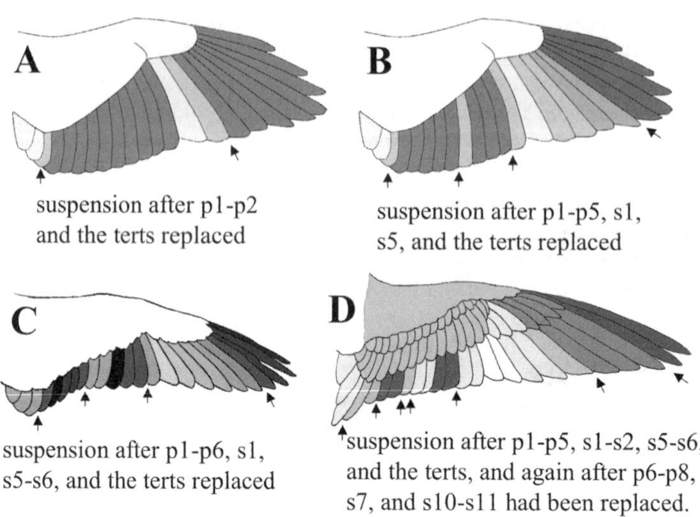

FIGURE 15. Examples of **suspension limits** among primaries and secondaries of birds. These develop after suspension of definitive prebasic molts for breeding, migration, and/or winter, and indicate AHY/ASYs in definitive cycles and, often, individuals that bred the previous season (*cf.* Figs. 289, p. 393, & 458, p. 635). Suspension limits are characterized by a marked contrast between adjacent feathers, the earlier feather in sequence being substantially more worn than the subsequent feather, indicating elapsed time between the replacement of the two feathers (see Pyle 2005c for more information). Among pp, note that suspension limits can be separated from staffelmauser patterns by the distal p across the break being fresher than the adjacent proximal p, whereas breaks defining sets in staffelmauser have the distal p more worn (Fig. 16**D-H**, p. 24). However, care might be needed in shorebirds to separate suspension limits from eccentric replacement patterns of first-cycle SYs (Fig. 376**A**, p. 504). **A-B** show suspension limits that can occur in diurnal raptors after a molt suspension for incubation and following completion of molt after breeding (see Fig. 289 for more details). **C** shows a Mississippi Kite (p. 405) that has suspended molt for migration after six inner pp and five ss had been replaced, in this case indicating a non-breeding bird late in its second cycle (TY); older breeding birds typically suspend after only 1-2 pp have been replaced (see Fig. 302, p. 407, for details). **D** represents a definitive-cycle ASY shorebird that has suspended molt of pp twice, once for southbound migration (after p1-p5 had been replaced on or near breeding grounds) and a second time for winter (after p6-p8 had been replaced following migration). See Figure 492 (p. 693) for patterns resulting from similar suspensions in terns, and Figure 344**C** (p. 457) for suspension patterns in falcons. Note that suspension limits can also occur among rectrices (*cf.* Fig. 17, p. 25), but patterns of suspension have not been investigated in detail. More study is needed on suspension limts and their use in ageing.

these AHY/ASYs can be separated from first-cycle HY/SYs of the same species by the lack of molt limits, along with shapes and other characters of basic *vs.* juvenal feathers (*cf.* Fig. 19**A-L**, p. 28). Birds that undergo complete molts in typical sequence may show an uninterrupted "**molt cline**" and "**s1-p1 contrast**" among primaries and secondaries, based on gaps in replacement times of these feathers (Fig. 14**B**). Birds with protracted prebasic molts, such as many seabirds and species or individuals that molt in the tropics or southern Hemisphere, will show more pronounced molt clines and s1-p1 contrasts than those with more-rapid prebasic molts, typically including species that molt on the breeding grounds or on north-temperate winter grounds (*cf.* pp. 16-18 and 501-507). When assessing molt clines beware of "**wear clines**" that may obscure sequential replacement patterns, especially among outer primaries. Wear clines result from certain feathers being more exposed than adjacent feathers and becoming sequentially more worn. Wear clines are most evident proximally among secondaries (resulting in more-worn tertials) and distally among primaries (*cf.* Fig. 13**D**), and are thus usually opposite to molt clines in these ares of the wing.

Prebasic molts can often be incomplete, and the retention of either juvenal feathers during the second prebasic molt (Fig. 14**C**) or definitive feathers during subsequent prebasic molts (Fig. 14**D**) can be used to identify second-cycle SY/TYs and later-cycle ASY/ATYs, respectively. Some species may suspend the definitive prebasic molt for breeding, migration, or winter, and these can show "**suspension limits**" after completion of the molt (Fig. 15). Suspension limits can often be used to infer breeding during the previous season (*cf.* Figs. 289, p. 393; Fig. 344**C**, p. 457; Fig. 458, p. 635; and Pyle 2005c), in turn resulting in age-determination to AHY/ASY, ASY/ATY, or older, depending on age of first breeding (*cf.* Figs. 15**C** & 302, p. 407). More study is needed on the use of suspension limits to determine age and life-history patterns in birds.

Staffelmauser

Many large and long-winged birds that need to maintain flight to survive, but do not have time to undergo complete, sequential remegial molts between breeding seasons, have developed a molting strategy termed "**staffelmauser**" (Stresemann & Stresemann 1966), also known as "stepwise molt" or "serial molt". During staffelmauser, two or more simultaneous "waves" (replacement sequences) can develop among primaries and secondaries (Fig. 16, p. 24). Staffelmauser likely evolved due to time constraints (Shugart & Rohwer 1996, Rohwer 1999) but results in multiple small gaps in the wing, allowing continued ability for flight during molt (Hedenström & Sunada 1999; Pyle 2005c, 2006). Staffelmauser results in multiple "sets" (series of sequentially replaced feathers between arrested waves) among primaries, and the number of sets can be used to determine minimum ages up to the fourth (A4Y/A5Y) or possibly fifth (A5Y/A6Y) cycles (Fig. 16, p. 24; Clark 2004, Pyle 2006a). Extent of feather replacement varies according to annual events and food availability. Within species exhibiting Staffelmauser, furthermore, there can be varying proportions of individuals that undergo complete sequential molts within a season, lacking staffelmauser patterns during the ensuing cycle (Fig. 14**B**; *cf.* Pyle 2005b). Molt terminology for species exhibiting staffelmauser follows that recommended by Pyle (2006a).

Staffelmauser typically begins with an incomplete 2nd prebasic molt (PB2), during which primary and secondary replacement proceeds in typical sequence (*cf.* Fig. 12**B**, p. 19) but then arrests before all feathers are replaced (Fig. 16**B**; see also Fig. 14**C**). Juvenal outer primaries and medial secondaries are thus retained by SY/TYs through the second molt cycle. The third prebasic molt (PB3) begins where the PB2 arrested the year before, while another molt wave typically commences again from the molt centers at p1, s1, s5, and the tertials, resulting in two waves of replacement simultaneously (Fig. 16**C**). Larger birds may continue to retain some juv feathers during the PB3 allowing the identification of TY/4Ys through their third cycle (Fig. 16**D**). Other individuals of these or other species may complete replacement of all juvenal primaries and secondaries during the PB3, resulting in two sets of basic feathers (Fig. 16**E**). These are in at least their third cycle (ASY/ATY), although certain patterns of replacement within a given species (e.g., sets at p1-p2 and p3-p10) may not be possible after the PB3, and may indicate fourth cycle or older (ATY/A4Y). More study is needed on the use of precise set placement to infer age-groups within species exhibiting staffelmauser.

Subsequent molts commence again where previous molts arrested, while additional waves also begin at molt centers. As long as fewer than all 10 primaries are replaced during each molt, and molt waves only occur once per cycle (year), the number of resulting sets allows age-determination through at least the fourth (ATY/A4Y), fifth (A4Y/A5Y), or possibly even the sixth (A5Y/A6Y) cycles (Fig. 16**F**-**H**). However, many older individuals may undergo complete or more-complete molts, perhaps due either to lack of breeding or presence of substantial resources in a given year, and the number of sets can become reduced. Thus, individuals with fewer than the maximum number of sets observed in a species cannot be assigned to younger age groups. When interpreting staffelmauser patterns, beware that some individuals of certain species (such as Swainson's Hawk, p. 436) may suspend molt for breeding and/or migration and that suspensions may partially obscure staffelmauser patterns (see Fig. 15, p. 22, for discussion).

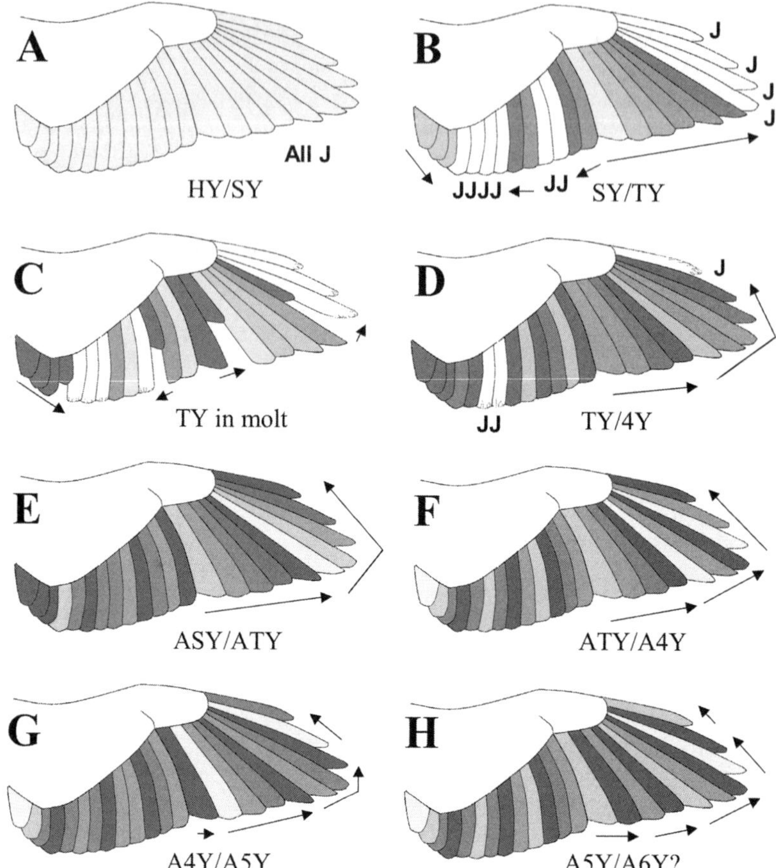

FIGURE 16. Typical patterns of **staffelmauser** exhibited by large N.Am birds, including tropicbirds, boobies, pelicans, cormorants, frigatebirds, herons, egrets, condors, ospreys, hawks, eagles, cranes, and noddy terns. Darker shading indicates fresher feathers. Arrows indicate sequence of replacement and "sets" of post-juvenal feathers, whereas "J" indicates juv feathers. These illustrations show 13 ss; many species exhibiting staffelmauser have more ss, up to 30 or more in larger species (*cf.* Fig. 182, p. 240). Sets among pp are defined by the distal p across a break being contrastingly more worn than the adjacent proximal p, as opposed to the other way around in suspension limits (Fig. 15, p. 22), which may also occur within the wings of species exhibiting staffelmauser. During the first cycle, HY/SYs retain their juv pp and ss (**A**). During the PB2, replacement of pp proceeds distally from p1 and the tertials, and proximally from s1 and s5 (**B**). Molt typically arrests after 4-7 pp and 4-9 or more ss have been replaced, leaving juv outer pp and juv ss among s3-s4 and/or in a block between s6 and the terts (**B**; see also Fig. 14**C**, p. 21). In larger species up to 10 or more ss can be retained among, e.g., s11-s20 (*cf.* Fig. 182**B**). These patterns can be used to identify SY/TYs. The PB3 begins where the PB2 arrested and starts again at p1, the terts, s1, and/or s5 (**C**). In some larger species or individuals, the PB3 can again arrest before all juvenal feathers have been replaced, often with the juvenal p10 and 1-3 ss retained between the terts and s7 (**D**). Other species or individuals may replace all juvenal feathers during this molt, resulting in two sets of basic feathers, and allowing age determination of ASY/ATY (**E**), although inferring older minimum age groups may be possible for certain set placements (see text). Assuming fewer than 10 pp are replaced each cycle (year), the number of sets of basic feathers indicates the minimum age in years. Thus individuals with three sets (**F**) can be aged ATY/A4Y and individuals with four sets (**G**) can be aged A4Y/A5Y. Look for occasional hawks or other large birds with slow molts to display five sets of pp (**H**) and be aged A5Y/A6Y. Secondaries maintain their replacement sequence but arrest at different positions, resulting in mixed generations in variable patterns following the PB3 or PB4 (**E-H**). See text and Pyle (2005c, 2006a) for more information.

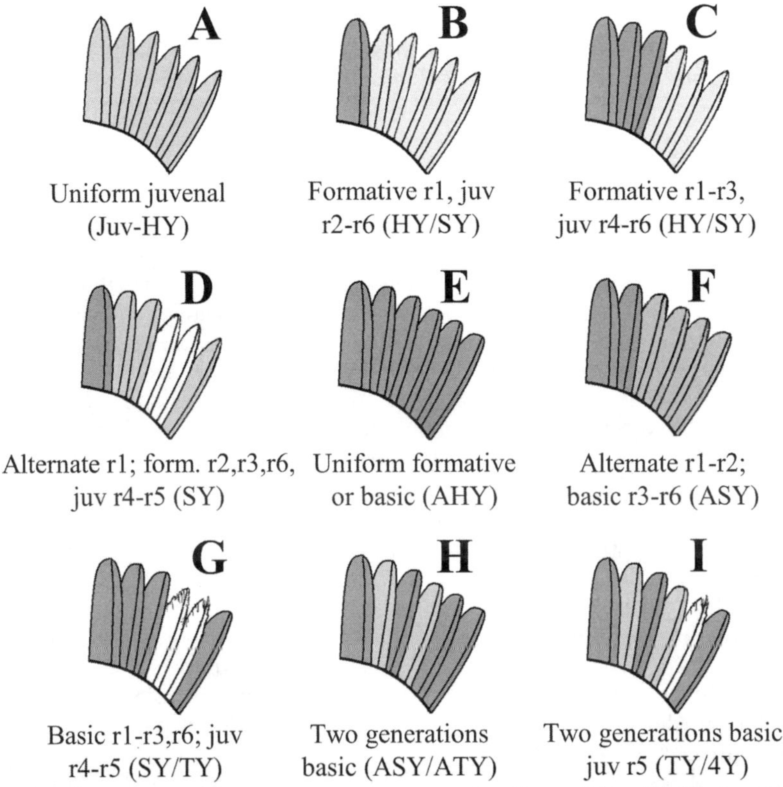

FIGURE 17. Molt patterns and limits among rectrices; see also Figures 26 (p. 48), 190 (p. 251), 288 (p. 392), and 379 (p. 507). Juvs have uniformly juv rects (**A**), which are more pointed, paler and/or duller, and tend to wear more quickly than basic or formative rects (*cf.* Fig. 19**M-P**, p. 28). Rects are often replaced in sequences such as r1-r2-r6-r3-r4-r5 (order among r2-r4 can be variable), such that the last feathers replaced are often feathers among r2-r4, followed by r5. Following incomplete PFs, first-cycle HY/SYs can exhibit mixed generations of formative and juvenal rects (**B-C**), and in certain small species (such as *Calidris* sandpipers), the tail may include juv, formative, and first alternate rects following the PA1 in first-cycle SYs (**D**). Some taxa can replace rects completely during the PF (see text), resulting in uniformly formative rects (**E**) or mixed formative and alternate rects (**F**). These cannot be distinguished from uniformly basic rects of definitive-cycle AHY/ASYs following complete DPBs (**E**) or mixed basic and alternate rects following DPAs (**F**); however, the presence and/or number of alternate feathers can sometimes be used to indicate ASY. Incomplete prebasic molts can result in mixed basic and juv feathers indicating second-cycle SY/TYs (**G**), two generations of basic feathers indicating definitive-cycle ASY/ATYs (**H**), or rarely in the largest of birds (such as eagles), two generations of basic feathers plus 1-2 remaining juv feathers indicating third-cycle TY/4Ys (**I**). Note that suspension limits for migration, breeding, and/or winter can also occur among rects (*cf.* Fig. 15, p. 22); as in pp and ss, suspension limits can be identified by later feathers in sequence being substantially fresher, rather than more worn, than earlier feathers in sequence. In all cases, juv rects are more tapered and pointed, and wear more quickly than do basic rects, especially when retained for a year or more (Fig. 19**M-P**).

Molt Limits among Rectrices

As with primaries and secondaries, rectrices can or may not be replaced incompletely during preformative, prealternate, or prebasic molts, and patterns of replaced and retained feathers, along with characteristics of the rectrices themselves (Fig. 19**M-P**, p. 28), can be used to help determine a bird's age (Fig. 17). Rectrix replacement during the PF varies from absent in many taxa (e.g., Procellariiformes, most Pelecaniformes, most herons and egrets, ibis, vultures, diurnal raptors, cranes, and most gulls), to incomplete in many taxa (e.g., among waterfowl, rails, limpkins, shorebirds, and alcids), to complete in other taxa (e.g., many waterfowl, loons, rails, shorebirds, terns, and jaegers). As with molt of primaries and secondaries, migratory species and individuals wintering in the tropics or southern Hemisphere generally have more complete rectrix molts. Thus, first-cycle HY/SYs can vary from having completely juvenal rectrices (Fig. 17**A**) to mixed juvenal and formative rectrices (Fig. 17**B-C**), to completely formative rectrices (Fig. 17**E**). Occasional individuals (primarily among ducks and shorebirds) can replace r1 during the PA1, resulting in three generations of feathers in SYs that retain juvenal rectrices (Fig. 17**D**), or two generations in those with complete PFs (Fig. 17**F**). The definitive prebasic molt is complete in most taxa, resulting in uniformly basic rectrices (Fig. 17**E**); individuals among ducks and Charadriiformes can replace 1-4 (occasionally more) central rectrices during DPAs and show two generations in spring (Fig. 17**F**). In most species with PAs, more feathers are typically replaced during DPAs than during PA1s (the latter often not including any rectrices), so the occurrence and number of alternate rects can often be used to age spring ASYs. Molting individuals with protracted complete PFs and DPBs can be aged by the shape and condition of unmolted feathers until the molt is complete, often as late as winter or spring.

Larger birds (e.g., among geese, swans, Procellariiformes, ibis, storks, vultures, diurnal raptors, and cranes) can also exhibit incomplete rectrix replacement during prebasic molts. Juvenal feathers retained during the second prebasic molt are then very worn and frayed (Fig. 17**G**), allowing identification of second-cycle SY/TYs; basic or formative feathers retained during incomplete prebasic molts contrast less in shape and wear with replaced feathers (Fig. 17**H**). Depending on the extent of the preformative molt, individuals with retained non-juvenal feathers can either be aged ASY/ATY (most of the above taxa) or AHY/ASYs (e.g., geese, that could be exhibiting mixed basic and formative feathers). A few individuals of very large species, such as eagles and possibly other large diurnal raptors, storks, vultures, and cranes, may occasionally retain 1-2 juvenal feathers through the third prebasic molt and, along with two generations of basic feathers, be identified as third-cycle TY/4Ys (Fig. 17**I**).

FAULT BARS

Fault bars are small pigment or structural anomalies in flight feathers, resulting from trauma or inconsistencies in a bird's diet when the feathers were growing (Grubb 1989, Shawkey et al. 2003); major stress or diet deficiencies can cause actual breaks in the feather vein (Fig. 18, p. 26). Among species treated here, fault bars have been most widely used to age diurnal raptors (Hamerstrom 1967, Machmer et al. 1992, Negro et al. 1994); but, because chicks of many larger species grow slowly and often rely on protein-rich diets, fault bars likely have wider application for identifying first-cycle (HY/SY) waterbirds than is currently recognized. Because juvenal flight feathers grow simultaneously, fault bars in first-cycle HY/SYs are found uniformly across primaries, primary coverts, secondaries, and rectrices, at the positions where feathers were erupting at the time of nutritional stress or trauma (Fig. 18**A**). In the many species with partial first-cycle molts and sequential prebasic molts (see Fig. 18), second-cycle or older AHY/ASYs can be identified by having symmetrical fault bars that reflect the sequence and duration of previous molts (Fig. 18**B**). Beware that AHY/ASYs of species exhibiting synchronous flight-feather replacement during second and definitive prebasic molts (Fig. 12**A**, p. 19; including waterfowl, loons, grebes, anhingas, rails, and some alcids) will show similar fault-bar patterns to first-cycle individuals, and thus cannot be aged by fault bars. In addition, first-cycle SYs of species exhibiting complete preformative rectrix or flight-feather molts (including some shorebirds, gulls, and terns) cannot be aged by fault bars in these tracts after the molts have completed. Finally, individuals that have lost their tails accidentally usually replace rectrices simultaneously and may show a fault-bar pattern typical of a first-cycle HY/SY.

FLIGHT-FEATHER SHAPE AND WEAR

In species for which the first prebasic molt is partial or incomplete, the shape (*cf.* Prum & Williamson 2001) and the amount of wear and bleaching of flight feathers can serve as very use-

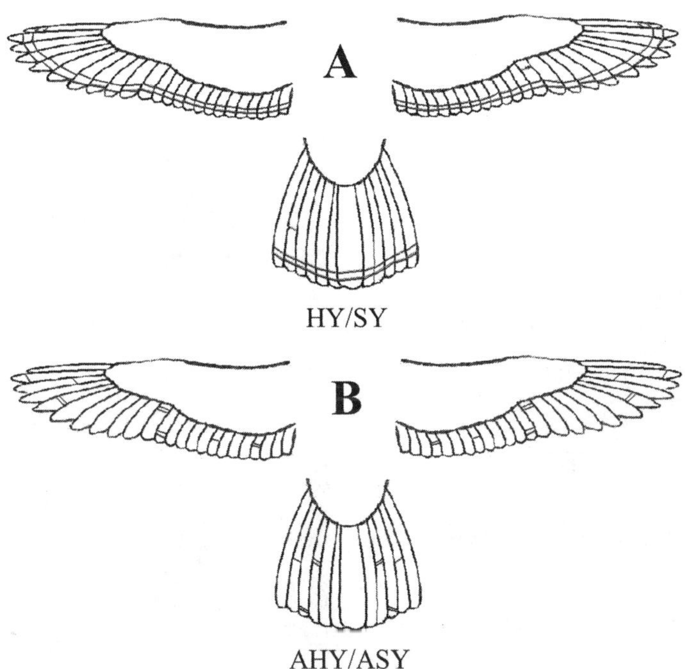

FIGURE 18. Fault-bar patterns among flight feathers to assist in ageing large birds. "**Fault bars**" are feather deficiencies that appear as visible pale bars or, sometimes breaks across barbs, occurring at points of flight-feather eruption from follicles during moments of trauma or lack of nutrient availability. Fault bars are most common among juvenal flight feathers retained by HY/SYs, resulting from food deficiency or other stressful moments when a chick was developing its first feathers. Because all feathers grow simultaneously during the prejuvenal (PB1) molt, fault bars occur in the same place across all feathers on both sides of the wing and tail in first-cycle HY/SYs (**A**). Occasionally other breaks can result from other causes, such as interaction with vegetation or predators (*cf.* left r5 and right s1 in **A**), but these often appear different from other fault bars and are not found symmetrically on both sides of the wings or tail. In definitive-cycle AHY/ASYs, the position of fault bars reflect duration and sequence of molts. Thus, in **B**, a fault bar developed when p6 was about a third grown, s1 was mostly grown, s2 and r4 had just erupted from the follicle, and s11 and r3 were about half grown. These feathers are often replaced at the same time during a typical complete DPB (*cf.* Fig. 12**B**, p. 19). Another fault bar developed in **B** when p8 was about three-fourths grown, p9 had just erupted from the sheath, and s7 and r5 were about half grown, again reflecting feathers that are typically replaced contemporaneously. Note that fault bars may also be detected among primary coverts, often at the same location along the feathers at which they occur in corresponding primaries. Note also that the illustration depicts breaks across feathers but fault bars represented by subtle pigment deficiencies can also be detected and can assist with ageing. These are easiest to see when feathers are held at an angle and with a strong source of back-lighting. Fault bars are most helpful in ageing species that exhibit partial PF/PA1s but complete DPBs, such as certain Procellariiformes, ibis, storks, vultures, diurnal raptors, cranes, and Charadriiformes. For more information, see Grubb (1989), Hamerstrom (1967), Machmer et al. (1992), Negro et al. (1994), Pyle (1997), and Shawkey et al. (2003).

ful clues for age determination (Fig. 19, p. 28). Juvenal feathers typically are thinner and more tapered than adult, are of a less durable quality, and thus become abraded and worn at a quicker pace (compare **A-B** with **C-D** in Fig. 19). The best feathers to examine for shape differences by age are typically the outer primaries (Fig. 19**A-D**), medial secondaries (Fig. 19**E-H**), outer primary coverts (Fig. 19**I-J**), medial greater coverts (Fig. 19**K-L**), and outer rectrices (Fig. 19**M-P**).

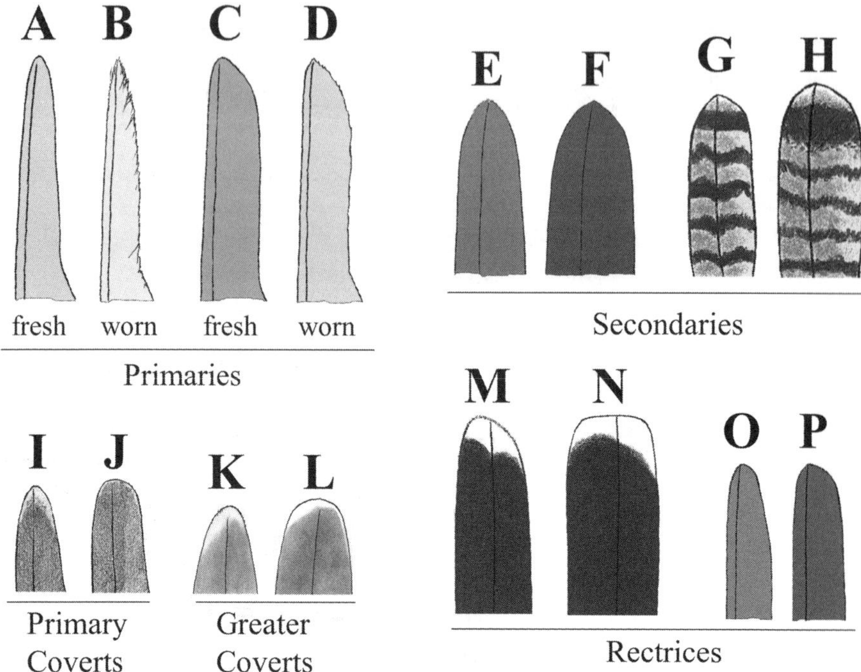

FIGURE 19. Examples of feather shapes by age in birds. Shown are the primaries of waterfowl (**A-D**; Fig. 25, p. 47), the secondaries of Plain Chachalaca (**E-F**; Fig. 113, p. 163) and *Buteo* hawks (**G-H**; Fig. 322, p. 431), the primary coverts of American Bittern (**I-J**; Fig. 248, p. 342), the greater coverts of Greater White-fronted Goose (**K-L**; Fig. 30, p. 55), and the rectrices of Plain Chachalaca (**M-N**; Fig. 112, p. 163) and Black Storm-Petrel (**O-P**; Fig. 214, p. 288). In all cases juv feathers or pair of feathers (**A-B**) are to the left of basic feathers. Note that juv feathers are narrower and tend to be more tapered toward the tip, whereas basic feathers are broader and often somewhat truncated at tip. Because juv feathers are of poorer quality, they wear down quicker than basic feathers, accentuating these shape differences with wear (*cf.* **A-B** *vs* **C-D**). Note also that juv feathers tend to be a bit paler in coloration than basic feathers, because of reduced pigment saturation coupled with increased wear and bleaching due to their poorer quality. Formative feathers tend to resemble basic feathers, although at times they can be intermediate in shape, especially in Galliformes, in which preformative molt of these feathers occur when juveniles are quite young. Other illustrations of shape differences by age in these feather tracts can be found throughout the species accounts.

Other feathers within these tracts can show similar shape differences by age, and these differences can also be observed among back feathers (*cf.* Figs. 32, p. 57; 153, p. 201, 187, p. 248; & 236, p. 319) and axillars (*cf.* Fig. 191, p. 251). When using feather shape and wear for age determination, it is best to carefully consider the molting strategies of the species in question (*cf.* Figs. 10-17) and to look accordingly for retained juvenal feathers, at times contrasting with replaced formative or basic feathers (Figs. 13-17).

PLUMAGE ASPECT BY AGE AND SEX

The most apparent method for determining both the age and the sex of many birds is often by examining plumage-aspect characters. As explained on pp. 12-13, the term "**plumage**" refers to the existing feather coat (consisting of one or more feather generations) based on previous molts, whereas plumage "**aspect**" refers to the appearance of the bird based on pattern and color deposition during molt, and as also affected by other factors such as bleaching and wear. Plumage-aspect patterns generally do not vary as widely by age and sex among North American waterbirds, raptors, and Galliformes as they do among passerines (Pyle 1997). However, in certain species among ducks, Galliformes, raptors, and shorebirds, ages and/or sexes can differ markedly in aspect, and aspect can also vary markedly by plumage (e.g., basic *vs* alternate). In addition, several groups (e.g., among albatross, eagles, condors, gulls, and jaegers) exhibit delayed plumage-aspect maturation and take up to several years or more to reach definitive plumage aspect (see p. 13). Plumage aspects in predefinitive cycles become more variable with age in these species, such that overlap can exist between aspects of different age-groups (see pp. 41-42 concerning age terminology), complicating the age-determination process.

The interaction between hormonal cycles, color-deposition, and plumage aspect is a fascinating and under-studied subject that is beyond the scope of this guide (see Voitkevich 1966 and Kimball 2006 for reviews). In birds that have protracted molts, the concept that color change can occur throughout the process of a single molt is relevant to age and sex determination. During a PF or PB2, for example, earlier-replaced feathers can show more juvenal-like aspect and later-replaced feathers more definitive-like aspect within a single generation of feathers (*cf.* Beebe 1914; Howell et al. 2004; Pyle 2005a, 2005b). Additionally, feathers replaced adventitiously or early or late within molts, and apart from hormonal periods that typically occur during peak molt, may exhibit aspects that do not reflect that age or sex (*cf.* Gromadzka 1985, Howell & Dunn 2007, Pyle 1997:19). Finally, it should be noted that non-breeding, first-cycle SYs may display alternate feathers that have basic-like aspect because hormones have not elevated to those of breeding, definitive-cycle ASYs; e.g., over-summering SY shorebirds can show basic-like aspect, even though they have undergone the prealternate molt (Loftin 1962, Chandler & Marchant 2001, Johnson & Johnson 1983, Chu 1994). These are commonly misclassified as being in "basic plumage". Hormone-aspect interactions should be considered when classifying birds to plumage, age, and sex, especially individuals exhibiting variably protracted molts.

In this guide, a substantial proportion of the species accounts are comprised of characters related to plumage aspect. Criteria are given only when clearly defined and consistent age/sex-related plumage-aspect patterns occur. However, it is important that users understand the variable nature of plumage aspect—that variation can occur both within each defined age/sex plumage-aspect association, and among the different age and sex classes, even in species with no clearly defined, age-specific and/or sex-specific plumage-aspect patterns.

In species otherwise displaying little plumage-aspect variation, males (or females in polyandrous species) and definitive-aspect AHY/ASYs often exhibit slightly brighter and more-contrasting plumage aspects than females (males) and first-cycle HY/SYs. Thus, in many cases, when either age or sex is known from other criteria, the relative brightness or distinctness of plumage aspect may assist in determining the other class. Bright or well-marked first-cycle individuals may be males (or females in polyandrous species), bright females may be in their definitive cycle, and the same might work in reverse for particularly dull or indistinctly marked individuals. In many cases, a small to moderate proportion of extremes may be accurately aged or sexed, especially in combination with species familiarity.

On the other hand, plumage-aspect variation within each age/sex class often is such that intermediates or overlapping aspects between age/sex groups occur. In these cases it is again best to incorporate other ageing and sexing information. When plumage-aspect overlap exists, it is most often between young males (or females in polyandrous species) and adult females (males), and in many species this is an adaptive pattern (see Rohwer et al. 1980, Pyle 1997). Plumage-aspect exceptions can also occur, even in species that normally exhibit no overlap between age/sex classes. In many cases these are senescent females which can acquire male-like plumage aspect, especially among ducks and Galliformes (*cf.* Buchanan & Parkes 1948, Owens & Short 1995, Swennen et al. 1989) exhibiting estrogen-dependent dichromatism (Voitkevich 1966, Kimball 2006).

Males with plumage aspect typical of females are less common, but these or even individuals with both male and female characters (*cf.* Lillie 1931, Brodkorb 1935, Parrish et al. 1987, Patten 1993a) may also be encountered. When ageing and/or sexing, users are encouraged to always confirm plumage-aspect characters with all other available criteria.

Finally, it should be noted that plumage aspects, and thus many aspect-related ageing and sexing criteria, change during periods of molt. This is especially important concerning species treated in this guide, many of which undergo suspended and/or protracted molts, that can be quite extended and may vary substantially among different individuals of the same species. Generally, the aspect of outgoing plumages will be more instructive for ageing than the aspect of incoming plumages. Users should always consider how molt might affect the reliability of the plumage-aspect criteria when ageing and sexing individuals in transitional plumages, undergoing active molt.

BREEDING AND CLOACAL CHARACTERS

The development of breeding characters, in particular brood patches and distended cloaca during the nesting season, along with differences in the cloacal region that can be appreciated on live birds in at least some taxa year-round, can be very important criteria for ageing and sexing larger species treated in this guide. Unlike passerines (Pyle 1997), males of species treated in this guide do not develop visible cloacal protuberances. Most previous research on age and sex determination using cloacal features has been performed on waterfowl and gamebirds (e.g., Hochbaum 1942, Quinn & Burrows 1936, Stromberg 1977) but it is likely that some or all of these methods can also be used on other large taxa treated here (*cf.* Hamerstrom & Skinner 1971).

Brood Patch

Incubation or **brood patches** are developed by incubating birds as a means of transferring as much body heat as possible to eggs in the nest (Bailey 1952, Pyle 1997). In many birds, females perform all or most of the incubating and develop more complete brood patches than males; however, in many other species (e.g., loons, grebes, Procellariiformes, ibis, vultures, most shorebirds, gulls, terns, jaegers, and alcids) both sexes incubate and develop patches (in some cases more developed in females than in males); in polyandrous species (e.g., Eurasian Dotterel, p. 533; jacanas, and phalaropes) males but not females can incubate and develop brood patches; and in some species (e.g. among Pelecaniformes) eggs are incubated with the feet and thus no brood patches develop. Among taxa treated in this guide, brood patches are most useful in identifying females of sexually monochromatic species such as geese, swans, chachalacas, most diurnal raptors, polygynous shorebirds, and a few other species. The presence of brood patches also usually indicates breeding and, combined with typical age of first reproduction, can be used to help identify minimum ages. However, individuals of pre-breeding age, in their 2nd-4th or later cycles, may also develop partial or full brood patches (*cf.* Ainley et al. 1995, Bailey 1952, Gaston & Jones 1998, Tranquilla et al. 2003) so caution is advised in using brood patches for minimum-age determinations. In this guide, conservative minimum ages as determination by brood patch are indicated, often reflecting cycles just previous to known ages of first reproduction.

Breeding individuals of most bird species develop a single medial brood patch along the medio-ventral apterum in the center of the abdomen (Fig. 20**A**), but many waterbirds can also develop bilateral brood patches along lateral-ventral aptera on the sides of the abdomen under the wings (Fig. 20**B**; Manuwal 1974). Some species that can lay three or more eggs (e.g., among falcons and Charadriiformes) can develop both bilateral and medio-ventral brood patches simultaneously, with the latter patch often located closer to the vent than in birds with a single medial patch. It is not always well documented what types of brood patches can develop in waterbirds and further study is thus needed.

The development of a brood patch begins with the loss of the feathers of the abdomen, about 3-5 days before the first egg is laid. Shortly thereafter, especially with medial brood patches (Fig. 20**A**), the blood vessels of the region begin to increase in size and the epidermis becomes thicker and more fluid filled, occasionally folding into wrinkles. Less-developed bilateral brood patches can

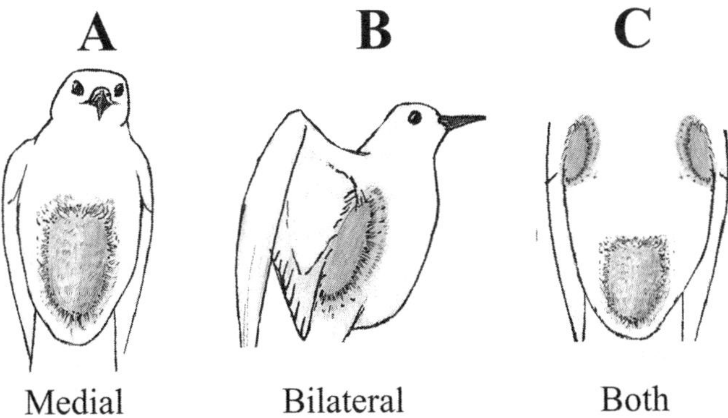

FIGURE 20. Examples of brood patches in larger birds, usually an indication of active breeding (but see text concerning older individuals of pre-breeding age) and most often used to sex females of sexually monochromatic species in the hand. Many species develop a single **medial brood patch** in the center of the abdomen (**A**). Other species, primarily among Charadriiformes, can develop **bilateral brood patches** along lateral-ventral aptera under each wing (**B**) or occasionally more centrally, on either side of the keel. Occasional species (among falcons, gulls, and perhaps shorebirds), that can lay three or more eggs, can develop both bilateral patches and a third medial patch located toward the vent (**C**). To examine a bird for one or more brood patches, simply part the feathers through blowing or with the fingers. With experience, brood patches are relatively easy to detect and to score for developmental phases (*cf.* Bailey 1952, Manuwal 1974, Tranquilla et al. 2003).

appear like small pouches of bare skin, with little or no vascularization (Fig. 20**B**). Once fledglings hatch or leave the nest, a hardening of the epidermal surface often ensues, and downy refeathering of these patches can commence. If a second clutch of eggs is laid, the patches may (or may not; Manuwal 1974) remain and/or become reinvigorated. A complete new coat of feathers usually does not develop over brood patches until the prebasic molt following completion of breeding. More study is needed on the use of partially refeathered brood patches for reliable sex determinations.

In many species males may assist with incubation and develop a partial, incomplete, or complete brood patch. In some of these species complete brood patches can be used to sex females but partial brood patches may represent males or be found in females at certain stages, so caution is warranted. Many females that have brood patches also exhibit distended cloacae (Fig. 21, p. 32) at the same time, a more reliable indication that an individual is a female. Of course, brood patches should only be expected during nesting season(s) which, for most North American birds, are restricted to periods in April-August. In a few species in southern North America, brood patches may occur for year-round.

Distended Cloaca

A reliable method of identifying female birds during the nesting season is by the presence of a **distended cloaca**, or vent, which results from recent egg laying (Fig. 21, p. 32). Although studied specifically in only a handful of taxa treated in this guide (e.g., petrels, Serventy 1956; storm-petrels and coots, Boersma & Davies 1987; pelicans, Lingle & Sloan 1979; and plovers, Jackson & Jackson 2006), this should be a reliable method for sexing females of all medium-sized and large birds. Both width and length of cloacal openings can be measured and values determined to separate the sexes. For example, studies by Boersma & Davies (1987) and Jackson & Jackson (2006) calculated that cloacal lengths > 7.0 mm and widths > 4.4 mm indicated female Fork-tailed Storm-Petrels (p. 279) after stimulated contraction, lengths of > 4.4 mm and widths of > 3.5 mm indicated female American Coots (p. 488) after simulated contraction, and widths of > 4.5 mm indicated female Killdeer (p. 530). Values for other species need to be calculated individually, although visual examination of the condition of the cloaca is usually enough to sex individuals (especially of

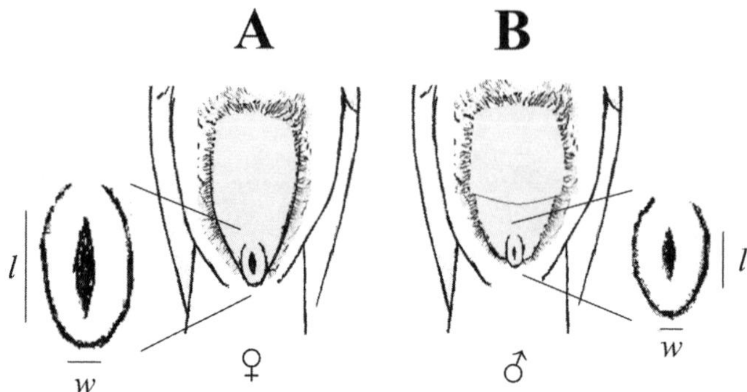

FIGURE 21. Cloacal region in ♀ (**A**) and ♂ (**B**) birds during the breeding season. Distended cloacae can be used to identify breeding ♀♀; dimensions (*l* and *w*) of the cloaca can be measured with calipers or a ruler to include the inside portion of the opening. See Fork-tailed Storm-Petrel (p. 279), American Coot (p. 488), and Killdeer (p. 530) for sex-specific measurements; similar measures likely can be used to sex most species treated here (study needed). Artificially contracting the cloaca with alcohol (*cf.* Boersma & Davies 1987) may produce more standardized measures. See also Hamerstrom & Skinner (1971) for techniques on prolapsing the cloacae of raptors to identify sex. In addition to the difference in cloacal size, note the subtle difference in shape of the abdomen, most apparent during the breeding season. ♀♀ tend to have smoothly oblong abdomens (stretched for egg laying) whereas ♂♂ often have a step at the diaphram and a more truncated base near the cloaca.

mated pairs), with experience, during periods up to several weeks following egg-laying. In addition to the expanded cloacal opening, note that the shape of the abdomen is usually distended in females, whereas in males the diaphram is often more pronounced and the end of the abdomen is more truncated (Fig. 21). Beware, however, that some males may also develop slightly swollen cloacal regions during the breeding season, which may superficially resemble these regions in females during times of cloacal distension. Cloacal dimensions and abdominal shape cannot be used to sex individuals outside of the breeding season or to reliably sex males during the breeding season, as non-breeding females can exhibit similar characters to males.

Cloacal Examination

In waterfowl, the presence and size of the penis in males or the closed or opened oviduct in females has long been used to accurately determine sex of live birds (including chicks), and to help determine age through at least mid-winter in first-cycle (HY/SY) ducks and second-cycle (SY/TY) large geese (Hochbaum 1942, Hanson 1949, Bellrose et al. 1961). The presence and depth of the **bursa of Fabricius** (hereafter "**bursa**"), which opens in the cloaca, has been used to age waterfowl, gamebirds, and a few other taxa through the first-cycle and for larger birds into or through the second cycle as well (Gower 1939). The presence and status of the sexual organs and bursa are easily examined on live waterfowl by angling the tail toward the back on an upside-down bird, parting the cloacal region with the thumb and forefinger, and using a probe or nasal speculum if necessary to view the inside of the cloaca (Hochbaum 1942; Elder 1946; Hanson 1949, 1953; Larson & Taber 1980; Fig. 22). In certain taxa (such as shorebirds) the bursa does not reach the cloaca and cannot be used in ageing (McNeil & Burton 1972, Petrides 1950), and in other taxa besides waterfowl, presence and status of sexual organs may be difficult to assess (Hochbaum 1942; *cf.* Hamerstrom & Skinner 1971), but these methods of ageing and sexing need to be explored more fully in most taxa treated in this guide.

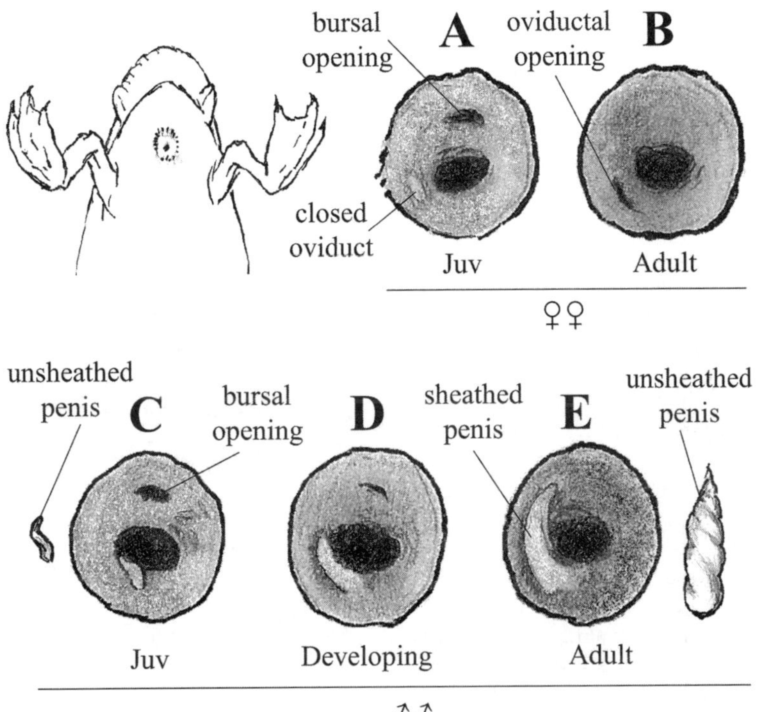

FIGURE 22. Cloacae of live waterfowl and gamebirds for age and sex determination according to presence and condition of sexual organs and bursa of Fabricius (Fig. 23, p. 34); further study is needed on the use of these characters in other large birds. To view the cloaca hold the subject bird upside down as shown, cock the tail toward the back, and part the cloacal region with thumb and forefinger. The cloaca may need to be partially inverted for optimal viewing, and a probe or speculum can greatly facilitate examination; e.g., to determine if an oviductal opening is closed or not. The illustrations (**A-E**) orient the cloaca as shown in the upper-left illustration, dorso-ventrally from below. The cloaca is translucent in Juvs (**A**, **C**) but often becomes darker and reddish (to blackish in some species) as adults (**B**, **E**). The bursal opening is toward the top, and is usually present in Juvs, first-cycle HY/SYs (**A**, **C**) and some developing second-cycle SY/TYs of species that do not breed until two years or older (**D**), but absent in adults of definitive-cycle AHY/ASYs or ASY/ATYs (**B**, **E**). See Figure 23 for more details on the bursa. In Juvs and first-cycle ♀ ducks and gamebirds (and some second-cycle ♀ geese and swans), the oviductal opening is covered by a membrane (**A**) and may not be detectable until sometime during late winter or early spring in SYs (or TY geese and swans), after which it opens and appears as a conspicuous slit on the left side of the cloacal wall (**B**). Juv and HY/SY ♂ waterfowl exhibit a smaller translucent penis along the lower portion of the cloacal wall (**C**); caution that it can easily be missed in some species (*cf.* Henny et al. 1981). When inverted (inset) it is no longer than 8-12 mm in length. The penis develops at variable rates such that, in adults, the penis is enveloped by a redder sheath (**D-E**) and is spiraled and typically 50-90 mm in length during the breeding season when unsheathed (inset). In ducks development of a mature penis (**E**) may occur by December-May in HY/SYs but some SYs may only develop a reduced penis (**D**). In larger species such as geese and swans it takes much longer to develop, such that TYs can often be identified in the breeding season (Feb-Jun in N.Am) by an intermediate-sized penis, 15-50 mm in length (**D**). In the non-breeding season (Jul-Jan) AHY/ASYs typically show reduced penises (**D**) and should not be aged to SY/TY or ASY/ATY by this character alone. More precise calculations of oviductal opening by species and age, and penile length by species, age, and season may enable more refined age-determination in waterfowl and other birds; further study is needed.

The cloaca consists of the intestinal opening in the center, a bursal opening in younger birds toward the head of the bird, and the sex organs on the left side, when viewing from the outside and ventrally as shown in Figure 22. Besides the presence of sexual organs and bursal opening, the cloaca can become more pigmented by age, from pale pinkish in juveniles to dark reddish or even blackish in older geese, at least (Elder 1946, Hanson 1949); study is needed on more precise pigmentation rates by age and species. The presence of an oviduct and whether or not it is covered by an occluding membrane can be used to identify and infer age in females (Fig. 21**A**-**B**), and the presence and size of the penis can be used to identify and infer age in males (Fig. 21**C**-**E**). With experience, sex can be quickly and accurately determined in live waterfowl and, based on the condition of the sexual organs, age can be inferred through at least December in first-cycle HYs and often into or through the second-cycle (SY/TY) in larger species. Note that penis size can also vary by season in adults (Johnson 1961), being full in Feb-Jun (Fig. 22**E**) and regressed in Jul-Jan (Fig. 22**D**). More study is needed on the precise timing that the oviduct opens and the penis develops; in waterfowl, development appears to be correlated with age of first breeding, occurring during the first-cycle in most ducks but during the second cycle or later in larger ducks, geese, and swans, that do not begin breeding until age 2 or older.

The bursa of Fabricius is a sac-like lymphoid organ extending from the dorsal wall of the cloaca in juvenile birds of certain species (Boyden 1922, Glick 1983; Figs. 22 & 23). Within the first two to three years of life, the bursa regresses such that it is absent in adults. Thus, length of the bursal sac (*cf.* Fig. 23**A**-**B**) can be used to age live birds of certain species through the first cycle (HY/SYs) and often into or through the second cycle (SY/TYs). As with development and appearance of sexual organs in the cloaca, the use of the bursa to age live birds of many taxa needs further investigation.

The bursal opening can be examined and measured in live waterfowl and gamebirds, with experience, in a similar manner as other cloacal features are examined (Elder 1946, Gower 1939, Hanson 1949, Hochbaum 1942, Kirkpatrick 1944, Linduska 1943). A blunt probe or gauge is needed to investigate the bursal opening, above the intestinal opening when viewed from the outside and ventrally (Fig. 22**A**, **C**). An anesthetic may be useful in relaxing the area surrounding the bursal opening (Elder 1946). Gently rotate the probe or gauge and carefully insert it into the bursal opening until the depth can be read or estimated. If the bursal opening cannot be found it typically indicates that it has fully regressed (Figs. 22**C** & 23**C**), indicating an adult individual.

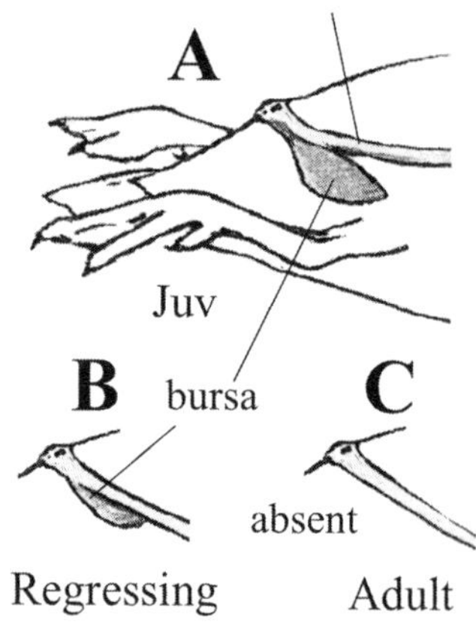

FIGURE 23. Variation in the size and length of the bursa of Fabricius, a sac-like lymphoidal organ, by age and maturity in birds. See Figure 22 (p. 33) for a good hold to view the bursa and the placement of the bursal opening within the cloaca given a dorso-ventral orientation from below. In Juvs (**A**) the bursa reaches maximum length at about the time of fledging, ranging from 8-10 mm to 30-50 mm depending on bird size (see text). It regresses at variable rates, depending on age of first reproduction, and is absent or < 5 mm long in breeding adults (**C**). Bursal length can be measured in at least some taxa (e.g., waterfowl and gamebirds) but not others (e.g., shorebirds) with a probe or gauge (see text). For species first breeding at one year of age, bursal presence and length (**A**-**B**) can be used to age HY/SYs through late winter or spring, and to age some SYs (**B**) through the first cycle or so. In species first breeding at two years of age or older, SY/TYs can be identified by having intermediate-length bursae (**B**), 8-20 mm in most larger species (see text). In very large species with older ages of first breeding (such as albatrosses) it may take up to four years or longer for the bursa to fully regress. More study is needed both on the ability to age live birds by bursal length, and the rates of bursal recrudence in most species treated in this guide.

Bursal lengths appear also to be correlated with age of first breeding. Information from the few species for which data has been collected suggest that juveniles (Fig. 23**A**) typically have bursal sacs that range from 8-10 mm in smaller species such as California Quail (p. 206; Lewin 1963) to 30-50 mm in larger species such as geese (Elder 1946, Hanson 1949). In species that breed during their first cycle, including dabbling ducks (Esler & Grand 1994, Hochbaum 1942, Ward & Middleton 1971), pheasants (Kirkpatrick 1944), and quail (Lewin 1963), the bursa tends to regress by the first spring and thus can only be used to separate HY/SYs through Jan-May and AHYs through December. In species that do not breed until two years or older, such as geese (Elder 1946, Hanson 1949, Higgins 1969), diving ducks (Anderson et al. 1969, Henny et al. 1981, Iverson et al. 2003, Mather & Esler 1999, Peterson & Ellarson 1978), grebes (Storer & Jehl 1985), shearwaters (Gould et al. 1998), cormorants (Siegel-Causey 1989, 1990), and gulls (Johnston 1956), the bursa appears to take up to two years to regress, such that SY/TYs can potentially be identified by having bursae that are 8-20 mm in length (Fig. 23**B**). In albatross, bursal regression according to examination of fresh dead birds may take 4-5 years, coinciding with age of first breeding (Broughton 1994), but it is unknown if bursal length can be determined on live Procellariiformes or most taxa other than waterfowl and Galliformes in the hand. As mentioned above, bursal length cannot be used to age live shorebirds as the opening does not pass through the cloacal wall, and this condition may extend to all Charadriiformes. Further study is needed on the use of the bursae to age most birds treated in this guide, especially those that do not commence breeding until two years or more. Once cloacal criteria have been established for these species, they have the potential to provide excellent independent assessments of age, with which to cross-check plumage-related and other criteria.

OTHER TECHNIQUES

Many other techniques exist for ageing and sexing birds in the hand. Some of these, such as direct gonadal examination (*cf.* Larson & Taber 1980), can only be performed on dead or recently deceased birds. Others, such as those involving surgical techniques, biochemical analysis, or DNA extraction may require expensive equipment and may not be practical for use in all studies. In certain species treated in this guide, mated pairs or birds on the breeding grounds can be sexed by voice (e.g., Brooke 1978a, 1988; Carlson & Trost (1992); Nelson 1978a, 2005) or behavior (e.g., Burger & Beer 1975, Butler & Janes-Butler 1983, Southern 1981), but a full treatment of these differences are beyond the scope of this guide. Here a few of these laboratory techniques are briefly summarized, and a selection of references are provided for further research if desired.

Ageing and Sexing Juveniles

Growing chicks and juveniles are usually aged by developmental criteria and often are indistinguishable to sex; thus, their treatment here is often restricted to a brief description of juvenal plumage aspects and to the months of the year in which they usually are found. In passerines, juvenal plumage can be looser in texture and more streaked or spotted than that of birds in formative or basic plumage (Pyle 1997), but for species treated in this guide this only applies to gallinaceous birds (Fig. 116, p. 166) and perhaps a few other species. However, certain species including ducks (*cf.* Fig. 110, p. 159); grebes (Fig. 175, p. 230); spoonbills, storks, and vultures (pp. 374-390), and Killdeer (Fig. 394, p. 530) can retain downy feathers or downy nessoptile feather tips well into the first cycle or longer. For birds that develop stronger juvenal plumage, the uniform freshness of feathers often indicates a juvenile bird (*cf.* Fig. 14**A**, p. 21) as compared to a worn post-breeding adult, and juvenal upperpart feathers often display more conspicuous fringing than formative or basic feathers. See Figures 30 (p. 55), 169 (p. 222), 187 (p. 248), 236 (p. 319), 252 (p. 348), 291 (p. 394), 397 (p. 536), and 436 (p. 587) for examples in different families. This often gives juveniles a finely scaled appearance, not present in subsequent plumage aspects of the same species.

In addition, nestling characters are often evident in juveniles and can be helpful in separating them from adults. The legs of nestlings or chicks and recently fledged juveniles can be more swollen and fleshier than those of adults, and the bill, and sometimes the wing, can take up to a month or more after fledging to reach full size. The gape of nestlings or chicks can be swollen and more brightly colored than it is in adults. These traits often are still present in fledged juveniles. The inside of the mouth can be brighter in juveniles than in adults. Most of these characters rapidly become less evident as the juvenile ages, although some can be used through the first cycle (HY/SYs) in certain species. Iris color of juveniles in many species can be duller, darker, or less colorful than is found in adults, especially in those species with brightly colored eyes. In contrast, several characters useful for separating first-year birds from adults can also be applied to juveniles. Molt-related criteria such as the absence or occurrence of molting flight feathers, the pattern of fault bars (Fig. 18, p. 27), and differences in flight-feather shape and wear (Fig. 19, p. 28) are applicable to the separation of juveniles from older birds.

In most species treated in this guide, birds in juvenal plumage cannot be reliably sexed by in-hand criteria alone. Cloacal examination (Fig. 22, p. 33) can be used to sex juvenile and even nestling waterfowl and, in several species, sexual size-dimorphism will apply to full-grown juveniles, especially individuals of the larger sex, which can be either female or male for species treated here. In a few species that are sexually dichromatic in formative plumage, such as ducks and gallinaceous birds, brighter male characters can be expressed in the juvenal plumage aspect of at least some individuals (*cf.* Fig. 156, p. 206).

Filoplumes

Filoplumes are poorly-understood, modified hair-like feathers that are typically whitish and more filamentous than pinnate feathers (Chandler 1916, Clark & de Cruz 1989). In cormorants, filoplumes have been modified into secondary sexual characters (Nelson 2005) and average much more extensive in definitive-cycle ASY/ATYs than in first-cycle HY/SYs; second-cycle SY-TYs may show intermediate amounts of filoplume development. Procellariiformes also tend to exhibit filoplumes in older but not first-cycle individuals (Fig. 193, p. 252; Imber 1971, James 1986, Plant 1989). Although filoplumes are more detectable on species with black plumage aspect, it is possible that they may also occur and be detectable in other species, and further study is needed on their relationship to age in birds.

Skull Pneumatization

The extent of skull pneumatization, as viewed on live birds through "skulling" has proven a very useful method for ageing live passerine birds up to six months or more in age (Pyle 1997) but thus far has not been applicable to non-passerines. When a juvenile bird fledges, the section of the skull overlying the brain (frontals and parietal) consists of a single layer of bone. During the first months or year of life a second layer develops underneath the first, the two layers being slightly separated by spaces or air pockets, and joined by small columns of bone. The process by which this second layer, the air pockets, and the columns develop is referred to as skull pneumatization.

Whereas most passerines complete the pneumatization process, such that two layers of bone cover the entire skull, most to all non-passerines do not complete pneumatization (Davis 1947, Harrison 1957, Johnston 1958, McNeil & Burton 1972, Siegel-Causey 1989, Winkler 1979). It is possible, however, that the relative sizes of "windows" (unpneumatized areas) in the skull are age-specific in certain species (*cf.* Harrison 1957, Johnston 1958, McNeil & Burton 1972, Sugimora et al. 1985) despite physiological reasons (related to brain size) that cause the skull pneumatization process to slow substantially when a juvenile non-passerine has reached full size (Jenni & Winkler 1994). More study is needed on rates and degree of skull pneumatization in non-passerines birds. The above-cited studies have all been performed on skeletal material from specimens; even if pneumatization rates are found to vary with age among waterbirds, raptors, and/or gamebirds, however, it is doubtful that skulling live birds of these species will be feasible, except perhaps with the smallest species, due to the thickness of the epidermis or initial layer of bone covering the cranium (*cf.* Pyle 1997). The use of electromagnetic radiation (x-ray) techniques (*cf.* Harrison 1957, Sugimora et al. 1985) to assess skull pneumatization on live birds could be further investigated.

Surgical and Biochemical Techniques

Several other surgical or biochemical techniques may be used to age or sex live birds in the hand, in given situations. Most of these require special equipment and/or experience, and descriptions of these are beyond the scope of this guide. Techniques for sexing live birds include laparotomy (e.g., Bailey 1953, Fiala 1979, Risser 1971, Wingfield & Farner 1976) and the less intrusive laparoscopy (Bush 1986, Richner 1989), various methods of DNA examination (e.g., Lessells & Mateman 1998, Longmire et al. 1993, Norris-Caneda & Elliott 1998, Nota & Takenaka 1999, Rasch & Kertin 1976, Sabo et al. 1994, Tomasulo et al. 2002), examination of fecal steroids (e.g., Bercovitz et al. 1978, Dieter 1973, Stavy et al. 1979), analysis of flow cytometry (e.g., Ellegren & Sheldon 1997), and ultrasonography (e.g., Hildebrandt et al. 1995). Laboratory techniques for ageing live birds include analysis of levels of skin pentosidine (e.g., Chaney et al. 2003, Fallon et al. 2006) and telomere length from blood chromosomes (e.g., Haussmann & Mauck 2008, Haussmann & Vleck 2002, Haussmann et al. 2003, Juola et al. 2006), whereas techniques for ageing freshly killed birds include quantifying endosteal layers in the tibia (e.g., Klomp & Furness 1992, but see Nelson & Bookhout 1980) and examination of other osteological criteria (e.g., Broughton et al. 2002, Jannett 1983, Stone & Morris 1981, Van Soust & Van Utrecht 1971).

HYBRIDS

An attempt was made to list all reported hybrids involving the species treated in this guide. This was greatly facilitated by the recent thorough compilation of hybrid birds by McCarthy (2006; see Pyle 2006b). Additional references are cited when they include substantial information on plumage-aspect variation in hybrids and parental species. Unless the parental species are known directly, the identity of hybrids is difficult to confirm; thus, many of the reports should be considered unconfirmed. Hybrids can take various plumage-aspect combinations of parental species, and hybridization also can revive ancestral characters causing hybrids to resemble unrelated species. On the other hand, beware of pure individuals showing totally or partially amelanistic or other anomalous plumage-aspect coloration (*cf.* Davis 2007), which may coincidentally cause them to resemble a suspected hybrid with another species. Hybrids are of substantial interest to ornithologists and should be documented carefully when encountered. See Gray (1958), McCarthy (2006), and Sibley (1994) for more information.

GEOGRAPHIC VARIATION

Geographic variation within species takes many forms among North American birds. Size, plumage aspect, and other phenotypic parameters vary with climate, habitat, altitude, migratory strategy, and other factors (Barrowclough 1990, James 1970, Zink & Remsen 1986). Overall, geographic variation is much more developed among North American passerines and near passerines (Pyle 1997) than it is among waterbirds, owing primarily to the more-sedentary habits of most landbird species; for taxa treated here, geographic variation is most developed among diurnal raptors and Galliformes. Knowledge of geographic variation can assist with ageing and sexing, especially as it relates to differences in molt strategies (see p. 501-507 for discussion of this subject in shorebirds). Thus, geographic variation should be considered when identifying, ageing, and sexing birds.

Unlike in Part 1 (Pyle 1997), some taxonomic recommendations have been made in the **Geographic variation** sections of this guide, in an attempt to standardize recognition of morphological subspecies and to add more objectivity to diagnoses (see Cicero & Johnson 2006, Patten & Unitt 2002 for discussion). Generally this has resulted in previously named subspecies being synonymized, according to the precept that 75% of individuals within a subspecies are diagnosable from similar subspecies (Amadon 1949, Amadon & Short 1992); note, however, that the concept of "diagnosis" is vaguely defined and biased by variation in observer acuity. This conservative approach is most evident among shorebirds, where differences in measurement means enabling diagnosis of far less than 75% of individuals have been used to name subspecies (*cf.* Engelmoer & Roselaar 1998, Tomkovich & Serra 1999), and where reported subspecific differences in plumage aspect may result from effects of environmental factors on molt. See Pyle (1997) for more details about patterns of geographic variation in North American passerines and near-passerines, applicable to a few species treated here.

DIRECTIONS FOR USE

In this section, the abbreviations, definitions, and format used in the species accounts are described in detail.

COLORS

Strictly defined and standardized color names (Paclt 1983; Ridgway 1886a, 1912; Smithe 1975, 1981; Tucker et al. 1991) are not used in this guide. Rather, the names used for colors are considered in a relative context within comparative phrases (p. 4) between species, subspecies, or age/sex classes. Geographic and seasonal variation in coloration, along with variable appearances that colors can assume under different molting, dietary, and lighting circumstances (*cf.* Endler 1990; Voitkevich 1966; Hill & Mcgraw 2006, 2007), considerably lessen the usefulness of strictly defined color names. Thus, simplified color names found in current ornithological literature and field guides are found here. Modified color names should be interpreted as the second color tinged with the first (*i.e.*, grayish brown is brown with a gray tinge). The modifiers "dark", "medium-dark", "medium", "medium-pale", and "pale" are used to indicate dark to light tints, respectively. The suffix "-ish" (e.g., "grayish"), when not modifying another color, indicates that more variability can be expected in the nature of the color than is indicated by unmodified color names (e.g., "gray").

MONTHS

All months are abbreviated by their first three letters. Month ranges indicate that the described event or condition may be encountered within the indicated time period, but is usually not found or reliably used during excluded months. Note that not all birds will exhibit an indicated plumage aspect or condition for the entire period indicated (especially during the two extreme months), and that exceptions are always possible. A slash between months (e.g., "Apr/Jul") indicates that the condition may begin or (more often) end within the indicated time frame (Apr through Jul), varying by individual (see further discussion on **Molt**, below). As with ranges in measurements, month ranges should be considered in terms of 95% confidence intervals (p. 4), with the indicated criteria or conditions occurring outside of the given temporal ranges in 5% of individuals.

TAXONOMIC SUMMARIES

Higher-order taxonomic summaries are provided that cover structure, flight-feather counts, criteria for age and sex determinations, and molt. Summaries are given for all families and, for large families such as Anatidae and Scolopacidae, summaries are further subdivided by subfamily and tribe. Characters are summarized that generally apply to all species within the taxonomic subdivision.

SPECIES ACCOUNT FORMAT

The species accounts are broken into the following sections:

Headings

For each species account, the heading includes the English and scientific names, an alpha (four-letter) code derived from the English name, the "AOU number" or "species number", and the recommended band size. English and scientific names (except for some gulls; see pp. 2 & 629) follow those of the AOU (1998) Check-list, as modified by AOU supplements through Banks et al. (2007). Alpha codes follow those recommended by Pyle & DeSante (2003, 2005, 2006). Species numbers and band sizes are those recognized and recommended by the BBL and CWS (CWS and USFWS 1991), as revised through 2007 (D. Bystrak and L.-A. Howes, pers. comm.). When two or more band sizes are given, the first usually indicates the size which best fits a majority of the individuals of the species. With polytypic species, banders should check the **Geographic variation** section and use an appropriate band size for the subspecies in their area. To increase efficiency, several closely related species pairs (and one triplet) are lumped into single species accounts. Species were combined only when molt patterns and age/sex-determination criteria apply similarly to all species. Names, alpha codes, species numbers, and in some cases band sizes are provided for subspecies, morphs, hybrids, or distinct populations that are recognized as species subunits by the CWS and BBL (see Pyle & DeSante 2003).

Species

Entries for identifying birds to species are given in all accounts. Unlike in Part 1, more details are given than absolutely essential, because (1) anomalous individuals and hybrids may be encountered that necessitate synthesis of all criteria to reach an identification; and (2) it is anticipated that this guide may be used during beach, wind-generator, or other surveys, or during "wing bees", where only a portion of a carcass may be available to aid in species identification. Size characters are generally listed first, followed by plumage aspect and/or other characters, in the form of comparative phrases (p. 4), and in descending order of diagnosability. To assist with identifications, users should refer to field guides in conjunction with the species-identification accounts.

Geographic Variation

Many species treated here have consistently been considered monotypic (no recognized subspecies), others have well-marked subspecies (polytypic), and others fall in between, having named subspecies considered valid by some but not all taxonomists. For species considered monotypic here but polytypic by other authors, justification is provided for synonymization. In all cases, an attempt has been made to reference all subspecies recognized by Peters (1931a, 1934a, 1937) and subsequent authors, and to provide a brief indication of characters used to diagnose synonymized populations. Historical references treating the identification of subspecies are listed, whether or not the subspecies under discussion has been synonymized here.

For species with recognized subspecies, all subspecies documented from North America (north of Mexico) are listed, along with brief descriptions which may assist in their identification. As in other sections, comparative phrases (p. 4) are provided among listed subspecies, and characters are ordered according to diagnosability. Among species with many subspecies, "**subspecies groups**" are also defined, representing geographically concordant groups of subspecies (occasionally a single subspecies) with shared characters (Amadon & Short 1992). Subspecific ranges include the terms resident (**res**), breeding (**br**), wintering (**wint**), and/or **vagrant**, and are defined in North America based on two-letter postal abbreviations for United States and standard abbreviations for each province in Canada (see Fig. 23 in Pyle 1997). Small-case letters (e.g., "e.", "nw.", "sc.", etc.) indicate locations ("eastern", "northwestern", "south-central", respectively) within the state or province. Other abbreviations include **Co** (County), **Cos** (Counties), **I** (Island), and **Is** (Islands). It should be noted that the boundaries for ranges of many subspecies may be inexact or temporally unstable, and that ranges for vagrants may not be comprehensive; thus, the ranges given for each subspecies should be considered only in a general context. Pyle and Desante (2003) provide rules for the derivation of six-letter codes for species and subspecies based on scientific name.

Molt

Molt accounts begin with indication of which of the four basic molt strategies (p. 16) is most likely employed by the species, based on available data. Other possible strategies are often given, along with the need for more study on molt in these species. Identified molts for all cycles through the definitive molt cycle (p. 13) are listed with abbreviations (e.g., **PF** for preformative molt, **PA1** for first prealternate molt, **PB2** for second prebasic molt, **DPB** for definitive prebasic molt, etc., defined on pp. 13-15), followed by information on extent and timing. In certain species for which age of first breeding is variable, breeding status is also indicated (e.g., as "non-breeding SYs" and "breeding AHYs"), as breeding individuals often exhibit a different strategy than non-breeding individuals for a given molt. Extent of each molt is indicated by one or more of the following:

Absent – No molt or feather replacement occurs.

Limited – Some but not all body feathers and no **flight feathers** (primaries, primary coverts, secondaries, and rectrices) are replaced.

Partial – Most or all body feathers and sometimes the tertials and/or central rectrices, but no other flight feathers, are replaced.

Incomplete – Most to all body feathers and some but not all flight feathers (excluding tertials and central rectrices) are replaced.

Complete – All body and flight feathers are replaced.

Extents of molts are subject to individual, geographic, and interannual variation, particularly in species for which more than one extent is indicated. Given ranges are intended to include what is typical of 95% of the population (see p. 4); 5% of individuals may replace fewer or more feathers than indicated.

Timing of each molt is indicated by month ranges covering a period in which 95% (see pp. 4 & 38) of feathers are molted within the population. Note that individuals often take less time to molt and thus some percentage will exhibit no molt during indicated periods, particularly in species whose molting grounds extend over a wide range of latitudes (*cf.* shorebirds, pp. 501-505). A slash between months, e.g., "Sep-Jan/May", indicates that the timing of the beginning or (more often) end of the molt is variable among individuals by at least a period of three months; the above example indicates that the molt typically begins in Sep (some to most may begin in Oct or Nov) and can complete anywhere from Jan to May among individuals. Less than 5% of individuals may be expected to begin molt in Aug, or complete it in Dec or Jun. Molt timings (hence temporal periods for reliable age determinations; see below) refer to populations that breed in North America north of Mexico; breeding populations of wide-ranging species usually exhibit varying molt strategies, often more extended in tropical populations, and often during opposite times of the year in populations breeding in the Southern Hemisphere.

Localities of molt are indicated next, expressed by the terms "**breeding grounds**", "**molting grounds**", "**non-breeding grounds**", and "**stopover sites**". Note that breeding and non-breeding grounds for molt may pertain to overall population ranges and not necessarily to breeding or non-breeding territories of individuals. Molting grounds generally refer to areas where a substantial proportion of a breeding population concentrates to molt, most notable in waterfowl (p. 47). Stopover sites refer to areas between breeding and non-breeding grounds in which individuals are not necessarily concentrated. Further study is needed on exact localities of molt, especially of definitive prebasic molts relative to breeding territories during post-breeding time periods; see p. 12 regarding the use of stable isotopes to investigate molt locations.

Further details on extent, timing, and sequence of each molt are then given for each species. Modifiers used to indicate proportions of the populations displaying given molt conditions include: **rarely** (1-4% of the populations), **occasionally** (5-20%), **sometimes** (21-50%), **often** (51-75%), and **usually** (76-95%). No modifier indicates that > 95% of the population (p. 4) can be expected to have the indicated molting condition. Additional information on extent and sequence can be found in the taxonomic summaries (see p. 38) beginning each family or lower-order section.

Age/Sex

Specific mensural, plumage-aspect, and bare-part criteria, in the form of comparative phrases (p. 4), are given for ageing and sexing each species. For most species in this guide, **Age** and **Sex** are separated into different sections, but these sections are combined under **Age/Sex** for some species in which plumage-aspect variation interacts substantially with both age and sex. Ageing and sexing criteria should be combined before either age or sex determinations are made, particularly regarding measurement values, which often vary by both age and sex (p. 5). Thus, even when **Age** and **Sex** sections are separated, users are encouraged to consider them simultaneously. Field guides can provide additional helpful illustrations of age/sex classes but note that some age/sex representations in field guides may not be entirely reliable.

Age and/or sex accounts begin with a brief description of juvenal (**juv** or B1) plumage aspect and bare-part colors typical of juveniles (**Juvs**), along with information on sexing juveniles (not possible in most cases; pp. 35-36). Information on the use and timing of brood patches (**BP**s; Fig. 20, p. 31) and distended cloacae (Fig. 21, p. 32), and the usefulness of measurements for sexing are also given for all species. **Banders should not use wing chord or tail length data alone to designate sex codes in data submissions to the CWS and BBL (see pp. 45-46), unless mensural information is given in sex-specific comparative phrases (p. 4), indicating substantial ability to diagnose sex by measurements.** Where available, information on sexing by discriminant function analyses (DFAs; p. 5) or ageing or sexing based on less traditional techniques (pp. 35-37) are often given in this section.

Calendar-based age categories follow those of (Pyle 1997), as based on the system used by the CWS and BBL (CWS & USFWS 1991). **HY** represents a bird in its first calendar ("hatching") year. **SY**, **TY**, **4Y**, **5Y**, etc. indicate birds in their second, third, fourth, fifth, etc. calendar years of life. Birds with delayed plumage-aspect maturation can exhibit overlap in age-determination criteria between adjacent cohorts (see p. 29), and some seabird and other species can breed in Dec-Jan, making it difficult to determine which calendar-year class applies. In such cases the terms, e.g., **H-SY**, **S-TY**, **T-5Y**, etc., can be used to indicate individuals that are either HY or SY; SY or TY; TY, 4Y, or 5Y; etc., respectively, but have not yet reached a definitive state. The terms, **AHY**, **ASY**, **ATY**, **A4Y**, etc., indicate individuals in definitive cycles that can be designated as older than (or "After") their HY, SY, TY, 4Y, etc. These individuals are of unknown exact age but can be assigned a minimum age at which the youngest of individuals reach the definitive cycle. The age-code **U** ("unknown") is occasionally used in this guide and indicates that a definitive cycle or state has been reached but it is unknown if an individual is in its first (hatching) or subsequent year of life.

Identifiable age categories usually represent plumage cycles, which typically span two calendar years; thus, two calendar-based categories (separated by a slash) are usually given, followed by month ranges spanning the plumage cycle and including the end of the first calendar year and beginning of the yext year. For example, **HY/SY (Oct-Sep)** indicates a bird in its first cycle that can be aged HY in Oct-Dec and SY in Jan-Sep. A single age-code is given only when the described plumage aspect or condition occurs within, or coincides with, a calendar year; i.e., "**SY (Jul-Dec)**" indicates that the given age-determination criteria apply through Dec but not into Jan. For species that breed and/or molt year-round, month ranges track plumage cycles for the majority of individuals, but beware that some individuals will have plumage cycles that may not be synchronous with month spans following age-group designations.

For convenience, the cycle and different plumages within the cycle (pp. 12-16) are also given for each identifiable age category. For example, **HY/SY (1st cycle, F1-A1; Oct-Sep)** indicates a bird in its first cycle that can be aged HY from Oct-Dec and SY from Jan-Sep. The preformative molt occurs (or at least begins) on the breeding grounds and full juvenal plumage is excluded from the month range. By contrast, **Juv-HY/SY (1st cycle, Juv/B1-F1-A1; Sep-Aug)** indicates that the species typically migrates in juvenal plumage or can retain complete juvenal plumage for a substantial proportion of the first cycle. In either case, the month range for full juvenal plumage is given in the text above the age-group accounts. "F1-A1" in both examples indicates that the species typically undergoes both a preformative and a first prealternate molt, and that formative and first alternate plumages can thus be expected. **SY/TY (2nd cycle, B2; Oct-Sep)** indicates a bird in its second cycle that can be aged SY from Oct-Dec and TY from Jan-Sep. The "B2" alone indicates that the species remains in second basic plumage throughout the cycle and that no second prealternate molt or alternate plumage occurs. **TY/4Y (3rd cycle, B3-A3; Sep-Aug)** indicates a third-cycle bird, aged TY in Sep-Dec and 4Y in Jan-Aug, in which some or or all individuals have a third alternate plumage. **T-4Y (3rd-4th cycles, B3-B4; Jan-Dec)** and **4-6Y (4th-6th cycles, B4-B6; Jan-Dec)** are examples designating predefinitive two-year or three-year age-category periods in which the precise cycle is unknown (see p. 41). Note that, for clarity, month ranges in these cases are simply designated "Jan-Dec"; it might be anticipated that individuals in the second half of a calendar year may more often be of younger indicated age designations (TY or 4Y in the above examples) whereas those in earlier portions of the year may be of older designations (4Y or 6Y in the above examples).

AHY/ASY (Def. cycle, DB-DA; Oct-Sep), **ASY/ATY (Def. cycle, DB; Oct-Sep)**, and **ATY/A4Y (Def. cycle, DB; Oct-Sep)** are examples of definitive age designations of individuals in at least their second, third, and fourth cycles, respectively, that can be given the first age code in Oct-Dec and the second age code in Jan-Sep. In the first case the species can exhibit a definitive alternate plumage aspect. Designations such as **U/AHY (Def. cycle, DB-DA; Nov-Oct)** are occasionally used, indicating that the cycle cannot always be determined (and aspect equates to that of definitive plumage), individuals of unknown age being coded U in Nov-Dec and AHY in Jan-Oct.

Terminal months in the range indicate the point at which individuals can no longer be identified to given cycles or age groups, based on the progress of prebasic molts. End dates for age determination can vary substantially among individuals according to variable timings of molts (see pp. 40-41). During periods before, during, and after terminal months, it is best to consider how molt affects reliability of plumage-aspect criteria. If an individual has completed the molt, for instance, the criteria may no longer apply in the final month or two of the given period. Alternatively, given criteria may enable ageing of molting birds a month or more after the period given. Both incoming and outgoing plumages should be considered carefully when categorizing molting birds to age; the aspect of an outgoing plumage is typically more informative. In some cases age designations cannot be assigned throughout a cycle or year, resulting in designations such as **SY/TY (2nd cycle, B2; Sep-May)** or **ASY/ATY (Def. cycle, DB; Oct-Mar)**. These are typically found in species with protracted second or definitive prebasic molts, respectively, in which at least some individuals can be identified by aspect of the previous feather generation until the molts are completed. Note in the first example that the plumage designation is second basic (B2), based on the definition of cycles as beginning with the initial replacement of primaries (p. 13).

In many cases, some individuals of a given age-group (e.g., TYs) can be aged by predefinitive aspect characters whereas other individuals of the same age group have reached their definitive plumage aspect. These cases can be recognized by designations for, e.g., both SY/TY and AHY/ASY, or both TY/4Y and ASY/ATY, indicating that some individuals can be aged SY/TY or TY/4Y whereas others must be aged by the more conservative designations AHY/ASY or ASY/ATY, respectively.

Sex-specific descriptions are often designated under the single symbols ♀ and ♂, indicating that all individuals showing post-juvenal plumage aspects can be sexed (refer to **Age** account for sexing Juvs in these cases). In other cases these symbols are accompanied by age designations and/or month ranges, to indicate age-specific or temporal limitations for sex determinations. For example, **AHY/ASY ♀** indicates that only AHY/ASYs (as defined under **Age**) can be sexed, and **ASY ♂ (Mar-Aug)** indicates that males can only be sexed as ASYs in Mar-Apr; e.g., only individuals in definitive alternate plumage aspect and/or in breeding condition, can be reliably sexed. In a few species, age and sex sections are combined under **Age/Sex** (see above), leading to designations such as **Juv-HY/SY ♂ (1st cycle, Juv/B1-F1-A1; Sep-Aug)** or **ASY/ATY ♀ (Def. cycle, DB; Oct-Sep)**. Most age designations in these cases have counterparts for both ♀ and ♂; occasionally certain age groups (e.g. SY/TYs) can be identified for males but not females.

Age and/or sex characters are listed in order of diagnosability; thus, earlier-listed criteria typically have more strength in making determinations than later-listed criteria. Regardless, they should always be used not only in combination with each other but also in combination with molt status, measurements, time of year, breeding characters, and the previous experience of the user with the species at hand (see p. 4). Measurements (pp. 4-11) are here listed in tables for convenience and should be consulted when making age/sex determinations.

Hybrids Reported

All species reported to have hybridized in the wild with the species being treated are listed. When both parent taxa are treated in this guide, pertinent references (p. 37) are listed only under the first species and are cross-referenced by page number under the second species. Use of the word "reported" indicates that a degree of uncertainty is usually present concerning identification of parental species (see p. 37). The phrase "in the wild" following the listings indicate that other hybrids are known with the species in captivity; see McCarthy (2006) for details on such hybrids and their parental combinations.

References

References for geographic variation and hybrids are listed separately under those sections. All other references, including those pertaining to species identification, molt, and age/sex determination, or including extensive measurement data, are listed at the end of the account. References derive largely from the North American literature, with Cramp & Simmons (1977, 1980, 1983, 1985), Dement'ev & Gladkov (1951a, 1951b, 1951c, 1952), Higgins & Davies (1996), Marchant & Higgins (1990, 1993), and Portenko (1972, 1973) cited as summaries for other literatures pertaining to species that occur in both North America and Europe, northern Asia, Australia, and Siberia, respectively. Birds of North America (BNA) accounts (Poole & Gill 1993-2002, Poole et al. 1992-1993), now available on line, provided useful summaries of information. To save space, the many citations to BNA accounts are listed in abbreviated rather than full format in the Literature Cited section. Unpublished manuscripts have only been cited in cases where completed drafts are in review or are ready for submission to a scientific journal. There is much other useful information contained in unpublished form (e.g., university theses) which should be published. A total of 3189 references is listed in the **Literature Cited** section. The author would appreciate receiving reprints or electronic copies of any relevant references that were overlooked (see www.SlateCreekPress.com).

BAR GRAPHS

Bar graphs (Fig. 24) indicate our ability to age and sex live birds in the hand and are found within each species account. The bar graphs have two primary purposes: 1) To present information (some of which is additional to that of the text) on the degree to which users can be expected to reliably age and sex birds throughout the year, and 2) to represent the age and sex codes currently accepted by the Canadian Wildlife Service (CWS) and Bird Banding Laboratory (BBL) in data submissions. Referring to Figure 24, the following sections provide information on how to interpret and use the bar graphs.

Ageing and age coding

Reliable ageing and age coding is represented by the horizontal bars, as broken down into monthly segments. Solid black segments indicate that > 95% of birds of that age group (essentially all) generally should be aged as indicated when using all available criteria; cross-hatched segments indicate that 25-95% of birds should be aged as indicated; stippled segments indicate that 5-25% of birds should be aged as indicated; and solid white segments indicate that < 5% of birds (usually none) should be aged as indicated. Note that these proportions indicate the reliability of identifying all birds of the given age class, not the proportion of birds that should be assigned that age code. For example, only a small proportion of Horned Grebes (p. 229) will be aged Juv-HY in June (because few have fledged), but > 95% of birds that have fledged by the end of June should be identifiable as juv-HYs. Question marks (*cf.* the bar graph for Greater White-fronted Goose, p. 56) indicate that it may be possible to reliably apply the age code during those months (and often ensuing months during the following calendar year; e.g., for TY in Greater White-fronted Goose), depending on the results of further study.

The proportions indicated by the cross-hatched and stippled segments should be regarded as general, and were assigned based on the experience of the author with live birds and specimens. These proportions may vary substantially among users of the accounts, based on their previous experience with age-determination in general and with the species in question. An attempt was made to assign proportions representing those of a user with an "average" amount of experience ageing a particular species. To make bar graphs easier to use, the "AHY-U" bar of Pyle (1997) has been split into separate U and AHY bars, as in Horned Grebe.

Proportions indicated by age-bar patterns attempt to represent the species as a whole. In

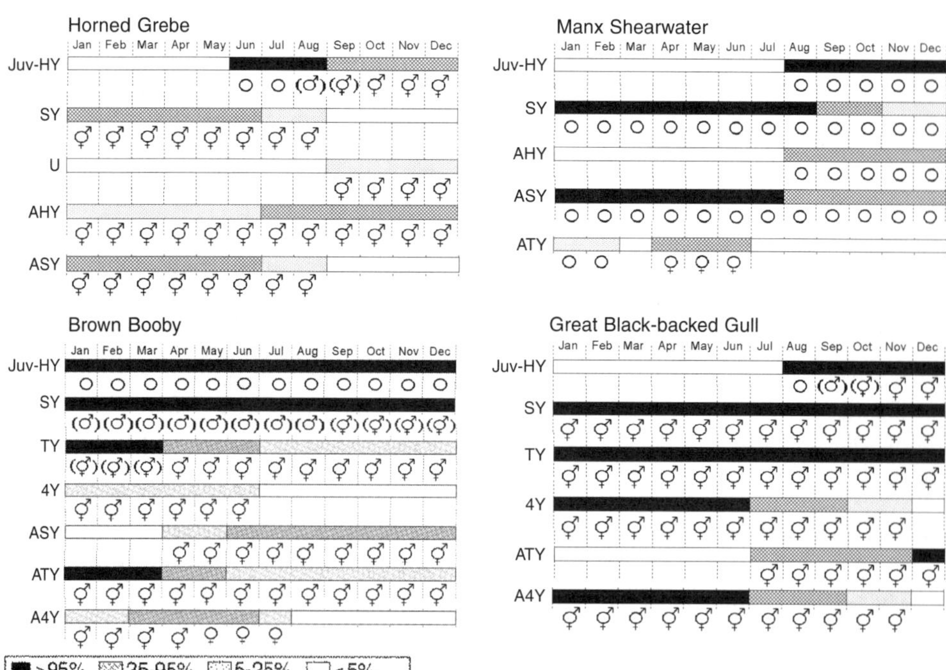

FIGURE 24 - Four examples of bar graphs indicating the reliability of ageing, sexing, and age/sex-code assignment. See text for complete explanation.

months when 5-95% of birds should be aged as indicated (stippled and cross-hatched segments), note that proportion of uncertainty can depend on temporal factors, geographic variation, sex-specific differences, and/or individual variation in the criteria used for reliable ageing (see also Pyle 1997). These periods sometimes apply to an entire cycle; e.g., 25-95% of first-cycle Horned Grebes can be aged HY or SY in Sep-Jun but 5-25% of these may be difficult to determine, and should be aged U or AHY. Ageing with 5-95% certainty usually also applies to periods of transitional plumage aspect due to molts. Such is the case during July-August in Horned Grebe, August-October in Manx Shearwater (p. 271), and July-November in Great Black-backed Gull (p. 671). For ATY Manx Shearwaters in April-June and A4Y Brown Boobies (p. 305) in March-July, the proportion of reliably aged birds increases due to the presence of distended cloacae (Fig. 21, p. 32) in females of these age groups.

Note that, by comparing bars of different age codes, the ageing proportions can often be refined further than is indicated by cross-hatched and stippled patterns alone. For Manx Shearwater in August, for example, 25-95% of individuals should be aged either AHY or ASY, indicating that 25-75% of each should be aged when these two bar segments are used together (as more than 75% is not possible for one age class given that at least 25% of the other can be determined). In September, 25-75% of SYs can also be identified, indicating that the proportion of AHYs that should be aged is only 25-50% (at least 25% each being aged SY and ASY). By comparing bar patterns for ASY Brown Boobies in June, it can be calculated that 25-40% should be aged TY, ATY, and A4Y (hatched pattern), and 5-20% should be aged 4Y and ASY (stippled pattern). In reality the system is not this precise; however, further study and increased experience should allow continued refinement of these proportional concepts.

Sexing and sex coding

Reliable sexing and sex coding is represented by the symbols under the monthly age-bar segments. A female symbol, ♀, a male symbol, ♂, or a "female-male symbol", ⚥, indicate that > 75% of live birds in the hand can be sexed as indicated for that age group and month. Parentheses around these symbols indicate that approximately 5-75% of individuals can be sexed as indicated. A "neither-sex" symbol, ○ indicates that < 5% of birds should be sexed. Sexing proportions are based on the sexing criteria indicated in the text, primarily those of plumage aspect and breeding characters; measurement criteria are incorporated only when all or nearly all individuals within the entire North American range of the species can be sexed based on morphology, as indicated by the inclusion of mensural characters in comparative phrases (p. 4) under **Sex** (see also p. 41).

As with the ageing proportions, sexing proportions can reflect individual, geographic, or temporal variation (within the given month) in our ability to reliably sex birds. In Horned Grebe, reliable sexing can be performed only by bill measurements; thus, for first-cycle juveniles and HYs, < 25% should be reliably sexed in June-July (when bills are not fully developed), 25-75% of males (but not females) can be reliably sexed in August, 25-75% of both sexes can be reliably sexed in September, and > 75% of both sexes can be sexed in October onwards, when bills in all birds are fully developed. Juvenile and HY Great Black-backed Gulls exhibit a similar progression of sexing certainty, based on development and use of head-bill length (Fig. 453, p. 630) for sexing this species. For Manx Shearwater, < 25% (typically none) can be sexed for most age groups throughout the season, with the exception of breeding ATY females in April-June, which exhibit distended cloacae following egg-laying (Fig. 21, p. 32). In such cases mates of known-breeding females may also be reliably sexed male, but this is not indicated in the bar graphs. For Brown Booby, first-cycle juveniles and HYs typically cannot be sexed, but some (5-75%) SY males of the subspecies *S.l. brewsteri* can be sexed in January-August. By September of the second cycle (in SYs) 5-75% of both sexes and of all subspecies can be sexed by bare-part color, and by April of the second cycle onwards, > 75% can be sexed by bare-part color. As with bar patterns for age-code reliability, further study and increased experience should allow continued refinement of these proportions.

CWS and BBL acceptance criteria

The bar graphs represent what is currently accepted by the CWS and BBL on data submissions from banders. For ageing, the CWS and BBL will accept all codes indicated with a solid black bar (> 95% should be aged as indicated) or a cross-hatched bar (25-95% should be aged as indicated). It is up to the bander to be conservative in cases indicated with cross-hatched segments, generally only ageing 25-95% of birds; however, > 95% of individuals may be aged by banders experienced with the species. For segments with the stippled pattern (5-25% of birds being reliably aged as indicated), the CWS and BBL will accept these age codes during these months, but may query certain banders that do not have adequate experience, or who are ageing more than 25% of birds without supplying documentation. **When using the "Juv-HY" bar, note that the CWS and BBL do not accept "Juv" as an age designation. Use "L" for "Local" birds that have not fledged (or have not become flighted for precocial species), and "HY" for birds in juvenal plumage that have fledged and become flighted.** For sexing, all codes indicating that > 75% of birds can be sexed will be accepted in submissions. Banders may be queried if they submit a high proportion of sexed birds where a symbol in parentheses (indicating a 5-75% sexing proportion) is given. Banders may also be queried if they are not ageing or sexing most or all birds, when > 95% ageing or > 75% sexing proportions are indicated. **The CWS and BBL will not accept aged birds during a month-segment indicated by a solid white bar (including those with question marks), or sexed birds during a month indicated by a neither-sex symbol, ○, without accompanying documentation from the bander**. This includes some cases where banders are sexing birds solely by measurements, DFAs (p. 5), or behavioral cues. Certain age-sex combinations are also unacceptable to the CWS and BBL, such as HY-♀ Horned Grebes in August or ATY-♂ Manx Shearwaters in April-June (including mates of known-females sexed by distended cloaca), even though a code for the opposite sex may be accepted. If banders are able to age and/or sex birds in situations where the bar graphs indicate otherwise, they must document their methods when submitting their schedules. They are also urged to provide a copy of their documentation to the author of this guide (see www.SlateCreekPress.com) or to publish their results. In this way, our knowledge of ageing and sexing, as represented by the bar graphs, will continue to be updated and refined.

SPECIMEN COLLECTIONS

The author spent approximately 900 hours in museum collections (95% at the California Academy of Sciences, San Francisco, and Museum of Vertebrate Zoology, Berkeley), and examined over 20,000 specimens in preparation for this guide. The value of these collections in providing and checking information presented here cannot be overestimated. Currently, however, many ornithologists assume that there is little left to learn from specimens, and funding for museum and other collections, and the staff to maintain them, has decreased (see Pyle 1997). Although data on specimen tags, especially concerning sex, should be interpreted with some caution (see Clench 1976, Parkes 1989, Lee & Griffiths 2003), banders, birders, and other ornithologists, are strongly encouraged to utilize specimens in answering questions about identification, molt, and plumage aspect, and to support the continued maintenance of museum and other collections.

Non-targeted collecting of birds in North America is no longer necessary; however, the full utilization of collections will point out areas where judicious collecting to answer specific questions may be warranted. Additional specimens can always help with existing questions, and banders and birders are strongly encouraged (with the appropriate local permits) to save specimens that perish during banding operations or are found under windows or on the road (*cf.* Jett 1991), to carefully note the date, location, and any other pertinent information, and to donate them to the nearest specimen collection.

Species Accounts

DUCKS, GEESE, AND SWANS *ANATIDAE*

Forty-three North American species. Family characters include heavy bodies, broad wings, short tails, and strong legs with webbed feet. North American ducks, geese, and swans ("waterfowl") have 10 functional primaries, 14-26 secondaries (one absent between s4 and s5; see Fig. 12**B**, p. 19), and 14-24 rectrices (variable both among and within species). Ageing through the first cycle (to SY and ASY), and occasionally the second cycle (to TY and ATY) in males, can be accomplished by plumage aspect, primary shape (Fig. 25), and shape and condition of the rectrices (Fig. 26); in certain species SY/TYs can be determined to age by retained juvenal feathers or characteristics. In many species females and males are easily sexed by plumage aspect. Breeding females may also be recognized during the incubation period by partial medial brood patches (Fig. 20**A**, p. 31); usually just bare patches created by feather removal) and transversly distended cloaca (Fig. 21; p. 32), and most individuals can be aged and sexed through AHY/ASY (and possibly SY/TY in many species) by cloacal examination (Figs. 22-23; pp. 32-35). Males average larger than females in all species and this can be useful for sexing mated pairs (of monochromatic species) or juveniles and HYs in certain other species.

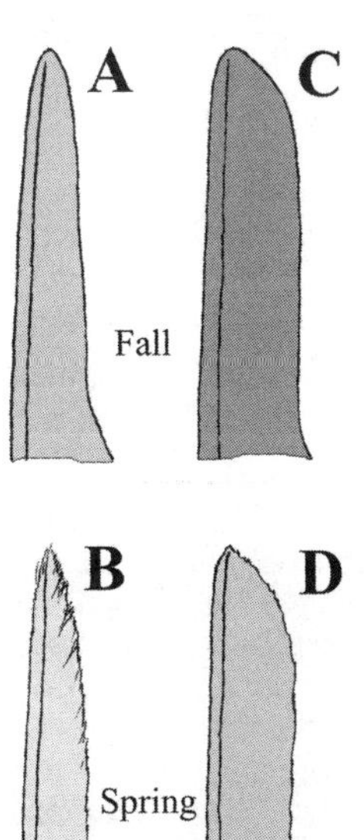

FIGURE 25. Outer primary shapes in waterfowl by age and season. Note that juvenal feathers (**A-C**) become progressively more worn (and thus narrower at the tip) than basic feathers (**C-D**) by spring.

In molting, North American whistling-ducks, geese, and swans exhibit the Complex Basic Strategy (CBS; Fig. 10**B**, pp. 13-16), with a formative plumage but no alternate plumages, whereas ducks exhibit the Complex Alternate Strategy (CAS; Fig. 10**F**), with a formative plumage and alternate plumages in all molt cycles. Preformative molts are partial to incomplete, up to many secondary coverts, one or more tertials, and/or the two central to all rectrices being replaced. During prebasic molts, waterfowl replace most primaries, secondaries, and wing coverts synchronously (or nearly so), becoming flightless for 3-5 weeks, followed by a complete or near-complete molt of the body feathers, tertials, and rectrices (see Pyle 2005 for molt terminology). Many species or individuals, especially males, migrate to "molting grounds", specific protective localities (up to 1000 km from breeding sites), to perform this molt (Salomonsen 1968, Hohman et al. 1992a). In ducks, an added prealternate molt occurs in spring ♀♀ of some species) or summer, often resulting in a cryptic plumage aspect for nesting ♀♀ and for wing molt in both sexes. Age of first breeding varies from 1 to 6 years; prebasic molts of non-breeding AHYs, failed breeders, and breeding males average earlier than those of breeding females within each population. See also subfamily and tribal accounts for more information.

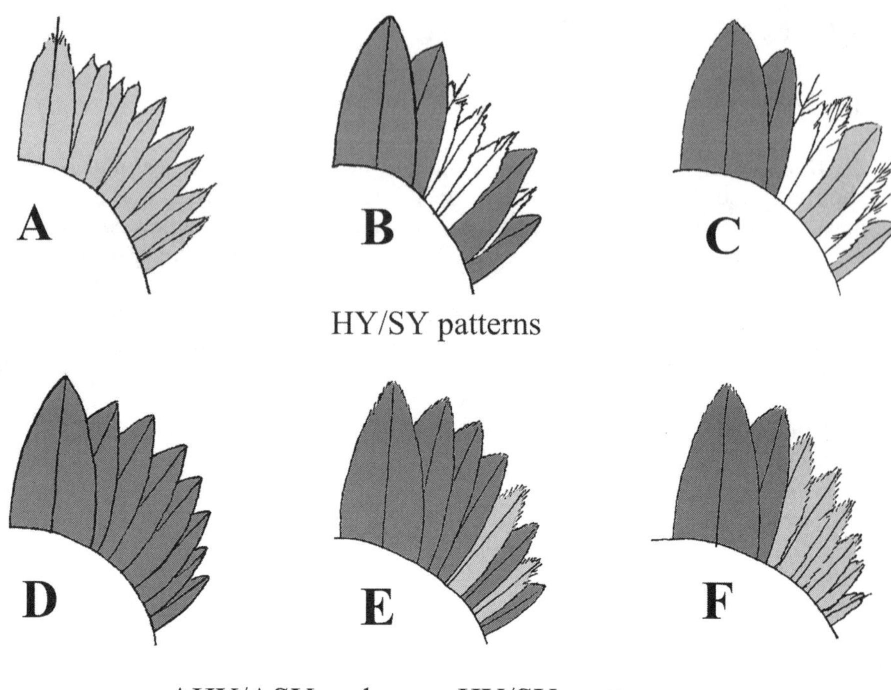

FIGURE 26. Rectrices and rectrix replacement patterns by age in waterfowl. **A** Uniform juv, as found in most HY waterfowl in fall, swans throughout the year, and many HY/SY ♀ ducks through spring. Note the notched tips to r2 and r3, which result from the breaking off of natal plumes attached to the feather tip (see also Figs. 67, p. 105, & 110, p. 159). **B** Formative r1-r2, r6, and r8 contrasting with juvenal r3-r5 and r7, as found in many HY/SY geese in winter-spring, HY/SY ♂ ducks in winter, and SY ♀ ducks in spring. By spring, juvenal feathers often become worn to a bare shaft, as shown here in r3. **C** Alternate r1-r2, formative r6 and r8, and juvenal r3-r5 and r7, as found in many SY female ducks in spring and some SY male ducks in summer. Alternate feathers are weaker in structure than formative and basic feathers. **D** Uniform basic or formative rectrices, as found in many AHY/ASY waterfowl throughout the year and some SY ducks (especially ♀♀) in spring. Note that the basic rectrices are broader and better-constructed than juvenal rectrices. **E** Most rectrices alternate contrasting with basic/formative r5 and r7, as shown by many ASY ♀♀ ducks in spring and some SY ♂♂ ducks in summer. Note that retained basic feathers contrast less with alternate feathers than do retained juvenal feathers. **F** Alternate r1-r2 contrasting with basic/formative r3-r8, as found in some ASY ♀♀ ducks in spring and many ASY and some SY ♂♂ ducks in summer.

General references for determination of age, sex, and subspecies in waterfowl include Bellrose (1980), Delacour (1954, 1956, 1959, 1964), Kear (2005), Kortright (1942), Madge & Burn (1988), Ogilvie (1978), Phillips (1922, 1923, 1925, 1926), and Taber (1969). See Nelson (1993a) and references therein for information on identifying the downy young of waterfowl. For convenience this family is divided into three subfamilies and seven tribes, reflecting groups with differing structures, molts, plumage aspects, and reproductive strategies.

Whistling-Ducks *Anatidae, Dendrocygninae, Dendrocygnini*

Two North American species. See Family Account (p. 47) for traits found throughout Anatidae. Subfamily/Tribal characters include long necks, long legs, and flattened, even-width bills. North American whistling-ducks have 10 functional primaries (p10 extending 10-20 mm short of the longest, p9-p8, and with p6-p10 both notched and emarginated), 16 secondaries (including 3 tertials), and 14-18 (usually 16) rectrices. Ageing through the first cycle (to SY and ASY) can be accomplished for most individuals through plumage aspect, molt limits, shape of the wing feathers and rectrices, and (for Black-bellied Whistling-Duck) bare part colors. Sexes are similar in plumage aspect and size (males averaging slightly larger than females). Partial medial brood patch (Fig. 20**A**, p. 31) is developed by both sexes, but these can remain feathered and not visible externally (Rylander et al. 1980).

In molting, North American whistling-ducks exhibit a Complex Basic Strategy (CBS; Fig. 10**B**, pp. 13-16), with a formative plumage but no alternate plumages in any molt cycles (see Family Account). Synchronous wing-feather molt occurs on the non-breeding grounds (*cf.* Petrie 1998), unusual among North American waterfowl. Age at first breeding appears to be 1 year in most individuals, the second prebasic molt and second basic plumage being definitive.

BLACK-BELLIED WHISTLING-DUCK

Dendrocygna autumnalis

BBWD
Species # 1770
Band size: 7A

Species—From other waterfowl by medium-large size with long legs (Table 1, p. 50); bill gray (HY) to red (AHY); plumage aspect gray, brown, reddish brown, black, and white; legs gray (HY) to pink (AHY).

Geographic variation—See Banks (1978), Blake (1977), Friedmann (1947), Hellmayr & Conover (1948a), James & Thompson (2001), Monroe (1968), Palmer (1976a), Pitelka (1948). One other subspecies occurs in Panama-S.Am (of which escapes and vagrants may occur in N.Am).

D.a. fulgens (br & wint N.Am): Upper back brown (HY) to reddish brown (AHY), uniform in aspect with nape and lower back (*vs* grayish, contrasting with browner nape and lower back in *autumnalis* of Panama-S.Am); center breast without (AHY) or with an indistinct (HY) gray band (*vs* with a distinct gray band in HY and AHY *autumnalis*). Populations of nw.Mex (and probably to s.CA-NM), "*lucida*", may average blacker bellies but difference confused by age/sex-related variation.

Molt—CBS. PF limited-incomplete (Aug/Oct-Jan/Mar in HY/SYs), DPB complete (Aug-Oct/Dec in AHYs); PA absent. The above timing pertains to N.Am populations. Most molting appears to occur on non-breeding grounds. The PF varies from a few body feathers only (in late-hatching HYs) to all body feathers, 0-3 terts, some proximal les and med covs, and all rects; most or all rects appear to be replaced in most SYs by Mar. See Family Account (p. 47) for more details.

Age—Juv (B1; Jun-Nov) has nape, back, and breast dull brownish to brownish gray, abdomen grayish to whitish with sparse blackish mottling, and bill and legs gray. Juv ♀=♂ by plumage aspect, but see Figures 22-23 (pp. 32-35) for cloacal characteristics useful in ageing and sexing (including Juvs). The following month ranges pertain to N.Am populations.

Juv-HY/SY (1st cycle, Juv/B1-F1; Nov-Oct): Pp and ss with indistinct whitish bases (Fig. 27**A**, p. 50); rects short, abraded, and with r1-r4 sometimes notched at tip in Nov-Feb (Fig. 26**A**);

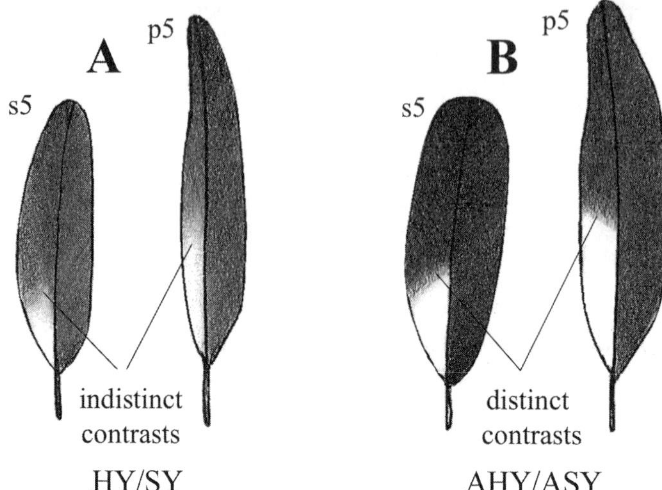

FIGURE 27. Medial secondary (s5) and primary (p5) by age in Black-bellied Whistling-Duck. Some intermediates may be found. Juv feathers (**A**) are retained by SYs through the PB2 in Aug-Oct/Dec.

back and breast brown to dull reddish brown; rump and abdomen mixed brownish and blackish; outer pp narrow at tips, averaging shorter by sex (Table 1), and abraded in Feb-Oct (Fig. 25**A**-**B**, p. 47); s covs and terts narrow, rounded, and worn (Fig. 28**A**-**B**, p. 52) often mixed with some replaced proximal feathers (see Fig. 13**D**, p. 20). **Note: Some SYs may be identifiable through Dec by retained juv feathers on the lower underparts. See AHY/ASY.**

AHY/ASY (Def. cycle, DB; Nov-Oct): Pp and ss with distinct white bases (Fig. 27**B**); rects broad, fresher, and without notches in Nov-Mar (Fig. 26**D**, p. 48); back and breast bright reddish brown; rump and abdomen blackish to black; outer pp broad at tips, averaging longer by sex (Table 1), and fresher in Feb-Oct (Fig. 25**C**-**D**); s covs and terts uniformly broad, squared, and fresher (Fig. 28**C**-**D**). **Note: See HY/SY. Some AHY/ASYs may retain a few body feathers and/or s covs but this appears unhelpful for ageing SY/TYs or ASY/ATYs.**

TABLE 1. Measurements (mm) of North American whistling-ducks to assist in identification, ageing, and sexing. Species summaries are in **bold**. See pp. 4-11 for methods of measurement. Values were derived from 95% confidence intervals as based (for wing, exposed culmen, and tarsus) approximately on the indicated sample sizes (see pp. 4- 5); sample sizes for tail length and bill depth were often smaller but included at least 10 of each sex. Thus, midpoints of ranges approximate means, and S.D. is approximated by 25% of the range.

Taxon/Sex	*n*	wing chord AHY/ASY	wing chord (HY/SY)[1]	tail length	exp culmen	bill depth[2]	tarsus
Black-bellied Wh.-Duck		**237-260**	**(231-252)**	**65-76**	**46-56**	**21.2-24.2**	**55-65**
♀	80	237-256	(231-248)	65-76	46-55	21.2-23.7	55-63
♂	80	243-260	(235-252)	65-76	48-56	21.6-24.2	56-65
Fulvous Whistling-Duck		**200-224**	**(194-219)**	**42-59**	**42-49**	**18.9-21.9**	**52-61**
♀	100	200-222	(194-216)	42-56	42-48	18.9-21.5	52-60
♂	100	204-224	(198-219)	45-59	43-49	19.3-21.9	53-61

[1] Wing chord differs substantially by age; other measurments less age-specific and given values refer to all age groups.

[2] Bill depth measured at the distal end of forehead feathering (Fig. 8**A**, p. 10).

Sex—Partially feathered medial BP (Fig. 20**A**, p. 31) developed by both sexes but distended cloaca (Fig. 21, p. 32) indicates AHY ♀ in Jan-May. Measurements unhelpful for sexing (Table 1). AHY/ASY ♀♀ average browner auriculars, duller plumage aspect, and darker (pinkish vs. whitish-pink or yellowish-pink) legs, which may be helpful for sexing mated pairs. Otherwise, sexing is reliably accomplished only through cloacal examination (Figs. 22-23, pp. 32-35).

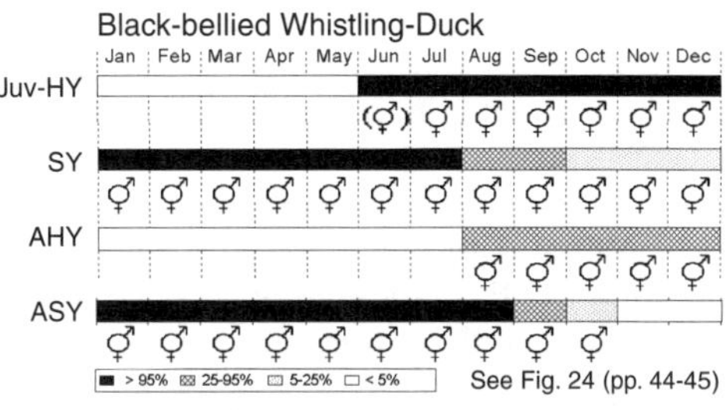

Hybrids reported—None in the wild.

References—Banks (1978), Bent (1925), Bolen (1964), Cain (1970), Carney (1992), James & Thompson (2001), Oberholser (1974), Palmer (1976a), Rylander et al. (1980).

FULVOUS WHISTLING-DUCK

Dendrocygna bicolor

FUWD
Species # 1780
Band size: 7A-6

Species—From other waterfowl by medium-small size with long legs (Table 1); bill dark gray; plumage aspect primarily brown, tan, and chestnut; feathers of neck corrugated buff and dusky; legs gray. West Indian Whistling-Duck (*D. arborea*), an escape and a potential vagrant to se.N.Am, averages longer wing and legs (wg chord 230-270, tarsus 62-75); s covs brownish without chestnut; breast darker brown; flanks with white spots. See Madge & Burn (1988) for separation of other whistling-ducks, which could occur in N.Am as escapes.

Geographic variation—Monotypic (P.A. Johnsgard *in* Mayr & Cottrell 1979). Populations of N.Am to Mex-W.Indies ("*D.b. helva*") may average paler and with smaller bills than populations of S.Am and elsewhere but differences, if present, are insufficient; see Friedmann (1947), Hellmayr & Conover (1948a), Monroe (1968), Oberholser (1974), Palmer (1976a), Wetmore & Peters (1922).

Molt—CBS. PF partial-incomplete (Aug/Oct-Jan/Mar in HY/SYs), DPB complete (Jul-Oct/Jan in AHY/ASYs); PA absent. The above timing pertains to N.Am populations. Most molting appears to occur on non-breeding grounds. The PF includes most to all body feathers (occasional late hatchlings may retain most of the juv body feathers), 0-3 terts, some proximal les and med covs, and the rects; most or all rects appear to be replaced in most SYs by Mar. Occasional body feathers and/or s covs can be retained during DPBs. See Family Account (p. 47) for more details.

Age—Juv (B1; Jun-Nov) resembles HY/SY in Oct-Dec; Juv ♀=♂ by plumage aspect but see Figures 22-23 (pp. 32-35) for cloacal characteristics useful for sexing Juvs and for ageing. The following month ranges pertain to N.Am populations.

Juv-HY/SY (1st cycle, Juv/B1-F1; Nov-Oct): S covs and terts narrow, brown, and relatively worn (Fig. 28**A-B**, p. 52), often mixed with some replaced, blackish proximal feathers (see Fig. 13**D**, p. 20), the retained les covs brownish with dull chestnut tips; rects short, abraded, and with r1-r4 sometimes notched at tip in Nov-Mar (Fig. 26**A**, p. 48); rump and uppertail covs often with worn brownish feathers with buff tips (sometimes without brown feathers in Feb-Oct); outer pp narrow at tips, averaging shorter by sex (Table 1, p. 50), and abraded in Feb-Oct (Fig. 25**A**-**B**, p. 47). **Note: Some intermediates may be difficult to age. Occasional SYs may be identifiable through Dec (and perhaps some TYs through Jan) by retained juv feathers on the lower underparts.**

AHY/ASY (Def. cycle, DB; Nov-Oct): S covs and terts uniformly broad, blackish, and fresher (Fig. 28**B**-**C**), the les covs chestnut or blackish with broad chestnut tips; rects broad, fresh, and without notches in Nov-Mar (Fig. 26**D**); rump and uppertail covs blackish, often with rusty tips; outer pp broad, averaging longer by sex (Table 1), and fresher in Feb-Oct (Fig. 25**C**-**D**). **Note: See HY/SY. Some AHY/ASYs may retain a few body feathers and/or s covs but this appears unhelpful for ageing SY/TYs or ASY/ATYs.**

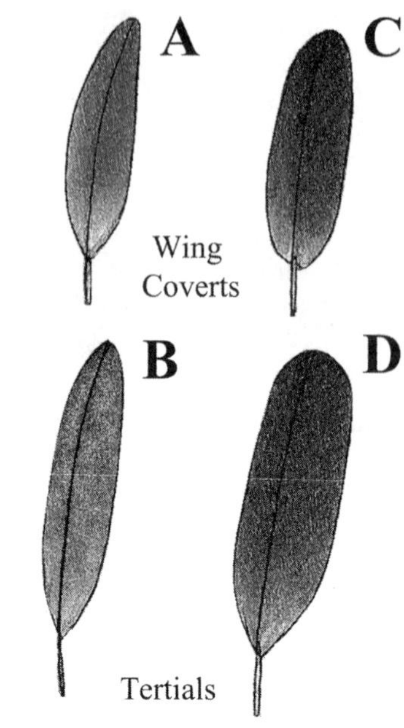

FIGURE 28. Shape of the tertials and wing coverts by feather generation in Fulvous Whistling-Ducks. Juv feathers (**A**-**B**) are often (but not always) retained by SYs through the PB2 in Jul-Oct/Dec.

Sex—♀ = ♂ by plumage aspect. Partially feathered medial BP (Fig. 20**A**, p. 31) occurs in both sexes but distended cloaca (Fig. 21, p. 32) indicates AHY ♀ in Jan-May. Measurements unhelpful for sexing (Table 1, p. 50). ♀♀ may average darker crown and nape than ♂♂ (Palmer 1976a) but too much overlap occurs for sexing (except perhaps some mated pairs). Reliable sexing is only accomplished through cloacal examination (Figs. 22-23, pp. 32-35).

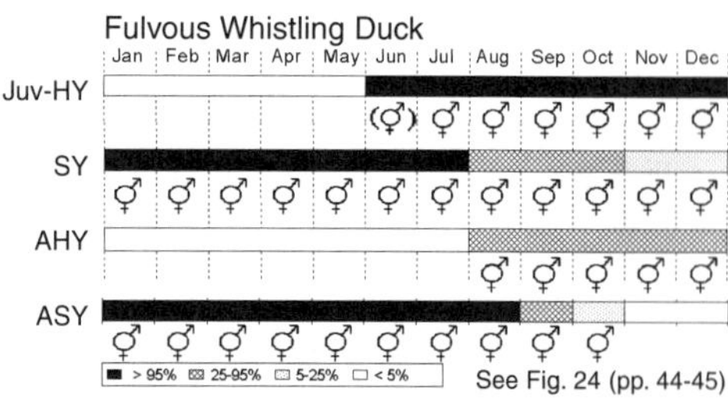

Hybrids reported—With White-faced Whistling-Duck (*D. viduata*) in the wild (Clark 1974).

References—Acosta Cruz et al. (1989), Bent (1925), Carney (1992), Dickey & van Rossem (1923a), Flickinger (1975), Hohman & Lee (2001), Hohman & Richard (1994), Oberholser (1974), Palmer (1976a), Rylander et al. (1980).

Geese and Swans *Anatidae, Anserinae*

Nine North American species. See Family Account (p. 47) for traits found throughout Anatidae. Subfamily characters include large, heavy bodies and legs. Ageing through the first cycle (to SY and ASY) and often through the seecond cycle (to TY and ATY) can be accomplished through plumage aspect, bare part colors, retained body feathers and wing coverts, and (in swans) bill morphology. Sexes are alike (for the most part) in plumage aspect. Within each population males are larger than females, and this can be used to sex some mated pairs.

In molting, North American geese and swans exhibit a Complex Basic Strategy (CBS; Fig. 10**B**, pp. 13-16), with a formative plumage but apparently no alternate plumages. See Family Account for more details. The preformative molt is protracted over winter and includes some to most of the upperpart and breast feathers, no to a few proximal wing coverts, occasionally 1-2 tertials, and no to (occasionally) all rectrices. During DPBs, synchronous wing molt occurs in Jun-Aug and body molt occurs primarily in Aug-Sep on molting grounds (p. 47), with replacement of some scapulars and rectrices occurring in Oct-Nov on non-breeding grounds. Scattered body feathers, secondary coverts, and rectrices can occasionally (geese) or often (swans) be retained during prebasic molts. Age at first breeding can be 1 year in some geese (e.g., Sedinger et al. 2004) but is more often 2-3 years (to as old as 4-6 years in swans); prebasic molts of non-breeding AHYs average earlier in timing than those of breeding adults.

Geese *Anatidae, Anserinae, Anserini*

Six North American species. See Family (p. 47) and Subfamily (above) accounts for traits found throughout Anatidae and Anserinae. Tribal characters include heavy bodies, medium-long to short and stocky necks, and proportionally small bills with narrow tips. North American geese have 10 functional primaries (p10 extending 0-15 mm short of the longest, p9-p8, when fully grown), 14-19 secondaries (including 3 tertials), and 14-20 rectrices. An enlarged and exposed area at the bend of the wing (carpometacarpus), resulting from aggressive intraspecific encounters, indicates ASY male in Canada Geese (p. 63; see Hanson 1962, Baker 1993) and should be considered in ageing and sexing other species. See Dzubin & Cooch (1992) for measurement techniques for geese.

GREATER WHITE-FRONTED GOOSE
Anser albifrons

GWFG
Species # 1710
Band size: 7B-8

Tule White-fronted Goose (TWFG) Species # 1719

Species—From other N.Am geese by variably large size (Table 2, p. 58); upper and undertail covs and lower abdomen white; shafts of pp whitish (vs. dark in other dark N.Am geese); AHYs with white feathers around base of bill (Fig. 29, p. 54), and abdomen with black patches or barring; bill and legs pinkish to orangish.

Taiga Bean-Goose (*A. fabalis*) and Tundra Bean-Goose (*A. serrirostris*), visitors, vagrants, or escapes in N.Am., average larger, especially wing length (wg chord 410-510, tl 100-145, exp culmen 49-80, tarsus 69-90; see Palmer 1976a, Cramp & Simmons 1977); AHYs without white to forehead or blackish to abdomen; bill blackish with yellow to orange subterminal band. Pink-footed Goose (*A. brachyrhynchus*), a vagrant or escape to N.Am is larger but with a proportionally shorter bill (wg chord 402-457, tl 112-149, exp culmen 40-52, tarsus 65-80); AHYs without white to forehead or blackish to abdomen; bill blackish with pink subterminal band. Lesser White-fronted Goose (*A. erythropus*), a vagrant or escape in N.Am, is smaller and with a much shorter bill (wg chord 329-390, tl 80-111, exp culmen 28-37, tarsus 65-80); AHY with white of forehead more extensive (see Fig. 30); orbital skin dull (HY) to bright (AHY) orange (*vs* dark to dull orange in Greater; see **Geographic variation**); underparts average less black by age.

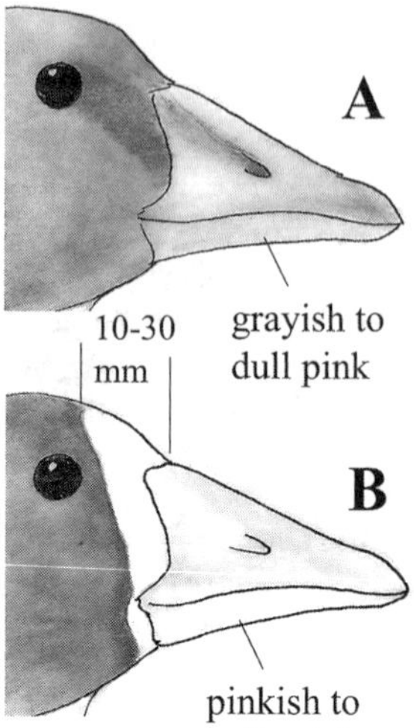

Geographic variation—See A.M. Bailey (1928a), Browning (1990), Dalgety & Scott (1948), Delacour & Ripley (1975), Elgas (1970), Ely & Dzubin (1994), Ely et al. (2005), Hellmayr & Conover (1948a), Kaufman (1994), Kemp (2001), Krogman (1978, 1979), Kuroda (1929), McAtee (1944), Moffitt (1926), Orthmeyer et al. (1995), Patten et al. (2003), A. Dzubin and R.S. Palmer *in* Palmer (1976a), Phillips et al. (1964), Portenko (1972), Salomonsen (1948), Swarth & Bryant (1917), Timm & Sellers (1981), Todd (1950a, 1963). One other subspecies occurs in Eurasia (escapes or vagrants could occur in N.Am). In addition to the following, see Takekawa & Orthmeyer (1993) for a DFA (p. 5) using bill measurements from live, known-sex individuals that separated 95% of *A.a. frontalis* from *elgasi* in CA non-breeding populations.

FIGURE 29. Head pattern in Greater White-fronted Goose by species and age. During the preformative molt in Sep-Apr, white feathering gradually develops at the base of the bills of HY/SYs and the bill color gradually brightens. AHY Lesser White-fronted Geese can be separated by a greater amount of white on the forehead, usually extending 25-40 mm from the base of the bill and beyond the eye (*vs.* not behind the eye in White-fronted Goose).

A.a. frontalis (br sw-n.AK-Nunavut tundra, wint sw.BC-s.CA to LA; visitor to Nfl-FL): Smaller (Table 2, p. 58); head and neck medium-pale brown; orbital skin usually dark; bill of AHY pinkish to orangish pink. Populations of sw.AK (Bristol Bay vicinity) average slightly larger than populations of n.AK and may warrant subspecific recognition (Orthmeyer et al. 1995). Populations of Eurasia (*albifrons*), potential vagrants or escapes to N.Am, are similar in size and plumage aspect but have shorter (exp culmen 40-49) and brighter pink (less orange) bills. **Note: See *A.a. gambeli*.**

A.a. elgasi (br sc.AK taiga, wint c.CA): Larger (Table 2); head and neck dark brownish; orbital skin sometimes dull yellow; bill of AHY pinkish to orangish pink. **Note: differences between this subspecies and *A.a. gambeli* are slight; these may represent just one subspecies with widely disjunct ranges.**

A.a. gambeli (="*gambelli*"; br NWT-Nunavut taiga, wint AZ-LA; vagrant Nfl-FL): Medium-large (Table 2); head and neck medium-dark brownish; orbital skin usually dark; bill of AHY pinkish to orangish pink. **Note: See *A.a. elgasi*. Also, appears to be broadly clinal with *frontalis* in size; intermediates may be impossible to determine to subspecies.**

A.a. flavirostris (br Greenland, wint nw.Europe; vagrant Nfl-NC): Medium-small (Table 2); head and neck dark brownish; orbital skin usually dark; back feathers, terts, and s covs with indistinct pale tips when fresh (vs with distinct tips in other subspecies); white edging to flank feathers narrower when fresh (usually < 5 mm wide vs > 7 mm in other subspecies); bill of AHY yellowish to orangish.

Molt—CBS. PF limited-incomplete (Sep/Nov-Jan/Apr in HY/SYs), PB2 complete (Jun-Oct in non-breeding SYs), DPB complete (Jul-Nov in breeding AHYs); PA absent. The PF occurs on non-breeding grounds whereas DPBs occur primarily on molting grounds (p. 47) but can complete on non-breeding grounds. The PF includes most to all head and neck feathers, scattered back and underpart feathers, no to a few proximal les covs, occasionally 1-2 terts, and no to (rarely?) all rects. Wing feathers molt synchronously and a few body feathers, s covs, and/or rects rarely may be retained during DPBs. See Family (p. 47) and Subfamily (p. 53) accounts for more details. Reports of a limited DPA (Cramp & Simmons 1977) may have been based on the protracted PF and require confirmation.

Age—Juv (B1; Jul-Oct) resembles HY/SY (see below) in Oct-Nov and has bill dusky yellowish with blackish nail, and feet dull yellow; Juv ♀ = ♂ by plumage aspect. See Figures 22-23 (pp. 32-35) for cloacal characteristics useful for sexing Juvs and ageing, perhaps to TY and ATY.

Juv-HY/SY (1st cycle, Juv/B1-F1; Sep-Aug): Feathers at base of bill without white in Aug-Sep (Fig. 29**A**), becoming whitish by Dec-Jan; underparts without blackish (Aug-Nov) or with < 10% blackish feathering by Mar (Fig. 31**A-B**); gr covs narrow, without distinct white fringe (Fig. 30**A**); back and breast feathers narrow and rounded, mixed with fresher and broader feathers in Dec-Aug (*cf.* Fig. 32**A-B**, p. 57); outer pp narrow at tips, averaging shorter by sex (Table 2, p. 58), and abraded in Apr-Jul (Fig. 25**A-B**, p. 47); some to all rects usually short, abraded, and often with notches to the tips of r1-r4 (Fig. 26**A-B**, p. 48); bill yellowish with dusky nail (Fig. 29**A**), becoming pinkish or orangish with whitish nail by Apr; legs yellowish, becoming orange by Apr.

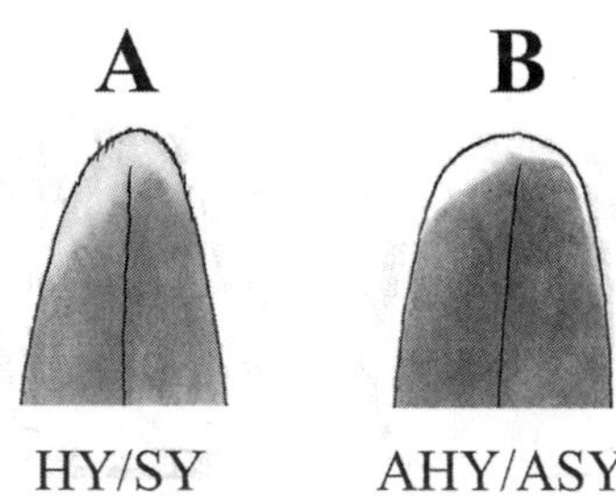

FIGURE 30. Juvenal (**A**) and basic (**B**) greater coverts in Greater White-fronted Goose. Note the shape difference and more distinct white fringing to the basic coverts, when fresh. Juv gr covs (**A**) are retained by SYs through the PB2 in Jun-Oct.

AHY/ASY (Def. cycle, DB; Sep-Aug): Feathers at base of bill white (Fig. 29**B**); underparts with > 10% blackish (Fig. 31**C-D**); gr covs broad and with distinct white fringe (Fig. 30**B**); back and breast feathers uniformly broad and squared (*cf.* Fig. 32**C-D**); outer pp broad at tips, averaging longer by sex (Table 2), and fresher in Apr-Jul (Fig. 25**C-D**); rects uniformly large and without notches when fresh (Fig. 26**D**); bill bright pinkish or orangish (Fig. 29**B**), with whitish nail; legs orange. **Note: See Figure 31 for more information on the extent of black**

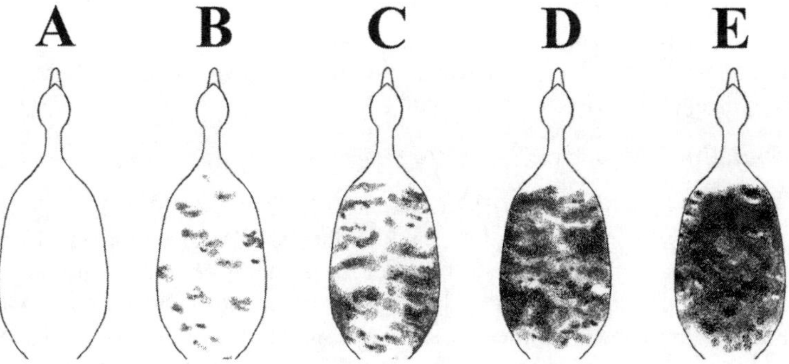

FIGURE 31. Variation in the amount of black on the abdomen of Greater White-fronted Goose by age and sex. HY/SYs have no to < 10% black (**A-B**) whereas AHY/ASYs usually have > 10% black (**C-D**). The extent of the black may continue to increase with age, such that AHY/ASYs with mostly to entirely black underparts (**D**) may be aged ASY/ATYs or older, but this also varies by sex (see **Sex**), and more study is needed to determine the limits of variation within each age group.

to the abdomen by age in AHY/ASYs. Also, some AHY/ASYs possibly can be aged SY/TY or ASY/ATY by retained gr covs; more study needed.

Sex—Partial medial BP (Fig. 20**A**, p. 31) and/or distended cloaca (Fig. 21, p. 32) indicates AHY ♀ in May-Aug. Measurements somewhat helpful for sexing within subspecies (Table 2, p. 58), with size comparison reliable for sexing mated pairs. The color of the orbital skin averages brighter yellow or orange in ♂♂ than in ♀♀ (especially in Apr-Jul) by subspecies, and the amount of black in the underparts averages greater in AHY/ASY ♂♂ (often Fig. 31**D**) than in AHY/ASY ♀♀ (usually Fig. 31**C**) but reliable sex-determination is confounded by variation in these characters by subspecies, age, and individual. Otherwise, no characters known; sexing is most reliably accomplished through cloacal examination (Figs. 22-23, pp. 32-35).

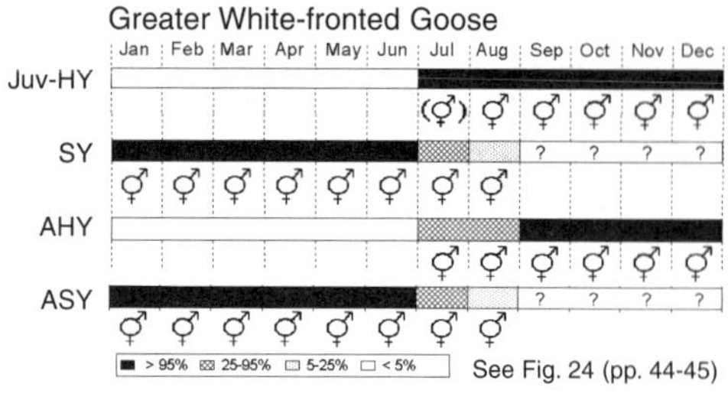

Greater White-fronted Goose

Jan Feb Mar Apr May Jun Jul Aug Sep Oct Nov Dec

Juv-HY

SY

AHY

ASY

■ > 95% ▨ 25-95% □ 5-25% □ < 5%

See Fig. 24 (pp. 44-45)

Note: Sexing reliable only through cloacal examination.

Hybrids reported—With Graylag Goose *Anser anser*, Bean Goose *A. fabalis*, and Lesser White-fronted Goose *A. erythropus* (McCarthy 2006, Voous & Wattel 1967), Snow Goose (Dzubin 1964, Lahrman 1970), Canada Goose (Craven & Westemeier 1979, Eckert 1970, Kuroda 1953), Barnacle Goose *Branta lecopsis* (Mauer 1980), and possibly Brant (McCarthy 2006) in the wild.

References—Ainley et al. (1994), Baker (1993), Bent (1925), Cramp & Simmons (1977), Dement'ev & Gladkov (1952), Ely & Dzubin (1994), Fox et al. (1995), Kristiansen et al. (1999), Oberholser (1974), R.S. Palmer & A. Dzubin *in* Palmer (1976a), Roberts (1955).

EMPEROR GOOSE

Chen canagica

EMGO
Species # 1760
Band size: 7B

Species—From other N.Am geese (including dark-morph Snow Goose, p. 59) by medium-small size (Table 2, p. 58); body feathers bluish gray, barred thinly dark and white (Fig. 32), without large white patches; hindneck of AHY white; chin of Juv dusky; bill dusky (HY) to pale pink (AHY); legs dull yellowish (HY) to bright orange (AHY).

Geographic variation—Monotypic.

Molt—CBS. PF limited-incomplete (Oct/Nov-Jan/Mar in HY/SYs), PB2 complete (Jun-Oct in non-breeding SYs), DPB complete (Jul-Nov in breeding AHYs); PA absent. The PF occurs primarily on non-breeding grounds whereas DPBs occur primarily on molting grounds (p. 47) but can complete on non-breeding grounds. The PF includes the head and neck, no to most breast and back feathers, few if any les or med covs, no gr covs or terts, and no to all rects. Wing feathers molt synchronously. Look for a few body feathers, s covs, and/or rects rarely to be retained during DPBs. See Family (p. 47) and Subfamily (p. 53) accounts for more details.

Age—Juv (B1; Jul-Oct) has an entirely dusky head, dusky bill, and grayish-yellow legs; Juv ♀ = ♂ by plumage aspect. See Figures 22-23 (pp. 32-35) for cloacal characteristics useful for sexing Juvs and for ageing.

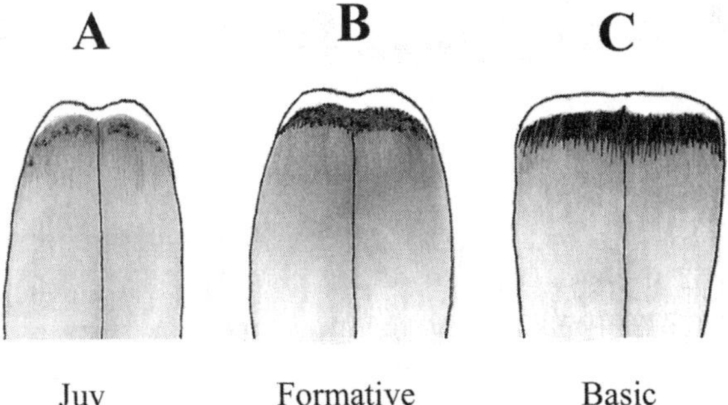

FIGURE 32. Variation in the shape and pattern of back and breast feathers of Emperor Geese by feather generation. Other species of geese show similar differences in shape to these feathers but have less distinct patterns. The mixture of worn juvenal feathers (**A**) and fresher formative feathers (**B**) creates a mottled appearance to the back and breast of HY/SYs in Dec-Aug, whereas AHY/ASYs have a more uniform look with even lines created by the pale tips to the broader basic feathers (**C**). Juv (**A**) and formative (**B**) feathers are retained by SYs through the 2nd PB in Aug-Oct.

Juv-HY/SY (1st cycle, Juv/B1-F1; Oct-Sep): Head and hindnape dusky in Oct-Nov, becoming mostly whitish with black flecking in lores and (often) auriculars in Dec-Sep (Fig. 33); back and breast feathers narrow and rounded, with indistinct dusky and whitish terminal bands (Fig. 32**A**), mixed with fresher and broader feathers with moderately distinct terminal bands (Fig. 32**B**) in Dec-Aug; outer pp narrow at tips, averaging shorter by sex (Table 2, p. 58), and abraded in Apr-Aug (Fig. 25**A-B**, p. 47); some to all rects usually short, abraded, and often with notches to the tips of r1-r4 (Fig. 26**A-B**, p. 48); throat washed or mottled brownish; bill dusky to pinkish dusky, becoming bright pinkish by Apr; legs yellowish, becoming orangish by Apr. **Note: Breast feathers appear to be among the last replaced during the PB2 and can be used to age many SYs in Aug-Oct, after wing feathers have been replaced.**

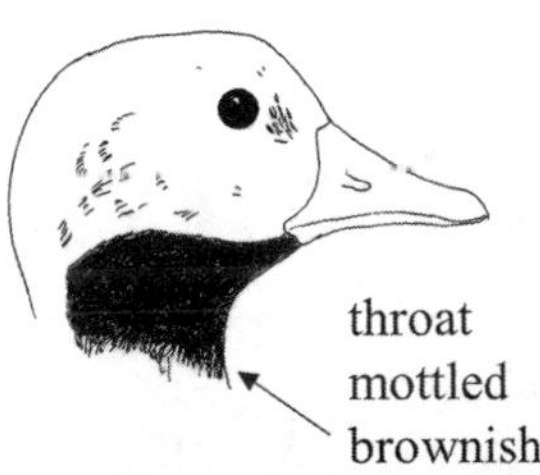

FIGURE 33. Head plumage aspect of HY/SY Emperor Goose in Dec-Sep showing dark flecking to auriculars and (especially) loral region. Dark marks often occur on earlier-replaced formative feathers showing juv-like aspect (see p. 29) rather than on retained juv feathers.

AHY/ASY (Def. cycle, DB; Oct-Sep): Head and hindnape white, without dark flecking (*cf.* Fig. 33); back and breast feathers uniformly broad and squared, with distinct black and white terminal bands (Fig. 32**C**); outer pp broad at tips, averaging longer by sex (Table 2), and fresher in Apr-Aug (Fig. 25**C-D**); rects uniformly large and without notches when fresh (Fig. 26**D**); throat black, without brown wash; bill pinkish; legs orange. **Note: Some SY/TYs might be identified by uniform upperparts and underparts, bright bill and legs, back and breast feathers intermediate in breadth and pattern between HY/SY and AHY/ASY (*cf.* Fig. 32B), and slight brown wash to the throat, but more study is needed to confirm this.**

Sex—♀ = ♂ by plumage aspect. Partial medial BP (Fig. 20**A**, p. 31 and/or distended cloaca (Fig. 21, p. 32) indicates AHY ♀♀ in May-Aug. Measurements helpful for sexing, especially bill size

(Table 2), with size comparison reliable for sexing mated pairs. Sexing is most reliably accomplished through cloacal examination (Figs. 22-23, pp. 32-35).

Hybrids reported—None in the wild.

References—Ainley et al. (1994), Bent (1925), Blaauw (1916), Conover (1926), Palmer (1976a), Petersen et al. (1994).

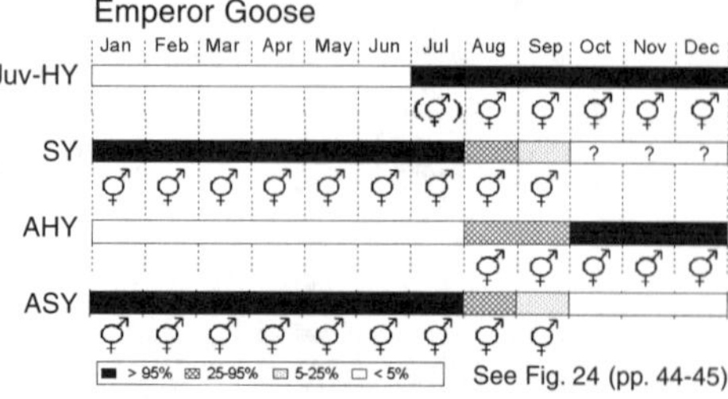

TABLE 2. Measurements (mm) of North American geese to assist in identification, ageing, and sexing. See pp. 4-11 for methods of measurement. Species summaries are in **bold** and subspecies summaries in ***italics***. Values were derived from 95% confidence intervals as based (for wing, exposed culmen, and tarsus) approximately on the indicated sample sizes (see pp. 4-5); sample sizes for tail length and bill depth were often smaller but included at least 10 of each sex. Thus, midpoints of ranges approximate means, and S.D. is approximated by 25% of the range. See Table 3 (p. 66) for measurements of Cackling and Canada geese.

Taxon/Sex	n	wing chord AHY/ASY	wing chord (HY/SY)[1]	tail length	exp culmen	bill depth[2]	tarsus
Gr. White-fronted Goose		**363-468**	**(351-452)**	**101-147**	**43-64**	**18.5-32.2**	**64-88**
A.a. frontalis		***363-448***	***(351-432)***	***109-138***	***43-58***	***18.5-28.1***	***64-83***
♀	100	363-426	(351-411)	109-130	43-55	18.5-26.4	64-79
♂	100	380-448	(367-432)	115-138	46-58	21.0-28.1	69-83
A.a. elgasi		***400-468***	***(386-452)***	***121-147***	***51-64***	***23.5-32.2***	***73-88***
♀	50	400-441	(387-425)	121-144	51-61	23.5-30.2	73-85
♂	70	426-468	(415-452)	124-147	54-64	25.2-32.2	76-88
A.a. gambeli		***399-465***	***(386-449)***	***118-146***	***50-63***	***23.3-30.6***	***71-85***
♀	40	399-441	(386-425)	118-142	50-59	23.3-29.4	71-82
♂	40	418-465	(405-449)	123-146	52-63	24.4-30.6	73-85
A.a. flavirostris		***393-453***	***(379-437)***	***101-135***	***44-59***	***19.8-27.9***	***66-83***
♀	100	393-450	(379-433)	101-132	44-58	19.8-26.6	66-82
♂	100	396-453	(383-437)	105-135	46-59	21.0-27.9	67-83
Emperor Goose		**364-403**	**(349-389)**	**97-131**	**31-43**	**22.0-25.1**	**61-72**
♀	20	364-390	(349-376)	97-122	31-40	22.0-24.5	61-70
♂	20	375-403	(362-389)	106-131	34-43	22.9-25.1	63-72
Snow Goose		**398-479**	**(377-456)**	**105-150**	**49-73**	**27.8-38.7**	**75-98**
C.c. caerulescens		***398-461***	***(377-440)***	***105-148***	***49-63***	***27.8-37.4***	***75-91***
♀	100	398-449	(377-426)	105-140	49-60	27.8-36.0	75-87
♂	100	413-461	(403-440)	112-148	52-63	29.3-37.4	78-91
C.c. atlanticus		***421-479***	***(397-456)***	***118-150***	***58-73***	***29.1-38.7***	***80-98***
♀	68	421-471	(397-437)	118-142	58-70	29.1-37.2	80-93
♂	73	429-479	(412-456)	125-150	61-73	31.0-38.7	85-98
Ross's Goose		**344-396**	**(330-385)**	**105-131**	**35-47**	**20.6-26.6**	**62-76**
♀	70	344-380	(330-370)	105-124	35-44	20.6-25.9	62-72
♂	70	356-396	(346-385)	110-131	37-47	21.1-26.6	65-76
Brant[3]		**302-342**	**(283-326)**	**84-106**	**27-38**	**15.5-20.7**	**53-66**
♀	100	302-330	(283-312)	84-101	27-36	15.5-19.4	53-62
♂	100	314-342	(300-326)	87-106	29-38	16.6-20.7	57-66

[1] Wing chord differs substantially by age; other measurments less age-specific and given values refer to all age groups.
[2] Bill depth measured at the distal end of forehead feathering (Fig. 8**A**, p. 10).
[3] Includes all subspecies, which do not differ appreciably in size (see **Geographic variation**).

SNOW GOOSE SNGO
Chen caerulescens Species # 1694
Band size: 7B

Lesser Snow Goose White-morph (LSGW)	Species # 1690
Lesser Snow Goose Blue-morph (LSGB)	Species # 1698
Lesser Snow Goose Intermediate-morph (LSGI)	Species # 1695
Greater Snow Goose Light-morph (GSGW)	Species # 1699
Greater Snow Goose Blue-morph (GSBG)	Species # 1698

Species—White morph ("Snow Goose") from most other geese and waterfowl by medium-large size (Table 2); body, s covs, and ss whitish and dusky (HY) to white (AHY); p covs grayish; pp black; bill and legs dusky brownish (HY) to bright reddish pink (AHY). Dark morph ("Blue Goose") from other geese and waterfowl (including Emperor Goose) by medium size (Table 2); back and underparts without paler or darker barring (*cf.* Fig. 32, p. 57); hindneck of AHY without white and chin of Juv whitish (*cf.* Fig. 33, p. 57); bill and legs dusky reddish (HY) to bright pink (AHY). Beware of hybrids between other species of geese that may resemble dark-morph Snow Goose (Harrison & Harrison 1969).

White and dark morph from corresponding morphs of Ross's Goose (p. 62) by larger size (Table 2); bill larger, pinkish without grayish or protuberances at base, with malar feathering extending distally beyond tip of forehead feathers, and with gap between upper and lower mandibles forming wider black stripe along tomia (Fig. 34**A-B**); outer ss of white-morph HYs average duskier centers (Fig. 36**A-B**, p. 61); dark morph with crown, neck, and abdomen mixed white and dusky grayish; legs reddish pink. Beware of intermediate-morph Snow Geese ("Snow X Blue Goose Intergrade") that may show plumage aspect more closely resembling dark-morph Ross's Goose, and of hybrid Snow X Ross's Geese with intermediate characters (Fig. 34**C**); see

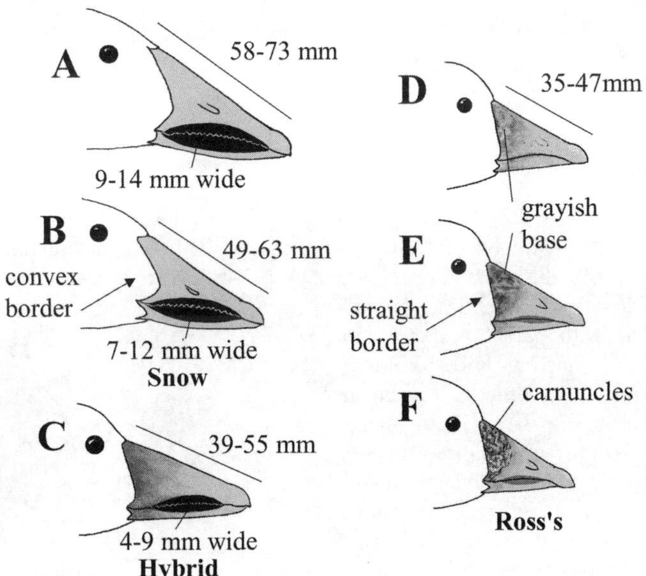

FIGURE 34. Size, shape, and other features of the bills of Snow and Ross's geese, and their hybrids, by species, subspecies, and age. Values indicate exposed culmen (Fig. 7**A**, p. 9); Table 2). **A** = Greater Snow Goose (*C.c. atlantica*); **B** = Lesser Snow Goose (*C.c. caerulescens*); **C** = typical hybrid Lesser Snow X Ross's Goose; **D-F** = Ross's Geese by age: HY/SY (**D**), AHY/ASY (**E**), and probable ASY/ATY in which ♂♂ average a greater amount of carnuncles than ♀♀ (**F**).

Kaufman et al. (1979), Matteson (1988), McLandress & McLandress (1979), Roberson (1993), Scott (1995), and Trauger et al. (1971), for more information.

Geographic variation—See Cooke et al. (1995), Dement'ev & Gladkov (1952), Kennard (1927), Palmer (1976a), Pittaway (1992a), Salomonsen (1933), and Todd (1963). See Cooch (1961), Cooke & Cooch (1968), Cooke & Mirsky (1972), Cooke et al. (1995), Manning (1942), and Portenko (1972) for discussions on morphs as related to taxomony. No other subspecies occur.

C.c. caerulescens (br n.AK-nw.Que tundra, wint BC-CA and TX-MD-FL): Lesser Snow Goose. Smaller (Table 2, p. 58; Fig. 34**B**); black stripe along tomia narrower (7-12 mm; Fig. 34**B**, p. 59); both dark-morph and white-morph individuals (as well as intermediate morphs) common. White-morph individuals formerly known as "*C.[c.] hyperborea*".

C.c. atlantica (br n.Nunavut-w.Greenland, wint coastal se.NY-NC): Greater Snow Goose. Larger (Table 2; Fig. 34**A**); black stripe along tomia broader (9-14 mm wide; Fig. 34**A**); virtually all individuals of white-morph (rare dark-morph individuals may be anomalous or represent intergrades).

Molt—CBS. PF partial-incomplete (Sep/Nov-Jan/Apr in HY/SYs), PB2 complete (Jun-Oct in non-breeding SYs), DPB complete (Jul-Nov in breeding AHYs); PA absent. The PF occurs primarily on non-breeding grounds whereas DPBs occur primarily on molting grounds (p. 47) but can complete on non-breeding grounds. The timing and extent of the PF appears to vary with subspecies and morph: in dark-morph Lesser Snow Geese the PF occurs primarily in Sep-Jan and includes some to all of the head and neck, no to some (up to 50%) of the back and breast, few if any s covs or terts, and 0-2 c. rects; whereas in white-morph Lesser Snow Geese it occurs from Sep-Apr and includes most to all of the body, no to some proximal s covs, sometimes 1-3 terts, and occasionally 1-2 central rects. The PF of Greater Snow Goose may be more similar to dark-morph Blue Goose in timing and extent. Wing feathers molt synchronously. Look for a few body feathers, s covs, and/or rects rarely to be retained during DPBs, especially in dark-morph Lesser Snow Geese. See Family (p. 47) and Subfamily (p. 53) accounts for more details.

Age—Juvs (Jul-Oct) resemble HY/SYs (see below) in Oct-Nov and have bill and legs dusky to brownish; Juv ♀=♂ by plumage aspect. See Figures 22-23 (pp. 32-35) and Higgins (1969) for cloacal characteristics useful for sexing Juvs and for ageing. Ageing criteria differ between the morphs; use a combination of the following to age intermediate-morph individuals.

Dark Morph ("Blue Goose")

Juv-HY/SY (1st cycle, Juv/B1-F1; Sep-Aug): Head and neck dusky in Sep-Oct, becoming variably mottled white in Nov-Sep; bill and legs dusky-reddish, becoming dull pinkish red (upper mandible often with dusky smudges; *cf*. Fig. 29**A**, p. 54) by Apr; gr covs brown with indistinct or no pale fringe (Fig. 35**A**); les covs dull brownish gray with pale tips; back and breast feathers narrow and rounded, mixed with fresher and broader feathers in Dec-Aug (*cf*. Fig. 32**A-B**, p. 57); outer pp narrow at tips, averaging shorter by sex (Table 2, p. 58), and abraded in Apr-Jul (Fig. 25**A-B**, p. 47); most to all rects short, abraded, and often with notches to the tips of r1-r4 (Fig. 26**A-B**, p. 48).

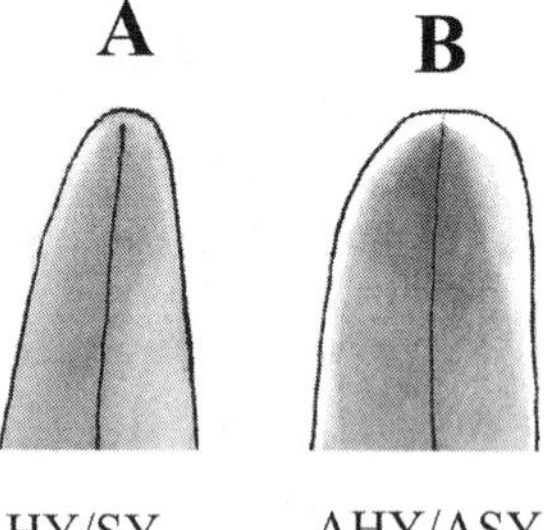

FIGURE 35. Greater covert shape and pattern by age in dark-morph Lesser Snow Goose ("Blue Goose"). Juv covs (**A**) are retained by SYs through the PB2 in Jun-Oct.

AHY/ASY (Def. cycle, DB; Sep-Aug): Head and neck mostly white (medial crown and nape feathers often contrastingly blackish); bill and legs reddish pink; gr covs dusky with distinct white edging (Fig. 35**B**); les covs gray; back and breast feathers uniformly broad and squared (*cf.* Fig. 29**C-D**); outer pp broad at tips, averaging longer by sex (Table 2), and fresher in Apr-Jul (Fig. 25**C-D**); rects uniformly large and without notches when fresh (Fig. 26**D**); **Note: Some AHY/ASYs may retain a few body feathers and/or les covs but this appears unhelpful for separating SY/TYs or ASY/ATYs. A few SYs with dusky smudging to the uppper mandible may be aged through Dec but more study is needed.**

White Morph ("Snow Goose")

Juv-HY/SY (1st cycle, Juv/B1-F1; Sep-Aug): Crown, nape, and back washed dusky, becoming whiter (through molt and bleaching) by Apr-Aug; most s covs and ss narrow and with dusky wash or feather centers (Fig. 36**A-B**), sometimes mixed with fresher and whiter terts and proximal s covs in Dec-Aug; outer pp (Fig. 25**A-B**), rects (Fig. 26**A-B**), bill (*cf.* Fig. 29**A**), and legs as in Dark Morph. **Note: See AHY/ASY. In Apr-Aug, SYs can become difficult to separate from AHYs due to molt and bleaching; the outer ss (Fig. 36) are the best feathers to examine at this time.**

AHY/ASY (Def. cycle, DB; Sep-Aug): Crown, nape, and back, white, without dusky wash; s covs and ss uniformly broad, white, and fresher (Fig. 36**D**); outer pp (Fig. 25**C-D**), rects (Fig. 26**D**), bill (*cf.* Fig. 29**B**), and legs as in Dark Morph. **Note: See HY/SY. AHY/ASYs sometimes have one or more scapulars, humerals, ss (especially s1; Fig. 36E), or other feathers with distinct dusky centers; this may indicate SY/TYs but it appears to occur in some ASY/ATYs as well, perhaps due to molt timing (see p. 29), pigment anomalies, or traces of intergradation with dark morph; more study needed. See also Dark Morph AHY/ASY.**

Sex—♀=♂ by plumage aspect. Partial medial BP (Fig. 20**A**, p. 31 and/or distended cloaca (Fig. 21, p. 32) indicates AHY ♀♀ in May-Aug. Measurements somewhat helpful for sexing within subspecies (Table 2), with size comparison reliable for sexing mated pairs. Sexing is most reliably accomplished through cloacal examination (Figs. 22-23, pp. 32-35).

Hybrids reported—Snow Geese from native populations with Greater White-fronted Goose (p. 53), Lesser White-fronted Goose *A. erythropus* (McCarthy 2006), Ross's Goose (Collins 1986, Cooke et al. 1995, Delnicki 1974, Hatch & Shortt 1976, Roberson 1993, Trauger et al. 1971), Canada Goose (Bailey 1949, McGlauchlin 1971, Nelson 1952, Prevett & MacInnes 1973), and possibly Brant (Brimley 1927) in Siberia and N.Am in the wild. Snow geese from naturalized

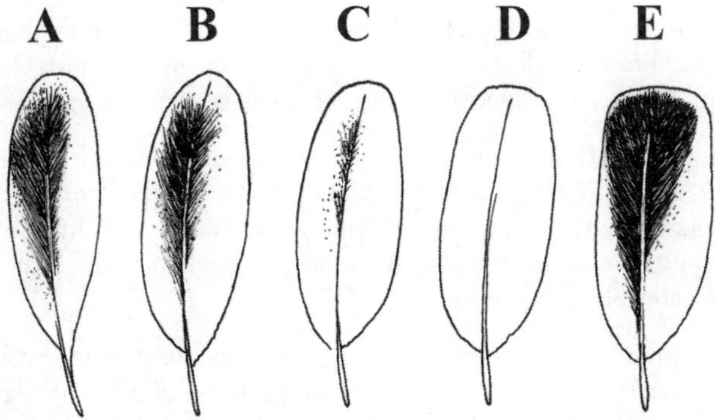

FIGURE 36. The amount of dusky to the outer secondary (s1) by age in Light-morph Snow and Ross's geese. HY/SYs usually have slightly narrower and more rounded feathers with dusky (**A-C**) whereas most AHY/ASYs have broader feathers lacking dusky (**D**). Occasional AHY/ASYs show extensive dusky (**E**; see text for discussion). HY/SY Snow Geese average more dusky to s1 (**A-B**) than HY/SY Ross's Geese (**B-C**).

populations with Barnacle Goose *Branta leucopsis* in Europe (Lebret 1983).

References—Abraham (1980), Ainley et al. (1994), Baker (1993), Bent (1925), Blaauw (1904), Cooch (1961), Cramp & Simmons (1977), Dement'ev & Gladkov (1952), Dzubin (1965), Kelsall (1974), McLandress & McLandress (1979), Mowbray et al. (2000), Oberholser (1974), F.G. Cooch & R.S. Palmer *in* Palmer (1976a), Roberts (1955), Scott (1995), Simon (1978), Trauger et al. (1971).

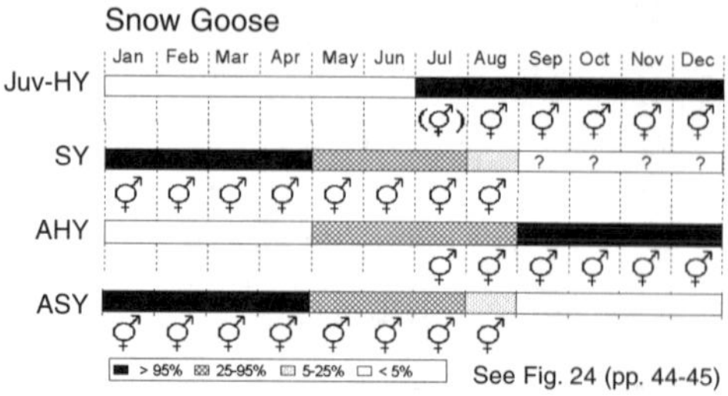

Snow Goose

Juv-HY, SY, AHY, ASY — Jan Feb Mar Apr May Jun Jul Aug Sep Oct Nov Dec

■ > 95% ▩ 25-95% ▭ 5-25% □ < 5% See Fig. 24 (pp. 44-45)

Note: Sexing reliable only through cloacal examination.

ROSS'S GOOSE

Chen rossii

ROGO
Species # 1720
Band size: 7B

Species—See Snow Goose (p. 59) for separation of white and dark morphs from other geese. White and (rare) dark morph from corresponding morphs of Snow Goose by smaller size (Table 2, p. 58); bill smaller, pinkish with grayish base and swelling or wart-like caruncles (see **Age** and **Sex**) at base, with malar feathering not extending distally beyond tips of forehead feathers, and with gap between mandibles narrower, forming no or thinner dusky stripe along tomia (Fig. 34**D**-**F**, p. 59); outer ss of white-morph HYs average less dusky (Fig. 36**B**-**C**, p. 61); dark morph with crown, neck, and abdomen blackish; legs pinkish. See Snow Goose for information on intermediate-morph geese and hybrids. Dark-morph Ross's Geese are very rare and may represent hybrids or back-crosses with dark-morph Snow Geese (see Cooke & Ryder 1971, Kaufman et al. 1979, McLandress & McLandress 1979, Williamson 1957).

Geographic variation—Monotypic. See Palmer (1976a).

Molt—CBS. PF partial-incomplete (Sep/Nov-Jan/Apr in HY/SYs), PB2 complete (Jun-Oct in non-breeding SYs), DPB complete (Jul-Nov in breeding AHYs); PA absent. The PF occurs primarily on non-breeding grounds whereas DPBs occur primarily on molting grounds (p. 47) but can complete on non-breeding grounds. The PF includes most to all body feathers, some proximal s covs, 0-4 terts, and most to all rects. Wing feathers molt synchronously during PBs. See Family (p. 47) and Subfamily (p. 53) accounts for more details.

Age—Juvs (Jul-Oct) resemble HY/SYs (see below) in Oct-Nov and have bill and legs dusky; Juv ♀ = ♂ by plumage aspect. See Figures 22-23 (pp. 32-35) for cloacal characteristics useful for sexing Juvs and for ageing. The following criteria applies to white-morph individuals only. See Snow Goose (p. 59) for information on ageing dark morphs, some of which may apply to dark-morph Ross's Goose (more study needed).

Juv-HY/SY (1st cycle, Juv/B1-F1; Sep-Aug): Crown, nape, and back white with pale grayish wash, becoming whiter (primarily through molt) by Jan-Aug; bill and legs dusky to dusky pinkish, becoming pinkish by Apr, the base of bill with little or no swelling and without caruncles (Fig. 34**A**, p. 59); most s covs and ss narrow and with pale grayish wash or feather centers (Fig. 36**B**-**C**, p. 61), sometimes mixed with fresher and whiter terts and proximal s covs in Dec-Aug; outer pp narrow at tips, averaging shorter by sex (Table 2, p. 58), and abraded in Apr-Jul (Fig. 25**A**-**B**, p. 47); some rects often short, washed grayish, abraded, and with notches to the tips of r1-r4 (Fig. 26**A**-**B**, p. 48; many replace all rects by Dec). **Note: In Feb-**

Aug, SYs can become difficult to separate from ASYs due to molt and bleaching; the outer ss (Fig. 36), especially s1-s5, are the best feathers to examine at this time. See also AHY/ASY.

AHY/ASY (Def. cycle, DB; Sep-Aug): Crown, nape, and back, white, without pale grayish wash; bill and legs brighter pinkish, the base of bill often with caruncles (Fig. 34**E-F**; see **Sex**); s covs and ss uniformly broad, white, and fresher (Fig. 36**D**); outer pp broad at tips, averaging longer by sex (Table 2), and fresher in Apr-Jul (Fig. 25**C-D**); rects uniformly large and without notches when fresh (Fig. 26**D**). **Note: See HY/SY. AHY/ASYs often have occasional scapulars, humerals, ss (especially s1; Fig. 36E), or other feathers with distinct grayish centers or black shaft streaks; this may be indicative of SY/TYs but it appears to occur in ASY/ATYs as well (see Snow Goose). Also, AHY/ASYs with extensive caruncles at base of bill (e.g., Fig. 34F or more) are probably reliably aged ASY/ATY but more study is needed (also, see Sex).**

Sex—♀=♂ by plumage aspect. Partial medial BP (Fig. 20**A**, p. 31 and/or distended cloaca (see Fig. 21, p. 32) indicates AHY ♀♀ in May-Aug. Measurements somewhat helpful for sexing (Table 2, p. 58), with size comparison reliable for sexing mated pairs. AHY/ASY ♂♂ average more extensive caruncles by age at the base of the bill than ♀♀ (see **Age**, Fig. 34**E-F**, and McLandress 1983) but there is near-complete overlap. Otherwise, no criteria known. Sexing is most reliably accomplished through cloacal examination (Figs. 22-23, pp. 32-35).

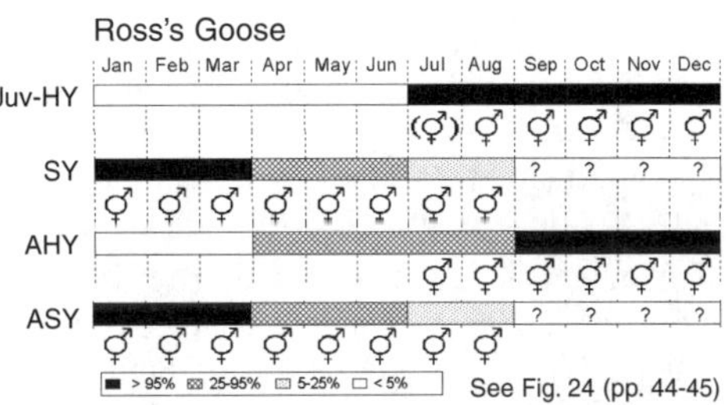

Hybrids reported—With Snow Goose (p. 59) in the wild.

References—Ainley et al. (1994), Bent (1925), Blaauw (1905), Dzubin (1965), Matteson (1988), McLandress & McLandress (1979), Oberholser (1974), J.P. Ryder, A. Dzubin, & R.S. Palmer *in* Palmer (1976a), Ryder & Alisauskas (1995), Scott (1995), Simon (1978), Trauger et al. (1971).

CACKLING GOOSE

Branta hutchinsii

CACG
Species # 1729
Band size: 7A-7B

Aleutian Crackling Goose (ACGO) Species # 1721, Band size: 7B
***Minima* Crackling Goose (MCGO)** Species # 1721, Band size: 7B

CANADA GOOSE

Branta canadensis

CANG
Species # 1720
Band size: 7B-8

Species—From other geese and waterfowl by head black; auricular and throat patch white; uppertail coverts whitish; breast and abdomen brown; vent white; bill and legs black. Size variable (Table 3, p. 66). Beware that partially amelanistic ("leucistic") individuals and hybrids (see below) occur regularly and can resemble other species of geese. Barnacle Goose (*B. leucopsis*), a vagrant to ne.N.Am and frequent escape, is smaller than Canada Goose and most subspecies of Cackling Goose (wg chord 295-352, tl 85-102, exp culmen 29-38, tarsus 54-68); white patch of head extends through forehead; breast black.

Cackling Goose separated from Canada Goose by smaller size, especially bill and neck lengths (Table 3; Figs. 37-38); see Fig. 38 for cautions measurements of neck length in "relaxed position". Criteria for separation of individual subspecies can also be used to separate the two species. See **Geographic variation** (especially *B.h. taverneri* and *hutchinsii vs B.c. parvipes*).

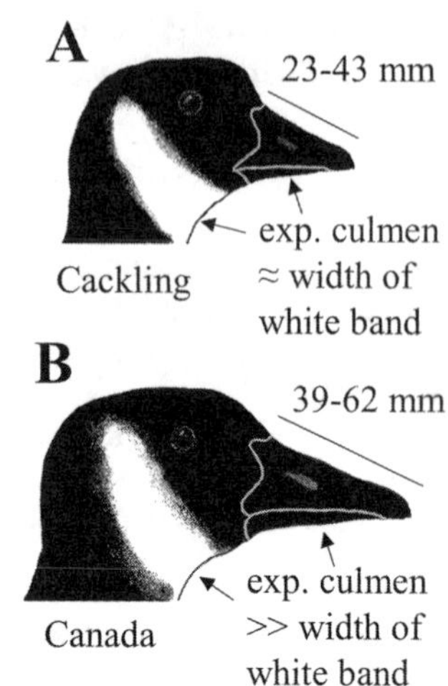

FIGURE 37. Head shape and bill length in Cackling (**A**) and Canada (**B**) geese. Values indicate exposed culmen (Fig. 7**A**, p. 9; Table 3, p. 66). Note the steeper forehead of Cackling Goose.

Geographic variation—See Abraham (2005), Aldrich (1946a), Bailey & Trapp (1984), Batty & Lowe (2001), Batty et al. (2001), Behle (1985), Brooks (1914, 1926a), Chapman (1970), Cramp & Simmons (1977), Delacour (1951), Dickson (2000), Figgins (1920, 1922, 1926), Grieb (1970), Hanson (1951, 1997), Hanson & Smith (1950), Hatch & Hatch (1983), Hellmayr & Conover (1948a), Johnson et al. (1979), Kaminski (1980), Leafloor & Rusch (1997), Macpherson & McLaren (1959), MacInnes (1966), Meredino et al. (1994), Moffitt (1937), Moser & Rolley (1990), Mowbray et al. (2002), Oberholser (1974), R.S. Palmer & C.D. MacInnes *in* Palmer (1976a), Patten et al. (2003), Pearce & Bollinger (2003), Pearce et al. (2000), Pierson et al. (2000), Ratti et al. (1977), Raveling (1977, 1978), Scribner et al. (2003), Shields & Wilson (1987), Spitzkeit & Tacha (1986), Sutton (1932a), Swarth (1913, 1920), Talbot et al. (2003), Taverner (1931), Thompson et al. (1999), Todd (1938, 1963), Van Wagner & Baker (1986), Yocom (1972). No other subspecies occur. See Rasmussen et al. (2001) for a discussion of measurement errors as related to subspecific determination in this species. Beware of frequent intergradation or hybridization based on the occurrence of naturalized populations. Most of the following criteria related to plumage aspect pertain to AHY/ASYs; HY/SYs generally show the same characters but less distinctly. The occurrence of a black stripe on the chin (*cf.* Fig. 38) may vary geographically but it also varies by age and is thus of reduced use in subspecific determination.

Cackling Goose

B.h. leucopareia (Aleutian, Chagulak, & Semidi Is, AK; wint Japan & sc.OR-c.CA): Aleutian Goose. Medium-small with short neck (Table 3; Fig. 38**E**; neck length in "relaxed position" usually 65-85 mm); upperparts medium grayish brown; base of neck without diffuse pale band and usually with distinct and narrow to wide, complete white ring (Fig. 38**A**-**B**); breast medium-pale grayish brown. An extinct taxon that bred in ne.Siberia ("*asiatica*") may have averaged paler but differences apparently insufficient for subspecific recognition.

B.h. minima (br coastal w.AK, wint c.CA; vagrant to NWT & NV-AZ): Small with very small bill and short neck (Table 3; Fig. 38**A**; neck length in "relaxed position" usually 65-85 mm); upperparts medium-dark to dark brown; base of neck sometimes with broad diffuse whitish band (Fig. 38**E**) but usually with variable narrow and distinct to broad and complete white ring (Fig. 38**A**-**C**); breast medium-dark to dark brown, often tinged pinkish to rufous.

B.h. taverneri (br interior nc.AK, wint interior WA-CA): Medium-small with medium-short neck (Table 3; Fig. 38**C**; neck length in "relaxed position" usually 80-105 mm); upperparts medium-dark to medium brown; base of neck usually with broad whitish band (Fig. 38**D**-**E**); breast dark brown.

B.h. hutchinsii (br coastal Nunavut, wint e.NM-LA; vagrant to AK-CA & ME-FL): Medium-small with short neck (Table 3; Fig. 38**C**; neck length in "relaxed position" usually 75-100 mm); upperparts medium brown; base of neck usually with broad diffuse whitish band and with incomplete or no distinct white ring (Fig. 38**D**-**E**); breast pale brownish gray to silvery or whitish.

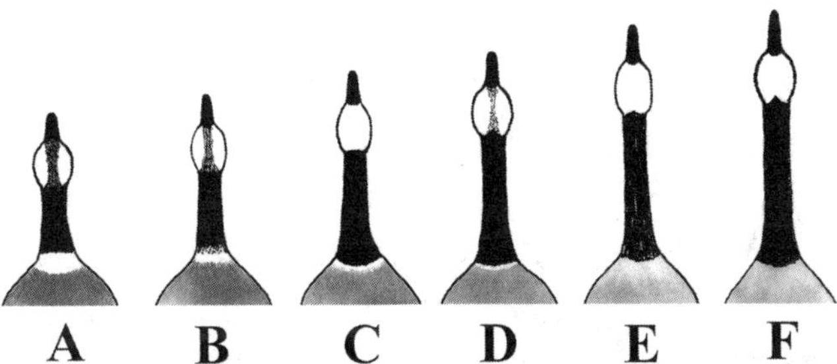

FIGURE 38. Neck lengths, throat patterns, and upper breast patterns in Cackling and Canada geese. Length from the base of the culmen to the lower edge of the black neck ("neck length"), as shown here with the neck in "relaxed position", is a good feature to separate the species (Cackling 65-105 mm, **A**-**C**; Canada 115-230 mm, **D**-**F**) and subspecies (see **Geographic variation**) but beware of variation related to degree of neck stretching, which can affect this measure by 40% or more. Plumage aspect varies substantially within each population: dark throat bands (**A**-**B** and **D**; see also **Age**) and distinct white neck rings (**A**-**C**) occur more commonly in w.subspecies of Cackling Geese than in other subspecies but these subspecies can also lack these features and they sometimes occur in other subspecies.

Canada Goose

B.c. occidentalis (br coastal s.AK-BC, wint to OR; vagrant to ND and c.CA-NV): Medium-sized with long bill, tarsus, and neck (Table 3; Fig. 38**D**; neck length in "relaxed position" usually 120-170 mm); upperparts dark brown; base of neck usually with broad diffuse whitish band (Fig. 38**E**), occasionally with narrow and incomplete white ring (Fig. 38**D**); breast dark brown, sometimes tinged chestnut to rufous. Populations breeding in coastal se.AK-BC ("*fulva*") average larger (especially in bill length) but differences are clinal and overlap broadly.

B.c. moffitti (br interior BC-ne.CA to s.Ont-w.TN, molt-migration to Nunavut, wint to s.CA-LA; naturalized, in part, WI-NH to FL): Large Canada Goose. Large and with long neck (Table 3; Fig. 38**F**; neck length in "relaxed position" usually 175-230 mm); upperparts medium brown; base of neck with broad diffuse whitish band but no distinct white ring (Fig. 38**E**); breast medium-pale grayish brown. Populations breeding (at least formerly) in ND-KS to WI-TN ("*maxima*") average larger but variation is clinal.

B.c. parvipes (br n.AK to Nunavut-n.Man, wint NM-LA; vagrant to CA & NJ-n.FL): Medium-large and with medium-long neck (Table 3; Fig. 38**D**; neck length in "relaxed position" usually 115-150 mm); upperparts medium-pale brown; base of neck usually with broad diffuse whitish band (Fig. 38**E**); breast medium-pale brown.

B.c. interior (br ne.Man to e.Nunavut-w.Que, wint IA-se.TX to NY-n.FL): Large with proportionally shorter legs and long neck (Table 3; Fig. 38**E**-**F**; neck length in "relaxed position" usually 170-220 mm); upperparts variably medium to medium-pale brown; base of neck with or without broad diffuse whitish-gray band (Fig. 38**E**-**F**); breast medium-pale grayish brown.

B.c. canadensis (br n.Que-Nfl to ME, wint coastal Nfl-NC; vagrant to MI & FL): Medium-large with proportionally longer legs and long neck (Table 3; Fig. 38**E**; neck length in "relaxed position" usually 155-200 mm); upperparts medium-pale brown; base of neck without broad diffuse whitish band or distinct white ring (Fig. 38**A**); breast pale grayish brown.

Molt—CBS. PF partial-incomplete (Sep/Nov-Jan/Apr in HY/SYs), PB2 complete (Jun-Nov in non-breeding SYs), DPB complete (Jul-Dec in breeding AHYs); PA absent. The PF occurs primarily on non-breeding grounds whereas DPBs occur primarily on molting grounds (p. 47) but can complete on non-breeding grounds. The PF includes some to all body feathers; no to ~50% of proximal les and med covs, 0-5 proximal gr covs, few if any terts, and the 2 central to all (in ~40% of HY/SYs) rects. The PF averages more complete in Cackling Goose (e.g., rects are often completely replaced) than Canada Goose (rects usually not completely replaced). During DPBs, wing feathers molt synchronously and a few body feathers, s covs, and occasionally 1-4 rects can be retained. See Family (p. 47) and Subfamily (p. 53) accounts for more details.

TABLE 3. Measurements (mm) of Cackling and Canada geese to assist in subspecific identification, ageing, and sexing. See pp. 4-11 for methods of measurement. Species summaries are in **bold** and subspecies summaries in ***italics***. Values were derived from 95% confidence intervals as based (for wing, exposed culmen, and tarsus) approximately on the indicated sample sizes (see pp. 4-5); sample sizes for tail length and bill depth were often smaller but included at least 10 of each sex. Thus, midpoints of ranges approximate means, and S.D. is approximated by 25% of the range. See Table 2 (p. 58) for measurements of other N.Am geese.

Taxon/Sex	*n*	wing chord AHY/ASY	(HY/SY)[1]	tail length	exp culmen	bill depth[2]	tarsus
Cackling Goose		**348-436**	**(337-422)**	**93-139**	**23-43**	**14.8-22.9**	**60-83**
B.c. leucopareia		***362-416***	***(351-405)***	***101-131***	***30-41***	***16.5-22.8***	***68-81***
♀	100	362-405	(351-394)	101-125	30-38	16.5-21.4	68-77
♂	100	373-416	(362-405)	107-131	32-41	18.0-22.8	72-81
B.c. minima		***345-400***	***(335-389)***	***93-127***	***23-34***	***14.8-20.6***	***60-76***
♀	100	345-384	(335-373)	93-121	23-32	14.8-19.0	60-72
♂	100	359-400	(351-389)	99-127	25-34	16.3-20.6	64-76
B.c. taverneri		***380-436***	***(365-413)***	***112-133***	***32-42***	***17.7-21.8***	***67-81***
♀	100	380-429	(365-389)	112-128	32-40	17.7-20.4	67-75
♂	100	401-436	(381-413)	116-133	34-42	18.9-21.8	72-81
B.c. hutchinsii		***369-436***	***(357-422)***	***103-139***	***31-43***	***17.3-22.9***	***64-83***
♀	100	369-420	(357-407)	103-131	31-41	17.3-21.9	64-78
♂	100	383-436	(370-422)	110-139	34-43	18.4-22.9	69-83
Canada Goose		**413-548**	**(400-533)**	**108-188**	**39-62**	**20.2-34.0**	**69-103**
B.c. occidentalis		***413-497***	***(400-482)***	***118-164***	***39-57***	***21.4-29.5***	***77-100***
♀	100	413-479	(400-459)	118-156	39-54	21.4-27.8	77-93
♂	100	440-497	(422-482)	125-164	41-57	24.0-29.5	84-100
B.c. parvipes		***424-476***	***(408-453)***	***125-148***	***37-47***	***20.2-24.8***	***71-85***
♀	100	424-449	(408-429)	125-143	37-44	20.2-23.4	71-81
♂	100	445-476	(424-453)	130-148	39-47	21.4-24.8	76-85
B.c. moffitti		***466-548***	***(451-533)***	***130-188***	***46-66***	***23.1-34.0***	***80-103***
♀	100	466-525	(451-510)	130-177	46-62	23.1-31.9	80-99
♂	100	492-548	(478-533)	141-188	50-66	24.9-34.0	85-103
B.c. interior		***444-524***	***(427-509)***	***108-165***	***44-60***	***21.7-31.1***	***69-87***
♀	100	444-501	(427-484)	108-157	44-55	21.7-28.5	69-83
♂	100	469-524	(452-509)	119-165	48-60	23.9-31.1	74-87
B.c. canadensis		***435-506***	***(418-488)***	***130-172***	***49-60***	***23.4-32.1***	***82-98***
♀	100	435-483	(418-467)	130-166	49-56	23.4-29.7	82-93
♂	100	448-506	(430-488)	136-172	51-60	25.9-32.1	87-98

[1] Wing chord differs substantially by age; other measurments less age-specific and given values refer to all age groups.
[2] Bill depth measured at the distal end of forehead feathering Fig. 8**A**, p. 10).

Reports of a limited DPA (Delacour 1954, Cramp & Simmons 1977, Marchant & Higgins 1990) may be based on the protracted PF and DPB (see Gates et al. 1993) and require confirmation.

Age—Juv (B1; Jul-Oct) resembles HY/SY (see below) in Oct-Nov and has head washed brownish and white cheeks speckled brown; Juv ♀=♂ by plumage aspect. See Figures 22-23 (pp. 32-35), Elder (1946), Hanson (1949, 1962), and Higgins (1969) for cloacal characteristics useful for sexing Juvs and for ageing.

Juv-HY/SY (1st cycle, Juv/B1-F1; Oct-Sep): Back and breast feathers narrow and rounded (*cf.* Fig. 32**A**, p. 57), mixed with fresher and broader feathers in Dec-Aug (*cf.* Fig. 32**B**); most to all terts and s covs narrow and worn (*cf*, Fig. 30, p. 55), the distal gr covs with indistinct or no pale tips; outer pp narrow at tips, averaging shorter by subspecies and sex (Table 3), and abraded in Apr-Jul (Fig. 25**A-B**, p. 47); some to all (sometimes none in Cackling Goose) rects short, brownish, abraded, and often with notches to the tips of r1-r4 (Fig. 26**A-B**, p. 48). **Note: In addition, a black stripe on the chin (Fig. 38A-B, D) may be more characteristic of HY/SYs than of AHY/ASYs and the underwing les covs may average paler or whiter in HY/SYs than in AHY/ASYs, by subspecies (see Fig. 38), but more study is needed. See also AHY/ASY.**

AHY/ASY (Def. cycle, DB; Sep-Aug): Back and breast feathers uniformly broad and squared (*cf.* Fig. 32**C**); terts and s covs uniformly broad and fresher, the distal gr covs with distinct pale tips (*cf.* Fig. 30**B**); outer pp broad at tips, averaging longer by sex (Table 3), and fresher in Apr-Jul (Fig. 25**C-D**); rects uniformly large, blackish, and without notches when fresh (Fig. 26**D**). **Note: See HY/SY. An enlarged and exposed area at the bend of the wing (carpometacarpus) usually indicates ASY ♂ (Hanson 1962, Baker 1993) but only a small proportion of ♂♂ show this. A few AHY/ASYs can be aged SY/TY by retention of 1-4 very worn juv rects (Fig. 26B-C). AHY/ASYs with retained definitive rects (*cf.* Fig. 26F), not contrasting as much in shape or wear, could be SY/TYs that had replaced rects during the PF and thus should be aged AHY/ASY.**

Sex—♀=♂ by plumage aspect. Partial medial BP (Fig. 20**A**, p. 31 and/or distended cloaca (Fig. 21, p. 32) indicates AHY ♀ in May-Aug. Measurements somewhat helpful for sexing, but only with individuals of known species and subspecies (Table 3), size comparison being reliable for sexing mated pairs. An enlarged and exposed area at the bend of the wing indicates ASY ♂♂ (see **AHY/ASY**, above), and the bill shape of AHY ♀♀ averages more concave than that of AHY ♂♂ (Turner 1953). More study is needed on sexing by skin transparency (Bench et al. 1976). Otherwise, sexing most reliably accomplished through cloacal examination (Figs. 22-23, pp. 32-35).

Hybrids reported—See Mowbray et al. (2002) and Sibley (1938) for reports of hybridization between Cackling (*B.h. taverneri* and *hutchinsii*) and Canada (*B.c. parvipes*) geese in the wild. Canada Geese from native populations in N.Am with Greater White-fronted Goose (p. 53), Snow Goose (p. 59), and Brant (McCarthy 2006, Ransom 1927) in the wild. Canada Geese from naturalized populations in Europe with Graylag Goose (*Anser anser*), Bean Goose (*A. fabalis*), Barnacle Goose (*B. bernicla*), Mute Swan, and possibly Pink-Footed Goose (*A. brachyrhynchus*) in the wild (McCarthy 2006).

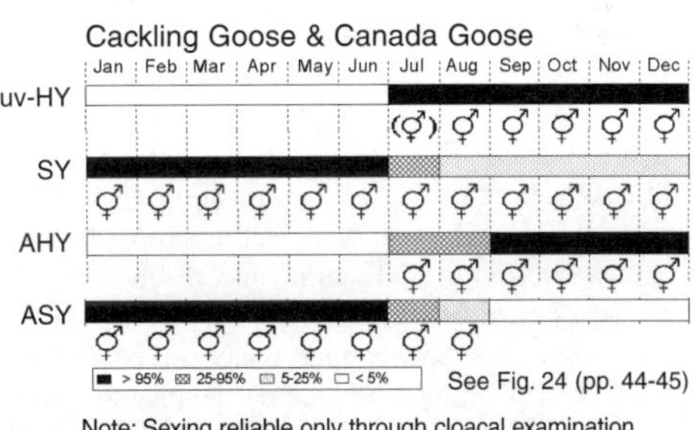

Note: Sexing reliable only through cloacal examination.

References—Abraham et al. (1999), Ainley et al. (1994), Baker (1993), Bent (1925), Brooks (1914), Caithamer et al. (1993), Cramp & Simmons (1977), Davis et al. (1985), Dement'ev & Gladkov (1952), Elder (1946), Gates et al. (1993), Hanson (1949, 1959, 1962, 1997), Higgins & Schoonover (1969), Krohn & Bizeau (1979), Kuyt (1966), Lawrence et al. (1998), Marchant & Higgins (1990), Marquardt (1962), Mowbray et al. (2002), Oberholser (1974), Palmer (1976a), Raveling (1977), Raveling & Zezulak (1991), Roberts (1955), Sterling & Dzubin (1967), Tacha et al. (1989), Taverner (1931), Turner (1953), Williams & Kendeigh (1982), Zicus (1981).

BRANT
Branta bernicla

BRAN
Species # 1734
Band size: 7A-7B

Black Brant (BLBR) Species # 1740
Brant Intergrade (BRIN) Species # 1731
Atlantic Brant (ATBR) Species # 1730

Species—From other geese and waterfowl by medium-small size (Table 2, p. 58); head, neck, and breast blackish to brownish black except for variable white tipping to feathers of lower neck (Fig. 39); upperparts dark brownish to dusky; uppertail covs and vent whitish; breast pale grayish brown to dusky; bill and legs black.

Geographic variation—See Boyd & Maltby (1979), Boyd et al. (1988), Browning (2002), Buckley & Mitra (2002), Buckley et al. (2004), Cramp & Simmons (1977), Tourgarinov (1941 *in* Dement'ev & Gladkov 1952), Delacour & Zimmer (1952), Ebels (1997), Garner & Millington (2001), Jourdain (1936), Maltby-Prevett et al. (1975), Manning et al. (1956), Martin (2002), Millington (1997), Mlodinow & Axelson (2006), Oberholser (1974), Palmer (1976a), Portenko (1972), Reed et al. (1989, 1998), Sangster (2000), Syroechkovski et al. (1998), Wilson & Guthrie (1999), Wynn (2003), Zöckler et al. (2000). No other subspecies occur.

B.b. nigricans (br coastal n.AK-nc.Nunavut, wint coastal s.AK-sw.CA; vagrant interior N.Am and to coastal MA-NJ): Black Brant. Back, scapulars and s covs, dusky brown to brown; tipping of neck feathers in AHYs more extensive by age and sex (Fig. 39**C**-**E**); breast brownish black, not or only slightly and indistinctly darker than the abdomen; flank feathers dusky brown with moderately wide (4-12 mm) and distinct white tips. Populations of nw.Siberia ("*orientalis*") may average paler, browner, and with less extensive white tipping to neck feathers but differences slight and confounded by individual variation.

B.b. hrota (br coastal nc-ne.Nunavut, wint coastal MA-n.FL; vagrant interior N.Am and to coastal BC-sw.CA): Atlantic Brant. Back and s covs medium to medium-dark brownish; tipping of neck feathers in AHYs reduced by age and sex (Fig. 39**B**-**D**); breast blackish, contrasting distinctly with whitish abdomen; flank feathers pale grayish brown with wide (5-15 mm) and distinct white tips. Populations variably intermediate in plumage aspect between *nigricans* and *hrota* (br Melville and Prince Patrick Is, Nunavut; wint sw.BC-nw.WA) may represent intergradation or a separate subspecies; more study is needed. Beware that SYs of *nigricans* in Mar-Jul become bleached and can resemble paler subspecies or intermediates (e.g., see Hoffman & Elliott 1974).

B.b. bernicla (br and wint Eurasia, vagrant to Que-VA): Dark-bellied Brant. Back, scapulars, and s covs blackish tinged grayish; tipping of neck feathers in AHYs moderately extensive by age and sex (Fig. 39**C**-**D**); breast blackish, distinctly darker than brownish abdomen; flank feathers brown with narrow (2-6 mm) and indistinct whitish to buff-white tips.

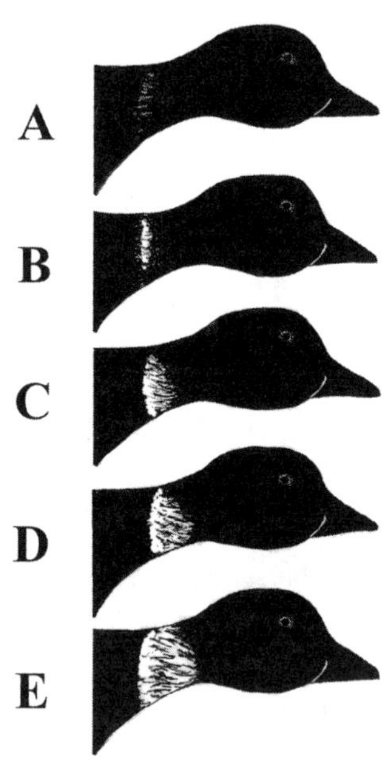

FIGURE 39. Variation in the white neck patch of Brant by subspecies, age, and sex. Western N.Am Brant (*B.b. nigriscens*) average larger white patches than e.N.Am Brant (*hrota*), AHY/ASYs average larger patches than HY/SYs, and ♂♂ average larger patches than ♀♀, so all three factors need to be considered when using this criterion.

Molt—CBS. PF partial-incomplete (Sep/Nov-Jan/May in HY/SYs), PB2 complete (Jun/Aug-Oct/Dec in non-breeding SYs), DPB complete (Jul-Nov in breeding AHY/ASYs); PA absent. The PF occurs primarily on non-breeding grounds whereas DPBs occur primarily on molting grounds (p. 47) but can complete on non-breeding grounds. The PF includes some to all body feathers, no to a few proximal s covs, 1-3 terts, and no to (sometimes) all rects. During DPBs, wing feathers molt synchronously; individual SYs that over-summer on non-breeding grounds complete a protracted PB2 in Jun-Dec. See Family (p. 47) and Subfamily (p. 53) accounts for more details. Reports of a limited DPA in Jan-Apr (Delacour 1954, Cramp & Simmons 1977, Baker 1993, Wynn 2003) may be based on changes in plumage aspect due to wear, or on the protracted PF, and require confirmation.

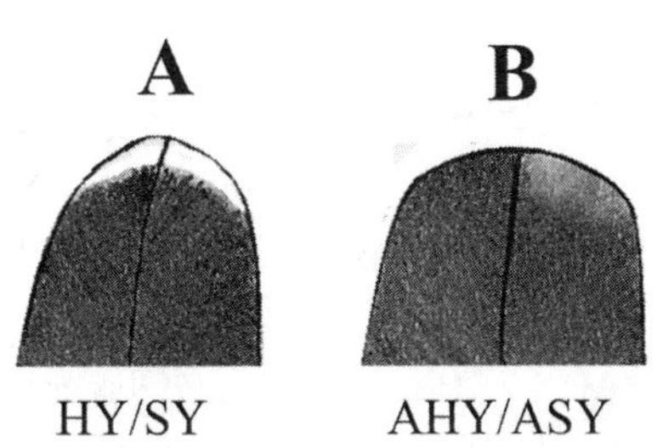

FIGURE 40. Juvenal secondary coverts and inner primary coverts have distinct white tips (**A**) whereas basic feathers have indistinct or no pale tips (**B**) in Brant. This age-specific difference is unique to Brant among N.Am geese, the other species showing white tips in both or neither age groups. Juv covs (**A**) are retained by SYs through the PB2 in Jun-Aug/Dec (see Fig. 41).

Age—Juv (B1; Jul-Oct) resembles HY/SY (see below) in Oct-Nov, lacks or has a rudimentary white neck patch (Fig.39**A**), and has uniformly colored flanks; Juv ♀ = ♂ by plumage aspect. See Figures 22-23 (pp. 32-35) for cloacal characteristics useful for sexing Juvs and for ageing. See Penkala (1977; also Boyd 1978) for ageing fresh SY/TY ♀♀ specimens by ovary condition, and Summers & Smith (1990) for age-related variation in the nasal gland.

Juv-HY/SY (1st cycle, Juv/B1-F1; Sep-Aug): Outer s covs narrow and rounded, and these and inner p covs with white tips (Fig. 40**A**); back and breast feathers narrow and rounded (*cf.* Fig. 32**A**, p. 57), mixed with fresher and broader feathers in Dec-Aug (*cf.* Fig. 32**B**); outer pp narrow at tips, averaging shorter by sex (Table 2, p. 58), and abraded in Apr-Jul (Fig. 25**A-B**, p. 47); some to all (sometimes no) rects short, abraded, often with notches to the tips of r1-r4 (Fig. 26**A-B**, p. 48), and tipped white when fresh; white neck patch reduced by sex and subspecies (Fig. 39**A-C** in ♀♀, Fig. 39**B-D** in ♂♂).

AHY/ASY (Def. cycle, DB; Sep-Aug): Outer s covs broad, and these and the inner p covs not distinctly tipped white (Fig. 40**B**); back and breast feathers uniformly broad and squared (*cf.* Fig. 32**C**); outer pp broad at tips, averaging longer by sex (Table 2), and fresher in Apr-Jul (Fig. 25**C-D**); rects uni-

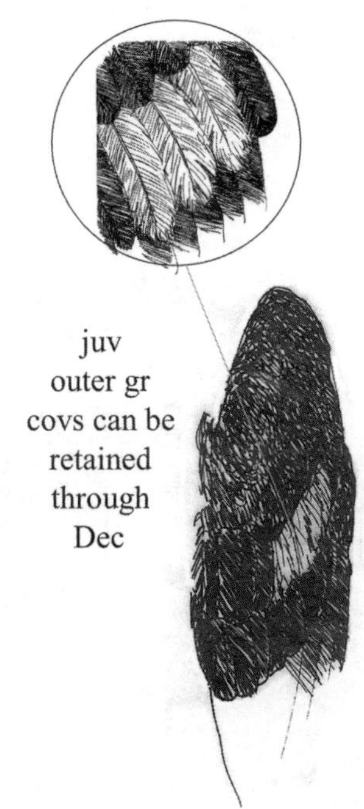

FIGURE 41. Some SY/TY Brant that over-summer on winter grounds retain outer gr covs or other s covs until Dec (possibly Jan in some) and can be aged through the fall or early winter. See also Figure 40.

formly large and without notches when fresh (Fig. 26**D**); white neck patch larger by sex and subspecies (Fig. 39**B-D** in ♀♀, Fig. 39**C-E** in ♂♂).

SY/TY (2nd cycle, B2; Sep-Jan): Like AHY/ASY but one or more s covs retained into winter, whitish to pale brown and extremely worn (Fig. 41, p. 69); one or more juv rects occasionally retained, contrastingly narrow, and extremely worn (*cf*. Fig. 26**D-E**, p. 64). **Note: SY/TYs with these characters likely over-summered on non-breeding grounds (see Molt).**

Sex—Partial medial BP (Fig. 20**A**, p. 31 and/or distended cloaca (Fig. 21, p. 32) indicates AHY ♀ in May-Aug. Measurements somewhat helpful for sexing (Table 2, p. 58), with size comparison reliable for sexing mated pairs. The extent of the white neck patch varies by sex, averaging greater in AHY ♂♂ (Fig. 39**D-E**, p. 68) than AHY ♀♀ (Fig. 39**C-D**), but this criterion is confused by variation in age (see **Age**) and subspecies (see **Geographic variation**). Otherwise, no criteria known, sexing best accomplished through cloacal examination (Figs. 22-23, pp. 32-35).

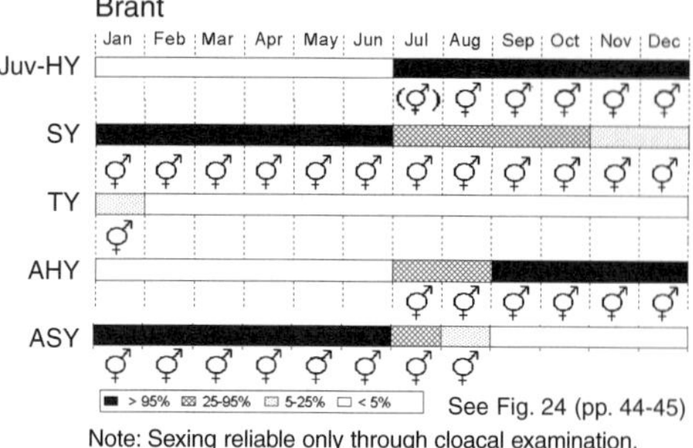

Note: Sexing reliable only through cloacal examination.

Hybrids reported—With Snow Goose (p. 59), Canada Goose (p. 63), and Barnacle Goose *B. bernicla* (Johnsgard 1960a, McCarthy 2006) in the wild.

References—Abraham et al. (1983), Ainley et al. (1994), Ankney (1984), Baker (1993), Bent (1925), Bollinger & Derksen (1996), Boyd (1978), Boyd & Maltby (1980), Cramp & Simmons (1977), Dement'ev & Gladkov (1952), Harris & Shepherd (1965), Martin (2002), Oberholser (1974), Palmer (1976a), Reed et al. (1988, 1998), Stone (1900), Taylor (1995), Wynn (2003).

Swans *Anatidae, Anserinae, Cygnini*

Three North American species. See Family (p. 47) and Subfamily (p. 53) accounts for traits found throughout Anatidae and Anserinae. Tribal characters for N.Am swans include very large size, large and even-width bills, very heavy bodies, very long necks, and entirely whitish to white plumage aspect. North American swans have 10 functional primaries (p 10 extending 10-30 mm short of the longest, p8-p9, when fully grown), 22-26 secondaries (including 3 tertials), and 20-24 rectrices. Ageing through the second cycle (to TY and ATY) is possible with many individuals through retained body feathers, wing coverts, and/or rectrices and, in Mute Swan, the development of the ornamental protuberance at the base of the bill.

MUTE SWAN
Cygnus olor

MUSW
Species # 1782
Band size: 9C

Species—From Trumpeter (p. 73) and Tundra (p. 75) swans by proportionally long tail and short bill (Table 4, p. 75); tail more graduated (r1 – outer rect > 90 mm); upper mandible with concave culmen, dusky-pink to orange, with swelling or rounded protuberance to proximal portion, and with bill nail elongated (Fig. 42); legs black (dark-morph HYs and AHYs) to pinkish brown (light-morph HYs and AHYs).

Geographic variation—Monotypic.

Molt—CBS. PF partial-incomplete (Aug/Oct-Jan/Mar in HY/SYs), PB2 incomplete-complete (May-Oct/Dec in SYs), DPB incomplete-complete (Jun-Nov/Jan in breeding ASY/ATY ♀♀, Jul-Jan in breeding ASY/ATY ♂♂); PA absent. The PF occurs primarily on non-breeding grounds whereas DPBs occur primarily on molting grounds (p. 47) but can complete on non-breeding grounds. The PF includes some to all body feathers, few if any s covs, and no terts or rects. During DPBs, wing feathers molt synchronously and a few body feathers, s covs, and up to 6 rects sometimes can be retained. See Family (p. 47) and Subfamily (p. 53) accounts for more details. Reports of a limited DPA (*cf.* Cramp & Simmons 1977) may have been based on the protracted PF, and require confirmation.

Age—Juv (B1; Jul-Oct) has brownish-olive head and neck (replaced with brownish-gray feathers during PF) and has upper mandible grayish (dark morph; Fig. 42) or pinkish (white morph); Juv ♀=♂ by plumage aspect. See Figures 22-23 (pp. 32-35) for cloacal characteristics useful for sexing Juvs and for ageing.

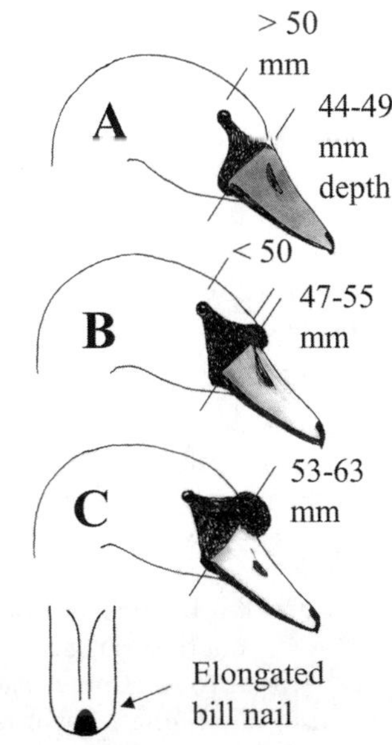

FIGURE 42. Bill characteristics by species and age in Mute Swan. Values indicate distance from eye to top of forehead feathers, and bill depth (Fig. 8**A**-**B**, p. 10) at distal and forehead feathers (**A**) or deepest point of ornamental swelling (**B**). **A** Typical HY/SY showing dusky coloration to the bill, no swelling at base, and forehead feathers extending > 50 mm distal to eye. **B** Typical SY/TY showing paler bill and moderate swelling to base. **C** Typical ASY/ATY showing bright bill and extensive ornamental knob at base. ASY/ATY ♂♂ average larger knobs than ASY/ATY ♀♀ which may help to sex some mated pairs.

HY/SY (1st cycle, Juv/B1-F1; Sep-Aug): Upper mandible grayish pink to dull dark pinkish, without swelling at base, and with downy forehead feathers extending > 50 mm distal to eye (Fig. 42**A**, p. 71; *cf.* Fig. 44, p. 76); body feathers, wing covs, and terts of dark morph narrow and brownish olive to brownish gray, the back increasingly mixed with broader white feathers in Dec-Aug (juv feathers elsewhere becoming bleached by May-Aug); outer pp narrow, with brownish-gray tips in dark-morph, averaging shorter by sex (Table 4, p. 75), and abraded in Apr-Jul (Fig. 25**A-B**, p. 47); rects uniformly juv (*cf.* Fig. 17**A**, p. 25), short, rounded, washed brownish gray, and often with notches to the tips of r1-r6 (Fig. 26**A-B**, p. 48). **Note: These ageing criteria pertain to dark-morph individuals only; less-common white-morph HY/SYs lack gray in the plumage aspect and have pinker bills but can be aged by other bill characters (Fig. 42), primary shape (Fig. 25), scapular width (< 50 mm for juv feathers on HY/SYs, > 50 mm in AHY/ASYs), and rect shape (Fig. 26).**

SY/TY (2nd cycle, B2; Sep-Aug): Upper mandible dull pinkish to yellowish, with slight to moderate swelling at base, and with downy forehead feathers extending < 50 mm distal to eye (Fig. 42**B**); plumage aspect white, often (dark-morph individuals) with scattered brown-streaked feathers in head and neck and/or gray-washed feathers on rump or among s covs in Sep-Mar; outer pp broad at tips, uniformly white, averaging longer by sex (Table 4), and fresher in Apr-Jul (Fig. 25**C-D**); most to all rects large, broad, and truncate (Fig. 26**D**), 1-6 juv rects sometimes retained (*cf.* Fig. 17**G**), narrow, washed grayish brown (if not bleached), and extremely abraded (*cf.* Fig. 26**B-C**). **Note: See ASY/ATY.**

ASY/ATY (Def. cycle, DB; Sep-Aug): Upper mandible primarily orange and with rounded protuberance at base (Fig. 42**C**; see **Sex**); plumage aspect uniformly white; outer pp as in SY/TY (Fig. 25**C-D**); rects large, broad, and truncate (Figs. 17**E** & 26**D**), sometimes with basic rects retained, not as worn as retained juv rects (*cf.* Figs. 17**H** & 26**E**). **Note: Some TY/4Ys might be reliably aged by bill orange (Fig. 42C) but with reduced knob (Fig. 42C-D); more study is needed.**

Sex—♀ = ♂ by plumage aspect. Partial medial BP (Fig. 20**A**, p. 31 and/or distended cloaca (see Fig. 21, p. 32) indicates AHY ♀ in May-Aug. Measurements somewhat helpful (Table 4, p. 75), with size comparison reliable for sexing mated pairs. The size of the rounded protuberance at the base of the culmen also varies by age, sex, and season, being largest in breeding ATY ♂♂ during Mar-Jul (Fig. 42**C**). Among mated pairs the protuberance of the bill in ♂♂ is usually larger and the bill deeper orange than in ♀♀, throughout the year, and these criteria can be used to sex some mated pairs. Otherwise, no criteria known, reliable sexing best accomplished through cloacal examination (Figs. 22-23, pp. 32-35).

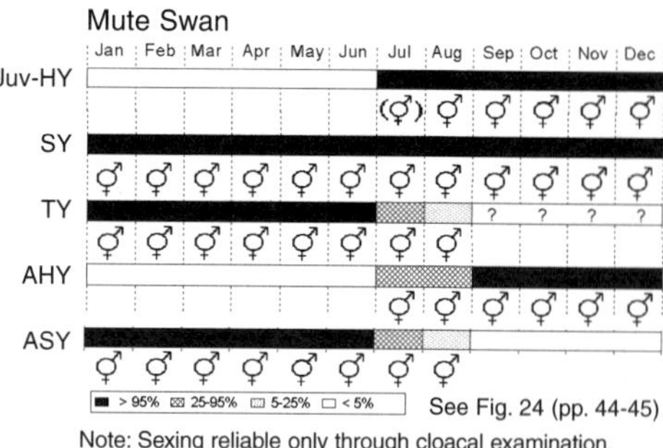

Hybrids reported—With Graylag Goose (*Anser anser*), naturalized populations of Canada Goose (p. 63), and Whooper Swan (*C. cygnus*) in the wild (McCarthy 2006).

References—Baker (1993), Bent (1925), Ciaranca et al. (1997), Cramp & Simmons (1977), Dement'ev & Gladkov (1952), Enright (1994), Marchant & Higgins (1990), Palmer (1976a), Perrins & McCleery (1995), Stejneger (1882), Wilmore (1979).

TRUMPETER SWAN
Cygnus buccinator

TRUS
Species # 1810
Band size: 9-9C

Species—From Mute Swan (p. 71) by proportionally short tail and long bill (Table 4, p. 75); tail less graduated (r1 – outer rect < 90 mm); upper mandible black and without swelling or rounded protuberance (Fig. 44**A-B**, p. 76); legs brownish (HY) to black (ASY). From Tundra Swan (p. 75) by larger average size (Table 4); bill nail larger and more triangular (Fig. 43**A**); distal end of nare to bill tip 49-59 mm and bill with straighter culmen, straighter border between loral feathers and bill, and without yellow (rarely with some whitish) at base (Fig. 44**A-B**); HY/SYs with grayish juv body feathers and s covs more extensively retained (or unbleached) through Feb-Jun (see **Molt** and **Age**); legs and feet dull pinkish (Juv) or yellowish to olive-gray (AHY).

Whooper Swan (*C. cygnus*), a vagrant to w.N.Am and escape elsewhere, is similar in size with shorter average tail (AHY/ASY wg chord 557-636, HY/SY wg chord 537-614, tl 134-185, exp culmen 103-115, tarsus 106-130) and has extensive pale whitish (HY) to yellow (AHY) loral skin and cere, usually extending to a point well beyond proximal end of nares (more yellow than in Fig. 44**E**).

Geographic variation—Monotypic. See Barrett & Vyse (1982), Hansen et al. (1971).

Molt—CBS. PF partial (Aug/Oct-Jan/Mar in HY/SYs), PB2 incomplete-complete (May-Nov/Jan in SY/TYs), DPB incomplete-complete (Jun-Nov/Jan in breeding ASY/ATY ♀♀, Jul-Feb in breeding ASY/ATY ♂♂); PA absent. The PF occurs primarily on non-breeding grounds whereas DPBs occur primarily on molting grounds (p. 47) but can complete on non-breeding grounds. The PF includes some to all body feathers, few if any s covs, and no terts or rects. During DPBs, wing feathers molt synchronously and a few body feathers, s covs, and up to 6 rects often (~75% of ASY/ATYs but fewer SY/TYs) can be retained. See Family (p. 47) and Subfamily (p. 53) accounts for more details.

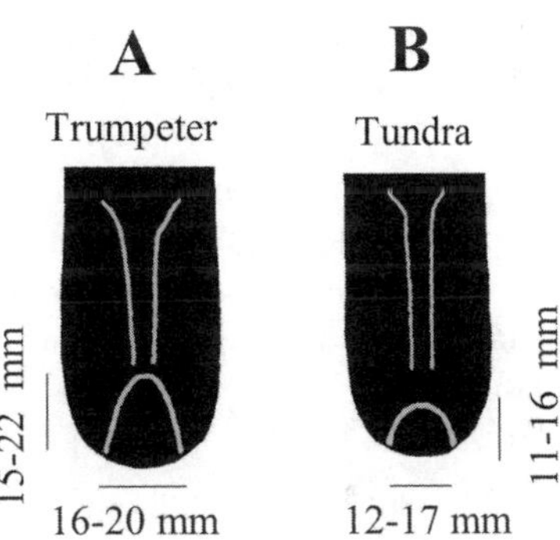

FIGURE 43. Bill nail in Trumpeter (**A**) and Tundra (**B**) swans to assist with identification.

Age—Juv (B1; Jul-Oct) has brownish head and neck (replaced with grayish feathers during PF) and has upper mandible with pinkish patch (Fig. 44**A**, p. 76); Juv ♀ = ♂ by plumage aspect. See Figures 22-23 (pp. 32-35) for cloacal characteristics useful in sexing Juvs and in ageing.

HY/SY (1st cycle, Juv/B1-F1; Sep-Aug): Body feathers, wing covs, and terts washed brownish gray, the back increasingly mixed with white in Dec-Aug (grays elsewhere becoming bleached by May-Aug); upper mandible mixed blackish and pink (becoming mostly blackish by Aug) and forehead with downy feathers extending > 40 mm distal to eye (Fig. 44**A** & **F**); outer pp narrow, with grayish tips, averaging shorter by sex (Table 4, p. 75), and abraded in Apr-Jul (Fig. 25**A-B**, p. 47); rects uniformly juv (*cf.* Fig. 17**A**, p. 25), short, rounded, washed gray, and often with notches to the tips of r1-r6 (Fig. 26**A-B**, p. 48); mouth lining pinkish to pinkish orange; legs and feet dull yellowish to olive-gray. **Note: These ageing criteria pertain to dark-morph individuals only; rare white-morph HY/SYs (see McEneaney 2005) can be aged by extension of forehead feathers, primary shape, scapular width (< 55 on juv feathers in HY/SYs *vs* > 55 in AHY/ASYs), rect shape, and leg color, with bill varying from mostly pinkish to dull grayish pink.**

AHY/ASY (Def. cycle, DB; Sep-Aug): Plumage aspect uniformly white; upper mandible black and forehead with feathers extending < 40 mm distal to eye (Fig. 44**B** & **G**); outer pp broad at tips, uniformly white, averaging longer by sex (Table 4), and fresher in Apr-Jul (Fig. 25**C-D**); rects uniformly large, squared, white, fresh, and without notches (Figs. 17**E** & 26**D**); mouth lining orange to red; legs and feet grayish (rarely olive-gray, pinkish, or orange) to black. **Note: See HY/SY, SY/TY and ASY/ATY. AHY/ASYs, with uniformly basic feathers, may be rare, especially in Sep-Jan. Individuals with entirely white plumage aspect might be reliably aged ASY through at least Nov and perhaps ATY through Jan or later but more study is needed. Some AHY/ASYs have occasional scapulars, humerals, ss, or other feathers with grayish shaft streaks through spring and summer; this may be a reliable criterion for ageing SY/TYs but more study is needed.**

SY/TY (2nd cycle, B2; Sep-Aug): Like AHY/ASY but scattered grayish feathers present on body (especially rump) and among s covs; one or more juv rects retained, narrow, washed grayish (if not bleached), and extremely abraded (*cf.* Figs. 17**G** & 26**B-C**); upper mandible sometimes with some pinkish or grayish pink through Dec (*cf.* Fig. 44**A**); mouth lining often tinged pinkish through Dec; legs sometimes tinged yellowish or olive through Dec. **Note: Retained juvenal or formative grayish feathers may be replaced during a protracted PB2 such that few TYs may be distinguishable after Jan (see Molt). See AHY/ASY regarding individuals with grayish shaft streaks. Some SY/TYs may be reliably aged by having gray tips to 2nd basic pp; more study is needed.**

ASY/ATY (Def. cycle, DB; Sep-Aug): Like AHY/ASY but 1-6 basic rects retained, broad, and white, contrasting only moderately in wear with replaced rects (*cf.* Figs. 17**H** & 26**E-F**). **Note: A few s covs may also be retained but basic feathers can be difficult to separate from juvenal feathers. See AHY/ASY and SY/TY.**

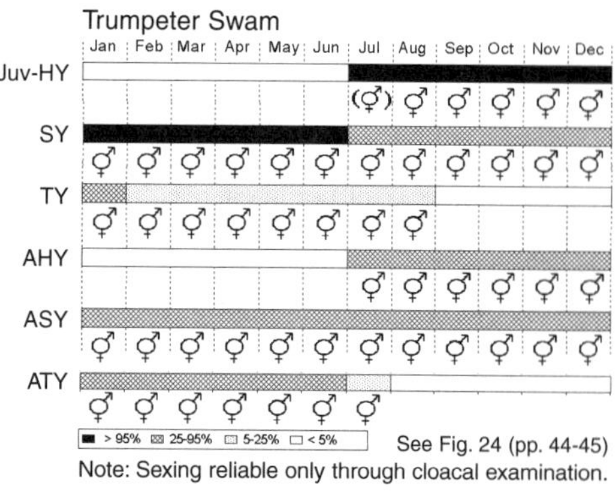

Sex—♀ = ♂ by plumage aspect. Partial medial BP (Fig. 20**A**, p. 31 and/or distended cloaca (Fig. 21, p. 32) indicates AHY ♀ in May-Aug. Measurements somewhat helpful (Table 4), with size comparison reliable for sexing mated pairs. Otherwise, no criteria known, sexing best accomplished through cloacal examination (Figs. 22-23, pp. 32-35).

Hybrids reported—None in the wild.

References—Bailey (1988), Banko (1960), Bent (1925), Blaauw (1904), Drewien & Bouffard (1994), Hansen et al. (1971), Johnsgard (1974), Jordan (1988), McEneaney (2005), Mitchell (1994), Oberholser (1974), R.S. Palmer & W.E. Banko *in* Palmer (1976a), Patten & Heindel (1994), Roberts (1955), Scott et al. (1972), Stejneger (1882), Tobish (1991), Wilmore (1979).

TABLE 4. Measurements (mm) of North American swans to assist in identification, ageing, and sexing. See pp. 4-11 for methods of measurement. Species summaries are in **bold** and subspecies summaries in ***italics***. Values were derived from 95% confidence intervals as based (for wing, exposed culmen, and tarsus) approximately on the indicated sample sizes (see pp. 4-5); sample sizes for tail length and bill depth were often smaller but included at least 10 of each sex. Thus, midpoints of ranges approximate means, and S.D. is approximated by 25% of the range.

Taxon/Sex	*n*	wing chord AHY/ASY	(HY/SY)[1]	tail length	exp culmen[2]	bill depth[3]	tarsus
Mute Swan		**524-634**	**(495-597)**	**187-248**	**72-84**	**23.3-33.13**	**97-121**
♀	28	524-593	(495-558)	187-235	72-79	23.3-29.7	97-113
♂	25	575-634	(543-597)	200-248	77-84	26.6-33.1	105-121
Trumpeter Swan		**559-690**	**(534-663)**	**164-234**	**96-129**	**40.7-53.4**	**106-138**
♀	30	559-649	(534-623)	164-221	96-123	40.7-50.2	106-133
♂	30	599-690	(574-663)	176-234	102-129	44.8-53.4	112-138
Tundra Swan		**468-574**	**(444-556)**	**126-190**	**78-120**	**33.8-51.7**	**86-124**
C.c. bewickii		***468-561***	***(444-538)***	***126-166***	***78-105***	***33.8-45.1***	***86-117***
♀	100	468-544	(444-521)	126-160	78-101	33.8-42.8	86-113
♂	100	489-561	(469-538)	132-166	82-105	36.0-45.1	90-117
C.c. columbianus		***483-574***	***(467-556)***	***149-190***	***87-120***	***39.6-51.7***	***96-124***
♀	100	483-556	(467-539)	149-183	87-116	39.6-49.6	96-119
♂	100	511-574	(493-556)	155-190	92-120	41.9-51.7	101-124

[1] Wing chord differs substantially by age; other measurments less age-specific and given values refer to all age groups (except see 2).

[2] Exposed culmen values are from ASY/ATYs only. HY/SYs and SY/TYs have smaller and more variable values due to variably receding distal extensions of forehead feathering (Fig. 44, p. 76) rather than bill size.

[3] Bill depth measured at the distal end of nares (Fig. 8**C**, p. 10; *cf.* Fig. 42, p. 71) for adult Mute Swans or forehead feathering (Fig. 8**A**) for other adult swans (not including downy extension of Juvs; Fig. 44).

TUNDRA SWAN
Cygnus columbianus

TUSW
Species # 1804
Band size: 9

Bewick's Swan (BESW) Species # 1801
Whistling Swan (WHSW) Species # 1800

Species—See Trumpeter Swan (p. 73) for separation from Mute and Whooper swans. From Trumpeter Swan by smaller average size (Table 4); bill nail smaller and more rounded (Fig. 43**B**, p. 73); distal end of nare to bill tip 39-47 mm and bill with more concave culmen, more convex border between loral feathers and bill, and often with at least some yellowish at base (Fig. 44**C-E**, p. 76); HY/SYs with grayish juv body feathers and s covs usually replaced by Jan-Feb (see **Molt** and **Age**); legs and feet grayish to black.

Geographic variation—See Dement'ev & Gladkov (1952), Tourgarinov (1941 *in* Dement'ev & Gladkov 1952), Evans & Sladen (1980), Johnsgard (1974), Kemp (1999), Knapton (2000), Mikami (1989), Palmer (1976a), Patten & Heindel (1994), Portenko (1972), Scott (1981), Stejneger (1882). No other subspecies occur.

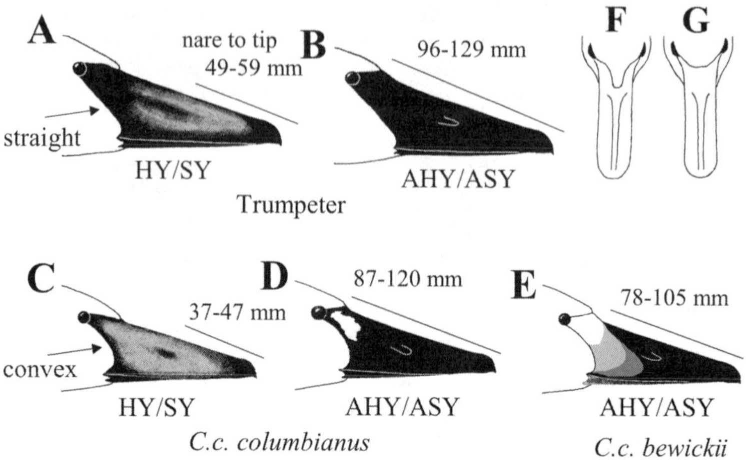

FIGURE 44. Bill and bill-feather features in Trumpeter (**A-B**) and Tundra (**C-E**) swans by species, subspecies, and age. Values indicate distal end of nares to bill tip (**A**, **C**) and exposed culmen (**B**, **D** & **E**; Fig. 7**A**, p. 9, Table 4, p. 75); the former measure is diagnostically longer in Trumpeter than in Tundra swan. HY/SY Trumpeter Swans have less pink in the bill than HY/SY Tundra Swans at the same time of year. In both species, HY/SYs (**F**) also have feathers extending further in front of the eye than AHY/ASYs (**G**). Among Tundra Swans, *C.c. columbaianus* of N.Am has a longer culmen and less yellow at the base of the bill (maximum extent shown in **D**) than *bewickii*. Illustration **E** shows *bewickii* with a minimum (palest shading), typical (intermediate shading), and maximum (darkest shading) amount of yellow.

C.c. bewickii (br & wint Eurasia, vagrant or escape AK-CA to Nfl-MD): Bewick's Swan. Averages smaller (Table 4, p. 75); upper mandible with more whitish pink (HYs) or yellow (AHYs), ranging from 22-42% of bill and extending to within 25 mm of, to slightly beyond, proximal end of nares, and lower mandible often washed yellow (Fig. 44**E**). Populations of e.Siberia (*"jankowskii"*) may have bills averaging larger and with less amount of yellow but differences, if present, are insufficient and variable, and may indicate intergradation with *columbianus*.

C.c. columbianus (br & wint N.Am): Whistling Swan. Averages larger (Table 4); upper mandible with no or less pink (HYs) or yellow (AHYs), ranging from 0-16% of bill and not extending to within 25 of proximal end of nares, and lower mandible black (Fig. 44**C-D**).

Molt—CBS. PF partial (Aug/Oct-Jan/Mar in HY/SYs), PB2 complete (May-Nov/Jan in SY/TYs), DPB incomplete-complete (Jun-Dec in breeding ASY ♀♀, Jul-Dec in breeding ASY ♂♂); PA absent. The PF commences on breeding grounds and completes on non-breeding grounds whereas DPBs occur primarily on molting grounds (p. 47) but can complete on non-breeding grounds. The PF includes some to all body feathers, few if any s covs, and no terts or rects. During DPBs, wing feathers molt synchronously and a few body feathers, s covs, and up to 6 rects sometimes (~40% of ASY/ATYs but fewer SY/TYs) can be retained. See Family (p. 47) and Subfamily (p. 53) accounts for more details.

Age—Juv (B1; Jul-Oct) has brownish head and neck (replaced by grayish feathers during PF) and has upper mandible mostly pinkish (*cf.* Fig. 44**C**); Juv ♀ = ♂ by plumage aspect. See Figures 22-23 (pp. 32-35) for cloacal characteristics useful for sexing Juvs and for ageing.

HY/SY (1st cycle, Juv/B1-F1; Sep-Aug): Body feathers, wing covs, and terts washed brownish gray, increasingly mixed with white in Dec-Aug (grays becoming mostly replaced or bleached by May-Aug); upper mandible mixed blackish and pink (becoming mostly blackish with variable amounts of straw-yellow at base by Aug) and forehead with downy feathers extending > 35 mm distal to eye (Fig. 44**C** & **F**); outer pp narrow, with grayish tips, averaging shorter by sex (Table 4, p. 75), and abraded in Apr-Jul (Fig. 25**A**-**B**, p. 47); rects uniformly juv (Fig. 17**A**, p. 25), short, rounded, washed gray, and often with notches to the tips of r1-r6 (Fig. 26**A**-**B**, p. 48); mouth lining pinkish to pinkish orange.

AHY/ASY (Def. cycle, DB; Sep-Aug): Plumage aspect uniformly white; upper mandible black with variable amounts of yellow at base, and forehead with feathers extending < 35 mm distal to eye (Fig. 44**D** & **G**); outer pp broad at tips, uniformly white, averaging longer by sex (Table 4), and fresher in Apr-Jul (Fig. 25**C**-**D**); rects uniformly large (Fig. 17**E**), squared, white, fresh, and without notches (Fig. 26**D**); mouth lining orange to red. **Note: ASYs with entirely white plumage aspect may be reliably aged through at least Nov and perhaps ATY through Jan or later but more study is needed. Some AHY/ASYs have occasional scapulars, humerals, ss, or other feathers with grayish shaft streaks through spring and summer; this may be a reliable criterion for ageing SY/TYs but more study is needed. See also SY/TY and ASY/ATY.**

SY/TY (2nd cycle, B2; Sep-Aug): Like AHY/ASY but scattered grayish feathers present on body (especially rump) and among s covs; one or more juv rects retained, narrow, washed grayish (if not bleached), and extremely abraded (*cf.* Figs. 17**G** & 25**B**-**C**); upper mandible blackish to black, sometimes with some pinkish or grayish pink mottling; mouth lining often tinged pinkish through Dec. **Note: Retained juvenal or formative grayish feathers appear to be replaced during a protracted PB2 such that few TYs are usually distinguishable after Jan (see Molt). See AHY/ASY regarding individuals with grayish shaft streaks.**

ASY/ATY (Def. cycle, DB; Sep-Aug): Like AHY/ASY but 1-6 basic rects retained, broad, and white, contrasting only moderately in wear with replaced rects (*cf.* Figs. 17**G** & 25**E**-**F**). **Note: A few s covs may also be retained but these can be difficult to identify. See AHY/ASY and SY/TY.**

Sex—♀ = ♂ by plumage aspect. Partial medial BP (Fig. 20**A**, p. 31 and/or distended cloaca (Fig. 21, p. 32) indicates AHY ♀ in May-Aug. Measurements somewhat helpful (Table 4, p. 75), with size comparison reliable for sexing mated pairs. See Miller et al. (1988) for DFAs (p. 5) using a variety of external and internal measures and weights from fresh specimens, that correctly sexed 74-91% of wintering adults collected in n.CA. Otherwise, no criteria known, sexing best accomplished through cloacal examination (Figs. 22-23, pp. 32-35).

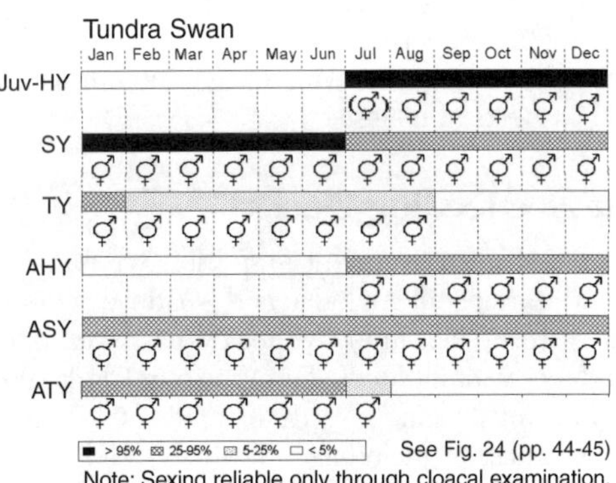

Hybrids reported—Tundra Swan (*C.c. columbianus*) with vagrant Whooper Swan (*C. cygnus*) in the wild (Garrett & Wilson 2003).

References—Ainley et al. (1994), Bailey (1988), Baker (1993), Bent (1925), Cramp & Simmons (1977), Dement'ev & Gladkov (1952), Earnst (1992), Evans & Kear (1978), Johnsgard (1974), Jordan (1988), Limpert & Earnst (1994), Limpert et al. (1987), Miller et al. (1988), Oberholser (1974), Palmer (1976a), Patten & Heindel (1994), Roberts (1955), Scott et al. (1972), Stejneger (1882), Tobish (1991), Wilmore (1979).

True Ducks *Anatidae, Anatinae*

Thirty-five species. See Family (p. 47) account for traits found throughout Anatidae. Subfamily characters include small to medium-large but heavy bodies and colorful aspects in basic-plumaged males of most species (see Pyle 2005a for molt and plumage terminology). P10 alone is notched, and p9 emarginated. Ageing through the first cycle (to SY and ASY) can be accomplished for most individuals through plumage aspect; in a few species males can be aged through the 2nd cycle (to SY/TY and ASY/ATY). Shape and pattern of the distal wing coverts often provide the best means for ageing, as these are retained during both preformative and prealternate molts (Fig. 45). Other feathers that are retained during molts and useful in ageing include the medial secondaries forming the speculum and the outer primaries (Fig. 25, p. 47). Differences among tertials and outer rectrices (Fig. 26, p. 48) can also be useful for ageing, although criteria are complicated by variable and sex-specific replacement during preformative and prealternate molts (Fig. 45). Sexes differ in non-juvenal plumage, although alternate-aspect males (most often found in June and July) can resemble females to varying extents, at which time wing-feather criteria often provides the best means for sexing. Also beware that older or senescent females can acquire male-like plumage criteria, the result of suppressed estrogen levels (Owens & Short 1995, Swennen et al. 1989, Voitkevich 1966). These colors in females tend to be muted and evenly washed, in contrast to the bolder colors and/or mixture of brown and colorful feathers in noncolorful males. Females with male-like aspects likely can be aged at least ATY but more study is needed to confirm this. Carney (1992) provides a good summary and shows excellent photographs of wings for ageing and sexing ducks by tertials, wing coverts, and secondaries; however, there can be more variation in both the extent of molts (*cf.* Figs. 26 & 45) and the appearance of feathers than the single examples per age/sex group in Carney (1992) might suggest. Cloacal differences (Figs. 22-23, pp. 32-35) provide consistent criteria for ageing and sexing live waterfowl (including juveniles) through the first cycle, and these should be used, if possible, to confirm aspect-related criteria.

In molting, North American ducks exhibit a Complex Alternate Strategy (CAS; Fig. 10**F**, pp. 13-16), with a formative plumage and alternate plumages in all molt cycles. An auxilliary preformative molt (PFa) may occur prior to the PF in some species (see Pyle 2005a and pp. 14-15). Molt strategies differ between the sexes: males have a more extensive preformative molt than females, in order to acquire a colorful plumage aspect for courting (*cf.* Ashley et al. 2007) whereas females have an earlier and more extensive prealternate molt than males, to produce a cryptic plumage aspect for nesting (Fig. 11**A**, p. 17). In both sexes the alternate plumage also provides cryptic aspect during the synchronous wing molt. As in geese, the complete prebasic body molt occurs following wing molt, often occurs more rapidly in females, and produces colorful aspects in males.

Surface-feeding Ducks *Anatidae, Anatinae, Anatini*

Twelve North American species. See Family (p. 47) and Subfamily (above) accounts for traits found throughout Anatidae and Anatinae. Tribal characters include small to medium-large bodies, spatulate bills in many species (narrower at tip in Wood Duck, p. 80, and wigeons, p. 84), and hind toes without lobes (Humphrey & Clark 1964). North American surface-feeding ducks have 10 functional primaries (p10 extending 0-10 mm short of the longest, p9, when fully grown), 14-15 secondaries (including 4-5 tertials), and 14-18 (usually 16) rectrices. Ageing through the first cycle (to SY and ASY) can be accomplished for most individuals through plumage aspect, particularly that of the secondary coverts. Sexing of most individuals (including juveniles of many species) can be accomplished through plumage aspect, bare part colors (particularly bill color), and measurements (males averaging larger than females by age).

Age at first breeding occurs at one year in most individuals; therefore, molt patterns are similar among age groups and the second prebasic molts and second basic plumages are definitive. A rudimentary auxilliary preformative molt and auxilliary formative plumage (resembling juvenal plumage and included under "Juv" in the following accounts) may precede the preformative molt in males (at least) of some or all species; but this may also represent a protracted first prebasic (prejuvenal) molt, as body size develops during the juvenile period. See Pyle (2005a) for more information. Molts occur primarily on breeding or molting (p. 47) grounds, although preformative and prebasic molts can complete on non-breeding grounds and the prealternate molt of females can commence on non-breeding grounds.

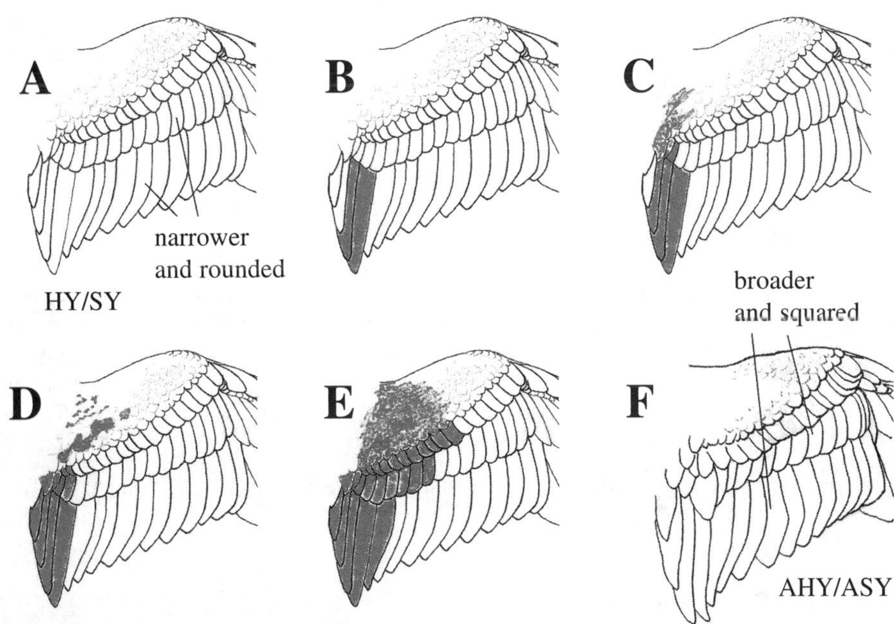

FIGURE 45. Variation in feather shapes and molt extents in the wing by age in ducks. Darker shading indicates fresher feathers. Note that the juvenal wing coverts in **A** are smaller and more rounded at the tips than formative or alternate coverts (shaded feathers in **C**-**E**), or basic wing coverts in **F**. Molt limits between replaced formative and retained juvenal wing coverts can be found in the wings of many HY/SYs in Sep-Mar, with ♂♂ averaging more replacement (typically **C**-**D**) than ♀♀ (**B**-**C**). By contrast, AHY/ASYs during this time have uniformly basic feathers (**F**). Both age groups can exhibit limits with replaced alternate feathers in Mar-Aug (♀♀) or May-Aug (♂♂), with ♀♀ typically exhibiting more molt (e.g., **D**-**E**) than ♂♂ (**B**-**C**). During these months the distal coverts and medial ss (forming the "speculum") can be examined for age- and sex-specific shape and color patterns. Alternate tertials and coverts are typically weaker and structure than basic and formative feathers, and have more distinct buff edging which creates crypsis for simultaneous wing molt.

WOOD DUCK

Aix sponsa

WODU
Species # 1440
Band size: 5A

Species—Juvs and ♀♀ from other N.Am ducks by medium-small size with proportionally long tail and short bill (Table 5, p. 93); head with ovate brownish-white to whitish eye patch or white stripes through auriculars (*cf.* Fig. 46); outer webs of p5-p9 edged silver (unique among ducks); bill and iris of ♂ with red (Fig. 46); legs yellowish to orangish. Mandarin Duck (*A. galericulata*) a frequent escape in N.Am, is similar in ♀♀ and Juv ♂♂ but has a smaller bill but longer average legs (wg chord 200-240, tl 90-113, exp culmen 27-31, tarsus 35-40); border of bill and face straight (*vs* convex in Wood Duck; Fig. 46); medial ss (e.g., s2-s4) brownish with little or no blue; ss distal to terts (s8-s9) with white chevrons at tips and often other white marks (*vs* rounder spots, located only at tip, in ♀ Wood Ducks; s11 < s10 and s12 (*vs* s11 > s10 and s12 in Wood Duck); underwing les covs brown (*vs* white with black spots in Wood Duck).

Geographic variation—Monotypic.

Molt—CAS. PFa absent-limited? (Jul-Aug in HYs), PF partial-incomplete (Aug-Nov in HYs), DPA limited-incomplete (Jan-Apr in AHY ♀, May-Jul in AHY ♂♂), DPB complete (Jun-Nov in AHYs). Molt occurs primarily on breeding or molting (p. 47) grounds. The PFa, if not part of the PB1 (prejuvenal molt; see p. 79), appears to include only a few head feathers (Bellrose & Holm 1994:336-337). The PF includes some to all of the body feathers, 1-4 terts, some to most proximal s covs (occasionally all?), and few if any rects. During PBs, wing feathers molt synchronously. The DPA includes some to all of the upperpart feathers, from no to many (up to 60%) proximal wing covs and 0-5 terts but few if any rects. ♂♂ replace more feathers during the PF whereas ♀♀ replace more during the DPA (Fig. 45, p. 79). See Family (p. 47), and Subfamily and Tribal (pp. 78-79) accounts for more details.

Age/Sex—Juv (B1; May-Oct) has distinct dark eyeline and whitish-brown supercilium, rects completely juv (Fig. 26**A**, p. 48), and bill, iris, and legs washed grayish or dusky. Juv ♂♂ have indistinct white stripes through auriculars (Fig. 46), lacking in ♀♀, and can also be sexed by wing-feather characters and iris and bill color as in HY/SYs. Partial medial BP (Fig. 20**A**, p. 31) and/or distended cloaca (Fig. 21, p. 32) developed by ♀♀ in Mar-Jun. See Figures 22-23 (pp. 32-35) for cloacal and molt-related characteristics useful in ageing and sexing, Table 5 (p. 93) for measurements by age and sex, and Carney (1992) for useful photographs.

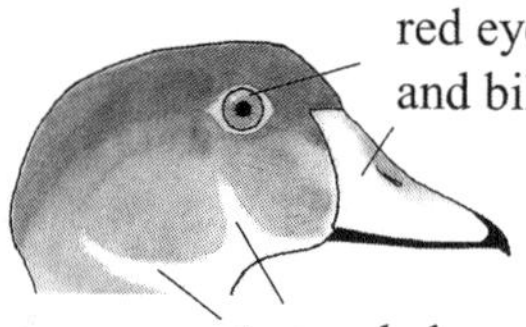

red eye and bill

two pale bars

FIGURE 46. Facial plumage aspect and bare part colors to separate Juv and alternate-aspect ♂ from ♀ Wood Ducks. Most ♀♀ lack two bars in the face and have dark eye and bill (although beware senescent ♀♀ that can show ♂-like characters).

HY/SY ♀ (1st cycle, F1-A1; Sep-Aug): Head and body gray and brown; face with abbreviated whitish eye-patch (usually extending < 20 mm posterior to eye) and without white stripes through auricular (*cf.* Fig. 46); most to all s covs narrow, rounded, and worn (Fig. 45**A-E**, p. 79), the juv les covs brown tinged greenish and the juv gr covs dull greenish blue and brown (Fig. 47**A**); base of bill blackish to gray, tinged yellowish or pinkish in Jan-Aug; iris dark; legs dull dusky yellow; most to all rects juv (Fig. 26**A**, p. 48); outer pp narrow (Fig. 25**A-B**, p. 47), shorter by sex (Table 5), and brown without sheen. **Note: Sexing reliable in all plumages but individuals of both sexes can sometimes be difficult to age by plumage aspect alone.**

AHY/ASY ♀ (Def. cycle, DB-DA; Sep-Aug): Head and body gray and brown, with few or no multi-colored feathers (see p. 78 regarding senescent ♀♀); face with extensive whitish eye-patch (usually extending > 20 mm posterior to eye) but without white stripes through auricular (*cf*. Fig. 46); s covs broad and fresher (Fig. 45**F**), the les covs brown tinged bluish and the gr covs with moderately bright bluish sheen and blackish tip (Fig. 47**B**); base of bill gray, washed yellowish or pinkish; iris dark; legs bright yellowish with blackish webs; most to all rects basic (Fig. 26 **D-E**; see **Molt**); outer pp broader (Fig. **C-D**), longer by sex (Table 5), and brown with slight greenish gloss. **Note: See HY/SY ♀.**

A B C

♀♂ ♀ ♂

Juv Form/Basic

FIGURE 47. Patterns in medial gr covs (corresponding to s6-s8) by feather generation and sex in Wood Duck. Note the thinner shape and lack or near-lack of bluish sheen to juv feathers (**A**) and the broader shape and increased sheen (♂ > ♀) in basic feathers (**B-C**). Note that these coverts can occasionally all be replaced during the PF (especially in HY/SY ♂♂; feathers intermediate in shape and aspect) or DPA (especially in ♀♀; feathers browner). Otherwise juv covs (**A**) are retained by SYs until the PB2 in Jun-Nov.

HY/SY ♂ (1st cycle, F1-A1; Sep-Aug): Head and body multi-colored (often with dull brownish tinge or feathers) in Nov-May; face without whitish eye-patch but with white stripes through auricular (Fig. 46); s covs as in HY/SY ♀ (Figs. 45**A-E** & 47**A**); base of bill grayish, becoming reddish in Nov-Aug; iris brown, becoming dull pinkish orange by Nov-Jan; legs dull dusky yellow, becoming moderately bright in Jan-Apr; outer rects (Fig. 26**A**) and pp (Fig. 25**A-B**, Table 5) as in HY/SY ♀. **Note: See HY/SY ♀. Intermediate ♂♂ should be aged U/AHY (Sep-Aug). Also. beware of occasional HY/SYs (especially in s.N.Am) that may replace all s covs during the PF and can only be aged by bare part color and criteria of the outer pp and rects.**

AHY/ASY ♂ (Def. cycle, DB-DA; Sep-Aug): Head and body bright multi-colored in Sep-May and often with traces or tinges of these colors in Jun-Aug; face as in HY/SY ♂ (Fig. 46); s covs broad and fresher (Fig. 45**F**), the les covs tinged bluish and the gr covs with bright bluish sheen and black tip (Fig. 47**C**); base of bill and iris bright red; legs bright yellowish to orangish; rects (Fig. 26 **D-E**; see **Molt**) and outer pp (Fig. 25**C-D**, Table 5) as in AHY/ASY ♀. **Note: See HY/SY ♀ and HY/SY ♂.**

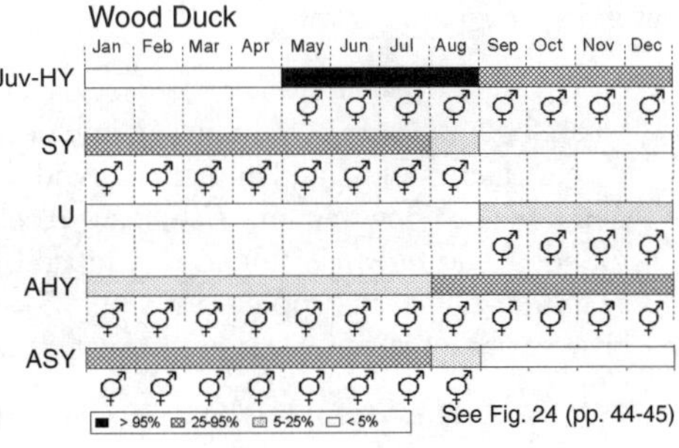

Hybrids reported—With Mallard (McCarthy 2006), Ring-necked Duck (Di Labio & Gosselin 1994), Hooded Merganser (Bouvier 1974, Russell 1978), and possibly Common Goldeneye (McCarthy 2006) in the wild. Reports with Redhead have been questioned (see McCarthy 2006).

References—Baldwin (1965), Bellrose & Holm (1994), Bent (1923), Carney (1964, 1992), Gilmer et al. (1977), Harvey et al. (1989), Hepp & Bellrose (1995), Hipes & Hepp (1995), Holt (1984), Johnsgard (1968), Miller (1925), Palmer (1972, 1976b), Oberholser (1974), Roberts (1955), Shurtleff & Savage (1996), Vrtiska et al. (1997), Zicus (1982).

GADWALL
Anas strepera

GADW
Species # 1350
Band size: 6

Species—Juvs and ♀♀ from other N.Am ducks by medium-large size with proportionally short tail (Table 5, p. 93); les covs usually with chestnut (Fig. 48); ss black, brown, and white, without blue or green (Fig. 49); underwing covs mostly to entirely white; bill yellowish orange with variable dark center (blackish in ♂♂ in Nov-Jun); legs dull yellowish to dark orange, without reddish tones. Falcated Duck (*A. falcata*), a vagrant to w.N.Am, averages shorter wing and tail (wg chord 224-263, tl 68-80, exp culmen 36-47, tarsus 35-43); face with dusky stripe extending posterior to eye; lateral undertail covs distinctly buff to yellowish; outer webs to s5-s10 with green and distinct white tips; abdomen not contrastingly white; bill and legs grayish to slate.

Geographic variation—An extinct population of *Anas*, formerly resident on Washington I, c.Pacific Ocean, is usually regarded as a smaller subspecies, *A.s. couesi* (wg chord 203, exp culmen 37, bill height at distal end of forehead feathering 14.0, tarsus 35.5); see Palmer (1976a), Streets (1876, 1877). No other (extant) subspecies occur.

Molt—CAS. PFa absent-limited? (Jul-Sep in HYs), PF partial-incomplete (Aug-Dec in HYs), DPA limited-incomplete (Jan-Apr in AHY ♀♀, May-Jul in AHY ♂♂), DPB complete (Jul-Nov in AHYs). Molt occurs primarily on breeding or molting (p. 47) grounds, although in ♀♀ the DPB can complete or take place on the non-breeding grounds. The PFa, if not part of the PB1 (prejuvenal molt; see p. 79), appears to include only a few body feathers (Oring 1968). The PF includes some to all body feathers, few to some proximal s covs, 0-4 terts and tert covs, and no to all 16 rects. During DPBs, wing feathers molt synchronously. The DPA includes some to all of the upperpart feathers, 0-5 terts/inner ss, up to 60% of the proximal s covs, and no to all rects. ♂♂ replace more feathers during the PF whereas ♀♀ replace more during the DPA (Fig. 45, p. 79). See Family (p. 47), and Subfamily and Tribal (pp. 78-79) accounts for more details.

Age/Sex—Juv (B1; Jun-Oct) resembles HY/SY ♀ (below) and has rects fully juv (Fig. 26**A**, p. 48) and legs and bill washed dusky. Juv ♀♀ average heavier spotting on abdomen than ♂♂, and the sexes can be separated by tert-cov (*cf.* Fig. 54, p. 88) and other wing-feather characters, as in HY/SYs. Partial medial BP (Fig. 20**A**, p. 31) and/or distended cloaca (Fig. 21, p. 32) developed by ♀♀ in Apr-Jun. See Figures 22-23 (pp. 32-35) for cloacal characteristics useful in ageing and sexing (including Juvs), Table 5 (p. 93) for measurements by age and sex, and Carney (1992) for useful photographs of wings.

HY/SY ♀ (1st cycle, F1-A1; Sep-Aug): Head and body brown and buff, without grayish or blackish; most to all s covs narrow, rounded, and worn (Fig. 45**A-E**, p. 79), the lower row of les covs and the juv med and gr covs with little or no chestnut or blackish (Fig. 48**A-B**); bill dull orange-yellow moderate to heavy blackish mottling (Fig. 55**A-C**, p. 89); juv s9 narrow, rounded, and brown with narrow whitish fringe (Fig. 49**A**; sometimes replaced by alternate s9 in Mar-Aug); outer pp narrow (Fig. 25**A-B**, p. 47), averaging shorter by sex (Table 5), and brown without sheen; rects juv, formative, and/or alternate (Fig. 26**A-D**; see **Molt**).

AHY/ASY ♀ (Def. cycle, DB-DA; Sep-Aug): Head and body brown and buff, with little or no grayish or blackish (see p. 78 regarding senescent ♀♀); s covs broad and fresher (Fig. 45**F**), the lower row of les covs and med and gr covs with moderate chestnut and dusky (Fig. 48**B-C**); bill bright orange-yellow (duller in Jun-Aug) with moderate blackish mottling (Fig. 55**B-D**); s9 broad, sinuous at tip, and with grayish tip and inner web (Fig. 49**B**; sometimes replaced by alternate s9 in Mar-Aug); outer pp broader (Fig. 25**C-D**), averaging longer by sex (Table 5), and brown with slight sheen; rects basic and/or alternate (Fig. 26**D-F**; see **Molt**).

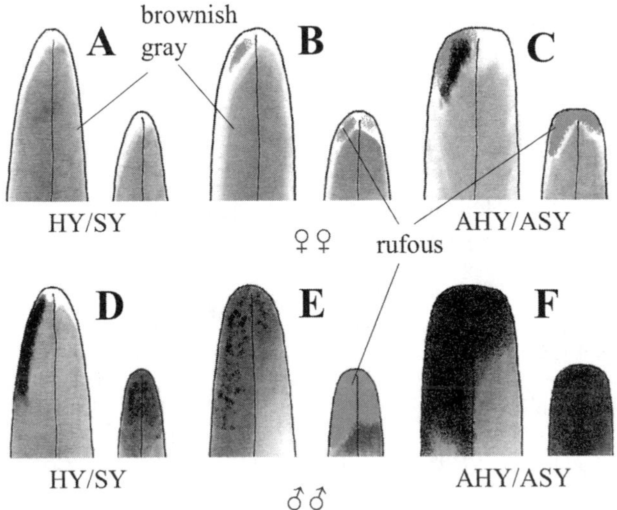

FIGURE 48. Pattern and shape of medial greater coverts (left) and med covs (right) by sex and age in Gadwall. The feathers represent the 4th to 5th coverts from the inside. In each row, the left-hand group (**A**, **D**) represent patterns found on juv feathers of HY/SYs, right-hand feathers (**C**, **F**) represent patterns found on definitive feathers of AHY/ASYs, and central feathers (**B**, **E**) represent intermediate patterns that can be found in both feather and age groups. A few ♀♀ may replace these feathers during the DPA. Otherwise, juv covs are retained by SYs through the PB2 in Jul-Nov.

HY/SY ♂ (1st cycle, F1-A1; Sep-Aug): Head and body with gray and black (often with dull brownish tinge or feathers) in Nov-May; most to all s covs narrow, rounded, and worn (Fig. 45**A-D**), the lower row of les covs and juv med and gr covs with little to moderate chestnut and blackish (Fig. 48**D-E**); bill dull orange-yellow with reduced dusky mottling (Fig. 55**D**), to blackish in Mar-Aug (*cf.*, Fig. 55**E**); s9 narrow and brownish with broad white fringe, especially to inner web (Fig. 49**C**); outer pp (Fig. 25**A-B**, Table 5) and rects (Fig. 26 **A-C**; see **Molt**) as in HY/SY ♀; 1-4 juv undertail covs occasionally retained, whitish with brown bars.

AHY/ASY ♂ (Def. cycle, DB-DA; Sep-Aug): Head and body bright gray and black in Sep-May and often with traces or tinges of this plumage aspect in Jun-Aug; s covs broad and fresher (Fig. 45**F**), the lower row of les covs and med and gr covs with an extensive amount of chestnut and dusky (Fig. 48**D-E**); bill black (*cf.* Fig. 55**E**), with narrow orange-yellow edges in Jun-Aug; s9 broad, sinuous, and with tip and inner web primarily white (Fig. 49**D**); outer pp

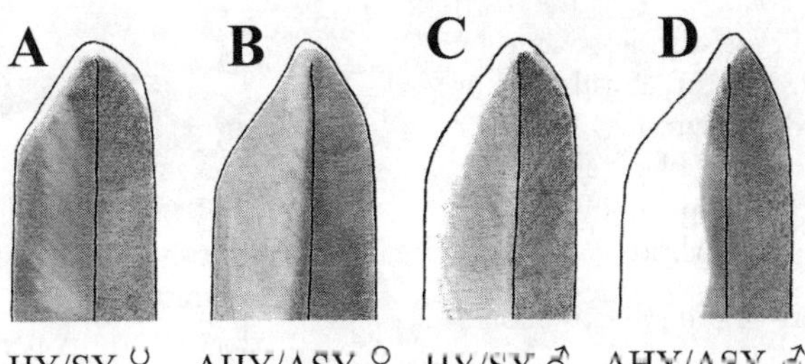

FIGURE 49. Pattern and shape of s9 by age and sex in Gadwall. ♀♀ sometimes replace s9 during the PA, resulting in a buff-fringed feather in Mar-Aug which is similar in both SYs and ASYs. See also Figure 48.

(Fig. 25**C**-**D**, Table 5) and rects (Fig. 26**D**-**F**) as in AHY/ASY ♀; undertail covs uniformly blackish.

Hybrids reported—With Falcated Duck *A. falcata* (McCarthy 2006), Eurasian Wigeon (McCarthy 2006), Mallard ("Brewer's Duck"; McIlhenny 1937, Merrifield 1998, Randler 2001b), Northern Shoveler (McCarthy 2006), Northern Pintail (McIlhenny 1937, McCarthy 2006), and possibly Green-winged Teal (McCarthy 2006) and Hooded Merganser (Sibley 1994) in the wild. Reports with American Wigeon have been questioned (McCarthy 2006).

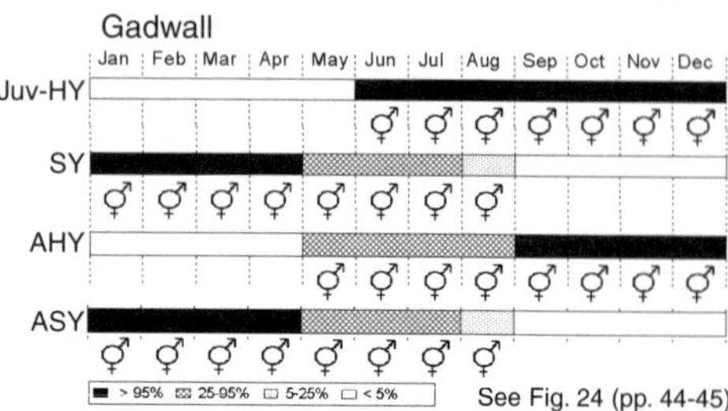

References—Bent (1923), Boyd et al. (1975), Carney (1964, 1992), Chabreck (1966), Cramp & Simmons (1977), Dement'ev & Gladkov (1952), Leschack et al. (1997), Oberholser (1974), Oring (1964, 1968), Palmer (1976a), Paulus (1984), Pyle (2005a), Roberts (1955).

EURASIAN WIGEON
Anas penelope

EUWI
Species # 1360

AMERICAN WIGEON
Anas americana

AMWI
Species # 1370
Band size: 6

Species—Juvs and ♀♀ from other N.Am ducks by medium size with proportionally short bill (Table 5, p. 93); most body feathers brown to reddish brown; les and med covs brownish to white; s3-s9 dusky to black, usually with green bases to outer webs and with narrow or reduced white tips; abdomen white; bill dusky to bluish with black nail.

Juv and ♂ Eurasian Wigeon from corresponding plumages of American Wigeon by slightly smaller average size (Table 5); base of bill usually without black border (*vs* with black border in most ♂♂ and some ♀♀ American Wigeon); axillars and proximal underwing med covs darker and less contrasting (Fig. 50); head, neck, and breast tinged reddish (*vs* grayish contrasting with brown breast); les and med covs with less white by age/sex (Fig. 51); chin and throat with little or no spotting (*vs* with dusky spotting). Look for one or more vermiculated black and white flank or back feathers to help identify Juv-HY ♂ in Aug-Sep. Beware of hybrids.

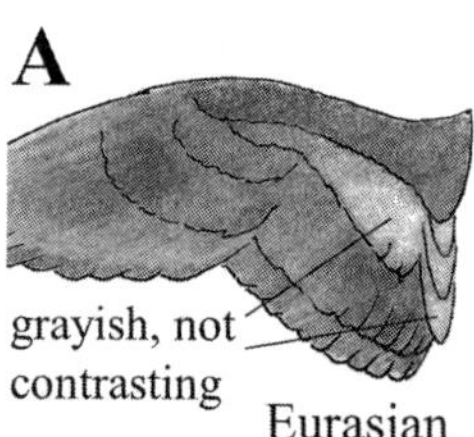

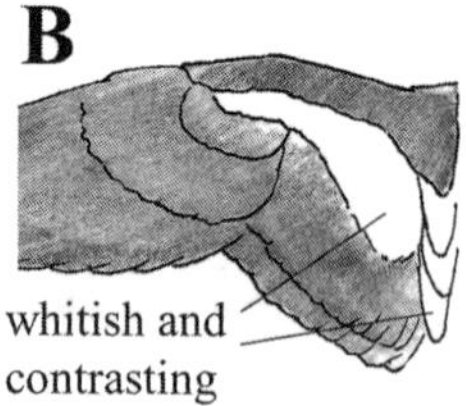

FIGURE 50. Axillars and underwing coverts of Eurasian Wigeon (**A**) and American Wigeon (**B**) to assist with separation of ♀♀ and Juv ♂♂.

Geographic variation—Both species monotypic.

Molt—CAS. PF partial-incomplete (Aug-Dec in HYs), DPA limited-incomplete (Feb-May in AHY ♀♀, Jun-Aug in AHY ♂♂), DPB complete (Jul-Dec in AHYs). The PF occurs primarily on non-breeding grounds, the DPBs commence on non-breeding to breeding or molting (p. 47) grounds and complete on non-breeding grounds, and the DPA occurs on the breeding (♀♀) or molting (♂♂) grounds. There is no evidence for a PFa (see p. 79) in wigeons. The PF includes some to all of the body feathers, few to some proximal s covs, 0-4 terts and tert covs, and no to all 16 rects (~20% of ♂♂ but few ♀♀ replace all). During DPBs, wing feathers molt synchronously, and timing in Eurasian Wigeon averages about one month later than in American wigeon by sex. The DPA includes some to all of the upperpart feathers, 0-4 terts, up to 10% of the proximal s covs, and no to all rects. ♂♂ replace more feathers during the PF whereas ♀♀ replace more during the DPA (Fig. 45, p. 79). See Family (p. 47), and Subfamily and Tribal (pp. 78-79) accounts for more details.

Age/Sex—Juv (B1; Jun-Oct) is like HY/SY ♀, with rects fully juv (Fig. 26**A**, p. 48) and bill washed dusky. Juvs are reliably sexed by the upper and under wing-cov characters by species, as described under HY/SY; also, the outer webs to the terts are uniformly brown in Juv ♀ and with a distinct dusky to blackish border in Juv ♂, and the undertail covs have indistinct rounded spots in ♀♀ and more distinct bars in ♂♂. Partial medial BP (Fig. 20**A**, p. 31) and/or distended cloaca (Fig. 21, p. 32) developed by ♀♀ in Apr-Jul. See Figures 22-23 (pp. 32-35) for cloacal characteristics useful in ageing and sexing (including Juvs), Table 5 (p. 93) for measurements by age and sex, and Carney (1992) for useful photographs of wings.

Juv-HY/SY ♀ (1st cycle, Juv/B1-F1-A1; Sep-Aug): Head and body brown, without pinkish or black; most to all s covs narrow, rounded, and worn (Fig. 45**A-D**, p. 79), brown with pale tips and little or no dusky to outer web by species (Fig. 51**A-B**); s3-s9 with little or no green and with white tips extending to outer web (Fig. 52**A**, p. 86); tert covs tipped whitish to buff (*cf.* Fig. 54**A**, p. 88); bill base dusky to dull grayish; underwing marginal covs brownish with white tips; outer pp narrow (Fig. 25**A-B**, p. 47), averaging shorter by sex (Table 5), and brown without sheen; rects juv and formative and/or alternate (Fig. 26 **A-C**; see **Molt**).

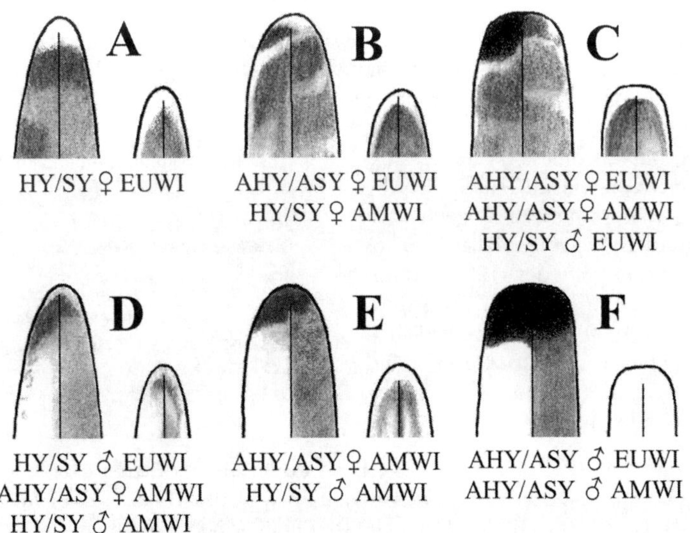

FIGURE 51. Pattern of greater coverts (left) and med covs (right) by species, age, and sex in Eurasian and American wigeon. Note that, for juv and female feathers, Eurasian Wigeon averages less white in these feathers, especially to the inner web. Juv gr and (often) med covs are retained by SYs through the PB2 in Jul-Dec.

AHY/ASY ♀ (Def. cycle, DB-DA; Sep-Aug): Head and body brown, with few or no pinkish or blackish (see p. 78 regarding senescent ♀♀); s covs broad and fresher (Fig. 45**F**), variably brown, whitish, and dusky by species (Fig. 49**B**-**C** in European Wigeon, 49**C**-**E** and nearly white in some variant American Wigeons); s3-s9 usually with dull dusky green; tert covs tipped white to buff (*cf.* Fig. 54**B**); bill base dull grayish blue; underwing marginal covs brownish with white tips; outer pp broader (Fig. 25**C**-**D**), averaging longer by sex (Table 5), and brown with slight sheen; rects basic and/or alternate (Fig. 26**D**-**F**; see **Molt**).

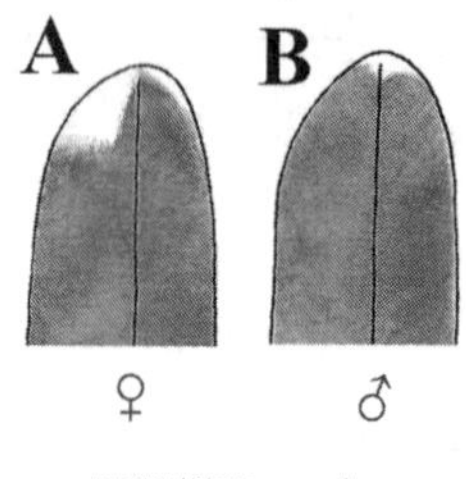

FIGURE 52. Pattern to tips of juv medial secondaries (s9 shown) by sex in HY/SY wigeon. Note that ♀♀ typically have more on the inner (left) web whereas ♂♂ have more white on the outer (right) web.

Juv-HY/SY ♂ (1st cycle, Juv/B1-F1-A1; Sep-Aug): Head and body with gray, reddish, pink, and/or blackish (often with dull brownish tinge or feathers, especially in rump) in Nov-May; most to all s covs narrow, rounded, and worn (Fig. 45**A**-**C**), variably mixed pale brown, whitish, and dusky by species (Fig. 51**C**-**E**); s3-s9 with variable amount of bright green, and with reduced white tip to outer web (Fig. 52**B**); tert covs with narrow or no pale tips (*cf.* Fig. 54**C**); bill base dull grayish blue to bluish; outer pp (Fig. 25**A**-**B**, Table 5) and rects (Fig. 26**A**-**D**; see **Molt**) as in Juv-HY/SY ♀; 1-4 juv undertail covs often retained, whitish with brown bars.

AHY/ASY ♂ (Def. cycle, DB-DA; Sep-Aug): Head and body bright gray, reddish, pink, and/or black in Sep-May; s covs broad and fresher (Fig. 45**F**), mostly to entirely white and/or with distinct black tips extending to both webs of gr covs (Fig. 51**F**); s3-s9 with extensive bright green; tert covs without pale tips (*cf.* Fig. 54**D**); bill base grayish blue to bright bluish; underwing marginal covs vermiculated and without white tips; outer pp (Fig. 25**C**-**D**, Table 5) and rects (Fig. 26 **D**-**F**; see **Molt**) as in AHY/ASY ♀; undertail covs uniformly blackish.

Hybrids reported—Eurasian Wigeon with Gadwall (p. 82), Falcated Duck *A. falcata* (McCarthy 2006), American Wigeon (Bailey 1919, Hamilton 1996, Hubbard 1971, Jiguet 1999, Merrifield 1993, Randler 2001b, Sibley 1994, Votier et al. 2003, Watson 1970b), Mallard (Kuroda 1960), and Northern Shoveler, Northern Pintail, Garganey (*A. querquedula*), Baikal Teal (*A. formosa*), and Green-winged Teal (McCarthy 2006) in the wild. American Wigeon with Gadwall, Eurasian Wigeon, Mallard (Elliot 1892, Fedynich & Rhodes 1993), Blue-winged Teal (McCarthy 2006), Northern Pintail (Gantlett 1989), Green-winged Teal (Johnsgard 1960a, Aubrey et al. 1987), and probably Canvasback (Edscorn 1974) in the wild; see also Gadwall.

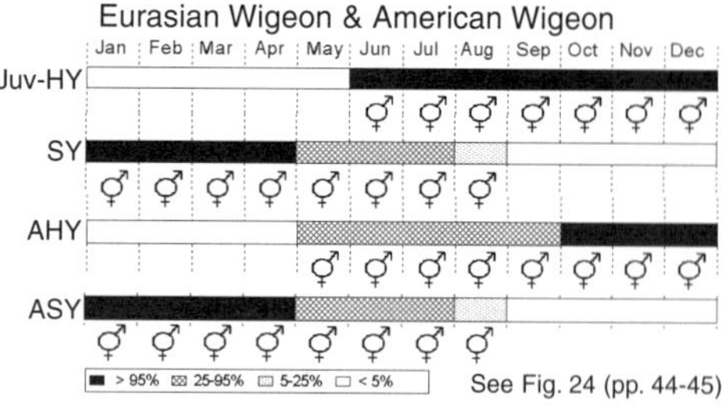

References—Alström (1985a), Bent (1923), Boyd et al. (1975), Carney (1964, 1992), Cox & Barry (2005), Cramp & Simmons (1977), Dement'ev & Gladkov (1952), Esler & Grand (1994), Harrop (1994), Heitmeyer (1995), Kemp (1990), Larkin (2000), Mowbray (1999), Oberholser (1974), Oring (1964), Palmer (1976a), Pyle (2005a), Roberts (1955), Votier et al. (2003), Wishart (1981, 1985), Wallace (1983).

AMERICAN BLACK DUCK
Anas rubripes

ABDU
Species # 1330
Band size: 7A

Species—From other N.Am ducks including Mallard (p. 89), Mottled Duck (p. 94), Steller's Eider (p. 117), and Black Scoter (p. 138) by large size (Table 5, p. 93); body dusky-brown, lacking buff tones, the feathers with indistinct or no internal markings (*cf.* Fig. 58**A**, p. 90); les covs without gray wash; gr covs with little or no white (Fig. 53, p. 88); s3-s9 with dark blue to purple at base and narrow or no white tips (Fig. 56**A**-**B**, p. 90); underwing p covs washed pale gray or with dusky centers (Fig. 57**A**, p. 90); outer rects dark brown, with few or no pale marks (Fig. 58**A**, p. 90); central uppertail covs not recurved (beware some Mallard hybrids with recurved feathers); bill grayish olive to dull greenish yellow, without distinct black border to base of proximal-ventral corner (*cf* Fig. 60, p. 94); legs bright orange to reddish.

Beware of hybrids with Mallard which are relatively common in the wild (see Figs. 53-54 & 56-59). For discussions on the relationships of American Black Duck, Mallard, and Mottled Duck (including incidence of hybridization) see Alison & Prevett (1976), Ankney et al. (1986), Brodskey & Weatherhead (1984), Delacour & Mayr (1945), Elliot (1892), Fedynich (1975), Hanson & Ankney (1994), Hepp et al. (1988), Heusmann (1974), Hubbard (1977), Johnsgard (1960b, 1961a, 1967), Kirby et al. (2000), Livezey (1991), McCarthy (2006), Morgan et al. (1984), Parkes (1954, 1958a), Phillips (1912, 1915a, 1921), and Weller (1980).

Geographic variation—Monotypic (P.A. Johnsgard *in* Mayr & Cottrell 1979). Populations breeding in WI to Nfl-MD ("*A.r. tristis*") may average slightly larger and paler than populations breeding to the northwest but differences, if present, are insufficient and broadly clinal. See Bent (1923), Brewster (1902a, 1909a, 1910), Dwight (1909), Farrand (1990), Hellmayr & Conover (1948a), Oberholser (1917b, 1974), Phillips (1920), Shortt (1943), and Townsend (1912).

Molt—CAS. PFa absent-limited? (Jul-Sep in HYs), PF partial-incomplete (Aug-Nov in HYs), DPA limited-incomplete (Feb-May in AHY ♀♀, May-Jul in AHY ♂♂), DPB complete (Jun-Oct in AHYs). Molt strategies appear similar to those of Mallard (p. 89).

Age/Sex—Juv (B1; Jun-Oct) is like HY/SY ♀, the underpart feathers with medial pale breaks giving streaked appearance, the rects entirely juv (Fig. 26**A**, p. 48), and the bill and legs grayish or washed dusky. Some Juvs can be sexed by the tert-cov, gr-cov, and s3-s4 characters as described under HY/SY. Partial medial BP (Fig. 20**A**, p. 31) and/or distended cloaca (Fig. 21, p. 32) indicate ♀ in Mar-Jun. See Figures 22-23 (pp. 32-35) for cloacal characteristics useful in ageing and sexing (including Juvs), Table 5 (p. 93) for measurements by age and sex, and Carney (1992) for useful photographs of wings.

HY/SY ♀ (1st cycle, F1-A1; Sep-Aug): Most to all s covs narrow, rounded, and worn (Fig. 45**A**-**D**, p. 79), the juv gr covs with indistinct or no pale band and/or dusky tip (Fig. 53**A**, p. 88); longest tert usually retained juv, short, rounded, and brown with pale fringe but without dusky, and the tert covs pointed and fringed pale (Fig. 54**A**, p. 88); bill dull grayish to greenish yellow with moderate blackish mottling (Fig. 55**B**-**C**, p. 89); legs dusky to dull dark orange; outer webs of s3-s4 with little or no iridescent purple; outer pp and p covs narrow (Fig. 25**A**-**B**, p. 47), the pp averaging shorter by sex (Table 5), and brown without sheen; rects juv and formative and/or alternate (Fig. 26**A**-**C**; see **Molt**); crown without greenish. **Note: Some intermediates may be difficult to age and/or sex. Sex-specific differences in underpart-feather markings (Godfrey 1986) show variation by age and feather generation and are generally unreliable for sexing. See HY/SY ♂.**

AHY/ASY ♀ (Def. cycle, DB-DA; Sep-Aug): S covs broad and fresher (Fig. 45**F**), the gr covs with indistinct pale brownish bands and broad blackish-purple tips (Fig. 53**B**); longest tert medium in length, rounded, fringed pale, and often with dusky to the outer web, and the tert covs rounded and fringed pale (Fig. 54**B**); bill dull greenish yellow to yellowish variably mottled blackish (Fig. 55**A-D**); legs dull dark orange to dull reddish; outer webs of s3-s4 usually with indistinct iridescent purple; outer pp and p covs broader (Fig. 25**C-D**), the pp averaging longer by sex (Table 5), and brown with slight sheen; rects basic and/or alternate (Fig. 26**C**; see **Molt**); crown without greenish. **Note: See HY/SY ♀.**

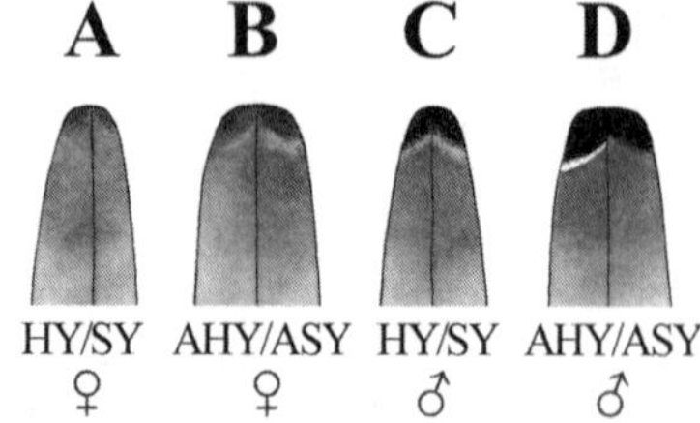

FIGURE 53. Shape and pattern to medial greater covert (corresponding to s5) by age/sex group in American Black and Mottled ducks. The pale bands in Mottled Ducks average slightly wider and more cinnamon in Mottled Duck. American Black Duck X Mallards may show intermediate patterns between this and those in Figure 59 (p. 91) by age/sex group. Juv covs (**A**, **C**) are retained by SYs through the PB2 in Jun-Oct.

HY/SY ♂ (1st cycle, F1-A1; Sep-Aug): Most to all s covs narrow, rounded, and worn (Fig. 45**A-C**), the juv gr covs with indistinct pale brownish bands and blackish-purple tips (Fig. 53**C**); most to all juv terts usually replaced in Sep-Nov, the longest formative tert long, pointed, curved medially, and grayish brown with dusky iridescence on outer web, and the tert covs pointed and without or with narrow and broken pale fringe (Fig. 54**C**); bill olive to dull greenish yellow, with diminishing dusky mottling (Fig. 55**C-D**); legs dull dusky orange to dull red; outer webs of s3-s4 with dull iridescent purple; outer pp (Fig. 25**A-B**, Table 5), p covs, and rects (Fig. 26**A-D**; see **Molt**) as in HY/SY ♀; crown usually without greenish. **Note: See HY/SY ♀. Note that a small proportion of HY ♂♂ retain juv terts during the PF, which resemble those of HY ♀♀ (Fig. 54A); however, the tert-cov character is reliable with juv, formative, and alternate feathers.**

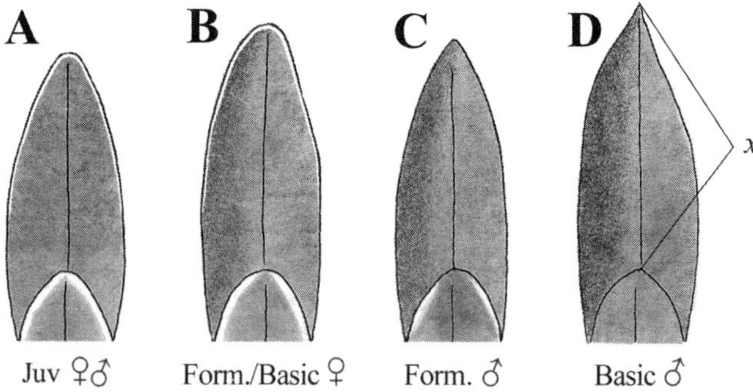

FIGURE 54. Shape, size, and pattern to longest tertial and corresponding tertial covert, by feather generation and sex, in American Black Duck; criteria are very similar in Mottled Duck and Mallard (especially *A.p. diazi*). ♀♀ of both age groups have complete fringing to the tert cov whereas ♂♂ usually lack fringing (can be partial in HY/SY ♂, up to the pattern shown in **C**). Note that the terts of Juv ♂♂ resemble those of ♀♀ (**A**) but are usually replaced during the PF in Oct-Nov (**C**), whereas ♀♀ retain juv terts through at least Apr and often Jun in SYs. In American Black Duck, the distance between the tip of the tert and the tip of the tert cov (*x* in **D**) varies by sex, with Juv (HY/SY) ♀ (**A**) < 85 mm, formative (HY/SY) ♂ (**C**) > 85 mm, formative and basic (AHY) ♀ (**B**) < 90 mm, and basic (AHY/ASY) ♂ (**D**) > 90 mm. Other ducks may show similar shape of terts and pattern to tert covs, but can differ in the pattern to the terts and the distance between the tips of the two feathers.

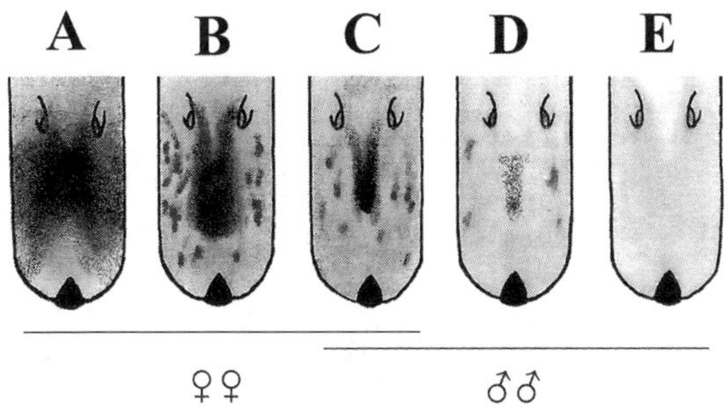

FIGURE 55. Patterns of bills by age and sex in certain *Anas* ducks. HY/SY ♀♀ usually show the most markings (**A-B**), followed by AHY/ASY ♀♀ (**B-C**), HY/SY ♂♂ (**C-D**), and AHY/ASY ♂♂ (**D-E**). The base color of the bill varies from dull orange, to olive, to bright yellowish in the Mallard group or to blackish in ♂ Gadwalls (p. 82) and Blue-winged Teal (p. 95).

AHY/ASY ♂ (Def. cycle, DB-DA; Sep-Aug): S covs broad and fresher (Fig. 45**F**), the gr covs with distinct pale brown to whitish bands and broad purplish tips (Fig. 53**D**); longest tert elongated, pointed, curved medially, and grayish with iridescent purplish on outer web, and the tert covs rounded and without pale fringe (Fig. 54**D**); bill bright greenish yellow (duller in Jun-Aug) with little to no dusky mottling (Fig. 55**D-E**); legs bright red (duller in Jun-Aug); outer webs of s3-s4 with bright iridescent purple; outer pp (Fig. 25**C-D**, Table 5), p covs, and rects (Fig. 26 **D-F**; see **Molt**) as in AHY/ASY ♀; crown usually tinged greenish in Sep-Jun. **Note: See HY/SY ♀.**

American Black Duck

Jan | Feb | Mar | Apr | May | Jun | Jul | Aug | Sep | Oct | Nov | Dec

Juv-HY

SY

U

AHY

ASY

■ > 95% ▨ 25-95% ▭ 5-25% □ < 5%

See Fig. 24 (pp. 44-45)

Note: Cloacal examination needed for reliable sexing of some HY/SYs.

Hybrids reported—With Mallard and Mottled Duck (see references in Species Account, p. 87) and Northern Pintail (Alison & Prevett 1976) in the wild.

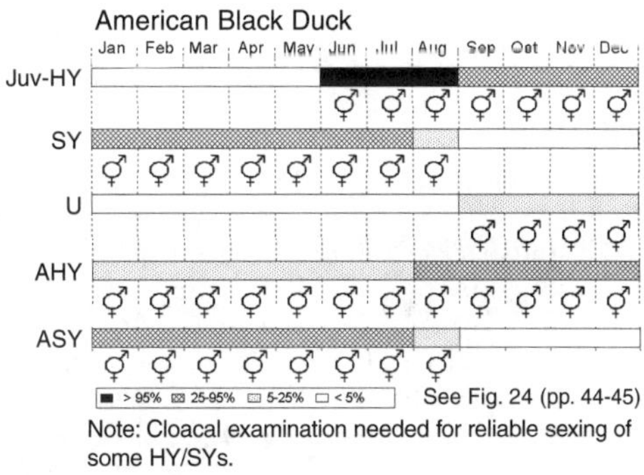

References—Ashley et al. (2006, 2007), Barnes (1989), Belanger et al. (1988), Bent (1923), Carney (1964, 1992), Cramp & Simmons (1977), Godfrey (1986), Hanson & Ankney (1994), Johnsgard (1961a), Longcore et al. (2000), Oberholser (1974), Palmer (1972, 1976a), Pyle (2005a), Reed & Boyd (1972), Roberts (1955), Shortt (1943).

MALLARD

Anas platyrhynchos

MALL
Species # 1320
Band size: 7A

Mexican Duck (MEDU)

Species # 1331

Species—Juvs, ♀♀, and Mexican Duck (*A.p. diazi*) from other N.Am ducks including American Black (p. 87) and Mottled (p. 94) ducks by large size (Table 5, p. 93); body washed buff, the feathers with distinct internal markings (*cf.* Fig. 58**C-D**, p. 90); les covs washed grayish; gr covs with distinct and wide white bands (Fig. 59); s3-s9 with bright blue to outer webs and wide and distinct white tips (Fig. 56**C-F**, p. 90); underwing covs white (Fig. 57**C**); outer rects primarily whitish or with substantial buff to whitish internal markings (Fig. 58**B-D**); central uppertail covs recurved in non-Juv ♂♂; bill partly to entirely dull orange-yellow (Juvs) to orange (♀) or bright

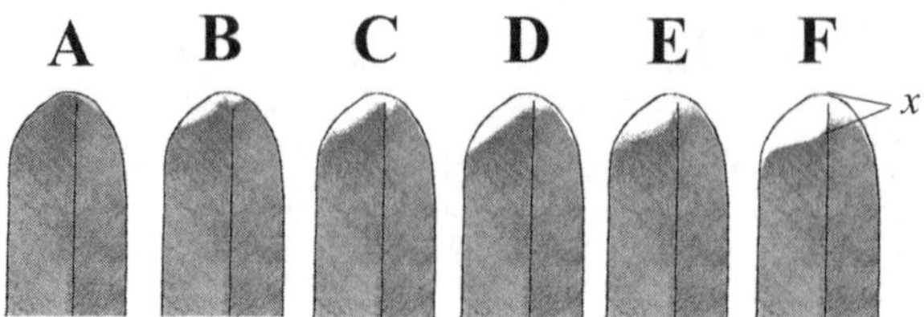

FIGURE 56. Amount of white to the tip of s5 by species among ducks of the "Mallard group". The amount varies by age and sex within each taxon, with HY/SYs averaging less white than AHY/ASYs (perhaps as much due to wear as age). The breadth of white along the shaft of the outer web (*x* in illustration **F**) varies by taxon: American Black Duck (**A-B**) 0-2 mm, Mottled Duck (**B-C**) 1-4 mm, "Mexican Duck" (**C-E**) 4-9 mm, nominate Mallard (**E-F**) 8-13 mm. American Black Duck X Mallard shows variable amounts of white (**B-E**).

greenish yellow (AHY ♂), without a distinct black border to the base or proximal-ventral corner (*cf* Fig. 60, p. 94); legs dull to bright orange, without red tones. Beware of hybrids with American Black Duck which are common in the wild (see American Black Duck, p. 87).

Geographic variation—See Aldrich & Baer (1970), Browning (1974, 1978), Byers & Cary (1991), Cramp & Simmons (1977), Hellmayr & Conover (1948a), Hubbard (1977), Huber (1920), Huey (1961), Johnsgard (1961a, 1961b), Kulikova et al. (2005), Lindsey (1946), Oberholser (1974), Palmer (1976a), A.R. Phillips (1959, 1961), A.R. Phillips et al. (1964), J.C. Phillips (1912), Pitelka (1948), Rea (1983a), Scott & Reynolds (1984). One other subspecies resident in Greenland.

A.p. platyrhynchos (br AK-sw.CA to s.ME-VA; wint to se.CA-s.TX-FL; domesticated individuals br throughout N.Am): Averages slightly larger (Table 5, p. 93); basic-plumaged ♂ green, gray, rusty and black; gr covs with wider and more distinct white bands by age and sex (Fig. 59**A-D**); s3-s9 with wider white tips (Fig. 56**E-F**); outer rects paler at base (Fig. 58**C-E**); undertail covs primarily whitish. Populations of N.Am ("*neobora*") average slightly larger and grayer than populations of Eurasia but differences, if present, are insufficient to warrant subspecific separation. Also, domesticated strains of nominate Mallard have larger bills and legs than wild strains (Byers & Cary 1991).

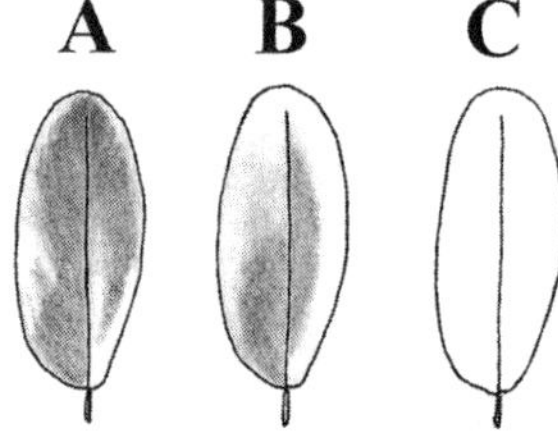

FIGURE 57. Distal underwing primary coverts in American Black Duck (**A**), Mottled Duck (**B**), and Mallard (**C**), including "Mexican" Duck. Patterns are similar by age, sex, and feather generation. American Black Duck X Mallard may show intermediate amounts of white (**B**).

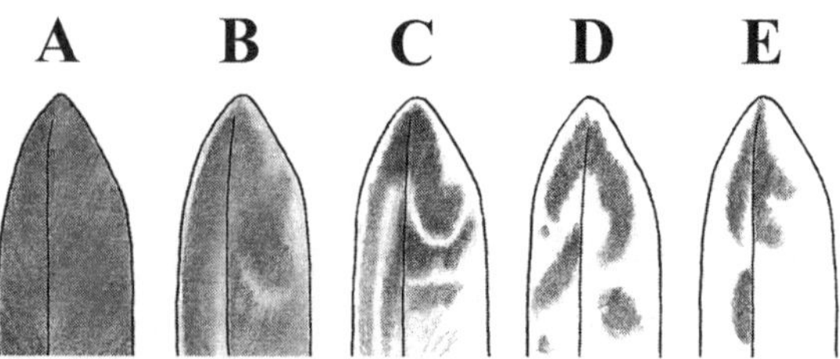

FIGURE 58. Outer rectrix (r8) in American Black Duck (**A-B**), Mottled Duck (**B**), "Mexican" Duck (**B-C**), and nominate Mallard (**C-E**). Patterns are similar by age, sex, and feather generation. Note that body feathers often show similar differences in pattern by species, except that light areas are buff to pale brown as opposed to whitish. American Black Duck X Mallards show variable amounts of white (**B-D**).

A.p. diazi (res se.AZ-s.TX to c.Mex, vagrant to NE): Mexican Duck. Averages slightly smaller (Table 5); basic-plumaged ♂ brown (similar to ♀♀); gr covs with narrower and less-distinct white bands by age and sex (Fig. 59**E**-**H**); s3-s9 with narrower white tips (Fig. 56**C**-**E**); outer rects darker at base (Fig. 58**B**-**C**); undertail covs primarily dark. Populations in N.Am ("*novimexicana*") may average paler and grayer with redder tinge to breast in AHY ♂♂ than populations in Mexico, but differences insufficient and/or due to intergradation with introduced *platyrhynchos*.

Molt—CAS. PFa absent-limited? (Jul-Sep in HYs), PF partial-incomplete (Aug-Dec in HYs), DPA limited-incomplete (Jan-May in AHY ♀♀, May-Jul in AHY ♂♂), DPB complete (Jun-Nov in AHYs). See Figure 11**A** (p. 17). Most molting occurs on breeding or molting (p. 47) grounds, although in ♀♀ the PB can complete or take place on non-breeding grounds. The PFa, if not part of the PB1 (prejuvenal molt; see p. 79), appears to include only a few body feathers. The PF includes some to all of the body feathers, few to some proximal s covs, 0-4 terts (all in most ♂♂ but 1-2 in most ♀♀), and no to all 16 rects (all in ~40% of ♂♂ but few in ♀♀). During DPBs, wing feathers molt synchronously. The DPA includes some to all of the upperpart feathers, 0-4 terts, up to 10% of the proximal s covs, and no to all rects. ♂♂ replace more feathers during the PF whereas ♀♀ replace more during the DPA (Fig. 45, p. 79). See Family (p. 47), and Subfamily and Tribal (pp. 78-79) accounts for more details.

Age/Sex—Juv (B1; Jun-Oct) is like HY/SY ♀, the underpart feathers with medial pale breaks giving streaked appearance, the rects entirely juv (Fig. 26**A**, p. 48), and the bill and legs washed dusky. Most Juvs can be reliably sexed by s-cov characters (especially the tert covs; Fig. 54**A** *vs* **C**, p. 88) as in HY/SY. Partial medial BP (Fig. 20**A**, p. 31) and/or distended cloaca (Fig. 21, p. 32) indicate ♀ in Feb-Jun. See also Figures 22-23 (pp. 32-35), Johnson (1961), and Ward & Middleton (1971) for cloacal characteristics useful in ageing and sexing (including Juvs), Table 5 (p. 93) for measurements by age and sex, and Carney (1992) for useful photographs of wings.

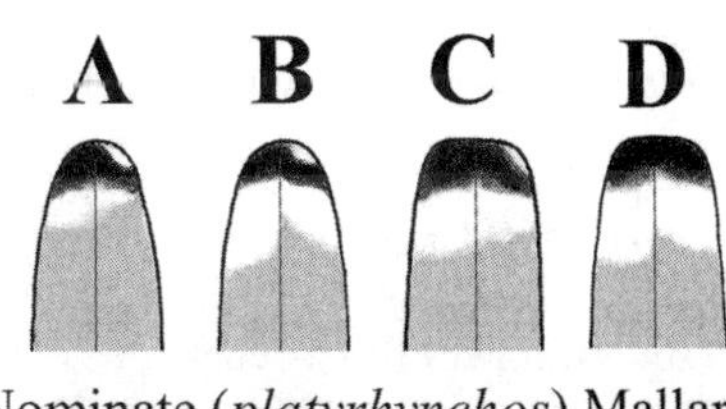

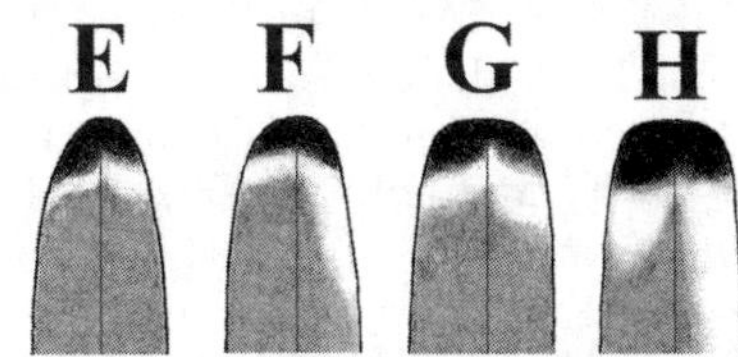

FIGURE 59. Shape and pattern to medial greater coverts (corresponding to s5) by subspecies, age, and sex in Mallards. The width of the white band (outer web, at shaft) typically as follows: Mallard HY/SY ♀ (**A**) 8-10 mm, AHY/ASY ♀ (**B**) 9-12 mm, HY/SY ♂ (**C**) 9-11 mm, AHY/ASY ♂ (**D**) 11-13 mm; Mexican Duck HY/SY ♀ (**E**) 5-7 mm, AHY/ASY ♀ (**F**) 7-9 mm, HY/SY ♂ (**G**) 6-8 mm, AHY/ASY ♂ (**H**) 8-10 mm. Juv covs (**A C E G**) are usually retained by SYs through the PB2 in Jul-Nov. American Black Duck X Mallards may show intermediate patterns between this and Figure 53 (p. 88) by age/sex group.

HY/SY ♀ (1st cycle, F1-A1; Sep-Aug): Head and body brown; most to all terts and s covs narrow, rounded, and worn (Fig. 45**A**-**D**, p. 79), the les, med, and tert covs brown with pale fringes or tips (*cf.* Fig. 54**A**), and the juv gr covs with indistinct whitish bands and blackish tips (Fig. 59**A**,**E**); bill dull greenish yellow to orange-yellow with moderate blackish mottling (Fig. 55**B**-**C**, p. 89); outer webs of s2-s3 with little or no iridescent bluish; outer pp narrow (Fig. 25**A**-**B**, p. 47), averaging shorter by sex (Table 5), and brown without sheen; rects juv and formative and/or alternate (Fig. 26**A**-**C**; see **Molt**); central uppertail covs not recurved.

AHY/ASY ♀ (Def. cycle, DB DA; Sep-Aug): Head and body brown, with little or no green, gray, reddish, or black (see p. 78 and Post 1992 regarding senescent ♀♀); terts and s covs broad and fresher (Fig. 45**F**), the les covs grayish brown with out distinct fringes, the tert covs fringed or tipped white to buff (*cf.* Fig. 54**B**), and the gr covs with moderately distinct white bands and black tips (Fig. 59**B**, **F**); bill orangish (duller in Jul-Sep) with variable blackish mottling (Fig. 55**A**-**D**); outer webs of s2-s3 sometimes washed with dull iridescent bluish; outer pp broader (Fig. 25**C**-**D**), averaging longer by sex (Table 5), and brown with slight sheen; rects basic and/or alternate (Fig. 26**D**-**F**; see **Molt**); central uppertail covs not recurved.

HY/SY ♂ (1st cycle, F1-A1; Sep-Aug): Head and body (*A.p. platyrhynchos*) primarily green, gray, reddish, and black (often with dull brownish tinge or feathers) in Nov-May; most to all s covs narrow, rounded, and worn (Fig. 45**A**-**C**), the juv les, med, and tert covs brown with indistinct or no pale buff fringes or tips (*cf.* Fig. 54**C**), and the medial gr covs with indistinct whitish bands and blackish tips (Fig. 59**C**, **G**); bill dull greenish yellow to yellow with little or no dusky mottling (Fig. 55**C**-**D**); outer web of s2 usually washed with dull iridescent bluish; outer pp (Fig. 25**A**-**B**, Table 5) and rects (Fg. 26**A**-**D**; see **Molt**) as in HY/SY ♀; central uppertail covs recurved in Nov-Aug.

AHY/ASY ♂ (Def. cycle, DB-DA; Sep-Aug): Head and body (*A.p. platyrhynchos*) bright green, gray, reddish, and black in Sep-May; terts and s covs broad and fresher (Fig. 45**F**), the les, med, and tert covs grayish brown without pale fringes or tips (*cf.* Fig. 54**D**), and the gr covs with distinct white band and black tip (Fig. 59**D**, **H**); bill bright greenish yellow (duller in Jun-Aug) usually without dusky mottling (Fig. 55**D**-**E**); outer web of s2 with glossy bluish; outer pp (Fig. 25**C**-**D**, Table 5) and rects (Fig. 26**D**-**F**; see **Molt**) as in AHY/ASY ♀; central uppertail covs recurved (slightly in Jun-Aug).

Hybrids reported—Native Mallards in the wild with Canada Goose (p. 63), Barnacle Goose *Branta bernicla* (McCarthy 2006), Wood Duck (p. 80), Gadwall (p. 82), Falcated Duck *A. falcata* (Kuroda 1960), Eurasian and American wigeons (p. 84), American Black and Mottled ducks (see American Black Duck, p. 87, for references), Hawaiian Duck *A. wyvilliana* (possibly with naturalized populations only; Engilis et al. 2002), Spot-billed Duck *A. poecilorhyncha* (McCarthy 2006), Northern Shoveler (Johnsgard 1960a), Northern Pintail (Gunther 1941, Mactavish 1979, McCarthy 2006, Sharpe & Johnsgard 1966), Green-winged Teal (Stone 1903, Trautman & Trautman 1968), Common Pochard *Aythya ferina* (McCarthy 2006), Tufted Duck (Clegg 1971, McCarthy 2006), and Red-crested Pochard *Netta rufina*, Comb Duck *Sarkidironis melanotos*, Common Eider, and Common Goldeneye (McCarthy 2006); probably Laysan Duck *A. laysanensis* (Moulton & Marshall 1996), and possibly Canvasback, Steller's Eider, Common Merganser, and Red-breasted Merganser (McCarthy 2006) in the wild. A hybrid with Cinnamon Teal (Maillard 1902) in the wild has been questioned (McCarthy 2006). See McCarthy (2006) for hybrids between naturalized Mallards and several other duck species around the world.

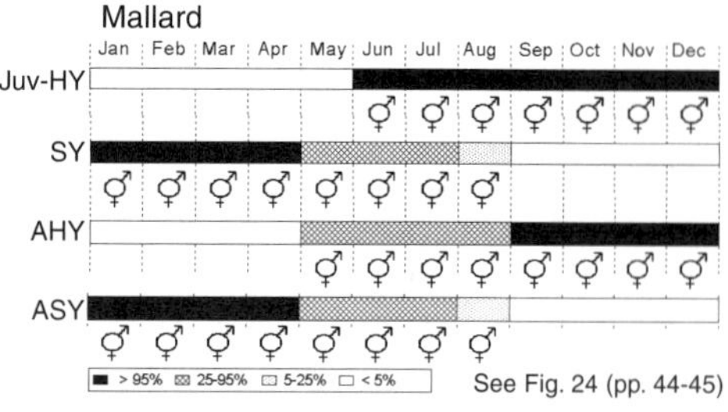

References—Baker (1993), Barnes (1989), Belanger et al. (1988), Bent (1923), Boyd et al. (1975), Carney (1964, 1992), Carney & Geis (1960), Combs & Fredrickson (1995), Cramp & Simmons (1977), Dement'ev & Gladkov (1952), Drilling et al. (2002), Gatti (1983), Gilmer et al. (1977), Hanson & Ankney (1994), Heitmeyer (1987, 1995), Hopper & Funk (1970), Hubbard (1977), Humphrey & Parkes (1959), Johnsgard (1961a), Klint (1982), Krapu et al. (1979), Leafloor et al. (1996), Marchant & Higgins (1990), Oberholser (1974), Oring (1964), Owen & Cook (1977), Palmer (1972, 1976a), Pehrsson (1987), Pyle (2005a), Richardson & Kaminski (1992), Roberts (1955), Scott & Reynolds (1984), Yarris et al. (1994), Young & Boag (1981).

TABLE 5. Measurements (mm) of North American surface-feeding ducks to assist in identification, ageing, and sexing. See pp. 4-11 for methods of measurement. Species summaries are in **bold** and subspecies summaries in ***italics***. Values were derived from 95% confidence intervals as based (for wing, exposed culmen, and tarsus) approximately on the indicated sample sizes (see pp. 4-5); sample sizes for tail length and bill depth were often smaller but included at least 10 of each sex. Thus, midpoints of ranges approximate means, and S.D. is approximated by 25% of the range.

		wing chord		tail	exp	bill	
Taxon/Sex	*n*	AHY/ASY	(HY/SY)[1]	length	culmen	depth[2]	tarsus
Wood Duck		**195-239**	**(188-233)**	**87-119**	**31-36**	**13.5-18.3**	**32-38**
♀	30	195-232	(188-226)	87-113	31-36	13.5-17.5	32-36
♂	30	217-239	(208-233)	94-119	32-38	14.3-18.3	34-38
Gadwall		**235-278**	**(228-270)**	**68-92**	**36-48**	**14.7-18.0**	**36-43**
♀	70	235-261	(228-253)	68-87	36-44	14.7-16.7	36-41
♂	70	252-278	(246-270)	74-92	39-48	15.8-18.0	38-43
Eurasian Wigeon		**229-271**	**(220-262)**	**73-112**	**30-38**	**14.4-17.8**	**35-42**
♀	40	229-254	(220-245)	73-100	30-37	14.4-17.0	35-40
♂	40	245-271	(238-262)	82-112	32-38	15.2-17.8	37-42
American Wigeon		**228-271**	**(224-263)**	**86-127**	**31-41**	**14.4-18.0**	**35-43**
♀	80	228-258	(224-247)	86-113	31-39	14.4-17.1	35-41
♂	100	247-277	(240-266)	96-127	33-41	15.3-18.0	37-43
American Black Duck		**255-300**	**(249-294)**	**81-103**	**47-59**	**18.6-23.6**	**40-50**
♀	100	255-283	(249-277)	81-98	47-55	18.6-22.6	40-47
♂	100	271-300	(265-294)	85-103	50-59	19.4-23.6	42-50
Mallard		**247-303**	**(239-295)**	**75-103**	**46-59**	**18.2-23.6**	**40-50**
A.p. platyrhyncos[3]		***255-303***	***(249-295)***	***80-103***	***48-59***	***18.6-23.6***	***41-50***
♀	100	255-287	(249-279)	80-98	48-55	18.6-22.6	41-47
♂	100	271-303	(265-295)	84-103	52-59	19.4-23.6	43-50
A.p. diazi		***247-297***	***(239-289)***	***75-93***	***46-57***	***18.2-22.6***	***40-48***
♀	45	247-279	(239-270)	75-91	46-54	18.2-21.8	40-46
♂	100	264-297	(257-289)	78-93	48-57	19.1-22.6	42-48
Mottled Duck		**230-267**	**(223-260)**	**78-93**	**48-61**	**18.1-22.5**	**40-47**
♀	50	230-253	(223-248)	78-90	48-57	18.1-21.2	40-47
♂	60	242-267	(235-260)	81-93	51-61	19.4-22.5	43-49
Blue-winged Teal		**167-195**	**(161-188)**	**56-71**	**35-45**	**13.6-16.8**	**28-35**
♀	36	167-183	(161-176)	56-68	35-42	13.6-15.8	28-33
♂	41	179-195	(173-188)	59-71	37-45	14.6-16.8	30-35
Cinnamon Teal		**178-202**	**(171-196)**	**61-78**	**39-49**	**14.6-17.7**	**29-38**
♀	93	178-193	(171-186)	61-75	39-47	14.6-16.4	29-36
♂	74	187-202	(180-196)	63-78	41-49	15.9-17.7	32-38
Northern Shoveler		**223-255**	**(216-248)**	**69-90**	**57-71**	**17.8-23.9**	**33-42**
♀	67	223-242	(216-235)	69-84	57-66	17.8-22.7	33-40
♂	72	235-255	(229-248)	76-90	60-71	18.9-23.9	35-42
Northern Pintail		**247-286**	**(241-277)**	**92-226**	**43-56**	**17.1-21.5**	**39-45**
♀	100	247-273	(241-264)	92-126	43-52	17.1-19.9	39-43
♂	100	259-286	(253-277)	167-226	46-56	18.7-21.5	40-45
Green-winged Teal		**167-194**	**(162-193)**	**59-75**	**31-40**	**12.0-15.6**	**28-34**
A.c. crecca		***167-197***	***(163-193)***	***59-74***	***31-40***	***12.0-15.5***	***28-34***
♀	77	167-191	(163-187)	59-71	31-38	12.0-14.2	28-32
♂	91	174-197	(170-193)	61-74	33-40	13.0-15.5	29-34
A.c. carolinensis		***168-194***	***(162-190)***	***60-75***	***32-40***	***12.1-15.6***	***28-34***
♀	30	168-188	(162-185)	60-72	32-38	12.1-14.4	28-33
♂	30	173-194	(171-190)	63-75	34-40	13.2-15.6	29-34

[1] Wing chord and tail length differ substantially by age; wing data are separated by age since juv primaries are retained through the second PB whereas tail lengths pertain to formative and basic feathers only, as the juvenal central rects are usually replaced by Oct-Dec in HYs. Other measures pertain to all age groups.

[2] Bill depth measured at the distal end of forehead feathering Fig. 8**A**, p. 10).

[3] Measures from N.Am populations only.

MOTTLED DUCK
Anas fulvigula

MODU
Species # 1340
Band size: 7A

Species—From other N.Am ducks including American Black Duck (p. 87) and Mallard (p. 89) by medium-large size with proportionally large bill (Table 5, p. 93); body dark brown, the feathers usually with cinnamon markings and indistinct darker chevrons (*cf*. Fig. 58**B**, p. 90); les covs dark brownish without gray wash; gr covs with little or indistinct cinnamon to whitish bands (Fig. 53, p. 88); s3-s9 with bright greenish blue at base and moderately narrow white tips (Fig. 56**B**-**C**, p. 90); underwing p covs variably whitish or washed pale gray and occasionally with dusky centers (Fig. 57**B**, p. 90); outer rects with moderate pale internal markings (Fig. 58**B**, p. 90); central uppertail covs not recurved; bill olive (Juvs), orange-yellow (AHY/ASY ♀♀), or bright greenish yellow (AHY/ASY ♂♂), with distinct black tip to the proximal-ventral corner (Fig. 60); legs dull to bright orange, without red tones. See American Black Duck (p. 87).

Geographic variation—Considered monotypic here. Populations of coastal se.TX ("*A.f. maculosa*") may average darker overall and with a slightly larger bill, but differences appear insufficient for subspecific recognition. See Delacour & Mayr (1945), Hellmayr & Conover (1948a), Johnsgard (1961a), Palmer (1976a), Phillips (1923), and Sennett (1889) for more information.

Molt—CAS. PFa absent-limited? (Jun-Aug in HYs), PF partial-incomplete (Jul-Dec in HYs), DPA limited-incomplete (Jan-May in AHY ♀♀, May-Aug in AHY ♂♂), DPB complete (May-Oct in AHYs). Most molting occurs on breeding or molting (p. 47) grounds. The PFa, if not part of the PB1 (prejuvenal molt; see p. 79), appears to include only a few body feathers. The PF includes some to all of the body feathers, few to some proximal s covs, 0-4 terts and tert covs, and no to all 16 rects (all in ~50% of ♂♂ but few ♀♀). During DPBs, wing feathers molt synchronously. The DPA includes some to all of the upperpart feathers, 0-4 terts, up to 10% of the proximal s covs, and no to all rects. ♂♂ replace more feathers during the PF whereas ♀♀ replace more during the DPA (Fig. 45, p. 79). See Family (p. 47), and Subfamily and Tribal (pp. 78-79) accounts for more details.

Age/Sex—Juvs (Jun-Oct) are like HY/SYs, the underpart feathers with medial pale breaks giving streaked appearance, rects entirely juv (Fig. 26**A**, p. 48), and bill and legs washed dusky. Partial medial BP (Fig. 20**A**, p. 31) and/or distended cloaca (Fig. 21, p. 32) indicate ♀ in Feb-May. Except for the iridescent aspect to the outer webs of s3-s4 (greenish blue in Mottled Duck) and slight differences in the timing of plumage-related characters (see Bar Graph), ageing and sexing criteria parallel those of American Black Duck (p. 87). In addition, the sexes of Mottled Duck can be reliably separated by the pattern of black to the base of the bill: more restricted in ♀♀ than in ♂♂ (Fig. 60).

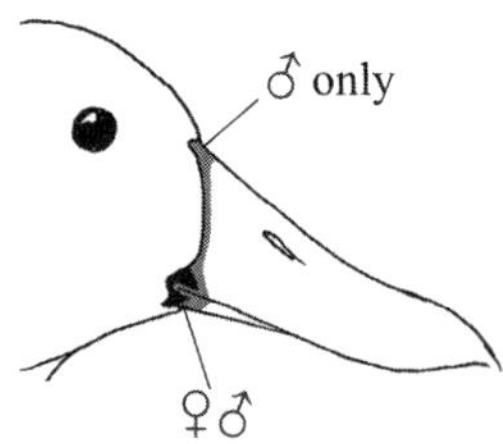

FIGURE 60. Pattern to base of bill by sex in Mottled Duck. Both sexes show black (indicated as gray in ♂), with that of ♀♀ being restricted to the corner

Hybrids reported—With Muscovy Duck *Cairina moschata* (Stutzenbaker 1988) and American Black Duck and Mallard (see references under American Black Duck, p. 87) in the wild.

References—Carney (1964, 1992), Johnsgard (1961a), T.W. Johnson (1973), Moorman & Gray (1994), Moorman et al. (1993), Oberholser (1974), Palmer (1976a), Pyle (2005a), Stutzenbaker (1988).

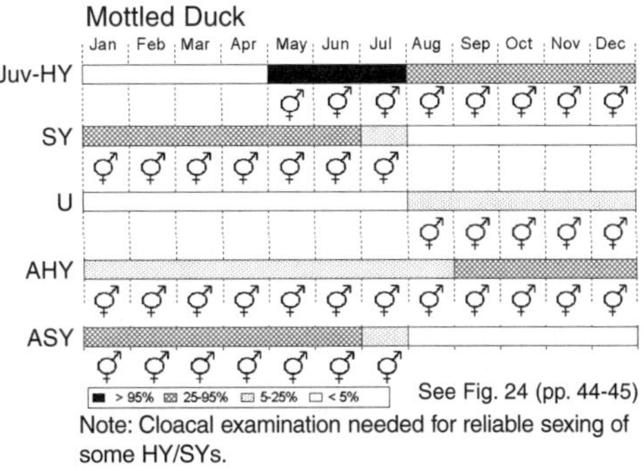

Note: Cloacal examination needed for reliable sexing of some HY/SYs.

BLUE-WINGED TEAL
Anas discors

BWTE
Species # 1400
Band size: 4A ♀, 5 ♂

Species—Juvs and ♀♀ from other N.Am ducks (particularly Cinnamon Teal, p. 97) by small to medium-small size (Table 5, p. 93); bill narrow (width at widest point 14.2-16.2 mm); body primarily brownish with moderately distinct facial features (Fig. 61) and little or no cinnamon or warm buff to breast; les and med covs mostly to entirely pale blue; p covs brown; distal gr covs partly to entirely white (Fig. 62, p. 96), without cinnamon; outer webs of s5-s10 with green, and narrow or no white tips (< 5 mm wide, if present); shafts to pp brownish; outer rects brownish; bill primarily dusky to black; iris dark brown, tinged reddish brown in AHY/ASY ♂; legs yellowish. Garganey (*A. querquedula*), a vagrant throughout N.Am, has a longer average wing (wg chord 177-206, tl 56-73, exp culmen 36-43, tarsus 28-33); les, med, and p covs grayish brown to silvery; outer webs to s2-s10 with green, and broad white tips (> 5 mm wide); shafts to pp whitish; iris dark to pale brown; legs grayish.

Geographic variation—Monotypic (P.A. Johnsgard *in* Mayr & Cottrell 1979). Populations breeding in s.TX-LA ("*A.d. albinucha*") may average more white tipping to feathers of the lateral crown and nape in basic-plumaged ♂♂ but this difference, if present, confounded by both temporal and individual variation. Populations breeding in coastal PEI-NC ("*orphna*") may average slightly darker and grayer (less brown) plumage aspect but difference, if present, confounded by individual variation. See Arthur (1920), Cramp & Simmons (1977), Kennard (1919), Oberholser (1974), Palmer (1976a), Stewart & Aldrich (1956), and Wetmore (1965) for more information.

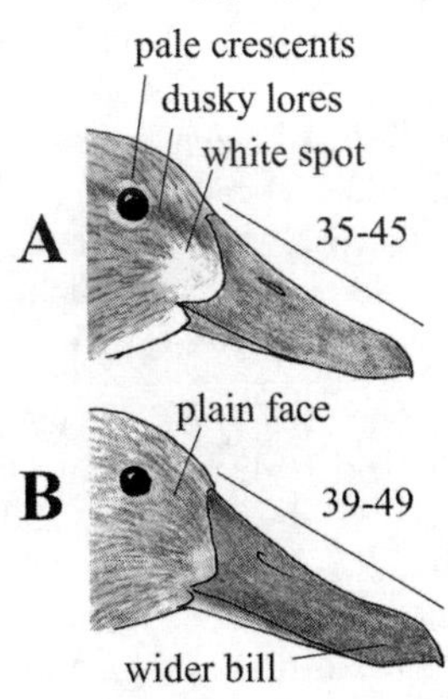

FIGURE 61. Facial and bill features of Blue-winged (**A**) and Cinnamon (**B**) teals in juv and ♀ plumages for identification. Values indicate exposed culmen (Fig. 7**A**, p. 9; Table 5, p. 93).

Molt—CAS. PFa limited-partial? (Jul-Sep in HYs), PF partial (Sep-Mar in HY/SYs), DPA partial-incomplete (Mar-May in AHY ♀♀, Jun-Sep in AHY ♂♂), DPB complete (Aug-Feb in AHY/ASYs). The PF occurs primarily on non-breeding grounds. During DPBs, synchronous replacement of wings usually occurs on molting grounds (p. 47), whereas the body molt occurs on non-breeding grounds. The DPA occurs on non-breeding to breeding (♀♀) or molting (♂♂) grounds. The PFa may be more extensive in this species than in most other ducks (see p. 79), including at least the head, due to the later timing of the PF; a similar, DPS may also occur in AHYs during the fall. The PF includes some to all body feathers, few to some proximal s covs, 1-4 terts and tert covs, and no to all 16 rects (all in ~60% of ♂♂ and a smaller proportion of ♀♀), and the DPA includes some to all of the upperpart feathers and 0-4 terts but few if any s covs or rects. More study needed on the occurrence and extent of molts during the fall. See Family (p. 47), and Subfamily and Tribal (pp. 78-79) accounts for more details.

Age/Sex—Juv (B1; Jun-Oct) resembles HY/SY ♀, with entirely juv rects (Fig. 26**A**, p. 48), and legs and bill washed dusky. Juvs are reliably sexed by the tert cov, gr-cov, and s5-s10 characters, as described under HY/SY. Partial medial BP (Fig. 20**A**, p. 31) and/or distended cloaca (Fig. 21, p. 32) developed by ♀ in Mar-Jun. See Figures 22-23 (pp. 32-35) for cloacal characteristics useful in ageing and sexing (including Juvs), Table 5 (p. 93) for measurements by age and sex, and Carney (1992) for useful photographs of wings.

Juv-HY/SY ♀ (1st cycle, Juv/B1-F1-A1; Oct-Sep): Head and body brown; most to all s covs narrow, rounded, and worn (Fig. 45**A-C**, p. 79), the les and med covs dull grayish blue washed brown, the tert covs tipped whitish to buff (Fig. 54**A-B**, p. 88), and the tips of the juv gr covs brown or with irregular whitish markings (Fig. 62**A-B**); bill with small blackish spots (Fig. 55**C-D**, p. 89); outer webs of s5-s10 with little or no dusky to greenish-dusky sheen; outer pp narrow (Fig. 25**A-B**, p. 79), averaging shorter by sex (Table 5), and brown; rects juv, formative, and/or alternate (Fig. 26**A-D**; see **Molt**). **Note: Beware HY/SY ♂♂ often do not acquire blue and rusty feathering until Mar. Some SYs and ASYs may be identifiable by wing-feather criteria (e.g., Fig. 62) through Dec; study needed.**

AHY/ASY ♀ (Def. cycle, DB-DA; Oct-Sep): Head and body brown, with little or no white, grayish blue, or rusty (see p. 78 regarding senescent ♀♀); s covs broad and fresher (Fig. 45**F**), the les and med covs grayish blue tinged dusky, the tert covs tipped white to buff (Fig. 54**A-B**), and the gr covs brown with irregular whitish or bluish markings or tips (Fig. 62**B-C**); bill with large dusky spots (*cf.* Fig. 55**B-C**); outer webs of s5-s10 usually with greenish-dusky sheen; outer pp broader (Fig. 25**C-D**), averaging longer by sex (Table 5), and brown with slight sheen; rects basic and/or alternate (Fig. 26**D-F**; see **Molt**). **Note: See Juv-HY/SY ♀.**

Juv-HY/SY ♂ (1st cycle, Juv/B1-F1-A1; Oct-Sep): Head and body brown in Oct-Feb and with white, grayish blue, and rusty (often with dull brownish tinge or feathers) in Mar-Jun; most to all s covs narrow, rounded, and worn (Fig. 45**A-C**), the les and med covs grayish blue tinged dusky, the tert covs with narrow or no pale tips (Fig. 54**C-D**), and the juv gr covs with broad white tips and brownish markings (Fig. 62**D-E**); bill slate with some spots (Fig. 55**D**), to blackish in Mar-Jun (*cf.* Fig. 55**E**);

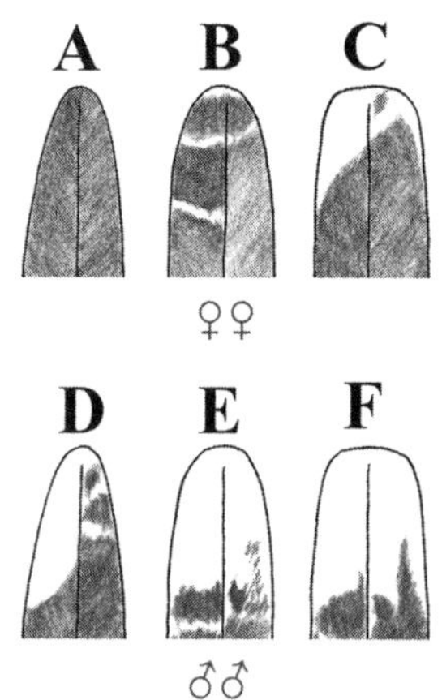

FIGURE 62. Distal greater coverts (corresponding to s1-s3) by age and sex in Blue-winged and Cinnamon teals. Within each sex, the left illustrations (**A**, **D**) are typical of HY/SYs, the right illustrations (**C**, **F**) are typical of AHY/ASYs, and the center illustrations (**B**, **E**) can be either age group. Juv covs are retained by SYs through the PB2 in Aug-Dec.

outer web of s4 with dusky-green sheen and those of s5-s10 with moderately bright green sheen; outer pp (Fig. 25**A**-**B**, Table 5) and rects (Fig. 26**A**-**D**) as in Juv-HY/SY ♀; iris dark grayish brown to brown. **Note: See Juv-HY/SY ♀. Some ♂♂ can be difficult to age by the s-cov characters; intermediates should be aged U/AHY without cloacal examination (Figs. 22-23, pp. 32-35).**

AHY/ASY ♂ (Def. cycle, DB-DA; Oct-Sep): Head and body primarily brown in Oct-Feb and bright grayish blue and rusty in Mar-Aug; s covs broad and fresher (Fig. 25**F**), the les and med covs bright bluish with little or no dusky tinge, the tert covs without pale tips (Fig. 54**D**), and the gr covs with broad white tips and little or no brown (Fig. 62**E**-**F**); bill blackish, without spots (*cf.* Fig. 55); outer webs of s4-s10 bright green; outer pp (Fig. 25**C**-**D**, Table 5) and rects (Fig. 26**D**-**F**; see **Molt**) as in AHY/ASY ♀; iris dark brown tinged reddish. **Note: See Juv-HY/SY ♀ and Juv-HY/SY ♂.**

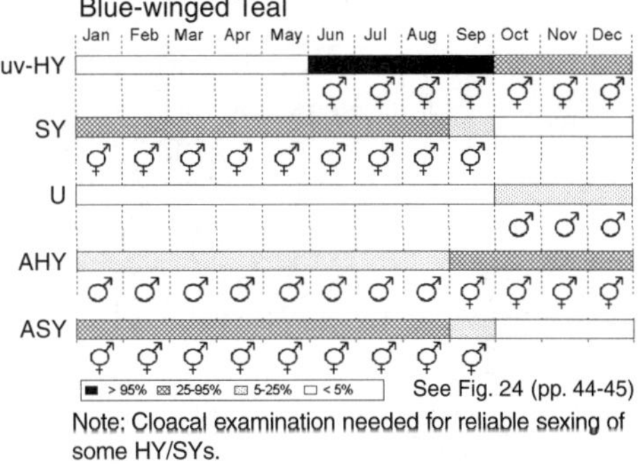

Hybrids reported—With American Wigeon (p. 84), Cinnamon Teal (Anderson & Miller 1953, Bolen et al. 1978, Wilson & Van den Akker 1948), Northern Shoveler (Childs 1952, Cooper & Graham 1985, David 1988, Deane 1905, Kemp 2000), and Green-winged Teal (Carlson 1979, Scrosati 1990) in the wild.

References—Baker (1993), Bent (1923), Carney (1964, 1992), Dane (1968), Dickey & van Rossem (1938), DuBowy (1985), Field (1965), Greij (1973), Hohman et al. (1995, 1997), Jackson (1991), Kaufman (1988), Oberholser (1974), Oring (1964, 1968), Palmer (1976a), Pyle (2005a), Roberts (1955), Rohwer et al. (2002), Wallace & Ogilvie (1977, 1985), White & Andrews (1985).

CINNAMON TEAL
Anas cyanoptera

CITE
Species # 1410
Band size: 4A ♀, 5 ♂

Species—Juvs and ♀♀ from most other N.Am ducks (particularly Blue-winged Teal) by medium-small size (Table 5, p. 93); bill relatively broad (width at widest point 15.3-17.0 mm); body brown to cinnamon-brown, without distinct facial features (Fig. 61, p. 95), and cinnamon wash to breast; les and med covs mostly to entirely pale blue; p covs brown; distal gr covs partly to entirely white (Fig. 62); outer webs of s5-s10 with green and narrow or no white tips (< 5 mm wide, if present); shafts of pp pale brownish; outer rects mostly brownish; bill dusky to black; iris dark, brown to bright reddish; legs yellowish.

Geographic variation—See Blake (1977), Madge & Burn (1988), Oberholser (1906a, 1974), Snyder & Lumsden (1951). Four other subspecies in S.Am.

A.c. *septentrionalium* (br & wint N.Am): Medium in size (Table 5, p. 93); basic-aspect ♂ pale chestnut with little or no sooty spotting on breast or flanks; ♀ variable in plumage aspect but pale. Subspecies in S.Am are either similar in plumage aspect but larger, or similar to slightly smaller in size but darker, often with sooty brown spotting to breast and flanks in ♂.

Molt—CAS. PFa limited-partial? (Jun-Sep in HYs), PF partial-incomplete (Sep-Feb in HY/SYs), DPA partial-incomplete (Jan-Mar in AHY ♀♀, May-Aug in AHY ♂♂), DPB complete (Jul-Jan in AHY/ASYs). The above timing pertains to N.Am populations. Except for slightly earlier periods of replacement, molt extents and strategies are similar to those of Blue-winged Teal (p. 95).

Age/Sex—Juv (B1; Jun-Oct) is pale brown, usually without cinnamon-brown, rects entirely juv (Fig. 26**A**, p. 48), and legs and bill washed dusky. Juvs are reliably sexed by tert cov, gr-cov, and ss characters; in addition, the undertail covs have indistinct rounded spots in Juv ♀ and more distinct bars in Juv ♂. Except for plumage aspect in ♂♂ (chestnut rather than white, grayish blue, and rusty), redder iris color by age/sex group, and more reliable ageing and sexing (see Bar Graph), age/sex criteria (including those of wing-feathers; Fig. 62, p. 96), are similar to those of Blue-winged Teal.

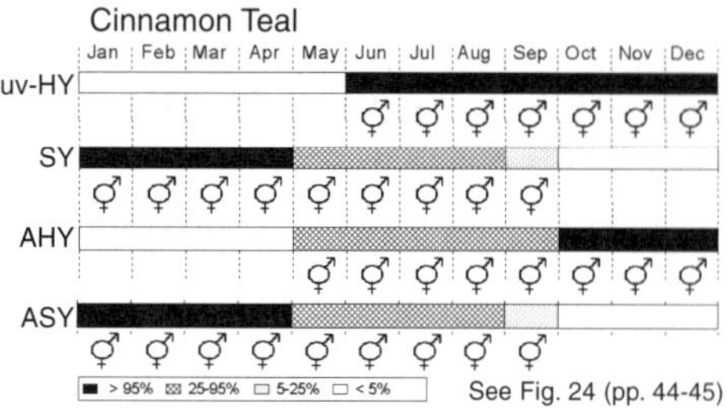

Hybrids reported—With Blue-winged Teal (p. 95), Argentine Red Shoveler *A. platalea* (McCarthy 2006), Northern Shoveler (Swarth 1915, Cooper & Graham 1985), Speckled Teal *A. flavirostris* (McCarthy 2006), and Green-winged Teal (Lockwood & Cooper 1999) in the wild. See also Mallard.

References—Bent (1923), Carney (1964, 1992), Gammonley (1996), Hohman et al. (1995), Jackson (1991), Kaufman (1988), Oberholser (1974), Oring (1964), Palmer (1976a), Pyle (2005a), Snyder & Lumsden (1951), Wallace & Ogilvie (1977, 1985), White & Andrews (1985).

NORTHERN SHOVELER
Anas clypeata

NSHO
Species # 1420
Band size: 5♀, 6♂

Species—Juvs and ♀♀ from other N.Am ducks by medium size with proportionately large bill (Table 5, p. 93); bill spatulate (> 25 mm wide at widest point); les and med covs variably washed bluish brown to bluish; distal gr covs distinctly tipped white (Fig. 63); outer web to s5-s10 with green; shafts of pp and ss white; outer rects pale buff to white; bill variably orangish to slate; iris pale brown to yellowish; legs orange.

Geographic variation—Monotypic.

Molt—CAS. PFa limited-partial? (Jul-Oct in HYs), PF partial-incomplete (Sep-Apr in HY/SYs), DPA partial-incomplete (Feb-May in AHY ♀♀, Jun-Aug in AHY ♂♂), DPB complete (Jul-Mar in AHY/ASYs). Timing and extents of molts are similar to those of Blue-winged Teal (p. 95).

Age/Sex—Juv (B1; Jun-Oct) resembles HY/SY ♀, with rects entirely juv (Fig. 26**A**, p. 48) and legs and bill washed dusky. Juvs are reliably sexed by the tert cov, gr-cov, and ss characters described under HY/SY and by the undertail covs, whitish with very indistinct or no rounded spots in Juv ♀ and indistinct brown bars in Juv ♂. Partial medial BP (Fig. 20**A**, p. 31) and/or distended cloaca (Fig. 21, p. 32) developed by ♀♀ in Apr-Jul. See Figures 22-23 (pp. 32-35) for cloacal characteristics useful in ageing and sexing (including Juvs), Table 5 (p. 93) for measurements by age and sex, and Carney (1992) for useful photographs of wings.

Juv-HY/SY ♀ (1st cycle, Juv/B1-F1-A1; Oct-Sep): Head and body brown; most to all s covs narrow, rounded, and worn (Fig. 45**A-C**, p. 79), the les and med covs brown washed grayish, the tert covs tipped whitish to buff (*cf.* Fig. 54**A**-**B**, p. 88), and the juv gr covs with narrow on no whitish tips (Fig. 63**A**); iris grayish; bill dull yellow-orange with small blackish spots (Fig. 55**C**-**D**, p. 89); outer webs of s5-s10 with little or no dull greenish sheen; outer pp narrow (Fig. 25**A**-**B**, p. 47), averaging shorter by sex (Table 5), and brown without sheen; rects juv, formative, and/or alternate (Fig. 26**A**-**D**; see **Molt**). **Note: Some SYs and ASYs may be aged by wing-feather criteria (e.g., Fig. 63) through Dec or later.**

AHY/ASY ♀ (Def. cycle, DB-DA; Oct-Sep): Head and body brown, with little or no green or sooty (see p. 78 regarding senescent ♀♀), sometimes with pale rufous wash to flanks; s covs broad and fresher (Fig. 45**F**), the les and med covs dusky brown washed bluish, the tert covs fringed white to buff (*cf.* Fig. 54**A**-**B**), and the gr covs with broad and distinct white tips (Fig. 63**B**); iris brown to brownish yellow; bill orange with variable dusky spots (Fig. 55**B**-**D**); outer webs of s5-s10 with little to a moderate amount of bright green sheen; outer pp broader (Fig. 25**C**-**D**), averaging longer by sex (Table 5), and brown with slight sheen; rects basic and/or alternate (Fig. 26**D**-**F**). **Note: See Juv-HY/SY ♀.**

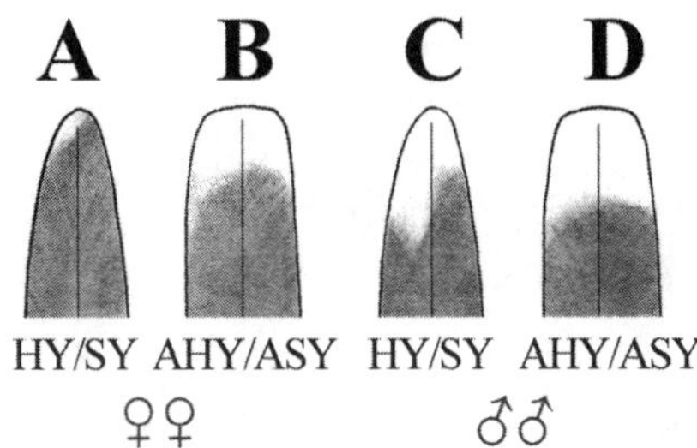

FIGURE 63. Distal greater coverts (corresponding to s1-s3) by age and sex in Northern Shoveler. Juv covs (**A**, **C**) are usually retained by SYs through the PB2 in Aug-Dec.

Juv-HY/SY ♂ (1st cycle, Juv/B1-F1-A1; Oct-Sep): Head and body primarily brown (sometimes with whitish loral crescent) in Oct-Mar, or with green, sooty, and rufous (often with dull brownish tinge or feathers) in Nov-May; most to all s covs narrow, rounded, and worn (Fig. 45**A**-**C**), the les and med covs dull bluish washed dusky, the tert covs with narrow or no pale tips (*cf.* Fig. 54**C**) in Oct-Jun (alternate covs in Jun-Sep can have broad buff tips), and the juv gr covs with indistinct and moderately broad whitish tips (Fig. 63**D**); iris brownish yellow to dull yellow; bill slaty orange with some spotting at base (Fig. 55**D**), to blackish (*cf.* Fig. 55) in Feb-Aug; outer web to s3 with little or no green and outer webs of s5-s10 with brightish green sheen; outer pp (Fig. 25**A**-**B**, Table 5) and rects (Fig. 26**A**-**C**) as in Juv-HY/SY ♀; 1-4 juv undertail covs often retained, whitish with brown bars; **Note: See Juv-HY/SY ♀. Head and body plumage in ♂♂ is highly variable due to protracted and complex molts. Generally, HY/SY ♂♂ are duller or have more sooty to the aspect than AHY/ASY ♂♂, especially in Sep-Jan, but extensive overlap may occur. It is best to rely on the s-cov, iris, and s3 characters for ageing.**

AHY/ASY ♂ (Def. cycle, DB-DA; Oct-Sep): Head and body bright green, sooty, and rufous in Sep-May; s covs broad and fresher (Fig. 45**F**), the les and med covs bluish, the tert covs without pale tips (*cf.* Fig. 54**D**) in Oct-Jun (alternate covs in Jun-Sep can have buff tips), and the gr covs with distinct and wide white tips (Fig. 63**D**); iris bright yellow; bill slaty orange to blackish, without spotting (Fig. 55**E**); outer webs of s3-s10 with brightish green sheen; outer pp (Fig. 25**C**-**D**, Table 5) and rects (Fig. 26**D**-**F**) as in AHY/ASY ♀; undertail covs blackish or mixed blackish, grayish, and/or rusty. **Note: See Juv-HY/SY ♀ and Juv-HY/SY ♂.**

Hybrids reported—With Muscovy Duck *Cairina moschata* (McCarthy 2006), Gadwall (p. 82), Eurasian Wigeon (p. 84), Mallard (p. 89), Blue-winged Teal (p. 95), Cinnamon Teal (p. 97), Northern Pintail (McCarthy 2006), Garganey *A. querquedula* (Childs 1952, Johnsgard 1960a), Baikal Teal *A. formosa* (McCarthy 1996), and Green-winged Teal (Johnsgard 1960a) in the wild.

References—Baker (1993), Bent (1923), Boyd et al. (1975), Carney (1964, 1992), Cramp & Simmons (1977), Dement'ev & Gladkov (1952), DuBowy (1985, 1996), Heitmeyer (1995), Hohman et al. (1995), Marchant & Higgins (1990), Oberholser (1974), Oring (1964), Palmer (1976a), Pyle (2005a), Roberts (1955), Smith (1977).

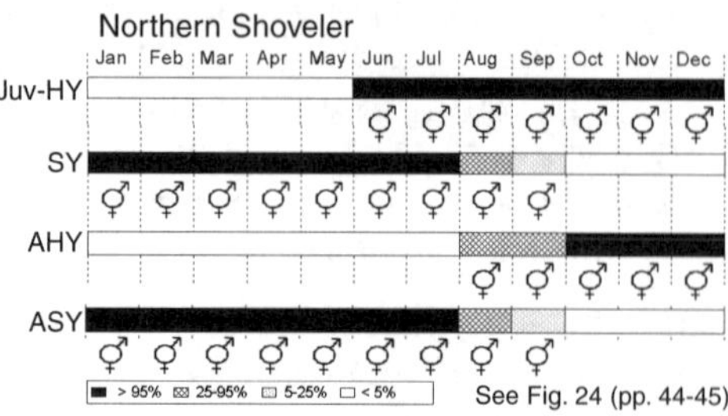

NORTHERN PINTAIL
Anas acuta

NOPI
Species # 1430
Band size: 6

Species—Juvs and ♀♀ from other N.Am ducks by medium-large size with proportionately long tail (Table 5, p. 93); central rects relatively long and attenuated (extremely so in ♂♂ in Oct-May); head with little or no eyeline or supercilium; les and med covs brown, sometimes with buff tips or fringes; distal gr covs brown with whitish to cinnamon tips (Fig. 64); outer web to s5-s10 with dull cinnamon to glossy bronze (Fig. 65); underwing covs grayish; bill grayish to slate; iris dark brown; legs grayish.

Geographic variation—Monotypic (P.A. Johnsgard *in* Mayr & Cottrell 1979). Populations of N.Am ("*A.a. tzitzihoa*") may average slightly larger and with a greener (*vs* bronzy) wash to the outer web of s5-s10 but differences, if present, are confounded by individual variation. See Dement'ev & Gladkov (1952), Hellmayr & Conover (1948a), Palmer (1976a), Portenko (1972).

Molt—CAS. PFa absent-limited? (Jul-Sep in HYs), PF partial-incomplete (Aug-Dec in HYs), DPA partial-incomplete (Jan-Apr in AHY ♀♀, May-Aug in AHY ♂♂), DPB complete (Jun-Oct in AHYs). The PF occurs primarily on non-breeding grounds. During DPBs, synchronous replacement of wings usually occurs on molting grounds (p. 47), whereas the body molt occurs on non-breeding grounds. The DPA occurs on non-breeding to breeding (♀♀) or molting (♂♂) grounds. The PFa, if not part of the PB1 (prejuvenal molt; see p. 79), appears to include only a few body feathers. The PF includes some to all of the body feathers, few to some proximal s covs, 0-4 terts and tert covs, and no to all 16 rects (all in a small proportion of ♂♂ and ♀♀). The DPA includes some to all of the upperpart feathers, 0-4 terts, up to 20% of the proximal s covs, and no to all rects. ♂♂ replace more feathers during the PF whereas ♀♀ replace more during the DPA (Fig. 45, p. 79). See Family (p. 47), and Subfamily and Tribal (pp. 78-79) accounts for more details.

Age/Sex—Juv (B1; Jun-Oct) is like HY/SY ♀, with rects entirely juv (Fig. 26**A**, p. 48). Juvs are reliably sexed by the tert cov, s-cov, s5-s10, and underwing characters described under HY/SY. Partial medial BP (Fig. 20**A**, p. 31) and/or distended cloaca (Fig. 21, p. 32) developed by ♀♀ in Apr-Jul. See Figures 22-23 (pp. 32-35) for cloacal characteristics useful in ageing and sexing (including Juvs), Table 5 (p. 93) for measurements by age and sex, and Carney (1992) for useful photographs of wings.

Juv-HY/SY ♀ (1st cycle, Juv/B1-F1-A1; Sep-Aug): Head and body pale brown; most to all s covs narrow, rounded, and worn (Fig. 45**A-C**, p. 79), the les and med covs brown fringed pale buff to whitish, the tert covs tipped whitish to buff (*cf.* Fig. 54**A-B**, p. 88), and the juv gr covs brown with narrow and indistinct buff tips (Fig. 64**A**); outer webs of s5-s10 dull cinnamon without sheen (Fig. 65**A**); outer pp narrow (Fig. 25**A**-**B**, p. 47), averaging shorter by sex (Table 5), and brown without sheen; rects juv, formative, and/or alternate (Fig. 26**A**-**B**; see **Molt**); bill grayish, with spots developing in center (*cf.* Fig. 55**C**-**D**, p. 89).

AHY/ASY ♀ (Def. cycle, DB-DA; Sep-Aug): Head and body brown, with little or no chocolate, white, or black (see p. 78 regarding senescent ♀♀); s covs broad and fresher (Fig. 45**F**), the les and med covs brown with distinct white tips, the tert covs tipped white to buff (*cf.* Fig. 54**A**-**B**), and the gr covs brown with narrow and distinct white to whitish tips (Fig. 64**B**); outer webs of s5-s10 dull cinnamon to dusky, sometimes with dull bronze sheen (Fig. 65**B**); outer pp broader (Fig. 25**C**-**D**), averaging longer by sex (Table 5), and brown with slight sheen; rects basic and/or alternate (Fig. 26**D**-**F**); bill grayish with variable blackish spotting down center (*cf.* Fig. 55**B**-**D**).

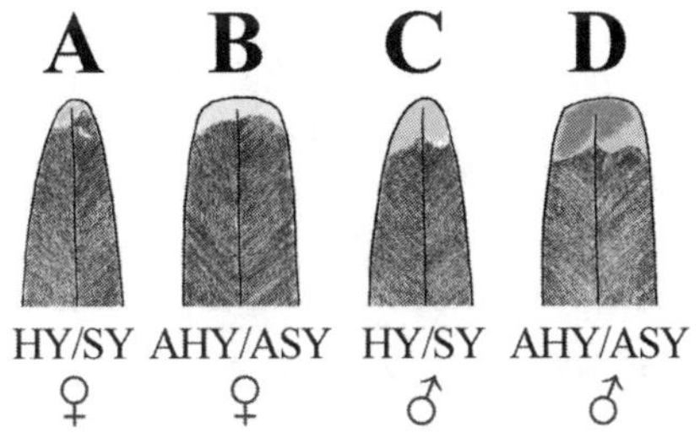

FIGURE 64. Distal greater coverts (corresponding to s1-s3) by age and sex in Northern Pintail. Tips are variably buff in HY/SYs (**A** & **C**), whitish in AHY/ASY ♀ (**B**), and tawny in AHY/ASY ♂ (**D**). Juv covs (**A**, **C**) and ss (Fig. 65**A**, **C**) are retained by SYs through the PB2 in Jun-Oct.

Juv-HY/SY ♂ (1st cycle, Juv/B1-F1-A1; Sep-Aug): Head and body with chocolate, white, and black (often with dull brownish tinge or feathers) in Nov-May; most to all s covs narrow, rounded, and worn (Fig. 45**A**-**C**), the les and med covs grayish brown, often with indistinct pale tips on proximal feathers, the tert covs with narrow or no pale tips (*cf.* Fig. 54**C**-**D**), and the juv gr covs with indistinct broad buff to cinnamon tips (Fig. 64**C**); outer webs of s5-s10 with dull purplish to bronzy green sheen (Fig. 65**C**); outer pp (Fig. 25**A**-**B**, Table 5) and rects (Fig. 26**A**-**D**) as in Juv-HY/SY ♀ except that replaced central rects elongated; 1-4 juv undertail covs often retained, whitish with brown bars; bill dusky without spots and with grayish fringes (*cf.* Fig. 55**E**).

AHY/ASY ♂ (Def. cycle, DB-DA; Sep-Aug): Head and body bright chocolate, white, and black in Sep-May; s covs broad and fresher (Fig. 45**F**), the les and med covs brownish gray, usually without pale tips (with slight tips when fresh), the tert covs without pale tips (*cf.* Fig. 54**D**); and the gr covs with distinct broad cinnamon tips (Fig. 64**D**); outer webs of s5-s10 with substantial dark purplish to bronzy green sheen (Fig. 65**D**); outer pp (Fig. 25**C**-**D**, Table 5) and rects (Fig. 26**D**-**F**) as in AHY/ASY ♀ except that central rects elongated; undertail covs uniformly blackish; bill blackish with grayish fringes (*cf.* Fig. 55**E**).

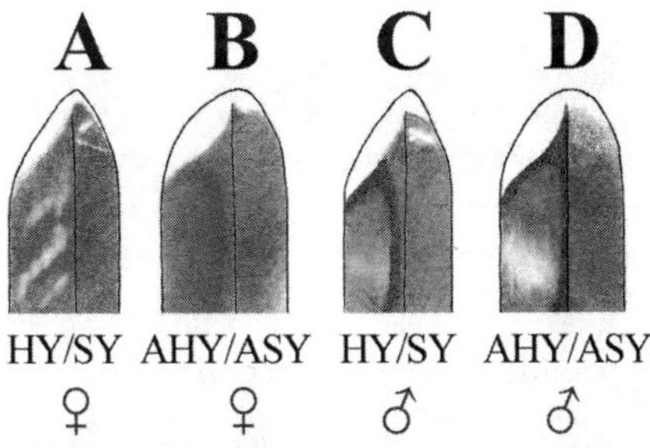

FIGURE 65. Width and pattern to s8 by age/sex group in Northern Pintail. ♂♂ (**C**-**D**) have more bronze sheen to the inner web (and dusky border to the sheen) than ♀♀ (**A**-**B**), age for age. See also Figure 64.

Hybrids reported—With Gadwall (p. 82), Eurasian and American wigeons (p. 84), American Black Duck (p. 87), Mallard (p. 89), Pacific Black Duck *A. superciliosa* (McCarthy 2006), Northern Shoveler (p. 98), Yellow-billed Duck *A. undulata* (McCarthy 2006), Garganey *A. querquedula* (McCarthy 2006), Baikal Teal *A. formosa* (McCarthy 2006), Green-winged Teal (Gantlett 1989, Howell 1959), Common Pochard *Aythya ferina* (McCarthy 2006), Red-crested Pochard *Netta rufina* (Harrop 1993a), and Common Eider (McCarthy 2006) in the wild. Reports with Redhead have been questioned (see McCarthy 2006).

References—Austin & Miller (1995), Baker (1993), Bent (1923), Boyd et al. (1975), Carney (1964, 1992), Conover (1926), Cramp & Simmons (1977), Dement'ev & Gladkov (1952), Duncan (1985), Esler & Grand (1994), Heitmeyer (1995), Marchant & Higgins (1990), Miller (1986), Miller et al. (1992), Oberholser (1974), Oring (1964), Palmer (1976a), Pyle (2005a), Roberts (1955), Sibley (1994), Smith (1977), Smith & Sheeley (1993), Sorenson & Derrickson (1994).

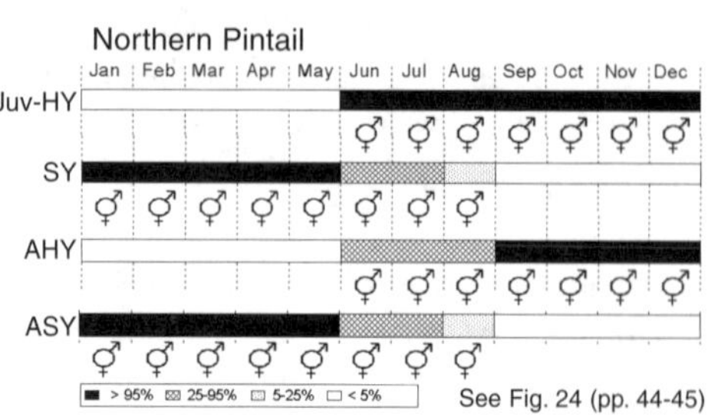

GREEN-WINGED TEAL

Anas crecca

GWTE
Species # 1394
Band size: 4♀, 4A♂

American Green-winged Teal (AGWT) Species # 1390
Eurasian Green-winged Teal (EGWT) Species # 1380

Species—Juvs and ♀♀ from other N.Am ducks by small size (Table 5, p. 93); les and med covs without bluish; distal gr covs with whitish to cinnamon tips (Fig. 66); outer webs to s7-s10 with green and narrow to no white tips (< 5 mm wide, if present); pp and ss shafts brown; lateral uppertail covs with distinct buff to whitish stripe; bill brownish to blackish, sometimes with dusky-orange fringes; iris dark brown; legs grayish to blackish.

Baikal Teal (*A. formosa*), a vagrant to w.N.Am, is larger (wg chord 186-225, tl 73-87, exp culmen 33-40, tarsus 31-39); Juvs and ♀♀ with small distinct white loral spot, dark crescent extending ventrally from eye, and supercilium broken at eye; wing-feather characters as in Green-winged Teal but les and med covs brown without grayish tinge; legs grayish to dull yellowish gray.

Geographic variation—See Browning (2002), Friedmann (1948), Gibson & Kessel (1997), Millington (1998), Oberholser (1919b, 1974), Palmer (1976a), Parkes (1958a), Patten et al. (2003), Sangster et al. (2001), Scott (1999), Vinicombe (1994). Some Juvs and ♀♀ are difficult or impossible to distinguish to subspecies.

A.c. crecca (br & wint Eurasia and Aleutian Is, AK, vagrant to w. and e.N.Am): Terts usually with dusky shaft streaks; basic and formative ♂♂ with green and rufous of head usually separated by distinct pale borders, whitish vermiculation of back and scapulars wide (> 0.5 mm), scapulars with distinct white stripe, and breast without white; Juvs and ♀♀ with lores and throat paler and more distinctly defined, and distal gr covs (*cf* Fig. 66) tipped white, with little or no buff tinge. Populations of the Aleutian Is, AK ("*nimia*"), may average larger than populations of Eurasia but difference slight.

A.c. carolinensis (br & wint throughout most of N.Am range): Terts with little or no dusky shaft streaks; basic-plumaged ♂♂ without pale borders in head and with whitish vermiculation of back and scapulars indistinct (often tinged brownish) and narrow (< 0.5 mm wide), scapulars without white stripe, and breast (near bend of wing) with vertical white stripe; Juvs and ♀♀ with lores and throat darker and less distinctly defined, and distal gr covs (*cf.* Fig. 66) tipped whitish cinnamon to cinnamon.

Molt—CAS. PFa absent-limited? (Jul-Sep in HYs), PF partial-incomplete (Aug-Dec in HYs), DPA partial-incomplete (Feb-Apr in AHY ♀♀, Jun-Aug in AHY ♂♂), DPB complete (Jul-Nov in AHYs). The PF occurs primarily on non-breeding grounds, the DPB commences on molting grounds (p. 47), but can complete on non-breeding grounds, and the DPA occurs on non-breeding to breeding (♀♀) or molting (♂♂) grounds. The PFa, if not part of the PB1 (prejuvenal molt; see p. 79), appears to include only a few body feathers. The PF includes some to all of the body feathers, few to some proximal s covs, 0-4 terts and tert covs, and no to all 16 rects (all in ~50% of ♂♂ but few if any ♀♀). During DPBs, wing feathers molt synchronously. The DPA includes some to all of the upperpart feathers, 0-4 terts, up to 25% of the proximal s covs, and no to all rects. ♂♂ replace more feathers during the PF whereas ♀♀ replace more during the DPA (Fig. 45, p. 79). See Family (p. 47), and Subfamily and Tribal (pp. 78-79) accounts for more details.

Age/Sex—Juv (B1; Jun-Oct) is like HY/SY ♀, with rects completely juv (Fig. 26**A**, p. 48); most Juvs are reliably sexed by the tert-cov and s5-s6 characters described under HY/SYs. Partial medial BP (Fig. 20**A**, p. 31) and/or distended cloaca (Fig. 21, p. 32) developed by ♀♀ in Apr-Jul. See Figures 22-23 (pp. 32-35) for cloacal characteristics useful in ageing and sexing (including Juvs), Table 5 (p. 93) for measurements by age and sex, and Carney (1992) for useful photographs of wings.

Juv-HY/SY ♀ (1st cycle, Juv/B1-F1-A1; Sep-Aug): Head and body (including breast) brown; most to all s covs narrow, rounded, and worn (Fig. 45**A-D**, p. 79), the tert covs tipped whitish to buff (*cf.* Fig. 54**A-B**, p. 88) and the juv gr covs with indistinct whitish to cinnamon (Fig. 66**A**); s5-s6 with little or no bright green; outer pp narrow (Fig. 25**A-B**, p. 47), averaging shorter by sex (Table 5), and brown without sheen; rects juv and formative and/or alternate (Fig. 26**A-C**; see **Molt**); bill grayish, with spots developing in center (Fig. 55**C-D**, p. 89).

AHY/ASY ♀ (Def. cycle, DB-DA; Sep-Aug): Head and body (including breast) brown, with little or no rufous, green, or grayish (see p. 78 regarding senescent ♀♀); s covs broad and fresher (Fig. 45**F**), the tert covs tipped white to buff (*cf.* Fig. 54**A-B**), and the gr covs with distinct white to cinnamon tips (Fig. 66**B**); s5-s6 with little or no bright green; outer pp broader (Fig. 25**C-D**), averaging longer by sex (Table 5), and brown with slight sheen; rects basic and/or alternate (Fig. 26**D-F**; see **Molt**); bill grayish with variable blackish spotting down center (Fig. 55**B-D**).

Juv-HY/SY ♂ (1st cycle, Juv/B1-F1-A1; Sep-Aug): Head and body rufous, green, and grayish (often with dull brownish tinge or feathers) in Nov-May; breast often tinged rufous in Jun-Aug; most to all s covs narrow, rounded, and worn (Fig. 45**A-C**), the tert covs with narrow or no pale tips (*cf.* Fig. 54**C-D**) and the juv gr covs with indistinct whitish to buffy tips (Fig. 66**A**); s5-s6 with bright green but that of s4 often with little or no green; outer pp (Fig. 25**A-B**, Table 5) and rects (Fig. 26**A-D**) as in Juv-HY/SY ♀; bill dusky without spots and with grayish fringes (*cf.* Fig. 55).

AHY/ASY ♂ (Def. cycle, DB-DA; Sep-Aug): Head and body bright rufous, green, and grayish in Sep-May or brown, the breast often tinged rufous and with distinct blackish spots in Jun-Aug; s covs broad and fresher (Fig. 45**F**), the tert covs without pale tips (*cf.* Fig. 54**D**), and the gr covs with distinct white to pale cinnamon tips (Fig. 66**B**); s4-s6 usually with bright green; outer pp (Fig. 25**C-D**, Table 5) and rects (Fig. 26**D-F**) as in AHY/ASY ♀; bill blackish with pale grayish fringes (*cf.* Fig. 55).

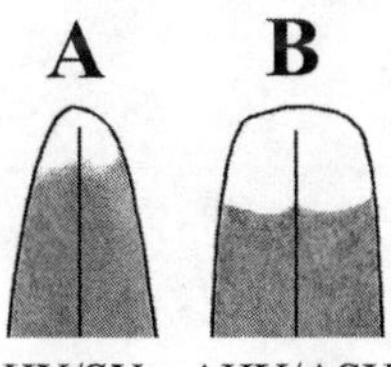

FIGURE 66. Width and pattern of the outer greater coverts (corresponding to s1-s5) by age in Green-winged Teal. The tips vary in coloration by subspecies, white to pale buff in *A.c. crecca* and pale buff to cinnamon in *carolinensis*, useful in differentiating some Juvs and ♀♀. Juv covs (**A**) are retained by SYs through the PB2 in Jul-Nov.

Hybrids reported—With Gadwall (p. 82), Eurasian and American wigeons (p. 84), Mallard (p. 89), Blue-winged Teal (p. 95), Cinnamon Teal (p. 97), Northern Shoveler (p. 98), Northern Pintail (p. 100); and Garganey *A. querquedula*, Baikal Teal *A. formosa*, and Common Pochard *Aythya ferina* (McCarthy 2006) in the wild.

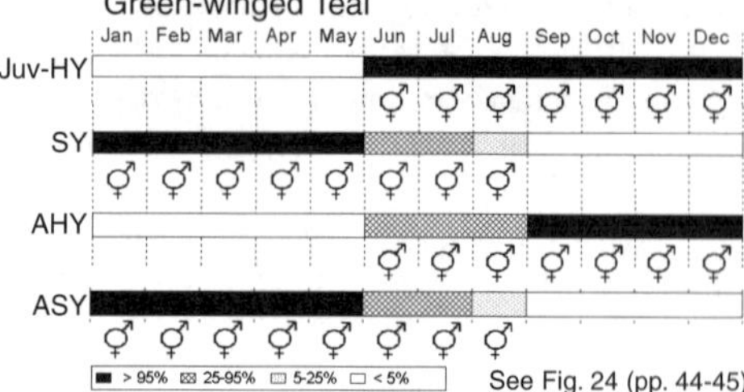

References—Anderson et al. (2000), Baker (1993), Bent (1923), Boyd et al. (1975), Carney (1964, 1992), Cramp & Simmons (1977), Dement'ev & Gladkov (1952), Fox et al. (1992), Jackson (1991, 1992), Johnson (1993), Oberholser (1974), Oring (1964), Palmer (1976a), Pyle (2005a), Roberts (1955), Rogers (1967).

Pochards *Anatidae, Anatinae, Aythyini*

Six North American species. See Family (p. 47) and Subfamily (p. 78) accounts for traits found throughout Anatidae and Anatinae. Tribal characters include medium-sized bodies, medium-small and spatulate bills (less spatulate in Canvasback), and lobed hind toes. North American pochards have 10 functional primaries (p10 often longest when fully grown, extending 5 mm longer to 3 mm shorter than p9), 14-16 secondaries (including 4 tertials), and (usually) 14 rectrices. The rectrices are stiffer and more durable than those of puddle ducks (Fig. 67), perhaps in part because they are replaced less frequently throughout the year. Ageing through the first cycle (to SY and ASY) can be accomplished with plumage-aspect criteria. Molt strategies in pochards are similar to those of surface-feeding ducks (p. 78-79), although there appear to be no auxilliary preformative molts and the prealternate molts are less extensive, to absent in some AHY/ASY males. Age of first breeding can occur at one year in most individuals of some species (e.g., Lesser Scaup) but is two years in most individuals overall; prebasic molts of non breeding AHYs average earlier in timing than those of breeding adults.

A

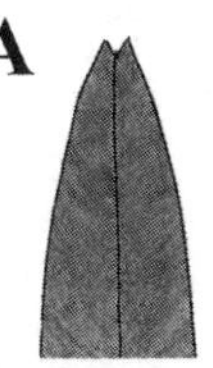

Juvenal

B

Formative /Basic

FIGURE 67. Rectices of Aythyini and Mergini ducks, by age, showing longer and narrower shape and more durable structure than are found in the rectices of Anatini (Fig. 26, p. 48). Because they are durable, the tips appear to break off more frequently in basic rects of AHY/ASYs, so caution is advised in using notches to tips of rects in ageing. Replacement patterns parallel those found in Anatini, except that fewer rects are typically replaced during both preformative and prealternate molts. Thus, most juv rects (**A**) are retained by SYs through the PB2 in Jul-Nov.

CANVASBACK
Aythya valisineria

CANV
Species # 1470
Band size: 7A

Species—Juvs and ♀♀ from other N.Am ducks, including Redhead, by large size, especially bill and legs (Table 6, p. 106); bill uniformly dusky to black, lacking hook at tip (hooked in other N.Am species of *Aythya*), narrowing distally, and with bill nail small and elongated (Fig. 69, p. 108); head pale brown with indistinct or no eye ring, stripes or white at base of bill; s covs with no to moderately heavy vermiculation (Fig. 70**A-E**, p. 109); outer ss brownish to pale gray by age/sex, contrasting slightly with darker gr covs (*cf.* Fig. 68, p. 107); iris dark (tinged reddish in some Juv ♂♂). See Redhead (p. 108) for separation from Common Pochard (*A. ferina*) and hybrid Canvasback X Redhead.

Geographic variation—Monotypic.

Molt—CAS. PF partial-incomplete (Sep-Mar in HY/SYs), DPA absent(?)-limited (Mar-May in AHY ♀♀, May-Jul in AHY ♂♂), DPB complete (Jul-Nov in AHYs). The PF occurs primarily on non-breeding grounds whereas the DPB and DPA occur primarily on breeding (♀♀) or molting (♂♂) grounds (p. 48). The PF includes some to most body feathers, sometimes 1-3 terts, often 1-5 tert covs or inner gr covs (*cf.* Fig. 68, p. 107), sometimes scattered other s covs, and occasionally the 2 central to all 14 rects. During DPBs, wing feathers molt synchronously. The DPA includes a few to most of the upperpart and breast feathers, few if any terts or wing covs, and 0-2 rects. ♂♂ replace more feathers during the PF whereas ♀♀ replace more during the DPA (Fig. 45, p. 79). The DPA may average less extensive with age in ♂♂; more study is needed. See Family (p. 47), and Subfamily (p. 78), and Tribal (above) accounts for more details.

TABLE 6. Measurements (mm) of North American pochards to assist in identification, ageing, and sexing. See pp. 4-11 for methods of measurement. Species summaries are in **bold**. Values were derived from 95% confidence intervals as based (for wing, exposed culmen, and tarsus) approximately on the indicated sample sizes (see pp. 4-5); sample sizes for tail length and bill depth were often smaller but included at least 10 of each sex. Thus, midpoints of ranges approximate means, and S.D. is approximated by 25% of the range.

Taxon/Sex	*n*	wing chord AHY/ASY	(HY/SY)[1]	tail length[1]	exp culmen	bill depth[2]	tarsus
Canvasback		**216-243**	**(211-238)**	**53-61**	**55-66**	**22.1-28.1**	**43-47**
♀	30	216-234	(211-228)	53-60	55-63	22.1-26.1	43-46
♂	30	224-243	(219-238)	54-61	57-66	23.6-28.1	44-47
Redhead		**214-237**	**(208-231)**	**53-63**	**43-51**	**18.0-22.4**	**38-45**
♀	100	213-227	(208-222)	53-61	43-49	18.0-21.7	38-43
♂	100	221-237	(216-232)	54-63	45-51	18.8-22.4	40-45
Ring-necked Duck		**180-205**	**(176-201)**	**47-63**	**42-50**	**18.0-22.3**	**31-37**
♀	100	180-196	(176-192)	47-61	42-48	18.0-20.9	31-36
♂	100	189-205	(185-201)	49-63	44-50	19.3-22.3	33-37
Tufted Duck		**186-209**	**(182-205)**	**45-59**	**36-44**	**15.5-20.1**	**33-38**
♀	80	186-202	(182-198)	45-58	36-42	15.5-18.8	33-37
♂	70	193-209	(189-205)	47-59	37-44	16.5-20.1	34-38
Greater Scaup[3]		**205-230**	**(200-225)**	**50-62**	**41-49**	**19.0-22.9**	**35-42**
♀	100	205-224	(200-219)	50-60	41-48	19.0-22.2	35-40
♂	100	211-230	(206-225)	52-62	42-49	19.6-22.9	36-42
Lesser Scaup[3]		**187-212**	**(182-206)**	**46-59**	**38-45**	**17.2-21.2**	**30-38**
♀	100	187-205	(182-199)	46-57	38-44	17.2-20.5	30-36
♂	100	194-212	(188-206)	47-59	39-45	17.7-21.2	32-38

[1] Wing chord and tail length differ substantially by age; wing data are separated by age since juv primaries are retained through the second PB whereas tail lengths pertain to formative and basic feathers only, as the juvenal central rects are often replaced by Oct-Dec in HYs. Other measures pertain to all age groups.

[2] Bill depth measured at the distal end of forehead feathering (Fig.8**A**, p. 10).

[3] Measures from N.Am populations (*A.m. nearctica*) only; size of Palearctic *A.m. marila* does not differ substantially. See Table 7 (p. 113) for additional measures in scaup.

Age/Sex—Juv (B1; Jun-Oct) resembles HY/SY ♀, with heavier brown wash to head and back and rects entirely juv (Figs. 67**A**, p. 105, & 26**A**, p. 48). Juv ♂ often has the head dark brown with slight rusty or cinnamon tinge (*vs* pale brown in Juv ♀) and iris tinged reddish; many Juvs can also be sexed by s-cov and underwing-cov characters as in Juv-HY/SYs. Partial medial BP (Fig. 20**A**, p. 31) and/or distended cloaca (Fig. 21, p. 32) developed by ♀♀ in May-Jul. See Figures 22-23 (pp. 32-35) for cloacal characteristics useful in ageing and sexing (including Juvs), Table 6 for measurements by age and sex, and Carney (1992) for useful photographs of wings.

Juv-HY/SY ♀ (1st cycle, Juv/B1-F1-A1; Oct-Sep): Head and body brown; iris brown; most to all s covs narrow, rounded, and worn (Fig. 45**A-B**, p. 79), brown, with little or no vermiculation (Fig. 70**A-B**, p. 109), the inner 1-3 gr covs sometimes replaced and paler (Fig. 68); outer pp shorter by sex (Table 6); rects juv and/or formative, (Figs. 67**A** & 26**A-B**; see **Molt**). **Note: The shape and wear of the outer pp does not seem as useful for ageing Canvasbacks as other duck species.**

AHY/ASY ♀ (Def. cycle, DB-DA; Oct-Sep): Head and body primarily brownish, often with slight rusty, whitish, and/or blackish tinge (see p. 78 regarding senescent ♀♀); iris brown; s covs broad and fresher (Fig. 45**F**), uniformly (*cf.* Fig. 68) blackish to dark gray, often with some vermiculation concentrated at tip (Fig. 70**A-D**); outer pp longer by sex (Table 6); rects usually uniformly basic (Figs. 76**B** & 26**D**), sometimes with r1 alternate in Mar-Sep. **Note: See Juv-HY/SY ♀. It is possible that the degree of vermiculation in AHY/ASY ♀♀ can be used to separate some SY/TYs (Fig. 70A-B) and ASY/ATYs (Fig. 70C-D), but more study is needed.**

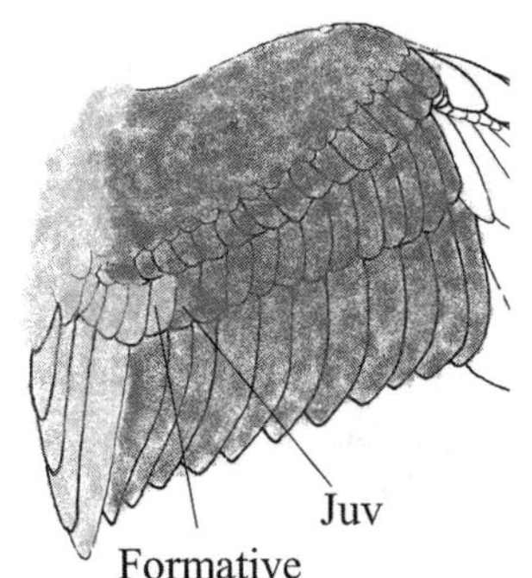

FIGURE 68. Molt limits in the s covs following the preformative molt in some *Aythya* ducks. Paler shading indicates fresher feathers. Replaced formative coverts can be paler or frostier than retained juvenal coverts, the result of increased amounts of vermiculation (*cf.* Fig. 70, p. 109). ♂♂ typically replace more inner gr covs than ♀♀, species by species.

Juv-HY/SY ♂ (1st cycle, Juv/B1-F1-A1; Oct-Sep): Head and body primarily brownish, becoming increasingly dull rusty, whitish, and black in Nov-Sep; iris brownish yellow, becoming dull reddish in Jan-Sep; most to all s covs narrow, rounded, and worn (Fig. 45**A-C**), grayish brown, often with slight to moderate vermiculation (Fig. 70**B-C**), the inner 1-5 gr covs often replaced and whiter (Fig. 68); outer pp shorter by sex (Table 6); rects (Figs. 67**A** & 26**A-B**) as in Juv-HY/SY ♀. **Note: See Juv-HY/SY ♀.**

AHY/ASY ♂ (Def. cycle, DB-DA; Oct-Sep): Head and body bright rusty, whitish, and black, the upperparts and breast variably mottled grayish in Jun-Sep; iris bright reddish; s covs broad and fresher (Fig. 45**F**), uniformly (*cf.* Fig. 68) dark gray with moderate to heavy vermiculation (Fig. 70**C-F**); outer pp longer by sex (Table 6); rects (Figs. 67**B** & 26**D**) similar to AHY/ASY ♀. **Note: See Juv-HY/SY ♀. As with ♀♀, the degree of vermiculation in AHY/ASY ♂♂ might be useful in separating some SY/TYs (Fig. 70C-D) and ASY/ATYs (Fig. 70F), but more study is needed.**

Hybrids reported—Canvasbacks from native populations with American Wigeon (p. 84), Mallard (p. 89), Redhead (Haramis 1982, Hochbaum 1944, Jorgensen 1997, McIlhenny 1937), Ring-necked Duck (Elliot 1892, Palmer 1976b, Weller 1957), Greater and Lesser scaups (McCarthy 2006) in the wild. Vagrant Canvasbacks with Common Pochard *A. ferina*, Tufted Duck, and Ferruginous Duck *A. nyroca* in Europe (McCarthy 2006, Vinicombe 2003).

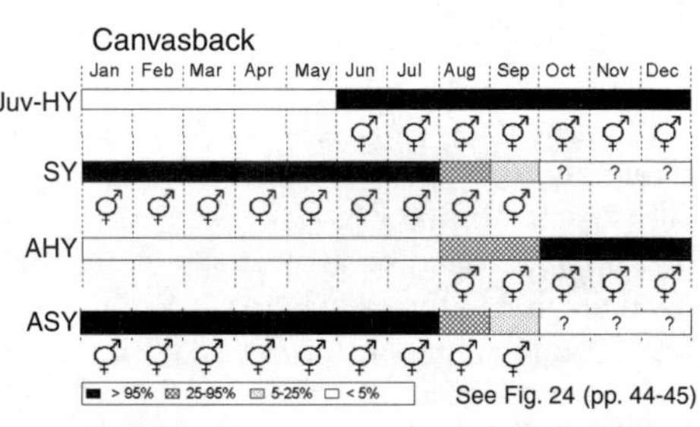

References—Ainley et al. (1994), Baker (1993), Bent (1923), Carney (1964, 1992), Dzubin (1959), Haramis et al. (1982), Hochbaum (1944), Lovvorn & Barzen (1988), Madge (1991), Mowbray (2002b), Oberholser (1974), Palmer (1976b), Patten (1993b), Roberts (1955), Serie et al. (1982), Thompson & Drobney (1995).

REDHEAD
Aythya americana

REDH
Species # 1460
Band size: 6

Species—Juvs and ♀♀ from other N.Am ducks, including Canvasback (p. 105) and Ring-necked Duck (p. 110), by medium size with proportionately long wings and tail (Table 6, p. 106); bill grayish to bluish, often with narrow pale band (AHYs), black tip, and large and triangular nail (Fig. 69**C**); head rounded, pale brown, with little or no eye ring or stripe posterior to eye, and usually with an indistinct pale loral spot; s covs brown to grayish brown with slight to no whitish vermiculation (Fig. 70**A-C**); outer ss grayish to grayish white, contrasting with darker gr covs (*cf.* Fig. 73, p. 115); iris dark (tinged yellowish in some Juv ♂♂).

Common Pochard (*A. ferina*) a vagrant to w.N.Am and occasional escape, is smaller, especially in wing chord and tail length (wg chord 185-223, tl 46-58, exp culmen 43-51, tarsus 36-42); bill with straight or slightly convex culmen, blackish to dusky with broad, pale grayish to bluish band (AHYs), black tip, and small nail (Fig. 69); iris reddish (*vs* whitish to yellowish in Redhead); AHY ♂ without dusky wash to head (*vs* with dusky wash around bill in Canvasback) and reddish iris (vs. whitish to yellowish in Redhead). Hybrids between Canvasback and Redhead may resemble Common Pochard in bill structure but have longer wings, tails, and tarsi, near in size to those of Canvasback (Table 6). Also, beware that hybrids between Common Pochard and Tufted Duck may resemble Redheads.

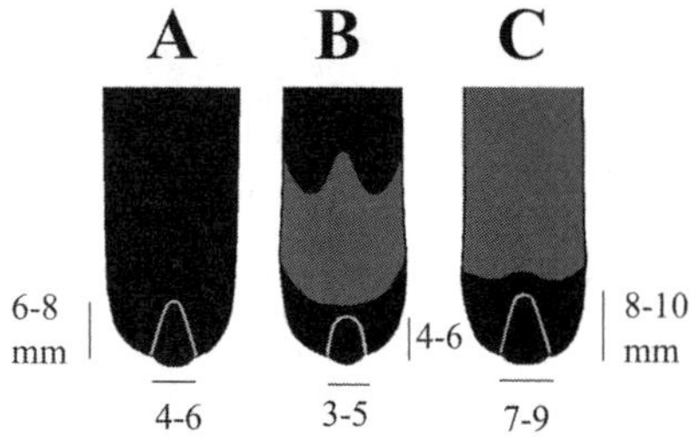

FIGURE 69. Bill shape and color pattern, and nail size and shape in Canvasback (**A**), Common Pochard (**B**), and Redhead (**C**). Patterns of pale blue shown in **B** and **C** are absent in Juvs and more distinct in AHY/ASYs and ♂♂ than in HY/SYs and ♀♀. Note also the difference in nail shape and size.

Geographic variation—Monotypic.

Molt—CAS. PF partial-incomplete (Sep-Mar in HY/SYs), DPA limited (Apr-May in AHY ♀♀, Jun-Jul in AHY ♂♂), DPB complete (Jul-Nov in AHYs). The PF occurs primarily on nonbreeding grounds whereas the DPB and DPA occur primarily on breeding (♀♀) or molting (♂♂) grounds (p. 47). The PF includes some to most body feathers, occasionally 1-3 terts, sometimes 1-3 tert covs and other s covs (*cf.* Fig. 68, p. 107), and occasionally the 2 central to all 14 rects. During PBs, wing feathers molt synchronously. The DPA includes a few to most of the upperpart and breast feathers, few if any terts or s covs, and 0-2 rects. ♂♂ replace more feathers during the PF whereas ♀♀ replace more during the DPA (Fig. 45, p. 79). See Family (p. 47), and Subfamily (p. 78), and Tribal (p. 105) accounts for more details.

Age/Sex—Juv (B1; Jun-Oct) resembles HY/SY ♀, with heavier brown wash to head and back, rects entirely juv (Figs. 67**A**, p. 105, & Fig. 26**A**, p. 48), and bill dusky with little or no pattern. Juv ♂ often has the head dark brown with slight reddish or cinnamon tinge (*vs* pale brown in Juv ♀) and iris tinged yellowish; many Juvs can also be sexed by s-cov and underwing-cov characters as in Juv-HY/SYs. Partial medial BP (Fig. 20**A**, p. 31) and/or distended cloaca (Fig. 21, p. 32) developed by ♀♀ in Apr-Jul. See Figures 22-23 (pp. 32-35) for cloacal characteristics useful in ageing and sexing (including Juvs), Table 6 (p. 106) for measurements by age and sex, and Carney (1992) for useful photographs of wings.

Juv-HY/SY ♀ (1st cycle, Juv/B1-F1-A1; Oct-Sep): Head and body brown; iris brown; most to all s covs narrow, rounded, and worn (Fig. 45**A-B**, p. 79), brown without vermiculation (Fig. 70**A**), the inner 1-2 gr covs sometimes replaced and paler (Fig. 68, p. 107); outer pp narrow

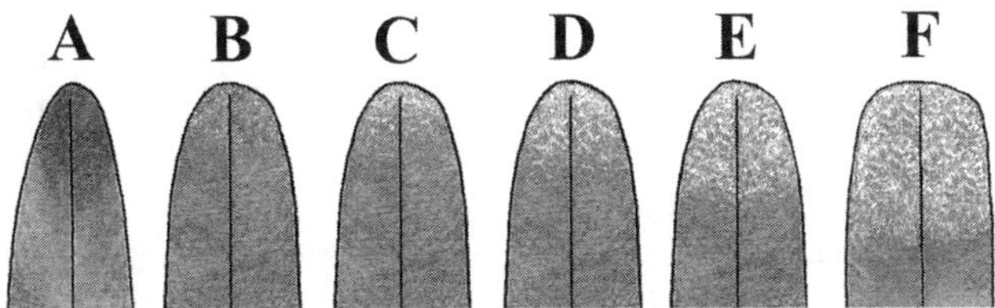

FIGURE 70. Variation in the extent of whitish vermiculation to the greater coverts by species and sex, in *Aythya* ducks. Typically, HY/SY ♀ show the least amount of vermiculation and AHY/ASY ♂ the most, but extent of age/sex-specific variation itself varies substantially among the six species of *Aythya* treated here (see Accounts), with Ring-necked Duck showing the least amount of variation (**A** in all groups) and Canvasback the most (**A-F**). The cumulative effect of increased vermiculation (as in **F**) is of a whitish to white aspect to the upperparts.

(Fig. 25**A-B**, p. 47), shorter by sex (Table 6), and brown without sheen; rects juv and/or formative (Figs. 67**A** & 26**A-D**; see **Molt**). **Note: Beware that both juv and definitive-basic rects can become extremely worn by Mar-Jun, such that age-specific differences become obscured.**

AHY/ASY ♀ (Def. cycle, DB-DA; Oct-Sep): Head and body primarily brownish, with little or no rufous, blackish, or gray (see p. 78 regarding senescent ♀♀); iris brown, sometimes tinged yellowish; s covs broad and fresher (Fig. 45**F**), grayish, sometimes with some vermiculation concentrated at tip (Fig. 70**A-B**); outer pp broader (Fig. 25**C-D**), longer by sex (Table 6), and with slight sheen; rects completely basic (Figs. 67**B** & 26**D**), sometimes with r1 alternate in Mar-Sep. **Note: See Juv-HY/SY ♀.**

Juv-HY/SY ♂ (1st cycle, Juv/B1-F1-A1; Oct-Sep): Head and body primarily brownish, becoming increasingly dull rufous, blackish, and gray in Nov-Sep; iris brownish yellow, becoming dull yellowish in Jan-Sep; most to all s covs narrow, rounded, and worn (Fig. 45**A-B**), brown, often with some vermiculation (Fig. 70**A-B**), the inner 1-3 gr covs often replaced and paler (Fig. 68); outer pp (Fig. 25**A-B**, Table 6) and rects (Figs. 67**A** & 26**A-D**) as in Juv-HY/SY ♀. **Note: See Juv-HY/SY ♀ and AHY/ASY ♂.**

AHY/ASY ♂ (Def. cycle, DB-DA; Oct-Sep): Head and body bright rufous, blackish, and gray, the upperparts and breast variably mottled grayish in Jun-Sep; iris bright yellow; s covs broad and fresher (Fig. 45**F**), dark gray with moderate vermiculation (Fig. 70**C-D**); outer pp (Fig. 25**C-D**, Table 6) and rects (Figs. 67**B** & 26**D**) as in AHY/ASY ♀. **Note: Individuals with substantial vermiculation to s covs may possibly be aged ASY/ATY but more study is needed.**

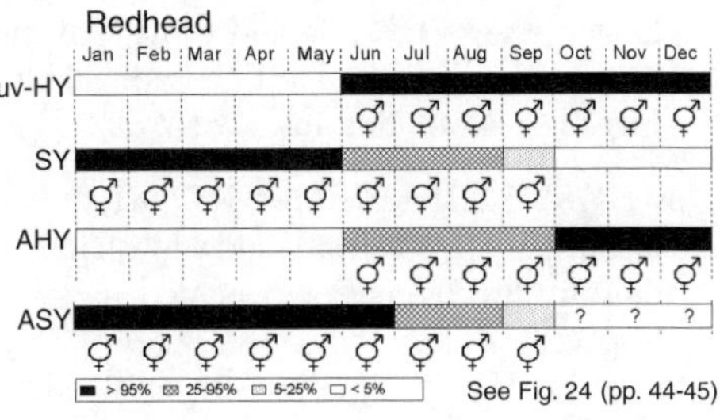

Hybrids reported—In the wild with Wood Duck (p. 80), Canvasback (p. 105), Ring-necked Duck (Palmer 1976b, Sibley 1938, Weller 1957), Greater Scaup (Johnsgard 1960a, Sibley 1938), and possibly Lesser Scaup (Palmer 1976b) in the wild. See also Northern Pintail (p. 100).

References—Ainley et al. (1994), Baker (1993), Bent (1923), Carney (1964, 1992), Dane & Johnson (1975), Madge (1991), Oberholser (1974), Palmer (1976b), Patten (1993b), Roberts (1955), Sayler (1995), Weller (1957, 1970), Woodin & Michot (2002).

RING-NECKED DUCK
Aythya collaris

RNDU
Species # 1500
Band size: 6

Species—Juvs and ♀♀ from other N.Am ducks by medium-small size (Table 6, p. 106); bill slate to dark grayish blue with narrow pale to white band, black tip, and moderately large and somewhat triangular nail (Fig. 71**A**, p. 114); head peaked but without tuft, pale brown to grayish brown with a distinct eye ring and stripe posterior to eye, and an indistinct and large, whitish loral spot; s covs dark brown, without vermiculation (Fig. 70**A**, p. 109); outer ss dark grayish, not contrasting distinctly with gr covs (*cf.* Fig. 73, p. 115); iris dark (tinged yellowish in some Juv ♂♂ and AHY ♀♀). Beware of hybrids (especially those between Tufted Duck and scaup; see p. 113) that may resemble Ring-necked Duck.

Geographic variation—Monotypic.

Molt—CAS. PF partial-incomplete (Sep-Mar in HY/SYs), DPA limited (Apr-May in AHY ♀♀, Jun-Aug in AHY ♂♂), DPB complete (Aug-Dec in AHYs). Molt strategies and extents are similar to those of Redhead (p. 108), with the PF perhaps averaging slightly less extensive.

Age/Sex—Juv (B1; Jun-Oct) resembles HY/SY ♀, with buffier brown wash to head and back, little or no pale eye ring and stripe posterior to the eye, rects uniformly juv (Figs. 67**A**, p. 105, & 26**A**, p. 48), and bill dusky with little or no pattern (*cf.* Fig. 71**A**, p. 114). Juv ♂♂ sometimes with head dark brown or dusky (*vs* paler brown in Juv ♀♀) and iris tinged yellowish; many Juvs can also be sexed by degree of sheen to s covs and terts as in Juv-HY/SYs. Partial medial BP (Fig. 20**A**, p. 31) and/or distended cloaca (Fig. 21, p. 32) developed by ♀♀ in May-Jul. See Figures 22-23 (pp. 32-35), Anderson et al. (1969), and Hohman & Cypher (1986) for cloacal characteristics useful in ageing and sexing (including Juvs); Table 6 (p. 106) for measurements by age and sex; and Carney (1992) for useful photographs of wings.

Juv-HY/SY ♀ (1st cycle, Juv/B1-F1-A1; Oct-Sep): Head and body brown; iris brown; s covs narrow, rounded, and worn (Fig. 45**A**, p. 79), brown without sheen; outer pp narrow (Fig. 25**A-B**, p. 47), averaging shorter by sex (Table 6), and without sheen; rects juv and/or formative (Figs. 67**A** & 26**A-D**; see **Molt**); bill dusky with no to indistinct pale band (*cf.* Fig. 71**A**). **Note: Some intermediate ♀♀ may be difficult to age by plumage aspect alone; confirm above criteria with cloacal characteristics (p. 32-35), if possible.**

AHY/ASY ♀ (Def. cycle, DB-DA; Oct-Sep): Head and body brown, with little or no blackish or whitish (see p. 78 regarding senescent ♀♀); iris brown to dull yellowish; s covs broad and fresher (Fig. 45**F**), dark brown with slight greenish sheen; outer pp broader (Fig. 25**C-D**), longer by sex (Table 6), and with slight sheen; rects usually basic (Figs. 67**B** & 26**D**), sometimes with r1 replaced in Feb-Sep; bill bluish slate with moderately distinct whitish band (*cf.* Fig. 71**A**). **Note: See Juv-HY/SY ♀.**

Juv-HY/SY ♂ (1st cycle, Juv/B1-F1-A1; Oct-Sep): Head and body primarily brownish, becoming increasingly dull blackish and whitish in Nov-Sep; iris brown, becoming yellowish in Dec-Sep; most to all s covs narrow, rounded, and worn (Fig. 45**A-B**), brown, with slight greenish sheen (especially to tips of gr covs); outer pp (Fig. 25**A-B**, Table 6) and rects (Figs. 67**A** & 26**A-D**) as in Juv-HY/SY ♀; bill dusky bluish with indistinct to moderately distinct whitish band (*cf.* Fig. 71**A**).

AHY/ASY ♂ (Def. cycle, DB-DA; Oct-Sep): Head and body bright glossy purplish, black, and white in Oct-May (flanks can be mottled gray through Dec) or variably mottled grayish in Jun-Sep; iris bright yellow; s covs broad and fresher (Fig. 45**F**), blackish with substantial greenish gloss; outer pp (Fig. 25**C**-**D**, Table 6) and rects (Figs. 67**B** & 26**D**) as in AHY/ASY ♀; bill grayish blue (brighter in Nov-May) with distinct white band (Fig. 71**A**).

Hybrids reported—With Wood Duck (p. 80), Canvasback (p. 105), Redhead (p. 108), Lesser Scaup (Anderson & Timken 1969, McIlhenny 1937), and Greater Scaup (Gosselin 1979) in the wild. Vagrant Ring-necked Ducks with Common Pochard (*A. ferina*) and Tufted Duck in the wild in Europe (McCarthy 2006, Vinicombe 1982).

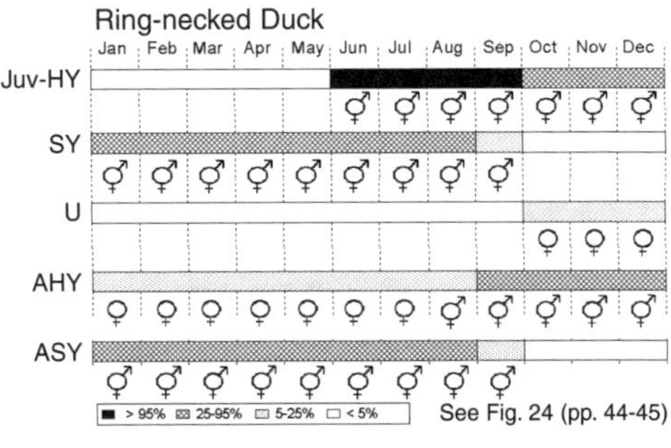

References—Anderson & Warner (1969), Baker (1993), Bent (1923), Carney (1964, 1992), Hohman & Crawford (1995), Hohman & Cypher (1986), Hohman & Eberhardt (1998), Mendall (1958), Oberholser (1974), Palmer (1976b), Roberts (1955), Vinicombe (1982).

TUFTED DUCK
Aythya fuligula

TUDU
Species # 1491
Band size: 5

Species—Juvs and ♀♀ from other N.Am ducks by smaller size and bill (Table 6, p. 106); bill slate to pale grayish blue with indistinct pale to whitish band. black tip, and small and somewhat triangular nail (Fig. 71**B**, p. 114); head peaked, often with elongated occipital plumes ("tuft"; see **Age/Sex**), dark brown to blackish, without eye ring or stripe posterior to eye, and sometimes with a small and indistinct white patch at base of bill, not extending below gape; s covs dark brown to blackish without vermiculation (Fig. 70**A**, p. 109); outer ss (and p1-p4) with substantial white (*cf.* Fig. 73, p. 115), contrasting markedly with darker gr covs; iris dark, to yellowish in some Juv ♂♂ and AHY ♀♀. Beware of hybrids, especially those involving scaup (p. 113), that may resemble Tufted Duck.

Geographic variation—Monotypic.

Molt—CAS. PF partial-incomplete (Sep-Mar in HY/SYs), DPA limited (Mar-May in AHY ♀♀, Jun-Aug in AHY ♂♂), DPB complete (Aug-Dec in AHYs). Except for a more extensive PF on average (most ♂♂ and many ♀♀ replace 1-3 terts and tert covs), molt strategies and extents are similar to those of Redhead (p. 108). Tuft feathers appear to be formative or basic, being replaced once per year in Aug-Sep and developing slowly to full length by Jan-Feb (SYs) or Dec-Jan (AHY/ASYs).

Age/Sex—Juv (B1; Jun-Oct) resembles HY/SY ♀, with rects entirely juv (Figs. 67**A**, p. 105, & 26**A**, p. 48) and bill dusky with little or no pattern (*cf.* Fig. 71**B**, p. 114). Juv ♂♂ sometimes have the head darker brown or dusky (*vs* paler brown in Juv ♀♀) and iris tinged yellowish, but wing-feather characters are not as reliable as in other duck species for sexing and most Juvs cannot be reliably sexed without cloacal examination. Partial medial BP (Fig. 20**A**, p. 31) and/or distended cloaca (Fig. 21, p. 32) developed by ♀♀ in May-Jul. See Figures 22-23 (pp. 32-35) for cloacal characteristics useful in ageing and sexing (including Juvs), Table 6 (p. 106) for measurements by age and sex, and Carney (1992) for useful photographs of wings.

Juv-HY/SY ♀ (1st cycle, Juv/B1-F1-A1; Oct-Sep): Head and body brown; iris brown; occipital tuft reduced or absent in Oct-Nov and short when fully grown in Feb-Aug (longest feather 15-30 mm from base); most to all s covs narrow, rounded, and worn (Fig. 45**A**, p. 79; *cf.* Fig. 68, p. 107), brown without sheen or vermiculation (Fig. 70**A**, p. 109); outer pp narrow (Fig. 25**A**-**B**, p. 47), averaging shorter by sex (Table 6), and without sheen; rects juv and/or formative (Figs. 67**A** & 26**A**-**D**; see **Molt**); bill dusky with indistinct or no pale band (*cf.* Fig. 71**B**). **Note: Beware that some HY/SY ♂♂ may not acquire blackish or white in plumage aspect until Nov-Dec or later and may be difficult or impossible to sex by plumage aspect alone in Oct-Nov (see Juv, above). Also, some intermediate ♀♀ may be difficult to age by plumage aspect alone; confirm all age and sex criteria with cloacal characteristics (p. 32-35), if possible.**

AHY/ASY ♀ (Def. cycle, DB-DA; Oct-Sep): Head and body brown to blackish brown, with little or no blackish or whitish, the head sometimes washed dull purplish (see p. 78 regarding senescent ♀♀); iris yellowish brown to moderately bright yellow; occipital tuft moderate in length when fully grown in Jan-Aug (longest feather 25-45 mm); s covs broad and fresher (Fig. 45**F**), dark brown with slight greenish sheen but without vermiculation (Fig. 70**A**); outer pp broader (Fig. 25**C**-**D**), longer by sex (Table 6), and with slight sheen; rects usually basic (Fig. 26**D**), sometimes with r1 replaced alternate in Feb-Sep; bill bluish slate with indistinct whitish band (Fig. 71**B**). **Note: See Juv-HY/SY ♀.**

Juv-HY/SY ♂ (1st cycle, Juv/B1-F1-A1; Oct-Sep): Head and body primarily brownish, becoming increasingly dull purplish, blackish, and whitish in Nov-Sep; iris brown, becoming yellowish in Dec-Sep; occipital tuft washed brownish, reduced in Oct-Nov, and moderately long when fully grown in Feb-Aug (longest feather 35-55 mm); most to all s covs narrow, rounded, and worn (Fig. 45**A**-**B**; *cf.* Fig. 68), brown, without greenish sheen or vermiculation (Fig. 70**A**); outer pp (Fig. 25**A**-**B**, Table 6) and rects (Fig. 26**A**-**D**) as in Juv-HY/SY ♀; bill dusky bluish to pale grayish blue, with indistinct whitish band (Fig. 71**B**). **Note: See Juv-HY/SY ♀.**

AHY/ASY ♂ (Def. cycle, DB-DA; Oct-Sep): Head and body bright glossy purplish, black, and white in Nov-May (flanks can be mottled brown through Jan), variably mottled brownish in Jul-Sep; iris bright yellow; occipital tuft purple, extensive when fully grown in Jan-Aug (longest feather 50-75 mm); s covs broad and fresher (Fig. 45**F**), blackish with moderate to substantial greenish sheen and sometimes with sparse vermiculation (Fig. 70**A**-**B**); outer pp (Fig. 25**C**-**D**, Table 6) and rects (Figs. 67**B** & 26**D**) as in AHY/ASY ♀; bill pale grayish blue (brighter in Nov-May) with moderately distinct white band (Fig. 71**B**). **Note: See Juv-HY/SY ♀**

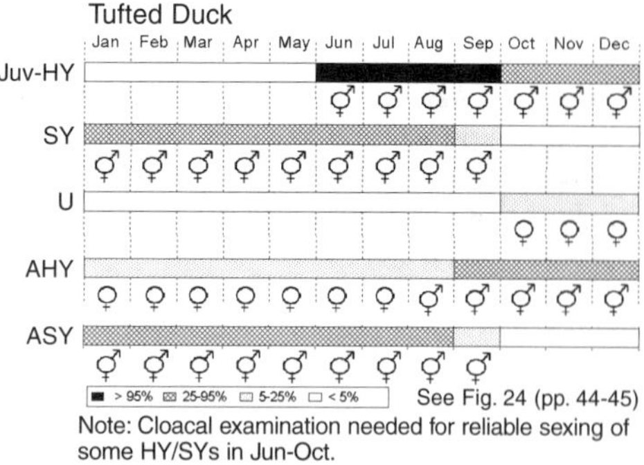

Note: Cloacal examination needed for reliable sexing of some HY/SYs in Jun-Oct.

Hybrids reported—With Mallard (p. 89), Common Pochard *A. ferina*, and Ferruginous Duck *A. nyroca* (McCarthy 2006); Canvasback (p. 105); Ring-necked Duck (p. 110); Greater Scaup (Gillham et al. 1965, McCarthy 2006); and probably Lesser Scaup (McCarthy 2006, Sibley 1938) in the wild.

References—Baker (1993), Boyd et al. (1975), Cramp & Simmons (1977), Dement'ev & Gladkov (1952), Palmer (1976b), Toochin (1998).

GREATER SCAUP
Aythya marila

GRSC
Species # 1480
Band size: 6-5

LESSER SCAUP
Aythya affinis

LESC
Species # 1490
Band size: 6-5

Species—Juvs and ♀♀ from other N.Am ducks by medium-large (Greater) to smaller (Lesser) size with proportionately long wings (Table 6, p. 106); bill slate to pale grayish blue with no or indistinct pale bluish band, black tip, and variable nail size by species (Fig. 71**C**-**D**, p. 114); head dark brown, without tuft, eye ring, or stripe posterior to eye, and with an extensive white patch at base of bill extending below gape; s covs dark brown to blackish with no to moderate whitish vermiculation (Fig. 70**A**-**D**, p. 109); outer ss white to grayish white (Fig. 73, p. 115), contrasting distinctly with darker gr covs; iris dark, to yellowish in AHY ♀♀ and some Juv ♂♂. Beware of hybrids among all species of *Aythya* (including both scaup), that may resemble scaup; hybrid Tufted Duck X Greater Scaup or Tufted Duck X Common Pochard can resemble Lesser Scaup (*cf.* Perrins 1961, Palmer 1976b, Clarke et al. 1995, Harrop 1998).

Greater Scaup from Lesser Scaup by larger overall size and larger bill (Tables 6 & 7); bill nail and black of bill tip wider (Fig. 71**C**-**D**); head larger (Table 7) and rounder (longest crown feather 7-12 mm when fresh *vs* 12-16 mm in Lesser); p2-p4 whiter by sex (Fig. 73), contrasting with darker s1; underwing gr covs pale gray to whitish (*vs* medium to dark gray in Lesser); AHY/ASY ♂ with greenish gloss to auriculars (*vs* purplish in Lesser; both species can have either green or purple gloss to crown and nape). Beware of hybrids (see below). See **Geographic variation** for size differences among populations of Greater Scaup, and Nelson (1996) for separating ducklings and younger Juvs.

TABLE 7. Certain measurements (mm) for the separation of Greater and Lesser scaup, by sex. Values were derived from 95% confidence intervals as based on data presented by Wilson & Ankney (1988); thus midpoints of ranges approximate means, and S.D. is approximated by 25% of the range. See also Table 6 (p. 106) for other standard measurements in these two species.

	Greater Scaup		Lesser Scaup	
	♀(n61)	♂(n81)	♀(n80)	♂(n140)
Middle toe length	63-71	64-73	56-66	58-68
Head bill length[1]	92-100	94-105	82-91	85-95
Head width at widest point	29.4-34.0	29.8-35.6	24.8-30.0	25.8-31.6
Bill height[2]	23.2-28.0	24.5-28.9	18.8-24.4	19.8-25.2
Bill width				
at widest point	24.1-27.7	24.5-27.9	21.5-25.2	21.8-26.2
at distal end of nares	21.9-24.7	22.4-25.2	18.0-23.2	19.3-23.9
Nail width[3]	6.4-8.5	6.5-8.7	4.5-6.8	4.7-6.9
Lamellar spacing[4]	1.21-1.65	1.22-1.66	1.02-1.44	1.07-1.46
Distance between nares[5]	10.1-11.9	10.4-12.2	8.4-10.6	8.6-11.0

[1] See Figure 453 (p. 630).
[2] Taken at distal end of feathering along underside of lower mandible. See Table 6 for bill depth taken from distal end of forehead feathering.
[3] Measured at the tip of the bill from points even with the notches separating the nail from the bill.
[4] Calculated by taking the inverse of the number of lamella over the 10 mm distance distal to the point directly below the distal end of the nares.
[5] Distance between the distal ends of each nare.

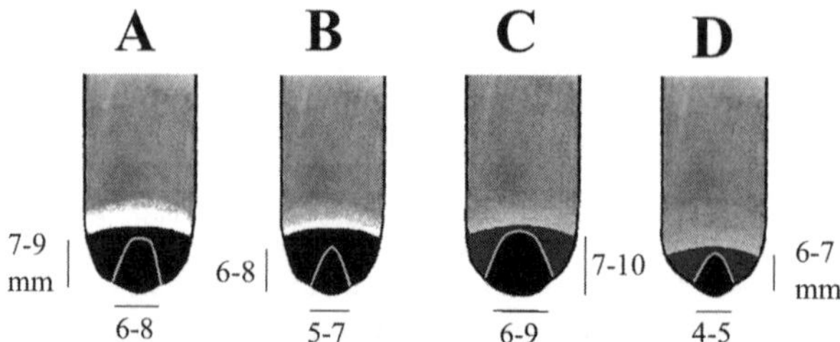

FIGURE 71. Bill shape and color pattern, and nail size and shape in Ring-necked Duck (**A**), Tufted Duck (**B**), Greater Scaup (**C**), and Lesser Scaup (**D**). Pale subterminal bands (especially in **A-B**) are absent in Juvs and more distinct in AHY/ASYs and ♂♂ than in HY/SYs and ♀♀. Note also the difference in nail shape and size, especially between the two scaups.

Geographic variation—Lesser Scaup is monotypic. For Greater Scaup, see Banks (1986a), Hellmayr & Conover (1948a), Palmer (1976b), Parkes (1958a), Portenko (1972), Stejneger (1885). No other subspecies occur.

Greater Scaup

A.m. marila (br & wint Iceland and throughout Palearctic range; vagrant to w.AK, Greenland, and potentially ne.N.Am): Back feathers and scapulars of AHY/ASY ♂♂ with fine blackish vermiculation (Fig. 72**A**); p1-p4 average whiter by sex (*cf.* Fig. 73**A-B**). Populations of e.Asia ("*mariloides*") may average smaller but difference, if present, is too small to warrant subspecific separation.

A.m. nearctica (br & wint N.Am): Back feathers and scapulars of AHY/ASY ♂♂ with coarser blackish vermiculation (> 1 mm wide; Fig. 72**B**); p1-p4 average less white by sex (*cf.* Fig. 73).

Molt—CAS. PF partial-incomplete (Sep-Mar in HY/SYs), DPA limited (Apr-May in AHY ♀♀, Jun-Aug in AHY ♂♂), DPB complete (Jul-Nov in AHYs). Molt strategies in both species of scaup appear to be similar to those of Redhead (p. 108).

Age/Sex—Juv (B1; Jun-Oct) resembles HY/SY ♀, with less distinct whitish at base of bill and sometimes with indistinct white mottling in auriculars, flanks with browner wash, and rects entirely juv (Figs. 67**A**, p. 105, & 26**A**, p. 48). Juv ♂♂ often have a yellowish tinge to the iris (*vs* olive or brownish in ♀♀), and many Juvs can be sexed by s-cov and inner ss characters, as in Juv-HY/SYs. Partial medial BP (Fig. 20**A**, p. 31) and/or distended cloaca (Fig. 21, p. 32) developed by ♀♀ in Apr-Jul. See also Figures 22-23 (pp. 32-35) and Anderson et al. (1969) for cloacal characteristics useful in ageing and sexing (including Juvs), Tables 6 (p. 106) and 7 (p. 113) for measurements by age and sex, and Carney (1992) for useful photographs of wings.

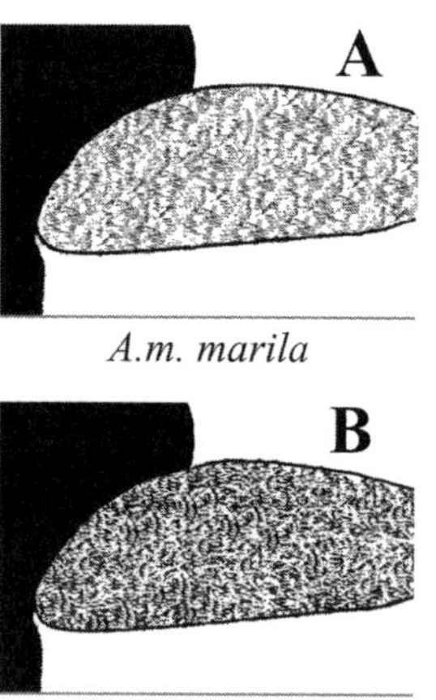

FIGURE 72. Degree of vermiculation in the back and scapulars by subspecies in Greater Scaup. The black bars on the back are usually < 1 mm wide in *A.m. marila* (**A**) and > 1 mm wide in *nearctica* (**B**).

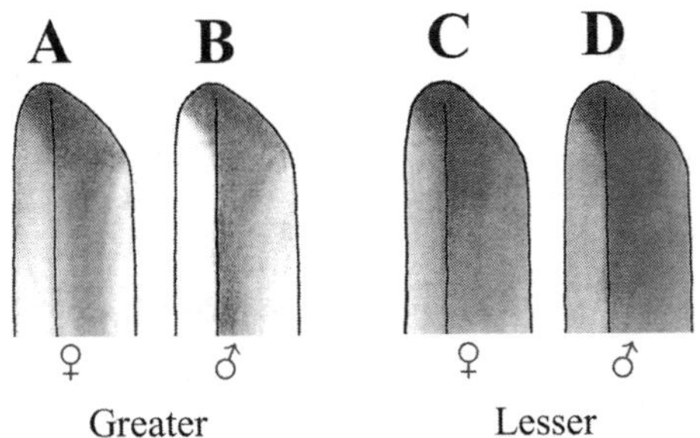

FIGURE 73. Pattern to s3 by species and sex in Greater (**A-B**) and Lesser (**C-D**) scaup. In Greater Scaup s3 is contrastingly whiter than s1 whereas in Lesser Scaup these two feathers are similar in shade. The degree of whiteness also varies slightly by age (AHY/ASY whiter than HY/SY) within each sex, but variation by sex is greater than that of age. Figures **A-B** represent N.Am Greater Scaups (*A.m. nearctica*); the Palearctic subspecies (*nearctica*) shows whiter feathers in each sex. Tufted Dick shows a similar amount of white (or more) as Greater Scaup (**A-B**).

Juv-HY/SY ♀ (1st cycle, Juv/B1-F1-A1; Oct-Sep): Head and body brown; iris brown, becoming olive brown by Jan-May; most to all s covs narrow, rounded, and worn (Fig. 45**A-B**, p. 79; *cf.* Fig. 68, p. 107), brown, without sheen and with little or no vermiculation (Fig. 70**A**, occasionally to **B** in Greater Scaup; p. 109); outer pp narrow (Fig. 25**A-B**, p. 47), averaging shorter by sex (Table 6), and without sheen; abdomen worn and pale brown to whitish, not contrasting distinctly with breast; rects juv and/or formative (Figs. 67**A** & 26**A-D**; see **Molt**).

AHY/ASY ♀ (Def. cycle, DB-DA; Oct-Sep): Head and body brown, with little to no purplish/greenish, black, and/or white in back (see p. 78 regarding senescent ♀♀); iris yellowish brown (SY/TYs?) to moderately bright yellow; s covs broad and fresher (Fig. 45**F**), dark brown, with slight sheen, and with slight to moderate vermiculation (Fig. 70**B-D**); outer pp broader (Fig. 25**C-D**), longer by sex (Table 6), and with slight sheen; abdomen fresher and medium-dark brown, contrasting distinctly with darker breast; rects usually basic (Figs. 67**D** & 26**D**), sometimes with r1 replaced alternate in Feb-Sep. **Note: ♀♀ with bright yellow eyes might reliably be aged ASY/ATY (see Trauger 1974) but experience may be required.**

Juv-HY/SY ♂ (1st cycle, Juv/B1-F1-A1; Oct-Sep): Head and body brownish, becoming increasingly dull purplish/greenish, blackish, and whitish in Nov-Sep; iris yellowish brown, becoming yellow by Oct-Feb; most to all s covs narrow, rounded, and worn (Fig. 45**A-C**), brown, without greenish sheen (sometimes a slight sheen to gr covs) and usually with a slight amount of vermiculation (Fig. 70**B-C**); outer pp (Fig. 25**A-B**, Table 6) and rects (Figs. 67**A** & 26**A-D**) as in Juv-HY/SY ♀.

AHY/ASY ♂ (Def. cycle, DB-DA; Oct-Sep): Head and body bright glossy purplish/greenish, black, and white in Nov-May (flanks can be mottled brown through Dec), variably mottled brownish (and with a whitish loral spot often present) in Jul-Sep; iris bright yellow to orangish yellow; s covs broad and fresher (Fig. 45**F**), dark brown with moderate to substantial greenish sheen (especially to gr covs) and vermiculation (Fig. 70**C-E**); outer pp (Fig. 25**C-D**, Table 6) and rects (Figs. 67**B** & 26**D**) as in AHY/ASY ♀.

Hybrids reported—Greater Scaup with Canvasback (p. 105), Redhead (p. 108), Common Pochard *A. ferina* (Gillham 1993), Ferruginous Duck *A. nyroca* (McCarthy 2006), Ring-necked

Duck (p. 110), Tufted Duck (p. 111), Common Goldeneye (McCarthy 2006), and probably Lesser Scaup (Bradshaw 2005, Eigenhuis 1985, Johnsgard 1960a, Sibley 1938) in the wild. Lesser Scaup from native populations with Canvasback, Ring-necked Duck, probably Tufted Duck and Greater Scaup, and possibly with Redhead in the wild. Vagrant Lesser Scaup with Common Pochard (*A. ferina*) in the wild in Europe (McCarthy 2006).

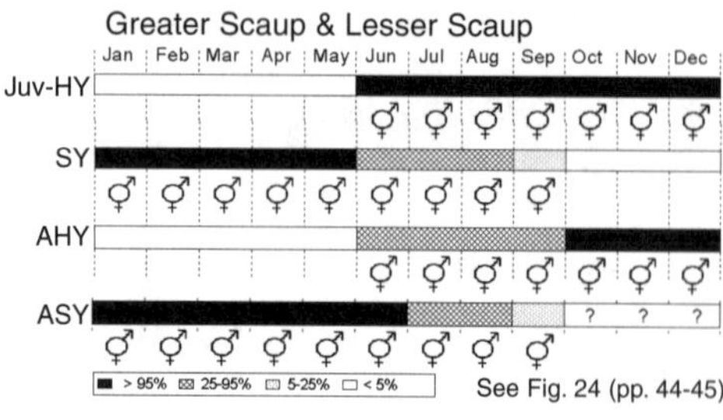

References—Ainley et al. (1994), Anderson & Warner (1969), Austin (1987), Austin & Fredrickson (1986), Austin et al. (1998), Baker (1993), Banks (1986a), Bent (1923), Billard & Humphrey (1972), Boyd et al. (1975), Bradshaw (2005), Carney (1964, 1992), Clarke et al. (1995), Cramp & Simmons (1977), Dement'ev & Gladkov (1952), Fix (1985), Garner (2002a), Holian & Forley (1992), Kaufman (1999), Kessel et al. (2002), C.H. Nelson (1997), Oberholser (1974), Oring (1964), Palmer (1976b), Roberts (1955), Todd (1963), Trauger (1974), Wilson & Ankney (1988).

Seaducks and Mergansers *Anatidae, Anatinae, Mergini*

Fifteen North American species. See Family (p. 47) and Subfamily (p. 58) accounts for traits found throughout Anatidae and Anatinae. Tribal characters include small to large bodies, even-width to narrow-tipped bills, and lobed hind toes. North American seaducks and mergansers have 10 functional primaries (p10 often longest when fully grown, extending 5 mm longer to 5 mm shorter than p9); 14-18 (usually 16) secondaries including 3 (most *Mergini*), 4-5 (Hooded Merganser; p. 149), or 7 (eiders) tertials or tertial-like feathers; and 14-20 rectrices. Ageing through the first cycle (to SY and ASY) can be accomplished for most individuals through plumage aspect, particularly of the wing, while in males of eiders and a few other species, ageing can be accomplished through the second cycle (to TY and ATY) by plumage-aspect characters. Condition of the rectrices (Figs. 26, p. 48, & 67, p. 105) can be used for ageing; however in certain species (e.g., eiders), feathers can become abraded by salt water and tips of basic feathers can break off, obscuring age-related differences. Sexing of most individuals (including juveniles of many species) is accomplished through plumage aspect and measurements, males being larger than females (definitively so in some species).

Molt strategies are similar to those of other ducks although, except in eiders, the timing of the definitive prealternate molt appears not to differ as much between the sexe, and Scoters exhibit a Simple Alternate Strategy (Fig. 10**C**, pp. 13-16). There is no auxilliary preformative molt during the first cycle and there is probably not a presupplemental molt in the definitive cycle of Long-tailed Ducks (p. 140), as often reported (see Molt under that species). In addition, preformative molts are usually more protracted and may supersede the need for first prealternate molts in many individuals and perhaps all scoters. Age at first breeding occurs at 2-3 years in most individuals of most species but up to 3-5 years in some eiders; prebasic molts of SYs and non-breeding ASYs average earlier in timing than those of breeding adults. In certain species a substantial proportion of SYs (and often some ASYs) over summer on non-breeding grounds; more study is needed on the molts and plumage aspects of these individuals and how they might differ from SYs that migrate north for the summer.

STELLER'S EIDER
Polysticta stelleri

STEI
Species # 1570
Band size: 6-7A

Species—Juvs and ♀♀ from other N.Am ducks and eiders by medium-small size with proportionally long tail and large bill (Table 8, p. 122); bill narrow at tip, slate to pale grayish blue with a paler nail, and with unique flaps to underside (Fig. 74); base of bill without feather extensions as in other eiders (*cf.* Fig. 80, p. 123); body primarily dark brown with an indistinct pale patch around eye; terts and medial ss with blackish, blue, and white (Figs. 77**A-B** & 78**A**, p. 119); axillars white; underwing covs grayish and white; legs dusky to dark grayish.

Geographic variation—Monotypic.

Molt—CAS. PF limited (Oct-Mar in HY/SYs), PA1 absent-limited (May-Jun in SYs), PB2 complete (Jul-Oct in SYs), DPA limited-partial (May-Jul in ASYs), DPB complete (Sep-Dec in ASYs). The PF occurs on non-breeding grounds, the PAs occur on breeding grounds, and the PBs occur primarily on molting

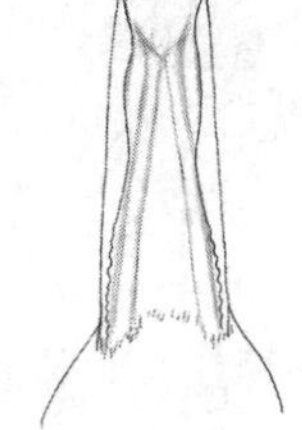

FIGURE 74. Underside of bill of Steller's Eider; note unique flaps on sides.

grounds (p. 47) between the breeding and non-breeding grounds. Both the PF and the PA1 include some to most body feathers but few if any rump or abdomen feathers, terts, s covs, or rects. Wing feathers are replaced synchronously during PBs. The DPA includes most body feathers but few if any terts or rects. See Family (p. 47), Subfamily (p. 78), and Tribal (p. 117) accounts for more details.

Age/Sex—Juv (B1; Jul-Oct) resembles HY/SY ♀♀ but plumage aspect tinged pale grayish and rects uniformly juv (Figs. 26**A**, p. 48, & 67**A**, p. 105). Juv ♂♂ often have small whitish spots to the breast feathers, absent in Juv ♀♀ (Fig. 75); Juvs can also be sexed by the combination of the tert and proximal ss characters, as in Juv-HY/SYs. Partial medial BP (Fig. 20**A**, p. 31) and/or distended cloaca (Fig. 21, p. 32) developed by ASY ♀♀ in May-Jul. See Figures 22-23 (pp. 32-35) for cloacal characteristics useful in ageing and sexing (including Juvs), Table 8 (p. 122) for measurements by age and sex, and Carney (1992) for useful photographs of wings.

Juv-HY/SY ♀ (1st cycle, Juv/B1-F1-A1; Oct-Sep): Head and body brown; s covs brown (Fig. 78**A**), the proximal gr covs long and rounded and with narrow and indistinct whitish tips (Fig. 76**A**); terts rounded, brown fringed buff, with little or no bluish or whitish (Fig. 77**A**); s8-s12 with thin white tips, confined primarily to outer web; outer pp narrow (Fig. 25**A**-**B**, p. 47), averaging shorter by sex (Table 8), and without sheen; rects juv (Figs. 26**A** & 67**A**). **Note: Beware that some HY/SY ♂♂ do not acquire whitish on the breast or other colorful plumage aspect until Mar-Apr; use gr-cov, tert, and s8-s12 characters to sex these.**

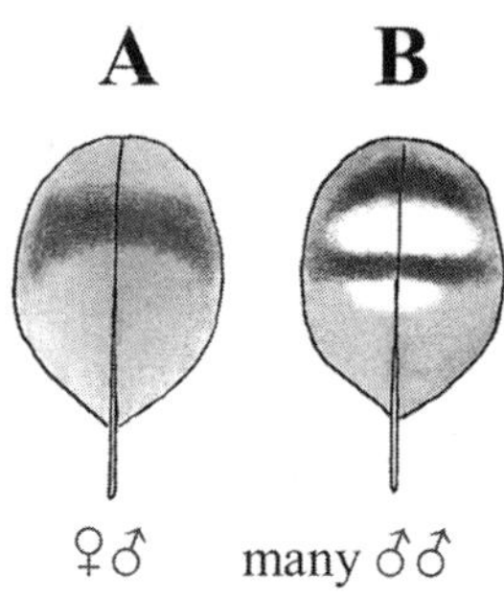

FIGURE 75. Juvenal breast feathers by sex in Steller's, King, and Common eiders. Note that not all Juv ♂♂ show white; thus, other criteria should be used to sex Juvs without white in the breast feathers. The feathers with white in ♂♂ may either be later-developed juvenile feathers or earlier-replaced formative feathers (more study needed).

AHY/ASY ♀ (Def. cycle, DB-DA; Oct-Sep): Head and body primarily brown, with little or no whitish, blackish, or cinnamon (see p. 78 regarding senescent ♀♀); s covs brown (Fig. 78**A**),

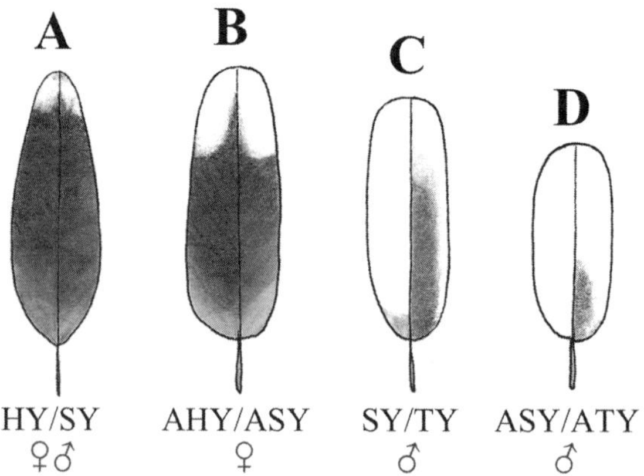

FIGURE 76. Shape, size, and color pattern of proximal gr covs (corresponding to s7-s9) by age and sex in Steller's Eider. Note rounded tip to juvenal covert (**A**) as compared to that of AHY/ASY ♀♀ (**B**) and that size of the covert becomes smaller with age in ♂♂ (**C**-**D**). Juv covs (**A**) are retained by SYs through the PB2 in Jul-Oct and 2nd basic covs (**C**) are retained by TY ♂♂ through the DPB in Sep-Dec.

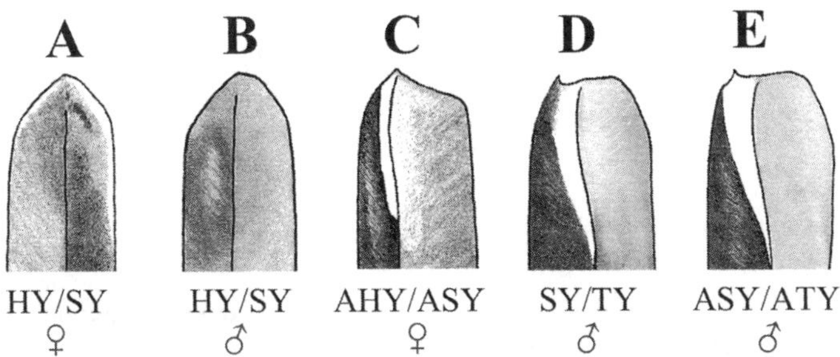

FIGURE 77. Shape and pattern of the tertials by age and sex in Steller's Eider. Note the buff fringe in terts of Juv ♀ (**A**) as compared to the hint of definitive pattern usually present those of Juv ♂ (**B**). The white stripe is thinner in AHY/ASY ♀ terts (**C**) and less distinct (sometimes washed dusky) in SY/TY ♂ terts (**D**) than in ASY/ATY ♂ terts (**D**). Juv terts (**A-B**) are retained by SYs through the PB2 in Jul-Oct and 2nd basic terts (♀) are retained by TY ♂♂ through the DPB in Sep-Dec.

the proximal gr covs long and squared with distinct white tips (Fig. 76**B**); terts pointed and with blue, silver, and brown (Fig. 77**C**); s8-s12 with wide white tips across both webs; outer pp broad (Fig. 25**C-D**), averaging longer by sex (Table 8), and with slight sheen; rects basic (Figs. 26**D** & 67**B**). **Note: See Juv-HY/SY ♀.**

Juv-HY/SY ♂ (1st cycle, Juv/B1-F1-A1; Oct-Sep): Head and body dark brown, usually with small amounts of whitish on breast (Fig. 75**B**), and becoming partially blackish and cinnamon in Dec-Sep; s covs brown (Fig. 78**A**), the proximal gr covs long and rounded with narrow and indistinct whitish tips (Fig. 76**A**); terts rounded, grayish, often with slight bluish and whitish tinge (Fig. 77**B**); s8-s12 narrow with a moderately thin white tip across both webs; outer pp (Fig. 25**C-D**) and rects (Figs. 26**A** & 67**A**) as in Juv-HY/SY ♀. **Note: See Juv-HY/SY ♀.**

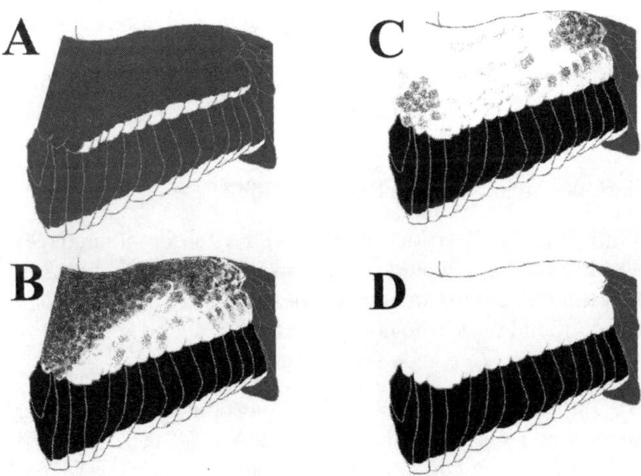

FIGURE 78. Upperwing patterns by age and sex in Steller's, Spectacled, and Common eiders. Entirely dark s covs (**A**) indicate ♀♀ and Juv-HY/SY ♂♂. The white tipping to the ss represents that found in Steller's Eider; Spectacled Eider has little to no white and the white tips of Common Eider are confined primarily to the outer webs (*cf.* Fig. 81, p. 124). SY/TY ♂♂ can have variable amounts of dark to the white wing patch (**B-C**), with some TY/4Y ♂♂ possibly showing some dusky to the marginal les covs (**C**), especially in Common Eider (more study needed). Entirely white coverts (**D**) indicates ASY/ATY ♂♂ (possibly ATY/A4Y ♂♂ in Spectacled and Common eiders).

SY/TY ♂ (B2-A2; Oct-Sep): Head and body primarily whitish, blackish, and cinnamon in Oct-Jun or washed brown in Jul-Sep; s covs mixed white and blackish (Fig. 78**B-C**), the proximal gr covs medium in length and with moderately broad and distinct white tips (Fig. 76**C**); terts with indistinct blue and white pattern (Fig. 77**D**). **Note: See ASY/ATY ♂.**

ASY/ATY ♂ (Def. cycle, DB-DA; Oct-Sep): Head and body bright white, black, and cinnamon in Oct-Jun or washed brown in Jul-Sep; s covs white (Fig. 78**D**), the proximal gr covs small (Fig. 76**D**); terts bright blue and white (Fig. 77**E**). **Note: Some TY/4Y ♂♂ may show reduced amount of blackish in marginal les covs (e.g., Fig. 78C); more study needed.**

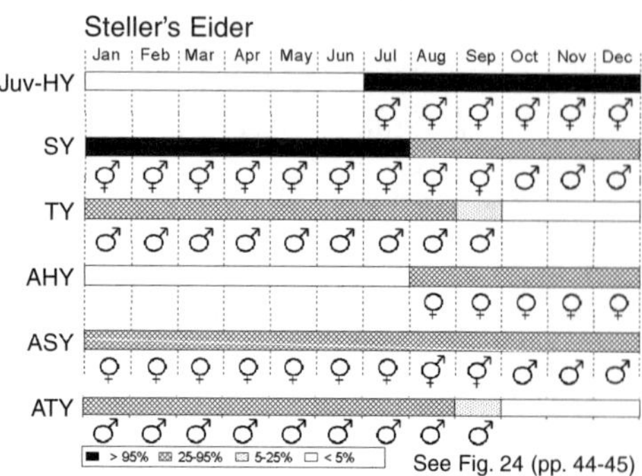

Hybrids reported—With Common Eider (Forsman 1995) and possibly with Mallard (p. 89) in the wild.

References—Ainley et al. (1994), Bent (1925), Conover (1926), Cramp & Simmons (1977), Dement'ev & Gladkov (1952), Fredrickson (2001), K.C. Parkes & R.S. Palmer *in* Palmer (1976b), Petersen (1980, 1981), Portenko (1952, 1972), Stejneger (1885), Stone (1900).

SPECTACLED EIDER
Somateria fischeri

SPEI
Species # 1580
Band size: 7A-7B

Species—Juvs and ♀♀ from other N.Am ducks and eiders by medium size (Table 8, p. 122); bill slate with pale nail (to pale pinkish yellow or orangish in ♂♂), forehead feathers extended, and bill process absent (Fig. 80**A**, p. 123); head with unique patch of specialized velvet-like feathers around eye in all plumages; outer webs to ss without bluish and with indistinct or no whitish tips in AHY ♀♀ (*cf.* Fig. 81**D**, p. 124); flanks with distinct black bars; axillars and underwing covs dusky.

Geographic variation—Monotypic. See Palmer (1976b), Petersen et al. (2000), Portenko (1972).

Molt—CAS. PF limited-partial (Oct-Mar in HY/SYs), PA1 absent-limited (May-Jul in SYs), PB2 complete (Jul-Oct in SYs), DPA limited-partial (Apr-Jun in ASY ♀♀, Jun-Aug in ASY ♂♂), DPB complete (Sep-Dec in ASYs). Molt strategies appear similar to those of King Eider (p. 123). The specialized feathers around the eye do not appear to be replaced at the PF or DPA, but become soiled (cryptic) in summer.

Age/Sex—Juv (B1; Jul-Nov) resembles HY/SY ♀♀ but plumage aspect paler brown and more mottled (less barred) and rects uniformly juv (Figs. 26**A**, p. 48, & 67**A**, p. 105); Juvs can be sexed by combination of scapular, gr-cov, and tert characters, as in Juv-HY/SYs. Partial medial BP (Fig. 20**A**, p. 31) and/or distended cloaca (Fig. 21, p. 32) developed by ASY ♀♀ in May-Jul. See Figures 22-23 (pp. 32-35) for cloacal characteristics useful in ageing and sexing (including Juvs), and Table 8 (p. 122) for measurements by age and sex.

Juv-HY/SY ♀ (1st cycle, Juv/B1-F1-A1; Oct-Sep): Head and body pale brown; bill dull slate; s covs brown (Fig. 78**A**, p. 119), the proximal gr covs (and ss) rounded with narrow and indistinct buffy tips (Fig. 81**A**, p. 124); terts brown, with little or no attenuation (Fig. 79**A**); longest scapulars with little broadening to inner web (Fig. 86**A**, p. 128); outer pp narrow (Fig. 25**A**-**B**, p. 47), averaging shorter by sex (Table 8), and without sheen; iris dark brown; rects juv (Figs. 26**A** & 67**A**). **Note: Beware that some HY/SY ♂♂ may not acquire multi-colored ♂ plumage aspect until Mar-Apr; use scapular, gr-cov, tert, and (especially) bill-color characters to sex these.**

AHY/ASY ♀ (Def. cycle, DB-DA; Oct-Sep): Head and body dark brown, with little or no whitish, greenish, or blackish (see p. 78 regarding senescent ♀♀); bill bluish slate; s covs brown (Fig. 78**A**), the proximal gr covs (and ss) squared and often with narrow and indistinct whitish tips (*cf.* Fig. 81**D**); terts washed dusky, with moderate attenuation (Fig. 79**C**); longest scapulars with little to a slight amount of broadening to inner web (Fig. 86**A**-**B**); outer pp broad (Fig. 25**C**-**D**), averaging longer by sex (Table 8), and with slight sheen; iris dark brown to grayish brown; rects basic (Figs. 26**D** & 67**B**). Note: See Juv-HY/SY ♀.

Juv-HY/SY ♂ (1st cycle, Juv/B1-F1-A1; Oct-Sep): Head and body dark brown, usually with small amounts of whitish, greenish, and/or blackish in Dec-Sep; bill dull slate, becoming tinged dull yellow or orangish by Oct-Dec; s covs brown (Fig. 78**A**), the proximal gr covs (and

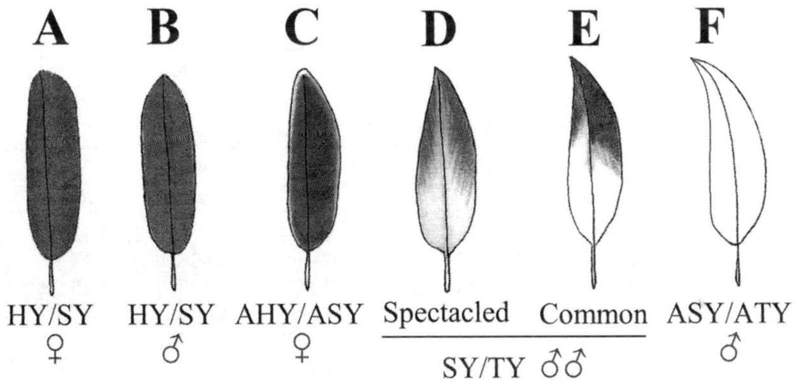

FIGURE 79. Shape and pattern to the tertials in Spectacled and Common eiders by age and sex. Note cline in shape, becoming more attenuated and curved from Juv ♀ (**A**) to ATY ♂ (**F**). The terts of King Eider are similar in shape and pattern of Juvs and ♀♀ (**A**-**C**) but are entirely blackish in AHY/ASY ♂♂ (**D**).

ss) rounded and with thin or no buff fringe (Fig. 81**C**); terts brown to dusky, usually with slight attenuation (Fig. 79**B**); longest scapulars with slight broadening to inner web (Fig. 86**B**); outer pp (Fig. 25**A**-**B**) and rects (Figs. 26**A** & 67**A**) as in Juv-HY/SY ♀; iris dark brown, becoming paler and grayer by Jan-Mar. **Note: See Juv-HY/SY ♀.**

SY/TY ♂ (B2-A2; Oct-Sep): Head and body primarily whitish, greenish, and blackish in Oct-Jun or with heavy brown mottling (but back partially white) in Jul-Sep; bill brightish orange (Oct-Mar) to dull pinkish yellow (Apr-Sep); s covs mixed white and brownish (Fig. 78**B**-**C**; terts moderately attenuated and curved and whitish washed gray (Fig. 79**D**); longest scapulars with slight to moderate broadening to inner web (Fig. 86**C**-**D**); iris dull to bright pale bluish. **Note: See ASY/ATY ♂.**

ASY/ATY ♂ (Def. cycle, DB-DA; Oct-Sep): Head and body bright white, green, and black in Oct-Jun, heavy mottled dusky (but back partially white) in Jul-Nov; bill bright orange (Oct-Mar) to pinkish yellow (Apr-Sep); s covs uniformly white (Fig. 78**D**); terts attenuated, curved, and white (Fig. 79**F**); longest scapulars with moderate broadening and modification to inner web (Fig. 86**C-D**); iris bright pale bluish. **Note: It is possible that ♂♂ with reduced blackish in the s covs (e.g., Fig. 78C) can be aged TY/4Y and that ♂♂ with the above characters (including entirely white terts and s covs) can be aged ATY/A4Y but more study is needed.**

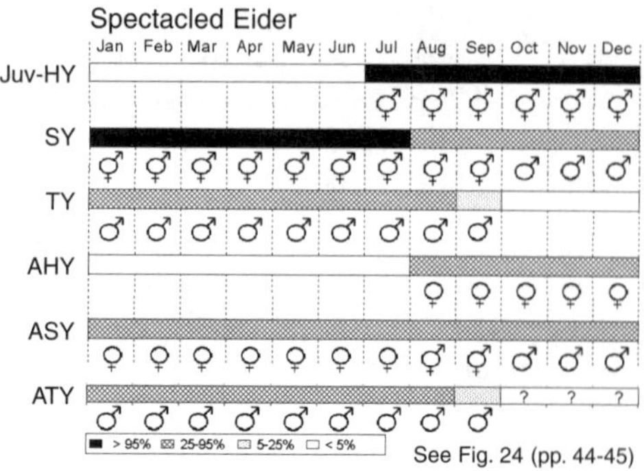

Hybrids reported—None.

References—Ainley et al. (1994), Bent (1925), Conover (1926), Cramp & Simmons (1977), Dement'ev & Gladkov (1952), K.C. Parkes & R.S. Palmer *in* Palmer (1976b), Petersen et al. (1999), Portenko (1952, 1972), Stejneger (1885), Stone (1900).

TABLE 8. Measurements (mm) of North American eiders to assist in identification, ageing, and sexing. See pp. 4-11 for methods of measurement. Species summaries are in **bold** and subspecies summaries in ***italics***. Values were derived from 95% confidence intervals as based (for wing, exposed culmen, and tarsus) approximately on the indicated sample sizes (see pp. 4-5); sample sizes for tail length and bill depth were often smaller but included at least 10 of each sex. Thus, midpoints of ranges approximate means, and S.D. is approximated by 25% of the range.

Taxon/Sex	*n*	wing chord AHY/ASY	wing chord (HY/SY)[1]	tail length[1]	bill length[2]	bill depth[2]	tarsus
Steller's Eider		**199-223**	**(194-218)**	**74-94**	**20-28**	**13.2-15.6**	**36-42**
♀	38	199-218	(194-214)	74-89	20-25	13.2-15.3	36-41
♂	46	204-223	(199-218)	79-94	22-28	13.4-15.6	37-42
Spectacled Eider		**246-266**	**(233-260)**	**72-87**	**30-35**	**14.8-17.6**	**45-51**
♀	30	246-259	(233-254)	72-85	31-35	14.8-17.5	45-49
♂	30	251-266	(238-260)	74-87	30-34	14.9-17.6	46-51
King Eider		**251-286**	**(243-278)**	**75-89**	**32-36**	**15.8-18.5**	**44-51**
♀	80	251-279	(243-272)	75-87	32-36	15.8-18.5	44-49
♂	90	260-286	(250-278)	76-89	32-35	16.1-18.2	46-51
Common Eider		**261-319**	**(254-309)**	**76-102**	**30-42**	**16.0-22.2**	**47-57**
S.m. v-nigra		***281-319***	***(271-309)***	***87-102***	***30-41***	***16.0-19.8***	***49-57***
♀	88	281-308	(271-298)	87-100	30-37	16.0-19.1	49-55
♂	82	292-319	(282-309)	89-102	35-41	16.6-19.8	50-57
S.m. borealis		***261-297***	***(254-288)***	***76-95***	***33-42***	***18.6-22.2***	***47-54***
♀	86	261-289	(254-280)	76-91	33-41	19.7-22.2	47-53
♂	71	272-297	(265-288)	81-95	34-42	18.6-20.5	48-54
S.m. sedentaria		***285-320***	***(278-315)***	***85-100***	***34-40***	***18.7-21.0***	***48-56***
♀	46	285-315	(278-305)	85-97	34-37	18.7-20.6	48-55
♂	30	296-320	(289-315)	89-100	36-40	19.1-21.0	49-56
S.m. dresseri		***268-299***	***(260-290)***	***78-96***	***31-39***	***16.6-20.8***	***47-55***
♀	45	268-288	(260-280)	78-92	31-36	16.6-20.4	47-53
♂	37	279-299	(271-290)	82-96	34-39	16.9-20.8	49-55

[1] Wing chord and tail length differ substantially by age; wing data are separated by age since juv primaries are retained through the second PB whereas tail lengths pertain to formative and basic feathers only, as the juvenal central rects are often replaced by Oct-Dec in HYs. Other measures pertain to all age groups.

[2] Bill length and depth measured from/at the proximal end of the nares (Fig. 8**C**, p. 10). The distal end of the forehead feathering varies too much among species and subspecies (Fig. 80) to provide comparable bill-depth values.

KING EIDER
Somateria spectabilis

KIEI
Species # 1620
Band size: 6

Species—Juvs and ♀♀ from other N.Am ducks and eiders by medium size with proportionately small exposed culmen (Table 8); bill grayish (to yellowish orange in ♂♂) with over-hanging hook, swelling at base, forehead feather-extension moderate, and bill process reduced (Fig. 80**B**); outer webs to medial ss without bluish but with white tips spanning both webs in AHY ♀♀ (Figs. 81**D** & 82**A**, p. 124); anterior scapulars of AHY ♀ without distinct indentations (Fig. 84**B**, p. 127); flanks without distinct blackish bars in Sep-Apr; axillars and underwing covs dusky (whitish in AHY/ASY ♂).

Geographic variation—Monotypic.

Molt—CAS. PF partial (Oct-Mar in HY/SYs), PA1 absent-limited (May-Jul in SYs), PB2 complete (Jul-Oct in SYs), DPA limited-partial (Apr-May in ASY ♀♀, Jun-Jul in ASY ♂♂), DPB complete (Sep-Dec in ASYs). The PF occurs on non-breeding grounds, the PAs occur on breeding grounds, and the PB occurs primarily on molting grounds (p. 47) between the breeding and non-breeding grounds. Both the PF and the PA1 include some to most body feathers but few if any rump or abdomen feathers, terts, s covs, or rects. Wing feathers are replaced synchronously during PBs. The DPA includes most body feathers and can include some proximal s covs in ♀♀ but not ♂♂. See Family (p. 47), Subfamily (p. 78), and Tribal (p. 117) accounts for more details.

Age/Sex—Juv (B1; Jul-Nov) resembles HY/SY ♀♀ but plumage aspect tinged grayish and rects uniformly juv (Figs. 26**A**, p. 48, & 67**A**, p. 105); Juv ♂♂ often have small whitish spots to the breast feathers, absent in Juv ♀♀ (Fig. 75, p. 118); Juvs can also be sexed by combination of scapular, gr-cov, tert, and bill-color characters, as in Juv-HY/SYs. Partial medial BP (Fig. 20**A**, p. 31) and/or distended cloaca (Fig. 21, p. 32) developed by ASY ♀♀ in May-Jul. See Figures 22-23 (pp. 32-35) for cloacal characteristics useful in ageing and sexing (including Juvs), and Table 8 for measurements by age and sex.

Juv-HY/SY ♀ (1st cycle, Juv/B1-F1-A1; Oct-Sep): Head and body pale brown (*cf.* Fig. 83**A**, p. 125); bill dusky to blackish (sometimes tinged grayish or olive) and without swelling at base (Fig. 83**A**); s covs brown (Fig. 82**A**, p. 124), the proximal gr covs (and ss) rounded and usu-

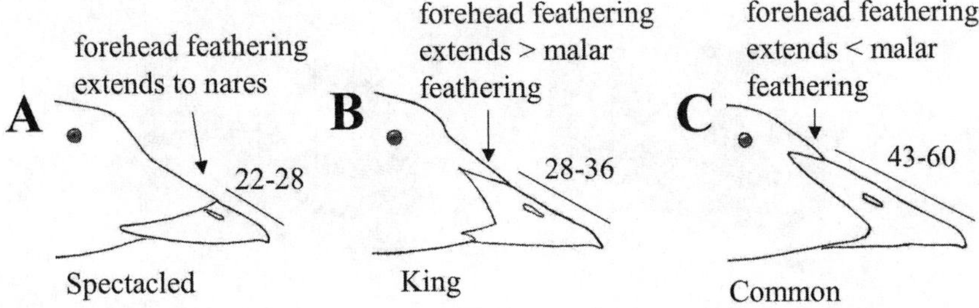

FIGURE 80. Bill size and shape, and pattern of feathering by species in Spectacled, King, and Common eiders. See also Figure 86 (p. 128) for geographic variation in feather patterns in Common Eider. Values indicate exposed culmen (Fig. 7**A**, p. 9). The "bill process" refers to the proximal extension of the bill toward the eye, absent in Spectacled, reduced in King, and variably extensive in Common (see also Fig. 86) eiders.

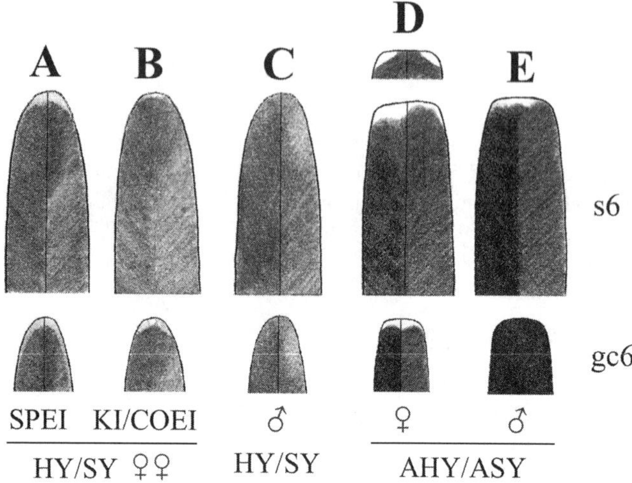

FIGURE 81. Shape and pattern to the medial secondaries (s6 shown) and corresponding greater coverts, by age and sex, in Spectacled, King, and Common eiders. For juv ♀ feathers (**A**) Spectacled Eider shows a buffier fringe than King and Common Eiders. For basic ♀ feathers (**D**), King Eider shows broader white tips than Common Eider (typically as in inset) and Spectacled Eider (indistinct or no whitish tips). These feathers occasionally can be replaced during the DPA in ♀♀ (*cf.* Fig. 45**D**-**E**, p. 79), the alternate feathers resembling illustration **A**, but more distal feathers are retained and can be used for ageing and sexing through the PB2 in ♀ King Eiders with very broad and distinct white tips to the ss (more so than shown in **D**) are possibly ASY/ATYs (see Boyd et al. 1975, Palmer 1976b) but more study is needed to confirm this.

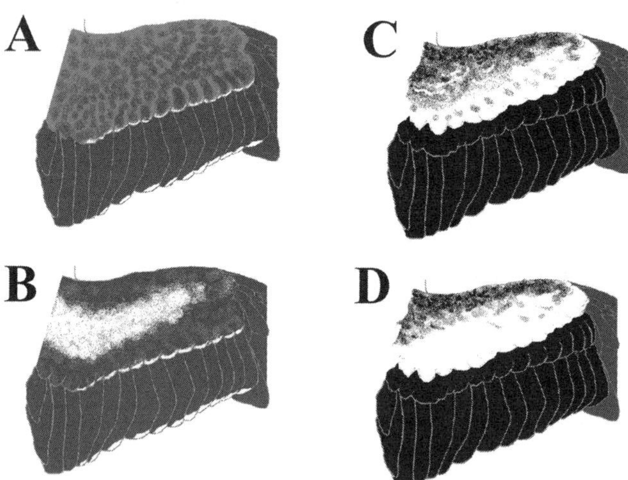

FIGURE 82. Upperwing patterns by age and sex in King Eider. Entirely dark s covs (**A**) indicate ♀♀ and Juv-HY/SY ♂♂; note the thin white tipping to the ss, less distinct than that of Steller's Eider (Fig. 78**A**) but more distinct than those of Spectacled and Common eiders (*cf.* Fig. 81). SY/TY ♂♂ often just show whitish gr covs (**B**) but may also show more white, perhaps as much as **C**. Additionally, some TY/4Y ♂♂ may be reliably aged by having some dusky to the med covs (**C**) but more study is needed. **D** represents ASY/ATY (possibly ATY/A4Y) ♂♂.

ally tipped narrowly and indistinctly with whitish (Fig. 81**B**); terts brown, with little or no attenuation (Fig. 79**A**, p. 121); longest scapulars with slight to moderate broadening to inner web (Fig. 86**B**-**C**, p. 128); outer pp narrow (Fig. 25**A**-**B**, p. 47), averaging shorter by sex (Table 8), and without sheen; rects juv (Figs. 26**A** & 67**A**). **Note: Beware that some HY/SY ♂♂ do not acquire whitish on the breast or other multi-colored feathers until Mar-Apr; use scapular, gr-cov, tert, and bill-color characters to sex these.**

AHY/ASY ♀ (Def. cycle, DB-DA; Oct-Sep): Head and body dark brown, usually with small amounts of whitish on breast (Fig. 75**B**), and with little or no bluish, blackish, or whitish (see p. 78 regarding senescent ♀♀); bill grayish, tinged yellowish or greenish, and with no or slight swelling at base (Fig. 83**A**-**B**); s covs brown (Fig. 82**A**), the proximal gr covs (and ss) squared and tipped broadly and distinctly with white (Fig. 81**D**); terts washed dusky, with moderate attenuation (Fig. 79**C**); longest scapulars with moderate modification to inner web (Fig. 86**C**-**D**); outer pp broad (Fig. 25**C**-**D**), averaging longer by sex (Table 8), and with slight sheen; rects basic (Figs. 26**D** & 67**B**). **Note: See Juv-HY/SY ♀.**

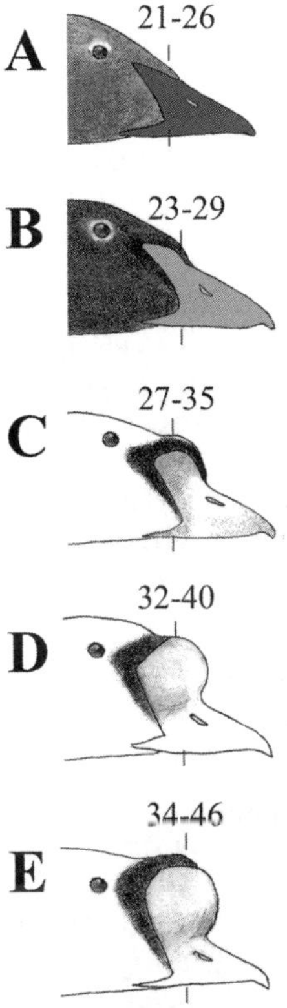

A 21-26

B 23-29

C 27-35

D 32-40

E 34-46

FIGURE 83. Bill color and swelling at base by age and sex in King Eider. Values indicate bill depth at distal end of feathers (Fig. 8**A**, p. 10). Most ♀♀ exhibit no swelling at the base (**A**) although ASY ♀♀ can exhibit some swelling (**B**) but still exhibit a dark bill, as in **A**. ♂♂ of all ages obtain more swollen bill knobs in Nov-Apr (e.g., **C** for SY/TYs, **D** for ASY/ATYs) than in May-Oct (**D** for TYs, **E** for ATYs).

Juv-HY/SY ♂ (1st cycle, Juv/B1-F1-A1; Oct-Sep): Head and body primarily dark brown, usually with small amounts of bluish, blackish, and whitish in Dec-Sep; bill dusky, becoming grayish and dusky orange, and swelling slightly at base by Oct-Dec (Fig. 83**B**); s covs uniformly brown (Fig. 82**A**), the proximal gr covs (and ss) rounded, with no or a narrow and indistinct pale or whitish fringe (Fig. 81**C**); terts brown to dusky, usually with slight attenuation (Fig. 79**B**); longest scapulars with moderate broadening to inner web (Fig. 86**C**-**D**); outer pp (Fig. 25**A**-**B**) and rects (Figs. 26**A** & 67**A**) as in Juv-HY/SY ♀. **Note: See Juv-HY/SY ♀.**

SY/TY ♂ (B2-A2; Oct-Sep): Head and body dull bluish, blackish, and whitish, often with dusky mottling (especially in nape and face) in Oct-Jun, or with heavy dusky mottling (but breast and back partially white) in Jul-Sep; bill variably orange (Oct-Mar) to orange-yellow (Apr-Sep), with moderate swelling at base (Fig. 83**C**-**D**); med and les covs dusky mixed variably with whitish feathers, especially among medial med covs (Fig. 82**B**-**C**); terts dusky to blackish, with moderately strong attenuation and curvature (*cf.* Fig. 79**D**-**E** for shape); longest scapulars with moderate to substantial modification to inner web (Fig. 86**D**-**E**). **Note: See ASY/ATY ♂.**

ASY/ATY ♂ (Def. cycle, DB-DA; Oct-Sep): Head and body bright bluish, blackish, and white (breast often with pinkish hue), heavily mottled dusky (but breast and back partially white) in Jul-Nov; bill bright orange to yellowish orange with extensive (Nov-Apr) to moderate (May-Oct) swelling at base (Fig. 83**E-D**); lower les and med covs white with little or no dusky mottling (Fig. 82**D**); terts blackish, with strong attenuation and curvature (*cf.* Fig. 79**E** for shape); longest scapulars with substantial modification to inner web (Fig. 84**E-F**). **Note: It is possible that ♂♂ with the above characters (with full bill knob and entirely white lower les and med covs) can be aged ATY/A4Y, and that ♂♂ with moderate dusky mottling to the white wing patch (Fig. 82D) and relatively undeveloped knobs in Nov-Apr (Fig. 83D) can be aged TY/4Y but more study is needed.**

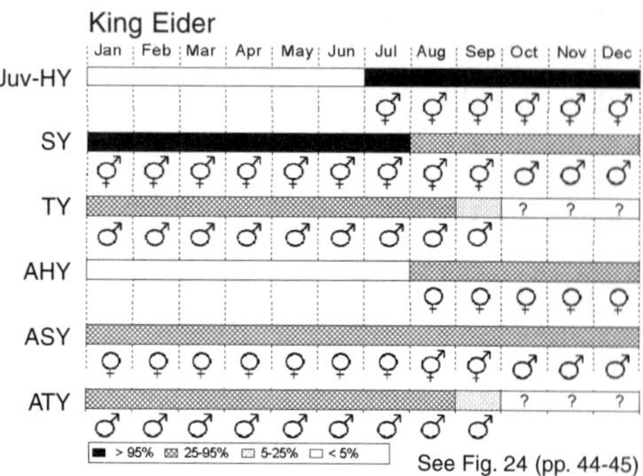

Hybrids reported—With Common Eider (Palmer 1973, 1976b, 1977; Pettingill 1959, 1962; Portenko 1952, Trefry et al. 2007).

References—Ainley et al. (1994), Baker (1993), Bent (1925), Carney (1992), Chandler (1987a), Cramp & Simmons (1977), Dawson (1994), Dement'ev & Gladkov (1952), Ellis (1994), Frimer (1994), Manning et al. (1956), K.C. Parkes & R.S. Palmer *in* Palmer (1976b), Phillips & Powell (2006), Portenko (1952, 1972), Stone (1900), Suddaby et al. (1998), Sutton (1932a), Suydam (2000).

COMMON EIDER

Somateria mollissima

COEI
Species # 1590
Band size: 7A

Species—Juvs and ♀♀ from other N.Am ducks and eiders by large size, especially exposed culmen (Table 8, p. 122); bill blackish or olive (to yellowish or orangish yellow in ♂♂), without over-hanging hook or swelling at base, and with malar feathering extended creating elongated bill process (Fig. 80**C**, p. 123); outer webs to medial ss without bluish but with white tips confined mostly to outer web in AHY ♀♀ (Fig. 81**D**, p. 124); anterior scapulars of AHY ♀ with distinct indentations (Fig. 84**C**); flanks with distinct black bars; axillars whitish to pale gray; underwing covs brownish gray.

Geographic variation—See Dement'ev & Gladkov (1952), Freeman (1970), Gibson & Kessel (1997), Godfrey (1986), Goudie et al. (2000), Hellmayr & Conover (1948a), Knapton (1997), Manning et al. (1956), Mendall (1980, 1986), Palmer (1976b), Portenko (1972), Rand (1948a), Snyder (1941), Todd (1963). Three other subspecies occur in s.Greenland-Europe.

Pacific *(S.m. v-nigrum)* Subspecies Group. Large, bill bright, throat with black lateral stripes in ASY ♂♂.

S.m. v-nigrum (br coastal w.AK-NWT, wint coastal AK-BC, vagrant to WA-IA, KS, Man, & Nfl): Large with long bill (Table 8, p. 122; eye to nares 53-61 mm *vs* 42-54 in the other subspecies); bill with malar feather extension broad and rounded and process abbreviated and acutely pointed (Fig. 85**A**), yellow

(HYs, Jun-Sep) to yellow-orange (AHYs, Oct-May) in ♂♂; ♀♀ dark brown fringed pale brown in Oct-Apr; AHY/ASY ♂ with distinct black lateral stripes (forming "V") to throat in Oct-Jun.

Atlantic *(S.m. mollissima)* Subspecies Group. Small to medium-large, bill dull to medium-bright and throat usually without black stripes in ♂♂.

S.m. sedentaria (br & wint coastal Nunavut-n.Ont-w.Lab; vagrant to NE & NY): Medium large with moderately short bill (Table 8); bill with malar feather extension short and pointed and bill process somewhat elongated, narrow, and rounded (Fig. 85**C**), medium-dull greenish yellow (HYs, Jun-Sep) to yellowish (AHYs, Oct-May) in ♂♂; ♀♀ pale brown fringed pale grayish in Oct-Apr; throat of AHY/ASY ♂ without black lateral stripes in Oct-Jun.

S.m. borealis (br coastal e.Nunavut-Que-nw.Lab, wint coastal Lab-CT, vagrant to Sask & n.AK): Small with moderately short bill (Table 8); bill with malar feather extension moderately pointed and bill processes moderately elongated, narrow, and rounded (Fig. 85**B**), medium-bright yellow (HYs, Jun-Sep) to orangish yellow (AHYs, Oct-May) in ♂♂; ♀♀ dark brown fringed buff in Oct-Apr; throat of AHY/ASY ♂ without or with indistinct black lateral stripes in Oct-Jun. Populations of s.Greenland (*islandica*), marginally distinct from *borealis*, average buffier coloration aspect in ♀♀ and duller coloration to the napes and bills of ♂♂. European subspecies may also average smaller "sails" (Fig. 86, p. 128) than N.Am subspecies by age and sex; study needed.

S.m. dresseri (br coastal n.Que-ne.Lab-ME, wint to coastal MD, vagrant to CO & FL): Medium-large with short bill (Table 8); bill with malar feather extension long, narrow, and pointed and bill processes elongated, broad, and rounded (Fig. 85**C**), medium-dull, greenish (HYs, Jun-Sep) to yellowish (AHYs, Oct-May) in ♂♂; ♀♀ dark brown fringed rusty in Oct-Apr; throat of AHY/ASY ♂ without black lateral stripes in Oct-Jun.

A **B** **C**

Both Species | King | Common

Juv ♀ | Form./Basic ♀♀

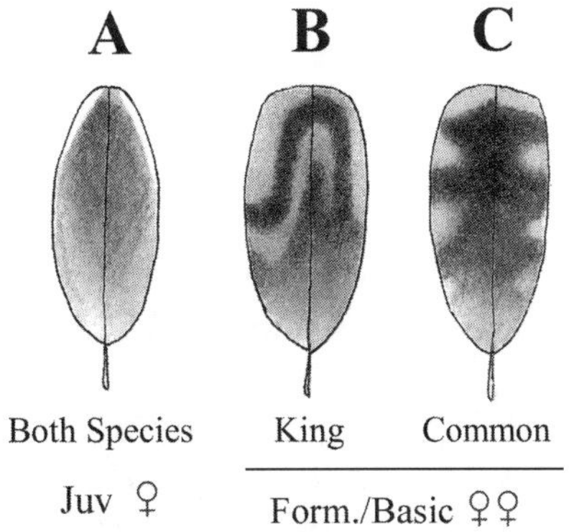

FIGURE 84. Upper scapular pattern by feather generation and species in ♀ King and Common eiders. Juv scapulars of both species, some of which are usually retained by SYs, are similar (**A**) but formative (SY) and basic (ASY) feathers show species-specific patterns.

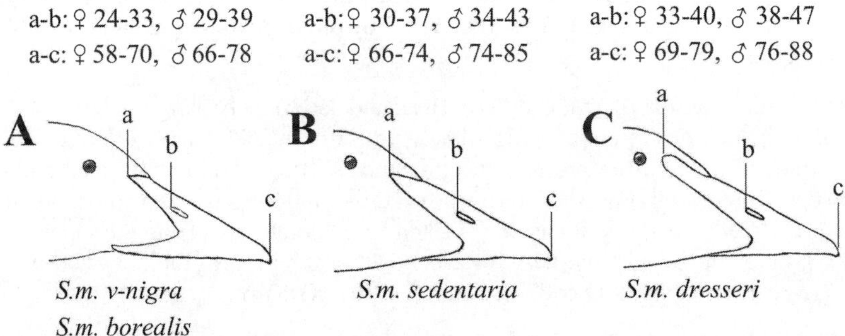

FIGURE 85. Differences in the feathering of the bill and the size and shape of the bill process by subspecies in Common Eider. Valuable measures include the proximal tip of the bill process (a) to the proximal end of the nare (b) and tip of the bill process (a) to the tip of the bill (c). These are based largely on published data of Mendall (1980, 1986) supplemented with specimen data. Note also the variation in the shape and extension of the malar feathering; illustration **A** shows wide malar feathering typical of *v-nigra*; the extension of *borealis* tends to be thinner, as in illustration **C**. Combine these criteria with those of size (Table 8, p. 122), plumage aspect, and bill color in ♂♂.

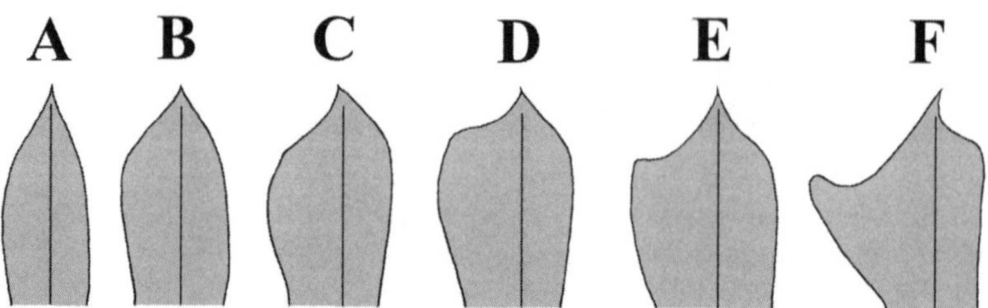

FIGURE 86. Shape of the modified scapulars, or "sails", in Spectacled, King, and Common eiders by species, age, and sex. These feathers are located near the terts and can sometimes be obscured by other feathers. Variation occurs both by species (Spectacled **A-D**, King **B-F**, Common **A-E**) and by age/sex group (HY/SY ♀ **A-C**, AHY/ASY ♀ **A-D**, HY/SY ♂ **B-D**, AHY/ASY ♂ **D-F**); see text.

Molt—CAS. PF partial (Oct-Mar in HY/SYs), PA1 absent-limited (May-Jul in SYs), PB2 complete (Jul-Oct in SYs), DPA limited-partial (Apr-May in ASY ♀♀, Jun-Jul in ASY ♂♂), DPB complete (Sep-Dec in ASYs). Molt strategies appear similar to those of King Eider (p. 123).

Age/Sex—Juv (B1; Jul-Nov) resembles HY/SY ♀♀ but plumage aspect tinged grayish and rects uniformly juv (Figs. 26**A**, p. 48, & 67**A**, p. 105). Juv ♂♂ often have small whitish spots to the breast feathers, absent in Juv ♀♀ (Fig. 75, p. 118); Juvs can also be sexed by combination of scapular, gr-cov, tert, and bill-color characters, as in HY/SYs. Partial medial BP (Fig. 20**A**, p. 31) and/or distended cloaca (Fig. 21, p. 32) developed by ASY ♀♀ in May-Jun. See Figures 22-23 (pp. 32-35) for cloacal characteristics useful in ageing and sexing (including Juvs) and Table 8 (p. 122) for measurements by age and sex.

Juv-HY/SY ♀ (1st cycle, Juv/B1-F1-A1; Oct-Sep): Head and body pale brown; bill dusky to grayish, sometimes tinged grayish or olive; s covs brown (Fig. 78**A**, p. 119), the proximal gr covs (and ss) rounded and usually tipped narrowly and indistinctly with whitish to outer web (Fig. 81**B**, p. 124); terts brown, with little or no attenuation (Fig. 79**A**, p. 121); longest scapulars with little to a slight amount of broadening to inner web (Fig. 86**A-B**); outer pp narrow (Fig. 25**A-B**, p. 47), averaging shorter by sex (Table 8), and without sheen; rects juv (Figs. 26**A** & 76**A**). **Note: Beware that some HY/SY ♂♂ may not acquire whitish feathers until Mar-Apr and may be difficult to distinguish from HY/SY ♀♀ by plumage aspect alone; check bill color on these.**

AHY/ASY ♀ (Def. cycle, DB-DA; Oct-Sep): Head and body dark brown, with little or no greenish, blackish, or whitish (see p. 78 regarding senescent ♀♀); bill grayish, often tinged olive; s covs brown (Fig. 78**A**), the proximal gr covs (and ss) squared and with broad and distinct white tips to outer web (Fig. 81**D**); terts washed dusky and fringed pale, with moderate attenuation (Fig. 79**C**); longest scapulars with slight to moderate broadening to inner web (Fig. 86**B-C**); outer pp broad (Fig. 25**A-B**), averaging longer by sex (Table 8), and with slight sheen; rects basic (Figs. 26**D** & 67**B**). **Note: See Juv-HY/SY ♀.**

Juv-HY/SY ♂ (1st cycle, Juv/B1-F1-A1; Oct-Sep): Head and body primarily dark brown in Oct-Nov, usually with small amounts of greenish, blackish, and whitish in Dec-Sep; bill grayish, becoming tinged greenish or yellowish by Oct-Dec; s covs brown (Fig. 78**A**), the proximal gr covs (and ss) rounded, with no or indistinct pale to whitish fringe (Fig. 81**C**); terts brown to dusky, with slight attenuation (Fig. 79**A-B**), and sometimes with whitish tips; longest scapulars with slight to moderate broadening to inner web (Fig. 86**B-C**); outer pp (Fig. 25**A-B**) and rects (Figs. 26**A** & 76**A**) as in Juv-HY/SY ♀. **Note: See Juv-HY/SY ♀.**

SY/TY ♂ (B2-A2; Oct-Sep): Head and body primarily greenish, blackish and whitish with indistinct or no whitish medial crown stripe in Oct-Jun, heavily mottled blackish to dark brown (but breast and back partially white) in Jul-Sep; bill olive to bright orangish yellow (see **Geographic variation**); s covs whitish with variable dusky mottling, especially among distal les covs (Fig. 78**B-C**); terts white, attenuated, and curved, and with distinct dark tip (Fig. 79**E**); longest scapulars with moderate modification to inner web (Fig. 86**C-D**). **Note: See ASY/ATY ♂.**

ASY/ATY ♂ (Def. cycle, DB-DA; Oct-Sep): Head and body bright greenish, blackish, and whitish with distinct and white medial crown stripe in Oct-Jun, heavily mottled blackish to dark brown (but breast and back partially white) in Jul-Nov; s covs uniformly white (Fig. 78**D**); terts white, attenuated, and and curved (Fig. 79**F**); scapulars pointed, with moderate to substantial modification to inner web (Fig. 86**D-E**). **Note: It is possible that ♂♂ with light dusky mottling to the marginal les covs (e.g., Fig. 78C) and/or small dusky tips to the terts can be aged TY/4Y, and that ♂♂ with the above characters (including entirely white les and med covs) can be aged ATY/A4Y but more study is needed.**

Common Eider

	Jan	Feb	Mar	Apr	May	Jun	Jul	Aug	Sep	Oct	Nov	Dec
Juv-HY							⚥	⚥	⚥	⚥	⚥	⚥
SY	⚥	⚥	⚥	⚥	⚥	⚥	⚥	⚥	⚥	♂	♂	♂
TY	♂	♂	♂	♂	♂	♂	♂	♂	♂	?	?	?
AHY								♀	♀	♀	♀	♀
ASY	♀	♀	♀	♀	♀	♀	♀	⚥	⚥	♂	♂	♂
ATY	♂	♂	♂	♂	♂	♂	♂	♂	♂	?	?	?

■ > 95% ▩ 25-95% ▒ 5-25% □ < 5% See Fig. 24 (pp. 44-45)

Hybrids reported—With Mallard (p. 89), Northern Pintail (p. 100), Steller's Eider (p. 117), King Eider (p. 123), Shelduck *Tadorna tadorna* (McCarthy 2006, Wakernagel 1972), and probably Common (but possibly Red-breasted) merganser (Tenovuo & Tenovuo 1983) in the wild. Has nested with Velvet Scoter (*Melanitta fusca*) but hybrids not observed (McCarthy 2006).

References—Ainley et al. (1994), Baker (1993), Bent (1925), Boyd et al. (1975), Carney (1992), Cramp & Simmons (1977), Dement'ev & Gladkov (1952), Goudie et al. (2000), Macpherson & McLaren (1959), Manning et al. (1956), Oliver (1989), K.C. Parkes & R.S. Palmer *in* Palmer (1976b), Portenko (1952, 1972), Stone (1900), Swennen et al. (1989).

HARLEQUIN DUCK

Histrionicus histrionicus

HADU
Species # 1550
Band size: 5

Species—Juvs and ♀♀ from other N.Am ducks by medium-small size with proportionally long tail and short bill (Table 10, p. 146); plumage aspect primarily dark brown with distinct white patches on forehead, lores, and auriculars; axillars and underwing covs blackish brown; bill slate to pale grayish blue with brownish to yellowish nail; eye dark.

Geographic variation—Monotypic (P. Johnsgard *in* Mayr & Cottrell 1979). Populations of w.N.Am ("*H.h. pacificus*") may average slightly smaller, larger billed, and with more chestnut in head and reduced and paler chestnut on sides of ♂♂, but differences are insufficient and confounded by individual variation. See Brooks (1915), Dement'ev & Gladkov (1952), Dickinson (1953), Hellmayr & Conover (1948a), Palmer (1976b), and Robertson & Goudie (1999).

Molt—CAS. PF limited-partial (Sep-Mar in HY/SYs), PA1 absent-partial (Jun-Aug in SYs), PB2 complete (Jul-Sep in SYs), DPA limited-partial (May-Jul in ASYs), DPB complete (Aug-Oct in ASYs). The PF and PBs occur primarily on non-breeding grounds and the PAs occur on breeding grounds. The PF includes a few to most body feathers, 1-3 terts, and sometimes the 2 central to some or (rarely) all rects, but few if any s covs. Wing feathers are replaced synchronously during PBs. The PA1 includes some body feathers in most SYs but few if any s covs, terts, or rects. The DPA includes some to most of the body feathers, sometimes 1-4 terts, and occasionally a few proximal s covs, but few if any rects. ♂♂ replace more feathers during the PF whereas ♀♀ replace more during the DPA. See Family (p. 47), Subfamily (p. 78), and Tribal (p. 117) accounts for more details.

Age/Sex—Juv (B1; Jul-Dec) resembles HY/SY ♀♀ but breast feathers with whitish fringing, rects uniformly juv (Figs. 26**A**, p. 48, & 67**A**, p. 105), and legs tinged olive or yellowish; Most Juv ♂♂ show a dull pale medial stripe to the longest tert (*cf.* Fig. 87**C**), absent in ♀♀ (Fig. 87**A**). Partial medial BP (Fig. 20**A**, p. 31) and/or distended cloaca (Fig. 21, p. 32) developed by ASY ♀♀ in May-Jul. See Figures 22-23 (pp. 32-35) and Mather & Esler (1999) for cloacal characteristics useful in ageing and sexing (including Juvs), Table 10 (p. 146) for measurements by age and sex, and Carney (1992) for useful photographs of wings. In addition to the following, Mather & Esler (1999) indicate length of the bursa (Fig. 23) in Aug-Sep can be used to age HY/SY (bursal length > 10 mm), SY/TY (bursal length 4-10 mm), and ASY/ATY (bursal length < 3 mm) in both sexes, although overlap precluded accuracy at 95%.

Juv-HY/SY ♀ (1st cycle, Juv/B1-F1-A1; Nov-Oct): Upperparts and breast primarily brown, contrasting distinctly with pale brown to whitish abdomen; s covs rounded (Fig. 45**A**, p. 79), relatively worn, brown without sheen; longest tert juv and brown, without a pale stripe (Fig. 87**A**), occasionally replaced, longer, and with or without an indistinct stripe (Fig. 87**B**); s2-s9 without dark glossy purplish; outer pp narrow (Fig. 25**A-B**, p. 47), averaging shorter by sex (Table 10), and without sheen; rects juv, formative, and/or alternate (see Figs. 26**A-D** & 67**A-B**). **Note: Beware that some HY/SY ♂♂ may not acquire colorful plumage aspect until Mar-Apr and can be difficult or impossible to distinguish from HY/SY ♀♀; check measurements on these and note that ♂♂ more often replace the terts with white-striped feathers (Fig. 87D).**

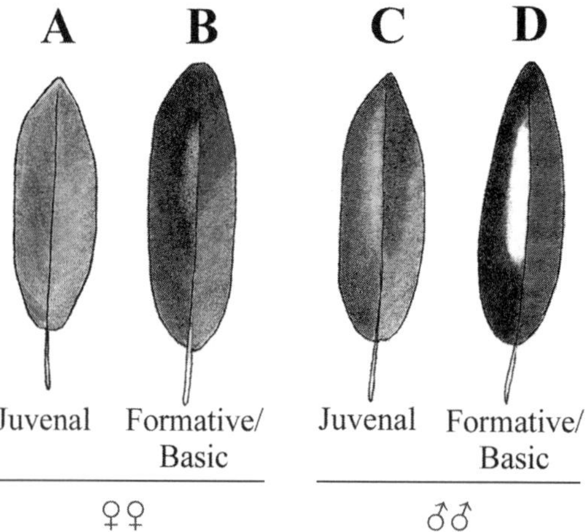

FIGURE 87. Shape, size, and pattern of the longest tertial by feather generation and sex in Harlequin Duck. Note that about 50% of HY ♂♂ replace juv terts (**B**) with formative terts in Oct-Mar; these are longer than the juv terts and can vary from dark brown with a hint of a pale stripe (as in **B**) to blackish with a distinct stripe (**D**). Fewer HY/SY ♀♀ replace terts; the formative feathers also may resemble those of AHY/ASY ♀ (**B**). Juv terts are otherwise retained by SYs through the PB2 in Jul-Sep.

AHY/ASY ♀ (Def. cycle, DB-DA; Nov-Oct): Upperparts and breast brown, with little or no bluish or reddish (see p. 78 regarding senescent ♀♀), not contrasting distinctly with dark brownish abdomen; s covs uniformly squared (Fig. 45**F**), fresher, and dark brown with slight sheen; longest tert dusky and elongated, sometimes with indistinct pale stripe to outer web (Fig. 87**B**); s2-s9 without dark glossy purplish; outer pp broad (Fig. 25**C-D**), averaging longer by sex (Table 10), and with slight sheen; rects basic and/or alternate (see Figs. 26**D-F** & 67**B**). **Note: See Juv-HY/SY ♀.**

Juv-HY/SY ♂ (1st cycle, Juv/B1-F1-A1; Nov-Oct): Upperparts and breast brown, increasingly mixed with dull slate-blue and reddish feathering in Nov-Jun, (often mottled brown in Jul-Sep), contrasting distinctly with pale brown to whitish abdomen; s covs rounded (Fig. 45**A-C**), worn, and brown with little or no sheen, the med covs without distinct white spots; longest tert juv and brown, sometimes with an indistinct pale stripe (Fig. 87**A**, **C**) or replaced and usually with a moderately distinct to distinct white stripe (*cf.* Fig. 87**D**); s2-s9 without dark glossy purplish; outer pp (Fig. 25**A-B**) and rects (Figs. 26**A-D** & 67**A-B**) as in Juv-HY/SY ♀. **Note: See Juv-HY/SY ♀. About 50% of HY/SY ♂♂ appear to acquire white-striped terts during the PF.**

AHY/ASY ♂ (Def. cycle, DB-DA; Nov-Oct): Upperparts and breast bright slate-blue and reddish in Nov-Jun (mottled brownish and often with bluish tinge in Jul-Sep); abdomen dark brown to blackish; s covs broad and fresher (Fig. 45**F**), slate blue, 1-3 proximal med covs with distinct white spots; longest tert black with distinct white stripe (Fig. 87**D**); s2-s9 with dark glossy purplish; outer pp (Fig. 25**C-D**) and rects (Figs. 26**D-F** & 67**B**) as in AHY/ASY ♀.

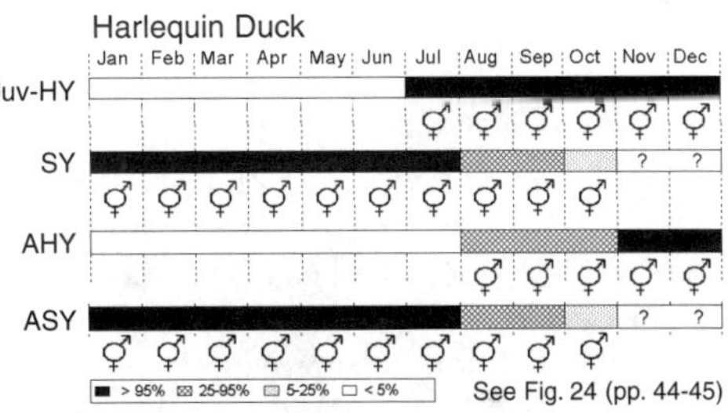

Hybrids reported—None.

References—Bent (1925), Cooke et al. (1997, 2000), Cramp & Simmons (1977), Dement'ev & Gladkov (1952), Palmer (1976b), Robertson & Goudie (1999), Robertson et al. (1997), Smith et al. (1998).

SURF SCOTER
Melanitta perspicillata

SUSC
Species # 1650
Band size: 7A

Species—Juvs and ♀♀ from other N.Am ducks and scoters by medium size (Table 9, p. 134); bill large with straight or convex culmen and swelling along sides at base, gray (♀) to dull orange and white (HY/SY ♂♂), the malar feathering truncated (Fig. 88**A-B**, p. 132); p10 > p8 by > 10 mm, and not emarginated (*cf.* Fig. 95, p. 140); head with cap dark brown, distinctly darker than lower auriculars and whitish or pale patches in lores, upper auriculars, and/or nape (Fig. 88**A-B**); iris brownish to white (Fig. 88); ss and gr covs without white.

Geographic variation—Monotypic.

Molt—SAS. PF limited-incomplete (Oct-May in HY/SYs), PA1 absent, PB2 complete (Jul-Oct in SYs), DPA absent-limited? (Jun-Aug in ASYs), DPB complete (Sep-Nov in ASYs). The single inserted 1st-cycle molt appears to be homologous with a PF rather than a PA1 (Fig. 10**C**, pp. 13-16). The PF occurs on non-breeding grounds, the DPA occurs on breeding grounds, and the

PBs occur primarily on molting grounds (p. 47) or the PB2 can occur on non-breeding grounds in over-summering SYs. The PF occasionally includes 1-3 terts and/or some proximal s covs, and often the 2 central to all 14 rects. Wing feathers are replaced synchronously during PBs. The DPA appears to be absent in many ASYs but includes a few feathers of the nape, upper back, breast, and flanks in others. There is little evidence for an extensive molt in ASY ♂♂ in Mar-May, as reported by Dwight (1914) and Palmer (1976b); see Pyle (2005a). See Family (p. 47), Subfamily (p. 78), and Tribal (p. 117) accounts for more details.

Age/Sex—Juv (B1; Jul-Nov) resembles HY/SY ♀♀, with rects uniformly juv (Figs. 26A, p. 48, & 67A, p. 105); Juv ♀=♂ by plumage aspect, although look for average differences in the terts (as described under HY/SY), and bill size, if fully grown, can be used to sex Juvs (Table 9). Partial medial BP (Fig. 20**A**, p. 31) and/or distended cloaca (Fig. 21, p. 32) developed by ASY ♀♀ in May-Jul. See Figures 22-23 (pp. 32-35) for cloacal characteristics useful in ageing and sexing (including Juvs), Table 9 (p. 134) for measurements by age and sex, and Carney (1992) for useful photographs of wings.

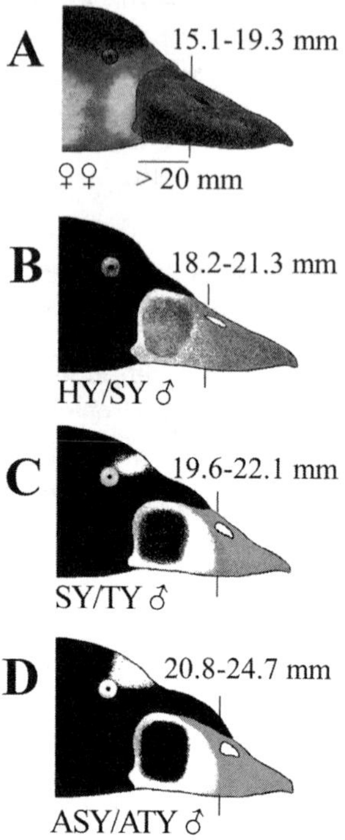

FIGURE 88. Bill color and shape, and iris color by age and sex, in Surf Scoter. Measures indicate bill depth at the proximal end of the nares (Fig. 8**C**, p. 10), and, in ♀♀, the distance between the malar feathers and nares *vs* other scoters (see Figs. 91, p. 136, & 94, p. 139).

Juv-HY/SY ♀ (1st cycle, Juv/B1-F1; Oct-Sep): Culmen from proximal end of nare < 32 mm (Table 9); bill dusky-olive to olive and without swelling, and iris brownish (Fig. 88**A**); upperparts and breast brown, increasingly mixed with dark brown feathering in Nov-Sep, contrasting distinctly with pale brownish abdomen, the latter wearing to whitish by May-Sep; forecrown and nape without whitish (Fig. 90**A**); most to all s covs rounded and worn (Fig. 45**A-C**, p. 79; *cf.* Fig. 92**A**, p. 137), pale brown; terts short and without dusky tinge to the outer webs (Fig. 89**A**; occasionally replaced and resembling Fig. 89**B**); outer pp narrow (Fig. 25**A-B**, p. 47), averaging shorter by sex (Table 9), and without sheen; rects juv and/or formative (Figs. 26**A-D** & 67**A-B**). **Note: Beware that dark brown feathering emerging on face of HY ♀♀ in Nov-Dec can resemble the black feathering of HY ♂♂. Also beware that some HY/SY ♂♂ may not acquire blackish or white plumage aspect until Jan-Apr or later and may not be distinguishable from HY/SY ♀♀ by plumage aspect alone; confirm sex with measurements and color pattern of bill.**

AHY/ASY ♀ (Def. cycle, DB-DA; Oct-Sep): Culmen from proximal end of nare < 32 mm (Table 9); bill olive to blackish and without swelling (Fig. 88**A**); iris grayish white (*cf.* Fig. 88**B**); upperparts and breast dark brown, with little or no blackish or bright white (see p. 78 regarding senescent ♀♀), not contrasting distinctly with brown abdomen, the latter wearing to slightly paler brown by May-Sep; forecrown and nape dark (Fig. 90**A**), sometimes with whitish tinge to nape (*cf.* Fig. 90**B**); s covs squared and fresher (Fig. 45**F**; *cf.* Fig. 92**B**), dark brown with slight sheen; terts elongated and dark brown (Fig. 89**B**); outer pp broad (Fig. 25**C-D**), averaging longer by sex (Table 9), and with slight sheen; rects uniformly basic (Figs. 26**D** & 67**B**). **Note: See Juv-HY/SY ♀.**

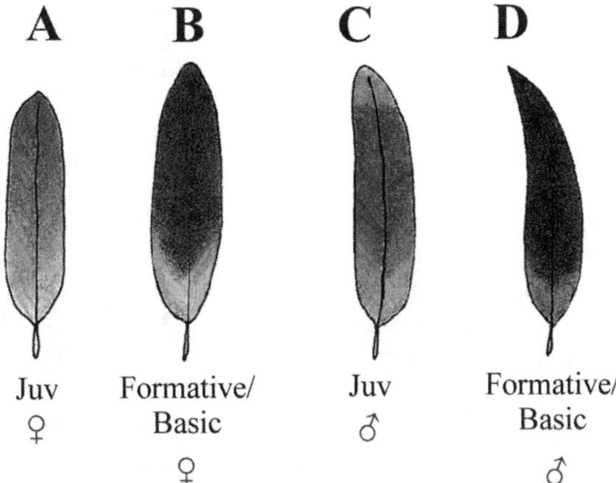

FIGURE 89. Length, curvature, and pattern to the tertials by feather generation and sex in Surf, White-winged, and Black scoters. Note that a small proportion of HY/SYs replace terts in Oct-Mar, which resemble basic terts in each sex (**B**, **D**). Otherwise, juv terts are usually retained by SYs until the PB2 in Jul-Oct. Some HY/SY ♂♂ exhibit juv terts more like those of HY/SY ♀♀ (**A**), especially when worn.

Juv-HY/SY ♂ (1st cycle, Juv/B1-F1; Oct-Sep): Culmen from proximal end of nare > 32 mm (Table 9); bill moderately swollen at base and dusky to dull orange, and iris grayish brown becoming whitish by Jan-Jun (Fig. 88**A-B**); upperparts and breast brown, increasingly mixed with blackish feathering in Nov-Sep, contrasting distinctly with paler abdomen, the latter bleaching to whitish by May-Sep; forecrown and nape brown (Fig. 90**A**), the nape becoming tinged whitish by Mar-Sep (*cf.* Fig. 90**B**); most to all s covs rounded and worn (Fig. 45**A-C**), pale brown; terts slightly curved and often with a dusky tinge to the outer webs (Fig. 89**C**); outer pp (Fig. 25**A-B**) and rects (Figs. 26**A-D** & 67**A-B**) as in Juv-HY/SY ♀. **Note: See Juv-HY/SY ♀.**

SY/TY ♂ (B2-A2; Oct-Sep): Upperparts and breast black, contrasting moderately with dark brown abdomen, the latter wearing to paler brown by May-Sep (sometimes with retained and bleached juvenal feathers); bill moderately swollen and dull to brightish orange, and iris

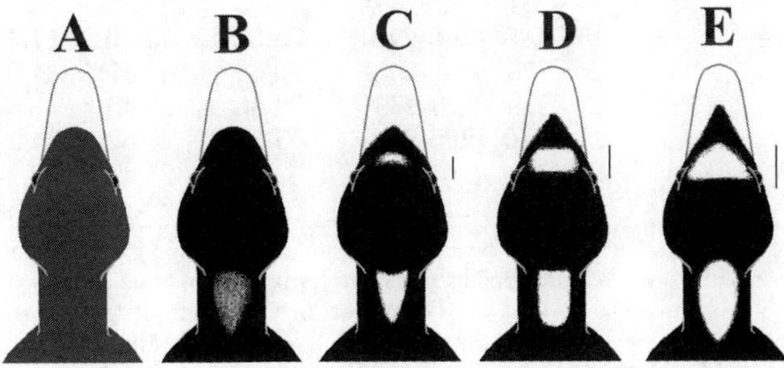

FIGURE 90. Variation in the extent of white on the forehead and nape in Surf Scoter by age and sex. Juvs and most ♀♀ show no white to the nape (**A**) although many AHY/ASY ♀♀ can obtain a white-tinged nape (**B**). The length of the forehead patch (along mid-line of forehead, as shown with lines) is the best means for ageing AHY/ASY ♂♂: SY/TYs have this patch averaging smaller (**C-D**; length 5-22 mm) than in ASY/ATYs (**D-E**; length 17-33 mm). ♂♂ vary from little to no white on the nape as Juvs and in alternate plumage aspect (**A-B**) to a large white patch in basic-aspect ATYs (**E**).

white (Fig. **C**); forecrown and nape with small to moderate white patches (Fig. 90**C-D**; nape patch sometimes obscured in Jun-Sep); s covs broad and black; terts black and curved (Fig. 89**D**). **Note: Some individuals may show intermediate features (*cf*. Fig. 90D) and should be aged AHY/ASY.**

ASY/ATY ♂ (Def. cycle, DB-DA; Oct-Sep): Upperparts and breast glossy black, not contrasting markedly with blackish to black abdomen, the latter wearing (slightly) to brownish black by May-Sep; bill swollen at base and bright orange, red, and white (duller in May-Aug), and iris bright white (Fig. 88**D**); forecrown and nape with extensive white patches (Fig. 90**D-E**; nape patch sometimes obscured in Jun-Sep). **Note: See SY/TY ♂.**

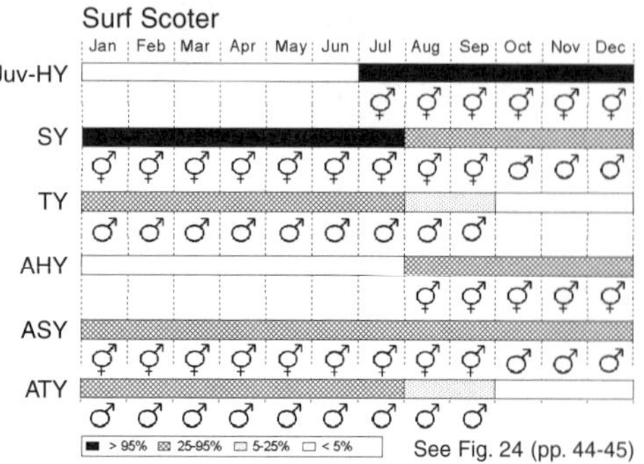

Hybrids reported—None. A report of a hybrid with White-winged Scoter was likely based on an aberrant Surf Scoter (Palmer 1976b).

References—Ainley et al. (1994), Baker (1993), Bent (1925), Brown (1992), Carney (1964, 1992), Cramp & Simmons (1977), Dwight (1914), Iverson et al. (2003), Kaufman (1990a), Miller (1926), Oberholser (1974), Palmer (1976b), Pyle (2005a), Roberts (1955), Savard et al. (1998).

TABLE 9. Measurements (mm) of North American scoters to assist in identification, ageing, and sexing. See pp. 4-11 for methods of measurement. Species summaries are in **bold**. Values were derived from 95% confidence intervals as based (for wing, exposed culmen, and tarsus) approximately on the indicated sample sizes (see pp. 4-5); sample sizes for tail length and bill depth were often smaller but included at least 10 of each sex. Thus, midpoints of ranges approximate means, and S.D. is approximated by 25% of the range.

Taxon/Sex	*n*	wing chord AHY/ASY	(HY/SY)[1]	tail length[1]	exp culmen[2]	bill depth[2]	tarsus
Surf Scoter		**218-251**	**(210-244)**	**63-90**	**37-37**	**15.1-24.7**	**38-47**
♀	100	218-235	(210-227)	66-82	27-32	15.1-19.3	38-45
♂	100	233-251	(225-244)	73-90	32-37	18.2-24.7	41-47
White-winged Scoter[3]		**255-289**	**(246-279)**	**70-88**	**32-40**	**17.3-20.6**	**45-55**
♀	100	255-273	(246-263)	70-84	32-37	17.3-20.6	45-52
♂	100	270-289	(261-279)	74-88	35-40	19.5-24.5	48-55
Black Scoter[4]		**213-240**	**(205-232)**	**65-99**	**25-32**	**14.2-17.3**	**40-50**
♀	50	213-231	(205-222)	65-82	25-29	14.2-15.7	40-47
♂	60	223-240	(214-232)	83-99	29-32	15.8-17.3	43-50

[1] Wing chord and tail length differ substantially by age; wing data are separated by age since juv primaries are retained through the second PB whereas tail lengths pertain to formative and basic feathers only, as the juvenal central rects are usually replaced by Jan-May in SYs. Other measures pertain to all age groups.

[2] Culmen length and bill depth measured from/at the proximal end of the nares (Figs. 7**C**, p. 9, & 8**C**, p. 10; variation in extent of forehead feathering leads to greater variation in bill measures if taken from that point) and includes external protuberances in ♂ Surf and White-winged but not Black scoters. See Figs. 88, p. 132, 91, p. 136, & 94, p. 139 for variation in bill depth by age in ♂.

[3] Includes both subspecies occurring in N.Am, which are similar in size.

[4] Includes N.Am subspecies only (see **Geographic variation**).

WHITE-WINGED SCOTER
Melanitta deglandi

WWSC
Species # 1650
Band size: 7A

Species—Juvs and ♀♀ from other N.Am ducks and scoters by large size with short exposed culmen (Table 9); bill with swelling along ridge at nares, black (♀) or dull orange without white (HY/SY ♂♂), the malar feathers extended (Fig. 91**A**-**B**, p. 136); p10 > p8 by > 10 mm, and without distinct emargination (*cf.* Fig. 95, p. 140); head with cap dark brown, similar in aspect to lower auriculars and with pale patches in lores and upper auriculars (Fig. 91**A**-**B**); iris brownish to white (Fig. 91); s1-s11 and gr covs with white (Figs. 92-93, p. 137).

Velvet Scoter (*M. fusca*, a vagrant to Greenland (and potentially to ne.N.Am), averages shorter wing chord (♀ 236-269, ♂ 248-286); malar feather extension abbreviated (tip of feathers to proximal end of nares > 5 mm *vs* 1-4 mm in White-winged Scoter; *cf.* Fig. 91**A**); ASY ♂♂ with nares smaller and with reduced protuberance (*cf.* Fig. 91**D**), upper mandible yellow (with little or no orange), and flanks blackish tinged brown, contrasting only slightly with blacker back and breast.

Geographic variation—See Brooks (1915), Cramp & Simmons (1977), Dement'ev & Gladkov (1952), Dwight (1914), Garðarsson (1997), Garner (1999a), Garner et al. (2004), Hellmayr & Conover (1948a), Palmer (1976b), Proctor (1997), Rand (1946). No other subspecies occur.

M.d. stejnegeri (br & wint ne.Asia, vagrant to w.AK Is): Bill slightly tapered at tip (Fig. 91**E**, p. 136); AHY/ASY ♂ with black on ridge of culmen narrow and elongated and nares smaller and within squared protuberance (Fig. 91**E**), sides of upper mandible yellowish (contrasting with more orange top), and flanks dusky to black when fresh, contrasting slightly, if at all, with breast and back.

M.d. deglandi (br & wint N.Am): Bill rounded at tip (Fig. 91**D**); AHY/ASY ♂ with black on ridge of culmen wider and more abbreviated and nares larger and within rounded protuberance (Fig. 91**D**; occasional older ♂♂ can show squared protuberance as in Fig. 91**E**), upper mandible uniformly orangish, and flanks olive-brown, contrasting distinctly with blacker breast and back. Populations of AK ("*dixoni*") may average slightly shorter and broader bills than in e.N.Am populations but this difference, if present, is confounded by individual variation.

Molt—SAS. PF limited-incomplete (Oct-May in HY/SYs), PA1 absent, PB2 complete (Jul-Oct in SYs), DPA absent-limited (Jun-Aug in AHYs), DPB complete (Sep-Nov in ASYs). Molt strategies appear similar to those of Surf Scoter (p. 131).

Age/Sex—Juv (B1; Jul-Dec) resembles HY/SY ♀♀, with rects uniformly juv (Figs. 26A, p. 48, & 67A, p. 105), bill dusky and not swollen at nares (Fig. 91**A**, p. 136), and iris dark grayish brown. Juv ♀=♂ by plumage aspect, although bill size, if fully grown, can be used to sex many Juvs (Table 9) and look for average differences in the gr covs, terts, and s1 (as described under HY/SY). Partial medial BP (Fig. 20**A**, p. 31) and/or distended cloaca (Fig. 21, p. 32) developed by ASY ♀♀ in May-Jul. See Figures 22-23 (pp. 32-35) for cloacal characteristics useful in ageing and sexing (including Juvs), Table 9 for measurements by age and sex, and Carney (1992) for useful photographs of wings.

Juv-HY/SY ♀ (1st cycle, Juv/B1-F1; Oct-Sep): Bill blackish (without orange), with little or no protuberance around nares (Fig. 91**A**); iris brownish, sometimes becoming grayish brown by Jan-Jun (Fig. 91**A**); upperparts and breast brown, increasingly mixed with dark brown to blackish feathering in Dec-Sep, contrasting distinctly with pale brownish abdomen, the latter wearing to whitish by May-Sep; s1 narrow and with indistinct or no white fringe to inner web (Fig. 92**A**, p. 137); most to all s covs rounded and worn (Fig. 45**A**-**C**, p. 79), brown, the proximal gr covs narrow and with reduced and indistinct white tips (Fig. 93**A**, p. 137); terts short and without dusky tinge to the outer webs (Fig. 89**A**, p. 133; occasionally replaced and resembling Fig. 89**B**); outer pp narrow (Fig. 25**A-B**), averaging shorter by sex (Table 9), and paler brown without sheen; rects juv and/or formative (Figs. 26**A-D** & 67**A-B**). **Note: Beware that dark brown to blackish feathering emerging on face of HY ♀♀ in Nov-Dec can resemble the black feathering of HY ♂♂; back and underpart feathers that emerge later show a greater difference in aspect between the sexes. Also beware that some HY/SY ♂♂ may not acquire blackish feathers until Jan-Apr or later and can be difficult or impossible to distinguish from HY/SY ♀♀ by plumage aspect alone; confirm sex with bill measurements and color, or cloacal examination if possible.**

AHY/ASY ♀ (Def. cycle, DB-DA; Oct-Sep): Bill blackish (without orange but sometimes with pinkish tinge to sides of upper mandible), with little to no protuberance at nares (Fig. 91**A**); iris brownish to grayish white (Fig. 91**A-B**); upperparts and breast dark brown to blackish, with little or no bright white around eye (see p. 78 regarding senescent ♀♀), and not contrasting distinctly with dark brown abdomen, the latter wearing to slightly paler brown by May-Sep; s1 broad and with distinct white to inner web (Fig. 91**C**); s covs squared and fresher (Fig. 45**F**), the proximal gr covs blackish brown and with moderately extensive and distinct white tips (Fig. 93**B**); terts elongated and blackish brown (Fig. 89**B**); outer pp broad (Fig. 25**C-D**), averaging longer by sex (Table 9), and dark brown with slight sheen; rects uniformly basic (Figs. 26**D** & 67**B**). **Note: See Juv-HY/SY ♀.**

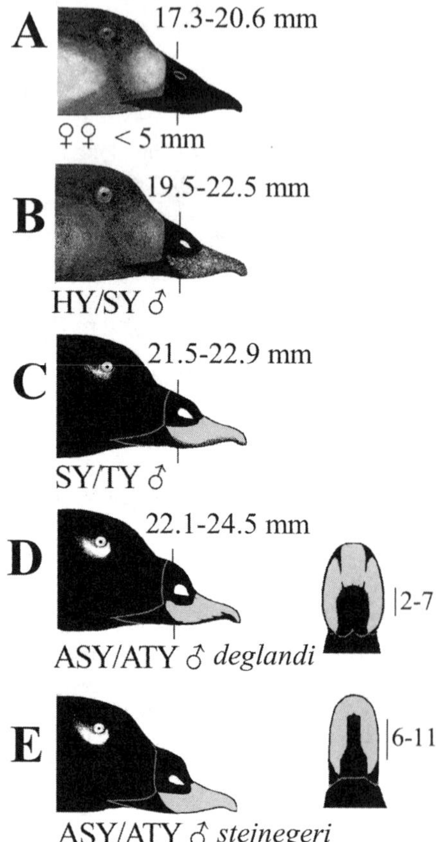

FIGURE 91. Bill color and shape and iris color by age, sex, and subspecies in White-winged Scoter. AHY/ASY ♀♀ can show paler iris, as in **B**. Measures shown are the depth at the proximal end of the nares (Fig. 8**C**, p. 10), and, in ♀♀, distance between malar feathers and nares *vs* other scoters (see Figs. 88, p 132, and 94, p. 139 and below). Note more rounded bill and shorter extension of black (2-7 mm > nares) in *deglandi* (**D** inset) than in *stejnegeri* (6-11 mm > nares; **E** inset). Nostril size also averages larger and more rounded in ASY ♂ *deglandi* (~3 X 6-7 mm; **D**) than in ASY ♂ *stejnegeri* (~2 X 5 mm; **E**). Velvet Scoter (*M. fusca*) of Europe shows the distance between the malar feather extent and the nares > 5 mm and, in ASY/ATY ♂♂, has less pronounced protuberance and smaller nostril (as in **B**) and a rounded bill tip (as in **D** inset).

Juv-HY/SY ♂ (1st cycle, Juv/B1-F1; Oct-Sep): Bill dusky, with sides of upper mandible becoming tinged orangish by Oct-Dec, and with protuberance beginning to develop (Fig. 91**A-B**); iris grayish brown, becoming whitish or yellowish by Jan-Jun (Fig. 91**B**); upperparts and breast brown, increasingly mixed with blackish feathering and small whitish patch below (rarely behind) eye, and contrasting distinctly with pale brownish abdomen, the latter wearing to whitish by May-Sep; s1 narrow and with indistinct white to inner web (Fig. 92**B**); most to all s covs rounded and worn (Fig. 45**A-C**), the proximal gr covs brown with moderately extensive but indistinct white tips (Fig. 93**C**); terts slightly curved and often with a dusky tinge to the outer webs (Fig. 89**C**); outer pp (Fig. 25**A-B**) and rects (Figs. 26**A-D** & 67**A-B**) as in Juv-HY/SY ♀; **Note: See Juv-HY/SY ♀.**

SY/TY ♂ (B2-A2; Oct-Sep): Upperparts and breast black, with reduced white behind eye (Fig. 91**C**), contrasting moderately with dark brown abdomen, the latter wearing to paler brown by May-Sep (sometimes with retained and bleached juvenal feathers); bill blackish and dull orange with moderate protuberance over nares (Fig. 91**C**); iris dull white to pale bluish (Fig. 91**C**); s1 broad and with distinct white to inner web (Fig. 92**C**); proximal gr covs blackish with extensive and distinct white tips (Fig. 93**D**); terts black and curved (Fig. 89**D**); outer pp (Fig. 25**C-D**) and rects (Figs. 26**D** & 67**B**) as in AHY/ASY ♀ but blacker. **Note: Some individuals may show intermediate features with ASY/ATY ♂ and should be aged AHY/ASY.**

ASY/ATY ♂ (Def. cycle, DB-DA; Oct-Sep): Upperparts and breast glossy black with extensive white behind eye (Fig. 91**D-E**), not contrasting distinctly with blackish abdomen, the latter wearing to brownish black by May-Sep; bill black and bright orangish to pale purplish with prominent protuberance over nares (Fig. 91**D-E**); iris bright white to pale bluish (Fig. 91**D-E**). **Note: See SY/TY ♂.**

Hybrids reported—Possibly with Common Goldeneye (McCarthy 2006, Palmer 1976b). See also Common Eider (p. 126) and Surf Scoter (p. 131).

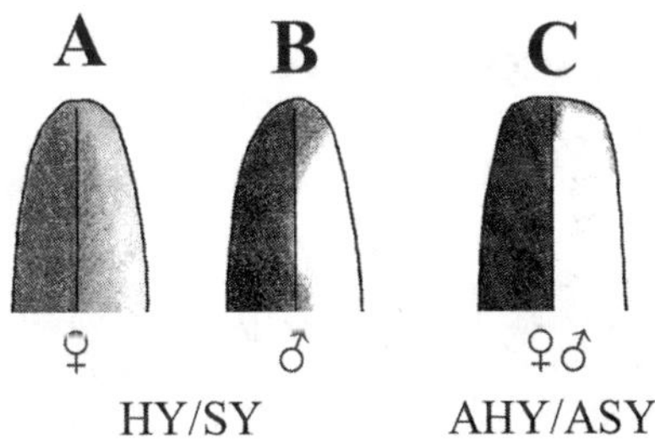

FIGURE 92. Shape and pattern of the medial greater coverts (corresponding to s5-s7) in White-winged Scoter by age and sex. Note that Surf Scoter shows a similar difference in shape and background color (paler in HY/SY ♀ than in the other age-sex groups) but lacks the whitish to white patterns. Juv covs (**A-B**) and ss (Fig. 93**A** & **C**) are retained by SYs through the PB2 in Jul-Oct.

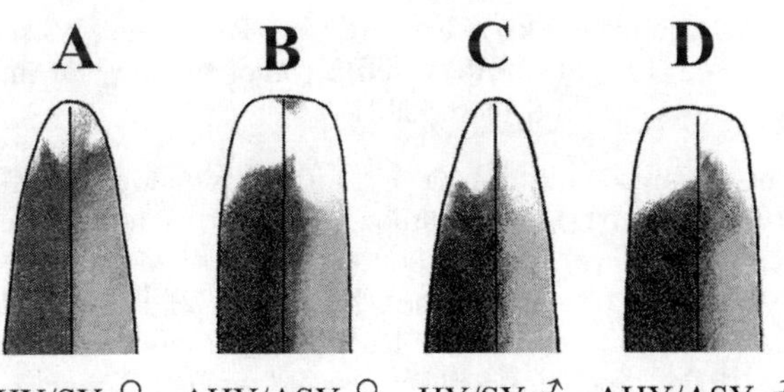

FIGURE 93. Shape and pattern of s1 by age and sex in White-winged Scoter. Note differences in brown coloration (paler in HY/SY ♀, darker in AHY/ASYs) as well as in the pattern of whitish to white. See Figure 92.

References—Ainley et al. (1994), Baker (1993), Bent (1925), Boyd et al. (1975), Brown (1992), Brown & Fredrickson (1997), Carney (1964, 1992), Cramp & Simmons (1977), Dement'ev & Gladkov (1952), Dwight (1914), Kaufman (1990a), Miller (1926), Oberholser (1974), Palmer (1976b), Pyle (2005a), Roberts (1955).

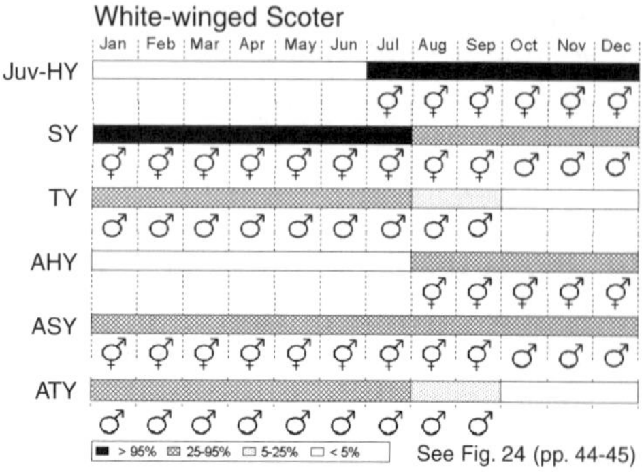

White-winged Scoter

	Jan	Feb	Mar	Apr	May	Jun	Jul	Aug	Sep	Oct	Nov	Dec
Juv-HY							⚥	⚥	⚥	⚥	⚥	⚥
SY	⚥	⚥	⚥	⚥	⚥	⚥	⚥	⚥	⚥	♂	♂	♂
TY	♂	♂	♂	♂	♂	♂	♂	♂	♂			
AHY								⚥	⚥	⚥	⚥	⚥
ASY	⚥	⚥	⚥	⚥	⚥	⚥	⚥	⚥	⚥	♂	♂	♂
ATY	♂	♂	♂	♂	♂	♂	♂	♂	♂			

■ > 95% ▨ 25-95% □ 5-25% □ < 5%

See Fig. 24 (pp. 44-45)

BLACK SCOTER

Melanitta nigra

BLSC
Species # 1630
Band size: 7A

Species—Juvs and ♀♀ from other N.Am ducks and scoters by medium-small size with long exposed culmen (Table 9, p. 134); bill small, narrowing at tip, blackish, and with swelling and dull yellow or orange at base in HY/SY ♂♂, the feathers of culmen and sides of bill not extended (Fig. 94**A**-**B**); p10 > p8 by < 10 mm (♀♀ and HY/SYs; < p8 in AHY/ASY ♂) and substantially emarginated by age/sex (Fig. 95, p. 140); cap dark brown to blackish, contrasting distinctly in aspect with pale brownish face, the latter with no or very indistinct pale patches (Fig. 94**A**-**B**); iris dark (Fig. 94); ss and gr covs without white.

Geographic variation—See Alderfer (1992), Astins (1992), Cramp & Simmons (1977), Dean (1989), Dement'ev & Gladkov (1952), Dwight (1914), Garner (1989), Oberholser (1974), Palmer (1976b), Waring (1993). One other subspecies occurs in n.Europe-nw.Asia.

M.n. americana (br & wint ne.Asia & N.Am): From European *nigra* (a potential vagrant to ne.N.Am) by bill shorter (exp culmen 39-46 *vs* 42-50 in *nigra*), broader (Fig. 94**D**-**E** insets), and with longer and more decurved bill nail (Fig. 94**D**-**E**); AHY/ASY ♂♂ with rounded protuberance at base of bill longer and more sloping, yellowish (*vs* blackish, divided by yellowish line in *nigra*; Fig. 94**D**-**E**). Bill length and shape (Fig. 94 **D**-**E**) are the only known criteria for separating ♀♀.

Molt—SAS. PF limited-incomplete (Oct-May in HY/SYs), PA1 absent, PB2 complete (Jul-Oct in SYs), DPA absent-limited (Jun-Aug in ASYs), DPB complete (Sep-Nov in ASYs). Molt strategies appear similar to those of Surf Scoter (p. 131).

Age/Sex—Juv (B1; Jul-Nov) resembles HY/SY ♀♀, with rects uniformly juv (Figs. 26A, p. 48, & 67A, p. 105). Juv ♀ = ♂ by plumage aspect, although the p10 and tert characters (as in HY/SYs), along with bill size (if fully grown) can be used to sex Juvs (Table 9, Figs. 94-96). Partial medial BP (Fig. 20**A**, p. 31) and/or distended cloaca (Fig. 21, p. 32) developed by ASY ♀♀ in May-Jul. See Figures 22-23 (pp. 32-35) for cloacal characteristics useful in ageing and sexing (including Juvs), Table 9 (p. 134) for measurements by age and sex, and Carney (1992) for useful photographs of wings.

Juv-HY/SY ♀ (1st cycle, Juv/B1-F1; Oct-Sep): Culmen from proximal end of nare < 29 mm (Table 9); bill blackish, without swelling at base (Fig. 94**A**); upperparts and breast brown, increasingly mixed with darker brown feathers in Nov-May, contrasting distinctly with pale brownish abdomen, the latter wearing to whitish by May-Sep; outer pp average shorter by sex (Table 9), brown without sheen, the tip of p10 tapered and not notched (Fig. 95**A**, p. 140); s covs rounded and worn (Fig. 45**A-C**, p. 79; *cf*. Fig. 92**A**, p. 137), pale brown without sheen, the distal gr covs without white tips; terts short and without dusky tinge to the outer webs (Fig. 89**A**, p. 133; occasionally replaced and resembling Fig. 89**B**); rects juv and/or formative (Figs. 26**A-D** & 67**A-B**). **Note: Beware that dark brown to blackish feathering emerging on HY/SY ♀♀ in Nov-Dec can resemble the black feathering of HY ♂♂; confirm sex with bill measurements and color, or cloacal examination if possible.**

AHY/ASY ♀ (Def. cycle, DB-DA; Oct-Sep): Culmen from proximal end of nare < 29 mm (Table 9); bill blackish (sometimes with a tinge of yellowish at base) and with little or no swelling (Fig. 94**A**); upperparts and breast dark brown with little or no blackish (see p. 78 regarding senescent ♀♀), not contrasting distinctly with dark brown abdomen, the latter wearing to slightly paler brown by May-Sep; outer pp averaging longer by sex (Table 9), dark brown with slight sheen, the tip of p10 truncate and with slight to moderate notch (Fig. 95**C**); s covs squared and fresher (Fig. 45**F**; *cf*. Fig. 92**B**), dark brown with slight sheen, the distal gr covs sometimes tipped white; terts elongated and blackish brown (Fig. 89**B**); rects uniformly basic (Figs. 26**D** & 67**B**). **Note: See Juv-HY/SY ♀.**

Juv-HY/SY ♂ (1st cycle, Juv/B1-F1; Oct-Sep): Culmen from proximal end of nare > 29 mm (Table 9); bill blackish becoming dull yellowish at base and with swelling developing by Dec-Feb (Fig. 94**A-B**); upperparts and breast brown, increasingly mixed with blackish feathering (to nearly completely blackish in some individuals) in Dec-Sep, contrasting distinctly with pale brownish abdomen, the latter wearing to whitish by May-Sep; outer pp averaging shorter by sex (Table 9), brown without sheen, the tip of p10 tapered and moderately notched (Fig. 95**B**); terts slightly curved and often with a dusky tinge to the outer webs (Fig. 89**C**); s covs 45**A-C**; *cf*. Fig. 92**B**) and rects (Figs. 26**A-D** & 67**A-B**) as in Juv-HY/SY ♀. **Note: See Juv-HY/SY ♀.**

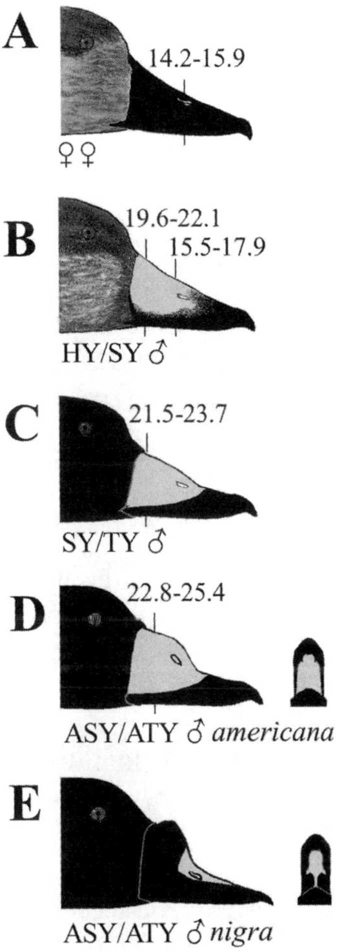

A 14.2-15.9 ♀♀

B 19.6-22.1 15.5-17.9 HY/SY ♂

C 21.5-23.7 SY/TY ♂

D 22.8-25.4 ASY/ATY ♂ *americana*

E ASY/ATY ♂ *nigra*

FIGURE 94. Bill color and shape by age, sex, and subspecies in Black Scoter. Measures indicate bill depth at the proximal end of the nares in ♀♀ and HY/SY ♂ (**A-B**) and maximum depth (approximately at distal end of forehead feathers) in ♂ *americana* by age (**B-D**). See Figure 8 (p. 10). Note narrower bill shape (from above) and shorter and straighter nail at tip in *niger* than in *americana* (**D-E** insets); bill features are the only known criteria for identifying ♀♀ to subspecies.

SY/TY ♂ (B2-A2; Oct-Sep): Upperparts and breast black, contrasting moderately with brownish-washed chin and throat and dark brown abdomen, the latter wearing to pale brown by May-Sep; bill with moderate dull-yellowish swelling at base (Fig. 94**C**); outer pp average longer by sex (Table 9), blackish, the tip of p10 moderately to extensively notched (Fig. 95**B**, **D**); s covs broad (Fig. 45**F**; *cf.* Fig. 92**D**), and black, the distal gr covs sometimes tipped whitish. **Note: Many individuals may show intermediate features and should be aged AHY/ASY.**

ASY/ATY ♂ (Def. cycle, DB-DA; Oct-Sep): Upperparts and breast glossy black, not contrasting with black chin, throat, and abdomen, the latter wearing to brownish black by May-Sep; bill with extensive, yellow-orange swelling at base (Fig. 94**D**); pp and s covs as in SY/TY ♂, the tip of p10 extensively notched (Fig. 94**D**). **Note: See SY/TY ♂.**

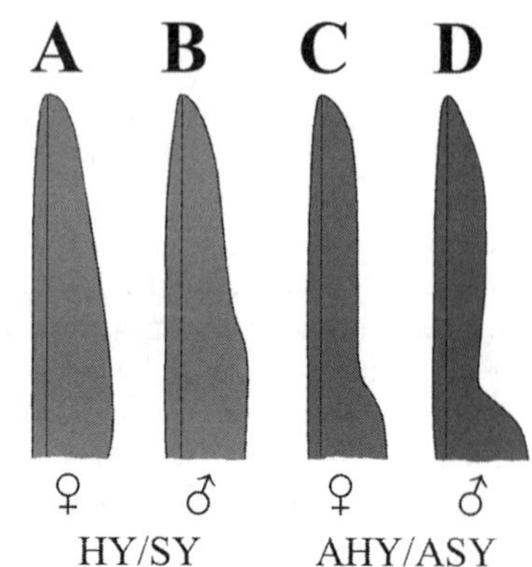

FIGURE 95. Degree of notching to p10 by age and sex in Black Scoter. There may be some overlap between groups; e.g., SY/TY ♂♂ may show a notch pattern between **B** and **D**. The juv p10 (**A-B**) is retained by SYs until wing molt during the PB2 in Jul-Sep.

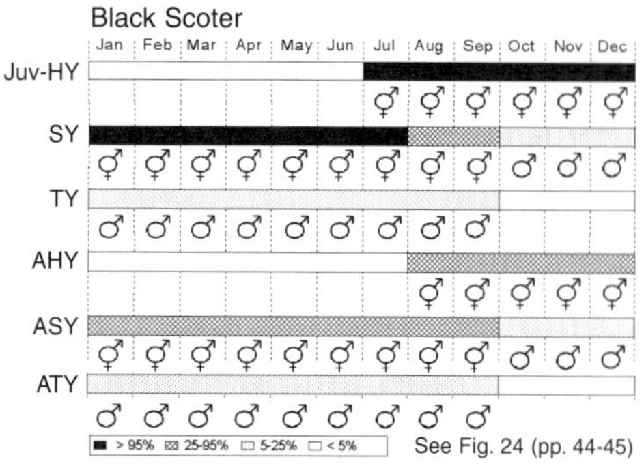

Hybrids reported—None in the wild.

References—Ainley et al. (1994), Alderfer (1992), Baker (1993), Bent (1925), Bordage & Savard (1995), Boyd et al. (1975), Carney (1964, 1992), Cramp & Simmons (1977), Dement'ev & Gladkov (1952), Dwight (1914), Fox et al. (2008), Hoffman & Bancroft (1984), Miller (1926), Oberholser (1974), Palmer (1976b), Pyle (2005a), Roberts (1955).

LONG-TAILED DUCK
Clangula hyemalis

LTDU
Species # 1540
Band size: 5-6

Species—From other N.Am ducks by medium-small size with proportionally short bill (Table 10, p. 146); body white, black, and brown; scapulars variably short to elongated and white to black with brown fringes (Fig. 96); upperwing and underwing covs uniformly dark brown to blackish; c.rects short to elongated (Fig. 97, p. 142); bill dusky to pale grayish or pinkish with a black nail; legs pale grayish with darker tips to webs and toes.

Geographic variation—Monotypic.

Molt—CAS. PF partial-incomplete (Nov-Mar in HY/SYs), PA1 absent-limited (Jun-Aug in non-breeding SYs), DPA limited-incomplete (Mar-Aug in AHYs), DPB complete (Aug-Dec in breeding AHYs). The PF occurs primarily on non-breeding grounds, the PA1 occurs primarily on breeding grounds, the DPA can commence on non-breeding grounds and complete on breeding grounds, and the DPB occurs primarily on molting grounds (p. 47) near breeding grounds. The PF includes some to most body feathers, few if any terts or s covs, and sometimes 2-6 medial rects. Wing feathers are replaced synchronously during PBs. The PA1 includes a few to some body feathers but no terts, s covs, or rects, and the DPA includes some to most body feathers, occasionally 1-4 terts and/or a few proximal s covs, and sometimes 1-4 c.rects. See Family (p. 47), Subfamily (p. 78), and Tribal (p. 117) accounts for more details. A reported DPS in this species (Salomonsen 1941, 1949) is likely based on individual variation in the appearance of alternate feathers with variation in the timing of the DPA (possibly as related to age). Alternate feathers developed in Apr-May appear to be longer and whiter than those developed in Jun-Jul (Fig. 96). See also Stresemann (1948), Pyle (2005a).

Age/Sex—Juv (Jul-Dec) has face, throat, and breast washed dusky, rects entirely juv (Fig. 97**A-B**, p. 142), and bill dusky; most Juv ♂♂ can be separated from most Juv ♀♀ by the length of the central rects relative to other rects (Fig. 97**A-B**). Partial medial BP (Fig. 20**A**, p. 31) and/or distended cloaca (Fig. 21, p. 32) developed by AHY ♀♀ in May-Jul. See also Figures 22-23 (pp. 32-35) and Peterson & Ellarson (1978) for cloacal characteristics useful in ageing and sexing (including Juvs), Table 10 (p. 146) for measurements by age and sex, and Carney (1992) for useful photographs of wings.

Juv-HY/SY ♀ (1st cycle, Juv/B1-F1-A1; Oct-Sep): Crown and breast dusky; back and scapulars brownish, without bright white (Fig. 96**A-C**; replaced formative scapulars can have whitish fringes); bill dusky, becoming primarily dull grayish by Dec-Mar; rects usually grayish brown, notched, and with r1 not elongated (Fig. 97**A**, occasionally as in **C**); s covs rounded and worn (Fig. 45**A**, p. 79), medium-pale brown without sheen; outer pp narrow (Fig. 25**A-B**, p. 47), averaging shorter by sex (Table 10), and paler brown without sheen. **Note: Beware some HY/SY ♂♂ may not acquire substantial white in the upperparts or dark brown in the breast until Jan-Mar; use the central rect length (Fig. 97A-B) and bill color to sex these. Also beware that all plumage aspects are extremely variable.**

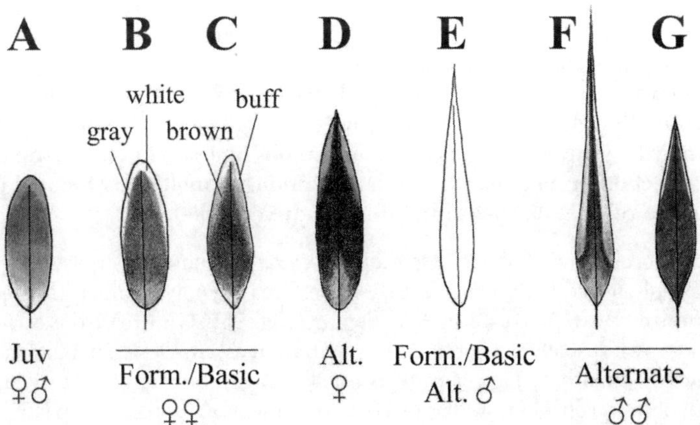

FIGURE 96. Shape, length, and pattern of the longest scapular by age, sex, and feather generation in Long-tailed Duck (see also Salomonsen 1941, 1949). Note that the color of the formative scapulars is a good way to distinguish HY/SY ♀♀ (**B**) from HY/SY ♂♂ (**E**) in Nov-Mar, once the upper scapulars (usually not including the longest feather) have been replaced during the PF. Salomonsen considered variation in the shape and coloration of scapulars in summer AHY ♂♂ (**E-G**) to indicate a DPS but it appears that this represents individual variation, with alternate scapulars replaced earlier in the molting season being white (**E**), those replaced mid-season being brown and whitish (**F**), and those replaced later in the season being dark brown and shorter in length (**G**).

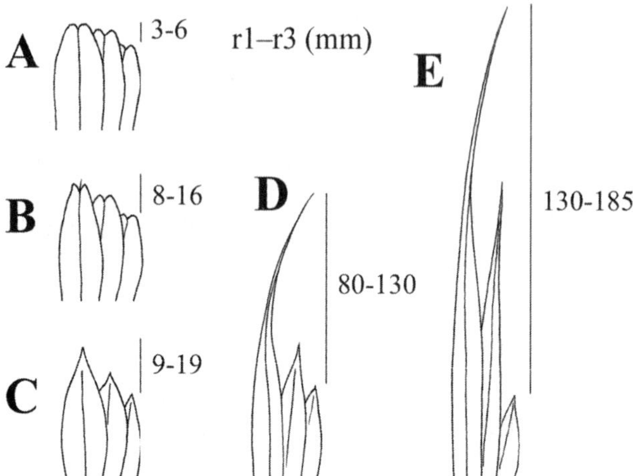

FIGURE 97. Shape and size of r1-r3 by age and sex in Long-tailed Duck: Juv ♀ (**A**), Juv ♂ (**B**), formative/basic ♀ (**C**), formative/2nd basic(?) ♂ (**D**), and definitive basic (AHY/ASY) ♂ (**E**). Measures indicate r1 – r3 as r3 is roughly the same length in all age/sex groups: note that, in Juvs and ♀♀, this distance can be used for sexing and ageing but that occasional HY/SYs will replace the central 1-3 rects during the PF in Oct-Mar, which will subsequently resemble **B** (♀♀) or **D** (♂♂). Some ASYs may replace these feathers during the DPA in Apr-Jun and show variably shorter feathers in Jun-Sep. Note also that ♂♂ showing full-grown rectrices as in **D** may be SY/TYs and that those with rectrices as in **E** may be ASY/ATYs but more study is needed.

AHY/ASY ♀ (Def. cycle, DB-DA; Oct-Sep): Crown white, contrasting with dusky breast in Oct-May, or mottled brownish in Jun-Sep; back and scapulars fringed brownish to grayish, without bright white (Fig. 96**B-C**; usually mottled dusky brownish in Jun-Sep); bill pale grayish to grayish blue (sometimes tinged pinkish across saddle); s covs squared and fresher (Fig. 45**F**), dark brown with slight sheen; outer pp broad (Fig. 25**C-D**), averaging longer by sex (Table 10), and with slight sheen. **Note: See Juv-HY/SY ♀. The color to the scapular fringes in Oct-Apr may be grayer in SY/TYs and more rufous in ASY/ATYs (Peterson & Ellarson 1978), but aspect differences may also relate to timing of molt (see Molt and p. 29), and thus may not be reliable on their own. More study is needed.**

Juv-HY/SY ♂ (1st cycle, Juv/B1-F1-A1; Oct-Sep): Crown dusky and upperparts brownish (Fig. 96**A**), increasingly mixed with white feathers (e.g., Fig. 96**E**) in Dec-Sep (head, neck, and scapulars often mottled chocolate in May-Sep; *cf.* Fig. 96**F-G**); breast dusky, increasingly mottled dark brown (usually not extending to central breast) in Dec-Sep; bill dusky, becoming primarily dull pinkish by Dec-Mar; rects usually grayish brown, with r1 slightly elongated (Fig. 97**B**; occasionally elongated as in **D**); s covs (Fig. 45**A**) and outer pp (Fig. 25**A-B**) as in Juv-HY/SY ♀. **Note: See Juv-HY/SY ♀.**

AHY/ASY ♂ (Def. cycle, DB-DA; Oct-Sep): Crown, upper back, and scapulars white in Oct-Apr (Fig. 96**E**) or mottled dark brown and with buff-edged scapulars in May-Sep (Fig. 96**F-G**); breast with chocolate brown patch (extending to center breast) in Oct-Apr; bill primarily bright pinkish (becoming blackish in some ASYs in Jun-Sep); rects blackish (r1-r3) and whitish (r5-r7), with r1 substantially elongated (Fig. 97**E**); s covs (Fig. 45**F**) and outer pp (Fig. 25**C-D**) as in AHY/ASY ♀. **Note: See Juv-HY/SY ♀. Length of the central**

rects (Fig. 97D-E), extent of pale clay aspect to face, retained coverts or abdomen feathers, or possibly other plumage-related criteria (perhaps depending on timing of PB2; p. 29) might be useful in determining some SY/TY and/or ASY/ATY ♂♂ (in combination with bursal length; Fig. 23, p. 34) but more study is needed.

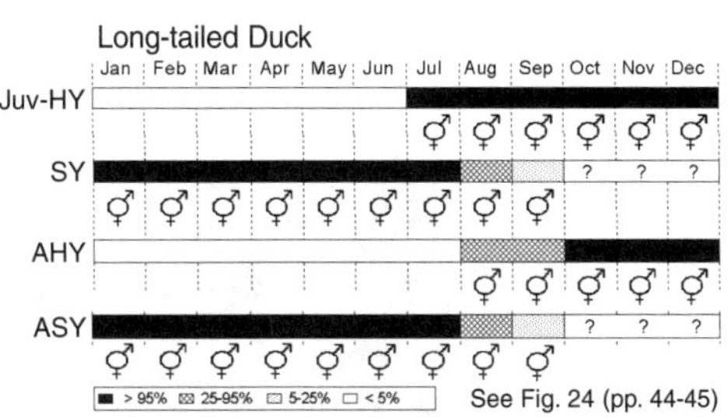

Hybrids reported—None in the wild.

References—Ainley et al. (1994), Alison (1975), Baker (1993), Bent (1925), Boyd et al. (1975), Carney (1964, 1992), Cramp & Simmons (1977), Delacour & Mayr (1946), Dement'ev & Gladkov (1952), M.D. Howell et al. (2003), Manning et al. (1956), Oberholser (1974), Palmer (1976b), Peterson & Ellarson (1978), Portenko (1972), Roberts (1955), Robertson & Savard (2002), Stone (1900), Sutton (1932a, 1932b).

BUFFLEHEAD
Bucephala albeola

BUFF
Species # 1530
Band size: 5

Species—Juvs and ♀♀ from other N.Am ducks by small size (Table 10, p. 146); bill small and narrowing toward tip, dusky to grayish; cheek with distinct, elongated white patch; les and med covs uniformly dusky to blackish; s6-s10 and corresponding gr covs with white in outer webs (Fig. 98, p. 144); axillars and underwing covs gray and whitish; legs dusky to pinkish with dusky webs.

Geographic variation—Monotypic (P. Johnsgard *in* Mayr & Cottrell 1979). Juvs and ♀♀ of BC-n.CA populations may average browner backs, but reported differences may be due to effects of bleaching. See Erskine (1972) and Palmer (1976b).

Molt—CAS. PF incomplete (Aug-Mar in HY/SYs), PA1 absent-limited (Jun-Aug in SYs), DPB complete (Aug-Oct in AHYs), DPA partial (Jun-Jul in ASYs). The PF commences on breeding grounds and completes on non-breeding grounds, the PAs occur primarily on breeding grounds, and the DPB occurs primarily on molting grounds (p. 47). The PF includes some to most body feathers, few if any terts or s covs, and usually all rects. Wing feathers are replaced synchronously during the DPB. The PA1 includes a few head and back feathers in a few SYs (perhaps ♂♂ only). The DPA includes some to most body feathers but few if any terts, s covs, or rects. The PF and DPA average more extensive in ♂♂ than in ♀♀. See Family (p. 47), Subfamily (p. 78), and Tribal (p. 117) accounts for more details.

Age/Sex—Juv (Jul-Oct) has face and throat washed pale brownish, merging into indistinct whitish cheek patch, scapulars narrow and brown (Fig. 99**A**, p. 145), and rects juv (Figs. 26A, p. 48, & 67A, p. 105). Juv ♂♂ can be separated from Juv ♀♀ by wing chord (Table 10, p. 146; if fully grown) and the patterns of the gr covs, s5, and rump as described under HY/SY (below). Partial medial BP (Fig. 20**A**, p. 31) and/or distended cloaca (Fig. 21, p. 32) developed by AHY ♀♀ in May-Jul. See Figures 22-23 (pp. 32-35) and Henny et al. (1981) for cloacal characteristics useful in ageing and sexing (including Juvs), Table 10 for measurements by age and sex, and Carney (1992) for useful photographs of wings. See also Henny et al. (1981) for foot web measures reliable for sexing, including Juvs.

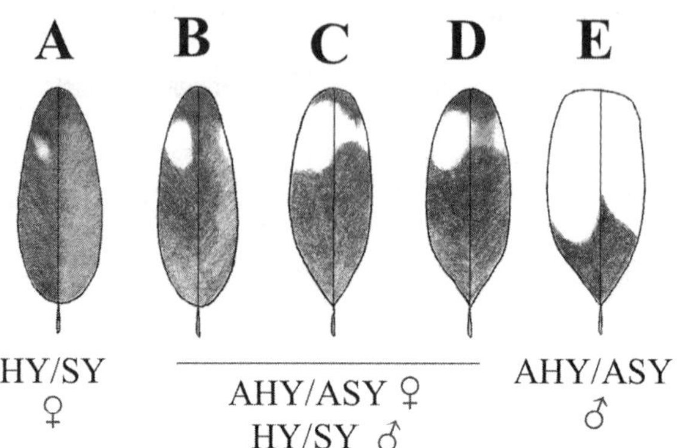

FIGURE 98. Pattern of white on the medial greater coverts by age and sex in Bufflehead. The illustrations represent the cov with the most amount of white, usually among those corresponding to s5-s8. Many HY/SY ♀♀ show no whitish at all, and some SY/TY ♂♂ may show a pattern intermediate between **D** and **E**; more study is needed. Juv covs are retained by SYs through the PB2 in Aug-Oct.

Juv-HY/SY ♀ (1st cycle, Juv/B1-F1-A1; Sep-Aug): Wing chord < 159 (Table 10); crown and throat dusky; s covs rounded and worn (Fig. 45**A**, p. 79), brownish without sheen, the gr covs with no or a small white spot (Fig. 98**A**); scapulars gray without whitish (Fig. 99**A-B**); s5 without white; uppertail covs and rump dusky, contrasting indistinctly with darker back; longest occipital feathers (of hind crown) short (usually < 15 mm); outer pp narrow (Fig. 25**A-B**, p. 47), averaging shorter by sex (Table 10), and without sheen. **Note: The size of the white cheek patch varies by age, averaging smaller in HY/SYs than AHY/ASYs by sex, and smaller in SY/TY ♂♂ than ASY/ATY ♂♂, but exceptions occur and variation in the shape of the patch with head posture makes comparisons difficult.**

AHY/ASY ♀ (Def. cycle, DB-DA; Sep-Aug): Wing chord < 160 (Table 10); crown and throat dusky; s covs squared and fresh (Fig. 45**F**), dusky to blackish and often with a slight sheen, the gr covs with some white (Fig. 98**B-D**); scapulars gray (Fig. 99**B-C**), sometimes slightly paler than back; s5 with little or no white; uppertail covs and rump dusky, contrasting indistinctly with darker back; longest occipital feathers short (usually < 15 mm); outer pp broad (Fig. 25**C-D**), averaging longer by sex (Table 10), with slight sheen. **Note: See Juv-HY/SY ♀.**

Juv-HY/SY ♂ (1st cycle, Juv/B1-F1-A1; Sep-Aug): Wing chord > 159 (Table 10); crown and throat dusky, increasingly mixed with glossy blackish in Nov-Jun; s covs rounded and worn (Fig. 45**A**), dusky without sheen, the gr covs with some white (Fig. 98**B-D**); formative scapulars pale gray to whitish (Fig. 99**C-E**); s5 with distinct white patch to inner web; uppertail covs pale grayish, contrasting distinctly with darker back; longest occipital feathers (both juvenal and formative?) long (usually > 15 mm); outer pp (Fig. 25**A-B**) as in Juv-HY/SY ♀. **Note: See Juv-HY/SY ♀.**

AHY/ASY ♂ (Def. cycle, DB-DA; Sep-Aug): Wing chord > 160 (Table 10); crown and throat glossy purplish and bronze in Sep-Jun; gr covs squared and with broad white tips (Fig. 98**E**); scapulars white in Sep-May or pale grayish in Jun-Aug (Fig. 99**D-E**); s5 with distinct white

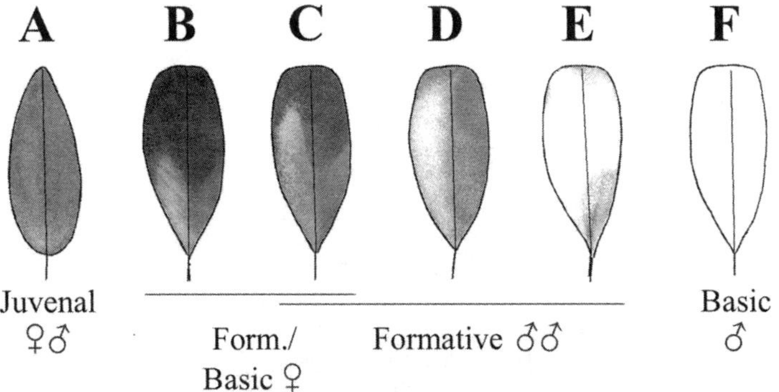

FIGURE 99. Pattern of the scapulars by feather generation and sex in Bufflehead. The scapulars may or may not be replaced during the PF but are usually replaced during the DPA; alternate scapulars (Jul-Sep) resemble **B** in ♀♀ and **C**-**D** in ♂♂. In HY/SY ♂♂, formative scapulars vary from only partially whitish (**C**) to nearly fully white (**E**), depending in part on whether they were replaced early or late during the PF, respectively (see p. 29). Generally, in ♀♀ the scapulars are the same color or only slightly paler than the back feathers, whereas in ♂♂ (except for HYs with completely juv scapulars) they are whiter than the back feathers.

patch to inner web; distal les and proximal med covs white; marginal les covs (at bend of wing) black (uniform in aspect with proximal les covs) or whitish; outer pp (Fig. 25**C**-**D**) as in AHY/ASY ♀. **Note: See Juv-HY/SY ♀ and SY/TY♂.**

SY/TY ♂ (2nd cycle, B2-A2; Sep-Aug): Like AHY/ASY ♂ but throat washed dusky or brownish; distal les and proximal med covs sometimes with thin dusky mottling; marginal les covs dull blackish, contrasting with blacker proximal les covs; proximal gr covs average less white (*cf.* Fig. 98**D**-**E**). **Note: See Juv-HY/SY ♀.**

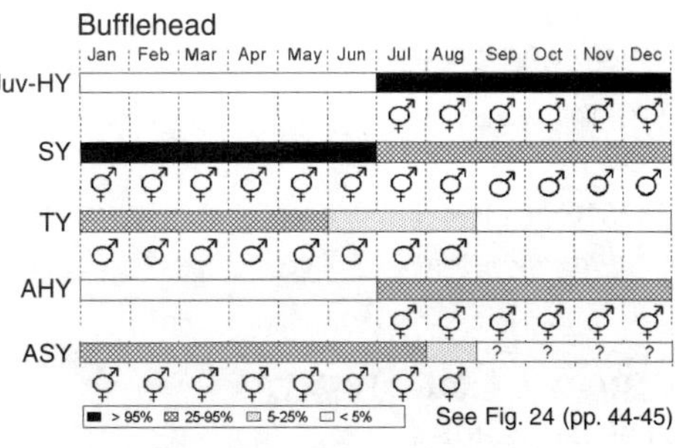

Hybrids reported—With Hooded Merganser (Marcisz 1981) and goldeneye sp. (probably Common Goldeneye; Palmer 1976b) in the wild.

References—Ainley et al. (1994), Bent (1925), Carney (1964, 1992), Cramp & Simmons (1977), Dement'ev & Gladkov (1952), Erskine (1972), Gauthier (1993), Henny et al. (1981), Oberholser (1974), Palmer (1976b), Roberts (1955).

TABLE 10. Measurements (mm) in assorted North American diving ducks to assist in identification, ageing, and sexing. See pp. 4-11 for methods of measurement. Species summaries are in **bold** and subspecies summaries in ***italics***. Values were derived from 95% confidence intervals as based (for wing, exposed culmen, and tarsus) approximately on the indicated sample sizes (see pp. 4-5); sample sizes for tail length and bill depth were often smaller but included at least 10 of each sex. Thus, midpoints of ranges approximate means, and S.D. is approximated by 25% of the range.

Taxon/Sex	*n*	wing chord AHY/ASY	wing chord (HY/SY)[1]	tail length[1]	exp culmen	bill depth[2]	tarsus
Harlequin Duck		**182-210**	**(173-200)**	**78-107**	**23-31**	**13.1-16.9**	**34-42**
♀	100	182-201	(173-191)	78-89	23-29	13.1-15.4	34-40
♂	100	193-210	(183-200)	90-107	25-31	14.5-16.9	35-42
Long-tailed Duck		**195-232**	**(185-220)**	**58-265**	**24-30**	**13.3-17.7**	**32-38**
♀	100	195-216	(185-206)	58-74	24-28	13.3-16.1	32-36
♂	100	208-232	(196-220)	180-265	25-30	14.9-17.7	33-38
Bufflehead		**146-176**	**(143-170)**	**60-80**	**23-30**	**12.6-15.8**	**30-35**
♀	100	146-160	(143-156)	60-71	23-27	12.6-14.6	30-33
♂	90	164-176	(159-170)	69-80	26-30	13.6-15.8	32-35
Common Goldeneye		**183-239**	**(177-231)**	**69-97**	**28-41**	**16.0-23.6**	**33-42**
B.c. clangula		***183-232***	***(177-224)***	***69-91***	***28-38***	***16.0-22.0***	***33-41***
♀	44	183-222	(177-205)	69-82	28-35	16.0-18.5	33-37
♂	52	205-232	(198-224)	77-91	31-38	18.2-22.0	36-41
B.c. americana		***193-239***	***(187-231)***	***74-97***	***31-41***	***17.7-23.6***	***34-42***
♀	100	193-219	(187-212)	74-88	31-37	17.4-19.6	34-39
♂	100	215-239	(208-231)	83-98	33-41	19.8-23.6	37-42
Barrow's Goldeneye		**202-248**	**(196-237)**	**79-93**	**29-36**	**18.4-24.5**	**37-44**
♀	100	202-224	(196-213)	79-89	29-33	18.4-20.8	37-41
♂	66	228-248	(220-237)	83-93	32-36	20.9-24.5	39-44

[1] Wing chord and tail length differ substantially by age; wing data are separated by age since juv primaries are retained through the second PB whereas tail lengths pertain to formative and basic feathers only, as the juvenal central rects are often replaced by Oct-Dec in HYs (see Fig. 97, p. 142. regarding Long-tailed Duck). Other measures pertain to all age groups.

[2] Bill depth measured at the distal end of forehead feathering (Fig. 8**A**, p. 10).

COMMON GOLDENEYE
Bucephala clangula

COGO
Species # 1510
Band size: 6

BARROW'S GOLDENEYE
Bucephala islandica

BAGO
Species # 1520
Band size: 7A

Species—Juvs and ♀♀ from other N.Am ducks by medium to medium-large size by species (Table 10); head primarily chocolate brown to blackish; bill blackish (♂♂) to mostly or entirely yellow (♀♀ in Nov-May; Fig. 100); med and lower les covs usually with white; s5-s11 mostly to entirely white; axillars and underwing covs dusky brown; legs olive to yellowish with dusky webs.

Common from Barrow's goldeneye by smaller average size except for larger average bill (Table 10, Fig. 100); bill rougher, with smaller nail, sloping evenly from tip to crown, and with less yellow in ♀♀ by season (Fig. 100); s covs with more white by age and sex (Fig. 101, p. 148); AHY ♂ with rounded loral patch (Fig. 100) and scapulars with white streaks (*vs* white patches in Barrow's). Use caution in separating Juvs and alternate-aspect ♀♀, and beware of hybrids (see Martin & Di Labio 1994a, 1994b). See Nelson (1993b) for identification of duckling goldeneyes.

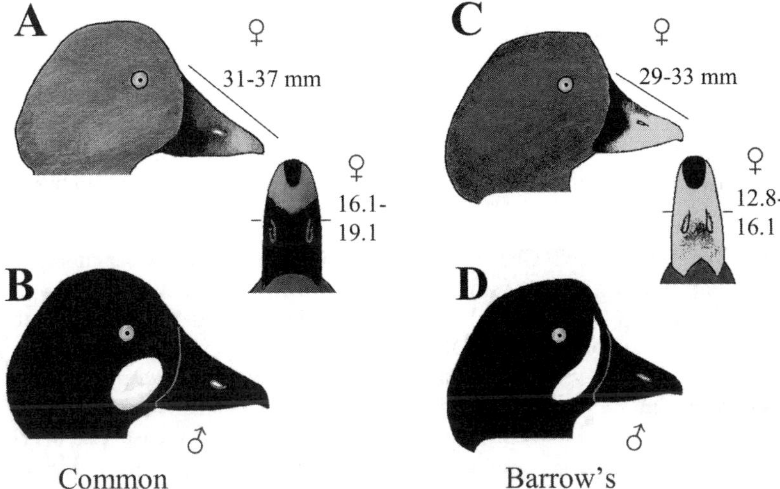

FIGURE 100. Head shape, plumage aspect, and bill and nail features by species in Common and Barrow's goldeneyes. Measures indicate exposed culmen (Fig. 7**A**, p. 9; Table 10) and bill width at proximal end of nares (*cf.* Fig. 8**C**, p. 10). Note that the bill profile of ♀♀ Common Goldeneye shows a maximum amount of yellow (often found on HYs and in Jul-Sep) and that of Barrow's Goldeneye shows a minimum amount of yellow (often for Icelandic populations). The insets show more typical bill patterns in both species. Note that anomalous Common Goldeneyes can show entirely yellow bills but in these individuals the nail is often yellow as well. Note differences in bill shape (thinner at tip in Barrow's Goldeneye) and nail size and shape: usually about 6x10 mm in Common and 9x12 mm in Barrow's. Note also that these bill measures represent the N.Am subspecies of Common Goldeneye (*B.c. americana*); the nominate Eurasian subspecies has smaller bill dimensions (see **Geographic variation**).

Geographic variation—Barrow's Goldeneye is monotypic (P. Johnsgard *in* Mayr & Cottrell 1979), although ♀♀ of Iceland have less yellow in the bill in Nov-May than those of N.Am (Di Labio & Pittaway 1987, Di Labio et al. 1997; Fig. 100); extirpated or anomalous breeding populations from Greenland may have been intermediate (Sherony 2006). For Common Goldeneye, see Browning (2002), Cramp & Simmons (1977), Dement'ev & Gladkov (1952), Palmer (1976b). No other subspecies occur.

Common Goldeneye

B.c. clangula (br & wint throughout Eurasia; vagrant to w.AK Is): Size, especially bill, averages smaller (Table 10); bill depth at distal end of nares 3.7-5.9 (♀) or 5.6-8.8 (♂).

B.c. americana (br & wint N.Am): Size, especially bill, averages larger (Table 10, Fig. 100); bill depth at distal end of nares 5.7-8.7 (♀) or 8.5-11.4 (♂).

Molt—CAS. PF incomplete (Aug-Mar in HY/SYs), PA1 absent-limited (Jun-Aug in SYs), DPB complete (Jul-Nov in AHYs), DPA partial (Jun-Jul in ASYs). The PF commences on breeding grounds and completes on non-breeding grounds, the PAs occur primarily on breeding grounds, and the PB occurs primarily on molting grounds (p. 47) near breeding grounds. The PF includes some to most body feathers, sometimes 1-4 terts and a few proximal s covs, and the central 6 to (often) all rects. Wing feathers are replaced synchronously during the DPBs. The PA1 includes a few head and back feathers in a few birds (perhaps ♂♂ only). The DPA includes some to all of the body feathers but few if any terts, s covs, or rects. The PF and DPA average more extensive in ♂♂ than in ♀♀. See Family (p. 47), Subfamily (p. 78), and Tribal (p. 117) accounts for more details.

Age/Sex—Juv (Jul-Nov) has plumage aspect washed brownish, scapulars narrow and brown, and rects entirely juv (Figs. 26**A**, p. 48, & 67**A**, p. 105). Some Juv ♂♂ have a dusky wash to the head and/or whitish-tipped breast and flank feathers; Juvs can also be sexed by wing chord (Table 10, p. 146), bill depth, and the amount of white in the s covs and ss, as in HY/SYs. Partial medial BP (Fig. 20**A**, p. 31) and/or distended cloaca (Fig. 21, p. 32) developed by AHY ♀♀ in May-Jul. See Figures 22-23 (pp. 32-35) for cloacal characteristics useful in ageing and sexing (including Juvs), Table 10 for measurements by age and sex, and Carney (1992) for useful photographs of wings.

Juv-HY/SY ♀ (1st cycle, Juv/B1-F1-A1; Oct-Sep): Bill shallower and wing shorter by species (Table 10); head brown; bill blackish, becoming partially dull yellowish in Dec-Jun (*cf.* Fig. 100, p. 147); most to all s covs narrow, rounded, and worn (Fig. 45**A-B**, p. 79), the gr covs with less white by species (Fig. 101**A**, **E**); iris brownish, becoming pale yellowish in Jan-Sep; upper scapulars without white; terts usually short and brownish; outer pp narrow (Fig. 25**A-B**, p. 47), averaging shorter by sex (Table 10), and without sheen. **Note: Beware HY/SY ♂♂ may not be distinguishable by plumage until Dec; sex these by measurements (Table 10), extent of white in the wing, and bill color. Also beware that bill color can be blackish in ♀♀ in Jun-Sep.**

AHY/ASY ♀ (Def. cycle, DB-DA; Oct-Sep): Bill shallower and wing shorter by species (Table 10); head usually brown (see p. 78 regarding senescent ♀♀); bill with bright yellowish in Oct-Jun (*cf.* Fig. 100); s covs uniformly broad, squared, and fresh (Fig. 45**F**), the gr covs with moderate white by species (Fig. 101**B**, **F**); iris bright pale yellowish; scapulars with distinct white tips; terts long and blackish; outer pp broad (Fig. 25**C-D**), averaging longer by sex (Table 10), and with slight sheen. **Note: See Juv-HY/SY ♀.**

Juv-HY/SY ♂ (1st cycle, Juv/B1-F1-A1; Oct-Sep): Bill deeper and wing longer by species (Table 10); head brown, increasingly mixed with blackish in Dec-Sep; bill black, without yellowish (*cf.* Fig, 100); most to all s covs narrow, rounded, and worn (Fig. 45**A-B**), the gr covs with

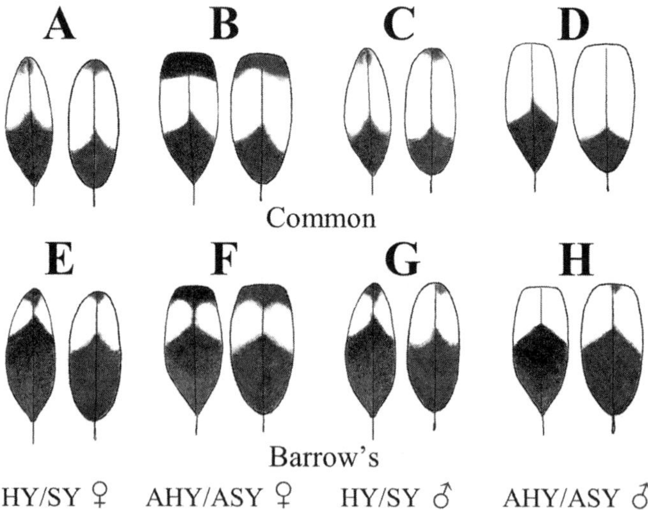

FIGURE 101. Pattern of white in the gr covs by age/sex group in Common and Barrow's goldeneyes. The left-hand feather represents a proximal gr cov corresponding to s8 and the right-hand feather a medial gr cov corresponding to s5. Juv covs are usually retained by SYs through the PB2 in Jul-Nov, although the cov corresponding to s8 might sometimes be replaced. during the PF in Nov-Mar.

moderate white by species (Fig. 101**C**, **G**); iris brownish, becoming pale yellowish in Jan-Sep; formative scapulars with distinct white tips in Nov-Sep; terts usually short and brownish; outer pp (Fig. 25**A-B**) as in Juv-HY/SY ♀. **Note: See Juv-HY/SY ♀.**

AHY/ASY ♂ (Def. cycle, DB-DA; Oct-Sep): Bill deeper and wing longer by species (Table 10); head glossy in Oct-Jun (heavily mottled grayish in Jul through Oct-Dec); bill black (can be tipped dull yellow in Jul-Nov); gr covs squared and with substantial white by species (Fig. 101**D**, **H**); iris bright yellow; scapulars distinctly black and white in Oct-Jun; terts elongated and black; outer pp (Fig. 25**C-D**) as in AHY/ASY ♀. **Note: The plumage aspect (especially of the head) may average duller, the white loral patch smaller by species, and the white wing patch with more dusky (see Bufflehead, p. 143) in SY/TYs than in ASY/ATYs and it is possible that some SY/TY and ASY/ATY ♂♂ can be identified in combination with bursal depth (Fig. 23, p. 34); more study needed.**

Hybrids reported—Common Goldeneye with Mallard (p. 89), Greater Scaup (p. 113), Barrow's Goldeneye (Fjeldså 1973b; Gochfeld & Tudor 1976; Jackson 1959; Martin & Di Labio 1994a, 1994b; Sibley 1994; Snyder 1953), Smew *Mergus albellus* (Ball 1934, Fjeldså 1973b, McCarthy 2006), Hooded Merganser (Ball 1934, Janssen 1980, Martin 1991, Scheider 1966), Common Merganser (Ball 1934, Sibley 1938), probably Bufflehead (p. 143), and possibly Wood Duck (p. 80), Common Pochard *Aythya ferina* (McCarthy 2006), White-winged Scoter (p. 135), and Red-breasted Merganser (McCarthy 2006) in the wild. Barrow's Goldeneye with Common Goldeneye, Hooded Merganser (Morlan 2005), and possibly Bufflehead.

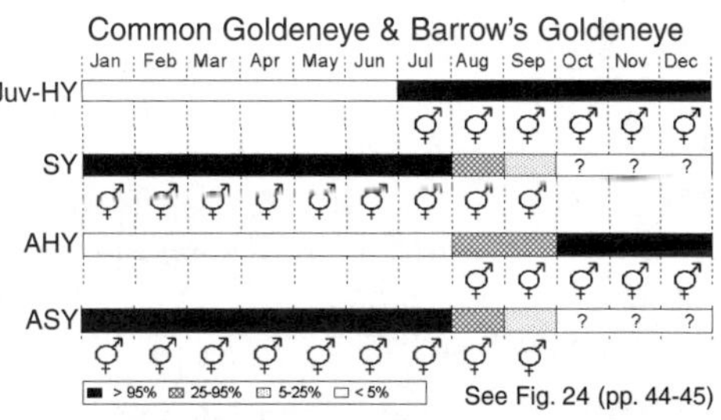

References—Ainley et al. (1994), Baker (1993), Bent (1925), Boyd et al. (1975), Brewster (1909b), Brooks (1920), Carney (1964, 1983, 1992), Cramp & Simmons (1977), Dement'ev & Gladkov (1952), Di Labio et al. (1997), Eadie et al. (1995, 2000), Fjeldså (1973b), Garner (1991), Godfrey (1986), Kraft & Frede (1997), Munro (1939), Nelson (1983), Oberholser (1974), Palmer (1976b), Robert et al. (2002), Roberts (1955), Ruusila et al. (2001), Tobish (1986), van de Wetering & Cooke (2000), Sherony (2006).

HOODED MERGANSER
Lophodytes cucullatus

HOME
Species # 1310
Band size: 5-6

Species—Juvs and ♀♀ from other N.Am ducks and mergansers by medium size with proportionally long tail and short legs (Table 11, p. 152); bill narrow, pointed, and highly serrated along tomium (*cf.* Fig. 104, p. 153), dusky to yellowish (♀♀) or black (♂♂); hind crown feathers elongated (35-50 mm in all age/sex groups) forming single broad crest; s covs grayish except for medial gr covs variably tipped white (Fig. 102, p. 150); s5-s9 with white fringe to outer web; legs yellowish to reddish with dusky webs.

Geographic variation—Monotypic.

Molt—CAS. PF incomplete (Aug-Mar in HY/SYs), PA1 absent-limited (Jun-Aug in non-breeding SYs), DPB complete (Aug-Oct in breeding AHYs), DPA partial (May-Jul in AHYs). Molt strate-

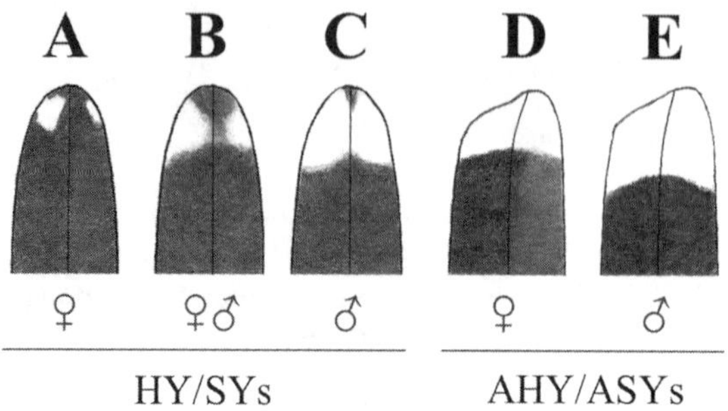

FIGURE 102. Shape and pattern to the distal greater coverts (that corresponding to s3 shown) by age and sex in Hooded Merganser. HY/SYs with patterns resembling **B** can be found on either ♀♀ or ♂♂. Juv covs (**A-C**) are retained by SYs through the PB2 in Aug-Oct.

gies and extents appear similar to those of Common and Red-breasted mergansers (p. 152). The PAs in this species are very poorly known (more study is needed).

Age/Sex—Juv (Jul-Oct) has hind-crest somewhat reduced, plumage aspect washed brownish, and rects entirely juv (Figs. 26A, p. 48, & 67A, p. 105); many Juvs can be sexed by wing chord (Table 11, p. 152) and, less reliably, by the amount of white in the medial gr covs, as described under HY/SY. Partial medial BP (Fig. 20**A**, p. 31) and/or distended cloaca (Fig. 21, p. 32) developed by AHY ♀♀ in May-Jul. See Figures 22-23 (pp. 32-35) for cloacal characteristics useful in ageing and sexing (including Juvs), Table 11 for measurements by age and sex, and Carney (1992) for useful photographs of wings.

Juv-HY/SY ♀ (1st cycle, Juv/B1-F1-A1; Oct-Sep): Hind-crest brownish chestnut; most to all s covs rounded and worn (Fig. 45**A-B**, p. 79), brown without sheen, the distal gr covs without

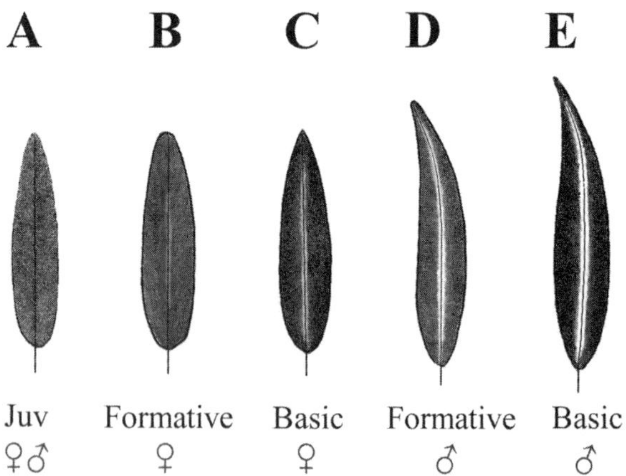

FIGURE 103. Shape and pattern to the longest tertial by feather generation and sex in Hooded Merganser. Many HY/SY ♀♀ and some HY/SY ♂♂ retain juv terts (**A**) throughout the first year, whereas formative terts are acquired by some HY/SY ♀♀ (**B**) and many HY/SY ♂♂ (**D**) in Oct-Mar. These formative terts will be contrastingly darker than the proximal ss. AHY/ASYs likely keep basic terts (♀, **C**; ♂, **E**) throughout the year although some individuals may replace these during the DPA (more study is needed).

whitish or with indistinct whitish tips primarily on outer web (Fig. 102**A-B**); longest tert short and brown (Fig. 103**A**) or sometimes replaced, contrastingly dusky with little or no whitish shaft streak (Fig. 103**B**); iris dark, becoming paler brown by Jan-Mar; outer pp narrow (Fig. 25**A-B**, p. 47), averaging shorter by sex (Table 11), and without sheen; rects juv and/or formative (Figs. 26**A-D** & 67**A**). **Note: Beware that some HY/SY ♂♂ may not acquire black or white feathers until Nov-Dec and are difficult to sex by plumage aspect alone; check wing chord and gr covs, and look for blackish in the chin and side of the breast (at the bend of the wing), often the first blackish feathers to develop during the PF.**

AHY/ASY ♀ (Def. cycle, DB-DA; Oct-Sep): Hind-crest chestnut, with little or no black or white (see p. 78 regarding senescent ♀♀); s covs uniformly squared and fresh (Fig. 45**F**), blackish with slight sheen, the distal gr covs blackish with distinct white tips across both webs (Fig. 102**D**); longest tert elongated, blackish, and with a pale to whitish medial streak (Fig. 103**C**); iris pale brownish or tinged yellowish; outer pp broad (Fig. 25**C-D**), averaging longer by sex (Table 11), and with slight sheen; rects uniformly basic (Figs. 26**D** & 67**B**).

Juv-HY/SY ♂ (1st cycle, Juv/B1-F1-A1; Oct-Sep): Hind-crest brownish chestnut (as in HY ♀) in Oct-Nov, increasingly mixed with black and white feathering in Dec-Sep; most to all s covs rounded and worn (Fig. 45**A-B**), brown without sheen, the medial gr covs with white tips primarily on outer web (Fig. 102**B-C**); longest tert short and brown (Fig. 103**A**), or often contrastingly blackish with distinct white shaft streaks (Fig. 103**D**); iris dark, becoming dull yellowish by Jan-Mar; outer pp (Fig. 25**A-B**) and rects (Figs. 26**A-D** & 67**A**) as in Juv-HY/SY ♀. **Note: See Juv-HY/SY ♀.**

AHY/ASY ♂ (Def. cycle, DB-DA; Oct-Sep): Crest bright black and white in Oct-Jun, or chestnut in Jul-Sep; s covs uniformly squared and fresh (Fig. 45**F**), the distal les and med covs pale grayish and the distal gr covs with broad and distinct white tips (Fig. 102**E**); terts elongated and glossy black with distinct white shaft streak (Fig. 103**E**); iris bright yellow; outer pp (Fig. 25**C-D**) and rects (Figs. 26**D** & 67**B**) as in AHY/ASY ♀.

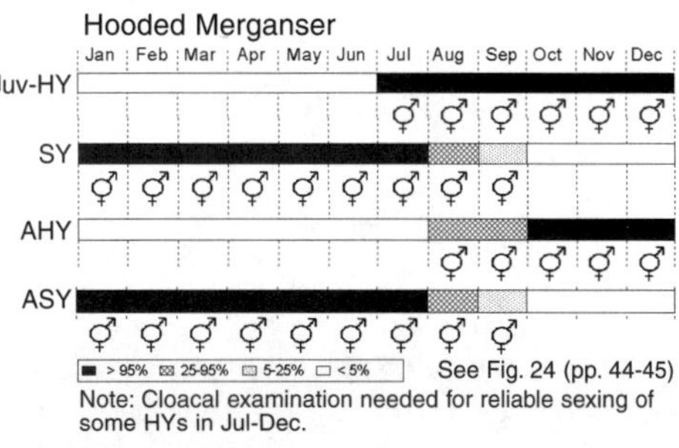

Hybrids reported—With Wood Duck (p. 80), Bufflehead (p. 143), Common and Barrow's Goldeneyes (p. 148), probably Red-breasted (but possibly Common) merganser (Erickson 1952), and possibly with Gadwall (p. 82) in the wild.

References—Bent (1925), Carney (1964, 1992), Cramp & Simmons (1977), Dugger et al. (1994), Oberholser (1974), Palmer (1976b), Roberts (1955).

TABLE 11. Measurements (mm) of North American mergansers to assist in identification, ageing, and sexing. See pp. 4-11 for methods of measurement. Species summaries are in **bold**. Values were derived from 95% confidence intervals as based (for wing, exposed culmen, and tarsus) approximately on the indicated sample sizes (see pp. 4-5); sample sizes for tail length and bill depth were often smaller but included at least 10 of each sex. Thus, midpoints of ranges approximate means, and S.D. is approximated by 25% of the range.

Taxon/Sex	*n*	wing chord AHY/ASY	(HY/SY)[1]	tail length[1]	exp culmen	bill depth[2]	tarsus
Hooded Merganser		**173-203**	**(163-194)**	**80-96**	**35-42**	**11.1-13.2**	**29-34**
♀	40	173-187	(163-178)	80-91	35-40	11.1-12.6	29-33
♂	40	185-203	(175-194)	85-96	37-42	11.6-13.2	30-34
Common Merganser[3]		**236-284**	**(226-274)**	**87-106**	**44-59**	**12.5-18.3**	**42-54**
♀	100	236-257	(226-248)	87-99	44-52	12.5-14.3	42-49
♂	100	261-284	(252-274)	94-106	50-59	15.2-18.3	47-54
Red-breasted Merganser		**207-252**	**(198-243)**	**68-88**	**49-64**	**11.6-15.9**	**40-46**
♀	63	207-227	(198-218)	68-81	49-57	11.6-14.3	40-46
♂	79	228-252	(219-243)	76-88	56-64	13.6-15.9	44-50

[1] Wing chord and tail length differ substantially by age; wing data are separated by age since juv primaries are retained through the second PB whereas tail lengths pertain to formative and basic feathers only, as the juvenal central rects are often replaced by Oct-Dec in HYs. Other measures pertain to all age groups.
[2] Bill depth measured at the distal end of forehead feathering (Fig. 8**A**, p. 10).
[3] Measurments include N.Am subspecies *(C.m. americanus)* only; those of nominate Eurasian subspecies are similar (perhaps averaging slightly larger) except for bill depth (Fig. 104).

COMMON MERGANSER

Mergus merganser

COME
Species # 1290
Band size: 7A

RED-BREASTED MERGANSER

Mergus serrator

RBME
Species # 1300
Band size: 6-5

Species—Juvs and ♀♀ from most other N.Am ducks by medium-large to large size (Table 11); bill long, narrow, pointed, highly serrated along tomium (Fig. 104), and dull reddish to bright red; head with elongated (> 40 mm in AHYs) hind-crown feathers; s5-s9 and s covs with extensive white (Figs. 105-107, pp. 153-155); legs brownish orange to red.

Common Merganser from Red-breasted Merganser by larger average size but shorter average bill (Table 11); bill deeper and with nares extending farther distally (Fig. 104); white tips on ss more extensive (Fig. 105); les covs gray (*vs* duskier in Red-breasted Merganser; Fig. 107); chin and throat white, distinctly defined from chestnut face and neck (*vs* whitish to pale rufous or grayish, not distinctly defined in Red-breasted Merganser; Fig. 104); back gray with dusky shaft streaks (*vs* dusky with few or no shaft streaks); iris brownish in AHY ♂ (*vs* reddish in Red-breasted Merganser). Chinese Merganser (*M. squamatus*), a possible vagrant to w.AK, is similar to Common Merganser but smaller (wg chord 238-265, exp culmen 43-57, tarsus 44-48); bill nail paler; upperparts with distinct black shaft streaks; breast and flank feathers with broad gray fringes creating scaly appearance.

Geographic variation—Red-breasted Merganser is monotypic; see Cramp & Simmons (1977), Gibson & Kessel (1997), Palmer (1976b), and Rand (1947b). For Common Merganser, see Cramp & Simmons (1977), Garner (1999b), Palmer (1976b), and Stejneger (1885). One other subspecies of Common Merganser occurs in c.Asia.

Common Merganser

M.m. merganser (br & wint Iceland and n. Eurasia; vagrant to w.AK Is): Bill averages deeper by sex, with nail deeply hooked (Fig. 104**A**); white tips to ss and gr covs more extensive by age/sex group (Fig. 105**A**; *cf*. Fig. 106, p. 154), the dark bases of the gr covs usually not visible beyond tips of med covs (*cf*. Fig. 107**A-C**, p. 155); AHY/ASY ♂ with elongated feathers across entire nape (sometimes with bilateral extensions) and bill darker red.

M.m. americanus (br & wint N.Am): Bill averages shallower by sex, with nail not deeply hooked (Fig. 104**B**); white tips to ss and gr covs less extensive by age/sex group (Fig. 105**B**; see also Fig. 106), the dark bases of the gr covs visible beyond tips of med covs (Fig. 107**A-C**); AHY/ASY ♂ with elongated feathers confined to medial nape (forming only a single extension) and bill brighter scarlet red.

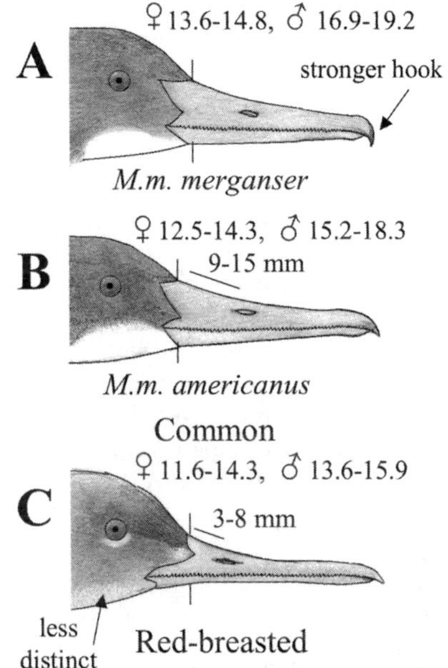

FIGURE 104. Head plumage aspect and bill size and shape by subspecies and species in Common and Red-breasted mergansers. Measures given are bill depth at distal end of forehead feathers (Fig. 8**A**, p. 10) and distance from malar feather extension to proximal end of nares.

Molt—CAS. PF incomplete (Aug-Mar in HY/SYs), PA1 absent-limited (Jun-Aug in SYs), PB2 complete (Jul-Oct in SYs), DPA partial (May-Jul in ASYs), DPB complete (Aug-Dec in ASYs). The PF commences on breeding grounds and completes on non-breeding grounds, the PAs occur primarily on breeding grounds, and the PBs occur primarily on molting grounds (p. 47) but can complete on non-breeding grounds. The PF includes some to most body feathers, sometimes 1-4 terts and a few proximal s covs, and usually the central 2 to all (18-20) rects. Wing feathers are replaced synchronously during PBs. The PA1 includes head and back feathers in some SYs (perhaps ♂♂ only). The DPA includes some

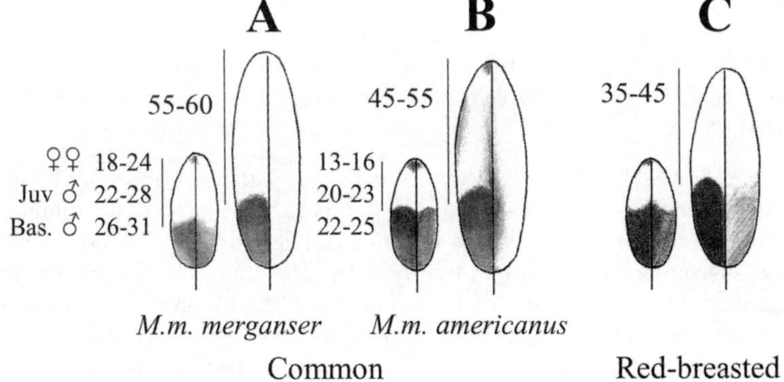

FIGURE 105. Pattern of white to the proximal gr covs and secondaries (gr cov 7 and s7 shown) by species and subspecies in Common and Red-breasted mergansers. Measures are the extent of white along the outer web at the shaft of each feather. Note also the more extensive dusky shaft in N.Am Common Mergansers (**B**) than in the nominate Eurasian subspecies (**A**). See also Figs. 106 (p. 154) & 107 (p. 155).

to all of the body feathers but few if any terts, s covs, or rects. The PF and DPA average more extensive in ♂♂ than in ♀♀. See Family (p. 47), Subfamily (p. 78), and Tribal (p. 117) accounts for more details.

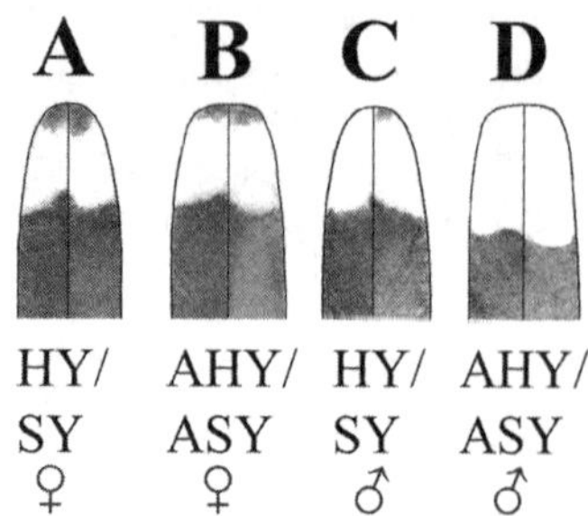

FIGURE 106. Pattern of white to the proximal greater covertss (corresponding to s7-s9) by age/sex group in Common and Red-breasted mergansers. Juv feathers (**A**, **C**) are retained by SYs through the PB2 in Jul-Oct. See also Figs. 105 (p. 153) and 107.

Age/Sex—Juv (Aug-Dec) has hind-crest feathers reduced (< 40 mm), body washed brownish, lores with indistinct white stripe, scapulars brown and narrow, and rects uniformly juv (Figs. 26A, p. 48, & 67A, p. 105). Juvs can be sexed by wing chord and bill depth (Table 11, p. 152), if fully grown, and by the s-cov characters as in Juv-HY/SYs. Partial medial BP (Fig. 20**A**, p. 31) and/or distended cloaca (Fig. 21, p. 32) developed by ASY ♀♀ in May-Jul. See Figures 22-23 (pp. 32-35) and Anderson & Timken (1971) for cloacal characteristics useful in ageing and sexing (including Juvs), Table 11 for measurements by age and sex, and Carney (1992) for useful photographs of wings.

Juv-HY/SY ♀ (1st cycle, Juv/B1-F1-A1; Oct-Sep): Wing chord and bill depth smaller by species and age (Table 11); body pale brownish and gray; bill and legs brownish to dull orange; iris dark; most to all s covs rounded and worn (Fig. 45**A-B**, p. 79), the les and med covs without sheen, and the proximal gr covs with indistinct white tips and often indistinctly grayish at very tip (Figs. 106**A** & 107**A**, **D**); longest tert brownish gray or occasionally contrastingly dark with whitish wash to center; outer pp narrow (Fig. 25**A-B**, p. 47) and without sheen; rects juv and/or formative (Figs. 26**A-D** & 67**A**). **Note: Beware some HY/SY ♂♂ do not acquire greenish, blackish, or white feathers until at least Feb-May (and sometimes Sep) and can be difficult to sex by plumage aspect; use wing chord for reliable sexing.**

AHY/ASY ♀ (Def. cycle, DB-DA; Oct-Sep): Wing chord and bill depth smaller by species and age (Table 11); body deep brownish and grayish, with little or no dark green, blackish, or white (see p. 78 regarding senescent ♀♀); bill and legs moderately bright red; iris dark; s covs uniformly squared and fresher (Fig. 45**F**), the les and med covs dark gray with slight sheen, and the proximal gr covs with reduced but distinct white bands and often with distinct gray tips (Figs. 106**B** & 107**B**, **E**); longest tert blackish, sometimes with whitish wash to center; outer pp broad (Fig. 25**C-D**) and with slight sheen; rects uniformly basic (Figs. 26**D** & 67**B**). **Note: See Juv-HY/SY ♀.**

Juv-HY/SY ♂ (1st cycle, Juv/B1-F1-A1; Oct-Sep): Wing chord and bill depth larger by species and age (Table 11); body pale brownish and gray in Oct-Dec, with increasing numbers of dark green, blackish, and/or white feathers in Jan-Sep; bill and legs brownish to reddish orange; iris dark, becoming dull reddish in Red-breasted Merganser by Jan-Mar; most to all s covs rounded and worn (Fig. 45**A-B**), the les and med covs grayish brown (often with paler grayish wash or centers) without sheen, and the proximal gr covs with indistinct white tips and sometimes grayish at tip (Figs. 106**C** & 107**A**, **C**); longest tert brownish gray or occasionally contrastingly dark with whitish outer webs; outer pp (Fig. 25**A-B**) and rects (Figs. 26**A-D** & 67**A**) as in Juv-HY/SY ♀. **Note: See Juv-HY/SY ♀.**

AHY/ASY ♂ (Def. cycle, DB-DA; Oct-Sep): Wing chord and bill depth larger by species and age (Table 11); body dark green, black, and white in Oct-Jul, or washed gray (resembling AHY/ASY ♀) in Aug-Nov; bill and legs (both species) and iris (Red-breasted Merganser) bright red; les and med covs largely white, the proximal gr covs with extensive white tips

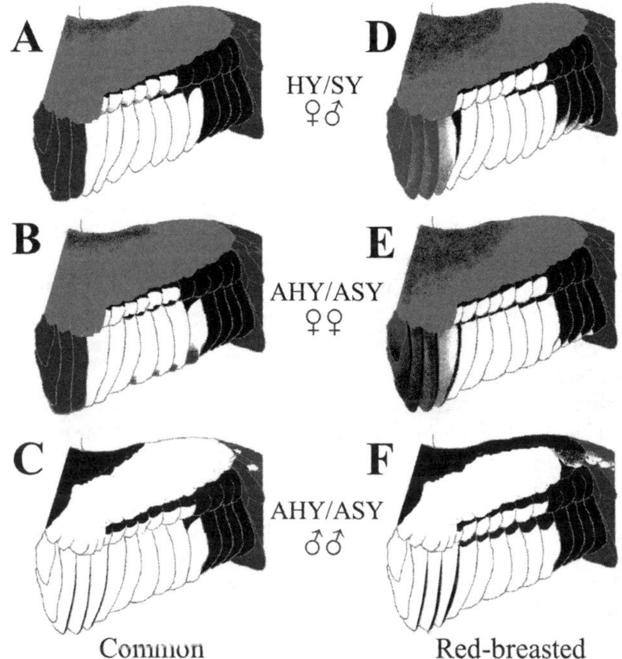

FIGURE 107. Pattern of white in the wing by age/sex group in N.Am (*M.m. americanus*) Common (**A-C**) and Red-breasted (**D-F**) mergansers. Note that white on the gr covs extends more distally on Red-breasted (typically to s5) than on Common (to s6), but that the white is more extensive among the les covs of Common than Red-breasted merganser. Note also the visible dark at the base of the gr covs of AHY/ASYs of both species, forming a dark bar; on nominate Eurasian subspecies of Common Merganser the white tips are more extensive, and there is no visible dark bar (see also Figs. 105, p. 153, & 106).

(Figs. 106**D** & 107**C**, **F**); longest tert black with bright white outer webs; outer pp (Fig. 25**C-D**) and rects (Figs. 26**D** & 67**B**) as in AHY/ASY ♀. **Note: Plumage aspect (especially of the head) and bill color may average duller in SY/TYs than in ASY/ATYs; more study is needed in combination with amount of white in wing (see Bufflehead, p. 143) and bursal depth (Fig. 23, p. 34).**

Hybrids reported—Common Merganser with Common Goldeneye (p. 148), Red-breasted Merganser (Blaser 1978), probably with Common Eider (p. 126), and possibly with Mallard (p. 89) and Hooded Merganser (p. 149) in the wild. Red-breasted Merganser with Common Merganser, probably with Hooded Merganser, and possibly with Mallard, Common Eider, and Common Goldeneye in the wild.

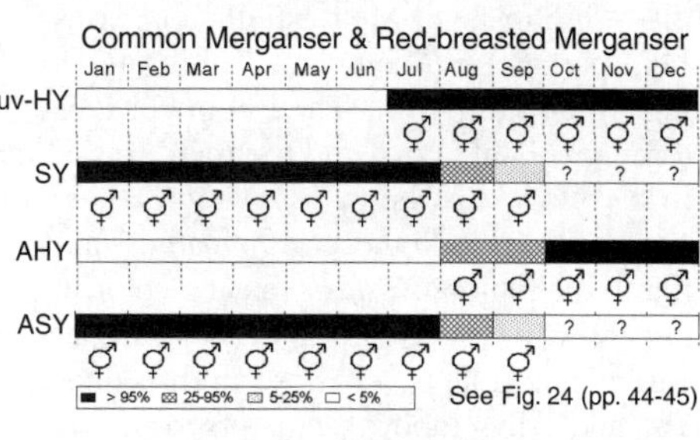

References—Ainley et al. (1994), Anderson & Timken (1971), Baker (1993), Bent (1925), Boyd et al. (1975), Carney (1964, 1992), Cramp & Simmons (1977), Dement'ev & Gladkov (1952), Erskine (1971), Kaufman (1990a, 1990b), Little & Furness (1985), Mallory & Metz (1999), Oberholser (1974), Palmer (1976b), Roberts (1955), Robinson (1999), Titman (1999).

Stiff-tailed Ducks *Anatidae, Anatinae, Oxyurini*

Two North American species. See Family (p. 47) and Subfamily (p. 78) accounts for traits found throughout Anatidae and Anatinae. Tribal characters include small bodies, very short wings, proportionally large and spatulate bills (reflecting bright blue in breeding males), more colorful alternate plumage aspects in males (as opposed to more colorful basic aspects in other tribes), narrow, rigid, and pointed rectrices, and lobed hind toes. North American stiff-tailed ducks have 10 functional primaries (p10 often longest when fully grown, extending 3 mm longer to 3 mm shorter than p9), 16 secondaries (including 3 tertials), and 18 (usually) rectrices. Ageing through the first cycle (to SY and ASY) and possibly the second cycle (to TY and ATY) can be accomplished by plumage aspect as related to the variable timing of the prebasic and prealternate molts. Sexing of AHYs can be accomplished by plumage aspect, and males average slightly larger than females. Medial brood patches (Fig. 20**A**, p. 31) are developed but the abdomen remains feathered during incubation (Siegfried et al. 1976).

Molt strategies still need to be determined in stiff-tailed ducks; it is possible that they exhibit a Simple Alternate Strategy (SAS; Fig. 10**C**-**E**, pp. 13-16). The second prebasic molt possibly may occur 3-5 months earlier than the definitive prebasic molt, in Ruddy Duck at least, leading to reports of a "double-wing molt" per year (see Siegfried 1973, Hohman 1996, Hobson et al. 2000, Jehl 2004, Pyle 2005a). Among adult Ruddy Ducks (but possibly not Masked Ducks), variation in pigment-deposition cycles rather than molting cycles appear to account for the difference in plumage-aspect strategies from other ducks (Pyle 2005a). Age at first breeding usually occurs at 2 years; prebasic molts of SYs and non-breeding ASYs average earlier in timing than those of breeding adults.

MASKED DUCK
Nomonyx dominicus

MADU
Species # 1680
Band size: 5

Species—Juvs and ♀♀ from Ruddy and other N.Am ducks by small bill and short legs but proportionally long tail (Table 12, p. 160); bill nail triangular and broad (> 5 mm wide at bill tip); supercilium distinct; feathers of back with broad, pale buff to cinnamon bands and tips (Fig. 108); gr covs and distal med covs tipped white and proximal ss with white outer webs (Fig. 109); rects narrow and stiff (Fig. 110, p. 159); bill dark to pale grayish, or pale blue with black tip in breeding ♂♂.

Geographic variation—Monotypic.

Molt—CAS or SAS. Molt extents appear as follows: PF/PA1 partial-incomplete, PB2 complete, DPA partial, DPB complete. Timing and locations of molts relative to breeding and non-breeding grounds unknown. The PF and/or PA1 appear to include most body feathers, 0-2 terts, scattered proximal s covs, and the rects; it is unknown whether or not feathers are replaced once or twice during the 1st cycle. Wing feathers are replaced synchronously during PBs. The DPA appears to include most body feathers and most to all terts and rects. In ASY ♂♂ it is possible that basic-plumage aspect may be colorful (molt into this plumage being complete and following the wing molt) and alternate-plumage aspect is cryptic, as in other N.Am ducks except Ruddy Duck; however, more study is needed to confirm this. See Family (p. 47), Subfamily (p. 78), and Tribal (above) accounts for more details on molt in waterfowl.

Age/Sex—Juv (Jan-Jun) is similar to HY/SY ♀♀ but has back and body feathers washed brownish, back feathers tipped buff (Fig. 108**A**), and rects entirely juv (Figs. 26**A**, p. 48, & 110**A**, p. 159); juvs can apparently be sexed by the pattern of s1 (Fig. 109). BP may not develop. See

Figures 22-23 (pp. 32-35) for cloacal characteristics useful in ageing and sexing (including Juvs), and Table 12 (p. 160) for measurements by age and sex.

Juv-HY/SY ♀ (1st cycle, Juv/B1-F1-A1; Mar-Feb): Head and body brown and buff; longest scapulars usually juv, brown with distinct buff markings and complete buff tip (Fig. 108**A**); s1 narrow, with broad dark tip to outer web (Fig. 109**A**); bill dusky; most to all s covs rounded and worn (Fig. 45**A-B**, p. 79), pale brownish, the proximal med and gr covs tipped buff; outer pp narrow (Fig. 25**A-B**, p. 47) and without sheen. **Note: Timing for age-code assignment in this species assumes year-round breeding and molting, and completion of the PF or PB2 at 8-10 months of age as in Ruddy Duck; more study is needed on all aspects of ageing and sexing in this species.**

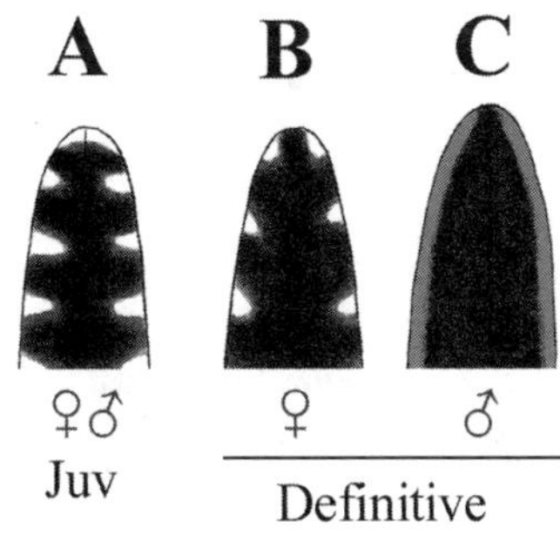

FIGURE 108. Longest scapular by feather generation and sex in Masked Duck. All juv scapulars (**A**) may or may not be replaced during the PF/PA in HY/SYs; formative scapulars may resemble definitive scapulars (**B**-**C**) by sex. Also, cryptic scapulars in ♂♂ (see **Molt**) may resemble definitive scapulars in ♀♀ (**B**), although often the longest scapular, at least, appears to be retained (**C**) and can be used for sexing AHY/ASYs throughout the year. More study is needed on molts and plumage aspects of Masked Duck.

U/AHY ♀ (Def. cycle, DB-DA; Oct-Sep): Head and body (including breast) primarily cinnamon and buff, with little or no black or rufous (see p. 78 regarding senescent ♀♀); longest scapulars brown, with indistinct buff indentations and broken buff tip (Fig. 108**B**); s1 broad, with broad dark tip to outer web (Fig. 108**A**); bill dusky; s covs uniformly squared and fresh (Fig. 45**F**), dark brownish, the proximal med and gr covs tipped white; outer pp broad (Fig. 25**C-D**) and with slight sheen. **Note: See Juv-HY/SY ♀. It is possible that individuals in this plumage aspect, with fresh wing feathers not suffused with rufous, can be aged AHY/ASY (Apr-Mar) and that individuals with worn and cinnamon-tinged wing feathers might be reliably aged SY/TY (Apr-Mar), as in Ruddy Duck (p. 158), but more study is needed.**

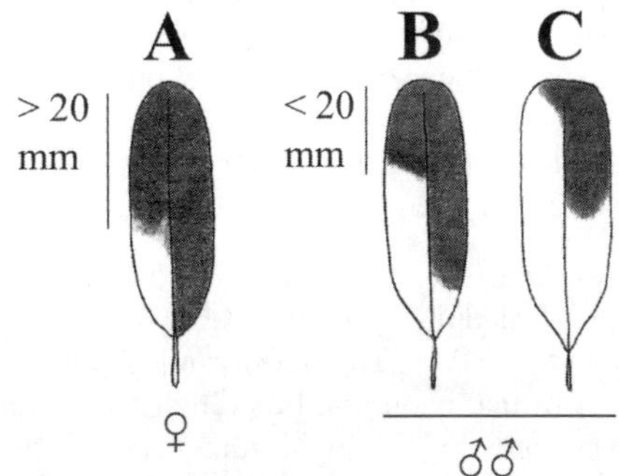

FIGURE 109. Outer secondary (s1) by sex (and age) in Masked Duck. ♀♀ of all ages show patterns similar to **A**, with the dark on the outer web along the shaft extending over 20 mm from the feather tip, but shape is narrower and more rounded in HY/SYs (as in **A**) than in AHY/ASYs (which resemble **C** in shape). ♂♂ vary in extent of white; most juv feathers on HY/SYs resemble **B** whereas most basic feathers on AHY/ASYs resemble **C**; there appears to be some overlap in the extent of white, in which case shape can be used, as shown in **B** (HY/SY) and **C** (AHY/ASY).

Juv-HY/SY ♂ (1st cycle, Juv/B1-F1-A1; Mar-Feb): Head and body brown and buff (as in Juv-HY/SY ♀), increasingly mixed with black (crown and face) and/or dull rufous feathering; longest scapulars (Fig. 108**A**), s covs (Fig. 45**A-B**), and outer pp (Fig. 25**A-B**) as in Juv-HY/SY ♀; s1 narrow, with narrow dark tip to outer web (Fig. 109**B**); bill dusky bluish to moderately bright bluish with indistinct dusky nail. **Note: See Juv-HY/SY ♀.**

U/AHY ♂ (Def. cycle, DB-DA; Dec-Nov): Head and body glossy black and rufous, or primarily brown and cinnamon (as in U/AHY ♀) except for rufous tinge to breast; longest scapular usually black with rufous fringe (Fig. 108**C**); s-covs (Fig. 45**F**) and outer pp (Fig. 25**C-D**) as in U/AHY ♀; s1 broad, with little or no dark tip to outer web (Fig. 109**B-C**); bill bright bluish with distinct black nail and (sometimes) other markings. **Note: See Juv-HY/SY ♀ and U/AHY ♀.**

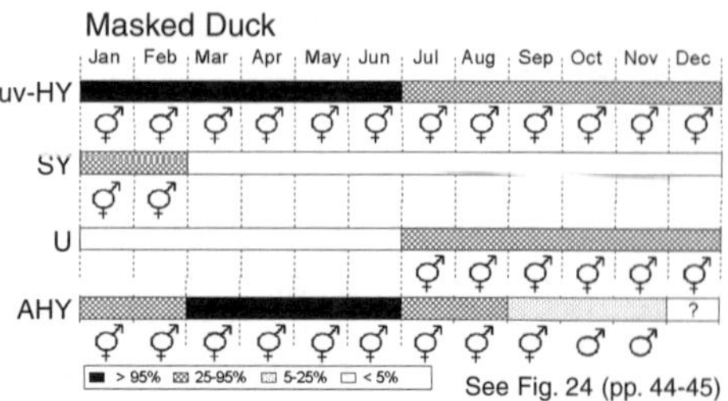

Hybrids reported—None.

References—Eitniear (1999), Johnsgard & Carbonell (1996), Wetmore (1965), Oberholser (1974), Palmer (1976b).

RUDDY DUCK
Oxyura jamaicensis

RUDU
Species # 1670
Band size: 6♀-7A♂

Species—From other N.Am ducks by small size with short wings but large bill (Table 12, p. 160); bill spatulate, slate to bright pale blue, and with ovate and narrow nail (< 5 mm wide at bill tip); supercilium indistinct or lacking; lores and auricular white or whitish with brown stripe (Fig. 111); upperwing brown, without white; rects narrow and stiff (Fig. 110).

Geographic variation—Considered monotypic here. Populations breeding in N.Am ("*O.j. rubida*") average slightly larger and with paler breast in alternate-plumaged ♂♂ than in nominate populations of the W.Indes, but differences insufficient and perhaps related to timing of molt (see p. 29). See Adams & Slavid (1984), Blake (1977), Brua (2002), Fjeldså (1986), Hellmayr & Conover (1948a), Lehmann V. (1916), Palmer (1976b), and Siegfried (1976) for more information.

Molt—SAS or CAS. PF/PA1 limited-complete? (Oct-Mar in HY/SYs); PB2 complete (Apr-Jul in non-breeding SYs), DPA partial (Feb-May in breeding AHYs), DPB complete (Jul-Nov in breeding AHYs). The above timing pertains to N.Am populations. The PF/PA1 and DPA occur primarily on non-breeding grounds and the PBs occur primarily on breeding or molting grounds (p. 47); replacement rects during the DPA (see below) and sometimes the DPB of ♀♀ can occur on non-breeding grounds. In many HY/SYs, the PF/PA1 includes some to most of the body feathers but few if any terts, s covs, or rects. Some SYs appear to replace wing feathers in Mar-May (Pyle 2005a), as in Eared Grebe (p. 234); whether this is part of a complete PF/PA1 (Fig. 10**D**, pp. 13-16) or an advanced PB2 requires further study. If the former, it is likely that some feathers are replaced twice during the first cycle, indicating both a PF and PA1 (and CAS), but details of nomenclature would need to be resolved. During DPBs, wing feathers are replaced synchronously, and rectrices are replaced alternately over a protracted period. The DPA includes most body feathers and no to (often) all rects (which can begin replacement as early as Jan); this molt may average less extensive in TYs than in ATYs. See Family (p. 47), Subfamily(p. 78), and Tribal (p. 156) accounts for more details. The timing of molt exhibits variation relative to the timing of bright pigment deposition, resulting in variable plumage aspects (see Pyle 2005a and p. 29).

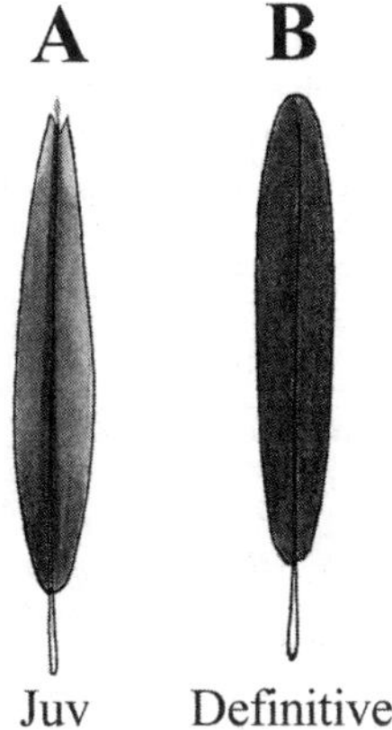

FIGURE 110. Rectrices of Masked and Ruddy ducks by feather generation; note the paler color and nub at tip, often present in juv rectices. In Ruddy Duck, juv rects are usually retained by HY/SYs until Apr-Jul (see **Molt**). Thereafter most to all rects are usually replaced twice per year, during the DPB and the DPA. But replacement can be protracted, occurring during most of the non-breeding season, at which time they can be replaced alternately.

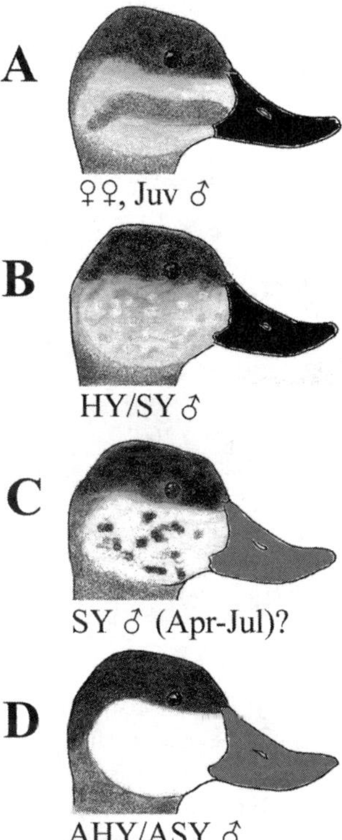

FIGURE 111. Face pattern of Ruddy Duck by age and season: **C** represents certain individuals that acquire blackish in the white cheeks in Apr-Jul. It is possible that these represent SYs that had replaced some feathers early during the PB2, the molt offset with the hormonal cycle governing pigment deposition (see p. 29).

Age/Sex—Juv (B1; Jul-Oct) is similar to Juv-HY/SY ♀♀ in Oct-Dec, with entirely juv rects (Fig. 110). Juv ♀=♂ by plumage aspect until the PA1 of cheek feathers commences in Nov-Dec. Visible BP does not develop. See Figures 22-23 (pp. 32-35 for cloacal characteristics useful in ageing and sexing (including Juvs), Table 12 (p. 160) for measurements by age and sex, and Carney (1992) for photographs of wings.

Juv-HY/SY ♀ (1st cycle, Juv/B1-A1; Oct-Sep): Head and body brown; cheeks pale brownish with indistinct facial stripe (Fig. 111**A**); some juv rects usually remaining brownish and often with notch and nub at tip (Fig. 110); s covs rounded and worn in Oct-May (Fig. 45**A**, p. 79), pale brown without sheen; outer pp narrow (Fig. 25**A-B**, p. 47), averaging shorter by sex (Table 12), and without sheen in Oct-Mar, often being replaced in Apr-May and (if so) fresh and often suffused with a cinnamon wash in May-Sep; bill blackish (Fig. 111**A**). **Note: Many HY/SY ♂♂ do not acquire whitish in the cheeks until Dec or later and can be difficult if not impossible to sex without cloacal examination. ♀♀ also can be difficult to age by plumage aspect alone.**

AHY/ASY ♀ (Def. cycle, DB-DA; Oct-Sep): Head and body brown (often tinged cinnamon), with little or no rufous (see p. 78 regarding senescent ♀♀); cheeks pale brownish with indis-

TABLE 12. Measurements (mm) North American *Oxyura* ducks to assist in identification, ageing, and sexing. See pp. 4-11 for methods of measurement. Species summaries are in **bold**. Values were derived from 95% confidence intervals as based (for wing, exposed culmen, and tarsus) approximately on the indicated sample sizes (see pp. 4-5); sample sizes for tail length and bill depth were often smaller but included at least 10 of each sex. Thus, midpoints of ranges approximate means, and S.D. is approximated by 25% of the range.

Taxon/Sex	*n*	wing chord AHY/ASY	(HY/SY)[1]	tail length[1]	exp culmen	bill depth[2]	tarsus
Masked Duck		**132-147**	**(128-143)**	**73-88**	**31-36**	**15.3-16.8**	**24-29**
♀	30	132-144	(128-139)	73-86	31-35	15.3-16.2	24-28
♂	30	135-147	(131-143)	75-88	32-36	15.8-16.8	26-29
Ruddy Duck[3]		**133-152**	**(129-147)**	**64-78**	**36-43**	**17.4-21.2**	**30-37**
♀	100	133-147	(129-140)	64-74	36-42	17.4-20.5	30-35
♂	100	138-152	(133-147)	68-78	38-43	18.0-21.2	32-37

[1] Wing chord and tail length differ substantially by age; wing data are separated by age since juv primaries are retained through the second PB whereas tail lengths pertain to formative and basic feathers only, as the juvenal central rects are often replaced by Oct-Dec in HYs. Other measures pertain to all age groups.

[2] Bill depth measured at the distal end of forehead feathering (Fig. 8**A**, p. 10).

[3] Values are for N.Am populations *(O.j. rubida)* only; see **Geographic variation**.

tinct facial stripe (Fig. 111**A**); rects basic and/or alternate, dark brown and usually without notch (Fig. 110**B**); s covs squared and fresh (Fig. 45**F**), dark brown with slight sheen; outer pp broad (Fig. 25**C-D**), averaging longer by sex (Table 12), dark brown (without cinnamon wash) and with slight sheen, relatively worn in May-Jul, and being replaced in Aug-Sep; bill blackish (Fig. 111**A**). **Note: See Juv-HY/SY ♀. It is possible that some SY/TYs can be aged by having pp, relatively worn, brownish, and variably infused with pale cinnamon to rufous (Pyle 2005a), characters that may result from the wing being replaced in Apr-Jun, and retained for 14-17 months before molting again during the PB3. More study needed.**

Juv-HY/SY ♂ (1st cycle, Juv/B1-A1; Oct-Sep): Head and body brown in Oct-Nov, increasingly suffused dull rufous in Nov-Sep; cheeks as in Juv-HY/SY ♀ in Oct-Dec (Fig. 111**A**), increasingly mottled white in Dec-Sep (Fig. 111**B**) and sometimes with blackish marks in Apr-Sep (Fig. 111**D**); rects (Fig. 110**A**), s covs (Fig. 45**A**), and outer pp (Fig. 26**A-B**), including replacement patterns, as in Juv-HY/SY ♀; bill blackish, often tinged dull bluish in Feb-Jun (Fig. 111**B-C**). **Note: See Juv-HY/SY ♀.**

AHY/ASY ♂ (Def. cycle, DB-DA; Oct-Sep): Body brown or with some dark rufous (e.g., to the bases of the lower scapulars and/or flank feathers) in Oct-Feb, or primarily bright rufous in Mar-Sep; cheeks bright white (Fig. 111**D**); rects (Fig. 110**B**), s covs (Fig. 45**F**), and outer pp (Fig. 26**C-D**) including replacement patterns, as in AHY/ASY ♀; bill bright bluish in Mar-Jul, and sometimes tinged bluish in Aug-Feb (Fig. 111**D**). **Note: See AHY/ASY ♀ regarding possibility of ageing SY/TYs. It is possible that AHY/ASY ♂♂ showing these characters, with fresh wing feathers, not suffused with rufous, and rufous-based (as opposed to rufous-tipped) aspect to basic feathers, can be aged ASY/ATY but more study is needed to confirm this.**

Hybrids reported—Ruddy Ducks from native populations with Andean Duck (*O. ferruginea*) in S.Am (Fjeldså 1986) and Ruddy Ducks from naturalized populations with White-headed Duck (*O. leucocephala*) in Europe (Gantlett 1993, McCarthy 2006), in the wild.

References—Baker (1993), Bent (1925), Brua (2002), Carney (1964, 1992), Cramp & Simmons (1977), Fjeldså (1986), Hays & Haberman (1969), Hobson et al. (2000), Hohman (1993, 1996), Hohman et al. (1992b), Jehl & Johnson (2004), Johnsgard & Carbonell (1996), Joyner (1978), Oberholser (1974), Orr (1938), Palmer (1972, 1976b), Pyle (2005a), Roberts (1955), Siegfried (1973), Siegfried et al. (1976), Stresemann (1948).

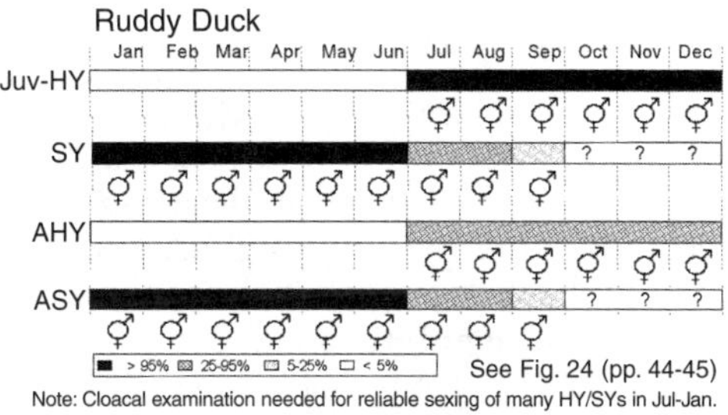

CURASSOWS, GUANS, AND CHACHALACAS *CRACIDAE*

One species. Family characters include small heads, often with unfeathered ornamentation; small bills; heavy bodies, shortish, broad, and bowed wings; long tails in most species; and sturdy legs and feet with well-developed hind toes. North American chachalacas have 10 functional primaries (p10 angled proximally and extending 60-80 mm short of the longest, p4-p6, when fully grown), 12-15 secondaries (including 4 tertials and without one absent between the 4th and 5th as in other taxa; Fig. 12**B**, p. 19), and 12 rectrices. Ageing through the second cycle (to TY and ASY/ATY) can be accomplished through bill color, tracheal development, and replacement patterns among primaries. Sexes are alike in plumage aspect, males are moderately larger than females, and adults can be sexed by tracheal development (Fig. 114, p. 164). Females can also be sexed during incubation periods by medial (occasionally bilateral) brood patches (Fig. 20, p. 31), and distended cloacae (Fig. 21, p. 32), and cloacal examination (Figs. 22-23, pp. 32-35) is useful for both ageing and sexing (Quinn & Burrows 1936, Stromberg 1977).

In molting, chachalacas exhibit the Complex Basic Strategy (CBS; Fig. 10**B**, pp. 13-16), including a formative plumage but lacking alternate plumages. Unlike most other N.Am gamebirds, the preformative molt can be complete (although protracted), including the outer two primaries and primary coverts. Prebasic molts can exhibit staffelmauser (Fig. 16, pp. 23-24) in some but not all individuals, with at most two sets present in adults. Age of first breeding appears to occur at two years (more study needed); thus, the second prebasic molt averages earlier than subsequent prebasic molts in timing.

Gamebirds should not be banded with federal bands; thus, no band sizes are recommended.

PLAIN CHACHALACA
Ortalis vetula

PLCH
Species # 3110

Species—From other N.Am birds by medium-large size, short and decurved bill, and long tail (Table 13, p. 166); tarsus and feet strong, the middle front toe > 10 mm longer than adjacent toes; tail rounded (r1–r6 40-70 mm); gular region on sides of throat naked; body primarily olive-brown; underwing covs tawny; basic lateral rects (r2-r6) of N.Am population blackish with white tips (Fig. 112). From other species of chachalacas, which could occur in N.Am as escapes from captivity, by smaller size and proportionally short wings (Table 13); ornamental feathers on forehead short (< 20 mm); lanceolate feathers on sides of neck not tipped pale; tips of lateral rects white to whitish (Fig. 112); ventral underparts pale brownish to whitish (without dark rufous or white).

Geographic variation—See Blake (1977), J. Bond (1936), Brodkorb (1942), Delacour & Amadon (1973), Griscom (1932), Hellmayr & Conover (1942), Howell & Webb (1995), Miller & Griscom (1921b), Monroe (1968), Moore & Medina (1957), Paynter (1955), Peters (1913), Peterson (2000), Ridgway & Friedmann (1946), Vaurie (1965, 1968), Vuilleumier (1965), Wetmore (1943). Three other subspecies in se.Mexico-C.Am.

O.v. mccalli (res s.TX-ec.Mex): Wing and tail long (Table 13, p. 166; *vs* wg chord 175-213, tl 197-248 in *vetula* of se.Mex-C.Am and wg chord 173-214, tl 197-252 in *pallidiventris* of Yucatan); head tinged grayish and upperparts medium olive-brown (*vs* head and upperparts darker brown in *vetula* and paler grayish brown in *pallidiventris*); tips to rects whitish (Fig. 112, *vs* pale brownish or grayish in *vetula* and buff in *pallidiventris*); ventral underparts pale brownish white to brownish (*vs* tinged rufous in *vetula* and whiter in *pallidiventris*).

Molt—CBS. PF incomplete?-complete (Jul?-Mar? in HY/SYs), DPB complete (Mar?-Nov? in AHYs); PA absent. The above timing pertains to N.Am populations. Pp are replaced distally and ss are apparently replaced proximally from s1 and distally from the terts (s10-s12). Some indi-

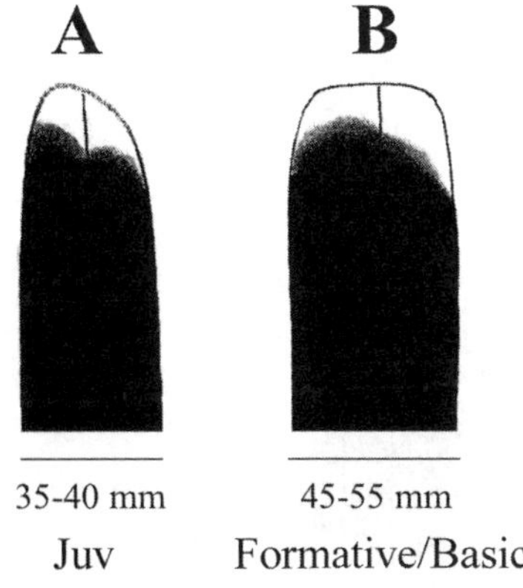

FIGURE 112. Width and shape of the rectrices by feather generation in Plain Chachalaca. Values indicate maximum width of the medial rects (r2-r5). The last juvenal rects replaced on HY/SYs are usually among r1 and r6 (see **Molt**) in Dec-Mar. Look for some SYs to retain 1-2 of these rects through Jun-Sep.

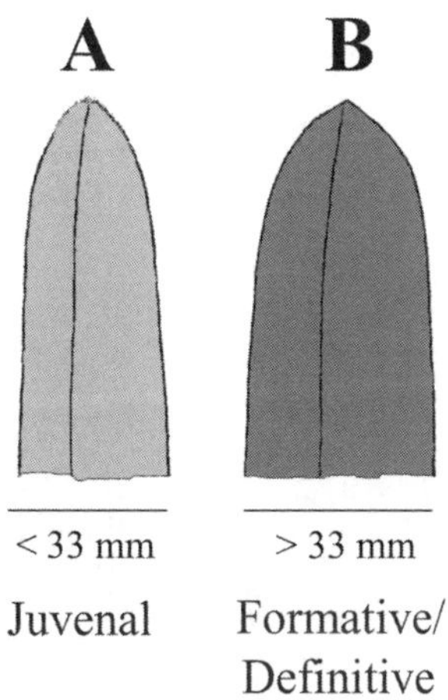

FIGURE 113. Width and shape of secondaries by feather generation in Chachalaca. Width measure indicates feather at widest point. The last juvenal ss replaced on HY/SYs are usually among s5-s9 in Dec-Mar. Look for some SYs to retain 1-2 of these ss through Jun-Sep.

viduals exhibit staffelmauser, presumably established through incomplete PFs and DPBs or perhaps by a DPB commencing before a prior molt completes (more study needed). Others undergo uninterupted complete molts. During the PF, rects are replaced centrifugally on both sides from r3 to r1 and r4 to r6, such that the outer rects are usually the last juv rects replaced, sometimes as late as Mar.

Age/Sex—Juvs (Apr-Aug) are similar to AHYs but have loosely-textured feathers and duller plumage aspect, indistinctly barred rumps, and dark culmens. Medial and/or occasionally bilateral BPs (Fig. 20, p. 31) and/or distended cloaca (Fig. 21, p. 32) indicates ASY ♀ in Feb-May. Measurements (especially wing chord) somewhat helpful for sexing (Table 13, p. 166). See Figures 22-23 (pp. 32-35) for cloacal characteristics useful in ageing and sexing (including Juvs). The following month ranges pertain to N.Am populations.

Juv-HY/SY ♀ (1st cycle, Juv/B1-F1; Apr-Mar): Rects, outer pp, and medial ss uniformly juv (Fig. 16**A**, p. 24), retained through Dec-Mar, narrow, tapered, and worn (Figs. 112**A** & 113**A**); upper mandible tipped dusky; loop of trachea 0-30 mm from thorax (*cf.* Fig. 114**A**, p. 164). **Note: See Juv-HY/SY ♂.**

AHY/ASY ♀ (Def. cycle, DB; Apr-Mar): Rects, outer pp, and medial ss uniformly basic (Fig. 14**B**, p. 21), fresh and broad (Figs. 112**B** & 113**B**), upper mandible bluish gray, without dusky tip; loop of trachea 30-45 mm from thorax (*cf.* Fig. 114**B**). **Note: See Juv-HY/SY ♂.**

Juv-HY/SY ♂ (1st cycle, Juv/B1-F1; Apr-Mar): Rects, pp, and ss, as in Juv-HY/SY ♀ (Figs. 16**A**, 112**A**, & 113**A**); upper mandible tipped dusky; loop of trachea 15-70 mm from thorax (*cf.* Fig. 114). **Note: Tracheal-loop length increases slowly during the first year in ♂♂, from 15-40 mm at 9-10 weeks of age, to 40-60 in Feb-Mar; some ♂♂ with tracheal loop < 70 mm can be reliably aged SY through Jun.**

AHY/ASY ♂ (Def. cycle, DB; Apr-Mar): Rects, pp, and ss uniformly basic as in AHY/ASY ♀ (Figs. 14**B**, 112**B**, & 113**B**); loop of trachea 70-90 mm from thorax (Fig. 114**C**); upper mandible bluish, without dusky tip.

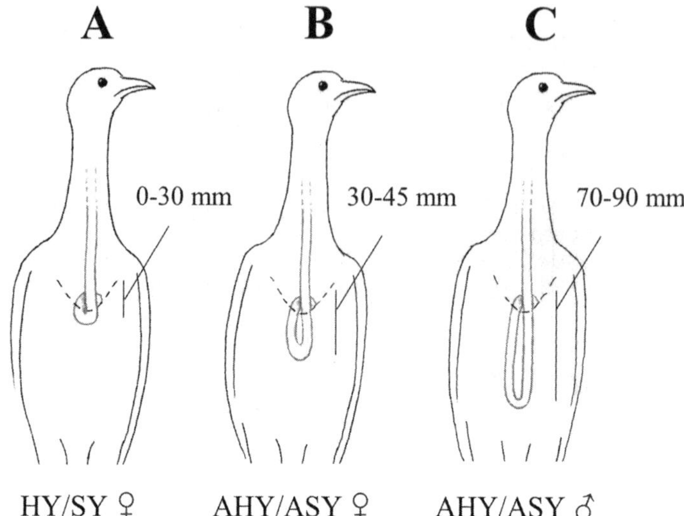

FIGURE 114. Tracheal loop extension by age and sex in Plain Chachalaca. The tracheal loop is located between epidermus and breast muscles and thus can be felt through the skin. Measurements are taken from the thorax (dashed line). In HY/SY ♂, note that tracheal-loop length increases slowly, from 15-40 mm at 9-10 weeks of age, to 40-60 in Feb-Mar; thus, some AHY ♂ with tracheal loop < 70 mm can be reliably aged SY through Jun.

ASY/ATY ♀ & ♂ (Def. cycle, DB; Apr-Mar): Like AHY/ASY ♀ & ♂ but pp with 2 sets of basic pp (Fig. 16**E**, p. 24).

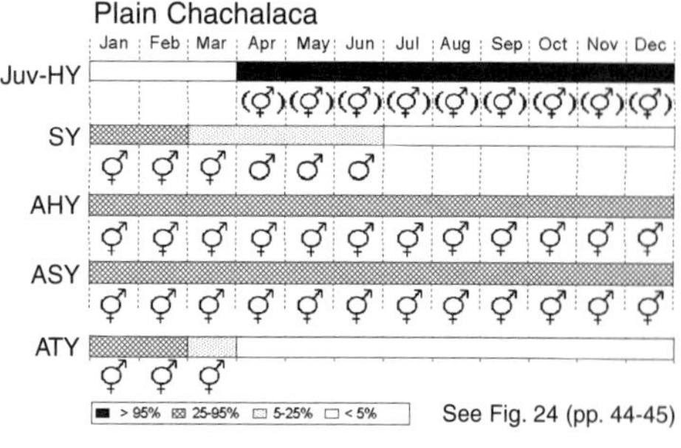

Hybrids reported—None in the wild (but see Vaurie 1965, McCarthy 2006).

References—Bent (1932), Delacour & Amadon (1973), Dickey & van Rossem (1938), Howell & Webb (1995), Leopold (1959), Marion (1977), Oberholser (1974), Peterson (2000), Petrides (1942, 1945), Ridgway & Friedmann (1946), Stresemann & Stresemann (1966), Vaurie (1965, 1968).

PARTRIDGES, PHEASANTS, GROUSE, & TURKEYS *PHASIANIDAE*

Fifteen species. Family characters include heavy (often large) bodies with small heads; small bills without serrations; shortish, broad, and bowed wings; short tails in most species; and sturdy legs and feet, with the hind claw reduced and tarsi often feathered (Fig. 123, p. 173) or sometimes spurred (Fig. 122, p. 172). North American partridges, pheasants, grouse, and turkeys (hereafter "gamebirds") have 10 functional primaries (p10 extending 20-70 [> 100 in Wild Turkey] mm short of the longest, p8-p7, when fully grown), 10 primary coverts (the 10th minute and lying distal to p10), 12-21 secondaries (including 3-5 terials and without one absent between the 4th and 5th as in other taxa; Fig. 12**B**, p. 19), and 12-22 rectrices. Ageing through the first cycle (to SY and ASY) can be accomplished by condition of the outer primaries and primary coverts (Fig. 115), thinner and/or shorter rectrices in some species, plumage aspect in some species, and length of spurs and/or ornamental feathers in other species. Freshly dead individuals can often be aged by suspending the carcass by the beak to see whether (HY/SY) or not (AHY/ASY) the lower mandible breaks (Petrides 1942). Males are moderately to substantially larger than females, and most species can be sexed by plumage aspect or bare part differences. Breeding females during the incubation period have medial brood patches (Fig. 20**A**, p. 31) and distended cloacae (Fig. 21, p. 32), and most individuals of all ages (including juveniles) can be aged and sexed through SY and ASY (and possibly to TY; more study needed) by cloacal examination (Figs. 22-23, pp. 32-35; Gower 1939).

In molting, some species exhibit the Complex Alternate Strategy (CAS; Fig. 10**F-H**, pp. 13-16), including formative and alternate plumages in all cycles, whereas most species exhibit the Complex Basic Strategy (CBS; Fig. 10**B**), including 1-2 formative plumages but lacking alternate plumages; an auxilliary preformative molt (PFa; pp. 14-15) occurs in Wild Turkey (p. 198) and may also occur in ptarmigan and other species. In most species the preformative molt includes all feathers except the outer two primaries (p9-p10) and primary coverts (Dwight 1900a, Petrides 1942; Fig. 115**A**) and it is protracted throughout the period of chick growth, initially replaced feathers being brown and streaked, and subsequently replaced feathers resembling basic plumage (Fig. 116, p. 166). Primaries are replaced distally and secondaries are replaced both distally and

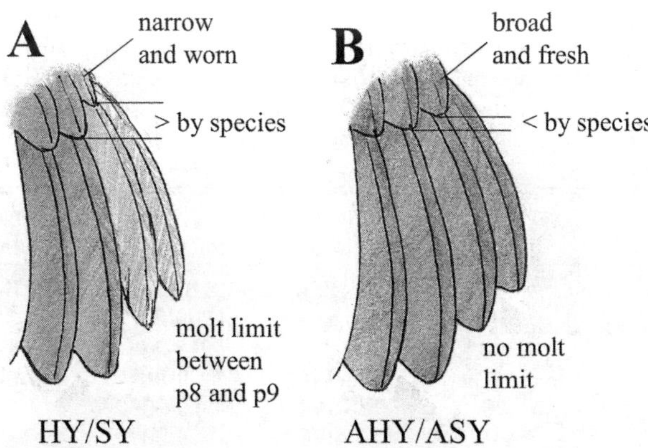

FIGURE 115. Outer primaries and primary coverts by age in most N.Am gamebirds. Darker shading indicates fresher feathers. HY/SYs retain the juvenal p9-p10 and corresponding p covs (the outer p cov is rudimentary and not shown; see also Fig. 118, p. 168), which are noticeably more pointed and worn than replaced formative p7-p8 and corresponding coverts. The juvenal p9 cov is noticeably shorter than that of the p8 cov in HY/SYs (see accounts for species-specific differences) whereas the basic p8 and p9 covs are more similar in length (see also Figs. 118, p. 168, & 129, p. 178). Most Ring-necked Pheasants and some Wild Turkeys may replace some or all of these juvenal feathers and cannot be aged by this criterion following completion of the PF. The juv p9-p10 (**A**) are retained by SYs through the PB2, usually in Jul-Aug.

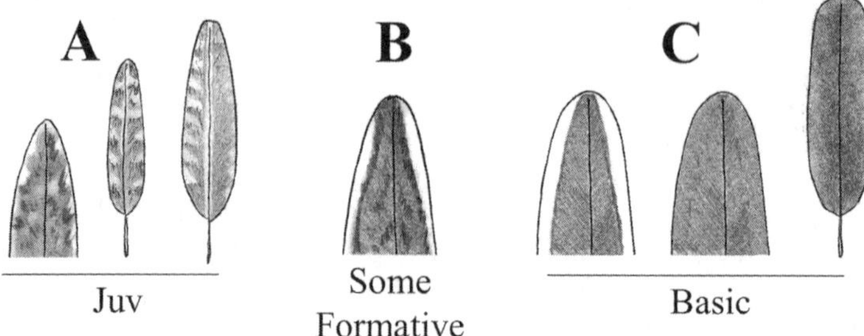

FIGURE 116. Patterns of feathers by feather generation (scapulars and rectrices shown) in gamebirds. All species have similarly patterned feathers in juv plumage aspect (**A**). It is possible that some species may have an extra replacement of some rects during a PFa (as occurs in Wild Turkey; Fig. 150, p. 199); auxillary formative rects may show hints of juvenile patterns (**A**), or juv rects may continue to grow until replaced (more study needed). In smaller species, juv feathers developed later during the prejuvenal (1st prebasic) molt can appear intermediate between juv and formative aspect (**B**). Basic and most formative feathers (see Fig. 140, p. 191, regarding s3) lack patterning but can have distinct pale edges to the scapulars in some species (**C**).

proximally from s3 (*cf.* Warren & Gordon 1935) and distally from the tertials. Rectrices are replaced in various sequences (see **Molt** under each species). Age of first breeding occurs at one year in most species (but can be two years in males of larger species); thus, the second prebasic molt and second-basic plumage are usually definitive. The three species of ptarmigan exhibit presupplemental molts (Dwight 1900a; Salomonsen 1938, 1939; Pyle 2007).

General references or summaries for species, age, and sex determinations in Phasianidae include Clark (1898), Grinnell et al. (1918), Koskimies (1956), Taber (1969), Johnsgard (1973, 1983), Larson & Taber (1980), Brown (1989), Dimmick & Pelton (1996), and Madge & McGowan (2002). Gamebirds should not be banded with federal bands; thus, no band sizes are recommended.

TABLE 13. Measurements (mm) of North American chachalacas, chukars, partridges, pheasants, and turkeys to assist with identification and sexing. See pp. 4-11 for methods of measurement. Species summaries are in **bold**. Values were derived from 95% confidence intervals as based approximately on the indicated sample sizes (see pp. 4-5); thus midpoints of ranges approximate means, and S.D. is approximated by 25% of the range.

Taxon/Sex	*n*	wing chord[1]	tail length[1]	exposed culmen	tarsus
Plain Chachalaca[2]		**185-225**	**213-266**	**17.5-27.5**	**49-67**
♀	100	185-217	209-257	18.5-25.9	47-63
♂	100	196-228	218-266	19.1-27.5	51-67
Chukar[2]		**136-176**	**69-90**	**17.9-22.4**	**41-50**
♀	20	136-162	69-86	20.3-22.4	41-47
♂	20	148-176	74-90	17.9-21.1	44-50
Gray Partridge[2]		**144-165**	**67-84**	**10.9-14.3**	**36-45**
♀	77	144-165	67-78	10.9-13.7	36-43
♂	100	148-168	73-84	11.5-14.3	38-45
Ring-necked Pheasant[2]		**188-273**	**203-556**	**25.5-33.8**	**60-77**
♀	20	188-229	230-293	25.5-30.3	60-67
♂	100	215-273	403-556	28.5-33.8	68-77

[1] Wing chord and tail lengths indicate birds with formative or basic flight feathers; juvenal primaries and rectrices (on HYs in Jun-Oct) average shorter by species and sex.

[2] Measures represent N.Am populations only (see **Geographic variation**).

CHUKAR CHUK
Alectoris chukar Species # 2882

Species—Juvs from other N.Am gamebirds by breast and flanks often with black markings (as in AHYs); tail usually with 14 rects, the outer feathers washed rufous; legs and bill dull reddish. Non-juvs from other gamebirds by medium-small size and proportionally short tail (Table 13); face and breast with distinct black necklace; flanks with brown and black barring; outer 4 rects rufous; legs and feet bright red, the tarsi unfeathered (*cf.* Fig. 123**A**, p. 173). From Rock Partridge (*A. graeca*), Red-legged Partridge (*A. rufa*), and other congeners, which could occur in N.Am as escapes or releases for propagation, by upperparts pale grayish brown (*vs* darker and grayer in Rock Partridge and browner in Red-legged Partridge); bars on flanks sparser (< 10) and blacker; throat washed cream or buff (*vs* white). Beware of hybrids among this genus (Watson 1962a).

Geographic variation—See Cramp & Simmons (1980), Dement'ev & Gladkov (1952), Hellmayr (1929), Madge & McGowan (2002), Shuskin (1927). Fifteen other subspecies occur in Asia. Note that populations in N.Am may be derived from a mixture of subspecies (Long 1981, Christensen 1996), and some influence from the paler and grayer *A.c. kleini*, *koroviakovi*, *pallescens*, *cypriotes*, and/or *kurdistancea* may possibly still be in evidence (especially in CA).

A.c. chukar (res e.Afghanistan-Nepal; introduced throughout N.Am range): Upperparts dark and brownish (*vs* paler and grayer in other subspecies); barring on flanks black and distinct (*vs* browner and less distinct in most other subspecies).

Molt—CBS. PF incomplete (Jun-Nov in HYs), DPB complete (Jun-Nov in AHYs); PA absent. See Family Account (p. 165) for replacement sequence of pp and ss. Rects are replaced distally during both the PF and DPB. The PF includes all feathers except the outer 2 pp (p9-p10) and p covs; occasional HY/SYs may also retain s1.

Age—Juv (B1; Jun-Sep) plumage aspect develops from brown and streaked to grayish with hints of black breast stripe and flank barring of AHYs and with short (< 60 mm) and narrow rects (Fig. 116**A-B**), ss fringed and marked buff, and legs and bill dull reddish. Juv ♀ = ♂ by plumage aspect although see Figures 22-23 (pp. 32-35), Campbell & Tomlinson (1962), and Siopes & Wilson (1973) for cloacal characters reliable for sexing hatchlings and Juvs.

HY/SY (1st cycle, F1; Oct-Sep): Outer 2 pp (p9-p10) narrow and contrastingly worn (Fig. 115**A**, p. 165), p9 with indistinct to no buff markings to outer web (Fig. 117**A**); p9 cov contrastingly narrow, pointed, short, and mottled or spotted buff (Fig. 118**A**, p. 168); formative rects relatively narrow and rounded (Fig. 119**A**, p. 169). **Note: Some intermediates (especially in Aug with p8 growing) may be difficult to age.**

AHY/ASY (Def. cycle, DB; Oct-Sep): Outer pp uniformly basic, broad, and truncate (Fig. 115**B**), p9 with distinct buff rectangle to outer web (Fig. 117**B**); outermost p covs uniformly broad, rounded, long, and with

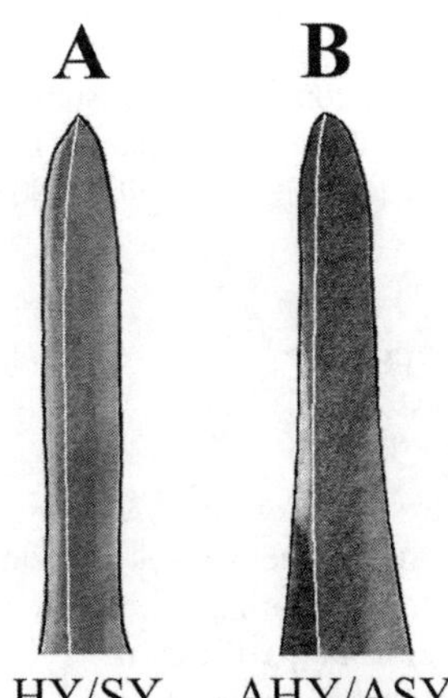

FIGURE 117. Shape and pattern of p9 by age in Chukar. HY/SYs retain the juv p9 which has an indistinct or no buff fringe to outer web (**A**), compared to more distinct buff section to outer web in the basic p9 of AHY/ASYs (**B**).

few or no buff markings (Fig. 118**B**); basic rects relatively broad and squared (Fig. 119**B**). **Note: See HY/SY.**

Sex— ♀ = ♂ by plumage aspect. Medial BP (Fig. 20**A**, p. 31) and/or distended cloaca (Fig. 21, p. 32) indicates AHY ♀ in Feb-May; see also Figures 22-23 (pp. 32-35), Campbell & Tomlinson (1962), and Siopes & Wilson (1973) for cloacal characteristics useful in ageing and sexing (including Juvs). The following is reliable for sexing virtually all N.Am individuals; see also Woodard et al. (1986) for sex-specific differences in shank length:

♀: Wg chord usually < 161 (Table 13, p. 166); bend of wing to tip of p1 < 120 mm and to tip of p3 < 136 mm. **Note: Individuals with these measures 160-162, 118-120, and 134-136 mm, respectively, are likely HY/SY ♂♂ and AHY/ASY ♀♀ and can probably be reliably sexed in combination with age.**

♂: Wg chord usually > 161 (Table 13); bend of wing to tip of p1 > 118 mm and to tip of p3 > 134 mm. **Note: See ♀.**

Hybrids reported— With Przevalski's (*A. magna*), Rock (*A. graeca*), and Red-legged (*A. rufa*) partridges in the wild, the last two with Chukars from naturalized populations in Europe (Watson 1962a, McCarthy 2006).

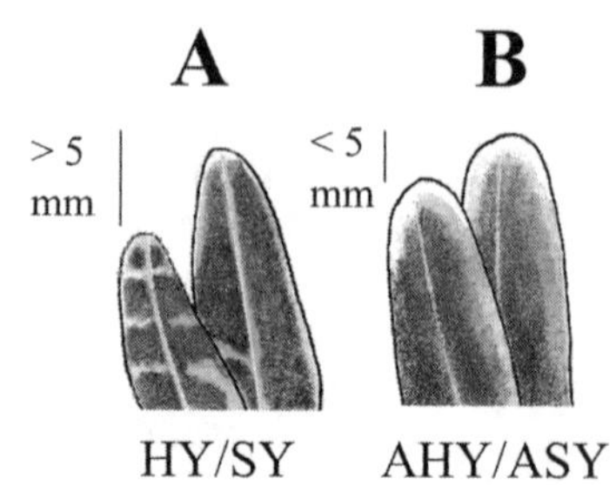

FIGURE 118. Shape and pattern to outer primary coverts by age in Chukar and Gray Partridge. These are the coverts corresponding to p9 (left) and p8 (right); the outermost covert is vestigial. Measure indicates tip of p8 cov to tip of p9 cov. Most N.Am gamebird species retain the juv p9 cov during the preformative molt and it is shorter and more patterned (**A**) than replaced outer p covs of adults (**B**).

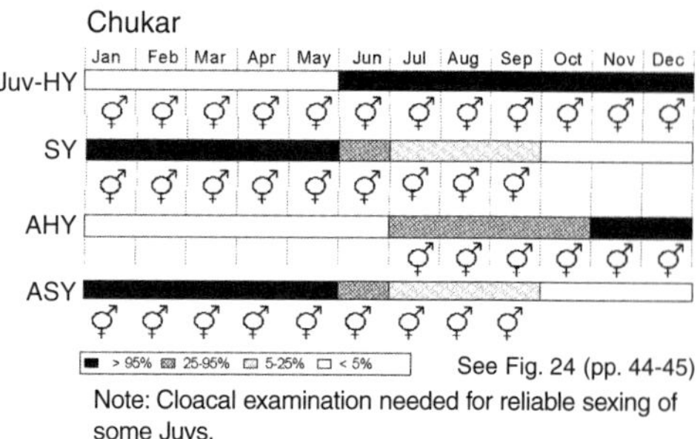

References— Alkon (1982), Christensen (1996), Cramp & Simmons (1980), Dement'ev & Gladkov (1952), Galbreath & Moreland (1953), Marchant & Higgins (1993), Petrides (1942, 1945), Siopes & Wilson (1973), Smith (1961), Watson (1962a, 1963b), Weaver & Haskell (1968).

GRAY PARTRIDGE
Perdix perdix

GRAP
Species # 2881

Species— Juvs from other N.Am gamebirds by nape and breast clay-colored with distinct buff streaks; flanks without black markings; outer rects washed rufous; legs dull grayish to olive. Non-juvs from other gamebirds by medium-small size and proportionally short tail (Table 13, p. 166); tail usually with 18 rects, the outer 4 rufous; face and throat pale brown to orangish; flanks with rufous barring; abdomen with chestnut in ♂♂; legs and feet dull olive, the tarsi unfeathered (*cf.* Fig. 123**A**, p. 173).

Geographic variation— See Cramp & Simmons (1980), Dement'ev & Gladkov (1952), Madge & McGowan (2002). Six other subspecies in Eurasia. Some mixing from other subspecies may have occurred in native range and in N.Am (e.g., Long 1981, specimen examination by author), especially with the paler *P.p. lucida*, but the majority of introductions appear to have involved relatively pure *perdix* (Carroll 1993).

P.p. perdix (res Britain-w.Europe; introduced throughout N.Am range): Upperparts generally grayish brown with slight reddish tinge (*vs* darker and reddish-brown or blackish in other European subspecies, and paler in Asian subspecies); abdomen patch reduced and pale chestnut by sex (*vs* larger and darker maroon in other subspecies).

Molt—CAS (CBS?). PF incomplete (Jul-Nov in HYs), DPA absent-limited? (Mar-May in AHYs); DPB complete (Jun-Oct in AHYs). See Family Account (p. 165) for replacement sequence of pp and (12) ss; rects are generally replaced distally (r1 to r6) during both the PF and the PB. The PF includes all feathers except the outer 2 pp (p9-p10) and p covs. The DPA, if it exists, includes feathers of the head; more study needed.

Age—Juv (B1; Jun-Sep) plumage aspect develops from heavily streaked to grayish with darker streaks to upperparts, whitish ventral underparts, and rects short (tail < 60 mm) and narrow (*cf.* Fig. 116**A**-**B**, p. 166). Juv ♀=♂ by plumage aspect although abdomen patch of ♂ (see **Sex**) is acquired early during the PF, and see Figures 22-23 (pp. 32-35) for cloacal characters reliable for sexing hatchlings and Juvs.

HY/SY (1st cycle, F1-A1; Oct-Sep): Outer 2 pp (p9-p10) and p covs narrow, pointed, and contrastingly worn (Fig. 115**A**, p. 165), the p9 cov short and mottled or spotted buff (Fig. 118**A**,); rects relatively rounded at tip (Fig. 119**A**); beak and legs brownish through Jan-Mar. **Note: In addition, HY/SYs average smaller and less distinct chestnut abdomen patches by sex (see Sex).**

AHY/ASY (Def. cycle, DB-DA; Oct-Sep): Outer pp uniformly basic, broad, and truncate (Fig. 115**B**), the p covs uniformly long and with few or no buff markings (Fig. 118**B**); rects relatively squared at tip (Fig. 119**B**); beak and legs grayish. **Note: See HY/SY.**

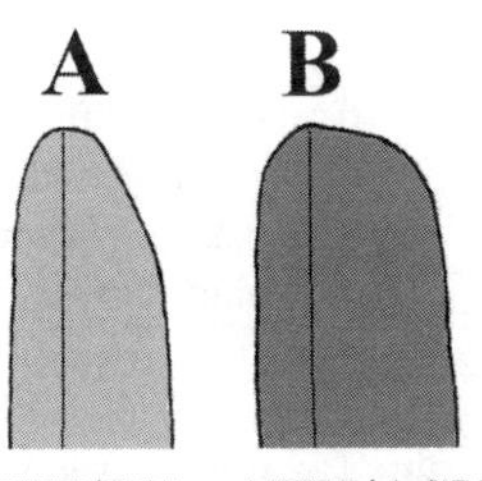

FIGURE 119. Shape of formative (**A**) and basic (**B**) rectrices in certain gamebirds that lack modified rectrices. Despite being replaced at the preformative molt (see Fig. 116, p. 166, regarding juv rects), the formative rects in HY/SYs (**A**) are narrower and more rounded than the basic rects of AHY/ASYs (**B**).

Sex—Medial BP (Fig. 20**A**, p. 31) and/or distended cloaca (Fig. 21, p. 32) indicates AHY ♀ in Feb-May. Measurements somewhat helpful for sexing (Table 13, p. 166). See Figures 22-23 (pp. 32-35) for cloacal characteristics useful in ageing and sexing (including Juvs).

♀: Upper back brown with slight gray mottling; inner webs to scapulars, les covs, and med covs brown with buff to cinnamon barring (Fig. 120**A**); forehead and eyeline with little to no pale cinnamon; abdomen with little to no chestnut patch by age (see **Age**). **Note: Some overlap in plumage aspect may occur; combine with age, measurements, and cloacal examination if possible.**

♂: Upper back gray with slight brown mottling; inner webs to scapulars, les covs, and med covs dark brown to maroon with little or no buff mottling (Fig. 120**B**); forehead and eyeline with substantial orangish; abdomen with substantial and distinct chestnut patch by age (see **Age**). **Note: See ♀.**

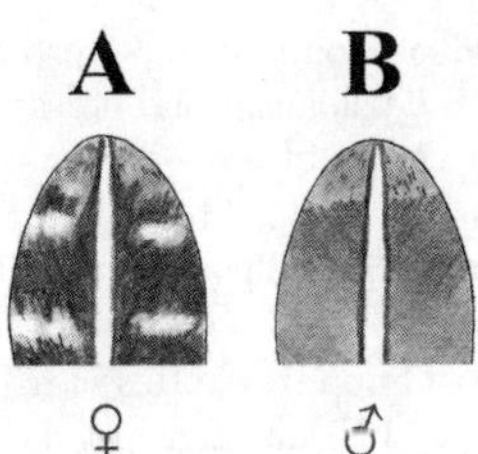

FIGURE 120. Pattern to the median coverts by sex in Gray Partridge. Some intermediates may occur; these are AHY/ASY ♀ or HY/SY ♂ so combine with age for reliable sexing.

Hybrids reported—With Daurian Partridge (*P. dauricae*) and possibly with Rock (*Alectoris graeca*) and Red-legged (*A. rufa*) partridges and Willow Ptarmigan in the wild (McCarthy 2006).

References—Bent (1932), Carroll (1993), Cramp & Simmons (1980), Dement'ev & Gladkov (1952), Hickey & McCabe (1953), McCabe & Hawkins (1946), Petrides (1942, 1945, 1951), Ridgway & Friedmann (1946), Roberts (1955), Thompson & Taber (1948).

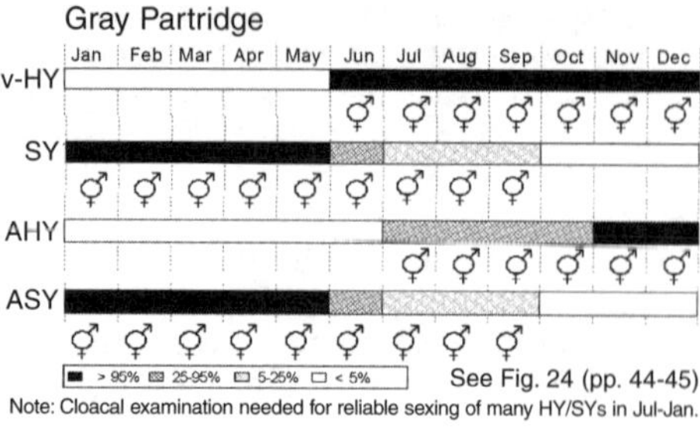

RING-NECKED PHEASANT
Phasianus colchicus

RNEP
Species # 3091

Species—Juvs from other N.Am gamebirds by large tarsus (> 25 mm by 2-3 weeks of age); rects graduated (r1-outer rect > 25 mm); back feathers dark with pale fringing but no shaft-streaks; cheeks with short and abbreviated (♀) or no (♂) feathers. Non-juv ♀♀ from other gamebirds by medium-large size including very long tail (Table 13, p. 166) with 16-18 rects; rects with distinct dark brown to blackish bars; plumage aspect primarily buffy brown to tawny with blackish markings.

Geographic variation—See Cramp & Simmons (1980), Delacour (1977), Dement'ev & Gladkov (1952), Giudice & Ratti (2001), Johnsgard (1999), Madge & McGowan (2002), Marchant & Higgins (1993), Niewoonder et al. (1998), Prince et al. (1988), Ridgway & Friedmann (1946), Sibley (2000), Wollard et al. (1977). Thirty-two subspecies in Eurasia. Note that frequent mixing of subspecies and continued release of specially bred varieties in N.Am (Long 1981, Giudice & Ratti 2001) has confounded subspecies distinctions and has essentially eliminated reliable recognition of individual subspecies. Therefore N.Am taxa are here summarized in the form of subspecies groups. Size varies slightly and clinally in the species' natural range (averaging slightly larger in the *P.c. colchicus* than the other groups) but is generally geographically discordant with respect to subspecies, except that the *P.c. versicolor* group averages smaller (see below). Otherwise, mixing of types and selective breeding have made size comparisons within N.Am populations unhelpful with respect to taxonomic determination.

P.c. torquatus Group (res Mongolia-China to se.Siberia-Taiwan; *P.c. torquatus* and to lesser extent *karpowi* introduced throughout N.Am range): AHY ♂ with pale supercilium reduced or absent, nape (but usually not breast) with narrow white collar, and marginal les covs gray; ♀♀ medium-pale buff to rufous-brown.

P.c. mongolicus Group (res Kazakhstan-n.China; *P.c. mongolicus* introduced BC): AHY ♂ with supercilium broad and pale, nape and breast with wide white collar, and marginal les covs white; ♀♀ medium-dark buff to rufous-brown.

P.c. chrysomelas Group (res Turkestan-Afghanistan; *P.c. chryosmelas* introduced TX): AHY ♂ with supercilium broad and pale, nape and breast with little or no white collar, and marginal les covs white; ♀♀ medium pale buff to brownish.

P.c. colchicus Group (res se.Russia-n.Turkey; introduced throughout Europe and *P.c. colchicus* sporadically throughout N.Am range, primarily e.N.Am): AHY ♂ with pale supercilium absent, nape and breast without white collar, and marginal les covs buffy rufous; ♀♀ dark brownish.

P.c. versicolor Group (res Japan; *P.c. versicolor* introduced DE-VA): Smaller than other subspecies (wg chord 173-256, tl 215-430; *cf.* Table 13); AHY ♂ with back, rump, and underparts dark green to bluish; nape and breast without white collar, and marginal les covs grayish; ♀♀ dark brownish.

Molt—CBS. PF complete (Jul-Nov in HYs), DPB complete (Jun-Oct in AHYs); PA absent. See Family Account (p. 165) for replacement sequence of pp and (12) ss; the rects are replaced irregularly but often centrifugally within each half. Occasional HY/SYs may retain the outer p (p10) and p cov during the PF; more study is needed on populations within N.Am.

Age—Juvs (Jun-Oct) resemble AHY ♀♀ in plumage aspect but have ss boldly fringed and marked buff, and rects soft, short (tl < 80 mm), and narrow (*cf.* Fig. 116**A**, p. 166). Juvs and most hatchlings can be sexed by pattern to the outer pp (Fig. 121); ovate region surrounding eye unfeathered in ♂♂ but with short feathers in ♀♀ (Woehler & Gates 1970); some juv back, breast, and/or flank feathers washed rufous or orange (green in *P.c. versicolor*) in ♂♂; see also Lassen et al. (1955) and Wentworth et al. (1967) for aspect differences in natal down, and Figures 22-23 (pp. 32-35) for cloacal characters reliable for sexing hatchlings and Juvs. See Greenberg et al. (1972) and Wishart (1969) for ageing by proximal pp length and shaft diameters on detached primaries. It is possible that measurements of the inner pp (e.g., p2; see Wishart 1969) or shaft diameter on live individuals may be useful for ageing many individuals, and iris color may also average paler cinnamon in HY/SYs and darker brown or orange in AHY/ASYs, but more study is needed. The following is reliable for ♂♂. Following the complete PF, most ♀♀ can only be aged by length of the bursa (Fig. 23, p. 34: 5-55 mm indicates HY/SY through Jan-Apr). Occasional ♀♀ with retained juv p10 (see below) can be aged HY/SY and ♀♀ with short spurs (Fig. 122**B-C**) are probably AHY/ASYs (if not ASY/ATYs); more study is needed to confirm this.

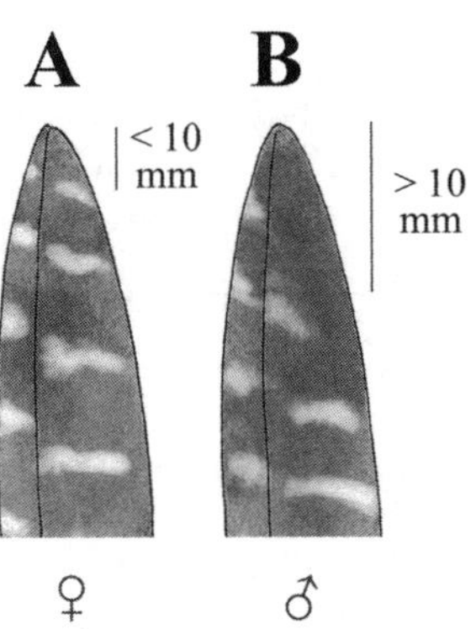

FIGURE 121. Pattern of pale bars to the juv outer primaries (particularly p9-p10) by sex in Ring-necked Pheasant. Measures represent the distance from the tip of the feather to the first pale bar on the inner web.

HY/SY ♂ (1st cycle, F1; Oct-Sep): Spur usually obtusely pointed, grayish, and < 10 mm in length through Jan-Jun (Fig. 122**A-B**, p. 172); plumage aspect sometimes suffused or washed buff. **Note: Look for occasional individuals (both sexes) to retain the juvenal outer p and/or p cov (*cf.* Fig. 115A, p. 165), that may be aged HY/SY as in other gamebirds.**

AHY/ASY ♂ (Def. cycle, DB; Oct-Sep): Spur usually sharply pointed, glossy blackish, and > 10 mm in length (Fig. 122**C-E**); plumage aspect fully colored, without buff suffusion or wash. **Note: See HY/SY. It is likely that ♂♂ with spurs > 13 mm (Fig. 122D-E) can be aged ASY/ATY or older but more study is needed to determine range of variation within each age group. See also Wild Turkey, p. 198).**

Sex—See **Age** for sexing of Juvs. Measurements (Table 13, p. 166) reliable for sexing (those of *P.c. versicolor* shorter by sex; see **Geographic variation**). Medial? BP (Fig. 20**A**, p. 31) and/or distended cloaca (Fig. 21, p. 32) indicates AHY ♀ in May-Jul. The following is reliable for all individuals in formative and basic plumages (see **Age** for criteria useful in sexing hatchlings and Juvs):

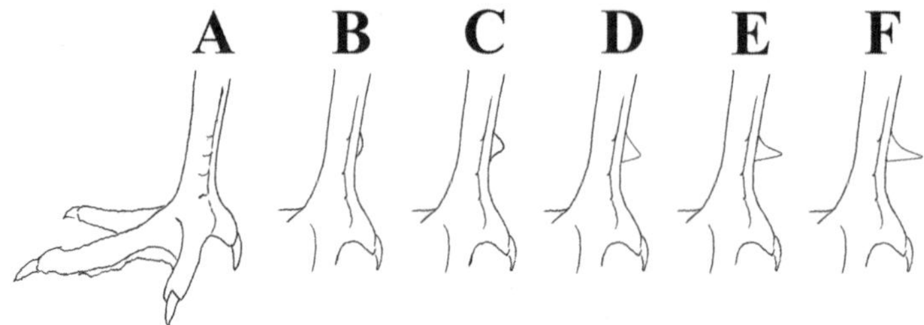

FIGURE 122. Variation in spur length and shape by age in Ring-necked Pheasant and Wild Turkey. Spurs are exhibited primarily by ♂, with juvs lacking spurs (**A**), HY/SY ♂ showing small spurs (**B**-**D**; < 10 mm in pheasants, 5-20 mm in turkeys), and AHY/ASY ♂ exhibiting larger spurs (**D**-**F**; > 10 mm in pheasants, 10-30 mm in turkeys). ♂ with very long spurs (**F** or greater; > 13 mm in pheasants, > 30 mm in turkeys) are probably older (ASY/ATY pheasants or ATY/A4Y turkeys). Occasional ♀♀ may develop small spurs as well (**B**-**C**; < 5 mm in pheasants, < 15 mm in turkeys) and these may also be ASY/ATYs; more study needed.

♀: Tail < 350 and tarsus < 68 (Table 13, p. 166); plumage aspect primarily brown; legs usually without spurs (Fig. 122**A**). **Note: Occasional older ♀♀ may acquire spurs and/or incomplete ♂-like plumage aspect; confirm sex of these with measurements and other criteria.**

♂: Tail > 350 and tarsus > 67 (Table 13); plumage aspect multi-colored and iridescent; AHYs with spurs (Fig. 122**B**-**F**). **Note: See ♀.**

Hybrids reported—Ring-necked Pheasants from naturalized populations with Black Grouse *Lyrurus tetrix* and Western Capercaillie *Tetrao urogallus* (McCarthy 2006), Ruffed Grouse (Bump et al. 1947, Peterle 1951), Dusky Grouse (Anthony 1899, Blackburn & Gray 1977, Hachisuka 1928, Hudson 1955, Jewett 1932, Johnsgard 1983a, Lincoln 1950), Greater Prairie-Chicken (Lincoln 1950, Peterle 1951), Wild Turkey (McCarthy 2006), and possibly Willow and Rock ptarmigan (McCarthy 2006) in the wild.

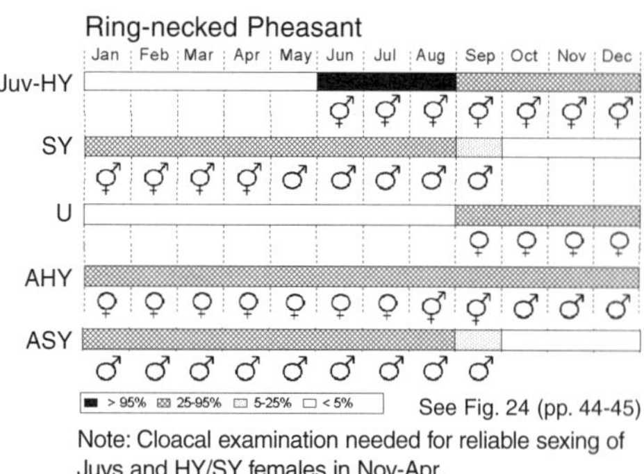

References—Bent (1932), Cramp & Simmons (1980), Dement'ev & Gladkov (1952), Domm (1939), Etter et al. (1970), Gates (1966), Giudice & Ratti (2001), Kabat et al. (1950), Kirkpatrick (1944), Linder et al. (1971), Linduska (1943, 1945), Marchant & Higgins (1993), Oberholser (1974), Papeschi et al. (2000, 2003), Petrides (1942, 1945), Roberts (1955), Stokes (1957), Thompson & Taber (1948), Wishart (1969), Wright & Hiatt (1943).

RUFFED GROUSE
Bonasa umbellus

RUGR
Species # 3000

Species—Juvs from other N.Am gamebirds by crown without cinnamon or rufous; upperparts with distinct spots and bars; rects without whitish tips; breast without distinct spots; flanks with distinct dark bars; tarsus feathering variably partial (as in adults; Fig. 123**B**-**D**) but feathers

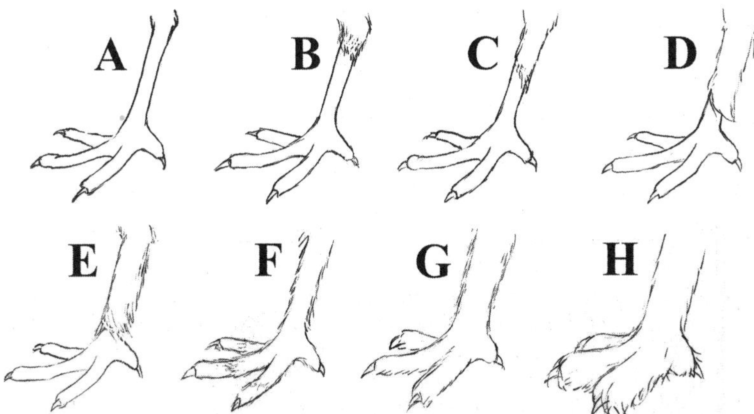

FIGURE 123. Variation in the extent of feathering to the tarsus in gamebirds, by species and subspecies (especially for Ruffed Grouse). See text for more information. In all species feathers become denser in winter than summer; in ptarmigan the density differs markedly (**G** in summer and **H** in winter). Note that chicks and Juvs show similar variation but feathers are downy plumaged in winter rather than filamentous.

downy. Non-juvs from other N.Am grouse by small size with proportionally long tarsus (Table 14, p. 176); tail usually with 18 rects and rounded (r1–r9 15-25 mm; HY/SY > AHY/ASY); sides of upper breast with fan-shaped, ornamental feathers but without inflatable sacs; rects with distinct dark brown subterminal band (*cf.* Fig. 125**D**-**F**, p. 175); tarsus partially feathered (Fig. 123**B**-**D**); toes with fleshy pectinations in Sep-Apr (Trainer 1947). Hazel Grouse (*B. bonasia*) of Eurasia, a possible escape in N.Am, is smaller (wg chord 159-187, tl 107-130, exp culmen 9.1-11.2, tarsus 31-36); tail usually with 16 rects; breast without ornamental feathers; throat partly to entirely black; breast mottled blackish.

Geographic variation—See Aldrich (1963), Aldrich & Friedmann (1943), Bailey (1941), Bangs (1912), Browning (2002), Conover (1935), Dickinson (1953), Godfrey (1986), Grinnell (1916), Hellmayr & Conover (1942), Hubbard & Banks (1970), Jewett et al. (1953), Ouellet (1990), Parkes (1954), Ridgway & Friedmann (1946), Rusch et al. (2000), Snyder & Shortt (1946), Swarth (1922), Todd (1940, 1947, 1963), Trainer (1947), Uttal (1941). No other subspecies occur. E. subspecies average slightly longer wing and tarsus and Pacific Coastal subspecies average longer toes and tarsus but these differences are unhelpful in subspecific determinations (Aldrich & Friedmann 1943). Note that some introduction of non-native subspecies has occurred (e.g., *B.u. umbelloides* to WA and CT, and *monticola* to MO; Long 1981) that may have influenced the characters of native subspecies.

Pacific Coastal (*P.u. sabini*) Group. Dark, brownish, tarsus ≤ 1/2 feathered (Fig. 123**B**-**C**).

B.u. brunnescens (res sw.BC): Upperparts dark brownish with little to no rufous or grayish wash; tail dark brownish tinged rufous to grayish; barring to flanks dark brownish and distinct; breast and abdomen without buff; unfeathered portion of tarsus 20-29 mm (Fig. 123**B**).

B.u. castenea (res coastal WA-nw.OR): Upperparts and tail dark chestnut with little or no grayish wash; barring to flanks dark brown and distinct; breast tinged buff; unfeathered portion of tarsus 16-29 mm (Fig. 123**B**-**C**).

B.u. sabini (res interior sc.BC-nw.CA): Upperparts medium-dark brown to bright rufous-brown without grayish; tail dark cinnamon to grayish; barring to flanks dark brown to chestnut and distinct; breast and abdomen washed buff; unfeathered portion of tarsus 16-29 mm (Fig. 123**B**-**C**).

Interior Western (*B.u. unbelloides*) Group. Pale, grayish, tarsus ≥ 1/2-feathered (Fig. 123**B**-**D**).

B.u. yukonensis (res AK to NWT-nw.Sask): Upperparts pale brownish gray; tail gray to brownish; barring to flanks dark brown and distinct; breast with little to no buff; abdomen whitish; unfeathered portion of tarsus 7-16 mm (Fig. 123**D**).

B.u. phaia (res sw.BC-ne.OR to w.MT): Upperparts medium pale grayish, dark grayish brown, or dark brownish; tail pale brown to grayish; barring to flanks dark brown and moderately distinct; breast washed buff; abdomen with little to no buff; unfeathered portion of tarsus 14-29 mm (Fig. 123**B**-**D**). Populations of e.WA-e.OR ("*affinis*" in part) may average browner and with less feathering on the tarsus than populations of ID-MT but differences are broadly clinal and confounded by polychromatism.

B.u. umbelloides (res BC-e.ID to Que): Upperparts medium grayish brown to brownish gray; tail grayish to clay-colored; barring to flanks dark brown and moderately indistinct; breast and abdomen without buff; unfeathered portion of tarsus 10-25 mm (Fig. 123**C**-**D**). Populations of interior BC ("*affinis*" in part) may average darker but differences slight, clinal, and confounded by polychromatism. Populations of Ont-Que ("*canescens*" or "*obscura*") average darker and populations of Lab-n.Quebec ("*labradorensis*") average darker, buffier, and with longer tarsi, but differences insufficient and due in part to intergradation with *togata*.

B.u. incana (res s.Sask-UT to ND-CO): Upperparts gray with brownish tinge and reduced white markings; tail pale gray to cinnamon; barring to flanks grayish brown and moderately indistinct; breast tinged buff; unfeathered portion of tarsus 12-22 mm (Fig. 123**C**-**D**).

Eastern (*B.u. unbellus*) Group. Medium dark, bright, tarsus < 1/2-feathered (Fig. 123**B**).

B.u. togata (res s.Ont-n.MN to Nfl-NH): Upperparts medium-dark brown tinged reddish or grayish; tail dark brownish to grayish; barring to flanks dark brown to chestnut and moderately distinct; breast and abdomen with little to no buff; unfeathered portion of tarsus 20-31 mm (Fig. 123**B**). Populations of NS ("*thayeri*") average slightly darker but difference is insufficient.

B.u. umbellus (res sw.MN-w.KS to se.MI-AR and w.NY-MA to e.MD): Upperparts medium-pale brown to cinnamon-brown, the head with slight to no grayish wash; tail clay-colored to grayish; barring to flanks brownish and indistinct; breast and abdomen washed buff; unfeathered portion of tarsus 19-32 mm (Fig. 123**B**). Populations of the w. (disjunct) portion of the range ("*mediana*") may average paler and grayer with slightly redder tails but differences insufficient and confounded by individual variation. Populations of Long I, NY ("*helmei*"), may average darker (less grayish) and with blacker streaks to the flanks but differences insignificant.

B.u. monticola (res montane se.MI-w.PA to nw.AL): Upperparts medium-dark brown to reddish brown, with little or no grayish wash; tail rufous or grayish; barring to flanks dusky brown and moderately indistinct; breast and abdomen washed buff; unfeathered portion of tarsus 19-34 mm (Fig. 123**B**).

Molt—CBS (CAS?). PF incomplete (Jun-Oct in HYs), DPB complete (May-Oct in AHYs); PA absent? See Family Account (p. 165) for replacement sequence of pp and (15-16) ss; rects are generally replaced proximally (r9 to r1) during the PF and distally (r1 to r9) during the DPB. The PF includes all feathers except the outer 2 pp (p9-p10) and p covs. Loss of feathers by breeding AHYs in Apr-May (likely related to thermoregulation) probably involves feathers not replaced until fall (Runkles 1989) and is thus part of the DPB rather than a DPA.

Age/Sex—Juvs (Jun-Sep) are like ♀♀ but plumage aspect buffier with less-distinct markings, outer web to ss barred buff, and rects short (tail < 90 mm) and narrow (*cf.* Fig. 116**A**-**B**, p. 166). Juv ♀ = ♂ by plumage aspect although see Figures 22-23 (pp. 32-35) for cloacal characters reliable for sexing hatchlings and Juvs. Medial BP (Fig. 20**A**, p. 31) and/or distended cloaca (Fig. 21, p. 32) indicates AHY ♀ in May-Jul. Measurements (especially tail length; see below) somewhat useful for sexing (Table 14, p. 176). See also Dorney & Holzer (1957), Davis (1968, 1969), and Rodgers (1979) for p shaft-width measurements, Fallon et al. (2006) for pentosidine accumulation in skin tissue, and Palmer (1959) for color differences in unfeathered skin above eye, that may assist with age and/or sex determinations.

HY/SY ♀ (1st cycle, F1; Oct-Sep): Tail length 118-141; outer 2 pp (p9-p10) contrastingly narrow, pointed, and worn (Fig. 115**A**, p. 165), p9 with less-distinct buff mottling than p8; p9 cov contrastingly narrow, pointed, and short (p8 cov – p9 cov often > 8 mm), often with buff shaft-streak or other markings (*cf.* Fig. 118**A**, p. 168); ornamental neck-feathers short (33-49 mm); rump feathers with single white dot (Fig. 124**A**); central rect (r1) with indistinct or no subterminal band (Fig. 125**B**-**C**); outer rect (r9) narrow (width at center of subterminal band area 18-23 mm) and rounded (Fig. 119**A**, p. 169).

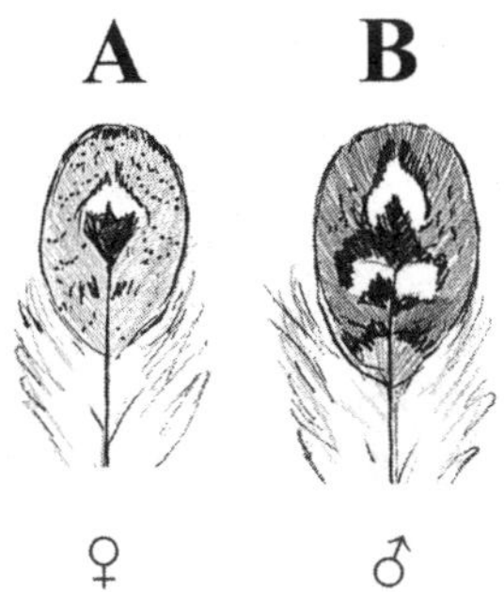

FIGURE 124. Pattern to the rump feathers by sex in Ruffed Grouse, with one pale mark in ♀ and 2-3 in ♂. The uppertail coverts show similar patterns but the feathers and marks are longer.

AHY/ASY ♀ (Def. cycle, DB; Oct-Sep): Tail length 125-148; outer pp uniformly broad and truncate (Fig. 115**B**), p9 and p8 with similar amounts of buff mottling; outermost p covs uniformly broad, rounded, and long (p8 cov – p9 cov often < 8 mm) and with few or no buff markings (*cf.* Fig. 118**B**); ornamental neck-feathers short (33-49 mm); rump feathers with single white dot (Fig. 124**A**); central rect (r1) with indistinct subterminal band (Fig. 125**C**-**D**); outer rect (r9) moderately narrow (width at center of subterminal band area 21-26 mm) and truncate (Fig. 119**B**).

HY/SY ♂ (1st cycle, F1; Oct-Sep): Tail length 139-172; outer pp and p covs as in HY/SY ♀ (Fig. 115**A**); ornamental neck-feathers long (51-76 mm); rump feathers with 2-3 white dots (Fig. 124**B**); central rect (r1) with partial to full subterminal band (Fig. 125**D**-**E**); outer rect (r9) moderately broad (width at center of subterminal band 23-29 mm) and rounded (Fig. 119**A**).

AHY/ASY ♂ (Def. cycle, DB; Oct-Sep): Tail length 146-171; outer pp and p covs as in AHY/ASY ♀ (Fig. 115**B**); ornamental neck-feathers long (51-76 mm); rump feathers with 2-3 white dots (Fig. 124**B**); central rect (r1) usually with full subterminal band (Fig. 125**E**-**F**); outer rect (r9) broad (width at center of subterminal band 27-34 mm) and truncate (Fig. 119**B**).

Hybrids reported—With Ring-necked Pheasant (p. 170), Spruce Grouse (Ouellet 1974) and Dusky Grouse (Tufts 1975) in the wild.

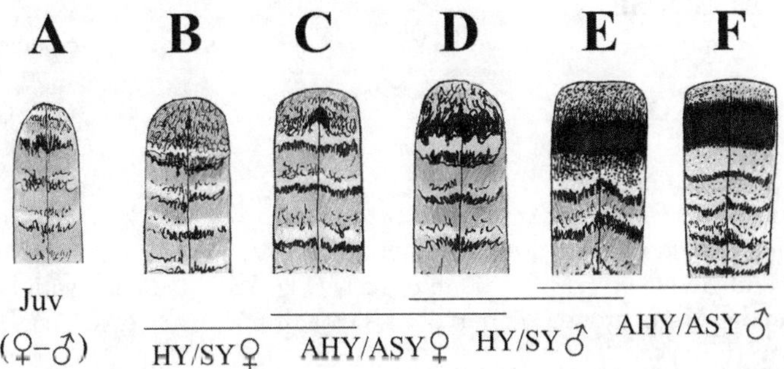

FIGURE 125. Variation in the subterminal band and other markings of the central rect (r1), by age and sex in Ruffed Grouse. The other rects (r2-r9) show fuller black bands (*cf.* **D**-**F**) in formative and basic feathers of both sexes.

References—Aldrich & Friedmann (1943), Bent (1932), Bump et al. (1947), Cramp & Simmons (1980), Dorney (1966), Dorney & Holzer (1957), Dwight (1900a), Garbutt & Middleton (1974), Hale et al. (1954), Palmer (1959), Petrides (1942, 1945), Ridgway & Friedmann (1946), Roberts (1955), Roussel & Ouellet (1975), Rusch et al. (2000), Servello & Kirkpatrick (1986), Short (1967), Wenstrom et al. (1972).

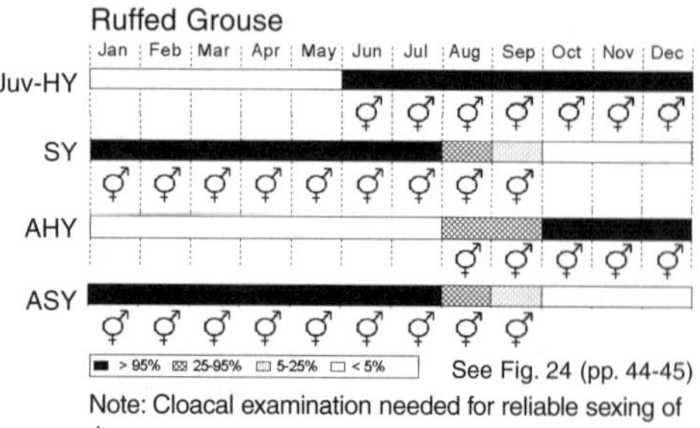

TABLE 14. Measurements (mm) of certain North American grouse to assist with identification and sexing. See pp. 4-11 for methods of measurement. Species summaries are in **bold**. Values were derived from 95% confidence intervals as based approximately on the indicated sample sizes (see pp. 4-5); thus midpoints of ranges approximate means, and S.D. is approximated by 25% of the range.[1]

Taxon/Sex	*n*	wing chord	tail length	exposed culmen	tarsus
Ruffed Grouse[2]		**167-191**	**139-171**	**12.9-16.4**	**49-67**
♀	100	167-186	118-148	12.9-15.2	37-46
♂	100	173-191	139-171	13.8-16.4	40-48
Greater Sage-Grouse[3]		**254-349**	**175-333**	**32.6-42.7**	**59-79**
♀	100	254-295	175-219	32.6-38.3	59-69
♂	100	303-349	276-363	37.2-42.7	69-79
Gunnison Sage-Grouse[3]		**239-310**	**160-328**	**24.6-35.5**	**55-73**
♀	100	239-266	160-202	24.6-30.7	55-63
♂	100	264-310	260-328	28.9-35.5	64-73
Spruce Grouse[2]		**164-194**	**94-144**	**12.8-20.7**	**31-39**
♀	100	164-190	94-122	12.8-20.0	31-38
♂	100	168-194	109-144	13.3-20.7	32-39

[1] Measurements pertain to birds in formative and definitive plumages; juveniles vary greatly in size but are substantially smaller.
[2] Measures represent all N.Am subspecies; see **Geographic variation**.
[3] Wing and tail lengths vary substantially between formative and definitive plumages; see Table 15.

GREATER SAGE-GROUSE
Centrocercus urophasianus

GRSG
Species # 3090

GUNNISON SAGE-GROUSE
Centrocercus minimus

GUSG
Species # 3091

Species—Juvs from juvs of other N.Am grouse by abdomen with black patch. Non-juv sage-grouse from other grouse by large size and stout bill (Table 14); tail with 16-20 (usually 18) acutely pointed and graduated (r1–r9 > 60 mm) rects (Fig. 127); abdomen with bold blackish patch (unique among N.Am grouse); undertail covs with distinct white tips; tarsus feathered to toes (Fig. 123**E**, p. 173).

Greater from Gunnison's sage-grouse by larger size (Tables 14-15), especially bill by tarsus (Fig. 126); black nuchal plumes of ♂♂ shorter (90-115 mm *vs* 120-173 mm in Gunnison when fully grown in Jan-Jun) and with more white at bases (> 20 mm *vs* < 20 mm in Gunnison); rects

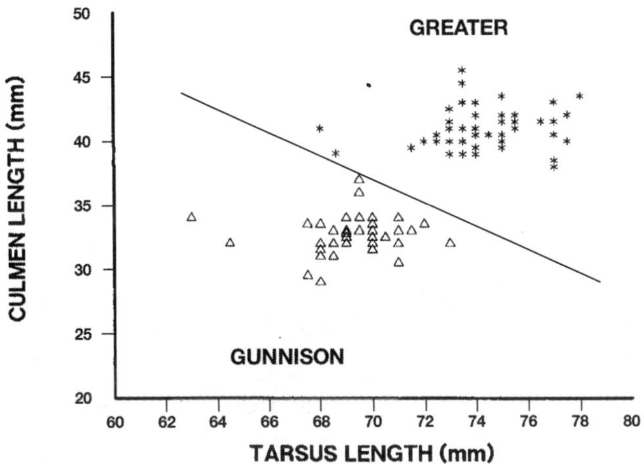

FIGURE 126. Exposed culmen vs. tarsus lengths in Greater and Gunnison sage-grouse for identification. Modified from Hupp and Braun (1991).

with less distinct pale bars (Fig. 127). See Hupp & Braun (1991) and Young et al. (1994, 2000) for more information on species determination among live sage-grouse.

Geographic variation—Both species considered monotypic here. Greater Sage-Grouse of WA-CA ("*C.u. phaios*") may average darker and perhaps slightly smaller but differences are insufficient. See Aldrich (1946b, 1963), Ottomeier & Crawford (1996), and Schroeder et al. (1999) for more information.

Molt—CAS. PF incomplete (Jun-Oct in HYs), DPA limited (May-Aug, in ♂♂ only?), DPB incomplete-complete (May-Oct in AHYs). See Family Account (p. 165) for replacement

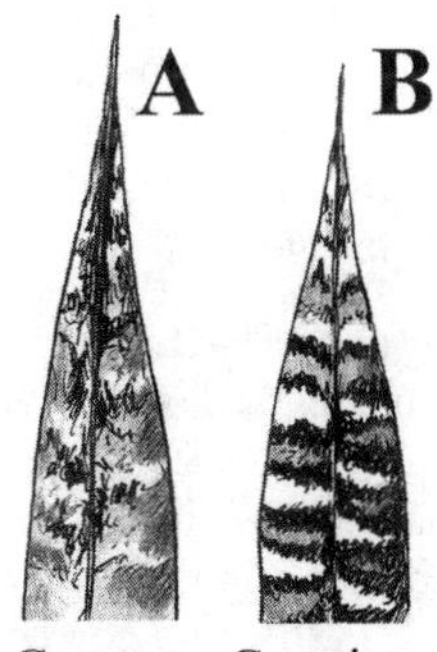

FIGURE 127. Pattern to the rectrices as reflected by the central rectrix (r1) in Greater (**A**) and Gunnison (**B**) sage-grouse.

TABLE 15. (Measurements mm) of Greater and Gunnison sage-grouse to assist with species, age, and sex determination. See pp. 4-11 for methods of measurement. Values were derived from 95% confidence intervals as based approximately on the indicated sample sizes (see pp. 4-5); thus midpoints of ranges approximate means, and S.D. is approximated by 25% of the range. See Table 14 for summary information.

	wing chord		tail length	
	HY/SY	AHY/ASY	HY/SY	AHY/ASY
Greater Sage-Grouse				
♀	254-285	264-295	175-206	188-219
♂	303-331	316-349	276-321	314-363
Gunnison Sage-Grouse				
♀	239-257	248-266	160-190	182-202
♂	264-297	275-310	260-298	289-328

sequence of pp and ss; rects are generally replaced proximally (r9 to r1) during both the DPF and the DPB. The PF includes all feathers except the outer 2 pp (p9-p10) and p covs; look for occasional HY/SYs to also retain s1. The DPA includes some to most feathers of the head, neck, and throat but does not involve replacement of ornamental plumes in ♂♂; more study need on the absence or presence of this molt in ♀♀. The PB2 and DPB can be incomplete in some AHYs, with p10 and up to 7 ss among s1-s2 and s7-s12 retained, especially in ♂♂.

Age—Juvs (Jun-Sep) are like ♀♀ in plumage aspect but have ss fringed and marked buff (*cf.* Fig. 140**A**, p. 191), and rects short (tail < 100 mm), soft, and narrow (*cf.* Fig. 116**A**, p. 166). Juv ♀=♂ by plumage aspect although see Figures 22-23 (pp. 32-35) for cloacal characters reliable for ageing and sexing (including hatchlings and Juvs), Ottomeier & Crawford (1996) for measurements of p4, and Patterson (1952), Eng (1955), and Dalke et al. (1963) for information on length of the bursa (Fig. 23, p. 34) by age.

HY/SY (1st cycle, F1-A1; Oct-Sep): Wing chord and tail length shorter by species and sex (Table 15); outer 2 pp (p9-p10) contrastingly narrow, pointed, and worn (Fig. 115**A**, p. 165), the outer web of p9 with buff mottling (Fig. 128**A**); p9 cov contrastingly narrow, pointed, short, and usually (especially ♀♀) with pale shaft-streak at tip (Fig. 129**A**); ss without retained feathers (except occasionally s1; see **Molt**); s3 sometimes with buff marks (*cf.* Fig. 140**A**, p. 191); throat of ♂ heavily mottled whitish in Jan-Jun.

AHY/ASY (Def. cycle, DB-DA; Oct-Sep): Wing chord and tail length longer by species and sex (Table 15); outer pp uniformly broad and truncate (Fig. 115**B**), the outer web of p9 without buff mottling (Fig. 128**B**); outermost p covs uniformly broad, rounded, long, and with white spots to tips of outer webs but no pale shaft-streaks (Fig. 129**B**); ss sometimes

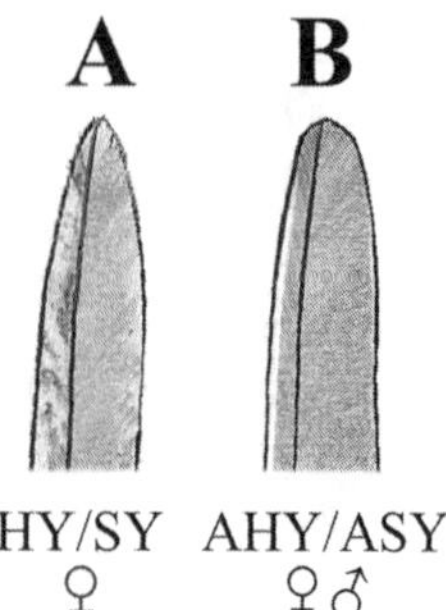

FIGURE 128. Pattern to the outer web of p9 by age and sex in sage-grouse. HY/SY ♂ can have either pattern or (often) something in between. There is usually noticeably more buff mottling on p9 than p8 in HY/SYs, whereas in AHY/ASYs these two pp appear to similarly lack buff. Similar patterns by age can be found in Spruce, Dusky, and Sooty grouse. Juv pp (**A**) are retained by SYs until the PB2 in Jul-Oct.

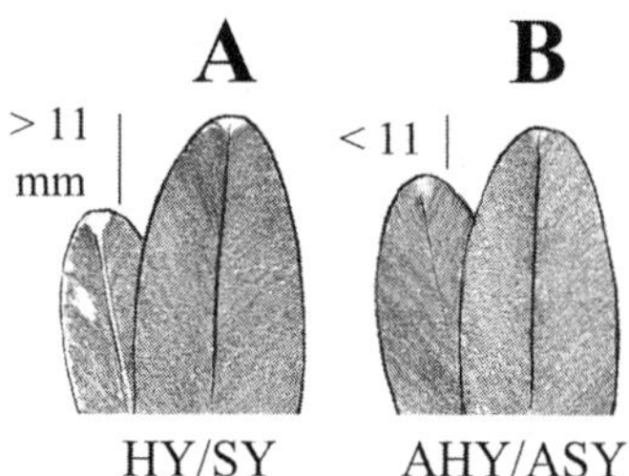

FIGURE 129. Shape, pattern, and morphology to outer primary coverts by age in sage-grouse. These are the coverts corresponding to p9 (left) and p8 (right); the outermost covert is vestigial. Measure indicates tip of p9 cov to tip of p8 cov. The patterning in HY/SY averages more pronounced in ♀ than in ♂. See also Figure 128. Similar patterns can be found in Spruce, Dusky, and Sooty grouse.

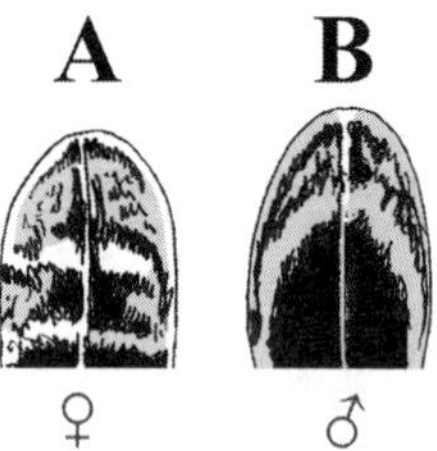

FIGURE 130. Pattern of the lesser coverts (and to some extent other secondary coverts) by sex in sage-grouse.

with retained feathers among p10, s1-s2, and/or s7-s12 (see **Molt**); s3 without buff marks (*cf.* Fig. 140**B**); throat of ♂ uniformly black in Jan-Jun. **Note: AHY/ASYs that retain p10 can possibly be aged to SY/TY or ASY/ATY by the age and condition of this feather; more study is needed.**

Sex—Medial BP (Fig. 20**A**, p. 31) and/or distended cloaca (Fig. 21, p. 32) indicates AHY ♀ in May-Jul. Measurements (especially tail and tarsal lengths) reliable for sexing each species (Tables 14-15). See Figures 22-23 (pp. 32-35) for cloacal characteristics useful in ageing and sexing (including Juvs).

♀: Wing, tail, and tarsal lengths shorter by species and age (Tables 14-15, pp. 176-177); les covs with bars and extensive buff mottling to edges (Fig. 130**A**); throat grayish to whitish, without black; breast brownish, without specialized plumes or inflatable pouches; longer undertail covs usually with buff marks proximal to white tips.

♂: Wing, tail, and tarsal lengths longer by species and age (Tables 14-15); les covs without bars but with buff subterminal fringe (Fig. 130**B**); throat entirely (Oct-Apr) or partially (May-Sep) black; breast completely or partially white and with attenuated plumes and inflatable pouches at sides; longer undertail covs without buff marks proximal to white tips.

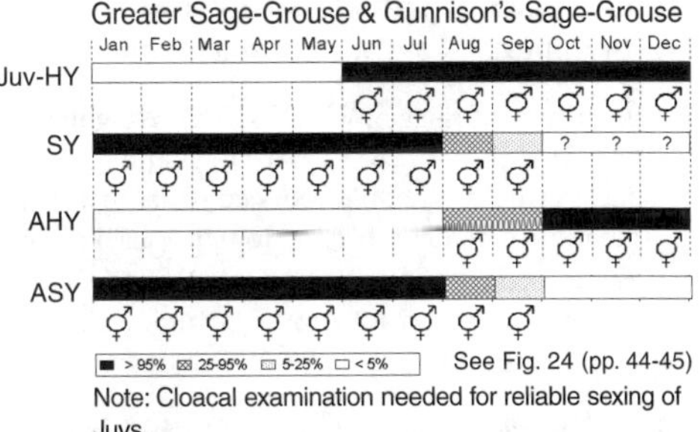

Hybrids reported—Greater Sage-Grouse with Dusky Grouse (Rensel & White 1988) and Sharp-tailed Grouse (Aldridge et al. 2001, Eng 1971, Johnsgard 1981a, Behle 1985, Kohn & Kobriger 1986) in the wild.

References—Beck et al. (1975), Bent (1932), Brooks (1930), Crunden (1963), Dalke et al. (1963), Dwight (1900a), Eng (1955), Girard (1937), Patterson (1952), Petrides (1942, 1945), Pyle (2007), Ridgway & Friedmann (1946), Short (1967), Young et al. (2000).

SPRUCE GROUSE

Falcipennis canadensis

SPGR
Species # 2980

Species—Juvs from other N.Am gamebirds by crown washed cinnamon; upperparts with small and indistinct spots and bars; rects with whitish tips; breast dark buff with distinct spots; flanks without distinct dark bars; tarsus feathering as in adults (Fig. 123**F**, p. 173) but feathers downy. Non-juvs from other grouse by small size, especially tail and tarsus lengths (Table 14, p. 176); tail usually with 16 rects and rounded (r1–r8 10-30 mm; HY/SY > AHY/ASY); plumage aspect without bright white; head often with thin white eyeline and subauricular streak; sides of breast without ornamental feathers or substantial inflatable sacs; rects dark brown to blackish, with chestnut tips in n.populations (see **Geographic variation**); tarsus and proximal half of toes feathered (Fig. 123**F**).

Geographic variation—See Aldrich (1963), Dickerman & Gustafson (1996), Gibson & Kessel (1997), Grinnell (1910), Hellmayr & Conover (1942), Jewett et al. (1953), Rand (1946, 1948b), Ridgway & Friedmann (1946), Swarth (1922), Uttal (1939). No other subspecies occur. Beware of foxing in older specimens, emphasizing brown aspect. In addition to the following, size (*cf.* Table 14, p. 176) is slightly clinal, n.populations being longer-winged but shorter-tailed than s.populations, but this difference is generally unhelpful for subspecific determinations.

Canadian (*F.c. canadensis*) Group. Grayish to sooty; lateral rects usually with broad chestnut tips; longer uppertail covs with indistinct whitish or gray tips.

F.c. canadensis (res w.AK-c.BC to Nfl-c.Que): Lateral rects blackish, usually with chestnut tips; longest uppertail covs with narrow whitish to gray tips by age (Fig. 131**A-B**); ♀ medium-dark with moderate cinnamon barring to upper back; ♂ with upperpart fringing gray, slightly tinged olive. ♀♀ of w.AK-NWT to n.BC-n.Sask ("*osgoodi*") average grayer and populations of sc.AK (Bristol Bay to Prince William Sound; "*atratus*") may average darker and grayer but differences are slight and confounded by plumage-aspect dichromatism.

F.c. canace (res s.Man-n.MN to NB-n.NY): Lateral rects and longest uppertail covs as in *canadensis* (Fig. 131**A-B**); ♀ pale with substantial bright cinnamon barring to back; ♂ with upperpart fringing gray without olive. ♀♀ of NB-NS ("*torridus*") may average redder but difference, if present, insufficient and confused by dichromatism.

Franklin's *(F.c. franklinii)* Group. Brownish; lateral rects with thin or no chestnut tips; longer uppertail covs with distinct white tips.

F.c. isleibi (res Prince of Wales Is, AK): Wing may average shorter but tail longer than *franklinii* (wg chord 168-170, tl ♂ 114-128, ♀ 98-105); lateral rects blackish, with little or no chestnut in tips; longest uppertail covs with distinct but reduced white tips (1-4 mm wide in ♂) by age (*cf.* Fig. 131**C-D**); ♀ dark with little to no cinnamon barring to upper back; ♂ with upperpart fringing dark olive-gray.

F.c. franklinii (res c.BC-sc.Alb to n.OR-nw.WY): Lateral rects as in *isleibi*; longest uppertail covs with distinct and extensive white tips (6-11 mm wide in ♂) by age (Fig. 131**C-D**); ♀ as in *isleibi*; ♂ with upperpart fringing dark gray without olive tinge.

Molt—CBS. PF incomplete (Jun-Oct in HYs), DPB complete (Jun-Oct in AHYs); PA absent. See Family Account (p. 165) for replacement sequence of pp and (17) ss; the rects are generally replaced proximally (within r8-r2 with r1 often replaced earlier and r9 often replaced later) during the PF and distally (r1 to r9) during the DPB. The PF includes all feathers except the outer 2 pp (p9-p10) and p covs. Reports that juvenal feathers can be retained in the head through the PB2 (Parkes 1954) requires verification; these may represent earlier-replaced formative feathers with juvenal characteristics.

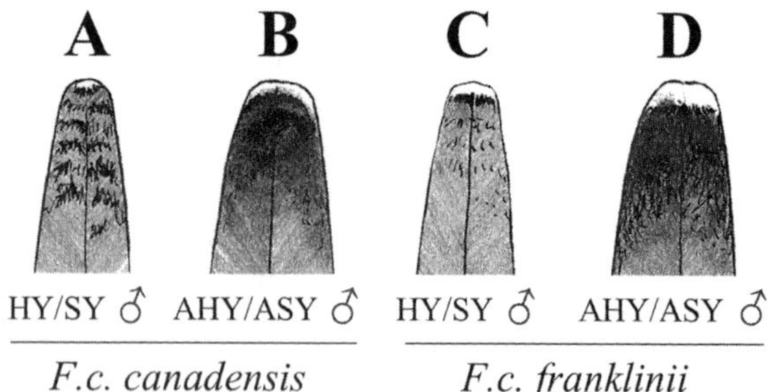

FIGURE 131. Pattern to the uppertail coverts by subspecies and age in ♂ Spruce Grouse. ♀ show similar patterns regarding the white tips but have more patterning to bases of feathers. The subspecies *F.c. isleibi* of the Franklin's group has distinct white tips narrower than those shown in **C-D**.

Age/Sex—Juv (Jun-Sep) is like ♀♀ but plumage aspect buffier with more distinct pale shaft-streaks to upperparts and dark spots on breast, outer web to ss barred buff (*cf.* Fig. 140**A**, p. 191), and rects short (tail < 60) and narrow (*cf.* Fig. 116**A-B**, p. 166). Juv ♀ = ♂ but see Figures 22-23 (pp. 32-35) for cloacal characters reliable for sexing hatchlings and Juvs. Medial BP (Fig. 20**A**, p. 31) and/or distended cloaca (Fig. 21, p. 32) indicates AHY ♀ in May-Jul. Measurements (except tail) unhelpful for sexing (Table 14, p. 176). See also McKinnon (1983), Szuba et al. (1987), and Boag & Schroeder (1992) for shaft-width measurements of detached primaries and other feathers, possibly useful for age and sex determinations of live individuals.

HY/SY ♀ (1st cycle, F1; Oct-Sep): Throat, breast, and bases to rects barred; supercilium without air sacs; outer 2 pp (p9-p10) contrastingly narrow, pointed, and worn (Fig. 115**A**, p. 165), p9 with substantial buff mottling to outer web (*cf.* Fig. 128**A**, p. 178); p9 cov contrastingly narrow, pointed, and short (p8 cov – p9 cov often > 7 mm), often with buff shaft streak or other markings (Fig. 129**A**, p. 178); s3 sometimes with buff marks (*cf.* Fig. 140**A**, p. 191); longer uppertail covs narrow and with less distinct pale tips by subspecies (*cf.* Fig. 131**A**, **C**); rects narrow (width of r2 15-18 mm) and rounded (Fig. 119**A**, p. 169).

AHY/ASY ♀ (Def. cycle, DB; Oct-Sep): Throat, breast, and bases to rects barred; supercilium without air sacs; outer pp uniformly broad and truncate (Fig. 115**B**), p9 with slight buff mottling to outer web (Fig. 128**B**); outermost p covs uniformly broad, rounded, long (p8 cov – p9 cov often < 7 mm), and with few or no buff markings (Fig. 129**B**); s3 without buff marks (*cf.* Fig. 140**B**); longer uppertail covs broad and with more distinct pale tips by subspecies (*cf.* Fig. 131**B**, **D**); rects moderately narrow (width of r2 17-21 mm) and truncate (Fig. 119**B**).

HY/SY ♂ (1st cycle, F1; Oct-Sep): Throat, breast, and bases to rects blackish; supercilium with red air sacs in Mar-Jul; outer 2 pp and p covs and s3 as in HY/SY ♀ (Figs. 115**A**, 128**A**, & 129**A**; *cf.* Fig. 140**A**); longer uppertail covs narrow and with less distinct pale tips by subspecies (Fig. 131**A**, **C**); rects moderately narrow (width of r2 17-21 mm) and rounded (Fig. 119**A**).

AHY/ASY ♂ (Def. cycle, DB; Oct-Sep): Throat, breast, and bases to rects black; supercilium with bright red air sacs in Mar-Jul; outer pp and p covs and s3 as in AHY/ASY ♀; (Figs. 115**B**, 128**B**, and 129**B**; *cf.* Fig. 140**B**) longer uppertail covs broad and with more distinct pale tips by subspecies (Fig. 131**B**, **D**); rects broad (width of r2 20-25 mm) and truncate (Fig. 119**B**).

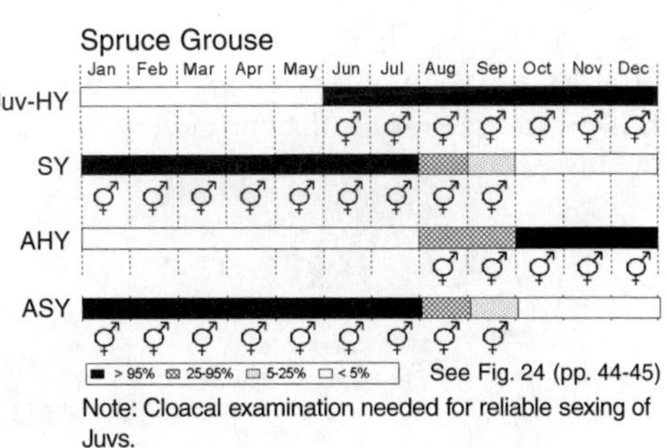

Hybrids reported—Spruce Grouse (*F.c. canadensis* group) with Ruffed Grouse (p. 172), Willow Ptarmigan (Lincoln 1950, Lumsden 1969, Taverner 1930a), and Dusky Grouse (Johnsgard 1981a); and Spruce Grouse (*franklinii* group) with Dusky Grouse (Jollie 1955).

References—Bent (1932), Boag & Schroeder (1992), Dwight (1900a), Ellison (1968), Lumsden & Weeden (1963), Parkes (1954), Petrides (1942, 1945), Ridgway & Friedmann (1946), Roberts (1955), Robinson (1980), Short (1967), Zwickel & Martinsen (1967).

WILLOW PTARMIGAN WIPT
Lagopus lagopus Species # 3010

ROCK PTARMIGAN ROPT
Lagopus mutus Species # 3020

WHITE-TAILED PTARMIGAN WTPT
Lagopus mutus Species # 3050

Species—Ptarmigan from other N.Am grouse by medium-small size with short bill and tarsus (Table 16, p. 185); tail with 14 rects (plus two medial feathers resembling rects, here considered modified uppertail coverts) and rounded (r1-r7 5-20 mm; HY/SY > AHY/ASY); pp, ss, and distal wing covs white in all plumages; tarsi and feet completely feathered (Fig. 123**G**-**H**, p. 173).

Willow from other ptarmigan by larger size (Table 16), bill stout (Fig. 132**A**); outer pp often with distinct dusky shafts and moderate to extensive dark mottling to webs (Figs. 134**B**-**G** & 137**A**, **C**, p. 187; see **Geographic variation**); rects primarily blackish; lores in basic plumage (Oct-Mar) white (Fig. 135**A**, p. 184); non-basic plumages primarily rufous or chestnut and/or brown tinged reddish (Fig. 133**A**).

Rock from other ptarmigan by medium size (Table 16), bill slender (Fig. 132**B**); outer pp sometimes with distinct dusky shafts and occasionally with reduced dark mottling to webs (Figs. 134**C**-**H** & 137**B**, **D**); rects primarily blackish; lores in basic plumage (Oct-Mar) usually with blackish (Fig. 135); non-basic plumages variably blackish, reddish brown, or clay-colored with heavy blackish vermiculation and/or grayish to buff with little to no reddish (Fig. 133**B**).

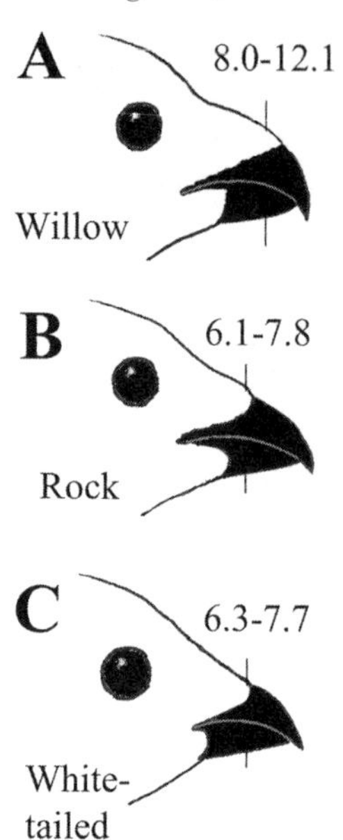

FIGURE 132. Bill shape and depth by species in Ptarmigan. Measures indicate bill depth at distal end of nares (Fig. 8**C**, p. 10). AHY/ASYs and ♂ average slightly thicker bills than HY/SYs and ♀ (*cf.* Table 16). See also Figure 135 (p. 184).

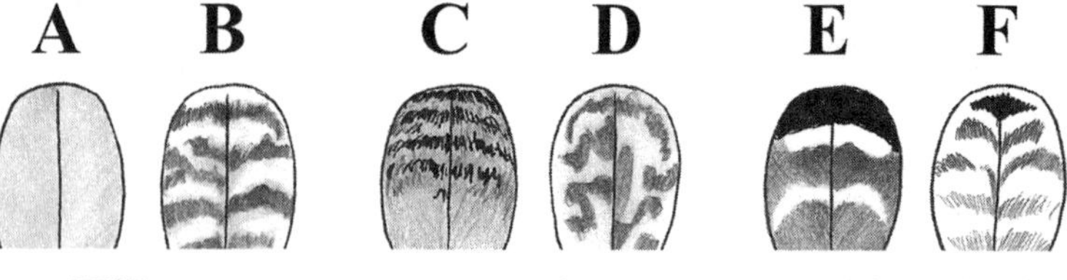

FIGURE 133. Typical patterns of supplemental (left) and alternate (right) body feathers in ptarmigan, emphasizing species-specific differences. Coloration various substantially for supplemental feathers but is generally rufous in Willow Ptarmigan; pale brown or reddish brown to dusky in Rock Ptarmigan; and dusky and white in White-tailed Ptarmigan (see text for more details). Alternate feathers are more similar in aspect across species, generally being buff and brownish. Despite the sex-specific sequence in plumage aspects (♀ are in alternate plumage in May-Jul and supplemental plumage Jul-Aug; ♂♂ in supplemental plumage in Apr-May and alternate plumage in Jun-Aug), plumage-aspect patterns are similar by season (Pyle 2007).

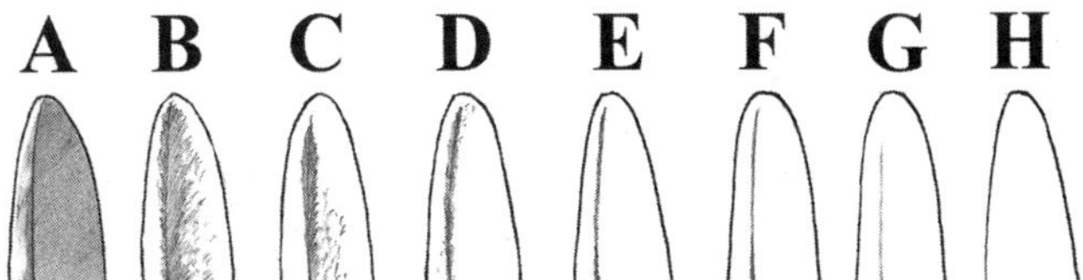

FIGURE 134. Variation in the amount of dusky mottling and/or dark shaft to the tip of p8 in ptarmigan by species, subspecies, and age. The juv p8, which is replaced in Aug-Oct in HYs in all three species, resembles **A**. Thereafter, formative feathers (in HY/SYs) average more dusky mottling and darker shafts than basic feathers (in AHY/ASYs) and, age-for-age, Willow and Rock ptarmigans (**B**-**G**) average more dusky mottling and darker shafts than White-tailed Ptarmigan (**D**-**H**), but there is also substantial geographic variation. See text for details.

White-tailed Ptarmigan from other ptarmigan species by smaller size (Table 16), bill slender (Fig. 132**C**); outer pp with white to pale dusky shafts and occasionally with reduced dark mottling to webs (Figs. 134**D**-**H** & 136**B**, **D**); rects white (rarely blackish; Scott 1984); lores in basic plumage (Oct-Mar) without blackish (Fig. 135**A**); non-basic plumages blackish with buff bars, spots, and vermiculation (Fig. 133**C**).

Geographic variation: White-tailed Ptarmigan here considered monotypic (see Braun et al. 1993). Compared to most Canadian populations, those of sc.AK ("*L.l. peninsularis*") may average paler and grayer in Apr-Sep, those of Vancouver I, BC ("*saxatalis*") may average larger and longer-billed, those of c.WA ("*rainierensis*") may average paler and grayer in Apr-Sep, and those of MT-NM ("*altipetens*") may average larger, shorter-billed, and with coarser black markings in Apr-Sep but in all cases differences are slight, broadly clinal, confounded by individual variation, and complicated by the different plumage aspects displayed by this genus (see **Molt** and **Sex**). See Chapman (1902), Cowan (1939), Hellmayr & Conover (1942), Osgood (1901), Ridgway & Friedmann (1946), Swarth (1912), and Taylor (1920) for more information. An understanding of molt and plumage-aspect changes by sex (see **Molt** and **Sex**) is needed to assess variation among Willow and Rock ptarmigans. In the following accounts descriptions of non-basic plumages includes supplemental (Feb-Jul in ♂ and Jul-Sep in ♀) and alternate (Apr-Jul in ♀, Jul-Sep in ♂) plumage aspects.

Willow Ptarmigan

See Cramp & Simmons (1980), Dement'ev & Gladkov (1952), Gabrielson & Lincoln (1949), Gibson & Kessel (1997), Grinnell (1909), Hannon et al. (1998), Hellmayr & Conover (1942), Portenko (1972), Ridgway & Friedmann (1946), Riley (1911), Swarth (1924, 1926), Taverner (1930b), Todd (1963), West et al. (1970). Ten other subspecies occur in Eurasia. Individuals from Norway (*L.l. lagopus*) introduced to MI in 1905-1906, probably did not survive to interbreed with native populations (Long 1981). In addition to the following, size (*cf.* Table 16, p. 185) is slightly clinal, wing length increasing and tail length decreasing from sw-ne.populations (e.g., West et al. 1970), but (except for wg chord in *L.l. leucopterus*; see below) these differences are small and broadly overlapping.

L.l. alexandrae (res coastal sw.AK-nw.BC): Bill medium-wide (width at gape ♀ 12.1-13.7, ♂ 13.2-14.8); pp with distinct blackish shafts (shaft to p4 1/2 to 3/4 dusky at base) and sometimes with moderate dark mottling to webs (Fig. 134**D**-**F**); non-basic plumage aspect medium-dark rufous and/or brownish to reddish with fine blackish markings. Populations of the c.Aleutian Is ("*muriei*") may average paler and brighter reddish in non-basic plumages but differences (if present) insufficient or based on mislabeled specimens.

L.l. alascensis (br & wint n-sc.AK to sw.Yuk): Bill medium-wide (width at gape ♀ 12.0-13.5, ♂ 13.0-14.7); pp with indistinct brownish shafts (shaft to p4 white to 1/3 dusky at base) with little to no dark mottling to webs (Fig. 134**G**); non-basic plumage aspect medium-bright rufous and/or reddish brown with moderately coarse blackish markings.

L.l. albus (br & wint ne.AK-c.BC to sc.Que; vagrant to MT-ME): Bill slender (width at gape ♀ 10.7-13.0, ♂ 11.5-13.9); pp with distinct dusky shafts (shaft to p4 white to 1/3-2/3 dusky at base) but with little or no dark mottling to webs (Fig. 134**E-F**); shafts to ss white; non-basic plumage aspect medium-bright rufous and/or reddish brown with moderately coarse blackish markings. **Note: This subspecies may not be distinguishable from L.l. lagopus of w.Europe (Hellmayr & Conover 1942, Dickinson 1952).**

L.l. leucopterus (br & wint Nunavut): Wing averages longer than in other species (wg chord ♀ 187-205 ♂ 196-216); bill broad (width at gape ♀ 12.3-14.0, ♂ 13.2-15.0); pp with indistinct on no brownish shafts (shaft to p4 white to 1/3 dusky at base) with little to no dark mottling to webs (Fig. 134**F-G**); shafts to ss white; non-basic plumage aspect medium-dark rufous and/or reddish brown with moderately coarse blackish markings.

L.l. ungavus (br & wint n.Que-Lab): Bill broad (width at gape ♀ 12.5-14.3, ♂ 13.4-15.3); pp with brownish shafts (shaft to p4 to 3/4 dusky at base) with little to some dark mottling to webs (Fig. 134**D-F**); shafts to ss white; non-basic plumage aspect medium-dark rufous and/or reddish brown to grayish brown with moderately coarse blackish markings.

L.l. alleni (res Nfl): Bill medium-slender (width at gape ♀ 11.7-13.1, ♂ 12.2-14.3); pp with distinct dusky shafts (shaft to p4 3/4 to fully dusky at base) with substantial dark mottling to webs (Fig. 134**B-C**); shafts to ss usually with dusky bases; non-basic plumage aspect bright, medium-pale rufous and/or dark brown with reddish barring and vermiculation.

Rock Ptarmigan

See Bent (1912), Browning (1979a), Clark (1907), Cramp & Simmons (1980), Dement'ev & Gladkov (1952), Gabrielson & Lincoln (1951, 1953a), Gibson & Kessel (1997), Grinnell (1909), Hantzsch (1929), Hellmayr & Conover (1942), Holder & Montgomerie (1993), Jacobsen et al. (1983), Murie (1944), Ridgway & Friedmann (1946), Swarth (1924, 1926), Taverner (1928), Todd (1963). Approximately 18 other subspecies occur in Greenland, Iceland, and Eurasia. Size among N.Am subspecies shows little variation (Ridgway & Friedmann 1946) and is unhelpful for subspecific determinations. Many individuals in formative and basic plumage (Oct-Mar) cannot be identified to subspecies, although proportions of dark feathers in basic plumage (see **Molt** for Willow Ptarmigan) may be higher in coastal and insular than in continental populations.

L.m. evermanni (res Attu I, Aleutian Is, AK): Bill slightly stouter than other subspecies (bill depth at base 7.2-8.3 mm); outer pp with pale brown shaft and little to no dusky mottling (Fig. 134**G**, p. 183); non-basic plumage aspect blackish brown (sometimes tinged rufous) and/or brownish with thick blackish bars (usually 4-5 mm wide on lower scapulars).

L.m. townsendi (res Kiska I, Aleutian Is, AK): Outer pp with dusky shaft and substantial dusky mottling (Fig. 134**C-D**); non-basic plumage

FIGURE 135. Variation in the extent of black in the lores of basic-aspect Rock Ptarmigan by age and sex. Entirely white lores (**A**) are found in all Willow and White-tailed ptarmigan but only in some HY/SY ♀ Rock Ptarmigan. Among Rock Ptarmigan, slight blackish mottling is found in some HY/SY ♀, some AHY/ASY ♀, and some HY/SY ♂; extensive blackish mottling (**C**) is found in some AHY/ASY ♀, some HY/SY ♂, and some AHY/ASY ♂; and completely black lores (**D**) are found only in some AHY/ASY ♂.

aspect dull buff to grayish with fine blackish vermiculation and/or brownish with moderately thin blackish bars (usually 2-4 mm wide on lower scapulars). Populations of Amchitka I ("*gabrielsoni*") may average browner and with more and broader black bars in non-basic plumage aspect but differences are insufficient.

L.m. atkhensis (res Atka I, Aleutian Is, AK): Outer pp with dusky shaft and little to some dusky mottling (Fig. 134**D-F**); non-basic plumage aspect dull buff to grayish with fine blackish vermiculation and/or brownish with thin blackish bars (usually 1-3 mm wide on lower scapulars). Populations of Tanaga I ("*sanfordi*") may average paler and grayer and populations of Adak I ("*chamberlaini*") may average darker and grayer in non-basic plumage aspects but differences are insufficient.

L.m. nelsoni (res n.AK-e.Aleutian Is to w.NWT; also e.Siberia): Outer pp with dusky shaft and little to no dusky mottling (Fig. 134**E-F**); non-basic plumage aspect blackish with olive-brown to reddish vermiculation and/or brownish with moderately thin blackish bars (usually 2-4 mm wide on lower scapulars). Populations of Yunaskensa I, Aleutian Is ("*yunaskensis*"), may average paler and grayer and populations of the Montague Is, sc.AK ("*kelloggae*"), may average darker and with coarser blackish markings but differences are slight and confounded by individual variation.

L.m. dixoni (res coastal se.AK-nw.BC): Outer pp with dusky shaft and little to no dusky mottling (Fig. 134**E-F**); non-basic plumage aspect blackish brown with fine pale brown vermiculation and/or brownish with thick blackish bars (usually 4-5 mm wide on lower scapulars).

L.m. rupestris (res n.NWT-c.BC to Nunavut-Lab): Outer pp with indistinct brownish to white shaft and no dusky mottling (Fig. 134**G-H**); non-basic plumage aspect blackish with fine brownish to grayish vermiculation and/or grayish brown with thick blackish bars (usually 4-5 mm wide on lower scapulars).

L.m. captus (res n.Ellesmere I, Nunavut; also n.Greenland): Outer pp with white shaft and no dusky mottling (Fig. 134**H**); non-basic plumage aspect brownish with fine blackish vermiculation and/or pale brownish with thin blackish bars (usually 1-3 mm wide on lower scapulars).

L.m. welchi (res Nfl): Outer pp with dusky shaft and substantial dusky mottling (Fig. 134**B-C**); non-basic plumage aspect blackish brown with substantial gray vermiculation and/or pale brown with moderately thin blackish bars (usually 2-4 mm wide on lower scapulars).

Molt—CAS. PFa absent-limited? (Jun-Jul in HYs), PF incomplete (Jul-Oct in HYs), DPS in AHY ♂♂ limited-incomplete (Feb-May), DPA in AHY ♂♂ limited-incomplete (Jul-Sep), DPA in AHY ♀♀ partial-incomplete (Apr-Jun), DPS in AHY ♀♀ limited (Jul-Sep), DPB complete (Jun-Oct in AHYs). See Pyle (2007) for molt terminology including explanation of a novel sex-specific sequence to the DPS and DPA. The auxilliary PF (PS1?), if present, includes scattered body

TABLE 16. Measurements (mm) of North American ptarmigan to assist with identification and sexing. See pp. 4-11 for methods of measurement. Species summaries are in **bold**. Values were derived from 95% confidence intervals as based approximately on the indicated sample sizes (see pp. 4-5); thus midpoints of ranges approximate means, and S.D. is approximated by 25% of the range.[1]

Taxon/Sex	*n*	wing chord[1]	tail length[1]	culmen from dist. nares	tarsus
Willow Ptarmigan[2,3]		**168-210**	**95-135**	**8.7-12.8**	**37-47**
♀	100	168-204	95-123	8.7-12.0	37-44
♂	100	181-210	109-135	9.4-12.8	39-47
Rock Ptarmigan[3]		**168-191**	**85-124**	**8.2-11.5**	**33-41**
♀	100	168-191	85-114	8.2-10.8	33-39
♂	100	178-202	95-124	8.9-11.5	35-41
White-tailed Ptarmigan		**168-201**	**86-124**	**7.9-11.1**	**30-37**
♀	100	168-190	86-113	7.9-11.1	30-35
♂	100	178-201	96-124	8.7-11.8	31-37

[1] Measurements pertain to birds in formative and definitive plumages, juveniles vary greatly in size but are substantially smaller.

[2] Wing chord excludes *L.l. leucopterus*; see **Geographic variation**.

[3] Measures represent N.Am populations only (see **Geographic variation**).

feathers; alternatively, this replacement may represent later-acquired juvenal feathers with formative-like aspect (see pp. 14-15); more study needed. See Family Account (p. 165) for replacement sequence of pp and ss; the rects are generally replaced proximally (r8 to r1) during both the PF and the DPB. The PF includes all feathers except the outer 2 pp (p9-p10) and p covs.

The DPS in ♂♂ is variable, including few to no upperpart and throat feathers in some high-arctic populations (*cf.* Montgomerie et al. 2001) and up to all upperpart and breast feathers in some individuals of other populations. The DPA in ♀♀ is similar in timing to the DPS of ♂♂ but averages much more extensive, including most to all body feathers, the modified central uppertail covs, up to half the proximal wing covs, and 1-5 inner ss (replaced proximally). The DPA in ♂♂ is similar in extent to that of ♀♀, although occurring later in the season; some feathers of the breast and back replaced during the DPS may not be replaced again. The DPS in ♀♀ occurs at the same time as the DPA in ♂♂ but is much less extensive, including scattered feathers of the head, back, and breast. Due to differing hormonal cycles, alternate feathers in both sexes are similar in aspect (despite being replaced at different times of the season), generally brownish heavily mottled with black, buff, and white to provide camouflage (Fig. 133, p. 182). Similarly, supplemental feathers are also similar in aspect despite being replaced at different times of the season, generally being reddish and plain in Willow Ptarmigan or highly vermiculated in Rock and White-tailed ptarmigans (Fig. 133). See **Geographic variation** for further descriptions of this plumage aspect by taxon.

In both sexes the DPB can commence (with replacement of inner pp) before the DPS (♀) or DPA (♂) has completed. Formative and basic plumage is usually completely white in both sexes; however, occasional individuals may display darker feathers, which could represent earlier-replaced basic feathers displaying atypical aspect (see p. 29); this perhaps may occur more frequently in SYs and/or non-breeding ASYs.

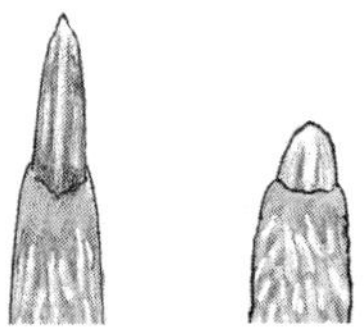

Age—Juvs (Jun-Sep) have buff body plumage; pp, ss, and p covs (except for whitish p9-p10 and corresponding p covs) dark brown, often with white fringes (Fig. 134**A**); rects short (tail < 80 mm), narrow, and brownish with buff barring (*cf.* Fig. 116**A**, p. 166); and toenails without grooves gained from shedding during winter (Fig. 136**A**; see Petrides 1942). Juv ♀ = ♂ by plumage aspect but see Figures 22-23 (pp. 32-35) for cloacal characters reliable for sexing hatchlings and Juvs. In addition to the following, see Fig. 135 (p. 184) for variation in lore color by age and sex in Rock Ptarmigans, that can assist with more accurate ageing in Oct-May.

FIGURE 136. Shape and length of the toenails in Jul-Oct, by age, in ptarmigan. AHYs shed the toenails in summer and exhibit short or growing nails during Jul-Oct (Stejneger (1884). By Nov, the toenails of both age groups are similar in shape and length. Petrides (1942) also reported that AHY/ASYs have grooves in the toenails (a result of replacement) that HY/SYs lack, but this could not be confirmed with specimen examination; more study is needed.

HY/SY (1st cycle, F1-S1-A1; Oct-Sep): Outer 2 pp (p9-p10) contrastingly narrow, pointed, lacking gloss (Fig. 115**A**, p. 165), and usually with more blackish mottling to inner webs of p9 than p8 (Fig. 137**A-B**); p9 cov contrastingly narrow, pointed, dull (lacking gloss), short and often mottled blackish (Fig. 137**A-B**).

AHY/ASY (Def. cycle, DB-DS-DA; Oct-Sep): Outer pp uniformly broad, truncate, glossy (Fig. 115**B**), and usually with similar amounts of blackish mottling to inner webs of p9 and p8 (Fig. 137**C-D**); outermost p covs uniformly broad, rounded, glossy, long, and white with few or no black markings (Fig. 137**C-D**).

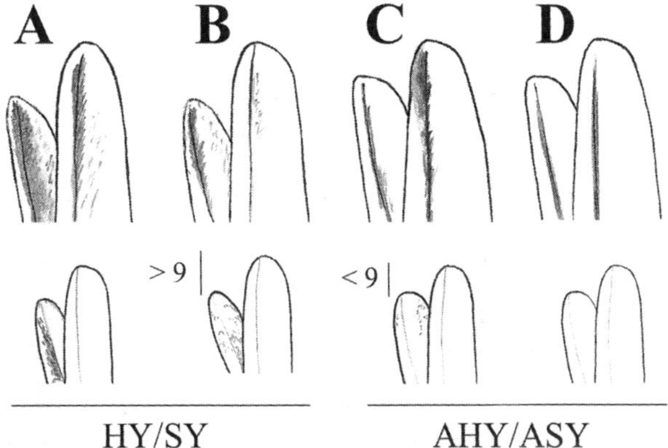

FIGURE 137. P9 and p8 (upper row) and corresponding p covs (lower row) by age in ptarmigan. Measure indicates tip of p8 cov to tip of p9 cov. Note that in HY/SYs, the juvenal p9 and p9 cov are narrower, more tapered, relatively shorter, more worn, and usually have more dusky mottling than the replaced formative p8 and p8 cov. In AHY/ASYs, the basic pp and p covs are more uniform in shape and wear, and p8 often has more dusky mottling than p9. Generally, most Willow Ptarmigan show patterns resembling **A** and **C**, whereas most Rock and White-tailed ptarmigan show patterns resembling **B** and **D**, but there is substantial variation by subspecies as well (see **Geographic variation**). Juv outer pp and p covs (**A**-**B**) are retained by SYs through the PB2 in Aug-Oct.

Sex—Medial BP (Fig. 20**A**, p. 31) and/or distended cloaca (Fig. 21, p. 32) indicates AHY ♀ in Jun-Aug. Measurements somewhat helpful for sexing (Table 16, p. 185); see Gruys & Hannon (1993) for DFAs (p. 5), using wing chord and outer rectrix length from dead individuals, that correctly sexed > 80% of Willow Ptarmigan from a BC population. See also Figures 22-23 (pp. 32-35) for cloacal characteristics useful in ageing and sexing (including Juvs). Formative-plumaged and basic-plumaged individuals are not reliably sexed by plumage aspect, except for some Rock Ptarmigans by the amount of blackish in the lores in combination with age (Fig. 135, p. 184). Otherwise, the following pertains to AHYs in non-basic plumages only. See **Molt** for an understanding of plumage sequences helpful for accurate sex determinations, and **Geographic variation** for more precise descriptions of plumage aspect by taxon.

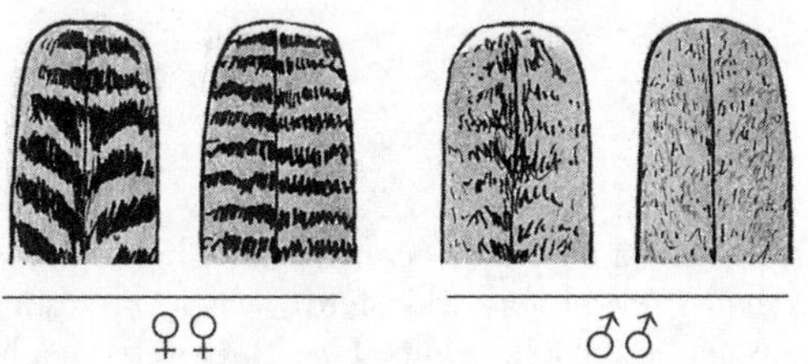

FIGURE 138. Variation in the alternate longest uppertail covert by sex in AHY ptarmigan. There is much intrasexual variation in the coloration of these feathers but generally ♀ show more distinct barring than ♂ (beware of some overlap). The difference in pattern may relate somehow to the timing of replacement of this feather (see **Molt**): typically Apr-May in ♀ and Jun-Jul in ♂. These feathers are not replaced during presupplemental molts and the basic covs are entirely white, so this difference is reliable for sexing ♀♀ in May-Sep and ♂♂ in Jul-Sep. HYs with juv uppertail covs cannot be sexed reliably by plumage. aspect

AHY ♀ (Apr-Sep): Modified central uppertail cov (resembling r1) dark brownish with distinct buff bars (Fig. 138**A-B**); head, upper back, and breast brownish to buff with distinct black mottling or bars in Apr-Jun, often mixed with rufous (Willow Ptarmigan), or vermiculated (Rock and White-tailed ptarmigans) feathering in Jul-Sep; supercilium without or with reduced red air sacs in Apr-Jul. **Note: In Jul-Sep, the alternate (brownish) feathers of the back and breast of ♀♀ are more worn than the (reddish or vermiculated) supplemental feathers, whereas the opposite is the case in ♂♂, and this distinction can be useful in sexing.**

AHY ♂ (Apr-Sep): Modified central uppertail cov dusky with fine reddish barring (Fig. 138**C-D**); head, upper back, and breast rufous (Willow Ptarmigan) or vermiculated (Rock and White-tailed ptarmigans) in Apr-Jun, becoming primarily brownish with distinct black mottling or bars in Jul-Sep; supercilium with noticeable red air sacs in Apr-Jul. **Note: AHY ♀.**

Hybrids reported—Willow Ptarmigan with Black Grouse *Lyrurus tetrix*, Western Capercaillie *Tetrao urogallus*, and Hazel Grouse *Bonasa bonasia* (Hachisuka 1928, Johnsgard 1981a, 1983a; McCarthy 2006); Spruce Grouse (p. 179); and possibly Gray Partridge (p. 168), Ring-necked Pheasant (p. 170), and Rock Ptarmigan (Harper 1953, Todd 1963) in the wild. Rock Ptarmigan with Black Grouse (Johnsgard 1981a, McCarthy 2006), and possibly Ring-necked Pheasant, Hazel Grouse (McCarthy 2006), and Willow Ptarmigan in the wild. White-tailed Ptarmigan with Sharp-tailed Grouse in the wild (McCarthy 2006).

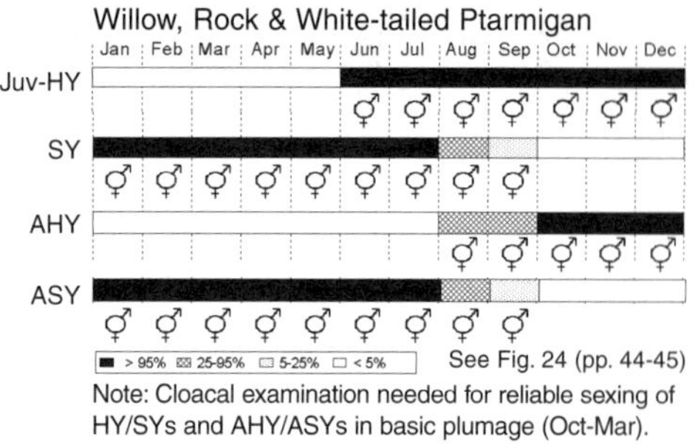

References—Bent (1932), Bergerud et al. (1963), Braun & Martin (2001), Braun & Rogers (1967), Braun et al. (1993), Cramp & Simmons (1980), Dement'ev & Gladkov (1952), Dwight (1900a), Godfrey (1986), Gruys & Hannon (1993), Hannon & Roland (1983), Hannon et al. (1998), Holder & Montgomerie (1993), Höst (1942), Jacobsen et al. (1983), Montgomerie et al. (2001), Petrides (1942, 1945), Pyle (2007), Ridgway & Friedmann (1946), Salomonsen (1938, 1939), Short (1967), Stejneger (1885), Sutton (1932a), Swarth (1926), Weeden (1961, 1966), Weeden & Watson (1967), West et al. (1968, 1970), Westerskov (1956).

DUSKY GROUSE
Dendragapus obscurus

DUGR
Species # 2970

SOOTY GROUSE
Dendragapus fuliginosus

SOGR
Species # 2970

Species—Juvs from other N.Am gamebirds by crown washed pale rufous; rects indistinctly barred and with terminal shaft-streak; breast whitish to grayish with distinct spots; flanks without distinct dark bars; tarsus feathering as in adults (Fig. 123**E-F**) but feathers downy. Non-juvs from other grouse by medium-large size (Table 17); tail usually with 18-20 rects, variably squared to graduated (r1–r9 or r1–r10 2-60 mm; see **Geographic variation**), and with gray tip in most subspecies (*cf.* Fig. 139); wings and lower underparts without white spotting; ♂ with yellowish to pale reddish inflatable sacs on sides of breast; flanks and undertail covs often with distinct white tips; rects blackish, often with grayish tips (Fig. 139, p. 190); tarsus feathered to toes (Fig. 123**E-F**, p. 173).

Dusky from Sooty grouse by medium size (compared to larger and smaller subspecies in Sooty Grouse; Table 17); plumage aspect paler grayish (*vs* darker sooty); s covs with whitish streaks/tips (*vs* grayish in Sooty Grouse); inflatable sacs on breast of ♂♂ thin and reddish purple (*vs* thick and yellowish in Sooty Grouse); tail with 18-20 squared rects *vs* usually 18 more rounded rects in Sooty Grouse (*cf.* Figs. 139 & 141, pp. 190-191). See **Geographic variation** for other criteria useful at the subspecies level.

Geographic variation—See Aldrich (1963), Barrowclough et al. (2004) Behle & Selander (1951), Bendell & Zwickel (1984), Brooks (1926b), Browning (2002), Chapman (1904a), Dickey & van Rossem (1923b), Gibson & Kessel (1997), Griscom (1923), Hellmayr & Conover (1942), Ridgway & Friedmann (1946), Short (1967), Swarth (1921, 1922, 1926, 1931b), Taverner (1914), van Rossem (1925), Zwickel et al. (1991). No other subspecies occur. Beware of foxing in older specimens, emphasizing brown aspect. See Moffitt (1938) for differences in chick plumage aspect by subspecies. Reported differences in undertail-cov pattern and extent of mottling to the back (especially in ♀♀), are confounded by individual, age-related, and seasonal variation.

TABLE 17. Measurements (mm) of Dusky and Sooty grouse for identification and sexing. See pp. 4-11 for methods of measurement. Species summaries are in **bold** and subspecies summaries are in ***italics***. Values were derived from 95% confidence intervals as based approximately on the indicated sample sizes (see pp. 4-5); thus midpoints of ranges approximate means, and S.D. is approximated by 25% of the range.[1]

Taxon/Sex	*n*	wing chord	tail length	exposed culmen	tarsus
Dusky Grouse		**182-250**	**109-205**	**16.0-25.6**	**38-46**
D.o. richardsonii		***195-240***	***122-175***	***16.9-22.4***	***39-45***
♀	100	195-222	122-156	16.9-20.8	39-43
♂	100	211-240	141-175	17.0-22.4	41-45
D.o. pallidus		***197-238***	***125-180***	***17.2-21.8***	***40-45***
♀	50	197-223	125-149	17.2-21.0	40-43
♂	45	214-238	149-180	18.4-21.8	42-45
D.o. obscurus		***198-248***	***130-185***	***17.5-22.9***	***40-45***
♀	50	198-226	130-156	17.5-22.3	40-43
♂	60	219-248	151-185	18.7-22.9	41-45
D.o. oreinus		***198-246***	***131-183***	***17.3-21.7***	***39-45***
♀	40	198-223	131-155	17.3-21.1	39-43
♂	45	220-246	152-183	18.6-21.7	40-45
Sooty Grouse		**195-248**	**122-185**	**16.9-22.9**	**39-45**
D.o. fuliginosus		***190-235***	***115-163***	***16.4-21.0***	***39-45***
♀	80	190-218	115-139	16.4-19.6	39-43
♂	90	207-235	135-163	17.5-21.0	41-45
D.o. sitkensis		***182-230***	***109-161***	***16.0-20.0***	***38-43***
♀	20	182-208	109-134	16.0-18.8	38-41
♂	25	204-230	132-161	17.1-20.0	40-43
D.o. sierrae		***196-241***	***116-166***	***17.0-22.5***	***39-44***
♀	60	196-224	116-140	17.0-21.2	39-43
♂	55	213-241	129-166	18.2-22.5	41-44
D.o. howardi		***202-250***	***129-205***	***19.0-25.6***	***41-46***
♀	15	202-230	129-166	19.0-22.1	41-44
♂	20	220-250	171-205	20.4-25.6	42-46

[1] Measurements pertain to birds in formative and definitive plumages; juveniles vary greatly in size but are substantially smaller.

Dusky Grouse

D.o. richardsonii (res interior s.Yuk-BC to n.ID-nw.WY): Medium-sized (Table 17, p. 189); tail usually with 20 rects, squared (r1–r10 2-17 mm; HY/SY > AHY/ASY), the outer rects (r2-r10) with indistinct to no gray tips (Fig. 139**A-B**); plumage aspect moderately pale. Populations of Yuk-NWT to n.BC ("*flemingi*") may average darker but differences are slight and confounded by individual variation.

D.o. pallidus (res sw.BC-ne.OR): Medium-large (Table 17); tail usually with 20 rects, squared (r1–r10 2-24 mm; HY/SY > AHY/ASY), the outer rects (r2-r10) with moderately indistinct (♀) to no (♂) gray tips (Fig. 139**A-C**); plumage aspect moderately pale.

D.o. obscurus (res montane c.WY-w.SD to n.AZ-NM): Medium-large (Table 17); tail usually with 18 rects, moderately squared (r1–r9 10-22 mm; HY/SY > AHY/ASY), the outer rects (r2-r9) with distinct and broad gray tips (Fig. 139**E-F**); plumage aspect moderately pale.

D.o. oreinus (res s.ID to ne.NV-nw.UT): Medium-large (Table 17); tail with 18-20 rects, moderately squared (r1–r9 or r1–r10 8-20 mm; HY/SY > AHY/ASY), the outer rects (r2-r9 or r2-r10) with distinct and broad gray tips (Fig. 139**F**); plumage aspect pale.

Sooty Grouse

D.f. fuliginosus (res coastal se.AK-sw.Yuk to nw.CA): Medium-small (Table 17); tail moderately graduated (r1–r9 12-32 mm; HY/SY > AHY/ASY), the outer rects (r2-r9) with distinct and narrow gray tips (Fig. 139**C**); plumage aspect moderately dark.

D.f. sitkensis (res Is off se.AK-BC): Small (Table 17); tail moderately graduated (r1–r9 10-28 mm; HY/SY > AHY/ASY), the outer rects (r2-r9) with distinct and narrow gray tips (Fig. 139**C**); plumage aspect dark. Populations of the Queen Charlotte Is, BC ("*munroi*") may average darker but difference insufficient.

D.f. sierrae (res montane c.WA to w.NV-ce.CA, Fresno Co): Medium-sized (Table 17); tail graduated (r1–r9 14-40 mm; HY/SY > AHY/ASY), the outer rects (r2-r9) with distinct and broad grayish (with black mottling) tips (Fig. 139**D**); plumage aspect medium in shade.

D.f. howardi (res montane se.CA, Fresno-Kern Cos): Large and long-tailed (Table 17); tail highly graduated (r1–r9 ♀ 18-31, ♂ 27-45 mm; HY/SY > AHY/ASY), the outer rects (r2-r9) with distinct and broad gray tips (Fig. 139**E-F**); plumage aspect medium in shade.

Molt—CBS. PF incomplete (Jun-Oct in HYs), DPB incomplete-complete (May-Oct in AHYs); PA absent. See Family Account (p. 165) for replacement sequence of pp and (15) ss; rects are generally replaced proximally during both the PF and the DPB. The PF includes all feathers except the outer 2 pp (p9-p10) and p covs. The DPB possibly can be incomplete in occasional AHYs, especially among outer pp, ss among s7-s10, and underwing gr covs of ♂♂ (see Bendell 1955); more study is needed.

Age—Juv (Jun-Sep) like ♀♀ but feathers with more distinct pale shaft streaks, outer web to ss barred buff (*cf.* Fig. 140**A**), rects short (tail < 100) and narrow (*cf.* Fig. 116**A**, p. 166), and breast buff with dark spotting; see Buss & Schottelius (1954) and Bendell (1955) for informa-

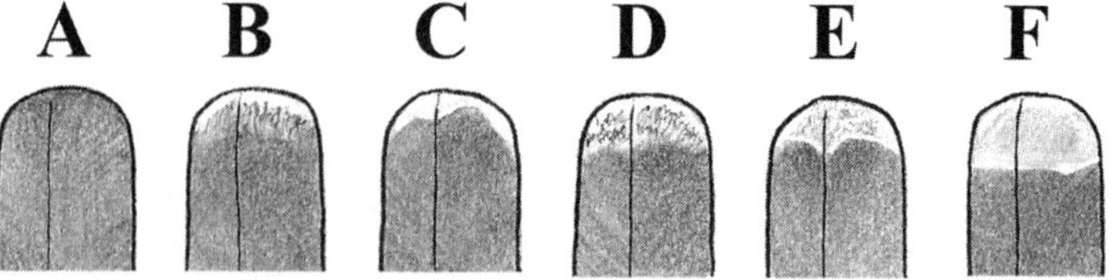

FIGURE 139. Variation in the pattern of the outer rectrix (r9 or r10) by subspecies in Dusky and Sooty grouse. Some Dusky Grouse lack distinct pale tips (**A-B**), some Sooty Grouse have narrow and distinct pale gray tips (**C**), and some of each species have variably distinct and broad grayish tips (**D-F**). Note that the shape of these feathers varies by age/sex group and species, with Sooty Grouse generally having broader and squarer rects than Dusky Grouse (Fig. 141).

tion on the length of the bursa (Fig. 23, p. 34). Juv ♀ = ♂, but see Figures 22-23 (pp. 32-35) for cloacal characters reliable for sexing hatchlings and Juvs, and Hoffman (1983) for a DFA (p. 5) using lengths of p9 and p10 to determine sex in 92% of Juvs (with fully grown outer pp) in a CO population (*D.o. obscurus*). Also, some Juv ♂♂ may be identifiable by having grayish areas to the bases of the c.rects (uniformly brown with buff bars in Juv ♀♀; *cf.* Fig. 142, p. 192); more study needed. In addition to the following, note that HY/SYs average substantially shorter wing and tail than AHY/ASYs but this also varies by subspecies and sex (Table 17, p. 189). In ♂♂, the skin of the inflatable sacs on the breast also average thicker and rougher in AHY/ASYs than in HY/SYs.

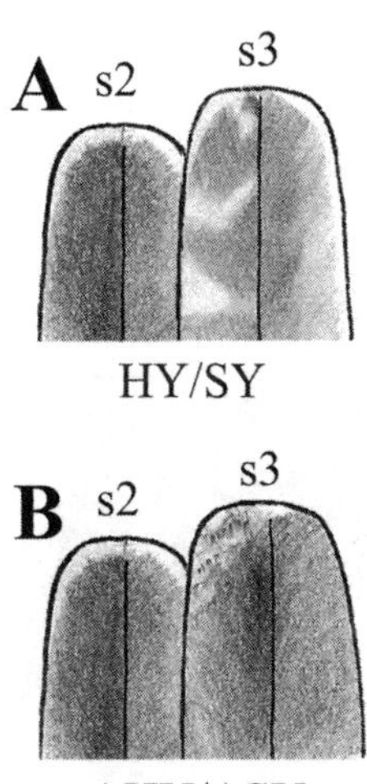

FIGURE 140. Outer secondaries (s2-s3) by age in Dusky and Sooty grouse. Note that, because s3 is the first secondary replaced during the preformative molt, it often shows some juv characteristics (buff bars) whereas s2, replaced much later, is more basic-like in aspect. S3 often may appear slightly more worn than s2, especially in HY/SYs. Other gamebirds can show this same relative pattern, with s3 showing juv characteristics, but the patterns may be slightly different than shown here. These are retained by SYs and ASYs through the PB2 in Jul-Oct.

HY/SY (1st cycle, F1; Oct-Sep): Outer 2 pp (p9-p10) contrastingly narrow, pointed, and worn (Fig. 115**A**, p. 165), with substantial (♀) to moderate (♂) buff mottling to outer web (*cf.* Fig. 128**A**, p. 178), greater than on p8; p9 cov contrastingly narrow, pointed, and short (p8 cov – p9 cov > 10 mm), often (especially ♀♀) with buff markings (*cf.* Fig. 129**A**, p. 178); s3 often barred buff, contrasting with s2 (Fig. 140**A**); outer rect rounded and narrower by sex (Fig. 141**A**, **C**).

AHY/ASY (Def. cycle, DB; Oct-Sep): Outer pp uniformly broad and truncate (Fig. 115**B**), with slight (♀) to no (♂) buff mottling to outer web (*cf.* Fig. 128**B**), the amount on p8 and p9 roughly equal; outermost p covs uniformly broad, rounded, and long (p8 cov – p9 cov < 10

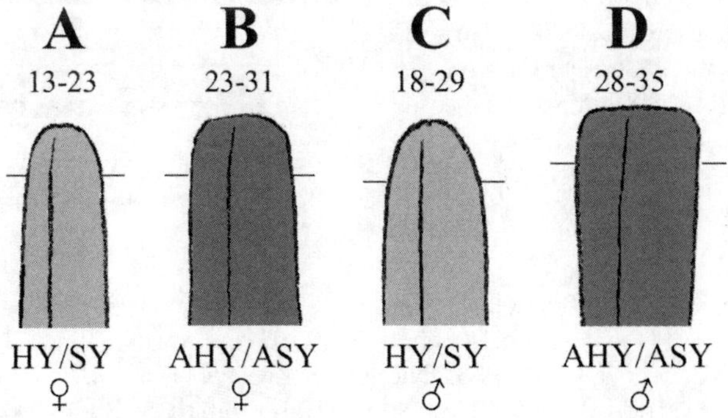

FIGURE 141. Width and shape of the outer rectrix by age/sex group in Dusky and Sooty Grouse. Note that, within each age/sex group, Sooty Grouse average squarer tips than Dusky Grouse. Measures are for the feather width at widest point.

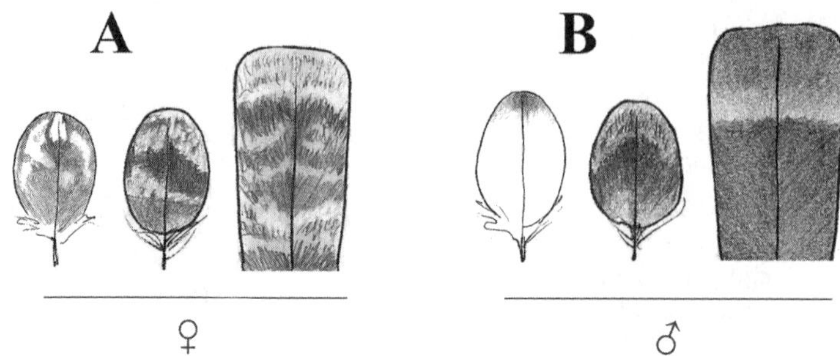

FIGURE 142. Lateral breast feather (near inflatable air sacs), back feather, and central rectrix by sex in Dusky and Sooty grouse. These characters are reliable for sexing HY/SYs in formative plumage and AHY/ASYs in basic plumage but not for Juvs, although some Juv ♂♂, may show areas of solid gray at the bases of the rects and can be sexed.

mm), with few (♀) or no (♂) buff markings (*cf.* Fig. 129**B**); s3 and s2 with little or no barring (Fig. 140**B**); outer rect squarer and broader by sex (Fig. 141**B**, **D**). **Note: Occasional AHY/ASYs may retain outer pp, medial ss, or underwing covs (see Molt) and might be aged to SY/TY or ASY/ATY; more study is needed.**

Sex—Medial BP (Fig. 20**A**, p. 31) and/or distended cloaca (Fig. 21, p. 32) indicates AHY ♀ in Apr-Jul. In addition to the following, note that ♀♀ average substantially shorter wings and tails than ♂♂ but this also varies by subspecies and age (Table 17). See Mussehl & Leik (1963) for a DFA (p. 5) using pp lengths of freshly dead individuals to determine sex of 93% of individuals in a MT population of Dusky Grouse (*D.o. richardsonii*).

♀: Feathers on sides of neck (around air sacs) gray with dark barring and back feathers, uppertail covs, and r1 with brown barring (Fig. 142**A**); outer rect narrower by age (Fig. 141**A**-**B**, p. 191).

♂: Feathers on sides of neck (around air sacs) white with dusky tips and back feathers, uppertail covs, and r1 with pale fringes or vermiculation and with little or no brown barring (Fig. 142**B**); outer rect broader by age (Fig. 141**C**-**D**).

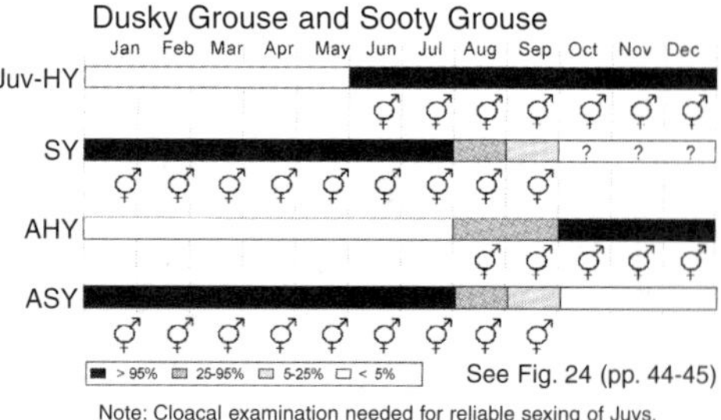

Hybrids reported—Dusky Grouse with Ring-necked Pheasant (p. 170), Ruffed Grouse (p. 172), Greater Sage-Grouse (p. 176), Spruce Grouse (p. 179), Sooty Grouse (Jewett et al. 1953, Munro & Cowan 1947), and Sharp-tailed Grouse (Brooks 1907). Sooty Grouse only with Dusky Grouse (see above).

References—Bendell (1955), Bendell & Zwickel (1984), Bent (1932), Boag (1965), Braun (1971), Bunnell et al. (1977), Buss & Schottelius (1954), Caswell (1954), Dwight (1900a), Hoffman (1983), Mussehl & Leik (1963), Nietfeld & Zwickel (1983), Pyle (2007), Ridgway & Friedmann (1946), Petrides (1942, 1945), Short (1967), Smith & Buss (1963), van Rossem (1925), Zwickel (1992), Zwickel & Dake (1977).

SHARP-TAILED GROUSE

Tympanuchus phasianellus

STGR
Species # 3080

Species—Juvs from other N.Am gamebirds by crown mottled rufous and brown; back with pale streaks; rects whitish with dark markings; tarsus feathering as in adults (Fig. 123**F**, p. 173) but feathers abbreviated. Non-juvs from other grouse and prairie-chickens by medium size with proportionally short tail (Table 18, p. 196); tail usually with 18 rects, the central two rects extended (r1–r2 27-33 mm; HY/SY > AHY/ASY) and the outer rects whitish with inward extension (Fig. 143; unique among N.Am gamebirds); upperparts brownish with dusky and whitish spots and mottling; nape without elongated ornamental plumes (*cf.* Fig. 147, p. 196); sides of breast of ♂ with purplish inflatable sacs; underparts whitish to white with dark chevrons; tarsus and proximal half of toes feathered (Fig. 123**F**). Beware that hybrids with Greater Prairie-Chicken (p. 195) occur regularly in areas of contact.

Geographic variation—See Aldrich (1963), Connelly et al. (1998), Dickerman & Hubbard (1994), Friedmann (1943a), Hellmayr & Conover (1942), Lincoln (1917), Miller & Graul (1980), Pittaway (1997), Ridgway & Friedmann (1946). No other subspecies occur. The following refers to individuals with fresh plumage aspect (Oct-Jan); worn individuals (Feb-Sep) are difficult to differentiate.

T.p. phasianellus (br & wint AK-nw.Sask to c.Que): Upperparts darker brown with large and moderately distinct white spotting. Populations from AK-nw.Sask ("*caurus*") and NWT ("*kennicotti*") may average paler and/or with broader shaft streaks to breast feathers but differences slight.

T.p. columbianus (br and wint e.BC-nc.Alb to se.Man-MI): Upperparts paler brown with small and moderately indistinct white spotting. Populations of nc.Alb-ec.Sask to ne.CO-w.NE ("*jamesi*") may average longer-winged and paler; populations formerly of se.CO-ne.NM ("*hueyi*") may have averaged larger, redder, and with fewer markings to throat; and populations of se.Man-sw.ON to WI-MI ("*campestris*") may have averaged longer tarsus and paler but in all cases differences slight.

Molt—CBS. PF incomplete (Jun-Oct in HYs), DPB complete (May-Oct in AHYs); PA absent. See Family Account (p. 165) for replacement sequence of pp and (18) ss; the rects are generally replaced proximally during both the PF and the DPB. The PF includes all feathers except the outer 2 pp (p9-p10) and p covs.

Age—Juv (Jun-Sep) is like ♀♀ but plumage aspect grayer and with more distinct pale shaft-streaks, outer web to ss barred buff (*cf.* Fig. 140**A**, p. 191), rects short (tail < 60 mm), narrow (*cf.* Fig. 116**A**, p. 166), whitish, and with little or no extension (*cf.* Fig. 143), breast buff with dark spotting. Juv ♀=♂ but see Figures 22-23 (pp. 32-35) for cloacal characters reliable for sexing Juvs. See also Gower (1939) for length of the bursa by age (Fig. 23), and Caldwell (1980) for shaft-width measurements of detached p9 that are possibly helpful to age and sex live individuals. Intermediates between the following, especially in Mar-Sep, may be difficult to age due to wear.

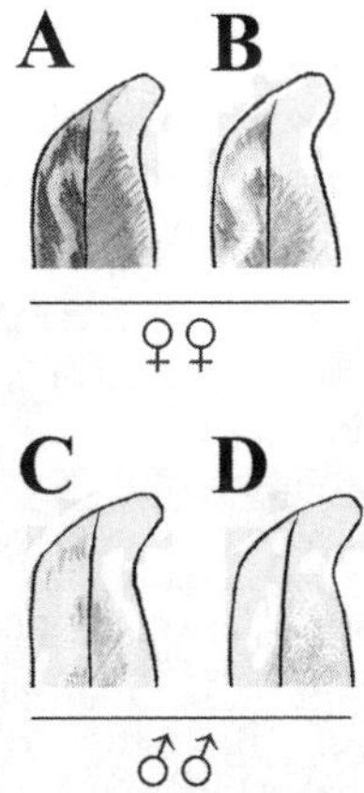

FIGURE 143. Outer rectrix on right side of tail by sex in Sharp-tailed Grouse. There can be some overlap; individuals with rects appearing between **B** and **C** should not be sexed by this criterion alone. These may more often be HY/SY ♂ or AHY/ASY ♀; more study is needed. The medial (inward) extension to the rects is unique among Galliformes.

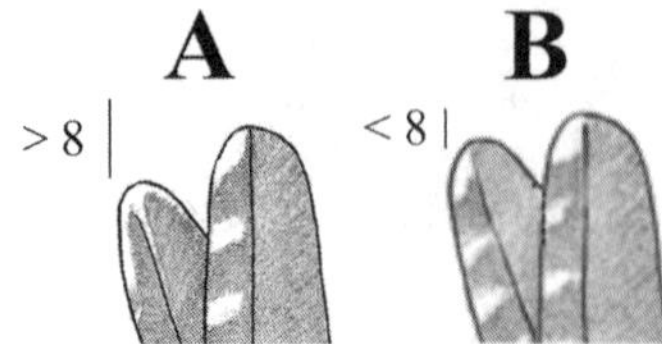

FIGURE 144. Shape, pattern and morphology to outer primary coverts by age in Sharp-tailed Grouse and prairie-chickens. These are the coverts corresponding to p9 (left) and p8 (right); the outermost covert is vestigial. Measure indicates tip of p8 cov to tip of p9 cov. For prairie-chickens, the cut-off for the distance between the tips of the coverts by age is 9 rather than 8 mm.

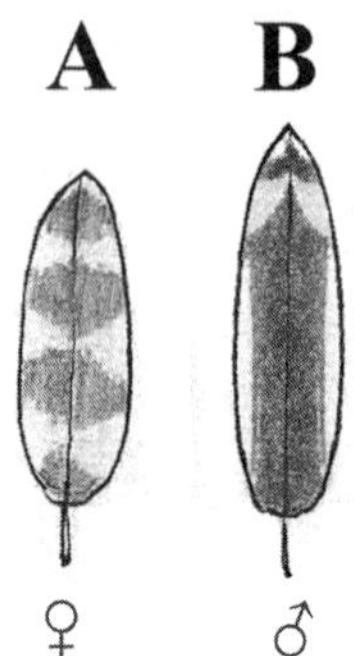

FIGURE 145. Size and pattern of the crown feathers by sex in Sharp-tailed Grouse and prairie-chickens.

HY/SY (1st cycle, F1; Oct-Sep): Outer 2 pp (p9-p10) contrastingly narrow, pointed, and worn (Fig. 115**A**, p. 165); p9 cov contrastingly narrow, pointed, short, often with pale shaft-streak at tip (Fig. 144**A**); s3 often with buff mottling between bars, more than on s2 (*cf.* Fig. 140**A**, p. 191).

AHY/ASY (Def. cycle, DB; Oct-Sep): Outer pp uniformly broad and truncate (Fig. 115**B**); outermost p covs uniformly broad, rounded, long, and with white spot to tips of outer webs but no pale shaft-streaks (Fig. 144**B**); s2 and s3 with similar amounts of buff mottling between bars (*cf.* Fig. 140**B**), usually less than s3 of HY/SY.

Sex—Medial BP (Fig. 20**A**, p. 31) and/or distended cloaca (Fig. 21, p. 32) indicates AHY ♀ in Apr-Jul. Measurements unhelpful for sexing (Table 18, p. 196). A few intermediates may be difficult to sex by the following; these are likely HY/SY ♂♂ or AHY/ASY ♀♀ so combine with age.

♀: Elongated crown feathers with pale brown bars (Fig. 145**A**); outer rects with extensive brown bars (Fig. 143**A**-**B**, p. 193); inflatable sacs on supercilium and side of neck reduced in Feb-Jul.

♂: Elongated crown feathers fringed pale brown (Fig. 145**B**); outer rects whitish, with little or no brownish (Fig. 143**C**-**D**); inflatable sacs on supercilium and side of neck enlarged in Feb-Jul.

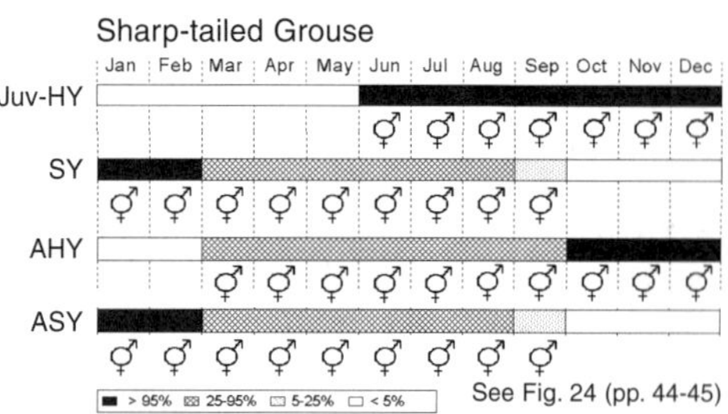

Hybrids reported—With Greater Sage-Grouse (p. 176), White-tailed Ptarmigan (p. 182), Dusky Grouse (p. 188), and Greater Prairie-Chicken (Brewster 1877, Evans 1966, Johnsgard & Wood 1968, Lincoln 1918, Rowan 1926, Sparling 1980).

References—Ammann (1944), Bent (1932), Connelly et al. (1998), Dwight (1900a), Hart et al. (1950), Henderson et al. (1967), Manweiler (1939), Petrides (1942, 1945), Ridgway & Friedmann (1946), Roberts (1955), Short (1967), Snyder (1935), Tsuji et al. (1994), Wright & Hiatt (1943).

GREATER PRAIRIE-CHICKEN
Tympanuchus cupido

GRPC
Species # 3050

LESSER PRAIRIE-CHICKEN
Tympanuchus pallidicinctus

LEPC
Species # 3070

Species—Juv prairie-chickens from other N.Am gamebirds by crown uniformly chestnut; upperparts with buff spots or streaks; rects indistinctly barred and with whitish shaft-streaks or tips; breast and flanks buff with dark bars; tarsus feathering as in adults (Fig. 123**D**-**E**, p. 173) but feathers abbreviated. Non-juvs from other gamebirds by medium size with proportionally short tails (Table 18, p. 196); tail usually with 18 rects, moderately graduated (r1–r9 32-48 mm; HY/SY > AHY/ASY), but with central pair not elongated (r1–r2 0-5 mm), and outer feathers without medial extensions (*cf.* Fig. 143, p. 193); upperparts dark brownish with buff bars; nape with elongated ornamental plumes (Fig. 147, Table 18; p. 196); sides of breast of ♂ with yellowish to reddish-orange inflatable sacs; breast and flanks whitish with straight dark bars; rects dark brown with distinct buff bars and whitish tips; tarsus feathered to toes (Fig. 123**D**-**E**, p. 173). Hybrids of Greater Prairie-Chicken with Sharp-tailed Grouse (p. 193) occur regularly; these have r1–r2 10-20 mm and shallow, chevron-shaped bars to underparts.

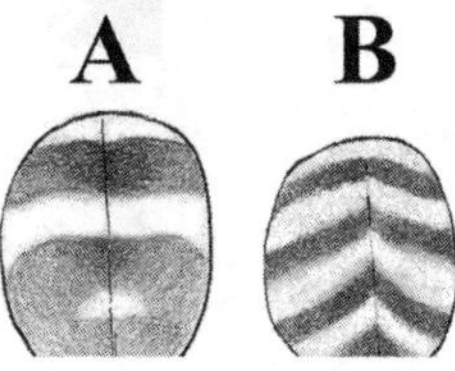

FIGURE 146. Typical central breast feather in Greater (**A**) and Lesser (**B**) prairie-chickens for identification. The subterminal dark bar is usually > 4 mm wide in Greater and < 4 mm wide in Lesser; in each species, ♂ have wider bars than ♀.

Greater from Lesser prairie-chicken by longer bill and tarsus (Table 18); ornamental nape plumes (*cf.* Fig. 147) greater in number by subspecies (12-20 *vs* 10-16 in Lesser) and longer (*T.p. pinnatus*) or shorter (*attwateri*) by sex (Table 18); breast feathers with broader bars (*vs* narrower in Lesser Prairie-Chicken; Fig. 146); plumage aspect darker brown with slight reddish tinge (*vs* paler brown with slight grayish tinge in Lesser Prairie-Chicken); inflatable sacs of ♂ in Mar-Jul yellowish (*vs* reddish orange in Lesser Prairie-Chicken).

Geographic variation—Lesser Prairie-Chicken is monotypic. For Greater Prairie-Chicken, see Bendire (1894), Brewster (1885), Gross (1928), Hellmayr & Conover (1942), Lehman (1941), Oberholser (1974), Ridgway & Friedmann (1946), Short (1967). No other subspecies occur.

Greater Prairie-Chicken

T.c. pinnatus (res ND-MN to OK-IL): Wing and tail longer by sex (Table 18, p. 196); ornamental nape plumes (*cf.* Fig. 147) usually numbering 12-17 and longer by sex (Table 18); plumage aspect reddish brown; proximal side of tarsus feathered to toes (Fig. 123**E**, p. 173). Populations formerly of MA-PA to VA (*T.c. cupido*, "Heath Hen") now extinct, had shorter wing (♀ 198-218, ♂ 206-228), longer tail (♀ 90-107, ♂ 99-115), darker and redder brownish bars, buffy spots on scapulars, 16 uppertail covs (*vs* 18 in the other subspecies), and narrower and fewer (8-13) ornamental nape plumes.

T.c. attwateri (res se.TX): Wing and tail shorter by sex (Table 18); ornamental nape plumes (*cf.* Fig. 147) usually numbering 15-20 and shorter by sex (Table 18); plumage aspect brown with slight reddish tinge; tarsus feathering shorter and proximal side unfeathered (*cf.* Fig. 123**D**).

Molt—CBS. PF incomplete (Jun-Oct in HYs), DPB complete (May-Oct in AHYs); PA absent? See Family Account (p. 165) for replacement sequence of pp and (18) ss; the rects are generally replaced proximally during both the PF and the DPB. The PF includes all feathers except

TABLE 18. Measurements (mm) of North American *Tympanuchus* grouse to assist with identification and sexing. See pp. 4-11 for methods of measurement. Species summaries are in **bold** and subspecies summaries are in ***italics***. Values were derived from 95% confidence intervals as based approximately on the indicated sample sizes (see pp. 4-5); thus midpoints of ranges approximate means, and S.D. is approximated by 25% of the range.[1]

Taxon/Sex	*n*	wing chord	tail length	exp culmen	tarsus	nape plume[2]
Sharp-tailed Grouse[3]		**188-219**	**97-132**	**13.8-16.7**	**38-48**	**12-16**
♀	100	188-211	97-126	13.8-16.3	38-46	12-15
♂	100	194-219	101-132	14.0-16.7	40-48	13-16
Greater Prairie-Chicken		**195-238**	**77-105**	**16.6-20.4**	**46-53**	**19-84**
T.c. pinnatus		***208-238***	***82-105***	***16.6-21.0***	***46-53***	***27-84***
♀	46	208-228	82-99	16.6-20.5	46-51	27-43
♂	53	216-238	89-105	17.0-21.0	47-53	65-84
T.c. attwateri		***195-217***	***77-92***	***16.9-20.4***	***46-52***	***19-68***
♀	30	195-210	77-85	16.9-19.8	46-51	19-32
♂	30	202-217	84-92	17.4-20.4	48-52	52-68
Lesser Prairie-Chicken		**195-226**	**80-95**	**15.0-18.3**	**41-47**	**26-77**
♀	100	195-216	80-88	15.0-17.7	41-45	26-39
♂	100	204-226	87-95	15.5-18.3	43-47	62-77

[1] Measurements pertain to birds in formative and definitive plumages; juveniles vary greatly in size but are substantially smaller.

[2] Measurement is of the longest ornamental nape plume (prairie-chickens; Fig. 147) or feather (Sharp-tailed Grouse) from point of insertion to tip. See text for variation in the number of these plumes by subspecies and sex in prairie-chickens.

[3] See **Geographic variation** for information on nominal average differences among certain subspecies.

the outer 2 pp (p9-p10) and p covs. A limited DPA may include a few feathers of the chin and head in Mar-Apr (Dwight 1900a), but confirmation needed.

Age—Juvs (Jun-Sep) have distinct pale streaks or tips to the upperpart feathers, outer web to ss barred buff (*cf.* Fig. 140**A**, p. 191), and rects short (tail < 90) and narrow (*cf.* Fig. 116**A**, p. 166). Juvs can be sexed by the presence (♀♀) or absence (♂♂) of bars to the outer portion of the outer rect (Fig. 148); See also Figures 22-23 (pp. 32-35) for cloacal characters reliable for sexing Juvs.

HY/SY (1st cycle, F1; Oct-Sep): Outer 2 pp (p9-p10) contrastingly narrow, pointed, and worn (Fig. 115**A**, p. 165), with substantial (♀) to slight (♂) buff mottling to tips of outer web (*cf.* Fig. 128**A**, p. 178), substantially more than on p8; p9 cov contrastingly narrow, pointed, short (p8 cov – p9 cov > 9 mm), and usually (especially ♀♀) with pale shaft-streak at tip (*cf.* Fig. 144**A**, p. 194); s3 often with buff mottling between bars, more than on s2 (*cf.* Fig. 140**A**).

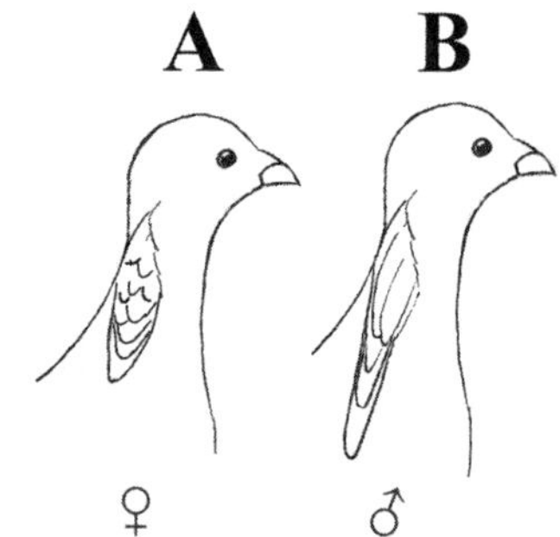

FIGURE 147. Typical length of "nape plumes" by sex in prairie-chickens. Although apparent on the sides of the neck, these plumes originate from the nape. Lengths exhibited are typical of nominate Greater Prairie-Chicken; *T.c. attwateri* and Lesser Prairie-Chicken exhibit shorter plumes by sex. These plumes are long enough in HY ♂ by Nov-Dec to be reliable for sexing. See text and Table 18 for variation in the number and length (respectively) of these plumes by species, subspecies, and sex.

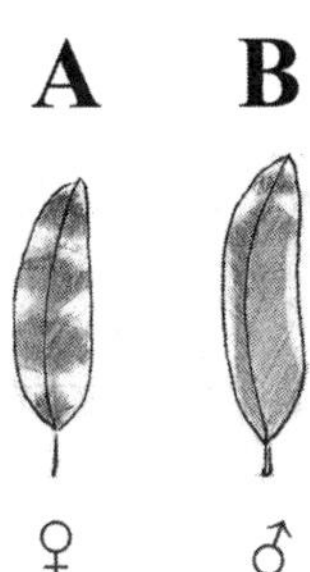

FIGURE 148. Pattern to the juv outer rectrix by sex in Juv prairie-chickens.

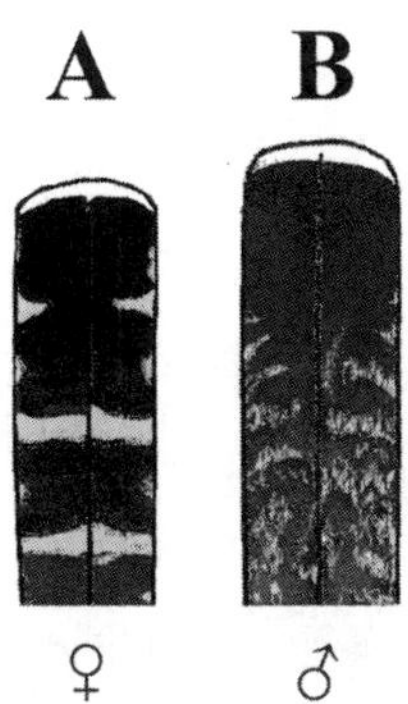

FIGURE 149. Pattern to the central rectrix by sex in prairie-chickens.

AHY/ASY (Def. cycle, DB; Oct-Sep): Outer pp uniformly broad and truncate (Fig. 115**B**), with slight (♀) to no (♂) buff mottling to tips of outer web (*cf.* Fig. 128**B**), similar to that on p8; outermost p covs uniformly broad, rounded, long (p8 cov – p9 cov < 9 mm), and with white spots to tip of outer webs but no pale shaft-streak (*cf.* Fig. 144**B**); s2 and s3 with similar amounts of buff mottling between bars (*cf.* Fig. 140**B**), usually less than s3 of HY/SY.

Sex—Medial BP (Fig. 20**A**, p. 31) and/or distended cloaca (Fig. 21, p. 32) indicates AHY ♀ in Apr-Jul. Tail length helpful for sexing within taxa (Table 18).

♀: Elongated crown feathers with pale brown bars (Fig. 145**A**, p. 194); inflatable sacs on supercilium and side of neck reduced in Feb-Jul; ornamental nape plumes shorter by species and subspecies (Fig. 147**A**, Table 18); r1 and the distal portion of the outer rect with distinct buff bars (Fig. 149**A**); undertail covs with dark bars.

♂: Elongated crown feathers fringed pale brown (Fig. 145**B**); inflatable sacs on supercilium and side of neck enlarged in Feb-Jul; ornamental nape plumes longer by species and subspecies (Fig. 147**B**, Table 18); r1 and the distal portion of the outer rect without distinct buff bars (Fig. 149**B**); undertail covs without dark bars.

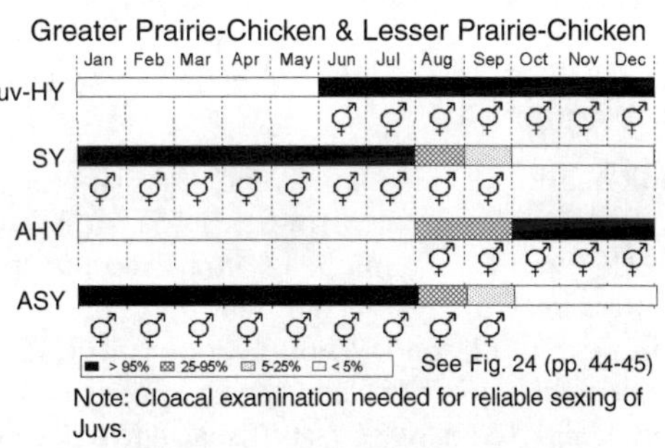

Hybrids reported—Greater Prairie-Chicken with Ring-necked Pheasant (p. 170), Sharp-tailed Grouse (p. 193), and Lesser Prairie-Chicken (Bain & Farley 2002, J.A. Crawford 1978) in the wild. Greater with Lesser prairie-chicken possibly in the wild (McCarthy 2006).

References—Baker (1953), Bent (1932), Campbell (1972), Copelin (1963), Dwight (1900a), Giessen (1998), Jones (1964), Oberholser (1974), Petrides (1942, 1945), Pitman et al. (2005), Ridgway & Friedmann (1946), Roberts (1955), Schroeder & Robb (1993), Short (1967), Sutton (1964, 1977).

WILD TURKEY WITU
Meleagris gallopavo Species # 3100

Species—Juvs from other N.Am gamebirds by large legs and feet; plumage aspect brown to dusky with pale fringing; longer scapulars barred blackish and cinnamon. Non-juv from other gamebirds by much larger by size (Table 19); pp and ss with distinct black-and-white barring; rects and uppertail covs with distinct whitish or rufous tips (see **Geographic variation**); breast of ♂♂ and some ♀♀ with keratin fibers ("beard"). Domestic strains of turkeys may show variable white areas to plumage aspect.

Geographic variation—See Aldrich (1967), Hellmayr & Conover (1942), Moore (1938), Nelson (1902), Oberholser (1974), Phillips (1962), Phillips et al. (1964), Ridgway & Friedmann (1946), Scott (1890), Schorger (1957, 1961, 1966, 1970), Sennett (1892), Stangel et al. (1992), Stevenson & Anderson (1994). Two other subspecies occur in Mexico. Subspecific differences have been confounded by millenia of domestication and re-introduction programs involving non-indigenous subspecies and modified, semi-domestic forms (Long 1981). Re-introductions have included *T.g. gallopavo* of Mexico to several N.Am locations prior to 1900, *merriami* and *intermedius* into e.N.Am during the 1940-1950s, and *silvestris* into w.N.Am during the 1950s.

M.g. merriami (res CO to AZ-sw.TX, introduced WA-ND to WY & CA): Large (Table 19); pp with dark bars slightly broader than white bars in width (Fig. 151, p. 200); uppertail covs and rects with whitish to cinnamon tips; filamentous fibers on breast (forming "beard") and spurs in ♂ average shorter by age/sex than in other subspecies (measures needed). Populations of nw.Mex (*mexicana*), which may have inhabited s.AZ in historic times (prior to re-introductions of *merriami*), average slightly larger (wg chord 405-544, tl 313-433), have golden and reddish iridescence to rump, and have whiter tips to the uppertail covs and rects. See Schorger (1961, 1970) for information on probable semi-domestic specimens found in NM, named "*tularosa*".

M.g. intermedia (res nc-s.TX, introduced s.KS-OK): Medium-small (Table 19); pp with dark bars slightly broader than white bars in width (Fig. 151); uppertail covs and rects with buff to pale rufous tips.

M.g. silvestris (res se.NE-LA to s.MA-GA, introduced ND): Large but with proportionally short tarsus (Table 19); pp with dark bars slightly broader than white bars in width (Fig. 151); uppertail covs and rects with rusty-buff tips; filamentous fibers on breast (forming "beard") average longer by age/sex than in other subspecies (measures needed).

M.g. osceola (res FL): Small but with long tarsus (Table 19); pp with dark bars substantially broader than white bars (*cf.* Fig. 151); uppertail covs and rects with rusty buff tips; filamentous fibers on breast (forming "beard") average thinner by age/sex and spurs average longer in ♂♂ than in other subspecies (measures needed).

Molt—CBS. PF incomplete-complete (Jun-Sep in HYs), PFa absent-incomplete (Aug-Nov in HYs), PB2 complete (Apr-Sep in SY ♂♂), DPB complete May-Nov in ASY ♂♂, Jun-Nov in AHY ♀♀); PA absent. See Family Account (p. 165) for replacement sequence of pp and (18-19) ss; rects are replaced distally (r1 to r8) during the PF and irregularly during the DPB, often from r8 to r2, followed by r9 and r1. The PF can be complete in ~10% of N.Am HYs (from s.populations or domestic lineage) but usually includes all feathers except the outer 1-2 pp (p9-p10) and p covs; some rects (usually up to 6 central feathers, occasionally more) can be replaced at least three times during the first molt cycle, here considered PFa (see pp. 14-15). following the PF (Fig. 150). It is possible that the PFa may also include body feathers or other rects, as reported, although it appears more likely that feathers replaced during a protracted prejuvenal molt (PB1) have been mistaken for a separate molt (see pp. 14-15). A reported DPA (Leopold 1943) probably does not exist (Williams & McGuire 1971).

Age/Sex—Juvs (Jun-Sep) are primarily dusky brown and have the outer web to ss barred buff (*cf.* Fig. 140**A**, p. 191) and rects short (tail < 150), narrow, and barred rusty and brown (*cf.* Fig. 116**A-B**, p. 166). Juv ♀=♂ but see Figures 22-23 (pp. 32-35) for cloacal characters reliable for

TABLE 19. Measurements (mm) of North American Wild Turkeys to assist with subspecific identification, ageing, and sexing. See pp. 4-11 for methods of measurement. Species summary is in **bold** and subspecies summaries are in ***italics***. Values were derived from 95% confidence intervals as based approximately on the indicated sample sizes (see pp. 4-5); thus midpoints of ranges approximate means, and S.D. is approximated by 25% of the range.

Taxon/Sex	n	wing chord[1]	tail length[1]	exposed culmen[2,3]	tarsus[3]
Wild Turkey		**345-535**	**215-425**	**27-40**	**122-173**
M.g. merriami		***395-535***	***260-425***	***30-40***	***123-173***
HY/SY ♀	11	395-435	260-310	---	---
AHY/ASY ♀	23	415-455	320-360	30-35	123-139
HY/SY ♂	12	470-510	315-375	---	---
AHY/ASY ♂	26	495-535	375-425	34-40	155-173
M.g. intermedia		***360-490***	***215-380***	***28-38***	***123-171***
HY/SY ♀	14	360-395	215-270	---	---
AHY/ASY ♀	29	385-410	275-320	28-32	123-137
HY/SY ♂	17	440-470	305-330	---	---
AHY/ASY ♂	36	460-490	335-380	32-38	156-171
M.g. silvestris		***390-535***	***250-410***	***29-38***	***122-173***
HY/SY ♀	18	390-430	250-300	---	---
AHY/ASY ♀	36	410-450	310-350	29-34	122-140
HY/SY ♂	28	460-510	300-360	---	---
AHY/ASY ♂	47	485-535	360-410	32-38	153-173
M.g. osceola		***345-475***	***215-370***	***27-35***	***126-173***
HY/SY ♀	10	345-375	215-270	---	---
AHY/ASY ♀	21	360-390	275-310	27-31	126-139
HY/SY ♂	11	420-455	260-320	---	---
AHY/ASY ♂	24	440-475	320-370	31-35	159-173

[1] Measurements of HY/SYs pertain to birds with formative rectrices; those with auxillary formative rects (Fig. 150) have full-length rects, similar to AHY/ASYs.
[2] Culmen measured from tip of cere (Fig. 7**B**, p. 9).
[3] Culmen and tarsus lengths vary only slightly by age and thus are not separated here.

sexing hatchlings and Juvs. Bilateral BPs (Fig. 20**B**, p. 31) and/or distended cloaca (Fig. 21, p. 32) indicates ASY ♀ in May-Jul. Measurements (Table 19) are reliable for sexing within each subspecies. See also Rumble et al. (1996) for toe and toe-pad measurements by age and sex, and Bailey (1956) for sex-specific differences in shape of droppings.

HY/SY ♀ (1st cycle, F1; Oct-Sep): Tarsus < 145 mm and wing and tail shorter by subspecies (Table 19); head and throat grayish with downy brown feathering; outer 1-2 pp (p9-p10) usually contrastingly narrow, pointed, worn (Fig. 115**A**, p. 165), and with tip unbarred (Fig. 151**A**, p. 200); gr covs shorter (Fig. 152**A**, p. 200); back feathers narrow and rounded with dull sheen and indistinct subterminal bar (Fig. 153**A**, p.

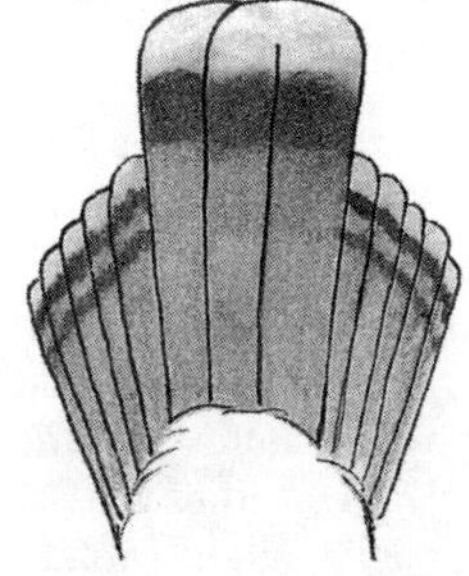

FIGURE 150. Tail morphology in HY/SY Wild Turkeys representing interesting, auxilliary preformative molt (pp. 14-15) in some individuals. The juv rects are completely replaced during the PF, followed by a second replacement during the PFa of up to 6 central rects (2 shown here) with auxillary formative feathers which are longer, broader, and have a broader and more distinct subterminal band; these characters resemble those of basic rects on AHY/ASYs (see also Fig. 153, p. 201). Look for other gamebirds to replace rects more than twice during the first cycle (*cf.* Fig. 116, p. 166).

201); most to all rects narrow (width < 55 mm), rounded, and with narrow and indistinct subterminal band, the central 1-3 or more pairs often longer and broader than the other rects (Fig. 150); keratin fibers on breast ("beard") absent or very short in Apr-Sep (< 50 mm from base, not protruding past breast feathers); tarsus dusky pinkish and without spurs (Fig. 122**A**, p. 172).

AHY/ASY ♀ (Def. cycle, DB; Oct-Sep): Tarsus < 145 mm and wing and tail medium-short by subspecies (Table 19); head and throat grayish to bluish gray with downy brown feathering; outer pp uniformly broad, truncate (Fig. 115**B**), and with tip barred (Fig. 151**B**); gr covs long (Fig. 152**B**); back feathers triangular with moderately bright sheen and distinct subterminal band (Fig. 153**B**); rects broad (width > 55 mm), squared, with broad and distinct subterminal band, and even in length (*cf.* Fig. 150); keratin fibers on breast sometimes present but moderately short (20-100 mm from base, rarely to 200 mm) and thin (fewer strands); tarsus reddish and usually without spurs (Fig. 122**A**). **Note: ♀♀ with keratin fibers > 50 mm and/or with short spurs (Fig. 122B-C) are probably ASY/ATYs but more study is needed to confirm this.**

HY/SY ♂ (1st cycle, F1; Oct-Sep): Tarsus > 145 mm and wing and tail medium-long by subspecies (Table 19); head and throat skin becoming bluish and red by Nov and with little to no downy feathering or caruncles by Jan; outer pp (Fig. 151**A**), gr covs (Fig. 152**A**), and rects (Fig.150) as in HY/SY ♀; back feathers broad and rounded with dull sheen and moderately distinct subterminal band (Fig. 153**C**); keratin fibers on breast short (to 20-100 mm from base by Sep) but thick (more strands); tarsus pinkish dusky with short (5-20 mm), rounded, and grayish spurs developing by May (Fig. 122**B-D**).

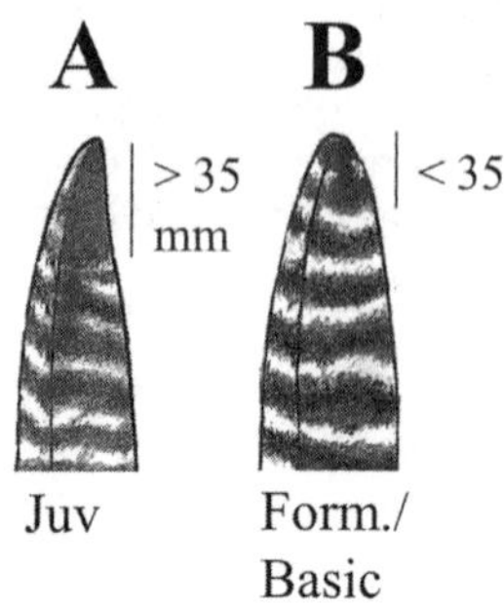

FIGURE 151. Juv (**A**) and formative/basic (**B**) p10 in Wild Turkey. The measure is to the first white bar along the shaft of the inner web (in mm). Most HY/SY turkeys from wild N.Am populations retain p10 and/or p9 during the preformative molt but some (~10%) individuals of s.populations or domestic lineage replace both pp and should be aged by other criteria. Note that the dark bars are slightly wider than the whitish bars, a feature of most N.Am populations, whereas in *G.p. osceola* (of FL) the dark bars are substantially wider than the whitish bars.

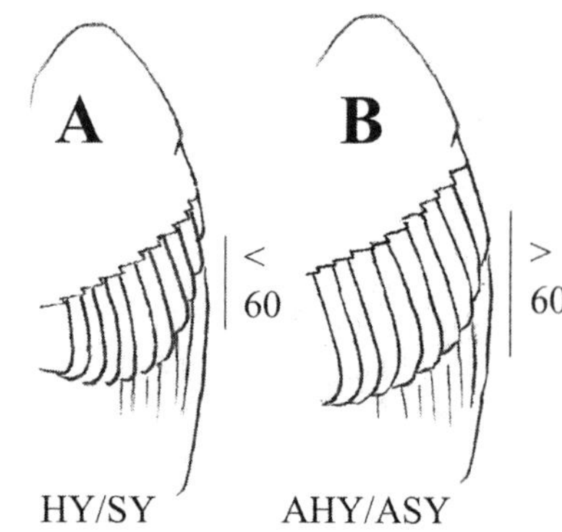

FIGURE 152. Proportional lengths of the greater coverts by age in Wild Turkey. The measure indicates the greatest distance (in mm) from the tip of a med cov and the tip of the corresponding gr cov, usually occurring among the medial feathers (gr cov 5-6) of these tracts.

AHY/ASY ♂ (Def. cycle, DB; Oct-Sep): Tarsus > 145 mm and wing and tail long by subspecies (Table 19); head and throat bright bluish and reddish with some caruncles but without downy feathering; outer pp (Fig. 151**B**), gr covs (Fig. 152**B**), and rects (*cf.* Fig. 150) as in AHY/ASY

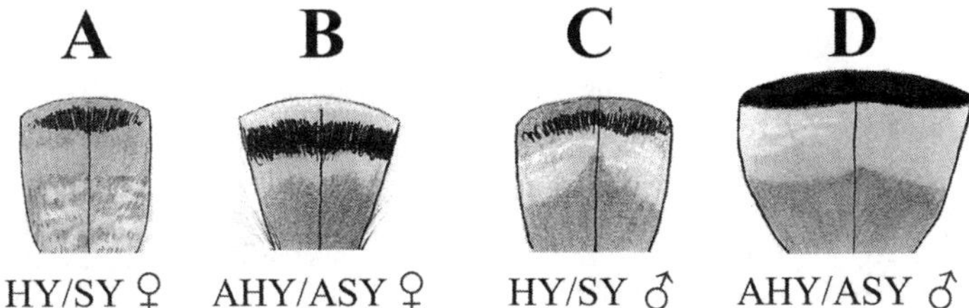

FIGURE 153. Shape, size, and pattern of the back and breast feathers by age/sex group in Wild Turkey. This is often the best criterion for sexing HYs, as it can be used as soon as the first formative breast or back feather has developed. See also Fig. 150 (p. 199) for similar pattern to the subterminal band in the rects.

♀; back feathers broadly triangular with bright sheen and distinct subterminal band (Fig. 153**D**); keratin fibers on breast moderately long (75-200 mm from base); tarsus bright reddish with moderately long (10-30 mm), recurved, and glossy blackish spurs (Fig. 122**D**-**E**). **Note: Some ♂♂ with keratin-fiber lengths of 75-150 mm and with amber tips, and spur lengths of 25-30 mm (Fig. 122D), probably can be aged SY/TY but more study needed.**

ASY/ATY ♂ (Def. cycle, DB; Oct-Sep): Like AHY/ASY but head with extensive caruncles, keratin fibers on breast > 200 mm and with broken tips, and tarsal spurs > 30 mm (Fig. 122**F**). **Note: It is possible that some ♂♂ may be aged ATY/A4Y or older by these criteria but more study needed.**

Wild Turkey
Jan Feb Mar Apr May Jun Jul Aug Sep Oct Nov Dec
Juv-HY
SY
AHY
ASY
ATY
■ > 95% ▩ 25-95% ▨ 5-25% □ < 5%
See Fig. 24 (pp. 44-45)

Hybrids reported—With Ring-necked Pheasant (p. 170) in the wild.

References—Bailey & Rinell (1967), Baldwin (1947), Bent (1932), Cobb (1994), Eaton (1970, 1992), Healy & Nenno (1980), Kelly (1975), Leopold (1943, 1944), J.B. Lewis (1966), J.C. Lewis (1967), Marchant & Higgins (1993), Nixon (1962), Oberholser (1974), Pattee & Beasom (1977), Pelham & Dickson (1992), Petrides (1942, 1945), Ridgway & Friedmann (1946), Rumble et al. (1996), Schmutz & Hoffman (1991), Schorger (1957, 1966), Steffen et al. (1990), Stresemann & Stresemann (1966), Wakeling et al. (1997). Wallin (1982), Warren & Gordon (1935), Williams (1961, 1971), Williams & Austin (1970, 1988), Williams & McGuire (1971).

NEW WORLD QUAIL *ODONTOPHORIDAE*

Six species. Family characters include compact bodies; small heads; small serrated bills; shortish, broad, and bowed wings; short tails; and sturdy legs and feet. North American quail have 10 functional primaries (the 10th extending 15-30 mm short of the longest, p6-p7, when fully grown), 10 primary coverts (p10 minute and distal to p10; Ohmart 1967), 12 secondaries (including 3 tertials and none absent between the 4th and 5th as in other N.Am taxa; *cf.* Fig. 12**B**, p. 19), and 12-14 rectrices. Ageing through the first cycle (to SY and ASY) can be accomplished by replacement patterns to the primaries (Fig. 115, p. 165), and by the retained juvenile primary coverts (Fig. 154). Males are only slightly larger than females but can be distinguished by plumage aspect and/or length of ornamental plumes in most if not all species; females with partial male-like plumage aspect occur occasionally (Domm 1939, Buchanan & Parkes 1948, Crawford et al. 1987, Hagelin & Kimball 1997). Both sexes can develop medial brood patches (Fig. 20**A**, p. 31), although those of females are more fully developed than in males; females also develop distended cloacae during breeding (Fig. 21, p. 32), and most individuals of all ages (including juveniles) can be aged and sexed through ASY by cloacal examination (Figs. 22-23, pp. 32-35; see Gower 1939).

In molting, most North American quail exhibit the Complex Basic Strategy (CBS; Fig. 10**B**, pp. 13-16), including a formative but no alternate plumages; one species (Northern Bobwhite, p. 209), apparently has a limited prealternate molt and thus exhibits the Complex Alternate Strategy (CAS; Fig. 10**F**). In most HYs, the preformative molt includes all feathers except the outer two primaries (p9-p10) and all ten primary coverts (van Rossem 1925, Leopold 1939); individuals of certain species retain p8 during this molt. The preformative molt is protracted throughout the period of chick growth, with initial feathers being brown and streaked, and subsequent feathers intermediate toward definitive plumage (Fig. 116**A-B**, p. 166). Primaries are replaced distally; secondaries are replaced both distally and proximally from s3 and distally from the tertials, such that the last ss replaced are usually among s8-s10; and rectrices are generally

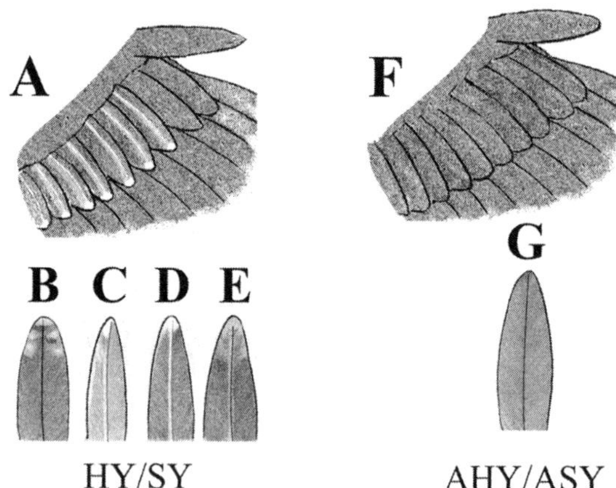

FIGURE 154. Pattern to the primary coverts by age in most N.Am species of quail. During the PF, all 10 p covs are usually retained and the inner 7 juv p covs variably (by species) show whitish or pale shaft streaks and/or tips (**A**). The p covs corresponding to p8-p9 are also retained but tend to lack pale markings (the p10 cov is minute or vestigial). The alula must be pulled aside (as shown) to view this area of the wing. Adults show uniformly fuller and unmarked p covs (**F-G**). By species, juv p covs resemble **B** in Mountain Quail (p. 203), **C** in Scaled Quail (p. 204), **D** in California (p. 206) and Gambel's (p. 207) quails, and **E** in Northern Bobwhite (p. 209).

replaced distally on both sides of the tail. Age of first breeding occurs at 1 year; thus, the second prebasic molt is similar in timing to subsequent molts and is considered the definitive prebasic molt.

General references or summaries for species, age, and sex determinations in New World quail include Grinnell et al. (1918), Taber (1969), Johnsgard (1973), Larson & Taber (1980), Brown (1989), Dimmick & Pelton (1996), and Madge & McGowan (2002). Gamebirds should not be banded with federal bands; thus, no band sizes are recommended.

MOUNTAIN QUAIL — MOUQ

Oreortyx pictus — Species # 2920

Species—Younger juvs from other N.Am quail by crown with white spots and two elongated ornamental plumes. Non-juvs from other quail by larger size but proportionally shorter tail (Table 20, p. 209); crown with two elongated (47-99 mm; see **Sex**) and narrow blackish ornamental plumes; upperparts and breast plain grayish; throat chestnut; flanks chestnut and white; undertail covs black and rufous. Beware of hybrids (see below).

Geographic variation—Considered monotypic here (*cf.* Gutiérrez & Delehanty 1999). Populations of coastal sw.BC-wc.CA ("*O.p. palmeri*") average slightly darker upperparts, populations of interior se.WA-w.ID to w.NV-ce.CA, ("*pictus*") average slightly more olive tinged upperparts, most populations of s.CA "*eremophilus*") average slightly grayer upperparts, and populations of the San Bernadino Mts, CA ("*russelli*") may average slightly darker underparts but in all cases differences are slight and broadly clinal; subspecies taxonomy has also been confused by specimen foxing and nomenclatural problems. See also Browning (1977a, 1979b, 2002), Hellmayr & Conover (1942), Miller (1946), Oberholser (1923), Ridgway (1894), Ridgway & Friedmann (1946), and van Rossem (1937).

Molt—CBS. PF incomplete (Jun-Nov in HYs), DPB complete (Jun-Oct in AHYs); PA absent. See Family Account (p. 202) for replacement sequence of pp, ss, and rects. The PF includes all feathers except the outer 2 pp (p9-p10), most to all p covs, and often one or more alula; rarely up to four medial p covs may be replaced.

Age—Juv (B1; Jun-Sep) plumage aspect develops from brown and streaked to basic-like but having upperparts with brownish vermiculations, breast with whitish spotting, ss barred brownish, and rects short (tl < 70) and barred brownish (*cf.* Fig. 116**A-B**, p. 166). Juv ♀=♂ but see Figures 22-23 (pp. 32-35) for cloacal characters reliable for sexing hatchlings and Juvs.

HY/SY (1st cycle, F1; Oct-Sep): Outer 2 pp (p9-p10) contrastingly narrow, pointed, and worn (Fig. 115**A**, p. 165); proximal 7 p covs shorter, fringed with brown mottling, and tipped or streaked whitish (Fig. 154**B**), contrasting with longer and dark brown outermost 2 large p covs (*cf.* Fig. 154**A**).

AHY/ASY (Def. cycle, DB; Oct-Sep): Outer pp uniformly broad and truncate (Fig. 115**B**); p covs uniformly dark brown, without whitish tips or streaks (Fig. 154**F-G**).

Sex—Full medial BP (Fig. 20**A**, p. 31) and/or distended cloaca (Fig. 21, p. 32) indicates AHY ♀ in Apr-Jul; ♂♂ can develop partial BPs. Measurements unhelpful for sexing (Table 20, p. 209). Intermediates between the following are likely HY/SY ♂♂ or AHY/ASY ♀♀ so combine with age-determination criteria, measurements, and cloacal examination (Figs. 22-23, pp. 32-35) if possible.

♀: Ornamental crown plumes shorter (longest plume 47-83 mm when fully grown); upper back primarily olive-brown, often slightly mottled gray. **Note: Length of longest ornamental crest plume may be more reliable for sex determinations within populations than overall (e.g., populations from a c.CA population exhibited only 7% overlap, with ♀ 64-83 and ♂ 81-99; Pine 1981); more study needed.**

♂: Ornamental crown plumes longer (longest plume 72-99 mm when fully grown); upper back uniformly gray or sometimes slightly mottled olive-brown. **Note: See ♀.**

Mountain Quail

Jan Feb Mar Apr May Jun Jul Aug Sep Oct Nov Dec

Juv-HY

SY

AHY

ASY

■ > 95% ▩ 25-95% □ 5-25% □ < 5%

See Fig. 24 (pp. 44-45)

Note: Cloacal examination needed for reliable sexing of Juvs and some non-Juvs.

Hybrids reported—With California Quail (V. Bailey 1928; Hachisuka 1928; Johnsgard 1970, 1973; Peck 1911; Peterle 1951).

References—Arnold (1972a), Bent (1932), Brennan & Block (1985), Collins (1974a), Delehanty & Turek (2003), Delehanty et al. (1995), Dwight (1900a), Gutiérrez & Delehanty (1999), Leopold (1939), Miller & Stebbins (1964), Petrides (1942, 1945), Pine (1981), Ridgway (1894), Ridgway & Friedmann (1946), van Rossem (1925, 1937).

SCALED QUAIL

Callipepla squamata

SCQU
Species # 2930

Species—Younger juvs from other N.Am quail by crown feathers (including two slightly elongated ornamental plumes) with distinct white streaks and rects gray with dusky bars. Non-juvs from other quail by medium-large size (Table 20, p. 209); tail with 14 rects; crown with short (17-28 mm from base) crest feathers tipped white; plumage aspect pale grayish and clay, the upper-back and underpart feathers finely tipped blackish; flanks grayish with short white marks. Beware of hybrids (see below).

Geographic variation—See Bangs (1914), Browning (1990), Oberholser (1974), Rea (1973), and Ridgway & Friedmann (1946). One other subspecies occurs in Mexico. In addition to the following, see Ridgway & Friedmann (1946) and Rea (1973) for slight differences in measurements (n.subspecies > s.subspecies), and beware that differences could be confounded by propagation of non-indigenous subspecies throughout range (Rea 1973, Long 1981).

C.s. pallida (res se.UT-sw.CO to s.AZ-sw.TX; introduced e.WA & NV): Back and rump medium gray with slight brown tinge; abdomen pale grayish buff without chestnut.

C.s. hargravei (res c.CO-nw.NW to sw.KS-cw.TX): Back pale grayish; scaling to breast less distinct (usually < 1 mm wide); abdomen whitish, without chestnut.

C.s. castanogastris (res s.TX, Maverick-Atascosa to Hidalgo Cos.): Back and rump brown with slight gray tinge; scaling to breast more distinct (usually > 1 mm wide); abdomen brownish buff, often with chestnut patch (see **Sex**).

Molt—CBS. PF incomplete (Jun-Sep in HYs), DPB complete (Jun-Oct in AHYs); PA absent? See Family Account (p. 202) for replacement sequence of pp, ss, and rects. The PF includes all feathers except the outer 2-3 pp (p8-p10 or p9-p10), all p covs, and often one or more alula; p8 can apparently be retained in < 20% of HY/SYs (Smith & Cain 1984) and look for 1-4 medial p covs to rarely be replaced, as in other quail. Occurrence of a limited DPA in Feb-Apr (Dwight 1900a) requires confirmation.

Age—Juv (B1; May-Aug) plumage aspect develops from brown and streaked to basic-like but having upperparts with brownish vermiculations, ss mottled brownish, breast with whitish spots, and rects short (tl < 70), narrow, and grayish (*cf.* Fig. 116**A**-**B**, p. 166). Juv ♀ = ♂ but see Figures 22-23 (pp. 32-35) for cloacal characters reliable for sexing hatchlings and Juvs.

HY/SY (1st cycle, F1; Oct-Sep): Outer 2-3 pp (among p8-p10) contrastingly narrow, pointed, and worn (Fig. 115**A**, p. 165); proximal p covs shorter and brownish with distinct white tips and/or shaft streaks (Fig. 154**C**, p. 202), contrasting with longer and more uniformly pale brown outermost 2 p covs (*cf.* Fig. 154**A**).

AHY/ASY (Def. cycle, DB; Oct-Sep): Outer pp uniformly broad and truncate (Fig. 115**B**); p covs uniformly pale brown and without white tips or streaks (Fig. 154**F**-**G**).

Sex—Full medial BP (Fig. 20**A**, p. 31) and/or distended cloaca (Fig. 21, p. 32) indicates AHY ♀ in Apr-Jul; ♂♂ possibly can develop partial BPs. Measurements unhelpful for sexing (Table 20, p. 209). Intermediates between the following may occur; these are likely HY/SY ♂♂ or AHY/ASY ♀♀ so combine with age-determination criteria and cloacal examination (Figs. 22-23, pp. 32-35) if possible.

♀: Crest averages shorter (17-23 mm from base); auriculars and throat brownish white with dusky streaks (Fig. 155**A**); abdomen of *C.s. castanogastris* (see **Geographic variation**) with little or no chestnut.

♂: Crest averages longer (21-28 mm from base); auriculars and throat pale buff without dusky streaks (Fig. 155**B**); abdomen of *C.s. castanogastris* with substantial chestnut patch.

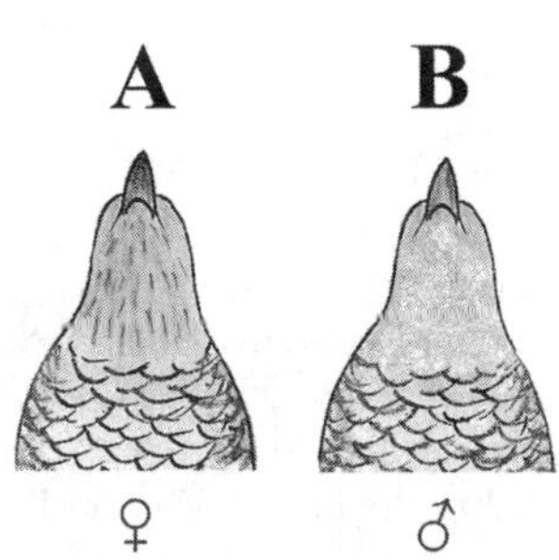

FIGURE 155. Throat streaking in ♀ (**A**) *vs* ♂ (**B**) Scaled Quail. Intermediates may occur that are likely HY/SY ♂ or AHY/ASY ♀ so combine with age for reliable sexing.

Hybrids reported—Scaled Quail from native populations with Gambel's Quail (V. Bailey 1928; Hachisuka 1928; Hubbard 1966; Johnsgard 1970, 1973; McCabe 1954; Phillips et al. 1964), Elegant Quail *C. douglasi* (Banks & Walker 1964), and Northern Bobwhite (Johnsgard 1970, 1973; McCabe 1954; Schemnitz 1961; Shupe 1990; Sutton 1963; Webb & Tyler 1988) in the wild. Scaled Quail from naturalized populations with naturalized California Quail (Jewett et al. 1953; Johnsgard 1970, 1971, 1973) in the wild.

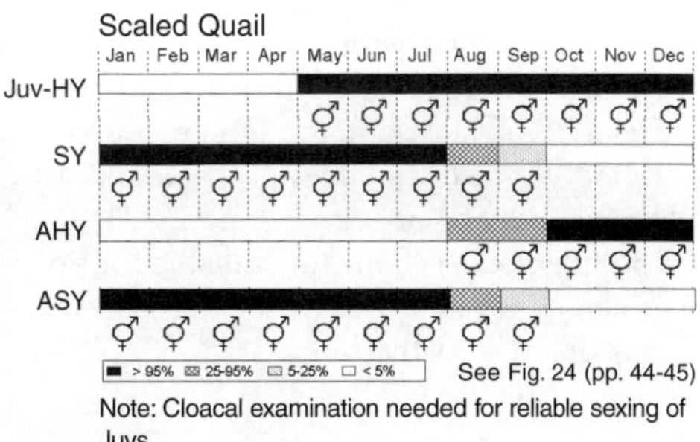

References—Bent (1932), Campbell & Lee (1956), Collins (1974b), Dwight (1900a), Leopold (1939, 1959), Oberholser (1974), Ohmart (1967), Petrides (1942, 1945), Rea (1973), Ridgway & Friedmann (1946), Schemnitz (1994), Smith & Cain (1984), van Rossem (1925), Wallmo (1956).

CALIFORNIA QUAIL CAQU
Callipepla californica Species # 2940

Species—Younger juvs from other N.Am quail (including Gambel's Quail) by crown with two elongated ornamental plumes, brownish; longest scapulars with distinct blackish subterminal fringes; breast grayish and often with indistinct dusky spots. Non-juvs from Gambel's and other quail by medium-small size and proportionally short tail (Table 20, p. 209); crown (♂) and flanks dull brown to olive-brown, the crown with moderately long (13-37 mm; see **Sex**) blackish ornamental plumes (widening distally), and the flanks with thin white streaks; lores pale grayish (♀) or tan (♂); abdomen without black (but with rufous in ♂♂), the feathers fringed black forming scaled appearance; ♂ with hind crown brown and throat black. Beware of hybrids with Gambel's Quail.

Geographic variation—Considered monotypic here based on results of Zink et al. (1987; see also Calkins et al. 1999) suggesting greater variation within current populations than between them; differences may also have been confounded by frequent propagation of non-indigenous subspecies for millenia (Figgins 1914, Long 1981). Compared to widespread "*C.c. californicus*," populations originally indigenous to coastal sw.OR-nw.CA ("*C.c. brunnescens*") averaged slightly darker and browner, those of sc.OR ("*orecta*") may have averaged slightly paler and grayer, those of ec.CA-wc.NV ("*canfieldae*") averaged slightly paler, and those of Santa Catalina I, CA ("*catalinensis*") averaged slightly larger and more contrasting in plumage aspect but all differences were/are weak, broadly clinal, and largely confounded by individual variation. Other populations from Baja CA average smaller but differences are slight and clinal. See also Behle (1985), Bent (1932), Browning (2002), Dickey & van Rossem (1922), Grinnell (1906, 1926), Hellmayr & Conover (1942), Leopold (1977), Oberholser (1917b, 1932), Ridgway & Friedmann (1946), van Rossem (1939c, 1946).

Molt—CBS. PF incomplete (Jun-Sep in HYs), DPB complete (Jun-Oct in AHYs); PA absent. See Family Account (p. 202) for replacement sequence of pp, ss, and rects. The PF usually includes all feathers except the outer 2 pp (p9-p10), all p covs, and often one or more alula; 1-4 medial p covs rarely can be replaced (Leopold 1939). The DPB averages slightly earlier in ♂♂ than in ♀♀. There is no evidence for a PA (*cf.* Dwight 1900a, Raitt 1961).

Age—Juv (B1; May-Sep) plumage aspect develops from brown and streaked to basic-likebut having upperparts with brownish vermiculations, breast with whitish spotting, ss mottled brownish, and rects short (tl < 70) and barred brownish (*cf.* Fig. 116**A**-**B**, p. 166). Older Juv ♂♂ can have blackish in the forecrown, lores, and face (especially below eye; Fig. 156). Juvs without blackish should not be sexed by plumage aspect but see Figures 22-23 (pp. 32-35) for cloacal characters reliable for sexing hatchlings and Juvs. See also Lewin (1963) for size of the bursa (Fig. 23, p. 34) by age.

FIGURE 156. Some Juv ♂ California Quail show dark auricular patches and can be sexed. Other Juv ♂♂ resemble ♀♀, so Juvs without blackish here cannot be sexed by plumage aspect.

HY/SY (1st cycle, F1; Oct-Sep): Outer 2 pp (p9-p10) contrastingly narrow, pointed, and worn (Fig. 115**A**, p. 165); proximal p covs shorter, fringed with brown mottling, and with prominent shaft streaks, contrasting with longer and more uniformly olive-brown outermost 2 large p covs (Fig. 154**A** & **D**, p. 202).

AHY/ASY (Def. cycle, DB; Oct-Sep): Outer pp uniformly broad and truncate (Fig. 115**B**); p covs uniformly olive-brown and without shaft streaks (Fig. 154**F**-**G**).

Sex—Full medial BP (Fig. 20**A**, p. 31) and/or distended cloaca (Fig. 21, p. 32) indicates AHY ♀ in Apr-Jul; ♂♂ can develop partial BPs. Measurements unhelpful for sexing (Table 20, p. 209). The following is reliable after commencement of the PF (in the head and face) in Jul (and for some Juv ♂♂; Fig. 156); see also Figures 22-23 (pp. 32-35) for cloacal examination criteria.

♀: Auriculars and throat dull brownish and dusky grayish, without distinct black or white feathering; occipital ornamental plumes short (longest plume 13-18 mm from base); abdomen without rufous.

♂: Auriculars and throat distinctly black and white; occipital ornamental plumes long (longest plume 27-37 mm from base); abdomen with rufous patch.

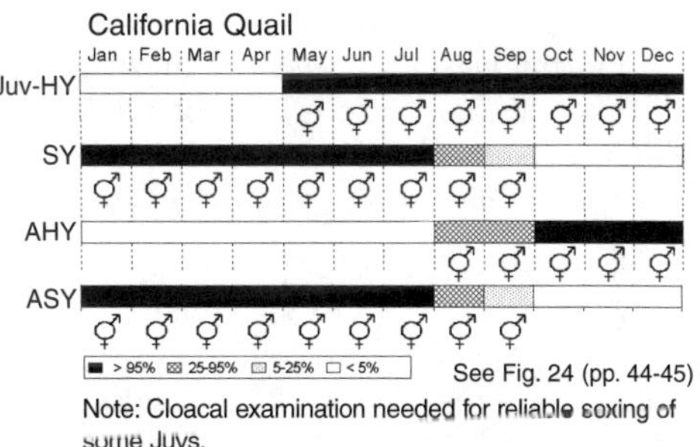

Hybrids reported—California Quail from native populations with Mountain Quail (p. 203) and Gambel's Quail (Gee 2004, Gee et al. 2003, Hachisuka 1928, Henshaw 1885, and Miller & Stebbins 1964, Hess 2005) in the wild. California Quail from naturalized populations with Scaled Quail (p. 204) and Bobwhite (Aiken 1930, Compton 1932, Peterle 1951) in the wild.

References—Bent (1932), Calkins et al. (1999), Collins (1974c), Dwight (1900a), Genelly (1955), Leopold (1939, 1959, 1977), Marchant & Higgins (1993), Ohmart (1967), Petrides (1942, 1945), Raitt (1961), Ridgway & Friedmann (1946), Stresemann & Stresemann (1966), Sumner (1935), van Rossem (1925), Williams (1959).

GAMBEL'S QUAIL — GAQU

Callipepla gambelii — Species # 2950

Species—Younger juvs from other N.Am quail (including California Quail) by crown with two elongated ornamental plumes, rusty-brown to chestnut; longest scapulars with indistinct subterminal fringes; breast pale grayish brown with very indistinct or no darker spots. Non-juvs from California and other quail by medium-small size but proportionally long tail (Table 20, p. 209); crown (♂) and flanks cinnamon-brown to chestnut, the crown with moderately long (22-44 mm; see **Sex**) black ornamental plumes (widening distally), and the flanks with thin white streaks; lores dark grayish (♀) or black (♂); abdomen pale buff, without scaled appearance, and with black patch in ♂. Beware of hybrids with California Quail.

Geographic variation—Considered monotypic here, following the opinions of Hellmayr & Conover (1942) and Phillips (1958), who between them have synonymized or questioned all described subspecies except a weakly differentiated and biogeographically unlikely Mexican race (Phillips 1958). Compared to widespread "*C.g. gambelii*", populations originally indigenous to se.AZ ("*fulvipectus*") averaged darker, browner, and larger; populations of se.UT-sw.CO ("*sana*", possibly introduced from CA) may have averaged darker and grayer; and populations of s.NM-w.TX ("*ignoscens*") may have averaged paler, but differences in all cases are/were slight, broadly clinal, and confounded by individual variation and propagation of non-indigenous subspecies throughout range (*cf.* California Quail, p. 206). The best differentiated of these populations, "*fulvipectus*", shows widespread intergradation with "*gambelii*" (van Rossem 1932, Pitelka 1948). See also Behle (1985), Brown et al. (1998), Figgins (1914), Friedmann (1943b), Mearns (1914), Nelson (1899), Phillips et al. (1964), Ridgway & Friedmann (1946).

Molt—CBS. PF incomplete (Jun-Oct in HYs), DPB complete (Jun-Nov in AHYs); PA absent. See Family Account (p. 202) for replacement sequence of pp, ss, and rects. The PF usually includes all feathers except the outer 2 pp (p9-p10), all p covs, and often one or more alula; 1-4 medial p covs rarely can be replaced (Leopold 1939). The DPB averages slightly earlier in ♂♂ than in ♀♀. There is no evidence for a PA (*cf.* Dwight 1900a, Raitt & Ohmart 1966).

Age—Juv (B1; May-Sep) plumage aspect develops from brown and streaked to basic-like but having upperparts with brownish vermiculations, breast with whitish spotting, ss mottled brownish, and rects short (tl < 70) and barred brownish (*cf.* Fig. 116**A-B**, p. 166). Older Juv ♂♂ can have blackish in the lower abdomen; Juvs without blackish should not be sexed by plumage aspect but see Figures 22-23 (pp. 32-35) for cloacal characters reliable for sexing hatchlings and Juvs.

HY/SY (1st cycle, F1; Oct-Sep): Outer 2 pp (p9-p10) contrastingly narrow, pointed, and worn (Fig. 115**A**, p. 165); proximal p covs shorter, fringed with brown mottling, and with pale shaft streaks, contrasting with longer and more uniformly olive-brown, outermost 2 large p covs (Fig. 154**A** & **D**, p. 202).

AHY/ASY (Def. cycle, DB; Oct-Sep): Outer pp uniformly broad and truncate (Fig. 115**B**); p covs uniformly olive-brown and without pale streaks (Fig. 154**F-G**).

Sex—Full medial BP (Fig. 20**A**, p. 31) and/or distended cloaca (Fig. 21, p. 32) indicates AHY ♀ in Apr-Jul; ♂♂ possibly can develop partial BPs. Measurements unhelpful for sexing (Table 20). The following is reliable after commencement of the PF (in the head and face) in Jul (and for some Juv ♂♂ with blackish in vent; see **Age**); see also Figures 22-23 (pp. 32-35) for reliable cloacal criteria.

♀: Auricular and throat dull brownish gray, without distinct black or white feathering; occipital ornamental plumes short (longest plume 24-33 mm from base); abdomen sometimes with indistinct dusky streaking but without blackish.

♂: Auricular and throat black and white; occipital ornamental plumes long (longest plume 34-44 mm from base); abdomen without indistinct streaks but with blackish patch.

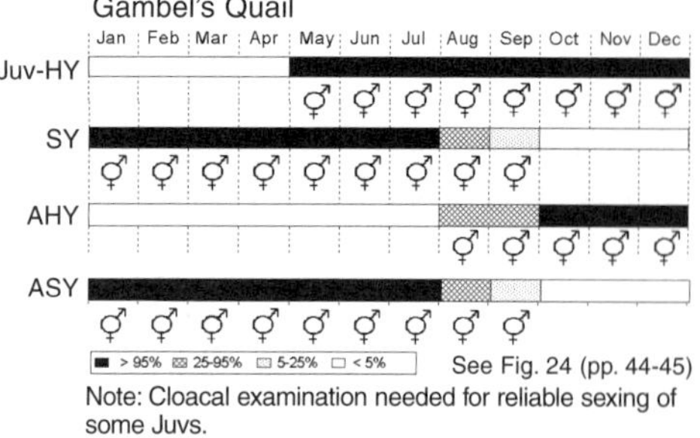

Hybrids reported—With Scaled Quail (p. 204), Elegant Quail *C. douglasi* (McCarthy 2006), and California Quail (p. 206) in the wild.

References—Bent (1932), Brown et al. (1998), Collins (1974d), Dwight (1900a), Hagelin (2003), Hagelin & Kimball (1997), Leopold (1939, 1959, 1977), Oberholser (1974), Ohmart (1967), Petrides (1942, 1945), Raitt & Ohmart (1966), Ridgway & Friedmann (1946), van Rossem (1925).

TABLE 20. Measurements (mm) of North American quail to assist with identification and sexing. See pp. 4-11 for methods of measurement. Species summaries are in **bold** and subspecies summaries are in ***italics***. Values were derived from 95% confidence intervals as based approximately on the indicated sample sizes (see pp. 4-5); thus midpoints of ranges approximate means, and S.D. is approximated by 25% of the range.[1]

Taxon/Sex	*n*	wing chord	tail length	exposed culmen	tarsus
Mountain Quail		**124-142**	**70-89**	**13.0-17.5**	**32-41**
♀	100	124-140	70-86	13.0-17.4	32-39
♂	100	125-142	74-89	13.1-17.5	34-41
Scaled Quail[2]		**107-124**	**76-91**	**12.3-15.1**	**26-35**
♀	80	107-121	76-87	12.3-14.7	26-33
♂	80	111-124	79-91	12.8-15.1	28-35
California Quail[2]		**104-119**	**80-96**	**11.1-12.8**	**28-35**
♀	100	106-116	80-93	11.1-12.5	28-34
♂	100	104-119	84-96	11.5-12.8	30-35
Gambel's Quail[2]		**105-121**	**85-106**	**11.5-13.4**	**26-33**
♀	60	105-119	85-103	11.5-13.0	26-32
♂	70	107-121	89-106	11.8-13.4	27-33
Northern Bobwhite[2]		**99-119**	**50-69**	**11.6-15.9**	**26-37**
C.v. ridgwayi		***102-112***	***54-68***	***11.6-14.0***	***27-33***
♀	10	102-111	54-65	11.6-13.1	27-32
♂	33	103-112	57-68	12.4-14.0	28-33
C.v. taylori		***105-118***	***53-69***	***12.7-15.1***	***28-35***
♀	10	105-116	53-67	12.7-14.4	28-34
♂	30	106-118	56-69	13.3-15.1	29-35
C.v. texanus		***101-113***	***52-67***	***13.0-15.6***	***26-33***
♀	20	101-112	52-64	13.0-14.8	26-32
♂	60	102-113	56-67	13.6-15.6	27-33
C.v. virginianus		***102-119***	***50-69***	***12.4-15.9***	***28-37***
♀	100	102-117	50-66	12.4-14.9	28-35
♂	100	104-119	54-69	13.2-15.9	30-37
C.v. floridanus		***99-111***	***50-64***	***12.8-15.6***	***26-33***
♀	20	99-110	50-62	12.8-14.7	26-32
♂	70	100-111	52-64	13.6-15.6	27-33
Montezuma Quail		**112-130**	**49-63**	**12.8-15.1**	**26-32**
♀	70	111-126	48-62	12.8-14.7	26-31
♂	90	116-130	49-63	13.1-15.1	27-32

[1] Measurements pertain to birds in formative and definitive plumages; Juvs vary greatly in size but are substantially smaller.

[2] Measures from N.Am populations only; see **Geographic variation**.

NORTHERN BOBWHITE
Colinus virginianus

NOBO
Species # 2890

Species—Younger juvs from other N.Am quail by underparts usually with cinammon and crown without elongated ornamental plumes. Non-juvs from other quail by small size with proportionally short tail and long bill (Table 20); crown without crest or ornamental plumes; plumage aspect variably brown, gray, and rusty, with distinctly defined buff (♀) to white (♂) lores, supercilium, and throat of most subspecies (see **Geographic variation**).

Geographic variation—See Aldrich (1942, 1946c), Banks (1975), Brennan (1999), Browning (2002), Hellmayr & Conover (1942), Howe (1904), Howell & Webb (1995), Leopold (1959), Lincoln (1915), Nelson (1899, 1902), Oberholser (1974), Phillips (1915b), Ridgway & Friedmann (1946), Ripley (1960), Rosene (1969), Stoddard (1931). About 15 other subspecies in Mex-n.C.Am and Cuba. Propagation of non-indigenous subspecies (Long 1981) may also have affected differences.

Western Mexican *(C.v. coyolcos)* Group. ♂ with black head and uniformly rufous underparts; ♀ pale and mottled.

C.v. ridgwayi (res. se.AZ): Masked Bobwhite. Averages medium-small with short bill (Table 20, p. 209); ♀ with upperparts uniformly checkered pale buff, dusky, and white, with little or no dark vermiculated feathers; ♂ with head and throat blackish, with indistinct or no whitish supercilium, and underparts uniformly rufous.

Northern (*C.v. virginianus*) Group. ♂ with distinct white supercilium and white throat; ♀ with dark vermiculated feathers in upperparts.

C.v. taylori (res se.WY-sc.SD to n.TX-nw.AR; introduced se.WA-ne.OR to w.ID): Averages medium-large (Table 20); hind crown dark pinkish with little to moderate blackish mottling by sex (♀<♂); upper breast and sides variably pinkish to orangish rufous with moderately thick blackish barring and vermiculation.

C.v. texanus (res. se.NM-s.TX): Averages medium-small (Table 20); hind crown buff with variable black mottling by sex (♀<♂); upper breast and sides dusky pinkish with little to no blackish markings.

C.v. virginianus (res e.SD-e.TX to MA-n.FL): Variably large (Table 20); hind crown pale rusty with little to moderate blackish mottling by sex (♀<♂); upper breast and sides variably dusky pinkish to pale rufous with thin blackish barring and vermiculation. Populations of MA-n.FL ("*marilandicus*") average slightly larger, redder, and more richly colored in aspect, and populations of e.SD-e.TX to NY-AL ("*mexicanus*") average grayer, but differences are slight, broadly clinal, and greatly confounded by individual variation. Near-complete rufous (carotenistic) morphs occur rarely within this subspecies.

C.v. floridanus (res s.FL): Averages small but with proportionally large bill (Table 20); hind crown dark rusty with moderate to heavy blackish mottling by sex (♀<♂); upper breast and sides blackish with white and rufous mottling and spotting. Populations of Key West ("*insularis*"), now extirpated (if ever existed), may have been smaller and with a darker crown, but distinctions can not be confirmed (Aldrich 1946c).

Molt—CAS. PF incomplete (Jun-Nov in HYs), DPA absent(?)-partial (Feb-May in AHYs). DPB complete (Jun-Nov in AHYs). See Family Account (p. 202) for replacement sequence of pp, ss, and rects. The PF usually includes all feathers except the outer 2-3 pp (among p8-p10, often p9-p10) all p covs, and often one or more alula; 1-4 medial p covs rarely can be replaced (Leopold 1939). The DPB rarely can be incomplete (more often in n.populations), with p10 and 2-3 ss among s7-s10 retained. The PA is apparently variable, absent or restricted to head and throat feathers in n. populations, but can include feathers throughout the body in s. populations (e.g., Cuba; Watson 1962b). More study is needed on the DPA in this species and other Galliformes.

Age—Juv (B1; May-Sep) plumage aspect develops from brown and streaked (*cf.* Fig. 116**A**-**B**, p. 166) to basic-like but showing brownish and reddish vermiculations to upperparts, whitish spotting on breast, short and barred brownish rects (tl < 70) and ss with brownish mottling. Juv ♀=♂ but see Figures 22-23 (pp. 32-35) for cloacal characters reliable for sexing hatchlings and Juvs. In addition to the following, see Thompson & Robel (1968) for age-related differences in skeletal parameters and tissue decomposition, and Roseberry & Verts (1963) for age-related variation in ocular-lens weights.

HY/SY (1st cycle, F1-A1; Oct-Sep): Outer 2-3 pp (p8-p10 or p9-p10) contrastingly narrow, pointed, and worn (Fig. 115**A**, p. 165); proximal p covs shorter and tipped or streaked with rufous to whitish buff (Fig. 154**E**, p. 202), contrasting with longer and more uniformly brown outermost 2 large p covs (*cf.* Fig. 154**A**).

AHY/ASY (Def. cycle, DB-DA; Oct-Sep): Outer pp uniformly broad and truncate (Fig. 115**B**); p covs uniformly brown and without rufous to whitish-buff streaks (Fig. 154**F**-**G**).

Sex—Full medial BP (Fig. 20**A**, p. 31) and/or distended cloaca (Fig. 21, p. 32) indicates AHY ♀ in Apr-Jul; ♂♂ can develop partial BPs. Measurements unhelpful for sexing (Table 20, p. 209). The following is reliable after commencement of the PF (in the head and face) in Jun-Jul; see also Figures 22-23 (pp. 32-35) for cloacal criteria reliable for sexing.

♀: Forehead, lores, and neck collar (usually incomplete) with reduced blackish by subspecies (see **Geographic variation**); supercilium and throat washed buff; les and med covs rufous to grayish with pale bars or corners; base of lower mandible yellowish.

♂: Forehead, lores, and neck collar (usually complete) with extensive blackish by subspecies; supercilium and throat white (or black in *C.v. ridgwayi*); les and med covs rufous with variable dark vermiculation but without white bars or distinct white corners; base of lower mandible black.

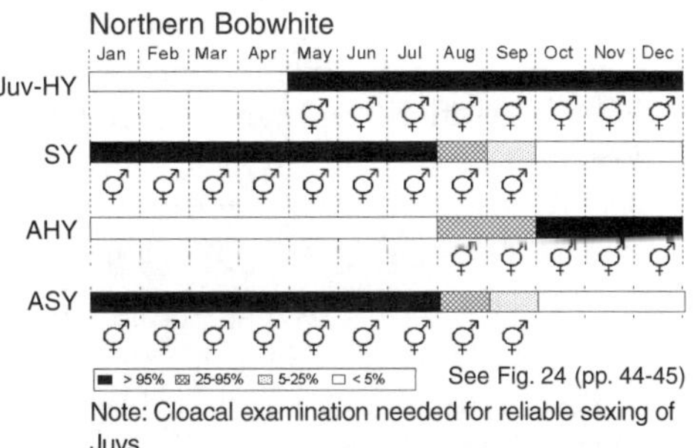

Hybrids reported—Bobwhite from native populations with Scaled Quail (p. 204) in the wild. Bobwhite from naturalized populations with California Quail (p. 206) in the wild.

References—Bent (1932), Brennan (1999), Buchanan & Parkes (1948), Dwight (1900a), Haugen (1957), Leopold (1939, 1959), Loveless (1958), Lyon (1962), Oberholser (1974), Petrides (1942, 1945), Petrides & Nestler (1943, 1952), Ridgway & Friedmann (1946), Rosene (1969), Rosene & Fitch (1956), Stoddard (1931), Thomas (1969), Thompson & Taber (1948), Thompson & Kabat (1950), Tomlinson (1975), van Rossem (1925), Watson (1962b).

MONTEZUMA QUAIL
Cyrtonyx montezumae

MONQ
Species # 2960

Species—Younger juvs from other N.Am quail by crown without elongated plumes, plumage aspect washed pinkish with distinct shaft streaks to upperparts, and rects very short (Table 20, p. 209). Non-juvs from other quail by medium-large size but short tail (Table 20); crown with short, broad crest but without ornamental plumes; pp, ss, and wing covs with distinct white bars or spots (Fig. 157, p. 212); ♀ brownish, pinkish, and dull rufous with distinct white streaks through upperparts.

Geographic variation—See Hellmayr & Conover (1942), Howell & Webb (1995), Leopold (1959), Leopold & McCabe (1957), Nelson (1902), Phillips (1966), Pitelka (1948), Ridgway & Friedmann (1946), Stromberg (2000), van Rossem (1942b). Three other subspecies occur in Mex.

Northern (*C.m. montezumae*) Group. ♂ with posterior flank spots white, *vs* cinnamon to rufous in Southern (*sallei*) Group of s.Mexico.

C.m. mearnsi (res. N.Am): Paler; ♀ with streaks on upperparts buff (*vs* whitish in *montezumae* of c.Mex); ♂ with crest pale buff (*vs* darker and browner), upperparts brownish (*vs* blackish), and flanks with wider white spots (> 4 mm, *vs* < 4 mm in *montezumae*).

Molt—CBS (CAS?). PF incomplete (Jun-Nov in HYs), DPB complete (Jun-Nov in AHYs); PA absent?. See Family Account (p. 202) for replacement sequence of pp, ss, and rects. The PF usually includes all feathers except the outer 1-2 pp (p9-p10), all p covs, and often one or more alula. A limited PA in Feb-Apr has been reported (Dwight 1900a, Oberholser 1974) but requires verification.

Age—Juv (B1; May-Sep) plumage aspect develops from brown and streaked (*cf.* Fig. 116**A**, p. 166) to resembling ♀ but with mottled brownish ss. Juvs with blackish or dark rufous in vent can be reliably sexed ♂; otherwise, Juv ♀ = ♂ until commencement of the PF. See also Figures 22-23 (pp. 32-35) for cloacal characters reliable for sexing hatchlings and Juvs.

HY/SY (1st cycle, F1; Oct-Sep): Outer 2 pp (p9-p10) contrastingly narrow, pointed, and worn (Fig. 115**A**, p. 165); proximal p covs shorter and with 2-3 buff bars and a buff tip (Fig. 157**A**), contrasting with longer outermost 2 large p covs with buff to whitish spots (*cf.* Fig. 154**A**, p. 202).

AHY/ASY (Def. cycle, DB; Oct-Sep): Outer pp uniformly broad and truncate (Fig. 115**B**); p covs uniformly broad and blackish with whitish marks (Fig. 157**B**-**C**).

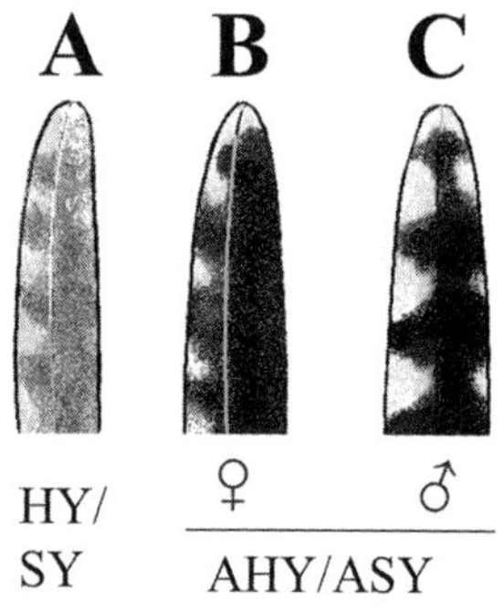

A B C

HY/SY ♀ ♂ AHY/ASY

FIGURE 157. Variation in the shape and color pattern to the primary coverts by age and (for AHY/ASYs) sex in Montezuma Quail.

Sex—Full medial BP (Fig. 20**A**, p. 31) and/or distended cloaca (Fig. 21, p. 32) indicates AHY ♀ in Apr-Jul; ♂♂ can develop partial BPs. Measurements unhelpful for sexing (Table 20, p. 209). The following is reliable after commencement of the PF in Jul (and for juv ♂♂ with blackish or rufous in vent; see **Age**); see also Figures 22-23 (pp. 32-35) for cloacal criteria.

♀: Face brown and dull dusky pinkish; flanks pinkish with dark streaks and pale spots; vent without black; AHY/ASY with narrow white marks to p covs (Fig. 157**B**).

♂: Face with distinct black and white pattern; flanks blackish with white spots; vent with black; AHY/ASY with broad white marks to p covs (Fig. 157**C**).

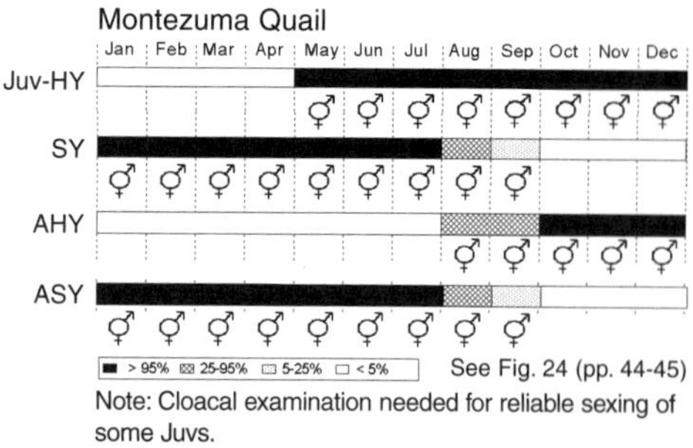

Montezuma Quail

Jan Feb Mar Apr May Jun Jul Aug Sep Oct Nov Dec

Juv-HY

SY

AHY

ASY

■ > 95% ▨ 25-95% ▤ 5-25% □ < 5% See Fig. 24 (pp. 44-45)

Note: Cloacal examination needed for reliable sexing of some Juvs.

Hybrids reported—None.

References—Bent (1932), Dwight (1900a), Leopold (1939, 1959), Leopold & McCabe (1957), Oberholser (1974), Petrides (1942, 1945), Ridgway & Friedmann (1946), Stromberg (2000), van Rossem (1925).

Five species. Family characters include heavy bodies, relatively small and pointed wings, strong pointed beaks, laterally compressed tarsi, and lobed front and back toes. Loons have 10 functional primaries (p10 longest or next to longest, 5 mm shorter to 12 mm longer than p9 when fully grown), 22-24 secondaries (including 4-5 tertials and one absent between s4 and s5; *cf.* Fig. 12B, p. 19), and 16-20 rectrices. Ageing through the second plumage cycle (to TY and ATY) can be accomplished by upperpart plumage aspect and iris color, although overlap may exist between second-cycle SY/TYs and retarded third-cycle TY/4Ys (see pp. 41-42). Sexes are alike in plumage aspect; males average larger and larger billed than females. Partial medial brood patches (Fig. 20**A**, p. 31) are developed by both sexes but distended cloacae (Fig. 21, p. 32) indicate breeding ATY females and other cloacal characters (Figs. 22-23, pp. 32-35) should be investigated

In molting, loons exhibit the Simple Alternate Strategy (SAS; Fig. 10**E**, pp. 13-16), with alternate plumages in definitive molt cycles but only one inserted molt during the first cycle, apparently a first prealternate rather than a preformative molt. The definitive molt cycle of Red-throated Loon differs from that of the other loons, flight feathers being replaced during a complete prebasic molt in fall, and alternate plumage gained by a partial prealternate molt in spring. In the other species, definitive prebasic molts commence with synchronous replacement of wing feathers in spring, concurrent with a partial prealternate molt of body feathers, followed by suspension for breeding and complete (or near-complete) replacement of body feathers in fall (see **Molt** under Arctic/Pacific Loon, p. 218, and Howell & Pyle 2005 for nomenclature). First-cycle molts are similar in all loons; a variably absent to incomplete (including rectrices) prealternate molt in spring is followed quickly by the complete second prebasic molt in summer. In subsequent predefinitive molt cycles the prebasic wing-feather molt of Red-throated Loon averages later in the summer/fall each year, whereas those of the other four species average earlier each year. The definitive strategy is achieved by first breeding, usually at 3-7 years but occasionally at 2 years in Red-throated Loon.

RED-THROATED LOON

Gavia stellata

RTLO
Species # 0110
Band size: 7B

Species—From other species of loons in basic and first alternate plumages by small size and short, shallow, and recurved bill (Table 21, p. 218; Fig. 158, p. 214); face grayish (often in Oct-Dec) to white (often in Mar-Aug), contrasting distinctly with the dark cap (Fig. 158); back feathers and wing covs uniform in appearance in Oct-Mar, gray with pale subterminal ovals (Figs. 159**A**-**C** & 161**A**-**B**, pp. 214-215), or back feathers unmarked or virtually so in Apr-Sep (Fig. 159**D**-**E**; *cf.* Fig. 161**C**).

Geographic variation—Monotypic (R.W. Storer *in* Mayr & Cottrell 1979). Populations of Spitzbergen and Franz Joseph Land, n.Norway ("*G.s. squammata*") may average paler and grayer but differences, if present, confounded by individual variation. See Baker (1993), Cramp & Simmons (1977), Dement'ev & Gladkov (1951a), Portenko (1972), Storer (1978).

Molt—SAS. PF absent, PA1 limited-incomplete (Nov-May in HY/SYs), PB2 complete (Jun-Oct in SYs), PA2 partial-incomplete (Mar-May in TYs), PB3 complete (Jul-Dec in non-breeding TYs), DPA partial-incomplete (Feb-May in ATYs), DPB complete (Aug-Dec in ATYs). The single inserted 1st-cycle molt appears to be homologous with a PA1 rather than a PF (Fig. 10**E**, pp. 13-16). The PAs occur on non-breeding grounds, the PB2 and DPB of non-breeding AHYs occur on non-breeding grounds or at staging areas near breeding grounds, and the DPBs of breeding adults can begin on breeding grounds but are primarily completed at staging areas or on non-breeding grounds. The PA1 is variable, being limited (perhaps absent?) in some HY/SYs and including up to most or all back feathers, les and med covs, and rects in others; HY/SYs in n.portions of non-breeding range may replace fewer feathers on average. During PBs, the pp and ss are replaced synchronously in Jun-Aug (SYs), Jul-Sep (non-breeding TYs), or Aug-Oct (breeding ATYs) and a few body feathers and s covs can be retained. The PA2 and DPA include most to all upperpart and throat feathers, often a few marginal les covs, and the rects. Most SYs and possibly some TYs over-summer on non-breeding grounds and exhibit less-complete (or no) PA1-PA2s and advanced PB2-PB3s (see p. 18).

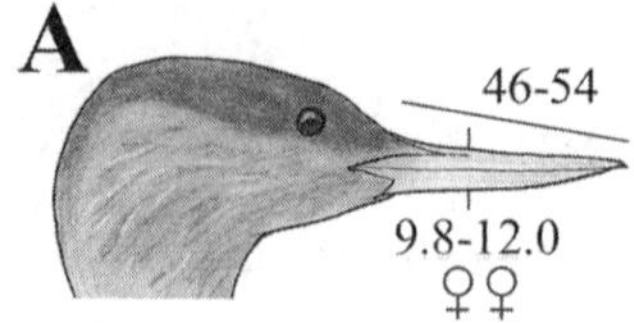

FIGURE 158. Head plumage aspect and bill features for identification and age determination in Red-throated Loon in juvenile, formative, and basic plumages, and bill size and shape by sex (indicated ageing and sexing criteria are independent of each other). Measures represent exposed culmen (Fig. 7**A**, p. 9) and bill depth at the distal end of the nares (Fig. 8**C**, p. 10) by sex; the bills of ♀♀ also average more recurvature than those of ♂♂. Note that there is some overlap in plumage aspects by age: some AHY/ASYs (perhaps non-breeders?) can have sullied faces whereas bleaching of the face can cause SYs to resemble ASYs in Mar-Aug.

Age—Juv (B1; Jul-Dec) is described under HY/SY (Oct-Dec), below; Juv ♀ = ♂. Beware of overlapping plumage aspects due to protracted molts in this species, especially in non-breeding AHYs (*cf.* Fig. 161).

Juv-HY/SY (1st cycle, Juv/B1-A1; Oct-Sep): S covs and back feathers rounded with whitish subterminal chevrons in Oct-Dec (Fig. 159**A**), becoming variably mixed with worn, unmarked les and med covs (Fig. 159**D**), and fresh black feathers with ovate to round spots in Jan-Sep (Fig. 159**B-C**), at least some juv wing covs retained and worn (Fig. 161**A**); outer pp relatively worn and narrow at tips in Oct-Jun (Fig. 160**A**), being replaced in Jun-Aug, and relatively fresh in Aug-Sep; face often washed grayish in Oct-Feb (Fig.

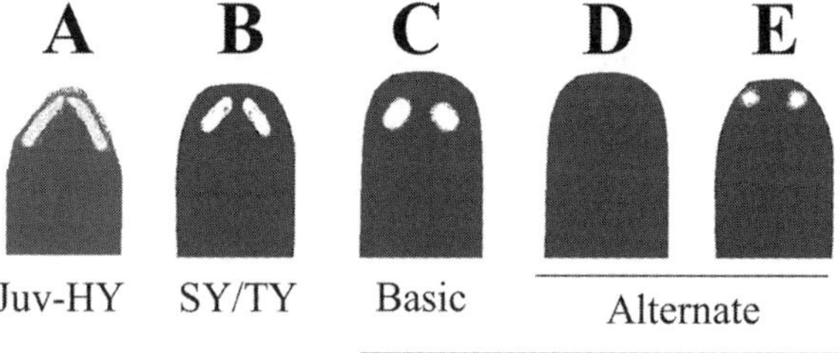

FIGURE 159. Secondary coverts and back feathers by feather generation and age in Red-throated Loon. Juv and basic gr covs are retained year-round and resemble **A** (HY/SYs), **B** (SY/TYs), or **E** (ASY/ATYs); les and med covs, replaced during the PA1, can be unmarked (**D**). Juv feathers resemble **A** when fresh, but first lose the dark fringe and often then the pale markings if retained until Mar or later. First alternate back feathers, which begin to appear in SYs in Jan-Mar, are variable but can appear like **B** and/or **C**; see also Figure 161**A**. Back feathers in second cycle in SY/TYs generally show spots, which are more ovate in basic (**B**) than in alternate (**C**) aspects; see also Figure 161**B**. Definitive basic back feathers have rounded spots (**C**), and most definitive alternate feathers are unmarked (**D**), while some (primarily in upper back, replaced earlier during the DPB?) can show small subterminal spots (**E**); see also Figure 161**C**.

158**A**); throat whitish or sometimes mottled grayish and reddish in Apr-Sep; iris brownish to dull reddish; bill pale gray to whitish gray (Fig. 158**A**). **Note: Most SYs remain on non-breeding grounds for the first summer.**

SY/TY (2nd cycle, B2-A2; Oct-Sep): Med and gr covs with whitish oval-shaped subterminal spots (Fig. 159**B**); back feathers truncate with variable whitish subterminal rectangles, oval-shaped spots, or rounded spots in Oct-Apr (Fig. 159**B-C**), mixed with fresher feathers with distinct round spots or unmarked in Apr-Sep (Figs. 159**C-E** & 161**B**); outer pp relatively fresh and broad at tips (Fig. 160**B**), being replaced in Jul-Sep; face often whitish to white in Oct-Feb (Fig. 158**B**); throat white in Oct-Mar or variably mixed grayish and reddish in Apr-Sep; iris reddish brown to brownish red; bill medium-pale gray (*cf.* Fig. 158**A**). **Note: Intermediates with ASY/ATY might occur (showing rounded white spots on s covs; Fig. 159C) that should be aged AHY/ASY. In addition, SY/TYs may average more dusky (*vs* white) feathering to face and throat (due to earlier PBs; see Fig. 158), and TYs (and 4Ys) may average more white spots to the back feathers in Apr-Sep than older age groups. See also ASY/ATY.**

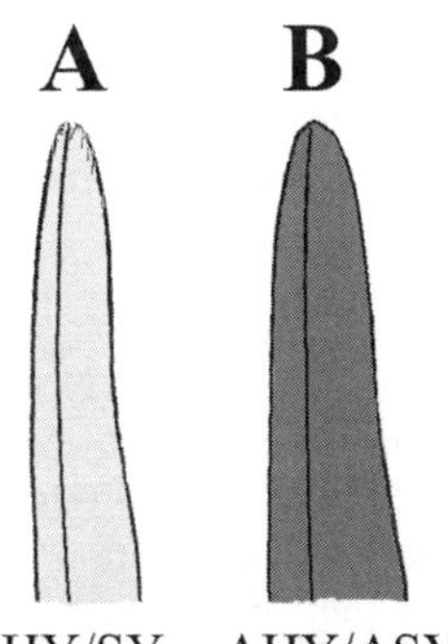

FIGURE 160. Width and shape of the outer primaries by age in loons. The figure illustrates fresh feathers; juvenal feathers of HY/SYs (**A**) become progressively more worn in Feb-Aug than basic feathers of AHY/ASYs (**B**); *cf.* Figure 25 (p. 47).

ASY/ATY (Def. cycle, DB-DA; Oct-Sep): Med and gr covs with white subterminal round spots (Fig. 159**C**); back feathers truncate, with white subterminal round spots in Oct-Dec (Fig. 159**C**), or most to all feathers unmarked in Mar-Sep (Figs. 159**D-E** & 161**C**); outer pp relatively fresh, broad at tips (Fig. 160**B**), and being replaced in Aug-Oct; throat often with

FIGURE 161. Variation in the appearance of back feathers in spring (Feb-May or later) Red-throated Loons by age. In SYs (**A**) more-worn juvenal feathers can show pale fringes (Fig. 159**A**) or have these completely worn off, whereas fresher 1st-alternate feathers tend to have larger ovate or rounded spots (Fig. 159**B**). In TYs (**B**), aspects of more-worn second-basic and fresher 2nd-alternate feathers each tend to have spots, those of the latter being more rounded (Fig. 159**B-C**). In ATYs, fresher definitive alternate feathers show little or no spots (Fig. 159**D-E**), and these contrast with more worn basic feathers with rounded spots (Fig. 159**C**); in many ASYs all basic feathers are replaced during the prealternate molt, such that the back lacks spots completely in May-Aug.

some reddish feathers in Oct-Dec or later, or uniformly reddish in Mar-Sep (often mottled due to molt in Mar and Sep); iris reddish to red; bill dark gray to blackish (Fig. 158**B**). **Note: See SY/TY. Some 4Ys possibly acquire less than full red throats in May-Aug, overlapping in appearance with advanced TYs; these could be aged T-4Y (see pp. 41-42) but more study needed.**

Sex—♀=♂ by plumage aspect. Medial BP (Fig. 20**A**, p. 31) developed by both sexes but distended cloaca (Fig. 21, p. 32) in Jun-Aug indicates ASY ♀. The number of white and black stripes on the hindneck in ASY/ATYs in Apr-Sep may average greater in ♂♂ than ♀♀ (Reimchen & Douglas 1985) but there appears to be broad overlap between the sexes, and number of stripes varies with proximal-distal position on the neck. Measurements, especially of bill, somewhat useful for sexing (Table 21, p. 218; Fig. 158, p. 214). See Okill et al. (1989) for a DFA (p. 5), using wing chord, exp culmen, and tarsus, that reliably separated the sexes in a Scottish population (which may average larger than N.Am populations). The following can be used to sex most N.Am individuals:

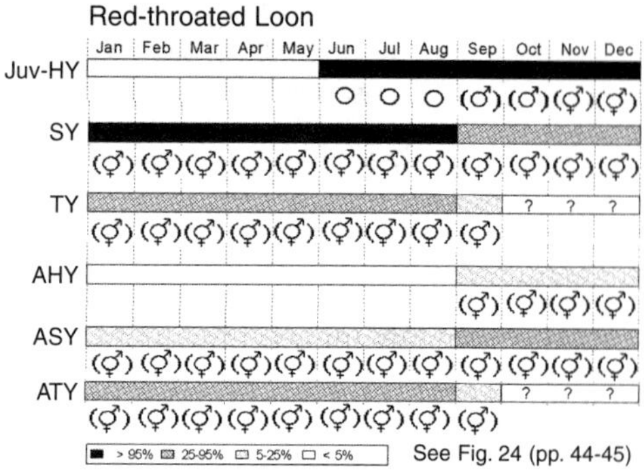

♀: Bill smaller and more recurved (Table 21, Fig. 158**B**). **Note: Some individuals with intermediate measurements and bill shape are not reliably sexed by bill features alone.**

♂: Bill larger and less recurved (Table 21, Fig.158**A**). **Note: See ♀.**

Red-throated Loon

Jan Feb Mar Apr May Jun Jul Aug Sep Oct Nov Dec

Juv-HY

SY

TY ? ? ?

AHY

ASY

ATY ? ? ?

■ > 95% ▩ 25-95% ▢ 5-25% □ < 5%

See Fig. 24 (pp. 44-45)

Hybrids reported—Possibly with Common Loon (McCarthy 2006).

References—Ainley et al. (1994), Appleby et al. (1986), Baker (1993), Barr et al. (2000), Bent (1919a), Carlson (1971), Cramp & Simmons (1977), Dement'ev & Gladkov (1951a), Godfrey (1986), Kaufman (1990a), Manning et al. (1956), Oberholser (1974), W.E. Godfrey *in* Palmer (1962), Phillips et al. (1983), Reimchen & Douglas (1985), Roberts (1955), Stone (1900), Storer (1978), Sutton (1943), Walsh (1988), Woolfenden (1967).

ARCTIC LOON
Gavia arctica

ARLO
Species # 0090

PACIFIC LOON
Gavia pacifica

PALO
Species # 0100
Band size: 7B

Species—From Red-throated (p. 213) and Common (p. 221) loons in basic and first alternate plumages by medium size and relatively short, shallow, and not or slightly recurved bill (Table 21, p. 218; Fig. 162); forehead without protrusion (*cf.* Fig. 167, p. 221); crown darker than or uniform with nape; white of face reduced and distinctly defined (Fig. 162); back feathers in Oct-Mar gray with pale terminal tips (HY/SY) to unmarked, contrasting in appearance with spotted wing covs (AHY/ASY; Figs. 165-166, pp. 218-219); or most feathers with white spots in Apr-Sep (Fig. 166).

Pacific Loon from Arctic Loon by smaller average size and bill size (Table 21, Fig. 162); central toe from joint usually < 110 (*vs* usually > 110 in Arctic Loon); upper flanks and proximal femoral feathers dark (*vs* white in Arctic Loon; Fig. 164); throat and vent with more complete dusky bands by age (Fig. 163); HY/SY with crown and nape grayish (*vs* blackish when fresh in Arctic Loon; Fig. 162); AHY/ASY in Apr-Sep with nape and neck pale silvery gray and with 5-7 indistinct and/or incomplete white neck stripes (*vs* darker gray and with 4-6 bold and complete white neck stripes in Arctic Loon) and throat sheen usually purplish (*vs* usually greenish in Asian populations of Arctic Loon). In nestlings, the natal down is grayish brown in Pacific Loon *vs* sooty in Arctic Loon. See Birch & Lee (1995, 1997), Douglas & Sowl (1993), Evered (1985), McCaskie et al. (1990), Reinking & Howell (1993), Roberson (1989), Schulenberg 1989), and Walsh (1984, 1988), for more information.

Geographic variation—See Bent (1919b), Dement'ev & Gladkov (1951a), Dwight (1918), Portenko (1972), Storer (1978). One other subspecies occurs in Eurasia.

G.a. viridigularis (br w.AK, vagrant to CA). From *arctica* of Eurasia (a potential vagrant to N.Am) by slightly larger size (Table 21, p. 218; *vs* wg chord 277-341, exp culmen 50-70, tarsus

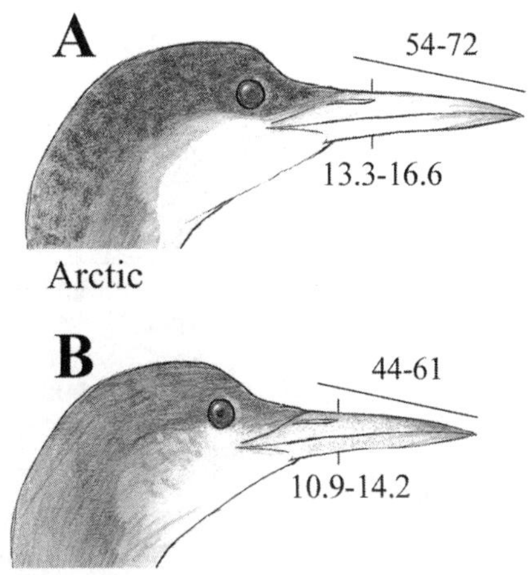

FIGURE 162. Head plumage aspect and bill size and shape for identification of Arctic (**A**) and Pacific (**B**) loons in juvenile, formative, and basic plumages. Measures refer to exposed culmen (Fig. 7**A**, p. 9) and bill depth at distal end of nares (Fig. 8**C**, p. 10). Note that Arctic Loons average darker crowns and more distinct white faces than Pacific Loons, although this varies by age and season; most plumage-aspect features are obscured by bleaching in Mar-Aug SYs. Note the lack of pale areas in the orbital region, *vs.* Common and Yellow-billed loons (Fig. 167, p. 221).

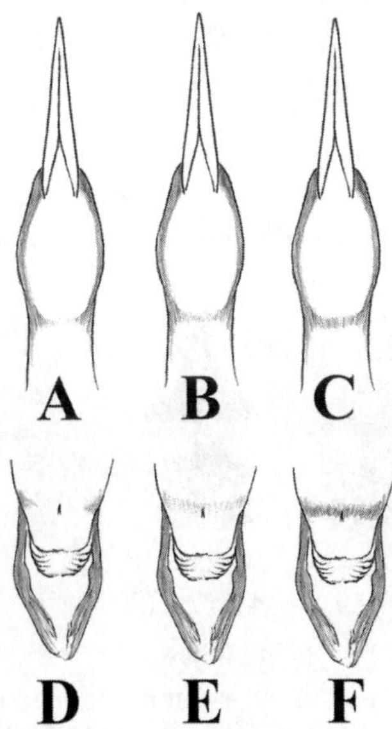

FIGURE 163. Variation in distinctness of chin and vent straps by species and age in Arctic and Pacific loons. Arctic Loon and HY/SYs average less complete and/or paler straps (**A-B**, **D-E**) than Pacific Loon and AHY/ASYs (**B-C**, **E-F**). Illustrations based on those of Reinking & Howell (1993), which see for more information.

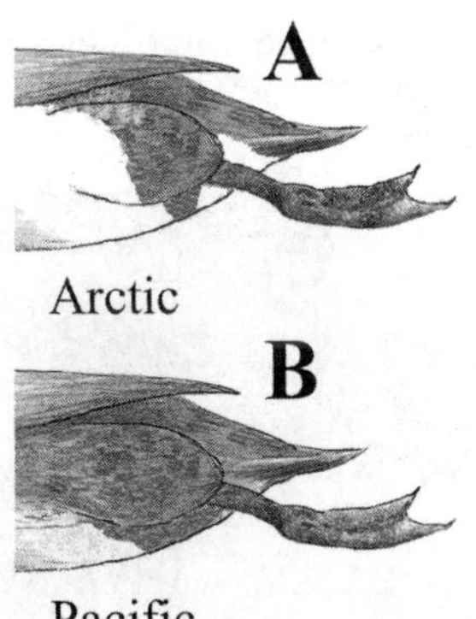

FIGURE 164. Plumage of the femoral tract in Arctic Loon (**A**) showing white proximal half, and Pacific Loon (**B**) showing completely dark feathers. Also, the maximum dorsal extension of white usually occurs near the femoral tract in Arctic loon and more centrally along the sides in Pacific Loon. A similar difference can be found in Townsend's (**A**) *vs* Black-vented (**B**) shearwaters (p. 273).

TABLE 21. Measurements (mm) of North American loons to assist in identification and sexing. See pp. 4-11 for methods of measurement. Species summaries are in **bold**. Values were derived from 95% confidence intervals as based (for wing, tail, exposed culmen, and tarsus) approximately on the indicated sample sizes (see pp. 4-5); sample size for bill depth was often smaller but included at least 10 of each sex. Thus, midpoints of ranges approximate means, and S.D. is approximated by 25% of the range.

Taxon/Sex	*n*	wing chord	tail length	exp culmen	bill depth[1]	tarsus
Red-throated Loon[2]		**253-297**	**42-57**	**46-59**	**9.8-13.7**	**64-80**
♀	68	253-287	42-53	46-54	9.8-12.0	64-74
♂	73	266-297	45-57	49-59	11.3-13.7	68-80
Arctic Loon[2]		**293-348**	**59-71**	**54-72**	**13.3-16.6**	**53-65**
♀	8	293-332	59-68	54-66	13.3-15.1	53-62
♂	15	306-348	61-71	59-72	14.4-16.6	56-65
Pacific Loon		**274-313**	**52-62**	**44-61**	**10.9-14.2**	**65-79**
♀	49	274-305	52-58	44-56	10.9-12.6	65-76
♂	73	280-313	55-62	48-61	12.0-14.2	69-79
Common Loon[2]		**331-401**	**70-100**	**69-97**	**16.3-24.7**	**77-103**
♀	100	331-388	70-96	69-93	16.3-21.7	77-99
♂	100	341-401	74-100	74-97	19.4-24.7	83-103
Yellow-billed Loon		**358-403**	**78-100**	**80-97**	**20.6-28.2**	**85-100**
♀	30	358-389	78-95	80-94	20.6-24.6	85-96
♂	33	366-403	82-100	84-97	23.1-28.2	89-100

[1] Bill depth measured at distal end of nares (Figs. 8**C**, p. 10; 158, p.214; 162, p. 217; & 167, p. 221).
[2] Measurements from N.Am breeding populations only; see **Geographic variation**.

67-92 in *arctica*); throat sheen in alternate plumage usually greenish (*vs* purplish in *arctica*). Populations breeding in nc.Siberia ("*suschkini*") may average slightly larger and paler but differences, if present, are insufficient for subspecific recognition.

Molt—SAS. PF absent, PA1 absent-incomplete (Dec-May in HY/SYs), PB2 complete (May-Oct in SYs), DPA incomplete (Feb-May in AHY/ASYs), PB3 complete (Apr-Sep in non-breeding TYs), DPB complete (Mar-May & Sep-Nov in breeding ASYs). See Figure 11**B** (p. 17). The single inserted first-cycle molt appears to be homologous with a PA1 rather than a PF (Fig.

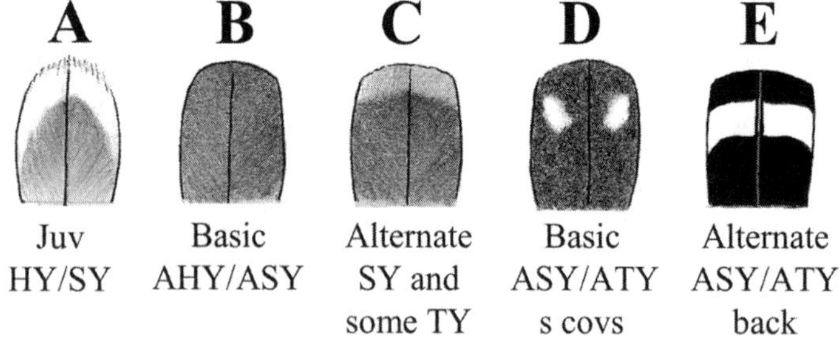

FIGURE 165. Secondary coverts and back feathers by feather generation and age in Pacific and Arctic loons. Juv and basic s covs are retained year-round and resemble **A** (HY/SYs), **B** or occasionally **D** (SY/TYs), or **D** (ASY/ATYs); in SY/TYs these are replaced in fall whereas in ASY/ATYs these are replaced in spring, prior to breeding. Juv feathers resemble **A** when fresh, but can lose the pale fringes if retained until Mar or later. First alternate back feathers, which begin to appear in SYs in Jan-Mar, are often unmarked (**B**) but can also have pale tips (**C**) or spots (**D**); see also Figure 166**A**. Second basic back feathers are unmarked in aspect or occasionally can have spots (**B**, **D**), and second alternate back feathers are often fringed pale (**C**); see also Figure 166**B**. Definitive-basic back feathers are found in Oct-Feb and are unmarked in aspect (**B**) whereas definitive alternate back feathers are well marked (**E**); see also Figure 166**C**.

10**E**, pp. 13-16). The PAs occur on non-breeding grounds and/or during northbound migration, the PB2 and DPBs of non-breeding AHYs occur on non-breeding grounds, and the DPBs of breeding adults can begin on breeding grounds but are primarily completed on non-breeding grounds. The PA1 can be absent or limited to a few back feathers, but usually includes some to most body feathers and the rects. During DPBs, pp and ss are replaced synchronously in Jun-Aug (SYs), Apr-Jun (non-breeding TYs), or Mar-May (breeding ATYs). DPBs are offset, with pp, ss, and wing covs replaced on non-breeding grounds (concurrent with the DPA) followed by breeding, and replacement of most to all body feathers and rects in Sep-Nov. Some body feathers are usually retained during DPBs. The PA2 and DPA include most to all upperpart and throat feathers and often a few marginal les covs and the rects. Most SYs and some TYs over-summer on non-breeding grounds and exhibit less-complete (or no) PA1-PA2s and advanced PB2-PB3s (see p. 18).

Various molt terminologies have been proposed for this strategy, which is also found in Common and Yellow-billed loons (p. 221; see also Horned Puffin, p. 784). The complete molt in spring has been considered the DPB and the partial molt in fall the DPA (Cramp & Simmons 1977, Baker 1993), and the DPB has been presumed to begin with body feathers in fall and complete with wing feathers the following spring, concurrent with the DPA (W.E. Godfrey *in* Palmer 1962, Woolfenden 1967, McIntyre & Barr 1997). Consideration of apparent homologous molts in the more primitive (Storer 1978) Red-throated Loon (p. 213) and the tracing of molts through the 1st and 2nd cycles results in the above interpretation, that wing-feather replacement during the DPB has been advanced forward in time, beginning in spring (concurrent with the previous PA) and completing in fall (see Howell & Pyle 2005 and Fig. 11**B**, p. 17).

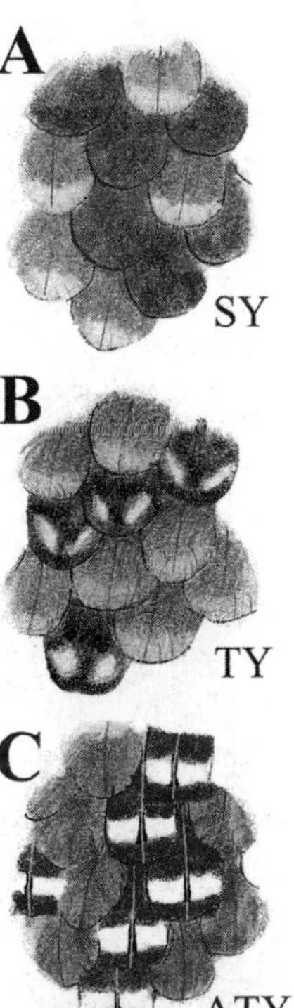

FIGURE 166. Variation in the appearance of back feathers in spring (Feb-May or later) Pacific and Arctic loons by age. In SYs (**A**) more-worn juvenal feathers can show pale fringes (*cf.* Fig. 165**A**) or have these completely worn off, whereas fresher 1st alternate feathers tend to be unmarked (*cf.* Fig. 165**B**). In TYs (**B**), more-worn second basic back feathers are primarily unmarked (Fig. 165**B**), although some individuals can have a few feathers with distinct white spots (Fig. 165**C**), while most fresher alternate feathers are fringed pale (Fig. 165**D**). ATYs (**C**) show unmarked basic back feathers (Fig. 165**B**), usually mixed with some retained alternate feathers (Fig. 165**E**) in Jan-Apr, to uniformly alternate feathers in May-Aug.

Age—Juv (B1; Jul-May) is described below under HY/SY; Juv ♀=♂. Beware of overlapping plumage aspects due to protracted molts in this species, especially in non-breeding AHYs. The following refers to Pacific Loon. Ageing of Arctic Loon is similar except for slight variation in the occurrence and color of chin and vent bands by age (Fig. 163, p. 217). In addition to the following, note that confirmed breeding adults can be aged ATY.

Juv-HY/SY (1st cycle, Juv/B1-A1; Sep-Aug): S covs rounded with narrow, distinct pale tips (Fig. 165**A**); back feathers rounded with narrow pale fringes (Fig. 165**A**), often mixed with a few to many fresher, unmarked (sometimes pale-tipped or indistinctly spotted) feathers in Feb-Aug (Figs. 165**B** & 166**A**); outer pp narrow at tips (Fig. 160**A**, p. 215), worn in Mar-Jun and being replaced in Jul-Aug; chin and vent often with partial and/or paler dark band by species in Sep-Apr (Fig. 163**A-B**, **D-E**); neck without stripes and throat with few or no blackish feathers in Apr-Aug; iris brownish to reddish brown; sides of bill medium-pale gray (*cf.* Fig. 158**A**, p. 214). **Note: Most SYs remain on non-breeding grounds for the first summer. See also SY/TY.**

SY/TY (2nd cycle, B2-A2; Sep-Aug): S covs truncate and unmarked or sometimes with small whitish spots (Fig. 165**B** & **D**); back feathers truncate and unmarked or with small whitish spots in Sep-Apr (Fig. 165**B** & **D**), mixed with fresher feathers with indistinct pale fringes in Apr-Aug (Figs. 165**C** & 166**B**); outer pp broad at tips (Fig. 160**B**), being replaced in Apr-May and fresh in May-Aug; chin and vent usually with complete and/or medium-dark band by species in Sep-Mar (Fig. 163**B** & **E**); neck with variably indistinct black-and-white stripes and throat variably mottled dull blackish and white in Apr-Aug; iris reddish brown to reddish; sides of bill grayish (*cf.* Fig. 158). **Note: Beware some SY/TYs may be difficult to separate from HY/SYs or ASY/ATYs, especially when worn or in transitional plumages. See also ASY/ATY.**

ASY/ATY (Def. cycle, DB-DA; Sep-Aug): S covs with bold white spots (Fig. 165**C**); back feathers truncate, unmarked (Fig.165**B**), often with retained, boldly patterned feathers (Fig. 165**E**) in Sep-Mar (*cf.* Fig. 166**C**), or uniformly patterned in Mar-Aug (Fig. 165**E**); chin and vent with complete and/or dark brown bands by species in Sep-Mar (Fig. 163 **B-C** & **E-F**); neck with distinct black-and-white stripes and throat uniformly glossy blackish in Apr-Aug; iris reddish to red; sides of bill dark grayish, to black in Mar-Aug (*cf.* Fig. 158**B**). **Note: Occasional retarded 4Ys may have mottled alternate plumage aspect in Apr-Aug, overlapping in appearance with the most advanced TYs; these possibly are best aged T-4Y (see pp. 41-42) but more study is needed.**

Sex—♀=♂ by plumage aspect. Partial, Medial BP (Fig. 20**A**, p. 31) developed by both sexes but distended cloaca (Fig. 21, p. 32) in Jun-Aug indicates ATY ♀. Measurements, especially of bill (Table 21, p. 218), could be useful for sexing extremes or mated pairs; otherwise, no criteria known.

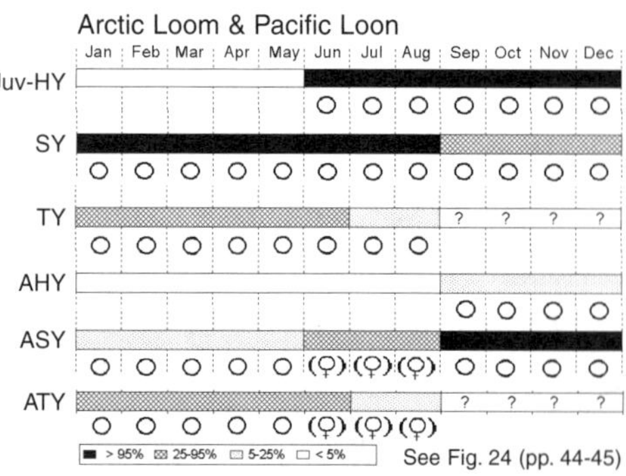

Hybrids reported—Arctic and Pacific loons have likely interbred (Bailey 1943, Manning et al. 1956, Storer 1978) and both species probably with Common Loon (Hunter & Dennis 1972, Robertson & Fraker 1974, McCarthy 2006).

References—Ainley et al. (1994), Appleby et al. (1986), Baker (1993), Bent (1919a), Carlson (1971), Cramp & Simmons (1977), Dement'ev & Gladkov (1951a), Dwight (1918), Godfrey (1986), Kaufman (1990a), Langridge (1984), Manning et al. (1956), McIntyre & McIntyre (1974), Mullarney (1980), Oberholser (1974), W.E. Godfrey *in* Palmer (1962), Phillips et al. (1983), Portenko (1972), Reinking & Howell (1993), Russell (2002), Stone (1900), Storer (1978), Sutton (1943).

COMMON LOON
Gavia immer

COLO
Species # 0070
Band size: 8-9

YELLOW-BILLED LOON
Gavia adamsii

YBLO
Species # 0080
Band size: 9

Species—From Red-throated (p. 213) and Arctic and Pacific (p. 216) loons in first alternate and basic plumages by larger size (Table 21, p. 218); bill large and with straight culmen, forehead often with a protrusion, crown paler than or uniform with nape in aspect, orbital region usually with white, and white cheek indistinctly defined (Fig. 167); back feathers with broad, indistinct pale tips (HY/SY) or squarish spots (AHY/ASY; Fig. 169, p. 222), contrasting with white-spotted s covs in Oct-Mar ASY/ATYs.

Common Loon from Yellow-billed Loon in juvenal, formative, and basic plumages by bill darker (especially along culmen toward tip) and shallower (Table 21), the lower mandible distinctly angled at gonydeal (*vs* recurved in Yellow-billed Loon), medial groove along ventral side of bill extending further distally, chin feathering abbreviated, forehead with less substantial protuberance (especially in AHY/ASYs), and head grayer (*vs* browner) with less distinct auricular patch (Fig. 167); shaft of outer pp (p5-p10) distal to p covs dusky *vs* pale horn in Yellow-billed Loon (Fig. 168). In definitive alternate plumage (ASY/ATYs), largest white spots in back feathers

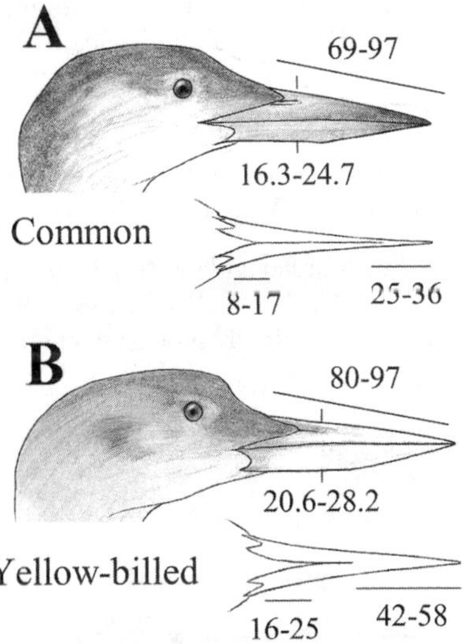

A
69-97
16.3-24.7
Common
8-17
25-36
B
80-97
20.6-28.2
Yellow-billed
16-25
42-58

FIGURE 167. Head plumage aspect and bill size, shape, and color for identification of Common (**A**) and Yellow-billed (**B**) loons in juvenal, formative, and basic plumages. Measures refer to exposed culmen (Fig. 7**A**, p. 9) and bill depth at distal end of nares (Fig. 8**C**, p. 10) and, on insets of underside of bills, distance from tips of malar to chin feathering, and from the end of the medial groove to the tip of the bill (Godfrey 1986). Common Loon has a dark grayish bill with dark culmen to tip whereas in Yellow-billed it is pale yellowish including culmen to tip. Note also that Common Loons have sharper gonydeal angles, more rounded foreheads, darker (less brownish) crowns, and auricular patches. Note also the pale areas in the orbital region, *vs.* Pacific and Arctic loons (Fig. 162, p. 217).

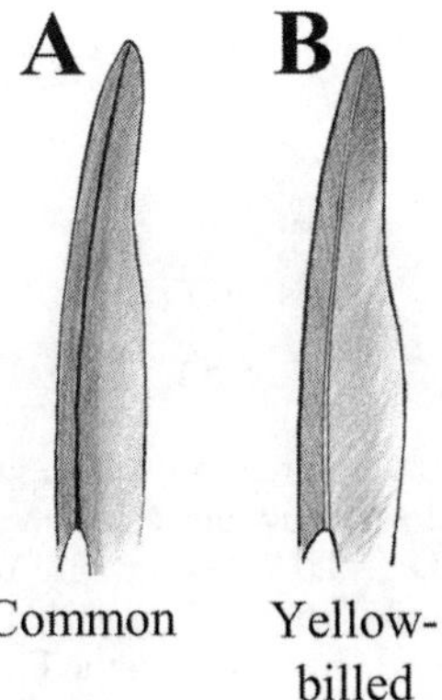

FIGURE 168. Color of shaft on the outer primary (p10) in Common (**A**) and Yellow-billed (**B**) loons. Note that the color difference is more pronounced just distal to the tip of the p10 cov.

(Fig. 169**F**) usually < 10 mm wide in Common Loon *vs* usually > 10 mm wide in Yellow-billed Loon.

Geographic variation—Monotypic in both species (R.W. Storer *in* Mayr & Cottrell 1979). Common Loons breeding from BC to WI ("*G.i. elasson*") may average smaller but differences are discordant, broadly clinal, and/or confounded by substantial individual variation. See Bishop (1921), Gabrielson & Lincoln (1953b), McIntyre & Barr (1997), Oberholser (1974), Rand (1947a), Storer (1978, 1988).

Molt—SAS. PF absent, PA1 absent-incomplete (Dec-May in HY/SYs), PB2 complete (May-Oct in SYs), PA2 partial-incomplete (Mar-May in non-breeding TYs), PB3 complete (Apr-Sep in non-breeding TYs), DPA incomplete (Jan-Apr in breeding ASY/ATYs), DPB complete (Mar-May & Sep-Nov in breeding ATYs). The single inserted 1st-cycle molt appears to be homologous with a PA1 rather than a PF (Fig. 10**E**, pp. 13-16). Location, extent, and terminology of molts similar to that of Pacific Loon (p. 218). Most SYs and possibly some TYs over-summer on non-breeding grounds and exhibit less-complete (or no) PA1-PA2s and advanced PB2-PB3s (see p. 18).

Age—Juv (B1; Jul-May) is described below under HY/SY; Juv ♀=♂. Beware of overlapping plumages due to protracted molts in this species, especially in non-breeding AHYs. In addition to the following, note that confirmed breeding adults can be aged ATY (and probably A4Y).

Juv-HY/SY (1st cycle, Juv/B1-A1; Sep-Aug): S covs rounded with broad and indistinct pale tips (Fig. 169**A**); back feathers rounded with broad and indistinct pale tips (Fig. 169**A**), often mixed with a few to many fresher, unmarked, pale-tipped, or indistinctly spotted feathers in Feb-Aug (Figs. 169**B-D** & 170**A**); outer pp narrow at tips (Fig. 160**A**, p. 215), worn in Mar-Jun, and being replaced in Jun-Aug; head without blackish-green feathering in Apr-Sep; iris brownish to dull reddish; sides of bill in Common Loon medium-pale gray (*cf.* Fig. 158**A**, p.

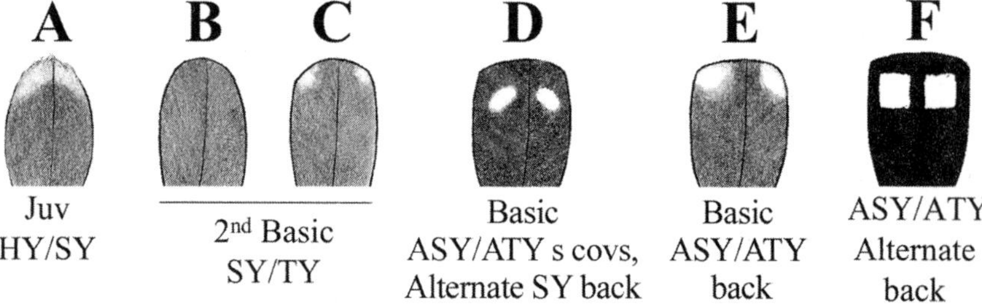

FIGURE 169. Secondary coverts and back feathers by feather generation and age in Common and Yellow-billed loons. Juv and basic s covs are retained year-round and resemble **A** (HY/SYs), **B-C** (SY/TYs), or **D** (ASY/ATYs); in SY/TYs these are replaced in fall whereas in ASY/ATYs these are replaced in spring, prior to breeding. Juvenal feathers resemble **A** when fresh, but can lose the pale fringes if retained until Mar or later. First alternate back feathers, which begin to appear in SYs in Jan-Mar, are often unmarked in aspect (**B**) but can also have indistinct subterminal spots (**C**); see also Figure 170**A**. Second basic back feathers are also unmarked or can have indistinct spots (**B-C**), and second alternate back feathers often have moderately distinct and small ovate spots (**D**); see also Figure 170**B**. Definitive basic back feathers are found in Oct-Feb and have indistinct squarish spots whereas definitive alternate back feathers are well marked in aspect (**F**); see also Figure 170**C**. The white squares in **F** are typical of Common Loon, usually < 10 mm wide; these squares in Yellow-billed Loon are usually larger, > 10 mm wide.

214). **Note: Most SYs remain on non-breeding grounds for the first summer. See SY/TY. Bill color in Yellow-billed Loon shows little age-related variation.**

SY/TY (2nd cycle, B2-A2; Sep-Aug): S covs truncate and unmarked or with indistinct ovals or squarish spots (Fig. 169**B-C**); back feathers unmarked or with ovals or squarish spots in Sep-Apr (Fig. 169**B-C**), mixed with fresher feathers with moderately distinct spots in Apr-Aug (Figs. 169**D** & 170**B**); outer pp broad at tips (Fig. 160**B**), being replaced in Mar-May, and fresh in May-Aug; head gray with light to moderately heavy blackish-green mottling in Mar-Sep; iris reddish brown to brownish red; sides of bill in Common Loon grayish, often mixed blackish in Mar-Aug (*cf.* Fig. 158**B**). **Note: Beware some SY/TYs may be difficult to separate from ASY/ATYs, especially when worn or in transitional plumage states.**

ASY/ATY (Def. cycle, DB-DA; Sep-Aug): S covs glossy blackish with distinct white spots (Fig. 169**D**); back feathers usually blackish with diffuse square spots (Fig. 169**E**) mixed with a few worn black feathers with distinct white spots in Sep-Mar (Fig. 170**C**), or uniformly glossy blackish with distinct white spots in Apr-Sep (Fig. 169**C** & **F**); head completely blackish green in Apr-Sep; iris reddish to red; sides of bill dark grayish, to black in Mar-Aug. **Note: Some to all 4Ys may have mottled alternate plumage aspect in Apr-Aug, overlapping in appearance with the most advanced TYs; these possibly could be aged T-4Y (see pp. 41-42). More study needed on variation in alternate plumage aspect in known-age TYs, 4Ys, and 5Ys.**

Sex—♀ = ♂ by plumage aspect. Partial medial BP (Fig. 20**A**, p. 31) developed by both sexes but distended cloaca (Fig. 21, p. 32) in Jun-Aug indicates ATY ♀. Measurements, especially of bill, somewhat useful for sexing (Table 21, p. 218). Also, ♂♂ may display (on average) a larger protrusion on the forehead than ♀♀, especially in Yellow-billed Loon (Fig. 167**B**, p. 221); more study needed. Otherwise, no sexing criteria known.

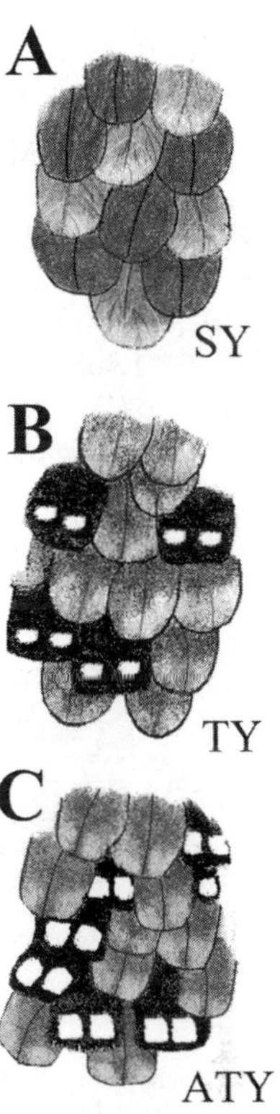

FIGURE 170. Variation in the appearance of back feathers in spring (Feb-May or later) Common and Yellow-billed loons by age. In SYs (**A**) more-worn juvenal feathers show pale fringes (*cf.* Fig. 169**A**) or have these completely worn off, whereas fresher 1st alternate feathers tend to be unmarked in aspect or have indistinct whitish subterminal areas (Fig. 169**B-C**). In TYs (**B**), more-worn second basic back feathers are unmarked or have indistinct pale patches (Fig. 169**B-C**), while most fresher alternate feathers have small and moderately distinct spots (Fig. 169**D**). ATYs (**C**) have basic back feathers with indistinct squarish spots (Fig. 169**E**) mixed with some retained alternate feathers with distinct spots (Fig. 169**F**) in Jan-Apr, to uniformly alternate feathers in May-Aug.

Hybrids reported—Common Loon with Arctic Loon (p. 216), Yellow-billed Loon (Godfrey 1986), probably with Pacific Loon (p. 216), and possibly with Red-throated Loon (p. 213).

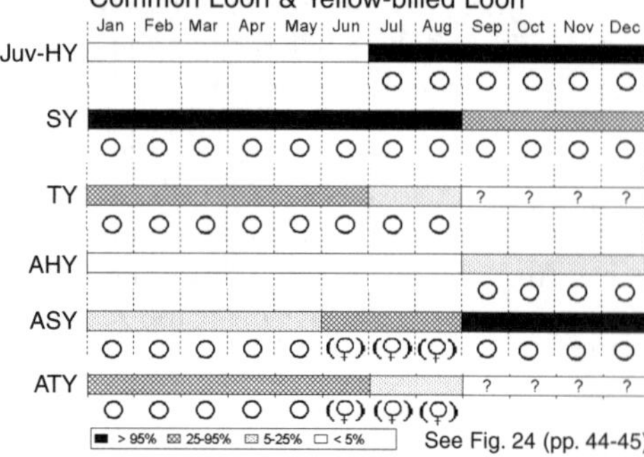

References—Ainley et al. (1994), Appleby et al. (1986), Baker (1993), Bent (1919a), Binford & Remsen (1974), Bishop (1921), Brodkorb (1953), Burn & Mather (1974), Carlson (1971), Cramp & Simmons (1977), Dement'ev & Gladkov (1951a), Gabrielson & Lincoln (1953b), Godfrey (1986), Heubeck et al. (1993), Kaufman (1990a), Langridge (1984), May (1930), McIntyre (1988), McIntyre & Barr (1997), McIntyre & McIntyre (1974), Mullarney (1980), North (1994), Oberholser (1974), W.E. Godfrey *in* Palmer (1962), Phillips (1990), Phillips et al. (1983), Rand (1947a), Roberts (1955), Stejneger (1885), Stone (1900), Storer (1978, 1988), Sutton (1943), Woolfenden (1967).

GREBES *PODICIPEDIDAE*

Seven North American species. Family characters include moderately heavy bodies, small and pointed wings, long necks, unfeathered lores, generally slender beaks, laterally compressed tarsi, and lobed front toes. Grebes have 11 functional primaries (p11 longest or next to longest, 5 mm shorter to 5 mm longer than p10 when fully grown, and with an extra primary on the metacarpus; Stresemann 1963a) and 17-22 secondaries (including 3-4 tertials and one absent between s4 and s5 in N.Am species; *cf.* Fig. 12B, p. 19). Rectrices are absent or rudimentary, the central pair slightly more developed in juveniles (Fjeldså 2004). Ageing through the first cycle (to SY and ASY) is reliable with most individuals by upperpart plumage aspect, wing/back contrasts, ss shape, bill color, and iris color. Ageing by the roughness to the posterior edge of the tarsus (Baker 1993, Storer & Nuechterlein 1985, Marchant & Higgins 1990) appears to be difficult at best with North American taxa. Sexes are alike in plumage aspect, alternate-plumaged females averaging slightly duller than males in some species and males average larger than females, especially in bill dimensions. Medial brood patch (Fig. 20**A**, p. 31) developed by both sexes but distended cloacae (Fig. 21, p. 32) indicates breeding AHY females and other cloacal characters (Figs. 22-23, pp. 32-35) should be further investigated: the presence and length of the bursa (Fig. 23, p. 34) is useful in ageing some (and probably all) species. In addition to cited references, see Fjeldså (2004) for information on the identification, molts, and plumages of grebes.

Most or all N.Am grebes exhibit a Complex Alternate Strategy (CAS; Fig. 10**F**, pp. 13-16), with both formative and alternate plumages during the first cycle and alternate plumages during subsequent cycles. Presupplemental molts may also occur in some species (Piersma 1988, Fjeldså 2004). The preformative molts are limited or partial and protracted into winter, with some juv body feathers retained at least until the first prealternate molt in spring. Some HY/SYs of certain species might replace primaries and secondaries during the preformative molt in late winter or spring; more study is needed. Primaries and secondaries are replaced synchronously during prebasic molts. Flank feathers can be continually replaced due to plucking for digestive purposes (see Storer 1969, Storer & Nuechterlein 1985, Fjeldså 2004), and should not be considered part of molt. Age at first breeding can be 1-2 years (smaller species < larger species); prebasic molts of non-breeding AHYs average earlier in timing than those of breeding adults (see p. 18).

LEAST GREBE
Tachybaptus dominicus

LEGR
Species # 0050
Band size: 4

Species—From Pied-billed Grebe (p. 227) by smaller overall size (Table 22, p. 232); bill much shallower (Table 22), pointed, and horn-colored to dusky without blackish ring (*cf.* Fig. 173, p. 228); face and neck grayish or dusky; pp with bold white patches (*cf.* Fig. 171, p. 226); iris yellowish brown to yellow (see **Age**). Little Grebe (*T. ruficollis*) a potential vagrant from Eurasia, averages larger (wg chord 92-107, tarsus 30-38); auriculars and nape washed rufous (*vs* dusky in Least Grebe); gape with whitish to yellow swelling; inner pp without white; underparts whiter.

Geographic variation—See Blake (1977), Brewster (1902b), Chapman (1899), Dickey & van Rossem (1938), Hellmayr & Conover (1948a), Palmer (1962), Paynter (1955), Storer & Getty (1985), Todd & Worthington (1911), van Rossem & Hachisuka (1937a), Wetmore (1943, 1965). Two other subspecies in S.Am. In all subspecies ♂♂ average larger than ♀♀, especially in bill length (see **Sex**). Reported differences in upperpart aspect seem slight, at best, and reported differences may have been based on comparison of individuals in different states of wear.

T.d. bangsi (res s.Baja CA-Sonora Mex, vagrant to CA-AZ): Size averages smaller (Table 22, p. 232; also, bill from base 10.6-14.5); flanks dusky, with little to no white.

T.d. brachypterus (res s.TX-C.Am, vagrant to LA): Size intermediate (Table 22; also, bill from base 11.2-16.4); flanks brownish with no to a slight amount of whitish mottling.

T.d. dominicus (br W.Indes, possible vagrant to FL): Size averages larger (Table 22; also, bill from base 11.2-18.2); flanks dusky with a slight to moderate whitish mottling.

Molt—CAS. PF partial-complete? (Jun-May? in HY/SYs), PA1 limited (Feb-May in non-breeding SYs), DPB complete (Jun-Nov in breeding AHYs), DPA limited (Dec-Apr in AHY/ASYs). The above timing pertains to most N.Am populations; some adults may breed year-round and exhibit different molt timing. The PF includes most to all body feathers; it is possibly complete in some HY/SYs (pp replaced in Mar-May) as in Eared Grebe (p. 234); study needed. During DPBs, pp and ss are replaced synchronously, usually in Jun-Oct, but in Mar-May in some (SYs?), and at any time of year in other AHY/ASYs. The PAs are limited to some throat feathers, at most. More study needed on molt patterns in adults that replace pp and ss in Mar-May (Storer & Jehl 1985) and those that show alternate plumage aspect in Sep-Mar.

Age—Juv (B1; Apr-Nov, Dec-Mar in some) has rufous in crown, indistinct whitish stripes in face and upper back, and whitish underparts; Juv ♀=♂. See Storer (1967) for plumage aspects of downy young. The following month ranges pertain to N.Am populations.

HY/SY (1st cycle, F1-A1; Sep-Aug): Crown washed brownish, becoming mottled with dusky in Mar-Aug; pp and ss uniformly narrow (Fig. 13**A**, p. 20), with less extensive and distinct whitish by sex (Fig. 171**A** & **C**); throat pale, with little or no dusky in Sep-Apr, and often with reduced dusky patch (confined to center of throat) in Apr-Aug; iris brownish (Sep-Dec) to brownish yellow (Mar-Aug). **Note: Intermediates occur that are best aged U/AHY. See also AHY/ASY.**

AHY/ASY (Def. cycle, DB-DA; Sep-Aug): Crown uniformly dusky to glossy blackish; pp and ss uniformly broad and squared (*cf.* Fig. 14**A**, p. 21), with more extensive and distinct white by sex (Fig. 171**B** & **D**); throat often blackish or mottled blackish in Sep-Mar, and extensively blackish in Apr-Aug (see **Molt**); iris yellow to orange-yellow. **Note: See HY/SY. Adults with black in the throat or replacing pp in Sep-Feb are reliably aged as AHY/ASYs.**

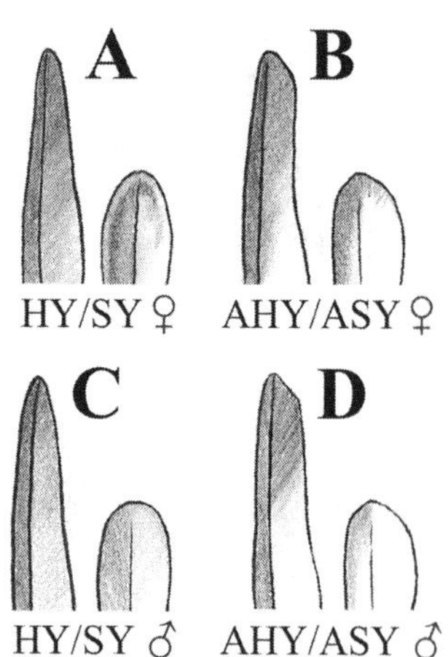

FIGURE 171. Shape and color pattern of p10 (the second from outermost) and s4 by age and sex in Least Grebe. Shape differences in p10 as illustrated here reflect similar differences in shape of outer pp in all grebes. More study is needed to confirm sexing by pattern to these feathers in Least Grebe.

Sex—Medial(?) BP (Fig. 20**A,** p. 31) developed by both sexes but distended cloaca (Fig. 21, p. 32) indicates AHY ♀ (primarily in Feb-May but possible all year). Measurements (especially bill size) fairly useful for sexing, especially with mated pairs in direct comparison (Table 22, p. 232). The amount and distinctness of white in the pp and ss may be reliable for sexing known-age individuals (Fig. 171); more study is needed. Otherwise, no criteria known.

Hybrids reported—None.

References—Bent (1919a), Dickey & van Rossem (1938), Gross (1949), Howell & Webb (1995), Oberholser (1974), Palmer (1962), Storer (1992), Storer & Getty (1985), Storer & Jehl (1985).

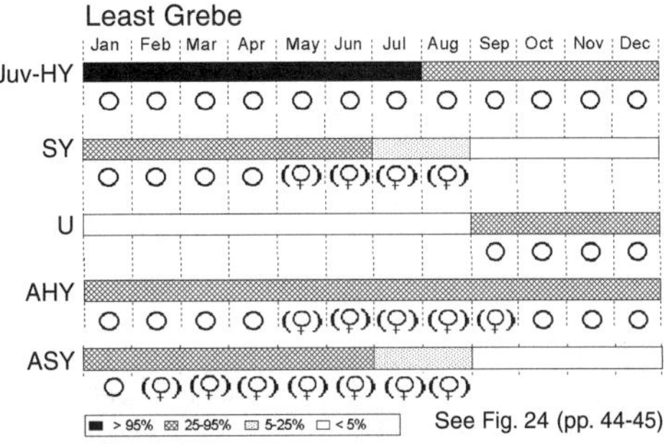

PIED-BILLED GREBE

Podilymbus podiceps

PBGR
Species # 0060
Band size: 5-6

Species—From Least Grebe (p. 225) by larger overall size (Table 22, p. 232); bill deeper (Table 22), blunt, and grayish with blackish to black ring, primarily in in Mar-Sep (Fig. 173, p. 228); face and neck brownish; inner pp with little or no white; iris brown to hazel. See Least Grebe for separation from Little Grebe.

Geographic variation—See Bangs (1913), Blake (1977), Hellmayr & Conover (1948a), Monroe (1968), Palmer (1962), Todd (1916a), Wetmore (1965). Two other subspecies in the Antilles and C.Am-S.Am.

P.p. podiceps (br & wint N.Am): From other subspecies by intermediate size (Table 22, p. 232) *vs* smaller in *antillarum* of the Antilles (wg chord 102-126, tarsus 33-42) and larger in *antarcticus* of C.Am-S.Am (wg chord 119-144, tarsus 39-47); bill short (Table 22; *vs* 19.3-26.2 in the other subspecies); nape washed medium-pale brown (*vs* blackish in the other subspecies); abdomen whitish with slight to moderate dusky mottling (*vs* heavily mottled dusky to blackish in the other subspecies); AHYs in Mar-Aug with black throat patch often > 20 mm wide (*vs* often < 20 mm wide in *antillarum*) and ring around bill black and complete (*vs* dusky and/or incomplete in *antillarum*).

Molt—CAS. PF partial (Jun-Oct in HYs), PA1 limited-partial (Feb-Jun in non-breeding SYs), DPB complete (Jun-Oct in breeding AHYs), DPA limited-partial (Dec-Apr in AHY/ASYs). The above timing pertains to N.Am populations. The PBs occur on breeding grounds and the PAs occur on non-breeding grounds. The PF includes most to all body feathers but no terts and few if any s covs. The DPAs include the head and neck feathers, although a variable number of other body feathers may also be replaced; more study needed. During DPBs, pp and ss are usually replaced synchronously in Jun-Sep (N.Am populations) before body molt commences; breeding adults can drop these feathers while incubating.

Age—Juv (B1; Apr-Nov) has plumage aspect washed buff and face and upper back with distinct whitish stripes; Juv ♀ = ♂ although bill depth can be used for sexing, once fully grown (see **Sex**). See Storer (1967) for plumage aspects of downy young. The following month ranges pertain to N.Am populations.

HY/SY (1st cycle, F1-A1; Sep-Aug): Upperparts mixed brownish and blackish; nape, breast, and flanks brownish to buffy brown; face sometimes with remnant juv stripes in Sep-Mar; pp and ss uniformly brownish and worn (Fig. 13**A**, p. 20), the outer pp narrow and tapered

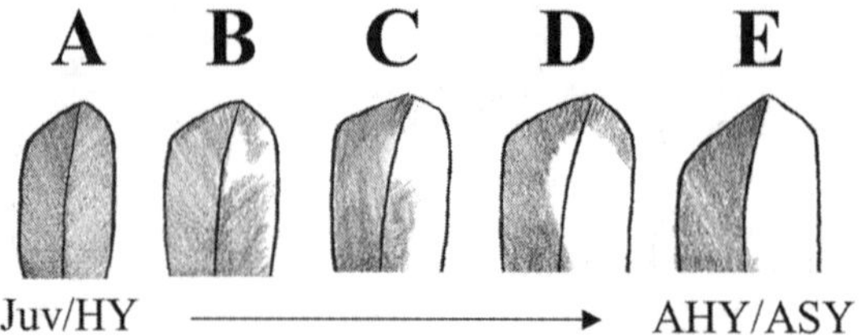

FIGURE 172. Shape and color pattern to the medial secondaries (s5-s7) by age in Pied-billed Grebe; note clinal differences in feather shape as well as the amount and distinctness of white coloration. Most Juv/HY/SYs resemble **A-C** (rarely **D**?) whereas most AHY/ASYs resemble **C-E** (rarely **B**?). It is also possible that ♂♂ average more white than ♀♀, age for age, but more study is needed.

(*cf.* Fig. 171**A** & **C**) and the medial ss (s5-s7) rounded and with reduced and/or mottled whitish tips (Fig. 172**A-C**); throat usually without black in Sep-Mar and blackish, mottled brownish, in Apr-Aug; bill brownish gray with incomplete to complete black ring in Apr-Aug; iris brown (Sep-Dec) to yellowish brown (Mar-Aug). **Note: Some or all of these characters may show overlap with those of AHY/ASY; only individuals showing consistent characters should be aged with confidence. More study needed on throat plumage aspect, as some Juv/HYs may show black.**

AHY/ASY (Def. cycle, DB-DA; Sep-Aug): Upperparts uniformly blackish; nape, breast, and flanks brownish to reddish brown; face without remnant stripes; pp and ss uniformly grayish and fresh (*cf.* Fig. 14**A**, p. 21), the outer pp broad and truncate (Fig. 171**B** & **D**) and the medial ss (s5-s7) truncated and with more extensive and distinct whitish to white tips (Fig. 172**C-E**); throat sometimes mottled blackish in Sep-Feb and uniformly black in Mar-Aug; bill bluish gray, with complete black ring in Feb-Sep; iris yellowish brown to hazel. **Note: See HY/SY.**

Sex—♀=♂ by plumage aspect. Medial(?) BP (Fig. 20**A,** p. 31) developed by both sexes but distended cloaca (Fig. 21, p. 32) indicates ♀ in Apr-Jun. Measurements useful for sexing (Table 22, p. 232); once fully grown (including most in juv plumage) most N.Am individuals (*P.p. podiceps*) can be sexed reliably by bill depth:

♀ Bill shallower (Fig. 173**A**). **Note: Individuals with bill depth 10.0-10.1 are AHY/ASY ♀♀ or HY/SY ♂♂ so combine with age to reliably sex these. In addi-**

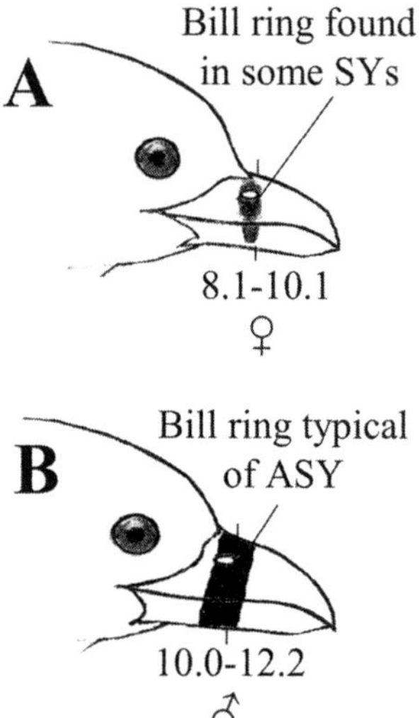

FIGURE 173. Bill shape by sex, and extent of the black ring in Apr-Aug by age, in Pied-billed Grebe. Age and sex characters shown here are independent. Measures pertain to the bill depth at distal end of nares (Fig. 8**C**, p. 10); exposed culmen and bill depth at proximal end of nares also are greater in ♂♂ than ♀♀ (Table 22, p. 232). AHY/ASYs can show a bill ring as in **A** during Oct-Jan but typically have a fuller ring, as in **B**, during Mar-Aug. The ring is usually absent in HY/SYs during Sep-Mar but can vary from partial, as in **A**, to almost full, as in **B**, during Apr-Aug. Bill ring also varies slightly by sex, being less full in ♀♀ than in ♂♂ by season, but substantial overlap and confounding by age and season precludes use of this in sexing.

tion, ♀♀ average slightly duller plumage aspect and bill ring, by season, than ♂♂.

♂ Bill deeper (Fig. 173**B**). **Note: See ♀.**

Hybrids reported—Probably with Atitlan Grebe *P. gigas* (Cade & Temple 1995); vagrants with Little Grebe (*Tachybaptus ruficollis*) in Europe (Fjeldså 2004).

References—Bent (1919a), Cramp & Simmons (1977), Muller & Storer (1999), Munro (1941), Oberholser (1974), Otto & Strohmeyer (1985), Palmer (1962), Roberts (1955), Storer & Jehl (1985), Stresemann & Stresemann (1966), Zusi & Storer (1969).

Pied-billed Grebe

	Jan	Feb	Mar	Apr	May	Jun	Jul	Aug	Sep	Oct	Nov	Dec
Juv-HY				O	O	(♂)	(⚥)	(⚥)	⚥	⚥	⚥	⚥
SY	⚥	⚥	⚥	⚥	⚥	⚥	⚥	⚥				
U									⚥	⚥	⚥	⚥
AHY	⚥	⚥	⚥	⚥	⚥	⚥	⚥	⚥	⚥	⚥	⚥	⚥
ASY	⚥	⚥	⚥	⚥	⚥	⚥	⚥	⚥				

■ > 95% ▩ 25-95% ▤ 5-25% □ < 5%

See Fig. 24 (pp. 44-45)

HORNED GREBE

Podiceps auritus

HOGR
Species # 0030
Band size: 6-5

Species—From Red-necked (p. 231), and Western and Clark's (p. 236) grebes by much smaller size (Table 22, p. 232); pp without white; bill without yellow or greenish tones; iris orange to red. From Eared Grebe (p. 234) in formative and basic plumages by longer average wing and tarsus (Table 22); bill shorter, deeper, and not recurved, with depth > width at distal end of nares, and usually with a pale tip (Table 22, Fig. 174); lores usually with a whitish spot and cheeks mostly (HY/SY) to entirely (AHY/ASY) white, the dark cap extending < 5 mm below the eye (within 5 mm proximal to the eye; Fig. 174**A**; beware of molting AHYs in Sep-Oct showing remaining black alternate or dusky juv feathering in cheeks; Fig. 174**B**); p1-p3 without white tips (*cf.* Fig. 179, p. 235); iris pinkish orange (HY) to red (ASY).

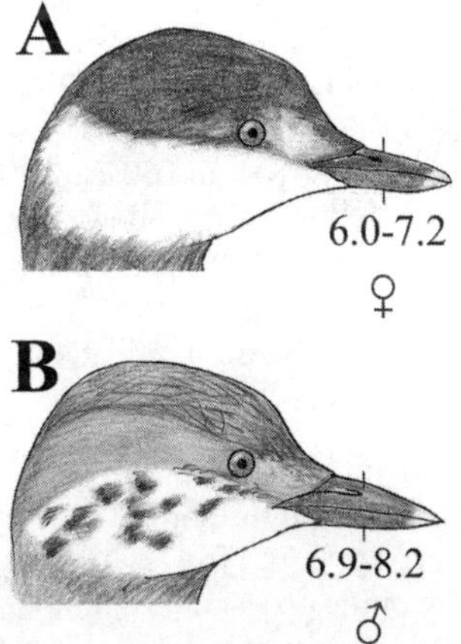

FIGURE 174. Head shape and plumage aspect for identification, and bill shape by sex, in Horned Grebe. Measures pertain to bill depth at distal end of nares (Fig. 8**C**, p. 10), where the depth is greater than the width in this species. Compared to Eared Grebe (Figure 178, p. 234), note the stouter and straighter bill with pale tip, more distinct cap with black extending < 5 mm below eye, and pale area in lores. Beware molting AHYs in Aug-Sep and Mar-Apr that can show black feathering in cheeks (**B**); however, this should not obscure characteristics separating Horned from Eared grebes. Note that variation in plumage aspect shown here does not relate to age or sex.

Geographic variation—Considered monotypic (Patten et al. 2003). Populations of N.Am ("*P.a. cornutus*") may average grayer (less blackish) upperparts than nominate populations of Eurasia but differences insufficient and confounded by feather bleaching and wear. See also Cramp & Simmons (1977), Fjeldså (1973a), Mayr & Short (1970), Palmer (1962), Parkes (1952a).

Molt—CAS. PF partial (Oct-Jan in HY/SYs), PA1 absent-partial (Mar-May in non-breeding SYs), DPB complete (Jun-Oct in breeding

AHYs), DPA partial (Feb-Apr in ASYs). The PF begins on breeding grounds and completes on non-breeding grounds, the PBs occur at stopover sites and/or on non-breeding grounds, and the PA occurs mostly or entirely on non-breeding grounds. The PF includes most of the body feathers but few if any s covs; some juv body feathers may not be replaced until the PA1. The DPA includes most or all body feathers and no to some s covs. The pp and ss are replaced synchronously during DPBs in Jun-Sep. Replacement of flank and other feathers may be the result of plucking rather than molt (see Family Account, p. 225). A limited presupplemental molt in Jun-Jul (resulting in cinnamon-buff auriculars) has been reported (Munro 1941); however, it is possible that this plumage aspect results from late prealternate or early prebasic molts (see p. 29).

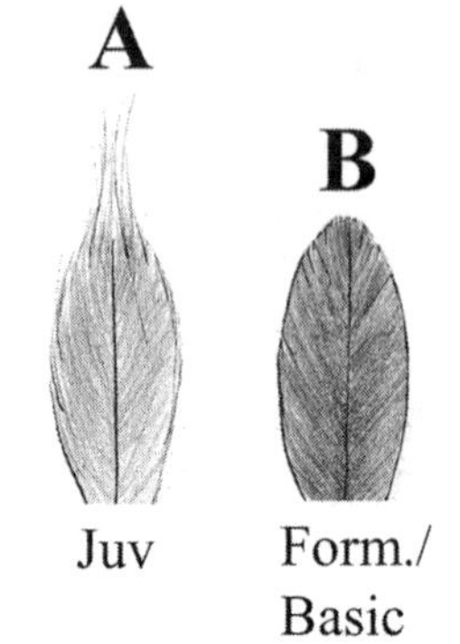

A B

Juv Form./ Basic

FIGURE 175. Scapulars by feather generation in Horned, Red-necked, and Eared grebes. The filamentous tips to the juvenal feathers (**A**) can wear or break off but a loose aspect to the tips of juv feathers remains, which can often be retained until Mar or later in HY/SYs.

Age—Juv (B1; Jun-Sep) has head with indistinct dusky and white streaking and cheek washed dusky; Juv ♀=♂. See Storer (1967) for plumage aspects of downy young. In addition to the following, Fjeldså (1973a) found that the pp constituted 55.2-61.6% of the wing length in HY/SYs and 60.7-65.9% of the wing length in AHY/ASYs, allowing ageing of >95% of individuals from European populations (*P.a. auritus*). More study is needed on this method in N.Am populations and in other grebe species.

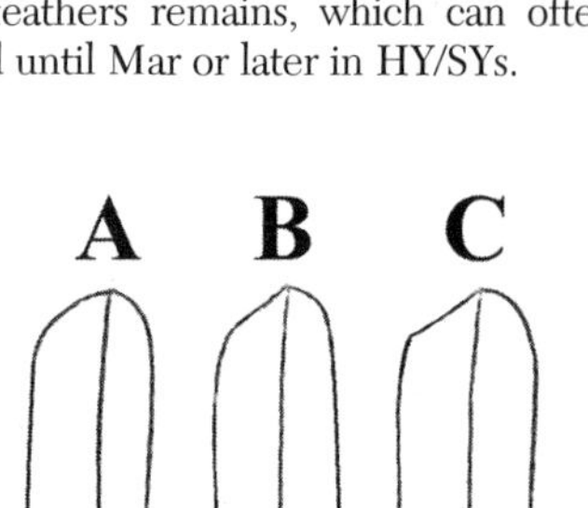

FIGURE 176. Shape of the medial ss (s5-s10) by age in Horned, Red-necked, and Eared grebes. Juv ss vary from rounded (**A**) to blunt (**B**), whereas basic ss vary from blunt (**B**) to squared (**C**).

HY/SY (1st cycle, F1-A1; Sep-Aug): Crown and back washed or mottled brownish; longest scapulars with downy/frayed tips in Sep-Nov through Mar (Fig. 175**A**); pp, ss, and most or all wing covs brownish and worn (Fig. 13**A**, p. 20), the outer pp narrow and tapered (Fig. 171**A** & **C**, p. 226) and the medial ss (~s5-s10) rounded to blunt at tip (Fig. 176**A-B**); bill pale horn with dusky culmen (Sep-Oct) to dusky (Mar-Aug); cheeks whitish mottled gray in Sep-Mar to dull or mottled gold and blackish in Mar-Aug; iris grayish brown (Sep-Oct) to medium-bright reddish (Mar-Aug). **Note: In addition, the amount of white in the ss averages less in HY/SYs than in AHY/ASYs but more study needed to determine limits of variation. A few intermediates (SY/TYs?) may be difficult or impossible to age based on these criteria.**

AHY/ASY (Def. cycle, DB-DA; Sep-Aug): Crown and back uniformly blackish in Sep-Mar or black in Mar-Aug; longest scapulars without downy/frayed tips (Fig. 175**B**); pp, ss, and wing covs uniformly dusky and fresh (*cf.* Fig. 14**A**, p. 21), the outer pp broad and truncate (Fig. 171**B** & **D**) and the medial ss (~s5-s10) blunt tipped to truncate (Fig. 176**B-C**); cheeks white in Sep-Mar to uniformly bright gold and black in Mar-Aug; bill grayish to black; iris bright red. **Note: See HY/SY. In addition, some older AHY/ASYs can acquire whitish in the proximal les covs (Fjeldså 1973a); more study is needed on the relationship of this with age and sex.**

Sex—♀=♂ by plumage aspect. Medial(?) BP (Fig. 20**A**, p. 31) developed by both sexes but distended cloaca (Fig. 21, p. 32) indicates ♀ in May-Jun. Measurements (especially those of bill) generally helpful for sexing (Table 22, p. 232; Fig. 174, p. 229), with mated pairs (in direct comparison) separable. In addition to the following, length of the ornamental head plumes average longer in ASY ♂♂ (29-36 mm) than ASY ♀♀ (25-32 mm) during Apr-Jun; SYs average shorter by sex. Also, whitish in the proximal les coverts, acquired by some older individuals (see **Age**), may be more evident in ♂♂ than ♀♀; more study is needed.

♀ Bill shallower (Fig. 174**A**). **Note: individuals with bill depths 6.9-7.2 can be sexed in combination with age, HY/SYs being ♂♂ and AHY/ASYs being ♀♀.**

♂ Bill deeper (Fig. 174**B**). **Note: See ♀.**

Horned Grebe

	Jan	Feb	Mar	Apr	May	Jun	Jul	Aug	Sep	Oct	Nov	Dec
Juv-HY						O	O	(♂)	(⚥)	⚥	⚥	⚥
SY	⚥	⚥	⚥	⚥	⚥	⚥	⚥	⚥				
U									⚥	⚥	⚥	⚥
AHY	⚥	⚥	⚥	⚥	⚥	⚥	⚥	⚥	⚥	⚥	⚥	⚥
ASY	⚥	⚥	⚥	⚥	⚥	⚥	⚥	⚥				

■ > 95% ▩ 25-95% ▤ 5-25% □ < 5%

See Fig. 24 (pp. 44-45)

Hybrids reported—With Eared Grebe (*P.a. auritus* with *P.n. nigricollis*; Dennis 1973, McCarthy 2006).

References—Ainley et al. (1994), Baker (1993), Bent (1919a), Cramp & Simmons (1977), Dement'ev & Gladkov (1951a), Fjeldså (1973a, 1980), Godfrey (1986), Kaufman (1992), Munro (1941), Oberholser (1974), Palmer (1962), Phillips et al. (1983), Stedman (2000), Storer (1967), Stout & Cooke (2003).

RED-NECKED GREBE

Podiceps grisegena

RNGR
Species # 0020
Band size: 7A

Species—From other N.Am grebes in basic and first alternate plumages by medium large size and bill (Table 22, p. 232; Fig. 177, p. 233); pp without white and s1-s3 tipped white; cheeks and neck brownish, bill straight and yellowish to yellow (at least at base), and iris dark (Fig. 177).

Geographic variation—See Cramp & Simmons (1977), Fjeldså (1982), Palmer (1962), Storer (1996), Stejneger (1885). No other subspecies.

P.g. holboellii (br & wint N.Am): Substantially larger (Table 22, p. 232).

P.g. grisegena (br & wint Europe; vagrant to Greenland and potential vagrant to ne.N.Am): Substantially smaller (Table 22).

Molt—CAS. PF partial (Sep-Jan in HY/SYs), PA1 absent-partial (Mar-Jun in non-breeding SYs), PB2 complete (May-Sep in non-breeding SYs), DPA partial (Feb-Apr in ASYs), DPB complete (Jun-Oct in breeding ASYs). The PF can begin on breeding grounds but occurs primarily on non-breeding grounds, the DPBs occur at stopover sites or on non-breeding grounds, and the PA occurs mostly or entirely on non-breeding grounds. The PF and PA1 combined include most body feathers but few if any s covs. The definitive DPA includes body feathers and none to a few proximal s covs. The pp and ss are replaced synchronously during DPBs, during May-Jul in SYs, Jun-Aug in non-breeding ASYs, and Jul-Sep in breeding ASYs. Replacement of flank and other feathers may be the result of plucking rather than molt (see Family Account, p. 225).

Age—Juv (B1; Jun-Sep) has indistinct, dusky and pale stripes on head (especially cheeks), rusty wash to neck and breast, and dull yellowish bill; Juv ♀=♂. See Storer (1967) for plumage aspects of downy young. Note that confirmed breeders can probably be aged ASY.

TABLE 22. Measurements (mm) of North American grebes to assist in identification and sexing. See pp. 4-11 for methods of measurement. Species summaries are in **bold** and subspecies summaries in ***italics***. Values were derived from 95% confidence intervals, as based (for wing, tail, exposed culmen, and tarsus) approximately on the indicated sample sizes (see pp. 4-5); sample size for bill depth was often smaller but included at least 10 of each sex. Thus, midpoints of ranges approximate means, and S.D. is approximated by 25% of the range.

Taxon/Sex	*n*	wing chord	bill from nares[1]	bill depth[2]	tarsus
Least Grebe[3]		**83-105**	**4.1-6.8**	**5.8-8.0**	**29-36**
T.d. bangsi		***83-97***	***4.1-5.6***	***5.8-7.3***	***29-33***
♀	20	83-94	4.1-5.2	5.8-6.6	29-31
♂	20	86-97	4.4-5.6	6.4-7.3	31-33
T.d. brachypterus		***85-103***	***4.3-6.2***	***5.8-8.0***	***29-35***
♀	100	85-97	4.3-5.4	5.8-6.9	29-33
♂	100	88-103	4.7-6.2	6.7-8.0	30-35
T.d. dominicus		***91-104***	***4.3-6.8***	***6.1-8.0***	***29-36***
♀	20	91-101	4.3-6.1	6.1-7.1	29-33
♂	20	94-105	4.9-6.8	6.9-8.0	31-35
Pied-billed Grebe[3]		**115-143**	**11.7-16.8**	**8.7-13.9**	**35-46**
♀	100	115-129	11.7-14.3	8.7-11.8	35-42
♂	100	127-143	13.4-16.8	10.7-13.9	38-46
Horned Grebe[3]		**126-147**	**12.7-17.6**	**7.0-9.2**	**40-49**
♀	36	126-144	12.7-16.1	7.0-8.3	40-46
♂	43	133-147	14.3-17.6	7.7-9.2	43-49
Red-necked Grebe[3]		**153-212**	**25-43**	**8.7-15.3**	**49-71**
P.g. holboellii		***180-212***	***28-43***	***10.7-15.3***	***55-71***
♀	68	180-203	28-41	10.7-14.1	55-67
♂	88	185-212	30-43	11.3-15.3	58-71
P.g. grisgena		***153-188***	***25-33***	***8.7-14.0***	***49-60***
♀	43	153-181	25-31	8.7-12.4	49-57
♂	49	159-188	37-33	9.6-14.0	52-60
Eared Grebe[3]		**120-142**	**12.7-18.5**	**5.7-7.9**	**38-46**
♀	100	120-139	12.7-16.1	5.7-6.9	38-45
♂	100	126-142	15.2-18.5	6.6-7.9	40-46
Western Grebe[3]		**165-213**	**48-68**	**9.3-14.6**	**67-83**
♀	64	165-193	48-58	9.3-11.6	67-76
♂	100	186-213	56-68	11.8-14.6	73-83
Clark's Grebe[3]		**164-210**	**46-66**	**8.9-14.0**	**69-84**
♀	20	164-193	46-56	8.9-11.3	69-75
♂	36	184-210	54-66	11.6-14.0	72-84

[1] Bill length measured from distal end of nares (*cf.* Figs. 7**C**, p. 9 & 178, p. 234).
[2] Bill depth measured at posterior end of nares (*cf.* Figs. 8**D**, p. 10 & 178).
[3] Measurements from N.Am populations only; see **Geographic variation**.

HY/SY (1st cycle, F1-A1; Sep-Aug): Crown and back washed or mottled brownish in May-Aug; longest scapulars with downy/frayed tips in Sep-Dec (Fig. 175**A**, p. 230); upper cheeks mottled white and brownish in Sep-Mar, bill dull yellowish (with a darker tip in Mar-Aug) and iris yellowish to brownish with yellow ring (Fig. 177**A**); pp, ss, and wing covs brownish and worn, contrasting with replaced dusky back feathers (Fig. 13**B**, p. 20), the outer pp narrow and tapered (*cf.* Fig. 171**A** & **C**, p. 226) and the medial ss (~s5-s10) rounded to blunt (Fig.

176**A**-**B**, p. 230); upper cheeks dull whitish or mottled dusky and breast dull rufous mottled whitish in Mar-Aug. **Note: The amount of white in the ss also averages less in HY/SYs than in AHY/ASYs but more study needed to determine limits of variation. Pale rufous on the necks can be found in Nov-Jan in some individuals of all ages. Some individuals (SY/TYs?) may show intermediate characters and should be aged U/AHY.**

AHY/ASY (Def. cycle, DB-DA; Sep-Aug): Crown and back uniformly blackish; longest scapulars without downy/frayed tips (Fig. 175**B**); upper cheeks uniformly washed gray in Sep-Mar, bill blackish with dull to bright yellow base, and iris brown (Fig. 177**B**); pp, ss, and wing covs dusky and fresh, not contrasting in quality and wear with back feathers (*cf.* Fig. 14**A**, p. 21), the outer pp broad and truncate (Fig. 171**B** & **D**) and the medial ss (~s5-s10) blunt to truncate (Fig. 176**B**-**C**); upper cheeks bright white and breast uniformly bright rufous in Mar-Aug. **Note: See HY/SY.**

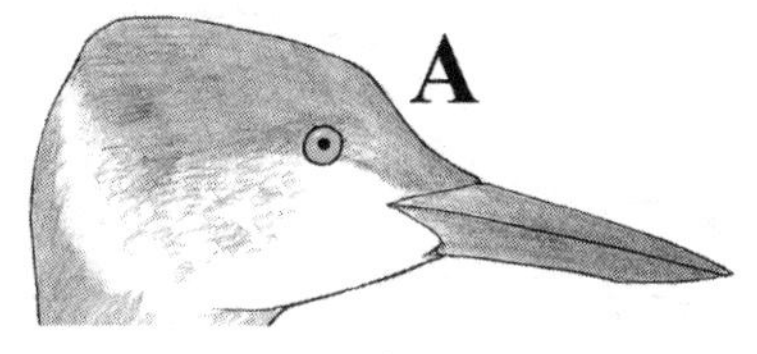

HY/SY

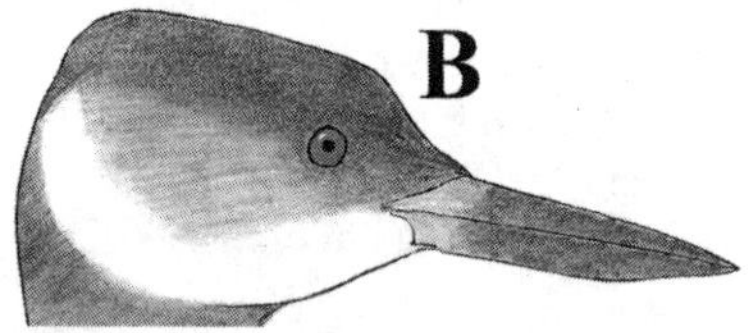

AHY/ASY

FIGURE 177. Head plumage aspect and eye color by age in Red-necked Grebes during formative and basic plumage (Oct-Mar). Many SYs may continue to show dusky mottling in cheeks through Apr-Aug. Note that Red-necked is the only grebe in which iris color becomes darker with age, with approximate shades of HYs (**A**) and ASYs (**B**) shown; SYs average an intermediate shade in Apr-Aug. Bill color becomes slightly darker with age and shows a more distinct yellow base in AHY/ASYs.

Sex—♀ = ♂ by plumage aspect. Medial BP (Fig. 20**A**, p. 31) developed by both sexes but distended cloaca (Fig. 21, p. 32) indicates ASY ♀ in May-Jul. Measurements generally unhelpful for sexing (Table 22, p. 232), although some mated pairs (in direct comparison) are probably separable. Otherwise, no criteria known.

Hybrids reported—With Great Crested Grebe *P. cristatus* (McCarthy 2006). Has reportedly nested and laid eggs with Eurasian Coot (*Fulica atra*; Dittberner & Dittberner 1992).

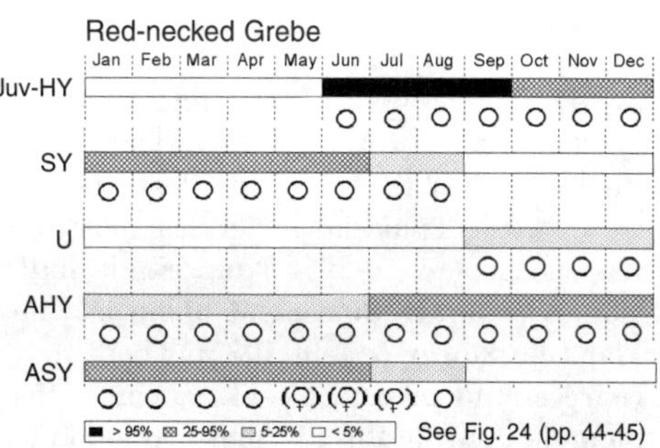

References—Ainley et al. (1994), Baker (1993), Bent (1919a), Cramp & Simmons (1977), Dement'ev & Gladkov (1951a), Fjeldså (1980), Munro (1941), Oberholser (1974), Palmer (1962), Roberts (1955), Storer (1967), Stout & Cooke (2003), Stout & Nuechterlein (1999), Walser & Barthel (1994).

EARED GREBE EAGR
Podiceps nigricollis Species # 0040
Band size: 5

Species—From Red-necked (p. 231), and Western and Clark's (p. 236) grebes by smaller overall size (Table 22, p. 232); white of pp confined to wash on p1-p3 in some N.Am individuals (Fig. 179); bill without yellow or greenish tones; iris brownish yellow to red. From Horned Grebe (p. 229) in formative and basic plumages by shorter average wing and legs (Table 22); bill longer, narrower, and recurved, with depth < width at the distal end of nares, and without a pale tip (Table 22, Fig. 178); lores without a white spot and cheeks variably dusky (often with a distinct white spot), with the dark cap usually extending > 5 mm below the eye (within 5 mm proximal to the eye; Fig. 178); p1-p3 usually (HY/SY) to sometimes (AHY/ASY) with white tips (Fig. 179); iris yellowish tan (HY) to orangish red or red (ASY).

Geographic variation—See Cramp & Simmons (1977), Palmer (1962). Three other subspecies occur in Eurasia, Africa, and S.Am.

P.n. californicus (br & wint N.Am): From *nigricollis* of Eurasia (which could occur as a vagrant to N.Am) by longer average bill (exp culmen 19.3-28.6, *vs* 19.0-25.4 in *nigricollis*); white on p1-p3 absent or confined to tips of feathers (Fig. 179**A-D**) *vs* more extensively or entirely white in *nigricollis* (Fig. 179**E**).

Molt—CAS. PF partial-incomplete? (Aug-Dec in HYs), PA1 absent-partial (Mar-Jun in SYs), PB2 complete (May-Sep in SYs), DPA partial (Feb-May in ASYs), DPB complete (Jul-Oct in ASYs). The PF and DPB begin on breeding grounds but occur primarily at stopover sites, and the PAs occur mostly or entirely on non-breeding grounds but can complete during migration or on breeding grounds. The PF includes most body feathers but few if any s covs. The PA1 is variable, including no or only a few feathers in some SYs, to most or all body feathers and most s covs in others. The DPA includes all body feathers and most to all wing covs. The pp and ss are replaced synchronously during the DPB, in May-Jul (SYs), Jul-Aug (non-breeding ASYs) or Aug-Oct (breeding ASYs). Replacement of flank and other feathers may be the result of plucking rather than molt (see Family Account, p. 225). **Note: Some individuals exhibit replacement of pp in Jan-Mar (see Storer & Jehl 1985). These may represent full or partial replacement of the pp and ss during the PF (more common in HY/SYs wintering south of N.Am?), as occurs in some Western and Clark's grebes (p. 236). The premise that HY/SYs retain pp for 18 months before molt (M.A. Traylor *in* Stresemann & Stresemann 1966) seems less likely.**

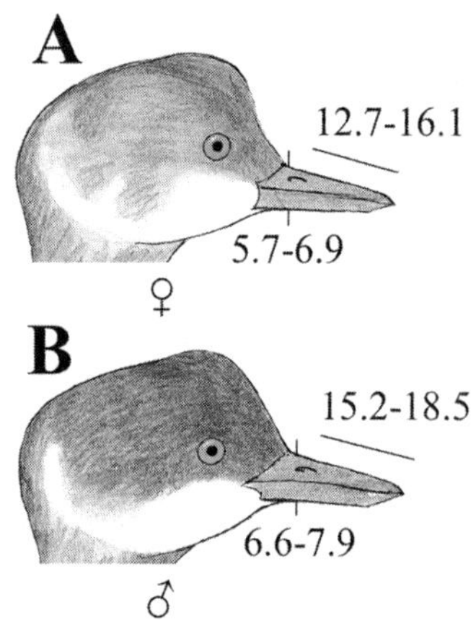

FIGURE 178. Head shape and plumage aspect for identification, and bill shape by sex, in Horned Grebe. Measures pertain to exposed culmen (Fig. 7**A**, p. 9) and bill depth at proximal end of nares (Fig. 8**C**, p. 10); at the distal end of nares width is greater than depth, unlike in Horned Grebe. Compared to Horned Grebe (Figure 174, p. 229), note the slimmer and slightly recurved bill without pale tip, less distinct cap with dusky extending > 5 mm below eye, and entirely dark lores. See Figure 174**B** regarding molting Horned Grebes. Note that variation in plumage aspect shown here does not relate to age or sex.

Age—Juv (B1; Jun-Sep) has pale brownish tips to upperpart feathers, cheek washed with brownish dusky, and iris brownish; Juv ♀=♂ but see **Sex** for culmen measurements allowing separation of many full-grown Juvs. See Storer & Jehl (1985), Winkler & Cooper

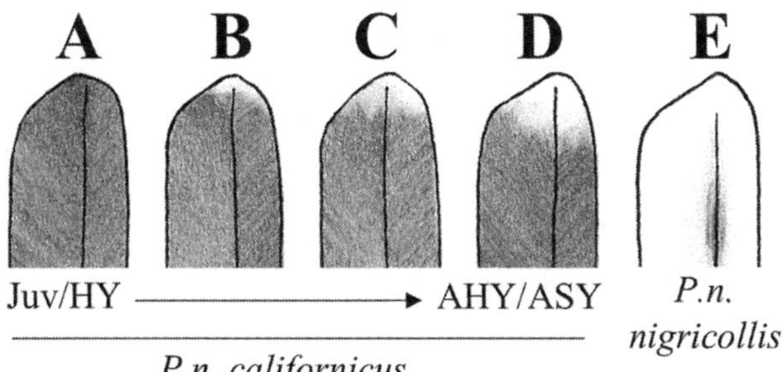

FIGURE 179. Shape and color pattern to the inner primary (p1) by age and subspecies in Eared Grebe. Similar patterns may be expected among the medial ss (s5-s10). Variation in the juv p1 in HY/SYs of N.Am populations (*P.n. californicus*) is reflected by **A-C** whereas variation in the basic p1 in AHY/ASYs is reflected by **B-D**. Note also the shape difference between **A-B** (typical of HY/SY) and **D-E** (typical of AHY/ASY). The p1 of Eurasian populations (*nigricollis*) is extensively white (**E**); it varies little by age-sex group in color but likely shows similar shape differences as found in N.Am populations; the shape shown for **E** is that of an AHY/ASY.

(1986), and Henny et al. (1990) for information on ageing by the bursa (Fig. 23, p. 34), and Storer (1967) for plumage aspects of downy young.

HY/SY (1st cycle, F1-A1; Sep-Aug): Crown and back washed brownish or with mixed brownish and dusky or blackish feathers; longest scapulars often with downy/frayed tips in Sep-Dec (Fig. 175**A**, p. 230); pp, ss, and most to all s covs brownish and worn, contrasting with replaced dusky back feathers (and sometimes some wing covs in Mar-Aug; Fig. 13**B-C**, p. 20), the outer pp narrow and tapered (*cf.* Fig. 171**A** & **C**, p. 226), the inner pp relatively rounded and with little to a reduced amount of white at tips (Fig. 179**A-C**), and the medial ss (~s5-s10) rounded to blunt tipped (Fig. 176**A-B**, p. 230); les covs seldom washed rufous, cheeks and breast variably grayish to blackish, and head with reduced yellow plumes in Mar-Aug; iris brownish yellow (Sep-Dec) to orangish red (May-Aug); legs dull yellowish green to greenish black. **Note: Some individuals may be difficult or impossible to age based on these criteria; these may be SY/TYs but should be aged U/AHY. Look also for occasional individuals to replace some or all pp and ss in Jan-Mar, that may be SYs (see Molt).**

AHY/ASY (Def. cycle, DB-DA; Sep-Aug): Crown and back uniformly blackish to black; longest scapulars without downy/frayed tips (Fig. 175**B**); pp, ss, and wing covs dusky and fresh, not contrasting in quality and wear with back feathers (*cf.* Fig. 14**A**, p. 21), the outer pp broad and truncate (*cf.* Fig. 171**B** & **D**), the inner pp blunt to truncate and usually with moderate white at tips (Fig. 179**B-D**), and the medial ss (~s5-s10) blunt tipped to truncate (Fig. 176**B-C**); les covs often washed rufous, cheeks and breast black, and head with extensive yellow plumes in Mar-Aug; iris orangish red to red; legs blackish, sometimes tinged yellowish or bluish. **Note: See HY/SY.**

Sex—♀=♂ by plumage aspect. Medial BP (Fig. 20**A**, p. 31) developed by both sexes but distended cloaca (Fig. 21, p. 32) in Apr-Jun indicates ♀. Measurements (except those of bill; see below) largely unhelpful for sexing (Table 22, p. 232). The following can be used to sex many N.Am individuals (*P.n. californicus*), including mated pairs in direct comparison, once fully grown (by Dec in HYs):

♀: Bill from distal end of nares < 15.2 and/or bill depth at proximal end of nares < 6.6 (Table 22, Fig. 178**A**). **Note: Individuals with bill-tip length 15.2-16.1 and depth 6.6-6.9 can be**

reliably sexed in combination with age, HY/SYs being ♂♂ and AHY/ASYs being ♀♀.

♂: Bill from distal end of nares < 16.1 and/or bill depth at proximal end of nares > 6.9 (Table 22, Fig. 178**B**). **Note: See ♀.**

Hybrids reported—With Horned Grebe (p. 229).

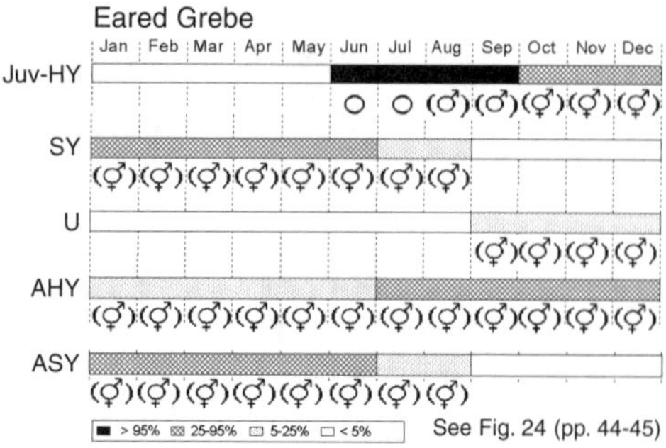

References—Ainley et al. (1994), Baker (1993), Bent (1919a), Cramp & Simmons (1977), Cullen et al. (1999), Dement'ev & Gladkov (1951a), Godfrey (1986), Jehl (1988, 1990), Jehl et al. (1998), Kaufman (1992), Munro (1941), Oberholser (1974), Palmer (1962), Phillips et al. (1983), Roberts (1955), Storer & Jehl (1985), Stresemann & Stresemann (1966), Winkler & Cooper (1986).

WESTERN GREBE

Aechmophorus occidentalis

WEGR
Species # 0010
Band size: 7A-7B

CLARK'S GREBE

Aechmophorus clarkii

CLGR
Species # 0011
Band size: 7A-7B

Species—From Horned (p. 229), Red-necked (p. 231), and Eared (p. 234) grebes by larger size (Table 22, p. 232); p1-p7 with white bases to inner webs; cheeks and foreneck uniform white; bill recurved (Fig. 181, p. 238) and greenish yellow to yellow; iris brownish yellow to orangish red.

Western from Clark's grebe by crown patch extensive by age and usually encompassing eye (Fig. 180**A-D**) *vs* usually not encompassing eye in Clark's Grebe (Fig. 180**D-E**); black of hindneck usually 15-20 mm wide at narrowest point (*vs* usually 10-15 mm in Clark's Grebe); mottled gray of flanks usually irregularly defined and extending below the folded pp in natural position (*vs* more distinctly defined at or near the folded pp in Clark's Grebe); bill and lores dingy greenish yellow to yellowish with indistinctly defined dusky culmen (Fig. 180**A-C**) *vs* brighter yellow to yellow orange, with redder base and lores and distinctly defined blackish culmen in Clark's Grebe (Fig. 180**D-E**). Note that some intermediates (possibly hybrids) are difficult or impossible to identify; bill color may be the most reliable feature on these. See Storer (1965) and Storer & Nuechterlein (1985) for other average characters.

Geographic variation—Considered monotypic here. Western Grebes breeding in c.Mexico ("*A.o. ephemeralis*") average smaller than those of N.Am, and Clark's Grebes breeding in N.Am ("*A.c. transitionalis*") average larger than those of c.Mexico, but in both cases differences are slight and broadly clinal. See Dickerman (1963, 1973a, 1986) and Storer & Nuechterlein (1985) for more information.

Molt—CAS. PF partial-incomplete (Oct-May in HYs), PA1 absent-limited (Mar-Jun in non-breeding SYs), PB2 complete (May-Sep in non-breeding SYs), DPA limited (Feb-May in ASYs), DPB complete (Jun-Oct in breeding ASYs). The PF probably begins on breeding grounds but occurs primarily on non-breeding grounds, the PBs occur at stopover sites or on non-breeding grounds, and the PAs occur mostly or entirely on non-breeding grounds. In some HY/SYs (that migrate farther south?) the PF can include the pp and ss (synchronously in Jan-

Feb) but otherwise this molt includes some to all body feathers and no to a few s covs, and a PA1 can involve a variable number of head feathers for a second time during the 1st cycle. The DPA includes feathers of the head (including elongated lateral crown feathers) and throat. Pp and ss are replaced synchronously during the PBs, in May-Aug (SYs) or Jul-Oct (ASYs; probably earlier in nonbreeding individuals); thus, some SYs (that molt pp and ss during the PF) probably molt their pp and ss twice within a six-month period (more study needed). Replacement of flank and other feathers may be the result of plucking rather than molt (see Family Account, p. 225).

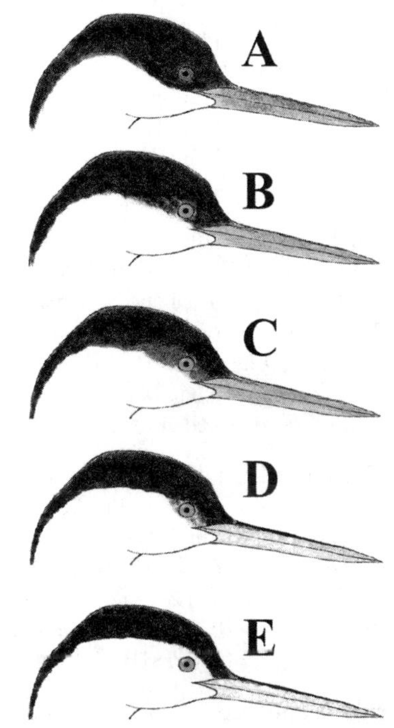

FIGURE 180. Loral patterns and bill shades in Western and Clark's grebes by species, age, and season. Loral patterns in Western Grebe vary from **A** to **D**, generally with AHY/ASYs (**A**-**B**) showing darker lores than HY/SYs (**B**-**D**) and ASYs can show alternate aspect (**A**-**C**) darker crown and lores than those in basic aspect (**A**-**D**); see text. Loral pattern in Clark's Grebe varies from **D** to **E**, with most age-plumage groups showing **E**, but some Juv-HY/SYs showing **D**. Figure based on information and illustrations in Storer & Nuechterlein (1985). Bill color is brighter in Clark's Grebe (**D**-**E**) than Western Grebe (**A**-**C**) and brighter in breeding ASYs by species.

Age—Juv (B1; Jun-Nov) has crown washed grayish (sometimes restricted in Western Grebe; Fig. 180**D**) and pale tips to upperpart feathers; Juv ♀=♂ but see **Sex** for culmen measurements allowing separation of full-grown Juvs. See Storer & Nuechterlein (1985) and Henny et al. (1990) for ageing by the bursa (Fig. 23, p. 34), and Storer (1967) for plumage aspects of downy young.

Juv-HY/SY (1st cycle, Juv/B1-F1-A1; Oct-Sep): Lores often with dusky wash in Oct to Mar-Sep (Fig. 180**D**); crown and back washed brownish or with mixed worn brownish and fresh dusky feathers, the crown without elongated lateral feathers and the back feathers with wide pale fringes; juv outer pp narrow and tapered (*cf.* Fig. 171**A** & **C**, p. 226); juv medial ss (~s5-s10) rounded to blunt tipped (Fig. 176**A**-**B**, p. 230); pp and ss sometimes molting in Jan-Feb; iris brownish (Oct-Dec) to orangish red (Mar-Sep). **Note: Those HY/SYs that do not replace pp in Jan-Feb can be recognized by very worn and brownish pp, contrasting distinctly with replaced back feathers and/or some les covs (Fig. 13B-C, p. 20). Some intermediates may be difficult to age; these may be SY/TYs but should be aged U/AHY.**

AHY/ASY (Def. cycle, DB-DA; Mar-Feb): Loral region darker in Western Grebe (Fig. 180**A**-**B**) or paler in Clark's Grebe (Fig. 180**E**); crown and back uniformly dusky to blackish, the crown with elongated lateral feathers and the back feathers with narrow pale fringes; outer pp broad and truncate (*cf.* Fig. 171**B** & **D**); medial ss (~s5-s10) blunt tipped to truncate (Fig. 176**B**-**C**); pp and ss not molting in Jan-Feb; iris orangish red to red. **Note: See Juv-HY/SY. ASYs are not reliably aged following Feb due to some SYs having replaced pp and ss; however, it is possible that some ASYs can be aged in Mar-Jul or later by presence of elongated crown feathers and iris color; more study needed.**

Sex—♀ = ♂ by plumage aspect. Medial BP (Fig. 20**A**, p. 31) developed by both sexes but distended cloaca (Fig. 21, p. 32) in Apr-Jun indicates ASY ♀. Measurements reliable for sexing (Table 22, p. 232). The following can be used to sex most individuals in N.Am, once fully grown (by at least Dec in HYs):

♀: Bill length from distal end of nares < 59 in Western Grebe or < 57 in Clark's Grebe; bill depth at proximal end of nares < 11.7 in Western Grebe or < 11.5 in Clark's Grebe (Table 22, Fig. 181**A**); bill depth at distal end of nares < 10.5 in both species and culmen more recurved (Fig. 181**A**).

♂: Bill length from distal end of nares > 55 in Western Grebe or > 53 in Clark's Grebe; bill depth at proximal end of nares > 11.7 in Western Grebe or > 11.5 in Clark's Grebe (Table 22, Fig. 181**B**); bill depth at distal end of nares > 10.5 in both species and culmen straighter (Fig. 181**B**).

Hybrids reported—Western Grebe with Clark's Grebe (Ratti 1979, Nuechterlein 1981, Storer & Nuechterlein 1985, Eichhorst & Parkin 1991, Sibley 1994, Tallman & Hanson 1997, Fjeldså 2004); however, beware that suspected hybrids may also represent individual variation within parental species as currently defined (see Fig. 180, p 237, and **Age**).

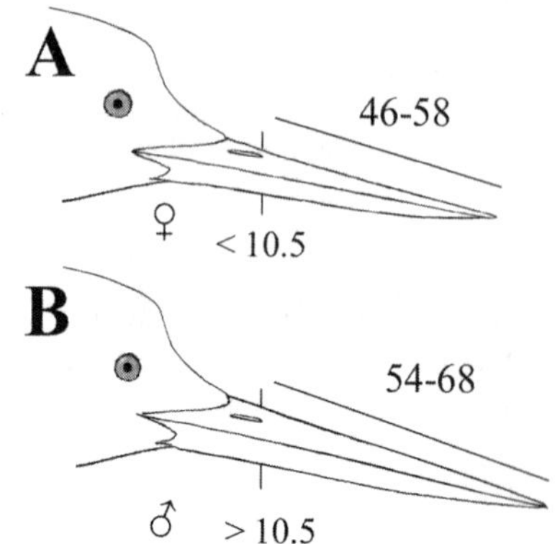

FIGURE 181. Bill size and shape by sex in Western and Clark's grebes. Indicated measures are culman from distal end of nares (Fig. 7**C**, p. 9) and bill depth at the distal ends of the nares (Fig. 8**C**, p. 10); see Table 22 (p. 232) and **Sex** for differences by species.

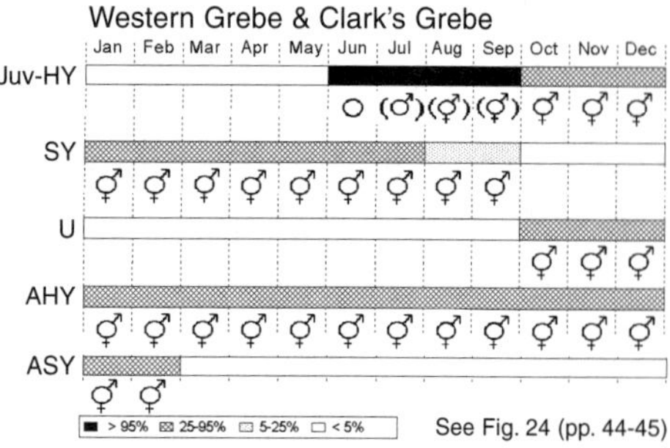

References—Ainley et al. (1994), Bent (1919a), Eckert (1989, 1993, 1995), Eichhorst & Parkin (1991), Gilliland (1984), Henny et al. (1990), Henshaw (1881), Kaufman (1979a, 1990a), Munro (1941), Oberholser (1974), Palmer (1962), Phillips et al. (1983), Ratti (1979, 1981), Ratti et al. (1983), Roberts (1955), Sibley (1970), Storer (1967), Stout & Cooke (2003), Storer & Nuechterlein (1985, 1992).

ALBATROSSES *DIOMEDEIDAE*

Three North American species. Family characters include large and heavy bodies; extremely long wings; powerful, hooked bills with short and laterally separated tubenares, opened distally (Figs. 183 & 185, pp. 242-244); and webbed feet without rear toes. North Pacific albatrosses have 10 functional primaries (p10 longest by 5-35 mm when fully grown), 25-29 secondaries (including 3-4 tertials and one absent between s4 and s5; *cf.* Fig. 12**B**, p. 19), and 12 rectrices. The humerals are well developed and extend distally to form the inner portion of the wing. Ageing through at least the 2nd cycle (to TY and ATY) can be accomplished by primary and secondary molt patterns, and minimum age-groups up to the 20th cycle (A10Y) or older can be distinguished in Black-footed (p. 243) and Short-tailed (p. 245) albatrosses due to substantially delayed plumage aspect maturation. Sexes are alike in plumage aspect and both develop medial brood patches (Fig. 20**A**, p. 31) but individuals often can be sexed by size, males larger and larger billed than females (*cf.* Figs. 183-185). Breeding females are also reliably sexed during the incubation period by distended cloacae (Fig. 21, p. 32; Serventy 1956); see Figures. 22-23 (pp. 32-35) for other cloacal characters possibly useful for ageing and sexing albatrosses. In addition to cited references, Brooke (2004), Harrison (1983a, 1987), and Tickell (2000) provide an overview of taxonomy and species determination in this group.

In molting, North Pacific albatrosses reportedly exhibit a Simple Basic Strategy (SBS; Fig. 10**A**, pp. 13-16), lacking a formative plumage and alternate plumages in all molt cycles; however, the presence or absence of a limited preformative molt needs to be confirmed. The prebasic molt is incomplete, and varies in timing and extent with age, breeding status, and interannual variation in food availability. Following successful breeding some adults lack the time and resources for a sufficient molt and forego breeding the following year to finish molt; for Short-tailed Albatross this appears to occur after every successful breeding attempt. Age at first breeding can be as early as 4 years but averages 8-10 years and can be as late as 16 or more years in some individuals; prebasic molts of S-4Ys and pre-courting individuals (usually 4-10Ys) average earlier in timing than those of courting pre-breeders (usually 6-12Y), which in turn average earlier and more complete than those of breeding adults (A5Ys or older; see p. 248-252 and Table 24).

Albatrosses exhibit unique sequences of primary replacement, with separate strategies among the inner (p1-p6 or p1-p7) and outer (p7-p10 or p8-p10) feathers (Howell 2006a, Langston & Rohwer 1995, Rohwer & Edwards 2006); see Figure 182 (p. 240) for more information. Replacement of secondaries also exhibits consistent but more complex patterns, with centers at s1, s5, the tertials, and possibly elsewhere (Fig. 182; Edwards & Rohwer 2005). Primary coverts are usually (but not always) replaced with corresponding primaries while greater and median coverts appear to be replaced independently of secondaries. Rectrices are often replaced completely during prebasic molts but up to five retained feathers, among r2-r5 (*cf.* Fig. 17**G-H**, p. 25), can occasionally be found in breeding adults. Several adjacent primaries and secondaries may molt synchronously, or nearly so, perhaps inhibiting flight for a short time in Aug-Sep.

In Black-footed and Laysan (p. 241) albatrosses the second prebasic molt includes some to most body feathers and secondary covs, p8-p10, sometimes/occasionally p7 and p6, no other primaries, 1-6 consecutive inner secondaries, sometimes s1-s2 and/or s5-s6 (*cf.* Fig. 182**B**), and the rectrices. Subsequent prebasic molts are quite variable, including at least half of the body feathers, p8-p10, most or all of the rectrices, and 3-10 secondaries in successful breeders, to all body feathers, primaries, and rectrices, most to all secondary coverts, and up to 50% of the secondaries in non-breeders. Primaries appear to be replaced distally from p8 and proximally from p6, with the inner primaries exhibiting staffelmauser-like waves (Fig. 16, pp. 23-24) progressing proximally; whether or not p7 is aligned with the distal or proximal wave has been debated (Howell 2006a, Rohwer & Edwards 2006). Replacement of secondaries also proceeds in waves that span cycles, usually proximally from s1 and s5 (possibly linked to replacement of inner primaries; Edwards & Rohwer 2005) and distally from the tertials, with irregular replacement among s12-s20 (of 25-30

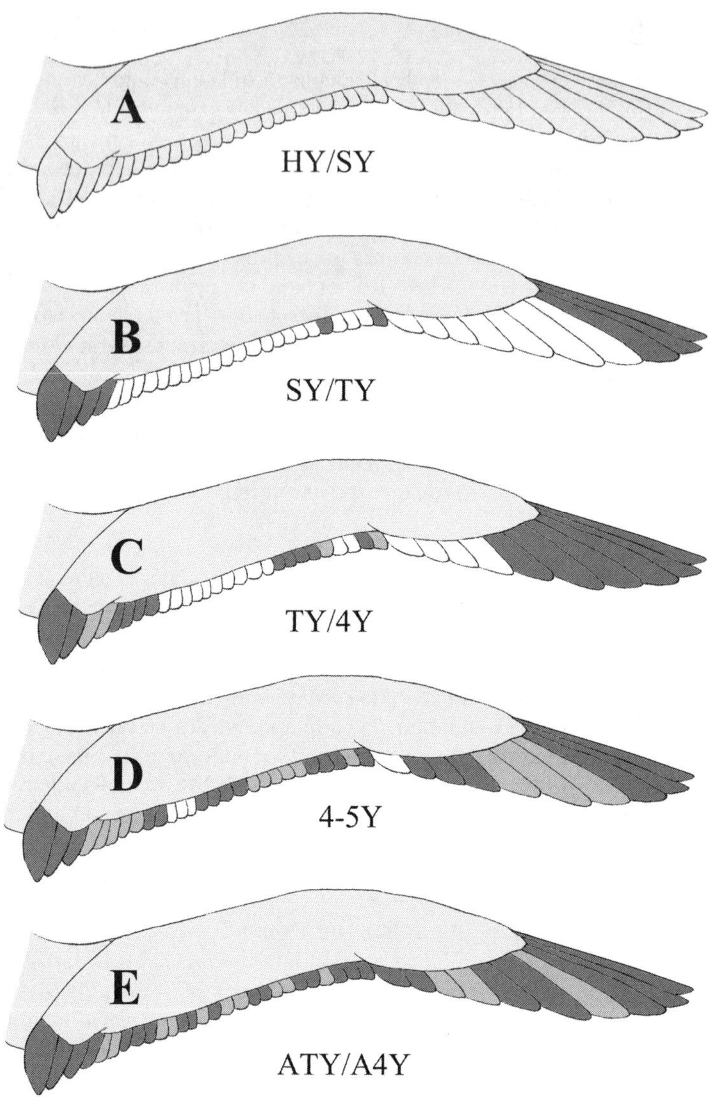

FIGURE 182. Molt patterns by age in Laysan and Black-footed albatrosses; darker shading indicates fresher feathers. Pp are replaced distally from p7 or p8 and proximally from p6 or p7 (see Howell 2006,a Rohwer & Edwards 2006), and ss are replaced distally from the tertials and proximally from s1 and s5, with replacement becoming irregular in the area where the two waves come together among s12-s20 (of 25-32 ss). HY/SYs retain all pp and ss (**A**). The PB2 typically includes p8-p10 (occasionally p7 and/or p6), and 1-10 ss (among inner ss, s1-s2, and s5-s6), resulting in patterns similar to **B** in SY/TYs. Thereafter, each prebasic molt can exhibit substantial variation in the number of primaries and secondaries replaced, with p8-p10 and the terts usually replaced every year but other feathers retained in Staffelmauser-like patterns (*cf.* Fig. 16, pp. 23-24). TY/4Ys can retain from many (e.g., p1-p4, s3-s4, and 8-12 ss among s8-s22 as in **C**), to few juv feathers (e.g., p1 and 2-3 ss among s13-s20 as in **D**) and some 4Y/5Ys may also retain a few juvenal ss; thus, birds showing patterns as in **D** should probably be aged 4-5Y (pp. 41-42) to be safe. Individuals exhibiting irregular patterns of retained and replaced basic pp and ss can be aged ATY/A4Y, although certain patterns may indicate A4Y/A5Y or older (study needed). Molt patterns of Short-tailed Albatross are likely similar but fewer feathers are replaced each year; thus, some 4Y/5Ys (with juv plus three generations of definitive feathers retained) may be identifiable in combination with body plumage aspect (Fig. 186, p. 246) and individuals with mixed generations of basic feathers (as in **E**) may be safely aged A4Y/A5Y or older; more study is needed. Note the expanded humeral tract proximal to the s covs and terts.

secondaries). Thus, the last juvenal primaries and secondaries to be replaced, during the 3rd or 4th prebasic molts, are most often among p1-p4 and s12-s20 (Fig. 182**C**-**D**).

Molt patterns among primaries, secondaries, and rectrices in Short-tailed Albatross (p. 245) are unknown. In contrast to Laysan and Black-footed albatrosses, successful breeding occurs biennially, so prebasic molts of breeding adults may occur in two phases, as proposed for s.Hemisphere species that breed biennially (see Prince et al. 1993, 1997), and requiring an additional year (on average) to replace all juvenal primaries and secondaries. Thus, a typical HY/SY may show no primaries, p8 only, or p8-p9 replaced during the PB2, most to all of p8-p10 and perhaps p6 or p6-p7 replaced during the PB3, some to all of p5-p7, p8-p10 again, and 1-2 feathers among p1-p4 replaced during the PB4, etc., but more study is needed. Replacement of primaries during subsequent PBs likely depends on breeding status and combinations of previous molts, although p8-p10 and p6-p7 may be replaced every other year, in alternating years, as in some s.Hemisphere albatrosses (Prince et al. 1997). Secondaries are probably replaced in a sequence similar to that described above, but at a slower pace, perhaps taking 5-6 years to replace all juvenal feathers.

LAYSAN ALBATROSS

Phoebastria immutabilis

LAAL
Species # 0821
Band size: 7B

Species—From other albatrosses by small size (Table 23, p. 245); back, upperwings, and rump uniformly dark brown; underwing feathers white except for axillars and les p covs variably blackish; bill dusky pink to pinkish with a grayish tip; legs dusky pinkish to pale pink. Beware of hybrids and variants with abnormal plumage aspect and/or bare part colors (McKee & Pyle 2002). On breeding colonies, the first down of Laysan Albatross averages darker brown than that of Black-footed Albatross (p. 243) which is tipped frosty, and the bill is narrow and grayish (*vs* stout and black in Black-footed Albatross).

Geographic variation—Monotypic.

Molt—SBS (CBS?). PF absent(?), PB2 incomplete (Apr-Nov in SYs), DPB incomplete (Apr-Nov in ASYs); PA absent. Most to all molting occurs at sea, away from breeding grounds. A limited PF of head and back feathers may occur in Aug-Oct; more study is needed. See Family Account (pp 239-241), Figure 182, and Table 24 (p. 249) for more information on molting in albatrosses.

Age—Juv (B1; Mar-Feb) is described below under HY/SY; Juv ♀ = ♂. See Broughton (1994) and Langston & Rohwer (1995) for ageing by bursal length (Fig. 23, p. 34). Note that confirmed-breeding adults (including ♀♀ with distended cloacae) can be reliably aged A4Y.

Juv-HY/SY (1st cycle, Juv/B1; Sep-Aug): Auricular and face below eye white to whitish, not contrasting in aspect with crown and neck (Fig. 183**A**, p. 242); pp and ss (Fig. 182**A**), s covs, and probably body feathers (Fig. 187**A**, p 248; see **Molt**) entirely of one generation and uniform in wear through at least Apr (at which point back and pp molt can commence), the outer pp relatively narrow and worn (Fig. 189**A**, p. 250); bill grayish (Jul-Aug), dusky pinkish (Aug-Jan), or pink with a gray tip (Dec-Jun).

SY/TY (2nd cycle, B2; Sep-Aug): Auricular and face below eye gray, contrasting in aspect with white crown and neck (Fig. 183**B**); back feathers with mixed levels of wear indicating protracted molt and (usually) retained juv feathers (Fig. 187**C**); consecutive 3-5 outer pp (among p6-p10, often just p8-p10) and 1-10 ss among s1-s2, s5, and the proximal 6 ss (including terts) fresh and blackish, contrasting with browner and more worn juv inner pp and outer ss (Fig. 182**B**), the outer pp relatively broad and fresh (Fig. 189**B**); bill pink with a gray tip.

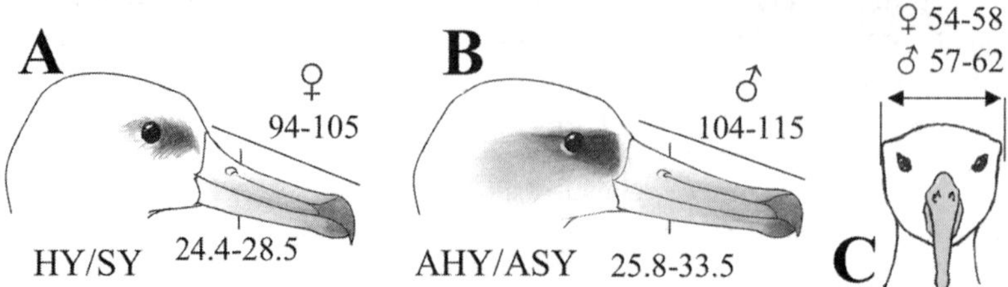

FIGURE 183. Auricular coloration by age and bill size by sex in Laysan Albatross (age and sex features shown are independent). Measures by sex refer to proximal end of gape angle to bill tip and bill depth at distal end of nasal groove (**A-B**; see also Table 23, p. 245, for exposed culmen differences), and width of head at widest point, just behind eye (**C**). Direct comparison of relative bill proportions can be used to sex many but not all individuals of mated pairs. Auricular color appears to be reliable for separating HY/SYs through the PB2 (May-Aug in SYs), although beware of worn adults during this period with bleached plumage aspect.

TY/4Y (3rd cycle, B3; Sep-Aug): Auriculars (Fig. 183**B**) and bill as in SY/TY; back feathers without juv feathers and with mixed levels of wear indicating protracted molt and retained feathers (Fig. 187**D**); p1-p5 exhibiting two generations, with 1-4 consecutive juv feathers among p1-p4 retained and very worn, and ss with three generations including some very worn and frayed juv feathers occurring irregularly among s12-s20 (Fig. 182**C-D**). **Note: Beware older individuals that may coincidentally exhibit similar patterns of ss retention (but with less-worn retained feathers); age these ASY/ATY if unsure. Some 4Y/5Ys may retain a few juv ss and pp (Fig. 182E) and these should probably be aged 4-5Y (pp. 41-42); more study needed.**

ATY/A4Y (Def. cycle, DB; Sep-Aug): Auriculars (Fig. 183**B**), back feathers (Fig. 187**D**), and bill coloration as in TY/4Y; pp and ss including 1-3 generations of basic feathers in irregular patterns (e.g., Fig. 182**E**). **Note: See TY/4Y. Certain patterns of p retention (e.g. among p1-p5) may enable ageing to A4Y/A5Y or older; study needed.**

Sex—♀=♂ by plumage aspect. Medial BP (Fig. 20**A,** p. 31) developed by both sexes but distended cloaca (Fig. 21, p. 32; Serventy 1956) in Nov-Jan indicates A4Y ♀. Measurements can be helpful (Table 23, p. 245) and the following is useful for sexing many individuals.

♀: Bill shorter and shallower (Table 23, Fig. 183**A**) and head narrower (Fig. 183**C**). **Note: These measures are predominantly independent of each other so most individuals should be reliably sexed.**

♂: Bill longer and deeper (Table 23, Fig. 183**B**) and head broader (Fig. 183**C**). **Note: See ♀.**

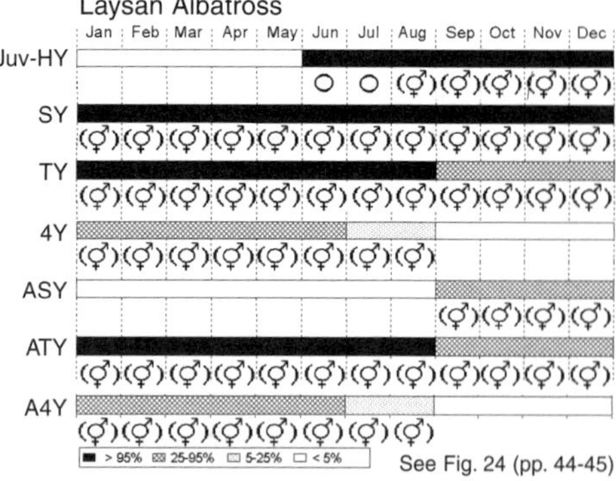

Hybrids reported—With Black-footed Albatross (Fisher 1972, McKee & Pyle 2002).

References—Ainley et al. (1994), Bent (1922), Dement'ev & Gladkov (1951a), Edwards (2002), Edwards & Rohwer (2005), Frings & Frings (1961), Howell (2006a), Langston & Hillgarth (1995), Langston & Rohwer (1995, 1996), Loomis (1918), McKee & Pyle (2002), Palmer (1962), Rice & Kenyon (1962), Rohwer & Edwards (2006), Tickell (2000), Whittow (1993a).

BLACK-FOOTED ALBATROSS BFAL
Phoebastria nigripes Species # 0810
Band size: 7B

Species—From other albatrosses by medium-small size (Table 23); plumage aspect primarily dark brown except for white at base of bill, and on uppertail and undertail covs in A6Ys (Fig. 184); bill pinkish dusky to blackish; legs black. Beware of hybrids and variants with abnormal plumage aspect and/or bare part colors (see McKee & Pyle (2002). See Laysan Albatross (p. 243) regarding separation of chicks.

Geographic variation—Monotypic.

Molt—SBS (CBS?). PF absent(?), PB2 incomplete (Apr-Nov in SYs), DPB incomplete (May-Nov in ASYs); PA absent. Most to all molting occurs at sea, away from breeding grounds. A limited PF of head and back feathers may occur in Aug-Oct; more study is needed. P6 is rarely replaced during the PB2. The DPB is defined based on molt rather than plumage aspect (see p. 29). See pp. 248-252 and Table 24 (p. 249) for more information on molting in albatrosses and seabirds.

Age—Juv (B1; Mar-Feb) is described below under HY/SY; Juv ♀ = ♂. See Broughton (1994) and Langston & Rohwer (1995) for ageing through SY/TY by bursa (Fig. 23, p. 34). Due to slow maturation of the undertail-cov plumage aspect (Fig. 184), age-groups (see p. 13) can be determined up to A10Y. More precise determination of older age-groups may be possible, especially in combination with sex, but more study is needed on undertail plumage aspect succession in this species by sex (change is slower in ♀♀ than in ♂♂; see **Sex**). Note that confirmed-breeding adults (including ♀♀ with distended cloacae) can be aged A4Y.

Juv-HY/SY (1st cycle, Juv/B1; Oct-Sep): Feathers at base of bill with dark brown tips in Jul-Sep, wearing off by Feb-Jun to create reduced amount of whitish at base of bill; pp and ss (Fig. 182**A**, p. 240), s covs, and probably body feathers (Fig. 187**A**, p 248; see **Molt**) entirely of one generation and uniform in wear through at least Apr (at which point back and pp molt can commence), the outer pp relatively narrow and worn (Fig. 189**A**, p. 250); undertail covs and rump dark (Fig. 184**A**). **Note: HYs are separated from SYs in Aug-Oct by much fresher feathering and absence of body molt.**

SY/TY (2nd cycle, B2; Oct-Sep): Feathers at base of bill pale brown to whitish; back feathers with mixed levels of wear indicating protracted molt and (usually) retained juv feathers (Fig. 187**C**); consecutive 3-4 outer pp (among p7-p10, often just p8-p10) and 1-8 ss among s1-s2, s5, and the proximal 6 ss (including terts) fresh and blackish, contrasting with browner and more worn inner pp and outer ss (Fig. 182**B**), the outer pp broad and fresh (Fig. 189**B**); undertail covs and rump dark (Fig. 184**A**).

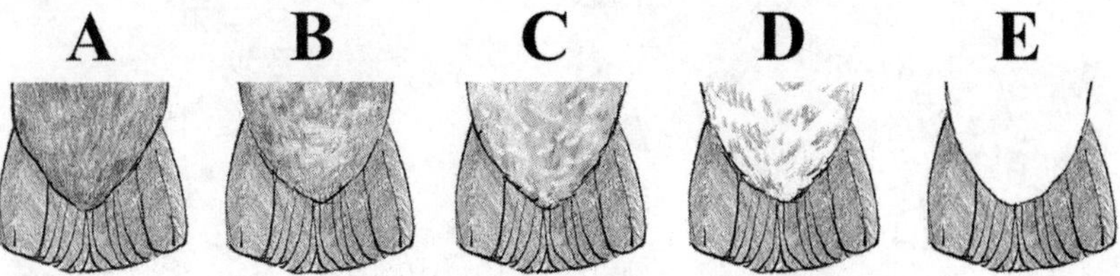

FIGURE 184. Coloration of the undertail coverts by age and sex in Black-footed Albatross. Details need to be worked out, but individuals through at least A4Y apparently retain dark undertail coverts (**A**), A5Y-A10Ys or older slowly acquire paler undertail covs (**B-D**), and individuals with entirely white undertail covs (**E**) can be reliably classified as A10Y ♂♂. It is possible that ♀♀ showing **D** and ♂♂ showing **E** can be aged A15Y or older but more study is needed on the maturation of undertail-cov color by age and sex.

TY/4Y (3rd cycle, B3; Oct-Sep): Like SY/TY in face and bill; back feathers without juv feathers and with mixed levels of wear indicating protracted molt and/or retained basic feathers (Fig. 187**D**); p1-p5 showing two generations, with 1-4 consecutive juv feathers among p1-p4 retained and very worn, and ss with three generations including some very worn and frayed juv feathers occurring irregularly among s12-s20 (Fig. 182**C-D**); undertail covs and rump dark (Fig. 184**A**). **Note: Beware older individuals that may coincidentally exhibit similar patterns of ss retention (but with less-worn retained feathers); if undertail covs dark (Fig. 184A), age these T-6Y if unsure.**

4-6Y (3rd-6th cycles, B3-B6; Jan-Dec): Like TY/4Y (undertail covs dark; Fig. 184**A**) but pp and ss including 1-3 generations of basic feathers in irregular patterns (e.g., Fig. 182**E**). **Note: See TY/4Y. Individuals with bleached heads in Apr-Aug are likely breeding (McKee & Pyle 2002).**

A5Y (Def. cycle, DB; Jan-Dec): Like 4-6Y but undertail covs mixed dark and whitish (Fig. 184**B-D**). **Note: See 4-6Y and Sex. ASYs with patterns as shown in 184C and 184D may be reliably placed in older age groups (e.g., A7Y or A8Y), especially in ♀♀, but more study is needed.**

A10Y (Def. cycle, DB; Jan-Dec): Like 4-6Y but undertail covs uniformly white (Fig. 184**E**), sometimes with dark tips when fresh (Nov-Jan). **Note: See 4-6Y, A5Y, and Sex. This age-group probably only occurs in ♂♂ and may indicate A15Y or older; more study is needed.**

Sex—♀=♂ by plumage aspect. Medial BP (Fig. 20**A**, p. 31) developed by both sexes but distended cloaca (Fig. 21, p. 32; Serventy 1956) in Nov-Jan indicates A4Y ♀. Measurements generally helpful for sexing (Table 23) and the following is reliable for sexing most if not virtually all individuals. In addition, older (A10-A15Y) ♂♂ average more white in the undertail covs than older ♀♀, and those with complete or near-complete white undertail covs (Fig. 184**E**; see **Age**) can probably be reliably sexed ♂♂.

♀: Bill shorter and shallower (Table 23; Fig. 185**A**) and head narrower (Fig. 185**C**); exp culmen + bill depth at distal end of nasal groove usually < 134 mm. **Note: These measures are predominantly independent of each other so most individuals should be reliably sexed.**

♂: Bill longer and deeper (Table 23; Fig. 185**B**) and head broader (Fig. 185**C**); exp culmen + bill depth at distal end of nasal groove usually > 134 mm. **Note: See ♀.**

Hybrids reported—With Laysan Albatross (p. 2241). No known hybridization with Short-tailed Albatross (*contra* McCarthy 2006).

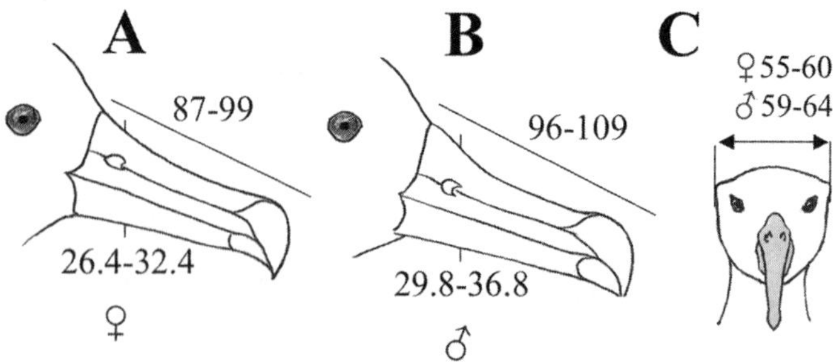

FIGURE 185. Bill size and head width by sex in Black-footed Albatross. Measures refer to proximal end of gape angle to bill tip and bill depth at distal end of nasal groove (**A-B**; see also Table 23, for exposed culmen differences), and width of head at widest point, just behind eye (**C**). In addition, exposed culmen (Table 23) plus bill depth as above is usually < 134 in ♀♀ and > 134 in ♂♂. Direct comparison of relative bill proportions can be used to sex virtually all individuals of mated pairs.

References—Ainley et al. (1994), Bent (1922), Bourne (1982), Dement'ev & Gladkov (1951a), Edwards (2007), Edwards & Rohwer (2005), Frings & Frings (1961), Howell (2006a), Loomis (1918), Langston & Rohwer (1995, 1996), McKee & Pyle (2002), Miller (1940), Palmer (1962), Rice & Kenyon (1962), Rohwer (1999), Rohwer & Edwards (2006), Stone (1900), Streets (1877), Tickell (2000), Whittow (1993b).

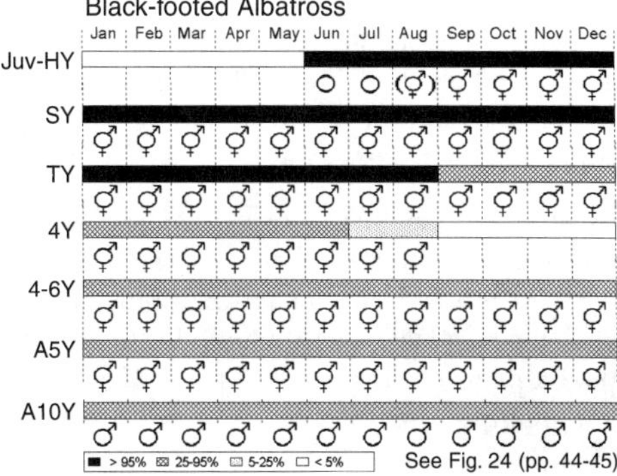

TABLE 23. Measurements (mm) of albatross that occur in North America to assist in identification and sexing. See pp. 4-11 for methods of measurement. Species summaries are in **bold**. Values are derived from 95% confidence intervals based approximately on the indicated sample sizes (see pp. 4-5); thus midpoints of ranges approximate means, and S.D. is approximated by 25% of the range.

Taxon/Sex	*n*	wing chord	tail length	exp culmen	bill depth[1]	tarsus
Laysan Albatross		**460-513**	**135-161**	**94-113**	**24.4-33.3**	**77-87**
♀	10	460-505	135-157	94-105	24.4-28.5	77-84
♂	10	467-513	139-161	102-113	25.8-33.5	80-87
Black-footed Albatross		**481-536**	**132-153**	**95-113**	**26.4-36.8**	**84-95**
♀	60	481-529	132-149	95-107	26.4-32.4	84-91
♂	40	487-536	136-153	102-113	29.8-36.8	87-95
Short-tailed Albatross		**518-593**	**144-170**	**122-145**	**36.5-46.8**	**90-103**
♀	8	518-564	144-158	122-139	36.5-41.1	90-98
♂	6	538-593	153-170	129-145	40.0-46.8	94-103

[1] Bill depth measured at distal end of nasal groove (*cf*.. Figs. 183, p. 242, & 185, p. 244).

SHORT-TAILED ALBATROSS

Phoebastria albatrus

STAL
Species # 0820
Band size: 8

Species—From other albatrosses by medium-large size (Table 23); plumage aspect variable by age, from entirely dark brown to mostly or completely white backed and golden headed (Fig. 186, p. 246); bill dull pink (Juv, Jul-Sep) to bright pink with grayish or bluish tip; legs pale grayish to bright pink. Beware of aberrant or hybrid Laysan and Black-footed albatrosses that can show plumage-aspect features resembling Short-tailed Albatross (McKee & Pyle 2002).

Geographic variation—Monotypic.

Molt—Little known in this species; adults breed biennially rather than annually and strategies may follow other s.Hemisphere species that breed every other year (see p. 241). SBS?. PF absent(?), PB2 partial-incomplete? (Apr-Nov in SYs), DPB incomplete (May-Nov in ASYs); PA absent. A limited PF of head and back feathers may occur in some HYs in Aug-Oct; more study needed. Replacement strategies of pp and ss are probably similar to Laysan and Black-footed albatrosses but rate likely slower (*cf*. Fig. 182, p. 240). The PB2 appears to include some to most head and body feathers and 0-3 pp, being partial in some to many SYs and including p8, p8-p9, or possibly p8-p10, and up to 4 innermost ss in others. Subsequent molts of pp and ss require further study (see p. 241). Most to all molting occurs at sea, away from breeding grounds. Note that the DPB is defined by molts rather than plumage aspect (p. 13). See Family Account, pp 239-241, and Table 24 (p. 249) for more information on molting in albatrosses and seabirds.

Age—Juv (B1; Jun-May) is described below under HY/SY and has dusky-pink bill; Juv ♀ = ♂. Due to the slow maturation of plumage aspect, age-groups (see pp. 41-42) can be determined up to A12Y or later. More precise determination of older age-groups may be possible, especially in known-sex individuals (see **Sex**), but more study is needed on plumage-aspect succession and p molt patterns of pp in this species. Note that plumage-aspect maturity in ♀♀ averages slower than in ♂♂ (see **Sex**).

Juv-HY/SY (1st cycle, Juv/B1; Oct-Sep): Plumage aspect (including face) entirely dark brown (Fig. 186**A**); pp and ss (Fig. 182**A**, p. 240) and probably body feathering (Fig. 187**A**, p. 248; see **Molt**) entirely of one generation and uniform in wear through at least Apr, the outer pp relatively narrow and worn (Fig. 189**A**, p. 250). **Note: HYs separated from SYs in Aug-Oct by much fresher feathering, absence of molt, and slightly duskier or duller bill color.**

SY/TY (2nd cycle, B2; Oct-Sep): Plumage aspect entirely dark brown, with small crescent of white in the face below eye and/or slight white mottling to lores or chin (Fig. 186**A-B**); body feathers with mixed levels of wear indicating protracted molt, and with retained juv feathers (Fig. 187**C**); pp and ss uniformly juvenal and very worn (*cf.* Fig. 182**A**) or 1-3 pp (p8, p8-p9, or p8-p10) and 1-4 innermost ss replaced, blackish, and broader (Fig. 189**B**), contrasting with browner and more worn inner pp and outer ss (*cf.* Fig. 182**B**). **Note: See Juv-HY/SY.**

TY/4Y (3rd cycle, B3; Oct-Sep): Face, breast, and flanks with sparse white mottling (Fig. 186**B-C**); back feathers without juv feathers and with mixed levels of wear indicating protracted molt and retained feathers (Fig. 187**D**); pp and ss likely with 1-2 generations of basic feathers among p6-p10 and the ss, with p1-p5, s3-s4, and s7-s25 (at least) still juv and very worn (*cf.* Fig. 182 **B-C**).

FIGURE 186. Plumage aspect by age in Short-tailed Albatross. Details need to be worked out and there is likely a sex-specific difference in plumage-aspect maturation (see **Sex**), but evidence suggests that **A** represents H-TYs, **B** represents S-4Ys, **C** represents 4-7Ys, **D** represents 5-9Ys, **E** represents 7-15Ys (possibly some ♀♀ to 17Y or older), and **F** represents A10Ys (possibly A15Y in ♀♀). The amount of white in the les covs and elsewhere appears to increase with age and it may be possible to age whiter individuals (especially ♀♀) to A20Y or older.

4-7Y (3rd-7th cycles, B3-B7; Jan-Dec): Plumage aspect brown but with varying amounts of white on face, abdomen, flanks, underwing covs, rump, and in humerals but no white on back or yellow on crown (Fig. 186**C-D**); pp and ss with three or more generations of basic feathers (*cf.* Fig. 182**E**). **Note: It is possible that some juv pp (among p2-p4) and/or juv ss (among s12-s20) may be retained through 3 or more PBs, allowing more precise ageing within subadult age-groups (see p. 241), but more study is needed to confirm this.**

5-11Y (4th-11th cycles, B4-B11; Jan-Dec): Crown mixed yellow and brown, nape and les covs brown, back blackish with some white mottling, and underparts white, sometimes with some brown mottling (Fig. 186**D-E**). **Note: ♀♀ showing this plumage aspect are possibly older (e.g., 7-13Y) but more study needed.**

8-15Y (7th-15th cycles, B7-B15; Jan-Dec): Crown yellow with little or no brown, nape and les covs with varying amounts of brown, back white with blackish mottling, and underparts mostly to entirely white (Fig. 186**E**). **Note: ♀♀ with this plumage aspect are possibly older (e.g., 10-17Y) but more study needed.**

A10Y (Def. cycle, DB; Jan-Dec): Crown and nape yellow, without brown, les covs with variable amounts of white, back entirely or almost entirely white, and underparts entirely white (Fig. 186**F**). **Note: ♀♀ showing this plumage aspect are possibly older (e.g., A15Y) but more study needed. The amount of white in the les covs continues to increase (proximally) with age; it might be possible to age certain individuals with more extensive white (e.g., extending to within 100 mm of the bend of the wing) A20Y or more but more study needed to confirm this.**

Sex—♀=♂ by plumage aspect; although plumage-aspect maturation appears to be slower in ♀♀ than in ♂♂, both sexes can reach full definitive plumage (Fig. 186**F**). Medial BP (Fig. 20**A,** p. 31) developed by both sexes but distended cloaca (Fig. 21, p. 32; Serventy 1956) in Nov-Jan indicates A5Y ♀. Measurements (especially tail length and bill depth) apparently useful for sexing (Table 23) but more precise ranges needed to determine reliable limits.

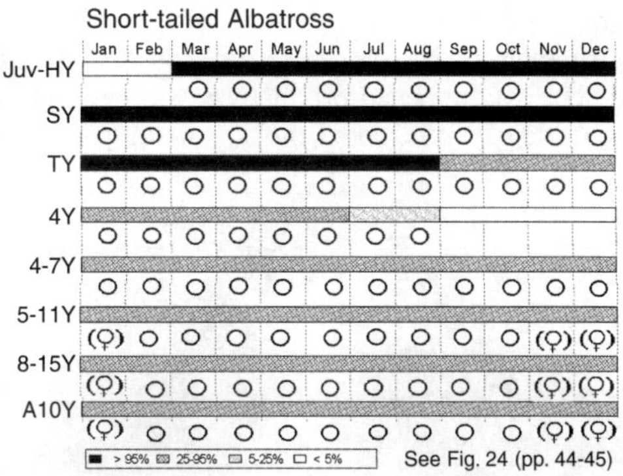

Hybrids reported—None. No known hybridization with Black-footed Albatross (*contra* McCarthy 2006).

References—Ainley et al. (1994), Bent (1922), Dement'ev & Gladkov (1951a), Hasegawa & Grange (1982), Iliff (2007), McKee & Pyle (2002), Palmer (1962), Stresemann & Stresemann (1966), Tickell (2000); H. Hasegawa (*pers. comm.*).

Molt and age determination in Procellariiformes

Adult Procellariiformes (albatrosses, fulmars, petrels, shearwaters, and storm-petrels) molt primarily at sea during non-breeding periods and precise strategies are unknown. The timing and extent of molts in these species are further complicated by individual variation with age, breeding status, and latitude of occurrence— factors that themselves vary interanually with climate cycles and availability of food resources (*cf.* Bridge 2006). Within each species, three groups of individuals with varying annual constraints can be identified with respect to molting strategies: 1) first-cycle HY/SYs, 2) pre-breeding and non-breeding AHY/ASYs, and 3) breeding adults.

Procellariiformes have been assumed to follow the Simple Basic Strategy (SBS; Fig. 10**A**, pp. 13-16), lacking formative and alternate plumages in all molt cycles; however, recent study suggests that limited to partial preformative molts occur in at least some HY/SYs of certain species that migrate across the equator to temperate or subarctic latitudes during the first six months of life; preformative molts should be looked for in other species as well. Some or all Wilson's (p. 277) and Least (p. 288) storm-petrels may undergo a complete molt during their first 6-8 months, perhaps best considered a preformative molt. These species thus exhibit the Complex Basic Strategy (CBS; Fig. 10**B**). On the other hand, many first cycle HY/SYs of most species appear to retain their complete juvenal (first basic) plumage until the onset of the second prebasic molt, usually 8-10 months after fledging.

Adults of species that breed annually appear to undergo complete or near-complete prebasic molts within regular annual molt cycles. Body molt (and occasionally replacement of inner primaries; Monteiro & Furness 1996; *cf.* Barbrand & Chastel 1998) can begin during the chick-feeding period, followed by replacement of most or all primaries, secondaries, and rectrices at sea during the non-breeding season (Table 24). Adults that migrate to high-latitude summers, including Southern-Hemisphere breeders that spend the non-breeding season in north-temperate and subarctic North American waters, replace primaries and secondaries rapidly, and more often undergo complete molts. Species or individuals that molt at tropical latitudes or during winter at high-latitudes, where ocean productivity is poorer and day-lengths (for diurnal species) shorter, more often undergo protracted molts, sometimes spanning the non-breeding period, and can retain

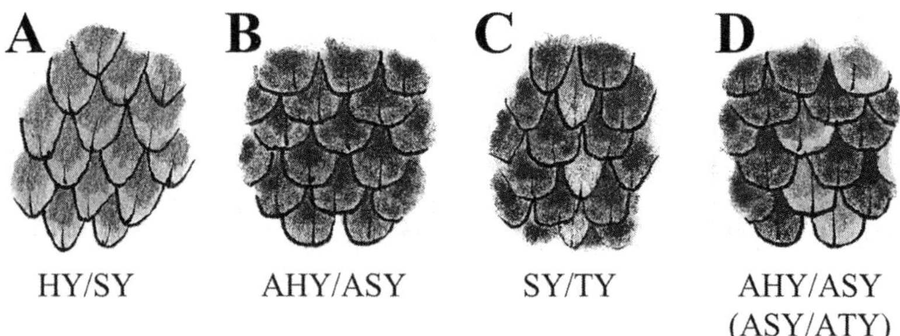

FIGURE 187. Variation in back-feather wear patterns by age in Procellariiformes. Juvenal feathers are narrower than formative and basic feathers, with HY/SYs of most species showing uniformly worn feathers throughout the first cycle (**A**). AHY/ASYs of many species, especially those that undergo rapid molts at temperate or subarctic latitudes, show uniformly broader, squarer, and darker feathers (**B**). SY/TYs of many species can retain some juv feathers during the 2nd prebasic molt, which are contrastingly narrow and very worn (**C**); however, some species undergo a fairly extensive preformative molt and can show similar patterns (with less-worn retained juv feathers) in HY/SYs or SYs during the second half of the first cycle. Patterns resembling **D** result from retained basic feathers on ASY/ATYs. However, it can also result from protracted or suspended prebasic molts, or from mixed basic and retained formative feathers of certain species; thus, it is generally not safe to age ASY/ATYs by this trait alone.

TABLE 24. Month ranges of breeding and molt in Procellariformes that occur in North America. Note that these should be used as a guideline for the timing of peak molting in a majority of individuals; some individuals of all species may exhibit peak molt at any time of year, and within individuals, low-level molt may occur year-round. Species that molt in productive temperate or subarctic waters will complete feather replacement more rapidly than those that molt in less-productive tropical waters.

		Prebasic Molts		
Species	Breeding Season[1]	Second[2]	Older non-breeders[2,3]	Breeding adults[2]
Laysan Albatross[4]	Nov-Jul	Apr-Nov	May-Nov	Jul-Nov
Black-footed Albatross[4]	Oct-Jul	Apr-Nov	May-Nov	Jul-Oct
Short-tailed Albatross[4]	Oct-Aug	Apr-Nov	May-Nov	Jul-Oct
Northern Fulmar	Mar-Sep	Apr-Nov	Jun-Nov	Aug-Jan
Murphy's Petrel[4,5]	May-Dec	Sep-Feb	Oct-Mar	Nov-Apr
Mottled Petrel[5]	Nov-May	Feb-Aug	May-Oct	Jun-Oct
Black-capped Petrel[4,5]	Nov-May	Mar-Aug	May-Aug	Jun-Sep
Cook's Petrel[5]	Sep-Apr	Jan-Jun	Mar-Jul	Apr-Aug
Cory's Shearwater	Apr-Nov	Apr-Jan	Aug-Jan	Oct-Feb
Pink-footed Shearwater	Oct-Apr	Jan-Jun	Mar-Aug	May-Aug
Flesh-footed Shearwater[5]	Oct-Apr	Jan-Jul	Mar-Aug	May-Sep
Greater Shearwater[6]	Oct-Apr	Jan-Aug	Mar-Sep	May-Sep
Buller's Shearwater[6]	Sep-May	Feb-Jun	Mar-Jul	May-Aug
Sooty Shearwater	Sep-Apr	Feb-Jul	Apr-Aug	May-Oct
Short-tailed Shearwater	Oct-May	Mar-Aug	May-Sep	Jul-Oct
Manx Shearwater	Mar-Oct	Jun-Dec	Jul-Jan	Sep-Feb
Black-vented Shearwater	Jan-Aug	Apr-Sep	Jun-Oct	Aug-Nov
Audubon's Shearwater[5]	Jan-Jul	Apr-Oct	Jun-Nov	Aug-Dec
Wilson's Storm-Petrel[6]	Nov-Apr	Jun-Nov?	Apr-Sep	May-Sep
Fork-tailed Storm-Petrel	Apr-Sep	May-Oct	Jul-Nov	Aug-Dec
Leach's Storm-Petrel[7]	Mar-Sep	May-Dec	Jul-Feb	Sep-Apr
Leach's Storm-Petrel[5,8]	Oct-Apr	Dec-Jun	Feb-Oct	Apr-Nov
Ashy Storm-Petrel	Apr-Oct	May-Nov	Jul-Feb	Aug-Mar
Band-rumped Storm-Petrel[5,9]	Sep-Mar	Dec-Jul	Feb-Aug	Mar-Sep
Black Storm-Petrel[5]	Apr-Oct	Jul-Dec	Sep-Feb	Oct-Mar
Least Storm-Petrel[5,6]	May-Nov	Apr-Aug	Nov-Mar	Dec-Apr

[1] Defined as month of peak return to colony to month of peak fledging.
[2] Breeding birds often start body molt 1-3 months earlier than molt of primaries begins, during the latter stages of incubation or chick feeding. However, the majority of body molt occurs during the period of primary molt, as indicated here
[3] Includes SY/TYs, pre-breeding ASY/ATYs, adults that skip a year of breeding, and (possibly) breeders that fail early.
[4] Some or all birds may routinely skip a year of breeding, leading to variable molting strategies among breeding adults.
[5] Molt strategies little-known or may be substantially more variable than indicated.
[6] These species show evidence that a preformative molt may occur (see text). For Wilson's (p. 277) and Least (p. 288) storm-petrels what is listed under 2nd PB may be a PF (see p. 248 and **Molt** under these species).
[7] Includes all taxa of Leach's Storm-Petrel (p. 280) except *O.l. cheimomnestes* of Guadalupe Is, Mexico. See **Molt** for Leach's Storm-Petrel.
[8] *O.l. cheimomnestes* only. See [7].
[9] Refers to winter-breeding populations, from which Atlantic North American birds appear to originate. See **Molt** for this species.

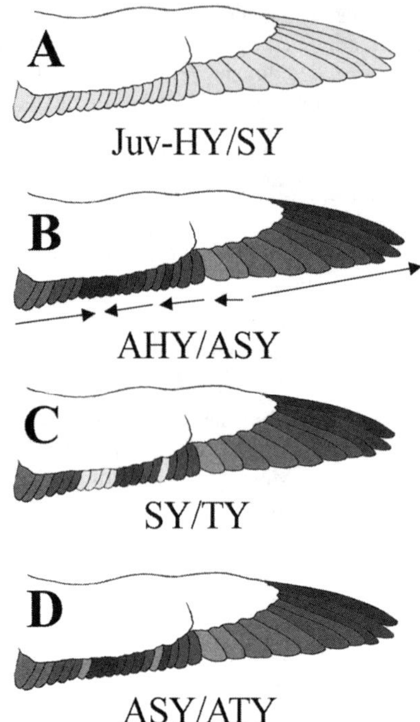

FIGURE 188. Molt patterns by age in fulmars, petrels, and shearwaters. Darker shading indicates fresher feathers. Sequence is shown in **B**; pp are apparently replaced both distally and proximally from p2 (at least in some species) and ss are replaced distally from the tertials and proximally from s1 and s5, with replacement becoming irregular in the area where the two waves come together among s8-s14 (of 18-22 ss). HY/SYs retain all pp and ss (**A**) and AHYs that undergo a complete prebasic molt (typically non-breeders or individuals that molt in productive temperate or subarctic waters) have uniformly basic feathers showing molt clines reflecting replacement sequence (**B**); see Figure 189 for differences in shape and wear between juv and basic pp. Note that a contrast between s1 and p1 can often be used to infer previous complete molts in many species or individuals (*cf.* Fig. 14**B**, p. 21). Some AHYs with prolonged breeding seasons, that molt in less-productive tropical regions, or that encounter decreased productivity during molts, can retain ss (most often among s8-s14) and can be aged as SY/TY (**C**; with retained juvenal s4 and s10-s13) or ASY/ATY (**D**; with retained basic s5 and s13). Beware of suspension limits which can result in the appearance of retained feathers; note that retained ss should be more worn than adjacent ss, both proximally and distally.

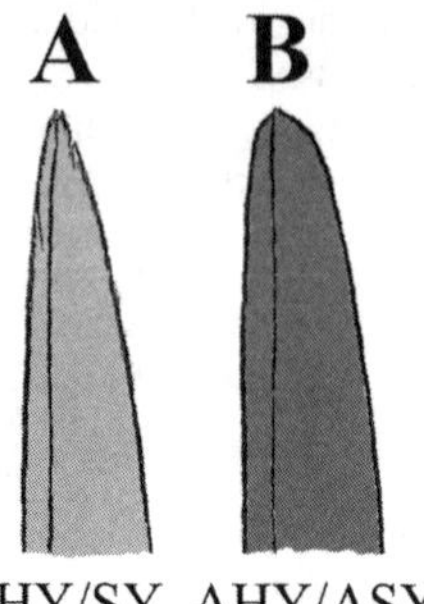

FIGURE 189. Outer primary shape and wear by age in Procellariiformes. Most species retain the juv outer pp for 8-11 months after fledging and can be aged by this criterion, although differences can be subtle. See also Figure 188.

body feathers, wing coverts, secondaries and/or rectrices. Smaller species (including most storm-petrels and many shearwaters) usually have complete molts, presumably because of the lower costs involved with replacing all feathers. In many larger species (including albatross, fulmars, and larger petrels and shearwaters), HY/SYs typically have uniformly narrow and rounded back feathers (Fig. 187**A**, p. 248), primaries and secondaries (Figs. 188**A** & 189**A**, p. 248), and rectrices (Fig. 190**A**), whereas AHY/ASYs can be determined to age by uniformly broader and squarer feathers or mixed degrees of wear resulting from protracted and incomplete molts (Figs. 187**B**-**D**, 188**B**, 189**B**, & 190**B**). Larger and some smaller species also can retain juvenal or basic feathers during the 2nd and later prebasic molts and can be aged as SY/TYs or ASY/ATYs (Figs. 187**C**-**D**, 188**C**-**D**, 190**C**-**D**, & 209**B**-**C**).

First-year Procellariiformes often occur in regions away from breeding colonies, either remaining on non-breeding grounds for a year or more after hatching, or migrating to an area separate from that occupied at the time by breeding adults. Migration strategies and non-breeding ranges (including hemispheres) can differ among species and individuals within species, sometimes leading to non-breeding individuals of a given species being in molt at any time of year. Generally, however, replacement of primaries tends to begin 3-4 months earlier and finish 1-2 months earlier in HY/SYs than that in breeding adults (Table 24, p. 249).

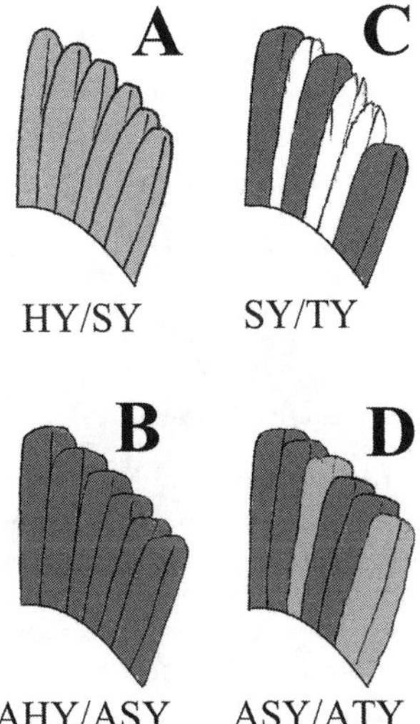

FIGURE 190. Shape and molt patterns among the rectices of Procellariiformes (half-tails shown, from below). Note that juvenal feathers (**A**) average narrower than basic feathers (**B**). AHYs that molt in less-productive situations (see Fig. 188) may retain one or more rects, typically among s2-s5, and can be aged SY/TY (with retained juv rects; e.g., r2, r4, and r5, as in **C**) or ASY/ATY (with retained definitive rects; e.g., r3 and r6, as in **D**). Note that Northern Fulmars (p. 253) typically have 14 rects whereas other N.Am Procellariiformes have 12 rects.

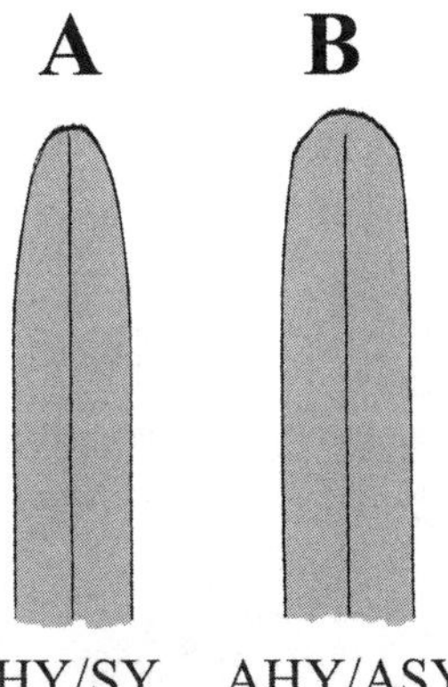

FIGURE 191. Shape of the longest axillar by age in Procellariiformes. Many species also can show difference by age in the amount of dark coloration (*cf.* Fig. 197, p. 258; 200, p. 264; 205, p. 272; & 206, p. 273). Differences in shape can be subtle and this criterion should not be relied upon alone.

Uniformity of plumage (*cf.* Fig. 187**A**) can thus be used to determine juveniles of most species up to eight months after fledging, and the timing of primary molt may be helpful in determining age of some individuals.

Age at first breeding varies from 3 to 10 years or more in Procellariiformes and thus there is a substantial population of pre-breeding AHY/ASYs, aged 2-6 or more years, for which migratory patterns and molting strategies may vary substantially. As Procellariiformes age they increasingly show distribution, migration, and molting patterns resembling those of breeding adults (*cf.* Table 24), although typically they spend less time at or near breeding colonies. Little is known about this process, however, or how much individual variation occurs. Non-breeding ASYs may show molt timing at variance with that of breeding adults (perhaps even at the opposite time of the year). Occurrence patterns at different latitudes and hemispheres may result in variable, photoperiod-induced trigger times for the onset of molts.

Primaries and primary coverts of fulmars and shearwaters appear to be replaced distally and proximally from p2, and secondaries are replaced distally from the tertials and proximally from s1 and s5 (Fig. 188**B**). Replacement can become irregular in the area in which the two waves of ss come together, among s8-s14 (of 19-22 ss; *cf.* Fig. 188**C-D**). Molt-related contrasts between s1 and p1 ("s1-p1 contrast") and between s4 and s5 can usually be used to infer a previous complete molt in AHY/ASYs (Fig. 188**B**), and position and quality of retained feathers can be used to age some SY/TYs and ASY/ATYs (Fig. 188**C-D**). Albatrosses can take several cycles to complete molt of primaries and secondaries, and have unique replacement patterns within these feather groups (Fig. 182, p. 240), whereas most storm-petrels can complete the molt more rapidly and show less-distinct contrasts in feather wear.

Several other clues may assist with the ageing of Procellariiformes that show intermediate plumage-related characters. Shape of the primaries, rectrices, and axillars (Figs. 189-191) can be used to separate juveniles from AHY/ASYs of most species, although differences between juvenal and basic feathers can be subtle. Breeding (and thus older) adults of burrowing species can often

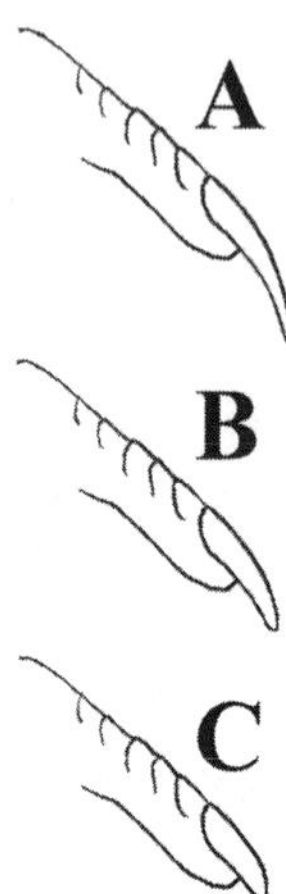

FIGURE 192. Degree of wear to the claws, by age, in Procellariiformes that dig burrows for breeding, including fulmars and many but not all species of petrels, shearwaters, and storm-petrels (see species accounts). HY/SYs and prebreeding ASYs typically have sharper claws (**A**), which can become more worn with age (**B**-**C**). Individuals with very worn claws (**C**) may be much older but more study is needed to determine reliability of age determination within each species. This difference may also be of use in ageing other bird taxa; further study needed.

FIGURE 193. Filoplumes in the head of Procellariiformes. The presence of these indicates at least AHY/ASY; extensive numbers may indicate breeding adults and thus ASY/ATYs or older among many species (Imber 1971; *cf.* James 1986). More study is needed.

be recognized by increasingly duller or blunter claws with age (Fig. 192), the result of digging burrows (Wynne-Edwards 1939, Murphy 1952, Todd 1963). Filoplumes (Fig. 193), small white plumes most easily seen on the crown and nape of darker-headed shearwaters and petrels (Imber 1971, James 1986), are absent in HY/SYs and are more abundant in breeding than in non-breeding individuals. Individuals found at sea during the breeding seasons with distended cloacae (Fig. 21, p. 32; Serventy 1956) are breeding adult females, and therefore can be aged at least ATY or older (see **Age** under each species). Finally, Sugimora et al. (1985) found that skull ossification in the Short-tailed Shearwater (p. 269) develops in several ways, which may be potentially useful in separating HY/SYs from older individuals. Examination of live individuals is needed to determine whether or not these differences can be appreciated through skulling (Pyle 1997).

Fifteen North American species. Family characters include medium-large and ovate bodies, long pointed wings, hooked bills with single tubenare separated by a septum and opened distally in fulmars (Fig. 194, p. 253) and petrels (Fig. 195, p. 256) but dorsally in most shearwaters (Fig. 198, p. 261), and webbed feet with vestigial rear toes and strong claws for digging (Fig. 192). North American shearwaters and petrels have 10 functional primaries (p10 longest by 2-10 mm when fully grown), 19-22 secondaries (including 3 tertials and one absent between s4 and s5; *cf.* Fig. 12B, p. 19), and 12 (or 14 in Northern Fulmar) rectrices. Ageing through AHY/ASY can be accomplished in most individuals through plumage-related characters, molt patterns (Fig. 188, p. 250), claw condition (Fig. 192), and/or the occurrence of filoplumes (Fig. 193). AHYs of certain species with incomplete molts can be aged through the second cycle (to TY and ATY) by the quality and shape of retained feathers (Fig. 188**C-D**). Sexes are alike in plumage aspect but some species can be separated by head and bill size, males having wider heads and deeper bills (especially at the nail) than females (Figs. 194, 195, & 198). Head-bill length (Fig. 453, p. 630) should also be investigated for sexing (*cf.* Thalmann et al. 2007). Both sexes develop medial brood patches (Fig. 20**A**, p. 31) but breeding females can be recognized during the incubation period by distended cloacae (Fig. 21, p. 32; Serventy 1956); other cloacal characters (Figs. 22-23, pp. 32-35) should be further investigated. Vocalizations show differences that enable sexing on the breeding colonies in at least two species (Brooke 1978a, 1988) and probably many others; more study is needed. In addition to cited references, Brooke (2004), Harrison (1983a, 1987), Onley & Scofield (2007), and Warham (1990, 1996) provide overviews of taxonomy and species determination in this group.

In molting, most shearwaters and petrels exhibit a Simple Basic Strategy (SBS; Fig. 10**A**, pp. 13-16) or a Complex Basic Strategy (CBS; Fig. 10**B**). See pp 248-252 and Table 24 (p. 249) for sequence and timing of molt, by age and breeding status, in petrels and shearwaters.

NORTHERN FULMAR

Fulmarus glacialis

NOFU
Species # 0860
Band size: 6

Species—From other petrels and shearwaters by medium size (Table 25, p. 255); tarsus rounded in cross-section; bill stout, with elongated tubes (Fig. 194), yellowish to pale greenish; plumage soft and aspect uniformly gray or patterned gray and white; tail with 14 (rather than 12) rects. Southern (Antarctic) Fulmar (*F. glacialoides*), a possible vagrant to N.Am, averages larger, with a longer bill and slightly shorter legs (wg chord 323-355, tail 114-136 exp culmen 39-49, tarsus 46-52); tip of tubes to base of bill nail > 10 mm (*vs* < 8 mm in Northern Fulmar); outer webs of pp blackish to black (*vs* dusky or grayish); inner webs to pp and ss mostly to entirely white (*vs* gray with pale fringes); bill pinkish with bluish tubenares and dark tip (*vs* greenish or yellowish with little or no dark coloration in Northern Fulmar).

Geographic variation—See Camphuysen et al. (1995), Cramp & Simmons (1977), Fisher (1952), Hatch (1991), Hatch & Nettleship

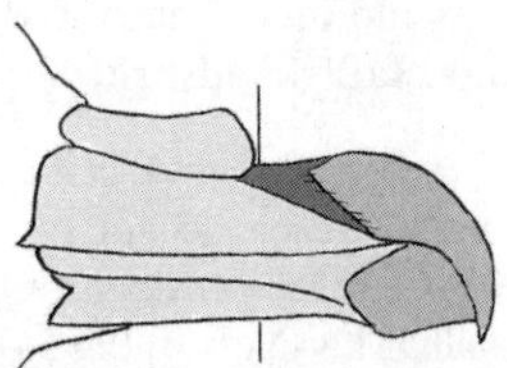

FIGURE 194. Bill shape and depth in Northern Fulmar as compared to petrels (Fig. 195, p. 256) and shearwaters (Fig. 198, p. 261). Note shorter and deeper saddle as compared with the other groups. Bill depth distal to tubes (as indicated) may be useful for sexing mated pairs and perhaps many individuals of known populations (see **Geographic variation**). More study is needed.

(1998), Mathiasson (1963), Portenko (1972), Salomonsen (1950, 1965), Stejneger (1885), Todd (1963), van Franeker (1986, 1995), van Franeker & Wattel (1982), Voous (1949), Watson (1957), and Wynne-Edwards (1952a). No other subspecies occur. In addition to the following, bill size and other biometrics vary geographically in the Atlantic but this variation is broadly clinal and not entirely correlated with subspecies according to plumage morph (see van Franeker & Wattel 1982). Note that dark-morph individuals can appear intermediate in plumage aspect in Apr-Sep, when bleached.

F.g. rodgersii (br & wint throughout Pacific range): Smaller with shorter wing (Table 25); dark morph predominant, medium-dark dusky gray in aspect; while morph without yellow tinge to head.

F.g. glacialis (br and wint throughout Atlantic range): Larger with longer wing (Table 25); white morph predominant, often with yellow tinge to head; dark morph medium bluish gray. Populations breeding in Nfl-n.Greenland ("*auduboni*") average slightly larger and have a greater proportion of dark-morph individuals but differences insufficient for subsppecific recognition.

Molt—SBS (CBS?). PF absent(?), PB2 incomplete-complete? (Apr-Nov in SYs), DPB incomplete-complete (Jun-Jan in breeding ASY/ATYs); PA absent. See pp. 248-252 and Table 24 (p. 249). The PB2 usually includes all pp (occasionally p9-p10 or p10 can be retained) and rects but usually not all body feathers, s covs, and/or (especially) ss. Ss retained during the PB2 vary from just s8-s10 or s8-s11, to 13 or more in 1-2 blocks among s3-s16 (*cf.* Fig. 188**C**, p. 250). Incomplete DPBs result in variable patterns of replaced and retained ss in ASYs (*cf.* Fig. 188**D**). Individuals with a complete DPB (Fig. 188**B**) may be rare, and could indicate pre-breeding AHYs or non-breeding adults.

Age—Juv (B1; Aug-Jul) is described below under HY/SY; Juv ♀=♂. See also Klomp & Furness (1992) for ageing fresh dead birds by the number of endosteal layers in the tibia. Note that confirmed-breeding adults (including ♀♀ with distended cloacae) can be reliably aged A4Y.

Juv-HY/SY (1st cycle, Juv/B1; Dec-Nov): Back feathers (Fig. 187**A**, p. 248), pp and ss (Figs. 188**A** & Fig. 189**A**, p. 250), and rects (Fig. 190**A**, p. 251) uniform in wear, narrower, and more tapered or rounded, the pp and ss usually molting in Apr-Nov (Table 24, p. 249); longest axillar averages narrower and more rounded (Fig. 191**A**, p. 251); legs and feet grayish (Oct) to grayish pink (Jun-Sep); claws sharp (Fig. 192**A**, p. 252); head of white morph without yellow tinge;

AHY/ASY (Def. cycle, DB; Dec-Nov): Back feathers (Fig. 187**B**), pp and ss (Figs. 188**B** & 189**B**, **D**), and rects (Fig. 190**B**) squarer and showing molt clines and contrasts, the pp and ss usually molting in May-Jan (Table 24); longest axillar averages broader and squarer (Fig. 191**B**); legs and feet pinkish; claws sharp (Fig. 192**A**); head of white morph without yellow tinge. **Note: Individuals without retained feathers may be rare (see Molt).**

SY/TY (2nd cycle, B2; Nov-Oct): Like AHY/ASY but ss with 2-13 retained, worn, and narrow juv feathers in 1-2 blocks among s3-s16 (Fig. 188**C**); back (Fig. 187**B-C**), s covs, and/or rects (Fig. 190**B-C**) often with contrastingly worn and narrow, retained juv feathers; replacement of pp usually May-Nov (Table 24); claws sharp (Fig. 192**A**).

ASY/ATY (Def. cycle, DB; Dec-Nov): Like AHY/ASY but one or more basic ss retained, square, and not contrasting markedly with adjacent feathers, and not necessarily showing the placement of retained juv feathers (Fig. 188**D**); back (Fig. 187**D**), s covs, and/or rects (Fig. 190**D**) with retained basic feathers, squarer, contrasting less with newer feathers; replacement of pp usually Jun-Jan (Table 24); claws often showing wear (Fig. 192**A-C**); head of light-morph *F.g. glacialis* often with yellow tinge. **Note: AHYs with very dull claws (Fig. 192C) can likely be aged ATY/A4Y or older but more study is needed.**

Sex—♀=♂ by plumage aspect. Medial BP (Fig. 20**A**, p. 31) developed by both sexes but distended cloaca (Fig. 21, p. 32; Serventy 1956) in Apr-Jun indicates A4Y ♀. Measurements (especially bill depth; Fig. 194) can be helpful for sexing some individuals including mated pairs (Table 25). DFAs (p. 5) using head-bill length (Fig. 453, p. 630), tarsus, exposed culmen, middle toe and claw length, and bill depth at nail and tube, and can be used to correctly sex 93-98% of various Atlantic populations (Dunnet & Anderson 1961, MacDonald 1977, Mallory & Forbes 2005, van Franeker & ter Braak 1993). Similar analyses are likely useful for sexing Pacific populations, especially mated pairs, but more study is needed.

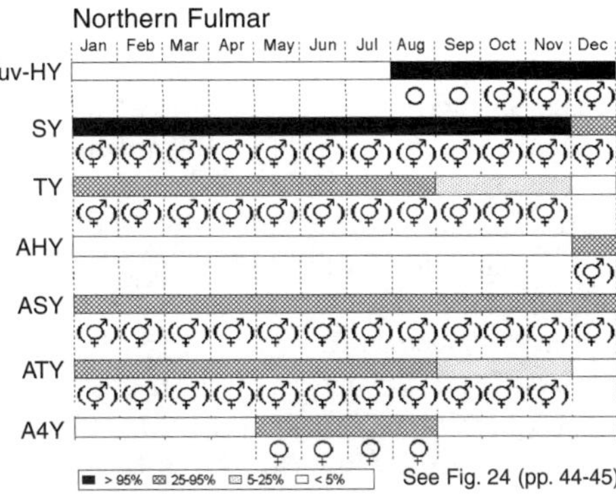

Hybrids reported—None.

References—Ainley et al. (1994), Baker (1993), Bent (1922), Brown (1988), Cramp & Simmons (1977), Fisher (1952), Harrington-Tweit (1979), Hatch & Nettleship (1998), Loomis (1918), Palmer (1962), Thompson et al. (2000), Voous (1949), Wynne-Edwards (1935, 1939).

TABLE 25. Measurements (mm) of fulmars and petrels that occur in North America to assist in identification and sexing. See pp. 4-11 for methods of measurement. Species summaries are in **bold** and subspecies summaries in ***italics***. Values are derived from 95% confidence intervals based approximately on the indicated sample sizes (see pp. 4-5); thus midpoints of ranges approximate means, and S.D. is approximated by 25% of the range.

Taxon/Sex	*n*	wing chord	tail length	exp culmen	bill depth[1]	tarsus
Northern Fulmar		**284-348**	**100-135**	**31-45**	**12.8-18.0**	**47-57**
F.g. rodgersii		***284-330***	***100-132***	***34-41***	***13.1-16.3***	***47-55***
♀	100	284-322	100-124	34-39	13.1-15.3	47-53
♂	100	291-330	108-132	36-41	14.5-16.3	49-55
F.g. glacialis		***305-348***	***109-135***	***31-45***	***12.8-18.0***	***48-57***
♀	100	305-339	109-129	31-40	12.8-17.3	48-54
♂	100	317-348	115-135	33-45	14.2-18.0	50-57
Murphy's Petrel		**267-296**	**104-123**	**28-32**	**8.6-10.0**	**36-41**
♀	44	267-296	104-119	28-31	8.6-9.3	36-40
♂	50	268-296	105-123	28-32	9.1-10.0	36-41
Mottled Petrel		**243-270**	**93-111**	**25-29**	**8.3-9.8**	**33-38**
♀	40	245-270	93-109	25-29	8.3-9.5	33-37
♂	46	243-269	94-111	25-29	8.7-9.8	33-38
Black-capped Petrel		**264-297**	**113-140**	**30-34**	**10.6-14.0**	**36-43**
♀	8	264-288	113-134	30-33	10.6-13.1	36-41
♂	9	268-297	119-140	31-34	11.7-14.0	38-43
Cook's Petrel		**223-246**	**86-97**	**24-30**	**6.5-7.4**	**28-33**
♀	45	223-239	86-94	24-29	6.5-7.1	28-32
♂	43	229-246	88-97	25-30	6.7-7.4	30-33

[1] Bill depth taken distal to tubenares (Figs. 194, p. 253 & 195, p. 256). Samples for bill depths are smaller than those given for other metrics but include > 10 individuals for each taxon/sex.

MURPHY'S PETREL MUPE
Pterodroma ultima Species # 1001
Band size: 3

Species—From other petrels and shearwaters by medium-small size (Table 25, p. 255); bill stout (Fig. 195) and black; tarsus somewhat rounded in cross-section (*vs* shearwaters); plumage aspect brownish gray, often with light sheen and sometimes with indistinct upperwing pattern at certain angles; forehead with little or no white when fresh (can be whiter when worn); throat mottled white (whiter when worn); underwing p covs and bases to pp slightly paler and more silvery than remainder of underwing; shafts of pp dark; legs and feet pale pinkish or bluish with black toes. Solander's (*P. solandri*) and Great-winged (*P. macroptera*) petrels, vagrants or visitors to the N.Pacific, are much larger (wg chord 285-320, tail 116-143, exp culmen 31-40, tarsus 39-47), often show glossier heads than backs and undeparts (creating hooded effect, absent in Murphy's Petrel except perhaps individuals in head molt), legs and feet dusky to black, and underwing pp and p covs with distinct whitish bases in Solander's Petrel. See Bailey et al. (1989a), Spear et al. (1992), and Marchant & Higgins (1990) for more information and separation from other extralimital species.

Geographic variation—Monotypic.

Molt—Timing and sequences unknown. Presumably SBS but possibly CBS, as in other Procellariiformes (see pp. 248-252 and Table 24, p. 249). Wear patterns of individuals occurring in the n.Hemisphere and timing of breeding suggest that the DPB may occur in Sep-Apr in the N.Pacific but confirmation needed; molting strategies may vary if the species breeds biennially as in certain other larger *Pterodroma* petrels (Murphy & Pennoyer 1952). Most AHYs appear to retain ss and sometimes gr covs during the DPB (*cf.* Fig. 188**C**-**D**, p. 250).

Age—Juv (B1; Dec-Sep?) is described below under HY/SY; Juv ♀=♂. Note that confirmed-breeding adults (including ♀♀ with distended cloacae) can be reliably aged ASY (probably ATY; more study needed).

Juv-HY/SY (1st cycle, Juv/B1; Feb-Jan?): Back feathers (Fig. 187**A**, p. 248), pp and ss (Figs. 188**A** & Fig. 189**A**, p. 250), and rects (Fig. 190**A**, p. 251) uniform in wear, narrower, and more tapered or rounded, the pp and ss possibly molting in Sep-Feb (Table 24, p. 249); longest axillar averages narrower and more rounded (Fig. 191**A**, p. 251); filoplumes (*cf.* Fig. 193, p. 252) absent.

AHY/ASY (Def. cycle, DB; Feb-Jan?): Back feathers (Fig. 187**B**), pp and ss (Figs. 188**B** & 189**B**, **D**), and rects (Fig. 190**B**) squarer and uniform in wear or showing molt clines and contrasts, the pp and ss possibly molting in Oct-Mar (Table 24); longest axillar averages broader and squarer (Fig. 191**B**); filoplumes (Fig. 193) often present.

SY/TY (2nd cycle, B2; Feb-Jan?): Like AHY/ASY but ss with 1-7 retained, worn, and narrow juv feathers among s4 and/or s6-s12 (*cf.* Fig. 188**C**).

ASY/ATY (Def. cycle, DB; Feb-Jan?): Like AHY/ASY but 1-5 basic ss retained, square,

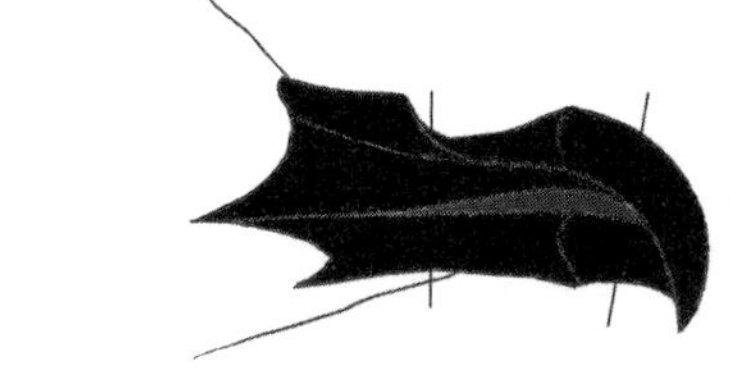

FIGURE 195. Bill shape and depth in petrels as compared to Northern Fulmar (Fig. 194, p. 253) and shearwaters (Fig. 198, p. 261). Note shorter and narrower saddle as compared with the other groups. Bill depth distal to tubes and "maximum nail depth" (as indicated) can be useful for sexing many petrels, including mated pairs (see also Fig. 198). Maximum nail depth may also vary by age (HY < AHY); more study needed.

and not contrasting markedly with adjacent feathers, and not necessarily showing the placement of retained juv feathers (*cf.* Fig. 188**D**).

Sex—♀ = ♂ by plumage aspect. Medial BP (Fig. 20**A,** p. 31) developed by both sexes but distended cloaca (Fig. 21, p. 32; Serventy 1956) in Jun-Aug indicates ASY ♀. Most measurements unhelpful for sexing, although bill depth distal to tubenares (Table 25, p. 255) may be useful for some individuals or mated pairs; more study needed.

Murphy's Petrel

	Jan	Feb	Mar	Apr	May	Jun	Jul	Aug	Sep	Oct	Nov	Dec
Juv-HY												
	O	O	O	O	O	O	O	O	O	O	O	O
SY												
	O	O	O	O	O	O	O	O	O	O	O	O
AHY												
	O	O	O	O	O	O	O	O	O	O	O	O
ASY												
	O	O	O	O	O	O	(♀)	(♀)	(♀)	O	O	O

■ > 95% ▩ 25-95% ▤ 5-25% □ < 5% See Fig. 24 (pp. 44-45)

Hybrids reported—None.

References—Ainley et al. (1994), Bailey et al. (1989a), Murphy (1949), Murphy & Pennoyer (1952), Spear et al. (1992), Zimmer (1992).

MOTTLED PETREL

Pterodroma inexpectata

MOPE
Species # 0990
Band size: 3

Species—From other petrels and shearwaters by medium-small size with short legs (Table 25, p. 255); bill stout (Fig. 195) and black; tarsus somewhat rounded in cross-section (*vs* shearwaters); upperparts (including rump) gray with indistinct to moderately distinct dusky pattern to upperwing; black underwing ulnar bar broad and distinct; abdomen washed dusky to blackish; outer rects (Fig. 196) and axillars (Fig. 197, p. 258) gray and whitish.

Geographic variation—Monotypic.

Molt—SBS (CBS?). Little known but possibly as follows: PF absent(?), PB2 complete (Feb?-Aug? in SYs), DPB complete (May-Oct in breeding ASYs); PA absent. See pp. 248-252 and Table 24 (p. 249). The DPB likely takes place in the n.Hemisphere for many AHYs. Non-breeding individuals may be in molt at any time of year, and a limited PF may occur in this species. Few if any AHYs appear to retain ss during DPBs.

Age—Juv (B1; Apr-Mar) is described below under HY/SY; Juv ♀ = ♂. Note that confirmed-breeding adults (including ♀♀ with distended cloacae) can be reliably aged ATY.

Juv-HY/SY (1st cycle, Juv/B1; Sep-Aug): Rects narrower, more rounded, more worn, and with more white to r4-r6 (Fig. 196**A**); longest axillar tapered, rounded, and with distal portion gray, often mottled white (Fig. 197**A** p. 258); back feathers (Fig. 187**A**, p. 248) and pp and ss (Figs. 188**A** &

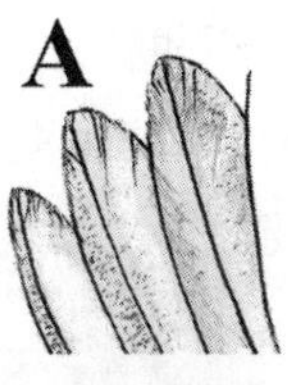

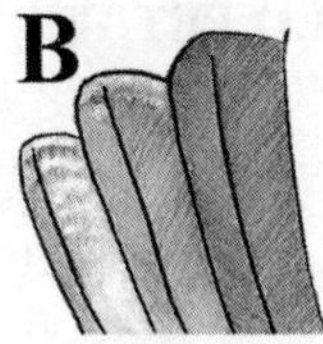

FIGURE 196. Shape and pattern of outer rectrices (r4-r6) by age in Mottled Petrel. Note increased amount of white and less distinct patterns by rectrix in juv feathers (**A**).

Fig. 189**A**, p. 250) uniform in wear, narrower, and more tapered or rounded, the pp and ss probably molting in Feb-Sep (Table 24, p. 249); claws sharp (Fig. 192**A**, p. 252); filoplumes (*cf.* Fig. 193, p. 252) absent.

AHY/ASY (Def. cycle, DB; Oct-Sep): Rects broader, more squared, fresher, and with less white to r4-r6 (Fig. 196**B**); longest axillar squared and with distal portion usually solid gray tipped white (Fig. 197**B**); back feathers (Fig. 187**B**) and pp and ss (Figs. 188**B** & 189**B**, **D**) broader, squarer, and uniform in wear or showing slight molt clines and contrasts, the pp and ss usually molting in Jun-Sep (Table 24); claws often worn (Fig. 192**B-C**); filoplumes (Fig. 193) often present. **Note: AHYs with very dull claws (Fig. 192C) can likely be aged ASY/ATY or older but more study is needed.**

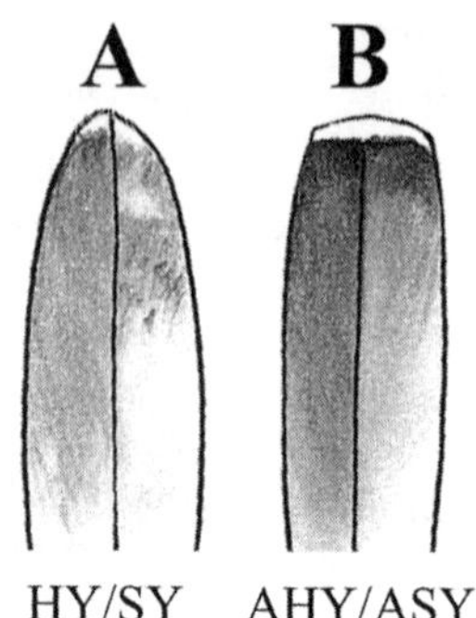

FIGURE 197. Shape and pattern of longest axillar by age in Mottled Petrel. Typical patterns are shown; some intermediates may be encountered.

Sex—♀=♂ by plumage aspect. Medial BP (Fig. 20**A,** p. 31) developed by both sexes distended cloaca (Fig. 21, p. 32; Serventy 1956) in Dec-Feb indicates ATY ♀. Most measurements unhelpful for sexing (Table 25, p. 255), although the following appears useful for sexing most AHYs:

♀: Maximum nail depth (*cf.* Fig. 195, p. 256): 8.8-10.0. **Note: SYs may average shallower nail depths than ASYs; combine with age for individuals with depth 9.6-10.0 mm.**

♂: Maximum nail depth (*cf.* Fig. 195): 9.6-10.8. **Note: See ♀.**

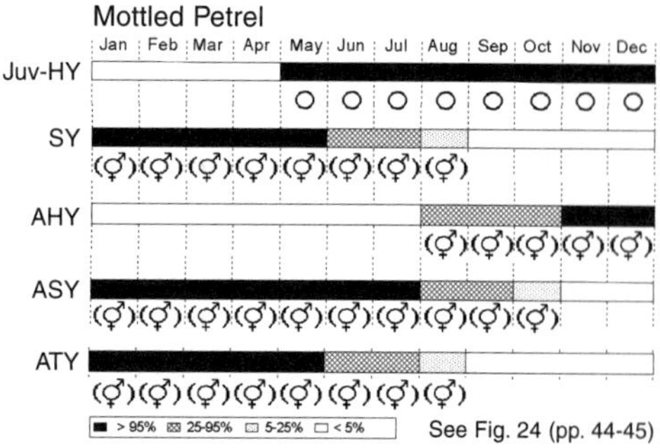

Mottled Petrel
Jan Feb Mar Apr May Jun Jul Aug Sep Oct Nov Dec
Juv-HY
SY
AHY
ASY
ATY
> 95% 25-95% 5-25% < 5%
See Fig. 24 (pp. 44-45)

Hybrids reported—None.

References—Ainley & Manolis (1979), Ainley et al. (1994), Bent (1922), Loomis (1918), Marchant & Higgins (1990), Murphy & Pennoyer (1952), W.R.P. Bourne *in* Palmer (1962), Richdale (1964), Spear & Ainley (1998), Warham et al. (1977), Watson (1975).

BLACK-CAPPED PETREL
Pterodroma hasitata

BCPE
Species # 0980
Band size: 3

Species—From most other petrels and shearwaters by medium size with long and graduated tail (Table 25, p. 255; r1 > r6 by 35-55 mm); bill stout (Fig. 195, p. 256) and black; tarsus somewhat rounded in cross-section (*vs* shearwaters); cap dusky, contrasting with white forehead and (usually) white hind collar; upperparts brown with indistinct or no darker pattern to upperwing; uppertail covs mostly to entirely white; black underwing ulnar bar broad and distinct; abdomen and flanks white.

Bermuda Petrel (*P. cahow*), a visitor to se.N.Am, is smaller but with a proportionately longer tail (wg chord 260-262, tl 118-124, exp culmen 27-30, bill depth at distal end of nares

8.8-9.9, tarsus 34-38), lacks a white hind collar, and has uppertail covs grayish to whitish with black tips.

Geographic variation—No extant subspecies recognized (C. Jouanin & J.-L. Mougin *in* Mayr & Cottrell 1979); several previously recognized Pacific subspecies are now considered separate species. A dark-morph taxon (*P. [h.] caribbaea*) from Jamaica is poorly known and presumably extinct. See also Murphy (1936), W.R.P. Bourne *in* Palmer (1962).

Molt—SBS (CBS?). Little known but possibly as follows: PF absent(?), PB2 complete (Mar?-Aug? in SYs), DPB complete (May-Sep in breeding ASYs); PA absent. See pp. 248-252 and Table 24 (p. 249). Look for some AHYs to retain ss during DPBs and be aged SY/TY or ASY/ATY (Fig. 188**C**-**D**).

Age—Juv (B1; Apr-Mar) is described below under HY/SY; Juv ♀ = ♂. Note that confirmed-breeding adults (including ♀♀ with distended cloacae) can be reliably aged ASY/ATY.

Juv-HY/SY (1st cycle, Juv/B1; Aug-Jul): Back feathers (Fig. 187**A**, p. 248), pp and ss (Figs. 188**A** & Fig. 189**A**, p. 250), and rects (Fig. 190**A**, p. 251) uniform in wear, narrower, and more tapered or rounded, the pp and ss probably molting in Mar-Aug (Table 24, p. 249); longest axillar averages narrower and more rounded (Fig. 191**A**, p. 251); claws sharp (Fig. 192**A**, p. 252).

AHY/ASY (Def. cycle, DB; Nov-Oct): Back feathers (Fig. 187**B**), pp and ss (Figs. 188**B** & 189**B**, **D**), and rects (Fig. 190**B**) broader, squarer, and often showing molt clines and contrasts, the pp and ss usually molting in May-Sep (Table 24); longest axillar averages broader and squarer (Fig. 191**B**); claws often worn (Fig. 192**B**-**C**). **Note: AHYs with very dull claws (Fig. 192C) can likely be aged ASY/ATY or older but more study is needed.**

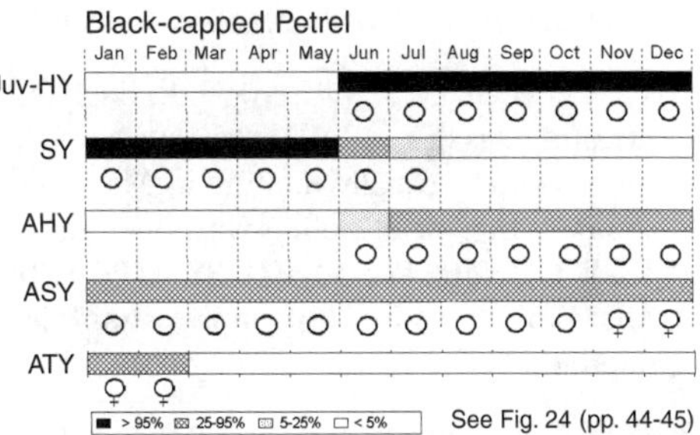

Sex—♀ = ♂ by plumage aspect. Medial BP (Fig. 20**A,** p. 31) developed by both sexes but distended cloaca (Fig. 21, p. 32; Serventy 1956) in Nov-Feb indicates ASY/ATY ♀. Most measurements unhelpful for sexing (Table 25, p. 255), although maximum nail depth (Fig. 195, p. 256) may be of use: ~11.3-12.9 in ♀♀, ~12.5-14.2 in ♂♂.

Hybrids reported—None.

References—Bangs & Penard (1919), Bent (1922), Lee (1984), Murphy (1936), Murphy & Mowbray (1951), Noble (1916), W.R.P. Bourne *in* Palmer (1962), Wingate (1964).

COOK'S PETREL
Pterodroma cookii

COOP
Species # 0983
Band size: 3

Species—From most other petrels and shearwaters by small size (Table 25, p. 255); bill stout (Fig. 195, p. 256) and black; tarsus somewhat rounded in cross-section (*vs* shearwaters); upperparts including cap pale gray (when fresh) with distinct dusky pattern to upperwing; pp with wedge-shape white patches on inner webs; black underwing ulnar bar narrow and indistinct; abdomen white; legs and feet pale bluish with dusky toes.

Stejneger's Petrel (*P. longirostris*), an occasional visitor off w.N.Am, is smaller (wg chord 198-226, tl 97-107, exp culmen 23-26, tarsus 26-30); cap and nape blackish, contrasting distinctly in aspect with white face and gray back; underwing ulnar bar slightly wider (> 15 mm wide *vs* < 13 mm in Cook's Petrel). See Austin (1952), Falla (1942), Fleming (1941), Howell et al. (1996), Marchant & Higgins (1990), Murphy (1929), Roberson & Bailey (1991), and Spear et al. (1992) for separation of these and other small *Pterodroma* petrels, including De Filippi's (*P. defillipiana*) and Pycroft's (*P. pycrofti*) petrels, potential vagrants to Pacific N.Am.

Geographic variation—Monotypic; several previously recognized subspecies are now considered species. Individuals off S.Am identified as "*P.c. orientalis*," represented nominate Cook's Petrels in fresher plumage; see Bourne (1983), Falla (1942), Murphy (1929, 1936), W.R.P. Bourne *in* Palmer (1962), Tyler & Burton (1986).

Molt—SBS (CBS?). Little known but probably as follows: PF absent(?), PB2 complete (Jan?-Jun? in SYs), DPB complete (Mar-Aug in breeding ASYs); PA absent. See pp. 248-252 and Table 24 (p. 249). Molting may occur primarily in the n.Hemisphere, although it is possible that the PB2 can commence in the s.Hemisphere and/or that some AHYs remain in the s.Hemisphere to molt. As such, non-breeding individuals may be in molt at any time of year. A limited PF may also occur in this species. Few if any ss are retained during DPBs.

Age—Juv (B1; Mar-Feb) is described below under HY/SY; Juv ♀ = ♂. Note that confirmed-breeding adults (including ♀♀ with distended cloacae) can be reliably aged ASY/ATY.

Juv-HY/SY (1st cycle, Juv/B1; Jul-Jun): Back feathers (Fig. 187**A**, p. 248), pp and ss (Figs. 188**A** & Fig. 189**A**, p. 250), and rects (Fig. 190**A**, p. 251) uniform in wear, narrower, and more tapered or rounded, the pp and ss usually molting in Jan-Jun (Table 24, p. 249); longest axillar averages narrower and more rounded (Fig. 191**A**, p. 251), often entirely white; claws sharp (Fig. 192**A**, p. 252). **Note: Look for age-related differences in the amount of white mottling in r4-r6, as in Mottled Petrel (Fig. 196, p. 257).**

AHY/ASY (Def. cycle, DB; Aug-Jul): Back feathers (Fig. 187**B**), pp and ss (Figs. 188**B** & 189**B**, **D**), and rects (Fig. 190**B**) broader, squarer, and often showing slight molt clines and contrasts, the pp and ss usually molting in Mar-Aug (Table 24); longest axillar averages broader and squarer (Fig. 191**B**), often with fine gray vermiculations near the tip; claws often dull (Fig. 192**B-C**). **Note: See Juv-HY/SY. AHYs with very dull claws (Fig. 192C) can likely be aged ASY/ATY or older but more study is needed.**

Cook's Petrel

	Jan	Feb	Mar	Apr	May	Jun	Jul	Aug	Sep	Oct	Nov	Dec
Juv-HY			O	O	O	O	O	O	O	O	O	O
SY	O	O	O	O	O	O						
AHY			O	O	O	O	O	O	O	O	O	O
ASY	O	O	O	O	O	O	O				♀	♀
ATY	♀											

■ > 95% ▨ 25-95% □ 5-25% □ < 5% See Fig. 24 (pp. 44-45)

Sex—♀ = ♂ by plumage aspect. Medial BP (Fig. 20**A,** p. 31) developed by both sexes but distended cloaca (Fig. 21, p. 32; Serventy 1956) in Nov-Jan indicates ASY/ATY ♀. Most measurements unhelpful for sexing (Table 25, p. 255) including maximum nail depth (Fig. 195, p. 256): ♀ 7.4-8.3, ♂ 7.7-8.8.

Hybrids reported—None.

References—Ainley et al. (1994), Bourne (1983), Falla (1933, 1942), Fleming (1941), Howell et al. (1996), Loomis (1918), Marchant & Higgins (1990), Murphy (1929, 1936), W.R.P. Bourne *in* Palmer (1962), Roberson & Bailey (1991), Spear et al. (1992), Tyler & Burton (1986).

CORY'S SHEARWATER
Calonectris diomedea

COSH
Species # 0880
Band size: 4

Species—From most other petrels and shearwaters by large size and bill (Table 26, p. 265); bill moderately long and slender (Fig. 198; but relatively stout for a shearwater), yellowish to pinkish yellow, tipped dusky, with moderately elongated tubes opened distally more like fulmar (Fig. 194, p. 253) *vs* dorsally (Fig. 198) in other shearwaters; tarsus laterally compressed in cross-section (*vs* petrels); upperparts uniformly grayish brown (without black cap or white nape); underparts (including undertail covs and underwing covs) uniformly white.

Cape Verde Shearwater (*C. edwardsii*), a vagrant to e.N.Am, is smaller (wg chord 285-320, tl 114-127, tarsus 44-50), with bill shorter, shallower (exp culmen 39-49, depth at distal end of tubenares 10.4-12.7), and grayish to yellowish, and has duskier upperparts with crown more distinctly separated from the white face and throat (see Porter et al. 1997, Patterson & Armistead 2004). Pattern of the under primaries resembles that of *C.d. borealis* (Fig. 199**C**, p. 262).

Geographic variation—See Baker (1993), Bannerman (1915), Bourne (1955, 1986), Camphuysen & van der Meer (2001), Cramp & Simmons (1977), Fisher & Flood (2004), Granadeiro (1993), Gutiérrez (1998), Mathews (1937a, 1937b), Murphy (1922, 1923, 1924), Murphy & Chapin (1929), Palmer (1962), Patterson & Armistead (2004), Randi et al. (1989), Thibault & Bretagnolle (1998). No other subspecies (although see Species regarding *C. edwardsii*); The name *"flavirostris"* (=*"disputans"*) was based on the assumption that the species bred in the Kerguelen Is (*cf.* Bourne 1955). Intermediates between the following may be encountered that perhaps represent intergrades.

C.d. borealis (br Atlantic Is off w.Europe, visitor throughout Atlantic N.Am range): Size and bill larger (Table 26, p. 265; also, flat wing length (Fig. 3**B**, p. 6) 347-388, bill depth at end of forehead feathering 18.5-24.0); white extension on inner web of outer pp absent or reduced (Fig. 199**A-B**, p. 162); upperparts medium-dark grayish brown when fresh. See Granadeiro (1993) for variation in biometrics within *borealis*.

C.d. diomedea (br Mediterranean Is, visitor NY-TX): Size and bill smaller (Table 26; also flat wing length 330-366), bill depth at end of forehead feathering 15.6-18.8); white extension on inner web of outer pp elongated (Fig. 199**C**); upperparts medium-pale grayish brown when fresh.

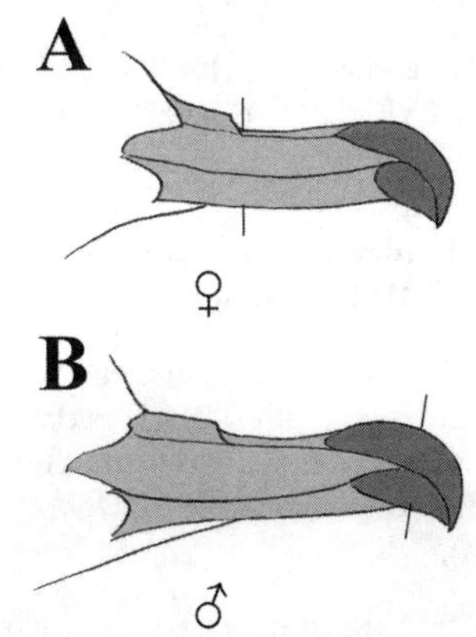

FIGURE 198. Bill shape and depth in shearwaters by sex and as compared to Northern Fulmar (Fig. 194, p. 253) and petrels (Fig. 195, p. 256). Note longer and narrower saddle as compared with the other groups. Bill depth distal to tubes (indicated for ♀♀ in **A**) and especially "maximum nail depth" (as indicated for ♂♂ in **B**) can be useful for sexing shearwaters, including mated pairs. Maximum nail depth may also vary by age (HY < AHY); more study needed.

Molt—SBS (CBS?). PF absent(?), PB2 incomplete-complete (Apr-Jan in SYs), DPB incomplete-complete (Aug-Feb in breeding ASYs); PA absent. The DPB begins during breeding (body feathers and occasionally 1-4 inner primaries during incubation), suspends for southbound migration, and completes in the s.Hemisphere. See pp. 248-252 and Table 24 (p. 249). PBs are incomplete in ~15% of AHYs, with some body feathers, rects, s covs, and/or ss (among s3-s4 and s8-s15) retained during the PB2 (*cf.* Fig. 188**C**, p. 250) or

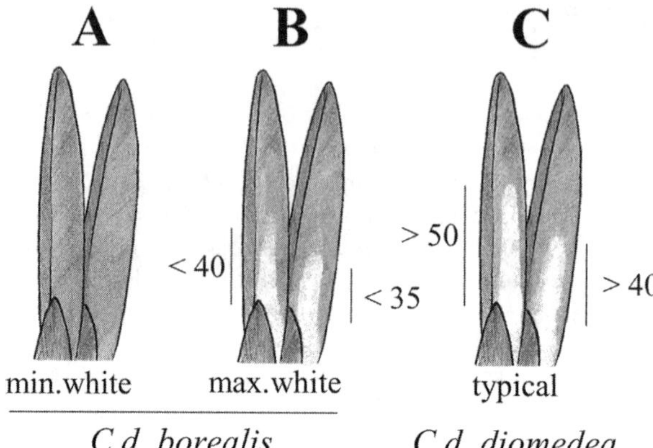

FIGURE 199. Extent of white to p9 (left) and p10 (right) by subspecies in Cory's Shearwater. Measure indicates distance of white "tongue" from tip of underwing p cov of corresponding p. The extent of white on p9 is more reliable but that on p10 is better to use in the field. A few intermediates, possibly intergrades, may be encountered.

among s3-s17 (of 22 ss) during subsequent PBs (*cf.* Fig. 188**D**). ♀♀ average earlier DPB than ♂♂ in breeding individuals. A limited PF may occur in at least some HYs that spend Aug-Oct in more productive n.Hemisphere waters.

Age—Juv is described below under SY; Juv ♀=♂. Note that confirmed-breeding adults (including ♀♀ with distended cloacae) can be reliably aged A4Y.

Juv-HY/SY (1st cycle, Juv/B1; Oct-Sep): Back feathers (Fig. 187**A**, p. 248), pp and ss (Figs. 188**A** & Fig. 189**A**, p. 250), and rects (Fig. 190**A**, p. 251) uniform in wear, narrower, and more tapered or rounded, the pp and ss usually molting in Apr-Nov (Table 24, p. 249); longest axillar averages narrower and more rounded (Fig. 191**A**, p. 251). **Note: SYs and ASYs may be determined with these criteria (especially outer pp shape and wear) until the PB2 or DPB is complete in Nov-Jan (see also SY/TY and ASY/ATY).**

AHY/ASY (Def. cycle, DB; Oct-Sep): Back feathers (Fig. 187**B**), pp and ss (Figs. 188**B** & 189**B**, **D**), and rects (Fig. 190**B**) broader, squarer, and showing molt clines and contrasts, the pp and ss usually molting in Aug-Jan (Table 24); longest axillar averages broader and squarer (Fig. 191**B**). **Note: See HY/SY. Most ASYs show these characters (resulting from a complete DPB).**

SY/TY (2nd cycle, B2; Oct-Sep): Like AHY/ASY but ss with 1-9 retained, worn, and narrow juv feathers among s3-s4 and/or s8-s14 (*cf.* Fig. 188**C**); back (Fig. 187**B-C**), s covs, and/or rects (Fig. 190**B-C**) sometimes with contrastingly worn and narrow, retained juv feathers; replacement of pp usually Jun-Dec (Table 24). **Note: Only ~15% of SY/TYs and ASY/ATYs have incomplete PBs and can be aged following completion of the molts, in Nov-Jan.**

ASY/ATY (Def. cycle, DB; Oct-Sep): Like AHY/ASY but 1-5 basic ss among s3-s17 retained, square, and not contrasting markedly with adjacent feathers (*cf.* Fig. 188**D**); back (Fig. 187**D**), s covs, and/or rects (Fig. 190**D**) sometimes with retained basic feathers, squarer, contrasting less with newer feathers; replacement of pp often Oct-Jan (Table 24). **Note: See SY/TY.**

Sex—♀=♂ by plumage aspect. Medial BP (Fig. 20**A**, p. 31) developed by both sexes but distended cloaca (Fig. 21, p. 32; Serventy 1956) in Apr-Jun indicates A4Y ♀. Most measurements unhelpful for sexing (Table 26, p. 265). See Granadeiro (1993) for DFAs (p. 5) using exp culmen, bill height at tip of forehead feathering, and bill height at gonys that separated 96-97% of *C.d. borealis* in the hand. See Lo Valvo (2001) and Ristow & Wink (1980) for similar data useful for sexing populations of *C.d. diomedea*. The following will separate most individuals of known-subspecies. Use caution in sexing individuals of unknown subspecies.

♀: Maximum nail depth 11.9-13.7 in *C.d. borealis* or 10.5-12.1 in *diomedea* (*cf.* Fig. 198**A**, p. 261); bill depth at tip of forehead feathering 18.5-20.9 in *borealis*. **Note: HY/SYs may average shallower bill depths than AHY/ASYs; combine with age for individuals with intermediate depths.**

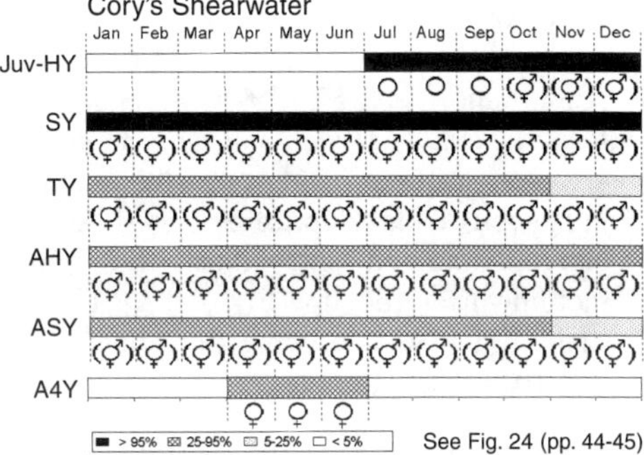

♂: Maximum nail depth 13.5-15.5 in *C.d. borealis* or 11.8-13.4 in *diomedea* (Fig. 198**B**); bill depth at tip of forehead feathering 20.0-24.0 in *borealis*. **Note: See ♀.**

Hybrids reported—Doubtfully with Greater Shearwater (McCarthy 2006; *cf.* Pyle 2006b).

References—Baker (1993), Bent (1922), Bourne (1986), Brown (1988, 1990), Camphuysen & van der Meer (2001), Cramp & Simmons (1977), Forsythe (1980), Granadeiro (1993), Kuroda (1954), Marchant & Higgins (1990), Monteiro & Furness (1996), Monteiro et al. (1996), Mougin et al. (1986), Murphy (1924), Palmer (1962), Porter et al. (1997), Pulich (1982), Ramos et al. (unpublished ms.), Robertson & James (1988).

PINK-FOOTED SHEARWATER
Puffinus creatopus

PFSH
Species # 0910
Band size: 4

Species—From most other petrels and shearwaters by medium-large size with relatively short tail (Table 26, p. 265); bill slender (Fig. 198, p. 261), pinkish tipped dusky; tarsus laterally compressed in cross-section (*vs* petrels); upperparts uniformly brownish gray (without black cap or white nape); inner webs of pp dusky; underparts largely white with variable amounts of dusky on the sides, flanks, and underwing covs; undertail covs dusky to white tipped dusky (*cf.* Fig. 204**D-F**, p. 272); legs pinkish with dusky toes. Rare dark-morph Pink-footed Shearwaters similar to Flesh-footed Shearwater (p. 266) but plumage aspect grayer (*vs* browner in Flesh-footed Shearwater) and often with hint of bicolored pattern; bill base usually duskier pink (*vs* bright pink with a more distinctly defined dark tip in Flesh-footed Shearwater). Light-morph Wedge-tailed Shearwater (*P. pacificus*), a vagrant to w.N.Am, can be separated by smaller size but longer tail (wg chord 298-326, tl 123-148, tarsus 48-54); tail graduated (r6 – r1 45-58 mm *vs* 14-26 in Pink-footed Shearwater); bill shallower (depth distal to tubenares 8.2-10.2) and grayish, usually with less distinct dark tip; underparts variable, often with less dusky mottling to head and flanks; undertail covs entirely dark (*cf.* Fig. 204**F**).

Geographic variation—Monotypic.

Molt—CBS. PF absent-limited (Oct-Jan in HY/SYs), PB2 complete (Jan-Jun in SYs), DPB complete (Mar-Aug in breeding ASYs); PA absent. See pp. 248-252 and Table 24 (p. 249). The PB2 likely commences in the s.Hemisphere and completes in the n.Hemisphere whereas DPBs take place primarily in the n.Hemisphere. A limited PF (consisting of at least some upperpart feathers) can occur in at least some HY/SYs that remain in the n.Hemisphere during Oct-Apr. One or more ss can rarely be retained during DPBs.

Age—Juv (B1; Mar-Feb) is described below under HY/SY; Juv ♀=♂. Note that confirmed-breeding adults (including ♀♀ with distended cloacae) can be reliably aged ATY/A4Y.

Juv-HY/SY (1st cycle, Juv/B1-F1; Jul-Jun): Most to all back feathers (Fig. 187**A**, p. 248) and all pp and ss (Figs. 188**A** & 189**A**, p. 250) and rects (Fig. 190**A**, p. 251) uniform in wear, narrower, and more tapered or rounded, the pp and ss usually molting in Jan-Jun (Table 24, p. 249); longest axillar tapered, rounded, and whitish with gray mottling near the tip (Fig. 200**A**); claws sharp (Fig. 192**A**, p. 252); filoplumes (*cf.* Fig. 193, p. 252) absent.

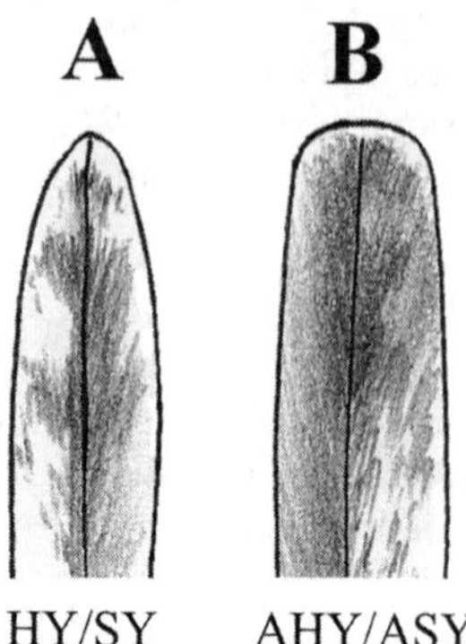

FIGURE 200. Shape and pattern of longest axillar by age in Pink-footed Shearwater. Typical patterns are shown; some intermediates may be encountered.

AHY/ASY (Def. cycle, DB; Aug-Jul): Back feathers (Fig. 187**B**), pp and ss (Figs. 188**B** & 189**B**, **D**), and rects (Fig. 190**B**) broader, squarer, and often showing molt clines and contrasts, the pp and ss usually molting in Mar-Aug (Table 24); longest axillar squared and primarily gray at tip (Fig. 200**B**); claws often dull (Fig. 192**B**-**C**); filoplumes (Fig. 193) often present. **Note: Occasional AHYs retain one to a few ss and/or rects during the PB2 or DPB and can be aged SY/TY or ASY/ATY (respectively), as in other shearwaters (Figs. 188C-D & 190C-D). In addition, AHYs with very dull claws (Fig. 192C) can likely be aged ASY/ATY or older but more study is needed.**

Sex—♀=♂ by plumage aspect. Medial BP (Fig. 20**A,** p. 31) developed by both sexes but distended cloaca (Fig. 21, p. 32; Serventy 1956) in Nov-Jan indicates ATY/A4Y ♀. Most measurements unhelpful for sexing (Table 26); however, the following is reliable for sexing many individuals:

♀: Maximum nail depth 11.1-12.5 (*cf.* Fig. 198**A**, p. 261). **Note: HY/SYs may average shallower bill depths than AHY/ASYs; combine with age for individuals with depth 12.1-12.5 mm.**

♂: Maximum nail depth 12.1-14.1 (*cf.* Fig. 198**B**). **Note: See ♀.**

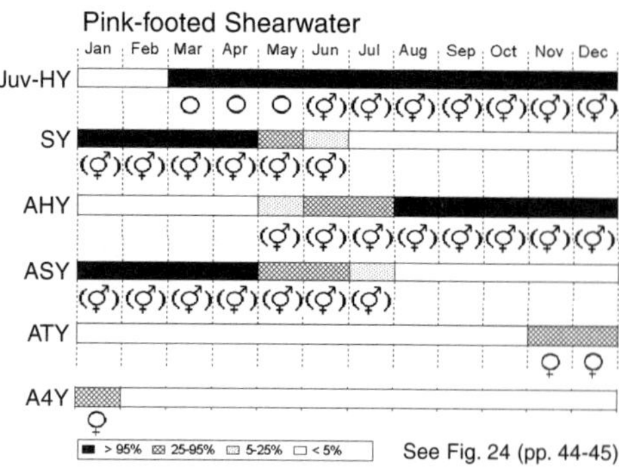

Hybrids reported—None. Darker underparts on certain individuals (see **Species**) apparently represent individual variation or melanism; reported hybridism with Flesh-footed Shearwater (*cf.* Marchant & Higgins 1990) has not been adequately documented.

References—Ainley et al. (1994), Bent (1922), Blake (1977), Bull et al. (2005), Loomis (1918), Kuroda (1954), Marchant & Higgins (1990), Murphy (1936), Palmer (1962).

TABLE 26. Measurements (mm) of shearwaters that occur in North America to assist in identification and sexing. See pp. 4-11 for methods of measurement. Species summaries are in **bold** and subspecies summaries in ***italics***. Values were derived from 95% confidence intervals as based (for wing, tail, exposed culmen, and tarsus) approximately on the indicated sample sizes (see pp. 4-5); sample size for bill depth was often smaller but included at least 10 of each sex. Thus, midpoints of ranges approximate means, and S.D. is approximated by 25% of the range.

Taxon/Sex	*n*	wing chord	tail length	exp culmen	bill depth[1]	tarsus
Cory's Shearwater		**319-367**	**117-144**	**45-62**	**11.2-16.7**	**46-61**
C.d. borealis		***328-367***	***121-144***	***49-62***	***13.0-16.7***	***50-61***
♀	100	328-361	121-141	49-58	13.0-15.2	50-58
♂	100	333-367	123-144	52-62	14.5-16.7	53-61
C.d. diomedea		***319-355***	***117-135***	***45-54***	***11.2-14.6***	***46-57***
♀	100	319-350	117-132	45-51	11.2-13.8	46-54
♂	100	323-355	120-135	48-54	12.0-14.6	49-57
Pink-footed Shearwater		**319-345**	**106-124**	**40-46**	**11.0-13.8**	**51-58**
♀	100	319-343	107-122	40-44	11.0-13.2	51-56
♂	100	321-345	106-124	41-46	11.6-13.8	52-58
Flesh-footed Shearwater		**308-334**	**108-122**	**39-45**	**10.6-13.2**	**52-58**
♀	80	308-332	108-120	39-45	10.6-11.9	52-57
♂	80	311-334	109-122	40-46	11.4-13.2	53-58
Greater Shearwater		**310-341**	**106-126**	**42-50**	**9.8-12.3**	**55-63**
♀	64	310-337	106-120	42-47	9.8-11.6	55-61
♂	67	317-341	108-126	44-50	10.5-12.3	58-63
Buller's Shearwater		**276-304**	**115-135**	**38-45**	**9.6-11.2**	**48-54**
♀	66	276-302	115-133	38-43	9.6-10.6	48-52
♂	100	278-304	116-135	39-45	10.0-11.2	50-54
Sooty Shearwater		**281-319**	**83-97**	**38-46**	**8.3-10.5**	**52-60**
♀	100	281-315	83-96	38-44	8.3-9.9	52-58
♂	100	287-319	84-97	40-46	8.8-10.5	53-60
Short-tailed Shearwater		**261-286**	**74-87**	**29-35**	**6.9-8.6**	**48-56**
♀	100	261-284	75-87	29-34	6.9-8.0	48-55
♂	100	262-286	74-87	29-35	7.4-8.6	49-56
Manx Shearwater		**219-241**	**67-85**	**31-38**	**7.1-9.5**	**41-48**
♀	100	220-238	67-83	31-37	7.1-8.6	41-47
♂	100	219-241	68-85	32-38	8.0-9.5	42-48
Black-vented Shearwater		**223-248**	**69-82**	**33-40**	**7.3-8.9**	**42-49**
♀	100	223-246	69-80	33-38	7.3-8.4	42-48
♂	100	225-248	70-82	35-40	7.9-8.9	42-49
Audubon's Shearwater[2]		**192-212**	**80-94**	**26-31**	**5.9-7.8**	**37-43**
♀	100	192-210	80-94	26-30	5.9-7.3	37-42
♂	100	193-212	81-95	28-31	6.3-7.8	38-43

[1] Bill depth taken distal to tubenares (*cf.*. Fig. 198, p. 261).

[2] Populations occurring in N.Am only (see **Geographic variation**).

FLESH-FOOTED SHEARWATER

Puffinus carneipes

FFSH
Species # 0951
Band size: 4

Species—From most other petrels and shearwaters by medium-large size (Table 26, p. 265); bill slender (Fig. 198, p. 261), pale pink with complete blackish tip; tarsus laterally compressed in cross-section (*vs* petrels); plumage aspect uniformly brown, without pale coloration to the axillars (*cf.* Fig. 200, p. 264) or underwing covs (*cf.* Fig. 203, p. 270); legs and feet pinkish with dusky toes. See Pink-footed Shearwater (p. 262) for information concerning rare dark morphs of that species.

Dark-morph Wedge-tailed Shearwater, a vagrant to w.N.Am, can be separated by smaller size but longer tail (wg chord 298-326, tl 123-148, tarsus 48-54); bill shallow (depth distal to tubenares 8.2-10.2) and grayish with less distinct darker tip; tail graduated (r6 – r1 45-58 mm *vs* 13-25 mm in Flesh-footed Shearwater). Parkinson's Petrel (*Procellaria parkinsoni*), a visitor to w.N.Am, averages longer wing but shorter tail length (wg chord 330-360, tail 93-106, exp culmen 40-45, tarsus 50-55); bill proportionally stouter (*cf.* Fig. 195, p. 256); legs and feet black; plumage aspect darker with little or no feather fringing; and bill pale whitish or tinged green, with nail often only partially dusky (*cf.* Marchant & Higgins 1990, Howell 2006b).

Geographic variation—Monotypic. Populations breeding in New Zealand ("*P.c. hullianus*") may average larger and shorter-billed than those of Is off Australia, but differences are insufficient and clinal. See Marchant & Higgins (1990), Murphy (1930, 1936), W.R.P. Bourne *in* Palmer (1962).

Molt—SBS (CBS?). PF absent(?), PB2 complete (Jan?-Jul? in SYs), DPB complete (Mar-Sep in breeding ASYs); PA absent. See pp. 248-252 and Table 24 (p. 249). Non-breeding individuals may be in molt at any time of year and a limited PF may occur in this species. Look for some individuals to retain one or more ss during PBs (see Fig. 188**C**-**D**, p. 250).

Age—Juv (B1; Mar-Feb) is described below under HY/SY; Juv ♀ = ♂. Note that confirmed-breeding adults (including ♀♀ with distended cloacae) can be reliably aged ATY/A4Y.

Juv-HY/SY (1st cycle, Juv/B1; Aug-Jul): Back feathers (Fig. 187**A**, p. 248), pp and ss (Figs. 188**A** & Fig. 189**A**, p. 250), and rects (Fig. 190**A**, p. 251) uniform in wear, narrower, and more tapered or rounded, the pp and ss probably molting in Jan-Jul (Table 24, p. 249); longest axillar averages narrower and more rounded (Fig. 191**A**, p. 251); claws sharp (Fig. 192**A**, p. 252); filoplumes (*cf.* Fig. 193, p. 252) absent.

AHY/ASY (Def. cycle, DB; Sep-Aug): Back feathers (Fig. 187**B**), pp and ss (Figs. 188**B** & 189**B**, **D**), and rects (Fig. 190**B**) broader, squarer, and often showing molt clines and contrasts, the pp and ss usually molting in Mar-Sep (Table 24); longest axillar averages broader and squarer (Fig. 191**B**); claws often dull (Fig. 192**B**-**C**); filoplumes (Fig. 193) often present. **Note: Occasional AHYs may retain ss and/or rects during DPBs (Figs. 188C-D & 190C-D) and be aged SY/TY or ASY/ATY, as in other shearwaters, but most AHYs appear to have complete DPBs (see Molt). AHYs with very dull claws (Fig. 192C) can likely be aged ASY/ATY or older but more study is needed.**

Sex—♀ = ♂ by plumage aspect. Medial BP (Fig. 20**A,** p. 31) developed by both sexes but distended cloaca (Fig. 21, p. 32; Serventy 1956) in Nov-Jan indicates ATY/A4Y ♀. Most measurements unhelpful for sexing although bill depth can be used to sex some individuals (Table 26, p. 265); see also Thelmann et al. (2007) for a DFA (p. 5) including head-bill length (Fig. 453, p. 630), minimum bill depth above tubenares, and width of bill nail that correctly sexed 91% of live individuals.

♀: Maximum nail depth 10.5-12.1 (*cf.* Fig. 198**A,** p. 261); head-bill length (*cf.* Fig. 453) 89-97.

Note: HY/SYs may average shallower bill depths than AHY/ASYs; combine with age for individuals with bill depth 11.4-12.1 and head-bill length 95-97 mm.

♂: Maximum nail depth 11.4-13.1 (*cf.* Fig. 198**B**); head-bill length 95-101. **Note: See ♀.**

Hybrids reported—None. See Pink-footed Shearwater (p. 262).

References—Bent (1922), Bull et al. (2005), Kuroda (1954), Loomis (1918), Marchant & Higgins (1990), Murphy (1930, 1936), W.R.P. Bourne *in* Palmer (1962), Thalmann et al. (2007), Watson (1975).

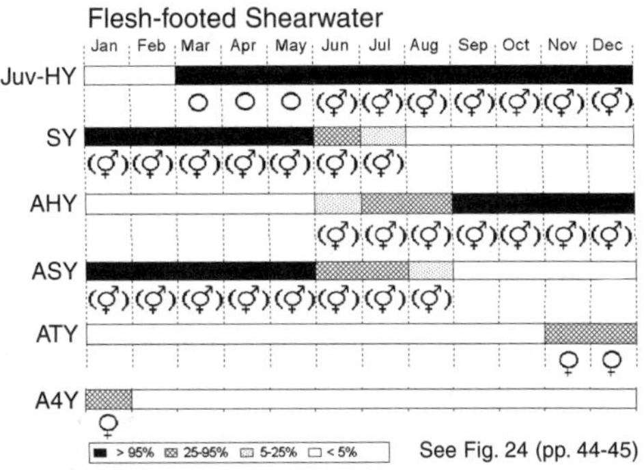

GREATER SHEARWATER

Puffinus gravis

GRSH
Species # 0890
Band size: 6

Species—From other petrels and shearwaters by large size (Table 26, p. 265); bill slender (Fig. 198, p. 261) and black; tarsus laterally compressed in cross-section (*vs* petrels); crown black, usually separated from grayish back by white nape collar (Fig. 201; see **Age**); underparts white with dusky abdomen and undertail covs; underwing feathers white with black markings in covs and axillars.

Geographic variation—Monotypic.

Molt—CBS. PF absent-limited (Jul-Sep in HYs), PB2 complete (Jan-Aug in SYs), DPB complete (Mar-Sep in breeding ASYs); PA absent. See pp 248-252 and Table 24 (p. 249). The PF (if present) and PBs in breeding ASYs occur in productive waters in the n.Hemisphere; the PB2 (and PBs of non-breeders?) can begin at sea in the s.Hemisphere, suspend, and complete in the n.Hemisphere. The PF includes some head and back feathers in some HYs. Few individuals retain ss or other feathers during DPBs.

Age—Juv (B1; Mar-Feb) is described below under HY/SY; Juv ♀=♂. Note that confirmed-breeding adults (including ♀♀ with distended cloacae) can be reliably aged ATY/A4Y.

Juv-HY/SY (1st cycle, Juv/B1-F1; Aug-Jul): Nape with indistinct to incomplete white collar (Fig. 201**A-B**); most to all back feathers (Fig. 187**A**, p. 248) and all pp and ss (Figs. 188**A** & Fig. 189**A**, p. 250) and rects (Fig. 190**A**, p. 251) uniform in wear, narrower, and more tapered or rounded, the pp and ss usually molting in Jan-Aug (Table 24, p. 249); longest axillar tapered and rounded (Fig. 191, p. 251), perhaps averaging more gray near tip; claws sharp (Fig. 192**A**, p. 252); filoplumes (*cf.* Fig. 193, p. 252) absent.

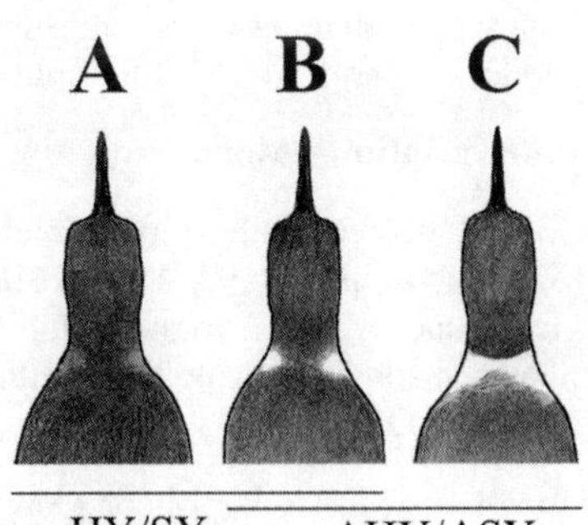

FIGURE 201. Variation in the completeness of the white nape collar in Greater Shearwater as an indication of age. More study is needed to determine ranges of variation; it is possible that AHY/ASYs resembling **C** can be reliably aged ASY/ATY or older.

AHY/ASY (Def. cycle, DB; Aug-Jul): Nape with indistinct to distinct white collar (Fig. 201**B-C**); back feathers (Fig. 187**B**), pp and ss (Figs. 188**B** & 189**B**, **D**), and rects (Fig. 190**B**) broader, squarer, and sometimes showing molt clines and contrasts, the pp and ss usually molting in Mar-Sep (Table 24); longest axillar broad and squared (Fig. 191**B**), perhaps averaging less gray near tip; claws often dull (Fig. 192**B-C**); filoplumes (Fig. 193) usually present. **Note: AHYs with very dull claws (Fig. 192C) can likely be aged ASY/ATY or older but more study is needed.**

Sex—♀=♂ by plumage aspect. Medial BP (Fig. 20**A,** p. 31) developed by both sexes but distended cloaca (Fig. 21, p. 32; Serventy 1956) in Nov-Jan indicates ATY/A4Y ♀. Most measurements unhelpful for sexing (Table 26, p. 265); maximum nail depth (*cf.* Fig. 198, p. 261) ♀ 9.7-11.5, ♂ 10.6-12.4. See Brooke (1988) for sex-specific differences in vocalizations useful for sexing individuals on breeding grounds.

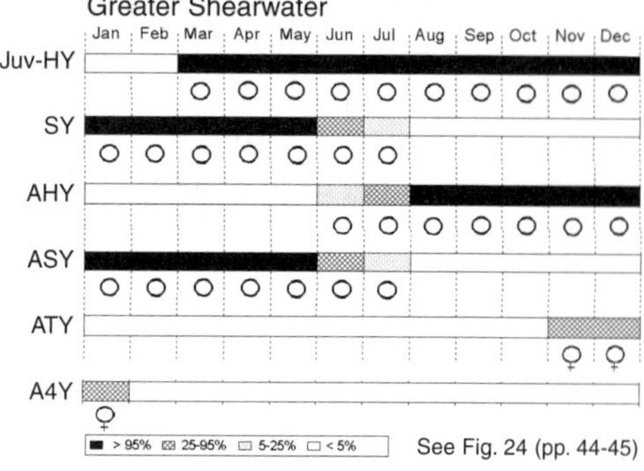

Hybrids reported—Doubtfully with Cory's Shearwater (p. 261).

References—Bent (1922), Blake (1977), Brown (1988, 1990), Bull et al. (2005), Cramp & Simmons (1977), Kuroda (1954), Marchant & Higgins (1990), Murphy (1936), W.R.P. Bourne *in* Palmer (1962), Stresemann & Stresemann (1970), Watson (1970a, 1971), Wynne-Edwards (1935).

BULLER'S SHEARWATER

Puffinus bulleri

BULS
Species # 0962
Band size: 4

Species—From other petrels and shearwaters by medium size with relatively long tail (Table 26, p. 265); bill slender (Fig. 198, p. 261) and gray; tarsus laterally compressed in cross-section (*vs* petrels); upperparts bluish gray to gray with dusky cap and well-marked blackish pattern to upperwings; pp with inner webs extensively white; underparts (including undertail covs) bright white; underwing covs white without ulnar bar.

Geographic variation—Monotypic.

Molt—CBS. PF absent-limited (Aug-Nov in HYs), PB2 complete (Feb-Jun in SYs), DPB complete (Mar-Aug in breeding ASYs); PA absent. See pp. 248-252 and Table 24 (p. 249). The PF occurs in productive waters in the n.Hemisphere whereas PBs occur in the s.Hemisphere. The PF can include some head and back feathers in some HYs. Few if any AHYs retain ss or other feathers during DPBs.

Age—Juv (B1; Apr-Mar) is described below under HY/SY; Juv ♀=♂. Note that confirmed-breeding adults (including ♀♀ with distended cloacae) can be reliably aged ATY.

Juv-HY/SY (1st cycle, Juv/B1-F1; Jul-Jun): Most to all back feathers (Fig. 187**A**, p. 248) and all pp and ss (Figs. 188**A** & Fig. 189**A**, p. 250) and rects (Fig. 190**A**, p. 251) uniform in wear, narrower, and more tapered or rounded, the pp and ss usually molting in Feb-Jun (Table 24, p. 249); longest axillar averages narrower and more rounded (Fig. 191**A**, p. 251); claws sharp (Fig. 192**A**, p. 252). **Note: Intermediates can be difficult to age.**

AHY/ASY (Def. cycle, DB; Sep-Aug): Back feathers (Fig. 187**B**), pp and ss (Figs. 188**B** & 189**B**, **D**), and rects (Fig. 190**B**) broader, squarer, and often showing molt clines and contrasts, the pp and ss usually molting in Mar-Aug (Table 24, p. 249); longest axillar averages broader and squarer (Fig. 191**B**). **Note: See Juv-HY/SY. Also, AHYs with very dull claws (Fig. 192C) can likely be aged ASY/ATY or older but more study is needed.**

Sex—♀ = ♂ by plumage aspect. Medial BP (Fig. 20**A,** p. 31) developed by both sexes but distended cloaca (Fig. 21, p. 32; Serventy 1956) in Oct-Dec indicates ATY ♀. Most measurements unhelpful for sexing (Table 26, p. 265), although maximum nail depth (*cf.* Fig. 198, p. 261; ♀ 8.4-10.2, ♂ 9.4-11.0) might be useful for some individuals including mated pairs.

Hybrids reported—With Sooty Shearwater (Warham 1996).

Buller's Shearwater
Jan Feb Mar Apr May Jun Jul Aug Sep Oct Nov Dec
Juv-HY
SY
U
AHY
ASY
ATY
■ > 95% ▩ 25-95% ▭ 5-25% □ < 5%
See Fig. 24 (pp. 44-45)

References—Ainley et al. (1994), Bent (1922), Bull et al. (2005), Gould et al. (1998) Loomis (1918), Marchant & Higgins (1990), Murphy (1930, 1936), W.R.P. Bourne *in* Palmer (1962).

SOOTY SHEARWATER
Puffinus griseus

SOSH
Species # 0950
Band size: 4-5

SHORT-TAILED SHEARWATER
Puffinus tenuirostris

STTS
Species # 0960
Band size: 4

Species—From most other petrels and shearwaters by medium size with short tail and long legs (Table 26, p. 265); bill slender (Fig. 198, p. 261) and dusky; tarsus laterally compressed in cross-section (*vs* petrels); plumage aspect brownish to grayish with underwing covs variably washed whitish to grayish, paler than pp and ss (Fig. 203, p. 270); legs and feet blackish.

Sooty from Short-tailed shearwater, with caution, by larger size (especially longer tail; Table 26), bill longer and deeper (Fig. 202; Table 26); distal underwing gr, med, and p covs silvery gray to white, usually with distinct shaft streaks, and contrasting distinctly with darker pp and ss (Fig. 203**A-B**), *vs* gray, without distinct shaft streaks, and contrasting less with darker pp and ss in Short-tailed Shearwater (Fig. 203**C**).

Geographic variation—Monotypic in both species. See Mathews & Iredale (1915), Murphy (1930), and Richdale (1963) regarding Sooty Shearwater.

Molt—CBS. PF absent-limited (Jul-Nov in HYs), PB2 incomplete-complete (Feb-Aug in SYs), DPB incomplete-complete (May-Oct in breeding ASYs); PA absent. Timing of molt averages about a month later in Short-tailed than in Sooty Shearwater (Table 24); see pp 248-252 and Table 24 (p. 249). The PF appears to include some feathers of the head, back, and breast on at least some HYs in the n.Hemisphere. It is possible that the PB2 occurs primarily in the s.Hemisphere (suspended and completed in the n.Hemisphere?) whereas the DPB (of successful breeders at least) occurs in the n.Hemisphere (see Cooper et al. 1991); more study needed. The DPBs are sometimes (10-20% of ASYs) incomplete with 1-9 ss among s3-s4 and/or s6-s14, often s9 and/or s10 (*cf.* Fig. 188**C-D**, p. 250) retained.

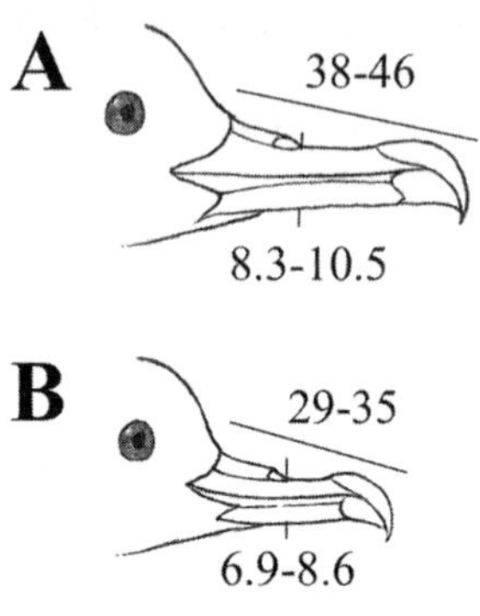

FIGURE 202. Comparison of bills for identification of Sooty and Short-tailed Shearwaters. Measures include exposed culmen and bill depth distal to tubenares. Note also the steeper forehead of Short-tailed Shearwater as compared with Sooty.

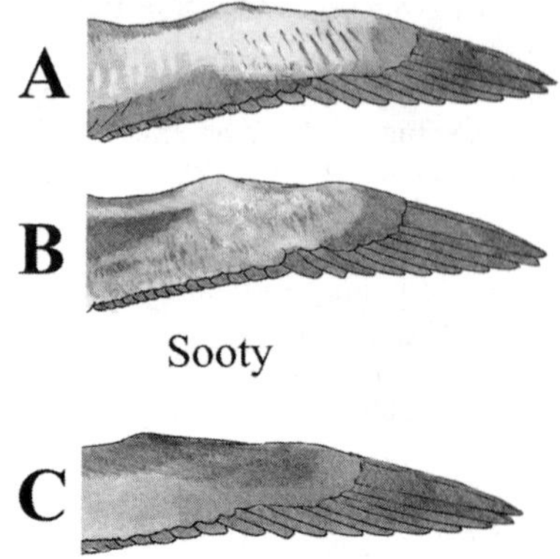

FIGURE 203. Variation in underwing covert coloration for identification of Sooty (**A** = paler example, **B** = darker example) and Short-tailed (**C**) shearwaters. Note that the distal underwing gr and med covs and proximal p covs are the tracts that display the greatest differences; these tend to contrast with the color of the undersides of distal ss in Sooty but not Short-tailed Shearwater. In addition, the coverts in this region usually show distinct shaft streaks in Sooty Shearwater, lacking in Short-tailed Shearwater In Sooty Shearwater, look for HY/SYs to possibly average paler underwings (**A**) than AHY/ASYs (**B**).

Age—Juv (B1; Mar-Feb) is described below under HY/SY; Juv ♀=♂. In addition to the following, the amount of whitish to the underwing covs of Sooty Shearwater (*cf.* Fig. 203**A-B**) may vary by age (paler in younger individuals?) but more study needed. Note that confirmed-breeding adults (including ♀♀ with distended cloacae) can be reliably aged ASY/ATY (probably ATY/A4Y). In addition to the following, see Sugimora et al. (1985) for information on the patterns of skull ossification by age in the Short-tailed Shearwater, potentially useful in separating HY/SYs from older AHY/ASYs.

Juv-HY/SY (1st cycle, Juv/B1-F1; Aug-Jul): Most to all back feathers (Fig. 187**A**, p. 248) and all pp and ss (Figs. 188**A** & Fig. 189**A**, p. 250) and rects (Fig. 190**A**, p. 251) uniform in wear, narrower, and more tapered or rounded, the pp and ss usually molting Mar-Jul (Table 24, p. 249); longest axillar averages narrower and more rounded (Fig. 191**A**, p. 251); lower abdomen feathers often with pale fringes; claws sharp (Fig. 192**A**, p. 252).

AHY/ASY (Def. cycle, DB; Aug-Jul): Back feathers (Fig. 187**B**), pp and ss (Figs. 188**B** & 189**B**, **D**), and rects (Fig. 190**B**) broader, squarer, and often showing molt clines and contrasts, the pp and ss usually molting Jun-Oct (Table 24); longest axillar averages broader and squarer (Fig. 191**B**); lower abdomen feathers without pale fringes; claws often dull (Fig. 192**B-C**). **Note: See SY/TY and ASY/ATY. Most AHY/ASYs show these characters (resulting from a complete DPB). AHY/ASYs with very dull claws (Fig. 192C) can likely be aged ASY/ATY or older but more study is needed.**

SY/TY (2nd cycle, B2; Aug-Jul): Like AHY/ASY but ss with 1-9 retained, worn, and narrow juv feathers among s3-s4 and/or s6-s14 (*cf.* Fig. 188**C**); back (Fig. 187**B-C**), s covs, and/or rects (Fig. 190**B-C**) sometimes with contrastingly worn and narrow, retained juv feathers. **Note: See AHY/ASY. Only a small proportion (~10-20%) of AHYs appear to have incomplete DPBs and can be identified as SY/TYs or ASY/ATYs.**

ASY/ATY (Def. cycle, DB; Sep-Aug): Like AHY/ASY but 1-5 basic ss among s3-s12 retained, square, and not contrasting markedly with adjacent feathers (*cf.* Fig. 188**D**); back (Fig. 187**D**), s covs, and/or rects (Fig. 190**D**) sometimes with retained basic feathers, squarer, contrasting less with newer feathers. **Note: See AHY/ASY and SY/TY.**

Sex— ♀ = ♂ by plumage aspect. Medial BP (Fig. 20**A,** p. 31) developed by both sexes but distended cloaca (Fig. 21, p. 32; Serventy 1956) in Oct-Jan indicates ASY/ATY ♀. Most measurements unhelpful for sexing (Table 26, p. 265); however, the following can be used to sex many Sooty Shearwaters and some Short-tailed Shearwaters:

♀: Maximum nail depth 8.3-9.4 in Sooty Shearwater and 6.9-8.3 in Short-tailed Shearwater (*cf.* Fig. 198**A**, p. 261). **Note: HY/SYs may average shallower nail depths than AHY/ASYs; combine with age for intermediate depths.**

♂: Maximum nail depth 9.1-10.4 in Sooty Shearwater and 7.6-8.8 in Short-tailed Shearwater (*cf.* Fig. 198**B**). **Note: See ♀.**

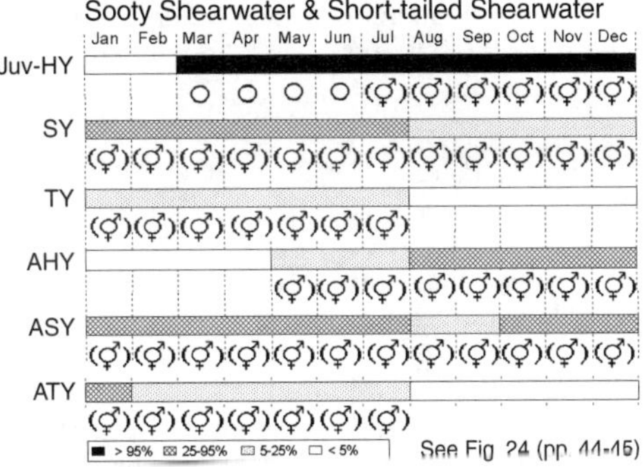

Hybrids reported—Sooty Shearwater with Buller's (p. 268) and Short-tailed (Kuroda 1967) shearwaters.

References—Ainley et al. (1994), Bent (1922), Brown (1988), Bull et al. (2003), Chu (1984), Cooper et al. (1991), Cramp & Simmons (1977), Eisenmann & Serventy (1962), Kratter & Steadman (2003), Kuroda (1954, 1967), Loomis (1918), Marchant & Higgins (1990), Marshall & Serventy (1956), McKee & Terrill (2004), Murphy (1930, 1936), Oberholser (1974), Ogi et al. (1981), W.R.P. Bourne and D.L. Serventy *in* Palmer (1962), Richdale (1963), Wahl (1982), Watson (1975).

MANX SHEARWATER
Puffinus puffinus

MASH
Species # 0900
Band size: 4A-4

Species—From most other petrels and shearwaters by medium-small size (Table 26, p. 265); bill slender (Fig. 198, p. 261) and grayish with a blackish culmen; tarsus laterally compressed in cross-section (*vs* petrels); upperparts uniformly blackish; white of auriculars often extending in crescent proximal to eye; inner webs to outer pp (p7-p10) grayish; underparts including undertail covs and most underwing feathers white (Figs. 204**A-B** & 205, p. 272; see **Age**); base of bill often with thin white band; legs and feet pinkish with blackish toes. From Audubon's Shearwater (p. 275) by larger size except for tail length (Table 26); upperparts blacker; base of bill often with white band; undertail covs mostly to entirely white (Fig. 205**A-B**; see **Age**). See Black-vented Shearwater (p. 273) for information on separating Townsend's and Newell's shearwaters.

Little Shearwater (*P. assimilis*), a vagrant to e.N.Am, is much smaller (wg chord 169-191, tl 64-83, exp culmen 23-29, tarsus 35-40); dark of cap usually does not extend below eye; inner webs to outer pp (p7-p10) white, contrasting with darker outer webs; legs and feet usually bluish. See Baker (1993), Bourne et al. (1988), Cramp & Simmons (1977), Curtis et al. (1985), Dunn (1988), Howell et al. (1994), Jehl (1982), Kinsky & Fowler (1973), Lee & Haney (1996), Loomis (1918), Marchant & Higgins (1990), Mathews (1935), Murphy (1930, 1952), W.R.P.

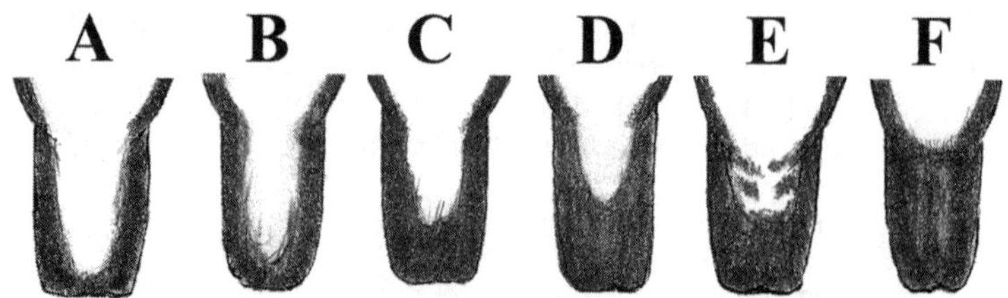

FIGURE 204. Variation in the amount of white and blackish to the undertail covs in small shearwaters. By species, typical patterns are Manx and Little **A-B**, Newell's **C-E**, Townsend's and Black-vented **E-F**, and Audubon's **C-F** shearwaters. Also, light-morph Wedge-tailed Shearwater has entirely dark undertail covs (**F**) *vs* more white here in most Pink-footed Shearwaters (**D-F**).

Bourne *in* Palmer (1962), Roberson (1996), and Yésou et al. (1990) for separation of Manx Shearwater from other similar species worldwide.

Geographic variation—Monotypic. Several related taxa (formerly considered conspecific) now considered separate species.

Molt—SBS (CBS?). PF absent(?), PB2 complete (Jun-Dec in SYs), DPB complete (Jul-Feb in breeding ASY/ATYs); PA absent. See pp. 248-252 and Table 24 (p. 249). Body and primary molt can begin on adults during late incubation or chick-rearing; otherwise, all molting occurs at sea, primarily in the s.Hemisphere (at least for breeding adults). Non-breeding individuals may be in molt at any time of year, and a limited PF may occur in this species. Occasional AHYs may retain ss and/or other feathers during DPBs.

Age—Juv (B1; Sep-Aug) is described below under HY/SY; Juv ♀ = ♂. Note that confirmed-breeding adults (including ♀♀ with distended cloacae) can be reliably aged ATY.

Juv-HY/SY (1st cycle, Juv/B1; Dec-Nov): Back feathers (Fig. 187**A**, p. 248), pp and ss (Figs. 188**A** & Fig. 189**A**, p. 250), and rects (Fig. 190**A**, p. 251) uniform in wear, narrower, and more tapered or rounded, the pp and ss usually molting in Jun-Dec (Table 24, p. 249); longest axillar tapered and rounded, with substantial black at tip (Fig. 205**A**); undertail covs sometimes with thin black tips; claws sharp (Fig. 192**A**, p. 251); filoplumes (*cf.* Fig. 193, p. 252) absent.

AHY/ASY (Def. cycle, DB; Sep-Aug): Back feathers (Fig. 187**B**), pp and ss (Figs. 188**B** & 189**B**, **D**), and rects (Fig. 190**B**) broader, squarer, and often showing molt clines and contrasts, the pp and ss usually molting in Jul-Feb (Table 24); longest axillar squared and entirely white or with reduced black subterminal band or marking (Fig. 205**B-C**); undertail covs usually without black tips; claws often dull (Fig. 192**B-C**); filoplumes (Fig. 193) often present. **Note: See ASY/ATY. Occasional AHYs may retain ss (Fig. 188C-D) or other feathers and can be aged SY/TY and ASY/ATY (see Fig. 288C-D, p. 250). Also, AHYs with very dull claws (Fig. 192C) can likely be aged ASY/ATY or older but more study is needed.**

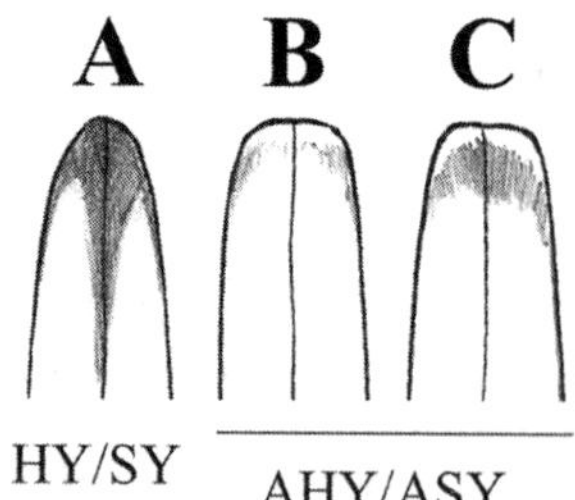

FIGURE 205. Shape and pattern of longest axillar by age in Manx Shearwater. Juv feathers (**A**) average narrower and darker at the tip than basic feathers (**B-C**).

ASY/ATY (Def. cycle, DB; Sep-Feb): Like AHY/ASY but pp being replaced and outer pp broad and truncate (Fig. 189**B**).

Sex—♀ = ♂ by plumage aspect. Medial BP (Fig. 20**A,** p. 31) developed by both sexes but distended cloaca (Fig. 21, p. 32; Serventy 1956) in Apr-Jun indicates ATY ♀. Most measurements unhelpful for sexing (Table 26, p. 265), although maximum nail depth appears useful for many individuals: ♀ 5.9-6.8, ♂ 6.4-8.0 (*cf.* Fig. 198, p. 261). See Brooke (1978a) for differences in vocalizations useful in sexing individuals on breeding grounds.

Manx Shearwater

Jan Feb Mar Apr May Jun Jul Aug Sep Oct Nov Dec

Juv-HY

SY

AHY

ASY

ATY

■ > 95% ▩ 25-95% ▤ 5-25% □ < 5%

See Fig. 24 (pp. 44-45)

Hybrids reported—None.

References—Ainley et al. (1994, 1997), Baker (1993), Bent (1922), Brooke (1978a, 1978b, 1996), Brown (1988), Bull et al. (2005), Cramp & Simmons (1977), Dement'ev & Gladkov (1951a), Dwight (1927), James (1986), King & Gould (1967), Kuroda (1954), Lee (1995), Lee & Haney (1996), Marchant & Higgins (1990), Monteiro et al. (1996), Murphy (1930, 1936, 1952), W.R.P. Bourne *in* Palmer (1962).

BLACK-VENTED SHEARWATER
Puffinus opisthomelas

BVSH
Species # 0930
Band size: 4

Species—From most other petrels and shearwaters by medium-small size, short tail (Table 26, p. 265); bill slender (Fig. 198, p. 261) and grayish; tarsus laterally compressed in cross-section (*vs* petrels); upperparts uniformly dusky brown; auriculars without pale crescent extending proximal to eye; underparts white with dusky-brownish wash to flanks, underwing covs, and axillars (Fig. 206); undertail covs mostly to entirely dark (Fig. 204**E-F**); legs and feet pinkish with dusky toe. Townsend's (*P. auricularis*) and Newell's (*P.[a.] newellii*) shearwaters, potential visitors to w.N.Am, have similar measurements but are blacker-backed with more distinct contrasts with white underparts; femoral region with extensive white patches (*cf.* Fig. 164**A**, p. 217) *vs* restricted in Black-vented Shearwater (*cf.* Fig. 164**B**); undertail covs with white bases in Newell's Shearwater (Fig. 204**C-E**). See Howell (2007a) for information on occurrence and identification of a dark-morph Black-vented Shearwater.

Geographic variation—Monotypic.

Molt—CBS. PF absent-limited (Jul-Oct in HYs), PB2 incomplete-complete (Apr-Sep in SYs), DPB incomplete-complete (Jun-Nov in breeding ASY/ATYs); PA absent. See pp. 248-252 and Table 24 (p. 249). The PF appears to occur in only a small proportion of HY/SYs

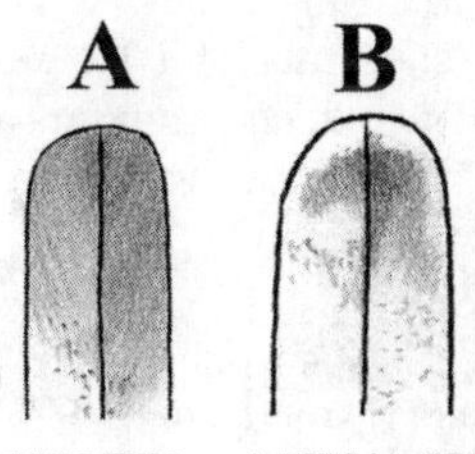

FIGURE 206. Shape and pattern of longest axillar by age in Black-vented Shearwater. Juv feathers (**A**) average narrower and darker at the tip than basic feathers (**B**), but intermediates occur and some individuals cannot be aged by this feature alone.

and includes a few head and upperpart feathers. The DPBs are sometimes (~25%) incomplete, with 1-6 ss and occasionally other feathers (including rects) retained (Fig. 188**C**-**D**, p. 250; Fig. 190**C**-**D**, p. 251).

Age—Juv (B1; Jul-Jun) is described below under HY/SY; Juv ♀=♂. Note that confirmed-breeding adults (including ♀♀ with distended cloacae) can be reliably aged ATY.

Juv-HY/SY (1st cycle, Juv/B1; Dec-Nov): Back feathers (Fig. 187**A**, p. 248), pp and ss (Figs. 188**A** & Fig. 189**A**, p. 250), and rects (Fig. 190**A**, p. 251) uniform in wear, narrower, and more tapered or rounded, the pp and ss usually molting in Apr-Sep (Table 24, p. 249); longest axillar averages narrower, more rounded, and darker at tip (Fig. 206**A**, p. 273); claws sharp (Fig. 192**A**, p. 252); filoplumes (*cf.* Fig. 193, p. 252) absent.

AHY/ASY (Def. cycle, DB; Dec-Nov): Back feathers (Fig. 187**B**), pp and ss (Figs. 188**B** & 189**B**, **D**), and rects (Fig. 190**B**) broader, squarer, and often showing molt clines and contrasts, the pp and ss usually molting in Jun-Dec (Table 24); longest axillar averages broader, squarer, and paler at tip (Fig. 206**B**); claws often dull (Fig. 192**B**-**C**); filoplumes (Fig. 193) often present. **Note: See SY/TY and ATY; most AHY/ASYs show these characters, resulting from a complete DPB. Also, AHYs with very dull claws (Fig. 192C) can likely be aged ASY/ATY or older but more study is needed.**

SY/TY (2nd cycle, B2; Dec-Nov): Like AHY/ASY but ss with 1-6 retained, worn, and narrow juv feathers among s3-s4 and/or s9-s14 (*cf.* Fig. 188**C**); back (Fig. 187**B**-**C**), s covs, and/or rects (Fig. 190**B**-**C**) sometimes with contrastingly worn and narrow, retained juv feathers. **Note: Only a small proportion (~25%) of AHYs appear to have incomplete DPBs and can be identified as SY/TYs or ASY/ATYs.**

ATY (Def. cycle, DB; Jan-Dec): Like AHY/ASY but 1-5 basic ss among s3-s12 retained, square, and not contrasting markedly with adjacent feathers (*cf.* Fig. 188**D**); back (Fig. 187**D**), s covs, and/or rects (Fig. 190**D**) sometimes with retained basic feathers, squarer, contrasting less with newer feathers. **Note: See SY/TY.**

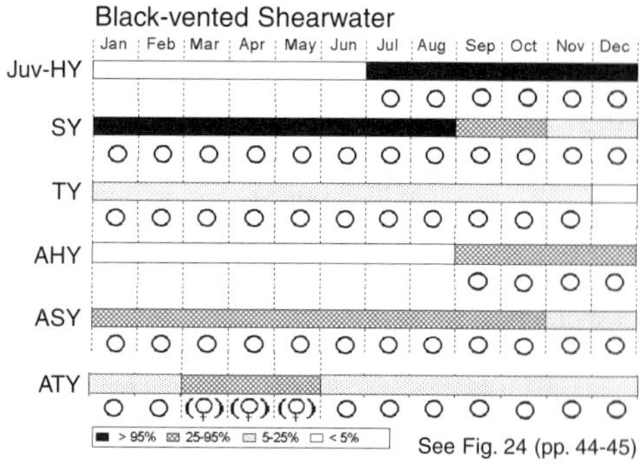

Black-vented Shearwater

Jan Feb Mar Apr May Jun Jul Aug Sep Oct Nov Dec

Juv-HY

SY

TY

AHY

ASY

ATY

(♀) (♀) (♀)

■ > 95% ▩ 25-95% ▥ 5-25% □ < 5%

See Fig. 24 (pp. 44-45)

Sex—♀=♂ by plumage aspect. Medial BP (Fig. 20**A,** p. 31) developed by both sexes but distended cloaca (Fig. 21, p. 32; Serventy 1956) in Mar-May indicates ATY ♀. Most measurements unhelpful for sexing (Table 26, p. 265) including maximum nail depth: ♀ 6.9-8.1, ♂ 7.6-8.5 (*cf.* Fig. 198, p. 261).

Hybrids reported—None.

References—Ainley et al. (1994), Bent (1922), Bourne et al. (1988), Bull et al. (2005), Everett (1988), Jehl (1982), Keitt et al. (2000), Kuroda (1954), Loomis (1918), Murphy (1952), W.R.P. Bourne *in* Palmer (1962).

AUDUBON'S SHEARWATER
Puffinus lherminieri

AUSH
Species # 0920
Band size: 3A-3B

Species—From most other petrels and shearwaters by small size (Table 26, p. 265; see **Geographic variation**); bill slender (Fig. 198, p. 261) and grayish (or washed yellowish in HYs) with a blackish culmen; tarsus laterally compressed in cross-section (*vs* petrels); upperparts uniformly blackish brown to dusky brown; inner webs to outer pp (p7-p10) uniformly grayish; underparts white with dusky-brownish wash to flanks and underwing covs; undertail covs mostly dark brownish (Fig. 204**C**-**F**, p. 272); legs and feet dusky pinkish with blackish toes. From Manx Shearwater (p. 271) by smaller size except for tail length (Table 26); upperparts browner; base of bill without white band; undertail covs partly to entirely dusky brown (Fig. 204**C**-**F**; see **Age**). See Manx and Black-vented shearwaters for separation from other extralimital species.

Geographic variation—Considered monotypic here, following (in part) the species and subspecies recommendations of Austin et al. (2004); see also Blake (1977), Murphy (1927), W.R.P. Bourne *in* Palmer (1962), Wetmore (1959, 1965). Populations of Caribbean Is off Panama ("*P.l. loyemilleri*") average smaller than other populations but this difference appears insufficient for subspecies recognition. Other populations throughout the Pacific and Indian Oceans, formerly considered subspecies of Audubon's Shearwater, are considered separate species (Austin et al. 2004), along with the much smaller *P. boydi* and *P. baroli* (wg chord 163 190, tl 67-84, exp culmen 23-28, tarsus 35-39) of the e.Atlantic.

Molt—SBS (CBS?). PF absent(?), PB2 incomplete-complete (Apr?-Oct? in SYs), DPB incomplete-complete (Jun-Dec in breeding ASY/ATYs); PA absent. See pp. 248-252 and Table 24 (p. 249). The DPBs usually involve most to all feathers but are occasionally incomplete, with 1-6 ss and rarely other feathers (including rects) retained (Figs. 188**C**-**D** & 189**C**-**D**, p. 250).

Age—Juv (B1; Jun-May) is described below under HY/SY; Juv ♀ = ♂. Note that confirmed-breeding adults (including ♀♀ with distended cloacae) can be reliably aged ATY.

Juv-HY/SY (1st cycle, Juv/B1; Oct-Sep): Back feathers (Fig. 187**A**, p. 248), pp and ss (Figs. 188**A** & Fig. 189**A**, p. 250), and rects (Fig. 190**A**, p. 251) uniform in wear, narrower, and more tapered or rounded, the pp and ss probably molting in Apr-Oct (Table 24, p. 249); longest axillar averages narrower and more rounded (Fig. 191**A**, p. 251), perhaps averaging more dark near tip (*cf.* Fig. 206**A**, p. 273); lower mandible tinged yellowish through Oct-Dec; claws sharp (Fig. 192**A**, p. 252); filoplumes (*cf.* Fig. 193, p. 252) absent.

AHY/ASY (Def. cycle, DB; Dec-Nov): Back feathers (Fig. 187**B**), pp and ss (Figs. 188**B** & 189**B**, **D**), and rects (Fig. 190**B**) broader, squarer, and often showing molt clines and contrasts, the pp and ss usually molting in Jun-Dec (Table 24); longest axillar averages broader and squarer (Fig. 191**B**), perhaps averaging less dark near tip (*cf.* Fig. 206**B**); lower mandible grayish; claws often dull (Fig. 192**B**-**C**); filoplumes (Fig. 193) often present. **Note: See SY/TY and ATY; Most AHY/ASYs show these characters (resulting from a complete DPB).**

SY/TY (2nd cycle, B2; Nov-Oct): Like AHY/ASY but ss with 1-6 retained, worn, and narrow juv feathers among s3-s4 and/or s9-s14 (*cf.* Fig. 188**C**); back (Fig. 187**B**-**C**), s covs, and/or rects

(Fig. 190**B-C**) sometimes with contrastingly worn and narrow, retained juv feathers. **Note: Only a small proportion of AHYs appear to have incomplete DPBs and can be identified as SY/TYs or ASY/ATYs.**

ATY (Def. cycle, DB; Jan-Dec): Like AHY/ASY but 1-5 basic ss among s3-s12 retained, square, and not contrasting markedly with adjacent feathers (*cf.* Fig. 188**D**); back (Fig. 187**D**), s covs, and/or rects (Fig. 190**D**) sometimes with retained basic feathers, squarer, contrasting less with newer feathers. **Note: See SY/TY.**

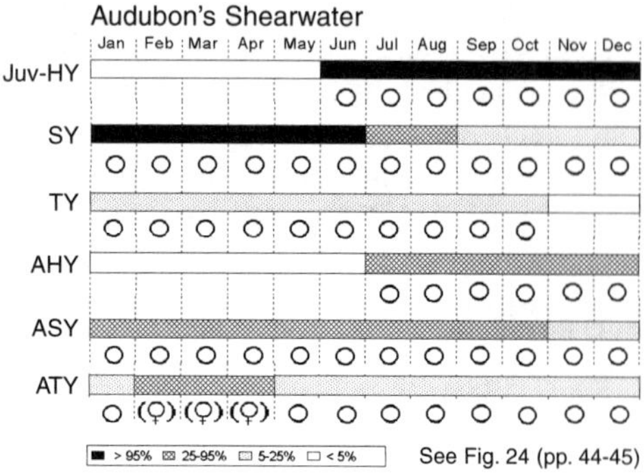

Audubon's Shearwater

Jan Feb Mar Apr May Jun Jul Aug Sep Oct Nov Dec

Juv-HY

SY

TY

AHY

ASY

ATY

■ > 95% ▨ 25-95% □ 5-25% □ < 5%

See Fig. 24 (pp. 44-45)

Sex—♀=♂ by plumage aspect. Medial BP (Fig. 20**A,** p. 31) developed by both sexes but distended cloaca (Fig. 21, p. 32; Serventy 1956) in Feb-Apr indicates ATY ♀. Most measurements unhelpful for sexing (Table 26, p. 265) including maximum nail depth: ♀ 5.4-6.7, ♂ 5.9-7.2 (*cf.* Fig. 198, p. 261).

Hybrids reported—None. See McCarthy (2006) regarding Audubon's and Little shearwaters.

References—Bent (1922), Bretagnolle et al. (2000), Bull et al. (2005), Kuroda (1954), Loomis (1918), Murphy (1927, 1936), Oberholser (1974), W.R.P. Bourne *in* Palmer (1962), Wetmore (1959).

STORM-PETRELS *HYDROBATIDAE*

Seven North American species. Family characters include small size, somewhat rounded wings, hooked bills with prominent tubenares separated by septa and opened distally, and webbed feet with vestigial rear toes and strong claws for digging. North American storm-petrels have 10 functional primaries (p10 extending 3-15 mm short of p9, when fully-grown), 14 secondaries (including 3 tertials and one absent between s4 and s5; *cf* Fig. 12**B**, p. 19), and 12 rectrices. Ageing through the first cycle (to SY and ASY) and occasionally the second cycle (to TY and ATY) can be accomplished through plumage aspect, molt patterns, presence or absence of filoplumes (Plant 1989), and claw condition. Sexes are alike in plumage aspect and most measurements; in many species, females average slightly longer wings and tarsi but slightly shorter and shallower bills than males. Both sexes develop medial brood patches (Fig. 20**A**, p. 31) but breeding females can be recognized during the incubation period by distended cloacae (Fig. 21, p. 32; Boersma & Davies 1987, Copestake et al. 1988, Huntington et al. 1996); other cloacal characters (Figs. 22-23, pp. 32-35) should be further investigated. Brooke (2004), Harrison (1983a, 1987), and Naveen (1981, 1982a, 1982b, 1982c) provide overviews of species determination in this group.

In molting, storm-petrels are reported to undergo a Simple Basic Strategy (SBS; Fig. 10**A**, pp. 13-16), lacking a formative plumage and lacking alternate plumages in all molt cycles. However, preformative molts may occur in some species, especially those (e.g., Wilson's Storm-Petrel, p. 277) that cross the equator to productive feeding grounds during their first six months of life. Least Storm-Petrel (p. 288) may also have a complete inserted preformative molt during the first cycle (and thus exhibit the Complex Basic Strategy; CBS, Fig. 10**B**) but more study is needed. One storm-petrel (Fork-tailed, p. 279) regularly retains secondaries during prebasic molts; otherwise, these molts are typically complete. Molt of the rectrices often begins with the outer pair. See pp. 248-252 for a detailed account of the sequence and timing of molt, by age and breeding status, in Procellariiformes including storm-petrels.

WILSON'S STORM-PETREL
Oceanites oceanicus

WISP
Species # 1090
Band size: 1A-1B

Species—From other storm-petrels by medium-small size but longer legs (Table 27, p. 284; see **Geographic variation**); tarsus >> foot with claws; plumage aspect blackish brown with pale upperwing ulnar bar; uppertail covs short, white, and with white shafts, and tail unforked (Fig. 210**A**, p. 281; Table 27); undertail covs with extensive white; outer rect with little or no white at base (< 25 mm when present); underwing gr and med covs silvery, contrasting somewhat with darker underwing les and p covs (Fig. 213**A**, p. 285); webs of feet pale, often yellowish.

European Storm-Petrel (*Hydrobates pelagicus*), a visitor to ne.N.Am, is much smaller with shorter tarsus (wg chord 114-127, tl 47-62, exp culmen 9.8-11.8, tarsus 20.1-23.8); upperwing ulnar bar less distinct; underwing covs with distinct white feathering (*vs* silvery in Wilson's; *cf.* Fig. 213**A**); webs of feet dark.

Geographic variation—See Beck & Brown (1972), Blake (1977), Bourne (1964), Copestake & Croxall (1985), Flood and Thomas (2007), Marchant & Higgins (1990), Murphy (1918, 1936, 1960), Murphy & Snyder (1952), W.R.P. Bourne *in* Palmer (1962), Roberts (1940), Spear & Ainley (2007). One other subspecies (*O.o. chilensis*) breeds in sw.S.Am and may occur in Pacific N.Am waters but this has yet to be confirmed.

O.o oceanicus (br Antarctica and surrounding Is, disperses to N.Am waters): Larger than *chilensis* breeding in sw.S.Am (Table 27, p. 284); plumage aspect may average blacker (*vs* browner in *chilensis*). Breeding populations of Is off Antarctica ("*exasperatus*") may average smaller but differences insufficient for subspecific recognition.

Molt—CBS (SBS?). PF complete? (Jul-Dec? in HYs), PB2 complete (Mar?-Sep? in SYs), DPB complete (Apr-Sep in breeding ASYs); PA absent. See pp. 248-252 and Table 24 (p. 249). It appears that a complete molt occurs in the n.Hemisphere or in equatorial regions in HYs during the first 6-8 months of life, which is provisionally considered a PF (see also Least Storm-Petrel, p. 288), but might also be considered a PB2 that has been advanced forward; more study needed. Non-breeding individuals in the s.Hemisphere may be in molt at any time of year.

Age—Juv (B1; Mar-Aug) is described below under HY/SY; Juv ♀=♂. The following assumes that HYs have a complete molt during their first 6-8 months of life (see **Molt**); it is possible that HY/SYs can be identified through the second spring, summer, or fall by molt patterns or wear but more study is needed. Note that confirmed-breeding adults (including ♀♀ with distended cloacae) can be reliably aged ATY. In addition to the following some HY/SYs may show whiter bases to feathers of the lores but this appears to be uncommon and/or unreliable.

Juv-HY (1st cycle, Juv/B1; Apr-Nov): S1-p1 contrast absent (Fig. 188**A**, p. 250); outer pp average narrower near tip (Fig. 189**A**); outer rects narrow, rounded, and worn (Fig. 207**A**); claws sharp (Fig. 192**A**, p. 252); filoplumes (*cf.* Fig. 193, p. 252) absent. **Note: White fringes to abdomen feathers and wider and whiter tips to the gr covs and terts, appear to reflect feather freshness, rather than age of the bird as has been reported. See AHY/ASY.**

U/AHY (Def. cycle, DB; Oct-Sep): S1-p1 contrast present (Fig. 188**B**); outer pp average broader near tip (Fig. 189**B**); outer rects broad, truncate, and fresh (Fig. 207**B**); claws often dull (Fig. 192**B-C**); filoplumes (Fig. 193) sometimes present. **Note: Characteristics related to timing of molt (e.g. individuals completing molt in May-Jun) possibly may be used for more reliable ageing but more study needed.**

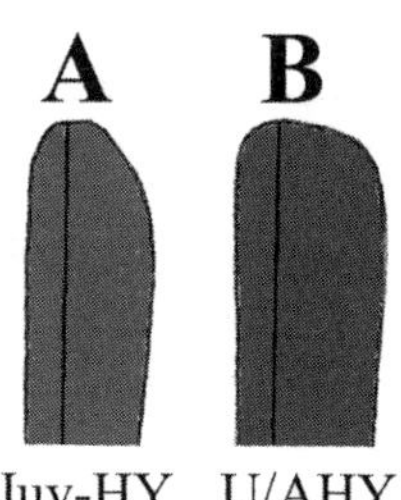

FIGURE 207. Shape of the outer rectrices by age in Wilson's Storm-Petrel. Note that age designations assume a complete molt in HYs; see **Molt**.

Sex—♀=♂ by plumage aspect. Medial BP (Fig. 20**A,** p. 31) developed by both sexes but distended cloaca (p. 32; > 5 mm, Copestake et al. 1988) in Dec-Feb indicates ATY ♀. Measurements are generally unhelpful for sexing (Table 27, p. 284). See Copestake & Croxall (1985) for a DFA (p. 5), based on live individuals, using flat wing length (Fig. 3**B**, p. 6) culmen, and tarsus, that separated 85-94% of the sexes of a South Georgia I breeding population (*O.o. oceanicus*). It is doubtful that individuals in N.Am can be reliably sexed by such analyses due to unknown source populations and variation in size among breeding populations (see **Geographic variation**).

Wilson's Storm-Petrel

Jan Feb Mar Apr May Jun Jul Aug Sep Oct Nov Dec

Juv-HY ?

U

AHY

ASY ♀

ATY ♀ ♀

■ > 95% ▨ 25-95% □ 5-25% □ < 5%

See Fig. 24 (pp. 44-45)

Hybrids reported—None.

References—Ainley et al. (1994), Beck (1970), Beck & Brown (1972), Bent (1922), Copestake & Croxall (1985), Copestake et al. (1988), Cramp & Simmons (1977), Flood and Thomas (2007), Harrison (1983b), Huber (1971), Marchant & Higgins (1990), Murphy (1918, 1936), Oberholser (1974), W.R.P. Bourne *in* Palmer (1962), Roberts (1940), Watson (1975).

FORK-TAILED STORM-PETREL
Oceanodroma furcata

FTSP
Species # 1050
Band size: 1B

Species—From all other storm-petrels by medium to large size with longer and more forked tail by age (Table 27, p. 284; Fig. 208); plumage aspect pale bluish gray to grayish with blackish to dusky les covs and underwing covs; uppertail covs without white.

Geographic variation—See Boersma & Silva (2001), Grinnell & Test (1939), W.R.P. Bourne *in* Palmer (1962). No other subspecies recognized.

O.f. furcata (br Aleutian Is-sc.AK, wint primarily in nw.Pacific): Larger (Table 27, p. 284); plumage aspect medium-pale bluish gray; throat whitish, distinctly paler than breast; gr covs edged white to whitish when fresh.

O.f. plumbea (br se.AK-nw.CA, wint primarily in ne.Pacific): Smaller (Table 27); plumage aspect medium-dark grayish; throat pale grayish, blending with breast; gr covs edged grayish when fresh.

Molt—SBS (CBS?). PF absent(?), PB2 incomplete-complete (May-Oct in SYs), DPB incomplete-complete (Jul-Dec in breeding ASYs); PA absent. See pp 248-252 and Table 24 (p. 249). During DPBs, 1-5 ss among s4-s9 are retained in most (~90-95%) AHYs (*cf.* Fig. 209, p. 280). More study is needed on the proportion of AHYs that can have a complete PB2 and DPB; it is unlikely that breeding adults have complete PBs whereas pre-breeders (ages 2-4 or more years) and failed breeders may be more likely to undergo complete feather replacement. Look for a limited PF to occur in Aug-Oct in some HYs.

Age—Juv (B1; Aug-Jul) is described below under HY/SY; Juv ♀ = ♂. Note that confirmed-breeding adults (including ♀♀ with distended cloacae) can be reliably aged ATY.

Juv-HY/SY (1st cycle, Juv/B1; Nov-Oct): Outer rects rounded and tail fork shallower (Fig. 208**A-B**); ss uniform in wear, without s1-p1 contrast (Figs. 188**A**, p. 250, & 209**A**, p. 280); outer pp average narrower near tip and more worn in Feb-Oct (Fig. 189**A**); replacement of pp usually May-Oct (Table 24, p. 249); feathers of lower abdomen usually with subtle, narrow pale fringes, wearing off or becoming difficult to see in Feb-Oct; claws sharp (Fig. 192**A**, p. 252).

AHY/ASY (Def. cycle, DB; Nov-Oct): Outer rects pointed and tail fork deeper (Fig. 208**C-D**); ss showing s1-p1 contrast but otherwise uniform in wear (Figs. 188**B** & Fig. 209**A**); outer pp average broader near tip and fresher in Feb-Oct (Fig. 189**B**); replacement of pp often Jul-Dec (Table 24); feathers of lower abdomen without narrow pale fringes; claws often dull (Fig. 192**B-C**); filoplumes (Fig. 193) sometimes present. **Note: See SY/TY and ASY/ATY. Only a**

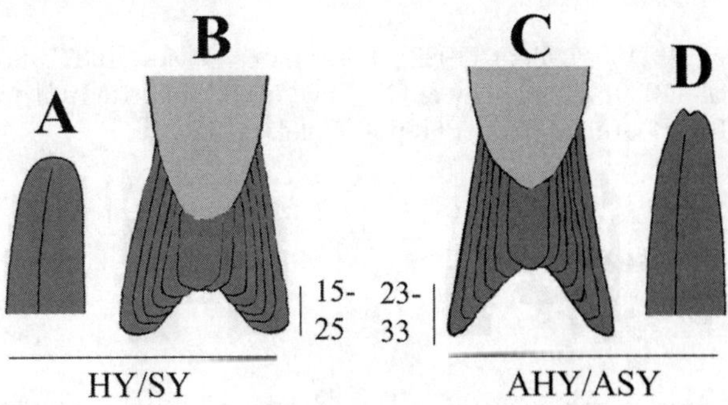

FIGURE 208. Outer rect (r6) shape and tail fork (*cf.* Fig. 6, p. 9) by age in Fork-tailed Storm-Petrel. The measure refers to r1 – r6.

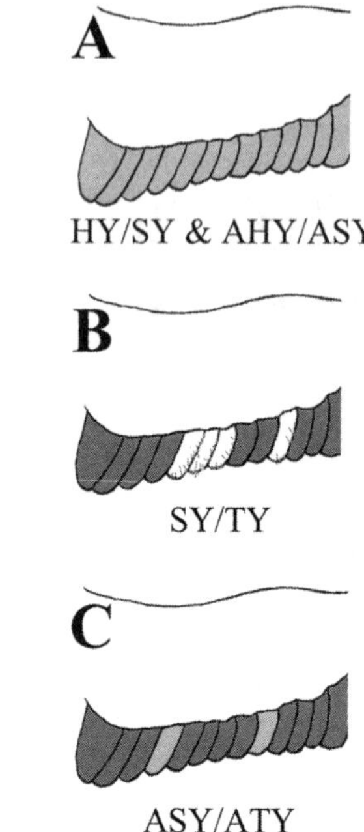

FIGURE 209. Patterns of secondary retention in Fork-tailed Storm-Petrel by age. HY/SYs and occasional AHY/ASYs exhibit uniform ss (**A**) and need to be separated by other characters. Most AHY/ASYs (~90%) retain ss and can be identified as SY/TYs (**B**) with retained juv ss, typically among s3-s4 and s7-s10 (here s4 and s7-s9) or ASY/ATYs (**C**) with retained basic ss, not necessarily the same feathers as in SY/TYs (here s5 and s10). Retained juv feathers are contrastingly, narrow, brownish, and worn whereas retained basic feathers contrast less in shape and wear.

small proportion of individuals may show characters indicating AHY/ASY (resulting from a complete DPB; see Molt).

SY/TY (2nd cycle, B2; Dec-Nov): Like AHY/ASY but 1-5 juv ss retained among s4 and consecutively among s6-s9, brown, contrasting distinctly with adjacent replaced feathers (Fig. 209**B**); replacement of pp usually Jul-Nov (Table 24).

ATY (Def. cycle, DB; Jan-Dec): Like AHY/ASY but 1-3 basic ss retained among s4-s9, grayish brown, contrasting only moderately with adjacent replaced feathers (Fig. 209**C**); replacement of pp often Aug-Dec (Table 24).

Fork-tailed Storm-Petrel
Jan Feb Mar Apr May Jun Jul Aug Sep Oct Nov Dec
Juv-HY
SY
TY
AHY
ASY
ATY
(♀) (♀) (♀)
■ > 95% ▨ 25-95% ▭ 5-25% □ < 5%
See Fig. 24 (pp. 44-45)

Sex—♀=♂ by plumage aspect. Medial BP (Fig. 20**A,** p. 31) developed by both sexes but distended cloaca (p. 32; width > 5 mm, length > 7 mm, or length + width > 11.5 mm, Boersma & Davies 1987) in May-Jul indicates ATY ♀. Measurements generally unhelpful for sexing (Table 27, p. 284) and no other criteria known.

Hybrids reported—None.

References—Ainley et al. (1994), Bent (1922), Boersma & Davies (1987), Boersma & Silva (2001), Boersma et al. (1980), Dement'ev & Gladkov (1951a), Harris (1974), Loomis (1918), Osborne (1985), W.R.P. Bourne *in* Palmer (1962), Willett (1912).

LEACH'S STORM-PETREL

Oceanodroma leucorhoa

LESP
Species # 1060
Band size: 1B

Species—From other storm-petrels by medium size with longer bill and shorter legs (Table 27, p. 284; see **Geographic variation**); tarsus < foot with claws; plumage aspect dark brownish with pale brown upperwing ulnar bar; tail moderately forked and uppertail covs moderately long and with variable white coloration (and dark shafts) present in most individuals (Fig. 210**D-G** &

212**A**, p. 285: see **Geographic variation**); outer rect with little or no white at base (< 25 mm when present); undertail covs with little or no white; underwing gr and med covs dark brown, not contrasting with underwing les and p covs (Fig. 213**B**, p. 285); webs of feet black. Wedge-rumped Storm-Petrel (*O. tethys*), an occasional visitor to sw.N.Am, is smaller except for tarsal length (wg chord 117-139, tl 54-64, exp culmen 11.3-14.0, depth distal to tubenares 2.9-3.6, tarsus 20.6-24.2); tarsus > feet with claws; white uppertail covs longer and tail fork shallower (Fig. 210**C**). See Wilson's Storm-Petrel (p. 277) for separation from European Storm-Petrel.

Pacific forms of Leach's with dark uppertail covs (primarily *O.l. chapmani*; see **Geographic variation**) from Ashy (p. 283), Black (p. 287), and Least (p. 288) storm-petrels by medium-small size with long bill and shorter legs (Table 27); plumage aspect brownish with pale-brown upperwing ulnar bar; underwing gr and med covs dark brown, not contrasting with underwing les covs (Fig. 213**B**); tail moderately forked (Table 27; Fig. 212**A**, p. 285). Swinhoe's Storm-Petrel (*O. monorhis*), a possible visitor to e.N.Am and sw.AK has long wings (similar to nominate Atlantic but > Pacific dark forms) but shorter tail and bill (wg chord 147-165, tl 66-81, exp culmen 13.5-15.5); uppertail covs dark (*vs* white in Atlantic Leach's); pale shafts to the pp average more extensive (often extending beyond p covs but some Leach's can show overlap in the amount of pale); more study is needed.

Geographic variation—See Ainley (1980, 1983), Anthony (1898), Austin (1952), Bourne & Jehl (1982), Bourne & Simmons (1997), Bretagnolle et al. (1991), Browning (1990), Crossin (1974), Emerson (1906), Grinnell (1928), Hubbs (1960), Huey (1930), Huntington et al. (1996), Jehl & Everett (1985), Loomis (1918), Oberholser (1917a), W.R.P. Bourne *in* Palmer (1962), Patten et al. (2003), Power & Ainley (1986), Slud (1979), Townsend (1890), van Rossem (1942a), von Berlepsch (1906), Willett (1915). No other subspecies occur.

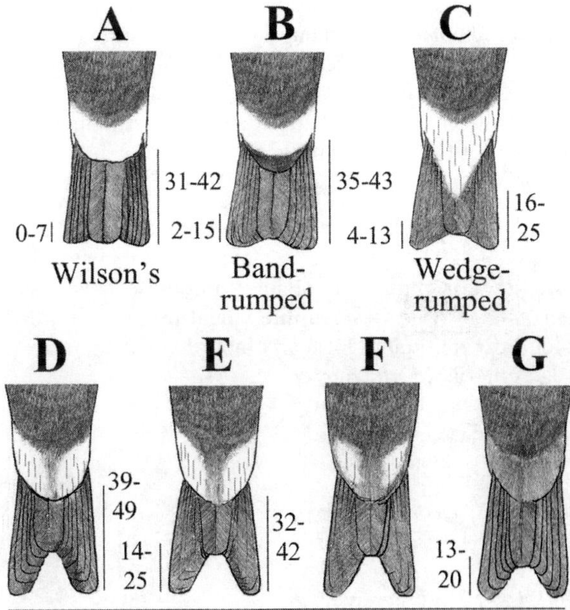

FIGURE 210. Tails and rumps by storm-petrels for specific and subspecific identification. Measures include tail fork (r1 – r6; *cf.* Fig. 6, p. 9) to left of each illustrations and distance from tip of white uppertail-covert feathering to tip of tail to the right of illustration. The former measure is longer in nominate Leach's Storm-Petrels (*O.l. leucorhoa*; *cf.* **D**) than in the other subspecies (*cf.* **G**) whereas the latter measure is smaller in *O.l. soccoroensis* (and possibly *cheimomnestes*; *cf.* **E**) than the other subspecies. Note that the shaft streaks on the uppertail coverts are white in Wilson's (**A**) and Band-rumped (**B**) storm-petrels but dark to partially dark in Wedge-rumped (**C** and Leach's (**D-G**) storm-petrels.

O.l leucorhoa (br AK-c.CA & n.Atlantic Is, wint throughout Pacific and Atlantic ranges): Averages larger (Table 27, p. 284); uppertail covs with extensive white (Fig. 210**D**, p. 281) in >95% of individuals, with intermediate amount of white (Fig. 210**B-C**) in some individuals of c-s.CA, the distance from the white to the tail tip larger (*cf.* Fig. 210**D**); tail fork deeper (Table 27, *cf.* Fig. 210**E**). Populations breeding in the n.Pacific (*"beali"* of w-s.AK) and (*"beldingi"* of se.AK-nw.CA) average slightly smaller than Atlantic populations and with more dark in the uppertail covs (especially *"beldingi"*) but differences insufficient and broadly clinal.

O.l. chapmani (br San Benito-Coronado Is, c-n.Baja CA; wint to c.CA): Averages medium-small (Table 27); uppertail covs dark (Fig. 210**G**) in most (~95%) individuals, intermediate (Fig. 210**F**) in some (~5%); tail fork shallower (Table 27, Fig. 210**G**). Populations of the Coronado Is (*"willetti"*) average grayer and with paler aspect to the uppertail covs than those of the San Benito Is, but differences insufficient for subspecific recognition.

O.l. soccoroensis (=*"kaedingi"*; br. Guadalupe I, Mex, May-Sep; wint to s.CA): Averages smaller (Table 27); uppertail covs with variable amount of white (Fig. 210**D-G**, most frequently **D** and **F**), the distance between the white and the tail tip shorter (*cf.* Fig. 210**E**); tail fork shallower (Table 27, *cf.* Fig. 210**G**). See also **Molt** and *O.l. cheimomnestes*.

O.l. cheimomnestes (br. Guadalupe I, Mex, Oct-Apr; non-breeding range to s.CA): Averages medium-small (Table 27); uppertail covs with intermediate to extensive amount of white (Fig. 210**D-E**); tail fork shallower (Table 27, *cf.* Fig. 210**G**). See also **Molt**; it is possible that the timing of molt by age could help distinguish Guadalupe I subspecies.

Molt—SBS (CBS?). Timing complicated by variable breeding seasons (see Table 24, p. 249). For nominate and most other subspecies: PF absent(?), PB2 complete (May-Dec in SYs), DPB complete (Jul-Apr in breeding ASY/ATYs); PA absent. See pp. 248-252 and Table 24. Molt of rects is usually complete by Dec but pp molt can extend through spring. The timing of (breeding and) molt in Pacific populations averages 1-2 months earlier, by age, than in Atlantic populations. Timing of molt also varies by subspecies in the Pacific, with pp replacement of *soccoroensis* and *chapmani* extending later in the spring than that of *leucorhoa* (Crossin 1974). For *O.l. cheimomnestes*, which breeds Oct-Apr on Guadalupe I, Mex, the PB2 may occur in Dec-Jun and the DPB in Feb-Nov but more study is needed. Also, the annual cycle and molt of individuals breeding in the s.Hemisphere (*c.f.* Imber & Lovegrove 1982) might be opposite to that of n.Hemisphere breeders. Look for a limited PF to occur in Aug-Oct in some HYs (see p. 288).

Age—Juv (B1; Jul-Jun) is described below under HY/SY; Juv ♀=♂. See Haussmann and Mauck (2008) and Haussmann et al. (2003) for ageing by telomere fragments on chromosomes. The timing for the following criteria applies to nominate and most other Leach's Storm-Petrels. Criteria for *O.l. cheimomnestes* (see **Geographic variation**), which breeds in Oct-Apr, are likely similar except for different timings for molt (Table 24, p. 249), relative wear of feathers, and thus timing of age criteria. More study needed. Note that confirmed-breeding adults (including ♀♀ with distended cloacae) can be reliably aged ATY.

Juv-HY/SY (1st cycle, Juv/B1; Dec-Nov): S1-p1 contrast absent (Fig. 188**A**, p. 250); outer pp average narrower near tip and worn in Mar-Nov (Fig. 189**A**, p. 250); outer rects average narrower and more tapered and worn in Mar-Nov (Fig. 211**A-B**); replacement of pp usually May-Dec (Table 24); claws sharp (Fig. 192**A**, p. 252); filoplumes absent (cf. Fig. 193, p. 252). **Note: Beware of winter-breeding *O.l. cheimomnestes*,**

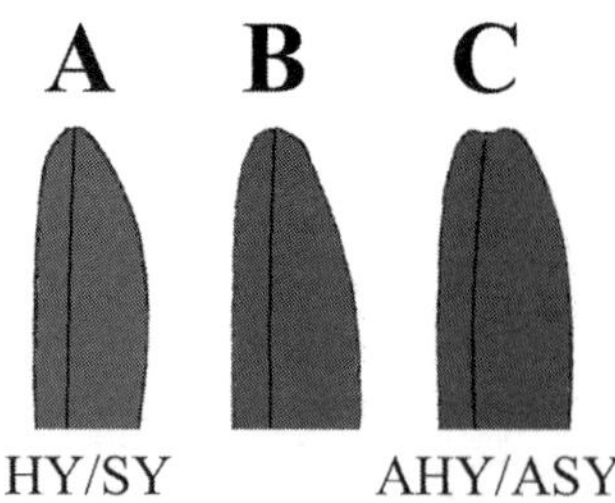

FIGURE 211. Rectrix shape in Leach's and Ashy storm-petrels by age. Differences between juv rects (**A**) and basic rects (**C**) can be subtle, and some intermediates (**B**) cannot be reliably aged.

which likely show differing molt strategies (see Table 24) and, thus, seasonal timing for age classification. Wider and whiter tips to the gr covs and terts appear to reflect feather freshness, rather than age of the bird as has been reported. Intermediates occur that can be difficult to age. See AHY/ASY.

AHY/ASY (Def. cycle, DB; Dec-Nov): S1-p1 contrast present (Fig. 188**B**); outer pp average broader near tip and fresh in Mar-Nov (Fig. 189**B**); outer rects average broader and fresher in Mar-Nov (Fig. 211**B-C**); replacement of pp often Jul-Apr (Table 24); claws often dull (Fig. 192**B-C**); filoplumes (Fig. 193) sometimes present. **Note: See Juv-HY/SY. Look for occasional AHYs to retain ss and possibly be aged SY/TY or ASY/ATY (see Fig. 209, p. 280).**

ASY/ATY (Def. cycle, DB; Dec-Mar): Like AHY/ASY but pp being replaced and outer pp broad at tip (Fig. 189**B**).

Sex—♀=♂ by plumage aspect. Medial BP (Fig. 20**A**, p. 31) developed by both sexes but distended cloaca (p. 31, > 4.5 mm, Huntington et al. 1996) in Apr-Jul (Nov-Dec in *O.l. cheimomnestes*) indicates ATY ♀. Measurements unhelpful for sexing (Table 27, p. 284) and no other criteria known.

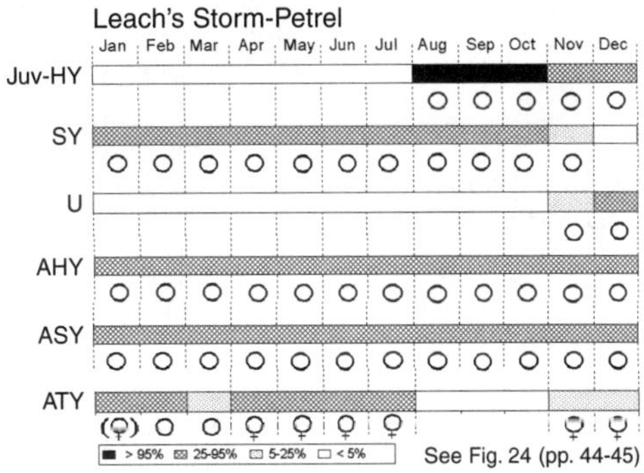

Leach's Storm-Petrel
Jan Feb Mar Apr May Jun Jul Aug Sep Oct Nov Dec
Juv-HY
SY
U
AHY
ASY
ATY
> 95% 25-95% 5-25% < 5%
See Fig. 24 (pp. 44-45)

Hybrids reported—None.

References—Ainley (2005), Ainley et al. (1974, 1976, 1994), Austin (1952), Baker (1993), Bent (1922), Bourne & Simmons (1997), Cramp & Simmons (1977), Crossin (1974), Dement'ev & Gladkov (1951a), Flood and Thomas (2007), Harris (1974), Harrison (1983b), Huey (1930), Lee (1984), Loomis (1918), Marchant & Higgins (1990), Murphy (1936), Oberholser (1917a), W.R.P. Bourne *in* Palmer (1962).

ASHY STORM-PETREL
Oceanodroma homochroa

ASSP
Species # 1080
Band size: 1B

Species—From other storm-petrels including dark-morph Leach's (p. 280) by medium size with moderately long tail and short legs (Table 27, p. 284); tarsus ≈ foot with claws; plumage aspect dark grayish to grayish brown with paler gray to whitish upperwing ulnar bar; uppertail covs without white and tail deeply forked (Fig. 212**B**, p. 285; Table 27); underwing gr and med covs silvery to whitish, contrasting with darker underwing les and p covs (Fig. 213**A**, p. 285).

Geographic variation—Monotypic.

Molt—SBS (CBS?). PF absent(?), PB2 complete (May-Nov in SYs), DPB complete (Jul-Mar in breeding ASY/ATYs); PA absent. See pp. 248-252 and Table 24 (p. 249). Look for a limited PF to occur in Aug-Nov in some HYs (see p. 288).

Age—Juv (B1; Aug-Jul) is described below under HY/SY; Juv ♀=♂. Note that confirmed-breeding adults (including ♀♀ with distended cloacae) can be reliably aged ATY.

Juv-HY/SY (1st cycle, Juv/B1; Nov-Oct): S1-p1 contrast absent (Fig. 188**A**, p. 250); outer pp average narrower near tip and worn in Mar-Oct (Fig. 189**A**, p. 250); outer rects average nar-

TABLE 27. Measurements (mm) of storm-petrels occurring in North America to assist in identification. See pp. 4-11 for methods of measurement. Species summaries are in **bold** and subspecies summaries in ***italics***. Values were derived from 95% confidence intervals as based (for wing, tail, exposed culmen, and tarsus) approximately on the indicated sample sizes (see pp. 4-5); sample sizes for bill depth and tail fork were often smaller but included at least 10 of each sex. Thus, midpoints of ranges approximate means, and S.D. is approximated by 25% of the range.

Taxon/Sex	*n*	wing chord	tail length	exp culmen	bill depth[1]	tarsus	tail fork (r6r1)[2]
Wilson's Storm-Petrel[3]		**132-162**	**58-76**	**10.4-13.5**	**3.8-4.7**	**33-38**	**0-7**
O.o. oceanicus		***143-162***	***63-76***	***11.8-13.5***	***4.1-4.7***	***33-38***	---
♀	100	145-162	63-74	11.8-13.3	---	34-38	---
♂	100	143-158	65-76	12.0-13.5	---	33-37	---
O.o. chilensis		***132-148***	***56-66***	***10.4-12.2***	***3.8-4.4***	***32-37***	---
♀	10	132-145	68-66	10.4-12.2	---	34-37	---
♂	10	135-148	56-64	10.6-12.0	---	33-36	---
Fork-tailed Storm-Petrel		**144-167**	**79-100**	**13.9-16.5**	**4.6-5.4**	**24-29**	**15-33**
O.f. furcata		***150-167***	***82-100***	***14.0-16.5***	***4.8-5.4***	***26-29***	***19-33***
♀	30	153-167	85-100	14.0-16.0	---	26-29	---
♂	30	150-163	82-96	14.3-16.5	---	26-28	---
O.f. plumbea		***144-159***	***74-96***	***13.9-16.0***	***4.6-5.2***	***24-27***	***15-28***
♀	30	147-159	83-96	13.9-15.7	---	25-27	---
♂	30	144-156	79-93	14.1-16.0	---	24-27	---
Leach's Storm-Petrel		**140-169**	**69-93**	**13.4-17.6**	**3.7-5.2**	**19-26**	**11-25**
O.l leucorhoa		***139-169***	***72-93***	***13.6-17.3***	***4.0-5.2***	***22-26***	***18-25***
♀	100	141-169	75-93	13.6-17.0	---	22-26	---
♂	100	139-166	72-90	13.9-17.3	---	21-25	---
O.l. chapmani		***140-154***	***74-84***	***13.9-16.4***	***3.8-4.4***	***20-24***	***13-20***
♀	70	143-154	75-84	14.1-16.5	---	20-24	---
♂	75	140-152	74-82	14.0-16.4	---	20-23	---
O.l. soccoroensis		***131-153***	***67-80***	***13.0-15.4***	***3.7-4.2***	***19-22***	***11-18***
♀	100	134-153	68-80	13.0-15.4	---	19-23	---
♂	100	131-150	67-79	13.0-15.4	---	19-22	---
O.l. cheimomnestes		***140-152***	***71-81***	***13.7-15.9***	***3.8-4.3***	***21-24***	***13-20***
♀	30	142-152	73-84	13.9-15.9	---	21-24	---
♂	32	140-150	71-81	13.7-15.7	---	21-23	---
Ashy Storm-Petrel		**132-148**	**72-84**	**13.1-15.2**	**3.7-4.3**	**21-25**	**17-27**
♀	68	135-148	74-84	13.1-15.1	---	21-25	---
♂	87	132-145	72-82	13.2-15.2	---	21-25	---
Band-rumped Storm-Petrel		**143-165**	**62-81**	**13.4-16.0**	**4.1-5.1**	**21-25**	**2-15 2**
♀	78	147-165	64-81	13.5-15.8	---	22-25	---
♂	75	143-161	62-78	13.4-16.0	---	21-25	---
Black Storm-Petrel		**163-181**	**77-94**	**14.0-16.3**	**5.2-5.9**	**29-34**	**20-33**
♀	100	165-181	79-94	14.0-16.0	---	29-34	---
♂	100	163-179	77-93	14.2-16.3	---	29-34	---
Least Storm-Petrel		**113-129**	**50-58**	**10.5-11.8**	**3.2-3.7**	**20-22**	**-7to-13**
♀	30	116-129	52-58	10.5-11.8	---	20-22	---
♂	30	113-126	50-56	10.6-11.7	---	20-22	---

[1] Bill depth taken distal to tubenares (*cf.* Fig. 194, p. 253).

[2] Tail fork length (see Figs. 210, p. 281, & 212, p. 285) varies by age in some species

[3] Measures for both subspecies are shown due to the possibility that *O.o. chilensis* occurs in Pacific N.Am waters.

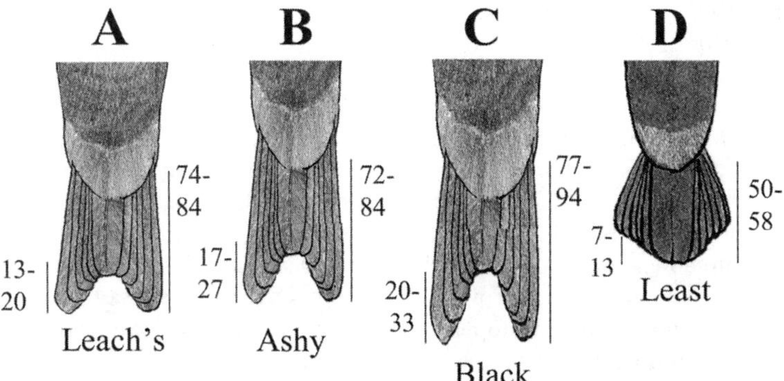

FIGURE 212. Size and degree of tail fork (*cf.* Fig. 6, p. 9) in dark Leach's (primarily *O.l. chapmani*; **A**), Ashy (**B**), Black (**C**), and Least (**D**) storm-petrels for identification. Measures represent tail fork (r1 – r6) to left (r6 – r1 in Least Storm-Petrel) and tail length to right.

row and more tapered and worn in Mar-Oct (Fig. 211**A**-**B**, p. 282); replacement of pp usually May-Nov (Table 24, p. 249); claws sharp (Fig. 192**A**, p. 252); filoplumes absent (cf. Fig. 193, p. 252). **Note: Intermediates occur that can be difficult to age. See AHY/ASY.**

AHY/ASY (Def. cycle, DB; Dec-Nov): S1-p1 contrast present (Fig. 188**B**); outer pp average broader near tip and fresh in Mar-Oct (Fig. 189**B**); outer rects average more rounded and fresh in Mar-Oct (Fig. 211**B**-**C**); replacement of pp often Jul-Mar (Table 24); claws often dull (Fig. 192**B**-**C**); filoplumes (Fig. 193) sometimes present. **Note: See Juv-HY/SY. Look for occasional AHYs to retain ss and possibly be aged SY/TY or ASY/ATY (see Fig. 209, p. 280).**

Sex—♀=♂ by plumage aspect. Medial BP (Fig. 20**A,** p. 31) developed by both sexes in Apr-Jul but distended cloaca (Fig. 21, p. 32; Serventy 1956) in Apr-Jun indicates ATY ♀ in Apr-Jun. Measurements unhelpful for sexing (Table 27) and no other criteria known.

Hybrids reported—None.

References—Ainley (1995, 2005), Ainley et al. (1974, 1976, 1994), Bent (1922), Crossin (1974), Loomis (1918), W.R.P. Bourne *in* Palmer (1962).

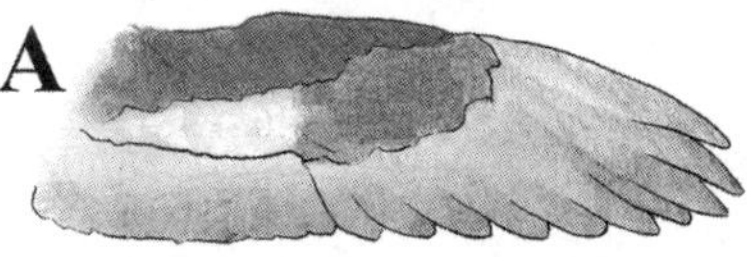

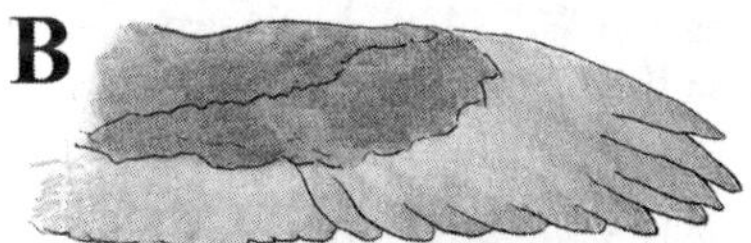

FIGURE 213. Pattern to the underwing covs in storm-petrel by species, showing silvery underwing med and gr covs of Ashy Storm-Petrel and (less distinctly) in Wilson's Storm-Petrel contrasting with darker underwing les and p covs (**A**); in the other N.Am species the underwing covs are more uniformly dark (**B**). European Storm-Petrel shows whiter underwing med and gr covs than are shown in **A**.

Ashy Storm-Petrel

Jan Feb Mar Apr May Jun Jul Aug Sep Oct Nov Dec

Juv-HY

SY

U

AHY

ASY

ATY

■ > 95% ▨ 25-95% ▫ 5-25% □ < 5%

See Fig. 24 (pp. 44-45)

BAND-RUMPED STORM-PETREL

Oceanodroma castro

BSTP
Species # 1062
Band size: 2

Species—From other storm-petrels by medium size (Table 27, p. 284; see **Geographic variation**); plumage aspect dark brown with pale grayish-brown upperwing ulnar bar; uppertail covs moderately long and white (including shafts) with distinct dark tips (forming band) and tail slightly forked (Fig. 210**B**, p. 281; Table 27; see **Age**); outer rect with white > 25 mm at base; undertail covs with a moderate amount of white; underwing gr and med covs dark brown, not contrasting with underwing les and p covs (Fig. 213**B**, p. 285); webs of feet black. See Wilson's Storm-Petrel for separation from European Storm-Petrel, and Leach's Storm-Petrel for separation from Wedge-rumped Storm-Petrel.

Geographic variation—Treated as monotypic here following C. Jouanin & J.-L. Mougin *in* Mayr & Cottrell (1979) but recent work suggests 3-4 different taxa may be recognized based on biochemical evidence, timing and behavior of breeding and, perhaps, average dimensions (Monteiro & Furness 1998, Friesen et al. 1998, Bolton 2007). Molt timing may help distinguish adults of populations that breed in different seasons but variable timing of pre-breeding birds (*cf.* Table 24, p. 249) may make this difficult. Historically, various subspecies have been named, but morphological differences appear to be insufficient and/or confounded by substantial individual variation to diagnose subspecies at this time. For more information, suggested trinomials, and/or reported differences in measurements from various populations see Austin (1952), Cramp & Simmons (1977), Crossin (1974), Harris (1969), Loomis (1918), Mathews (1934, 1938), Monteiro et al. (1996), Murphy (1936), Nichols (1914), Robertson & James (1988).

Molt—SBS (CBS?). Timing complicated by variable breeding seasons, both winter-breeding and summer-breeding populations occurring at Atlantic-breeding colonies (e.g., see Harris 1969, Monteiro & Furness 1998, Friesen et al. 1998, Bolton 2007). Most individuals off e.N.Am appear to originate from winter-breeding populations (Table 24, p. 249) and molt as follows: PF absent(?), PB2 complete (Dec-Jul in SYs), DPB complete (Feb-Sep in breeding ASYs); PA absent. Summer-breeding individuals (including both Atlantic and Pacific populations, the former probably occurring in N.Am waters at least occasionally) may molt on a schedule more similar to that of Leach's Storm-Petrel (Crossin 1974). See pp. 248-252 and Table 24 (p. 249). Nonbreeding individuals may be in molt at any time of year and look for a limited PF in HY/SYs within the first six months after fledging (see p. 288).

Age—Juv (B1; Feb-Jan) is described below under HY/SY; Juv ♀ = ♂. The timing for the following criteria applies to winter-breeding populations including those that appear to occur most frequently in e.N.Am waters. Note that confirmed-breeding adults (including ♀♀ with distended cloacae) can be reliably aged ASY/ATY.

Juv-HY/SY (1st cycle, Juv/B1; Aug-Jul): S1-p1 contrast absent (Fig. 188**A**, p. 250); outer pp average narrower near tip and worn in Oct-Jul (Fig. 189**A**, p. 250); outer rects average narrower and more rounded and worn in Oct-Jul (Fig. 211**A-B**, p. 282); tail fork averages shallower (r6-r1 3-10 mm); replacement of pp usually Jan-Jul (Table 24, p. 249); claws sharp (Fig. 192**A**, p. 252); filoplumes absent (cf. Fig. 193, p. 252). **Note: Beware of individuals from summer-breeding populations, which likely show differing molt strategies (see Molt) and, thus, seasonal timing for age classification. Intermediates occur that can be difficult to age.**

AHY/ASY (Def. cycle, DB; Sep-Aug): S1-p1 contrast present (Fig. 188**B**); outer pp average broader near tip and fresh in Oct-Jul (Fig. 189**B**); outer rects average broader and more truncate and fresh in Oct-Jul (Fig. 211**B-C**); tail fork averages deeper (r6-r1 6-15 mm); replacement of pp usually Feb-Sep (Table 24); claws often dull (Fig. 192**B-C**); filoplumes (Fig. 193) sometimes present. **Note: See Juv-HY/SY. Look for occasional AHYs to retain ss and possibly be aged SY/TY or ASY/ATY (see Fig. 209, p. 280).**

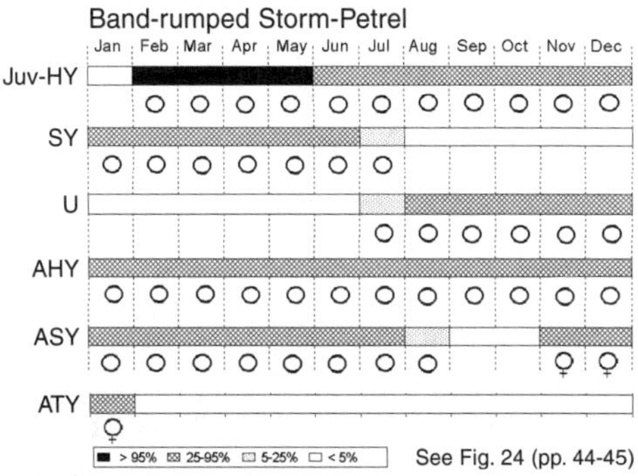

Sex— ♀ = ♂ by plumage aspect. Medial BP (Fig. 20**A,** p. 31) developed by both sexes but distended cloaca (Fig. 21, p. 32; Serventy 1956) indicates ASY/ATY ♀ in Nov-Jan. Measurements appear unhelpful for sexing (Table 27, p. 284) and no other criteria known.

Band-rumped Storm-Petrel

Jan Feb Mar Apr May Jun Jul Aug Sep Oct Nov Dec

Juv-HY

SY

U

AHY

ASY

ATY

■ > 95% ▨ 25-95% ▫ 5-25% □ < 5%

See Fig. 24 (pp. 44-45)

Hybrids reported—None.

References—Ainley et al. (1994), Allan (1962), Austin (1952), Bent (1922), Crossin (1974), Cramp & Simmons (1977), Flood and Thomas (2007), Harris (1969), Harrison (1983b), Lee (1984), Loomis (1918), Monteiro et al. (1996), Murphy (1936), W.R.P. Bourne *in* Palmer (1962), Robertson & James (1988), Slotterback (2002), Woolfenden et al. (2001).

BLACK STORM-PETREL

Oceanodroma melania

BLSP
Species # 1070
Band size: 1A

Species—From other storm-petrels by large size (Table 27, p. 284); tarsus ≈ foot with claws, plumage aspect brownish black with brownish-gray upperwing ulnar bar; uppertail covs without white, tail fork deep, and outer rect tapered (Figs. 212**C**, p. 285, & 214, p. 288; Table 27); underwing gr and med covs dark brown, not contrasting with underwing les and p covs (Fig. 213**B**, p. 285). Markham's Storm-Petrel (*O. markhami*), a possible visitor to w.N.Am, has a longer tail (wg chord 164-181, tl 85-111), longer but shallower bill (exp culmen 16.7-19.0, depth distal to tubenares 4.6-5.3), and much shorter legs (tarsus 22.9-25.0, shorter than middle toe with claw *vs* longer in Black); plumage aspect averages browner with paler and more extensive upperwing ulnar bar; uppertail covs with gray bases (*vs* entirely blackish in Black Storm-Petrel), and tail more deeply forked (r6 – r1 27-37). Tristram's Storm-Petrel (*O. tristrami*), a vagrant to w.N.Am, is larger (wg chord 182-192, tail 92-114, exp culmen 16.8-19.5) but with a shorter tarsus (26.6-30.4); tarsus < foot with claws; legs thick and grayish (*vs* thin and black in Black Storm-Petrel); p10 shorter (p9 – p10 12-18 and p10 usually < p7, *vs* p9 – p10 7-9 mm and p10 > p7 in Black Storm-Petrel); plumage aspect ashy when fresh, wearing to brown (except head) when worn.

Geographic variation—Monotypic.

Molt—SBS (CBS?). PF absent(?), PB2 complete (Mar?-Nov? in SYs), DPB complete (Oct-Mar in breeding ASY/ATYs); PA absent. See pp 248-252 and Table 24 (p. 249).. Most molting appears to occur in the Humboldt Current off S.Am. Look for a limited PF to occur in some HY/SYs in Nov-Jan (see p. 288).

Age—Juv (B1; Sep-Aug) is described below under HY/SY; Juv ♀ = ♂. Note that confirmed-breeding adults (including ♀♀ with distended cloacae) can be reliably aged ATY.

Juv-HY/SY (1st cycle, Juv/B1; Dec-Nov): S1-p1 contrast absent (Fig. 188**A**, p. 250); outer pp average narrower near tip and worn in Mar-Sep (Fig. 189**A**, p. 250); outer rects narrow and tapered (Fig. 214**A**), and worn in Mar-Sep; replacement of pp usually Jul-Dec (Table 24, p.

249); claws sharp (Fig. 192**A**, p. 252); filoplumes absent (cf. Fig. 193, p. 252). Some intermediates occur that are difficult to age. See also AHY/ASY.

AHY/ASY (Def. cycle, DB; Oct-Sep): S1-p1 contrast present (Fig. 188**B**); outer pp average broader near tip and fresher in Mar-Dec (Fig. 189**B**); outer rects broad and truncate (Fig. 214**B**), and fresh in Mar-Dec; replacement of pp usually Aug-Mar (Table 24); claws often dull (Fig. 192**B-C**); filoplumes (Fig. 193) sometimes present. **Note: See Juv-HY/SY. Look for occasional AHYs to retain ss and be reliably aged SY/TY or ASY/ATY (see Fig. 209, p. 280).**

ASY/ATY (Def. cycle, DB; Oct-Mar): Like AHY/ASY but pp being replaced and outer pp broad near tip (Fig. 189**B**).

Sex—♀ = ♂ by plumage aspect. Medial BP (Fig. 20**A,** p. 31) developed by both sexes but distended cloaca (Fig. 21, p. 32; Serventy 1956) in May-Jul indicates ATY ♀. Measurements unhelpful for sexing (Table 27, p. 284) and no other criteria known.

A B

HY/SY AHY/ASY

FIGURE 214. Shape of the outer rectrix (r6) by age in Black Storm-Petrel.

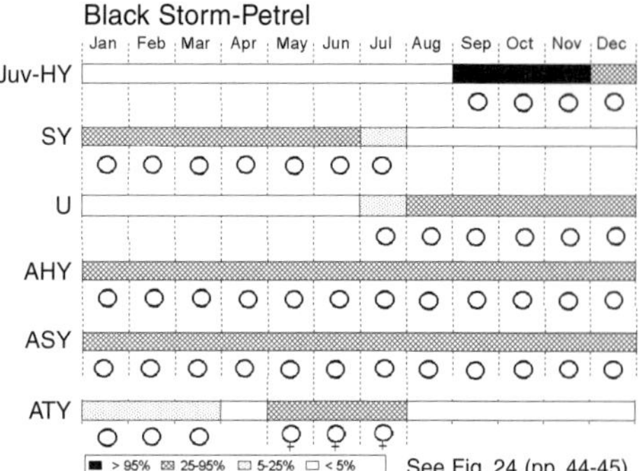

Hybrids reported—None.

References—Ainley (2005), Ainley & Everett (2001), Ainley et al. (1994), Austin (1952), Bent (1922), Loomis (1918), Murphy (1936), W.R.P. Bourne *in* Palmer (1962).

LEAST STORM-PETREL
Oceanodroma microsoma

LSTP
Species # 1030
Band size: 1B

Species—From other storm-petrels by small size (Table 27, p. 284); plumage aspect brownish black with brownish-gray upperwing ulnar bar; uppertail covs without white and tail wedge-shaped (Fig. 212**D**, 285; Table 27); underwing gr and med covs dark brown, not contrasting with underwing les and p covs (Fig. 213**B**, p. 285).

Geographic variation—Monotypic.

Molt—CBS (SBS?). PF absent-complete? (Mar?-Aug? in HYs), PB2 complete (Aug?-Jan? in HY/SYs); DPB complete (Dec-Apr in breeding AHY/ASYs); PA absent. Molts in this species are confusing and may indicate populations breeding at different times or the possible presence of a complete PF in some HYs. Molting periods appear to occur in both Mar-Aug and in Aug-Jan. See also Wilson's Storm-Petrel (p. 277). It is possible that other storm-petrels may have PFs, although a complete PF may be more likely in some Least Storm-Petrels due to small size and the need to replace feathers more frequently with increased solar exposure. See pp. 248-252 and Table 24 (p. 249) for more information on molt in Procellariiformes.

Age—Juv (B1; Sep-Dec) is described below under Juv-HY/SY; Juv ♀=♂. The following assumes a complete PF as described above; it is possible that AHYs can be aged through SY/TY and ASY/ATY, as in other storm-petrels, but more study is needed. Note that confirmed-breeding adults (including ♀♀ with distended cloacae) can be reliably aged ATY.

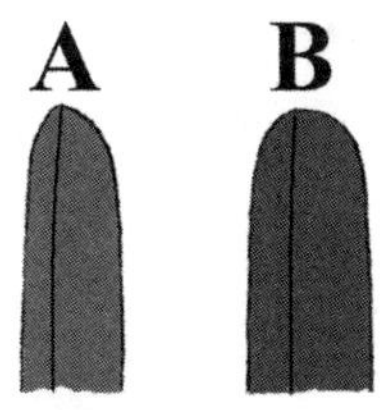

FIGURE 215. Shape of the outer rectrix (r6) by age in Least Storm-Petrel.

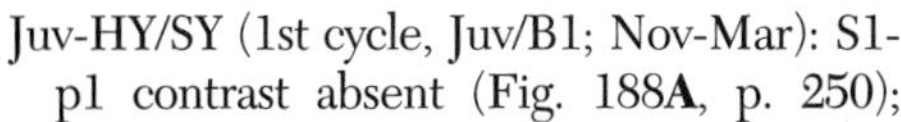

Juv-HY/SY (1st cycle, Juv/B1; Nov-Mar): S1-p1 contrast absent (Fig. 188**A**, p. 250); outer pp average narrower near tip (Fig. 189**B**, p. 250); outer rects narrower and more rounded (Fig. 215**A**); replacement of pp usually Nov-Mar (Table 24, p. 249); claws sharp (Fig. 192**A**, p. 252); filoplumes absent (cf. Fig. 193, p. 252). **Note: Some intermediates occur that are difficult to age. See also AHY/ASY.**

AHY/ASY (Def. cycle, DB; May-Apr): S1-p1 contrast present (Fig. 188**B**); outer pp average broader near tip (Fig. 189**B**); outer rects broad and truncate (Fig. 215**B**); replacement of pp often Nov-Apr (Table 24); claws often dull (Fig. 192**B-C**); filoplumes (Fig. 193) sometimes present. **Note: See HY/SY.**

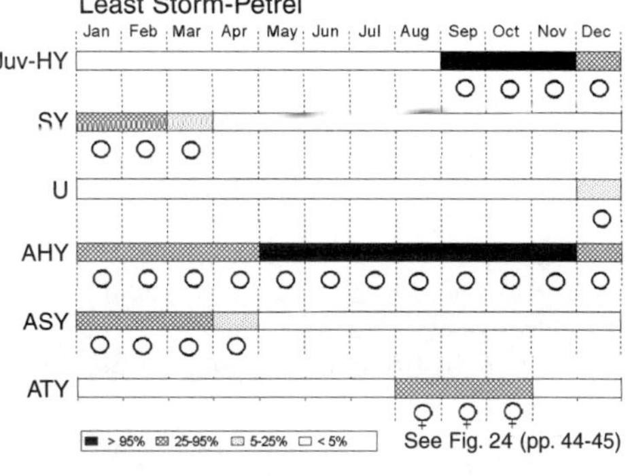

Sex—♀=♂ by plumage aspect. Medial BP (Fig. 20**A**, p. 31) developed by both sexes but distended cloaca (Fig. 21, p. 32; Serventy 1956) indicates ATY ♀ in Aug-Oct. Measurements unhelpful for sexing (Table 27, p. 284) and no other criteria known.

Hybrids reported—None.

References—Ainley & Everett (2001), Ainley et al. (1994), Bent (1922), Loomis (1918), Murphy (1936), W.R.P. Bourne *in* Palmer (1962).

TROPICBIRDS *PHAETHONTIDAE*

Three species. Family characters include medium-large, elongated bodies, moderately long and pointed wings, strong and slightly decurved bills (*cf.* Fig. 218, p. 291, & Fig. 224, p. 297) with serrated tomia, greatly elongated central rectrices in adults, and weak, posteriorly located legs and feet with webbing between all four toes. Tropicbirds have 10 functional primaries (p10 longest by 0-10 mm when fully grown), 14-18 secondaries (including 3-4 tertials and one absent between s4 and s5; *cf.* Fig. 12**B**, p. 19), and 12-14 (occasionally 16) rectrices. Ageing through the third (to TY and ATY) or fourth (to 4Y and A4Y) cycle can be accomplished through plumage aspect, length of

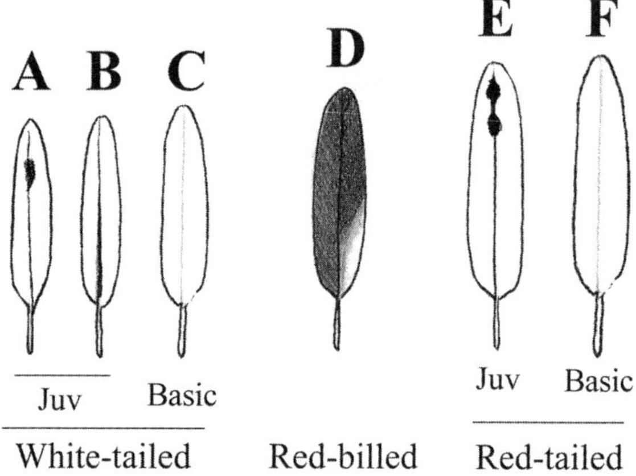

FIGURE 216. The 8th primary covert (third from outside, including the reduced 10th covert) by species and age in tropicbirds. This cov in Juv White-tailed and Red-tailed tropicbirds can be white with a black shaft (**B**) or sometimes have 1-2 spots (**A, E**), *vs* white with a white shaft in basic covs (**C, F**). Juv and definitive covs are similar in Red-billed Tropicbird.

the central rectrices, molt patterns among primaries, and bill color. Sexes are alike in plumage aspect and size, males averaging slightly larger than females; brood patches are not developed (eggs tucked into feathered abdomens) but distended cloacae (Fig. 21, p. 32) indicate breeding females; other cloacal features (Figs. 22-23, pp. 32-35) should be investigated.

Molt patterns in tropicbirds are complicated by year-round breeding cycles that can be < 1 year in many (but not all) populations, resulting in year-round molting patterns among individuals over time (Gould et al. 1974). Tropicbirds exhibit the Complex Basic Strategy (CBS; Fig. 10**B**, pp. 13-16), including a formative plumage but lacking alternate plumages. Replacement of primaries and secondaries exhibits staffelmauser (Fig. 16, pp. 23-24; Pyle 2006a). The second prebasic molt often includes 6-7 inner primaries and up to 3 or 4

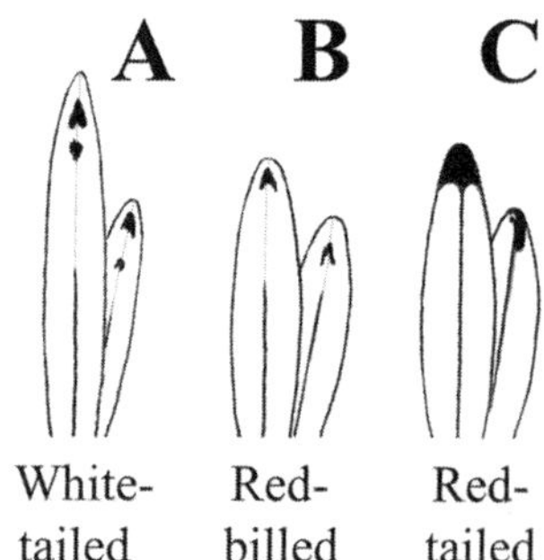

FIGURE 217. Juv central rectrices (r1-r2) by species in tropicbirds. In addition to usually having two black marks at the tip (**A**), the juv central rects of White-tailed Tropicbird are longer than in the other two species. Red-billed Tropicbird has black subterminal marks (**B**) whereas Red-tailed Tropicbird shows black tips (**C**). The pattern to the remaining juv rects (r3-r6, r7, or r8) generally resemble that of the juv r2.

sets of pp can be found in ATY/A4Ys (Fig. 16**F-G**), at least of Red-tailed Tropicbird (p. 296). Secondaries are replaced proximally from s1 and s5 and distally from the tertials, such that the last feathers replaced are among s9-s11 in White-tailed Tropicbird (with 14 secondaries) to s11-s14 in Red-tailed Tropicbird (with 17-18 secondaries). Rectrices appear to be replaced both distally and proximally on each side, with r3-r4 the last feathers replaced, although variation may occur; e.g., the central rectrices appear to be replaced alternately in adults, several months apart (see **Molt** under Red-tailed Tropicbird). Age of first breeding is presumably 3-4 years; prebasic molts of S-TYs and non-breeding ASYs average earlier in timing italicsthan those of breeding adults (see p. 18). Molt and predefinitive plumages are usually only encountered at sea and much needs to be learned about each.

WHITE-TAILED TROPICBIRD

Phaethon lepturus

WTTR
Species # 1120
Band size: 4-3A-3B-3

Species—From other tropicbirds by smaller size (especially bill) but longer tail excluding r1 (Table 28, p. 296); bill olive and black (Juv) to bright yellowish (Fig. 220, p. 292); outer p covs white or sometimes with small black spots in Juv-HY/SY (Fig. 216**A-C**); outer pp (p8-p10) with extensive black on outer webs by subspecies and age (Fig. 218); Juv-HYs with abbreviated dusky eyeline (Fig. 220**A**), r1 relatively long and with two spots (Fig. 217**A**), and back feathers with fewer black chevrons (Fig. 219); AHYs with back mostly white to white, terts, med covs, and larger les covs black or tipped black (*cf.* Fig. 221**B-E**), and r1 with white webs distally.

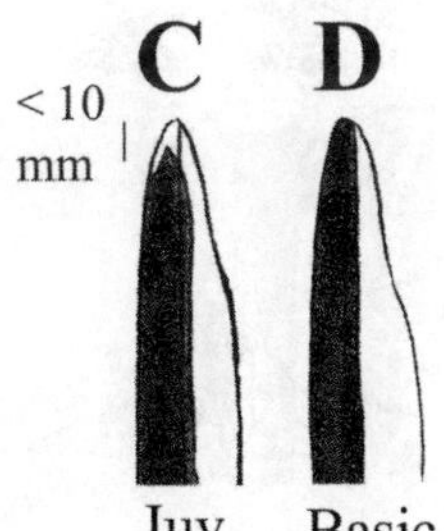

FIGURE 218. P8 by subspecies and age in White-tailed Tropicbird. In both subspecies the black stripe usually extends ≥ 4 mm onto the inner web in juv feathers (Juv-HY/SYs and some TYs, **A** & **C**) *vs* < 4 mm on basic feathers (AHY/ASYs, **B** and **C**).

Geographic variation—See Blake (1977), Hellmayr & Conover (1948a), Le Corre & Jouvetin (1999), Lee & Walsh-McGehee (1998), Mathews (1915), Oberholser (1919a), Olson (1974), M.A. Traylor *in* Palmer (1962). Four other subspecies breed in the s.Atlantic and Indian oceans.

P.l. dorotheae (br & wint c-s.Pacific, vagrant to CA & AZ): Smallest of all subspecies (Table 28, p. 296); p8 with less-extensive black by age (Fig. 218**A-B**) and p6 with less-extensive black (> 50 mm from tip, if present); Juv-HYs with broader black barring to back (Fig. 219**A**); AHYs with bill greenish yellow.

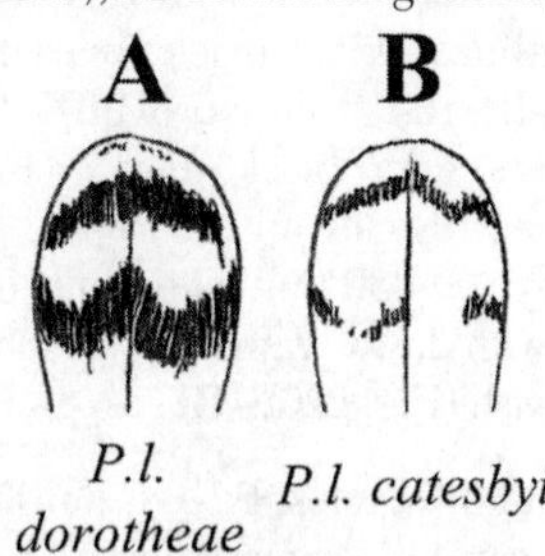

FIGURE 219. Juvenal back feathers in White-tailed Tropicbird by subspecies. Some Juvs of each subspecies can show one bar but most show two.

P.l. catesbyi (br Caribbean, visitor NS-FL): Largest of all subspecies (Table 28); p8 with more-extensive black by age (Fig. 218**C-D**) and p6 with more-extensive black (within 50 mm of tip); Juv-HYs with sparser black barring to back (Fig. 220**B**); AHYs with bill orangish yellow. *P.l. asenscionis* of s.Atlantic, a possible visitor to se.N.Am, is smaller (wg chord 248-280, tl excluding r1 95-116, exp culmen 41-53, tarsus 19.1-23.5), has pattern to the outer pp like *dorotheae* (Fig. 218**A-B**), and has AHYs with bill greenish yellow to yellow.

Molt—CBS (SBS?). Molt patterns little studied and complicated (see Family Account, pp. 290-291). Molts appear as follows: PF limited-partial? (5-8 months after hatching), PB2 incomplete (9-18 months after hatching), DPB incomplete-complete (requiring 4-6 months during non-breeding periods); PA absent. N.populations breed primarily in Mar-Sep and molt primarily in Aug-Feb. The PF may include some to most of the body feathers and some to most s covs, but no terts or rects. During DPBs, replacement of pp and ss exhibits staffelmauser (Fig. 16, pp. 23-24, resulting in 2-4 sets of pp in adults. The PB2 appears to include 6-7 inner pp and most to all ss and rects. The central rects appear to molt alternately in adult; see Red-tailed Tropicbird (p. 296).

Age—Juv (B1; Jun-Nov) is similar to Juv-HY/SY (below); Juv ♀ = ♂. The following month ranges assume a n.breeding cycle; use caution in assigning age codes within tropical populations, where breeding can occur year-round (base age assignments on molting information; see **Molt**). Note that confirmed-breeding adults can be reliably aged ATY.

Juv-HY/SY (1st cycle, Juv/B1-F1; Sep-Aug): Back with extensive black markings (Figs. 219, p. 291, & 221**A**); terts white with variable black barring (Fig. 221**A**); pp uniformly juv (Fig. 16**A**, p. 24) or inner (up to p7) feathers being replaced, the outer pp juv, with reduced black by subspecies (Fig. 218**A** & **C**, p. 291), and the outer p covs white with white to dusky shaft and sometimes with black markings (Fig. 216**A-B**, p. 290); r1 short and all to some rects marked with black (Fig. 217**A**, p. 290); bill olive, washed dusky, and tipped black (Fig. 220**A**).

SY/TY (2nd cycle, B2; Sep-Aug): Back with moderate black markings and terts black with white fringing (Fig. 221**B-C**); pp and p covs with 2 generations (Fig. 16**B**), the outer pp juv, worn, with reduced black by subspecies (Fig. 218**A** & **C**), and the outer p covs white, often with dusky shaft, and sometimes with black markings (Fig. 216**A-B**); r2-r7 white or with 1-4 worn juv feathers with black marks (Fig. 217**A**) retained (usually among r3-r4); longest r1 usually 200-350 mm when fully grown; bill olive with dusky wash to lower mandible, to yellowish (Fig. 220**B-C**).

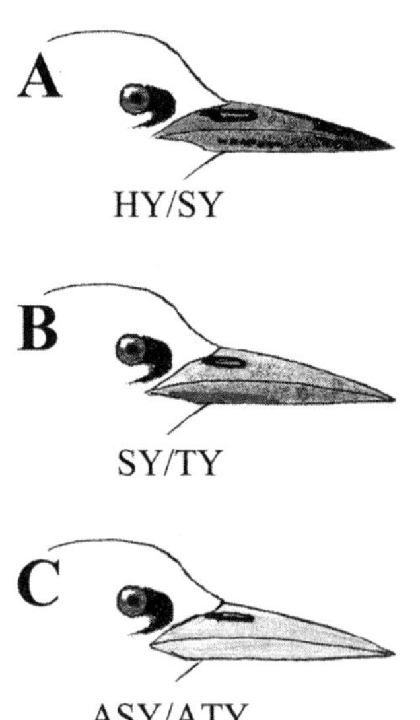

FIGURE 220. Bill color pattern by age in White-tailed Tropicbird. Note also that Juv-HY/SYs (**A**) tend to show a smaller black mark around the eye than in Juv-HY/SY Red-billed and Red-tailed tropicbirds (Fig. 225**A**, p. 297) and older White-tailed Tropicbirds (**B-C**).

T-4Y (2nd-4th cycles, B2-B4; Jan-Dec): Back with sparse black markings (Fig. 221**C-D**); pp with 2-3 sets of basic feathers in staffelmauser patterns (Fig. 16**E-F**), the outer pp with extensive black by subspecies (Fig.

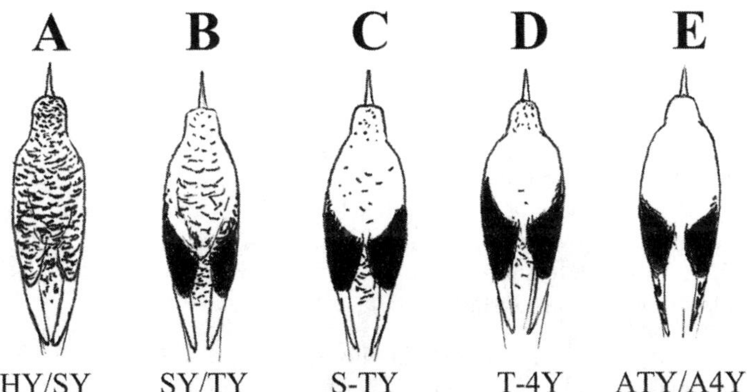

FIGURE 221. Variation in the amount of black in the back of White-tailed Tropicbirds by age. The amount of black shown here is intermediate between the two subspecies (*cf.* Figs. 218, p. 291, & 220); thus, *P.l. dorotheae* will show a bit more black and *catesbyi* a bit less black, by age, than what is shown. Note also that there may be individual as well as age-related variation; e.g., the most advanced SY/TYs may overlap the most retarded TY/4Ys in the amount of black, as shown in **C**. More study may reveal more precise age determinations based on this character.

218**B** & **D**) and the outer p covs white (Fig. 216**C**); , r2-r7 white; longest r1 usually 250-400 mm when fully grown; bill yellowish (Fig. 220**C**). **Note: Individuals with 3 sets of basic feathers (Fig. 16F) can be aged 4Y.**

ATY/A4Y (Def. cycle, DB; May-Apr): Back white (Fig. 221**E**), often tinged yellowish or pinkish; pp with 2-3 sets of basic feathers in staffelmauser patterns (Fig. 16**E**-**F**); longest r1 usually 400-550 mm or greater when fully grown; bill yellowish (Fig. 220**C**). **Note: AHYs showing these characters but with some barring to rump might be 4-5Ys and those with completely white backs and rumps might be A4Y/A5Ys, but more study is needed.**

Sex—♀=♂ by plumage aspect. BP not developed but distended cloaca (Fig. 21, p. 32) indicates ATY ♀ (primarily Mar-Aug in n.populations). Measurements unhelpful for sexing (Table 28, p. 296). ♂♂ appear to average a greater amount of pink or yellow plumage-aspect bloom (by age) and brighter and yellower bills than ♀♀, at least in some populations. It is possible that mated pairs (in direct comparison), at least, can be sexed using these criteria; more study needed.

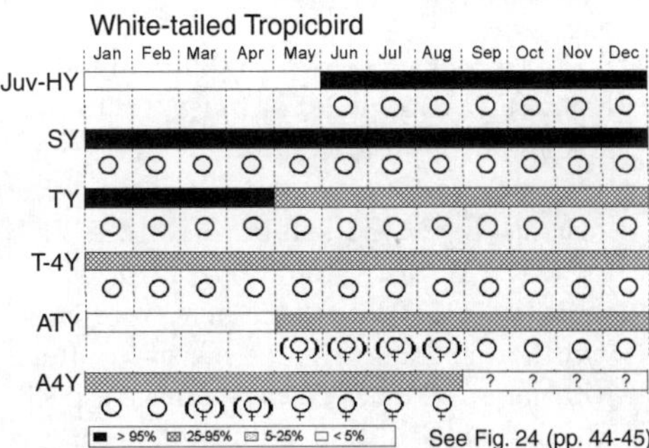

Hybrids reported—None.

References—Bent (1922), Chasen (1933), Diamond (1975), Gibson-Hill (1947), Howell & Webb (1995), Kinsky & Yaldwyn (1981), Lee & Walsh-McGehee (1998), Lee et al. (1981), Marchant & Higgins (1990), Murphy (1936), M.A. Traylor *in* Palmer (1962), Plath (1914), Spear & Ainley (2005), Stonehouse (1962), Stresemann & Stresemann (1966).

RED-BILLED TROPICBIRD
Phaethon aethereus

RBTR
Species # 1130
Band size: 4A

Species—From other tropicbirds by medium-large size (Table 28, p. 296); bill reddish (Juv) to bright red (*cf.* Fig. 225, p. 297); outer p covs mostly black (Fig. 216**D**, p. 290); outer pp (p8-p10) with extensive black on outer and inner webs by age (Fig. 222); Juv-HYs with extensive blackish eyeline, extending to or across nape (*cf.* Fig. 225**A**, p. 297), r1 short and with subterminal chevron (Fig. 217**B**, p. 290), and back feathers with more, and more distinct, black bars (Fig. 223**A**); AHYs with back feathers with fine black bars (Fig. 223**B**), terts and s covs primarily white, and r1 with white webs distally.

Geographic variation—See Blake (1977), Cramp & Simmons (1977), Hellmayr & Conover (1948a), Knox (1994), Murphy (1936), M.A. Traylor *in* Palmer (1962), Peters (1930a). Two other subspecies breed in the s.Atlantic and Indian oceans.

P.a. mesonauta (br & wint throughout n.Atlantic & Pacific ranges): Bill long (Table 28, p. 296; *vs* 50-62 in *indicus* of the Indian Ocean); outer p covs and pp primarily black (*vs* frosty grayish when fresh in *aethereus* of the s.Atlantic); dusky or blackish eyeline distinct and extending to or across nape (*vs* less distinct or lacking in *indicus*); bill entirely red (*vs* orangish with black stripe along tomium in *indicus*). Populations of Tower I., Galapagos ("*limatus*") are indistinguishable from other populations of *mesonauta*.

Molt—CBS (SBS?). Molts appear to be as follows: PF limited-partial? (5-8 months after hatching), PB2 incomplete (9-18 months after hatching), DPB incomplete-complete (requiring 4-6 months during non-breeding periods); PA absent. Molt strategies include staffelmauser (Fig. 16, pp. 23-24), and are similar to those of White-tailed Tropicbird (p. 292), as far as known.

Age—Juv (B1; Jun-Nov) has back feathers with broader dusky bars (Fig. 223**A**), central rects short with black subterminal chevrons (Fig. 217**B**, p. 290), and bill grayish to yellowish; Juv ♀ = ♂. The following month ranges pertain to individuals within boreal breeding cycles; use caution in assigning age codes within tropical populations, where breeding can occur year-round (base age assignments on molting information; see **Molt**). Note that confirmed-breeding adults can be reliably aged ATY.

HY/SY (1st cycle, F1; Sep-Aug): Pp uniformly juv (Fig. 16**A**, p. 24) or inner (up to p7) feathers being replaced, the outer pp juv, with more extensive black on inner web near tip (Fig. 222**A**); all to some rects juv, marked with black, the juv r1 (if present) short (Fig. 217**B**); back feathers and s covs with thicker bars (Fig. 223**A**); nape often with complete black collar; plumage aspect without pinkish tinge; bill yellowish to orangish (*cf.* Fig. 225**B**-**C**, p. 297).

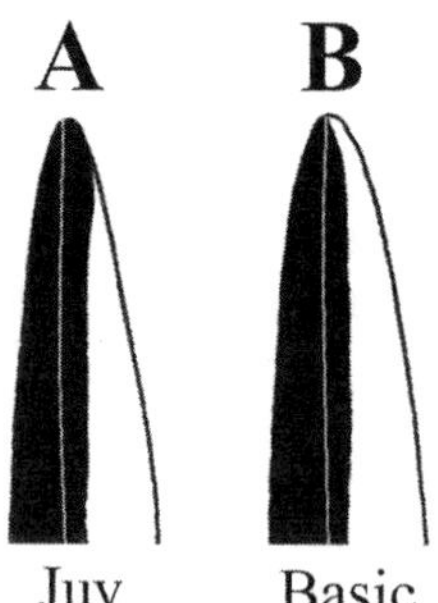

FIGURE 222. P8 by age in Red-billed Tropicbird. The juv p8 (present in Juv-HY/SYs and some TYs) averages more black extending onto the inner web near the tip (**A**) than basic feathers (**B**).

SY/TY (2nd cycle, B2; Sep-Aug): Pp with 2 generations (Fig. 16**B**), the outer p juv, worn, and averaging more extensive black on inner web near tip (Fig. 222**A**); rects without blackish markings or with 1-4 worn

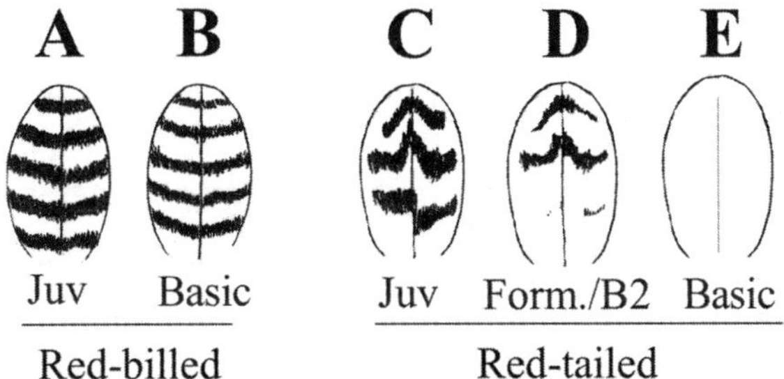

FIGURE 223. Back feathers and secondary coverts by age and species in Red-billed and Red-tailed tropicbirds. Red-billed Tropicbird typically shows 5-6 black bars on both juv (**A**) and basic feathers (**B**), with those of juv feathers averaging slightly thicker. Red-tailed Tropicbird shows fewer and less organized bars on juv feathers (**C**). It appears that formative and 2nd basic feathers on Red-tailed can show thinner bars (**D**), at least those replaced earlier during the PF and PB2 (typically among upper back feathers and les covs) whereas later-replaced feathers (e.g., among rump feathers and gr covs) can be entirely white (**E**).

juv feathers retained (usually among r3-r4), with black marks (Fig. 217**B**), the longest r1 usually 200-350 mm when fully grown; back feathers and s covs with thinner black bars (Fig. 223**B**); nape often with incomplete black collar; plumage aspect sometimes with pale pinkish tinge; bill orangish to orangish red.

ASY/ATY (Def. cycle, DB; May-Apr): Pp with 2 sets of basic feathers in staffelmauser patterns (Fig. 16**E**), the outer pp with less extensive black on inner web near tip (Fig. 222**B**); rects (except r1) without blackish markings, the longest r1 usually 400-550 mm or greater when fully grown; nape without black collar; plumage often tinged pinkish; bill red (*cf.* Fig. 225**D**).

ATY/A4Y (Def. cycle, DB; May-Apr): Like ASY/ATY but pp with 3 sets of basic pp (Fig. 16**F**).

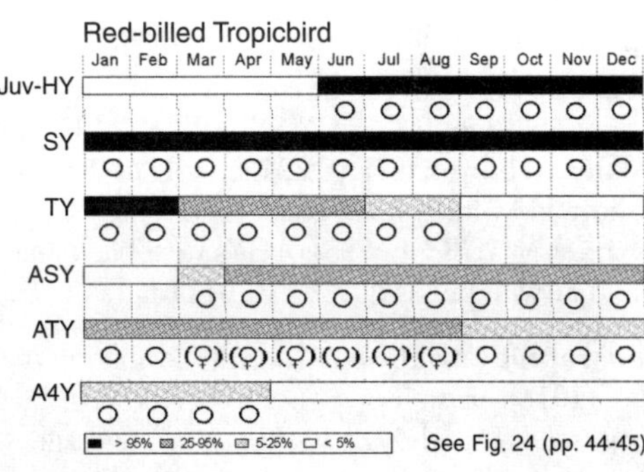

Sex—♀=♂ by plumage aspect. BP not developed but distended cloaca (Fig. 21, p. 32) indicates ATY ♀ (primarily Mar-Jul in N.Am). Measurements unhelpful for sexing (Table 28, p. 296). ATY ♂♂ may average pinker bloom than ATY ♀♀ but more study is needed. Otherwise, no criteria known.

Hybrids reported—None.

References—Ainley et al. (1994), Bent (1922), Gifford (1913), Howell & Webb (1995), Lee et al. (1981), Murphy (1924, 1936), M.A. Traylor *in* Palmer (1962), Spear & Ainley (2005), Stonehouse (1962).

TABLE 28. Measurements (mm) of North American tropicbirds to assist in identification and sexing. See pp. 4-11 for methods of measurement. Species summaries are in **bold** and subspecies summaries in ***italics***. Values were derived from 95% confidence intervals as based (for wing, tail, exposed culmen, and tarsus) approximately on the indicated sample sizes (see pp. 4-5); sample size for bill depth was often smaller but included at least 10 of each sex. Thus, midpoints of ranges approximate means, and S.D. is approximated by 25% of the range.

Taxon/Sex	*n*	wing chord	tail length[1]	exp culmen	bill depth[2]	tarsus
White-tailed Tropicbird[3]		**251-299**	**99-128**	**42-56**	**14.8-19.0**	**18-24**
P.l. dorotheae		***251-279***	***99-125***	***42-51***	***14.8-17.7***	***18-21***
♀	14	251-274	99-122	42-49	14.8-17.2	18-20
♂	15	254-279	102-125	43-51	15.3-17.7	19-21
P.l. catesbyi		***267-299***	***99-128***	***47-56***	***16.5-19.0***	***21-24***
♀	53	267-296	99-125	47-53	16.5-18.4	21-23
♂	51	269-299	101-128	49-56	16.9-19.0	22-24
Red-billed Tropicbird[3]		**287-329**	**98-118**	**58-70**	**18.8-21.7**	**26-31**
♀	64	287-326	98-116	58-67	18.8-21.8	26-30
♂	70	292-329	101-118	59-70	20.4-22.7	27-31
Red-tailed Tropicbird[3]		**294-349**	**70-92**	**56-69**	**19.9-22.9**	**28-33**
♀	100	294-348	70-88	56-68	19.9-21.7	28-32
♂	100	296-349	73-92	57-69	21.0-22.9	28-33

[1] Tail length excludes the elongated central rects.
[2] Bill depth taken at distal tip of forehead feathering or skin (Fig. 8**A-B**, p. 10).
[3] Measurements from N.Am populations only; see **Geographic variation**.

RED-TAILED TROPICBIRD

Phaethon rubricauda

RTTR
Species # 1131
Band size: 5

Species—From other tropicbirds by larger size but shorter tail excluding r1 (Table 28, p. 296); bill black (Juv) to bright red (Fig. 225); outer p covs white, with elongated black central mark or double-spot in Juv-HY/SY (Fig. 216**E-F**, p. 290); outer pp (p8-p10) with little to no black on outer web by age (Fig. 224); Juv-HYs with moderately short blackish eyeline (Fig. 225**A**), r1 short and with distinct black tip (Fig. 217**C**, p. 290), and back feathers with a few disorganized bars (Fig. 223**C**, p. 295); AHYs with back feathers and s covs white, terts white or virtually so, and r1 with pinkish or red webs distally.

Geographic variation—Considered monotypic here after Tarburton (1989); see also Gould et al. (1974), Schreiber & Schreiber (1993), Stager (1964). Populations of the c-n.Pacific ("*P.r. rothschildi*" and "*melanorhynchos*") average smaller (see Table 28) than populations of the sw.Pacific ("*roseotinctus*") but differences appear to be broadly clinal. Populations of the w.Indian ("*rubricauda*") and e.Indian ("*westralis*") ocean do not appear to differ substantially in size from each other or from Pacific populations. Differences in the average intensity of pinkish bloom occur within both Pacific and Indian Ocean populations, but this character is age-specific and unlikely related to genotype.

Molt—CBS (SBS?). Molts appear as follows: PF limited-partial? (5-8 months after hatching), PB2 incomplete (9-18 months after hatching), DPB incomplete-complete (requiring 4-6 months during non-breeding periods); PA absent. The PF appears to include most to all body feathers and a few to most s covs but no terts or rects. Molt strategies include staffelmauser (Fig. 16, pp. 23-24) and are otherwise similar to those of White-tailed Tropicbird (p. 291), as far as known. See Gould et al. (1974). In n.populations, the ornamental central rectrices of breeding ASYs molt alternately, with one feather usually shed in Mar-Apr (just after egg-laying) and the other in Aug-Sep, such that both are fully grown during courtship in Jan-Mar (Veit & Jones 2004).

Age—Juv (B1; Jun-Nov) has back feathers with thick blackish bars (Fig. 223**C**, p. 295), central rects short with black tip (Fig. 217**C**, p. 290), and bill black (Fig. 225**A**); Juv ♀ = ♂. The following month ranges refer to populations with boreal breeding cycles; use caution in assigning age codes within tropical populations, where breeding can occur year-round (base age assignments on molting information; see **Molt**). Note that confirmed-breeding adults can be reliably aged ATY.

HY/SY (1st cycle, F1; Sep-Aug): Most to all upperpart feathers with black bars (Fig. 223**C-D**); bill black to dusky reddish (Fig. 225**A-B**); pp and p covs uniformly juv (Fig. 16**A**, p. 24) or inner (up to p7) feathers being replaced, the outer feathers juv, with more extensive black near tip of p8-p9 (Fig. 224**A**) and with black marks to p covs (Fig. 216**E**, p. 290); all to some rects juv, marked with black, the juv r1 short (Fig. 217**C**).

SY/TY (2nd cycle, B2; Sep-Aug): Upperparts often with some black spotting or barring (Fig. 223**D**) to nape, les covs, belly, and/or rump (possibly elsewhere); bill dusky to dull reddish (Fig. 225**B-C**); pp and p covs with 2 generations (Fig. 16**B**), the outer feathers juv, worn, with more extensive black near tip of p7-p9 (Fig. 224**A**) and with black marks to p covs (Fig. 216**E**); r1-r7 without blackish markings or with 1-4 worn juv feathers retained (usually among r3-r4) and with black marks (Fig. 217**C**); longest r1 usually 150-250 mm when fully grown, and with pinkish to orangish (bleaching to whitish) outer webs distally; plumage aspect with little or no pinkish tinge. **Note: See ASY/ATY.**

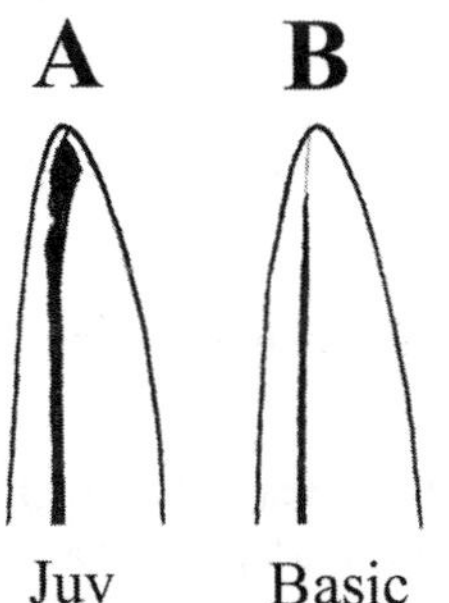

FIGURE 224. P8 by feather generation in Red-tailed Tropicbird. The juv p8 (present in Juv-HY/SYs and some TYs) averages more black along shaft near tip (**A**) than basic feathers (**B**).

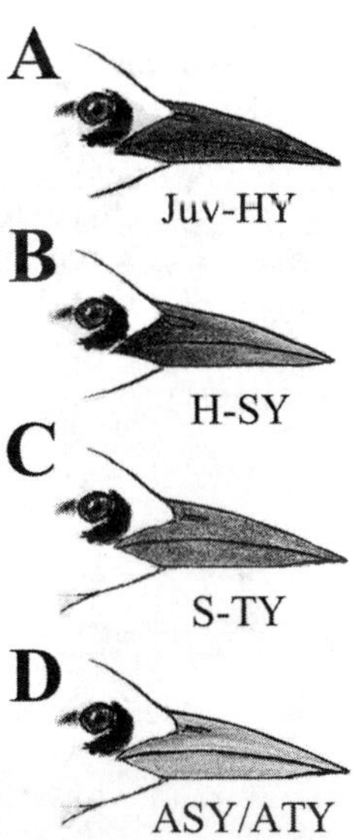

FIGURE 225. Bill color by age in Red-tailed Tropicbird, varying from black to blackish in Juvs and HYs (**A**), dusky with dull red distally in HYs and SYs (**B**), dull red in SYs and TYs (**C**), and bright red in ASY/ATYs (**D**). Red-billed Tropicbird shows similar variation but bill color matures more quickly. Note that the black mark around the eye in Juv-HY/SYs (**A**) is more extensive than that of Juv-HY/SY White-tailed Tropicbird (Fig. 220**A**, p. 292).

ASY/ATY (Def. cycle, DB; May-Apr): Upperparts white, occasionally with some black spotting or barring to les covs; bill red (Fig. 225**D**); pp and p covs with 2 sets of basic feathers in staffelmauser patterns (Fig. 16**E**), the outer feathers, with black restricted to shaft of p7-p9 (Fig. 224**B**) and with p covs without black marks (*cf.* Fig. 216**F**); r2-r7 without blackish markings; longest r1 usually 250-450 mm or greater when fully grown and with red outer webs; plumage aspect often tinged pink. **Note: Some ASY/ATYs show some black spotting to some les covs or other feathers, which could indicate TY/4Y, although it could also result from early or late definitive molts (see p. 29); more study needed.**

ATY/A4Y (Def. cycle, DB; May-Apr): Like ASY/ATY but pp with 3 sets of basic pp (Fig. 16**F**). **Note: Look for some ATYs with 4 sets of pp, that can possibly be aged A4Y/A5Y, but confirmation is needed.**

Sex—♀=♂ by plumage aspect. BP not developed but distended cloaca (p. 32; Veit & Jones 2004) indicates ATY ♀ (primarily Mar-Aug in n.populations). Measurements (including length of c.rect; Veit & Jones 2003) unhelpful for sexing (Table 28, p. 296) and the strength of the plumage-aspect bloom also appears unrelated to sex. No other criteria known.

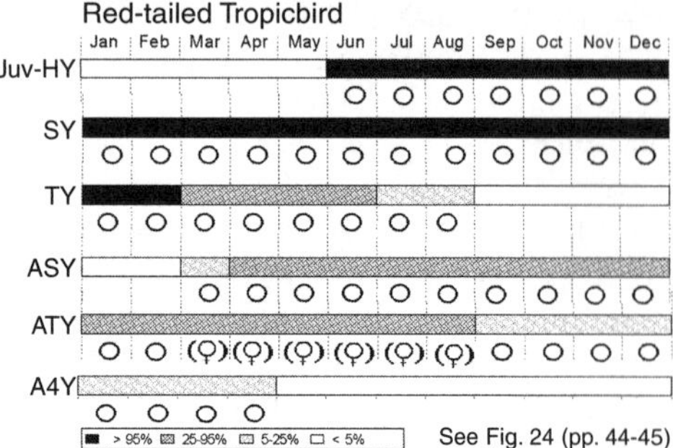

Hybrids reported—None.

References—Bent (1922), Boland et al. (2004), Chasen (1933), Diamond (1975), Fleet (1974), Gibson-Hill (1947), Gould et al. (1974), Howell & Webb (1995), LeValley & Pyle (2007), Marchant & Higgins (1990), Murphy (1936), Schreiber & Ashmole (1970), Schreiber & Schreiber (1993), Spear & Ainley (2005), Stresemann & Stresemann (1966), Stokes (1990), Tarburton (1989), Veit & Jones (2003, 2004).

Five North American species. Family characters include large, elongated bodies, long and pointed wings and tails, large conical bills (Fig. 226) lacking external nares and with serrations along tomia, unfeathered facial skin and gular areas, and short but strong legs and feet, with webbing between the three front toes and a combed middle toenail. Boobies have 10 functional primaries (p10 longest or next to longest, 3 mm shorter to 20 mm longer than p9, when fully grown), 24-28 secondaries (including 3 tertials and one absent between s4 and s5; *cf* Fig. 12**B**, p. 19), and 12-16 rectrices. Ageing through the third (to TY and ATY) or later (to 4-6Y and A4Y) cycles can be accomplished through molt patterns and plumage aspect; definitive plumage aspect can take three to six years fully develop. Sexes are alike in plumage aspect but differ in some species in bare part colors and/or size, females averaging slightly to moderately larger than males. Brood patches are not developed (eggs incubated with feet) but distended cloacae (Fig. 21, p. 32) indicate breeding females; other cloacal features (Fig. 22-23, pp. 32-35) should be further investigated. The best clue to sexing live AHY/ASYs of Masked (p. 300), Blue-footed (p. 303), and Brown (p. 305) boobies in the hand or on the breeding colony is by voice (see Murphy 1936:834 for differences in tracheal structure): ♀♀ and HY/SY ♂♂ give a goose-like bray whereas AHY/ASY ♂♂ give a hissing whistle (Nelson 1978a, 2005; Lormée et al. 2000).

In molting, boobies and gannets appear to exhibit a Simple Basic Strategy (SBS; Fig. 10**A**, pp. 13-16), lacking formative and alternate plumages, but the possible presence of a limited preformative molt (indicating the Complex Basic Strategy) has not been fully investigated. Molting strategies are complicated by year-round breeding in most species. Prebasic molts occurs primarily at sea, and year-round breeding and variation in individual breeding histories result in individuals at all stages of molt at any time of year (Diamond 1974; Dorward 1962; Nelson 1978a, 2005). Replacement of primaries and secondaries exhibits staffelmauser (Fig. 16, pp. 23-24). The second prebasic molt typically begins at age 8-10 months, with subsequent waves commencing at 12-month intervals. Replacement of secondaries proceeds distally from the tertials and proximally from both s1 and s5 (Fig. 16**B-C**); in some individuals the juvenal outer primary and one to a few juvenal secondaries among s10-s19 may not be replaced until the third prebasic molt or later (*cf* Fig. 16**D**). Up to 3 sets

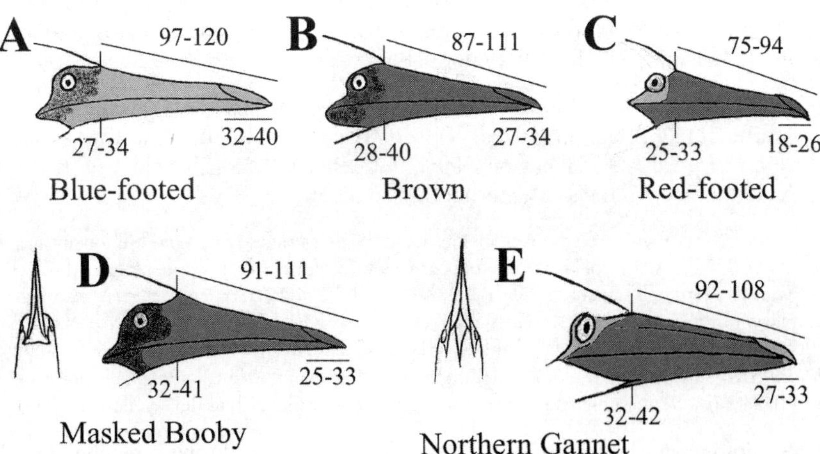

FIGURE 226. Shape, size, and color patterns of bills for identification of HY boobies and Northern Gannet. Indicated measures represent exposed culmen (Fig. 7**A-B**, p. 9), bill depth at tip of forehead feathers or skin (Fig. 8**A-B**, p. 10), and length of bill nail. Note also that Northern Gannet (**E**) differs from Masked and the other boobies by having more extensive forehead feathering (> 15 mm from eye, *vs* < 10 mm in boobies) and malar feathering (forward of eye, *vs* usually behind eye in boobies. Also note the unique shape to the gular pouch in Northern Gannet (**E**, inset) *vs* Masked (**D**, inset) and the other boobies.

of pp (Fig. 16**F**) can be encountered in ATY/A4Ys. The rectrices are replaced in irregular sequences, sometimes alternately, each feather replaced about once per cycle. Age at first breeding is 3-6 years and breeding may not occur at annual intervals. Prebasic molts of S-TYs and non-breeding ASYs average earlier in timing than those of breeding adults (see p. 18).

See Harrison (1983a, 1987), Nelson (1978a, 2005) for general information on taxonomy, molts, and plumages of boobies.

MASKED BOOBY
Sula dactylatra

MABO
Species # 1140
Band size: 7B-8

Species—From other boobies by large size but short tail (Table 29, p. 302); bill large and deep with medium-length nail and gular not elongated (Fig. 226**D**, p. 299); central rects not elongated at tip (Fig. 228**A**, p. 303); Juv-HY with head and back uniformly brown except nape usually white, underparts (including breast) and underwing p covs largely white, bill grayish, quickly becoming yellowish, and legs and feet grayish to dull grayish green (see **Geographic variation**); ASY white except for blackish pp, p covs, ss (including terts), and rects, unfeathered facial skin blackish, bill yellow, iris yellow, and feet orangish, yellow, or grayish blue (see **Geographic variation**). See Northern Gannet (p. 309) for more information on separating ASYs.

Nazca Booby (*S. granti*), a potential vagrant to sw.CA, separated with caution. Nazca Boobies average slightly longer wing and bill but slightly shorter tarsus (wg chord 404-493, tl 162-197, exp culmen 96-113, tarsus 48-63); AHY with orange bill (*vs* yellow in Masked); ASY with central rects white or with substantial white (*vs* primarily dark, rarely entirely white in Masked). Juv/HYs may not be separable: Nazca Boobies have upperparts averaging grayer brown (*vs* more chocolate in Masked); white hind collar more often absent and averaging less complete (*vs* usually present and more complete in Masked); central rects with more white at bases, often extending beyond uppertail covs (*vs* central rects dark or with small amount of white, usually concealed by uppertail covs in Masked); beware limits of individual variation within each species have not been fully defined. Bill color can begin to tinge orange in Nazca Booby at 4-8 months of age and is the most diagnostic criterion at any age. See Gifford (1913), Pitman & Jehl (1998), and Roberson (1998) for more information.

Geographic variation—See Gifford (1913), Marchant & Higgins (1990), Mathews & Iredale (1931), Murphy (1936), Nelson (1978a), O'Brien & Davies (1990), M.A. Traylor *in* Palmer (1962), Pitman & Jehl (1998), Roberson (1998), Rothschild (1915a), Shaughnessy (1993). Three other subspecies breed in the sw.Pacific and Indian oceans.

S.d. personata (br & wint throughout n.Pacific range): Size averages larger and bill longer and deeper (Table 29, p. 302); ASY with bill bright yellow, iris yellow (*vs* dark in some populations of the sw.Pacific), and legs and feet grayish blue to greenish. Populations of the ne.Pacific ("*californicus*") average smaller, have yellower or greener tones to the legs and feet, and may have less white to the collar in juv plumage, but differences are confounded by individual variation and are insufficient to warrant subspecific status.

S.d. dactylatra (br & wint throughout Atlantic range): Size averages smaller and bill shorter and shallower (Table 29); ASY with bill straw yellow and legs and feet orangish to olive-yellow.

Molt—SBS. Molting can be continuous except when suspended during breeding (see Family Account, p. 299): PF absent, PB2 incomplete (age 8-22 months), PB3 incomplete (age 18-30 months), DPB incomplete-complete (active 10 months between periods of breeding); PA absent. Replacement of pp and ss exhibits staffelmauser (Fig. 16, pp. 23-24), resulting in 2-4 sets among pp of adults. See Family Account for more details.

Age—Juv (B1; year-round) is described under HY/SY, below; Juv ♀=♂. Note that confirmed-breeding adults can be reliably aged A4Y.

Juv-HY/SY (1st cycle, Juv/B1; year-round): Head, neck, back, and scapulars brown, becoming mostly to entirely white by end of 1st cycle; s covs and rump brown (Fig. 227**A**), becoming partly white by end of 1st cycle (Fig. 227**B**); molt of pp and ss begins at age 8-10 months and completes at age 20-22 months, the juv outer pp brown and pointed (Fig. 19**A-B**, p. 28), and remaining juv ss (among s11-s12 and s14-s19; *cf.* Fig. 16**B**, p. 24) worn, brown, and lacking slight silvery blush of replaced ss; bill dusky to dull olive; iris brown to grayish; legs and feet grayish to dull grayish green. **Note: It is best to estimate age in months (see Molt and Fig. 227) and to then assign HY or SY based on this estimate. Juvs that have not dropped p1 can be aged HY in Aug-Dec and HY or SY in Jan-Jul, depending on plumage freshness and occurrence of tufts of down, which can remain 5-7 months post-hatching. First-cycle individuals that have dropped p5 but not p6 can be aged SY (Jan-Dec).**

SY/TY (2nd cycle, B2-B3; year-round): Head, neck, back, and scapulars mostly to entirely white; wing covs and rump mixed white and brown (Fig. 227**B-C**); juv outer pp and medial ss (usually among s12-s16) completing replacement (Figs. 16**C-D** & 19**B**), after which 2 sets of basic pp present in staffelmauser patterns (Fig. 16**E**); bill olive to yellowish; iris dull grayish to yellow; legs and feet as in ASY/ATY (below) but duller. **Note: See HY/SY. According to progress of molt, AHYs showing these characters that have juv p7 dropped and p1 dropped for a second time (cf. Fig. 16C) can be aged SY/TY (May-Apr), and those with all juv pp replaced and p5 dropped for a second time can be aged TY (Jan-Dec).**

ATY/A4Y (Def. cycle, DB; Jul-Jun): Head, neck, back, scapulars, s covs, and rump entirely white (Fig. 227**E**); pp and ss with 2-3 sets of basic feathers in staffelmauser patterns (Fig. 16**E-F**), the outer pp broad and truncate (Fig. 19**C-D**); bill yellowish or yellow; iris yellow; legs and feet bright, grayish blue to greenish (*S.d. personata*) or orangish to olive-yellow (*dactylatra*). **Note: Look for ASYs with 4 sets of pp (Fig. 16F) that probably can be aged A4Y/A5Y. Also, see 4-5Y.**

4-5Y (3rd-5th cycles, B3-B5; Jan-Dec): Like ATY/A4Y but s covs and/or rump lightly mottled brown or with a few brown feathers remaining (Fig. 227**D**). **Note: See pp. 41-42 for age-code terminology.**

Sex—♀ = ♂ by plumage aspect. BP not developed but distended cloaca (Fig. 21, p. 32) indicates A4Y ♀ (primarily Mar-Aug in n.populations). Populations breeding in the Atlantic (*S.d. dactylatra*) with bright orange legs and feet are reliably sexed ♂♂ but individuals with duller (yellow or yellow-olive legs and feet) cannot be sexed due to individual and age-related variation in leg

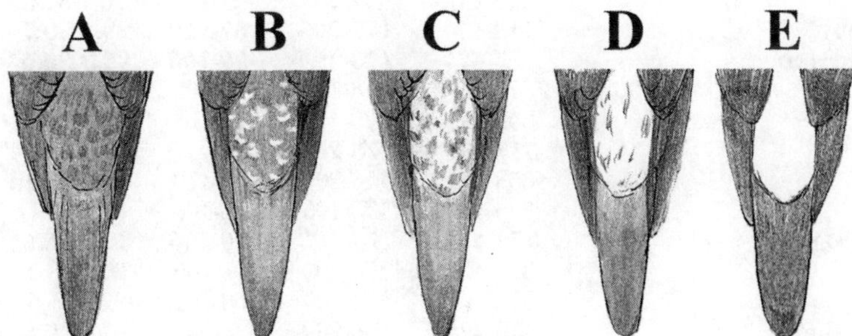

FIGURE 227. Extent of brown and white feathering on the rump by age in Masked Booby; Northern Gannet shows similar variation to the rump plumage aspect but differs in developing partially to entirely white terts and rects by the time the rump is partly (**C**) to entirely (**E**) white, respectively. Masked Boobies can breed and molt year-round and age is best estimated in months: **A** = 1-6 months, **B** = 8-15 months, **C** = 12-26 months, **D** = 20-36 months, and **E** = 30 months or greater. Northern Gannet undergoes more defined breeding and molting seasons and can be aged as follows: **A** = Juv-HY/SY, **B** = SY/TY, **C** = advanced SY/TY or retarded TY/4Y, **D** = advanced TY/4Y or retarded 4Y/5Y, and **E** = A4Y/A5Y.

color of ♂♂; Pacific populations (*personata*) appear to show less sex-specific difference in leg color. ♂♂ (of all populations) also average brighter bills and smaller size than ♀♀ (Table 29), resulting in reliable sexing of some mated pairs (in direct comparison) but not individuals. Otherwise, the best clue to sexing live AHY/ASYs in the hand is voice (see Family Account, p. 299).

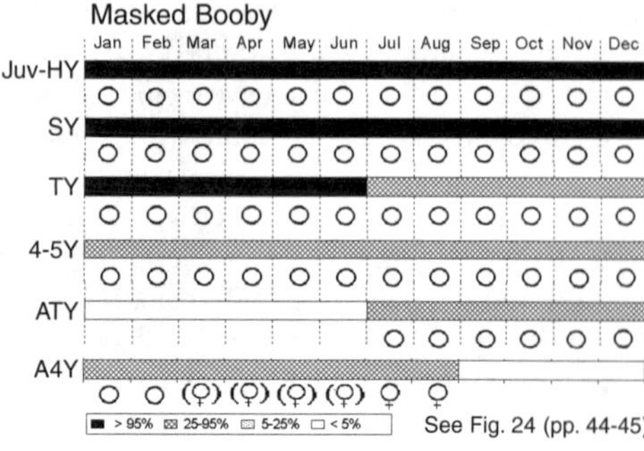

Hybrids reported—With Brown Booby (Dorward 1962, Nelson 1978a, Castillo-Guerrero et al. 2005); suspected with Nazca Booby *S. granti* (Pitman & Jehl 1998).

References—Ainley et al. (1994), Anderson (1993), Bent (1922), Dorward (1962), Gifford (1913), Howell & Webb (1995), Kepler (1969), Marchant & Higgins (1990), Murphy (1936), Oberholser (1974), M.A. Traylor *in* Palmer (1962).

TABLE 29. Measurements (mm) of North American boobies and gannets to assist in identification and sexing. See pp. 4-11 for methods of measurement. Species summaries are in **bold** and subspecies summaries in ***italics***. Values were derived from 95% confidence intervals as based (for wing, tail, exposed culmen, and tarsus) approximately on the indicated sample sizes (see pp. 4-5); sample size for bill depth was often smaller but included at least 10 of each sex. Thus, midpoints of ranges approximate means, and S.D. is approximated by 25% of the range

Taxon/Sex	*n*	wing chord	tail length	exp culmen	bill depth[1]	tarsus
Masked Booby[2]		**392-480**	**147-206**	**91-111**	**31.8-40.7**	**51-66**
S.d. personata		***394-480***	***148-206***	***95-111***	***32.9-40.7***	***51-66***
♀	36	400-480	159-206	95-111	35.5-40.7	52-66
♂	41	394-471	148-203	95-110	32.9-38.2	51-65
S.d. dactylatra		***392-442***	***147-180***	***91-102***	***31.8-38.6***	***51-57***
♀	30	399-442	148-180	92-102	34.7-38.6	52-57
♂	30	392-437	147-180	91-99	31.8-36.1	51-56
Blue-footed Booby		**396-470**	**172-251**	**97-120**	**26.7-34.4**	**49-55**
♀	71	427-470	175-251	107-120	30.3-34.4	51-56
♂	64	396-451	172-250	97-114	26.7-31.7	48-54
Brown Booby[2]		**358-430**	**173-203**	**87-110**	**28.3-39.7**	**43-63**
S.l. brewsteri		***377-427***	***173-195***	***90-105***	***28.3-35.6***	***43-50***
♀	100	377-427	176-195	95-105	31.0-35.6	45-50
♂	100	359-399	173-193	90-101	28.3-33.2	43-48
S.l. plotus		***358-430***	***173-200***	***83-110***	***33.4-39.7***	***50-63***
♀	65	358-401	176-200	97-110	33.4-37.0	47-59
♂	60	378-430	173-196	93-106	36.0-39.7	50-63
S.l. leucogaster		***372-422***	***174-203***	***90-106***	***32.5-38.0***	***43-51***
♀	30	384-422	176-203	94-106	35.3-38.0	45-51
♂	30	372-409	174-200	90-101	32.5-36.5	43-49
Red-footed Booby		**359-422**	**188-234**	**75-94**	**25.5-32.8**	**32-45**
♀	100	366-422	188-230	81-94	26.9-32.8	34-45
♂	100	359-416	191-234	75-89	25.5-31.7	32-42
Northern Gannet		**459-525**	**197-244**	**92-108**	**31.6-41.8**	**57-65**
♀	100	459-520	197-238	92-105	31.6-39.4	57-64
♂	100	465-525	200-244	95-108	32.9-41.8	57-65

[1] Bill depth taken at distal tip of forehead feathering or skin (Fig. 8**A-B**, p. 10).
[2] Measurements from N.Am populations only; see **Geographic variation**.

BLUE-FOOTED BOOBY BFBO
Sula nebouxii Species # 1141
Band size: 7A-7B

Species—From other boobies by medium-large size with long legs (Table 29); bill and nail long and relatively shallow (Fig. 226**A**, p. 299); feathers of head and neck narrow and stiff resulting in ridged feathering (unique among boobies); central rects elongated at tip (Fig. 228**B**); HY with head, neck, and upperparts dark grayish brown (the back sometimes with pale barring), abdomen white (not cut off sharply from dark breast), underwing p covs dark, and bill and feet dark grayish; ASY with white head variably streaked dusky, back dark with whitish bars, rects primarily blackish with white bases, bill bluish gray, iris yellowish, and feet bright blue.

Geographic variation—Considered monotypic after Nelson (1978a); see also Murphy (1936), M.A. Traylor *in* Palmer (1962), Todd (1948), Wetmore (1965). Populations of the Galapagos Is. ("*S.n. excisa*") may average slightly larger and with more white in the head, but differences are insufficient and confounded by individual variation.

Molt—SBS. PF absent, PB2 incomplete (8-22 months after fledging), PB3 incomplete (18-30 months after fledging), DPB incomplete-complete (active 10 months between periods of breeding); PA absent. Replacement of pp and ss exhibits staffelmauser (Fig. 16, pp. 23-24). See Family Account (p. 299) for more details.

Age—Juv (B1; year-round) is described under HY/SY, below; Juv ♀=♂. Note that confirmed-breeding adults can be reliably aged A4Y.

Juv-HY/SY (1st cycle, Juv/B1; year-round): Head and neck dark brown, becoming mottled white by end of 1st cycle; breast grayish brown (Fig. 229**A**), becoming flecked white by end of 1st cycle (Fig. 229**B**); molt of pp and ss begins at age 8-10 months and completes at age 20-22 months, the juv outer pp brown and pointed (Fig. 19**A-B**, p. 28), and remaining juv ss (among s11-s12 and s14-s19; *cf.* Fig. 16**B**, p. 24) worn, brown, and

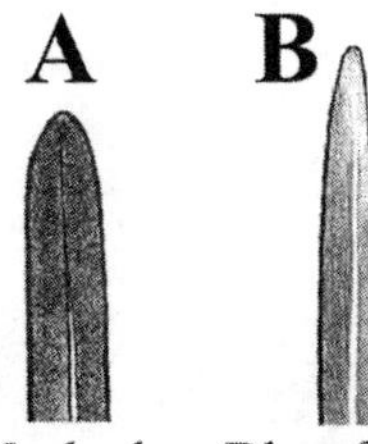

FIGURE 228. Central rectrix by species in N.Am boobies. Blue-footed and Red-footed boobies have longer, stiffer, paler, and more pointed central rects than Masked and Brown boobies.

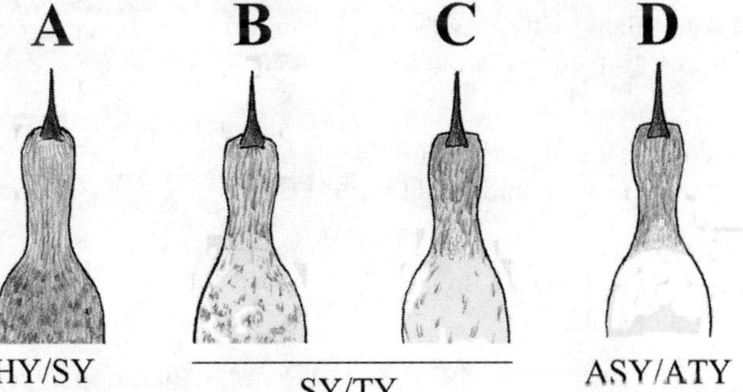

FIGURE 229. Breast pattern by age in Blue-footed Booby. Approximate ages in months are **A** 6-8 months, **B** 10-14 months, **C** 20-28 months, and **D** > 30 months. Juvs < 6 months old resemble **A** but may be slightly darker and show tufts of down to the underparts. Note the pale extensions into the streaked neck (**C-D**) as compared with Brown Booby (Fig. 231, p. 306).

lacking slight silvery blush of replaced ss; bill dark grayish; iris brownish to grayish tinged yellow; legs and feet grayish to dull bluish gray. **Note: It is best to estimate age in months (see Molt and Fig. 227, p. 301) and to then assign HY or SY based on this estimate, although Blue-footed Booby in N.Am may exhibit more seasonality than other species (cf. Northern Gannet, p. 309). See Masked Booby (p. 300) for more details.**

FIGURE 230. Eye pattern by sex in AHY/ASY Blue-footed Boobies. This characteristic probably becomes reliable at 10-14 months of age (more study needed). The variable brown markings to the inner portion of the female iris (**A**) results in the pupil appearing to be larger than is found in males (**B**). Certain populations of Brown Booby may show similar sex-specific differences, with both sexes averaging more brown markings than found in Blue-footed Booby; study needed.

SY/TY (2nd cycle, B2; year-round): Head and neck streaked grayish brown and white, to white with dusky streaking; breast mixed pale grayish brown and white (Fig. 229**B-C**) becoming mostly to entirely white by end of 2nd cycle (Fig. 229**C-D**); juv outer pp and medial ss (usually among s12-s16) completing replacement (Figs. 16**C-D** & 19**B**), after which 2 sets of definitive pp present in staffelmauser patterns (Fig. 16**E**); bill dark to pale grayish tinged blue; iris grayish yellow to yellowish; legs and feet dull bluish gray to blue. **Note: See HY/SY and ASY/ATY.**

ASY/ATY (Def. cycle, DB; Jul-Jun): Head and neck white with dusky streaking; breast white (Fig. 229**D**); pp and ss with 2 sets of basic feathers in staffelmauser patterns (Fig. 16**E**), the outer pp broad and truncate (Fig. 19**C-D**); bill bluish gray; iris yellow; legs and feet bright blue. **Note: It is possible that some TY/4Ys might retain brown feathers in the breast; more study is needed.**

ATY/A4Y (Def. cycle, DB; May-Apr): Like ASY/ATY but pp with 3 sets of basic pp (Fig. 16**F**).

Sex— ♀ = ♂ by plumage aspect. BP not developed but distended cloaca (Fig. 21, p. 32) indicates A4Y ♀ (primarily Feb-Jun in n.populations). Wing chord and bill measurements moderately useful for sexing (Table 29, p. 302). The following is reliable for sexing AHY/ASYs; no means (except measurements) known for sexing Juv-HY/SYs or specimens by plumage aspect alone. See also Family Account (p. 299) for sexing live AHY/ASYs by voice.

AHY/ASY ♀: Iris pale yellow, with irregular brownish markings or splotches around pupil (Fig. 230**A**).

AHY/ASY ♂: Iris pale yellow, without brownish markings or splotches around pupil (Fig. 230**B**).

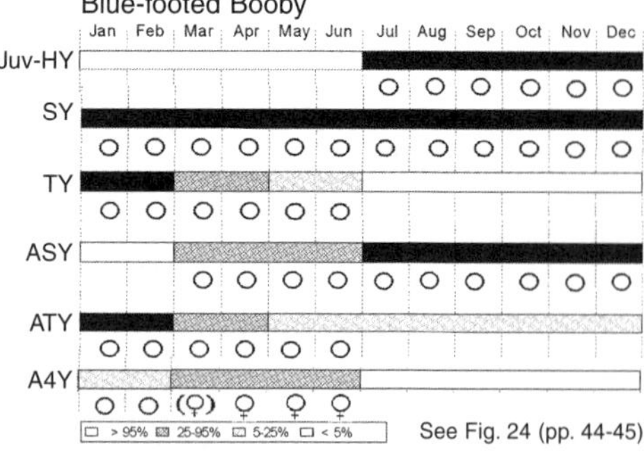

Hybrids reported— With Brown Booby (Castillo-Guerrero et al. 2005).

References— Ainley et al. (1994), Bent (1922), Coker (1919), Gifford (1913), Howell & Webb (1995), Murphy (1936), M.A. Traylor *in* Palmer (1962).

BROWN BOOBY BRBO
Sula leucogaster Species # 1150
Band size: 7B

Species—From other boobies and Northern Gannet (p. 309) by medium-small size and short tail (Table 29, p. 302); bill and nail intermediate in length and depth (Fig. 226**B**); central rects not elongated at tip (Fig. 228**A**, p. 303); head, upperparts, and breast entirely brown (except for ♂ *S.l. brewsteri* with whitish head; see **Geographic variation**); abdomen brownish (HY) to white (ASY), cut off sharply and horizontally from uniform brown breast (Fig. 231, p. 306; border can be subtle or virtually absent in Juvs); proximal underwing s covs whitish to white; underwing p covs brown; bill and feet grayish to pinkish (HY) to bright yellowish or greenish (ASY); facial skin yellow to bluish by sex (Fig. 232, p. 306).

Geographic variation—See Cramp & Simmons (1977), Heller & Snodgrass (1901), Murphy (1936), Nelson (1978a, 2005), M.A. Traylor *in* Palmer (1962), Thayer & Bangs (1905), van Rossem (1938a), Wetmore (1939, 1965). No other subspecies occur. Caution when using bare part color differences as these vary by age, sex, and population within subspecies. The following applies to ASYs only; HY/SYs may be difficult or impossible to distinguish except, perhaps, by measurements for some individuals.

S.l. brewsteri (br w.Mex-Clipperton I, visitor to cw-sw.CA, vagrant to NV-AZ): Averages smaller, especially bill depth (Table 29, p. 302; Fig. 232, p. 206); AHYs with bill pale yellowish to whitish (sometimes tinged pink), iris pale yellow, and legs and feet pale yellowish to greenish; AHY ♀ with brown head and neck slightly paler and grayer than back; ASY ♂ with whitish head (sometimes including foreneck and upper breast). Populations of the Tres Marias Is, Mex ("*albiceps*") and Clipperton I ("*nesiotes*") may average smaller and with whiter forenecks and upper breasts but differences are insufficient.

S.l. plotus (br HI-Indian Ocean, probable visitor to w.CA): Size as in *leucogaster* (perhaps averaging shorter wing chord and longer tl) but variable (Table 29; Fig. 232); ASY ♂ and ♀ with brown head and breast concolor with (or slightly darker than) back; bill yellow to greenish, sometimes tinged pink; iris pale yellow; legs and feet dark yellow to greenish.

S.l. leucogaster (br throughout Atlantic and Caribbean range, visitor to NB-TX): Averages larger (Table 29); ASY ♂ and ♀ with brown head and breast slightly darker or more blackish than back; bill yellow with bluish tip; iris pale bluish; legs and feet pale yellowish to greenish.

Molt—SBS. PF absent, PB2 incomplete (8-22 months after fledging), PB3 incomplete 18-30 months after fledging, DPB incomplete-complete (active 10 months between periods of breeding); PA absent. Replacement of pp and ss exhibits staffelmauser (Fig. 16, pp. 23-24). See Family Account (p. 299) for more details.

Age—Juv (B1; year-round) is described under HY/SY, below; Juv ♀=♂. Note that confirmed-breeding adults can be reliably aged A4Y.

Juv-HY/SY (1st cycle, Juv/B1; year-round): Abdomen brown with slight (sometimes ~absent) horizontal demarcation from darker brown breast (Fig. 231**A**, p. 306), becoming partly whitish by end of 1st cycle (Fig. 231**B-C**); longest axillar brown; molt of pp and ss begins at age 8-10 months and completes at age 20-22 months, the juv outer pp brown and pointed (Fig. 19**A-B**, p. 28), and remaining juv ss (among s11-s12 and s14-s19; *cf.* Fig. 16**B**, p. 24) worn, brown, and lacking slight silvery blush of replaced ss; bill and unfeathered facial skin dark grayish; iris dark brownish to grayish; legs and feet dark grayish to dull yellowish or greenish; ♂♂ of e.Pacific populations (including *S.l. brewsteri*) with head entirely brown or with whitish coming in on forehead at age 6 months. **Note: It is best to estimate age in months (see Molt and Fig. 227, p. 301) and to then assign HY or SY based on this estimate. See Masked Booby (p. 300) for more details.**

SY/TY (2nd cycle, B2-B3; year-round): Abdomen partly whitish (Fig. 231**B-C**), becoming mostly (to fully?) white by end of 2nd cycle (Fig. 231**C-D**); longest axillar dingy brownish white; juv outer

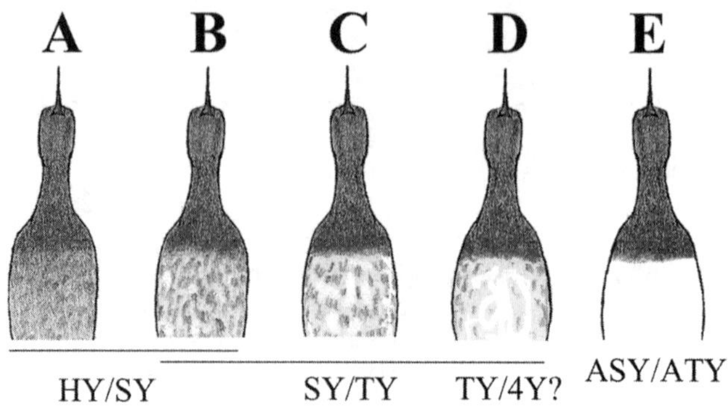

FIGURE 231. Breast pattern by age in Brown Booby. Approximate ages in months are **A** 6-10 months, **B** 10-15 months, **C** 18-24 months, **D** 24-36 months, and **E** > 30 months. Juvs < 8 months old resemble **A** but are darker on the belly; in some Juvs the demarcation line between breast and belly can be extremely subtle or absent. Juvs may also show tufts of down to the underparts.

pp and medial ss (usually among s12-s16) completing replacement (Figs. 16**C-D** & 19**B**), after which 2 sets of basic pp present in staffelmauser patterns (Fig. 16**E**); bill and unfeathered facial skin dark to pale grayish, tinged yellow or olive; iris dusky grayish to yellowish; legs and feet dull yellowish to greenish; ♂♂ of e.Pacific populations with crown and auriculars mixed brown and whitish. **Note: See HY/SY**.

ASY/ATY (Def. cycle, DB; Jul-Jun): Abdomen white, without brown (Fig. 231**E**); longest axillar white; pp and ss with 2 sets of basic feathers in staffelmauser patterns (Fig. 16**E**), the outer pp broad and truncate (Fig. 19**C-D**); bill bright yellowish to whitish; unfeathered facial skin yellowish or bluish (see **Sex**); iris bright pale bluish to yellow; legs and feet bright yellowish to greenish; ♂♂ of e.Pacific populations with crown and auriculars whitish to white. **Note: See TY/4Y**.

TY/4Y (3rd cycle, B3-B4; Jul-Jun): Like ASY/ATY (with 2 sets of basic pp in wings; Fig. 16**E**) but abdomen slightly mottled brownish to grayish or with a few brownish feathers, particularly along sides and flanks (Fig. 231**D**); longest axillar white tinged brownish. **More study needed on variation in the loss of brown on the abdomen; it is possible that some 4Y/5Ys might retain brown, in which case individuals showing above characters should be aged 4-5Y (see pp. 41-42).**

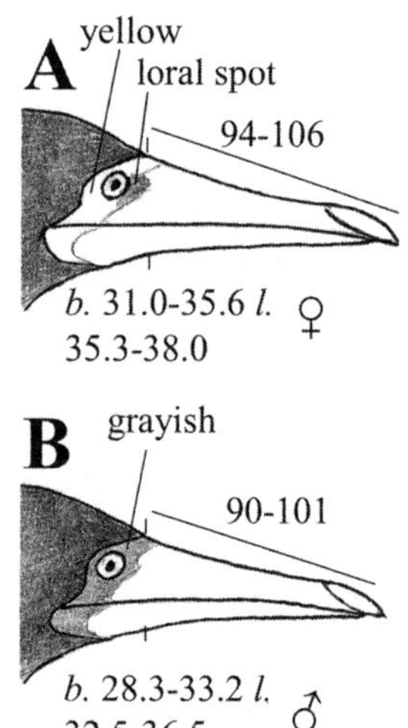

FIGURE 232. Facial color and bill size and shape in Brown Booby. Measures represent exposed culmen (Fig. 7**A-B**, p. 9) and bill depth at distal end of forehead feathers or skin (Fig. 8**A-B**, p. 10). Note that bill depth varies substantially by subspecies, with *S.l. brewsteri* of the e.Pacific (*b.*) exhibiting much shallower bills, by sex, than *leucogaster* of the Atlantic (*l.*). Note also that ♀♀ typically show a dusky loral spot (in AHYs > 10 months old) that is not prominent in ♂♂, and look for slight sex-specific eye color differences as in Blue-footed Booby (Fig. 230, p. 304) but not as marked.

ATY/A4Y (Def. cycle, DB; May-Apr): Like ASY/ATY but pp with 3 sets of basic pp (Fig. 16**F**); ♂♂ of e.Pacific populations with crown, auriculars, neck, and upper breast extensively white.

Sex—BP not developed but distended cloaca (Fig. 21, p. 32) indicates A4Y ♀. Measurements somewhat helpful for sexing, within each population (Table 29, p. 302). The following is reliable for sexing HY/SY *brewsteri* and AHY/ASYs of all populations; no means (except for size) known for sexing Juv *brewsteri* or HY/SYs of the other subspecies. In addition, look for iris-color differences as in Blue-footed Booby (Fig. 230, p. 304) but with more brown markings by sex, and see Family Account (p. 299) for sex-specific differences in voice. Slight differences in bare part color between *brewsteri* and *leucogaster* (see **Geographic variation**) should be considered when using the following.

AHY/ASY ♀: Unfeathered facial skin yellowish (with distinct dusky patch distal to eye), not contrasting markedly with bill color (Fig. 232**A**); crown, auriculars, and breast dark chocolate in all populations; legs and feet yellowish. **Note: See AHY/ASY ♂.**

AHY/ASY ♂: Unfeathered facial skin (including lores) uniformly greenish to bluish gray or dark bluish, contrasting with color of bill (Fig. 232**B**); crown and auriculars whitish and breast medium brown to whitish in e.Pacific populations (including *S.l. brewsteri*); legs and feet greenish. **Note: Some HY/SYs can possibly be sexed by bare part characters but more study is needed. Some HY/SY ♂♂ of *brewsteri* begin to acquire white on the forehead at six months of age (e.g., by the time p1 has been shed during the PB2) and can be sexed at this time; ♀♀ *brewsteri* should not be sexed until the PB2 has reached p5, at least.**

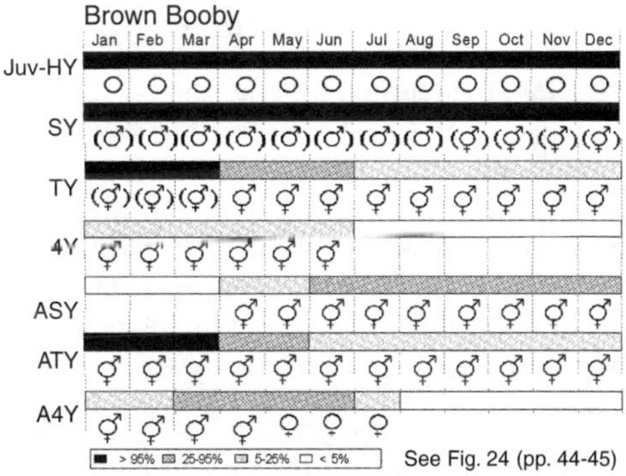

Brown Booby
Jan Feb Mar Apr May Jun Jul Aug Sep Oct Nov Dec
Juv-HY
SY
TY
4Y
ASY
ATY
A4Y
■ > 95% ▨ 25-95% ▧ 5-25% □ < 5%
See Fig. 24 (pp. 44-45)

Hybrids reported—With Masked (p. 300) and Blue-footed (p. 303) boobies.

References—Ainley et al. (1994), Bent (1922), Chasen (1933), Cramp & Simmons (1977), Dorward (1962), Gibson-Hill (1947), Gifford (1913), Howell (2006c), Howell & Webb (1995), Marchant & Higgins (1990), Murphy (1924, 1936), M.A. Traylor *in* Palmer (1962), Schreiber & Norton (2002), Stager (1964).

RED-FOOTED BOOBY

Sula sula

RFBO
Species # 1160
Band size: 7B-7A

Species--From other boobies and Northern Gannet (p. 309) by small size and short legs but with long tail (Table 29, p. 302); bill short and shallow and bill nail short (Fig. 226**C**, p. 299); central rects elongated (Fig. 228**B**, p. 303); HY grayish brown (including upperparts and all underwing covs) with variable whitish underparts, bill and unfeathered facial skin dark grayish, and legs and feet dull pinkish to pinkish; ASY variable in plumage aspect but with bill pale bluish with pink base, facial skin pinkish with blue around eye, iris dark brown to dark yellowish, and legs and feet bright red (all unique among boobies). Because of variation in plumage aspect (see **Geographic variation**) the best means of identifying Red-footed Boobies are often by measurements and the pinkish (HY) to red (AHY/ASY) legs and feet.

Geographic variation—Subspecific status uncertain but treated as monotypic here in lieu of further data. Proportions of "white-tailed light-morph," "dark-tailed white morph," "white-tailed dark-morph," and "dark-tailed dark-morph" individuals vary geographically but subspecific designations are obscured and complicated by substantial individual variation, intermediate morphs, and age-related variation. Populations of the e.Pacific ("*S.s. websteri*") consist primarily of dark-tailed white-morph and dark-tailed dark-morph ASYs (perhaps averaging darker brown than dark-morphs from other populations), with a smaller proportion of white-tailed white-morph ASYs. Populations of the Atlantic ("*S.s. sula*") are primarily of white-tailed dark-morph ASYs with a moderately small proportion of white-tailed white-morph ASYs. A third subspecies of the c.Pacific-Indian Ocean ("*rubripes*") has not been reported from N.Am but could occur: it consists largely of white-tailed white-morph ASYs with smaller proportions of the other morphs. Intermediate-morph individuals also occur to varying degrees among these populations. Bare part color may vary slightly but is confounded by individual and age-related variation. Size also varies slightly among these populations but exhibits little concordance with subspecies as defined. See Grant & Mackworth-Praed (1933), Hellmayr & Conover (1948a), and Murphy (1936) for more information.

Molt—SBS. PF absent, PB2 incomplete (8-22 months after fledging), PB3 incomplete 18-30 months after fledging, DPB incomplete-complete (active 10 months between periods of breeding); PA absent. Replacement of pp and ss exhibits staffelmauser (Fig. 16, pp. 23-24). See Family Account (p. 299) for more details.

Age—Juv (B1; year-round) is described under HY/SY, below; Juv ♀ = ♂. Due to variation in both plumage aspect (see **Geographic variation**) and rates of plumage-aspect acquisition (see Woodward 1972), with ASY/ATYs of certain populations resembling Juv/HYs, and intermediate-morph ASY/ATYs resembling SY/TY white-morph individuals, the best means to age individuals are by wing-molt patterns and bare part colors. In populations dominated by white-morph individuals, plumage-aspect acquisition (from dark to white head, back, and s covs) can possibly be used for ageing as in Masked Booby (Fig. 227, p. 301), although rates of plumage-aspect maturation may be quicker. Note that confirmed-breeding adults can be reliably aged ATY.

Juv-HY/SY (1st cycle, Juv/B1; year-round): Molt of pp and ss begins at age 8-10 months and completes at age 20-22 months, the juv outer pp brown and pointed (Fig. 19**A-B**, p. 28), and remaining juv ss (among s11-s12 and s14-s19; *cf.* Fig. 16**B**, p. 24) worn, brown, and lacking slight silvery blush of replaced ss; bill, unfeathered facial skin, and gular dark grayish to blackish, becoming pinkish and bluish by the end of the 1st cycle); iris dark brown; legs and feet dull pinkish. **Note: It is best to estimate age in months (see Molt and Fig. 227, p. 301) and to then assign HY or SY based on this estimate. See Masked Booby (p. 300) for more details.**

SY/TY (2nd cycle, B2-B3; Jul-Jun): Juv outer pp and medial ss (usually among s12-s16) completing replacement (Figs. 16**C-D** & 19**B**), after which 2 sets of basic pp present in staffelmauser patterns (Fig. 16**E**); bill pink with dusky tip to mixed pinkish and bluish; unfeathered facial skin primarily bluish; iris brownish yellow; legs and feet reddish. **Note: See HY/SY.**

ASY/ATY (Def. cycle, DB; Jul-Jun): Pp and ss with 2 sets of basic feathers in staffelmauser pattern (Fig. 16**E**), the outer pp broad and truncate (Fig. 19**C-D**); bill bright bluish; iris brownish yellow to pale yellow; unfeathered facial skin bright blue and pinkish; legs and feet bright red. **Note: Look for occasional ASYs possibly to have 3 sets of basic feathers (Fig. 16F) and be reliably aged ATY/A4Y.**

Sex—♀ = ♂ by plumage aspect. BP not developed but distended cloaca (Fig. 21, p. 32) indicates ATY ♀. Measurements not as helpful for sexing as in other boobies (Table 29, p. 302), although increased samples may reveal stronger dimorphism within populations, especially for bill dimensions. Otherwise, no other criteria known for sexing; unlike other boobies, voice does not differ markedly between the sexes.

Hybrids reported—None.

References—Ainley et al. (1994), Bent (1922), Chasen (1933), Dement'ev & Gladkov (1951b), Diamond (1974), Gibson-Hill (1947), Gifford (1913), Harrington (1977), Howell & Webb (1995), Marchant & Higgins (1990), Murphy (1936), Nicoll (1904), M.A. Traylor *in* Palmer (1962), Schreiber et al. (1996).

Red-footed Booby

Juv-HY / SY / TY / ASY / ATY — Jan Feb Mar Apr May Jun Jul Aug Sep Oct Nov Dec

■ > 95% ▨ 25-95% ▭ 5-25% □ < 5%

See Fig. 24 (pp. 44-45)

NORTHERN GANNET
Morus bassanus

NOGA
Species # 1170
Band size: 8A-8-9

Species—From all boobies by larger size (Table 29, p. 302); bill large and deep, with proportionally short nail, with malar and forehead feathering extending further in front of eye, and gular extended ventrally (Fig. 226**E**, p. 299); HY dark grayish with white flecks and streaks, white uppertail covs, paler (usually) abdomen and proximal underwing covs, and dark to blackish bill, facial skin, iris, and legs; ATY white except head washed buffy yellow and pp and p covs (but not ss or rects) blackish, unfeathered facial skin blackish, bill grayish blue, iris pale grayish to yellowish, and feet blackish with paler yellowish or greenish ridges to the toes. ATYs occasionally can show blackish ss and rects (see **Age**) but are readily separated from Masked Booby (p. 300) by other features.

Geographic variation—Monotypic.

Molt—SBS. PF absent, PB2 incomplete (Apr-Mar in SYs), PB3 incomplete-complete (Apr-Mar in non-breeding TYs), DPB incomplete-complete (May-Apr in ATY/A4Ys); PA absent. Replacement of pp and ss exhibits staffelmauser (Fig. 16, pp. 23-24). Timing, extent, and sequence of molt follows that of boobies but is suspended during winter periods, resulting in slower rate of replacement. Thus, all pp and ss may not be replaced until the PB3 in many SY/TYs. See Family Account (p. 299) for more details.

Age—Juv (B1; Aug-Jul) is described under HY/SY, below; Juv ♀ = ♂. Note that confirmed-breeding adults can be reliably aged A4Y (and probably A5Y).

Juv-HY/SY (1st cycle, Juv/B1; Oct-Sep): Head, neck, and underparts mostly dark grayish, becoming partly whitish in some SYs by Jul-Sep; back, scapulars, s covs, and rump dark grayish with white flecks (Fig. 227**A**, p. 301); pp and ss uniformly juv (Fig. 16**A**, p. 24) in Oct-Apr, or with 1-7 inner pp and 1-8 (of 28) ss (among s1, s5, and s24-s28) often replaced in May-Sep (Fig. 16**B**), the juv outer pp pointed and worn (Fig. 19**A-B**, p. 28), and the replaced ss dark sooty brown, contrasting with the paler brown retained juv ss; rects dark grayish or blackish; bill and iris blackish to dusky gray.

SY/TY (2nd cycle, B2; Oct-Sep): Head, neck, and underparts partly white, becoming entirely white in most TYs by Nov (head often tinged buffy yellow); back, scapulars, s covs, and rump brown with a variable amount of white coming in by Jul (Fig. 227**B-C**); pp and ss with 2 generations, with 1-6 outer pp and 1-6 ss (among s13-s20) juv, being replaced in Mar-Jul, and very faded and worn (Fig. 16**C**), the juv ss replaced by sooty-brown or (in Apr-Jul) whitish feathers; rects sooty brown, mixed with whitish feathers in Apr-Jul; bill and iris dull gray to bluish gray. **Note: Some SYs can remain all brown in Aug-Dec; these separated from HYs by much more worn feathering, with white flecks of juv feathers usually worn off). See also TY/4Y.**

TY/4Y (3rd cycle, B3; Oct-Sep): Head, neck, and underparts white (head washed buffy yellow); back, scapulars, s covs, and rump partly to mostly white (Fig. 227**C-D**); pp and ss with 2 sets of basic feathers in staffelmauser pattern (Fig. 16**E**), or the juv p10 and/or 1-3 ss among s14-s19 sometimes retained (Fig. 16**D**); ss and rects mixed blackish and white, becoming mostly white in most 4Ys by Jul; bill and iris pale grayish blue. **Note: Retarded TY/4Ys may overlap in plumage aspect with advanced SY/TYs; use all characters (including molt patterns and bare part colors) to make determinations, and age individuals S-TY or T-4Y (see pp. 41-42) if unsure.**

ATY/A4Y (Def. cycle, DB; Oct-Sep): Head, neck, back, scapulars, s covs, rump, underparts, ss, and rects entirely white (Fig. 227**E**; head washed buffy yellow); pp and ss with 2-3 sets of basic feathers in staffelmauser patterns (Fig. 16**E-F**); bill and iris bright grayish blue. **Note: See 4-6Y. Occasional ATYs might exhibit 4 sets of basic feathers (Fig. 16G) and be reliably aged A4Y/A5Y.**

4-6Y (3rd-6th cycles, B3-B6; Jan-Dec): Like A4Y/A5Y but one to a few medial ss and/or rects (especially central rects) dark brownish or blackish; s covs and/or rump lightly mottled brown or with a few brown feathers remaining (Fig. 227**D**). **Note: See pp. 41-42 for age-code terminology. It is possible that some advanced TY/4Ys or retarded 7Ys may also show these characters; more study needed. In addition to these criteria, check p1 and the proximal 2-3 p covs, which appear to whiten with age in A4Y/A5Ys. Occasional individuals can show entirely white body but ss and rects entirely blackish (cf. Brinkley et al. 2001), or have anomalous black feathers among the ss and rects; these should probably be aged ATY/A4Y, as they may be older individuals showing anomalous (molt-related?) plumage aspects. See also ATY/A4Y.**

Sex—♀=♂ by plumage aspect. BP not developed but distended cloaca (Fig. 21, p. 32) indicates A4Y ♀ in May-Jul. Measurements not as helpful for sexing as in boobies (Table 29, p. 302), voice does not differ markedly by sex, and no other criteria known. Head may average paler yellow in breeding ♀♀ than ♂♂ (Nelson 1978b, Redman et al. 2005); color of webbing along toes (Nelson 1978b) appears unreliable (Redman et al. 2005).

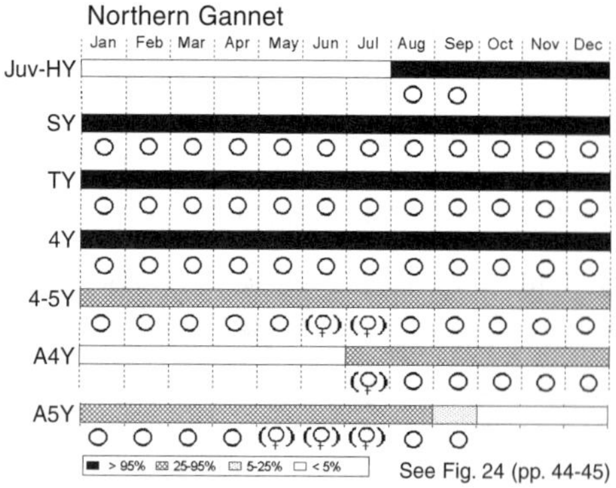

Northern Gannet

Jan Feb Mar Apr May Jun Jul Aug Sep Oct Nov Dec

Juv-HY

SY

TY

4Y

4-5Y

A4Y

A5Y

■ > 95% ▨ 25-95% □ 5-25% □ < 5%

See Fig. 24 (pp. 44-45)

Hybrids reported—None.

References—Baker (1993), Bent (1922), Brinkley et al. (2001), Cramp & Simmons (1977), Dement'ev & Gladkov (1951b), Mowbray (2002a), Nelson (1978b), Oberholser (1974), Palmer (1962), Wynne-Edwards (1935).

Two North American species. Family characters include huge bodies, broad and rounded wings, immense, hooked bills with fully developed gular pouches, and short but strong legs with totipalmate feet (webbing between all four toes). Pelicans have 10 functional primaries (p10 extending 25-50 mm short of the longest, p9, when fully grown), 28-33 secondaries (including 3-5 tertials and one absent between s4 and s5; Fig. 12**B**, p. 19), and 20-24 rectrices. Ageing through the third (to TY and ATY) or later (to 4-5Y and A4Y) cycles can be accomplished through molt patterns and plumage aspect; definitive plumage aspect can take four to six years to be fully acquired. Breeding American White Pelicans (p. 312) develop a keratinous appendage on the bill (Fig. 234, p. 313), which can be used to help age older individuals. Sexes are alike in plumage aspect but differ slightly in bare part colors and, markedly, in size (especially of bill) allowing sexing of mated pairs (in direct comparison) and many individuals in the hand. Brood patches do not develop (incubation performed with feet) but a distended cloaca (Fig. 21, p. 32) can be used to sex breeding ASY females; other cloacal features (Figs. 22-23, pp. 32-35) should be investigated.

In molting, pelicans appear to exhibit a Simple Alternate Strategy (SAS; Fig. 10**C**, pp. 13-16), apparently with a formative (but no alternate) plumage during the first cycle and alternate plumages during subsequent cycles. Feather replacement is extremely slow, with 2-3 or more years required to replace all wing feathers. It is possible that feathers of the head and breast may be replaced three times per year, thus involving a presupplemental molt. But it is also possible that ornamental feathers emerge from specialized follicles activated at the end of the prebasic molt, that the prealternate molt is protracted, suspended, and involves individual variation in molt timing, extent, and color deposition, and/or that the "supplemental plumage" is simply downy feathers exposed for a short time in summer (see p. 15 and Schreiber et al. 1989:30-33). More study is needed. Replacement of primaries and secondaries exhibits staffelmauser (Fig. 16, pp. 23-24), resulting in 2-4 sets of primaries in adults; replacement sequence of rectrices appears to be variable. The preformative molt includes scattered body feathers and wing coverts and the prebasic molt includes some to all body feathers and a variable number of primaries, secondaries, and rec-

TABLE 30. Measurements (mm) of North American pelicans to assist in identification and sexing. See pp. 4-11 for methods of measurement. Species summaries are in **bold** and subspecies summaries in ***italics***. Values are derived from 95% confidence intervals as based approximately on the indicated sample sizes (see pp. 4-5); thus midpoints of ranges approximate means, and S.D. is approximated by 25% of the range.

Taxon/Sex	*n*	wing chord	tail length	exp culmen	tarsus
American White Pelican		**529-635**	**135-170**	**264-366**	**109-131**
♀	20	529-590	135-157	264-320	109-123
♂	20	578-635	150-170	316-366	115-131
Brown Pelican[1]		**444-583**	**116-198**	**243-369**	**62-90**
P.o. californicus		***487-583***	***128-198***	***291-369***	***71-90***
♀	30	487-553	128-195	291-333	71-83
♂	40	516-583	132-198	324-369	78-90
P.o. carolinensis		***480-551***	***121-158***	***280-348***	***68-90***
♀	30	480-428	121-155	280-335	68-85
♂	30	501-551	123-158	292-348	70-90
P.o. occidentalis		***444-514***	***116-134***	***243-310***	***62-77***
♀	14	444-478	116-131	243-281	62-72
♂	16	461-514	119-134	266-310	66-77

[1] Measurements from N.Am populations only; see **Geographic variation**.

trices, from none (sometimes, apparently) to most feathers. Age at first breeding is 3-6 years and adults frequently skip years of breeding; prebasic molts of and non-breeding ASYs average earlier in timing and more complete italicsthan those of breeding adults (see p. 18).

See Harrison (1983a, 1987) and Nelson (2005) for general information on taxonomy, molts, and plumages of pelicans.

AMERICAN WHITE PELICAN
Pelecanus erythrorhyncos

AWPE
Species # 1250
Band size: 9-9C

Species—From Brown Pelican (p. 315) by larger size but shorter bill (Table 30, p. 311); back, s covs, and breast primarily white; bill and legs of AHY orange-yellow to pinkish orange. From extralimital white pelicans and Wood Stork (p. 377) by the combination of mensural characters (Table 30); pp and distal ss (at least s1-s22) black; wing covs, terts, and rects white.

Geographic variation—Monotypic.

Molt—SAS. Molt patterns little studied but possibly as follows: PF limited-partial (Aug-Jun in HY/SYs), PA1 absent, PB2 incomplete (Jun-May in SY/TYs), DPA limited (Jan-Jul breeding ASYs), PB3 incomplete (Jul-Feb in non-breeding TY/4Ys), DPB incomplete (Aug-Feb in ATY/A4Ys). See Family Account (p. 311) regarding the possibility of presupplemental molts. The single inserted 1st cycle molt appears to be homologous with a PF rather than a PA1 (Fig. 10**C**, pp. 13-16). In breeding adults, the DPA completes during incubation and the DPB begins during the chick-rearing stage; otherwise, molting is protracted and occurs on non-breeding grounds. The PF includes some to most body feathers and some s covs. During DPBs, replacement of pp and ss exhibits staffelmauser (Fig. 16, pp. 23-24), resulting in 2-4 sets among pp of adults; the last juv ss (among s12-s20 of 30-33 total) are not typically replaced until the PB3 or PB4. Elongated crown feathers that are acquired in Dec-Mar may be part of a DPA or may represent specialized follicles activated at the end of the DPB. If the latter, replacement of crown (with short brown feathers) in May-Jul represents part of the DPA (or may simply be exposed down); otherwise, replacement of certain crown feathers for a third time within a cycle might represent a DPS (p. 15). More study is needed.

Age—Juv (B1; Aug-Oct) resembles HY/SY in Oct-Feb, as described below; Juv ♀=♂. Note that confirmed-breeding adults can be reliably aged ATY.

Juv-HY/SY (1st cycle, Juv/B1-F1; Oct-Sep): Head, neck, and back dusky brownish, the crown whitish in May-Aug; les covs spatulate with brownish centers (Fig. 233**A**), some replaced by stiffer, whiter, and semi-elongated feathers in May-Sep (Fig. 233**B**); pp and ss uniformly juv (Fig. 16**A**, p. 24), or 1-5 inner pp and 1-6 ss (among s1, s5, and/or terts) often replaced by Sep (*cf.* Fig. 16**B**); unreplaced (juv) distal gr covs with distinct blackish centers (Fig. 233**F**); breast feathers not elongated; bill, facial skin, and gular grayish to dull olive-yellow or pinkish, without appendage on culmen near distal end (*cf.* Fig. 234); iris dark brown, becoming paler grayish brown by Sep.

SY/TY (2nd cycle, B2-A2; Oct-Sep): Head, neck, and back white, often mixed with brownish feathers, the crown whitish to pale grayish in May-Aug; les covs mixed spatulate to semi-elongated, most with indistinct brownish centers (Fig. 233**A-C**); pp and ss with 2 generations, the 1-5 outer pp and/or 1-6 ss (among s12-s20) juv, very faded and worn (Fig. 16**C-D**); distal gr covs with indistinct dusky centers (Fig. 233**G-H**); ornamental breast feathers often present,

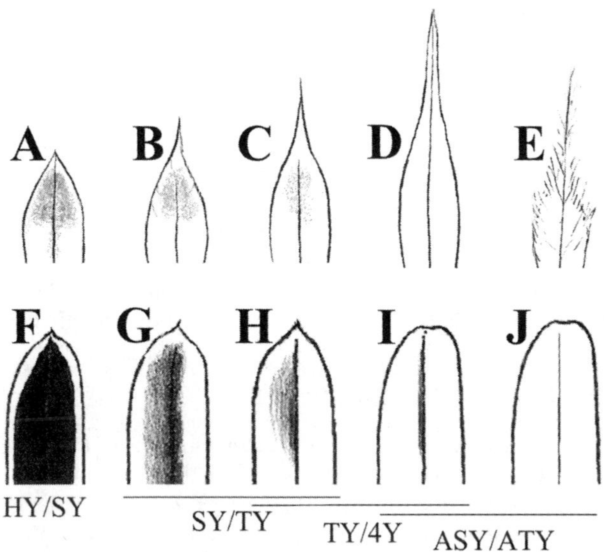

FIGURE 233. Variation in the lesser (**A**-**E**) and distal greater (**F**-**J**) coverts by age in American White Pelican. Les covs have a slight curvature (not shown), are white when fresh in Sep-Dec, become yellowish with oil in Jan-Apr in older AHYs (**C**-**D**), and become quite frayed when worn in May-Jul (compare **D** with **E**). Gr covs refer primarily to those covering s1-s4, often retained during the PF (and later molts); the feather covering s1 can often resemble **H** in ASY/ATYs. Note that ss can exhibit mixed generations, those of previous generations (e.g., B2) showing more dark than those of subsequent generations (e.g. B3). In addition, within feather generations, feathers can become more elongated (les covs) and show less brown or dusky with timing of replacement due to protracted molts.

semi-elongated; bill, facial skin, and gular pale fleshy yellow to dull orange, usually without but occasionally with a reduced appendage on culmen Mar-Jun (*cf.* Fig. 234); iris pale grayish brown to whitish. **Note: Much variation and overlap between age-groups may occur; intermediates should be aged H-SY or S-TY (see p. pp. 41-42); more study needed. TYs in Jan-Jun with buff elongated crest feathers and small appendages on the culmen appear more often to be ♂♂ than ♀♀; see Sex. See also T-4Y and ASY/ATY.**

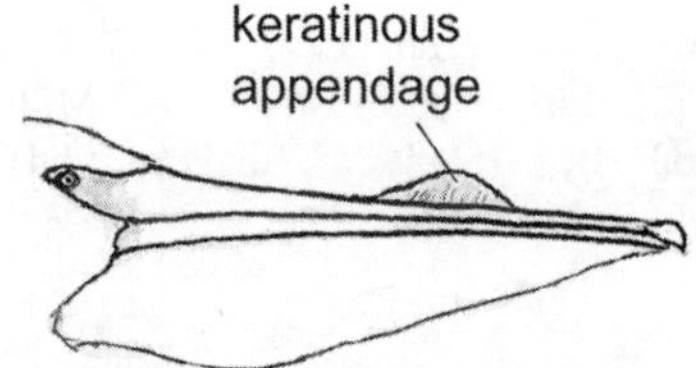

FIGURE 234. Keratinous appendage on the bill of adult American White Pelican, usually developed in Dec-Apr and shed in Aug. Maximum development is illustrated and indicates ATYs, at least. Some TYs develop appendages about half what is shown, 4Ys may also display reduced appendages, and ♂♂ may exhibit larger appendages by age. More study is needed on maximum size of this appendage by season, age, and sex.

T-4Y (2nd-4th cycles, B2/A3-B4/A4; Jan-Dec): Head, neck, and back white, occasionally mixed with a few brownish feathers, the crown grayish in May-Aug; les covs white and semi-elongated to elongated, sometimes with indistinct brownish centers (Fig. 233**C**-**E**); pp and ss with 2-3 generations, 1-3 juv outer pp and/or 1-3 juv ss (among s14-s18) sometimes retained through Sep and very faded and worn (Fig. 16**D**); distal gr covs white or with very indistinct blackish centers or shaft streaks (Fig. 233**H**-**I**); ornamental breast feathers present and semi-elongated to elongated; bill, facial skin, and gular bright yellow to orange, with a reduced to enlarged appendage on culmen in Mar-Jun (Fig. 234); iris pale grayish brown to whitish. **Note: ♂♂ may be more advanced than ♀♀ so combine with Sex when assessing the age of intermediate individuals.**

ASY/ATY (Def. cycle, DB-DA; Oct-Sep): Head and neck white, the crown dark grayish to dusky in May-Aug; les covs white and elongated (Fig. 233**D-E**); pp and ss with 2 sets of basic feathers in staffelmauser patterns (Fig. 16**E**); distal gr covs (except sometimes that covering s1) white or with dark along shaft (Fig. 233**I-J**); elongated ornamental breast feathers present (becoming yellow with oil in Mar-Apr); bill, facial skin, and gular bright yellow (Sep-Jan) to orange-yellow (Jan-Aug) with large appendage on culmen in Feb-May (Fig. 234); iris bright whitish. **Note: It is possible that these individuals can be reliably aged ATY/A4Y.**

ATY/A4Y (Def. cycle, DB-DA; Oct-Jul): Like ASY/ATY but pp with 3 sets of basic feathers in staffelmauser patterns (Fig. 16**F**). **Note: See ASY/ATY.**

Sex—♀ = ♂ by plumage aspect. BP not developed but distended cloaca (p. 32; Lingle & Sloan 1979) indicates ATY ♀ in Jan-Apr. For TYs and 4Ys on breeding grounds, ♂♂ appear to be more advanced in acquiring breeding characteristics than ♀♀; e.g., TYs with elongated crest feathers or a appendage on the culmen (see **Age**) are likely ♂♂. Measurements generally helpful for sexing (Table 30, p. 311); the following can be used to reliably sex most individuals in the hand as well as mated pairs (in direct comparison) in the field:

♀: Bill shorter (exp culmen < 321; Table 30). **Note: Individuals with exposed culmen 316-320 are reliably sexed in conjunction with age, HY/SYs being ♂♂ and AHY/ASYs being ♀♀.**

♂: Bill longer (exp culmen > 315; Table 30). **Note: See ♀.**

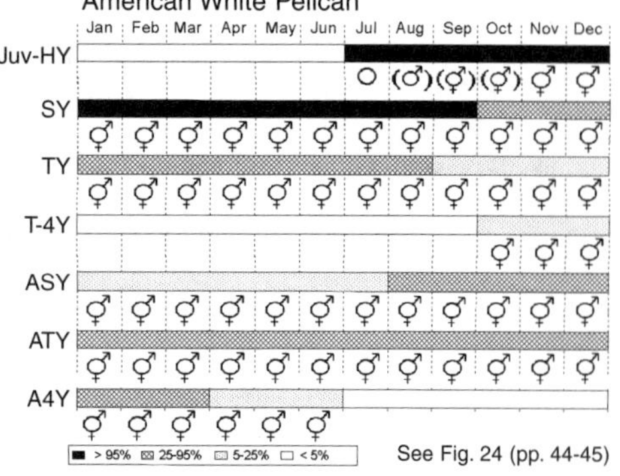

Hybrids reported—None in the wild.

References—Behle (1958), Bent (1922), Evans & Knopf (1993), Johnsgard (1993), Knopf (1975), Lingle & Sloan (1979), Miller (1977), Oberholser (1974), M.A. Traylor *in* Palmer (1962), Roberts (1955), Shaller (1964).

BROWN PELICAN BRPE
Pelecanus occidentalis Species # 1260
Band size: 8A-9-8

Species—From American White Pelican (p. 312) by smaller size but longer bill (Table 30, p. 311); back, wings, and breast brownish to ashy; bill mostly dark horn to pinkish; legs and feet dark.

Geographic variation—See Blake (1977), Dickey & van Rossem (1938), Forbes (1914), Hellmayr & Conover (1948a), Johnsgard (1993), Murphy (1936), Oberholser (1918a, 1974), M.A. Traylor *in* Palmer (1962), Schreiber et al. (1989), Swarth (1931a), Wetmore (1945). Three other subspecies in w.S.Am. The following applies to ASYs in alternate plumage only. HY/SYs and AHY/ASYs in basic plumage may be difficult or impossible to separate by plumage aspect; use measurements for these.

P.o. californicus (br sw.CA-w.Mex, disperses to w.WA, vagrant BC-ID to AZ): Larger (Table 30, p. 311); alternate-aspect ASYs with hindneck dark chocolate to blackish; proximal portion of gular brownish to bright red in breeding adults (Dec-Jul).

P.o. carolinensis (br & wint MD-FL-se.TX to w.C.Am-ne.S.Am, vagrant NE-NY to c.TX-n.FL): Medium in size (Table 30); upperparts medium-pale ashy brown; alternate-aspect ASYs with hindneck medium-dark reddish brown and underparts medium-dark brown; proximal portion of gular olive-brown to blackish.

P.o. occidentalis (res W.Indies; visitor s.FL): Smaller (Table 30), plumage aspect and gular color as in *carolinensis* except upperparts medium-dark ashy brown; alternate-aspect ASYs with underparts chocolate brown.

Molt—SAS. PF limited (Sep-Dec in HYs), PA1 absent, PB2 partial-complete (Apr-Jan in SY/TYs), DPA limited (Jan-Jul in breeding ASYs), DPB incomplete-complete (May-Feb in breeding ASY/ATYs). See Schreiber et al. (1989) for details. The above timing pertains to N.Am populations. The single inserted 1st cycle molt appears to be homologous with a PF rather than a PA1 (Fig. 10**C**, pp. 13-16). In breeding adults, the DPA completes during incubation and the DPB begins during the chick-rearing stage; otherwise, molting is protracted and occurs on non-breeding grounds. The PF includes some body feathers and s covs. Replacement of pp and ss exhibits staffelmauser (Fig. 16, pp. 23-24), resulting in 2-4 sets of pp in adults; the last juv ss (among s12-s19 of 28-30) are replaced during the PB3 or PB4. During the PB2, replacement of pp and p covs begins with p1 (in Apr-May in many SYs) and often proceeds distally to p10 by Dec. Some SY/TYs apparently can molt no or few primaries or secondaries during the PB2, and during subsequent PBs replacement varies from some to most pp and ss. The definitive PA includes the neck (and possibly the crown) in Jan-May and the crown in May-Jul. It is possible that some feathers of the crown may be replaced for a third time within a cycle in Jun-Jul, as part of a DPS (new feathers brown in aspect, *vs* yellow in basic feathers and white in alternate feathers grown in May-Jun), but it is also possible that the DPA is protracted, suspended, and involves individual variation in molt timing, extent, and/or color deposition (see pp. 15 & 29, and Schreiber et al. 1989:30-33) or that brown feathers simply are exposed down. More study needed.

Age—Juv (B1; Aug-Oct) resembles HY/SY as described below; Juv ♀=♂. Note that the following month ranges pertain to individuals from N.Am populations (see **Molt**); in tropical populations it may be best to estimate age in months and assign age codes accordingly (*cf.* Masked Booby, pp. 301-302). Note that confirmed-breeding adults can be reliably aged ATY.

HY/SY (1st cycle, F1; Oct-Sep): Head and neck uniformly dark brown; medial back feathers and les covs not elongated and fringed pale brown (Figs. 235**A** & **E**, p. 316); abdomen white

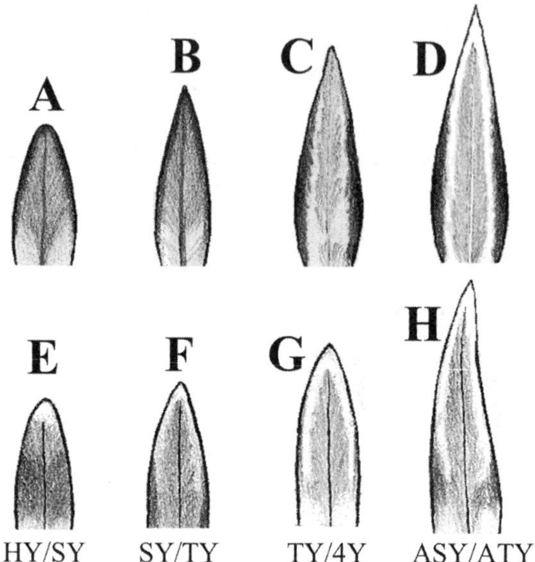

FIGURE 235. Central back feathers (**A-D**) and lesser coverts (**E-H**) by age in Brown Pelican. Juv feathers shown by HY/SYs are brown, whereas older feathers become increasingly adorned with a silvery bloom. Note that the les covs typically exhibit mixed generations and that, even within feather generations, both back feathers and les covs can become more elongated and display more of a silver bloom with timing of replacement due to protracted molts. Note also that there may be some overlap in appearance between feather generations, so caution with the use of these criteria.

without brown; pp and ss uniformly juv (Fig. 16**A**, p. 24), 1-5 inner pp and 1-6 ss (among s1, s5, and the terts) often replaced by Sep (*cf.* Fig. 16**B**); iris dark brown, becoming paler grayish brown by Sep. **Note: In Aug-Sep, HYs resemble SYs in plumage aspect but are much fresher and lack molt. HY/SYs also can be similar in plumage aspect to SY/TYs in Oct-Apr but are easily separated by combination of plumage aspect, molt patterns, and iris-color characters, as described.**

SY/TY (2nd cycle, B2-A2; Oct-Sep): Head and neck grayish brown, often with white patches on head (e.g., near eye) in May-Sep; medial back feathers somewhat elongated and grayish with dusky fringes (Fig. 235**B**); les covs mixed, brown and worn (Fig. 235**E**) with somewhat elongated and grayish brown feathers (Fig. 235**F**); abdomen white, often with sparse brownish streaks; pp and ss with 2 generations, the outer 1-5 pp and 1-6 ss (among s12-s20) juv, often retained through Sep, and very faded and worn (Fig. 16**B**); iris pale grayish brown to bluish or yellowish. **Note: See HY/SY.**

TY/4Y (3rd cycle, B3-A3; Oct-Sep): Head grayish brown with paler white patches in Oct-Jan, or crown white (sometimes tinged yellow) and hind neck medium-dark brown contrasting with whitish side neck in Feb-Sep; medial back feathers somewhat pointed and ashy with narrow black fringes (Fig. 235**C**); les covs mixed with shorter and grayish-brown to more elongated and ashy feathers (Fig. 235**F-G**); pp and ss with 2 sets of basic feathers in staffelmauser patterns (Fig. 16**E**), sometimes with 1-2 outer juv pp and/or 1-4 juv ss (among s12-s16) remaining (Fig. 16**D**); abdomen varying from mostly white to mostly brown; iris pale bright bluish to yellowish. **Note: Advanced, alternate-plumaged 4Ys may be difficult to distinguish from A4Ys in Mar-Sep (and should be aged ATY), although most will show at least some white**

to the abdomen, and the head pattern averages less distinct and with paler yellow to the crown. On the other hand, some individuals approaching definitive plumage-aspect probably should be aged T-4Y, 4-5Y, or 5-6Y (see pp. 41-42) as retarded 4Y/5Ys and possibly 5Y/6Ys may overlap advanced TY/4Ys in alternate-plumage characters.

ATY/A4Y (Def. cycle, DB-DA; Oct-Sep): Head white with pale (Oct-Jan) to dark (Feb-May) yellow crown; hind neck white (Oct-Jan), or dark brown contrasting with white side neck (Jan-Sep); medial back feathers elongated and blackish with distinct silvery centers (Fig. 235**D**); les covs very elongated and with strong silver blush when fresh (Fig. 235**H**); pp and ss with 2-3 sets of basic feathers in staffelmauser patterns (Fig. 16**E-F**); abdomen entirely dark brown; iris pale bright bluish to yellowish. **Note: See TY/4Y. ATYs showing full definitive aspect possibly can be aged A4Y/A5Y; more study needed.**

Sex—♀=♂ by plumage aspect. BP not developed but distended cloaca (Fig. 21, p. 32) indicates A4Y ♀ in Jan-May. Measurements helpful with individuals of known subspecies (Table 30, p. 311). Otherwise, ♂♂ average brighter bill and gular colors and more distinct head-plumage aspect (including more extensive white at base of neck) than ♀♀ during Jan-Jun and, along with direct size comparison (especially of bill length), this can be used to reliably sex most mated pairs. Otherwise, no criteria known for individuals.

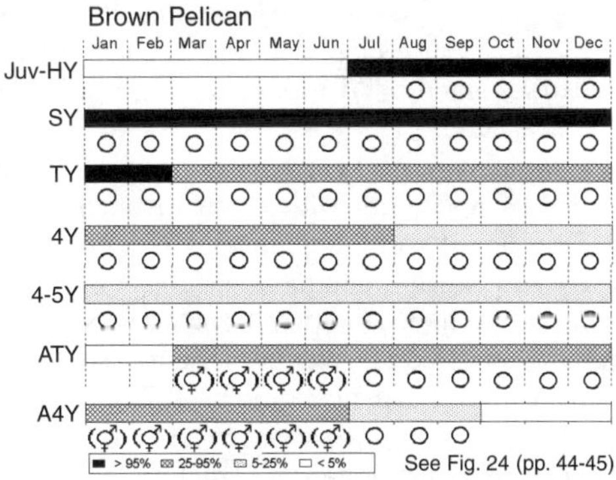

Brown Pelican

Jan Feb Mar Apr May Jun Jul Aug Sep Oct Nov Dec

Juv-HY

SY

TY

4Y

4-5Y

ATY

A4Y

■ > 95% ▨ 25-95% ▭ 5-25% □ < 5%

See Fig. 24 (pp. 44-45)

Hybrids reported—None in the wild.

References—Ainley et al. (1994), Bent (1922), Blus & Keahey (1978), Brewster (1902b), Coker (1919), Forbes (1914), Johnsgard (1993), Murphy (1936), Oberholser (1974), M.A. Traylor *in* Palmer (1962), Schreiber (1976, 1980), Schreiber & Schreiber (1983), Schreiber et al. (1989), Shields (2002), Stresemann & Stresemann (1966), Williams & Joanen (1974).

CORMORANTS *PHALACROCORACIDAE*

Six North American species. Family characters include large and elongated bodies, long necks, rounded wings, long and rounded tails with stiff rectrices, strong and hooked bills, gular pouches, short but strong legs, and totipalmate feet (with webbing between all four toes). North American cormorants have 10 functional primaries (p10 the longest or next to longest, extending 5 mm shorter to 15 mm longer than p8-p9, when fully grown), 17-20 secondaries (including 3 tertials and one absent between s4 and s5 in N.Am species; *cf.* Fig. 12**B**, p. 19), and 12-14 rectrices. Ageing through the third or fourth cycle (to ATY and 4Y) can be accomplished through molt patterns and plumage aspect. Filoplumes (p. 36) are prevalent in some adult cormorants and certain ornamental plumes in the head may be modified filoplumes. See Siegel-Causey (1989) for information on age-related aspects of cranial pneumatization (p. 36) and bursa (Fig. 23, p. 34) in cormorants. Sexes are generally alike in plumage aspect (females average slightly duller and with less extensive ornamental plumes) while males average larger than females, resulting in reliable sexing in some species. Brood patches are not developed (eggs incubated with feet) but distended cloaca (Fig. 21, p. 32) can be used to sex breeding ATY females in the hand; other cloacal features (Figs. 22-23, pp. 32-35) should be investigated.

In molting, most cormorants appear to exhibit a Simple Alternate Strategy (SAS; Fig. 10**C**, pp. 13-16), apparently with a formative plumage but no first alternate plumage in most 1st-cycle individuals and alternate plumages in definitive molt cycles; Neotropical Cormorant (p. 320) may have a first prealternate molt and thus exhibit the Complex Alternate Strategy (CAS; Fig. 10**F**). Preformative molts and prealternate molts in non-breeding AHYs are variable (often dependent on variation in food resources): absent in some individuals but sometimes including a few to many feathers on the head, neck, and back. The ornamental plumes may be basic feathers, replaced just once per year from specialized follicles or representing modified filoplumes, rather than alternate feathers (replacing non-ornamental basic feathers (*cf.* Newell and Sutton 1982) but more study is needed to determine this. Replacement of primaries and secondaries exhibits staffelmauser (Fig. 16, pp. 23-24; see also Filardi & Rohwer 2001; Nelson 2005; Potts 1971; Pyle 2006a; Rasmussen 1987, 1988), resulting in 2-4 sets of primaries in adults; rects are replaced in irregular sequences, sometimes alternately, each feather replaced ~once per cycle. Age at first breeding can be as young as 2 years but more often occurs at 3-5 years; prebasic molts of second-cycle SYs and prebreeding ASYs average earlier in timing and more complete italicsthan those of breeding adults (see p. 18). See Harrison (1983a, 1987) and Nelson (2005) for general information on taxonomy, molts, and plumages of cormorants.

BRANDT'S CORMORANT

Phalacrocorax penicillatus

BRAC
Species # 1220
Band size: 8

Species—From other N.Am cormorants by medium size but shorter tail (Table 31, p. 323); back feathers and les covs moderately pointed by age, with narrow and indistinct dark fringes (Fig. 236) creating somewhat scaled appearance; facial skin reduced and blackish, gular dull gray (HYs) to bright blue (ASYs in Feb-Jun), upper mandible moderately hooked, lower mandible blackish, and feathers of chin and sides of lower face buff to grayish brown; AHY with head and back with moderate greenish/purplish sheen, uniform in aspect with wings and tail, neck and back with sparse white plumes, crest without tufts, and femoral feathers without white in Jan-Jul.

Geographic variation—Monotypic.

Molt—SAS. PF absent-partial (Sep-Feb in HY/SYs), PA1 absent, PB2 incomplete (Feb-Nov in SYs), DPA absent-partial (Dec-Mar in AHY/ASYs), DPB incomplete-complete (Jun-Dec in breeding ASYs). The single inserted first-cycle molt appears to be homologous with a PF rather than a PA1 (Fig. 10**C**, pp. 13-16). Most molting occurs at sea, away from breeding grounds. The PF includes no to many feathers on the head, neck, and back. Replacement of pp and ss exhibits staffelmauser (Fig. 16, pp. 23-24), resulting in 2-4 sets of pp in adults. The DPA includes no to most feathers of the head and neck and no to some feathers of the back and breast. The ornamental plumes of the head and neck may be basic feathers. See Family Account (p. 318) for more details.

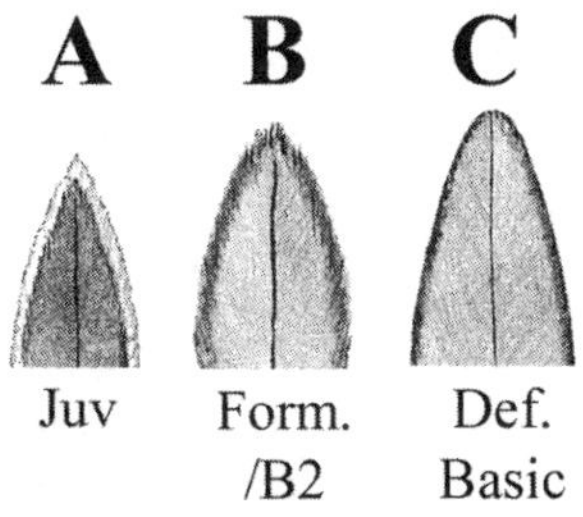

A B C

Juv Form. /B2 Def. Basic

FIGURE 236. Shape, size, and degree of gloss to central back feathers and secondary coverts by species in Brandt's Cormorant. Compared with other N.Am cormorants these feathers are semi-pointed and with a thinner darker fringe, resulting in a semi-scaled appearance. Feathers become larger and glossier with age, and lose the distinct pale fringes found on juv feathers (**A**); this pale fringe also wears off by Jan-Mar.

Age—Juv (B1; Jul-Feb) resembles HY/SY in Oct-Feb, as described below; Juv ♀ = ♂.

Juv-HY/SY (1st cycle, Juv/B1-F1; Oct-Sep): Crown and upperparts brown, the back feathers and les covs pointed and with pale fringes (Fig. 236**A**), becoming bleached and mottled with scattered semi-glossy blackish feathers (Fig. 236**B**) by Jan-Apr; breast pale brown, becoming bleached by Apr and mottled with replaced dark brown feathers in May-Sep; pp and ss uniformly juv (Fig. 16**A**, p. 24), with 2-7 inner pp and 4-10 (of 19) ss often replaced by Sep, the retained juv outer pp and medial ss tapered, brownish, and abraded (Fig. 19**A-B**, p. 28); whitish ornamental plumes of neck and back absent or rudimentary in Mar-Aug; gular grayish to dull bluish gray; iris dark brown, becoming greenish by Sep.

SY/TY (2nd cycle, B2-A2; Oct-Sep): Crown and upperparts variably mixed with dark brown (fading to pale brown by Mar) and bluntly-pointed, semi-glossy blackish feathers (Fig. 236**B**); breast dark brown (bleaching to paler brown by Mar), often with a few semi-glossy blackish feathers in Jun-Sep; pp and ss with 1-2 generations, 1-2 juv outer pp and/or 1-3 juv ss (among s4 and s7-s10) sometimes retained through Sep, very faded and worn (Fig. 16**B**); whitish ornamental plumes of neck and back usually reduced in Feb-Aug; gular dull bluish gray to grayish blue; iris medium-bright blue. **Note: See T-4Y.**

ASY/ATY (Def. cycle, DB-DA; Oct-Sep): Crown, upperparts, and breast uniformly black with purple/green sheen, the back feathers and les covs rounded and glossy (Fig. 236**C**); pp and ss with 2 sets of basic feathers in staffelmauser patterns (Fig. 16**E**), the outer pp broad and truncate (Fig. 19**C-D**); gular dull (Jul-Jan) to bright (Feb-Jun) blue; whitish ornamental plumes of neck and back extensive in Jan-Aug; iris bright blue. **Note: ATYs showing the above characters possibly can be aged A4Y in Jan-Aug; see also T-4Y.**

T-4Y (2nd-4th cycles, B2/A2-B4/A4; Jan-Dec): Like ASY/ATY but upper breast washed dark brownish (without pale brown feathers as in SY/TY); pp with 2 sets of basic feathers in staffelmauser patterns (Fig. 16**E**) or with the juv p10 and/or 1-3 ss among s4 and s7-s10 sometimes retained, very brown and faded (*cf.* Figs. 16**D** & 19**B**). **Note: T-4Ys also average less extensive ornamental plumes by sex (see Sex) in Jan-Aug but this difference too variable to be of use. Retained juv outer pp and/or ss probably indicates TY/4Y (Oct-Sep), whereas some 4Y/5Ys might be recognized by 3 sets of basic feathers but brown remaining in the body; more study is needed.**

ATY/A4Y (Def. cycle, DB-DA; Oct-Sep): Like ASY/ATY but pp with 3 sets of basic feathers in staffelmauser patterns (Fig. 16**F**). **Note: See T-4Y regarding 4Y/5Ys.**

A4Y/A5Y (Def. cycle, DB-DA; Oct-Jun): Like ASY/ATY but pp with 4 sets of basic feathers in staffelmauser patterns (Fig. 16**G**). **Note: This pattern may be rare in this species.**

Sex—BP not developed but distended cloaca (Fig. 21, p. 32) indicates ASY ♀ in Mar-Jul. Measurements (Table 31, p. 323) besides bill (see below) only somewhat useful for sexing. In addition to the following, the extensiveness of ornamental plumes averages larger and the plumage aspect brighter in ♂♂ than in ♀♀ in Jan-Aug, but these differences are confounded by variation with age (see **Age**) and in the development of these plumes. The following can be used to reliably sex most individuals in the hand and mated pairs (in direct comparison) in the field:

♀: Bill small (Table 31; exp culmen 61-69, bill from gape 88-98, depth at distal end of forehead feathers 15.4-18.9, depth at shallowest point 9.2-10.9). **Note: Individuals with intermediate values likely can be sexed in combination with age, HY/SYs being ♂♂ and AHY/ASYs being ♀♀.**

♂: Bill large (Table 31; exp culmen 67-77, bill from gape 94-108, depth at distal edge of forehead feathers 18.4-21.6, depth at shallowest point 10.6-13.3). **Note: See ♀.**

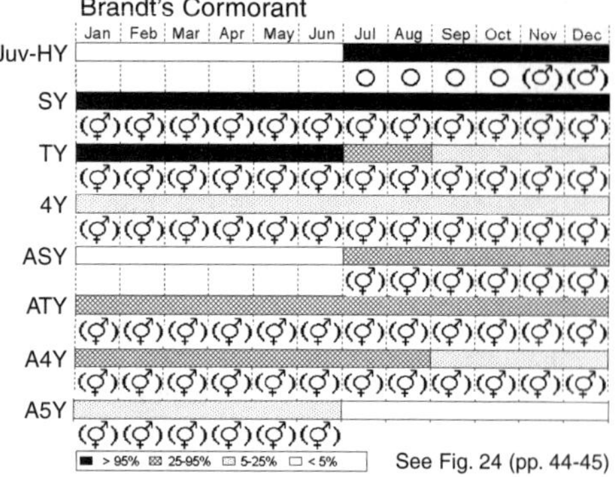

Hybrids reported—None.

References—Ainley et al. (1994), Bent (1922), Boekelheide & Ainley (1989), Johnsgard (1993), Palmer (1962), Wallace & Wallace (1998), Williams (1942).

NEOTROPIC CORMORANT
Phalacrocorax brasilianus

NECO
Species # 1210
Band size: 7A

Species—From other N.Am cormorants by small size with relatively long tail (Table 31, p. 323; Fig. 238**A**, p. 324); back feathers and les covs pointed by age and with distinct but narrow darker fringes (Fig. 237) creating scaled appearance in AHYs; upper mandible moderately hooked and gular and unfeathered facial skin reduced in size, dull yellowish to brownish yellow, and bordered proximally by grayish to white feathering (Fig. 238**A**); lower mandible grayish to brownish; HY/SY with head, breast, and abdomen medium-dark brown when fresh; ASY with head and back with slight purplish sheen, head and neck with a few ornamental plumes at sides, and femoral feathers without white. HY/SYs from HY/SY Double-crested Cormorant (p. 322) with caution, especially regarding larger nominate (extralimital) *P.b. brasilianus*: use size, back-feather shape (Fig. 237), head and breast aspect, and details of the bill and facial skin (Fig. 238**A**).

Geographic variation—See Blake (1977), Hellmayr & Conover (1948a), Murphy (1936), Patten et al. (2003), and van Rossem & Hachisuka (1939). One other subspecies occurs in C-S.Am.

The following applies to ASYs only; HY/SYs may be difficult or impossible to separate except by measurements for some individuals.

P.b. mexicanus (br & wint N.Am): Smaller (Table 31, *vs* wg chord 263-305, tl 148-191, exp culmen 50-61, tarsus 50-59 in *brasilianus* of C-S.Am); centers to upperpart feathers in AHY/ASYs grayish black when fresh (*vs* blacker in *brasilianus*). Populations recorded in se.CA-sw.NM ("*chancho*") may average smaller (especially bill and legs) and with paler and bronzier (*vs* greener) gloss to plumage aspect in AHYs but differences are slight and variable.

Molt—CAS (SAS?). PF absent-partial (Aug-Jan? in HY/SYs), PA1 absent-limited (Mar?-Apr in SYs), PB2 incomplete (Jan?-Dec? in SYs), DPA absent-limited (Dec-Mar in AHY/ASYs), DPB incomplete-complete (Apr-Dec in ASY/ATYs). The above timing pertains to N.Am populations, which have a prolonged breeding season. The PF includes no to many feathers on the head, neck, and back. It is possible that only a single insert molt occurs within the first cycle, perhaps best considered a "PF/PA1" (Fig. 10**D**, pp. 13-16), in which case the species would exhibit SAS. During DPBs, replacement of pp and ss exhibits staffelmauser (Fig. 16, pp. 23-24), resulting in 2-3 sets of primary molt in adults. Due to protracted seasons some SYs may replace the inner pp more than once during the 2nd year as in vultures (Fig. 276, p. 381) but confirmation is needed; reports of SYs with 3 waves of p molt (Fig. 16**F**) by Jul may be based on TYs. The PA1 appears to include scattered feathers of the head in some SYs (replacing formative and/or juvenal feathers). The DPA includes no to most feathers of the head and neck and no to some feathers of the back and breast. The ornamental plumes of the head and neck may be basic feathers. See Family Account (p. 318) for more details.

Age—Juv (B1; May-Oct) resembles HY/SY in Jul-Nov, as described below; Juv ♀=♂.

Juv-HY/SY (1st cycle, Juv/B1-F1-A1; Jul-Jun): Crown and upperparts brown, the back feathers and les covs with indistinct pale fringes (Fig. 237**A**), becoming bleached and mottled with scattered semi-glossy feathers (Fig. 237**B**) by Nov-Feb; breast pale brown, becoming bleached by Feb and mottled with replaced dark brown feathers by Mar-Jun; pp and ss uniformly juv (Fig. 16**A**, p. 24), with 2-8 inner pp and 4-10 (of 17) ss often replaced by Jun, the retained juv outer pp and medial ss tapered, brownish, and abraded (Fig. 19**A-B**, p. 28); whitish ornamental plumes of neck absent or rudimentary in Feb-Jun; iris dark brown, becoming greenish by Sep.

SY/TY (2nd cycle, B2-A2; Jul-Jun): Crown and upperparts variably mixed with dark brown (fading to pale brown by Feb) and semi-glossy blackish feathers (Fig. 237**B**); breast dark brown (bleaching to paler brown by Mar), often with a few blackish feathers by Mar-Jun; pp and ss with 1-2 generations, 1-2 juv outer pp and/or 1-3 juv ss (among s4 and s7-s10) occasionally retained through Jun, very faded and worn (Figs. 16**B** & 19**B**); whitish ornamental plumes of neck usually reduced in Jan-Jun; iris medium-bright green.

ASY/ATY (Def. cycle, DB-DA; Jul-Jun): Crown, upperparts, and breast uniformly

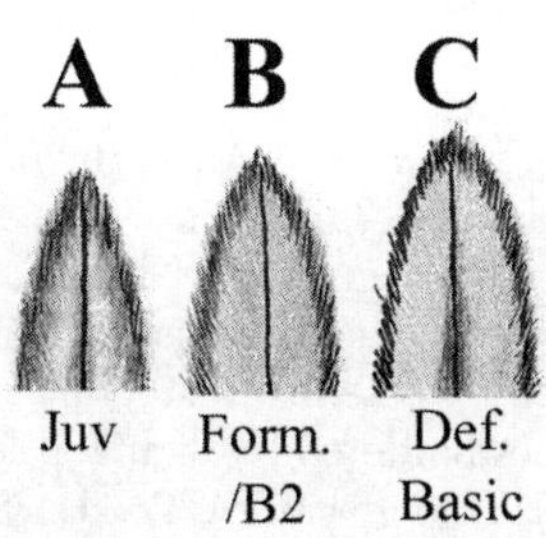

FIGURE 237. Shape, size, and degree of gloss to central back feathers and secondary coverts by age in Neotropic Cormorant. Compared with other N.Am cormorants these feathers are pointed and with a more distinct darker fringe, resulting in a scaled appearance. Feathers become larger and glossier with age, and lose the indistinct pale fringes found on juv feathers (**A**); this pale fringe also wears off quickly in this species, by Sep-Dec in most individuals.

black with purplish sheen, the back feathers and les covs glossy (Fig. 237**C**); pp and ss with 2 sets of basic feathers in staffelmauser patterns (Fig. 16**E**), the outer pp broad and truncate (Figs. 16**D** & 19**B**); whitish ornamental plumes of neck relatively extensive in Dec-Jun; iris bright green.

ATY/A4Y (Def. cycle, DB-DA; Jul-Jun): Like ASY/ATY but pp with 3 sets of basic feathers in staffelmauser patterns (Fig. 16**F**). **Note: Caution assigning this code; due to the possibility of year-round breeding and molting, some ASY/ATYs may attain three sets of pp toward the end of the 3rd cycle.**

Sex—♀=♂ by plumage aspect. BP not developed but distended cloaca (Fig. 21, p. 32) indicates ASY ♀ in Jan-May. Measurements (Table 31, p. 323), especially those of bill, somewhat useful for sexing but not as much as in some other N.Am cormorants. The number and size of ornamental plumes likely average larger in ♂♂ than in ♀♀ in Dec-Jun but this difference is confounded by variation with age (see **Age**) and season. Otherwise, no criteria known for sexing.

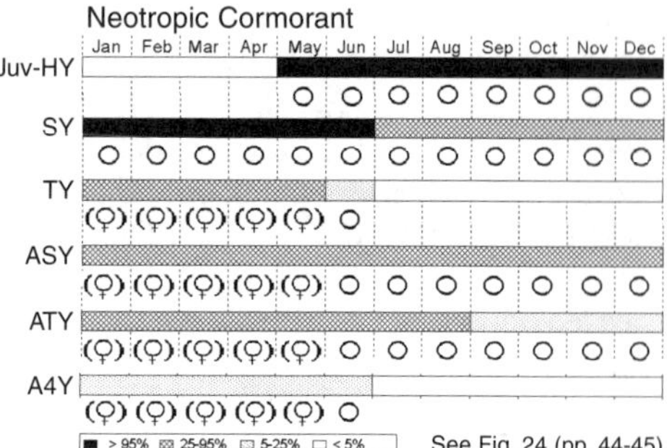

Hybrids reported—None.

References—Bent (1922), Bó (1956), Clark (1992), Dickey & van Rossem (1938), Howell & Webb (1995), Johnsgard (1993), Morrison (1979), Murphy (1936), Newell & Sutton (1982), Oberholser (1974), Palmer (1962), Patten (1993c), Telfair & Morrison (1995), Watson et al. (1991).

DOUBLE-CRESTED CORMORANT

Phalacrocorax auritus

DCCO
Species # 1200
Band size: 8-7B

Species—From other N.Am cormorants by medium-large size with relatively long wing and short bill (Table 31, p. 323; Fig. 238**B**, p. 324); back feathers and les covs rounded by age and with distinct darker fringes (Fig. 239, p. 325) creating scaled appearance in AHYs; upper mandible strongly hooked and gular and unfeathered facial skin moderately extensive and truncated proximally, not bisected by feathering below bill, dull (HY) to bright (AHY) orangish yellow, and sometimes bordered by slightly paler feathering below gape (Fig. 238**B**); lower mandible yellowish (HY) to grayish (AHY); HY/SY with head, breast, and abdomen medium-pale brown to whitish, contrasting with darker abdomen; ASY with head and back with slight bluish/greenish sheen, ornamental crests located proximal to eyes, and femoral feathers without white in Dec-Jul. HY/SYs from HY/SY Neotropical Cormorant (p. 320) with caution, especially regarding smaller *P.b. heuretus* (see **Geographic variation**): use size, details of the bill and facial skin (Fig. 238**B**), back-feather shape (Fig. 239), and head and breast aspect. See also HY/SY under Great Cormorant (p. 326) regarding *P.c. sinensis*).

Geographic variation—See Hatch (1995), Hatch & Weseloh (1999), Johnsgard (1993), Lewis (1929), Oberholser (1974), R. Arbib *in* Palmer (1962), Pittaway & Burke (1996a), Watson et al. (1991). One other subspecies breeds on San Salvador I, Bahamas. The following applies primarily to ASYs; HY/SYs and non-breeding ASYs are difficult or impossible to separate due to

TABLE 31. Measurements (mm) of North American cormorants to assist in identification and sexing. See pp. 4-11 for methods of measurement. Species summaries are in **bold** and subspecies summaries in ***italics***. Values were derived from 95% confidence intervals as based (for wing, tail, exposed culmen, and tarsus) approximately on the indicated sample sizes (see pp. 4-5); sample size for bill depth was often smaller but included at least 10 of each sex. Thus, midpoints of ranges approximate means, and S.D. is approximated by 25% of the range.

Taxon/Sex	*n*	wing chord	tail length	exp culmen	bill depth[1]	tarsus
Brandt's Cormorant		**255-304**	**98-138**	**61-77**	**15.4-21.6**	**58-72**
♀	44	255-284	98-123	61-69	15.4-18.9	58-67
♂	49	271-304	114-138	67-77	18.4-21.6	63-72
Neotropic Cormorant[2]		**238-281**	**155-181**	**37-51**	**12.6-16.1**	**45-56**
♀	46	238-271	155-174	37-49	12.6-14.4	45-54
♂	54	246-281	161-181	39-51	13.3-16.1	47-56
Double-crested Cormorant		**267-359**	**122-172**	**46-65**	**13.2-23.0**	**53-74**
P.a. cincinatus		***308-359***	***133-172***	***53-65***	***16.8-23.0***	***61-73***
♀	20	308-350	133-164	53-63	16.8-19.5	61-71
♂	23	319-359	140-172	55-65	18.9-23.0	63-73
P.a. albociliatus		***277-331***	***125-159***	***51-63***	***15.1-20.2***	***58-69***
♀	73	277-317	125-150	51-61	15.1-18.3	58-68
♂	69	291-331	134-159	53-63	17.9-20.2	59-69
P.a. auritus		***280-350***	***127-171***	***48-65***	***14.8-19.8***	***57-74***
♀	44	280-330	127-160	48-63	14.8-17.6	60-74
♂	37	291-350	138-171	50-65	16.0-19.8	57-72
P.a. floridanus		***267-333***	***122-158***	***46-61***	***13.2-17.9***	***53-68***
♀	20	267-309	122-153	46-58	13.2-15.8	53-66
♂	20	279-333	130-158	50-61	15.1-17.9	56-68
Great Cormorant[2]		**326-380**	**134-171**	**62-86**	**18.2-25.3**	**65-79**
♀	28	326-361	134-166	62-76	18.2-22.9	65-75
♂	26	345-380	140-171	72-86	22.1-25.3	68-79
Red-faced Cormorant		**249-302**	**132-173**	**51-64**	**10.3-15.9**	**51-62**
♀	28	249-284	132-165	51-60	10.3-13.6	51-58
♂	33	270-302	144-173	54-64	12.8-15.9	54-62
Pelagic Cormorant[2]		**220-301**	**121-152**	**41-55**	**8.3-14.2**	**42-58**
♀	54	220-281	121-142	41-53	8.3-11.1	42-55
♂	60	231-301	133-152	44-55	10.5-14.2	44-58

[1] Bill depth measured at distal end of forehead feathering or skin (Fig. 8**A-B**, p. 10). Note that in most species (particularly Red-faced Cormorant) the feathering can recede with age during the first few cycles and the measure should be taken at the distal end of the loral skin.

[2] Measurements pertain to N.Am subspecies only (see **Geographic variation**).

greatly overlapping measurements (Table 31). Beware also individual variation, within each subspecies, in crest-feather color and form.

P.a. cincinatus (br coastal sw-s.AK, wint to w.BC): Larger (Table 31); feathers of crest usually straight and white.

P.a. albociliatus (br & wint coastal sw.BC-sw.CA): Medium small (Table 31); feathers of crest usually straight and white or mixed white and black.

P.a. auritus (br Alb-Nfl to se.CA-MA, wint to sw.CA-s.FL): Medium large (Table 31); feathers of crest usually curled and black, occasionally white or mixed with some white.

P.a. floridanus (br & wint se.TX to NC-s.FL): Smaller (Table 31); feathers of crest curled and black. *P.a. heuretus* of the Bahamas (which could occur in FL?) is similar in appearance but much smaller (wg chord 255-281, tl 118-134, exp culmen 42-49, tarsus 49-58).

Molt—SAS. PF absent-partial (Sep-Mar in HY/SYs), PA1 absent, PB2 incomplete (Feb-Dec in SYs), DPA absent-limited (Jan-Apr in ASYs), DPB incomplete-complete (Apr-Jan in breeding ASY/ATYs). The single inserted first-cycle molt appears to be homologous with a PF rather than a PA1 (Fig. 10**C**, pp. 13-16). The PF includes no to many feathers of the head, neck, and back. Replacement of pp and ss exhibits staffelmauser (Fig. 16, pp. 23-24), resulting in 2-4 sets of pp in adults. Replacement of pp and ss may be more rapid and extensive in coastal and s.populations (e.g., *P.a. albociliatus* and *floridanus*) than in n.populations (*cincinatus* and *auritus*). Due to protracted seasons in the former group, some SYs may replace the inner pp more than once during the 2nd year as in vultures (Fig. 276, p. 381) but confirmation is needed. The DPA includes no to most feathers of the head and neck and no to some feathers of the back and breast. The ornamental plumes of the head and neck may be basic feathers. Many SYs may over-summer on non-breeding grounds and average less-complete PA2 and advanced PB2 (p. 18). See Family Account (p. 318) for more details.

Age—Juv (B1; Jun-Oct) resembles HY/SY in Aug-Dec, as described below; Juv ♀=♂. Many SYs may remain on non-breeding grounds during the first summer. The number of endosteal lamellae in tarsal bones (see Klomp & Furness 1992) does not seem well correlated with age in this species (Broughton et al. 2002) but see Fallon et al. (2006) for ageing by pentosidine accumulation in skin tissue.

Juv-HY/SY (1st cycle, Juv/B1-F1; Aug-Jul): Crown and upperparts brown and with pointed feathers (Fig. 239**A**), becoming bleached and mottled with scattered, rounded semi-glossy feathers (Fig. 239**B**) by Dec-Mar; breast pale brown to whitish, becoming bleached by Feb and mottled with replaced dark brown feathers in Mar-Jun; pp and ss uniformly juv (Fig. 16**A**, p. 24), with 1-6 inner pp and 2-6 (of 18-19) ss often replaced by Jul, the retained juv outer pp and medial ss tapered, brownish, and abraded (Fig. 19**A**-**B**, p. 28); ornamental

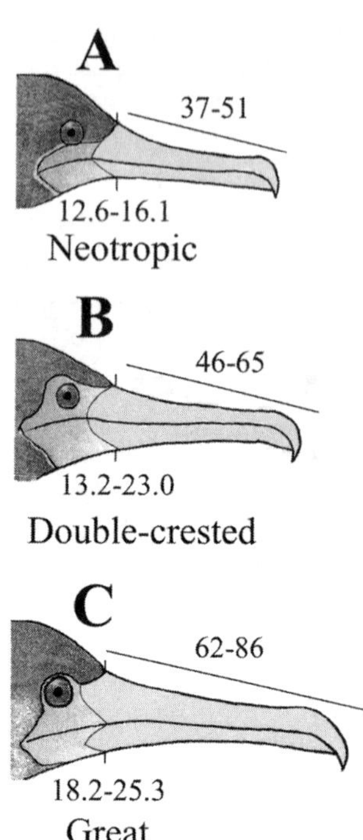

FIGURE 238. Facial features and bill size in HY/SY Neotropic, Double-crested, and Great cormorants for identification. Indicated measures represent exposed culmen and bill depth at distal end of forehead feathering (Figs. 7**A**-**B**, p. 9, & 8**A**-**B**, p. 10) in N.Am populations (see **Geographic variation** in Neotropic and Great cormorants). In Great Cormorant and within subspecies of Double-crested Cormorant bill depth also varies substantially by sex (see Table 31, p. 323) so knowing the sex can assist with identification. Note the differences in the shape of the facial skin: in Neotropic Cormorant (**A**) it is restricted below the eye, in Double-crested Cormorant (**B**) it extends relatively far behind and above the eye, and in Great Cormorant (**C**) it is intermediate; note also the differences in shape along the proximal border. HY/SY Neotropic begin (variably) to develop pale feathering along the entire border of the facial skin whereas in Double-crested Cormorant it is less evident and found only below the gape. HY/SY Great Cormorants usually have paler (whitish) patches proximal to the facial skin. Extralimital Great Cormorants may exhibit features closer to Double-crested Cormorant; see **Geographic variation**). In Great Cormorant but not the other two species the chin feathering extends distally to bisect the gular.

plumes of crest absent or rudimentary in Apr-Jul; lower mandible yellowish at base (Fig. 238**B**); iris dark brown, becoming greenish by Sep.

SY/TY (2nd cycle, B2-A2; Aug-Jul): Crown and upperparts variably mixed with dark brown (fading to pale brown by Feb) and semi-glossy and rounded blackish feathers (Fig. 239**B**); breast dark brown (bleaching to paler brown by Mar), often with a few blackish feathers by Mar-Jul; pp and ss with 1-2 generations, 1-4 juv outer pp and/or 1-6 juv ss (among s3-s4 and s7-s10) often retained through Jul, very faded and worn (Figs. 16**B** & 19**B**); ornamental plumes of crest usually reduced in Mar-Jul; lower mandible grayish at base; iris medium-bright green.

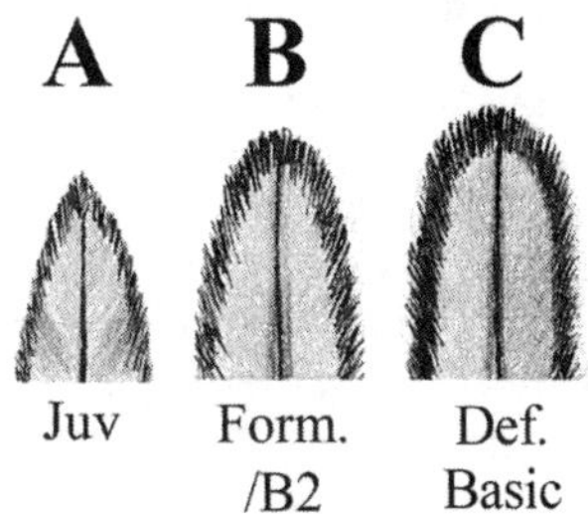

FIGURE 239. Shape, size, and degree of gloss to central back feathers and secondary coverts by age in Double-crested Cormorant. Compared with other N.Am cormorants these feathers are rounded and with very distinct darker fringes, resulting in a distinct scaled appearance. Feathers become larger and glossier with age; note that juv feathers have a darker fringe and less distinct (to no) pale fringe as compared with other species.

ASY/ATY (Def. cycle, DB-DA; Aug-Jul): Crown, upperparts, and breast uniformly black with bluish/greenish sheen, the back feathers and les covs glossy (Fig. 239**C**); pp and ss with 2 sets of basic feathers in staffelmauser patterns (Fig. 16**E**), the outer pp broad and truncate (Fig. 19**C-D**); ornamental plumes of crest relatively extensive in Feb-Jul; iris bright green. **Note: See T-4Y.**

T-4Y (2nd-4th cycles, B2/A2-B4/A4; Jan-Dec): Like ASY/ATY but upper breast washed dark brownish (without pale brown feathers as in SY/TY); pp with 2 sets of basic feathers in staffelmauser patterns (Fig. 16**E**) or with the juv p10 and/or 1-3 ss among s4 and s7-s10 occasionally retained, very brown and faded (*cf.* Figs. 16**D** & 19**B**). **Note: T-4Ys also average less extensive ornamental plumes by sex (see Sex) in Jan-Aug but this difference too variable to be of use. Retained juv outer pp and/or ss probably indicates TY/4Y (Oct-Sep), whereas some 4Y/5Ys might be recognized by 3 sets of basic pp but brown remaining in the body; more study is needed.**

ATY/A4Y (Def. cycle, DB-DA; Aug-Jul): Like ASY/ATY but pp with 3 sets of basic feathers in staffelmauser patterns (Fig. 16**F**). **Note: See T-4Y regarding 4Y/5Ys.**

A4Y/A5Y (Def. cycle, DB-DA; Aug-Jun): Like ASY/ATY but pp with 4 sets of basic feathers in staffelmauser patterns (Fig. 16**G**). **Note: This pattern may be rare in this species.**

Sex—♀=♂ by plumage aspect (although ASY ♀♀ average duller and with smaller ornamental plumes than ASY ♂♂). BP not developed but distended cloaca (Fig. 21, p. 32) indicates ASY ♀ in Feb-Jun. Measurements (Table 31, p. 323), especially those of bill, somewhat useful for sexing (especially in Pacific coast subspecies), but not as much as in some other cormorant species. The size of ornamental plumes averages larger in ♂♂ than in ♀♀ in Feb-Jul but this difference is confounded by variation with age (see **Age**) and season. See Bédard et al. (1995) for DFAs (p. 5), using flat wing length (Fig. 3**B**, p. 6) and width of the central rects on specimens, that correctly sexed 94-97% of individuals in Quebec populations (*P.a. auritus*), and Glahn & McCoy (1995) for an analysis using flat wing length, exposed culmen, and bill depth at distal end of nares that correctly sexed 95-98% of wintering individuals in Mississippi (*P.a. auritus*); similar formula can probably be used to sex individuals of other subspecies. Otherwise, no criteria known for sexing.

Hybrids reported—None in the wild.

References—Ainley et al. (1994), Alström (1991), Bent (1922), Clark (1992), Glahn & McCoy (1995), Johnsgard (1993), Lewis (1929), Morrison (1979), Newell & Sutton (1982), Oberholser (1974), R. Arbib *in* Palmer (1962), Patten (1993c), Pittaway & Burke (1996a), Roberts (1955), Watson et al. (1991), Williams (1996).

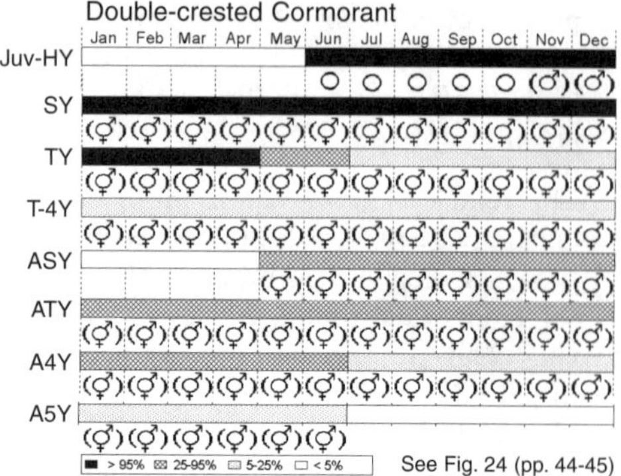

GREAT CORMORANT

Phalacrocorax carbo

GRCO
Species # 1190
Band size: 8

Species—From other N.Am cormorants by larger size (Table 31, p. 323; Fig. 238**C**, p. 324); back feathers and les covs rounded to truncate by age and with distinct darker fringes (Fig. 240) creating scaled appearance in AHYs; upper mandible strongly hooked, gular and unfeathered facial skin moderately restricted, and with feathering bisecting gular on chin, dull (HY) to bright (AHY) yellow to orange, and with feathering proximal to facial skin whitish to white (Fig. 238**C**); lower mandible grayish; tail usually with 14 rects (*vs* 12 in the other species); HY/SY with breast medium pale gray, contrasting with paler abdomen; ASY with head and back with slight purplish/bronze sheen, sides of head and nape with whitish plumes, and femoral feathers white in Feb-Jul. Beware HY/SY of extralimital *P.c. sinensis* (see **Geographic variation**) may resemble Double-crested Cormorant (p. 322) in size, facial features, and plumage aspect; bill color may be the best criterion to separate these.

Geographic variation—See Alström (1985b), Cramp & Simmons (1977), Dement'ev & Gladkov (1951b), Hatch et al. (2000), Koffijberg & Van Eerden (1995), Marchant & Higgins (1990), Marion (1995), Newson et al. (2004), Palmer (1962), Sellers (1993), Stokoe (1958). Five other subspecies in Eurasia, Africa, and Australasia. Note that the following applies primarily to ASYs; HY/SYs may be difficult or impossible to separate except, perhaps, by measurements in some individuals (look also for differences in sheen color on rump).

P.c. carbo (br & wint N.Am): Larger than other subspecies (see Table 31, p. 323); AHY with purplish sheen (*vs* more greenish in other subspecies), ornamental plumes reduced, and white of throat restricted (Fig. 238**C**, p. 324; *vs* extending to throat and breast in other subspecies). *P.c. sinensis* of Eurasia, a possible vagrant to ne.N.Am and w.AK, is smaller-billed (exp culmen 52-73, depth at distal tip of forehead feathers/skin 16.8-22.9; see Newson et al. 2004 for DFAs, p. 5); ventral angle of gular pouch relative to gape < 73 0; ASY with more extensive ornamental plumes (head sometimes whitish), and sheen to head and back plumage aspect greener; HY/SYs also may average more brownish or blackish feathering to the abdomen.

Molt—SAS. PF absent-limited (Sep-Feb in HY/SYs), PA1 absent, PB2 incomplete (Apr-Dec in SYs), DPA absent-limited (Feb-Apr in ASYs), DPB incomplete-complete (May-Dec in breeding ASYs). The above timing pertains to N.Am populations. The single inserted first-cycle molt appears to be homologous with a PF rather than a PA1 (Fig. 10**C**, pp. 13-16). The PF includes no to many feathers on the head, neck, and back. Replacement of pp and ss exhibits staffelmauser (Fig. 16, pp. 23-24), resulting in 2-4 sets of pp in adults. The DPA includes no to most feathers of the head and neck and no to some feathers of the back and breast; the ornamental plumes of the head, neck, and femoral region may be basic feathers (study needed). Many SYs may over-summer on non-breeding grounds and average less-complete PA2 and advanced PB2 (p. 18). See Family Account (p. 318) for more details.

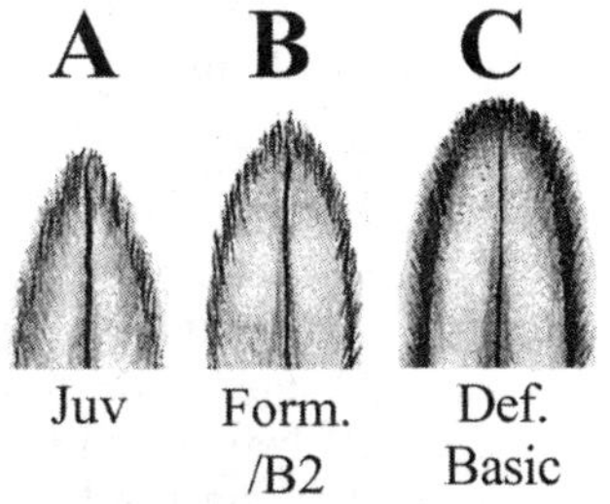

A B C

Juv Form. /B2 Def. Basic

FIGURE 240. Shape, size, and degree of gloss to central back feathers and secondary coverts by age in Great Cormorant. Compared with other N.Am cormorants these feathers are broader and with very distinct darker fringes, resulting in a distinct scaled appearance. Feathers become larger and glossier with age; note that juv feathers have a darker fringe and a very narrow paler outer fringe present only when fresh.

Age—Juv (B1; Jul-Dec) resembles HY/SY in Sep-Feb, as described below; Juv ♀=♂. Many SYs may remain on non-breeding grounds during the first summer. The following month ranges and molt-related criteria pertain to N.Am populations.

Juv-HY/SY (1st cycle, Juv/B1-F1; Oct-Sep): Crown and upperparts brown and with somewhat pointed feathers (Fig. 240**A**), becoming bleached and mottled with scattered, rounded semi-glossy feathers (Fig. 240**B**) by Feb-May; breast pale brown to grayish (becoming bleached by Feb) and contrasting with white belly; pp and ss uniformly juv (Fig. 16**A**, p. 24), with 1-6 inner pp and 2-6 (of 19) ss often replaced by Sep, the retained juv outer pp and medial ss tapered, brownish, and abraded (Fig. 19**A-B**, p. 28); whitish ornamental plumes of head, neck, and femoral region absent or rudimentary in Apr-Jul; iris dark brown, becoming tinged greenish by Sep.

SY/TY (2nd cycle, B2-A2; Oct-Sep): Crown and upperparts variably mixed with dark brown (fading to pale brown by Feb) and semi-glossy and rounded blackish feathers (Fig. 240**B**); breast and belly dark brown (bleaching to paler brown by Mar), often with a few blackish feathers by Mar-Jul; pp and ss with 2 generations, 1-6 juv outer pp and/or 1-8 juv ss (among s3-s4 and s6-s12) retained through Sep, very faded and worn (Figs. 16**B** & 19**B**); whitish ornamental plumes of head, neck, and femoral region usually reduced in Mar-Jul; iris medium-bright green.

ASY/ATY (Def. cycle, DB-DA; Oct-Sep): Crown, upperparts, and breast uniformly black with purplish-bronze sheen, the back feathers and les covs glossy (Fig. 240**C**); pp and ss with 2 sets of basic feathers in staffelmauser patterns (Fig. 16**E**), the outer pp broad and truncate (Fig. 19**C-D**); ornamental plumes of crest relatively extensive in Feb-Jul; iris bright green. **Note: It is possible that individuals showing this plumage aspect can be aged ATY/A4Y but more study is needed. See also T-4Y.**

T-4Y (2nd-4th cycles, B2/A2-B4/A4; Jan-Dec): Like ASY/ATY but upper breast washed dark brownish (without pale brown feathers as in SY/TY); pp with 2 sets of basic feathers in staffelmauser patterns (Fig. 16**E**) or with the juv p9-p10 and/or 1-5 ss among s4 and s7-s11 occasionally retained, very brown and faded (*cf.* Figs. 16**D** & 19**B**). **Note: T-4Ys also average less extensive ornamental plumes by sex (see Sex) in Jan-Aug but this difference too variable to be of use. Retained juv outer pp and/or ss probably indicates TY/4Y (Oct-Sep), whereas some 4Y/5Ys might be recognized by 3 sets of basic feathers but brown remaining in the body; more study is needed.**

ATY/A4Y (Def. cycle, DB-DA; Oct-Sep): Like ASY/ATY but pp with 3 sets of basic feathers in staffelmauser patterns (Fig. 16**F**). **Note: See ASY/ATY, and see T-4Y regarding 4Y/5Ys.**

A4Y/A5Y (Def. cycle, DB-DA; Oct-Jun): Like ASY/ATY but pp with 4 sets of basic feathers in staffelmauser patterns (Fig. 16**G**). **Note: This pattern may be uncommon in this species.**

Sex— ♀=♂ by plumage aspect (Childress & Bennum 2002). BP not developed but distended cloaca (Fig. 21, p. 32) indicates ASY ♀ in Apr-Jul. Measurements (Table 31, p. 323), especially those of bill, can be useful for sexing. The number and size of ornamental plumes average larger in ♂♂ than in ♀♀ in Feb-Jul but this difference is confounded by variation with age (see **Age**) and season. See Koffijberg & Van Eerden (1995) for DFAs (p. 5), using wing chord, exp culmen, depth of bill at proximal end of nares, and body length on specimens, that correctly sexed 82-100% of individuals in a Netherlands population (*P.c. sinensis*). The following is reliable for sexing most individuals of N.Am populations (*P.c. carbo*):

AHY ♀: Bill depth at tip of forehead feathering < 22.1 mm (Table 31; Fig. 238**C**, p. 324). **Note: Individuals with bill depth 22.1-22.9 can be sexed in combination with age, HY/SYs being ♂♂ and AHY/ASYs being ♀♀.**

AHY ♂: Bill depth at tip of forehead feathering > 22.9 mm (Table 31, Fig. 238**C**). **Note: See AHY ♀.**

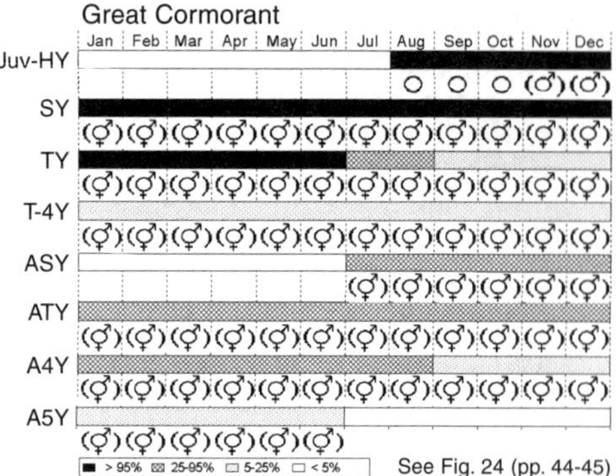

Hybrids reported—None in the wild.

References—Alström (1985b, 1991), Baker (1993), Bent (1922), Childress & Bennum (2002), Cramp & Simmons (1977), Dement'ev & Gladkov (1951b), Hatch et al. 2000, Johnsgard (1993), Koffijberg & Van Eerden (1995), Marchant & Higgins (1990), Palmer (1962), Stokoe (1958), Van Eerden & Munsterman (1995), Williams (1996), Winkler (1987).

RED-FACED CORMORANT

Phalacrocorax urile

RFCO
Species # 1240
Band size: 8

Species—From other N.Am cormorants by medium size with relatively long tail and shallow bill (Table 31, p. 323; Fig. 241**A**); back feathers and les covs pointed by age and relatively uniform in aspect (Fig. 242, p. 331), not creating distinct scaled appearance; lower mandible yellowish (HY) to grayish (ASY) and upper mandible weakly hooked (Fig. 241**A**); gular bluish gray and inconspicuous and unfeathered facial skin extensive and with little or no feathering along malar apterium; Fig. 241**A**), and yellowish or pinkish (HYs) to bright red (ASYs); plumage aspect of HY/SY dark brownish with slight purplish sheen to back; ASY with head and back glossy purplish, lower back glossy greenish, and femoral feathers usually white in Apr-Aug. HY/SY from HY/SY Pelagic Cormorant (p. 330) with caution (measurements can nearly overlap given variation in size of Pelagic Cormorant); use extent and color of loral skin and bill color (Fig. 241**A**) and scapular color (purplish in Red-faced Cormorant, greenish in Pelagic Cormorant). Nestling Red-faced Cormorants are grayish with whitish mottling whereas nestling Pelagic Cormorants are dark. See Pelagic Cormorant regarding "Kenyon's Shag".

Geographic variation—Monotypic. See Causey (2002).

Molt—SAS. PF absent-limited (Feb-Apr in SYs), PA1 absent, PB2 incomplete (May-Oct in SYs), DPA absent-limited (Feb-Apr in ASYs), DPB incomplete-complete (May-Dec in breeding ASYs). The single inserted first-cycle molt appears to be homologous with a PF rather than a PA1 (Fig. 10**C**, pp. 13-16). The PF includes no to many feathers on the head, neck, and back. Replacement of pp and ss exhibits staffelmauser (Fig. 16, pp. 23-24), resulting in 2-3 sets of pp in adults. The DPA includes no to most feathers of the head and back and no to some feathers of the back and breast. The ornamental plumes of the head and femoral region may be basic feathers (see Pelagic Cormorant, p. 330). See Family Account (p. 318) for more details.

Age—Criteria for age determination follow those of Pelagic Cormorant (p. 330), with slight differences in the timing of reliable age determination (see bar graphs). In addition, the bill and facial skin is yellowish to pinkish in HY/SY Red-faced Cormorants, becoming red (facial skin) or grayish (bill) by ASY, and the feathering of the forehead is more extensive in HY/SYs (Fig. 241**A**) and SY/TYs than in ASY/ATYs. The number of primaries and secondaries replaced during DPBs may also average fewer than in s.populations of Pelagic Cormorant.

Sex—♀=♂ by plumage aspect. BP not developed but distended cloaca (Fig. 21, p. 32) indicates ASY ♀ in May-Jul. Measurements not as useful as in other cormorants (Table 31, p. 323) and no other characters known for reliable sexing.

Hybrids reported—None.

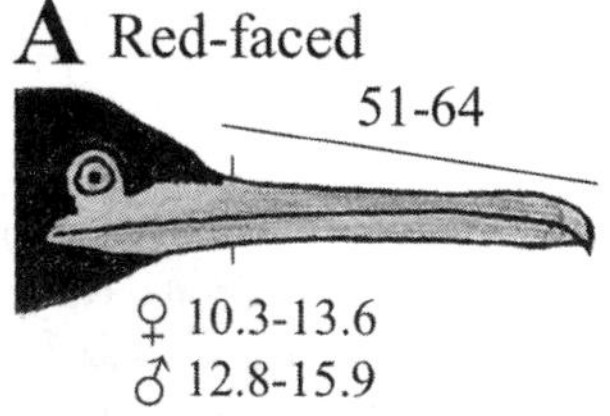

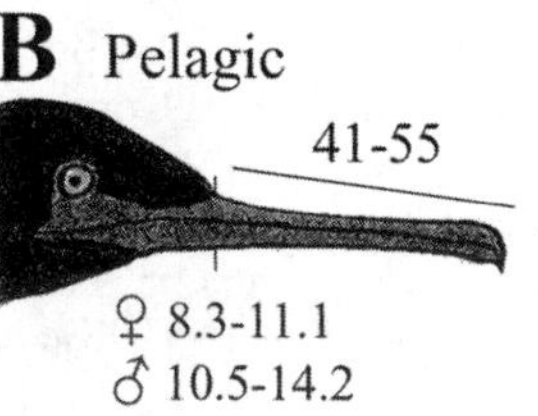

FIGURE 241. Facial features and bill size and color of HY/SY Red-faced and Pelagic cormorants by species and sex. Indicated measures represent exposed culmen and bill depth at distal end of forehead feathers or skin (Figs. 7**A-B** & 8**A-B**, pp. 9-10) by sex. Note that Red-faced Cormorant averages more exposed loral skin than Pelagic Cormorant, and that the skin and bill are yellowish in HY/SY Red-faced Cormorant and dark in HY/SY Pelagic Cormorant. With age, the extent of loral skin increases in both species (but more so in Red-faced Cormorant) and the coloration becomes red, brighter in Feb-Aug than in Sep-Jan.

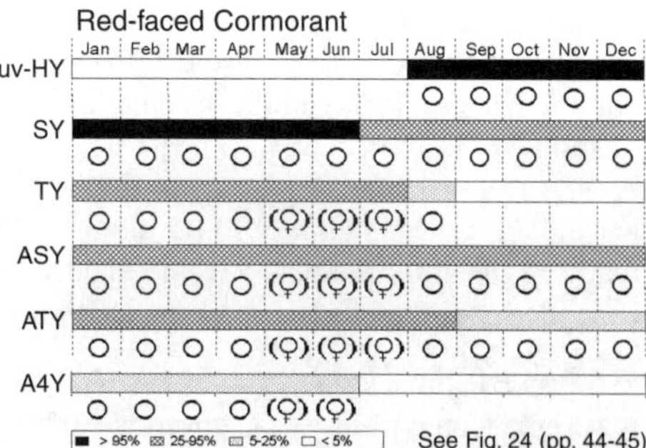

References—Ainley et al. (1994), Bent (1922), Causey (2002), Davis (2005), Dement'ev & Gladkov (1951b), Johnsgard (1993), J. Verner *in* R.S. Palmer (1962), W. Palmer (1899), Stejneger (1885, 1889).

PELAGIC CORMORANT PECO
Phalacrocorax pelagicus Species # 1230
Band size: 7B-7A

Species—From other N.Am cormorants by smaller size (Table 31, p. 323; Fig. 241**B**, p. 329); back feathers and s covs pointed by age and relatively uniform in aspect (Fig. 242), not creating distinct scaled appearance; lower mandible dark grayish, upper mandible weakly hooked, gular blackish and inconspicuous, and unfeathered facial skin reduced (Fig. 241**B**), blackish (HYs) to red (ASYs); plumage aspect of HY/SY dark brownish with slight greenish sheen to back and abdomen; ASY with glossy purplish head, glossy greenish back, and femoral feathers white in Feb-Jul. See Red-faced Cormorant (p. 328) regarding separation of HY/SYs and nestlings from that species.

Populations that formerly (at least) bred on Amchitka I, AK ("Kenyon's Shag, *P. kenyoni*"), have been described as a separate species based on skeletal measures, but re-analysis suggests that these may be ♀ Pelagic Cormorants from a population of smaller individuals (for more information see Gibson & Kessel 1997, Rohwer et al. 2000, Siegel-Causey 1991, and **Geographic variation**).

Geographic variation—Considered monotypic here (*cf.* Rohwer et al. 2000). Populations breeding in Siberia ("*P.p. aeolus*") may average larger than populations of AK-BC ("*pelagicus*"), which in turn may average larger than populations breeding in WA-CA ("*resplendens*") but populations of the Aleutian Is, AK, appear to be smaller than those of other n.populations (being similar in size to s.populations) and size differences appear generally to be broadly clinal. See also Bent (1922), Godfrey (1986), Johnsgard (1993), J. Verner *in* Palmer (1962), Portenko (1972), and Siegel-Causey (1991).

Molt—SAS. PF absent-partial (Jan-Apr in SYs), PA1 absent, PB2 incomplete (Mar-Nov in SYs), DPA absent-limited (Feb-Apr in ASYs), DPB incomplete-complete (May-Dec in breeding ASYs). The single inserted first-cycle molt appears to be homologous with a PF rather than a PA1 (Fig. 10**C**, pp. 13-16). The PF includes no to many feathers on the head, neck, and back. Replacement of pp and ss exhibits staffelmauser (Fig. 16, pp. 23-24), resulting in 2-3 sets of pp in adults. Due to protracted seasons some SYs may replace the inner pp more than once during the 2nd year as in vultures (Fig. 276, p. 381) but confirmation is needed. Note that the extent and timing of the PF and DPB vary geographically in this species, with n.populations commencing molt later and replacing fewer feathers, on average, than s.populations. The DPA includes no to most feathers of the head and back and no to some feathers of the back and breast. The ornamental plumes of the head and femoral region may be basic feathers (black basic flank feathers appear to be retained and covered up by the white ornamental femoral feathers, the latter perhaps developed once per year from specialized follicles), but more study is needed. See Family Account (p. 318) for more details.

Age—Juv (B1; Jun-Oct) resembles HY/SY in Aug-Dec, as described below; Juv ♀ = ♂. Many SYs may remain on non-breeding grounds during the first summer. The number of endosteal lamellae in tarsal bones (see Klomp & Furness 1992) does not seem well correlated with age in this species (Broughton et al. 2002).

Juv-HY/SY (1st cycle, Juv/B1-F1; Aug-Jul): Crown and upperparts brown and with smaller feathers with dark fringe when fresh (Fig. 242**A**), becoming somewhat bleached and mottled with scattered semi-glossy feathers (Fig. 242**B**) by Dec-Mar; breast brownish, bleaching to paler brown by Feb and usually mottled with replaced dark brown feathers in Mar-Jun; pp and ss uniformly juv (Fig. 16**A**, p. 24), with 1-8 inner pp and 2-9 (of 17-18) ss often replaced by Jul, the retained juv outer pp and medial ss tapered, brownish, and abraded (Fig. 19**A**-**B**,

p. 28); femoral region with little or no white in Mar-Jul; facial skin blackish (Fig. 241**A**, p. 329); iris dark brown, becoming greenish yellow by Sep.

SY/TY (2nd cycle, B2-A2; Aug-Jul): Crown and upperparts variably mixed with dark brown and medium-sized, semi-glossy and blackish feathers (Fig. 241**B**); breast dark brown, often with a few blackish feathers by Mar-Jul; pp and ss with 1-2 generations, 1-3 juv outer pp and/or 1-4 juv ss (among s4 and s7-s10) often retained through Jul, very faded and worn (Figs. 16**B** & 19**B**); femoral region with reduced white in Mar-Jul; facial skin dark dull red; iris medium-bright greenish or yellowish.

A B C

Juv Form./B2 Def. Basic

FIGURE 242. Shape and degree of gloss to central back feathers and secondary coverts by age in Red-faced and Pelagic cormorants. Compared with other N.Am cormorants these feathers are more pointed and lack darker fringes (except for fresh juv feathers), resulting in the lack of a scaled appearance. Feathers become larger and glossier with age; note that juv feathers have a slightly darker fringe when fresh, which wears off by Oct-Dec.

ASY/ATY (Def. cycle, DB-DA; Aug-Jul): Crown and head uniformly glossy purplish, the back feathers and les covs large and glossy greenish (Fig. 239**C**); pp and ss with 2 sets of basic feathers in staffelmauser patterns (Fig. 16**E**), the outer pp broad and truncate (Fig. 19**C**-**D**); femoral region with extensive white patch in Feb-Jul; facial skin bright red; iris bright yellowish green. **Note: Individuals with these criteria but a slight brownish cast to breast might be reliably aged TY/4Y but more study is needed.**

ATY/A4Y (Def. cycle, DB-DA; Aug-Jul): Like ASY/ATY but pp with 3 sets of basic feathers in staffelmauser patterns (Fig. 16**F**). **Note: This pattern may be uncommon in this species.**

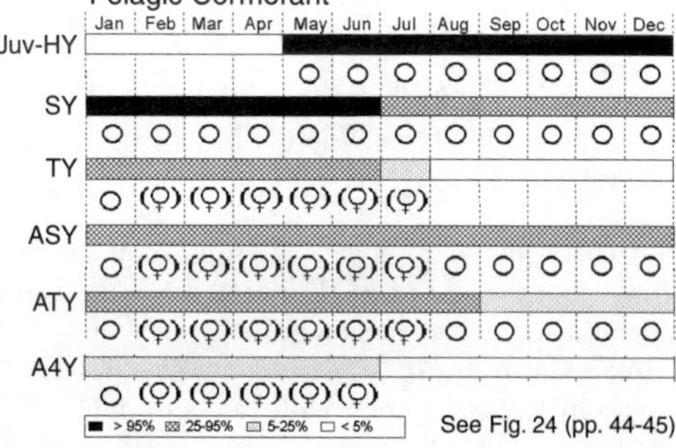

Sex—♀=♂ by plumage aspect. BP not developed but distended cloaca (Fig. 21, p. 32) indicates ASY ♀ in Feb-Jul. Measurements not useful for sexing due to substantial interpopulation variation (Table 31, p. 323; see also Hobson 1997) and no other criteria known.

Hybrids reported—None.

References—Ainley et al. (1994), Bent (1922), Dement'ev & Gladkov (1951b), Filardi & Rohwer (2001), Hobson (1997), Johnsgard (1993), Owre (1967), J. Verner *in* Palmer (1962), Rohwer (1999), Stejneger (1885).

DARTERS *ANHINGIDAE*

One North American species. Family characters include elongated bodies; very long necks and small heads; broad wings; long and broadly rounded tails with transversely corrugated central rectrices in ASYs (Fig. 243); narrow, straight, and unhooked bills with serrated tomia; short but strong legs; and totipalmate feet (webbing between all four toes). Anhingas have 10 functional primaries (p10 extending 15-30 mm short of the longest, p8, when fully grown), 15-16 secondaries (including 3-4 tertials and one absent between s4 and s5; *cf.* Fig. 12**B**, p. 19), and 12 rectrices. Ageing through the second cycle (to TY and ATY) can be accomplished in most ♀♀ and all ♂♂ through plumage aspect and degree of corrugation to the tertials and rectrices (Fig. 243). Sexes are similar in plumage aspect in Juvs but differ markedly in ASY/ATYs, with SY/TY males and, perhaps, some TY/4Y males identifiable. Males average slightly larger in most measurements. Brood patches probably not developed (eggs apparently incubated with feet), but distended cloacae (Fig. 21, p. 32) indicate breeding ATY females and other cloacal characters (Figs. 22-23, pp. 32-35) should be investigated.

In molting, Anhingas exhibit a Simple Alternate Strategy (SAS; Fig. 10**C**, pp. 13-16), with a formative plumage in most first cycle individuals and alternate plumages in definitive molt cycles. Primaries and secondaries are replaced synchronously during prebasic molts. Age at first breeding is not well-documented but appears to be 2-4 years; prebasic molts of SYs and non-breeding ASYs likely average earlier in timing italicsthan those of breeding adults (see p. 18).

ANHINGA

Anhinga anhinga

ANHI
Species # 1180
Band size: 8

Species—From cormorants and other birds by long wings, tail, and bill but relatively short legs (Table 32, p. 335); bill narrow and very pointed; scapulars, humerals, and gr covs with pale to silvery white stripe by age (*cf.* Fig. 243); rects elongated and with pale to whitish tip by age (Fig. 243); iris yellowish (HYs) to bright red (AHY ♂♂).

Geographic variation—See Blake (1977), Frederick & Siegel-Causey (2000), Griscom & Greenway (1941), Gyldenstolpe (1951), Oberholser (1974), Palmer (1962), Phillips et al. (1964), van Rossem (1939a), Wetmore (1943, 1965). One other subspecies occurs in S.Am.

A.a leucogaster (br & wint N.Am): From nominate *anhinga* of S.Am by smaller average size (Table 32, p. 335; *vs* wg chord 307-365, tl 217-292, exp culmen 76-100, tarsus 37-47 in *anhinga*). Reported differences in extent of buff on breast and tail tip appear to be minimal or obscured by variation. Populations of w.Mex-C.Am (possible vagrants to CA-w.TX; "*minima*") may average smaller but this difference is insufficient and inconsistent.

Molt—SAS (CBS?). PF partial (Aug-May in HY/SYs), PA1 absent, PB2 complete (May-Nov in SYs), DPA limited? (Jan-Apr in ASYs), DPB complete (Jul-Dec in breeding ASYs). The above timing pertains to (most) N.Am populations; some adults in FL may breed year-round and exhibit different molt timing. The single inserted first-cycle molt appears to be homologous with a PF rather than a PA1 (Fig. 10**C**, pp. 13-16). The PF includes most to all body feathers and often some to many les, med, and proximal gr covs. During the PBs, pp, ss, p covs, and rects are replaced synchronously, or nearly so. The DPA appears to be limited to feathers of the head and neck, possibly including renewal of ornamental plumes on the neck (although ornamental plumes may involve specialized follicles that are activated just once per cycle, in which case they would be part of the basic plumage). More study is needed on the extent of the DPA, which may be absent altogether.

Age/Sex—Juv (B1; Jun-Oct) has head, neck, and breast with weak, pale-brown feathers; Juv ♀=♂. BP apparently not developed but distended cloaca (Fig. 21, p. 32) indicates ASY ♀ in Feb-Jul (most N.Am populations). Measurements unhelpful for sexing (Table 32, p. 335). Note that the following month ranges pertain to most N.Am populations (see **Molt**); in tropical populations (and in some populations of FL) it may be best to estimate age in months and assign age codes accordingly (see Masked Booby, p. 300).

Juv-HY/SY ♀ (1st cycle, Juv/B1-F1; Aug-Jul): Head, neck, and upper breast uniformly pale brownish; lower abdomen dark brownish; subscapulars with indistinct and dull silver medial stripes and little to no corrugations (Fig. 243**A**); rects narrow, with no or indistinct buff when fresh (becoming brown without buff tips when worn), and without corrugations (Fig. 243**A**); iris brown. **Note: Some HY/SYs may be difficult or impossible to sex, particularly in Aug-Nov.**

SY/TY ♀ (2nd cycle, B2-A2?; Aug-Jul): Head, neck, and upper breast uniformly pale brownish to buffy cinnamon; lower abdomen mixed brown and blackish; subscapulars with indistinct to moderately distinct pale medial stripes and moderate corrugations (Fig. 243**B**); rects moderately narrow with indistinct buff tips and r1 with reduced or no corrugations (Fig. 243**B**); iris brown to dull yellowish brown. **Note: Intermediates with ASY/ATY ♀ may occur that should be aged AHY/ASY; more study is needed.**

ASY/ATY ♀ (Def. cycle, DB-DA; Aug-Jul): Head, neck, and upper breast uniformly cinnamon; lower abdomen blackish; subscapulars with distinct silver medial stripes and moderately extensive corrugations (Fig. 243**C**); rects moderately broad with distinct buff tips and r1 with moderately extensive corrugations (Fig. 243**C**); iris brownish, yellowish, or reddish brown. **Note: See SY/TY ♀.**

HY/SY ♂ (1st cycle, Juv/B1-F1; Oct-Sep): Like HY/SY ♀ (Fig. 243**A**) but lower abdomen mixed brownish and blackish; breast often mixed with some blackish-brown feathers in Oct-Jul; iris brown, often tinged reddish in Jan-Jul. **Note: See HY/SY ♀.**

SY/TY ♂ (2nd cycle, B2-A2; Oct-Sep): Head, neck, and upper breast variably mixed brownish and black; lower abdomen blackish; subscapulars with moderately distinct silver medi-

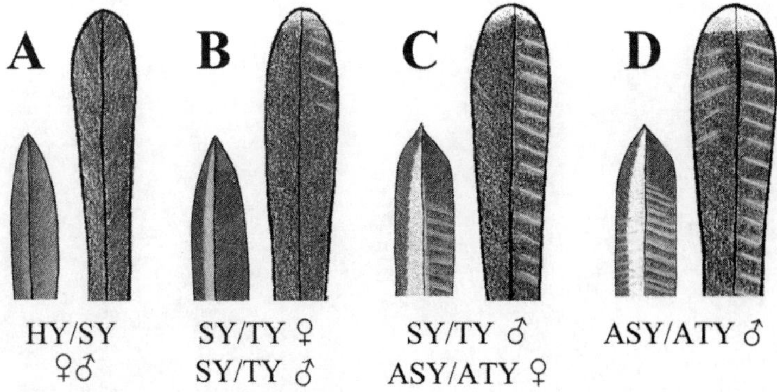

FIGURE 243. Shape, pattern, and extent of corrugations to the subscapulars (left) and central rectrices (right) in Anhingas by age and sex. The transverse pale bars represent corrugations. The width and truncation of the feathers, the extent of corrugations, and the distinctness of the white stripe to the subscapulars and whitish tip to the central rects increases with age and sex, from juv feathers on HY/SYs of both sexes (**A**) to definitive basic feathers on ASY/ATY ♂♂ (**D**). SY/TY ♂♂ can vary from **B** to **C**. The tertials show similar variation in corrugations and distinctness of the white stripe as is found on the subscapulars.

al stripes and corrugations (Fig. 243**C**); rects moderately broad with buff tips and r1 often with reduced or moderately extensive corrugations (Fig. 243**B-C**); iris reddish brown to dull reddish.

ASY/ATY ♂ (Def. cycle, DB-DA; Oct-Sep): Head, neck, upper breast, and lower abdomen uniformly black with slight greenish sheen; subscapulars with distinct silver medial stripes and extensive corrugations (Fig. 243**D**); rects broad with distinct buff tips and r1 with extensive corrugations (Fig. 243**D**); iris bright red. **Note: Individuals showing these characters but with slight brownish mottling to the head and throat are possibly TY/4Ys or T-4Y/4-5Ys (see pp. 41-42), but could also be ATY/A4Ys in fresh basic plumage; more study is needed.**

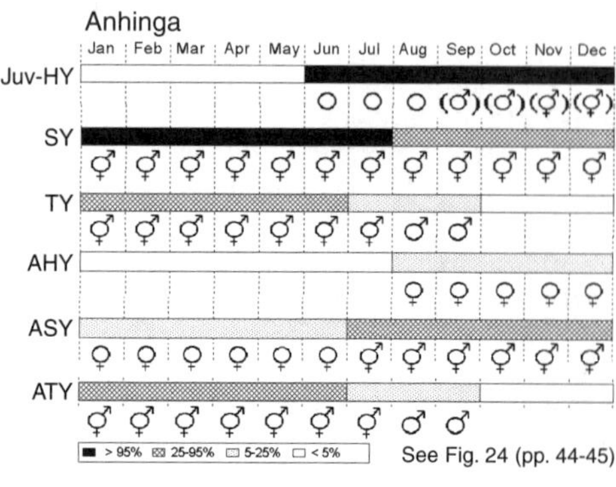

Hybrids reported—None.

References—Bent (1922), Dickey & van Rossem (1938), Frederick & Siegel-Causey (2000), Howell & Webb (1995), Johnsgard (1993), Nelson (2005), Oberholser (1974), Owre (1967), Palmer (1962), Stresemann & Stresemann (1966), van Rossem (1939a), Wetmore (1920).

FRIGATEBIRDS *FREGATIDAE*

One North American species. Family characters include light and slender bodies with short necks, extremely long and pointed wings, long and deeply forked tails, large and strongly hooked bills, moderately sized but highly distendable gular pouches in adult males, and weak legs and feet with four long, crooked, and semipalmated toes, the longest with a comb-like nail. Frigatebirds have 10 functional primaries (p10 longest by 20-60 mm when fully grown), 22-24 secondaries (including 3-4 tertials and one absent between s4 and s5; Fig. 12**B**, p. 19), and 12 rectrices. Ageing through at least the sixth cycle or later (to 4-8Y and A6Y) in females or the eighth cycle or later (to 6-10Y and A8Y) in males can be accomplished through plumage aspect (*cf.* Valle et al. 2006), although degree of overlap between "retarded" and "advanced" individuals in aspect maturation necessitates the use of age-group coding (see pp. 41-42). Sexes differ in plumage aspect among ATY age-groups and most individuals can be sexed by measurements (especially bill size), females being larger. Brood patches are not developed (eggs apparently incubated with feet); other cloacal features (Figs. 21-23, pp. 32-35) can be investigated to help age and sex live frigatebirds in the hand, although plumage-aspect patterns are diagnostic in adults.

In molting, frigatebirds appear to exhibit a Complex Basic Strategy (CBS; Fig. 10**B**, pp. 13-16), with a formative plumage but lacking alternate plumages in all molt cycles. Biennial breeding and molt cycles may occur (in females at least) and molt strategies are further complicated by year-round breeding, which results in individuals at all stages of molt at any time of year. Replacement of primaries and secondaries exhibits staffelmauser (Fig. 16, pp. 23-24), resulting in 2-4 sets of primaries in adults. The second prebasic molt appears to begin with p1 at age 12-15 months, with subsequent waves thereafter commencing at 12-16 month intervals. Replacement of secondaries proceeds distally from the tertials and proximally from s1 and s5 (Fig. 16**B**); in some individuals, the juvenal outer primary and juvenal secondaries among s10-s19 may not be replaced until the third prebasic molt or later (Fig. 16**D**). Age at first breeding likely does not occur until at least 7 years of age (potentially to 15 years or older in some individuals) and breeding is biennial (in females at least) when successful; molt strategies of non-breeding 5-6Ys and adults likely differ from those of breeding adults (see p. 18). More study is needed on molt patterns in frigatebirds.

TABLE 32. Measurements (mm) of North American anhingas and frigatebirds to assist in identification and sexing. See pp. 4-11 for methods of measurement. Species summaries are in **bold**. Values were derived from 95% confidence intervals as based approximately on the indicated sample sizes (see pp. 4-5); sample size for bill depth was often smaller but included at least 10 of each sex. Thus, midpoints of ranges approximate means, and S.D. is approximated by 25% of the range.

Taxon/Sex	*n*	wing chord	tail length	exp culmen	bill depth[1]	tarsus
Anhinga[2]		**220-301**	**121-152**	**41-55**	**13.7-16.5**	**42-58**
♀	100	301-346	215-266	70-85	13.7-16.3	37-43
♂	100	310-349	216-268	74-89	14.0-16.5	38-43
Magnificent Frigatebird		**583-690**	**389-498**	**100-133**	**23.8-30.1**	**21-26**
♀	78	610-690	419-498	113-133	25.0-30.1	21-26
♂	100	583-661	389-478	100-118	23.8-27.2	21-25
Great Frigatebird		**510-650**	**320-440**	**95-125**	**19.3-25.6**	**19-24**
♀	100	545-650	353-440	107-125	21.8-25.6	19-24
♂	100	510-614	320-416	95-113	19.3-24.7	19-23

[1] Bill depth measured at distal end of forehead feathering or skin (Fig. 8**A-B**, p. 10).
[2] Measurements pertain to N.Am subspecies only (see **Geographic variation**).

MAGNIFICENT FRIGATEBIRD
Fregata magnificens

MAFR
Species # 1280
Band size: 7B-7A short

Species—From other frigatebirds by generally long wings and tail (Table 32, p. 335; see **Geographic variation**); white of head and/or breast without cinnamon tinge or wash; axillars usually without white (Fig. 245, p. 338); legs and feet of HY/SYs and all ♂♂ bluish (pinkish in SY/TY? and older ♀♀); replaced back feathers of ♀♀ and S-TY ♂♂ lacking extensive glossy sheen (Fig. 246**A**, p. 339); ATY ♀♀ with crown (but not back) with elongated glossy feathers, throat and upper breast black (Fig. 245**G**), and orbital skin bluish; ATY ♂♂ with pale upperwing ulnar bar absent or restricted (Fig. 244**C**-**D**), scapulars moderately glossy purplish (Fig. 246**B**-**D**), contrasting indistinctly with blackish rump and s covs, and legs and feet gray to blackish. See Figure 245 for further information on variation in underpart pattern by age, sex, and species.

Great Frigatebird (*F. minor*), a vagrant to w.N.Am, averages smaller with shorter tail and shallower bill (Table 32); white of head and/or breast usually tinged or washed cinammon in H-TYs (and probably T-5Ys) and axillars with white patch or (more typically) narrow vermiculated bars (Fig. 245**B**-**C**); legs and feet pink in all age/sex groups; non-juv back feathers of ♀♀ and S-TY ♂♂ glossy green and purple (*cf.* Fig. 246); ATY ♀♀ with both crown and back feathers glossy, the back feathers semi-elongated (*cf.* Fig. 246**B**-**C**), chin and throat pale gray, upper breast white, and orbital skin reddish in e.Pacific and s.Atlantic populations (can be bluish in w.Pacific populations); ATY ♂♂ with more extensive pale ulnar upperwing bar (Fig. 244**A**-**B**), scapulars glossy green and purple, contrasting distinctly with blackish rump and s covs (*cf.* Fig. 246**D**), and legs and feet pinkish. See also Fig. 245 and Howell (1994) for species-specific variation in underpart patterns by age and sex. Lesser Frigatebird (*F. ariel*), a vagrant to N.Am, is much smaller (wg chord 520-580, tl 280-350, exp culmen 79-92; ♀>♂), has white patches in the axillars in most plumage aspects (including that of definitive ♂), and red orbital ring in adult ♀. Ascension Frigatebird (*F. aquila*), a possible vagrant to e.N.Am, is medium small (wg 552-613, exp culmen 87-108) with a shallower bill (depth at midpoint of bill in ♀♀ ~13.5-15.5 *vs* ~15.5-18.0 in Magnificent Frigatebird), and axillar region usually with white. See Chalmers (2002), Harrison (1983a, 1987), Howell (1994), James (2004), and Walbridge et al. (2003) for more details on the identification of frigatebirds.

Geographic variation—Monotypic (J. Dorst & J.-L. Mougin *in* Mayr & Cottrell 1979). Populations of the Galapagos Is ("*F.m. magnificens*") and the Cape Verde Is ("*lowei*") may average larger and/or larger-billed than populations of N.-S.Am ("*rothschildi*") but differences, if present, are slight and greatly confounded by individual variation; more study is needed. See Bannerman (1927), Bourne (1957), Diamond & Schreiber (2002), Hellmayr & Conover (1948a), Lowe (1924), Mathews (1914), Murphy (1936), Rothschild (1915b), Swarth (1933a), and Wetmore (1965) for more information.

Molt—CBS? Little studied, especially within the first 3-4 cycles; the following is proposed: PF limited? (age 6-15 months), PB2 incomplete (age 12-21 months), PB3 incomplete (age 24-32 months), DPB incomplete-complete (active 10 months between breeding attempts which, if successful, are 12-16 months duration within a biennial breeding cycle, in ♀♀ at least); PA absent. Note that the DPB is here defined based on the molt cycle rather than attainment of definitive plumage aspect (see p. 13). The PF appears to consist of scattered body feathers, replaced well before the onset of p1 replacement during the PB2. Replacement of pp and ss of frigatebirds exhibits staffelmauser (Fig. 16, pp. 23-24), resulting in 2-4 sets of pp in adults. See Family Account (p. 335) for more details.

Age/Sex—Juv (B1; year-round) resembles H-SY ♀♂ (Fig. 245**A**, p. 338), as described below; Juv ♀=♂ by plumage aspect. BP not developed but distended cloaca (Fig. 21, p. 32) indicates A5Y ♀. Note that confirmed-breeding adults can be reliably aged A5Y, and measurements (especially of bill) are useful for sexing (Table 32, p. 335). The length of molt cycles (hence rate of plumage-aspect change) in this species is very poorly known (see **Molt**), and individual variation likely results in overlapping plumage aspects between different cycles and ages, in predefinitive plumages. Thus, a conservative approach based on age-group coding (see pp. 41-42) is presented. It is best to sex by bill length, then age by plumage aspect:

H-SY ♀♂ (1st-2nd cycles, Juv/B1-B2; Jan-Dec): Head and breast white with dark-brown patches on sides of breast (Fig. 245**A**); back feathers rounded and blackish brown (Fig. 246**A**, p. 339); molt of pp and ss begins at age 12-15 months, the juv outer pp brown and pointed (Fig. 19**A-B**, p. 28), and the remaining juv ss (among s11-s19) worn and brown (Fig. 16**A-B**, p. 24); **Note: More precise ageing might be possible according to rates of pp and ss molt but more study is needed. Individuals with exp culmen > 118 can be reliably sexed ♀, but ♂♂ should not be sexed by bill length until the bill is fully grown.**

S-TY ♀ (2nd-3rd cycles, B2-B3; Jan-Dec): Bill long (exp culmen 113-133); head, breast, and abdomen white, without or with hints of blackish nape collar and/or mottling in abdomen (Fig. 245**D**); back feathers rounded and blackish (Fig. 246**A**); juv outer pp and medial ss (usually among s12-s16) completing replacement (Fig. 16**C-D**), after which pp and ss with 2 sets of basic feathers in staffelmauser patterns (Fig. 16**E**). **Note: See H-SY ♀♂ and S-TY ♂.**

A

Some HY/SY Magnificents
Most Greats

B

Most Magnificents (see text)
Some ASY/ATY M Greats

C

T-8Y M Magnificents

D

A6Y M Magnificents

FIGURE 244. Extent of upperwing ulnar bar by species and age in Magnificent and Great frigatebirds. Within age/sex groups, Great Frigatebird shows paler coloration to the terts, proximal gr and med covs, and les covs than Magnificent Frigatebird, all ♀♀ and H-TY ♂♂ showing extensive pale brownish as in **A** and many ASY/ATY ♂♂ showing patterns resembling **B**. In Magnificent Frigatebird, some HY/SYs of both sexes show patterns resembling **A**, many HY/SYs, AHY/ASY ♀♀, and most S-5Y ♂♂ show slightly less paling (**B**), and older ♂♂ gradually lose most of the paling (**C-D**). For most A6Y ♂ Magnificent Frigatebirds the paling is limited to the terts and most proximal gr covs (**D**). Thus, it is best to combine age and sex-related criteria for the underparts (Fig. 245, p. 338) and back feathers (Fig. 246, p. 339) to reliably separate these two species, especially S-8Y ♂♂.

T-5Y ♀ (2nd-5th cycles, B2-B5; Jan-Dec): Bill long (exp culmen 113-133); head, breast, and abdomen primarily white but with a dusky collar and mottling on abdomen but no blackish in central breast (Fig. 245**E**); back feathers rounded and blackish (Fig. 246**A**); pp with 2-3 sets of basic feathers in staffelmauser patterns (Fig. 16**E-F**); upperwing ulnar bar moderately distinct (Fig. 244**B**); gular grayish; legs and feet pink. **Note: Individuals with 3 sets of basic feathers (Fig. 16F) can be aged 4-5Y.**

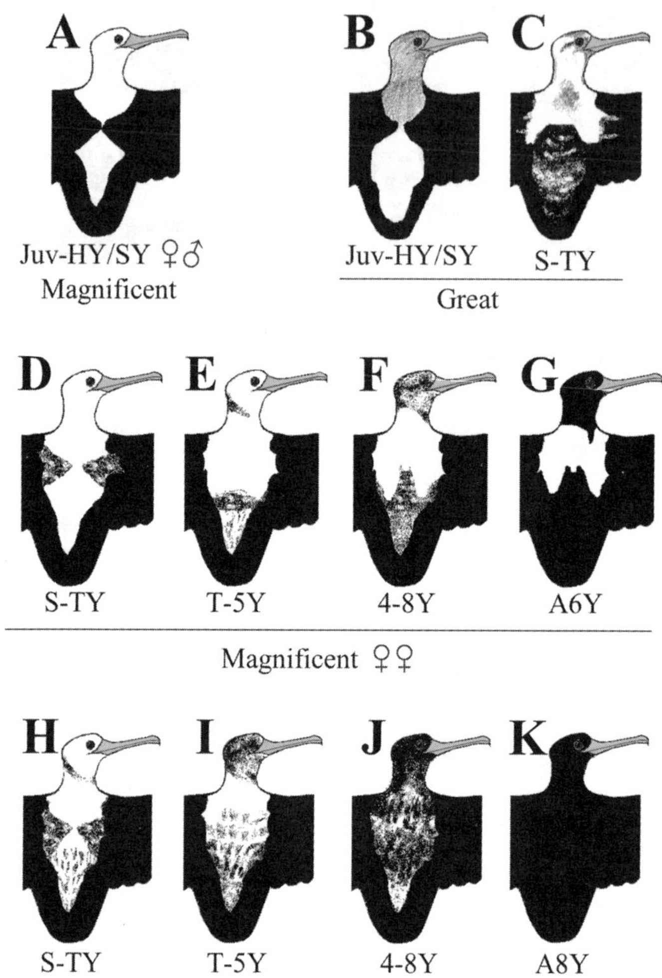

FIGURE 245. Patterns to the underparts by age and sex in Magnificent Frigatebird, with reference to younger Great Frigatebirds for identification. Note that the length of molt cycles and plumage-aspect variation within each cycle is poorly known, necessitating designation by overlapping age-group codes (see pp. 41-42). Note that Juv-HY/SY and S-TY Magnificent Frigatebirds (**A**, **D**, **H**) lack rufous in the head, whereas correspondingly aged Great Frigatebirds show rufous (**B**-**C**), with the last vestige tending to occur on the upper breast (**C**). More study is needed to determine in which cycle the rufous aspect is lost. Note also the more rounded belly patch and the development of white spurs in the axillars of Great Frigatebird (**B**-**C**) whereas Magnificent Frigatebirds show more triangular patches and usually lack white spurs. For sexing Magnificent Frigatebirds, note that ♀♀ (**D**-**G**) tend to develop black in the plumage aspect more slowly than like-aged ♂♂ (**H**-**J**), and that T-5Y ♂♂ can begin to show blackish in the area of the central breast (**I**-**J**), where ♀♀ always lack black (**E**-**G**). Sex of H-5Ys is best confirmed in conjunction with length of the exposed culmen and other measurements (Table 32, p. 335). See Howell (1994) for further information, including more on age and sex determination in Great Frigatebird.

4-8Y ♀ (3rd-8th cycles, B3-B8; Jan-Dec): Bill long (exp culmen 113-133); head, throat, and abdomen mottled white and blackish, and breast white (Fig. 245**F**); back feathers rounded and blackish (Fig. 246**A**); pp with 2-4 sets of basic feathers in staffelmauser patterns (Fig. 16**E-G**); upperwing ulnar bar moderately distinct (Fig. 244**B**); gular grayish; legs and feet pink. **Note: Individuals with 4 sets of basic feathers (Fig. 16G) can be aged 5-8Y.**

A6Y ♀ (Def. cycle, DB; Jan-Dec): Bill long (exp culmen 113-133); head, throat, and abdomen black (without white mottling) and breast white (Fig. 245**G**); back feathers rounded and blackish (Fig. 246**A**); pp with 2-4 sets of basic feathers in staffelmauser patterns (Fig. 16**E-G**); upperwing ulnar bar more distinct (Fig. 244**B**); gular grayish; legs and feet pink. **Note: It is possible that individuals showing these characters can be aged A7Y or older but more study is needed.**

S-TY ♂ (2nd-3rd cycle, B2-B3; Jan-Dec): Bill short (exp culmen 100-118); head, breast, and abdomen white, without or with slight blackish collar and/or mottling in abdomen, but with extensions on sides of breast (Fig. 245**H**); back feathers rounded and blackish (Fig. 246**A**); pp and ss as in S-TY ♀. **Note: See H-SY ♀♂. Check also for legs and feet becoming dusky pink in ♂♂ but remaining pink in ♀♀ in this age-group.**

T-5Y ♂ (2nd-5th cycles, B2-B5; Jan-Dec): Bill short (exp culmen 100-118); head, breast, and abdomen primarily white but with blackish side extensions on breast and a dusky collar and mottling on abdomen (Fig. 245**I**); back feathers rounded to slightly pointed and blackish or tinged glossy purplish (Fig. 246**A-B**); pp and ss as in T-5Y ♀; gular grayish or tinged pinkish; legs and feet dusky pink.

4-8Y ♂ (3rd-8th cycles, B3-B8; Jan-Dec): Bill short (exp culmen 100-118); head, throat, center breast, and abdomen white mottled blackish (Fig. 245**J**); back feathers slightly to moderately pointed and tinged to washed glossy (Fig. 246**B-C**); upperwing ulnar bar less distinct (Fig. 244**C-D**); gular pinkish to red; legs and feet pinkish dusky to dusky.

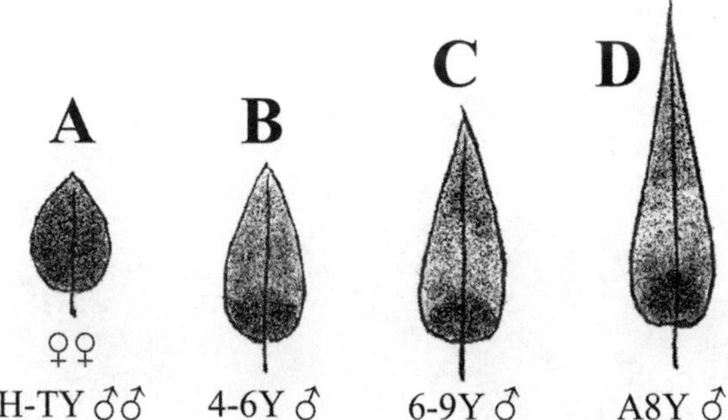

FIGURE 246. Back feather size, shape, and degree of sheen by age and sex in Magnificent Frigatebird. All ♀♀ and younger ♂♂ (with white heads; Fig. 245**A**, **D-G**) exhibit rounded and blackish back feathers without gloss (**A**). As ♂♂ become older the feathers become elongated and display increasing amounts of glossy purplish sheen (**B-C**), with A8Y ♂♂ showing a moderately strong sheen. Great Frigatebird differs in exhibiting more elongated feathers and more extensive sheen by age/sex group, from a slight to moderate greenish and purplish sheen in ♀♀ and H-SY ♂♂ to a much more extensive and bright greenish sheen in A8Y ♂♂; the strong greenish sheen contrasts more with the black aspects to the upperparts than does the moderate purplish sheen in A8Y ♂ Magnificent Frigatebirds. ASY/ATY ♀ Great Frigatebirds can also exhibit more elongated back feathers, as in **B-C**.

6-10Y ♂ (5th-10th cycles, B5-B10; Jan-Dec): Bill short (exp culmen 100-118); head, throat, abdomen and breast black with slight white mottling, especially to vent (*cf.* Fig. 245**J**-**K**); back feathers moderately to fully elongated and washed glossy purplish (Fig. 246**C**-**D**); upperwing ulnar bar usually absent (Fig. 244**C**-**D**); gular red; legs and feet dusky to blackish.

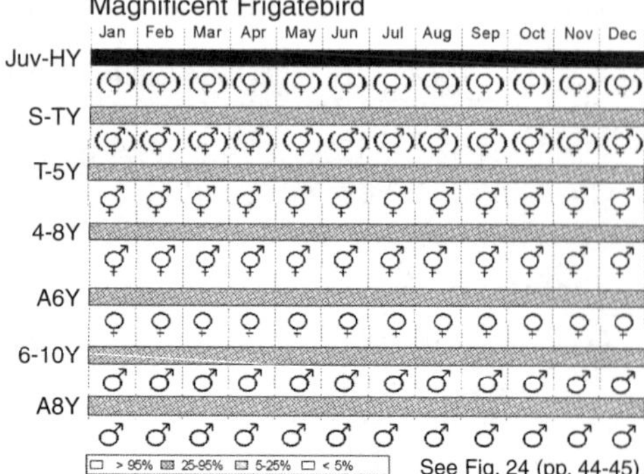

A8Y ♂ (Def. cycle, DB; Jan-Dec): Bill short (exp culmen 100-118); head, throat, abdomen and breast black without white mottling (Fig. 245**K**); back feathers elongated and with purplish gloss (Fig. 246**D**); upperwing ulnar bar absent (Fig. 244**D**); gular red; legs and feet dusky to blackish. **Note: It is possible that individuals showing these characters can be aged A9Y or older but more study is needed.**

Hybrids reported—None.

References—Ainley et al. (1994), Bent (1922), Cramp & Simmons (1977), DeKorte & DeVries (1978), Diamond (1972), Diamond & Schreiber (2002), Harrison (1983a, 1987), Howell (1994), Howell & Webb (1995), James (2004), Lowe (1924), Metz & Schreiber (2002), Murphy (1936), Nelson (1975, 2005), Oberholser (1974), Palmer (1962), Parker et al. (1987), Schreiber & Schreiber (1988), Swarth (1931a, 1933a), Valle et al. (2006), Wetmore (1965).

HERONS, BITTERNS, AND ALLIES *ARDEIDAE*

Twelve North American species. Family characters include light and slender bodies with long necks, rounded wings, occipital, pectoral, and/or scapular ornamental plumes in adults of many species (Fig. 254, p. 349; Bock 1956) reaching maximum length during the breeding season, short tails, long and dagger-like bills, and long and strong legs without extensive palmations between the toes. Bitterns and Herons have 10 functional primaries (p10 extending 5-25 mm short of the longest, p8-p9, when fully grown), 15-19 secondaries (including 3-4 tertials and one absent between s4 and s5; Fig. 12**B**, p. 19), and 8-12 rectrices. Ageing through the 3rd (to TY and ATY), 4th (to 4Y and A4Y) or occasionally later (to A5Y) cycles can be accomplished in most species by plumage aspect and molt patterns among pp and ss. Sexes are alike in plumage aspect in all but one species (Least Bittern, p. 344), although in some species females average slightly duller plumage aspect and shorter ornamental plumes than males. Measurements are generally unhelpful for sexing (males averaging slightly larger in most species). Medial brood patches (Fig. 20**A**, p. 31) usually develop in both sexes, but distended cloacae (Fig. 21, p. 32) indicate breeding ATY females, and other cloacal characters (Figs. 22-23, pp. 32-35) should be investigated. Bare part coloration (especially that of the loral skin, bill, and iris) vary more by season (becoming brighter during breeding) than with age or sex (Meyerriecks 1960) and can be quite ephemeral (e.g., Kent 1986), although certain bare part colors can also vary by age or (less commonly) sex in a few species. See Hancock & Kushlan (1984), Kushlan & Hancock (2005), and Voisin (1991) for general information on identification, molts, and plumages of bitterns and herons.

In molting, bitterns and herons exhibit a Complex Basic Strategy (CBS; Fig. 10**B**, pp. 13-16), with a formative plumage but lacking alternate plumages in all molt cycles (Pyle & Howell 2004). Primaries and primary coverts are replaced distally except that p9 or p8-p9 can be replaced subsequent to p10; replacement of secondaries proceeds proximally from s1 and s5 and both proximally and distally from the longest tertials (*cf.* Fig. 12**B**, p. 19); and rectrices appear to be replaced in irregular sequences, all feathers often replaced once per cycle, but not always in the larger species. One species (Least Bittern) appears to replace flight feathers synchronously. Larger species can exhibit staffelmauser (Fig. 16, pp. 23-24), resulting in 1-4 sets of primaries in adults. Age at first breeding can be 1 year in most species (commonly in the smaller species and rarely in the larger species), with individuals of some small and most large species initiating breeding at 2-3 years; prebasic molts of non-breeding AHYs average earlier in timing and often more complete italicsthan those of breeding adults (see p. 18).

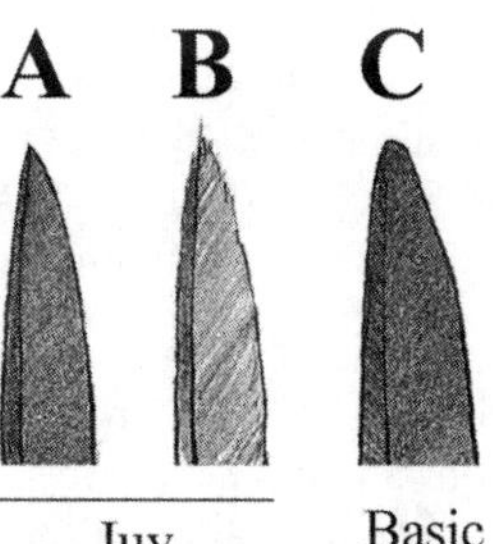

FIGURE 247. Shape of the outer primaries (p8-p10) by age in bitterns, herons, and egrets. Juv pp on HY/SYs are more pointed and relatively fresh in fall-winter (**A**) but very worn and abraded on spring SYs, or (especially) when this feather is retained during incomplete prebasic molts (**B**) on SYs, TYs, and occasionally 4Ys. Basic primaries on AHY/ASYs are broad and fresh. Smaller species often replace the outer pp during the PB2 but large species may retain p9-p10 or p10 until the PB3 or (rarely) the PB4.

AMERICAN BITTERN
Botaurus lentiginosus

AMBI
Species # 1900
Band size: 6♀, 7A♂

Species—From other N.Am bitterns and herons (including Juv-HY night-herons) by medium size with proportionately short tail (Table 33, p. 346); outer pp not notched (*cf.* Fig. 4**B**, p. 7); breeding plumes (*cf.* Fig. 254, p. 349) absent; back and s covs without well-defined pale spots and contrasting distinctly with blacker pp; malar stripe well defined (*cf.* Fig. 2, p. 3); bill yellowish; legs and feet blackish. Great Bittern (*B. stellaris*) of Eurasia, a possible vagrant, is larger but with shorter average bill (wg chord 296-357, tl 96-126, exp culmen 60-74, tarsus 98-132); culmen mostly pale (*vs* mostly dusky in American Bittern); gape dull greenish to bluish (*vs* bright yellow); crown glossy blackish (*vs* rusty); back and s covs with distinct black centers; pp and ss mottled brown (*vs* blackish in American Bittern). Pinnated Bittern (*B. pinnatus*) and Juv/HY tiger-herons (*Tigrisoma*), possible vagrants to s-se.N.Am, are larger in most measures (see Blake 1977), have heavily barred or marked upperparts, and lack distinct malar stripe or streaking to the underparts.

Geographic variation—Monotypic (R.B. Payne *in* Mayr & Cottrell 1979). Populations of BC-Alb to CA-NM ("*B.l. peeti*") may average slightly larger and brighter (less grayish) but differences, if present, are insufficient. See Brodkorb (1936), Hellmayr & Conover (1948a), Oberholser (1974), Parkes (1955a), Todd (1963).

Molt—CBS. PF partial (Jul-Nov in HYs), PB2 incomplete-complete (May-Oct in non-breeding SYs), DPB incomplete-complete (Jun-Nov in breeding ASYs); PA absent. Most or all molting occurs on breeding grounds, with replacement of some back feathers commencing during breeding. The PF includes most or all body feathers and can include some marginal les covs, but no pp, ss, or rects. The PBs appear usually to be incomplete, most (~75-80%) AHYs exhibiting staffelmauser (Fig. 16, pp. 23-24), resulting in 2-3 sets among pp of adults. One to 4 outer pp and 1-6 (of 15) ss (among s3-s4 and s7-s10) can be retained during the PB2 (*cf.* Fig. 16**B**), and occasional TYs may retain the juv p9, p10, and/or 2-3 ss (among s4 and s7-s9) during the PB3 (Fig. 16**D**).

Age—Juv (B1; Jul-Oct) has crown dull brown, bars of back and streaks of underparts less distinct and buffier, and malar streak dusky and indistinct; Juv ♀=♂, although some ♂♂ and full-grown ♀♀ may be reliably sexed by bill depth (see **Sex**). In addition to the following, the juv inner ss (s11-s17, including the terts) and outer rects average more cinnamon barring than definitive feathers but there is substantial variation within both age groups.

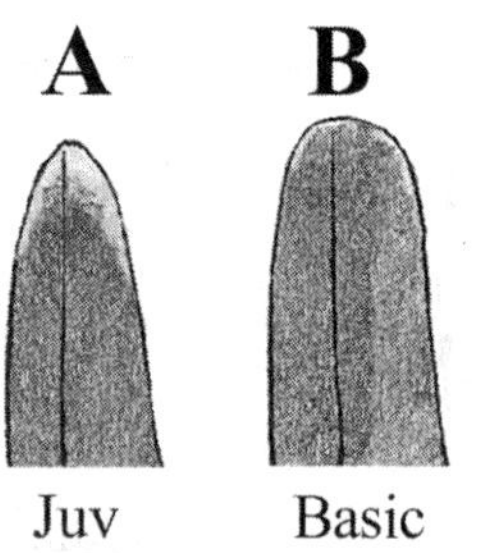

FIGURE 248. Shape and degree of buff-cinnamon fringing to the outer primary coverts (corresponding to p8-p10) by age in American Bittern, showing wider and more extensive fringing in juv (**A**) than basic (**B**) feathers. Juv outer p covs are retained by HY/SYs and some SY/TYs whereas basic covs indicate AHY/ASY (uncommon?) or perhaps ASY/ATY.

HY/SY (1st-cycle, F1; Oct-Sep): Pp and ss uniformly juv and not showing s1-p1 contrast (Fig. 13**A**, p. 20), or 1-5 inner pp and/or 1-6 ss (among s1, s5, and the terts) often replaced in May-Sep, the juv outer pp pointed and worn (Fig. 247**A-B**, p. 341), and the outer p covs narrow with wider buffy-cinnamon fringes or tips to inner webs (Fig. 248**A**); back, scapulars, humerals, and some marginal les covs replaced, contrasting with worn, juv les (most), med, and gr covs (Fig. 13**B**, p. 20); outer rects narrow and rounded (Fig. 256**A**, p. 351).

AHY/ASY (Def. cycle, DB; Oct-Sep): Pp, p covs, and ss uniformly basic and showing uninterrupted replacement cline and s1-p1 contrast (Fig. 14**B**, p. 21), the outer pp broad and relatively fresh (Fig. 247**C**), and the outer p covs broad and with narrow or no buffy-cinnamon fringes (Fig. 248**B**); back, scapulars, humerals, and s covs uniform in wear (*cf.* Fig. 14**B**); outer rects broad and truncate (Fig. 256**B**). **Note: These characters, resulting from a complete PB, may be uncommon in this species.**

SY/TY (2nd cycle, B2; Oct-Sep): Like AHY/ASY but pp and ss with 2 generations, 1-4 juv outer pp and/or 1-6 juv ss (among s3-s4 and s7-s10 of 15 ss) retained through Sep, very faded and worn (Fig. 16**B**, p. 24; Fig. 247**B**); note that p10 can be replaced before p9). **Note: Rarely some TY/4Ys may retain 1-2 juv pp or ss and can be identified by the presence of two sets of basic feathers in staffelmauser patterns as well (Fig. 16D).**

ASY/ATY (Def. cycle, DB; Oct-Sep): Like AHY/ASY but pp and ss with 2 sets of basic feathers in staffelmauser patterns (Fig. 16**E**).

ATY/A4Y (Def. cycle, DB; Oct-Jun): Like ASY/ATY but pp with 3 sets of basic feathers in staffelmauser patterns (Fig. 16**F**). **Note: this age designation may be uncommon in this species.**

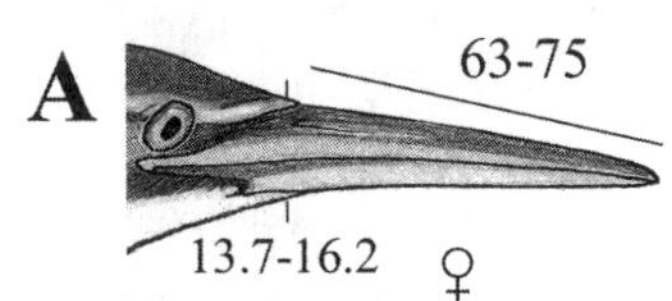

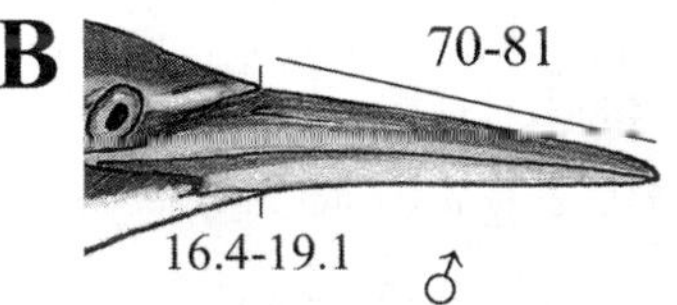

FIGURE 249. Bill size by sex in American Bittern. See also Table 33 (p. 346). Measures refer to exp culmen (Fig. 7**A**, p. 9) and bill depth at tip of forehead feathers (Fig. 8**A**, p. 10).

Sex— ♀ = ♂ by plumage aspect. Medial BP (Fig. 20**A**, p. 31) apparently developed by ♀ only and distended cloaca (Fig. 21, p. 32) indicates ASY ♀♀ in Apr-Aug. Measurements are generally useful (Table 33, p. 346); see Azure et al. (2000) for DFAs (p. 5), primarily using tarsus length and bill from distal end of nares, that correctly sexed 76-86% of live individuals from a MN population. The following appears to be reliable for sexing most or all individuals:

♀: Bill shallow (Table 33; Fig. 249**A**; also, depth at distal end of nares 11.9-14.5).

♂: Bill deep (Table 33; Fig. 249**B**; also, depth at distal end of nares 14.5-16.8).

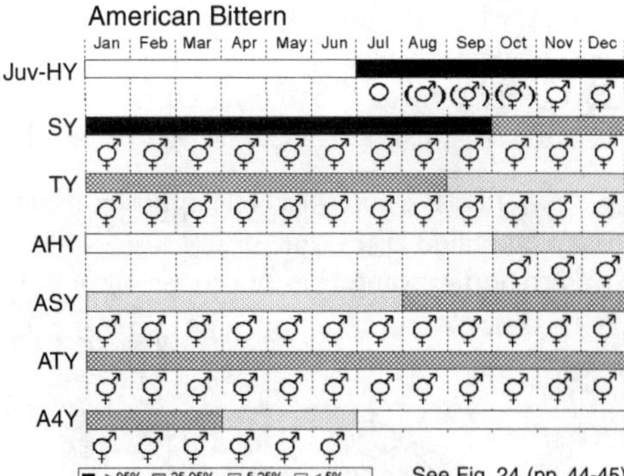

Hybrids reported—None.

References—Azure et al. (2000), Baker (1993), Bent (1926), Cramp & Simmons (1977), Gibbs et al. (1992a), Lansdown (2000), Oberholser (1974), Palmer (1962), Roberts (1955), Wood (1986).

LEAST BITTERN LEBI
Ixobrychus exilis Species # 1910
Band size: 4

Species—From other N.Am bitterns and herons (including Green Heron) by much smaller size (Table 33); outer pp not notched (*cf.* Fig. 4**B**, p. 7); breeding plumes absent (*cf.* Fig. 254, p. 349); back uniformly blackish (♂) to brown (♀); face, nape, and les covs primarily buff to buffy yellow (*cf.* Fig. 250); bill yellowish. Local, carotenistic (erythristic) morph "Cory's" Least Bittern, formerly known as "*I.e. neoxena*", has buffy yellow feathering replaced by chestnut, rusty, and/or black, and bill brown; see Cory (1886), Scott (1892), Chapman (1896a), Bangs (1915a), Carpenter (1948), Teixeira & Alvarenga (1985), and Pittaway & Burke (1996b) for more information.

Little Bittern (*I. minutus*), a vagrant to the Caribbean and potentially to N.Am, is larger with proportionally shorter bill (wg chord 142-158, tl 48-53, exp culmen 43-53, tarsus 39-51); proximal scapulars without white or buff stripes (*vs* with stripes in Least); s covs brighter yellow (less brownish or buff). Yellow Bittern (*I. sinensis*), a vagrant to w.AK, is larger (wg chord 129-150, tl 40-50, exp culmen 47-57, tarsus 44-51); nape straw yellow (*vs* bright buff to rufous in Least); s covs and terts uniformly straw yellow (*vs* mixed buff, rufous, and blackish in Least Bittern).

Geographic variation—See Blake (1977), Brodkorb (1943a), Chapman (1914), Dickerman (1973b), Dickey & van Rossem (1924a), Griscom (1932), Norton (1965), Palmer (1962), Patten et al. (2003), van Rossem (1930a, 1945). Note that plumage-aspect polychromatism occurs occasionally (see **Species**) which might confuse subspecific designations. Five other subspecies in Mex-S.Am.

I.e. exilis (br & wint N.Am): From other subspecies of Mex-S.Am by auriculars, s covs, and underparts washed buff to yellowish (*vs* ochre to chestnut in other subspecies); ♂♂ with upperparts blackish with greenish sheen (*vs* brownish black with little or no sheen in other subspecies). Populations breeding in CA-se.AZ ("*hesperis*") average slightly larger (especially in tarsal length) but differences insufficient for subspecific recognition. Populations of s.Sonora, Mex (*pullus*), possible visitors to sw.N.Am (if still extant or not just erythristic morphs of *exilis*), average smaller (wg chord 108-114, tl 37-42, exp culmen 43-48, tarsus 38-41); nape browner; s covs grayish brown, similar in aspect to pp and ss; underparts washed grayish brown.

Molt—CBS. PF incomplete (Sep-Feb? in HY/SYs), DPB complete (Jul-Sep in AHYs), PA absent. The above timing pertains to N.Am populations. The PF occurs primarily on non-breeding grounds whereas DPBs occur on breeding grounds. The PF includes the body feathers, a few to many wing covs, and sometimes 1-3 terts and the rects. Pp and ss appear to be replaced synchronously (or nearly so) during DPBs. There appears to be no evidence of a DPA, as previously reported (e.g., Palmer 1962; *cf.* Pyle & Howell 2004; but see also Pezzo & Gosler 2005).

Age/Sex—Juv (B1; Jun-Nov) has upperpart feathers brown to chestnut with distinct buff fringes (creating scaled appearance); Juv ♀ = ♂ until first back feathers are replaced during the PF, as early as Sep in some HYs but more often in Oct or later (also, some individuals may be sexed

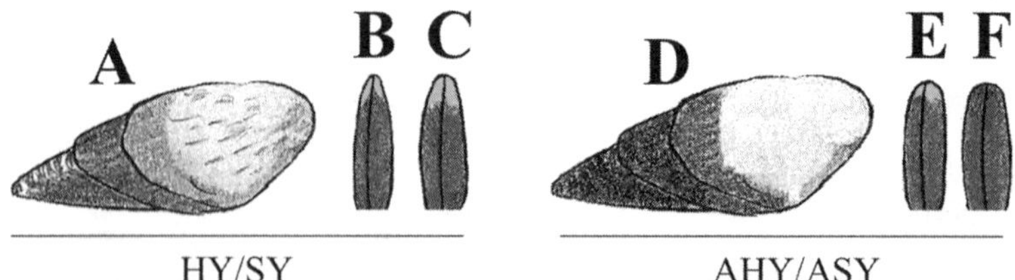

FIGURE 250. Secondary coverts (**A**, **D**) and outer primary coverts (**B-C**, **E-F**) by age in Least Bittern. The streaked and duller juv les covs and paler rufous juv med covs (as shown in **A**) variably get replaced during the PF in Sep-Feb on non-breeding grounds; usually at least some juv feathers are still retained in spring. The juv outer p covs (**B-C**) are retained until Jul-Aug when they are replaced synchronously during the PB2 on breeding grounds. Note that the cinnamon tips are broader and more symmetrical on the juv feathers whereas on basic feathers (**E-F**) they are absent or, if present, broader on the outer web.

by the color of the juv terts and/or rects, as described under HY/SY of each sex, but more study is needed). Medial(?) BP (Fig. 20**A**, p. 31) developed by both sexes but distended cloaca (Fig. 21, p. 32) indicates ♀ in Mar-Jul. Measurements unhelpful for sexing (Table 33, p. 346). Note that the following month ranges pertain to individuals from N.Am populations (see **Molt**); in tropical populations it may be best to estimate age in months and assign age codes accordingly (see Masked Booby, p. 300).

HY/SY ♀ (1st cycle, F1; Oct-Sep): Outer p covs narrow with broad and symmetrical pale rufous tips (Fig. 250**B-C**); some or all les covs worn and with dusky centers (Fig. 250**A**), often contrasting with replaced covs in Dec-Oct (*cf.* Fig. 13**B-C**, p. 20); terts worn and indistinctly patterned brown and pale rufous (Fig. 251**A**) or one or more terts replaced in Oct-Feb and contrastingly fresh, brown, and rufous (Fig. 251**B**); outer pp brown and pointed at tip (Fig. 247**A-B**, p. 341); back feathers mixed juv (with buff fringes) and formative (brown, without buff fringes) in Nov-Feb, becoming completely brown by Mar; rects (if retained juv) narrow (*cf.* Fig. 256**A**, p. 351) and dusky to dusky brown, without sheen. **Note: Some HYs do not replace back feathers until reaching the non-breeding grounds and thus cannot be sexed during autumn migration; see also HY/SY ♂.**

AHY/ASY ♀ (Def. cycle, DB; Oct-Sep): Outer p covs broad with narrow or no rufous tips (Fig. 250**E-F**); les covs uniform (Fig. 12**A**, p. 19) and without dusky centers (Fig. 250**D**); terts fresh and distinctly patterned brown and rufous (Fig. 251**B**); outer pp uniformly dusky, broader at tip, and relatively fresh (Figs. 12**A** & 247**C**); back feathers uniformly brown or tinged rufous, without buff fringes; rects broad (*cf.* Fig. 256**B**) and blackish with slight greenish sheen.

HY/SY ♂ (1st cycle, F1; Oct-Sep): Outer p covs (Fig. 250**B-C**), les covs (Figs. 13**B-C** & 250**A**), and outer pp (Fig. 247**A-B**) as in Juv-HY/SY ♀; terts worn and moderately patterned dark brown and rufous (Fig. 251**C**) or one or more replaced in Oct-Feb and contrastingly fresh, brownish black, and rufous (Fig. 251**D**); back feathers mixed juv (with buff fringes) and formative (blackish) in Nov-Feb, becoming completely blackish (with slight green gloss) by Mar; rects (if retained juv) narrow (*cf.* Fig. 256**A**) and blackish with slight greenish sheen. **Note: In fall, Juv-HY ♂♂ can be sexed as soon as one or more blackish formative feathers appears in the back but some ♂♂ completely retain these feathers through migration; see Juv-HY/SY ♀.**

AHY/ASY ♂ (Def. cycle, DB; Oct-Sep): Outer p covs (Fig. 250**E-F**), les covs (Figs. 12**A** & 250**D**), and outer pp (Figs. 12**A** & 247**C**) as in AHY/ASY ♀; terts fresh and distinctly patterned blackish and rufous with a slight sheen (Fig. 251**D**); back feathers uniformly black with glossy

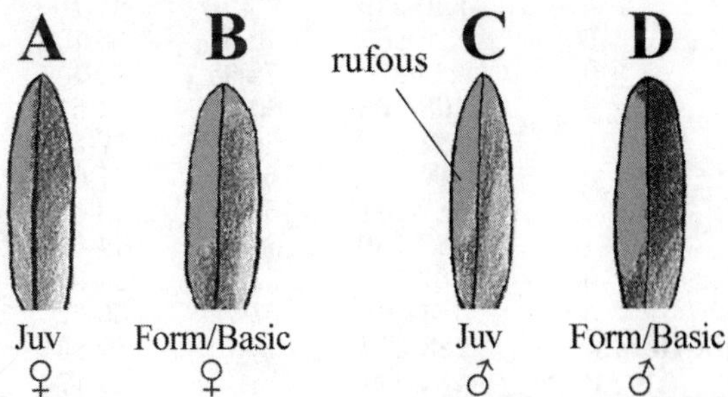

FIGURE 251. Shape and color pattern to the tertials by feather generation and sex in Least Bittern. On ♀♀, juv terts (**A**) are narrow and indistinctly patterned brown and pale rufous, whereas formative and basic terts (**B**) are broader and have a more distinctly defined rufous patch. The juv terts of ♂♂ resemble formative and basic terts of ♀♀ except for being narrower (**C**). Formative and basic terts are broader with blackish outer web, an extensive and well-defined rufous patch to the inner web (**D**), and a slight sheen absent in juv ♂ and ♀ terts. HY/SYs retain juv terts through at least the fall migration but often will replace 1-2 terts (and occasionally all 3) during the PF in Oct-Feb.

greenish sheen; rects (*cf.* Fig. 256**B**) broad and blackish with glossy green sheen.

Hybrids reported—None.

References—Baker (1993), Bent (1926), Cramp & Simmons (1977), Gibbs et al. (1992b), Marchant & Higgins (1990), McVaugh (1975), Oberholser (1974), Palmer (1962), Pittaway & Burke (1996b), Roberts (1955).

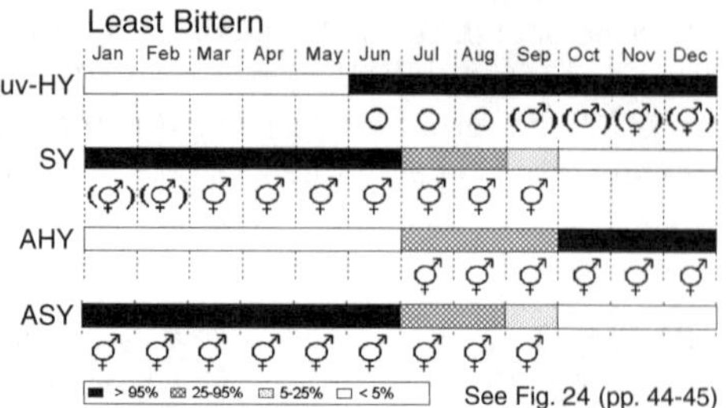

TABLE 33. Measurements (mm) of North American bitterns and dark herons to assist in identification and sexing. See pp. 4-11 for methods of measurement. Species summaries are in **bold** and subspecies summaries in ***italics***. Values were derived from 95% confidence intervals as based (for wing, tail, exposed culmen, and tarsus) approximately on the indicated sample sizes (see pp. 4-5); sample size for bill depth was often smaller but included at least 10 of each sex. Thus, midpoints of ranges approximate means, and S.D. is approximated by 25% of the range.

Taxon/Sex	*n*	wing chord	tail length	exp culmen	bill depth[1]	tarsus
American Bittern		**229-298**	**71-103**	**63-81**	**13.7-19.1**	**81-98**
♀	70	229-266	71-90	63-75	13.7-16.2	81-88
♂	100	259-298	84-103	70-81	16.4-19.1	86-98
Least Bittern[2]		**107-131**	**36-48**	**41-50**	**8.5-9.8**	**37-46**
♀	85	107-128	36-47	41-49	8.5-9.3	37-45
♂	90	109-131	37-48	42-50	9.0-9.8	37-46
Great Blue Heron		**432-515**	**149-203**	**114-174**	**23.9-34.2**	**139-228**
A.h. fannini		***444-507***	***169-203***	***114-146***	***23.9-28.9***	***139-176***
♀	50	444-483	169-194	114-133	23.9-27.1	139-165
♂	50	462-507	178-203	120-146	25.7-28.9	148-176
A.h. herodias		***432-495***	***159-190***	***123-156***	***24.2-31.0***	***156-193***
♀	50	432-471	159-184	123-148	24.2-28.7	156-184
♂	50	441-495	166-190	129-156	25.7-31.0	166-193
A.h. wardi		***438-515***	***162-196***	***129-171***	***24.8-32.7***	***159-224***
♀	100	438-415	162-189	129-160	24.8-30.0	159-214
♂	100	450-527	169-196	136-171	26.5-32.7	168-224
A.h. occidentalis[3]		***462-514***	***160-196***	***134-172***	***27.1-34.2***	***175-225***
♀	50	448-500	160-186	134-166	27.1-31.7	175-212
♂	40	462-514	168-196	151-172	30.4-34.2	188-225
Tricolored Heron[2]		**226-279**	**73-96**	**88-108**	**14.1-17.1**	**86-105**
♀	30	226-265	73-87	88-103	14.1-15.9	86-97
♂	35	239-279	78-96	93-108	15.5-17.1	94-105
Green Heron		**168-203**	**60-79**	**54-67**	**10.3-13.6**	**48-57**
B.v. anthonyi		***182-203***	***64-79***	***57-65***	***10.5-13.6***	***49-57***
♀	35	182-197	64-75	57-64	10.5-13.1	49-55
♂	30	188-203	67-79	58-65	11.0-13.6	51-57
B.v. virescens		***168-189***	***60-72***	***54-67***	***10.3-13.3***	***48-56***
♀	30	167-185	60-70	54-65	10.3-12.8	48-54
♂	30	174-191	61-72	56-67	10.8-13.3	50-56
Black-crowned Night-Heron[2]		**283-314**	**108-129**	**69-83**	**20.7-24.1**	**74-89**
♀	30	283-309	108-124	69-77	20.7-23.1	74-87
♂	30	288-314	111-129	74-83	21.7-24.1	75-89
Yellow-crowned Night-Heron[2]		**271-309**	**100-121**	**64-78**	**21.7-26.5**	**90-108**
♀	50	271-303	100-118	64-75	21.7-25.6	90-106
♂	60	279-309	102-121	66-78	22.5-26.5	92-108

[1] Bill depth measured at distal end of forehead feathering or skin see Fig. 8**A-B**, p. 10).

[2] Measurements pertain to N.Am populations only (see **Geographic variation**).

[3] See also Table 34 (p. 356).

GREAT BLUE HERON
Ardea herodias

GBHE
Species # 1940
Band size: 7B-8

Great White Heron (GWHE)

Species # 1920

Species—Dark morph from other N.Am herons by large size (Table 33); crown blackish to black and white (Fig. 253, p. 349); AHYs with elongated lanceolate black occipital (Fig. 254**A**, p. 349), grayish scapular (Fig. 254**B**), and whitish pectoral (Fig. 254**C**) plumes; plumage aspect primarily medium-pale grayish, the marginal les covs and femoral feathering cinnamon to rufous. White-plumaged Great Blue Herons (Great White Heron) from Great Egret (p. 350) by larger overall size (Table 34, p. 356; Fig. 257**A**, p. 352); ornamental crown feathers usually present (longest feather > 40 mm); AHY with occipital (Dec-May), pectoral, and straight lanceolate scapular plumes (*cf.* Fig. 254), the last not extending beyond tail; bill without black tomial stripe, malar feathering extends 24-28 mm proximal to eye, and unfeathered loral skin grayish to bluish (Fig. 257**A**); legs and feet pale brownish to yellowish.

Grey Heron (*A. cinerea*), a vagrant from Eurasia, averages shorter wing, bill and legs (wg chord 428-485, tl 157-187, exp culmen 101-131, tarsus 132-172); marginal les covs and femoral feathering grayish or whitish (tinged brownish pink in some Juv/HYs; beware some HY or worn AHY Great Blue Herons with whitish-cinnamon feathering); HY/SY with lateral breast plumes (at bend of wing) mixed indistinctly with white and gray (*vs* boldly marked white, dark gray, and usually cinnamon in Great Blue Heron) and neck pale whitish gray with dark streaking (*vs* dark gray with light cinnamon mottling in Great Blue Heron); unfeathered loral skin medium-bright to bright yellow (*vs* dusky or with dull yellow wash in HY/SY Great Blue Heron). HY/SYs with uniformly dull greenish legs (*vs* yellow tibia and blackish tarsus in Great Blue Heron). See Lethaby & McLaren (2002) and Renner & Linegar (2007) for other average bare part and plumage-aspect differences.

Geographic variation—See Blake (1977), Bond (1935), Chapman (1901), Court (1908), Dickerman (2004a, 2004b), Hellmayr & Conover (1948a), Oberholser (1912a, 1974), Palmer (1962), Parkes (1955a), Thayer & Bangs (1912), Todd (1916a). Uncertainty remains as to whether or not "*A.h. occidentalis*" (see below) is best treated as a subspecies or a morph; see discussions by Bangs (1915a), Bent (1926), Bond (1950a), Holt (1928), Mayr (1956), Mayr & Short (1970), McGuire (2002), McHenry & Dyes (1983), Meyerriecks (1957), Payne & Risley (1976), Paynter (1955), Ridgway (1882), and Stevenson & Anderson (1994). One other subspecies occurs on the Galapagos Is.

A.h. fannini (br & wint coastal se.AK-Queen Charlotte Is, BC): Medium-sized with proportionally long tail, small bill, and short tarsus (Table 33, p. 346); plumage aspect dark, the upperparts medium-dark, dull gray.

A.h. herodias (br & wint interior s.BC-e.WA to Que-SC): Medium-small (Table 33); plumage aspect dark, the upperparts medium gray to bluish gray; occipital plumes lanceolate and medium long (longest 90-200 mm when fully grown).

A.h. wardi (br & wint interior sw.BC-s.CA to FL): Medium-large to large (Table 33); plumage aspect dark, the upperparts medium-pale gray to bluish gray; occipital plumes lanceolate and long (longest 110-230 mm when fully grown). Populations of coastal w.OR-cw.CA ("*hyperonica*"), the Channel Is, CA ("*oligista*"), sw.CA-Baja CA ("*santilucae*"), and interior BC-ID to se.CA-w.TX ("*treganzai*") may average smaller than populations of se.N.Am but differences, if present, are slight and clinal. See *occidentalis* regarding "*würdemanni*".

A.h. occidentalis (br & wint s.FL, vagrant? TX-AL & MA-PA to GA): Great White Heron. Large but with a proportionally short tail (Table 33); plumage aspect primarily or entirely white; occipital plumes filamentous and short (longest 60-120 mm when fully grown). Individuals with intermediate plumage aspects (formerly named "*würdemanni*") may represent intergrades between *wardi* and *occidentalis*. Beware occasional leucistic (amelanistic) individuals of *herodias* and *wardi* (including reported vagrants?) which may be difficult or impossible to distinguish from *occidentalis*.

Molt—CBS. PF partial (Sep-Apr in HY/SYs), PB2 incomplete (Mar-Nov in SYs), PB3 incomplete (May-Nov in non-breeding TYs), DPB incomplete (Jun-Dec in breeding ASYs); PA absent. The PF occurs primarily on non-breeding grounds whereas PBs occur primarily on or N of breeding grounds. The PF includes most to all of the crown, head, and neck, scattered other body feathers (ornamental plumes develop in Nov-Apr) and possibly some med and les covs. The PBs exhibit staffelmauser (Fig. 16, pp. 23-24), resulting in 2-3 sets among pp of adults. Four to 7 juv outer pp and 6-12 (of 18) juv ss (often among s2-s4 and s6-s13) are retained during the PB2, and some TYs may retain 1-2 juv outer pp and/or 1-4 juv ss among s3-s4 and s7-s10 during the PB3. White-aspect individuals may replace more feathers per cycle due to longer molting seasons and less nutrients required to replace white feathers (see Great Egret, p. 350); more study is needed.

Age—Juv (B1; Jun-Feb) resembles HY/SY in Sep-Feb, as described below; Juv ♀=♂. The following applies to dark-aspect Great Blue Herons. White-aspect individuals (primarily *A.h. occidentalis*; see **Geographic variation**) can be aged only by molt patterns among pp and ss (Fig. 16, p. 24) and rect shape (Fig. 256, p. 351), which may proceed quicker (more feathers replaced per cycle) than in dark-aspect individuals. Until further study, it is probably best to age white-aspect individuals according to the criteria presented under Great Egret (adjusting for ornamental-plume differences in the two species).

Juv-HY/SY (1st cycle, Juv/B1-F1; Oct-Sep): Most or all med and gr covs with distinct cinnamon or white tips or shaft streak (Fig. 252**A**-**B**); crown uniformly grayish dusky (Fig. 253**A**), with variable grayish to whitish feathers medially in Nov-Sep (Fig. 253**B**-**C**); neck grayish, lightly mottled cinnamon in Sep-Feb; pp and ss uniformly juv (Fig. 16**A**), or inner pp and ss being replaced in Mar-Sep, the juv outer pp and medial ss tapered, brownish, and relatively worn (Fig. 247**A**-**B**, p. 341); lateral breast feathers grayish with white and/or cinnamon centers. **Note: In addition, the ornamental occipital, pectoral, and scapular plumes (Fig. 254A-C) average shorter by season (absent in Sep-Oct, emerging and/or short in Nov-Aug) than in SY/TYs and older age groups, but this criterion shows substantial seasonal, sex-specific (see Sex), and individual variation.**

SY/TY (2nd cycle, B2; Oct-Sep): Med and gr covs gray without pale tips (Fig. 252**C**) or some med covs sometimes with cinnamon shaft streaks (Fig. 252**B**); medial crown stripe mixed blackish and white (Fig. 253**C**-**D**); neck lilac, without mottled cinnamon; pp and ss with 2 generations, 1-2 juv outer pp (p10 can molt < p9) and 1-6 juv ss (among s4 and s7-s11) being replaced in Apr-Sep, very faded and worn (Figs. 16**B**-**D** & 247**B**); lateral breast feathers black. **Note: See Juv-HY/SY.**

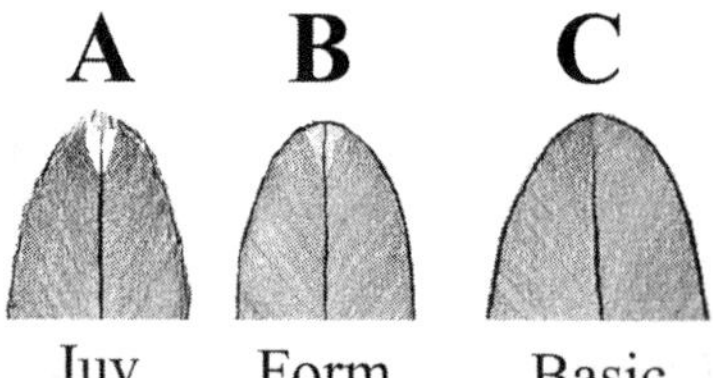

FIGURE 252. Outer median coverts by age in dark-morph Great Blue Heron. At least some juv median covs with distinct whitish-cinnamon tips (**A**) are retained by HY/SYs until the PB2 in Jul-Aug. **B** represents some (but not all) formative feathers (earlier replaced?) that show indistinct cinnamon tips; many SY/TYs may exhibit one or more covs resembling **B**, likely formative feathers retained during the PB2. Some formative covs (later replaced?) and basic covs lack pale tips (**C**). Tricolored Heron and dark-morph Reddish Egret also show cinnamon to whitish tips to juv feathers (**A**) but uniformly dark formative and basic feathers (**C**).

ASY/ATY (Def. cycle, DB; Oct-Sep): Med covs gray, without cinnamon (Fig. 252**C**); medial crown stripe mostly to entirely white (Fig. 253**E**-**F**); pp and ss with 2 sets of basic feathers in staffelmauser patterns (Fig. 16**E**), the outer pp broad and relatively fresh (Fig. 247**C**). **Note: See Juv-HY/SY and TY/4Y. It is possible that ASYs with fully white crowns can be reliably aged ATY/A4Y (see below) but more study is needed.**

TY/4Y (3rd cycle, B3; Oct-Jul): Proximal med covs gray (Fig. 252**C**); medial crown stripe

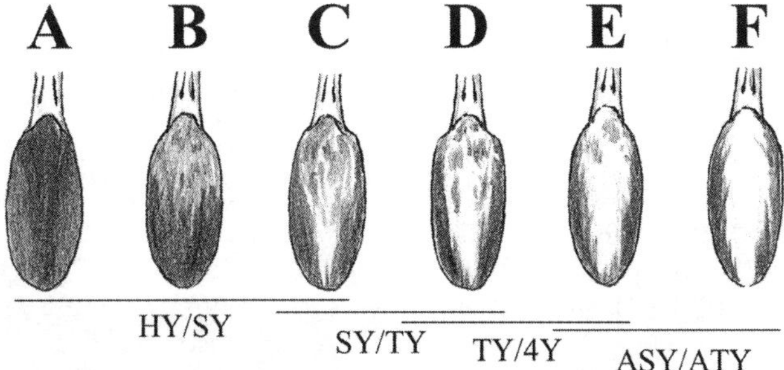

FIGURE 253. Crown plumage aspect by age in dark-morph Great Blue Herons. Juvs have completely dark crowns (**A**) but white formative feathers develop during Nov-Mar, resulting in mixed crowns in HY/SYs (**B-C**). Thereafter there is substantial individual variation within SY/TYs and TY/4Ys (**C-E**). Individuals with completely white crowns (**F**) are possibly ATY/A4Ys but without more study of known-age individuals these should be aged ASY/ATY. See **Age** for more information on variation in crown plumage aspect with age.

white with some blackish in forehead (Fig. 253**D-E**); pp and ss with 2 sets of basic feathers in staffelmauser patterns and with 1-2 outer juv pp (p10 can molt < p9) and/or 1-4 juv ss (among s12-s16) remaining and very tapered, brownish, and worn (Figs. 16**D** & 247**B**). **Note: Only individuals with retained juv feathers as described should be aged TY/4Y, although it is possible that individuals with two sets of basic pp and ss (Fig. 16E) and some black in crown (as in Fig. 253D-E) can be aged TY/4Y or 4-5Y (see pp. 41-42), but more study of marked, known-age individuals is needed to determine age criteria in predefinitive plumages.**

ATY/A4Y (Def. cycle, DB; Oct-Jun): Like ASY/ATY but pp with 3 sets of basic feathers in staffelmauser patterns (Fig. 16**F**).

Sex—♀ = ♂ by plumage aspect. Medial(?) BP (Fig. 20**A**, p. 31) developed by both sexes but distended cloaca (Fig. 21, p. 32) indicates ASY ♀ in Jan-May. Measurements somewhat helpful for sexing when subspecies is known (Table 33, p. 346). The lengths of the ornamental plumes (Fig. 254**A-C**) average longer in ♂♂ than in ♀♀ in Jan-May but extensive variation by season, age, and individual precludes reliable sexing; dark-aspect individuals with longest occipital plume (Fig. 254**A**) > 190 mm, longest scapular plume (Fig. 254**B**) > 230 mm, and/or longest

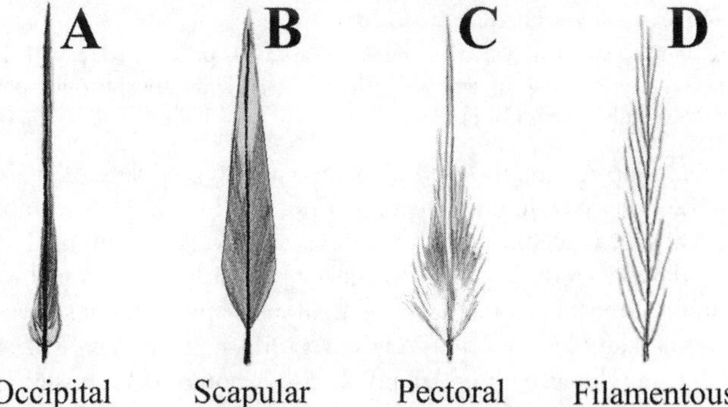

FIGURE 254. Types of ornamental plumes found in herons and egrets. Lanceolated feathers (**A-C**) can show wide variation in form by body region whereas filamentous feathers (**D**) are similar and can be found in all three regions of the body (occipital, scapular, and pectoral). The types and number of ornamental feathers found in each region varies by species (see text).

pectoral plume (Fig. 254**C**) > 240 mm (usually in Dec-May) can be sexed ♂. Otherwise, no criteria known.

Hybrids reported—With Great Egret (Malosh 2004).

References—Baker (1993), Bent (1926), Butler (1992, 1997), Butler et al. (1990), Cramp & Simmons (1977), Gantlett (1998), Lethaby & McLaren (2002), Meyerriecks (1960), Oberholser (1912a, 1974), Palmer (1962), Parkes (1955a), Pratt (1973), Pyle (2006a), Pyle & Howell (2004), Roberts (1955), Shanahan (2001), Simpson & Kelsall (1978).

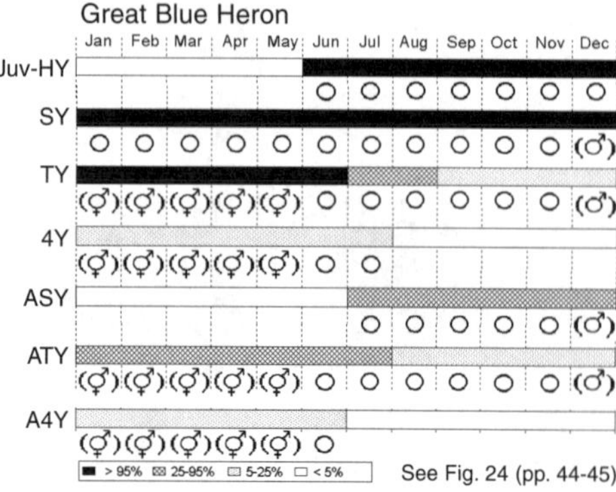

GREAT EGRET

Ardea alba

GREG
Species # 1960
Band size: 7A-7B

Species—From other N.Am white herons and egrets by medium-large size (Table 34, p. 356; Fig. 257**B**, p. 352); ornamental crown feathers absent (longest < 40 mm); AHYs with pectoral plumes absent and scapular plumes filamentous (*cf.* Fig. 254**D**, p. 349) and up to 480 mm in length, often beyond tail tip; bill medium-bright to bright yellow with short black stripe at base of upper mandible, malar feathering extending > 30 mm proximal to eye, and unfeathered loral skin yellow to greenish (Fig. 257**B**); legs and feet black (often greenish or grayish in Juvs).

Geographic variation—See Amadon & Woolfenden (1952), Cramp & Simmons (1977), Dement'ev & Gladkov (1951a), McCrimmon et al. (2001). Oberholser (1919a). Three other subspecies in Eurasia, Africa, and Australasia.

A.a. modesta (br & wint Asia, vagrant to w.AK Is): Smaller (wg chord 345-390, tl 117-147, exp culmen 92-117, tarsus 128-170); AHY with bill black or substantially tipped black year-round; tibia pinkish or yellowish to reddish in Jan-Jul and usually with yellowish in Aug-Dec; filamentous scapular plumes (Fig. 254**D**, p. 349) averaging shorter when fully grown in Feb-Aug (often not exceeding tail tip). Populations of Europe (*alba*), potential vagrants to e.N.Am, generally resemble *modesta* but are larger (wg chord 406-480, tl 130-185, exp culmen 110-135, tarsus 165-215).

A.a. egretta (br & wint N.Am): Intermediate in size (Table 34, p. 356); AHY with bill yellow-orange (sometimes washed dusky) in Jan-Jun; tibia blackish or black; filamentous scapular plumes (Fig. 254**D**) averaging longer when fully grown in Feb-Aug (up to 100 mm > tail tip).

Molt—CBS. PF partial (Sep-Apr in HY/SYs), PB2 incomplete-complete (Apr-Nov in SYs), PB3 incomplete-complete (May-Nov in non-breeding TYs), DPB incomplete-complete (Jul-Dec in breeding ASYs); PA absent. The above timing pertains to N.Am populations. The PF occurs primarily on non-breeding grounds whereas PBs occur primarily on or N of breeding grounds. The PF includes some to most body feathers (filamentous scapular plumes develop in Nov-Apr) and some proximal med and les covs but no gr covs, terts, or rects. The PBs are usually complete but can exhibit staffelmauser (Fig. 16, pp. 23-24) in some ASYs, resulting in up to 2 sets of basic feathers, especially among the ss.

Age—Juv (B1; Jun-Feb) resembles HY/SY (below) and has iris dull or pale yellowish and legs dusky-greenish or grayish to blackish in Jul-Sep; Juv ♀ = ♂. The following month ranges pertain to N.Am populations.

Juv-HY/SY (1st cycle, Juv/B1-F1; Oct-Sep): Scapulars small and filamentous (or worn) along edges (Fig. 255**A**); outer rects narrow and rounded (Fig. 256**A**); filamentous scapular plumes absent in Oct-Jan and developing in Jan-Jul but reduced, not extending beyond tail; molt limits can occur among the humerals, les covs, and med covs (Fig. 13**A-B**, p. 20), the replaced formative feathers glossier white; pp and ss uniformly juv and not showing s1-p1 contrast (Fig. 13**A**), or inner pp and inner and outer ss being replaced in Mar-Sep, the juv outer pp and medial ss tapered and relatively worn (Fig. 247**A-B**, p. 341).

AHY/ASY (Def. cycle, DB; Oct-Sep): Scapulars larger and less filamentous (or worn) along edges (Fig. 255**B**); outer rects broad and truncate (Fig. 256**B**); filamentous scapular plumes developing in Oct-Dec and elongated, extending beyond tail in Dec-Jul; les and med covs uniform in gloss and wear, and pp and ss uniformly basic and showing uninterrupted replacement cline and s1-p1 contrast (Fig. 14**B**), the outer pp broad and relatively fresh (Fig. 247**C**). **Note: See SY/TY.**

SY/TY (2nd cycle, B2; Oct-Jul): Like AHY/ASY but 1-3 outer pp (p9 can molt < p10) and/or 1-5 ss (among s4 and s7-s10) retained juv, tapered, and worn (Figs. 16**B**, p. 24, & Fig. 247**B**). **Note: Most SYs appear to replace all pp and ss during the PB2. It can be difficult to assess wear patterns among the white pp and ss of this and other white egrets; thus, AHY/ASY should be designated if uncertainty exists.**

ASY/ATY (Def. cycle, DB; Oct-Jul): Like AHY/ASY but pp and ss with 2 sets of basic feathers in staffelmauser patterns (Fig. 16**E**). **Note: See SY/TY.**

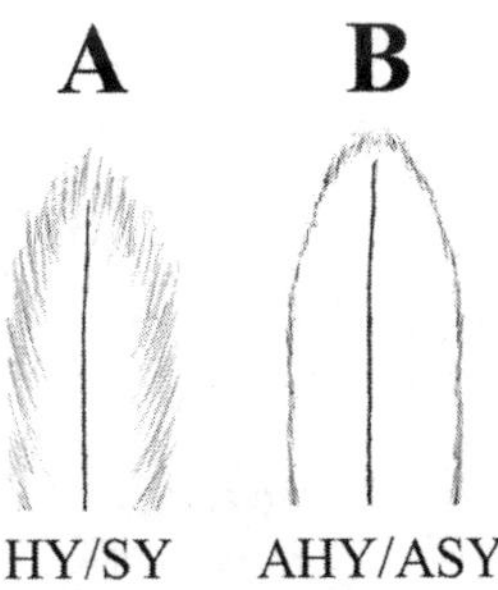

FIGURE 255. Size and condition of longest (non-ornamental) scapular by age in Great Egret. Note that juv feathers, retained by HY/SYs until the PB2 in Apr-Nov, are smaller and more filamentous along edges than basic feathers on AHY/ASYs.

Sex—♀ = ♂ by plumage aspect. Medial BP (Fig. 20**A**, p. 31) developed by both sexes but distended cloaca (Fig. 21, p. 32) indicates ASY ♀ in Jan-Jun. Measurements somewhat helpful for sexing (Table 34, p. 356). Ornamental plumes may average longer in ♂♂ than in ♀♀ in Jan-May but more study is needed to determine reliable measures by sex. Otherwise, no criteria known.

Hybrids reported—With Gray Heron *Ardea cinerea* (Lippens & Burggraeve 1983, Eigenhuis 1984), Great Blue Heron (p. 347), and Rufous Night-Heron *Nycticorax caledonicus* (McCarthy 2006).

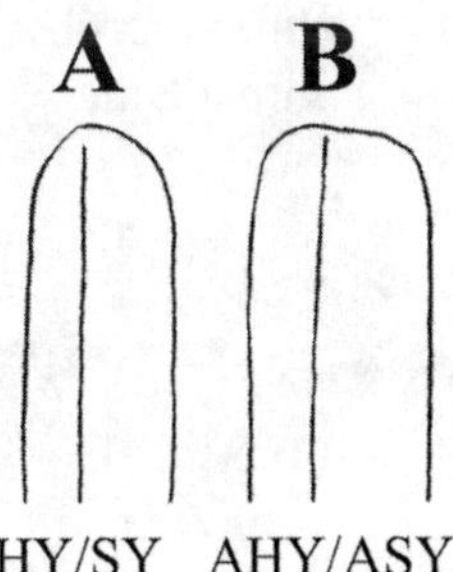

FIGURE 256. Rectrix shape by age in herons and egrets. This criterion is more valuable for egrets than for herons, due to the lack of other plumage-aspect criteria as are found in herons.

References—Bent (1926), Cramp & Simmons (1977), Dement'ev & Gladkov (1951a), Hancock (1984), Marchant & Higgins (1990), McCrimmon et al. (2001), McVaugh (1972), Oberholser (1974), Palmer (1962).

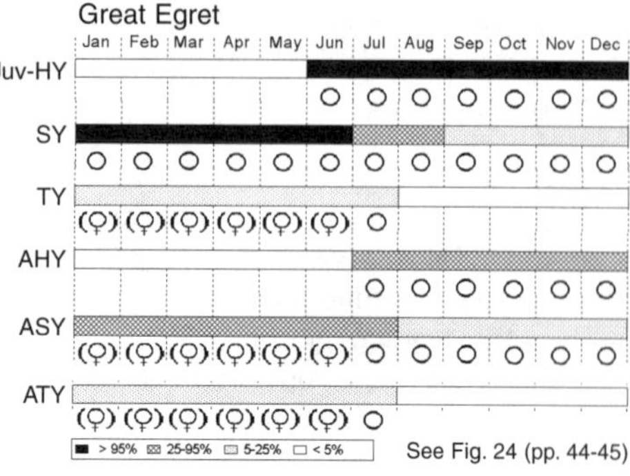

SNOWY EGRET
Egretta thula

SNEG
Species # 1970
Band size: 6

Species—From other N.Am white herons and egrets by medium-small size with proportionally long bill and legs (Table 34, p. 356; Fig. 257**D**); AHYs with elongated, filamentous occipital, pectoral, and recurved scapular plumes (*cf.* Fig. 254**D**, p. 349) in Dec-Sep; pp entirely white (*cf.* Fig. 259, p. 355); bill grayish blending to dark tip (HY/SY) to bluish black (AHY/ASY), malar feathering extending 10-16 mm proximal to eye, and unfeathered loral skin bright yellow (grayish in some Juvs; see **Age**) to reddish in breeding ASYs (Fig. 257**D**); legs greenish yellow ventrally and dusky to black dorsally (HY) to black (ASY) and feet yellowish to yellow (Fig. 258**A-C**).

Little Egret (*E. garzetta*), a visitor to e.N.Am, averages larger except for leg length (wg chord 238-303, tl 81-114, exp culmen 70-95, bill depth at distal end of forehead feathers 14-18, tarsus 86-115; Fig. 257**E**); tarsus thicker (4.3-5.1 mm at center *vs* 3.8-4.7 in Snowy Egret; Fig. 258);

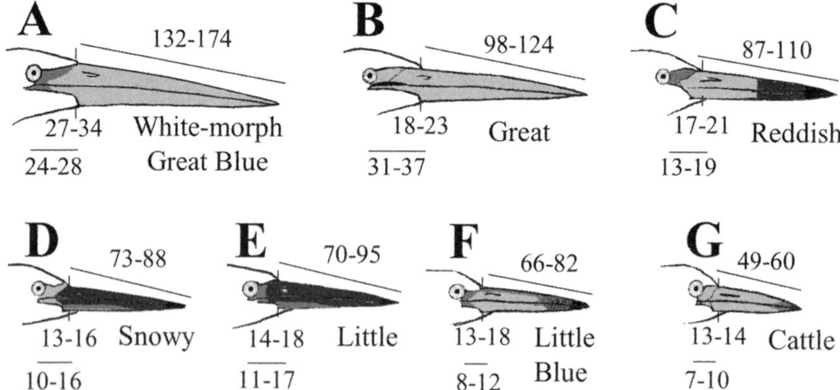

FIGURE 257. Bill shade and dimensions and loral shade and patterns in egrets and white herons to assist with identification. Indicated measures represent exposed culmen (Fig. 7**A**, p. 9), bill depth at distal end of forehead feathers (Fig. 8**A**, p. 10), and distance from front of eye to distal end of malar feathering. This latter measure may be especially helpful in identifying Great Egret (proportionally long), white-morph Reddish Egret (proportionally short), and Juv-HY/SY Little Blue Heron (proportionally short). Note also the distinct black tomial stripe at the base of the bill in Great Egret, absent in the other pale-billed species.

loral skin variably grayish or greenish, becoming pale yellow to reddish in Feb-Apr (occasionally in May-Jan), and not connecting across forehead (Fig. 257**E**), *vs* brighter yellow to orange-yellow and connecting across the forehead in Snowy Egret (Fig. 257**D**); AHYs with two elongated, lanceolate (*cf.* Fig. 254**A**) occipital plumes (*vs* many filamentous plumes, although occasional Snowy Egrets or hybrids can also have one or more lanceolate plumes in Jan-Aug); dorsal side of tarsus blackish or with a reduced amount of yellowish extending partially up tarsus in HYs and soles of feet greenish yellow, duller than tops of feet (Fig. 258**D-E**), *vs* legs extensively greenish yellow including most or all of tarsus and part of tibia in HYs and some AHYs, and soles and tops of feet uniformly bright yellow in Snowy Egret (Fig. 258**A-C**). See Cramp & Simmons (1977), Godfrey (1986), Grant et al. (1980), Jackson (2004), Massiah (1996), McLaren (1989), Oreel (1979), Palmer (1962), and Scott et al. (1983) for more information and beware of hybrids (*cf.* Perkins 1995).

Geographic variation—Considered monotypic here. Individuals of w.populations ("*E.t. brewsteri*" and "*arileuca*") average slightly larger than those of e.populations but difference is broadly clinal and not substantive enough for subspecific recognition. See A.M. Bailey (1928b), Behle (1985), Browning (1974, 1978, 1990), Oberholser (1974), Parsons & Master (2000), Phillips et al. (1964), Rea (1983a), and Thayer & Bangs (1909) for more information.

Molt—CBS. PF partial (Sep-Jan in HY/SYs), PB2 complete (Apr-Oct in non-breeding SYs), DPB complete (Jun-Nov in breeding AHYs); PA absent. The PF occurs primarily on non-breeding grounds whereas PBs occur primarily near or N of breeding grounds. The PF includes most to all body feathers (ornamental plumes develop in Oct-Mar) and some proximal les, med, and (occasionally) gr covs but no terts. Look for occasional incomplete molts in staffelmauser patterns (Fig. 16, pp. 23-24 in breeding ASYs, as in other herons and egrets.

Age—Juv (B1; Jun-Feb) resembles HY/SY (below) but has loral skin grayish, upper mandible pale yellowish to grayish at base, and legs entirely olive to greenish in Jul-Sep; Juv ♀=♂. The following month ranges pertain to N.Am populations.

Juv-HY/SY (1st cycle, Juv/B1-F1; Oct-Sep): Pp and ss uniformly juv and not showing s1-p1 contrast (Fig. 13**A**, p. 20) or being replaced in Apr-Oct, the juv outer pp tapered and relatively worn (Fig. 247**A-B**, p. 341); molt limits usually occur among the humerals and s covs (Fig.

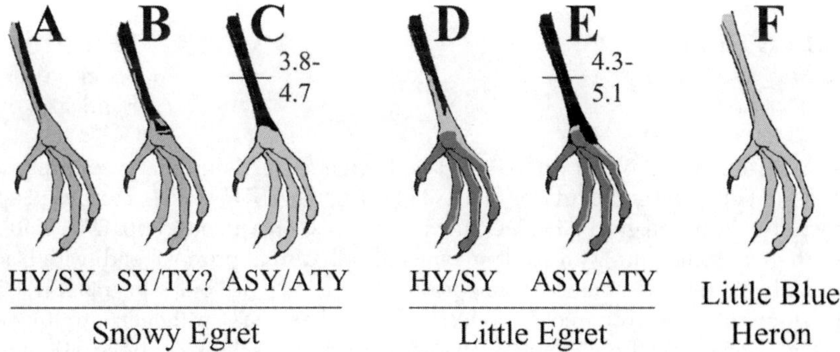

FIGURE 258. Foot and tarsal color by species and age in Snowy Egret, Little Egret, and Little Blue Heron. Indicated measure represents tarsal width (from side to side) at center, narrower in Snowy Egret than in Little Egret (and Little Blue Heron). Note that average differences in leg and foot coloration in the two egrets are indicated and that there is moderate individual variation within species/age groups. Little Blue Heron shows little variation in foot and leg color, although in some adults they darken during the breeding season.

13**B-C**), the replaced formative feathers glossier white; outer rects narrow and rounded (Fig. 256**A**, p. 351); legs dull olive to greenish ventrally indistinct dusky to blackish dorsally (increasing by May-Aug), not contrasting distinctly with greenish-yellow foot color (Fig. 258**A-B**, p. 353); filamentous occipital, scapular, and pectoral plumes (Fig. 254**D**, p. 349) absent in Oct-Jan, developing in Jan-Apr, and reduced in length in Mar-Aug.

AHY/ASY (Def. cycle, DB; Oct-Sep): Pp and ss uniformly basic and showing s1-p1 contrast, and s covs uniform in gloss and wear (Fig. 14**B**, p. 21), being replaced in Jun-Nov, the outer pp broad and relatively fresh (Fig. 247**C**); outer rects broad and truncate (Fig. 256**B**); legs black with little or no yellow on ventral surface (if present, restricted to distal portion of tarsus) and feet bright yellow (Fig. 258**C**); filamentous occipital, scapular, and pectoral plumes (Fig. 254**D**) developing in Oct-Jan and full and elongated in Dec-Aug. **Note: Some SY/TYs might be recognized by intermediate leg and foot color, the legs blackish with variable amounts of yellow ventrally (Fig. 258B). Confirmation is needed.**

Sex—♀=♂ by plumage aspect. Medial(?) BP (Fig. 20**A**, p. 31) developed by both sexes but distended cloaca (Fig. 21, p. 32) indicates ♀ in Feb-May. Measurements somewhat unhelpful for sexing (Table 34, p. 356). Ornamental plumes may average longer in ♂♂ than in ♀♀ in Jan-May but more study is needed to determine reliable measures by sex. Otherwise, no criteria known.

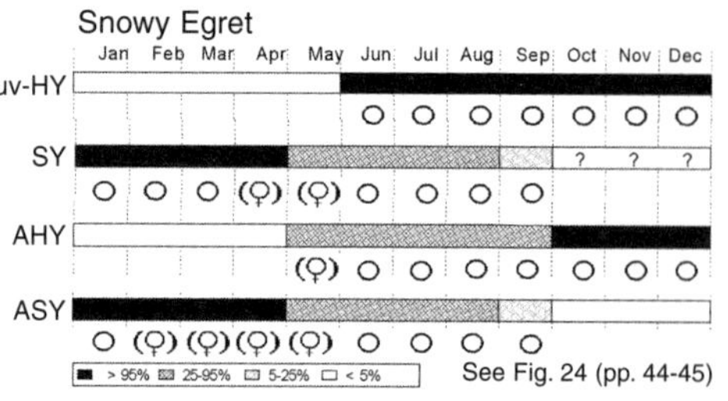

Hybrids reported—With Little Blue Heron (Sprunt 1954, but see Payne & Risley 1976:69-70), Tricolored Heron (Dickerman & Parkes 1968, Meeks et al. 1996), Cattle Egret (Paul & Schnapf 1998), and possibly Little Egret (Perkins 1995, McCarthy 2006) in the wild.

References—Bent (1926), Cramp & Simmons (1977), Hancock (1984), Kaufman (1990a, 1991), Massiah (1996), McVaugh (1975), Meyerriecks (1960), Murphy (1992), Oberholser (1974), Palmer (1962), Parsons & Master (2000).

LITTLE BLUE HERON
Egretta caerulea

LBHE
Species # 2000
Band size: 6

Species—HY/SY from other N.Am white herons and egrets by medium-small size with proportionally short but deep bill and short legs (Table 34, p. 356; Fig. 257**F**, p. 352); crown and upperpart feathers usually tinged grayish in Dec-Mar; juv outer 7-8 pp with dusky tips (Fig. 259); base of bill bluish gray (sometimes with small amounts of yellowish at proximal end) with blackish tip, the malar feathering extending 8-12 mm proximal to eye, and the loral skin gray (Fig. 257**F**); legs and feet uniformly olive or greenish to blackish (breeding ASYs), without contrastingly yellow feet (Fig. 258**F**). AHY from other N.Am dark herons by smaller size (Table 34); plumage aspect, including filamentous occipital (Fig. 254**D**, p. 349) and lanceolate scapular (Fig. 254**B**) and pectoral (Fig. 254**C**) plumes, blue and purple, without reddish; base of bill bluish gray; legs and feet olive to greenish.

Geographic variation—Monotypic (see Monroe 1968; Parkes 1955a; Todd 1916a, 1963).

Molt—CBS. PF partial (Sep-Apr in HY/SYs), PB2 complete (Apr-Dec in non-breeding SYs), DPB complete (Jul-Dec in breeding AHYs). PA absent. The above timing pertains to N.Am populations. The PF occurs primarily on non-breeding grounds whereas PBs can occur either on or N of breeding grounds or on non-breeding grounds. The PF includes most to all body feathers (ornamental plumes develop in Nov-Apr), some to many les and med covs, and up to 4 ss/terts (among s12-s15). Look for occasional incomplete molts in staffelmauser pattern (Fig. 16, pp. 23-24) in breeding ASYs, as in other herons and egrets; SYs can rarely show a few white (retained or earlier-replaced?) feathers, especially among underwing covs, during the PB2.

Age—Juv (B1; Jun-Feb) resembles HY/SY in Nov-Dec (below) and has lores tinged greenish and iris cream to whitish in Jun-Oct; Juv ♀=♂. The following month ranges pertain to N.Am populations.

Juv-HY/SY (1st cycle, Juv/B1-F1; Nov-Oct): Plumage aspect primarily white (the crown tinged bluish) in Nov-Dec, increasingly mixed with gray-washed feathers in Dec-Mar and dark blue feathers in Apr-Oct; ornamental plumes (mixed blue and white) absent or reduced and developing in Dec-Apr. **Note: Beware of possible white-morph AHY/ASYs in this species (presumably with full basic ornamental plumes), especially at s.latitudes, although reports of these (cf. Bangs 1915a, Bent 1926) may represent mis-aged HY/SYs or leucistic (amelanistic) individuals.**

AHY/ASY (Def. cycle, DB; Oct-Sep): Plumage aspect (including elongated breeding plumes) bright, dark purplish (head and neck) and slate-blue, without white. **Note: See Juv-HY/SY and SY/TY. It is possible that individuals showing these characters can be reliably aged ASY/ATY but separation from SY/TY can be subtle and more study is needed.**

SY/TY (2nd cycle, B2); Oct-Aug): Like AHY/ASY but plumage aspect duller, the underparts washed sooty, and sometimes with some white mottling or feathers on chin, throat, underparts, and/or underwing. **Note: See Juv-HY/SY and AHY/ASY.**

Sex—♀=♂ by plumage aspect. Medial BP (Fig. 20**A**, p. 31) developed by both sexes but distended cloaca (Fig. 21, p. 32) indicates ♀ in Feb-May. Measurements generally unhelpful for sexing (Table 34). The lengths of the ornamental plumes average longer in ♂♂ than in ♀♀ in Jan-May but extensive variation by season, age, and individual precludes reliable sexing of most individuals; those with longest occipital plume (Fig. 254**D**) > 100 mm, longest scapular plume (Fig. 254**B**) > 210 mm, and/or longest pectoral plume (Fig. 254**C**) > 95 mm (usually in Dec-May) can be sexed ♂. Otherwise, no criteria known.

Hybrids reported—With Snowy Egret (p. 352) and Cattle Egret (Bailey et al. 1989b). Possibly with Little Egret (McCarthy 2006) and Black-crowned Night Heron (Sibley 1994). Reports of hybrids with Tricolored Herons are likely based on anomalous Little Blue Herons (Dickerman & Parkes 1968, Payne & Risley 1976).

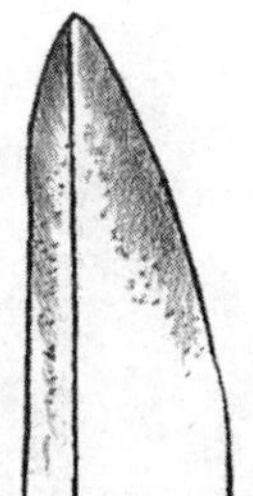

HY/SY
Little Blue Heron

FIGURE 259. Juv outer primaries (p8-p10) in Little Blue Heron for purposes of identification. Snowy and other egrets show entirely white outer pp.

References—Bent (1926), Dickerman & Parkes (1968), Kaufman (1990a, 1991), McVaugh (1972), Oberholser (1974), Palmer (1962), Pyle & Howell (2004). Rodgers (1978a, 1980), Rodgers & Smith (1995), Stresemann & Stresemann (1966).

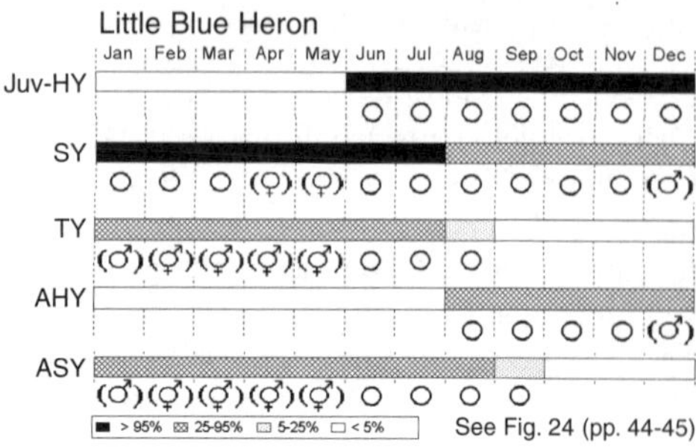

TABLE 34. Measurements (mm) of North American egrets and herons with white plumage aspects to assist in identification and sexing. See pp. 4-11 for methods of measurement. Species summaries are in **bold** and subspecies summaries in ***italics***. Values were derived from 95% confidence intervals as based (for wing, tail, exposed culmen, and tarsus) approximately on the indicated sample sizes (see pp. 4-5); sample size for bill depth was often smaller but included at least 10 of each sex. Thus, midpoints of ranges approximate means, and S.D. is approximated by 25% of the range.

Taxon/Sex	*n*	wing chord	tail length	exp culmen	bill depth[1]	tarsus
"Great White" Heron[2]						
A.h. occidentalis[3]		***462-514***	***160-196***	***134-172***	***27.1-34.2***	***175-225***
♀	50	448-500	160-186	134-166	27.1-31.7	175-212
♂	40	462-514	168-196	151-172	30.4-34.2	188-225
Great Egret[3]		**329-414**	**123-166**	**98-124**	**18.0-22.7**	**127-178**
♀	30	329-400	123-155	98-116	18.0-21.6	127-162
♂	25	346-414	136-166	107-124	19.2-22.7	150-178
Snowy Egret		**228-283**	**80-103**	**73-88**	**12.6-15.5**	**85-115**
♀	100	228-273	80-98	73-84	12.6-14.6	85-109
♂	100	237-283	83-103	76-88	13.3-15.5	90-115
Little Blue Heron		**241-274**	**82-103**	**66-82**	**13.0-18.0**	**81-103**
♀	35	241-264	82-99	66-79	13.0-16.0	81-98
♂	50	251-274	87-103	70-82	14.2-18.0	88-103
Reddish Egret		**281-344**	**91-127**	**87-110**	**17.3-20.8**	**124-156**
♀	50	281-324	91-119	87-106	17.3-19.3	124-144
♂	60	298-344	98-127	92-110	18.8-20.8	137-156
Cattle Egret		**226-263**	**75-98**	**49-66**	**13.0-14.8**	**70-91**
B.i. coromanda		***231-263***	***76-98***	***54-66***	***13.6-14.8***	***77-91***
♀	20	231-256	76-93	54-62	13.6-14.4	77-87
♂	20	236-263	80-98	57-66	13.9-14.8	79-91
B.i. ibis		***226-260***	***75-98***	***49-60***	***13.0-14.1***	***70-84***
♀	50	226-255	75-94	49-57	13.0-13.8	70-81
♂	55	232-260	79-98	52-60	13.3-14.1	72-84

[1] Bill depth measured at distal end of forehead feathering or skin see Fig. 8**A-B**, 10).
[2] See also Table 33 (p. 346).
[3] Measurements pertain to N.Am populations only (see **Geographic variation**).

TRICOLORED HERON TRHE
Egretta tricolor Species # 1990
Band size: 6

Species—From other N.Am herons and egrets by medium to medium-small size with long bill (Table 33, p. 346); AHYs with brownish lanceolate occipital (*cf.* Fig. 254**A**, p. 349), brownish filamentous scapular (Fig. 254**D**, and purplish lanceolate pectoral (Fig. 245**C**) plumes; upperparts primarily dark blue (AHY) to reddish and blue (HY); rump, uppertail covs, abdomen, and underwing covs white; bill primarily yellowish (HY) to bluish with a black tip (AHY); legs and feet yellowish (to orangish in breeding AHYs).

Geographic variation—See Frederick (1997), Hellmayr (1906), Hellmayr & Conover (1948a), Huey (1927a). Two other subspecies in Trinidad-S.Am.

E.t. ruficollis (br & wint N.Am): Larger (Table 33, p. 346; *vs* wg chord 216-253, exp culmen 84-104 in the other subspecies); upperparts of AHY medium-dark bluish slate (paler in *tricolor* of S.Am and duskier in *rufimentum* of Trinidad); chin and throat whitish to cinnamon (chestnut in *rufimentum*). Populations of Baja to s.CA ("*occidentalis*") may average larger but difference is slight and broadly clinal.

Molt—CBS. PF partial (Sep-Apr), PB2 incomplete-complete (May-Dec in non-breeding SYs), DPB incomplete-complete (Jul-Jan in breeding AHYs); PA absent. The above timing pertains to N.Am populations. The PF occurs primarily on non-breeding grounds whereas PBs occur primarily near or N of breeding grounds. The PF includes most to all body feathers (ornamental plumes develop in Nov-Apr), some proximal les and med covs, and rarely the 2 innermost terts. The PBs are usually complete but can exhibit staffelmauser in some ASYs (Fig. 16, pp. 23-24), especially among the ss, resulting in up to 2 sets of basic feathers in adults.

Age—Juv (B1; Jun-Feb) resembles HY/SY (below) in Nov-Jan and has legs and feet grayish olive; Juv ♀=♂. The following month ranges pertain to N.Am populations.

Juv-HY/SY (1st cycle, Juv/B1-F1; Nov-Oct): Crown, head, hind neck, upper back, and les covs reddish or brownish, increasingly mottled with incoming dull slate-blue feathers in Dec-Oct; med and gr covs with rufous tips (Fig. 252**A**, p. 348); occipital and scapular plumes absent in Oct-Jan, developing in Jan-Apr, and reduced in length in Mar-Aug; pp and ss uniformly juv and not showing s1-p1 contrast (Fig. 13**A**, p. 20), or inner pp and ss being replaced in May-Sep, the juv outer pp and medial ss tapered, brownish, and relatively worn (Fig. 247**A-B**, p. 341); molt limits occur within the humerals, s covs, and (rarely) terts (Fig. 13**B-C**); iris yellowish (Nov-Dec) to orange-red (Sep-Oct).

AHY/ASY (Def. cycle, DB; Nov-Oct): Crown, head, hind neck, upper back, and most to all s covs uniformly dull slate-blue, without brown or reddish(Fig. 252**C**); occipital and pectoral plumes elongated in Jan-Aug; pp and ss uniformly basic and showing uninterrupted replacement cline and s1-p1 contrast, and s covs uniform in wear (Fig. 14**B**, p. 21), being replaced in Jun-Nov, the outer pp broad and relatively fresh (Fig. 247**C**); iris orange-red or red.

SY/TY (2nd cycle, B2; Nov-Aug): Like AHY/ASY but pp and ss with 2 generations, 1-2 juv outer pp (p10 can molt < p9) and/or 1-6 juv ss (among s4 and s7-s11) retained and very faded and worn (Figs. 16**B**, p. 24, &. 247**B**); iris orange-red to red. **Note: SY/TYs having retained pp and ss during the PB2 may be rare.**

ASY/ATY (Def. cycle, DB; Nov-Sep): Like AHY/ASY but pp and ss with 2 sets of basic feathers in staffelmauser patterns (Fig. 16**E**); iris red.

Sex— ♀ = ♂ by plumage aspect. Medial(?) BP (Fig. 20**A**, p. 31) developed by both sexes but distended cloaca (Fig. 21, p. 32) indicates ♀ in Feb-May. Measurements (especially bill depth and tarsus) helpful for sexing (Table 33, p. 346). Ornamental plumes may average longer in ♂♂ than in ♀♀ in Jan-May but more study is needed to determine reliable measures by sex. During courtship in Feb-May, the bluish loral skin and red iris color may average brighter in ♂♂ than ♀♀, which can perhaps be used to sex some mated pairs (in combination with size and leg length). Otherwise, no criteria known.

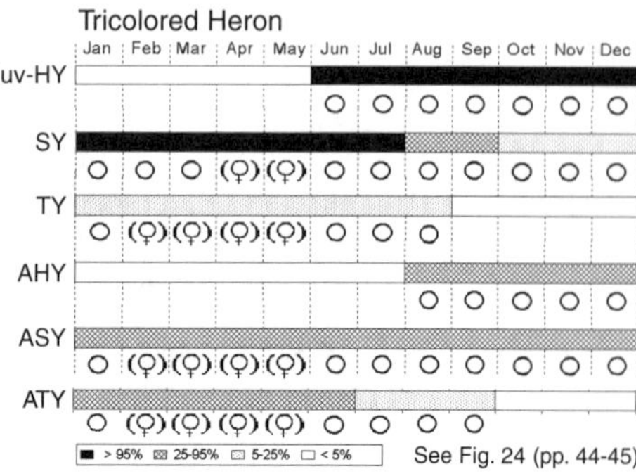

Hybrids reported— With Snowy Egret (p. 352) and possibly with Black-crowned Night Heron (Sibley 1994). See Little Blue Heron.

References— Bent (1926), Frederick (1997), McVaugh (1972), Oberholser (1974), Palmer (1962), Rodgers (1978b).

REDDISH EGRET

Egretta rufescens

REEG
Species # 1980
Band size: 7A

Species— From other N.Am herons by medium-large size with deep bill (Table 34, p. 356; Fig. 257**C**, p. 352); dark morph with head and neck grayish cinnamon (HY/SY) to purplish rufous (AHY/ASY) and back, underparts, and underwing covs without white; AHY (including white morph) with elongated lanceolate occipital (*cf.* Fig. 254**A**, p. 349) and pectoral (Fig. 254**C**) plumes (extending anteriorly to nape) and with filamentous and lanceolate scapular plumes (Fig. 254**B**, **D**); bill grayish pink (HY) to bright pink with a distinct black tip (AHY), the malar feathering extending 13-19 mm proximal to eye, and the loral skin dusky gray to bluish (Fig. 257**C**); legs and feet dusky to slate.

Geographic variation— Considered monotypic here. Populations of Baja CA-sw.CA ("*E.r. dickeyi*") may average darker heads and napes (dark morph) than other populations but difference not substantive enough for subspecific recognition. See Blake (1977), Griscom (1926), Hellmayr & Conover (1948a), Palmer (1962), Paynter (1955), and van Rossem (1926a) for more information.

Molt— CBS. PF partial (Sep-Apr in HY/SYs), PB2 incomplete-complete (Apr-Nov in non-breeding SYs), DPB incomplete-complete (Jun-Jan in breeding AHY/ASYs); PA absent. The PF occurs primarily on non-breeding grounds whereas PBs can occur N of breeding grounds and/or on non-breeding grounds. The PF includes some to most body feathers (ornamental plumes develop in Nov-Apr) and some proximal med and les covs but no gr covs or terts. The PBs are usually complete but can exhibit staffelmauser in some ASYs (Fig. 16, pp. 23-24), resulting in up to 2 sets of basic feathers in adults, especially among the ss. White-morph and dark-morph individuals appear to display similar molt patterns, although a greater proportion of dark-morph individuals might exhibit incomplete molts.

Age—Juv (B1; Jun-Feb) dark-morph is like HY/SY (below) in Nov-Dec but has bill, legs, and feet blackish (white morph differs only in leg and bill color); Juv ♀=♂. Most of the following plumage-aspect characters refer to dark-morph individuals; white-morph individuals can be aged by molt and feather-shape characters.

Juv-HY/SY (1st cycle, Juv/B1-F1; Nov-Oct): Crown, head, and neck feathers short, pale grayish and brown, increasingly mottled with incoming dull pinkish-brown (and more elongated) feathers in Dec-Oct; abdomen dull grayish or washed rufous; most to all s covs, p covs, and large scapulars dull gray with whitish-brown to pale rufous tips (Fig. 252**A**, p. 348); pp and ss uniformly juv and not showing s1-p1 contrast (Fig. 13**A**, p. 20), or inner pp and ss being replaced in Apr-Sep, the juv outer pp and medial ss tapered, brownish, and relatively worn (Fig. 247**A-B**); molt limits occur among the humerals, les covs, and med covs (Fig. 13**B-C**); base of bill dusky or with an indistinct pinkish wash in Apr-Oct; rects narrow and rounded (Fig. 256**A**, p. 351); legs blackish to grayish.

AHY/ASY (Def. cycle, DB; Nov-Oct): Crown, head, and neck bright pinkish brown, the neck feathers elongated; abdomen bluish gray; s covs, p covs, and longest scapulars uniformly bright bluish gray, without pale tips (Fig. 252**C**); pp and ss uniformly basic and showing uninterrupted replacement cline and s1-p1 contrast, and s covs uniform in wear (Fig. 14**B**, p. 21), the outer pp broad and relatively fresh (Fig. 247**C**); base of bill uniformly pinkish to pink, distinctly cut off from black tip; rects broad and truncate (Fig. 256**B**); legs bluish (brighter in Feb-Jun). **Note: AHY/ASYs with these characters (especially the bare part colors) may be reliably aged ASY/ATY but more study is needed.**

SY/TY (2nd cycle, B2; Nov-Aug): Like AHY/ASY but crown, head, and neck duller pinkish brown; abdomen dull grayish or washed dusky; pp and ss with 2 generations, 1-2 juv outer pp (p10 can molt < p9) and/or 1-6 juv ss (among s4 and s7-s11) retained and very faded and worn (Figs. 16**B**, p. 24, & 247**B**); base of bill mixed blackish and pink (the culmen and ventral side of lower mandible often blackish); legs dusky-slate to slate.

ASY/ATY (Def. cycle, DB; Nov-Jul): Like AHY/ASY but pp and ss with 2 sets of basic feathers in staffelmauser patterns (Fig. 16**E**).

Sex—♀=♂ by plumage aspect. Medial(?) BP (Fig. 20**A**, p. 31) developed by both sexes but distended cloaca (Fig. 21, p. 32) indicates ASY ♀ in Jan-Apr. Measurements (especially tail length and bill depth) somewhat helpful for sexing (Table 34, p. 356). Ornamental plumes may average longer in ♂♂ than in ♀♀ in Jan-May but more study is needed to determine reliable measures by sex. Otherwise, no criteria known.

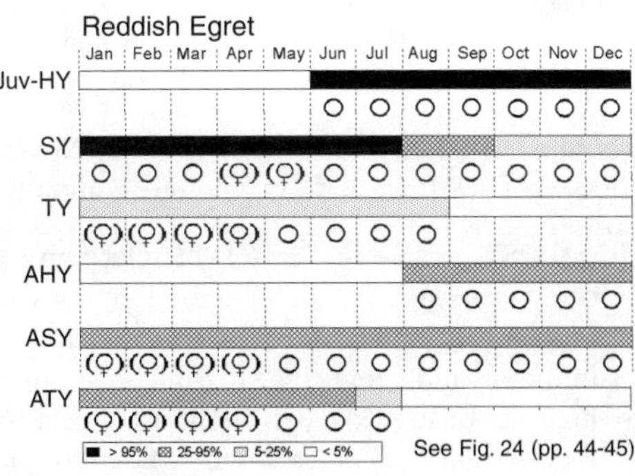

Hybrids reported—None.

References—Bent (1926), Kaufman (1990a, 1991), Lowther & Paul (2002), Meyerriecks (1960), Oberholser (1974), Palmer (1962), Payne & Risley (1976).

CATTLE EGRET
Bubulcus ibis

CAEG
Species # 2001
Band size: 6

Species—From other N.Am white herons and egrets by smaller size, especially bill and legs (Table 34, p. 356; Fig. 257**G**, p. 352); filamentous occipital, scapular, and pectoral plumes (Fig. 254**D**, p. 349) extending to the throat and becoming buff to buffy orange (through externally acquired pigment) in Feb-Jun; bill and loral skin yellowish (to greenish or pinkish in Mar-Jun) and malar feathering extends 7-10 mm proximal to eye (Fig. 257**G**); legs blackish (without yellow feet).

Geographic variation—See Cramp & Simmons (1977), Drury et al. (1953), Heather (1982), Marchant & Higgins (1990), Payne & Risley (1976), Telfair (1994), Tucker (1985). No other subspecies occur. Note that differences in extent of buff or orange coloration may be based on external pigment acquisition rates rather than geographic variation in plumage-aspect patterns (see also Sandhill Crane, p. 494).

B.i. coromanda (br & wint Asia, vagrant to sw.AK): Larger, especially bill and legs (Table 34, p. 356); exposed portion of tibia longer (from tibiotarsal joint to tips of thigh feathers ~30-50 mm); ornamental plumes, face, neck, and throat stained dark orange in Feb-Jun.

B.i. ibis (br & wint Africa and N.Am): Smaller, especially bill and legs (Table 34); exposed portion of tibia shorter (from tibiotarsal joint to tips of thigh feathers ~15-35 mm); ornamental plumes stained pale buff to buffy orange and face, neck, and throat white to whitish in Feb-Jun.

Molt—CBS. PF partial (Sep-Apr in HY/SYs), PB2 incomplete-complete (Apr-Dec in non-breeding SY/TYs), DPB incomplete-complete (Jul-Jan in breeding AHY/ASYs); PA absent. The above timing pertains to N.Am populations. The PF occurs primarily on non-breeding grounds whereas PBs can occur N of breeding grounds and/or on non-breeding grounds; flight-feather molt during the PB2 can be suspended for northward migration (often around p6 and s11) in SYs that breed. The PF includes most to all body feathers (ornamental plumes develop in Nov-Apr) and some proximal les covs but no gr covs or terts. The PBs can be complete but often exhibit staffelmauser (Fig. 16, pp. 23-24), resulting in up to 2 sets of basic feathers among pp and ss of adults. One to 4 outer pp and 2-6 (of 15) ss (often among s2-s4 and s6-s10) can be retained during the PB2. Pigmentation appears to result from topical application or oxidation rather than molt (Pyle & Howell 2004).

Age—Juv (B1; Jun-Feb) is like HY/SY in Nov-Mar (below) but with bill and loral skin dusky to dusky yellow; Juv ♀ = ♂. The following month ranges pertain to N.Am populations.

Juv-HY/SY (1st cycle, Juv/B1-F1; Oct-Sep): Crown white, becoming pale buff in Oct-Mar; occipital, scapular, and pectoral plumes absent in Oct-Jan, developing in Jan-Apr, and reduced in length and whitish to buffy orange in Mar-Aug; molt limits occur among the humerals and s covs (Fig. 13**B-C**, p. 20), replaced feathers glossier white; pp and ss uniformly juv and not showing s1-p1 contrast (Fig. 13**A**), or inner pp and ss being replaced in Mar-Sep, the juv outer pp and medial ss tapered and worn (Fig. 247**A-B**, p. 341); bill dusky yellow through Nov-Jan. **Note: Rect shape (Fig. 256, p. 351) does not appear as useful for ageing in this species as in other egrets.**

AHY/ASY (Def. cycle, DB; Oct-Sep): Crown pale to rich buff; occipital, scapular, and pectoral plumes elongated and buffy orange in Feb-Jun; s covs uniform in wear gloss, and pp and ss uniformly basic and showing uninterrupted replacement cline and s1-p1 contrast (Fig. 14**B**, p. 21), the outer pp broad and fresh (Fig. 247**C**); bill yellow to pale orangish in Apr-Jun. **Note: See HY/SY.**

SY/TY (2nd cycle, B2; Oct-Aug): Like AHY/ASY but pp and ss with 2 generations, 1-2 juv outer pp (p10 can molt < p9) and/or 1-6 juv ss (among s4 and s7-s11) retained and very faded and worn (Figs. 16**B**, p. 24, & Fig. 247**B**).

ASY/ATY (Def. cycle, DB; Oct-Jul): Like AHY/ASY but pp and ss with 2 sets of basic feathers in staffelmauser patterns (Fig. 16**E**).

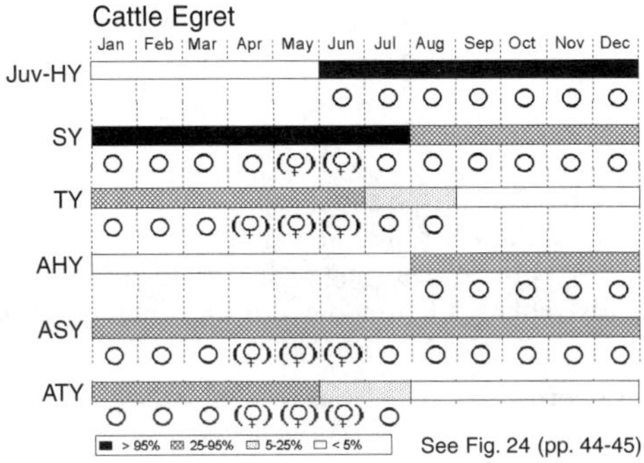

Sex—♀=♂ by plumage aspect. Medial(?) BP (Fig. 20**A**, p. 31) developed by both sexes but distended cloaca (Fig. 21, p. 32) indicates ♀ in Mar-Jun. Measurements generally unhelpful for sexing (Table 34, p. 356). Ornamental plumes may average longer in ♂♂ than in ♀♀ in Jan-May but more study is needed to determine reliable measures by sex. Otherwise, no criteria known.

Hybrids reported—With Snowy Egret (p. 352) and Little Blue Heron (p. 354) in the wild.

Cattle Egret

	Jan	Feb	Mar	Apr	May	Jun	Jul	Aug	Sep	Oct	Nov	Dec
Juv-HY						O	O	O	O	O	O	O
SY	O	O	O	O	(♀)	(♀)	O	O	O	O	O	O
TY	O	O	O	(♀)	(♀)	(♀)	O	O				
AHY								O	O	O	O	O
ASY	O	O	O	(♀)	(♀)	(♀)	O	O	O	O	O	O
ATY	O	O	O	(♀)	(♀)	(♀)	O					

■ > 95% ▨ 25-95% ▭ 5-25% □ < 5%

See Fig. 24 (pp. 44-45)

References—Bent (1926), Cramp & Simmons (1977), Dement'ev & Gladkov (1951a), Heather (1982), Lancaster (1970), Maddock (1989), Marchant & Higgins (1990), McKilligan (1985), Oberholser (1974), Palmer (1962), Payne & Risley (1976), Pyle & Howell (2004), Siegfried (1971), Telfair (1994).

GREEN HERON
Butorides virescens

GRHE
Species # 2010
Band size: 5

Species—From other N.Am herons by smaller overall size and from Least Bittern (p. 344) by larger overall size (Table 33, p. 346); plumage aspect greenish, grayish, and rufous, without buff or yellowish; outer pp slightly notched (*cf.* Fig. 4**B**, p. 7). See Least Bittern regarding erythristic (carotenistic) ("Cory's") plumage aspects that might be confused with Green Heron. Occasional erythristic individuals of Green Heron also occur (head entirely reddish brown), especially in se.N.Am (more regularly in Caribbean region). Striated Heron (*B. striatus*), a potential vagrant to se.N.Am, is smaller (wg chord 150-180, tarsus 44-52) and has auriculars, nape, and neck grayish (auriculars sometimes tinge rufous) and occipital plume longer. Beware of hybrids (see Hayes 2006 and Payne 1974 for more information).

Geographic variation—See Brewster (1888), Dickey & van Rossem (1938), Fisher & Wetmore (1931), Hayes (2002, 2006), Hellmayr & Conover (1948a), Mearns (1895), Monroe (1968), Monroe & Browning (1992), Oberholser (1912b, 1912c, 1974), Parkes (1955a), Payne (1974), Peters (1931b), Phillips et al. (1964), Todd (1916a), Todd & Worthington (1911), van Rossem (1934), Voous (1986). Two other subspecies occur in s.Baja CA and the Bahamas. Note that variation can be confounded by occasional plumage-aspect erythrism (carotenism).

B.v. anthonyi (br & wint OR to s.CA-AZ, visitor to se.AK-w.TX): Averages larger, especially in wing length (Table 33, p. 346); AHYs with more white to tips of inner pp and outer ss (Fig. 260**B-C**, p. 362); back and rump feathers average slightly grayer green; underparts of HY/SY with sparser and more distinct brown streaks.

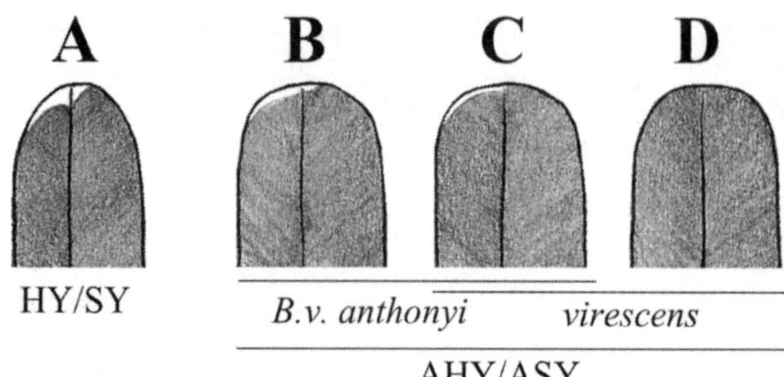

FIGURE 260. Shape and amount of white to the tips of the inner primaries and outer secondaries by age and subspecies in Green Heron. Juv feathers (**A**) have roughly the same amount of white by subspecies (perhaps averaging slightly more in *B.v. anthonyi* than in *virescens*). Note that the juv s3 and/or s4 (resembling **A** but more worn) can often be retained by SY/TYs. See also Figure 261.

B.v. virescens (br & wint ND-NB to NM-FL; visitor to Sask-Nfl): Averages smaller, especially in wing length (Table 33); AHYs with little or no white to tips of inner pp and outer ss (Fig. 260**C**-**D**); back and rump feathers average slightly greener (less grayish); underparts of HY/SY with denser and more diffuse brownish-gray streaks.

Molt—CBS. PF partial-incomplete (Sep-Apr in HY/SYs), PB2 incomplete-complete (Jul-Mar in non-breeding SY/TYs), DPB incomplete-complete (Sep-Mar in breeding AHY/ASYs); PA absent. The PF and PBs can begin on breeding grounds (including replacement of up to 7 inner pp and 5 inner ss during PBs) but are usually suspended, with most molting protracted and completing on non-breeding grounds. The PF includes most to all body feathers (ornamental plumes develop in Oct-Apr), a few to most or all les, med, and/or proximal gr covs, up to 5 terts and ss (among s11-s15 of 15 ss), and up to 6 rects (often none, occasionally all?). The PBs are often incomplete, exhibiting staffelmauser (Fig. 16, pp. 23-24), resulting in up to 2 sets among pp and ss of adults. One to 3 outer pp and 1-6 (of 15) ss (often among s3-s4 and s7-s10) can be retained during the PB2.

Age—Juv (B1; Jun-Feb) is like HY/SY (below) in Jul-Jan but bill primarily dull yellow with brownish culmen; Juv ♀ = ♂. The following month ranges pertain to N.Am populations.

Juv-HY/SY (1st cycle, Juv/B1-F1; Nov-Oct): Neck and underparts streaked dull rufous and white in Nov-Jan; most or all s covs dull slate with whitish tips or fringes (Fig. 261**A**), contrasting with a few to many (rarely all) green feathers with narrow fringes (Fig. 261**B**) in Dec-Oct (Fig. 13**B**-**C**, p. 20); inner pp and outer ss dull slate with extensive white tips along shafts (Fig. 260**A**); pp and ss uniformly juv and not showing s1-p1 contrast (Fig. 13**A**) or with 1-5 inner ss replaced and contrastingly fresh, the juv outer pp narrow at the tips and relatively worn (Fig. 247**A**-**B**, p. 341); rects narrow (*cf.* Fig. 256**A**, p. 351) and dull slate with little or no green sheen (sometimes contrasting with greener, replaced feathers); lower mandible primarily yellow.

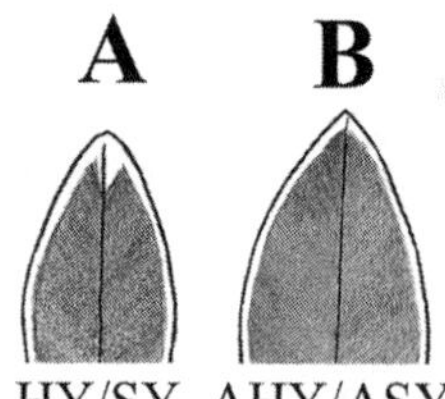

FIGURE 261. Relative size, shape, and color pattern to the secondary coverts by age in Green Heron. Juv feathers with white tips (**A**) are shown by HY/SYs and can be mixed with formative covs (resembling **B**) in Dec-Oct. Some SYs may rarely replace all s covs during the PF so confirm age of AHY/ASYs with patterns to the inner pp and outer ss (Fig. 260) if possible.

AHY/ASY (Def. cycle, DB; Nov-Oct): Neck and breast dark rufous, without whitish streaks; s covs uniformly green with narrow fringes (Fig. 261**B**); inner pp and outer ss blackish green with reduced or no white fringes by subspecies (Fig. 260**B-D**; see **Geographic variation**); pp and ss uniformly basic and showing uninterrupted replacement clines and s1-p1 contrast and the s covs uniform in wear (Fig. 14**B**, p. 21), the outer pp broad and fresh (Fig. 247**C**); rects uniformly broad (*cf.* Fig. 256**B**) and black with a green sheen; lower mandible primarily black.

SY/TY (2nd cycle, B2; Nov-Oct): Like AHY/ASY but pp and ss with 2 generations, 1-2 juv outer pp (p10 can molt < p9) and/or 1-5 juv ss (among s3-s4 and s7-s10) retained, abraded and pointed (Figs. 16**B**, p. 24, & Fig. 247**B**), the retained ss (especially s3-s4) brownish slate with white tips (Fig. 260**A**, can wear off by spring); lower mandible primarily brownish to blackish.

ASY/ATY (Def. cycle, DB; Nov-Oct): Like AHY/ASY but pp and ss with 2 sets of basic feathers in staffelmauser patterns (Fig. 16**E**).

Sex—♀ = ♂ by plumage aspect. Medial(?) BP (Fig. 20**A**, p. 31) developed by both sexes but distended cloaca (Fig. 21, p. 32) indicates ♀ in Apr-Jun. Measurements unhelpful for sexing (Table 33, p. 346). ♀♀ may average duller in plumage aspect than ♂♂ but there is extensive overlap. The lengths of the lanceolate occipital and scapular plumes (*cf.* Fig. 254**A-B**, p. 349) average longer in ♂♂ than in ♀♀ in Jan-May but extensive variation by season, age, and individual precludes reliable sexing of most individuals; those with longest occipital plume > 52 mm and/or longest scapular plume > 105 mm (usually in Dec-May) can be sexed ♂. Otherwise, no criteria known.

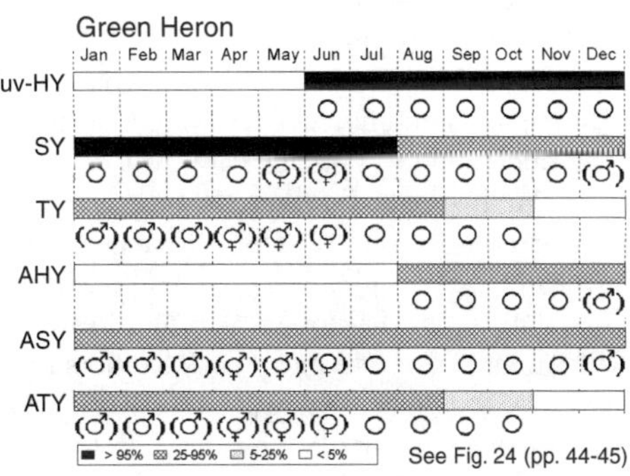

Hybrids reported—With Striated Heron *B. striatus* (Payne 1974, Monroe & Browning 1992, Hayes 2002, 2006).

References—Bangs (1915a), Bent (1926), Blake (1977), Cramp & Simmons (1977), Davis & Kushlan (1994), Gaviño & Dickerman (1972), Hayes (2002, 2006), McVaugh (1975), Meyerriecks (1960), Oberholser (1912b, 1912c, 1974), Palmer (1962), Payne (1974), Payne & Risley (1976), Pyle & Howell (2004), Roberts (1955).

BLACK-CROWNED NIGHT-HERON
Nycticorax nycticorax

BCNH
Species # 2020
Band size: 7A

Species—From American Bittern and most other N.Am herons by medium-large size with short wing, long tail, and deep bill (Table 33, p. 346; Fig. 262**A**, p. 364; depth at distal end of nares > 17 mm); HY/SYs with feathers of upperparts (especially s covs) brownish with well-defined pale spots or streaks (Figs. 263-264, pp. 364-365), not contrasting distinctly in aspect with brownish pp; outer pp notched (Fig. 4**B**, p. 7); bill brown with yellow base (HY), to black (ASY); legs and feet yellowish. HY/SY from HY/SY Yellow-crowned Night Heron (p. 366) by larger size but shallower bill and shorter legs (Table 33; Fig. 262**A**); bill paler at base (Fig. 262**A**); loral skin yellowish; nares longer (Fig. 262**A**); s covs rounded and these, inner ss, and p covs with larger and wider whitish spots or streaks (Figs. 263-264); pp and ss brown; SY with crown becoming dusky blackish and throat and breast becoming whitish by Jan-Mar.

Geographic variation—See Bangs & Penard (1918), Blake (1977), Cramp & Simmons (1977), Hellmayr & Conover (1948a), Peters (1930b). One other subspecies in s.S.Am.

N.n. nycticorax (br & wint Eurasia and N.Am): Smaller than *obscurus* of s.S.Am (Table 33, p. 346; *vs* wg chord 283-320, exp culmen 73-103 in *obscurus*); ASY/ATY with forehead and underparts whitish to pale gray (*vs* washed darker gray); HY/SY with spots and fringes of upperparts whitish (*vs* buff in *obscurus*). Populations of N.Am ("*hoactli*") may average slightly larger and with shorter supercilium and duller reddish legs during the breeding season than populations of Eurasia, but differences are insufficient for subspecific diagnosis.

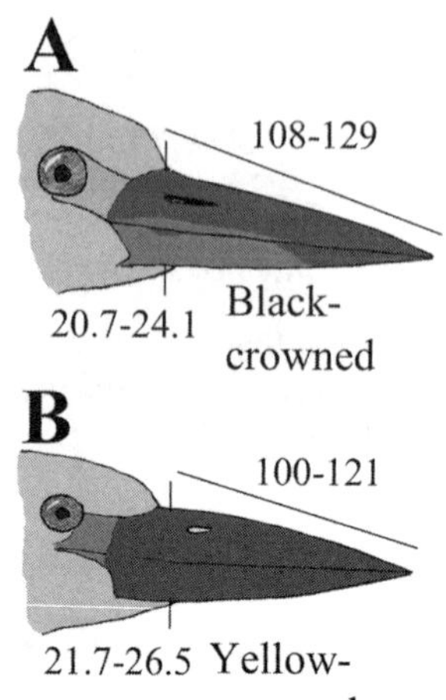

FIGURE 262. Bill size and proportions in Black-crowned and Yellow-crowned night-herons for identification of Juv-HY/SYs. Indicated measures are exposed culmen and bill depth at distal end of forehead feathers (Figs. 7**A** & 8**A**, pp. 9-10); see **Geographic variation** regarding Yellow-crowned Night-Heron. In both species bill depth at distal end of nares is > 17 mm, *vs* < 17 mm in all other N.Am bitterns and herons. Note elongated nares/nasal groove of Black-crowned Night-Heron (> 10 mm) as compared to Yellow-crowned Night-Heron (< 10 mm).

Molt—CBS. PF limited (Oct-Apr in HY/SYs), PB2 incomplete-complete (May-Nov in SYs), PB3 incomplete-complete (May-Dec in non-breeding TYs), DPB incomplete-complete (Jul-Jan in breeding ASY/ATYs); PA absent. The above timing pertains to N.Am populations. Molting occurs on both the breeding and non-breeding grounds. The PF appears to involve most to all of the crown (reduced occipital plumes develop in Nov-Mar in some HY/SYs) and some to many back feathers but no s covs, terts, or underpart feathers. The PBs can be complete but often exhibit staffelmauser (Fig. 16, pp. 23-24), resulting in 2-3 sets among pp of adults. One to 7 outer pp and 1-12 (of 16) ss (often among s2-s4 and s6-s10) can be retained during the PB2, and some TYs can retain 1-2 juv outer pp and/or 1-4 juv ss among s3-s4 and s7-s10 during the PB3. During DPBs, successful breeders appear to replace 2-5 pp and non-breeders and/or failed breeders appear to replace 7-10 pp per cycle.

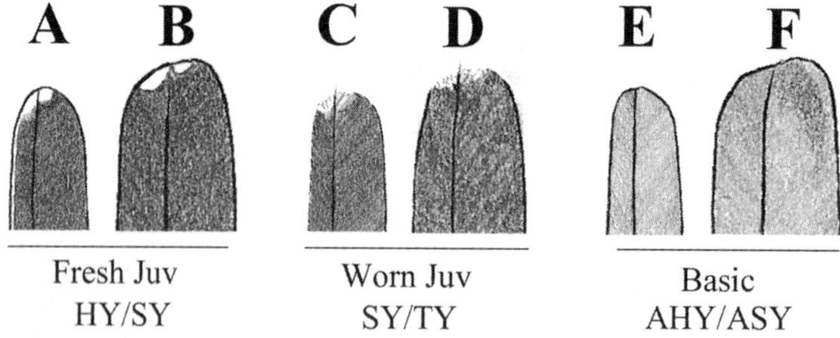

FIGURE 263. Shape and pattern to juv and basic primary coverts (left; p cov 9 shown) and inner secondaries (right; s4 shown) by age in Black-crowned Night-Heron; the inner primaries also show these characters. The PB2 is typically incomplete, resulting in juv outer p covs and inner ss (especially s3 and/or s4) being retained in SY/TYs and becoming worn (**C-D**); the white tips sometimes can become worn off in spring TYs. Rarely the outermost juv p covs and/or ss (among s3-s4 and s7-s10) can be retained during the PB3 and shown by TY/4Ys. Definitive basic feathers (**E-F**) lack pale tips, with 2nd basic and sometimes 3rd basic feathers washed brownish.

Age—Juv (B1; Jun-Feb) is like HY/SY in Nov-Jan (below) but with bill primarily dull yellow with brownish culmen; Juv ♀ = ♂. The following month ranges pertain to N.Am populations.

Juv-HY/SY (1st cycle, Juv/B1-F1; Oct-Sep): Crown, back, and s covs brown with distinct white streaks or spots (Fig. 264**A**), some replaced by dusky-brown to grayish feathers in May-Sep; face and upper breast with heavy brown streaking, becoming pale grayish in May-Sep; pp, p covs, and ss uniformly juv (Fig. 13**A**, p. 20) or inner pp and ss being replaced in May-Sep, the juv outer pp and medial ss tapered, brownish, and worn (Fig. 247**A**-**B**, p. 341) and the p covs, inner pp, and outer ss with white tips (Fig. 263**A**-**B**); bill brownish with yellow or pale grayish base to lower mandible; iris yellow to dull orange-red.

SY/TY (2nd cycle, B2; Oct-Sep): Crown, back, and s covs dusky brown to grayish, the crown and back being replaced by dull black feathers in May-Sep, and the proximal med and other covs often with diffuse pale streaks or spots (Fig. 264**B**); face and upper breast grayish white with indistinct dusky streaks; pp, p covs, and ss with 2 generations, 1-7 juv outer pp and/or 1-10 juv ss (among s2-s4 and s6-s12) retained, very faded and worn (Figs. 16**B**, p. 24, & Fig. 247**B**), and with white tips (Fig. 263**C**-**D**) if not worn off; bill grayish yellow with a black tip to black; iris orange to orange-red. **Note: See TY/4Y.**

ASY/ATY (Def. cycle, DB; Oct-Sep): Crown and back black with bluish sheen; face and upper breast white to pearly gray; s covs gray without brown tinge or pale tips (Fig. 264**D**); pp uniformly basic (Fig. 14**B**, p. 21) or with 2 sets of basic feathers in staffelmauser patterns (Fig. 16**E**), the inner pp, p covs, and ss without white tips (Fig. 263**E**-**F**); bill blackish, to black in Feb-Jun; iris bright orange-red to red. **Note: See TY/4Y. Individuals in this plumage, without brown wash to the wing feathers (Fig. 264C & *cf.* Fig. 263) may be ATY/A4Ys; study needed.**

TY/4Y (3rd cycle, B3; Oct-Sep): Crown and back dull black, sometimes tinged grayish or brownish; face and upper breast whitish; s covs mostly gray with slight brown tinge, sometimes with very diffuse pale tips to the proximal med covs (Fig. 264**C**); pp, p covs, and ss with 2 sets of basic feathers in staffelmauser patterns (Fig. 16**E**), sometimes also with 1-2 outer juv pp and/or 1-4 juv ss (among s3-s4 and s7-s10) remaining (Fig. 16**D**), very abraded, brown, worn, and with white tips occasionally remaining (Figs. 247**B** & 263**C**-**D**); bill blackish to black (sometimes with paling at the base); iris bright orange-red. **Note: It is possible that some advanced SY/TYs or retarded 4Y/5Ys may also show this plumage aspect; intermediate individuals (e.g., those with intermediate aspect and complete pp and ss replacement) may be best aged S-TY, T-4Y, or 4-5Y (see pp. 41-42); more study is needed.**

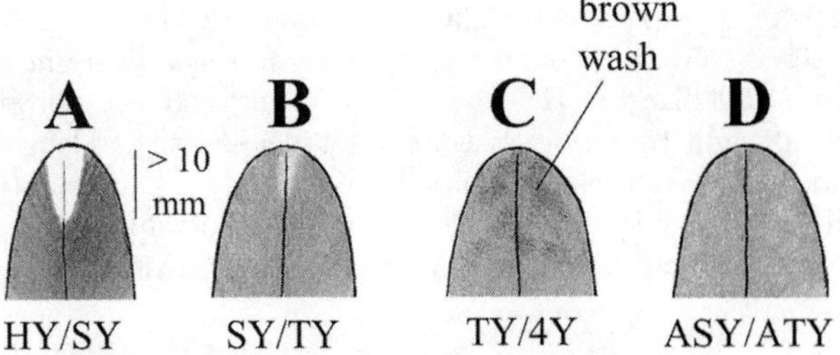

FIGURE 264. Secondary coverts by age in Black-crowned Night-Heron (inner median covert shown). In HY/SYs (**A**), the length of the pale feather tips is > 10 mm and note different feather shape and patterns by age as compared with Yellow-crowned Night-Heron (Fig. 265, p. 367).

ATY/A4Y (Def. cycle, DB; Aug-Jul): Like ASY/ATY but pp with 3 sets of basic feathers in staffelmauser patterns (Fig. 16**F**).

A4Y/A5Y (Def. cycle, DB; Oct-Jul): Like ASY/ATY but pp with 4 sets of basic feathers in staffelmauser patterns (Fig. 16**G**). **Note: This age designation may be rare.**

Sex— ♀ = ♂ by plumage aspect. Medial BP (Fig. 20**A**, p. 31) developed by both sexes but distended cloaca (Fig. 21, p. 32) indicates ASY ♀ in Mar-Jun. Measurements generally unhelpful for sexing (Table 33, p. 346). See Dieter (1973) for sexing Black-crowned Night-Herons by plasma steroid hormones. The following appears to be reliable for sexing most N.Am ASY/ATYs in Feb-Jul but beware of ♂♂ that have dropped their longest plume; it is probable that some SY/TYs may also be reliably sexed (plume length reduced in both sexes) but more study is needed:

ASY/ATY ♀ (Feb-Jul): Longest occipital plume 113-171 mm from base.

ASY/ATY ♂ (Feb-Jul): Longest occipital plume 162-225 mm from base.

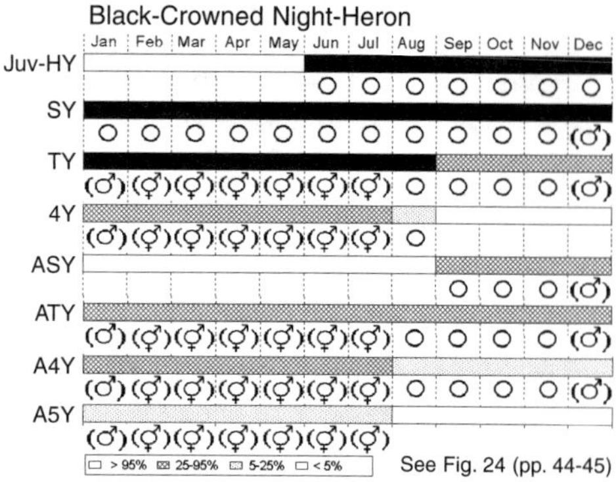

Black-Crowned Night-Heron

See Fig. 24 (pp. 44-45)

Hybrids reported—With Rufous Night-Heron *N. caledonicus* (Hubbard 1976), either Little Blue Heron (p. 354) or Tricolored Heron (p. 357), and possibly with Yellow-crowned Night-Heron (Monson & Phillips 1981) in the wild.

References—Adams (1955), Bent (1926), Cramp & Simmons (1977), Custer & Davis (1982), Davis (1993, 1999), Dement'ev & Gladkov (1951a), Fasola et al. (2001), Gross (1923), McVaugh (1972), Noble et al. (1938), Palmer (1962), Payne & Risley (1976), Roberts (1955), Rohwer (1999), Shugart & Rohwer (1996).

YELLOW-CROWNED NIGHT-HERON

Nyctanassa violacea

YCNH
Species # 2030
Band size: 7A

Species—From American Bittern and most other N.Am herons by medium-large size with short wing and deep bill (Table 33, p. 346; Fig. 262**B**, p. 364; depth at distal end of nares > 17 mm); HY/SYs with feathers of upperparts (especially s covs) brownish with well-defined white triangular spots (Figs. 265 & 266), not contrasting distinctly in shade with grayish pp; outer pp notched (Fig. 4**B**, p. 7); bill blackish (HY), to black (ASY); legs and feet yellowish. HY/SY from HY/SY Black-crowned Night-Heron by smaller size but deeper bill and longer legs (Table 33; Fig. 262**B**); bill darker (Fig. 262**B**); loral skin dull olive to grayish; nares shorter (Fig. 262**B**); s covs triangular and these, ss, and p covs with smaller whitish spots at tip (Figs. 265-266; *cf.* Fig. 264, p. 365); pp and ss dark gray; SY with crown brownish and throat and breast not becoming whitish by Jan-Mar.

Geographic variation—See Blake (1977), Dickey & van Rossem (1938), Hellmayr & Conover (1948a), Huey (1927b), Monroe (1968), Palmer (1962), van Rossem (1943), Wetmore (1946a, 1946b, 1965). Two other subspecies in Panama-S.Am and the Galapagos Is.

N.v. bancrofti (br & wint nw.Mex-West Indies, visitor to s.AZ-s.CA; potential visitor to s.FL): Bill deeper (depth at distal end of nares 21.5-27.5); plumage aspect may average darker.

N.v. violacea (br & wint N.Am): Bill narrower (depth at distal end of nares 18.9-22.6); plumage aspect may average paler.

Molt—CBS. PF limited (Oct-Apr in HY/SYs), PB2 incomplete-complete (May-Nov in SYs), PB3 incomplete-complete (May-Dec in nonbreeding TYs), DPB incomplete-complete (Jul-Jan in breeding ASY/ATYs); PA absent. Molt strategies appear to be similar to those of Black-crowned Night-Heron (p. 363), the PBs possibly averaging more complete.

Age—Juv (B1; Jun-Feb) is like HY/SY in Nov-Jan (below) and with some yellowish or greenish to base of lower mandible; Juv ♀=♂. The following month ranges pertain to N.Am populations.

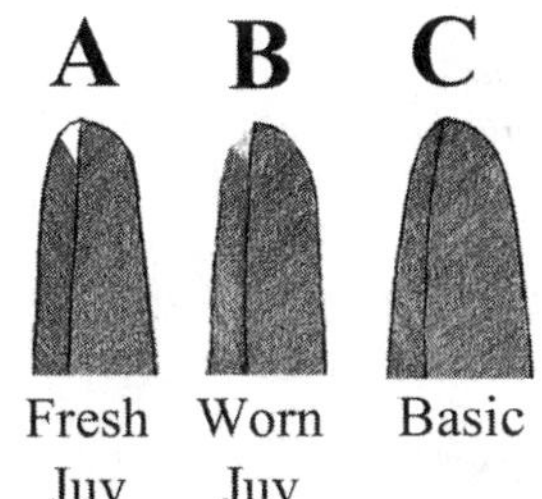

FIGURE 265. Shape and pattern to juv and basic primary coverts (p cov 9 shown) by age in Yellow-crowned Night-Heron. The PB2 is typically incomplete, resulting in juv outer p covs being retained in SY/TYs and becoming worn (**B**); the white tips sometimes can become worn off in spring TYs. Rarely the outermost juv p covs can be retained during the PB3 and shown by TY/4Ys. Basic feathers (**C**) lack pale tips. See Fig. 263 (p. 364) for similar patterns among ss; Yellow-crowned Night-Heron differs by having smaller or no white tips to the juv inner ss and outer pp.

Juv HY/SY (1st cycle, Juv/B1-F1; Oct-Sep): Crown and back brownish with whitish streaks; chin, throat, and upper breast brown with diffuse whitish streaking; les covs rounded with distinct white triangular spots (Fig. 266**A**); pp, p covs, and ss uniformly juv (Fig. 16**A**, p. 24), or inner pp and ss being replaced in May-Sep, the juv outer pp and medial ss tapered, brownish, and worn (*cf.* Figs. 263**B**, **D**, p. 364; & 247**A-B**, p. 341), and the p covs with distinct white tips (Fig. 265**A-B**); iris dull orange.

SY/TY (2nd cycle, B2; Oct-Sep): Crown black with variably brown to whitish forecrown; back grayish brown with diffuse dusky streaks; chin and throat grayish brown with narrow white streaks; upper breast brownish gray with diffuse pale streaks; les covs moderately elongated and brown with diffuse dusky centers (Fig. 266**B**); pp and ss with 2 generations (Fig. 16**B**), 1-7 juv outer pp and p covs and/or 1-10 juv ss (among s2-s4 and s6-s12) retained or being replaced in Apr-Sep, very faded and worn (Fig. 247**B**), the juv p covs often with white tips (*cf.* Fig. 263**D**; Fig. 266**B**); iris orange-red. **Note: See TY/4Y.**

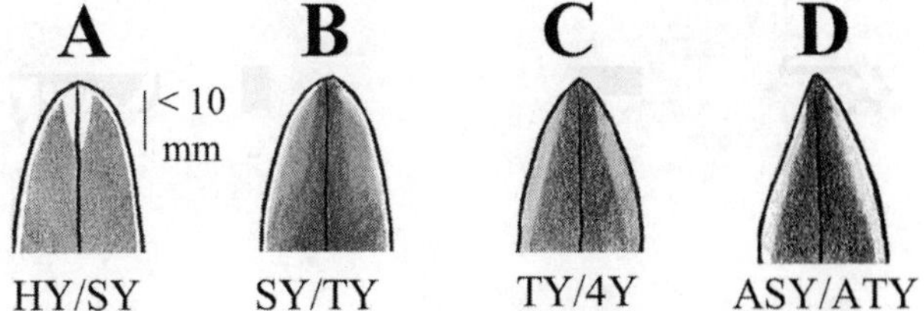

FIGURE 266. Shape and pattern to the secondary coverts by age in Yellow-crowned Night-Heron (lesser covert shown). In HY/SYs (**A**), the length of the pale feather tips is < 10 mm and note different feather shape and patterns by age as compared with Black-crowned Night-Heron (Fig. 264, p. 365).

ASY/ATY (Def. cycle, DB; Oct-Sep): Head black and white, the forecrown whitish without brown; back dark gray with distinct black streaks; chin black; throat gray without pale mottling (sometimes with dusky streaks); upper breast gray; les covs elongated and gray with distinct blackish centers (Fig. 266**D**); pp with 2 sets of basic feathers in staffelmauser patterns (Fig. 16**E**), the outer pp broad and fresh (Fig. 247**C**) and retained p covs without white tips (Fig. 265**C**); iris bright orange-red to red. **Note: It is possible that birds in full definitive basic plumage can be aged ATY/A4Y but more study is needed; see TY/4Y.**

TY/4Y (3rd cycle, B3; Oct-Aug): Like ASY/ATY but forecrown sometimes with brown smudging; chin and throat mottled pale whitish; upper breast gray with slight brown tinge; les covs slightly tinged brownish and with less distinct blackish centers (Fig. 266**C**); pp, p covs, and ss sometimes with 1-2 outer juv pp and/or 1-4 juv ss (among s4 and s7-s9) remaining (Fig. 16**D**), very abraded, brown, worn (Fig. 247**B**), and sometimes with white tips remaining to p covs (Fig. 265**C**); iris orange-red. **Note: It is possible that some advanced SY/TYs or retarded 4Y/5Ys may also show this plumage aspect; intermediate individuals (e.g., those with intermediate aspect and complete pp and ss replacement) may be best aged S-TY, T-4Y, or 4-5Y (see pp. 41-42); more study is needed.**

ATY/A4Y (Def. cycle, DB; Aug-Jul): Like ASY/ATY but pp with 3 sets of basic feathers in staffelmauser patterns (Fig. 16**F**).

A4Y/A5Y (Def. cycle, DB; Oct-Jul): Like ASY/ATY but pp with 4 sets of basic feathers in staffelmauser patterns (Fig. 16**G**). **Note: This age designation may be rare.**

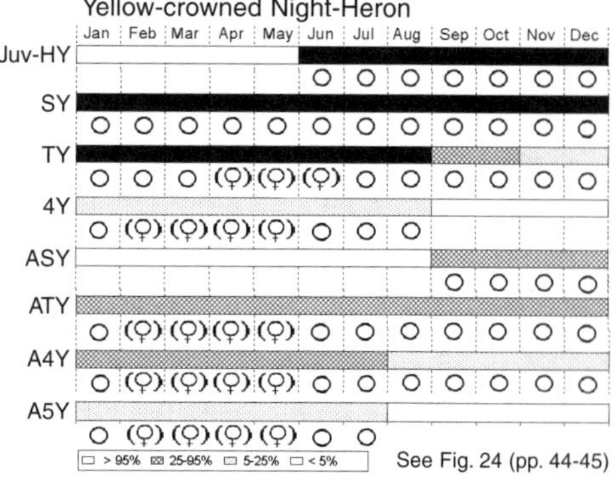

Sex—♀ = ♂ by plumage aspect. Medial(?) BP (Fig. 20**A**, p. 31) developed by both sexes but distended cloaca (Fig. 21, p. 32) indicates ASY ♀ in Feb-May. Measurements unhelpful for sexing (Table 33, p. 346). Ornamental plumes may average longer in ♂♂ than in ♀♀ in Jan-May but more study is needed to determine reliable measures for sexing. Otherwise, no criteria known.

Hybrids reported—Possibly with Black-crowned Night-Heron (p. 363) in the wild.

References—Adams (1955), Bent (1926), Davis (1999), Dickey & van Rossem (1938), Gifford (1913), McVaugh (1975), Palmer (1962), Payne & Risley (1976), Watts (1995), Wingate (1982).

IBISES AND SPOONBILLS *THRESKIORNITHIDAE*

Four North American species. Family characters include somewhat heavy bodies, fairly long necks, rounded wings, short tails, specialized bills (long and decurved or spatulate), and strong legs without extensive palmations between the toes. North American ibises and spoonbills have 10 functional primaries (p10 extending 5-20 mm short of the longest, p9, when fully grown), 15-18 secondaries (including 3-4 tertials and one absent between s4 and s5; Fig. 12**B**, p. 19), and 12 rectrices. Ageing through the second cycle (to TY and ATY) can be accomplished in most species through bare part colors, plumage aspect, and molt patterns among primaries and secondaries. Plumage aspect is similar in females and males but size is reliable for sexing ibises and is helpful in spoonbills, males being larger than females. Medial brood patches (Fig. 20**A**, p. 31) are developed by both sexes but distended cloacal can be used to sex ASY females and other cloacal features (Figs. 22-23, pp. 32-35); should be investigated further.

In molting, ibises and spoonbills exhibit the Simple Alternate Strategy (SAS; Fig. 10**C-E,** pp. 13-16), with a single molt and plumage within the first cycle, and alternate plumages within definitive molt cycles. The single inserted first-cycle molt may have resulted from a merging of preformative and first-prealternate molts but more study needed; it is limited to head, neck, and a few other feathers. During prebasic molts, primaries are replaced distally and secondaries are replaced proximally from s1 and s5 and distally from the longest terts (s13-s17); see Figure 12**B**. Definitive prebasic molts are usually complete; occasionally 1-2 outer primaries and 1-4 secondaries (among s2-s3 and s6-s9) can be retained by ASYs, although staffelmauser replacement patterns (Fig. 16, pp. 23-24) do not appear to follow. Definitive prealternate molts include much of the body feathers in ibises but only a few ornamental feathers (if alternate feathers) in Roseate Spoonbill. Age at first breeding appears to be 2-4 years; prebasic molts of SYs and non-breeding ASYs average earlier in timing italicsthan those of breeding adults (see p. 18).

WHITE IBIS

Eudocimus albus

WHIB
Species # 1840
Band size: 6-7A

Species—HY/SY from Glossy and White-faced ibises (p. 371) by longer average wing and bill (Table 35, p. 374); rump, underwing covs, most of underparts, and bases of pp and ss white; bill and legs pale yellowish to salmon. From Wood Stork by much smaller size (Table 35); bill narrow (depth at tip of forehead feathering or skin < 25; Table 35) and decurved throughout.

Scarlet Ibis (*E. ruber*), a possible vagrant to se.N.Am, has a shorter average tail (tl 84-97 *vs* 89-120 in White Ibis); AHYs with pinkish to red plumage aspect. Juv-HY/SY Scarlet and White ibises may not be distinguishable by plumage aspect until the first formative feathers (pink or white) appear in Oct-Feb, usually on the back.

Geographic variation—Monotypic. See Hubbard & Banks (1970), Stangel et al. (1991). White and Scarlet ibises are sometimes considered subspecies (Hancock et al. 1992, Ramo & Busto 1987) but see AOU (1998).

Molt—SAS. PF/PA1 limited-partial (Oct-Apr in HY/SYs), PB2 complete (Apr-Oct in SYs), DPA limited-partial (Feb-Apr in ASYs), DPB incomplete-complete (Jul-Oct in ASYs). The above timing pertains to N.Am populations. The single inserted first-cycle molt may be a merged PF and PA1 Fig. 10**D**, pp. 13-16). The PF/PA1 begins on breeding grounds and completes on non breeding grounds, PBs occur primarily on breeding grounds, and PAs occur on non-breeding grounds. The PF/PA1 can include most body feathers and up to 2 terts and 4 c.rects but no s covs. PBs are nearly always complete, a few outer pp and medial ss occasionally retained by breeding ASYs. The DPA includes at least the head and neck; more study is needed. See Family Account (p. 369) for additional details on extent and sequence.

Age—Juv (Jun-Dec) has head and neck feathers brownish, bill pinkish with dusky bands, and iris and legs dusky; Juv ♀ = ♂. The following month ranges pertain to N.Am populations.

Juv-HY/SY (1st cycle, F1/A1; Sep-Aug): Head, neck, back, wing covs, pp, ss, and rects mostly to entirely brown, the head and neck increasing mixed with grayish-fringed feathers in Oct-Sep and the back and scapulars mixed with white feathers in Dec-Sep; bill, loral skin, and legs brownish yellow to pale salmon; iris brown to pale grayish blue.

SY/TY (2nd cycle, B2-A2; Sep-Aug): Head and neck brown with gray fringing, being replaced by white feathers in Feb-Jun; back, wings, and tail white except for black tips to p7-p10; bill, loral skin, and legs salmon; iris pale blue. **Note: Occasional ♀♀ with p7 (on either or both wings) completely white or with mixed black and white tips are possibly SY/TYs (see also Sex); more study needed.**

ASY/ATY (Def. cycle, DB-DA; Sep-Jul): Head, neck, back, wing covs, pp, ss, and rects bright white except for black tips to p7-p10; bill, loral skin, and legs salmon, to red in Feb-Jun; iris bright pale blue. **Note: A few individuals (TY/4Ys?) may occasionally have light brown mottling to the head and neck in Oct-Feb; more study is needed.**

Sex—♀ = ♂ by plumage aspect. Medial(?) BP (Fig. 20**A**, p. 31) developed by both sexes but distended cloaca (Fig. 21, p. 32) indicates ASY ♀ in Feb-Jun. Measurements useful for sexing (Table 35, p. 374) and all individuals should be reliably sexed by the following. In addition, the gular pouches of ♀♀ may average larger than those of ♂♂ during breeding (*cf.* Hancock et al. 1992).

♀: Exposed culmen (chord) < 135 mm (Table 35); tip of p7 (either or both wings) occasionally white or mixed white and black (see **Age**). **Note: See Table 35 for other measures useful for sexing.**

♂: Exposed culmen > 134 mm (Table 35); tip of p7 black. **Note: See ♀.**

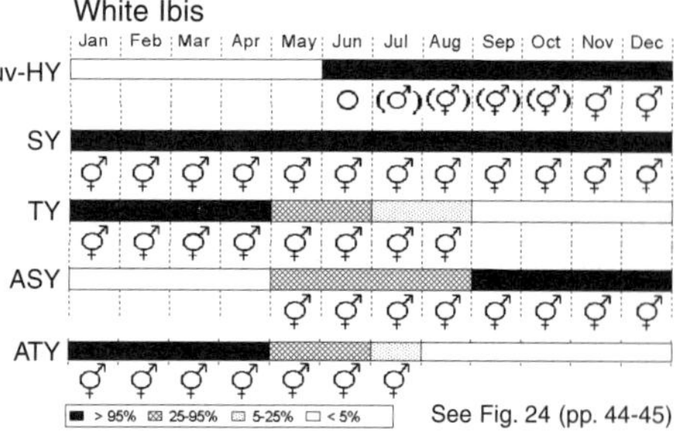

Hybrids reported—With Scarlet Ibis (*E. ruber*) in the wild (Maehr & Hintermeister 1982, Ramo & Busto 1987).

References—Beebe (1914), Bent (1926), Bildstein (1984, 1987, 1993), De Santo et al. (1990), Hancock et al. (1992), Kushlan (1977), Kushlan & Bildstein (1992), Oberholser (1974), Palmer (1962), Todd (1916a), van Wieringen & Brouwer (1990).

GLOSSY IBIS
Plegadis falcinellus

GLIB
Species # 1860
Band size: 6

WHITE-FACED IBIS
Plegadis chihi

WFIB
Species # 1870
Band size: 6

Species—From HY/SY White Ibis (p. 369) by shorter average wing and bill (Table 35, p. 374); rump, bases of pp and ss, underwing covs, and underparts entirely dark; bill and legs dark grayish (often with reddish tinge in Feb-Jul). AHY Glossy Ibis from White-faced Ibis by larger average wing but similar or smaller average exposed culmen by sex (Table 35); loral skin blackish to blue with well-defined, grayish to bluish borders in Glossy Ibis, *vs* grayish to reddish with indistinct or no paler borders in White-faced Ibis (Fig. 267); feathers around eye without white in Glossy Ibis, *vs* with white in Mar-Aug (and sometimes in sep-Feb) in White-faced Ibis (Fig. 267); eye grayish brown to brown in Glossy Ibis, *vs* reddish brown to reddish in White-faced Ibis. Beware of hybrids with intermediate features. Some HYs in Jun-Oct may not be identifiable until development of the pale stripes in the loral skin of HY Glossy Ibis (in Jul-Oct) or the reddish eye in HY White-faced Ibis (in Sep-Dec). See Figure 267, Arterburn & Grzybowski (2003), Fall (1995), Howell & de Montes (1989), Kaufman (1990a), Patten & Lasley (2000), and Pratt (1976, 1980) for more information.

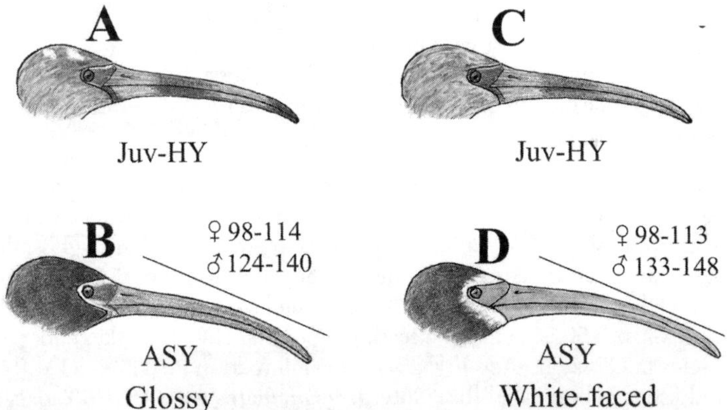

FIGURE 267. Bill length by sex and facial features by species in Juv-HY and ASY Glossy (**A**-**B**) and White-faced (**C**-**D**) ibises. Measures indicate bill chord, from the distal end of the forehead feathering or skin to the tip of the bill in a direct line (Fig 7**C**, p. 9). Note that bills can take up to six months to develop full length. Glossy Ibis is best separated by the pale whitish to bluish lines on the blackish to bluish loral skin, which are indistinct but present in many Juv-HYs as well (**A**). Juv-HY White-faced Ibis (**C**) can sometimes show a very indistinct pale line but the loral skin quickly becomes unmarked and tinged reddish. ASY White-faced Ibis also show white feathers bordering the loral skin (**D**), absent in Glossy Ibis; some Juv-HY White-faced can show contrastingly pale feathers as well. Color of the iris is dark brown in Glossy Ibis and Juv-HY White-faced Ibis but quickly (by Sep-Dec in HYs) becomes reddish brown. Note also the bands to the bill and whitish feathering (shown on the forehead in **A**) of Juv-HYs. See Arterburn & Grzybowski (2003), Fall (1995), Howell & de Montes (1989), Kaufman (1990a), Patten & Lasley (2000), and Pratt (1976, 1980) for more information.

Geographic variation—Both species are monotypic (J. Steinbacher *in* Mayr & Cotrell 1979, Amadon & Woolfenden 1952), see also Cramp & Simmons (1977), Marchant & Higgins (1990). Some authors (e.g., Amadon & Woolfenden 1952, Dement'ev & Gladkov 1951a, Palmer 1962, Parkes 1955a) consider Glossy and White-faced ibises to be subspecies of a single species.

Molt—SAS. PF/PA1 limited-partial (Aug-Apr in HY/SYs), PB2 complete (May-Nov in SYs), DPA partial (Jan-Apr in ASYs), DPB incomplete-complete (Jul-Nov in ASYs). The above timing pertains to N.Am populations. The single inserted first-cycle molt may be a merged PF and PA1 (Fig. 10**D**, pp. 13-16). The PF/PA1 begins on breeding grounds and completes on non-breeding grounds, DPBs occur primarily on breeding grounds, and DPAs occur primarily on non-breeding grounds. The PF/PA1 includes some to most body feathers, often scattered s covs, and occasionally 1-2 terts but no rects. PBs are nearly always complete, a few outer pp and medial ss occasionally retained by breeding ASYs. The DPA includes most to all upperpart and breast feathers and some to most les covs but few to no other wing covs, terts, rects, or feathers of the lower underparts. See Family Account (p. 369) for additional details on extent and sequence.

Age—Juv (B1; Jun-Aug) has head and neck pale brown, without streaks and often with scattered white feathers or patches in head and throat, and bill pinkish with dusky bands (Fig. 267**A**, **C**); Juv ♀ = ♂. The following month ranges pertain to N.Am populations.

HY/SY (1st cycle, F1/A1; Sep-Aug): Bill pinkish, becoming grayish by Oct-Dec; head and neck grayish brown with whitish streaks, often mixed with worn juv brown feathers through Jan; rects rounded and without glossy sheen (Fig. 268**A**); upperparts including les and med covs uniformly greenish olive with dull sheen (Fig. 269**A**), the s covs often with one to many dull maroon-centered or semi-glossy feathers in Dec-Aug (Fig. 269**B**); med covs with little or no purplish sheen (Fig. 269**A**); breast with no to a few dull maroon-centered feathers in Feb-Aug; loral skin dull slate within indistinct pale stripes in Glossy Ibis (Fig. 267**A**), or dusky to dull reddish in White-faced Ibis (Fig. 267**C**); iris brownish in White-faced Ibis, becoming reddish brown by Sep-Dec.

SY/TY (2nd cycle, B2-A2; Sep-Aug): Bill grayish; head and neck brown with white streaks, variably mixed (5-95%) with maroon alternate feathers in Feb-Aug; rects truncate and with substantial glossy purplish sheen (Fig. 268**B**); upperparts greenish with bluish gloss, the les covs mixed with some dull maroon-centered feathers in Sep-Feb (Fig. 269**B-C**) or some to many bright maroon feathers in Feb-Aug (Fig. 268**C-D**); med covs with moderate purplish sheen (Fig. 269**C**); breast with 50-95% maroon feathering in Mar-Aug; loral skin dark grayish with distinct pale lines in Glossy Ibis (*cf.* Fig. 267**B**), or dull reddish in White-faced Ibis (*cf.* Fig. 267**D**); iris reddish in White-faced Ibis. **Note: Intermediates with ASY/ATY, e.g., individuals with full maroon bodies but les covs indicating SY/TY (Fig. 269B-C) or intermediate (Fig. 269D-E), are perhaps best aged T-4Y (see pp. 41-42) but more study is needed.**

ASY/ATY (Def. cycle, DB-DA; Sep-Jul): Head and neck brown with white streaks, becoming uniformly maroon in Feb-Sep; les covs mixed with many maroon feathers in Sep-Feb (Fig. 269**D-E**) or with full maroon patch in Feb-Aug (Fig. 269**F**); med covs with full purplish gloss (Fig. 269**F**); breast with 95-100% maroon feath-

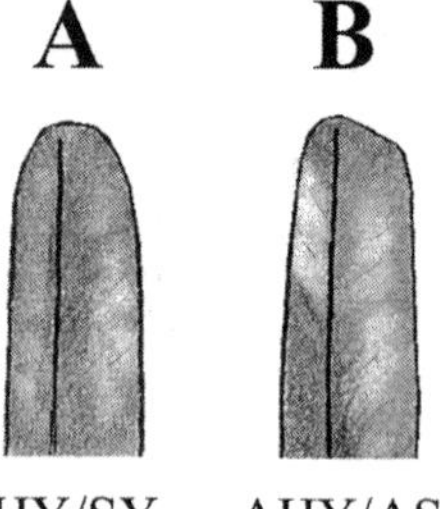

FIGURE 268. Shape of the outer rectrices and degree of sheen to these feathers by age in Glossy and White-faced ibises.

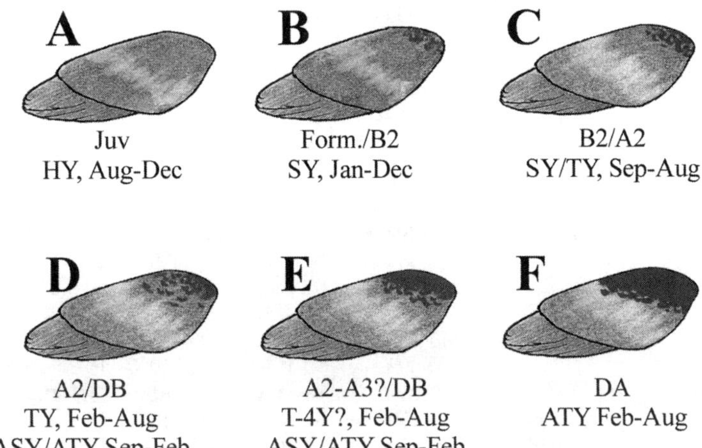

FIGURE 269. Extent of rufous feathers among the les covs, and degree of sheen to the med covs, by age and season in Glossy and White-faced ibises. The PF/PA1, PA2, and DPA include replacement of variable numbers of les covs, resulting in observed differences in number of maroon feathers. Few med covs are replaced during the PF/PA1 and few to none during subsequent PAs; thus, color and sheen of the med covs is represented best by **A-B** (olive, juv med covs, sometimes with a few semi-glossy feathers), **C** (bronzy, 2nd basic med covs), and **D-F** (bronzy maroon, definitive basic med covs).

ering in Mar-Aug; loral skin blackish to bluish with bright pale-bluish lines in Glossy Ibis (Fig. 267**B**), or reddish in White-faced Ibis (Fig. 267**D**); iris bright reddish in White-faced Ibis. **Note: See SY/TY.**

Sex--♀=♂ by plumage aspect. Medial BP (Fig. 20**A**, p. 31) developed by both sexes but distended cloaca (Fig. 21, p. 32) indicates ASY ♀ in Feb-Jun. Measurements useful (Table 35, p. 374). In the field, individuals of both species can be sexed by relative size and, in flight, whether or not just the toes (♀♀) or part of the legs and the entire feet (♂♂) extend beyond the tail. In the hand, all individuals should be reliably sexed by the following (Table 35):

♀: Wing chord < 270 (Glossy Ibis) or < 253 (White-faced Ibis); exposed culmen (chord) < 120 mm (Fig. 267); tarsus < 93 mm.

♂: Wing chord > 269 (Glossy Ibis) or > 253 (White-faced Ibis); exposed culmen (chord) > 120 mm (Fig. 267); tarsus > 93 mm.

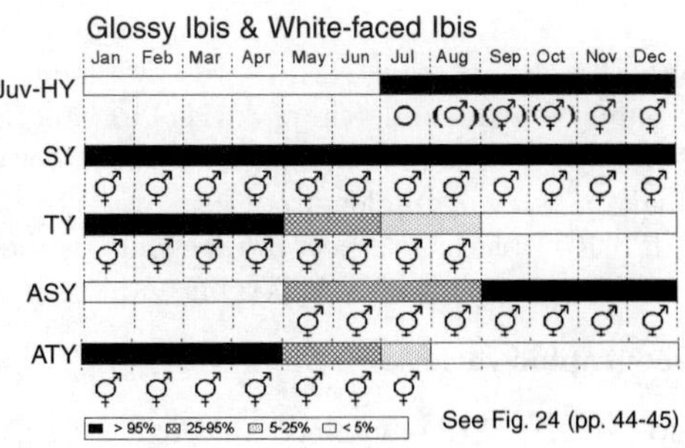

Hybrids reported—Glossy Ibis with White-faced Ibis in the wild (Arterburn & Grzybowski 2003, Faulkner 2005, Sibley 2000).

References—Arterburn & Grzybowski (2003), Bent (1926), Cramp & Simmons (1977), Davis & Kricher (2000), Dement'ev & Gladkov (1951a), Hancock et al. (1992), Howell & de Montes (1989), Kaufman (1990a), Marchant & Higgins (1990), Oberholser (1974), Palmer (1962), Patten & Lasley (2000), Pratt (1976), Roberts (1955), Ryder & Manry (1994), Wilson et al. (2002).

TABLE 35. Measurements (mm) of North American ibises, spoonbills, storks, and flamingoes to assist in identification and sexing. See pp. 4-11 for methods of measurement. Species summaries are in **bold**. Values were derived from 95% confidence intervals as based (for wing, tail, exposed culmen, and tarsus) approximately on the indicated sample sizes (see pp. 4-5); sample size for bill depth was often smaller but included at least 10 of each sex. Thus, midpoints of ranges approximate means, and S.D. is approximated by 25% of the range.

Taxon/Sex	*n*	wing chord	tail length	exp culmen[1]	bill depth[2]	tarsus
White Ibis		**259-308**	**89-120**	**114-165**	**17.9-20.7**	**79-111**
♀	56	252-286	89-106	108-130	17.9-20.7	79-97
♂	52	281-308	98-120	132-165	20.2-23.0	92-111
Glossy Ibis[3]		**245-302**	**91-109**	**98-140**	**16.0-20.8**	**76-112**
♀	53	245-269	91-101	98-114	16.0-18.7	76-90
♂	58	270-302	99-109	124-140	17.8-20.8	95-112
White-faced Ibis		**228-279**	**83-104**	**98-149**	**15.1-19.5**	**79-110**
♀	56	228-250	83-96	98-113	15.1-17.4	79-91
♂	52	256-279	92-104	133-148	17.1-19.5	95-110
Roseate Spoonbill		**314-362**	**85-110**	**147-177**	**15.2-19.4**	**98-118**
♀	21	314-348	85-106	147-167	15.2-17.4	98-108
♂	23	327-362	89-110	155-177	17.1-19.4	105-118
Wood Stork		**427-491**	**137-164**	**190-238**	**47.0-54.5**	**174-213**
♀	20	427-465	137-154	190-212	47.0-50.5	174-198
♂	20	454-491	152-164	216-238	51.1-54.5	194-213
Greater Flamingo[3]		**363-465**	**120-175**	**114-139**	—	**236-366**
♀	49	363-458	120-163	114-135	—	236-316
♂	52	380-465	124-175	118-139	—	287-366

[1] Exposed culmen (e.g., of ibis, flamingo) measured as the chord (Figs. 7**C**, p. 9 and 267, p. 371). Beware that bills may not become fully developed in HY/SYs until Oct-Jan.
[2] Bill depth measured at distal end of forehead feathering or skin (see Fig. 8**A-B**, p. 10).
[3] Measurement data from North American populations only (see **Geographic variation**).

ROSEATE SPOONBILL

Ajaia ajaja

ROSP
Species # 1830
Band size: 7B

Species—From other N.Am birds by medium-large size (Table 35); bill spatulate (Fig. 270); plumage white and pale pink (HY) to pink (AHY); legs brown to reddish; front toes not fully webbed. Eurasian Spoonbill (*Platalea leucorodia*), a potential escape or vagrant to e.N.Am, is larger, especially in length of legs (wg chord 345-411, tl 107-127, exp culmen 170-232, tarsus 123-161); plumage aspect mostly white (without pink); feathered crown with elongated yellowish occipital plumes in AHYs; bill and legs pinkish (HYs) to black.

Geographic variation—Monotypic.

Molt—SAS. PF/PA1 limited (Aug-Apr in HY/SYs), PB2 complete (Apr-Oct in SYs), DPA limited (Jan-Apr in ASYs), DPB incomplete-complete (Jul-Nov in ASYs). The above timing pertains to N.Am populations. The single inserted first-cycle molt may have resulted from a merging of a PF and PA1 in ancestral species (Fig. 10**D**, pp. 13-16) but study is needed. The PF/PA1 begins on breeding grounds and completes on non-breeding grounds, PBs occur primarily on breeding grounds, and the DPA occurs primarily on non-breeding grounds but may complete on breeding grounds. The PF/PA1 includes some body feathers but no wing covs, terts, or rects. PBs are nearly always complete; occastional ASYs may retain 1-2 outer pp and a few medial ss during DPBs. The DPA includes ornamental feathers of the les covs, uppertail covs, breast, and undertail covs but apparently few if any other feathers. See Family Account (p. 369) for additional details on extent and sequence.

Age—Juv (B1; Jul-Oct) resembles Juv-HY/SY (below); Juv ♀=♂. The following month ranges pertain to N.Am populations.

Juv-HY/SY (1st cycle, Juv/B1-F1/A1; Oct-Sep): Crown and nape with short white feathering and bill smooth (Fig. 270**A**); plumage aspect (including pp and ss) primarily whitish and pale pink; outer pp and p covs narrow with substantial brown tips (Fig. 271**A**); les covs, uppertail covs, breast, and undertail covs without filamentous reddish feathers (Fig. 272**A**, p. 376); bill yellowish to yellowish gray; iris yellowish to orangish; legs brownish.

SY/TY (2nd cycle, B2-A2; Oct-Sep): Crown and nape with short white feathering and bill moderately smooth (Fig. 270**A**), becoming defeathered with narrow black band and little to no scaling by Apr-Sep (Fig. 270**B**); plumage aspect (including pp and ss) pale to dark pink; outer pp and p covs broad with narrow brown tips (Fig. 271**B**); les covs, uppertail covs, breast, and undertail covs with reduced or no filamentous reddish feathers in Feb-Sep (Fig. 272**A-B**); bill grayish to greenish gray; iris orangish to dull red; legs brownish to dull reddish. **Note: Intermediates between this and ASY/ATY (especially in head features and with some brown on p10; Fig. 272C), may best be aged S-TY or T-4Y**

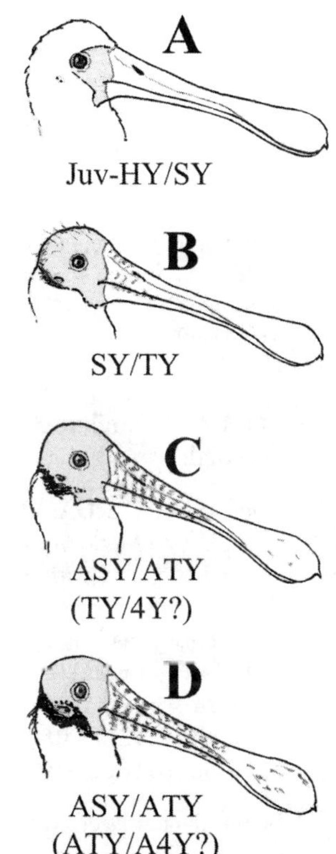

FIGURE 270. Extent of head feathering, markings, and bill corrugations in Roseate Spoonbill by age. As individuals age, the head feathering and smooth bill of Juv-HY/SY (**A**) gradually gives way to a naked head with a well-marked black band posteriorly, and a roughly corrugated base to the bill. ASY/ATYs showing extensive corrugation (as in **D** or more) might be reliably aged ATY/A4Y but more study is needed. -

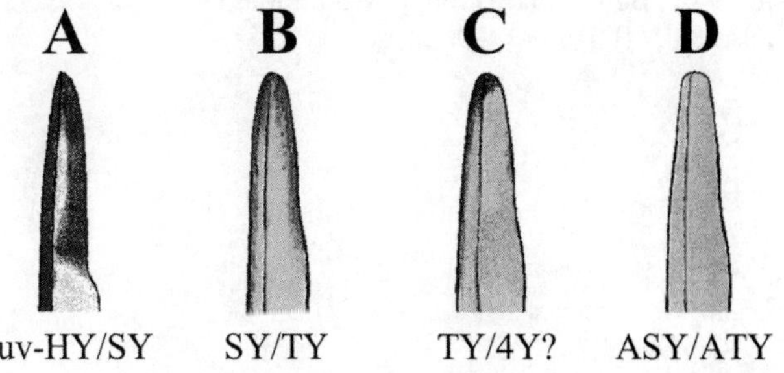

FIGURE 271. Shape and degree of brown edging to p10 by age in Roseate Spoonbill.

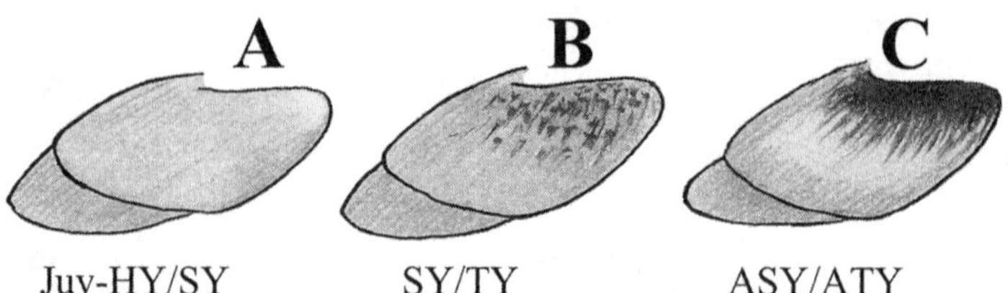

FIGURE 272. Extent of ornamental feathering among the lesser coverts by age in Roseate Spoonbills in Jan-Sep. HY/SYs (**A**) display no ornamental feathering. In addition to displaying less-extensive reddish feathering in alternate aspect, SY/TYs (**B**) also develop the feathering later in the season (Feb-Jun) than do ASY/ATYs (Jan-Apr).

(see pp. 41-42), although it is also possible that these can be reliably aged TY/4Ys. More study is needed.

ASY/ATY (Def. cycle, DB-DA; Oct-Sep): Crown and nape unfeathered, with broad blackish band, and slightly to moderately scaled (Fig. 270**C**-**D**); plumage aspect dark pink to orangish pink; outer pp and p covs without brown tips (Fig. 271**D**); les covs, uppertail covs, breast, and undertail covs with extensive filamentous reddish feathers in Jan-Sep (Fig. 272**C**); bill bright grayish to greenish; iris bright cherry-red to red; legs dark reddish. Note: See SY/TY. **Note that extent of ornamental feathering also varies by season and possibly sex (see Sex). It is possible that some TY/4Ys, with intermediate features, may be identified, and it is probable that ASY/ATYs with heavily scaled base to bill (Fig. 270D) can be reliably aged ATY/A4Y, but more study is needed.**

Sex—♀ = ♂ by plumage aspect. Medial(?) BP (Fig. 20**A**, p. 31) developed by both sexes but distended cloaca (Fig. 21, p. 32) indicates ASY/ATY ♀ in Dec-May. Measurements (especially bill depth) somewhat helpful for sexing, perhaps reliably so with mated pairs in direct comparison (Table 35, p. 374). Also check the maximum width of the bill: ♀ 44-53, ♂ 49-58 (Oberholser 1974). The extent of ornamental plumes appears to average greater in ♂♂ than ♀♀ but age-related and seasonal variation obscures sex-related variation. Otherwise, no criteria known for sexing.

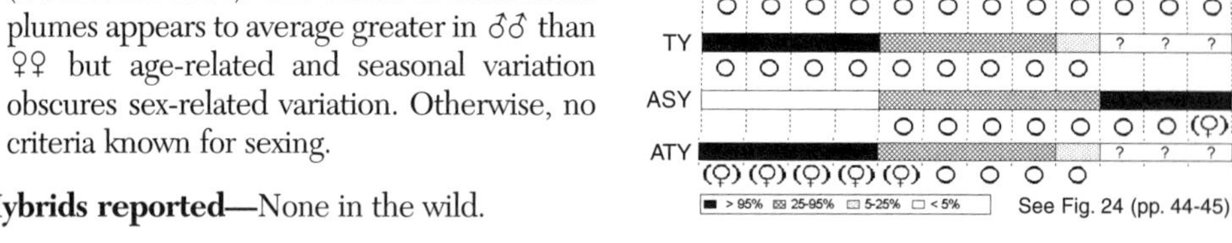

Hybrids reported—None in the wild.

References—Allen (1942), Bent (1926), Cramp & Simmons (1977), Dumas (2000), Hancock et al. (1992), Oberholser (1974), Palmer (1962).

STORKS *CICONIIDAE*

One North American species. Family characters include large bodies with unfeathered heads; longish necks; rounded wings; short tails; large, conical bills; and strong legs without extensive palmations between the toes. North American storks have 11 functional primaries (p11 70-100 mm short of the longest, p9, when fully grown, and with an extra primary on the metacarpus; Stresemann 1963), 20-21 secondaries (including 3 tertials and one absent between s4 and s5; Fig. 12**B**, p. 19), and 12 rectrices. Ageing through the third cycle (to T-4Y and A4Y) can be accomplished through plumage aspect, bare part colors, and feathering and scaling of the head and neck. Sexes are alike in plumage aspect but size is a reliable criterion for sexing, males being larger than females. It is unknown whether or not brood patches (Fig. 20, p 31) develop; incubation is performed by both sexes. Distended cloacae (Fig. 21, p. 32) indicate breeding A4Y females and other cloacal features (Figs. 22-23, pp. 32-35); should be further investigated.

In molting, North American storks may exhibit a Complex Basic Strategy (CBS; Fig. 10**B**, pp. 13-16), with a formative plumage but without alternate plumages; the preformative molt may not exist, development of a few head feathers instead representing a protracted prejuvenal (PB1) molt, in which case the Simple Basic Strategy (SBS) is exhibited. During prebasic molts, primaries are replaced distally and secondaries are replaced proximally from s1 and s5 and distally from the longest terts (s18-s20); see Figure 12**B**. Prebasic molts appear most often complete but may sometimes exhibit staffelmauser (Fig. 16, pp. 23-24), especially among secondaries. Age at first breeding appears to be at least 4 years; prebasic molts of SYs, TYs, 4Ys and non-breeding A4Ys may average earlier in timing italicsthan those of breeding adults (see p. 18).

WOOD STORK
Mycteria americana

WOST
Species # 1880
Band size: 8

Species—From White Pelican by different bill, leg, and foot characters; inner ss and rects black. From White Ibis and other N.Am waders by large size (Table 35, p. 374); bill very large and deep (Table 35; Fig. 273, p. 378); plumage aspect white except pp, ss, p covs and rects black; legs grayish with paler (often yellow to pinkish) feet.

Geographic variation—Monotypic.

Molt—CBS (SBS?). PF absent-limited? (Jul?-Mar? in HY/SYs), PB2 incomplete-complete (Apr?-Feb? in SY/TYs), DPB incomplete-complete (Jun-Feb in ASY/ATYs); PA absent. The above timing pertains to N.Am populations. Molts begin on breeding grounds but complete on non-breeding grounds. The PF, if it exists (see Family Account), may be limited to feathers of the head. PBs can be complete, or up to 2 outer pp, 6 medial ss (among s2-s3 and s7-s12), and 1-4 rects (among r3-r5) can be retained. Staffelmauser patterns (Fig. 16, pp. 23-24) may be exhibited by some ASYs; more study is needed.

Age—Juv (B1; Jul-Jun) has crown and neck feathered dusky to yellowish (Fig. 273**A**); Juv ♀ = ♂. The following month ranges pertain to N.Am populations.

Juv-HY/SY (1st cycle, Juv/B1; Oct-Sep): Crown and neck with short dusky to yellowish feathering (Fig. 273**A**, p. 378), increasingly mixed with some white feathers, the crown becoming partially defeathered by Sep (Fig. 273**B**); outermost underwing p covs mostly blackish (Fig. 274**A**, p. 378); longest scapulars dusky or with dusky tips; pp and ss uniformly juv and without sheen or s1/p1 contrast (Fig. 13**A**, p. 20), the inner pp and ss being replaced in Apr-Sep, and the juv outer pp and ss tapered, (*cf.* Fig. 19**A**-**B**, p. 28); undertail covs short, not reaching tip of tail; bill yellowish (Fig. 273**A**); iris pale bluish; legs and feet dull grayish to yellowish gray.

SY/TY (2nd cycle, B2; Oct-Sep): Head with short white feathering (Fig. 273**B**), continuing to defeather (the skin smooth and with indistinct or no scales, approaching Fig. 273**C** in some TYs) through Sep; outermost underwing p covs blackish with some whitish (Fig. 274**B**); longest scapulars white; pp and ss with 1-2 generations (Figs. 14**B**-**C** or 16**C**-**D**, pp. 22-24), the inner pp and most ss black with a bluish sheen, and the juv outer pp and/or 1-6 juv ss (among s2-s3 and s7-s12) retained or being replaced in Oct-Feb, very faded, brown, and worn (Fig. 19**B**); undertail covs moderate in length, often reaching tip of tail; bill brownish with variable yellowish tinge (Fig. 273**B**-**C**); iris dusky; legs and feet blackish. **Note: See T-4Y**.

T-4Y (3rd-4th cycles, B3-B4; Oct-Sep): Head defeathered (neck sometimes with small patches of white feathering), the skin smooth to partially scaled and wrinkled (Fig. 273**C**); outermost underwing p covs mixed white with some blackish, occasionally all white (Fig. 274**C**-**D**); pp usually uniformly definitive, with broad tips (Fig. 19**C**-**D**); pp and ss uniform or with two generations of basic feathers but no juv feathers remaining (*cf.* Figs. 14**D** & 16**E**); undertail covs long, extending beyond tail tip when fully grown; bill brownish to grayish (Fig.

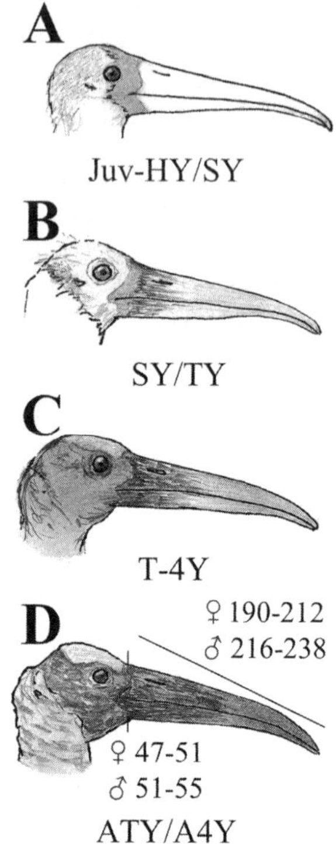

FIGURE 273. Extent of head feathering, neck features, and bill color change by age, along with bill measures by sex in Wood Stork. Measures pertain to exposed culmen and bill depth at base from distal end of forehead skin (Figs **7B** & 8**B**, pp. 9-10), indicating little to no overlap between the sexes, although it may take up to a full year for Juv-HY/SYs to develop full bill size. ATY/A4Ys showing extensive corrugation to the neck, head, and bill base (as in **D** or more) might be reliably aged A4Y/A5Y but more study is needed.

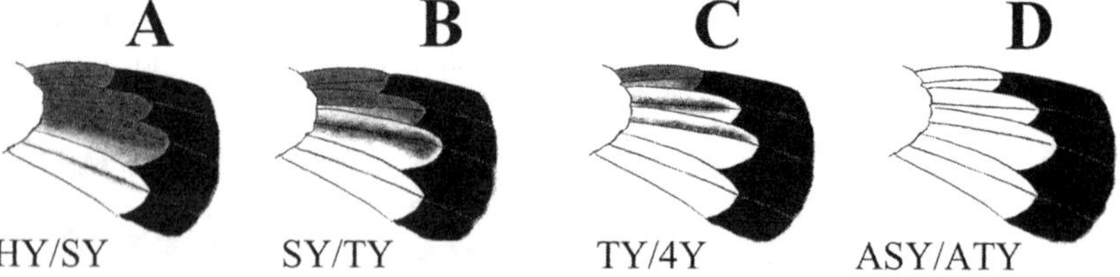

FIGURE 274. Pattern of the outer four underwing primary coverts by age in Wood Stork. Darker feathers of Juv/HY-SYs (**A**) gradually become white with age; more study is needed on ages at which fully white covs are acquired; it could indicate ATY/A4Y or older.

273**C**); iris dark brown; legs and feet blackish to bluish black. **Note: Contrasts between retained and replaced basic feathers can be subtle and best viewed at certain angles of light. Intermediates between this and the following may best be aged 4-5Y (see pp. 41-42); more study is needed.**

ATY/A4Y (Def. cycle, DB; Oct-Sep): Like T-4Y but crown and neck defeathered, the skin heavily scaled and wrinkled (Fig. 273**D**); outermost underwing p covs white (Fig. 274**D**). **Note: See T-4Y. It is possible that some individuals may be reliably aged A4Y/A5Y or older by extent of scaled and wrinkled skin but more study is needed.**

Sex—♀ = ♂ by plumage aspect. BP (Fig. 20, p. 31) possibly developed by both sexes but distended cloaca (Fig. 21, p. 32) indicates A4Y ♀ in Jan-Apr. Measurements useful for sexing (reliable with mated pairs in direct comparison; Table 35, p. 374). The following is reliable for sexing AHYs (use with caution on HYs as bills may not become fully developed for several months after fledging):

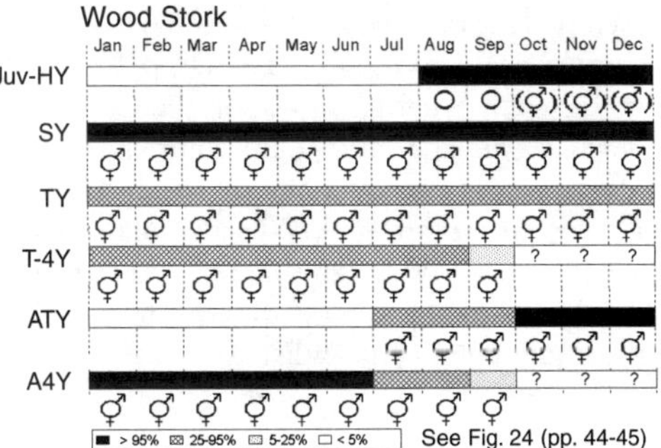

♀: Exp culmen < 213 and bill depth at distal end of forehead skin < 50 (Table 35, Fig. 273) when fully grown.

♂: Exp culmen > 213 and bill depth at distal end of forehead skin > 50 (Table 35, Fig. 273) when fully grown.

Hybrids reported—None.

References—Bent (1926), Coulter et al. (1999), Hancock et al. (1992), Oberholser (1974), Palmer (1962).

FLAMINGOS *PHOENICOPTERIDAE*

One North American species. Family characters include ovate bodies, extremely long necks, broad wings, short tails, a uniquely shaped bill with a distinct angle to the culmen, and extremely long legs without extensive palmations between the toes. North American flamingos have 11 functional primaries (p11 longest or next to longest, 10 mm shorter to 10 mm longer than p10 when fully grown, and with an extra primary on the metacarpus; Stresemann 1963), 21-23 secondaries (including 4-5 tertials and one absent between s4 and s5; Fig. 12**B**, p. 19), and 14 rectrices. Ageing through the 3rd-4th cycles (to T-4Y and ATY) can be accomplished through plumage aspect, retained coverts, and bare part colors, although there is overlap between age groups, necessitating the use of age-group codes (see pp. 41-42) for some individuals. Sexes are alike in plumage aspect but size (especially leg length) might be used to sex some individuals (including mated pairs), males being larger and taller than females. Medial brood patches (Fig. 20**A**, p. 31) are developed in both sexes but distended cloacae (Fig. 21, p. 32) indicate breeding A4Y females, and other cloacal features (Figs. 22-23, pp. 32-35) should be further investigated.

In molting, flamingos exhibit the Complex Basic Strategy (CBS; Fig. 10**B**, pp. 13-16), with a formative plumage but without alternate plumages. The preformative molt includes some body feathers and les covs but no primaries, secondaries or rectrices. During PBs, primaries, secondaries, and wing coverts are replaced synchronously, or nearly so, although wing-covert replacement may not coincide with that of primaries and secondaries. Age at first breeding appears to be at least 4 years and may be as late as 7-8 years; prebasic molts of SYs, TYs, 4Ys and non-breeding A4Ys average earlier in timing italicsthan those of breeding adults (see p. 18).

GREATER FLAMINGO
Phoenicopterus ruber

GREF
Species # 1820
Band size: 8

Species—From Roseate Spoonbill and other N.Am birds by long wing chord and extremely long legs (Table 35, p. 374); bill unique, grayish (HY) to pink and red (AHY) with black tip and distinct angle to culmen (Fig. 275); head feathered; neck extremely long (> 250 mm); body and legs grayish (HY) to bright red (ATY); front toes not fully webbed.

Chilean Flamingo (*P. chilensis*), escapes of which occur in N.Am, is smaller (wg chord 345-466, tl, exp culmen 90-117, tarsus 130-265); bill whitish with extensive black tip (including the bill angle on both upper and lower mandibles; cf Fig. 275); ASYs with body medium-pale pink (*vs* reddish and deeper pink in N.Am Greater Flamingos); legs and feet grayish to grayish yellow with pink joints and webs. Lesser Flamingo (*Phoeniconaias minor*), escapes of which occur in N.Am, is smaller (wg chord 305-354, tl 107-142, exp culmen 91-118, tarsus 190-247); base of bill dusky to blackish (*vs* pale grayish to pinkish in Greater; *cf.* Fig. 275); ASYs with deep-pinkish plumage aspect (usually with contrastingly redder patches in the wings). See Allen (1956) and Blake (1977) for information on identifying other flamingos.

Geographic variation—See Allen (1956), Cramp & Simmons (1977), Ridgway (1897). One other subspecies occurs in Eurasia and Africa (escapes occur in N.Am).

P.r. ruber (br & wint W.Indies-S.Am; visitor to se.N.Am): Averages larger with larger bill (Table 35, p. 374; *vs* wg chord 351-438, tl 118-166, exp culmen chord 110-127, tarsus 226-353 in *roseus* of Eurasia); ATY with upper and under wing covs, terts, neck, and vent bright reddish and rest of body deep pink (*vs* upper and under wing covs reddish and rest of body pale pink in *roseus*); bill with base of mandible bright yellowish to reddish (*vs* pale pinkish in *roseus*) and black tip not extending proximally to angle of culmen (*cf.* Fig. 275).

Molt—CBS. PF limited-partial (Aug-Feb? in HY/SYs), PB2 incomplete (Apr-Jul in SYs), PB3

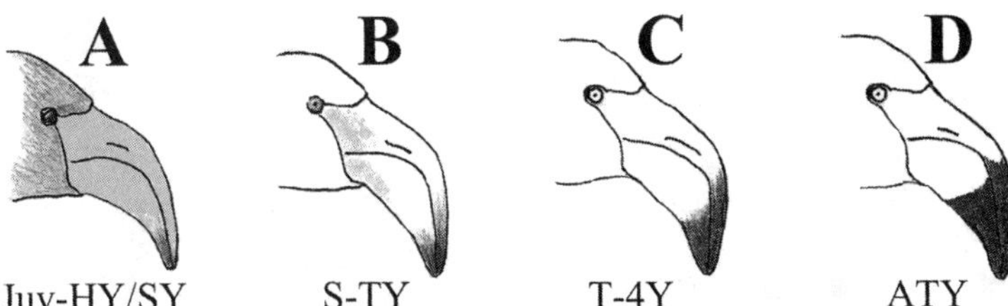

FIGURE 275. Bill patterns and head plumage aspect by age in Greater Flamingo. Note that the bill can take up to four years to develop a bright pink base and distinct black tip as in **D**; however, there is substantial individual variation in the rate of bill-color change, resulting in age-group designations for each of the above stages. In Chilean Flamingo the dark tip includes the bill angle, and in Lesser Flamingo the base of the bill is dusky at all ages. In European Greater Flamingos (*P.r. roseus*), the black tip often extends proximally past the angle in the upper mandible.

incomplete-complete (May-Aug in TYs), DPB incomplete-complete (Jul-Sep in ATYs); PA absent. The above timing pertains to N.Am (Caribbean) populations. The PF includes a few to many body feathers and no to all les covs, but few if any gr or med covs and no primaries, secondaries, or rectrices. During PBs, molt of pp and ss may be rapid, approaching synchronous, as is molt of the s covs (but often on a separate schedule). The PB2 commences with the med and other s covs in Apr-May, with pp and ss replaced in May-Jul. Some or all underwing covs and axillars appear to be retained during the PB2 and may be replaced roughly every other year beginning with the PB3 (some juv underwing covs retained in some individuals until the PB4). A reported DPA appears to be based on pigmentation added through preening rather than molt; more study is needed on this and the (unlikely) possibility of an additional presupplemental molt of these feathers (as reported) as well.

Age—Juv (B1; Jul-Nov) resembles Juv-HY/SY in Sep-Nov and may have dark gray down remaining on the head and nape through Oct-Dec; Juv ♀ = ♂. See Figures 22-23 (pp. 32-35) regarding cloacal characters possibly useful for ageing live flamingos in the hand. The following month ranges pertain to N.Am populations.

Juv-HY/SY (1st cycle, Juv/B1-F1; Sep-Aug): Head, neck, and back pale pink tinged brownish (increasingly mixed with pale pinkish feathers in Nov-Aug) and base of bill dull yellowish with indistinct dusky tip (Fig. 275**A**-**B**); p covs brownish with pink bases to inner webs (Fig. 276**A**); les covs whitish with extensive dusky shaft streaks (Fig. 276**A**), mixed with some or all pinkish feathers with narrow shaft streaks (Fig. 276**B**) in Dec-Aug; underwing gr covs uniformly

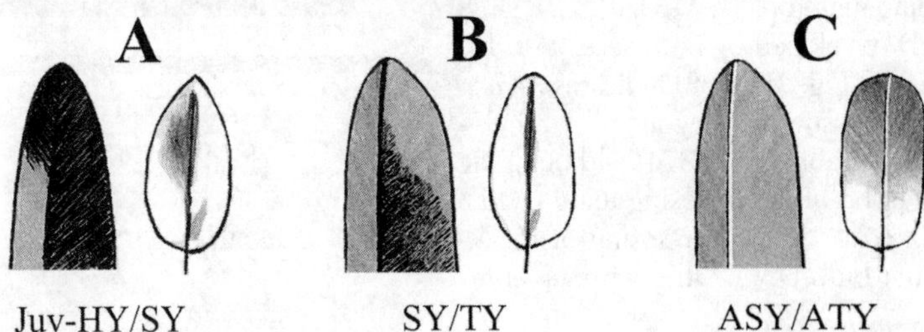

FIGURE 276. Shape and pattern to primary coverts (left; p10 covert, of 11, shown) and lesser coverts (right) by age in Greater Flamingo. **A** represents juvenal feathers. Some (occasionally all) les covs can be replaced during the preformative molt and resemble patterns in between **A** and **B** in SYs. Most 2nd basic feathers resemble **B**; the amount of dark usually decreases distally such that some outer les covs and p covs can approach **C** in appearance. ASY/ATYs typically have basic coverts uniformly resembling **C** (showing a richer salmon color); look for some TY/4Ys to show some dark coloration on medial p covs (e.g., p4-p6 covs).

brown with indistinct pinkish tips (Fig. 277**A**); med and gr covs whitish with dusky tips; legs grayish to grayish pink; iris brown.

SY/TY (2nd cycle, B2; Sep-Aug): Head, neck, and back whitish to pale pinkish; base of bill dull yellowish to pinkish with indistinct dusky smudging at base and tip (Fig. 275**B**); p covs variably mixed brownish and pink (Fig. 276**B**), les covs pinkish; some often with narrow black shaft streaks (Fig. 276**B-C**); most or all underwing gr covs juv, brown with pinkish tips (Fig. 277**A**), and worn; med and gr covs salmon-pink without dusky tips; legs grayish pink to dull pinkish red; iris brown, becoming pale yellow in Sep-Mar. **Note: See TY/4Y**.

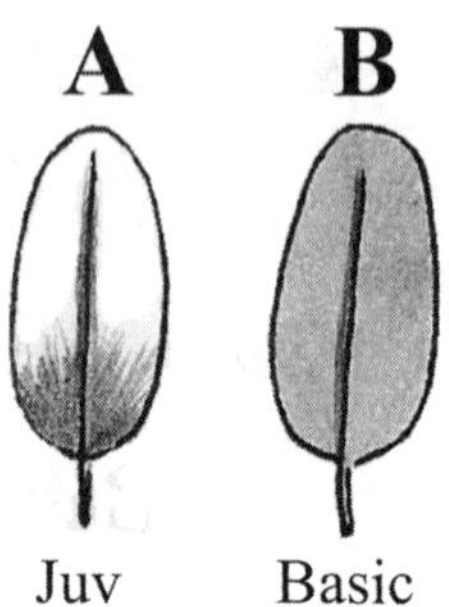

FIGURE 277. Underwing greater coverts by feather generation in Greater Flamingo. Juv covs (**A**), pink with brown tips, are retained through the 2nd prebasic molt and sometimes through the 3rd prebasic molts and thus can be used to identify SY/TYs and some TY/4Ys. ASY/ATYs show uniformly brown underwing covs (**B**).

ASY/ATY (Def. cycle, DB; Sep-Aug): Head, neck, and back pinkish to reddish; base of bill pinkish to reddish, sharply cut off from black tip (Fig. 275**D**); p, les, med, and gr covs uniformly salmon-pink, without dusky shaft streaks or other marks (Fig. 276**C**); underwing gr covs uniformly brown (Fig. 276**B**); legs usually dull to bright reddish; iris pale yellow. **Note: It is possible that individuals showing this plumage aspect can be aged ATY/A4Y but more study is needed (see TY/4Y). Occasional ATY/A4Ys keep grayish legs**.

TY/4Y (3rd cycle, B3; Sep-Aug): Like ASY/ATY but base of bill sometimes dull pinkish with indistinct cut-off with black tip (Fig. 275**C**); medial p covs sometimes with brownish (*cf.* Fig. 276); at least one to most underwing gr covs retained juv, brown with pinkish tips (Fig. 277**A**), very worn. **Note: Some advanced SY/TYs or retarded 4Y/5Ys may also show these features; intermediates are best aged S-TY, T-4Y, or 4-5Y (see pp. 41-42). Note that ♂♂ of these age groups may show more advanced plumage aspect than ♀♀ and this could help with the ageing of intermediates (more study needed). See also ASY/ATY.**

Sex—♀=♂ by plumage aspect although AHY/ASY ♂♂ appear to average slightly brighter and redder than AHY/ASY ♀♀ by age (see TY/4Y, above), and this might be of use in ageing mated pairs. Medial(?) BP (Fig. 20**A,** p. 31) developed by both sexes but distended cloaca (Fig. 21, p. 32) indicates A4Y ♀ in Jan-Apr. Measurements generally unhelpful for sexing (Table 35, p. 374), although leg length might be of use in sexing mated pairs. See Balkiz et al. (2007) for sexing of chicks using feather-bulb DNA. Otherwise, no criteria known.

Greater Flamingo
Jan Feb Mar Apr May Jun Jul Aug Sep Oct Nov Dec
Juv-HY
SY
TY
4Y
ASY
ATY
A4Y
(♀) (♀) (♀) (♀)
■ > 95% ▨ 25-95% ▭ 5-25% □ < 5%
See Fig. 24 (pp. 44-45)

Hybrids reported—None in the wild.

References—Allen (1956), Bent (1926), Chapman (1905), Cramp & Simmons (1977), Fox (1975), Gifford (1913), Johnson et al. (1993), Kear & Duplaix-Hall (1975), Oberholser (1974), Palmer (1962), Richter & Bourne (1990), Richter et al. (1991), Rooth (1965), Shannon (2000), Stresemann & Stresemann (1966).

NEW WORLD VULTURES *CATHARTIDAE*

Three North American species. Family characters include large, ovate bodies with unfeathered heads, short necks, broad and expansive wings, hooked bills with extensive ceres, and weak legs with reduced palmations among the outer toes. North American vultures and condors have 10 functional primaries (p10 extending 50-100 mm short of the longest, p7-p8, when fully grown), 16 (vultures) to 22 (condors) secondaries (including 3 tertials and one absent between s4 and s5; Fig. 12**B**, p. 19), and 12-14 rectrices. Ageing through at least the second cycle (to TY and ATY) in vultures and the seventh cycle (to 5-8Y and A7Y) in condors can be accomplished through the color and condition of the head and bill, and molt patterns among the primaries and secondaries. Sexes are alike in plumage aspect and size, females averaging slightly larger than males. Bilateral brood patches (Fig. 20**B**, p. 31) are developed by both sexes but distended cloacae (Fig. 21, p. 32) indicate ATY to A5Y females during breeding; see also Fry (1983) for biochemical and surgical techniques for sexing vultures. Other cloacal criteria (Figs. 22-23, pp. 32-35) should be investigated.

In molting, North American vultures exhibit a Simple Basic Strategy (SBS; Figs. 10**A** & 11**C**, pp. 13-17), without formative or alternate plumages. Replacement of primaries proceeds distally and that of secondaries proceeds proximally from s1 and s5 and both proximally and distally from the tertials (Fig. 12**B**). New-World vultures exhibit an interesting strategy among North American birds for the replacement of primaries, whereby p1-p3 is typically replaced twice during the first year and molting period, after which each primary (and secondary?) is replaced once per year during subsequent prebasic molts; some cormorants and hawks may exhibit similar strategies. Following Chandler et al. (unpublished ms.) the second replacement of p1-p3 that occurs in Aug-Nov of the first year (in SYs) is considered the initiation of the third prebasic molt, advanced forward and overlapping with completion of the second prebasic molt (Fig. 11**C**, p. 17). In the California Condor (p. 388), molt exhibits more typical staffelmauser patterns (Fig. 16, pp. 23-24), beginning with an incomplete second prebasic molts (see species accounts for more details). Age at first breeding appears to be at least 3 years (vultures) to at least 5 years (condors); prebasic molts of SYs and non-breeding ASYs are earlier in timing and often more complete than those of breeding adults (see p. 18).

BLACK VULTURE

Coragyps atratus

BLVU
Species # 3260
Band size: 7 Special

Species—From Turkey Vulture (p. 385) by shorter wing and tail but longer legs (Table 36, p. 385); longest p – longest s < 40 mm; tail squared or slightly notched (outer rect usually > r1); bill blackish to dull yellowish with shorter slit-like nares, crown and cere skin blackish (HY) to dusky gray (AHY), and neck skin looser and more wrinkled by age (Fig. 278, p. 384); plumage aspect mostly black, contrasting with paler p5-p10; legs and feet grayish. From Juv-HY/SY California Condor (p. 388) by much smaller size (Table 36); gr covs and underwing les covs without whitish. From dark species or morphs of hawks by bill and head features (Fig. 278); feet with elongated middle toe (> 20 mm beyond next longest toe) and short claws (chord < 25 mm and claw < 35% of toe-claw length).

Geographic variation—Monotypic (E. Stresemann & D. Amadon *in* Mayr & Cottrell 1979). See Blake (1977), Brodkorb (1943b), Brown & Amadon (1968), Friedmann (1933a, 1950), Monroe (1968), Oberholser (1974), Rea (1998), Swann (1922a), Wetmore (1926, 1965), and Wheeler (2003a, 2003b) for information on slight variation in tropical populations.

Molt—SBS. PF absent, PB2 complete (Jan-Oct in SYs), PB3 complete (Aug-2nd Oct in SY/TYs), DPB incomplete-complete (Oct-Oct in ASYs); PA absent. Molt strategies appear to be similar to those of Turkey Vulture (p. 385).

FIGURE 278. Head and bill features by age in Black Vulture. Note slit-like nares (distal end of nares to bill tip 33-36 mm) compared with Turkey Vulture (Fig. 279, p. 386). Progression of development is from feathered head and darker bill (**A**) to an un-feathered and wrinkled head with paler bill (**D**). It is possible that full development of these features may take longer than indicated, with **C** representing TY/4Ys and **D** representing ATY/A4Ys, but more study is needed.

Age—Juv (B1; Jul-Jun) is described under Juv-HY/SY (below); Juv ♀=♂. The following month ranges pertain to N.Am populations.

Juv-HY/SY (1st cycle, Juv/B1; Sep-Aug): Crown and nape with downy gray and whitish feathering, cere brownish dusky (Sep-Dec) to blackish (May-Aug), and bill blackish to dull yellowish gray with dusky wash near tip (Fig. 278**A-B**); body feathering dull brownish black to black, often with white down remaining (especially around bend of wing) through Nov-Feb; gr covs and rects juv, narrow and rounded (*cf.* Fig. 280**A-B**, p. 386); pp and ss uniform in wear, being replaced in Dec-Aug, the outer pp pointed at tips and abraded (Fig. 281**A**, p. 387).

SY/TY (2nd cycle, B2; Sep-Aug): Crown, nape, and cere blackish, the intra-orbital area with sparse to some blackish bristle-like feathers, the bill dull yellowish with a blackish smudge near the tip, and the neck skin smooth to moderately wrinkled (Fig. 278**C**); body feathering black with moderate glossy tinge; gr covs and rects broad and squared (*cf.* Fig. 280**C-D**); pp and ss with replacement clines, the inner pp (often p1-p3) fresher than adjacent medial pp (e.g., p4), and with outer pp broad at tips and relatively fresh (Fig. 281**B**). **Note: Intermediates between this and ASY/ATYs are perhaps best aged S-TY or T-4Y (see. pp. 41-42). Look for occasional AHY/ASYs also to retain juv gr covs (Fig. 280A), rects (Fig. 280C), and/or ss (among s7-s12).**

ASY/ATY (Def, cycle, DB; Sep-Aug): Crown, nape, and cere grayish, the intra-orbital area unfeathered, the bill bright ivory without blackish (can have yellowish or brownish tinged tip), and the neck skin heavily wrinkled (Fig. 278**D**); body black with heavy glossy greenish tinge; gr covs and rects with 1-2 generations of basic feathers, broad and squared (Fig. 280**C-D**); pp and ss as in SY/TY, more often showing mixed generations (Fig. 281**B**). **Note: See SY/TY. It is quite possible that AHY/ASYs with substantially wrinkled necks can be reliably aged ATY/A4Y but more study is needed**.

Sex—♀=♂ by plumage aspect. Bilateral(?) BPs (Fig. 20**B**, p. 31) developed by both sexes but distended cloaca (Fig. 21, p. 32) indicates ATY ♀ in Feb-May. Measurements unhelpful for sexing (Table 36, p. 385) and no other criteria known.

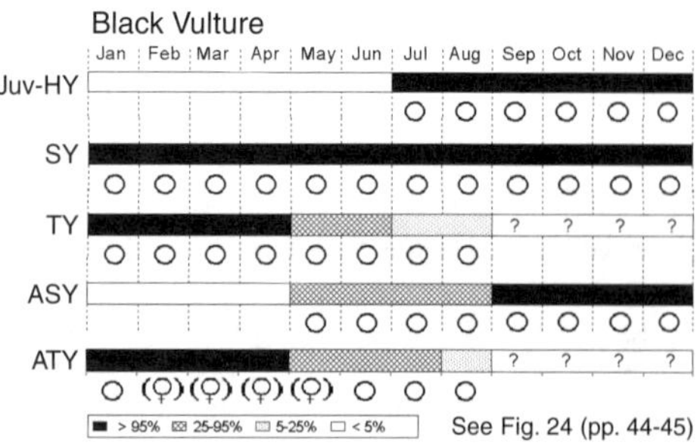

Hybrids reported—None. Reports of a Black X Turkey vulture appear to be unreliable (McCarthy 2006, Palmer 1988a).

References—Bent (1937), Brown & Amadon (1968), Buckley (1999), Friedmann (1950), Kirk & Gosler (1994), Oberholser (1974), J.A. Jackson *in* Palmer (1988a), Wheeler (2003a, 2003b).

TABLE 36. Measurements (mm) of North American vultures and condors to assist in identification and sexing. See pp. 4-11 for methods of measurement. Species summaries are in **bold** and subspecies summaries in ***italics***. Values were derived from 95% confidence intervals as based approximately on the indicated sample sizes (see pp. 4-5); thus, midpoints of ranges approximate means, and S.D. is approximated by 25% of the range.

Taxon/Sex	*n*	wing chord	tail length	bill from nares[1]	bill depth[2]	tarsus
Black Vulture		**406-451**	**167-194**	**24.4-30.8**	**16.0-17.6**	**71-90**
♀	25	406-451	167-211	24.8-30.8	16.0-17.5	71-90
♂	25	408-450	170-214	24.4-30.5	16.1-17.6	72-89
Turkey Vulture		**463-553**	**227-294**	**25.3-32.9**	**15.7-18.4**	**57-73**
C.a. meridionalis		***488-530***	***238-277***	***26.8-32.9***	***16.2-18.2***	***61-68***
♀	25	492-535	243-277	27.5-32.9	16.6-18.2	62-68
♂	35	488-530	238-272	26.8-31.2	16.2-17.7	61-67
C.a. aura		***463-502***	***227-256***	***25.3-30.1***	***15.7-17.5***	***57-67***
♀	31	464-502	230-256	26.7-30.1	15.8-17.5	58-67
♂	35	461-498	227-253	25.3-28.8	15.7-17.3	57-66
C.a. septentrionalis		***508-553***	***248-294***	***27.1-31.8***	***16.4-18.4***	***60-73***
♀	40	516-553	256-294	27.8-31.8	16.7-18.4	60-73
♂	50	508-544	248-286	27.1-31.2	16.4-17.9	59-72
California Condor		**725-825**	**295-380**	**58-72**		**108-130**
♀	10	740-825	320-380	62-72	—	113-130
♂	10	725-810	295-360	58-69	—	108-127

[1] Bill length and depth measured from/at the distal end of the nares (Figs. 7**C** & 8**C**, pp. 9-10).

TURKEY VULTURE

Cathartes aura

TUVU
Species # 3250
Band size: 7 Special

Species—From Black Vulture (p. 383) by longer wing and tail but shorter legs (Table 36, p. 385); longest p longest s > 70 mm; tail rounded (r1 > outer rect by > 30 mm); bill blackish to bright ivory, with larger ovate nares, crown and cere skin purplish gray (HY) to bright reddish (ATY), and neck skin less wrinkled by age (Fig. 279, p. 386); plumage aspect largely brownish, contrasting with paler underwing gr covs and blacker pp and p covs; legs and feet pinkish. See Black Vulture for separation from California Condor and dark species or morphs of hawks.

Yellow-headed Vulture (*C. burrovianus*) of Mexico (a possible vagrant to s.TX) is smaller (wg chord 428-462, tl 192-231, exp culmen from cere 19.4-24.0, tarsus 51-61) than N.Am populations of Turkey Vulture; unfeathered head skin yellow to orangish and bluish (on crown), with wart-like papillae on the neck; plumage aspect blacker with stronger and greener gloss in AHYs (*vs* bluer or purplish in Turkey Vulture).

Geographic variation—See Amadon (1949, 1977), Blake (1977), Brown & Amadon (1968), Friedmann (1933a, 1950), Hellmayr & Conover (1949), Kirk & Gosler (1994), Rea (1983b, 1998), Swann (1922a), Todd (1916a), Wetmore (1946a, 1964, 1965), and Wheeler (2003a, 2003b). Three other subspecies in C.Am-S.Am.

C.a. meridionalis (="*teter*"; br & wint w.BC-s.Ont to s.CA-e.TX). Medium-large to large (Table 36, p. 385); head with few to some whitish tubercles in front of eye (*cf.* Fig. 279**D**, p. 386); les covs with slight and indistinct sheen to centers.

C.a. aura (br se.CA-s.TX, possibly s.FL): Smaller (Table 36); head with few to some whitish tubercles in front of eye (*cf.* Fig. 279**D**); les covs with distinct purple gloss to centers.

FIGURE 279. Head and bill features by age in Turkey Vulture. Note ovate nares (distal end of nares to bill tip 27-32 mm) compared with Black Vulture (Fig. 278, p. 384). Progression of development is from feathered head and blackish bill (**A**) to an un-feathered and wrinkled head and ivory bill (**D**). It is possible that full development of these features may take longer than indicated, with **C** representing TY/4Ys and **D** representing ATY/A4Ys, but more study is needed. Note on **D** the whitish tubercles in front of eye. These vary by subspecies, being reduced in *C.a. aura* and *meridionalis* and more extensive in *septentrionalis* (see **Geographic variation**).

C.a. septentrionalis (br & wint s.Ont-ME to e.TX-FL): Larger (Table 36); head with more-extensive whitish tubercles in front of eye (*cf.* Fig. 279**D**); les covs with distinct bluish gloss to centers.

Molt—SBS. PF absent, PB2 complete (Jan-Oct in SYs), PB3 complete (Aug-2nd Oct in SY/TYs), DPB incomplete-complete (Oct-Oct in ASYs); PA absent. See Figure 11**C** (p. 17). The above timing pertains to N.Am populations. The PB2 begins on non-breeding grounds and can complete on breeding or non-breeding grounds. The PB3 and DPB typically begin with p1-p3 in Aug-Oct, concurrent with completion of the previous PB (p8-p10), suspend for winter, and resume during incubation (Feb-Apr); in breeding adults, molt may also suspend during chick feeding. Most N.Am ASYs suspend molt in Nov-Mar but some s.N.Am ASYs may exhibit sporadic feather replacement through Nov-Feb. 1-6 ss (and corresponding gr covs, usually among s2-s4 and s7-s11, of 16 ss), and 1-6 rects (often among r2-r5) can be retained during DPBs in breeding adults.

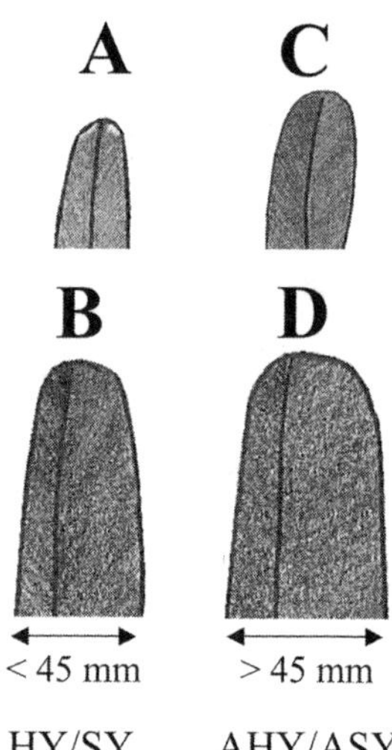

FIGURE 280. Shape and size of greater coverts (**A**,**C**) and outer rectrices (r2-r6; **B**,**D**) of Black and Turkey vultures by age. Measure indicates outer-rectrix width at widest point. Rectrices in Black Vulture are slightly narrower by age, with a cut-off of 40 mm as opposed to 45 mm in Turkey Vulture; in California Condor, the cut-off is 75 mm in width.

Age—Juv (B1; Jul-Jun) is described under Juv-HY/SY (below); Juv ♀=♂. The following month ranges pertain to N.Am populations.

Juv-HY/SY (1st cycle, Juv/B1; Oct-Sep): Crown and nape with downy gray and whitish feathering, cere brownish dusky to dull purplish, and bill blackish to whitish with blackish spot near tip (Fig. 279**A**-**B**); body dull blackish to brownish black, white down often remaining (especially around bend of wing) through Nov-Feb, the upperpart feathers uniform in wear and with distinct pale fringing; gr covs and rects narrow and rounded (Fig. 280**A**-**B**); pp and ss uniform in wear, being replaced in Jan-Aug, the outer pp pointed at tips and abraded (Fig. 281**A**). **Note: Beware head and cere color often becomes ashen during handling of live individuals.**

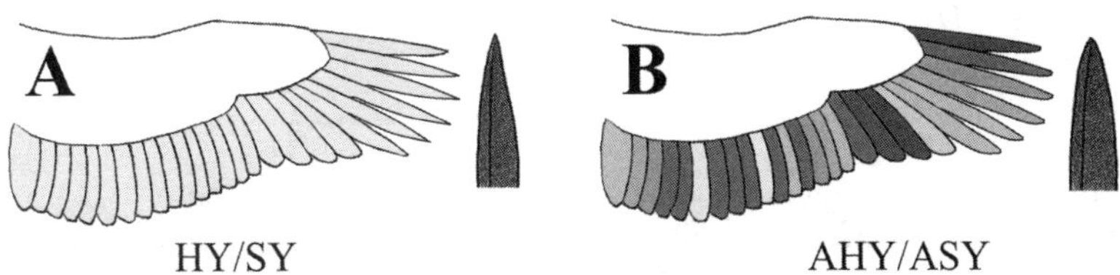

FIGURE 281. Molt clines among the primaries and secondaries, and outer primary shape by age in Black and Turkey vultures. Darker shading indicates fresher feathers. Juvs (**A**) exhibit evenly worn pp and ss, which begin to be replaced in Jan/Mar and complete replacement in Aug/Oct. Outer primaries are narrow and pointed. Prebasic molts begin in Sep-Nov, usually with replacement of p1-p3, then continue the following Mar-Apr with replacement of outer pp (usually p4-p10). P1-p3 and p9-p10 are often in molt simultaneously (see Chandler et al., unpubl. ms. for more information). This results in a suspension limit within the inner pp, usually between p3 and p4 (**B**). Outer primaries are broader and more squared. 1-4 ss can occasionally be retained during DPBs (e.g., s7 and s11 in **B**); this likely does not occur during the PB2 and thus it may indicate ASY/ATY or older.

SY/TY (2nd cycle, B2; Oct-Sep): Crown, nape, and cere dark purplish to reddish, the intra-orbital area and crown with some blackish bristle-like feathers, and the bill dull whitish, occasionally with a blackish smudge near the tip in Oct-Jan (Fig. 279**B-C**); body blackish, slightly tinged purplish or greenish (especially on neck and back), the upperpart feathers variable in wear (resulting from protracted molt) and without distinct pale fringing; gr covs and rects broad and squared (Fig. 280**C-D**); pp and ss with replacement clines, the inner pp (often p1-p3) fresher than adjacent medial p (e.g., p4), and with outer pp broad at tips and relatively fresh (Fig. 281**B**). **Note: See Juv-HY/SY. Intermediates between this and ASY/ATYs are perhaps best aged S-TY or T-4Y (see. pp. 41-42). Look for occasional SY/TYs also to retain juv gr covs (Fig. 280A), rects (Fig. 280C), and/or ss (among s7-s12).**

ASY/ATY (Def. cycle, DB; Oct-Sep): Crown, nape, and cere reddish to orangish, the intra-orbital area and crown with sparse bristles, and the bill bright ivory without blackish (Fig. 279**D**); body blackish tinged glossy greenish or purplish (especially on neck and back); gr covs and rects with 1-2 generations of basic feathers, broad and squared (Fig. 280**C-D**); pp and ss as in SY/TY, more often showing mixed generations of ss (Fig. 281**B**). **Note: See Juv-HY/SY and SY/TY. It is possible that some individuals with especially bright and feather-less heads can be reliably aged ATY/A4Y but more study is needed.**

Turkey Vulture

Jan Feb Mar Apr May Jun Jul Aug Sep Oct Nov Dec

Juv-HY / SY / TY / ASY / ATY

■ > 95% ▨ 25-95% ▭ 5-25% □ < 5% See Fig. 24 (pp. 44-45)

Sex—♀ = ♂ by plumage aspect. Bilateral(?) BPs (Fig. 20**B**, p. 31) developed by both sexes but distended cloaca (Fig. 21, p. 32) indicates ASY ♀ in Feb-May. Measurements unhelpful for sexing (Table 36, p. 385) and no other criteria known.

Hybrids reported—None. See Black Vulture (p. 383).

References—Bent (1937), Friedmann (1950), Henckel (1981), Kirk & Gosler (1994), Kirk & Mossman (1998), Oberholser (1974), J.A. Jackson *in* Palmer (1988a), Rea (1983b, 1998), Roberts (1955), Wheeler (2003a, 2003b).

CALIFORNIA CONDOR
Gymnogyps californianus

CACO
Species # 3240
Band size: 7[V]

Species—From N.Am storks, vultures and all other birds by extremely large size (Table 36, p. 385); unfeathered head blackish to bright orange and pinkish by age; bill with elongated cere (extending to forehead), enlarged nares, and upper mandible moderately hooked (Fig. 282); plumage aspect sooty black with whitish tips to proximal gr covs and underwing les covs in AHY/ASYs (Figs. 283-284); base of neck and breast with elongated ornamental plumes.

Geographic variation—Monotypic.

Molt—SBS. PF absent, PB2 incomplete (Feb-Oct in SYs), DPB incomplete (Mar-Nov in ASYs); PA absent. Note that a definitive molt cycle is here defined (in terms of timing and extent) prior to attainment of definitive plumage aspect (see p. 13). Limited molting of primaries, secondaries, and rectrices can also occur in some ASYs in Nov-Jan. The PBs exhibit staffelmauser (Fig. 16, pp. 23-24), resulting in 3-5 sets of basic feathers among the pp of adults. The PB2 includes 2-6 inner pp, 2-6 ss (often among s1, s5, and s17-s20 of 22 ss), and 0 (usually) to 4 c.rects. During the PB3, some TYs can retain 1-3 juv outer pp and most or all TYs retain 3-12 juv ss (usually among s3-s4, s6-s8, and s11-s15). 3-7 pp and 6-12 ss are usually replaced during subsequent PBs. Body feathers and wing covs can take 2-3 years to be replaced.

Age—Juv (B1; Jul-Jun) is described under Juv-HY/SY (below); Juv ♀ = ♂. Note that slow and variable rates of head-color, bill-color, and plumage-aspect maturation necessitates the use of age-

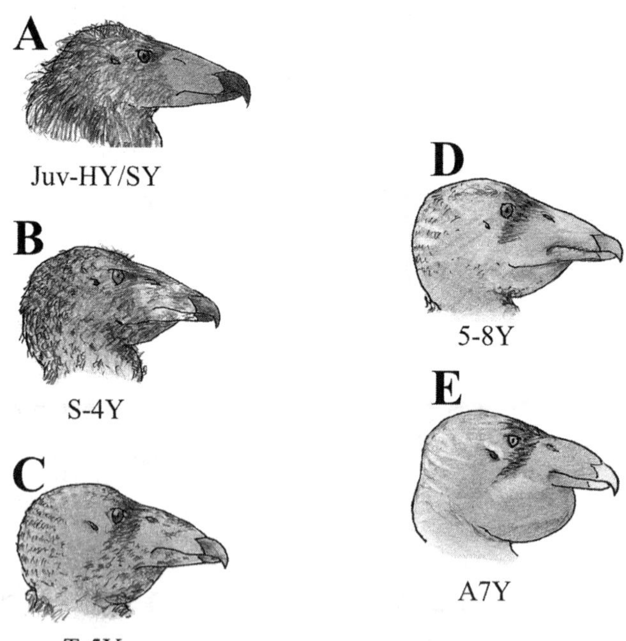

FIGURE 282. Extent and color of head and neck feathering and bill patterns by age in California Condor. The progression is from a dark head and neck with extensive feathers, a dusky cere, and a blackish bill in Juvs (**A**) to a bright orange and pink head and neck with no or a few bristle-like feathers on the forehead, a bright orange cere, and an ivory bill in A7Ys (**E**). See **Age** for more details. Because of the slow and variable rate of maturation in these features, age-group coding is necessary (see pp. 41-42).

group coding (see p. 41-42) on individuals with predefinitive head and bill colors and without juv pp or ss remaining.

Juv-HY/SY (1st cycle, Juv/B1; Oct-Sep): Head and neck with downy blackish feathers, cere dusky to slate, and bill usually dusky (Fig. 282**A**); body uniformly dull blackish to brownish, white down often remaining (especially around bend of wing) through Nov-Feb; proximal gr covs brownish, usually without pale tips or edging (Fig. 283**A**); underwing les covs uniformly brownish or with indistinct pale fringes (Fig. 284**A-B**); axillars brownish; pp and ss uniformly juv (Fig. 16**A**, p. 24), or inner pp and ss (among s1, s5, and s17-s20) being replaced in Feb-Sep, the juv outer pp and (most) ss tapered (*cf.* Fig. 281**A**, p. 387) and brownish; rects uniformly narrow (usually < 75 mm at widest; *cf.* Fig. 280**B**, p. 386); iris dull olive to olive-brown.

SY/TY (2nd cycle, B2; Oct-Sep): Head dusky with slight pinkish tinge to skin, with moderately dense downy and bristle-like blackish feathers, cere dusky or tinged dull orange, and bill variably dull pale to dark grayish (Fig. 282**A-B**); body mixed with worn juv and fresher blackish (with slight sheen) feathers; most to all proximal gr covs retained juv (Fig. 283**A**), 1-3 sometimes replaced and with indistinct whitish tips (Fig. 283**B**); most to all underwing les covs and axillars brownish or with indistinct pale fringes (Fig. 284**A-B**); pp and ss with 2 generations (Fig. 16**B**), 4-7 juv outer pp and 14-20 ss (often among s2-s4 and s6-s16) retained, very faded brownish and worn; rects juvenal, narrow (< 75 mm at widest; *cf.* Fig. 280**C**), and abraded, sometimes mixed with 1-4 fresher and broader (> 75 mm wide; *cf.* Fig. 280**D**) central feathers; iris dull brown to reddish brown.

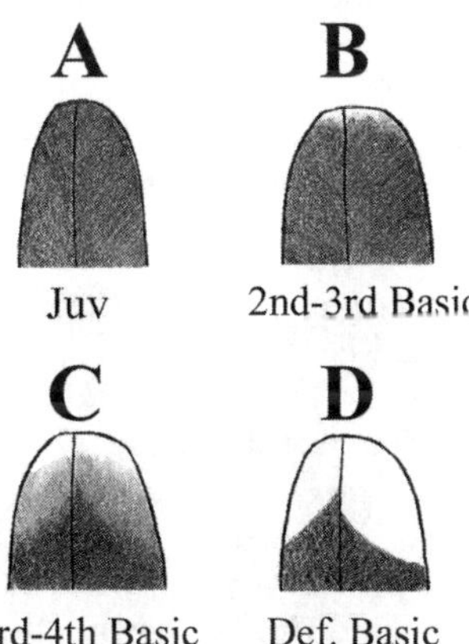

FIGURE 283. Shape and pattern to the proximal (innermost 3-6) greater coverts by feather generation in California Condor. These feathers are frequently retained during prebasic molts, resulting in mixed generations and patterns on pre definitive T-8Ys; e.g., juv feathers (**A**) can be retained through the third cycle and thus still be present on TY/4Ys, and 3rd-basic feathers resembling **C** can occur in 5-8Ys.

TY/4Y (3rd cycle, B3; Oct-Sep): Head dusky (sometimes tinged orange) with brighter pink to orange skin at base of neck, and with sparse (crown) to dense (neck) bristle-like blackish feathers, cere dusky orange, and bill grayish to pale bluish gray (Fig. 282**B**-

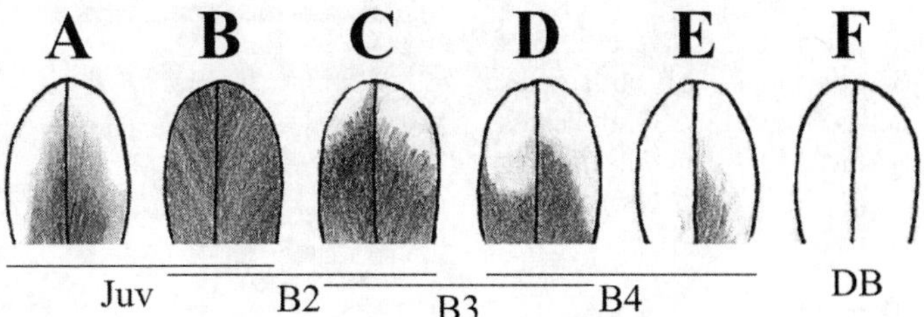

FIGURE 284. Pattern to the lesser underwing coverts in California Condor by feather generation. Note that 2nd-basic feathers are often darker than juv feathers, before slowly becoming white in succeeding generations. These feathers are frequently retained during prebasic molts, resulting in mixed generations and patterns on predefinitive T-8Ys; e.g., juv feathers (**A**) can be retained through the third cycle and thus still be present on TY/4Ys, and 4th-basic feathers resembling **D-E** can occur in 5-8Ys.

C); body without juv feathers remaining, blackish with sheen; proximal gr covs mixed brownish (juv), brownish with indistinct tips, and blackish with silver bloom and moderately distinct whitish tips (Fig. 283**A-C**); underwing les covs and axillars mixed brownish, dusky with pale fringes, and whitish with dusky base and shaft streak (Fig. 284**A-D**); pp and ss with 2 generations of basic feathers and 1-3 outer juv pp and/or 3-12 juv ss (among s3-s4, s6-8, and s11-s15) remaining (Fig. 16**D**); rects with 2-3 generations, often including 1-4 retained juv feathers, narrow (< 75 mm wide at widest; *cf.* Fig. 280**C**) and abraded, often among s3-s5; iris reddish brown.

4-6Y (3rd-6th cycles, B3-B6; Jan-Dec): Head dull dusky orange with bright pink to orange skin at base of neck, with moderately sparse bristle-like blackish feathers, cere dull to bright orange, and bill usually pale bluish gray (Fig. 282**C-D**); proximal gr covs mixed brownish with moderately distinct white tips and silvery black with distinct white tips (Fig. 284**C-D**); underwing les covs and axillars varying from white with black shaft streaks (most feathers) to dusky with indistinct pale fringes (Fig. 284**B-E**); pp and ss with 3-4 generations of basic feathers but no juv feathers (Fig. 16**F-G**); rects with 2-3 generations of wide (*cf.* Fig. 280**D**) feathers; iris reddish brown to reddish. **Note: More accurate ageing of some individuals showing these characters may be possible but more study is needed; e.g., look for 1-2 very worn juv ss remaining on individuals with dull orange heads, perhaps indicating 4Y/5Y.**

5-8Y (4th-8th cycles, B4-B8; Jan-Dec): Head moderately bright orange with moderately bright pinkish to orange neck, with sparse bristle-like blackish feathers and/or dusky patches in forehead and hind crown, cere brightish orange, and bill pale grayish to whitish (Fig. 282**D**); proximal gr covs mixed blackish with moderately distinct white tips and silvery black with distinct white tips (Fig. 284**C-D**); underwing les covs and axillars mostly white (Fig. 284**F**), a few feathers dusky centered or with blackish shaft streaks (Fig. 284**D-E**); pp and ss with evidence of 3-5 generations of basic but no juv feathers (Fig. 16**F-H**); rects with 2-3 generations of wide feathers (*cf.* Fig. 280**D**); iris reddish brown to reddish. **Note: More accurate ageing of some individuals showing these characters may be possible but more study needed**.

A7Y (Def. cycle, DB; Jan-Dec): Head bright reddish orange and/or pink, with sparse or no bristle-like feathers distal to eyes, cere bright orange, and bill whitish to bright ivory (Fig. 283**E**); proximal gr covs silvery black with distinct white tips (Fig. 284**D**; silver bloom can wear off of older feathers); underwing les covs and axillars white (Fig. 284**F**), a few sometimes with blackish shaft streaks (Fig. 284**E**); pp and ss with evidence of 3-5 generations of basic but no juv feathers (Fig. 16**F-H**); rects with 2-3 generations of wide feathers (*cf.* Fig. 280**D**); iris reddish.

California Condor

	Jan	Feb	Mar	Apr	May	Jun	Jul	Aug	Sep	Oct	Nov	Dec
Juv-HY						O	O	O	O	O	O	O
SY	O	O	O	O	O	O	O	O	O	O	O	O
TY	O	O	O	O	O	O	O	O	O	O	O	O
4Y	O	O	O	O	O	O	O	O	O	O	O	O
4-6Y	O	O	O	O	O	O	O	O	O	O	O	O
5-8Y	O	(♀)	(♀)	(♀)	(♀)	O	O	O	O	O	O	O
A7Y	O	(♀)	(♀)	(♀)	(♀)	O	O	O	O	O	O	O

■ > 95% ▨ 25-95% □ 5-25% □ < 5% See Fig. 24 (pp. 44-45)

Sex—♀ = ♂ by plumage aspect. Bilateral(?) BPs (Fig. 20**B**, p. 31) developed by both sexes but distended cloaca (Fig. 21, p. 32) indicates A5Y ♀ in Feb-May. Measurements largely unhelpful for sexing (Table 36, p. 385) and no other criteria known.

Hybrids reported—None.

References—Bent (1937), Brown & Amadon (1968), Finley (1910), Harris (1941), Johnson et al. (1983), Koford (1953), Miller (1937), Miller & Fisher (1938), N.F.R. Snyder *in* Palmer (1988a), Snyder & Johnson (1985), Snyder & Schmitt (2002), Snyder & Snyder (2000), Snyder et al. (1987), Todd (1974), Todd & Gale (1970), Wheeler (2003a, 2003b), Wilbur (1975).

HAWKS, KITES, EAGLES, AND ALLIES *ACCIPITRIDAE*

Twenty-four species. Family characters include large heads, moderately broad and pointed wings, rounded back feathers and strong decurved bills without tomial teeth in N.Am species (Fig. 285**A**), and feet with long, sharp talons. Hawks, kites, and eagles have 10 functional primaries (p10 extending 60-150 mm short of the longest, p6-p9, when fully grown), 13-19 secondaries (including 3 terials and one absent between s4 and s5; Fig. 12**B**, p. 19), and 12 rectrices. Several species are polymorphic, with light, dark, and sometimes intermediate morphs, and monomorphic species can have rare melanistic individuals (*cf.* Howell et al. 1992, Patten & Wilson 1996, Clark 1998). Ageing through the first cycle (to SY and ASY) and often through later cycles (up to 4-5Y and A5Y) can be accomplished through plumage aspect, fault bars (Fig. 18, p. 27), staffelmauser and other replacement patterns among pp and ss (Figs. 14-16, p. 21-24, & 289, p. 393), and retained rectrices (Fig. 288, p. 392). Females are larger than males (for theories see Hill 1944, Mosher & Matray 1974, Reynolds 1972, Snyder & Wiley 1976, and Storer 1966), often without overlap, and sex-specific plumage-aspect differences (sometimes subtle or overlapping) can be found in about half of the species. Medial brood patches (Fig. 20**A**, p. 31) are developed only by females in many species, and partially by males in some species, distended cloacae (Fig. 21, p. 32) indicate breeding AHY or ASY females, and other cloacal characters (Figs. 22-23, pp. 32-35) appear to be of some use in ageing and sexing (*cf.* Fletcher 1981, Hamerstrom & Skinner, 1971). See Swann (1922a, 1925), Brown & Amadon (1968), Dunne et al. (1988), Johnsgard (1990), Snyder & Snyder (1991), Clark & Wheeler (1987), Wheeler & Clark (1995), and Wheeler (2003a, 2003b) for general references on determination of species, age, and sex.

In molting, most to all species of Accipitridae exhibit the Complex Basic Strategy (CBS; Fig. 10**B**, pp. 13-16), including a limited formative plumage (absent in many HY/SYs of most species) but lacking alternate plumages (see Pyle 2005b for details). Sequence of primary and secondary replacement is fixed (Miller 1941): primaries are replaced distally from p1 to p10, secondaries are replaced proximally from s1 and s5 and distally from the tertials (s11-s13 in most species; *cf.* Fig. 12**B**), and rectrices are typically replaced in sequence r1-r6-r3-r4-r2-r5, with minor individual variation. Prebasic molts can (but do not always) involve retained secondaries or exhibit staffelmauser (Figs. 14-16; *cf.* Clark 2004, Pyle 2005c, Pyle 2006a), with larger species requiring 3-4 years to replace all juvenal feathers. Suspension limits among inner primaries (p1-p7) and sometimes among tertials, s1-s2, s5-s6, and/or central rectrices, are detectable in several species and indicate breeding the previous season, or suspension for

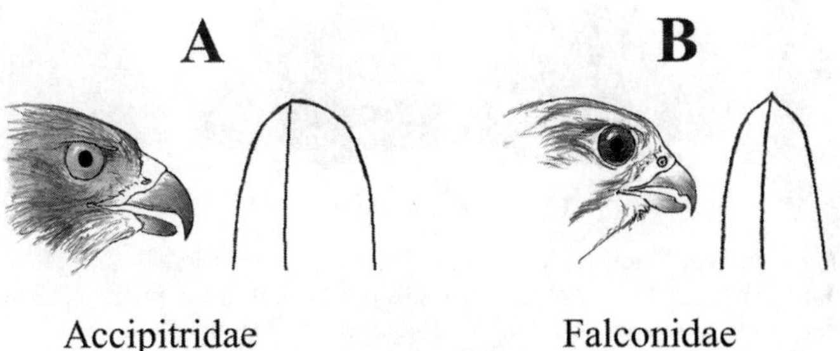

Accipitridae Falconidae

FIGURE 285. Bill structure and back feather shape in Accipitridae (Osprey, kites, hawks, and eagles) and Falconidae (caracaras and falcons) for the separation of certain species (e.g., Sharp-shinned Hawk from Merlin) in the hand. Note the lack of a tooth to the cutting edge of the upper mandible, and the broader and more rounded upperpart feathers in Accipitridae (**A**) *vs* the presence of a tooth to the mandible and the narrower and more pointed upperpart feathers in Falconidae (**B**).

migration (Fig. 289). Thus, four replacement strategies among primaries and secondaries can be detected and used to help ascertain age and breeding status in definitive aspect hawks, kites, and eagles: complete replacement, suspension of molt during breeding and/or migration, retention of secondaries, and staffelmauser (Pyle 2005c). Age of first breeding can be 1-2 years in some species but as old as 4-6 years in others; prebasic molts of non-breeding AHYs average earlier in timing italicsthan those of breeding adults (see p. 18).

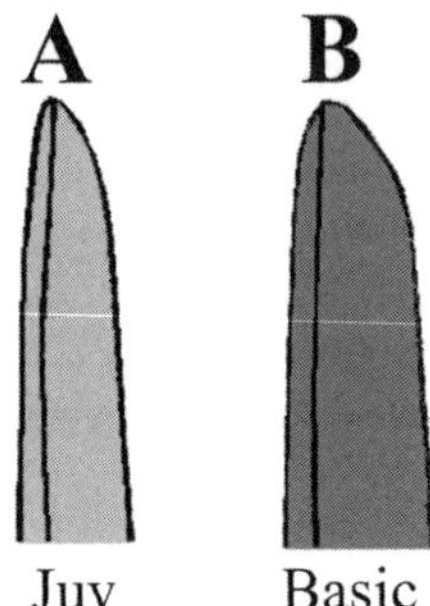

FIGURE 286. Width and shape of the outer primaries (p9 in this case) by feather generation in ospreys, kites, hawks, eagles, and falcons. Depending on the species, the juvenal p9-p10 can be retained by SY/TYs and typically replaced during the third prebasic molt or later (e.g., in Osprey, larger *Buteo* species, and eagles). In addition to being narrower and more tapered, juvenal feathers (**A**) become increasingly more faded and worn than basic feathers (**B**) with time of retention.

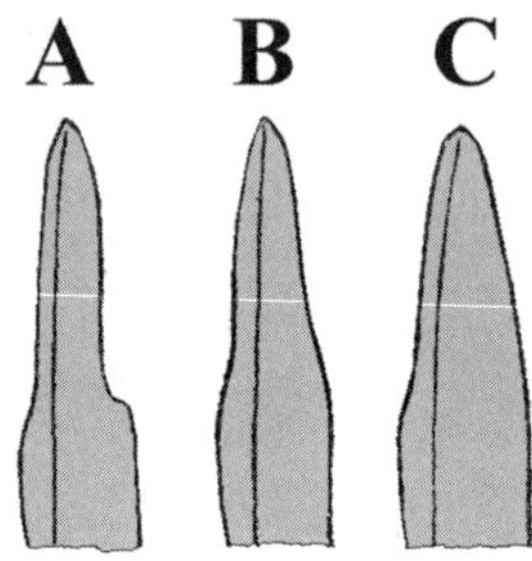

FIGURE 287. Variation in the extent of notching (to right) and emargination (to left) to the outer primaries (of the left wing) in Accipitridae and Falconidae. Different pp can show varying levels of notching, from extensive (**A**) to slight (**B**) to lacking (**C**), and either can be emarginated (as in all three feathers shown) or not, and this can assist with identifications. Typically, feathers among p7-p10 are notched and those among p6-p9 are emarginated but extent of notching and emargination among individual feathers (often p7) differ by species (see **Species** accounts for details).

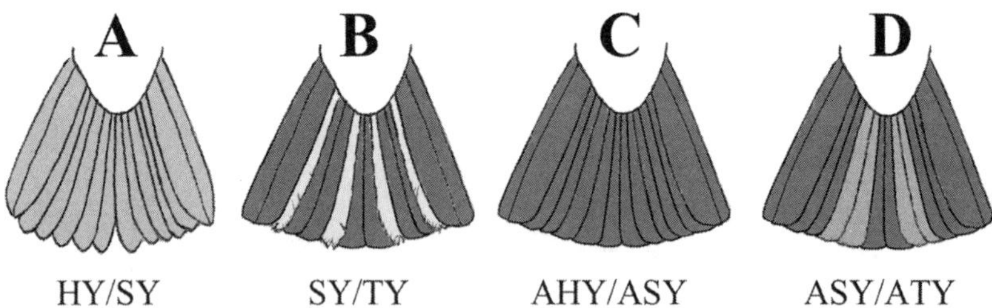

FIGURE 288. Shape and retention patterns among the rectrices of hawks and falcons by age; the underside of the tail is shown. HY/SYs of most species exhibit uniformly juv rects (**A**) which are narrower, more pointed, and often paler in coloration than basic rects found in AHY/ASYs (**C**). SY/TYs of many species can retain 1-6 narrow and very worn juv rects, with r2 and/or r5 the feathers most often retained (**B**). ASY/ATYs of many species can be identified by the retention of broader and slightly worn basic rects, which may not always involve r2 and r5 (**D**). Beware that the outer rect (r6) can show different color patterns and sometimes can appear to be retained, when in fact it is of the same generation. Beware also that suspension limits (see Fig. 289) can also occur among rects, resulting in r1 and/or r6 appearing either fresher or more worn than other rects of the same generation, depending on state of molt.

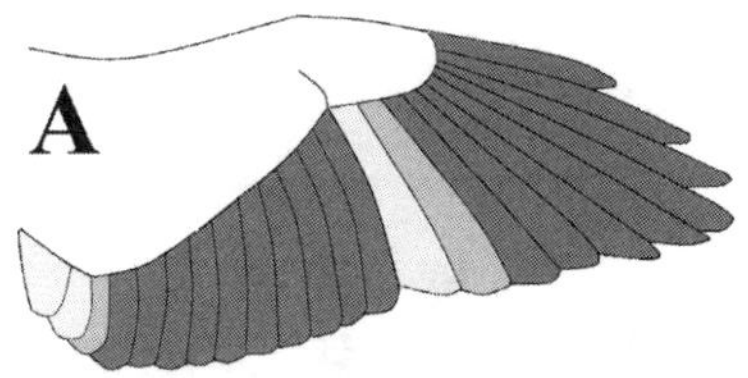

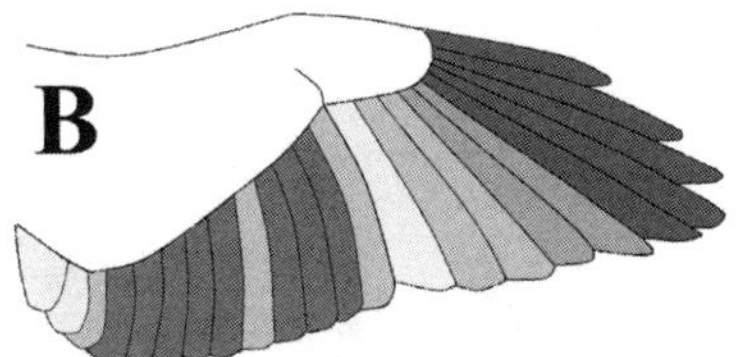

FIGURE 289. Suspension limits among the primaries and secondaries as found in many species of kites and hawks (see also Fig. 15, p. 22). Darker shading indicates fresher feathers. These limits can result from some flight feathers being replaced during incubation, followed by suspension for chick feeding, and resumption of molt after breeding and/or fall migration. ♀♀ often replace more feathers than ♂♂ during incubation and this can sometimes be used to assist in sexing; these limits can also be used to infer breeding status the prior year (Newton & Marquiss 1982, Pyle 2005c). In some species, molt can begin during the summer, suspend for southbound migration, and resume on the winter grounds. In these species, SYs often replace more feathers than ASYs, and the position of the limits can be used to distinguish SY/TYs from ASY/ATYs, respectively (*cf.* Fig. 302, p. 407). **A** exhibits suspension limits after only p1-p2 and the terts had been replaced prior to suspension, as can be found in ♂ kites and hawks after breeding, or ASY/ATYs after suspension for southbound migration. **B** exhibits suspension limits after p1-p5, s1, s5, and the terts had been replaced prior to suspension, as can be found in ♀ kites and hawks after breeding, or SY/TYs after suspension for southbound migration. In each case note that more worn feathers replaced before suspension (paler) contrast with the fresher (darker) feathers replaced following suspension. Note that ASY/ATYs with retained basic feathers (Fig. 14**D**, p. 21) may look similar but have the retained feathers in different positions (typically among s3-s4 and s7-s11). Species that exhibit staffelmauser (Fig. 16, pp. 23-24) can also suspend molt for chick-feeding and/or migration, but limits following suspension are obscured by those related to staffelmauser.

OSPREY
Pandion haliaetus

OSPR
Species # 3640
Band size: 8 Lock-on

Species— From other hawks by medium-large size with proportionally long (Table 37, p. 405) and pointed (usually p8≈p9>p7>p10>p6>p5) wings; p7-p10 notched and p6-p9 emarginated (*cf.* Fig. 287, p. 392); upperparts dark brown and eyeline and underparts white (Fig. 290, p. 394); underwing s covs white and brown, many barred; medial rects (r2-r5) with 6-8 dusky bars (Fig. 292, p. 395); cere and bill blackish; iris brownish orange (Juv) to yellowish (AHY); feet grayish, the underside of the toes with sharp spicules (unique to Osprey among N.Am raptors).

Geographic variation— See Blake (1977), Blanco & Rodriguez-Estrella (1999), Cramp & Simmons (1980), Friedmann (1950), Hellmayr & Conover (1949), C.J. Henny *in* Palmer (1988a), Poole (1989), Poole et al. (2002), Prevost (1983a), Stevenson & Anderson (1994). Two other subspecies breed in Eurasia and Australasia.

P.h. carolinensis (br N.Am, wint to S.Am): Larger with a proportionally shorter bill (Table 37, p. 405); forecrown and eyeline mostly dark (Fig. 290**B-D,** p. 294); breast with no (occasional ♂♂) to extensive (♀♀) blackish streaks by sex (Fig. 290**B-E**); underwing gr covs primarily dark. Populations of Baja CA may average whiter (more bleached?) heads than those of n.populations (*cf.* Fig. 290**E**); more study is needed. *P.h. haliaetus* of Eurasia (a potential vagrant to N.Am) is similar in size but has breast band more heavily streaked by sex (Fig. 290**A-B** in ♀♀ and **B-C** in ♂♂) and underwing gr covs primarily whitish.

P.h. ridgwayi (res W.Indies and possibly to s.FL): Smaller with a proportionally longer bill (Table 37); forecrown and eyeline with little or no blackish (Fig. 290**E**); breast with little to no blackish streaking by sex (Fig. 290**D-E** in ♀♀, **E** in ♂♂); underwing gr covs primarily dark.

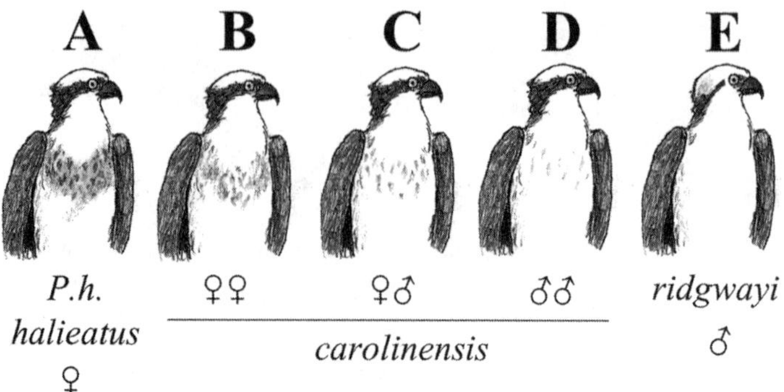

FIGURE 290. Extent of breast band in North American (*P.h. carolinensis*) and extralimital subspecies of Osprey by sex. Within each subspecies, ♀♀ average heavier breast bands than ♂♂. *P.h. haliaetus* of Europe averages darker breast bands by sex (**A** in ♀♀, **B** in ♂♂) and *ridgwayi* of the Caribbean region averages whiter breast bands by sex (**D-E** in ♀♀, **E** in ♂♂). In *carolinensis*, occasional ♀♀ may be as dark as **A** and occasional ♂♂ may lack breast markings (**E**). Also, some Juv ♂ *carolinensis* may show darker breast bands, as in **B**.

Molt—CBS. PF absent?-limited (Sep-Mar in HY/SYs), PB2 incomplete-complete (Dec-Jul in HY/SYs), PB3 incomplete (Apr-Dec in non-breeding TYs), DPB incomplete (May-Feb in breeding ASY/ATYs); PA absent. The above timing pertains to N.Am populations. The PF and PB2 occur primarily on non-breeding grounds, the 3rd PB may commence on non-breeding grounds and complete on breeding grounds, and DPBs commence on breeding grounds (often during incubation) and complete on non-breeding grounds. The PF may be absent but usually includes some body feathers (up to 35%). The PB2 may be continuous (or nearly so) with the 3rd PB. The DPBs exhibit staffelmauser (Fig. 16, pp. 23-24), resulting in 2-4 sets of basic feathers present among pp of adults. One to 4 outer pp and 1-8 (of 18-19) ss (often among s3-s4 and s7-s14) sometimes retained during the PB2, although in most SYs the PB2 appears to be complete. Subsequent PBs are typically incomplete; approximately half the rects are replaced each year. Suspension of the DPB likely occurs during breeding but limits (Fig. 289, p. 393) are difficult to distinguish. See Family Account (pp. 391-392) for more information.

Age—Juv (B1; Jul-Mar) is described under Juv-HY/SY, below; Juv ♀=♂ by plumage aspect. The following month ranges pertain to N.Am populations. See also Machmer et al. (1992) for information on ageing by fault bars in Ospreys. Note that confirmed breeders can be reliably aged ATY.

Juv-HY/SY (1st cycle, Juv/B1-F1; Aug-Jul): Most to all upperpart feathers fringed or tipped buff to whitish (Fig. 291**A-B**); rects uniformly narrow and tapered (Fig. 288**A**, p. 392), r2-r5 with 7-8 distinct dusky bars and a distinct white tip when fresh (Fig. 292**A**); underwing covs with buff or tawny wash; pp and ss uniformly juv, not showing p1/s1 contrast (Fig. 13**A**, p. 20), and being replaced in Dec-Jul, the juv outer pp

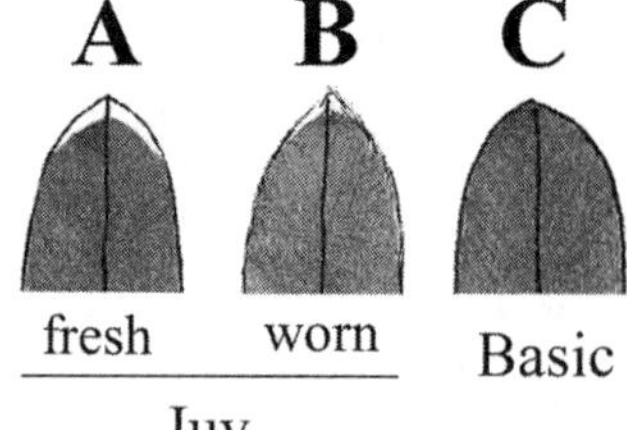

FIGURE 291. Shape and extent of pale fringing to back feathers by age in Osprey and other diurnal raptors. The fringing found on fresh juv feathers (**A**) can often wear away by Apr-Aug (**B**), sometimes completely.

tapered (Fig. 286**A**, p. 392, brownish, and fringed whitish when fresh; fault bars (if present) as in Figure 18**A** (p. 27); iris brownish orange to grayish, becoming dull yellow by Oct-Apr. **Note: Most SYs and possibly some TYs over-summer on non-breeding grounds and exhibit advanced PB2-PB3s (see p. 18).**

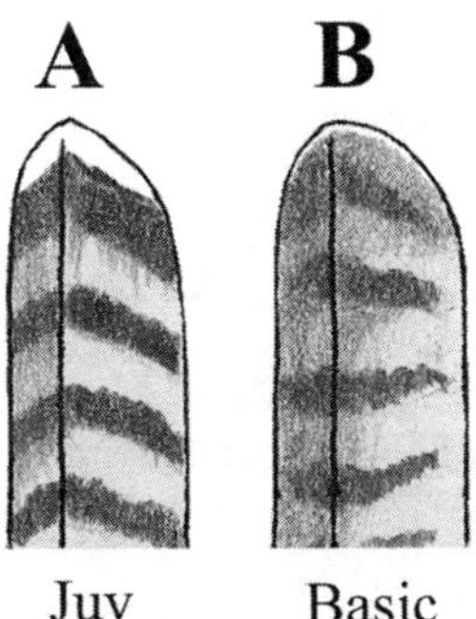

FIGURE 292. Shape and pattern of the rectrices by feather generation in Osprey. The distinct white tips to the juv rects (**A**) often wear off by Apr-Aug in SYs. R5 is shown and is usually the last feather replaced during molts and the most likely to be retained during the PB2 and DPB (*cf.* Fig. 288, p. 392).

AHY/ASY (Def. cycle, DB; Aug-Jul): Upperpart feathers and upperwing covs without pale fringing or tipping (Fig. 291**C**); rects uniformly broad and truncate (Fig. 288**C**), r2-r5 with 6-7 indistinct dusky bars and an indistinct pale tip (Fig. 292**B**); underwing covs without buff or tawny wash; pp and ss basic, showing replacement cline and p1/s1 contrast (Fig. 14**B**, p. 21), and being replaced in Apr-Feb, the outer pp broad (Fig. 291**C**), fresh, and without white fringes; fault bars (if present) as in Figure 18**B**; iris olive-yellow to orange-yellow. **Note: AHY/ASYs with uniformly replaced pp and ss are more likely SY/TYs.**

SY/TY (2nd cycle, B2; Aug-Jul): Like AHY/ASY but underwing sometimes with a few retained buff s covs; pp and ss with 2 generations, 1-4 juv outer pp (Fig. 286**A**) and 1-8 juv ss (*cf.* Fig. 322**A**, p. 431; among s3-s4 and s7-s14) retained, very faded and worn (Fig. 16**B**-**C**, p. 24); rects sometimes with 1-4 juv feathers (Fig. 292**A**) retained, narrow, rounded, and very abraded (Fig. 288**B**); iris yellowish. **Note: See Juv-HY/SY and AHY/ASY**.

ASY/ATY (Def. cycle, DB; Aug-Jul): Like AHY/ASY but pp and ss with 2 sets of basic and no juv feathers (Figs. 16**E**, 286**B**, & 322**B**); rects with 1-2 generations of basic feathers (Figs. 288**D** & 292**B**); iris yellow to orange-yellow. **Note: See AHY/ASY**.

ATY/A4Y (Def. cycle, DB; Aug-Apr): Like ASY/ATY but pp with 3 sets of basic and no juv feathers (Fig. 16**F**).

Sex—Full medial BP (Fig. 20**A**, p. 31) and/or distended cloaca (Fig. 21, p. 32) indicates ATY ♀ in Feb-May; ♂♂ can develop a partial BP. Measurements, especially culmen, somewhat helpful for sexing (Table 37, p. 405). The following should be used only in combination with measurements or direct size comparison of mated pairs; many HY/SYs (Sep-Feb) and some AHY/ASYs (especially those in s. portions of N.Am, where ♀♀ average paler breasts) are not reliably sexed (see **Geographic variation**). The following refers to the widespread N.Am subspecies (*P.h. carolinensis*) only. In addition, ♂♂ average brighter yellow or yellow-orange eyes than ♀♀ but this is also confounded by age-related variation.

♀: Breast with moderately heavy to moderately sparse streaking (Fig. 289**B**-**D**).

AHY ♂: Breast with moderately sparse to no streaking (Fig. 289**C**-**E**).

Hybrids Reported—None.

References—Bent (1937), Blanco & Rodriguez-Estrella (1999), Bretagnolle et al. (1994), Cramp & Simmons (1980), Dement'ev & Gladkov (1951b), Edelstam (1984), Ewins (1995), Forsman (1999), Friedmann (1950), Macnamara (1977), Marchant & Higgins (1993), Oberholser (1974), C.J. Henny *in* Palmer (1988a), Poole et al. (2002), Prevost (1983b), Pyle (2005b, 2005c), Roberts (1955).

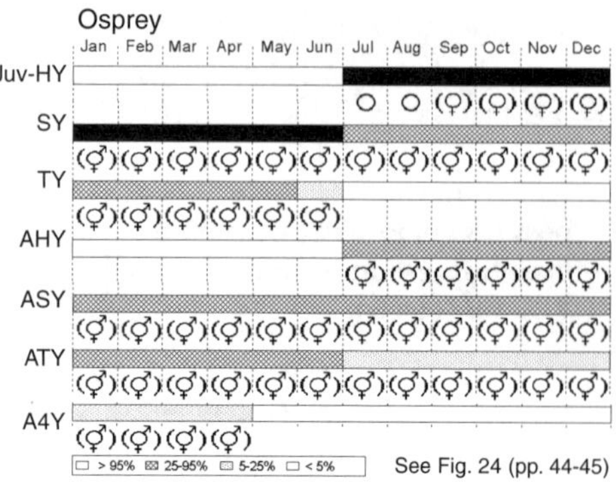

HOOK-BILLED KITE
Chondrohierax uncinatus

HBKI
Species # 3271
Band size: 6♂, 7A♀ Lock-on

Species—From other N.Am hawks by medium-small size, proportionally short wings, and long, hooked bill (Table 37, p. 405); wings rounded (usually p7≈p6>p5≈p8>p6≈p9>p5>p4>p3>p1≈p10) and with p6-p10 notched and p7-p9 emarginated (*cf.* Fig. 287, p. 392); plumage aspect variable (see **Age/Sex**) but hindcrown feathers always with white bases; lores and supra-orbital area without feathers, greenish to orangish; pp and ss with distinct blackish bars; uppertail covs with pale gray to white tips; medial rects (r2-r5) black with 1-3 dark bands both dorsally and ventrally (Fig. 293); cere yellowish and black; iris pale grayish to whitish or yellowish (see **Age**); legs and feet yellow to orange-yellow.

Geographic variation—See Amadon (1960, 1964), Blake (1977), Friedmann (1934a, 1950), Gurney (1880), Hellmayr & Conover (1949), T.B. Smith *in* Palmer (1988a), Smith & Temple (1982). Two other subspecies, possibly extinct, occur in the W.Indes.

C.u. uncinatus (res s.Tx-S.Am): Large (Table 37, p. 405; *vs* wg 234-274 in other subspecies); culmen dusky to blackish (*vs* yellowish in *wilsonii* of Cuba); ASYs with bases to back feathers uniformly dark (*vs* with white bars in *wilsonii*); plumage aspect variable but vivid and including a melanistic morph (*vs* more subdued and possibly without melanistic morph in other subspecies); ♂♂ without brownish hind collar (*vs* often with hind collar in *mirus* of Grenada). ♂♂ of s.TX-c.Mex ("*aquilonis*") may average paler than other populations but differences are subtle and variable.

Molt—CBS. PF limited-partial (Oct?-Mar? in HY/SYs), PB2 incomplete(?)-complete (Mar?-Dec? in non-breeding SYs), DPB incomplete-complete (May-Dec? in breeding AHYs); PA absent. The above timing pertains to N.Am populations. The PF includes some to most body feathers and occasionally r1 but no wing feathers. Up to 6 ss and 1-4 rects can be retained during PBs (≈25% of ASY/ATYs; probably a smaller proportion in SY/TYs), and occasional ASYs exhibit staffelmauser (Fig. 16, pp. 23-24), resulting in 2-3 sets of basic feathers present among pp of adults. Look for suspension limits (Fig. 289, p. 393) to occur in breeding adults. See Family Account (pp. 391-392) for more information.

Age/Sex—Juv (B1; Jun-Jan) has upperpart feathers barred white at base; sides of nape whitish, often forming hind collar; underparts whitish with thin brown to buff bars (blackish and whitish in dark morph), and iris brown to grayish; Juv ♀=♂. Medial BP (Fig. 20**A**, p. 31) may be developed by both sexes but distended cloaca (Fig. 21, p. 32) indicates ♀ in Dec-Jun. Measurements largely unhelpful for sexing (Table 37, p. 405). The following month ranges and criteria pertain to N.Am populations.

HY/SY ♀ (1st cycle, F1; Oct-Sep): Rects uniformly narrow (Fig. 288**A**, p. 392), rounded, and with more dark bands by morph (Fig. 293**A-B**); crown and upperparts dull brown mixed with darker brown feathers (light morph) or blackish brown with rufous fringing (dark morph); sides of nape and underparts primarily white mixed with rufous formative feathers (light morph), or black with white bases or indistinct white bars (*cf.* Fig. 329**A-B**, p. 441; dark morph); pp and ss juv and not showing s1-p1 contrast (Fig. 13**A**, p. 20), the juv inner pp without rufous tinge and the juv outer pp tapered (Fig. 286**A**, p. 392), relatively worn, and distinctly barred; iris brown to grayish, becoming dull whitish, yellowish, or grayish by Jan-Apr. **Note: Dark-morph individuals of all age groups are not reliably sexed. Also, light-morph HY/SYs can only be sexed after the PF has begun, as late as Oct-Jan in some individuals.**

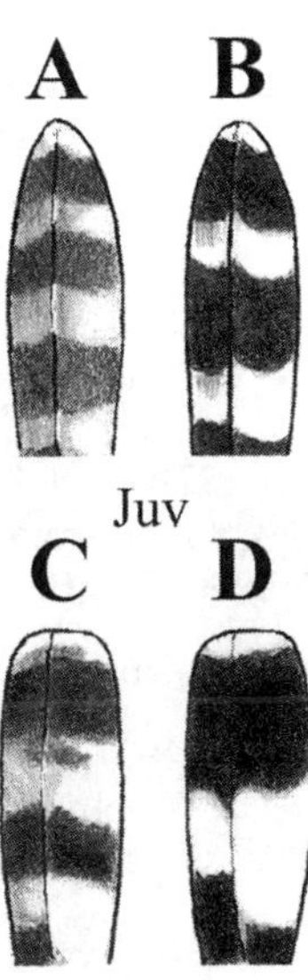

FIGURE 293. Rectrices by feather generation and morph in Hook-billed Kite. R5 is shown and is usually the last feather replaced during molts and the most likely to be retained during the PB2 and DPB (*cf.* Fig. 288, p. 392). There can be substantial variation within each morph and generation, and exceptions in pattern may be encountered.

AHY/ASY ♀ (Def. cycle, DB; Oct-Sep): Rects uniformly broad and truncate (Fig. 288**C**), with fewer dark bands by morph (Fig. 293**C-D**); crown dark grayish and upperparts uniformly blackish brown, sometimes tinged grayish and/or cinnamon (light morph), or crown and upperparts blackish to grayish black, without rufous (dark morph); sides of nape cinammon (often forming hind collar) and underparts barred rufous and white (light morph), or sides of nape and underparts uniformly blackish without white (*cf.* Fig. 329**C**; dark morph); pp and ss basic and showing s1-p1 contrast (Fig. 14**B**, p. 21), p1-p4 washed rufous, and the outer pp broad (Fig. 286**B**), relatively fresh, and without distinct bars; iris bright white or yellowish to grayish. **Note: See HY/SY ♀.**

HY/SY ♂ (1st cycle, F1; Oct-Sep): Like HY/SY ♀ but light morph with crown, upperparts, nape and underparts mixed with juv (brown and white) and bluish gray formative feathers. **Note: See HY/SY ♀.**

AHY/ASY ♂ (Def. cycle, DB; Oct-Sep): Like AHY/ASY ♀ but crown and upperparts uniformly bluish gray and underparts grayish with sparse whitish mottling or barring. **Note: See HY/SY ♀.**

SY/TY ♀ and ♂ (2nd cycle, B2; Oct-Sep): Like AHY/ASY ♀ and ♂ but pp and/or ss with 2 generations, 1-4 juv outer pp and 1-8 juv ss (among s3-s4 and s7-s14; *cf.* Fig. 322**A**, p. 431) retained (Fig. 288**B**), very faded and worn (Figs. 14**C** & 16**B**); juv r5 (Fig. 293**A-B**) occasionally retained, very worn. **Note: See HY/SY ♀. The PB2 may often be complete, rarely**

resulting in retained juv pp and ss. Also, some AHY/ASY ♂♂ have rufous-tinged underparts or some rufous feathers; these could be SY/TYs but more study is needed.

ASY/ATY ♀ and ♂ (Def. cycle, DB; Oct-May): Like AHY/ASY ♀ and ♂ but pp and ss with 2 sets of basic and no juv feathers (Figs. 16**E**, 286**B**, & 322**B**); rects occasionally with 2 generations of basic feathers (Figs. 288**D** & 293**C-D**). **Note: See HY/SY ♀.**

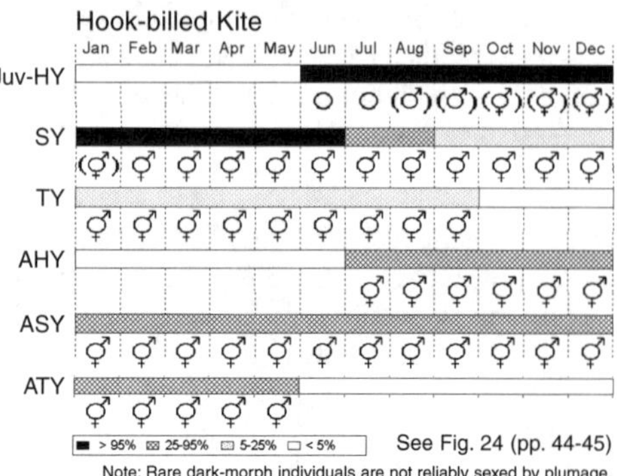

Hybrids Reported—None.

References—Blake (1977), Dickey & van Rossem (1938), Friedmann (1934a, 1950), Gurney (1880), Howell & Webb (1995), T.B. Smith *in* Palmer (1988a), Smith & Temple (1982), Wetmore (1965).

SWALLOW-TAILED KITE

Elanoides forficatus

STKI
Species # 3270
Band size: 6

Species—From other N.Am kites and hawks by medium size and proportionally very long wings and tail (Fig. 294) but short bill and tarsus (Table 37, p. 405); wings pointed (usually p8>p9>p7>p10>p6>p5) and with p9-p10 notched and p8-p9 emarginated (Fig. 295; *cf.* Fig. 287, p. 392); tail deeply forked (Fig. 294); head, underparts, and underwing covs white; back, upper wings, pp, ss, and rects grayish black to glossy black; cere dark gray; iris dark brown to red; legs and feet gray.

Geographic variation—See Blake (1977), Friedmann (1950), Hellmayr & Conover (1949), W.B. Robertson *in* Palmer (1988a). One other subspecies in s.Mex-S.Am.

E.f. forficatus (br N.Am-ne.Mex, wint s.Mex-n.S.Am): Larger and longer tailed (Table 37, p. 405; *vs* wing chord 390-445, tail 275-330 in *yetapa* breeding in s.Mex-S.Am); scapulars, lower back, and les covs usually with purplish or dark bluish sheen (seldom greenish), *vs* usually with greenish (seldom purplish) sheen in *yetapa*.

Molt—CBS. PF partial (Oct-Mar in HY/SYs), PB2 incomplete-complete (Apr-Nov in non-breeding SYs), DPB incomplete-complete (Jun-Dec in breeding AHYs); PA absent. The above timing pertains to N.Am populations. Most molting occurs on non-breeding grounds although the DPBs usually commence on breeding grounds and suspend for migration. The PF includes most body feathers (some juv scapulars usually retained), a few to some s covs, and sometimes r1 but no pp or ss. During DPBs, occasional AHYs can retain 1-4 ss, usually among s7-s11. Suspension of the DPB for the fall migration usually occurs among p6-p8, s1-s2, s5-s6, and the terts during the PB2 and among p3-p6 and occasionally s1-s2 and/or s5-s6 during subsequent PBs (*cf.* Fig. 302, p. 407). See Family Account (pp. 391-392) for more information.

Age—Juv (B1; Jul-Dec) resembles HY/SY in Nov (see below); Juv ♀=♂. The following month ranges pertain to N.Am populations.

Juv-HY/SY (1st cycle, Juv/B1-F1; Nov-Oct): Tail shorter, dull black, and less-deeply forked (Fig. 294**A**); inner pp with white tips; outer pp narrower (Fig. 295**A**) and worn; pp and ss uniformly juv (Fig. 13**A**, p. 20); upperparts and s covs dull blackish to brownish black, increasingly mixed with glossy black feathers in Nov-Mar (some juv scapulars usually retained through Oct in SYs); head, breast, and underwing covs tinged buff and/or with dusky shaft streaks, increasingly mixed with white feathers in Nov-Mar (buff underwing p covs retained through Oct in SYs); iris dark brown, becoming dark reddish by Jan-Apr.

AHY/ASY (Def. cycle, DB; Nov-Oct): Tail longer, glossy black, and more deeply forked (Fig. 294**B**); inner pp without white tips; outer pp broader (Fig. 295**B**) and fresher; pp and ss with molt clines but without retained feathers (Fig. 14**B**, p. 21) and with suspension limits absent or among p4-p7 (*cf.* Fig. 302, p. 407); upperparts and s covs uniformly glossy black; head, breast, and underwing covs white; iris red.

SY/TY (2nd cycle, B2; Nov-Oct): Like AHY/ASY but molt of pp often completing in Nov-Dec and outer pp narrow (Fig. 195**A**) and very worn; 1-4 juv ss (among s8-s11) sometimes retained, brownish and narrow (*cf.* Fig. 14**C**); suspension limit present among p7-p8 and the ss (*cf.* Fig. 302**A**). **Note: Only occasional AHY/ASYs retain ss during DPBs.**

ASY/ATY (Def. cycle, DB; Nov-Oct): Like AHY/ASY but molt of pp often completing in Nov-Dec and outer pp broad (Fig. 195**B**) and fresher; 1-4 basic ss sometimes retained, blackish and broad (Fig. 14**D**); suspension limit present among p3-p4 (Fig. 302**B**). **Note: See SY/TY.**

Sex—♀=♂ by plumage aspect. A Full medial BP (Fig. 20**A**, p. 31) and/or distended cloaca (Fig. 21, p. 32) indicates AHY ♀ in Mar-Jun; ♂♂ can develop a partial BP. Measurements

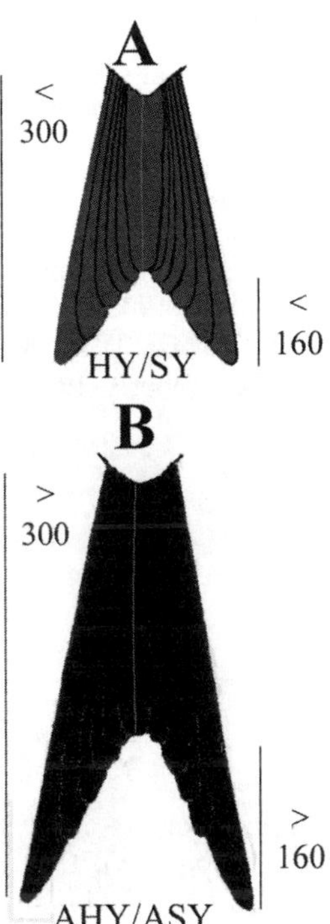

FIGURE 294. Tail length and fork (Fig. 5**C**, p. 8) by age in Swallow-tailed Kite. Juv rects (**A**) are also duller black than basic rects (**B**). Measures indicate tail fork (r1-r6) in N.Am breeding populations; shape is proportionally similar in *E.f. yetapa* of Mex-S.Am but measures differ (tail length 275-330 in AHY/ASYs).

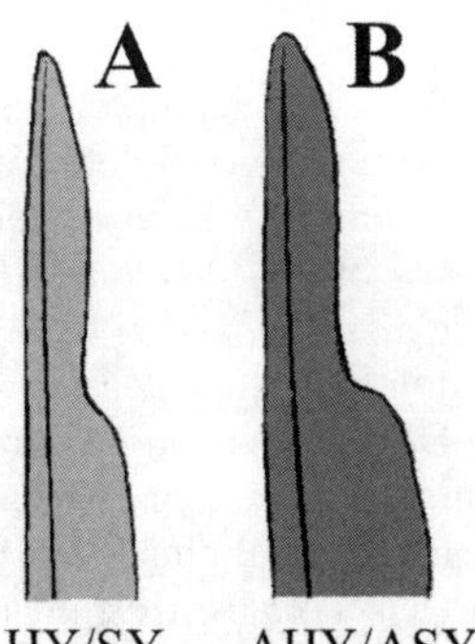

FIGURE 295. Shape of the outer primary (p10) by age in Swallow-tailed Kite. Note more extensive notch to basic feathers (**B**) than on juv feathers (**A**). Some SYs can retain the juv p10 until Nov-Dec or later, after all rects have been replaced.

generally unhelpful for sexing (Table 37, p. 405), although tail length might be reliable for sexing some mated pairs. Otherwise, no criteria known.

Hybrids Reported—None.

References—Bent (1937), Friedmann (1950), Lee & Clark (1993), Meyer (1995), Oberholser (1974), W.B. Robertson *in* Palmer (1988a), Roberts (1955).

Swallow-tailed Kitc

	Jan	Feb	Mar	Apr	May	Jun	Jul	Aug	Sep	Oct	Nov	Dec
Juv-HY							O	O	O	O	O	O
SY	O	O	O	O	O	O	O	O	O	O	O	O
TY	O	O	(♀)	(♀)	(♀)	(♀)	O	O	O	O		
AHY										O	O	O
ASY	O	O	(♀)	(♀)	(♀)	(♀)	O	O	O	O	O	O
ATY	O	O	(♀)	(♀)	(♀)	(♀)	O	O	O			

■ > 95% ▨ 25-95% ▢ 5-25% □ < 5%

See Fig. 24 (pp. 44-45)

WHITE-TAILED KITE
Elanus leucurus

WTKI
Species # 3280
Band size: 6-5 Lock-on

Species—From other N.Am kites and hawks by medium-small size (Table 37, p. 405); wings pointed (usually p9>p8>p10>p7>p6>p5) and with p9-p10 notched and p8-p9 emarginated (*cf.* Fig. 287, p. 392); tail double-rounded (r2 usually longest; r2 – r1 9-16 mm and r2 – r6 13-22 mm); upperparts largely pale gray; wing covs black; underparts white (often washed cinnamon in Juvs); distal underwing covs with variable black patch; rects primarily whitish (Fig. 296); cere, legs, and feet yellow; iris brownish to bright red.

Geographic variation—Considered monotypic here but more study needed. Populations of N-C.Am ("*E.l. majusculus*") average longer-tailed (170-192 mm) than those of S.Am (150-174 mm) but reliability, distinctness, and taxonomic significance of this difference requires study. See Bangs & Penard (1920), Blake (1977), Clark & Banks (1992), Friedmann (1950), Palmer (1988a), Parkes (1958b), and Patten et al. (2003) for more information.

Molt—CBS. PF partial-incomplete (Aug-Jan in HY/SYs), PB2 incomplete-complete (Mar-Sep in SYs); DPB incomplete-complete (Apr-Nov in AHYs); PA absent. The above timing pertains to N.Am populations. The PF includes most to all body feathers, no to some les covs, 2-12 rects (all 12 in ~20% of HY/SYs), rarely 1-3 inner pp, and occasionally (~15% of HY/SYs from CA) 1-6 ss among s1-s3, s5, and s11-s12; body feathers are replaced by Nov whereas rect replacement can extend into Jan. Occasional ASYs retain p10 and or 1-6 ss (usually among s4 and s6-s10) during DPBs. Breeding ASYs replace 3-6 pp, often 1-3 terts, and occasionally s1 and/or s5 during incubation, creating suspension limit (Fig. 289**A-B**, p. 393); ♀♀ average more pp replaced than ♂♂. Staffelmauser (Fig. 16, pp. 23-24) can occasionally occur in Black-shouldered Kites (*E. caeruleus*; Herremans 2000) and should be looked for in White-tailed Kite. See Family Account (pp. 391-392) for more information.

Age—Juv (B1; Jun-Nov) has crown and nape feathers dusky with cinnamon to tawny fringing, back feathers brownish gray with broad cinnamon tips, and breast feathers washed cinnamon or tawny; Juv ♀ = ♂. The following month ranges pertain to N.Am populations.

HY/SY (1st cycle, F1; Nov-Oct): Gr covs, p covs, inner pp, and most or all ss with whitish tips, and one or more rects usually juv, narrow, rounded, and with dusky spots or bands (Fig. 296**A-B**); pp and ss usually uniformly juv (Fig. 13**A**, p. 20), or occasionally 1-3 inner pp and/or

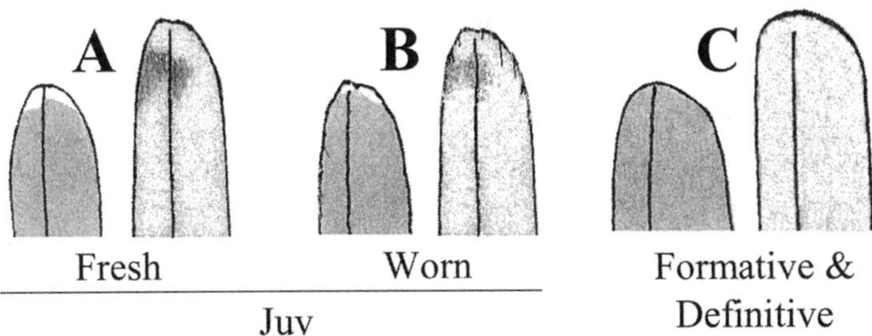

FIGURE 296. Shape and pattern to the secondaries (left) and rectrices (right) in White-tailed Kites by feather generation; shown are s8 and r5, among the last feathers typically replaced during molts and the most likely to be retained during the PB2 and DPB (*cf.* Figs. 14**C**-**D**, p. 22, & 288**C**-**D**, p. 392). The juv inner pp and p covs also show white tips as in **A**. 1-6 ss and 2-12 rects can be replaced during the PF (see **Molt**) and resemble feathers shown in **C** in HY/SYs, but most ss (including s8) will show white tips and most HY/SYs will show dusky markings to some rects (including r5), as in **A**-**B**. Occasional SY/TYs can retain ss (including s8) during the PB2 (usually still showing whitish tips, as in **B**), and some ASY/ATYs will retain some ss (often including s8) during the DPB (Fig. 14**C**-**D**).

1-6 ss replaced during the PF (see **Molt**), the juv outer pp tapered, brownish, and relatively worn (Fig. 286**A**, p. 392); iris brownish, becoming dull orangish red by Jan-Apr.

AHY/ASY (Def. cycle, DB; Nov-Oct): Gr covs, p covs, inner pp, and ss without whitish tips, and rects broad, truncate, and without dusky spots or bands (Fig. 296**C**); pp and ss basic, showing replacement clines and/or s1-p1 contrast but without suspension limits (Fig. 14**B**, p. 21), the outer pp broader and fresher (Fig. 286**B**); iris bright orange to red.

SY/TY (2nd cycle, B2; Oct-Sep): Like AHY/ASY but the juv p10 (Fig. 286**A**) and/or 1-4 juv ss (among s4 and s8-s10) retained, very faded and worn (Figs. 14**C** & 296**B**); pp and ss not showing suspension limits (*cf.* Fig. 289, p. 393). **Note: Only occasional AHYs retain pp and ss during DPBs.**

ASY/ATY (Def. cycle, DB; Oct-Sep): Like AHY/ASY but pp and ss showing suspension limits among p3-p6 and occasionally the ss (Fig. 289**A**-**B**); basic p10 (Fig. 286**B**) and/or 1-6 basic ss (among s1-s12) occasionally retained (Figs. 14**D** & 296**C**). **Note: See SY/TY. Look for occasional ASYs also to show staffelmauser patterns, with two generations of basic feathers, as in Fig. 16E (pp. 23-24).**

Sex—Medial BP (Fig. 20**A**, p. 31) and/or distended cloaca (Fig. 21, p. 32) indicates ♀ in

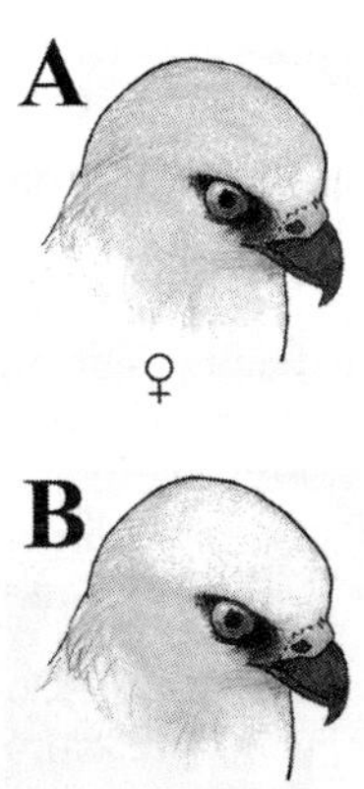

FIGURE 297. Extent of pale feathering to the crown and ocular area by sex in White-tailed Kites; note especially difference in contrast between crown and auriculars. This character is useful in sexing most individuals, including mated pairs, but some intermediates may be encountered. HY/SY ♂♂ usually gain enough pale feathering to the crown to be reliably sexed by Dec-Jan. Thereafter, intermediates are likely SY ♂♂ or ASY ♀♀ and can often be sexed in combination with age. Beware of bleaching in ♀♀ in May-Oct.

Feb-Jul. Measurements unhelpful for sexing (Table 37, p. 405). The following is reliable for sexing most individuals in formative and basic plumage, with experience or for mated pairs; intermediates are likely SY ♂♂ or ATY ♀♀ so combine with age for reliable sexing.

♀: White of forehead and ocular region reduced (Fig. 297**A**, p. 401); ASYs with suspension limits often among p5-p6 (*cf.* Fig. 289**B**).

♂: White of forehead and ocular region extensive (Fig. 297**B**); ASYs with suspension limits often among p3-p4 (*cf.* Fig. 289**A**).

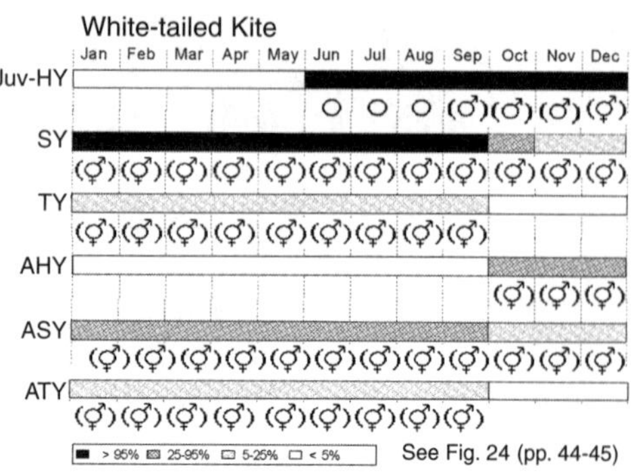

Hybrids Reported—None.

References—Bent (1937), Cramp & Simmons (1980), Dunk (1995), Forsman (1999), Friedmann (1950), Hawbecker (1942), Herremans (2000), Marchant & Higgins (1993), Oberholser (1974), Palmer (1988a), Pyle (2005b, 2005c), Underhill (1986).

SNAIL KITE
Rostrhamus sociabilis

SNKI
Species # 3300
Band size: 6 Lock-on

Species—From other N.Am kites and hawks by medium-large size (especially bill and tarsus) but proportionally short tail (Table 37, p. 405); tip of upper mandible extends 7-9 mm beyond tip of lower mandible; wings somewhat rounded (usually p8≈p7>p6>p9>p5>p10>p4) and with p8-p10 notched and p5-p9 emarginated (*cf.* Fig. 287, p. 392); tail squared (r6 > r1 by 10-25 mm); upperparts and underparts largely dark brown to blackish (see **Age/Sex**); uppertail covs and vent contrastingly white; rects white with broad dusky to black band (Fig. 298); cere yellowish to red; iris brownish to bright orange or red; legs and feet yellow to red by age/sex.

Geographic variation—See Amadon (1975), Blake (1977), Brodkorb (1943a), Friedmann (1933b, 1950), Hellmayr & Conover (1949), Monroe (1968), Nelson & Goldman (1933), S.R. Beissinger *in* Palmer (1988a), Sykes et al. (1995). Two other subspecies in Mex-S.Am.

R.s. plumbeus (res sc.FL-W.Indes): Averages medium in size (Table 37, p. 405; culmen with cere 27-35), *vs* wing chord 336-380, tail 161-221, and culmen with cere 33-39 in *major* of Mex-n.C.Am (possible vagrant to s.TX), and wing chord 308-348, tail 152-185, and culmen with cere 28-34 in *sociabilis* of C.Am-S.Am. Populations of Cuba ("*levis*") may average slightly longer bills but difference slight.

Molt—CBS. PF partial-incomplete (Aug-Feb in HY/SYs), PB2 incomplete-complete (Mar-Aug in SYs); DPB incomplete-complete (Apr-Nov in AHYs); PA absent. The above timing pertains to N.Am populations. The PF includes some (up to 50%) of the body feathers and sometimes 1-4 c.rects but few if any wing feathers. The DPBs can be complete but sometimes exhibit staffelmauser (Fig. 16, pp. 23-24), resulting in 2 (occasionally 3) sets of basic feathers present among pp of adults. One to 2 juv outer pp, 1-4 juv ss (among s3-s4 and s8-s10), and one or more juv rump feathers can occasionally be retained until the 3rd PB. Suspension of the DPB likely occurs during breeding but limits (Fig. 289, p. 393) are difficult to distinguish. See Family Account (pp. 391-392) for more information.

Age/Sex—Juv (B1; Jun-Oct) has crown and head tawny or buff to whitish except for dark eyeline, and upperpart feathers uniform in wear and broadly fringed cinnamon; Juv ♀=♂. A Full medial BP (Fig. 20**A**, p. 31) and/or distended cloaca (Fig. 21, p. 32) indicates ♀ in Feb-Aug; ♂♂ may develop a partial BP. Measurements unhelpful for sexing (Table 37, p. 405). The following month ranges pertain to N.Am populations.

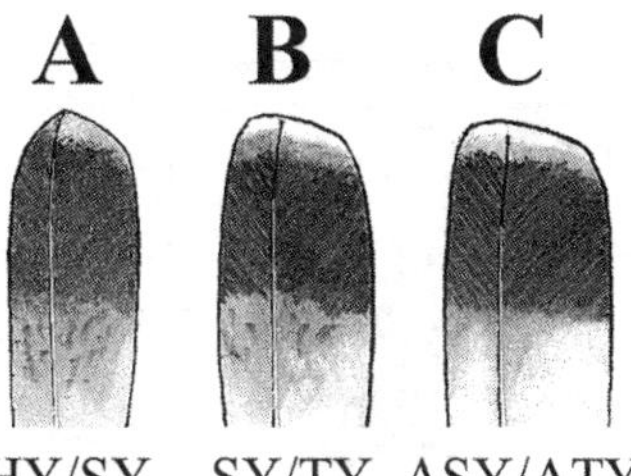

FIGURE 298. Shape and pattern of the rectrices by age in Snail Kite. R5 is shown and is usually the last feather replaced during molts (*cf.* Fig. 288, p. 392); rectrices are rarely if ever retained during PBs in this species.

HY/SY ♀♂ (1st cycle, F1; Sep-Aug): Head and throat mixed buff and brown with distinct buff eyeline (usually broad); upperparts brown; underparts whitish to buff with heavy brown streaking; rects uniformly narrow and rounded (Fig. 288**A**, p. 392), r2-r5 with indistinct dusky band (Fig. 298**A**); pp and ss uniformly juv and not showing s1-p1 contrast (Fig. 13**A**, p. 20), the juv outer pp tapered, brownish, relatively worn, and barred pale underneath (Fig. 299**A**), and the juv medial ss with distinct bars (Fig. 300**A**, p. 404); cere and legs dull yellowish; iris brown, becoming dull orangish red in some ♂♂ by Jan-Apr. **Note: It may be possible to sex males as early as Dec and females as early as Jan by the aspect of incoming formative feathers on the upperparts and underparts (see SY/TY ♀ and ♂) and by the iris color; more study is needed.**

SY/TY ♀ (2nd cycle, B2; Sep-Aug): Head dark brown with indistinct whitish eyeline, auriculars, and throat; upperparts dark brown; underparts dusky brown with diffuse whitish mottling; rects moderately broad and truncate, r2-r5 with semi-distinct blackish band (Fig. 298**B**); pp and ss basic and showing s1-p1 contrast (Fig. 14**B**, p. 21), the juv outer pp with diffuse bars underneath (Fig. 299**B**), and the juv medial ss with moderately distinct bars (Fig. 300**B**), or 1-2 juv outer pp (Fig. 299**A**) and 1-4 juv ss (Fig. 300**A**) among s3-s4 and s8-s10 retained, very faded and worn (*cf.* Fig. 16**B**, p. 24); cere and legs bright yellowish; iris dark brown. **Note: SY/TYs following a complete PB2 (without retained juv feathers) can be aged by aspect of the body feathers, ss, and rects.**

ASY/ATY ♀ (Def. cycle, DB; Sep-Aug): Head dark brown to grayish brown, with small whitish eyeline and throat patch extending to auriculars; upperparts brownish to grayish brown; underparts dusky brown with sparse brownish or whitish mottling on abdomen; rects uniformly broad and truncate (Fig. 288**C**), r2-r5 with distinct blackish band (Fig. 298**C**); pp and ss with 1-2 sets of basic but no juv feathers (Figs. 14**B** & **D**, & Fig. 16**E**), the underside of p10 somewhat pale at base and with diffuse bands (Fig. 299**B**) and the medial ss with moderately diffuse bars (Fig. 300**C**); cere and legs bright yellowish; iris dark brown to reddish brown. **Note: See SY/TY ♀.**

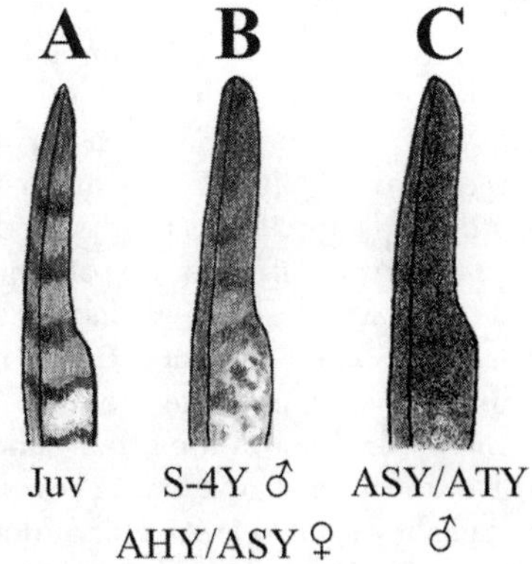

FIGURE 299. Underside of the outer primary (p10) by feather generation, age, and sex in Snail Kite. Note that occasional SY/TYs of both sexes can retain the juv outer p (**A**), and that ♂♂ can retain 2nd basic feathers through the PB3 or PB4 and can thus be identified as 4-5Ys (see **Age**).

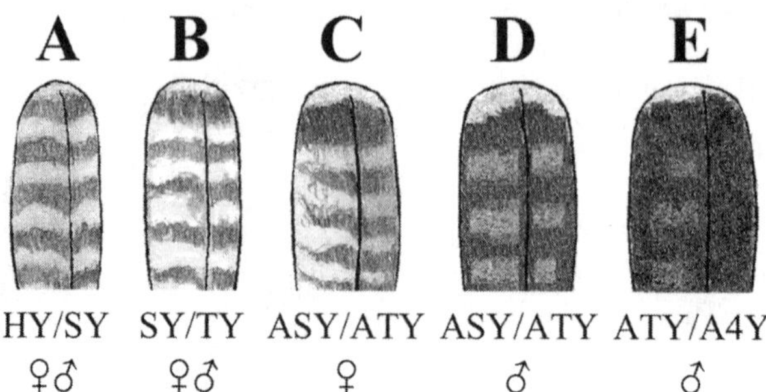

FIGURE 300. Shape and pattern to the undersides of the medial secondaries (s7 shown) by age and sex in Snail Kite. Note that some of these ss (especially s4 and s7-s8) can be retained during PBs, and can be used to help age SY/TYs, TY/4Ys, and ATY/A4Ys.

ATY/A4Y ♀ (Def. cycle, DB; Sep-Mar): Like ASY/ATY ♀ but upperparts grayish brown; pp with 3 sets of basic feathers (Fig. 16**F**), the retained pp with diffuse bands (Fig. 299**B**) and retained ss with moderately diffuse bars (Fig. 300**C**).

SY/TY ♂ (2nd cycle, B2; Aug-Jul): Head primarily brownish slate, with variably indistinct whitish eyeline (usually narrow), auriculars, and throat; upperparts brownish slate with sparse whitish to buff markings; underparts dusky brown with diffuse whitish streaks ventrally; rects (Fig. 298**B**) and pp and ss (Figs. 14**B**, 299**A-B**, & 300**A-B**) as in SY/TY ♀; cere and legs orangish; iris dull orangish to orange-red. **Note: See SY/TY ♀. Beware SY ♂♂ can resemble AHY/ASY ♀♀; use iris color to confirm sex and age.**

T-4Y ♂ (3rd-4th cycle, B3-B4; Jan-Dec): Head, upperparts, throat, breast, and abdomen slaty black with indistinct pale streaking, most often present on breast; rects (Fig. 298**C**) and pp and ss (Figs. 14**B**, **D**, & Fig. 16**E**) as in ASY/ATY ♀ but the underside of p10 can be duskier (Fig. 299**B-C**) and medial ss dusky with diffuse squarish spots (Fig. 300**D**); cere, legs, and iris bright orange-red to red. **Note: See ATY/A4Y ♂.**

ATY/A4Y ♂ (Def. cycle, DB; Aug-Jul): Head, upperparts, throat, breast, and abdomen uniformly slaty, without white; pp and ss with 1-3 sets of basic but no juv feathers (Figs. 14**B** & **D**, & Fig. 16**E-F**), the underside of p10 dusky (Fig. 299**C**) and the medial ss dusky with very diffuse or no pale squarish spots (Fig. 300**E**); cere, legs, and iris bright red. **Note: Some ♂♂ apparently can retain indistinct pale barring to the undersides of the pp for life; on the other hand, ♂♂ with entirely black underwing covs might be reliably aged A4Y/A5Y or older but more study is needed. Some intermediate ♂♂ may best be aged ASY/ATY.**

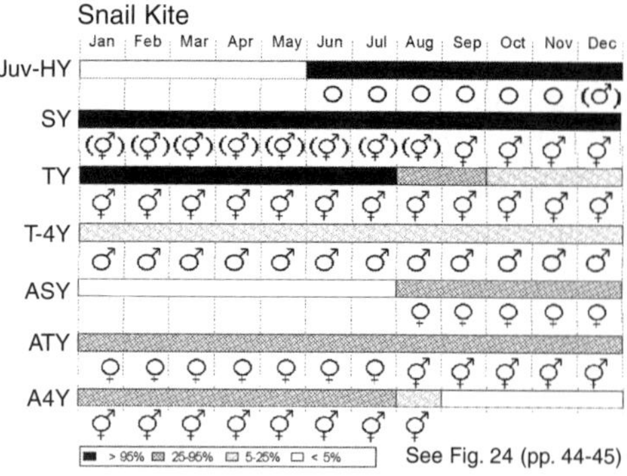

Hybrids Reported—None.

References—Bent (1937), Friedmann (1950), Howell & Webb (1995), S.R. Beissinger *in* Palmer (1988a), Pyle (2005b, 2005c), Sykes (1979), Sykes et al. (1995), Wetmore (1926).

TABLE 37. Measurements (mm) of North American ospreys and kites to assist in identification and sexing. See pp. 4-11 for methods of measurement. Species summaries are in **bold** and subspecies summaries in ***italics***. Values were derived from 95% confidence intervals as based approximately on the indicated sample sizes (see pp. 4-5); thus midpoints of ranges approximate means, and S.D. is approximated by 25% of the range.

Taxon/Sex	*n*	wing chord	tail length	culmen from cere[1]	tarsus
Osprey		**433-526**	**184-238**	**30.4-36.4**	**52-59**
P.h. carolinensis		***455-526***	***212-238***	***30.4-36.1***	***53-59***
♀	100	478-526	212-238	32.2-36.1	54-59
♂	85	455-492	194-223	30.4-33.9	53-58
P.h. ridgwayi		***433-505***	***184-228***	***32.1-36.4***	***52-57***
♀	7	453-505	200-228	33.1-36.4	53-57
♂	6	433-482	184-211	32.1-35.3	52-56
Hook-billed Kite[2,3]		**262-318**	**172-222**	**27.2-36.8**	**31-37**
♀	35	266-318	183-222	28.0-36.8	31-36
♂	30	262-313	172-210	27.2-36.0	32-37
Swallow-tailed Kite[2,4]		**423-449**	**322-368**	**18.8-20.9**	**32-34**
♀	20	432-449	338-368	19.2-20.9	32-34
♂	20	423-439	322-354	18.8-20.4	32-33
White-tailed Kite[2]		**297-327**	**170-192**	**16.8-20.6**	**36-41**
♀	100	298-327	171-192	17.7-20.6	37-41
♂	100	297-326	170-191	16.8-19.5	36-40
Snail Kite[2]		**324-377**	**158-196**	**22.1-26.9**	**48-57**
♀	74	324-370	166-196	22.7-26.9	48-57
♂	55	329-377	158-188	22.1-26.2	47-56
Mississippi Kite		**284-320**	**148-172**	**14.3-17.1**	**35-41**
♀	20	299-320	154-172	14.9-17.1	37-41
♂	20	284-305	148-166	14.3-16.4	34-38

[1] Culmen from cere represents the chord (Fig. 7**B**, p. 9).
[2] Values are for N.Am populations only; see **Geographic variation**.
[3] Bill size in Hook-billed Kites varies substantially among both sexes, with "large-billed" and "small-billed" forms (see Smith & Temple 1982).
[4] Tail length in Swallow-tailed Kites varies by age: values represent AHY/ASYs; those for HY/SYs are 180-260 (Fig. 294, p. 399).

MISSISSIPPI KITE
Ictinia mississippiensis

MIKI
Species # 3290
Band size: 5 Lock-on

Species—From other N.Am kites and hawks by medium-small size, especially tail and bill lengths (Table 37); wings pointed (usually p9>p8>p7>p6>p10≈p5) and with p9-p10 notched and p9 emarginated (*cf.* Fig. 287, p. 392); tail notched (r6 – r1 4-25 mm); plumage aspect largely slate and gray (washed brown in Juvs); outer webs of ss pale gray, contrasting with blackish wing covs and pp; inner webs of p1-p9 with indistinct or no rufous; medial rects (r2-r5) dusky, with or without indistinct white bands (Fig. 301, p. 406); HY/SYs with some to all underwing covs rufous and white; cere, legs, and feet dull grayish to yellow; iris brownish to bright red. Plumbeous Kite (*I. plumbea*), a possible vagrant from Mex-S.Am, has tail proportionately short (138-165, < half the wing chord); pp with substantial rufous; ss blackish, uniform in aspect with pp and wing covs; medial rects (r2-r5) with distinct pale bands on inner webs in all plumage aspects (*cf.* Fig. 301**C**); HY/SYs with underwing covs primarily dark; dorsal surface of legs and feet bright yellow to orange.

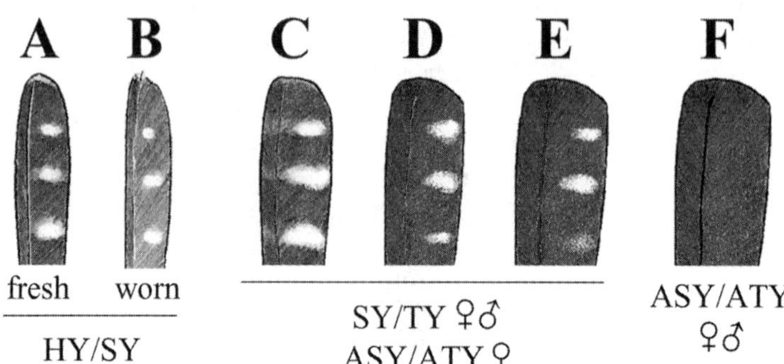

FIGURE 301. Shape and pattern of the rectrices by age in Mississippi Kite; r5 is shown, which can be the last feather replaced during molts, in Dec (SYs) or Jan (ATYs). Note that some SYs can show mixed juv (**A-B**) and formative (resembling **C-D**) rects in Jan-Oct. The extent of white shows substantial individual variation among AHY/ASYs: in SY/TY ♀♀ it varies from **C** to **D**, in ASY/ATY ♀♀ it varies from **D** to **E** (occasionally **F**), and in SY/TY ♂♂ it varies from **C** to **E**. Most ASY/ATY ♂♂ show no white (**F**) but some individuals can show small and indistinct white spots, as in **E**, on some feathers. Thus, sexing by the amount of white in the rectrices (by age) is not reliable; reports that ASY/ATY ♀♀ have paler shafts to r6 than ASY/ATY ♂♂ requires further study.

Geographic variation—Monotypic.

Molt—CBS. PF partial-incomplete (Oct?-Jul? in HY/SYs), PB2 complete (Feb?-Nov? in non-breeding SYs), DPB complete (Jun-Jan? in breeding AHY/ASYs); PA absent. Most molting occurs on non-breeding grounds although the DPBs usually commence on breeding grounds and suspend for migration. The PF includes most body feathers (some juv underwing covs usually retained), some to all s covs, and sometimes 1-6 rects but no other pp or ss. See Family Account (pp. 391-392) for replacement sequence of pp and ss during DPBs. Molt suspension for fall migration typically occurs among p6-p7, the terts, and often s1 and/or S5-s6 during the PB2 and among p2-p3 during subsequent PBs (Fig. 302).

Age—Juv (B1; Jul-Oct) has plumage aspect washed brownish and underwing covs with heavy rufous to whitish mottling; Juv ♀=♂.

Juv-HY/SY (1st cycle, Juv/B1-F1; Nov-Oct): Body and underwing s covs with rufous and/or whitish mottling, becoming mostly to entirely dull grayish by Mar-Jul (at least some juv underwing covs usually retained through Oct); rects usually uniformly narrow and rounded (Fig. 288**A**, p. 392), r2-r5 grayish with 3-4 whitish bands to inner webs and white tips (Fig. 301**A-B**), sometimes with 1-6 c.rects replaced and broader (Fig. 301**C-D**); pp and ss juv and without contrasts (Fig. 14**A**, p. 20; *cf.* Fig. 302), with white tips when fresh, the inner pp without rufous and the outer pp narrow (Fig. 286**A**, p. 392), brownish, and relatively worn; iris brownish, becoming dull orangish red by Jan-Apr.

AHY/ASY (Def. cycle, DB; Nov-Oct): Body and underwing s covs uniformly gray; rects uniformly broader (Fig. 288**C**), r2-r5 dusky to blackish with indistinct pale bands or tips (Fig. 301**D-E**); pp and ss basic, without white tips, and with suspension limit evident among p4-p5 (*cf.* Fig. 302), the outer pp broad (Fig. 286**B**), and the inner pp with little to no rufous; iris bright orangish red. **Note: See SY/TY and ASY/ATY.**

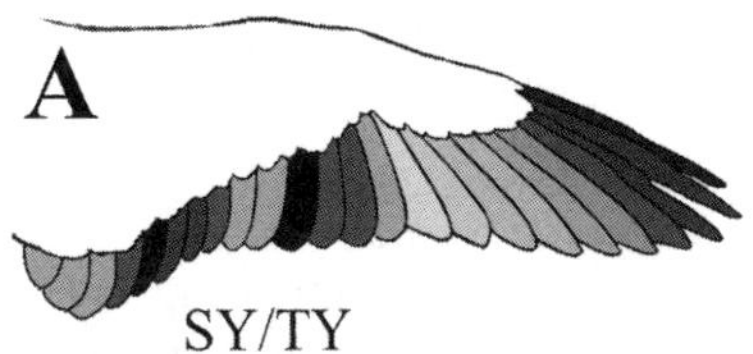

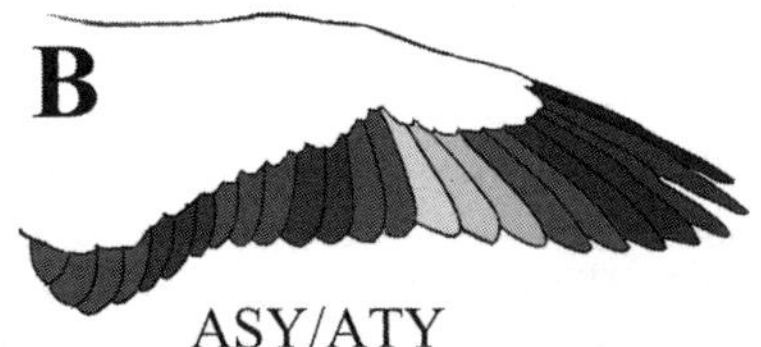

FIGURE 302. Replacement patterns among the primaries and secondaries in SY/TY and ASY/ATY Mississippi Kites in Nov-Oct. Darker shading indicates fresher feathers. These patterns result from molt suspension for southbound migration, which typically occurs after 6-7 pp and 3-6 ss had been replaced prior to suspension in SYs but after only 2-3 pp and no ss had been replaced prior to suspension in ASYs. Thus, there is a cline in freshness within each smaller series and a suspension limit apparent where molt was suspended. See Figures 15, (p. 23) & 289, (p. 393) for more information. Individuals with suspension limits among p4-p5 should be aged AHY/ASY by this criterion alone.

SY/TY (2nd cycle, B2; Nov-Oct): Like AHY/ASY but r2-r5 can be paler with more distinct pale bands or tips (Fig. 301**C-E**; some SYs can retain 1-2 juv rects, as in Fig. 301**B**, through Dec); pp and ss with suspension limits evident among p6-p7 and the ss (Fig. 302**A**); iris dull to bright orangish red.

ASY/ATY (Def. cycle, DB; Nov-Oct): Like AHY/ASY but r2-r5 dusky to black, without or with indistinct pale bands or tips (Fig. 301**D-F**; some ASY/ATYs can retain 1-2 basic rects through Jan); pp and ss with suspension limit evident among p2-p3 (Fig. 302**B**); iris bright orange-red to red.

Sex—A Full medial BP (Fig. 20**A**, p. 31) and/or distended cloaca (Fig. 21, p. 32) indicates ♀ in Mar-Jul; ♂♂ possibly may develop a partial BP. Measurements (especially wing chord and tarsus) somewhat helpful for sexing (Table 37, p. 405). Among breeding ASYs, ♂♂ average paler whitish heads, throats, and medial ss, and perhaps darker undertail covs and rects (see Fig. 301) than ♀♀ but age-related overlap in these features prevents reliable sexing of most individuals, perhaps with the exception of some mated pairs. More study is needed. Otherwise, no criteria known for sexing.

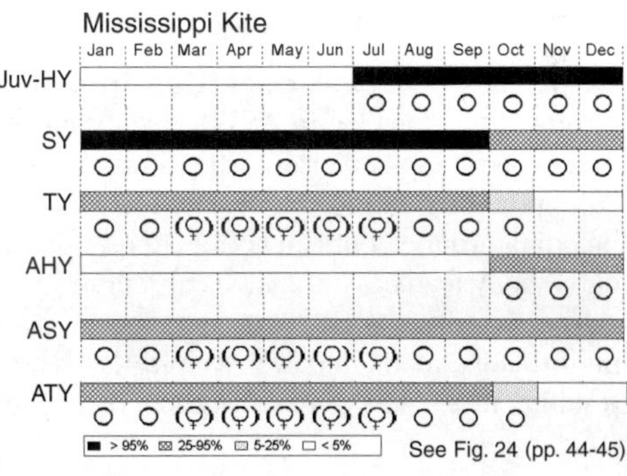

Hybrids Reported—None.

References—Bent (1937), Eisenmann (1963), Fitch (1963), Friedmann (1950), Oberholser (1974), J.W. Parker *in* Palmer (1988a), Parker (1981, 1999), Sutton (1939, 1944), Wetmore (1946a), Wheeler (2004).

BALD EAGLE BAEA
Haliaeetus leucocephalus Species # 3520
Band size: 9 Riveted

Species—From most other N.Am raptors (including Golden Eagle, p. 453) by large size and proportionally large bill (Table 38, p. 419; bill depth at base 32-38); wings somewhat rounded (usually p8≈p7>p9≈p6>p10≈p5>4) and with p5-p10 notched and p5-p9 emarginated (*cf.* Fig. 287, p. 392); crown and nape without cinnamon or buff; S-4Ys with head, back, wing covs, abdomen, and/or (especially) axillars and underwing covs mixed with at least some white (Fig. 303); proximal pp and distal ss without distinct white bases (can be mixed indistinctly with whitish; Fig. 305, p. 410); rects without well-defined white bases or indistinct bands (Fig. 304); cere grayish; bill black (Juv) to yellow (A4Y); iris dark brown (Juv) to pale yellowish (A4Y); legs and feet yellow, the tarsus without feathering to toes (Fig. 334**A**, p. 448).

White-tailed Eagle (*H. albicilla*), a visitor to w.AK islands and vagrant to ne.N.Am, is larger by age/sex (wg chord 550-700, tl 245-375, culmen from cere 47-66, tarsus 93-107; Atlantic > Pacific populations); upperparts paler tan; upperwing covs with more whitish but underwing and undertail covs with less whitish by age; rects of Juv/HY/SYs with completely dark outer webs (*vs* with whitish in Bald Eagle; Fig. 304**A**); iris brown to yellowish brown. Steller's Sea-Eagle (*H. pelagicus*), a vagrant to AK, is longer-tailed and larger-billed (tl 270-390, culmen from cere 50-75, bill depth 40-50); tail wedge-shaped (r1-r6 > 110 mm *vs* < 110 in Bald Eagle); cere dull (Juv) to bright (ATY) yellowish; H-4Ys with tail mostly to entirely white; ATYs with les covs contrastingly whitish to white.

Geographic variation—Considered monotypic here, following information presented by R.S. Palmer & J.M. Gerrard *in* Palmer (1988a). Populations breeding in nw.N.Am ("*H.l. alascanus*" = "*washingtoniensis*") average larger than those in s.N.Am ("*leucocephalus*" and "*floridana*") but size variation appears to be broadly clinal throughout range. See also Amadon (1983), Behle (1985), Bent (1937), Buehler (2000), Friedmann (1950), Hellmayr & Conover (1949), Hubbard & Banks (1970), Mengel (1953), Oberholser (1974), Patten et al. (2003), Peters (1931a), Stalmaster (1987), and Stejneger (1885) for more information.

Molt—CBS. PF absent-limited (Dec-Apr in HY/SYs), PB2 incomplete (Feb-Nov in SYs), DPB incomplete (Mar-Dec in ASYs); PA absent. Note that a definitive molt cycle is here defined (based on timing and extent) that occurs prior to attainment of definitive plumage aspect (see p. 13). Sporadic molting can occasionally continue through Jan-Feb. Molt largely takes place on breeding grounds but can complete on non-breeding grounds. The PF can include up to 40% of the body feathers but may be absent in some HY/SYs. Formative feathers may or may not be replaced during the PB2; however, the PF (as described above) appears to be homologous with preformative molts in other Accipitridae. The DPBs exhibit staffelmauser (Fig. 16, pp. 23-24), resulting in 2-4 sets of basic feathers present among pp of adults. Four to 8 pp and 5-12 ss are

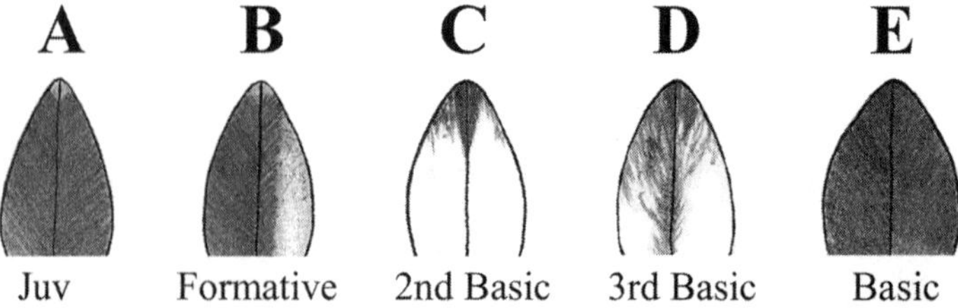

FIGURE 303. Shape and color pattern to feathers of the underparts by feather generation in Bald Eagle. Note that these feathers are frequently retained during the PF and PBs, such that Juv-HY/SYs exhibit **A** or a mixture of **A** (old) and **B** (new), SY/TYs exhibit a mixture of **A-B** (old) and **C** (new), TY/4Ys exhibit a mixture of **C** (old) and **D** (new), 4-5Ys exhibit a mixture of **D** (old) and **E** (new), and A4Y/A5Ys exhibit **E**.

typically replaced during each molt; 3-5 juv outer pp and 1-5 juv ss among s3-s4 and s7-s11 are usually retained until the 3rd PB, and 1-2 juv pp and/or ss (among p10 and s8-s10) can occasionally be retained until the 4th PB. Five to (often) all 12 rects are replaced per molt, the last juv rects (among r2-r5) occasionally retained until the 3rd PB. Body feathers and wing covs are rarely (if ever) completely replaced during DPBs. See Family Account (pp. 391-392) for more information.

Age—Juv (B1; Jul-May) is described under Juv-HY/SY, below, with the breast feathers uniformly pointed and dark (Fig. 303**A**); Juv ♀=♂.

Juv-HY/SY (1st cycle, Juv/B1-F1; Sep-Aug): Body feathers pointed and even in wear, primarily blackish brown (can bleach to buffy brown by Mar-Jul), with little or no exposed white (Fig. 303**A**; some breast feathers can be replaced in Mar-Jul, resembling Fig. 303**B**); axillars and underwing covs mostly brown with some whitish; rects uniformly narrow and elongated (Fig. 288**A**, p. 392), dark with extensive white mottling to inner web (Fig. 304**A**); pp and ss uniformly juv (Fig. 16**A**, p. 24), the outer pp tapered (Fig. 286**A**, p. 392), brownish, and relatively worn, and the juv ss narrow, long, and brown or with some indistinct whitish mottling (Fig. 305**A-B**, p. 410); iris dark brown becoming pale brown by Jan-Apr; bill dusky.

SY/TY (2nd cycle, B2; Sep-Aug): Body feathers uneven in shape and wear, the head and nape largely pale to medium-dark brownish (sometimes with some whitish), contrasting with darker brown auriculars, and the upper back and underparts variably mixed with brownish to mostly whitish feathers (Fig. 303**A**-**C**); axillars and underwing covs mostly white with some brownish; rects broad and variably mottled whitish with darker tips (Fig. 304**B-C**), 1-4 juv rects (Fig. 304**A**) among r2 and r5 occasionally retained (*cf.* Fig. 288**B**); pp and ss with 2 generations, 3-6 juv outer pp (Fig. 286**A**) and 3-10 juv ss (among s2-s4 and s7-s12; Fig. 305**A-B**) retained, very faded and worn (Fig. 16**B**), the retained juv ss longer and usually with less whitish (Fig. 304**A-B**), and the replaced ss shorter and with increased white mottling (Fig. 304**C**); iris pale brown, sometimes becoming brownish yellow by Jan-Jul; bill grayish, sometimes tinged dull yellowish by Jan-Jul. **Note: Some individuals, intermediate in plumage aspect, molt extent, and bare part color between this and TY/4Y, might best be aged S-TY or T-4Y (see pp. 41-42).**

TY/4Y (3rd cycle, B3; Sep-Aug): Body feathers uneven in wear, the head and nape variably mixed brownish and whitish, usually contrasting with darker brownish auriculars; upper back and underparts primarily brown, with variable amounts of retained whitish feathers and feathers with whitish bases (Fig. 303**C-D**); axillars and underwing covs mostly brown with some whitish; most or all rects with white at bases and dark tips (Fig. 304**B-C**); pp and ss with

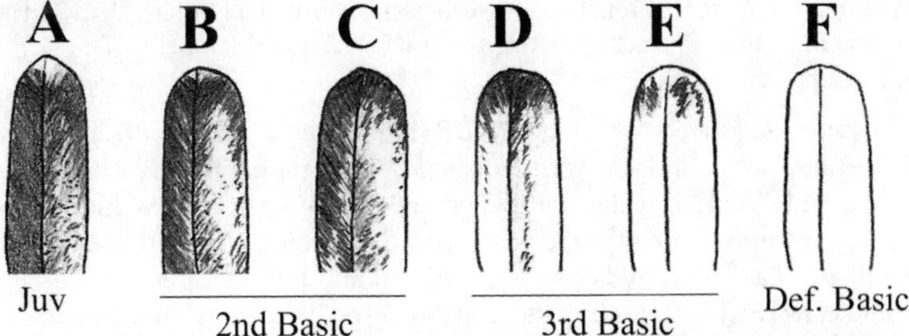

FIGURE 304. Shape and color pattern to the rectrices by feather generation in Bald Eagle. R5 is shown and is usually the last feather replaced during molts and the most likely to be retained during the PB2 and DPB (*cf.* Fig. 288, p. 392). These feathers are frequently retained in this species, such that Juv-HY/SYs exhibit **A** (Fig. 288**A**, p. 392), SY/TYs often exhibit a mixture of older **A** and newer **B-C** (Fig. 288**B**), TY/4Ys exhibit a mixture of older **B-C** and newer **D-E** (Fig. 288**D**), 4-5Ys exhibit a mixture of **D-E** (old) and **F** (new), and A4Y/A5Ys exhibit one or more generations of white feathers (**F**).

2 sets of basic and no juv feathers (Figs. 16**E** & 286**B**), or occasionally with 1-3 juv outer pp (Fig. 286**A**) and 1-5 juv ss (Fig. 305**A**; among s3-s4 and s8-s11) retained (Fig. 16**D**), most to all ss brownish with white mottling to inner webs (Fig. 305**C-D**); iris pale brownish yellow to dull yellowish; bill yellowish gray. **Note: See SY/TY and 4-5Y**.

4-5Y (3rd-5th cycles, B3-B5; Jan-Dec): Head and nape mostly white with brown flecking to crown and auriculars; upper back and abdomen dark brown (Fig. 303**E**), the breast often with some retained feathers with white bases (Fig. 303**D**); axillars and underwing covs brown, often with some whitish flecking; rects white or with sparse brown mottling (Fig. 304**D-E**); pp and ss with 2-3 sets of basic feathers (Figs. 16**E-F**), the ss brown with white mottling (Fig. 305**D**) to entirely brown (Fig. 305**E**); uppertail covs white with brown mottling; iris dull pale yellow; bill yellowish, usually with some grayish to upper mandible. **Note: See TY/4Y. Beware of occasional older individuals with sparse grayish flecking in head; see A4Y/A5Y**.

A4Y/A5Y (Def. cycle, DB; Sep-Aug): Head, nape, uppertail covs, and rects (Fig. 304**E**) entirely white, without brown mottling or flecking; upper back, underparts (Fig. 303**E**), ss (Fig. 305**E**), axillars, and underwing covs brown, without whitish mottling or flecking; pp and ss with 2-4 sets of basic feathers (Fig. 16**F-G**); iris, cere, and bill entirely bright yellow. **Note: A few older individuals can show small amounts of pale brownish to grayish flecking in head (even as A8Y/A9Ys), especially in crown and around eyes; if all other characters are definitive it is best to age these as A4Y/A5Y. Also, individuals in complete definitive plumage possibly can be aged A5Y/A6Y; more study is needed.**

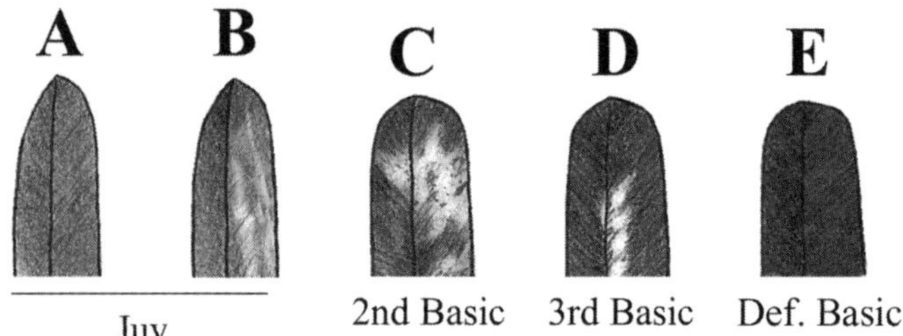

FIGURE 305. Shape and color pattern to the medial secondaries by feather generation in Bald Eagle. S8 is shown and is often one of the last feather replaced during molts and likely to be retained during the PB2 and DPB (*cf.* Fig. 14**B** & **D**, p. 21). These feathers are frequently retained in this species, such that Juv-HY/SYs exhibit **A-B**, SY/TYs exhibit a mixture of **A-B** (old) and **C** (new), TY/4Ys exhibit a mixture of **C** and sometimes **A-B** (old) and **D** (new), 4-5Ys exhibit a mixture of **C-D** (old) and **E** (new), and A4Y/A5Ys exhibit **E**. Note that retained juv feathers are substantially longer than 2nd and 3rd basic feathers, resulting in an uneven trailing edge to the ss in SY/TYs and some TY/4Ys.

Sex— ♀ = ♂ by plumage aspect. A Full medial BP (Fig. 20**A**, p. 31) and/or distended cloaca (Fig. 21, p. 32) indicates A4Y ♀ in Dec-Apr; ♂♂ can develop a partial BP. Measurements (Table 38, p. 419) somewhat helpful for sexing within populations but broadly clinal increases in size with latitude (see **Geographic variation**) obscures overall differences. In addition to the following, see Bortolotti (1984a) for a predictive model, including bill depth at distal end of cere and length of hind claw (Fig. 342, p. 455), that reliably sexed " northern" individuals, Dieter (1973) for sexing Bald Eagles by plasma steroid hormones, and Garcelon et al. (1985) for sexing by karyotyping and laparoscopy. See also Bortolotti (1984b) for sexing of nestlings and fledglings. The following can be used to sex individuals of "northern" populations (those that breed north of 40° N), especially mated pairs. More study needed on these measures in southern breeding populations, where no reliable criteria known. On the winter grounds, ♀♀ can be sexed by the following criteria but not ♂♂.

♀: Wing chord in ASY > 604 mm; bill depth at distal end of cere > 34 mm; hallux length (Fig. 342, p. 455) > 43.2 mm. **Note: Wing chords of H-TYs that have retained the juv p8 are longer and cannot be used for sexing according to the above criteria. Individuals with wing chord 590-604, bill depth 33-34, and hind claw length 41.3-43.2 cannot be reliably sexed.**

♂: Wing chord in ASY < 590 mm; bill depth at distal end of cere < 33 mm; hallux length (Fig. 342) < 41.3 mm. **Note: See ♀.**

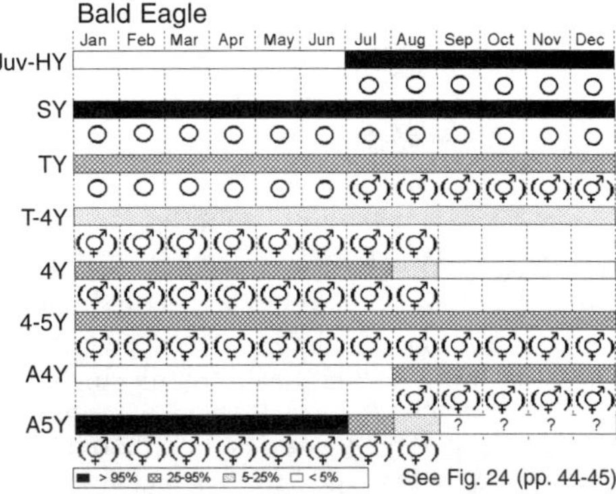

Hybrids Reported—Possibly with Steller's Sea Eagle (Cecile 2005).

References—Bent (1937), Bortolotti (1984a, 1984c), Bortolotti & Honeyman (1983), Buehler (2000), Clark (1983a, 2001a), Cramp & Simmons (1980), Crandall (1941), Dement'ev & Gladkov (1951b), Edelstam (1984), Forsman (1999), Friedmann (1950), Gerrard & Bortolotti (1988), Gerrard et al. (1978), McClelland et al. (1998), McCollough (1989), Mengel (1953), Oberholser (1906b, 1974), R.S. Palmer & J.M. Gerrard *in* Palmer (1988a), Pyle (2005b, 2005c), Roberts (1955), Sherrod et al. (1976), Southern (1964, 1967), Stalmaster (1987).

NORTHERN HARRIER
Circus cyaneus

NOHA
Species # 3310
Band size: 5♀, 4♂ Lock-on

Species—From other N.Am hawks by medium-large size with proportionally long wing and tail (Table 38, p. 419); wings somewhat rounded (usually p7>p8>p6>p9>p5>p10≈p4) and with p7-p10 notched and p6-p9 emarginated (*cf.* Fig. 287, p. 392); plumage aspect variably brownish to pale gray by age/sex class (see **Age/Sex**) but with white uppertail covs contrasting with dark tail and back in all plumage aspects; medial rects (r2-r5) with 3-5 dusky to dark brown bands (Fig. 307, p. 412); bill blackish; cere yellowish; iris brown (Juv) to yellow (ATY); legs and feet bright yellow. See Baker (1993), Cramp & Simmons (1980), Dement'ev & Gladkov (1951b), and Forsman (1999) for separation from other Eurasian harriers including Marsh Harrier, a potential vagrant to N.Am.

Geographic variation—See Cramp & Simmons (1980), Grant (1980, 1983), Oberholser (1919b), K.L. Bildstein *in* Palmer (1988a), Picozzi (1981), Scharf & Hamerstrom (1975), Thorpe (1988), Todd (1963), van Krueningen (1981), Wallace (1971, 1998). One other subspecies in Eurasia (a potential vagrant to N.Am).

C.c. hudsonius (br & wint N.Am): Juv-HY/SY and ♀♀ from *cyaneus* of Eurasia by darker and warmer brown to rufous feathering, less streaking to underwing covs and underparts, and more and more distinct bars to p8 (Fig. 306**A**, *vs* **C** in *cyaneus*) and rects (Fig. 307**A**, *vs* **B** in *cyaneus*); AHY/ASY ♂♂ with more white to bases of p6-p10 (Fig. 306**B**, *vs* **D** in *cyaneus*) and underwing covs and underparts streaked and spotted rufous (*vs* with few or no streaks in *cyaneus*).

Molt—CBS. PF absent-limited (Dec-Apr in HY/SYs), PB2 incomplete-complete (Apr-Nov in non-breeding SYs), DPB incomplete-complete (Jun-Dec in breeding AHYs); PA absent. The PF occurs primarily on non-breeding grounds whereas DPBs occur primarily on breeding grounds. The PF can include up to 50% of the body feathers but is absent in most individuals.

The DPBs can be incomplete in ~15% of individuals, with 1-6 ss (among s3-s4 and s7-s10) and one or more les covs and/or rump feathers retained. Look also for some underwing covs to be retained. Retained feathers appear to be less frequent during the PB2 than during subsequent PBs. Suspension of molt during breeding sometimes occurs among p2-p5 the terts, and rarely s1 and/or s5 (Fig. 289**A**-**B**, p. 393); ♀♀ average more feathers replaced than ♂♂. See Family Account (pp. 391-392) for more information.

Age/Sex—Juv (B1; Jul-May) is described under Juv-HY/SY, below, and can have a tawny wash to uppertail covs (which bleach to white by Sep-Oct). Juv ♀=♂ by plumage aspect although both size (including depth of tarsus) and eye color, as in Juv-HY/SY below, allows reliable sexing of Juvs and most nestlings (Hamerstrom 1968, Saunders & Hansen 1988). Medial BP (Fig. 20**A**, p. 31) and/or distended cloaca (Fig. 21, p. 32) indicates ♀ in Apr-Jul. Measurements reliable for sexing all individuals (Table 38, p. 419).

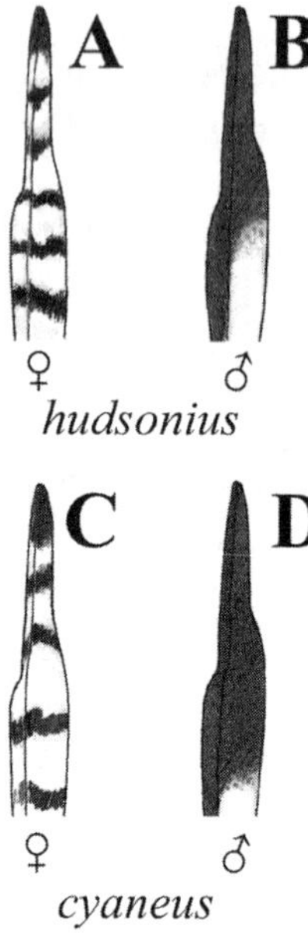

FIGURE 306. Underside of p8 by subspecies and sex in Northern Harrier. In N.Am populations (*C.c. hudsonius*) this feather in ♀♀ usually has 5-6 dusky bands (**A**) and in ♂♂ it has substantial white at the base of the feather (**B**), whereas in European populations (*C.c. cyaneus*) ♀♀ have 4-5 bands (**C**) and ♂♂ have less white at the base (**D**).

Juv-HY/SY ♀ (1st cycle, Juv/B1-F1; Oct-Sep): Wg chord > 361 and depth of tarsus > 6 mm; upperparts brown, including scattered newer feathers sometimes present in May-Sep; pp and ss uniformly juv (Fig. 13**A**, p. 20), the juv outer pp tapered (Fig. 286**A**, p. 392), brownish, and relatively worn, and

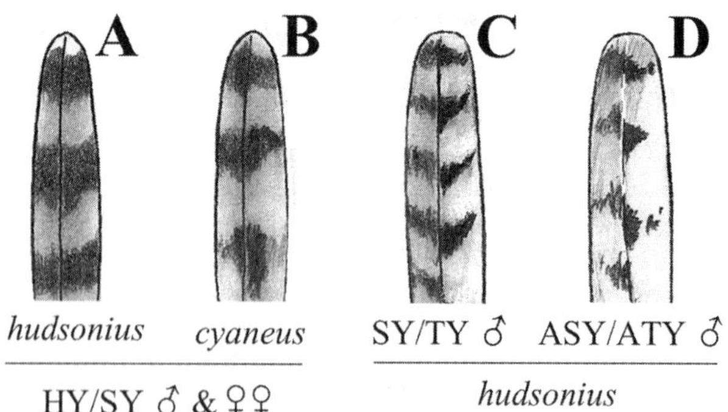

FIGURE 307. Pattern to the rectrices by age, sex, and subspecies in Northern Harrier. R5 is shown and is usually the last feather replaced during molts (*cf.* Fig. 288, p. 392); rectrices are rarely if ever retained during PBs in this species. In N.Am populations (*C.c. hudsonius*), HY/SY ♂♂ and all ages of ♀♀ exhibit a similar pattern (**A**), although shape averages narrower in HY/SYs than in AHY/ASY ♀♀ (*cf.* Fig. 311, p. 417). These age/sex groups in European populations (*cyaneus*) average fewer, less-distinct bars (**B**). Males of *hudsonius* continue to exhibit fewer and less-organized bars to the rects by age (**C**-**D**). This pattern difference by age is similar in *cyaneus*, which in turn averages fewer and less distinct bands than *hudsonius*.

the outer ss with indistinct, slightly paler bars (Fig. 308**A**); p covs dark brown with broad (> 1.5 mm wide) tawny to whitish tips; rects uniformly narrow and rounded (Fig. 288**A**, p. 392), r2-r5 with 3-4 wide and indistinct dark brown bands (Fig. 307**A**); underpart feathers cinnamon-brown to buff (can wear to whitish by spring) with narrow or no streaking (Fig. 309**A**, p. 414); iris dark brown.

AHY/ASY ♀ (Def. cycle, DB; Oct-Sep): Wg chord > 361 and depth of tarsus > 6 mm; upperparts brown or slightly washed grayish; pp and ss basic and with replacement clines and/or s1-p1 contrast (Fig. 14**B**, p. 21), the outer pp broader (Fig. 286**B**) and fresher, and the outer ss grayish brown to brown with distinct paler bars (Fig. 308**B**); p covs grayish brown with narrow (< 1.5 mm wide) or no white tips; rects uniformly broad and truncate (Fig. 288**C**), r2-r5 with 3-4 wide and indistinct dark brown bands (Fig. 307**A**); underpart feathers beige to whitish with distinct, brown, teardrop-shaped spots (Fig. 309**B**); iris yellow with variable amount of brown mottling or flecking. **Note: It is possible that ♀♀ with > 50% yellow in the iris can be reliably aged ASY/ATY but more study is needed. Also, individuals showing suspension limits (Fig. 289, p. 393) are likely ASY/ATYs but more study is needed to confirm this.**

SY/TY ♀ (2nd cycle, B2; Oct-Sep): Like AHY/ASY ♀ but 1-6 juv ss among s3-s4 and s6-s9 occasionally retained, contrastingly narrow, worn, and with distinct bars (Figs. 14**C** & 308**A**); pp usually without suspension limit (*cf.* Fig. 289); one to many juv les covs and/or rump feathers sometimes retained, pale brown, sometimes with distinct pale fringing if not worn off, contrasting markedly with replaced fresher feathers in wear (Fig. 313**A**, p. 418); iris brown with < 50% yellow flecking, to dull yellow with brown flecking. **Note: Retained ss and/or rump feathers appear to occur in only ~15% of AHY/ASYs. See ASY/ATY.**

ASY/ATY ♀ (Def. cycle, DB; Oct-Sep): Like AHY/ASY ♀ but 1-6 basic ss among s2-s4 and s6-s10 sometimes retained, broad, with indistinct bars (Figs. 14**D** & 308**B**); pp often with suspension limit among p2-p5 (*cf.* Fig. 289**A**; rarely among ss as well); one to a few les covs and/or rump feathers sometimes retained, brownish gray without pale fringing, and contrasting only slightly with replaced feathers in wear (Fig. 313**B**); iris yellow with < 50% brown flecking. **Note: See SY/TY. In addition, look for ASY/ATY ♀♀ to have an increasingly gray cast to upperpart feathers (especially p covs) with some ATY/A4Ys perhaps diagnosable (see ASY/ATY ♂).**

Juv-HY/SY ♂ (1st cycle, Juv/B1-F1; Oct-Sep): Wg chord < 361 and depth of tarsus < 6 mm; upperparts brown, sometimes with scattered newer grayish feathers in May-Sep; pp, ss, and rects as in Juv-HY/SY ♀ (Figs. 307**A** & 308**A**); underpart feathers cinnamon-brown to buff (can wear to whitish by spring), often with dark teardrop markings along shaft (Fig. 309**C**); iris

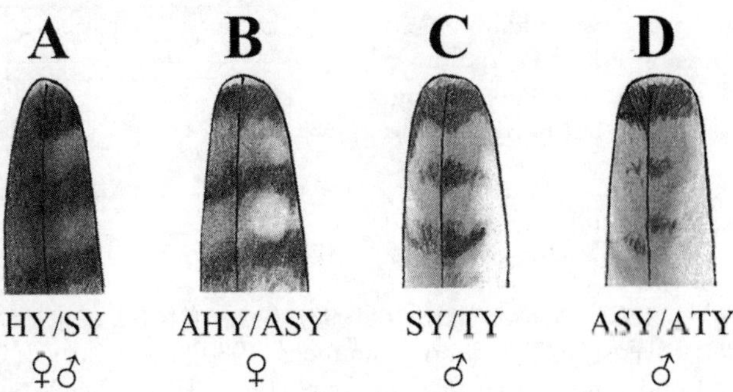

FIGURE 308. Shape and pattern to the outer secondaries (s1-s4) by age and sex in Northern Harrier. S3 and s4 can be retained during PBs and this can help with ageing of SY/TYs, ASY/ATYs, and possibly TY/4Y ♂♂ (more study needed).

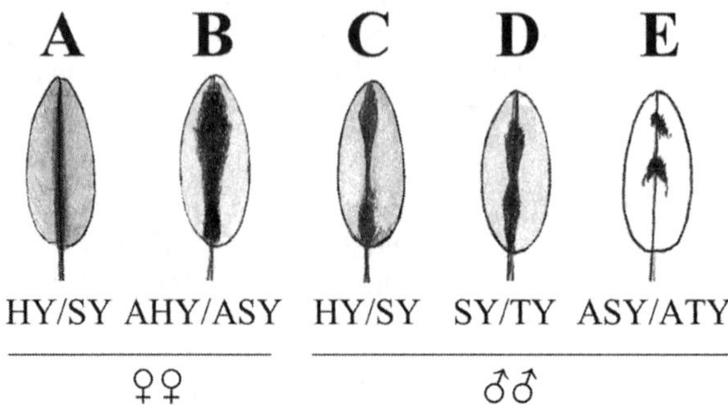

FIGURE 309. Pattern to the underpart feathers by age and sex in Northern Harrier; a breast feather is shown. Note that there can be variation both among individuals and according to location of the feather on the underparts, but generally this pattern is reliable for determining age and sex.

usually pale grayish to brownish, becoming yellowish with some brown flecking by Nov-Mar.

SY/TY ♂ (2nd cycle, B2 Oct-Sep): Wg chord < 361 and depth of tarsus < 6 mm; upperparts dull grayish to grayish brown; auriculars washed rufous; p5-p9 with dark dusky-brown tips, sometimes sparsely mottled pale; ss grayish with 2-3 distinct dusky bands (Fig. 308**C**), sometimes with 1-6 juv ss retained among s3-s4 and s6-s9 (Figs. 14**C** & 308**A**); retention patterns of les covs and rump as in SY/TY ♀ (Fig. 313**A**); rects broad and truncate, r2-r5 with 4-5 distinct dusky bands (Fig. 307**C**); lower underparts and underwing les covs white, spotted or streaked rufous (Fig. 309**D**); iris dull to brightish yellow, sometimes with reduced brown flecking. **Note: Some intermediates between this and ASY/ATY ♂ may best be aged AHY/ASY, S-TY, or T-4Y (more study needed).**

ASY/ATY ♂ (Def. cycle, DB; Oct-Sep): Upperparts gray with little or no brown tinge; auriculars gray with little or no rufous; p5-p9 with uniformly blackish tips; ss gray with indistinct or no dusky bands (Fig. 308**D**), sometimes with 1-6 basic ss retained among s2-s4 and s6-s10 (Figs. 14**C** & 308**C**-**D**); retention patterns of les covs and rump as in ASY/ATY ♀ (Fig. 313**B**); rects with 3-4 indistinct bands (Fig. 307**D**); lower underparts and underwing les covs spotted dusky (Fig. 309**E**), with little or no rufous; iris bright yellow. **Note: ♂♂ with paler gray and white plumage aspect, no hints of brown in nape or breast, and bright yellow irises are reliably aged ASY/ATY and possibly ATY/A4Y, and those with retained ss (Fig. 14D) as in Fig. 308C could be TY/4Ys, but more study is needed.**

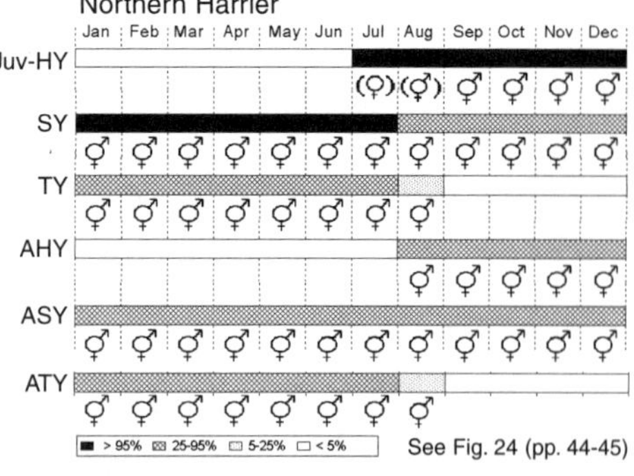

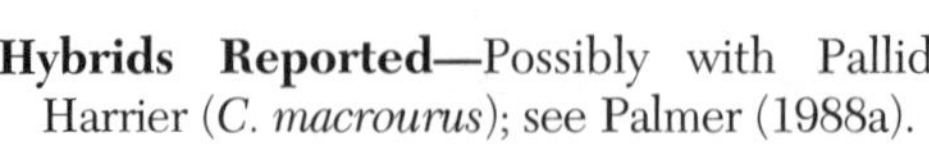

Hybrids Reported—Possibly with Pallid Harrier (*C. macrourus*); see Palmer (1988a).

References—Amadon (1961), Arroyo & King (1996), Baker (1993), Bent (1937), Bildstein & Hamerstrom (1980), Blake (1977), Cramp & Simmons (1980), Dement'ev & Gladkov (1951b), Forsman (1999), Friedmann (1950), Hamerstrom (1968, 1986), MacWhirter & Bildstein (1996), Oberholser (1974), R.S. Palmer & K.L. Bildstein *in* Palmer (1988a), Picozzi (1981), Pyle (2005b, 2005c), Roberts (1955), Schmutz & Schmutz (1975), Simmons (2000), Simmons et al. (1986), Temeles (1986).

SHARP-SHINNED HAWK
Accipiter striatus

SSHA
Species # 3320
Band size: 3A-3B♀, 2-3♂ Lock-on

COOPER'S HAWK
Accipiter cooperii

COHA
Species # 3330
Band size: 5-6♀, 4♂ Lock-on

Species—From other N.Am hawks by small to medium-small size and proportionally long tail and tarsus (Table 38, p. 419); wings rounded (usually p6>p7>p5≈p8>p9>p4>p3>p2>p10≈p1 in Sharp-shinned Hawk (Fig. 4, p. 7) and p7≈p6>p8>p5>p9>p4>p3>p2>p10≈p1 in Cooper's Hawk) and with p6-p10 notched and p5-p9 emarginated (*cf.* Fig. 287, p. 392); medial rects (r2-r5) with 4-6 even and dusky bands (Fig. 311, p. 417); bill grayish; cere yellowish; iris brownish yellow (Juv) to red (ATY); legs and feet bright yellow. Juv-HY/SY Cooper's Hawk from Juv-HY/SY Northern Goshawk (p. 420) by smaller size (Table 38); narrowest tarsus depth 5.3-7.0 mm; bands of medial rects even and without narrow pale borders (Fig. 311; *cf.* Fig. 315, p. 421); upperparts with little or no whitish mottling. Sharp-shinned Hawk from Merlin by bill without tooth and back feathers and terts rounded (Fig. 285**A**, p. 391); tarsus longer (Table 38); wing rounded (p6-p7 longest, >p8); underwing covs paler than underside of pp and ss; iris pale grayish to yellowish.

Sharp-shinned from Cooper's hawk by smaller size (Table 38; slight overlap in wing chord occurs only between ♀♀ Sharp-shinned and ♂♂ Cooper's in w.N.Am); narrowest tarsus depth 4.1-4.9 mm (*vs* 5.3-7.0 in Cooper's Hawk); p8<p5 (*vs* p8 > p5 in Cooper's Hawk; see above); tail squared (r1-r6 2-12 mm) *vs* rounded (r1-r6 20-30 mm) in Cooper's Hawk (beware of molting rects); white tip to rects 1-4 mm wide *vs* 4-10 mm in Cooper's Hawk (Fig. 311); Juv-HY/SYs often with hourglass-shaped streaks or spots to underparts (Fig. 310**B**, p. 416) *vs* narrow or teardrop shaped streaks (Fig. 310**A**) in Cooper's Hawk; AHY/ASYs with crown not contrasting distinctly with back (*vs* duskier or blacker than back in Cooper's Hawk).

Eurasian Sparrowhawk (*A. nisus*), a potential vagrant, is intermediate betwen Sharp-shinned and Cooper's hawks in size (wg chord ♀ 232-250, ♂ 195-212; tl 142-186; cere from culmen 10.6-15.5; tarsus 51-63); wing more pointed (p8 > p5 and longest p–p10 75-95 *vs* 55-75 in Sharp-shinned Hawk and 65-85 in Cooper's Hawk); tail somewhat squared (r1-r6 7-15 mm); upperparts average grayer by age; underpart and underwing covs barred in both Juv-HY/SYs and AHY/ASYs (*cf.* Fig. 310**E**); AHY/ASY ♀ with underpart barring brownish (*vs* rufous in Cooper's and N.Am subspecies of Sharp-shinned Hawks).

Geographic variation—Cooper's Hawk considered monotypic. Populations of w.N.Am ("*A.c. mexicanus*") average smaller (Smith et al. 1990), may have heavier streaking to the underparts of HY/SYs, and develop redder irises more rapidly by age and sex, but differences appear to be broadly clinal and insufficient for subspecific recognition (see also Hellmayr & Conover 1949; Henny et al. 1985; Mueller et al. 1981; Palmer 1988a; Patten et al. 2003; Rosenfeld et al. 2003; Smith et al. 1990; Swann 1922a; van Rossem 1931, 1945; Whaley & White 1994).

For Sharp-shinned Hawk, see Bildstein & Meyer (2000), Blake (1977), Clark & Wheeler (1998), Dickerman (2004c), Friedmann (1950), Hellmayr & Conover (1949), Monson & Phillips (1981), Palmer (1988a), Patten & Wilson (1996), Pearlstine & Thompson (2004), Phillips et al. (1964), Snyder (1938), Storer (1952a), Sutton & Burleigh (1941), Todd (1963), van Rossem (1939b), Wattel (1973), Webster (1988), and Wetmore (1914). See also Smith et al. (1990) for slight geographic variation in size among N.Am populations (*A.s. velox*). Nine to 11 other subspecies (depending on species taxonomy) occur in the W.Indes and Mex-S.Am.

Sharp-shinned Hawk

A.s. perobscurus (br Queen Charlotte Is and coastal sw.AK-w.BC, possibly wint to CA-NM): Upperparts dark brownish sooty (Juv) to slaty with sooty barring (AHY/ASY); Juv-HY/SY with underparts primarily dark brown (tinged rufous) with heavier markings (Fig. 310**C**); AHY/ASY with underparts dark brownish rufous with indistinct whitish bars and elongated femoral and leg feathers dark rufous with little or no whitish barring; iris yellowish to red.

A.s. *velox* (br & wint throughout most of N.Am range): Upperparts medium brown (Juv) to bluish (AHY/ASY); Juv-HY/SY with underparts primarily whitish with indistinct narrow dark brown to rufous streaks (Fig. 310**A-B**); AHY/ASYs with underparts rufous and white and elongated femoral and leg feathers pale rufous, usually barred white; iris yellowish to red. Populations of w.N.Am ("*pacificus*") may average more rufous to underparts in AHY/ASYs but difference, if present, is insufficient. Populations of Cuba (*fringilloides*), possible vagrants to s.FL, average paler upperparts and underparts, and have rufous tinge to forehead and brown barring to lower underparts in AHY/ASYs. Populations of Puerto Rico (*venator*) average darker, have more distinct black and white tail banding, and have AHY/ASYs with leg feathers uniformly washed pale rufous.

A.s. *suttoni* (br & wint se.AZ-sw.NM, possibly to sw.TX): Averages slightly larger than *velox* (wg chord 170-229, tl 131-177); HY/SY with distinct brownish streaking to breast (*cf.* Fig. 310**C**); AHY/ASY with sparse rufous barring to underparts; elongated femoral and leg feathers uniformly cream (HY/SY) to rufous (AHY/ASY); iris yellowish brown to reddish brown.

Molt—CBS. PF absent-limited (Dec-Apr in HY/SYs), PB2 incomplete-complete (Apr-Aug in non-breeding SYs), DPB incomplete-complete (May-Oct in breeding AHYs); PA absent. The PF occurs primarily on non-breeding grounds whereas DPBs occur primarily on breeding grounds (but may complete during migration or on non-breeding grounds in some individuals). The PF can include up to 45% (Sharp-shinned Hawk) or 10% (Cooper's Hawk) of the body feathers but is absent in most individuals. The DPBs can be incomplete in ~30-40% of individuals, scattered wing covs and rump feathers, 1-6 ss (usually among s3-s4 and s7-s10), and (rarely) 1-2 rects (among r2-r5) retained. Retention of ss (but not rump feathers) is less frequent during the PB2 than during DPBs. Suspension of molt among p2-p6 the terts, and sometimes s1 and/or ss during breeding often occurs (Fig. 289**A-B**, p. 393; ♀♀ average more feathers replaced than ♂♂). See Family Account (pp. 391-392) for more information.

Age—Juv (B1; Jul-May) is described under Juv-HY/SY (below) and has grayish to grayish-yellow iris. Juv ♀=♂ by plumage aspect but size (see **Sex**) can be used to reliably sex full-grown juvs. When using the following, note that iris color can show substantial variation with season and with individual over time, so should be used with caution.

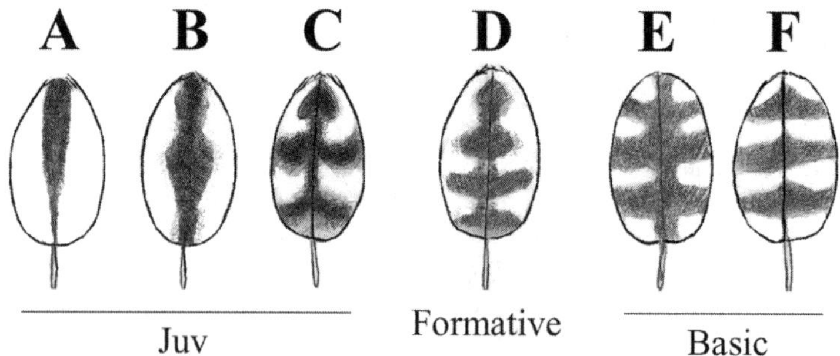

FIGURE 310. Pattern to the underpart feathers by species, subspecies, and feather generation in Sharp-shinned and Cooper's Hawks; a typical breast feather is shown. Note that there can be substantial variation both among individuals and according to location of the feather on the underparts. Most Juv-HY/SY Cooper's Hawks have juv feathers resembling **A** and sometimes scattered formative feathers resembling **D** in Jan-Oct, and AHY/ASYs have basic feathers resembling **F**, so age determination is straightforward. Underpart feathers of Sharp-shinned Hawks are more variable, juv feathers (in Juv-HY/SYs) varying from **A** to **C** (the last typical of *A.s. perobscurus* and to a lesser extent *suttoni*), sometimes scattered formative feathers resembling **D** in Jan-Oct, and basic feathers (in AHY/ASYs) resembling **E-F**. Beware some well-marked Juv-HY/SY Sharp-shinned Hawks can resemble less well-marked AHY/ASYs in underpart pattern.

Juv-HY/SY (1st cycle, Juv/B1-F1; Nov-Oct): Upperparts mostly to entirely brown, the feathers with distinct rufous to buff fringing when fresh, sometimes with scattered bluish feathers in Feb-Oct; underparts and underwing covs with brownish or rufous streaks (Fig. 310**A**-**C**), sometimes with scattered semi-barred feathers (Fig. 310**D**) in Jan-Oct; rects unformly narrow and rounded (Fig. 288**A**, p. 392), r2-r5 with 4-6 distinct and narrow dark brown bands by species (Fig. 311**A**-**B**); les covs and rump feathers with distinct white spots (Fig. 312**A**-**B**, p. 418); iris yellow to orangish yellow. **Note: Some HY/SYs (especially Sharp-shinned Hawk) can have underpart patterns approaching those of AHY/ASYs (see Fig. 310).**

AHY/ASY (Def. cycle, DB; Nov-Oct): Upperparts uniformly grayish (♀) to slaty blue (♂), the feathers without pale fringing; underparts and underwing covs reddish, generally patterned in bars (Fig. 310**E**-**F**); rects uniformly broad and truncate (Fig. 288**C**), r2-r5 usually with 3-4 indistinct and broad dusky bands (Fig. 311**C**-**D**); les covs and rump feathers with indistinct or no white spots (Fig. 312**C**-**D**) and without retained feathers (Fig. 313**B**); ss uniformly basic (Fig. 14**B**, p. 21; *cf.* Fig. 322**B**, p. 431); iris orangish to reddish (♂♂ average redder than ♀♀). **Note: See HY/SY. AHY/ASYs not retaining ss or rump feathers can often be aged more precisely by iris color, as in SY/TY or ASY/ATY (see below).**

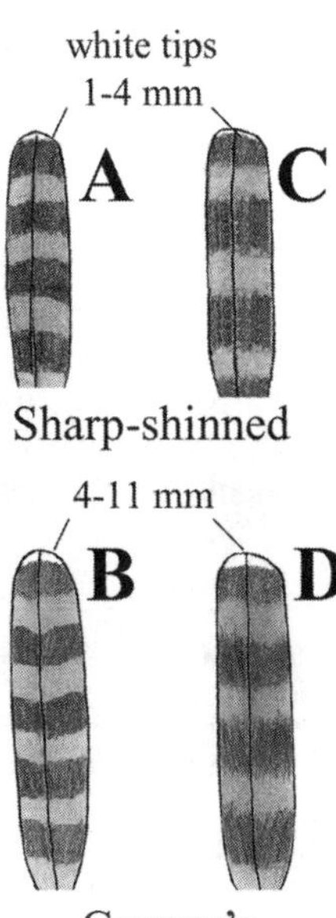

FIGURE 311. Shape and pattern (including number of bars) on the rectrices by species and age in Sharp-shinned and Cooper's hawks. R5 is shown and is usually the last feather replaced during molts and the most likely to be retained during the PB2 and DPB (*cf.* Fig. 288, p. 392). Note that the number of dusky bars is generally greater in Cooper's Hawk than in Sharp-shinned Hawk by age, and greater in HY/SYs than AHY/ASYs by species (see **Age**). Note also the difference in the distinctness of the bars (more distinct in HY/SYs than in AHY/ASYs), a feature also found among medial ss of these species (*cf.* Fig. 322, p. 431).

SY/TY (2nd cycle, B2; Nov-Oct): Like AHY/ASY but one to many les covs and/or rump feathers sometimes retained, brown, with distinct white spots (Fig. 312**B**) and/or cinnamon fringing, and contrastingly worn (Fig. 313**A**); 1-2 juv rects occasionally retained (Figs.288**B** & 311**A**-**B**). 1-6 juv ss among s3-s4 and s6-s9 occasionally retained, contrastingly narrow and worn (Figs. 14**C** & 322**A**), and with distinct bars; pp usually without suspension limits among p2-p6 (*cf.* Fig. 289, p. 393); iris yellowish orange to pale reddish by sex and species. **Note: Among SY/TYs, iris color often is yellowish in ♀ Cooper's Hawks, yellowish orange in ♀ Sharp-shinned and ♂ Cooper's hawks, and pale orangish to reddish in ♂ Sharp-shinned Hawks.**

ASY/ATY (Def. cycle, DB; Nov-Oct): Like AHY/ASY but one to a few les covs and/or rump feathers sometimes retained, gray without distinct white spots (Fig. 312**C**-**D**) or pale fringing, and only slightly worn (Fig. 313**C**); 1-4 basic rects occasionally retained (Figs. 288**D** & 311**C**-**D**), 1-6 basic ss among s2-s4 and s6-s10 sometimes retained (Figs. 14**D** & 322**B**), pp often with suspension limits among p2-p6 and sometimes the ss (Fig. 289**A**-**B**); iris yellow-orange to dark red (♂♂ average redder than ♀♀). **Note: Among ASY/ATYs, iris color often is reddish orange in ♀ Cooper's Hawks, orangish red in ♀ Sharp-shinned and ♂ Cooper's hawks, and dark reddish in ♂ Sharp-shinned Hawks (see also Sex). Individuals**

in definitive plumage aspect and deep red irises can possibly be aged ATY/A4Y or older; more study is needed.

Sex—Medial BP (Fig. 20**A**, p. 31) and/or distended cloaca (Fig. 21, p. 32) indicates ♀ in Apr-Jul. Measurements reliable for sexing all age classes of both species (Table 38); Cooper's Hawks exhibit sufficient geographic variation such that sexing is best accomplished regionally, in w.populations *vs* e.populations, essentially as divided by longitude 100° W. See also **Age** for sex-related differences in back and iris color.

Sharp-shinned Hawk

♀: Wg chord > 183; tl > 143; AHY/ASYs with back and terts grayish (occasionally tinged bluish) and iris usually yellowish-orange to pale red by age.

♂: Wg chord < 183; tl < 143; AHY/ASYs with back and terts bluish and iris usually orange to dark red by age.

Cooper's Hawk

♀: Wg chord > 239 (w.populations) or > 253 (e.populations); tl > 200 (w.populations) or > 205 (e.populations); AHY/ASYs with back and terts grayish (sometimes washed brownish) and iris usually yellowish to reddish orange with age (occasionally dark red; A5Ys?).

♂: Wg chord < 239 (w.populations) or < 253 (e.populations); tl < 200 (w.populations) or < 205 (e.populations); AHY/ASYs with back and terts bluish and iris usually reddish orange to dark red by age.

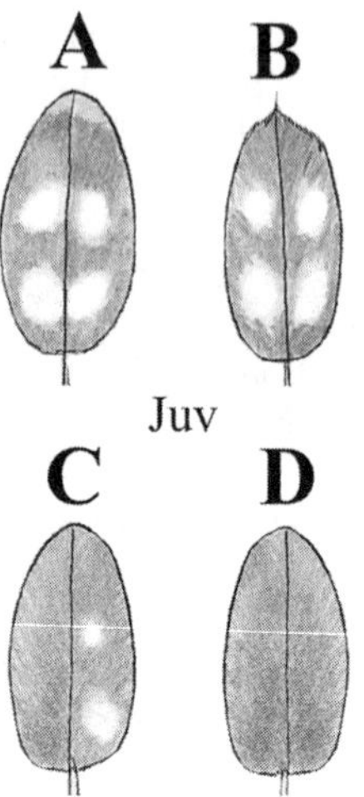

FIGURE 312. Pattern to the les covs and central rump feathers by feather generation in Sharp-shinned and Coopers hawks. On the rump, the size and shape of the white spots varies by feather position, becoming more extensive and squarer in the larger distal feathers in both feather-generation groups. See Figure 313 for approximate position of rump feathers indicated above. SY/TYs can retain worn rump feathers resembling **B**. Those resembling **C** may indicate formative feathers or perhaps some 2nd basic feathers in SY/TYs; more study needed. In Northern Goshawk a few juv feathers can show indistinct buff spots.

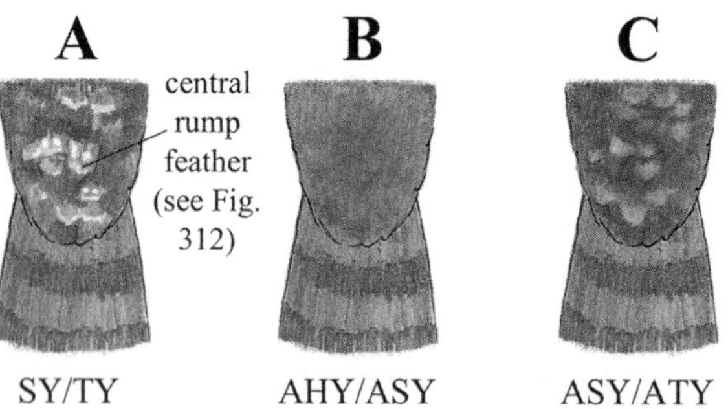

FIGURE 313. Rump and uppertail covs exhibiting retained feathers by age in AHY/ASY hawks. In *Accipiter*, juv feathers have distinct white spots whereas basic feathers usually lack spots (Fig. 312), which can assist in separating SY/TYs (**A**) and ASY/ATYs (**C**). Other species that exhibit this character lack white spots in juv feathers and age groups must be separated by the extent of wear, coloration, and in some species pale tips of retained feathers. Each species exhibits a different proportion of individuals that typically retain feathers during the PB2 and DPB molts (see **Molt** accounts); individuals not retaining rump feathers (**B**) must be aged AHY/ASY based on this criterion alone.

Hybrids Reported—Powers (1905) reported a hybrid between Broad-winged Hawk and either Cooper's or Sharp-shinned Hawk. An old report of a Cooper's Hawk X Northern Goshawk (McCarthy 2006) has been questioned (Palmer 1988a).

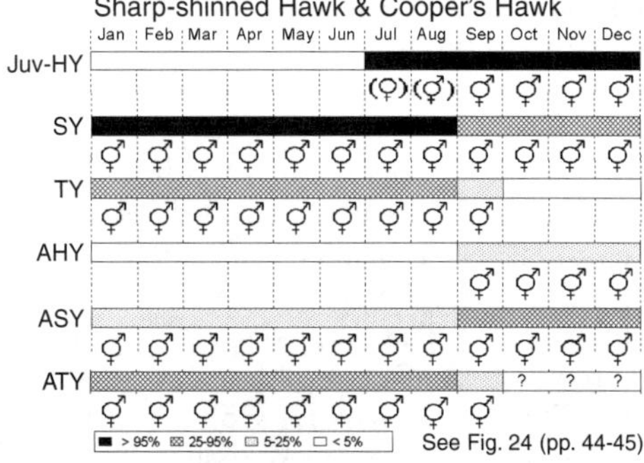

References—Baker (1993), Bent (1937), Cramp & Simmons (1980), Dement'ev & Gladkov (1951b), Forsman (1999), Friedmann (1950), Henny et al. (1985), Hoffman et al. (1990), Kaufman (1990a), Miller (1941), Mueller et al. (1979a, 1979b, 1981, 2004), Newton & Marquiss (1982), Oberholser (1974), Palmer (1988a), Pearlstine & Thompson (2004), Pyle (2005b, 2005c), J.O.L. Roberts (1967), T.S. Roberts (1955), Robertson (1970), Rosenfield & Bielefeldt (1993, 1997), Rosenfield & Wilde (1981), Rosenfield et al. (1992, 2003), Sheppard & Klimkiewicz (1976), Storer (1955, 1966), Smith et al. (1990), Snyder & Snyder (1974), Wattel (1973), Wood (1969).

TABLE 38. Measurements (mm) of North American eagles, harriers, and *Accipiters* to assist in identification, sexing, and ageing (Bald Eagle). See pp. 4-11 for methods of measurement. Species summaries are in **bold**. Values were derived from 95% confidence intervals as based approximately on the indicated sample sizes (see pp. 4-5); thus midpoints of ranges approximate means, and S.D. is approximated by 25% of the range.

Taxon/Sex	*n*	wing chord	tail length	culmen from cere[1]	tarsus
Bald Eagle (adult)[2]		**509-652**	**228-331**	**43.9-60.4**	**90-109**
♀	84	551-652	257-331	46.8-60.4	96-109
♂	89	509-594	228-301	43.9-55.5	90-104
Bald Eagle (Juv)[2]		**533-678**	**259-392**	—	—
♀	100	586-678	287-392	—	—
♂	100	533-629	259-363	—	—
Northern Harrier[3]		**322-400**	**195-254**	**14.9-20.5**	**68-86**
♀	90	362-400	223-254	17.6-20.5	75-86
♂	70	322-360	195-229	14.9-17.7	68-78
Sharp-shinned Hawk[3]		**160-214**	**124-165**	**9.0-13.6**	**47-61**
♀	100	188-210	148-165	10.9-13.6	52-61
♂	100	160-180	124-142	8.8-11.0	47-54
Cooper's Hawk[4]		**215-283**	**197-235**	**13.8-19.0**	**58-75**
♀	100	244-283	197-235	16.1-19.0	65-75
♂	100	215-248	171-205	13.8-16.5	58-68
Northern Goshawk[3]		**302-387**	**207-288[5]**	**19.6-26.0**	**69-87**
♀	100	336-387	242-288[5]	21.9-26.0	74-87
♂	100	302-346	207-250[5]	19.6-22.1	69-81
Golden Eagle[3]		**551-680**	**316-389**	**37.1-47.3**	**102-125**
♀	70	595-680	337-389	40.9-47.3	105-125
♂	60	551-631	316-364	37.1-43.0	102-122

[1] Culmen from cere represents the chord (Fig. 7**B**, see p. 9).
[2] In Bald Eagle, wing chord and tail differ substantially by age; "Juv" represents those indivduals with the juvenal longest primary (p8) or rectrix (r1) retained, which varies by age in this species. See **Molt** and **Age** for more information. Measures for Bald Eagle also vary substantually and clinally by latitude (see **Geographic variation** and **Sex**).
[3] Measures represent N.Am populations only (see **Geographic variation**).
[4] Cooper's Hawks of w.N.Am are smaller than those of e.N.Am (see **Geographic variation**).
[5] Tail lengths of AHY/ASYs only; those of Juv-HY/SYs are longer, being 250-299 in ♀♀ and 217-260 in ♀♀.

NORTHERN GOSHAWK NOGO
Accipiter gentilis Species # 3340
Band size: 7A-7B♀, 6♂ Lock-on

Species—From other N.Am hawks by medium-large size with proportionally long tail and tarsus (Table 38, p. 419); wings rounded (usually p7>p8≈p6>p5>p9>p4>p3>p2>p10≈p1) and with p6-p10 notched and p5-p9 emarginated (*cf.* Fig. 287, p. 392); underside of pp and ss with wide (> 4 mm wide) distinct dusky bands; underparts streaked, without spots (Fig. 314); medial rects (r2-r5) with 4-6 uneven and moderately distinct to indistinct dusky bands (Fig. 315); bill grayish; cere yellowish; iris brownish yellow (Juv) to red (ATY); legs and feet bright yellow. From Juv-HY/SY Cooper's Hawk (p. 415) by larger size (Table 38); narrowest tarsus depth 7.5-10.3 mm; bands of medial rects uneven with narrow pale borders proximally (Fig. 315**A**); upperparts mottled white (due to exposed pale feather bases). Juv-HY/SY from dark-morph Gyrfalcon by longer tarsus (Table 38); p9 < p7 and p10 < p5; bill without tooth and back feathers and terts rounded (Fig. 285**A**-**B**, p. 391); rects with 4-6 dark bands (Fig. 315); throat heavily streaked; iris pale.

Geographic variation—See Bond & Stabler (1941), Cramp & Simmons (1980), Dement'ev & Gladkov (1951b), Friedmann (1950), Hellmayr & Conover (1949), Hubbard (1972), Johnson (1989), Monson & Phillips (1981), Munro & Cowan (1947), Oberholser (1918b, 1974), Palmer (1988a), Phillips et al. (1964), Swarth (1926), Taverner (1940), Todd (1963), van Rossem (1936, 1938b), Wattel (1973), Whaley & White (1994). Six other subspecies occur in Eurasia.

A.g. atricapillus (br & wint throughout most of N.Am range): AHY/ASYs with cap blackish, contrasting with grayish (♀) to bluish (♂) back, and underparts whitish with fine dusky vermiculations (Fig. 314**C**-**D**); Juv-HY/SY with underparts cream with sparse and distinct brown streaks and spots (Fig. 314**A**-**B**). Populations of w.N.Am ("*striatulus*") may average more finely barred than populations of e.N.Am, populations of coastal BC Is ("*laingi*") may average darker and with more streaks to back, and populations of se.AZ-wc.Mex ("*apache*") may average longer-winged, darker, and with sparser markings to underparts but, in all cases, differences are insufficient and confounded by age-related and individual variation. The Eurasian (*A.g. gentilis*) Subspecies Group (possible vagrant to Canada; see Taverner 1940, Todd 1963) has AHY/ASYs with cap brownish gray (♀) to dusky (♂), uniform in aspect or only slightly darker than back, and underparts white with distinct streaks or bars (Fig. 314**D**-**E**).

Molt—CBS. PF absent-limited (Dec-Apr in HY/SYs), PB2 incomplete-complete (Apr-Sep in non-breeding SYs), DPB incomplete-complete (May-Nov in breeding ASYs); PA absent. DPBs occur primarily on breeding grounds. The PF is usually absent but can include up to 10% of the body feathers. The DPBs occasionally may be complete but are usually incomplete, scattered wing covs and body feathers, 1-6 ss among s3-s4 and s7-s10, and 1-8 rects among r2-r5 retained.

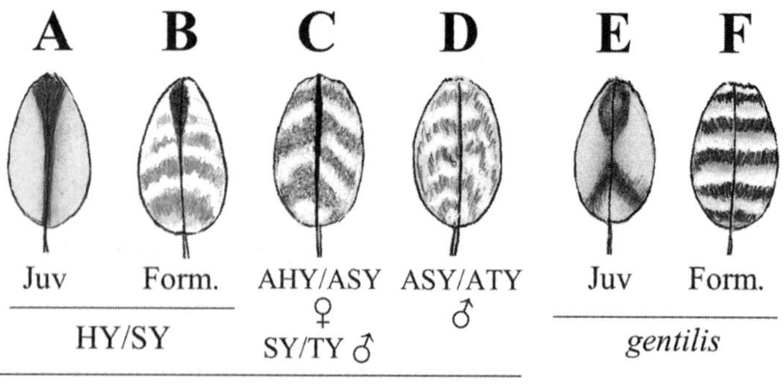

FIGURE 314. Pattern to breast feathers by subspecies, feather generation, and age in Northern Goshawk. Note the broader blackish shaft streaks found in some breast feathers of AHY/ASY ♀♀ and SY/TY ♂♂ (**C**) than are found in ASY/ATY ♂♂ (**D**).

Occasional individuals may also retain the juv outer p9-p10 during the PB2, leading to staffelmauser patterns (Fig. 16, pp. 23-24) among pp of AHYs. It is possible that complete replacement of ss and body-feathers occurs only in non-breeding individuals including many SYs and perhaps some TYs. Suspension of molt among p2-p4 during breeding sometimes occurs (Fig. 289**A**, p. 393; more often in ♀♀ than ♂♂). See Family Account (pp. 391-392) for more information.

Age—Juv (B1; Jul-May) is described under Juv-HY/SY (below) and has grayish to grayish-yellow iris. Juv ♀=♂ by plumage aspect but size (see **Sex**) is reliable for sexing full-grown juvs.

Juv-HY/SY (1st cycle, Juv/B1-F1; Nov-Oct): Forehead and upperparts primarily brown with white streaks and marks; rects uniformly narrow and rounded (Fig. 288**A**, p. 392), r2-r5 brown with 5-6 distinct dusky-brown bands (Fig. 315**A**); les covs and rump feathers often with indistinct buff spots (*cf.* Fig. 312**B-C**, p. 418); underparts and underwing covs buff with brown streaking and spotting (Fig. 314**A**), occasionally with scattered indistinctly vermiculated feathers in Feb-Oct (Fig. 314**B**); iris yellow to orangish yellow.

AHY/ASY (Def. cycle, DB; Nov-Oct): Forehead uniformly dusky or with sparse whitish streaks; upperparts bluish to grayish blue; rects uniformly broad and truncate (Fig. 288**C**), r2-r5 grayish with 4-5 indistinct dusky bands (Fig. 315**B**); les covs and rump feathers without spots (Fig. 312**D**) or retained feathers (Fig. 313**B**, p. 418); underparts and underwing covs whitish with dusky vermiculation (Fig. 314**C-D**); pp and ss uniformly basic (Fig. 14**B**, p. 21); iris yellowish orange to pale orange. **Note: Individuals with uniformly replaced pp, ss, and rects may be rare and could often be SY/TYs; check iris color.**

SY/TY (2nd cycle, B2; Nov-Oct): Like AHY/ASY but forehead with substantial white streaking; upperparts washed brownish by sex (see **Sex**); one to many les covs and/or rump feathers often retained and contrastingly worn (Fig. 313**A**), brown, or with indistinct buff spots (Fig. 312**B-C**) and/or cinnamon fringing; 1-6 juv ss among s3-s4 and s6-s9 often retained, contrastingly narrow, worn, and brown (Fig. 14**C**); pp without suspension limit (Fig. 289, p. 393); 1-8 juv rects occasionally retained, narrower, contrasting markedly in wear, and more distinctly barred (Figs. 288**B** & 315**A**); ♂♂ with darker vermiculation and wider streaks on breast (Fig. 314**C**); iris yellowish orange to pale orange. **Note: See AHY/ASY.**

ASY/ATY (Def. cycle, DB; Oct-Sep): Like AHY/ASY but forehead uniformly dusky, without white streaks; upperparts with little or no brownish (see **Sex**); one to a few les covs and/or rump feathers often retained, slightly worn (Fig. 313**C**), and gray without distinct white spots (Fig. 312**C-D**) or pale fringing; 1-6 basic ss among s2-s4 and s6-s10 often retained, broad and slightly worn (Fig. 14**D**); suspension limit among p2-p4 sometimes occurs (Fig. 289**A**); 1-6 basic rects (among r2-r5) often retained, broad, contrasting moderately in wear, and indistinctly barred (Figs. 288**D** & 315**B**); ♂♂

FIGURE 315. Shape and pattern to the rectrices by feather generation in Northern Goshawks. R5 is shown and is usually the last feather replaced during molts and the most likely to be retained during the PB2 and DPB (*cf.* Fig. 288, p. 392). These feathers are frequently retained in this species, such that Juv-HY/SYs exhibit **A**, SY/TYs can exhibit a mixture of **A** (old) and **B** (new), AHY/ASYs exhibit feathers like **B** uniform in wear, and ASY/ATYs can exhibit a mixture of old and new feathers resembling **B**. Note also the pale narrow borders proximal to the darker bands on juv rects (**A**), usually not (or indistinctly) found in Cooper's Hawk (Fig. 311**B**, p. 417).

with paler vermiculation and narrower streaks on breast (Fig. 314**D**); iris pale orange to orange-red. **Note: See Rust & Kechele (1996) for reported identification of older age classes in Europe by bar patterns among pp; more study is needed on the reliability of this method in N.Am populations.**

Sex—Medial BP (Fig. 20**A**, p. 31) and/or distended cloaca (Fig. 21, p. 32) indicates ♀ in Apr-Jun. Measurements reliable for sexing most individuals (Table 38, p. 419). The following applies to N.Am populations.

♀: Wg chord > 340 and tail > 260 (Juv-HY/SYs) or wg chord > 346 and tail > 250 (AHY/ASYs); culmen from cere > 21.9; AHY/ASYs with upperparts grayer, breast-feather streaking wide (Fig. 314**C**, p. 420), and iris with paler orange tinge by age.

♂: Wg chord < 336 and tail < 250 (Juv-HY/SYs) or wg chord < 342 and tail < 242 (AHY/ASYs); culmen from cere < 22.1; AHY/ASYs with upperparts bluer, breast-feather streaking wide to narrow by age (Fig. 314**C**-**D**), and iris with deeper red tinge by age.

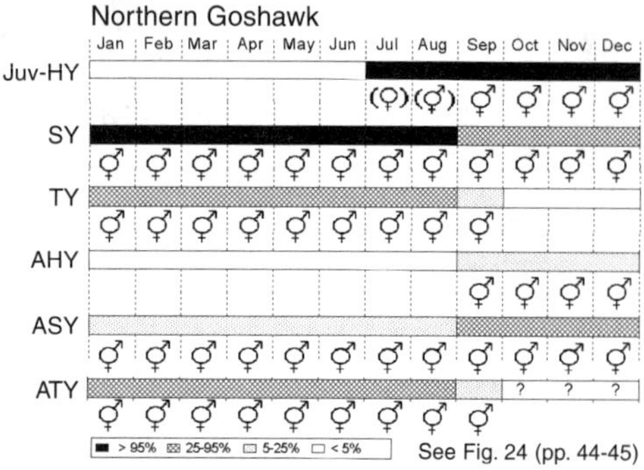

Hybrids Reported—See Cooper's Hawk (p. 415). Otherwise, none in wild.

References—Bährmann (1974) Baker (1993), Bent (1937), Bond & Stabler (1941), Brooks (1927), Cramp & Simmons (1980), Dement'ev & Gladkov (1951b), Forsman (1999), Friedmann (1950), Henny et al. (1985), Hoffman et al. (1990), Kaufman (1990a), McGowan (1975), Mueller & Berger (1968), Mueller et al. (1976), Oberholser (1974), Palmer (1988a), Pyle (2005b, 2005c), Reading (1990), Roberts (1955), Robertson (1970), Rust & Kechele (1996), Smith et al. (1990), Snyder & Snyder (1974), Squires & Reynolds (1997), Storer (1955, 1966), Swarth (1926), Todd (1963), Wattel (1973).

COMMON BLACK-HAWK

Buteogallus antracinus

COBH
Species # 3450
Band size: 7A-6 Lock-on

Species—From other N.Am hawks, including dark-morph *Buteo* hawks, by medium size with proportionally large bill and long tarsus (Table 40, p. 443); wings rounded (usually p8≈p7≈p6>p5>p9>p4>p10≈p3) and with p6-p10 notched (p6 slight) and p5-p9 emarginated (p5 slight; *cf.* Fig. 287, p. 392); ss washed (Juv-HY/SY) to tinged (ASY/ATY) rufous (*cf.* Fig. 317, p. 424); AHY/ASY with whitish bases to undersides of pp extending 0-40 mm > p covs; rects whitish with 6-8 distinct dark bands in Juv-HY/SYs, to black with a single distinct white band in AHY/ASYs (Fig. 316); facial skin and cere yellow; iris dark; bill dusky with yellowish at base; tarsus without dense feathering to toes (Fig. 334**A**, p. 448); crown of Juv-HY/SY with cream streaking.

Great Black-Hawk (*B. urubitinga*), a possible vagrant to sw.N.Am, averages larger with much longer tarsus (wg chord 363-415, tl 221-258, culmen from cere 29-36, tarsus 114-128); wing tip shorter (longest s to longest p < 80 mm *vs* > 80 mm in Common Black-Hawk); r2-r5 grayish with 10-14 dusky bands (Juv-HY/SY) or with extra white band at base (AHY/ASYs); bill uniformly dark (*vs* pale yellowish at base in Common Black-Hawk); loral skin grayish; uppertail covs of ASY/ATY with broader white barring and tips (10-25 mm *vs.* 3-6 mm in Common Black-Hawk); Juv-HY/SY and SY/TY without or with indistinct malar stripe. Mangrove Hawk (*B. sub-*

tilis), a possible escape, sometimes considered conspecific, averages smaller (wg 315-370, tl 175-205, culmen from cere 24-29) and lacks brownish in the ss. See **Geographic variation** for separation from Cuban Black-Hawk (*B. gundlachii*), now considered a species.

Geographic variation—See Blake (1977), Clark (1905), Daniels et al. (1989), Friedmann (1950), Hellmayr & Conover (1949), Howell & Webb (1995), Monroe (1963), Monson & Phillips (1981), Palmer (1988a), Twomey (1956), van Rossem & Hachisuka (1937b), Wetmore (1965), Wiley & Garrido (2005). One other resident subspecies occurs in Cuba and the Isle of Pines.

B.a. anthracinus (br & wint most of N.Am-S.Am range): Averages larger (Table 40, p. 443; *vs* wg chord 330-380, tail 175-210, culmen from cere 25-30, tarsus 81-86 in *gundlachii* of Cuba); AHY/ASYs with plumage aspect blackish (*vs* brownish black), head uniformly black (*vs* with whitish malar streak), and base of primaries grayish-white (*vs* white in *gundlachii*). Populations of AZ-nw.Mex ("*micronyx*") may average larger and browner, but differences are slight and confounded by individual variation.

Molt—CBS. PF absent-limited (Sep?-Mar? in HY/SYs), PB2 incomplete-complete (Apr-Dec? in SYs), DPB incomplete (May-Feb in ASY/ATYs); PA absent. The above timing pertains to N.Am populations. The PF is occasionally absent or can include up to 50% of the body feathers. The DPBs exhibit staffelmauser (Fig. 16, pp. 23-24), with 2-4 sets of basic feathers present among pp of adults. The PB2 occasionally can be complete but usually 1-3 outer pp, 1-6 ss (among s3-s4 and s6-s9), and 1 or more rump feathers retained; 1-4 rects can occasionally be retained during DPBs. Suspension during breeding (Fig. 289, p. 393) likely occurs but limits are difficult to distinguish. See Family Account (pp. 391-392) for more information.

Age—Juv (B1; Jul-May) has upperparts dark brown with buff to whitish eyeline and auriculars and underparts cream to whitish with blackish streaks and/or spots; Juv ♀=♂ by plumage aspect. The following month ranges pertain to N.Am populations.

Juv-HY/SY (1st cycle, Juv/B1-F1; Oct-Sep): Upperparts dark brown and buff and underparts cream with brownish streaks and/or spots, increasingly mottled blackish in Nov-Mar; rects uniformly narrow and rounded, r2-r5 whitish with 6-8 distinct blackish bands (Fig. 316**A**); pp and ss juv (Fig. 16**A**, p. 24) or being replaced in Apr-Sep, the juv outer pp tapered (Fig. 286**A**, p. 392), brownish with variable dark bars or markings, and relatively worn, and the medial ss narrow and buff with distinct dark bars (Fig. 317**A**, p. 424).

SY/TY (2nd cycle, B2; Oct-Sep): Upperparts and underparts sooty to black, sometimes with indistinct pale streaks; rects black with white band and often other white markings (Fig. 316**B**), occasionally with 1-2 retained juv feathers (Figs. 288**C** & Fig. 316**A**); pp and ss basic and with uninterrupted replacement clines (Fig. 14**B**, p. 21) or (more often) with 1-3 juv outer pp (Fig. 286**A**) and/or 1-6 juv ss (Fig. 317**A**; among s3-s4 and s6-s9) retained, narrow, worn, and pale with distinct dusky bars (Fig.

FIGURE 316. Shape and color pattern to the rectrices by feather generation in Common Black-Hawk. R5 is shown and is usually the last feather replaced during molts and often is retained during the PB2 and DPB; thus, Juv-HY/SYs exhibit **A** (Fig. 288**A**, p. 392), SY/TYs can exhibit a mixture of **A** and **B-C** (Fig. 288**B**), individuals exhibiting uniform feathers resembling **B** are AHY/ASYs (Fig. 288**C**), and ASY/ATYs exhibit one or more generations of feathers resembling **C** (Fig. 288**C-D**). Second basic feathers on SY/TYs may more often exhibit additional white markings to the base, as in **B**, but this might vary geographically as well; more study needed.

16**B**), and the replaced (2nd basic) medial ss often washed rufous and with moderately distinct dark bars (Fig. 317**B**); one to many lower back and/or rump feathers often retained, brown, and very worn (Fig. 313**A**, p. 418); **Note: Occasional intermediates (following complete PB2) may exist that should be aged AHY/ASY**.

ASY/ATY (Def. cycle, DB; Oct-Sep): Upperparts and underparts uniformly sooty; rects black with a single white band (Fig. 316**C**), sometimes showing 2 generations of basic feathers (Fig. 288**D**); pp and ss with 2 sets of basic feathers in staffelmauser patterns (Fig. 16**E**), the outer pp broader (Fig. 286**B**), dusky without distinct pale markings, and fresher, and the medial ss dusky with little or no rufous and very indistinct whitish or buff mottling (Fig. 317**C**). **Note: Some ATYs show more substantial rufous tinge to medial ss; these may be TY/4Ys but study is needed.**

ATY/A4Y (Def. cycle, DB; Oct-Sep): Like ASY/ATY but pp with 3 sets of basic feathers (Fig. 16**F**).

A4Y/A5Y (Def. cycle, DB; Oct-Apr): Like ASY/ATY but pp with 4 sets of basic feathers (Fig. 16**G**).

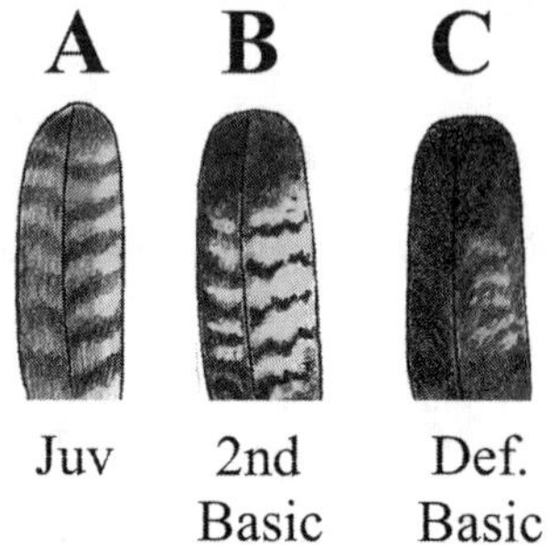

A B C

Juv 2nd Basic Def. Basic

FIGURE 317. Medial secondaries by feather generation in Common Black-Hawk. S5 is shown and is usually the first secondary replaced during molts and the most likely to exhibit juvenal characteristics in SY/TYs, as in **B**; following the PB2 it may contrast with a more basic-like (**C**) s4. The paler coloration on each feather represents rufous.

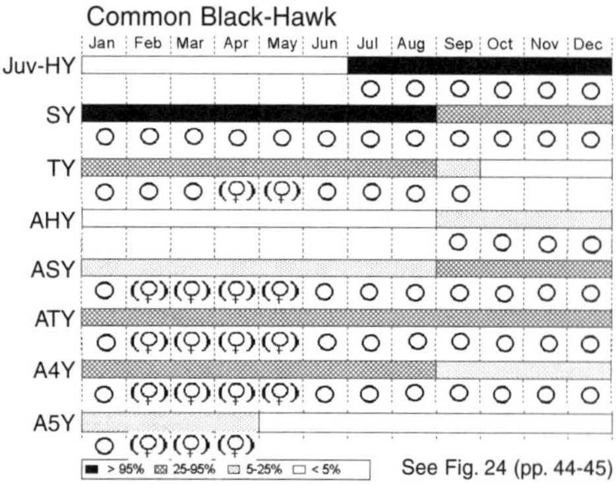

Common Black-Hawk

■ > 95% ▨ 25-95% □ 5-25% □ < 5% See Fig. 24 (pp. 44-45)

Sex—A Full medial BP (Fig. 20**A**, p. 31) and/or distended cloaca (Fig. 21, p. 32) indicates ASY ♀ in Feb-Jun; ♂♂ possibly may develop a partial BP. Measurements somewhat helpful for sexing a small proportion of individuals and probably most mated pairs (Table 40, p. 443). Otherwise, no criteria known.

Hybrids reported—None.

References—Bent (1937), Clark & Wheeler (1985), Daniels et al. (1989), Dickey & van Rossem (1938), Friedmann (1950), Howell & Webb (1995), Oberholser (1974), Palmer (1988a), Pyle (2005b, 2005c), Schnell (1994), Stresemann & Stresemann (1966).

HARRIS'S HAWK

Parabuteo unicinctus

HRSH
Species # 3350
Band size: 7A-7B Lock-on

Species—From other N.Am hawks, including dark morphs of other *Buteo* hawks, by medium size but long tail and culmen (Table 39, p. 427); wings rounded (usually p6>p7>p5≈p8>p9>p4>p3>p2>p10) and with p6-p10 notched and p5-p9 emarginated (*cf.* Fig. 287, p. 392); les covs, underwing gr and p covs, and elongated femoral feathers with chestnut (see **Age**); longest uppertail covs and vent whitish to white; r2-r5 grayish with indistinct dark markings or bars in

Juv-HY/SY, to blackish with broad white bases and moderately narrow white tips in AHY/ASY (Fig. 318); iris dark; tarsus without dense feathering to toes (Fig. 334**A**, p. 448).

Geographic variation—See Bednarz (1988, 1995), Blake (1977), Dickey & van Rossem (1938), Friedmann (1950), Hamerstrom & Hamerstrom (1978), Hellmayr & Conover (1949), Monson & Phillips (1981), Palmer (1988a), Patten et al. (2003), van Rossem (1942b), Webster (1973). One other subspecies occurs in c-s.S.Am.

P.u. harrisi (br & wint s.N.Am-n.S.Am): Averages longer-tailed and longer-billed (Table 39, p. 427; *vs* tail 194-240, culmen from cere 19.9-26.4 in *unicinctus* of S.Am); AHY/ASYs with breast uniformly brown (*vs* streaked pale in *unicinctus*). Populations of s.CA-sw.NM ("*superior*") average slightly larger and darker than populations of se.NM-TX but differences are confounded by individual variation throughout range of *harrisi*.

Molt—CBS. PF limited (Sep-Mar in HY/SYs), PB2 incomplete-complete (Feb-Oct in SYs), DPB incomplete-complete (Apr-Jan in ASY/ATYs); PA absent. The above timing pertains to most N.Am populations; occasional N.Am individuals that breed in fall-winter likely exhibit different molt strategies (more study needed). The PF includes up to 30% of the body feathers but may be absent in some individuals. The PB2 appears most often to be incomplete, with up to 4 outer pp (p7-p10), 1-6 juv ss among s3-s4 and s6-s9, 1-4 rects among r2-r5, and scattered wing covs and body feathers (especially on rump) retained. Replacement of pp and ss exhibits staffelmauser (Fig. 16, p. 23-24), resulting in 1-4 sets of basic feathers present within the pp of adults. Suspension during breeding (Fig. 289, p. 393) likely occurs but limits are difficult to distinguish. See Family Account (pp. 391-392) for more information.

Age—Juv (B1; Jun-Apr) has variable whitish streaking to head and underparts and elongated femoral feathers with indistinct barring or mottling. Juv ♀ = ♂ by plumage aspect but size (see **Sex**) is reliable for sexing full-grown juvs. The following month ranges pertain to most N.Am populations (see **Molt**); beware occasional breeding in winter resulting in HYs in Feb-May.

HY/SY (1st cycle, F1; Oct-Sep): Head and underparts with indistinct whitish streaking, increasingly mottled with darker brown feathers in Sep-Mar; rects uniformly narrow and rounded, r2-r5 grayish with indistinct dark markings or bars and white tips (Fig. 318**A**); pp and ss juv or being replaced in Feb-Sep, the juv outer pp tapered (Fig. 286**A**, p. 392), brownish mottled grayish ventrally, and relatively worn, and the medial ss narrow and grayish with indistinct blackish barring (*cf.* Fig. 322**A**, p. 431); feathers of tibia mixed pale rufous and whitish.

SY/TY (2nd cycle, B2; Oct-Sep): Head and underparts blackish brown, with little to no whitish streaking; rects broad and truncate, r2-r5 dark with indistinct white base and distinct white tip (Fig. 318**B**), sometimes with 1-4 juv rects retained (Figs. 288**B** &

FIGURE 318. Shape and color pattern to the rectrices by feather generation in Harris's Hawk. R5 is shown and is usually the last feather replaced during molts and the most likely to be retained during the PB2 and DPB. R5 and other rects are often retained in this species, such that Juv-HY/SYs exhibit **A** (Fig. 288**A**, p. 392), SY/TYs can exhibit a mixture of **A** and **B** (Fig. 288**B**), individuals exhibiting uniform feathers resembling **B** are AHY/ASYs (Fig. 288**C**), and ASY/ATYs exhibit one or more generations of feathers resembling **B** (Fig. 288**C-D**). Look for some second basic feathers on SY/TYs to exhibit intermediate patterns.

318**A**); pp and ss basic and uniformly dark ventrally, 1-4 juv outer pp (Fig. 286**A**) and/or 1-6 juv ss (Fig. 322**A**; among s3-s4 and s6-s9) usually retained, contrastingly narrow, worn, and pale brownish or grayish with indistinct markings (Figs. 16**B** & 322**A**); one to many juv les covs and/or rump feathers retained, pale brown, very worn (Fig. 313**A**, p. 418); feathers of tibia rufous, sometimes with indistinct whitish streaking. **Note: Individuals with uniformly replaced pp and ss occasionally occur (possibly only in SY/TYs) and usually can be aged by body-plumage aspect.**

ASY/ATY (Def. cycle, DB; Oct-Sep): Head and underparts blackish brown, without whitish streaking; rects basic, dark with indistinct white base and distinct white tip (Fig. 318**B**), sometimes showing 2 generations (Fig. 288**D**); pp and ss with 1-2 sets of basic feathers in staffelmauser patterns or among ss (Figs. 14**B** & 16**E**), the outer pp broader (Fig. 286**B**), fresher, and dark ventrally, and retained ss broad, and dark brownish to blackish with little or no barring (Fig. 322**B**); rump sometimes with retained basic feathers, dark brown and slightly worn (Fig. 313**C**); feathers of tibia uniformly chestnut. **Note: See SY/TY.**

ATY/A4Y (Def. cycle, DB; Oct-Sep): Like ASY/ATY but pp with 3 sets of basic feathers (Fig. 16**F**).

A4Y/A5Y (Def. cycle, DB; Oct-Apr): Like ASY/ATY but pp with 4 sets of basic feathers (Fig. 16**G**).

Sex—♀ = ♂ by plumage aspect. Medial BP (Fig. 20**A**, p. 31) and/or distended cloaca (Fig. 21, p. 32) indicates ASY ♀ at any time of year (but primarily in Feb-Jun). Measurements useful for sexing most of individuals (Table 39) and all mated pairs; the following is reliable with N.Am populations (*P.u. harrisi*):

♀: Wg chord > 329 (Juv-HY/SY) or > 342 (AHY/ASY); footpad length (Fig. 342, p. 455) 92-100. **Note: A few individuals with intermediate wing lengths can be sexed by foot-pad length.**

♂: Wg chord < 328 (Juv/HY/SY) or < 340 (AHY/ASY); footpad length (Fig. 342) 85-90.

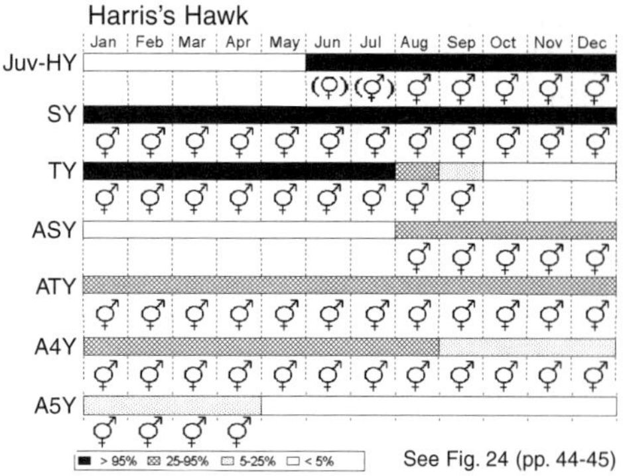

Harris's Hawk

Jan Feb Mar Apr May Jun Jul Aug Sep Oct Nov Dec

Juv-HY, SY, TY, ASY, ATY, A4Y, A5Y

■ > 95% ▩ 25-95% ▭ 5-25% □ < 5%

See Fig. 24 (pp. 44-45)

Hybrids reported—With Red-tailed Hawk (McCarthy 2006) in the wild.

References—Bednarz (1995), Bednarz & Hayden (1991), Bent (1937), Dickey & van Rossem (1938), Friedmann (1950), Hamerstrom & Hamerstrom (1978), Mader (1976), Oberholser (1974), Palmer (1988a), Pyle (2005b, 2005c).

RED-SHOULDERED HAWK

Buteo lineatus

RSHA
Species # 3390
Band size: 6-7A Lock-on

Species—From other N.Am hawks by medium size with proportionally long tarsus among *Buteo* (Table 39); wings rounded (usually p7>p6>p8>p9>p5>p4>p10≈p3) and with p7-p10 notched and p6-p9 emarginated (*cf.* Fig. 287, p. 392); les covs usually with extensive rufous; bases to p5-p10 whitish, forming distinct pale crescent distal to dark p covs (unique among N.Am *Buteo* hawks); breast and underwing covs whitish with hourglass and/or anchor-shaped brown spots

TABLE 39. Measurements (mm) of smaller North American *Buteos* and allies to assist in identification and sexing. See pp. 4-11 for methods of measurement. Species summaries are in **bold** and subspecies summaries in ***italics***. Values were derived from 95% confidence intervals as based approximately on the indicated sample sizes (see pp. 4-5); thus midpoints of ranges approximate means, and S.D. is approximated by 25% of the range.

Taxon/Sex	*n*	wing chord	tail length[1]	culmen from cere[1]	tarsus
Harris's Hawk[3]		**298-385**	**211-274**	**24.0-30.4**	**80-91**
♀	100	329-385	234-274	24.9-29.5	81-91
♂	100	298-342	211-251	24.0-30.4	80-90
Red-shouldered Hawk		**272-360**	**163-236**	**18.2-25.1**	**70-85**
B.l. elegans		***276-322***	***180-215***	***19.6-23.7***	***71-80***
♀	65	290-322	185-215	20.2-23.7	73-80
♂	55	276-309	180-210	19.6-22.5	71-78
B.l. lineatus		***306-360***	***196-236***	***20.5-25.1***	***74-85***
♀	70	324-360	207-236	22.3-25.1	77-85
♂	75	306-341	196-223	20.5-23.1	74-82
B.l. alleni		***288-340***	***173-211***	***19.4-24.3***	***73-83***
♀	50	294-340	182-211	21.2-24.3	76-83
♂	65	278-323	173-202	19.4-23.3	73-81
B.l. extimus		***272-315***	***163-204***	***18.2-23.6***	***70-82***
♀	23	287-315	173-204	19.9-23.6	73-82
♂	19	272-301	163-194	18.2-21.9	70-79
Broad-winged Hawk[3]		**246-296**	**140-188**	**16.5-20.8**	**58-67**
♀	100	258-296	152-188	17.3-20.8	59-67
♂	95	246-282	140-175	16.5-19.9	58-65
Gray Hawk[3]		**239-293**	**153-195**	**18.8-25.7**	**66-76**
♀	70	256-293	165-195	21.6-25.7	68-76
♂	100	239-273	153-180	18.8-22.9	66-73
Short-tailed Hawk[3]		**267-342**	**133-188**	**16.4-22.5**	**55-64**
♀	53	287-342	146-188	17.9-22.5	58-64
♂	49	267-318	133-173	16.4-21.1	55-61

[1] Tail length values include birds of all ages; in most *Buteo* species the juvenal rects average up to 15% longer than adult rects, sex for sex.

[2] Culmen from cere represents the chord (Fig. 7**B**, p. 9).

[3] Measures represent N.Am populations only (see **Geographic variation**).

(Juv-HY/SY; Fig. 320**D-E**, p. 430) or barred to washed reddish (AHY/ASY); medial rects (r2-r5) brown with 5-9 pale bands in Juv-HY/SYs or blackish with 4-6 distinct white bands and white tip in AHY/ASYs (Fig. 319, p. 428); tarsus without feathering to toes (Fig. 334**A**, p. 448); Juv-HY/SY with uppertail covs whitish with brown spots, auriculars primarily dark, and elongated femoral feathers unmarked to distinctly barred brownish.

Roadside Hawk (*B. magnirostris*), a vagrant to s.TX, is shorter-winged but longer-tailed (wg 218-249, tl 155-178, culmen from cere 16.5-21.1, tarsus 64-69), wings very rounded (usually p7≈p6>p8>p5>p9>p4>p3>p2>p10); Juv/HY-SY with breast mottled or streaked grayish, contrasting with reddish barring to abdomen, and uppertail covs barred rufous and whitish; rects brown with 4-6 indistinct (Juv-HY/SY) to distinct (AHY/ASY) dusky-brownish bands; inner webs to pp and ss pale buff to rufous with distinct brownish bands ventrally.

Geographic variation—See Bangs (1920), Bishop (1912), Friedmann (1950), Hellmayr & Conover (1949), Johnson & Peeters (1963), Palmer (1988a), Pyle et al. (2004), Wheeler (2003a, 2003b). No other subspecies occur.

Western (*B.l. elegans*) Subspecies Group. Aspect bright; rects with 3-6 white bands.

B.l. elegans (br & wint coastal sw.OR-s.CA; vagrant to BC to UT-AZ): Medium small with proportionally long tail (Table 39, p. 427); throat and auriculars not distinctly darker than breast; Juv-HY/SY with upperparts dark brown and r2-r5 brownish black with 4-6 whitish bands (Fig. 319**A**); AHY/ASY with upperparts blackish brown, bright rufous, and white, underparts uniformly to heavily washed (breast) and barred (abdomen) bright rufous, with very narrow or no dark streaks, and r2-r5 black with 3-4 broad white bands (Fig. 319**C**).

Eastern (*B.l. lineatus*) Subspecies Group. Aspect dull; rects with 4-9 white bands.

B.l. lineatus (br MN-NS to OK-NC, wint to TX-FL; vagrant to c.CA): Large (Table 39); throat and auriculars usually distinctly darker than breast; Juv-HY/SY with upperparts medium brown and r2-r5 brown with 7-9 narrow whitish bands (Fig. 319**B**); AHY/ASY with upperparts brown, pale rufous, and whitish, underparts barred pale rufous with numerous narrow blackish streaks, and r2-r5 black with 4-5 narrow white bands (Fig. 319**D-E**).

B.l. alleni (br & wint OK-s.TX to SC-c.FL): Medium large with proportionally long culmen (Table 39); throat and auriculars not distinctly darker than breast; Juv-HY/SY with upperparts medium-dark brown (sometimes tinged grayish), underparts with dense brown streaks and spots (Fig. 320**B**), and r2-r5 brownish with 6-8 narrowish whitish bands (Fig. 319**B**); AHY/ASY with upperparts pale brown with grayer head and slight pale rufous fringing and white mottling, underparts barred pale rufous with some very narrow blackish streaks, and r2-r5 black with 4-5 narrow white bands (Fig. 319**D-E**). Populations of c-s.TX ("*texanus*") may average slightly larger and darker but differences are insufficient for subspecific recognition.

B.l. extimus (res. s.FL): Small (Table 39); throat and auriculars not distinctly darker than breast; Juv-HY/SY with upperparts medium-pale brown, underparts with sparse brownish streaks (Fig. 320**D**), and r2-r5 brownish with 5-7 narrowish whitish bands (Fig. 319**B**); AHY/ASY with upperparts pale brownish gray with paler (to whitish) head and reduced pale rufous and white, underparts barred pale rufous with few very narrow blackish streaks, and r2-r5 black with 4-5 wide white bands (Fig. 319**D-E**).

Molt—CBS. PF limited (Sep-Mar in HY/SYs), PB2 complete (Apr-Sep in non-breeding SYs), DPB complete (May-Oct in breeding AHYs); PA absent. The PF occurs primarily on non-

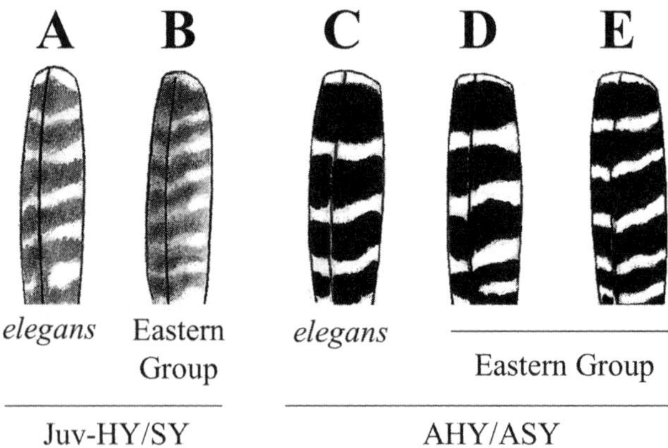

FIGURE 319. Shape and color pattern to the rectrices by feather generation and subspecies in Red-shouldered Hawk. R5 is shown and is usually the last feather replaced during molts; however, it is rarely retained during PBs. *B.l. elegans* (**A**, **C**) average few bars by age than subspecies of the Eastern Subspecies Group (**B**, **D-E**), consisting of *B.l. lineatus, alleni*, and *extimus*. Note also the difference in the width of the subterminal black band, usually 9-14 mm in *elegans* and 5-8 mm in the Eastern Group, and broader in ♂♂ than in ♀♀ in each subspecies. *B.l. alleni* averages slightly more bars by age (more AHY/ASYs with **E**) than *lineatus* and *extimus*, but overlap is extensive.

breeding grounds and the DPBs occur primarily on breeding grounds. The PF includes up to 10% of the body feathers but appears to be absent in most individuals. Occasional individuals may retain one or more ss or rump feathers during the PB2 or (more likely) DPBs. Suspension of molt among p2-p6, the terts, and sometimes s1 and/or s5 often occurs during breeding (Fig. 289**A**-**B**, p. 393; ♀♀ average more feathers replaced than ♂♂). See Family Account (pp. 391-392) for more information.

Age—Juv (B1; Jul-May) is described under Juv-HY/SY (below) and has grayish to pale grayish-brown iris. Juv ♀=♂ by plumage aspect. See Hawfield (1986) for information on fault bars in this species.

Juv-HY/SY (1st cycle, Juv/B1-F1; Oct-Sep): Breast and abdomen whitish with variable brownish to rufous-brown spots, barring, and/or streaks (Fig. 320**D**-**E**, p. 430), sometimes mottled with reddish feathers in Oct-Mar; rects narrow and rounded, r2-r5 brownish with more indistinct bands by subspecies (Fig. 319**A**-**B**); pp and ss juv (Fig. 13**A**, p. 20), the outer pp narrow at tip (Fig. 286**A**, p. 392) and the juv ss narrow with narrow (usually < 20 mm wide) and indistinct subterminal bands (*cf.* Fig. 322**A**, p. 431); iris usually pale grayish brown to medium-dark brown.

AHY/ASY (Def. cycle, DB; Oct-Sep): Breast and abdomen with rufous wash and/or barring; rects broad and truncate, r2-r5 blackish to black with fewer distinct white bands by subspecies (Fig. 319**C**-**E**); pp and ss basic (Fig. 14**B**, p. 21), the outer pp broad at tip (Fig. 286**B**) and the ss broad with distinct and wide (usually > 20 mm) subterminal bands (*cf.* Fig. 322**B**); iris dark brown. **Note: Look for occasional individuals with retained ss, rump feathers, or rects that can be aged to SY/TY or ASY/ATY, as in other hawks (Figs. 14C, 288B & D, & 313, p. 418). Also, individuals showing suspension limits among p1-p6 and sometimes the ss (Fig. 289A-B, p. 393; see Molt) are likely ASY/ATYs because SYs seldom breed but more study is needed to confirm this.**

Sex—♀=♂ by plumage aspect. Medial BP (Fig. 20**A**, p. 31) and/or distended cloaca (Fig. 21, p. 32) indicates ASY ♀ in Feb-Jun. Measurements (especially wg chord) somewhat helpful for sexing mated pairs of known subspecies (Table 39, p. 427). The following can be used to sex some but not all AHY/ASYs (combine with measurements and see also Fig. 323, p. 432); most Juv-HY/SYs are probably not reliably sexed:

AHY/ASY ♀: Width of subterminal blackish band broader by subspecies, usually 12-14 mm in *B.l. elegans* (*cf.* Fig. 319**C**) or 7-8 mm in the Eastern Subspecies Group (Fig. 319**D**).

AHY/ASY ♂: Width of subterminal blackish band narrower by subspecies, usually 9-11 mm in *B.l. elegans* (*cf.* Fig. 319**C**) or 5-6 mm in the Eastern Subspecies Group (Fig. 319**E**).

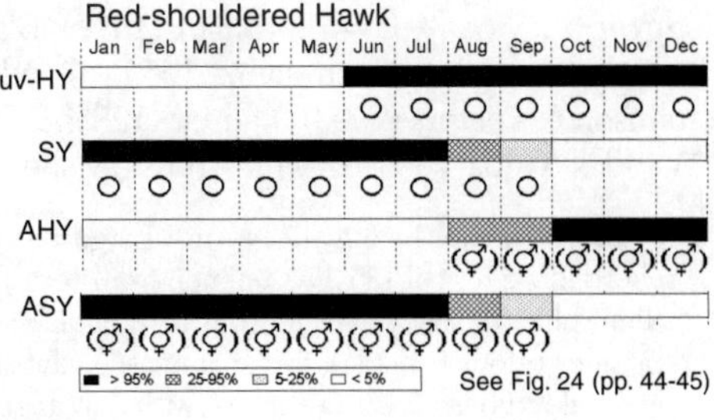

Hybrids reported—With Gray Hawk (Lasley & Sexton 1989). Possibly with Red-tailed Hawk (VT, March 2007).

References—Bent (1937), Crocoll (1994), Friedmann (1950), Johnson & Peeters (1963), Oberholser (1974), Palmer (1988a), Pyle (2005b, 2005c), Roberts (1955), Sheppard & Klimkiewicz (1976), Wood (1969).

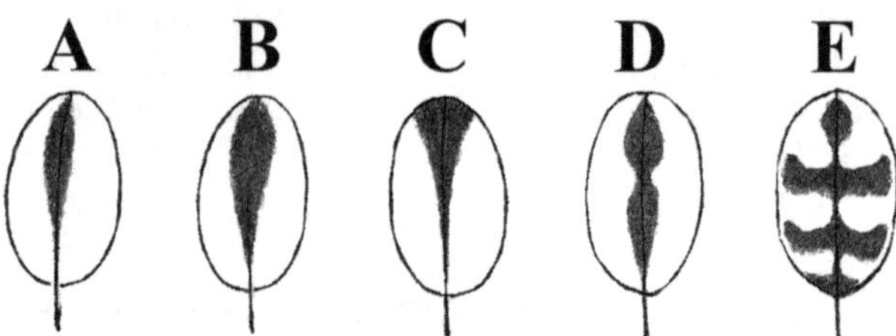

FIGURE 320. Variation in the underpart feathers (breast and underwing coverts) of Juv feathers in small *Buteo* species. Juv-HY/SY Red-shouldered Hawk typically exhibits patterns resembling **D-E**, Juv-HY/SY Broad-winged Hawk exhibits **A-C**, Juv-HY/SY Gray Hawk exhibits **B-C**, and Juv-HY/SY Short-tailed Hawk exhibits few or no markings, those present exhibiting thin streaks as in **A**. Note that there is generally quite a bit of variation, both between individuals and among underpart feathers on a single individual, but the above patterns are typically found on each species. Note also that variable numbers of underpart feathers might be replaced during the preformative molt and exhibit more basic-like patterns (generally more barred in all species, as in **E**).

BROAD-WINGED HAWK

Buteo platypterus

BWHA
Species # 3430
Band size: 5-6 Lock-on

Species—From other N.Am hawks by medium-small size (Table 39, p. 427); wings rounded (usually p8≈p7>p6>p9>p5>p4>p3>p10) and with p8-p10 notched and p7-p9 emarginated (*cf.* Fig. 287, p. 392); r2-r5 with 5-7 indistinct dusky bands and wider terminal band in Juv-HY/SY, or dark brown to blackish with 2-3 indistinct whitish bands in AHY/ASY (Fig. 321); tarsus without feathering to toes (Fig. 334**A**, p. 448); light morph with auriculars paler brown than crown, les covs with little or no rufous, inner webs of p1-p5 not contrastingly paler than those of outer ss dorsally, breast with a light to heavy amount of markings by age, and Juv-HY/SY with uppertail covs dark brown (narrowly tipped white when fresh), elongated femoral feathers with brown spots, and underwing covs white with sparse brownish or rufous-brown streak-like marks (Fig. 320**A-C**); rare dark morph with plumage aspect brownish black, without white flecking to lores; inner webs of pp and ss grayish ventrally; abdomen and underwing covs of Juv-HY/SY without white spotting (*cf.* Fig. 329**C**, p. 441).

Geographic variation—See Bailey (1917), Blake (1977), Burns (1911), Clark (1905), Danforth & Smythe (1935), Friedmann (1950), Goodrich et al. (1996), Hellmayr & Conover (1949), Johnson & Peeters (1963), Palmer (1988b), Riley (1908). Five other resident subspecies in the W.Indes (Cuba-Tobago), which possibly should be synonymized; more study needed.

B.p. platypterus (br & wint N.Am): Large but with proportionally small bill (Table 39, p. 427; *vs* wg chord 227-273, tail 135-170, culmen from cere 18.4-21.3, tarsus 53-62 in resident W.Indies subspecies); dimorphic (*vs* solely light morphs in W.Indian subspecies); upperparts with little or no rufous (*vs* with broader rufous fringing); throat primarily whitish (*vs* primarily dark); underparts of AHY/ASYs whitish and pale rufous (*vs* buff or tawny with darker rufous markings in W.Indian subspecies). Populations of Alb-Man to IA ("*B.p. iowensis*") have a higher proportion of dark-morph individuals.

Molt—CBS?. PF absent-limited? (Oct?-Mar? in HY/SYs), PB2 incomplete-complete (Apr-Sep in SYs), DPB incomplete-complete (May-Dec in ASYs); PA absent. The DPBs occur primarily on breeding grounds but can commence on or just before northbound spring migration in SYs, and can occasionally complete during southbound migration or on non-breeding grounds in ASYs. A limited PF probably occurs in a small proportion of individuals. The PB2 can be complete or 1-2 outer pp, 1-6 ss among s3-s4 and s6-s9, 1-4 rects among r2-r5, and one or more rump feathers can be retained until the PB3; later PBs are more often incomplete. Replacement of pp and ss usually exhibits staffelmauser (Fig. 16, pp. 23-24; in ~75% of AHY/ASYs), resulting in 1-4 sets of basic feathers present among pp of adults. Suspension during breeding (Fig. 289, p. 393) likely occurs but limits are difficult to distinguish. See Family Account (pp. 391-392) for more information.

Age—Juv (B1; Jul-May) is described under Juv-HY/SY (below) and has grayish to pale grayish-brown or yellowish iris. Juv ♀=♂ by plumage aspect. See Hawfield (1986) for information on fault bars in this species.

Juv-HY/SY (1st cycle, Juv/B1-F1; Oct-Sep): Underparts of light morph creamy white with sparse brownish to reddish-brown streaking (Fig. 320**A-C**); r2-r5 brownish with 5-7 narrow dusky bands (Fig. 321**A**); pp and ss uniformly juv (Fig. 16**A**, p. 24), the outer pp narrow at tip (Fig. 286**A**, p. 392), and the medial ss narrow with narrower subterminal dusky bands (Fig. 322**A**); rump and underpart feathers of dark morph with variable rufous-brown streaking or fringes; iris pale grayish brown to yellowish brown. **Note: Some SYs may over-summer on non-breeding grounds and exhibit advanced PB2s (see p. 18).**

AHY/ASY (Def. cycle, DB; Oct-Sep): Underparts of light morph white with rufous mottling (breast) and barring (abdomen); rects broad and truncate, r2-r5 dark brown to blackish with 3-5 white to whitish bands (Fig. 321**B**); pp and ss uniformly basic

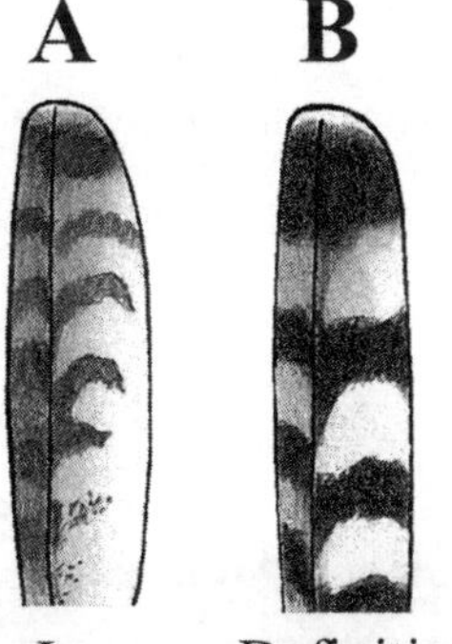

FIGURE 321. Shape and color pattern to the rectrices by feather generation in Broad-winged Hawk. R5 is shown and is usually the last feather replaced during molts and the most likely to be retained during the PB2 and DPB. R5 and other rects are sometimes retained in this species, such that Juv-HY/SYs exhibit **A** (Fig. 288**A**, p. 392), SY/TYs can exhibit a mixture of **A** and **B** (Fig. 288**B**), individuals exhibiting uniform feathers resembling **B** are AHY/ASYs (Fig. 288**C**), and ASY/ATYs can exhibit one or more generations of feathers resembling **B** (Fig. 288**C-D**). Second basic feathers on SY/TYs may be somewhat intermediate toward **A** from **B**; more study is needed.

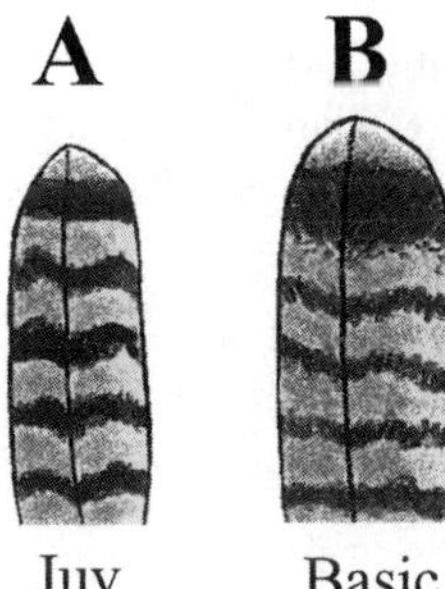

FIGURE 322. Typical difference between juvenal and basic medial secondaries (s8 shown here) in *Buteo* hawks. In addition to narrower shape and shorter length to juv feathers (**A**), note the more distinct and wider proximal dark bars but narrower subterminal dark bar as compared to basic feathers (**B**). Second basic feathers on SY/TYs may exhibit somewhat intermediate characters, especially those replaced earlier in the molt such as s1 and s5. S8 is usually among the last ss replaced during molts and the most likely to be retained during the PB2 and DPB. In most *Buteo* species, Juv-HY/SYs exhibit uniform ss resembling **A** (Fig. 14**A**, p. 21); SY/TYs can exhibit newer feathers resembling **B** and 1-6 older feathers resembling **A**, contrastingly paler (worn) and short (Fig. 14**C**); and ASY/ATYs exhibit one or more generations of feathers resembling **B**, the older feathers contrasting in wear and faded but not contrasting markedly in shape, pattern, or length (Fig. 14**D**).

(Fig. 14**B**, p. 21), the outer pp broader (Fig. 286**B**), and the medial ss broad with wider subterminal dark bands (Fig. 322**B**); rump and underpart feathers of dark morph without rufous-brown streaking or fringes; iris pale to dark brownish. **Note: Individuals with uniformly replaced pp and ss are most likely SY/TYs; look also for intermediate patterns to the underparts and rects (see SY/TY).**

SY/TY (2nd cycle, B2; Oct-Sep): Like AHY/ASY but 1-3 juv outer pp (Fig. 286**A**) and/or 1-6 juv ss (Fig. 322**A**; among s3-s4 and s6-s9) retained, contrastingly narrow, worn, and brownish with distinct bars (Figs. 14**C** & 16**B**); one to many lower back and/or rump feathers often retained, pale brown, sometimes with distinct pale fringing, and very worn (Fig. 313**A**, p. 418); 1-4 juv rects (Fig. 321**A**; among r2-r5) occasionally retained, brown and narrow (Fig. 288**B**, p. 392); breast often mixed with streaking and barring (*cf.* Fig. 320); iris often pale brownish. **Note: In addition, look for intermediate patterns to the rects (*cf.* Fig. 321).**

ASY/ATY (Def. cycle, DB; Oct-Sep): Like AHY/ASY but pp and ss with 2 sets of basic feathers in staffelmauser patterns or among ss only (Figs. 16**E**, 286**B**, & 322**B**); one to a few scattered lower back and/or rump feathers sometimes retained, dark brown without pale fringing, and slightly worn (Fig. 313**B**); rects basic (Fig. 321**B**), sometimes showing 2 generations (Fig. 288**D**); breast barred, without streaking; iris usually dark brownish to reddish brown. **Note: See SY/TY.**

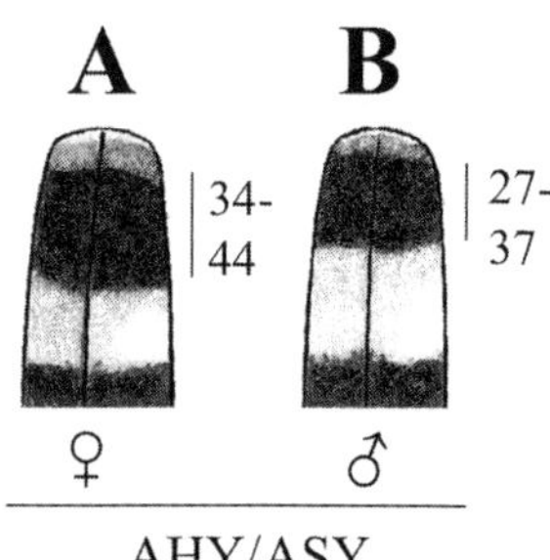

FIGURE 323. Width of the subterminal band by sex in AHY/ASY Broad-winged Hawks. More study is needed on the reliability of this feature for sexing this and other *Buteo* species.

ATY/A4Y (Def. cycle, DB; Oct-Sep): Like ASY/ATY but pp with 3 sets of basic feathers in staffelmauser patterns (Fig. 16**F**).

A4Y/A5Y (Def. cycle, DB; Oct-Apr): Like ASY/ATY but pp with 4 sets of basic feathers in staffelmauser patterns (Fig. 16**G**).

Sex—♀ = ♂ by plumage aspect. Medial BP (Fig. 20**A**, p. 31) and/or distended cloaca (Fig. 21, p. 32) indicates ASY ♀ in Apr-Jun. Measurements unhelpful for sexing, except possibly with some mated pairs (Table 39, p. 427). Otherwise, no reliable criteria known for sexing, although the width of the subterminal dark tail band averages larger in ♀♀ than in ♂♂ (Fig. 323) and this could be useful in sexing some individuals including mated pairs.

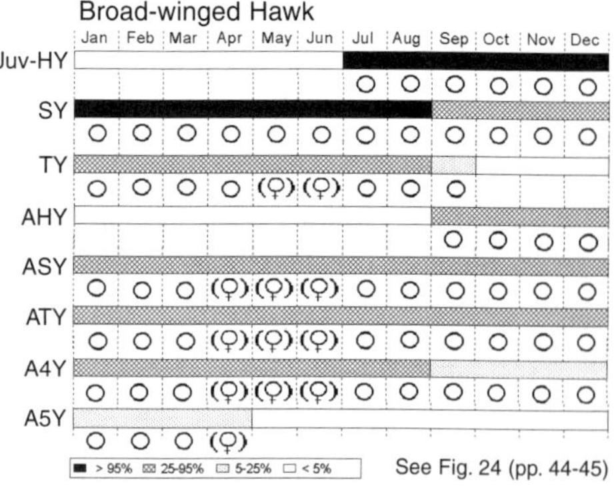

Hybrids reported—See Sharp-shinned/Cooper's hawk (p. 415).

References—Bent (1937), Burns (1911), Clark & Anderson (1984), Friedmann (1950), Goodrich et al. (1996), Howell & Webb (1995), Johnson & Peeters (1963), Kaufman (1979b), Matray (1974), Mosher & Matray (1974), Oberholser (1974), R.S. Palmer & J.A. Mosher *in* Palmer (1988b), Pyle (2005b, 2005c), Roberts (1955), Sheppard & Klimkiewicz (1976), Wood (1969).

GRAY HAWK GRHA
Buteo nitida Species # 3460
Band size: 6-7A Lock-on

Species—From other N.Am hawks by medium-small size (Table 39, p. 427); wings rounded (usually p8>p7>p6>p9>p5>p4>p3>p2>p10) and with p7-p10 notched and p6-p9 emarginated (*cf.* Fig. 287, p. 392); r2-r5 with 8-10 narrow dusky bands widening distally in Juv-HY/SY, to black with 2-3 distinct white bands in AHY/ASY (Fig. 324); underwing covs whitish with sparse barring or spotting; underwing p covs with narrow bars and without dusky tips; Juv-HY/SYs with auriculars and longest uppertail covs primarily whitish, breast creamy to whitish with narrow to broad, teardrop-shaped spots (Fig. 320**B-C**, p. 430), and elongated femoral feathers barred (N.Am populations).

Geographic variation—See Amadon (1982), Bibles et al. (2002), Blake (1977), Dickey & van Rossem (1938), Friedmann (1950), Hellmayr & Conover (1949), Johnson & Peeters (1963), Miller & Griscom (1921a), Monroe (1968), Palmer (1988a), Peters (1929), van Rossem (1930b, 1934). Three other subspecies in C.Am-S.Am.

A.n. plagiata (br & wint N.Am to n.C.Am): Longer-winged and longer-tailed (Table 39, p. 427; *vs* wg chord 228-260, tail 147-179, culmen from cere 19.7-24.7, tarsus 67-74 in the other subspecies); Juv-HY/SYs with upperpart feathers fringed rufous (*vs* whitish), elongated femoral feathers barred (*vs* streaked or without markings), and r2-r5 with 5-9 visible dusky bands distal to uppertail covs (Fig. 324**A**; *vs* 3-5 in the *nitida* Group of S.Am); AHY/ASYs with upperparts paler gray without whitish barring and r2-r5 with 1-2 complete white bands (Fig. 324**B**; *vs* 0-1 complete bands in the other subspecies). Populations of nw.Mex ("*maxima*") may average larger, paler, and with less white in the tail but differences, if present, are broadly clinal and confounded by individual variation.

Molt—CBS. PF absent-limited (Dec?-Mar? in HY/SYs), PB2 incomplete-complete (Apr-Nov? in SYs), DPB incomplete-complete (May-Feb in ASY/ATYs); PA absent. The above timing pertains to N.Am populations. The PF includes up to 10% of the body feathers but appears to be absent in most individuals. The DPBs often exhibit staffelmauser (Fig. 16, p. 23-24; in ~70% of ASY/ATYs), resulting in 1-3 sets of basic feathers present among pp of adults. The PB2 is often complete, but the juv outer 1-2 pp, 1-4 ss among s3-s4 and s8-s10, 1-4 rects among r2-r5, and 1 or more rump feathers can be retained. Suspension during breeding (Fig. 289, p. 393) likely occurs but limits are difficult to distinguish. See Family Account (pp. 391-392) for more information.

FIGURE 324. Shape and color pattern to the rectrices by feather generation in Gray Hawk. R5 is shown and is usually the last feather replaced during molts and the most likely to be retained during the PB2 and DPB. These feathers are occasionally retained in this species, such that Juv-HY/SYs exhibit **A** (Fig. 288**A**, p. 392), SY/TYs can exhibit a mixture of **A** and **B** (Fig. 288**B**), individuals exhibiting uniform feathers resembling **B** AHY/ASYs (Fig. 288**C**), and ASY/ATYs can exhibit one or more generations of feathers resembling **B** (Fig. 288**C-D**).

Age—Juv (B1; Jul-May) is described under Juv-HY/SY (below) and has grayish to pale-brown iris. Juv ♀=♂ by plumage aspect. The following month ranges pertain to N.Am populations.

Juv-HY/SY (1st cycle, Juv/B1-F1; Oct-Sep): Upperparts brown; underparts and underwing covs buff to whitish with brown teardrop-shaped spots (Fig. 320**B-C**, p. 430); rects narrow and rounded, r2-r5 brown with 8-10 dusky-brown bands (Fig.

324**A**); ss uniformly narrow with narrow bands (Fig. 322**A**, p. 431); outer pp narrow (Fig. 286**A**, p. 392) and brownish; iris usually pale brownish.

AHY/ASY (Def. cycle, DB; Oct-Sep): Upperparts uniformly gray; underparts barred gray and whitish; rects uniformly broad and truncate, r2-r5 black with white bands (Fig. 324**B**); ss broad with wide bands (Fig. 322**B**); outer pp broad (Fig. 286**B**) and dusky; iris usually dark brownish.

SY/TY (2nd cycle, B2; Oct-Sep): Like AHY/ASY but 1-3 outer juv pp (Fig. 286**A**) and 1-6 juv ss (Fig. 322**A**; among s3-s4 and s6-s9) retained (Figs. 14**C**, p. 21 & 16**B**, p. 24); one to many lower back and/or rump feathers retained, brown, and very worn (Fig. 313**A**, p. 418); 1-4 juv rects (among r2-r5) occasionally retained, brown, with 7-9 bands (Figs. 288**B**, p. 392, & 324**B**).

ASY/ATY (Def. cycle, DB; Oct-Sep): Like AHY/ASY but pp and ss with 2 sets of basic feathers in staffelmauser patterns or among ss only (Figs. 14**D** & 16**E**), the outer pp broad and fresh (Fig. 286**B**) and retained ss broad with wide bands (Fig. 322**B**); one to a few lower back and/or rump feathers retained, gray, and slightly worn (Fig. 313**C**); 1-4 basic rects occasionally retained (Figs. 288**D** & 324**B**).

ATY/A4Y (Def. cycle, DB; Oct-Apr): Like ASY/ATY but pp with 3 sets of basic feathers in staffelmauser patterns (Fig. 16**F**).

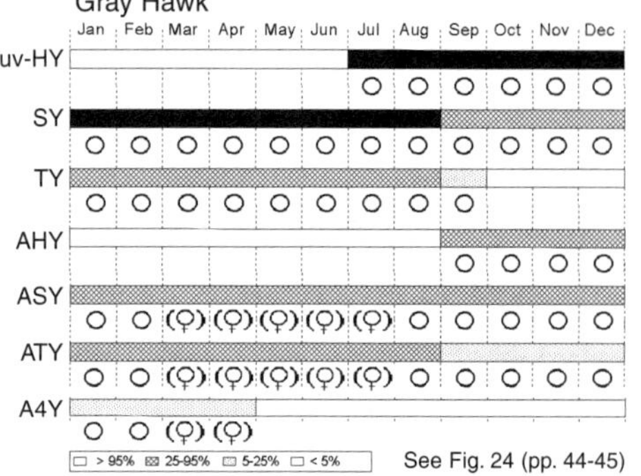

Sex—♀ = ♂ by plumage aspect. Medial BP (Fig. 20**A**, p. 31) and/or distended cloaca (Fig. 21, p. 32) indicates ASY ♀ in Mar-Jul. Measurements (especially culmen from cere) somewhat helpful for sexing some individuals and most mated pairs (Table 39, p. 427). Otherwise, no reliable criteria known for sexing.

Hybrids reported—With Red-shouldered Hawk (p. 426).

References—Bent (1937), Bibles et al. (2002), Dickey & van Rossem (1938), Friedmann (1950), Howell & Webb (1995), Johnson & Peeters (1963), Oberholser (1974), Palmer (1988a), Pyle (2005b, 2005c), Roberts (1955).

SHORT-TAILED HAWK

Buteo brachyurus

STHA
Species # 3440
Band size: 6 Lock-on

Species—From other N.Am hawks by medium-small size (Table 39, p. 427); wings rounded (usually p7>p8>p6>p9≈p5>p4>p3>p2≈p10>p1) and with p6 (slightly) to p10 notched and p6-p9 emarginated (*cf.* Fig. 287, p. 392); middle toe (without claw) longer than other small *Buteo* hawks (> unfeathered portion of tarsus); r2-r5 pale with 9-11 dark brown bands in Juv-HY/SY, or 6-7 bands in AHY/ASY (Fig. 325); light morph with auriculars and crown uniformly dark, inner webs of p1-p5 not contrastingly paler than those of outer ss dorsally; breast and elongated femoral feathers and underwing covs with little to no dark marking by age (*cf.* Fig. 320, p. 430), and uppertail covs of Juv-HY/SY uniformly dark brown; dark morph from dark-morph Broad-winged Hawk (p. 430) and other *Buteo* species by plumage aspect black, sometimes with white flecking to lores; inner webs to underwing pp and s5 dusky; Juv-HY/SY with feathers of underpart feathers and underwing covs with distinct white bases or indistinct whitish bars (*cf.* Fig. 329**A**-**B**, p. 441).

Geographic variation—See Blake (1977), Miller & Meyer (2002), Palmer (1988b), Rand (1960). One other subspecies occurs in S.Am.

B.b. fuliginosus (br & wint N.Am): Larger (Table 39, p. 427) and proportionally long-winged (wg chord/tl 49.5-55.0; *vs* wg chord 255-315, tail 133-170, and wg chord/tl 48.5-51.0 in *brachyurus* of n.S.Am); light morph with upperparts brown (*vs* slaty black), sides of breast and rump washed rufous (*vs* blackish, with slight to no rufous tinge in *brachyurus*).

Molt—CBS. PF absent-limited? (Sep?-Mar? in HY/SYs), PB2 incomplete-complete (Apr-Sep? in SYs), DPB incomplete-complete (May-Dec in ASYs); PA absent. The above timing pertains to N.Am populations. A limited PF could occur in a small proportion of individuals; more study is needed. The PB2 probably can be complete but 1-4 outer pp, 1-6 ss among s3-s4 and s6-s9, possibly 1-4 rects (more study needed), and 1 or more rump feathers can be retained until the PB3; later PBs are more often incomplete. Replacement of pp and ss usually exhibits staffelmauser (Fig. 16, pp. 23-24), resulting in 1-3 sets of basic feathers present among pp of adults. Suspension during breeding (Fig. 289, p. 393) likely occurs but limits are difficult to distinguish. See Family Account (pp. 391-392) for more information.

Age—Juv (B1; Jun-May) is described under Juv-HY/SY (below) and has grayish to pale grayish-brown or yellowish iris. Juv ♀=♂ by plumage aspect. The following month ranges pertain to N.Am populations.

Juv-HY/SY (1st cycle, Juv/B1-F1; Oct-Sep): Rects narrow and rounded, r2-r5 brownish with 9-11 dark brown bands (Fig. 325**A**); pp and ss juv (Fig. 16**A**, p. 24), or being replaced in Apr-Sep, the juv outer pp tapered (Fig. 286**A**, p. 392) and brownish, and the juv ss narrow with narrow subterminal bands (Fig. 322**A**, p. 431); iris usually pale grayish brown to brownish or yellowish brown; light morph with auriculars streaked pale; dark morph with white bases or bars to underpart and underwing feathers (*cf.* Fig. 329**A-B**, p. 441).

AHY/ASY (Def. cycle, DB; Oct-Sep): Rects broad and truncate, r2-r5 pale with 6-7 dusky and narrow (light morph) or blackish and broad (dark morph) bands (Fig. 325**B-C**); pp and ss basic and showing uninterrupted replacement clines (Fig. 14**B**, p. 21), the outer pp broader (Fig. 286**B**) and dusky, and the medial ss broad with wide subterminal bands (Fig. 322**B**); iris dark brownish (can be yellower in populations of Mex-C.Am); light morph with auriculars uniformly brown; dark morph without white bases or bars to underpart feathers (*cf.* Fig. 329**C**). **Note: Individuals with uniformly replaced pp and ss may be rare in this species and likely are SY/TYs.**

SY/TY (2nd cycle, B2 Oct-Sep): Like AHY/ASY but 1-3 juv outer pp (Fig. 286**A**) and/or 1-6 juv ss (Fig. 322**A**; among s3-s4 and s6-s9) retained, contrastingly narrow, worn, and brownish with distinct bars (Figs. 14**C** & 16**B**); one to a few lower back and/or rump feathers sometimes retained, pale brown, and very worn (Fig. 313**A**, p. 418). **Note: Look also for some SY/TYs and ASY/ATYs also to retain rects (Figs. 288C & D, & 325).**

ASY/ATY (Def. cycle, DB; Oct-Sep): Like AHY/ASY but pp and ss with 2 sets of basic feathers in staffelmauser patterns (Fig.

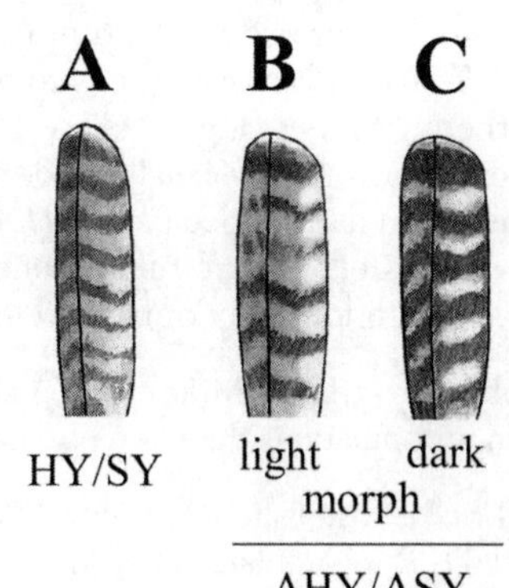

FIGURE 325. Shape and color pattern to the rectrices by age and morph in Short-tailed Hawk. Juv feathers (**A**) are similar among the two morphs. R5 is shown and is usually the last feather replaced during molts and the most likely to be retained during the PB2 and DPB. Some AHYs likely retain rects during these PBs (*cf.* Fig. 288, p. 392) but more study is needed.

16**E**); one to a few scattered lower back and/or rump feathers sometimes retained, dark brown, and slightly worn (Fig. 313**C**). **Note: See SY/TY**.

ATY/A4Y (Def. cycle, DB; Oct-May): Like ASY/ATY but pp with 3 sets of basic feathers in staffelmauser patterns (Fig. 16**F**). **Note: look for occasional individuals with 4 sets of pp (Fig. 16G), reliably aged A4Y/A5Y**.

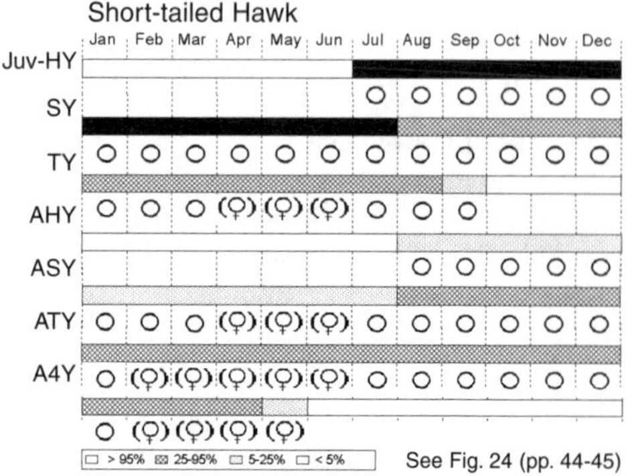

Sex—♀ = ♂ by plumage aspect. Medial BP (Fig. 20**A**, p. 31) and/or distended cloaca (Fig. 21, p. 32) indicates ASY ♀ in Feb-Jun. Measurements generally unhelpful for sexing, although some mated pairs are possibly reliably sexed (Table 39, p. 427). Otherwise, no reliable criteria known.

Hybrids reported—None.

References—Bent (1937), Friedmann (1950), Howell & Webb (1995), Miller & Meyer (2002), Ogden (1973), J.C. Ogden *in* Palmer (1988b), Rand (1960).

SWAINSON'S HAWK

Buteo swainsoni

SWHA
Species # 3420
Band size: 7A Lock-on

Species—From other N.Am hawks by medium size with proportionally long wings, small bill, and short tarsus (Table 40, p. 443; bill width at distal end of cere 10-12 mm); wings pointed (usually p8>p7>p6>p5>p9>p4≈p10>p3) and with p8-p10 notched and p7-p9 emarginated (*cf.* Fig. 287, p. 392); inner webs of p1-p5 dark grayish ventrally and not contrastingly paler than those of outer ss dorsally; rump and uppertail covs dark; r2-r5 grayish, without reddish, and with 7-10 evenly spaced dusky to blackish bands and 1 wider band (Fig. 326); tarsus without feathering to toes (Fig. 334**A**, p. 448); light morphs with heavier markings on breast than abdomen, undertail covs usually paler than abdomen, and underwing covs predominantly pale to whitish, with dark-tipped p covs (*cf.* Fig. 332, p. 444); dark morphs with plumage aspect primarily chocolate, without rufous tones to upperparts, often with squarish white patch to throat, and with lower abdomen and undertail covs paler than abdomen.

Geographic variation—Monotypic. A slightly higher proportion of dark-morph individuals are found in w.populations than in e.populations.

Molt—CBS. PF absent-limited (Sep?-Mar? in HY/SYs), PB2 incomplete-complete (Feb?-Jan? in SY/TYs), DPB incomplete (May-Mar? in ASY/ATYs); PA absent. The DPBs can occur virtually year round, commencing in spring on breeding grounds and continuing on non-breeding grounds after suspensions for chick feeding and migration (see Fig. 289, p. 393); the PB2 commences on non-breeding grounds in some individuals. The PF includes up to 40% of the body feathers but can be absent in some individuals. The PB2 may be complete, or 1-5 outer pp, 1-7 ss (among s3-s4 and s6-s10), 1-4 rects among r2-r6, and/or 1 or more rump feathers can be retained until the PB3. Replacement of pp and ss usually (in ~90% of AHY/ASYs) exhibits staffelmauser (Fig. 16, pp. 23-24), resulting in 1-4 sets of basic feathers present among pp of adults, but identification of sets may be complicated by year-round molting interrupted by suspensions. See Family Account (pp. 391-392) for more information.

Age—Juv (B1; Jul-May) is described under Juv-HY/SY (below) and has grayish to grayish-yellow iris. Juv ♀=♂.

Juv-HY/SY (1st cycle, Juv/B1-F1; Oct-Sep): Rects uniformly narrow and rounded (Fig. 288**A**, p. 392), r2-r5 with 7-10 distinct narrow bands and indistinct dusky subterminal band (Fig. 326**A**); pp and ss uniformly juv (Fig. 16**A**, p. 24), or being replaced in Feb-Sep, the juv outer pp tapered (Fig. 386**A**, p. 392) and brownish, and the juv ss narrow with narrower bands (Fig. 322**A**, p. 431); iris usually yellowish brown; light morph with underparts uniformly streaked or spotted; dark morph with upperparts fringed buff and breast and underparts with pale mottling or large teardrop-shaped spots. **Note: Some SYs may over-summer on non-breeding grounds and exhibit advanced PB2s (see p. 18). This species can be more difficult to age than other *Buteo* hawks; intermediates should be aged AHY/ASY or H-SY or S-TY (see p. 41-42).**

SY/TY (2nd cycle, B2; Oct-Sep): Rects uniformly broad and truncate (Fig. 288**C**), r2-r5 with diffuse brownish bands and broader, blackish subterminal band (Fig. 326**B-C**), or 1-4 juv rects (Fig. 326**A**) sometimes retained (Fig. 288**B**); pp and ss uniformly basic and showing s1-p1 contrast (Fig. 14**B**, p. 21), or 1-5 juv outer pp (Fig. 286**A**; often p8-p10) and/or 1-7 juv ss (Fig. 322**B**; among s3-s4 and s6-s10) retained, contrastingly narrow, worn, and brownish (Figs. 14**C** & 16**B**); one to many les covs, lower back, and/or rump feathers retained, pale brown, and very worn (Fig. 313**A**, p. 418); iris often pale brownish; light morph with streaking concentrated across chest in form of a band and sides of abdomen with sparse markings; dark morph with upperparts and underparts uniformly or near-uniformly dark. **Note: See HY/SY.**

ASY/ATY (Def. cycle, DB; Oct-Sep): Rects broad and truncate (Fig. 288**C**), r2-r5 with diffuse brownish bands and broader, blackish subterminal band (Fig. 326**B-C**), sometimes showing 2-3 generations of basic feathers (Fig. 288**D**); pp and ss with 2 sets of basic feathers in staffelmauser patterns (Fig. 16**E**), the outer pp broad and fresh (Fig. 286**B**), and retained ss broad with somewhat wide and distinct band (Fig. 322**B**); one to a few lower back and/or rump feathers often retained, grayish to dark brown, and slightly worn (Fig. 313**B**); iris usually dark brownish to reddish brown; light morph with complete dark breast band and sides of abdomen with sparse to no markings; dark morph uniformly dark. **Note: See Juv-HY/SY and SY/TY. Reports that some TY/4Ys show distinct predefinitive plumage aspects require verification.**

ATY/A4Y (Def. cycle, DB; Oct-May): Like ASY/ATY but pp with 3 or 4 sets of basic feathers in staffelmauser patterns (Fig. 16**F-G**). **Note: It is possible that individuals with 4 sets of basic pp can be aged A4Y/A5Y, in consideration of suspension limits, but more study is needed.**

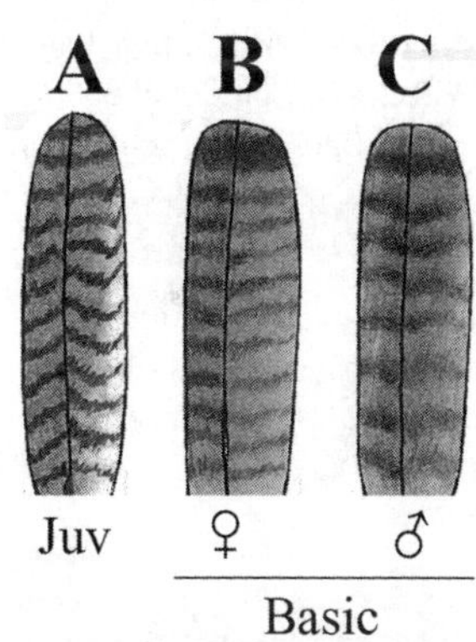

FIGURE 326. Shape and color pattern to the rectrices by feather generation and sex in Swainson's Hawk. Sexes are similar in juv feathers (**A**). R5 is shown and is usually the last feather replaced during molts and the most likely to be retained during the PB2 and DPB; these are sometimes retained in this species, such that Juv-HY/SYs exhibit **A** (Fig. 288**A**, p. 392), SY/TYs can exhibit a mixture of **A** and **B-C** (Fig. 288**B**), individuals exhibiting uniform feathers resembling **B** or **C** are AHY/ASYs (Fig. 288**C**), and ASY/ATYs can exhibit one or more generations of feathers resembling **B-C** (Fig. 288**C-D**), although beware of suspension limits (*cf.* Fig. 289, p. 393), prevalent in this species. There is some overlap between the patterns of the sexes, which might relate to age; confirm sex with measures, if possible, or restrict sex determination to mated pairs; see also Figure 327 (p. 438).

Sex—♀ = ♂ by plumage aspect. Medial BP (Fig. 20**A**, p. 31) and/or distended cloaca (Fig. 21, p. 32) indicate ASY ♀ in Mar-Jul. Measurements unhelpful for sexing, although some mated pairs are possibly reliably sexed (Table 40, p. 443). ♀♀ may average more or darker markings on the underparts than ♂♂ but this difference is confounded by individual variation. In addition to the following, see Sarasola & Negro (2004) for a DFA (p. 5) using forearm length (wrist to proximal end of ulna; *cf.* Fig. 522, p. 744), tail and wg chord that separated 89-94% of live birds in Argentina. Juv-HY/SYs are not reliably sexed.

AHY/ASY ♀: Rects with more distinct bars and wider subterminal dark bar (Figs. 326**B**, p. 437, & 327**A**).

AHY/ASY ♂: Rects with less distinct bars and narrower subterminal dark bar (Figs. 326**C** & 327**B**).

A B
♀ ♂
AHY/ASY

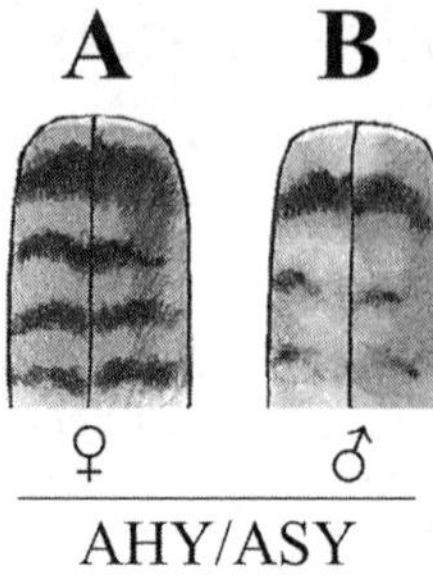

FIGURE 327. Underside of the central rectrices (r1) by sex in Swainson's Hawk. The width of the subterminal band (along the shaft) is usually > 15 mm in ♀♀ and < 15 mm in ♂♂, but beware that there may be overlap in this feature (see also Fig. 326).

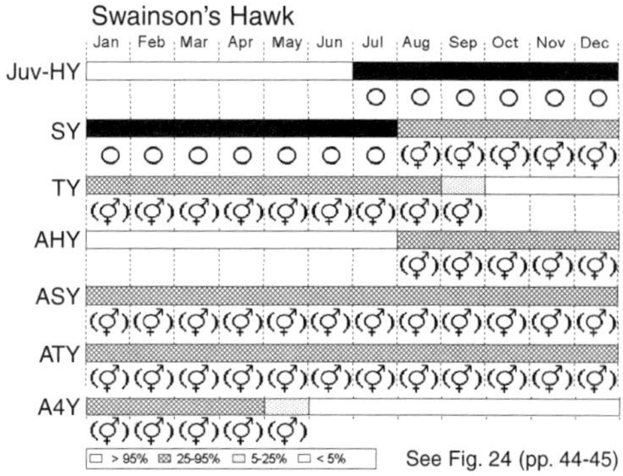

Swainson's Hawk
Jan Feb Mar Apr May Jun Jul Aug Sep Oct Nov Dec
Juv-HY
SY
TY
AHY
ASY
ATY
A4Y
□ > 95% ▨ 25-95% □ 5-25% □ < 5%
See Fig. 24 (pp. 44-45)

Hybrids reported—With Rough-legged Hawk (Clark & Witt 2006, Clark et al 2005) and with non-native Red-backed Buzzard (*B. polyosoma*), of unknown origin, in CO (Clark et al. 2005).

References—Bent (1937), Cameron (1908, 1913), England et al. (1997), Friedmann (1950), Goldstein et al. (1999), Kaufman (1979b), Oberholser (1974), Palmer (1988b), Pyle (2005b, 2005c, 2006a), Sarasola & Negro (2004), Schmutz (1992).

WHITE-TAILED HAWK
Buteo albicaudatus

WTHA
Species # 3410
Band size: 7A-7B Lock-on

Species—From most other N.Am hawks by large size but proportionally short tail (Table 40, p. 443); wings moderately rounded (usually p7>p8>p6>p9>p5>p4≈p10) and with p8-p10 notched and p7-p9 emarginated (*cf.* Fig. 287, p. 392); inner webs of pp and ss dark grayish ventrally; rump and uppertail covs primarily to entirely white; rects pale gray with 12-16 indistinct dusky bands in Juv-HY/SY, to white with distinct blackish band in ASY/ATY (Fig. 328); tarsus without feathering to toes (Fig. 334**A**, p. 448); Juv-HY/SYs and SY/TYs with underparts heavily mottled blackish, the breast paler than the abdomen and with a distinct white patch in SY/TYs; AHY/ASYs with les covs and proximal scapulars reddish.

Geographic variation—See Blake (1977), Friedmann (1950), Hellmayr & Conover (1949), Lehmann V. (1960), Stresemann (1925), Voous (1968), Webster (1973). Two other subspecies in S.Am.

B.a. hypospodius (br & wint N.Am-nw.S.Am): Large (Table 40, p. 443; *vs* wg 360-440, tl 141-215 in *colonus* of ne.S.Am); dark morph absent (*vs* regular in *colonus* and rare in *albicaudatus* of S.Am); upperparts and auriculars medium gray (*vs* sooty to blackish in *albicaudatus* and pale grayish in *colonus*).

Molt—CBS. PF absent-limited (Oct?-Mar? in HY/SYs); PB2 incomplete-complete (Jan?-Nov? in SYs), DPB incomplete (May-Jan in ASY/ATYs); PA absent. The above timing pertains to N.Am populations, which may also include migrants from the S. The PF includes up to 50% of the body feathers but may be absent in some individuals. It is possible that up to 3 pp (p1-p3) and r1 can be replaced for a 2nd time in SYs during the first molt period (W.S. Clark pers. comm.), as part of the PB3 pulled forward (see Turkey Vulture, p. 385, for a similar molt strategy). In most individuals 1-3 outer pp, 1-5 ss among s3-s4 and s7-s9, and 1-4 rects among r2-r5 can be retained until the PB3. Replacement of pp and ss exhibits staffelmauser (Fig. 16, pp. 23-24) with 2-4 sets of basic feathers among pp of adults. Suspension during breeding (Fig. 289, p. 393) likely occurs but limits are difficult to distinguish. See Family Account (pp. 391-392) for more information.

Age—Juv (B1; May-Apr) is described under Juv-HY/SY (below). Juv ♀ = ♂. The following month ranges pertain to N.Am populations.

Juv-HY/SY (1st cycle, Juv/B1-F1; Sep-Aug): Upperparts brown, the les covs sometimes with narrow rufous fringing; underparts and underwing covs heavily mottled blackish, the breast and some underwing covs often mixed with white feathers in Oct-Aug; rects narrow and rounded, brownish white with 12-16 narrow dark brown bands (Fig. 328**A**); pp and ss juv (Fig. 16**A**, p. 24), or being replaced in Dec-Aug, the juv outer pp tapered (Fig. 286**A**, p. 392) and brownish, and the juv ss narrow with a narrow and indistinct band (Fig. 322**A**, p. 431). **Note: Caution that underpart plumage aspect in this species can overlap between age groups, the most advanced formative plumage aspects and most retarded 3rd basic aspects potentially overlapping with 2nd basic aspects. Confirm age with other characters.**

SY/TY (2nd cycle, B2; Sep-Aug): Upperparts blackish, the les covs washed rufous and with dark shaft streaks; underparts and underwing covs variably mottled blackish with distinct white patch in breast and scattered rufous-barred underwing covs; rects broad and truncate, brownish white with variable dusky markings and indistinct subterminal band (Fig. 328**B**), sometimes with 1-4 juv rects (Fig. 328**A**) retained (288**B**, p. 392),; pp and ss uniformly basic

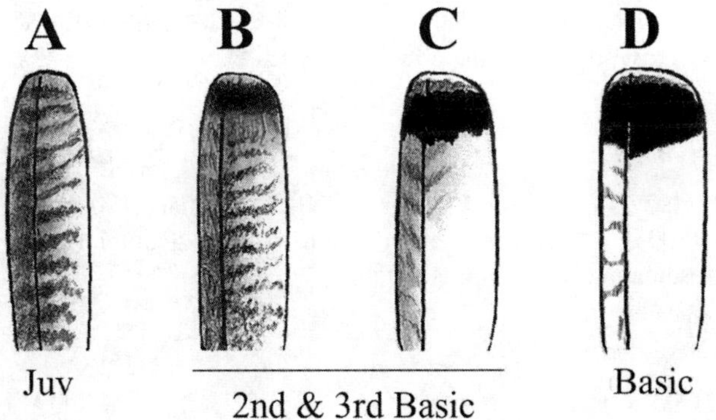

FIGURE 328. Shape and color pattern to the rectrices by feather generation in White-tailed Hawk. R5 is shown and is usually the last feather replaced during molts and the most likely to be retained during the PB2 and DPB. R5 and other rects are sometimes retained in this species, such that Juv-HY/SYs exhibit **A** (Fig. 288**A**, p. 392), SY/TYs can exhibit **B C** or a mixture of **A** and **B-C** (Fig. 288**B**), TY/4Ys can exhibit a mixture of **B-C** (old) and **D** (new), and ATY/A4Ys can exhibit one or more generations of feathers resembling **D** (Fig. 288**C-D**). For 2nd basic rects, earlier-replaced feathers (often r1 and r6) may resemble **B** whereas later-replaced feathers (e.g., r2, r5) may resemble **C**, and for 3rd basic rects, early-replaced feathers can resemble **C** whereas later-replaced feathers resemble **D**. More study is needed on this.

(Fig. 14**B**, p. 21) or with 1-3 juv outer pp (Fig. 286**A**) and/or 1-5 juv ss (Fig. 322**B**; among s3-s4 and s7-s9) retained or being replaced in May-Aug, very faded and worn (Fig. 16**B**). **Note: See Juv-HY/SY. Look for some SY/TYs with pp uniformly basic and p1-p3 replaced for a 2nd time (see Molt).**

TY/4Y (3rd cycle, B3; Sep-Aug): Upperparts sooty, the les covs uniformly rufous; underparts mostly white, with sparse to moderate blackish and rufous mottling or streaking to the throat and abdomen; underwing covs white with fine to heavy rufous and blackish barring; rects white with moderately distinct to distinct dusky band and sometimes with indistinct markings proximally (Fig. 328**C-D**), often with 1-4 2nd-basic rects (Fig. 328**B-C**) retained; pp and ss with 2 sets of basic feathers in staffelmauser patterns (Fig. 16**E**), the outer pp broad (Fig. 286**B**) and retained ss broad with somewhat wide bands (Fig. 322**B**). **Note: See Juv-HY/SY. Some intermediates between this and SY/TY should be aged S-TY or T-4Y (see pp. 41-42); note that ♀♀ may exhibit slower plumage-aspect maturation than ♂♂.**

ATY/A4Y (Def. cycle, DB; Sep-Aug): Upperparts sooty, the les covs uniformly rufous; underparts white, with little or no dark mottling; underwing covs white with fine rufous barring; rects white with distinct black band and usually without indistinct markings proximally (Fig. 328**D**); pp with 2-3 sets of basic feathers in staffelmauser patterns (Fig. 16**E-F**). **Note: Some ATY/A4Ys (perhaps ♀♀ only) may still retain some dark to throat, abdomen, and base of rects; intermediates (with 2 sets of pp) should be aged ASY/ATY.**

A4Y/A5Y (Def. cycle, DB; Sep-May): Like ASY/ATY but underparts and base of rects without dark markings (Fig. 328**D**), the rects often with 2 generations (Fig. 288**D**); pp with 3-4 sets of basic feathers in staffelmauser patterns (Fig. 16**F-G**). **Note: See ATY/A4Y.**

Sex—A full medial BP (Fig. 20**A**, p. 31) and/or distended cloaca (Fig. 21, p. 32) indicates ASY ♀ in Jan-Jun; ♂♂ possibly may develop a partial BP. Measurements unhelpful for sexing, although some mated pairs are possibly reliably sexed (Table 40, p. 443). ♀♀ may average more darkish to throat than ♂♂ of the same age but more study needed on the reliability of this for sexing. Otherwise, no reliable criteria known.

White-tailed Hawk
Jan Feb Mar Apr May Jun Jul Aug Sep Oct Nov Dec
Juv-HY
SY
TY
ASY
ATY
A4Y
A5Y
■ > 95% ▩ 25-95% ▨ 5-25% □ < 5%
See Fig. 24 (pp. 44-45)

Hybrids reported—None.

References—Bent (1937), Clark & Wheeler (1989), Farquhar (1992), Friedmann (1950), Howell & Webb (1995), Oberholser (1974), M. Kopeny *in* Palmer (1988b), Pyle (2005c), Stresemann & Stresemann (1960), Voous (1968).

ZONE-TAILED HAWK

Buteo albonotatus

ZTHA
Species # 3400
Band size: 7A Lock-on

Species—From other N.Am hawks, including dark morphs of other *Buteo* species, by medium size with proportionally long wing and short tarsus (Table 40, p. 443); wings somewhat pointed (usually p7>p6>p8>p9≈p5>p4>p3>p10) and with p7-p10 notched and p6-p9 emarginated (*cf.* Fig. 287, p. 392); body, underwing covs, and undertail covs uniformly blackish with bluish tinge (with white marks to some feathers in Juv-HY/SYs; Fig. 329); inner webs of pp and ss pale grayish ventrally with distinct narrow dusky bands (Fig. 330); r2-r5 grayish with 6-8 indistinct dusky bands and wider terminal tip in Juv-HY/SY or blackish with 2-3 white bands, the subterminal band wider in AHY/ASY (Fig. 331, p. 442); facial skin grayish, contrasting with yellow cere; iris dark in all ages; tarsus without feathering to toes (Fig. 334**A**, p. 448).

Geographic variation—Monotypic (E. Stresemann & D. Amadon *in* Mayr & Cottrell 1979). Populations of e.Panama-S.Am ("*B.a. abbreviatus*") may average smaller and with reduced bluish tinge but differences are insufficient. See Friedmann (1950), Hellmayr & Conover (1949), Monroe (1968), Van Tyne & Sutton (1937), Wetmore (1965).

Molt—CBS. PF limited (Sep?-Mar? in HY/SYs), PB2 incomplete (Mar-Dec in SYs), DPB incomplete (Apr-Feb in ASY/ATYs); PA absent. The above timing pertains to N.Am populations. The PF includes up to 55% of the body feathers. The PB2 is usually if not always incomplete, 1-4 outer pp, 1-6 ss among s3-s4 and s6-s9, 1-4 rects among r2-r5, and 1 or more rump feathers retained until the PB3. Replacement of pp and ss exhibits staffelmauser (Fig. 16, pp. 23-24) with 2-4 sets of basic feathers present among pp of adults. Suspension during breeding (Fig. 289, p. 393) likely occurs but limits are difficult to distinguish. See Family Account (pp. 391-392) for more information.

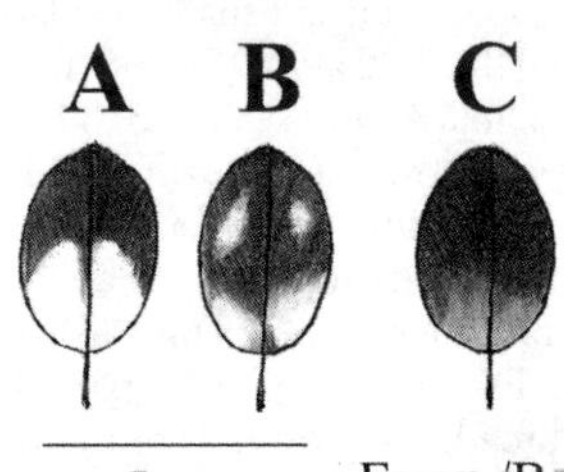

FIGURE 329. Breast feather by age in Zone-tailed Hawk. Juv feathers (**A-B**) exhibit variable amounts of distinct whitish, which is usually visible in the field. Formative and basic feathers have paler but not whitish bases (**C**). Some SYs can replace some breast feathers during the PF but always retain at least a few feathers with distinct white bases or markings. Beware heavily molting AHY/ASYs that can display exposed whitish down feathers. Similar patterns are found in dark-morph Hook-billed Kites and Short-tailed Hawks.

Age—Juv (B1; Jun-Apr) has brown-tinged plumage aspect and some to most underpart (and occasionally upperpart) feathers with extensive white bases or indistinct white bars (Fig. 329**A-B**). Juv ♀=♂ by plumage aspect but size (see **Sex**) is reliable for sexing full-grown juvs. The following month ranges pertain to N.Am populations.

HY/SY (1st cycle, F1; Oct-Sep): Body brownish black, some to most underpart (sometimes upperpart) feathers with white bases or markings (Fig. 329**A-B**); rects narrow and rounded, r2-r5 grayish with 6-8 indistinct dusky bands (Fig. 331**A**, p. 442); pp and ss juv or being replaced in Dec-Sep, the juv outer pp tapered, brownish, relatively worn, and with barring to the tip (Fig. 330**A**), and the ss narrow with narrower bands (*cf.* Fig. 322**A**, p. 431).

SY/TY (2nd cycle, B2; Oct-Sep): Body black, with bluish or grayish tinge, the feathers without white bases or markings (Fig. 329**C**); rects moderately wide and truncate, r2-r5 black with 2-5 white to pale grayish bands (Fig. 331**B-C**), 1-4 juv rects (Fig. 330**A**) sometimes retained (Fig. 288**B**, p. 392); pp and ss with 2 generations, 1-4 juv outer pp (Fig. 330**A**) and 1-6 juv ss (*cf.* Fig. 322**A**; among s3-s4 and s6-s9) retained or being replaced in May-Sep, very faded and worn (Fig. 16**B**, p. 24). **Note: Rare indi-**

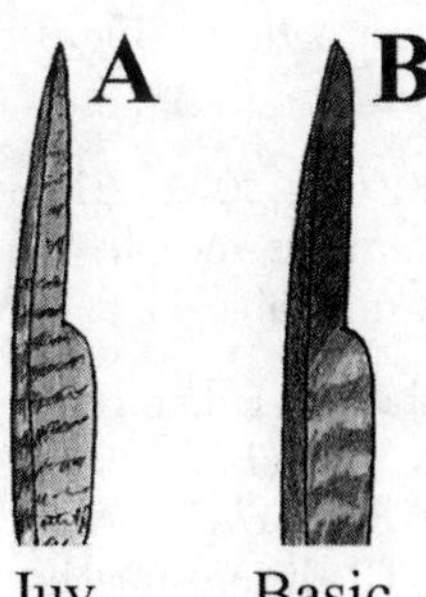

FIGURE 330. Underside to outer primary (p10) by feather generation in Zone-tailed Hawk. Juv feathers (**A**) are usually (if not always) retained during the PB2 and are thus present on SY/TYs as well as Juv-HY/SYs. In basic feathers (**B**) ♂♂ average darker tips than ♀♀, but there is overlap, perhaps related to age.

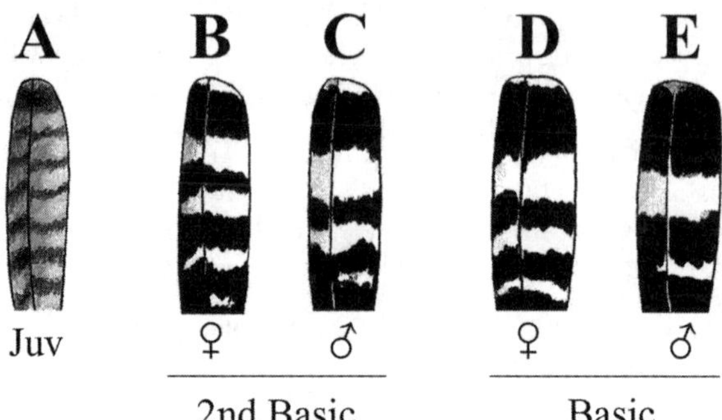

FIGURE 331. Shape and color pattern to the rectrices by feather generation and sex in Zone-tailed Hawk. R5 is shown and is usually the last feather replaced during molts and the most likely to be retained during the PB2 and DPB. R5 and other rects are sometimes retained in this species, such that Juv-HY/SYs exhibit **A** (Fig. 288**A**, p. 392), SY/TYs can exhibit **B-C** or a mixture of **A** and **B-C** (Fig. 288**B**), TY/4Ys can exhibit a mixture of **B-C** (old) and **D-E** (new), and ATY/A4Ys can exhibit one or more generations of feathers resembling **D-E** (Fig. 288**C-D**). A sex-specific difference in the number of white bands in the rects begins to appear in 2nd basic feathers (**B-C**; typically 3-4 bands in ♀♀ and 3 in ♂♂) and becomes more diagnostic in definitive basic feathers (**D-E**; 3 bands in ♀♀ and 2-3 bands in ♂♂). ASY/ATY ♂♂ with 3 bands typically have the proximal band narrow and not extending to r6, whereas it is broader and extends to r6 in ♀♀.

viduals with uniformly replaced pp and ss (Fig. 14B, p. 21) may be encountered; these should be aged AHY/ASY but are likely SY/TYs.

ASY/ATY (Def. cycle, DB; Oct-Sep): Like SY/TY but pp and ss with 2 sets of basic feathers in staffelmauser patterns (Fig. 16**E**), the outer pp broad, fresh, and dark at tip (Fig. 330**B**), and retained ss broad with somewhat wide bands (Fig. 322**B**); rects basic (Fig. 331**D-E**), sometimes showing 2 generations (Fig. 288**D**). **Note: See SY/TY. It is possible that some TY/4Ys with retained 2nd basic rects (Fig. 331B-C) can be aged; study needed.**

ATY/A4Y (Def. cycle, DB; Oct-Sep): Like ASY/ATY but pp with 3 sets of basic feathers in staffelmauser patterns (Fig. 16**F**). **Note: See SY/TY.**

A4Y/A5Y (Def. cycle, DB; Oct-Apr): Like ASY/ATY but pp with 4 sets of basic feathers in staffelmauser patterns (Fig. 16**G**). **Note: See SY/TY. This age designation may be rare in this species.**

Sex—Medial BP (Fig. 20**A**, p. 31) and/or distended cloaca (Fig. 21, p. 32) indicates ASY ♀ in Feb-Jun. Measurements reliable for sexing individuals in N.Am (Table 40, p. 443).

♀: Wg chord > 400, culmen from cere > 23.3, and tarsus > 72 (Table 40); rects with 3-4 (SY/TY) to 3 (ASY/ATY) white bands (Fig. 331**B**, **D**), if 3, the proximal band broad and extending to r6.

♂: Wg chord < 400, culmen from cere < 23.3, and tarsus < 72 (Table 40); rects with 3 (SY/TY) to 2-3 (ASY/ATY) white bands (Fig. 331**C**, **E**), if 3, the proximal band narrow and not extending to r6.

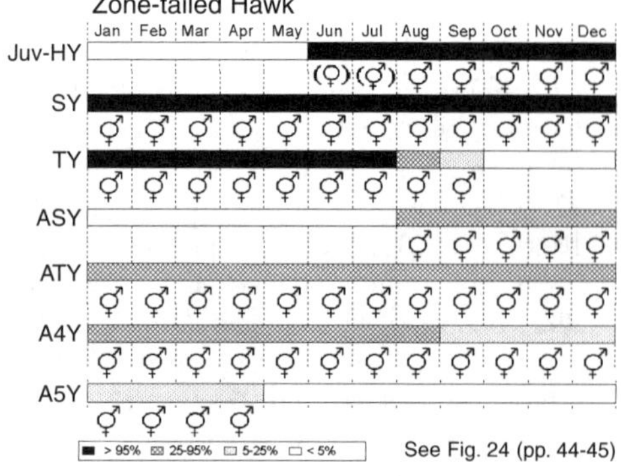

Hybrids reported—None.

References—Bent (1937), Dunne et al. (2000), Friedmann (1950), Howell & Webb (1995), Johnson et al. (2000), Oberholser (1974), Palmer (1988b), Pyle (2005b, 2005c).

TABLE 40. Measurements (mm) of larger North American *Buteo* hawks and allies to assist in identification and sexing. See pp. 4-11 for methods of measurment. Species summaries are in **bold** and subspecies summaries are in ***italics***. Values were derived from 95% confidence intervals as based approximately on the indicated sample sizes (see pp. 4-5); thus midpoints of ranges approximate means, and S.D. is approximated by 25% of the range.

Taxon/Sex	*n*	wing chord	tail length[1]	culmen from cere[2]	tarsus
Common Black-Hawk[3]		**343-395**	**180-238**	**23.5-31.5**	**83-95**
♀	47	357-395	189-238	25.0-31.5	84-95
♂	43	343-378	180-229	23.5-29.2	83-94
Swainson's Hawk		**360-432**	**185-233**	**19.6-26.2**	**59-77**
♀	70	382-432	195-233	21.2-26.2	64-77
♂	100	360-408	185-222	19.6-24.6	59-73
White-tailed Hawk[3]		**397-457**	**151-225**	**22.3-30.6**	**84-95**
♀	40	413-457	163-225	23.8-30.6	86-95
♂	51	397-437	151-212	22.3-28.7	84-93
Zone-tailed Hawk[3]		**374-436**	**196-253**	**20.9-25.9**	**65-78**
♀	30	404-436	213-253	23.6-25.9	71-78
♂	30	374-399	196-236	20.9-23.2	65-72
Red-tailed Hawk[3]		**321-455**	**187-263**	**22.3-31.0**	**75-99**
Interior Western ssp.[4]		***355-450***	***199-263***	***22.3-30.3***	***78-97***
♀	100	380-450	210-263	23.4-30.3	81-97
♂	100	355-421	199-250	22.3-28.0	78-93
B.j. alascensis		***321-391***	***189-246***	***22.3-28.2***	***75-91***
♀	17	339-391	200-246	23.3-28.2	77-91
♂	17	321-367	189-235	22.3-26.1	75-88
B.j. fuertesi		***370-455***	***189-250***	***22.8-30.8***	***83-99***
♀	30	395-455	202-250	23.9-30.8	86-99
♂	30	370-430	189-237	22.8-28.5	83-94
B.j. borealis		***332-437***	***187-259***	***22.5-30.8***	***76-95***
♀	100	356-437	199-259	23.6-30.8	79-95
♂	100	332-409	187-244	22.5-28.9	76-91
B.j. umbrinus		***338-433***	***206-262***	***24.1-31.0***	***82-95***
♀	14	362-433	218-262	26.2-31.0	85-95
♂	16	338-405	206-249	24.1-27.8	82-91
Ferruginous Hawk		**417-466**	**217-264**	**25.1-32.8**	**80-92**
♀	50	434-466	226-264	27.0-32.8	83-92
♂	40	417-446	217-255	25.1-30.8	80-88
Rough-legged Hawk[3]		**378-448**	**194-250**	**20.3-25.8**	**64-76**
♀	100	420-448	208-250	21.4-25.8	66-76
♂	100	378-425	194-234	20.3-24.5	64-73

[1] Tail length values include birds of all ages; in most *Buteo* species the juvenal rects average up to 15% longer than adult rects, sex for sex.

[2] Culmen from cere represents the chord (Fig. 7**B**, p. 0).

[3] Measures represent N.Am populations only (see **Geographic variation**).

[4] In Red-tailed Hawk "Interior western subspecies" includes *B.j. harlani, calurus*, and "*kriderii*". See **Geographic variation** for more information, including values for the shorter tail length of *harlani*.

RED-TAILED HAWK
Buteo jamaicensis

RTHA
Species # 3370
Band size: 7B-7D-7A Lock-on

Harlan's Hawk (HALH) Species # 3380, Band size: 7B-7A Lock-on

Species—AHY/ASYs of most subspecies from other N.Am raptors by rects primarily rufous (*cf.* Fig. 333, p. 446). Harlan's Hawk and Juv/HY-SYs of all subspecies from other N.Am hawks by medium-large to large size (Table 40, p. 443; bill width at distal end of cere 10-13 mm); wings somewhat rounded (usually p7>p6>p8>p9>p5>p4>p10≈p3) and with p7-p10 notched and p6-p9 emarginated (*cf.* Fig. 287, p. 392); inner webs of pp and ss white to pale grayish ventrally and light morph with underwing marginal les covs and tips to p covs contrastingly dark (Fig. 332); les covs without rufous; uppertail covs dark; medial rects (r2-r5) with 10-12 evenly spaced and distinct dusky brownish bands (Juv-HY/SY) or indistinctly mottled grayish in AHY/ASY Harlan's Hawk (Fig. 333); tarsus without feathering to toes (Fig. 334**A**, p. 448); Juv-HY/SY with inner webs of p1-p5 contrastingly paler than those of outer ss dorsally; light morph with abdomen usually with distinct teardrop-shaped streaks, often forming band, and usually contrasting with paler breast; dark morph dark brown, often washed rufous (heaviest on breast), the throat and undertail covs dark.

Common Buzzard (*Buteo buteo*), a potential vagrant to w.AK or elsewhere, is smaller in size, especially bill (wg chord 320-410, tl 175-235, culmen from cere 18.1-24.9, tarsus 69-80); middle toe without claw < 37 mm (*vs* > 37 mm in Red-tailed Hawk); bases to underside of pp mostly white, without rufous, dusky, or gray markings; plumage aspect of Asian subspecies washed pale brown; rects of AHY/ASY mostly dusky, gray, and whitish, with no to some rufous.

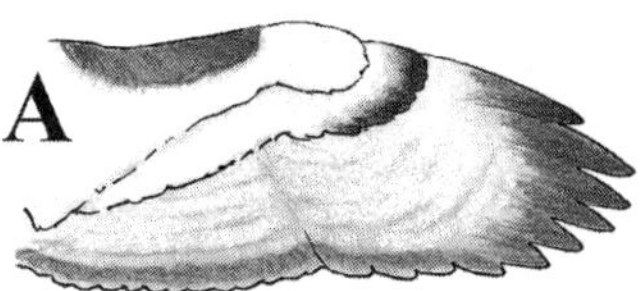

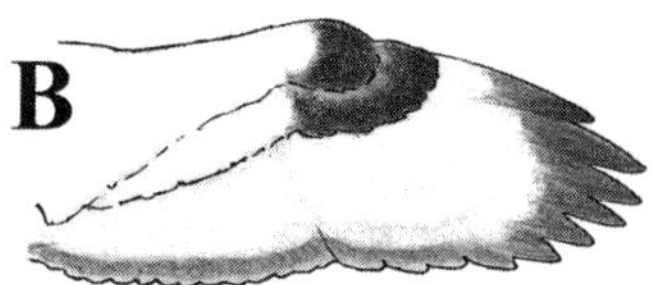

FIGURE 332. Underwing patterns of Red-tailed (**A**) and Rough-legged (**B**) hawks for identification in the hand. Note dark underwing marginal les covs and tips to p covs in Red-tailed Hawk as opposed to pale marginal coverts but completely dark p covs in Rough-legged Hawk. These patterns pertain to all age groups of all but the darkest morphs. Light-morph Swainson's and Ferruginous hawks typically exhibit pale to whitish underwing covs with dark tips to the p covs; some intermediate-morph Swainson's Hawks can have largely dark p covs (as in **B**) and some intermediate-morph Ferruginous Hawks can have dark mottling to the marginal les covs (as in **A** but not as completely dark).

Geographic variation—See Bangs (1901), Behle (1985), Blake (1977), Brewster (1902b), Clark & Wheeler (1987), Collins & Bloom (2000), Dickerman (1989, 1994), Dickerman & Parkes (1987), Dickey & van Rossem (1938), Eifrig (1928), Fitzpatrick & Dunk (1999), Friedmann (1950), Gibson & Kessel (1997), Green (1967), Grinnell (1909), Hellmayr & Conover (1949), Julian (1967), Lavers (1975), Liguori (2001), Lish (2007), Lish & Voelker (1986), Mindell (1983, 1985), Oberholser (1974), Palmer (1988b), Parkes (1996), Patten et al. (2003), Pearlstine & Thompson (2004), Phillips et al. (1964), Pittaway (1993a), Preston & Beane (1993), Sibley (2000), Storer (1962), Sutton & Van Tyne (1935), Swarth (1926, 1928), Taverner (1927, 1936), Todd (1950b, 1963), Van Tyne & Sutton (1937), Wheeler (2003a, 2003b), and Wood (1932). Nine other subspecies in W.Indes and Mex-C.Am. Beware that zones of intergradation between the following subspecies can be broad.

Harlan's *B.j. harlani* Subspecies Group. Both light and dark morphs; rects of AHY/ASYs variably washed gray and white, sometimes with rufous mottling.

B.j. harlani (br c.AK-Yuk to n.BC, wint e.WA-ne.CA to IA-LA, vagrant to s.CA-AZ and WI-FL): Harlan's Hawk. Medium to large in size (Table 40, p. 443) but tail proportionally short (♀ 197-253, ♂ 187-235); dark morph sooty, without reddish or brownish tones; underparts and underwing covs of light morph with blackish mottling, spotting, or streaking throughout and underwing gr covs darkish gray with dusky bars; rects of AHY/ASYs variably washed whitish, brown, and dusky with little to no rufous mottling, often with a dusky terminal band (Fig. 333**H**, p. 446).

Western (*B.j. calurus*) Subspecies Group. Both light and dark morphs; underparts and underwing covs of light morph with heavy markings; tail of AHY/ASY primarily rufous.

B.j. alascensis (br & wint coastal se.AK-sw.BC): Small (Table 40); dark morph blackish with brownish tinge; underparts and underwing covs of light morph buff to pale rufous with heavy brownish spotting or streaking to throat and abdomen, indistinct rufous streaking to the elongated femoral feathers, and underwing gr covs washed dusky; rects of AHY/ASYs dark rufous with irregular cross bands and complete and wide subterminal band (Fig. 333**D-E**).

B.j. calurus (br sc.AK-w.Sask to s.CA-NM, wint to MN-LA, vagrant to Ont-MS): Medium to large in size (Table 40); dark morph washed rufous or warm brown; underparts and underwing covs of light morph buff to pale rufous with heavy dusky streaking to throat, light to heavy dusky spotting or streaking to abdomen, moderately heavy brown to rufous streaking to the elongated femoral feathers, and underwing gr covs gray with dusky bars; rects of AHY/ASYs medium-pale rufous with variable dusky markings and usually complete and moderately wide dusky band (Fig. 333**D-F**).

Eastern (*B.j. borealis*) Subspecies Group. Mostly or entirely light morph; underparts and underwing covs with no to some dark markings.

B.j. fuertesi (br & wint se.CA-e.UT to se.TX): Medium-large with proportionally long wing and short tail (Table 40); underparts and underwing covs white to cream with sparse to heavy, dusky to rufous streaking to throat, sparse to no dusky spotting or streaking to abdomen, little or no pale brown streaking to elongated femoral feathers, and whitish underwing gr covs with sparse or no dusky markings; rects of AHY/ASYs pale rufous with little to no markings except (sometimes) a very incomplete blackish band (Fig. 333**G**). **Note: This could be considered in a different subspecies group.**

B.j. borealis (br & wint ne.Alb-Lab to TX-n.FL): Medium in size (Table 40); underparts and underwing covs white to pale buff, with little to moderate dark streaking to throat and/or buff to dusky streaking to elongated femoral feathers, sparse to moderate and distinct black spotting or streaking to abdomen, and cream underwing gr covs with sparse but distinct dark barring; rects of AHY/ASYs medium-dark rufous with little or no markings except an incomplete to complete, narrow to moderately wide band (Fig. 333**F-G**). Populations of ne.Alb-Lab ("*abieticola*") may average darker markings to the underparts and underwing covs and a wider blackish band to rects but these differences are confounded by substantial individual variation. **Note: The above description excludes white-morph individuals, "Krider's Red-tailed Hawk" ("*krideri*"), that br in sc.Alb-e.Man to n.CO-nw.NE, wint to TX, and occur as vagrants to CA-AZ and PA-FL. These are medium to large in size (Table 40); crown and nape primarily whitish; underparts and underwing covs white with no dusky streaking to throat or buff streaking to elongated femoral feathers, moderately sparse to no black spotting or streaking to abdomen, and white underwing gr covs with little or no dark markings; rects of Juv-HY/SY pale brown to whitish with distinct bands (Fig. 333B) and those of AHY/ASY whitish, often with pale rufous distally, and with an incomplete to complete dusky band (Fig. 333F-G). Krider's Red-tailed Hawk is here considered a white morph of borealis (Wheeler 2003a, 2003b), although, based on size, it may also be a morph of calurus (Dickerman 1989) or of both subspecies.**

B.j. umbrinus (res c-s. FL, vagrant to NC): Medium-large (Table 40); underparts and underwing covs white to pale buff, with moderate dusky streaking to throat, distinct black spotting to streaking to abdomen, whitish elongated femoral feathers often with small brown marks, and whitish underwing gr covs with sparse but distinct dark barring; rects of AHY/ASYs rufous with variable dusky markings and usually complete and moderately narrow dusky band (Fig. 333**D**). Populations of the W.Indes (*solitudinis* and *jamaicensis*), possible vagrants to s.FL, are similar in plumage aspect but average smaller (wg 330-371, tl 189-215, culmen from cere 25.5-29.1, tarsus 80-87).

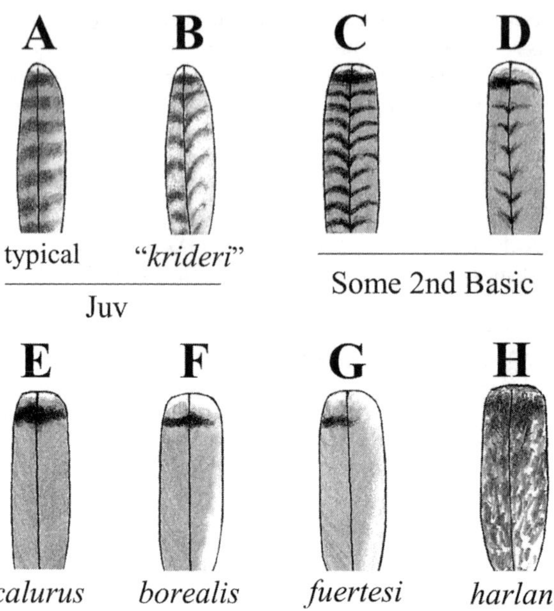

FIGURE 333. Shape and color pattern to the rectrices by feather generation, subspecies, and age in Red-tailed Hawk. R5 is shown and is usually the last feather replaced during molts and the most likely to be retained during the PB2 and DPB. R5 and other rects are occasionally retained in this species, such that Juv-HY/SYs exhibit **A-B** (Fig. 288**A**, p. 392), SY/TYs can exhibit **C-D** or **E-H**, occasionally with 1-2 feathers resembling **A-B** retained (Fig. 288**B**), and ATY/A4Ys can exhibit one or more generations of feathers resembling **E-H** (Fig. 288**C-D**). Second basic rects exhibiting bars basally (**C-D**) are often those replaced earlier during the PB2, including r1 and r6, and are rarely retained during the PB3. Note that there is individual variation within all subspecies/age groups; typical examples are shown.

Molt—CBS. PF absent-limited (Sep-Mar in HY/SYs), PB2 incomplete-complete (Feb-Oct in SYs), DPB incomplete (Apr-Nov in ASYs); PA absent. The above timing pertains to N.Am populations. The PF occurs primarily on non-breeding grounds whereas the DPBs occur primarily on breeding grounds but can complete on non-breeding grounds in ASYs. The PF can include up to 20% of the body feathers, but appears to be absent in many individuals. The PB2 is typically incomplete (but can be complete in 5-10% of individuals), with 1-4 outer pp, 1-6 ss among s3-s4 and s6-s9, 1 or more rump feathers, occasionally 1 or more rects among r2-r5, and/or scattered other feathers retained until the PB3. Replacement of pp and ss exhibits staffelmauser (Fig. 16, pp. 23-24) with 2-4 sets of basic feathers present among pp of adults. Suspension during breeding (Fig. 289, p. 393) likely occurs but limits are difficult to distinguish. See Family Account (pp. 391-392) for more information.

Age—Juv (B1; Jul-May) is described under Juv-HY/SY (below) and has grayish to grayish-yellow iris. Juv ♀=♂. See Hawfield (1986) for additional information on fault bars in this species. The following month ranges pertain to N.Am populations.

Juv-HY/SY (1st cycle, Juv/B1-F1; Oct-Sep): Rects narrow, rounded, with 10-12 dusky brownish bands (Fig. 333**A-B**), and without reddish; pp and ss juv (Fig. 16**A**, p. 24), or being replaced in Feb-Sep, the juv outer pp tapered (Fig. 286**A**, p. 392), relatively worn, and with indistinct dusky bars and tips, and the ss narrow with narrower band (Fig. 322**A**, p. 431); inner webs of p1-p5 mottled pale brown to whitish (*cf.* Fig. 336**A**, p. 450), contrastingly paler than those of outer ss dorsally; iris usually grayish to yellowish. **Note: See SY/TY.**

SY/TY (2nd cycle, B2; Oct-Sep): Rects broad and truncate, r2-r5 dull to bright rufous with a dusky band (Fig. 333**E-H**), one or more often distinctly barred blackish basally (Fig. 333**C-D**), and/or with 1-2 juv feathers (Fig. 333**A-B**) occasionally retained (Fig. 288**B**, p. 392); pp and ss with 2 generations, 1-4 juv outer pp (Fig. 286**A**) and/or 1-6 juv ss (Fig. 322**A**, among s3-s4 and s6-s9) retained (Fig. 16**B**) or being replaced in May-Sep; inner webs of p1-p5 brown (*cf.* Fig. 336**E**), slightly paler or uniform in aspect with those of outer ss dorsally; one to many lower back and/or rump feathers retained, pale brown, and very worn (Fig. 313**A**, p. 418); iris usually yellowish to brownish yellow (often darker below than above). **Note: SY/TY Harlan's Hawk and "Krider's" Red-tailed Hawk (see Geographic variation) can lack red in the rects; use other characters to age these forms. Occasional individuals with uniformly replaced pp and ss (Fig. 14B, p. 21) may be encountered; these should be aged AHY/ASY but are often SY/TYs.**

ASY/ATY (Def. cycle, DB; Oct-Sep): Rects broad and truncate, r2-r5 primarily bright rufous with a dusky band, sometimes with sparse basal markings (Fig. 333**D-H**), and occasionally with 2 generations (Fig. 288**D**); pp and ss with 2 sets of basic feathers in staffelmauser patterns (Fig. 16**E**), the outer pp broad (Fig. 286**B**), fresh, and with distinct blackish bars and tips, and retained ss broad and with somewhat wider band (Fig. 322**B**); inner webs of p1-p5 dusky brown (*cf.* Fig. 336**F**), uniform in aspect with those of outer ss dorsally; one to a few lower back and/or rump feathers sometimes retained, dark brown, and slightly worn (Fig. 313**C**); iris usually brownish yellow to brown. **Note: See SY/TY**.

ATY/A4Y (Def. cycle, DB; Oct-Sep): Like ASY/ATY but pp with 3 sets of basic feathers in staffelmauser patterns (Fig. 16**F**).

A4Y/A5Y (Def. cycle, DB; Oct-Apr): Like ASY/ATY but pp with 4 sets of basic feathers in staffelmauser patterns (Fig. 16**G**).

Sex—♀=♂ by plumage aspect. Medial BP (Fig. 20**A**, p. 31) and/or distended cloaca (Fig. 21, p. 32) indicates ASY ♀ in Feb-Jun. Measurements unhelpful for sexing, although some mated pairs may be reliably sexed assuming subspecies is known (Table 40, p. 443); see also O'Leary (1994) for information on sexing this species by hallux (hind claw; Fig. 342, p. 455) depth. The width of the band on the rects may average wider in AHY/ASY ♀♀ than in AHY/ASY ♂♂, as in other *Buteo* hawks (*cf.* Fig. 327, p. 438), but this difference is confounded by geographic variation. Otherwise, no reliable criteria known for sexing.

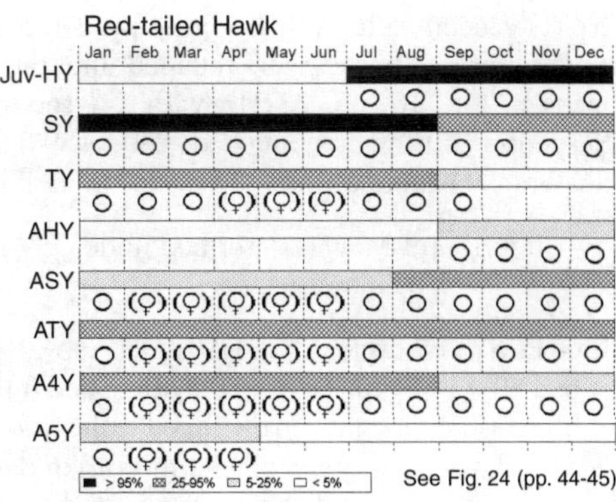

Hybrids reported—With Harris's Hawk (p. 424) and Rough-legged Hawk (Clark et al. 2005) in the wild. Possibly with Red-shouldered Hawk (p. 426). A released Red-tailed Hawk with Common Buzzard (*B. buteo*) in Scotland in the wild (Murray 1970).

References—Baker (1993), Bent (1937), Bierregaard (1974), Cramp & Simmons (1980), Dement'ev & Gladkov (1951b), Forsman (1999), Friedmann (1950), Hamerstrom (1971), Kaufman (1979b, 1989), Mindell (1985), Oberholser (1974), Palmer (1988b), Pearlstine & Thompson (2004), Preston & Beane (1993), Pyle (2005b, 2005c), Roberts (1955), Sheppard & Klimkiewicz (1976), Taverner (1927), Wood (1969).

FERRUGINOUS HAWK
Buteo regalis

FEHA
Species # 3480
Band size: 7D-8-7B Lock-on

Species—From other N.Am hawks by medium-large to large size with large bill (Table 40, p. 443; bill width at distal end of cere 13-17 mm, bill depth at base 20.3-22.1 mm); wings rounded (usually p8≈p7>p6>p9>p5>p4>p10≈p3) and with p7-p10 notched (p6 slightly notched) and p6-p9 emarginated (*cf.* Fig. 287, p. 392); les covs fringed (Juv-HY/SY) to predominantly (AHY/ASY) bright rufous; inner webs of pp and ss white ventrally; r2-r5 whitish with 1-5 very indistinct dusky bands (Juv-HY/SY) or with variable gray wash and rufous fringes in AHY/ASY (Fig. 335); tarsus with dense feathering to base of toes (Fig. 334**A**); Juv-HY/SYs with inner webs of p1-p5 contrastingly paler than those of outer ss dorsally (*cf.* Fig. 336, p. 450); light morph with abdomen usually more densely streaked than breast, elongated femoral feathers usually darker, and underwing covs whitish variably mottled rufous and with dark tips to the p covs (*cf.* Fig. 332, p. 444); uncommon dark morph dark brown with rufous wash (heaviest on breast) and elongated femoral and leg feathers.

Geographic variation—Monotypic. W.populations have a higher proportion of dark-morph individuals and may average slightly larger but these differences insufficient for subspecific recognition. See Bechard & Schmutz (1995), Palmer (1988b), Schmutz & Fyfe (1987), and Schmutz & Schmutz (1981) for more information.

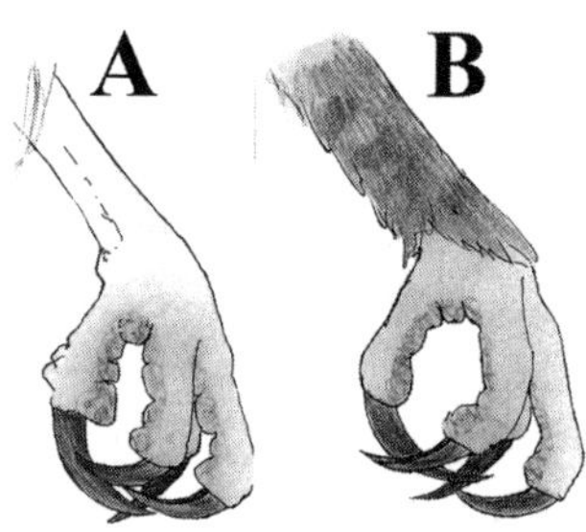

FIGURE 334. Extent of feathering to tarsus by species in diurnal raptors. Most species exhibit unfeathered tarsus (**A**), whereas feathered tarsus (**B**) is exhibited by Ferruginous Hawk, Rough-legged Hawk, and Golden Eagle.

Molt—CBS. PF absent-limited (Sep-Mar in HY/SYs), PB2 incomplete (Apr-Oct in SYs), DPB incomplete (May-Dec in ASYs); PA absent. The PF occurs primarily on non-breeding grounds and the DPBs occur primarily on breeding grounds but can complete on non-breeding grounds in ASYs. The PF includes up to 5% of the body feathers but appears to be absent in most individuals. The PB2 is typically incomplete, with 1-4 outer pp, 1-6 ss among s3-s4 and s6-s9, and sometimes 1-4 rects and scattered other feathers retained until the PB3. Replacement of pp and ss exhibits staffelmauser (Fig. 16, pp. 23-24), with 2-4 sets of basic feathers present among pp of adults. Suspension during breeding (Fig. 289, p. 393) likely occurs but limits are difficult to distinguish. See Family Account (pp. 391-392) for more information.

Age—Juv (B1; Jul-May) is described under Juv-HY/SY (below) and has grayish to grayish-yellow iris. Juv ♀=♂ by plumage aspect.

Juv-HY/SY (1st cycle, Juv/B1-F1; Oct-Sep): Rects uniformly narrow and rounded (Fig. 288**A**, p. 392), r2-r5 with 1-5 very indistinct and often incomplete dusky bands (Fig. 335**A**); les covs brownish (dark morph), fringed pale rufous in light morph; elongated femoral feathers whitish with dusky spots (light morph) or dark brown (dark morph); pp and ss juv (Fig. 16**A**, p. 24), or being replaced in Apr-Sep, the juv outer pp tapered (Fig. 286**A**, p. 392), brownish, and relatively worn, and the medial ss pale brown with 2-3 narrow and indistinct dark brown bands to the outer webs (*cf.* Fig. 322**A**, p. 431); inner webs of p1-p5 whitish brown (*cf.* Fig. 336**A**, p. 450), contrastingly paler than those of the outer ss dorsally; iris usually grayish to yellowish.

SY/TY (2nd cycle, B2; Oct-Sep): Rects broad and squared, r2-r5 primarily white or dull gray, sometimes fringed rufous, with little or no indistinct dusky bands (Fig. 335**B**), and sometimes with 1-2 juv feathers (Fig. 335**A**) retained (Figs. 288**B** & 335**A**); les covs bright rufous, sometimes with dusky shaft streaks (light morph) or dark brown with brightish rufous fringing (dark morph); elongated femoral feathers rufous with dusky barring; pp and ss with 2 generations, 1-4 juv outer pp (Fig. 286**A**) and 1-6 juv ss (Fig. 322**A**; among s3-s4 and s6-s9) retained or being replaced in May-Sep, very faded and worn (Fig. 16**B**); inner webs of p1-p5 brown (*cf.* Fig. 336**E**), slightly paler than those of the outer ss dorsally; iris usually yellowish to brownish yellow (often darker below than above). **Note: Rare individuals with uniformly replaced pp and ss (Fig. 14B, p. 21) may be encountered; these should be aged AHY/ASY but are often SY/TYs.**

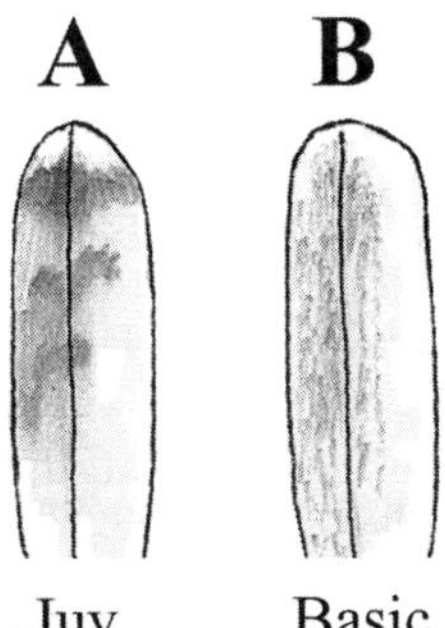

FIGURE 335. Shape and color pattern to the rectrices by feather generation in Ferruginous Hawk. R5 is shown and is usually the last feather replaced during molts and the most likely to be retained during the PB2 and DPB. R5 and other rects are sometimes retained in this species, such that Juv-HY/SYs exhibit **A** (Fig. 288**A**, p. 392), SY/TYs exhibit **B** or sometimes both **A** and **B** (Fig. 288**B**), and ATY/A4Ys can exhibit one or more generations of feathers resembling **B** (Fig. 288**C**-**D**). Look for some 2nd basic rects in some SY/TYs to be intermediate.

ASY/ATY (Def. cycle, DB; Oct-Sep): Rects uniformly broad and squared (Fig. 288**C**), r2-r5 whitish with variable gray wash and rufous fringing and without dusky bands (Fig. 335**B**), sometimes with 2 generations (Fig. 288**D**); les covs and femoral feathers as in SY/TY; pp and ss with 2 sets of basic feathers in staffelmauser patterns (Fig. 16**E**), the outer pp broad (Fig. 286**B**) and fresh, and the medial ss gray with 2 narrow and 1 broader and distinct dusky bands to the outer web (*cf.* Fig. 322**B**); inner webs of p1-p5 dusky brown (*cf.* Fig. 336**F**), uniform in aspect with those of the outer ss dorsally; iris usually brownish. **Note: See SY/TY.**

ATY/A4Y (Def. cycle, DB; Oct-Sep): Like ASY/ATY but pp with 3 sets of basic feathers in staffelmauser patterns (Fig. 16**F**).

A4Y/A5Y (Def. cycle, DB; Oct-May): Like ASY/ATY but pp with 4 sets of basic feathers in staffelmauser patterns (Fig. 16**G**).

Sex—♀=♂ by plumage aspect. A Full medial BP (Fig. 20**A**, p. 31) and/or distended cloaca (Fig. 21, p. 32) indicates ASY ♀ in Mar-Jun; ♂♂ possibly may develop a partial BP. Measurements unhelpful for sexing, although some mated pairs are possibly reliably sexed (Table 40, p. 443). Otherwise, no reliable criteria known for sexing.

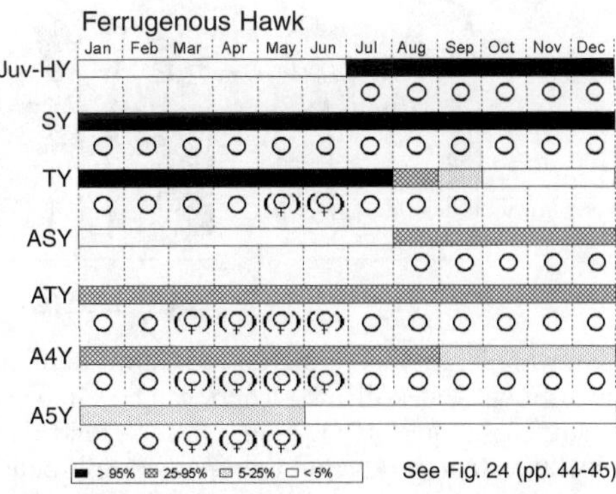

Hybrids reported—None.

References—Bechard & Schmutz (1995), Bent (1937), Eckert (1982), Friedmann (1950), Kaufman (1989), Oberholser (1974), Palmer (1988b), Pyle (2005b, 2005c), Roberts (1955), Schmutz (1992).

ROUGH-LEGGED HAWK

Buteo lagopus

RLHA
Species # 3470
Band size: 7A-7B Lock-on

Species—From other N.Am hawks by medium to medium-large size with proportionally small bill and tarsus (Table 40, p. 443; bill width at distal end of cere 9-11 mm, bill depth at base 16.8-20.3 mm); wings pointed (usually p7>p8>p9>p6>p5>p4>p3>p10≈p2) and with p6-p10 notched (p6 slightly) and p6-p9 emarginated (*cf.* Fig. 287, p. 392); inner webs of pp and ss pale grayish to white ventrally (Fig. 336); rects with variably indistinct dusky banding and (usually) a distinct dusky to blackish subterminal band (Fig. 338, p. 452); underwing les and gr p covs broadly tipped to entirely dusky to blackish (Fig. 332**B**, p. 444); tarsus with dense feathering to toes (Fig. 334**B**, p. 448); light morph with lower breast whitish, variably spotted or streaked dark, usually contrasting with dusky or more heavily marked abdomen; dark morph uniformly brown, sometimes with slight rufous tones (usually heaviest on elongated femoral feathers) to blackish, often with pale mottling dorsally in Juv-HY/SYs, the throat and undertail covs not distinctly paler.

Geographic variation—See Bailey (1942), Bechard & Swem (2002), Cade (1955), Chapman (1904b), Cramp & Simmons (1980), Dement'ev & Gladkov (1951b), Friedmann (1934b, 1950), Gibson & Kessel (1997), Millington (2001), D.P. Mindell *in* Palmer (1988b), Portenko (1972), Todd (1963). One other subspecies occurs in Europe-w.Asia. Reported variation in the amount of white to the undersides of the pp as a subspecific character is confounded by age-related and individual variation.

B.l. kamtschatkensis (br c-ne.Asia, probable vagrant to w.AK): Plumage aspect averages paler and dark morph absent (intermediates may occur); Juv-HY/SY with white to pale cream breast.

B.l. sanctijohannis (br & wint N.Am): Plumage aspect averages darker and dark morph occurs; Juv-HY/SY pale morph with buff breast. Within N.Am, w.populations (west of 80° W) average slightly larger and with less contrasting plumage aspect (especially to the rects of AHY/ASY ♂♂; see also **Sex**) than e.populations (east of 80° W) but differences are broadly clinal and insufficient for subspecific recognition.

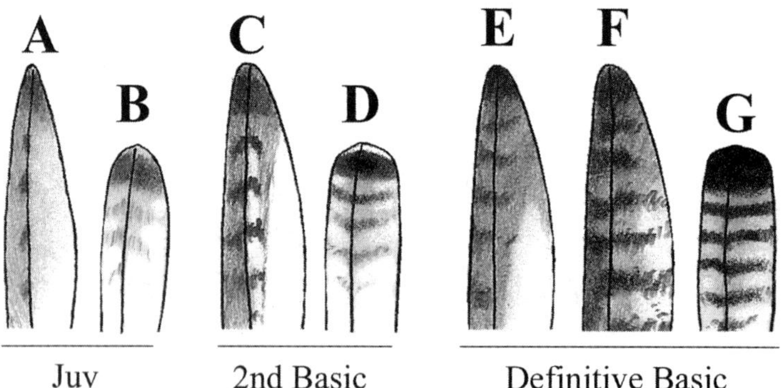

FIGURE 336. Medial primaries (p5 shown here) and secondaries (s4 shown here) by feather generation in Rough-legged Hawk. There can be some overlap in pattern between feathers of different generations, based in part on timing of molt, and dark-morph individuals average slightly darker inner webs by feather generation than pale-morph individuals. Note that 2nd-basic feathers (**C**-**D**), often among p3-p8, s3-s4, and s7-s10, can be retained during the PB3, resulting in blocks of paler feathers in the wings of TY/4Ys (see Clark & Bloom 2005). Red-tailed and Ferruginous hawks also exhibit variation to the amount of white to the inner webs of the inner and medial pp, the juv p1-p5 generally resembling **A** or **C**, the 2nd basic p1-p5 resembling **E**, and the definitive basic p1-p5 resembling **F**. In Juv-HY/SYs these contrast distinctly with the outer ss dorsally, which are darker in color.

Molt—CBS. PF absent-partial (Sep-Mar in HY/SYs), PB2 incomplete (Apr-Sep in SY/TYs), DPB incomplete (May-Oct in ASY/ATYs); PA absent. The PF occurs primarily on non-breeding grounds whereas the DPBs occur primarily on breeding grounds. The PF includes up to 10% of the body feathers but appears to be absent in some individuals. Reports that the pp can be replaced from p4 to p1 during PBs are apparently invalid. The PB2 is typically incomplete, with 1-4 outer pp, 1-6 ss among s3-s4 and s6-s9, occasionally 1-4 rects among r2-r5, and 1 or more rump feathers retained until the PB3. Replacement of pp and ss exhibits staffelmauser (Fig. 16, pp. 23-24) with 2-4 sets of basic feathers present among pp of adults. Suspension during breeding (Fig. 289, p. 393) likely occurs but limits are difficult to distinguish. See Family Account (pp. 391-392) for more information.

Age—Juv (B1; Jul-May) is described under Juv-HY/SY (below) and has cere dull olive and iris grayish to grayish yellow. Juv ♀ = ♂ by plumage aspect.

Juv-HY/SY (1st cycle, Juv/B1-F1; Oct-Sep): Pp and ss juv (Fig. 16**A**, p. 24) or being replaced in Apr-Sep, the juv outer pp tapered (Fig. 286**A**, p. 392), brownish, and relatively worn, the juv medial pp with substantial white to inner web (Fig. 336**A**), and the ss narrow and whitish with indistinct and band (Fig. 336**B**); uppertail covs with diffuse barring (Fig. 337**A**); rects uniformly narrow and rounded (Fig. 288**A**, p. 392), r2-r5 with indistinct dusky tip and little if any band (Fig. 338**A**, p. 452); iris usually yellowish brown; light morph with abdomen heavily streaked to completely blackish, more heavily marked than breast; dark morph with body washed brownish, the underparts often with pale mottling (some feathers with large tear-shaped spots, *cf.* Fig. 339**D**, p. 452). **Note: A few ♀♀ (see Sex) can show intermediate plumage-aspect characters with SY/TY; use pp and ss replacement characters to age these.**

SY/TY (2nd cycle, B2; Oct-Sep): Pp and ss with 2 generations, 1-4 juv outer pp (Fig. 286**A**) and 1-6 juv ss (Fig. 336**B**; among s3-s4 and s6-s9) retained or being replaced in May-Sep, very faded and worn (Fig. 16**B**), the replaced medial pp and ss with moderately white inner webs (Fig. 336**B-C**); uppertail covs distinctly barred (Fig. 337**B**), usually with 1 or more juv feathers (Fig. 337**A**) retained and very worn (Fig. 313**A**, p. 418); rects broad and truncate, with moderately distinct blackish band (Fig. 338**B-E**), 1-4 juv feathers (Fig. 338**A**) occasionally retained (Fig. 288**B**); iris often pale brownish; light morph with abdomen moderately streaked to heavily mottled blackish, usually more heavily marked than breast; dark morph with body blackish, the underparts usually without pale mottling. **Note: See Juv-HY/SY**.

ASY/ATY (Def. cycle, DB; Oct-Sep): Pp and ss with 2 sets of basic feathers in staffelmauser patterns (Fig. 16**E**), the outer pp broad and fresh (Fig. 286**B**), the basic medial pp with reduced white inner webs (Fig. 336**E-F**), and the ss broad with distinct bands and dark tips (Fig. 336**G**); uppertail covs distinctly barred (Fig. 337**B**), often with two generations (Fig. 313**C**); rects broad and truncate, r2-r5 with subterminal bars (Fig. 338**B-E**), sometimes showing 2 generations (Fig. 288**D**); iris dark brown; light morph with abdomen lightly to moderately streaked blackish, the breast often more heavily marked than abdomen (especially in ♂♂; see **Sex**); dark morph with body blackish, the underparts without pale mottling. **Note: See TY/4Y**.

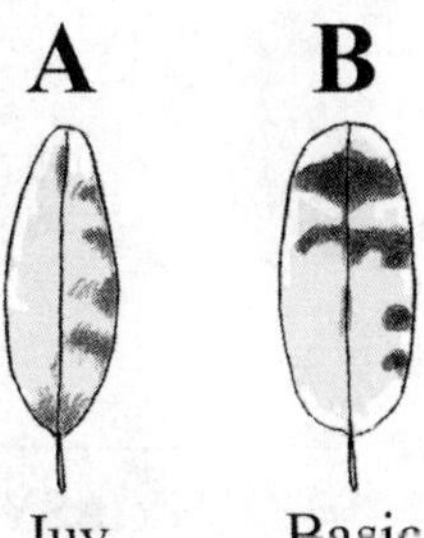

FIGURE 337. Shape and color pattern to the uppertail covs by feather generation in Rough-legged Hawk. Juv feathers are often retained during the PB2 and thus present in SY/TYs.

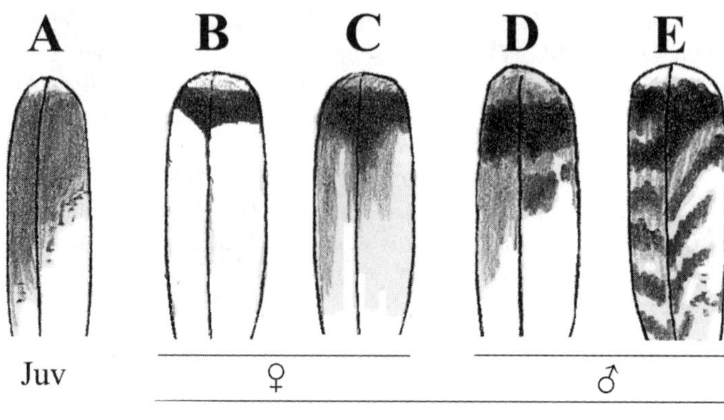

FIGURE 338. Shape and color pattern to the rectrices by feather generation and sex in Rough-legged Hawk. R5 is shown and is usually the last feather replaced during molts and the most likely to be retained during the PB2 and DPB. R5 and other rects are occasionally retained in this species, such that Juv-HY/SYs exhibit **A** (Fig. 288**A**, p. 392), SY/TYs exhibit **B**-**D**, occasionally with 1-2 feathers resembling **A** retained (Fig. 288**B**), and ATY/A4Ys can exhibit one or more generations of feathers resembling **B**-**D** (Fig. 288**C**-**D**). Generally, rects in dark-morph individuals average darker by sex (**C**, **E**) than light-morph individuals (**B**, **D**) but much variation occurs.

TY/4Y (3rd cycle, B3; Oct-Sep): Like ASY/ATY but pp and ss with 2 sets of basic feathers in staffelmauser patterns (Fig. 16**E**), including a block of retained 2nd basic pp among p3-p8 with whitish inner webs (Fig. 336**C**), contrasting with replaced inner and outer (often p1-p3 and p8-p10) feathers with darker webs (Fig. 336**E**-**F**), and with some ss among s3-s4, and s7-s10 paler and with indistinct bands (Fig. 336**D**), contrasting with darker ss with distinct bands (Fig. 336**G**). **Note: Individuals with intermediate color to the inner webs of retained pp and ss should be aged ASY/ATY**.

ATY/A4Y (Def. cycle, DB; Oct-Sep): Like ASY/ATY but pp with 3 sets of basic feathers in staffelmauser patterns (Fig. 16**F**).

A4Y/A5Y (Def. cycle, DB; Oct-May): Like ASY/ATY but pp with 4 sets of basic feathers in staffelmauser patterns (Fig. 16**G**).

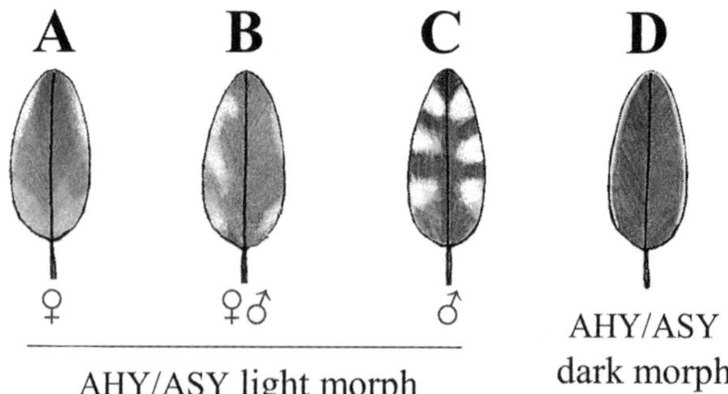

FIGURE 339. Central back feathers by sex in AHY/ASY Rough-legged Hawks. Juv back feathers can exhibit broader fringes in light-morph (*cf.* Fig. 291**A**, p. 394) and pale tear-drop-shaped spots in dark morph. In pale-morphs, intermediate feathers (**B**) appear to occur more regularly in SY/TY ♂♂ and older ♀♀. Back feathers in dark-morphs (**D**) exhibit little to no sex-specific variation in AHY/ASYs.

Sex—Medial BP (Fig. 20**A**, p. 31) and/or distended cloaca (Fig. 21, p. 32) indicates ASY ♀ in Mar-Jul. Measurements (especially wing chord) helpful for sexing (Table 40, p. 443). In addition to the following, dark-morph ♀♀ average browner than ♂♂ (blacker) but overlap occurs, with a minority of each sex showing the full range of variation. Juv-HY/SYs and most if not all SY/TYs are not reliably sexed by plumage aspect.

♀: Wing chord > 425 (Table 40); back feathers of AHY/ASY pale morphs without or with indistinct grayish bars (Fig. 339**A-B**); rects of AHY/ASYs usually with diffuse dusky tip and with or without indistinct darker subterminal band (Fig. 338**B-C**); flanks of AHY/ASYs often uniformly black. **Note: Beware a small proportion of each sex shows back-feather and rect patterns of the other sex, especially among S-TYs and T-4Ys; sex-specific differences are more consistent among e.populations than among w.populations. Dark-morphs, Juv-HY/SYs, SY/TYs, and intermediate-aspect ASY/ATYs with wing chord 421-425 are not reliably sexed.**

♂: Wing chord < 421 (Table 40); back feathers of ASY/ATY pale morphs indistinctly to distinctly barred grayish (Fig. 339**C-D**); rects of AHY/ASYs usually with multiple bands (Fig. 338**D-E**); flanks of AHY/ASYs mixed whitish and blackish. **Note: See ♀.**

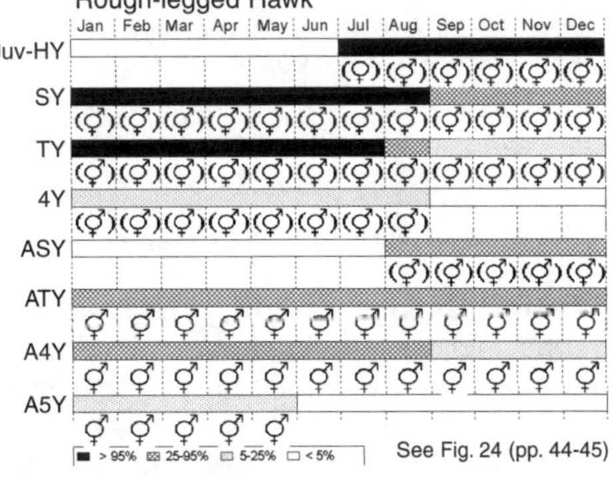

Hybrids reported—With Swainson's Hawk (p. 436) and Red-tailed Hawk (p. 444); possibly with Common Buzzard *B. buteo* (McCarthy 2006).

References—Bechard & Swem (2002), Bent (1937), Clark & Bloom (2005), Cramp & Simmons (1980), Dement'ev & Gladkov (1951b), Forsman (1999), Friedmann (1950), Hamerstrom & Weaver (1968), Kaufman (1989), Manning et al. (1956), Oberholser (1974), Palmer (1988b), Porter (1981), Pyle (2005b, 2005c), Roberts (1955).

GOLDEN EAGLE
Aquila chrysaetos

GOEA
Species # 3490
Band size: 9 Riveted

Species—From most other N.Am raptors (including Bald Eagle, p. 408) by very large size and proportionally small bill (Table 38, p. 419; bill depth at base 31-35 mm); wings rounded (usually p6≈p7>p8≈p5>p9>p4>p10) and with p5-p10 notched and p4-p8 emarginated (*cf.* Fig. 287, p. 392); crown and nape brown to cinnamon, bleaching to pale brown or buff in Apr-Sep; head, back, wing covs, abdomen, and/or (especially) axillars and underwing covs with little or no white; proximal juv pp and distal juv ss with distinct white bases; juv rects with well-defined white bases and rects of AHY/ASYs often with indistinct bands (Fig. 340, p. 454); cere yellowish; bill gray with black distal half; iris dark brown (Juv) to yellowish (A4Y); legs and feet yellow, the tarsus with dense feathering to the toes (Fig. 334**B**, p. 448). See Bald Eagle for separation from extralimital eagles.

Geographic variation—See Cramp & Simmons (1980), Dement'ev & Gladkov (1951b), Friedmann (1950), Hellmayr & Conover (1949), Palmer (1988b), Watson (1997). Four other subspecies in Eurasia.

A.c. canadensis (br & wint N.Am): Medium-sized (Table 38, p. 419; *vs* larger in *chrysaetos* of n.Europe and *daphanea* of c.Asia and smaller in *japonica* of e.Asia); plumage aspect dark brown with darker crown (*vs* paler without darker crown in *chrysaetos*); tarsal plumes brown, usually dark (*vs* mottled whitish in *chrysaetos*).

Molt—CBS. PF absent-limited (Dec-Mar in HY/SYs), PB2 incomplete (Mar-Oct in SYs), DPB incomplete (Apr-Dec in ASYs); PA absent. Sporadic molting can continue through Nov-Mar in some individuals. The PF occurs on non-breeding grounds whereas the DPBs largely occur on breeding grounds but can complete on non-breeding grounds. The PF includes up to 5% of the body feathers but appears to be absent in most individuals. Replacement of pp and ss exhibits staffelmauser (Fig. 16, pp. 23-24) with 3-7 pp, 1-9 ss, and 2-8 rects typically replaced during each molt, and 2-4 sets of basic feathers present among pp of adults. Three to 7 juv outer pp, 4-14 juv ss (including at least s3-s4 and s7-s10), and 4-12 juv rects are retained until the PB3 (Apr-Nov in TYs), and 1-3 juv outer pp, 1-6 juv ss (among s3-s4 and s7-s11), and 1-4 juv rects (usually among r3-r5) are usually retained until the PB4. Body feathers and wing covs are not completely replaced during DPBs. Suspension during breeding (Fig. 289, p. 393) possibly occurs but limits are difficult to distinguish. See Family Account (pp. 391-392) for more information.

Age—Juv (B1; Jul-May) is described under Juv-HY/SY (below); Juv ♀ = ♂. See **Sex** for slight variation in eye color by sex. Note that confirmed breeders can be reliably aged ATY.

Juv-HY/SY (1st cycle, Juv/B1-F1; Oct-Sep): Rects uniformly juv, narrow, basally white with distinct, variably wide, blackish band and no to slight dusky mottling (Fig. 340**A**); body and wing covs even in wear, uniformly blackish brown except for elongated crown and nape feathers rusty-cinnamon (bleaching to buffy brown by Mar-Jul); pp and ss uniformly juv (Fig. 16**A**, p. 24), or being replaced in Mar-Sep, the juv outer pp tapered (Fig. 286**A**, p. 392), brownish, and relatively worn, and the juv outer ss narrow and usually with distinct white bases; iris dark brown becoming paler brown by Jun-Sep.

SY/TY (2nd cycle, B2; Oct-Sep): Rects mixed juv with white bases and relatively worn (Fig. 340**A**; often 4-8 feathers among r2-r5), and 2nd basic broader and fresher with one or more

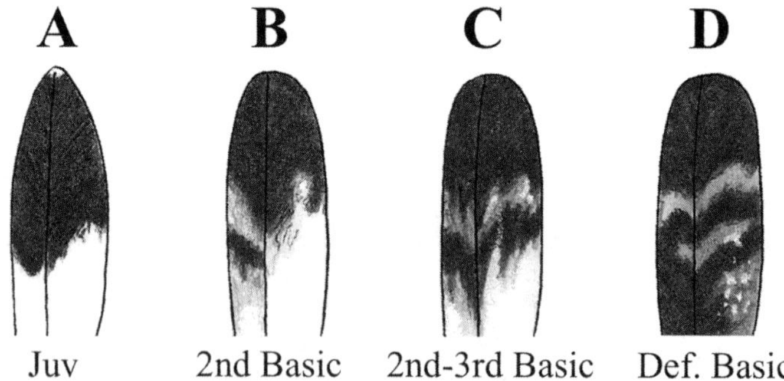

FIGURE 340. Shape and color pattern to the rectrices by feather generation in Golden Eagle. R5 is shown and is usually the last feather replaced during molts and the most likely to be retained during the PB2 and DPB. R5 and other rects are typically retained in this species, sometimes for two molts, such that Juv-HY/SYs exhibit **A** (Fig. 288**A**, p. 392), SY/TYs exhibit **B-C** with 4-8 feathers resembling **A** retained (Fig. 288**B**), TY/4Ys exhibit **B-C**, sometimes with 1-4 feathers resembling **A**, 4-5Ys show at least 4 rects resembling **B-C**, and ATY/A4Ys can exhibit two or more generations of feathers resembling **D** (Fig. 288**D**). **D** represents definitive basic feathers found in ♂♂; ♀♀ typically show less barring (see also Fig. 341, p. 455).

indistinct bars basally (Fig. 340**B**-**C**); body and wing covs uneven in wear, mottled with fresh and bleached brownish feathers, the elongated crown and nape feathers with cinnamon to buff tips; pp and ss with 2 generations, 1-7 juv outer pp (Fig. 286**A**) and 4-14 juv ss among s2-s4 and s7-s15 retained (Fig. 16**B**) or being replaced in May-Sep, very faded and worn; iris medium-pale brown, sometimes becoming yellowish brown by Jan-Jul.

TY/4Y (3rd cycle, B3; Oct-Sep): Rects with 2-3 generations, with 1-4 juv rects (Fig. 340**A**; primarily among r3-r5) sometimes retained, contrasting with 2 sets of 2nd-3rd basic feathers (Fig. 340**B**-**D**); pp and ss with 2-3 generations of basic feathers and 1-3 juv outer pp and 1-5 juv ss (among s3-s4 and s8-s11) retained (Fig. 16**D**), narrow, and very worn; iris medium-dark brownish to medium-pale yellowish brown.

ATY/A4Y (Def. cycle, DB; Oct-Sep): Rects with 2-3 generations of basic feathers with little or no white at base (Fig. 340**D**); pp and ss with 2 sets of basic feathers in staffelmauser patterns (Fig. 16**E**), the outer pp broad (Fig. 286**B**) and fresh, and the outer ss brown, without white bases; iris medium-pale brownish to amber. **Note: See TY/4Y and 4-5Y**.

4-5Y (3rd-5th cycles, B3-B5; Jan-Dec): Like ATY/A4Y but 4 or more rects retained with substantial white at base (Fig. 340**B**-**C**). **Note: some older individuals (up to A20Y) can show 1-3 white-based rects, perhaps based on the timing of replacement (see p. 29).**

A4Y/A5Y (Def. cycle, DB; Oct-Apr): Like ATY/A4Y but pp with 4 sets of basic feathers in staffelmauser patterns (Fig. 16**G**).

Sex—A Full medial BP (Fig. 20**A**, p. 31) and/or distended cloaca (Fig. 21, p. 32) indicates ATY ♀ in Jan-Jul; ♂♂ can develop a partial BP. Measurements (except perhaps bill length) unhelpful for sexing (Table 40, p. 443). Juv-HY/SYs are not reliably sexed by plumage aspect alone. Some intermediates occur between the following, especially among SY/TYs, but sexing of most individuals should be possible.

♀: Footpad length (Fig. 342) > 138.5 mm; culmen from cere by hallux (rear claw) length (Fig. 342) larger by age (Fig. 343, p. 456); ATY/A4Ys with bases to rects grayish, usually with little or no banding proximal to the dark band (Fig. 341**A**); iris dark brown (SY)

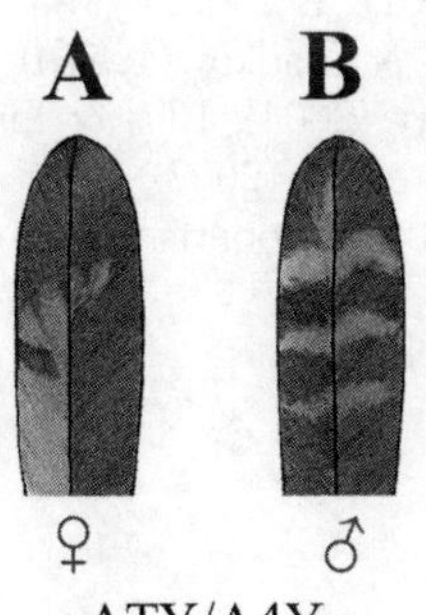

FIGURE 341. Aspect pattern to the definitive central rectrices by sex in ATY/A4Y Golden Eagle. Look for similar differences among 2nd basic and 3rd basic rects (*cf.* Fig. 340).

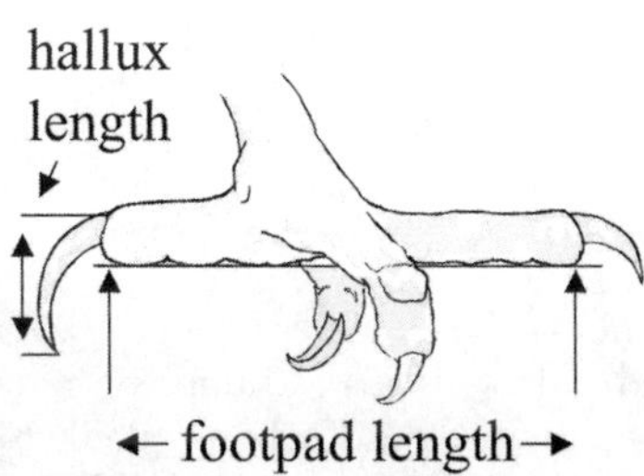

FIGURE 342. Footpad and hallux (rear claw) lengths, useful measures for sexing Bald Eagle, Harris' Hawk, and Golden Eagle (shown here). Footpad length is from the end of the pad at hallux (rear claw) to the end of the pad at middle claw. Hallux length represents the vertical length of the claw rather than the chord. Foot size may be more sexually dimorphic than other measures in raptors due to sex-specific hunting strategies during nesting; look for other species of raptors to exhibit differences that may be useful for sexing. Illustration and measures based on Bortolotti 1984a, 1984b).

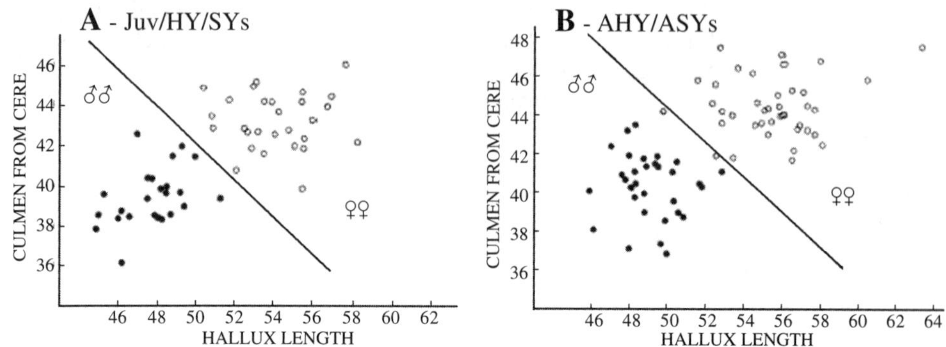

FIGURE 343. Graph of culmen from cere (see also Table 38, p. 419) against hind-claw (hallux) length (*cf.* Fig. 342, p. 455) by sex in Juv-HY/SY (**A**) and AHY/ASY (**B**) Golden Eagles. Based on Bortolotti (1984d).

to medium-dark yellowish brown (ATY). **Note: The central rects in SY/TYs and TY/4Ys (*cf.* Fig. 340B-C, p. 454) may also show sex-specific patterns similar to those of basic feathers.**

♂: Footpad length (Fig. 342) < 138.5 mm; culmen from cere by hallux length (Fig. 342) smaller by age (Fig. 343); ATY/A4Ys with bases to rects pale grayish, usually with 2-3 incomplete or complete dark bands proximal to the dark band (Figs. 340**D** & 341**B**, pp. 454-455); iris medium-dark brown (SY) to amber (ATY).

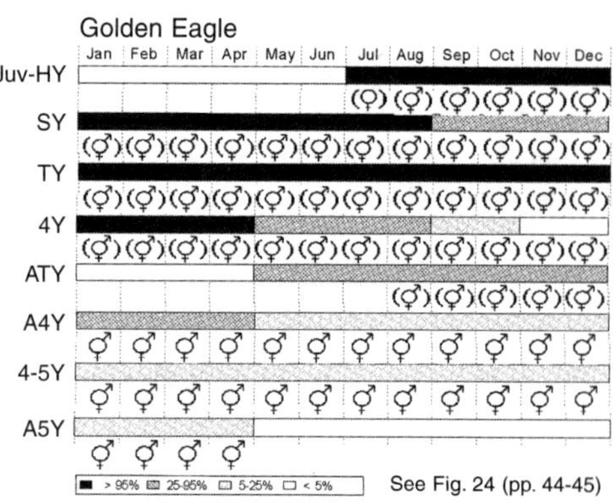

Hybrids reported—With Imperial (*A. heliaca*) and Lesser Spotted (*A. pomarina*) eagles in the wild (Corso & Forsman 1997).

References—Baker (1993), Bent (1937), Bloom & Clark (2001), Bortolotti (1984a,, 1984b, 1984d), Clark (1983a), Cramp & Simmons (1980), Dement'ev & Gladkov (1951b), Edelstam (1984), Edwards & Kochert (1986), Ellis (2004), Ellis & Kéry (2004), Ellis & Lish (2006), Forsman (1999), Friedmann (1950), Jollie (1947), Kochert et al. (2002), Liguori (2004), Oberholser (1906b, 1974), Palmer (1988b), Pyle (2005b, 2005c), Roberts (1955), Spofford (1946), Tjernberg (1988).

CARACARAS AND FALCONS *FALCONIDAE*

Seven species. Family characters include relatively large heads, long and very pointed wings, pointed back feathers and strong decurved bills with tomial teeth (Fig. 285**B**, p. 391) in all N.Am species except Crested Caracara, and powerful legs and feet with long, sharp talons. North American falcons have 10 functional primaries (p10 extending 0-35 mm short of the longest, usually p9, when fully grown), 12-13 secondaries (including 3 tertials and one absent between s4 and s5; Fig. 12**B**, p. 19), and 12 rectrices. Ageing through the first cycle (to SY and ASY) can be accomplished through plumage aspect, fault bars (Fig. 18, p. 27), shape and pattern to the outer primaries (Fig. 351, p. 466), and replacement patterns among pp and ss (Fig. 344); occasional individuals of larger species can be aged to SY/TY or ASY/ATY through the presence of retained secondary coverts or body feathers. Females are larger than males, sometimes without overlap, and sex-specific plumage aspects (sometimes subtle or overlapping) can be found in most North American species. Bilateral and medial brood patches (Fig. 20**C**, p. 31) are developed by both sexes (usually to a greater extent in females) but distended cloacae (Fig. 21, p. 32) indicate breeding AHY females; other cloacal characters (Figs. 22-23, pp. 32-35) should be investigated. See Accipitridae (p. 391) and Cade (1982) for general references on species, age, and sex determination in falcons.

In molting, falcons exhibit the Complex Basic Strategy (CBS; Fig. 10**B**, pp. 13-16)), including formative plumages but lacking alternate plumages. Sequence of primary and secondary replacement is unusual, proceeding both proximally and distally within each tract from centers at p4-p5 and s5 (R.M. Bond 1936, Miller 1941, Willoughby 1966), such that the last feathers replaced are p10, p1, s1, and secondaries among s9-s13, depending on total number of secondaries (Fig. 344**B**). Replacement of rectrices typically occurs distally (r1 to r6), with r6 sometimes replaced before r4-r5. Prebasic molts are usually complete, although some lesser coverts or body feathers can occasionally be retained in some of the larger species. Suspension limits (Fig. 344**C**) can be detected in all species and indicate breeding the previous season. Age of first breeding can be 1-2 years in some species and as old as 3-4 years in others; prebasic molts of non-breeding AHYs average earlier in timing italicsthan those of breeding adults (see p. 18).

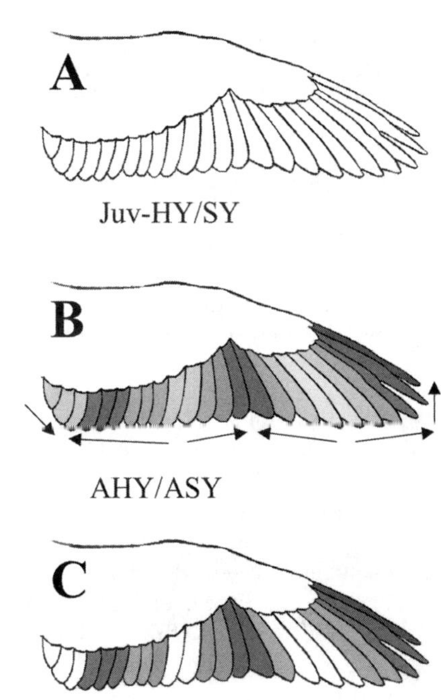

FIGURE 344. Replacement patterns among the primaries and secondaries in falcons by age. Darker shading indicates fresher feathers. Both pp and ss are replaced proximally and distally from centers at p4-p5 and s5, as shown in **B**. This results in molt clines in AHY/ASYs, most obvious among p4-p1 and s5-s1, where feathers are more protected (**B**); Juv-HY/SYs exhibit uniformly juv and more worn feathers (**A**). Breeding adults (indicating ASY/ATY in larger species) can suspend molt for chick feeding, after replacing up to 5 pp (among p3-p7), 3 medial ss (among s4-s6) and 1-3 terts, resulting in suspension limits (**C**; suspension after p3-p5, s4-s5, and the terts had been replaced, as shown). In falcons, both sexes replace roughly equal numbers of feathers prior to suspension, except for Merlin, where ♂♂ average more feathers replaced than ♀♀. See also Figures 15 (p. 23) and 289 (p. 393) regarding suspension limits.

CRESTED CARACARA CRCA
Caracara cheriway Species # 3620
Band size: 7B(♀)-7A(♂) Lock-on

Species—From other hawks and falcons by medium-large size with proportionally large bill and long tarsus (Table 41, p. 469); wings rounded (usually p7≈p6>p8>p9≈p5>p4>p10) and with p7-p10 notched and p6-p9 emarginated (*cf.* Figs. 289, p. 393, & 351, p. 466); plumage aspect brownish to blackish with whitish face, uppertail covs, and vent, and streaked to barred upper back and breast by age (Fig. 346); rects whitish with indistinct narrow barring and a distinct band (Fig. 345); pp and ss largely dark brown, with indistinct barring to bases of p5-p10; facial skin and cere bright pinkish to red and bill pale grayish to bluish; legs grayish to bright yellow by age.

Geographic variation—Monotypic. See Dove & Banks (1999), Power (1980), and Vuilleumier (1970) for information on taxa formerly considered subspecies. Populations of TX-AZ ("*C.c. ammophilus*") may average smaller-billed and more heavily barred, and populations of sc.FL ("*audubonii*") may average smaller and paler but differences confounded by age-related and individual variation. See also Blake (1977), Friedmann (1950), Grant (1965), Hellmayr & Conover (1949), Oberholser (1974), Palmer (1988b), and van Rossem (1939a) for more information.

Molt—CBS. PF limited (Dec?-Mar? in HY/SYs), PB2 incomplete-complete (Jan-Nov in SYs), DPB incomplete-complete (Mar-Dec in ASYs); PA absent. The above timing pertains to N.Am populations. The PF can include up to 25% of the body feathers; look also for some individuals to replace r1 (see below). The PB2 and DPB are complete except sometimes s1-s2, 1 or more rump feathers, and occasionally wing covs or other body feathers can be retained. Reports that r1 can be replaced twice during a definitive basic cycle (thus involving a PA) require confirmation; this may have been based on replacement of these feathers in some individuals during the PF. In breeding ATYs, the DPB can occasionally suspend after 1-5 pp, 1-3 medial ss, and/or the terts have been replaced (*cf.* Fig. 344**C**, p. 457). See Family Account (p. 457) for more information.

Age—Juv (B1; Jun-May) is described under Juv-HY/SY (below) and has whitish bill, dull (usually pale pinkish) cere and facial skin, dark iris, and dull gray legs; Juv ♀=♂. The following month ranges pertain to N.Am populations. In addition to the following, bare parts (e.g., cere, facial skin, and legs) are paler in Juv-HY/SYs but this color can change rapidly in all age groups; e.g., becoming paler when live individuals are handled.

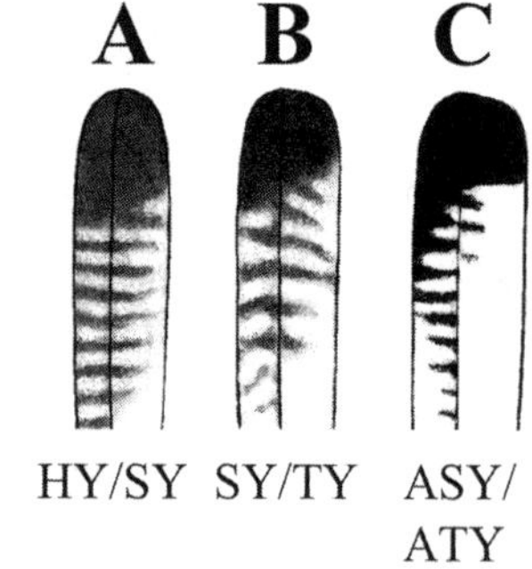

FIGURE 345. Shape and pattern to the rectrices by age in Crested Caracara (r5 shown). Note that some SY/TYs show patterns resembling **C** (especially among r2 and r5) and some ASY/ATYs may show patterns resembling **B** but many show those indicated above.

Juv-HY/SY1st cycle, Juv/B1-F1; Oct-Sep): Crown, lower back, wing covs, and abdomen brownish, the wing covs with whitish tips (*cf.* Fig. 291**A-B**, p. 394); rects narrow and rounded, r2-r5 with complete brown bars basally and broad brown tips (Fig. 345**A**); nape and neck buff; back and breast brown with indistinct buff streaks (Fig. 346**A-B**), usually mixed with some

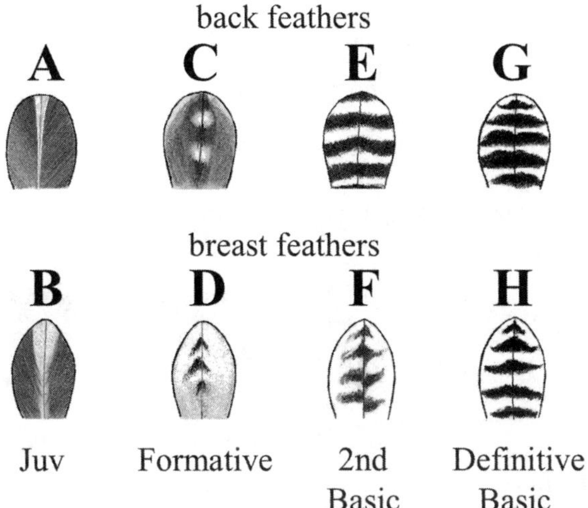

FIGURE 346. Pattern to the upper back and upper breast feathers by feather generation in Crested Caracara. Juv-HY/SYs exhibit **A**-**B**, mixed with formative feathers (**C**-**D**) in Jan-Sep; SY/TYs exhibit **E**-**F**; and ASY/ATYs exhibit **G**-**H**. There may be some overlap between these patterns in SY/TYs and ASY/ATYs, as in the rects (see Fig. 345).

partially barred feathers in Jan-Sep (Fig. 346**C**-**D**); pp and ss uniformly juv (Fig. 344**A**, p. 457), the outer pp narrower at tip and worn (*cf.* Fig. 351**A**, p. 466), and the ss narrow (*cf.* Fig. 322**A**, p. 431) and brown with moderately distinct pale bars; iris brownish or tinged orange.

SY/TY (2nd cycle, B2; Nov-Oct): Crown, lower back, wing covs, and abdomen brownish black, the crown with paler brown streaking and the wing covs without whitish tips (*cf.* Fig. 291**C**); rects moderately broad and truncate, r2-r5 often with indistinct and incomplete blackish bars basally and indistinct blackish tips (Fig. 345**B**); nape and neck cream to whitish; back and breast with moderately distinct brown and whitish barring (Fig. 346**E**-**F**); rump often with retained juv feathers, pale brown to whitish and very worn (Fig. 313**A**, p. 418); pp and ss basic and showing molt clines but without suspension limits (Fig. 344**B**; 1-2 ss among s1-s2 can occasionally be retained), the outer pp broad at tip and fresh (Fig. 351**B**) and the ss broad (*cf.* Fig. 322**B**) and brownish-black with indistinct pale bars; iris orangish brown. **Note: Intermediates between this and ASY/ATY should be aged T-4Y (see pp. 41-42).**

ASY/ATY (Def. cycle, DB; Oct-Sep): Crown, lower back, wing covs, and abdomen blackish, the crown without brownish streaking; rects broad and truncate, r2-r5 with distinct partial black bars and black tips (Fig. 345**C**); nape and neck whitish to white; back and breast with distinct black and white barring (Fig. 346**G**-**H**); rump often with retained basic feathers, grayish brown and slightly worn (Fig. 313**C**); pp, ss, and rects as in SY/TY except suspension limits often present among p3-p7 and s4-s6 (Fig. 344**C**); iris brownish orange to dull orangish. **Note: See SY/TY.**

Sex—♀=♂ by plumage aspect. BP of unknown type (Fig. 20, p. 31) may be developed by both sexes but distended cloaca (Fig. 21, p. 32) indicates ASY ♀ in Jan-Jun. Measurements (Table 41, p. 469) not helpful for sexing. See Morrison & Maltbie (1999) for biochemical methods of sexing this species and a logistic-regression model separating 41% of live individuals to sex based on wg chord and bill depth at cere. Otherwise, no criteria known for sexing.

Hybrids Reported—Possibly with Southern Caracara *C. plancus* (Dove & Banks 1999).

References—Bent (1938), Clark (2001b), Dickey & van Rossem (1938), Friedmann (1950), Layne (1986), Morrison (1996), Morrison & Maltbie (1999), Oberholser (1974), Palmer (1988b), Pyle (2005b, 2005c).

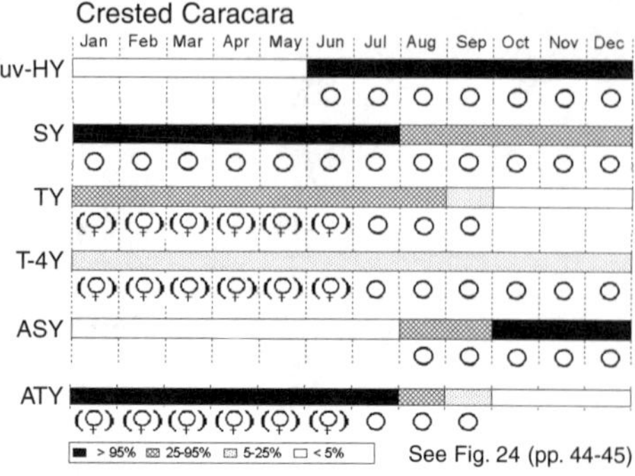

AMERICAN KESTREL

Falco sparverius

AMKE
Species # 3600
Band size: 3B Lock-on

Species—From other falcons and hawks by small size (Table 41, p. 469); wings pointed (usually p9>p8>p7>p10>p6) and with p9-p10 notched and p8-p9 emarginated (*cf.* Figs. 289, p. 393, & 351, p. 466); crown with grayish, and back and rects with rufous; wing covs mostly rufous (♀) or bluish (♂); moustachial stripe and posterior auriculars with blackish stripes; pp and ss with distinct blackish barring; rects barred in ♀♀ or with subterminal band in ♂♂ (Fig. 347).

Eurasian Kestrel (*F. tinnunculus*), a vagrant to N.Am, is larger (wg chord 224-272, tl 141-186, culmen from cere 12.4-16.9, tarsus 36-42); moustachial area and auriculars without blackish; Juv-HY/SYs and ♀♀ with crown, head, and breast pale brown with narrow dark streaks, and subterminal tail band wider (> 20 mm *vs* < 20 in American Kestrel; *cf.* Fig. 347); AHY/ASY ♂ without rufous in crown and with bluish bases to rects.

Geographic variation—See Bent (1938), Bond (1943), Chapman (1915), Friedmann (1950), Griscom (1930), Hellmayr & Conover (1949), Holt & Sutton (1926), Howell (1965), Jewett et al. (1953), Layne & Smith (1992), Mearns (1892), Miller & Smallwood (1997), Monson & Phillips (1981), Moore & Bond (1946), Palmer (1988b), Patten et al. (2003), Pearlstein & Thompson (2004), Phillips et al. (1964), Power (1980), Rea (1983a), Smallwood et al. (1999), Stevenson & Anderson (1994), Todd (1916a), Tomkins (1948), van Rossem (1931). Fifteen other subspecies occur in the W.Indes and Mex-S.Am.

F.s. sparverius (br & wint throughout most of N.Am range): Larger but bill proportionally small (Table 41, p. 469); rufous crown patch averages larger; ♂♂ with upper scapulars (near bend of wing) with black bars or spots and abdomen with moderate to heavy black spotting, often across center; cere and legs duller yellow by season, age, and sex.

F.s. peninsularis (="*phalaena*;" br & wint nw.Mex; visitor or breeder to s.CA-s.AZ): Small (Table 41); plumage aspect as in *sparverius*; cere and legs duller yellow by season, age, and sex.

F.s. paulus (br & wint LA to s.GA-FL): Smaller but bill proportionally large (Table 41); rufous crown patch averages smaller (sometimes absent); non-Juv ♂♂ with upper scapulars (near bend of wing) with little or no black marks and abdomen with little to no black spotting, confined to sides if present; cere and legs brighter yellow by season, age, and sex. Subspecies of the W.Indes (e.g., *sparveroides* of Cuba, possibly recorded s.FL Is) differ in having a dusky morph in certain populations; ♂♂ with heavier barring to the upperparts, and reduced spotting to the underparts by age.

Molt—CBS. PF partial-incomplete (Sep-Jan in HY/SYs), DPB complete (Apr-Nov in AHYs); PA absent. The above timing pertains to N.Am populations. The PF and DPBs occur primarily on breeding grounds but can complete on non-breeding grounds. The PF includes most to all body feathers (up to 25% of juv feathers can be retained), no to all les covs, occasionally 0-3 inner med covs, and perhaps rarely 1-2 c.rects, but no gr covs, pp, or ss. In breeding ASY ♀♀, the DPB can occasionally suspend after 1-2 pp, 1-2 medial ss, and/or the terts have been replaced (*cf.* Fig. 344**C**, p. 457). See Family Account (p. 457) for more information.

Age/Sex—Juvs dimorphic as in HY/SYs: ♀♀ (Jun-Oct) similar in plumage aspect to HY/SY ♀♀ (below) whereas Juv ♂♂ have more heavily barred upper backs and streaked breasts than HY/SY ♂♂ by subspecies (see **Geographic variation**); The following month ranges pertain to N.Am populations. See Negro et al. (1994) for information on fault bars in this species, and Brodkorb (1935) and Parrish et al. (1987) for examples of ♀♀ showing partial ♂-like plumage aspect. Full bilateral and medial BPs (Fig. 20**C**, p. 31) and/or distended cloaca (Fig. 21, p. 32) indicates ♀ in Feb-Jun; ♂♂ can develop partial BPs. See Table 41 (p. 469) for measurements by sex.

HY/SY ♀ (1st cycle, F1; Sep-Aug): Wing covs rufous, some les covs and occasionally 1-3 inner med covs usually replaced, contrastingly fresh in luster (Fig. 13**B-C**, p. 20); r2-r5 narrow and rounded with blackish bars, the subterminal bar 7-10 mm in width, not substantially wider than the proximal bars (Fig. 347**A-B**); pp and ss uniformly juv, without replacement clines (Fig. 344**A**, p. 457), the outer pp narrower, with moderately ovate spots, and more worn (Fig. 351**A**, p. 466); fault bars (if present) as in Fig. 18**A** (p. 27); legs and feet duller yellow. **Note: Some intermediates of both sexes may be difficult to age.**

AHY/ASY ♀ (Def. cycle, DB, Sep-Aug): Wing covs uniformly rufous (*cf.* Fig. 14**B**, p. 21); r2-r5 uniformly broad and truncate with blackish bars, the subterminal bar 9-14 mm in width, substantially wider than the proximal bars (Fig. 247**C**); pp and ss basic and showing replacement clines and sometimes suspension limits (Fig. 344**B-C**), the outer pp broader, with moderately squared spots, and fresher (Fig. 351**B**); fault bars (if present) as in Fig. 18**B**; legs and feet brighter yellow. **Note: See HY/SY ♀.**

HY/SY ♂ (1st cycle, F1; Sep-Aug): Wing covs bluish, some les covs and sometimes 1-3 inner med covs usually replaced, contrastingly fresh in luster and aspect (Fig. 13**B-C**); r2-r5 narrow and rounded with single broad blackish band (Fig. 347**D**); pp and ss (Fig. 344**A**), fault bars (Fig. 18**A**), and leg color as in **HY/SY ♀. Note: See HY/SY ♀.**

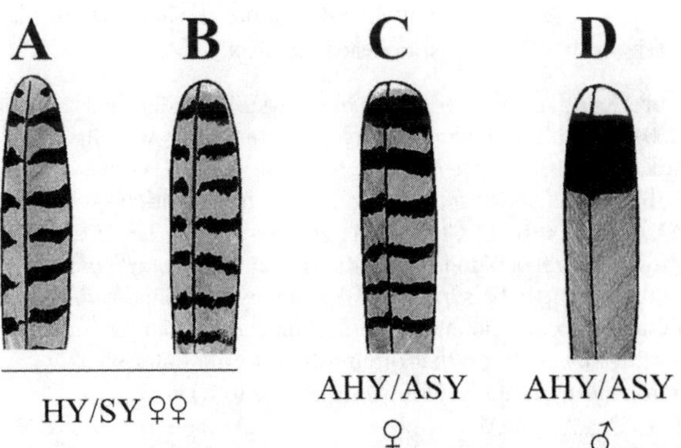

FIGURE 347. Shape and pattern to the rectrices by age in American Kestrel (r5 shown). Note that juv ♀♀ (**A-B**) show more bars and narrower subterminal bands (7-10 mm wide) that are more-or-less the same width as the other bars, whereas AHY/ASY ♀♀ (**C**) show subterminal bands that are wider than the other bands (9-14 mm). Rects of HY/SY ♂♂ show a very different pattern than those of ♀♀ but a similar pattern by age (but note shape difference, as in ♀♀). In Eurasian Kestrels, ♀♀ show a wider subterminal band (> 20 mm) at all ages and ♂♂ have bluish bases to the rects.

AHY/ASY ♂ (Def. cycle, DB; Sep-Aug): Wing covs uniformly bluish (*cf.* Fig. 14**B**); r2-r5 uniformly broad and truncate with single broad black band (Fig. 347**D**); pp and ss (Fig. 344**B-C**), fault bars (Fig. 18**B**), and leg color as in AHY/ASY ♀. **Note: See HY/SY ♀.**

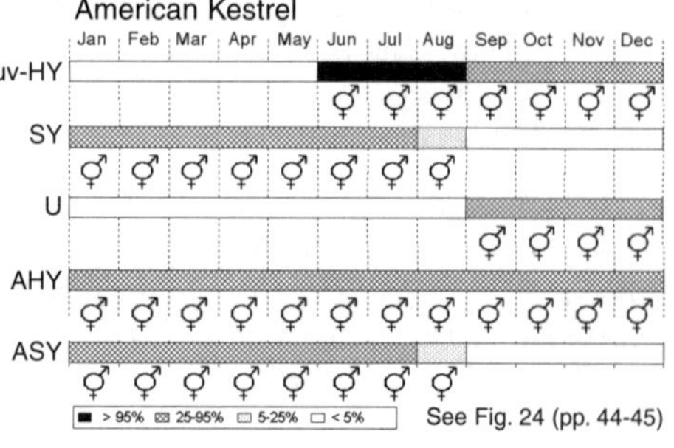

Hybrids Reported—None in the wild.

References—Baker (1993), Balgooyen (1976), Bent (1938), Bloom (1973), Bond (1943), Friedmann (1950), Layne & Smith (1992), MacFarlane (1973), Mearns (1892), Miller & Smallwood (1997), Oberholser (1974), Palmer (1988b), Parkes (1955b), Pearlstein & Thompson (2004), Pyle (2005b, 2005c), Roberts (1955), Roest (1957), Smallwood (1989), Smallwood & Bird (2002), Smallwood et al. (1999), Willoughby (1966), Willoughby & Cade (1964), Wood (1969).

MERLIN
Falco columbarius

MERL
Species # 3570
Band size: 4-3A♀, 3-3B♂ Lock-on

Species—From other falcons and hawks by medium-small size (Table 41, p. 469); wings pointed (usually p9>p8>p7>p10>p6) and with p9-p10 notched and p8-p9 emarginated (*cf.* Figs. 289, p. 393, & 351, p. 466); upperparts variably blackish, brownish, or grayish; pp, ss, and rects with moderately distinct pale spotting or barring (Fig. 348). From Juv-HY/SY Sharp-shinned Hawk (p. 415) by bill with tooth and back feathers and terts pointed (Fig. 285**B**, p. 391); tarsus shorter (Table 41); wing pointed (p8-p9 longest, >p6 by 20+ mm); underwing covs not paler than underside of pp and ss; iris dark.

Geographic variation—See Behle (1985), Blake (1977), Campainolo & Pitocelli (1990), Cramp & Simmons (1980), Dement'ev & Gladkov (1951b), Donahue (1987), Friedmann (1950), Garner (2002b), Hamilton & Schmitt (2000), Hellmayr & Conover (1949), Oberholser (1974), Palmer (1988b), Peters (1927), Pittaway (1994), Rand (1946), Swann (1922b), Swarth (1924, 1935), Temple (1972a). Six other subspecies in Eurasia.

F.c. columbarius (br AK-Nfl to e.OR-ME, wint to s.CA-s.FL): Wing chord and tail length average shorter (Table 41, p. 469); rects blackish with 4 (rarely 5) distinct narrow white bands (Fig. 348**A-B**); upperparts medium-dark, brownish (Juv & AHY ♀) to bluish slate (AHY ♂); undersides of pp brown with pale bars or ovals; breast and abdomen with moderately heavy dark brownish to reddish brown streaks. Populations of AK-Sask to OR-ID (*"bendirei"*) average slightly larger and paler but differences are insufficient for subspecies recognition. Populations of ne.Asia (*pacificus*), potential vagrants to w.AK, average paler and have 6-7 pale bars to rects. Populations of Iceland (*subaesalon*) and n.Eurasia (*aesalon*), vagrants to Greenland and potentially ne.N.Am, average darker (*subaesalon*) or paler (*aesalon*), with grayer (less white) bands to pp that often extend to the outer webs (*vs* seldom in *columbarius*), sparser streaking to underparts, and wider whitish bands to rects.

F.c. suckleyi (br coastal se.AK-nw.WA, wint to coastal s.CA; vagrant to TX & NY-FL): Wing chord and tail length average shorter (Table 41); rects blackish with no to 3-4 indistinct pale bands (Fig. 348**C-D**); upperparts blackish (Juv & AHY ♀) to dark slate (AHY ♂); undersides of pp dark, with reduced and indistinct pale markings; breast and abdomen with heavy blackish streaking or mottling. **Note: melanistic individuals of other subspecies may occur rarely and be difficult to separate from *suckleyI*.**

F.c. richardsonii (br Alb-sw.Man to CO, wint to s.CA-w.TX; vagrant to ON-MO): Wing chord and tail length average longer (Table 41); rects dusky with 5 (rarely 4) indistinct broad whitish bands (Fig. 348**E-F**);

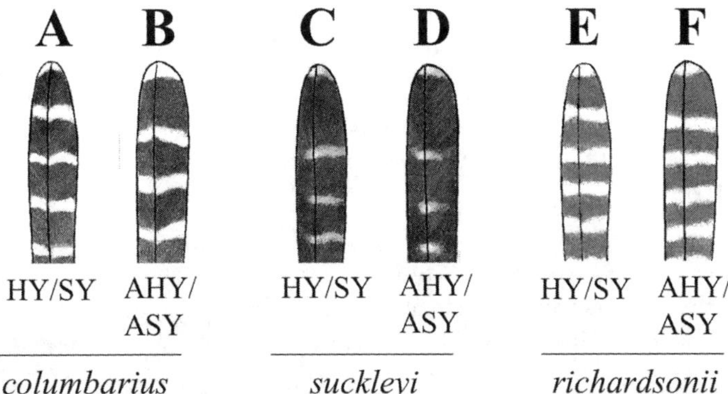

FIGURE 348. Shape and pattern to the rectrices by subspecies and age in North American Merlins (r5 shown). Note that, within each subspecies, HY/SYs (**A**, **C**, & **E**) average more and more distinct bars than AHY/ASYs (**B**, **D**, & **F**). Sexes show similar patterns, although in HY/SYs, ♀♀ average buffier pale bands than ♂♂. See **Geographic variation** for information on rect patterns in extralimital subspecies of Merlin.

upperparts pale brownish (Juv and AHY ♀) to pale grayish blue (AHY ♂); undersides of pp pale cream with brown barring; breast and abdomen with sparser and paler reddish to brownish streaks.

Molt—CBS. PF absent-limited (Nov-Apr in HY/SYs), DPB complete (Apr-Oct in AHYs); PA absent. The PF occurs primarily on non-breeding grounds (but can commence on breeding grounds) whereas DPBs occur primarily on breeding grounds (but can complete on non-breeding grounds). The PF can include up to 50% of the body feathers but appears to be absent in some individuals. In breeding ASYs, the DPB usually suspends after 1-4 pp, 1-3 ss, and/or the terts have been replaced (*cf.* Fig. 344**C**, p. 457, and Espie et al. 1996); ♂♂ average more feathers replaced than ♀♀. See Family Account (p. 457) for more information.

Age/Sex—Juvs (B1; Jul-May) similar to HY/SYs of each sex, as described below; Juvs reliably sexed by size and plumage aspect, as in HY/SYs. Full bilateral and/or medial BPs (Fig. 20**A-C**, p. 31), and/or distended cloaca (Fig. 21, p. 32) indicates ♀ in Apr-Jul; ♂♂ can develop partial BPs. See Table 41 (p. 469) for measurements by sex.

Juv-HY/SY ♀ (1st cycle, Juv/B1-F1; Nov-Oct): Wg > 201 (or > 209 in *F.c. richardsonii*); upperparts brownish to dusky brown (see **Geographic variation**), the feathers with very indistinct or no dusky shaft streaks; rects narrow and rounded, the pale bands of r2-r5 washed buff and often more frequent and/or distinct by subspecies (Fig. 348**A**, **C**, & **E**); pp and ss uniformly juv, without replacement clines or suspension limits (Fig. 344**A**, p. 457), the outer pp narrower, more worn, and often showing rounder pale markings (Fig. 351**A**, p. 466); fault bars (if present) as in Fig. 18**A** (p. 27). **Note: ♀♀ can be difficult to age; replacement clines among p1-p5 and s1-s5 are the best characters (Fig. 344B) although some intermediates should be aged U/AHY. Some SYs may over-summer on non-breeding grounds and exhibit advanced PB2s (see p. 18).**

AHY/ASY ♀ (Def. cycle, DB; Nov-Oct): Wg > 201 (or > 209 in *F.c. richardsonii*); upperparts brownish to dusky brown (see **Geographic variation**), often with moderately distinct dusky shaft streaks and grayer tinge to rump; rects broad and truncate, the pale bands of r2-r5 tinged grayish, with little or no buff, and often less frequent and/or distinct by subspecies (Fig. 348**B**, **D**, & **F**); pp and ss basic, showing replacement clines and often suspension limits (Fig. 344**B-C**), the outer pp broader, fresher, and often showing squarer pale markings (Fig. 351**B**); fault bars (if present) as in Fig. 18**B**. **Note: See HY/SY ♀.**

Juv-HY/SY ♂ (1st cycle, Juv/HY-F1; Nov-Oct): Wg < 199 (or < 209 in *F.c. richardsonii*); upperparts brownish, sometimes mixed with scattered bluer feathers; pp, ss, and rects (Figs. 348**A**, **C**, & **E**; 344**A**, and 351**A**) as in HY/SY ♀ except that pale bands to the rects grayer or whiter. **Note: See HY/SY ♀.**

AHY/ASY ♂ (Def. cycle, DB; Nov-Oct): Wg < 199 (or < 209 in *F.c. richardsonii*); upperparts bluish gray to slaty blue (see **Geographic variation**), the feathers with shaft streaks; pp, ss, and rects (Figs. 348**B**, **D**, & **F**; 344**B**, and 351**B**) as in AHY/ASY ♀. **Note: Reports that the edging to the alula might be paler in SY/TYs than in ASY/ATYs (Baker 1993) require confirmation in N.Am populations.**

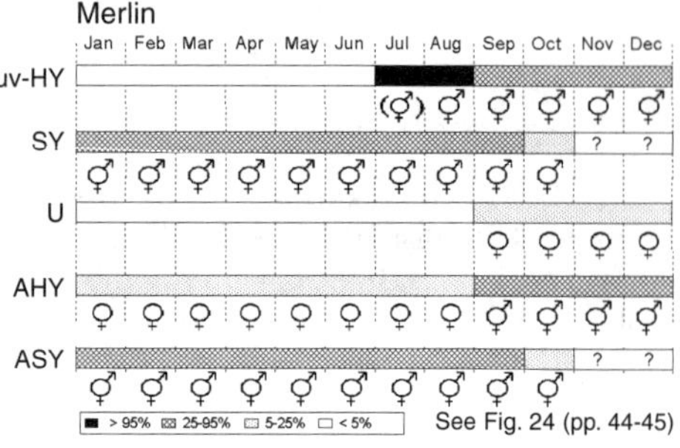

Hybrids Reported—Possibly with Eurasian Kestrel (*F. tinnunculus*) in the wild (McCarthy 2006).

References—Baker (1993), Bent (1938), Clark (1983b), Cramp & Simmons (1980), Dement'ev & Gladkov (1951b), Espie et al. (1996), Forsman (1999), Fox (1964), Friedmann (1950), Garner (2002b), Hamilton & Schmitt (2000), Mueller et al. (2002), Oberholser (1974), Palmer (1988b), Pyle (2005b, 2005c). Roberts (1955), Sodhi et al. (1993), Temple (1972b), Warkentin et al. (1990, 1992), Wiklund (1996).

APLOMADO FALCON
Falco femoralis

APFA
Species # 3590
Band size: 5 Lock-on

Species—From other falcons and hawks by medium size with long tail (Table 41, p. 469); wings moderately pointed (usually p8>p9>p7>p10≈p6>p5) and with p10 > p9 by > 30 mm, p9-p10 notched, and p8-p9 emarginated (*cf.* Figs. 289, p. 393, & 351, p. 466); upperparts dusky to slaty with distinct pale supercilium, connecting or nearly connecting across nape; pp, ss, and rects dusky with distinct narrow white barring (Fig. 349); underparts with distinct blackish abdomen band and predominantly buffy orange to rufous vent and undertail covs.

Geographic variation—See Blake (1977), Chapman (1925), Friedmann (1950), Hellmayr & Conover (1949), Keddy-Hector (2000), D.P. Hector *in* Palmer (1988b), Todd (1916b). Two other subspecies in s.C.Am-S.Am.

F.f. septentrionalis (res Mex-n.C.Am, former or recent res and visitor to se.AZ-s.TX): Intermediate in wing length (Table 41, p. 469; *vs* wg chord 220-280 in *femoralis* of s.C.Am-e.S.Am and 241-313 in *pichinchae* of e.S.Am); throat medium-pale buff to white (*vs* darker buff in *pichinchae*); abdomen band usually complete (*vs* narrower and often incomplete in *pichinchae*).

Molt—CBS. PF limited-partial (Sep?-Feb? in HY/SYs), DPB complete (Apr-Nov? in AHYs); PA absent. The above timing pertains to N.Am populations. The PF can include up to 40% of the body feathers but is possibly absent in some individuals; more study is needed. In breeding ATYs, the DPB often suspends after 1-5 pp, 1-3 medial ss, and/or the terts have been replaced (*cf.* Fig. 344**C**, p. 457). See Family Account (p. 457) for more information.

Age—Juvs (B1; Jun-Mar) have upperpart feathers fringed tawny and head and breast washed darker buff, the breast with triangular spots (Fig. 350**A**); full-grown Juvs reliably sexed by wg chord (see **Sex**). The following month ranges pertain to N.Am populations.

Juv-HY/SY1st cycle, Juv/B1-F1; Oct-Sep): Some to most upperpart feathers grayish brown fringed tawny or pale (*cf.* Fig. 291**A-B**, p. 394); rects narrow and rounded, r2-r5 dusky brown with 7-8 distinct buff to whitish bars (Fig. 349**A**); most to some breast feathers with triangular spots (Fig. 350**A**); pp and ss uniformly juv, without replacement clines or suspension limits (Fig. 344**A**, p. 457), the outer pp narrower, more worn, and with rounder pale markings (Fig. 351**A**, p. 466).

AHY/ASY (Def. cycle, DB; Oct-Sep): Upperpart feathers slate to bluish, without tawny fringing (*cf.* Fig. 291**C**); rects broad and truncate, r2-r5 blackish with 5-7 distinct white bars (Fig. 349**B**); breast with moderately broad to no blackish streaks by sex (Fig. 350**B-C**); pp and ss basic, showing replacement clines and often suspension limits (Fig. 344**B-C**), the outer pp broader, fresher, and with squarer markings (Fig. 351**B**).

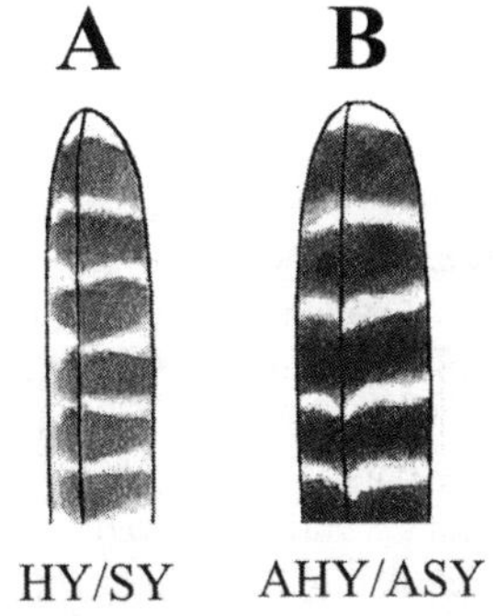

A **B**

HY/SY AHY/ASY

FIGURE 349. Shape and pattern to the rectrices by age in Aplomado Falcons (r5 shown). Note that HY/SYs (**A**) average more bars than AHY/ASYs (**B**).

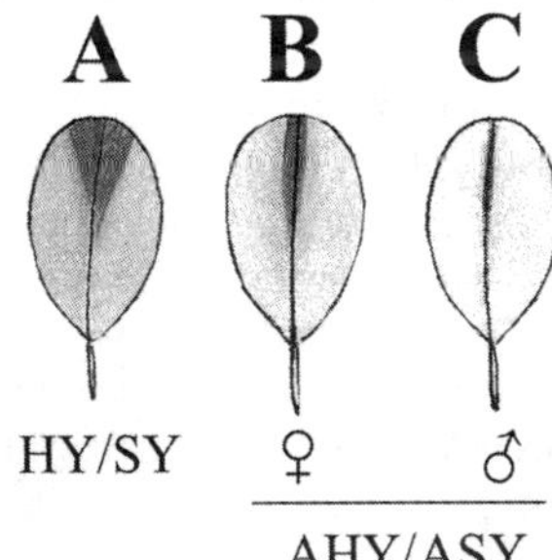

FIGURE 350. Pattern and coloration to the breast feathers by age in Aplomado Falcon. Juv feathers (**A**) are buffy, those of AHY/ASY ♀♀ are pale buff or cream colored, and those of AHY/ASY ♂♂ are whitish. SYs can exhibit a mixture of juv and formative breast feathers in Jan-Sep, the latter intermediate in color and pattern between **A** and **B** or **C**. Some AHY/ASY ♂♂ can have a plain breast, without any streaks.

Sex—Full bilateral(?) BPs (Fig. 20**B**, p. 31) and/or distended cloaca (Fig. 21, p. 32) indicates ♀ in Apr-Jul; ♂♂ can develop partial BPs. The following can be used to reliably sex all individuals of N.Am populations (see Table 41, p. 469, for other measures useful in sexing):

♀: Wg chord > 278; AHY/ASYs with moderately broad black streaks to breast (Fig. 350**B**).

♂: Wg chord < 279; AHY/ASYs with narrow or no black streaks to breast (Fig. 350**C**).

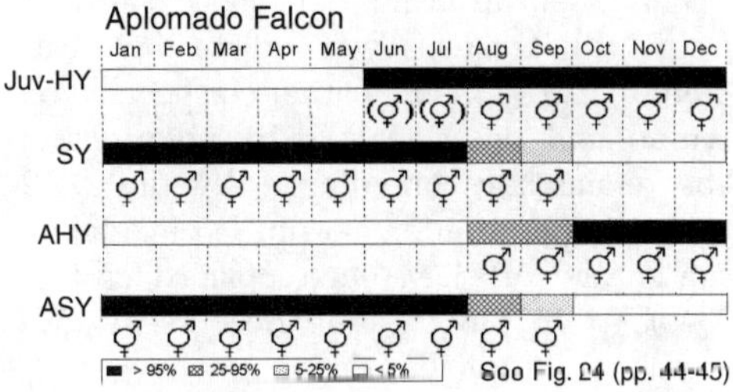

Aplomado Falcon

	Jan	Feb	Mar	Apr	May	Jun	Jul	Aug	Sep	Oct	Nov	Dec
Juv-HY						(⚥)	(⚥)	⚥	⚥	⚥	⚥	⚥
SY	⚥	⚥	⚥	⚥	⚥	⚥	⚥	⚥	⚥			
AHY								⚥	⚥	⚥	⚥	⚥
ASY	⚥	⚥	⚥	⚥	⚥	⚥	⚥	⚥	⚥			

■ > 95% ▩ 25-95% ▧ 5-25% □ < 5% See Fig. 24 (pp. 44-45)

Hybrids Reported—None in the wild.

References—Bent (1938), Friedmann (1950), Keddy-Hector (2000), Montoya et al. (1997), Oberholser (1974), D.P. Hector *in* Palmer (1988b).

GYRFALCON
Falco rusticolus

GYRF
Species # 3540
Band size: 7B Lock-on

Species—From other falcons and hawks by large size, especially tail and tarsus lengths (Table 41, p. 469); wings pointed (usually p9>p8>p10>p7>p6) and with p10 > p9 by 12-25 mm, p9-p10 notched and p8-p9 emarginated (*cf.* Figs. 289, p. 393, & 351); dark (gray and brown) "variants" (*cf.* Flann 2003) with crown and upperparts generally uniform in aspect (crown can be slightly paler), eyeline and moustachial stripe dusky, narrow (usually < 12 mm wide), and indistinct relative to auricular; pp, ss, and rects (including r1) "softer" in texture (less stiff), with 7-12 indistinct dusky bars (Figs. 351**A** & 352**A-C**); axillars and underwing covs uniform in aspect but darker than pp and ss ventrally; underparts marked in dark variants to predominantly white in white variant (Fig. 352), uniform in tone with upperparts; elongated femoral feathers usually extend to feet. Dark variants from Juv-HY/SY Northern Goshawk (p. 420) by shorter tarsus (Table 41); p9 > p7 and p10 > p5; back feathers and terts pointed (Fig. 285**B**, p. 391); rects with 9-12 dark bands (Fig. 252**A-C**); throat with indistinct or no streaking; iris dark.

Geographic variation—Monotypic (following Cade 1960, Cramp & Simmons 1980, and Palmer 1988b); see also Dement'ev & Gladkov (1951b), Flann (2003), Friedmann (1950), Hantzsch (1929), Hellmayr & Conover (1949), Koelz (1929), Manning et al. (1956), Mattox (1969), Portenko (1972), Swann (1922b), Todd (1963), Todd & Friedmann (1947). Size variation within Eurasian populations (*cf.* Dement'ev & Gladkov 1951b) insufficient for subspecific recognition. Populations of w.AK ("*F.r. uralensis*" or "*alascanus*") average more rounded wings (p10 – p7 longer) than populations elsewhere in N.Am ("*obsoletus*"), but this difference is slight and variable. In N.Am, higher proportions of whiter variants ("*candicans*") are found at higher latitudes, grayer variants are widespread, and higher proportions of darker variants occur in humid areas along both coasts (Palmer 1988b), but these patterns are discordant.

Molt—CBS. PF absent-limited (Nov-Mar), PB2 incomplete-complete (Mar-Oct in non-breeding SYs), DPB incomplete-complete (Apr-Nov in breeding AHYs); PA absent. The PF occurs on non-breeding grounds whereas DPBs occur primarily on breeding grounds but can complete on non-breeding grounds. The PF can include up to 30% of the body feathers but appears to be absent in many individuals. The PB2 and DPB are usually complete, but scattered les covs, body feathers (especially on rump) and (occasionally) p10 and/or s1 can be retained. In breeding ASYs, the DPB often suspends after 1-4 pp, 1-3 medial ss, and/or the terts have been replaced (*cf.* Fig. 344**C**, p. 457). See Family Account (p. 457) for more information.

Age—Juvs (B1; Aug-May) described below; Juv ♀=♂.

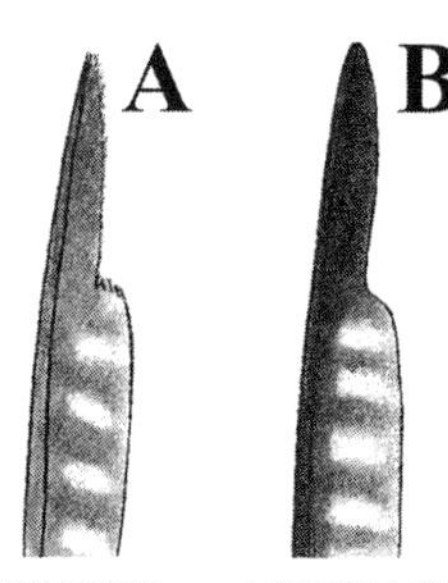

FIGURE 351. Shape and pattern to the outer primary (p10) by age in most N.Am falcons (Crested Caracara shows similar differences in shape but not pattern). Note that juv feathers (**A**) show narrower and paler tips and deeper notches than basic feathers (**B**), and are often more noticeably worn in Apr-Sep. Note also that the pale spots on juv feathers tend to be more restricted and rounded than those of basic feathers. The illustration shows patterns typical of most Gyrfalcons and Aplamado, Peregrine, and Prairie falcons; some white ASY/ATY Gyrfalcons may show very indistinct or no pattern to the primaries and Merlin and American Kestrel show more subtle differences.

Juv-HY/SY (1st cycle, Juv/B1-F1; Oct-Sep): Upperpart feathers without barring (dark variants) or blackish with white fringing (white variant); rects narrow and rounded, r2-r5 brown with 9-12 rounder pale bars (dark variants), or white, often with dark marks on outer web (white variant) and longitudinal streaks to underparts (Fig. 352**A**, **D**); pp and ss uniformly juv, without replacement clines or suspension limits (Fig. 344**A**), the outer pp narrower, more worn, and with rounder pale markings (Fig. 351**A**); fault bars (if present) as in Fig. 18**A** (p. 27); cere and legs dull grayish to greenish yellow. **Note: Some dark variants have intermediate features (*cf.* Fig. 352B) and may be difficult to age.**

AHY/ASY (Def. cycle, DB; Oct-Sep): Upperpart feathers with indistinct pale barring (dark variants) or black chevrons (white variant); rects broad and truncate, r2-r5 with 7-11 squarer pale bars (dark variants) or white without dark marks (white variant) and underpart markings reduced and rounded or absent (Fig. 352**C**, **E**); pp and ss basic, showing replacement clines but without suspension limits (Fig. 344**B**), the outer pp broader, fresher, and with squarer markings if present (Fig. 351**B**); cere and legs dull to bright yellow. **Note: See Juv-HY/SY and SY/TY.**

SY/TY (2nd cycle, B2; Oct-Sep): Like AHY/ASY but 1 to a few juv wing covs and/or body feathers (especially on rump) retained (Fig. 313**A**, p. 418), narrow, worn, and without darker barring or chevrons; p10 and/or s1 occasionally retained, narrow and very worn; one or more rects often with semi-rounded spots (dark variant; Fig. 352**B**) or limited blackish on outer web (white variant), underpart markings sometimes intermediate, variably streaked to semi-rounded (Fig. 352**B**); cere and legs dull to bright yellow. **Note: Individuals should only be aged SY/TY or ASY/ATY by the presence of retained feathers or suspension limits (ASY/ATYs); intermediate plumage aspect to rects or underpart feathers can be used as secondary characters.**

ASY/ATY (Def. cycle, DB; Oct-Sep): Like AHY/ASY but 1 to many basic wing covs, body feathers, and/or rump feathers retained (Fig. 313**B**), broad, fresh, and with darker barring or chevrons; pp and ss often with suspension limits among p3-p6 and s4-s6 (Fig. 344**C**); p10 and/or s1 occasionally retained, broad and slightly worn; cere and legs bright yellow. **Note: See SY/TY.**

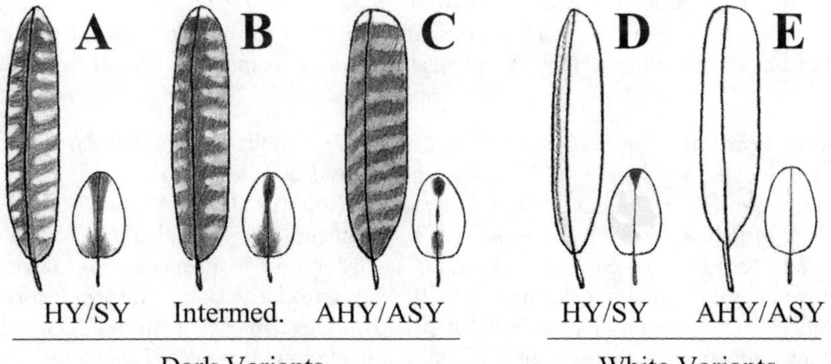

FIGURE 352. Shape and pattern to the rectrices (left, r5 shown) and underpart feathers (right) by age in Gyrfalcon. Note that some intermediates can occur (e.g., **B** in dark variants) and that some Juv-HY/SY white variants can lack dark markings to the outer webs of the rects, especially when worn

Sex— ♀ = ♂ by plumage aspect. Full bilateral BPs (Fig. 20**B**, p. 31) and/or distended cloaca (Fig. 21, p. 32) indicates ASY ♀ in Apr-Jul; ♂♂ can develop partial BPs. Measurements (Table 41, p. 469) can be used to sex a majority of full-grown individuals including all mated pairs:

♀: Wg chord > 387 and/or tarsus > 65 (Table 41). **Note: Individuals with wing chord 380-387 and tarsus 64-65 are not reliably sexed except, potentially, among mated pairs where ♀ > ♂ in both of the above measures.**

♂: Wg chord < 380 and/or tarsus < 64 (Table 41). **Note: See ♀.**

Gyrfalcon
Jan Feb Mar Apr May Jun Jul Aug Sep Oct Nov Dec
Juv-HY
SY
TY
AHY
ASY
ASY
■ > 95% ▨ 25-95% ▭ 5-25% □ < 5%
See Fig. 24 (pp. 44-45)

Hybrids Reported—With Saker *F. cherrug* (Fox & Potapov 2001) and Peregrine Falcon (Gantlett & Millington 1992) in the wild.

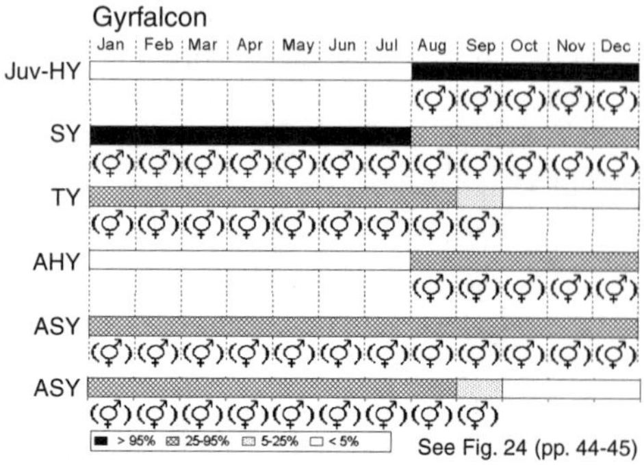

References—Bent (1938), Clum & Cade (1994), Cramp & Simmons (1980), Dement'ev & Gladkov (1951b), Forsman (1999), Friedmann (1950), Gantlett & Millington (1992), Koelz (1929), Mattox (1969, 1970), Nicoletti & Benson (2000), C.M. White *in* Palmer (1988b), Pyle (2005b, 2005c), Roberts (1955), Wheeler (2000).

PEREGRINE FALCON
Falco peregrinus

PEFA
Species # 3560
Band size: 6♂, 7A-7B♀ Lock-on

Species—From other falcons and hawks by medium-large size (Table 41, p. 469); wings pointed (usually p9>p10>p8>p7>p6) and with p10 notched and p9 emarginated (*cf.* Figs. 289, p. 393, & 351, p. 466; p8 can be slightly emarginated); upperparts brownish to blackish brown (most Juv-HY/SYs) or dusky to bluish (AHY/ASYs); moustachial stripe dark blackish to black and broad (10-25 mm wide; see **Geographic variation**), contrasting distinctly with cream to white throat; pp, ss, and rects (including r1) "harder" in texture (stiffer), with moderately distinct dusky barring (Fig. 353, p. 470); axillars and underwing covs uniformly dusky brown to grayish, similar in aspect to pp and ss ventrally; underparts whitish, with variable brown streaking (Juv-HY/SY) or blackish barring (AHY/ASY); elongated femoral feathers usually extend 10-20 mm short of feet.

Geographic variation—See Beebe (1960), Blake (1977), Brooks (1926c), Cramp & Simmons (1980), Dement'ev & Gladkov (1951b), Earnheart-Gold & Pyle (2001), Friedmann (1950), Gibson & Kessel (1997), Harrop (2004), Hellmayr & Conover (1949), Manning et al. (1956), C.M. White *in* Palmer (1988b), Portenko (1972), Stejneger (1885), Todd (1963), White (1968, 1972), White & Boyce (1988), White et al. (2002). Sixteen other subspecies worldwide. Note that captive breeding programs during the 1970-1980s introduced other subspecific forms into North American populations, particularly *F.p. peregrinus* and *brookei* of Europe. The influence of these introductions are still evident, especially among e.populations of *F.p. anatum* (Tordoff & Redig 2001; Wheeler 2003a, 2003b).

TABLE 41. Measurements (mm) of North American caracaras and falcons to assist in identification and sexing. See pp. 4-11 for methods of measurements. Species summaries are in **bold** and subspecies summaries are in ***italics***. Values were derived from 95% confidence intervals as based approximately on the indicated sample sizes (see pp. 4-5); thus midpoints of ranges approximate means, and S.D. is approximated by 25% of the range.

Taxon/Sex	*n*	wing chord	tail length[1]	culmen from cere[2]	tarsus
Crested Caracara[3]		**353-416**	**204-242**	**29.7-36.6**	**86-96**
♀	100	362-418	210-242	30.7-36.6	87-96
♂	100	350-406	204-233	29.7-35.5	86-93
American Kestrel[3]		**166-204**	**99-144**	**10.1-14.0**	**31-42**
F.s. sparverius		***176-204***	***116-144***	***10.6-14.0***	***34-42***
♀	100	182-204	118-144	11.1-14.0	35-42
♂	100	176-198	116-142	10.6-13.4	34-41
F.s. peninsularis		***161-183***	***111-131***	***10.8-13.4***	***34-41***
♀	15	167-183	115-131	11.2-13.4	36-41
♂	20	161-178	111-126	10.8-12.9	34-39
F.s. paulus		***166-191***	***99-122***	***10.1-13.2***	***31-37***
♀	39	175-191	102-122	10.8-13.2	32-37
♂	45	166-185	99-119	10.1-12.5	31-36
Merlin[3]		**178-227**	**108-142**	**11.7-15.1**	**33-43**
F.c. columbarius & suckleyi		***178-221***	***108-137***	***11.7-15.1***	***33-43***
♀	100	199-221	120-137	13.3-15.1	36-43
♂	100	178-201	108-124	11.7-13.3	33-41
F.c. richardsonii		***186-227***	***114-142***	***11.8-14.9***	***34-43***
♀	90	209-227	126-142	13.3-14.9	37-43
♂	100	186-209	114-129	11.8-13.3	34-41
Aplomado Falcon[3]		**248-314**	**172-211**	**15.9-19.6**	**48-59**
♀	20	279-314	188-211	16.9-19.6	52-59
♂	20	248-278	172-196	15.9-17.1	48-54
Gyrfalcon		**344-422**	**183-246**	**20.3-27.9**	**61-70**
♀	79	380-422	207-246	22.7-27.9	64-70
♂	59	344-387	183-216	20.3-25.2	61-65
Peregrine Falcon[3]		**291-376**	**129-194**	**17.2-26.5**	**38-58**
F.p. tundrius		***291-369***	***131-190***	***19.8-25.3***	***39-56***
♀	100	331-369	157-190	21.1-25.3	44-56
♂	100	291-328	131-167	19.8-24.3	39-50
F.c. anatum		***296-373***	***129-194***	***17.2-26.1***	***39-58***
♀	80	338-373	156-194	21.7-26.1	45-58
♂	70	296-330	129-163	17.2-22.0	39-52
F.c. pealei		***308-376***	***141-191***	***18.1-26.5***	***38-56***
♀	35	352-376	169-191	22.3-26.5	44-56
♂	30	308-330	141-162	18.1-22.1	38-50
Prairie Falcon		**291-360**	**154-200**	**17.3-24.1**	**52-64**
♀	100	329-360	176-200	20.5-24.1	57-64
♂	100	291-320	154-178	17.3-20.3	52-59

[1] Tail length values include birds of all ages; in most falcons the juvenal rects can average 5-10% longer than adult rects, sex for sex.

[2] Culmen from cere represents the chord (Fig. 7**B**, p. 9).

[3] Measures represent N.Am populations only only (see **Geographic variation**).

F.p tundrius (br interior nw.AK-n.Nfl, wint Mex-S.Am): Averages smaller (Table 41, p. 469); moustachial stripe narrow (10-17 mm wide); Juv-HY/SY with crown washed buff, upperparts medium-pale brown, rects with distinct bars (Fig. 353**A**), and underparts cream with medium-sparse brown streaking; AHY/ASY with blackish crown and hood contrasting with medium-pale grayish-blue back, and breast white with few or no black spots.

F.p. anatum (br & wint wc.AK-s.Nfl to CA-FL): Variable in size (Table 41; note that populations of e.N.Am average larger than those of w.N.Am); moustachial stripe moderately broad (13-22 mm wide); Juv-HY/SY with crown usually without buff, upperparts medium-dark brown (sometimes tinged rufous), rects with distinct bars (Fig. 353**A**), and underparts whitish with moderately heavy to heavy brown streaking; AHY/ASY with crown and hood dusky, contrasting indistinctly with medium-dark bluish-gray back, and breast washed cinnamon with narrow or no black spots or streaks. **Note: In e.populations breast can be moderately streaked due to infusion of European subspecies (see above).**

F.p. pealei (br coastal sw.AK Is-sw.BC, wint to wc.CA): Averages larger (Table 41); moustachial stripe broad (16-25 mm wide); Juv-HY/SY crown without buff, upperparts medium-pale brown to blackish, rects with indistinct bars (Fig. 353**B**), and underparts dark brown to blackish with narrow white streaks; AHY/ASY with dusky crown and hood, contrasting little or not with medium-dark grayish back, and breast white with distinct black spotting or streaking concentrated ventrally. Populations of ne.Asia (*japonensis*), potential vagrants to w.AK Is, are similar in plumage aspect but smaller (the size of *tundrius*; Table 41), and may have more extensive PFs.

Molt—CBS. PF absent-limited (Oct-Mar in HY/SYs), PB2 incomplete-complete (Apr-Nov in non-breeding SYs), DPB incomplete-complete (May-Nov in breeding AHYs); PA absent. The PFs occur primarily on non-breeding grounds whereas DPBs commence on breeding grounds and complete on non-breeding grounds. The PF can include up to 25% of the body feathers but can be absent in some individuals (extralimital subspecies, e.g. *F.p. japonensis*, may have more extensive PFs). The DPB completes later in *P.f. tundrius* (Jan-Mar) than in other N.Am subspecies (Nov-Jan). A few wing covs and body feathers (especially on rump) can be retained during DPBs. In breeding ASYs, the DPB often suspends after 1-5 pp, 1-3 medial ss, and/or the terts have been replaced (*cf.* Fig. 344**C**, p. 457). See Family Account (p. 457) for more information.

Age—Juvs (B1; Jul-May) similar to HY/SYs in Sep-Oct, as described below; Juv ♀=♂.

Juv-HY/SY1st cycle, Juv/B1-F1; Oct-Sep): Upperparts brown, often mixed with scattered brownish-gray feathers in Nov-May; underparts streaked brown, often mixed with barred feathers in Nov-May; rects narrow and rounded, r2-r5 with rounded buff to indistinctly pale markings by subspecies (Fig. 353**A-B**); pp and ss uniformly juv, without replacement clines or suspension limits (Fig. 344**A**, p. 457), the outer pp narrower, more worn, and with rounder pale markings (Fig. 351**A**, p. 466); cere dull grayish to greenish yellow. **Note: Some SYs may over-summer on non-breeding grounds and exhibit advanced PB2s (see p. 18).**

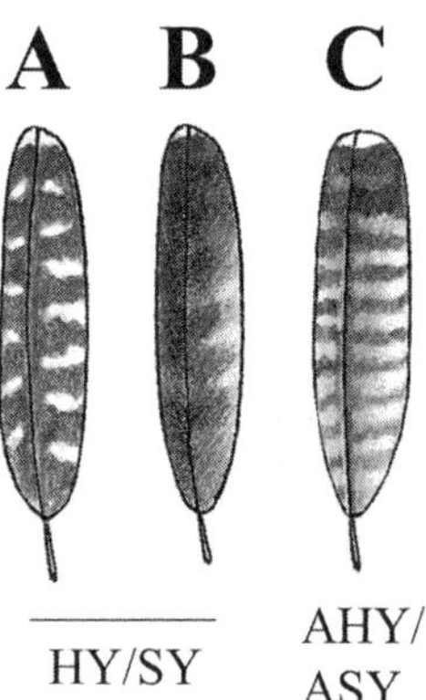

FIGURE 353. Shape and pattern to the rectrices (r5 shown) by age and subspecies in Peregrine Falcon. Among Juv-HY/SYs, the rects of *F.p. tundrius* and *anatum* have more distinct patterns (**A**) than those of *pealei* (**B**). Rects of AHY/ASYs are similar among all 3 N.Am subspecies.

AHY/ASY (Def. cycle, DB; Oct-Sep): Upperparts uniformly gray; lower underparts barred blackish; rects broad and truncate, r2-r5 with squared grayish bars (Fig. 353**C**); pp and ss, basic, showing replacement clines but not suspension limits (Fig. 344**B**), the outer pp broader, fresher, and with squarer pale markings (Fig. 351**B**); cere yellow to yellowish orange. **Note: See SY/TY.**

SY/TY (2nd cycle, B2; Oct-Sep): Like AHY/ASY but 1 to many juv wing covs and/or body feathers (especially on rump) retained, brown, and worn (Fig. 313**A**, p. 418); p4-p6 and s4-s6 sometimes distinctly browner (in aspect, not wear) than other wing feathers; pp and ss usually without suspension limits (Fig. 344**B**). **Note: Some SY/TY tundrius also may not complete the PB2 until Jan-Apr and can be aged by the retained juv p10 (Fig. 344A) and outer and/or inner ss. Retention of juv feathers subsequent to completion of the PB2 may be rare. Look also for a brownish wash to the upperparts and intermediate back, underpart, and rect (cf. Fig. 353) characters in SY/TYs. See also ASY/ATY.**

ASY/ATY (Def. cycle, DB; Oct-Sep): Like AHY/ASY but 1 to many basic wing covs and/or body feathers (especially on rump) retained, grayish, slightly worn (Fig. 313**C**); pp and ss often showing suspension limits (Fig. 344**C**), but uniform in pattern. **Note: Beware that retained basic feathers can become faded and worn, resembling juv feathers. Most individuals with suspension limits are reliably aged ASY/ATY, as SYs seldom breed.**

Sex—AHY/ASY ♀♀ average darker and more brown-tinged upperparts and warmer and more heavily marked underparts than AHY/ASY ♂♂, but differences are confounded by geographic and age-related variation. Otherwise, ♀ = ♂ by plumage aspect. Full bilateral BPs (Fig. 20**B**, p. 31) and/or distended cloaca (Fig. 21, p. 32) indicates ♀ in Mar-Jul; ♂♂ can develop partial BPs. Other measures in addition to the following can be used to sex most individuals (Table 41, p. 493).

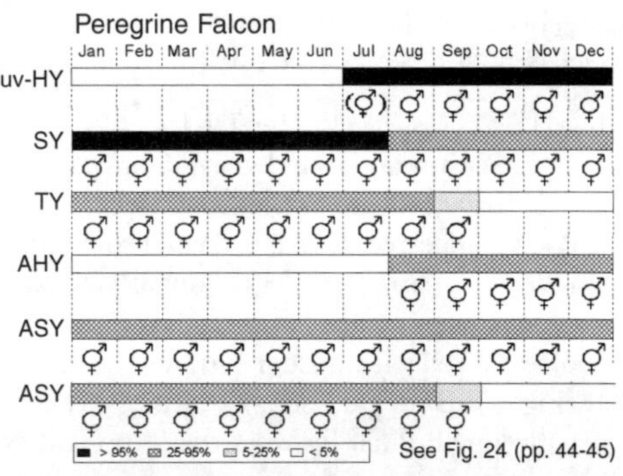

♀: Wg chord > 330; footpad length (Fig. 342, p. 455) > 90.

♂: Wg chord < 331; footpad length < 90.

Hybrids Reported—With Lanner *F. biarmicus* and Saker *F. cherrug* falcons (McCarthy 2006), Gyrfalcon (p. 466), and Prairie Falcon (Oliphant 1991) in the wild.

References—Baker (1993), Bent (1938), R.M. Bond (1936), Cade (1960), Cramp & Simmons (1980), Dement'ev & Gladkov (1951b), Enderson et al. (1973), Forsman (1999), Friedmann (1950), Henny & Clark (1982), Hunt et al. (1975), Marchant & Higgins (1993), Oberholser (1974), Palmer (1988b), Pyle (2005b, 2005c), Roberts (1955), Stresemann & Stresemann (1966), Swarth (1933b), White (1968), White et al. (2002).

PRAIRIE FALCON
Falco mexicanus

PRFA
Species # 3550
Band size: 6-5♂, 7A-6♀ Lock-on

Species—From other falcons and hawks by medium size with proportionally long tail and tarsus (Table 41, p. 469); wings pointed (usually p9>p8>p10>p7>p6) and with p9-p10 notched and p8-p9 emarginated (*cf.* Figs. 289, p. 393, & 351, p. 466); crown and upperparts moderately pale brownish to grayish brown, the back feathers with indistinct markings (Fig. 355); eyeline and moustachial stripe dark brown, the latter narrow (5-10 mm wide); postocular area whitish; pp, ss, and rects "softer" in texture (less stiff), with indistinct pale brown barring (Fig. 354), r1 with little or no barring dorsally; axillars and underwing covs extensively blackish (Fig. 356); underparts whitish, with sparse dark brownish streaking (Juv-HY/SY) or spotting (AHY/ASY); elongated femoral feathers usually extend 10-20 mm short of feet.

Geographic variation—Monotypic. The name "*F.m. polyagrus*" for populations of nw. or w.N.Am (Oberholser 1974) is without merit (Browning 1978, Rea 1983a).

Molt—CBS. PF absent-limited (Oct-Jan in HY/SYs), PB2 complete (Apr-Oct in non-breeding SYs), DPB complete (Apr-Nov in breeding AHYs); PA absent. The PFs occur primarily on non-breeding grounds whereas DPBs commence on breeding grounds and complete on non-breeding grounds. The PF can include up to 20% of the body feathers but can be absent in some individuals. In breeding ASY ♀♀, the DPB often suspends after 1-5 pp, 1-3 medial ss, and/or the terts have been replaced (*cf.* Fig. 344**C**, p. 457, and Steenhof & McKinley 2006). See Family Account (p. 457) for more information.

Age—Juvs (B1; Jun-Apr) similar to HY/SYs in Oct-Nov, as described below; Juv ♀=♂.

Juv-HY/SY (1st cycle, Juv/B1-F1; Oct-Sep): Rects narrow and rounded, r2-r5 brown with oval-shaped or triangular buff spots (Fig. 354**A**); upperparts medium-dark brown with little or no barring but with cinnamon to pale brown fringe or tips when fresh (Fig. 355**A**), often mixed with fresher formative feathers (Fig. 355**B**) in Dec-Sep; underparts whitish with longitudinal brown streaks; pp and ss uniformly juv, without replacement clines or suspension limits (Fig. 344**A**, p. 457), the

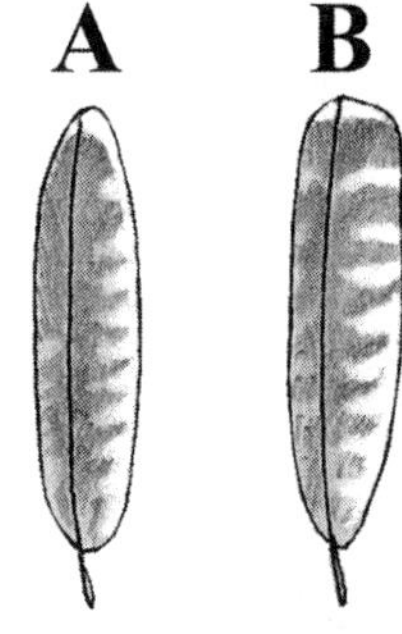

FIGURE 354. Shape and pattern to the rectrices (r5 shown) by age in Prairie Falcon.

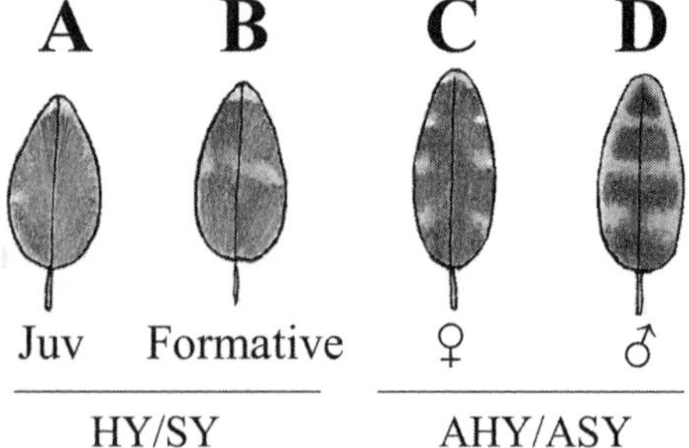

FIGURE 355. Shape and pattern to the back feathers by age, and by sex in AHY/ASY Prairie Falcons. Some overlap may occur between the sexes in AHY/ASYs. Juvs are not reliably sexed by back-feather pattern, although average differences in formative feathers, toward the patterns found in AHY/ASYs, may occur (more study needed).

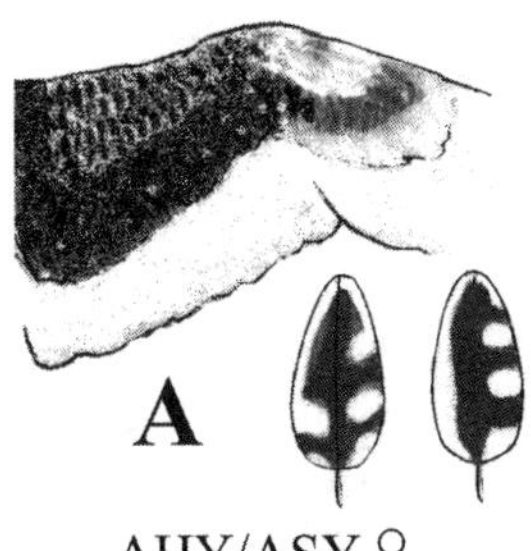

AHY/ASY ♀

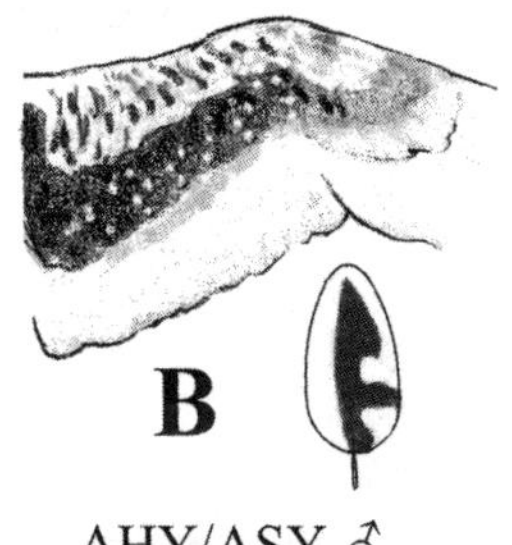

AHY/ASY ♂

FIGURE 356. Extent of blackish coloration to the underwings and pattern to the outermost underwing greater covert by sex in AHY/ASY Prairie Falcons. Intermediates will be encountered that are not reliably sexed by underwing plumage aspect alone. Juv-HY/SY ♀♀ also average more dark coloration than Juv-HY/SY ♂♂ but are probably not reliably sexed by this criterion alone due to extensive overlap; more study needed.

outer pp narrower, more worn, and with rounder pale markings (Fig. 351**A**, p. 466); fault bars (if present) as in Fig. 18**A** (p. 27); cere and legs dull grayish to greenish yellow.

AHY/ASY (Def. cycle, DB; Oct-Sep): Rects broad and truncate, r2-r5 grayish with distinct dusky bars (Fig. 354**B**); upperparts uniformly pale brown to grayish brown with indistinct to distinct dark brown barring by sex (Fig. 355**C-D**); underparts white with distinct dark brown spots or horizontal bars; pp and ss; basic, showing replacement clines but not suspension limits (Fig. 344**B**), the outer pp broader, fresher, and with squarer pale markings (Fig. 351**B**); fault bars (if present) as in Fig. 18**B**; cere and legs bright yellow.

ASY/ATY (Def. cycle, DB; Oct-Sep): Like AHY/ASY but pp showing suspension limits (Fig. 344**C**).

Sex—Full bilateral(?) BPs (Fig. 20**B**, p. 31) and/or distended cloaca (Fig. 21, p. 32) indicates ♀ in Mar-Jul; ♂♂ can develop partial BPs. Other measures in addition to the following can be used to sex most individuals (Table 41, p. 469; Steenhof & McKinley 2006). In addition to the following, look for AHY/ASY ♂♂ to average longer and bolder white supercilia than AHY/ASY ♀♀ (see Wheeler 2003a; this difference may not be as appreciable in museum specimens).

♀: Wg chord > 325; footpad length (Fig. 342, p. 455) > 83; AHY/ASY with more extensive blackish to the underwing (Fig. 356**A**), indistinct and broken dusky bars or spots to back feathers and wing covs (Fig. 355**C**), and r1 usually without indistinct dusky barring dorsally. **Note: Juv-HY/SY ♀♀ also average more extensive dark to the underwing gr covs than Juv-HY/SY ♂♂, but these are reliably sexed only by measurements.**

♂: Wg chord < 325; footpad length < 83; AHY/ASY with less extensive dark coloration to the underwing (Fig. 356**A**), distinct and complete dusky bars to back feathers and wing covs (Fig. 355**D**), and r1 usually with indistinct dusky barring dorsally. **Note: See ♀.**

Prairie Falcon

Jan | Feb | Mar | Apr | May | Jun | Jul | Aug | Sep | Oct | Nov | Dec

Juv-HY

SY

AHY

ASY

ATY

■ > 95% ▨ 25-95% ▢ 5-25% □ < 5%

See Fig. 24 (pp. 44-45)

Hybrids Reported—With Peregrine Falcon (p. 468) in the wild.

References—Anderson & Squires (1997), Bent (1938), Enderson (1964), Friedmann (1950), Oberholser (1974), Palmer (1988b), Pyle (2005b, 2005c), Roberts (1955), Steenhof (1998), Steenhof & McKinley (2006).

RAILS, GALLINULES, AND COOTS *RALLIDAE*

Nine species. Family characters include thin bodies, variably shaped bills with ornamental shields in three species, shortish and broad wings (Fig. 357) with sharp spicules ("claws") at the bends, short tails, sturdy legs, and large feet, with short but functional hind toe, and without webbing (American Coot, p. 488, has lobed toes). North American rails, gallinules, and coots have 10 functional primaries (p10 extending 12-25 mm short of the longest, p7-p9, when fully grown), 10-13 secondaries (including 3 tertials and one absent between the 4th and 5th in N.Am species; *cf.* Fig. 12**B**, p. 19), and 12 rectrices. Ageing through the first cycle (to SY and ASY) can be accomplished by plumage aspect, molt limits among wing feathers (Fig. 357) and tail, shape of the outer primaries (Fig. 358), medial ss in some species (Fig. 475), and rectrices (when retained), color changes to the iris and legs, and structural changes to the ornamental bill shield in gallinules and coots. Males are only slightly larger than females and plumage-aspect distinctions by sex are slight in most species. Both sexes develop medial brood patches (Fig. 20**B**, p. 31) in most species but females can be sexed by distended cloacae (Fig. 21, p. 32; Boersma & Davies 1987). Other cloacal differences (Figs. 22-23, pp. 32-35) should be investigated, although length of the bursa (Fig. 23, p. 34) appears not to be useful for ageing American Coots (Gullion 1952, Fredrickson 1968, Eddleman & Knopf 1985). Further study needed.

In molting, North American rails, gallinules, and coots appear to exhibit the Complex Basic Strategy (CBS; Fig. 10**B**, pp. 13-16), including a formative but no alternate plumages; limited prealternate molts have been reported for many species but these seem more likely to be based on protracted preformative molts, or aspect changes due to wear, as opposed to feather replacement.

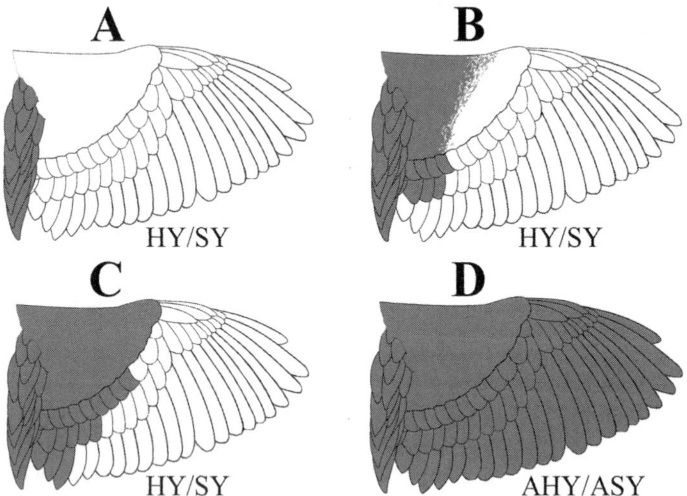

FIGURE 357. Molt limits by age in rails. The PF can vary (by individual and species) from no s covs or terts replaced, resulting in uniformly juv wing feathers contrasting with newer formative humerals on some Juv-HY/SYs (**A**), to including most les and med covs, some proximal gr covs, and 1-3 terts replaced, resulting in molt limits in the wing of some HY/SYs (**C**). AHY/ASYs have uniformly basic wing feathers (**D**), which are relatively fresh and lustrous (by season) compared to juv wing feathers and are also uniform in wear and quality with the humerals. Beware that humerals can be a different color than s covs, perhaps resulting in pseudolimits (p. 19). Note also that the outer pp of HY/SYs are relatively narrow and worn compared to those of AHY/ASYs (Fig. 358) and that juv medial ss can be more pointed than basic feathers in some species (Fig. 359). Beware that the wings of both age groups can become very worn in May-Aug, rendering age-determination by wing-related criteria difficult.

Preformative molts are partial to incomplete, including a few to most secondary coverts and 1-3 tertials in some species (Fig. 357**A**-**C**), and some to all rectrices in most species. Primaries, secondaries, and rectrices are replaced synchronously (or nearly so) during definitive prebasic molts, on breeding grounds, following breeding in July to September. Age of first breeding occurs at 1 year in most individuals resulting in similar timing of the second and subsequent prebasic molts.

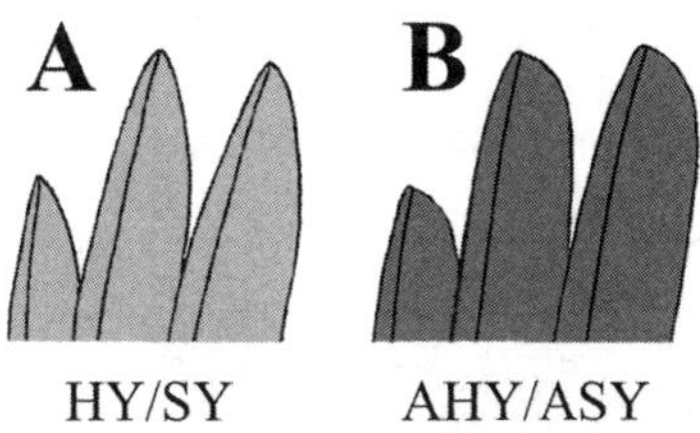

FIGURE 358. Shape to the outer primaries (p8-p10) by age in rails. Note that this difference can be subtle, and many intermediates are not reliably aged by this character alone.

YELLOW RAIL
Coturnicops noveboracensis

YERA
Species # 2150
Band size: 2

Species—From Juv gamebirds and other N.Am rails by medium-small size (Table 42, p. 480); plumage aspect blackish brown, buffy ochre, and dull yellowish with narrow white markings (*cf.* Fig. 360, p. 476); proximal ss (s1-s6) with white (Fig. 359); axillars and proximal underwing covs white; bill brown (juv) to yellow (AHY); iris brownish-red; legs dull pinkish. Swinhoe's Rail (*C. exquisitus*), a possible vagrant to w.AK Is, averages smaller (wg 75-81, tl 29-35, tarsus 20-24) and has face plainer and washed gray, plumage aspect redder, and underparts with indistinct barring.

Geographic variation—See Dickerman (1971), Taylor (1998), Hellmayr & Conover (1942), Hubbard & Banks (1970), Nelson (1904), Ridgway & Friedmann (1941), Ripley (1977). One other subspecies occurs in c.Mex.

C.n. noveboracensis (br & wint N.Am): Smaller (Table 42, p. 480; *vs* wg 87-93, tarsus 24-28 in *goldmani* of c.Mex); upperparts brownish black (*vs* blacker in *goldmani*); Juv with white speckling to face and flanks (*vs* often unflecked in *goldmani*). The names "*richii*" for populations of e.N.Am and "*emersoni*" for populations of OR-CA are not valid.

Molt—CBS (CAS?). PF partial-incomplete (Jul-Sep in HYs), DPB complete (Jul-Sep in AHYs); PA absent(?). The above timing refers to N.Am populations. All molts occur on breeding grounds. The PF includes most to all body feathers, some proximal s covs, occasionally 1-2 terts, and no to all rects. During DPBs, pp, ss, and rects are replaced synchronously in Aug. There is little evidence for a PA, despite reports (see Family Account).

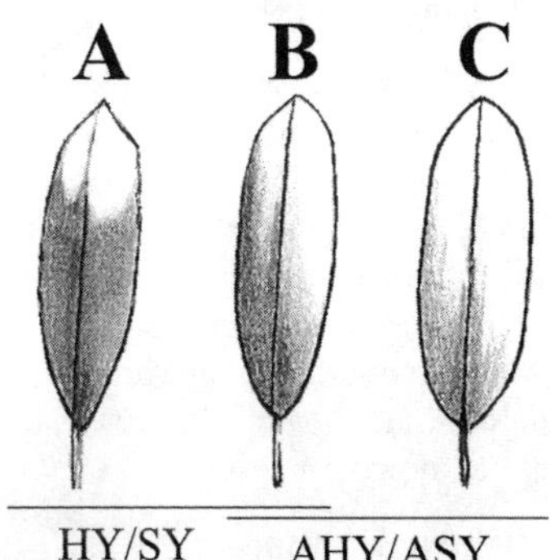

FIGURE 359. Shape and color pattern to the medial secondaries (s5 shown) by age in Yellow Rail. The cumulative result is of a more restricted and less distinct white patch in the wings of HY/SYs than in AHY/ASYs. The color pattern shown in **B** can be found in both HY/SYs (perhaps more often in ♂♂) and AHY/ASYs (perhaps more often in ♀♀); note that some intermediates are best aged U/AHY. The pointed shape in juv ss (**A**) *vs.* blunter shape in basic ss (**C**) is also found in Black Rail and Sora among N.Am crakes (see also Green 2004, Green et al. 2001).

Age—Juv (B1; Jun-Sep) has duller plumage aspect, reduced white barring, and iris grayish brown to brownish. Juv ♀ = ♂ by plumage aspect. The following month ranges pertain to N.Am populations. Intermediates between the following occur that may be difficult to age.

HY/SY (1st cycle, F1; Oct-Sep): Medial ss narrower, acutely pointed, and with reduced and indistinct white patch (Fig. 359**A-B**, p. 475); p covs without white spots; some to all rects often narrow (*cf.* Fig. 17**A-C**, p. 25) without white or with narrow white spots or bars (Fig. 360**A-B**); molt limits occur between back and wing or among s covs and (occasionally) terts (Fig. 357**A-C**, p. 474), the replaced scapulars, humerals, and proximal s covs glossy and blackish (fringed ocher), contrasting with the duller and brown (fringed buff) retained juv distal s covs, and the juv outer pp more pointed (Fig. 358**A**, p. 475) and brownish; breast without tawny wash; iris brownish red to reddish. **Note: Some intermediates may best be aged U/AHY**.

AHY/ASY (Def. cycle, DB; Oct-Sep): Medial ss broader, more rounded, and with large and distinct white patch (Fig. 359**C**); one or more p covs often with white spots near tip; rects uniformly broad (Fig. 17**E**) with broad white bars (Fig. 360**C**); scapulars, humerals, and s covs uniform in wear (Fig. 357**D**), glossy and blackish fringed ocher, the outer pp blunter (Fig. 358**B**) and dusky; breast sometimes washed tawny; iris deep reddish. **Note: See HY/SY.**

A B C

Juv Formative/ Basic

FIGURE 360. Shape and color pattern to the outer rectrices (r2-r6) by feather generation in Yellow Rail. Note that some HY/SYs can replace all rects with formative feathers showing shape and pattern as in **C**.

Sex—♀ = ♂ by plumage aspect. Medial BP (Fig. 20**A**, p. 31) possibly reliable for sexing ♀♀; distended cloaca (Fig. 21, p. 32) indicates AHY ♀ in Mar-May. Measurements generally unhelpful for sexing (Table 42, p. 480). Bill averages brighter yellow in ♂♂ than in ♀♀ during Mar-Jun and this might help sex some individuals or mated pairs. Otherwise, no reliable criteria known for sexing.

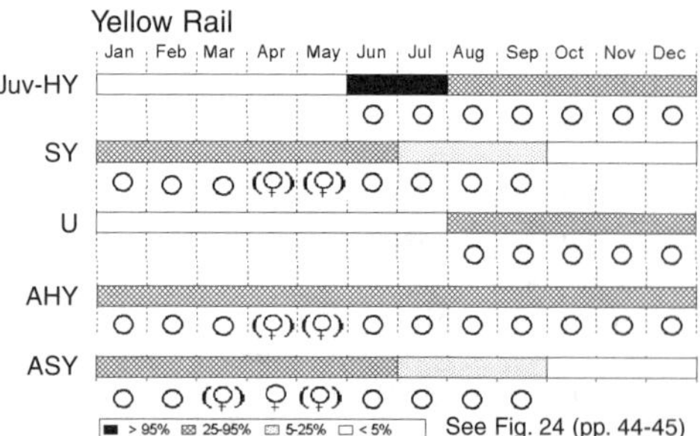

Hybrids Reported—None.

References—Bent (1926), Bookhout (1995), Dickerman (1971), Oberholser (1974), Ridgway & Friedmann (1941), Roberts (1955), Stalheim (1975), Taylor (1998), Walkinshaw (1939).

BLACK RAIL

Laterallus jamaicensis

BLRA
Species # 2160
Band size: 2-1A

Species—From other N.Am rails by small size (Table 42, p. 480); plumage aspect largely sooty blackish with dusky brown back and chestnut hind collar; pp, ss, and upperparts with white spots (*cf.* Fig. 361); bill blackish; iris reddish; legs dusky brownish to pinkish.

Geographic variation—See Blake (1977), Brewster (1907), Coale (1923), Dickerman (1971), Hellmayr & Conover (1942), Oberholser (1918a, 1974), Ridgway (1890), Ridgway &

Friedmann (1941), Ripley (1977), Russell (1966), Taylor (1998), Wayne (1923). Three other subspecies occur in S.Am.

L.j. coturniculus (br & wint CA-sw.AZ): Smaller (Table 42, p. 480); bill slender (width at proximal end of nares often < 2.5 mm) and tapered at tip; crown washed brown; hind collar bright chestnut.

L.j. jamaicensis (br & wint KS-TX to NY-FL): Larger (Table 42); bill stouter (width at proximal end of nares often > 2.5 mm) and rounded at tip; crown sooty, sometimes with slight brown wash; hind collar dull chestnut. Populations of N.Am ("*stoddardi*" or "*pygmaeus*") may average shorter-billed and with larger white markings than nominate populations of Jamaica but differences, if present, are insufficient for subspecific recognition.

Molt—CBS (CAS?). PF partial-incomplete (Jul-Sep in HYs), DPB complete (Jul-Sep in AHYs); PA absent(?). The above timing refers to N.Am populations. All molts occur on breeding grounds. The PF includes most to all body feathers, some proximal s covs, and most to all rects. During DPBs, pp, ss, and rects are replaced synchronously in Aug. A reported PA (e.g., Flores & Eddleman 1993) requires confirmation (see Family Account, p. 474).

Age—Juv (B1; Jun-Sep) has dull-brown nape, grayish underparts, and brownish iris. Juv ♀ = ♂ by plumage aspect. The following month ranges pertain to N.Am populations; intermediates may occur that are difficult to age:

HY/SY (1st cycle, F1; Oct-Sep): Medial ss acutely pointed (cf. Fig. 359**A**, p. 475) outer pp, p covs, and alula tapered and brownish (Fig. 358**A**, p. 475) with smaller or no white spots (Fig. 361**A**); molt limits occur between back and wing or among s covs (Fig. 357**A-B**, p. 474), the replaced scapulars, humerals, and proximal s covs glossy and blackish, contrasting with duller and browner retained juv distal s covs; iris brownish-red to reddish.

AHY/ASY (Def. cycle, DB; Oct-Sep): Medial ss broader and more rounded (*cf.* Fig. 359**C**); outer pp, p covs, and alula blunt and dusky (Fig. 358**B**), usually with distinct white spots (Fig. 361**B**); scapulars, humerals, and wing covs uniform in wear (Fig. 357**D**), glossy and blackish; iris deep reddish.

FIGURE 361. Shape and pattern to outer primary (p10) by age in Black Rail. Caution that intermediates occur, with smaller and indistinct white spots, that should not be aged by this character alone.

Sex—♀ = ♂ by plumage aspect. Medial BP (Fig. 20**A**, p. 31) developed by both sexes but a distended cloaca (Fig. 21, p. 32) indicates AHY ♀ in Feb-May. Measurements generally unhelpful for sexing (Table 42, p. 480). The following appears reliable for sexing after completion of the PF (Aug-Sep); intermediates are likely AHY/ASY ♀♀ or HY/SY ♂♂ (confirmation needed):

♀: Throat whitish or pale gray; breast and abdomen often washed or streaked grayish.

♂: Throat sooty; breast and abdomen sooty to blackish.

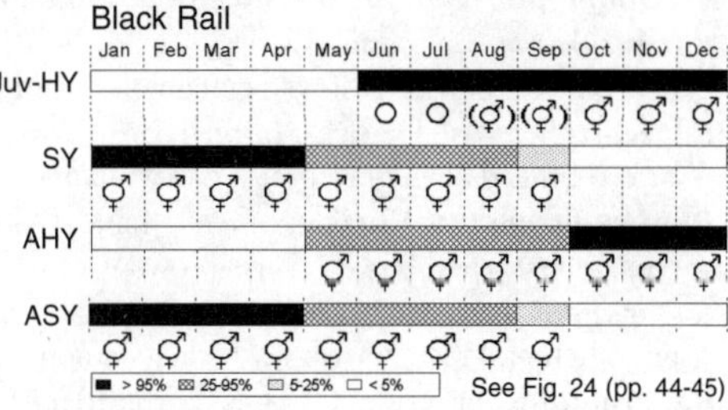

Hybrids Reported—None.

References—Bent (1926), Eddleman et al. (1994), Flores & Eddleman (1993), Oberholser (1974), Ridgway & Friedmann (1941), Russell (1966), Taylor (1998).

CLAPPER RAIL
Rallus longirostris

CLRA
Species # 2110
Band size: 5

KING RAIL
Rallus elegans

KIRA
Species # 2080
Band size: 5

Species—From other N.Am rails by larger size (Table 42, p. 480); upperparts brownish with grayish to ochre fringing; breast tinged cinnamon to bright rufous; bill of AHYs yellowish; eye brownish to orange; legs grayish to pinkish. Clapper Rail distinguished from King Rail with caution and consideration of geographic variation (see below). Clapper Rails of e.subspecies groups, generally sympatric with King Rail, average shorter wing and tarsus (Table 42); p10 usually < p4 (*vs* usually > p4 in King Rail); upperparts fringed grayish (*vs* tawny in King Rail); s covs dull brown to olive-brown (*vs* bright tawny in King Rail); breast of AHY pale brownish tinged cinnamon (*vs* bright cinnamon to rufous in King Rail); flanks grayish with indistinct whitish bars (*vs* dark brown with distinct white bars in King Rail). Clapper Rails of w.subspecies groups (perhaps King Rails; Olson 1997), resemble King Rails more closely in plumage aspect, although wing morphology (p10 *vs* p4) and aspect of back fringing and flanks (as above) can be used for identification. Juv King Rails can be identified by richer buff edging to terts and extensive blackish mottling to breast (*vs* grayish or washed sooty in Clapper Rail). Beware of hybrids, usually found in brackish areas where breeding ranges meet.

Geographic variation—See Banks & Tomlinson (1974), Bent (1926), Blake (1977), Dickerman (1971), Dickey (1923), Eddleman & Conway (1998), Hellmayr & Conover (1942), Oberholser (1937, 1974), Olson (1997), Ridgway & Friedmann (1941), Riley (1913), Ripley (1977), Stevenson & Anderson (1994), Taylor (1998), Todd (1916a), van Rossem (1929), Warner & Dickerman (1959). Thirteen other subspecies of Clapper Rail occur in Baja CA and the W.Indes-S.Am (including another subspecies group in S.Am) and two other subspecies of King Rail occur in Mexico and Cuba. See **Species** for further information.

Clapper Rail, Western North American (*R.l. obsoletus*) Subspecies Group. Medium-large; plumage aspect richer; auriculars brownish; upperparts fringed olive.

R.l. obsoletus (br & wint San Francisco Bay, CA): Larger (Table 42, p. 480); upperparts dark brown fringed grayish olive; breast bright, medium-pale cinnamon; flanks dull grayish with indistinct whitish bars.

R.l. levipes (br & wint coastal sw.CA, Ventura-San Diego Cos): Medium-large (Table 42); upperparts dark brown fringed dark olive; breast bright, medium-dark cinnamon; flanks brown with bright white bars.

R.l. yumanensis (br se.CA-sw.AZ): Medium-small (Table 42); upperparts blackish fringed olive-gray; breast bright, pale cinnamon; flanks dull grayish with whitish bars.

Clapper Rail, Eastern North American and Caribbean (*R.l. crepitans*) Subspecies Group. Small; plumage aspect subdued; auriculars grayish; upperparts grayish.

R.l. saturatus (br coastal TX-AL, wint to nw.FL): Medium-small (Table 42); upperparts dark brown fringed olive-gray; breast pale cinnamon tinged brown; flanks medium-dark brown with white bars.

R.l. scotti (br coastal nw.FL-Martin Co, ec.FL; wint to AL): Small (Table 42); feathers of upperparts dark brown fringed olive-gray; breast dark cinnamon washed sooty; flanks grayish brown with white bars.

R.l. insularum (res FL Keys): Small (Table 42); upperparts blackish fringed gray; breast medium-dark cinnamon washed brown; flanks brown with white bars.

R.l. waynei (br & wint coastal se.NC-ce.FL, Martin Co): Small (Table 42); upperparts brown fringed grayish; breast pale grayish washed cinnamon; flanks pale brownish gray with whitish bars.

R.l. crepitans (br coastal CT-ce.NC, wint to n.FL; vagrant to VT-NS): Medium-sized (Table 42); upperparts brown indistinctly fringed gray; breast whitish tinged gray and cinnamon; flanks brownish gray with whitish bars.

King Rail

R.e. elegans (br and wint N.Am): Upperparts dark brown with ochre to tawny fringes (*vs* brownish with grayish-cinnamon fringes in *tenuirostris* of c.Mex and *ramsdeni* of Cuba); breast and abdomen bright dark cinnamon (*vs* paler cinnamon and whitish ventrally in *tenuirostris* and *ramsdeni*); bars of flanks white (*vs* buff in *tenuirostris*).

Molt—CBS (CAS?). PF partial-incomplete (Jul-Oct in HYs), DPB complete (Jul-Sep in AHYs); PA absent(?). The above timing refers to N.Am populations. All molts occur on breeding grounds. The PF includes most to all body feathers, often a few proximal s covs, and occasionally 1-4 (at least) central rects. During DPBs, the pp, ss, and rects are replaced synchronously in Aug-Sep. There is little evidence for a PA; scattered body feathers may be replaced in Feb-Mar (Eddleman & Conway 1998) but confirmation required (see Family Account, p. 747).

Age—Juv (B1; Jun-Sep) is duller with black mottling to lateral underparts, buff bars to flanks, brownish bills, and brownish-olive iris. Juv ♀=♂ by plumage aspect. Intermediates between the following occur and are difficult to age.

HY/SY (1st cycle, F1; Oct-Sep): Molt limits occur between back and wing or among s covs (Fig. 357**A-B**, p. 474), the replaced scapulars, humerals, and sometimes some proximal s covs glossy and more richly colored, contrasting with the duller, browner, and more worn retained juv distal s covs; outer pp browner and more pointed (Fig. 358**A**, p. 475); rects narrower, more pointed, and relatively abraded, with 1-4 or more central rects sometimes contrastingly fresh (*cf.* Fig. 17**A-C**, p. 25); bill brownish yellow to dull yellow-orange; iris brownish to dull orange through Dec-Feb.

AHY/ASY (Def. cycle, DB; Oct-Sep): Scapulars, humerals, and wing covs uniform in wear (Fig. 357**D**), glossy and rich in aspect; outer pp duskier and blunter (Fig. 358**B**); rects uniformly broader, more rounded, and relatively fresh (*cf.* Fig. 17**E**); bill brightish yellow-orange; iris orange to reddish orange.

Sex—Medial BP (Fig. 20**A**, p. 31) developed by both sexes but a distended cloaca (Fig. 21, p. 32) indicates AHY ♀ in Feb-May. Wing chord and other measurements relatively helpful for sexing, especially in Western Subspecies Group (Table 42, p. 480). ♀♀ average paler throats and duller breasts by subspecies and age but overlap precludes reliable sexing.

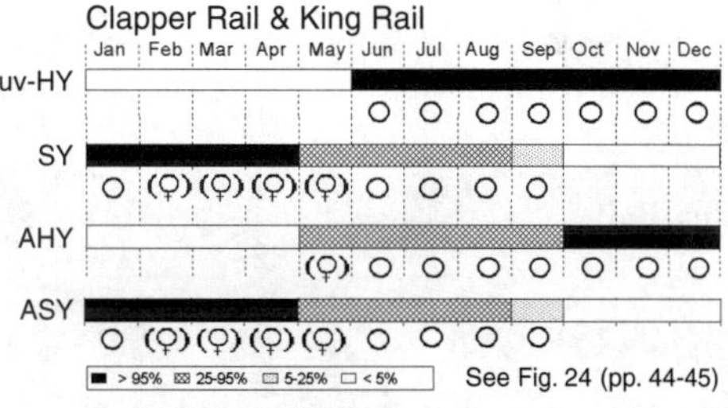

Hybrids Reported—Clapper Rail with King Rail (Bledsoe 1988, Meanley 1988, Meanley & Wetherbee 1962, Olson 1997).

References—Adams & Quay (1958), Bent (1926), Dickerman (1971), Eddleman & Conway (1998), Meanley (1969, 1985, 1992), Meanley & Meanley (1958), Oberholser (1937, 1974), Olson (1997), Ridgway & Friedmann (1941), Roberts (1955), Taylor (1998).

TABLE 42. Measurements (mm) of North American rails for identification and sexing. See p. 4-11 for methods of measurement. Species summaries are in **bold** and subspecies summaries are in ***italics***. Values were derived from 95% confidence intervals as based approximately on the indicated sample sizes (see pp. 4-5); sample sizes for bill depth were often smaller but included at least 10 of each sex. Thus, midpoints of ranges approximate means, and S.D. is approximated by 25% of the range.

Taxon/Sex	*n*	wing chord	tail length	exposed culmen	bill depth[1]	tarsus
Yellow Rail[2]		**78-92**	**28-37**	**11.9-15.6**	**5.7-7.5**	**20-27**
♀	40	78-89	28-36	11.9-14.5	5.7-7.1	20-25
♂	40	80-92	29-37	12.7-15.6	6.0-7.5	22-27
Black Rail[2]		**62-80**	**28-38**	**11.8-15.9**	**5.1-6.2**	**19-26**
L.j. coturnculus		***63-73***	***28-36***	***11.8-15.7***	***5.1-6.0***	***19-24***
♀	100	63-72	28-36	11.8-14.6	5.1-5.9	19-23
♂	100	64-73	28-36	12.6-15.7	5.2-6.0	19-24
L.j. jamaicensis		***69-80***	***29-38***	***12.0-15.9***	***5.3-6.2***	***21-26***
♀	50	69-79	29-37	12.0-15.0	5.3-6.1	21-25
♂	65	69-80	30-38	12.8-15.9	5.4-6.2	22-26
Clapper Rail[2]		**127-169**	**53-79**	**48-68**	**10.1-16.0**	**41-60**
R.l. obsoletus		***143-169***	***60-79***	***50-67***	***10.7-15.5***	***46-60***
♀	64	143-159	60-74	50-61	10.7-12.9	46-56
♂	74	153-169	66-79	55-67	12.0-15.5	52-60
R.l. levipes		***137-166***	***56-73***	***48-65***	***10.7-16.0***	***47-60***
♀	44	137-154	56-68	48-59	10.7-13.3	47-55
♂	47	153-166	62-73	53-65	12.4-16.0	52-60
R.l. yumanensis		***133-162***	***55-73***	***53-67***	***10.9-13.8***	***42-56***
♀	57	133-147	55-67	49-61	10.9-12.1	42-52
♂	83	143-162	59-73	53-67	11.6-13.8	47-56
R.l. saturatus		***134-160***	***55-69***	***56-67***	***10.1-14.3***	***43-55***
♀	43	134-149	55-66	56-64	10.1-12.6	43-52
♂	52	143-160	58-69	58-67	11.5-14.3	47-55
NC-FL Subspecies[3]		***127-154***	***53-71***	***52-65***	***10.6-13.7***	***41-55***
♀	100	127-145	53-64	52-62	10.6-12.0	41-50
♂	100	135-154	56-71	55-65	11.7-13.7	44-55
R.l. crepitans		***137-160***	***55-70***	***56-68***	***11.0-14.4***	***43-55***
♀	78	137-152	55-67	54-64	11.0-12.6	43-53
♂	93	143-160	57-70	57-68	12.3-14.4	47-55
King Rail[2]		**149-173**	**57-73**	**55-67**	**11.2-14.9**	**50-64**
♀	32	149-166	57-70	55-64	11.2-13.4	50-59
♂	38	158-175	59-73	57-67	12.5-14.9	55-64
Virginia Rail[2]		**93-113**	**35-52**	**32-46**	**8.2-10.4**	**29-38**
♀	66	93-107	35-48	32-42	8.2-9.5	29-36
♂	75	99-113	38-52	35-46	9.0-10.4	31-38
Sora		**96-115**	**38-54**	**16-23**	**7.2-9.9**	**27-36**
♀	40	96-109	38-49	16-22	7.2-9.3	27-34
♂	79	101-115	42-54	17-23	7.9-9.9	29-36

[1] Bill depth measured at tip of forehead feathering (Fig. 8**A**, p. 10).

[2] Measures from N.Am populations only; see **Geographic variation**.

[3] Includes similar-sized *R.l. scottii, insularum,* and *waynei*.

VIRGINIA RAIL VIRA
Rallus limicola Species # 2120
Band size: 3 Above joint

Species—From other N.Am rails by medium size with proportionally long bill (Table 42, p. 480); upperparts sooty with dull-rufous fringing; wing covs chestnut to rufous (sometimes barred dusky and white); auriculars gray; breast mottled blackish (Juv) to cinnamon-rufous; bill, eye, and legs of AHYs red. Water Rail (*R. aquaticus*), a possible vagrant to n.Am, is larger with proportionally shorter bill (wg chord 111-131, tl 44-58, exp culmen 34-45, tarsus 36-46); upperparts and wing covs without rufous; breast and abdomen grayish.

Geographic variation—See Blake (1977), Dickerman (1966), Dickey (1928), Fjeldså (1990), Hellmayr & Conover (1942), Ridgway & Friedmann (1941), Ripley (1977), Taylor (1998). Three other subspecies occur in Mex and S.Am.

R.l. limicola (br & wint N.Am): Upperparts fringed dark rufous (*vs* paler olive-rufous in *friedmanni* of Mex); les and med covs bright rufous (*vs* paler and duller in *friedmanni*); underparts rich cinnamon-rufous (*vs* paler and redder in *friedmanni*). Subspecies of S.Am are smaller and duller. Populations of the Pacific coast ("*pacificus*" or "*zetarius*") average slightly larger than other N.Am populations but differences are broadly clinal and insufficient for subspecific designation.

Molt—CBS (CAS?). PF partial-incomplete (Jun-Oct in HYs), DPB complete (Jul-Sep in AHYs); PA absent(?). The above timing refers to N.Am populations. All molts occur on breeding grounds. The PF includes most to all body feathers, some proximal s covs, sometimes 1-2 terts, and no to all rects. During DPBs, pp, ss, and rects are replaced synchronously in Aug. There is little evidence for a PA, despite reports (see Family Account, p. 474).

Age—Juvs (B1; Jun-Sep) duller with heavy blackish mottling to the breast and flanks, brownish bills, and greenish irises; Juv ♀=♂ by plumage aspect. Intermediates between the following occur that may be difficult to age.

HY/SY (1st cycle, F1; Oct-Sep): Molt limits occur between back and wing or among s covs and terts (Fig. 357**A-C**, p. 474), the replaced proximal s covs glossy and uniformly rufous, contrasting with the duller and pale-tipped, retained juv distal s covs; outer pp browner and more pointed (Fig. 358**A**, p. 475); abdomen feathers narrowly edged whitish when fresh; bill brownish to dull reddish in Oct-Mar; iris brownish red to dull red through Dec-Apr.

AHY/ASY (Def. cycle, DB; Oct-Sep): Wing covs and terts uniform in wear (Fig. 357**D**), the s covs rufous (without pale tips), sometimes with dusky and white barring; outer pp duskier and blunter (Fig. 358**B**); abdomen feathers without whitish edging; bill brightish red to orangish red; iris bright red.

Sex—Medial BP (Fig. 20**A**, p. 31) developed by both sexes but a distended cloaca (Fig. 21, p. 32) indicates AHY ♀ in Feb-May. Measurements unhelpful for sexing (Table 42). ♀♀ average slightly duller s covs and duller red bills than ♂♂, but differences confounded by age-specific and seasonal variation. Otherwise, no criteria known for sexing.

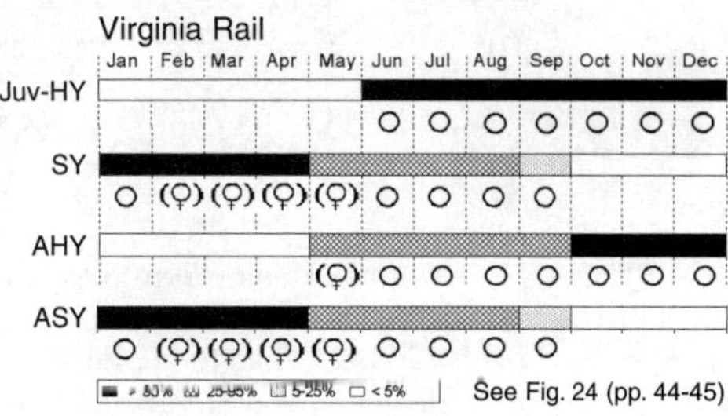

Hybrids Reported—None.

References—Bent (1926), Conway (1995), Oberholser (1974), Pospichal & Marshall (1954), Ridgway & Friedmann (1941), Roberts (1955), Taylor (1998).

SORA
Porzana carolina

SORA
Species # 2140
Band size: 2 Above joint

Species—From other N.Am rails by medium size with proportionally short bill (Table 42, p. 480); upperparts brown and blackish with narrow white streaks; AHYs with lores and throat mottled blackish to black (Figs. 362-363); proximal ss without white; axillars and proximal underwing covs gray; bill brownish (Juv-HY) to yellow (AHY); eye brown; legs greenish yellow. Black in lores and throat of older HYs and AHYs unique among *Porzana* crakes; Juv-HYs (lacking black in face) from Baillon's Crake (*P. pusilla*), a possible vagrant to w.AK, and Spotted Crake (*P. porzana*), a possible vagrant to ne.N.Am, by medium size (*vs* wg chord 84-96, exp culmen 14.8-18.4, tarsus 25-31 in smaller Baillon's Crake and wg chord 112-128, exposed culmen 16.5-22.1, tarsus 30-37 in larger Spotted Crake); marginal les covs mostly brown (*vs* white or mottled whitish in Spotted Crake); upper breast buff washed brown and without spots (*vs* white in Baillon's Crake and with distinct white spots in Spotted Crake); bill brownish yellow (*vs* dull olive in Baillon's Crake and greenish with dull-orange base in Spotted Crake).

Geographic variation—Monotypic.

Molt—CBS. PF partial-incomplete (Jul-Feb in HY/SYs), DPB complete (Jul-Sep in AHYs); PA absent. The PF can occur on either the breeding or non-breeding grounds, or it can be suspended for migration; the DPB occurs on breeding grounds. The PF includes most to all body feathers, often some proximal s covs, sometimes 1-3 terts, and no to all rects. During DPBs, the pp, ss, and rects are replaced synchronously in Aug. There is little evidence for a PA, despite reports.

Age/Sex—Juvs (B1; Jun-Dec) lack black in the lores and throat (Fig. 362**A**) and have buff face and breast and brownish eyes and bill; Juv ♀=♂ by plumage aspect. Medial BP (Fig. 20**A**, p. 31) developed by both sexes but a distended cloaca (Fig. 21, p. 32) indicates AHY ♀ in Feb-May. Measurements somewhat helpful for sexing (Table 42, p. 480). Intermediates may occur

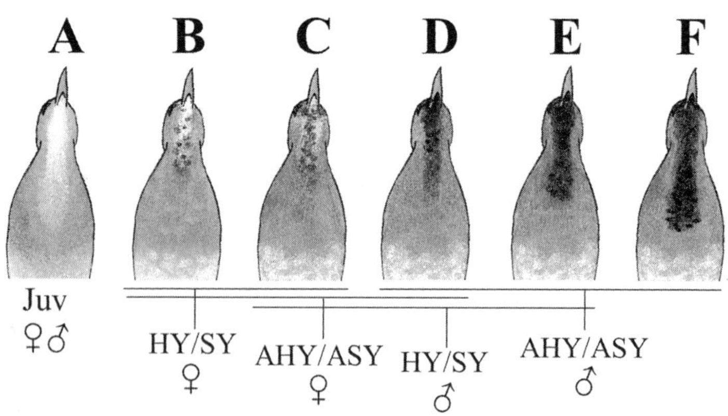

FIGURE 362. Extent of black coloration to the face and throat by age and sex in Sora. Juvs (**A**) can lack black through fall migration but gain variable amounts of black during the preformative molt, averaging less in HY/SY ♀♀ (**B-C**) than in HY/SY ♂♂ (**C-E**). AHY/ASYs have the black coloration veiled with buff to grayish fringing in Sep-Dec, resembling **B-C** in AHY ♀♀ and **D-E** in AHY ♂♂. By spring the veiling wears off such that ASY ♀♀ resemble **D** and ASY ♂♂ resemble **F**. Although a DPA has been reported there is little evidence that seasonal color change in head and throat plumage aspect is due to molt rather than the wearing of feather fringing. See also Figure 363.

between the following that are difficult to age and/or sex; combine with measurements to confirm.

Juv-HY/SY ♀ (1st cycle, Juv-F1; Oct-Sep): Face and throat buff or mixed gray and buff in Oct-Feb (Figs. 362**A** & 363**A**), becoming slightly mottled with blackish and whitish by Jan-Sep (Figs. 362**B-C** & 363**B**); pale supercilium often connected across forehead and bill brownish to dull greenish without pale band at base (Fig. 363**A-B**); medial ss acutely pointed (*cf.* Fig. 359**A**, p. 475); molt limits occur between back and wing or among s covs and terts (Fig. 357**A-C**, p. 474), the replaced scapulars, humerals, and proximal s covs glossy and black, fringed brown, contrasting with the duller, dusky and olive-fringed retained juv distal s covs; outer pp browner, narrower, and more pointed (Fig. 358**A**, p. 475); iris brown to brownish red. **Note: See AHY/ASY ♀.**

AHY/ASY ♀ (Def. cycle, DB; Oct-Sep): Face and throat gray, with some blackish and whitish mottling in Oct-Feb (Figs. 362**B-C** & 363**A-B**), becoming moderately washed blackish in Jan-Sep (Figs. 362**C-D** & 363**B-C**); pale supercilium sometimes connected across forehead and bill medium-dull greenish yellow with little to no pale band at base (Fig. 363**B-C**); medial ss broader and more rounded (*cf.* Fig. 359**C**); scapulars, humerals, and wing covs uniform in wear (Fig. 357**D**), glossy and black fringed brown; outer pp duskier and blunter (Fig. 358**B**); iris reddish to dark red. **Note: Gray tips to lore and throat feathers wear off, resulting in blacker appearance to these areas by May-Sep (Fig. 362).**

Juv-HY/SY ♂ (1st cycle, Juv-F1; Oct-Sep): Face and throat buff or mixed gray and buff in Oct-Feb (Figs. 362**A** & 363**B**), becoming mottled with moderate to substantial blackish and sometimes whitish by Jan-Sep (Figs. 362**C-E** & 363**C-D**); pale supercilium often but not always broken across forehead and bill brownish to yellowish, often with pale band at base (Fig. 363**B-D**); molt limits in back and wing (Fig. 357**A-B**, p. 474) and outer pp (Fig. 358**A**) as in HY/SY ♀; iris brownish to brownish red. **Note: See AHY/ASY ♀.**

AHY/ASY ♂ (Def. cycle, DB; Oct-Sep): Face and throat gray with substantial blackish mottled gray in Oct-Feb (Figs. 362**D-E** & 363**C**), becoming extensively blackish in Jan-Sep (Figs. 362**F** & 363**D**); pale supercilium broken across forehead and bill bright yellow with pale band at base (Fig. 363**C-D**); scapulars, humerals, and wing covs (Fig. 357**D**), and outer pp (Fig. 358**B**) as in AHY/ASY ♀; iris reddish to dark red. **Note: See AHY/ASY ♀.**

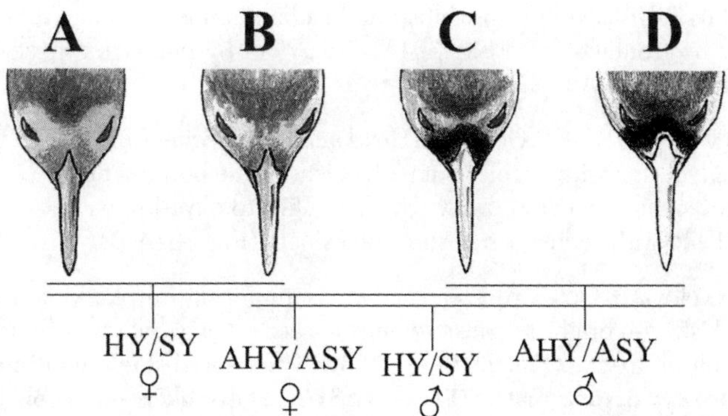

FIGURE 363. Patterns of brown, black, and white on the forehead and brightness of bill by age and sex in Sora. The extent of black increases through winter and spring in HY/SYs and is veiled with buff to grayish fringing in AHY/ASYs in Sep-Dec (see Fig. 362). Note that the bill becomes brighter yellow with age and sex (and probably brighter in Mar-May than at other times of year) and the white band to the forehead immediately above the bill is more distinct in AHY/ASY ♂♂.

Hybrids Reported—None.

References—Bent (1926), Cramp & Simmons (1980), Melvin & Gibbs (1996), Oberholser (1974), Pospichal & Marshall (1954), Ridgway & Friedmann (1941), P.J. Roberts (1984), T.S. Roberts (1955), Taylor (1998), Uyehara (2004), Vinicombe (1985).

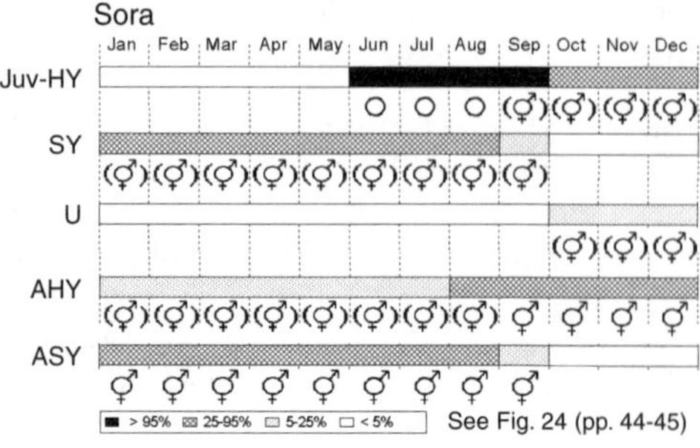

PURPLE GALLINULE
Porphyrula martinica

PUGA
Species # 2180
Band size: 4-5

Species—From other N.Am rails, gallinules, and coots by large size and stout bill (Table 43, p. 487); upperparts primarily olive to greenish; underparts buff (Juv) to purple (AHY/ASY); undertail covs white; bill brownish horn (Juv) to red tipped yellow (AHY), with ovate, grayish to pale-blue frontal shield (Fig. 364); legs bright yellow. Allen's Gallinule (*P. alleni*) of Africa, a potential vagrant to N.Am, is smaller and with a shorter bill (wg chord 140-163, tl 60-70, exp culmen 22-26, tarsus 46-56); middle toe without claw > tarsus; Juv-HY with dark centers to upperpart feathers forming scaled appearance; undertail covs with blackish at base; legs and feet reddish.

Geographic variation—Monotypic.

Molt—CBS. PF partial (Oct-Apr in HY/SYs), DPB complete (May-Aug in AHYs); PA absent. The above timing pertains to N.Am populations. The PF occurs primarily on non-breeding grounds whereas the DPB occurs on breeding grounds. The PF includes most to all body feathers but no wing covs, terts, or rects. During DPBs, the pp, ss, and rects are replaced nearly synchronously in Jun-Aug. The PB2 averages slightly earlier than subsequent PBs. There is little evidence for a PA, despite reports.

Age—Juvs (B1; May-Feb) have buff to whitish on head and underparts and dull-brownish bills with reduced or no frontal shield (Fig. 364**A**). Juv ♀=♂ by plumage aspect. The following month ranges pertain to N.Am populations.

Juv-HY/SY (1st cycle, Juv/B1-F1; Oct-Sep): Head and breast primarily buff and whitish in Oct-Nov, increasingly mixed with purple (but with at least some buff mottling to head and throat) in May-Sep; terts and wing covs dusky with dull olive to olive-brown edging; bill brownish red to dull red and with reduced grayish frontal shield (Fig. 364**A**-**B**).

AHY/ASY (Def. cycle, DB; Oct-Sep): Head and breast uniformly purple, without buff; terts and wing covs blackish with bright-greenish to bluish-green edging; bill red with bright-yellow tip and extensive bluish frontal (Fig. 364**C**-**D**). **Note: The frontal shield continues to develop through the 3rd cycle, such that SY/TYs and ASY/ATYs are likely separable (see Fig. 364), sex for sex, but this also varies by season, being duller and perhaps smaller in each age/sex group in Jul-Dec than in Jan-Jun; more study is needed.**

Sex—♀=♂ by plumage aspect. Medial BP (Fig. 20**A**, p. 31) developed by both sexes but a distended cloaca (Fig. 21, p. 32) indicates AHY ♀ in Jan-May. Measurements unhelpful for sexing (Table 43, p. 487). The frontal shield averages larger in ♂♂ than in ♀♀ by age (see Fig. 364

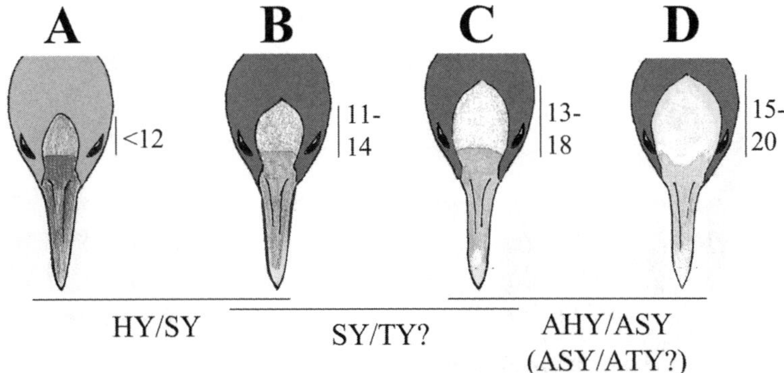

FIGURE 364. Size and coloration of bill and ornamental shield by age in Purple Gallinule. The measure indicates the distance (in mm) between the top of the shield and the color change between the shield (dusky to bright pale bluish) and the bill base (dull brownish to bright red). The bill tip varies from dull yellowish in Juvs to bright yellow in AHY/ASYs. Note that both shield size and shield and bill coloration among AHY/ASYs appears to vary by sex and season, as well as age. Tentatively, the above measure may be 11-14 mm in SY/TY ♀♀ (**B**), 13-18 mm in ASY/ATY ♀♀ and SY/TY ♂♂ (**C**), and 15-20 mm in ASY/ATY ♂♂ (**D**), but more study is needed to define these limits by season.

and **Age**) and it is likely possible to sex some individuals by season; more study is needed.

Hybrids Reported—None.

References—Bent (1926), Cramp & Simmons (1980), Helm (1994), Oberholser (1974), Ridgway & Friedmann (1941), Taylor (1998), West & Hess (2002).

Purple Gallinule

Jan Feb Mar Apr May Jun Jul Aug Sep Oct Nov Dec

Juv-HY

SY

AHY

ASY

■ > 95% ▩ 25-95% ▢ 5-25% □ < 5%

See Fig. 24 (pp. 44-45)

COMMON MOORHEN

Gallinula chloropus

COMO
Species # 2190
Band size: 5-6

Species—From other N.Am rails, gallinules, and coots by medium-large size (Table 43, p. 487); head and underparts grayish (Juv-HY) to blackish (AHY); back and wing covs brown; ss without white tips; flank feathers streaked buff (Juv) to white; undertail covs white laterally; bill brownish yellow (Juv) to bright red with yellow tip (AHY/ASY), and with truncated red shield (Fig. 365, p. 486); legs bright greenish yellow; toes not lobed.

Geographic variation—See Bangs (1915b), Blake (1977), Cramp & Simmons (1980), Dement'ev & Gladkov (1951c), Dickey & van Rossem (1924b, 1938), Hellmayr & Conover (1942), Ridgway & Friedmann (1941), Ripley (1977), Taylor (1998). Eleven other subspecies worldwide, including oceanic islands.

G.c. cachinnans (br & wint N.Am): Larger than most subspecies but smaller than S.Am subspecies (Table 43, p. 487); head and breast slate-gray (*vs* blacker in S.Am subspecies); wing covs browner than

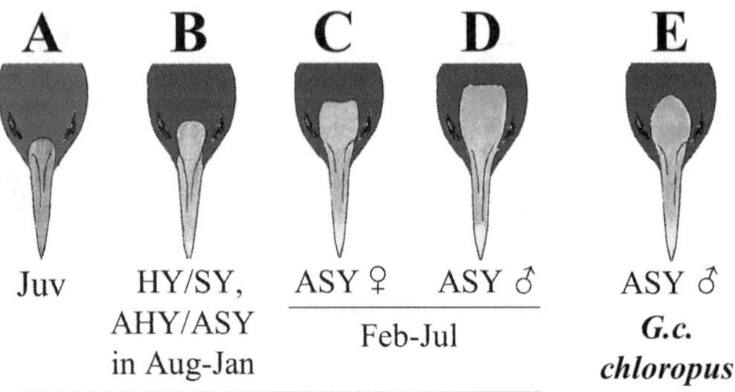

FIGURE 365. Size and coloration of bill and ornamental shield by age and subspecies in Common Moorhen. In the N.Am subspecies, bill and shield color vary from dull brownish red in Juvs (**A**) to bright red with a yellow tip to the bill in ASYs (**C-D**). The top of the bill shield is 6-11 mm in width in ASY ♀♀ (**C**) and 9-14 mm in width in ASY ♂♂ (**D**). It is possible some AHYs may be sexed by bill characters in Jul-Dec, but this may also vary by age (SY *vs.* ASY); more study is needed.

other subspecies; frontal shield truncate in ASYs, widest anteriorly (Fig. 365**C-D**). Populations of Europe (*chloropus*), possible vagrants to e.N.Am, have frontal shield smaller and elliptical in ASYs, being widest medially (Fig. 365**E**). Populations of the W.Indes (*cerceris* & *barbadensis*), possible vagrants to se.N.Am, have head, breast, and/or les covs brighter and grayer.

Molt—CBS. PF incomplete (Sep-Apr in HY/SYs), DPB complete (Jul-Oct in AHYs); PA absent. The above timing pertains to N.Am populations. The PF occurs primarily on non-breeding grounds whereas the DPB occurs on breeding grounds. The PF includes most to all body feathers, some proximal wing covs, sometimes 1-2 terts, and most or all rects. During DPBs, pp, ss, and rects are replaced nearly synchronously in Aug. There is little evidence for a PA, despite reports.

Age—Juvs (B1; Jun-Mar) are dull grayish with whitish throat and have dull brownish bills with reduced or no frontal shield (Fig. 365**A**) and grayish iris. Juv ♀ = ♂ by plumage aspect.

Juv-HY/SY (1st cycle, Juv/B1-F1; Oct-Sep): Head and breast grayish in Oct-Nov, increasingly mixed with sooty in May-Sep (but throat often with pale mottling); bill brownish yellow to dull red and with reduced frontal shield (Fig. 365**A-B**); molt limits occur between back and wing or among s covs and terts (Fig. 357**A-C**, p. 474), the replaced scapulars, humerals, proximal s covs, and (sometimes) terts glossy and dark brown, contrasting with paler brown and fringed whitish or buff (Oct-Feb) or very abraded (Mar-Sep) distal s covs; outer pp brown, narrow, and relatively pointed (Fig. 358**A**, p. 475); iris brownish to brownish red through Dec-Mar.

AHY/ASY (Def. cycle, DB; Oct-Sep): Head and breast uniformly sooty to blackish (chin and throat feathers sometimes narrowly fringed whitish when fresh); bill bright red with larger frontal shield by season and sex (Fig. 365**B-D**); scapulars, humerals, s covs, and terts uniform in wear (Fig. 357**D**), glossy and dark brown; outer pp dusky, broad, and relatively blunt (Fig. 358**B**); iris red.

Sex—♀ = ♂ by plumage aspect. Medial BP (Fig. 20**A**, p. 31) developed by both sexes but a distended cloaca (Fig. 21, p. 32) indicates AHY ♀ in Feb-May; other cloacal characters may not be reliable for sexing (Anderson 1975). Measurements generally unhelpful for sexing (Table 43, p. 487); but see Anderson (1975) for DFAs (p. 5), using tarsus and middle toe length, wing chord, exposed culmen (including shield), and weight, that reliably sexed 84-88% of individuals within a British population. See Lee & Griffiths (2003) for molecular sexing techniques. The following can be used to sex most ASYs in Jan-Jun, especially when combined with measurements; plumage aspect differences (as described below) occur but are probably unreliable for sexing AHYs in Oct-Dec, due to feather veiling, without combining with bill shield differences.

ASY ♀ (Jan-Jun): Frontal shield smaller (Fig. 365**C**); plumage aspect averages duller and sootier, sometimes with pale mottling to underparts.

ASY ♂ (Jan-Jun): Frontal shield larger (Fig. 365**D**); plumage aspect averages glossier and blacker, without pale mottling to underparts.

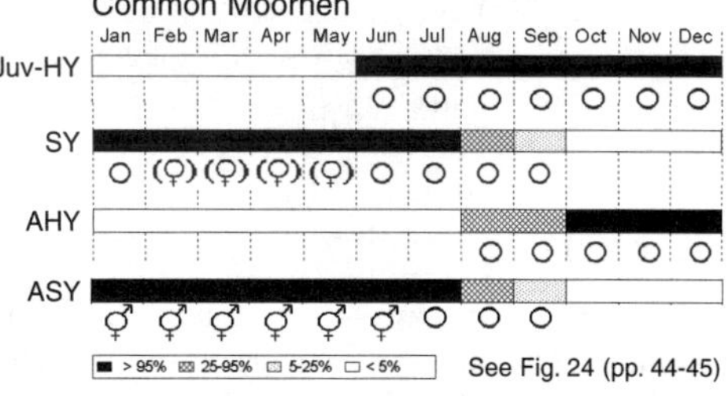

Hybrids Reported—With European Coot *Fulica atra* (Moore & Piotrowski 1983, Flower 1983) and American Coot (McIlhenny 1937) in the wild.

References—Anderson (1975), Baker (1993), Bannor & Kiviat (2002), Bent (1926), Cramp & Simmons (1980), Dement'ev & Gladkov (1951c), Fenoglio et al. (2002), Grant (1914), Loncarich & Krementz (2004), Oberholser (1974), Ridgway & Friedmann (1941), Roberts (1955), Stresemann & Stresemann (1966), Taylor (1998), Trautman & Glines (1964).

TABLE 43. Measurements (mm) of North American gallinules and coots for identification and sexing. See pp. 4-11 for methods of measurement. Species summaries are in **bold**. Values were derived from 95% confidence intervals as based approximately on the indicated sample sizes (see pp. 4-5); sample sizes for bill depth were often smaller but included at least 10 of each sex. Thus, midpoints of ranges approximate means, and S.D. is approximated by 25% of the range.

Taxon/Sex	*n*	wing chord	tail length	exposed culmen[1]	bill depth[2]	tarsus
Purple Gallinule		**160-185**	**60-78**	**41-52**	**13.6-16.1**	**51-66**
♀	100	160-181	60-77	41-50	13.6-15.3	51-64
♂	100	163-185	61-78	44-52	14.3-16.1	53-66
Common Moorhen[3]		**157-182**	**60-78**	**36-47**	**9.5-11.3**	**45-56**
♀	30	157-171	60-71	36-44	9.5-10.7	45-51
♂	30	167-182	66-78	39-47	10.0-11.3	49-56
American Coot[3,4]		**162-204**	**45-59**	**37-55**	**12.8-15.8**	**52-64**
♀	100	162-192	45-56	37-51	12.8-15.1	48-59
♂	100	176-204	47-59	40-55	13.4-15.8	52-64

[1] Includes frontal shield and measures are for AHY/ASYs only. HY/SYs average shorter shield/bill lengths by taxa (Figs. 364-366).

[2] Measured at base end of lower mandible.

[3] Measures from N.Am populations only, see **Geographic variation**.

[4] Shield/callus plus culmen averages shorter in w.population (♀ 37-47, ♂ 40-50) than in e.populations (♀ 40-51, ♂ 44-55) of American Coots; see **Geographic variation**.

AMERICAN COOT
Fulica americana

AMCO
Species # 2210
Band size: 6

Species—From other N.Am rails and gallinules by large size but proportionally short tail (Table 43, p. 487); plumage aspect grayish (Juvs) to blackish; ss tipped white; flank feathers without white; undertail covs white (bisected by black vent feathers); bill grayish (Juv) to white (occasionally tinged yellow) with dusky to blackish subterminal ring in AHYs and reddish or pale yellow callus anteriorly (Fig. 366); legs dull greenish to greenish yellow; toes lobed.

European Coot (*F. atra*), a vagrant to w.AK and ne.Canada, is larger, especially in wing length (wg chord 190-222, tl 49-61, bill with shield/callus in AHY/ASY 41-62, tarsus 54-65); undertail covs black; bill without dusky ring; frontal shield white, without reddish or yellowish tip; eye of AHY/ASY duller and orangish. Caribbean Coot (*F. caribaea*), a possible vagrant to FL, is shorter-winged but with a bigger bill (wg chord 165-191, tl 40-56, culmen and shield/callus 43-60, tarsus 50-64), has bill, shield, and callus yellowish and wrinkled, the bill usually without a dark band; legs and feet duller olive. Beware of variant American Coots that can show bill features resembling Caribbean Coot (Bolte 1974, Clark 1985, Payne & Master 1983, Roberson & Baptista 1988).

Geographic variation—See Blake (1977), Chapman (1914), Fjeldså (1983), Gill (1964), Hellmayr & Conover (1942), Ridgway & Friedmann (1941), Riley (1916), Ripley (1977), Taylor (1998). One other subspecies occurs in S.Am.

F.a. americana (br & wint N.Am): From *columbiana* of S.Am by larger average size but smaller bill and frontal shield (wg chord 174-208, exposed culmen with shield 29-40, tarsus 58-67); plumage aspect paler; white tips of ss broader (*vs* narrower and restricted to inner web in *columbiana*). Within N.Am, e.populations may average larger bills and frontal shields than w.populations (Fredrickson 1968, Alisauskas 1987, Brisbin et al. 2002), and s.populations may average longer tarsus and blacker plumage aspect than n.populations (Patten et al. 2003) but these differences probably too slight and/or broadly clinal for subspecific recognition; more study needed.

Molt—CBS. PF partial (Sep-Jan in HY/SYs), DPB complete (Jun-Dec in AHYs); PA absent. The above timing pertains to N.Am populations. The PF commences on breeding grounds and completes on non-breeding grounds whereas DPBs occur primarily on breeding grounds, molt of body feathers sometimes completing on non-breeding grounds. The PF includes most to all body feathers and a few to some proximal wing covs but few if any terts or rects. During DPBs, pp, ss, and rects are replaced nearly synchronously in Jul-Sep. The PB may average earlier in SYs than in ASYs. There is little evidence for a PA; winter replacement probably pertaining to the protracted PF and DPB (McKnight & Hepp 1999).

Age—Juv (B1; Jun-Mar) is dull grayish with white throat and has dull brownish bill with reduced or no frontal shield (Fig. 366**A**) and grayish iris and legs. Juv ♀ = ♂ by plumage aspect. Length of the bursa (Fig. 23, p. 34) may not be reliable for ageing (Eddleman & Knopf 1985, Fredrickson 1968, Gullion 1952); width of bursal wall (> 3 mm in HY/SYs) may be reliable but cannot be determined in live individuals. The following month ranges pertain to N.Am populations. In addition to the following, see Alisauskas (1987) for differences in average measurements between age groups, within each sex.

Juv-HY/SY (1st cycle, Juv/B1-F1; Oct-Sep): Head and breast grayish to whitish in Oct-Nov, increasingly mixed with sooty in Dec-Feb, often completely sooty in Mar-Sep (but throat usually with pale mottling); bill grayish to whitish with reduced frontal shield and callus and indistinct dusky subterminal band (Fig. 366**A**-**B**); molt limits occur between back and wing or among s covs (Fig. 357**A**-**B**, p. 474), the replaced scapulars, humerals, and a few to some proximal s covs glossy and gray, contrasting with browner and fringed whitish or

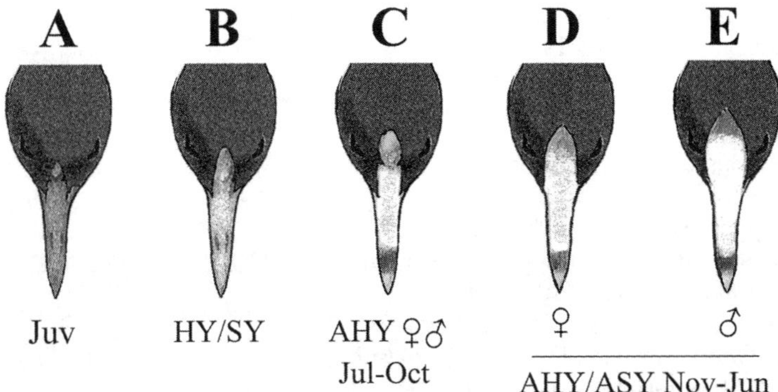

FIGURE 366. Size and coloration of bill and ornamental shield by age and sex in American Coot. Note that some AHY ♀♀ may resemble **B** in Jul-Nov and that some SY ♂♂ may resemble **D** in Mar-Jun. Unlike in Purple Gallinule (Fig. 364, p. 485) and Common Moorhen (Fig. 365, p. 486), the "shield" is not part of the mandibular structure but callus that fluctuates more substantially in size by season (Ridgway & Friedmann 1941, Gullion 1952). Thus, once it is fully developed in adults, the shield reduces in Jul-Nov (**C**) and expands in Nov-Jun (**D-E**). In Feb-Jul, ♀♀ tend to have shields that are 6-11 mm in maximum width (**D**; but beware of SY ♂♂; see above) and ♂♂ have shields that are 9-14 mm in maximum width (**E**). Bill color varies from brownish in Juvs (**A**) to brownish white in HY/SYs (**B**) to whitish in AHYs (**C-D**), and the dusky ring becomes more distinct with age.

buff (Oct-Feb) and/or worn (Mar-Sep) retained distal s covs; white tips to ss indistinctly defined; outer pp brown, narrow, and pointed (Fig. 358**A**, p. 475); iris brownish to brownish red through Nov-Jan; legs dull grayish green to greenish. **Note: In all age groups leg color becomes duller in Jun-Nov and it also varies with breeding hormone levels and other endochronological factors; experience may be needed for reliable use in ageing.**

AHY/ASY (Def. cycle, DB; Oct-Sep): Head and breast uniformly blackish; bill whitish to white with distinct blackish subterminal band, and reduced frontal shield in Jul-Nov (Fig. 366**C**) or extensive frontal shield and callus and in Dec-Jul (Fig. 366**D-E**); scapulars, humerals, and s covs uniform in wear (Fig. 357**D**), glossy dark gray; white tips to ss distinctly defined; outer pp dusky, broad, and blunt (Fig. 358**B**); iris reddish to red; legs brighter greenish yellow or yellow (becoming duller in Jun-Nov). **Note: See HY/SY. It is possible that some individuals with definitive plumage aspect but dull greenish legs can be aged SY/TY but more study is needed.**

ASY/ATY (Def. cycle, DB; Oct-Sep) like AHY/ASY but legs strongly washed orange or reddish (becoming duller in Jun-Nov). **Note: See HY/SY and AHY/ASY.**

Sex—♀=♂ by plumage aspect. Medial BP (Fig. 20**A**, p. 31) developed by both sexes but a distended cloaca > 4.6 mm (p. 32; see Boersma & Davies 1987) indicates AHY ♀ in Feb-May. Measurements generally unhelpful for sexing (Table 43, p. 487), although see Eddleman & Knopf (1985) for DFAs (p. 5) using up to 13 variables that reliably sexed 90-93% of individuals throughout e.N.Am. range. See also Gullion (1950) for sex-specific differences in voice. The following can be used to sex many AHY/ASYs in Dec-Jul, especially when combined with measurements; no criteria known for sexing individuals in Aug-Nov.

AHY/ASY ♀ (Dec-Jul): Frontal shield smaller, with maximum width 6-11 mm (Fig. 366**D**).

AHY/ASY ♂ (Dec-Jul): Frontal shield larger, with maximum width 9-14 mm (Fig. 366**E**).

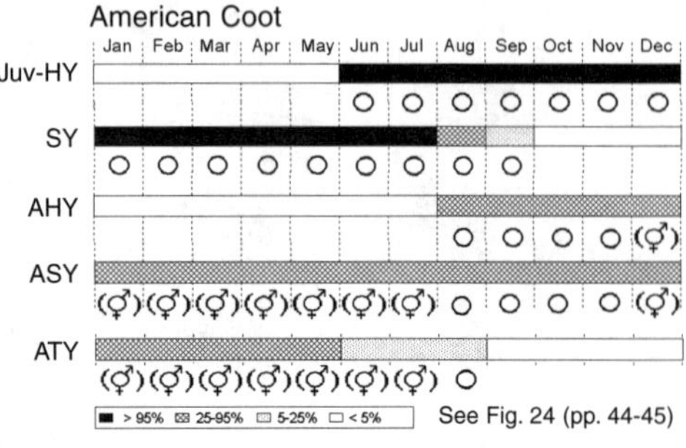

Hybrids Reported—With Common Moorhen (p. 485), Caribbean Coot (Bond 1950b, Payne & Master 1983), and Andean Coot (*F. ardesiaca*; Gill 1964) in the wild.

References—Alisauskas (1987), Baker (1993), Bent (1926), Brisbin et al. (2002), Burton (1959), Cramp & Simmons (1980), R.D. Crawford (1978), Eddleman & Knopf (1985), Fredrickson (1968), Gullion (1951, 1952, 1953), Hutchinson et al. (1984), McKnight & Hepp (1999), Oberholser (1974), Payne & Master (1983), Ridgway & Friedmann (1941), Roberts (1955), Stresemann & Stresemann (1966), Taylor (1998).

LIMPKINS *ARAMIDAE*

One species. Family characters include a heavy body; long, laterally compressed, and slightly recurved bill with tip angled to right; shortish and broad wings; short tail; and large and sturdy legs and feet (four toes) without webbing. Limpkins have 10 functional primaries (p10 extending 60-100 mm short of the longest, p6-p8, when fully grown), 12 secondaries (including 3 tertials and one probably absent between the 4th and 5th; *cf.* Fig. 12**B**, p. 19), and 12 rectrices. Ageing through the second cycle (to TY and ATY) can be accomplished by replacement patterns to the primaries and secondaries, combined with the shape of the modified outer primary and the shape of the rectrices (Figs. 368-370, pp. 492-493). The sexes are similar in plumage aspect but males average larger than females, especially in tarsus. Both sexes develop medial (?) brood patches (Fig. 20**A**, p. 31) but females can be sexed by distended cloacae (Fig. 21, p. 32) during the breeding season; other cloacal characters (Figs. 22-23, pp. 32-35) should be investigated.

In molting, Limpkins exhibit the Complex Basic Strategy (CBS; Fig. 10**B**, pp. 13-16), including a formative plumage during the first molt cycle but no alternate plumages. The preformative molt is incomplete, including most to all of the body feathers and some to all rectrices but no primaries or secondaries. Replacement sequence of the primaries and secondaries exhibit a staffelmauser-like pattern, but opposite to that of most birds, the primaries being replaced proximally and the secondaries generally both proximally and distally from s8-s9, with frequent irregularities (Fig. 369). Molt can be suspended during breeding and otherwise may occur somewhat continuously throughout the year. Age of first breeding is usually one year; the second prebasic molt is similar in timing to subsequent prebasic molts.

LIMPKIN
Aramus guarauna

LIMP
Species # 2070
Band size: 6

Species—From other N.Am birds by combination of medium-large size (Table 44, p. 495); bill long and laterally compressed (width at base 10-13 mm, depth at base 18-21 mm), slightly recurved, angled to right at tip, and primarily yellowish to pink; plumage aspect primarily dark olive-brown with whitish streaks to head, neck, breast, back, and wing covs (Fig. 367); legs and feet dusky olive, the hind toe well-developed.

Geographic variation—See Blake (1977), Bryan (2002), Hellmayr & Conover (1942), Oberholser (1974), Peters (1925a), Ridgway & Friedmann (1941), Todd (1916a), Wetmore (1965). Two other subspecies occur in the W.Indes and S.Am.

Northern (*A.g. pictus*) Subspecies Group. Larger than Southern (*A.g. guarauna*) Group; back and wing covs with white markings.

A.g. pictus (br and wint N.Am): Plumage aspect primarily dull brownish olive with little or no gloss; back with white streaks; white marks on scapulars, humerals, and wing covs narrower (Fig. 367**A**); base of ss with little or no white. Populations of Hispaniola-Puerto Rico (*elucus*), possible vagrant to FL, are darker and have white marks on scapulars, humerals, and wing covs reduced to narrow shaft streaks (*cf.* Fig. 367).

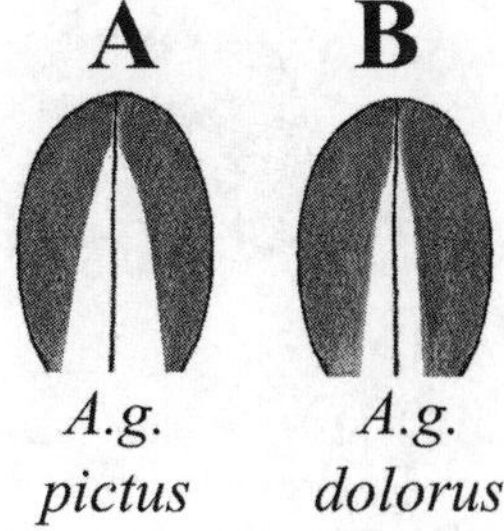

FIGURE 367. Extent of white in secondary coverts (medial gr cov shown) by subspecies in Limpkin. *A.g. pictus* is found in se.N.Am. whereas *dolorus* is found in Mexico and could occur in s.TX. A third subspecies from Puerto Rico (*elucus*), a potential vagrant to FL, has narrower streaks than *pictus*.

A.g. dolosus (br and wint c.Mex-C.Am; possible vagrant to s.TX): Plumage aspect primarily dark olive-brown with slight to moderate gloss; back with few or no white streaks; white marks on scapulars, humerals, and wing covs broader (Fig. 367**B**); base of ss with white extension along shaft.

Molt—CBS. PF incomplete (Sep?-Jan? in HY/SYs), DPB incomplete (Mar/Jun-Nov in AHYs); PA absent. The above timing pertains to N.Am populations. The PF includes most to all body feathers and some to all rects. During DPBs, pp are replaced proximally (from p10 to p1) and ss also appear to be replaced in reverse of typical sequence, both proximally and distally from s8-s9 of 14 ss (Fig. 368**B**), such that the last juv ss replaced are s1-s2, but replacement of ss may be irregular. Up to 3 sets of basic feathers can be present among pp of adults, in proximal sequence (Fig. 368**C-D**). Molt can commence during incubation, be suspended for chick-rearing, and otherwise may occur somewhat continuously throughout the year; look for occasional individuals to exhibit a complete DPB. More study needed.

Age—Juvs (B1; Jun-Mar) are dull olive-brown with narrower white streaks to upperparts (by subspecies), rects narrow and tapered (Fig. 370**A**), and bill shorter and dusky; Juv ♀=♂ by plumage aspect. The following month ranges pertain to N.Am populations.

HY/SY (1st cycle, F1; Nov-Oct): Pp and ss uniformly juv (Fig. 368**A**), or being replaced in Apr-Oct (Fig. 368**B**), the juv p10 tapered and without modification to the inner web (Fig. 369**A**), and the juv ss narrower and more worn; rects juv, narrow and rounded (Fig. 370**A**), some to all being replaced by squarer feathers in Dec-Feb (Fig. 370**B**); base of bill dusky-yellow, becoming yellowish pink in Jan-Apr.

SY/TY (2nd cycle, B2; Nov-Oct): Pp and ss with 2 sets of basic feathers (Fig. 368**C**), or with the innermost pp and outermost ss juv (*cf.* Fig. 368**B**), the p10 with moderate modification to the

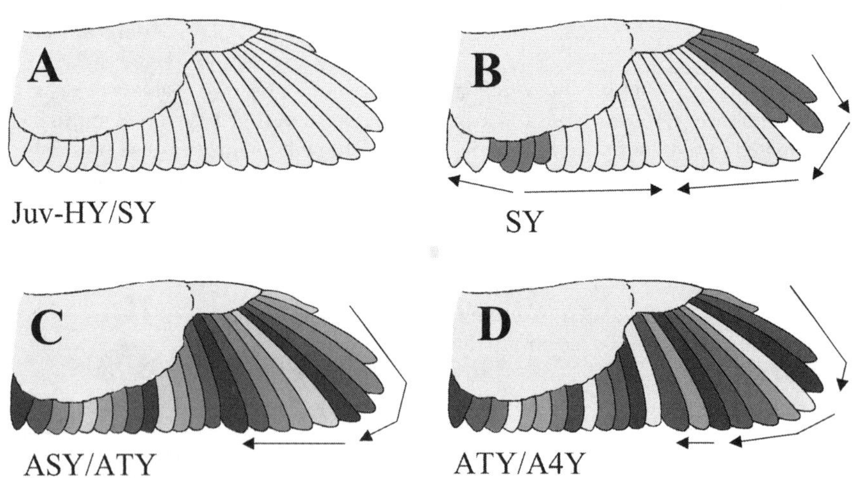

FIGURE 368. Molt patterns among the primaries and secondaries to help with age determination in Limpkin. Darker shading indicates fresher feathers. Limpkins exhibit a staffelmauser-like pattern (*cf.* Fig. 16, pp. 23-24) except that replacement sequence of the pp is opposite to that of most other birds, proceeding from p10 to p1 (**B**). It may also be opposite among ss, proceeding both proximally and distally from s8-s9 (**B**; study needed). Molt clines among pp thus proceed proximally rather than distally, with two sets of pp found in ASY/ATYs (**C**) and three sets found in ATY/A4Ys (**D**). Occasional HY/SYs may exhibit complete PFs and should be aged AHY/ASY or by the shape of p10 (Fig. 369), and beware also of suspension limits (*cf.* Fig. 15, p. 22), with proximal pp markedly fresher than the adjacent distal pp of the same generation. More study is needed.

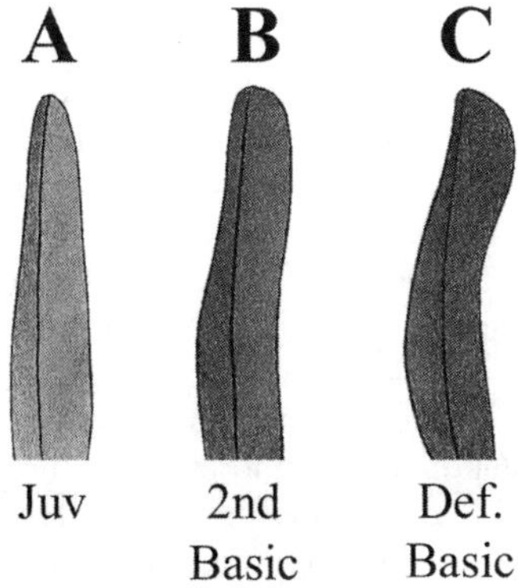

FIGURE 369. Shape of the outer primary (p10) by feather generation in Limpkin. Combine this with replacement patterns among pp (Fig. 368) for accurate age determination.

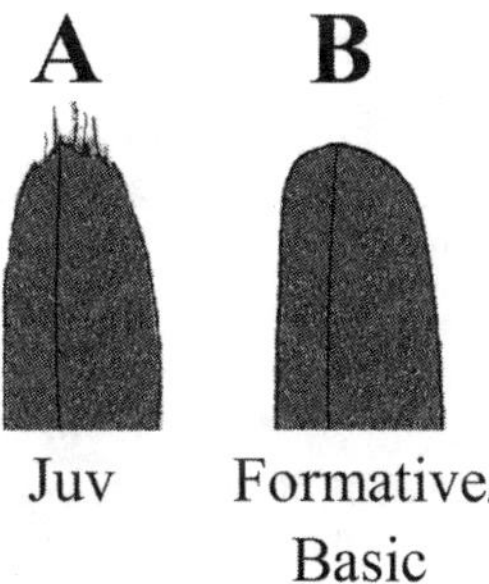

FIGURE 370. Shape and condition of the rectrices by feather generation in Limpkin, including presence of downy filaments on juvenal rectrices when fresh (**A**). Note that all Juv rects (**A**) can be replaced during the PF in Sep-Jan but many HY/SYs exhibit a mixture of juv and formative (**B**) rects through Jul-Sep. AHY/ASYs exhibit uniformly basic rects (**B**).

inner web (Fig. 369**B**), and the replaced ss broader and fresher; rects uniformly broad and square (Fig. 370**B**); base of bill pinkish. **Note: Individuals with 2 generations of basic pp and ss and an intermediate shape to p10 should be aged AHY/ASY.**

ASY/ATY (Def. cycle, DB; Nov-Oct): Pp and ss with 2 sets of basic feathers (Fig. 368**C**), the p10 with substantial modification to the inner web (Fig. 369**C**); base of bill pink to pinkish orange. **Note: See SY/TY.**

ATY/A4Y (Def. cycle, DB; Nov-Apr): Like ASY/ATY but pp with 3 sets of basic feathers (Fig. 368**D**).

Sex—♀ = ♂ by plumage aspect. Medial(?) BP (p. 31) developed by both sexes (♀♀ may average fuller BPs; more study needed) but a distended cloaca (Fig. 21, p. 32) indicates ASY ♀ in Feb-May. Measurements, especially tarsus, somewhat helpful for sexing (Table 44, p. 495). A loop in the trachea (related to display vocalizations) is present in adult ♂♂ (Wetmore 1965); more study is needed on use of this character for sexing live individuals, as in chachalacas (Fig. 114, p. 164). ♂♂ may average larger white marks on gr covs than ♀♀ but this difference is confounded by age-related and geographic variation.

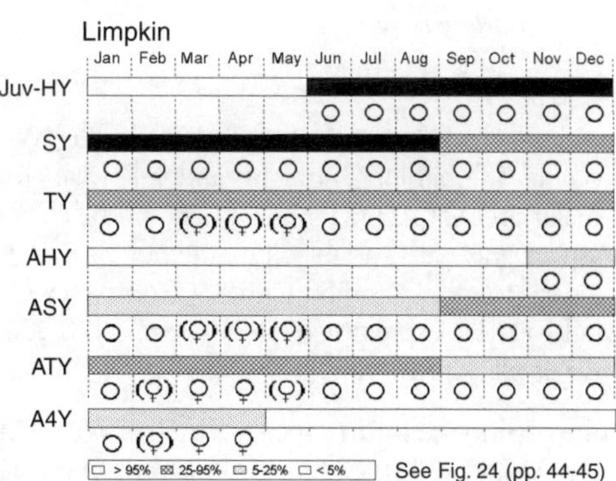

Hybrids Reported—None.

References—Bent (1926), Bryan (2002), Oberholser (1974), Ridgway & Friedmann (1941), Stresemann & Stresemann (1966).

CRANES GRUIDAE

Two species. Family characters include large bodies; moderately long, straight, and sharp bills; large and broad wings; short tails; and large and sturdy legs and feet, without webbing and with elevated hind toes. North American Cranes have 10 functional primaries (p10 extending 20-40 mm short of the longest, p7-p9, when fully grown), 16-18 secondaries (including 4 tertials and modified ss and one absent between the 4th and 5th; *cf.* Fig. 12**B**, p. 19), 3-5 elongated ornamental humerals in AHY/ASYs, and 12 rectrices. Ageing through the second cycle (to TY and ATY) and sometimes older (to ASY) can be accomplished by plumage aspect, shape and width of wing feathers and rectrices (Fig. 372, p. 497), retained feathers during prebasic molts, and development of ornamental head features (Fig. 371, p. 496). In Sandhill Crane, pigmentation is added to plumage through staining (Taverner 1929a, Portenko 1972, Miller & Hatfield 1974), or perhaps (more likely?) an oxidation process (see Cattle Egret, p. 360). The sexes are similar in plumage aspect, males average only slightly larger than females, and both sexes develop bilateral brood patches (Fig. 20**B**; p. 31) more fully by females), but females can be sexed by distended cloacae (Fig. 21, p. 32) during the breeding season; other cloacal methods (Figs. 22-23, pp. 32-35) should also be investigated.

In molting, cranes exhibit the Complex Basic Strategy (CBS; Fig. 10**B**, pp. 13-16), including a formative plumage during the first molt cycle but apparently no alternate plumages. The preformative molt is limited to some body feathers but no wing feathers or rectrices. In Whooping Crane (p. 498) the definitive prebasic molt is synchronous and occurs once every 2-4 years. Some migratory Sandhill Cranes may follow this strategy, while others exhibit staffelmauser patterns (Fig. 16, pp. 23-24), and still others may replace all secondaries and inner primaries while retaining outer primaries. Resident southern populations exhibit staffelmauser, resulting in 2-4 sets of basic feathers present among the primaries of adults. Scattered wing coverts and rectrices can also be retained during prebasic molts. Age of first breeding varies from 3 to 9 years; prebasic molts in S-TYs and non-breeding ATYs average earlier and more complete than molts of breeding individuals (see p. 18). More study is needed on these interesting patterns of molt in cranes, e.g., in Sandhill Crane, whether variation is taxonomically based, or is related only indirectly to subspecies as driven by confounding environmental factors.

SANDHILL CRANE

Grus canadensis

SACR
Species # 2060
Band size: 8-9

Species—From other N.Am birds including Whooping Crane (p. 498) by moderately large size (Table 44); bill long, straight, and yellowish (Juv) to grayish or black (AHY); forecrown (but not malar area) of AHYs with red skin and black bristle-like feathers (Fig. 371**B-D**, p. 496); plumage aspect gray with variable cinnamon or rust (Fig. 372, p. 497); legs and feet grayish black; eye yellowish to red. Common Crane (*G. grus*), a vagrant to N.Am, averages larger (wg chord 410-480, tail 150-190, exp culmen 82-110, tarsus 176-230) and has hindcrown, nape, and throat with blackish or black feathering.

Geographic variation—See Aldrich (1972, 1979), Browning (1990), Cramp & Simmons (1980), Du Mont (1933), Gaines & Warren (1984), Hellmayr & Conover (1942), Johnson & Stewart (1973), Oberholser (1974), Peters (1925b), Ridgway & Friedmann (1941), Todd (1916a), Walkinshaw (1949, 1965, 1973). One other subspecies occurs in Cuba. Beware that many individuals of migratory subspecies may not be reliably distinguished by measurements (Oberholser 1921, Tacha et al. 1985). In addition to the following, see **Molt** for geographic variation in strategies there.

G.c. canadensis (br AK-Nunavut, wint s.CA-TX; vagrant to PEI-FL): Small, especially in bill and tarsal lengths (Table 44); plumage aspect including hind crown and nape paler gray, contrasting minimally with paler malar area; pp and ss blacker by age.

G.c. tabida (br se.AK Is-n.CA to Ont-OH, wint CA-FL; vagrant to Ont-DC): Large, especially in wing and bill lengths (Table 44); plumage aspect including hind crown and nape paler gray, contrasting minimally with paler malar area; pp and ss browner by age. Populations breeding in Canada ("*rowani*") average larger and with proportionally longer legs than populations breeding in the U.S. but differences are slight, broadly clinal, and represent intergradation toward *canadensis* (with which *tabida* might better be considered a synonym). Populations of the Great Lakes region ("*woodi*") were described primarily on the basis of increased rusty pigment deposition rather than genetic variation (*cf.* Hubbard & Banks 1970).

G.c. pratensis (res se.GA to FL): Large, especially in tarsal length (Table 44); plumage aspect medium-pale gray, the hind crown and nape slightly darker gray, contrasting somewhat with paler malar area.

G.c. pulla (res s.MS): Large, especially in tarsal length (Table 44); plumage aspect dark gray, contrasting markedly with paler malar area.

Molt—CBS. PF limited-partial (Oct-Apr in HY/SYs), PB2 partial-incomplete (May-Aug in SYs), DPB incomplete-complete (Jun-Sep in ASYs); PA absent. Molt strategies differ by subspecies and/or migratory status (Nesbitt & Schwikert 2005). More study is needed on the interesting variation and the evolution of wing molt patterns in this species.

In resident populations (*pratensis* and *pulla*) the DPBs exhibit staffelmauser (Fig. 16, p. 23-24), resulting in 2-4 sets of basic feathers present among pp of adults. The PF includes most of the head and neck and scattered other body feathers but few if any wing covs and no terts or rects. The PB2 can be partial (include no pp, ss, or rects) or can include 1-5 proximal ss (among s12-s16) and occasionally 1-2 distal ss (s1-s2). Some to many juv s covs are also typi-

TABLE 44. Measurements (mm) of North American limpkins and cranes for identification and sexing. See pp. 4-11 for methods of measurement. Species summaries are in **bold** and subspecies summaries are in ***italics***. Values were derived from 95% confidence intervals as based approximately on the indicated sample sizes (see pp. 4-5); sample sizes for bill depth were often smaller but included at least 10 of each sex. Thus, midpoints of ranges approximate means, and S.D. is approximated by 25% of the range.

Taxon/Sex	*n*	wing chord	tail length	exposed culmen	bill depth[1]	tarsus
Limpkin[2]		**298-337**	**124-153**	**108-132**	**17.4-22.1**	**112-142**
♀	20	298-320	124-143	108-123	17.4-20.4	112-130
♂	20	311-337	130-153	116-132	18.9-22.1	123-142
Sandhill Crane[2]		**421-573**	**154-204**	**84-163**	**19.6-42.4**	**166-264**
G.c. canadensis		***421-495***	***154-177***	***84-109***	***19.6-28.1***	***166-213***
♀	55	421-471	154-171	84-106	19.6-27.1	166-200
♂	95	443-495	157-177	88-109	20.2-28.1	177-213
G.c.tabida		***460-573***	***173-199***	***107-163***	***25.9-37.3***	***207-256***
♀	100	460-554	173-191	107-149	25.9-35.4	207-240
♂	100	483-573	180-199	119-163	27.3-37.3	221-256
G.c.pratensis/pulla		***455-526***	***167-204***	***118-141***	***24.4-42.4***	***223-264***
♀	20	455-491	167-191	118-134	24.4-30.9	223-247
♂	30	488-526	184-204	124-141	25.2-32.4	239-264
Whooping Crane		**540-645**	**195-246**	**126-151**	**30.6-38.2**	**263-304**
♀	20	540-630	195-238	126-149	30.6-36.9	263-299
♂	30	555-645	202-246	129-151	31.8-38.2	268-304

[1] Measured at tip of forehead feathering or skin. (Fig. 8**A**-**B**, p. 10)

cally retained during the PB2. Usually, 3-8 juv outer pp (among p3-p10) and 1-6 juv medial ss (among s3-s4 and s7-s10) can be retained during the PB3, and look for occasional individuals to retain 1-2 juv outer pp (p9-p10) during the PB4 (more study needed).

In migratory populations (*G.c. canadensis* and *tabida*), the PF occurs primarily on non-breeding grounds whereas the DPB occurs primarily on the summer grounds but usually completes (body feathers, wing coverts, and rectrices) on non-breeding grounds; replacement of pp has also been reported during northbound migration in March (*cf.* Hobson et al. 2006). The PF appears to be similar in extent to that of resident populations. The PB2 may typically include only some to most s covs and no pp, ss, or rects (*cf.* Whooping Crane), or it may include some proximal ss as in resident subspecies; more study is needed. DPBs can apparently take one of three forms: 1) staffelmauser as in resident populations (Fig. 16 and see above); 2) synchronous replacement of all flight feathers during a complete molt as in Whooping Crane; or 3) synchronous replacement of ss and inner pp with 1-5 outer pp retained. Whether or not the latter group can retain inner pp during subsequent molts requires further study.

A DPA probably does not occur in Sandhill Crane (*cf.* Bent 1926, Dement'ev & Gladkov 1951a); neck-feather replacement year-round (Nesbitt & Schwikert in press), at least in resident populations, may be part of a protracted DPB (more study is needed).

Age—Juv (B1; Jun-Dec) has forecrown feathered (Fig. 371**A**), upperpart feathers with tawny to cinnamon tips, bill yellowish, eye brownish, and legs olive to grayish; Juv ♀=♂ by plumage aspect. Juv plumage is retained longer in migratory than in resident populations. Ageing criteria differs with subspecies and/or migratory status (see **Molt**).

Juv-HY/SY (1st cycle, Juv/B1-F1; Oct-Sep): Forecrown feathered to partially feathered (Fig. 371**A**-**B**); pp, ss, and s covs uniformly juvenal (Fig. 16**A**, p. 24), the ss and s covs narrow and tipped buff to cinnamon when fresh (Fig. 372**A**-**C**) and the outer pp brownish and tapered (Fig. 19**A**-**B**, p. 28); rects narrow and rounded (Fig. 372**D**); iris brownish yellow to dull yellowish orange.

SY/TY (2nd cycle, B2; Oct-Sep): Forecrown partially feathered to smooth and without pinnate feathers (Fig. 371**B**-**C**); pp, most to all ss, and usually one or more wing covs and rects retained, narrow, very worn, and tipped pale cinnamon (Fig. 172**A**-**D**), 1-5 inner ss often replaced and contrastingly fresh and broad (Fig. 371**F**); iris dull yellow-orange to orange. **Note: See Molt for details of wing-feather replacement during the PB2, leading to molt limits among SY/TYs.**

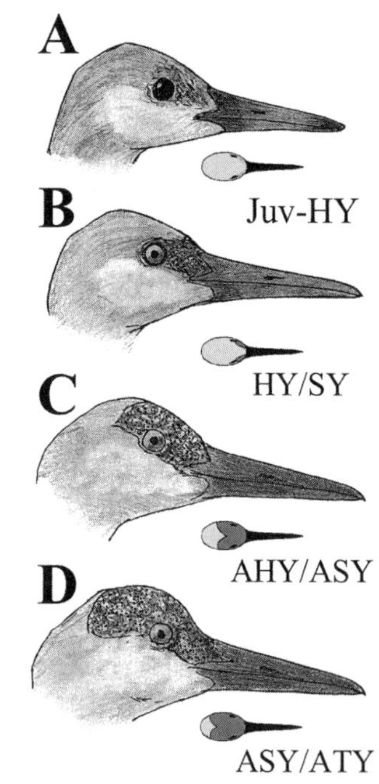

FIGURE 371. Development of crown feathers and orbital area by age in Sandhill Crane. Full development (**D**) may represent older age groups than ATY/A4Y (more study needed). Note that development of these areas in Whooping Crane follows similar age-related patterns, except that bare-skin areas include the malar region below the gape.

ASY/ATY (Def. cycle, DB; Oct-Sep): Forecrown without pinnate feathers and with rougher skin and denser bristles (Fig. 371**C-D**); pp and ss uniformly basic (Figs. 14**A**, p. 22; 19**C-D**; & 372**E-F**); s covs and rects basic and without buff tips but often with tawny marks (Fig. 372**G-H**); iris yellow-orange to reddish orange. **Note: Individuals showing these characters typically occur only among migratory populations (see Molt). It is possible that individuals with highly developed ornamental crown features (Fig. 371D) can be aged ATY/A4Y or older but more study is needed.**

TY/4Y (3rd cycle, B3; Oct-Sep): Like ASY/ATY but 3-8 outer pp retained juv, brownish, and very worn (Figs. 16**B** & 19**B**); ss with 2-3 generations, 3-8 ss (among s3-s4 and s7-s10) often retained, juv, narrow (Fig. 371**A**) and worn (*cf.* Fig. 16**D**); iris often dull yellow-orange to orange. **Note: These patterns occur in s. resident subspecies and some n. migratory subspecies (see Molt). Look for occasional 4Y/5Ys to have two generations of basic pp and 1-2 outer pp (p9-p10) retained (*cf.* Fig. 16D).**

ATY/A4Y (Def. cycle, DB; Oct-Sep): Like ASY/ATY but pp with 2-3 sets of basic feathers in staffelmauser patterns (Fig. 16**E-F**). **Note: See TY/4Y.**

A4Y/A5Y (Def. cycle, DB; Oct-May): Like ASY/ATY but pp with 4 sets of basic feathers in staffelmauser patterns (Fig. 16**G**). **Note: See TY/4Y. Individuals showing 4 sets may be rare.**

Sex—♀ = ♂ by plumage aspect. Bilateral BPs (Fig. 20**B**, p. 31) developed by both sexes (fuller in ♀♀ than in ♂♂) but a distended cloaca (Fig. 21, p. 32) indicates ATY ♀ in Apr-Jun. Measurements possibly helpful for sexing mated pairs but not useful overall (Table 44, p. 495). See Rasch & Kertin (1976) for sexing by karyotype analysis. The possibility of sexing by tracheal length (see Fig. 114, p. 164) should be investigated.

Hybrids Reported—With naturalized and cross-fostered Whooping Crane in the wild (Lewis 1995).

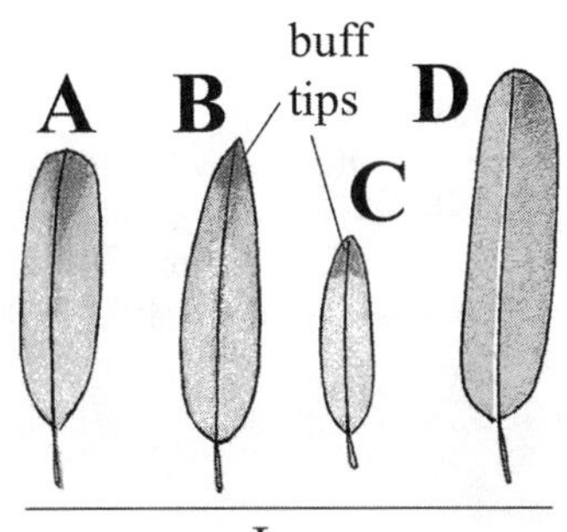

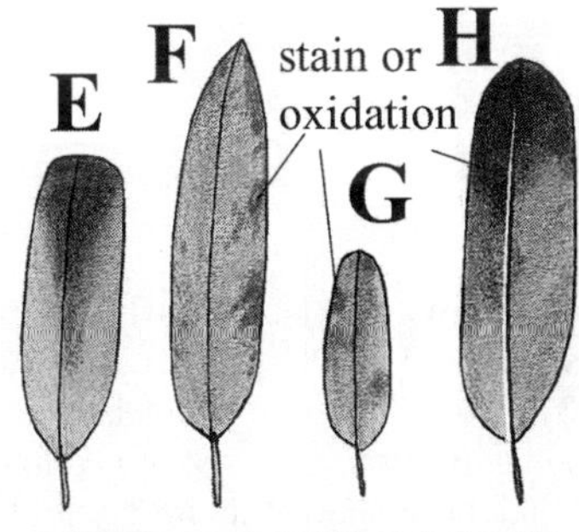

FIGURE 372. Shape and pigmentation patterns to the outer secondaries (**A**, **E**; s3 shown), inner secondaries (**B**, **F**; s18 shown), greater coverts (**C**, **G**), and rectrices (**D**, **H**) by feather generation in Sandhill Crane. Maximum width or the rectrices is usually < 43 mm in juv feathers (**D**) but > 43 mm in basic feathers (**H**). Note that in juv feathers, buff to cinnamon tips represent true feather pigmentation whereas basic feathers develop uniformly gray but gain tawny coloration through staining or oxidation. SY/TYs from northern migratory populations (see **Geographic variation**) replace most or all of these feathers during the PB2, such that those with uniformly basic feathers can only be aged AHY/ASY by feather shape and coloration alone. Many individuals can retain juv or basic feathers during incomplete PBs, however, and can be aged SY/TY or ASY/ATY, respectively. ASYs from southern resident populations exhibit staffelmauser patterns (Fig. 16, pp. 23-24) and can be aged to TY/4Y or A4Y/A5Y, depending on the number of sets within the pp and whether or not the outer pp are juv or basic. See **Age** for more information.

References—Bent (1926), Blaauw (1897), Dement'ev & Gladkov (1951a), Hobson et al. (2006), Johnsgard (1983b), Layne (1981), Lewis (1979a, 1979b), Littlefield (1970), Nesbitt (1987), Nesbitt & Schwikert (1998, 2005, in press), Oberholser (1974), Portenko (1972), Ridgway & Friedmann (1941), Roberts (1955), Tacha & Vohs (1984), Tacha et al. (1992), Walkinshaw (1949, 1973).

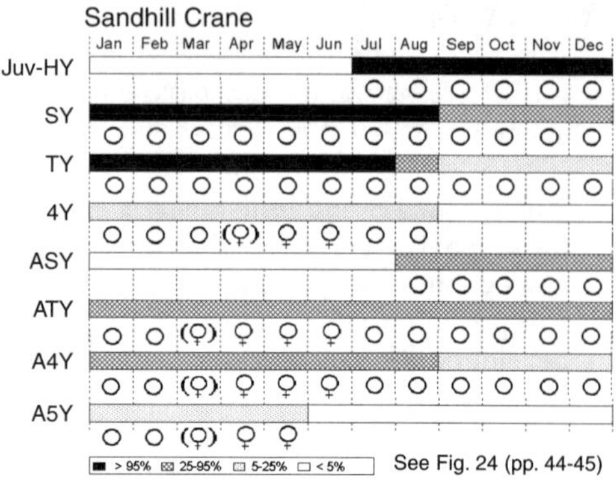

WHOOPING CRANE

Grus americana

WHCR
Species # 2040
Band size: 9

Species—From other N.Am birds including Sandhill Crane (p. 494) by large size and very long tarsus (Table 44, p. 495); bill straight with pinkish to yellowish base; crown and malar region (*cf.* Fig. 371) with red skin and blackish bristle-like feathers; plumage aspect primarily white (washed cinnamon in Juvs), with contrastingly black pp, p covs and alula (p1 and the inner 4 p covs white or washed grayish); eye and feet yellowish; legs black.

Geographic variation—Monotypic.

Molt—CBS. PF limited-partial (Sep-Mar in HY/SYs), PB2 partial (May-Aug in SYs), DPB partial-complete (May-Sep in ASYs); PA absent. The PF occurs primarily on non-breeding grounds whereas the DPB occurs primarily on breeding grounds but can complete on non-breeding grounds. The PF includes some to most feathers of the head and body but no wing feathers or rects. During DPBs, most to all body feathers replaced annually but pp, ss, and wing covs are replaced synchronously, once every 2-4 (often 3) years in May-Jun, followed by body-feather replacement in Jun-Sep. This is based on resident populations in FL (Folk et al. in press) but specimen evidence indicates that individuals in migratory populations also skip wing-feather replacement for one or more years. There is little evidence for a PA (see Sandhill Crane).

Age—Juv (B1; Jul-Mar) has forecrown and malar region feathered (*cf.* Fig. 371**A**), upperparts extensively tawny to dull orangish, iris dull olive, and base of bill dusky. Juv ♀ = ♂ by plumage aspect.

Juv-HY/SY (1st cycle, Juv-B1/F1; Sep-Aug): Forecrown and malar region feathered to partially feathered (*cf.* Fig. 371**A-B**); some to most feathers of crown and upperparts cinnamon or fringed cinnamon, increasingly mixed with replaced or bleached whitish feathers in Dec-Aug (can become whitish except for cinnamon-washed head); pp, ss, s covs, and rects uniformly juv, fresh, the outer pp tapered (Figs. 16**A**, p. 24, & 19**A-B**, p. 28), and the ss, s covs, and rects narrow and tipped cinnamon (*cf.* Fig. 372**A-D**); base of bill dusky, becoming pinkish to dull yellowish by Jun-Sep.

SY/TY (2nd cycle, B2; Sep-Aug): Like Juv-HY/SY but forecrown and malar partially feathered (through Dec) or without pinnate feathers (*cf.* Fig. 371**B-C**); hind crown and upperparts with little or no cinnamon (scattered cinnamon feather tipping can be present when fresh); pp, ss, s covs, and rects juv, very worn or broken, and tipped pale cinnamon where intact (Fig. 372**A-D**); base of bill duller yellow. **Note: A few ss, s covs, and rects can be replaced (adventitiously) and appear contrastingly fresh and white.**

ASY/ATY (Def. cycle, DB; Sep-Aug): Forecrown and malar region without pinnate feathers and smooth (*cf.* Fig. 371**C-D**); hindcrown and upperparts white; pp, ss, and s covs uniformly basic (Fig. 14**A**, p. 21), fresh, the outer pp truncate (Fig. 19**C**), and the ss, s covs, and rects broad and without cinnamon tipping (*cf.* Fig. 372**E-H**); base of bill brighter yellow.

ATY/A4Y (Def. cycle, DB; Sep-Aug): Like ASY/ATY but basic pp, ss, s covs, and rects much more worn and/or broken (Fig. 19**D**), the ss, s covs, and rects not tipped pale cinnamon (Fig. 372**E-H**). **Note: It is possible that individuals with highly developed ornamental crown features can be aged ATY/A4Y or older; more study is needed. See SY/TY.**

Sex—♀ = ♂ by plumage aspect. Bilateral(?) BPs (Fig. 20**B**, p. 31) developed by both sexes (fuller in ♀♀ than in ♂♂) but a distended cloaca (Fig. 21, p. 32) indicates ATY ♀ in Apr-Jun. Measurements possibly helpful for sexing mated pairs but are not useful overall (Table 44, p. 495). See Carlson & Trost (1992) and Fitch & Kelley (2000) for sex-specific differences in behavior and vocalization pitch; the possibility of sexing by tracheal length (*cf.* Fig. 114, p. 164) should be investigated.

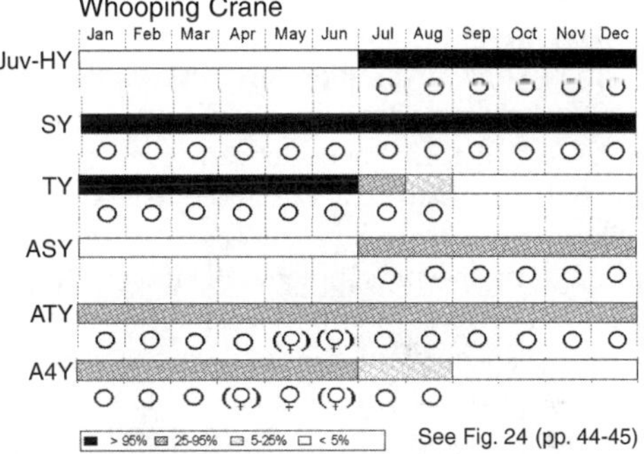

Hybrids Reported—Cross-fostered Whooping Crane, from naturalized population, with Sandhill Crane (p. 494, in the wild.

References—Allen (1952), Bent (1926), Blaauw (1897), Folk et al. (in press), Johnsgard (1983b), Lewis (1995), Oberholser (1974), Ridgway & Friedmann (1941), Roberts (1955), Stevenson & Griffith (1946), Walkinshaw (1973).

SHOREBIRDS *CHARADRII*

Fifty-eight species. Suborder characters include variable sizes and body shapes, relatively long bills and legs with the hind toe poorly developed and sometimes absent (Fig. 373), and webbing usually present between the bases of the fore toes (Fig. 374). North American shorebirds have 10 functional primaries, 12-19 secondaries (including 3-5 tertials and one absent between the 4th and 5th in all but American Woodcock; *cf.* Fig. 12**B**, p. 19), and 12 rectrices in all species except Northern Jacana (10) and Wilson's Snipe (usually 16). Ageing through the first (to SY and ASY) and sometimes the second (to TY and ATY) cycles can be accomplished through plumage aspect in combination with molt or feather-retention patterns among the wings and tail. Degree of cranial pneumatization patterns may be useful for ageing some individuals, but species-specific details need to be investigated (McNeil & Burton 1972). Sexing can be accomplished in some species by plumage aspect (often only in definitive alternate plumage) and in others by size, either females or males being larger (Jehl & Murray (1986). Bilateral or (sometimes) medial brood patches (Fig. 20**A**-**B**, p. 31) are most often developed by both sexes, but in certain species they can be used to sex either females or males; distended cloacae (Fig. 21, p. 32) indicate AHY (sometimes ASY or ATY) females during the breeding season. Other cloacal differences (Figs. 22-23, pp. 32-35) should be investigated, although length of the bursa (Fig. 23, p. 34), cannot be measured on live birds due to the lack of an opening in the cloaca (McNeil & Burton 1972)

In molting, many shorebirds exhibit the Complex Alternate Strategy (CAS; Fig 10**F**-**H**, pp. 13-16), including a formative plumage and alternate plumages in all molt cycles. Some larger species (e.g., oystercatchers, curlews, and godwits) may exhibit a Simple Alternate Strategy (SAS; Fig. 10**C**), in which only one molt occurs during the first cycle, and several species of various families appear to lack prealternate molts and exhibit the Complex Basic Strategy (CBS; Fig 10**B**). A definitive presupplemental molt (p. 15) involving some body feathers has been proposed for several species (of different families) and could occur in many others; more study is needed. As in other species that exhibit dyastataxy, most shorebirds replace pp distally from p1 to p10 and replace ss proximally from s1 and s5 and distally from the tertials, such that the last ss replaced are typically among s4 and s7-s10 (Fig. 375**E**, p. 503); rectrices are generally replaced distally although the outer rectrix is usually replaced prior to r4 and r5. Molt strategies exhibit substantial variation, apparently dependent on non-breeding latitude rather than taxonomic affinity (Table 45, Figs. 375-376, pp. 503-504). Plumage-aspect variation based on different molt strategies (p. 29), as affected more by environmental than phylogenetic factors, has possibly led to over-splitting of subspecies within highly migratory species such as Ruddy Turnstone and Red Knot. Age of first breeding occurs at 1-2 years in smaller species and 2-4 years in larger species; non-breeding AHYs often remain on or near non-breeding grounds and exhibit later and less-extensive prealternate molts and earlier prebasic molts (p. 18). See the following section for details on molt and ageing in shorebirds, and the family, subfamily, and tribal accounts for more specific information

General references for determination of age, sex, and subspecies in North American shorebirds include Chandler (1989), Gratto (2004), Haig et al. (1997), Hayman et al. (1986), Johnsgard (1981b), O'Brien et al. (2006), Palmer (1967a), Paulson (1993, 2005), Prater et al. (1977), Rosair & Cottridge (1995); Dwight (1900b) and Jackson (1919 and related accounts in British Birds) provided initial accounts of shorebird molts, Holmes (1966) detailed pterylography, and Jehl (1968a) provided criteria for

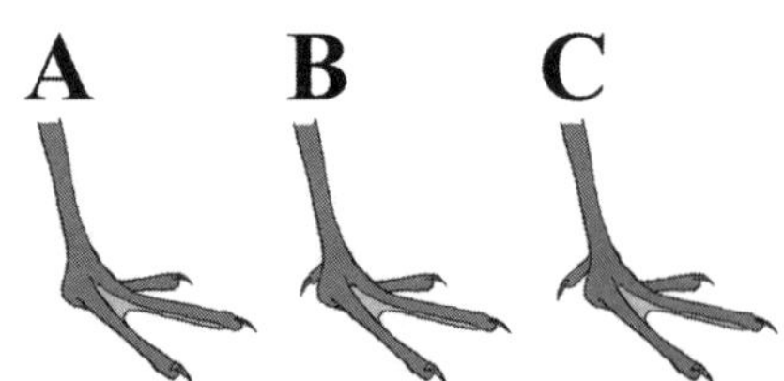

FIGURE 373. Variation in presence and size of hind toe among shorebirds. Different species can have the hind toe absent (**A**), rudimenatry (**B**), or more fully developed (**C**).

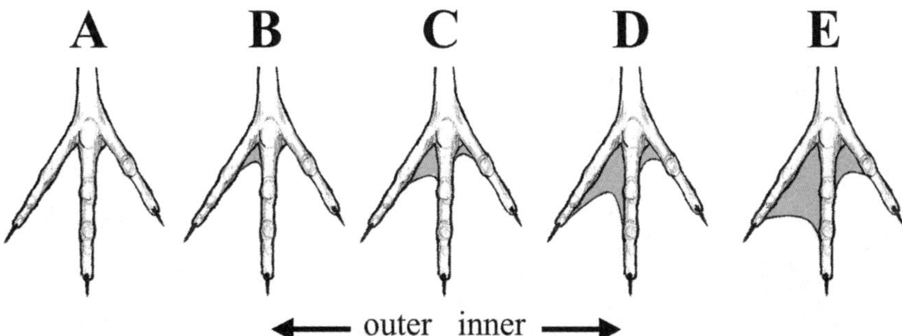

FIGURE 374. Variation in the extent of webbing to the toes in shorebirds. The right foot is shown; thus, the outer toe is to the right and the inner toe is to the left.

separation of chicks based on patterns and color of the natal down. This suborder is divided into five families, one of which (Scolopacidae) has 40 species and, for convenience, is further separated into two subfamilies and eight tribes, reflecting groups with differing structures, molts, and plumage-aspect patterns.

Molts, plumages, and age determination in shorebirds

Shorebird molts and plumages

Shorebirds exhibit a wide variety of molt and plumage-aspect patterns, many of which relate to specific migratory and breeding strategies (Table 45, Figs 375-376; *cf.* Prater 1981, Bridge 2006). Whereas most species breed in arctic or subarctic regions, non-breeding ("winter") grounds vary from northern North American coasts to the southern tip of South America, the tropical Pacific, and Australasia. In some species (e.g., Black-bellied Plover, Wandering Tattler, Willet, Whimbrel, Ruddy Turnstone, Red Knot, and Red Phalarope) the non-breeding range encompasses all of these areas, and intra-specific molt strategies are correspondingly variable. Here, two broad molt strategies within Charadrii are defined, correlating more with non-breeding latitude than with taxonomic group (Table 45), and thus appearing to be driven more by environmental than phylogenetic factors

Many species and individuals with non-breeding grounds in the Northern Hemisphere, and in some cases the tropics, follow a "**n.Hemisphere strategy**" (Table 45, Fig. 375; *cf.* Fig. 11**E**, p. 17). This strategy is typically characterized by partial to incomplete preformative molts (not including primaries or outer secondaries) and relatively rapid prebasic molts occurring in Jul-Aug to Oct-Nov. Prealternate molts are well defined and often take place on non-breeding grounds, prior to northward migration in spring. This strategy is apparently adaptive for species or individuals with less daylight and fewer prey resources during the winter months with which to garner nutrition to molt. A few individuals of the larger species can suspend prebasic molt during winter (completing it in spring) or arrest this molt until the following prebasic molt (*cf.* Jukema 1982), but this appears to be relatively uncommon and is thus not a substantial factor in ageing shorebirds by molt-replacement patterns among flight feathers (see below)

Species and individuals with non-breeding grounds in the Southern Hemisphere, and in some cases the tropics, follow a "**s.Hemisphere strategy**" (Table 45, Fig. 376; *cf.* Fig. 11**D**). This strategy is characterized by incomplete to complete preformative molts (including primaries and secondaries, often in eccentric sequence) and relatively protracted prebasic molts. Body feathers are often replaced during Aug-Oct whereas replacement of flight feathers may begin during these months but is protracted, completing in Jan-Apr or later. Prealternate and/or presupplemental

TABLE 45. Molt strategies shown by North American Shorebirds, apparently reflecting non-breeding range as opposed to taxonomic affinity. See text for details. Two species (Northern Jacana, p. 542, and Bristle-thighed Curlew, p. 562) show unique strategies among shorebirds and are excluded from the table.

Northern Hemisphere Strategy	Southern Hemisphere Strategy	Both Strategies
Pacific Golden-Plover[1]	American Golden-Plover[c]	Black-bellied Plover[b]
Snowy Plover	Lesser Sand-Plover[2,e]	Wilson's Plover[e]
Semipalmated Plover[1,e]	Lesser Yellowlegs[e]	Common Ringed Plover[e]
Piping Plover	Solitary Sandpiper[e]	Eurasian Dotterel[e]
Killdeer	Spotted Sandpiper[1,e]	Wandering Tattler[e]
Mountain Plover	Hudsonian Godwit[?]	Whimbrel[t]
American & Black oystercatchers	Semipalmated Sandpiper[e]	Bar-tailed Godwit[e]
Black-necked Stilt	Red-necked Stint[e]	Ruddy Turnstone[t]
American Avocet	White-rumped Sandpiper[c]	Red Knot[e]
Greater Yellowlegs	Baird's Sandpiper[c]	Sanderling[e]
Willet	Curlew Sandpiper[e]	Least Sandpiper[e]
Upland Sandpiper	Stilt Sandpiper[e]	Red Phalarope[e]
Long-billed Curlew	Buff-breasted Sandpiper[c]	Wilson's Phalarope[e]
Marbled Godwit		Red-necked Phalarope[c,e]
Black Turnstone		
Surfbird[1?]		
Western Sandpiper		
Purple & Rock Sandpiper		
Dunlin		
Ruff[1,e]		
Short-billed[1,e] & Long-billed dowitchers		
Common Snipe		
American Woodcock		

[1] The majority of individuals show this strategy but a small proportion shows or may show the other strategy.
[2] Strategy shown by North American populations; other populations may show the opposite strategy.
Replacement strategies of pp and ss during the PF are shown by superscripts:
[e] Eccentric Replacement Pattern (Fig. 376**A**, p. 504)
[t] Typical Replacement Pattern (Fig. 376**D**)
[b] Individuals can show either eccentric or typical patterns
[c] Preformative molt complete

molts are more variable, can overlap flight-feather replacement at the end of prebasic molts, and/or can begin on non-breeding grounds but complete or take place at stopover sites to the north of non-breeding grounds (Fig. 11**D**, p. 17). This strategy appears to be adaptive in species or individuals with more daylight and prey resources for molting during the boreal winter (Austral summer). The protracted replacement of primaries may also result in greater amounts of melanin in these feathers to protect them from increased amounts of solar exposure experienced throughout the annual cycle (Serra 2001); they also may result in more distinct s1-p1 contrasts (Fig. 375**E**).

The preformative and definitive prebasic molts in shorebirds usually take place primarily on non-breeding grounds but can begin (and even complete) at stopover sites in some species. Breeding individuals of many species can begin the prebasic molt during incubation and suspend it for migration (*cf.* Fig. 11**D-E**). Molt on breeding grounds usually involves only a few body feathers, but in some individuals (perhaps more typically first-cycle SYs and/or non-breeders) up to 5 inner primaries can be replaced before suspension for migration, resulting in suspension limits (caution that suspension limits in ASYs can resemble eccentric molt patterns in SYs of certain species).

In certain species (exhibiting both molt strategies), a variable proportion of first-cycle individuals (SYs) can over-summer on non-breeding grounds or move to stopover sites away from

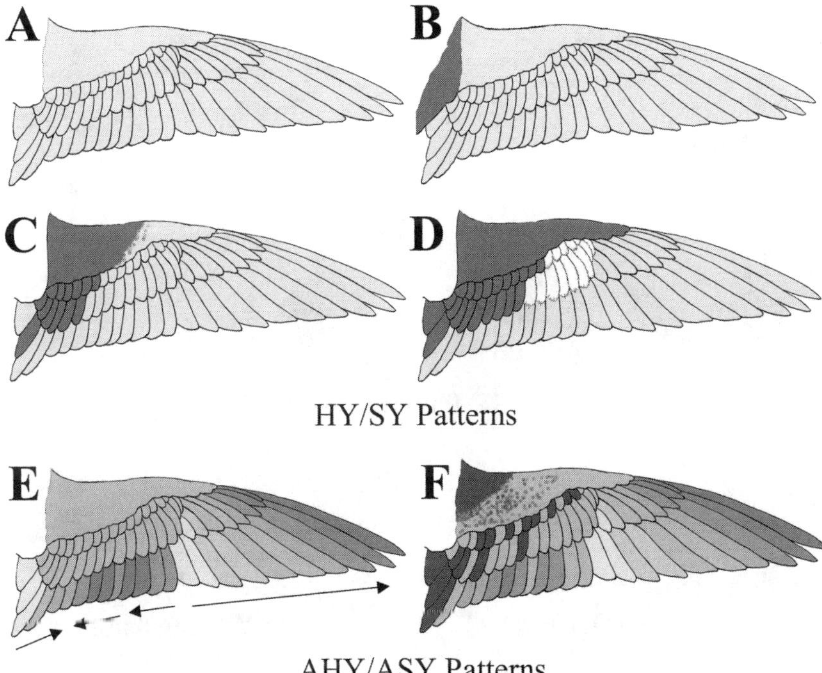

FIGURE 375. Replacement patterns among the wing feathers of shorebirds by age, stressing differences among wing coverts and tertials useful in ageing species exhibiting a n.Hemisphere molt strategy (Table 45). Darker shading indicates fresher feathers. Juv shorebirds have uniformly juv wing feathers (**A**); most species tend to keep these through the southbound migration (Jul-Sep) but some can begin the PF and exhibit molt limits with fresher formative humerals, scapulars, and/or s covs, as in **B** or **C**, before reaching non-breeding grounds, and others may complete the molt before migration. Species or individuals wintering in the n.Hemisphere often exhibit molt limits among the humerals, s covs, and terts in winter (**B**-**D**), and can exhibit very bleached and frayed, retained juv outer med and gr covs and outer pp by their first spring (**D**). AHY/ASYs of most species typically have worn flight feathers and scattered alternate feathers during breeding and southbound migration in Apr-Sep/Nov (**F**). After molt, they exhibit uniformly basic s covs, replacement clines (see Fig. 12**B**, p. 19), and p1-s1 contrasts (see Fig. 12**B**) because s1 is typically not replaced until p6-p7 are replaced; Dwight 1900b. Pp are replaced distally from p1 to p10 and ss are usually replaced proximally from s1 and s5, and distally from the terts (**E**). Effective ageing of shorebirds by wing patterns combines these molt patterns with shape, wear, and patterns of the pp and p covs (Figs. 377-378, p. 506). See also Figure 376 (p. 504).

breeding grounds while skipping their first breeding season. The proportion of these "**over-summering**" individuals appears to relate to body size, longevity, reproductive parameters, and migratory strategy; in some species individuals that winter farther to the south are more likely to over-summer. Individuals of larger species may over-summer for more than one year (i.e., during second and third cycles as TY-4Ys) before breeding (*cf.* Johnson & Johnson 1983, Marks 1993). Over-summering individuals, especially SYs in their first cycle, typically have either reduced or late prealternate molts, usually resulting in basic-plumage aspect during the breeding season (Loftin 1962, Chandler & Marchant 2001, Johnson & Johnson 1983, Chu 1994), although the feathers themselves may be alternate (see p. 29). Over-summering individuals also can begin the prebasic molt much earlier than breeding individuals, often obtaining complete basic-plumage aspect by the time breeding adults return to non-breeding grounds in worn alternate-plumage aspect. In

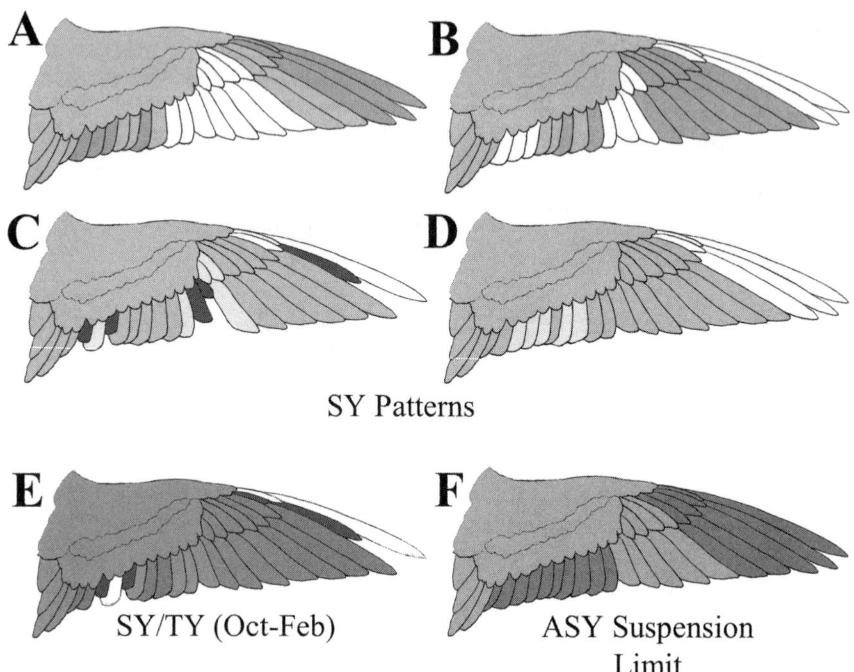

FIGURE 376. Replacement patterns among the wing feathers of shorebirds by age, stressing differences among primaries and secondaries useful in ageing species exhibiting a s.Hemisphere molt strategy (Table 45, pp. 501-505) in the spring and summer. Darker shading indicates fresher feathers. The PF is often eccentric (p. 18) in these species (Table 45), with all s covs, 3-8 outer pp, and 5-12 inner ss (including terts) typically replaced, resulting in identifiable patterns among the wings of SYs (**A**-**B**); **A** exhibits five inner primaries and two outer ss retained and **B** exhibits two inner pp and one outer s retained as juv feathers and contrastingly faded and worn. Sometimes this molt can be arrested, with outer pp and medial ss (typically among s7-s11) also retained (**B**), and sometimes (especially in SYs over-summering on non-breeding grounds) the PF can continue into May-Jun, overlapping the beginning of the PB2 (**C**). A few shorebirds can exhibit PFs in typical sequence (Table 45) that can arrest, resulting in retained juv outer pp and medial ss among s3-s4 and s6-s11 (**D**). In Oct-Feb, some shorebirds may have a protracted over-winter molt and still be identifiable as SY/TYs by the retained juv outer pp and medial ss, very worn and abraded by this time (**E**). ASY/ATYs also undergo protracted molts, but often cannot be aged beyond AHY/ASY because SY/TYs may have replaced outer pp during eccentric PFs. Several species may suspend PBs for southbound migration, replacing 1-6 inner pp and the terts on breeding grounds and finishing the molt on non-breeding grounds, resulting in suspension limits (**F**; see also Fig. 15, p. 22). These can be aged ASY in spring (many are likely TYs). Effective ageing of shorebirds by wing patterns combines these molt patterns with shape, wear, and patterns of the pp and p covs (Figs. 377-378, p. 506). See also Figure 375 (p. 503).

some first-cycle SYs the beginning of the second prebasic molt (of inner primaries) can overlap the end of the preformative molt (of outer primaries) resulting in two waves of primary molt occurring simultaneously within the wings (*cf.* Fig. 376**C**). Some definitive-cycle ASYs are reported to have an inserted molt of outer primaries in eccentric sequence during January-May of second or later cycles (*cf.* Pearson 1984, Marks 1993, Higgins & Davies 1996, Balachandran & Hussain 1998) but more study is needed to confirm and/or understand this pattern; it is possible that it occurs only in over-summering TYs.

In species exhibiting the s.Hemisphere strategy, the molt of primaries during December-May of the first cycle, often in eccentric patterns but sometimes in typically patterns or completely (Table 45, Fig. 376**A-D**), is here considered part of the preformative molt. Because it often occurs later than (and sometimes does not overlap with) replacement of body feathers, other interpretations have been suggested: that it be considered part of the first prealternate molt or that it has evolved separately under specialized circumstances and be considered a presupplemental molt (*cf.* Marchant & Higgins 1993, Higgins & Davies 1996). However, replacement of wing coverts and rectrices can apparently span the entire period of molt, suggesting that it is a single preformative molt that has adapted in timing in accordance with resource availability, in the same manner that some protracted definitive prebasic molts have adapted. Furthermore, some species that otherwise appear to lack a first prealternate molt (e.g., Whimbrel) can replace primaries during their first December-May, as in related species that do have prealternate molts. However, if it is confirmed that later-cycle individuals (ASYs) also can replace outer primaries during an inserted molt in January-May (see above), terminology of inserted molts in all cycles may warrant reconsideration

Age determination in shorebirds

The variation in molts and plumages among shorebirds, described above, complicates ageing criteria, which rely substantially on replacement patterns in the wings and tail. During the boreal fall, Juv-HYs of almost all species are readily separated from AHYs by upperpart plumage aspect and condition of the flight feathers and wing coverts. Several species regularly have complete preformative molts (Table 45, p. 502), and in these it is not possible to separate first-cycle SYs from definitive-cycle ASYs following completion of preformative or prebasic molts, typically in February-April. For most of the remaining species, however, molt patterns (Table 45, Figs. 375-376 & 379) can be carefully considered and combined with criteria related to retained feathers (Figs. 377-379) to accurately separate first-cycle SYs from definitive-cycle ASYs in boreal winter, spring, and summer.

Figures 375 (p. 503), 376, and 379 (p. 507) illustrate various replacement patterns among wing coverts, primaries, secondaries, and rectrices that result from preformative and prebasic molts. In fall, the wings and tail of first-cycle individuals (HYs) are comparatively fresh, with thinner and more tapered feathers (Figs. 375**A**, 377**A**, & 379**A**). Wing coverts are smaller, more rounded, and typically show distinct juvenal patterns, with relatively broad buff or rufous fringing (e.g. Figs. 387**A-B**, p. 520; 397, p. 536; 417, p. 556; & 437, p. 587). Preformative molts result in variable proportions of wing coverts, tertials, and rectrices being replaced during fall and winter, from none of these feathers in some individuals employing the n.Hemisphere strategy to all tertials and most or all wing coverts and rects in those employing the s.Hemisphere strategy (Figs. 375**B-D**, 376, and 379**A-D**). In many species at least some of the distal greater and/or median coverts are retained, becoming very frayed by spring (Fig. 375**D**). In most *Calidris* sandpipers and some other species, formative proximal greater, median, and some lesser coverts retain the rufous fringing typical of juvenal feathers (Fig. 437, p. 588) and, because these feathers are relatively protected, this is a good ageing criterion in spring and summer

In species or individuals exhibiting a n.Hemisphere strategy, the juvenal primaries, primary coverts, most secondaries (other than the tertials), and some to all rectrices in first-cycle HY/SYs are typically retained until the second prebasic molt (Fig. 376**A-D**), becoming very brownish and abraded by spring (Figs. 377**B**, 378**B**, & 379**D**). In species exhibiting the s.Hemisphere strategy, molt of primaries and medial secondaries exhibits varying patterns, from no replacement in some individuals (Fig. 376**A-D**), to incomplete replacement in typical sequence or full or arrested eccentric sequence in other individuals (Fig. 376**A-D**). Evidence of these patterns indicates a first-cycle individual (SY). Rectrices are usually replaced in SYs that replace primaries, and these are generally indistinguishable from definitive rectrices of ASYs (Fig. 379**E**)

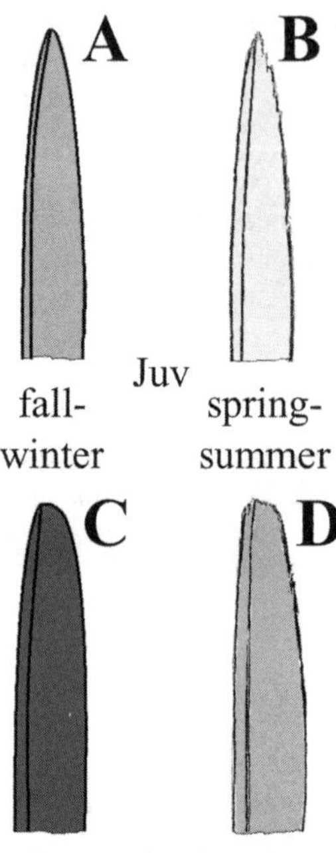

FIGURE 377. Shape of the outer primaries by feather generation and season in shorebirds. Note that many HY/SY shorebirds wintering in the s.Hemisphere can replace juv outer pp (**A**) during the PF (*cf.* Fig. 376, p. 504), after which they attain definitive aspects as SYs (**C**). Note also that retained juv pp in spring/summer SYs (**B**) are typically much more worn and bleached than retained basic pp of spring/summer ASYs (**D**).

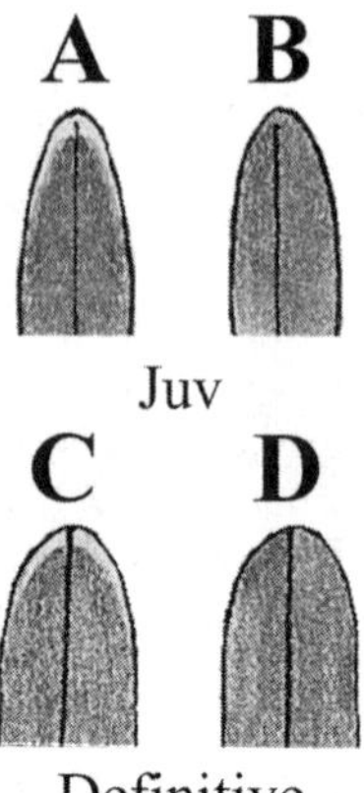

FIGURE 378. Variation in the shape and pattern to the primary coverts by feather generation in shorebirds. Note that many HY/SY shorebirds wintering in the s.Hemisphere can replace juv outer p covs (**A**-**B**) during the PF (*cf.* Fig. 376, p. 504), after which they attain basic characteristics as SYs (**C**-**D**). Within species, juv covs tend to have more pronounced pale fringing (e.g., **A**) than basic covs (**B**-**C**).

In contrast to first-cycle HYs, most definitive-cycle AHYs exhibit worn primaries (Fig. 377**D**), secondaries, and rectrices (*cf.* Fig. 379**F**) in late summer and early fall. These flight feathers are completely replaced in July-October (n.Hemisphere strategy) or September-March (s.Hemisphere strategy) in typical sequence (*cf.* Fig. 375**E**). Thus, most definitive-cycle ASY shorebirds in spring and early summer exhibit uniform wing feathers with replacement clines reflecting a complete molt (Fig. 375**E**); some may exhibit suspension limits if they had undergone migration after a suspended molt (Fig. 376**F**; see also Fig. 15, p. 22). Wing coverts of definitive-cycle AHY/ASYs are uniformly rather fresh and lack the distinct rufous or buff fringing characteristic of juvenal feathers in many species (*cf.* Figs. 387**C**, 520, and 437**B**, p. 588). In spring-summer these can be mixed with scattered fresher alternate feathers, concentrated medially (Fig. 375**F**), as opposed to the more consistent, proximal to distal replacement patterns resulting from preformative molts (Fig. 375**C**-**D**). Relative to juvenal feathers, outer primaries are broad and fresh by season (Fig. 377**C**-**D**), primary coverts are broader and often show less pale fringing (Fig. 378**C**-**D**), and rectrices are uniformly broader and fresher (Fig. 379**E**), sometimes with replaced alternate central feathers (Fig. 379**F**)

Some individuals or species exhibiting the s.Hemisphere molting strategy have partial preformative molts but protracted prebasic molts, allowing the determination of second-cycle SY/TYs through late fall or winter, by the retention of juvenal outer primaries or medial secondaries until completion of the 2nd prebasic molt in October-February (Fig. 376**E**; *cf.* Gratto & Morrison

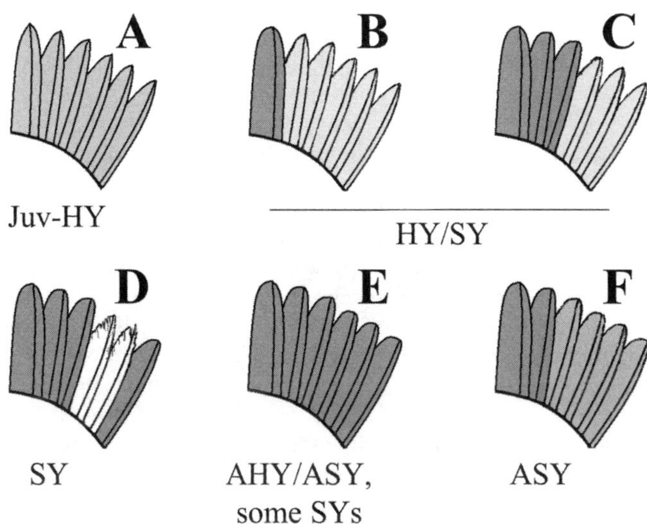

FIGURE 379. Patterns to the rectrices by age and season in shorebirds. In fall, Juv-HYs have uniformly juv rects (**A**) which are weaker and more pointed than basic rects found in AHYs at this time (**E**). Many HY/SYs can replace one or more rects during the PF, exhibiting mixed generations in fall-winter (**B-C**) and spring (**D**). Some SYs (including most that undergo a s.Hemisphere strategy and replace pp; Fig. 376, may) may exhibit completely formative rects in winter-spring, that resemble those of AHY/ASYs (**E**). Some ASYs may replace 1-2 central rects during the prealternate molt (**F**) and this may be a reliable criterion for age in most species, as rects are seldom if ever replaced during the PA1. Note that retained basic rects in spring ASYs (r3-r6 in **F**) are fresher and broader compared to retained juvenal rects in spring SYs (r4-r5 in **D**).

1981). However, most of these species can also replace outer primaries during eccentric preformative molts; thus, molting definitive-cycle ASY/ATYs typically cannot be reliably aged by shape and condition of the outer primaries, as basic and formative feathers are similar (Fig. 377**C-D**).

In many (especially smaller) species, some first-cycle SYs may attempt to breed whereas others remain to over-summer on non-breeding grounds. The prealternate molt and/or extent of alternate aspect obtained by these SYs are variable, tending to be greater in individuals migrating north, but usually not as complete as in definitive alternate ASYs. SYs remaining on non-breeding grounds in April-July are often characterized by having reduced or no alternate-plumage aspect. In larger species, some TYs and older individuals can also over-summer and typically obtain substantial but not full alternate aspect (*cf.* Johnson & Johnson 1983)

To age shorebirds in spring and summer it is best to first determine range of variation in the species' preformative molt and thus the different replacement patterns that can be exhibited by first-cycle SYs in the wings and tail (Figs. 375**A-D**, 376**A-D**, & 379**A-D**). Consider differences in the timing of flight-feather replacement during preformative, second prebasic, and definitive prebasic molts, and how this might affect feather wear. Be aware of over-summering strategies; e.g., in some species almost all first-cycle SYs exhibiting a s.Hemisphere molting strategy may remain to over-summer, not occurring in the n.Hemisphere at all. Lastly, realize that the information presented here may be incomplete, especially concerning species exhibiting s.Hemisphere strategies, and that our understanding of age-specific molt patterns is still developing.

PLOVERS *CHARADRIIDAE*

Thirteen species. Family characters include stout bodies, proportionally short bills, long wings, and moderately sturdy legs and feet with the hind toe usually absent but occasionally present (Fig. 373**A-B**, p. 500), and with slight to moderate webbing between the fore toes (Fig. 374**B-D**, p. 501). North American plovers have 10 functional primaries (p10 longest by 2-10 mm, when fully grown), 14-17 secondaries (including 3-5 tertials), and 12 rectrices. Ageing in most species can be accomplished through the first cycle (to SY and ASY), and sometimes into the second cycle (to TY and ATY) through the following winter or spring by molt limits and other plumage-aspect criteria (pp. 500-507). Sexes are similar in size (♀♀ slightly larger) but can be separated by definitive plumage-aspect characters in some species. In molting, most N.Am plovers exhibit the Complex Alternate Strategy (CAS; Fig 10**F**, pp. 13-16), although the Complex Basic Strategy (CBS; Fig. 10**B**) is exhibited by Killdeer (p. 530), and Black-bellied Plover may possibly exhibit a Simple Alternate Strategy (SAS). Among species, both n.Hemisphere and/or s.Hemisphere molt strategies are employed (Table 45, pp. 501-505). Age of first breeding is 1-2 years in smaller species (most *Charadrius*) and 2-3 years in larger species (most *Pluvialis*). See pp. 500-507 for further information on molt and ageing in shorebirds.

BLACK-BELLIED PLOVER

Pluvialis squatarola

BBPL
Species # 2700
Band size: 3B

Species—From golden-plovers and other shorebirds by larger size (Table 46, p. 511); bill stout (depth at distal end of nares 5.8-7.1 mm) and black; upperparts primarily gray to brownish gray with white rump; bases to ss (outer webs) and inner pp white, forming distinct wing stripe; rects white with narrow black bars (Fig. 380); underparts whitish to largely black by age and season (Fig. 381; *cf.* Fig. 386, p. 517); most underwing covs whitish to pale gray, contrasting with black axillars; legs and feet dark gray to blackish, with hind toe present but small (Fig. 373**B**, p. 500) and with moderate webbing between fore toes (Fig. 374**C-D**, p. 501). Beware occasional HYs (especially from Asian populations; see **Geographic variation**) with brownish and yellowish tinge to upperparts, which can resemble that of some golden-plovers.

Geographic variation—Considered monotypic here. Populations of N.Am (*"P.s. cynosurae"*) average slightly smaller, populations of ne.Asia (*"hypomela"*) and perhaps nw.AK average slightly larger, and populations of Wrangel I, Siberia (*"tomkovichi"*), may average shorter bills and tarsi than European populations but differences are slight. HYs of Asian populations may also average browner and more golden upperparts than other populations, and ASY ♂♂ of e.Asian populations may average brighter than N.Am populations which, in turn, average more contrasting than those of N.Am populations, but in all cases differences are slight and confounded by age-related variation. See Byrkjedal & Thompson (1998), Cramp & Simmons (1983), Dement'ev & Gladkov (1951c), Engelmoer & Roselaar (1998), Low (1938), Manning et al. (1956), Oberholser (1974), Peters (1934b), Portenko (1972), Thayer & Bangs (1914), Tomkovich & Serra (1999), and Vaurie (1964) for more information.

Molt—CAS (SAS?). PF partial-incomplete (Sep-Jan/May in HY/SYs), PA1 absent-limited? (Mar-May in SYs), PB2 complete (May-Sep in SYs), DPA partial (Feb-Apr in TYs), DPB incomplete-complete (Aug-Oct/Feb in ASY/ATYs). A PA1 may or may not occur regularly in this species (Howell & Pyle 2002), or a single inserted first-cycle molt may have resulted from a merging of the PF and PA1 in ancestral species (Fig. 10**D**, p. 16); study is needed. Molting occurs primarily on non-breeding grounds, although the DPB can commence (body feathers, occasionally 1-

5 inner pp) and the DPA can complete on breeding grounds or at stopover sites. Most individuals exhibit a n.Hemisphere molt strategy but some exhibit a s.Hemisphere strategy (Table 45, pp. 501-505). The PF includes some to most body feathers, no to most proximal s covs, and often 1-5 terts and 2-6 c.rects in Oct-Dec; in some individuals (primarily among those with non-breeding grounds in the s.Hemisphere) it can also include all rects and 1-10 inner, medial, or outer pp and p covs, and 1-7 medial ss (distal to the terts), in either typical or eccentric sequence and often arrested (Fig. 376**A-B**, **D**, p. 504), in Jan-May. Commencement of the PB2 can occasionally overlap the end of the PF such that two waves of pp are molting simultaneously (Fig. 376**C**). The DPB completes by Nov among most individuals but sometimes can suspend at p7-p9 and complete in Feb-Apr in the n.Hemisphere and it occurs in Oct-Feb in the s.Hemisphere. One to 5 ss (among s6-s11) and/or 1-6 rects (among r3-r6) can occasionally be retained during DPBs. The DPA includes some to most body feathers, up to 30% (♀) or 60% (♂) of the medial s covs, and often 1-3 terts and 1-2 (occasionally 3-4) c.rects; ♂♂ average more replaced feathers than ♀♀ by age. Many SYs and some TYs over-summer on non-breeding grounds (especially in the tropics and s.Hemisphere) and average less-complete PA1-PA2s and advanced PB2-PB3s (Balachandran et al. 2000, Serra et al. 1999; see p. 18). See pp. 500-507 for more information on molt in shorebirds

Age—Juv (B1; Jul-Sep) has uniformly fresh plumage aspect, back feathers washed brownish or yellowish, s covs, terts, and pp uniformly juv and fresh (Figs. 375**A**, p. 503, & 384**A**, p. 515), and underpart feathers small and with wide pale fringes (Fig. 381**A**, p. 510); Juv ♀=♂.

Juv-HY/SY (1st cycle, Juv/B1-F1/A1; Oct-Sep): Rects uniformly juv and narrow (Fig. 379**A**, p. 507), with indistinct or no dusky bars (Fig. 380**A-B**), sometimes mixed with fresher formative c.rects in Jan-Sep (Fig. 379**B-D**); s covs and terts uniformly juv in Oct-Nov (Fig. 375**A**), narrower with indistinct scalloping and broken fringes at tip (Fig. 384**A**, p. 515), contrasting with fresher formative scapulars, humerals, terts, and/or proximal s covs (Fig. 384**B**) in Nov-Mar (Figs. 375**B-C**), the juv distal gr covs usually retained and becoming worn and frayed by Apr-Sep (Fig. 375**D**); pp, p covs, and ss usually uniformly juv and without s1-p1 contrast or suspension limit (Fig. 375**A**), the juv outer pp and p covs tapered, brownish, and relatively abraded (Figs. 377**A-B** & 378**A-B**, p. 506); feathers of underparts with thin shaft streaks or broad fringes in Oct-Dec (Fig. 381**A**), to whitish with no to many partially blackish feathers in Apr-Sep (Fig. 381**A-C**). **Note: Most SYs remain on non-breeding grounds during the first summer. Those that over-summer in the**

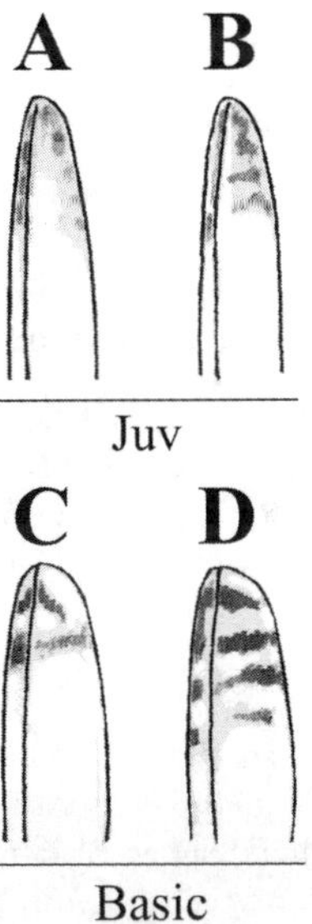

FIGURE 380. Outer rectrix (r6) by feather generation in Black-bellied Plover. The extent of barring shows variation in both juv (**A-B**) and basic (**C-D**) rects; among ASYs, ♀♀ may average less markings (**C**) than ♂♂ (**D**) but study is needed. In N.Am, the majority of HY/SYs retain juv outer rects (**A-B**) during the PF and can be aged by this feature. Those showing basic-like outer rects (**B-C**) in spring are likely ASYs but other criteria should be checked to confirm that they are not SYs that had replaced these during the PF. Most to all SYs that have replaced these feathers during the PF appear to remain on s.Hemisphere non-breeding grounds during boreal summer.

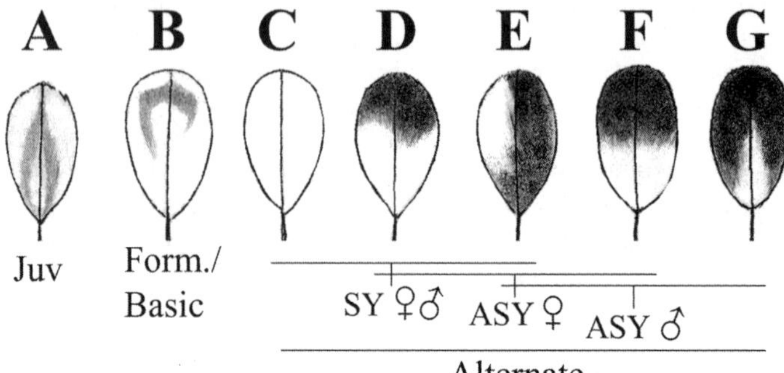

FIGURE 381. Relative size and patterns to the breast feathers by feather generation and sex in Black-bellied Plover and golden-plovers. Most to all juv feathers (**A**) are often replaced by formative feathers (**B**) by Jan-Feb, at which time SYs cannot be separated from ASYs by this character. For alternate feathers (**C-G**), pattern varies by position on the breast as well as age and sex, generally being blacker anteriorly and toward the center, especially in ♀♀. More study is needed on patterns to alternate feathers by age and sex in American Golden-Plover (p. 512). Note that SYs and ♀♀ also can retain faded basic feathers mixed with these variably-colored alternate feathers and that, in Black-bellied Plover, the PF and PA1 may be merged (see text).

s.Hemisphere can also exhibit replacement of all rects (Fig. 379E) and some to most pp and ss in typical or eccentric patterns (Fig. 376A-B, D; see Molt).

AHY/ASY (Def. cycle, DB-DA; Oct-Sep): Rects uniformly basic and broad (Fig. 379**E**) with more distinct black bars (Fig. 380**C-D**), occasionally with 1-4 fresher alternate c.rects in Mar-Sep (Fig. 379**F**); s covs and terts uniformly basic in Oct-Feb (Fig. 375**E**), the basic s covs broader and with more distinct scalloping and complete pale fringing at tip (Fig. 384**C**), mixed with fresh alternate feathers (Fig. 384**D**) in Mar-Sep (Figs. 375**F**); pp, p covs, and ss usually uniformly basic, sometimes with s1-p1 contrast (Fig. 375**E**) and/or occasionally with suspension limit among p1-p5 (Fig. 376**F**, p. 504), the outer pp and p covs broad, dusky, and relatively fresh (Figs. 377**C-D** & 378**C-D**); feathers of underparts with dusky chevrons in Oct-Mar (Fig. 381**B**; occasionally one or more feathers show black), mixed with some to all, partially to entirely black feathers by sex in Apr-Sep (Fig. 381**D-G**). **Note: See Juv-HY/SY. Over-summering AHY/ASYs with basic flight feathers and showing reduced alternate-plumage aspect in Apr-Aug can possibly be aged TY; more study needed.**

ASY/ATY (Def. cycle, DB-DA; Oct-Sep): Like AHY/ASY but 1-5 ss (among s3-s4 and s9-s11) and/or 1-4 rects (among r3-r5) occasionally retained (Figs. 14**C**, p. 21, & 17**D**, p. 26); underparts with one or more blackish feathers in Nov-Mar. **Note: Only a small proportion of individuals can be reliably aged ASY/ATY.**

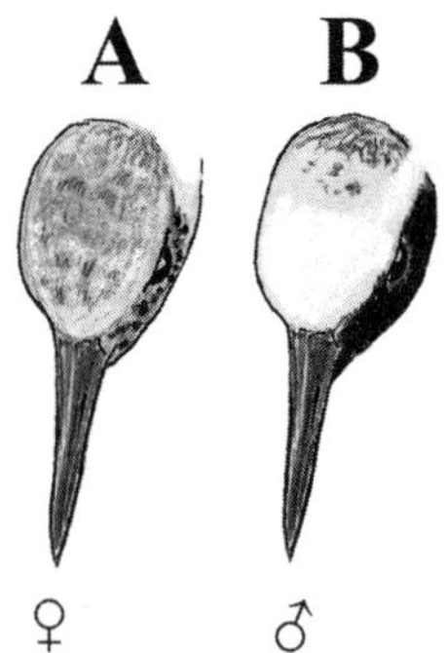

FIGURE 382. Crown pattern by sex in alternate-aspect (Apr-Aug) ASY Black-bellied Plovers. Some SY ♂♂ may be reliably sexed by showing mottled white foreheads or black lores; SY ♀♀ are not reliably sexed.

Sex—Bilateral BPs (Fig. 20**B**, p. 31) developed by both sexes but distended cloaca (Fig. 21, p. 32) indicates ASY ♀ in May-Jul. Measurements unhelpful for sexing (Table 46). The following is reliable for sexing most or all ASYs in Apr-Aug; HY/SYs and AHYs in Nov-Mar are not reliably sexed although some SY ♂♂ may be identifiable (*cf.* Fig. 382); further study needed.

ASY ♀ (Apr-Aug): Crown with brownish-gray mottling, and auriculars, throat, and breast with whitish and mixed blackish-and-white feathers (Figs. 381**B-F** & 382**A**; *cf.* Fig. 386, p. 517). **Note: On molting individuals check alternate feathers only, incoming and fresh in Mar-Apr or worn in Aug-Sep. See also Figure 380 (p. 509) for possible sex-specific differences in pattern to basic rects.**

ASY ♂ (Mar-Sep): Crown white, and auriculars, throat, and breast with black to extensively black feathers (Figs. 381**E-G** & 382**B**; *cf.* Fig. 386). **Note: See ASY ♀. Some ASY ♂♂ in the s.Hemisphere might be reliably sexed through Oct-Dec; more study is needed.**

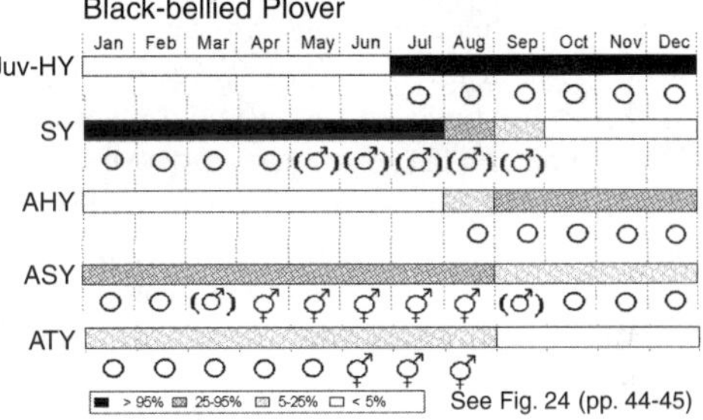

Hybrids reported—With European Golden-Plover *P. apricaria* (Kusters 1991).

References—Balachandran et al. (2000), Bent (1929), Byrkjedal & Thompson (1998), Cramp & Simmons (1983), Dement'ev & Gladkov (1951c), Dwight (1900b), Engelmoer & Roselaar (1998), Harrison (1980), Howell & Pyle (2002), Jukema et al. (2003), Loftin (1962), MacKay (1892), Marchant & Higgins (1993), McNeil (1970), Minton & Serra (2001), Oberholser (1974), Palmer (1967b), Paulson (1995), Pearson & Serra (2002), Prater et al. (1977), Ridgway (1919), Roberts (1955), Serra (2001), Serra & Rusticali (1998), Serra et al. (1999), Stone (1900), Todd (1916a).

TABLE 46. Measurements (mm) of North American *Pluvialis* plovers for identification and sexing. See pp. 4-11 for methods of measurement. Species summaries are in **bold**. Values were derived from 95% confidence intervals as based approximately on the indicated sample sizes (see pp. 4-5). Thus, midpoints of ranges approximate means, and S.D. is approximated by 25% of the range.

Taxon/Sex	*n*	wing chord	tail length	exposed culmen	tarsus
Black-bellied Plover[1]		**179-208**	**60-81**	**26.1-34.2**	**41-52**
♀	100	179-208	60-78	26.1-33.4	41-51
♂	100	179-208	62-81	26.9-34.2	42-52
American Golden-Plover		**168-183**	**57-73**	**19.8-25.8**	**38-47**
♀	60	168-183	57-72	19.8-25.4	38-45
♂	60	168-182	59-73	20.1-25.8	40-47
Pacific Golden-Plover		**154-171**	**54-69**	**21.0-27.6**	**40-49**
♀	100	154-170	54-68	21.0-27.2	40-47
♂	100	155-171	55-69	21.3-27.6	42-49

[1] Measures from N.Am populations only; see **Geographic variation**.

AMERICAN GOLDEN-PLOVER
Pluvialis dominica

AMGP
Species # 2720
Band size: 2-3

Species—From Black-bellied Plover (p. 508) and other N.Am shorebirds by medium-large size (Table 46, p. 511); bill moderately stout (depth at distal end of nares 4.5-5.4 mm) and blackish; upperparts washed brownish, with variable gold, and without white rump; bases to ss and inner pp with little or no whitish, forming very indistinct wing stripe; rects brownish with narrow buff to gold bars (Fig. 385, p. 516); underparts pale without breast band, or primarily black to blackish in ASYs in Mar-Aug (Figs. 381, p. 510, & 386, p. 517); underwing covs and axillars uniformly grayish; legs and feet gray, with hind toe absent (Fig. 373**A**, p. 500) and with small webbing between outer fore toes (Fig. 374**B**, p. 501). European Golden-Plover (*P. apricaria*), a vagrant to N.Am, has longer wing and tail but shorter tarsus (wg 173-197, tl 65-82, exp culmen 20.7-25.6, tarsus 38-43); bases to outer webs of proximal pp white (*vs* grayish in N.Am golden-plovers); underwing covs and axillars uniformly white to whitish; undertail covs and flanks white or mottled white in Apr-Aug (*vs* black in many American and some Pacific golden-plovers (*cf.* Fig. 386), but beware of molting individuals, SYs, and ♀♀.

American Golden-Plover from Pacific Golden-Plover (p. 515), with caution, by larger average size, especially wing chord (Table 46; also, maximum flattened wing 176-192); wing-tip morphology averages longer (Table 47, Fig. 383**A-B**); breast with little or no yellow wash in Sep-Mar; rump with gold spotting, contrasting with grayer spotting on back; ASY ♂♂ (and ♀♀ to a lesser extent) in Apr-Jul with undertail covs and flanks and sides (ventral to folded wing in natural position) black (*cf.* Fig. 386), and white stripe on breast wider (♀ 15-20 mm, ♂ 18-30 mm wide at bend of wing) but not extending to flanks (ventral to folded wing). See also **Molt** and Figure 11**D-E** (p. 17) for species-specific differences that may be helpful, especially in winter and spring. See Johnson & Johnson (2004a, 2004b) for information on other characters showing average inter-specific differences, and Barter (1988), Byrkjedal & Thompson (1998), Conover (1945a), Connors (1983), Connors et al. (1993), Cramp & Simmons (1983), Dunn et al. (1987), Evanich (1989), Golley & Stoddart (1991), Jaramillo (2004), Marchant & Higgins (1993), Ridgway (1919), and Roselaar (1990) for additional information.

Geographic variation—Monotypic. Breeding populations of AK average shorter wings and tarsi but longer bills than those of Canada (Johnson & Johnson 2004a, 2004b; Vaurie 1964), but differences are slight and broadly clinal.

TABLE 47. Wing-tip structure in American and Pacific golden-plovers to assist with identification. See also Figure 383. Measures taken from 100 specimens, 25 of each species/age group. Beware that measures from specimens may not reflect those of wild birds, exactly, due to variable prepartion methods. Values were derived from 95% confidence intervals; thus, midpoints of ranges approximate means, and S.D. is approximated by 25% of the range.

	# of pp > terts[1] Age		p projection[2] Age		wing tip-tail tip[3] Age	
	1st-yr	adult	1st-yr	adult	1st-yr	adult
American	4-5(5.2)	4-5(4.7)	42-62	32-52	10-19	14-22
Pacific	3-4(4.2)	3-4(3.6)	20-48	16-38	-1 to 6	4-11

[1] The number of primary tips beyond the longest tertial tip (range and mean presented). See also Figure 383. This includes p10, the tip of which which can sometimes be hidden behind p9 in the field. Beware that the longest tert may often be in molt, and that those of differing generations (juv, formative, basic, alternate; cf. Fig. 384, p. 515) may extend to different lengths, affecting this value.

[2] The distance between the tip of the wing to the tip of the longest tertial (Fig. 383).

[3] The distance from the tip of the wing to the tip of the tail. Note that this value may be the most affected by variation in specimen preparation (Fig. 383).

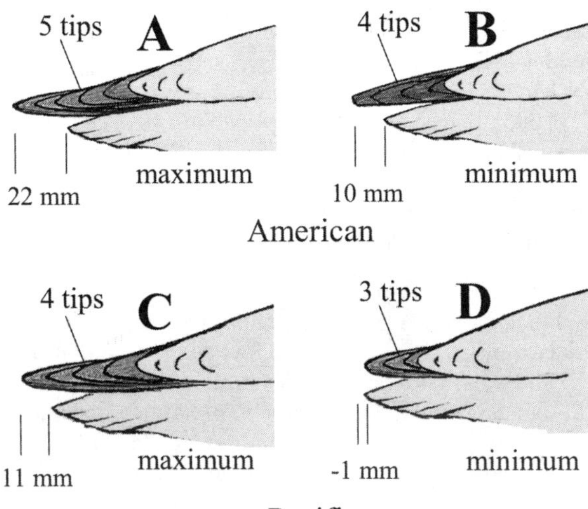

FIGURE 383. Wing-tip structure in American and Pacific golden-plovers for identification. Values indicate number of primary tips beyond tip of largest tertial and tip of wing to tip of tail in natural position; note that the number of primary tips extending beyond the tip of the longest tertial is confounded by feather generation and molt. Note also that the tip of p10 can sometimes be hidden behind p9. Generally, minimum values are found on HY/SYs and maximum values are found on AHY/ASYs (Table 47); see Figure 384 (p. 515) for differences in tertial pattern by feather generation.

Molt—CAS. PF complete (Oct-Mar/May in HY/SYs), PA1 limited-partial (Apr-Jun in SYs), DPB complete (Jul-Mar in AHY/ASYs), DPA partial (Mar-Jun in ASYs). See Figure 11**D** (p. 17). The PF and DPB can commence (body feathers only) on breeding grounds but occur primarily on non-breeding grounds, and the DPA occurs primarily at stopover sites but can complete on breeding grounds. Molt follows a s.Hemisphere strategy (Table 45, pp. 501-505). Occasional individuals may retain some medial ss (among s5-s10) during the PF or DPB (Fig. 14**C**, p. 21); more study is needed. DPAs include some to most body feathers, up to 90% of the s covs, often 1-5 terts, and sometimes 1-2 (occasionally 3-4) c.rects; ♂♂ replace more feathers than ♀♀ (e.g., up to 40% of the s covs in ♀♀ and up to 90% in ♂♂). Some SYs may over-summer on non-breeding grounds or at stopover sites and exhibit less-complete (or no) PA1s and advanced PB2s (see p. 18); more study is needed. See pp. 500-507 for more information on molt in shorebirds.

A limited DPS, including some underpart feathers on breeding grounds, has been reported (Byrkjedal & Thompson 1998, Jukema & Piersma 1987, Jukema et al. 2003). Alternatively, it is possible that replacement of these feathers at this time represents the beginning of the DPB (Johnson & Connors 1996) or the end of the DPA, with aspect changes varying individually and correlating with the timing of replacement (see p. 29 and Long-tailed Duck); more study is needed.

Age—Juv (B1; Jul-Oct) has uniformly fresh plumage aspect, the s covs, terts, and pp uniformly juv and fresh (Figs. 375**A**, p. 503, & 384**A**, p. 515), and the underpart feathers small and with wide pale fringes or thin shaft streaks (Fig. 381**A**, p. 510); Juv ♀=♂. See Johnson (1973, 1977) and Johnson & Johnson (1983) for information on ageing golden-plovers by bursa (Fig. 23, p. 34).

Juv-HY/SY (1st cycle, Juv/B1-F1-A1; Oct-May): Rects uniformly juv and narrow (Fig. 379**A**, p. 507), with indistinct or no pale bars by sex (Fig. 385**A-C**, p. 516), mixed with some to all fresher formative rects in Jan-May (Fig. 379**B-D**); s covs and terts uniformly juv in Oct-Nov

(Fig. 375**A**), narrower with indistinct scalloping and broken fringes at tip (Fig. 384**A**), contrasting with some to all fresher formative scapulars, humerals, terts, and/or proximal s covs (Fig. 384**B**) in Nov-May (Figs. 375**B**-**C**); pp, p covs, and ss juv and without s1-p1 contrast (Fig. 375**A**), the juv outer pp and p covs tapered, brownish, and relatively abraded (Figs. 377**A**-**B** & 378**A**-**B**, p. 506), being completely replaced in Dec-May; feathers of underparts with thin shaft streaks or broad fringes in Oct-Dec (Fig. 381**A**). **Note: It is possible that some SYs can be aged in Jun-Sep by less extensive alternate feathering (*cf.* Fig. 375F & 379F), more mottled underpart plumage aspect by sex (Fig. 381A-E), and/or the retention of juv ss in some individuals (Fig. 14C, p. 21) but further study is needed; see also AHY/ASY.**

AHY/ASY (Def. cycle, DB-DA; May-Apr): Rects uniformly basic and broad (Fig. 379**E**) with more distinct whitish bars by sex (Fig. 385**D**-**F**); s covs and terts uniformly basic (Fig. 375**E**-**F**), the s covs broader and with more distinct scalloping and complete pale fringing at tip (Fig. 384**C**), mixed with fresher alternate terts and s covs (Fig. 384**D**); pp, p covs, and ss basic, worn, with s1-p1 contrast, and mixed with alternate feathers in May-Dec (Fig. 375**E**-**F**), being replaced in Aug-Mar, the outer pp and p covs broad and dusky (Figs. 377**C**-**D** & 378**C**-**D**); feathers of underparts with dusky chevrons (Fig. 381**B**). **Note: See Juv-HY/SY. It is possible that some ASYs can be aged in Jun-Sep by more extensive alternate feathering (*cf.* Fig. 375F & 379F), blacker underpart plumage aspect by sex (Fig. 381E-G), and/or the retention of basic ss in some individuals (Fig. 14D) but further study is needed.**

Sex—Bilateral BPs (Fig. 20**B**, p. 31) developed by both sexes but distended cloaca (Fig. 21, p. 32) indicates ♀ in May-Jul. Measurements unhelpful for sexing (Table 46, p. 511). The following is reliable for some (Aug-Apr) to most (May-Jul) AHYs only; many intermediates occur that cannot be sexed by plumage aspect alone, and HY/SYs are probably not reliably sexed in Oct-Apr

AHY/ASY ♀ (May-Apr): Basic rects with indistinct barring (Fig. 385**D**-**E**, p. 516); auriculars, throat, and breast with many whitish or mixed blackish-and-white alternate feathers in Jun-Aug (Figs. 381**B**-**F**, p. 510, & *cf.* Fig. 386, p. 517). **Note: Use caution in sexing ♀♀ by plumage aspect in May-Sep as some SY ♂♂ may be similar; more study is needed.**

AHY/ASY ♂ (May-Apr): Basic rects with distinct barring (Fig. 385**E**-**F**); auriculars, throat, and breast with extensively black alternate feathers in May-Sep (Figs. 381**E**-**G**; *cf.* Fig. 386).

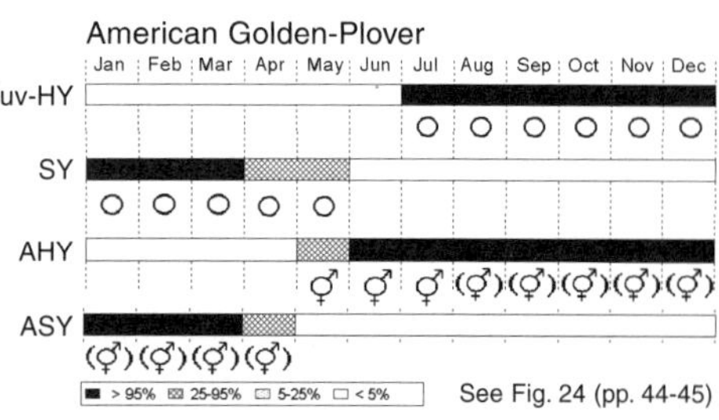

Hybrids reported—Possibly with Pacific Golden-Plover (Connors 1983, Johnson & Johnson 2004b, O'Brien et al. 2006) and Golden Plover *P. apricaria* (Borg 1976).

References—Barter (1988), Barter & Davidson (1990), Bent (1929), Byrkjedal & Thompson (1998), Connors (1983), Cramp & Simmons (1983), Dement'ev & Gladkov (1951c), Dwight (1900b), Henshaw (1910), Iliff et al. (2007), Jackson (1919), Johnson (1973, 1977, 1979, 1985), O.W. Johnson & Connors (1996), Johnson & Johnson (1983), Johnston & MacFarlane (1967), Jukema et al. (2003), Kinsky & Yaldwyn (1981), Marchant & Higgins (1993), Oberholser (1974), Palmer (1967b), Paulson & Lee (1992), Portenko (1972), Prater et al. (1977), Ridgway (1919), Roberts (1955), Sauer (1962), Stone (1900), Stresemann & Stresemann (1966).

PACIFIC GOLDEN-PLOVER PAGP
Pluvialis dominica Species # 2721
Band size: 2-3

Species—See American Golden-Plover (p. 512) for separation from other plovers. From American Golden-Plover, with caution, by smaller average size, especially wing chord (Table 46, p. 511; also, maximum flattened wing 163-180); wing morphology averages shorter (Table 47, p. 512; Fig. 383**C-D**, p. 513); breast usually washed yellow in Sep-Mar; spots on rump and back uniformly gold; ASY ♂♂ (and ♀♀ to a lesser extent) in Apr-Jul with undertail covs white or mottled white (*cf.* Fig. 386), and white stripe on breast narrower (♀ 7-14, ♂ 10-18 at bend of wing) but extending to flanks (below folded wing). See American Golden-Plover for additional information and references.

Geographic variation—Monotypic. Populations of w.AK average larger (except in wing length) than those of n.AK (Johnson & Johnson 2004a, 2004b; Vaurie 1964), but differences are slight and broadly clinal.

Molt—CAS. PF partial-incomplete (Sep-Dec/Mar in HY/SYs), PA1 limited-partial (Mar-May in SYs), PB2 complete (Jun-Oct in non-breeding SYs), DPA partial (Feb-Apr in ASYs), DPB complete (Jul-Oct/Feb in AHY/ASYs). See Figure 11**E** (p. 17). Molting occurs primarily on non-breeding grounds, although the DPB can commence (body feathers, occasionally 1-4 inner pp) and the DPA can complete on breeding grounds or at stopover sites. Molt generally follows a n.Hemisphere strategy (Table 45, pp. 501-505), although the DPB is protracted in individuals that migrate to the s.Hemisphere. The PF includes some to all body feathers, no to most proximal s covs, and often 1-5 terts and 1 to (occasionally) all 12 c.rects, but few if any pp, p covs, or ss (other than terts); body feathers are replaced primarily in Sep-Nov whereas some s covs, terts, and rects can be replaced in Jan-Mar. The DPA includes up to 40% of the s covs, often 1-4 terts, and occasionally 1-2 c.rects; ♂♂ replace more feathers than ♀♀ (e.g., up to 15% of the s covs in ♀♀ and up to 40% in ♂♂). Many SYs (and some TYs?) over-summer on non-breeding grounds and exhibit less-complete (or no) PA1s and advanced PB2s (Johnson & Johnson 1983; see p. 18). Occasional individuals with non-breeding grounds farther S may exhibit a

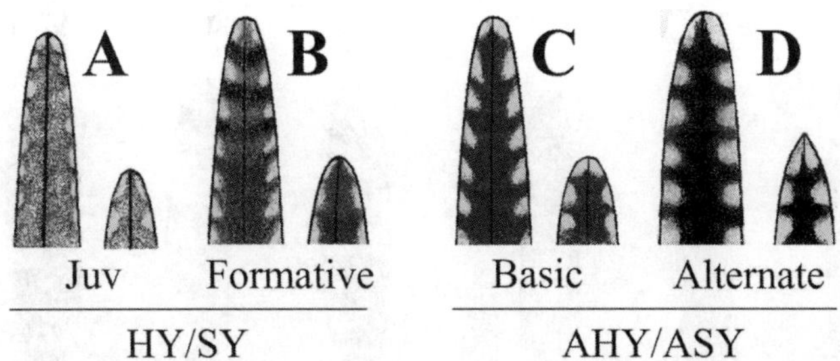

FIGURE 384. Shape and pattern to the tertials (left) and s covs (right) by feather generation in golden-plovers; Black-bellied Plover shows similar but often more distinct patterns by generation. HY/SYs have juv feathers (**A**) in fall but can replace some to all terts and some to most s covs with formative feathers (**B**) in Oct-Mar (Fig. 375**B-D**); American Golden-plover has a complete preformative molt, after which ages cannot be distingished; formative and basic feathers are probably too similar to reliably distinguish. AHY/ASYs exhibit mixed basic (**C**) and fresher alternate (**D**) feathers in Mar-Oct, and uniformly basic feathers (**D**) in Oct-Mar. Beware that formative, basic, and alternate feathers can show variation in patterns, depending on the timing of molts (p. 29).

s.Hemisphere molting strategy (pp. 501-505); more study is needed. See American Golden-Plover (p. 512) for information on a possible DPS in golden-plovers and pp. 500-507 for more information on molt in shorebirds.

Age—Juv (B1; Jul-Sep) has uniformly fresh plumage aspect, the s covs, terts, and pp uniformly juv and fresh (Figs. 375**A**, p. 503, & 384**A**, p. 515), and the underpart feathers small and with wide pale fringes or thin shaft streaks (Fig. 381**A**, p. 510); Juv ♀=♂. See O.W. Johnson (1973, 1977) and Johnson & Johnson (1983) for information on ageing by the bursa (Fig. 23, p. 34).

Juv-HY/SY (1st cycle, Juv/B1-F1-A1; Oct-Sep): Rects uniformly juv and narrow (Fig. 379**A**, p. 507), with indistinct or no pale bars by sex (Fig. 385**A-C**), often mixed with fresher formative c.rects in Jan-Sep (Fig. 379**B-D**; occasional individuals replace all rects by Mar); s covs and terts uniformly juv in Oct-Nov (Fig. 375**A**), narrower with indistinct gold scalloping and broken fringes at tip (Fig. 384**A**), contrasting with fresher formative scapulars, humerals, terts, and/or proximal s covs in Nov-Mar (Figs. 375**B-C** & Fig. 384**B**), the retained, juv distal gr covs becoming worn and frayed by Apr-Sep (Fig. 375**D**); pp, p covs, and ss uniformly juv and without s1-p1 contrast or suspension limit (Fig. 375**A**), the juv outer pp and p covs tapered, brownish, and relatively abraded (Figs. 377**A-B** & 378**A-B**, p. 506); feathers of underparts with thin shaft streaks or broad fringes in Oct-Dec (Fig. 381**A**), mixed with whitish to a few partially blackish feathers in Apr-Sep (Fig. 381**A-C**). **Note: Many SYs and some TYs remain on non-breeding grounds during the first summer (see p. 18)**.

AHY/ASY (Def. cycle, DB-DA; Oct-Sep): Rects uniformly basic and broad (Fig. 379**E**) with more distinct white bars by sex (Fig. 385**D-F**), occasionally with 1-2 fresher alternate c.rects in Mar-Sep (Fig. 379**F**); s covs and terts uniformly basic in Oct-Feb (Fig. 375**E**), the basic s covs broader and with more distinct lemon to whitish scalloping and complete pale fringing at tip (Fig. 384**C**), worn and mixed with fresher alternate feathers in Mar-Sep (Figs. 375**F** & Fig. 384**D**); pp, p covs, and ss uniformly basic, being replaced in Aug-Oct/Feb, sometimes with s1-p1 contrast (Fig. 375**E**) and/or occasionally with suspension limit among p1-p4 (Fig. 376**F**, p. 504), the outer pp and p covs broad, dusky, and relatively fresh (Figs. 377**C-D** & 378**C-D**); feathers of underparts with dusky chevrons in Oct-Mar (Fig. 381**B**;

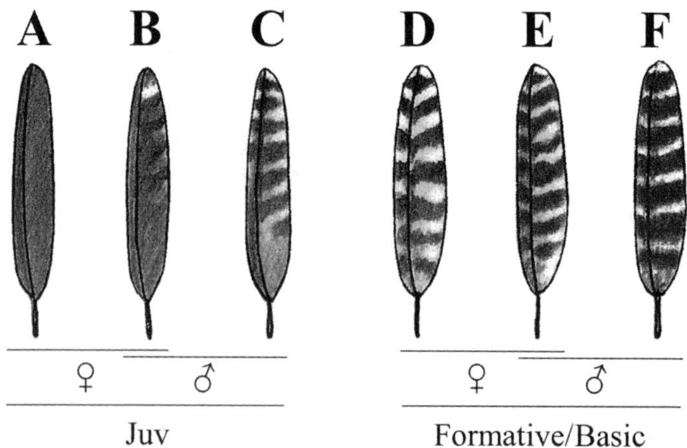

FIGURE 385. Pattern to the outer rectrix (r6) by age and sex in golden-plovers. Most (~80%) of Pacific Golden-Plovers retain the juv r6 until the 2nd PB (Jun-Aug in SYs) whereas in American Golden-Plover this feather is replaced during the complete PF by Mar-Apr, after which this species no longer can be reliably aged.

occasionally one or more feathers show black), mixed with some to all, partially to entirely black feathers by sex in Mar-Sep (Figs. 381**D-G** & 386). **Note: See Juv-HY/SY. Over-summering AHY/ASYs with basic flight feathers, showing reduced alternate-plumage aspect in Apr-Aug, and commencing p molt in Jun-Jul, might be reliably aged TY but more study is needed.**

SY/TY (2nd cycle, B2; Oct-Feb): Like AHY/ASY with molt of pp occurring, but outer pp and p covs juv, very pointed, and abraded (Fig. 376**E**). **Note: These typically include individuals in s.Hemisphere non-breeding areas only and may be uncommon.**

ASY/ATY (Def. cycle, DB-DA; Oct-Feb): Like AHY/ASY, with molt of pp occurring, and outer pp and p covs broad and only moderately worn (*cf.* Fig. 376**E**). **Note: See SY/TY.**

Sex—Bilateral BPs (Fig. 20**B**, p. 31) developed by both sexes but distended cloaca (Fig. 21, p. 32) indicates ♀ in May-Jul. Measurements unhelpful for sexing (Table 46, p. 511). The following is reliable for some AHY/ASYs only; many intermediates occur that cannot be sexed by plumage aspect alone, and HY/SYs (except perhaps some ♂♂) are not reliably sexed.

AHY/ASY ♀: Basic rects with indistinct barring (Fig. 385**D-E**); auriculars, throat, and breast with many whitish or mixed blackish-and-white, alternate feathers in May-Jul (Figs. 381**B-F**,p. 510 & *cf.* Fig. 386).

AHY/ASY ♂: Basic rects with distinct barring (Fig. 385**E-F**); auriculars, throat, and breast with extensively black alternate feathers in Apr-Aug (Figs. 381**E-G** & *cf.* Fig. 386).

Hybrids reported—Possibly with American Golden-Plover (p. 512).

References—See American Golden-Plover (p. 512).

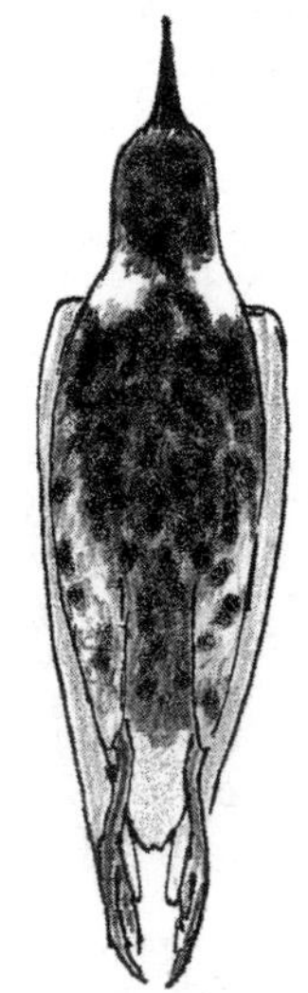

FIGURE 386. Extent of blackish to underparts on a hypothetical Pacific Golden-Plover to aid in sex determination. ASY ♀♀ typically show less black whereas ASY ♂♂ typically show more black than this illustration depicts. American Golden-Plover and Black-bellied Plover show similar sex-specific patterns but Black-bellied Plover (as well as European Golden-Plover) shows more extensive white to the lower belly and flanks, and American Golden-Plover shows more black to the undertail coverts. SY Pacific Golden-Plovers and Black-bellied Plovers typically cannot be sexed by underpart plumage aspect (except perhaps a few SY ♂♂) whereas SY American Golden-Plovers may resemble ASYs and be reliably sexed; more study is needed on variation in alternate aspect in American.

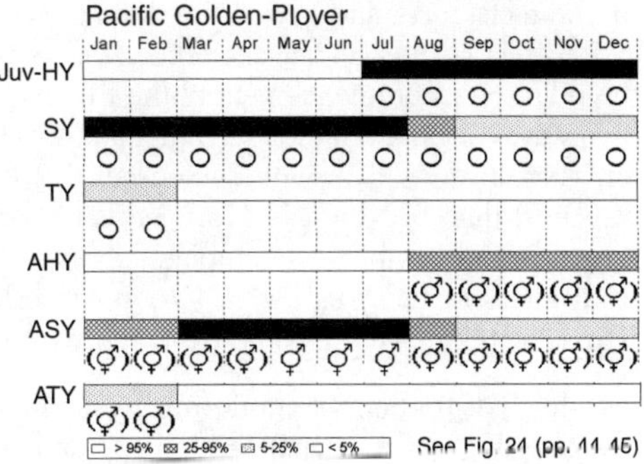

LESSER SAND-PLOVER LSAP
Charadrius mongolus Species # 2790
Band size: 3

Species—From other N.Am plovers and shorebirds by medium size with proportionally long wings (Table 48, p. 527), bill moderately stout (depth at tip of forehead feathers 5.3-6.5); upperparts grayish brown without pale or white hind-neck collar; throat white, contrasting with diffuse brownish band across breast (incomplete or complete and narrowing in center) in Sep-Mar; ASYs with breast and nape rufous in Apr-Jul; legs and feet usually blackish, with hind toe absent (Fig. 373**A**, p. 501) and with slight to moderate webbing between outer fore toes (Fig. 374**B**-**C**, p. 501).

Greater Sand-Plover (*C. leschenaulti*), a vagrant to w.N.Am, averages larger and has longer bill and tarsus (wg chord 132-151, tail 49-56, exp culmen 21.3-27.0, tarsus 34-40); bill more pointed and with larger nail (10-13 mm *vs* 6-10 mm in Lesser Sand-Plover); plumage aspect averages paler; legs usually dull olive to pinkish. See Abbott et al. (2001), Hirschfeld et al. (2000), and Taylor (1982) for more information.

Geographic variation—See Barter (1991), Cramp & Simmons (1983), Dement'ev & Gladkov (1951c), Hirschfeld et al. (2000), Lane (1986), Marchant & Higgins (1993), Portenko (1972), Prater et al. (1977), Taylor (1982). Four other subspecies occur in Eurasia.

Siberian (*C.m. mongolius*) Group. Wing relatively long and bill and tarsus relatively short; wing/exposed culmen usually > 7.7 *vs* < 7.7 in the West Asian (*C.m. atrifrons*) Group; exp culmen/bill depth at gonys < 3.8 (*vs* > 3.8 in the West Asian Group); white patch on forehead prominent and throat bordered with thin black band in Apr-Jul.

C.m. stegmanni (br w.AK): Wing averages longer, tarsus averages shorter (Table 48, p. 527), and exp culmen/bill depth at gonys averages smaller (3.0-3.5 *vs* 3.3-3.8) than *mongolus* of w.Siberia; plumage aspect averages darker; head with thicker black bands (by sex) in Apr-Jul. Vagrants to OR-CA to NJ-LA have not been critically identified to subspecies but are likely of the Siberian Group and *stegmanni*.

Molt—CAS. PF partial-incomplete (Oct-Jan/May in HY/SYs), PA1 absent(?)-limited (Mar-May in SYs), PB2 complete (Jun-Nov in non-breeding SYs), DPA partial (Apr-May in ASYs), DPB complete (Sep-Apr in breeding AHY/ASYs). Molting occurs primarily on non-breeding grounds, although the DPB can commence (body feathers, occasionally 1-3 inner pp) and the DPA usually completes on breeding grounds or at stopover sites. The Siberian Group (see **Geographic variation**) exhibits a s.Hemisphere strategy. The PF includes most to all body feathers, some proximal s covs, 1-3 terts, and 2-6 c.rects in Oct-Dec, usually followed by the rest of the rects, terts, and s covs (the distal gr covs usually retained), 2-8 outer pp and p covs, and 1-7 medial ss in eccentric sequence (Fig. 376**A**-**B**); sometimes arrested) in Dec-Jun. In non-breeding SYs, commencement of the PB2 can occasionally overlap the end of the PF such that two waves of pp are molting simultaneously (Fig. 376**C**). The DPA includes some body feathers, few if any s covs, and sometimes 1-2 terts or c.rects; ♂♂ may average more feathers replaced than ♀♀ by age. Most SYs and possibly some TYs over-summer on non-breeding grounds and exhibit less-complete (or no) PA1-PA2s and advanced PB2-PB3s (see p. 18). Individuals of the West Asian Group can exhibit a n.Hemisphere strategy (Balachandran & Hussain 1998). See pp. 500-507 for more information.

Age—Juv (B1; Jul-Sep) has uniformly fresh plumage aspect, the upperpart feathers with thin buff fringing (Fig. 387**A**, p. 520), and the pp and ss uniformly juv and fresh (Fig. 375**A**, p. 503); Juv ♀ = ♂. The following refers to N.Am populations (*C.m. stegmanni*):

Juv-HY/SY (1st cycle, Juv/B1-F1-A1; Oct-Sep): All to some upperpart feathers (Oct-Dec), terts, and/or distal s covs juv, with broader pale fringing when fresh (Fig. 387**A-B**), contrasting with fresher formative scapulars, humerals, terts, and proximal s covs (Fig. 375**B-C**), the juv distal gr covs usually retained and becoming worn and frayed by Apr-Sep (Fig. 375**D**); pp, p covs, and ss juv, fresh, and without s1-p1 contrast in Oct-Dec (Fig. 375**A**), usually being incompletely replaced in Dec-May and exhibiting eccentric replacement patterns in May-Sep (Fig. 376**A-C**), and being completely replaced in Jun-Nov, the juv outer pp and p covs (if present) tapered (Figs. 377**A-B** & 378**A-B**, p. 506); rects uniformly juv and narrow in Oct-Dec (Fig. 379**A**, p. 507), mixed with formative rects in Dec-Mar (Fig. 379**B-C**) and sometimes in Apr-Sep (Fig. 379**D**); forehead without blackish (*cf.* Fig. 391**A**, p. 525), and breast with no to a small amount of rufous mottling in Feb-Aug. **Note: Most SYs remain on non-breeding grounds during the first summer.**

AHY/ASY (Def. cycle, DB-DA; Oct-Sep): Upperpart feathers, terts, and s covs uniformly basic (Fig. 375**E**), the basic feathers broader and with thin or no pale fringing (Fig. 387**C**); pp, p covs, and ss worn and being completely replaced in Oct-Apr, or basic, fresh, and with replacement clines and s1-p1 contrast in Jan-Sep (Fig. 375**E**), the outer pp and p covs broad and truncate (Figs 377**C-D** & 378**C-D**); rects uniformly basic and broader (Fig. 379**E**); forehead with blackish (*cf.* Fig. 391**B-D**) and breast with an extensive amount of rufous in Feb-Sep (occasionally to Nov). **Note: See Juv-HY/SY. Over-summering individuals with basic flight feathers, showing reduced alternate-plumage aspect in Apr-Aug, and commencing p molt in Jun Jul, might bc rcliably aged TY but more study is needed.**

Sex—Bilateral BPs (Fig. 20**B**, p. 31) are presumably developed by both sexes but distended cloaca (Fig. 21, p. 32) indicates ♀ in May-Jul. Measurements unhelpful for sexing (Table 48, p. 527). The following is reliable for many but not all N.Am individuals (*C.m. stegmanni*); many intermediates cannot be reliably sexed. The sexes are more reliably separated in the West Asian (*atrifrons*) Group. Some SY ♂♂ in Apr-Aug and AHY/ASY ♂♂ in Oct-Mar may be identifiable by the presence of blackish in the face and lores (more study needed); otherwise, HY/SYs and AHY/ASYs in Sep-Mar cannot be reliably sexed by plumage aspect.

ASY ♀ (Apr-Aug): Forehead band and auriculars brownish or mixed brown, cinnamon, and blackish (*cf.* Fig. 391**B-C**, p. 525); rufous of nape usually absent and that of breast often reduced and/or mottled with pale cinnamon or whitish.

ASY ♂ (Mar-Sep): Forehead band and auriculars complctcly black (*cf.* Fig. 391**D**); rufous of nape usually present and that of breast usually extensive and without whitish mottling.

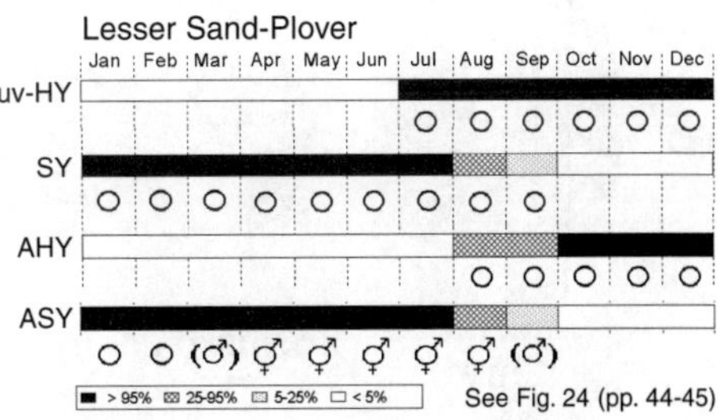

Hybrids reported—None.

References—Abbott et al. (2001), Barter (1991), Bent (1929), Cramp & Simmons (1983), Dement'ev & Gladkov (1951c), Marchant & Higgins (1993), Palmer (1967b), Prater et al. (1977), Ridgway (1919), Stejneger (1885).

SNOWY PLOVER
Charadrius alexandrinus

SNPL
Species # 2780
Band size: 1P

Species—From other N.Am plovers and shorebirds by small size, especially wing length (Table 48, p. 527), bill thin (depth at tip of forehead feathers 4.0-5.1; Fig. 388) and black; exp culmen usually > middle toe without claw; upperparts pale brown to grayish with pale to whitish hindneck collar (sometimes thin or indistinct); white of forehead contiguous with white supercilium (Figs. 388 & 389); sides of breast with brownish-gray to black marks, not connecting across breast (Fig. 388); legs and feet grayish, sometimes tinged pinkish, with hind toe absent (Fig. 373**A**, p. 500), and with slight to moderate webbing between outer fore toes (Fig. 374**B**-**C**, p. 501).

Geographic variation—See Binford (1989), Conover (1945b), Cramp & Simmons (1983), Hellmayr & Conover (1948b), Monroe (1968), Oberholser (1974), Prater et al. (1977), Ridgway (1919). Four other subspecies occur worldwide.

C.a. nivosus (br and wint N.Am): Smaller than other subspecies (Table 48, p. 527); lores of AHY/ASY ♂ pale or mottled dusky in Mar-Aug (Fig. 388**D**; *vs* with dark line in Old-World subspecies); cap with little or no cinnamon; legs grayish to dull pinkish (*vs* usually blackish in Old-World subspecies); breast band reduced (Fig. 388; *vs* expanded and sometimes almost complete in Asian populations). Populations of coastal LA-w.FL

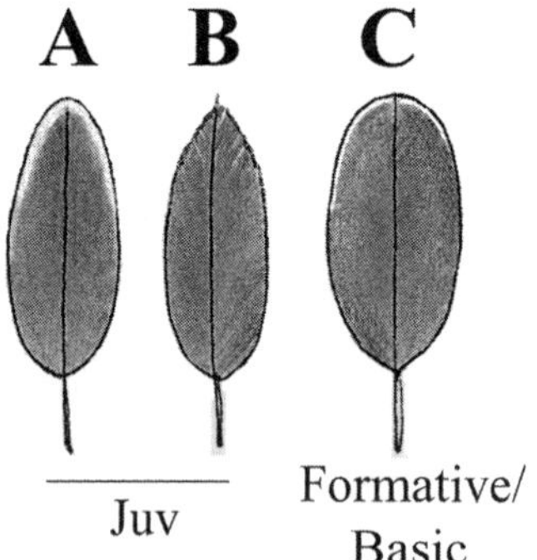

FIGURE 387. Back feathers and s covs by feather generation in *Charadrius* plovers. Juv-HY/SYs exhibit fresh juv feathers (**A**) with wider pale fringes through Aug-Oct, after which the s covs become mixed with worn juv (**B**) and formative (**C**) feathers (see also Fig. 375**A**-**D**, p. 503). AHY/ASYs exhibit uniformly basic feathers (**C**), with thinner and whiter fringes when fresh (see also Fig. 375**E**).

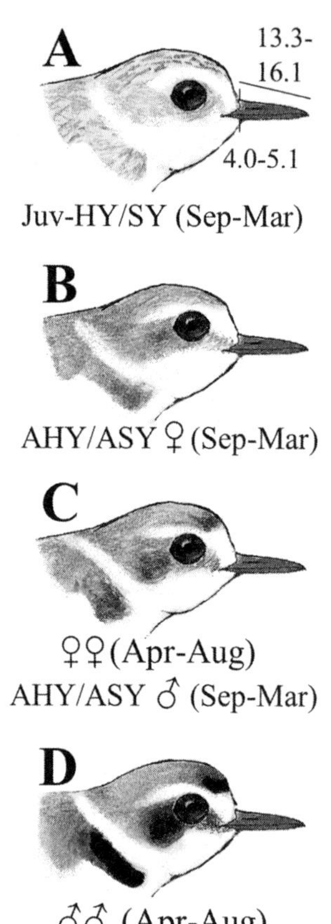

FIGURE 388. Bill size, and head pattern by age, sex, and season in Snowy Plover. Measures, given for species identification, are exposed culmen (Fig. 7**B**, p. 9) and bill depth at distal end of forehead feathers (Fig. 8**A**, p. 10). See also Figure 389. In addition to showing less dark alternate feathering by sex, SYs often retain bleached juv and/or formative feathers in these areas in Apr-Aug.

("*tenuirostris*) may average slightly paler and grayer upperparts than populations of w.N.Am (through coastal TX), but differences, if present, are slight and may simply be related to bleaching.

Molt—CAS. PF partial (Aug-Dec/Mar in HY/SYs), DPA limited-partial (Jan-Apr in AHYs), DPB complete (Jul-Nov in AHYs). The above timing and extent pertain to N.Am populations, which follow a n.Hemisphere strategy (Table 45, pp. 501-505). The PF and DPA occur primarily on non-breeding grounds whereas the DPB occurs primarily on breeding grounds but can complete on non-breeding grounds. The PF includes most to all body feathers, no to some proximal s covs, and sometimes 1-3 terts, but no rects. The DPA is primarily restricted to the head and breast (it may be more extensive in European populations; Cramp & Simmons 1983). See pp. 500-507 for more information on molt in shorebirds.

Age—Juv (B1; Jun-Sep) has uniformly fresh plumage aspect, the back feathers and s covs narrow and with thin whitish fringing (Fig. 387**A**), and the pp and ss uniformly juv and fresh (Fig. 375**A**, p. 503); Juv ♀ = ♂. The following month ranges pertain to N.Am populations.

Juv-HY/SY (1st cycle, Juv/B1-F1-A1; Oct-Sep): Forecrown, auriculars, and breast-bar pale grayish, without dusky or blackish in Oct-Mar (Fig. 388**A**; through Sep in some SYs), often mixed with bleached feathers in Apr-Sep; some to all distal s covs juv, narrower, and with broader pale fringing when fresh (Fig. 387**A-B**), contrasting with fresher formative scapulars, terts (sometimes), and proximal s covs (Fig. 375**B-C**), the retained juv distal s covs becoming worn and frayed in Apr-Sep (Fig. 375**D**); pp, p covs, and medial ss uniformly juv (Fig. 375**A**), the outer pp and p covs tapered, brownish, and relatively worn (Figs. 377**A-B** & 378**A-B**, p. 506); juv rects uniformly juv and narrow (Fig. 379**A**, p. 507). **Note: Many individuals in Jun-Sep are difficult to age due to bleaching.**

AHY/ASY (Def. cycle, DB-DA; Oct-Sep): Forecrown, auriculars, and breast-bar often mottled dusky or blackish in Oct-Mar (Fig. 388**B-C**; see **Sex**) and without bleached feathers in Apr-Sep; upperpart feathers, terts, and s covs uniformly basic (Fig. 375**E**), broader and with thin or no whitish fringing (Fig. 387**C**); pp, p covs, and medial ss uniformly basic and with s1-p1 contrast (Fig. 375**E**), the outer pp and p covs broad, truncate, and relatively fresh (Figs. 377**C-D** & 378**C-D**); rects basic and broad (Fig. 379**E**). **Note: See HY/SY.**

Sex—Medial or bilateral BPs (Fig. 20**A-B**, p. 31) developed by both sexes but distended cloaca (Fig. 21, p. 32) indicates ♀ in Mar-Jun. Measurements unhelpful for sexing (Table 48, p. 527). The following is reliable for many AHYs but some intermediates are not reliably sexed by plumage aspect alone. HY/SYs in Jun-Mar and SY ♀♀ in Apr-Sep are not reliably sexed by plumage aspect.

AHY/ASY ♀ (Sep-Aug): Forecrown, auriculars, and breast bar gray or with minimal dusky mottling (especially near eye) in Sep-Mar (Fig. 388**B**), or brownish, often mottled blackish and with narrower forehead band in Mar-Aug (Fig. 388**C** & 389**A**).

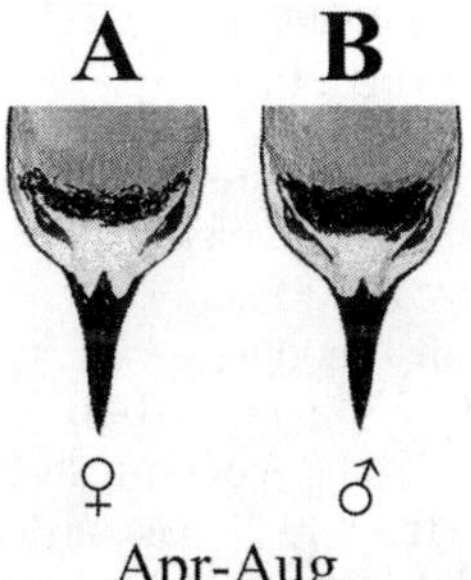

FIGURE 389. Extent of black forehead band by sex in definitive alternate aspect (Apr-Aug). Snowy Plovers. The width of the band at the midline is typically < 4 mm in ♀♀ and > 4 mm in ♂♂. Intermediates are likely SY ♂♂ or ASY ♀♀ so combine with age for most accurate sex determination. See also Figure 388.

AHY/ASY ♂ (Mar-Feb): Forecrown, auriculars, and breast bar variably mottled dusky to blackish in Sep-Feb (Fig. 388**C**), or black with broader forehead band in Feb-Aug (Figs. 388**D** & 389**B**).

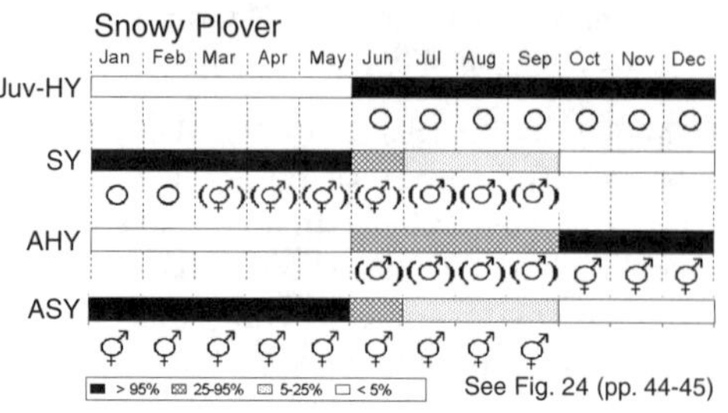

Hybrids reported—None.

References—Bent (1929), Cramp & Simmons (1983), Oberholser (1974), Page et al. (1995), Palmer (1967b), Prater et al. (1977), Ridgway (1919).

WILSON'S PLOVER

Charadrius wilsonia

WIPL
Species # 2800
Band size: 2-1A

Species—From other N.Am plovers and shorebirds by small size with proportionally long bill and tarsus (Table 48, p. 527), bill stout (depth at tip of forehead feathers 6.3-8.0 mm) and black; exp culmen > middle toe without claw; upperparts grayish brown with white to whitish hind-neck collar (sometimes broken at center); white of forehead contiguous with white supercilium; breast with complete brownish, cinnamon, or black band; legs and feet dull pinkish, with hind toe absent (Fig. 373**A**, p. 500) and with slight webbing between outer fore toes (Fig. 374**B**, p. 501).

Geographic variation—Considered monotypic here. Populations of Pacific coastal s.CA (vagrant) to Mex-S.Am ("*C.w. beldingi*") may average darker upperparts with less distinct facial features, and populations of the W.Indes ("*rufinucha*" and "*cinnamominus*") may average darker and more cinnamon (♀♀) than nominate populations of TX-FL-MD, but differences, if present, are slight and confounded by individual and seasonal variation. See Blake (1977), Conover (1945b), Corbat & Bergstrom (2000), Hellmayr & Conover (1948b), Monroe (1968), Patten et al. (2003), Prater et al. (1977), Ridgway (1919), Todd & Worthington (1911), and Wetmore (1965) for more information.

Molt—CAS. PF partial-incomplete (Aug-Nov/Mar in HY/SYs), DPA limited-partial (Dec-Apr in AHYs), DPB complete (Jun-Oct in AHYs). The above timing and extent pertain to N.Am populations. The PF and DPA occur primarily on non-breeding grounds and the DPB occurs primarily on breeding grounds. Molt can follow either a s.Hemisphere or n.Hemisphere strategy (Table 45, pp. 501-505). The PF includes most to all body feathers, rects, terts, and s covs (the distal gr covs usually retained), and often 4-6 outer pp and p covs and 2-8 medial ss (distal to the terts) in eccentric sequence (Fig. 376**A**, p. 504; seldom if ever arrested); body feathers, terts, and c.rects are replaced primarily in Aug-Nov whereas pp, ss, and outer rects are replaced in Dec-Mar. The DPA is variably restricted to the head and breast or can also include more upperpart and underparts feathers, 1-3 terts, and 1-4 c.rects; ♂♂ average earlier molt than ♀♀. Some SYs over-summer on non-breeding grounds or at stopover sites and exhibit less-complete (or no) PA1s and advanced PB2s (see p. 18). See pp. 500-507 for more information.

Age—Juv (B1; Jun-Sep) has uniformly fresh plumage aspect, the back feathers and s covs narrow and with thin whitish fringing (Fig. 387**A**, p. 520), and the pp and ss uniformly juv and fresh (Fig. 375**A**, p. 503); Juv ♀ = ♂. The following month ranges pertain to N.Am populations.

Juv-HY/SY (1st cycle, Juv/B1-F1-A1; Oct-Sep): Crown, auriculars, and breast band pale grayish, without dusky or cinnamon in Oct-Dec (*cf.* Fig. 391**A**, p. 525), or often with some dusky or cinnamon mixed with worn bleached feathers in Feb-Sep (*cf.* Fig. 391**B-C**); some upperpart feathers, terts, and/or distal s covs juv, narrower, and with broader pale fringing when fresh (Fig. 387**A-B**), contrasting with fresher formative scapulars, humerals, terts, and proximal s covs (Fig. 375**B-C**), the distal juv gr covs usually retained and becoming worn and frayed by Apr-Sep (Fig. 375**D**); pp, p covs, and ss uniformly juv in Oct-Nov (Fig. 375**A**), usually being incompletely replaced in Dec-Apr and exhibiting eccentric replacement patterns in May-Sep (Fig. 376**A**), the juv outer pp and p covs (if present) tapered (Figs. 377**A-B** & 378**A-B**, p. 506); rects uniformly juv and narrow in Oct-Dec (Fig. 379**A**, p. 507), mixed with formative rects in Dec-Mar (Fig. 379**B-C**) and occasionally in Apr-Sep (Fig. 379**D**). **Note: Some SYs over-summer on non-breeding grounds for the summer. Individuals can be difficult to age in Feb-Sep due to bleaching.**

AHY/ASY (Def. cycle, DB-DA; Oct-Sep): Crown, auriculars, and breast band often mottled with dusky or cinnamon in Oct-Mar (*cf.* Fig. 391**B-C**), or with extensive cinnamon or black by sex and without worn feathers in Apr-Sep (*cf.* Fig. 391**C-D**); upperpart feathers, terts, and s covs uniformly basic (Fig. 375**E**), broader and with thin or no whitish fringing (Fig. 387**C**), pp, p covs, and ss uniformly basic (Fig. 375**E**), the outer pp and p covs broad and truncate (Figs. 377**C-D** & 378**C-D**); rects uniformly basic and broader (Fig. 379**E**), sometimes with 1-4 fresher alternate c.rects in Apr-Sep (Fig. 379**F**). **Note: See Juv-HY/SY.**

Sex—Bilateral(?) BPs (Fig. 20**B**, p. 31) developed by both sexes but distended cloaca (Fig. 21, p. 32) indicates ♀ in Mar-Jun. Measurements unhelpful for sexing (Table 48, p. 527). The following is reliable for ASYs, many SYs in Jan-Sep, and some AHY ♂♂ in Sep-Dec; HYs, some SYs in Jan-Aug, and AHY ♀♀ in Sep-Dec are not reliably sexed by plumage aspect.

AHY ♀ (Jan-Sep): Forehead and breast band with brownish and/or cinnamon but no blackish feathers. **Note: SYs that lack cinnamon or blackish feathers are not reliably sexed.**

AHY ♂ (Jan-Dec): Forehead and breast band with dusky and/or black feathers in Dec-Sep; breast band sometimes with dusky or blackish mottling in Oct-Dec. **Note: See AHY ♀.**

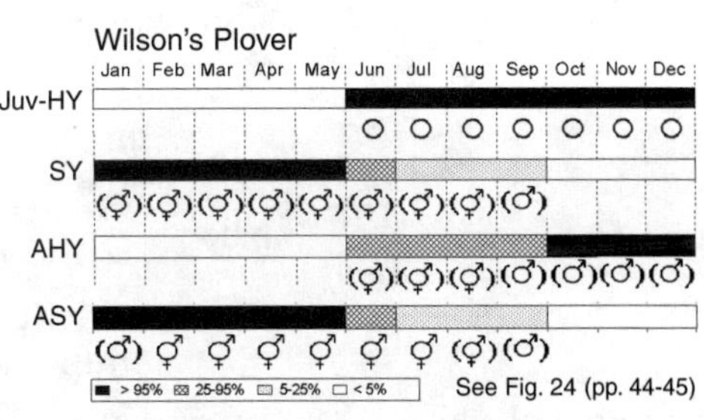

Hybrids reported—None.

References—Bent (1929), Corbat & Bergstrom (2000), Oberholser (1974), Palmer (1967b), Prater et al. (1977), Ridgway (1919).

COMMON RINGED PLOVER CRPL
Charadrius hiaticula Species # 2750

SEMIPALMATED PLOVER SEPL
Charadrius semipalmatus Species # 2740
Band size: 1A-1B

Species—From other N.Am plovers by medium-small size with proportionally short bill (Table 48, p. 527); bill moderately stout (depth at tip of forehead feathers 4.9-6.2 mm; Fig. 390), dusky (Juvs) to blackish with orange base (AHYs; orange confined to lower mandible in Oct-Feb); exp culmen < middle toe without claw; upperparts brown with white hind-neck collar, white of forehead usually not contiguous with white supercilium, and breast with complete or nearly complete brownish to black band (Figs. 390-391); legs orangish yellow with hind toe absent (Fig. 373**A**, p. 500) and variable webbing between fore toes by species (Fig. 374**A**-**D**, p. 501).

Common Ringed Plover from Semipalmated Plover, with caution, by longer average wing and larger average bill (Table 48, Fig. 390); outer fore toes with no to slight webbing (Fig. 374**A**-**B**) *vs* slight to moderate webbing in Semipalmated Plover (Fig. 374**C**-**D**); white of throat usually extends above gape (Fig. 390); orbital eye ring dull orange and inconspicuous *vs* brighter yellow

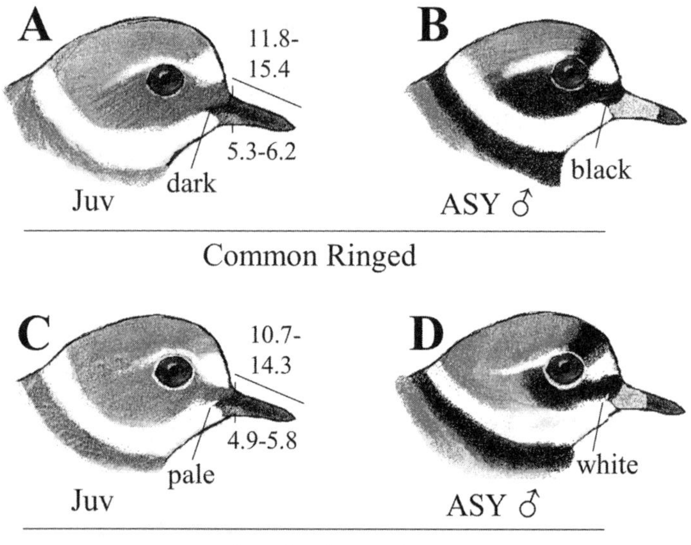

FIGURE 390. Bill size, and head pattern by species in juvenile and adult ♂ Common Ringed and Semipalmated plovers to assist in identification; HY/SYs and ♀♀ show similar differences (see also Fig. 391). Measures indicate exposed culmen (Fig. 7**B**, p. 9) and bill depth at distal end of forehead feathers (Fig. 8**A**, p. 10). In Juv Common Ringed plover the "gape line" is darker than in Juv Semipalmated Plover (Mullarney 1991) and this seems fairly consistent across age/sex groups but more study is needed to determine if exceptions occur. Note also the more distinct eye ring by age and sex in Semipalmated Plover, and the more extensive pale base to the bill in ASY ♂ Common Ringed Plover. Other indicative features to separate ASY ♂♂ (and to a lesser extent other age/sex groups) include a more distinct supercilium, larger white forehead patch, and thicker breast band in Common Ringed Plover, but these features exhibit individual variation, and width of the breast band is affected substantially by the posture of the breast and neck. Common Ringed Plover also averages larger (Table 48, p. 527) and has less extensive webbing in the toes (Fig. 374**A**-**B**, p. 501) than Semipalmated Plover (Fig. 374**C**-**D**).

and more conspicuous in Semipalmated Plover by age/sex (Figs. 390-391); distal ss and proximal pp with more white on outer web (e.g., s2-s5 with white *vs* gray in Semipalmated Plover); orange base to bill averages more extensive (Fig. 390). In addition, ♂♂ Common Ringed Plovers in Mar-Aug average larger white forehead patches and thicker breast bands but these characters are confounded by individual variation and (for breast band width) posture (see Sibley 2000). See Bock (1959), Chandler (1987b), Cramp & Simmons (1983), Dunn (1993), Engelmoer & Roselaar (1998), Laken & Rylands (1997), Lehman (2006), Manning et al. (1956), Marchant & Higgins (1993), Mullarney (1991), Nol & Blanken (1999), Oberholser (1974), Smith (1969), Vaurie (1964), Walsh (1985), and Wynne-Edwards (1952b) for more information.

Geographic variation—Both species considered monotypic here. Among Semipalmated Plovers, Canadian breeding populations may average slightly longer wing and tail than AK breeding populations, but differences are broadly clinal. Among Common Ringed Plovers, populations of Asia-w.AK ("*C.h. tundrae*") average slightly smaller and with darker brown (less grayish) upperparts (when fresh) than populations of both Europe (nominate) and e.Canada-Iceland ("*C.h. psammodroma*"), but differences are slight and confounded by individual variation; reported differences in molt strategies are based on non-breeding latitude (see **Molt** and pp. 501-505), and may not have taxonomic significance. See Bock (1959), Cramp & Simmons (1983), Dement'ev & Gladkov (1951c), Engelmoer & Roselaar (1998), Hellmayr & Conover (1948b), Marchant & Higgins (1993), Meissner (2007a), Portenko (1972), Prater et al. (1977), Tomkovich & Serra (1999), and Vaurie (1964) for more information.

Molt—CAS, PF partial-incomplete(complete?) (Sep-Nov/Mar in HY/SYs), DPA limited-partial (Feb-May in AHYs), PB2 complete (Jun-Oct in non-breeding SYs), DPB complete (Aug-Oct/Feb in breeding AHY/ASYs). Molting occurs primarily on non-breeding grounds. Molt exhibits both n.Hemisphere (e.N.Am Common Ringed and most Semipalmated plovers) and s.Hemisphere (Siberian Common Ringed and some Semipalmated plovers) strategies (Table 45, pp. 501-505). The PF includes most to all body feathers, no to some proximal s covs, and sometimes 1-3 terts, but no rects in Sep-Dec; individuals with non-breeding grounds in the s.Hemisphere also replace most to all remaining rects, terts, and s covs (the distal gr covs usually retained), 3-10 outer pp and p covs, and 3-8 medial ss (distal to the terts) in eccentric sequence (Fig. 376**A**-**E**, p. 504) in Jan-Jun. The DPB completes by Nov among most individuals but occurs in Oct-Feb among individuals with non-breeding grounds in the s.Hemisphere. The DPA is primarily restricted to the head and breast but can include 1-3 terts and 1-6 c.rects.

FIGURE 391. Head pattern by age, sex, and season in Semipalmated Plover; Common Ringed Plover shows similar variation (but with less distinct eye ring by age/sex/season; Figure 390). In addition to showing less dark alternate feathering by sex, SYs often retain bleached juv and/or formative feathers in these areas in Apr-Aug.

Some SYs over-summer on non-breeding grounds and exhibit less-complete (or no) PA1s and advanced PB2s (see p. 18). See pp. 500-507 for more information.

Age—Juv (B1; Jul-Sep) has uniformly fresh plumage aspect, the back feathers and s covs narrow and with thin whitish fringing (Fig. 387**A**, p. 520), pp and ss uniformly juv and fresh (Fig. 375**A**, p. 503), and bill dusky with little or no orangish; Juv ♀=♂. The following pertains to most Semipalmated Plovers and Common Ringed Plovers of e.Canada-Europe (see **Molt**). Some SYs remain on non-breeding grounds during the first summer. In addition to the following, p6 often has a white stripe near the shaft that averages larger in juvenal than in basic feathers by species (Burton & McNeil 1976) but there is substantial overlap in this character.

Juv-HY/SY (1st cycle, Juv/B1-F1-A1; Oct-Sep): Auriculars and breast band brownish with pale fringing and little to no dusky in Oct-Mar (through Sep in some individuals; Figs. 390**A** & **C**, p. 524, & 391**A**, p. 525) or often with some dusky (to blackish in ♂♂), mixed with worn bleached feathers in Apr-Sep (Fig. 391**A-C**); some upperpart feathers and/or distal s covs juv, narrower, and with broader pale fringing when fresh (Fig. 387**A-B**), contrasting with fresher formative scapulars, humerals, terts, and proximal s covs (Fig. 375**B-C**), the retained juv distal s covs usually retained and becoming worn and frayed by Apr-Sep (Fig. 375**D**); pp, p covs, and ss juv, fresh, and without s1-p1 contrast in Oct-Dec (Fig. 375**A**), the juv outer pp and p covs tapered (Figs. 377**A-B** & 378**A-B**, p. 506); rects uniformly juv and narrow (Fig. 379**A**, p. 507), occasionally mixed with formative rects in Dec-Mar (Fig. 379**B-C**); orbital ring and legs grayish to dull olive tinged yellow and bill dusky with indistinct orangish base to lower mandible (Fig. 391**A-B**) in Oct-Mar. **Note: Occasional SY Semipalmated, and Common Ringed Plovers from e.Asia, can exhibit eccentric replacement patterns in the wing in Feb-Sep (Fig. 376A-D).**

AHY/ASY (Def. cycle, DB-DA; Oct-Sep): Auriculars and breast band dusky or mottled blackish, without pale fringing in Oct-Mar (Fig. 391**B-C**), or with extensive dusky or black by sex and without worn feathers in Apr-Sep (Figs. 390**B** & **D**, & 391**C-D**); upperpart feathers, terts, and s covs uniformly basic (Fig. 375**E**), broader, and with thin or no pale fringing (Fig. 387**C**); pp, p covs, and ss worn and being completely replaced in Oct-Dec (Dec-Mar in s.Hemisphere), or fresh and occasionally with s1-p1 contrast in Jan-Sep (Fig. 375**E**), the outer pp and p covs broad and truncate (Figs 377**C-D** & 378**C-D**); rects uniformly basic and broader (Fig. 379**E**), sometimes with 1-6 fresher alternate c.rects in Apr-Sep (Fig. 379**F**); orbital ring and legs yellowish and bill with distinct orange base to lower mandible (Fig. 391**C-D**) in Oct-Mar. **Note: See HY/SY.**

Sex—Bilateral BPs (Fig. 20**B**, p. 31) developed by both sexes but distended cloaca (Fig. 21, p. 32) indicates ♀ in May-Jul. Measurements unhelpful for sexing (Table 48, p. 527). The following is reliable for most AHY/ASYs (some intermediates occur, especially in Sep-Mar, that cannot be reliably sexed by plumage aspect); HYs and SY ♀♀ in Jan-Sep are not reliably sexed by plumage aspect.

AHY/ASY ♀ (Apr-Mar): Forehead band and breast band brownish with little or no dusky in Sep-Mar (Fig. 391**B**, p. 525) or mottled brown and dusky, with > 8 brown feathers in band in Mar-Aug (Fig. 391**B-C**). **Note: It is best to determine age before sexing. SYs with > 8 brown feathers in breast band in Apr-Aug cannot be reliably sexed.**

AHY ♂ (Jan-Dec): Forehead band and breast band mottled dusky in Sep-Mar (Fig. 391**B-C**), or uniformly (ASYs) to mostly (SYs; < 8 brown feathers) black in Mar-Aug (Figs. 390**B** & **D** & Fig. 391**C-D**). **Note: See AHY/ASY ♀.**

Hybrids reported—Semipalmated Plover with Common Ringed Plover (Bock 1959, Smith 1969).

References—Bent (1929), Burton & McNeil (1976), Cramp & Simmons (1983), Dement'ev & Gladkov (1951c), Engelmoer & Roselaar (1998), Ferns (1978a), Loftin (1962), Marchant & Higgins (1993), McNeil (1970), Nol & Blanken (1999), Oberholser (1974), Palmer (1967b), Prater et al. (1977), Ridgway (1919), Roberts (1955), Spaans (1979), Stresemann & Stresemann (1966), Teather & Nol (1997), Wymenga et al. (1990).

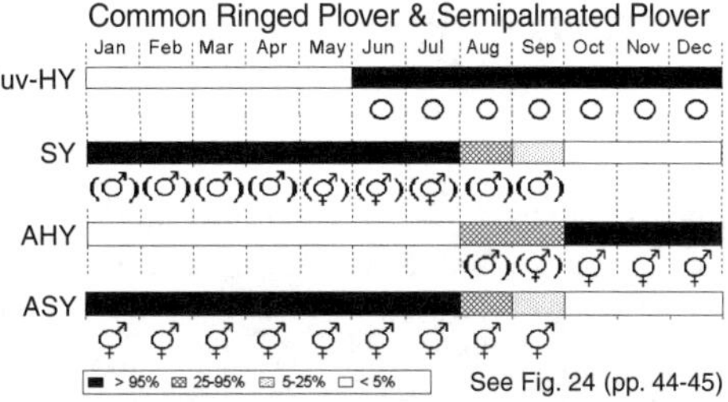

TABLE 48. Measurements (mm) of North American *Chardrius* plovers for identification and sexing. See pp. 4-11 for methods of measurement. Species summaries are in **bold**. Values were derived from 95% confidence intervals as based approximately on the indicated sample sizes (see pp. 4-5). Thus, midpoints of ranges approximate means, and S.D. is approximated by 25% of the range.

Taxon/Sex	*n*	wing chord	tail length	exposed culmen	tarsus
Lesser Sand-Plover[1]		**127-145**	**45-53**	**14.5-16.9**	**28-32**
♀	20	128-145	45-53	14.8-16.9	28-32
♂	20	127-144	45-53	14.5-16.3	28-32
Snowy Plover[1]		**98-111**	**39-51**	**13.3-16.1**	**22-29**
♀	100	98-110	39-50	13.3-15.6	22-27
♂	100	99-111	40-51	13.6-16.1	23-29
Wilson's Plover[1]		**110-125**	**44-53**	**19.4-23.1**	**28-32**
♀	50	111-125	44-52	19.9-23.1	28-32
♂	55	110-124	45-53	19.4-22.7	28-32
Common Ringed Plover[1]		**119-137**	**49-63**	**11.8-15.4**	**22-28**
♀	100	119-137	50-63	11.8-15.4	22-27
♂	100	119-137	49-61	12.0-15.6	23-28
Semipalmated Plover		**111-131**	**47-57**	**10.7-14.3**	**22-26**
♀	100	111-131	47-57	10.7-14.1	22-26
♂	100	110-130	47-57	10.9-14.3	22-26
Piping Plover		**110-126**	**46-59**	**11.1-14.6**	**21-25**
♀	50	110-119	46-55	11.1-14.3	21-24
♂	60	115-126	49-59	11.4-14.6	21-25
Killdeer[1]		**151-170**	**87-103**	**18.6-22.1**	**33-38**
♀	45	154-170	87-103	18.6-21.8	33-38
♂	50	151-167	87-103	18.9-22.1	33-37
Mountain Plover		**139-154**	**59-71**	**19.1-23.5**	**35-43**
♀	100	139-154	59-70	19.3-23.5	35-43
♂	100	139-154	59-71	19.1-23.2	36-43
Eurasian Dotterel		**135-157**	**60-74**	**14.4-18.7**	**32-39**
♀	80	141-157	61-74	15.3-18.7	33-39
♂	75	135-151	60-72	14.4-17.8	32-38

[1] Measures from N.Am populations only; see **Geographic variation**.

PIPING PLOVER PIPL
Charadrius melodus Species # 2770
Band size: 1A-1B

Species—From other N.Am plovers and shorebirds by small size (Table 48, p. 527), bill moderately stout (depth at tip of forehead feathers 4.8-6.1 mm; Fig. 392), blackish (Juvs) to orange with black tip (AHYs; Fig. 393; orange confined to lower mandible in Oct-Feb); exp culmen usually > middle toe without claw; upperparts very pale brownish to whitish with white hindneck collar, white of forehead usually contiguous with white supercilium, and sides of breast with pale gray to black marks (Figs. 392-393), not connecting across breast (except in some ♂♂ in Mar-Aug; see **Geographic variation**); legs yellowish gray (Juv) to orangish (AHY), with hind toe absent (Fig. 373**A**, p. 500) and with slight to moderate webbing between outer fore toes (Fig. 374**B-C**, p. 501).

Geographic variation—Monotypic (Haig & Oring 1988a, 1988b). AHY/ASY ♂♂ breeding in Alb-Man to NE ("*P.m. cicumcinctus*") average more black in lores and breast band (which is sometimes complete) in Mar-Aug than those of Atlantic coastal populations (breast band usually not complete) but differences are broadly clinal and confounded by individual (possibly age-related or molt-related) variation. See also Haig (1992), Moser (1942), and Wilcox (1959).

Molt—CAS. PF partial (Aug-Nov/Mar in HY/SYs), DPA limited-partial (Jan-Apr in AHYs), DPB complete (Jul-Nov in AHYs). Molting occurs primarily on non-breeding grounds (although the DPB, especially in SYs and non-breeders, can begin on breeding grounds) and exhibits a n.Hemisphere strategy (Table 45, pp. 501-505). The PF includes most to all body feathers, no to some proximal s covs, and sometimes 1-3 terts and 1-6 c.rects. The DPA is primarily restricted to the head and breast but can include scattered back and underpart feathers, 1-2 terts, and some medial s covs. See pp. 500-507 for more information on molt in shorebirds.

Age—Juv (B1; Jul-Sep) has uniformly fresh plumage aspect, the back feathers and s covs narrow and with thin whitish fringing (Fig. 387**A**, p. 520), and the pp and ss uniformly juv and fresh (Fig. 375**A**, p. 503); Juv ♀=♂.

Juv-HY/SY (1st cycle, Juv/B1-F1-A1; Oct-Sep): Forecrown and collar pale grayish, without dusky or blackish in Oct-Mar (Fig. 392**A**; through Sep in some ♀♀) and with reduced blackish by sex and often mixed with worn bleached feathers by Mar-Sep (Fig. 392**A-C**); some

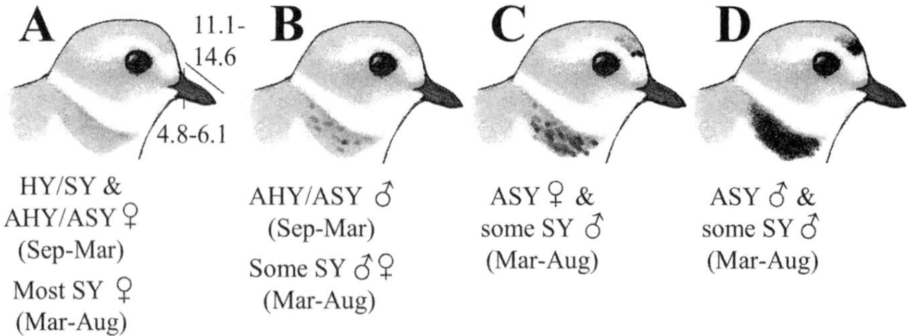

FIGURE 392. Bill size, and head pattern by age, sex, and season in Piping Plover. Measures, given for species identification, are exposed culmen (Fig. 7**B**, p. 9) and bill depth at distal end of forehead feathers (Fig. 8**A**, p. 10). See also Figure 393. In addition to showing less dark alternate feathering by sex, SYs often retain and bleached juv and/or formative feathers in these areas in Apr-Aug.

upperpart feathers and most s covs juv, narrower, and with whitish fringing when fresh (Fig. 387**A-B**, p. 520), contrasting with fresher formative scapulars, terts (sometimes), and proximal s covs (Fig. 375**B-C**), the retained juv distal s covs becoming worn and frayed by Apr-Sep (Fig. 375**D**); pp, p covs, and medial ss uniformly juv (Fig. 375**A**), the outer pp and p covs tapered, brownish, and relatively worn (Figs. 377**A-B** & 378**A-B**, p. 506); rects juv and narrower (Fig. 379**A**, p. 507); orbital ring and legs grayish tinged yellow, and bill blackish with orangish base to lower mandible in Oct-Mar. **Note: Individuals can be difficult to age in Feb-Sep due to bleaching.**

AHY/ASY (Def. cycle, DB-DA; Oct-Sep): Forecrown and collar often mottled with dusky or blackish in Oct-Mar (Fig. 392**B**) and with more extensive black by sex and without worn feathers in Mar-Sep (Fig. 392**C-D**); upperpart feathers, terts, and s covs uniformly basic or mixed basic and alternate (Fig. 375**E-F**), the feathers broader and with thin or no pale fringing (Fig. 387**C**); pp, p covs, and medial ss uniformly basic (Fig. 375**E**), the outer pp and p covs broad, truncate, and relatively fresh (Figs. 377**C-D** & 378**C-D**); rects basic and broader (Fig. 379**E**); orbital ring and legs yellow to orangish and bill with orange base to lower mandible in Oct-Mar. **Note: See HY/SY.**

Sex—Bilateral(?) BPs (Fig. 20**B**, p. 31) developed by both sexes but distended cloaca (Fig. 21, p. 32) indicates ♀ in Apr-Jun. Measurements largely unhelpful for sexing (Table 48, p. 527). The following is reliable in Apr-Aug and for some AHY/ASY ♂♂ in Sep-Mar only. Individuals without blackish in Sep-Mar cannot be reliably sexed by plumage aspect.

AHY ♀ (Apr-Aug): Forecrown with thin to no blackish bar, nape without complete blackish band, breast band mixed gray and dusky, and bill duller orange with indistinct blackish tip (Figs 392**C** & 393**A**). **Note: AHY/ASYs in Sep-Mar with gray breast bands (without dusky mottling (Fig. 392A) are not reliably sexed. Intermediates in Apr-Aug are ASY ♀♀ or SY ♂♂; combine with age for reliable sexing of these.**

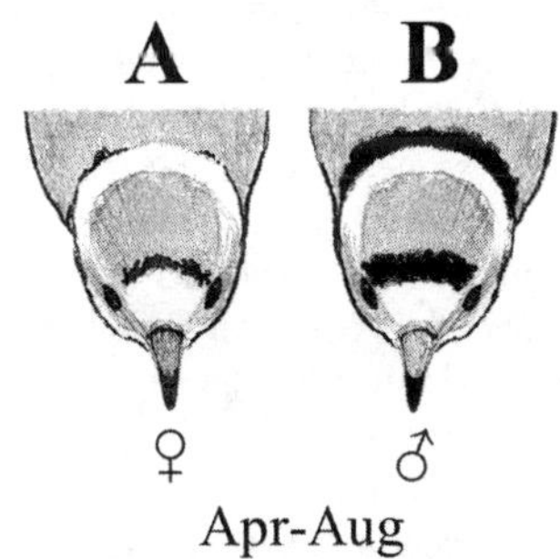

FIGURE 393. Extent of black forehead band and hind collar, and brightness of bill, by sex in definitive alternate aspect (Apr-Aug) Piping Plovers. See also Figure 392.

AHY/ASY ♂ (Mar-Feb): Forecrown with thick blackish bar, nape with complete or near-complete black collar, breast band completely black, and bill brighter orange with distinct black tip in Mar-Aug (Figs. 392**D** & 393**B**); breast band often with indistinct dusky mottling in Sep-Mar (Fig. 392**B**). **Note: See AHY ♀.**

Piping Plover

Jan Feb Mar Apr May Jun Jul Aug Sep Oct Nov Dec

Juv-HY
O O O O O O

SY
O O O (♀)(♀)(♀)(♂)(♂)(♂)

AHY
O O (♀)(♀)(♀)(♂)(♂)(♂)(♂)(♂)(♂)

ASY
(♂)(♂)(♀) ♀ ♀ ♀ ♀ (♀)(♂)

■ > 95% ▨ 25-95% ▤ 5-25% □ < 5%

See Fig. 24 (pp. 44-45)

Hybrids reported—None.

References—W.M. Tyler *in* Bent (1929), Haig (1992), Oberholser (1974), Palmer (1967b), Prater et al. (1977), Ridgway (1919), Roberts (1955), Wilcox (1959).

KILLDEER
Charadrius vociferus

KILL
Species # 2730
Band size: 2

Species—From other N.Am plovers by large size and long, graduated (r1 – r6 > 15 mm) tail (Table 48, p. 527); upperparts brown with variable rufous fringing to s covs and bright-rufous rump; breast white with one (some chicks) to two (Juvs and older individuals) complete blackish bands; legs dull pinkish, with hind toe absent (Fig. 373**A**, p. 500) and with slight webbing between outer fore toes (Fig. 374**B**, p. 501).

Geographic variation—See Blake (1977), Chapman (1920), Conover (1945b), Jackson & Jackson (2000), Ridgway (1919). Two other subspecies occur in the W.Indes and S.Am.

C.v. vociferus (br & wint N.Am): Larger (Table 48, p. 527; *vs* wg chord 137-161, tl 82-99, exp culmen 18.8-22.0, tarsus 32-36 in *ternominatus* of the W.Indes and *peruvianus* of w.S.Am); upperparts paler and browner (less grayish) with reduced rufous fringing to s covs.

Molt—CBS (CAS?). PF limited-partial (Aug-Nov/Mar in HY/SYs), DPB complete (Jun-Nov in AHYs); DPA absent(?). The PF begins on breeding grounds and completes on nonbreeding grounds whereas the DPB occurs primarily on breeding grounds. Molt follows a n.Hemisphere strategy (Table 45, pp. 501-505). The PF includes most to all body feathers and no to some proximal s covs but few in any terts or rects; body feathers are replaced primarily in Aug-Oct whereas some s covs, can be replaced in Nov-Mar. Despite reports (*cf.* Cramp & Simmons 1983) there is little or no evidence for a DPA in this species; more study is needed. See pp. 500-507 for more information on molt in shorebirds.

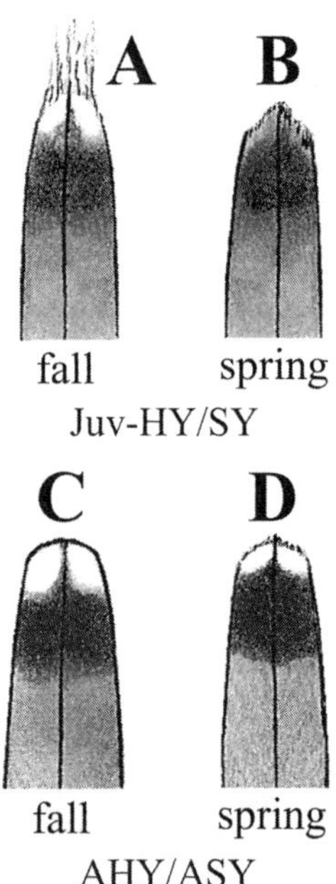

FIGURE 394. Central rectrix by age and season in Killdeer. Juv feathers have filamentous extensions when fresh (**A**), that wear off between Oct and Dec (**B**). Note that the subterminal band averages duskier and less distinct on juv feathers in HY/SYs (**A-B**) than on basic feathers in AHY/ASYs (**C-D**) but some overlap occurs. Look for occasional HY/SYs to have replaced the central rects during the PF; these would resemble basic feathers in pattern but would exhibit molt limits with juv outer rects (Fig. 379**B**).

Age—Juv (B1; Jun-Sep) has uniformly fresh plumage aspect, the back feathers and s covs narrow and with thin whitish to cinnamon fringing (Fig. 387**A**, p. 520), and the pp and ss uniformly juv and fresh (Fig. 375**A**, p. 503); Juv ♀ = ♂.

Juv-HY/SY (1st cycle, Juv/B1-F1; Oct-Sep): Rects uniformly juv and narrower (Fig. 379**A**, p. 507), r1 with filamentous extensions in Oct-Dec (wearing off by Jan-Sep) and less distinct subterminal band (Fig. 394**A-B**); some upperpart feathers (Oct-Nov) and most s covs juv, contrasting with fresher formative humerals, scapulars, and (sometimes) proximal s covs (Fig. 375**B-C**), the retained juv distal s covs becoming worn and frayed by Apr-Sep (Fig. 375**D**); pp, p covs, and ss uniformly juv (Fig. 375**A**), the outer pp and p covs tapered, brownish, and relatively worn (Figs. 377**A-B** & 378**A-B**, p. 506); orbital ring dull yellowish to orange in Oct-Feb.

AHY/ASY (Def. cycle, DB; Oct-Sep): Rects uniformly basic and broader (Fig. 379**E**), r1 without filamentous extensions and with more distinct subterminal band (Fig. 394**C-D**); upperpart feathers and s covs uniformly basic (Fig. 375**E**); pp, p covs, and ss uniformly basic and relatively fresh (Fig. 375**E**), the outer pp and p covs broad, truncate, and relatively fresh (Figs. 377**C-D** & 378**C-D**); orbital ring bright orange to reddish.

Sex—Medial or bilateral BPs (Fig. 20**A-B**, p. 31) developed by both sexes but distended cloaca (Fig. 21, p. 32) > 4.5 mm in width (Jackson & Jackson 2006) indicates ♀ in Apr-Jul. Measurements unhelpful for sexing (Table 48, p. 527). ♂♂ may average more distinct black forehead bar and breast bands and a brighter red orbital ring in Apr-Aug, but reliable sexing is precluded by individual (including age-related) variation, except perhaps with some mated pairs. No other criteria known.

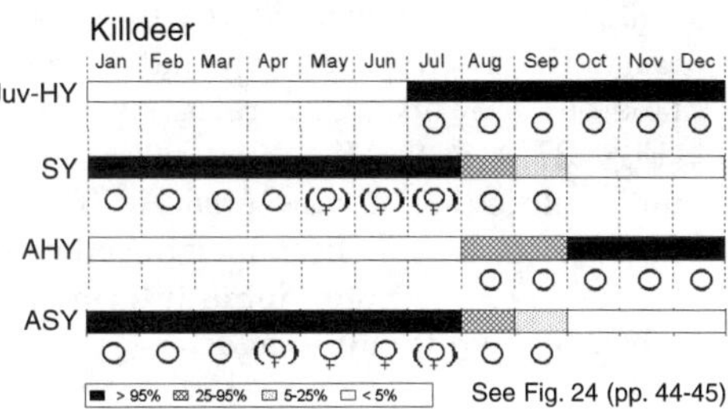

Hybrids reported—None.

References—Bent (1929), Cramp & Simmons (1983), Jackson & Jackson (2000, 2006), Oberholser (1974), Palmer (1967b), Prater et al. (1977), Ridgway (1919), Roberts (1955).

MOUNTAIN PLOVER

Charadrius montanus

MOPL
Species # 2810
Band size: 2-3

Species—From other N.Am plovers by medium-large size with long bill and tarsus (Table 48, p. 527); upperparts medium-pale brown with buff to rufous fringing (Fig. 395, p. 532) and little or no pale hind-neck collar; forehead pale brownish (Sep-Mar) to white (AHYs in Mar-Aug), contiguous with indistinct and pale (Sep-Mar) to distinct and white but short (Mar-Aug) eye-line; inner webs and tips to ss and inner pp white, forming narrow wing stripe; throat buff (Sep-Mar) to whitish (Mar-Aug), contrasting indistinctly with browner (Sep-Mar) or peach (Mar-Aug) breast; legs dull grayish olive to yellowish, with hind toe absent (Fig. 373**A**, p. 500) and with slight webbing between outer fore toes (Fig. 374**B**, p. 501).

Geographic variation—Monotypic.

Molt—CAS. PF partial (Aug-Nov/Jan in HY/SYs), DPA limited-partial (Feb-Apr in AHYs), DPB complete (Jul-Oct in AHYs). The DPB occurs on breeding grounds, the PF begins on breeding grounds and completes on non-breeding grounds, and the DPA occurs primarily on non-breeding grounds. Molt follows a n.Hemisphere strategy (Table 45, pp. 501-505). The PF includes most to all body feathers, some to most proximal s covs, and often 1-3 terts, but few if any rects. The DPA includes feathers of the head, nape, and breast, and usually scattered back feathers and s covs. See pp. 500-507 for more information on molt in shorebirds.

Age—Juv (B1; Jul-Sep) has uniformly fresh plumage aspect; back feathers and wing covs narrow and with thin buff fringing and subterminal dusky bands (Fig. 395**A**); pp and ss uniformly juv and fresh (Fig. 375**A**, p. 503); legs dull grayish. Juv ♀=♂.

Juv-HY/SY (1st cycle, Juv/B1-F1-A1; Oct-Sep): All to some upperpart feathers (Oct-Nov), terts, and/or distal s juv (Fig. 375**A**), narrower, and with pale fringes and subterminal dusky bands (Fig. 395**A-B**), contrasting with fresher formative scapulars, terts (often), and proximal s covs (Figs. 375**B-C**, 395**C**), the retained juv distal s covs becoming worn and frayed by Apr-Sep (Fig. 375**D**); pp, p covs, and medial ss uniformly juv and without s1-p1 contrast (Fig. 375**A**), the outer pp and p covs tapered, brownish, and relatively worn (Figs. 377**A-B** & 378**A-B**, p. 506); rects uniformly juv and narrower (*cf.* Fig. 379**A**, p. 507); legs grayish, becoming tinged yellow in Apr-Sep. **Note: Some intermediates may be difficult to age.**

AHY/ASY (Def. cycle, DB-DA; Oct-Sep): Upperpart feathers, terts, and s covs uniformly basic or mixed basic and alternate (Fig. 375**E-F**), with thin to no pale fringe and without dusky subterminal band (Fig. 395**C**), mixed with alternate feathers (Fig. 395**D**) in Apr-Sep; pp, p covs, and medial ss basic and with s1-p1 contrast (Fig. 375**E**), the outer pp and p covs broad, truncate, and relatively fresh (Figs. 377**C-D** & 378**C-D**); rects basic and broader (Fig. 379**E**); legs olive to yellowish, brighter in Mar-Aug. **Note: See Juv-HY/SY.**

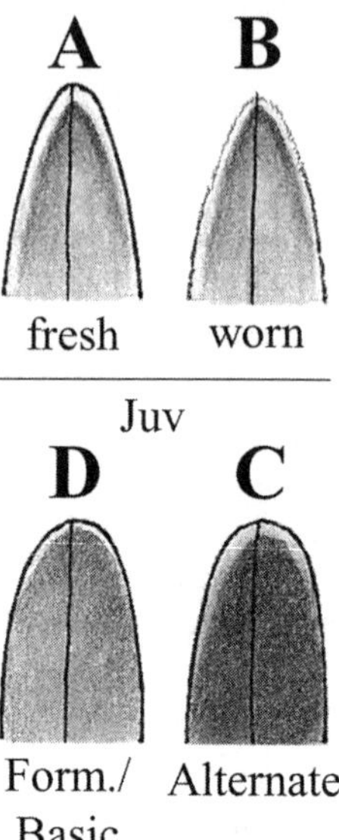

FIGURE 395. Shape and pattern to back feathers and secondary coverts by feather generation in Mountain Plover. The PF includes most to all back feathers and some to most proximal s covs in Aug-Nov/Jan, after which HY/SYs exhibit mixed juv (**A-B**) and formative (**C**) feathers (Fig. 375**B-D**, p. 503). AHY/ASYs have uniformly basic feathers (**C**) in Oct-Mar. Scattered alternate feathers (**D**) are present in Apr-Aug in both age groups, although averaging more frequent in ASYs than SYs.

Sex—♀ = ♂ by plumage aspect. Bilateral(?) BPs (Fig. 20**B**, p. 31) developed by both sexes but distended cloaca (Fig. 21, p. 32) indicates ♀ in Apr-Jun. Measurements unhelpful for sexing (Table 48, p. 527). ♂♂ average more black in the forehead during Apr-Aug than ♀♀ but reliable sexing is precluded by individual (including age-related) variation, except perhaps with some mated pairs. Otherwise, no criteria known for sexing.

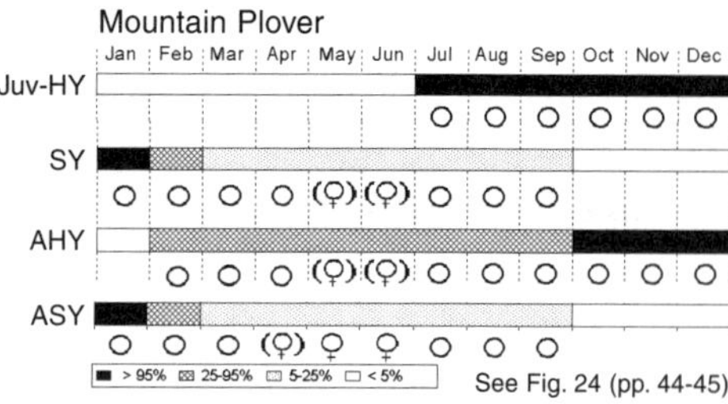

Hybrids reported—None.

References—Bent (1929), Iko et al. (2004), Knopf (1996), Oberholser (1974), Palmer (1967b), Prater et al. (1977), Ridgway (1919).

EURASIAN DOTTEREL
Charadrius morinellus

EUDO
Species # 2691
Band size: 1B-1A

Species—From other N.Am plovers and shorebirds by medium size (Table 48, p. 527); upperparts blackish and brown (Juvs and Oct-Mar) to grayish (AHYs in Apr-Sep) with buff, white, or tawny fringing and/or spots (brighter in ♀♀ than ♂♂); forehead and lores dark, contrasting with bold and long white to buff supercilia (joining or nearly joining at nape); bases to ss and inner pp without white; throat whitish; breast brown (Juvs) to gray (AHYs in Apr-Sep) with distinct buff to white band; abdomen with rich buff (Juv) to rufous and black (AHYs in Apr-Sep); legs yellowish, with hind toe absent (Fig. 373**A**, p. 500) and with moderate webbing between outer fore toes (Fig. 374**C**, p. 501).

Geographic variation—Monotypic.

Molt—CAS. PF partial-incomplete (Oct-Jan/Apr in HY/SYs), PA1 absent-limited (Apr-Jun in SYs), PB2 complete (Jun-Oct in non-breeding SYs), DPA partial-incomplete (Apr-May in ASYs), DPB complete (Jul-Oct/Dec in breeding AHYs). The PF occurs on non-breeding grounds, the PAs occur on non-breeding grounds or at stopover sites during migration, and the DPBs often commence on breeding grounds and complete on non-breeding grounds after suspension for migration. Molt exhibits both n.Hemisphere and s.Hemisphere strategies (Table 45, pp. 501-505). The PF includes some to all body feathers, some to most proximal s covs, and often 1-3 terts and 1-6 c.rects in Oct-Dec; in many individuals (with non-breeding grounds in the s.Hemisphere) the PF can also include the remaining rects, terts, and s covs (the distal med and gr covs sometimes retained), and 2-5 medial or outer pp and p covs and 1-3 medial ss (distal to the terts) in eccentric sequence (Fig. 376**A-D**, p. 504; sometimes arrested) in Dec-Apr. The PBs can suspend for migration after 4-8 pp (often during the PB2) or 2-5 pp (sometimes during the DPB) have been replaced on breeding grounds. The DPA includes most to all body feathers, some medial s covs, and often 1-3 terts and 1-8 c.rects. See pp. 500-507 for more information on molt in shorebirds.

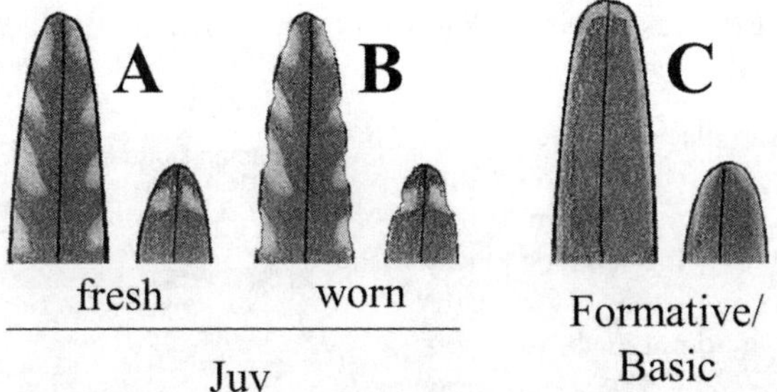

FIGURE 396. Shape and pattern to the tertials (left) and med covs (right) by feather generation in Eurasian Dotterel. For HY/SYs wintering in the n.Hemisphere the PF includes no to all terts and some to most proximal med covs; thus, HY/SYs exhibit a mixture of juv (**A-B**) and formative feathers in Nov-Sep. HY/SYs wintering in the s.Hemisphere typically replace all terts and most-to all s covs and exhibit feathers resembling those of AHY/ASYs in Mar-Sep. AHY/ASYs have uniformly basic feathers (**C**) in Oct-Mar and can have these mixed with similarly patterned but fresher alternate feathers in Mar-Sep; SYs replace few or no terts or s covs during the PA1.

Age—Juv (B1; Jul-Sep) has uniformly fresh plumage aspect, the back feathers and s covs narrow and with broad buff fringing, often broken or indented (Fig. 396**A**), and the pp uniformly juv and fresh (Fig. 375**A**, p. 503); Juv ♀=♂.

Juv-HY/SY (1st cycle, Juv/B1-F1-A1; Oct-Sep): All to some upperpart feathers (Oct-Dec), terts, and/or distal s covs juv, narrower, and with broad, often broken or indented, buff to whitish fringes (Fig. 396**A-B**), contrasting with fresher formative scapulars, humerals, terts, and proximal s covs (Figs. 375**B-C**, 396**C**), the retained juv distal gr covs becoming worn and frayed in Apr-Sep (Fig. 375**D**); pp, p covs, and ss uniformly juv and without s1-p1 contrast in Oct-Dec (Fig. 375**A**), sometimes being incompletely replaced in Dec-Apr and exhibiting eccentric replacement patterns in May-Sep (Fig. 376**A**), the juv outer pp and p covs (when present) tapered, brownish, and relatively worn (Figs. 377**A-B** & 378**A-B**, p. 506); rects uniformly juv and narrow in Oct-Dec (Fig. 379**A**, p. 507), mixed with formative rects in Dec-Sep (Fig. 379**B-C**) and sometimes in Apr-Sep (Fig. 379**D**); abdomen with indistinct (occasionally no) pale rufous or blackish in Apr-Sep by sex (see **Sex**).

AHY/ASY (Def. cycle, DB-DA; Oct-Sep): Upperpart feathers, terts, and s covs uniformly basic (Fig. 375**E**), broader, and with thin and complete pale fringing (Fig. 396**C**); pp, p covs, and ss worn and being completely replaced in Oct-Dec, or basic, fresh, and with replacement clines and s1-p1 contrast in Nov-Sep (Fig. 375**E**), the outer pp and p covs broad and truncate (Figs. 377**C-D** & 378**C-D**); rects uniformly basic and broader (Fig. 379**E**), often with 1-8 alternate c.rects in Apr-Sep (Fig. 379**F**); abdomen with variably distinct rufous and black aspect in Apr-Sep by sex (see **Sex**).

Sex—Full bilateral(?) BPs (Fig. 20**B**, p. 31) are reliable for sexing ♂♂ in May-Jul whereas distended cloaca (Fig. 21, p. 32) indicates ♀ in May-Jun; some ♀♀ may develop partial BPs. Measurements largely unhelpful for sexing (Table 48, p. 527). The following is reliable with ASYs (perhaps mated pairs) and some SY ♂♂ in Apr-Aug; some intermediates cannot be reliably sexed by plumage aspect alone. Otherwise, HY/SYs and AHY/ASYs in Oct-Feb are not reliably sexed by plumage aspect.

ASY ♀ (Apr-Aug): Cap uniformly blackish; breast gray with little to no brownish; abdomen dark rufous with extensive black patch (usually with completely black feathers) and little or no whitish mottling. **Note: See ASY ♂.**

ASY ♂ (Mar-Sep): Cap blackish, usually with some buff to whitish streaking; breast dull gray with buff to brownish mottling; abdomen pale rufous with reduced dusky patch (few or no completely black feathers), usually with moderate whitish mottling. **Note: Beware some SY ♀♀ can show this plumage aspect; only ASYs can be reliably sexed.**

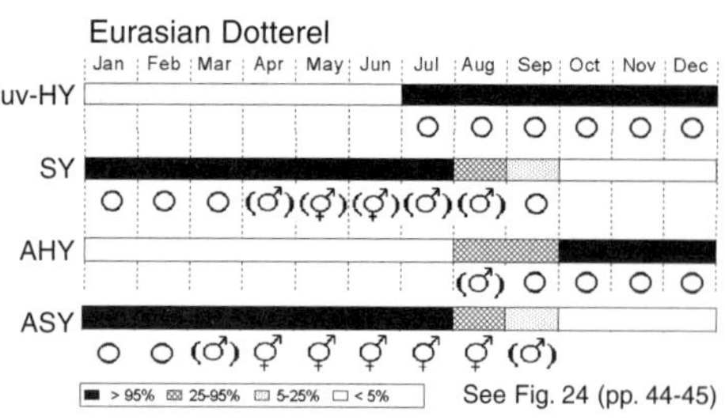

Hybrids reported—None.

References—Cramp & Simmons (1983), Kålås (1988), Nicoll & Kemp (1983), Palmer (1967b), Prater et al. (1977), Ridgway (1919), Stone (1900), Whitfield (1999).

OYSTERCATCHERS *HAEMATOPODIDAE*

Two species. Family characters include heavy bodies; proportionally short wings; sturdy legs and feet with hexagonal-shaped scales on the tarsi; no hind toes (Fig. 373**A**, p. 500); extensive webbing between fore toes (Fig. 374**E**, p. 501); and long, red bills (Fig. 399, p. 537), laterally compressed at the tip for opening bivalves. North American oystercatchers have 10 functional primaries (p10 longest by 0-12 mm when fully grown), 16-17 secondaries (including 4 tertials, and one absent between the 4th and 5th; *cf.* Fig. 12**B**, p. 19), and 12 rectrices. Ageing can be accomplished through the second cycle (to TY and ATY) by plumage aspect and bill color into at least spring, whereas sexes are similar in plumage aspect and size (♀♀ slightly larger). In molting, N.Am oystercatchers follow a n.Hemisphere strategy (Table 45, pp. 501-505) and appear to exhibit the Complex Basic Strategy (CBS; Fig. 10**B**, pp. 13-16), although a limited definitive prealternate molt may occur (as in Eurasian Oystercatcher), in which case N.Am species may exhibit a Simple Alternate Strategy (SAS; Fig. 10**E**). Age of first breeding is 2-5 years. See pp. 500-507 for further information on molt and ageing in shorebirds.

AMERICAN OYSTERCATCHER
Haematopus palliatus

AMOY
Species # 2860
Band size: 5

BLACK OYSTERCATCHER
Haematopus bachmani

BLOY
Species # 2870
Band size: 5

Species—Oystercatchers from other N.Am shorebirds by large size and long bill (Table 49, p. 541); head blackish, contrasting with brown back and rump; orbital ring and bill reddish (Juv) to red (Fig. 399, p. 537); iris yellow; legs pale pinkish, with hind toe absent (Fig. 373**A**, p. 500) and with extensive webbing between outer fore toes (Fig. 374**C**-**D**, p. 501). American from Black oystercatcher by larger average size and longer tail (Table 49); rects and ss with distinct white bases (*cf.* Fig. 398); breast and abdomen white (*vs* rects, ss, and abdomen dark brown in Black Oystercatcher). Hybridism between these two species occurs regularly in sw.CA-Baja CA; progeny can show complete range of variation in the amount of white to the wing, tail, and underparts (Jehl 1985). Eurasian Oystercatcher (*H. ostralegus*; a vagrant to ne.N.Am) from American Oystercatcher by shorter average bill and tarsus (wg chord 235-268, tail 99-112, exp culmen 61-89, tarsus 47-55); head and upper back uniformly black; lower back and rump white (*vs.* brown in American Oystercatcher); all rects with broad white bases (*vs* r1 without white and r2-r6 with narrower white bases in American Oystercatcher; *cf.* Fig. 398, p. 536); iris reddish.

Geographic variation—Black Oystercatcher monotypic, although populations in s.CA-Baja can show paler abdomens and white feathers due to introgression with American Oystercatcher (Jehl 1985). For American Oystercatcher, see Blake (1977), Brewster (1888), Gifford (1913), Hayman et al. (1986), Hellmayr & Conover (1948b), Jehl (1985), Murphy (1925, 1936), Ridgway (1919), and Wetmore (1965). Three other subspecies occur in S.Am.

American Oystercatcher

H.p. frazari (br w.Mex, visitor and former breeder sw.CA): Wing averages longer but bill and tarsus average shorter (Table 49, p. 541); breast with mottled division between dark and white; back and upperparts dusky; bases to p1-p4, uppertail covs, and underwing p covs dusky or mottled dusky; s10-s12 usually with some brown markings.

H.p. palliatus (br and wint coastal TX-FL-MA, vagrant to Oct-NS): Wing averages shorter but bill and tarsus average longer (Table 49); breast with clean division between dark and white; back and upperparts brown; bases to p1-p4, s10-s12, uppertail covs, and underwing p covs white. Populations of the Bahama Is (*"pratti"*), may average larger but difference slight.

Molt—CBS (SAS?). PF limited-incomplete (Sep-Dec in HYs), PB2 complete (Apr-Sep in non-breeding SYs), DPB incomplete-complete (Jun-Oct/Dec in breeding ASYs); PA absent(?). The PF includes some to most body feathers, no to a few proximal s covs, sometimes 1-3 terts, and often 1-2 c.rects (occasionally to all rects). The DPBs can be suspended in breeding ASYs, with 1-3 pp replaced during incubation in Jun, followed by the remainder in Sep-Dec. 1-3 medial ss (usually among s7-s12) can be retained by American Oystercatchers during DPBs. A limited DPA of head feathers may occur in some ASYs, as in Eurasian Oystercatcher, but see Webster (1942). See pp. 500-507 for more information on molt in shorebirds.

Age—Juv (B1; Jul-Oct) has back feathers and wing covs smaller and with rusty fringes or broken fringes (Fig. 397**A**), bill short and blackish (*cf.* Fig. 399**A**), and iris brownish; Juv ♀=♂.

HY/SY (1st cycle, F1; Oct-Sep): Bill dull to bright red with distinct dusky tip (Fig. 399**A**); all to some upperpart (e.g., rump) feathers and terts, and most s covs juv (Fig. 375**A**, p. 503), with cinnamon fringes or broken fringes when fresh (Fig. 397**A**), often bleaching to pale brown or whitish by Jan (Fig. 397**B**), and contrasting with fresher formative scapulars, terts (sometimes), and s covs (Figs. 375**B**-**C** & 397**C**), the retained distal juv s covs becoming worn and frayed by Apr-Sep (Fig. 375**D**); some to all juv rects usually retained (Fig. 379**A**-**D**, p. 507), contrastingly narrow, worn, and with reduced and less distinct white bases in American Oystercatcher (Fig. 398**A**); pp, p covs, and medial ss uniformly juv and without s1-p1 contrast (Fig. 375**A**), being replaced in May-Oct, the juv outer pp and p covs tapered, brownish, and relatively

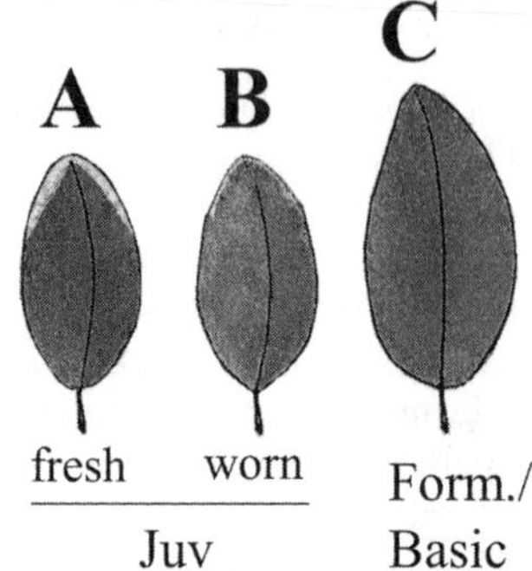

FIGURE 397. Size and pattern to the secondary coverts by feather generation in American and Black oystercatchers. Juv feathers have distinct cinnamon to rufous fringing when fresh (**A**); by Oct-Nov these become mixed with formative feathers (**C**) in HY/SYs and by Mar-Sep the remaining juv feathers become very worn, with little or no pale fringing remaining (**B**). AHY/ASYs exhibit uniformly broad basic covs (**C**).

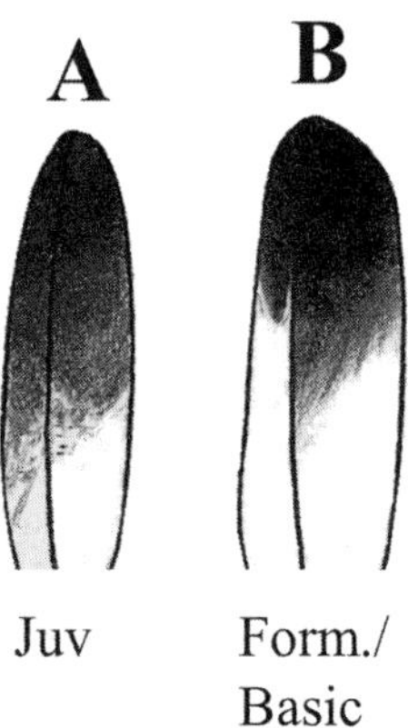

FIGURE 398. Size, shape, and pattern to the rectrices in American Oystercatcher; Black Oystercatcher exhibits similar differences in shape and size but have entirely dark feathers. The extent of white at the bases in American Oystercatcher varies but averages greater in formative and basic feathers than on juv feathers; note also the less distinct transition between dark and white in the juv feathers. Most HY/SYs retain all to some juv rects during the PF and can be aged through Aug-Sep; occasional HY/SYs replace all rects and cannot be distinguished from ASYs after Dec by this character alone.

worn (Figs. 377**A-B** & 378**A**, p. 506); iris brownish to dull yellow.

AHY/ASY (Def. cycle, DB; Oct-Sep): Bill red with yellow tip (Fig. 399**C**); upperpart feathers, terts, and s covs uniformly basic (Fig. 375**E**), without pale fringes or tips (Fig. 397**C**); rects uniformly basic and broader (Fig. 379**E**), with expanded and more distinct white bases in American Oystercatcher (Fig. 398**B**); pp, p covs, and ss worn and being replaced in Oct-Dec, or basic, fresher, and with uninterrupted replacement clines and slight s1-p1 contrast in Nov-Sep (Fig. 375**E**), the outer pp and p covs broad, truncate, and relatively fresh (Figs. 377**C-D** & 378**C-D**); iris bright yellow. **Note: It is possible that individuals fitting the above description can be reliably aged ASY/ATY but more study is needed.**

SY/TY (2nd cycle, B2; Oct-May): Like AHY/ASY (with uninterrupted replacement clines) but bill with dusky to brownish tinge and with dull yellow tip (Fig. 399**B**) through Feb-May; iris dull to bright yellow.

ASY/ATY (Def. cycle, DB; Oct-Sep): Like AHY/ASY but pp often with suspension limit among p1-p4 (Fig. 376**F**, p. 504); 1-3 ss among s7-s12 sometimes retained (Fig. 14**D**, p. 21; typically in American Oystercatcher only); bill bright red and yellow (Fig. 399**C**), often with orangish tinge to yellow tip; iris bright yellow.

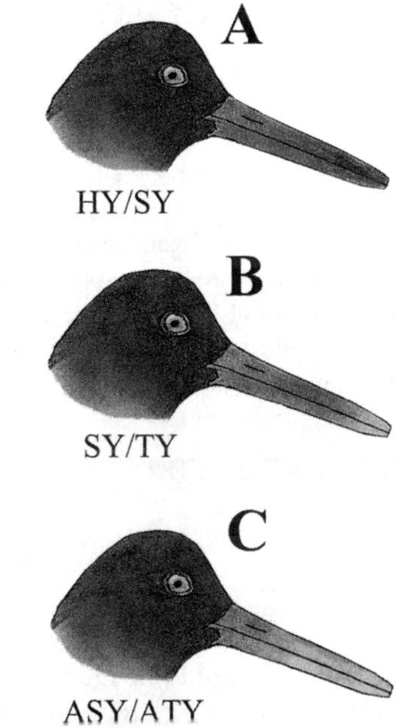

FIGURE 399. Bill color by age in American and Black oystercatchers. In Juvs the bill can be dusky with a dull reddish base; the dusky gradually disappears (**A-B**) such that by ASY it has been replaced by a bright red bill with a yellowish tip (**C**).

Sex—♀=♂ by plumage aspect. Bilateral BPs (Fig. 20**B**, p. 31) developed by both sexes but distended cloaca (Fig. 21, p. 32) indicates ASY ♀ in Apr-Jun. Measurements largely unhelpful for sexing (Table 49, p. 541). Otherwise, no criteria known.

Hybrids reported—American Oystercatcher with Black Oystercatcher (Bancroft 1927, Jehl 1985, Kenyon 1949, Wehtje 2005, Willett 1913) and with Blackish Oystercatcher *H. ater* (Fleming 1973, Happleston 1973, Jehl et al. 1973).

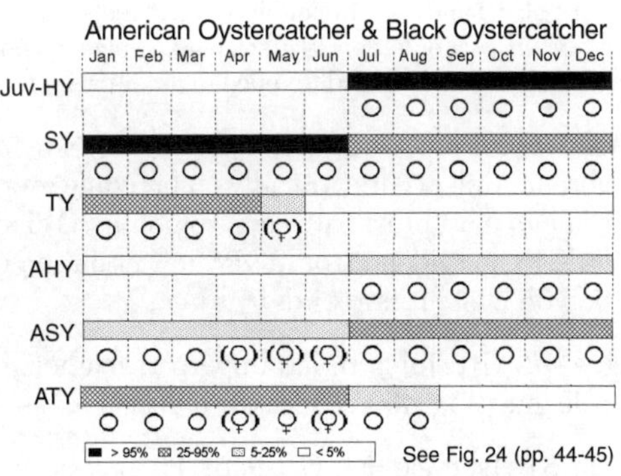

References—Andres & Falxa (1995), Bent (1929), Cramp & Simmons (1983), Jehl (1985), Murphy (1936), Oberholser (1974), Nol & Humphrey (1994), Palmer (1967b), Prater et al. (1977), Ridgway (1919), Webster (1942).

STILTS AND AVOCETS *RECURVIROSTRIDAE*

Two species. Family characters include thin bodies with long necks, extremely long legs, and long bills, recurved in avocets. North American stilts and avocets have 10 functional primaries (p10 longest by 10-15 [stilt] or 0-8 [avocet] mm when fully grown), 16-17 secondaries (including 4 tertials, and one absent between the 4th and 5th; *cf.* Fig. 12**B**, p. 19), and 12 rectrices. Ageing can be accomplished through the second cycle (to SY and ASY) by plumage aspect. Sexes are similar in size (♀♀ moderately smaller); stilts can be sexed by plumage aspect and avocets by bill morphology. In molting, N.Am stilts appear to exhibit the Complex Basic Strategy (CBS; Fig. 10**B**, pp. 13-16), avocets exhibit the Complex Alternate Strategy (CAS; Fig. 10**F**), and both species follow a n.Hemisphere strategy (Table 45, pp. 501-505). Age of first breeding is 1-2 years. See pp. 500-507 for further information on molt and ageing in shorebirds.

BLACK-NECKED STILT
Himantopus mexicanus

BNST
Species # 2260
Band size: 4-3A Above joint

Species—From other N.Am shorebirds by medium size with long tarsus (Table 49, p. 541); bill thin, tapered, and black; crown, nape, upper back, and upper and under wings (of N.Am subspecies; see **Geographic variation**) blackish brown to glossy black; rump, tail, sides of neck, and underparts white; iris brownish (juv) to red (ASY); legs pink to pinkish red, with hind toe absent (Fig. 373**A**, p. 500) and with slight webbing between outer fore toes (Fig. 374**B**, p. 501). Black-winged Stilt (*H. himantopus*), a vagrant to w.AK, has longer tail (72-86) and tarsus (104-137); crown and nape white, often with indistinct dusky cap. Beware of leucistic (partially amelanistic) Black-necked Stilts that can resemble other taxa of *Himantopus*.

Geographic variation—See Blake (1977), Hellmayr & Conover (1948b), Ridgway (1919), Robinson et al. (1999). Two other subspecies occur, in S.Am and in the Hawaiian Is.

H.m. mexicanus (br & wint N.Am): Smaller (Table 49, p. 541) *vs.* larger with longer tarsus in *knudseni* of the Hawaiian Is (wg 213-250, exp culmen 69-79, tarsus 165-220); crown blackish and extending to back (*vs* crown mostly to entirely white and black of neck separated from back by white bar in *melanurus* of S.Am); auriculars, sides of neck and throat white or slightly mottled black (*vs* mottled black to black in *knudseni*); uppertail covs and rects white (*vs* tipped dusky to blackish in *knudseni*). Within *mexicanus*, ♀♀ of FL populations may average darker and grayer upperparts than ♀♀ of other populations (Ridgway 1919) but difference slight, if present.

Molt—CBS. PF partial-incomplete (Aug-Nov in HYs), DPB complete (Jun-Sep in AHYs); PA absent. Molt occurs primarily on breeding grounds. The PF includes most to all body feathers, some to most proximal s covs, sometimes 1-3 terts, and often 2-4 (rarely to all) c.rects. There is little to no evidence for a DPA (*cf.* Robinson et al. 1999). See pp. 500-507 for more information on molt in shorebirds.

Age—Juv (B1; Jul-Sep) has upperpart feathers broadly fringed buff, ss and proximal pp tipped pale gray (Fig. 400**A**), rects with dusky marks (Fig. 401**A**), and iris brown.

HY/SY (1st cycle, F1; Oct-Sep): Pp, p covs, and medial ss juv (Fig. 375**A**, p. 503), the outer ss (s1-s5) and inner pp (p1-p5) tipped pale gray (Fig. 400**A**), and the outer pp and p covs tapered, brownish, and relatively worn (Figs. 377**A-B** & 378**A**, p. 506); some to all juv rects usually retained (Fig. 379**A-D**, p. 507), contrastingly narrow, worn, and with white indistinct dusky subterminal band or smudging (Fig. 401**A**); some to most s covs and/or terts juv, brownish with buff fringes when fresh, contrasting with fresher formative scapulars, humerals, terts, and/or proximal s covs (Fig. 375**B-C**), the retained distal juv s covs becoming worn and frayed by Apr-Sep (Fig. 375**D**); iris brownish red in Oct-Dec, becoming dull (♀) to medium-bright (♂) red in Jan-Sep (see **Sex**).

AHY/ASY (Def. cycle, DB; Oct-Sep): Pp, p covs, and medial ss basic and fresher (Fig. 375**E**), the outer pp and p covs broad and truncate (Figs. 377**C-D** & 378**C-D**), and the outer ss and inner pp without pale tips (Fig. 400**B**); rects uniformly basic and broader (Fig. 379**E**), without dusky subterminal band (Fig. 401**B**); upperpart feathers, terts, and s covs uniformly basic (Fig. 375**E**), without pale fringing; iris dull to bright red by sex and season (see **Sex**).

Sex—Bilateral(?) BPs (Fig. 20**B**, p. 31) developed by both sexes but distended cloaca (Fig. 21, p. 32) indicates ♀ in Apr-Jun. Measurements largely unhelpful for sexing (Table 49, p. 541). The following is reliable following commencement of the PF in HYs in Aug-Sep:

♀: Crown and nape blackish brown; back, humerals, scapulars, and terts brown, contrasting with blacker wing covs; AHY/ASYs with iris medium-dull (Aug-Feb) to medium-bright (Mar-Jul) red (see **Age**).

♂: Crown, nape, back, and terts uniformly glossy black; AHY/ASYs with iris medium-bright (Aug-Feb) to bright (Mar-Jul) red (see **Age**).

Hybrids reported—With American Avocet (Morlan 2004, O'Brien et al. 2006) in the wild (see also Principe 1977). A probable escaped Black-necked Stilt with Black-winged Stilt in the wild in Europe (Meininger 1993).

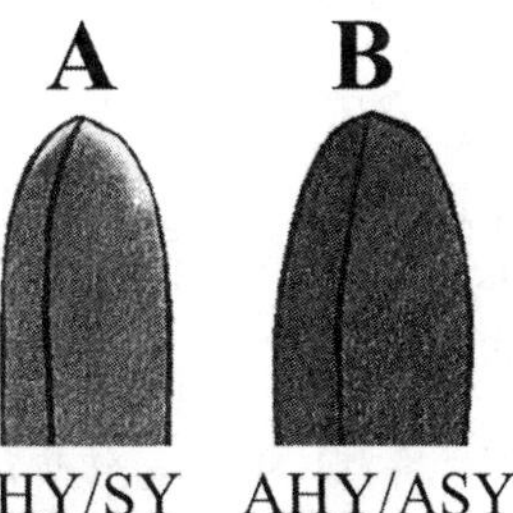

FIGURE 400. Shape and pattern to the outer secondaries (s1-s5) and inner primaries (p1-p5) by age in Black-necked Stilt. Juv feathers (**A**) are retained by SYs until the PB2 in Jun-Sep.

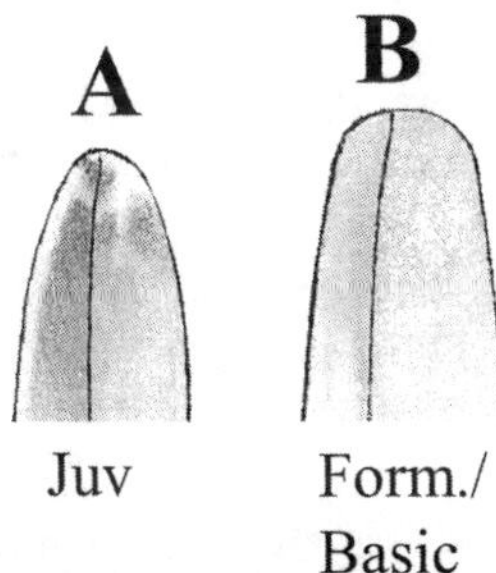

FIGURE 401. Shape and pattern to the outer rectrices (r6 shown) by feather generation in Black-necked Stilt. HY/SYs usually retain at least one juv rect (**A**, among r4-r6) until the PB2 in Jun-Sep; occasional HY/SYs show uniformly formative (**B**) rects..

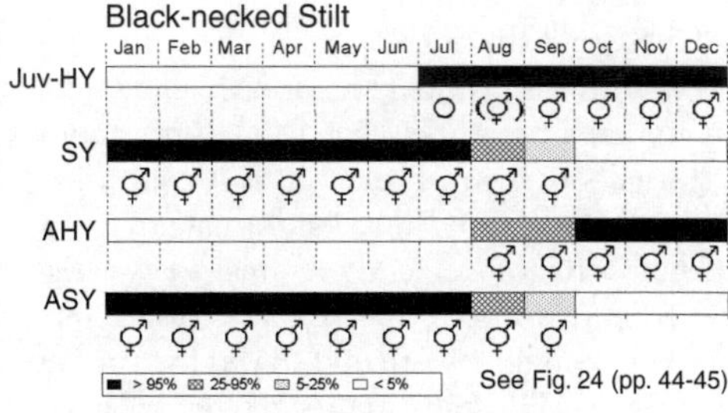

References—Bent (1927), Burger (1980), Cramp & Simmons (1983), Hamilton (1975), Oberholser (1974), Palmer (1967b), Prater et al. (1977), Ridgway (1919), Roberts (1955), Robinson et al. (1999).

AMERICAN AVOCET
Recurvirostra americana

AMAV
Species # 2250
Band size: 4-4A Above joint

Species—From other N.Am shorebirds by medium-large size, long bill, and relatively long tarsus (Table 49, p. 541); bill recurved and black (Fig. 403); head and neck pale gray (Sep-Feb) to cinnamon (Mar-Aug); back, rump, tail, scapulars, s11-s13, and underwing covs primarily white; les and med covs, pp, and p covs primarily blackish; iris dark; legs gray-blue, with small hind toe (Fig. 373**B**, p. 500) and substantial webbing between fore toes (Fig. 374**E**, p. 501).

Geographic variation—Monotypic.

Molt—CAS. PF partial-incomplete (Oct-Dec/Mar in HY/SYs), DPA limited (Feb-May in AHYs), DPB complete (Jun-Oct in AHYs). The PF commences on breeding grounds but completes on non-breeding grounds, the DPA occurs primarily on non-breeding grounds, and the DPB appears to occur primarily at stopover locations or molting grounds within the breeding range of the species. The PF includes most to all body feathers, up to 70% of the s covs, often 1-3 terts, and usually 2 to (sometimes) all 12 rects; body feathers are replaced primarily in Oct-Dec whereas some s covs, terts, and rects can be replaced in Jan-Mar. The DPA is primarily limited to feathers of the head and neck.

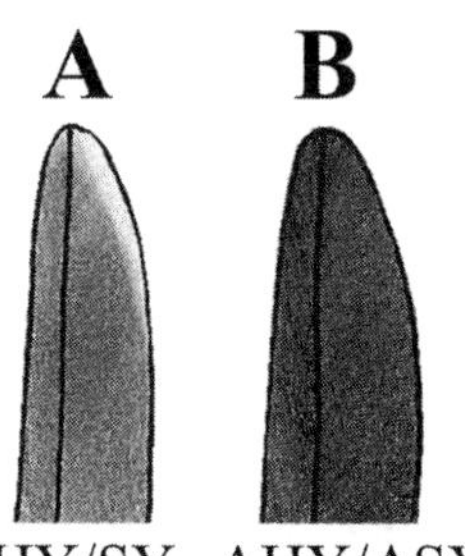

FIGURE 402. Shape and pattern to inner primaries (p4 shown) by age in American Avocet. The juv p1-p5 on HY/SYs have broad pale fringes as shown in **A**; the definitive p1-p3 can often show much thinner white fringes but p4-p5 lack (**B**) or occasionally have extremely thin pale fringes. The juv inner pp (**A**) are retained by SYs until the PB2 in Jun-Oct.

Age—Juv (B1; Jul-Sep) has head and neck cinnamon to buff, back brown, inner pp tipped white (Fig. 402**A**), and legs tinged olive; Juvs can be sexed by bill morphology (Fig. 403).

Juv-HY/SY (1st cycle, Juv/B1-F1-A1; Oct-Sep): Pp, p covs, and medial ss uniformly juv and without s1-p1 contrast (Fig. 375**A**), the outer pp and p covs tapered, brownish, and relatively worn (Figs. 377**A-B** & 378**A**, p. 506), and the inner pp (p1-p5) with inner web fringed white (Fig. 402**A**); all to some upperpart feathers (Oct-Dec), terts, and/or distal s covs juv, brownish, and contrasting with fresher and duskier formative scapulars, terts (often), and proximal s covs (Fig. 375**B-C**, p. 503), the retained distal juv s covs becoming worn and frayed by Apr-Sep (Fig. 375**D**); some juv rects often retained, contrastingly narrow and worn (Fig. 379**A-D**, p. 507).

AHY/ASY (Def. cycle, DB-DA; Oct-Sep): Pp, p covs, and medial ss basic and often with slight s1-p1 contrast (Fig. 375**E**), the outer pp and p covs broad, truncate, and relative-

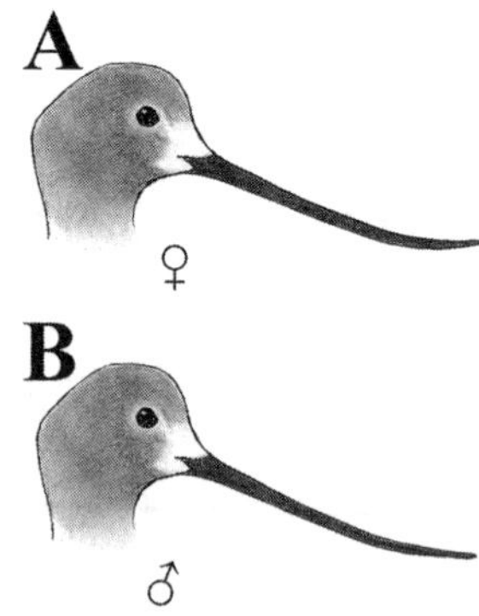

FIGURE 403. Bill shape by sex in American Avocet. See Hamilton (1975) for a statistical treatment of this difference.

ly fresh (Fig. 377**C-D** & 378**C-D**), and p1-p3 often with thin white fringes but p4-p5 without white (Fig. 402**B**); upperpart feathers, terts, and s covs uniformly basic (Fig. 375**E**), dusky to blackish; rects uniformly basic and broader (Fig. 379**E**).

Sex— ♀ = ♂ by plumage aspect. Bilateral(?) BPs (Fig. 20**B**, p. 31) developed by both sexes but distended cloaca (Fig. 21, p. 32) indicates ASY ♀ in Apr-Jun. Measurements largely unhelpful for sexing (Table 49, p. 541) but the following is reliable for all individuals (including Juvs):

♀: Bill strongly recurved (Fig. 403**A**).

♂: Bill slightly recurved (Fig. 403**B**).

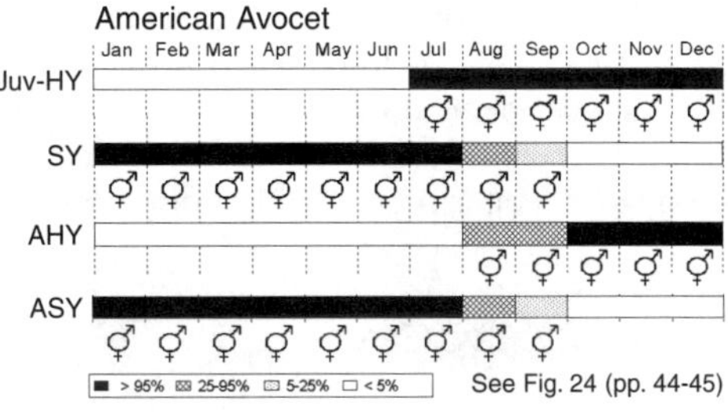

Hybrids reported— With Black-necked Stilt (p. 538) in the wild.

References— Bent (1927), Bucher (1978), Gibson (1971), Hamilton (1975), Oberholser (1974), Palmer (1967b), Prater et al. (1977), Ridgway (1919), Robinson et al. (1997), Sordhal (1988).

TABLE 49. Measurements (mm) of North American oystercatchers, stilts, avocets, and jacanas for identification and sexing. See pp. 4-11 for methods of measurement. Species summaries are in **bold** and subspecies summaries are in ***italics***. Values were derived from 95% confidence intervals as based approximately on the indicated sample sizes (see pp. 4-5). Thus, midpoints of ranges approximate means, and S.D. is approximated by 25% of the range.

Taxon/Sex	n	wing chord	tail length	exposed culmen	tarsus
American Oystercatcher		**238-273**	**91-110**	**69-97**	**50-65**
H.p. frazari		***245-273***	***94-110***	***69-92***	***50-60***
♀	40	250-273	97-110	77-92	52-60
♂	45	245-267	94-107	69-84	50-59
H.p. palliatus		***238-270***	***91-109***	***73-97***	***52-65***
♀	60	243-270	95-109	80-97	54-65
♂	65	238-263	91-105	73-90	52-63
Black Oystercatcher		**233-260**	**76-92**	**61-82**	**48-59**
♀	70	235-260	79-92	66-82	49-59
♂	85	233-257	76-89	61-75	48-57
Black-necked Stilt[1]		**206-239**	**64-78**	**59-69**	**96-119**
♀	80	206-229	64-74	59-69	96-112
♂	100	215-239	67-78	59-69	103-119
American Avocet[2]		**211-243**	**76-104**	**77-91**	**82-106**
♀	100	211-239	76-92	77-89	82-101
♂	100	215-243	87-104	79-91	86-106
Northern Jacana[3]		**111-140**	**37-45**	**40-50**	**47-59**
♀	40	127-140	42-51	43-50	50-59
♂	55	111-126	37-45	40-46	47-56

[1] Measures from N.Am populations only; see **Geographic variation**.
[2] Exposed culmen represents chord.
[3] Exposed culmen represents chord including frontal shield.

JACANAS

One species. Family characters include thin bodies, frontal shields to the bills (Fig. 404), small and rounded wings with metacarpal spurs (Fig. 406), and extremely long toes. North American jacanas have 10 functional primaries (p10 roughly equal in length to the 7th-9th, when fully grown), 12 secondaries (including 3 tertials, and one absent between the 4th and 5th; *cf.* Fig. 12**B**, p. 19), and 10 rectrices. Ageing can be accomplished through the second cycle (to SY/TY and AHY/ASY or ASY/ATY) by plumage aspect and development of the wing spurs and frontal shield. Sexes can be separated by size (♀♀ > ♂♂); in addition, only males incubate and develop brood patches. In molting, jacanas exhibit the Complex Basic Strategy (CBS; Fig. 10**B**, pp. 13-16); the preformative molt is protracted and often complete. Age of first breeding occurs at 1-2 years.

NORTHERN JACANA

Jacana spinosa

NOJA
Species # 2880
Band size: 3A

Species—From other N.Am shorebirds by medium size with proportionally short tail (Table 49, p. 541), wing rounded (p10 ≈ p7-p9); pp and ss primarily yellow (Fig. 405); AHY/ASY with blackish and chestnut plumage aspect; HY/SY with dull-olive upperparts and whitish supercilium and underparts; bill yellowish and with frontal shield (Fig. 404); iris dark; legs and feet olive-gray with extremely long fore toes (> 40 mm).

Geographic variation—Monotypic (Blake 1977). Populations of Mex ("*J.s. gymnostoma*" and "*lowi*") may average smaller and duller, and populations of the W.Indes ("*violacea*") may average brighter and with more maroon than populations of C.Am, but differences slight and broadly clinal. See Conover (1945b), Hellmayr & Conover (1948b), Todd (1916a), van Rossem (1938a), and Wetmore (1965) for more information.

Molt—CBS. PF incomplete-complete (Aug-May in HY/SYs), DPB complete (Jun-Dec/Mar in AHY/ASYs); PA absent. The above timing and extent pertain to N.Am populations; there is substantial variation in timing due to irregular and protracted breeding. 1-4 outer pp and p covs and 1-6 ss (among s3-4 and s7-s10) can be retained during the PF.

Age—Juv (B1; May-Sep) has brownish upperparts with cinnamon fringing, dull brownish bill with rudimentary frontal shield (Fig. 404**A**), and small and triangular wing spur (Fig. 406**A**); Juv ♀ = ♂ by plumage aspect, but wing chord is reliable for sexing (see **Sex**) once fully grown. The

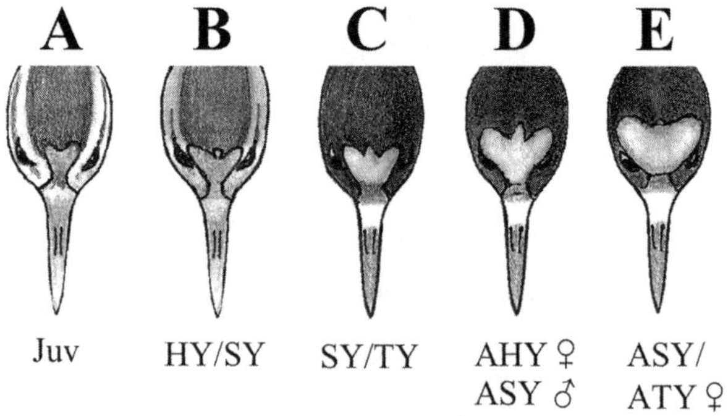

FIGURE 404. Size, shape and coloration of the frontal shield by age and sex in Northern Jacana. Note that ♀♀ may develop shields faster then ♂♂; thus, age determination of SY/TYs and ASY/ATYs should be undertaken after sex has been determined by measurements.

following month ranges pertain to N.Am populations.

HY/SY (1st cycle, F1; Jul-Jun): Upperparts grayish olive, increasingly mixed with blackish and chestnut in Sep-Jun; underparts mostly to entirely whitish; bill brownish yellow with reduced frontal shield (Fig. 404**A-B**); juv outer pp and p covs (when present), narrow, straight, and with indistinct pale-yellow centers (Fig. 405**A**); wing spur small and triangular (Fig. 406**A-B**).

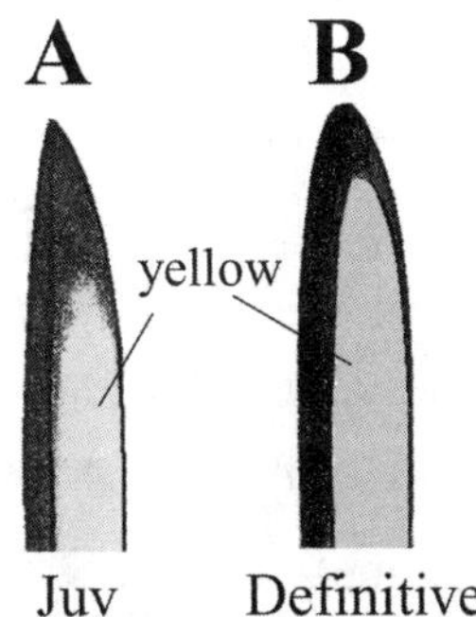

FIGURE 405. Shape and color pattern to the underside of the outer primary (p10) by feather generation in Northern Jacana. The juv p10 (**A**) is sometimes retained during the PF and can be used to age SY/TY through completion of the PB2, in Nov or later (more study needed).

AHY/ASY (Def. cycle, DB; Aug-Sep): Upperparts and underparts blackish and chestnut, with or without olive to lower back and scapulars; bill yellow and bluish, with moderately extensive frontal shield (Fig. 404**D**); outer pp and p covs basic, broad, slightly sinuate, and with distinct bright-yellow centers (Fig. 405**B**); wing spur moderately large and triangular (Fig. 406**D**). **Note: More study is needed on reliable age determination of SY/TYs and ASY/ATYs by size and shape of frontal shield and wing spur. Note also that ♀♀ may develop shields and spurs faster than ♂♂, so combine with sex for most accurate age determinations. See also ASY/ATY.**

SY/TY (2nd cycle, B2; Aug-Sep): Like AHY/ASY but lower back and scapulars with some olive feathering; chin mottled or tinged pale brownish; some underpart feathers with whitish fringing; frontal shield moderately small by sex (Fig. 404**C**); wing spur moderately small and triangular by sex (Fig. 406**C**); outer pp occasionally retained through Nov or later, very worn and with indistinct yellow centers (Fig. 405**A**). **Note: See AHY/ASY**.

ASY/ATY (Def. cycle, DB; Aug-Sep): Like AHY/ASY but lower back and scapulars without olive; frontal shield large (Fig. 404**E**); wing spur large and attenuated (Fig. 406**E**). **Note: See AHY/ASY. It is possible that only ♀♀ with maximum shield and spur development can be aged ASY/ATY; more study needed**.

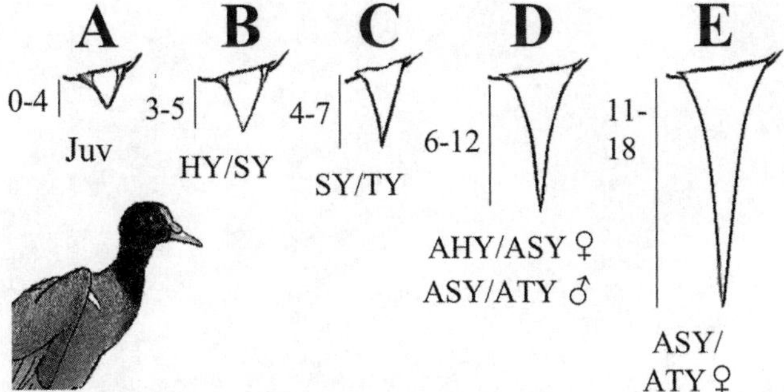

FIGURE 406. Variation in the shape and length of the wing spur (see inset) by age and sex in Northern Jacana. The spur is typically folded under the wing but can be everted when needed for territorial disputes or defense. Note that the spurs of ♀♀ grow longer and may develop quicker than those of ♂♂; thus, intermediates are likely younger ♀♀ or older ♂♂; lengths of >15 mm indicate ASY/ATY ♀♀.

Sex—♀ = ♂ by plumage aspect. Medial(?) BP (Fig. 19**A**, p. 28) indicates ♂ in Mar-Jul whereas a distended cloaca (Fig. 21, p. 32) indicates ASY ♀ in Feb-Jun. Measurements reliable for sexing (Table 49, p. 541; see below). In addition to the following, shield size and wing spurs average larger in ♀♀ by age (Figs. 404 & 406, pp. 542-543).

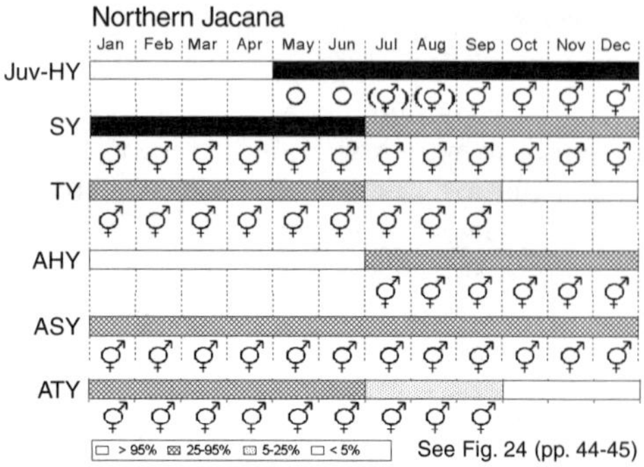

♀: Wing chord > 126, bill depth at base > 8.5.

♂: Wing chord < 126, bill depth at base < 8.5.

Hybrids reported—Possibly with Wattled Jacana *J. jacana* (Betts 1973, Hellmayr & Conover 1948b, Wetmore 1965; but see Jenni & Mace 1999).

Northern Jacana

	Jan	Feb	Mar	Apr	May	Jun	Jul	Aug	Sep	Oct	Nov	Dec
Juv-HY					O	O	(⚥)	(⚥)	⚥	⚥	⚥	⚥
SY	⚥	⚥	⚥	⚥	⚥	⚥	⚥	⚥	⚥	⚥	⚥	⚥
TY	⚥	⚥	⚥	⚥	⚥	⚥	⚥	⚥	⚥			
AHY							⚥	⚥	⚥	⚥	⚥	⚥
ASY	⚥	⚥	⚥	⚥	⚥	⚥	⚥	⚥	⚥	⚥	⚥	⚥
ATY	⚥	⚥	⚥	⚥	⚥	⚥	⚥	⚥	⚥			

> 95% 25-95% 5-25% < 5%

See Fig. 24 (pp. 44-45)

References—Bent (1929), Dickey & van Rossem (1938), Howell & Webb (1995), Jenni & Mace (1999), Oberholser (1974), Palmer (1967b), Ridgway (1919), Stresemann & Stresemann (1966), Todd (1916a).

SANDPIPERS, PHALAROPES, AND ALLIES *SCOLOPACIDAE*

Forty species. Family characters are variable; for convenience, this family is separated into two subfamilies and eight tribes, reflecting groups with differing structures, molts, and plumages.

Tringine Sandpipers *Scolopacidae, Scolopacinae, Tringini*

Six species. Tribal characters include small to medium-sized bodies, long wings, straight bills, proportionally long legs in several species, well-developed hind toes (Fig. 373**C**, p. 500), and slight to extensive webbing between fore toes (Fig. 374**B-E**, p. 501). North American tringine sandpipers have 10 functional primaries (p10 longest by 2-8 mm, when fully grown), 14-17 secondaries (including 4-5 tertials, and one absent between the 4th and 5th; *cf.* Fig. 12**B**, p. 19), and 12 rectrices. Ageing can be accomplished through the first cycle (to SY and ASY), and sometimes into the third cycle (TY) by plumage aspect and molt patterns among wing feathers; sexes are similar in plumage aspect and size (♀♀ slightly to moderately larger). In molting, N.Am tringine sandpipers exhibit the Complex Alternate Strategy (CAS; Fig 10**F**, pp. 13-16) and, among species, both n.Hemisphere and/or s.Hemisphere strategies (Table 45, pp. 501-505) are employed. Age of first breeding is 1-2 years in smaller species and 2-3 years in larger species. See pp. 500-507 for further information on molt and ageing in shorebirds.

SPOTTED SANDPIPER
Actitis macularia

SPSA
Species # 3630
Band size: 1B-1A

Species—From other N.Am shorebirds by medium-small size (Table 50, p. 549), bill straight or slightly decurved, and pale (often yellowish) with a dark tip; upperparts (including rump and c.rects) and breast pale brownish, the breast white with dusky sides; eyeline and supercilium distinct; inner pp and outer ss with white triangular patches to inner webs; AHYs with distinct black spots to underparts in Mar-Aug (Fig. 409, p. 547); underwing coverts with dark med and p covs contrasting with white lesser and gr covs (*cf.* Fig. 409); legs and feet yellowish to pinkish yellow, with hind toe relatively well developed (Fig. 373**C**, p. 500) and slight webbing between outer fore toes (Fig. 374**B**, p. 501).

Common Sandpiper (*A. hypoleucos*), a vagrant from Eurasia, averages larger (wg chord 103-113, tl 48-58, exp culmen 22-27, tarsus 23-27); white patches of pp and ss more extensive, the dark tip to p5 usually < 25 mm along shaft *vs* > 25 mm in Spotted Sandpiper) and s9 primarily white, without well-defined dark band (Fig. 407); inner web to r6 distinctly barred dusky and white (*vs* indistinctly washed or marked dusky in Spotted Sandpiper); breast with complete or near-complete dusky band in all plumage aspects; juv terts plain with dark subterminal marks (*vs* with white lateral scalloping in Spotted Sandpiper); underparts without spots in Mar-Aug (*cf.* Fig. 409); base of bill and legs grayish; legs grayish to dull pinkish.

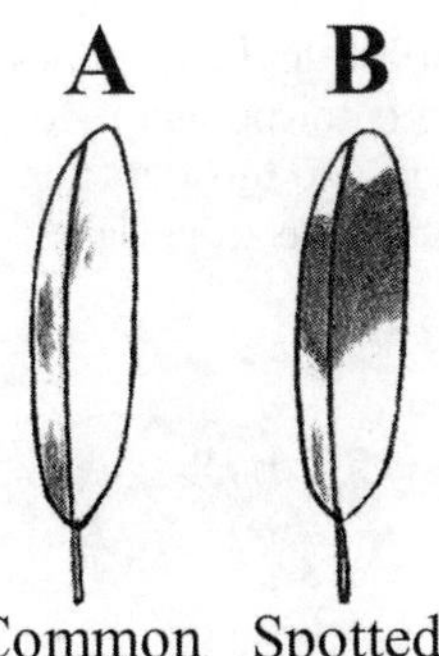

FIGURE 407. Typical color pattern to s9 to differentiate Common and Spotted sandpipers. Both species may exhibit substantial variation in the exact pattern but the amount of white is greater in Common Sandpiper than Spotted Sandpiper, with little or no overlap.

Geographic variation—Monotypic (Browning 1990). Populations of AK to OR-ID ("*A.m. rava*") may average darker and with less-distinct spots in Mar-Aug but differences, if present, insufficient. See also Burleigh (1960), Oberholser (1974).

Molt—CAS. PF incomplete (Oct-Feb/May in HY/SYs), PA1 limited-partial (Mar-Jun in SYs), DPB complete (Sep-Nov/Apr in AHY/ASYs), DPA partial (Mar-May in ASYs). Most to all molting occurs on non-breeding grounds, although the DPB sometimes commences (body feathers and up to 4 inner pp) on breeding grounds or at stopover sites. Molt of most individuals follows a s.Hemisphere strategy (Table 45, pp. 501-505). The PF includes some to all body feathers, rects, terts, and proximal s covs (the distal gr covs usually retained), and usually 3-7 outer pp and p covs and 1-5 medial ss (distal to the terts) in eccentric sequence (Fig. 376**A**, p. 504; seldom if ever arrested); body feathers, terts, and c.rects are replaced primarily in Sep-Nov whereas pp, ss, and outer rects are replaced primarily in Jan-Apr. The DPA includes most to all body feathers, sometimes a few medial s covs, usually 1-4 terts, and occasionally 1-2 c.rects. Some SYs over-summer on non-breeding grounds and may exhibit less-complete (or no) PA1s and advanced PB2s (see p. 18). See pp. 500-507 for more information on molt in shorebirds.

Age—Juv (B1; Jul-Nov) has uniformly fresh plumage aspect, the back feathers and wing covs with thin buff (fading to white by Nov) and dark fringing (Fig. 408**A-B**), and the pp and ss uniformly juv and fresh (Fig. 375**A**, p. 503); Juv ♀=♂.

Juv-HY/SY (1st cycle, Juv/B1-F1-A1; Oct-Sep): All to some upperpart feathers (Oct-Nov), terts, and/or distal s covs juv, the s covs with distinct whitish and dark fringing when fresh (Fig. 408**A-B**), contrasting with fresher formative scapulars, humerals, terts, and proximal s covs (Figs. 375**B-C** & 408**C**), the distal gr covs (if juv) becoming worn and frayed in Apr-Sep (Fig. 375**D**); pp, p covs, and ss juv, fresh, and without s1-p1 contrast in Oct-Dec (Fig. 375**A**), usually being incompletely replaced in Jan-Apr and exhibiting eccentric replacement patterns in May-Sep (Fig. 376**A**, p. 504); some to all juv rects often retained in Oct-Jan (sometimes through Feb-Sep) contrastingly narrow and worn (Fig. 379**A-D**, p. 507); underparts without dusky spotting in Nov-Mar. **Note: Some SYs remain on non-breeding grounds during the first summer.**

AHY/ASY (Def. cycle, DB-DA; Oct-Sep): Upperpart feathers, terts, and s covs basic (Fig. 375**E-F**), the basic s covs with thin or indistinct dark and pale fringing (Fig. 408**C-D**); pp, p covs, and ss worn, and being replaced in Sep-Apr, or fresh and with replacement clines, often s1-p1 contrast, and sometimes suspension limit among p1-p4 in Dec-Sep (Figs. 375**E** & 376**F**), the outer pp and p covs broad and truncate (Figs. 377**C-D** & 378**C-D**); rects uniformly basic, and broader (Fig. 379**E**), sometimes with 1-2 alternate c.rects in Apr-Sep (Fig. 375**F**); underparts (especially flanks and vent) sometimes with dusky spotting in Nov-Mar.

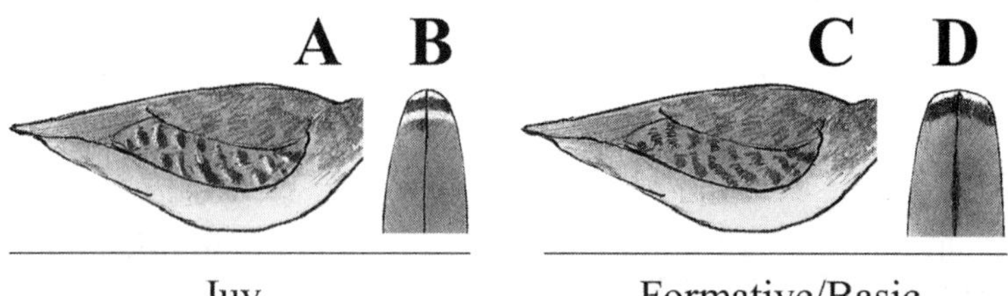

FIGURE 408. Shape and pattern to the secondary coverts by feather generation in Spotted Sandpiper (Common Sandpiper exhibits similar differences). Juv feathers have two sets of whitish/dusky fringing (**B**), which gives the overall effect of more barred s covs (**A**). Some to most SYs replace all s covs by Feb-Mar, at which time they can resemble ASYs by these characters, and in other SYs the overall effect can become obscured through feather wear (*cf.* Fig. 375**D**, p. 503). Formative and basic feathers have only one set of pale and dusky fringing, which is more subtle (**D**), leading to a muted overall pattern (**C**).

SY/TY (2nd cycle, B2; Oct-Feb): Like AHY/ASY with molt of pp occurring and outer pp and p covs juv, very pointed and abraded (Fig. 376**E**). **Note: These include SYs that did not replace outer pp during the PF, and are relatively uncommon (see pp. 506-507).**

Sex—Medial(?) BP (p. 31) developed by both sexes but distended cloaca (Fig. 21, p. 32) indicates ♀ in Apr-Jun. Measurements largely unhelpful for sexing (Table 50, p. 549). The following is reliable for sexing many individuals showing alternate-plumage aspect; no criteria known for sexing individuals in formative or basic plumages. Some intermediates occur that cannot be reliably sexed.

AHY ♀ (Apr-Aug): Dark spots on underparts denser, larger, and rounder (Fig. 409**A**). **Note: SYs may average fewer spots than ASYs, sex for sex; study needed.**

AHY ♂ (Apr-Aug): Dark spots on underparts sparser, smaller, and more triangular (Fig. 409**B**). **Note: See AHY ♀.**

Hybrids reported—None, but has been observed copulating with Common Sandpiper in Europe (Lawrence 1993).

References—Bent (1929), Cramp & Simmons (1983), Dwight (1900b), Hays (1972), McNeil (1970), Nicoll & Kemp (1983), Oberholser (1974), Oring et al. (1997), Palmer (1967b), Prater et al. (1977), Ridgway (1919), Roberts (1955), Spaans (1979).

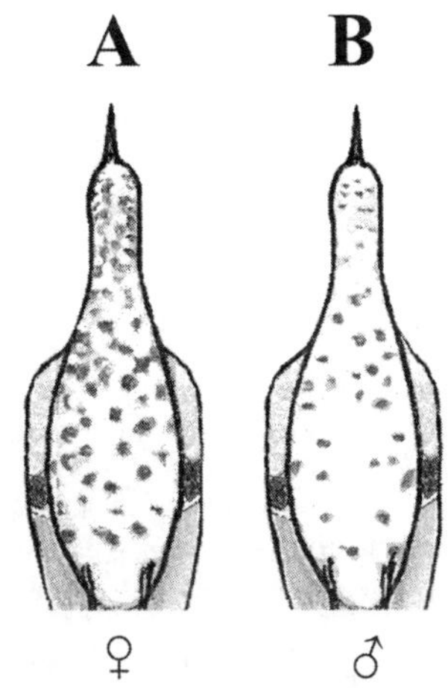

FIGURE 409. Typical size and extent to underpart spots by sex in alternate-aspect (Apr-Aug) Spotted Sandpipers. The largest spot is typically 4-6 mm wide in ♀♀ and 3-4 mm wide in ♂♂. Note that intermediates occur, possibly SY ♀♀ and ASY ♂♂; more study is needed. Note also the darker underwing p covs (and med covs) contrasting with the whiter les covs, unique to *Actitis* among shorebirds.

Spotted Sandpiper

	Jan	Feb	Mar	Apr	May	Jun	Jul	Aug	Sep	Oct	Nov	Dec
Juv-HY							O	O	O	O	O	O
SY	O	O	O	(⚥)	⚥	⚥	⚥	(⚥)	O	O	O	O
TY	O	O										
AHY								O	O	O	O	O
ASY	O	O	O	(⚥)	⚥	⚥	⚥	(⚥)	O			

■ > 95% ▨ 25-95% ▭ 5-25% □ < 5% See Fig. 24 (pp. 44-45)

SOLITARY SANDPIPER
Tringa solitaria

SOSA
Species # 2560
Band size: 1A

Species—From other N.Am shorebirds by medium-small size (Table 50, p. 549), bill thin, straight, and grayish with black tip; upperparts including lower back rump, and uppertail covs dusky with black and white spotting; pp and ss without white at bases; r1 gray and outer rects white with ≥ 3 broad black bands; breast gray with little or no streaking; underwing covs blackish with thin whitish bars or marks; legs and feet dull olive to dull yellowish, with hind toe relatively well developed (Fig. 373**C**, p. 500) and slight webbing between outer fore toes (Fig. 374**B**, p. 501). From Lesser Yellowlegs (p. 556) by smaller size and shorter legs (Table 50); rump, r1, and underwing covs primarily blackish; legs duller.

Wood Sandpiper (*T. glareola*), a vagrant from Eurasia, averages smaller in size but with longer legs (wg chord 116-132, tail 45-53, exp culmen 26-32, tarsus 35-42); supercilium more distinct; rump and uppertail covs white; outer rects with ≤ 3 thinner dark bands; underwing covs pale grayish; legs average brighter and yellower.

Geographic variation—See Blake (1977), Brewster (1890), Conover (1944a), Cramp & Simmons (1983), Hellmayr & Conover (1948b), Patten et al. (2003), Ridgway (1919), Swarth (1926, 1935), Taverner & Sutton (1934), Wetmore (1965). No other subspecies occur.

T.s. cinnamomea (br AK-nw.BC to ne.Man; wint w.Mex-S.Am): Averages larger (Table 50); upperparts and lores brownish, the back with buff spots in Juv; p10 with paler shaft and (often) whitish mottling to inner web.

T.s. solitaria (br se.Yuk-se.BC to Nfl-Que, wint coastal s.TX-FL-GA to S.Am, vagrant to n.AK): Averages smaller (Table 50); upperparts and lores dusky blackish, the back with whitish spots in Juv; p10 with darker shaft and without whitish mottling to inner web.

Molt—CAS. PF partial-incomplete (Sep-Dec/Apr in HY/SYs), DPA partial (Mar-May in AHYs), DPB complete (Jul-Nov/Jan in AHY/ASYs). Most molting occurs on non-breeding grounds. Molt follows a s.Hemisphere strategy (Table 45, pp. 501-505). The PF includes most to all body feathers, some to most proximal s covs (the distal gr covs usually retained), all 5 terts, 8 to (often) all rects, and usually 4-6 outer pp and p covs, and 1-5 medial ss (distal to the terts) in eccentric sequence (Fig. 376**A**, p. 504); body feathers, terts, and c.rects are replaced primarily in Sep-Nov whereas pp, ss, and outer rects are replaced primarily in Jan-Apr. The DPA includes most body feathers, sometimes a few (up to 20%) medial s covs, often 1-3 terts, and occasionally r1. See pp. 500-507 for more information on molt in shorebirds.

Age—Juv (B1; Jul-Nov) has uniformly fresh plumage aspect, the back feathers and s covs with buff to rusty scalloping (Fig. 410**A**), and the pp and ss uniformly juv and fresh (Fig. 375**A**, p. 503); Juv ♀=♂. In addition to the following, AHY/ASYs average more dark barring to undertail coverts (especially smaller lateral feathers) than HY/SYs but there is overlap.

Juv-HY/SY (1st cycle, Juv/B1-F1-A1; Oct-Sep): All to some upperpart feathers (Oct-Nov) and/or distal s covs juv, with buff scalloping when fresh (Fig. 410**A**), contrasting with fresher formative scapulars, humerals, terts, and proximal s covs (Figs. 375**B-C** & 410**C**), the distal gr covs usually retained and becoming worn and frayed by Apr-Sep (Figs. 375**D** & 410**B**); pp, p covs, and ss juv, fresh, and without s1-p1 contrast in Oct-Jan (Fig. 375**A**), usually being incompletely replaced in Jan-Apr and exhibiting eccentric replacement patterns in May-Sep (Fig. 376**A-C**, p. 504), the outer pp and p covs (before replacement) tapered (Figs. 377**A-B** & 378**A-B**, p. 506); some juv rects retained through Jan-Mar (sometimes Apr-Sep), contrastingly narrow and worn (Fig. 379**A-D**, p. 507).

AHY/ASY (Def. cycle, DB-DA; Oct-Sep): Upperpart feathers, terts, and s covs uniformly basic in Oct-Mar (Fig. 375**E**), the basic feathers with thin or no whitish fringing (Fig. 410**C**), mixed with alternate feathers in Apr-Sep (Fig. 375**F**); pp, p covs, and ss worn and being replaced in Oct-Jan, or basic, fresh, and with replacement clines and usually s1-p1 contrast in Dec-Sep (Fig. 375**E**), the outer pp and p covs broad and truncate (Figs. 377**C-D** & 378**C-D**); rects uniformly basic and broader (Fig. 379**E**).

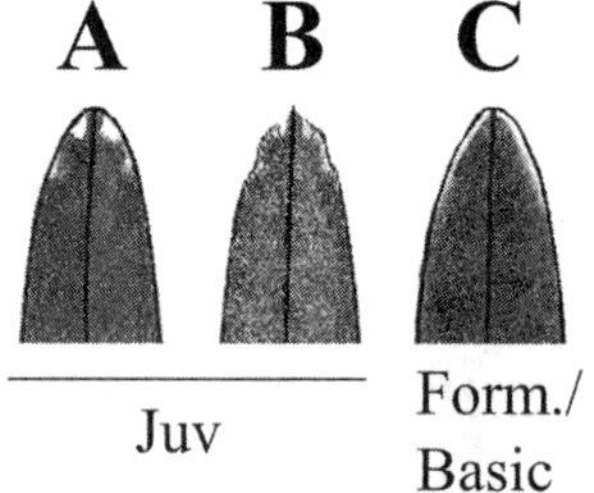

FIGURE 410. Shape and pattern to the greater coverts by feather generation and season in Solitary Sandpiper. Some distal juv coverts are usually retained during the PF (*cf.* Fig. 375**D**, p. 503) and become frayed and worn by spring (**B**).

SY/TY (2nd cycle, B2; Oct-Jan): Like AHY/ASY with molt of pp occurring, but outer pp and p covs juv, very pointed and abraded (Fig. 376**E**). **Note: These include SYs that did not undergo outer p molt during the PF and may be uncommon (see pp. 506-507).**

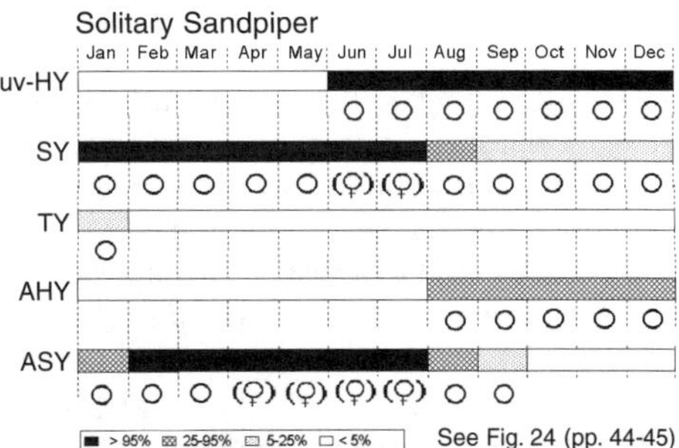

Sex—♀=♂ by plumage aspect. Bilateral BPs (Fig. 20**B**, p. 31) developed by both sexes but distended cloaca (Fig. 21, p. 32) indicates ♀ in Apr-Jul. Measurements largely unhelpful for sexing and confounded by geographic variation (Table 50); no other criteria known.

Hybrids reported—None.

References—Bent (1929), Cramp & Simmons (1983), Lethaby (1995), Moskoff (1995), Oberholser (1974), Palmer (1967b), Prater et al. (1977), Ridgway (1919), Roberts (1955), Spaans (1979).

TABLE 50. Measurements (mm) of North American tringine sandpipers for identification and sexing. See pp. 4-11 for methods of measurement. Species summaries are in **bold** and subspecies summaries are in ***italics***. Values were derived from 95% confidence intervals as based approximately on the indicated sample sizes (see pp. 4-5). Thus, midpoints of ranges approximate means, and S.D. is approximated by 25% of the range.

Taxon/Sex	*n*	wing chord	tail length	exposed culmen	tarsus
Spotted Sandpiper		**95-110**	**46-53**	**20-26**	**20-26**
♀	100	99-110	47-53	21-26	21-26
♂	100	95-105	46-52	20-25	20-25
Solitary Sandpiper		**121-147**	**49-62**	**27-34**	**28-33**
T.s. cinnamomea		***128-147***	***50-62***	***28-34***	***29-33***
♀	100	134-147	53-62	29-34	30-33
♂	100	128-140	50-59	28-32	29-32
T.s. solitaria		***121-138***	***49-59***	***27-32***	***28-33***
♀	100	126-138	51-59	28-32	29-33
♂	100	121-133	49-57	27-31	28-32
Wandering Tattler		**161-183**	**68-81**	**35-44**	**31-37**
♀	100	167-183	68-81	36-44	32-37
♂	100	161-177	66-78	35-42	31-36
Greater Yellowlegs		**177-200**	**69-83**	**50-61**	**55-67**
♀	55	179-200	69-83	50-60	55-66
♂	70	177-198	69-83	50-61	56-67
Willet		**174-225**	**61-88**	**50-67**	**51-74**
C.s. inornata		***190-225***	***73-88***	***55-67***	***60-74***
♀	60	198-225	75-88	57-67	63-74
♂	65	190-216	73-86	55-65	60-70
C.s. semipalmata		***174-200***	***61-76***	***47-61***	***51-62***
♀	45	183-200	64-76	49-61	53-62
♂	45	174-191	61-73	47-59	51-60
Lesser Yellowlegs		**145-167**	**57-66**	**32-40**	**46-56**
♀	100	148-167	58-66	32-39	47-56
♂	100	145-163	57-66	33-40	46-55

WANDERING TATTLER
Tringa incana

WATA
Species # 2590
Band size: 3-2

Species—From other N.Am shorebirds by medium size with proportionally short legs (Table 50, p. 549), bill straight, grayish and/or olive-based with black tip (Fig. 411**B**); upperparts, breast, pp, ss, and rects uniformly gray (feathers fringed pale in juv), or underparts (including ventral area and undertail covs) barred in ASYs in Mar-Aug; underwing covs dusky; legs and feet yellowish, with hind toe relatively well developed (Fig. 373**C**, p. 500) and moderate to extensive webbing between the outer fore toes (Fig. 374**C-E**, p. 501).

Gray-tailed Tattler (*T. brevipes*), a vagrant from Asia, averages smaller (wg chord 153-170, exp culmen 34-42, tarsus 29-34); nasal groove shorter (Fig. 411**A**); bill often with yellowish base; tarsus thinner (usually < 2.5 deep at shallowest point *vs* > 2.5 in Wandering Tattler) and with less-distinct scutes; upperparts (especially rump and tail) paler; supercilia often meet across forehead (*vs* seldom in Wandering Tattler; Fig. 411); Juv with bolder white scalloping to back feathers and s covs (Fig. 412**A**); underparts (especially flanks) whiter; ASYs in Apr-Aug with thinner dark scalloping confined to breast (vs. throughout underparts in Wandering). See Dement'ev & Gladkov (1951c), Gibson (1978), Higgins & Davies (1996), Lehman (2000, 2006), O'Brien et al. (2006), Paulson (1986, 1993, 2005), Prater et al. (1977), Serventy (1944), and Thorpe (1995) for more information.

Geographic variation—Monotypic.

Molt—CAS. PF partial-incomplete (Oct-Mar/Jun in HY/SYs), PA1 absent-limited (Apr-May in SYs), PB2 complete (Jun-Oct in SYs), PA2 limited-partial (Mar-May in over-summering TYs), PB3 complete (Jul-Nov in non-breeding TYs), DPA partial (Mar-Apr in breeding ASYs), DPB complete (Aug-Oct/Apr in breeding ASY/ATYs). Molting occurs primarily on non-breeding grounds and follows either a n.Hemisphere or s.Hemisphere strategy (Table 45, pp. 501-505). The PF includes most to all body feathers, some proximal s covs, 1-3 terts, and 2 to all 12 c.rects in Oct-Dec; in many HY/SYs with non-breeding grounds in the s.Hemisphere it can also include the remainder of the rects, terts, and s covs (the distal gr covs usually retained), and 1-7 medial or outer pp and p covs and 1-5 medial ss (distal to the terts) in eccentric sequence (Fig. 376**A-B**, p. 504; sometimes arrested) in Jan-Jun. Commencement of the PB2 can overlap the end of the PF such that two waves of pp are molting simultaneously (Fig. 376**E**). In the n.Hemisphere the DPB can suspend during Nov-Feb, after 3-7 pp and 1-5 medial ss have been replaced (Fig. 376**F**). The DPA includes some to most body feathers (all of the underparts), sometimes a few medial s covs, and 1-4 terts, but few or no rects. Most to all SYs and many TYs over-summer on non-breeding grounds and exhibit less-complete (or no) PA1-PA2s and advanced PB2-PB3s (Johnson 1977, Gill et al. 2002). See pp. 500-507 for more information on molt in shorebirds.

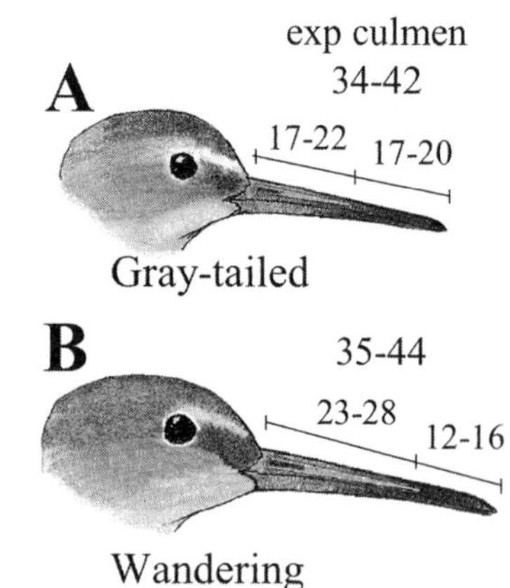

FIGURE 411. Bill dimensions, nasal groove lengths, and head plumage aspect in Gray-tailed and Wandering Tattlers for identification. Measures indicate exposed culmen (Fig. 7**B**, p. 9), length of nasal groove from distal end of forehead feathers, and distance from tip of nasal groove to tip of bill. Note also that the nostril averages smaller, the head aspect paler, and the supercilia more consistently meeting across the forehead in Gray-tailed Tattler than in Wandering Tattler.

Age—Juv (B1; Jul-Nov) has uniformly fresh plumage aspect, the back feathers and wing covs with thin whitish fringing (Fig. 412**B**), and the pp and ss uniformly juv and fresh (Fig. 375**A**, p. 503); Juv ♀=♂. See Johnson (1973, 1977) for information on ageing by the bursa (Fig. 23, p. 34).

Juv-HY/SY (1st cycle, Juv/B1-F1-A1; Oct-Sep): All to some upperpart feathers (Oct-Dec), terts, and/or distal s covs juv, with pale fringing and indistinct dusky subterminal band when fresh (Fig. 412**B**), contrasting with fresher formative scapulars, humerals, terts, and proximal s covs (Figs. 375**B-C** & 412**C**), the distal gr covs usually retained and becoming worn and frayed by Apr-Sep (Fig. 375**D**); pp, p covs, and ss juv, fresh, and without s1-p1 contrast in Oct-Dec (Fig. 375**A**), sometimes being incompletely replaced in Jan-Apr and exhibiting eccentric replacement patterns in May-Sep (Fig. 376**A-B**, p. 504; sometimes arrested), and being completely replaced in Jun-Oct, the juv outer pp and p covs (if present) tapered (Figs. 377**A-B** & 378**A-B**, p. 506); some to all juv rects retained through Jan-Mar (often Apr-Sep), contrastingly narrow and worn (Fig. 379**A-D**, p. 507); underparts with few to no dusky-barred feathers in Apr-Aug. **Note: Most SYs remain on non-breeding grounds during the first summer.**

AHY/ASY (Def. cycle, DB-DA; Oct-Sep): Upperpart feathers, terts, and s covs basic or mixed basic and alternate (Fig. 375**E-F**), the feathers with thin or no pale fringing or subterminal band (Fig. 412**C**); pp, p covs, and ss worn and being completely replaced in Oct-Dec (n.Hemisphere) to Oct-Apr (s.Hemisphere), or basic and with replacement clines, usually s1-p1 contrast, and/or suspension limit among p3-p7 in Jan-Sep (Fig. 375**E-F**), the outer pp and p covs broad and truncate (Figs. 377**C-D** & 378**C-D**); rects uniformly basic and broader (Fig. 379**E**); underparts with substantial barring in Mar-Sep. **Note: See Juv-HY/SY. Oversummering AHY/ASYs with completely basic flight feathers, showing reduced alternate-plumage aspect in Apr-Aug, and commencing p molt in Jun-Jul, might be reliably aged TY, but more study needed.**

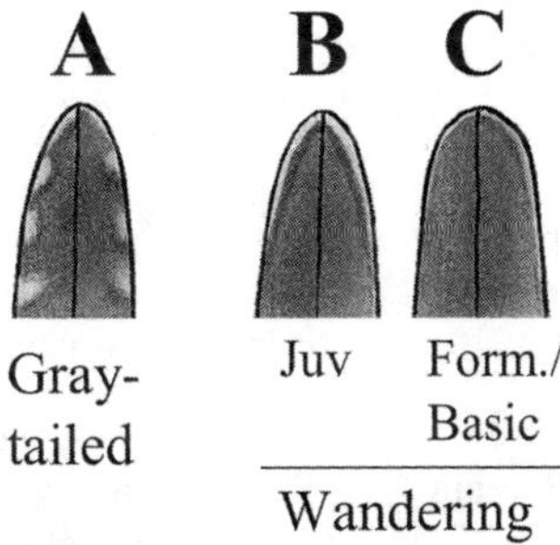

FIGURE 412. Shape and pattern to the secondary coverts in juvenile Gray-tailed Tattler, and in Wandering Tattler by feather generation, for identification and ageing. Most to all s covs are replaced during the preformative molt, but some distal gr covs are often retained through the PB2 (*cf.* Fig. 375**D**, p. 503). Similar variation in these feathers by age (**B-C**) is exhibited by Willet.

Sex—♀=♂ by plumage aspect. Bilateral BPs (Fig. 20**B**, p. 31) developed by both sexes but distended cloaca (Fig. 21, p. 32) indicates ASY ♀ in Apr-Jul. Measurements largely unhelpful for sexing (Table 50, p. 549) and no other criteria known.

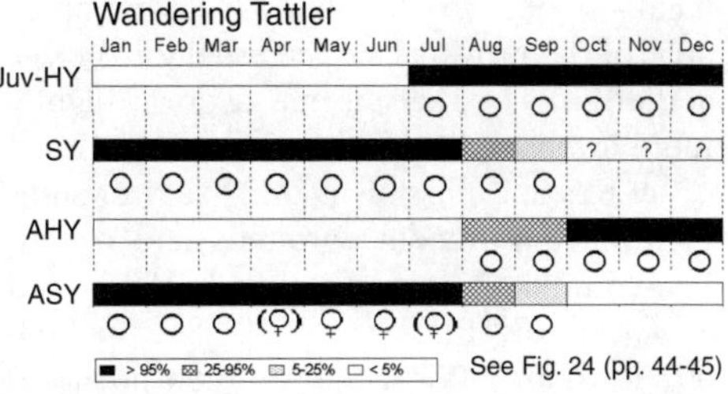

Hybrids reported—With Gray-tailed Tattler *H. brevipes* (Gill et al. 2002).

References—Bent (1929), Dement'ev & Gladkov (1951c), Gill et al. (2002), Higgins & Davies (1996), O.W. Johnson (1973, 1977, 1979), Kinsky & Yaldwyn (1981), Palmer (1967b), Paulson (1986), Prater & Marchant (1975), Prater et al. (1977), Ridgway (1919), Stejneger (1885).

GREATER YELLOWLEGS

Tringa melanoleuca

GRYE
Species # 2540
Band size: 3-3B

Species—From other N.Am shorebirds by medium large size with proportionally long legs (Table 50, p. 549), bill long, slightly recurved, and blackish with grayish base (Fig. 413**A**); upperparts including lower back variably grayish to blackish with whitish spotting; pp and ss without white bases (*cf.* Fig. 414); rump and tail whitish with thin black bars to outer rects; underwing covs white with sparse dusky chevrons; legs and feet bright yellow, with hind toe relatively well developed (Fig. 373**C**, p. 500) and moderate webbing between fore toes (Fig. 374**D**, p. 501). From Lesser Yellowlegs (p. 556) primarily by larger size (Table 50; wg chord > 170, exp culmen > 45, tarsus usually > 55); bill thicker, slightly recurved, grayer at base, and with shorter nasal groove (Fig. 413**A**); ss with white scalloping (Fig. 414); outer rect with > 6 distinct and even bars; breast with more distinct white and dusky streaking in Sep-Mar and heavier blackish mottling in Apr-Jul. See also **Molt** for differences in extent of the PF.

Common Greenshank (*T. nebularia*), a vagrant from Eurasia, is similar in size (wg chord 172-192, tail 66-83, exp culmen 48-63, tarsus 53-65) but has lower back white and legs olive to grayish. Spotted Redshank (*T. erythropus*), a vagrant from Eurasia, has shorter wings (wg chord 154-170, tail 59-68, exp culmen 52-64, tarsus 52-63), lower back white, and plumage aspect paler, less marked, and with abdomen and flanks washed grayish in Sep-Mar, or largely black in Apr-Aug; base of bill and legs reddish to red (beware of occasional yellowlegs with reddish legs).

Geographic variation—Monotypic. See Elphick & Tibbitts (1998), Prater et al. (1977), and Ridgway (1919) regarding slight variation in size.

Molt—CAS. PF partial-incomplete (Aug-Nov/Mar in HY/SYs), PA1 limited-partial (Mar-May in non-breeding SYs), PB2 complete (May-Sep in non-breeding SYs), DPB complete (Jul-Oct in breeding AHYs), DPA partial-incomplete (Feb-Apr in ASYs). Molting exhibits a n.Hemisphere strategy (Table 45, pp. 501-505) and occurs primarily at stopover sites (where it can complete) and on non-breeding grounds; occasional AHYs (non-breeders) may replace body feathers and 1-3 inner pp on breeding grounds. The PF includes most to all body feathers, some proximal s covs, 2-3 terts, and the 2 to (occasionally) all 12 c.rects; body feathers are replaced primarily in Aug-Nov whereas some s covs, terts, and rects can be replaced in Jan-Mar. The DPA includes some to most body feathers, up to 40% of the proximal s covs, usually 1-3 terts, and often 1-4 c.rects; it may average slightly more extensive in ♂♂ than ♀♀ by age. Most or all SYs and possibly some TYs over-summer on non-breeding grounds and exhibit less-complete (or no) PA1-PA2s and advanced PB2-PB3s (see p. 18). See pp. 500-507 for more information on molt in shorebirds. Occasional individuals with non breeding grounds in S.Am could exhibit a s.Hemisphere molting strategy (pp. 501-505); more study is needed.

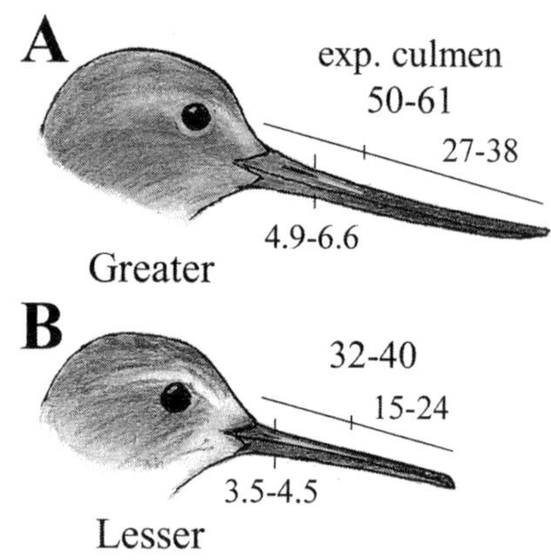

FIGURE 413. Head and bill features in Greater and Lesser yellowlegs for identification. Measures indicate exposed culmen (Fig. 7**B**, p. 9), distance from tip of nasal groove to tip of bill, and bill depth at distal end of nares (Fig. 8**C**, p. 10).

Age—Juv (B1; Jul-Nov) has uniformly fresh plumage aspect, the back feathers and s covs with broad buff scalloping (*cf.* Figs. 414**A** & 417**A**, p. 556), and the pp and ss uniformly juv and fresh (Fig. 375**A**, p. 503); Juv ♀ = ♂.

Juv-HY/SY (1st cycle, Juv/B1-F1-A1; Oct-Sep): Outer ss narrower and with broader scalloping (Fig. 414**A**); all to some upperpart feathers (Oct-Nov), terts, and/or distal s covs juv, contrasting with fresher formative scapulars, humerals, terts, and proximal s covs (Fig. 375**B**-**C**), the retained distal juv s covs becoming worn and frayed by Apr-Sep (Fig. 375**D** & *cf.* Fig. 417**B**, p. 556); pp, p covs, and ss juv (Fig. 375**A**), the outer pp and p covs tapered, brownish, and relatively abraded (Figs. 377**A**-**B** & 378**A**-**B**, p. 506); some juv rects usually retained, contrastingly narrow and worn (Fig. 379**A**-**D**, p. 507; all rects occasionally replaced and resembling Fig. 379**E**). **Note: SYs (and some TYs?) over-summering on non-breeding grounds and acquire less black mottling to plumage aspect than breeding ASYs.**

AHY/ASY (Def. cycle, DB-DA; Oct-Sep): Outer ss broader and with narrower scalloping (Fig. 414**B**); upperpart feathers, terts, and s covs uniformly basic or mixed basic and alternate (Fig. 375**E**-**F**); pp, p covs, ss, and terts basic, fresher, and occasionally showing suspension limit among p1-p3 (Fig. 375**E**-**F**), the outer pp and p covs broad and truncate (Figs. 377**C**-**D** & 378**C**-**D**); rects uniformly basic and broader (Fig. 379**E**), often mixed with 1-4 alternate c.rects in Apr-Sep (Fig. 379**F**).

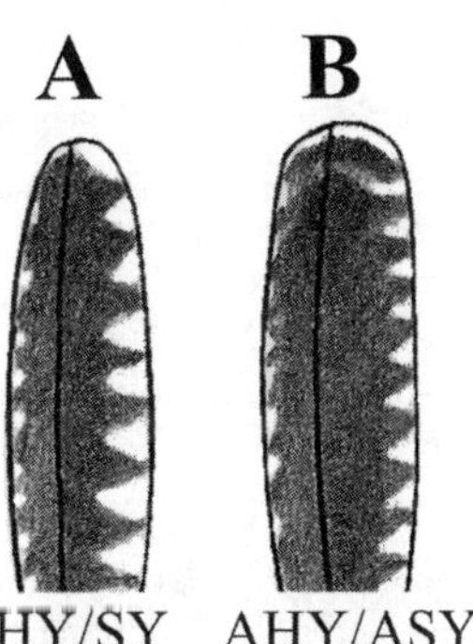

FIGURE 414. Outer secondaries (s1 shown) by age in Greater Yellowlegs. Juv feathers (**A**) are retained by SYs until the PB2 in May-Sep. Distal gr covs also exhibit similar variation but not as marked, basic covs overlapping substantially in pattern. Note that outer ss of Lesser Yellowlegs lack pale markings.

Sex—♀ = ♂ by plumage aspect. Bilateral(?) BPs (Fig. 20**B**, p. 31) developed by both sexes but distended cloaca (Fig. 21, p. 32) indicates ♀ in May-Jul. Measurements unhelpful for sexing (Table 50, p. 549). ASY ♂♂ may average more blackish alternate feathers to upperparts and s covs than ASY ♀♀ in Apr-Aug, which might be helpful in sexing some mated pairs. Otherwise, no criteria known.

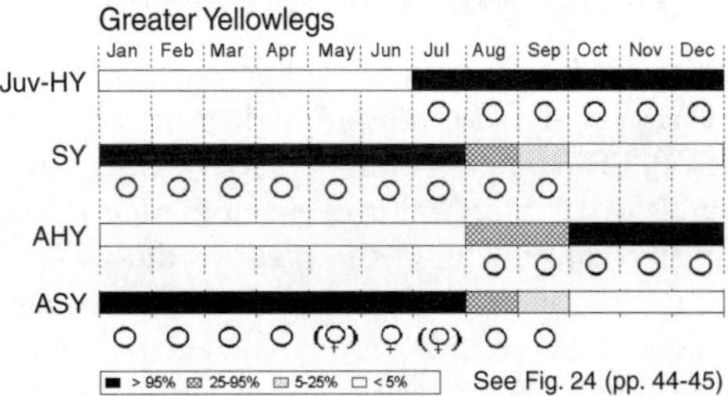

Hybrids reported—None.

References—Bent (1927), Burton & McNeil (1976), Cramp & Simmons (1983), Elphick & Tibbitts (1998), Jackson (1919), Kwater (1992), McNeil (1970), Oberholser (1974), Palmer (1967b), Prater et al. (1977), Ridgway (1919), Roberts (1955), Spaans (1979), Wilds (1982).

WILLET
Tringa semipalmata

WILL
Species # 2580
Band size: 4

Species—From other N.Am shorebirds by medium-large to large size (Table 50, p. 549), bill deep, straight, grayish to slate (Fig. 415); upperparts including lower back and breast grayish in Sep-Mar, often with dusky and buff to whitish spotting in Apr-Aug; pp and ss with broad white bases (*cf.* Fig. 416) forming distinct wing stripe; rump white (often with dusky markings); basic rects grayish centrally to whitish laterally; underwing covs primarily sooty; legs and feet grayish, with hind toe relatively well developed (Fig. 373**C**, p. 500) and extensive webbing between fore toes (Fig. 374**E**, p. 501).

Geographic variation—See Blake (1977), Brewster (1887), Hellmayr & Conover (1948b), Hess (1998), Lowther et al. (2001), O'Brien (2006), Paulson (1993, 2005), Prater et al. (1977), Ridgway (1919). In addition to the following, *C.s. semipalmatus* averages a more extensive DPA (often including more of the underparts and the c.rects) which results in reported differences in aspect patterns in Mar-Aug, but this difference shows broad overlap due substantial individual and age-related variation in molt extents (see **Molt**). More study needed on winter ranges of each subspecies.

C.s. inornata (br Alb-Sask to ne.CA-NE; wint coastal BC-CA, TX-FL-SC, and to n.S.Am?): Larger with longer legs (Table 50, p. 549; wg chord usually > 200 and tarsus usually > 60); bill longer, proportionally shallower, and usually with grayish-blue tinge to base (Fig. 415**A**); upperparts medium-dark brownish gray, usually with sparser but darker alternate barring in Mar-Aug.

C.s. semipalmata (br coastal TX-FL-NS; vagrant to Man; wint to C.S.Am): Smaller with shorter legs (Table 50; wing chord usually < 200 and tarsus usually < 60); bill shorter, proportionally deeper, and with pinkish tinge to base (Fig. 415**B**); upperparts medium-pale gray, usually with sparser but paler alternate barring in Mar-Aug.

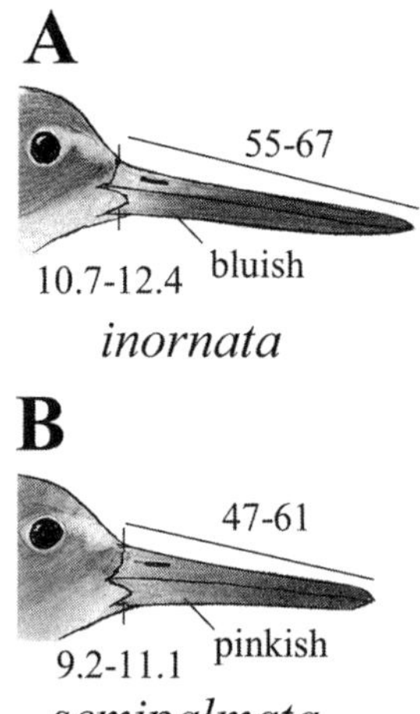

FIGURE 415. Shape, size, and coloration of the bill by subspecies in Willet. Measures pertain to exposed culmen (Fig. 7**B**, p. 9) and depth at distal end of forehead feathers (Fig. 8**A**, p. 10); the depth at the distal end of the nares (Fig. 8**C**) divided by the exposed culmen is typically < 0.18 in *T.s. inornata* and > 0.18 in *semipalmata*. In *inornata* the bill can be slightly recurved (as shown) but can also be slightly decurved; that of *semipalmata* tends to be straighter. Color to the base of the bill (grayish in *inornata*, pinkish in *semipalmata*) is more prominent in winter than in summer and beware of some overlap. Note also the slightly darker plumage aspect of *inornata*.

Molt—CAS. PF partial (Sep-Nov/Mar in HY/SYs), PA1 absent-limited (Apr-May in SYs), PB2 complete (Jun-Sep in SYs), PA2 limited-partial (Mar-May in over-summering TYs), PB3 complete (Jul-Oct in non-breeding TYs), DPA partial-incomplete (Feb-Apr in breeding ASYs), DPB complete (Aug-Nov/Jan in breeding ASY/ATYs). Molting occurs primarily on non-breeding grounds and exhibits a n.Hemisphere strategy (Table 45, pp. 501-505). The PF includes most to all body feathers, no to some (up to 40%) proximal s covs, 2-3 terts, and r1 to (sometimes) all 12 rects; body feathers are replaced primarily in Sep-Nov whereas some s covs, terts, and rects can be replaced in Jan-Mar. The DPA includes most to all body feathers, 10-80% of the proximal s covs, and often 1-5 terts and 1-6 c.rects; it may average slightly more extensive in ♂♂ than ♀♀ by age. All SYs and many TYs over-summer on non-breeding grounds and exhibit less-complete (or no) PA1-PA2s and advanced PB2-PB3s (see p. 18). The nominate subspecies may average a more-protracted PF and DPB a more-extensive DPA than *C.s. inornata*, and look for occasional nominate individuals to replace outer pp (*cf.* Fig. 376**A**, p. 504) during the PF.

Age—Juv (B1; Jul-Nov) has uniformly fresh plumage aspect, the back feathers with whitish fringing and subterminal band (*cf.* Fig. 412**B**, p. 551), and the pp and ss uniformly juv and fresh (Fig. 375**A**, p. 503); Juv ♀=♂.

Juv-HY/SY (1st cycle, Juv/B1-F1-A1; Oct-Sep): Inner pp with narrower and less-distinct dusky tips (Fig. 416**A**); all to some upperpart feathers (Oct-Nov), terts, and/or distal s covs juv, with whitish fringing and subterminal band when fresh (*cf.* Fig. 412**B**), contrasting with fresher and grayer formative scapulars, humerals, terts, and proximal s covs (Figs. 375**B-C** & 412**C**), the distal juv s covs becoming worn and frayed by Apr-Sep (Fig. 375**D**); pp, p covs, and ss uniformly juv and without s1-p1 contrast in Oct-Apr (Fig. 375**A**), being completely replaced in Jun-Sep, the outer pp and p covs tapered, brownish, and relatively abraded (Figs. 377**A-B** & 378**A-B**, p. 506); some juv rects usually retained, contrastingly narrow and worn (Fig. 379**A-D**); upperparts and breast with few to no dusky-barred alternate feathers in Apr-Aug. **Note: Most to all SYs remain on non-breeding grounds during the breeding season.**

AHY/ASY (Def. cycle, DB-DA; Oct-Sep): Inner pp with broader and more distinct blackish tips (Fig. 416**B**); upperpart feathers, terts, and s covs uniformly basic or mixed basic and alternate (Fig. 375**E-F**), the basic feathers with thin or no pale fringing (*cf.* Fig. 412**C**); pp, p covs, ss, and terts basic or mixed basic and alternate in Apr-Sep (Fig. 375**F**) sometimes with s1-p1 contrast (Fig. 375**E**), and being completely replaced in Aug-Nov, the outer pp and p covs broad and truncate (Figs. 377**C-D** & 378**C-D**); outer rects uniformly basic and broader, often mixed with 1-6 alternate c.rects in Apr-Sep (Fig. 379**E-F**); upperparts and breast usually with substantial dusky-barred alternate feathers in Apr-Aug. **Note: See Juv-HY/SY. Over-summering AHY/ASYs with basic flight feathers, showing reduced alternate-plumage aspect in Apr-Aug, and commencing p molt in Jun-Jul, might be reliably aged TY but more study is needed.**

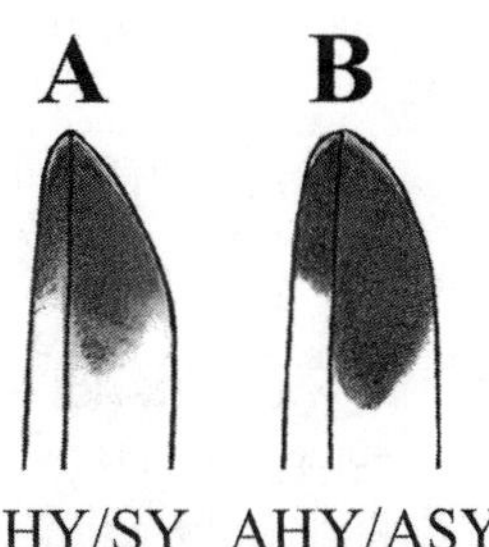

FIGURE 416. Shape and pattern to p4 by age in Willet. Juv feathers (**A**) are retained by SYs until the PB2 in Jun-Sep.

Sex—♀=♂ by plumage aspect. Bilateral BPs (Fig. 20**B**, p. 31) developed by both sexes but distended cloaca (Fig. 21, p. 32) indicates ASY (possibly ATY) ♀ in Apr-Jul. Measurements largely unhelpful for sexing and confounded by geographic variation (Table 50, p. 549). ASY ♂♂ may average more barring to the upperparts and underparts than ASY ♀♀ in Apr-Aug, which might be helpful in sexing some mated pairs. Otherwise, no criteria known.

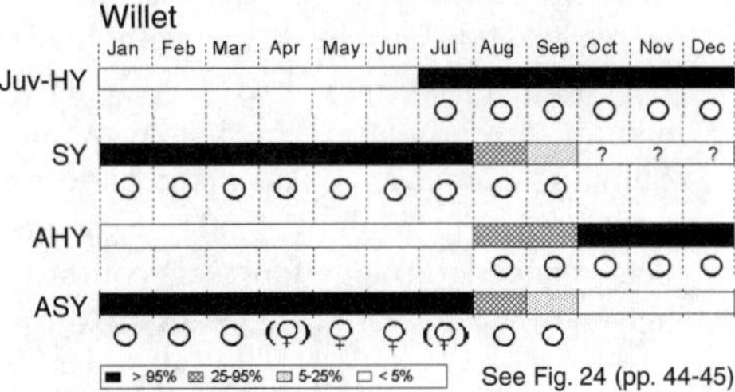

Hybrids reported—None.

References—Alexander & Gratto-Trevor (1997), Bent (1929), Lowther et al. (2001), McNeil (1970), Oberholser (1974), Palmer (1967b), Prater et al. (1977), Ridgway (1919), Roberts (1955), Wilcox (1980).

LESSER YELLOWLEGS
Tringa flavipes

LEYE
Species # 2550
Band size: 2

Species—See Greater Yellowlegs (p. 552) for separation from other shorebirds. From Greater Yellowlegs primarily by smaller size (Table 50; wg chord < 170, exp culmen < 45, tarsus usually < 55); bill straighter, thinner, without gray at base, and with longer nasal groove (Fig. 413**B**, p. 552); ss unmarked, without white scalloping (*cf.* Fig. 414, p. 553); r6 with < 5 indistinct and uneven bars; breast with less distinct dusky streaking in Sep-Mar and sparser blackish mottling in Apr-Jul. See also **Molt** for differences in extent of the PF. From Solitary Sandpiper (p. 547) by larger size and longer legs (Table 50); rump, r1, and underwing covs primarily whitish; legs brighter and yellower.

Geographic variation—Monotypic.

Molt—CAS. PF incomplete (Sep-Feb/Apr in HY/SYs), DPA partial (Mar-May in AHYs), DPB complete (Jul-Nov/Jan in AHY/ASYs). Most molting occurs on non-breeding grounds, although the DPB sometimes commences (body feathers and up to 5 inner pp and the terts in non-breeders or failed-breeders), and the DPA can complete, on breeding grounds or at stopover sites. Molt follows a s.Hemisphere strategy (Table 45, pp. 501-505). The PF includes most to all body feathers, rects, terts, and proximal s covs (the distal gr covs sometimes retained), 4-8 outer pp and p covs, and 1-6 medial ss (distal to the terts) in eccentric or arrested eccentric sequence (Fig. 376**A**-**B**, p. 504); body feathers, terts, and c.rects are replaced primarily in Sep-Nov whereas pp, ss, and outer rects are replaced primarily in Jan-Apr. The DPA includes some to most body feathers, a few to most proximal s covs, 1-4 terts, and 2-6 c.rects; it may average slightly more extensive in ♂♂ than ♀♀ by age. See pp. 500-507 for more information on molt in shorebirds.

Age—Juv (B1; Jul-Nov) has uniformly fresh plumage aspect, the back feathers and s covs with distinct buff to whitish scalloping (Fig. 417**A**), and the pp and ss uniformly juv and fresh (Fig. 375**A**, p. 503); Juv ♀ = ♂.

Juv-HY/SY (1st cycle, Juv/B1-F1-A1; Oct-Sep): All to some upperpart feathers (Oct-Nov), terts, and/or distal s covs juv, with distinct whitish scalloping (Fig. 417**A**-**B**), contrasting with fresher formative scapulars, humerals, terts, and proximal s covs (Figs. 375**B**-**C** & 417**C**), the distal gr covs sometimes retained and becoming worn and frayed by Apr-Sep (Figs. 375**D** & 417**B**); pp, p covs, and ss juv, fresh, and without s1-p1 contrast in Oct-Jan (Fig. 375**A**), being incompletely replaced in Jan-Apr, and exhibiting eccentric replacement patterns in May-Sep (Fig. 376**A**-**B**, p. 504); some juv rects retained through Jan-Mar, contrastingly narrow and worn (Fig. 379**A**-**D**).

AHY/ASY (Def. cycle, DB-DA; Oct-Sep): Upperpart feathers, terts, and s covs uniformly basic or mixed basic and alternate (Fig. 375**E**-**F**), the basic feathers with thin

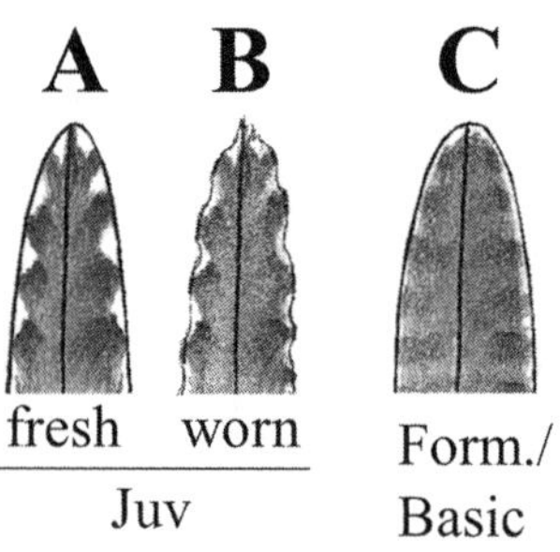

FIGURE 417. Shape and pattern to s covs by feather generation in Lesser Yellowlegs. Many HY/SYs replace all juv feathers (**A**-**B**) by Dec-Feb during the PF and can no longer aged by this character, although some SYs retain worn outer gr covs (**B**) through the PB2 in Jul-Nov/Jan (*cf.* Fig. 375**D**). Greater Yellowlegs exhibits similar patterns of wear but tends to have deeper scalloping in both juv and basic feathers, as in ss (*cf.* Fig. 414, p. 553).

or no white fringing or scalloping (Fig. 417**C**); pp, p covs, and ss worn and being completely replaced in Oct-Jan, or basic, fresh, and with replacement clines, usually s1-p1 contrast, and sometimes suspension limit among p1-p5 in Dec-Sep (Fig. 375**E**-**F**); outer rects uniformly basic and broader (Fig. 379**E**), mixed with 2-6 alternate c.rects in Apr-Aug (Fig. 375**F**).

Sex—♀=♂ by plumage aspect. Bilateral BPs (Fig. 20**B**, p. 31) developed by both sexes but distended cloaca (Fig. 21, p. 32) indicates ♀ in May-Jul. Measurements unhelpful for sexing (Table 50, p. 549) and no other criteria known.

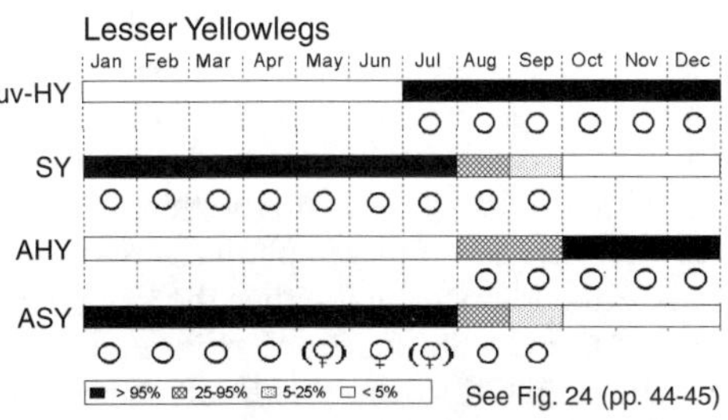

Hybrids reported—None.

References—Alexander & Gratto-Trevor (1997), Bent (1927), Burton & McNeil (1976), Cramp & Simmons (1983), Higgins & Davies (1996), Jackson (1919), Kwater (1992), McNeil (1970), Oberholser (1974), Palmer (1967b), Prater et al. (1977), Ridgway (1919), Roberts (1955), Spaans (1979), Tibbitts & Moskoff (1999), Wilds (1982).

Curlews *Scolopacidae, Scolopacinae, Numeniini*

Four species. Tribal characters include medium-sized to large bodies, long and decurved bills in most species, fleshy legs with hind toe relatively well developed (Fig. 373**C**, p. 500) and no to moderate webbing between fore toes (Fig. 374**A-C**, p. 501), and contrastingly pale shaft to outer primary. North American curlews have 10 functional primaries (p10 longest by 1-10 mm, when fully grown), 16-19 secondaries (including 4-5 tertials, and one absent between the 4th and 5th; *cf.* Fig. 12**B**, p. 19), and 12 rectrices. Ageing can be accomplished through the first cycle (to SY and ASY), and sometimes into the third cycle (to TY and ATY) through plumage aspect and molt patterns; sexes are similar in plumage aspect and size (♀♀ slightly to moderately larger). In molting, N.Am curlews exhibit either the Complex Basic Strategy (CBS; Fig. 10**B**, pp. 13-16) or the Simple Alternate Strategy (SAS; Fig. 10**C**) with a preformative molt but apparently no prealternate molt in the first cycle; both n.Hemisphere and s.Hemisphere strategies (Table 45, pp. 501-505) are employed. One species, Bristle-thighed Curlew (p. 562), evidently has unique molt strategies adapted to unique non-breeding environments (Marks 1993, Pyle 1999). Age of first breeding is 1-2 years in Upland Sandpiper and 2-4 years in larger species. See pp. 500-507 for further information on molt and ageing in shorebirds.

UPLAND SANDPIPER

Bartramia longicauda

UPSA
Species # 2610
Band size: 3

Species—From other N.Am shorebirds by medium size with proportionally long tail (Table 51, p. 562); tail graduated (r1 – r6 > 20 mm); bill straight, thin, and yellowish with a dark tip; crown, back, and wing covs dark brown with paler fringing; lower back and rump blackish; outer rects pale rufous with dark subterminal band; pp and ss brownish, without white at base; underparts whitish with distinct blackish chevrons to breast and flanks; axillars and underwing s covs finely barred blackish and white; legs and feet yellow, with hind toe relatively well developed (Fig. 373**C**, p. 500) and no to slight webbing between outer fore toes (Fig. 374**A-B**, p. 501).

Geographic variation—Monotypic. ♀♀ breeding in AK-KS may average larger than those in MN-ME (Cramp & Simmons 1983); more study needed.

Molt—SAS (CAS?). PF incomplete (Oct-Dec/Mar in HY/SYs), PA1 absent(?), DPB complete (Sep-Dec/Feb in AHY/ASYs), DPA absent-partial (Feb-Apr in ASYs). The single inserted first-cycle molt appears to be homologous with a PF rather than a PA1 (Fig. 10**C**, p. 14), although a few body feathers may be replaced twice, indicating the presence of both molts (and CAS, Fig. 10**F**); study needed. Most molting occurs on non-breeding grounds, although the DPB can commence (with some body feathers and occasionally 1-5 inner pp and the terts) on breeding grounds or at stopover sites. Molt largely follows a n.Hemisphere strategy (Table 45, pp. 501-505), despite non-breeding grounds in S.Am. The PF includes most to all body feathers and s covs (a few distal gr and occasionally med covs often retained), occasionally 1-2 terts, and most to (usually) all rects, but no pp, p covs or ss; body feathers and terts are usually replaced in Oct-Dec whereas some s covs and rects can be replaced in Jan-Mar. The DPA appears to be variable but can include up to most back feathers and some proximal s covs.

Age—Juv (B1; Jul-Nov) has uniformly fresh plumage aspect, the breast washed tawny, and the pp and ss uniformly juv and fresh (Fig. 375**A**, p. 503); Juv ♀ = ♂.

Juv-HY/SY (1st cycle, Juv/B1-F1; Oct-Sep): Medial ss (adjacent to terts) pointed and with indistinct pale brown centers and thin whitish tips (Fig. 418**A**), occasionally contrasting with fresher formative terts (Fig. 375**C-D**); all to some upperpart feathers (Oct-Dec) and/or distal s covs juv, fringed tawny or (distal gr covs) indistinctly barred when fresh (*cf.* Fig. 418**A**), contrasting with fresher formative humerals, scapulars, and proximal s covs (Fig. 375**B-C**), the retained distal juv s covs becoming worn and frayed by Apr-Sep (Fig. 375**D**; beware pseudolimit between buffier med and les covs and grayer gr covs in both age groups of this species); pp, p covs, and ss juv and without s1-p1 contrast (Fig. 375**A**), relatively fresh in Oct-Jan, and relatively worn in Jan-Sep, the outer pp and p covs tapered and brownish (Figs. 377**A-B** & 378**A-B**, p. 506); juv rects usually retained through Oct-Dec, narrower (Fig. 379**A**, p. 507).

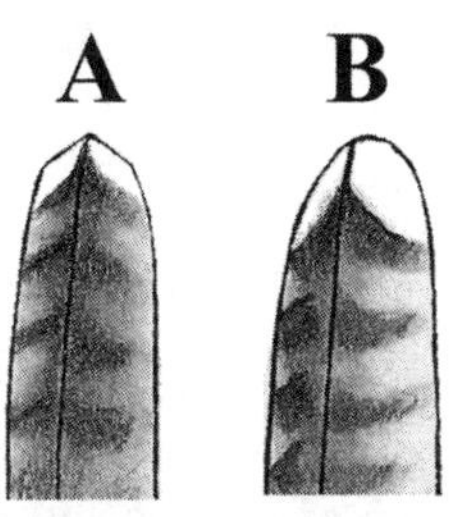

FIGURE 418. Shape and pattern to the medial secondaries (s8-s11, next to the tertials) by feather generation in Upland Sandpiper. Juv feathers (**A**) are retained by SY/TYs until the PB2 in Sep-Dec/Feb. S covs exhibit similar variation but without the white tips.

AHY/ASY (Def. cycle, DB-DA; Oct-Sep): Medial ss (adjacent to terts) more rounded and with distinct dusky brown centers and broader white tips (Fig. 418**B**), uniform in wear with terts (or fresher than terts due to wear cline; Fig. 375**E**); upperpart feathers and s covs uniformly basic or mixed basic and alternate (Fig. 375**E-F**), the basic feathers fringed buff to olive-brown; pp, p covs, and ss worn and being replaced in Oct-Feb, or basic and with replacement clines and slight s1-p1 contrast and/or suspension limit among p1-p5 in Jan-Sep (Figs. 375**E** & 376**F**, p. 504), the outer pp and p covs broad, dusky, and fresh (Figs. 377**C-D** & 378**C-D**); rects uniformly basic and broader (Fig. 379**E**).

SY/TY (2nd cycle, B2; Oct-Feb): Like AHY/ASY with molt of pp occurring, and outer pp and p covs very tapered, worn, and abraded (Fig. 376**E**). **Note: Intermediates between this and ASY/ATY should be aged AHY/ASY.**

ASY/ATY (Def. cycle, DB; Oct-Mar): Like AHY/ASY with molt of pp occurring, and outer pp and p covs broad and only moderately worn (*cf.* Fig. 376**E**). **Note: See SY/TY.**

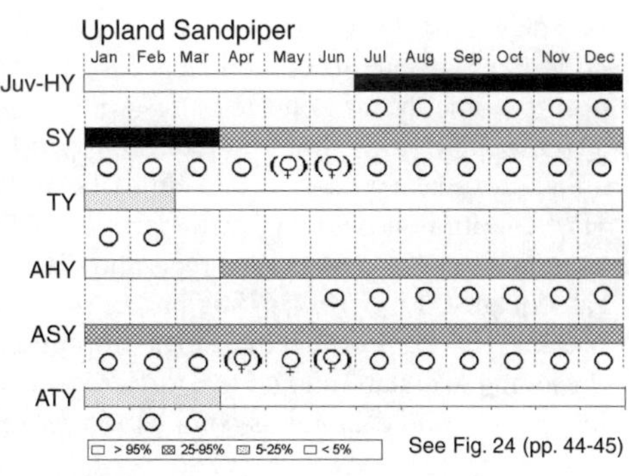

Sex—♀=♂ by plumage aspect. Bilateral(?) BPs (Fig. 20**B**, p. 31) presumably developed by both sexes but distended cloaca (Fig. 21, p. 32) indicates ♀ in Apr-Jun. Measurements largely unhelpful for sexing (Table 51, p. 562) and no other criteria known.

Hybrids reported—None.

References—Bent (1929), Cramp & Simmons (1983), Higgins & Davies (1996), Houston & Bowen (2001), Oberholser (1974), Palmer (1967b), Prater et al. (1977), Ridgway (1919), Roberts (1955).

WHIMBREL
Numenius phaeopus

WHIM
Species # 2650
Band size: 4

Species—From other N.Am shorebirds by large size (Table 51, p. 562), bill decurved, moderately long and thick, and blackish, often with a pinkish base to lower mandible; plumage aspect of N.Am individuals (see **Geographic variation**) uniformly brown with buff to pale-brown fringing and without cinnamon, the head with distinct dark-brown lateral crown stripes and the lower abdomen whitish; pp and ss brown with indistinct buff to whitish bands; ventral flank feathers without bristle-like tips (*cf.* Fig. 420, p. 563); legs and feet grayish, with hind toe relatively well developed (Fig. 373**C**, p. 500) and moderate webbing between fore toes (Fig. 374**C-D**, p. 501).

Geographic variation—See Bosanquet (2000), Cramp & Simmons (1983), Dement'ev & Gladkov (1951c), Engelmoer & Roselaar (1998), Heindel (1999), Hellmayr & Conover (1948b), Higgins & Davies (1996), Prater et al. (1977), Ridgway (1919), Skeel & Mallory (1996). One other subspecies occurs in c.Asia.

N.p. variegatus (br & wint e.Asia-Australia; vagrant to AK-CA): Wing and bill average shorter (Table 51, p. 562); upperpart fringing brownish gray; lower back whitish with variable brownish gray streaking, often contrasting with browner rump and uppertail covs; underwing covs whitish with distinct blackish bars; medial abdomen usually with distinct black streaks.

N.p. hudsonicus (br & wint N-S.Am): Wing medium in length and bill averages longer (Table 51); upperpart fringing buff; lower back, rump, and uppertail covs uniformly brown; underwing covs barred buff to tawny and dusky; medial abdomen without distinct black streaks. Populations breeding in AK-nw.NWT ("*rufiventris*") average longer-winged and grayer brown but differences slight.

N.p. phaeopus (br and wint Europe-Africa; vagrant to Nfl-FL): Wing averages longer and bill averages shorter (Table 51); upperpart fringing olive-brown to brown; lower back, rump, and uppertail covs uniformly white with sparse brown markings; underwing covs barred white and brown; medial abdomen sometimes with distinct black streaks. Populations breeding in Iceland ("*islandicus*"; with vagrants reported from Nfl-NS) average longer winged but difference slight, and continuous with broadly clinal trend in nw.Europe.

Molt—SAS. PF partial-incomplete (Oct-Dec/Jun in HY/SYs), PA1 absent, PB2 complete (Jun-Nov in non-breeding SYs), DPA absent-limited (Feb-Apr in ASYs), PB3 complete (Jul-Dec in non-breeding TYs), DPB complete (Aug-Oct/Mar in breeding ASY/ATYs). The single inserted first-cycle molt appears to be homologous with a PF rather than a PA1 (Fig. 10**C**, p. 14). Molting occurs primarily on non-breeding grounds and can exhibit either a n.Hemisphere (most) or s.Hemisphere (few) strategy (Table 45, pp. 501-505). The PF includes most body feathers, no to a few proximal s covs, and sometimes 1-2 terts and c.rects in Oct-Dec; in a small proportion of HY/SYs with non-breeding grounds in the s.Hemisphere, the PF can also include up to all rects, terts, and s covs (some medial rects and distal gr covs usually retained), and 1-5 inner pp in typical sequence (Fig. 376**D**, p. 504) in Jan-Jun; more study needed (see also Bristle-thighed Curlew, p. 562). The DPA occurs in a small proportion of ASYs and can include scattered body feathers (including scapulars) and up to 3 terts. Most to all SYs and many TYs over-summer on non-breeding grounds and exhibit less-complete (or no) PA2s and advanced PB2-PB3s (see p. 18).

Age—Juv (B1; Jul-Nov) has uniformly fresh plumage aspect, the back feathers and wing covs with broader buff scalloping (Fig. 419**A**), and the pp and ss uniformly juv and fresh (Fig. 375**A**, p. 503); Juv ♀=♂.

Juv-HY/SY (1st cycle, Juv/B1-F1; Oct-Sep): All to some upperpart feathers (Oct-Dec), terts, and/or distal s covs juv, with broader buff scalloping (Fig. 419**A-B**), contrasting with fresher formative scapulars, terts (sometimes), and proximal s covs (Figs. 375**B-C** & 419**C**), the distal gr covs usually retained and becoming worn and frayed by Apr-Sep (Figs. 375**D** & 419**B**);

pp, p covs, and ss juv, fresh, without s1-p1 contrast in Oct-Dec (Fig. 375**A**), and being replaced in Jun-Nov, the juv outer pp and p covs tapered and worn (Figs. 377**A-B** & 378**A-B**, p. 506); some juv rects retained through Jan-Feb (and usually Mar-Sep), contrastingly narrow and worn (Fig. 379**A-D**, p. 507). **Note: SYs typically remain to over-summer on non-breeding grounds. The above applies to HY/SYs with non-breeding grounds in the n.Hemisphere; those with non-breeding grounds in the s.Hemisphere can occasionally exhibit incomplete pp replacement in typical sequence (Fig. 376D, p. 504). See also AHY/ASY.**

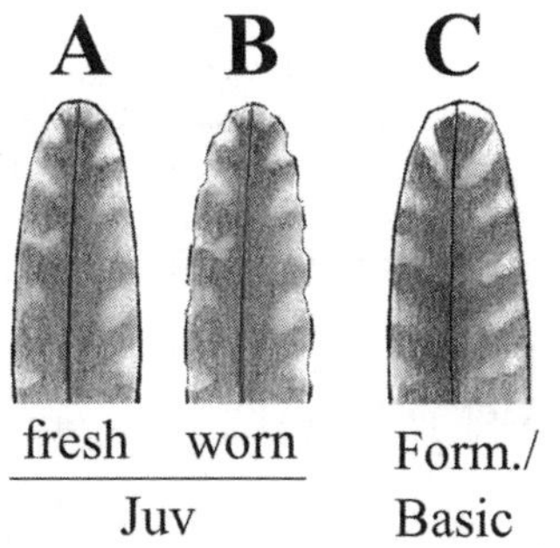

AHY/ASY (Def. cycle, DB-DA; Oct-Sep): Upperpart feathers, terts, and s covs uniformly basic or mixed basic and alternate (Fig. 375**E-F**), the basic feathers with narrower pale barring (Fig. 419**C**); pp, p covs, and ss worn and being completely replaced in Oct-Dec (n.Hemisphere) or Oct-Apr (s.Hemisphere), and/or basic, fresh, and with replacement clines and often s1-p1 contrast in Jan-Sep (Fig. 375**E**), the outer pp and p covs broad and truncate (Figs. 377**C-D** & 378**C-D**); rects uniformly basic and broader (Fig. 379**E**). **Note: See Juv-HY/SY. Look for patterns indicating incomplete PB2s in TYs over-summering on non-breeding grounds, as in Bristle-thighed Curlew.**

A B C

fresh worn Form./

Juv Basic

FIGURE 419. Shape and pattern to s covs by feather generation in Whimbrel and Bristle-thighed Curlew; the latter species averages slightly bolder pattern by feather generation. These differences can be subtle and exhibit overlap, so caution in warranted. Some HY/SYs replace all juv feathers (**A-B**) by Dec-Feb during the PF and can no longer be aged by this character, although most SYs retain worn outer gr covs (**B**) through the PB2 in Jun-Nov (*cf.* Fig. 375**D**).

SY/TY (2nd cycle, B2; Oct-Mar): Like AHY/ASY with molt of pp occurring or suspended in Nov-Mar and outer pp and p covs juv, narrow, tapered, and very worn (Fig. 376**E**, p. 504). **Note: Individuals that can be aged SY/TY or ASY/ATY usually occur only on the s.Hemisphere non-breeding grounds.**

ASY/ATY (Def. cycle, DB; Oct-Mar): Like AHY/ASY with molt of pp occurring or suspended in Nov-Mar, and outer pp and p covs basic, broad, and truncate (*cf.* Fig. 376**E**). **Note: See SY/TY.**

Sex— ♀ = ♂ by plumage aspect. Bilateral BPs (Fig. 20**B**, p. 31) developed by both sexes but distended cloaca (Fig. 21, p. 32) indicates ASY (possibly ATY) ♀ in May-Jul. Measurements largely unhelpful for sexing (Table 51, p. 562); see Skeel (1982) for a DFA (p. 5) using wing chord, tail, and exposed culmen lengths from dried specimens that correctly sexed 85% of Whimbrels from e.N.Am populations. No other criteria known.

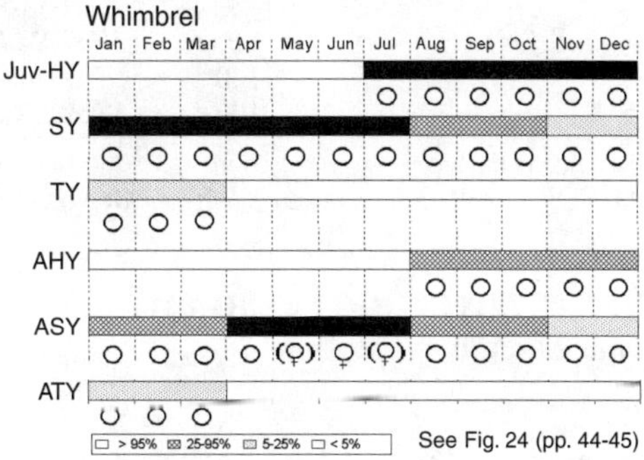

Whimbrel

Jan Feb Mar Apr May Jun Jul Aug Sep Oct Nov Dec

Juv-HY

SY

TY

AHY

ASY

ATY

□ > 95% ▨ 25-95% □ 5-25% □ < 5% See Fig. 24 (pp. 44-45)

Hybrids reported—Possibly with Slender-billed Curlew *N. tenuirostris* (McCarthy 2006).

References—Bent (1929), Cramp & Simmons (1983), Dement'ev & Gladkov (1951c), Higgins & Davies (1996), Johnson (1977, 1979), Oberholser (1974), Palmer (1967b), Prater et al. (1977), Ridgway (1919), Roberts (1955), Zwarts et al. (1990).

TABLE 51. Measurements (mm) of North American curlews and godwits for identification and sexing. See pp. 4-11 for methods of measurement. Species summaries are in **bold** and subspecies summaries are in ***italics***. Values were derived from 95% confidence intervals as based approximately on the indicated sample sizes (see pp. 4-5). Thus, midpoints of ranges approximate means, and S.D. is approximated by 25% of the range.

Taxon/Sex	*n*	wing chord	tail length	exposed culmen[1]	tarsus
Upland Sandpiper		**153-178**	**74-90**	**26-32**	**44-52**
♀	40	159-178	78-90	27-32	46-52
♂	40	153-170	74-88	26-31	44-51
Whimbrel		**219-269**	**84-103**	**69-99**	**49-65**
N.p. variegatus		***219-260***	***85-101***	***70-90***	***51-64***
♀	50	229-260	88-101	73-90	53-64
♂	50	219-251	85-98	70-86	51-62
N.p. hudsonicus		***224-265***	***84-100***	***76-99***	***49-65***
♀	100	234-265	88-100	83-99	52-65
♂	100	224-256	84-96	76-93	49-62
N.p. phaeopus		***223-269***	***85-103***	***69-93***	***52-65***
♀	70	232-269	87-103	73-93	54-65
♂	80	223-260	85-101	69-89	52-63
Bristle-thighed Curlew		**223-266**	**86-107**	**79-107**	**52-63**
♀	60	237-266	89-107	84-107	54-63
♂	65	223-255	85-103	79-102	52-61
Long-billed Curlew		**251-304**	**97-134**	**99-215**	**69-94**
♀	100	262-304	101-134	142-215	74-94
♂	80	251-293	97-130	99-155	69-89
Hudsonian Godwit		**195-222**	**68-83**	**68-95**	**52-70**
♀	30	207-222	72-83	81-95	57-70
♂	30	195-210	68-79	68-82	52-65
Bar-tailed Godwit[2]		**183-247**	**65-86**	**69-121**	**47-64**
L.l. baueri		***201-247***	***66-82***	***73-121***	***49-64***
♀	100	215-247	69-88	92-121	54-64
♂	100	201-232	67-83	73-93	49-59
L.l. lappoinca		***183-229***	***65-86***	***69-111***	***47-59***
♀	100	195-229	68-86	86-111	50-59
♂	100	183-217	65-82	69-88	47-56
Marbled Godwit		**201-244**	**76-94**	**80-132**	**58-82**
L.f. beringiae		***201-224***	***73-87***	***80-117***	***58-71***
♀	6	210-224	75-87	100-117	62-71
♂	8	201-215	73-85	80-96	58-66
L.f. fedoa		***207-244***	***76-94***	***85-132***	***63-82***
♀	100	219-245	78-94	105-132	69-82
♂	100	209-234	76-91	85-110	63-75

[1] Exposed culmen represents the chord.
[2] Measures from N.Am populations only; see **Geographic variation**.

BRISTLE-THIGHED CURLEW
Numenius tahitiensis

BTCU
Species # 2680
Band size: 4A

Species—See Whimbrel (p. 560) for separation from other N.Am shorebirds. From Whimbrel by longer average bill (Table 51); bill averages extensive pink base in Sep-Apr; back with coarser buff to cinnamon fringing; rump, uppertail covs, and tail buff to cinnamon, the rects with brown barring; ventral flank feathers with bristle-like tips (Fig. 420);

undertail covs unmarked (*vs* barred or marked in Whimbrel).

Geographic variation—Monotypic.

Molt—SAS. PF partial-complete? (Oct-Mar/Aug in HY/SYs), PA1 absent(?), PB2 incomplete-complete (May-Nov in non-breeding SYs), PA2 limited-incomplete(?), PB3 complete (Jun-Nov in non-breeding TYs), DPA partial-incomplete (Jan-Mar in ATYs), DPB complete (Aug-Dec in breeding ATYs). The single inserted first-cycle molt appears to be homologous with a PF rather than a PA1 (Fig. 10**C**, p. 14). All molting occurs on non-breeding grounds. Molt strategies unique, reflecting adaptation to non-breeding environment (Marks 1993, Pyle 1999). The PF includes most to all body feathers, some to most proximal s covs (the distal gr covs usually retained), 4-5 terts, usually 2 to (sometimes) all c.rects, and 3-10 inner pp and 1-9 distal ss (other than terts) in typical sequence (Fig. 376**D**, p. 504); body feathers, terts, and c.rects replaced primarily in Oct-Dec whereas pp, ss, and outer rects replaced primarily in Feb-Jul; some SYs may replace all feathers during a complete PF. The PB2 can be arrested (or suspended?) in some SYs, after 4-9 pp have been replaced. The DPB can involve blocks of pp and ss being replaced synchronously, resulting in flightlessness (Marks et al. 1990). An extra molt of outer pp may occur in some TYs as part of the PA2 (see p. 504); more study is needed. The DPA includes some to most of the body feathers, no to a few proximal s covs, and sometimes 1-2 terts and 1-6 c.rects. All SYs and TYs and some 4Ys over-summer on non-breeding grounds and exhibit less-complete (or no) PA2-PA3s and advanced PB2-PB4s (see p. 18).

FIGURE 420. Modified feather of ventral flanks in Bristle-thighed Curlew, displaying exposed shaft or "bristle". Note these feathers are not found on "thigh" (femoral tract).

Age—Juv (B1; Jul-Nov) has uniformly fresh plumage aspect, the back feathers and wing covs with broader rufous scalloping (Fig. 419**A**, p. 561), and the pp and ss uniformly juv and fresh (Fig. 375**A**, p. 503); Juv ♀ = ♂. Note that confirmed breeders can be reliably aged ATY.

Juv-HY/SY (1st cycle, Juv/B1-F1; Oct-Sep): All to some upperpart feathers (Oct-Dec), terts, and/or distal s covs juv, with broader rufous scalloping (Fig. 419**A-B**), contrasting with formative humerals, scapulars, proximal s covs, and terts (Figs. 375**C-D** & 419**C**), the distal gr covs usually retained and becoming worn and frayed by Apr-Sep (Figs. 475**D** & 419**B**); pp, p covs, and ss uniformly juv in Oct-Feb (Fig. 375**A**), being incompletely to completely replaced in typical sequence in Feb-Jul (Fig. 376**D**), and being completely replaced again (2 waves often present; Fig. 376**C**) in May-Sep, the juv outer pp and p covs (if present) tapered and relatively worn (Figs. 377**A-B** & 378**A-B**, p. 506); some juv rects retained through Feb-Mar (often Apr-Sep), contrastingly narrow and worn (Fig. 379**A-D**). **Note: See SY/TY.**

AHY/ASY (Def. cycle, DB-DA; Oct-Sep): Upperpart feathers and s covs uniformly basic or mixed basic and alternate (Fig. 375**E-F**), the basic feathers with narrower buff to cinnamon barring (Fig. 419**C**); pp, p covs, and ss uniformly basic (Fig. 375**E**), being replaced in Aug-Nov, the outer pp and p covs broad and truncate (Figs. 377**C-D** & 378**C-D**); rects uniformly basic and broader (Fig. 379**E**), sometimes with 1-6 alternate c.rects in Mar-Sep (Fig. 379**F**). **Note: See SY/TY. Adults found on breeding grounds can be reliably aged ATY in May-Aug but this age cannot be assigned by in-hand criteria.**

SY/TY (2nd cycle, B2-A2; Oct-Sep): Like AHY/ASY but the outer 1-6 pp and p covs and/or 1-9 medial ss retained juv (Fig. 375**D**), the outer pp very tapered, abraded, and worn (Figs. 375**E** & 377**B**). **Note: SY/TYs retaining juv pp may be uncommon. SYs and TYs, as well**

as some 4Ys over-summer on non-breeding grounds and thus are not encountered on migration or breeding grounds. See Molt regarding differences in strategies that might provide further clues to ageing on non-breeding grounds.

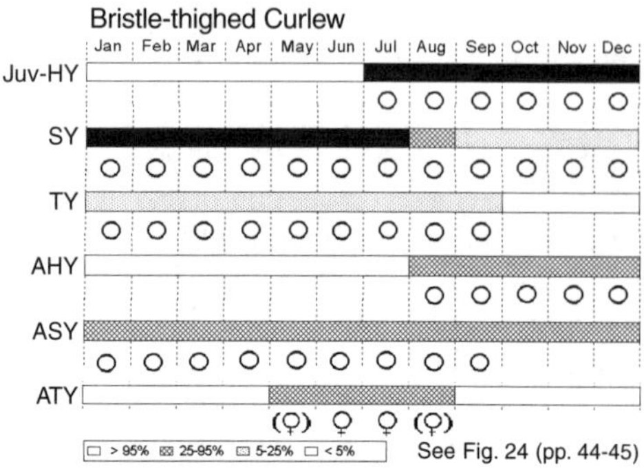

Sex—♀=♂ by plumage aspect. Bilateral BPs (Fig. 20**B**, p. 31) developed by both sexes but distended cloaca (Fig. 21, p. 32) indicates ATY ♀ in May-Jul. Measurements largely unhelpful for sexing (Table 51, p. 562). No other criteria known.

Hybrids reported—None.

Bristle-thighed Curlew
Jan Feb Mar Apr May Jun Jul Aug Sep Oct Nov Dec
Juv-HY
SY
TY
AHY
ASY
ATY
(♀) ♀ ♀ (♀)
> 95% 25-95% 5-25% < 5%
See Fig. 24 (pp. 44-45)

References—Higgins & Davies (1996), O.W. Johnson (1973, 1977, 1979), Kinsky & Yaldwyn (1981), Marks (1993), Marks & Underhill (1994), Marks et al. (1990, 2002). Mlodinow et al. (1999), Palmer (1967b), Patterson (1998), Prater et al. (1977), Pyle (1999), Ridgway (1919).

LONG-BILLED CURLEW

Numenius americanus

LBCU
Species # 2640
Band size: 5-6 Above joint

Species—From other N.Am shorebirds by large size and very long bill (Table 51, p. 562), bill decurved, dark brownish with a pinkish base, and with upper mandible with bulbous tip and extending beyond lower mandible by 5-12 mm (Fig. 422; unique among N.Am curlews); back fringing and underparts cinnamon (*cf.* Fig. 421); head with indistinct to no dark lateral crown stripes and eyeline; pp and ss brown with indistinct cinnamon bands; underwing covs dark cinnamon to rufous; legs and feet grayish, with hind toe relatively well developed (Fig. 373**C**, p. 500) and moderate webbing between fore toes (Fig. 374**C**-**D**, p. 501). Far Eastern Curlew (*N. madagascarensis*), a vagrant to w.AK, averages longer winged (wg chord 271-323); has upper mandible with less bulbous tip and not extending as far (3-8 mm) beyond lower mandible (*cf.* Fig. 422); back fringing whitish to pale buff; underwing covs whitish and brown, without cinnamon or rufous.

Geographic variation—Monotypic, following Hellmayr & Conover (1948b). Populations breeding in BC-Sask to NV ("*N.a. parvus*" or "*occidentalis*") average smaller and shorter billed than those of ID-SD to NM but differences are slight, probably broadly clinal, and confounded by age-related variation. See also Behle (1985), Bishop (1910), Dugger & Dugger (2002), Grinnell (1921), Oberholser (1918c), Patten et al. (2003), Phillips et al. (1964), and Ridgway (1919) for more information.

Molt—SAS. PF partial-incomplete (Oct-Dec/Mar in HY/SYs), PA1 absent; PB2 complete (May-Aug in non-breeding SYs), PA2 absent-limited? (Apr-May in TYs), PB3 complete (Jun-Sep in non-breeding TYs), DPA absent-limited (Mar-Apr in breeding ASYs), DPB complete (Aug-Nov in breeding ASYs). The single inserted first-cycle molt appears to be homologous with a PF rather than a PA1 (Fig. 10**C**, p. 14). Molting occurs primarily on non-breeding grounds, although the DPB can commence (with some body feathers) on breeding grounds; it exhibits a n.Hemisphere strategy (Table 45, pp. 501-505). The PF includes some to most body feathers, no to a few proximal s covs, usually 1-3 terts, and often 1-6 c.rects. The DPA occurs in a small proportion of ASYs and can include scattered body feathers (including scapulars), possibly some proximal s covs, and up to 2 terts. All SYs, most to all TYs, and probably some to many 4Ys over-summer on non-breeding grounds and exhibit less-complete (or no) PA2-PA3s and advanced PB2-PB4s (see p. 18). See pp. 500-507 for more information on molt in shorebirds.

Age—Juv (B1; Jul-Oct) has uniformly fresh plumage aspect, the back feathers and wing covs with broad cinnamon fringing (Fig. 421**A**), and the pp and ss uniformly juv and fresh (Fig. 375**A**, p. 503); Juv ♀ = ♂.

Juv-HY/SY (1st cycle, Juv/B1-F1; Oct-Sep): All to some upperpart feathers, terts, and/or distal s covs juv, with broad cinnamon fringing (Fig. 421**A-B**), contrasting with fresher formative scapulars, humerals, terts, and (sometimes) proximal s covs (Figs. 375**B-C** & 421**C**), and becoming worn and frayed by Apr-Sep (Figs. 375**D** & 421**B**); pp, p covs, and ss uniformly juv in Oct-Apr (Fig. 375**A**) and being completely replaced in Apr-Aug, the outer pp and p covs tapered, brownish, and relatively worn (Figs. 377**A-B** & 378**A**, p. 506); some juv rects retained, contrastingly narrow and worn (Fig. 379**A-D**, p. 507). **Note: SYs remain to over-summer on non-breeding grounds**.

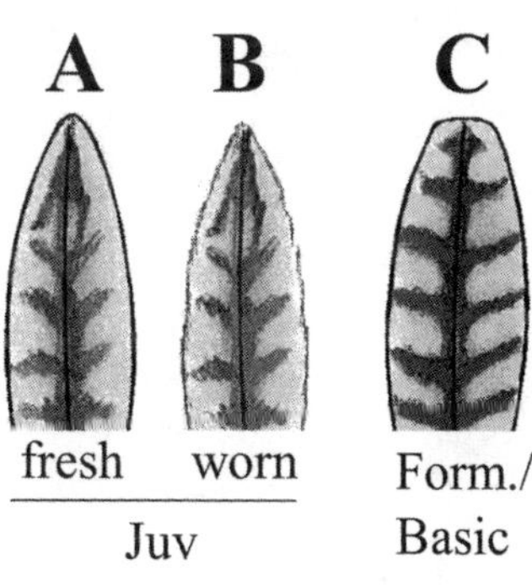

FIGURE 421. Shape and pattern to s covs by feather generation in Long-billed Curlew. SYs retain worn outer gr covs (**B**) through the PB2 in May-Aug (*cf.* Fig. 375**D**).

AHY/ASY (Def. cycle, DB-DA; Oct-Sep): Upperpart feathers, terts, and s covs uniformly basic or mixed basic and alternate (Fig. 375**B-C**), barred cinnamon and brown (Fig. 421**C**); pp, p covs, and ss uniformly basic (Fig. 375**E**), the outer pp and p covs broad and truncate (Figs. 377**C-D** & 378**C-D**); outer rects uniformly basic and broader (Fig. 379**E**). **Note: See Juv-HY/SY. Over-summering AHY/ASYs with basic flight feathers and commencing p molt in Jun-Jul, might be reliably aged TY or T-4Y (see pp. 41-42) but more study is needed.**

Sex—♀ = ♂ by plumage aspect. Bilateral(?) BPs (Fig. 20**B**, p. 31) developed by both sexes but distended cloaca (Fig. 21, p. 32) indicates ASY (probably ATY) ♀ in Apr-Jun. Measurements (especially exp culmen) helpful for sexing many individuals (Table 51, p. 562), although full development of bill may take up to a year or more.

AHY ♀: Exposed culmen > 155 and culmen averages flatter (Fig. 422**A**). **Note: Individuals with exposed culmen 142-155 likely represent HY/SY ♀♀ or AHY/ASY ♂♂, so combine with age and bill shape for more reliable sex determinations.**

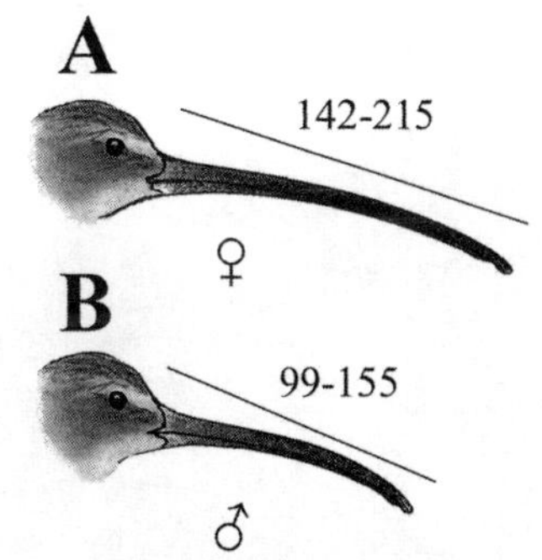

FIGURE 422. Bill shape and length by sex in Long-billed Curlew. Measure pertains to the chord of the exposed culmen (Fig. 7**C**, p. 9). ♀♀ have flatter profiles to the bill than ♂♂; some intermediates occur that are likely HY/SY ♀♀ or AHY/ASY ♂♂, as full bill development may take up to a year. Note also the abbreviated lower mandible and bulb-tipped upper mandible, unique among N.Am curlews.

AHY ♂: Exposed culmen < 142 and culmen more decurved (Fig. 422**B**). **Note: See AHY ♀.**

Hybrids reported—None.

References—Allen (1980), Bent (1929), Bucher (1978), Dugger & Dugger (2002), Oberholser (1974), Palmer (1967b), Prater et al. (1977), Ridgway (1919), Roberts (1955).

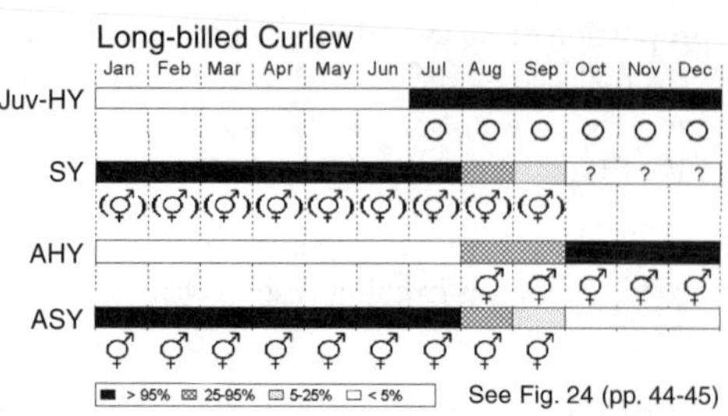

Godwits *Scolopacidae, Scolopacinae, Limosini*

Three species. Tribal characters include medium-large to large bodies; long, slightly recurved bills, expanded at tip; and fleshy legs with hind toe relatively well developed (Fig. 373**B**-**C**, p. 500) and slight webbing between fore toes (Fig. 374**B**, p. 501). North American godwits have 10 functional primaries (p10 longest by 3-10 mm, when fully grown), 16-19 secondaries (including 4-5 tertials, and one absent between the 4th and 5th; *cf.* Fig. 12**B**, p. 19), and 12 rectrices. Ageing can be accomplished through the first cycle (to SY and ASY) by plumage aspect and molt patterns, and sexes can be separated by alternate-plumage aspect and size (♀♀ larger). In molting, most godwits exhibit the Complex Alternate Strategy (CAS; Fig 10**F**, pp. 13-16) but Marbled Godwit appears to exhibit a Simple Alternate Strategy (SAS, Fig. 10**D**-**E**), perhaps with a merging of a PF and a PA1. Among godwits, both n.Hemisphere and/or s.Hemisphere strategies (Table 45, pp. 501-505) are employed. Age of first breeding is 2-4 years. See pp. 500-507 for further information on molt and ageing in shorebirds.

HUDSONIAN GODWIT
Limosa haemastica

HUGO
Species # 2510
Band size: 3A

Species—From other N.Am shorebirds and godwits by medium-large size with proportionally long bill (Table 51, p. 562), bill slightly recurved, moderately thick, and dull pink to orange with a dusky tip; upperparts grayish-brown (Oct-Mar) to dark brown with buff spots (Apr-Sep) and white rump and bases to uppertail covs; pp, ss, and rects dusky with white bases (Fig. 425, p. 568); lower breast and abdomen whitish to pale brown (Mar-Oct) or variably washed dark rufous with dusky bars (Mar-Oct); axillars and underwing covs dusky brown; legs and feet black, with hind toe relatively well developed (Fig. 373**C**, p. 500) and slight webbing between outer fore toes (Fig. 374**B**, p. 501).

Black-tailed Godwit (*L. limosa*), a vagrant from Eurasia, is similar (especially Juvs) but has proportionally longer bill and legs (wg chord 191-224, tl 70-85, exp culmen 80-120, tarsus 63-94; see Prater et al. 1977 and Cramp & Simmons 1983 for geographic variation); middle toe claw longer and straight (Fig. 423); axillars and underwing covs white; bill often with more distinct black tip; gr covs with distinct white tips (*vs* little or no white to corners in Hudsonian Godwit; Fig. 424, p. 568); auriculars, hind neck, and nape orangish in Apr-Oct (*vs* browner in Hudsonian Godwit); Juv with less black to outer rectrices (Fig. 425).

Geographic variation—Monotypic. See Haig et al. (1997).

Molt—CAS. PF partial-incomplete (Oct-Dec/Jun in HY/SYs), PA1 limited-partial (Mar-May in SYs), PB2 complete (May-Nov in non-breeding SYs), DPA partial (Jan-May in ASYs), DPB complete (Aug-Jan/Mar in ASY/ATYs). Molting occurs at stopover sites and on non-breeding grounds, and follows a s.Hemisphere strategy (Table 45, pp. 501-505). The extent of the PF is little-known but likely includes some to all body feathers, some to most proximal s covs, and some terts and/or rects in Oct-Dec, and it may

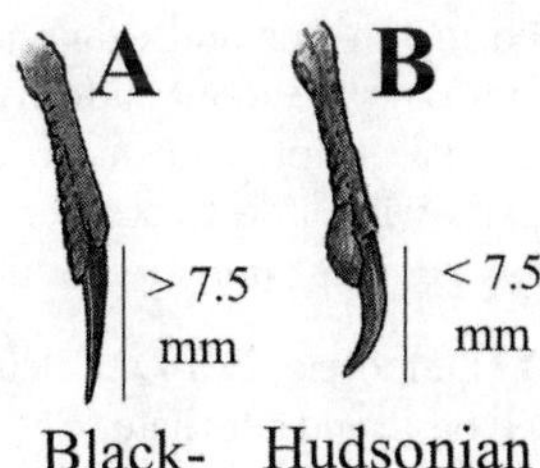

FIGURE 423. Shape and length of middle claw in Black-tailed and Hudsonian godwits for identification. Measure is vertical length of the claw from insertion along dorsal edge. The claw in Black-tailed Godwit can also be flanged.

include the remainder of the rects, pp, and ss in typical or eccentric sequence (Fig. 376**A**, **D**, p. 504) in Jan-Jun (as in some Bar-tailed Godwits); more study is needed. The DPA includes most to all body feathers, no to a few (up to 20%) s covs, 1-5 terts, and occasionally 1-2 c.rects. Most to all SYs and possibly some to many TYs over-summer on non-breeding grounds or at stopover sites and exhibit less-complete (or no) PA1-PA2s and advanced PB2-PB3s (see p. 18). See pp. 500-507 for more information on molt in shorebirds.

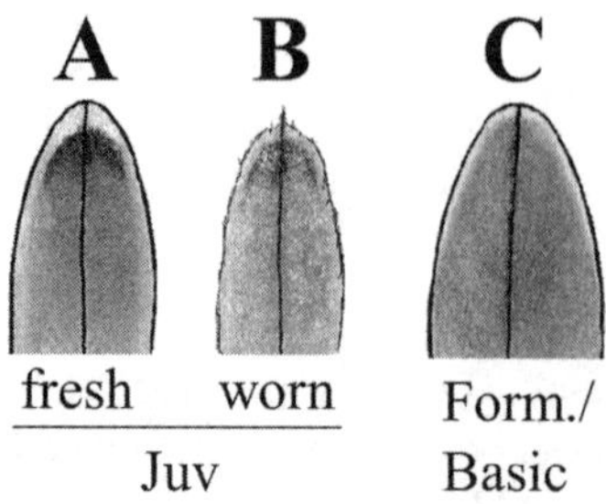

FIGURE 424. Shape and pattern to s covs by feather generation in Hudsonian Godwit. SYs may or may not retain worn outer gr covs (**B**) through the PB2 in May-Nov (*cf.* Fig. 375**D**); more study needed.

Age—Juv (B1; Jul-Nov) has uniformly fresh plumage aspect, the back feathers and wing covs distinctly fringed dusky and buff (Fig. 424**A**), and the pp and ss uniformly juv and fresh (Fig. 375**A**, p. 503); Juv ♀ = ♂.

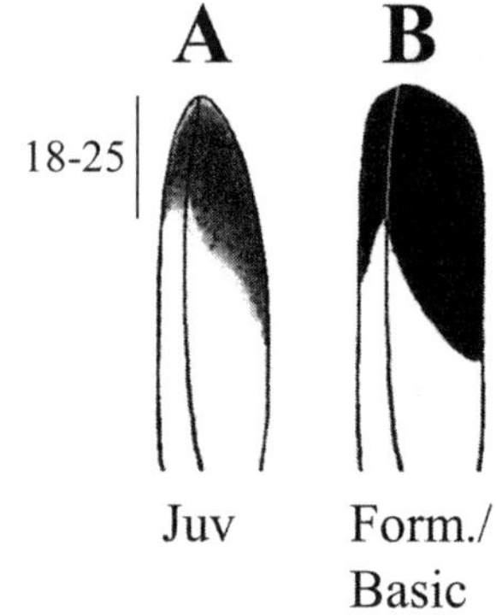

FIGURE 425. Shape and pattern to the outer rectrices (r6 shown) by feather generation in Hudsonian Godwit. Most HY/SYs appear to replace juv rects (**A**) by Dec-Feb but some SYs may retain these or r4-r5 until Sep or later (*cf.* Fig. 379**D**); more study needed. In Juv Black-tailed Godwit, the black tip to the outer web of r6 is 10-15 mm in length

Juv-HY/SY (1st cycle, Juv/B1-F1-A1; Oct-Sep): All to some upperpart feathers (Oct-Dec), terts, and/or distal s covs juv (Fig. 375**A**), distinctly fringed dusky and buff when fresh (Fig. 424**A**), contrasting with fresher and grayer formative scapulars, humerals, terts, and proximal s covs (Figs. 375**B-C** & 424**C**), the distal gr covs probably becoming worn and frayed by Apr-Sep (Figs. 375**D** & 424**B**); some juv rects retained through Jan-Mar (occasionally Apr-Sep), contrastingly narrow and worn (Fig. 379**A-D**, p. 507), the outer rects with indistinct brown and whitish pattern (Fig. 425**A**); pp, p covs, and ss juv, fresh, and without s1-p1 contrast in Oct-Jan (Fig. 375**A**), possibly being incompletely replaced in Jan-Apr and exhibiting typical or eccentric replacement patterns in May-Sep (Fig. 376**A**, **D**, p. 504; see **Molt**), the juv outer pp and p covs (if present) narrow and relatively abraded (Figs. 377**A-B** & 378**A-B**, p. 506); underparts with little to some rufous in Mar-Aug by sex (see **Sex**). **Note: Most SYs (and probably some TYs) over-summer on non-breeding grounds or at stopover locations.**

AHY/ASY (Def. cycle, DB-DA; Oct-Sep): Upperpart feathers, terts, and s covs uniformly basic or mixed basic and alternate (Fig. 375**E-F**), the basic feathers without distinct dusky and buff fringe (Fig. 424**C**); rects uniformly basic and broader (Fig. 379**E**), with distinct blackish and white pattern (Fig. 425**B**), occasionally with 1-2 alternate c.rects in Apr-Sep (Fig. 379**F**); pp, p covs, and ss worn and being replaced in Dec-Mar, or basic, fresh, and with replacement clines and s1-p1 contrast in Jan-Sep (Fig. 375**E**), the outer pp and p covs broad and truncate (Figs. 377**C-D** & 378**C-D**); underparts near-completely to completely rufous in Mar-Aug by sex (see **Sex**). **Note: See Juv-HY/SY. It is possible that SY/TYs and ASY/ATYs can be recognized by molt patterns and extent of alternate-plumage aspect in Mar-Aug, as in other large shorebirds, but a more-complete understanding of molt and plumage succession on non-breeding grounds is needed.**

Sex—Bilateral BPs (Fig. 20**B**, p. 31) developed by both sexes but distended cloaca (Fig. 21, p. 32) indicates ASY ♀ in Apr-Jun. Measurements helpful for sexing (Table 51, p. 562). The following is reliable once Juvs are fully grown in Aug-Sep.

♀: Exp culmen > 81, tarsus > 58 (Table 51); many underpart feathers of ASYs in Apr-Sep with broad (> 1 mm) buff to whitish tips in Apr-Aug; ASYs with base of bill dull pinkish in May-Jul. **Note: Beware SY, non-breeding, and molting ♂♂ that can resemble ♀♀ in alternate-plumage aspect.**

♂: Exp culmen < 82, tarsus < 59 (Table 51); underpart feathers of ASYs in Mar-Sep with few or no narrow white tips (< 1 mm, when fresh); ASYs with base of bill bright yellow-orange in May-Jul. **Note: See ♀.**

Hudsonian Godwit
Jan Feb Mar Apr May Jun Jul Aug Sep Oct Nov Dec
Juv-HY
SY
AHY
ASY
■ > 95% ▩ 25-95% ▤ 5-25% □ < 5%
See Fig. 24 (pp. 44-45)

Hybrids reported—None.

References—Alexander & Gratto-Trevor (1997), Baker et al. (1996), Bent (1927), Cox (1990a), Elphick & Klima (2002), Higgins & Davies (1996), Oberholser (1974), Palmer (1967b), Prater et al. (1977), Ridgway (1919), Roberts (1955), Stone (1900), Sutton (1968a).

BAR-TAILED GODWIT
Limosa lapponica

BTGO
Species # 2500
Band size: 4♂, 4A♀

Species—From other N.Am shorebirds by medium-large to large size with proportionally long bill (Table 51, p. 562), bill straight to slightly recurved, moderately long and thick, and dark with variable pinkish base; plumage aspect brown and buff to grayish without cinnamon in Sep-Mar and SYs, to largely dark rufous in Apr-Aug ASY ♂♂; rump, uppertail covs, axillars, and underwing covs variably whitish with dark barring (Fig. 426; see **Geographic variation**); pp and ss brown with little to no whitish at base; legs and feet grayish, with hind toe relatively well developed (Fig. 373**C**, p. 500) and slight webbing between outer fore toes (Fig. 374**B**, p. 501).

Geographic variation—See Barter (1989a), Cramp & Simmons (1983), Dement'ev & Gladkov (1951c), Engelmoer & Roselaar (1998), Hellmayr & Conover (1948b), Higgins & Davies (1996), McCaffery & Gill (2001), Nieboer et al. (1985), Prater et al. (1977), Portenko (1936), Ridgway (1919), Tomkovich & Serra (1999), Wilson et al. (2007). One other subspecies (*menzbieri*) occurs in c.Eurasia, intermediate between the following two taxa.

L.l. baueri (="*novaezealandiae*"; br Siberia-nw.AK; vagrant s.AK-NWT to CA): Averages larger (Table 51, p. 562); lower back dark; rump and uppertail covs grayish with indistinct whitish barring; axillars with heavy blackish markings (Fig. 426**A-B**). Populations of Siberia ("*anadyrensis*")

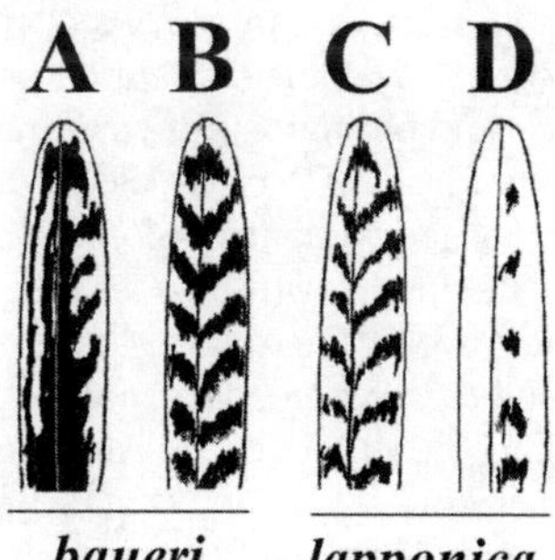

FIGURE 426. Pattern to the axillars by subspecies in Bar-tailed Godwit. Within each subspecies, w.populations average fewer and smaller black markings (**B**, **D**) than e.populations (**A**, **C**); the c.Eurasian subspecies *L.l. menzbieri* is intermediate.

may average smaller and with more whitish to axillars (Fig. 426**B**) than populations of AK but differences slight and broadly clinal.

L.l. lapponica (br Europe; vagrant to Nfl-FL): Averages smaller (Table 51); lower back primarily white; rump and uppertail covs white with distinct dark bars or marks; axillars with sparse black markings (Fig. 426**C-D**). Populations in the e. part of range ("*taymyrensis*") may average smaller and with more dark to rump, back, and axillars (Fig. 426**C**) but differences are slight.

Molt—CAS. PF partial-incomplete (Sep-Dec/Apr in HY/SYs), PA1 absent-partial (Mar-May in non-breeding SYs), PB2 complete (Jul-Oct in non-breeding SYs), DPA partial-incomplete (Feb-May in breeding ASYs), DPS absent-limited? (Apr-Jun in ASY ♂♂), DPB complete (Jul-Oct/Feb in breeding ASY/ATYs). Molting occurs primarily on non-breeding grounds, although the PF and DPB can commence and the DPA can complete on breeding grounds or at stopover sites. Molt exhibits either a n.Hemisphere or s.Hemisphere strategy (Table 45, pp. 501-505) depending on location of non-breeding grounds. The PF includes most body feathers, a few to some proximal s covs, 2-3 terts, and often 1-4 c.rects in Sep-Dec; in many SYs (primarily among *L.l. baueri*) the PF can also include up to all rects, terts, and s covs (the distal gr covs usually retained), and 4-10 medial or outer pp and p covs and 1-7 medial ss (distal to the terts) in eccentric sequence (Fig. 376**A-B**, p. 504; occasionally arrested) in Jan-Jun. The DPB completes earlier in *lapponica* (Oct-Nov) than in *baueri* (Dec-Feb). The PA1 includes scattered body feathers (few if any s covs, terts, or rects) and the DPA includes some to all body feathers, a few to some s covs, 1-5 terts, and 1-6 c.rects; ♂♂ average more feathers replaced than ♀♀ during the DPA by age. More study needed on a possible DPS in ASY ♂♂, during which some alternate breast feathers are reportedly replaced for a third time within the cycle (Piersma and Jukema 1993; see p. 15). Most to all SYs (and some TYs primarily *baueri*) over-summer on non-breeding grounds, and exhibit less-complete (or no) PA1-PA2s and earlier PB2-PB3s (see p. 18). See pp. 500-507 for more information on molt in shorebirds.

Age—Juv (B1; Jul-Nov) has uniformly fresh plumage aspect, the back feathers and wing covs with broader buff scalloping or barring (Fig. 427**A**), and the pp and ss uniformly juv and fresh (Fig. 375**A**, p. 503); Juv ♀=♂.

Juv-HY/SY (1st cycle, Juv/B1-F1-A1; Oct-Sep): All to some upperpart feathers (Oct-Dec), terts, and/or distal s covs juv, with buff scalloping or barring when fresh (Fig. 427**A**), contrasting with fresher and grayer formative scapulars, humerals, terts, and proximal s covs (Figs. 375**B-C** & 427**B**), the distal gr covs usually retained and becoming worn and frayed by Apr-Sep (Fig. 375**D**); pp, p covs, and ss uniformly juv and without s1-p1 contrast (Fig. 375**A**), the juv p4 with broader pale fringe to inner web (Fig. 428**A**), often being incompletely replaced in Jan-Apr and exhibiting eccentric or arrested replacement patterns in May-Sep (Fig. 376**A-B**, p. 504; regularly in *L.l. baueri* only), and being completely replaced in May-Oct, the juv outer pp and p covs (if present) tapered Figs. 377**A-B** & 378**A-B**, p. 506); some juv rects retained through Jan-Mar (often Apr-Sep, especially in *lapponica*), contrastingly

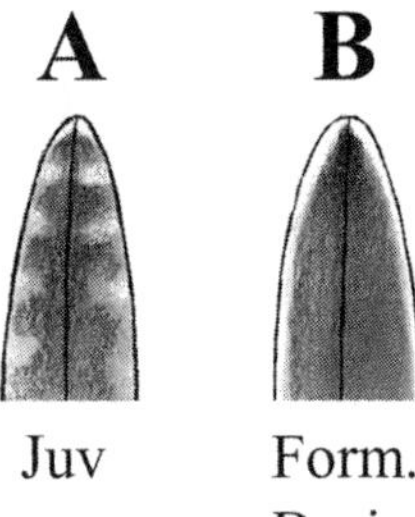

FIGURE 427. Shape and pattern to s covs by feather generation in Bar-tailed Godwit. Most SYs retain at least some gr covs through the PB2 in Jul-Oct (*cf.* Fig. 375**D**); some SYs of *L.l. baueri* may replace all covs during the PF, by Feb-Mar.

narrow and worn (Fig. 379**A-D**, p. 507); underparts with little to no rufous in Apr-Sep by sex. **Note: A small proportion of *baueri* may molt all pp and ss in Jan-Apr during the PF, but not enough to preclude reliable ageing of ASYs. Most or all SYs and some TYs remain to over-summer on non-breeding grounds.**

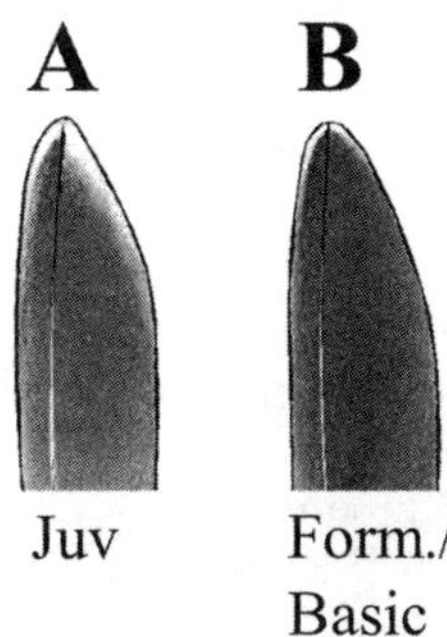

FIGURE 428. Pattern to p4 by feather generation in Bar-tailed Godwit. The pale fringe to the inner web is usually > 1.7 mm wide in juv feathers (when fresh) and < 1.7 mm wide in basic feathers. Most SYs retain the juv p4 (**A**) until the PB2 in Jul-Oct but occasional SYs (of *baueri*) replace it with formative p4 (**B**) in Feb-Apr. See Cronau et al. (1986) for more information.

AHY/ASY (Def. cycle, DB-DA; Oct-Sep): Upperpart feathers, terts, and s covs uniformly basic or mixed basic and alternate (Fig. 375**E-F**), the basic feathers with whitish fringing (Fig. 427**B**); pp, p covs, and ss worn and being completely replaced in Sep-Nov (*lapponica*) or Oct-Feb (*baueri*), or basic, fresher, and with replacement clines and often s1-p1 contrast in Nov-Sep in *lapponica* or Jan-Sep in *baueri* (Fig. 375**E**), the p4 with narrower fringe to inner web (Fig. 428**B**), and the outer pp and p covs broad and truncate (Figs. 377**C-D** & 378**C-D**); rects uniformly basic and broader (Fig. 370**E**), usually with 1-6 alternate c.rects in Mar-Sep (Fig. 379**F**); underparts with substantial rufous by sex in Apr-Aug (see **Sex**). **Note: See Juv-HY/SY. Over-summering AHY/ASYs with basic flight feathers, showing reduced alternate-plumage aspect in Apr-Aug, and commencing p molt in Jun-Jul, might be reliably aged TY but more study is needed.**

Sex—Bilateral BPs (Fig. 20**B**, p. 31 developed by both sexes but distended cloaca (Fig. 21, p. 32) indicates ASY ♀ in Apr-Jun. Measurements helpful for sexing (Table 51, p. 562). The following is reliable for sexing virtually all individuals of known subspecies and age:

♀: Exp culmen > 92 (*L.l. baueri*) or > 86 (*lapponica*); underparts of ASYs in Apr-Sep whitish with little to some (< 50%) pale rufous. **Note: Individuals with exposed culmen 92-93 (baueri) or 86-88 (lapponica) are HY/SY ♀♀ or AHY/ASY ♂♂; combine with age for reliable sexing.**

♂: Exp culmen < 93 (*baueri*) or < 88 (*lapponica*); underparts of ASYs in Apr-Sep extensively (> 50%) rufous. **Note: See ♀.**

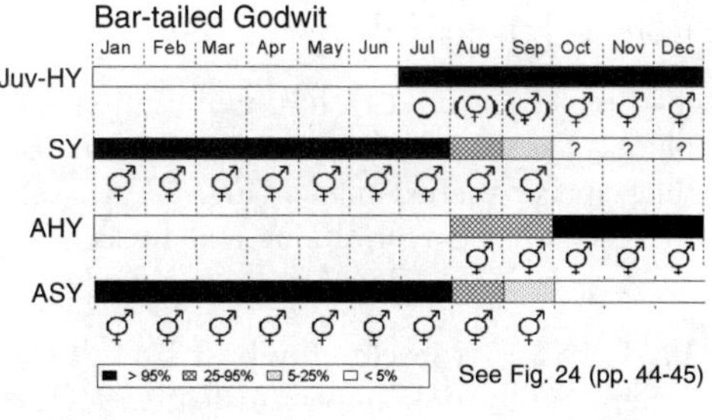

Hybrids reported—Doubtfully with Red Knot (McCarthy 2006, Pyle 2006b).

References—Barter (1989b), Barter et al. (1990), Bent (1927), Cramp & Simmons (1983), Cronau et al. (1986), Dement'ev & Gladkov (1951c), Higgins & Davies (1996), McCaffery & Gill (2001), Palmer (1967b), Piersma & Jukema (1993), Prater et al. (1977), Ridgway (1919), Wilson et al. (2007).

MARBLED GODWIT
Limosa fedoa

MAGO
Species # 2490
Band size: 4♂, 4A♀

Species—From other N.Am shorebirds and godwits by large size and proportionally long bill (Table 51, p. 562), bill slightly recurved and pink (tinged orangish in some ASYs in May-Jul) with a dusky tip; plumage aspect mixed brown, buff, and cinnamon, with barring to underparts in Apr-Aug ASYs (*cf.* Figs. 429-431); pp, ss, and underwing covs primarily cinnamon; feet grayish, with hind toe relatively well developed (Fig. 373**C**, p. 500) and slight webbing between outer fore toes (Fig. 374**B**, p. 501).

Geographic variation—See Gibson & Kessel (1989). No other subspecies occur.

L.f. beringiae (br sw.AK, wint coastal WA-n.CA): Smaller in dimensions (Table 51, p. 562) but greater in mass (lean weight [p. 12] of ♂♂ 293-373).

L.f. fedoa (br Alb-MT to Ont, wint coastal c-s.CA and TX-MD): Larger in dimensions (Table 51) but leaner in mass (lean weight of ♂♂ 263-345).

Molt—SAS (CAS?). PF/PA1 partial-incomplete (Sep-Dec/Mar in HY/SYs), PB2 complete (May-Sep in non-breeding SYs), PA2 limited (Apr-May in over-summering TYs), PB3 complete (Jun-Oct in non-breeding TYs), DPA partial (Mar-Apr in breeding ASYs), DPB complete (Aug-Nov in breeding ASY/ATYs). The single inserted first-cycle molt may have resulted from a merging of a PF and a PA1 in ancestral taxa (Fig. 10**D**, p. 14); study is needed. Molting occurs primarily on non-breeding grounds and exhibits a n.Hemisphere strategy (Table 45, pp. 501-505). The PF/PA1 includes some to all body feathers, no to some proximal s covs, usually 1-5 terts, and often 1-10 rects; body feathers are replaced primarily in Sep-Dec whereas some s covs, terts, and rects can be replaced in Jan-Mar. A few body feathers may be replaced twice in the first cycle, indicating the presence of both a PF and a PA1 (and CAS; Fig. 10**F**); study needed. The PA2 includes scattered underpart and upperpart feathers but no s covs, terts, or rects. The DPA includes most to all underpart feathers, some to most upperpart feathers, and often 1-4 terts, but few if any s covs or rects. All SYs, most TYs, and possibly some 4Ys over-summer on non-breeding grounds and exhibit less-complete (or no) PA2-PA3s and advanced PB2-PB4s (see p. 18). See pp. 500-507 for more information on molt in shorebirds. Occasional individuals with non-breeding grounds in S.Am may exhibit a s.Hemisphere molting strategy (pp. 501-505); more study is needed.

Age—Juv (B1; Jul-Oct) has uniformly fresh plumage aspect, the back feathers with indistinct anchor-shaped marks (Fig. 429**A**), and the pp and ss uniformly juv and fresh (Fig. 375**A**, p. 503); Juv ♀=♂.

Juv-HY/SY (1st cycle, Juv/B1-F1/A1; Oct-Sep): All to some upperpart feathers (Oct-Dec), terts, and/or distal s covs juv, with indistinct anchor-shaped marks (Fig. 429**A**), contrasting with fresher formative scapulars, humerals, terts, and proximal s covs (Figs. 375**B**-**C** & 429**B**), the retained distal juv s covs becoming worn and frayed by Apr-Sep (Fig. 375**D**); axillars and underparts without barring (Figs. 430**A** & 431**A**), occasionally with a small amount to flanks

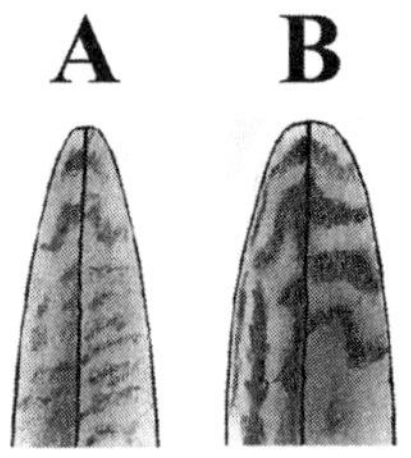

FIGURE 429. Shape and pattern to the back feathers and s covs by feather generation in Marbled Godwit. SYs retain at least some s covs and often some back feathers through the PB2 in May-Sep (*cf.* Fig. 375**D**).

and/or abdomen in Apr-Jun (Fig. 431**B**); pp, p covs, and ss uniformly juv and without s1-p1 contrast in Oct-May (Fig. 375**A**), being completely replaced in May-Sep, the outer pp and p covs tapered, brownish, and relatively worn (Figs. 377**A-B** & 378**A-B**, p. 506); some juv rects retained, contrastingly narrow and worn (Fig. 379**A-D**, p. 507); **Note: Most to all SYs remain on non-breeding grounds during summer**.

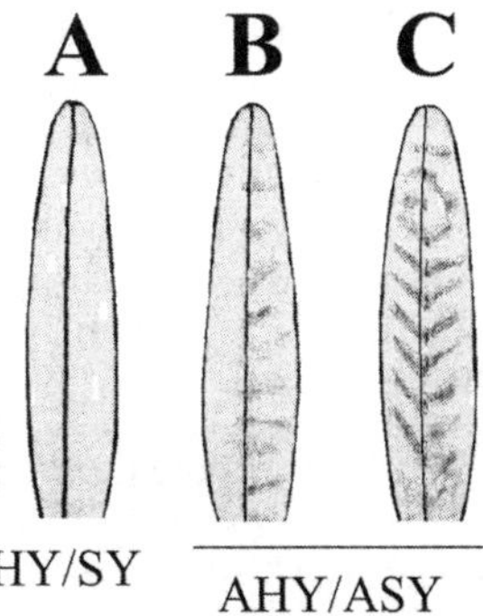

FIGURE 430. Pattern to the longest axillar by age in Marbled Godwit. See also Figure 431. Juv feathers lack markings (**A**) whereas basic feathers have variably distinct, dusky chevrons (**B-C**). Auxillars appear not to be replaced during the PF or DPA so these differences are valid year-round. It is possible that less distinct patterns (**B**) are more typical of SY/TYs and more distinct patterns (**C**) are more typical of ASY/ATYs; more study needed.

AHY/ASY (Def. cycle, DB-DA; Oct-Sep): Upperpart feathers, terts, and s covs uniformly basic or mixed basic and alternate (Fig. 375**E-F**), the basic feathers distinctly barred cinnamon and brown (Fig. 429**B**); axillars with indistinct to distinct barring (Fig. 430**B-C**); underparts with little to some dark barring in Oct-Mar (Fig. 431**A-B**) or moderate to full dark barring in Mar-Sep (Fig. 431**C-D**); pp, p covs, ss, and terts uniformly basic and often with slight s1-p1 contrast (Fig. 375**E**), the outer pp and p covs broad and truncate (Figs. 377**C-D** & 378**C-D**); outer rects uniformly basic and broader (Fig. 379**E**). **Note: See Juv-HY/SY. Oversummering AHY/ASYs with basic flight feathers, showing reduced barring to the axillars and underparts (Figs. 430A-B & 431B-C), and commencing p molt in Jun-Jul, might be reliably aged SY/TY, and individuals with more-extensive barring to the axillars (Fig. 430C) and underparts (Fig. 431B in Sep-Mar and Fig. 431D in Apr-Aug) might be reliably aged ASY/ATY, but further study is needed.**

Sex—♀=♂ by plumage aspect. Bilateral BPs (Fig. 20**B**, p. 31) developed by both sexes but distended cloaca (Fig. 21, p. 32) indicates ASY ♀ in Apr-Jun. Measurements helpful for sexing

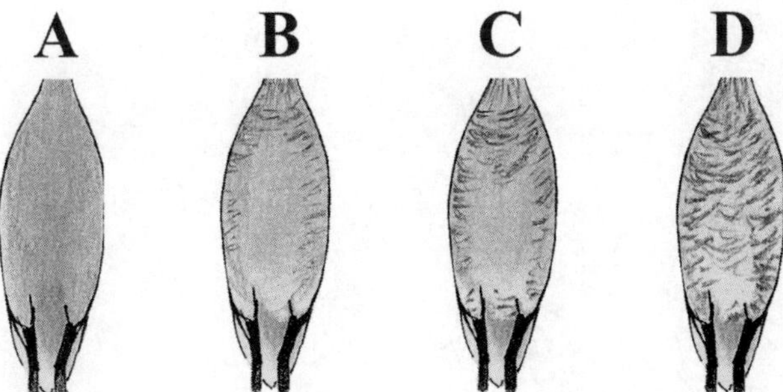

FIGURE 431. Variation in the extent to the underpart barring by age, sex, and season in Marbled Godwit. See also Figure 430. Juv-HY/SYs show no barring (**A**) in Sep-Mar and no to a small amount of barring, typically confined to flanks and abdomen, in Apr-Aug (**A-B**). SY/TYs likely show little to no barring in Sep-Mar (**A**, perhaps rarely to **B**), and some barring in Apr-Sep (**B-C**). ASY/ATYs show no to some barring in Oct-Mar (**A-C**) and full barring in Mar-Sep (**D**). More study is needed to determine if SY/TYs and ASY/ATYs can be reliably aged according to extent of underpart barring by season, combined with other criteria (see **Age**).

individuals of known subspecies (Table 51, p. 562). The following is reliable for sexing most but not all ASYs of known subspecies (usually only on breeding grounds), including mated pairs:

ASY ♀ (May-Jul): Exposed culmen > 110 (*L.f. fedoa*) or > 99 (*beringiae*); base of bill dull orange in May-Jul. **Note: Individuals of fedoa with exposed culmen 109-110 are not reliably sexed.**

ASY ♂ (May-Jul): Exposed culmen < 109 (*fedoa*) or < 100 (*beringiae*); base of bill bright orange in May-Jul. **Note: See ASY ♀.**

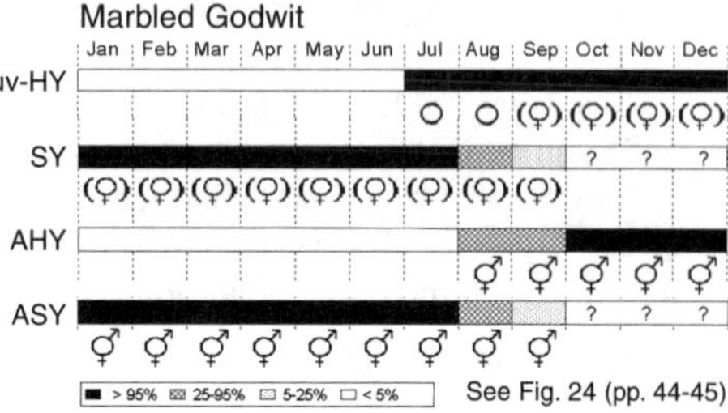

Hybrids reported—None.

References—Bent (1927), Gratto-Trevor (2000), Oberholser (1974), Palmer (1967b), Prater et al. (1977), Ridgway (1919), Roberts (1955).

Turnstones *Scolopacidae, Scolopacinae, Arenariini*

Two species. Tribal characters include medium-small bodies with proportionally short legs; short, slightly recurved, and pointed bills; and fleshy legs with hind toe relatively well developed (Fig. 373**C**, p. 500), and fore toes without webbing (Fig. 374**A**, p. 501) but margined with fleshy padding. Turnstones have 10 functional primaries (p10 longest by 0-5 mm, when fully grown), 14 secondaries (including 4 tertials, and one absent between the 4th and 5th; *cf.* Fig. 12**B**, p. 19), and 12 rectrices. Ageing can be accomplished through the first cycle (to SY and ASY) and sometimes into the second cycle (to TY) by plumage aspect and molt patterns. Sexes are similar in size (♀♀ slightly larger); some Ruddy Turnstones can be sexed by alternate-plumage aspect. In molting, turnstones exhibit the Complex Alternate Strategy (CAS; Fig. 10**F**, pp. 13-16) and follow a n.Hemisphere strategy (Black and many Ruddy turnstones) or a s.Hemisphere strategy (many Ruddy Turnstones); see Table 45 (pp. 501-505). Age of first breeding is 1-3 years. See pp. 500-507 for further information on molt and ageing in shorebirds.

RUDDY TURNSTONE
Arenaria interpres

RUTU
Species # 2830
Band size: 2-3

Species—From other N.Am shorebirds by medium-small size with proportionally short legs (Table 52, p. 578); bill black, short, slightly recurved, and pointed at tip; s8-s9, scapulars, rump, tips to gr covs (Fig. 432, p. 576), uppertail covs, and bases to rects white or primarily white; abdomen and underwing covs white; legs and feet brownish to orange, with hind toe relatively well developed (Fig. 373**C**, p. 500), and fore toes without webbing (Fig. 374**A**, p. 501) but margined with fairly well-developed padding. From Black Turnstone (p. 577) by upperpart feathers and s covs fringed buff to rufous; auricular and nape with pale markings; s6-s7 with more (> 35%) dark coloration; legs and feet brighter yellowish to orange and with smaller padded margins to toes.

Geographic variation—Considered monotypic here. Populations breeding in ne.AK-n.NWT ("*A.i. morinella*") may average a slightly shorter wing but longer bill and tarsus, and have ASYs with more extensive and brighter rufous to rufous-orange upperparts in Mar-Aug by sex, and populations breeding in nw.AK ("*cinclus*") may average darker, but differences are slight, confounded by substantial individual and sex-specific variation (*cf.* Ferns 1978b), and could be based on variation in non-breeding latitudes and molting patterns. See Bailey (1943), Conover (1945b), Cramp & Simmons (1983), Engelmoer & Roselaar (1998), Engelmoer et al. (1987), Godfrey (1953, 1986), Hellmayr & Conover (1948b), Higgins & Davies (1996), Jewett et al. (1953), Manning et al. (1956), Prater et al. (1977), Ridgway (1919), and Whitfield (1986) for more information.

Molt—CAS. PF partial-incomplete (Sep-Dec/May in HY/SYs), PA1 absent-limited (Apr-May in non-breeding SYs), PB2 complete (Jun-Sep in SYs), DPA partial-incomplete (Feb-Apr in AHYs), DPB complete (Aug-Oct/Feb in breeding AHY/ASYs). Molting occurs primarily on non-breeding grounds, although the PF and DPB can commence (body feathers only) and the DPA can occur or complete on breeding grounds or at stopover sites. Molt exhibits either a n.Hemisphere or s.Hemisphere strategy (Table 45, pp. 501-505) depending on location of non-breeding grounds. The PF includes most to all body feathers, a few to most proximal s covs, and often 1-4 terts and 1 to all 12 c.rects in Oct-Dec; in some HY/SYs (~30-50% of those with non-breeding grounds in the s.Hemisphere) it can also include 1-10 outer pp (often arrested among p5-p8) and 1-5 outer ss (among s1-s5) in typical sequence (Fig. 375**D**, p. 503) in Dec-May. The DPB completes by Nov among most AHYs (with non-breeding grounds in N.Am) but typically occurs in

Oct-Feb among AHY/ASYs with non-breeding grounds in the s.Hemisphere. The DPA includes some to most body feathers, some to most (up to 80%) proximal s covs, 1-4 terts, and occasionally r1 (rarely r2-r3 as well); ♂♂ average more feathers replaced than ♀♀ by age. Many SYs and some TYs over-summer on non-breeding grounds (primarily in the s.Hemisphere) and exhibit less-complete (or no) PA1-PA2s and advanced PB2-PB3s (Johnson 1977; see p. 18). See pp. 500-507 for more information on molt in shorebirds.

Age—Juv (B1; Jul-Oct) has uniformly fresh plumage aspect, the back feathers and wing covs with broad pale fringing, the pp and ss uniformly juv and fresh (Fig. 375**A**, p. 503), and the legs yellowish to brownish; Juv ♀=♂. See Johnson (1973, 1977) for information on age-related variation in the bursa (Fig. 23, p. 34). In addition to the following, check for p10 – p9 to be longer in Juv-HY/SYs (2-5 mm) than in AHY/ASYs (0-2 mm).

Juv-HY/SY (1st cycle, Juv/B1-F1-A1; Oct-Sep): Some to most upperpart feathers, terts, and distal s covs uniformly juv and fresh in Oct-Dec (Fig. 375**A**), the outer gr cov with narrower and less distinct mark to outer web (Fig. 432**A**), contrasting with fresher formative scapulars, terts, and proximal s covs (Fig. 375**B-C**), the distal gr covs becoming worn and frayed in Apr-Sep (Figs. 375**D** & 432**B**); sides of upper back and breast brown, sometimes mixed blackish in Apr-Sep; pp, ss, and p covs uniformly juv, fresh, and without s1-p1 contrast in Oct-Jan (Fig. 375**A**), the juv outer pp and p covs tapered and worn (Figs. 377**A-B** & 378**A-B**, p. 506); some juv rects often retained, contrastingly narrow and worn (Fig. 379**A-D**, p. 507); legs brownish to dull orange through Jan-Mar. **Note: In addition, SYs average less rufous and black to the plumage aspect (sometimes none), sex for sex, than ASYs in Apr-Aug, but some SYs can match ASYs in plumage aspect. SYs with non-breeding grounds in the s.Hemisphere also can exhibit replacement of inner pp (Fig. 375D; occasionally all pp), but these are uncommon in N.Am. Many SYs and some TYs remain on non-breeding grounds (particularly in the tropics or S.Am) during the first summer.**

AHY/ASY (Def. cycle, DB-DA; Oct-Sep): Upperpart feathers, terts, and s covs uniformly basic or mixed basic and alternate (Fig. 375**E-F**), the distal gr covs with wider and more distinct marks to outer webs (Fig. 432**C**); sides of upper back and breast often mixed brown and blackish in Oct-Mar, to entirely blackish in Apr-Sep; pp, p covs, and ss worn and being replaced in Oct-Nov (Oct-Feb in S.Am), or basic, fresh, and with slight replacement clines and sometimes s1-p1 contrast in Nov-Sep (Fig. 375**E**), the outer pp and p covs broad and truncate (Figs. 377**C-D** & 378**C-D**); rects basic and broad (Fig. 379**E**), occasionally with 1-3 alternate c.rects in Apr-Sep (Fig. 379**F**); legs bright orange. **Note: See Juv-HY/SY. Over-summering AHY/ASYs with basic flight feathers, showing intermediate to reduced amounts of alternate-plumage aspect in Apr-Aug, and commencing p molt in Jun-Jul, might be reliably aged TY but more study is needed.**

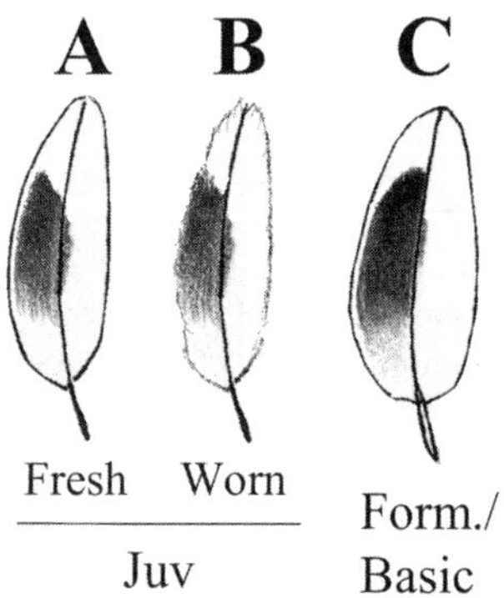

FIGURE 432. Shape and pattern to outer greater coverts by feather generation in Ruddy Turnstone. Note the less-distinct contrasts in juv (**A-B**) than in formative/basic (**C**) covs. Most to all SYs retain at least a few worn outer gr covs (**B**) through the PB2 in Jun-Sep (*cf.* Fig. 375**D**, p. 503). Black Turnstone exhibits similar variation by age, although differences are less appreciable.

SY/TY (2nd cycle, B2; Oct-Feb): Like AHY/ASY with molt of pp occurring, but outer pp and p covs juv, pointed and very abraded (Fig. 376**E**, p. 504). **Note: These are probably found in the s.Hemisphere only (see pp. 501-505).**

Sex—Bilateral BPs (Fig. 20**B**, p. 31) developed by both sexes but distended cloaca (Fig. 21, p. 32) indicates ♀ in May-Jul. Measurements unhelpful for sexing (Table 52, p. 578). The following is reliable for sexing some ASYs in Apr-Aug; HY/SYs and AHY/ASYs in formative and basic plumage aspects are not reliably sexed. In addition to the following, tongue color is reported to vary by sex, being blue-black in AHY/ASY ♂♂ and white with gray tip in AHY/ASY ♀♀; more study is needed on the reliability of this for sexing.

ASY ♀ (Apr-Aug): Forehead, lores, and sides of crown whitish and brown, contrasting indistinctly with blackish and brown crown, proximal auriculars, and breast; scapulars and wing covs brownish to dull rufous. **Note: On molting ASYs check alternate feathers only, incoming and fresh in Mar-Apr or worn in Aug-Sep. See AHY ♂.**

AHY ♂ (Mar-Sep): Forehead, lores, and sides of crown white, contrasting distinctly with black medial crown, proximal auriculars, and breast; scapulars and wing covs bright rufous to rufous-orange. **Note: See ASY ♀. Some but not all SY ♂♂ can be sexed but SY ♀♀ are not reliably sexed. Some ASY ♂♂, especially in the s.Hemisphere, might be reliably sexed in Oct-Nov or later by retained alternate feathers during protracted molts or rufous-colored basic feathers; more study is needed.**

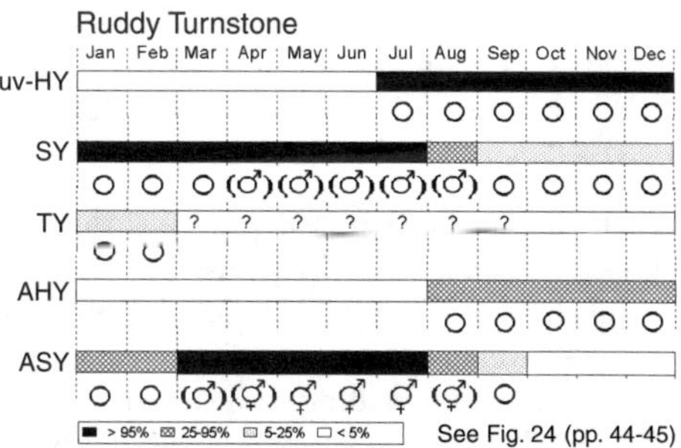

Hybrids reported—None.

References—Bent (1929), Cramp & Simmons (1983), Dement'ev & Gladkov (1951c), Engelmoer & Roselaar (1998), Ferns (1978a, 1978b), Higgins & Davies (1996), O.W. Johnson (1973, 1977, 1979), Kinsky & Yaldwyn (1981), McNeil (1970), Morrison (1975), Nettleship (2000), Oberholser (1974), Palmer (1967b), Prater et al. (1977), Ridgway (1919), Roberts (1955), Skewes et al. (2004). Spaans (1979), Summers et al. (1989).

BLACK TURNSTONE
Arenaria melanocephala

BLTU
Species # 2840
Band size: 2

Species—See Ruddy Turnstone (p. 575) for separation from other N.Am shorebirds. From Ruddy Turnstone by upperpart feathers and s covs blackish, with thin or no whitish fringing; auriculars and nape blackish, without pale markings; s6-s7 with little (< 35%) dark; legs and feet duller pinkish to brownish and with wider padded margins to toes.

Geographic variation—Monotypic.

Molt—CAS. PF partial (Sep-Nov/Apr in HY/SYs), PA2 absent-limited (Apr-May in non-breeding SYs), PB2 complete (Jun-Sep in non-breeding SYs), DPA limited (Mar-May in breeding AHYs), DPB complete (Aug-Nov in breeding AHYs). Most to all molting occurs on non-breeding grounds. Molt follows a n.Hemisphere strategy (Table 45, pp. 501-505). The PF includes most body feathers and often 1-3 terts but few if any s covs or rects; most molting occurs in Sep-Nov although replacement of terts can occur as late as Mar. The PA is limited to feathers of the head, breast, and back and includes few if any s covs, terts or rects. Some SYs over-summer on non-breeding grounds and exhibit less-complete (or no) PA1s and advanced PB2s. See pp. 500-507 for more information on molt in shorebirds.

Age—Juv (B1; Jul-Oct) has uniformly fresh plumage aspect, the pp and ss uniformly juv and fresh (Fig. 375**A**), and the legs dull to dark pinkish; Juv ♀=♂. In addition to the following, check for p10 – p9 to be longer in Juv-HY/SYs (2-5 mm) than in AHY/ASYs (0-2 mm).

Juv-HY/SY (1st cycle, Juv/B1-F1-A1; Oct-Sep): Some to most back feathers, s covs, and terts juv and fresh in Oct-Nov (Fig. 375**A**), brownish, the outer gr covs with narrower and less distinct marks to outer webs (*cf.* Fig. 432**A-B**, p. 576), contrasting with formative and blacker scapulars, proximal s covs, and 1-3 terts in Nov-Sep (Fig. 375**B-C**); pp, ss, and p covs juv (Fig. 375**A**), the outer pp and p covs tapered and more worn (Figs. 377**A-B** & 378**A-B**, p. 506); rects juv, narrow, and relatively worn (Fig. 379**A**, p. 507); legs dull to dusky pinkish through Jan-Mar. **Note: Some SYs but few ASYs over-summer on non-breeding grounds. Some intermediates in Jan-Sep are difficult to classify and should be aged AHY.**

AHY/ASY (Def. cycle, DB-DA; Oct-Sep): Upperpart feathers and s covs uniformly basic (Fig. 375**E**) and blackish, the outer gr covs with wider and more distinct marks to outer webs (*cf.* Fig. 432**C**); pp, p covs, ss, and terts uniformly basic (Fig. 375**E**), the outer pp and p covs broad and truncate (Figs. 377**C-D** & 378**C-D**); rects basic, broad, and relatively fresh (Fig. 379**E**); legs dark brownish or tinged reddish. **Note: See Juv-HY/SY.**

Sex—Bilateral BPs (Fig. 20**B**, p. 31) developed by both sexes but distended cloaca (Fig. 21, p. 32) indicates ♀ in May-Jul. Measurements largely unhelpful for sexing (Table 52). In Apr-Aug ♂♂ may average blacker alternate feathering and more white spotting to head and breast than ♀♀ by age, but overlap apparently precludes reliable sexing. Otherwise, no criteria known.

Black Turnstone
Jan Feb Mar Apr May Jun Jul Aug Sep Oct Nov Dec
Juv-HY
SY
AHY
ASY
(♀) ♀ (♀)
> 95% 25-95% 5-25% < 5%
See Fig. 24 (pp. 44-45)

Hybrids reported—None.

References—Bent (1929), Handel & Gill (2001). Palmer (1967b), Prater et al. (1977), Ridgway (1919).

TABLE 52. Measurements (mm) of North American turnstones, surfbirds, and knots for identification and sexing. See pp. 4-11 for methods of measurement. Species summaries are in **bold**. Values were derived from 95% confidence intervals as based approximately on the indicated sample sizes (see pp. 4-5). Thus, midpoints of ranges approximate means, and S.D. is approximated by 25% of the range.

Taxon/Sex	*n*	wing chord	tail length	exposed culmen	tarsus
Ruddy Turnstone[1]		**138-158**	**53-67**	**20.7-26.7**	**23-29**
♀	100	140-158	54-67	21.7-26.7	24-29
♂	100	138-156	53-65	20.7-24.5	23-28
Black Turnstone		**139-159**	**57-66**	**21.4-27.1**	**25-29**
♀	100	141-159	58-66	22.5-27.1	26-29
♂	100	139-154	57-64	21.4-25.8	25-28
Surfbird		**162-183**	**62-70**	**22.2-27.8**	**29-33**
♀	20	162-178	63-70	22.2-26.5	29-32
♂	20	167-183	62-69	23.4-27.8	30-33
Red Knot[1]		**148-175**	**60-70**	**29.4-40.4**	**28-36**
♀	100	152-175	61-70	31.5-40.4	29-36
♂	100	148-170	59-68	29.4-38.3	28-35

[1] Measures from N.Am populations only; see **Geographic variation**.

Calidridine Sandpipers *Scolopacidae, Scolopacinae, Calidridini*

Eighteen species. Tribal characters generally include medium-small to small bodies with proportionally long wings, short legs with hind toe present (Fig. 373**B**-**C**, p. 500) in all but one species (Sanderling), and fore toes with variable amounts of webbing (Fig. 374**A**-**E**, p. 501). Calidridine sandpipers have 10 functional primaries (p10 longest by 1-7 mm, when fully grown), 14-15 secondaries (including 4-5 tertials, and one absent between the 4th and 5th; *cf.* Fig. 12**B**, p. 19), and 12 rectrices. Ageing can be accomplished through the first cycle (to SY and ASY) and sometimes into the second cycle (to TY and ATY) by plumage aspect and molt patterns. A few species can be sexed by alternate (or supplemental) plumage aspect and/or size (♂♂ > ♀♀ in some, bill lengths of ♀♀ > ♂♂ in others); bilateral brood patches (Fig. 20**B**, p. 31) can be used to sex females of some species, in which lekking behavior is exhibited by males. In molting, most calidridine sandpipers exhibit the Complex Alternate Strategy (CAS; Fig. 10**F**, pp. 13-16); Buff-breasted Sandpiper (p. 608) may exhibit the Complex Basic Strategy (CBS; Fig. 10**B**) and, among species, both n.Hemisphere and/or s.Hemisphere strategies are employed (Table 45, pp. 501-505). Age of first breeding is 1-2 years, with variable proportions of SYs breeding at one year of age. See pp. 500-507 for further information on molt and ageing in shorebirds.

SURFBIRD SURF
Aphriza virgata Species # 2820
Band size: 2

Species—From other N.Am shorebirds and plovers by medium size with proportionally short bill and legs (Table 52); bill stout, with prominent rounded nail, and dusky with a yellow-orange base to lower mandible; upperparts and breast primarily gray fringed white, with variable amounts of rufous to scapulars in Apr-Aug; uppertail covs white; tips to gr covs and bases to ss (outer webs) and inner pp white, forming distinct wing stripe; rects with distinct white bases (Fig. 433, p. 580); abdomen and underwing covs white, with distinct dark spots on flanks; legs and feet yellow, with hind toe fairly well developed (Fig. 373**B**-**C**, p. 500) and fore toes without webbing (Fig. 374**A**, p. 501) but margined with well-developed fleshy padding.

Geographic variation—Monotypic.

Molt—CAS. PF partial (Sep-Nov/Mar in HY/SYs), PA1 absent-limited (Apr-May in non-breeding SYs), DPB complete (Jul-Nov in AHY/ASYs), DPA limited-partial (Feb-May in non-breeding AHYs). Most to all molting occurs on non-breeding grounds. Molt appears to follow a n.Hemisphere strategy, although look for some individuals to employ a s.Hemisphere strategy. The PF includes most to all body feathers, often 1-3 terts, and some proximal s covs but no rects; most molting occurs in Sep-Nov, although replacement of terts can occur as late as Mar. The DPA includes a few to most body feathers, sometimes 1-3 terts, and a few proximal s covs but no rects; it may average slightly more extensive in ♂♂ than ♀♀ by age. Some SYs over-summer on non-breeding grounds (primarily in the s.Hemisphere) and exhibit less-complete (or no) PA1s and more-advanced PB2s (see p. 18). See pp. 500-507 for more information on molt in shorebirds.

Age—Juv (B1; Jul-Oct) has uniformly fresh plumage aspect, the back feathers and wing covs with wide whitish fringing (*cf.* Fig. 436**A**, p. 587), the pp and ss uniformly juv and fresh (Fig. 375**A**, p. 503), and the legs grayish. Juv ♀ = ♂.

Juv-HY/SY (1st cycle, Juv/B1-F1-A1; Oct-Sep): Rects narrow and relatively worn (Fig. 379**A**, p. 507), with less-distinct subterminal marks and pale fringing when fresh (Fig. 433**A**, p. 580);

some to most upperpart feathers, terts, and/or distal s covs uniformly juv and fresh in Oct-Nov (Fig. 375**A**), with pale fringing (*cf.* Fig. 436**A**), contrasting with fresher formative scapulars, terts, and (sometimes) proximal s covs in Nov-Sep (Fig. 375**B**-**C**); pp, p covs, and ss juv (Fig. 375**A**), the outer pp and p covs tapered (Figs. 377**A**-**B** & 378**A**-**B**, p. 506); scapulars with no to some dull rufous fringing (by sex) in Apr-Sep. **Note: Some SYs over-summering in S.Am may exhibit evidence of molting or replaced pp in Jan-Sep; see Molt.**

AHY/ASY (Def. cycle, DB-DA; Oct-Sep): Rects basic, broad, and relatively fresh (Fig. 379**E**), usually with more-distinct subterminal band but little or no pale fringing (Fig. 433**B**-**C**); upperpart feathers, terts, and s covs uniformly basic or mixed basic and alternate (Fig. 375**E**-**F**), the basic feathers with thin or indistinct whitish fringes (*cf.* Fig. 436**B**); pp, p covs, and ss basic (Fig. 375**E**), the outer pp and p covs broad and truncate (Figs. 377**C**-**D** & 378**C**-**D**); scapulars with extensive bright rufous fringing (by sex) in Mar-Sep. **Note: See Juv-HY/SY**.

A B C

HY/SY AHY/ASY

FIGURE 433. Shape and pattern to the outer rectrices by age in Surfbird. Juv rects (**A**) are retained by HY/SYs until the PB2 in Jul-Nov and are easily distinguished from basic rects of AHY/ASY, which usually resemble **B** but can occasionally show variation toward **C**.

Sex—Bilateral(?) BPs (Fig. 20**B**, p. 31) presumably developed by both sexes but distended cloaca (Fig. 21, p. 32) indicates ♀ in May-Jul. Measurements largely unhelpful for sexing (Table 52, p. 578). ASY ♂♂ may average brighter and more chestnut fringing to the upperparts than ASY ♀♀ in Apr-Aug, which might be helpful in sexing some mated pairs. Otherwise, no criteria known.

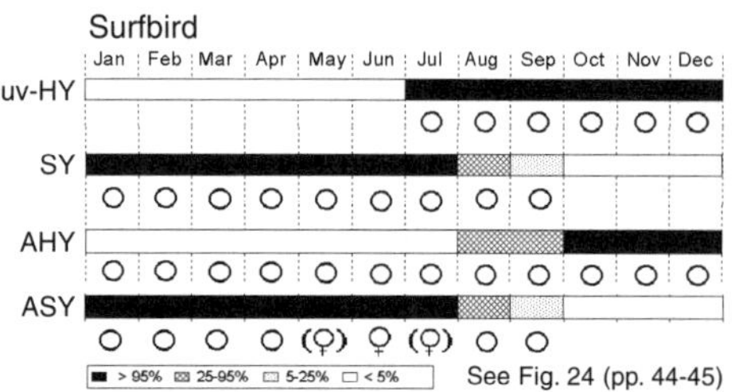

Hybrids reported—None.

References—Bent (1929), Chandler & Marchant (2001), Dixon (1927), Jehl (1968b), Palmer (1967b), Prater et al. (1977), Ridgway (1919), Senner & McCaffery (1997).

RED KNOT

Calidris canutus

REKN
Species # 2340
Band size: 2-3

Species—From other N.Am shorebirds and plovers by medium size with proportionally long wings and short tail (Table 52, p. 578); bill black, straight, and tapered at tip; upperparts gray (or blackish fringed white and salmon in ASYs in Apr-Aug) contrasting with whitish and gray rump and darker tail; gr covs broadly tipped white; underparts dusky (breast) and white (Sep-Mar), to salmon or rufous in Apr-Aug ASYs; central rects even in length with other rects (*vs* longer in other calidridine sandpipers); legs and feet dull olive, with hind toe moderately small but well developed (Fig. 373**B**-**C**, p. 500) and little to no webs between outer fore toes (Fig. 374**A**-**B**, p. 501). Great Knot (*C. tenuirostris*), a vagrant to W.N.Am, is larger (wg 166-182, tl 56-72, exp culmen 39-46, tarsus 33-38); bill slightly decurved; breast with distinct blackish spotting or mottling in all plumage aspects; uppertail covs white with dusky centers; underparts without reddish.

Geographic variation—Considered monotypic here. Populations breeding in AK ("*C.c. roselaari*") average longer wings, darker upperparts, and whiter vent in Apr-Aug ASYs; those breeding in NWT-w.Nunavut ("*rufa*") may average proportionally longer legs and bill, paler upperparts, and whiter vent in Apr-Aug ASYs; and those breeding in n.Nunavut and with non-breeding grounds in Europe ("*islandica*") may average paler upperparts and less white to the vent in Apr-Aug ASYs but measurement differences are slight and plumage-aspect differences are confounded by substantial individual, age-specific, and sex-specific variation, and may be based on variation in molting patterns rather than genetic differences (see p. 29), which are reported to be slight (Buehler et al. 2006). See also Barter et al. (1988a), Buehler & Baker (2005), Conover (1943), Cramp & Simmons (1983), Dick et al. (1976), Engelmoer & Roselaar (1998), Godfrey (1953, 1992), Harrington (2001), Hellmayr & Conover (1948b), Higgins & Davies (1996), Patten et al. (2003), Piersma (1994), Piersma & Davidson (1992), Portenko (1972), Prater et al. (1977), Roselaar (1983), Todd (1963), Tomkovich (1992, 2004), and Tomkovich & Serra (1999) for more information.

Molt—CAS. PF partial-incomplete (Oct-Dec/May in HY/SYs), PA1 absent-partial (Mar-May in non-breeding SYs), PB2 complete (May-Sep in non-breeding SYs), DPA partial-incomplete (Feb-May in breeding AHYs), DPB complete (Aug-Oct/Feb in breeding ASY/ATYs). Much molting occurs on non-breeding grounds, although the DPB can commence (body feathers only) and the DPA can complete on breeding grounds or at stopover sites. Molt exhibits either a n.Hemisphere or s.Hemisphere strategy (Table 45, pp. 501-505), depending on location of non-breeding grounds. The PF includes most to all body feathers, a few to some proximal s covs, usually 1-3 terts, and 2 to all 12 c.rects in Oct-Dec; in most SYs (among those with non-breeding grounds in the s.Hemisphere) the PF includes up to all rects, terts, and s covs (distal gr covs often retained), 1-7 medial or outer pp and p covs, and 1-4 medial ss (distal to the terts) in eccentric sequence (Fig. 376**A-B**; sometimes arrested) in Dec-May. In non-breeding SYs, commencement of the PB2 can overlap the end of the PF such that two waves of pp are molting simultaneously (Fig. 376**C**). The DPB completes by Nov among some AHYs (with non-breeding grounds in N.Am) but typically occurs in Oct-Feb among AHY/ASYs with non-breeding grounds in the s.Hemisphere. More study is needed on ASYs reportedly molting pp in Apr-Jul on non-breeding grounds (Higgins & Davies 1996); these may include TYs (primarily) or ATYs that had over-summered (see pp. 504-505). The DPA includes some to most body feathers, a few to some (up to 50%) of the proximal s covs, 1-4 terts, and sometimes 1-4 c.rects; ♂♂ average more feathers replaced than ♀♀ by age. Most to all SYs and some TYs over-summer on tropical and s.Hemisphere non-breeding grounds, and exhibit less-complete (or no) PA1-PA2s and advanced PB2-PB3s (see p. 18). See pp. 500-507 for more information on molt in shorebirds. A PS (see American Golden Plover, p. 512, and Bar-tailed Godwit, p. 569) might occur during Apr-Jun in ASYs of this species, as has been rported for Great Knot (Battley et al. 2005).

Age—Juv (B1; Jul-Oct) has uniformly fresh plumage aspect, the back feathers and wing covs with distinct dark and pale fringing (Fig. 436**A**, p. 587), the pp and ss uniformly juv and fresh (Fig. 375**A**, p. 503), and the legs dull yellowish; Juv ♀=♂.

Juv-HY/SY (1st cycle, Juv/B1-F1-A1; Oct-Sep): Some to most upperpart feathers, terts, and/or distal s covs juv and fresh in Oct-Dec (Fig. 375**A**), brownish with broad dark and pale fringing when fresh (Fig. 436**A**), contrasting with fresher and grayer formative scapulars, terts, and proximal s covs in Nov-Sep (Figs. 375**B-C** & 436**C**), the distal gr covs usually retained and becoming worn and frayed in Apr-Sep (Figs. 375**D** & 436**B**; see also Fig. 13**E**, p. 20); pp, p covs, and ss juv, fresh, and without s1-p1 contrast in Oct-Dec (Fig. 375**A**), often being incompletely replaced in Jan-May and exhibiting eccentric or arrested replacement patterns in May-Sep (Fig. 376**A-C**, p. 504), and being completely replaced in Jun-Oct, the juv outer pp and p covs (if present) tapered (Figs. 377**A-B** & 378**A-B**, p. 506); all to some juv rects retained through Jan-Mar (sometimes Apr-Sep), contrastingly narrow and worn (Fig. 379**A-D**, p. 507); breast with little to no pale rufous in Apr-Aug. **Note: Many SYs remain on non-breeding grounds during the first summer.**

AHY/ASY (Def. cycle, DB-DA; Oct-Sep): Upperpart feathers, terts, and s covs uniformly basic or mixed basic and alternate (Fig. 373**E-F**), the basic feathers gray, with thin or indistinct whitish fringes (Fig. 436**B**); pp, p covs, and ss worn and being completely replaced in Oct-Dec (n.Hemisphere) to Oct-Apr (s.Hemisphere), or basic, fresh, and with replacement clines and often s1-p1 contrast in Dec-Sep (Fig. 375**E**), the outer pp and p covs broad and truncate (Figs. 377**C-D** & 378**C-D**); rects basic and broad (Fig. 379**E**), sometimes mixed with 1-4 alternate c.rects in Apr-Oct (Fig. 379**F**); breast with substantial rufous feathering in Apr-Aug. **Note: See Juv-HY/SY**.

SY/TY (2nd cycle, B2; Oct-Feb): Like AHY/ASY with molt of pp occurring, but outer pp and p covs juv, pointed and very abraded (Fig. 376**E**). **Note: These usually occur in s.Hemisphere non-breeding areas only and may be uncommon (see pp. 506-507).**

Sex—Bilateral BPs (Fig. 20**B**, p. 31) developed by both sexes but distended cloaca (Fig. 21, p. 32) indicates ♀ in May-Jul. Measurements largely unhelpful for sexing (Table 52, p. 578). ASY ♂♂ average more-extensive and deeper rufous aspect to underparts and a blacker bill in Apr-Aug than ASY ♀♀, but these characters are unreliable for sexing most individuals due to substantial individual and age-related variation (Baker et al. 1999); however, some ♂♂ during migration (with extensive rufous to the upperparts and full rufous underparts) and most mated pairs on breeding grounds probably can be sexed by plumage aspect. See also Baker et al. (1999) for molecular sexing techniques.

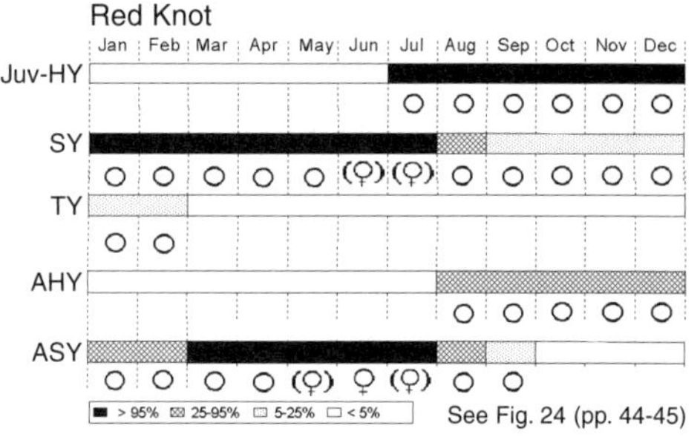

Hybrids reported—Doubtfully with Bar-tailed Godwit (p. 569).

References—Baker et al. (1996), Barter (1992), Barter et al. (1988b), Bent (1927), Chandler & Marchant (2001), Cramp & Simmons (1983), Dement'ev & Gladkov (1951c), Engelmoer & Roselaar (1998), Harrington et al. (2007). Higgins & Davies (1996), Morrison (1975), Morrison & Harrington (1992), Oberholser (1974), Prater et al. (1977), Palmer (1967b), Piersma & Davidson (1992), Ridgway (1919), Roberts (1955), Taylor (1981).

SANDERLING
Calidris alba

SAND
Species # 2480
Band size: 1A

Species—From other N.Am shorebirds by medium-small size (Table 53, p. 585); bill moderately short, somewhat tapered, and black; upperparts blackish (Juv-HY), pale gray (Oct-Mar), or mixed blackish, white, and rufous (Apr-Aug), the medial uppertail covs dark (Fig. 438**A**, p. 594); underparts white, the breast with little or no streaking and with buff cast in Juvs, and the throat and breast spotted dusky in Apr-Aug; legs and feet dull black, with hind toe absent (Fig. 374**A**, p. 501) and without webs between fore toes (Fig. 374**A**, p. 501). From smaller *Calidris* sandpipers by larger size (Table 53); tarsus without hind toe (Fig. 374**A**); marginal les covs marked dusky (*cf.* Fig. 434**A**), contrasting with paler med and gr covs (Fig. 434**B**) in Nov-Mar. Juvs and AHYs in alternate-plumage aspect from Red-necked Stint (p. 591) further by chin, throat, and breast with dusky spots. From Red Phalarope (p. 627) in Sep-Mar by shorter tail but longer bill and tarsus (Table 53); bill without yellowish at base; auriculars white with gray streaks; hind toe absent and fore toes without webs or lobes.

Geographic variation—Monotypic. Populations breeding in N.Am ("*C.a. rubidus*") average slightly larger than those of Eurasia (Engelmoer & Roselaar 1998, but see Tomkovich & Serra 1999, Patten et al. 2003); difference insufficient for subspecific recognition.

Molt—CAS. PF partial-complete (Sep-Dec/Apr in HY/SYs), PA1 limited-partial (Mar-May in non-breeding SYs), PB2 complete (Apr-Sep in non-breeding SYs), DPA partial (Feb-May in breeding AHYs), DPB complete (Aug-Oct/Feb in breeding AHY/ASYs). Most molting occurs on non-breeding grounds, although the PF and DPB can commence (body feathers only) and the DPA can complete on breeding grounds or at stopover sites. Molt exhibits either a n.Hemisphere or s.Hemisphere strategy (Table 45, pp. 501-505). The PF includes most to all body feathers, no to a few proximal s covs, 1-3 terts, and often 1-4 c.rects in Oct-Dec; in the tropics and s.Hemisphere it can also include most to all rects, terts, and s covs (the distal gr covs often retained), and often 2-10 outer pp and p covs and 1-10 medial ss (distal to the terts) in eccentric sequence (Fig. 376**A**, p. 504; occasionally arrested) in Dec-Apr. In non-breeding SYs, commencement of the PB2 can overlap the end of the PF such that two waves of pp are molting simultaneously (Fig. 376**C**). An unknown proportion of SYs following this strategy may have a complete PF (more study needed). The DPB completes by Nov among most AHYs (with non-breeding grounds in N.Am) but typically occurs in Oct-Feb among AHY/ASYs with non-breeding grounds in the tropics and s.Hemisphere. The DPA includes most body feathers, no to a few proximal s covs, usually 1-5 terts, and often 2-4 c.rects; ♂♂ average more feathers replaced than ♀♀ by age. Many SYs with non-breeding grounds in the s.Hemisphere and tropics (but few with non-breeding grounds in N.Am) over-summer on non-breeding grounds and exhibit less-complete (or no) PA1s and advanced PB2s (see p. 18). See pp. 500-507 for more information on molt in shorebirds.

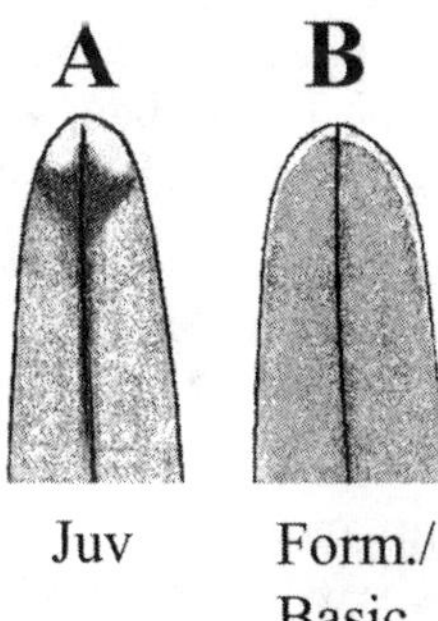

FIGURE 434. Shape and pattern to the back feathers and most secondary coverts by feather generation in Sanderling. The cumulative effect of the juv feathers is dark upperparts until back feathers are replaced by HYs during the PF in Sep-Nov/Dec; AHY/ASYs have worn paler backs mixed with basic and alternate feathers, molting to uniform gray appearance of basic feathers in Oct-Mar. The marginal les covs resemble **A** in both age groups year-round, unique to Sanderling among N.Am *Calidris* sandpipers. Most SYs (including all of those wintering in the n.Hemisphere) retain at least a few outer gr covs until the PB2 in Apr-Sep (*cf.* Fig. 375**D**, p. 503); some SYs wintering in the s.Hemisphere replace all s covs during a complete PF, after which they are indistinguishable from ASYs. See also Figure 436 (p. 587).

Age—Juv (B1; Jul-Oct) has uniformly fresh plumage aspect, the back feathers and wing covs with blackish patterning (Fig. 434**A**), and the pp and ss uniformly juv and fresh (Fig. 375**A**, p. 503); Juv ♀=♂. In addition to the following, SYs average less-extensive rufous to the head and underparts than ASYs by sex (see **Sex**) in Apr-Aug, but there is extensive overlap.

Juv-HY/SY (1st cycle, Juv/B1-F1-A1; Oct-Sep): Some to most upperpart feathers, terts, and s covs juv and fresh in Oct-Dec (Fig. 375**A**), with dusky patterning at tip when fresh (Fig. 434**A**), contrasting with fresher and grayer formative scapulars, terts, and s covs in Nov-Sep (Figs. 375**B-C** & 436**B**), the distal gr covs usually retained and becoming worn and frayed by Apr-Sep (Fig. 375**D**; see also Fig. 13**E**, p. 20); pp, p covs, and ss juv, fresh, and without s1-p1 contrast in Oct-Dec (Fig. 375**A**), sometimes being incompletely replaced in Jan-Apr and exhibiting eccentric or typical replacement patterns in May-Sep (Fig. 376**A-D**, p. 504), the juv outer pp and p covs (if present) tapered (Figs. 377**A-B** & 378**A-B**, p. 506); all to some juv rects often retained, contrastingly narrow and worn (Fig. 379**A-D**, p. 507; perhaps occasionally including an alternate r1 as well; Fig. 17**D**, p. 25). **Note: Some SYs remain on non-breeding grounds (usually S of N.Am) during the first summer, and average no or less rufous to the plumage aspect than ASYs in Apr-Aug (sex for sex). See also AHY/ASY.**

AHY/ASY (Def. cycle, DB-DA; Oct-Mar): Upperpart feathers, terts, and s covs uniformly basic or mixed basic and alternate (Fig. 375**E-F**), the basic feathers pale gray with narrow pale tipping (Fig. 434**B**); pp, p covs, and ss worn, being completely replaced in Aug-Oct (N.Am) to Oct-Feb (tropics and s.Hemisphere), or basic, fresh, and with replacement clines and sometimes s1-p1 contrast in Nov-Mar (Fig. 376**E**), the outer pp and p covs broad and truncate (Figs. 377**C-D** & 378**C-D**); rects uniformly basic and broad (Fig. 379**E**), often with 1-4 alternate c.rects in Apr-Aug (Fig. 379**F**). **Note: See Juv-HY/SY. Some AHY/ASYs in the n.Hemisphere probably can be aged by molt timing or extent of alternate feathering through Sep; however, an unknown proportion of HY/SYs with non-breeding grounds in the s.Hemisphere can have a complete PF and may become indistinguishable from AHY/ASYs in Apr-Sep. More study is needed.**

SY/TY (2nd cycle, B2; Oct-Jan): Like AHY/ASY with molt of pp occurring, but outer pp and p covs juv, pointed and very abraded (Fig. 376**E**). **Note: SY/TYs exhibiting this strategy usually occur in s.Hemisphere non-breeding areas only, and may be uncommon (see pp. 506-507).**

Sex—Bilateral BPs (Fig. 20**B**, p. 31) developed by both sexes but distended cloaca (Fig. 21, p. 32) indicates ♀ in May-Jul. Measurements largely unhelpful for sexing (Table 53). ASY ♂♂ average more-extensive and deeper rufous aspect to head and underparts than ASY ♀♀ but these characters are unreliable for sexing most individuals due to substantial age-related and individual variation; some ♂♂ during migration (with extensive rufous, extending to medial breast) and some mated pairs on breeding grounds possibly can be sexed by plumage aspect. See Maron & Myers (1984) for a DFA (p. 5) using maximum flattened wing length (*cf.* Fig. 3, p. 6) and bill from proximal end of nares, that reliably sexed 92% of individuals among a California non-breeding population, and Wood (1987) for an analysis using maximum flattened wing length and exposed culmen or bill, that reliably sexed 86% of individuals among a British non-breeding population.

Hybrids reported—With Dunlin (Clark 1987a).

References—Bent (1927), Chapman (1896b), Cramp & Simmons (1983), Dement'ev & Gladkov (1951c), Dwight (1900b), Gosbell & Minton (2001), Higgins & Davies (1996), MacWhirter et al. (2002). Manning et al. (1956), Myers et al. (1985), Oberholser (1974), Palmer (1967b), Prater et al. (1977), Ridgway (1919), Spaans (1980), Stone (1897), Underhill (1989).

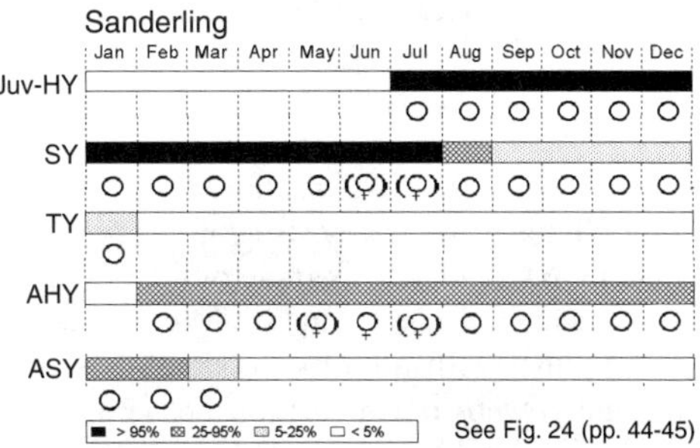

TABLE 53. Measurements (mm) of North American small Calidris sandpipers for identification and sexing. See pp. 4-11 for methods of measurement. Species summaries are in **bold**. Values were derived from 95% confidence intervals as based approximately on the indicated sample sizes (see pp. 4-5). Thus, midpoints of ranges approximate means, and S.D. is approximated by 25% of the range.

Taxon/Sex	*n*	wing chord	tail length	exposed culmen	tarsus
Sanderling[1]		**113-129**	**44-57**	**23.1-28.5**	**23-28**
♀	100	117-129	46-57	24.4-28.5	24-28
♂	100	113-125	44-54	23.1-27.1	23-27
Semipalmated Sandpiper		**89-102**	**35-45**	**15.4-23.1**	**19-23**
♀	100	92-102	36-45	17.5-23.1	20-23
♂	100	89-99	35-44	15.4-20.7	19-22
Western Sandpiper		**90-102**	**37-46**	**20.7-29.2**	**20-24**
♀	100	93-102	38-46	24.2-29.2	21-24
♂	100	90-99	37-45	20.7-24.4	20-23
Red-necked Stint		**93-105**	**38-49**	**15.7-21.2**	**18-21**
♀	100	97-105	39-49	16.8-21.2	19-21
♂	100	93-102	38-48	15.7-20.1	18-20
Least Sandpiper		**81-94**	**33-42**	**16.2-21.0**	**17-21**
♀	100	84-94	34-42	17.5-21.0	18-21
♂	100	81-90	33-41	16.2-19.0	17-20
White-rumped Sandpiper		**115-126**	**46-55**	**20.8-26.6**	**22-26**
♀	60	117-126	47-55	21.9-26.6	22-26
♂	80	115-124	46-54	20.8-24.5	22-26
Baird's Sandpiper		**114-127**	**45-54**	**20.5-25.2**	**21-25**
♀	30	117-127	47-54	21.8-25.2	21-25
♂	30	114-124	45-52	20.5-23.9	20-24

[1] Measures from N.Am populations only; see **Geographic variation**.

SEMIPALMATED SANDPIPER SESA
Calidris pusilla Species # 2460
Band size: 1B

Species—From other N.Am shorebirds by small size with proportionally short bill (Table 53, p. 585); bill black, relatively straight, proportionally deep at base, and rounded or bulbous at tip (Fig. 435**A**); medial uppertail covs dark (Fig. 438**A**, p. 594); throat white; breast with little or no streaking in Juvs and in Oct-Mar, streaked blackish in Apr-Aug; legs and feet black to dark grayish olive, with hind toe moderately small but well developed (Fig. 373**B**-**C**, p. 500) and substantial webs between fore toes (Fig. 374**D**-**E**, p. 501). From Sanderling by smaller size (Table 53), hind toe present (Fig. 373**B**-**C**), and webbing between fore toes extensive (Fig. 374**D**-**E**).

From other small *Calidris* sandpipers with caution, especially in Oct-Mar. From Western Sandpiper (p. 589; see also Cartar 1984, Kaufman 1990a, Ouellet et al. 1973, Phillips 1975, Portenko 1972, Stevenson 1975) by bill shorter by sex (Table 53), straighter, deeper at base, and more rounded at tip (Fig. 435**A**); exp culmen/wing usually < 0.19; exposed culmen usually < middle toe with claw; Juv (Aug-Oct) and AHYs (Apr-Aug) with scapulars and lateral back feathers usually fringed buff to pale rufous, not contrasting distinctly with wing covs, and flanks with less-distinct streaking; head and breast washed grayish in Oct-Mar; legs sometimes dark grayish olive in Oct-Mar (*vs* blacker in Western Sandpiper). A small proportion of ♀♀ Semipalmated Sandpipers (with bill depth 4.5-5.1 and exposed culmen 20.7-23.1) may not be reliably separated from ♂♂ Western Sandpipers in Oct-Mar. From Red-necked and Little (*C. minuta*) stints (p. 591) by fore toes with substantial webbing (Fig. 374**D**-**E**); tarsus averages longer (Table 53); bill deeper at base and more rounded at tip (Fig. 435**A**); Juv with supercilium usually narrow (unsplit) and distinct; Juv (Aug-Oct) and AHYs (Apr-Aug) usually with indistinct or no pale fringes to inner scapulars. See Red-necked Stint for more details on separation from Little Stint. From Least Sandpiper (p. 592) by longer wing and tarsus (Table 53); bill more rounded at tip (Fig. 435**A**); throat and breast primarily whitish in all plumage aspects; legs and feet black to grayish, with substantial webbing between fore toes (Fig. 374**D**-**E**). See Alström & Olsson (1989), Cramp & Simmons (1983), Garner (2005), Hayman et al. (1986), Jonsson & Grant (1984), O'Brien et al. (2006), Paulson (1993, 2005), Prater et al.

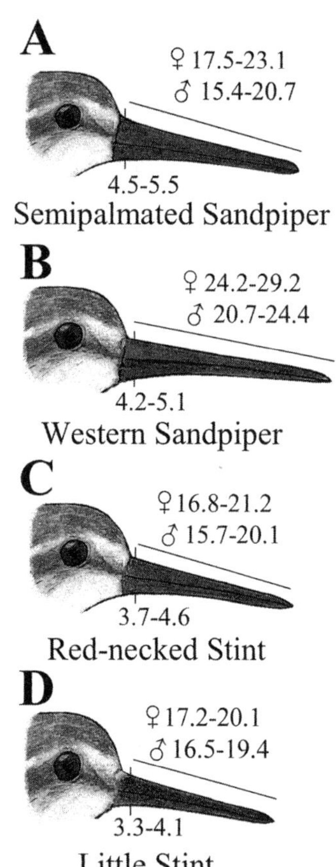

FIGURE 435. Bill size and shape in small, black-legged *Calidris* sandpipers for identification. Basic plumage is shown. Measures pertain to exposed culmen (Fig. 7**A**, p. 9) and bill depth at distal end of forehead feathers (Fig. 8**A**, p. 10). See text for identification details. Note that large ♀ Semipalmated Sandpipers can overlap small ♂ Western Sandpipers in bill dimensions and may not be separable in formative or basic plumage aspect (Oct-Mar/Apr). The bill size and shape of Least Sandpiper is closest to that of Little Stint (**D**).

(1977), Prowse (2006), Veit & Jonsson (1984), and Wallace (1974, 1979, 1986) for detailed accounts on the separation of small *Calidris* sandpipers.

Geographic variation—Monotypic. Populations breeding in AK average smaller (especially in exposed culmen length) than those breeding in e.Canada (Harrington & Morrison 1979, Manning et al. 1956, Palmer 1967b) but variation slight and apparently clinal.

Molt—CAS. PF partial-complete (Sep-Dec/Apr in HY/SYs), PA1 limited-partial (Mar-May in non-breeding SYs), PB2 complete (May-Nov in non-breeding SYs), DPA partial (Feb-Apr in breeding AHYs), DPB complete (Aug-Nov/Jan in breeding AHY/ASYs). Most molting occurs on non-breeding grounds, although the PF and DPB can commence (body feathers only) and the DPA can complete on breeding grounds or at stopover sites. Molt follows a s.Hemisphere strategy (Table 15, pp. 501-505). The PF includes most to all body feathers, rects, terts, and proximal s covs (the distal gr covs usually retained), often (~55% of HY/SYs) followed by 1-10 outer pp and p covs and 1-8 medial ss (distal to the terts) in eccentric sequence (Fig. 376**A**, p. 504; occasionally arrested); body feathers, terts, and c.rects are replaced primarily in Sep-Dec whereas pp, ss, and outer rects are replaced primarily in Jan-Apr. The PF may be complete in a small proportion of SYs. An extra molt of outer pp may occur in some TYs (as part of the PA2?); more study is needed (see pp. 504-505). The PA1 and DPA include some to most body feathers, a few to some (up to 15%) proximal s covs, and sometimes 1-3 terts and 1-4 c.rects; it averages slightly more extensive in ♂♂ than ♀♀ by age. Occasional SYs over-summer on non-breeding grounds and exhibit less-complete or no PA1s and advanced PB2s (see p. 18). See pp. 500-507 for more information on molt in shorebirds.

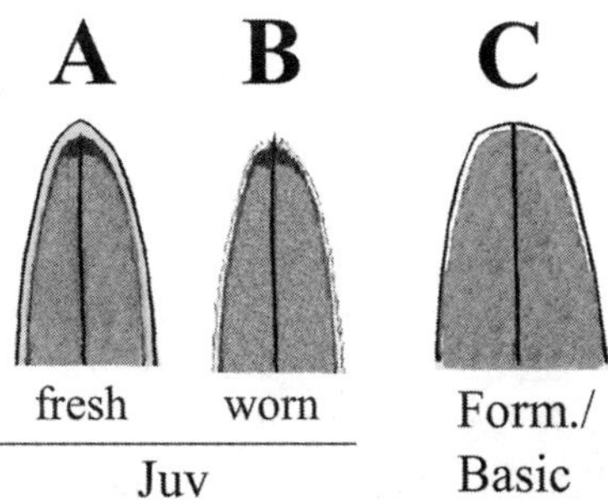

FIGURE 436. Shape and pattern to the back feathers and secondary coverts by feather generation in N.Am Calidridine sandpipers (all except Sanderling; Fig. 434, p. 583) and dowitchers. The cumulative effect of the pale (usually buff to rufous) fringing to the juv feathers is often a scaled appearance to the upperparts until back feathers are replaced by HYs during the PF in Sep-Nov/Dec; AHY/ASYs have mixed worn basic and alternate feathers at this time, molting to a uniform appearance of basic feathers in Oct-Mar. Most SYs retain at least a few outer gr covs until the PB2 in Apr-Sep (*cf.* Fig. 375**D**, p. 503); a small proportion of SY Semipalmated, Least, Curlew, and Stilt sandpipers wintering in the s.Hemisphere, along with White-rumped, Baird's, Pectoral, and Buff-breasted sandpipers, can replace all gr covs and wing feathers by Mar, during complete PFs, and cannot be distinguished from ASYs after molt has completed, except perhaps by fringe color to the proximal s covs (see Fig. 437, p. 588).

Age—Juv (B1; Jul-Oct) has uniformly fresh plumage aspect, the back feathers and wing covs fringed pale buff to cinnamon (Fig. 436**A**, p. 587), and the pp and ss uniformly juv and fresh (Fig. 375**A**); Juv ♀=♂. In addition to the following, SYs average less-extensive rufous to the upperparts than ASYs by sex (see **Sex**) in Apr-Aug, but there is extensive overlap.

Juv-HY/SY (1st cycle, Juv/B1-F1-A1; Oct-Sep): Some to most upperpart feathers and s covs uniformly juv and fresh in Oct-Nov (Fig. 375**A**), fringed buff (Fig. 436**A**), contrasting with fresher and grayer formative humerals, scapulars, proximal s covs, and terts in Nov-Sep (Figs. 375**B-C** & 436**C**), the distal gr covs usually retained and becoming worn and frayed by Apr-Sep (Figs. 375**D** & 436**B**; see also Fig. 13**E**, p. 20); some formative proximal s covs with thin rufous fringes (Fig. 437**A**, p. 588); pp, p covs, and ss juv, fresh, and without s1-p1 contrast in Oct-Jan (Fig. 375**A**), often being incompletely replaced in Jan-Apr and exhibiting eccentric replacement patterns in May-Sep (Fig. 376**A-C**, p. 504; occasionally arrested), the juv outer pp and p covs (if present) narrow and relatively abraded (Figs. 377**A-B** & 378**A-B**, p. 506);

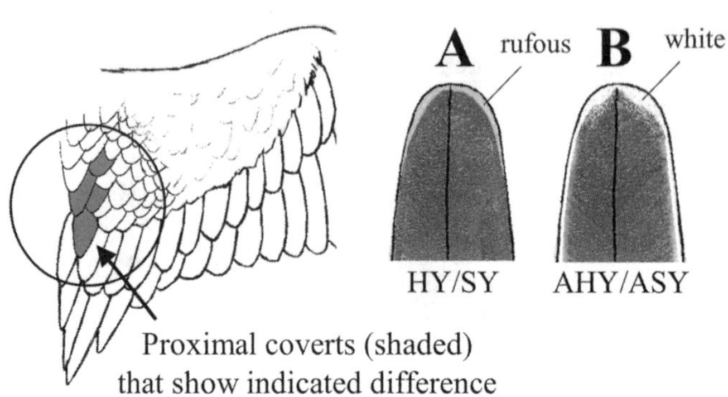

FIGURE 437. Many Calidridine sandpipers as well as dowitchers can show rufous or cinnamon fringing to proximal secondary coverts (including tertial coverts) in HY/SYs (**A**), whereas these feathers are usually fringed indistinctly with whitish in basic feathers of AHY/ASYs (**B**; alternate feathers can be fringed bright rufous). Note that in HY/SYs these appear to be formative rather than juv feathers, perhaps replaced early enough during the PF to retain juv-like pigmentation to the fringes. Some HYs may undergo a later PF and can show paler (buff) fringes, and some AHYs (typically SYs?) can undergo an earlier DPB (PB2?) and show buff-tinged fringes, so combine this criterion with others for effective age determinations. It is possible that this criterion may be the only method to reliably age species with complete PFs (e.g., White-rumped, Baird's, and Pectoral sandpipers) but study is needed to confirm this.

all to some juv rects retained through Jan-Mar (sometimes Apr-Sep), contrastingly narrow and worn (Fig. 379**A-D**, p. 507; perhaps occasionally including an alternate r1 as well; Fig. 17**D**, p. 25). **Note: In addition, some SYs in Apr-Aug average less rufous to the upperparts (sometimes none) than ASYs, sex for sex.**

AHY/ASY (Def. cycle, DB-DA; Oct-Sep): Upperpart feathers, terts, and s covs uniformly basic or mixed basic and alternate (Fig. 375**E-F**), the basic feathers with thin or indistinct whitish fringing (Figs. 436**C** & 437**B**); pp, p covs, and ss worn and being completely replaced in Oct-Jan or basic, fresh, and with replacement clines and often s1-p1 contrast in Dec-Sep (Fig. 375**E**), the outer pp and p covs broad and truncate (Figs. 377**C-D** & 378**C-D**); rects uniformly basic and broad (Fig. 379**E**), sometimes with 1-4 alternate c.rects in Apr-Aug (Fig. 379**F**). **Note: See Juv-HY/SY. A small proportion of HY/SYs may have a complete PF and become indistinguishable from AHY/ASYs in Apr-Sep except, perhaps, for the proximal s covs (Fig. 437), but the proportion appears to be sufficiently small (< 5%) to enable reliable ageing of ASYs through Sep.**

SY/TY (2nd cycle, B2; Oct-Jan): Like AHY/ASY with molt of pp occurring, but outer pp and p covs juv, pointed and very abraded (Fig. 376**E**). **Note: These usually occur in s.Hemisphere non-breeding areas only (see pp. 506-507).**

Sex— ♀ = ♂ by plumage aspect. Bilateral BPs (Fig. 20**B**, p. 31) developed by both sexes but distended cloaca (Fig. 21, p. 32) indicates ♀ in May-Jul. Measurements largely unhelpful for sexing (Table 53, p. 585). See Harrington & Taylor (1992) for analyses using wing chord and exposed culmen that reliably sexed 40% of individuals from a migratory population in MA, and Cartar (1984) for a DFA (p. 5) using wing and bill lengths as well as various skeletal measures, that reliably sexed 85% of individuals collected throughout range. ASY ♂♂ may average more and brighter rufous fringing to upperparts than ASY ♀♀ in Apr-Aug, which might be helpful in sexing some mated pairs. Otherwise, no criteria known.

Hybrids reported—None.

References—Bent (1927), Burton & McNeil (1976), Cramp & Simmons (1983), Gratto & Morrison (1981), Gratto-Trevor (1992), Jackson (1919), McNeil (1970), Oberholser (1974), Page & Bradstreet (1968), Palmer (1967b), Prater et al. (1977), Prowse (2006), Resende et al. (1989), Ridgway (1919), Roberts (1955), Sandercock (1998), Spaans (1979), Stone (1900).

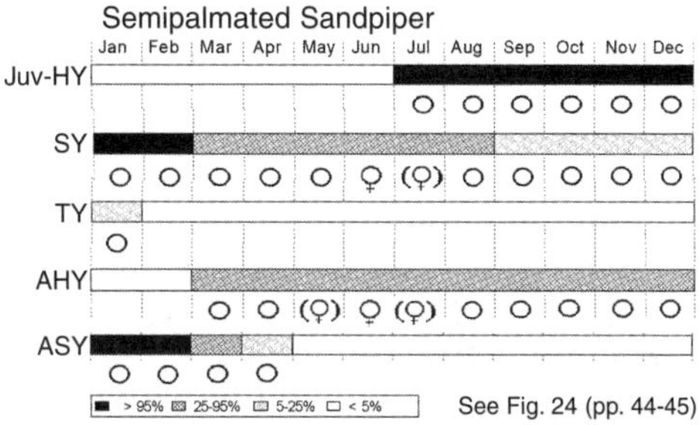

Semipalmated Sandpiper

	Jan	Feb	Mar	Apr	May	Jun	Jul	Aug	Sep	Oct	Nov	Dec
Juv-HY							○	○	○	○	○	○
SY	○	○	○	○	○	♀	(♀)	○	○	○	○	○
TY	○											
AHY			○	○	(♀)	♀	(♀)	○	○	○	○	○
ASY	○	○	○	○								

■ > 95% ▩ 25-95% ▤ 5-25% □ < 5%

See Fig. 24 (pp. 44-45)

WESTERN SANDPIPER

Calidris mauri

WESA
Species # 2470
Band size: 1B

Species—From other N.Am shorebirds by small size with proportionally long bill (Table 53, p. 585); bill black, slightly decurved, and proportionally narrow at base (Fig. 435**B**, p. 586); medial uppertail covs dark (Fig. 438**A**, p. 594); throat white; breast with little or no streaking in Juvs and in Oct-Mar, and streaked blackish in Apr-Aug; legs and feet black, with hind toe moderately well developed (Fig. 373**B**-**C**, p. 500) and with substantial webs between fore toes (Fig. 374**D**-**E**, p. 501). From Dunlin by shorter wing and shorter average bill and tarsus (Table 53); outer rects grayish; underwing covs primarily white; breast unstreaked in Sep-Mar; abdomen without dusky spots (Juv) or black patch (AHYs in Apr-Sep); fore toes with substantial webbing (Fig. 374**D**-**E**).

See Semipalmated Sandpiper (p. 586) for separation from other small *Calidris* sandpipers and for additional references. From Semipalmated Sandpiper by bill longer by sex (Table 53), decurved, narrower at base, and tapered at tip (Fig. 435**B**); exp culmen/wing usually > 0.19; exposed culmen > middle toe with claw; Juv (Aug-Oct) and AHYs (Apr-Aug) with scapulars and lateral back feathers fringed bright rufous, contrasting distinctly with grayer wing covs, and flanks with more-distinct blackish streaking; head and breast whiter in Oct-Mar. A small proportion of ♂♂ Western Sandpipers may be impossible to separate from ♀♀ Semipalmated Sandpipers in Oct-Mar.

Geographic variation—Monotypic. See Senner et al. (1981).

Molt—CAS. PF partial-incomplete (Aug-Dec/Feb in HY/SYs), PA1 limited-partial (Mar-May in non-breeding SYs), PB2 complete (May-Oct in non-breeding SYs), DPA partial (Feb-Apr in breeding AHYs), DPB complete (Jul-Nov in breeding AHYs). Molting occurs primarily on non-breeding grounds and exhibits a n.Hemisphere strategy (Table 45, pp. 501-505). The PF includes most to all body feathers, no to some proximal s covs, often 1-3 terts, and 2 to (occasionally) all 12 c.rects. The DPA includes some to most body feathers, up to 20% of the medial s covs, and sometimes 1-3 terts and 1-4 c.rects; it averages slightly more extensive in ♂♂ than ♀♀ by age. Most SYs with non-breeding grounds in the s.Hemisphere or tropics (but few with non-breeding grounds in N.Am) over-summer on non-breeding grounds and exhibit less-complete (or no) PA1s and advanced PB2s (O'Hara et al. 2002; see p. 18). Look for occasional individuals with non-breeding grounds in S.Am to exhibit a s.Hemisphere molting strategy. See pp. 500-507 for more information on molt in shorebirds.

Age—Juv (B1; Jul-Oct) has uniformly fresh plumage aspect, the back feathers and wing covs fringed rufous and pale buff (Fig. 436**A**, p. 587), and the pp and ss uniformly juv and fresh (Fig.

375**A**, p. 503); Juv ♀ = ♂. In addition to the following, SYs average less-extensive rufous to the upperparts than ASYs by sex (see **Sex**) in Apr-Aug, but there is extensive overlap.

Juv-HY/SY (1st cycle, Juv/B1-F1-A1; Oct-Sep): Some to most upperpart feathers, terts, and/or distal s covs juv and fresh in Oct-Dec (Fig. 375**A**), fringed pale buff to rufous when fresh (Fig. 436**A**), contrasting with fresher and grayer formative scapulars, terts, and s covs in Nov-Sep (Figs. 375**B-C** & 436**C**), the retained distal juv s covs becoming worn and frayed by Apr-Sep (Figs. 375**D** & 436**B**; see also Fig. 13**E**, p. 20); some formative proximal s covs with thin rufous to buff fringes (Fig. 437**A**, p. 588); pp, p covs, and ss uniformly juv (Fig. 375**A**), the outer pp and p covs tapered, brownish, and relatively worn (Figs. 377**A-B** & 378**A-B**, p. 506); some to most juv rects usually retained, contrastingly narrow and worn (Fig. 379**A**, p. 507; perhaps occasionally including an alternate r1 as well; Fig. 17**D**, p. 25). **Note: Some SYs remain on non-breeding grounds (usually S of N.Am) during the first summer and average less rufous to the plumage aspect (sometimes none) by sex than ASYs in Apr-Aug.**

AHY/ASY (Def. cycle, DB-DA; Oct-Sep): Upperpart feathers, terts, and s covs uniformly basic or mixed basic and alternate (Fig. 375**E-F**), the basic feathers with thin or indistinct whitish fringing (Figs. 436**C** & 437**B**); pp, p covs, and ss uniformly basic (Fig. 375**E**), the outer pp and p covs broad, truncate, and relatively fresh (Figs. 377**C-D** & 378**C-D**); rects basic and broader (Fig. 379**E**), sometimes with 1-4 alternate c.rects in Apr-Aug (Fig. 379**F**). **Note: See Juv-HY/SY.**

Sex—♀ = ♂ by plumage aspect. Bilateral BPs (Fig. 20**B**, p. 31) developed by both sexes but distended cloaca (Fig. 21, p. 32) indicates ♀ in May-Jul. Measurements (except for bill length) largely unhelpful for sexing (Table 53, p. 585). See Cartar (1984) for a DFA (p. 5) using wing and bill lengths (as well as various skeletal measures) that reliably sexed 100% of individuals collected throughout range. See Fernández & Lank for sex-specific (and age-specific) differences in wing morphology. In addition to the following, ASY ♂♂ may average more and brighter rufous fringing to upperparts than ASY ♀♀ in Apr-Aug, which might be helpful in sexing some mated pairs (see **Age**). The following is reliable for sexing > 90% of individuals (Page & Fearis 1971):

AHY ♀: Exposed culmen > 24.4. (Table 53). **Note: AHYs with exposed culmen 24.2-24.4 may represent SY ♀♀ or ASY ♂♂, so combine with age for reliable sex determinations.**

AHY ♂: Exposed culmen < 24.2 (Table 53). **Note: See AHY ♀.**

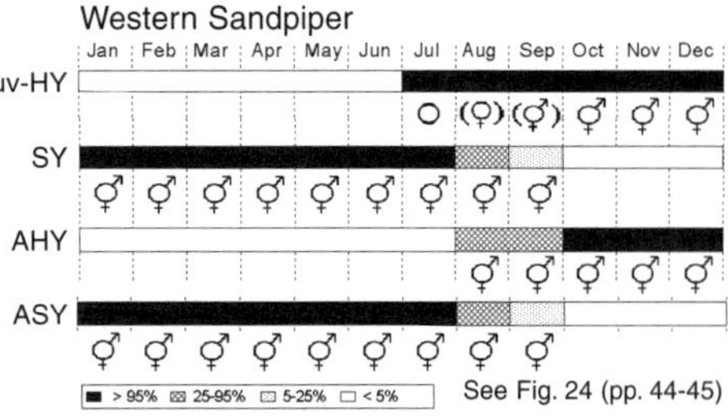

Hybrids reported—None.

References—Bent (1927), Buchanan (2002), Butler et al. (1987), Cramp & Simmons (1983), Fernández & Lank (2006, 2007), Fernández et al. (2004), Higgins & Davies (1996), Loftin (1962), McNeil (1970), Naranjo et al. (1994), Oberholser (1974), O'Hara et al. (2002, 2006), Page (1974a), Page & Fearis (1971), Page et al. (1972), Palmer (1967b), Prater et al. (1977), Prowse (2006), Ridgway (1919), Roberts (1955), Sandercock (1998), Spaans (1979), Wilson (1994).

RED-NECKED STINT RNST
Calidris ruficollis Species # 2422
Band size: 1B-1

Species—See Semipalmated Sandpiper (p. 586) for separation from other small *Calidris* sandpipers and for additional references. From Sanderling (p. 582) by smaller size (Table 53, p. 585); les and med covs uniformly dark with pale fringes; hind toe present (Fig. 373**B-C**, p. 500); Juv and alternate aspect without dusky spots to chin, throat, and breast. From other small *Calidris* sandpipers with caution, especially in Oct-Mar. From Semipalmated and Western sandpipers by shorter average bill and tarsus (Table 53); fore toes without webbing (Fig. 374**A**, p. 501); bill shallower at base and moderately attenuated at tip (Fig. 435**C**, p. 586); Juv with supercilium wider (especially in loral region) and less distinct, and scapulars and proximal wing covs fringed reddish, contrasting with grayer-fringed distal s covs.

From Little Stint (a vagrant to N.Am) with extreme caution, by shorter average wing but longer average tarsus (wg chord 88-100, tl 36-44, exp culmen 16.5-20.1, tarsus 18-23); flat wing length (Fig. 3**B**, p. 6) divided by tarsus length usually > 5.0 mm (*vs* usually < 5.0 in Little Stint); bill averages deeper and less attenuated at tip (Fig. 435**C-D**); Juv with scapulars and proximal wing covs fringed reddish, contrasting with grayer- to buff-fringed distal s covs and rump feathers (*vs* upperparts unformly fringed rufous and with blacker centers, and scapulars edged white forming more distinct streaks or "braces" in Little Stint); basic aspect with upperparts and breast washed reddish and streaking to lower breast and sides primarily dusky and white (*vs* breast white medially and with sides streaked or spotted dusky and washed reddish in Little Stint); basic aspect with paler grayish (*vs* dusky or blackish) centers to terts and wing covs. Many individuals may not be reliably identified, even in hand. See references under Semipalmated Sandpiper, as well as Altsröm & Olsson (1989), Iliff et al. (2004), Lehman (1998, 2006), McCaskie (1975), Parkes (1986), Riddington (1994), Szantyr (1997), Veit (1988), and Wilson (2005) for more information.

Geographic variation—Monotypic.

Molt—CAS. PF partial-incomplete (Sep-Nov/Apr in HY/SYs), PA1 limited-partial (Mar-May in non-breeding SYs), PB2 complete (Jun-Nov in non-breeding SYs), DPA partial (Feb-Apr in breeding AHYs), DPB complete (Aug-Nov/Jan in breeding AHY/ASYs). Most molting occurs on non-breeding grounds, although the DPB can commence (body feathers only) and the DPA can complete on breeding grounds or at stopover sites. Molt follows a s.Hemisphere strategy (Table 45, pp. 501-505). The PF includes most to all body feathers, some to all rects, terts, and proximal s covs (the distal gr covs usually retained), and sometimes (in ~50% of individuals) 4-7 outer pp and p covs and 1-8 medial ss (distal to the terts) in eccentric sequence (Fig. 376**A-C**, p. 504; occasionally arrested); body feathers, terts, and c.rects are replaced primarily in Sep-Nov whereas pp, ss, and outer rects are replaced primarily in Jan-Apr. The DPA includes most body feathers, no to a few medial s covs, usually 1-4 terts, and often 1-6 c.rects, and averages slightly more extensive in ♂♂ than ♀♀ by age. Most SYs and probably some TYs over-summer on non-breeding grounds and exhibit less-complete (or no) PA1s and advanced PB2s (Paton & Wykes 1978; see p. 18). See pp. 500-507 for more information on molt in shorebirds.

Age—Juv (B1; Jul-Oct) has uniformly fresh plumage aspect, the back feathers and wing covs fringed rufous and pale buff (Fig. 436**A**, p. 587), and the pp and ss uniformly juv and fresh (Fig. 375**A**); Juv ♀ = ♂.

Juv-HY/SY (1st cycle, Juv/B1-F1-A1; Oct-Sep): Some to most upperpart feathers, terts, and/or distal s covs juv and fresh in Oct-Nov (Fig. 375**A**), fringed rufous to pale buff (Fig. 436**A**), contrasting with fresher and grayer formative scapulars, terts, and proximal s covs in Nov-Sep (Figs. 375**B-C** & 436**C**; see also Fig. 13**E**, p. 20), the distal gr covs usually retained and becoming worn and frayed by Apr-Sep (Figs. 375**D** & 436**B**); some formative proximal s covs with thin rufous to buff fringes (Fig. 437**A**, p. 588); pp, p covs, and ss juv, fresh, and without s1-p1 contrast in Oct-Jan (Fig. 375**A**), and sometimes being incompletely replaced in Jan-Apr and exhibiting eccentric replacement patterns in May-Sep (Fig. 376**A-C**, p. 504; occasionally arrested), the juv outer pp and p covs (if present) narrow and relatively abraded (Figs. 377**A-B** & 378**A-B**, p. 506); all to some juv rects retained through Jan-Mar (sometimes Apr-Sep), contrastingly narrow and worn (Fig. 379**A-D**, p. 507; perhaps occasionally including an alternate r1 as well; Fig. 17**D**, p. 25). **Note: Many SYs remain on non-breeding grounds during the first summer and average less rufous to the plumage aspect (sometimes none) than ASYs in Apr-Aug, sex for sex.**

AHY/ASY (Def. cycle, DB-DA; Oct-Sep): Upperpart feathers, terts, and s covs uniformly basic or mixed basic and alternate (Fig. 375**E-F**), the basic feathers with thin or indistinct whitish fringing (Figs. 436**C** & 437**B**); pp, p covs, and ss worn and being completely replaced in Oct-Jan, or basic, fresher, and with replacement clines and often s1-p1 contrast in Jan-Sep (Fig. 375**E**), the outer pp and p covs broad and truncate (Figs. 377**C-D** & 378**C-D**); rects basic and broader (Fig. 379**E**), often with 1-6 alternate c.rects in Apr-Aug (Fig. 379**F**). **Note: See Juv-HY/SY.**

SY/TY (2nd cycle, B2; Oct-Jan): Like AHY/ASY with molt of pp occurring, but outer pp and p covs juv, pointed and very abraded (Fig. 376**E**). **Note: These usually occur in s.Hemisphere non-breeding areas only (see pp. 505-506).**

Sex—♀ = ♂ by plumage aspect. Bilateral(?) BPs (Fig. 20**B**, p. 31) presumably developed by both sexes but distended cloaca (Fig. 21, p. 32) indicates ♀ in May-Jul. Measurements largely unhelpful for sexing (Table 53, p. 585). ASY ♂♂ average brighter and more rufous aspect to the upperparts, head, and throat than ASY ♀♀ in Apr-Aug, which might be helpful in sexing some mated pairs. Otherwise, no criteria known.

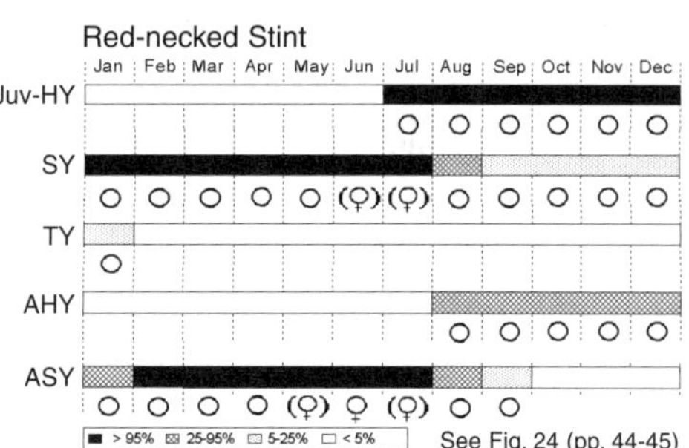

Hybrids reported—None.

References—Barter & Davidson (1990), Bent (1927), Cramp & Simmons (1983), Dement'ev & Gladkov (1951c), Forest (1982), Higgins & Davies (1996). Melville (1981), Palmer (1967b), Paton & Wykes (1978), Prater et al. (1977), Ridgway (1919).

LEAST SANDPIPER

Calidris minutilla

LESA
Species # 2420
Band size: 1-1B

Species—From other N.Am shorebirds by small size (Table 53, p. 585); bill dusky, relatively straight, and tapered at tip (*cf.* Fig. 435**D**, p. 586); upperpart feathers primarily brown to grayish brown (*vs* grayish or dusky in other N.Am small *Calidris*), the medial uppertail covs dark (Fig. 438**A**, p. 594); throat and breast with variable brown wash and dusky streaking; legs and feet greenish and yellowish, the hind toe present (Fig. 373**B-C**, p. 500) and fore toes without webs (Fig. 374**A**, p. 501). See Semipalmated Sandpiper (p. 586) for separation from other small *Calidris* sandpipers and for references.

Long-toed Stint (*C. subminuta*), a vagrant to w.N.Am, is similar in size but with proportionally long tarsus (wg chord 83-94, tl 35-42, exp culmen 16.2-20.4, tarsus 19-24); middle toe with claw longer (21.4-25.5 *vs* 18.0-20.6 in Least Sandpiper) and middle toe without claw longer than bill (*vs* usually shorter in Least); lores average paler; shafts of p1-p9 dark (*vs* pale in Least); underwing med, gr, and p covs primarily brownish gray (*vs* primarily white in Least and other small *Calidris* sandpipers). See references under Semipalmated Sandpiper, Alström & Olsson (1989), and Patten & Daniels (1991) for other characters. Temminck's Stint (*C. temminckii*), a vagrant to w.N.Am, has longer wing and tail (wg chord 90-101, tl 42-51, exp culmen 15.6-18.2, tarsus 17-19); upperpart aspect grayer and with little to no feather fringing; outer rects white (*vs* washed gray in Least and other small *Calidris* sandpipers); breast washed gray, without distinct streaks.

Geographic variation—Monotypic. Populations breeding in AK may average longer-billed than those breeding in e.Canada (Miller 1979, Cooper 1994) but variation slight.

Molt—CAS. PF partial-incomplete (Aug-Nov/Mar in HY/SYs), PA1 partial (Mar-May in SYs), DPB complete (Jul-Sep/Jan in AHY/ASYs), DPA partial-incomplete (Feb-Apr in ASYs). Molting occurs primarily at stopover sites (where it can complete) and on non-breeding grounds. Molt exhibits either a n.Hemisphere or s.Hemisphere strategy (Table 45, pp. 501-505). The PF includes most to all body feathers, no to a few proximal s covs, 1-3 terts, and 1-2 c.rects in Oct-Dec; in many HY/SYs (primarily among those with tropical and/or s.Hemisphere non-breeding grounds), the PF can include up to all rects, terts, and s covs (the distal gr covs usually retained), and 2-10 outer pp and p covs and 1-10 medial ss (distal to the terts) in eccentric sequence in Dec-Apr (Fig. 376**A**-**B**, p. 504). The PF apparently can be complete in a small proportion of SYs. The DPB completes by Nov among many AHYs (with non-breeding grounds in N.Am) but typically occurs in Oct-Feb in those with non-breeding grounds in the tropics and s.Hemisphere. An extra molt of outer pp may occur in some TYs (as part of the PA2); more study is needed (see pp. 504-505). The DPA includes most body feathers, no to a few proximal s covs, usually 1-4 terts, and often 1-8 c.rects. A small proportion of SYs over-summer on tropical non-breeding grounds and probably exhibit less-complete (or no) PA1s and advanced PB2s (see p. 18). See pp. 500-507 for more information on molt in shorebirds.

Age—Juv (B1; Jul-Oct) has uniformly fresh plumage aspect, the back feathers and wing covs broadly fringed rufous to pale buff (Fig. 436**A**, p. 587), and the pp and ss uniformly juv and fresh (Fig. 375**A**, p. 503); Juv ♀=♂.

Juv-HY/SY (1st cycle, Juv/B1-F1-A1; Sep-Aug): Some to most upperpart feathers, terts, and/or distal s covs juv and fresh in Oct-Dec (Fig. 375**A**), broadly fringed rufous to pale buff when fresh (Fig. 436**A**), contrasting with fresher formative scapulars, humerals, and proximal s covs in Nov-Sep (Figs. 375**B**-**C** & Fig. 436**C**), the distal gr covs usually retained and becoming worn and frayed by Apr-Sep (Figs. 375**D** & 436**B**); some formative proximal s covs with thin rufous to buff fringes (Fig. 437**A**, p. 588); pp, p covs, and ss juv and fresh in Oct-Dec (Fig. 375**A**), sometimes being incompletely replaced in Jan-Apr and exhibiting eccentric replacement patterns in May-Sep (Fig. 376**A**-**C**, p. 504), the juv outer pp and p covs (if present) tapered (Figs. 377**A**-**B** & 378**A**-**B**, p. 506); all to some juv rects retained through Jan-Mar (often Apr-Sep), contrastingly narrow and worn (Fig. 379**A**-**D**, p. 507; perhaps occasionally including an alternate r1 as well; Fig. 17**D**, p. 25). **Note: See AHY/ASY.**

AHY/ASY (Def. cycle, DB-DA; Oct-Sep): Upperpart feathers, terts, and s covs uniformly basic or mixed basic and alternate (Fig. 375**E**-**F**), the basic feathers with thinner pale fringing (Figs. 436**C** & 437**B**); pp, p covs, and ss worn and being completely replaced in Jul-Oct (n.Hemisphere) to Sep-Jan (tropics and s.Hemisphere), or basic and fresh in Nov-Sep (Fig. 375**E**), the outer pp and p covs broad and truncate (Figs. 377**C**-**D** & 378**C**-**D**); rects basic and broader (Fig. 379**E**), often with 1-8 alternate c.rects in Apr-Aug (Fig. 379**F**). **Note: A small proportion of HY/SYs may have a complete PF and become indistinguishable from AHY/ASYs in Apr-Sep but the proportion appears to be sufficiently small (< 5%) to enable reliable ageing of ASYs through Sep.**

SY/TY (2nd cycle, B2; Oct-Jan): Like AHY/ASY with molt of pp occurring, but outer pp and p covs juv, pointed and very abraded (Fig. 376**E**). **Note: These usually occur in tropical and s.Hemisphere non-breeding areas only and may be very rare (most SYs having replaced the outer pp and p covs during the PF).**

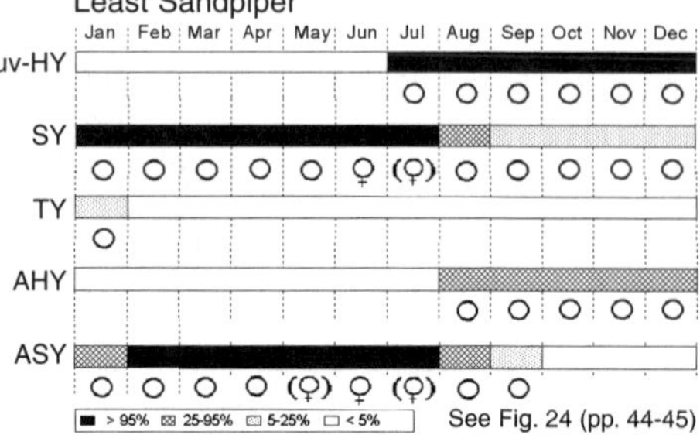

Sex—♀ = ♂ by plumage aspect. Bilateral BPs (Fig. 20**B**, p. 31) developed by both sexes but a distended cloaca (Fig. 21, p. 32) indicates ♀ in May-Jul. Measurements largely unhelpful for sexing (Table 53, p. 585) and no other criteria known.

Hybrids reported—Possibly with Baird's Sandpiper (OR, Sep 1998).

References—Alexander & Gratto-Trevor (1997), Bent (1927), Burton & McNeil (1976), Cramp & Simmons (1983), Cooper (1994), Dwight (1900b), Higgins & Davies (1996), Jehl (1970), McNeil (1970), Oberholser (1974), Page (1974a, 1974b), Page & Bradstreet (1968), Palmer (1967b), Prater et al. (1977), Ridgway (1919), Roberts (1955), Spaans (1976, 1979).

WHITE-RUMPED SANDPIPER
Calidris fuscicollis

WRSA
Species # 2400
Band size: 1A-1B

Species—From other N.Am shorebirds by medium-small size with proportionally long wings (Table 53, p. 585); bill dusky with pale brownish base to lower mandible, slightly decurved, moderately stout (depth at distal end of nares 4.0-5.2 mm), and somewhat rounded at tip; rump and medial uppertail covs mostly white (Fig. 438**B**-**D**; see **Age**); underparts white, the breast with indistinct (Sep-Mar) to distinct (Mar-Sep) streaking; legs and feet black, with hind toe present (Fig. 373**B**-**C**, p. 500) and without webbing between fore toes (Fig. 374**A**, p. 501); Juv with upperpart feathers fringed rufous contrasting with white-edged scapulars (forming streaks or "braces"). From all other shorebirds including Baird's Sandpiper (p. 596) by combination of size, white uppertail covs, and bill shape, depth, and color.

Geographic variation—Monotypic.

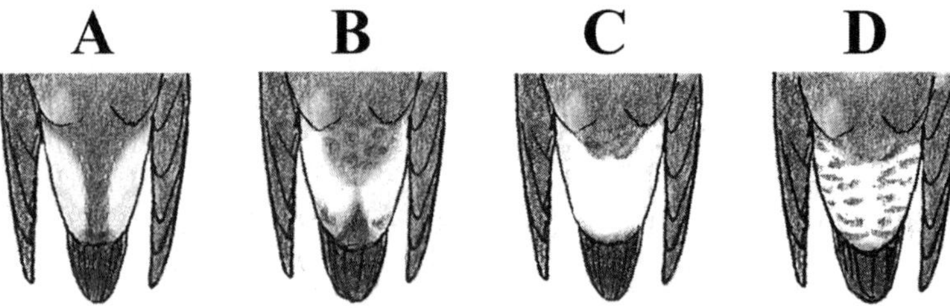

FIGURE 438. Pattern to the rump and medial uppertail coverts in Calidridine sandpipers for identification. Most species exhibit dark rump and medial uppertail covs (**A**). The exceptions are White-rumped Sandpiper (variable **B**-**D**), Curlew Sandpiper (**B**-**C**), Stilt Sandpiper (**B**-**C**), and Ruff (resembles **B** but with dark medial stripe tapering caudally). Wilson's Phalarope also displays white (**C**) *vs.* darker medially (**A**) in Red-necked and Red phalaropes. For the three sandpipers, patterns **B**-**C** are found in juv, formative, and basic plumage aspect (Oct-Mar) whereas **D** is found in definitive alternate aspect (ASYs in Apr-Sep). For Curlew and Stilt sandpipers, SYs in first alternate aspect average less barring (sometimes none) than ASYs in definitive alternate plumage aspect.

Molt—CAS. PF complete (Nov-Mar in HY/SYs), DPA partial (Feb-Apr in AHYs), DPB complete (Aug-Dec in AHYs). The PF occurs primarily at stopover sites although it can commence on breeding grounds and complete on non-breeding grounds, the DPB can commence (body feathers only) on breeding grounds but occurs primarily on non-breeding grounds, and the DPA usually commences on non-breeding grounds but can occur primarily at stopover sites and compete on breeding grounds. Molt exhibits a s.Hemisphere strategy (Table 45, pp. 501-505). The DPA includes some to most body feathers but few (if any) proximal s covs, terts, or rects, and may average slightly more extensive in ♂♂ than ♀♀. See pp. 500-507 for more information on molt in shorebirds.

Age—Juv (B1; Jul-Oct) has uniformly fresh plumage aspect, the back feathers and wing covs fringed tawny to buff (Fig. 436**A**, p. 587), and the pp and ss uniformly juv and fresh (Fig. 375**A**, p. 503); Juv ♀=♂.

Juv-HY/SY (1st cycle, Juv/B1; Oct-Feb): Some to most upperpart feathers and s covs juv (Fig. 375**A**) and fringed rufous to pale buff (Fig. 436**A-B**); some formative proximal s covs with thin rufous to buff fringes (Fig. 437**A**, p. 588); pp, p covs, and ss juv and fresh in Oct-Dec (Fig. 375**A**) and/or being completely replaced in Nov-Feb, the outer pp and p covs narrow and relatively abraded (Figs. 377**A-B** & 378**A-B**, p. 506); outer rects narrow (Fig. 379**A**, p. 507), relatively fresh in Jul-Oct, and being replaced in Nov-Feb. **Note: Some individuals can be difficult to age. It is possible that SYs can be separated from ASYs in Mar-Aug by the fringing to the proximal s covs (Fig. 437) but study is needed to confirm the reliability of this after completion of the PF. Otherwise, SYs may average less-extensive rufous to the upperparts and less black barring to the rump (Fig. 438B-C) than ASYs (Fig. 438D) in Apr-Aug by sex (see Sex), but there is extensive overlap. Thus, ageing is not reliable in Mar-Sep.**

AHY/ASY (Def. cycle, DB/DA; Feb-Jan): Upperparts and s covs basic or mixed basic and alternate (Fig. 375**E-F**), the basic feathers with thin or indistinct whitish fringing (Figs. 436**C** & 437**B**); pp, p covs, and ss worn and being completely replaced in Aug-Nov (usually not in Dec-Feb), the outer pp and p covs broad and truncate (Figs. 377**C-D** & 378**C-D**); outer rects broad (Fig. 379**E**), relatively worn in Jul-Oct, and being replaced in Sep-Dec (not Jan-Feb). **Note: See Juv-HY/SY.**

Sex—♀=♂ by plumage aspect. Bilateral BPs (Fig. 20**B**, p. 31) and/or distended cloaca (Fig. 21, p. 32) indicate ♀ in Jun-Aug. Measurements largely unhelpful for sexing (Table 53, p. 585). ASY ♂♂ may average brighter and more rufous fringing to upperparts (and perhaps more barring to the uppertail covs; Fig. 438**D**) than ASY ♀♀ in Apr-Aug, which might be helpful in sexing some mated pairs. In addition, some breeding ♂♂ may be reliably sexed in May-Jul by having swollen throats with thickened skin (Parmelee et al. 1968). Otherwise, no criteria known.

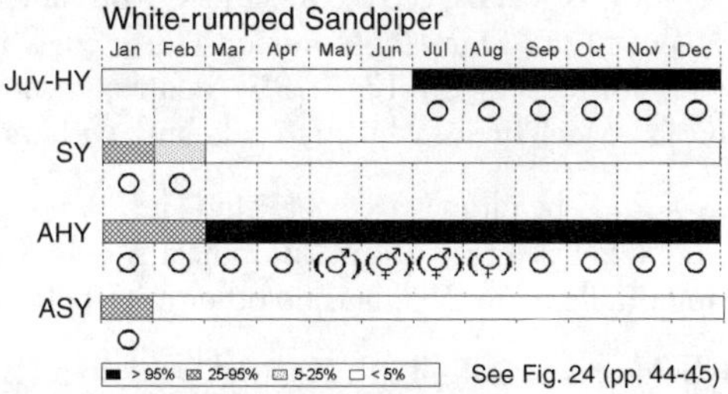

White-rumped Sandpiper
Jan Feb Mar Apr May Jun Jul Aug Sep Oct Nov Dec
Juv-HY
SY
AHY
(♂)(⚥)(⚥)(♀)
ASY
■ > 95% ▨ 25-95% ▤ 5-25% □ < 5%
See Fig. 24 (pp. 44-45)

Hybrids reported—With Dunlin (McLaughlin & Wormington 2000), Pectoral Sandpiper (Cox 1989, 1990b; Paulson 2005), Curlew Sandpiper (Golley 1999), and Buff-breasted Sandpiper (Mactavish 2001, 2004; Mactavish & Knowles 2004).

References— Alström (1987), Bent (1927), Burton & McNeil (1976), Cramp & Simmons (1983), Dement'ev & Gladkov (1951c), Dwight (1900b), Harrington et al. (1991), Higgins & Davies (1996), Jackson (1919), Manning et al. (1956), McNeil (1970), Oberholser (1974), Palmer (1967b), Parmelee (1968, 1992), Prater et al. (1977), Ridgway (1919), Roberts (1955).

BAIRD'S SANDPIPER
Calidris bairdii

BASA
Species # 2410
Band size: 1B-1A

Species—From other N.Am shorebirds by medium-small size with proportionally long wings (Table 53, p. 585); bill black, straightish, thin (depth at distal end of nares 3.1-4.0 mm); medial uppertail covs dark (Fig. 438**A**, p. 594); breast with dull buff to brownish wash and indistinct dusky to blackish streaking; legs and feet blackish, with hind toe present (Fig. 373**B**-**C**, p. 500) and without webbing between fore toes (Fig. 374**A**, p. 501); Juv with upperpart feathers fringed buff and scapulars with thin or no white edging. From all other shorebirds including White-rumped Sandpiper (p. 594) by combination of size, dark medial uppertail covs, and narrow bill.

Geographic variation—Monotypic.

Molt—CAS. PF complete (Nov-Mar in HY/SYs), DPA limited-partial (Feb-Apr in AHYs), DPB complete (Jul-Dec in AHYs). Most molting occurs on non-breeding grounds, although the DPB (and rarely the PF) can commence (body feathers only), and the DPA can complete on breeding grounds or at stopover sites. Molt exhibits a s.Hemisphere strategy (Table 45, pp. 501-505). The DPA includes some to most body feathers but few if any s covs, terts, or rects. See pp. 500-507 for more information on molt in shorebirds.

Age—Juv (B1; Jul-Oct) has uniformly fresh plumage aspect, the back feathers and wing covs fringed tawny to buff (Fig. 436**A**, p. 587), and the pp and ss uniformly juv and fresh (Fig. 375**A**); Juv ♀=♂.

Juv-HY/SY (1st cycle, Juv/B1; Oct-Mar): Some to most upperpart feathers and s covs juv and relatively fresh (Fig. 375**A**), fringed buff (Fig. 436**A**-**B**); some formative proximal s covs with thin rufous to buff fringes (Fig. 437**A**, p. 588); pp, p covs, and ss uniformly juv in Oct-Dec (Fig. 375**A**) and/or being completely replaced in Dec-Mar, the outer pp and p covs tapered (Figs. 377**A**-**B** & 378**A**-**B**, p. 506); outer rects narrow (Fig. 379**A**, p. 507), relatively fresh in Jul-Oct, and being replaced in Dec-Mar; breast with dark buff wash and indistinct dusky streaks in Oct-Jan. **Note: It is possible that SYs can be separated from ASYs in Mar-Aug by the fringing to the proximal s covs (Fig. 437) but study is needed to confirm the reliability of this after completion of the PF. Otherwise, SYs may average less-extensive black and gray centers to the upperpart feathers than ASYs in Apr-Aug by sex (see Sex), but there is extensive overlap. Thus, ageing is not reliable in Apr-Sep**.

AHY/ASY (Def. cycle, DB/DA; Feb-Jan): Upperpart feathers and s covs basic or mixed basic and alternate (Fig. 375**E**-**F**), the basic feathers with thin or indistinct whitish fringing (Figs. 436**C** & 437**B**); pp, p covs, and ss worn and being completely replaced in Aug-Dec (usually not in Jan-Mar), the outer pp and p covs broad and truncate (Figs. 377**C**-**D** & 378**C**-**D**); outer rects broad (Fig. 379**E**), relatively worn in Jul-Oct and being replaced in Sep-Dec (not Jan-Mar); breast whitish to pale buff, with more-distinct dusky streaks. **Note: See Juv-HY/SY.**

Sex—♀=♂ by plumage aspect. Medial(?) BP (Fig. 20**A**, p. 31) is developed by both sexes but distended cloaca (Fig. 21, p. 32) indicates ♀ in May-Jul. Measurements largely unhelpful for sexing (Table 53, p. 585) and no other criteria known.

Hybrids reported—With Pectoral Sandpiper (Bain 2006), Dunlin (O'Brien et al. 2006); possibly Least Sandpiper (p. 592) and Buff-breasted Sandpiper (Laux 1994, Robbins 2000; but see Alderfer 1995, Mactavish 2004).

References— Alström (1987), Bent (1927), Cramp & Simmons (1983), Higgins & Davies (1996), Jackson (1919), Jehl (1979), Manning et al. (1956), Moskoff & Montgomerie (2002), Oberholser (1974), Palmer (1967b), Prater et al. (1977), Ridgway (1919), Roberts (1955), Stone (1900), van Ijzendoorn (1982).

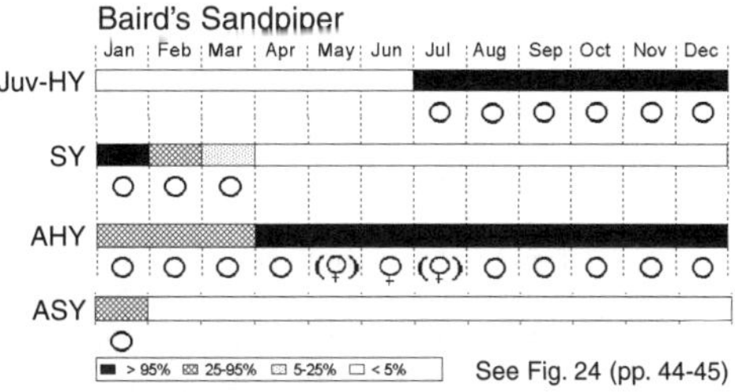

PECTORAL SANDPIPER

Calidris melanotos

PESA
Species # 2390
Band size: 1A

Species—From other N.Am shorebirds by medium-small to medium size (Table 54, p. 602); bill brown, with a yellowish base to lower mandible, and slightly decurved; medial uppertail covs dark (Fig. 438**A**, p. 594); breast washed brown to buff and with distinct streaking and sharp lateral contrast with white belly; legs and feet yellow, with hind toe present (Fig. 373**B-C**, p. 500) and without webbing between fore toes (Fig. 374**A**, p. 501). From Sharp-tailed Sandpiper (p. 598) by lower mandible with more extensive and yellower base; tail with broadly tapered (*cf.* Fig. 439, p. 599) and stepped rects (r2 – r3 > 5 mm); crown, back, and breast with less rufous or cinnamon, the breast streaking complete across center; p1-p9 with dull brownish shafts, contrasting with whiter shaft to p10; proximal p covs with thin (< 1.5 mm) white tips; breast with indistinct streaks and flanks white in Mar-Aug.

Geographic variation—Monotypic. ♂♂ from AK may average slightly smaller than ♂♂ from e.Canada (Manning et al. 1956).

Molt—CAS. PF complete (Oct-Jan in HY/SYs), DPA limited-partial (Feb-May in AHYs), DPB complete (Oct-Jan in AHY/ASYs). Most molting occurs on non-breeding grounds, although the DPB can commence (body feathers only), and the PA can complete on breeding grounds or at stopover sites. Molt exhibits a s.Hemisphere strategy (Table 45, pp. 501-505). The DPA includes some body feathers, few if any s covs or rects, and occasionally 1-3 terts. See pp. 500-507 for more information on molt in shorebirds.

Age—Juv (B1; Jul-Oct) has uniformly fresh plumage aspect, the pp and ss uniformly juv and fresh (Fig. 375**A**); Juv ♀ = ♂ by plumage aspect but sexes can be separated by wing chord when fully grown (Table 54, p. 602). Individuals are not reliably aged in Feb-Sep.

Juv-HY/SY (1st cycle, Juv/B1; Oct-Jan): Some to most upperpart feathers and s covs juv, with wide rufous and white fringing (Fig. 436**A-B**, p. 587); some formative proximal s covs with thin rufous to buff fringes (Fig. 437**A**, p. 588); pp, p covs, and ss relatively fresh, the outer pp and p covs tapered (Figs. 377**A-B** & 378**A-B**, p. 506); outer rects narrow (Fig. 379**A**, p. 507) and relatively fresh in Oct-Jan. **Note: It is possible that SYs can be separated from ASYs in Feb-Aug by the fringing to the proximal s covs (Fig. 437) but study is needed to confirm the reliability of this after completion of the PF. Otherwise, no criteria known for separating SYs from ASYs in Feb-Sep.**

AHY (Def. cycle, DB/DA; Jan-Dec): Upperpart feathers and s covs basic or mixed basic and alternate (Fig. 375**E-F**), the basic feathers with thin whitish fringing (Figs. 436**C** & 437**B**); pp, p covs, and ss relatively worn in Jul-Nov, the outer pp and p covs broad and truncate (Figs. 377**C-D** & 378**C-D**); outer rects broad and truncate (Fig. 379**E**), relatively worn in Oct-Jan. **Note: See Juv-HY/SY.**

Sex—♀ = ♂ by plumage aspect. Medial BP (Fig. 20**A**, p. 31) and/or distended cloaca (Fig. 21, p. 32) indicate ♀ in Jun-Aug. In addition, ♂♂ may be reliably sexed in May-Jul by having swollen breasts with thickened skin (Pitelka 1959). Measurements reliable for sexing (Table 54, p. 602):

♀: Wing chord < 133 (Table 54).

♂: Wing chord > 133 (Table 54).

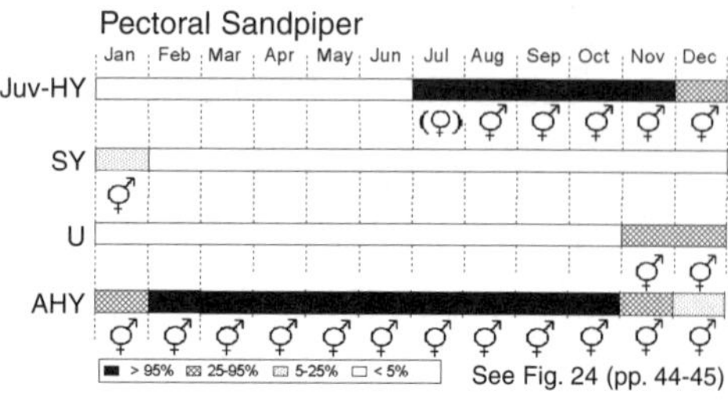

Hybrids reported—With White-rumped Sandpiper (p. 594), Baird's Sandpiper (p. 596), Curlew Sandpiper (Cox 1989, 1990b, 1990c; Cristidis et al. 1996; Higgins & Davies 1996; Stepanyan 1990, Vickery et al. 1987); possibly with Dunlin (Clark 1987a, Gauntlett & Grant 1989).

References—Alexander & Gratto-Trevor (1997), Bent (1927), Cramp & Simmons (1983), Harrop (1993b), Higgins & Davies (1996), Holmes & Pitelka (1998), Kaufman (1987, 1990a), Manning et al. (1956), Oberholser (1974), Palmer (1967b), Pitelka (1959), Prater et al. (1977), Ridgway (1919), Roberts (1955), Stone (1900), Webb & Conry (1979).

SHARP-TAILED SANDPIPER

Calidris acuminata

SHAS
Species # 2380
Band size: 1A

Species—See Pectoral Sandpiper (p. 597) for separation from other shorebirds. From Pectoral Sandpiper by lower mandible blacker, with less extensive and grayer pale base; tail with attenuated (Fig. 439; unique among N.Am *Calidris* sandpipers) and evenly graduated (r2 – r3 < 5 mm) rects; crown, back, and breast with more rufous or cinnamon in Apr-Sep, the breast streaking narrower and confined primarily to the sides; p1-p10 with uniformly pale shafts; proximal p covs with thicker (> 1.5 mm) white tips; sides of breast and flanks with dusky spots in Mar-Aug.

Geographic variation—Monotypic.

Molt—CAS. PF incomplete (Oct-Dec/Apr in HY/SYs), PA1 limited-partial (Feb-May in SYs), DPB complete (Aug-Nov/Jan in AHY/ASYs), DPA partial (Jan-Apr in ASYs). Molting occurs primarily on non-breeding grounds, although the DPB can commence (a few body feathers only) and the DPA can complete on breeding grounds or at stopover sites. Molt follows a s.Hemisphere strategy (Table 45, pp. 501-505). The PF includes most to all body feathers, rects, terts, and proximal s covs (the distal gr covs usually retained), and usually 4-8 outer pp and p covs and 1-7 medial ss (distal to the terts) in eccentric sequence (Fig. 376**A**, p. 504; sometimes arrested); body feathers, terts, and c.rects are replaced primarily in Oct-Dec whereas pp, ss, and outer rects are replaced primarily in Jan-Apr. The PF may occasionally be complete. The DPA includes most body feathers, a few to many proximal s covs, 1-4 terts, and often 1-6 c.rects. Occasional SYs over-summer on non-breeding grounds or at stopover sites and exhibit less-complete (or no) PA1s and advanced PB2s (see p. 18). See pp. 500-507 for more information on molt in shorebirds.

Age—Juv (B1; Jul-Oct) has uniformly fresh plumage aspect, the upperparts and breast with substantial rufous and cinnamon fringing (*cf.* Fig. 436**A**, p. 587), and the pp and ss uniformly juv and fresh (Fig. 375**A**); Juv ♀ = ♂ by plumage aspect.

Juv-HY/SY (1st cycle, Juv/B1-F1-A1; Oct-Sep): Some to most upperpart feathers, terts, and/or distal s covs juv and fresh in Oct-Dec (Fig. 375**A**), fringed rufous to buff (*cf.* Fig. 436**A**), contrasting with fresher formative scapulars, terts, and proximal s covs in Nov-Sep (Figs. 375**B-C** & 436**C**), the distal gr covs usually retained and becoming worn and frayed by Apr-Sep (Figs. 375**D** & 436**B**; see also Fig. 13**E**, p. 20); some formative proximal s covs with thin rufous to buff fringes (Fig. 437**A**, p. 588); pp, p covs, and ss juv, fresh, and without s1-p1 contrast in Oct-Dec (Fig. 375**A**), usually being incompletely replaced in Jan-Apr and exhibiting eccentric replacement patterns in May-Sep (Fig. 376**A-C**, p. 504; sometimes arrested), the juv outer pp and p covs (if present) narrow and relatively abraded (Figs. 377**A-B** & 378**A-B**, p. 506); all to some juv rects retained through Jan-Mar, contrastingly narrow and worn (*cf.* Figs. 379**A-C**, p. 507, & 439**A**); breast washed dark cinnamon in Oct-Dec. **Note: Some individuals may be difficult to age in Mar-Sep. See also AHY/ASY.**

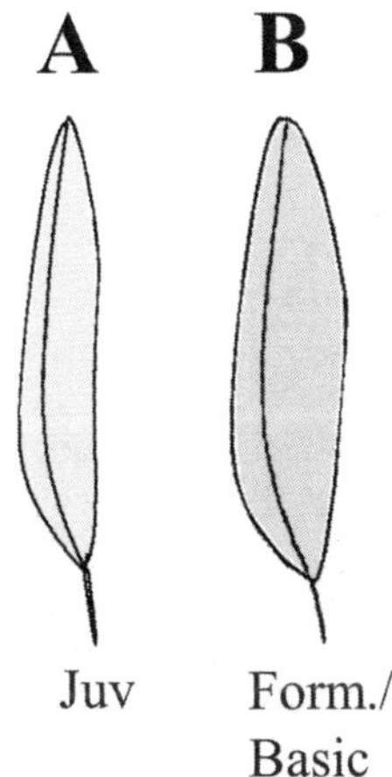

FIGURE 439. Shape of the rectrices by feather generation in Sharp-tailed Sandpiper. Juv rects are retained by SYs until the end of the PF, in Jan-Mar, after which rect shape is no longer useful for age determination.

AHY/ASY (Def. cycle, DB-DA; Oct-Sep): Upperpart feathers, terts, and s covs uniformly basic or mixed basic and alternate (Fig. 375**E-F**), the basic proximal s covs with thin or indistinct whitish fringes (Fig. 437**B**); pp, p covs, and ss worn and being completely replaced in Oct-Feb, or basic, fresh, and with replacement clines and often s1-p1 contrast in Dec-Sep (Fig. 375**E**), the outer pp and p covs broad and truncate (Figs. 377**C-D** & 378**C-D**); outer rects basic, and broader (Fig. 379**E**), often mixed with 1-6 alternate c.rects in Apr-Sep (Fig. 379**D**); breast with little to no cinnamon in Oct-Dec. **Note: See Juv-HY/SY. A small proportion of HY/SYs may have a complete PF and, except perhaps for the proximal s covs (Fig. 437), may become indistinguishable from AHY/ASYs in Apr-Sep, but the proportion appears to be sufficiently small (< 5%) to enable reliable ageing of ASYs through Sep.**

Sex—♀ = ♂ by plumage aspect. Type and status of BP (Fig. 20, p. 31) for sexing unknown but distended cloaca (Fig. 21, p. 32) indicates ♀ in May-Jul. Measurements (especially wing length) helpful for sexing some individuals (Table 54, p. 602); see also Rogers (1995) for a bivariate analysis using flat wing (Fig. 3**B**, p. 6) and head-bill length (see Fig. 453, p. 630) on live adults, that correctly sexed 80% of individuals.

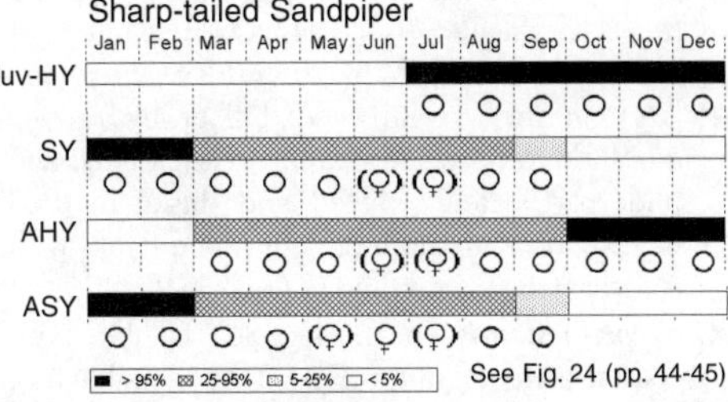

Hybrids reported—With Curlew Sandpiper (Cox 1989, 1990b, 1990c; Higgins & Davies 1996; Lane et al. 1981) but probably not with Ruff (Stepanyan 1990; *cf.* McCarthy 2006).

References—Barter & Davidson (1990), Bent (1927), Cramp & Simmons (1983), Dement'ev & Gladkov (1951c), Harrop (1993b), Higgins & Davies (1996), Kaufman (1987, 1990a), Palmer (1967b), Prater et al. (1977), Ridgway (1919), Webb & Conry (1979).

PURPLE SANDPIPER
Calidris maritima

PUSA
Species # 2350
Band size: 1A

ROCK SANDPIPER
Calidris ptilocnemis

ROSA
Species # 2360
Band size: 2

Species—From other N.Am sandpipers by medium-small size with proportionally medium long bill and short legs (Table 54, p. 602); bill dusky, with olive to orangish at base of both mandibles, and slightly decurved; medial uppertail covs dark (Fig. 438**A**, p. 594); breast dusky, mixed white (and rufous in Rock Sandpiper) in Apr-Aug; legs and feet yellowish to orangish yellow, with hind toe present (Fig. 373**B**-**C**, p. 500) and without webbing between fore toes (Fig. 374**A**, p. 501). Juv from juv Dunlin (p. 603) by longer average wings (Table 54); base of bill pale; upperparts and breast darker gray; legs and feet yellow to orangish.

Purple from Rock sandpiper with caution (and consideration of **Geographic variation** in Rock Sandpiper) by base of bill and legs usually tinged orangish (*vs* duller and olive to yellowish in Sep-Mar and blackish to black in Apr-Aug in Rock Sandpiper); white in pp/ss reduced, with little to none in outer web of s1 (Fig. 440**A**), *vs* substantial white in most populations of Rock Sandpiper (Fig. 440**B**-**C**; see **Geographic variation**); Juvs and alternate aspect with upperpart fringing thinner and whitish to pale rufous (*vs* broader and variably buff to dark rufous in Rock Sandpiper); Juv with underparts whitish with denser dusky streaking (*vs* washed buff and with sparser streaking in Juv Rock Sandpiper); abdomen without solid black patch in Apr-Sep.

Geographic variation—Purple Sandpiper considered Monotypic. Populations breeding on e.Hudson Bay Is, Que ("*C.m. belcheri*") may average smaller, populations from Greenland ("*groenlandica*") may average brighter fringing to upperparts in alternate plumage aspect, and populations from Iceland ("*littoralis*") average larger (except bill length), but differences slight and confounded by age-specific and individual variation. See Cramp & Simmons (1983), Engelmoer & Roselaar (1998), Lehman (2006), Payne & Pierce (2002), Prater et al. (1977), and Tomkovich & Serra (1999) for more information. For Rock Sandpiper see Aversa (2001), Conover (1944b), Gibson & Kessel (1997), Gill et al. (2002), Hellmayr & Conover (1948b), Portenko (1972), Prater et al. (1977), and Ridgway (1919). One other subspecies occurs in e.Asia.

Rock Sandpiper

C.p. quarta (br Commander Is, Siberia; vagrant to w.AK): Smaller (Table 54, p. 602); white in ss intermediate (Fig. 440**B**); Juvs dusky and white; AHYs in Apr-Sep with wide, dull, tawny fringing and little to no white tips to back feathers, and underpart patch reduced and dusky mottled whitish; back medium-dark gray and flanks with extensive dusky mottling in Oct-Mar.

C.p. ptilocnemis (br Bering Sea Is, AK; wint coastal s.AK; vagrant w.WA): Larger (Table 54); white in ss extensive (Fig. 440**C**); Juvs primarily buff to pale rufous; AHYs in Apr-Sep with medium-broad, pale, buff to tawny fringing and few or no white tips to back feathers, and underpart patch reduced and dusky mottled whitish; back medium-pale gray and flanks with little to no dusky mottling in Oct-Mar.

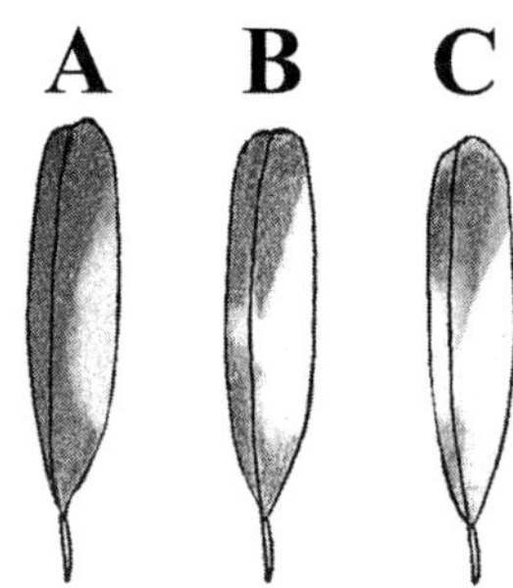

FIGURE 440. Pattern to the outermost secondary (s1) by species and subspecies in Purple and Rock sandpipers. Purple Sandpiper and Rock Sandpipers of the Aleutian Is (*C.p. couesi*) typically have no white in the outer web of this feather. Otherwise, Rock Sandpipers show more substantial white to the outer web of this feather, with the widespread *C.p. tschuktschorum*, along with *quarta* of Siberia, showing intermediate amounts of white (**B**), and populations breeding on Bering Sea Is (*ptilocnemis*) showing extensive white (**C**).

C.p. couesi (br & wint Aleutian Is-coastal w.AK): Smaller (Table 54); white in ss reduced (Fig. 440**A**); Juvs dusky and whitish; AHYs in Apr-Sep with moderately narrow, dull rufous fringing and distinct white tips to back feathers, and underpart patch reduced to absent and dusky (if present); back blackish dusky and flanks with extensive dusky mottling in Oct-Mar.

C.p. tschuktschorum (br ne.Siberia and coastal nw.AK, wint to coastal c.CA): Medium-small (Table 54); white in ss intermediate (Fig. 440**B**); Juvs dusky, buff, and white; AHYs in Apr-Sep with moderately narrow, bright, dark rufous fringing and distinct white tips to back feathers, and underpart patch extensive and uniformly black; back medium-dark dusky and flanks with moderately extensive dusky spotting in Oct-Mar.

Molt—CAS. PF partial (Aug-Oct in HYs), DPA partial (Mar-May in AHYs), DPB complete (Jul-Sep in AHYs). The PF and DPB occur primarily on breeding grounds but can complete (or occasionally occur entirely, in n.populations) on non-breeding grounds, whereas the DPA occurs primarily on non-breeding grounds but can complete on breeding grounds. Molt follows a n.Hemisphere strategy (Table 45, pp. 501-505). The PF includes most to all body feathers and often a few proximal s covs, 1-3 terts, and 1-4 c.rects. DPBs may average earlier in non-breeding AHYs (including many SYs). The DPA includes most body feathers and occasionally (Purple Sandpiper) to often (Rock Sandpiper) a few proximal s covs, 1-3 terts, and 1-2 (rarely 4) c.rects, and averages slightly more extensive in ♂♂ than ♀♀ by species and age. SYs rarely over-summer on non-breeding grounds and those that do may average a later and less-extensive DPAs than ASYs (see p. 18). See pp. 500-507 for more information on molt in shorebirds.

Age—Juv (B1; Jul-Sep) has uniformly fresh plumage aspect, the back feathers with crisp whitish to pale rufous fringing (Fig. 436**A**, p. 587) and the pp and ss uniformly juv and fresh (Fig. 375**A**); Juv ♀=♂. In addition to the following, SYs average less-extensive rufous to the upperparts and black to the underparts than ASYs by sex (see **Sex**) in Apr-Aug, but there is extensive overlap.

HY/SY (1st cycle, F1-A1; Oct-Sep): Most to all s covs juv, brownish, with broad pale rufous to whitish fringing when fresh (Fig. 436**A**), contrasting with fresher and duskier replaced scapulars, terts, and/or proximal s covs in Oct-Apr (Figs. 375**B-C** & 436**C**), the retained distal juv s covs becoming somewhat worn and frayed by Apr-Sep (*cf.* Figs. 375**D** & 436**B**, see also Fig. 13**E**, p. 20); some formative proximal s covs with thin rufous to buff fringes (Fig. 437**A**, p. 588); pp, p covs, and ss juv (Fig. 375**A**), the outer pp and p covs tapered, brownish, and relatively worn (Figs. 377**A-B** & 378**A-B**, p. 506); all to most juv rects retained, contrastingly narrow and worn (Fig. 379**A-C**, p. 507). **Note: Look also for juv rump feathers to be retained on some indivuals through Sep.**

AHY/ASY (Def. cycle, DB-DA; Oct-Sep): Upperpart feathers, terts, and s covs uniformly basic or mixed basic and alternate (Fig. 375**E-F**), the basic feathers dusky with grayish fringing (*cf.* Figs. 436**C** & 437**B**); pp, p covs, and ss basic (Fig. 375**E**), the outer pp and p covs broad, truncate, and relatively fresh (Figs. 377**C-D** & 378**C-D**); rects uniformly basic, broad, and relatively fresh (Fig. 379**E**), occasionally (in Rock Sandpiper) mixed with 1-4 alternate c.rects in Apr-Sep (Fig. 379**F**). **Note: See HY/SY.**

Sex—Medial(?) or bilateral(?) BPs (Fig. 20**A-B**, p. 31) developed by both sexes but a distended cloaca (Fig. 21, p. 32) indicates ♀ in May-Jul. Measurements largely unhelpful for sexing (Table 54, p. 602). For both species, ASY ♂♂ average brighter rufous fringing to upperparts and more black to underparts than ASY ♀♀ in Apr-Aug, which might be helpful in sexing some mated pairs (see **Age**). Otherwise the following is reliable for sexing alternate-aspect Rock Sandpipers; no criteria known for sexing Juv-HY/SYs, basic-aspect individuals, or any Purple Sandpipers by plumage aspect.

Rock Sandpiper

AHY ♀ (May-Jul): Supercilium, anterior portion of auriculars, and malar region whitish with extensive dusky streaking.

AHY ♂ (Apr-Aug): Supercilium, anterior portion of auriculars, and malar region white with little to no dusky streaking.

Hybrids reported—Purple Sandpiper with Dunlin (Millington 1994, O'Brien et al. 2006).

References—Bent (1927), Boere et al. (1984), Cramp & Simmons (1983), Gill et al. (2002), Lehman (2006), Morrison (1976), Palmer (1967b), Payne & Pierce (2002), Pittaway (1993b), Prater et al. (1977), Ridgway (1919), Summers et al. (2004).

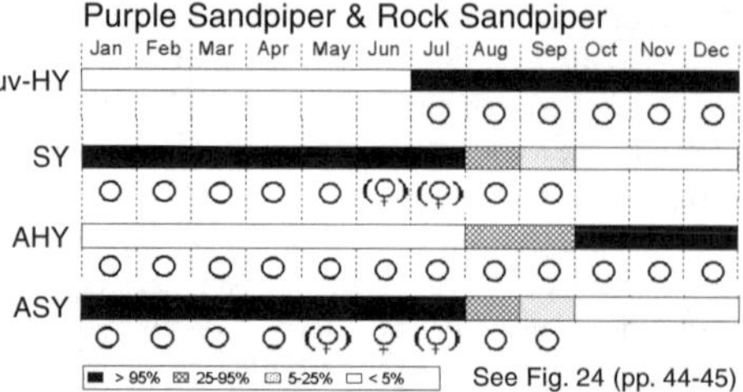

TABLE 54. Measurements (mm) of North American medium-sized *Calidris* sandpipers for identification and sexing. See pp. 4-11 for methods of measurement. Species summaries are in **bold** and subspecies summaries are in ***italics***. Values were derived from 95% confidence intervals as based approximately on the indicated sample sizes (see pp. 4-5). Thus, midpoints of ranges approximate means, and S.D. is approximated by 25% of the range.

Taxon/Sex	*n*	wing chord	tail length	exposed culmen	tarsus
Pectoral Sandpiper		**123-146**	**51-67**	**23.9-31.5**	**25-31**
♀	100	123-131	51-60	23.9-28.6	25-29
♂	100	135-146	57-67	26.3-31.5	27-31
Sharp-tailed Sandpiper		**119-140**	**48-62**	**21.9-27.0**	**26-33**
♀	100	119-132	48-58	21.9-25.7	26-31
♂	100	128-140	51-62	23.0-27.0	27-33
Purple Sandpiper[1,2]		**117-137**	**49-61**	**26.8-38.1**	**20-25**
♀	65	121-137	50-61	31.7-38.1	21-25
♂	75	117-133	49-60	26.8-33.4	20-24
Rock Sandpiper[1]		**111-139**	**46-65**	**23.9-38.5**	**20-27**
C.p. quarta		***114-126***	***46-57***	***23.9-33.0***	***20-25***
♀	20	116-126	47-57	28.2-33.0	21-25
♂	20	114-124	46-56	23.9-28.7	20-24
C.p. ptilocnemis		***119-140***	***52-65***	***26.9-38.5***	***22-27***
♀	80	123-139	54-65	29.7-38.5	23-27
♂	50	119-135	52-63	26.9-32.5	22-26
C.p. couesi		***111-129***	***47-59***	***24.6-34.2***	***21-26***
♀	90	113-129	48-59	28.6-34.2	22-26
♂	100	111-127	47-58	24.6-29.8	21-25
C.p. tschuktschorum		***113-131***	***48-60***	***24.5-34.0***	***20-26***
♀	55	116-131	49-60	28.4-34.0	21-26
♂	75	113-128	48-59	24.5-30.1	20-25
Dunlin[1]		**102-128**	**41-56**	**23.3-44.4**	**21-30**
E.a. sakhalina		***111-126***	***41-54***	***29.6-41.6***	***24-28***
♀	100	114-126	42-54	33.2-41.6	25-28
♂	100	111-122	41-53	29.6-38.2	24-27
E.a. pacifica/hudsonia		***113-128***	***45-56***	***32.9-44.4***	***25-30***
♀	100	116-128	45-56	36.6-44.4	26-30
♂	100	113-125	45-55	32.9-40.6	25-29
E.a. arctica		***102-115***	***41-53***	***23.3-34.2***	***21-25***
♀	100	106-115	41-53	26.7-34.2	22-25
♂	100	102-111	41-52	23.3-30.7	21-24
E.a. alpina		***106-120***	***41-54***	***27.1-37.4***	***23-28***
♀	100	110-120	42-54	30.6-37.4	24-28
♂	100	106-116	41-53	27.1-33.8	23-26
Curlew Sandpiper		**119-130**	**41-52**	**33.4-43.1**	**27-32**
♀	80	121-130	42-52	37.5-43.1	29-32
♂	100	119-128	41-51	33.4-39.0	27-31
Stilt Sandpiper		**122-139**	**44-53**	**36.4-44.8**	**39-46**
♀	100	125-139	45-53	38.4-44.8	41-46
♂	100	122-135	44-52	36.4-42.6	39-44

[1] Measures from N.Am populations only; see **Geographic variation**.
[2] Note that extralimital (European) populations of Purple Sandpiper average slightly smaller than N.Am populations.

DUNLIN DUNL
Calidris alpina Species # 2430
Band size: 1A-1B

Species—From other N.Am sandpipers including Western, Rock, and Curlew sandpipers by medium-small size with variably but proportionally long bill (Table 54; Fig. 441**A-B**); bill black, slightly to distinctly decurved, usually more at tip (Fig. 441**A-B**); underwing covs (including p covs) primarily pale gray; medial uppertail covs dark (Fig. 438**A**, p. 594); outer rects uniformly grayish brown; breast streaked dusky in Sep-Mar; abdomen with dusky spots (Juv) or black patch (AHYs in Apr-Sep); legs and feet black, the hind toe small but present (Fig. 373**B**, p. 500) and the fore toes without webbing (Fig. 374**A**, p. 501).

Geographic variation—See Browning (1977b, 1991), Buehler & Baker (2005), Conover (1945b), Cramp & Simmons (1983), Dement'ev & Gladkov (1951c), Engelmoer & Roselaar (1998), Gibson & Kessel (1997), Greenwood (1986), Hellmayr & Conover (1948b), Higgins & Davies (1996), MacLean & Holmes (1971), Meissner (2005), Nechaev & Tomkovich (1987), O'Brien et al. (2006), Patten et al. (2003), Paulson (1993, 2005), Portenko (1972), Prater et al. (1977), Ridgway (1919), Stejneger (1885), Todd (1953), Tomkovich (1986), and Tomkovich & Serra (1999). Three other subspecies occur in Greenland-Europe and e.Siberia. In addition to the following, the timing and location of the prebasic molt varies by subspecies (see **Molt**).

C.a. sakhalina (br ne.Siberia to n.AK-nw.NWT, wint se.Asia; vagrant to CA): Medium-large (Table 54); posterior flanks and undertail covs with few or no dusky streaks; upperpart feathers of AHYs in Apr-Sep with extensive, bright orange-rufous fringing. Populations of AK-NWT (*"articola"*) may average slightly larger, darker, and with less distinct black streaks to flanks but differences are slight and confounded by substantial individual variation. Populations of w.Kamchatka I (*kistchinski*) and Sakhalin I (*actites*), e.Siberia, possible vagrants to w.AK, are smaller (*actites*, wg chord 101-110) and have darker buff to cinnamon fringing and more distinct black spots to upperparts in Apr-Sep.

C.a. pacifica (br w.AK, wint coastal BC-CA): Larger (Table 54); posterior flanks and undertail covs with few or no dusky streaks; upperpart feathers of AHYs in Apr-Sep with extensive, moderately bright rufous fringing.

C.a. hudsonia (br Nun-n.Ont, wint TX-FL-MA; vagrant AZ): Larger (Table 54); posterior flanks and undertail covs with distinct dusky streaks; upperpart feathers of AHYs in Apr-Sep with extensive, moderately dull orange-rufous fringing.

C.a. arctica (br ne.Greenland; vagrant to ne.Canada-MA): Smaller (Table 54); upperpart feathers of AHYs in Apr-Sep with moderately dull cinnamon fringing and black of abdomen patch often mottled whitish. Populations that

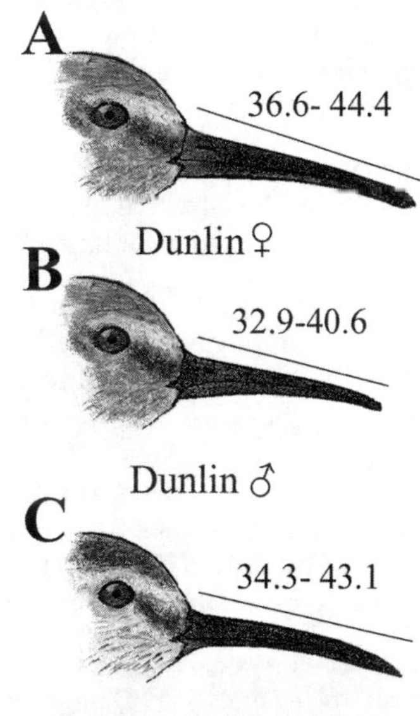

FIGURE 441. Variation in bill size and shape by sex in North American Dunlin (*C.a. pacifica/hudsonicus*) versus Curlew Sandpiper for identification. **A** shows a large ♀ and **B** shows a small ♂ Dunlin; there is some overlap in bill sizes between the sexes and note also that extralimital subspecies have smaller bills by sex (Table 54). Note in Dunlin that the bill is rather straight at the base, especially in ♀♀, before becoming decurved at the tip, whereas in Curlew Sandpiper the bill tends to be more decurved throughout its length. Beware of some overlap in bill shape, however; in both species ♀♀ may show straighter bills and ♂♂ may show more decurved bills (*cf.* also Fig. 422, p. 565). Note also the blunter tip to the bill and darker basic head plumage aspect in Dunlin than in Curlew Sandpiper.

breed in Iceland and w.Europe ("*schinzii*" if valid), potential vagrants to ne.N.Am, are slightly longer-billed (exp culmen 25-36) and average more extensive rufous-cinnamon fringing to upperparts in Apr-Sep.

C.a. alpina (br n.Europe; vagrant to MA-SC): Medium-small (Table 54); upperpart feathers of AHYs in Apr-Sep with moderate cinnamon-rufous fringing and black abdomen patch with little or no white mottling.

Molt—CAS. PF partial (Aug-Sep in HYs), DPA limited-partial (Mar-May in AHYs), DPB complete (Jul-Sep in AHYs in N.Am). The PF and DPB occur primarily on breeding grounds in N.Am populations (primarily at stopover sites and/or non-breeding grounds in Eurasian populations), but body molt can complete on non-breeding grounds. The DPA occurs primarily on non-breeding grounds but can complete at stopover sites. Molt follows a n.Hemisphere strategy (Table 45, pp. 501-505). DPBs begin during incubation in *C.a. sakhalina* but do not commence until after breeding in other subspecies, and the DPA averages later in n. than s.breeding populations. The PF includes most to all body feathers and sometimes a few proximal s covs and 1-2 c.rects but few if any terts. The DPA includes most body feathers and sometimes a few s covs, 1-2 terts, and 1-2 (rarely to 4) c.rects; it averages slightly more extensive in ♂♂ than ♀♀ by species and age. SYs rarely over-summer on non-breeding grounds and those that do may average a less-extensive and later PA1 than the DPA in ASYs. See pp. 500-507 for more information on molt in shorebirds.

Age—Juv (B1; Jul-Sep) has uniformly fresh plumage aspect, the back feathers with white and rufous fringing (Fig. 436**A**, p. 587), the pp and ss uniformly juv and fresh (Fig. 375**A**, p. 503), and the breast and abdomen buff with dusky spots; Juv ♀=♂.

HY/SY (1st cycle, F1-A1; Oct-Sep): Most to all terts and s covs juv and brownish with distinct rufous to buff fringing when fresh (Fig. 436**A**), contrasting with fresher and duskier replaced humerals, scapulars, and/or proximal s covs in Oct-Apr (Figs. 375**C-D** & 436**C**), the retained distal juv s covs becoming worn and frayed by Apr-Sep (Figs. 375**D** & 436**B**; see also Fig. 13**E**, p. 20); formative terts and some proximal s covs with thin rufous to buff fringes (Fig. 437**A**, p. 588); pp, p covs, and ss juv (Fig. 375**A**), the outer pp and p covs tapered, brownish, and relatively worn (Figs. 377**A-B** & 378**A-B**, p. 506); most to all rects narrow and relatively worn (Fig. 379**A-B**, p. 507), the juv rects washed pale brown. **Note: Look also for juv rump feathers to be retained on some individuals through Sep**.

AHY/ASY (Def. cycle, DB-DA; Oct-Sep): Upperparts and s covs uniformly basic or mixed basic and alternate (Fig. 375**E-F**); terts and basic proximal s covs dusky with indistinct gray fringes (Figs. 436**C** & 437**B**); pp, p covs, and ss basic (Fig. 375**E**), the outer pp and p covs broad, truncate, and relatively fresh (Figs. 377**C-D** & 378**C-D**); outer rects broad and relatively fresh (Fig. 379**E**), usually with 1-2 (rarely 4) alternate c.rects in Apr-Sep (Fig. 375**F**), the basic rects grayish. **Note: See HY/SY**.

Sex—Bilateral(?) or medial(?) BPs (Fig. 20**A-B**, p. 31) developed by both sexes but a distended cloaca (Fig. 21, p. 32) indicates ♀ in May-Jul. Measurements largely unhelpful for sexing (Table 54, p. 602), although bill length is useful for individuals of known subspecies (*cf.* Fig. 441, p. 603). ASY ♂♂ may average slightly brighter rufous fringing to upperparts and less white mottling to black abdomen patch than ASY ♀♀ in Apr-Aug; along with bill length this should enable sexing of most mated pairs on breeding grounds. See Brennan et al. (1984, 1991) for DFAs (p. 5) using exposed culmen and wing chord lengths and mass, from freshly dead specimens, that correctly sexed 91% of Dunlins (*C.a. pacifica*) on non-breeding grounds in WA.

Hybrids reported—With Sanderling (p. 582), White-rumped Sandpiper (p. 594), Baird's Sandpiper (p. 596), Purple Sandpiper (p. 600), and Curlew Sandpiper (McCarthy 2006); possibly with Pectoral Sandpiper (p. 597).

References—Bent (1927), Buchanan (2002), Chapman (1896b), Clark (1984, 1987b), Cramp & Simmons (1983), Dwight (1900b), Engelmoer & Roselaar (1998), Greenwood (1983), Gromadzka (1985), Gromadzka & Przystupa (1984), Higgins & Davies (1996), Holmes (1966, 1971), Holmgren et al. (1993), Kania (1990), Kus et al. (1984), Lehman (2000), Oberholser (1974), Page (1974a), Palmer (1967b), Prater et al. (1977), Ridgway (1919), Roberts (1955), Senner et al. (1981), Serra et al. (1998), Stone (1900), Tomkovich (1998), Warnock & Gill (1996).

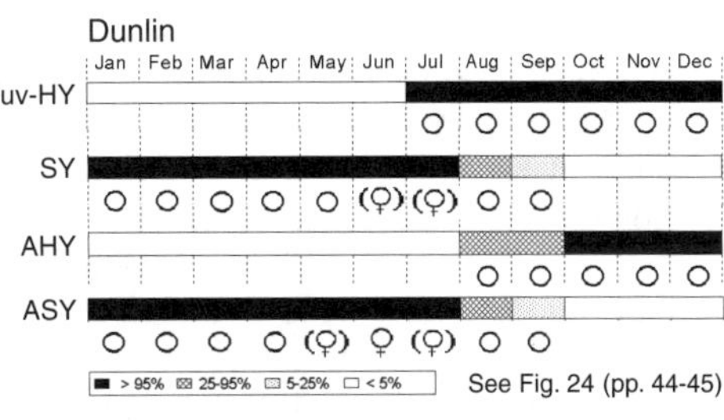

CURLEW SANDPIPER

Calidris ferruginea

CUSA
Species # 2440
Band size: 1A

Species—See Dunlin (p. 603) for separation from other shorebirds. From Dunlin by longer average wing and tarsus (Table 54, p. 602); bill black and decurved, often smoothly throughout length (Fig. 441**C**, p. 603); underwing covs (including p covs) primarily bright white; rump and medial uppertail covs mostly white (Fig. 438**C-D**, p. 594); outer rects mottled white and gray (Fig. 442, p. 606); breast with little or no streaking (Sep-Mar, Apr-Aug in some SYs) or variably chestnut in Apr-Aug; abdomen without black patch in Apr-Sep. From Stilt Sandpiper in basic plumage aspect (Sep-Mar) by smaller average size but longer average bill and shorter tarsus (Table 54); underwing covs primarily white; outer rects whitish with variable dusky tip (Fig. 442); legs black; fore toes without webbing.

Geographic variation—Monotypic (Portenko 1972, Engelmoer & Roselaar 1998).

Molt—CAS. PF incomplete (Oct-Dec/Apr in HY/SYs); PA1 absent-partial (Apr-Jun in non-breeding SYs), PB2 complete (Jun-Oct in non-breeding SYs), DPA partial (Feb-Apr in breeding AHYs), DPB complete (Aug-Nov/Jan in breeding AHY/ASYs). Molting occurs primarily at stopover sites and/or on non-breeding grounds, although the DPB can commence (body feathers and occasionally 1-3 inner pp), and the DPA can complete on breeding grounds. Molt follows a s.Hemisphere strategy (Table 45, pp. 501-505). The PF includes most to all body feathers, some to all rects, terts, and proximal s covs (the distal gr covs usually retained), and often 3-6 outer pp and p covs and 1-4 medial ss (distal to the terts) in eccentric sequence (Fig. 376**A**, p. 504, occasionally arrested); body feathers, terts, and c.rects are replaced primarily in Oct-Dec whereas pp, ss, and outer rects are replaced primarily in Jan-Apr. Proportion of HY/SYs replacing outer pp varies from ~25% on tropical non-breeding grounds to ~90% in the s.Hemisphere. The DPB and DPA average earlier in ♂♂ than in ♀♀. The PA1 can be absent or includes up to some body feathers but few if any terts or c.rects. The DPA includes some to most body feathers and often 1-3 terts, a few proximal s covs, and 1-4 c.rects. Most SYs and possibly some TYs over-summer on non-breeding grounds and exhibit less-complete (or no) PA1-PA2s and advanced PB2-PB3s (see p. 18). See pp. 500-507 for more information on molt in shorebirds.

Age—Juv (B1; Jul-Oct) has uniformly fresh plumage aspect, upperpart feathers with dusky centers and white fringing (Fig. 436**A**, p. 587), pp and ss uniformly juv and fresh (Fig. 375**A**, p. 503), and upper breast with buff wash and little or no streaking; Juv ♀ = ♂ by plumage aspect.

Juv-HY/SY (1st cycle, Juv/B1-F1-A1; Oct-Sep): Some to most upperpart feathers, terts, and distal s covs juv and fresh in Oct-Dec (Fig. 375**A**), fringed buff to whitish (Fig. 436**A**), contrasting with fresher formative scapulars, terts, and some proximal s covs in Nov-Sep (Figs. 375**B-C** & 436**C**), the distal gr covs usually retained and becoming worn and frayed by Apr-Sep (Figs. 375**D** & 436**B**); formative terts and some proximal s covs with thin buff fringes (Fig. 437**A**, p. 588); pp, p covs, and ss juv, fresh, and without s1-p1 contrast in Oct-Dec (Fig. 375**A**), often being incompletely replaced in Jan-Apr and exhibiting eccentric replacement patterns in May-Sep (Fig. 376**A-C**, p. 504; occasionally arrested), the juv outer pp and p covs (if present) narrow and relatively abraded (Figs. 377**A-B** & 378**A-B**, p. 506); all to some juv rects retained through Jan-Mar (occasionally Apr-Sep), contrastingly narrow and worn (Figs. 379**A-D**, p. 507), and usually with more white, contrasting less distinctly with dark coloration (Fig. 442**A**); underparts with no to some chestnut by sex (see **Sex**) and rump with less barring (*cf.* Fig. 438**D**, p. 594) in Apr-Sep. **Note: See AHY/ASY.**

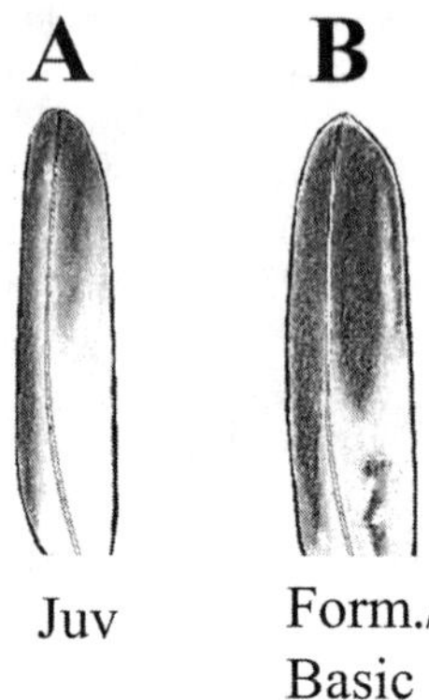

FIGURE 442. Typical shape and pattern to the outer rectrix (r6) by feather generation in Curlew Sandpiper. Some juv rects (**A**) are retained by HY/SYs through the PF in Jan-Apr, and occasionally by SYs through the PB2 in Jun-Oct.

AHY/ASY (Def. cycle, DB-DA; Oct-Sep): Upperpart feathers, terts, s covs, and rects uniformly basic or mixed basic and alternate (Fig. 375**E-F**), the basic feathers brownish gray with thin or indistinct whitish fringes (Figs. 436**C** & 437**B**); pp, p covs, and ss worn, being completely replaced in Oct-Feb, or basic, fresh, often with s1-p1 contrast, and occasionally with suspension limit among p1-p3 in Dec-Sep (Fig. 375**E-F**), the outer pp and p covs broad and truncate (Figs. 377**C**A-**D** & 378**C-D**); rects uniformly basic and broad (Figs. 379**E**), often with 1-4 alternate c.rects in Apr-Sep (Fig. 379**F**), the basic rects usually with less white, contrasting more distinctly with dark coloration (Fig. 442**B**); underparts with some to extensive chestnut by sex (see **Sex**) and rump with more barring (Fig. 438**D**) in Apr-Sep. **Note: A small proportion of HY/SYs may have a complete PF and become indistinguishable from AHY/ASYs in Apr-Sep, but the proportion appears to be sufficiently small (< 5%) to enable reliable ageing of ASYs through Sep.**

SY/TY (2nd cycle, B2; Oct-Jan): Like AHY/ASY with molt of pp occurring, but outer pp and p covs juv, pointed and very abraded (Fig. 376**E**). **Note: These usually occur in s.Hemisphere non-breeding areas only (see Molt and pp. 506-507).**

Sex—Bilateral(?) or medial(?) BPs (Fig. 20**A-B**, p. 31) apparently developed by both sexes but distended cloaca (Fig. 21, p. 32) indicates ♀ in May-Jul. Most measurements unhelpful for sexing, although bill length and shape may reliably differentiate some individuals to sex, including mated pairs (Table 54, p. 602; *cf.* Fig. 441**C**, p. 603). The following is reliable for sexing many ASYs in Apr-Aug, including most or all mated pairs in combination with culmen measurements and shape (Table 54, Fig. 441**C**); intermediate ASYs, AHY/ASYs in Sep-Mar, and HY/SY ♀♀ (and most HY/SY ♂♂) are not reliably sexed by plumage aspect.

ASY ♀ (Apr-Aug): Nape, throat, and breast varying from mostly grayish and whitish, to spotted dull rufous, black, and white.

AHY ♂ (Mar-Sep): Nape, throat, and breast mostly to entirely chestnut, with little or no black or white spotting, the black spotting, if present, confined to the sides and flanks.

Hybrids reported—With White-rumped Sandpiper (p. 594), Pectoral Sandpiper (p. 597), Sharp-tailed Sandpiper (p. 598), and Dunlin (p. 603); probably not with Ruff (Stepanyan 1990; *cf.* McCarthy 2006).

References—Barter (1985), Barter & Davidson (1990), Bent (1927), Cramp & Simmons (1983), Dement'ev & Gladkov (1951c), Figuerola & Bertolero (1995), Higgins & Davies (1996), Jackson (1919), Kaufman (1990c), Melville (1981), Palmer (1967b), Paton et al. (1982), Prater et al. (1977), Ridgway (1919).

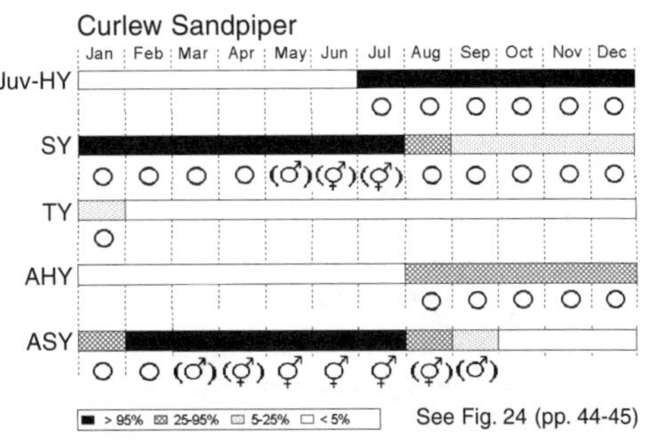

STILT SANDPIPER
Calidris himantopus

STSA
Species # 2330
Band size: 1A

Species—From other shorebirds (including Dunlin, p. 603 and Curlew Sandpiper, p. 605) by medium-small size with proportionally long legs (Table 54, p. 602); bill blackish with slight paling at base and slightly decurved at tip (*cf.* Fig. 441, p. 603); rump and medial uppertail covs primarily white (Fig. 438**C**-**D**, p. 594); outer rects mottled whitish to white with a dusky fringes; breast pale dusky (Sep-Mar, Apr-Aug in some SYs) or heavily barred blackish (without chestnut or distinct black patch) in Apr-Sep; legs and feet yellow to greenish, with hind toe present (Fig. 373**C**, p. 500) and with substantial webbing between fore toes (Fig. 374**D**-**E**, p. 501). From Wilson's Phalarope (p. 623) in basic plumage by longer wing, bill, and tarsus (Table 54); bill thicker (> 4 mm deep at base); back and s covs with dark shaft streaks; breast with indistinct dusky streaks.

Geographic variation—Monotypic.

Molt—CAS. PF incomplete (Oct-Dec/Apr in HY/SYs), PA1 limited-partial (Mar-May in non-breeding SYs), PB2 complete (Jun-Oct in non-breeding SYs), DPA partial (Feb-Apr in breeding AHYs), DPB complete (Aug-Nov in breeding AHYs). Molting occurs primarily at stopover sites and/or on non-breeding grounds, although the PF and DPB can commence (a few body feathers), and the PA can complete on breeding grounds. Molt follows a s.Hemisphere strategy (Table 45, pp. 501-505). The PF includes some to all body feathers, 2 to all c.rects, 2-4 terts, some proximal s covs (the distal gr covs usually retained), and usually 2-7 outer pp and p covs and 1-7 medial ss (distal to the terts) in eccentric sequence (Fig. 376**A**-**C**, p. 504; sometimes arrested); body feathers, terts, and c.rects are replaced primarily in Oct-Dec whereas pp, ss, and outer rects are replaced primarily in Jan-Apr. It is possible that some HY/SYs may undergo a complete PF; more study is needed. The PA1 includes up to some body feathers and 0-2 terts but few if any s covs or rects. The DPA includes some to most body feathers, usually 1-4 terts, and occasionally a few proximal s covs and 1-2 c.rects. Some SYs over-summer on non-breeding grounds and exhibit less-complete (or no) PA1s and advanced PB2s (see p. 18) See pp. 500-507 for more information on molt in shorebirds.

Age—Juv (B1; Jul-Dec) has uniformly fresh plumage aspect, the upperpart feathers with brownish centers and buff fringing (Fig. 436**A**, p. 587), and the pp and ss uniformly juv and fresh (Fig. 375**A**, p. 503); Juv ♀ = ♂ by plumage aspect.

Juv-HY/SY (1st cycle, Juv/B1-F1-A1; Oct-Sep): Some to most upperpart feathers, terts, and/or distal s covs juv and fresh in Oct-Dec (Fig. 375**A**), fringed buff to whitish (Fig. 436**A**), contrasting with fresher and grayer formative scapulars, terts, and some proximal s covs in Nov-Sep (Figs. 375**B-C** & 436**C**), the distal gr covs usually retained and becoming worn and frayed by Apr-Sep (Figs. 375**D** & 436**B**); some formative proximal s covs often with thin rufous fringes (Fig. 437**A**, p. 588); pp, p covs, and ss juv and fresh in Oct-Dec (Fig. 375**A**), usually being incompletely replaced in Jan-Apr and exhibiting eccentric replacement patterns in May-Sep (Fig. 376**A-C**, p. 504; sometimes arrested), the juv outer pp and p covs (if present) narrow and relatively abraded (Figs. 377**A-B** & 378**A-B**, p. 506); all to some juv rects retained through Jan-Mar (sometimes Apr-Sep), contrastingly narrow and worn (Fig. 379**A-D**, p. 507); rump (Fig. 438**C-D**, p. 594) and underparts with no to some dusky barring in Apr-Aug. **Note: See AHY/ASY.**

AHY/ASY (Def. cycle, DB-DA; Oct-Sep): Upperpart feathers, terts, and s covs uniformly basic or mixed basic and alternate (Fig. 375**E-F**), the basic feathers grayish with thin or indistinct whitish fringes (Figs. 436**C** & 437**B**); pp, p covs, and ss worn and being completely replaced in Oct-Jan, or basic and fresh in Dec-Sep (Fig. 375**E**), the outer pp and p covs broad and truncate (Figs. 377**C-D** & 378**C-D**); rects basic and broad (Fig. 379**E**), occasionally with 1-2 alternate c.rects in Apr-Sep (Fig. 379**F**); rump (Fig. 438**D**) and underparts usually with some to extensive blackish barring in Apr-Aug. **Note: It is possible that occasional HY/SYs may undergo a complete PF and be indistinguishable from AHY/ASYs in Mar-Sep, although the fringing to the proximal covs (Fig. 437) may allow reliable ageing; study needed.**

Sex—Bilateral(?) or medial(?) BPs (Fig. 20**A-B**, p. 31) developed by both sexes but distended cloaca (Fig. 21, p. 32) indicates ♀ in Jul-Sep. Measurements largely unhelpful for sexing (Table 54, p. 602). ASY ♂♂ in Apr-Aug average more-extensive and darker rufous feathering to crown, nape, and auriculars than ASY ♀♀ but there appears to be too much (age-related?) overlap for reliable sexing. Otherwise, no criteria known.

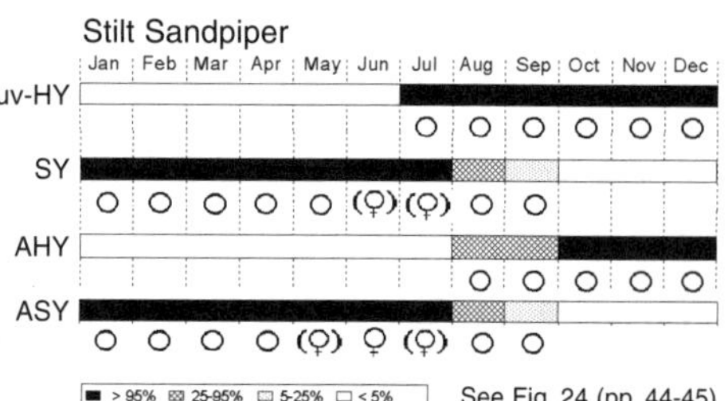

Hybrids reported—None.

References—Alexander & Gratto-Trevor (1997), Bent (1927), Chandler & Marchant (2001), Cramp & Simmons (1983), Higgins & Davies (1996), Jehl (1970, 1973), Klima & Jehl (1998), McNeil (1970), Oberholser (1974), Palmer (1967b), Prater et al. (1977), Ridgway (1919), Roberts (1955), Spaans (1979).

BUFF-BREASTED SANDPIPER

Tryngites subruficollis

BBSA
Species # 2620
Band size: 1A

Species—From other N.Am shorebirds by medium-small size with proportionally very short bill (Table 55, p. 612); bill black, sometimes with slight yellowish at base, and straight; upperpart feathers uniformly dark with distinct and wide buff to tawny fringes and without white; auriculars and throat washed buff; underside of p10 speckled to mottled dark and underwing p covs distinctly marked (Fig. 443); legs and feet yellow, with hind toe present (Fig. 373**B**, p. 500) and without webbing between fore toes (Fig. 374**A**, p. 501).

Geographic variation—Monotypic.

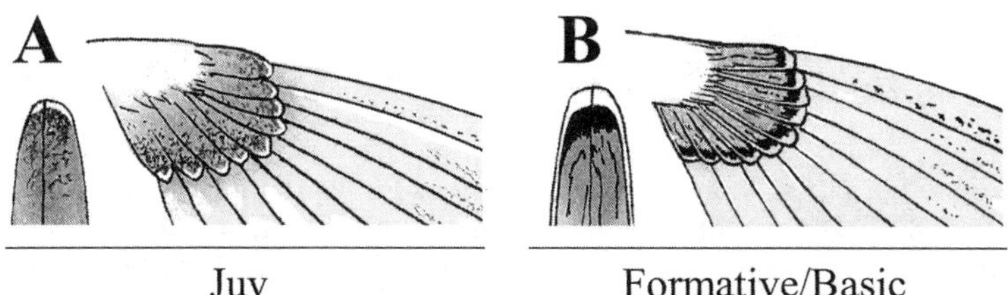

FIGURE 443. Underwing primary covert and pattern by feather generation in Buff-breasted Sandpiper. Juv p covs and underside of p10 (to a lesser extent other pp) have less-distinct patterning and speckling than formative and basic feathers (**B**). The PF is usually complete, such that this criterion can only be used for ageing until p10 and its corresponding p cov are replaced during the PF (SYs) or DPB (ASYs), in Jan-Feb.

Molt—CBS (CAS?). PF complete (Nov-Feb in HY/SYs), DPB complete (Oct-Feb in AHY/ASYs); PA absent(?). Most molting occurs on non-breeding grounds, although the DPB can commence with a few body feathers on breeding grounds or during migration. Molt exhibits a s.Hemisphere strategy (Table 45, pp. 501-505). Occasional HY/SYs may have an incomplete PF (see **Age**). A limited DPA (upperpart feathers) may occur in some AHYs; more study is needed. See pp. 500-507 for more information on molt in shorebirds.

Age—Juv (B1; Jul-Oct) has uniformly fresh plumage aspect, the wing covs tipped tawny to buff (Fig. 436**A**, p. 587), and the pp and ss uniformly juv and fresh (Fig. 375**A**, p. 503); Juv ♀=♂.

Juv-HY/SY (1st cycle, Juv/B1; Oct-Feb): Underside to pp and underwing p covs with indistinct dusky markings (Fig. 443**A**); some to most upperpart feathers and s covs juv, tipped tawny or buff to whitish (Fig. 436**A**); pp, p covs, and ss uniformly juv in Oct-Dec (Fig. 375**A**) and/or being completely replaced in Dec-Mar, the outer pp and p covs tapered (Figs. 377**A-B** & 378**A-B**, p. 506); all to some rects juv, narrow (Fig. 379**A-D**, p. 507), and relatively fresh in Jul-Dec. **Note: Occasional SYs might be identified in Mar-Sep by retained outer pp, medial ss, or back feathers; otherwise, no reliable criteria known.**

AHY/ASY (Def. cycle, DB; Mar-Feb): Underside to p10 and underwing p covs distinctly marked black (Fig. 443**B**); upperpart feathers and s covs uniform in wear, with clay-colored fringing (Fig. 436**C**); pp, p covs, and ss worn, being completely replaced in Sep-Jan (but not Feb-Mar), the outer pp and p covs broad and truncate (Figs. 377**C-D** & 378**C-D**); outer rects broad (Fig. 375**E**) and relatively worn in Jul-Dec. **Note: See Juv-HY/SY.**

Sex—♀=♂ by plumage aspect. Bilateral(?) or medial(?) BPs (Fig. 20**A-B**, p. 31) and/or distended cloaca (Fig. 21, p. 32) indicate ♀ in May-Jul. Measurements may be helpful for sexing some individuals, particularly mated pairs (Table 55, p. 612); otherwise, no criteria known.

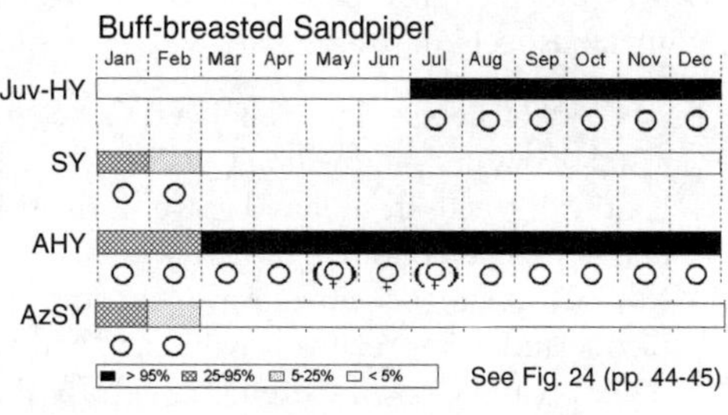

Hybrids reported—With White-rumped Sandpiper (p. 594) and possibly with Baird's Sandpiper (p. 596).

References—Bent (1929), Campbell & Gregory (1976), Cramp & Simmons (1983), Higgins & Davies (1996), Lanctot & Laredo (1994), Lanctot et al. (1998), Manning et al. (1956), Oberholser (1974), Palmer (1967b), Prater et al. (1977), Ridgway (1919), Roberts (1955).

RUFF RUFF
Philomachus pugnax Species # 2600
Band size: 3♀, 3B♂

Species—From other N.Am shorebirds by medium (♀) to medium-large (♂) size (Table 55, p. 612), bill blackish (Juv), and with variable amount of orange to red to base (AHY), and straight to slightly decurved; plumage aspect variably buff (Juv-HY), brown and white (Oct-Feb) and/or barred dusky (Mar-Aug), ASY ♂♂ with black, white, and/or rufous elongated ornamental plumes to upperparts and breast in Apr-Jul; underwing covs primarily bright white; uppertail covs white laterally and brown medially (*cf.* Fig. 438, p. 594); legs and feet yellow-olive to orange, with hind toe present (Fig. 373**C**, p. 500) and slight webbing between outer fore toes (Fig. 374**B**, p. 501).

Geographic variation—Monotypic.

Molt—CAS. PF partial-incomplete (Sep-Dec/Mar in HY/SYs), PA1 limited-partial (Mar-May in non-breeding SYs), PS1 absent-limited (May-Jun in SY ♂♂), PB2 complete (Jun-Oct in non-breeding SYs), DPA partial-incomplete (Dec-May in breeding AHY/ASYs), DPS limited (Apr-May in ASY ♂♂), DPB complete (Jul-Oct/Dec in breeding AHYs). The PF occurs primarily on non-breeding grounds, the DPA begins on non-breeding grounds but can complete at stopover sites (especially in ♀♀), the PS occurs primarily at stopover sites, and the DPB can occur on breeding grounds, non-breeding grounds, and/or at stopover sites, sometimes being suspended for migration after 1-6 pp, the terts, and occasionally s1 and/or s5 have been replaced. Molt follows either a n.Hemisphere (most individuals) or a s.Hemisphere (some ♀♀) strategy (Table 45, pp. 501-505). The PF includes most body feathers, a few to some proximal s covs, 2-4 terts, and often 1-4 c.rects in Sep-Dec; in occasional HY/SYs (more often ♀♀) the PF can also include 1-3 outer pp and 1-2 medial ss (distal to the terts) in eccentric sequence (Fig. 376**A**, p. 504) in Jan-Mar. The PA1 (and PS1 if present) includes scattered body feathers but few if any s covs, terts, or rects. The DPA includes some to all body feathers, a few to some proximal s covs, 1-5 terts, and 1-8 (occasionally all) c.rects; ♀♀ > ♂♂ in extent. The DPS includes some to most upperpart and breast feathers and sometimes 1-3 terts in ASY ♂♂, including development of the elongated ornamental plumes (Jukema & Piersma 2000). The DPS is apparently absent in ♀♀. Some to most SYs and probably some TYs over-summer on non-breeding grounds, and average less-complete (or no) PA1-PA2s and advanced PB2-PB3s (see p. 18). See pp. 500-507 for more information on molt in shorebirds.

Age—Juv (B1; Jul-Nov) has uniformly fresh plumage aspect, the back feathers and wing covs dusky with broad buff fringes (Fig. 436**A**, p. 587), the pp and ss uniformly juv and fresh (Fig. 375**A**, p. 503), the breast washed buff to cinnamon, and the legs dull olive; Juv ♀=♂ by plumage aspect but sexes separated by measurements (Table 55, p. 612), when Juvs fully grown.

Juv-HY/SY (1st cycle, Juv/B1-F1-A1; Oct-Sep): Some to most upperpart feathers, terts, and/or distal s covs juv and fresh in Oct-Dec (Fig. 375**A**), with buff fringing when fresh (Fig. 436**A**), contrasting with fresher and grayer formative scapulars, terts, and proximal s covs in Nov-Sep (Figs. 375**B-C** & 436**C**), the distal gr covs becoming worn and frayed by Apr-Sep (Figs. 375**D** & 436**B**); some formative proximal s covs often with thin buff fringes (Fig. 437**A**, p. 588); pp, p covs, and ss juv, relatively worn, and without s1-p1 contrast in Dec-Sep (Fig. 375**A**), the juv outer pp and p covs tapered (Figs. 377**A-B** & 378**A-B**, p. 506); all to some juv rects retained through Jan-Mar (often Apr-Sep), contrastingly narrow and worn (Fig. 379**A-D**, p. 507; perhaps occasionally including an alternate r1 as well; Fig. 17**D**, p. 25); bill dusky, often with dull yellowish to reddish base in Feb-Sep; legs olive to yellowish; ♂♂ with reduced to no elongated ornamental plumes in Apr-Aug. **Note: Some to most SYs remain to over-summer on non-breeding grounds and exhibit reduced PA1s and advanced PB2s. In addition, look for some ♀♀ to exhibit eccentric molt patterns (Fig. 376A, p. 504) in Mar-Sep.**

AHY/ASY (Def. cycle, DB-DA; Oct-Sep): Upperpart feathers, terts, and s covs basic or mixed basic and alternate/supplemental (Fig. 375**E-F**), the basic feathers with thin or indistinct whitish fringes (Fig. 436**C**); pp, p covs, and ss usually being replaced in Oct-Nov, fresher, and sometimes with slight s1-p1 contrast or suspension limit among p1-p6 in Nov-Sep (Fig. 375**E-F**), the outer pp and p covs broad and truncate (Figs. 377**C-D** & 378**C-D**); rects basic and broad (Fig. 379**E**), mixed with one or more (occasionally all) alternate c.rects in Apr-Sep (Fig. 379**F**); bill blackish with dull (Aug-Feb) to bright (Feb-Jul) orange to red at base; legs yellowish to reddish; ♂♂ usually with substantial elongated ornamental plumes in Apr-Aug. **Note: See Juv-HY/SY. Some to all ♂♂ with extensive and full ornamental plumes in Apr-Aug can probably be aged ASY/ATY but more study is needed. Although the color of ornamental-plumage aspect is correlated with size in ♂♂ (black > rufous > white), there appears to be no age effect (Höglund & Lundberg 1989). See footnote to Table 55 regarding "faeders".**

SY (2nd cycle, B2; Oct-Dec): Like AHY/ASY with molt of pp occurring, but outer pp and p covs juv, pointed and very abraded (Fig. 376**E**).

ASY ♂ (DB-DA; Oct-Dec): Like AHY/ASY with molt of pp occurring, but outer pp and p covs basic, broad and relatively fresh (Figs. 377**C-D** & 378**C-D**; *cf.* Fig. 376**E**). **Note: Most ♀♀ with these characters can probably be aged ASY as well but some SYs may have replaced outer pp in eccentric pattern during the PB2 and cannot be separated.**

Sex—Bilateral(?) BPs (Fig. 20**B**, p. 31) and/or distended cloaca (Fig. 21, p. 32) indicate ♀ in Apr-Jun. Measurements reliable for sexing (Table 55, p. 612).

♀: Wg chord < 165, tail < 61, tarsus < 46 (Table 55); upperparts and breast without elongated ornamental plumes in Apr-Aug. **Note: Some ♀♀ in Apr-Aug can show plumage aspect (presumably alternate) approaching that of the ornamental plumes in ♂♂; however, the feathers are not elongated. See also ♂.**

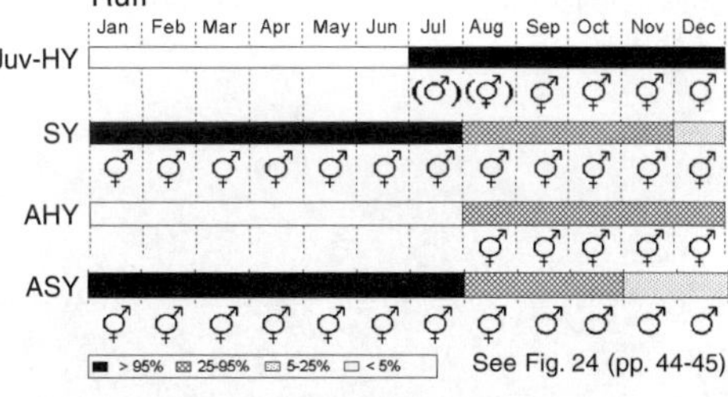

♂: Wg chord > 165, tail > 61, tarsus > 46 (Table 55); upperparts and breast of ASYs usually with elongated ornamental plumes in Apr-Aug. **Note: See ♀ and footnote to Table 55.**

Hybrids reported—Probably none in the wild (McCarthy 2006).

References—Bent (1929), Cramp & Simmons (1983), Dement'ev & Gladkov (1951c), Gill et al. (1995), Higgins & Davies (1996), Jukema & Piersma (2000, 2006), Karlionova et al. (2007), Koopman (1986), Oberholser (1974), Palmer (1967b), Prater et al. (1977), Ridgway (1919).

TABLE 55. Measurements (mm) of miscellaneous medium-sized shorebirds for identification and sexing. See pp. 4-11 for methods of measurement. Species summaries are in **bold** and subspecies summaries are in ***italics***. Values were derived from 95% confidence intervals as based approximately on the indicated sample sizes (see pp. 4-5). Thus, midpoints of ranges approximate means, and S.D. is approximated by 25% of the range.

Taxon/Sex	*n*	wing chord	tail length	exposed culmen	tarsus
Buff-breasted Sandpiper		**119-135**	**52-62**	**17.7-21.0**	**27-35**
♀	100	119-130	52-58	16.7-19.3	27-32
♂	100	126-135	55-62	18.4-21.0	30-35
Ruff[1]		**143-192**	**50-73**	**27.4-38.5**	**38-54**
♀	100	143-161	50-60	27.4-33.6	38-46
♂	100	171-192	62-73	31.7-38.5	46-54
Short-billed Dowitcher		**132-156**	**50-61**	**51.2-67.2**	**31-41**
L.g. caurinus		***141-156***	***52-61***	***52.7-67.2***	***33-40***
♀	100	142-156	54-61	56.8-67.2	34-40
♂	100	139-153	52-59	52.7-60.8	33-39
L.g. hendersoni		***137-152***	***51-59***	***53.4-66.6***	***34-41***
♀	60	139-152	53-59	58.3-66.6	35-41
♂	75	137-150	51-58	53.4-61.6	34-39
C.g. griseus		***132-147***	***50-59***	***51.2-63.2***	***31-37***
♀	55	134-147	52-59	56.1-63.2	32-37
♂	65	132-145	50-57	51.2-59.3	31-36
Long-billed Dowitcher		**133-152**	**51-61**	**58.0-77.9**	**35-45**
♀	100	137-152	53-61	68.2-77.9	38-45
♂	100	133-147	51-59	58.0-66.4	35-41
Wilson's Snipe		**118-135**	**50-62**	**57.3-70.3**	**28-33**
♀	100	118-133	50-59	59.6-70.3	29-33
♂	100	120-135	53-62	57.3-67.7	28-32
American Woodcock		**118-142**	**55-66**	**59.7-76.1**	**26-36**
♀	100	129-142	58-66	67.3-76.1	29-36
♂	100	118-129	55-63	59.7-68.3	26-33

[1] Smaller ♂ Ruffs (wg chord 163-173) are occasionally encountered and represent "faeders" which also may show ♀-like plumage aspect in May-Aug. See Jukema & Piersma 2006 and Karlionova et al. 2007 for more information.

Dowitchers *Scolopacidae, Scolopacinae, Limnodromini*

Two species. Tribal characters include medium-sized bodies with proportionally long and distally expanded bills, small hind toes (Fig. 373**B**, p. 500), and moderate webbing between outer (but not inner) fore toes (*cf.* Fig. 374**B-C**, p. 501). Dowitchers have 10 functional primaries (p10 longest by 1-6 mm, when fully grown), 15 secondaries (including 5 tertials, and one absent between the 4th and 5th; *cf.* Fig. 12**B**, p. 19), and 12 rectrices. Ageing can be accomplished through the first cycle (to SY and ASY) by plumage aspect and molt pattterns; sexes are similar in plumage aspect but differ in bill length (♀ > ♂). In molting, dowitchers exhibit the Complex Alternate Strategy (CAS; Fig. 10**F**, pp. 13-16) and, for the most part, follow a n.Hemisphere strategy (Table 45, pp. 501-505). Age of first breeding is 1-2 years. See pp. 500-507 for further information on molt and ageing in shorebirds.

SHORT-BILLED DOWITCHER SBDO
Limnodromus griseus Species # 2310

LONG-BILLED DOWITCHER LBDO
Limnodromus scolopaceus Species # 2320
Band size: 2

Species—From other N.Am shorebirds by medium size with proportionally long bills (Table 55), bill straight to slightly decurved and grayish to olive with dusky tip; lower back, rump, and uppertail covs white with variable black spotting or barring; p10 not edged whitish; rects distinctly barred black (Fig. 444, p. 614); underparts buff to cinnamon (Juvs), grayish and white (Oct-Mar), or variably washed orange-rufous (Apr-Sep); legs and feet olive to yellowish, with hind toe small but present (Fig. 373**B**, p. 500) and outer fore toes with slight to moderate webbing (Fig. 374**B-C**, p. 501). From Wilson's Snipe (p. 617) by longer wing and tarsus (Table 55); head and back without buff stripes; lower upperparts primarily white; tail with 12 rects, barred black and white (Fig. 444), the outer feather 8-10 mm wide.

Short-billed from Long-billed dowitcher, with caution (especially in basic, worn alternate, and transitional plumages), by shorter average bill and tarsus by sex (Table 55); wing tips usually > tail tip in natural closed position (*vs* usually < in Long-billed Dowitcher); white bars to outer rects average thicker and/or more irregular (Fig. 444**A-D** *vs* **C-F** in Long-billed Dowitcher); undertail covs with spots or sometimes with bars in Sep-Mar (*vs* with bars or occasionally spots in Long-billed Dowitcher); Juv (Jul-Dec) with back feathers, scapulars, and terts with variable buff to orange markings (Fig. 445**A-B**, p. 615) *vs* with pale fringes in Long-billed Dowitcher (Fig. 445**D**); gray breast usually spotted or mottled dusky in Sep-Mar (*vs* darker and more evenly colored in Long-billed); ASYs in Apr-Aug with lower scapulars tipped buff to orange (*vs* whitish in Long-billed Dowitcher), medial abdomen usually with whitish (see **Geographic variation**) and sometimes with distinct spots (*vs* usually uniformly rufous and with bars or without markings in Long-billed Dowitcher), alternate terts with more distinct orange bars (Fig. 445**C** *vs* **E** in Long-billed Dowitcher), and c.rects (*cf.* Fig. 444) usually basic and white and black (*vs* often alternate and black and rufous in Long-billed Dowitcher).

In addition, Short-billed Dowitcher may have larger primary extension (longest p – longest s ~15-30 mm *vs.* ~12-20 mm in Long-billed); further study needed. ASY Long-billed Dowitchers also undergo more extensive DPBs (including pp) at more northerly (often inland) stopover sites than Short-billed Dowitcher, thus showing grayer basic-plumage aspect during migration in N.Am (see **Molt**). See Chandler (1998), Conover (1941), Cramp & Simmons (1983), Jaramillo & Henshaw (1995), Jaramillo et al. (1991), Lee & Birch (2006), Newlon &

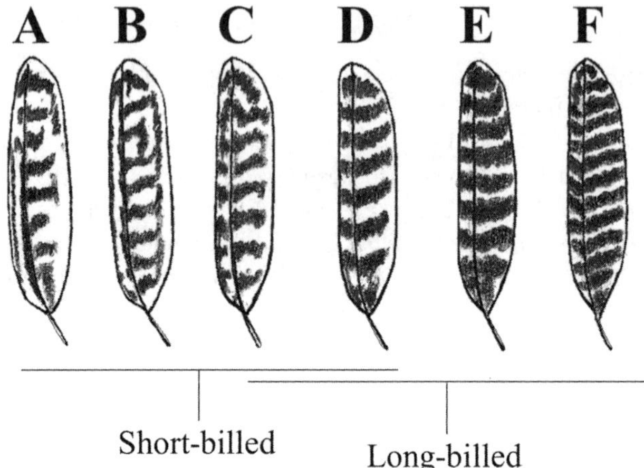

FIGURE 444. Pattern of dark and whitish to the rectrices (r6 shown) in Short-billed and Long-billed dowitchers for identification; note that Short-billed usually shows more whitish than dark and Long-billed usually shows more dark than whitish. These differences appear to be relatively consistent across feather generations (juv, formative, basic, and alternate). In Short-billed Dowitcher, the rectrices appear to vary by subspecies, averaging darkest in *L.g. caurinus* (**C-D**), intermediate in *hendersoni* (**B-C**), and palest in *griseus* (**A-B**).

Kent (1980), Oberholser (1974), O'Brien et al. (2006), Orr (1940), Paulson (1993, 2005), Putnam (2005), Rowan (1932), Wallace (1980), Wilds (1990), and Wilds & Newlon (1983) for more information on identifying dowitchers and for other, less-reliable, field marks.

Geographic variation—Long billed-Dowitcher is Monotypic. For Short-billed Dowitcher, see Aldrich (1948), Brodkorb (1933), Hellmayr & Conover (1948b), Jaramillo et al. (1991), Jaramillo & Henshaw (1995), Jehl (1963), Lee & Birch (2006), O'Brien et al. (2006), Orr (1940), Patten et al. (2003), Paulson (1993, 2005), Pitelka (1950), Pittaway (1992b), Rowan (1932), and Wilds (1990). Note that only a small proportion of Juvs and basic-aspect Short-billed Dowitchers can be identified; thus, non-breeding ranges, especially of *L.g. hendersoni* and *griseus*, are not well delineated; note also intergradation between these two e. subspecies.

Short-billed Dowitcher

L.g. caurinus (br s.AK-sw.Yuk & nw.BC, wint coastal CA-w.Mex): Averages larger (Table 55); Juv (Jul-Dec) with breast washed grayish; alternate-plumage aspect (Apr-Aug) with upperpart feathers fringed narrowly with whitish and rufous, face and underparts with bright cinnamon to rufous, abdomen with whitish mottling, and sides of breast and flanks with relatively heavy spotting and barring.

L.g. hendersoni (br nw.BC-e.Yuk to s.Nun-n.Ont, wint TX-FL-NC to S.Am): Medium-sized (Table 55); Juv (Jul-Dec) with breast washed buff to brownish; alternate-plumage aspect (Apr-Aug) with upperpart feathers fringed broadly with bright cinnamon to rufous, face and underparts with bright cinnamon to rufous (feathers fringed whitish when fresh), and sides of breast and flanks with relatively sparse spotting (occasionally barring).

L.g. griseus (br se.Nun-n.Ont to w.Lab, wint coastal VA-FL to S.Am): Averages smaller (Table 55); Juv (Jul-Dec) with breast washed buff to cinnamon; alternate-plumage aspect (Apr-Aug) with upperpart feathers fringed narrowly with whitish to pale cinnamon; breast cinnamon; face, throat, and abdomen whitish; and sides of breast and flanks with relatively heavy spotting to mottling.

Molt—CAS. PF partial-incomplete (Sep-Dec/Mar in HY/SYs), PA1 limited-partial (Mar-May in non-breeding SYs), PB2 complete (Jun-Oct in non-breeding SYs), DPA partial-incomplete (Feb-Apr in breeding ASYs), DPB complete (Jul-Nov in breeding ASYs). The PF often begins

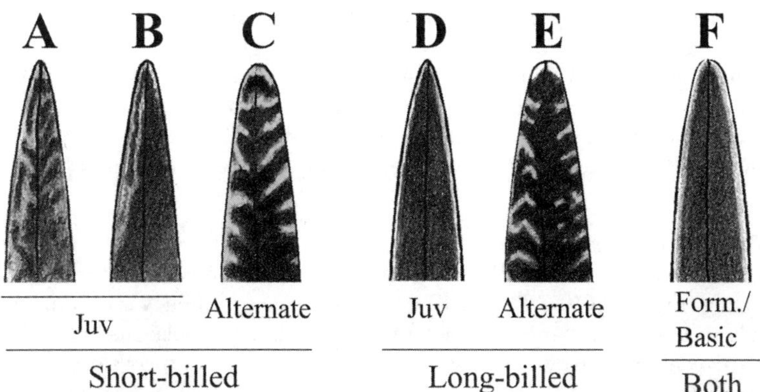

FIGURE 445. Shape and pattern to the tertials by species and feather generation in Short-billed and Long-billed dowitchers. During the PF in HY/SYs, the juv terts (**A-B**, **D**) are often (Short-billed Dowitcher) to sometimes (Long-billed Dowitcher) replaced with formative terts (**F**) in Oct-Jan. SYs retain juv and/or formative terts through the PB2 in Jun-Oct but ASYs usually replace most to all with alternate terts (**C**, **E**) during the DPA in Feb-Apr. Formative and basic terts are similar in both species (**F**).

on breeding grounds or at stopover sites and completes on non-breeding grounds, and the DPA begins on non-breeding grounds but can complete at stopover sites or breeding grounds. The DPB can begin on breeding grounds (body feathers only) and can complete at stopover sites (farther N and at inland locations in Long-billed Dowitcher *vs* farther S and at coastal locations in Short-billed Dowitcher) or on non-breeding grounds. Molt follows a n.Hemisphere strategy in most individuals, although occasional Short-billed Dowitchers with S.Am non-breeding grounds appear to follow a s.Hemisphere strategy (Table 45, pp. 501-505). The PF includes most to all body feathers, a few to some proximal s covs, and often (Short-billed Dowitcher) to sometimes (Long-billed Dowitcher) 1-4 terts and 1-4 c.rects (up to all rects in Short-billed Dowitcher). Occasional Short-billed Dowitchers can also replace 1-5 outer pp and 1-2 medial ss (distal to the terts) in eccentric sequence in Jan-Mar (Fig. 376**A**, p. 504). The PA1 includes some body feathers but few to no s covs, terts, or c.rects. The DPA includes most to all body feathers, a few to most proximal s covs, 2-4 terts and occasionally (Short-billed Dowitcher) to usually (Long-billed Dowitcher) 1-4 c.rects. Some to many SYs and probably some TYs (especially among Short-billed Dowitchers) over-summer on non-breeding grounds and average less-complete (or no) PA1s and advanced PB2s (see p. 18). See pp. 500-507 for more information on molt in shorebirds.

Age—Juv (B1; Jul-Nov) has uniformly fresh plumage aspect, the back feathers, terts, and s covs with variable (by species) cinnamon to rufous fringing (Figs. 436**A**, p. 587, & 445**A**-**B**, **D**), the pp and ss uniformly juv and fresh (Fig. 375**A**, p. 503), and the breast washed gray, buff, or cinnamon (see **Geographic variation**); Juv ♀ = ♂.

Juv-HY/SY (1st cycle, Juv/B1-F1-A1; Oct-Sep): Upperpart feathers, terts, and/or distal s covs juv and fresh in Oct-Nov (Fig. 375**A**), with variable whitish to cinnamon fringing when fresh (Figs. 436**A** & 445**A**-**B**, **D**), contrasting with fresher and grayish formative humerals, terts, and proximal s covs in Nov-Sep (Figs. 375**B**-**C**, 436**C**, & 445**F**), the distal gr covs becoming worn and frayed by Apr-Sep (Figs. 375**D** & 436**B**); some formative proximal s covs brownish with cinnamon to rufous tips (Fig. 437**A**, p. 588); pp and medial ss juv and without s1-p1 contrast (Fig. 375**A**), the outer pp and p covs relatively tapered and worn (Figs. 377**A**-**B** & 378**A**-

B, p. 506); all to some juv rects usually retained, contrastingly narrow and worn (Fig. 379**A-D**, p. 507); plumage aspect often with no to reduced bright reddish and terts without alternate feathers (*cf.* Fig. 445**C**, **E**) in Mar-Aug (see **Species** and **Geographic variation**). **Note: Some to most SYs over-summer on non-breeding grounds. Occasional SY Short-billed Dowitchers (with S.Am non-breeding grounds) replace the outer 1-3 pp and medial 1-2 ss during the PF and exhibit eccentric replacement patterns in Mar-Sep (Fig. 376A, p. 504).**

AHY/ASY (Def. cycle, DB-DA; Oct-Sep): Upperpart feathers, terts, and s covs basic or mixed basic and alternate (Fig. 375**E-F**), the basic feathers brownish gray with thin or indistinct pale fringing (Figs. 436**C**, 437**B**, & 445**F**); pp, p covs, and ss often worn and being replaced in Oct-Nov (Oct-Feb in S.Am), or basic, fresh, and with slight replacement clines and sometimes s1-p1 contrast in Nov-Sep (Fig. 375**E**), the outer pp and p covs broad and truncate (Figs. 377**C-D** & 378**C-D**); rects basic and broad (Fig. 379**E**), occasionally (Short-billed Dowitcher) to usually (Long-billed Dowitcher) with 1-4 reddish and dark alternate c.rects in Apr-Sep (Fig. 379**F**); upperparts and underparts usually with substantial reddish in Apr-Aug. **Note: See Juv-HY/SY**.

Sex— ♀ = ♂ by plumage aspect. Bilateral or medial(?) BPs (Fig. 20**A-B**, p. 31) developed by both sexes but distended cloaca (Fig. 21, p. 32) indicates ♀ in May-Jul. Except for bill length, measurements largely unhelpful for sexing (Table 55, p. 612). Some to many Short-billed Dowitchers (especially mated pairs of known subspecies) can be sexed by exposed culmen length (Table 55) whereas the following is reliable for sexing Long-billed Dowitchers:

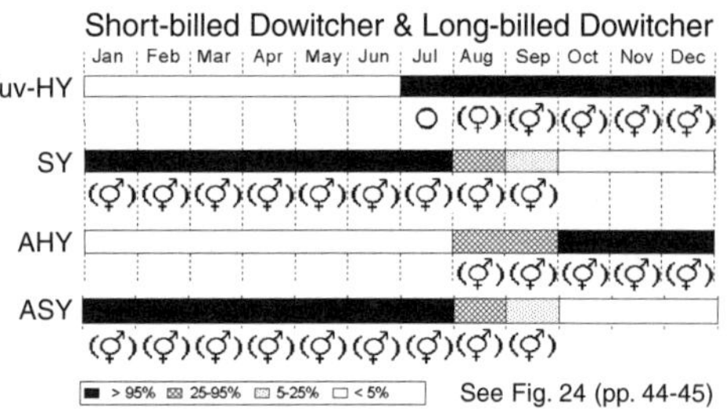

Long-billed Dowitcher

♀: Exposed culmen > 67.5 (Table 55).

♂: Exposed culmen < 67.5 (Table 55).

Hybrids reported—None; however, hybrids between the two dowitchers would be difficult to confirm.

References—Alexander & Gratto-Trevor (1997), Bent (1927), Chandler (1998), Cramp & Simmons (1983), Dunn (1999), Jehl et al. (2001), Kaufman (1990a), Lee & Birch (2006), Loftin (1962), McLaughlin & Pittaway (2003), McNeil (1970), Oberholser (1974), Palmer (1967b), Pitelka (1950), Prater et al. (1977), Putnam (2005), Ridgway (1919), Roberts (1955), Takekawa & Warnock (2000), Winger (2003).

Snipe *Scolopacidae, Scolopacinae, Gallinagini*

One species. Tribal characters include medium-sized bodies, proportionally long bills, and short legs with hind toe present (Fig. 373**C**, p. 500) and no webbing between the fore toes (Fig. 374**A**, p. 501). North American snipe have 10 functional primaries (p10 usually the longest, extending 2 mm shorter to 3 mm longer than p9, when fully grown), 14 secondaries (including 4 tertials, and one absent between the 4th and 5th; *cf.* Fig. 12**B**, p. 19), and 16 (rarely 14) rectrices. Ageing can be accomplished through the first cycle (to SY and ASY) in most individuals by plumage aspect and molt patterns; sexes are similar in size but differ in the characteristics of the outer rectrix. In molting, snipes exhibit the Complex Alternate Strategy (CAS; Fig. 10**F**, pp. 13-16) and follow a n.Hemisphere strategy (Table 45, pp. 501-505). Age of first breeding is typically 1 year. See pp. 500-507 for further information on molt and ageing in shorebirds.

WILSON'S SNIPE
Gallinago delicata

WISN
Species # 2300
Band size: 3

Species—From other N.Am shorebirds, including dowitchers (p. 613), by medium-small size with proportionally long bill and short legs (Table 55, p. 612); bill straight, tapered at tip, and grayish olive to brownish with a dusky tip; scapulars with broad white edging to outer webs forming distinct back stripes; ss (Fig. 446) and s covs (Fig. 448, p. 619) with distinct white tips; p10 edged whitish; tail typically with 16 rects (occasionally 14), the outer feather narrow (Figs. 446 & 449, p. 619); auriculars buff with distinct brown stripes; breast buff with brown mottling; legs and feet pale olive, with hind toe present (Fig. 373**C**, p. 500) and without webbing between fore toes (Fig. 374**A**, p. 501).

Pin-tailed Snipe (*G. stenura*), a vagrant to AK, has shorter bill and tail and longer average tarsus (wg chord 120-135, tl 44-51, exp culmen 53-68, tarsus 30-35); lower scapulars fringed pale brown (*vs* whitish to buff in Wilson's Snipe); ss with indistinct or no pale tips and tail with 24-28 rects, the outer rect very narrow and with distinct subterminal band (Fig. 446**A**). Common Snipe (*G. gallinago*) of Eurasia, a vagrant to w.AK and Lab, has ss with wider white

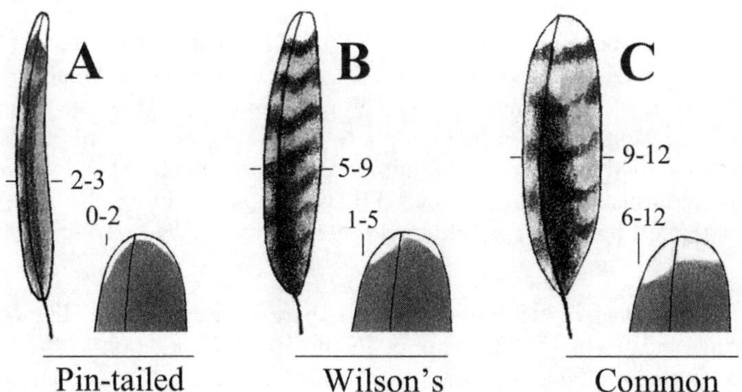

FIGURE 446. Pattern and shape to the outer rectrix and medial secondaries (s7 shown) in Pin-tailed, Wilson's, and Common snipes for identification. Measures indicate width of the outer rect at widest point and extent of white along the outer web at the shaft of s7. Note that the outer rect is usually r12-r14 in Pin-tailed Snipe (24-28 rects), r8 in Wilson's Snipe (usually 16 rects), and r7 in Common Snipe (14 rects). These differences hold for both juv and basic feathers; the outer rect is typically shorter and broader in ♀♀ than in ♂♂ by species (*cf.* Fig. 449, p. 619).

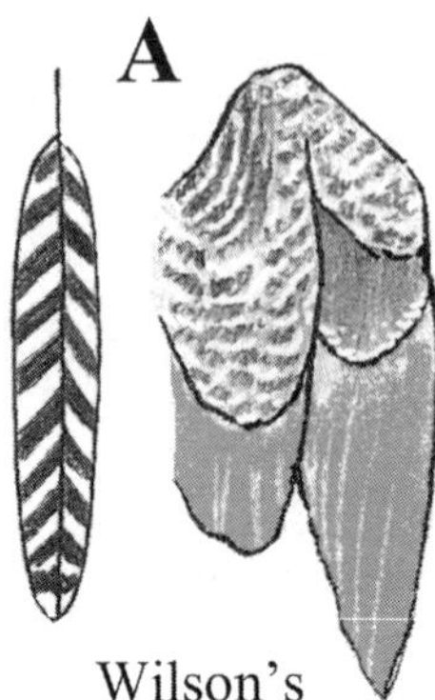

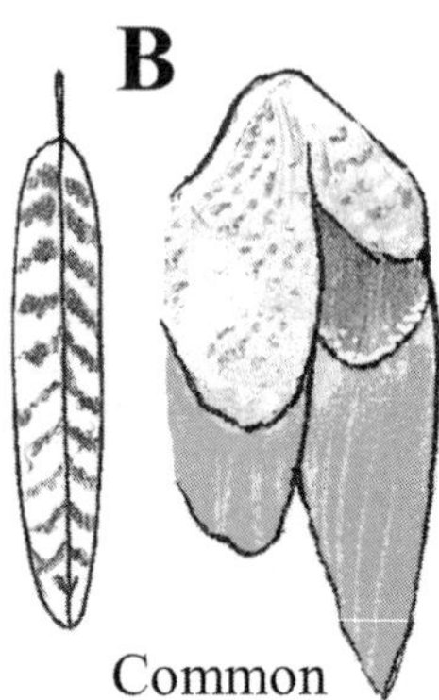

FIGURE 447. Pattern of blackish and whitish to the longest axillar (left) and the underwing (right) in Wilson's and Common snipes for identification. Typical examples are shown; caution that some Common Snipes vary toward overlap with the patterns of Wilson's Snipe. The proximal underwing med and gr covs tend to exhibit the greatest differences, being barred like the rest of the underwing in Wilson's Snipe and approaching bright white in Common Snipe.

tips (Fig. 446**C**); tail typically with 14 rects (rarely 16; *vs* usually 16 and rarely 14 in Wilson's Snipe), the outer feather broader and with less-distinct barring (Fig. 446**C**); axillars and proximal underwing s covs variably but usually broadly tipped white resulting in whitish underwing with irregular dark markings (Fig. 447**B**), *vs* dusky with narrow bars or tips resulting in even white bars in Wilson's Snipe (Fig. 447**A**). See Bland (1998, 1999), Carey & Olsson (1995), Dunn & Alderfer (2007), Gibson (1978), Leader (1999), Oberholser (1921), Portenko (1972), Prater et al. (1977), Ridgway (1919), Todd (1963), and Tuck (1972) for more information, including additional plumage-aspect differences that generally are confounded by individual variation.

Geographic variation—Monotypic; formerly considered a subspecies of *C. gallinago* (see **Species**).

Molt—CAS. PF partial-incomplete (Jul-Dec in HYs), DPA partial (Feb-May in AHYs), DPB complete (Jul-Nov in AHYs). The PF and DPB usually commence on breeding grounds and complete at stopover sites or on non-breeding grounds, and the DPA occurs primarily on non-breeding grounds. Molt follows a n.Hemisphere strategy (Table 45, pp. 501-505). The PF includes most to all body feathers (some humerals often retained), a few to some proximal s covs, 1-3 terts, and usually 1-6 c.rects. The DPB averages earlier in ♂♂ than in ♀♀. The DPA includes some to most body feathers and sometimes a few medial s covs, but few if any terts or rects.

Age—Juv (B1; Jul-Oct) has distinct buff tips to upperpart feathers (*cf.* Fig. 448**A-B**) and pp and ss uniformly juv and fresh (Fig. 375**A**, p. 503); Juv ♀=♂. In addition to the following, see McCloskey & Thompson (2000) for DFAs (p. 5) using lengths of the outer rect, r3, p5, p8, p10, and s1, and width of r1, r2, and r3, that reliably aged 70-84% of freshly dead individuals from non-breeding grounds in TX.

HY/SY (1st cycle, F1-A1; Oct-Sep): Some to most s covs juv, rounded, with complete buff to whitish tips (Fig. 448**A-B**), contrasting with fresher replaced humerals, terts, and/or proximal s covs in Oct-Apr (Fig. 375**B-C**), the distal s covs becoming worn and frayed by Apr-Sep (Fig.

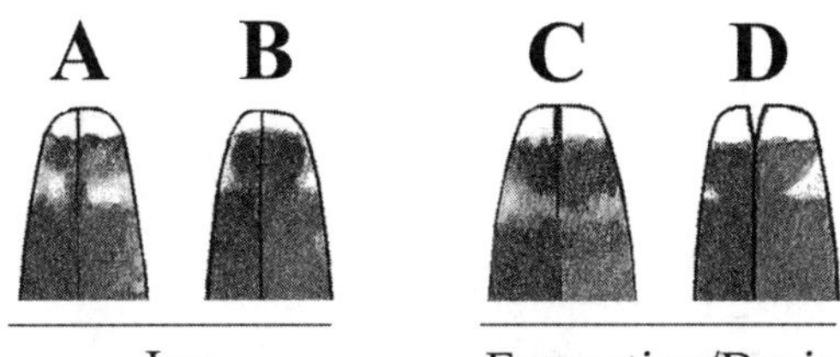

FIGURE 448. Shape and pattern to the secondary coverts by feather generation in Wilson's Snipe. Most juv s covs are usually retained during the PF, including some proximal feathers (*cf.* Fig. 437, p. 588), which usually are more protected and retain differences between HY/SY (**A-B**) and AHY/ASY (**C-D**) through spring and summer. Note the broader shaft streak, often split, on the formative/basic feathers. Caution that these differences can be subtle and many individuals may not be reliably aged, especially without experience.

375**D**); pp, p covs, and ss juv (Fig. 375**A**), the outer pp and p covs tapered, brownish, and relatively worn (Figs. 377**A-B** & 378**A-B**, p. 506); all to some juv rects usually retained, contrastingly narrow and worn (*cf.* Fig. 379**A-D**, p. 507; note unique shape to rects in this species; Figs. 446 & 449). **Note: Many intermediates occur which may not be reliably aged. See also AHY/ASY.**

AHY/ASY (Def. cycle, DB-DA; Oct-Sep): S covs uniformly basic or mixed basic and alternate (Fig. 375**E-F**), squared, with white tips usually interrupted by shaft streak and/or split at tip (Fig. 448**C-D**); pp, p covs, and ss basic (Fig. 375**E**), the outer pp and p covs broad, truncate, and relatively fresh (Figs. 379**C-D** & 378**C-D**); rects uniformly basic (*cf.* Fig. 379**E**; see HY/SY). **Note: See HY/SY. Contrasts among the humerals (*cf.* Fig. 375B) should be looked for and may indicate AHYs with suspended molt (*vs.* HYs) in Aug-Oct (Kaczmarek et al. 2007); more study needed.**

Sex—♀=♂ by plumage aspect. Bilateral(?) or medial(?) BPs (Fig. 20**A-B**, p. 31) and/or distended cloaca (Fig. 21, p. 32) indicate ♀ in May-Jul. Measurements largely unhelpful for sexing (Table 55, p. 612). See McCloskey & Thompson (2000) for DFAs (p. 5) using lengths of the outer rect, s1, p5, p10, and culmen, that reliably sexed 85-91% of freshly dead individuals from non-breeding grounds in TX. The following is reliable for separating many (but not all) individuals.

♀: Outer rect (usually r8) broader, shorter, and with 5-6 dark bars (Fig. 449**A**). **Note: Individuals with outer rect 47-49 mm in length are probably not reliably sexed.**

♂: Outer rect (usually r8) narrower, longer, and with 6-8 dark bars (Fig. 449**B**). **Note: See ♀.**

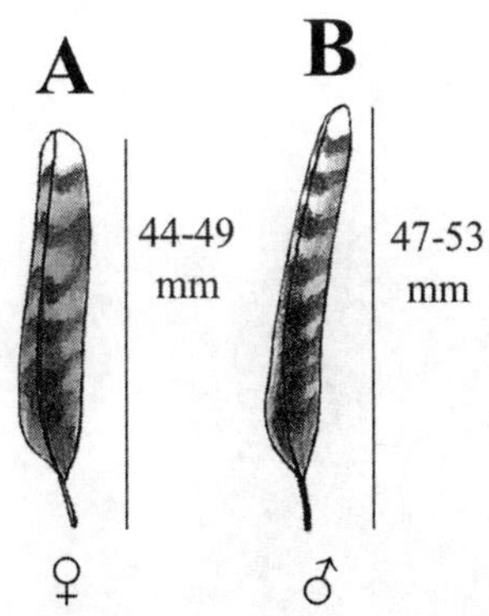

FIGURE 449. Size and shape of the outer rectrix (usually r8 but sometimes r7) by sex in Wilson's Snipe. The measure pertains to the length of the feather from point of insertion. Note also that ♀♀ usually show 5-6 dark bars and ♂♂ show 6-8 dark bars. Some intermediates (with length 47-49 mm and 6 dark bars) may be difficult to sex: combine with age; these are likely AHY/ASY ♀♀ or HY/SY ♂♂.

Hybrids reported—None.

References—Arnold (1972b), Bent (1927), Cramp & Simmons (1983), Dwyer & Dobell (1979), Hellmayr & Conover (1948b), Kaczmarek et al. (2007), McCloskey & Thompson (2000), Mueller (1999), Oberholser (1974), Palmer (1967b), Perry et al. (1972), Prater et al. (1977), Ridgway (1919), Roberts (1955), Sloan (1967), Tuck (1972).

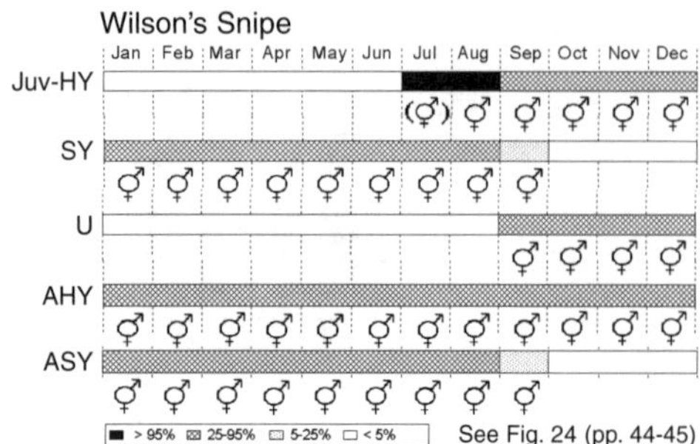

Woodcocks *Scolopacidae, Scolopacinae, Scolopacini*

One species. Tribal characters include medium-sized bodies with proportionally short and rounded wings (Fig. 450), long bills, and short legs with hind toe present (Fig. 373**C**, p. 500) and no webbing between fore toes (Fig. 374**A**, p. 501). North American Woodcocks have 10 functional primaries (p10 extending 5-10 mm short of the longest pp, p6-p7, when fully grown), 15 secondaries (including 3 tertials and none absent, unlike other shorebirds; *cf.* Fig. 12**B**, p. 19), and 12-14 rectrices. Ageing can be accomplished through the first cycle (to SY and ASY) by plumage aspect and molt patterns. Sexes are similar in plumage aspect but can be separated by size (♀ > ♂) and the shape of p10 (narrower in ♂ than ♀). In molting, Woodcocks exhibit the Complex Basic Strategy (CBS; Fig. 10**B**, pp. 13-16) and follow a n.Hemisphere strategy (Table 45, pp. 501-505). Age of first breeding is typically 1 year. See pp. 500-507 for further information on molt and ageing in shorebirds.

AMERICAN WOODCOCK
Scolopax minor

AMWO
Species # 2280
Band size: 3

Species—From other N.Am shorebirds by proportionally short wings, long bill, and short legs (Table 55, p. 612; Fig. 450); p8-p10 attenuated (Figs. 450 & 451, p. 622); bill straight, with overhanging upper mandible; pp, ss, and underparts without bars; medial ss brown with buff to cinnamon markings (Fig. 450**A**, **C**); tail with 12-14 rects, dark gray at tips; legs with hind toe present (Fig. 373**C**, p. 500) and without webbing between fore toes (Fig. 374**A**, p. 501). Eurasian Woodcock (*S. rusticola*), a former vagrant to e.N.Am, is larger (wg chord 179-200, tl 79-100, exp culmen 70-79, tarsus 33-39); p8-p10 full in length and p9-p10 longest; outer rect broader (13-15 mm wide vs 6-9 mm in American Woodcock); pp, ss, outer rects, and underparts distinctly barred.

Geographic variation—Monotypic.

Molt—CBS. PF incomplete (Jul-Oct in HYs), DPB complete (Jun-Oct in AHYs), PA absent. The PF and DPB occur primarily on breeding grounds. The PF includes most to all body

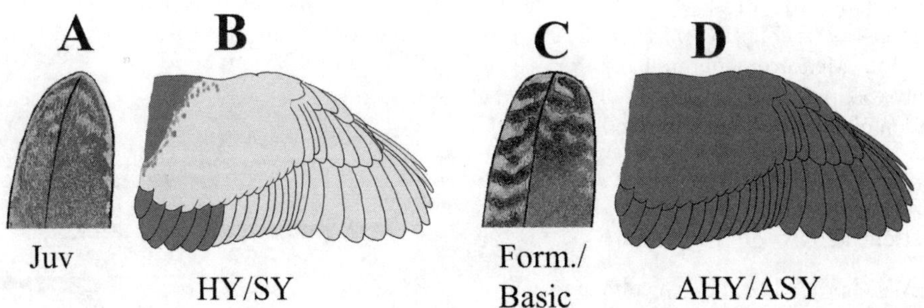

FIGURE 450. Medial ss (s9 shown) by feather generation, and molt limits within the wings by age, in American Woodcock. This species has a unique pattern to the PF among Scolopacidae, perhaps related to its being the only eutaxic (non-diastataxic) shorebird (*cf.* Fig. 12**B**, p. 19). The PF typically includes some proximal s covs and 4-9 proximal ss (**A**). The juv medial ss (**A**; among s8-s12) are less distinctly marked than formative and basic medial ss (**B**), such that HY/SYs can be identified by the limit between the two types of ss. Note also the unique wing morphology (p6-p7 longest *vs* p9-p10 longest in other shorebirds) and shape to the outer pp (*cf.* also Fig. 451, p. 622).

feathers, a few proximal s covs, 4-9 proximal ss, and most to all rects; 1-6 outer rects occasionally retained.

Age—Juv (B1; Jun-Oct) has duller plumage aspect, the upperpart feathers distinctly fringed buff to cinnamon, pp and ss uniformly juv and fresh (*cf.* Fig. 375**A**, p. 503), and throat usually with dark-gray band; Juv ♀=♂ but measures can be used to sex full-grown juvs (see **Sex**). See Greeley (1953) and Martin (1964) for information on use of the bursa (Fig. 23, p. 34) to age fresh dead individuals.

HY/SY (1st cycle, F1; Oct-Sep): Most distal juv s covs retained, washed cinnamon, contrasting with formative, fresher and duskier proximal covs and humerals (Fig. 450**B**, p. 621); molt limit occurs among s5-s16 (Fig. 450**B**), the distal ss retained juvenal, brown with buff fringing (Fig. 450**A**), contrasting with replaced proximal ss dusky with cinnamon markings (Fig. 450**C**); outer pp and p covs relatively tapered at tip by sex, brownish, and worn (Fig. 451**A**, **C**); 1-6 outer rects, occasionally retained (*cf.* Fig. 379**C**, p. 507), contrastingly worn. Beware of pseudolimits (p. 19) among inner terts and humerals, feathers with more black appearing fresher.

AHY/ASY (Def. cycle, DB; Oct-Sep): S covs and ss uniformly basic (Fig. 450**D**), the s covs dusky and gray with cinnamon vermiculations, and the medial ss uniformly dusky with cinnamon markings (Fig. 450**C**); outer pp and p covs relatively broad, dusky, and fresh (Fig. 451**B**, **D**); rects uniformly basic (*cf.* Fig. 379**E**). **Note: See HY/SY.**

FIGURE 451. Shape and coloration of p10 by age and sex in American Woodcock; in each sex juv feathers (**A**, **C**), paler and more tapered at tip, are shown to the left of basic feathers (**B**, **D**), darker and blunter at tip. The measure indicates the width at the narrowest point; the indicated difference by sex holds for both juv and basic feathers. Note also that the cumulative sum of this width value in p8, p9, and p10 (measured 20 mm proximal to tip) is > 12.5 mm in ♀♀ and < 12.5 mm in ♂♂.

Sex—♀=♂ by plumage aspect. Poorly developed medial BP (Fig. 20**A**, p. 31) and/or distended cloaca (Fig. 21, p. 32) indicate ♀ in Apr-Jul. Measurements reliable for sexing (Table 55, p. 612). See Glasgow (1957) for the design of a sex-determination tool.

♀: Wg chord > 129 and exp culmen usually > 68 (Table 55); outer pp broader and less attenuated by age (Fig. 451**A**-**B**).

♂: Wg chord < 129 and exp culmen usually < 68 (Table 55); outer pp narrower and more attenuated by age (Fig. 451**C**-**D**).

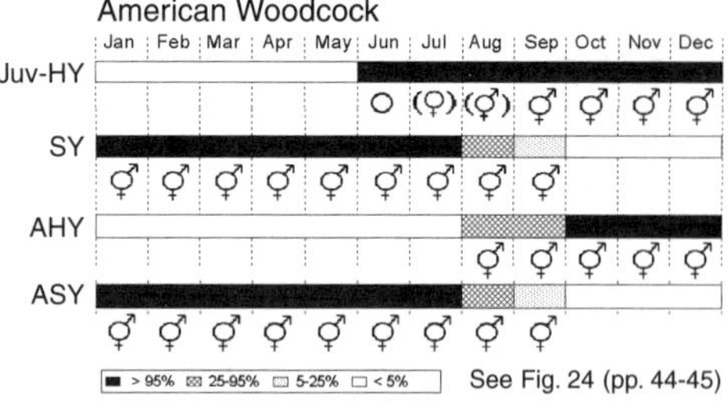

Hybrids reported—None.

References—Artmann & Schroeder (1976), Bent (1927), Blankenship (1957), Clark (1978), Duvall (1955), Dwight (1900b), Greeley (1953), Keppie & Redmond (1988), Keppie & Whiting (1994), Martin (1964), McAuley et al. (1993), Mendall & Aldous (1943), Oberholser (1974), Owen & Krohn (1973), Palmer (1967b), Petrides (1950), Pettingill (1936), Prater et al. (1977), Ridgway (1919), Roberts (1955), Sheldon (1967), Sheldon et al. (1958), Tufts (1940).

Phalaropes *Scolopacidae, Phalaropodinae*

Three species. Subfamily characters include medium-small to small bodies, laterally compressed tarsi with distinctly lobed toes (Fig. 452), and dense feathering to abdomens for floatation purposes. Phalaropes have 10 functional primaries (p10 usually the longest, extending 1 mm to 4 mm > p9, when fully grown), 14 secondaries (including 4 tertials and one absent between the 4th and 5th; *cf.* Fig. 12**B**, p. 19), and 12 rectrices. Ageing can be accomplished through the first cycle (to SY and ASY), and sometimes into the second cycle (to TY and ATY) through the following winter. Sexes can be separated by plumage aspect in Apr-Aug (♀♀ brighter than ♂♂) and by measurements in two species (♀♀ larger); bilateral brood patches (Fig. 20**B**, p. 31) are developed by males only (*cf.* Johns 1964, Johns & Pfeiffer 1963). In molting, phalaropes exhibit the Complex Alternate Strategy (CAS; Fig. 10**F**, pp. 13-16) and most follow a s.Hemisphere strategy (Table 45, pp. 501-505), although some Red Phalaropes (p. 627) can follow a n.Hemisphere strategy. Age of first breeding is 1-2 years. See pp. 500-507 for further information on molt and ageing in shorebirds.

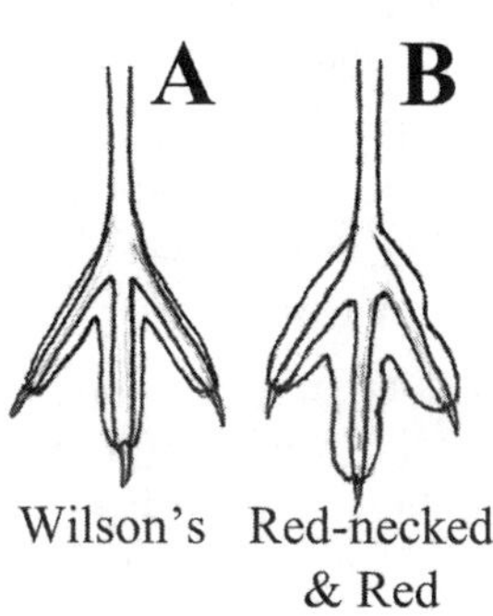

FIGURE 452. Diagrammatic illustration indicating toe webbing by species in phalaropes. Note that the proximal point of webbing extends less than half the length of the outer toe in Wilson's Phalarope (**A**) but more than half the length in Red-necked and Red phalaropes (**B**).

WILSON'S PHALAROPE
Phalaropus tricolor

WIPH
Species # 2240
Band size: 1A-2

Species—From other shorebirds and phalaropes by medium-small size with proportionally long tarsus (Table 56, p. 624); bill straight, thin, tapered at tip, and black with greenish tinge to base; upperpart feathers dusky with broad buff fringes (Juv), pale gray with narrow white fringes when fresh (Sep-Mar), or variably brownish or gray and rufous (most AHYs in Apr-Aug), the lateral rump feathers and medial uppertail covs white (Fig. 438**C**, p. 594); ss and gr covs completely grayish with little or no white (no wing stripe); underwing s covs white; outer rects white with gray subterminal fringe; legs and feet dull greenish yellow (Juv and Sep-Mar) to black (AHY in Apr-Aug), with hind toe present (Fig. 373**C**, p. 500) and fore toes narrowly flanged with moderately extensive webbing (Fig. 452**A**). From Stilt Sandpiper (p. 607) in basic plumage aspect by shorter wing, bill, and tarsus (Table 56); bill thinner (< 4 mm deep at base); back and s covs without dark shaft streaks; breast white, without indistinct dusky streaks.

Geographic variation—Monotypic.

Molt—CAS. PF incomplete-complete? (Sep-Mar in HY/SYs), PA1 limited (Apr-May in non-breeding SYs), PB2 complete (May-Nov in non-breeding SYs), DPA partial (Mar-May in breeding AHYs), DPB complete (Jun-Nov/Feb in breeding AHY/ASYs). The PF and DPB commence at stopover sites and complete on non-breeding grounds, and the DPA occurs on non-breeding grounds. Molt follows a s.Hemisphere strategy (Table 45, pp. 501-505). The PF includes some to all body feathers, all s covs, terts, and rects, and 2-7 outer pp and p covs and 1-5 medial ss (distal to the terts) in eccentric sequence (Fig. 476**A-C**, p. 504; occasionally arrested); body feathers, terts, and c.rects are replaced primarily in Sep-Oct on stopover grounds whereas pp, ss, and outer rects are replaced primarily in Jan-Mar on non-breeding grounds. Occasional HY/SYs may have a complete PF (more study needed). The PB2 and DPB include most to all body feathers and up to 6 pp, the terts, and 6 c.rects during Jun-Aug at stopover sites (SYs and ♀♀ average earlier and more pp replaced at stopover locations than ASYs and ♂♂), followed by suspension for migration and completion during Dec-Feb on non-breeding grounds. The DPA includes some to all head, back, and breast feathers but few if any s covs, terts, or c.rects. Some SYs over-summer on non-breeding grounds and exhibit less-complete (or no) PA1s and advanced PB2s (see p. 18).

Age—Juv (B1; Jul-Oct) has uniformly fresh plumage aspect, upperpart feathers, s covs, and rects with dusky centers and broad buff fringing, pp and ss uniformly juv and fresh (Fig. 375**A**, p. 503), and legs yellowish; Juv ♀=♂ by plumage aspect.

HY/SY (1st cycle, F1-A1; Oct-Sep): All to some s covs and terts juv in Oct-Dec (Fig. 375**A-C**), distinctly fringed buff to whitish; pp, p covs, and ss juv, fresh, and without s1-p1 contrast in Oct-Dec (Fig. 375**A**), being incompletely replaced in Jan-Mar and exhibiting eccentric replacement patterns in Apr-Sep (Fig. 376**A-C**, p. 504; occasionally arrested), the juv outer pp and p covs (when present) narrow and relatively abraded (Figs. 377**A-B** & 378**A-B**, p. 506); plumage aspect in Apr-Sep averages less-extensive gray and rufous by sex (see **Sex**). **Note: See AHY/ASY and ASY.**

AHY/ASY (Def. cycle, DB-DA; Oct-Sep): S covs and terts uniformly basic (Fig. 375**E**), brownish gray with thin or no pale fringing; pp, p covs, and ss basic, being completely replaced in Oct-Feb, and showing replacement clines, s1-p1 contrast, and/or suspension limits among p1-p6 in Feb-Sep (Figs. 375**E** & 376**F**), the outer pp and p covs broad and truncate (Figs. 377**C-D** & 378**C-D**) plumage aspect in Apr-Sep averages more-extensive gray and rufous by sex. **Note: A small proportion of HY/SYs may have a complete PF, becoming indistinguishable from ASYs in Apr-Sep; more study is needed.**

ASY (Def. cycle, DB; Oct-Dec): Like AHY/ASY but molt of pp occurring and suspension limits (Fig. 376**F**) present between p1 and p6. **Note: Distinguishing suspension limits from eccentric patterns can be difficult (see Fig. 376); some intermediates are best aged AHY in Feb-Sep.**

Sex—Bilateral(?) BPs (Fig. 20**B**, p. 31) indicate ♂ and distended cloaca (Fig. 21, p. 32) indicates ♀ in May-Jul. Measurements useful for sexing (Table 56); in addition to the following, see Jehl

TABLE 56. Measurements (mm) of North American phalaropes for identification and sexing. See pp. 4-11 for methods of measurement. Species summaries are in **bold**. Values were derived from 95% confidence intervals as based approximately on the indicated sample sizes (see pp. 4-5). Thus, midpoints of ranges approximate means, and S.D. is approximated by 25% of the range.

Taxon/Sex	*n*	wing chord	tail length	exposed culmen	tarsus
Wilson's Phalarope		**114-138**	**47-60**	**27.7-35.7**	**29-36**
♀	100	126-138	53-60	30.5-35.7	31-36
♂	100	114-126	47-54	27.7-32.5	29-34
Red-necked Phalarope		**101-117**	**44-54**	**19.7-24.1**	**18-22**
♀	100	105-117	46-54	20.5-24.1	18-22
♂	100	101-112	44-52	19.7-23.6	18-21
Red Phalarope		**119-139**	**58-72**	**19.8-24.9**	**19-23**
♀	100	128-139	61-72	20.6-24.9	20-23
♂	100	119-131	58-68	19.8-24.0	19-23

(1987a) for reliable formulae for sexing using wing chord, exposed culmen, and tarsus on live individuals.

♀: Wing chord > 126 (Table 56); ASYs and many SYs in Mar-Aug with upperparts and nape bright gray and rufous.

♂: Wing chord < 126; AHYs in Apr-Sep with upperparts brownish to dusky, often with dull rufous to sides of nape.

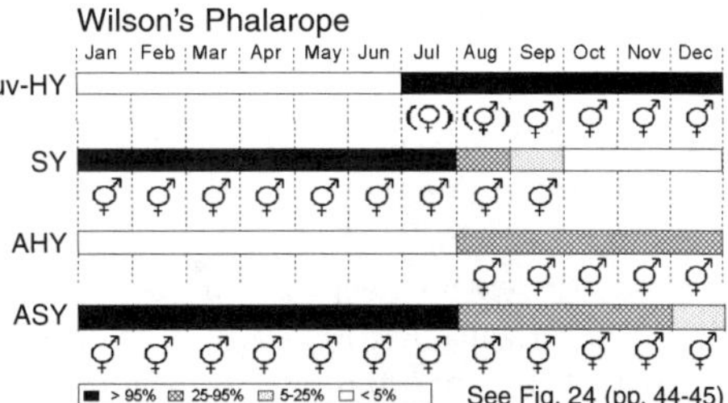

Hybrids reported—None.

References—Alexander & Gratto-Trevor (1997), Bent (1927), Burger & Howe (1975), Colwell & Jehl (1994), Cramp & Simmons (1983), Higgins & Davies (1996), Jehl (1987a, 1988), Murphy (1936), Oberholser (1974), Palmer (1967b), Prater et al. (1977), Ridgway (1919), Roberts (1955).

RED-NECKED PHALAROPE

Phalaropus lobatus

RNPH
Species # 2230
Band size: 1B

Species—From other shorebirds and phalaropes by small size with proportionally short legs (Table 56, p. 624); bill straight, thin, tapered at tip, and black; upperpart feathers black with tawny and gray fringes (Juv and AHY ♂ in Apr-Aug), gray and black with whitish fringes (Sep-Mar), or primarily dark gray (AHY ♀ in Mar-Aug), the rump and medial uppertail covs dark (Fig. 438**A**, p. 594); gr covs with broad white tips and medial ss (s9-s12) whitish, forming wing stripe; underwing s covs white; outer rects gray with thin white fringes; legs and feet dull dusky pinkish (Juv and Sep-Mar) to black (AHY in Apr-Aug), with hind toe present (Fig. 373**C**, p. 500) and fore toes broadly lobed with extensive webbing (Fig. 452**B**, p. 623).

From Red Phalarope (p. 627) by shorter wing and tail (Table 56); bill thinner (depth at distal end of nares 2.0-2.8 mm), tapered at tip, and without pale base; Juv with back feathers fringed tawny, forming distinct stripes, and breast washed dusky; formative and basic upperpart feathers dusky to blackish with white fringing in Sep-Mar; abdomen without reddish. In addition, HY Red-necked Phalaropes retain some to all juv feathers through migration whereas HY Red Phalaropes replace most of the juv feathering before migrating (see **Molt**).

Geographic variation—Monotypic.

Molt—CAS. PF incomplete-complete (Aug-Mar in HY/SYs), DPA partial (Mar-May in AHYs), DPB complete (Jun-Nov/Feb in AHY/ASYs). The PF and PB commence at stopover sites and complete on non-breeding grounds and the DPA occurs on non-breeding grounds. Molt follows a s.Hemisphere strategy (Table 45, pp. 501-505). The PF includes some body feathers and occasionally the c.rects at stopover sites in Aug-Oct, followed by the remainder of the body and flight feathers on non-breeding grounds in Dec-Mar. Occasional SYs may retain a few inner pp and/or outer ss in an eccentric replacement pattern (Fig. 476**A**, p. 504). The DPB usually includes some to most body feathers and occasionally 1-4 inner pp and some c.rects during Jun-Aug at stopover sites (SYs average earlier than ASYs and ♀♀ average earlier than ♂♂), followed by suspension for migration and completion during Sep-Jan on non-breeding grounds. The DPA includes some to all body feathers and occasionally 1-2 terts and c.rects but few if any s covs.

Age—Juv (B1; Jul-Dec) has uniformly fresh plumage aspect, the upperpart feathers with blackish centers and tawny to buff fringing, the pp and ss uniformly juv and fresh (Fig. 375**A**, p. 503), the breast washed dusky when fresh, and the legs pinkish to slate; Juv ♀ = ♂ by plumage aspect.

Juv-HY/SY (1st cycle, Juv/B1-F1-A1; Oct-Jul): All to some upperpart feathers, terts, and distal s covs juv in Oct-Dec (Fig. 375**A**-**C**), fringed tawny to buff; pp, p covs, and ss juv and fresh in Oct-Dec (Fig. 375**A**), being completely replaced in Jan-Apr or occasionally exhibiting eccentric replacement patterns in May-Sep (Fig. 376**A**, p. 504), the juv outer pp and p covs (when present) narrow and relatively abraded (Figs. 377**A**-**B** & 378**A**-**B**, p. 506); all to some juv rects retained through Jan-Mar, contrastingly narrow and worn (Fig. 379**A**-**D**, p. 507), and brown with broad buff fringing when fresh. **Note: Only occasional SYs can be aged by eccentric patterns in Mar-Jul. See also AHY/ASY.**

AHY/ASY (Def. cycle, DB-DA; Aug-Feb): Upperpart feathers, terts, and s covs basic or mixed basic and alternate (Fig. 375**E**-**F**), the basic feathers dark gray with thin or no white fringing; pp, p covs, and ss basic, worn in Aug-Oct, being completely replaced in Oct-Feb, and showing replacement clines, s1-p1 contrast, and/or occasionally suspension limits among p1-p4 in Feb-Sep (Figs. 375**E** & 376**F**), the outer pp and p covs broad and truncate (Figs. 377**C**-**D** & 378**C**-**D**); outer rects basic and broader (Fig. 379**E**), gray with narrow white fringing, occasionally mixed with 1-2 alternate c.rects in Apr-Sep (Fig. 379**F**). **Note: See HY/SY. Occasional ASYs possibly can be aged through Sep by exhibiting suspension limits (Fig. 376F) among p1-p4 (without corresponding limits in the ss, as in SYs exhibiting eccentric patterns; Fig. 376B); more study needed.**

Sex—Bilateral BPs (Fig. 20**B**, p. 31) indicate ♂ and distended cloaca (Fig. 21, p. 32) indicates ♀ in Jun-Aug. Measurements largely unhelpful for sexing (Table 56, p. 624). See Rubega (1996) for DFAs (p. 5) using wing chord, head length, exposed culmen, bill length from distal end of nares, and bill depth that separated 66-73% of the sexes in a migrant w.N.Am population. The following is reliable for separating AHYs in Apr-Aug; otherwise, no criteria known for sexing Juvs and individuals in Sep-Mar.

AHY ♀ (Mar-Aug): Crown blackish; back dark gray with tawny stripes in scapulars; nape and breast with extensive and uniform dark rufous. **Note: A small proportion of intermediates may occur (Reynolds 1987) that may not be reliably sexed; these are likely SY ♀♀ and ASY ♂♂. Occasional SYs may remain on non-breeding grounds and show duller plumage aspect, sex for sex; those resembling ♂♂ are probably not reliably sexed.**

AHY ♂ (Apr-Aug): Crown and back dusky with whitish mottling and indistinct or no tawny stripes in scapulars; nape and breast grayish, variably mottled pale rufous. **Note: See AHY ♀.**

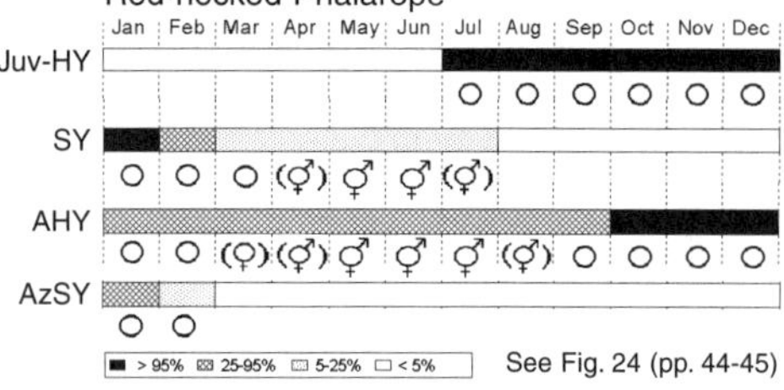

Hybrids reported—Possibly with Red Phalarope (McCarthy 2006).

References—Alexander & Gratto-Trevor (1997), Bent (1927), Cramp & Simmons (1983), Higgins & Davies (1996), Jehl (1986), Murphy (1936), Oberholser (1974), Palmer (1967b), Prater et al. (1977), Reynolds (1987), Ridgway (1919), Roberts (1955), Rubega et al. (2000), Schamel & Tracy (1988).

RED PHALAROPE
Phalaropus fulicarius

REPH
Species # 2220
Band size: 1A

Species—From other shorebirds and phalaropes by medium-small size with proportionally short legs (Table 56, p. 624); bill straight, moderately thick, moderately rounded at tip, and dusky with a pale base (Juvs and Sep-Mar) to yellow with a dusky tip (AHYs in Apr-Aug); upperpart feathers blackish with buff to tawny fringes (Juv and AHY ♂ in Apr-Jul), medium-pale gray (Aug-Mar), or black with bright buff fringes (AHY ♀ in Mar-Aug), the rump and medial uppertail covs dark (Fig. 438**A**, p. 594); gr covs with broad white tips and medial ss (s9-s12) whitish, forming wing stripe; underwing s covs white; outer rects gray with thin to no white fringes; legs and feet pinkish (Juv and Sep-Mar) to slate with yellowish feet (AHY in Apr-Aug), and with hind toe present (Fig. 373**C**, p. 500) and fore toes broadly lobed with extensive webbing (Fig. 452**B**, p. 623).

From Sanderling (p. 582) in Sep-Mar by shorter tail but longer bill and tarsus (Table 56); bill often with at least some yellowish at base; auriculars largely blackish; hind toe present and fore toes with substantial lobes. From Red-necked Phalarope (p. 625) by longer wing and tail (Table 56); bill thicker (depth at distal end of nares 3.1-4.1 mm), rounded at tip, and often with at least some yellowish to base; Juv with back feather fringing uniform, not showing distinct stripes, and breast washed pale brownish; formative and basic back feathers and scapulars medium-pale gray without white fringing in Sep-Mar. See Red-necked Phalarope for further differences related to the PF.

Geographic variation—Monotypic. Paler individuals breeding in Spitzbergen I, Iceland, and e.Greenland ("*P.f. jourdaini*") were described based on individuals collected in worn plumage aspect. See Jourdain (1934), Manning et al. (1956), and Peters (1934c) for more information.

Molt—CAS. PF partial-incomplete (Jul-Nov/Mar in HY/SYs), PA1 limited (Apr-May in non-breeding SYs), PB2 complete (May-Oct in non-breeding SYs); DPA limited-partial (Mar-Apr in breeding AHYs), DPB complete (Jun-Oct/Feb in AHY/ASYs). The PF and DPB commence on breeding grounds (most to all body feathers) and complete on non-breeding grounds, and the DPA occurs on non-breeding grounds. Molt can follow either a n.Hemisphere or s.Hemisphere strategy (Table 45, pp. 501-505). The PF includes most to all body feathers and sometimes some proximal s covs, terts, and c.rects on breeding grounds in Jul-Sep, followed by the remainder of the s covs, terts, rects and often 2-5 outer pp and 1-4 medial ss (distal to the terts) in eccentric sequence (Fig. 376**A-B**, p. 504; sometimes arrested) in Dec-Mar. The DPB includes some to most body feathers, occasionally p1-p4, and some c.rects on breeding grounds in Jun-Aug, followed by completion on non-breeding grounds in Oct-Mar; flight feather molt can be suspended (often among p6-p9) during Dec-Feb for individuals with non-breeding grounds in the n.Hemisphere. The DPA includes some to all body feathers and occasionally 1-2 terts and c.rects but few if any s covs. Some SYs over-summer on non-breeding grounds and exhibit less-complete PA1s and advanced PB2s (see p. 18).

Age—Juv (B1; Jul-Sep) has uniformly fresh plumage aspect, the upperpart feathers black with gold fringing, the pp and ss uniformly juv and fresh (Fig. 375**A**, p. 503), the breast washed purplish brown, and the legs pinkish; Juv ♀ = ♂ by plumage aspect.

HY/SY (1st cycle, F1-A1; Oct-Sep): All to some s covs and terts juv and fresh in Oct-Jan (Fig. 375**A-C**), blackish fringed tawny to buff, contrasting with fresher and grayer formative humerals and proximal s covs in Nov-Sep (Fig. 375**B-C**); pp, p covs, and ss juv, fresh, and without s1-p1 contrast in Oct-Dec (Fig. 375**A**), often being incompletely replaced in Jan-Mar and exhibiting eccentric replacement patterns among p5-p10 in Apr-Sep (Fig. 376**A-B**, p. 504; sometimes arrested), the juv outer pp and p covs (if present) narrow and relatively abraded (Figs. 377**A-B** & 378**A-B**, p. 506); some juv outer and/or medial rects retained through Nov-Feb (sometimes Mar-Sep), narrow and relatively worn (Fig. 379**A-D**, p. 507), and with buff fringes; underparts often with reduced to no reddish feathering (by sex) in Mar-Jul. **Note: See ASY/ATY**.

AHY/ASY (Def. cycle, DB-DA; Oct-Sep): Terts, s covs, and humerals uniformly basic or mixed basic and alternate (Fig. 375**E-F**), the basic feathers grayish with thin or no pale fringing; pp, p covs, and ss worn and/or being completely replaced in Oct-Mar, or basic and with replacement cline and sometimes s1-p1 contrast and/or suspension limit among p1-p4 or p6-p9 in Dec-Sep (Fig. 375**E** & 376**F**; see **Molt**), the outer pp and p covs broad and truncate (Figs. 377**C-D** & 378**C-D**); rects uniformly basic and broader (Fig. 379**E**), gray with white fringes, occasionally mixed with 1-2 alternate c.rects in Apr-Sep (Fig. 379**F**); underparts with extensive reddish feathering (by sex) in Mar-Jul.

SY/TY (2nd cycle, B2; Oct-Feb): Like AHY/ASY with molt of pp occurring, but suspension limits not present (*cf.* Fig. 376**F**) and outer pp and p covs juv, very pointed and abraded (Fig. 376**E**). **Note: Only a small proportion of SY/TYs (without eccentric PF or early PB2) can be aged in Oct-Feb.**

ASY/ATY (Def. cycle, DB; Oct-Jan): Like AHY/ASY but molt of pp occurring, suspension limits present among p1-p4 or p6-p9 (Fig. 376**F**), and outer pp broader and fresher (*cf.* Fig. 376**E**). **Note: Some SY/TYs can also show broader outer pp accompanied by eccentric patterns, but distinguishing these from suspension limits can be difficult (see Fig. 376); intermediates are best aged AHY/ASY in Feb-Jan.**

Sex—Bilateral BPs (Fig. 20**B**, p. 31) indicate ♂ and distended cloaca (Fig. 21, p. 32) indicates ♀ in Jun-Aug. Wing length may be helpful for sexing many individuals (Table 56, p. 624). The following is reliable for separating most AHYs in Apr-Aug; otherwise, no criteria known for sexing Juvs and individuals in Sep-Mar.

AHY ♀ (Mar-Aug): Crown, lores, and chin black; face distinctly white; neck, throat, and breast uniformly dark rufous; bill bright yellow with black tip. **Note: Bright ASY ♂♂ may approach dull SY ♀♀ in plumage aspect; combine with age and wing length (Table 56) to sex intermediates. Over-summering individuals are probably not reliably sexed.**

AHY ♂ (Apr-Aug): Crown, lores, and chin brown to blackish with whitish to pale brownish streaks; face indistinctly whitish; neck, throat, and breast variably whitish mottled rufous to pale rufous with some whitish mottling; bill dull yellow with dusky tip. **Note: See AHY ♀.**

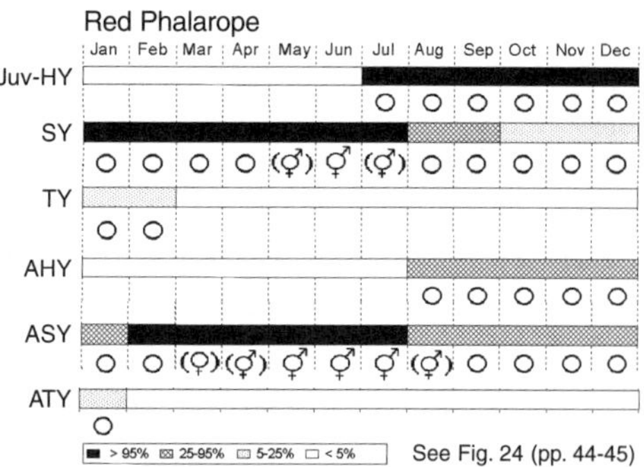

Hybrids reported—Possibly with Red-necked Phalarope (p. 625).

References—Bent (1927), Cramp & Simmons (1983), Higgins & Davies (1996), Murphy (1936), Oberholser (1974), Palmer (1967b), Portenko (1972), Prater et al. (1977), Ridgway (1919), Stone (1900), Tracy et al. (2002).

GULLS, TERNS, AND SKIMMERS *LARIDAE*

Forty species. Family characters include variable sizes, body shapes, and bill forms, relatively long wings, and relatively short legs with extensive webbing between the front toes. Ageing through the first (to SY and ASY), second (to TY and ATY) or third (to 4Y and A4Y) cycles can be accomplished primarily through plumage aspect (particularly of the outer primary coverts and primaries) in gulls, and by molt patterns among primaries in terns. Plumage aspect and bare part colors are similar between sexes, and both males and females develop brood patches. Males average larger than females in most species, and measurements, especially head-bill length (see Fig. 453, p. 630) can be used to determine sex in most individuals of many gull species; most terns cannot be sexed by size. In molting, gulls follow several strategies, most terns follow the Complex Alternate Strategy, and skimmers appear to follow the Simple Alternate Strategy (see Fig. 10, pp. 13-16). See Subfamily Accounts for more information on structure, age and sex determination, and molts.

Upperpart coloration in definitive-aspect gulls and terns varies from very pale gray to slaty blackish, and can be all shades of gray in between. Although often showing substantial intraspecific variation, upperpart color can be a useful character in separating species and subspecies. A useful way of describing shades of grays shown by gulls and terns is by comparison to a Kodak gray-scale chart (*cf.* Howell 2003c), available on line or at many photographic supply stores. This scale assigns stepped values to neutral gray tones, and varies from 1 (very pale gray) to 20 (blackish). Among North American gulls and terns, Kodak scales for upperparts vary from 3-4 in some Glaucous and Iceland gulls, and in Gull-billed and Royal terns, to 13-15 in Great Black-backed Gull and 16-17 in Sooty Tern. Qualifiers used here include: "very pale gray" (for Kodak 3-4), "pale gray" (4.5-6), "medium-pale gray" (6-7.5), "medium-dark gray" (8-9.5), "dark gray" (10-11.5), "very dark gray" (11.5-13), "blackish" (13-15) and black (16+). Kodak values are a convenient way of comparing shades between species, and subspecies and indicating the degree of overlap that may be encountered between groups (*cf.* Howell 2003c).

This family is divided into three subfamilies reflecting groups with differing structures, molts, and plumages.

Gulls *Laridae, Larinae*

Twenty-four species in two groups: smaller, more slender-billed sternine gulls and larger, stouter-billed larine gulls (Moynihan 1959, Chu 1998); taxonomy at the generic level generally follows that of Pons et al. (2005) in anticipation of adoption by the AOU. Family characters include medium to large size, relatively long wings, relatively short (and usually squared) tails, variably shaped bills with expanded gonydeal region in larger species, and three front toes connected by extensive webbing. Gulls have 10 functional primaries (10th longest by 0-10 mm, when full-grown), 16-23 secondaries (including 3 tertials and one absent between the 4th and 5th; *cf.* Fig. 12**B**, p. 19), and 12 rectrices. Ageing of small and medium gulls through the second cycle (to TY and ATY) and of large gulls through the third cycle (to 4Y and A4Y) can be accomplished by plumage aspect and color of the bare parts (although exceptions occur with bare part color). The outer primaries, outer primary coverts, greater coverts, tertials, alula, and underwing coverts generally vary from brown during the 1st cycle (HY/SYs) to gray, black, and white in definitive plumage (ASY/ATYs or ATY/A4Ys). See pp. 659-663 for more on ageing larger species of gulls. Many of the smaller species attain dark hoods for the breeding season and some have a variable pink flush to their underparts. Bills, legs, and orbital rings are often more brightly colored on breeding adults. Plumage aspect and bare part colors are similar between sexes, and both males and females develop bilateral and often medial brood patches (Fig. 20**B**-**C**, p. 31). Distended cloacae (Fig. 21, p. 32) indicate ASY or ATY females during breeding seasons, and other cloacal features should be examined (Figs. 22-23, pp. 32-35). Males average larger than females in most species, and measurements, especially head-bill length (Fig. 453, p. 630) can be used to determine sex in most individuals of many species.

In molting, North American gulls follow the Complex Alternate Strategy (CAS; Fig. 10**F**, pp. 13-16) in most small gulls, a Simple Alternate Strategy (SAS; Fig. 10**E**, *cf.* Fig. 11**F**, p. 17) in most large gulls, or the Simple Basic Strategy (Fig. 10**A**) in Ivory Gull (p. 636). The single inserted first-cycle molt in species exhibiting the Simple Alternate Strategy appears to be a prealternate rather than a preformative molt (Fig. 10**E**; Howell 2001a; Howell & Corben 2000a, 2000b). Primaries and primary coverts are replaced distally from p1 to p10 and rectrices are generally replaced rapidly and distally on each side, from r1 to r6. Secondaries are replaced rapidly and proximally from s1 and s5 and more slowly in a distal direction from the tertials, such that the last secondaries replaced are usually among 1-3 feathers near the tertials, e.g., s12-s14 in many smaller species with 17 secondaries. The preformative molt may be absent in most large species, is partial in most small species, can be complete in Sabine's Gull (p. 637), and can exhibit eccentric replacement patterns (*cf.* Fig. 376**A-B**, p. 504) in at least some Heermann's Gulls (p. 650). Replacement of outer primaries and inner secondaries during the preformative molt may occur occasionally in other species that inhabit tropical areas and/or regions of high insolation; study needed.

Prebasic molts are complete, replacement of primaries sometimes starting during incubation and suspending for chick-rearing. Extents of preformative and prealternate molts in many species, especially large gulls, still need to be determined because of overlapping molts as well as variable aspects of formative, alternate, and basic feathers and plumages; thus, it often is not possible to infer feather generation without tracking an individual through time. Second and third prealternate molts are often more extensive than first and definitive prealternate molts, commencing in the fall, concurrent with the completion of the second and third prebasic molts (Fig. 11**F**, p. 17), and showing more extensive replacement of secondary coverts, tertials, and rectrices. In larger (primarily non-migratory) species this can occur with definitive prealternate molts as well. The definitive prealternate molts are usually limited to partial, although they can be incomplete in Lesser Black-backed Gull (p. 668) and complete in Franklin's Gull (p. 648). Age of first breeding is variable (1-3 years in smaller species and 3-10 years in larger species); pre-breeding individuals often remain on non-breeding grounds and average earlier prebasic molts. See pp. 659-663 for more details on molt in larger species.

General references for identification, molt, and ageing in gulls include Dwight (1901, 1925), Grant (1986), Harrison (1983a, 1987), Howell & Dunn (2007), and Malling Olsen & Larsson (2003).

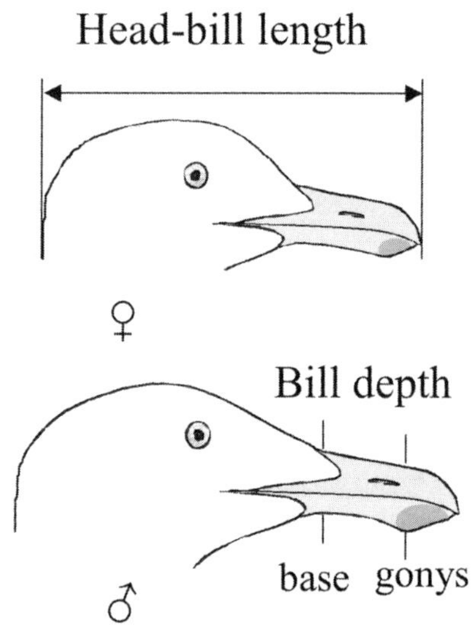

FIGURE 453. Head shape and head and bill measures by sex in larger species of gulls. Note more rounded head and slimmer bill of ♀. In the ♂ shown, bill depth at gonys is larger than bill depth at base, whereas in some species the depth at base is larger than the depth at gonys. The head-to-bill-tip measurement (hereafter "**head-bill" length**) is helpful for sex determination in many species of gulls, especially when used in DFAs (see p. 5). More study is needed on live, known-sex individuals of several species, in which differences in this measure are currently not known; it is unreliable for sexing specimens due to variation in the preparation of crania.

Sexing gulls

In most gulls, males average larger than females but there is usually considerable overlap. Researchers working in specific colonies have found that the distance between the back of the head and the bill tip (Figure 453), hereafter **head-bill length**, is useful for determining sex, especially when combined with other measurements in DFAs (p. 5). Head-bill length cannot be measured accurately from most specimens because of cranial preparation methods, but specimen measurements can suggest whether head-bill length is useful on a given species. Because of inter-population variation within most species, the use of head-bill length and any given DFA may be limited in potential geographic scope (Evans et al. 1993, McGowan & Zonfrillo 1995). Hence, it would be best for head-bill lengths and DFAs to be calculated for given populations under study (see also p. 5). Head shape also varies by sex in larger gulls, being rounder in ♀♀ and flatter or more wedge-shaped in ♂♂ (Fig. 453), and this can often be used to sex mated pairs, along with relative size (Pierotti 1981). Nesting gulls can also be sexed by behavior (e.g., Burger & Beer 1975, Southern 1981, Butler & Janes-Butler 1983), although presence of female-female pairs can confuse the sexing of mated adults (Hunt et al. 1980).

BLACK-LEGGED KITTIWAKE

Rissa tridactyla

BLKI
Species # 0400
Band size: 4A

Species—From other gulls including Red-legged Kittiwake (p. 633) and Mew Gull (p. 652) by medium size with proportionally longer bill (Table 57, p.635); bill shallower at gonys (♀ 9.3-11.7, ♂ 10.0-12.5) than at base (10.8-15.2; Table 57, *cf.* Fig. 453); iris dark; legs black; HY/SY with black ulnar bar, nape patch (extending to auriculars), distal tail band, and bill blackish or with yellowish base; ASY with upperparts medium pale gray (Kodak 6.5-8, p. 629), inner pp without distinct white tips, outer pp without white mirrors (Fig. 455, p. 632), underwing p covs white, and bill unmarked yellow.

Geographic variation—See Barrett et al. (1985), Coulson et al. (1983), Cramp & Simmons (1983), Dement'ev & Gladkov (1951c), Dwight (1925), Helfenstein et al. (2004), McGowan & Zonfrillo (1995), Portenko (1973), Ridgway (1919), Sluys (1982), Stejneger (1885). See Chardine (2002) for a DFA using the black tip lengths on p8-p10 which separated 98% of ASY/ATYs to subspecies, and see **Molt** for differences by subspecies in timing. No other subspecies occur.

R.t. pollicaris (br and wint n.Pacific): Averages larger (Table 57, p. 635); head-bill length (Fig. 453) 90-103 (see **Sex**); upperparts average darker gray (Kodak 7-8, p. 629); p5-p10 of ASY/ATYs more extensively black (e.g., 40% of ASY/ATYs have black subterminal band on p5, and only about 10% lack black on p5; Chardine 2002); black hind-collar of Juv-HY/SY may average thicker (study needed).

R.t. tridactyla (br and wint n.Atlantic): Averages smaller (Table 57); head-bill length (Fig. 453) 82-95 (see **Sex**); upperparts average paler gray (Kodak 6.5-7.5); p5-p10 of ASY/ATYs less extensively black (e.g., p5 has limited black marks on up to 40% of ASY/ATYs, and rarely has a narrow black subterminal band; Chardine 2002); black hind-collar of Juv-HY/SY may average thinner. Breeding populations of n.Europe average larger than British and N.Am populations (Chardine 2002).

Molt—SAS. PF absent, PA1 partial (Oct-May in HY/SYs), PB2 complete (May-Oct in SYs), PA2 partial (Feb?-May? in SYs), DPB complete (Jun-Feb in ASY/ATYs), DPA partial (Jan-May in ASYs). All molts occur primarily during migrations and/or on non-breeding grounds. The single inserted first-cycle molt appears homologous with a PA1 rather than a PF (Fig. 10**E**, p. 14). Timing of molts averages earlier in nominate *R.t. tridactyla* than in *pollicaris*; e.g., primarily Oct-Apr *vs* Jan-May for the PA1, Jun-Nov *vs* Jul-Jan for the DPB, and Jan-Apr *vs* Mar-May for the DPA, respectively. The DPB can also extend into spring during occasional years of poor food production; e.g., until May or later during El Niño conditions in *pollicaris* (Howell & Corben 2000c) and into Feb or later in *tridactyla* (Weir et al. 1996). The PA1 includes some body feathers but few if any s covs, terts, or rects. The DPA includes some body feathers and up to few med covs and proximal les covs but few if any terts or rects.

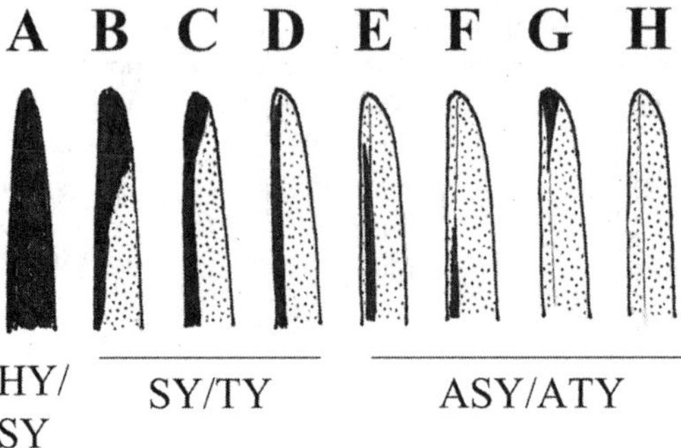

FIGURE 454. Pattern of outermost primary covert by age in Black-legged Kittiwake.

Age—Juv (B1; Jul-Jan) has upperpart feathers fringed whitish and cap, ear-spot, hind-collar, and bill blackish; Juv ♀ = ♂.

Juv-HY/SY (1st cycle, Juv/B1-A1; Oct-Sep): Outer p covs extensively brownish (Fig. 454**A**); outer webs of p8-p9 black (Fig. 455**A**); rects with black distal band; bill blackish, becoming grayish to yellow at base in Dec-Sep (occasionally unmarked yellow in Aug-Sep); nape with distinct black patch in Oct-Apr.

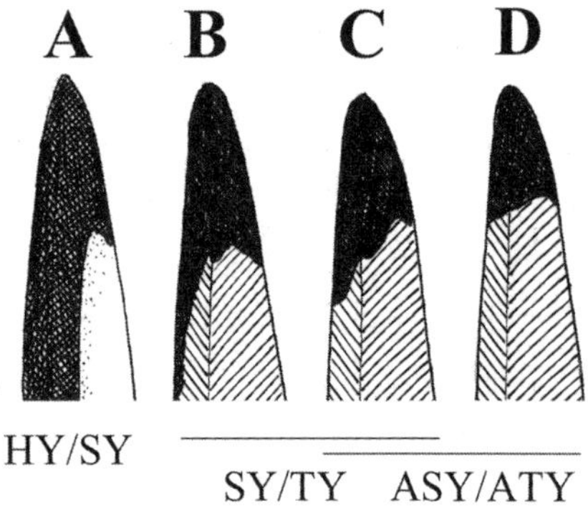

SY/TY (2nd cycle, B2-A2; Oct-Sep): Outermost p cov with brownish black on outer web usually extending to tip (Fig. 454**B-D**); p8-p9 with extensive black tip (Fig. 455**B-C**); bill yellow, usually with small dark tip in Oct-Apr or later; nape with indistinct grayish nape patch in Oct-Apr. **Note: Coulson (1959) aged SY/TYs in a British population with 90% confidence based on the extent of black on p8 (see Fig. 455), but this difference appears less useful for *R.t. pollicaris* (study needed).**

FIGURE 455. Pattern to p8 by age in nominate Black-legged Kittiwake (*R.t. trydactyla*). The difference between SY/TY (**B**) and ASY/ATY (**D**) appears not as helpful in ageing the Pacific subspecies (*pollicaris*), although study of known-age individuals is needed.

ASY/ATY (Def. cycle, DB-DA; Oct-Sep): Outermost p cov and alula with little or no black (Fig. 454**E-H**); p8-p9 average less extensive black, at least in *R.t. tridactyla* (Fig. 455**C-D**); bill unmarked yellow; nape with indistinct grayish or no nape patch in Oct-Apr. **Note: See SY/TY.**

TY/4Y (3rd cycle, B3; Oct-Mar): Like ASY/ATY with molt in pp occurring or suspended, outer p covs with brownish black on outer web usually extending to tip (Fig. 454**B-D**), and p8-p9 with extensive black tip (Fig. 455**B-C**). **Note: Suspended molt may only occur in breeding adults and, thus, ageing to TY/4Y beyond Nov may be rare.**

ATY/A4Y (Def. cycle, DB; Oct-Mar): Like ASY/ATY with molt in pp occurring or suspended, outermost p cov and alula with little or no black (Fig. 454**E-H**), and p8-p9 averaging less extensive black, at least in *R.t. tridactyla* (Fig. 455**C-D**). **Note: See TY/4Y. Also, some ATY/A4Ys may arrest molt (see Molt) and be reliably aged A4Y through Sep or later, but confirmation needed.**

Sex— ♀ = ♂ by plumage aspect. Bilateral and medial(?) BPs (p. 31) developed by both sexes but distended cloaca (Fig. 21, p. 32) indicates ATY ♀ in May-Jul. Measurements relatively unhelpful for sexing (Table 57, p. 635), but the following can be used to reliably sex most full-grown individuals (Coulson et al. 1983, Jodice et al. 2000):

♀: Head-bill length (Fig. 453, p. 630) 90-97 (Pacific *R.t. pollicaris*) or 82-89 (Atlantic *tridactyla*) mm. **Note: Individuals with head-bill length 95-97 (Pacific) or 88-89 (Atlantic) mm cannot be reliably sexed by this measure alone; see also McGowan & Zonfrillo (1995) for cautions on sexing individuals of unknown geographic origin.**

♂: Head-bill 95-103 (Pacific) or 88-95 (Atlantic) mm. **Note: See ♀.**

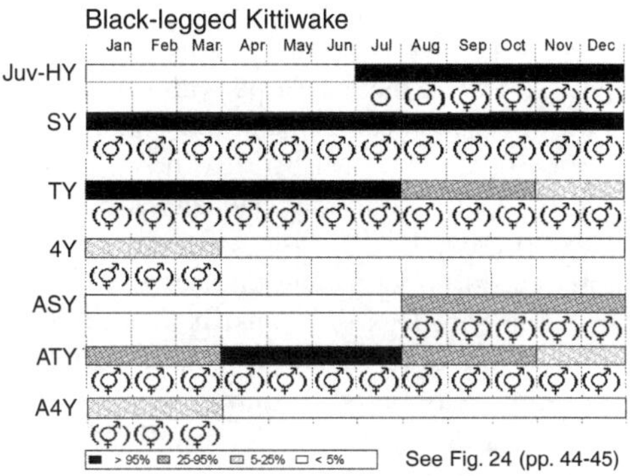

Black-legged Kittiwake

Jan Feb Mar Apr May Jun Jul Aug Sep Oct Nov Dec

Juv-HY

SY

TY

4Y

ASY

ATY

A4Y

■ > 95% ▨ 25-95% ▭ 5-25% □ < 5%

See Fig. 24 (pp. 44-45)

Hybrids Reported—None.

References—Baird (1994), Baker (1993), Bent (1921), Chardine (2002), Cottle (1987), Coulson (1959), Coulson et al. (1983), Cramp & Simmons (1983), Dement'ev & Gladkov (1951c), Dwight (1925), Helfenstein et al. (2004), Howell & Corben (2000c), Howell & Dunn (2007), Jodice et al. (2000), McGowan & Zonfrillo (1995), Oberholser (1974), Pennington et al. (1994), Ridgway (1919), Smith (1988), Stone (1900), Weir et al. (1996).

RED-LEGGED KITTIWAKE

Rissa brevirostris

RLKI
Species # 0410
Band size: 4A

Species—From other gulls including Sabine's Gull (p. 637) and Black-legged Kittiwake (p. 631) by combination of medium size with proportionally shorter bill (Table 57, p.635); bill shallower at gonys (♀ 9.6-11.4, ♂ 9.8-12.2) than at base (10.8-13.0; Table 57, *cf.* Fig. 453, p. 630); iris dark; Juv-HY/SY with legs dull pinkish to reddish, black ulnar bar and black in tail absent, and bill blackish with yellow base in Dec-Jun; ASY with upperparts medium-dark gray (Kodak 8.5-9.5, p. 629), legs red, inner pp with moderately distinct white tips, outer pp with small or no white mirrors, underwing p covs dusky, and bill unmarked yellow. HY/SY from Sabine's Gull further by larger size (Table 57), especially wing chord (> 288 mm) and bill depth (> 10 mm); tail fork shallow (r6-r1 < 13 mm); head and rects mostly to entirely white; p5-p6 mostly gray and white; outer ss and gr covs whitish to gray with white tips, not contrasting in pattern with inner ss and gr covs.

Geographic variation—Monotypic.

Molt—SAS. PF absent, PA1 partial (Feb?-May? in SYs), PB2 complete (May-Oct in SYs), DPA partial (Mar?-May? in ASYs), DPB complete (Jul-Mar in ASY/ATYs). The single inserted first-cycle molt appears homologous with a PA1 rather than a PF (Fig. 10**E**, p. 14). Molting occurs on non-breeding grounds and details poorly known. The DPB probably suspends during Dec-Mar and in some ASY/ATYs (probably during poor food years; see Howell & Corben 2000c) it can extend over almost a year and overlap the successive DPB (*cf.* Fig. 376**C**, p. 504). Both the PA1 and the DPA can include a few proximal s covs but probably no (or rarely 1-2) terts or c.rects; more study needed.

Age—Juv (B1; Jul-Feb) has upperparts fringed whitish, les covs with scattered black spots, and cap, ear-spot, hind-collar, and bill blackish; Juv ♀ = ♂.

Juv-HY/SY (1st cycle, Juv/B1-A1; Oct-Sep): Outer p covs (Fig. 456**A**) and p9 (Fig. 457**A**) extensively black; p5 with extensive brownish subterminal band (*cf.* Fig. 471**A**, p. 649); les covs usually(?) with scattered black spots; ss mostly whitish; auricular spot present; bill blackish, with yellow base in Mar-Jul, occasionally unmarked yellow in Aug-Sep; legs dull pinkish to reddish. **Note: Age-determination criteria in this species may need refining. Unlike in other gulls, Juv-HY/SYs usually show entirely white rects.**

SY/TY (2nd cycle, B2-A2; Oct-Sep): Outermost p cov (Fig. 456**B-C**) and p9 (Fig. 457**B**) with extensive black on outer web; p5 with narrow and complete to incomplete blackish subterminal band (*cf.* Fig. 471**C**); les covs without black spots; ss gray with distinct white tips; head with little or no auricular spot in Oct-Apr; bill unmarked yellow, often with small dark tip in Oct-Apr or later; legs reddish to bright red. **Note: See Juv-HY/SY.**

ASY/ATY (Def. cycle, DB-DA; Oct-Sep): Outermost p cov with little or no blackish (Fig. 456**C-D**); p9 with black on outer web restricted to distal third (Fig. 457**C**); p5 usually with reduced and incomplete black subterminal band (*cf.* Fig. 471**D**); head without auricular spot; bill unmarked yellow; legs bright red.

FIGURE 456. Pattern of the outermost primary covert by age in Red-legged Kittiwake: **A** 1st cycle (Juv-HY/SY), **B-C** 2nd cycle (SY/TY), **D** definitive cycle (ASY/ATY). Some ASY/ATYs can show a minimal amount of dusky to the outer web, between that shown in **C** and **D**. These may represent TY/4Ys but more study is needed.

FIGURE 457. Variation in the pattern of p9 by age in Red-legged Kittiwake. During the 2nd cycle (in SY/TYs), black on the outer web usually extends proximally to within 30 mm of the pp cov tips whereas in definitive plumage (ASY/ATYs) the black is restricted to the distal portion, not reaching to within 30 mm of the pp covs. Juv outer pp of Sabine's Gull resemble **A**.

TY/4Y (3rd cycle, B3; Oct-Mar): Like ASY/ATY with molt in pp occurring or suspended and outermost p cov (Fig. 456**B-C**) and p9 (Fig. 457**B**) with extensive black on outer web. **Note: Suspended molt may only occur in breeding adults and, thus, ageing to TY/4Y beyond Sep may be rare.**

ATY/A4Y (Def. cycle, DB; Oct-Mar): Like ASY/ATY with molt in pp occurring or suspended, outermost p cov with little or no blackish (Fig. 456**C-D**), and p9 with black on outer web restricted to distal third (Fig. 457**C**). **Note: See TY/4Y. Also, some ATY/A4Ys may arrest molt (see Molt) and be reliably aged A4Y through Sep or later, but confirmation needed.**

Sex—♀ = ♂ by plumage aspect. Bilateral and medial BPs (Fig. 20**C**, p. 31) developed by both sexes but distended cloaca (Fig. 21, p. 32) indicates ATY ♀ in May-Jul. Measurements unhelpful (Table 57) and head-bill length (Fig. 453, p. 630) probably not useful for sexing, but study needed on live individuals.

Hybrids Reported—None.

References—Bent (1921), Byrd & Williams (1993a), Dement'ev & Gladkov (1951c), Dwight (1925), Howell & Dunn (2007), Lehman (2006), Malling Olsen & Larsson (2003), Ridgway (1919).

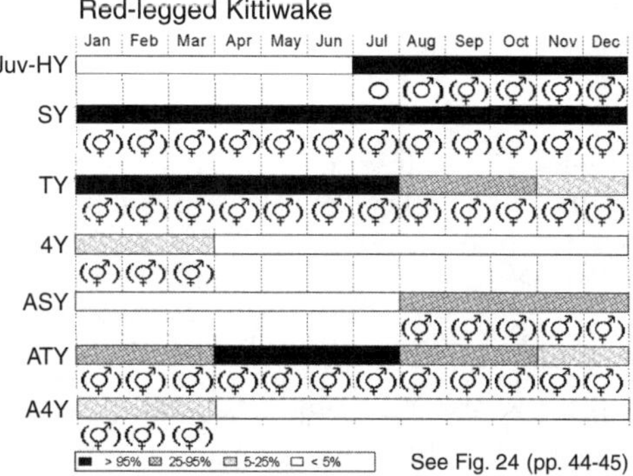

TABLE 57. Measurements (mm) of small North American gulls to assist in identification and sexing. See pp. 4-11 for methods of measurement. Species summaries are in **bold** and subspecies values are in ***italics***. Values were derived from 95% confidence intervals as based approximately on the indicated sample sizes; sample size (see pp. 4-5) for bill depth was often smaller but included at least 10 of each sex. Thus, midpoints of ranges approximate means, and S.D. is approximated by 25% of the range.

Taxon/Sex	*n*	wing chord[1]	tail length	exp culmen	bill depth[2]	tarsus
Black-legged Kittiwake		**283-335**	**114-141**	**31-42**	**10.8-15.2**	**29-36**
R.t. pollicaris		***301-335***	***124-141***	***33-42***	***11.0-15.2***	***30-36***
♀	85	301-332	124-137	35-42	11.0-13.4	30-34
♂	100	304-335	129-141	33-40	11.6-15.2	31-36
R.t. tridactyla[3]		***283-325***	***114-134***	***31-40***	***10.8-14.2***	***29-35***
♀	100	283-319	114-127	31-37	10.8-13.7	29-34
♂	100	292-325	121-134	33-40	12.0-14.2	30-35
Red-legged Kittiwake		**290-321**	**119-132**	**26-31**	**10.8-13.0**	**28-33**
♀	55	290-318	119-131	26-30	10.8-12.5	29-33
♂	55	294-321	119-132	27-31	11.1-13.0	28-32
Ivory Gull		**317-360**	**143-156**	**30-39**	**11.1-15.0**	**33-42**
♀	75	317-350	137-149	30-37	11.1-13.2	33-39
♂	100	326-360	143-156	32-39	11.5-15.0	35-42
Sabine's Gull		**246-286**	**109-124**	**22-28**	**6.8-9.4**	**30-36**
♀	75	246-276	109-121	22-27	6.8-8.6	30-35
♂	100	258-286	112-124	23-28	7.0-9.4	30-36
Bonaparte's Gull		**242-272**	**93-108**	**25-32**	**6.8-9.4**	**32-38**
♀	80	242-267	93-105	25-30	6.8-8.8	32-37
♂	100	247-272	96-108	27-32	7.0-9.4	33-38
Black-headed Gull		**275-325**	**102-124**	**28-39**	**7.3-10.5**	**39-50**
♀	100	275-314	102-119	28-38	7.3-9.0	39-46
♂	100	283-325	107-124	30-39	7.7-10.5	40-50
Little Gull		**209-231**	**82-97**	**20-25**	**5.2-7.1**	**24-28**
♀	75	209-229	82-94	20-24	5.2-6.8	24-27
♂	100	211-231	85-97	21-25	5.4-7.1	24-28
Ross's Gull		**240-271**	**113-133**	**17-21**	**5.8-6.6**	**29-34**
♀	55	238-270	113-128	17-20	5.8-6.5	29-33
♂	55	240-271	116-133	17-21	5.9-6.6	29-34

[1] Wing chord averages ~5% (10% in Ross's Gull) shorter in Juv-HY/SY than in AHY/ASY.
[2] Bill depth measured at distal end of forehead feathering (see Fig. 8**A**, p. 10).
[3] N.Am population only; n.European populations average slightly larger.

IVORY GULL
Pagophila eburnea

IVGU
Species # 0390
Band size: 4

Species—From other gulls by medium size (Table 57, p. 635); bill shallower at gonys (♀ 9.7-11.8, ♂ 10.5-13.1) than at base (11.1-15.0; Table 57; *cf.* Fig. 453, p. 630); plumage aspect ivory-white, spotted black in HY/SYs; bill greenish with dull yellowish to yellow-orange tip; legs and feet black with well-developed claws.

Geographic variation—Monotypic.

Molt—SBS. PF absent, PB2 complete (Apr-Aug in SYs), DPB complete (Mar-Sep in ASYs), PA absent. The DPB occurs primarily on breeding grounds but can occasionally be suspended during Oct-Feb, with p8-p10 not completing replacement until Mar-Apr (rarely arrested until following PB?). In breeding adults the DPB can start in Mar-May (up to 7 inner pp replaced), suspend during the chick-feeding period (Jun-Aug), and resume after breeding is completed (*cf.* Fig. 15, p. 22). See Howell (2001c) for more information.

Age—Juv (Aug-May) is described under Juv-HY/SY; Juv ♀=♂.

Juv-HY/SY (B1; Aug-Jul): Face mottled black; remainder of body (usually) and flight feathers variably spotted or tipped dusky to blackish; bill dull grayish and yellow.

AHY/ASY (Def. cycle, DB; Aug-Jul): Face and remainder of plumage aspect entirely ivory-white; outer pp without evidence of molt suspension among pp (*cf.* Fig. 458). **Note: AHY/ASYs with this plumage aspect but with fine dusky flecking on head (especially above eyes) may be SY/TY; confirmation from known-age individuals needed.**

ASY/ATY (Def. cycle, DB-DA; Aug-Jul): Like AHY/ASY but pp (especially among p7-p10) with suspended molt (mid Jun-early Aug; Fig. 458**A**), or with evidence of molt suspension (Fig. 458**B**).

Sex—♀=♂ by plumage aspect. Bilateral and medial BPs (Fig. 20**C,** p. 31) developed by both sexes but distended cloaca (Fig. 21, p. 32) indicates ASY ♀ in Jun-Jul. ♂♂ average larger (Table 57, p. 635), and mated pairs probably can be sexed reliably; also, head-bill length (Figure 453, p. 630) probably useful for sexing but study needed on live individuals.

Hybrids Reported—None.

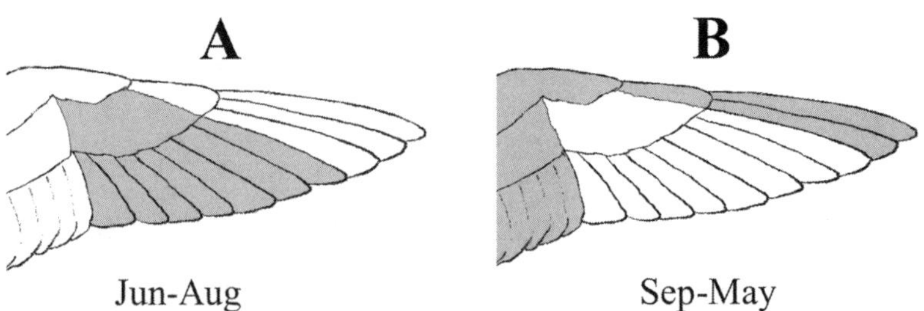

FIGURE 458. Molt-suspension pattern among the primaries in ASY/ATY Ivory Gull, here showing the two most common placements, between p7 and p8 (**A**) and between p8 and p9 (**B**); others can show limits between p9 and p10. Shading indicates fresher feathers. The suspension occurs for breeding (or chick-feeding, at least) after which it resumes, creating the suspension limit; thus, patterns resembling **A** are found in Jun-Aug and those resembling **B** are found after the molt is completed, in Sep-May. These patterns indicate not only a breeding-aged bird (ASY/ATY) but one that had bred the previous season. Individuals with definitive aspect and lacking limits may represent non-breeders and must be aged AHY/ASY. See Howell (2001c) for more information.

References—Bent (1921), Dement'ev & Gladkov (1951c), Dwight (1925), Haney & MacDonald (1995), Howell (2001c), Howell & Dunn (2007), Malling Olsen & Larsson (2003), Ridgway (1919), Stone (1900).

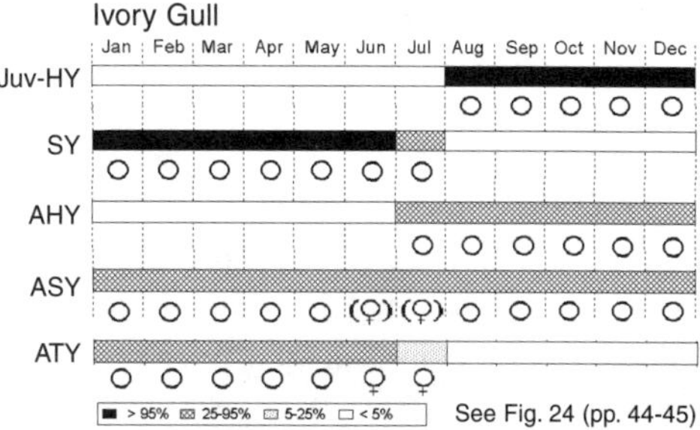

SABINE'S GULL

Xema sabini

SAGU
Species # 0620
Band size: 3

Species—From other gulls including Juv-HY/SY Ross's Gull (p. 643) by combination of medium-small to medium size (Table 57, p.635); bill depth at gonys (6.8-8.5) similar in size to that at base (6.8-9.4; *cf.* Fig. 453, p. 630); tail forked (r6 > r1 by 15-30 mm); upperparts medium-pale to medium-dark gray (Kodak 6.5-9, p. 629); inner pp, ss, and outer gr covs white, contrasting with gray proximal s covs and blacker outer pp; bill black, with yellow tip in most AHYs; iris dark; legs dull flesh to blackish. From HY/SY Red-legged Kittiwake further by smaller size (Table 57), especially wing chord (< 280 mm) and bill depth (< 10 mm); tail fork deeper (r6 – r1 ≥ 15 mm); HY/SY with head mostly dark and rects with black band; p5-p6 mostly sooty to blackish; outer ss and gr covs primarily whitish contrasting with grayer inner ss and gr covs.

Geographic variation—Monotypic, following Cramp & Simmons (1983). Populations of Siberia-w.AK ("*X.s. woznesenskii*") average darker upperparts (Kodak 7.5-9, p. 629) than those of e.N.Am and Europe (Kodak 6.5-8.5) but difference insufficient and probably clinal. See also Dement'ev & Gladkov (1951c), Patten et al. (2003), Portenko (1939, 1973), Todd (1963).

Molt—CAS (SAS?). PF complete (Oct-Apr in HY/SYs), PA1 absent-limited? (Apr-May in SYs), DPB complete (Jul-Mar in AHY/ASYs), DPA limited-partial (Mar-Apr in ASYs). The PF can begin during southbound migration (scattered head and back feathers), the PAs occur on non-breeding grounds, and the DPB often starts on or near breeding grounds or during migration (head feathers) and completes on non-breeding grounds. During the PF, body feathers are replaced primarily in Oct-Feb and flight feathers primarily in Jan-Apr; look for occasional SYs to retain 1-2 outer pp and p covs and/or medial ss. Extent of PA1 unknown: it may include a few to some body feathers in some SYs but may be absent (indicating SAS; Fig. 10**C**, p. 14); more study is needed. The DPA includes some body (primarily head) feathers but few if any s covs, terts, or rects. During the DPB, body feathers replaced primarily in Aug-Jan and flight feathers primarily in Dec-Mar, the latter overlapping with initiation of DPA.

Age—Juv (B1; Jul-Nov) has upperparts brownish, the feathers with distinct subterminal dark bands and buff tips creating scaled appearance, tail with black distal band, and bill black; Juv ♀ = ♂.

Juv-HY/SY (1st cycle, Juv/B1-F1-A1; Nov-Oct): Back and s covs brown or mixed gray and brown; juv rects with distinct black band in Nov-Mar (until juv feathers replaced); p10 with reduced and indistinct whitish until replaced in Mar-Apr (*cf.* Fig. 457**A**, p. 634); head whitish to partly slaty in Apr-Aug; bill black, sometimes with yellow tip in Apr-Oct. **Note: Look for a few SYs to also retain outer pp or medial ss. It is possible that some SYs may attain solid dark hoods and become indistinguishable from ASYs in May-Oct (study needed).**

AHY/ASY (Def. cycle, DB-DA; Nov-Oct): Back and s covs gray; rects without black; p10 with increased white to inner web and distinct black tip (*cf.* Fig. 464**A**, p. 642); head with complete slaty hood in Apr-Aug; bill black, usually with distinct yellow tip. **Note: See Juv-HY/SY. The pattern and amount of black on p5 may average more extensive on SY/TYs; more study needed.**

Sex—♀=♂ by plumage aspect. Bilateral and medial BPs (Fig. 20**C,** p. 31) developed by both sexes but distended cloaca (Fig. 21, p. 32) indicates ASY ♀ in May-Jul. Measurements largely unhelpful (Table 57, p. 635); head-bill length (Figure 453, p. 630) possibly useful for sexing but study needed on live individuals. Suggestions that ♂♂ usually lack subterminal black marks on p4 are not supported by specimen data.

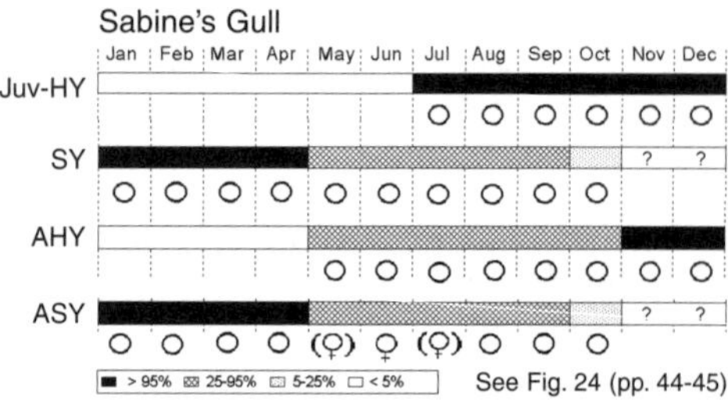

Hybrids Reported—None.

References—Bent (1921), Cramp & Simmons (1983), Day et al. (2001), Dement'ev & Gladkov (1951c), Dwight (1925), Higgins & Davies (1996), Howell & Dunn (2007), Malling Olsen & Larsson (2003), Manning et al. (1956), Oberholser (1974), Ridgway (1919), Stone (1900), Yésou (1997).

BONAPARTE'S GULL
Chroicocephalus philadelphia

BOGU
Species # 0600
Band size: 3-3B

Species—From other gulls by small size (Table 57, p. 635); bill shallower at gonys (6.0-7.6 mm) than at base (6.8-9.4; *cf.* Fig. 453, p. 630); upperparts medium-pale gray (Kodak 5-6, p. 629); underside of p7-p9 with extensive white tongues (Figs. 459**A** & 461); head with distinct black spot or partially to completely slaty blackish on ASYs in Apr-Aug; underwing covs white; bill black; legs pinkish to pale reddish. From Black-headed (p. 640) and Little (p. 642) gulls further by medium-sized wing chord (242-275), exposed culmen (25-32), and tarsus (32-38) (Table 57); p7-p9 with sharply defined pattern and relatively broad black tip (Fig. 459**A**, *cf.* Fig. 461); outer p covs of HY/SY with reduced black (Fig. 460); bill without reddish; legs paler.

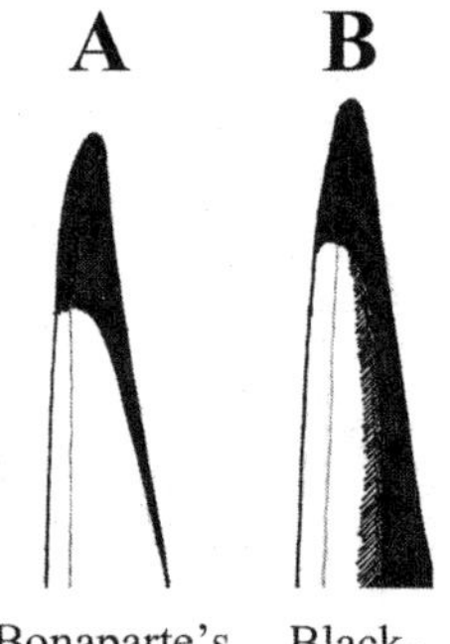

FIGURE 459. Typical pattern on the underside of (the outer primaries p7-p9) by species in definitive-aspect (AHY/ASY) Bonaparte's (**A**) and Black-headed (**B**) gulls, here showing p8. Black-headed Gull has more-extensive but less sharply defined dark on the inner web, and averages a shorter blackish tip. In the 1st cycle (HY/SYs) the inner web differences are similar to those of definitive plumage aspect, but the outer webs of both species are mostly to entirely blackish (see Fig. 461).

Geographic variation—Monotypic; e.N.Am populations average slightly larger than w.N.Am populations (Braune 1987a).

Molt—CAS. PF partial (Aug-Nov? in HY/SYs), PA1 partial-incomplete (Feb?-Jun in SYs), PB2 complete (Jun-Sep in SYs), DPA partial (Mar-May in ASYs), DPB complete (Jul-Oct in

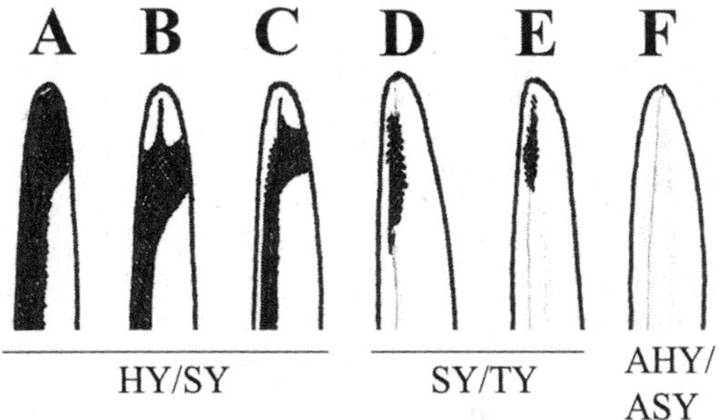

FIGURE 460. Pattern to the longest primary covert by age in Bonaparte's Gull. First-cycle HY/SYs always have extensive black (**A**-**C**) and most (to all?) 2nd-cycle SY/TYs have variable black markings (**D**-**E**). AHY/ASYs with no black markings (**F**) might be reliably aged ASY/ATY but study is needed.

ASYs). The PF and DPB usually start on or near breeding grounds and complete on non-breeding grounds, and the DPA starts on non-breeding grounds and often completes during northward migration. The PF and PA1 combined include most to all body feathers, often some med and proximal les covs, occasionally 1-3 terts, and sometimes one to all 12 c.rects; more study needed on extents of each molt. The DPA includes some body feathers but few if any s covs, terts, or rects.

Age—Juv (B1; Jul-Oct) has crown, face, and upperparts mottled and washed cinnamon-brown and back mottled cinnamon-brown; Juv ♀ = ♂.

HY/SY (1st cycle, F1-A1; Oct-Sep): Alula, outer p covs, and outer pp with extensive black (Figs. 460**A**-**C** & 461**A**); terts with blackish markings; rects with narrow blackish distal band; head with no or some slaty-blackish mottling in Apr-Aug (rarely if ever attains complete hood).

AHY/ASY (Def. cycle, DB-DA; Oct-Sep): Alula, outer p covs, terts, and rects without blackish (Fig. 460**F**); p8-p9 with little or no black on edge of outer web and with distinct tip when fresh (Fig. 461**D**-**E**); head with complete slaty black hood in Apr-Aug. **Note: See SY/TY. AHY/ASYs with no black on outer webs of p8-p9 (Fig. 461E), large white pp tips out to p9, and no black marks on rects, alula, and outer p covs (e.g., Fig. 460F) might be reliably aged ASY/ATY (study needed).**

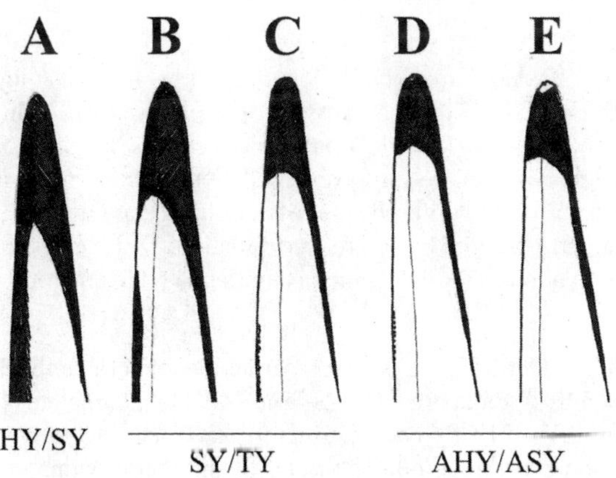

FIGURE 461. Variation in pattern of the outer primaries (p8-p9) by age in Bonaparte's Gull, here showing p9. AHYs with no black on the outer webs of p8-p9 and large white pp tips on p8-p9 (**E**) might be safely aged as ASY/ATY (Oct-Sep) but study is needed.

SY/TY (2nd cycle, B2-A2; Oct-Sep): Like AHY/ASY but alula and outer p covs with blackish distal marks (Fig. 460**D-E**); outer webs of p8-p9 with black medial edging but with reduced or no white tips (Fig. 461**B-C**); terts and rects sometimes with variable blackish marks; head sometimes with whitish mottling in May-Jun. **Note: See AHY/ASY; some to many SY/TYs may be indistinguishable from AHY/ASYs (more study needed).**

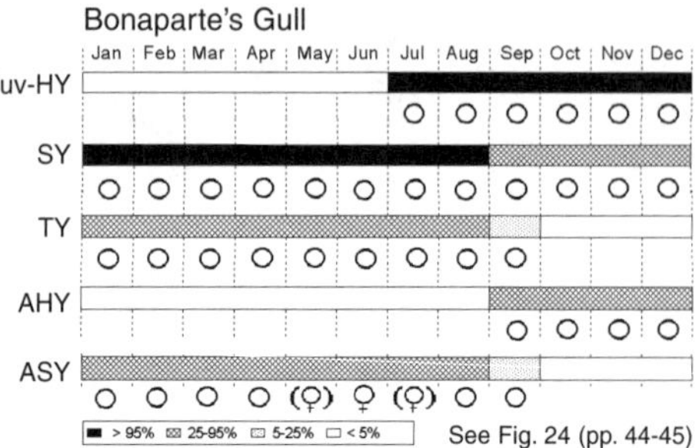

Sex—♀=♂ by plumage aspect. Bilateral and medial BPs (Fig. 20**C**, p. 31) developed by both sexes but distended cloaca (Fig. 21, p. 32) indicates ASY ♀ in May-Jul. Measurements unhelpful for sexing (Table 57, p. 635). Head-bill length (Figure 453, p. 630) possibly useful for sexing; study needed on live individuals. No other criteria known.

Hybrids Reported—None.

References—Bent (1921), Braune (1987a), Burger & Gochfeld (2000), Cramp & Simmons (1983), Dwight (1901, 1925), Howell & Dunn (2007). Malling Olsen & Larsson (2003), Oberholser (1974), Ridgway (1919), Roberts (1955).

BLACK-HEADED GULL
Chroicocephalus ridibundus

BHGU
Species # 0551
Band size: 5

Species—From other smaller gulls by medium-small size (Table 57, p. 635); bill depth at gonys (7.5-10.1) similar to depth at base (7.3-10.5; *cf.* Fig. 453, p. 630); upperparts pale gray (Kodak 4-5, p. 629); undersides of p7-p9 with fairly extensive white tongues (Fig. 459**B**, p. 638; *cf.* Fig. 461, p. 639); underwing covs pale to medium gray by age; head with distinct black spot or partially to completely dark brown in Apr-Aug ASYs; legs dusky pink to drab red. From Bonaparte's (p. 638) and Little (p. 642) gulls further by wing chord > 275, exp culmen ≥ 29, and tarsus > 38 (Table 57); p7-p9 with indistinct pattern and relatively narrow black tip (Fig. 459**B**); outer p covs of HY/SY with moderate black (Fig. 462); bill with extensive pinkish or reddish basally; legs darker.

Geographic variation—Considered monotypic here in lieu of further study; see Cramp & Simmons (1983), Dwight (1925), Gibson & Kessel (1997), Howell & Dunn (2007), Kozlova (1932), and Malling Olsen & Larsson (2003). Populations of e.Asia ("*L.r. sibiricus*") average larger (especially in bill size) than nominate European populations but difference appears too slight for subspecific recognition; reported differences in extent of black to outer pp (Malling Olsen & Larsson 2003) are slight and obscured by age-related variation. DPBs may also average later in Asian than European populations but this is probably more related to environmental than genetic factors (see pp. 16-18).

Molt—CAS. PF partial (Aug-Oct in HY/SYs), PA1 partial-incomplete (Feb-May in SYs), PB2 complete (May/Jul-Sep in SYs), PA2 partial (Jan-Apr in SYs), DPB complete (Jul-Nov in ASYs), DPA partial (Jan-Mar in ASYs). The PF occurs primarily on or near breeding grounds but completes on migration or non-breeding grounds, the DPB starts on breeding grounds or during migration and completes on non-breeding grounds, and the DPA starts on non-breeding grounds and often completes during northward migration. The PF and PA1 combined include some to most body feathers, no to most s covs, sometimes 1-3 terts, and occasionally 1-12 c.rects; more study needed to determine extents of each molt. The DPA includes few if any s covs, terts, or c.rects (more study needed). The DPBs and DPAs of w.Europe populations average earlier than those of e.Asia.

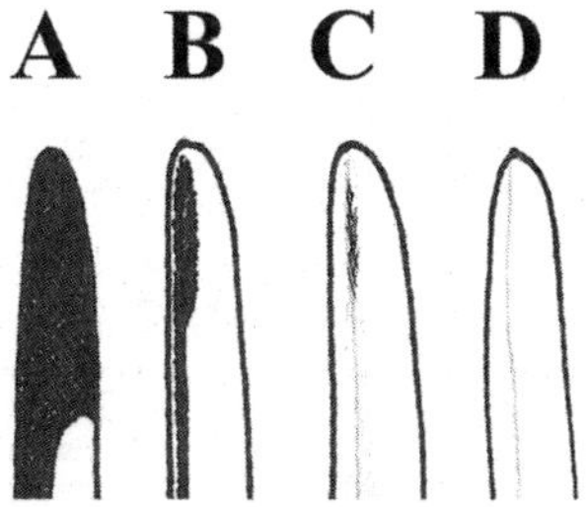

A B C D

FIGURE 462. Pattern to the outermost primary coverts by age in Black-headed Gull. Juv covs on 1st-cycle HY/SYs have extensive black markings (**A-B**), some 2nd-cycle birds (SY/TYs) show a variably small amount of blackish (e.g., **C**), and definitive plumage aspects (of AHY/ASYs and including many SY/TYs) shows no blackish (**D**).

Age—Juv (Jul-Sep) has crown, face, and hindcollar mottled and washed cinnamon-brown and back mottled cinnamon-brown; Juv ♀=♂.

HY/SY (1st cycle, F1-A1; Oct-Sep): Alula and inner p covs with variable blackish markings (Fig. 462**A-B**); outer pp with outer webs mostly blackish (*cf*. Figs. 459 & 461**A**, pp. 638-639); rects with narrow blackish distal band (*cf*. Fig. 486**E**, p. 661); underwing covs pale gray; head with no to (occasionally) complete dark brown hood in May-Jun.

AHY/ASY (Def. cycle, DB-DA; Oct-Sep): Alula and outer p covs without blackish distal marks (Fig. 462**D**); outer pp with little or no black to outer webs (*cf*. Figs. 459 & 461**B-D**); rects white; underwing covs medium gray; head with complete dark brown hood in Apr-Jul. **Note: See SY/TY; it is possible that some ASY/ATYs can be reliably aged but more study needed.**

SY/TY (2nd cycle, B2-A2; Oct-Sep): Like AHY/ASY but alula, outer p covs, and/or rects with variable blackish distal marks (Fig. 462**C-D**; *cf*. Fig. 486**F**); head occasionally mottled whitish in May-Jun. **Note: In addition, p9-p10 average more black (*cf*. Allaine & Lebreton 1990) and probably smaller white tips in SY/TY than ASY/ATY but reliability of this unclear; more study needed. Many SY/TY are not be distinguishable from AHY/ASY.**

Sex—♀=♂ by plumage aspect. Bilateral and medial BPs (Fig. 20**C,** p. 31) developed by both sexes but distended cloaca (Fig. 21, p. 32) indicates ATY ♀ in Apr-Jul. See Coulson et al. (1983), Allaine & Lebreton (1990), and Palomares et al. (1997) for DFAs (p. 5) using head-bill length (Fig. 453, p. 630) and bill depth at gonys, on specimens and fresh dead individuals, that correctly distinguished 92.2-94.5% of sexes in w.European populations. Most measurements largely unhelpful (Table 57, p. 635) but the following can be used to reliably sex most individuals:

♀: Head-bill length (Fig. 453) 72-84 mm. **Note: These head-bill lengths based on w.European populations and may not apply exactly to Siberian populations (see Geographic variation). Individuals with head-bill length 80-84 are not reliably sexed by this measure alone.**

♂: Head-bill length (Fig. 453) 80-92 mm. **Note: See ♀.**

Hybrids Reported—With Laughing Gull (Sibley 1994), Brown-headed Gull *L. brunnicephalus* (McCarthy 2006), Slender-billed Gull *L. genei* (McCarthy 2006), Mediterranean Gull *L. melanocephalus* (Langman 2000, Taverner 1970), Mew Gull *L.c. canus* (Balten et al. 1993, Moskoff & Bevier 2002), Ring-billed Gull (Weseloh & Mineau 1986), and Herring Gull (McCarthy 2006) in the wild.

References—Allaine & Lebreton (1990), Baker (1993), Bent (1921), Coulson et al. (1983), Cramp & Simmons (1983), Higgins & Davies (1996), Howell & Dunn (2007). Malling Olsen & Larsson (2003), Meissher (2007b), Oberholser (1974), Palomares et al. (1997), Paterson (1993), Ridgway (1919), Walters (1978, 1982).

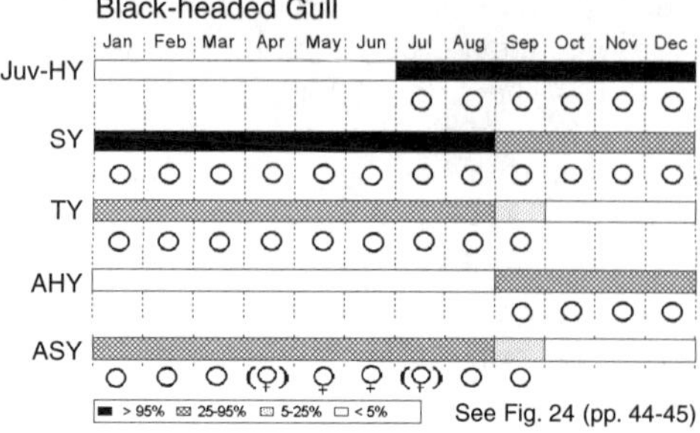

LITTLE GULL
Hydrocoloeus minutus

LIGU
Species # 0601
Band size: 3

Species—From all other gulls by smaller size (Table 57, p. 635), bill shallower at gonys (4.8-6.0 mm) than at base (5.2-7.1; *cf.* Fig. 453, p. 630); upperparts pale gray (Kodak 3.5-4.5, p. 629); head with black spot and blackish in crown in Sep-Mar, or mostly to entirely blackish in Apr-Aug; underwing s covs pale grayish to blackish by age; bill black; legs pinkish to bright red. From Bonaparte's (p. 638) and Black-headed (p. 640) gulls further by wing chord < 235, exposed culmen ≤ 25, and tarsus < 30 (Table 57); p7-p9 with pale grayish (rather than white) tongue, and reduced black tip in Juv-HY/SY (Fig. 464); HY/SY with outer p covs blackish (Fig. 463**A**). Juv-HY/SY from Juv-HY/SY Ross's Gull (p. 643) by shorter wing chord, tail, and tarsus, but longer bill (Table 57) and less graduated tail (r1 – r6 < 20 mm); crown with blackish; gr covs and ss grayish to dusky with distinct white tips; legs brighter.

Geographic variation—Monotypic.

Molt—CAS. PF partial (Aug-Nov? in HY/SYs), PA1 partial-incomplete (Feb?-May in SYs), PB2 complete (Jun-Oct in SYs), PA2 partial (Feb-May in TYs), DPB complete (Jul-Nov in ASYs), DPA partial (Mar-May in ATYs). The PF and DPB usually start on or near breeding grounds and complete on non-breeding

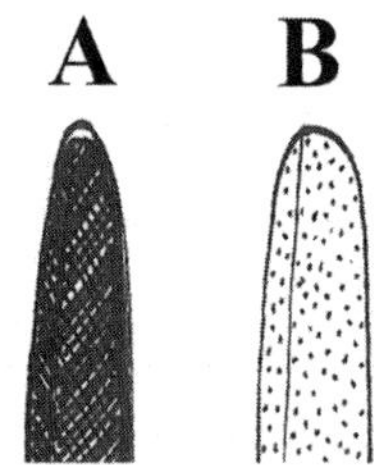

FIGURE 463. Pattern of outermost primary coverts by age in Little Gull; patterns in Ross's Gull appear to be similar but more study is needed on those of 2nd-cycle SY/TYs. AHY/ASYs with limited black markings can probably be aged SY/TY; compare with pattern to outer pp (Fig. 464**B**-**C**).

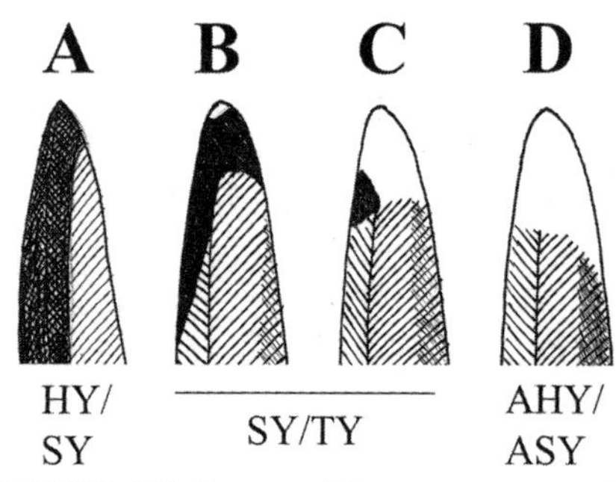

FIGURE 464. Pattern of the outer primaries by age in Little Gull, here showing p8. Note that definitive plumage aspect (in AHY/ASYs) can show dusky to the inner web but no black in the outer web. AHY/ASYs with extensive white as shown in **D** may be reliably aged ASY/ATY in Nov-Oct (*cf.* Allaine & Lebreton 1990) but study needed. Ross's Gull shows similar patterns in first-cycle Juv-HY/SYs; (**A**) and definitive-cycle AHY/ASYs; (**D**) cycles; more study needed to determine patterns of 2nd-cycle SY/TYs; (**B**-**C**?). Basic outer pp of Sabine's Gull resemble **A** but with white inner webs, extending closer to shaft.

grounds, and the DPA starts on non-breeding grounds and often completes during northward migration. The PF and PA1 combined include some s covs, sometimes 1-3 terts, and often 1-12 c.rects; more study needed to determine extents of each molt. The DPA includes no to a few s covs and sometimes 1-2 terts but few if any c.rects (confirmation needed).

Age—Juv (B1; Jul-Nov) has cap, auricular spot, and hindneck blackish brown, back mottled blackish brown, and legs dull pinkish; Juv ♀=♂.

HY/SY (1st cycle, F1-A1; Nov-Oct): Outer pp, p covs, and alula extensively blackish (Figs. 463**A** & 464**A**); rects with blackish distal band (*cf.* Fig. 486**F**, p. 661; sometimes mixed white and rarely all white in May-Oct); underwing covs whitish, often contrasting with dusky marginal les covs; legs pinkish (becoming reddish by Mar-Aug); head with no to (occasionally) complete blackish hood in May-Jun.

AHY/ASY (Def. cycle, DB-DA; Nov-Oct): Outer pp, p covs, and alula pale gray without blackish subterminal marks (Figs. 463**B** & 464**D**); rects white; underwing covs smoky gray to blackish; legs reddish; head with complete blackish hood in Apr-Jun. **Note: See SY/TY. It is possible that some AHY/ASYs with the above description may be reliably aged ASY/ATY but study needed.**

SY/TY (2nd cycle, B2-A2; Nov-Oct): Like AHY/ASY but one or more pp among p6-p10 often, and alula and p covs sometimes, with blackish subterminal marks (Fig. 464**B-D**; *cf.* Fig. 463); underwing covs grayish; forehead and lores sometimes with white spotting in May-Jun. **Note: Some to many SY/TYs may not be distinguishable from AHY/ASY (study needed).**

Sex—♀=♂ by plumage aspect. Bilateral and medial BPs (Fig. 20**C,** p. 31) developed by both sexes but distended cloaca (Fig. 21, p. 32) indicates ASY ♀ in Apr-Jul. Measurements largely unhelpful (Table 57, p. 635) but head-bill length (Figure 453, p. 630) possibly useful for sexing; study needed on live individuals.

Little Gull

Jan Feb Mar Apr May Jun Jul Aug Sep Oct Nov Dec

Juv-HY

SY

TY

AHY

ASY

■ > 95% ▨ 25-95% ▭ 5-25% □ < 5%

See Fig. 24 (pp. 44-45)

Hybrids Reported—None.

References—Baker (1993), Bent (1921), Cramp & Simmons (1983), Dement'ev & Gladkov (1951c), Dwight (1925), Ewins & Weseloh (1999), Howell & Dunn (2007), Malling Olsen & Larsson (2003), Murphy (1936), Ridgway (1919).

ROSS'S GULL

Rhodostethia rosea

ROGU
Species # 0610
Band size: 3

Species—From other smaller gulls including Sabine's Gull (p. 637) by medium-small size with short bill and long tail (Table 57, p. 635), the latter graduated (r1>r6 by 20-36 mm); bill similar to or slightly shallower at gonys (5.4-6.6 mm) than at base (5.8-6.6; *cf.* Fig. 453, p. 630); upperparts very pale gray (Kodak 3-4, p. 629); outer pp without white tongue (Fig. 464; *cf.* Fig. 450, p. 638); bill black; legs pinkish (Juv) to reddish (AHY); underwing covs grayish to dusky; Juv-HY/SY with outer p covs blackish (Fig. 463**A**); AHY with underparts increasingly suffused pink in Dec-Jun. Juv-HY/SY from Little Gull (p. 642) further by longer wing chord, tail, and tarsus but shorter bill (Table 57); tail graduated (r1>r6 by 20 mm); crown usually without blackish; gr covs and ss pale grayish with indistinct white tips.

Geographic variation—Monotypic.

Molt—CAS. PF partial (Aug-Oct? in HYs), PA1 partial (Mar?-May in SYs), PB2 complete (Jun-Sep in SYs), DPA partial (Mar-May in ASYs), DPB complete (Jul-Oct/Mar? in ASYs). The PF (often) and DPB start on breeding grounds and complete on non-breeding grounds or perhaps at staging areas. The DPA starts on non-breeding grounds and often completes during migration. The PF and PA1 combined include no to (often) all 12 c.rects but probably few if any s covs or terts; study needed to determine extents of each molt. The DPA includes some body feathers but few if any s covs, terts, or rects. The DPB can occasionally(?) be suspended or arrested, e.g., p9-p10 and s2-s11 retained until at least Mar-Apr. This likely indicates breeders and possibly occurs only in years of poor ocean productivity (see Black-legged Kittiwake and Howell and Corben 2000c).

Age—Juv (B1; Aug-Nov) has head and back mottled sooty brown, scapulars with bold, cinnamon-buff to pale buffy-gray tips, and legs dull pinkish; Juv ♀ = ♂.

Juv-HY/SY (1st cycle, Juv/B1-F1-A1; Oct-Sep): Outer pp, alula, and p covs extensively blackish (Figs. 463**A** & 464**A**, p. 642); inner rects (r1-r3/r4) with blackish tips (without blackish marks in Apr-Sep if all rects replaced); underwing covs pale grayish; legs pinkish, becoming reddish in Mar-Aug; head with dark auricular spot in Oct-Apr.

AHY/ASY (Def. cycle, DB-DA; Oct-Sep): Outer pp, alula, and p covs without blackish subterminal marks (Figs. 463**B** & 464**D**); terts and inner rects without subterminal marks; underwing covs dusky; legs reddish; head usually without dark auricular spot in Oct-Apr. **Note: See SY/TY. Look also for AHY/ASYs with retained outer pp and medial ss or suspension limits in these areas (see Fig. 458, p. 636) in Feb-Sep, possibly indicating breeding adults (ATYs).**

SY/TY (2nd cycle, B2-A2; Oct-Sep): Like AHY/ASY but alula and/or some p covs occasionally with dark markings (*cf.* Fig. 463); rects and terts occasionally with dark markings. **Note: Most SY/TYs probably indistinguishable from AHY/ASY (study needed).**

ASY/ATY (Def. cycle, DB; Oct-Mar): Like ASY/ATY with molt in pp occurring or suspended, and outer pp and p covs without blackish subterminal marks (Figs. 463**B** & 464**D**). **Note: Some ATYs may arrest molt (see Molt) and be reliably aged through Sep or later, and ASY/ATYs with suspended molt and outer pp and p covs as in SY/TY may possibly be reliably aged TY/4Y in Oct-Mar, but confirmation of these patterns needed.**

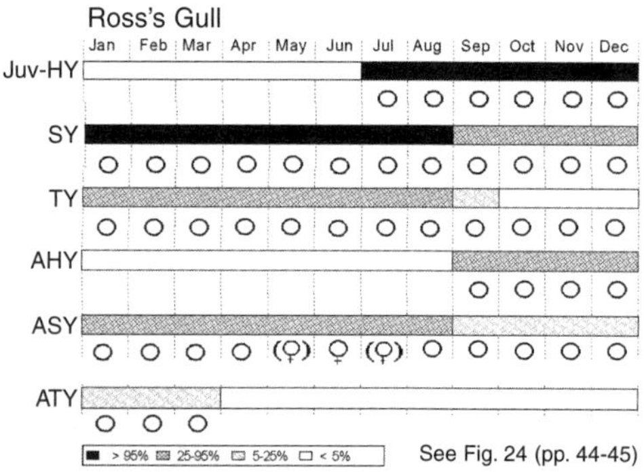

Ross's Gull
Jan Feb Mar Apr May Jun Jul Aug Sep Oct Nov Dec
Juv-HY
SY
TY
AHY
ASY
(♀) ♀ (♀)
ATY
■ > 95% ▨ 25-95% ▭ 5-25% □ < 5%
See Fig. 24 (pp. 44-45)

Sex—♀ = ♂ by plumage aspect. Bilateral and medial(?) BPs (Fig. 20**C**, p. 31) probably developed by both sexes but distended cloaca (Fig. 21, p. 32) indicates ASY ♀ in May-Jul. Measurements unhelpful (Table 57, p. 635) and head-bill length (Figure 453, p. 630) probably not useful for sexing.

Hybrids Reported—None.

References—Bent (1921), Cramp & Simmons (1983), Dwight (1925), Dement'ev & Gladkov (1951c), Lindström et al. (1998), Malling Olsen & Larsson (2003), Ridgway (1919), Stone (1900), Yésou (1994).

TABLE 58. Measurements (mm) of Laughing, Franklins, and Heermann's gulls to assist in identification and sexing. See pp. 4-11 for methods of measurement. Species summaries are in **bold** and subspecies values are in ***italics***. Values were derived from 95% confidence intervalsas based approximately on the indicated sample sizes (pp. 4-5); sample size for bill depth was often smaller but included at least 10 of each sex. Thus, midpoints of ranges approximate means, and S.D. is approximated by 25% of the range.

Taxon/Sex	*n*	wing chord[1]	tail length	exp culmen	bill depth[2]	tarsus
Laughing Gull		**288-354**	**110-134**	**32-43**	**9.9-14.0**	**41-56**
L.a. megalopterus		***296-354***	***115-134***	***32-43***	***10.3-14.0***	***44-56***
♀	100	296-338	115-130	32-40	10.3-13.3	44-52
♂	100	306-354	119-134	35-43	11.0-14.0	47-56
L.a. atricilla		***288-326***	***110-127***	***33-42***	***9.9-13.5***	***41-51***
♀	60	288-320	110-123	33-39	9.9-13.0	41-48
♂	100	292-326	114-127	36-42	11.1-13.5	43-51
Franklin's Gull		**258-299**	**94-112**	**25-35**	**8.8-11.2**	**38-46**
♀	100	258-290	94-111	25-33	8.1-10.2	38-45
♂	100	265-299	95-112	27-35	8.8-11.2	39-46
Heermann's Gull		**329-368**	**131-162**	**36-48**	**11.4-14.9**	**48-55**
♀	50	327-352	131-159	36-44	11.4-13.7	48-55
♂	60	335-368	133-162	38-48	12.0-14.9	50-58

[1] Wing chord averages ~5% shorter in Juv-HY/SY than in AHY/ASY.
[2] Bill depth measured at distal end of forehead feathering (see Fig. 8**A**, p. 10).

LAUGHING GULL
Leucophaeus atricilla

LAGU
Species # 0580
Band size: 4A-4-5 (a)

Species—From other gulls by medium to medium-large size (Table 58; bill depth at gonys 9.3-12.7 for N.Am populations); head washed dusky in Sep-Mar (and Apr-Aug in some SYs; Fig. 465**A**), or blackish with white eye crescents in most Feb-Aug AHYs; bill and legs blackish to dark red; ATY with upperparts medium-dark gray (Kodak 9-10.5, p. 629). From Franklin's Gull (p. 648) further by larger size and bill (Table 57, Fig. 465**A**); head without distinct black in Oct-Mar and with thinner eye crescents year-round (Fig. 465**A**); outer rect of juv-HY/SY usually with extensive black (Fig. 466**A**, p. 646); p9-p10 of ASY/ATY without white medial band or extensive white tips (Fig. 467, p. 646).

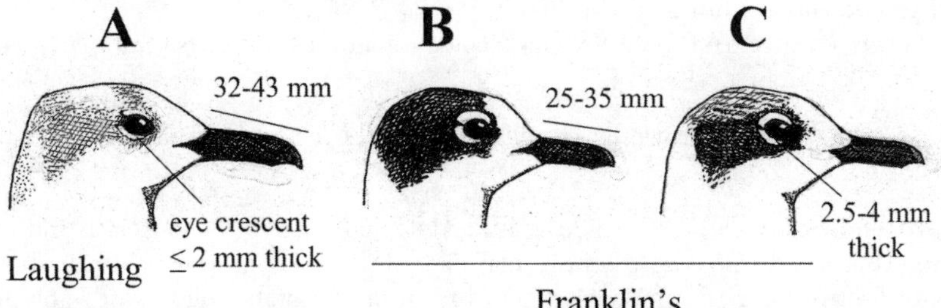

FIGURE 465. Typical head patterns of Laughing Gull (**A**) and Franklin's Gull (**B**-**C**) in basic aspect. Also note Laughing Gull's larger bill and narrower white eye-crescents (typical of all plumage aspects). Measures indicate exposed culmen (Fig. 7A, p. 9).

Geographic variation—See Burger (1996), Cramp & Simmons (1985), Dwight (1925), Hellmayr & Conover (1948b), Malling Olsen & Larsson (2003), Murphy (1936), Noble (1916), Oberholser (1974), and Parkes (1952b) for more information. No other subspecies occur. Within *L.a. megalopterus*, AHYs from NY breeding populations may average longer wing and shorter tarsus than AHYs from FL populations (Evans et al. 1993); further study needed. Perhaps this species should be treated as monotypic.

L.a. megalopterus (br throughout N.Am range, wint to S.Am): Averages larger but with proportionally shorter bill (Table 58, p. 645; bill depth at gonys 9.3-12.7); tips of p5-p7 on ASY/ATY average less extensive but more distinct black, and larger white tips (Fig. 467**A**).

L.a. atricilla (res? West Indies; probable visitor to s. FL): Averages smaller but with proportionally longer bill (Table 58; bill depth at gonys 8.3-11.6); tips of p5-p7 on ASY/ATY average more extensive but less distinct black, and smaller white tips (Fig. 467**B**).

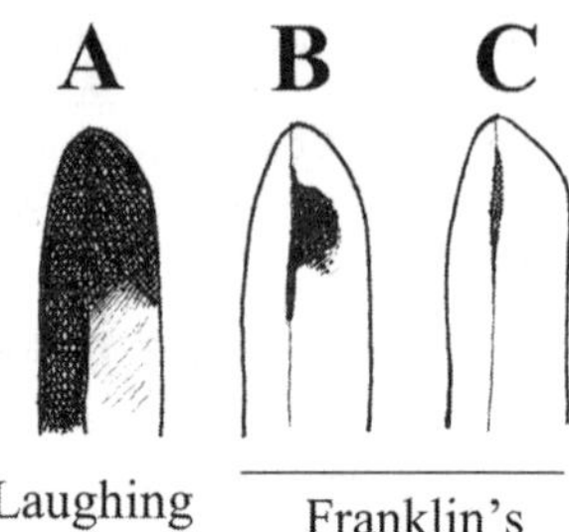

FIGURE 466. Patterns of the juvenal outer rectrix (r6) in 1st cycle Juv-HY/SY Laughing (**A**) and Franklin's (**B-C**) gulls. SY Franklin's Gulls typically replace the outer rectrices with white feathers in Mar-Apr, whereas SY Laughing Gulls can occasionally replace them during Dec-Mar, often with a feather resembling the pattern of Juv Franklin's (**B-C**).

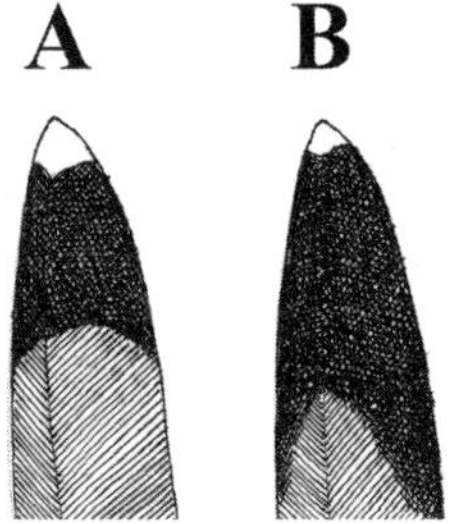

FIGURE 467. Typical patterns of p6 by subspecies in definitive-aspect (ASY/ATY) Laughing Gulls. The widespread *L. a. megalopterus* (**A**) averages less-extensive but more sharply defined black distally, and typically has a larger white tip (which often wears off by spring) than that of *atricilla* (**B**) of the W.Indies. Beware that 2nd-cycle (SY/TY) *megalopterus* often have a p6 pattern resembling *atricilla*, but with little or no white tip (*cf*. Fig. 469).

Molt—CAS. PF partial (Jul-Dec in HYs), PA1 partial-incomplete (Dec-Apr in HY/SYs), PB2 complete (May-Oct in SYs), DPA partial (Jan-Apr in ASYs), DPB complete (Jun-Nov in ASYs). The PF and DPB usually start on or near breeding grounds but complete on non-breeding grounds, whereas DPAs start on non-breeding grounds and may complete on breeding grounds. The PF and/or PA1 include a few to most s covs, sometimes 1-5 terts/inner ss, and sometimes 1-6 c.rects (occasionally all 12 rects); study needed to determine extents of each molt. The DPA includes no to a few proximal s covs, sometimes 1-4 terts, and occasionally 1-2 c.rects.

Age—Juv (B1; Jun-Oct) has brown head, neck, chest, and back, and scapulars with scaly buff to whitish edging; Juv ♀ = ♂.

Juv-HY/SY (1st cycle, Juv/B1-F1-A1; Aug-Jul): Alula and outer p covs blackish and relatively tapered (Fig. 468**A**); p6 with extensive black and little white at tip (Fig. 469**A**); bases to ss blackish brown; back and upperwing covs brownish or variably mixed with gray feathers; underwing s covs dusky brownish; rects with solid to broken black distal band (*cf*. Fig. 466**A**, occasionally without black in Feb-Jul); neck and sides of breast extensively brownish gray in Aug-Apr; head blackish mottled whitish (especially base of bill) and bill and legs blackish (sometimes tinged dark reddish) in Apr-Jul.

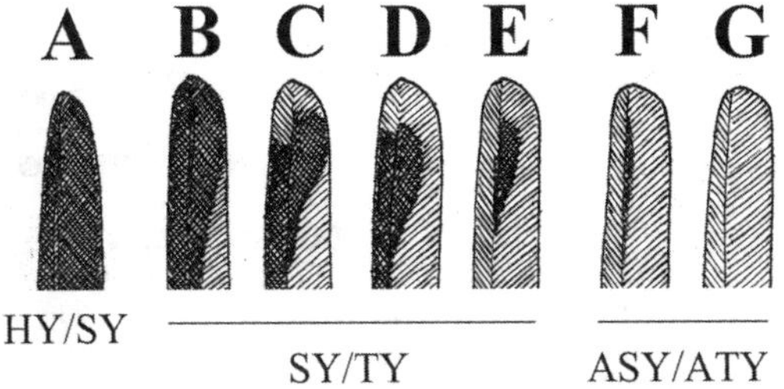

FIGURE 468. Variation in pattern of the longest primary covert by age in Laughing Gull. Note also more tapered shape of the juv cov (**A**).

SY/TY (2nd cycle, B2-A2; Aug-Jul): Alula and outer p covs usually with black to outer web (Fig. 468**B-E**); p6 with moderate black and small white tip (Fig. 469**B**); bases to ss slaty gray, sometimes with dark basal marks; back and upperwing covs slaty gray; underwing s covs whitish; rects white, often with black subterminal marks (rarely forming incomplete tail band); neck and sides of breast washed pale gray in Aug-Apr; head black (sometimes flecked whitish) and bill and legs dark reddish in Apr-Jul.

ASY/ATY (Def. cycle, DB-DA; Aug-Jul): Alula and outer p covs with little or no black (Fig. 468**F-G**); p6 with reduced black and relatively large white tip (Fig. 469**C**); ss slaty gray; rects white; neck and sides of breast white or tinged pale gray in Aug-Apr; head black and bill and legs dark reddish in Apr-Jul. **Note: Some TY/4Ys may be recognized by having the above plumage aspect but rects with limited dark markings and p5-p6 and p covs with moderate black (Fig. 468E-F) but study needed.**

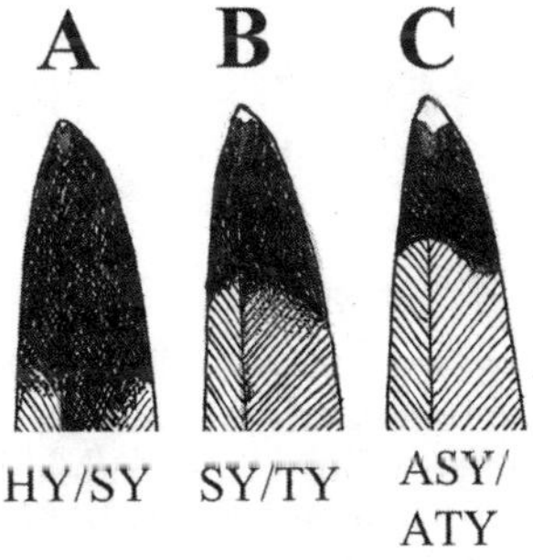

FIGURE 469. Typical patterns of black on p6 by age in N.Am Laughing Gulls (*L. a. megalopterus*); beware possible confounding effects of subspecies (at least in Florida; see **Geographic variation** and Fig. 467) and combine with pattern of longest p covs (Fig. 468). Some definitive-cycle ASY/ATYs have less black than shown here (see Belant & Dolbeer 1996 for details).

Sex—♀=♂ by plumage aspect. Bilateral and medial BPs (Fig. 20**C**, p. 31) developed by both sexes but distended cloaca (Fig. 21, p. 32) indicates ATY ♀ in Apr-Jun. Measurements somewhat helpful for sexing (Table 58, p. 645), especially mated pairs, and the following is reliable for sexing most N.Am *L.a. megalopterus*. In addition, see Hanners & Patton (1985) for DFA (p. 5) using head-bill length and bill depth at gonys that separated 95% of freshly dead adults from a FL breeding population, and Evans et al. (1993) for DFAs using bill length, total length, and flat wing length for sexing individuals in a NY breeding population.

♀: Head-bill length (Fig. 453, p. 630) 80-91 mm. **Note: Individuals with head-bill length 88-91 mm may not be reliably sexed (n.breeding populations average larger values than s.breeding populations).**

♂: Head-bill length 88 08 mm. **Note: See ♀.**

Hybrids reported—With Black-headed Gull (p. 640), Gray-hooded Gull *L. cirrocephalus* (Cramp & Simmons 1980, Erard et al. 1984), and Ring-billed Gull (Henshaw 1992, Sibley 1994) in the wild.

References—Belant & Dolbeer (1996), Burger (1996), Burger & Beer (1975), Cramp & Simmons (1983), Dinsmore & Schreiber (1974), Dolbeer & Bernhardt (2003), Dwight (1925), Evans et al. (1993), Hanners & Patton (1985), Higgins & Davies (1996), Howell & Dunn (2007), Kaufman (1990a), Malling Olsen & Larsson (2003), Murphy (1936), Noble (1916), Oberholser (1974), Parkes (1952b), Schreiber & Schreiber (1979).

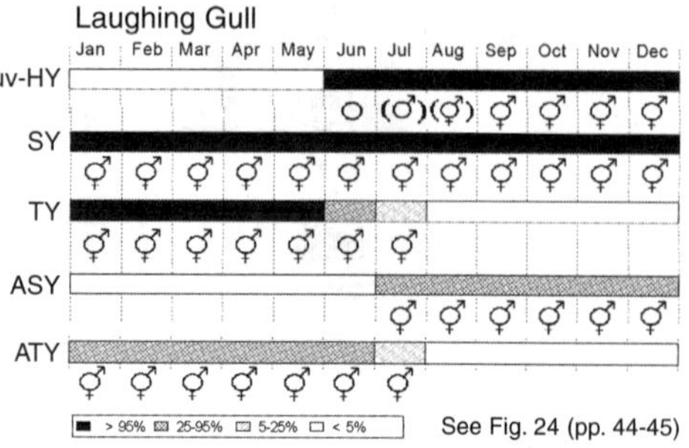

FRANKLIN'S GULL
Leucophaeus pipixcan

FRGU
Species # 0590
Band size: 4

Species—See Laughing Gull (p. 645) for separation from other gulls. From Laughing Gull by smaller size and bill (Fig. 465**B**-**C** & Table 58, p. 645; bill depth at gonys 8.0-9.7 mm); head and auriculars with distinct black in Oct-Mar and with thicker eye crescents year-round (Fig. 465**B**-**C**); outer rect of juv-HY/SY with little or no black (Fig. 466**B**-**C**, p. 646); ATY with upperparts medium to medium-dark gray (Kodak 8.5-10, p. 629) and p9-p10 with partial to complete white subterminal band and extensive white tips (Fig. 472**D**-**G**).

Geographic variation—Monotypic.

Molt—CAS. PF partial (Aug-Dec in HYs), PA1 partial-complete (Dec-May in HY/SYs), PB2 complete (Jun-Oct in SYs), DPA incomplete-complete (Dec-Apr in AHY/ASYs), DPB complete (Jun-Oct in ASYs). The PF and DPB occur primarily on or near breeding grounds whereas PAs occur primarily on non-breeding grounds. The PF includes some body feathers but few if any s covs, terts, or rects. Extent of the PAs (especially PA1) varies with wintering latitude and probably with interannual variation in food resources. The PA1 usually includes all s covs and rects but 0-10 pp and p covs and 3-17 outer to medial ss (n.wintering SYs may replace no pp; Hoogendoorn & van Ijzendoorn 1994). Most SYs replace at least p1-p7, p covs 1-4, and s1-s5 and s15-s17 (SYs can retain up to 3 juv outer p covs even when all pp replaced) and some individuals have a complete PA1. The DPA is usually complete, but some individuals can retain p9-p10 or p10, corresponding p covs, and/or up to six medial ss.

Age—Juv (B1; Jun-Oct) has neck and sides of breast mottled and washed dusky brownish, lower hindneck and back dark brown, and scapulars with scaly buff to whitish fringes; Juv ♀ = ♂.

Juv-HY/SY (1st cycle, Juv/B1-F1-A1; Aug-Jul): Outer p covs blackish (Fig. 470**A**) or sometimes gray with black distal marks in Apr-Jul (Fig. 470**B**-**D**); pp with substantial brownish in Aug-Feb and sometimes in Mar-Jul (Figs. 471**A** & 472**A**), or often with moderate black in Mar-Jul (Figs. 471**B**-**C** & 472**B**-**C**); rects (except r6) with dark subterminal band in Aug-Mar (*cf.* Fig. 486**E**, p. 661) or white, sometimes with black distal spots after replacement in Feb-Jul (*cf.* Fig. 486**F**-**G**); forehead and lores mottled white in Apr-Jul.

SY/TY (2nd cycle, B2-A2; Aug-Jul): Outer p covs often with black streaks in Aug-Mar (Fig. 470**C**-**D**; sometimes without streaks) or without black in Apr-Jul (Fig. 470**E**); p5 usually with black subterminal marks in Aug-Mar (Fig. 471**B**-**C**) and lacking black in Apr-Jul (Fig. 471**D**); p8-p10 with moderate black and reduced white (Fig. 472**B**-**C** in Aug-Mar, usually **D**-**E** in Apr-Jul); black hood usually complete in Apr-Jul; rects without black. **Note: In Apr-Jul indi-**

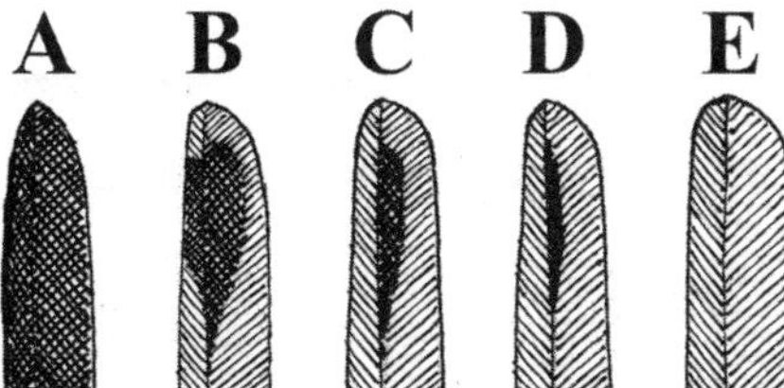

FIGURE 470. Variation in pattern of the longest primary coverts by age and feather generation in Franklin's Gull. Note that this feather may or may not be replaced during the PA1 but it is typically replaced during the DPA. Thus, 1st-cycle Juv-HY/SYs have juv covs (**A**) in Aug-Mar and sometimes through Jul, but many will replace this feather with covs resembling **B-D** in Apr-Jul. Second-cycle SY/TYs often have black streaks to this cov in Aug-Mar (**C-D**), but lack streaks in Apr-Jul (**E**) after replacement. In definitive aspect (ASY/ATYs) this cov lacks black year-round (**E**).

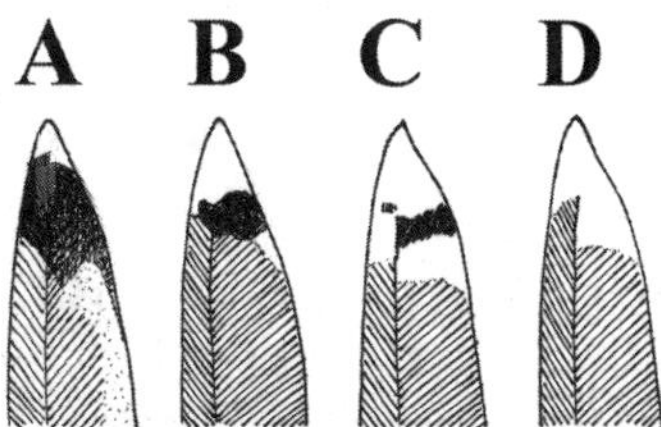

FIGURE 471. Variation in the pattern of p5 by age and feather generation in Franklin's Gull. See **Molt** and Fig. 470 regarding feather generations. The juv p5 in 1st-cycle HY/SYs resembles **A** in Aug-Mar and **A** (if retained) or **B-C** (if replaced formative) in Apr-Jul; p5 in 2nd-cycle SY/TYs resemble **B-C** in Aug-Mar (when basic) and **D** in Apr-Jul (when alternate); and p5 in definitive aspect (ASY/ATYs) resembles **D** year-round. Red-legged Kittiwake shows similar variation in the pattern to p5 year-round (no replacement during PAs).

viduals with complete PA and moderate black to the outer pp (Fig. 472E) are not reliably separable from ATYs and should be aged ASY.

ASY/ATY (Def. cycle, DB-DA; Aug-Jul): Outer p covs without black marks (Fig. 470**E**); p5 usually without black subterminal marks (Fig. 471**D**); p8-p10 with reduced black and more extensive white (Fig. 472**D-F** in Aug-Mar, usually **E-G** in Apr-Jul); black hood complete in Apr-Jul. **Note: See SY/TY.**

Sex— ♀ = ♂ by plumage aspect. Bilateral and medial BPs (Fig. 20**C,** p. 31) developed by both sexes but distended cloaca (Fig. 21, p. 32) indicates ATY ♀ in May-Jun. Measurements generally unhelpful (Table 58, p. 645) but head-bill length (Figure 453, p. 630) possibly useful for sexing; study needed on live individuals.

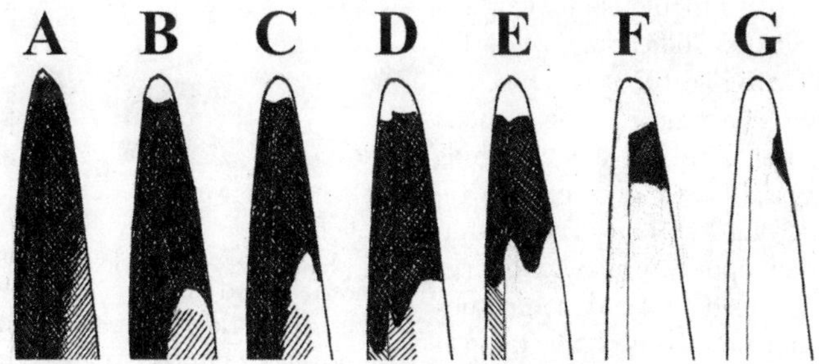

FIGURE 472. Variation in the pattern of p9 by age and season in Franklin's Gull. See **Molt** and Fig. 470 regarding feather generations. P9 during the 1st cycle (in Juv-HY/SYs) resembles **A** in Aug-Mar and **A** (if retained juv) or **B-C** (if replaced formative) in Apr-Jul; p9 during the 2nd cycle (in SY/TYs) resembles **B-C** in Aug-Mar and usually **D-E** (if replaced alternate) in Apr-Jul; and p9 in definitive aspect (in ASY/ATYs) resembles **D-F** in Aug-Mar and **E-G** (if replaced) in Apr-Jul. Note that individuals in Apr-Jul lacking black to the longest p cov (Fig. 470**E**) and p5 (Fig. 471**D**), and showing pattern **D** to p9, should be aged ASY.

Hybrids reported—With Gray-hooded Gull *L. cirrocephalus* (Erard et al. 1984) and Ring-billed Gull (Weseloh 1981).

References—Burger & Gochfeld (1994), Cramp & Simmons (1983), Dwight (1925), Erard et al. (1984), Higgins & Davies (1996), Hoogendoorn & van Ijzendoorn (1994), Howell & Dunn (2007), Kaufman (1990a), Malling Olsen & Larsson (2003), Murphy (1936), Oberholser (1974), Roberts (1955), Stresemann & Stresemann (1966), Weseloh (1981).

Franklin's Gull

	Jan	Feb	Mar	Apr	May	Jun	Jul	Aug	Sep	Oct	Nov	Dec
Juv-HY							O	O	O	O	O	O
SY	O	O	O	O	O	O	O	O	O	O	O	O
TY	O	O	O	O	O	O	O					
AHY								O	O	O	O	O
ASY	O	O	O	O	O	O	O	O	O	O	O	O
ATY	O	O	O	O	(♀)	♀	O					

■ > 95% ▨ 25-95% □ 5-25% □ < 5%

See Fig. 24 (pp. 44-45)

HEERMANN'S GULL

Larus heermanni

HEEG
Species # 0570
Band size: 4A

Species—From other gulls by medium-large size (Table 58, p. 645; bill depth at gonys 11.9-14.9); breast and abdomen dark brown (Juv-HY/SY) to sooty or gray (AHY); pp without white mirrors; bill pinkish (Juv) to red (ASY) at base; legs black; ATY with upperparts dark gray (Kodak 11-13, p. 629).

Geographic variation—Monotypic.

Molt—SAS (CAS?). PF absent?, PA1 partial-incomplete (Sep-Mar in HY/SYs), PB2 complete (Apr-Aug in SYs), PA2 partial-incomplete (Aug-Mar in SY/TYs); PB3 complete (May-Sep in TYs), DPA partial (Sep-Mar in ASY/ATYs), DPB complete (May-Oct in ATYs). The single inserted first-cycle molt appears homologous with a PA1 rather than a PF (Fig. 10**E**, p. 14), although some feathers may be replaced twice, indicating both a PF and a PA1 (and CAS; Fig. 10**F**). The PA1 and DPB commence on or near breeding grounds and complete on non-breeding grounds whereas DPAs occur primarily or entirely on non-breeding grounds. The PA1 often includes some to all upperwing covs and terts, especially in s.populations, and sometimes includes 1-10 outer pp (and probably outer p covs, inner ss, and rects), in eccentric sequence (Fig. 376**A**, p. 504), in some Mexican populations (Howell & Wood 2004). The extent of this molt needs further study and might include some to all rects and ss on

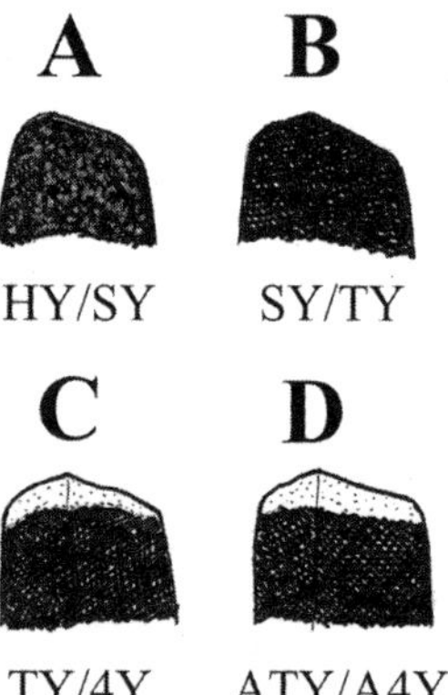

FIGURE 473. Typical patterns of the outer secondaries and inner primaries by age in Heermann's Gull, here showing s1. Note narrower, browner, and more rounded tips to HY/SY ss (**A**), generally getting darker, broader, and with broader white tips through ATY/A4Y (**D**). The range of inner pp with white tips also increases with age (e.g., p1-p5 or p6 in TY/4Ys, p1-p7 or p8 in ATY/A4Ys).

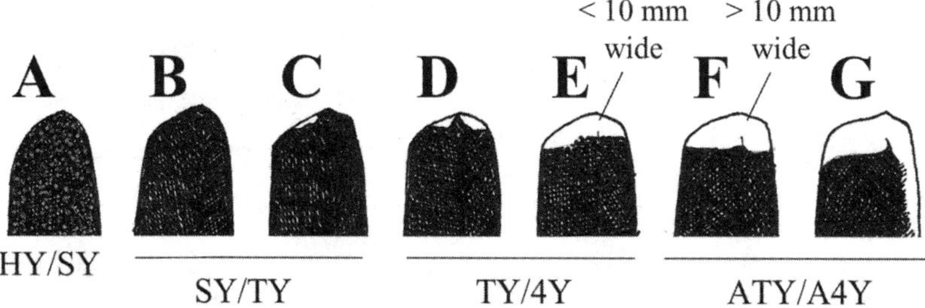

FIGURE 474. Pattern of the outer rectrix (r6) by age in Heermann's Gull. Note narrower, browner, and more rounded tips to the juv ss in HY/SYs (**A**), generally getting darker, broader, and with broader white tips by definitive aspect in ATY/A4Ys (**G**). Some SYs (and possibly some TYs) replace 1-4 c.rects during PAs in Feb-Apr, the patterns of new rects being contrastingly fresh and resembling **D-E**.

some HY/SYs, thus potentially complete. The PA2 can include some med covs and up to 1-4 c.rects (but no terts) whereas DPAs include few if any s covs, terts, or rects.

Age—Juv (B1; Jul-Sep) has plumage aspect uniform in freshness, back and upperwing covs with scaly buff fringes, and bill pink with an indistinct dusky tip; Juv ♀=♂.

Juv-HY/SY (1st cycle, Juv/B1-A1; Aug-Jul): Plumage aspect uniformly dark sooty brown; some to all s covs juv, with distinct buff to whitish fringes; pp, p covs, and ss uniformly juv, the outer ss and inner pp brownish, sometimes with fine whitish tips when fresh (Fig. 473**A**), and the outer pp and p covs relatively tapered and worn (Fig. 483**A**, p. 660), or the inner ss and outer pp occasionally replaced in Dec-Mar and exhibiting eccentric patterns in Jan-Sep (Fig. 376**A**, p. 504; see **Molt**); uppertail covs brown to gray-brown; rects narrow, rounded, and brownish (Fig. 474**A**); bill primarily dull flesh with indistinct blackish distal half to third, often tinged gray-green at base in Feb-Jul.

SY/TY (2nd cycle, B2-A2; Aug-Jul): Plumage aspect dark brown to brownish gray, the head mottled whitish in Mar-Jul; s covs without distinct pale edging; pp, p covs, and ss uniform in wear, the outer ss and inner pp blackish brown with indistinct or no whitish tips when fresh (Fig. 473**B**), and the outer pp and p covs relatively truncate and fresh (Fig. 483**B**); uppertail covs grayish to pale gray; rects moderately broad, blackish, and with indistinct or no whitish tips (Fig. 474**B-C**), sometimes with 1-4 contrastingly fresher inner rects broadly tipped white in Dec-Mar (Fig. 474**E**); bill primarily pinkish (Aug-Feb) to orange-red (Feb-Jul) with indistinct blackish distal third and blue-gray base in Feb-Jul.

TY/4Y (3rd cycle, B3-A3; Aug-Jul): Plumage aspect dark sooty gray-brown to slaty gray, the head uniformly white or white with dusky mottling in Jan-May; outer ss and inner pp (p1-p5 or p6) blackish with distinct whitish tips (Fig. 473**C**); rects with distinct but narrow (< 10 mm wide) whitish tips when fresh (Fig. 474**D-E**); bill primarily orange-red to red (sometimes with bluish or greenish patch to base in Jun-Jul) with moderately distinct blackish distal third. **Note: Some worn 4Ys may be indistinguishable from A4Ys in Jan-Jul and are best aged as ATY. See also ATY/A4Y.**

ATY/A4Y (Def. cycle, DB-DA; Aug-Jul): Plumage slaty gray, the head uniformly white in Dec-May; outer ss and inner pp (p1-p7 or p8) slaty black with broad whitish tips (Fig. 473**D**); rects with distinct and broad (> 10 mm wide) whitish tips (Fig. 474**F-G**); bill primarily red to bright red with distinct black tip. **Note: See TY/4Y.**

Sex—♀=♂ by plumage aspect. Bilateral and medial(?) BPs (Fig. 20**C**, p. 31) developed by both sexes but distended cloaca (Fig. 21, p. 32) indicates ATY ♀ in Apr-Jun. Measurements generally unhelpful (Table 58, p. 645) but head-bill length (Figure 453, p. 630) probably useful for sexing; study needed on live individuals.

Hybrids reported—With California Gull (Chisholm & Neel 2002).

Heermann's Gull

	Jan	Feb	Mar	Apr	May	Jun	Jul	Aug	Sep	Oct	Nov	Dec
Juv-HY						O	O	O	O	O	O	O
SY	O	O	O	O	O	O	O	O	O	O	O	O
TY	O	O	O	O	O	O	O	O	O	O	O	O
4Y	O	O	O	O	(♀)	(♀)	O					
ATY	O	O	O	(♀)	♀	(♀)	O	O	O	O	O	O
A4Y	O	O	O	(♀)	♀	(♀)	O					

■ > 95% ▨ 25-95% □ 5-25% □ < 5% See Fig. 24 (pp. 44-45)

References—Chisholm & Neel (2002), Dwight (1925), Howell (2001d), Howell & Dunn (2007), Howell & Wood (2004), Malling Olsen & Larsson (2003), Iron & Pittaway (2001), Islam (2002).

MEW GULL
Larus canus

MEGU
Species # 0550
Band size: 4A

Species—From other larger gulls including Ring-billed (p. 656) and California (p. 663) gulls by smaller size, especially bill and legs (Table 59, p. 657); bill slightly shallower at gonys (8.7-11.1 in N.Am) than at base (9.1-11.6; *cf.* Fig. 453, p. 630); Juv-HY with bill dull pink with black tip, les covs with indistinct or no dark centers (Fig. 475**A-C**), rects extensively brown or with reduced white bases (Fig. 476**C-D** n N.Am), inner pp extensively pale gray (Fig. 478**A-B**), and underwing s covs mostly brownish (in N.Am); AHY with upperparts pale gray (Kodak 6-7.5, p. 629), bill unmarked yellow to yellowish with dusky smudging, legs usually greenish or yellow, iris usually dark (occasionally pale), and outer pp with large pale to white mirrors and subterminal bands (Fig. 479, p. 655). The above applies to all subspecies of Mew Gull (see **Geographic variation**) but beware that HY/SYs of Eurasian subspecies can be more difficult

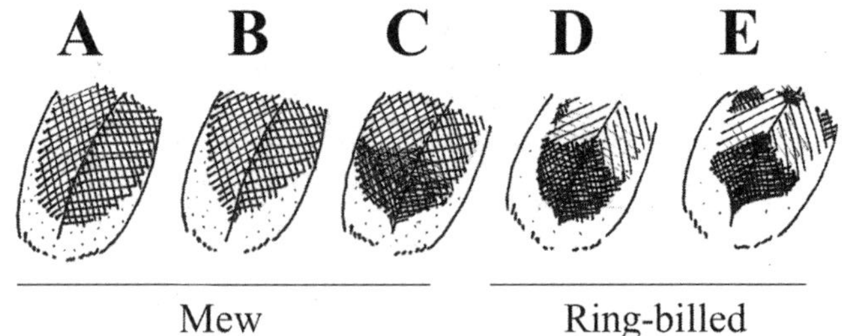

FIGURE 475. Variation in patterns of the juvenal lesser and median coverts in 1st-cycle (Juv-HY/SY) Mew and Ring-billed gulls. Mew Gulls average more solidly gray-brown, fairly rounded to V-shaped centers and narrower pale edging (**A-B**), sometimes with darker subterminal marks (**C**) that do not contrast strongly with the paler, gray-brown feather base. Ring-billed Gulls have distinct and angular dark subterminal marks contrasting more strongly with a paler grayish feather base or medial area (**D-E**). The whitish tips often abrade by late winter, resulting in a more-contrasting and checkered pattern in Ring-billed *vs* a more-uniform pattern overall on Mew Gull. Note that Ring-billed Gulls sometime replace these covs in their first winter with gray feathers, whereas Mew Gulls usually do not.

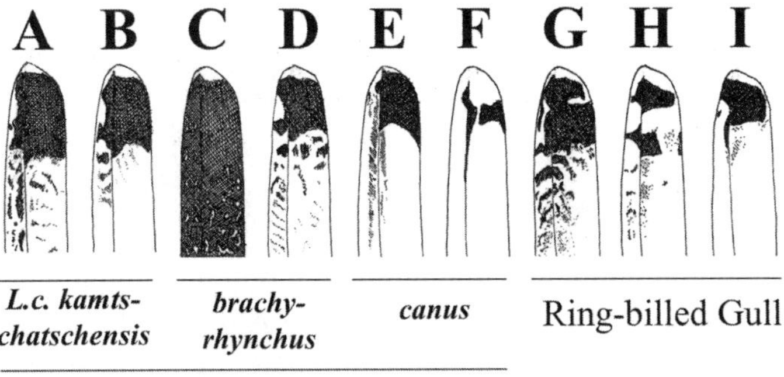

FIGURE 476. Variation in the typical patterns of the outer rectrix (r6) by subspecies and species in 1st cycle (Juv-HY/SY) Mew and Ring-billed gulls. Ring-billed Gulls typically have a coarser pattern with black distal bands broken by white markings. Second-cycle SY/TYs of these species can have entirely white rects but most show either a full black band (resembling **D-E** or **I**) or some distal markings (resembling **F**). Beware much interspecific and intraspecific variation in these patterns and, during ageing, that some ATY/A4Ys (including individuals known to be > 15 years of age) can occasionally show dark markings in the rects.

to separate from Ring-billed Gull; bill proportions, and dark underwing-covert color in *L.c. kamtschatschensis* are perhaps the best means of separating these from Ring-billed Gull.

Geographic variation—See Cramp & Simmons (1983), Dement'ev & Gladkov (1951c), Dwight (1925), Gibson & Kessel (1997), Grant (1986), Johansen (1961), Moskoff & Bevier (2002), Oberholser (1919b), Ridgway (1919), Shepard & Votier (1993), Stejneger (1885), and Tove (1993). One other subspecies occurs in Asia. In addition to the following, see **Molt** for subspecific differences in molt timing.

L.c. kamtschatschensis (br e.Asia; vagrant to w.AK): Averages larger and stouter billed (Table 59, p. 657; bill depth at gonys 9.2-13.3); HY/SY with rects washed or marked dusky at base, r6 with distinct black subterminal band (Fig. 476**A-B**), and underwing s covs dusky and whitish; ASY/ATY with upperparts averaging darker gray (Kodak 6.5-8.0, p. 629), head and breast markings relatively coarse, and distinct in Oct-Feb, inner pp with relatively narrow white tips (usually narrower than tips to outer ss), p4 usually lacking subterminal blackish mark, p8 with narrower white tongue-tip, p8-p10 with more extensive black, and p9 mirror averaging smaller (15-25 mm on p9; *cf.* Figs. 478-479, pp. 654-655).

L.c. brachyrhynchus (br and wint throughout N.Am range): Averages smaller, especially bill (Table 59; bill depth at gonys 8.7-11.1); HY/SY with rects variable but often mostly dark (Fig. 476**C-D**) and underwing s covs dusky; ASY/ATY with gray upperparts intermediate in tone (Kodak 6.0-7.5), head and breast markings relatively diffuse, smudgy, and indistinct in Nov-Feb, inner pp with relatively broad white tips (usually broader than tips to outer ss), p4 often with subterminal black, p8 often with white tongue-tip but lacking mirror, p8-p10 with less extensive black, and p9-p10 mirrors averaging larger (20-30 mm on p9; Figs. 478-479).

L.c. canus (br w.Asia, vagrant to ne.N.Am). Medium in size with bill averaging longer than *brachyrhynchus* (Table 59; bill depth at gonys 8.8-12.2); HY/SY with white bases and clean-cut blackish distal band or marks to rects (Fig. 476**D-E**) and underwing s covs whitish; ASY/ATY with upperparts averaging paler gray (Kodak 5.0-6.5), head and breast markings relatively fine and spotted in Nov-Feb, inner pp with relatively narrow white tips (usually narrower than tips to ss), p4 usually lacking subterminal black, p8 rarely with white tongue-tip but sometimes with small white mirror, p8-p10 with more extensive black, and p9-p10 mirrors larger (30-35 mm on p9; *cf.* Figs. 478-479).

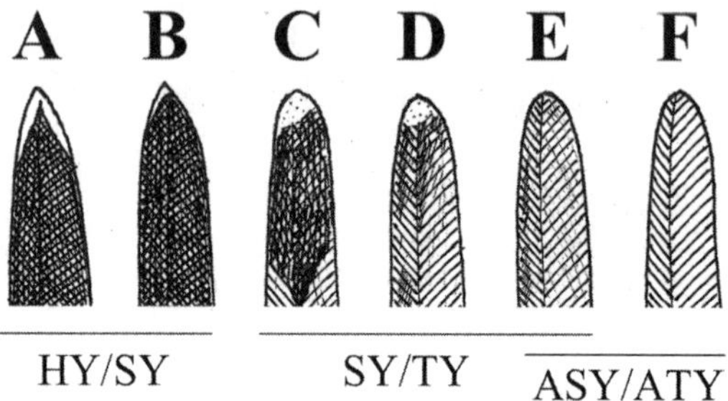

FIGURE 477. Variation in pattern of the longest primary covert by age in Mew Gull Also note more tapered shape of HY/SY covs (**A-B**).

Molt—SAS (CAS?). PF absent?, PA1 partial (Sep-Apr? in HY/SYs), PB2 complete (May-Sep in SYs), PA2 partial (Sep-May in SY/TYs), PB3 complete (Jun-Sep in TYs), DPA partial (Feb?-May in ASYs), DPB complete (Jun-Oct in ATYs). The single inserted first-cycle molt appears homologous with a PA1 rather than a PF (Fig. 10**E**, p. 14), although some feathers may be replaced twice, indicating both a PF and a PA1 (and CAS; Fig. 10**F**). The PA1 and DPB usually start on or near breeding grounds and complete on non-breeding grounds; the DPA occurs on non-breeding grounds or (often) during northward migration. The PA1 and DPA include some to most body feathers but few if any s covs, terts, or rects. The PA2 can include some med covs and proximal les covs but few if any terts or rects. The timing of the DPA requires study: molt of scapulars and upperwing covs may commence in fall, as in large white-headed gulls. The above extents and timing pertain to *L.c. brachyrhynchus* of N.Am; the DPB averages earlier in *canus* (Walters 1978) and later in *kamtschatschensis*.

Age—Juv (B1; mid Jul-Jan) has back gray-brown, scapulars with scaly buff to whitish fringes, and bill dull flesh with black tip; Juv ♀ = ♂. The following applies to N.Am Mew Gulls and generally to other subspecies; see Figures 476 (p. 653), 478, and 479 for further information on ageing Eurasian subspecies.

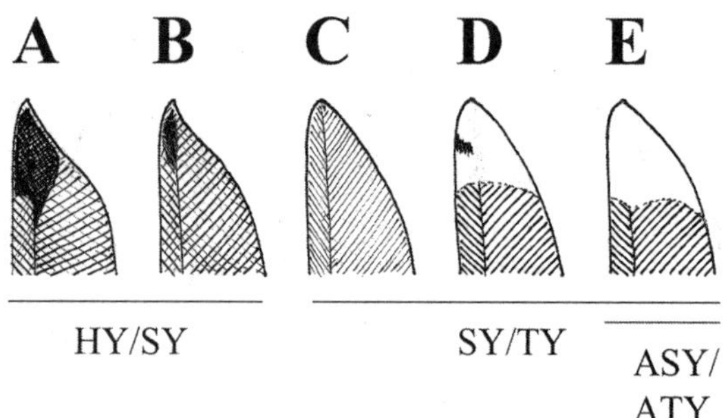

FIGURE 478. Variation in pattern of the inner primaries by age in N.Am Mew Gulls here showing p3. Note that some 2nd-cycle SY/TYs can show a similar pattern to definitive-aspect ASY/ATYs (**E**). The white tips in **D-E** are relatively broad (usually broader than tips to outer ss) whereas in Eurasian subspecies these tips are narrower than those of the ss. The juv p3 of Ring-billed Gull resembles that of Mew Gull (**A-B**) but averages less distinct and more extensive black.

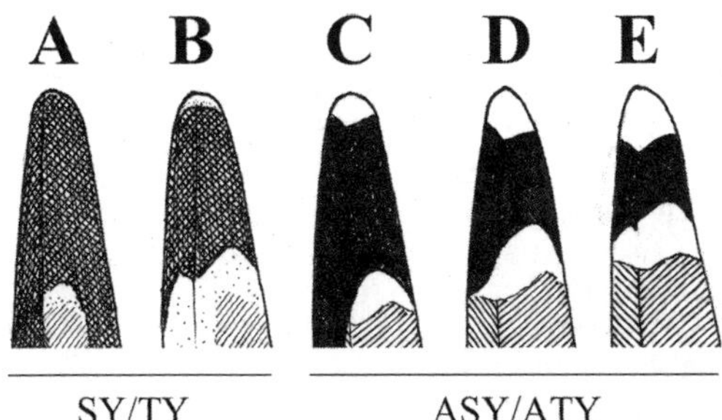

FIGURE 479. Variation in pattern to p7 by age in 2nd-cycle (SY/TY) and older (AHY/ASY) Mew Gulls. First-cycle HY/SYs have this feather entirely brown. ASY/ATYs with the least black (**E**) may be ATY/A4Ys (study needed). These illustrations reflect variation in N.Am Mew Gulls; Eurasian subspecies generally average less-extensive white tongue-tips, more extensive blackish to black coloration, and smaller mirrors by primary number and age (see **Geographic variation** for details).

Juv-HY/SY (1st cycle, Juv/B1-A1; Sep-Aug): Body plumage aspect heavily mottled brown, the upperparts usually mixed with gray feathers in Nov-Aug; outer pp and p covs relatively tapered, the alula and p covs dark brown with variable whitish tips (Fig. 477**A-B**) and the outer pp dark brown (Fig. 483**A**, p. 660); inner pp brownish gray with variable dark-brown subterminal marks (Fig. 478**A-B**); underwing s covs dark brown; uppertail covs with distinct brown barring (Fig. 485**A-D**, p. 661); rects brownish or with reduced whitish bases (Fig. 476**C-D** for N.Am populations); bill usually flesh to flesh-pink with blackish tip in Oct-Mar (rarely greenish at base by Mar-Jun); legs dull flesh to flesh-pink.

SY/TY (2nd cycle, B2-A2; Sep-Aug): Body plumage aspect whitish and grayish, with moderate dusky mottling to head and breast in Sep-Mar; outer pp and p covs relatively truncate, the alula and p covs usually with variable dark distal markings and diffuse pale tips (Fig. 477**C-E**), and the outer pp lacking bold black-and-white pattern (Fig. 479**A-B**); inner pp grayish, usually with distinct whitish tips and sometimes dark subterminal marks (Fig. 478**C-E**); proximal gr covs and terts usually with brown wash or markings; underwing s covs silvery brown; uppertail covs without distinct barring (*cf.* Fig. 485); rects often with some black distal markings (Fig. 486**F-H**; 12% of SY/TYs have solid black subterminal tail band, 13% have all-white tails; Howell & McKee 1998); bill usually greenish with blackish tip or marks in Sep-Mar, becoming yellowish with indistinct or no dusky in May-Aug; legs usually gray-green to yellowish, sometimes becoming yellow in May-Aug.

ASY/ATY (Def. cycle, DB-DA; Sep-Aug): Body plumage aspect white and gray, with sparse to moderate dusky mottling to head and breast in Sep-Feb; alula and outer p covs gray, without distinct black marks (Fig. 477**E-F**); outer pp with bold black-and-white pattern (Fig. 479**C-E**); inner pp gray with distinct white tips (Fig. 478**E**); proximal gr covs and terts without brown wash or dark marks; underwing s covs white; rects white (Fig. 483**H**); bill yellowish, sometimes with indistinct dusky ring in Sep-Mar; legs usually yellowish to yellow. **Note: Some TY/4Ys might be reliably aged by averaging more black and less white in wing-tips (Fig. 479C-D *vs* D-E), having white tips to p8-p10 reduced or absent, and having alula and outer p covs with some black markings (Fig. 477D-F). Also, ASY/ATYs with extensive white to outer pp (Fig. 479E) may be ATY/A4Ys; but confirmation of these criteria needed based on known-age individuals.**

Sex—♀=♂ by plumage aspect. Bilateral and medial(?) BPs (Fig. 20**C**, p. 31) developed by both sexes but distended cloaca (Fig. 21, p. 32) indicates ATY ♀ in May-Jul. Measurements (especially wing chord and exposed culmen) somewhat helpful for sexing (Table 59), perhaps especially with mated pairs. The following is reliable for sexing most individuals of European populations (*L.c. canus*) based on live birds (Coulson et al. 1983) and is presumed reliable for N.Am *brachyrhynchus* based on similarity in measures and degree of sexual dimorphism but confirmation needed.

♀: Head-bill length (Fig. 453, p. 630) 82-89 mm. **Note: Individuals with head-bill length 87-89 mm cannot be reliably sexed by this measure alone.**

♂: Head-bill length 87-98 mm. **Note: See ♀.**

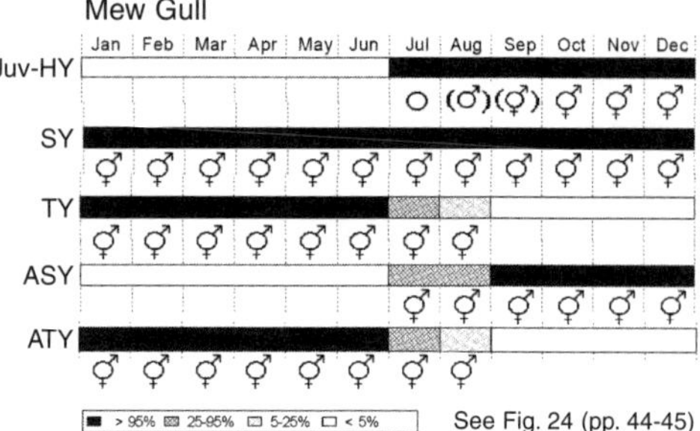

Hybrids reported—With Black-headed Gull (p. 640), Mediterranean Gull *L. melanocephalus* (Oddie 1994, Pullan & Martin 2004), Ring-billed Gull (Howell & Dunn 2007, Kehoe 1992); possibly with Lesser Black-backed Gull (Harrison 1965) and California Gull (Harrison 1983).

References—Baker (1993), Barth (1967), Coulson et al. (1983), Cramp & Simmons (1983), Dement'ev & Gladkov (1951c), Dwight (1925), Howell & Dunn (2007), Howell & McKee (1998), Lauro & Spencer (1980), Malling Olsen & Larsson (2003), Moskoff & Bevier (2002), Tove (1993), Walters (1978).

RING-BILLED GULL

Larus delawarensis

RBGU
Species # 0540
Band size: 4A

Species—From other gulls including Mew (p. 652) and California (p. 663) gulls by medium-small size (Table 59); bill depth at gonys (11.7-15.2) similar to depth at base (11.3-15.9; *cf.* Fig. 453, p. 630); Juv-HY with bill bright pink with dark tip, les covs with distinct blackish subterminal spots (Fig. 475**D-E**, p. 652), uppertail covs with relatively sparse bars (Fig. 485**D-E** & **H**, p. 661), inner pp pale gray, rects extensively white at bases (Fig. 476**E-F**, p. 653), and underwing s covs mostly whitish; AHYs with upperparts pale gray (Kodak 4-5; p. 629), bill yellow with distinct black ring, and iris and legs usually yellow. Beware of extralimital subspecies of Mew Gull which are larger and can be more difficult to separate from Ring-billed Gull (see Mew Gull).

Geographic variation—Monotypic. Populations of w.Canada average larger than those of e.Canada; see Termaat & Ryder 1984) for a DFA (p. 5) including skeletal characters (by sex) which correctly assigned 90-95% of individuals to geographic origin.

Molt—SAS (CAS?). PF absent?, PA1 partial (Aug-Apr in HY/SYs), PB2 complete (Apr-Sep in SYs), PA2 partial (Sep-Apr in SY/TYs), DPB complete (May-Oct in ASYs), DPA partial (Jan?-Apr in ASYs). The single inserted first-cycle molt appears homologous with a PA1 rather than a PF (Fig. 10**E**, p. 14), although some feathers may be replaced twice, indicating both a PF and a PA1 (and CAS; Fig. 10**F**). The PAs occur on non-breeding grounds, often completing during northward migration, and the DPA can be suspended during Nov-Feb. The PBs usually start on or near breeding grounds and complete on non-breeding grounds. The PA1 includes most to all body

TABLE 59. Measurements (mm) of North American medium-sized, yellow-legged gulls to assist in identification and sexing. See pp. 4-11 for methods of measurement. Species summaries are in **bold** and subspecies values are in ***italics***. Values were derived from 95% confidence intervals as based approximately on the indicated sample sizes (see pp. 4-5). Thus, midpoints of ranges approximate means, and S.D. is approximated by one-quarter of the range.

Taxon/Sex	*n*	wing chord[1]	tail length	exp culmen	bill depth[2]	tarsus
Mew Gull		**320-406**	**126-154**	**28-43**	**9.1-15.9**	**41-61**
L.c. kamtschatschensis		***337-406***	***135-154***	***32-43***	***10.2-15.9***	***48-61***
♀	50	337-385	135-143	32-40	10.2-14.6	48-58
♂	30	357-406	141-154	35-43	11.3-15.9	49-61
L.c. brachyrhynchus		***322-365***	***131-148***	***29-38***	***9.1-11.6***	***43-54***
♀	95	322-355	131-143	29-35	9.1-11.5	43-51
♂	100	331-365	136-148	32-38	9.8-11.6	45-54
L.c. canus		***320-365***	***126-143***	***28-39***	***9.9-13.5***	***41-51***
♀	100	320-365	126-133	28-36	9.4-12.0	43-53
♂	100	332-384	135-143	31-39	10.5-13.2	46-57
Ring-billed Gull		**330-392**	**132-161**	**33-46**	**11.3-15.9**	**49-62**
♀	100	330-369	132-150	33-42	11.3-14.5	49-59
♂	100	346-392	143-161	37-46	12.5-15.9	52-62
California Gull		**353-426**	**135-166**	**38-57**	**12.7-18.8**	**49-69**
L.c. californicus		***353-413***	***135-156***	***38-48***	***12.7-16.5***	***49-63***
♀	100	353-390	135-148	38-48	12.7-15.7	49-60
♂	100	368-413	143-156	40-54	13.8-16.5	51-63
L.c. albertaensis		***362-426***	***147-166***	***41-57***	***14.3-18.8***	***53-69***
♀	40	362-402	147-159	41-51	14.3-15.9	53-65
♂	50	378-426	154-166	47-57	16.1-18.8	57-69

[1] Wing chord averages ~5% shorter in Juv-HY/SY than in AHY/ASY.
[2] Bill depth measured at distal end of forehead feathering (see Fig. 8**A**, p. 10).

feathers and often a few med and proximal les covs but few if any terts or rects. The DPA includes most to all body feathers, often some med and proximal les covs, and sometimes 1-3 terts, but few if any rects. Median and some other upperwing covs often replaced Sep-Nov during PA2 and PA3, overlapping end of PB2 and PB3. The DPA may occasionally commence in fall; study needed.

Age—Juv (B1; Jul-Dec) has back dark brown to gray-brown, scapulars with scaly buff to whitish fringes, and bill dull pinkish with black tip; Juv ♀=♂.

Juv-HY/SY (1st cycle, Juv/B1-A1; Sep-Aug): Body plumage aspect whitish mottled brown, the upperparts usually mixed grayish in Nov-Aug; outer pp and p covs relatively tapered, the p covs dark brown with variable whitish tips (Fig. 480**A**, p. 658) and the outer pp brownish (483**A**, p. 660); inner pp grayish with variable dark-brown subterminal marks (*cf.* Fig. 478**A-B**, p. 654; Fig. 481); underwing s covs with brown mottling; uppertail covs with sparse bars (Fig. 485**D-E** & **H**, p. 661); rects with broad blackish subterminal band (Fig. 476**E-F**, p. 653); iris usually dark brown to pale gray-brown; bill flesh-pink with blackish tip, sometimes becoming pinkish yellow with indistinct black subterminal ring in Mar-Jun; legs flesh-pink.

SY/TY (2nd cycle, B2-A2; Sep-Aug): Body plumage aspect primarily whitish and gray, with sparse dusky mottling to head and breast in Sep-Mar; outer pp and p covs relatively truncate, the outer p covs grayish with variable dark distal markings (Fig. 480**B-D**) and the distal portions of the outer pp dark brown to blackish, often with small whitish to white mirror on p10

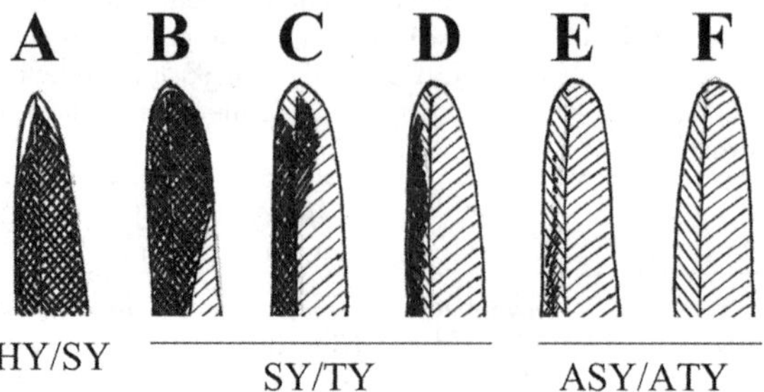

FIGURE 480. Variation in pattern of the longest primary covert by age in Ring-billed Gull. Note also more-tapered shape of HY/SY cov (**A**).

(Fig. 483**B-C**); inner pp pale gray with white tips to p1-p5/p6 and usually with dark subterminal mark to p4 (Fig. 481**A-B**); proximal gr covs and terts washed brownish; underwing s covs white, usually with sparse brown mottling; uppertail covs white; rects white, often with black distal markings or sometimes a solid black subterminal band (Fig. 486**E-G**, p. 661); iris usually pale brown to lemon; bill usually greenish yellow in Sep-Feb to yellow with broad black subterminal ring in Mar-Aug; legs usually grayish green to flesh in Sep-Feb, becoming yellowish in Mar-Aug.

ASY/ATY (DA-DB; Sep-Aug): Body plumage aspect white and gray, with sparse dusky mottling to head and breast in Sep-Feb; outer p covs with little or no black (Fig. 480**E-F**); outer pp boldly patterned black and white (*cf.* Fig. 483**D-E**); inner pp with white tips to p1-p7/p9 and without or with a small black subterminal spot to p4 (Fig. 481**C-D**); proximal gr covs and terts pale gray, without brownish wash; underwing s covs white; rects white (Fig. 486**G**, rarely with black marks as in **F**); iris usually pale lemon to whitish; bill yellow with distinct black ring; legs yellowish, brighter in Feb-Jul. **Note: TY/4Ys usually lack white to p9 and more often show blackish on p covs (Fig. 480D-E; see Blokpoel et al. 1985), but there appears to be too much variation among ATYs for reliable ageing.**

Sex—♀=♂ by plumage aspect. Bilateral and medial BPs (Fig. 20**C**, p. 31) developed by both sexes but distended cloaca (Fig. 21, p. 32) indicates ATY ♀ in May-Jun. Measurements somewhat helpful for sexing (Table 59, p. 657), especially mated pairs. In addition to the following, see Shugart (1977) for a DFA (p. 5) using head-bill length (Fig. 453, p. 630), wing chord, and total length in MI, and (Ryder 1978) for a similar analysis using bill length from gape and bill depth at gonys in ON, each of which correctly sexed 98% of freshly dead adults. The following can be used to sex most full-grown individuals:

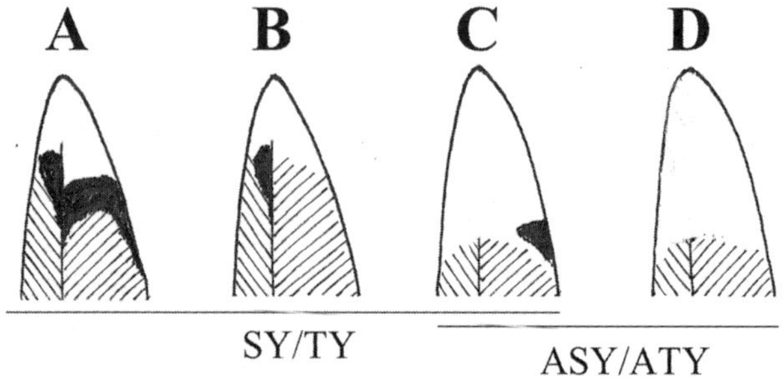

FIGURE 481. Variation in pattern of p4 by age in AHY/ASY Ring-billed Gulls. First-cycle HY/SYs have these feathers grayish with dusky marks (*cf.* Fig. 26**A-B**).

♀: Head-bill length (Fig. 453) 88-95 mm. **Note: Individuals with head-bill length 94-95 mm cannot be reliably sexed by this measure alone.**

♂: Head-bill length 94-103 mm. **Note: See ♀.**

Hybrids reported—With Black-headed (p. 640), Laughing (p. 645), Franklin's (p. 648), and Mew (p. 652) gulls; possibly with California Gull (Harrison 1983, Howell & Dunn 2007).

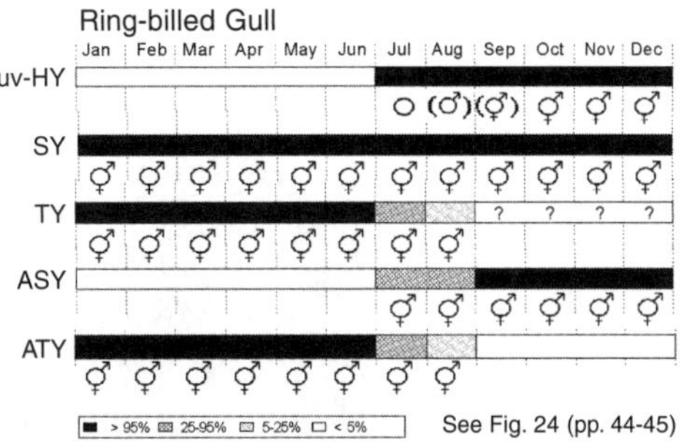

References—Blokpoel et al. (1985), Cramp & Simmons (1983), Dwight (1925), Howell & Dunn (2007), Kaufman (1990a), Lauro & Spencer (1980), Malling Olsen & Larsson (2003), McLaughlin (2001), Oberholser (1974), Roberts (1955), Ryder (1978, 1993), Shugart (1977), Southern (1981), Termaat & Ryder (1984).

Identification and ageing large white-headed gulls

Large white-headed gulls are a relatively homogeneous group of recently evolved and evolving taxa that include numerous unresolved taxonomic questions. Species-level identification can be very difficult, especially during the 2nd-3rd cycles, and frequent hybridization among some taxa, especially in w.N.Am, adds a confounding dimension. A good feature for separating 1st-cycle HY/SYs can be the contrast and pattern to the juvenal outer primaries when fresh (Fig. 482); however, bleaching (Howell 2001b) and intraspecific variation can obscure differences between

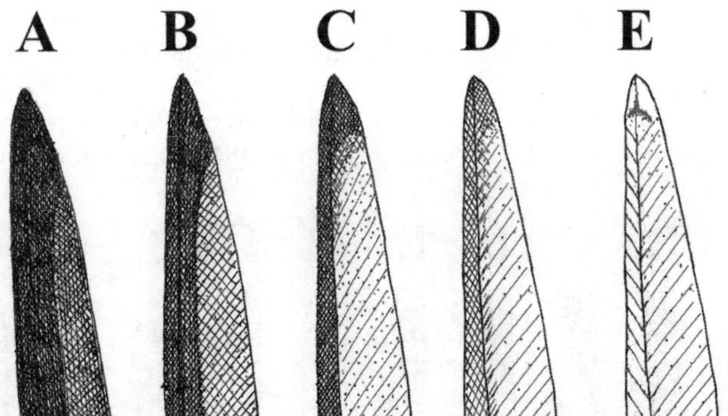

FIGURE 482. Typical patterns of the outer primaries (p7-p10) on first-cycle HY/SY large gulls by species, here showing p9. Contrast between the darker and paler areas can be changed by bleaching (especially on Slaty-backed, Glaucous-winged, and Thayer's gulls) and feathers can become quite faded by spring, with the inner webs often whitish overall (*cf.* Howell 2001b). **A**: Low-level contrast on the inner web about 30-50% out from the shaft as found in California, Western, Yellow-footed, and Lesser Black-backed gulls. **B**: Moderate contrast on the inner web about 20-30% out from the shaft, as found in Herring and Great Black-backed gulls. **C**: Strong contrast at or near the shaft, as found in Slaty-backed and Thayer's gulls. **D**: Moderate contrast near the shaft, as found in Glaucous-winged Gull. **E**: Whitish or pale brown with indistinct to distinct subterminal chevron as found in Glaucous and Iceland gulls.

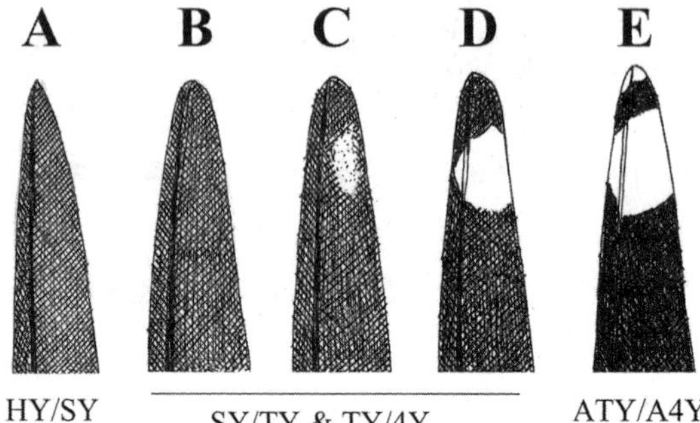

FIGURE 483. P10 by age in large, white-headed gulls. Note the difference in shape of the juv outer pp in first-cycle HY/SYs (**A**) *vs* 2nd basic pp of SY/TYs (**B**). By spring juv pp in SYs can become heavily worn and brownish whereas 2nd-basic and older pp (in ASYs) show relatively less wear and remain darker. This difference is useful in separating 1st-cycle HY/SYs from 2nd-cycle SY/TYs (which can otherwise be similar in plumage aspect). The outer pp of 2nd-cycle SY/TYs are typically dusky brown, those of 3rd-cycle TY/4Ys birds of larger species are washed brown, and those of definitive-aspect ASY/ATYs (medium-sized gulls) or ATY/A4Ys (large gulls) are blackish to black. The degree and distinctness of the white mirror to p9 and p10 varies extensively by both species and age (see text).

species. Species-level identification of individuals away from breeding colonies (and even in colonies where taxa hybridize) is not always possible.

Age determination of individuals in predefinitive plumage aspect can also be difficult, especially since advanced individuals of one age group (e.g. 2nd cycle SY/TYs) can overlap with retarded individuals of the next older age group (e.g., 3rd cycle TY/4Ys). Important points to check include shape and color pattern of the outer pp and longest p covs (Figs. 483-484), pattern of the uppertail covs (Fig. 485); pattern of the outer rectrices (Fig. 486), and pattern of the inner and middle pp (for separating 2nd-cycle SY/TYs from 3rd-cycle TY/4Ys; Fig. 487, p. 662). The underwing s covs typically vary from uniformly dark during the 1st cycle, to dark mottled whitish in the 2nd cycle, to white with sparse dark mottling in the 3rd cycle, to white in definitive cycles.

First-cycle HY/SYs are generally brownish or mottled brown and white in plumage aspect and have relatively tapered pp and p covs (Figs. 483**A** & 484**A**), the outer pp often becoming

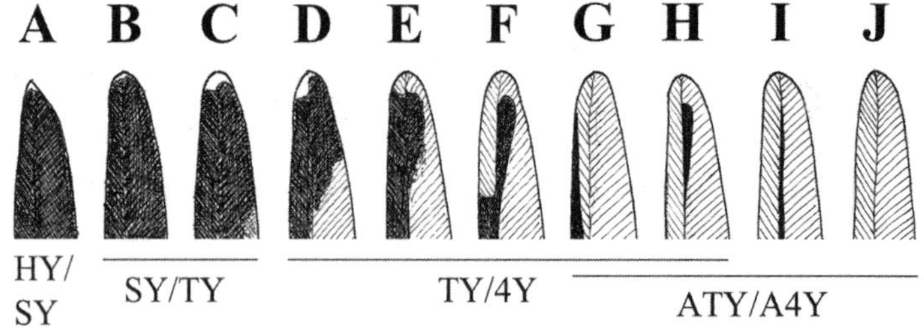

FIGURE 484. Typical patterns of the longest primary coverts by age in large white-headed gulls, here showing those of Herring Gull; other species may have slightly different ranges of variation within 3rd-cycle TY/4Ys and definitive-cycle ATY/A4Ys (see accounts). Also, other species will show a variable degree of darkness to the tips and bases; e.g., the distal marks of Glaucous-winged and Thayer's gulls are dark brown to gray-brown and those of Glaucous and Iceland gulls are pale brown to grayish, and the bases are darker gray in Slaty-backed, Western, Yellow-footed, and Black-backed gulls.

quite worn by late in the first cycle (Howell 2001b), usually distinct and more-regular dark barring on the uppertail covs (Fig. 485**A-D**) and outer rectrices (Fig. 486**A-D**, to **E** in some taxa), and underwing s covs darker and more uniformly brown than in 2nd cycle SY/TYs. Bill, leg, and eye color tends to be duller, darker, and/or pinker the 1st cycle HY/SYs but bare part colors in general can be variable and should only be used as supporting criteria to those of plumage aspect.

Second-cycle SY/TYs can be surprisingly difficult to separate from 1st-cycle HY/SYs, especially in larger species. They are also generally mottled brownish and whitish in plumage aspect, although alternate upperpart feathers replaced in Jan-Jun are usually pale to dark grayish, definitive in color. Second-cycle SY/TYs also have blacker and broader-tipped pp and p covs (Fig. 483**B**, 484**B-C**); less-regular dark markings on the tail coverts (Fig. 485**E-H**) and outer rects (Fig. 486**D-E** or **F**); and paler underwing s covs, often brown with variable silvery or

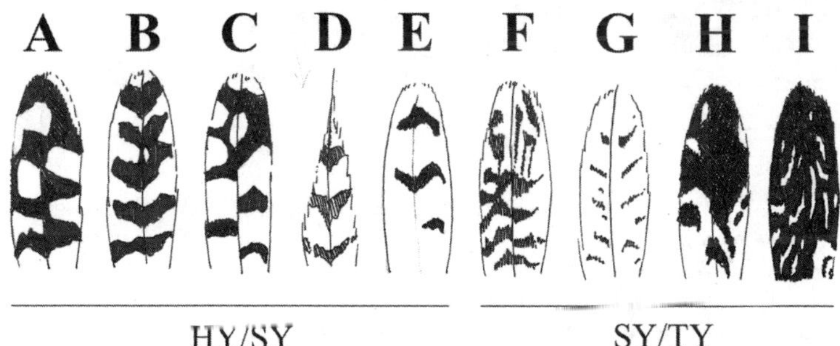

FIGURE 485. Variation in pattern to the longest uppertail covs by age in large white-headed gulls. These feathers are more evenly and more regularly barred overall in 1st cycle HY/SYs (**A-E**), with dark bars varying to pale brown in some taxa (such as Glaucous and Glaucous-winged gulls); patterns are usually apparent even on heavily worn SYs (**D**). The pattern shown in **E** occurs in 1st-cycle (HY/SY) Yellow-footed Gulls, as well as both 1st-cycle and 2nd-cycle (SY/TY) Lesser Black-backed Gulls. Second-cycle feathers (**F-I**) have more-irregular, often wavy, and usually finer patterning (again, paler in tone on the paler-winged species such as Glaucous and Glaucous-winged gulls).

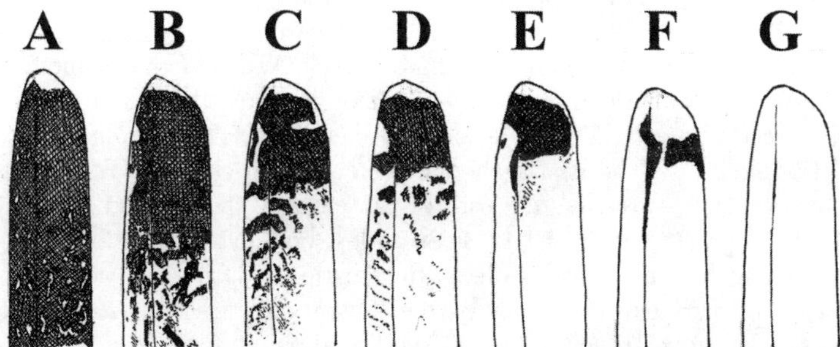

FIGURE 486. Pattern to the outer rectrices (generally r5-r6) by age in large, white-headed gulls. The degree of dark and white in 1st-cycle (HY/SY) rects varies considerably by species and individual (**A-D**), often averaging more white to the bases in Eurasian taxa than in N.Am counterparts. Second-cycle (SY/TY) rects of most large gulls continue to show substantial dark distally (**B-E**), in some cases showing as much as or more than is typical of 1st-cycle HY/SYs. Some species can replace rects during the PA2 (in TYs) and these are usually whiter or can be entirely white. During the 3rd cycle (TY/4Ys) most species retain at least some blackish markings and at times full black bands to the rects (**E-F**), although in some species at least some 3rd-cycle TY/4Ys can have entirely white rects. In definitive-aspect ATY/A4Ys, rects are typically white (**G**), but certain individuals (with early or late prebasic molts?) can show some black marks to some feathers, as in **E-F**.

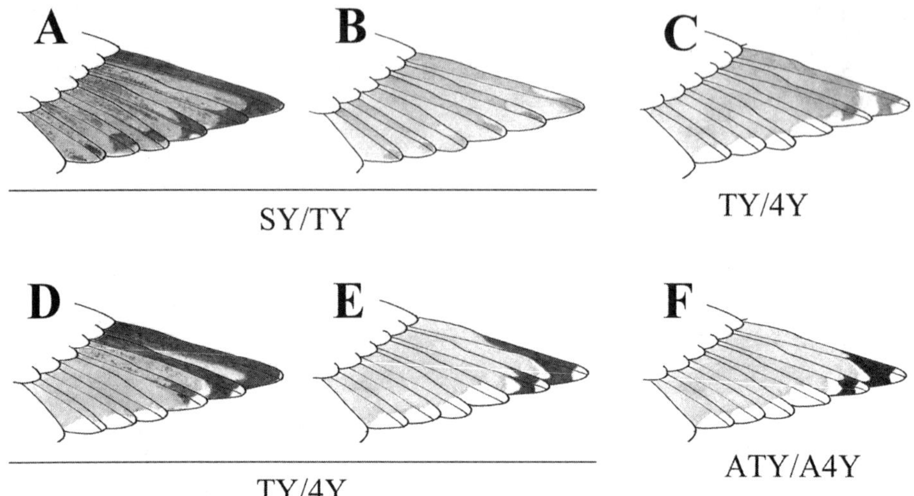

FIGURE 487. Typical patterns of the inner primaries (p1-p6) by age in AHY/ASY large white-headed gulls. In general, inner primaries of 2nd-cycle SY/TYs (**A-B**) are immature-like in appearance (resembling juv primaries), whereas those of 3rd-cycle TY/4Ys (**C-E**) are definitive in pattern; in particular note the distinct white tips on TY/4Ys, lacking in SY/TYs. ATY/A4Ys have sharper contrasts as in **F**. Patterns vary by species; shown here are typical Herring Gulls (**A** = SY/TY, **D** = retarded TY/4Y, **E** = advanced TY/4Y, **F** = ATY/A4Y) and Glaucous-winged Gull (**B** = SY/TY, **C** = TY/4Y). Note that 2nd-cycle (SY/TY) California Gulls occasionally show definitive patterns to the inner primaries and are best aged by other features. Beware also that some TY Yellow-footed Gulls and Lesser Black-backed Gulls (primarily in Europe) can replace inner primaries during the PA2, new feathers being definitivet-like in pattern, but molt limits between these and older (B2) primaries should be evident.

whitish mottling. Inner and medial pp also have patterns that can resemble first-cycle HY/SYs (Fig. 487**A-B**); very rarely, 1-2 inner pp (p1-p2) can be more definitive-like in pattern (e.g. Fig. 487**C-F**).

Third-cycle TY/4Ys generally resemble definitive-cycle ATY/A4Ys much more than they do 2nd-cycle SY/TYs, being primarily unmarked white and gray, but retarded 3rd-cycle TY/4Ys can be similar to advanced 2nd-cycle SY/TYs in some species (especially Herring, Glaucous-winged, Glaucous, and Iceland gulls). The best ageing character for 3rd-cycle TY/4Ys appears to be the pattern on p1-p6, which are usually gray with broad, clean-white tips and moderately distinct black markings on p4-p6 (Fig. 487**C-E**), versus with less-bold patterns on 2nd-cycle birds (Fig. 487**A-B**), and often with sharper and more distinct patterns during the definitive cycle (Fig. 487**F**). The longest primary coverts usually have extensive dark areas in 3rd cycle TY/4Ys (Fig. 484**D-G**), whereas definitive-aspect ATY/A4Ys tend to show little or no dusky markings (Fig. 484**H-J**). In addition, the upperwing coverts, tertials and secondaries are usually tinged brown in 3rd-cycle TY/4Ys (*vs* pure gray in definitive cycle ATY/A4Ys), and the rectrices may often show dark markings in 3rd-cycle TY/4Ys (Fig. 486**E-F**), whereas in definitive-aspect ATY/A4Ys they are usually (but not always) completely white (Fig. 486**G**).

Beware, however, that some retarded 4th-cycle 4Y/5Ys in some species (especially Great Black-backed Gull, p. 671) may be indistinguishable from 3rd-cycle TY/4Ys and should probably be aged "T-4Y/4-5Y" (see pp. 41-42); more study needed. Also note that some adults may retain predefinitive characters (especially dark markings in the tail) for life.

CALIFORNIA GULL
Larus californicus

CAGU
Species # 0530
Band size: 5

Species—From other gulls by the combination of medium size (Table 59, p. 657); bill slightly deeper at gonys (13.1-19.2) than at base (12.7-18.8; *cf.* Fig. 453, p. 630); Juv-HY/SY with bill pink with well-defined black tip, inner pp relatively dark brown, not contrasting strongly with p7-p10 (Fig. 482**A**, p. 659), rects mostly brownish with reduced white bases (Fig. 486**B-C**, p. 661), and underwing s covs dark brown; ASY with upperparts medium-pale gray (Kodak 5-7.5, p. 629), orbital ring reddish; bill yellow with red gonydeal spot and variable black subterminal ring (occasionally absent Jun-Aug on ATY/A4Y), distal portions of p5-p10 black with white mirrors on p9-p10 (Fig. 483**C-E**), and legs grayish, greenish, or yellowish.

Geographic variation—See Browning (1990), Jehl (1987b), Jehl et al. (1990), King (2000), Patten et al. (2003), Winkler (1996), Zink & Winkler (1983). No other subspecies occur. In addition to the following, see Jehl (1987b) for a DFA (p. 5) using exposed culmen, flat wing length (Fig. 3**B**, p. 6), and tarsus lengths on specimens that distinguished 87-95% of known-sex individuals to subspecies.

L.c. californicus (br c.CA to s.MT-CO; wint coastal w.WA-nw.Mexico). Averages smaller (Table 59, p. 657); definitive upperpart feathers darker gray (Kodak 6.0-7.5, p. 629); ASY/ATYs with black on outer pp extensive, that on outer web of p7 occasionally (~13% of individuals) and p8 often (~56%) reaching p covs.

L.c. albertaensis (br NWT to ne.MT-ND; wint CA-AZ to n.Mexico). Averages larger (Table 59); definitive upperpart feathers paler gray (Kodak 5.0-6.0); ASY/ATYs with black on outer pp reduced, that on outer web of p7 not reaching p covs and on p8 only occasionally (~15%) reaching p covs.

Molt—SAS (CAS?). PF absent?, PA1 partial (Aug-May in HY/SYs), PB2 complete (May-Sep in SYs), PA2 partial-incomplete (Sep-Mar in SY/TYs), PB3 complete (May-Oct in TYs), PA3 partial (Oct?-Apr in TY/4Ys), DPB complete (Jun-Oct in ATYs), DPA partial (Sep?-Apr in ATY/A4Ys). The single inserted first-cycle molt appears homologous with a PA1 rather than a PF (Fig. 10**E**, p. 14), although some feathers may be replaced twice, indicating both a PF and a PA1 (and CAS; Fig. 10**F**). The PAs occur primarily on non-breeding grounds or (often) during northward migration, and can suspend during Dec-Feb. The PB2 occurs on non-breeding grounds in many over-summering SYs. The DPB usually starts on or near breeding grounds and completes on non-breeding grounds. The PA1 often includes some med and proximal les covs, often 1-6 or more c.rects, and occasionally 1-2 terts. The PA2 includes some to many med and proximal les covs, sometimes 1-6 or more c.rects, and often 1-3 terts. The DPA sometimes includes a few med and proximal les covs, but appears to include few if any terts or rects. Med and some other s covs are often replaced Sep-Nov during PAs (PA2 and later), overlapping completion of PBs.

Age—Juv (B1; Jul-Dec) has plumage uniform in wear; scapulars dark brown with scaly to notched, cinnamon to whitish fringes, bill blackish or with variable extent of flesh basally, and legs dull pinkish; Juv ♀ = ♂. See pp. 659-663 for additional information on ageing gulls.

Juv-HY/SY (1st cycle, Juv/B1-A1; Sep-Aug): Body feathers heavily mottled brown; outer pp and p covs relatively tapered, p9-p10 brownish and without mirror (Fig. 483**A**, p. 660), and outer p covs dark brown with fine pale tips (Fig. 484**A**, p. 660); longest uppertail covs with coarse dark-barred pattern (Fig. 485**A-D**, p. 661); underwing s covs uniformly dark brown; rects primarily blackish brown with reduced whitish at bases (Fig. 486**B-C**, p. 661); bill flesh to pink with broad black tip in Sep-Aug, to yellowish flesh with broad black subterminal band in May-Aug; legs dull pinkish, sometimes tinged greenish in Mar-Aug.

SY/TY (2nd cycle, B2-A2; Sep-Aug): Body feathers mottled brown and white, the upperparts usually mixed with gray feathers in Nov-Aug; p1-p4 medium gray-brown to pale grayish (*cf.* Fig. 487**A**, p. 662), contrasting with mostly brownish-black p5-p10; outer pp and p covs relatively broad at tips, p9-p10 blackish brown or sometimes with diffuse mirror on p10 (Fig. 483**B-C**), and outer p covs dark brown, sometimes with small pale tips (Fig. 484**B-C**); longest uppertail covs with irregular markings (Fig. 485**F-H**); underwing s covs mottled silvery brown and whitish; rects variably mostly dark to mostly whitish (Fig. 486**B-E**), sometimes with entirely white feathers in Mar-Aug; bill bluish flesh, sometimes yellowish in Apr-Aug, with black subterminal band and dull orange to reddish gonydeal spot in Sep-Mar; legs usually greenish flesh (Sep-Feb) to dull yellowish (Mar-Aug).

TY/4Y (3rd cycle, B3-A3; Sep-Aug): Body feathers white and gray, with moderate dusky mottling to head and breast in Sep-Mar; p1-p6 gray with moderately distinct black tips (*cf.* Fig. 487**D-E**), not contrasting with p7-p10; p9-p10 gray and blackish with white mirrors on p10 and often p9 (Fig. 483**D**); outer p covs gray with variable blackish marks (Fig. 484**D-H**); proximal gr covs and terts often with brownish wash; underwing s covs white (occasionally with a few dark spots); rects white or sometimes with black distal marks (Fig. 486**F-G**); bill greenish (Sep-Apr) to yellow (Apr-Aug), with indistinct black band and reddish gonydeal spot (most distinct Mar-Aug); legs usually grayish green to yellow, brighter in Mar-Aug. **Note: See ATY/A4Y.**

ATY/A4Y (Def. cycle, DB-DA; Sep-Aug): Body feathers white and gray, with sparse to moderate dusky mottling to head and breast in Sep-Feb; p1-p6 distinctly gray, white, and black (*cf.* Fig. 487**F**); p9-p10 gray and black with larger white mirrors and often with distinct white tips (Fig. 483**E**); outer p covs uniformly gray or sometimes with limited dark marks (Fig. 484**I-J**); s covs and terts without brownish wash; rects white (Fig. 486**G**, rarely with black markings as in **E-F**); bill greenish yellow (Sep-Jan) to yellow or orange-yellow (Feb-Aug), with black and red gonydeal spots (rarely lacking in Jun-Aug); legs usually greenish to bright yellow. **Note: Some ATY/A4Ys with reduced blackish on alula, p covs (Fig. 484H-I), and rects (Fig. 486F) may be 4Y/5Ys, but occasional A4Y/A5Ys may also retain these characters; more study needed.**

Sex—♀ = ♂ by plumage aspect. Bilateral and medial(?) BPs (Fig. 20**C**, p. 31) developed by both sexes but distended cloaca (Fig. 21, p. 32) indicates ATY ♀ in Apr-Jul. Measurements somewhat helpful for sexing within subspecies (Table 59, p. 657). In addition to the following, see Rodriguez et al. (1996) for a DFA (p. 5) using head-bill length (Fig. 453, p. 630) tarsus length, and bill depth at base that distinguished 98% of live adults in *L.c. californicus*, and Schnell et al. (1985) for reliable sexing using four skeletal measures. The following is based on studies of live *californicus*; values for *albertensis* were inferred based on specimen examination and subspecific differences in bill size and need to be confirmed based on live birds in the field:

♀: Head-bill length (Fig. 453, p. 630) 94-107 (*californicus*) or ~99-113 (*albertensis*) mm. **Note: Known *californicus* with head-bill length 105-107 mm, and individuals of unknown subspecies with head-bill length 105-113 mm cannot be reliably sexed by this measure alone.**

♂: Head-bill length 105-116 (*californicus* or 111-123 (*albertensis*) mm. **Note: See ♀.**

Hybrids reported—With Herring Gull (Chase 1984) and possibly with Mew Gull (p. 652) and Ring-billed Gull (p. 656).

References—Behle & Selander (1953), Bent (1921), Howell & Dunn (2007), Jehl (1987b), Johnston (1956), King (2000), Oberholser (1974), Ridgway (1919), Rodriguez et al. (1996), Schnell et al. (1985), Winkler (1996), Zink & Winkler (1983).

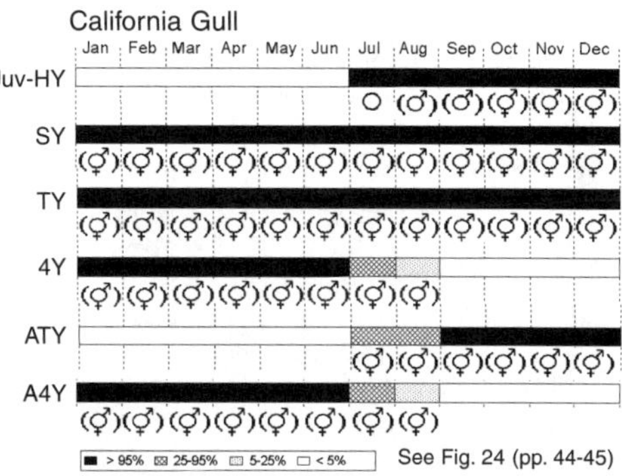

HERRING GULL

Larus argentatus

HERG
Species # 0510
Band size: 6

Species—From other species of gulls by the combination of medium-large size (Table 60, p. 668); bill depth at gonys (16.2-22.1) similar to that at base (16.0-21.8; *cf.* Fig. 453, p. 630); Juv-HY/SY with bill variably blackish with dull pink base to bright pink with well-defined black tip, inner pp pale to medium-pale brownish gray contrasting with darker p7-p10, the latter with moderately contrasting inner web (Fig. 482**B**, p. 659), and rects dark, often with reduced whitish basally (Fig. 486**A-B**, p. 661); ASY with upperparts pale gray (Kodak 4-5, p. 629; N.Am populations), outer pp with contrastingly black tips (Fig. 491**A-B**, p. 686), bill yellow with red gonydeal spot and without distinct black ring or spot, orbital ring yellow-orange, iris usually bright pale lemon, and legs pink. See Lesser Black-backed Gull (p. 668) and Howell & Dunn (2007) for separation of Yellow-legged Gull.

From Thayer's Gull (p. 688) further by larger average size (Table 60); Juv-HY with stronger contrast between paler inner and darker outer pp, and with darker inner webs to outer pp (Fig. 482**B**); ASY with upperparts paler gray (Kodak 4-5), outer pp tips blacker (Kodak 18-19) and more extensive, and p9 often without white mirror (Fig. 491**A-B**), orbital ring yellow-orange, and iris usually pale yellow. Beware of hybrids with Great Black-backed (p. 671), Glaucous-winged (p. 679), and Glaucous (p. 682) gulls; see Howell & Dunn (2007) for additional details of identification.

Geographic variation—See Adriaens & Mactavish (2004), Crochet et al. (2002), de Knijff et al. (2001, 2005), Dement'ev & Gladkov (1951c), Dwight (1925), Grant (1986), Hellmayr & Conover (1948b), Howell & Dunn (2007), Jonsson & Mactavish (2001), Kennerley et al. (1995), Liebers et al. (2001, 2004), Lonergan & Mullarney (2004), Macpherson (1961), Malling Olsen & Larsson (2003), Patten et al. (2003), Poor (1946), Portenko (1973), Ridgway (1919), Snell (1991a, 1991b, 1993), Weber (1981a), Yésou (2002). No other subspecies occur. In addition to the following, note that molt timing averages later in *L.a. smithsonianus* than in the Eurasian subspecies. ASYs within *smithsonianus* exhibit variation in pattern of outer pp and upperpart tone, suggesting that it may comprise more than one subspecies. Studies linking types to known breeding populations are needed.

L.a. vegae (br Siberia-St. Lawrence I, AK; ranges to w. AK; vagrant to CA, TX): Averages larger in size (Table 60, p. 668); Juv-HY/SYs average somewhat paler and with paler bases to rects (Fig. 486**C-D**, p. 661); ASYs with upperparts darker gray (Kodak 7-8), outer pp with relatively extensive black (averaging more than in Fig. 491**A-B**, p. 686), iris usually dirty pale lemon to brownish, and orbital ring orange-red.

L.a. smithsonianus (br and wint throughout most of N.Am range): Variably intermediate in size (Table 60); Juv-HY/SYs average darker and with darker bases to rects (Fig. 486**A-B**); ASYs with upperparts paler gray (Kodak 4-5), outer pp with intermediate extent of black (Fig. 491**A-B**); iris usually clear pale lemon or flecked dusky (primarily in w.N.Am), and orbital ring yellow-orange.

L.a. argentatus (br n.Europe, probable vagrant to e.N.Am): Larger (Table 60); Juv-HY/SYs average paler and with paler bases to rects (Fig. 486**C-D**); ASYs with upperparts darker gray (Kodak 5.5-7), outer pp with reduced black (averaging less extensive than in Fig. 491**A-B**), iris usually clear pale lemon, and orbital ring yellow-orange.

L.a. argenteus (br w. Europe, probable vagrant to e.N.Am): Averages smaller (Table 60); Juv-HY/SYs somewhat paler and with paler bases to rects (Fig. 486**C-D**); ASYs with upperparts paler gray (Kodak 4-5), outer pp with intermediate extent of black (Fig. 491**A-B**), iris usually clear pale lemon, and orbital ring yellow-orange.

Molt—SAS (CAS?). PF absent?, PA1 limited-partial (Sep/Feb-May in HY/SY), PB2 complete (Apr-Nov in SYs), PA2 partial (Sep-May in SY/TYs), PB3 complete (May-Dec in TYs), PA3 partial (Sep-May in TY/4Ys), DPB complete (Jun-Jan in ATY/A4Ys), DPA partial (Oct-Apr in ATY/A4Ys). The PA1 and DPA occur primarily on non-breeding grounds and the PAs can suspend during Nov-Feb. The PB2 occurs on non-breeding grounds in some over-summering SYs. The single inserted first-cycle molt appears homologous with a PA1 rather than a PF (Fig. 10**E**, p. 14), although some feathers may be replaced twice, indicating both a PF and a PA1 (and CAS; Fig. 10**F**). The DPB usually starts on or near breeding grounds and complete on non-breeding grounds. The PA1 includes some to most body (primarily back) feathers but few if any s covs, terts, or rects. The DPA includes most to all body feathers, a few to many med and proximal les covs, sometimes 1-2 terts, but few if any rects, with median and some other upperwing covs often replaced Sep-Nov (overlapping end of DPB). The above pertains primarily to *L.a. smithsonianus* (see **Geographic variation**): molts of migrants wintering in w.N.Am may average up to a month later than those wintering in e.N.Am.

Age—Juv (B1; Aug-Feb) has plumage uniform in wear; scapulars dark brown with scaly to notched, buff to whitish fringes, and bill blackish or with some pinkish basally; Juv ♀=♂. See pp. 659-663 for additional information on ageing gulls. The following pertains to N.Am Herring Gulls (*L.a. smithsonianus*); see **Geographic variation** for differences relative to certain ageing criteria in Eurasian subspecies.

Juv-HY/SY (1st cycle, Juv/B1-A1; Sep-Aug): Body feathers heavily mottled brown, to whitish with brown checkering; outer pp and p covs relatively tapered, p9-p10 brownish and without mirrors (Fig. 483**A**, p. 660), and outer p covs dark brown, sometimes with fine pale tips (Fig. 484**A**, p. 660); longest uppertail covs with coarse dark barring (Fig. 485**A-D**, p. 661); underwing s covs uniformly dark brown; rects dark brown or with reduced whitish bases (Fig. 486**A-B**, p. 661); bill blackish with variably paler, pinkish basal two-thirds.

SY/TY (2nd cycle, B2-A2; Sep-Aug): Body feathers whitish mottled brown, the upperparts usually mixed with pale gray feathers in Nov-Aug; p1-p6 medium gray-brown to pale grayish (Fig. 487**A**, p. 662; occasionally with 1-2 paler gray feathers), contrasting with mostly brownish-black p7-p10; outer pp and p covs relatively truncate, p9-p10 blackish and without mirrors (Fig. 483**B**), and outer p covs dark brown, usually with diffuse pale tips (Fig. 484**B-C**); longest uppertail covs with variable and irregular markings (Fig. 485**F** & **H-I**); underwing s covs mixed brown and whitish; rects mostly brown to white with dark subterminal band (Fig. 486**B-D**); bill blackish with yellowish to pink base, becoming yellow with dull orange-red gonydeal spot and dark subterminal mark by Jun-Aug.

TY/4Y (3rd cycle, B3-A3; Sep-Aug): Body feathers primarily white and gray, with moderate dusky mottling to head and breast in Sep-Mar; p1-p6 gray and white with moderately distinct blackish tips (Fig. 487**D-E**), not contrasting with p7-p10; p9-p10 gray and blackish usually with white mirror to p10 but without white tips (Fig. 483**C-D**); outer p covs grayish with blackish markings (Fig. 484**D-F**); proximal gr covs and terts usually washed brownish; underwing s covs white, often with sparse brown mottling; rects usually with blackish distally (Fig. 486**D-G**; ~30% as in **D** and ~13% white, as in **G**); bill yellowish with black subterminal band and dull red spot in Sep-Feb, to bright yellow with red gonydeal spot and little or no black in Apr-Aug. **Note: See ATY/A4Y. Many intermediates with ATY/A4Y may occur which may best be aged T-4Y or 4-5Y (see p. 41-42).**

ATY/A4Y (Def. cycle, DB-DA; Sep-Aug): Body feathers white and gray, with sparse dusky mottling to head and breast in Sep-Feb; p1-p6 gray and white with distinct black tips to p5-p6 (Fig. 487**F**, p. 662); p9-p10 with black tips, p10 with distinct white mirror and rarely white tip, and p9 occasionally with white mirror (Fig. 483**D-E**; see also 491**A-B**, primarily in ne.N.Am); outer p covs without black, or rarely with limited black marks (Fig. 484**I-J**); gr covs and terts without brownish wash; underwing s covs white; rects white (Fig. 486**G**, rarely with black marks as in **E-F**); bill bright yellow with red gonydeal spot, often also with blackish subterminal marks in Sep-Feb. **Note: Many 4Y/5Ys appear to retain dark markings on alula, p covs (Fig. 484G-I), and rects (Fig. 486E-F) but great individual variation makes age assignment unreliable (Poor 1946, Monaghan & Duncan 1979).**

Sex— ♀ = ♂ by plumage aspect. Bilateral and medial(?) BPs (Fig. 20**C**, p. 31) developed by both sexes but distended cloaca (Fig. 21, p. 32) indicates ATY ♀ in Apr-Jul. Most measurements somewhat helpful for sexing (Table 60, p. 668), especially with mated pairs. See Shugart (1977), Fox et al. (1981), Coulson et al. (1983), and Evans et al. (1995) for DFAs (p. 5) using (variously) head-bill length (Fig. 453, p. 630), exposed culmen, bill depth, wing chord, and tarsus, that correctly sexed 94-98% of North American or European Herring Gulls. The following can be used to sex many full-grown individuals:

♀: Head-bill length (Fig. 453) 108-121 mm. **Note: Individuals with head-bill length 119-121 mm cannot be reliably sexed by this measure alone.**

♂: Head-bill length 119-134 mm. **Note: See ♀.**

Hybrids reported—With Black-headed (p. 640), California (p. 663), Yellow-legged *L. michahellis* (Garner 1997, Yésou 1991), Caspian (*L. cachinnans*; Faber et al. 2001), Lesser Black-backed (Harris et al. 1978, Howell & Dunn 2007), Kelp *L. dominicanus* (Dittman & Cardiff 1998, 2005), Great Black-backed (Andrle 1972, Foxhall 1979, Godfrey 1973, Jehl 1960), Thayer's (Manning et al. 1956), Slaty-backed (King & Carey 1999, Portenko 1963), Glaucous-winged (Howell & Corben 2000d, Williamson & Peyton 1963), Glaucous (Dwight 1925, Ingolfsson 1987, Kessel 1989, Spear 1987); and possibly with Iceland (Davies 1978; see McCarthy 2006) gulls in the wild.

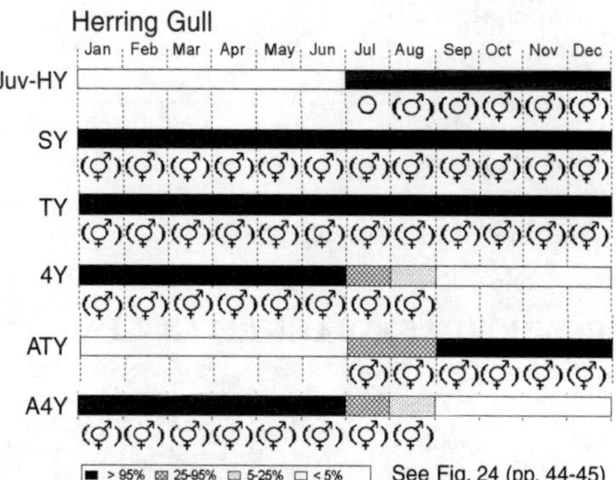

References—Adriaens & Mactavish (2004), Andrle (1972), Baker (1993), Barth (1967, 1974), Bent (1921), Boss (1943), Cramp & Simmons (1983), Dement'ev & Gladkov (1951c), Dwight (1901, 1925), Godfrey (1973), Howell & Corben (2000d), Howell & Dunn (2007), Howell et al. (1999), Jehl (1960, 1987c), Jonsson & Mactavish (2001), Kaufman (1990a), Macpherson (1961), Malling Olsen & Larsson (2003), Monaghan & Duncan (1979), Oberholser (1974), Pierotti & Good (1994), Poor (1946), Ridgway (1919), Roberts (1955), Threlfall & Jewer (1978), Verbeek (1977), Yésou (2002).

TABLE 60. Measurements (mm) of North American large, "dark-winged" gulls to assist in identification and sexing. See pp. 4-11 for methods of measurement. Species summaries are in **bold** and subspecies values are in ***italics***. Values were derived from 95% confidence intervals as based approximately on the indicated sample sizes. Thus, midpoints of ranges approximate means, and S.D. is approximated by one-quarter of the range.

Taxon/Sex	*n*	wing chord[1]	tail length	exp culmen	bill depth[2]	tarsus
Herring Gull		**369-468**	**148-188**	**42-63**	**16.0-21.8**	**56-73**
L.a. vegae		***402-468***	***160-188***	***45-62***	***16.9-21.3***	***60-72***
♀	30	402-447	160-181	45-59	16.9-20.5	60-70
♂	50	416-468	163-188	50-62	17.2-21.3	62-72
L.a. smithsonianus		***394-458***	***153-185***	***46-62***	***16.0-21.8***	***56-73***
♀	95	394-431	153-178	46-56	16.0-19.3	56-66
♂	100	412-458	160-185	51-62	17.9-21.8	60-73
L.a. argentatus		***392-462***	***154-190***	***45-63***	---	***59-72***
♀	100	392-433	154-175	45-60	---	59-67
♂	100	420-462	168-190	49-63	---	64-72
L.a. argenteus		***369-442***	***148-181***	***42-61***	---	***57-70***
♀	100	369-412	148-169	42-57	---	57-65
♂	100	398-442	159-181	46-61	---	62-70
Lesser Black-backed Gull[3]		**378-447**	**143-167**	**45-58**	**15.0-20.5**	**54-69**
♀	100	378-430	143-158	45-56	15.0-18.2	54-67
♂	100	392-447	153-167	48-58	16.1-20.5	57-69
Great Black-backed Gull		**442-511**	**171-207**	**54-72**	**20.6-27.6**	**67-84**
♀	100	442-490	171-194	54-65	20.6-25.1	67-78
♂	100	459-511	183-207	58-72	21.8-27.6	72-84
Slaty-backed Gull		**402-465**	**170-195**	**49-61**	**16.0-21.8**	**60-75**
♀	40	402-441	170-187	49-58	17.4-20.6	60-70
♂	40	429-465	177-195	52-61	18.6-22.8	64-75
Western Gull		**368-438**	**148-174**	**47-61**	**16.1-22.5**	**59-74**
L.o. occidentalis		***378-438***	***151-174***	***48-61***	***17.2-22.5***	***61-74***
♀	70	378-409	151-167	48-57	17.2-21.1	61-70
♂	60	399-438	157-174	52-61	19.0-22.5	63-74
L.o. wymani		***368-434***	***148-171***	***47-59***	***16.1-21.4***	***59-72***
♀	60	368-407	148-163	47-54	16.1-19.5	59-68
♂	70	398-434	155-171	51-59	17.8-21.4	62-72
Yellow-footed Gull		**390-450**	**154-177**	**49-61**	**16.0-21.8**	**60-75**
♀	45	390-431	154-169	49-57	16.9-20.9	60-71
♂	65	412-450	162-177	53-61	19.0-23.9	65-75

[1] Wing chord averages ~5% shorter in Juv-HY/SY than in AHY/ASY.

[2] Bill depth measured at distal end of forehead feathering (see Fig. 8**A**, p. 10).

[3] Measures refer to both subspecies of Lesser Black-backed Gull that occur in N.Am (see **Geographic variation**), which have similar values by sex.

LESSER BLACK-BACKED GULL
Larus fuscus

LBBG
Species # 0500
Band size: 6

Species—From other species of gull inclduing Yellow-footed (p. 678) by the combination of medium-large size with proportionally long wings (Table 60; bill usually deeper at gonys (14.3-19.3) than at base (15.0-20.5; Table 60; *cf.* Fig. 453, p. 630); Juv-HY/SY with bill blackish, inner pp dark brown, not contrasting strongly with p7-p10, the latter with indistinct inner webs (Fig. 482**A**, p. 659), uppertail covs whiter than most other species (Fig. 485**E**, p. 661), and rects with white base and black terminal band (Fig. 486**C-D**, p. 661); ASY with upperparts medium-dark to very dark gray (Kodak 9-13, p. 629; see **Geographic variation**), orbital ring orange-red, iris usually bright pale lemon, and legs usually yellow.

Kelp Gull (*L. dominicanus*, a vagrant to N.Am) averages larger (wing 387-456, exp culmen 45-57, tarsus 60-69); bill deeper at gonys (18.1-23.5) than at base (16.4-21.5); ATY with upperparts blackish (Kodak 14-15.5), legs usually greenish yellow, head with very limited dusky streaking in Oct-Mar (N.Am), and iris often dusky. Yellow-legged Gull (*L. michahellis*), a vagrant to e.N.Am, very similar to Lesser Black-backed Gull but averages larger (wing chord 400-463, exp culmen 45.5-59.9, tarsus 57-74); bill deeper at gonys (16.4-21.5) than at base (16.0-22.4); HY/SY often lacks black barring to white bases of r5-r6 (Fig. 486**D**-**E**); ASY with upperparts paler gray (Kodak 6-8.5). See Garner & Quinn (1997) and Howell & Dunn (2007) for further identification criteria.

Geographic variation—See Cramp & Simmons (1983), Crochet et al. (2002), de Knijff et al. (2001), Dement'ev & Gladkov (1951c), Dwight (1925), Eskelin & Pursiainen (1998), Kennerley et al. (1995), Post & Lewis (1995a, 1995b), Liebers & Helbig (2002), Liebers et al. (2001, 2004), Stevenson & Anderson (1994), and Yésou (2002). Three other subspecies occur in Eurasia.

L.f. graellsii (br w. Europe, wint e.N.Am, vagrant to w.N.Am): ASY with upperparts paler gray (Kodak 9-11), contrasting distinctly with black distal portions of p6-p10, inner webs to inner pp paler, and white lounge-tips to p6-p10 and mirrors on p9-p10 larger. Nominate subspecies of Lesser Black-backed Gull (*L.f. fuscus*), unrecorded in N.Am, has upperparts much darker (Kodak 13-15) and with darker inner webs and less white to pp (usually lacking white mirror on p9). *L.f. heuglini* and *taimyrensis*, possible vagrants to AK, similar to *graellsii* (although upperparts variably paler in *taimyrensis*) but average larger (wg chord 398-472, exp culmen 44-62, tarsus 62-78) and with smaller mirrors and black tips to outer pp. See Buzin (2002) and Eskelin & Pusiainen (1998) for more information.

L.f. intermedius (br Scandinavia; vagrant to e.N.Am): ASY with upperparts darker gray (Kodak 11-13), contrasting less distinctly with black distal portions of p6-p10, inner webs to inner pp darker, and white tongue-tips to p6-p10 and mirrors to p9-p10 smaller.

Molt—SAS (CAS?). PF absent?, PA1 partial (Sep-Apr in HY/SYs), PB2 complete (Apr-Nov in SYs), PA2 partial-incomplete (Sep?-Apr in SY/TYs), PB3 complete (May-Jan in TY/4Ys), PA3 partial-incomplete (Sep?-Apr in TY/4Ys), DPB complete (May-Mar in ATY/A4Ys), DPA partial? (Oct?-Apr in ATY/A4Ys). The single inserted first-cycle molt appears homologous with a PA1 rather than a PF (Fig. 10**E**, p. 14), although some feathers may be replaced twice, indicating both a PF and a PA1 (and CAS; Fig. 10**F**). The PAs occur primarily on non-breeding grounds and can suspend during Nov-Feb (in n.wintering individuals). The PB2 occurs on non-breeding grounds in some over-summering SYs. The DPB can start on or near breeding grounds and complete on non-breeding grounds. The PA1 and DPA in N.Am include some to most body feathers, sometimes a few to many s covs, and 1-3 terts, but few if any rects. Median and some other upperwing covs probably replaced Sep-Nov during PAs (PA2 and later), overlapping completion of PBs. In *L.f. fuscus* and *intermedius* (presumably longer-distance migrants) of Europe the PA2 and PA3 can include some to all c.rects and a variable number of ss and inner pp; look for occasional *graellsii* to replace rects and pp during these molts as well.

Age—Juv (B1; Aug-Feb) has plumage uniform in wear; scapulars dark brown with scaly to notched, cinnamon-buff to whitish edges, bill blackish, iris dark brown, and legs dull pinkish; Juv ♀=♂. See pp. 659-663 for additional information on ageing gulls.

Juv-HY/SY (1st cycle, Juv/B1-A1; Sep-Aug): Body feathers heavily mottled brown; outer pp and p covs relatively tapered, p9-p10 brownish and without mirrors (Fig. 483**A**, p. 660), and outer p covs blackish brown with indistinct fine pale tips (Fig. 484**A**, p. 660); longest uppertail covs with distinct, relatively regular but sparse dark-barred pattern (Fig. 485**C**-**E**, p. 661); underwing s covs uniformly dark brown; rects white with black distal band (Fig. 486**C**-**D**, p. 661); iris usually brown; bill blackish, with flesh base in Mar-Aug; legs dull pinkish.

SY/TY (2nd cycle, B2-A2; Sep-Aug): Body feathers washed brownish and white, the upperparts usually mixed with dark gray feathers in Nov-Aug; p1-p6 dark gray-brown to grayish (*cf.* Fig. 487**A**, p. 662), contrasting with mostly brownish-black p7-p10; outer pp and p covs relatively truncate, p9-p10 blackish and without mirrors (Fig. 483**B**), and outer p covs dark slaty brown, usually with broad pale tips (Fig. 484**B**-**C**); longest uppertail covs usually with narrow and sparse dark bars (Fig. 485**D** & **G**); underwing s covs variably mixed brown and white; rects whitish with blackish distal band (Fig. 486**B**-**D**, often broader than HY/SY and occasionally with completely white feathers in Mar-Aug); iris usually brown to yellowish with brown flecking; bill blackish with flesh to yellowish at base and pale tip, sometimes yellow with dull orange-red gonydeal spot and a dark subterminal band in May-Aug; legs usually pinkish, often tinged yellow by Mar-Aug.

TY/4Y (3rd cycle, B3-A3; Sep-Aug): Body feathers primarily white and gray with sparse to moderate dusky mottling to head and breast in Sep-Feb; p1-p6 dark gray with indistinct black tips (*cf.* Fig. 487**D**), not contrasting with p7-p10; p9-p10 gray and blackish with brownish wash and variable mirrors to p10 by subspecies (Fig. 483**B**-**C**; see **Geographic variation**); outer p covs grayish with variable black markings and often a distinct whitish tip to outer web (Fig. 484**C**-**G**); proximal gr covs and terts with brownish wash; longest uppertail covs white, rarely with faint dark bars; underwing s covs white, usually with sparse brown mottling; rects white, often with reduced blackish markings (Fig. 486**F**-**G**); iris usually yellowish, sometimes with brown flecking; bill blackish with yellowish at base and a large creamy tip, becoming yellow with an orange-red gonydeal spot and sometimes a dark subterminal band in Mar-Aug; legs usually pinkish yellow to yellowish. **Note: See ATY/A4Y.**

ATY/A4Y (Def. cycle, DB-DA; Sep-Aug): Body feathers white and gray, with sparse dusky mottling to head and breast in Feb-Sep; p1-p6 dark gray and white with distinct black tips to p5-p6 (*cf.* Fig. 487**F**); p9-p10 gray and black with distinct white mirrors (Fig. 483**E**); outer p covs slaty gray or with some blackish on outer webs (Fig. 484**G**-**J**); proximal gr covs and terts without brownish wash; longest uppertail covs white; underwing s covs white; rects white (Fig. 486**G**, rarely with black marks as in **E**-**F**); iris usually clear lemon yellow; bill bright yellow with red gonydeal spot, sometimes also with blackish markings in Sep-Feb; legs usually bright yellow. **Note: Some 4Y/5Ys that have completed molt may retain dark markings on alula, p covs (Fig. 484E-I), and rects (Fig. 486E-F) but substantial individual variation makes age assignment unreliable.**

4Y (4th cycle, B4; Sep-Dec): Like ATY/A4Y with molt in pp occurring or suspended, the outer p covs with substantial blackish and distinct whitish tips to outer webs (Fig. 484**C**-**F**), and p9-p10 with no or reduced mirrors by subspecies (Fig. 483**B**-**D**; see **Geographic variation**). **Note: A few individuals may suspend molt of outer pp until Jan-Mar and can be aged 5Y or A5Y.**

A4Y (Def. cycle, DB; Sep-Dec): Like ATY/A4Y with molt in pp occurring or suspended, the outer p covs slaty gray or with some blackish on outer webs (Fig. 484**H**-**J**), and p9-p10 with distinct white mirrors by subspecies (Fig. 483**E**). **Note: See 4Y.**

Sex—♀ = ♂ by plumage aspect. Bilateral and medial BPs (Fig. 20**C**, p. 31) developed by both sexes but distended cloaca (Fig. 21, p. 32) indicates ATY ♀ in Apr-Jul. Measurements largely unhelpful for sexing (Table 60, p. 668). See Coulson et al. (1983) for a DFA (p. 5) using head-and-bill length that correctly sexed 98% of freshly dead adults (*L.f. graellsii*) from Britain. The following can be used to sex many full-grown individuals of *graellsii* and probably *intermedius* as well:

♀: Head-bill length (Fig. 453, p. 630) 103-115 mm. **Note: Individuals with head-bill length 114-115 mm cannot be reliably sexed by this measure alone.**

♂: Head-bill length 114-127 mm. **Note: See ♀.**

Hybrids reported—With Herring (p. 665), Yellow-legged *L. michahellis* (Cottaar 2004, Yésou 1991) and Glaucous gulls (McCarthy 2006); and possibly with Mew Gull (p. 652) in the wild.

References—Baker (1993), Barth (1967, 1974), Bent (1921), Coulson et al. (1983), Cramp & Simmons (1983), Dwight (1925), Garner & Quinn (1997), Harris et al. (1978), Howell & Dunn (2007), Jiguet (2002), Malling Olsen & Larsson (2003), Ridgway (1919), Verbeek (1977), Winters (2006), Yésou 2002.

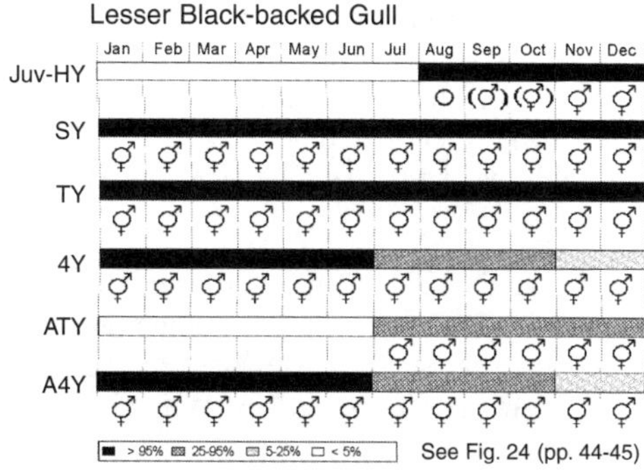

GREAT BLACK-BACKED GULL

Larus marinus

GBBG
Species # 0470
Band size: 7B-7A

Species—From other gulls by very large size (Table 60, p. 668); bill usually slightly deeper at gonys (♀ 21.0-26.5, ♂ 22.6-27.6) than at base (♀ 20.6-25.1, ♂ 21.8-27.6; *cf.* Fig. 453, p. 630); Juv-HY (and many SY/TYs) with head whitish, bill black, upperparts boldly checkered, inner pp gray-brown, contrasting slightly to moderately with p7-p10, the latter with moderately indistinct contrast to inner web (Fig. 482**B**, p. 659), uppertail covs white with sparse dark marks (Fig. 485**E**, p. 661), rects white, with wavy distal black band (Fig. 486**D**-**E**, p. 661), and often including a unique thin bar proximally; ATY with upperparts blackish (Kodak 13-15; see p. 629), p9-p10 tips with extensive white, orbital ring red, legs and feet pink, and iris usually bright whitish to grayish. Beware hybrids with Herring Gull (p. 665)

Geographic variation—Monotypic.

Molt—SAS (CAS?). PF absent?, PA1 limited-partial (Oct/Feb-May in HY/SYs), PB2 complete (Apr-Oct in SYs), PA2 partial (Sep-Apr in SY/TYs), PB3 complete (May-Nov in TYs), PA3 partial (Sep?-Apr in TY/4Ys), DPB complete (Jun-Jan in ATY/A4Ys), DPA partial (Oct?-Apr in ATY/A4Ys). The single inserted first-cycle molt appears homologous with a PA1 rather than a PF (Fig. 10**E**, p. 14), although some feathers may be replaced twice, indicating both a PF and a PA1 (and CAS; Fig. 10**F**). The PAs occur primarily on non-breeding grounds and can suspend during Nov-Feb, the PB2 occurs on non-breeding grounds in many over-summering SYs, and the DPB can start on or near breeding grounds and complete on non-breeding grounds. The PA1 includes some body feathers (primarily on the back) and sometimes a few med and proximal les covs but no terts or rects, the PA2 and PA3 probably include a few to many med and proximal les covs but no terts or rects, and the DPA occasionally includes a few med and proximal les covs but no terts or rects. Median and some other upperwing covs often replaced Sep-Nov during PAs (PA2 and later), overlapping end of PBs.

Age—Juv (B1; Aug-Feb) has plumage uniform in wear; scapulars dark brown with broad, notched, cinnamon-buff to whitish fringes, and bill black; Juv ♀ = ♂. See pp. 659-663 for additional information on ageing gulls.

Juv-HY/SY (1st cycle, Juv/B1-A1; Sep-Aug): Body feathers checkered and mottled grayish brown and whitish; gr covs with distinct black markings and broad whitish fringes (Fig. 488**A**-**B**, p. 672); ss with grayish and narrow whitish tips (width of whitish < 8 mm); outer pp and p covs relatively tapered, p9-p10 brownish and without mirrors (Fig. 483**A**, p. 660), and the outer p covs blackish brown (Fig. 484**A**, p. 660), with narrow pale to whitish tips (Fig. 489**A-C**); underwing s covs dark brown checkered whitish; rects white with black distal band (Fig. 486**D-E**, often including extra proximal bar); iris usually brownish; bill blackish, with grayish flesh base in Mar-Aug. **Note: Some HY/SY can be difficult to separate from SY/TYs; use caution.**

SY/TY (2nd cycle, B2-A2; Sep-Aug): Body feathers white with sparse to moderate grayish checkering and mottling (including breast), the upperparts mixed with sooty brown feathers in Nov-Aug; gr covs with narrow and indistinct blackish marks and whitish fringes (Fig. 488**C-D**); ss with broad (> 8 mm) whitish tips; p1-p6 grayish brown with dusky tips (*cf.* Fig. 487**A**, p. 662), contrasting with mostly brownish-black p7-p10; outer pp and p covs relatively truncate, p9-p10 blackish brown, sometimes with small and indistinct white mirror on p10 (Fig. 483**B-C**), and outer p covs blackish brown (Fig. 484**B-C**) with broad, pale brownish-gray to white tips (Fig. 489**D**); underwing s covs mixed silvery and brown; rects with broad dark tips (Fig. 486**B-D**, averaging more dark than in HY/SYs); iris usually pale brownish to grayish; bill blackish with pale base and tip in Sep-Feb, often dusky pinkish to yellowish with broad black subterminal band in Mar-Aug, and rarely with dull orange-red gonydeal spot in Jun-Aug. **Note: See Juv-HY/SY.**

TY/4Y (3rd cycle, B3-A3; Sep-Aug): Body feathers primarily white and blackish with sparse dusky mottling to head (but not breast) in Sep-Feb; p1-p6 dark gray with indistinct black tips (*cf.* Fig. 487**D**), not contrasting with p7-p10; p9-p10 gray and blackish, p10 with small but distinct white tip or mirror, and p9 sometimes with white mirror (Fig. 483**D**); outer p covs grayish to dusky with variable black markings (Fig. 484**D-G**); s covs and terts variably washed brownish; underwing s covs white with sparse brown mottling; rects white with reduced to moderate blackish subterminal band or markings (Fig. 486**C-E**); iris usually whitish; bill mostly flesh with black subterminal band, to yellowish with reddish gonydeal spot and black subterminal marks (occasionally lacking in Apr-Aug). **Note: Some to many individuals may best be aged T-4Y or 4-5Y (see pp. 41-42); see ATY/A4Y.**

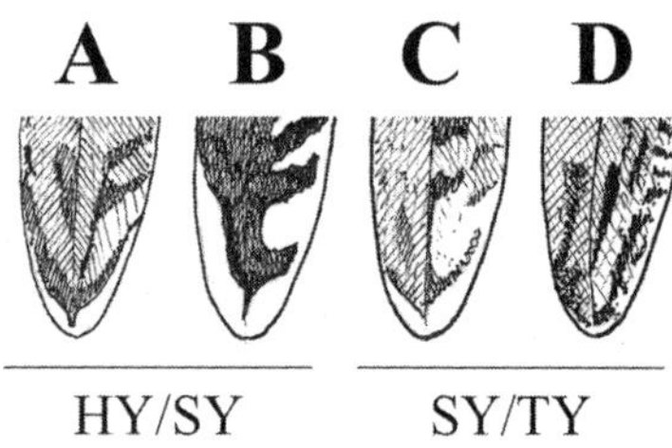

FIGURE 488. Typical patterns of the greater coverts by age in 1st-cycle (HY/SY) and 2nd-cycle (SY/TY) Great Black-backed Gulls. These two age groups can be surprisingly difficult to separate in this species.

ATY/A4Y (Def. cycle, DB-DA; Sep-Aug): Body feathers white and blackish with little or no gray mottling to crown and nape in Feb-Sep; p1-p6 dark gray and white with distinct black tips to p5-p6 (*cf.* Fig. 487**F**); p9-p10 gray and black with distinct white mirrors and tips (Fig. 483**D-E**; p8 also sometimes with mirror); outer p covs slaty gray or with some blackish on outer webs (Fig. 484**G-J**); proximal gr covs and terts without brownish wash; underwing s covs white; rects white (Fig. 486**G**, rarely with black marks as in **E-F**); iris usually bright whitish; bill bright yellow with red gonydeal spot, often with flesh tinge to base and blackish markings in Sep-Feb.

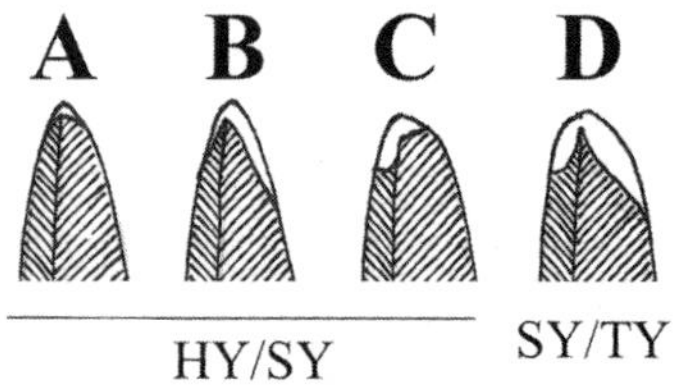

FIGURE 489. Typical patterns and shapes of the longest primary covert by age in 1st-cycle (HY/SY) and 2nd-cycle (SY/TY) Great Black-backed Gulls. Compare with Fig. 485, p. 661.

Note: Some to many (perhaps most?) 4Y/5Ys appear to retain dark markings on alula, p covs (Fig. 484E-I), and rects (Fig. 486E-F) but substantial individual variation makes age assignment unreliable. These may best be aged T-4Y or 4-5Y (see pp. 41-42). More study needed.

4Y (4th cycle, B4; Sep-Nov): Like ATY/A4Y with molt in pp occurring and outer p covs dusky to brownish gray with blackish on outer web (Fig. 484**D-F**), p9 with small to no whitish mirror (*cf.* Fig. 483**C**), and p10 with small white mirror (Fig. 483**D**).

A4Y (Def. cycle, DB; Sep-Nov): Like ATY/A4Y with molt in pp occurring and outer p covs gray, without blackish on outer web (Fig. 484**J**), p9 (and occasionally p8) with distinct white mirror (Fig. 483**D**), and p10 with large and distinct white mirror and tip (Fig. 483**E**).

Sex— ♀ = ♂ by plumage aspect. Bilateral and medial BPs (Fig. 20**C,** p. 31) developed by both sexes but distended cloaca (Fig. 21, p. 32) indicates ATY ♀ in Apr-Jul. Most measurements largely unhelpful for sexing (Table 60, p. 668). See Harris (1964) and Mawhinney & Diamond (1999) for DFAs (p. 5) using head-bill length (Fig. 453, p. 630), exposed culmen, and bill depth at gonys, that correctly 96-99% of live or freshly dead individuals from a NB population. The following can be used to reliably sex most full-grown individuals:

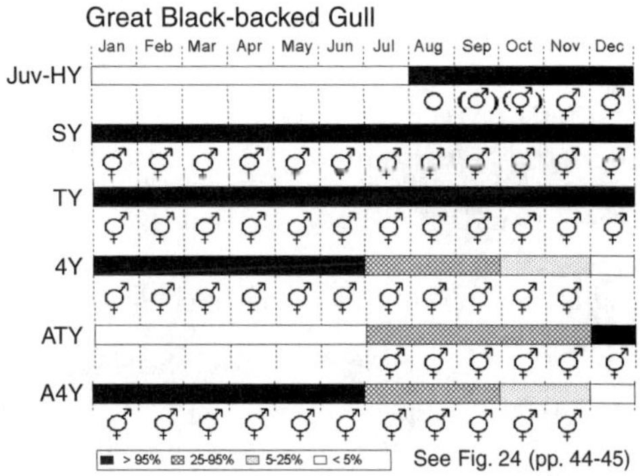

♀: Head-bill length (Fig. 453) 130-143 mm. **Note. Individuals with head-bill length 142-143 mm cannot be reliably sexed by this measure alone.**

♂: Head-bill length 142-156 mm. **Note: See ♀.**

Great Black-backed Gull

Jan | Feb | Mar | Apr | May | Jun | Jul | Aug | Sep | Oct | Nov | Dec

Juv-HY, SY, TY, 4Y, ATY, A4Y

■ > 95% ▨ 25-95% ▭ 5-25% ▭ < 5% See Fig. 24 (pp. 44-45)

Hybrids reported—With Herring (p. 665) and Glaucous gulls (Wilson 1951) in the wild.

References—Baker (1993), Barth (1967), Bent (1921), Butler & Janes-Butler (1983), Cramp & Simmons (1983), Dement'ev & Gladkov (1951c), Dwight (1925), Godfrey (1973), Good (1998), Harris (1964), Howell & Dunn (2007), Ingolfsson (1970), Malling Olsen & Larsson (2003), Ridgway (1919).

SLATY-BACKED GULL

Larus schistisagus

SBGU
Species # 0480
Band size: 7A

Species—From other large gulls, with caution, by the combination of large size with relatively long wings (Table 60, p. 668); bill usually similar in depth or deeper at gonys (♀ 17.7-20.9, ♂ 19.0-22.8) than at base (♀ 17.4-20.6, ♂ 18.6-22.8; *cf.* Fig. 453, p. 630); Juv-HY/SY with bill black, inner pp medium-pale gray-brown with variable dark subterminal marks, contrasting with darker brown p7-p10, the latter with moderate contrast to inner web (Fig. 482**B**, p. 659), and rects brownish with reduced to moderate whitish basally (Fig. 486**B-C**, p. 661); ASY with upperparts dark gray (Kodak 9.5-11.5, p. 629), p5-p7/p8 usually with distinct white tongue-tips, distal underside of p7-p10 dark slaty to silvery black, orbital ring reddish (at least in Apr-Jul), iris usually bright whitish, and legs dark pink. See Howell & Dunn (2007) for species identification details and beware the possibility of hybrids, especially with Glaucous-winged Gull (p. 679).

From Western Gull (p. 675) further by longer average wing and tail (Table 60); bill similar in depth at gonys and base (see above); iris clearer and whiter by age; Juv-HY/SY and SY/TY with paler body feathers (especially head and rump), contrasting more with dark marks around eye; definitive upperpart feathers average darker gray (Kodak 9.5-11.5); p5-p8 with well-defined white tongue-tips; distal underside to p7-p10 with broader and paler inner web; head and breast with dusky-brownish streaking in Sep-Feb; bill typically duller and with dark distal marks in Oct-Feb; orbital ring reddish (at least in Apr-Jul); legs darker pink.

Geographic variation—Monotypic.

Molt—SAS (CAS?). PF absent?, PA1 partial (Oct/Jan-May? in HY/SYs), PB2 complete (May-Nov in SYs), PA2 partial (Sep-Apr? in SY/TYs), PB3 complete (May-Nov in TYs), PA3 partial (Oct?-Apr in TY/4Ys), DPB complete (Jun-Jan in ATY/A4Ys), DPA partial (Jan?-Apr in ATY/A4Ys). The single inserted first-cycle molt appears homologous with a PA1 rather than a PF (Fig. 10**E**, p. 14), although some feathers may be replaced twice, indicating both a PF and a PA1 (and CAS; Fig. 10**F**). The PAs occur primarily on non-breeding grounds and can suspend during Dec-Feb. The PB2 probably can occur on non-breeding grounds in over-summering SYs. The DPB can start on or near breeding grounds and complete on non-breeding grounds. The PA1 appears to include a few to some body (primarily back) feathers but no s covs, terts, or rects, and subsequent PAs include a few to some med and proximal les covs but no terts or rects, as in other large gulls. Median and some other upperwing covs probably replaced Sep-Nov during PAs (PA2 and PA3, at least), overlapping completion of PBs.

Age—Juv (B1; Aug-Feb) has plumage uniform in wear; scapulars dark brown with scaly to notched, cinnamon-buff to whitish fringes, and bill blackish; Juv ♀=♂. See pp. 659-663 for additional information on ageing gulls.

Juv-HY/SY (1st cycle, Juv/B1-A1; Sep-Aug): Body feathers mottled brown and white; outer pp and p covs relatively tapered, p9-p10 brownish and without mirrors (Fig. 483**A**, p. 660), and outer p covs dark brown, usually without pale tips (Fig. 484**A**, p. 660); longest uppertail covs with distinct brown bars (Fig. 485**C**-**E**, p. 661); underwing s covs uniformly dark brown; rects blackish brown with variable whitish basally (Fig. 486**B**-**C**, p. 661); bill blackish or (primarily Mar-Aug) with reduced grayish to dull pinkish base; iris usually brownish.

SY/TY (2nd cycle, B2-A2; Sep-Aug): Body feathers mottled whitish and brown, the upperparts usually mixed with dark gray in Nov-Aug; p1-p5/p6 dark gray-brown to grayish (*cf.* Fig. 487**A**, p. 662), contrasting with darker p7-p10; outer pp and p covs relatively truncate, p9-p10 blackish brown and without mirrors (Fig. 483**B**), and outer p covs dark gray-brown with diffuse paler tips (Fig. 484**B**-**C**); longest uppertail covs with irregular brown bars and wavy markings (Fig. 485**F**-**H**); underwing s covs probably mixed brown and silvery or white; rects with variable whitish basally (Fig. 486**B**-**D**); bill blackish with reduced flesh to yellowish at base and a pale-yellowish tip, sometimes yellow with orange-red gonydeal spot and blackish subterminal band or marks in Jun-Aug; iris usually pale brown to whitish.

TY/4Y (3rd cycle, B3-A3; Sep-Aug): Body feathers primarily gray and white, with moderate dusky streaks to head and breast in Sep-Mar; p1-p6 dark gray with moderately distinct blackish tips (*cf.* Fig. 487**D**), not contrasting with p7-p10; p9-p10 gray and black with brownish wash and whitish mirror to p10 but not p9 (Fig. 483**C**-**D**); outer p covs grayish with variable black markings (Fig. 484**C**-**G**); s covs and terts variably washed brownish; longest uppertail covs white, rarely with faint dark bars; underwing s covs probably white with sparse dusky mottling; rects white, often with reduced blackish markings or occasionally completely white (Fig. 486**F**-**G**); bill pinkish to yellowish with a black subterminal band and sometimes a reddish gonydeal spot (Sep-Mar) to yellow with a reddish gonydeal spot (Apr-Aug); iris usually whitish. **Note: See ATY/A4Y.**

ATY/A4Y (Def. cycle, DB-DA; Sep-Aug): Body feathers gray and white, the head with sparse to moderate dusky streaking in Sep-Feb; p1-p6 dark gray with distinct black tips (*cf.* Fig. 487**F**); p10 or p9-p10 with distinct white mirrors (Fig. 483**E**); outer p covs slaty gray or with limited blackish on outer webs (Fig. 484**H-J**); proximal gr covs and terts without brownish wash; longest uppertail covs white; underwing s covs white; rects white (Fig. 486**G**, rarely with black marks as in **E-F**); bill yellow with reddish gonydeal spot, sometimes with flesh tinge on basal half and a blackish subterminal mark in Sep-Mar. **Note: Some 4Y/5Ys in Dec-Aug may retain dark markings on alula, p covs (Fig. 484E-I), and rects (Fig. 486E-F) but substantial individual variation makes age assignment unsafe.**

4Y (4th cycle, B4; Sep-Nov): Like ATY/A4Y with molt in pp occurring, outer p covs with more extensive black markings (Fig. 484**C-G**), and p9-p10 with small whitish mirror to p10 but not p9 (Fig. 483**C-D**).

A4Y (Def. cycle, DB; Sep-Nov): Like ATY/A4Y with molt in pp occurring and outer p covs slaty gray or with limited blackish on outer webs (Fig. 484**H-I**) and p10 or p9-p10 with distinct white mirrors (Fig. 483**D-E**).

Sex— ♀ = ♂ by plumage aspect. Bilateral and medial(?) BPs (Fig. 20**C**, p. 31) developed by both sexes but distended cloaca (Fig. 21, p. 32) indicates ATY ♀ in May-Jul. Measurements somewhat helpful for sexing (Table 60, p. 668), especially for mated pairs. Head-bill length (Figure 453, p. 630) likely useful for sexing (specimen evidence and comparison with similar species suggests ♀ 115-124 mm, ♂ 124-136 mm) but measures needed from live individuals.

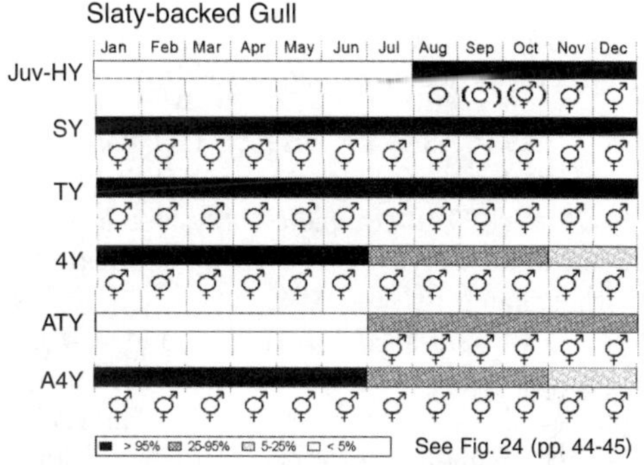

Hybrids reported—With Herring (p. 665) and Glaucous-winged (Firsova & Levada 1982, King & Carey 1999, Grabovsky et al. unpublished ms.) gulls.

References—Bent (1921), Cramp & Simmons (1983), Dement'ev & Gladkov (1951c), Dwight (1925), Gustafson & Peterjohn (1994), Howell & Dunn (2007), Kennerley et al. (1995), King & Carey (1999), McCaffery et al. (1997), Malling Olsen & Larsson (2003), Ridgway (1919), Stejneger (1885).

WESTERN GULL
Larus occidentalis

WEGU
Species # 0490
Band size: 6

Species—From other large gulls by large size with proportionally short wings and large bill (Table 60, p. 668); bill deeper at gonys (♀ 17.4-22.1, ♂ 19.1-23.8) than at base (♀ 16.1-21.1, ♂ 17.8-22.5; see Table 60 & Fig. 453, p. 630); Juv-HY/SY with bill black, inner pp dark brownish, not contrasting with paler p7-p10, the latter with indistinctly paler inner web (Fig. 482**A**, p. 659), and rects primarily blackish or with reduced whitish bases (Fig. 486**A-B**, p. 661); ATY with upperparts medium-dark to dark gray (Kodak 8-11, p. 629; see **Geographic variation**), distal underside of p7-p10 blackish (*vs* paler in most other species), head and breast with little or no dusky streaking in Sep-Jan, orbital ring orange-yellow to yellow, and legs bright pink (occasionally suffused yellow in spring). Beware frequent hybridization with

Glaucous-winged Gull (p. 679; Bell 1996). See Howell & Dunn (2007) for additional details of identification.

From Slaty-backed Gull (p. 673) further by shorter average wing and tail (Table 60); bill deeper at gonys than at base (see above); iris usually darker or yellower by age; Juv-HY/SY and SY/TY with darker body feathers, not contrasting markedly with darker eye marks, pp tips, and replaced back feathers; ATY with upperparts averaging paler gray (Kodak 8-11); white tongue tips narrow and indistinct on p5-p6 and lacking on p7-p8; distal underside to p7-p10 with narrower and blacker inner web; head and breast with little or no streaking in Sep-Feb; bill typically brighter and without dark distal marks in Oct-Feb; orbital ring orange-yellow to yellow; legs brighter and paler pink.

Geographic variation—See Bell (1996), Dickey & van Rossem (1925), Grant (1986), Patten et al. (2003), Unitt (2004), Weber (1981b). No other subspecies occur.

L.o. occidentalis (br coastal WA-c.CA; wint to sw.CA): Averages slightly larger (Table 60, p. 668; bill depth at gonys 17.6-23.8); upperparts of ASY average paler gray (Kodak 8-9.5); iris usually averages darker by age. Typical *occidentalis* breeds N to 42° N; populations in OR-WA average paler (Kodak 7-8), perhaps reflecting introgression with Glaucous-winged Gull (Bell 1996).

L.o. wymani (res coastal c-sw.CA and Baja CA; occasionally disperses N to c.CA): Averages slightly smaller, especially bill and tarsus (Table 60; bill depth at gonys 17.4-22.3); upperparts of ASY average darker gray (Kodak 9.5-11); iris usually averages paler by age. Typical *wymani* breeds in Channel Islands, s.CA to Baja California Sur; populations in Monterey and San Luis Obispo counties, CA (35-36.5° N) intermediate in upperpart tone (Kodak 9-10), presumably reflecting intergradation with *occidentalis*.

Molt—SAS (CAS?). PF absent?, PA1 partial (Sep-May in HY/SYs), PB2 complete (Apr-Oct in SYs), PA2 partial (Aug-Apr in SY/TYs), PB3 complete (May-Oct in TYs), PA3 partial (Sep-Mar in TY/4Ys), DPB complete (May-Dec in ATY/A4Ys), DPA partial (Oct/Jan-Feb in ATY/A4Ys). See Figure 11**F** (p. 17). The single inserted first-cycle molt appears homologous with a PA1 rather than a PF (Fig. 10**E**, p. 14), although some feathers may be replaced twice, indicating both a PF and a PA1 (and CAS; Fig. 10**F**). Molting can occur near or away from breeding grounds. Subsequent PAs can suspend during Nov-Dec. The PA1 includes some body feathers but few if any s covs, terts, or rects. The PAs include a few to many med and proximal les covs but few if any terts or rects. Median and some other upperwing covs often replaced Sep-Nov during PAs (PA2 and later), overlapping completion of PBs.

Age—Juv (B1; Jul-Nov) has plumage uniform in wear; scapulars dark brown with scaly to notched, buff to whitish fringes, and bill black; Juv ♀=♂. See pp. 659-663 for additional information on ageing gulls.

Juv-HY/SY (1st cycle, F1/A1; Sep-Aug): Body feathers primarily brownish; outer pp and p covs relatively tapered, p9-p10 brownish and without mirrors (Fig. 483**A**, p. 660), and outer p covs blackish brown with fine whitish tips (Fig. 484**A**, p. 660); longest uppertail covs with distinct dark-barred pattern (Fig. 485**A-D**, p. 661); underwing s covs uniformly dusky brown; rects blackish brown, often with reduced pale bases (Fig. 486**A-B**, p. 661); bill blackish, sometimes with reduced grayish-flesh base in Mar-Aug.

SY/TY (2nd cycle, B2-A2; Sep-Aug): Body feathers mottled brownish and whitish, the upperparts and s covs mixed with dark gray feathers in Nov-Aug; p1-p6 dark gray-brown to grayish (*cf.* Fig. 487**A**, p. 662), contrasting with darker p7-p10; outer pp and p covs relatively truncate, p9-p10 blackish and without mirrors (Fig. 483**B**), and outer p covs dark brownish with diffuse paler tips (Fig. 484**B-C**); longest uppertail covs with irregular brown bars and wavy markings (Fig. 485**F-I**); underwing s covs mixed dusky and pale grayish; rects mostly blackish brown, sometimes with extensive whitish bases (Fig. 486**B-C**); bill blackish with limited flesh to yellowish at base and a pale tip, sometimes yellowish with dull reddish gonydeal spot and blackish subterminal band in Jun-Aug.

TY/4Y (3rd cycle, B3-A3; Sep-Aug): Body feathers primarily dark gray and white, usually with sparse grayish mottling to head and breast in Sep-Feb; p1-p6 dark gray with moderately distinct black tips (*cf.* Fig. 487**D**), not contrasting with p7-p10; p9-p10 gray and black, p9 without mirror and p10 sometimes with whitish mirror (Fig. 483**B-D**); outer p covs dark grayish with variable black markings (Fig. 484**C-G**); s covs and terts with variable brownish wash; longest uppertail covs white, rarely with faint dark bars; rects white, often with blackish markings (Fig. 486**E-G**); bill pinkish to yellowish with a black subterminal band and sometimes a reddish gonydeal spot in Sep-Jan, to bright yellow in Feb-Aug. **Note: Occasional 4Ys completing molt can be aged by patterns to outer pp and p covs through Sep/Oct. See also ATY/A4Y.**

ATY/A4Y (Def. cycle, DB-DA; Sep-Aug): Body feathers gray and white, occasionally with sparse dusky mottling to head and breast in Sep-Nov; p1-p6 dark gray with distinct black tips (*cf.* Fig. 487**F**); p9-p10 without brownish wash, p10 and sometimes p9 with distinct white mirrors (Fig. 483**E**); outer p covs slaty gray or with limited blackish on outer webs (Fig. 484**H-J**); s covs and terts without brownish wash; longest uppertail covs and underwing s covs white; rects white (Fig. 486**G**, rarely with black marks as in **E-F**); bill bright yellow with red gonydeal spot, rarely with blackish subterminal marking in Sep-Feb. **Note: Some 4Y/5Ys may retain dark markings on alula, p covs (Fig. 484E-I), and rects but substantial individual variation makes age assignment unsafe**

A4Y (Def. cycle, DB; Sep-Oct): Like ATY/A4Y with molt in pp occurring and outer p covs slaty gray or with limited blackish on outer webs (Fig. 484**H-I**) and p10 or p9-p10 with distinct white mirrors (Fig. 483**D-E**).

Sex—♀=♂ by plumage aspect. Bilateral and medial BPs (Fig. 20**C,** p. 31) developed by both sexes but distended cloaca (Fig. 21, p. 32) indicates ATY ♀ in Apr-Jul. Most measurements (especially wing length) relatively helpful for sexing (Table 60, p. 668). The following can be used to sex most full-grown individuals (see Pierotti 1981):

♀: Head-bill length (Fig. 453, p. 630) 113-122 mm. **Note: Individuals with head-bill length 121-122 mm cannot be reliably sexed by this measure alone.**

♂: Head-bill length 121-134 mm. **Note: See ♀.**

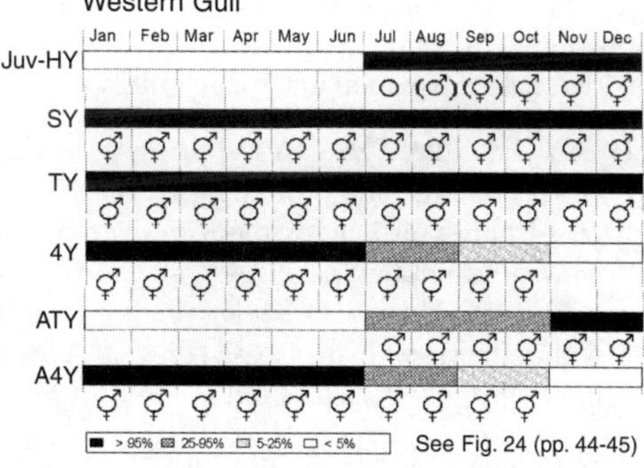

Hybrids reported—Extensively with Glaucous-winged Gull (p. 679), some colonies in WA and OR comprising up to 75% hybrids (Bell 1996, Hoffman et al. 1978, Scott 1971, Weber 1981b).

References—Bell (1996), Bent (1921), Dwight (1925), Hoffman et al. (1978), Howell & Corben (2000a, 2000b), Howell & Dunn (2007), Malling Olsen & Larsson (2003), Pierotti (1981), Pierotti & Annett (1995), Ridgway (1919), Scott (1971), Spear (1988).

YELLOW-FOOTED GULL
Larus livens

YFGU
Species # 0491
Band size: 6

Species—From Lesser Black-backed (p. 668), Western (p. 675), and other species of gull with caution, by the combination of large size (Table 60, p. 668); bill deeper at gonys (♀ 18.6-21.7, ♂ 20.5-24.0) than at distal end of forehead feathers (♀ 16.9-20.9, ♂ 19.0-23.9; *cf.* Figure 453, p. 630); iris usually yellowish with relatively heavy dark speckling by age; Juv-HY with bill black, inner pp dark brownish, not contrastingly paler than brownish p7-p10 (Fig. 482**A**, p. 659), uppertail covs with sparse dark bars (Fig. 485**C-E**, p. 661), rects primarily blackish (Fig. 486**A-B**, p. 661); SY and TY with most s covs and terts replaced in Feb-Jul (*vs* fewer replaced in Western Gull and other species); ASY/ATY with upperparts medium-dark to dark gray (Kodak 9.0-10.5, p. 629), whitish tongue tips narrow and indistinct on p5 and usually lacking on p6-p8; distal underside of p7-p10 blackish; head and breast with relatively extensive dusky markings in Aug-Oct or later, orbital ring orange-yellow, and legs usually yellow to orange-yellow. See Howell & Dunn (2007) for additional details of identification.

Geographic variation—Monotypic.

Molt—SAS (CAS?). PF absent?, PA1 partial (Jul-Mar? in HY/SYs), PB2 complete (Mar-Sep in SYs), PA2 partial-incomplete (Aug-Mar in SY/TYs), PB3 complete (Apr-Sep in TYs), PA3 partial-incomplete (Aug-Feb in TY/4Ys), DPB complete (Apr-Oct in ATY/A4Ys), DPA partial (Sep?-Feb in ATY/A4Ys). The single inserted first-cycle molt appears homologous with a PA1 rather than a PF (Fig. 10**E**, p. 14), although some feathers may be replaced twice, indicating both a PF and a PA1 (and CAS; Fig. 10**F**). Molting can occur near or away from breeding grounds and the PAs can suspend during Dec-Jan. The PA1 includes most body feathers (some uppertail covs usually retained), some to many med and proximal les covs, 1-3 terts, 1-12 c.rects, and sometimes up to 8 inner pp (but fewer or no p covs) and 2 (or more?) outer ss. The PA2-PA3 are similar and also sometimes includes up to 6 inner pp and possibly some ss and c.rects (needs study). The DPA includes some to many s covs but few if any terts or rects. Median and some other upperwing covs are often replaced Sep-Nov during PAs (PA2 and probably later), overlapping completion of PBs.

Age—Juv (B1; Jun-Sep) has plumage uniform in wear; scapulars dark brown with scaly to notched, cinnamon-buff to whitish fringes, and bill blackish; Juv ♀=♂. See pp. 659-663 for additional information on ageing gulls.

HY/SY (1st cycle, F1/A1; Aug-Jul): Body feathers mottled brownish and white, back and scapulars becoming darker (often brownish gray) in Nov-Jul; outer pp and p covs relatively tapered, p9-p10 brownish and without mirrors (Fig. 483**A**, p. 660), and outer p covs blackish brown with indistinct fine pale tips (Fig. 484**A**, p. 660); longest uppertail covs with sparse dark bars (Fig. 485**C-E**, p. 661); underwing s covs uniformly dark brown; rects blackish brown, often with reduced whitish at base (Fig. 486**A-B**, p. 661); bill blackish, with flesh to yellowish base in Dec-Aug; legs dull pinkish.

SY/TY (2nd cycle, B2-A2; Aug-Jul): Body feathers primarily mottled white and brownish in Aug-Oct, with substantial dark gray to s covs and back in Feb-Jul; p1-p6 dark gray-brown to grayish (*cf.* Fig. 487**A**, p. 662), or with one or more adult-like feathers proximally in Dec-Mar (see **Molt**); outer pp and p covs relatively truncate, p9-p10 blackish and without mirrors (Fig. 483**B**), and outer p covs blackish brown with narrow pale tips (Fig. 484**B-C**; occasionally with gray and dusky covs proximally in Dec-Mar); longest uppertail covs white, with few (Fig. 485**G**) or no dark marks; underwing s covs mixed dark brown and silvery; rects extensively blackish with white basally (Fig. 486**A-B**), one to all proximal rects often white or with variable blackish marks in Dec-Jul (Fig. 486**E**-**G**); bill flesh to yellowish with broad blackish tip in Aug-Dec, to yellow with orange-red gonydeal spot and blackish subterminal band in Feb-Aug; legs usually pinkish to pale yellowish.

TY/4Y (3rd cycle, B3-A3; Aug-Jul): Body feathers primarily gray and white, usually with moderate dusky mottling to head and breast in Sep-Jan; p1-p6 dark gray with relatively distinct black tips (*cf*. Fig. 487**D**); p9-p10 gray and black with brownish wash, p9 without mirror and p10 mirror small or absent (Fig. 483**B**-**C**); outer p covs dark gray with variable blackish markings (Fig. 484**D**-**H**, rarely mostly or entirely slaty gray as in **I**-**J**); longest uppertail covs white; rects white, sometimes with reduced blackish markings (Fig. 486**F**-**G**); bill bright yellow with reddish gonydeal spot, often with a variable black subterminal band in Aug-Jan; legs usually yellowish. **Note: A small proportion of TY/4Ys may be indistinguishable from ATY/A4Ys; study of known-age individuals needed. See also ATY/A4Y.**

ATY/A4Y (Def. cycle, DB-DA; Aug-Jul): Body feathers white and gray, with sparse dusky mottling to head and breast in Aug-Dec; p1-p6 dark gray with distinct black tips (*cf*. Fig. 487**F**); p9 occasionally with small white mirror and p10 mirror distinct (Fig. 483**D**-**E**); outer p covs slaty gray or with some blackish on outer webs (Fig. 484**F**-**J**); rects white (Fig. 486**G**); bill bright yellow with red gonydeal spot and usually without black subterminal marks; legs brightish yellow. **Note: Some A4Ys finishing molt can be aged through Aug by patterns to outer pp and p covs. Presumed 4Y/5Ys can retain dark markings on alula and p covs (Fig. 484F-I), but individual variation makes age assignment unsafe; blackish on p covs appears to be shown by all ages in this species.**

Sex—♀=♂ by plumage aspect. Bilateral and medial(?) BPs (Fig. 20**C**, p. 31) developed by both sexes but distended cloaca (Fig. 21, p. 32) indicates ATY ♀ in Mar-Jun. Measurements somewhat helpful for sexing (Table 60, p. 668), especially for mated pairs. Head-bill length (Figure 453, p. 630) likely useful for sexing (specimen evidence and comparison with similar species suggests ♀ 114-123 mm, ♂ 122-135 mm) but measures needed from live individuals.

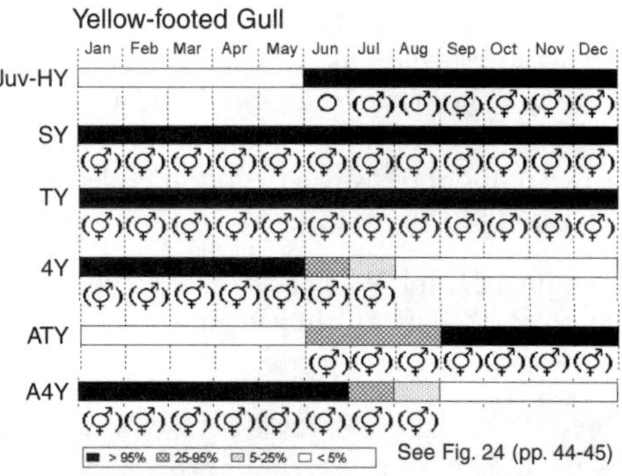

Hybrids reported—None.

References—Bent (1921), Dwight (1925), Howell & Dunn (2007), Malling Olsen & Larsson (2003), McCaskie (1983), Patten (1996), Ridgway (1919).

GLAUCOUS-WINGED GULL

Larus glaucescens

GWGU
Species # 0440
Band size: 7A

Species—From other large pale gulls by medium-large to large size (Table 61, p. 684); bill usually slightly deeper at gonys (♀ 17.4-20.6, ♂ 18.5-22.7) than at base (♀ 17.0-20.2, ♂ 17.9-22.1; *cf*. Fig. 453, p. 630); distal portions of p6-p10 medium-grayish, without blackish (Figs. 482**D**, p. 659, & 487**B**-**C**, p. 662); iris usually dark brown (Juv) to dull yellowish (ATY); Juv-HY/SY with bill black, Body feathers milky brown (usually bleaching to whitish by Mar-Jun), rects pale grayish (*cf*. Fig.

486**A**, p. 661), and outer pp with distinctly pale inner webs (Fig. 482**D**); ATY with upperparts pale to medium-pale gray (Kodak 5-6, p. 629), distal portions of outer pp medium-pale gray (Kodak 6-8; *cf.* Fig. 487**C**) with indistinct mirrors, orbital ring pinkish, and legs pink. HY/SYs from bleached HY/SY Thayer's Gull (p. 688), with caution, by larger size, especially bill dimensions (Table 62); inner pp without contrasting dark subterminal bands or marks; ATY with paler tips to outer pp (Kodak 6-8) and bases to rects. From Glaucous Gull (p. 682) by smaller average wing and tail but proportionally larger bill and tarsus (Table 62); tips of pp with grayish wash (Figs. 482**D** & 487**B**-**C**); Juv-HY/SYs and some SY/TYs (which can have bleached plumage aspect including pp; Howell 2001b) with bill black or with indistinct pinkish base. Because of frequent hybridization with Glaucous, Herring, and Western gulls, determining a pure Glaucous-winged Gull may not always be possible, at least away from core breeding areas (Bell 1996). See Howell & Dunn (2007) for additional details of identification.

Geographic variation—Monotypic. Breeding populations from n.BC-w.AK average paler mantles than populations from s.BC-WA, perhaps reflecting introgression of latter with Western Gull (Bell 1996; p. 675).

Molt—SAS (CAS?). PF absent?, PA1 limited-partial (Oct/Mar-May in HY/SYs), PB2 complete (Apr-Nov in SYs), PA2 partial (Sep-Apr in SY/TYs), PB3 complete (May-Nov in TYs), PA3 partial (Sep-Apr in TY/4Ys), DPB complete (May-Dec in ATY/A4Ys), DPA partial (Jan?-Apr in ATY/A4Ys). The single inserted first-cycle molt appears homologous with a PA1 rather than a PF (Fig. 10**E**, p. 14), although some feathers may be replaced twice, indicating both a PF and a PA1 (and CAS; Fig. 10**F**). The PAs occur primarily on non-breeding grounds and probably can suspend during Dec-Feb, the PB2 occurs on non-breeding grounds in many oversummering SYs, and the PB3 and DPB start on or near breeding grounds (often before egg-laying in breeding individuals) and complete on non-breeding grounds. The PA1 includes a few to some body (primarily back) feathers but no s covs, terts, or rects. Subsequent PAs include a few to many med and proximal les covs but few if any terts or rects. Median and some other upperwing covs often replaced Sep-Nov during PAs (PA2-PA3, at least), overlapping completion of PBs.

Age—Juv (B1; Jul-Nov) has plumage uniform in wear; scapulars medium gray-brown with scaly to notched, buff to whitish fringes, and bill black; Juv ♀=♂. See pp. 659-663 for additional information on ageing gulls.

Juv-HY/SY (1st cycle, Juv/B1-A1; Sep-Aug): Body feathers variably white with dusky checkering to uniformly grayish brown; outer pp and p covs relatively tapered, p9-p10 pale grayish and without mirrors (*cf.* Figs. 482**D**, p. 659, & 483**A**, p. 660), usually bleaching to white in Mar-Aug, and outer p covs dusky gray with whitish tips (*cf.* Fig. 484**A**, p. 660); longest uppertail covs with coarse grayish barring (Fig. 485**A**-**D**, p. 661); underwing s covs uniformly grayish brown; rects grayish (*cf.* Fig. 486**A**, p. 661); bill blackish, sometimes with grayish to pinkish base in Mar-Aug. **Note: See SY/TY.**

SY/TY (2nd cycle, B2-A2; Sep-Aug): Body feathers primarily mottled pale brownish and whitish, the s covs and back mixed with pale gray feathers in Nov-Aug; p1-p6 pale gray-brown to grayish (Fig. 487**B**, p. 662); outer pp and p covs relatively truncate, p9-p10 pale grayish and without mirrors (Fig. 483**B**; sometimes bleaching to white by Mar-Aug), and outer p covs dusky brownish gray, often with diffuse pale tips (Fig. 484**B**-**C**); longest uppertail covs white with moderately fine markings (Fig. 485**F**-**I**); underwing s covs pale grayish brown, usually with some white mottling; rects pale grayish brown with diffuse whitish bases (*cf.* Fig. 486**B**-**C**); bill blackish with flesh to yellowish base, sometimes becoming yellowish with dull orange-red gonydeal spot and blackish subterminal marks in Jun-Aug. **Note: Caution in separating HY/SY from SY/TY, especially in Sep-Nov before alternate feathers present; bill color often the best criterion.**

TY/4Y (3rd cycle, B3-A3; Sep-Aug): Body feathers primarily pale gray and white, with moderate to extensive grayish mottling to head and breast in Sep-Mar; p1-p6 pale gray with indistinct dusky tips (Fig. 487**C**); p9-p10 whitish and gray with brownish wash, p9 without mirror, and p10 with small diffuse mirror (*cf.* Fig. 483**C-D**); outer p covs pale grayish with variable dusky markings and distinct whitish tip to outer web (Fig. 484**C-G**); s covs and terts with variable brownish wash; longest uppertail covs white; underwing s covs usually white mottled pale brownish; rects white, usually with grayish subterminal band or markings (*cf.* Fig. 486**C-F**); bill pinkish to yellowish with a black tip in Sep-Mar, to yellow with a reddish gonydeal spot in Apr-Aug. **Note: Some 4Ys do not complete molt until Nov and are possibly aged 4Y (or ATY) based on the pattern to the outer pp and p covs, but bleaching likely makes this difficult, at best. See also ATY/A4Y.**

ATY/A4Y (Def. cycle, DB-DA; Sep-Aug): Body feathers white and gray, often with sparse to moderate grayish mottling to head and breast in Sep-Feb; p9-p10 grayish with relatively distinct white mirror on p10 and sometimes p9 (*cf.* Fig. 483**D-E**); outer p covs slaty gray or with some blackish on outer webs (Fig. 484**G-J**); s covs and terts without brownish wash (can appear brownish when worn); underwing s covs and rects white (Fig. 486**G**); bill bright yellow with red gonydeal spot, sometimes also with blackish subterminal mark in Sep-Feb. **Note: See TY/4Y. Some presumed 4Y/5Ys retain dusky markings on alula, p covs (*cf.* Fig. 484G-I), and rects (*cf.* Fig. 486D-E), and probably average less white on outer pp than A4Y/A5Ys (e.g., p9 lacks mirror, white tongue-tips to p6-p8 narrower), but individual variation makes age assignment unsafe.**

Sex—♀=♂ by plumage aspect. Bilateral and medial BPs (Fig. 20**C**, p. 31) developed by both sexes but distended cloaca (Fig. 21, p. 32) indicates ATY ♀ in May-Jul. Measurements somewhat helpful for sexing (Table 61, p. 684), especially for mated pairs. Head-bill length (Figure 453, p. 630) likely useful for sexing (specimen evidence and comparison with similar species suggests ♀ 113-123 mm, ♂ 121-135 mm) but measures needed from live individuals.

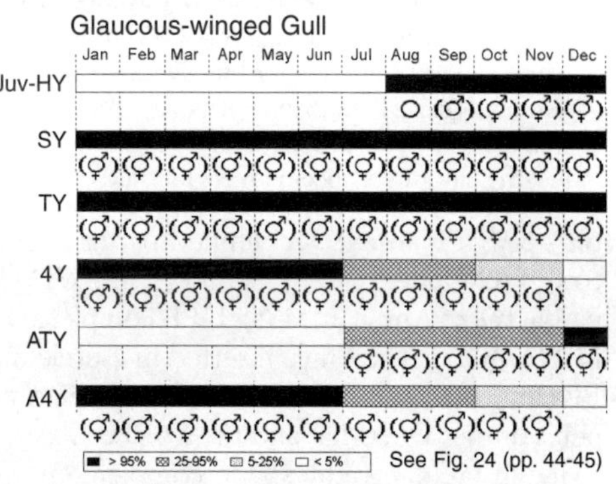

Hybrids reported—With Herring Gull (p. 665), Slaty-backed (p. 673), Western (p. 675), and Glaucous (McCaffery et al. 1997, Strang 1977, Swarth 1934) gulls.

References—Bell (1996), Bent (1921), Dement'ev & Gladkov (1951c), Dwight (1925), Hoffman et al. (1978), Howell (2001b), Howell & Corben (2000d), Howell et al. (1999), Howell & Dunn (2007), Kaufman (1990a), Malling Olsen & Larsson (2003), Ridgway (1919), Schultz (1951), Stone (1900), Verbeek (1979, 1993), Williamson & Peyton (1963).

GLAUCOUS GULL
Larus hyperboreus

GLGU
Species # 0420
Band size: 7A

Species—From other large gulls by large size with proportionally small bill and tarsus (Table 61, p. 684); bill usually shallower at gonys (♀ 17.9-21.4, ♂ 19.5-23.7 in N.Am populations; see **Geographic variation**) than at base (♀ 18.2-23.3, ♂ 19.2-25.4; Table 62; *cf.* Fig. 453, p. 630); iris dark brown (Juv) to pale lemon (ATY); Juv-HY/SY with bill pink with well-defined black tip, plumage aspect milky brown to white with light brown mottling, outer pp and p covs whitish to milky pale brown, often with fine brown subterminal chevrons or spots (Figs. 482**E**, p. 659, & 490**A-B**), and rects with pale gray to brownish mottling (*cf.* Fig. 486**A-B**, p. 661); ATY with upperparts very pale gray (Kodak 3-5, p. 629), distal portions of outer pp white, orbital ring orange-yellow to orange-red (can be pinkish in Aug-Mar), and legs pink.

From Glaucous-winged Gull (p. 679) by longer average wing and tail lengths (Table 62); tips of pp white when fresh; Juv-HY/SYs and SY/TYs with bill pink with distinct black tip. Beware bleached Glaucous-winged Gulls and hybrids with Glaucous-winged and Herring gulls, which show intermediate characters. See Howell & Dunn (2007) for details of identification.

Geographic variation—See Banks (1986b), Bishop (1927), Dement'ev & Gladkov (1951c), Dwight (1906, 1919, 1925), Gibson & Kessel (1997), Gilchrist (2001), Hellmayr & Conover (1948b), Malling Olsen & Larsson (2003), Oberholser (1918d, 1919c, 1974), Portenko (1939, 1973), Rand (1942), Ridgway (1886b), Snell (1991b), Taverner (1929b), Todd (1963). No other subspecies occur.

L.h. pallidissimus (br ne.Russia-Bering Sea Is, AK; wint to e Asia and rarely se.AK). Averages longer wing, shorter tarsus, and shorter but thicker bill (Table 61, p. 684); upperparts of ATY average paler gray (Kodak 3-4; see p. 629).

L.h. barrovianus (br coastal AK-n.Yuk, wint to coastal s.CA). Averages intermediate in size with shorter wing (Table 62); upperparts of ATY average darker gray (Kodak 4-5).

L.h. hyperboreus (br coastal NWT-Nfl to Europe, wint to MN-VA, vagrant to TX-FL). Averages longer wing and tarsus and longer but slenderer bill (Table 62); upperparts of ATY intermediate in gray tone (Kodak 3-4.5). Populations of N.Am ("*leuceretes*") may average slightly smaller and paler, and have fewer dusky head and breast markings in ATY in Oct-Mar than European populations but differences insufficient for subspecific recognition.

Molt—SAS. PF absent, PA1 limited-partial (Oct/Mar-May in HY/SYs), PB2 complete (May-Oct in SYs), PA2 limited-partial (Sep?-Apr in SY/TYs), PB3 complete (May-Nov in TYs), PA3 limited-partial (Oct?-Apr in TY/4Ys), DPB complete (May-Dec in ATYs), DPA limited-partial (Jan?-Apr in ATY/A4Ys). The single inserted first-cycle molt appears homologous with a PA1 rather than a PF (Fig. 10**E**, p. 14). The PAs occur primarily on non-breeding grounds and probably can suspend during Dec-Mar, and the DPB can start on or near breeding grounds (often before egg-laying in breeding adults) and complete on non-breeding grounds. The PA1 includes some to most body feathers and sometimes some med and proximal les covs but few if any terts or rects. Subsequent PAs include some to most body feathers but no s covs, terts, or rects.

Age—Juv (B1; Aug-Apr) has plumage uniform in wear; scapulars pale brown to creamy with variable brownish markings and bill dull pink with black tip; Juv ♀=♂. See pp. 659-663 for additional information on ageing gulls. Note that hybrids between Glaucous and Herring or Glaucous-winged gulls are regular and show age-related features intermediate between parental species.

Juv-HY/SY (1st cycle, Juv/B1-F1/A1; Sep-Aug): Body feathers white with moderate pale brown mottling or checkering; outer pp and p covs relatively tapered, p9-p10 milky brownish (when fresh), often with dusky subterminal markings, and without mirrors (*cf.* Figs. 482**E**, p. 659, & 483**A**, p. 660), usually bleaching to white in Mar-Aug, and outer p covs whitish to pale brownish, usually with broad whitish tips and dusky subterminal chevrons (Fig. 490**A-B**); longest uppertail covs with pale brownish barring (Fig. 485**A-D**, p. 661); underwing s covs uniformly pale brown; rects with very pale grayish-brown mottling (*cf.* Fig. 486**A-B**, p. 661); iris usually brown; bill flesh-pink with black tip. **Note: SYs can be difficult to separate from TYs when bleached (primarily Mar-Jul); check pattern of juv uppertail covs and bill and eye colors. In general, beware that bleaching may affect criteria of all age groups in May-Aug.**

SY/TY (2nd cycle, B2-A2; Sep-Aug): Body feathers white with slight pale brownish mottling when fresh (often bleaching to white by spring), the back mixed with very pale gray feathers in Nov-Aug; p1-p6 often with fine brown wash and sometimes with diffuse whitish tips (*cf.* Fig. 487**B**, p. 662); outer pp and p covs relatively truncate, p9-p10 pale grayish and without mirrors or (usually) dusky marks (*cf.* Fig. 483**B**; often bleaching to white by Mar-Aug), and outer p covs whitish to milky pale brown, with dusky marks and sometimes whitish tips (Fig. 490**C**); longest uppertail covs with irregular marbled markings (Fig. 485**F-G**); underwing s covs mixed pale brown and white; rects white with very pale gray-brown mottling to distal portions (*cf.* Fig. 486**B-C**); iris usually brown to pale grayish yellow; bill pink to yellowish pink with black tip, sometimes yellowish with pale red gonydeal spot and black subterminal mark in May-Aug. **Note: See Juv-HY/SY.**

TY/4Y (3rd cycle, B3-A3; Sep-Aug): Body feathers primarily pale gray and white, with slight to moderate pale grayish mottling to head and breast in Sep-Mar; p1-p6 pale gray with brownish wash to bases and broad white tips (*cf.* Fig. 487**C**); p9-p10 pale gray with brownish wash to bases and indistinct but relatively broad white tips; outer p covs pale gray, sometimes with pale brown markings, especially on outer webs (Fig. 490**C-D**); s covs and terts with variable pale brownish wash; longest uppertail covs white; underwing s covs white, often with very sparse brown mottling; rects white, with variable, very pale brownish markings (*cf.* Fig. 486**C-F**); iris usually pale lemon, often flecked dark; bill pink to pinkish yellow with black and pale tip in Sep-Mar, usually yellow with red gonydeal spot and sometimes black subterminal marks in May-Aug. **Note: See Juv-HY/SY.**

ATY/A4Y (Def. cycle, DB-DA; Sep-Aug): Body feathers clear white and gray, with little to no pale grayish mottling to head and breast in Sep-Feb (N.Am populations); pp pale gray without brownish wash or markings and with distinct white tips; outer p covs whitish without brownish markings (Fig. 490**D**); s covs and terts without brownish wash; underwing s covs and rects white (Fig. 486**G**); iris usually pale lemon; bill yellow with orange-red gonydeal spot, often with pinkish suffusion to base and dark subterminal marks in Apr-Aug. **Note: See Juv-HY/SY.**

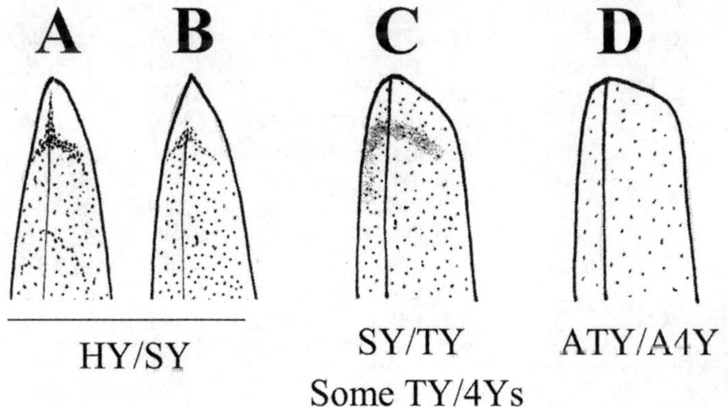

FIGURE 490. Typical patterns and shapes of the longest primary coverts by age in 1st-cycle (HY/SY) and 2nd-cycle (SY/TY) Glaucous Gulls. Paler-winged Iceland Gulls (i.e. most *L.g. glaucoides)* show similar patterns of variation.

Sex—♀ = ♂ by plumage aspect. Bilateral and medial BPs (Fig. 20**C**, p. 31) developed by both sexes but distended cloaca (Fig. 21, p. 32) indicates ATY ♀ in Jun-Jul. Measurements moderately useful for sexing (Table 61), especially mated pairs. Head-bill length (Figure 453, p. 630) likely useful for sexing (specimen evidence and comparison with similar species suggests ♀ 116-125 mm, ♂ 124-137 mm for *L.h. barrovianus* and ♀ 120-130 mm, ♂ 128-143 mm for *hyperboreus*) but measures needed from live individuals.

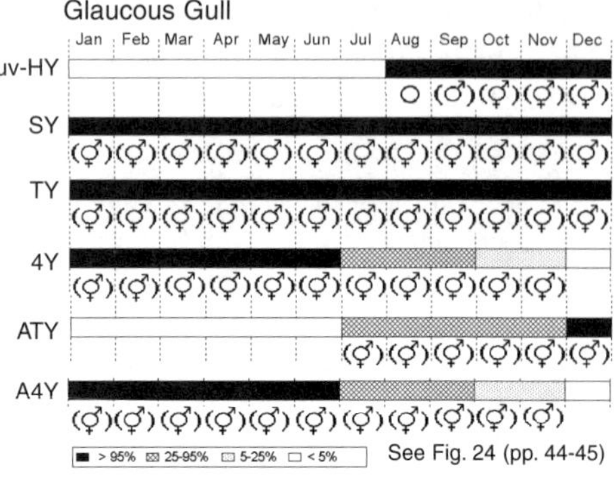

Hybrids reported—With Herring (p. 665), Lesser Black-backed (p. 668), Glaucous-winged (p. 679), Great Black-backed (p. 671), and Iceland (Swarth 1934, Taverner 1933) gulls.

References—Andresen & Thomas (1986), Banks (1986b), Bent (1921), Dement'ev & Gladkov (1951c), Dwight (1919, 1925), Gilchrist (2001), Howell & Dunn (2007), Ingolfsson (1970), Johnston (1961), Kaufman (1990a), Kessel (1989), Malling Olsen & Larsson (2003), Manning et al. (1956), Oberholser (1918d, 1919c, 1974), Ridgway (1919), Roberts (1955), Stejneger (1885), Stone (1900).

TABLE 61. Measurements (mm) of North American large, paler-winged gulls to assist in identification and sexing. See pp. 4-11 for methods of measurement. Species summaries are in **bold** and subspecies values are in ***italics***. Values were derived from 95% confidence intervals as based approximately on the indicated sample sizes (see pp. 4-5). Thus, midpoints of ranges approximate means, and S.D. is approximated by one-quarter of the range.

Taxon/Sex	*n*	wing chord[1]	tail length	exp culmen	bill depth[2]	tarsus
Glaucous-winged Gull		**390-455**	**165-191**	**49-63**	**17.0-22.1**	**60-75**
♀	70	390-435	165-184	48-58	17.0-20.2	60-71
♂	70	404-455	171-191	52-63	17.9-22.1	63-75
Glaucous Gull		**417-494**	**175-213**	**45-69**	**18.2-24.5**	**60-76**
L.h. pallidissimus		***428-490***	***181-213***	***45-62***	***19.3-24.5***	***60-72***
♀	20	428-466	181-206	56-65	19.3-24.1	67-76
♂	20	453-490	189-213	58-68	22.2-24.5	68-78
L.h. barrovianus		***417-475***	***175-207***	***49-65***	***18.2-23.9***	***61-75***
♀	35	417-455	175-200	49-60	18.2-21.2	61-71
♂	40	431-475	183-207	54-65	19.2-23.9	64-75
L.h. hyperboreus		***424-494***	***176-212***	***53-69***	***18.7-23.3***	***62-76***
♀	100	424-464	176-205	53-64	18.7-23.3	62-73
♂	100	446-494	184-212	57-69	20.4-25.4	64-76
Iceland Gull[3]		**379-435**	**152-184**	**37-50**	**13.3-17.7**	50-65
♀	100	379-415	152-179	37-46	13.3-16.7	50-61
♂	100	392-435	158-184	40-50	14.3-17.7	53-65
Thayer's Gull		**380-439**	**155-185**	**42-55**	**16.2-19.4**	53-68
♀	75	380-420	155-179	42-49	14.4-17.4	53-62
♂	60	397-439	161-185	47-55	16.2-19.4	58-68

[1] Wing chord averages ~5% shorter in Juv-HY/SY than in AHY/ASY.

[2] Bill depth measured at distal end of forehead feathering (see Fig. 8**A**, p. 10).

[3] Both subspecies of Iceland gull have similar measurements (see Geographic variation)

ICELAND GULL ICGU
Larus glaucoides Species # 0430
Band size: 6

Species—From Glaucous-winged (p. 679), Glaucous (p. 682), and other species of gull by the combination of medium size with proportionally small bill (Table 61); bill depth at gonys (13.3-17.7) similar to that at base (13.3-17.7; Table 62; *cf.* Fig. 453, p. 630); Juv-HY/SY with bill blackish or with dull pink base, plumage whitish with light brown mottling, outer pp and p covs whitish to pale brownish, often with fine brown subterminal chevrons or spots (Figs. 482**E**, p. 659, & 490**D**, p. 683); and rects with pale gray to dusky mottling (*cf.* Fig. 486**A-B**, p. 661); ATY with upperparts very pale gray (Kodak 3-5, p. 629), distal portions of outer pp white (*cf.* Fig. 491**E-F**, p. 686), orbital ring purplish pink (may be dark grayish, Sep-Mar), iris clear lemon, and legs pink.

N.Am populations (*L.g. kumlieni*) from Thayer's Gull (p. 688) with caution, by smaller average bill dimensions (Table 62); Juv-HY/SY with bases of ss paler and not contrasting strongly with gr covs, and underwing s covs paler brown; ASY with outer pp tips paler (Kodak 7-10) and often less extensive, p9 with mirror usually spanning both webs and dark usually not extending to inner web, and p10 without dark subterminal marks (*cf.* Fig. 491**E-F**), p5 without black marks, and iris clearer yellow. See Thayer's Gull for more information and citations.

Geographic variation—See Browning (2002), Cramp & Simmons (1983), Dement'ev & Gladkov (1951c), Dwight (1906, 1917, 1925), Godfrey (1986), Howell & Dunn (2007), Howell & Elliott (2001), Howell & Mactavish (2003), Macpherson (1961), Pittaway (1992c), Ridgway (1919), Smith (1966), Snell (1991b, 2003), Sutton (1968b), Weber (1981a), and Weir et al. (2000) for more information.

L.g. kumlieni (br ne.Canada; wint to MI-n.FL). Bill averages slightly larger by sex (exposed culmen 39-50, bill depth at gonys 14.0-17.7); Juv-HY/SYs with p1-p6 paler than p7-p10 and rects, outer pp, and underwing s covs washed dusky brown when fresh; ASYs with upperparts darker gray (Kodak 4-5) and distal portions of p6/p9-p10 usually with gray subterminal markings (Fig. 491**E-F**, p. 686), rarely all-white.

L.g. glaucoides (br Greenland; wint to NY and w.Europe, vagrant to CA). Bill averages slightly smaller by sex (exposed culmen 36-48, bill depth at gonys 13.3-17.2); Juv-HY/SYs with p1-p6 similar to p7-p10 in color and rects, outer pp, and underwing s covs washed pale brown when fresh; ASYs with upperparts paler gray (Kodak 3-4) and distal portions of p6-p10 white, without subterminal gray markings (*cf.* Fig. 491**E-F**).

Molt—SAS. PF absent, PA1 limited-partial (Oct/Mar-May in HY/SYs), PB2 complete (May-Oct in SYs), PA2 limited-partial (Sep?-Apr in SY/TYs), PB3 complete (May-Oct in TYs), PA3 limited-partial (Sep?-Apr in TY/4Ys), DPB complete (Jun-Dec in ATYs), DPA limited-partial (Oct?-Apr in ATY/A4Ys). The single inserted first-cycle molt appears homologous with a PA1 rather than a PF (Fig. 10**E**, p. 14). The PAs occur primarily on non-breeding grounds (timing of the PAs needs further study) and probably can suspend during Nov-Feb. The DPB can start on or near breeding grounds and complete on non-breeding grounds. The PAs include some body feathers but few if any s covs, terts, or rects (1-2 terts occasionally replaced at PA2); more study is needed.

Age—Juv (B1; Aug-Apr) has plumage overall uniform in wear; scapulars medium-pale brown to creamy with variably wavy brownish barring, checkering, and lacey patterning; and bill black; Juv ♀ = ♂. See pp. 659-663 for additional information on ageing gulls.

Juv-HY/SY (1st cycle, Juv/B1-A1; Sep-Aug): Body feathers whitish mottled or checkered pale grayish brown; outer pp and p covs relatively tapered, p9-p10 medium brown to whitish (when fresh), often with brownish subterminal markings, and without mirrors (*cf.* Figs. 482**E**, p. 659, & 483**A**, p. 660), usually bleaching to white in Mar-Aug, and outer p covs whitish to medium-pale brownish, usually with broad whitish tips and dusky subterminal chevrons (*cf.* Figs. 484**A**, p. 660, & 490**A-B**, p. 683); longest uppertail covs with pale brownish barring (Fig. 485**A-D**, p. 661); underwing s covs uniformly pale to medium-pale brown; rects with very pale brown to grayish-brown mottling (*cf.* Fig. 486**A-B**, p. 661); bill black, often with dull to bright pink base and a fine pale tip in Jan-Aug. **Note: SYs can be difficult to separate from TYs when bleached (primarily Mar-Jul); check pattern of juv uppertail covs and bill color. In general, beware that bleaching may affect criteria of all age groups in May-Aug.**

SY/TY (2nd cycle, B2-A2; Sep-Aug): Body feathers white with slight to moderate brownish mottling when fresh (sometimes bleaching to white by spring), the back mixed with very pale gray feathers in Nov-Aug; p1-p6 often with fine dusky speckling and sometimes with diffuse whitish tips (*cf.* Fig. 487**B**, p. 662); outer pp and p covs relatively truncate, p9-p10 of pale grayish brown, sometimes with indistinct whiter tongues (*cf.* Figs. 483**B** & 491**E-F**; often bleaching to white by Mar-Aug), and outer p covs whitish to brownish, with dusky marks and sometimes whitish tips (*cf.* Figs. 484**B-C** & 490**C**); longest uppertail covs with irregular marbled markings (Fig. 485**F-G**); underwing s covs mixed brown and white; rects white with pale gray-brown mottling to distal portions (*cf.* Fig. 486**B-C**); bill dull flesh to pale greenish with black distal third and pale tip, sometimes yellowish with reddish gonydeal spot and black subterminal marks in Jun-Aug. **Note: See Juv-HY/SY.**

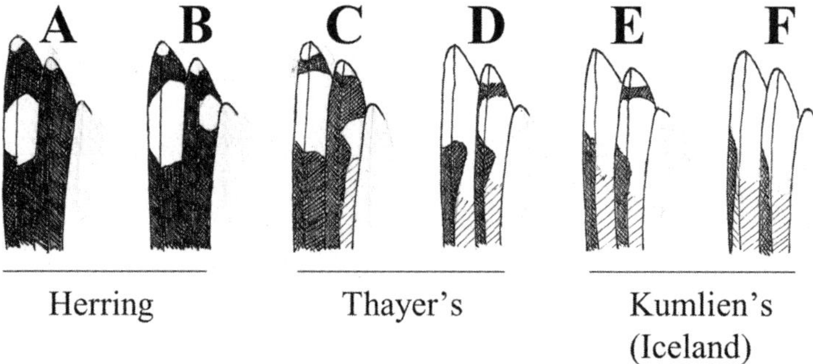

FIGURE 491. Variation in the typical patterns of outer primaries (p9-p10) in definitive-aspect (ASY/ATY or ATY/A4Y) N.Am Herring, Thayer's, and Kumlien's (Iceland) gulls. In w.N.Am (where most Thayer's Gulls winter), p9 of ASY/ATY Herring (*cf.* Fig. 483, p. 660) usually lacks a white mirror and has upperwing-tip more solidly black than almost all Thayer's, but outer pp of some ATY/A4Y Herrings in e.N.Am (**B**) have pattern similar to Thayer's (**C**). Compared to N.Am Herring Gulls (**A-B**), *L.a. vegae* averages more extensive black (but quite variable), *L.a. argentatus* averages more white (e.g., the white mirror on p9 extends across feather to form a band in about 50% of ATY/A4Ys), and *L.a. argenteus* shows a similar amount of black but less often lacks a mirror to p9. Beware of hybrids between N.Am Herring gulls and Glaucous-winged or Glaucous gulls, which can have outer pp patterns resembling those of Thayer's Gull.

TY/4Y (3rd cycle, B3-A3; Sep-Aug): Body feathers primarily pale gray and white, with moderate pale grayish mottling to head and breast in Sep-Mar; p1-p6 pale gray with brownish wash to bases and broad white tips (*cf.* Fig. 487**C**); p9-p10 pale gray with brownish wash to bases, variably dusky distal areas (*L.g. kumlieni*), and indistinct but relatively broad white tips; outer p covs pale gray with or without brownish to dusky markings, especially on outer webs (*cf.* Figs. 484**D-I** & 490**C-D**); s covs and terts with variable pale brownish wash; longest uppertail covs white; underwing s covs white, often with very sparse brown mottling; rects white, usually with variable pale brownish markings (*cf.* Fig. 486**C-F**); bill pinkish to yellowish with black distal third and pale tip, usually becoming yellow with reddish gonydeal spot and sometimes black subterminal marks in May-Aug. **Note: See Juv-HY/SY. Some 4Ys and A4Ys finishing molt may be reliably aged through Nov by characters of the outer pp and p covs.**

ATY/A4Y (Def. cycle, DB-DA; Sep-Aug): Body feathers clear white and gray, often with sparse pale grayish mottling to head and breast in Sep-Feb; p9-p10 variable in pattern, with gray subterminal markings (Fig. 491**E-F**) to all-white (see **Geographic variation**); outer p covs pale gray, usually without dusky markings (Figs. 484**I-J** & 490**D**); s covs and terts without brownish wash; underwing s covs and rects white (Fig. 486**G**); bill yellow with orange-red gonydeal spot, sometimes with dark subterminal marks in Apr-Aug. **Note: See TY/4Y.**

Sex—♀=♂ by plumage aspect. Bilateral and medial(?) BPs (Fig. 20C, p. 31) developed by both sexes but distended cloaca (Fig. 21, p. 32) indicates ATY ♀ in Jun-Jul. Most measurements somewhat helpful for sexing (Table 61, p. 684); head-bill length (Figure 453, p. 630) likely useful for sexing (specimen evidence and comparison with similar species suggests ♀ 97-107 mm, ♂ 105-116 mm) but measures needed from live individuals.

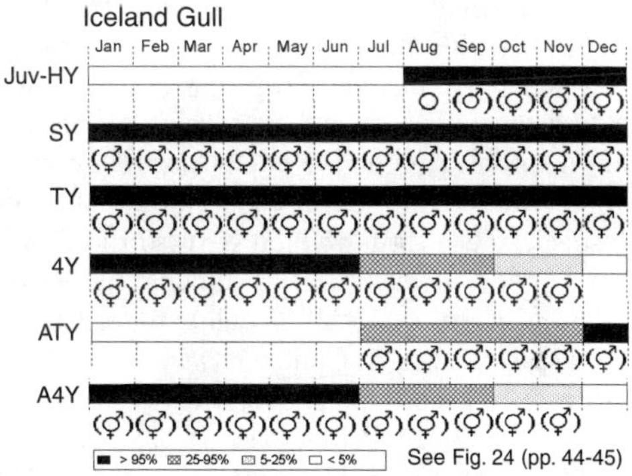

Iceland Gull

Jan Feb Mar Apr May Jun Jul Aug Sep Oct Nov Dec

Juv-HY, SY, TY, 4Y, ATY, A4Y

■ > 95% ▨ 25-95% ▭ 5-25% □ < 5% See Fig. 24 (pp. 44-45)

Hybrids reported—With Glaucous Gull (p. 682), possibly with Herring Gull (p. 665), and presumably with Thayer's Gull (see p. 688 for references) in the wild.

References—Andresen & Thomas (1986), Bent (1921), Browning (2002), Dwight (1925), Gaston & Decker (1985), Godfrey (1986), Howell & Dunn (2007), Howell & Elliott (2001), Howell & Mactavish (2003), Kaufman (1990a), Knudsen (1976), Malling Olsen & Larsson (2003), Ridgway (1919), Snell (1989, 2003), Weir et al. (1995, 2000), Zimmer (1991).

THAYER'S GULL THGU
Larus thayeri Species # 0431
Band size: 6

Species—From most other gulls by medium-large size (Table 61, p. 684); bill depth at gonys (♀ 14.4-17.4 ♂ 15.9-19.0) similar to that at base (14.3-19.4; Table 61; *cf.* Fig. 453, p. 630); Juv-HY/SY with bill blackish or with dull pink base, inner pp pale to medium-pale brownish gray, not contrasting markedly with pale and dark brown p7-p10 (Fig. 482**D**, p. 659), rects mostly dark brown (Fig. 486**A**, p. 661); ASY with upperparts pale to medium-pale gray (Kodak 5-6, p. 629), outer pp tipped blackish (Kodak 14.5-17; Fig. 491**C-D**, p. 686), bill yellow tinged greenish, orbital ring purplish pink, iris with variably moderate dusky flecking, and legs rich pink.

From Herring Gull (p. 665) further by smaller average size (Table 61); Juv-HY with paler inner webs to outer pp (Fig. 482**D**); ASY with upperparts darker gray (Kodak 5-6), outer pp tips paler (Kodak 14.5-17) and less extensive, and p9 usually with white mirror (Fig. 491**C-D**), orbital ring purplish pink, and iris usually dull yellow with dusky flecking. From Glaucous-winged Gull (p. 679), with caution, by smaller average size, especially bill; inner pp (p1-p7 in HY-TYs or p5-p7 in ATYs) with contrasting dark subterminal bands or marks; ASY with darker tips to outer pp (Kodak 14.5-17).

From Iceland Gull (p. 685), particularly *L.g. kumlieni*, with caution, by larger average bill dimensions (Table 61); Juv-HY/SY with bases of ss darker and contrasting with whiter gr covs and underwing s covs darker brown; ASY with outer pp tips darker (Kodak 14.5-17) and often more extensive, p9 with dark usually extending onto inner web and mirror often not extending across outer web, and p10 often with dark subterminal marks (Fig. 491**C-D**), and p5 often with subterminal black marks. Beware presumed hybrids with Iceland Gulls look intermediate and are not safely assigned to either taxon; beware also of bleached SY Thayer's Gulls (bases to ss a good criterion on these). Also beware that hybrids of other species can resemble Thayer's Gull (especially Glaucous-winged X Western and Glaucous-winged X Herring gulls, both of which are larger, especially in bill dimensions; Table 61). See Banks & Browning (1999), Brooks (1937), Browning (2002), Dwight (1906, 1917), Erickson & Hamilton (2001), Gibson & Kessel (1997), Hellmayr & Conover (1948b), Howell & Corben (2000d), Howell & Dunn (2007), Howell & Elliott (2001), Howell & Mactavish (2003), Macpherson (1961), McGowan & Kitchener (2001), Patten et al. (2003), Pittaway (1999), Rand (1942), Ridgway (1919), Smith (1966), Snell (1989, 1991c, 2003), Sutton (1968b), Taverner (1933), Taverner & Sutton (1934), Weber (1981a), and Weir et al. (2000) for more details on taxonomy and identification of Thayer's and Iceland gulls.

Geographic variation—Monotypic. Some n.populations may average paler gray outer pp markings and/or all-white distal portions to outer pp (Godfrey 1986, Parmelee & MacDonald 1960, Snell 2003), but taxonomic status of these unresolved (Howell & Mactavish 2003).

Molt—SAS. PF absent, PA1 limited-partial (Nov/Feb-May in HY/SYs), PB2 complete (May-Oct in SYs), PA2 partial (Sep?-Apr in SY/TYs), PB3 complete (May-Oct in TYs), PA3 partial (Sep?-Apr in TY/4Ys), DPB complete (Jun-Jan in ATY/A4Ys), DPA limited-partial (Oct?-Apr in ATY/A4Ys). The single inserted first-cycle molt appears homologous with a PA1 rather than a PF (Fig. 10**E**, p. 14). The PAs occur primarily on non-breeding grounds (timing needs further study) and probably can be suspended in Dec-Jan. The DPB usually starts on or near breeding grounds and complete on non-breeding grounds. The PAs include some body feathers but few if any s covs, terts, or rects; the PA2 and PA3 also include a few to some med and proximal les covs, occasionally 1-2 terts and 1 to (occasionally?) all c.rects. Median and some other upperwing covs probably can be replaced Sep-Nov during the PA2 and PA3, overlapping completion of PBs.

Age—Juv (B1; Aug-Apr) has plumage uniform in wear; scapulars dark brown to medium gray-brown with scaly to notched, buff to whitish fringes, and bill blackish; Juv ♀=♂. See pp. 659-663 for additional information on ageing gulls.

Juv-HY/SY (1st cycle, Juv/B1-F1-A1; Sep-Aug): Body feathers variably mottled brownish and whitish; outer pp and p covs relatively tapered, p9-p10 pale brownish and without mirrors (Fig. 483**A**, p. 660), and outer p covs dark gray-brown, usually with distinct whitish tips (Fig. 484**A**, p. 660); longest uppertail covs with coarse dark barring (Fig. 485**A-D**, p. 661); underwing s covs uniformly dark brown; rects brown with whitish bases (Fig. 486**B-C**, p. 661); bill blackish, often with dull grayish to pinkish base in Dec-Aug.

SY/TY (2nd cycle, B2-A2; Sep-Aug): Body feathers primarily whitish and brown, the s covs and back mixed with pale gray feathers in Nov-Aug; p1-p6 medium-pale gray-brown (*cf.* Fig. 487**A-B**, p. 662), contrasting with mostly brownish p7-p10; outer pp and p covs relatively truncate, p9-p10 blackish gray and without mirrors (Fig. 483**B**), and outer p covs gray-brown, often with diffuse paler tips (Fig. 484**B-C**); underwing s covs mottled white and brown; longest uppertail covs with irregular (often marbled) markings (Fig. 485**F-I**); rects brownish with white bases (Fig. 486**C-D**), sometimes replaced with whiter rects in Mar-Aug (Fig. 486**E-G**); bill dull flesh to pale greenish with black distal third and pale tip, sometimes yellowish with reddish gonydeal spot and extensive black subterminal marks in Jun-Aug.

TY/4Y (3rd cycle, B3-A3; Sep-Aug): Body feathers primarily gray and white, with moderate dusky mottling to head and breast in Sep-Feb; p1-p6 grayish and whitish (sometimes tinged brown) with moderately distinct black tips (*cf.* Fig. 487**D-E**), not contrasting with p7-p10; p9-p10 gray and brownish black, p9 sometimes with small mirror and p10 usually with mirror (Fig. 483**B-D**); outer p covs grayish with brownish markings (Fig. 484**D-H**); s covs and terts sometimes with brownish wash; longest uppertail covs gray; rects white, usually with variable dusky-gray markings (Fig. 486**E-G**); bill flesh to yellowish with black distal third and pale tip, usually becoming yellow with reddish gonydeal spot and sometimes reduced black subterminal marks in May-Aug. **Note: See ATY/A4Y.**

ATY/A4Y (Def. cycle, DB-DA; Sep-Aug): Body feathers clear gray and white, often with sparse dusky mottling to head in Sep-Jan; p1-p6 gray and white, without brownish wash, and with distinct slaty-blackish markings (*cf.* Fig. 487**F**); p9-p10 with distinct white mirrors (Figs. 483**D-E** & 491**C-D**); outer p covs gray, usually without dusky or dark markings (Fig. 484**I-J**); s covs and terts without brownish wash; rects white (Fig. 486**G**, rarely with dusky marks as in **E-F**); bill yellow with orange-red gonydeal spot, sometimes with pinkish suffusion to base and dark subterminal marks in Aug-Apr. **Note: Presumed 4Y/5Ys can retain dusky markings on alula, p covs (Fig. 484F-I), and rects (Fig. 486E-F), but individual variation makes age assignment unsafe based on plumage-related criteria.**

4Y (4th cycle, B4; Sep-Nov): Like ATY/A4Y but with molt in pp occurring and outer p covs grayish with brownish markings (Fig. 484**D-H**); p9 sometimes with small mirror and p10 usually with mirror (Fig. 483**B-C**).

A4Y (Def. cycle, DB; Sep-Nov): Like ATY/A4Y with molt in pp occurring and outer p covs gray without dusky or dark markings (Fig. 484**J**); p9-p10 with distinct white mirrors (Figs. 483**D-E** & 491**C-D**).

Sex—♀=♂ by plumage aspect. Bilateral and medial(?) BPs (Fig. **20C**, p. 31) developed by both sexes but distended cloaca (Fig. 21, p. 32) indicates ATY ♀ in Jun-Jul. Most measurements somewhat helpful for sexing (Table 61, p. 684), especially with mated pairs; head-bill length (Figure 453, p. 630) likely useful for sexing (specimen evidence and comparison with similar species suggests ♀ 102-112 mm, ♂ 110-121 mm) but measures needed from live individuals.

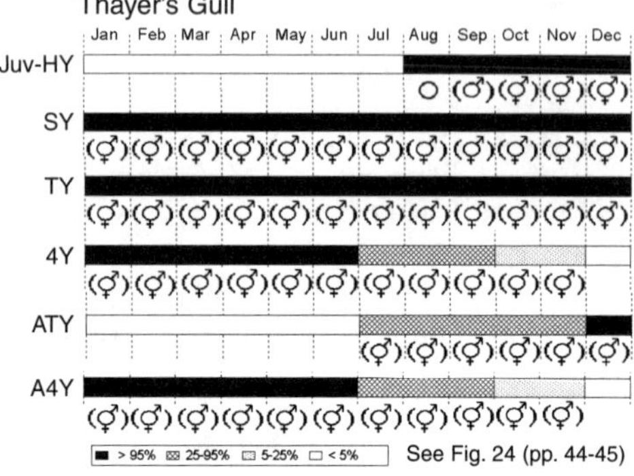

Hybrids reported—With Herring Gull (p. 665) and presumably with Iceland Gull *L.g. kumlieni* (Gaston & Decker 1985; Knudsen 1976; Snell 1989, 2003; Weir et al. 2000; but see Howell & Dunn 2007) and possibly with Iceland Gull *L.g. glaucoides* (Howell & Mactavish 2003).

References—Bent (1921), Dwight (1925), Gaston & Decker (1985), Godfrey (1986), Howell & Dunn (2007), Howell & Elliott (2001), Howell & Mactavish (2003), Howell et al. (1999), Kaufman (1990a), Knudsen (1976), Malling Olsen & Larsson (2003), Manning et al. (1956), Parmelee & MacDonald (1960), Ridgway (1919), Snell (1989, 2003), Sutton & Parmelee (1978).

Fifteen species. Subfamily characters include small to medium-large size; relatively straight, slender, and sharply pointed bills; long and pointed wings; short to medium-length tails that, on many species, have definitive alternate outer rectrix elongated and attenuated; and short legs with webbing between the three front toes. Terns have 10 functional primaries (p10 longest by 5-20 mm when fully grown), 16-23 secondaries (Table 62, p. 692; including 3 tertials and one absent between the 4th and 5th, *cf.* Fig. 12**B**, p. 19), and 12 rectrices. Ageing through the 2nd cycle (to TY and sometimes ATY) can be accomplished in many individuals of most species, by plumage aspect and molt patterns among primaries (Fig. 492, p. 693). The dorsal surface of the outer primaries in many species has a distinct frosting or silvery bloom when fresh, caused by elongated, curved, and frilled barbules on the distal sides of the barbs; when the barbules wear off, underlying black becomes conspicuous, such that fresh primaries are paler and grayer and worn feathers are darker and blacker dorsally (Dwight 1901, Voelker 1996). Many terns attain black caps for the breeding season, and at any age some species develop a variable pink flush to their underparts (see Hudon and Brush 1990, Hays et al. 2006). Bills and legs are often brightly colored, especially on breeding individuals. Plumage aspect and bare part color are similar between the sexes and both males and females develop brood patches (Fig. 20, p. 31) but distended cloacae (Fig. 21, p. 32) indicate ASY ♀♀ during the breeding season, and other cloacal characters (Figs. 22-23, pp. 32-35) should be investigated. Males average larger than females but measurements largely unhelpful to determine sex; head-bill length (*cf.* Fig. 453, p. 630) appears to be useful for sexing in some species (*cf.* Craik 1999) and should be evaluated on live individuals of all species. General references for identification, molt, and ageing in terns include Dwight (1901), Harrison (1983), and Malling Olsen & Larsson (1995).

Terns exhibit unique molt strategies, which can include complete preformative molts and incomplete definitive prealternate and presupplemental molts (Figs. 11**G**, p. 17, & 492; Table 62, pp. 691-695). Most North American species exhibit the Complex Alternate Strategy (CAS; Fig. 10**F-G**, pp. 13-16) with alternate plumages in both first and subsequent cycles; Forster's (p. 718), and possibly Bridled (p. 700) terns appear to exhibit the Simple Alternate Strategy (SAS; Fig. 10**E**), lacking a preformative molt but having a first prealternate molt, and Brown Noddy may lack a prealternate molt in all cycles and would thus exhibit the Complex Basic Strategy (CBS; Fig. 10**B**). Primaries are replaced proximally, secondaries are replaced proximally from s1 and s5 and distally from the tertials, and rectrix replacement usually commences with r1 after which sequence varies, r5 often being the last replaced. Primary replacement during the definitive prebasic molt can commence during incubation, suspend for chick feeding, and complete during autumn migration. The preformative molt can be incomplete in temperate-wintering and larger species but is complete in most North American species. Age of first breeding is 2-10 (primarily 3-6) years; the timing of prebasic molts averages earlier in non-breeders and failed breeders, although wide variation in timing presumably also reflects interannual and regional differences in food supply. Molt timings for several species are poorly known due to little or no information from non-breeding grounds, but available evidence suggests these species follow similar strategies to those of related terns. See Figures 11**G** & 492, Table 62, and the next section for more information on the unique primary, secondary, and rectrix molts in terns.

Molt and age determination in terns

Most terns can replace 1-9 inner primaries and 1-16 outer and inner secondaries for a second time within both the first and definitive molt cycles and, uniquely among birds, several species can replace up to five inner primaries and occasionally 1-5 outer and inner secondaries for a third time within the definitive (and occasionally the first) cycle (Fig. 492, Table 62). All North American species except Brown Noddy (p. 695) appear to exhibit similar replacement patterns, with the number of feathers replaced generally related to bird size, wintering latitudes, migration strategies, and other factors (see below). Primary coverts are typically replaced along with corresponding primaries, although 1-3 fewer coverts often may be replaced.

Replacement strategies of primaries in terns have received much descriptive attention (e.g., Bridge & Nisbet 2004; Cramp & Simmons 1985; Dwight 1901; Higgins & Davies 1996; Malling Olsen & Larsson 1995; Roselaar 1985; Ward 2000, 2002; Ward et al. 2004) but the naming of the inserted molts has not been consistent. Some (perhaps ancestral) species of terns (including Brown Noddy and White Tern *Gygis alba*) appear to exhibit Staffelmauser or another "multi-series" approach (Fig. 16, pp 23-24; see Ashmole 1968, Bridge et al. 2007, Dorward & Ashmole 1963, Higgins & Davies 1996) and it is possible that the replacement patterns of the more-advanced species (described here) represent a derived form of Staffelmauser that has become arrested to provide social signaling clues manifested by the number of inner primaries and secondaries replaced (Bridge & Nisbet 2004, Bridge et al. 2007, Pyle 2006a, Roselaar 1985). Although these molts may have originated from a prebasic Staffelmauser pattern, the first inserted replacement of primaries and secondaries is here considered part of a prealternate molt and the second replacement as a discrete presupplemental molt, as outlined by Higgins & Davies (1996); see also Figure 11**G** (p. 17).

Both the preformative and prebasic molts are complete in most individuals and species, although the preformative molt is partial in the temperate-wintering Bridled (p. 700) and Forster's (p. 718) terns and can be incomplete in some individuals among larger species such as Caspian (p. 707) and Royal (p. 720) terns (*cf.* Fig. 492**B**). Prealternate molts include most to all body feathers, a few to most or all lesser and median coverts, a few to (occasionally) all primaries, primary coverts, and secondaries (Fig. 492**D-F**), and some to (often) all rectrices. First prealternate molts often include fewer feathers than definitive prealternate molts, at times being partial (including no primaries and secondaries) while the definitive prealternate molt is incomplete. Presupplemental molts often overlap with prealternate molts (Fig. 11**G**) and can include 1-5 inner primaries and 1-5 inner and outer secondaries (Fig. 492**G-H**) along with 1-4 central rectrices; they may include some body feathers and lesser coverts as well but study is needed. Because non-

TABLE 62. Ranges in extent of primary, secondary, and rectrix replacement during definitive molts of North American terns. Numbers of primary coverts replaced are usually equal to or 1-2 less than those of primaries. See Figure 492 for replacement sequence of primaries and secondaries, as reflected by the numbers below; rectrix replacement commences with r1-r2, after which it becomes irregular, r4-r5 often the last replaced. Ranges represent molts within the second and later cycles; typically those of the first cycle are substantially less extensive and those of the non-breeders (e.g. in the second and third cycles) average more extensive than those of breeders in definitive cycles (see **Molt** accounts). Note that the following ranges are preliminary and exceptions will likely be found; however, they can be used as a starting point for further study.

	Definitive Prealternate Molt			Definitive Presupplemental Molt		
Tern Species	Primaries	Secondaries[1]	Rectrices	Primaries	Secondaries	Retrices
Sooty[2]	0-3	0-5/16	0-10	0-0	0-0	0-0
Bridled[2]	0-2	0-4/16	0-10	0-0	0-0	0-0
Aleutian[2]	4-6	4-7/17	12-12	0-0	0-0	0-0
Least	6-9	13-16/16	12-12	1-5	0-5	0-4
Gull-billed	1-6	3-6/19	0-12	0-0	0-0	0-0
Caspian	2-7	5-17/23	0-10	0-2	0-0	0-0
Black	2-8	4-10/16	2-12	0-3	0-2	0-2
Roseate	5-8	8-15/18	12-12	0-4	0-4	0-2
Common	3-7	5-13/19	10-12	0-5	0-4	0-2
Arctic	0-3	0-5/17	8-12	0-0	0-0	0-0
Forster's	0-7	0-8/19	2-12	0-0	0-0	0-0
Royal	2-6	0-8/23	8-12	0-2?	0-2?	0-2?
Sandwich	4-7	4-15/21	6-12	0-2	0-2	0-2
Elegant[2]	4-7	6-14/22	10-12	0-2?	0-2?	0-2?

[1] Ranges in extent/typical number of secondaries per species shown.

[2] Ranges in extent poorly known.

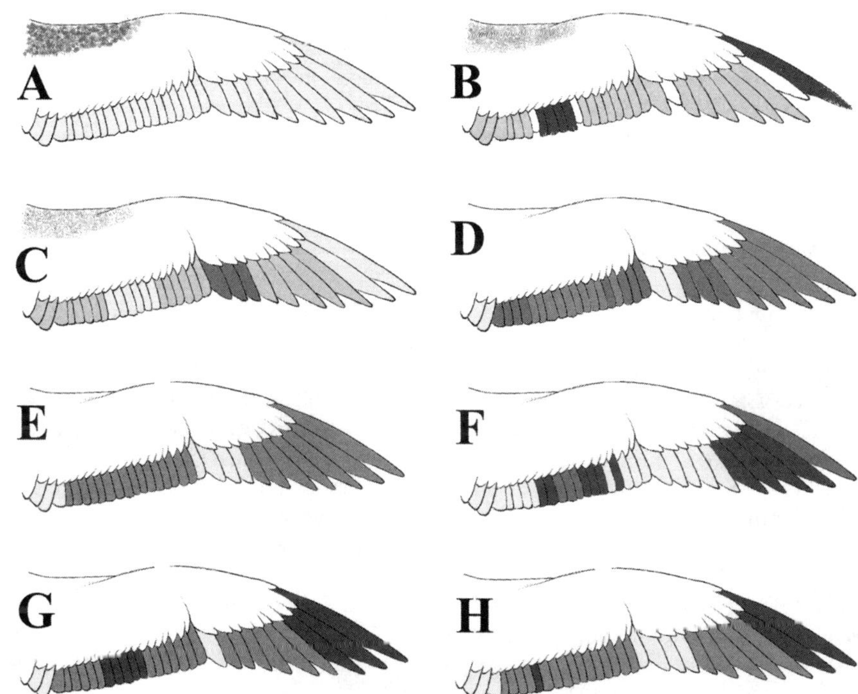

FIGURE 492. Molt patterns by age and plumage in terns. See also Figure 11**G** (p. 17). Darker shading indicates more worn feathers, as is typical of terns due to the loss of paler bloom (see p. 691). Pp are replaced distally from p1 and ss are replaced distally from the tertials and proximally from both s1 and s5, although the replacement of s1-s4 can occur rapidly, obscuring the differences in wear between s4 and s5 that are observed in other large species of birds (*cf.* Fig. 12**B**, p. 19). All N.Am species except Brown Noddy (which may exhibit staffelmauser; Fig. 16, pp. 23-24) appear to show similar sequences and strategies of pp and ss molt, although extent varies by body size and other factors (Table 62); Forster's and Bridled terns differ by having a partial rather than an incomplete-complete PF, but otherwise exhibit PAs as in many other species.

A represents a Juv or HY tern, before commencement of the PF. Note the uniform pp and ss, and dusky mottling to the les covs that can remain apparent throughout the first year of certain species (see text). **B** represents an SY nearing the end of its PF, in Jan-Aug of SYs, depending on the species. Note that the PB2 often commences (in this case p2 is growing) before the PF has completed. In some larger species (e.g., Caspian, Gull-billed, Royal, and other terns), the p10 and 1-5 medial ss may be retained. Many species that have blackish les covs as Juvs (**A**) attain partially dusky feathers after the PF and until the PB2 has completed in Aug-Oct in SYs (**B**). **C** represents an ASY with completely basic feathers; note that marginal les covs can be mottled dusky in a few species, perhaps in the 2nd cycle only (study needed). Note that contrasts in wear among both pp and ss can often result from suspensions of molt for migration or winter. In **C**, the primaries had suspended replacement after p1-p3 had been replaced (typically for fall migration), and again after p4-p8 had been replaced (typically for winter or northbound migration). Suspension limits can be identified by the fact that distal pp are fresher than proximal pp, whereas the opposite is the case for molt limits following an incomplete DPA or DPS (see below).

D-F represent SYs and ASYs following PAs (typically observed in Mar-Sep), with varying numbers of inner pp and inner and outer ss replaced. Note that suspension limits often occur as well among both pp and ss; in **D** one is shown between p5 and p6 (as can occur for suspension during fall migration in SYs and/or non-breeding ASYs) and in **F** one is present between p9 and p10 (as can occur for winter or northbound migration). **G** and **H** represent individuals after both a PA and PS had occurred (typically observed in May-Sep), showing varying extents of each; e.g., in **G**, seven pp and all but five ss were replaced during a DPA and p1 and the terts were replaced during a DPS; and in **H**, eight pp and all but one s had been replaced during a DPA and 4 pp and 5 ss had been replaced again during a DPS. Such extensive molts as in **H** may only occur in Least Terns among N.Am species (note 16 ss in **H**, *vs.* 21 ss in **A-G**; see Table 62 for numbers of ss per species).

breeders have more time to molt, SYs and TYs often exhibit more extensive inner primary and secondary molts than older age classes (*cf.* Bridge and Nisbet 2004).

Factors to consider in understanding tern molt strategies include wing length, migration distance, and wintering latitude and habitat (*cf.* Bridge et al. 2007). All else being equal, primary molts are completed more rapidly in shorter-winged terns (such as Least and Roseate) than longer-winged species (such as Caspian and Royal), and shorter-winged species will thus usually have more-extensive prealternate and presupplemental primary molts (Table 62). Larger species typically replace 1-4 primaries and 0-4 secondaries during the prealternate molt (Fig. SNGH**D-E**) and apparently lack a presupplemental molt, whereas Least Tern can replace up to eight (rarely nine) primaries and all secondaries during the prealternate molt and up to five primaries and secondaries during the presupplemental molt (Fig. 492**H**). Exceptions to this size-related pattern occur in certain species; e.g., the smaller Arctic Tern (p. 716) has a relatively reduced prealternate molt and no preformative molt of primaries and secondaries (Table 62), perhaps related to the time and resources needed for extensive migrations. Species that inhabit relatively unproductive tropical waters during the spring and summer (e.g., Sooty and Bridled terns) also appear to have fewer pp and ss replaced relative to their wing length (Table 62). On the other hand, Caspian Tern appears to have relatively extensive molts given its size (Table 62), for unstudied reasons at this time.

All North American terns can be aged at least to HY/SY by plumage aspect and molt timing, but precise ageing of older AHYs can be problematic due to individual variation in both molt timing and maturation rates of plumage aspect. In the well-studied Common Tern (p. 713) it was concluded that AHY/ASYs showing predefinitive characters could be either SY/TYs or TY/4Ys (*cf.* White & Kehoe 2001), and overlap was sufficient that these perhaps should be aged S-TY or T-4Y (see pp. 41-42). More study is needed on the other species of terns, as similar situations likely apply.

After loss of juvenal plumage the most helpful characters for age determination include wing molt patterns and relative wear of the outer primaries. The first prealternate molt usually includes no or many fewer primaries and secondaries than subsequent prealternate molts, which can result in SYs being recognized by the number of inner primaries and secondaries replaced. Molt patterns have to be interpreted with caution, however, due to frequent suspensions that can occur during complete preformative and prebasic molts (*cf.* Fig. 492**C-D** & **F**).

Several plumage-aspect features can also be helpful for ageing typical terns. The extent of black on the inner web of the outer primary (p10) averages greater in juvenal than in definitive primaries and can be used to age terns through much or all of the first cycle; see Figure 493 and Species Accounts for how this varies by both species and age. In spring and early summer (Feb-Jun, depending on species), aspect patterns of the crown and outer rectrices can also be helpful

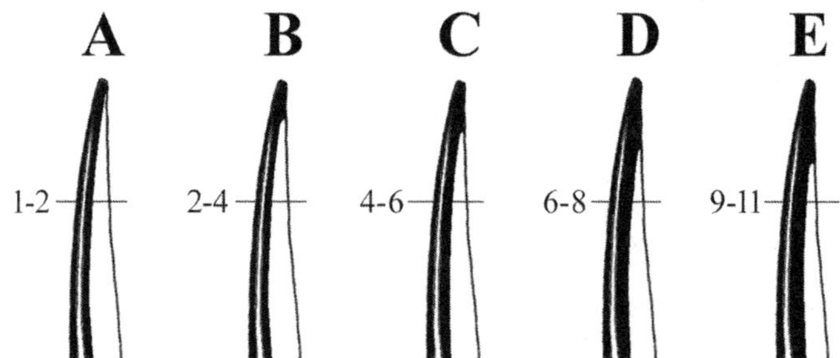

FIGURE 493. Variation in the width of black in the outer primary (p10) by species and age in many terns. Measure indicates width of black streak on inner web from shaft, 70 mm from tip (50 mm in Least Tern). Within each species, the amount of black extending to the inner web is (or at least averages) more extensive on juv feathers than on formative or basic feathers; see Species accounts for age-related ranges within each species.

(e.g., see Common Tern) but more study is needed in light of seasonal variation in these characters. Absent or incomplete black caps usually indicate SYs in Apr-Aug, but studies of known-age individuals have also reported nesting ATYs with white foreheads (Cullen 1957) so caution is warranted; also note that most species can start the prebasic head molt while incubating eggs, and can have white-spotted crowns as early as May-June (*cf.* Voelker 1996). Tail fork depth on most species reflects the length of the elongated r6 (the tip of which is often broken by Jul-Aug) and varies substantially with age, molt status, and season; however, it is usually greatest on breeding adults and shortest on juveniles and could be helpful for ageing some species. Several species can retain blackish (Fig. 492**A**, p. 693) or dusky (Fig. 492**B**) coloration in the marginal lesser coverts through the first-cycle molts. Dusky coverts are also found during Sep-Mar in AHY/ASYs of certain species (Fig. 492**C**), perhaps typically in SY/TYs but possibly also in ASY/ATYs due to variable timing of molt; study needed. Accurate age determination in terns can thus be complex and requires a synthesis of all available information on molt patterns and plumage aspect.

BROWN NODDY
Anous stolidus

BRNO
Species # 0790
Band size: 3

Species—From other dark terns by medium-large size with proportionally long tail (Table 63, p. 700); tail graduated (r1>r6 by > 50 mm), unique among N.Am terns; body plumage aspectdark brown to blackish (see **Geographic variation**) with paler gray to whitish caps in AHYs (Fig. 494, p. 696); bill black; legs brownish to blackish.

Black Noddy (*A. minutus*), a vagrant to se.N.Am, has shorter wing and tail lengths (wing chord 210-235, tail to longest rect 105-125, exp culmen 41-49, tarsus 20-25); bill slimmer (depth at gonys 5.8-7.2 *vs* 6.9-9.1 in Brown Noddy); tail slightly forked (r6>r1 by < 30 mm); body plumage aspect and s covs blacker, not contrasting in color with pp and ss (*vs* browner than pp and ss in most Brown Noddies; see **Geographic variation**); Caribbean populations with white subocular crescent restricted primarily behind midpoint of eye (*vs* spanning eye in Brown Noddy); HY/SY with contrasting white cap (*vs* less distinct in HY/SY Brown Noddy; Fig. 494**A**).

Geographic variation—See Blake (1977), Cramp & Simmons (1985), Hellmayr & Conover (1948b), Higgins & Davies (1996), Malling Olsen & Larsson (1995), Murphy (1936), Ridgway (1919), Stager (1964). Three other subspecies occur in tropical Pacific and Indian oceans.

A.s. *stolidus* (br and ranges se.N.Am-Atlantic S.Am): Size averages smaller and bill thinner than other subspecies (Table 63, p. 700); upperparts medium brown (*vs* medium-dark brown in other subspecies and blackish in *ridgwayi* of Pacific coastal Mexico-C.Am); crown with more extensive white in AHY/ASYs when fresh (Fig. 494**C**), *vs* more restricted (e.g., Fig. 494**B**) in other subspecies including *ridgwayi*.

Molt—CBS (CAS or SAS?). PF partial? (Oct-Sep in HY/SYs), PB2 complete (Aug?-Apr? in SY/TYs), DPB complete (Apr-Mar in ASY/ATYs); PAs absent? The above timing refers to N.Am populations. The PF occurs on non-breeding grounds at sea. The DPB starts on breeding grounds, can slow or suspend during breeding, and completes on breeding or non-breeding grounds, perhaps with suspensions for winter. Replacement of pp may occur primarily in May/Aug?-Feb/May during the PB2 and Apr/Jun-Mar during the DPB. The PF appears to include most body feathers, some les and med covs, and perhaps 1-2 terts and c.rects, but no pp or outer ss. The DPB can be completed during a single molt in many AHY/ASYs, but it appears that some individuals also can undergo Staffelmauser (Fig. 16, pp. 23-24), resulting in at least two sets of pp and ss in adults (Dorward & Ashmole 1963). PAs, if they occur, may include some to most head and body feathers, and some s covs but such a molt would be difficult to separate from protracted PBs. Further study needed on all aspects of molt in this species.

Age—Juv (B1; Jul-Oct) has back feathers and s covs with paler brown tips, and supraloral line distinct (Fig. 494**A**); Juv ♀=♂. The following month ranges refer to N.Am populations.

HY/SY (1st cycle, F1; Sep-Aug): Forecrown dusky to pale ashy gray, blending into brownish-gray hindcrown by subspecies (Fig. 494**A**-**B**); outer p covs relatively pointed and browner (Fig. 495**A**); juv pp and ss uniform in wear (Fig. 492**A**, p. 693), with p8-p10 relatively worn (*cf.* Fig. 492**B**); retained juv s covs contrastingly brown and worn in May-Aug (*cf.* Fig. 13**D**, p. 20).

AHY/ASY (Def. cycle, DB; Sep-Aug): Forehead and crown extensively pale ashy gray by subspecies (Fig. 494**B**-**C**; see **Geographic variation**); outer p covs relatively truncate and darker (Fig. 495**B**); basic pp and ss of one generation and exhibiting replacement clines and/or suspension limits (*cf.* Fig. 492**C**), the outer pp relatively fresh and replaced primarily in Dec-Mar; s covs uniform in wear (*cf.* Fig. 12**B**, p. 19). **Note: the timing for ageing of AHY/ASY, SY/TY, and ASY/ATY may be refined with more study.**

SY/TY (B2, 2nd cycle; Sep-Apr): Like AHY/ASY but basic pp, p covs, and ss with 2 generations, the outer pp and p covs and retained medial ss juv, rounded, worn, and very faded brown (Fig. 16**B**, p. 24; *cf.* Fig. 495**A**). **Note: See AHY/ASY**.

ASY/ATY (Def. cycle, DB; Sep-Aug): Like AHY/ASY but basic pp, p covs, and ss with 2-3 sets of basic feathers (Fig. 16**E**-**F**), the outer pp and p covs and retained ss basic, truncate, and contrasting less markedly with replaced feathers (*cf.* Fig. 495**B**). **Note: See AHY/ASY.**

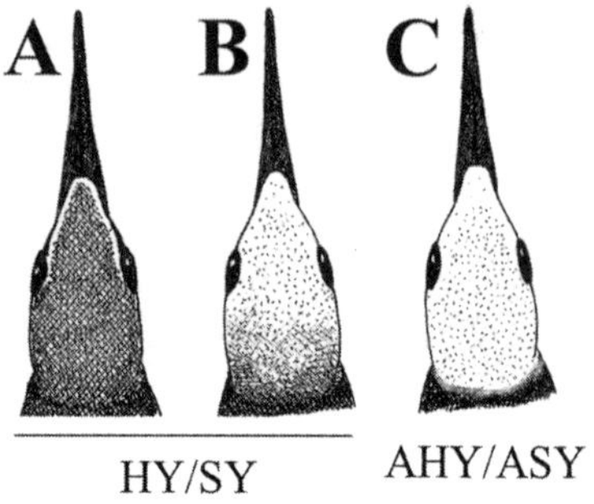

FIGURE 494. Variation in crown pattern by age in Brown Noddy. Note that these patterns apply to the nominate subspecies found off se.N.Am. In other subspecies (e.g., in the Pacific), HY/SYs may have crown patterns resembling **A** and AHY/ASYs may have patterns resembling **B**.

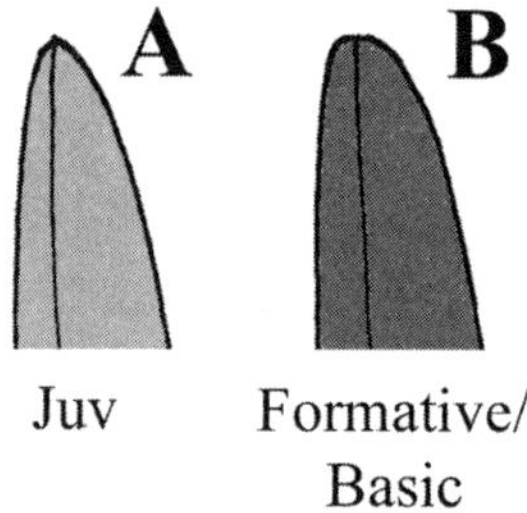

FIGURE 495. Shape and color of the outer primary coverts by feather generation in Brown Noddy. The juv outer pp and p covs (**A**) are brown and contrast more distinctly with replaced inner feathers, than do formative and basic pp and p covs (**B**). The juv outer pp and p covs are typically retained until the 2nd prebasic molt, being replaced in Nov-Apr in SY/TYs. By this time the outer feathers can become very faded brown.

Sex—♀=♂ by plumage aspect, although ♂♂ may average whiter crowns than ♀♀ by age (study needed). Bilateral BPs (Fig. 20**B**, p. 31) developed by both sexes but distended cloaca (Fig. 21, p. 32) indicates ASY ♀ in Feb-Jun. See Chardine & Morris (1989) for a DFA (p. 5) using head-bill length (*cf.* Fig. 453, p. 630) and straightened wing (*cf.* Fig. 3, p. 6), that correctly sexed 90% of live individuals from a Puerto Rico colony. Otherwise, measurements largely unhelpful for sexing (Table 63, p. 700) and no other criteria known.

Hybrids reported—None.

References—Bent (1921), Chardine & Morris (1989, 1996), Diamond & Prŷs-Jones (1986), Dorward & Ashmole (1963), Dunlop (1987), Gifford (1913), Higgins & Davies (1996), Malling Olsen & Larsson (1995), Murphy (1936), Ridgway (1919), Schreiber & Ashmole (1970), Stresemann & Stresemann (1966).

Brown Noddy

	Jan	Feb	Mar	Apr	May	Jun	Jul	Aug	Sep	Oct	Nov	Dec
Juv-HY							O	O	O	O	O	O
SY	O	O	O	O	O	O	O	O	O	O	O	O
TY	O	O	O	O								
AHY							O	O	O	O	O	O
ASY	O	O	O	O	O	(♀)	(♀)	O	O	O	O	O
ATY	O	O	O	O	(♀)	♀	(♀)	O				

■ > 95% ▨ 25-95% ▭ 5-25% □ < 5%

See Fig. 24 (pp. 44-45)

SOOTY TERN
Onychoprion fuscatus

SOTE
Species # 0750
Band size: 3

Species—From other dark-backed terns (including Bridled Tern, p. 700) by relatively large size with long wings (Table 63, p. 700); tail fork very deep (alternate r6 – r1 93-135 mm ASYs); upperparts uniformly black (Kodak 16-17, p. 629), undersides of outer pp sooty (Fig. 496**A**); r6 variably white and blackish by age (Fig. 497, p. 698), juv-HY completely blackish (*cf.* Fig. 498**A**, p. 699) with white tips to upperpart feathers (unique among terns); white forehead patch of AHYs with thin white extension to eyes (Fig. 498**B**-**C**); bill and legs black. Juv and molting Juvs from Black Tern (p. 709), which can be black mottled white in SYs or when molting, by much larger measures (Table 63); crown and back similar in coloration; upperpart feathers black tipped white; legs blackish.

Geographic variation—See Blake (1977), Cramp & Simmons (1985), Hellmayr & Conover (1948b), Higgins & Davies (1996), Murphy (1936), Ridgway (1919), Schreiber et al. (2001). Up to 6 other subspecies have been described from tropical oceans, some of which likely should be synonymized.

S.f. crissalis (br e.Pacific Is, rarely to s.CA): Underparts of ASY washed pale gray in alternate plumage; outer rects of ASYs average shorter and darker (by feather generation?) than in *oahuensis* of HI (*cf.* Fig. 497**E**-**F**).

S.f. fuscata (br Atlantic Is, to TX-FL): Underparts of ASY white in alternate plumage.

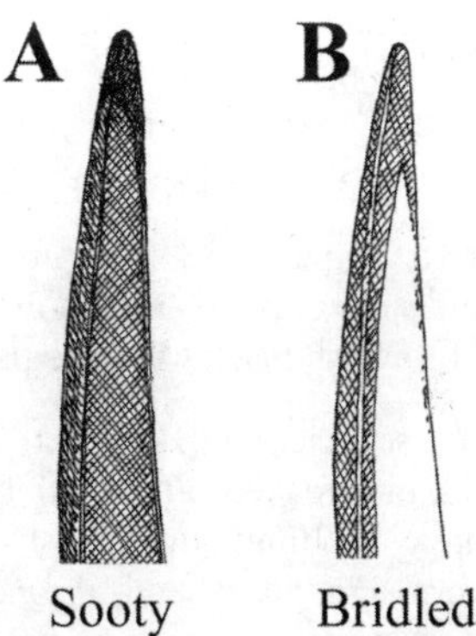

FIGURE 496. Pattern of underside of outer primaries in ASY/ATY Sooty and Bridled Terns, here showing p9. Note that the pattern for Bridled Tern shown here refers to Atlantic populations (*S.a. recognita*); Pacific populations (including *nelsoni*) show darker coloration, as in Figure 504**D**, p. 717). Gray-backed and Aleutian terns have distinct white tongues as well, which average less extensive than those of Bridled Tern (*cf.* Fig. 504**D**).

Molt—CAS (SAS?). PF complete (Nov?-Aug? in HY/SYs), PA1 partial-incomplete? (Jun?-Aug? in SYs), PB2 complete (Sep?-Apr? in SY/TYs), PA2 partial-incomplete? (Jan?-Apr? in TYs), DPB complete (Sep?-Mar? in ASY/ATYs), DPA partial-incomplete (Jan?-Mar? in ATYs); DPS absent. The above (provisional) timing refers to Caribbean populations breeding in N.Am; other populations breed and may molt on less-than-annual cycles. All

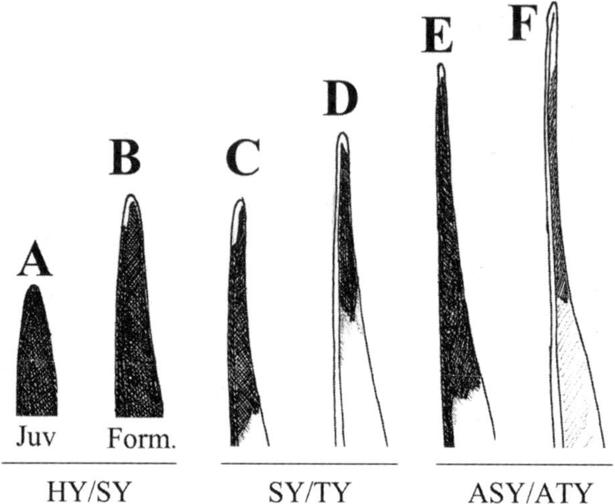

FIGURE 497. Variation in the pattern of the outer rectrix (r6) by feather generation and age in Sooty Tern. The juv r6 (**A**) is retained by HY/SYs provisionally until Dec-May, when replaced by the formative feather (**B**), which is retained until the PB2, provisionally in Sep-Nov. The outer rect in 2nd-cycle SY/TYs and definitive-cycle ASY/ATYs may get replaced once or twice (more study needed); in either case feathers replaced later in the cycles (**D**, **F**; alternate feathers?) appear to be longer and show more white than basic feathers replaced earlier in the cycles (**C**, **E**). See Figure 499 (p. 701) for comparison with Bridled Tern.

molts occur at sea, on non-breeding grounds. The PA1 may occasionally and the PA2 and DPA sometimes include 1-3 inner pp and 1-5 inner and outer ss (Table 62, p. 692; *cf.* Fig. 492**D**-**E**, p. 693), at least in some Pacific populations. Molt of rects needs study: r6 may be replaced once or twice per cycle, according to length of breeding cycles. It is possible that, in some populations, the basic r6 is long and white on breeding adults and mostly dark on non-breeding individuals (*cf.* Fig. 497**E**-**F**). Look for Staffelmauser (Fig. 16, p. 23-24) to occur among pp and (especially) the ss of some ASYs. See pp. 691-695 for more information.

Age—Juvs (B1; Aug-Oct in N.Am) are uniformly blackish brown (Fig. 498**A**, p. 699) with back feathers and s covs tipped cinnamon to whitish and r6 relatively broad, short (juv r6 – r1 < 50 mm), and brownish black with fine pale-buff tip when fresh (Fig. 497**A**); Juv ♀ = ♂.

Juv-HY/SY (1st cycle, Juv/B1-F1-A1; Oct-Sep): Upperparts sooty with forecrown patch lacking, indistinct, or streaked buff to whitish (Fig. 498**A**-**B**); throat and upper breast whitish with heavy dusky mottling; juv pp and ss uniform in wear (Fig. 492**A**, p. 693), with p8-p10 relatively worn (Fig. 492**B**) and replaced primarily in May-Aug, perhaps with 1-2 inner pp and 1-3 inner ss replaced again and fresh and paler in May-Aug (Fig. 492**D**); juv or formative r6 relatively short and blackish with small whitish tip (Fig. 497**A**-**B**); back feathers usually with pale gray to brownish edging in Feb-Sep.

SY/TY (2nd cycle, B2-A2; Oct-Sep): Upperparts blackish, the forehead patch white, often with some dusky streaking (Fig. 498**B**-**C**); throat and breast white with scattered dusky mottling; basic pp and ss showing molt clines and suspension limits (Fig. 492**C**), with p8-p10 relatively fresh and replaced primarily in Jan-Apr, and 1-3 inner pp and 1-5 inner and outer ss usually fresh and paler in Jan-Sep (Fig. 492**D**-**E**); r6 short (r6 – r5 < 45 mm) with moderate to extensive dark subterminal area on inner web (Fig. 497**C**-**D**); back feathers usually without

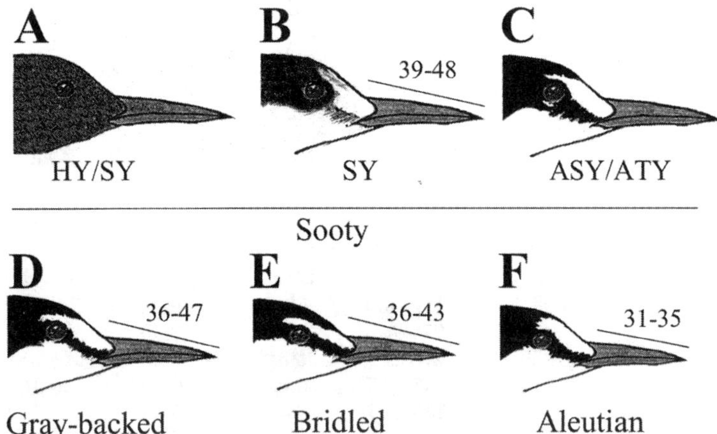

FIGURE 498. Head patterns and bill lengths by species and age in N.Am dark-backed terns. Measures refer to exposed culmen (Fig. 7**A**, p. 9). Head plumage aspect in Sooty Tern varies from juv (**A**) to formative/2nd basic (**B**) to definitive basic and alternate (**C**). The streaked forehead patch in SY Sooty Tern (**B**) is also found in SY Bridled and Aleutian terns, but (unlike Sooty Terns) note that these species also have definitive basic aspects (in ASYs) showing streaked forecrowns.

pale-gray edging in Feb-Sep. **Note: Intermediates between SY and ASY in Oct-Dec (with light dusky mottling to breast) may be TYs but should probably be aged AHY**.

ASY/ATY (Def. cycle, DB-DA; Oct-Sep): Upperparts glossy black with forehead patch white (Fig. 498**C**); throat and breast white to whitish; basic pp and ss as in SY/TY, with p8-p10 replaced primarily in Dec-Mar and 1-3 pp and 1-3 inner and outer ss only occasionally replaced and paler in Jan-Sep (Fig. 492**D-E**); r6 long (r6 – r5 > 45 mm when fresh), variably blackish with white tip (Fig. 497**E**; primarily Oct-Jan) to whitish with subterminal dark band on inner web (Fig. 497**F**; primarily Feb-Sep); back feathers without pale-gray edging in Feb-Sep. **Note: See SY/TY. More study needed on the length and pattern of r6 relative to season, breeding condition, and age (see Molt)**.

Sex— ♀ = ♂ by plumage aspect. Bilateral BPs (Fig. 20**B**, p. 31) developed by both sexes but distended cloaca (Fig. 21, p. 32) indicates ATY ♀ in Apr-Jun. Measurements generally unhelpful for sexing (Table 63, p. 700); see Reynolds et al. (2008) for a DFA (p. 5) including head-bill length (Fig. 453, p. 630), tarsus and wing lengths, and bill depth at gonys, that correctly sexed > 80% of live birds from Ascension I. Otherwise, no criteria known for sexing.

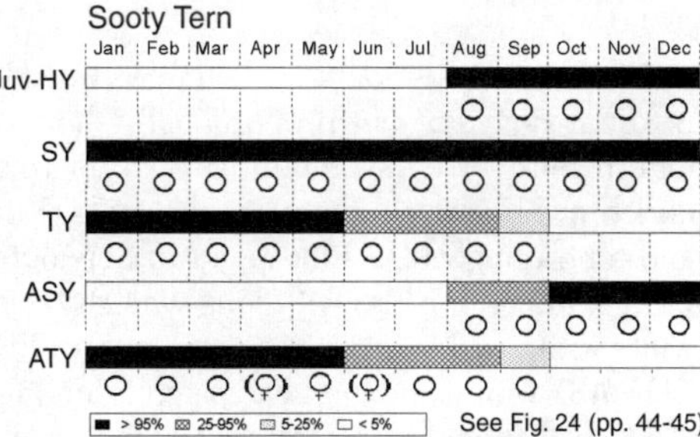

Hybrids reported—None.

References—Ashmole (1963a, 1963b, 1965), Bent (1921), Clancey (1977), Diamond & Prŷs-Jones (1986), Gifford (1913), Higgins & Davies (1996), Malling Olsen & Larsson (1995), Murphy (1936), Oberholser (1974), Ridgway (1919), Schreiber et al. (2002), Stresemann & Stresemann (1966).

TABLE 63. Measurements (mm) of North American dark-backed terns to assist in identification and sexing. See pp. 4-11 for methods of measurement. Species summaries are in **bold** and subspecies values are in ***italics***. Values were derived from 95% confidence intervals as based approximately on the indicated sample sizes (see pp. 4-5). Thus, midpoints of ranges approximate means, and S.D. is approximated by one-quarter of the range.

Taxon/Sex	*n*	wing chord[1]	tail length[2]	exp culmen	bill depth[3]	tarsus
Brown Noddy[4]		**256-289**	**128-157**	**38-46**	**9.5-12.2**	**22-25**
♀	100	256-279	128-145	38-43	9.5-11.4	22-25
♂	100	261-289	134-157	41-46	10.3-12.2	23-25
Sooty Tern[5]		**274-300**	**68-86**	**39-48**	**8.6-11.5**	**20-25**
♀	50	274-297	68-82	39-45	8.6-10.7	20-24
♂	50	275-298	69-86	40-48	9.1-11.5	21-25
Bridled Tern[4]		**245-267**	**63-75**	**36-43**	**8.6-10.8**	**19-23**
S.a. nelsoni		***253-267***	***64-75***	***36-43***	***9.3-10.6***	***20-23***
♀	2	253-266	64-70	36-40	9.3-9.8	20-21
♂	6	255-267	65-75	40-43	9.6-10.6	21-23
S.a. recognita		***245-262***	***63-75***	***37-42***	***8.6-10.8***	***19-23***
♀	17	245-261	63-74	37-40	8.6-9.9	19-22
♂	25	247-262	64-75	39-42	9.4-10.8	20-23
Aleutian Tern		**254-280**	**58-73**	**31-35**	**6.4-8.1**	**17-20**
♀	30	254-278	58-72	31-35	6.4-7.8	17-20
♂	30	259-280	58-73	31-35	6.8-8.1	17-20
Black Tern[4]		**190-224**	**51-59**	**24-30**	**6.1-7.5**	**14-18**
♀	100	190-218	51-58	24-29	6.1-7.3	14-17
♂	100	196-224	51-59	25-30	6.4-7.5	15-18

[1] Wing chord averages ~5% shorter in Juv-HY/SY than in AHY/ASY.

[2] Tail measured to tip of central rectrix (r1; Fig. 5**C**, p. 8). See text and Figure 6**A** (p. 9) for measures of tail fork (r6–r1), which varies substantially with plumage and molt, due to variable length of r6.

[3] Bill depth measured at distal end of forehead feathering (see Fig. 8**A**, p. 10).

[4] N.Am population only. See **Geographic variation**.

[5] Includes both N.Am subspecies, which are similar in measurments (Schreiber et al. 2002).

BRIDLED TERN
Onychoprion anaethetus

BRTE
Species # 0760
Band size: 2-3

Species—From other dark-backed terns including Sooty (p. 697) and Aleutian (p. 702) terns by medium-large size but proportionally short wings (Table 63, p. 700); tail fork medium deep (alternate r6 – r1 77-109 mm ASYs); upperparts (including rump, uppertail covs, and c. rects) dark brownish gray to sooty by subspecies (Kodak 11.5-13.5 in N.Am; p. 629) with whitish nape and contrastingly blackish cap in Apr-Sep; outer pp with moderately extensive black along shaft by age, the undersides with long whitish tongues (Figs. 493**D**, p. 694, & 496**B**, p. 697); r5-r6 white with variable amount of gray by age (Fig. 499); juv ss with gray centers (*cf.* Fig. 505**B**, p. 717); ASY with white forehead patch extending proximally to rear edge of eyes in Apr-Sep (Fig. 498**E**, p. 699) and underparts and underwing covs uniformly white; bill and legs black.

Gray-backed Tern (*S. lunata*) of tropical Pacific Ocean (possible vagrant to w.N.Am.) is slightly larger with relatively short tarsus (wg chord 250-280, exp culmen 36-47, tarsus 18-21) has upperparts paler and grayer (~ Kodak 9), contrasting more with pp; AHY with supercilium extending well behind eye (Fig. 498**D**); r5 gray and r6 more extensively gray on inner web (*cf.* Fig. 499); ss with dark centers (Fig. 505**A**, p. 717); underwing uniformly whitish (*vs* covs washed grayish contrasting with darker under pp and ss in Bridled Tern); and upperparts of Juv gray with extensive white feather fringing; see McKee & Erickson (2002) and Rauzon (2006) for more information.

Geographic variation—See Blake (1977), Cramp & Simmons (1985), Higgins & Davies (1996), Murphy (1936), Ridgway (1919). Two other subspecies occur in the Indian and sw.Pacific oceans; these generally show darker upperparts (13-14) and have darker outer rects.

S.a. nelsoni (br w Mexico to Panama, vagrant to sw.CA): Averages larger (Table 63); undersides of pp darker (*cf.* Fig. 504**D**, p. 717) upperparts sooty (Kodak 12-13.5); ASY with pale gray underparts in Mar-Aug.

S.a. recognita (br Caribbean region, visitor to pelagic TX-VA, vagrant to WI-Que): Averages smaller (Table 63); undersides of pp whiter (Fig. 496**B**, p. 697); upperparts dark brownish gray (Kodak 11.5-12.5); ASY with white underparts in Mar-Aug.

Molt—SAS or CAS. PF1/PA1 incomplete (Dec-Apr in HY/SYs), PB2 complete (May/Jun-Aug/Oct in SYs), PA2 incomplete (Jan?-May? in TYs), PB3 complete (May/Jul-Aug/Oct in TYs), DPA incomplete (Jan?-Apr? in ATYs), DPB complete (Jun/Sep-Sep?/Dec in ATYs); DPS absent. More study needed on the number of inserted first-cycle molts and whether they are homologous with a PF, a PA1, or both (Fig. 10**C**-**E**, pp. 13-16). Molts occur primarily on non-breeding grounds at sea, although the DPB can start with inner pp on breeding grounds. The PF1/PA1 includes most head and body feathers and some to all rects but no pp, ss, or s covs; more study needed on the extent of each molt (the PA1 may be absent). Subsequent PAs can include 1-2 inner pp and 1-4 ss (Fig. 492**C**-**D**, p. 693); the PA2 can include at least r6 and the DPA sometimes includes some to all rects. More study needed; the above timing and extent based on specimens of *O.a. recognita* and may not reflect molt in Pacific populations. See pp. 691-695 for more information.

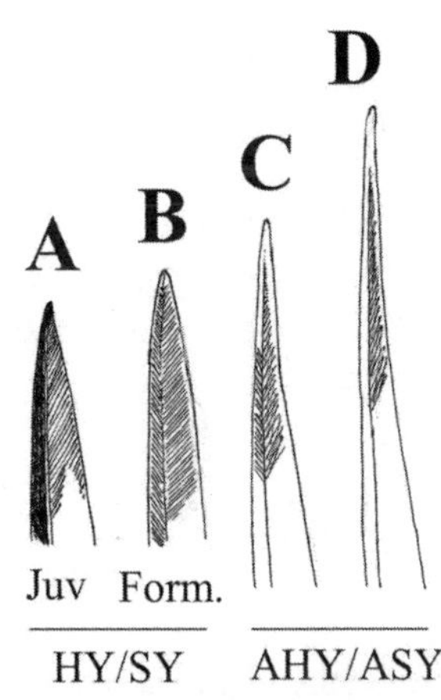

FIGURE 499. Variation in the pattern of the outer rectrix (r6) by feather generation and age in Bridled Tern. The juv r6 (**A**) is retained by HY/SYs provisionally until Dec-Apr, when replaced by a formative feather (**B**), which is retained by SYs until rect molt during the PB2 in Jul-Oct. It is possible that some SY/TYs may be separable by a combination of features including the length and pattern of r6 (as in **C**) but note that this feather often may be replaced during the PA2 in Jan-May, the replaced feather resembling **D**. See Figure 496 (p. 697) for comparison with Sooty Tern. Gray-backed Tern shows less-extensively white to the inner web by feather generation and age and Least Tern exhibits somewhat similar patterns by age.

Age—Juv (B1; Aug-Nov) has back, s covs, and terts with distinct whitish tips and narrow dark subterminal bars and r6 relatively short (r1 – r6 < 55 mm), broad, and dark distally with a contrasting blackish outer web (Fig. 499**A**).

Juv-HY/SY (1st cycle, Juv-B1/F1/A1; Sep-Aug): Juv pp and ss uniform in wear (Fig. 492**A**, p. 693), with p8-p10 relatively worn (cf. Fig. 492**B**) and replaced primarily in Jul-Aug; tail fork medium in depth (r1 – r6 usually 60-80 mm), with r6 usually extensively dusky across both webs (Fig. 499**A-B**); lores and crown with blackish mottling (cf. Fig. 498**B**, p. 699) and back usually with some whitish barring in Mar-Aug.

AHY/ASY (Def. cycle, DB-DA; Sep-Aug): Basic pp and ss showing molt clines and suspension limits (Fig. 492**C**), with p8-p10 relatively fresh and replaced primarily in Dec-Mar, and with 1-3 inner pp and 1-5 inner and outer ss sometimes replaced again and fresher and paler in Feb-Aug (Fig. 492**D**); tail fork deeper (r1 – r6 usually > 75 mm when fresh), r6 with reduced dusky usually not spanning both webs (Fig. 499**C-D**); cap black with white lores and forehead chevron (Fig. 498**D**) and back usually without whitish barring in Mar-Aug. **Note: Some SY/TYs and ASY/ATYs may be distinguishable by molt timing and patterns, plumage aspect, and length of r6 (as in other terns; Fig. 499C) but study needed.**

Sex—♀ = ♂ by plumage aspect. Bilateral BPs (Fig. 20**B**, p. 31) developed by both sexes but distended cloaca (Fig. 21, p. 32) indicates ATY ♀ in Apr-Jun. Measurements likely unhelpful for sexing (Table 63, p. 700), although head-bill length (Fig. 453, p. 630) should be investigated on live birds. Otherwise, no criteria known for sexing.

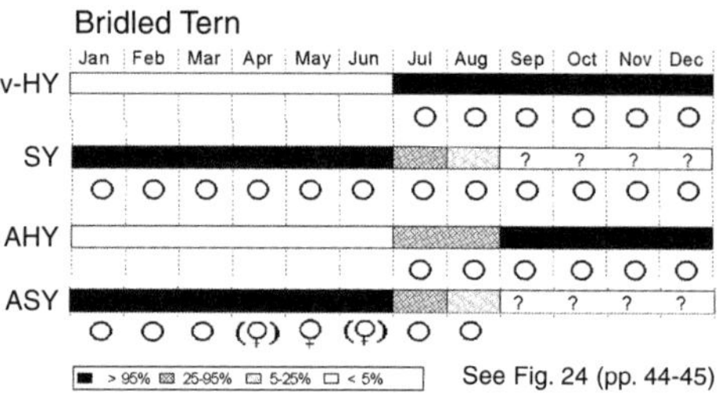

Hybrids reported—None.

References—Bent (1921), Diamond (1976), Haney et al. (1999), Higgins & Davies (1996), Malling Olsen & Larsson (1995), Murphy (1936), Ridgway (1919).

ALEUTIAN TERN
Onychoprion aleuticus

ALTE
Species # 0730
Band size: 2-1A

Species—From other dark-backed terns (including Sooty, p. 697, and Bridled, p. 700, terns) by smaller size and short legs (Table 63, p. 700); tail fork deep (alternate r6 – r1 74-119 mm ASYs); outer pp with moderately extensive black along shaft by age (Fig. 493**D**, p. 694), the undersides with white extending to tip (*cf.* Fig. 504**D**, p. 717); r5-r6 white or mostly white (Fig. 503**A-B**, p. 717); upperparts medium-dark gray (Kodak 8-9; p. 629), without brown tinge, and with white rump, uppertail covs, and c.rects; juv ss with blackish centers (Fig. 505**A**, p. 717); ASY with broad white forehead patch extending proximally to rear edge of eyes (Fig. 498**F**, p. 699) and underparts gray, contrasting with whiter underwing covs in Apr-Sep; bill black; legs dull orange (Juv) to black.

From darker Asian Common Terns (*S.h. longipennis*), p. 714, by slenderer average bill (Table 63); tail fork deeper (see above) and r5-r6 without dark outer web (Fig. 503**A-B**); upperparts darker gray (Kodak 8-9); ASY with white forehead patch in Apr-Sep (Fig. 498**F**). From Gray-backed Tern (see Bridled Tern) by shorter bill (exposed culmen < 36 mm *vs* > 36 mm in Gray-backed Tern); uppertail covs and rump white (*vs* gray, concolorous with back in Gray-backed Tern); ASY in Apr-Sep with white supercilium broader and shorter (Fig. 498**F** *vs*

E), underparts gray (*vs* white), ss with blacker centers (Fig. 505**A**), and r6 white (Fig. 503**A-B**) *vs* with dark on inner web (*cf.* Fig. 499**D**, p. 701) in Gray-backed Tern.

Geographic variation—Monotypic.

Molt—Poorly known, perhaps similar to Common Tern (see Leader 2000), as follows: CAS? PF complete (Oct?-Aug? in HY/SYs), PA1 partial-incomplete (May?-Aug? in SYs), PB2 complete (Aug?-Apr? in SY/TYs), PA2 incomplete (Jan?-May? in TYs), DPB complete (Aug?-Mar? in ASY/ATYs), DPA incomplete (Jan?-Apr? in ATYs); DPS absent. All molts apparently occur on non-breeding grounds. The DPA can include 4-6 inner pp and 4-7 ss (Table 62, p. 692; Fig. 492**E-F**, p. 693), and all rects. More study needed on extents of PF and PAs, and whether or not a PS of inner pp can occur (see Common Tern, p. 713). See pp. 691-695 for more information.

Age—Juv (B1; Aug-Oct) has upperpart feathers blackish brown with broad cinnamon edging and legs dull orange to brownish; Juv ♀=♂.

Juv-HY/SY (1st cycle, Juv/B1-F1-A1; Sep-Aug): Most to a few back feathers, terts, and s covs fringed cinnamon in Sep-Jan; juv pp and ss uniform in wear (Fig. 492**A**, p. 693), with p8-p10 relatively worn (Fig. 492**B**) and replaced primarily in Jun-Aug; 1-2 inner pp and 1-3 inner ss perhaps replaced again and fresher and paler in May-Aug (Fig. 492**C-D**); outer rects shorter and marked blackish in Sep-Jan (Fig. 503**A**, p. 717); anterior les covs mottled blackish to dusky (Fig. 492**A-B**); nape, lores, crown, and belly white or slightly mottled dark in Apr-Aug; legs dusky orangish through Nov-Jan.

AHY/ASY (Def. cycle, DB-DA; Sep-Aug): Back feathers, terts, and s covs without cinnamon fringes; basic pp and ss showing molt clines and/or suspension limits (*cf.* Fig. 492**C**), with p8-p10 relatively fresh and replaced primarily in Dec-Apr, and with 4-6 inner pp and 4-7 inner and outer ss fresh and paler in Feb-Aug (Fig. 492**E-F**); outer rects longer and white (Fig. 503**B**); anterior les covs gray, uniform with rest of upperwing (Fig. 492**D**); lores and crown black (Fig. 498**F**, p. 699) and belly uniformly gray in Apr-Aug; legs black. **Note: Some SY/TYs are probably distinguishable, as with Common Tern, but study needed.**

Sex—♀=♂ by plumage aspect. Bilateral(?) BPs (Fig. 20**B**, p. 31) developed by both sexes but distended cloaca (Fig. 21, p. 32) indicates ASY ♀ in Jun-Jul. Measurements unhelpful for sexing (Table 63) although head-bill length (Fig. 453, p. 630) should be investigated on live birds. Otherwise, no criteria known for sexing.

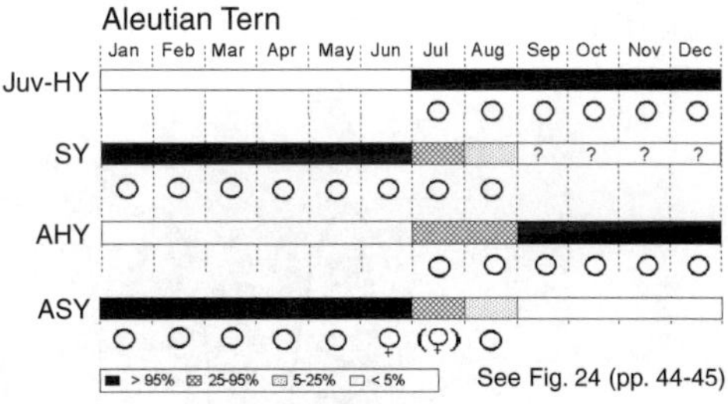

Hybrids reported—None.

References—Bent (1921), Cramp & Simmons (1985), Dement'ev & Gladkov (1951c), Leader (2000), Lee (1992), Malling Olsen & Larsson (1995), North (1997), Ridgway (1919), Stejneger (1885).

LEAST TERN
Sternula antillarum

LETE
Species # 0740
Band size: 1A-1B

Species—From other terns by very small size (Table 64, p. 713); tail fork shallow (alternate r6 – r1 30-48 mm in ASYs); outer pp with reduced black along shaft by age (Fig. 493**A-B**, p. 694), the undersides also with substantial black (Fig. 504**A-C**, p. 717, see **Age**); juv ss pale (*cf.* Fig. 505**E**, p. 717); r5-r6 white with black on inner web distally (*cf.* Fig. 499, p. 701); upperparts (including rump, medial uppertail covs, and c.rects) concolorous, medium-pale gray (Kodak 4-6; p. 629); bill and legs primarily blackish (Juv) to bright yellow (AHYs).

Little Tern (*S. albifrons*) of Eurasia, a possible vagrant to N.Am) is slightly larger (wing chord 165-180, tail to r1 39-48, exp culmen 27-33, tarsus 15-18); rump and uppertail covs white, contrasting with gray back; outer 1-2 pp usually retained during DPAs (*vs* outer 2-6 pp retained in Least Tern). See Pyle et al. (2001) for more information.

Geographic variation—Considered monotypic here, following Whittier et al. (2006); see also Burleigh & Lowrey (1942), Hellmayr & Conover (1948b), Johnson et al. (1998), Massey (1976, 1998), Mearns (1916), Monroe (1968), Oberholser (1974), Palacios & Mellink (1996), Patten & Erickson (1996), Patten et al. (2003), Ridgway (1919), Thompson et al. (1992, 1997), van Rossem & Hachisuka (1937a). Populations breeding in CA ("*S.a. browni*") may have paler upperparts and more-slender bills, those breeding in Baja CA and possible dispersing to se.CA ("*mexicanus*") may average smaller and darker, and those breeding in NE-IL to TX-LA ("*anthalassos*") may average darker and shorter-billed than (nominate) populations breeding in coastal TX-FL-MA, but differences appear insufficient for subspecific recognition.

Molt—CAS. PF complete (Aug-May in HY/SYs), PA1 incomplete (Feb?-Jun in SYs), PS1 incomplete (Apr?-Jun in SYs), PB2 complete (Jul-Feb in SY/TYs), PA2 incomplete (Jan?-Apr? in TYs), PS2 incomplete (Mar?-Apr? in TYs), DPB complete (May-Jan? in ASY/ATYs), DPA incomplete (Dec?-Mar in ATYs), DPS incomplete (Feb?-Mar? in ATYs). The PF and PBs start on or near breeding grounds, suspend for migration after some body feathers and occasionally (PF) to usually (PBs) 1-4 inner pp replaced, and complete on non-breeding grounds; the PAs occur primarily on non-breeding grounds and often overlap with completion of the PF and PBs (*cf.* Fig. 492**B**, p. 693). Replacement of pp occurs Sep?/Nov-Mar?/May during the

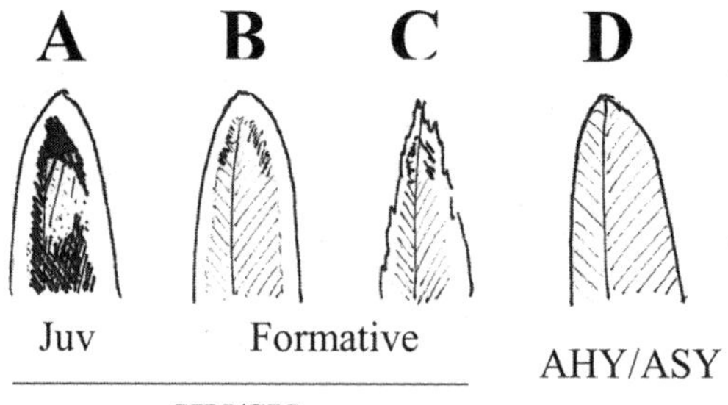

FIGURE 500. Variation in tertial pattern by age in Least Tern. Juv terts (**A**) are replaced by formative terts (**B**) in Sep-Oct. These can be retained by HY/SYs until the PA1 commences in Apr-May, at which point they are worn (**C**). Subsequent to the PA1, AHY/ASYs show plain gray terts (**D**) in all plumage aspects (basic, alternate, and supplemental when replaced). Similar patterns of age-related variation are exhibited by Caspian, Gull-billed, Roseate, Common, and Arctic terns, with juv and sometimes formative terts having variable brown markings and some formative and all basic and alternate terts being pale gray overall and without brown markings.

PF, Jul-Feb during the PB2, and May/Aug-Nov?/Jan? during the DPB. The PA1 includes most to all body feathers, some to most les and med covs, 3-9 inner pp, 5 to most or all ss, and most to all rects, and the PS1 sometimes can include 1-3 inner pp and occasionally 1-2 inner ss and c.rects again (Fig. 492**F**-**G**). These molts during the second and definitive cycles are similar but the PAs usually includes 6-8 outer pp, all ss (up to 4 ss among s7-s10 can be retained), and all rects, and the PS's usually includes 1-5 inner pp, 1-6 ss, and 1-4 c.rects (Table 62, p. 692; Fig. 492**G**-**H**). Body feathers are likely replaced during the PS as well but study needed to confirm this. See pp. 691-695 for more information.

Age—Juv (B1; Jul-Sep) has back feathers, terts, and outer rects with variable brown subterminal marks (Fig. 500**A**-**B**); Juv ♀ = ♂.

Juv-HY/SY (1st cycle, Juv/B1-F1-A1; Sep-Aug): Terts with brown subterminal marks in Sep-Apr (Fig. 500**A**-**C**); juv pp and ss uniform in wear (Fig. 492**A**, p. 693), with p8-p10 relatively worn (Fig. 492**B**), averaging more-extensively black (Fig. 493**B**, p. 694), and replaced primarily in Feb-May; 3-9 inner pp and most to all ss replaced again and fresher and paler in Mar-Aug (Fig. 492**D**-**F**), and 1-3 inner pp and 1-2 outer ss sometimes replaced for a third time and fresher and paler in May-Aug (Fig. 492**G**); anterior les covs mottled slaty blackish in Sep-Mar (Fig. 492**A**) or dusky in Mar-Aug (Fig. 492**B**); forecrown with indistinct white chevron in Mar-Aug; bill black in Sep-Mar to yellowish with indistinct black distal third in Apr-Aug.

AHY/ASY (Def. cycle, DB-DA; Sep-Aug): Terts without brown marks (Fig. 500**D**); basic pp and ss showing molt clines and/or suspension limits (*cf.* Fig. 492**C**), with p8-p10 relatively fresh, averaging less-extensively black (Fig. 493**A**), and replaced primarily in Nov-Feb; 6-8 pp and all ss usually fresher and paler in Dec-Apr, and 1-5 pp and 1-6 ss usually replaced for a third time and fresher and paler in Feb-Aug (Fig. 492**G**-**H**); anterior les covs often mottled dusky in Sep-Mar (Fig. 492**C**; SY/TYs only?) or unmarked gray in Mar-Aug (Fig. 492**D**); forecrown with distinct white chevron in Mar-Aug; bill bright yellow with distinct small black tip. **Note: Some retarded TYs might resemble advanced SYs in Mar-Aug (needs study).**

Sex—♀ = ♂ by plumage aspect. BP (Fig. 20, p. 31) may not develop (Thompson et al. 1997; but look for bilateral BPs, Fig. 20**B** in both sexes); distended cloaca (Fig. 21, p. 32) indicates ASY ♀ in May-Jul. Among breeding pairs, ♂♂ may average brighter and more orange-tinged bills than ♀♀ and this may be helpful for sexing mated pairs. Measurements unhelpful for sexing (Table 64, p. 713) although head-bill length (Fig. 453, p. 630) should be investigated on live birds. Otherwise, no criteria known for sexing.

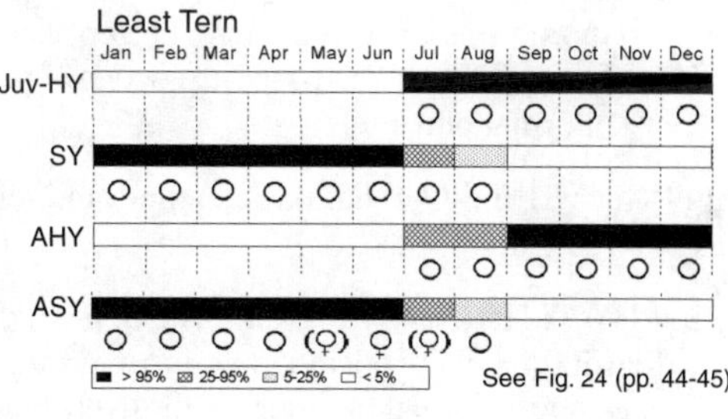

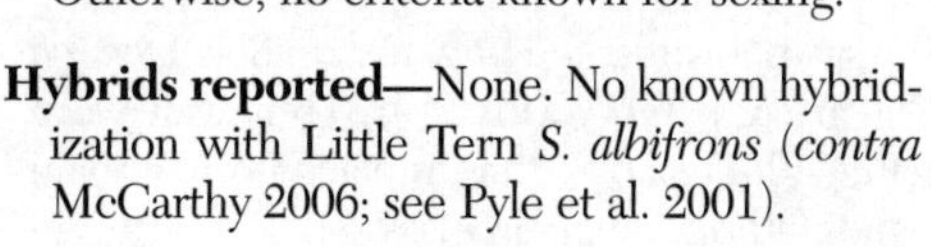

Hybrids reported—None. No known hybridization with Little Tern *S. albifrons* (*contra* McCarthy 2006; see Pyle et al. 2001).

References—Atwood & Massey (1982), Baker (1993), Bent (1921), Chandler & Wilds (1994), Cramp & Simmons (1985), Dement'ev & Gladkov (1951c), Higgins & Davies (1996), Malling Olsen & Larsson (1995), Massey & Atwood (1978), Murphy (1936), Oberholser (1974), Patten & Erickson (1996), Ridgway (1919), Thompson & Slack (1983), Thompson et al. (1992, 1997).

GULL-BILLED TERN
Gelochelidon nilotica

GBTE
Species # 0630
Band size: 3B

Species—From other terns by medium size with proportionally stout bill and long tarsus (Table 64, p. 713); tail fork shallow (alternate r6 – r1 31-45 mm ASYs); outer pp with substantial black along shafts by age (Fig. 493**D-E**), the undersides also substantially dark (*cf.* Fig. 504**D**, p. 717); outer rect white; upperparts pale gray (Kodak 3.5-4.5; p. 629); formative and basic aspect with white head and blackish auricular mask; AHY/ASY with black bill and legs.

Geographic variation—See Bancroft (1929), Blake (1977), Cramp & Simmons (1985), Dement'ev & Gladkov (1951c), Hellmayr & Conover (1948b), Higgins & Davies (1996), Monroe (1968), Murphy (1936), Patten et al. (2003), Rogers et al. (2005), Unitt (2004), Wetmore (1965). Four other subspecies occur in S.Am, Eurasia, and Australia.

S.n. aranea (br and wint throughout N.Am range): Variably smaller, bill thinner, and tail shorter than most extralimital subspecies; upperparts grayer (Kodak 3.5-4.5, p. 629), *vs.* paler (Kodak 3-4) in S.Am and Australian populations. Populations of s.CA-w.C.Am ("*vanrossemi*") may have bill averaging slightly wider (6.6-8.9 *vs* 6.1-8.7 mm at distal end of forehead feathers) and deeper (9.5-10.8 *vs* 8.8-10.3 at gonys) and tarsus longer than populations breeding in e.N.Am but differences too slight for subspecific recognition. Variation in N.Am Gull-billed Terns comparable to those of Royal Tern, not widely distinguished at the subspecies level.

Molt—CAS. PF complete (Aug-2nd Aug in HY/SYs), PA1 partial-incomplete? (Jun-Aug in SYs), PB2 complete (Aug-Apr? in SY/TYs), PA2 partial-incomplete (Dec?-Apr? in TYs), DPB complete (Jun-Feb in ASY/ATYs), DPA partial-incomplete (Dec-Mar in ATYs); DPS absent(?). The PF usually occurs on non-breeding grounds, often commencing (body feathers) during migration and suspending in Dec-Jan after 1-3 pp replaced; the DPB can start on or near breeding grounds (including crown feathers during incubation) or can occur completely on non-breeding grounds; and the PAs start on non-breeding grounds and (in breeding adults) can complete during migration. Replacement of pp occurs Dec-May/Aug during the PF and Jul/Sep-Feb during the DPB. The PF and DPB can rarely be incomplete, with p10 and some medial ss (among s7-s12) retained. The PA1 appears to include body feathers and some inner les covs and sometimes 1-4 rects; look for some SYs to replace 1-2 inner pp and outer ss as well. The PA2 and DPA include most to all body feathers, a few to some les and med covs, 1-6 inner pp and 1-6 inner and outer ss (Table 62, p. 692; Fig. 492**D-F**, p. 693), and some to (occasionally) all rects; more pp, ss, and rects may be replaced during the PA2 than during subsequent molts. Look for a PS2 or DPS (p1-p2) to occur in some ASYs, as in other terns. See pp. 691-695 for more information.

Age—Juv (B1; Jul-Oct) has back feathers and terts with brown subterminal marks (*cf.* Fig. 500**A-C**, p. 704); Juv ♀=♂.

Juv-HY/SY (1st cycle, Juv/B1-F1-A1; Sep-Aug): Terts variably marked brownish in Sep-Dec (*cf.* Fig. 500**A-C**); juv pp and ss uniform in wear (Fig. 492**A**, p. 693), with p8-p10 relatively worn (Fig. 492**B**), averaging more-extensively black (Fig. 493**E**, p. 694), and replaced primarily in Dec-Apr (juv p10 rarely retained; Fig. 492**B**), and without inner pp or ss replaced again in Jan-Aug (Fig. 492**C**); anterior les covs mottled slaty blackish in Sep-Mar (Fig. 492**A**) or dusky in Mar-Aug (Fig. 492**B**); cap white with cloudy smudging and sparse dark streaks year-round.

SY/TY (2nd cycle, B2-A2; Sep-Aug): Terts without brownish markings (*cf.* Fig. 500**D**); basic pp and ss showing molt clines and suspension limits (Fig. 492**C**), with p8-p10 relatively fresh, averaging less-extensively black (Fig. 493**D**), and replaced primarily in Mar-Aug; 3-6 inner pp and

3-6 inner and outer ss replaced again and fresher and paler in Jan-Aug (Fig. 492**E**-**F**); anterior les covs slightly mottled dusky in Sep-Mar (Fig. 492**C**) or unmarked gray in Apr-Aug (Fig. 492**D**); cap white with fine blackish streaks in Sep-Apr and mostly black in Mar-Jul (rarely completely black?). **Note: Intermediates between SY/TY and ASY/ATY, and are best aged AHY/ASY; characters of SY/TYs and TY/4Ys may also overlap (see Common Tern, p. 713).**

ASY/ATY (Def. cycle, DB-DA; Sep-Aug): Basic pp and ss showing molt clines and/or suspension limits (*cf.* Fig. 492**C**), with p8-p10 relatively fresh, averaging less-extensively black (Fig. 493**D**), and replaced primarily in Dec-Feb; 1-4 inner pp and 1-4 inner and outer ss usually fresh and paler in Jan-Aug (Fig. 492**C**-**E**); anterior les covs uniformly pale gray (Fig. 492**D**); cap white, sparsely streaked blackish in Sep-Mar or completely black in Mar-Aug. **Note: See SY/TY.**

Gull-billed Tern

Jan | Feb | Mar | Apr | May | Jun | Jul | Aug | Sep | Oct | Nov | Dec

Juv-HY

SY

TY

AHY

ASY

ATY

■ > 95% ▩ 25-95% ▭ 5-25% □ < 5%

See Fig. 24 (pp. 44-45)

Sex—♀=♂ by plumage aspect. Bilateral(?) BPs (Fig. 20**B**, p. 31) probably developed by both sexes but distended cloaca (Fig. 21, p. 32) indicates ATY ♀ in May-Jul. Measurements largely unhelpful for sexing (Table 64, p. 713) although head-bill length (Fig. 453, p. 630) should be investigated on live birds. Otherwise, no criteria known for sexing.

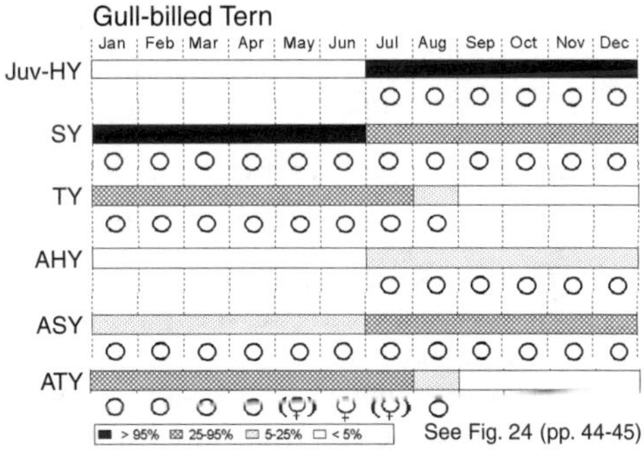

Hybrids reported—With Forster's Tern (McCarthy 2006).

References—Bancroft (1929), Bent (1921), Dement'ev & Gladkov (1951c), Higgins & Davies (1996), Malling Olsen & Larsson (1995), Murphy (1936), Oberholser (1974), Parnell et al. (1995), Ridgway (1919), Rogers et al. (2005), Unitt (2004).

CASPIAN TERN

Hydroprogne caspia

CATE
Species # 0640
Band size: 5-4A

Species—From other terns by very large size and stout bill (Table 65, p. 723; Fig. 507**A**, p. 721); tail fork shallow (alternate r6 – r1 25-48 mm ASYs); undersides of outer pp dark (*cf.* Fig. 496**A**, p. 697); head dusky streaked pale to black, without extensive white forehead (Fig. 507**A**); r5-r6 gray with black subterminal band in HYs (Fig. 501, p. 708); upperparts medium-pale gray (Kodak 5-6; p. 629); juv ss with dusky centers (*cf.* Fig. 505**C**, p. 717); bill primarily red; legs black.

Geographic variation—Monotypic. Populations of N.Am ("*S.c. imperator*") average slightly larger but difference insufficient for subspecific recognition. See Cramp & Simmons (1985), Hellmayr & Conover (1948b), Higgins & Davies (1996), Malling Olsen & Larsson (1995), and Ridgway (1919) for more information.

Molt—CAS. PF incomplete-complete (Aug-2nd Sep in HY/SYs), PA1 limited-partial? (Jun-Jul in SYs), PS1 absent, PB2 incomplete?-complete (Aug-Jun in SY/TYs), PA2 partial-incomplete (Feb-May in TYs), PS2 limited-incomplete (Apr-May in TYs), DPB incomplete-complete (Jul-Mar in ASY/ATYs), DPA partial-incomplete (Jan-Mar in ATYs), DPS limited-incomplete? (Mar-Apr in ATYs). The PF usually occurs on non-breeding grounds, often commencing (body feathers) during southbound migration and suspending for northbound migration after 7-8 pp replaced. The DPB can start on or near breeding grounds or can occur completely on non-breeding grounds and can suspend for winter after 7-8 pp replaced. The PAs start on non-breeding grounds and (in breeding adults) can complete during migration. Replacement of pp occurs Dec/Feb-Mar/May during the PF, Sep/Nov-Apr/Jun during the PB2, and Aug/Oct-Jan/Mar during the DPB. The PF and DPB can occasionally be incomplete, with p10 and some medial ss (among s9-s15) retained. The extent of the PA1 is poorly known and may include (at most?) some head and body feathers. The PA2 apparently includes some to most body feathers, a few to some les and med covs, 2-7 inner pp and 5-17 inner and outer ss (Table 62, p. 692; Fig. 492**D**-**G**, p. 693), and 2-8 or more rects, and an apparent PS2 occasionally includes 1-2 inner pp again (Fig. 492**G**) and perhaps body and other feathers (more study needed). The DPA is similar to the PA2 but averages less extensive, often including 1-4 inner pp, 1-5 inner and outer ss, and 1-4 c. rects. See pp. 691-695 for more information.

Age—Juv (B1; Jul-Oct) has back feathers, terts, and rects with variable brown subterminal marks (Fig. 501**A**-**C**; *cf.* Fig. 500**B**-**C**, p. 704); Juv ♀=♂.

Juv-HY/SY (1st cycle, Juv/B1-F1-A1; Sep-Aug): Terts (*cf.* Fig. 500**B**-**C**) and/or rects (Fig. 501**A**-**C**) usually with variable dusky subterminal marks in Sep-Mar, the rects often without marks but washed grayish in Apr-Aug (Fig. 501**D**); pp and ss uniform in wear (Fig. 492**A**, p. 693), with p8-p10 relatively worn (Fig. 492**B**) and replaced primarily in Apr-Aug (the juv p10 and some medial ss sometimes retained; Fig. 492**B**), and without inner pp or ss replaced again and paler in Jan-Aug (Fig. 492**C**); cap dusky with heavy white streaks year-round (Fig. 507**A**, p. 721).

SY/TY (2nd cycle, B2-A2; Sep-Aug): Terts grayish, usually with dusky centers or bases (*cf.* Fig. 505**C**, p. 717) or sometimes uniformly pale in Jan-Aug (*cf.* Fig. 500**D**); rects sometimes grayish and without dusky marks in Sep-Apr (Fig. 501**D**); basic pp and ss showing molt clines and/or suspension limits (Fig. 492**C**), with p8-p10 relatively fresh and replaced primarily in Feb-May, 2-7 pp and 5-7 ss replaced again and fresher and paler in Feb-Aug (Fig. 492**D**-**G**), and with 1-2 pp occasionally replaced for a third time and fresher and paler in Apr-Aug (Fig. 492**G**); cap blackish with variable white streaks or spots to forecrown (cf Fig. 507**A**; occasionally all black in Apr-Jun). **Note: Occasional TYs that have cap uniformly black in Apr-**

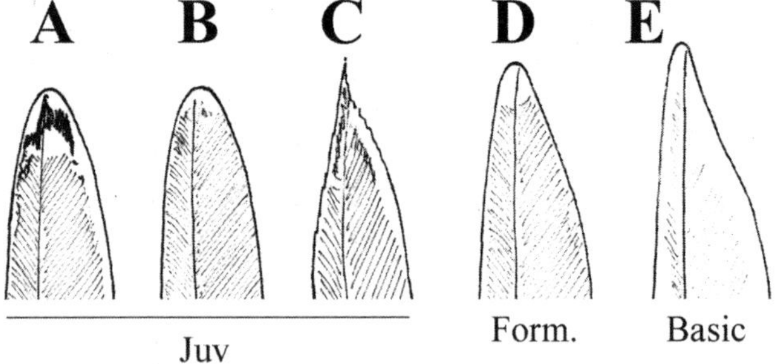

FIGURE 501. Shape and pattern to the outer rectrix (r6) by feather generation in Caspian Tern. Juv feathers on HY/SYs in Sep to Jan/May vary from showing strong dark subterminal marks (**A**) to less distinct marks (toward **B**), that can remain visible on worn feathers of SYs in May-Aug. Formative feathers (**D**) are washed grayish and some SYs may show similar second-basic rects in Sep-Apr (study needed). Both definitive basic and definitive alternate rects of ASY/ATYs have a silvery bloom and are more sinuate, as in **E**. Some ASY/ATYs in Sep-Mar may show outer rects resembling **D** so combine with other criteria for reliable ageing of SY/TYs.

Jun, may be aged by freshness of pp and extent of the PA2 and PS2 (see Molt), but some non-breeding ASY/ATYs may resemble SY/TYs in crown pattern and molt (needs study); some individuals are best aged AHY/ASY. Characters of SY/TYs and TY/4Ys may also overlap (see Common Tern, p. 713).

ASY/ATY (Def. cycle, DB-DA; Sep-Aug): Terts silvery gray, without dusky centers (*cf.* Fig. 505**C**); rects usually sinuate and silvery gray (Fig. 501**E**; some may resemble **D** in some birds in Sep-Mar); basic pp and ss showing molt clines and/or suspension limits (*cf.* Fig. 492**C**), with p8-p10 relatively fresh and replaced primarily in Dec-Feb, and with 1-4 inner pp and 1-5 inner and outer ss usually fresh and paler in Jan-Aug (Fig. 492**C-E**); cap white with dense black streaks in Sep-Feb (Fig. 507**A**); or completely black in Mar-Aug. **Note: See SY/TY. ATYs in Apr-Jul with a few white flecks in forecrown and adult-like wear and contrast in pp may be 4Ys or 5Ys (needs study).**

Sex—♀=♂ by plumage aspect. Bilateral BPs (Fig. 20**B**, p. 31) developed by both sexes but distended cloaca (Fig. 21, p. 32) indicates ATY ♀ in Apr-Jul. Measurements largely unhelpful for sexing (Table 65, p. 723); see Quinn (1990) for DFAs (p. 5) using bill depth and length, head-bill length (Fig. 453, p. 630), wing chord, and tarsus on live birds from a TX population, that separated 74-92% of the sexes. Otherwise, no criteria known for sexing.

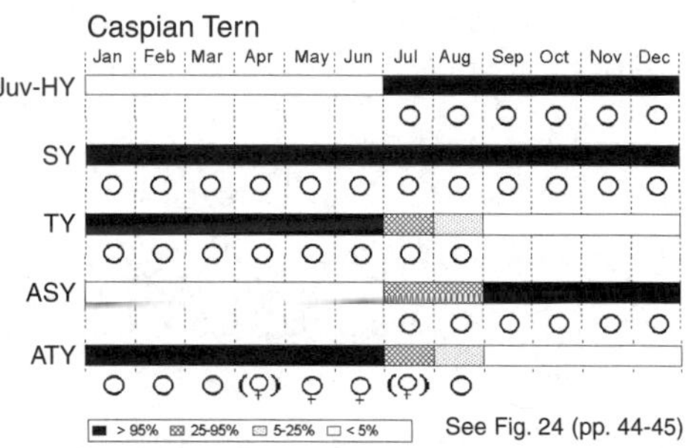

Hybrids reported—None.

References—Bent (1921), Cramp & Simmons (1985), Cuthbert & Wires (1999). Higgins & Davies (1996), Malling Olsen & Larsson (1995), Murphy (1936), Oberholser (1974), Quinn (1990), Ridgway (1919), Roberts (1955).

BLACK TERN
Chlidonias niger

BLTE
Species # 0770
Band size: 2-1A

Species—From other N.Am terns by small size (Table 63, p. 700); tail fork shallow (juv r6 – r1 11-17 mm and alternate r6 – r1 22-24 mm ASYs); upperparts dark smoky gray to blackish (Kodak 9-10 to basic aspect, 9.5-10.5 to alternate aspect, p. 629); outer pp, ss, and rects uniformly dusky to gray; legs dull brownish to dusky reddish; bill black (with paler orangish base in Juv). Molting adults from Juv Sooty Tern (p. 697) by much smaller measures (Table 63); back grayish, contrasting with blacker head; black feathers not tipped white; legs brownish to dusky reddish.

White-winged Black Tern (*C. leucopterus*), a vagrant to N.Am, has shallower tail fork (alternate r6 – r1 4-13 mm in ASYs); longer tarsus (17-21 mm); rects rounded and pale gray (formative/basic) to white (alternate) *vs* more pointed and darker gray in Black Tern; les and med covs paler than gr covs (*vs* concolorous in Black Tern); formative and basic plumage with underparts white, terts darker than back, and rump and uppertail covs paler than back (*vs* underparts pale gray and upperparts concolorous gray in Black Tern); alternate plumage with black underwings and back (Kodak 16-17) *vs* dark gray back and white underwings in Black Tern. See Alström (1989), Campbell (2000a, 2000b) for more information.

Geographic variation—See Adriaens (1999), Andrews et al. (2006), Cramp & Simmons (1985), Higgins & Davies (1996), McGeehan (2000), Ridgway (1919). One other subspecies occurs in Eurasia.

C.n. surinamensis (br throughout N.Am range; wint s.Mex-S.Am): From *niger* of Eurasia (a possible vagrant to N.Am) by slightly shorter wing (Table 63, p. 700; *vs* wg chord 203-224 in *niger*), sides and flanks with distinct dusky smudging in Sep-Mar (lacking in *niger*); head and underparts uniformly black in Apr-Aug (*vs* chest and belly sooty blackish gray, contrasting with blacker head in *niger*).

Molt—CAS. PF complete (Sep-Aug in HY/SYs), PA1 partial-incomplete (May-Aug? in SYs), PB2 complete (Jul-Apr? in SY/TYs), PA2 incomplete (Dec?-Apr? in SY/TY), DPS limited-incomplete? (Feb-Apr in ASYs), DPB complete (Jun-Mar in ASY/ATYs), DPA incomplete (Dec-Apr in ASY/ATYs). The PF occurs on non-breeding grounds and can be suspended in Jan-Feb; the DPB starts on or near breeding grounds (often with feathers of the head and p1-p4 replaced) and completes at stopover sites and/or on non-breeding grounds; and the PAs occur primarily on non-breeding grounds and often overlap with completion of the PF and PBs (*cf.* Fig. 492**B**, p. 693). Pp molt occurs Dec-May/Aug during the PF, Jul-Feb?/Apr? during the PB2, and Jun/Aug-Jan/Mar during the DPB. The PA1 includes some body feathers, sometimes 1-2 inner pp and outer ss, and often 2-8 rects. The PA2 and DPA usually include most to all body feathers, some to most les and med covs, 2-8 (often 4-5) inner pp and 4-10 inner and outer ss (Table 62, p. 692; Fig. 492**D**-**G**) and 2 to (occasionally) all rects. A DPS (primarily in TYs and 4Ys?) may include p1 (in nominate *niger*, at least; Cramp & Simmons 1985) and perhaps other feathers; more study needed. See pp. 691-695 for more information.

Age—Juv (B1; Jul-Oct) has back feathers, terts, and s covs with variable dark-brown to dark-rufous distal patches creating mottled aspect, brownish legs, and dull orange base to bill; Juv ♀ = ♂.

Juv-HY/SY (1st cycle, Juv/B1-F1-A1; Oct-Sep): Terts and s covs fringed brownish in Oct-Jan; juv pp and ss uniform in wear (Fig. 492**A**, p. 693), with p8-p10 relatively worn (Fig. 492**B**) and replaced primarily in May-Aug; 1-2 inner pp and 1-3 inner ss sometimes replaced again and fresher and paler in Jun-Aug (Fig. 492**C**-**D**); anterior les covs mottled slaty blackish in Oct-Jan (Fig. 492**A**) and dusky in Jan-Sep (Fig. 492**B**); underparts white, sometimes with scattered black feathers in May-Sep.

AHY/ASY (Def. cycle, DB-DA; Oct-Sep): Terts and s covs without brown fringing; basic pp and ss showing molt clines and/or suspension limits (*cf.* Fig. 492**C**; beware pseudolimit, p. 19, between p9 and p10), with p8-p10 relatively fresh and replaced primarily in Dec-Mar; 2-8 (often 4-5) inner pp and 4-10 inner and outer ss fresh and paler in Jan-Aug (Fig. 492**D**-**F**), and 1-3 inner pp sometimes replaced for a third time in Feb-Aug (Fig. 492**G**); anterior les covs gray, concolorous with rest of upperwing (Fig. 492**D**); underparts mostly to entirely black in Mar-Sep, sometimes mottled whitish in Jul-Sep. **Note: Some ASY/ATYs may be aged based on molt timing or by having entirely black plumage aspect in all or part of Mar-Sep but see SY/TY. More study is needed.**

SY/TY (2nd cycle, B2-A2; Oct-Sep): Like AHY/ASY but p8-p10 being replaced primarily in Jan-Apr; underparts black, variably mottled white in May-Sep. **Note: Many SY/TYs are probably not separable and are best aged AHY/ASY.**

Sex—♀ = ♂ by plumage aspect in N.Am populations (sexes differ in *C.n. niger*, with ♂ blacker than ♀ in alternate plumage). BP (Fig. 20, p. 31) may not develop (Dunn & Argo 1995; or look for bilateral BPs, Fig. 20**B**, in both sexes) but distended cloaca (Fig. 21, p. 32) indicates ASY ♀

in May-Jul. Measurements generally unhelpful for sexing (Table 63, p. 700) but see Stern & Jarvis (1991) and Shealer & Cleary (2007) for DFAs (p. 5), using head-bill (Fig. 453, p. 630), wg chord, exposed culmen, and tarsus lengths, that correctly sexed >80% of individuals in populations breeding in OR and WI respectively. Otherwise, no criteria known for sexing.

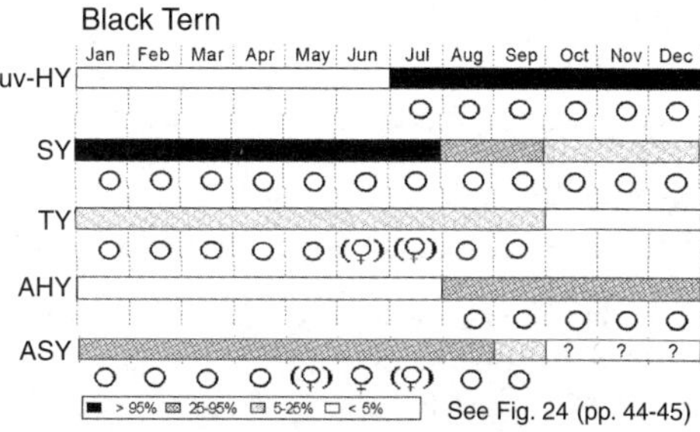

Hybrids reported—Both *C.n. surinamensis* and *niger* with White-winged Black Tern (Yank & Aubry 1985, McCarthy 2006).

References—Andrews et al. (2006), Baker (1993), Bent (1921), Dement'ev & Gladkov (1951c), Dunn & Argo (1995), Higgins & Davies (1996), Malling Olsen & Larsson (1995), Murphy (1936), Oberholser (1974), Ridgway (1919), Roberts (1955), Shealer & Cleary (2007), Tordoff (1962), Van der Winden (2002), van Rossem (1923), Walters (1987), Zenatello et al. (2002).

ROSEATE TERN

Sterna dougallii

ROST
Species # 0720
Band size: 2

Species—From other terns by small size with proportionally long and thin bill and long tarsus (Table 64, p. 713; Fig. 502**A**, p. 714); tail fork very deep (alternate r6 – r1 85-136 mm ASYs); outer pp with reduced black along shaft by age (Fig. 493**A-B**, p. 694), the undersides with white edge to inner web extending to tip (Fig. 504**A**, p. 717); r6 white with little or no dusky to outer web (Fig. 503**A-B**, p. 717); upperparts pale gray (Kodak 3.5-4.5, p. 629); Juv with crown and forehead mostly blackish (Fig. 502**A**) and medial ss white with gray mostly on outer web (Fig. 505**D**, p. 717); underparts of ASY white without smoky-gray wash in Mar-Aug; bill black (Fig. 502**A**, with variable red base in May-Jul); legs red.

Geographic variation—See Cramp & Simmons (1985), Gochfeld et al. (1998), Hellmayr & Conover (1948b), Higgins & Davies (1996), O'Neill et al. (2005), Tree & Klages (2003). Two other subspecies occur in Asia-Australia.

S.d. dougallii (br N.Am-Europe, wint S.Am-Africa). From *korustes* of Indian Ocean and *gracilis* of Australia by larger size (Table 64, p. 713; *vs* wg chord 200-218 in other subspecies) and longer bill (*vs* exp culmen 31-37 in *korustes*); bill blackish tinged red during breeding season (Mar-Aug) *vs* redder in other subspecies.

Molt—CAS. PF complete (Aug-Jul in HY/SYs), PA1 incomplete (Feb-May in SYs), PS1 limited-incomplete (Mar-Jun in SYs), PB2 complete (Jul-Apr? in SY/TYs), PA2 incomplete (Jan?-Apr? in TYs), PS2 limited-incomplete (Feb-May? in TYs), DPB complete (Jul-Mar? in ASY/ATYs), DPA incomplete (Jan?-Mar? in ATYs). DPS limited-incomplete? (Feb?-Apr? in ATYs). The PF usually occurs on non-breeding grounds, often commencing during migration; the DPB starts on or near breeding grounds, usually suspends for migration, and completes on non-breeding grounds; and the PAs start on non-breeding grounds (usually overlapping with the completion of the PF and PBs; *cf.* Fig. 492**B**, p. 693), and can complete during migration. Replacement of pp occurs Nov?-May/Jul during the PF, Jul-Jan?/Apr? during the PB2, and Jul-Dec?/Mar? during the DPB. The PA1 appears to include most body feathers, no to a few les covs, 1-7 inner pp and 1-10 inner and outer ss (Fig. 492**D-G**), and 2 to all(?) rects, and the

PS1 sometimes can include 1-3 inner pp and probably other feathers again (Fig. 492**G**). The PA2 and DPA usually include most to all body feathers, some to most les and med covs, 5-8 inner pp and 5-18 inner and outer ss (Table 62, p. 692; Fig. 492**F-H**), and the PS2 (and possibly the DPS or PS3) sometimes includes 1-4 inner pp, 1-4 inner and outer ss, and 1-2 c.rects again (Fig. 492**G-H**). See pp. 691-695 for more information.

Age—Juv (B1; Jul-Sep) has back feathers, s covs, and terts with highly variable brown subterminal marks (*cf.* Fig. 500**A**, p. 704) and r6 short and blunt (*cf.* Fig. 503**A**, p. 717); Juv ♀=♂.

Juv-HY/SY (1st cycle, Juv/B1-F1-A1; Sep-Aug): Terts and s covs fringed brownish in Sep-Dec; juv pp and ss uniform in wear (Fig. 492**A**, p. 693), with p8-p10 relatively worn (Fig. 492**B**), averaging more-extensively black (Fig. 493**B**, p. 694), and replaced primarily in Mar-Jun; 1-7 inner pp and 1-10 inner and outer ss replaced again and fresher and paler in Apr-Aug (Fig. 492**D-G**), and 1-3 inner pp sometimes replaced for a third time and fresher and paler in May-Aug (Fig. 492**G**); anterior les covs dark slaty in Sep-Mar (Fig. 492**A**) and slightly mottled dusky in Apr-Aug (Fig. 492**B**); cap and forecrown white, with limited black spotting in May-Aug.

AHY/ASY (Def. cycle, DB-DA; Sep-Aug): Terts and s covs without brown marks; basic pp and ss showing molt clines and/or suspension limits (Fig. 492**C**), with p8-p10 relatively fresh, averaging less-extensively black (Fig. 493**A-B**), and replaced primarily in Nov-Feb; 5-8 inner pp and 5-15 inner and outer ss replaced again and fresher and paler in Feb-Aug (Fig. 492**F-H**), and 1-4 pp and 1-4 ss occasionally replaced for a third time and fresher and paler in Apr-Aug (Fig. 492**G-H**); anterior les covs uniformly pale (Fig. 492**D**); cap and forecrown completely to mostly black in Mar-Aug, the forecrown becoming mottled whitish in Jul-Aug. **Note: See Juv-HY/SY and SY/TY.**

SY/TY (2nd cycle, B2-A2; Sep-Aug): Like AHY/ASY but anterior les covs often mottled dusky (Fig. 492**B**); p8-p10 replaced primarily in Dec-Mar; cap and forecrown sometimes with white-speckled foreheads (~35% of TYs show this). **Note: Many SY/TYs may not be reliably aged and should be aged ASY.**

Sex—♀=♂ by plumage aspect. Bilateral (and medial?) BPs (Fig. 20**C**, p. 31) developed by both sexes but distended cloaca (Fig. 21, p. 32) indicates ASY ♀ in May-Jul. Measurements unhelpful for sexing (Table 64). See Sabo et al. (1994) for sexing using genetic markers.

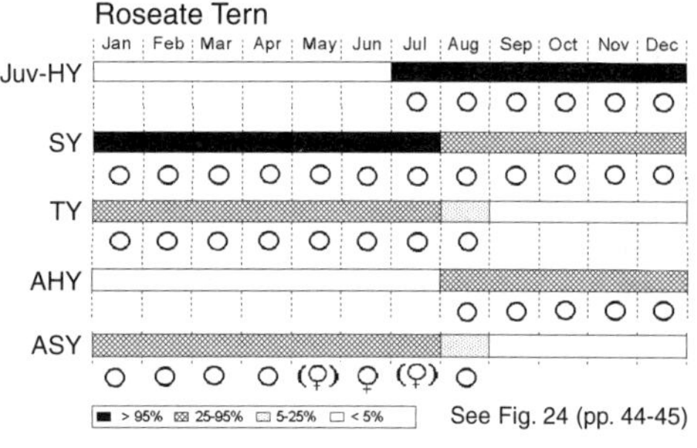

Hybrids reported—With Common Tern (Dennis & Harrop 1995, Hays 1975, McCarthy 2006) and Arctic Tern (Whittam 1998).

References—Bent (1921), Cormons (1976), Donaldson (1968), Gochfeld et al. (1998), Hays et al. (2006), Higgins & Davies (1996), Kaufman (1990a), Malling Olsen & Larsson (1995), Monticelli & Ramos (2007), Mullarney (1988), Murphy (1936), Oberholser (1974), O'Neill et al. (2005), Ridgway (1919), Stewart (1984), Tree & Klages (2003).

TABLE 64. Measurements (mm) of North American small to medium-sized terns to assist in identification and sexing. See pp. 4-11 for methods of measurement. Species summaries are in **bold**. Values were derived from 95% confidence intervals as based approximately on the indicated sample sizes (see pp. 4-5). Thus, midpoints of ranges approximate means, and S.D. is approximated by one-quarter of the range.

Taxon/Sex	*n*	wing chord[1]	tail length[2]	exp culmen	bill depth[3]	tarsus
Least Tern[4]		**156-177**	**37-45**	**23-31**	**6.3-8.1**	**13-17**
♀	100	156-173	37-44	23-30	6.3-7.9	13-16
♂	100	157-177	38-45	24-31	6.5-8.1	14-17
Gull-billed Tern[4]		**280-313**	**68-82**	**33-43**	**9.4-12.4**	**28-35**
♀	35	280-311	68-82	33-40	9.4-12.0	28-34
♂	55	285-313	73-84	36-43	10.1-12.4	29-35
Roseate Tern[4]		**216-241**	**53-69**	**35-42**	**6.7-8.9**	**19-21**
♀	100	216-241	53-65	35-41	6.7-8.7	19-21
♂	100	216-240	57-69	36-42	6.8-8.9	19-21
Common Tern[4]		**252-287**	**64-76**	**32-41**	**7.2-10.0**	**18-22**
♀	100	252-283	65-76	32-39	7.2-9.5	18-21
♂	100	252-281	64-75	34-41	7.6-10.0	18-22
Arctic Tern		**255-288**	**63-77**	**28-36**	**6.8-9.1**	**13-17**
♀	100	255-285	63-76	28-35	6.8-8.7	13-17
♂	100	257-288	65-77	29-36	7.2-9.1	14-17
Forster's Tern		**245-278**	**60-76**	**35-43**	**7.7-11.0**	**21-27**
♀	80	245-277	60-73	35-40	7.7-10.8	21-26
♂	90	246-278	62-76	37-43	9.0-11.0	22-27

[1] Wing chord averages ~5% shorter in Juv-HY/SY than in AHY/ASY.
[2] Tail measured to tip of central rectrix (r1; Fig. 5**C**, p. 8). See text and Figure 6**A** (p. 9) for measures of tail fork (r6–r1), which varies substantially with plumage and molt, due to variable length of r6.
[3] Bill depth measured at distal end of forehead feathering (see Fig. 8**A**, p. 10).
[4] N.Am population only. See **Geographic variation**.

COMMON TERN
Sterna hirundo

COTE
Species # 0700
Band size: 2

Species—From other terns by medium-small size with proportional bill and tarsus (Table 64, p. 713; Fig. 502**B**, p. 714); tail fork medium in depth (alternate r6 – r1 61-94 mm ASYs); outer pp with moderate black along shaft by age (Fig. 493**C-D**, p. 694), the undersides tipped broadly with dark (Fig. 504**B**, p. 717); r6 white with dark outer web (Fig. 503**C-D**, p. 717); upperparts in N.Am populations medium-pale gray (Kodak 4-5; see p. 629 and **Geographic variation**); Juv with crown dark and forehead mostly white (Fig. 502**B**) and medial ss with contrasting dark-slaty bases (Fig. 505**B**, p. 717); underparts of ASY washed grayish in Mar-Aug; bill with variable red base during Jan-Sep (Fig. 502**B**; rarely completely red in Apr-Jun and often completely black in Oct-Dec); legs red. See Craik & Harvey (1984) for distinguishing chicks of Common and Arctic (p. 716) terns.

Geographic variation—See Cramp & Simmons (1985), Dement'ev & Gladkov (1951c), Higgins & Davies (1996), Ridgway (1919). One other subspecies occurs in Asia.

S.h. hirundo (br throughout N.Am range, wint Mexico to S.Am): Averages shorter winged (Table 64, p. 713); bill proportionally tapered (Fig. 502**B**; depth at distal end of forehead feathers 7.2-10.0, depth at gonys 5.4-8.0) and red with black tip in Mar-Aug ASYs; upperparts (Kodak 4-5, p. 629) and underparts of AHY in Mar-Aug (Kodak 2-3) paler gray; tail fork may average shorter (alternate r6 – r1 61-94 in ASYs).

S.h. longipennis (br and wint e.Asia, vagrant to w AK): Averages longer winged (chord 261-287); bill less tapered (depth at distal end of forehead feathers 6.8-7.4, depth at gonys 7.4-8.4) and black in Mar-Aug ASYs; upperparts (Kodak 5-6) and underparts of AHY in Mar-Aug (Kodak 3-4) darker gray; tail fork may average longer (alternate r6 – r1 68-100 in ASYs).

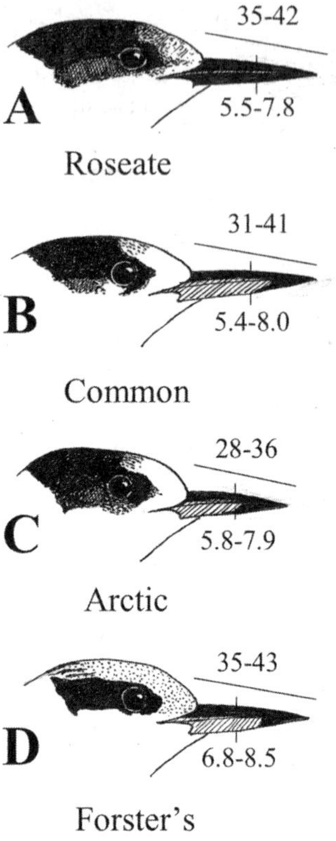

FIGURE 502. Typical head and bill patterns of Juv Roseate (**A**), Common (**B**), Arctic (**C**), and Forster's (**D**) terns. Note that Common Tern has extensive pale flesh at the mandible base and often a whitish area below the eyes, whereas Arctic Tern has limited pale flesh to the mandible base and extensive black in front of and below the eyes. Formative and basic plumage aspects of each species show similar patterns except that Roseate has an extensively white forehead, and the bills of all species are mostly to wholly black in winter.

Molt—CAS. PF complete (Nov-Aug in HY/SYs), PA1 partial-incomplete (May-Aug in SYs), PS1 absent, PB2 complete (Jul-May in SY/TYs), PA2 incomplete (Jan-May in TYs), PS2 limited-incomplete (Feb?-Apr in TYs), DPB complete (Jul-Mar in ASY/ATYs), DPA incomplete (Dec-May in ASY/ATYs), DPS limited-incomplete (Feb?-Mar? in ATYs). See Figure 11**G** (p. 17). The PF usually occurs on non-breeding grounds, rarely commencing during migration, and sometimes suspends in Feb-Apr; the PB2 and DPB start on breeding grounds or at stopover sites, suspend for migration (often after 1-4 inner pp replaced), and complete on non-breeding grounds; the PAs start on non-breeding ground (usually overlapping with the completion of the PF and PBs; *cf.* Fig. 492**B**, p. 693), and can complete during migration. Replacement of pp occurs Jan/Feb-May/Aug during the PF, Jul-Feb/May during the PB2, and Jul-Jan/Mar during the DPB. The PA1 includes a few to some body feathers, often 1-3 inner pp and 1-3 inner ss (Fig. 492**D**-**E**), and sometimes 1-2 c.rects. The PA2 and DPA usually include most to all body feathers, most les and med covs, 3-7 (often 4-6) inner pp and 5-13 inner and outer ss (Table 62, p. 692; Fig. 492**E**-**G**), and most to all rects (r4 and/or r5 occasionally retained). The PS2 often includes 1-5 inner pp and 1-4 inner and outer ss (Fig. 492**G**-**H**) and 1-2 c.rects, and the DPS occasionally includes at least p1 again (perhaps more likely in non-breeding T-5Ys); more study needed on replacement of body feathers and s covs during the PS in terns. See pp. 691-695 for more information.

Age—Juv (B1; Jul-Sep) has back feathers, s covs, and terts with variable brown subterminal marks (*cf.* Fig. 500**A-B**, p. 704) and r5-r6 short and blunt (Fig. 503**C**, p. 717); Juv ♀=♂. In addition to the following, see Haussmann et al. (2003) for information on ageing by length of chromosomal telomere fragments.

Juv-HY/SY (1st cycle, Juv/B1-F1-A1; Sep-Aug): Terts and s covs with brown marks in Sep-Oct (*cf.* Fig. 500**A-B**); juv pp and ss uniform in wear (Fig. 492**A**, p. 693), with p8-p10 relatively worn (Fig. 492**B**), averaging more-extensively black (Fig. 493**D**, p. 694), and replaced primarily in Apr-Aug; 1-3 inner pp and 1-3 inner ss often replaced again and fresher and paler in Mar-Aug (Fig. 492**C-E**); anterior les covs mottled slaty blackish (Fig. 492**A**); cap and forecrown white, with limited black spotting and outer rects shorter (alternate r6 – r1 usually < 70 mm) in May-Aug; bill black (usually with whitish tip by Dec), becoming dull reddish basally in Mar-Aug (Fig. 502**B**).

SY/TY (B2-B3/A2-A3; Sep-Aug): Terts and s covs without brown marks (*cf.* Fig. 500**D**); basic pp and ss showing molt clines and/or suspension limits (Fig. 492**C**), with p8-p10 relatively fresh, averaging less-extensively black (Fig. 493**C-D**), and replaced primarily in Jan-Apr; 3-7 pp and 5-13 ss replaced again and fresher and paler in Feb-Aug (Fig. 492**E-G**), and 1-5 pp and 1-4 inner and outer ss usually replaced for a third time and fresher and paler in Apr-Aug (Fig. 492**F-G**); anterior les covs mottled dusky in Sep-Mar (Fig. 492**B**) and sometimes slightly in Mar-Aug (Fig. 492**C**); cap and forecrown mostly to entirely black (about 35% of TYs have white-speckled foreheads), and outer rects average longer (alternate r6 – r1 usually > 65 mm) in Mar-Aug; bill black (occasionally with dull reddish at base) in Sep-Apr, to red with black tip in Apr-Oct (*cf.* Fig. 502**B**). **Note: Some retarded TY/4Ys can show characters overlapping advanced SY/TYs (White & Kehoe 2001) but these usually show little to no dark in the les covs, less white (usually none) on the crown, and a longer r6 in Mar-Aug; age these S-TY or T-4Y (pp. 41-42) if unsure. More study is needed on predefinitive plumages of Common and other terns.**

ASY/ATY (Def. cycle, DB-DA; Sep-Aug): Basic pp and ss showing molt clines and/or suspension limits (Fig. 492**C**) and replaced primarily in Dec-Mar; 3-7 pp and 5-13 ss replaced again and fresher and paler in Feb-Aug (Fig. 492**D-G**), and p1 occasionally replaced for a third time and fresher and paler in Apr-Aug (Fig. 492**F**); anterior les covs uniformly gray (Fig. 492**D**) and cap and forecrown entirely black (the forecrown often mottled white in Jul-Aug) in Mar-Aug; bill black with dull reddish at base in Sep-Apr, to bright red with black tip in Apr-Oct. **Note: See SY/TY.**

Sex—♀=♂ by plumage aspect. Bilateral and medial BPs (Fig. 20**C**, p. 31) developed by both sexes but distended cloaca (Fig. 21, p. 32) indicates ASY ♀ in Apr-Jun. See Coulter (1986), Craik (1999), and Nisbet et al. (2007) for DFAs (p. 5) using head-bill length (Fig. 453, p. 630), exposed culmen, bill depth (at distal end of forehead feathers), bill width, and mass, that correctly sexed 72-80% of adults in N.Am & European breeding colonies. See also Fletcher & Hamer (2003) for sexing mated pairs using measurements. Otherwise, measurements largely unhelpful for sexing single birds (Table 64, p. 713), although head-bill length (Fig. 453) should be investigated on live birds; Craik (1999) found it to be 78-79 mm in ♀♀ and 77-83 mm in ♂♂ of a European population. No other criteria known for sexing.

Hybrids reported—With Roseate (p. 711) and Little (*S. albifrons*) and Forster's (McCarthy 2006), terns. Has paired with Arctic Tern (McCarthy 2006).

References—Baker (1993), Bent (1921), Braune (1987b), Bridge & Nisbet (2004), Coulter (1986), Craik (1994, 1998, 1999), Cramp & Simmons (1985), Dement'ev & Gladkov (1951c),

Dwight (1901), Fletcher & Hamer (2003), Higgins & Davies (1996), Kaufman (1990a), Koopman (1996), Malling Olsen & Larsson (1995), Meissner & Krupa (2007), Murphy (1936), Nisbet (2002), Nisbet et al. (2007), Oberholser (1974), Palmer (1941), Ridgway (1919), Roberts (1955), Ullman (1989), Walters (1985, 1987), Ward (2000, 2002), Ward et al. (2004). White & Kehoe (2001), Wilds (1993).

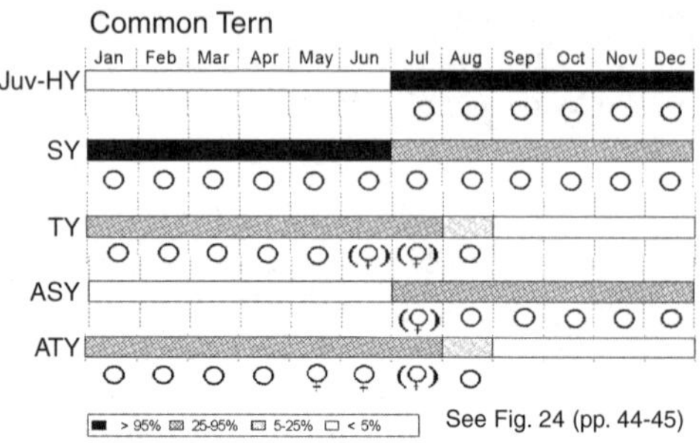

ARCTIC TERN

Sterna paradisaea

ARTE
Species # 0710
Band size: 2-1A

Species—From other terns by medium-small size with proportionally short bill and very short tarsus (Table 64, p. 713; Fig. 502**C**, p. 714); tail fork deep (alternate r6 – r1 72-133 mm in ASYs); outer pp average moderately less-extensively and with less distinct black along shaft (Fig. 493**C**, p. 694), the undersides of p7-p10 tipped narrowly with dark (Fig. 504**C**); r6 white with dark outer web (Fig. 503**C-D**); upperparts pale gray (Kodak 3.5-4.5; p. 629); Juv with crown dark and forehead mostly white (Fig. 502**C**) and medial ss mostly pale (Fig. 505**E**); underparts of ASY washed smoky gray in Mar-Aug; bill with variable red base during Jan-Sep (Fig. 502**C**; often completely red in Apr-Jun and sometimes completely black in Oct-Dec); legs red. See Craik & Harvey (1984) for distinguishing chicks of Arctic and Common (p. 713) terns.

Geographic variation—Monotypic.

Molt—CAS. PF complete (Oct-May in HY/SYs), PA1 limited-partial? (Mar?-May? in SYs), PB2 complete (Oct-Mar in SY/TYs), PA2 partial-incomplete (Feb-Mar in TYs), DPB complete (Oct-Mar in ASY/ATYs), DPA incomplete (Jan-Mar in ATYs); DPS absent. Most to all molting occurs on non-breeding grounds; PBs sometimes start (head feathers and sometimes outer rects during the PB2) during southbound migration, and DPAs can overlap with the completion of the DPBs (*cf.* Fig. 492**B**, p. 693). Replacement of pp occurs Jan-Mar/May during the PF and Dec-Mar during the DPB. The PA1 may occasionally include 1-2 inner pp, r1, and some head and body feathers but confirmation needed. The PA2 and DPA include a few to some body feathers, sometimes some les covs, occasionally 1-3 inner pp and 1-5 inner and outer ss (Table 62, p. 692; Fig. 492**C-E**), as well as some to all rects (although replacement of r4-r5 and possibly other rects may represent termination of PBs rather than PAs). See pp. 691-695 for more information.

Age—Juv (B1; Jul-Sep) has back feathers and terts with variable brown subterminal marks (*cf.* Fig. 500**A-B**, p. 704) and r5-r6 short and blunt (Fig. 502**C**, p. 714); Juv ♀ = ♂.

Juv-HY/SY (1st cycle, Juv/B1-F1-A1; Oct-Sep): Terts and s covs with brown marks in Oct-Nov (*cf.* Fig. 500**A-B**); juv pp and ss uniform in wear (Fig. 492**A**, p. 693), with p8-p10 relatively worn (Fig. 492**B**), averaging more-extensively black (dark 32-47 from tip; see also Fig. 493**D**, p. 694), and replaced primarily in Mar-May; pp or ss usually not replaced again and paler in Mar-Aug (Fig. 492**C**); anterior les covs mottled dusky (Fig. 492**A**); cap and forecrown white (often with limited black spotting), outer rects shorter (alternate r6 – r1 usually 65-75 mm), and underparts white or with a few smoky-gray patches in May-Sep; bill black (usually with fine whitish tip by Dec), with dull reddish basally in Mar-Aug (Fig. 502**C**, p. 714).

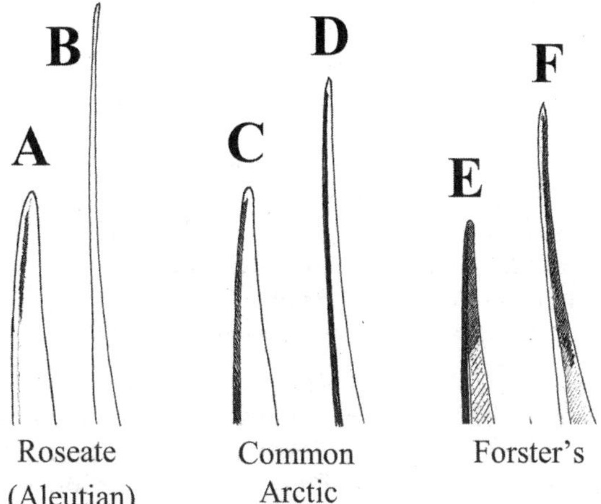

FIGURE 503. Typical patterns to the outer rectrix (r6) in Aleutian and Roseate terns (**A-B**), Common and Arctic terns (**C-D**), and Forster's Tern (**E-F**). In each case the feather to the left indicates juv, formative, 1st alternate, and/or some definitive basic rects and that to the right indicates definitive alternate (and sometimes some definitive basic) rects. The shape, length, and color pattern of the outer rectrix can vary substantially according to both feather generation and variable timing of replacement

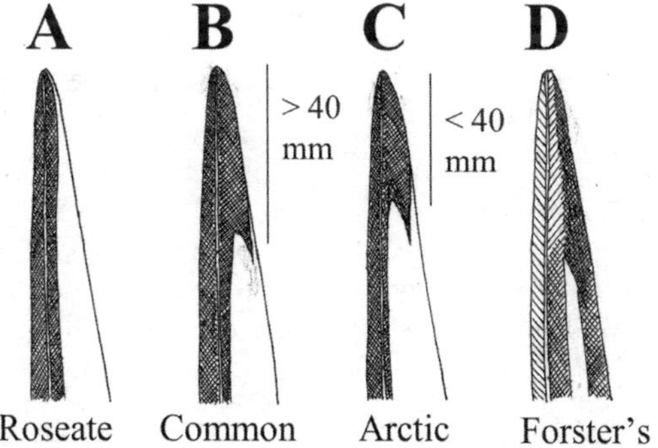

FIGURE 504. Typical pattern to the undersides of the outer primaries (p7-p10) in ASY/ATY Roseate, Common, Arctic, and Forster's terns, here showing p9. The measure is from the distal tip of the white tongue to the tip of the feather. Patterns on HY/SYs (and sometimes SY/TYs) are similar but the extent of black averages broader (see text and Fig. 493, p. 694). Patterns of Aleutian, Gray-backed, and Gull-billed terns resemble **D** and that of Least Tern varies from **A-B** (AHY/ASY) to **D** (HY/SY).

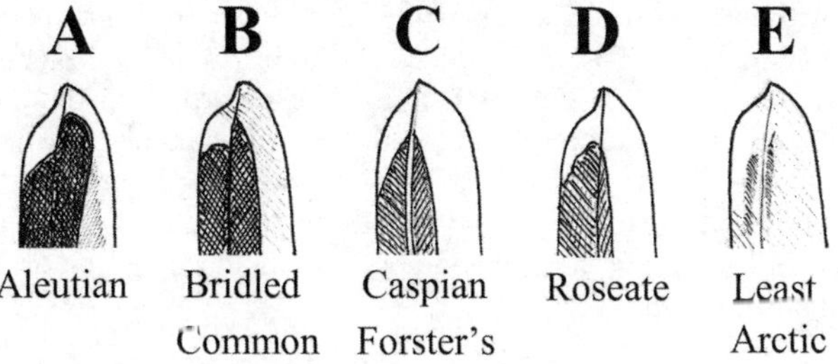

FIGURE 505. Typical patterns to the juvenal medial secondaries (~s6-s14) in terns by species. Note that formative and basic ss are often contrastingly pale at first but can approach these darker color patterns, as they become worn.

AHY/ASY (Def. cycle, DB-DA; Oct-Sep): Terts and s covs without brown marks (*cf.* Fig. 500**D**); basic pp and ss showing molt clines and/or suspension limits (*cf.* Fig. 492**C**), with p8-p10 relatively fresh, averaging less-extensively black (dark 27-32 mm from tip; see also Fig. 493**C**); 1-3 inner pp and 1-5 inner and outer ss occasionally fresh and paler in Feb-Aug (Fig. 492**C-E**); anterior les covs uniformly pale gray (Fig. 492**D**), sometimes mottled dusky in Sep-Mar (Fig. 492**C**; SY/TYs only?); cap and forecrown completely black, outer rects longer (basic r6 – r1 usually > 75 mm), and underparts completely smoky gray in Mar-Sep; bill black with dull reddish at base in Sep-Apr, to bright red in Apr-Oct (*cf.* Fig. 502**C**). **Note: Birds in Mar-Aug with some white mottling or brownish on forehead, traces of dark mottling on anterior les covs, darker bills and legs, and 1-3 inner pp replaced may be reliably aged TY but more study is needed (see also Common Tern, p. 713).**

Sex—♀=♂ by plumage aspect. Bilateral and medial BPs (Fig. 20**C,** p. 31) developed by both sexes but distended cloaca (Fig. 21, p. 32) indicates ASY ♀ in May-Jul. Measurements generally unhelpful for sexing (Table 64, p. 713), but see Craik (1999), Devlin et al. (2004), and Diamond & Saunders (2004) for DFAs (p. 5), using head-bill length (Fig. 453, p. 630) and bill depth at gonys, that separated 90% of breeding mated pairs in N.Am and Europe, and Fletcher & Hamer (2003) for more information on sexing mated pairs using measurements. Craik (1999) reported that head-bill length (Fig. 453) was 66-72 mm in ♀♀ and 69-77 mm in ♂♂ in a European population. Otherwise, no criteria are known for sexing.

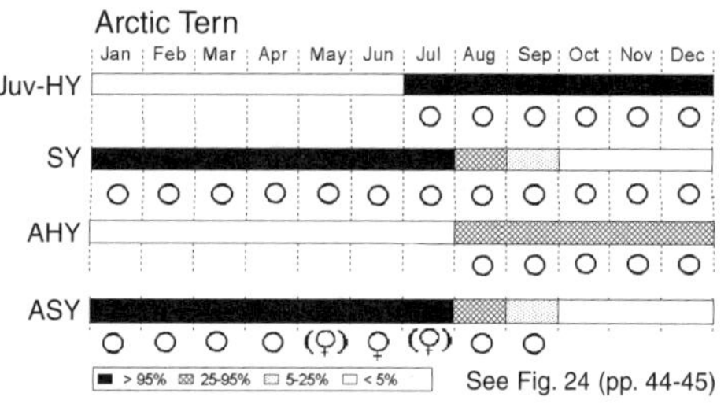

Hybrids reported—With Roseate (p. 711) and Forster's (Terrill et al. 2000) terns. See also Common Tern (p. 713).

References—Baker (1993), Bent (1921), Craik (1998, 1999), Cramp & Simmons (1985), Cullen (1957), Dement'ev & Gladkov (1951c), Fletcher & Hamer (2003), Hatch (2003), Higgins & Davies (1996), Kaufman (1990a), Malling Olsen & Larsson (1995), Manning et al. (1956), Murphy (1936), Ridgway (1919), Stone (1900), Ullman (1989), Voelker (1997).

FORSTER'S TERN
Sterna forsteri

FOTE
Species # 0690
Band size: 3

Species—From other terns by medium-small size with proportionally stout bill and very long tarsus (Table 64, p. 713; Fig. 502**D**, p. 714); tail fork medium in depth (basic r6 – r1 60-83 mm in AHYs); outer pp with more extensive silvery white bloom when fresh and moderate black along shaft by age (Fig. 493**C-D**, p. 694), the undersides with broad dusky tips (Fig. 504**D**, p. 717); r6 grayish with extensive dusky tip (Fig. 503**E-F**, p. 717); upperparts medium-pale gray (Kodak 4-5.5; see p. 629); with crown and forehead mostly pale and auricular mask black in Oct-Mar (Fig. 502**D**); Juv with medial ss grayish (Fig. 505**C**, p. 717); underparts of ASY white in Mar-Aug; bill with extensive orange to orange-red base during Jan-Sep (Fig. 502**D**; often completely black in Oct-Dec); legs orange-red. In addition, pp molt occurs primarily in N.Am *vs.* primarily S of N.Am in similar species.

Geographic variation—Monotypic, following AOU (1957). Populations breeding in coastal e.N.Am ("*S.f. litoricola*") may average smaller and with paler upperparts but differences insufficient for subspecific recognition. See Browning (1990), Hellmayr & Conover (1948b), McNicholl et al. (2001), Oberholser (1938, 1974), and Patten et al. (2003) for more information.

Molt—SAS (CAS?). PF absent(?), PA1 partial-incomplete (Aug-Nov/Apr in HY/SYs), PB2 complete (Mar-Sep in SYs), PA2 incomplete (Sep-Apr in SY/TYs), DPB complete (Jul-Nov in ASYs), DPA incomplete (Sep-Apr in ASY/ATYs); DPS absent. The single inserted first-cycle molt appears to be homologous with a PA1 rather than a PF (Fig. 10**E**, p. 14), although a few body feathers may be replaced twice, indicating the presence of both molts (and CAS; Fig. 10**F**-**G**); study needed. The PA1 can occur on breeding or non-breeding grounds, the DPB starts on or near breeding grounds, can suspend for migration, and completes on migration or non-breeding grounds, and the DPAs start on non-breeding grounds and can complete during migration; the PA2 can overlap with end of PB2 (*cf.*, Fig. 492**B**, p. 693). Replacement of pp occurs Mar/May-Sep during the PB2, and Jun/Aug-Sep/Nov during the DPB. The PA1 primarily includes head and back feathers, occasionally 1-2 terts, and sometimes 1-8 rects (often r1-r2 and r6). The PA2 includes some to most body feathers, a few to some les and med covs, usually 1-7 inner pp and 1-8 inner and outer ss (Table 62, p. 692; Fig. 492**C**-**G**), replaced primarily in Sep-Nov. The DPA is similar but 1-4 pp and 1-4 ss only sometimes replaced (Fig. 492**C**-**E**), and 1-8 rects usually replaced. See pp. 691-695 for more information.

Age—Juv (B1; Jul-Sep) crown and back variably washed cinnamon-brown, and rects (especially r6) relatively short and broad (Fig. 503**E**, p. 717); Juv ♀=♂.

Juv-HY/SY (1st cycle, Juv/B1-A1; Sep-Aug): Some to most back feathers and scapulars washed brown in Sep-Oct; one or more terts extensively dark, often worn and blackish (Fig. 506**A**-**B**); s covs and terts often mixed with worn juv and fresher formative feathers in Sep-May (*cf.* Fig. 13**C**-**D**, p. 20); pp and ss juv and uniform in wear (Fig. 492**A**, p. 693), with p8-p10 relatively worn (*cf.* Fig. 492**B**), averaging more-extensively black (Fig. 493**D**, p. 694), and without pp and ss replaced again and paler in Nov-Aug (Fig. 492**A**); anterior les covs mottled dusky (Fig. 492**B**); crown white or with limited dusky spotting in Mar-Aug; bill black, with variably dull orange-red base in Apr-Aug (Fig. 502**D**, p. 714); legs dusky to dull orange-red

SY/TY (2nd cycle, B2-A2; Sep-Aug): Back feathers and scapulars without brown wash; terts pale gray, with dusky basal area when worn (Fig. 506**C**-**D**); pp and ss showing molt clines and suspension limits (Fig. 492**C**), the basic p8-p10 relatively fresh, averaging less-extensively black (Fig. 493**C**-**D**), and replaced primarily in Mar-Aug; 1-7 inner pp and 1-8 inner and outer ss usually replaced, fresh and paler in Nov-Aug (Fig. 492**C**-**G**); anterior les covs often mottled dusky in Sep-Mar (Fig. 492**C**); crown black with variable white spotting to forehead in Apr-Aug; bill mostly black with limited dull orange at base, often orange-red with large black tip in Apr-Aug (*cf.* Fig. 502**D**); legs

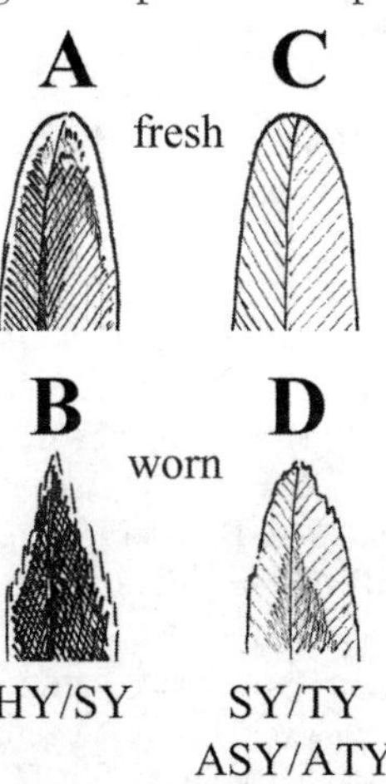

FIGURE 506. Variation in tertial pattern by age and season in Forster's Tern. Note that feathers are paler in Oct-Apr but get darker with wear through May-Aug. Most HY/SYs retain terts during the PA1 but some can replace 1-2 feathers, which appear contrastingly pale (as in **C**) in Apr-Aug. In AHY/ASYs, both basic and alternate terts resemble **C** when fresh and **D** when worn. Similar patterns may be found in other terns.

orange to orange-red. **Note: Characters of SY/TYs and TY/4Ys may overlap (see Common Tern, p. 713).**

ASY/ATY (Def. cycle, DB-DA; Sep-Aug): Basic pp and ss showing molt clines and/or suspension limits (*cf.* Fig. 492**C**), with p8-p10 relatively fresh and replaced primarily in Jul-Oct; 1-4 inner pp and 1-4 inner and outer ss sometimes fresh and paler in Jan-Aug (Fig. 492**C-E**); anterior les covs without dusky mottling (Fig. 492**D**); crown completely black in Apr-Aug (forehead sometimes flecked white in Jul-Aug); bill blackish with dull orange at base in Aug-Mar, or bright orange-red with narrow black tip in Mar-Aug; legs bright orange to orange-red.

Sex—♀=♂ by plumage aspect. Bilateral(?) BPs (Fig. 20**B**, p. 31) developed by both sexes but distended cloaca (Fig. 21, p. 32) indicates ASY ♀ in May-Jul. Measurements largely unhelpful for sexing (Table 64, p. 713), but see Bluso et al. (2006) for a DFA (p. 5) using head-bill length (Fig. 453, p. 630) and bill depth at gonys that accurately sexed 82-87% of freshly dead individuals from a c.CA population.

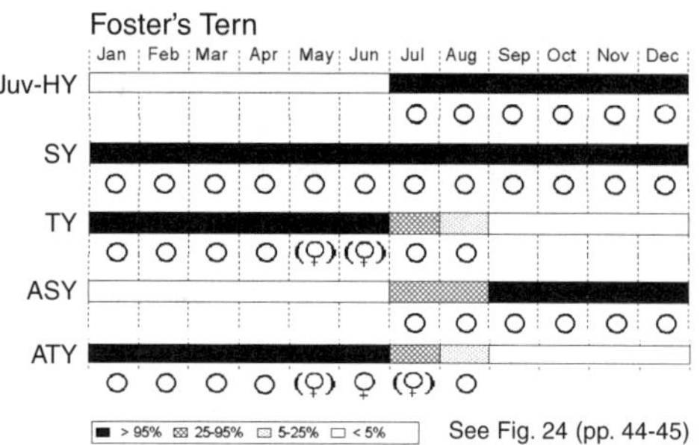

Hybrids reported—With Gull-billed (p. 706), Common (p. 713), and Arctic (p. 716) tern.

References—Bent (1921), Cramp & Simmons (1985), Malling Olsen & Larsson (1995), McNicholl et al. (2001), Oberholser (1974), Ridgway (1919), Roberts (1955), Wilds (1993).

ROYAL TERN
Thalasseus maximus

ROYT
Species # 0650
Band size: 4A

Species—From other terns by medium-large size with proportionally long tail (to r1) and long and thin bill (Table 65, p. 723; Fig. 507**B**); tail fork medium in depth (basic r6 – r1 53-89 mm and alternate r6 – r1 80-114 mm in AHY/ASYs); outer pp with extensive black along shaft by age (Fig. 493**D-E**, p. 694), the undersides with white edge to inner web extending to or near tip (*cf.* Fig. 504**A-B**, p. 717); forehead extensively white in all but definitive alternate plumage (Fig. 507**B**); r5-r6 white or with variable black or dusky markings distally (Fig. 509, p. 722); upperparts pale gray (Kodak 3.5-4.5, p. 629); juv ss with dusky centers (*cf.* Fig. 505**C**, p. 717); bill orange, without black marks; legs black or with yellow-orange patches in many Juv-HY/SY (s and some ASYs. From Elegant Tern (p. 725) further by longer wing, tail (to r1), and tarsus, and deeper bill (Table 65, Fig. 507**B**); crown with increased pale in most plumages (Fig. 507**B**); upperparts slightly paler (Kodak 3.5-4.5); PAs average less extensive (Table 62, p. 692). See Elegant Tern for separation from Lesser Crested Tern.

Geographic variation—See Cramp & Simmons (1985), Escalante (1985), Ridgway (1919). One other subspecies occurs in sw.Europe-nw.Africa (populations of se.S.Am also possibly referable to this subspecies).

S.m. maxima (br and wint throughout N.Am range): From *albididorsalis* of Europe and Africa by longer wing and proportionally shorter and thicker bill (Table 65, p. 723, bill depth at gonys 11.9-14.4; *vs* wg chord 335-355, exp culmen 62-70, and bill depth at gonys 11.0-13.2 in *albididorsalis*); bill orange (*vs* yellow-orange to yellowish in *albididorsalis*). Within N.Am, w.populations average slightly longer wing than e.populations (Ridgway 1919, Cramp & Simmons 1985) but no other differences evident.

Molt—CAS. PF incomplete-complete (Aug-2nd Aug in HY/SYs), PA1 partial (Apr-May in SYs), PB2 complete (Aug-Jul in SY/TYs), PA2 incomplete (Feb-Apr in TYs), DPB complete (May-Feb in ASY/ATYs), DPA incomplete (Nov-Feb in ASY/ATYs); DPS absent(?). The PF usually occurs on non-breeding grounds, often commencing during southbound migration and suspending for winter or northbound migration after 1-4 inner pp and 2-10 rects replaced; the PB2 and DPB can start on or near breeding grounds, usually suspend for migration (often after 3-5 pp have been replaced), and complete on non-breeding grounds; and the PAs start on non-breeding grounds, can complete during migration in breeding individuals, and usually overlap with the completion of the PF and PBs (Fig. 492**B**, p. 693). Replacement of pp occurs Oct/Feb-May/Aug during the PF, Aug/Oct-Feb/Jul during the PB2, and Jun/Aug-Nov/Feb during the DPB. The PF can be incomplete, with 1-3 outer pp and 1-9 medial ss (among s7-s15) sometimes retained. The PA1 includes some body feathers, possibly a few les covs, and occasionally r1 but few if any pp or ss (Fig. 492**A**). The PA2 and DPA usually include most to all body feathers, some les and med covs, 2-6 inner pp and usually 1-8 inner and outer ss (Fig. 492**D**-**F**), and most to all rects. A DPS of 1-2 inner pp (and possibly other feathers?) may occur in some ASYs, perhaps most likely in TYs. See pp. 691-695 for more information.

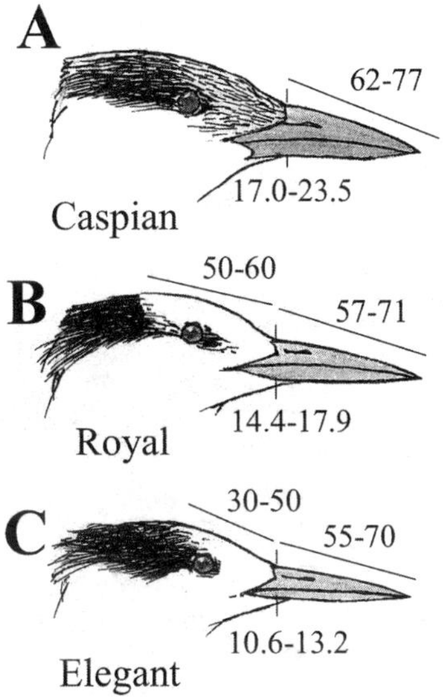

FIGURE 507. Head patterns in basic plumage aspect and relative bill size and pattern in Caspian, Royal, and Elegant terns. Measures include extent of white forehead (to point where black > white), (Fig. 8**A**, p. 10), exposed culmen (Fig. 7**A**, p. 9), and bill depth at tip of forehead feathers. Aspect shown occurs in all plumages except for definitive alternate, displayed in ASYs prior to breeding and during incubation, at which time the crown and forehead are entirely glossy black. Note that in formative, first-alternate, and basic plumage aspects Caspian Tern (**A**) has a dusky streaked forehead, Royal Tern has a white forehead that typically extends well behind the eye, and Elegant Tern has a white forhead that typically extends only moderately behind the eye.

Age—Juv (B1; Jul-Sep) has back feathers fringed brown, terts and gr covs with extensively dark bases (Figs. 506**A**, p. 719, & 508**A**, p. 722), anterior les covs washed dusky (Fig. 492**B**, p. 693), and rects extensively dark (Fig. 509**A**, p. 722); Juv ♀=♂. See Buckley & Buckley (1970) for variation in downy chicks.

Juv-HY/SY (1st cycle, Juv/B1-F1-A1; Aug-Jul): One or more terts and/or gr covs with extensively dark bases in Aug-May or later (Figs. 506**A** & 508**A**); r4-r6 extensively dark at bases in Aug-Dec (Fig. 509**A**), or short and with broad subterminal dusky areas in Jan-Jul (Fig. 509**B**); juv pp and ss uniform in wear (Fig. 492**A**), with p8-p10 relatively worn (Fig. 492**B**), averaging more-extensively black (Fig. 493**E**, p. 694), and replaced primarily in Mar-Aug or sometimes retained (*cf.* Fig. 492**B**); inner pp or ss not replaced and paler in Mar-Aug (Fig. 492**C**); marginal les covs washed dusky (Fig. 492**B**); cap and forecrown extensively white with sparse black streaks in Feb-Jul (Fig. 507**B**).

AHY/ASY (Def. cycle, DB-DA; Aug-Jul): Terts with reduced dusky on inner web at base (*cf.* Fig. 506**D**); gr covs uniformly pale gray (Fig. 508**B**); r4-r6 white with variable dusky gray in Aug-Dec (Fig. 509**B**) or elongated and mostly to entirely whitish in Dec-Jul (Fig. 509**C**);

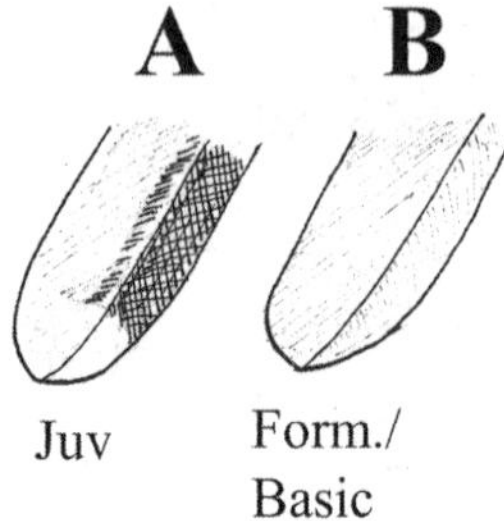

FIGURE 508. Patterns to the greater coverts by feather generation in Royal, Elegant, and Sandwich terns. Juv covs (**A**) are usually replaced during the preformative molt, but all juv covs have not typically been replaced until spring or summer in SYs (*cf.* Fig. 492**B**, p. 693). Completely gray covs (**B**) represent ASY/4TYs until at least Jan-Feb (more study needed); beware some basic ss may become darker with wear, but not as dark as juv covs.

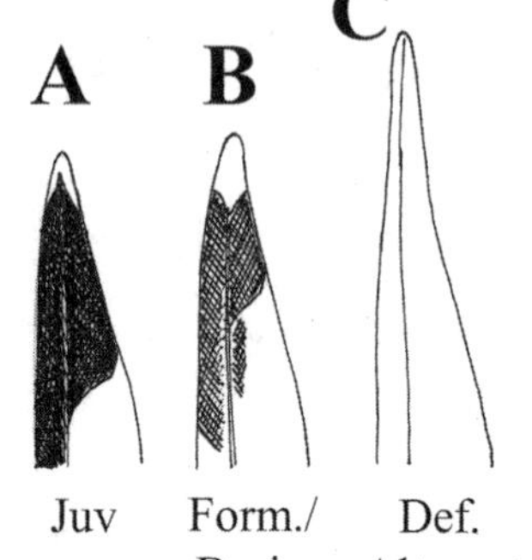

FIGURE 509. Typical patterns to the outer rectrix (r6) by feather generation in Royal, Sandwich, and Elegant terns, here showing r5. Juv feathers (**A**) are typically retained until Jan-May, at which time they are replaced by formative feathers (**B**). Basic feathers (and perhaps some 2nd alternate feathers in SYs) resemble **B**, whereas **C** is typical of definitive alternate feathers and perhaps indicates ATY.

basic pp and ss showing molt clines and/or suspension limits (*cf.* Fig. 492**C**), with p8-p10 relatively fresh, averaging less-extensively black (Fig. 493**D**-**E**). and replaced primarily in Jan-Apr; 2-6 inner pp and usually 1-8 inner and outer ss fresh and paler in Jan-Aug (Fig. 492**E**-**F**); marginal les covs uniformly pale gray (Fig. 492**D**); cap and forecrown completely to mostly black in Feb-Jun (*cf.* Fig. 507**B**), the forecrown becoming mottled whitish in May-Jul. **Note: Some to many TYs and ATYs may be identifiable by molt timing (p8-p10 replaced Jan-May in TYs, Dec-Feb in ATYs; see Molt), length of r4-r6 (longer in ATYs; *cf.* Fig. 509C), and extent of white streaking to crown in Feb-Jul (more extensive in TYs) but more study needed to confirm reliability of these criteria.**

Sex— ♀ = ♂ by plumage aspect. Bilateral BPs (Fig. 20**B**, p. 31) developed by both sexes but distended cloaca (Fig. 21, p. 32) indicates ATY ♀ in Apr-Jun. Measurements largely unhelpful for sexing (Table 65), although head-bill length (Fig. 453, p. 630) should be investigated on live birds. Otherwise, no criteria known for sexing.

Royal Tern

	Jan	Feb	Mar	Apr	May	Jun	Jul	Aug	Sep	Oct	Nov	Dec
Juv-HY							O	O	O	O	O	O
SY	O	O	O	O	O	O	O	?	?	?	?	?
AHY						O	O	O	O	O	O	O
ASY	O	O	O	O	O	O	O	O	O	O		
ATY	O	O	O	(♀)	♀	(♀)	O					

■ > 95% ▨ 25-95% □ 5-25% □ < 5%   See Fig. 24 (pp. 44-45)

Hybrids reported—None.

References—Bent (1921), Buckley & Buckley (1970, 2003), Cramp & Simmons (1985), Escalante (1968), Malling Olsen & Larsson 1995, Murphy (1936), Oberholser (1974), Ridgway (1919).

TABLE 65. Measurements (mm) of North American larger terns and Black Skimmer to assist in identification and sexing. See pp. 4-11 for methods of measurement. Species summaries are in **bold**. Values were derived from 95% confidence intervals as based approximately on the indicated sample sizes (see pp. 4-5). Thus, midpoints of ranges approximate means, and S.D. is approximated by one-quarter of the range.

Taxon/Sex	*n*	wing chord[1]	tail length[2]	exp culmen	bill depth[3]	tarsus
Caspian Tern[4]		**390-434**	**90-115**	**62-77**	**17.0-23.5**	**40-49**
♀	90	390-430	90-112	62-72	17.0-22.7	40-48
♂	90	394-434	91-115	67-77	19.0-23.5	41-49
Royal Tern[4]		**353-389**	**90-104**	**57-71**	**14.4-17.9**	**29-36**
♀	50	353-388	90-104	57-67	14.4-17.7	29-35
♂	50	354-389	90-104	60-71	14.9-17.9	30-36
Sandwich Tern[4]		**270-302**	**68-78**	**47-56**	**9.7-12.4**	**24-28**
♀	30	270-297	69-78	47-54	9.7-11.6	24-28
♂	50	271-302	68-77	49-56	10.0-12.4	25-28
Elegant Tern		**296-327**	**78-93**	**55-70**	**10.6-13.2**	**24-28**
♀	30	296-325	78-92	55-64	10.6-12.5	24-28
♂	30	300-327	78-93	59-70	11.3-13.2	25-28
Black Skimmer		**323-416**	**76-95**	**50-76**	**20.9-30.0**	**28-37**
♀	30	323-372	76-87	50-62	20.9-25.5	28-32
♂	30	374-416	86-95	63-76	25.9-30.0	32-37

[1] Wing chord averages ~5% shorter in Juv-HY/SY than in AHY/ASY.

[2] Tail measured to tip of central rectrix (r1; Fig. **5C**, p. 8). See text for measures of tail fork (r6–r1), which varies substantially with plumage and molt, due to variable length of r6.

[3] Bill depth measured at distal end of forehead feathering (see Fig. 8**A**, p. 10).

[4] N.Am population only. See **Geographic variation**.

SANDWICH TERN
Thalasseus sandvicensis

SATE
Species # 0670
Band size: 3B

Species—From other terns by medium size (Table 65); tail fork medium-shallow (alternate r6 – r1 39-68 mm ASYs); bill black with distinct yellow tip in AHYs (in N.Am); outer pp with moderate black along shaft by age (Fig. 493**D-E**, p. 694), the undersides with white edge to inner web extending to or near tip (*cf.* Fig. 504**A-B**, p. 717); forecrown extensively white in Sep-Mar; r5-r6 white or with variable black or dusky markings distally (Fig. 509); upperparts medium-pale gray (Kodak 4-5, p. 629); legs black. Yellow-billed subspecies (see **Geographic variation**) from Elegant Tern (p. 725) by shorter wing, tail (to r1), and bill (Table 65); bill usually yellow (rarely orange-red). Beware of hybrids with Elegant Tern.

Geographic variation—See Cramp & Simmons (1985), Dement'ev & Gladkov (1951c), Escalante (1970), Hayes (2004), Hellmayr & Conover (1948b), Malling Olsen & Larsson (1995). One other subspecies occurs in Europe.

S.s. acuflavida (br throughout N.Am range; wint to S.Am). Smaller than nominate European subspecies (Table 65; *vs* wg chord 295-313, exp culmen 51-58 in *sandvicensis*); bill black with yellow tip; white edge to p6-p8 narrower and abbreviated (~1 mm wide and not reaching feather tip *vs* > 2 mm and reaching feather tip when fresh in *sandwichensis*).

S.s. eurygnatha (br and wint Caribbean Is to S.Am, vagrant to se.N.Am). Wing and bill average longer (wing chord 277-305, exp culmen 53-61); bill yellow to yellow-orange, (rarely orange-red), and sometimes with dusky median patches. Size averages larger in S.Am populations than in Caribbean populations (Malling Olsen & Larsson 1995).

Molt—CAS. PF complete (Aug-2nd Aug in HY/SYs), PA1 partial-incomplete (Mar-Jun in SYs), PS1 absent, PB2 complete (Jul-Jun in SY/TYs), PA2 incomplete (Feb?-Jun in TYs), PS2 limited-incomplete (Feb-Mar in TYs), DPB complete (Jun-Mar in ASY/ATYs), DPA incomplete (Jan?-Apr in ATYs), DPS limited(?). The PF usually occurs on non-breeding grounds, often commencing during migration and suspending during Jan-Mar (typically after 1-4 inner pp and some to all rects replaced); the DPB starts on or near breeding grounds (forehead feathers during incubation and often 1-4 pp) and/or stopover sites, usually suspends for migration, and completes on non-breeding grounds; and the PAs start on non-breeding grounds, can complete during migration in breeding adults, and usually overlap with the completion of the PF and PBs (Fig. 492**B**, p. 693). Replacement of pp occurs Nov-Jun/Aug during the PF, Jul-Feb?/Jun during the PB2, and Jul-Dec/Mar during the DPB. The PA1 includes some to most body feathers and les and med covs, sometimes 1-6 inner pp and 1-10 inner and outer ss (Fig. 492**D-F**), and usually 2 to all 12 rects. The PA2 and DPA usually include most to all body feathers and les and med covs, 4-7 inner pp and 4-15 inner and outer ss (Table 62, p. 692; Fig. 492**F-G**), and most to all rects. The PS2 can include 1-2 inner pp (Fig. 492**G**) and possibly 1-2 terts and c.rects (along with body feathers? More study needed); occasional ASYs (TYs?) may replace p1-p2 during a DPS in Feb-Mar as well. See pp. 691-695 for more information.

Age—Juv (B1; Jul-Sep) back feathers fringed blackish and terts and gr covs with extensively dark bases (Figs. 506**A**, p. 719, & 508**A**, p. 722) and rects extensively dark (Fig. 509**A**, p. 722); Juv ♀=♂.

Juv-HY/SY (1st cycle, Juv/B1-F1-A1; Aug-Jul): One or more terts and/or gr covs with extensively dark bases in Aug-Jan or later (Figs. 506**A** & 508**A**); r4-r6 extensively dark at bases in Aug-Dec (Fig. 509**A**), or short and with broad subterminal dusky areas in Jan-Jul (Fig. 509**B**); juv pp and ss uniform in wear (Fig. 492**A**, p. 693), with p8-p10 relatively worn (Fig. 492**B**), averaging more-extensively black (Fig. 493**D-E**, p. 694); 1-6 inner pp and 1-10 inner and outer ss sometimes replaced again and fresher and paler in Mar-Aug (Fig. 492**D-F**); marginal les covs washed dusky (Fig. 492**B**); cap and forecrown extensively white with sparse black streaks or spotting in Jan-Jul.

AHY/ASY (Def. cycle, DB-DA; Aug-Jul): Terts with reduced or no dusky on inner web at base (*cf.* Figs. 500**D**, p. 704, and 506**D**); gr covs uniformly pale gray (Fig. 508**B**); r4-r6 white with variable dusky gray in Aug-Dec (Fig. 509**B**) or elongated and mostly to entirely whitish in Dec-Jul (Fig. 509**C**); basic pp and ss showing molt clines and/or suspension limits (*cf.* Fig. 492**C**), with p8-p10 relatively fresh, averaging less-extensively black (Fig. 493**D**) and replaced primarily in Oct-Mar; 4-7 inner pp and 4-12 inner and outer ss replaced, fresh and paler in Jan-Aug (Fig. 492**F-G**), and 1-2 pp occasionally replaced for a third time and fresher and paler in Apr-Aug (Fig. 492**G**); marginal les covs uniformly pale gray (Fig. 493**B**); cap and forecrown completely to mostly black in Feb-Jun, the forecrown becoming mottled whitish in May-Jul. **Note: See Juv-HY/SY. Some SY/TYs and ASY/ATYs may be identifiable by molt timing and extent of the PS (see Molt), length of r4-r6 (longer in ATYs; *cf.* Fig. 509C), and extent of white streaking to crown in Feb-Jul (more extensive in TYs) but more study needed to confirm reliability of these criteria.**

Sex—♀=♂ by plumage aspect. Bilateral BPs (Fig. 20**B**, p. 31) developed by both sexes but distended cloaca (Fig. 21, p. 32) indicates ATY ♀ in Apr-Jun. Measurements unhelpful for sexing (Table 65, p. 723), although head-bill length (Fig. 453, p. 630) should be investigated on live birds. Otherwise, no criteria known for sexing.

Hybrids reported—With Elegant Tern (Collins 1997, Paul et al. 2003, McCarthy 2006) and Lesser Crested Tern *S. bengalensis* (Dies & Dies 1998, Rogers et al. 1998).

References—Baker (1993), Bent (1921), Dement'ev & Gladkov (1951c), Hayes (2004), Malling Olsen & Larsson (1995), Meissner & Krupa (2007), Murphy (1936), Oberholser (1974), Ridgway (1919), Ward (2000).

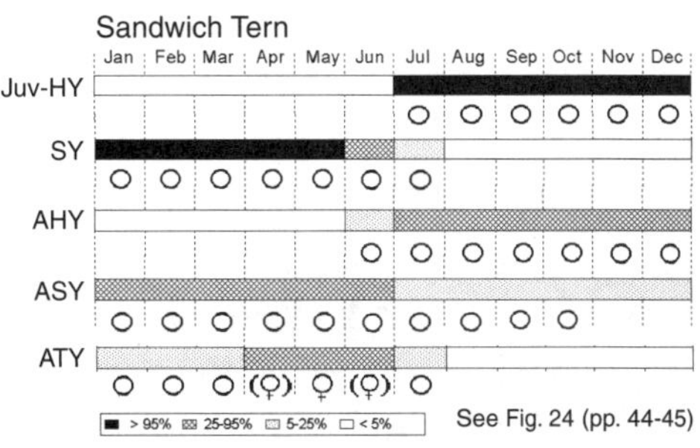

ELEGANT TERN

Thalasseus elegans

ELTE
Species # 0660
Band size: 3

Species—From other terns by medium to medium-large size with proportionally long and slender bill (Table 65, p. 723; Fig. 507**C**, p. 721); tail fork shallow (alternate r6 – r1 25-48 mm ASYs); outer pp with extensive black along shaft by age (Fig. 493**D-E**, p. 694), the undersides with white edge to inner web extending to or near tip (*cf.* Fig. 504**A-B**, p. 717); forehead white at most times (Fig. 507**C**); r5-r6 white or with variable black or dusky markings distally (Fig. 509, p. 722); upperparts medium-pale gray (Kodak 4-5, p. 629); juv ss with dusky centers (*cf.* Fig. 505**C**, p. 717); bill orange, without black distal marks (rarely with dusky lateral patches in HY/SYs); legs usually black, with patchy yellow-orange on many HY/SYs and some ASYs. From Royal Tern (p. 720) further by shorter wing, tail (to r1), and tarsus, and shallower bill (Table 65, Fig. 507**C**); crown with more black in most plumages (Fig. 507**C**); upperparts slightly darker (Kodak 4-5); PAs average more extensive (Table 62). From yellow-billed Sandwich Terns (p. 723) by longer wing, tail (to r1), and bill (Table 65); bill orange. Beware of hybrids with Sandwich Tern.

Lesser Crested Tern (*S. bengalensis*), a potential vagrant to e.N.Am, averages smaller (wing chord 275-320, exp culmen 47-61); bill slightly more even in depth, less tapered (depth at distal end of forehead feathers 10.1-13.3 mm, depth at gonys 8.0-10.9); upperparts slightly darker (Kodak 5-6) and concolorous with gray uppertail covs and tail (*vs* upperparts usually darker than uppertail covs and tail in Elegant and Royal terns).

Geographic variation—Monotypic.

Molt—CAS. PF complete (Jul-2nd Aug in HY/SYs), PA1 partial-incomplete (Apr-Sep in SYs), PB2 complete (Jul-Mar? in SY/TYs), PA2 incomplete (Dec?-Apr? in SY/TYs), DPB complete (May-Jan in ASY/ATYs), DPA incomplete (Nov-Feb in ASY/ATYs); PS absent(?). The PF occurs on non-breeding grounds, often commencing during migration and suspending, typically after 1-3 inner pp replaced; the DPB starts on breeding grounds (forehead feathers during incubation), usually suspends for northward dispersal in Jul-Aug, suspends again for southbound migration in Sep-Nov, and completes (with at least p7-p10) on S.Am non-breeding grounds; and the PAs start on non-breeding grounds, can complete during northward migration in breeding adults, and usually overlap with the completion of the PF and PBs (Fig. 492**B**, p. 693). Replacement of pp occurs Sep/Nov-May?/Aug during the PF, Jul/Sep-Mar? during the PB2, and Jun-Nov/Jan during the DPB. During the PF, some n.wintering HY/SYs may not start replacement of pp until Jan-Feb (needs study). The PA1 and PA2 include some to most body feathers and les and med covs, 1-6 inner pp and 1-6 inner and outer ss (Fig. 492**D**-**F**), and some to all rects, and the DPA includes most to all body feathers and les and med covs, 4-6 (rarely 7) inner pp and 6-14 inner and outer ss (Fig. 492**F**-**G**), and usually all rects. A DPS of 1-2 inner pp may occur in some ASYs in Feb-Mar (Fig. 492**F**), perhaps most likely in TYs. See pp. 691-695 for more information.

Age—Juv (B1; Jul-Sep) has terts and gr covs with extensively dark bases (Figs. 506**A**, p. 719, and 508**A**, p. 722), and rects extensively dark (Fig. 509**A**, p. 722) Juv ♀=♂.

Juv-HY/SY (1st cycle, Juv/B1-F1-A1; Aug-Jul): One or more terts and/or gr covs with extensively dark bases (Figs. 506**A** & 508**A**); r4-r6 extensively dark at bases in Aug-Dec (Fig. 509**A**), or short and with broad subterminal dusky areas in Jan-Jul (Fig. 509**B**); juv pp and ss uniform in wear (Fig. 492**A**, p. 693), with p8-p10 relatively worn (Fig. 492**B**), averaging more-extensively black (Fig. 493**E**, p. 694), and replaced primarily in Mar-Jul; 1-6 inner pp and 1-6 inner and outer ss replaced again and fresher and paler in Mar-Aug (Fig. 492**D**-**F**); marginal les covs washed dusky (Fig. 492**B**); cap and forecrown extensively white with sparse black streaks in Jan-Jul (Fig. 507**C**). **Note: See Molt and Table 62 (p. 692) for average differences in the number of pp and ss replaced during the PAs, which may assist with ageing some individuals.**

AHY/ASY (Def. cycle, DB-DA; Aug-Jul): Terts with reduced dusky on inner web at base (*cf.* Fig. 506**D**); gr covs uniformly pale gray (Fig. 508**B**); r4-r6 white with variable dusky gray in Aug-Dec (Fig. 509**B**) or elongated and mostly to entirely whitish in Dec-Jul (Fig. 509**C**); basic pp and ss showing molt clines and/or suspension limits (*cf.* Fig. 492**C**), with p8-p10 relatively fresh, averaging less-extensively black (Fig. 493**D**-**E**), and replaced primarily in Nov-Feb; 4-7 inner pp and 6-14 inner and outer ss fresh and paler in Jan-Aug (Fig. 492**E**-**F**); marginal les covs uniformly pale gray (Fig. 492**D**); cap and forecrown completely to mostly black in Jan-Jun (*cf.* Fig. 507**C**), the forecrown becoming mottled whitish in May-Jul. **Note: Some to many TYs and ATYs may be identifiable by molt timing (see Molt), length of r4-r6 (longer in ATYs; *cf.* Fig. 509C), and extent of white streaking to crown in Feb-Jul (more extensive in TYs) but more study needed to confirm reliability of these criteria.**

Sex—♀=♂ by plumage aspect. Bilateral(?) BPs (Fig. 20**B**, p. 31) developed by both sexes but distended cloaca (Fig. 21, p. 32) indicates ATY ♀ in Mar-May. Measurements largely unhelpful for sexing (Table 65, p. 723), although head-bill length (Fig. 453, p. 630) is likely useful and should be investigated on live birds. Otherwise, no criteria known for sexing.

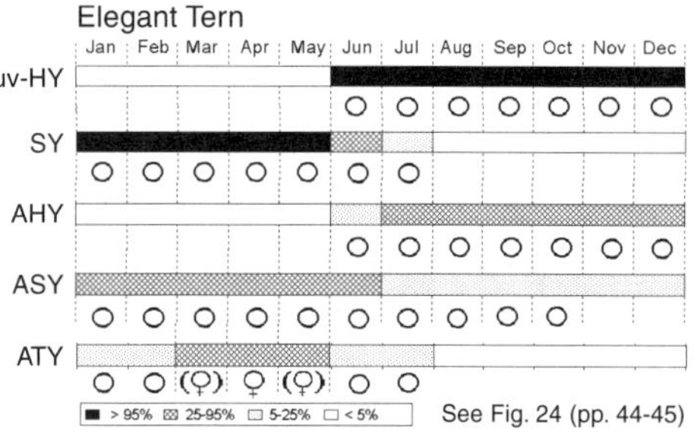

Hybrids reported—With Sandwich Tern (p. 723).

References—Bent (1921), Blokpoel et al. (1989), Burness et al. (1999), Malling Olsen & Larsson (1995), Murphy (1936), Oberholser (1974), Ridgway (1919).

Skimmers *Laridae, Rynchopinae*

One species. Subfamily characters include medium-large size, long and pointed wings, medium-length and forked tails, and medium-length legs with the three front toes connected by webbing. Highly specialized bills are relatively straight with mandibles laterally compressed distally, and tip of lower mandible projecting 20-30 mm beyond that of upper mandible in AHYs. Skimmers have 10 functional primaries (p10 longest, 10-15 mm > p9 when fully grown), 18-19 secondaries (including 3 tertials and one absent between the 4th and 5th; *cf.* Fig. 12**B**, p. 19), and 12 rectrices. Ageing can be accomplished through the first cycle (to SY and ASY) and perhaps sometimes the second cycle (to TY) by plumage-aspect and molt-related criteria. Molt strategy is probably Simple Alternate Strategy (SAS; Fig. 10**C**, pp. 13-16), with a preformative molt but without a first prealternate molt during the first cycle, but details need study. Definitive prebasic molts are typically complete and definitive prealternate molts limited to partial. Age of first breeding is 2-4 years; the timing of definitive prebasic molts in non-breeders and failed breeders averages earlier than that of breeders, and this variation may also reflect interannual and regional differences in food supply. Sexes are alike in plumage aspect but can be reliably sexed by measures (♂♂ larger than ♀♀), especially bill dimensions. Both sexes incubate and develop medial and bilateral brood patches.

BLACK SKIMMER
Rynchops niger

BLSK
Species # 0800
Band size: 4

Species—From other N.Am birds by medium-large size with proportionally large bill and short tarsus (Table 65, p. 723); bill with lower mandible extending beyond upper mandible and orange-red with black tip; tail fork shallow (r6 – r1 24-40); upperparts mostly black (Kodak 15-16, p. 629); underparts white; Juvs with broad, scaly-buff edging to the back feathers and s covs; legs bright orange-red. Other skimmers from S.Am and Africa have a white collar year-round, yellowish to orange bill, and/or brown underwing covs Harrison (1983).

Geographic variation—See Blake (1977), Gochfeld & Burger (1994), Griscom (1935), Hellmayr & Conover (1948b), Murphy (1936), Ridgway (1919), Wetmore (1965). Two other subspecies occur in S.Am.

R.n. niger (br and wint throughout N.Am range): Small (Table 65, p. 723; *vs* wg chord 350-430 exp culmen 58-89, tarsus 30-39 in S.Am subspecies); ss primarily white with black bases (vs. black with narrow to no white tips in S.Am subspecies); underwing covs white (*vs* dusky in S.Am subspecies); undertail covs and outer webs to outer rects white (*vs* dark in S.Am subspecies).

Molt—SAS (CAS?). PF complete (Oct-Sep in HY/SYs), PA1 absent?; PB2 complete (Oct?-Jun? in SY/TYs), PA2 limited (Mar?-May? in SYs), DPB complete (Jul-May in ASY/ATYs), DPA limited (Mar-May? in ASY/ATYs). The above timing pertains to N.Am populations. The single inserted first-cycle molt appears to be homologous with a PF rather than a PA1 (Fig. 10**C**, p. 14), although a few body feathers may be replaced twice, indicating the presence of both molts (and CAS; Fig. 10**F**); study is needed. Molts occur primarily on non-breeding grounds, although the DPB can start (inner pp) on or near breeding grounds. Replacement of pp occurs Jan/Apr-Jul/Sep during the PF, Oct?-May? during the PB2, and Jul/Sep-Feb/May during the DPB. The PF commences with head, back, sometimes some les and med covs, 1-3 terts, and most to all rects in Oct-Dec, followed by molt of pp and ss. The DPB can suspend for southbound migration after 1-4 inner pp are replaced (or p molt can occur entirely on non-breeding grounds); and often suspends again in Dec-Jan, with outer 1-4 pp (among p7-p10) retained until Mar-May. The DPAs appear to include some head and hindneck feathers (more study needed); a very limited PA1 may occur in some SYs.

Age—Juv (B1; Jul-Oct) has mandibles even in length at tips, plumage uniform in wear, crown and hindneck heavily streaked buffy and whitish, back feathers and s covs dark brown with bold buff to whitish edging, and base of bill and legs duller orange (*vs* red); Juv ♀ = ♂.

Juv-HY/SY (1st cycle, Juv/B1-F1; Sep-Aug): Crown dark sooty brown with pale-gray edging; molt limits occur among the s covs through May-Jun at least (Fig. 13**C-D**, p. 20), the juv distal feathers with buff fringing when fresh; hindneck white to mottled black and white in Mar-Aug; juv outer pp (p8-p10) and p covs relatively tapered (Fig. 19**A-B**, p. 28), the p covs brownish with whitish tips when fresh (Fig. 510**A**), being replaced primarily in Jun-Aug, the formative p covs brownish black and somewhat tapered (Fig. 510**B**).

AHY/ASY (Def. cycle, DB-DA; Sep-Aug): Crown black; s covs uniformly adult (Fig. 12**B**, p. 19), blackish without pale fringes; hindneck black in Mar-Aug. outer pp (p8-p10) and p covs relatively truncate (Fig. 19**C-D**), the p covs uniformly blackish (Fig. 510**B**), being replaced primarily Jan-Apr. **Note: Some AHY/ASYs with molt occurring in Sep-Apr may be aged SY/TY or ASY/ATY by condition of the outer pp and p covs (Fig. 510B *vs* C, respectively) but wear likely prevents accurate discrimination for most or all individuals (study needed). Also, some ASYs showing whitish mottled hindneck in May-Aug may be TYs; study needed.**

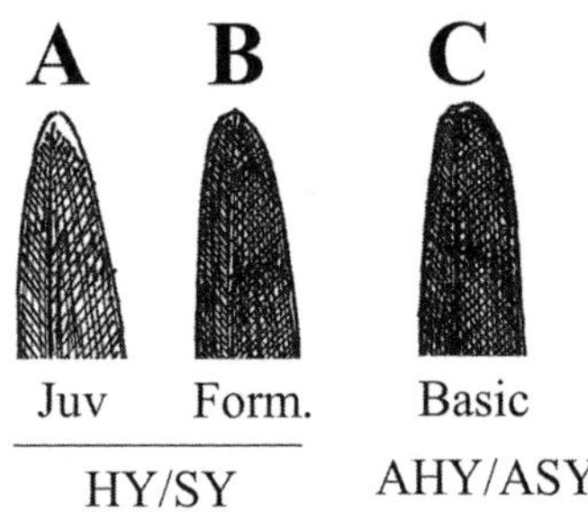

FIGURE 510. Shape and pattern of the outer primary coverts by age in Black Skimmer. The pale tips in HY/SYs (**A**) often can wear off by spring. By this time they are often replaced by formative covs (**B**), which average slightly more rounded and browner than basic covs (**C**); some SY/TYs and ASY/ATYs may be separated by this difference (along with molt timing) until the p covs are fully replaced in Feb-May, but confirmation based on known-aged individuals is needed.

Sex—♀ = ♂ by plumage aspect. Bilateral and medial BPs (Fig. 20**C**, p. 31) developed by both sexes but distended cloaca (Fig. 21, p. 32) indicates ASY ♀ in May-Jul. Measurements reliable for sexing (Table 65, p. 723; Quinn 1990), once Juvs are fully grown.

♀: Wing chord < 373; exposed culmen < 62; bill depth at distal end of forehead feathers < 25.7; tarsus < 32.

♂: Wing chord > 373; exposed culmen > 62; bill depth at distal end of forehead feathers > 25.7; tarsus > 32.

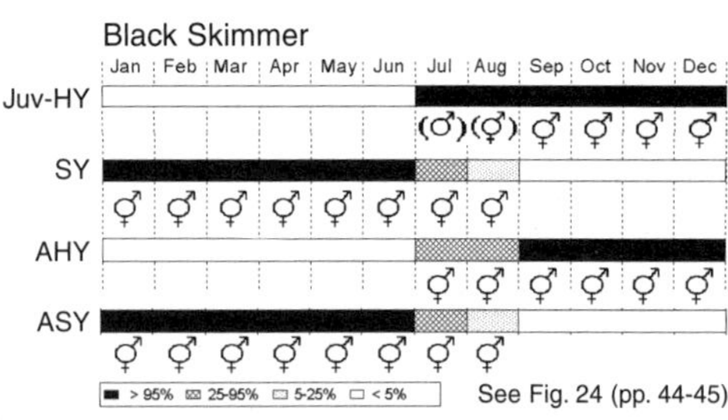

Hybrids reported—None.

References—Bent (1921), Gochfeld & Burger (1994), Mariano-Jelicich et al. (2007), Murphy (1936), Oberholser (1974), Quinn (1990), Ridgway (1919), Schew & Collins (1990).

Five species in two groups: larger skuas and smaller jaegers. Family characters include heavy to relatively heavy bodies; relatively stout, slightly hook-tipped bills with bill plates and sheathing of the nostrils ("false cere"); long and pointed wings with white to the bases of the underwing outer primaries; slightly graduated tails (with distinctly elongated central rectrices in jaegers); and webbed feet with strongly hooked claws. Skuas and jaegers have 10 functional primaries (the 10th longest by 5-15 mm, when fully grown), 17-22 secondaries (including 3 tertials and one missing between s4 and s5; *cf.* Fig. 12**B**, p. 19), and 12 rectrices. Plumage-aspect polymorphism (dark and light phases) is found to a variable degree among the five species. Ageing through the second cycle (to TY and ATY), and possibly the third cycle (to 4Y) in some jaegers, can be accomplished by plumage aspect, leg color, retained feathers during molt in skuas, and the length of r1 in jaegers. Older individuals develop hackles, finely attenuated and stiffer nape feathers that are absent or rudimentary during the first year of life (*cf.* Fig. 512, p. 732); study is needed on whether hackles are basic or alternate feathers and, if alternate, whether or not basic nape feathers can show ornamental characteristics. Sexes are generally similar in plumage aspect and size (♀♀ average larger than ♂♂), and both sexes develop bilateral brood patches (Fig. 20**B**, p. 31), but distended cloaca (Fig. 21, p. 32) indicates breeding ATY ♀♀, and other breeding characters (Figs. 22-23, pp. 32-35) should be investigated.

In molting, skuas and jaegers appear to employ a Simple Alternate Strategy (SAS; Fig. 10**E**, pp. 13-16) including a single first-cycle molt and prealternate molts in later cycles. The complete inserted first-cycle molt appears to be more homologous with a preformative than with a prealternate molt; however, limited first prealternate molts may also occur in at least some SYs (see below), in which case these species would employ the Complex Alternate Strategy (CAS; Fig. 10**F**). A definitive prealternate molt in skuas also needs confirmation (*cf.* Higgins & Davies 1996); it is possible that these employ the Complex Basic Strategy (CBS; Fig. 10**B**). Definitive prealternate molts are partial in jaegers, and definitive prebasic molts can be incomplete in skuas and perhaps larger jaegers. Age of first breeding is 3-7 years in jaegers, 4-10 years or older in skuas; non-breeding AHYs can remain on non-breeding grounds and average later and less-extensive prealternate molts and earlier prebasic molts (see p. 18).

Molt and age determination in skuas and jaegers

As with shorebirds (pp. 501-507), molt strategies among skuas and jaegers are complex, being similar among species but exhibiting variation among individuals reflecting factors such as migration distance and breeding and wintering hemispheres (Howell 2007b). In general, molt occurs at sea on non-breeding grounds, although some adults (especially non-breeders and failed breeders) start body molt (sometimes primary molt in Great Skua, p. 730), on or near breeding grounds. Primaries are replaced distally, secondaries appear to be replaced both proximally from s1 and s5 and distally from the tertials, and rectrices are generally replaced distally on both sides of the tail. Understanding molt in skuas and jaegers is complicated by factors such as the difficulty in following individuals at sea, and protracted molts spanning periods of hormonal development that, in jaegers at least, may affect both feather pigmentation and the length and shape of the ornamental central rectrices; e.g., earlier-replaced and/or later-replaced feathers may look more juvenal-like than those replaced during peak molting (and presumably hormonal) periods (see Howell 2007b and p. 29).

In jaegers, timing of the preformative molt exhibits considerable individual variation among first-cycle HY/SYs, presumably related to variation in migration distance and food resources. First-cycle molts in skuas are not as well documented. Juvenal plumage appears to be retained through fall migration, followed by a protracted preformative molt; a limited prealternate molt of some head and body feathers may occur in the first cycle but requires confirmation. Some first-cycle jaegers (especially those that complete molt earlier) migrate north in summer, at least to temperate latitudes if not to breeding grounds, whereas others remain on or near non-breeding grounds, primarily in tropical waters; molting strategies may differ according to location during the first summer, as in shorebirds (see pp. 501-507). The complete second prebasic molt closely follows and can overlap first-cycle molt(s), resulting in outer and inner primaries being replaced simultaneously, as can occur in some shorebirds (*cf.* Fig. 376**C**, p. 504).

The second prebasic molt is also protracted, occurring from late fall or winter into spring in jaegers, sometimes suspending in mid winter (especially in 1st-cycle HY/SYs wintering in temperate northern waters). The second and definitive prealternate molts appear to be partial in jaegers, but are poorly known in skuas, and may not exist. Complete on near-complete definitive prebasic molts (sometimes suspended) and partial to incomplete definitive prealternate molts in jaegers are similar to second-cycle molts but average slightly later and earlier (respectively) in timing. In jaegers, the definitive prebasic molt of head and body feathers generally proceeds quickly from fall to early or mid winter, and is mostly completed before primary replacement has advanced beyond the middle primaries. The ornamental central rectrices are often dropped during fall migration (especially in Long-tailed Jaeger, p. 743), followed by the remainder of molt on non-breeding grounds. Basic central rectrices may be short, followed by replacement by longer alternate feathers (Howell 2007b), but confirmation of this needed (*cf.* Cramp & Simmons 1983 regarding Parasitic Jaeger). The timing of prebasic molts in non-breeding (and failed breeding) adults also appears to be earlier than that of successful breeders.

Most jaegers, except the darkest-morph individuals, can be aged by plumage aspect, but no studies of plumage succession have involved known-age individuals, and the complex and protracted molts may produce intermediates that cannot be precisely aged. The second and third basic plumages can be especially variable, and may include individuals that overlap with those of younger or older cohorts in aspect (Howell 2007b) that should be aged S-TY or T-4Y (see pp. 41-42). Definitive plumage aspect apparently can be attained by completion of the third prebasic molt in some TY/4Ys, whereas other third-cycle TY/4Ys retain second-cycle characters. Pale markings on the tarsus are also useful in determining age groups, being extensive in juveniles but absent in adults (except in occasional Long-tailed Jaegers; Fig. 516, p. 738). Shape of the outer primaries and primary coverts is useful in skuas (Fig. 511, p. 731) but appears to be less useful in jaegers.

GREAT SKUA

Stercorarius skua

GRSK
Species # 0350
Band size: 7A-7B

Species—From other skuas (including extralimital taxa) with caution. From South Polar Skua (p. 733) by longer average wing and tarsus (Table 66, p. 735); r1 averages shorter (r1 – r2 7-12 mm) plumage aspect (including Juvs) with reddish tones; underwing covs dark brown; Juvs with head brown tinged reddish and upperparts with broad cinnamon edging when fresh, the ASYs with variegated, bold, buff, and reddish streaking on head and upperparts (Figs. 512**C** & 513**C**, p. 732). See also **Molt** for differences in timing that could assist with identification. Darkest Juv Great Skuas blackish brown and can be difficult to distinguish from dark-morph AHY South Polar Skua: on these compare with age, noting paler grayish bill base, relatively tapered juv pp, and pale blotches on tarsus shown by Juv Great Skuas. Juv from juv and dark-morph Pomarine Jaeger (p. 735) by larger size especially bill depth (Table 66); r1 only slightly elongated (r1 – r2 7-20 mm; *cf.* Fig. 517, p. 739); underwing covs and undertail covs without pale barring.

Brown Skua (*S. lonnbergi*, including taxa *antarctica* and *hamiltoni*) of the Subantarctic (with possible records in the n.Hemisphere) has similar measurements to South Polar Skua (*cf.* Table

66) except for longer average tarsus (60-82 mm, > 71 mm in nominate *lonnbergi*); wing/tarsus 4.91-5.52 (*vs* 5.35-6.43 in Great Skua); ASYs generally with reduced pale markings on s covs (Fig. 513**A-B**) contrasting distinctly with pale-mottled scapulars (Fig. 513**C**), *vs* upperwings and scapulars more uniformly patterned on ASY South Polar (Fig. 513**B**) and Great (Fig. 513**C**) skuas; ASYs of nominate *lonnbergi* generally with extensive dark hood, variable whitish to rufous streaking and mottling on back, and mottled brown underwing covs. Juvs perhaps not safely separable by measurements and plumage aspect (more study needed) but note timing of PF and plumage wear with respect to season (pp replaced primarily Jul-Jan in Brown Skua, Jun-Dec in South Polar Skua, and Dec-Sep in Great Skua). Chilean Skua (*S. chilensis*) of s.S.Am (possible vagrant to w.N.Am) has cap dark contrasting with cinnamon cheeks and throat; some to many underwing covs cinnamon-rufous. See Devillers (1977), Higgins & Davies (1996), Howell (2004, 2005), Malling Olsen & Larsson (1997), McLaren & Lucas (2004), Murphy (1936), and Votier et al. (2004) for more information on identifying skuas.

Geographic variation—Monotypic (see Cramp & Simmons 1983 for slight variation in measurements).

Molt—SAS (CBS or CAS?). PF complete (Dec-Oct in HY/SYs), PA1 absent-limited? (Apr?-May? in SYs), PB2 complete (Sep-Apr? in SY/TYs), PA2 limited? (Mar?-May? in TYs), DPB incomplete-complete (Jul-Mar in ASY/ATYs), DPA limited? (Mar?-Apr? in ATYs). The single inserted first-cycle molt appears to be homologous with a PF rather than a PA1 (Fig. 10**C**, p. 14), although a few head or body feathers may be replaced twice, indicating the presence of both molts (and CAS; Fig. 10**F**); study needed. Molting occurs primarily at sea, away from breeding grounds, although the DPB (body and inner pp) may commence on breeding grounds. The PF commences with body molt in Dec-Feb; replacement of pp occurs Feb/Apr-Aug/Oct and can overlap start of PB2 in Sep-Oct (two replacement waves occurring simultaneously; *cf.* Fig. 376**C**, p. 504). Molt of pp occurs Sep/Oct-Mar/May during the PB2 and Aug/Oct-Jan/Apr during the DPB, likely averaging earlier in TY/4Ys and other non-breeders (completing in Nov?). In all age groups p molt may be suspended in Dec-Jan. Some ASYs might retain 1-3 ss among s11-s14, as in South Polar Skua. A limited DPA (including head and neck feathers) reported to occur (e.g., Cramp & Simmons 1983), at least in second and subsequent cycles, but existence of DPA requires confirmation. See pp. 729-730 for more information on skua and jaeger molt.

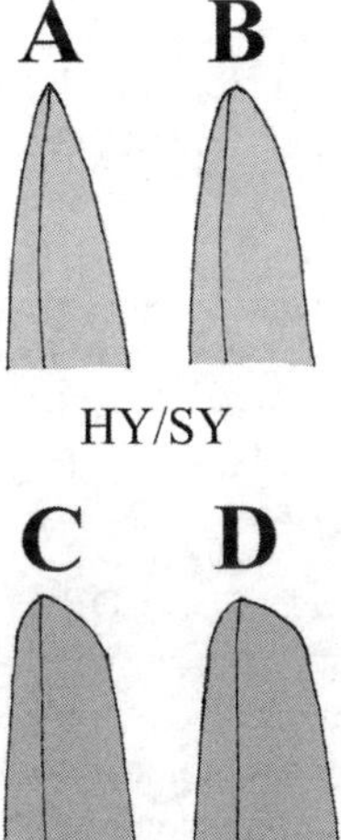

FIGURE 511. Variation in shape of the longest primary covert by age in skuas. Both pp and p covs average narrower and more tapered on juvenal (**A-B**) than basic (**C-D**) feathers (see also Fig. 518, p. 740). Abraded outer pp tips can make differences difficult to discern when worn, but the outer p covs, as shown here, are less prone to wear.

Age—Juv (B1; Aug-Feb) has variable pale-buff to cinnamon streaking and mottling on head, neck, and upperparts; bill grayish with dark tip; tarsus usually with grayish to bluish-white patches (*cf.* Fig. 516**C-D**, p. 738); Juv ♀=♂. See Klomp & Furness (1992) for ageing (up to 16 years) of corpses by number of endosteal lamellae in the tibia. In addition to the following, the average amount of white in the wing may increase with age (*cf.* Hahn & Peter 2003); more study needed.

Juv-HY/SY (1st cycle, Juv/B1-F1; Sep-Aug): Plumage uniform in wear, without distinct pale streaking and mottling (Fig. 513**A**); nape without hackles, the feathers soft, rounded, and without pale streaks (Fig. 512**A**); pp and ss uniformly juv and not showing s1-p1 contrast in Sep-Jan (Fig. 13**A**, p. 20), being replaced in Jan-Aug, the outer pp and p covs relatively tapered, faded, and worn at tips in Apr-Aug (Fig. 511**A-B**, p. 731); bill base grayish through Feb or later; tarsus with pale-gray markings (*cf.* Fig. 516**C-D**, p. 738). **Note: Juv and formative plumages not well known; more study needed.**

SY/TY (2nd cycle, B2-A2?; Sep-Aug): Plumage showing mixed degrees of wear, the head and neck coarsely spotted and streaked pale buff, and the scapulars with sparse and relatively narrow buff and cinnamon streaks (Fig. 513**B**); nape without hackles or with semi-elongated feathers with indistinct buff streaks (Fig. 512**A-B**); pp and ss basic and showing s1-p1 contrast (Fig. 14**B**, p. 21), being replaced in Sep-May or earlier, the outer pp and p covs relatively broad (Fig. 511**C-D**) and fresh; bill blackish to black; legs black, sometimes with pale markings (*cf.* Fig. 516**D**). **Note: See Juv-HY/SY.**

ASY/ATY (Def. cycle, DB-DA?; Sep-Aug): Plumage showing mixed degrees of wear, the head, neck, and scapulars with relatively extensive cinnamon-rufous to buff streaking and mottling (Fig. 513**C**); nape with hackles elongated and distinctly streaked buff (Fig. 512**C**); pp replaced Aug-Apr; bill and legs (Fig. 516**F**) black. **Note: Look for occasional ASY/ATYs to retain 1-3 ss among s11-s14; these may more often be ATY/A4Ys that bred the previous season (more study needed).**

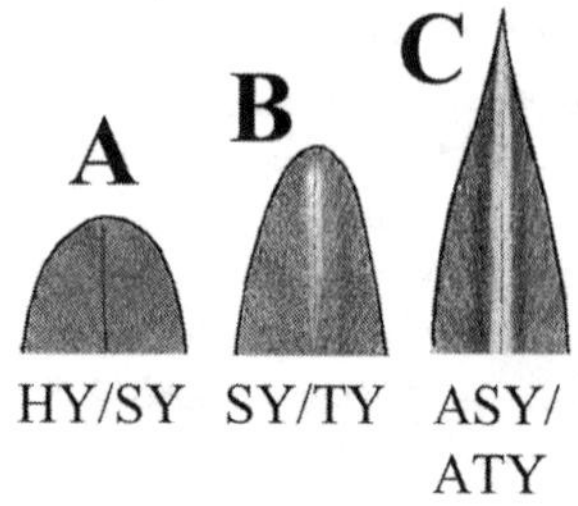

FIGURE 512. Nape feathers in Great Skua by age, illustrating the development of "hackles" (**C**), stiff ornamental feathers found in ASYs of all skuas and jaegers. In South Polar Skua these feathers show less distinct pale streaks (e.g., **B** in ASY/ATYs) and more golden coloration by age. In Long-tailed and light-morph Pomarine and Parasitic jaegers these feathers are mottled brown and pale in HY/SYs and bright pale golden in ASY/ATYs whereas in dark-morph ASY/ATYs they are blackish. More study needed on whether or not hackles are basic or alternate feathers; if the latter, attenuated feathers (**C**) may only be found in Mar-Oct.

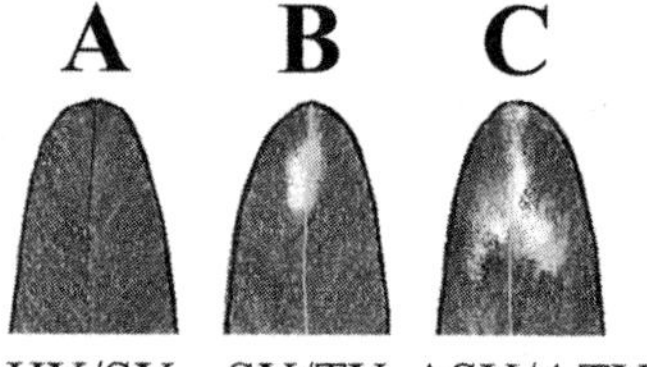

FIGURE 513. Patterns to scapulars by age in Great Skua. In South Polar Skua these feathers show less distinct pale streaks by age (e.g., **B** in ASY/ATYs).

Sex—♀=♂ by plumage aspect. Bilateral(?) BPs (Fig. 20**B**, p. 31) developed by both sexes but distended cloaca (Fig. 21, p. 32) indicates ATY ♀ in May-Jul. Measurements unhelpful for sexing (Table 66, p. 735). The amount of white in the wing may average more extensive in ♀♀ than in ♂♂ (*cf.* Hahn & Peter 2003) but this is unreliable for sexing. Otherwise, no criteria known.

Hybrids reported—None. See Andersson (1999) and Millington (2000).

References—Baker (1993), Bearhop et al. (1998), Bent (1921), Cramp & Simmons (1983), Dement'ev & Gladkov (1951c), Devillers (1977), Furness (1987), Godfrey (1986), Higgins & Davies (1996), Howell (2004), Jiguet (1997), Klomp & Furness (1992), Malling Olsen & Larsson (1997), Phillips et al. (2002), Ridgway (1919).

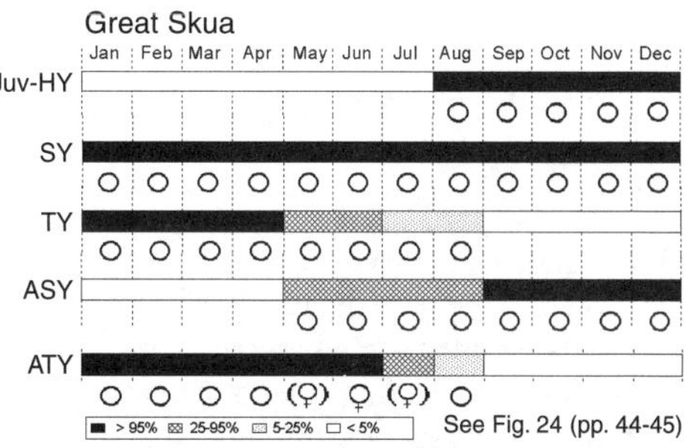

SOUTH POLAR SKUA

Stercorarius maccormicki

SPSK
Species # 0352
Band size: 7A-7B

Species—From other skuas with caution. From Great Skua (p. 730) by shorter average wing and tarsus (Table 66, p. 735); r1 averages longer (r1 – r2 10-26 mm); plumage aspect without reddish tones; underwing covs blackish; head brownish gray and upperparts with little or no cinnamon streaking by age (*cf.* Figs. 512**A-B** & 513**A-B**). Brown Skua (see Great Skua) has a longer average tarsus (> 71 mm in nominate *S.l. lonnbergi*), shorter wing/tarsus ratio 4.9-5.5 (*vs* 5.6-6.7 in South Polar Skua), and stouter average bill (bill length/height at proximal end of nares usually 2.2-2.8 in *lonnbergi vs* 2.4-3.1 in South Polar Skua); ASYs with crown darker (forming capped effect), back feathers more heavily marked with buff and rufous (*cf.* Fig. 513**C**), and underwing covs mottled brown and pale (vs. uniformly darker brown in South Polar Skua). Juv-HY/SYs may not be reliably separated although plumage averages warmer in Brown Skua than South Polar Skua. See Great Skua for more information and separation from Chilean Skua and dark-morph Pomarine Jaeger, and see **Molt** for differences in timing by age that could assist with identification.

Geographic variation—Monotypic. Populations in n.Antarctic Peninsula region are predominantly of dark morph whereas those farther south and around the Antarctic Continent are predominantly of pale morph (Devillers 1977).

Molt—SAS (CBS or CAS?). PF complete (Jun-Jan? in HY/SYs), PA1 absent-limited? (Nov?-Jan? in HY/SY), PB2 complete (Apr-Nov? in SYs), PA2 limited? (Sep?-Nov? in SYs), DPB incomplete-complete (Mar-Oct in ASY/ATY); DPA limited? (Sep?-Oct? in ASYs). The single inserted first-cycle molt appears to be homologous with a PF rather than a PA1 (Fig. 10**C**, p. 14), although a few head and/or nape feathers may be replaced twice, indicating the presence of both molts (and CAS; Fig. 10**F**); see below. Molting occurs primarily at sea, away from breeding grounds, although the definitive PB may commence on breeding grounds. The PF commences with body molt in Jul-Sep (often in the n.Hemisphere); replacement of pp occurs Jul/Sep-Nov/Jan (possibly extending later), with some HY/SYs suspending for southward migration and completing in the s.Hemisphere. Molt of pp occurs Apr/Jun-Aug/Oct during the PB2 and DPB, possibly averaging earlier in SYs and non-breeding ASYs. Some ASYs retain 1-3 ss among s11-s14. A limited DPA (including head and neck feathers) has been reported (Malling Olsen & Larsson 1997 but see Higgins & Davies 1996); confirmation needed. See pp. 729-730 for more information on skua and jaeger molt.

Age—Juv (B1; Feb-Jul) is uniformly brownish gray without pale streaks on neck but with narrow, pale-grayish tips to back and s covs, bill grayish with dark tip, and tarsus often with pale-gray to bluish-white patches (*cf.* Fig. 516**C-D**, p. 738); Juv ♀=♂. In addition to the following, the average amount of white in the wing may increase with age (*cf.* Hahn & Peter 2003); more study needed.

Juv-HY/SY (1st cycle, Juv/B1-F1; Jun-May): Head and underparts uniformly medium to dark brown, lacking distinct pale streaks or hackles on nape (Figs. 512**A** & 513**A**, p. 732) except for bleached tips of old feathers in Sep-Dec; pp and ss uniformly juv and not showing s1-p1 contrast in Feb-Jul (Fig. 13**A**, p. 20), being replaced primarily in Aug-Apr, the outer pp and p covs relatively tapered and worn at tips (Fig. 511**A-B**, p. 731); basal two-thirds of bill grayish through Oct or later; tarsus with pale markings (*cf.* Fig. 516**C-D**). **Note: Juv, formative, and 2nd-basic plumages poorly known. Some HYs may complete the PF in Dec and show the characters of SY (below).**

SY (2nd cycle, B2-A2?; Jun-Nov): Head and underparts medium-dark gray-brown to very dark brown, usually with paler nape but without or with reduced golden-brown hackles (*cf.* Fig. 512**A-B**); scapulars and s covs without pale-buff to pale-brownish streaks (Fig. 513**A**); pp and ss basic and showing s1-p1 contrast (Fig. 14**B**, p. 21), being replaced primarily in May-Oct, the outer pp and p covs broad and relatively fresh (Fig. 511**C-D**); bill blackish to black; legs black, sometimes with pale markings (*cf.* Fig. 517**D**). **Note: See Juv-HY and AHY/ASY. Some individuals may be aged SY/TY in Dec-May by these criteria but more study needed.**

AHY/ASY (Def. cycle, DB-DA?; Dec-Nov): Head and underparts dark brown to pale buff, the nape with elongated (*cf.* Fig. 512**C**) golden-brown hackles; scapulars and s covs usually with some pale-buff to pale-brownish streaks (Fig. 513**B**); bill and legs (Fig. 517**F**) black. **Note: See Juv-HY. It is possible that individuals (especially lighter morphs) showing these characters (including elongated hackles) can be aged ASY/ATY but further study needed.**

Sex—♀=♂ by plumage aspect but light-morph AHY/ASYs are more often ♀♀ within mixed-morph mated pairs (Ainley et al. 1985). Bilateral(?) BPs (Fig. 20**B**, p. 31) developed by both sexes but distended cloaca (Fig. 21, p. 32) indicates ASY/ATY ♀ in Nov-Jan. Measurements unhelpful for sexing (Table 66). The amount of white in the wing average more extensive in ♀♀ than in ♂♂ (*cf.* Hahn & Peter 2003) but this is unreliable for sexing. Otherwise, no criteria known.

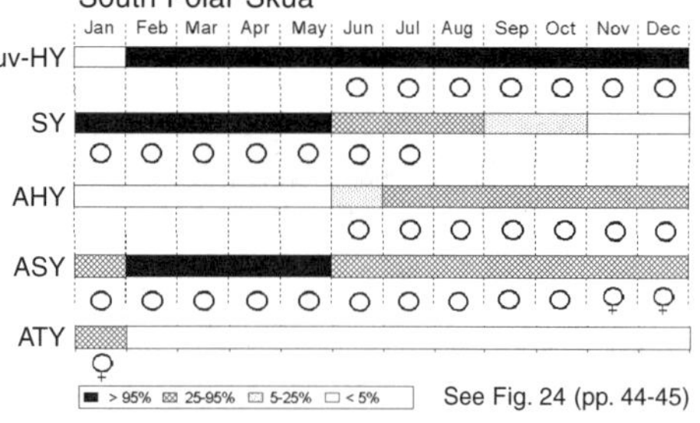

Hybrids reported—With Brown Skua *S. lonnbergi* (Hahn et al. 1998, Jiguet et al. 1999, Parmelee 1988) and Chilean Skua *S. chilensis* (Reinhardt et al. 1997); see also Andersson (1999) and Millington (2000).

References—Ainley et al. (1985), Bent (1921), Devillers (1977), Eigenhuis (1987), Higgins & Davies (1996), Howell (2004, 2005), Malling Olsen & Larsson (1997), McLaren & Lucas (2004), Murphy (1936), Phillips et al. (2002), Reinhardt et al. (1997), Ridgway (1919), Spellerberg (1970), Votier et al. (2004).

TABLE 66. Measurements (mm) of North American skuas and jaegers to assist in identification and sexing. See pp. 4-11 for methods of measurement. Species summaries are in **bold**. Values were derived from 95% confidence intervals as based approximately on the indicated sample sizes (see pp. 4-5); sample size for bill depth was often smaller but included at least 10 of each sex. Thus, midpoints of ranges approximate means, and S.D. is approximated by 25% of the range.

		wing	tail	exp	bill	
Taxon/Sex	*n*	chord[1]	length[2]	culmen	depth[3]	tarsus
Great Skua		**372-432**	**140-162**	**45-55**	**17.8-23.3**	**60-73**
♀	100	385-432	144-160	45-53	18.3-23.3	61-73
♀	100	372-420	140-162	46-55	17.8-21.6	60-72
South Polar Skua		**367-412**	**139-167**	**42-54**	**16.4-22.1**	**55-70**
♀	100	370-412	139-165	43-54	16.7-22.1	56-70
♀	100	367-408	142-167	42-52	16.4-21.5	55-68
Pomarine Jaeger		**331-376**	**120-138**	**35-43**	**14.1-16.7**	**50-59**
♀	100	331-376	122-137	35-42	14.4-16.7	50-59
♀	100	327-370	120-138	36-43	14.1-16.3	50-58
Parasitic Jaeger		**288-344**	**100-140**	**26-34**	**11.0-13.0**	**39-46**
♀	100	291-344	100-140	26-34	11.1-13.0	39-46
♀	100	288-338	103-137	25-33	11.0-12.7	38-45
Long-tailed Jaeger		**270-344**	**102-140**	**23-34**	**10.6-12.5**	**39-46**
♀	100	275-344	106-140	24-34	10.7-12.5	39-46
♀	100	270-318	102-135	23-30	10.6-12.3	39-46

[1] Wing chord averages 18-20% shorter in Juv-HY/SY than in AHY/ASY.

[2] Tail length includes r1 in skuas but is to the tip of r2 (or r3, if r2 elongated) in jaegers (Fig. 5**B**, p. 8).

[3] Bill depth measured at distal end of forehead feathering (see Fig.8**A**, p. 10).

POMARINE JAEGER

Stercorarius pomarinus

POJA
Species # 0360
Band size: 5

Species—From other jaegers, skuas, and gulls by medium-large size, intermediate between skuas and other jaegers (Table 66); r1 variably extended by age (Fig. 517, 739); plumage aspect polymorphic at all ages; uppersides of p3-p10 with creamy-white shafts (83% of ASY/ATYs with white limited to p5/p6-p10); bill black, with pinkish at base in all ages. Juv and dark morph from Great and South Polar skuas further by smaller size, especially bill depth (Table 66); r1 elongated (Figs. 517 and 519**A-B**, p. 740); underwing covs and undertail covs with variably distinct pale barring; bill base pinkish.

From Parasitic (p. 740) and Long-tailed (p. 743) jaegers by larger size and bill (Table 66; Fig. 514, p. 736); r1 broad with blunt tip, and twisted in Mar-Aug ASYs (Fig. 517 & 519**A-B**); Juv-HY with plumage aspect gray-brown (lacking reddish tones), hindneck without distinct streaking, underwing p covs usually with extensive whitish bases (Fig. 515**A**, occasionally to **B**), outer pp without distinct whitish fringes when fresh (Fig. 518**A**, p. 740), and uppertail covs with narrower, often broken bars (Fig. 520**A**, p. 741); ASY/ATY with bill pinkish to dull brownish flesh on basal two-thirds, blackish cap usually more extensive, and chest band (when present) barred or mottled (Fig. 514**A-B**). SYs and TYs variable in appearance; best separated by size (Table 66), r1 shape (Figs. 517 & 519**A-B**), cap shape if apparent (Fig. 514**C-D**), and pinkish bill base of TYs.

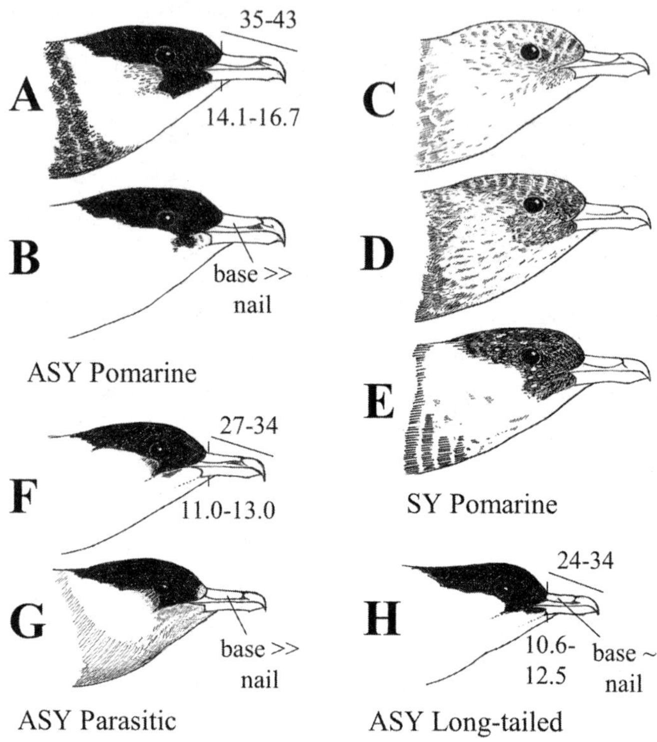

FIGURE 514. Head patterns and relative bill sizes in light-morph AHY jaegers in alternate plumage aspect (Apr-Oct) by species and age. Measures pertain to exposed culmen (Fig. 7**A**, p. 9) and bill depth at tip of forehead feathers (Fig. 8**A**, p. 10). Pomarine Jaegers (**A**-**E**) have a particularly large and stout bill. Plumage aspect can vary from extensively black in the malar region and with dark-mottled chest (**A**) to a more restricted cap and unmarked chest (**B**). The latter is closer in appearance to many ASY light-morph Parasitic Jaegers (**F**), whereas darker Parasitics show a dusky wash to the breast and throat (**G**). ASY Long-tailed Jaeger (**H**) is only found in light-morph and shows a restricted cap overlapping Parasitics only with the most reduced caps. SY Pomarines show substantial variation in head plumage aspect, perhaps reflecting the timing and extent of first-cycle molts. Variation in shape of the dark cap mimics that of ASYs in both Parasitic and Pomarine jaegers, and can be useful for the identification of SYs. Some retarded TYs may resemble **E** in cap development but most resemble ASYs (**A**-**B**, **F**-**G**). Note also that ASYs in basic plumage aspect (Aug-Mar) can resemble **D**-**E**; check underwing covs and tarsal coloration for help with ageing. Note difference in length of nail in proportion to bill length in Parasitic (**F**-**G**; exp culmen/bill nail 1.8-2.1) and Long-tailed (**H**; exp culmen/bill nail 1.6-1.9) jaegers. See Figures 518, 519, and 520 (pp. 740-741) for further clues to identify first-cycle jaegers, and Table 66 (p. 735) for measurements to separate Pomarine Jaegers, including dark-morph individuals.

Geographic variation—Monotypic. Populations breeding from e.Siberia to w.N.Am ("*S.p. camtschatica*") may average larger and darker, but differences confounded by individual variation and are probably insufficient for subspecific recognition. See Browning (1978, 1990) and Oberholser (1974) for more information.

Molt—SAS (CAS?). PF complete (Nov/Dec-Jul/Oct in HY/SYs), PA1 absent-limited? (Apr?-Jun? in SYs), PB2 complete (Jul/Oct-May in SY/TYs), PA2 partial-incomplete (Mar-May in TYs), DPB complete (Jul-Jan/Apr in ASY/ATYs), DPA partial-incomplete (Feb-May in ATYs). The

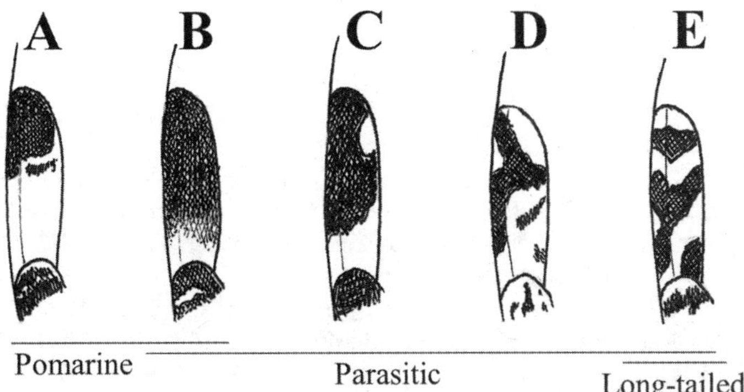

FIGURE 515. Variation in typical patterning of the outer underwing primary covert by species in juvenal jaegers. Most Juv Pomarine Jaegers have an extensive white base and distinct dark tip (**A**) although some light-morph and dark-morph Juvs usually show a more restricted white base (**B**). Some light-morph SY/TY Pomarine Jaegers can also show restricted pale at the base (**B**) but most SY/TYs (including all dark-morphs) and ASY/ATYs show a uniformly dark feather. The outer underwing p cov in Juv Parasitic Jaegers is the most variable (**B-E**), but often shows variegated pale markings (**C-D**). Juv Long-tailed and some Juv Parasitic jaegers show more structured pale markings or bars (**E**). In Parasitic and Long-tailed jaegers, SY/TYs show this feather dark but variably fringed or marked pale, and ASY/ATYs show an entirely dark feather, as in Pomarine Jaeger.

complete inserted first-cycle molt appears to be a PF rather than a PA1 (Fig. 10**C**, p. 14), although a limited PA1 of head and back feathers may also occur in some SYs indicating CAS (Fig. 10**F**). Most to all molting occurs on non-breeding grounds; the DPB can commence during southbound migration. The PF commences with body molt in Nov-Dec followed by molt of flight feathers in Dec/Feb-Jul/Oct, sometimes overlapping the beginning of the PB2 in Jul-Oct and resulting in two simultaneous waves (*cf.* Fig. 376**C**, p. 504). Molt of pp during the PB2 occurs Aug/Oct-Feb/May. During the DPB, body molt often completes by Dec and molt of pp occurs Aug/Nov-Dec/Apr; the ornamental r1 is usually replaced in Sep-Nov; occasional AHYs may retain one or more s covs or medial ss (among s7-s11) during the PB2 and/or DPB, as in skuas. The PB2 and DPB may occasionally suspend for Dec-Feb (more typically in individuals wintering in the n.Hemisphere?). Occurrence of a PA1 (overlapping flight-feather molt of PF) requires confirmation: it may include some head and body feathers. The PA2 and DPA include most body feathers, some to all les and med covs, no to some proximal gr covs, often 1-3 terts, possibly the ornamental c.rects (confirmation needed; variation in shape and length of r1 also could be related to variation in the timing of molts; see p. 29).

Age—Juv (B1; Aug-Jan) has pale-cinnamon to grayish-buff tips to back feathers and s covs (in all but darkest 10% of Juvs), bill grayish with dark tip, and tarsus and bases of feet pale gray to bluish white (Fig. 516**A**, p. 738); Juv ♀ = ♂. See also pp. 729-730 for ageing in jaegers.

Juv-HY/SY (1st cycle, Juv/B1-F1; Sep-Aug): Underwing p covs with extensive white bases (Fig. 515**A**); tarsus extensively to moderately pale (Fig. 516**A-C**); pale barring to axillars and underwing covs extensive (light morph) to moderate (dark morph); r1 not twisted, with blunt tip and short projection (4-19 mm) in Sep-Feb (Fig. 517**A-B** p. 739) or with pointed tip and moderately short projection (11-39 mm) in Feb-Aug (Fig. 517**C-D**); inner pp replaced primarily Jan-May; cap variably mottled or streaked whitish (Fig. 514**C-E**); hackles absent in Sep-Mar (*cf.* Fig. 512**A**, p. 732) to reduced in some SYs in Apr-Aug (*cf.* Fig. 512**A-B**). **Note: Darkest dark-morph HY/SYs difficult to separate from AHY/ASYs: note timing of inner**

p molt and check for barring on axillars and underwing covs, pale markings on tarsus (Fig. 516), and length of r1 (Fig. 517).

SY/TY (2nd cycle, B2-A2; Sep-Aug): Underwing p covs usually with reduced (Fig. 515**B**) or no white bases; tarsus usually with reduced pale blotching (Fig. 516**B-D**, occasionally to **E**); pale barring to axillars and underwing variably extensive to reduced (light morph) to reduced or absent (dark morph); r1 not twisted, with pointed tip, and probably with short projection (15-40 mm?) in Sep-Feb (Fig. 517**E-F**), or moderately twisted (0-60° from web plane), with blunt tip, and moderate projection by sex (26-82 mm) in Feb-Aug (Fig. 517**C-D**); inner pp replaced primarily Nov-Feb; cap usually uniformly dark (Fig. 514**A-B**; occasionally streaked as in **E**) and hackles moderate to extensive in Apr-Oct (*cf.* Fig. 512**B-C**). **Note: See Juv-HY/SY. Some dark-morph SY/TYs are not reliably separated from ASY/ATYs and should be aged AHY/ASY.**

ASY/ATY (Def. cycle, DB-DA; Sep-Aug): Underwing p covs without pale bases (*cf.* Fig. 515**A-B**); tarsus blackish, without pale markings (Fig. 516**E**); axillars and underwing covs without pale barring; r1 slightly twisted (5-60° from web plane), with pointed tip, and with moderate projection (21-60 mm) in Sep-Feb (Fig. 517**E-F**), or extensively twisted (40-90° from web plane), with blunt tip, and extensive projection by sex (46-110 mm) in Feb-Aug (Fig. 517**G-H**); inner pp replaced primarily Oct-Jan; cap uniformly black (Fig. 514**A-B**) and hackles extensive (*cf.* Fig. 512**C**) in Apr-Aug. **Note: See SY/TY. Plumage aspect in Nov-Mar includes streaked caps, dark barring to the underparts and other characters resembling those of SYs and TYs in Apr-Aug; check tarsus color and underwing patterns to confirm age at this time of year. Some TY/4Ys are probably reliably aged by scattered pale-barred underwing les covs, more-extensive dark barring and streaking to underparts in Apr-Jun, some barring to the uppertail covs, and shorter and less distinctly twisted r1,**

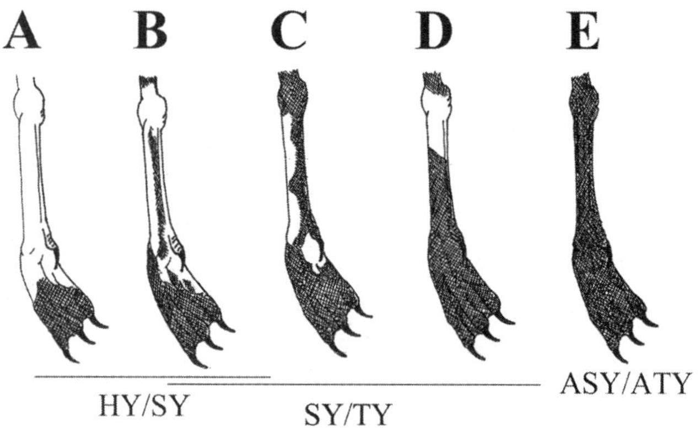

FIGURE 516. Tarsus pattern by age in Pomarine and Parasitic jaegers. Skuas also show variation in leg color with age (Juv-HY/SYs and some SY/TYs appearing as **C-D** and ASY/ATYs as **E**), but note that all ages of Long-tailed Jaeger show pale tarsal markings (**A-D**), those of HY/SYs averaging more extensive (**A-B**). Among Pomarine and Parasitic jaegers, tarsi appear to become blacker more quickly in dark morphs than in light morphs (study needed).

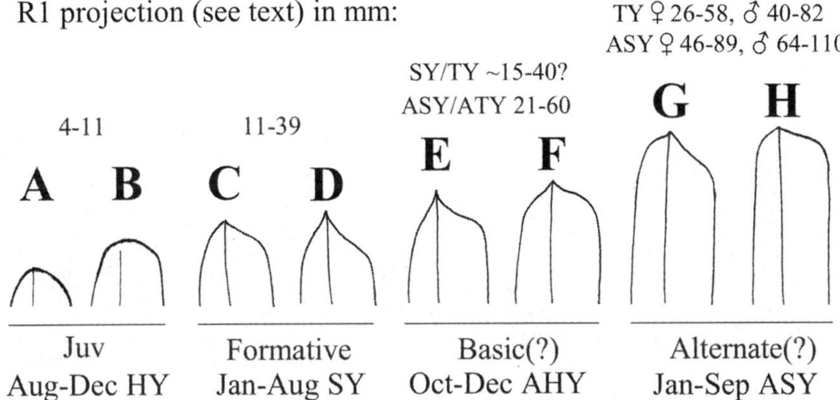

FIGURE 517. Shape and relative length of the r1 projection by feather generation, age, and sex in Pomarine Jaegers. R1 projection refers to the distance between the tip of r1 (when fully grown) and that of r2 (or from r1 to r3 if r2 is also elongated, as occurs in some individuals). Confirmation that the r1 is replaced twice per year is needed (see text). If so, predefinitive and basic feathers may be more pointed at the tip, whereas the definitive alternate r1 is blunter tipped, and the degree of twisting may average greater in the alternate than the basic r1, and greater in ATY than TY. But these differences also may represent individual variation as related to timing of molt (see p. 29); study needed.

but it is possible that some ASY/ATYs may also show these features; confirmation needed from known-age individuals.

Sex—♀ = ♂ by plumage aspect but light morph ♂♂ more often lack dark chest band. Bilateral BPs (Fig. 20**B**, p. 31) developed by both sexes but distended cloaca (Fig. 21, p. 32) indicates ATY ♀ in May-Jul. R1 appears to average longer in ASY ♂♂ than in ASY ♀♀ when fully grown in May-Aug (Fig. 517**G-H**), and this is likely useful for sexing some ♂♂, but length is also confounded by age, molt-related variation, and wear, so more study needed on the use of this character for sexing. Otherwise, measurements unhelpful for sexing (Table 66) and no other criteria known.

Pomarine Jaeger
Jan Feb Mar Apr May Jun Jul Aug Sep Oct Nov Dec
Juv-HY
SY
TY
AHY
ASY
ATY
(♀) ♀ (♀)
■ > 95% ▩ 25-95% ▨ 5-25% □ < 5%
See Fig. 24 (pp. 44-45)

Hybrids reported—None, but see Andersson (1999).

References—Bent (1921), Browning (1978), Cramp & Simmons (1983), Dement'ev & Gladkov (1951c), Higgins & Davies (1996), Howell (2007b), Jonsson (1984), Kaufman (1990a), Malling Olsen & Christensen (1984), Malling Olsen & Jonsson (1989), Malling Olsen & Larsson (1997), Manning et al. (1956), Murphy (1936), Oberholser (1974), Ridgway (1919), Stone (1900), Ullman (1984), Wiley & Lee (2000).

PARASITIC JAEGER
Stercorarius parasiticus

PAJA
Species # 0370
Band size: 4A

Species—From other jaegers, skuas, and gulls by medium-small size (Table 66, p. 735); r1 extended by age (Fig. 521); plumage aspect polymorphic at all ages; uppersides of p5-p10 with creamy-white shafts (95% of ASY/ATYs with white limited to p5/p7-p10); bill grayish to dusky with black tip.

From Pomarine Jaeger (p. 735) further by smaller size and bill (Table 66; Fig. 514**F**-**G**, p. 736); r1 narrow, untwisted, and with pointed tip (Figs. 519**C**-**D** & 521, p. 742); Juv-HY with warmer and browner (often reddish) plumage aspect, hindneck with distinct streaking, underwing p covs with reduced whitish bases or variable barred markings (Fig. 515**B**-**E**, p. 737), outer pp usually with distinct whitish fringes at tips when fresh (Fig. 518**B**-**D**, occasionally lacking), and uppertail covs with irregular or slightly checkered pattern (Fig. 520**B**); ASY/ATY with bill grayish to dusky on basal two-thirds, blackish cap not extending to malar region, and chest whitish or washed dusky (Fig. 514**F**-**G**). SYs and TYs variable in appearance; best separated by size (Table 66), r1 shape (Figs. 519**C**-**D** & 521), cap shape if apparent (*cf.* Fig. 514**C**-**D**), and grayish or dusky bill base.

From Long-tailed Jaeger (p. 743) further, with caution (especially Juv-HY/SYs), by bill nail proportionally shorter (Fig. 514**F**-**G**); forearm length longer (Fig. 522**A**, p. 743); p5-p8 usually with white shafts; Juv-HY with warmer brown plumage aspect (especially nape), outer pp usually with distinct and wider whitish fringes at tip (Fig. 518**C**-**D**), uppertail covs with less contrasting and more irregular and broken cinnamon-buff bars (Fig. 520**B**), r1 tips more pointed and r1 projection shorter (Fig. 519**C**-**D**), and underwing p covs variable in pattern (Fig. 515**B**-**E**); ASY/ATY

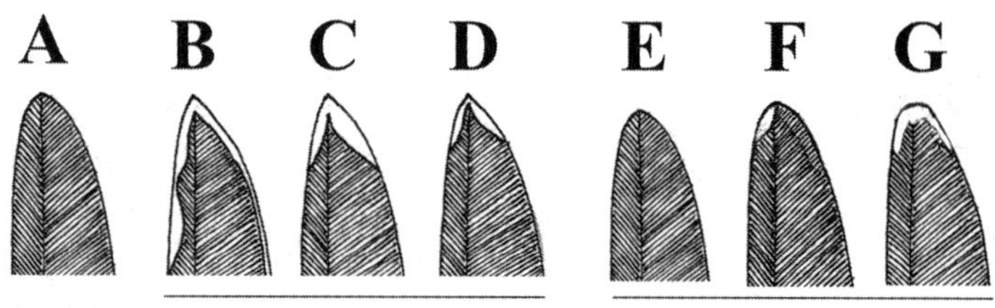

FIGURE 518. Variation in the pale tips to outer primaries in juvenile jaegers by species, here showing p8. These patterns are best seen in fresh plumage aspect and are often abraded by winter. Parasitic Jaeger can occasionally show reduced or no white fringes as found in Long-tailed Jaeger (**E**-**F**, occasionally **G**).

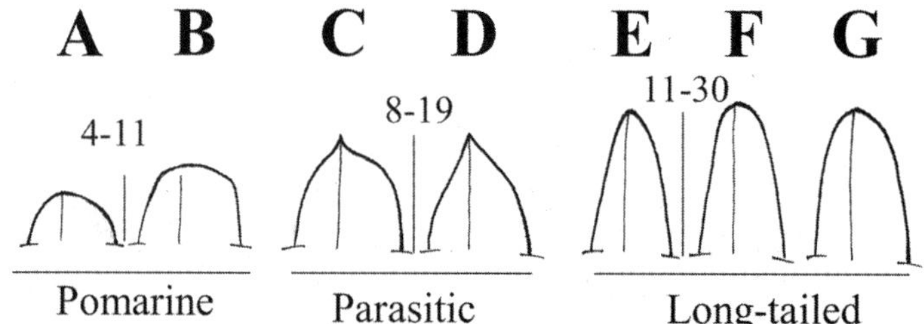

FIGURE 519. Typical shapes and projections of r1 by species in Juv jaegers. The indicated measure is the r1 projection (distance between the tips of r1 and r2). In Juv Pomarine Jaeger (**A**-**B**) r1 is relatively short, thick, and blunt-tipped. In Juv Parasitic Jaeger (**C**-**D**) r1 is intermediate in length and tapered to point); In Juv Long-tailed (**E**-**G**) it is relatively long and tapered, but blunt-tipped compared to Parasitic Jaeger.

with undersides of pp with distinct white bases, p9-p10 with darker shafts when fresh; upperparts and s covs darker brown and not contrasting distinctly with blackish secondaries, and r1 tips broader and r1 projection shorter by age (Figs. 519**C**-**D** & 521). SYs and TYs variable in appearance, best separated by bill and nail dimensions (Fig. 514**F**-**G**), r1 shape (Figs. 519**C**-**D** & 521); and p5-p8 with white shafts.

Geographic variation—Monotypic. Populations of e.Siberia ("*S.p. parallelus*") may average darker, slight mensural differences have been noted between populations, and dark-morph individuals apparently more frequent in s.parts of breeding range, but in all cases differences insufficient for subspecific recognition. See Bengston & Owen (1973), Cramp & Simmons (1983), Dement'ev & Gladkov (1951c), Portenko (1973), and Southern (1943) for more information.

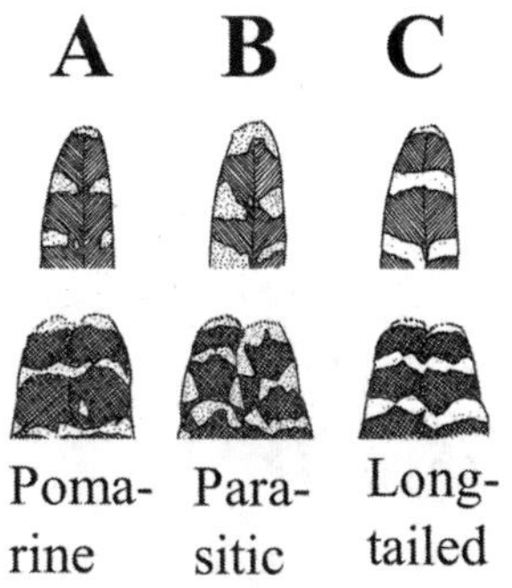

A B C

Poma-rine Para-sitic Long-tailed

FIGURE 520. Typical patterns of uppertail-covert barring for identification of Juv jaegers. The upper figure is of a single long covert, the lower figure shows the overall pattern created by the three distal rows of coverts. Juv Pomarine Jaeger (**A**) shows fairly broad cinnamon to whitish tips and slightly irregular, often broken median bands, creating a relatively evenly barred pattern. Juv Parasitic Jaeger (**B**) shows broad buff tips and notches, creating an irregular or slightly checkered pattern. Juv Long-tailed Jaeger (**C**) shows narrow whitish tips and broad median bands, creating a relatively even and broad-barred pattern.

Molt—SAS (CAS?) PF complete (Nov/Jan-Apr/Jul in HY/SYs), PA1 absent-limited? (Mar?-May? in SYs), PB2 complete (Aug/Oct-May in SY/TYs), PA2 incomplete (Mar-May in TYs), DPB complete (Aug-Dec/Apr in ASY/ATYs), DPA partial-incomplete (Feb-Apr in ATYs). The complete inserted first-cycle molt appears to be a PF rather than a PA1 (Fig. 10**C**, p. 14), although a limited PA1 of head and back feathers may also occur in some SYs indicating CAS (Fig. 10**F**). Most to all molting occurs on non-breeding grounds although the DPB can begin during southbound migration. The PF commences with body molt in Nov-Dec followed by molt of flight feathers in Dec/Feb-Apr/Jul. Molt of pp during the PB2 occurs Nov/Dec-Mar/May. During the DPB, body molt often completes by Dec and molt of pp occurs Oct/Nov-Feb/Apr (possibly beginning as early as Aug; Malling Olsen & Larsson 1997); the ornamental r1 is usually replaced in Oct-Nov. The PB2 and DPB may occasionally suspend for Dec-Feb (more typically in individuals wintering in the n.Hemisphere?). Occurrence of a PA1 (overlapping flight-feather molt of PF) requires confirmation: it may include some head and body feathers. The PA2 and DPA include some to most body feathers, most to all les and med covs, usually 1-3 terts, possibly the ornamental c.rects (confirmation needed; see Pomarine Jaeger **Molt**, p. 737).

Age—Juv (B1; Aug-Jan) has nape streaked cinnamon, back feathers and s covs tipped cinnamon to buff (sometimes with completely cinnamon marginal covs on light morphs, narrower in dark morph), bill grayish with dark tip, and tarsus and bases of feet pale gray to bluish white (Fig. 516**A**, p. 738); Juv ♀=♂. See also pp. 729-730 for ageing in jaegers.

Juv-HY/SY (1st cycle, Juv/B1-F1; Sep-Aug): Tarsus extensively to moderately pale (Fig. 516**A**-**C**); pale barring to axillars and underwing covs extensive in light morph to moderately indistinct in dark morph (Fig. 515**B**-**E**, p. 737); r1 broadly pointed and with moderately short projection (8-19) in Sep-Feb (Fig. 521**A**-**B**, p. 742) or pointed, occasionally pinched in, and with moderate projection (15-59 mm) in Feb-Aug (Fig. 521**C**-**D**); inner pp replaced primarily Jan-Apr; cap often mottled or streaked buff (*cf.* Fig. 514**C**-**E**, p. 736); hackles absent in Sep-Mar (*cf.* Fig. 512**A**, p. 732) to reduced in some SYs in Apr-Aug (*cf.* Fig. 512**A**-**B**). **Note: Darkest dark-morph HY/SYs may lack barring on underwing and be difficult to separate**

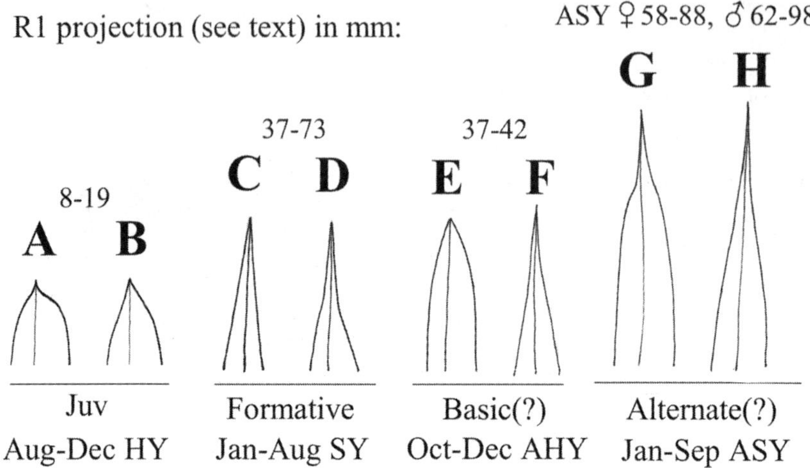

FIGURE 521. Shape and relative length of the r1 projection by feather generation and age in Parasitic Jaegers. R1 projection refers to the distance between the tip of r1 (when fully grown) and that of r2 (or from r1 to r3 if r2 is also elongated, as occurs in some individuals). Confirmation that the r1 is replaced twice per year is needed (see text). If so, predefinitive (and probably basic feathers; study needed) tend to be less pointed at the tip, whereas definitive alternate feathers are more pointed. Occasional feathers (uncommon or rare) can be tapered at tip or spatulate as in **E**. Long-tailed Jaeger shows moderately pointed juv c.rects (Fig. 519**E**-**G**, p. 740; projection 11-30 mm) and more attenuated (needle-like at tip) rects in subsequent generations. In Mar-Sep projection averages longer by age than in Parasitic Jaeger: 13-69 mm in SYs (shape as in **F** above), 43-167 in TYs (shape as in **H** above), and 136-231 mm in ATYs (shape more attenuated than **H**, evenly long and tapered). In both species, more study needed on the growth of these feathers in Nov-Mar and whether or not one or two generations are involved.

from AHY/ASYs: note molt timing for inner pp, pale markings on tarsus (Fig. 516A-C), and length of r1 (Fig. 521A-D).

SY/TY (2nd cycle, B2-A2; Sep-Aug): Tarsus with reduced to no pale blotching (Fig. 516**B**-**E**); pale barring to axillars and underwing covs variably extensive to reduced in light morph or reduced to absent in dark morph (*cf.* Fig. 515); r1 variably tapered to pointed, with moderate projection (37-42 mm) in Sep-Feb (Fig. 521**E**-**F**) to moderately long projection (37-73 mm) in Mar-Aug (Fig. 521**F**-**H**); inner pp replaced primarily Nov-Feb; cap usually uniformly dark (*cf.* Fig. 514**F**-**G**); hackles moderate to extensive in Apr-Oct (*cf.* Fig. 512**B**-**C**). **Note: See Juv-HY/SY. Some dark-morph SY/TYs are not reliably separated from ASY/ATYs and should be aged AHY/ASY.**

ASY/ATY (Def. cycle, DB-DA; Sep-Aug): Tarsus blackish, without pale markings (Fig. 516**E**); axillars and underwing covs without pale barring (*cf.* Fig. 515); r1 pointed and with moderately long projection (37-42 mm) in Sep-Mar (Fig. 521**F**) to long projection (58-98 mm) in Mar-Aug (Fig. 521**G**-**H**); inner pp replaced primarily Oct-Jan; cap uniformly dark (Fig. 514**F**-**G**); hackles extensive in Apr-Oct (*cf.* Fig. 512**C**). **Note: See SY/TY. Note that plumage aspect in Nov-Mar includes streaked caps, dark barring to the underparts, and other characters resembling those of SYs and TYs in Apr-Aug; check tarsus color and underwing patterns to confirm age at this time of year. Some TY/4Ys are perhaps reliably aged by scattered pale-barred underwing les covs and/or uppertail covs and shorter r1; more study needed.**

Sex— ♀ = ♂ by plumage aspect but light morph ♂♂ more often lack dark chest band. Bilateral BPs (Fig. 20**B**, p. 31) developed by both sexes but distended cloaca (Fig. 21, p. 32) indicates

ATY ♀ in May-Jul. Measurements unhelpful for sexing (Table 66, p. 735). R1 may average longer in ATY ♂♂ than in ATY ♀♀ in May-Aug (Fig. 521**F**-**G**) but this is also confounded by age and molt-related variation so is unlikely to be useful. See Phillips & Furness (1997) for DFAs (p. 5), using incubation body mass, wing length, head-bill length (Fig. 453, p. 630), bill length, and bill depth at gonys to sex 78-91% of adults breeding in Scotland.

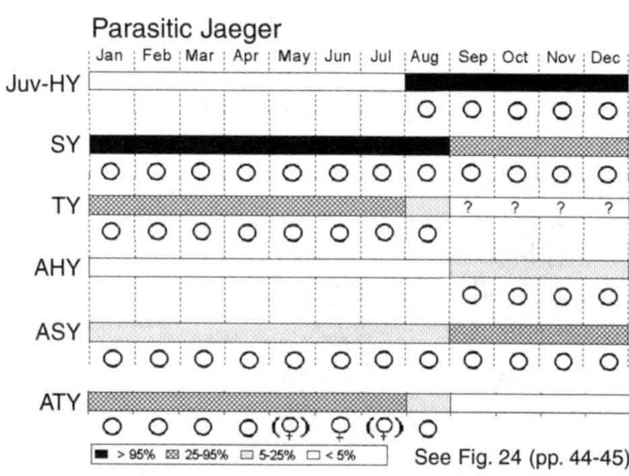

Hybrids reported—None, but see Andersson (1999).

References—Baker (1993), Bent (1921), Cramp & Simmons (1983), Dement'ev & Gladkov (1951c), Higgins & Davies (1996), Howell (2007b), Jonsson (1984), Kaufman (1990a), Malling Olsen & Christensen (1984), Malling Olsen & Jonsson (1989), Malling Olsen & Larsson (1997), Manning et al. (1956), Melville (1985), Murphy (1936), Parmelee et al. (1967), Phillips & Furness (1997), Ridgway (1919), Stone (1900), Wiley & Lee (1999), Willett & Howard (1934).

LONG-TAILED JAEGER
Stercorarius longicaudus

LTJA
Species # 0380
Band size: 4A-4

Species—From other jaegers and gulls by medium-small size (Table 66, p. 735); r1 extended by age (*cf.* Fig. 521); plumage aspect polymorphic in Juv-HY/SY/TY but ASY/ATY with light morph only; uppersides of p7-p10 (only) with creamy-white shafts (94% of ASY/ATYs with white limited to p8/p9-p10); ss blackish, contrasting distinctly with paler s covs in all except darkest HY/SYs; bill grayish to dusky with dark tip (Juv-HY) to black (ASY). See Parasitic Jaeger (p. 740) for separation from Pomarine Jaeger.

From Parasitic Jaeger, with caution (especially Juv-HY/SYs), by bill nail proportionally longer (Fig. 514**H**, p. 736); forearm length shorter (Fig. 522**B**); p5-p8 without white shafts; Juv-HY with colder brown plumage aspect (especially nape), outer pp without whitish tips or with narrow whitish fringes (Fig. 518**E**-**F**, occasionally **G**; p. 740); uppertail covs with more contrasting and even whitish markings (Fig. 520**C**, p. 741), r1 tips blunter and r1 projection longer (Fig. 519**E**-**G**, p. 740), and underwing p covs usually with bold pale bars (Fig. 515**E**, p. 737); ASY/ATY with undersides of pp without distinct white bases, p9-p10 with pale shafts when fresh;

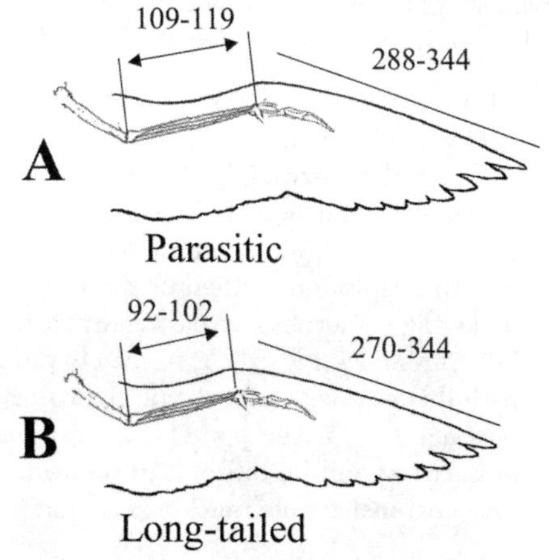

FIGURE 522. Wing structure in Parasitic and Long-tailed jaegers showing the shorter forearm length of Long-tailed. Forearm length is defined as the anterior edge of the ulna at the humeral joint (left) to the distal end of the ulna at the carpal joint (right). Accurate measures on live individuals can be achieved by feeling these skeletal points through the wing. The proportion of forearm length to wing chord, as indicated, is likely also diagnostic.

upperparts and s covs paler gray-brown contrasting distinctly with blackish ss, and r1 more attenuated and with longer projection by age (Fig. 519**E**-**G** & *cf.* Fig. 521, p. 742). See Parasitic Jaeger regarding separation of SYs and TYs.

Geographic variation—Monotypic (AOU 1957). Populations breeding in N.Am ("*S.l. pallescens*") average paler underparts than Eurasian populations but differences obscured by individual variation and may represent polymorphism rather than subspecific difference; more study needed. See Cramp & Simmons (1983), Dement'ev & Gladkov (1951c), Hellmayr & Conover (1948b), Løppenthin (1943), Malling Olson & Larsson (1997), Manning (1964), Portenko (1973), Stejneger (1885), and Wiley & Lee (1998) for more information.

Molt—SAS (CAS?). PF complete (Nov/Jan-Apr/Jul in HY/SYs), PA1 absent-limited? (Mar?-May? in SYs), PB2 complete (Aug/Oct-May in SY/TYs), PA2 incomplete (Mar-May in TYs), DPB complete (Aug/Nov-Feb/Apr in ASY/ATYs), DPA incomplete (Mar-May in ATYs). The complete inserted first-cycle molt appears to be homologous with a PF rather than a PA1 (Fig. 10**C**, p. 14), although a limited PA1 of head and back feathers may also occur in some SYs indicating CAS (Fig. 10**F**). Most to all molting occurs on non-breeding grounds although the DPB can begin during southbound migration. The PF commences with body molt in Nov-Dec followed by molt of flight feathers in Jan/Feb-Apr/Jul. Molt of pp during the PB2 occurs Oct/Dec-Apr/May. During the DPB, body molt often completes by Dec and molt of pp occurs Oct/Dec-Feb/Apr; the ornamental r1 is usually replaced in Aug-Oct during migration. Occurrence of PA1 (overlapping flight feather molt of PF) requires confirmation: it may include some head and body feathers. The PA2 and DPA include some to most body feathers, a few to most les and med covs, often 1-3 terts, and possibly the ornamental c.rects (confirmation needed; see Pomerine Jaeger **Molt**, p. 737).

Age—Juv (B1; Aug-Jan) has back feathers, s covs, and uppertail covs distinctly tipped pale buff to whitish, bill grayish with dark tip, and tarsus and bases of feet pale gray to bluish white (Fig. 516**A**, p. 738); Juv ♀=♂. See also pp. 729-730 for ageing in jaegers.

Juv-HY/SY (1st cycle, Juv/B1-F1; Sep-Aug): Polymorphic; outer pp and r6 usually with indistinct white bases and (r6) pale bars or markings to outer web (Fig. 523**A**-**B**); pale barring to axillars and underwing covs distinct (Fig. 515**E**, p. 737); r1 broadly pointed and with moderately short projection (11-30) in Sep-Jan (Fig. 519**E**-**G**, p. 740) or attenuated (*cf.* Fig. 521**F**, p. 742) and with moderate projection (13-69 mm) in Feb-Aug; inner pp replaced primarily Jan-Apr; cap often mottled or streaked buff (*cf.* Fig. 514**C**-**E**, p. 736) but uniformly dark in darker light-morphs and dark-morphs; tarsus extensively pale (Fig. 516**A**-**B**); hackles absent in Sep-Mar (*cf.* Fig. 512**A**, p. 732) to reduced in Apr-Aug (*cf.* Fig. 512**B**). **Note: Individuals with this plumage aspect but r1 projection > 100 mm in Apr-Aug could be TYs and are best aged S-TY (see pp. 41-42). Also, darkest dark-morph HY/SYs may lack barring on underwing and be difficult to separate from AHY/ASYs: note molt timing for inner pp, more extensive pale markings on tarsus (Fig. 516A-B), and length of r1 (*cf.* Fig. 521).**

SY/TY (2nd cycle, B2-A2; Sep-Aug): Polymorphic; outer pp and r6 uniformly dark or sometimes (outer pp) to usually (r6) with distinct white bases but few or no pale marks to outer web (Fig. 523**C**-**D**); pale barring to axillars and underwing covs variable (*cf.* Fig. 515); r1 projection probably 30-40 mm in Sep-Jan (study needed), or attenuated but with broader base (*cf.* Fig. 521**H**) and long projection (43-167 mm) in Apr-Aug; inner pp replaced primarily Nov-Feb; cap uniformly dark (*cf.* Fig. 514**H**); tarsus with variable pale markings (Fig. 516**A**-**D**); hackles moderate to extensive in Mar-Aug (*cf.* Fig. 512**B**-**C**). **Note: See Juv-HY/SY.**

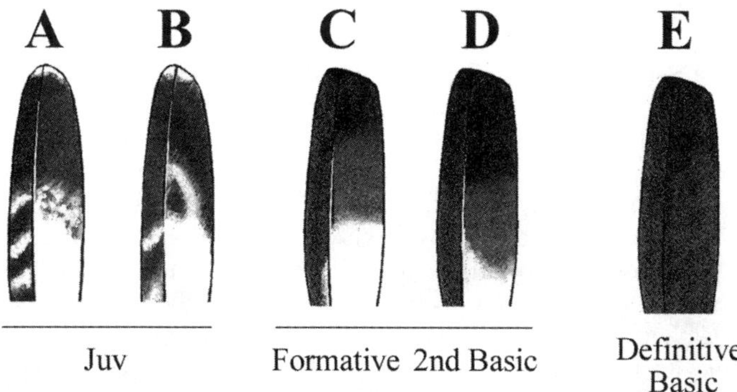

FIGURE 523. Shape and pattern to the outer rectrix (r6) by feather generation in Long-tailed Jaeger. Note that juv rects (**A-B**) are narrower and usually have increased but less distinct white bases than formative and 2nd basic rects (**C-D**), including barring or marking to the outer webs. Juv outer rects are retained until Apr-Jul in SYs. Some 3rd basic rects on TY/4Ys may also show reduced white bases (as in **D**); more study is needed. Definitive basic rects are mostly to entirely dark (**E**).

ASY/ATY (Def. cycle, DB-DA; Sep-Aug): Light morph only; outer pp and r6 uniformly dark (Fig. 523**E**); axillars and underwing covs without pale barring (*cf.* Fig. 515); r1 projection probably ~40 mm in Sep-Jan (study needed), or evenly attenuated throughout length and with very long projection (136-231 mm) in Apr-Aug; inner pp replaced primarily Nov-Feb; cap black (Fig. 514**H**); tarsus with variable pale markings (Fig. 516**A-D**, often **C-D**); hackles extensive in Apr-Aug (*cf.* Fig. 512**C**). **Note: See Juv-HY/SY. Plumage aspect in Nov-Mar includes streaked caps, dark barring to the underparts, and other characters resembling those of SYs and TYs in Apr-Aug; check tarsus color and underwing patterns to confirm age at this time of year. Some TY/4Ys may perhaps be distinguishable by some whitish to the base of r6 (*cf.* Fig. 523D), one or more pale-barred underwing les covs or uppertail covs, and shorter r1; more study needed.**

Sex—♀ = ♂ by plumage aspect although, within populations, ASY ♀♀ average more-extensively dusky on lower breast and belly than ♂♂ (Manning et al. 1956). Bilateral BPs (Fig. 20**B**, p. 31) developed by both sexes but distended cloaca (Fig. 21, p. 32) indicates ATY ♀ in May-Jul. Measurements unhelpful for sexing (Table 66, p. 735); length of r1 in ATYs in May-Aug also apparently not useful.

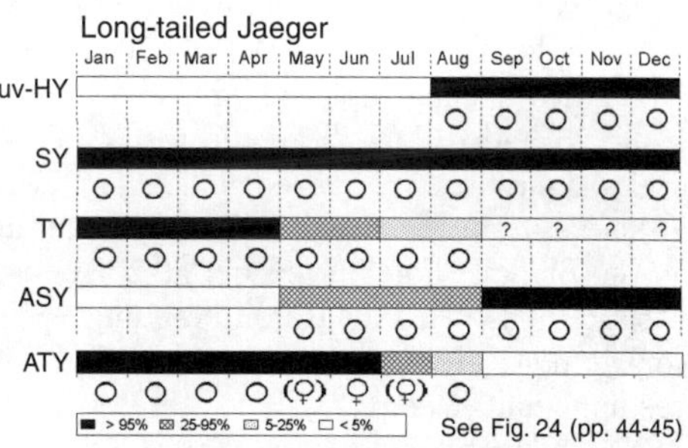

Hybrids reported—None.

References—Bent (1921), Cramp & Simmons (1983), Dement'ev & Gladkov (1951c), Higgins & Davies (1996), Howell (1999, 2007b), Kaufman (1990a), Løppenthin (1943), Malling Olsen & Christensen (1984), Malling Olsen & Larsson (1997), Manning (1964), Manning et al. (1956), Melville (1985), Murphy (1936), Parmelee & MacDonald (1960), Ridgway (1919), Stone (1900), Wiley & Lee (1998), Willett & Howard (1934).

AUKS, MURRES, AND PUFFINS *ALCIDAE*

Twenty species. Family characters include heavy bodies; proportionally short wings; sturdy, laterally compressed legs and feet with three fully webbed toes and claws; and variable, often highly modified bills, including deciduous ornamental processes in some species, shed in fall and re-developed in spring (cf. Stejneger 1885, Kozlova 1957). North American alcids have 10 functional primaries (p10 usually longest, by 0-8 mm, when fully grown), 15-20 secondaries (including 3 tertial-like feathers and one absent between the 4th and 5th in all species except *Aethia*; Fig. 12**B**, p. 19; see below), and 12-18 rectrices. Ageing can be accomplished through the first cycle (to SY and ASY) by plumage aspect, bill width at gape (Fig. 524), shape and patterns of retained feathers among flight feathers (Figs. 525-527, pp. 747-748), and bill color; some species can be aged through the third cycle (to TY and ATY) or later by eye color and/or bill characteristics. Sexes are alike in plumage aspect and most measurements (♂♂ average larger than ♀♀) but bill characters can be used to sex some individuals of certain species. Medial or bilateral brood patches (Fig. 20**A-B**, p. 31) are developed by both sexes but distended cloacae (Fig. 21, p. 32) indicate breeding ASY ♀♀; other cloacal characters (Figs. 22-23, pp. 32-35) should be investigated.

In molting, alcids exhibit Complex Basic (CBS; Fig. 10**B**, p. 14), Complex Alternate (CAS; Fig. 10**F**), and Simple Alternate (SAS; Fig. 10**C-F**) strategies. Species exhibiting the last strategy apparently can lack either a preformative molt or a first prealternate molt, or may have had these two molts from those of ancestral species merged (Fig. 10**D**). Prejuvenal molts (PB1) can occur partially or entirely at sea in six species but complete at the natal site in most. Preformative molts, when they occur, are partial and protracted over winter, and prealternate molts, when they occur, are primarily limited to body feathers. Ornamental filoplumes in several species appear to be formative or basic feathers developed slowly over winter, rather than alternate feathers that have replaced non-ornamental feathers of other generations. Several species replace all wing feathers synchronously (Fig. 525**D**; *cf.* Fig. 12**A**), some murrelets appear to replace primaries (at least) in blocks (Fig. 525**E**), and some auklets replace feathers sequentially (non-simultaneously), the primaries replaced distally from p1 to p10 and the secondaries usually replaced proximally from s1 and s5 and distally from the tertials. Two species (Least and Whiskered auklets, pp. 774-776) are eutaxic and may lack a molt center at s5. Age of first breeding occurs at 2-5 years; prebasic molts of SYs and non-breeding ASYs average more advanced in timing than those of breeding adults (see p. 18).

See Flint & Golovkin (1990), Gaston & Jones (1998), Harrison (1983a, 1987), Kozlava (1957), and Nettleship & Birkhead (1985) for more information on molts and age/sex determination in alcids.

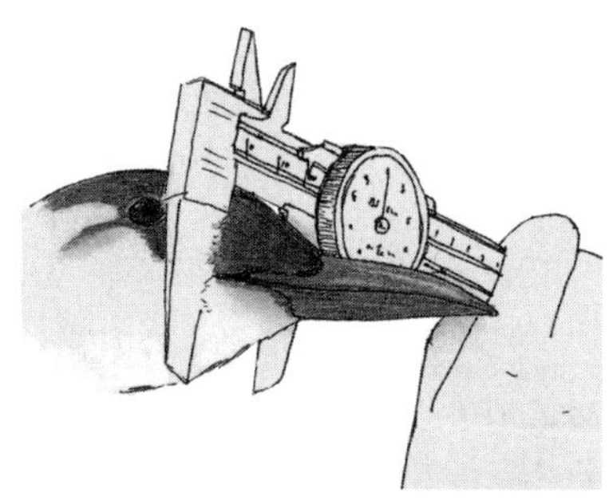

FIGURE 524. Technique for measuring "**bill width at gape**" for use in age-determination among alcids. Calipers should be held perpendicular to the axis of the bill. Measure is taken at the proximal end of the gape. Caution that measurement ranges presented in this guide are based on specimens and need verification on live birds in field. See Pyle (unpublished ms2) for more information.

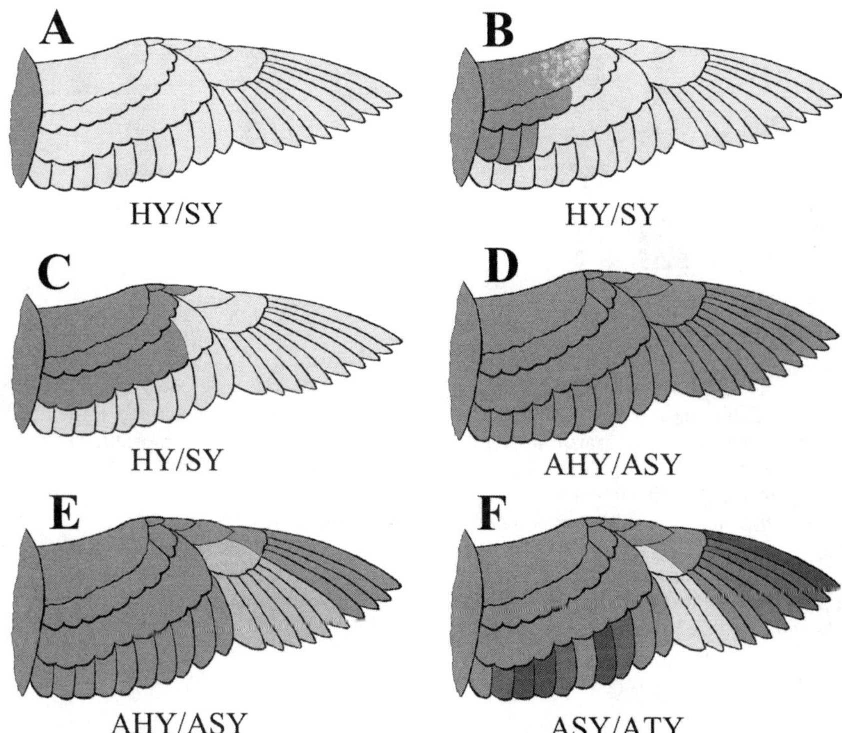

Figure 525. Wing shape and molt patterns by age in alcids. **A**-**C** exhibit thinner and more pointed wings (based on thinner pp; Fig. 526, p. 748) as well as molt limits found among wing coverts in HY/SYs after incomplete PFs. **A** shows a limit between formative humerals/scapulars and juvenal s covs (Juvs are similar but have entirely juv feathers without a limit) whereas **B**-**C** show molt limits among the wing covs. Note that at least one species (Cassin's Auklet) can show limits resembling **A**-**B** in ASYs in Mar-Sep, following partial DPAs. **E**-**F** show broader wings typical of AHY/ASYs. Wing-shape differences are not as pronounced in murres, razorbills, and some murrelets which undergo the PB1 (prejuvenal molt) at sea following fledging. Many species have synchronous or near-synchronous wing-feather replacement during DPBs, resulting in uniformly basic feathers in AHY/ASYs, as in **D**. A few species have sequential (non-synchronous) replacement patterns. **E** shows patterns that can be found in some AHY/ASY murrelets, after p1-p6 and p7-p10 had been replaced in blocks. **F** shows a pattern found in some post-breeding auklets, where the inner 1-3 pp had been replaced during incubation, molt was suspended for chick-feeding, and sequential replacement of remaining pp and ss resumed following breeding. Note the clines within ss and outer pp representing sequential rather than synchronous replacement. Individuals with the suspension limit can be assumed to be breeding ASY/ATYs, whereas individuals that lack the suspension limit but show s1-p1 contrast and sequential molt clines (*cf.* Fig. 14**B**, p. 21) may not have bred the previous year (as in SY alcids) and must be aged AHY/ASY.

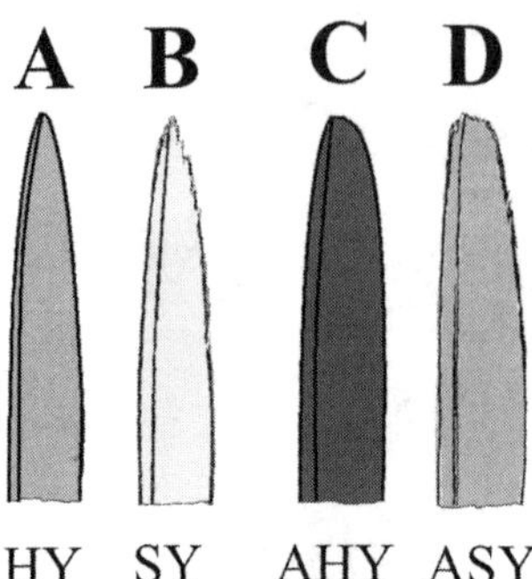

FIGURE 526. Shape of the outer primaries by age and season in alcids. See also Figure 525, p. 747. Note that differences in shape and wear are not as pronounced in murres, razorbills, and certain murrelets, which develop their juv pp at sea following breeding; the juv feathers in these species are stronger and more durable in structure. Also, ASY Atlantic and Horned puffins (p. 783) replace pp in spring and have a different seasonal pattern of wear. SY alcids retain their juv pp (**B**) until the PB2 in Jun-Aug.

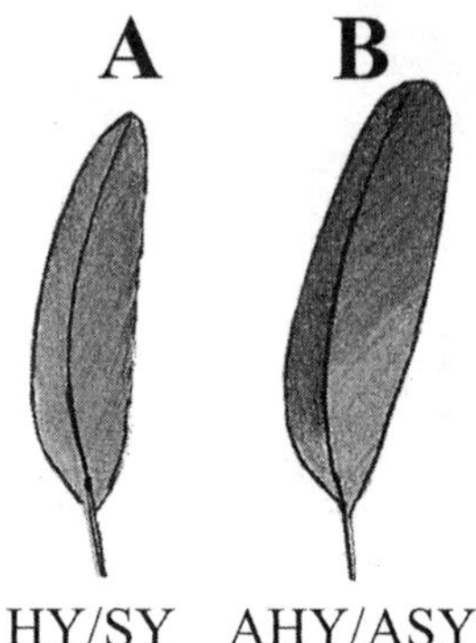

FIGURE 527. Shape and size of the outer rectrix (r6) by age in most alcids. In many species the juv rects (**A**) are developed at the natal site and are substantially shorter and weaker looking than basic rects (**B**). These are retained through the first cycle. In murres, razorbills, and some murrelets, the juv rects are developed at sea and do not differ as much from basic rects in size, shape, and structure; rects of Razorbill are also attenuated.

DOVEKIE

Alle alle

DOVE
Species # 0340
Band size: 3

Species—From other alcids by small size (Table 67, p. 754); bill black and stout with decurved culmen and extended mandible distal to gonys (Fig. 528); upperparts black, with white edges to longest scapulars and small white crescent often present near eye in Feb-Aug; ss with distinct white tips; sides of nape, throat, and breast black (Apr-Sep) to white (Sep-Mar); abdomen white; underwing covs dusky or with some whitish mottling; legs and feet grayish to slate with blackish toes.

Geographic variation—Considered monotypic here (*cf.* Bédard 1985). Populations breeding on Franz Joseph Land, n.Russia ("*A.a. polaris*") average larger than other subspecies but this difference is slight and may be broadly clinal; further study is needed. See also Day et al. (1988), Dement'ev & Gladkov (1951a), Kozlova (1957), Salomonsen (1944), Stempniewicz et al. (1996), Stenhouse (1930).

Molt—CAS. PF partial (Aug-Oct in HYs), PA1 absent-limited (Apr-May in SYs), PB2 complete (May-Aug in SYs), DPA limited (Jan-Apr in ASYs), DPB complete (Jul-Oct in ASYs). The PB1 (prejuvenile molt) commences at the natal site and can complete at sea, and the DPB can commence (body feathers only) during the later stages of nesting; otherwise, all molting occurs at sea, away from breeding grounds. The PF includes most to all body feathers and sometimes a few proximal les covs but no terts or rects. During DPBs, pp, p covs, and ss are replaced synchronously in Jun-Aug (SYs) or Aug-Oct (ASYs). The PAs are restricted primarily to feathers of the head, neck, and throat. Some SYs can over-summer on non-breeding grounds and these may exhibit reduced PA1s and advanced PB2s (see p. 18).

Age—Juv (B1; Jul-Oct) has small bill (depth at distal end of nares < 8 mm; *cf.* Fig. 528**A**), pp fresh and relatively pointed (Fig. 526**A**), upperparts brownish, and throat brownish or mottled white;

Juv ♀=♂. See Anker-Nilssen (1988) for information on ageing fresh dead individuals by bursal depth (Fig. 23, p. 34). Gular pouches may be developed and be useful for ageing as in Cassin's Auklet (Fig. 546, p. 770); study needed. In addition, confirmed breeding individuals can be reliably aged ASY.

Juv-HY/SY (1st cycle, Juv/F1-A1; Oct-Sep): Bill shallow (Fig. 528**A**-**B**); bill width at gape (Fig. 524, p. 746) ~10.5-13.0 mm; most to all wing feathers brownish, relatively worn, and lacking sheen, contrasting with the fresher, blacker and glossier scapulars, humerals, and sometimes some proximal s covs (Fig. 525**A**-**B**, p. 747), the juv outer pp and p covs somewhat narrow, pointed, and worn (Fig. 526**A**); outer rects relatively narrow and worn (Fig. 527**A**); throat white, often mottled brownish in Mar-Aug.

AHY/ASY (Def. cycle, DB-DA; Oct-Sep): Bill deep (Fig. 528**C**), bill width at gape (Fig. 524) ~11.5-14.0 mm; wing and back feathers uniformly black and glossy (Fig. 525**D**), the basic outer pp and p covs relatively broad, blunt, and fresh (Fig. 526**C**-**D**); outer rects relatively broad and fresh (Fig. 527**B**); throat uniformly black in Mar-Aug.

Sex—♀=♂ by plumage aspect. Bilateral BPs (Fig. 20**B**, p. 31) developed by both sexes but distended cloaca (Fig. 21, p. 32) indicates ASY ♀ in May-Jul. Measurements generally unhelpful for sexing (Table 67, p. 754; Fig. 528), although see Taylor (1994) and Jakubas & Wojczulanis (2007) for DFAs, based on bill width and head-bill length (Fig. 453, p. 630) that separated 70-80% of live breeding individuals. Amount of white mottling to the underwing may average greater in ♂♂ than ♀♀ but this appears to exhibit substantial individual (possibly age-related or geographic) variation; more study is needed. Otherwise, no criteria known for sexing.

Hybrids reported—None.

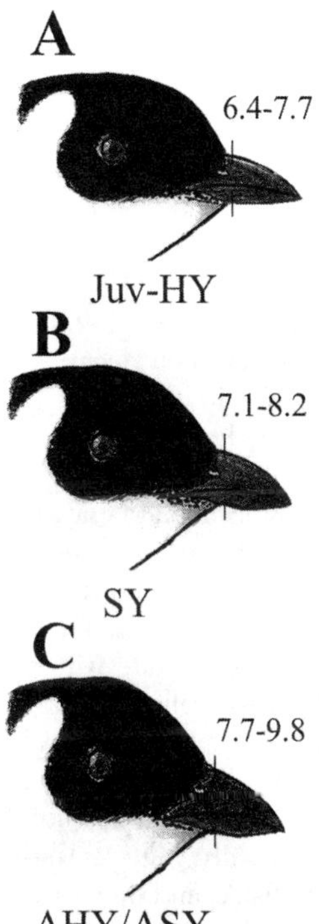

FIGURE 528. Bill size and depth by age in Dovekie. Measures indicate bill depth at distal end of nares (Fig. 8**C**, p. 10). **A** represents Juv-HYs in Jul-Dec; **B** represents SYs in Jan-Sep; **C** represents AHY/ASYs in Oct-Sep. In AHY/ASYs, note that bills are deeper in ♂♂ (depth at gonys 7.7-9.5 mm) than in ♀♀ (depth at gonys 7.3-9.1) but there is substantial overlap. Note also the distance between the gonydeal angle and the tip is longer in Dovekie (> 10 mm) than in murrelets (< 10 mm).

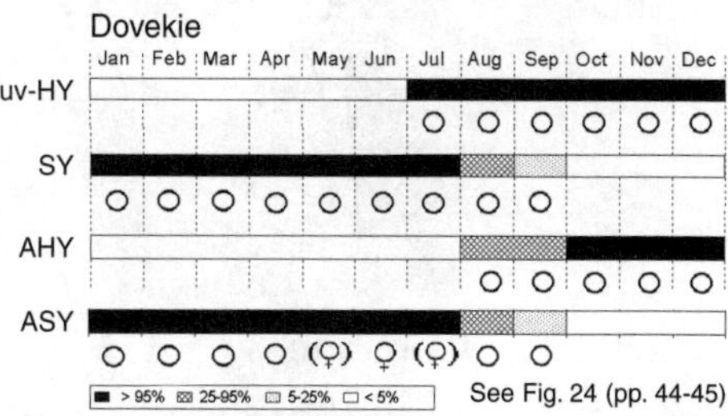

References—Anker-Nilssen et al. (1988), Bédard (1985), Bent (1919a), Camphuysen (1992), Cramp & Simmons (1985), Dement'ev & Gladkov (1951a), Heubeck & Suddaby (1991), Jakubas & Wojczulanis (2007), Kozlova (1957), Montevecchi & Stenhouse (2002), Pyle (unpublished ms.), Ridgway (1919), Roby et al. (1981), Salomonsen (1944), Stempniewicz (1989), Taylor (1994).

COMMON MURRE COMU
Uria aalge Species # 0300
Band size: 6M

THICK-BILLED MURRE TBMU
Uria lomvia Species # 0310
Band size: 6M-5R

Species—Murres from other alcids by longer wing, bill, and tarsus (Table 67, p. 754); bill with straight to moderately decurved culmen and mandible distal to gonys (Fig. 530), brownish with pale base (Juv) to black (ASY in Apr-Aug); mouth lining white to yellowish; upperparts brown to blackish with white tips to ss (Fig. 529**A-C**); s covs without white; underwing covs white, sometimes with dark mottling (*cf.* Fig. 532, p. 753; occasionally completely dark); legs and feet blackish posteriorly and grayish to brownish yellow anteriorly. From Juv and HY/SY Razorbills by shorter (Table 67) and squared (r1-r6 < 10) tail, the rects blunt; juv (filamentous) uppertail covs < 25 mm; bill proportionally thicker, shallower, and with longer tip to lower mandible (Fig. 530); ss narrower and usually with broader white tips (Fig. 529); forehead without loral stripes; underwing s covs white with at least some dusky mottling (*cf.* Fig. 532); legs and feet with brownish and/or yellowish. See Xantus' Murrelet regarding murre chicks.

Common Murre from Thick-billed Murre by shorter average wing and tail (Table 67); bill proportionally longer, thinner, and with darker tomium by age (Fig. 530); upperparts generally brown to brownish black when fresh (*vs* blacker in Thick-billed Murre); sides of head above gape usually with white in Aug-Jan (Fig. 530); ss of Pacific populations with thinner white tips (Fig. 529); flanks and underwing s covs streaked or mottled variably with dusky (*vs* flanks with few or no dusky streaks and underwing covs with slight dusky mottling in Thick-billed Murre). See Cooch & Collins (1982) for DFAs using tarsus and toe measurements that successfully separated 94% of fresh dead individuals. Beware of hybrids.

Geographic variation—See Ainley et al. (2002), Baker (1993), Bédard 1985), Cramp & Simmons (1985), Dement'ev & Gladkov (1951a), Gaston & Hipfner (2000), Johnson (1938), Kozlova (1957), Portenko (1973), Ridgway (1919), Salomonsen (1932, 1944), Southern (1941), Storer (1952b). No other subspecies occur.

Common Murre

U.a. californica (br and wint coastal AK-c.CA): Averages larger (Table 67, p. 754); upperparts medium-dark brown when fresh; bridled morph absent. Populations of coastal AK ("*inornata*") average longer

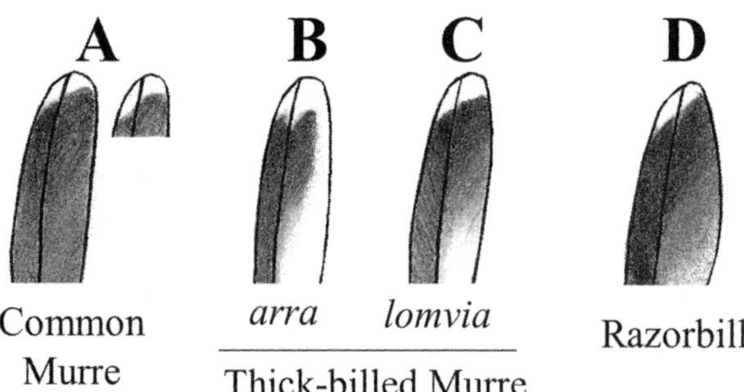

FIGURE 529. Shape and pattern to white at tip of s10 to help identify murres and Razorbill. The extent of the white at the tip of this feather, measured along outer web at shaft, varies as follows: 3-12 mm in Common Murres (**A**), 9-14 mm in Pacific Thick-billed Murres (*U.l. arra*; **B**), 4-8 mm in Atlantic Thick-billed Murres (*U.l. lomvia*; **C**), and 2-8 mm in Razorbill (**D**). Note also the whitish at the base of this feather in Thick-billed Murres, and the broader shape in Razorbills.

wing, shorter bill and tarsus, and paler underparts but differences are broadly clinal and confounded by individual variation.

U.a. aalge (br and wint ne.N.Am-nw.Europe): Averages smaller (Table 67); upperparts blackish brown when fresh; bridled morph with whitish eye ring and postocular streak (formerly considered "*U.a. ringvia*") occurs in ~20% of N.Am populations.

Thick-billed Murre

U.l. arra (br and wint n.Siberia, AK-BC & NWT): Averages larger (Table 67); ss with broader white tips and more white to inner web (Fig. 529**B**). Populations of ne.Siberia (probably occurring to w.AK; "*heckeri*") may average paler upperparts but difference, if present, insufficient for subspecific recognition.

U.l. lomvia (br and wint ne.N.Am-nw. Europe): Averages smaller (Table 67); ss with narrower white tips and less white to inner web (Fig. 529**C**). See Storer (1952b), Gaston et al. (1984) and Gaston & Hipfner (2000) for variation within Canadian populations of this subspecies.

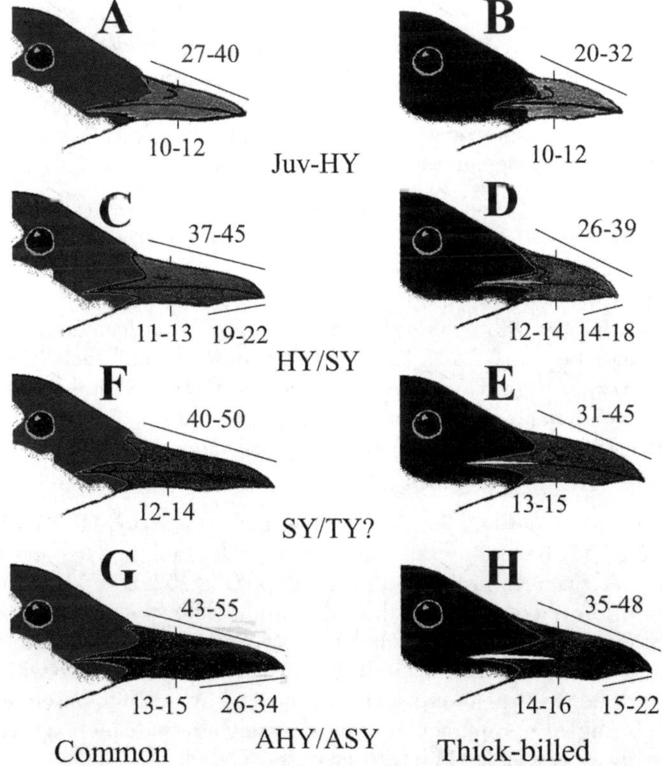

FIGURE 530. Head plumage (basic aspect) and bill dimensions for identification and ageing of Common and Thick-billed Murres. Measures indicate exposed culmen (Fig. 7**A**, p. 9), bill depth at distal end of nares (Fig. 8**C**, p. 10), and distance from gonydeal angle to tip. The last measure is often the best for identification, being reliable (by age) after Sep in the first cycle; exposed culmen ÷ bill depth at distal end of nares is usually > 3 in Common Murre and < 3 in Thick-billed Murre (overlap only in Juvs). Note that in Thick-billed Murre, exposed culmen averages longer in Pacific (*U.l. arra*) than Atlantic (*lomvia*) populations by age (Table 67, p. 754). In basic plumage-aspect, Common Murre usually has white extending above gape line whereas in Thick-billed Murre this area is entirely dark. Note also the increasingly distinct (with age) pale tomial stripe in Thick-billed but not Common murres; Juv-HY/SY Thick-billed Murres can lack this stripe into the first winter and ASY Common Murres can show an indistinct grayish stripe.

Molt—CAS. PF incomplete (Aug-Nov in HYs), PA1 absent-limited (Feb-May in SYs), PB2 complete (May-Sep in SYs), DPA limited (Nov-Apr in AHY/ASYs), DPB complete (Jul-Sep in ASYs). The PB1 (prejuvenile molt) commences at the natal site (body feathers, wing covs, rects) and completes at sea following fledging (pp and ss) concurrent with the PF. The DPB can commence (body feathers only) during the later stages of nesting; otherwise, all other molting occurs at sea, away from breeding grounds. The PF includes all body feathers and rects, some to all gr covs, and no ss, pp, or p covs (*cf.* Fig. 531, p. 753). Many Common Murres replace all gr covs (up to 4 outer juv feathers retained) whereas in Thick-billed Murre many retain 1-8 outer juv gr covs. During DPBs, pp, p covs, and ss are replaced nearly synchronously (apparently with centers at p4-p7 and possibly at s8) in Jun-Aug (SYs) or Jul-Oct (ASYs). The DPA in breeding ASYs occurs later in northernmost populations including all Thick-billed Murres (Feb-Apr) than in southernmost populations of Common Murre (Oct-Feb), and is primarily restricted to feathers of the head, neck, and throat. Most to all SYs and some TYs over-summer on non-breeding grounds and these may exhibit reduced PA1-PA2s and advanced PB2-PB3s (see p. 18).

Age—Juv (B1; Jun-Aug) is very small (< 1/2 mass of adult) and has loosely-textured feathers and no or developing pp, ss, and rects (see **Molt**); Juv ♀=♂. See Gaston (1984) and Nevins & Carter (2003) for information on the width of the supraorbital ridge by age, and Nevins & Carter (2003) for information on ageing by bursal depth (Fig. 23, p. 34). In addition to the following, confirmed breeding individuals can be reliably aged ATY (and likely A4Y).

HY/SY (1st cycle, F1-A1; Sep-Aug): Bill reduced in size (Fig. 530**A-D**); bill width at gape (Fig. 524, p. 746) ~15.5-21.0 (Common) or ~16.0-21.5 (Thick-billed) mm; p covs and sometimes some outer gr covs small, brownish, and worn, contrasting with most to all s covs and pp (Fig. 531**A**; see also Fig. 525**C**, p. 747); underwing p covs of Common Murre extensively white or with white tips (Fig. 532**A-C**); throat feathers completely white or some with dark tips in Mar-Aug. **Note: Shape of outer pp and rects (Figs. 526 & 527, p. 748) may average slightly narrower in HY/SY than AHY/ASY but differences are slight (due to development of these post-fledging; see Molt). Pattern of the underwing coverts (Fig. 632) in Thick-billed Murre appears too variable to be useful in ageing. See also AHY/ASY.**

AHY/ASY (Def. cycle, DB-DA; Sep-Aug): Bill full sized (Fig. 530**E-H**); bill width at gape (Fig. 524) ~19.5-24.0 (Common) or 20.5-24.5 (Thick-billed) mm; p covs and s covs uniformly broad and fresh, not contrasting in aspect with pp (Figs. 525**D** & 531**B**); underwing p covs of Common Murre completely dark or dark with white fringes (Fig. 532**D-E**); alternate throat feathers uniformly dark in Feb-Aug. **Note: See HY/SY. Some SY/TYs may be distinguishable by bill measures (Fig. 530E-F, but more study is needed with respect to geographic variation in size) and retention of some white or white-based feathers in throat during Feb-Aug. Also, Common Murres acquiring alternate plumage aspect in Nov-Jan are probably at least ASY/ATYs; further study needed.**

Sex—♀=♂ by plumage aspect. Medial BP (Fig. 20**A**, p. 31) developed by both sexes but distended cloaca (Fig. 21, p. 32) indicates ATY ♀ in Apr-Jul. Measurements generally unhelpful for sexing (Table 67, p. 754; Threlfall & Mahoney 1980); bill depth may be useful in separating small proportions of breeding individuals or mated pairs, but this criterion otherwise unreliable due to individual, age-related, and geographic variation within each species (*cf.* Fig. 530). See Parker et al. (1991) for sexing Common Murres by chromosome analysis. Otherwise, no criteria known.

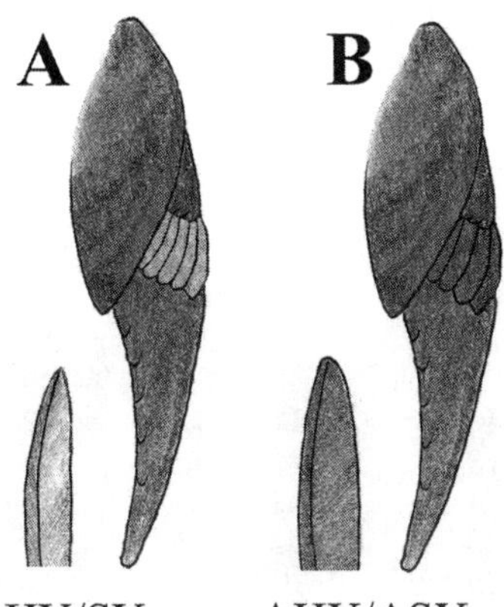

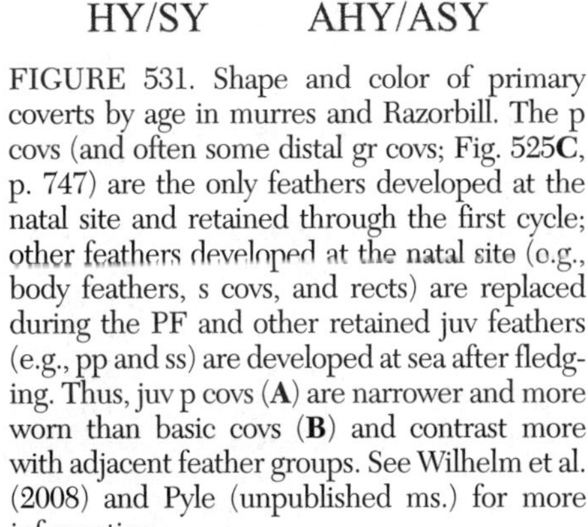

FIGURE 531. Shape and color of primary coverts by age in murres and Razorbill. The p covs (and often some distal gr covs; Fig. 525**C**, p. 747) are the only feathers developed at the natal site and retained through the first cycle; other feathers developed at the natal site (e.g., body feathers, s covs, and rects) are replaced during the PF and other retained juv feathers (e.g., pp and ss) are developed at sea after fledging. Thus, juv p covs (**A**) are narrower and more worn than basic covs (**B**) and contrast more with adjacent feather groups. See Wilhelm et al. (2008) and Pyle (unpublished ms.) for more information.

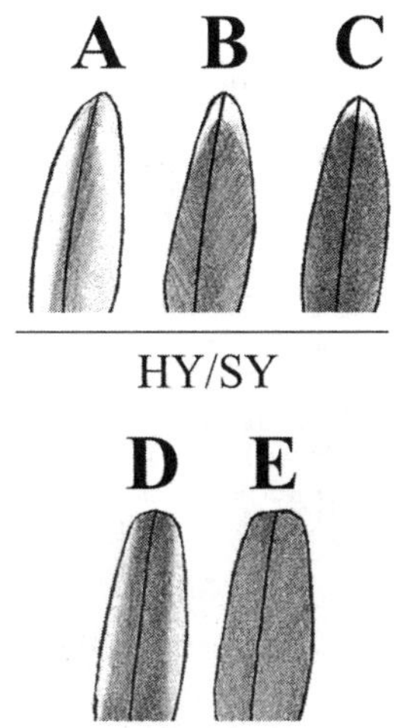

FIGURE 532. Shape and pattern to the outermost underwing primary covert by age in Common Murre; note especially the white tips on formative feathers of HY/SYs (**A-C**), not on basic feathers of AHY/ASYs (**D-E**). See Camphuysen (1995). In N.Am Thick-billed Murres, both age groups show patterns resembling **D-E**, although there may be a tendency for formative feathers to show more white than basic feathers.

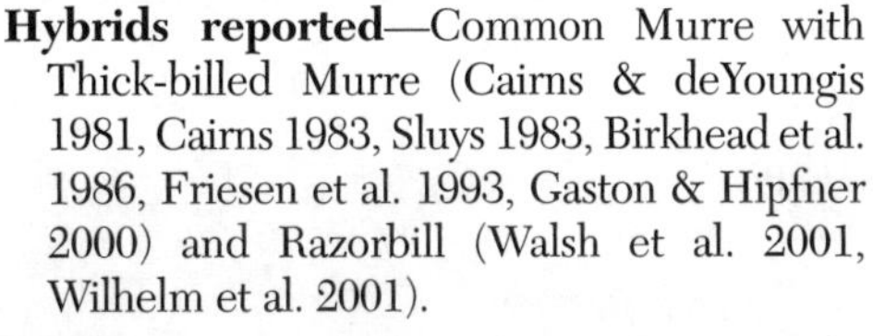

Hybrids reported—Common Murre with Thick-billed Murre (Cairns & deYoungis 1981, Cairns 1983, Sluys 1983, Birkhead et al. 1986, Friesen et al. 1993, Gaston & Hipfner 2000) and Razorbill (Walsh et al. 2001, Wilhelm et al. 2001).

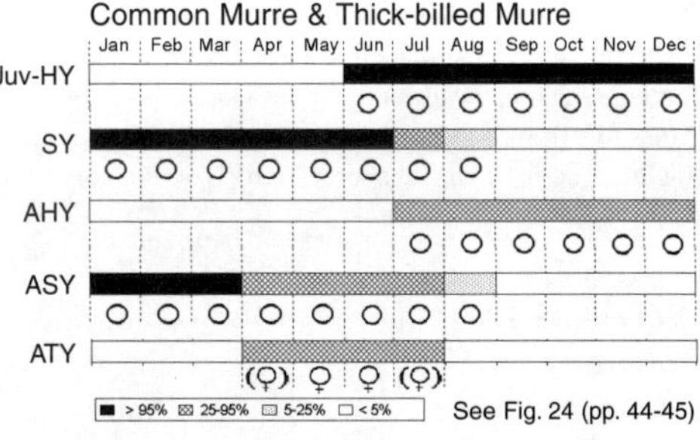

References—Ainley et al. (1994, 2002), Baker (1993), Bédard (1985), Bent (1919a), Birkhead & Nettleship (1985), Bridge (2004), Camphuysen (1995), Cooch & Collins (1982), Cramp & Simmons (1985), Dement'ev & Gladkov (1951a), Gaston (1984), Gaston & Hipfner (2000), Harris & Wanless (1990), Jones & Rees (1985), Kozlova (1957), Nevins & Carter (2003), Pyle (unpublished ms.), Ridgway (1919), Salomonsen (1944), Spring (1971), Stejneger (1885), Stewart (1993), Stone (1900), Storer (1952b), Swennen (1977), Thompson et al. (1998a, 1998b), Tuck (1960), Wilhelm et al. (2008).

TABLE 67. Measurements (mm) of North American dovekies, murres, razorbills, and guillemots for identification and sexing. See pp. 4-11 for methods of measurement. Species summaries are in **bold** and subspecies summaries are in ***italics***. Values were derived from 95% confidence intervals as based approximately on the indicated sample sizes (see pp. 4-5). Thus, midpoints of ranges approximate means, and S.D. is approximated by 25% of the range.

Taxon/Sex	*n*	wing chord[1]	tail length	exposed culmen[2]	tarsus
Dovekie[3]		**111-127**	**28-38**	**13.1-16.4**	**19-22**
♀	100	111-123	28-37	13.1-15.8	19-21
♂	100	112-127	29-38	13.8-16.4	19-22
Common Murre		**183-225**	**40-54**	**37.9-53.5**	**32-41**
U.a. californica		***194-225***	***43-54***	***41.5-53.5***	***32-41***
♀	100	194-225	44-54	41.5-51.2	32-40
♂	100	194-224	43-53	43.2-53.5	33-41
U.a. aalge[3]		***183-215***	***40-52***	***37.9-49.2***	***33-40***
♀	100	186-215	41-52	37.9-47.3	33-39
♂	100	183-212	40-51	39.6-49.2	34-40
Thick-billed Murre		**199-232**	**43-57**	**31.3-48.4**	**31-41**
U.l. arra		***211-232***	***45-57***	***38.1-48.4***	***34-41***
♀	100	211-231	46-57	38.1-45.2	34-40
♂	100	213-232	45-56	41.3-48.4	35-41
U.l. lomvia[3]		***199-226***	***43-53***	***31.3-42.4***	***31-39***
♀	100	199-225	44-53	31.3-40.6	32-38
♂	100	200-226	43-52	32.6-42.4	31-39
Razorbill[3]		**187-209**	**68-85**	**29.8-37.0**	**28-34**
♀	100	187-206	68-83	29.8-34.9	28-33
♂	100	190-209	70-85	31.3-37.0	29-34
Black Guillemot[3,4]		**150-168**	**43-53**	**26.1-34.8**	**28-33**
♀	80	151-168	43-53	26.1-34.3	28-33
♂	80	150-168	43-53	26.9-34.8	28-33
Pigeon Guillemot[3]		**160-187**	**45-58**	**29.6-38.3**	**31-37**
♀	100	164-187	45-58	29.9-38.3	32-37
♂	100	162-186	45-58	29.6-37.9	31-36

[1] Note that, in most alcids, wing chord of HY/SYs average 10-20% less than that of AHY/ASYs.
[2] Exposed culmen can take up to a year or more to reach full length. Also, see figures and text for bill depth values, which vary substantially by age.
[3] Measures from N.Am populations only; see **Geographic variation**.
[4] Includes both N.Am subspecies, which do not vary significantly by size.

RAZORBILL
Alca torda

RAZO
Species # 0320
Band size: 5R

Species—From other alcids by medium-large size with proportionally long tail (Table 67); bill proportionately deep, laterally compressed, with decurved culmen and mandible (distal to gonys), and with transverse grooves and white ring in ASYs (Fig. 533); mouth lining yellowish; upperparts black (when fresh) with white tips to ss (Fig. 529**D**, p. 750) white loral stripe (Fig. 533; concealed by dark feather tips in Sep-Jan); axillars and underwing covs white; legs and feet black. Juv from Juv murres by proportionally longer and more graduated (r1-r6 10-25 mm) tail, the rects pointed; juv (filamentous) uppertail covs > 25 mm; bill proportionally thinner and deeper, with shorter tip to lower mandible (Fig. 533**A**); ss truncate and usually with thinner white tips (Fig. 529**D**); underwing s covs white; legs and feet black (without brownish or yellowish).

Geographic variation—Considered monotypic here. Populations breeding in Iceland-w.Europe ("*A.t. islandica*") average smaller than those of N.Am and ne.Europe but differences somewhat clinal and insufficient for subspecific status. Separation of populations breeding in N.Am, Greenland, and nw.Russia ("*pica*") by more numerous and deeper bill grooves not warranted. See Anker-Nilssen et al. (1988), Barrett et al. (1997), Bédard (1985), Cramp & Simmons (1985), Dement'ev & Gladkov (1951a), P.H. Jones (1990), Jones et al. (1985), Kozlova (1957), and Salomonsen (1944) for more information.

Molt—CAS. PF incomplete (Aug-Nov in HYs), PA1 absent-limited (Mar-May in SYs), PB2 complete (Jun-Sep in SYs), DPA limited (Feb-Apr in ASYs), DPB complete (Aug-Sep in ASYs). The PB1 (prejuvenile molt) commences at the natal site (body feathers, wing covs, rects) and completes at sea following fledging (pp and ss) concurrent with the PF. The DPB can commence (body feathers only) during the later stages of nesting; all other molting occurs at sea, away from breeding grounds. The PF includes all body feathers, most to all s covs, and the rects, but no ss, pp, or p covs (*cf.* Fig. 531, p. 753); look for some HY/SYs to retain one or more outer gr covs (*cf.* Fig. 525**C**, p. 747), as in murres. During DPBs, pp, p covs, and ss are replaced near-synchronously in Jun-Aug (SYs) or Aug-Sep (ASYs). The DPA is primarily restricted to feathers of the head, neck, and throat. Most to all SYs and some TYs over-summer on non-breeding grounds and these may exhibit reduced PA1-PA2s and advanced PB2-PB3s (see p. 18). Bill sheathing may be molted in Aug-Oct; more study needed.

Age—Juv (B1; Jun-Aug) is very small (< 1/2 mass of adult) and has loosely-textured feathers and no or developing pp, ss, and rects (see **Molt**); Juv ♀ = ♂. In addition to the following, confirmed breeding individuals can reliably be aged ATY (and likely A4Y).

HY/SY (1st cycle, F1-A1; Oct-Sep): Bill shallow, without grooves or white ring in Oct-Jan (Fig. 533**A-B**), becoming deeper and developing an indistinct ring by Sep (Fig. 533**C**); bill width at gape (Fig. 524, p. 746) ~15.5-19.5 mm; p covs small, brownish, and worn, contrasting with s covs and pp (Fig. 531**A**, p. 753; look for some outer gr covs also to be retained as in Fig. 525**C**, p. 747); throat feathers completely white or some with white bases and dark tips in Apr-Aug. **Note: Shape of outer pp and rects (Figs. 526 & 527, p. 748) may average slightly narrower in HY/SY than AHY/ASY but differences are slight (due to development of**

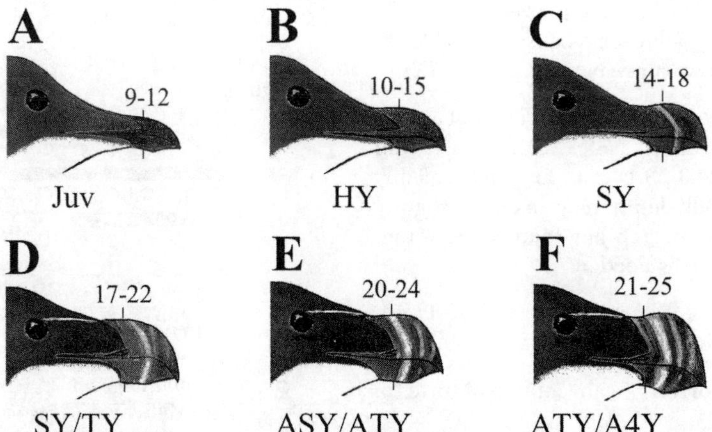

FIGURE 533. Shape and characters of the bill by age in Razorbill. Measure refers to bill depth at distal end of nares (Fig. 8**C**, p. 10). Juvs (**A**) and HYs (**B**) lack grooves to the bill and SYs in Jan-Jun (**C**) may develop a single indistinct whitish groove. In SY/TYs (**D**) a second groove develops proximal to the whitish groove and in ASY/ATYs (**E**) there is also a single groove distal to the whitish groove. Individuals with two grooves distal to the whitish groove (**F**) can be aged ATY/A4Y. See also Figure 534 (p. 756).

these post-fledging; see Molt). Pattern of the underwing coverts (Fig. 532, p. 753) may be too variable to be useful in ageing; study needed. See also AHY/ASY.

SY/TY (2nd cycle, B2-A2; Oct-Sep): Bill depth intermediate, with single indistinct whitish groove but no grooves distal to this (Fig. 533**D**); bill width at gape (Fig. 524) ~19-24 mm; p covs broad and fresh, not contrasting in aspect with s covs and pp (Figs. 525**D** & 531**B**); alternate throat feathers completely dark or a few with white bases in Mar-Aug. **Note: See HY/SY.**

ASY/ATY (Def. cycle, DB-DA; Oct-Sep): Bill deep, with distinct white groove and one full groove distal to this (Fig. 533**E**); bill width at gape (Fig. 524) ~22-27 mm; alternate throat feathers uniformly dark in Feb-Sep.

ATY/A4Y (Def. cycle, DB-DA; Oct-Sep): Like ASY/ATY but bill averages deeper and with two full grooves distal to white full groove (Fig. 533**F**); bill width at gape (Fig. 524) ~24-28 mm. **Note: Individuals with 3 distinct grooves distal to the white groove possibly can be aged A4Y/A5Y but further study needed.**

Sex—♀=♂ by plumage aspect. Medial BP (Fig. 20**A**, p. 31) developed by both sexes but distended cloaca (Fig. 21, p. 32) indicates ATY ♀ in May-Jul. Except for bill depth in ATYs, measurements generally unhelpful for sexing (Table 67, p. 754). See Grecian et al. (2003) for a DFA using wing chord, head-bill length (Fig. 453, p. 630), bill depth at gonys, and tarsus, from live ATYs, that correctly sexed 78-80% of Razorbills from a NB population. The following can be used to sex most ASY/ATY ♂♂ with 1 or more grooves and ATY/A4Y ♀♀ with 2 or more grooves distal to the white groove (Fig. 533**E-F**) including many breeding pairs; no reliable criteria are known for sexing HYs and SYs/TYs.

ATY/A4Y ♀: Maximum bill depth at ring < 22.3 (Fig. 534**A**). **Note: ASY/ATYs with bill depth 22.3-23.1 mm are not reliably sexed. Bill depth may average slightly shallower in Sep-Jan than in Feb-Aug; more study is needed.**

ASY/ATY ♂: Maximum bill depth > 23.1 (Fig. 534**B**). **Note: See ATY/A4Y ♀.**

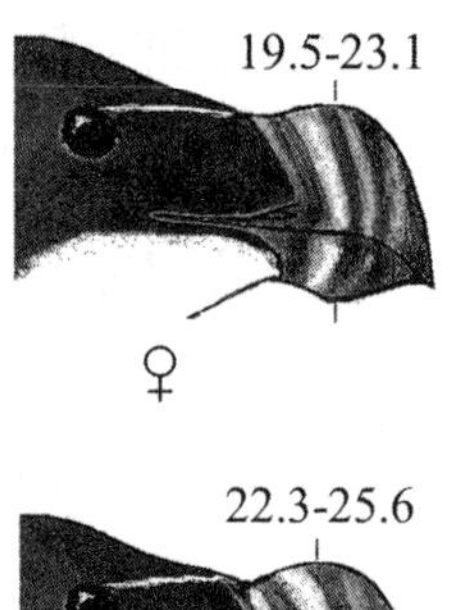

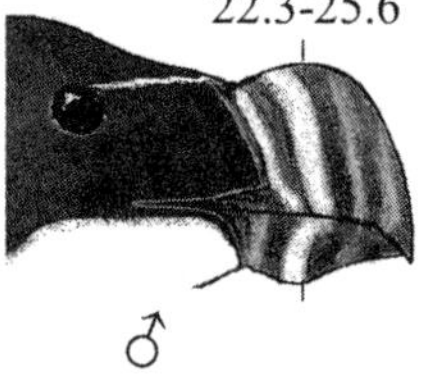

FIGURE 534. Maximum bill depth by sex in ATY/A4Y Razorbills. Note the two full grooves distal to the ring, indicating ATY/A4Y (Fig. 533, p. 755). ASY/ATYs with bill depth > 23.1 mm can be sexed ♂♂ but ASY/ATYs with bill depth < 22.3 mm might be TY/4Y ♂♂ and should be sexed unknown by this character alone.

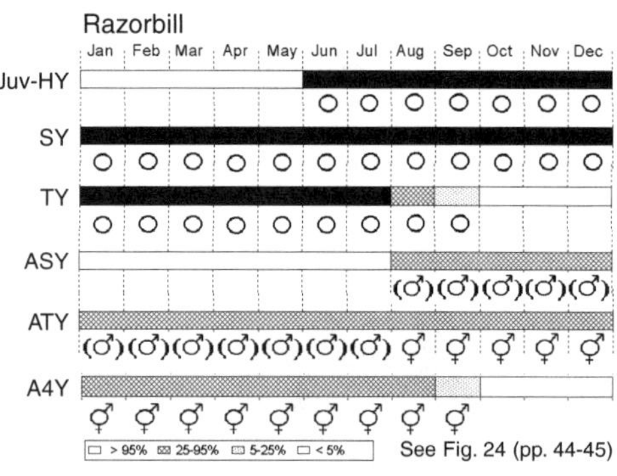

Hybrids reported—With Common Murre (p. 750).

References—Baker (1993), Bédard (1985), Bent (1919a), Birkhead & Nettleship (1985), Camphuysen (1995), Cramp & Simmons (1985), Dement'ev & Gladkov (1951a), de Wijs (1985), Harris & Wanless (1990), Hipfner & Chapdelaine (2002), Jones (1988), Jones & Rees (1985), Jones et al. (1985), Kozlova (1957), Pyle (unpublished ms.), Ridgway (1919), Salomonsen (1944), Storer (1952b), Swennen (1977), Taverner (1929c), Wilhelm et al. (2008).

BLACK GUILLEMOT BLGU
Cepphus grylle Species # 0270
Band size: 4

PIGEON GUILLEMOT PIGU
Cepphus columba Species # 0290
Band size: 4A

Species—Guillemots from other alcids by medium size (Table 67, p. 754); bill proportionately shallow (depth at distal end of nares 7-11 mm) and black; mouth lining pinkish to red; s covs with distinct white patterns (Figs. 537-538, p. 759); ss with little or no white at tips (*cf.* Fig. 536, p. 758); legs and feet pinkish (Sep-Jan) to bright red (Feb-Aug). Spectacled Guillemot (*C. carbo*), a potential vagrant to w.AK Is, is larger (wg chord 185-201, exp culmen 38-46, tarsus 35-40); s covs without white; plumage aspect browner with white patch around eye in Feb-Aug.

Black Guillemot from Pigeon Guillemot by smaller average size (Table 67); bill deeper (depth at distal end of nares 7.1-9.5 mm in Black Guillemot, 9.2-11.2 in Pigeon Guillemot); tail usually with 12 rects (usually 14 in Pigeon Guillemot); upperwing and underwing covs with more white (Figs. 535, 537, & 538).

Geographic variation—See Austin (1929), Bédard (1985), Browning (2002), Butler & Buckley (2002), Cramp & Simmons (1985), Dement'ev & Gladkov (1951a), Gross (1937), Hellmayr & Conover (1948b), Kozlova (1957), Portenko (1973), Ridgway (1919), Salomonsen (1944), Storer (1950, 1952b), Todd (1963), Udvardy (1963), Wynne-Edwards (1952b). Other subspecies of Black Guillemot may occur in Europe (*cf.* Bédard 1985) but more study is needed; one other subspecies of Pigeon Guillemot occurs in Siberia.

Black Guillemot

C.g. mandtii (br and wint n.AK-n.Lab to n.Man-Ont and arctic Eurasia): Crown, nape, and back white with sparse or no brown mottling in Oct-Feb; gr covs and ss with more extensive white by age (Figs. 536**A**-**B**, 537**A**, & 538**A**-**B**, pp. 758-759). Populations of Wrangel I, ne.Siberia (probably occurring to w.AK; "*tajani*") may average larger and with more greenish gloss in Apr-Aug, and populations of n.Man-Ont to Nun-n.Lab ("*ultimus*") may average more white in s covs and shorter bill, but in each case differences insufficient, confounded by individual variation, and/or represent intergradation toward *grylle*.

C.g. grylle (br and wint c.Lab-MA and w.Europe): Crown, nape, and back white with substantial brown mottling (to mostly brown) in Oct-Feb; gr covs and ss with reduced white by age (Figs. 536**C**-**D**, 537**B**, & 538**C**-**D**). Populations of N.Am ("*arcticus*" and/or "*atlantis*") may average smaller and with more white to the plumage aspect but differences are slight and represent intergradation toward *mandtii*.

FIGURE 535. Pattern to the underwing coverts in Black and Pigeon Guillemots. The distance from the tip of p10 to the tip of the white tongue on this feather is 35-65 mm in Black Guillemot (*C.g. mandtii* < *grylle*) and 50-80 mm in Pigeon Guillemot. Juv p10s appear to average less extensive white than basic p10s. The underwing of AHY/ASY Pigeon Guillemots average whiter in AK than in CA populations, but this variation is not consistent enough for subspecific recognition (see **Geographic variation**). See also Figures 536-538, pp. 758-759).

Pigeon Guillemot

C.c. columba (br and wint N.Am): S covs with substantial white (Figs. 537**D-F** & 538**E-G**) *vs* with reduced white in *snowi* of the Kurile Is (possible vagrant to w.AK but beware of melanistic individuals of other subspecies). Populations of ne.Siberia and w.Aleutian Is, AK ("*C.c. kaiurka*") average smaller and possibly average more white to the underwing and upperwing (*cf.* Figs. 535**B**, 537**E**, & 538**F**), populations of s.AK-WA ("*andianta*") average shorter wing and longer bill, and populations of OR-CA ("*eureka*") average larger and with less white to the underwing and upperwing (*cf.* Figs. 535**C**, 537**F**, & 538**G**); but in all cases differences are broadly clinal and confounded by individual variation.

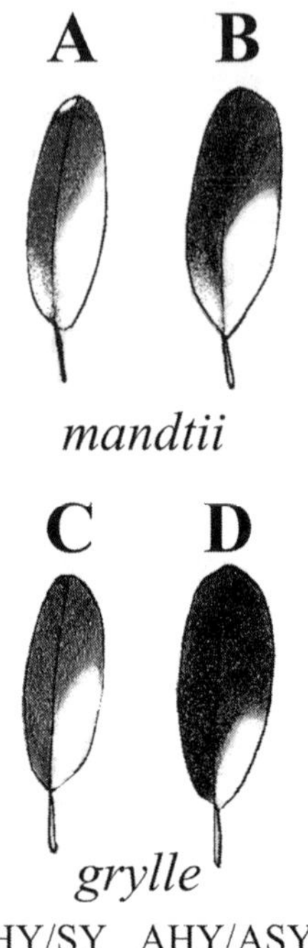

FIGURE 536. Shape and extent of white on the medial secondaries (s10 shown) by subspecies and age in Black Guillemot. See also Figures 537-538.

Molt—CAS. PF partial (Oct-Feb in HY/SYs), PA1 absent-limited (Mar-May in SYs), PB2 complete (Jun-Sep in SYs), DPA partial (Jan-Apr in ASYs), DPB complete (Jul-Oct in ASYs). The PB1 (prejuvenile molt) completes at the natal site; all subsequent molting occurs at sea, away from breeding grounds. The PF includes most to all body feathers but few if any s covs and no terts or rects. It generally appears to be continuous with the PA1, breast feathers replaced just once (with white or dark-tipped feathers) in Jan-Apr, and no to many back feathers replaced twice (more so in Black than in Pigeon Guillemot). Division of the PF and PA1 requires further study and comparison with other alcid species. During DPBs, pp, p covs, and ss are replaced nearly synchronously in Jun-Aug (SYs) or Aug-Oct (ASYs). The DPA includes most to all body feathers but few if any s covs and no terts or rects; it commences later in n.breeding populations than s.populations. Many SYs over-summer on non-breeding grounds and these may exhibit reduced PA1s and advanced PB2s (see also p. 18).

Age—Juv (B1; Jul-Dec) has pp fresh and pointed (Fig. 526**A**, p. 748), nape and sides of underparts white with brown mottling, s covs with dark tips (*cf.* Fig. 538**A**, **C**, & **E**), and legs dusky reddish to orangish; Juv ♀=♂. In addition to the following, confirmed breeding individuals can reliably be aged ATY and bill width at gape (Fig. 524, p. 746) varies by age (~13-14.5 mm in HY/SYs and ~14-15.5 in AHY/ASYs) but plumage-aspect characters diagnostic.

Juv-HY/SY (1st cycle, Juv/F1-A1; Oct-Sep): Juv s covs retained, variably tipped brown by species and subspecies (Figs. 537**A-B** & **D**; & 538**A**, **C**, & **E**); pp and ss brown and relatively worn, the juv outer pp relatively narrow, pointed and brownish (Fig. 526**A-B**), and the medial ss with more extensive white in Black Guillemot (Fig. 536**A** & **C**); outer rects narrow, brownish, and relatively worn (Fig. 527**A**, p. 748); underpart feathers with thin dusky fringing in Sep-Nov and sometimes through Mar (*cf.* Fig. 541**A**, p. 762); some feathers of head and underparts white or with broad white bases in Apr-Aug.

AHY/ASY (Def. cycle, DB-DA; Oct-Sep): S covs uniformly basic, with no or few brown tips (Figs. 537**C** & **D-E** & 538**B**, **D**, & **F-G**); pp and ss blackish and relatively fresh, the basic outer pp relatively broad, blunt, and blackish (Fig. 526**C-D**), and the medial ss with less extensive white in Black Guillemot (Fig. 536**B** & **D**); outer rects broad, blackish, and rela-

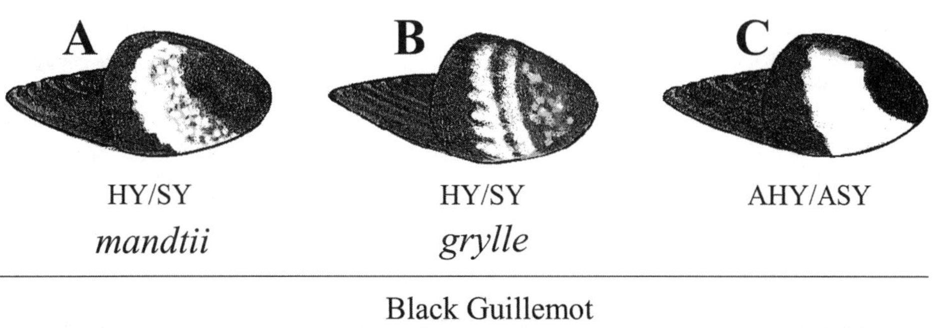

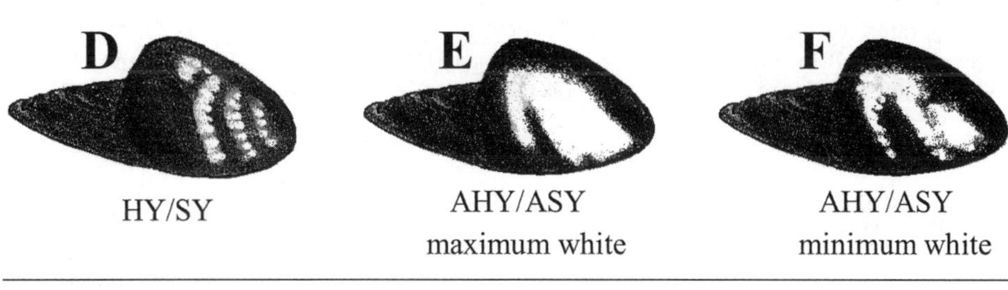

FIGURE 537. Variation in the pattern of white and black among upperwing s covs of Black and Pigeon guillemots for taxonomic identification and ageing. See Austin (1929) and Storer (1952) for more information. Shown are typical examples; there can be substantial variation within each species/subspecies/age group. As with white in the underwing (Fig. 535, p. 757), the upperwing of Pigeon Guillemot tends to show more white in AK than in CA populations, but variation is inconsistent. See also Figures 536 & 538.

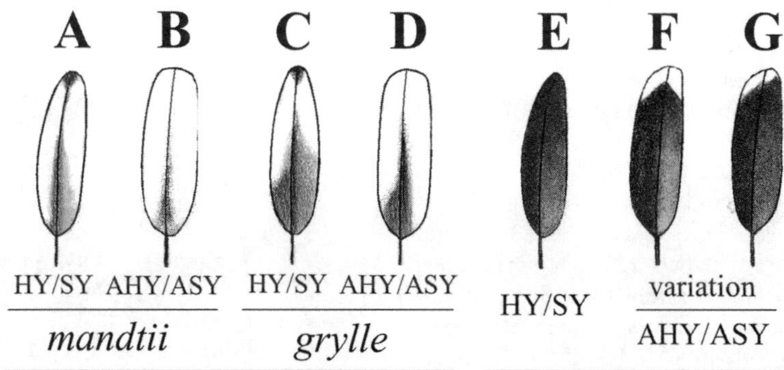

FIGURE 538. Variation in the extent of white on greater covert 3 (corresponding to s3) by taxa and age in guillemots. Extent of white on this feather in Pigeon Guillemot generally decreases from AK to CA (see also Fig. 537).

tively fresh (Fig. 527**B**); underparts white, without dusky mottling in Oct-Feb; feathers of head and underparts usually without white in Mar-Aug. **Note: Some SY/TYs might be identified by intermediate characters and perhaps some white to head and underparts in May-Jul; more study needed.**

Sex—♀ = ♂ by plumage aspect. Bilateral BPs (Fig. 20**B**, p. 31) developed by both sexes but distended cloaca (Fig. 21, p. 32) indicates ATY ♀ in May-Jul. Measurements generally unhelpful for sexing (Table 67, p. 754), although bill depth (at distal end of nares) may be useful for sexing AHY/ASY Black Guillemots: generally, ♀ 7.3-8.5 and ♂ 8.1-9.6, but more study is needed in conjunction with geographic variation in bill size. Otherwise, no other criteria known.

Hybrids reported—None. Pigeon Guillemots have been observed copulating with Black Guillemots (Ewins 1993).

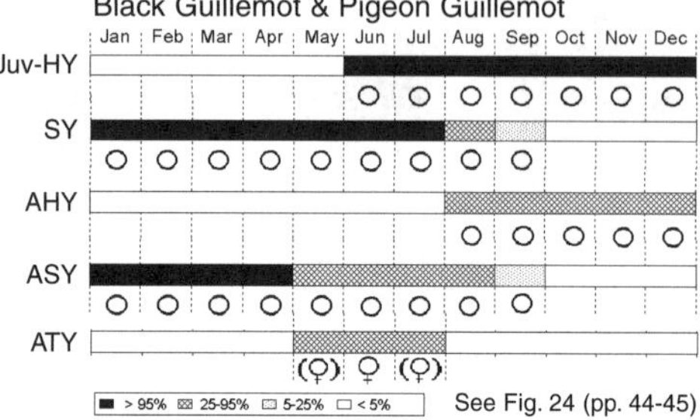

References—Ainley et al. (1994), Baker (1993), Bédard (1985), Bent (1919a), Butler & Buckley (2002), Cramp & Simmons (1985), Dement'ev & Gladkov (1951a), Ewins (1988, 1993), Kozlova (1957), Pyle (unpublished ms.), Ridgway (1919), Salomonsen (1944), Stone (1900), Storer (1952b).

MARBLED MURRELET
Brachyramphus marmoratus

MAMU
Species # 0230
Band size: 3B-3

Species—From other alcids by small size with proportionally short legs (Table 68, p. 764); bill thin (Fig. 539**B**) and black; tail with 14 rects; upperparts slate with white lores, sides of nape (Fig. 539**B**), and scapulars in Sep-Mar brown with rufous fringing in Mar-Aug; underparts mostly to entirely white (Sep-Mar; Fig. 541, p. 762), or variably marbled brown (Mar-Sep); underwing covs dark gray, with variable whitish to s covs and lesser p covs in HY/SYs (Fig. 540); legs and feet pinkish to grayish with dusky webs. From Kittlitz's Murrelet by longer bill (Table 68, Fig. 539); ss and rects with little to no white; back and rump uniformly dark gray to slate (Sep-Mar) or dark brown and rufous (Mar-Sep); auriculars surrounding eye dark (Fig. 539**B**); breast band incomplete in Sep-Mar; abdomen usually with brown marbling in Mar-Aug. See also Xantus' Murrelet (p. 764) regarding murre chicks.

Long-billed Murrelet (*B. perdix*), a visitor to w.N.Am from Siberia, is larger (wg chord 134-146, tl 31-38, exp culmen 17.9-23.1, tarsus 16-19), especially in wing and bill (Fig. 539**A**); exp culmen > tarsus (*vs* usually < tarsus in Marbled Murrelet); lores, auricular, and sides of nape darker, with straighter demarcation, and usually with isolated white patch at nape (Fig. 539**A**); outer rect sometimes with white edging to outer web; underwing covs

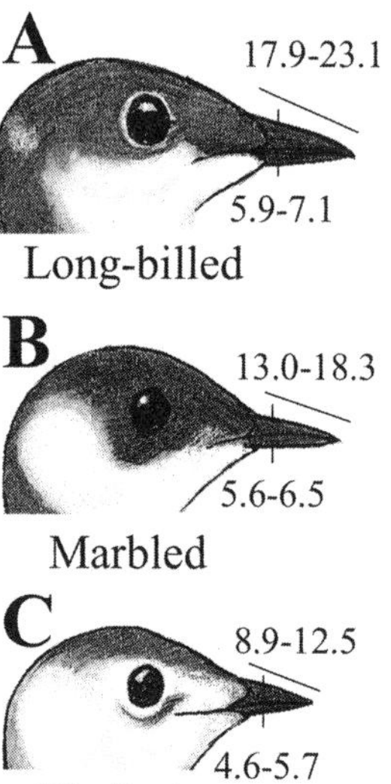

FIGURE 539. Basic-plumage head aspect and bill dimensions in *Brachyramphus* murrelets for identification. Measures indicate exposed culmen (Fig. 7**A**, p. 9) and bill depth at distal end of nares (Fig. 8**C**, p. 10). Note the more horizontal division between dark crown/face and white throat in Long-billed than in Marbled murrelet. This character is visible in most alternate and transitional plumage aspects as well, being obscured only in some Marbled Murrelets with full alternate aspect. The distinct white spot on the nape of Long-billed Murrelet is visible in most individuals with this plumage aspect.

may average more white by age (see **Age** & Fig. 540). See Dement'ev & Gladkov (1951a), Erickson et al. (1995), Friesen et al. (1996), Jehl & Jehl (1981), Konyukhov & Kitaysky (1995), Lethaby (2000), Mlodinow (1997), Patten (1997), Sealy et al. (1982, 1991), Sibley (1993), and Thompson et al. (2003) for more information.

Geographic variation—Monotypic. See Friesen et al. (1996), Hull et al. (2001), and Pitocchelli et al. (1995).

Molt—CAS. PF limited-partial (Sep-Feb in HY/SYs), PA1 absent-partial (Apr-Jun in SYs), PB2 complete (Jun-Sep in SYs), DPA partial (Mar-May in ASYs), DPB complete (Aug-Nov in ASYs). The PB1 (prejuvenile molt) completes at the natal site. Most or all subsequent molting occurs at sea, away from breeding grounds. The PF includes some to all body feathers, no to some proximal s covs, and no terts or rects. During DPBs, pp and ss are typically replaced in 2-3 blocks, often the inner 3-6 pp initially, followed by the outer 4-7 pp in one or two blocks. Replacement of ss can be much later than that of inner pp and appears also to occur in blocks, generally in a distal direction, although s1 (and probably s5) can be replaced prior to the medial ss. The PA1 is variable but can include up to most body feathers, and the DPA includes most to all body feathers but no s covs, terts, or rects. Some SYs over-summer on non-breeding grounds and these may exhibit reduced PA1s and advanced PB2s (see p. 18).

Age—Juv (B1; Jun-Nov) has pp fresh and pointed (Fig. 526**A**, p. 748), upperparts dark brownish, and breast feathers small with distinct and narrow brown fringing (Fig. 541**A**, p. 562); Juv ♀ = ♂. In addition to the following, confirmed breeding individuals can reliably be aged ASY.

Juv-HY/SY (1st cycle, Juv/F1-A1; Sep-Aug): Bill width at gape (Fig. 524, p. 746) ~8.5-12.5 mm; underwing covs usually with white and not uniformly dark brown (Fig. 540**A-B**); underpart feathers with thin dusky fringing in Sep-Nov and sometimes through May (Fig. 541**A**); most to all s covs, pp, and ss uniformly brown and relatively worn, contrasting with fresher and slatier scapulars, humerals, and some proximal s covs in Feb-Aug (Fig. 525**A-B**, p. 747), the

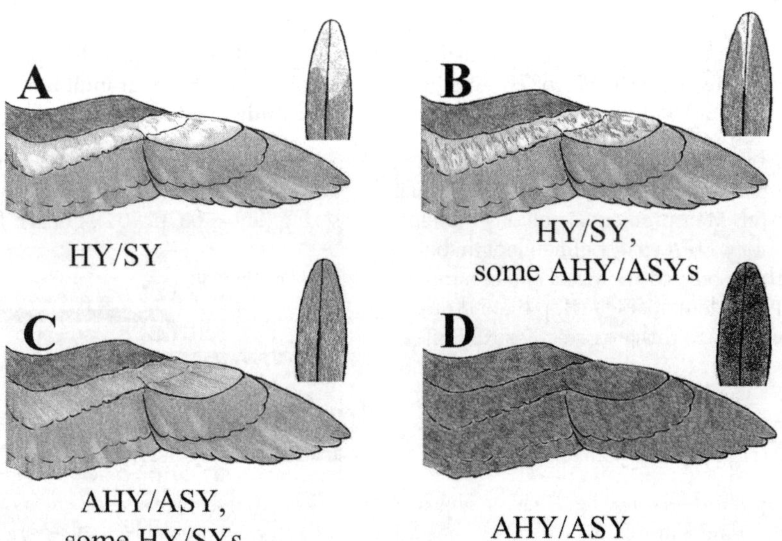

FIGURE 540. Pattern to the underwing coverts and 3rd underwing greater covert from the outside (inset) by age in *Brachyramphus* murrelets. In Marbled Murrelet; approximately 10-15% of AHY/ASYs (SY/TYs?) can show **B** and approximately 10-15% of HY/SYs can show **C**; Long-billed Murrelet may show more extensive pale coloration by age-group. This also appears to be helpful for ageing Kittlitz's Murrelet, but details need to be worked out.

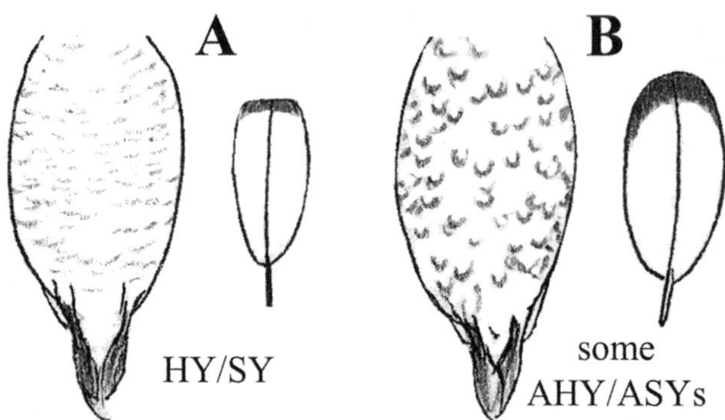

FIGURE 541. Underparts by age in basic-aspect Marbled and Kittlitz's murrelets. Juvs have finely mottled barring to the underparts (**A**), which can variably be lost by HY/SYs to bleaching and wear in Sep-Mar (occasionally visible through Jun). Most AHY/ASYs have entirely white underparts in Sep-Mar but some have distinct dark crescents, as in **B**, perhaps due to an early DPB (see p. 29). Thus, individuals with entirely white underparts cannot be aged by this criterion alone in Sep-Mar. Basic-aspect Kittlitz's Murrelet differs from Marbled Murrelet by having dark ventral extensions at sides of breast, sometimes forming a near-complete band.

outer pp (and p covs) relatively narrow and pointed (Fig. 526**A-B**, p. 748); outer rects narrow, brownish, and relatively worn (Fig. 527**A**, p. 748). **Note: In addition, many SYs have extensive white to the underparts in Mar-Aug but this is variable in both age groups, with some SYs acquiring full or near-full alternate aspect.**

AHY/ASY (Def. cycle, DB-DA; Sep-Aug): Bill width at gape (Fig. 524) ~11.5-13.5 mm; underwing covs completely dark or occasionally with some white (Fig. 540**B-C**); underparts completely white or some feathers with broad dusky fringing (Fig. 541**B**) in Nov-Feb; wing covs, pp, and ss blackish, relatively fresh, and not contrasting with scapulars or humerals (Fig. 525**D**), the pp and p covs often showing contrasts among p5-p6 and between s1 and p1 (Fig. 525**E**), and the outer pp relatively broad and blunt (Fig. 526**C-D**); outer rects broad, blackish, and relatively fresh (Fig. 527**B**). **Note: See HY/SY. It is possible that molt limits in the wing (Fig. 525E) might indicate breeding ASY/ATYs; study needed.**

Sex—♀ = ♂ by plumage aspect. Medial BP (Fig. 20**A**, p. 31) developed by both sexes (and may not indicate breeding; Tranquilla et al. 2003) but distended cloaca (Fig. 21, p. 32) indicates ATY ♀ in Apr-Jul. Measurements generally unhelpful for sexing (Table 68, p. 764); but see Hull et al. (2001) for a DFA using culmen length, bill height at base, bill width at distal end of nares, flattened wing length (Fig. 3**B**, p 6), and tarsus, from live ASYs, that correctly sexed 62-70% of Marbled Murrelets from a BC population. See Vanderkist et al. (1999) for sexing live individuals with molecular techniques from blood samples.

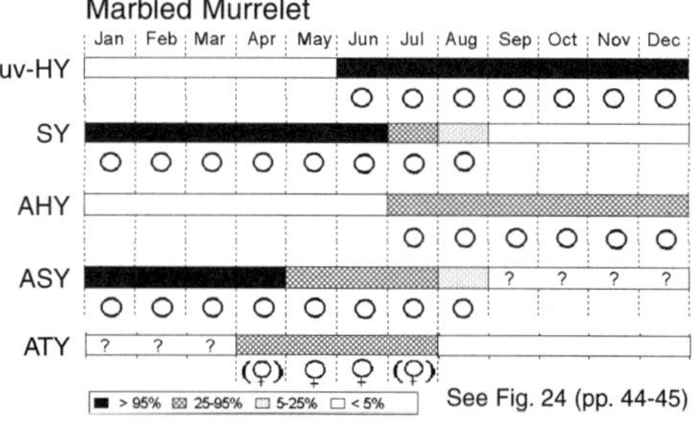

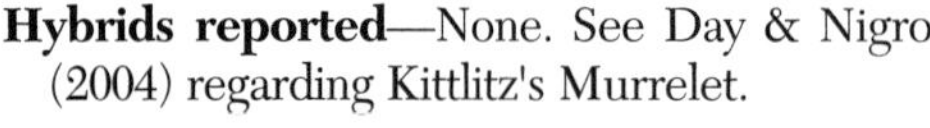
Hybrids reported—None. See Day & Nigro (2004) regarding Kittlitz's Murrelet.

References—Ainley et al. (1994), Bent (1919a), Carter & Stein (1995), Dement'ev & Gladkov (1951a), Kozlova (1957), Kuletz & Kendall (1998), S.K. Nelson (1997), Pyle (unpublished ms.), Ridgway (1919), Sealy (1975), Stresemann & Stresemann (1966), Strong (1998), Thompson et al. (2003).

KITTLITZ'S MURRELET
Brachyramphus brevirostris

KIMU
Species # 0240
Band size: 3B

Species—From other alcids including Marbled Murrelet by small size and very short legs (Table 68, p. 764); bill very small (Fig. 539**C**, p. 760) and black; ss with white tips and outer rects extensively white; underwing covs dark with variable whitish by age (see Fig. 540, p. 761); upperparts pale grayish and face and underparts entirely white in Sep-Apr (Fig. 539**C**), or upperparts, face, and breast feathers dark gray with buff to gold fringing, and belly primarily white in Apr-Aug; underparts with partial to near-complete breast band in Sep-Mar; legs and feet pale pinkish or yellowish to grayish with dusky webs between toes. See also Xantus' Murrelet (p. 764) regarding murre chicks.

Geographic variation—Monotypic, but see Friesen et al. (1996), Day et al. (1999).

Molt—CAS. PF limited-partial (Sep-Dec in HYs), PA1 absent-partial (May-Jun in SYs), PB2 complete (Jun-Aug in SYs), DPA partial (Mar-May in ASYs), DPB complete (Aug-Oct in ASYs). Molt strategies appear to be similar to those of Marbled Murrelet (p. 760).

Age—Juv (B1; Jul-Oct) has pp fresh and pointed (Fig. 526**A**, p. 748), upperparts dark grayish, and face and breast feathers with heavy gray fringing (*cf.* Fig. 541**A**); Juv ♀ = ♂. In addition to the following, confirmed breeding individuals can reliably be aged ASY.

Juv-HY/SY (1st cycle, Juv/F1-A1; Sep-Aug): Bill width at gape (Fig. 524, p. 746) ~10.0-12.5 mm; underpart feathers with thin dusky fringing in Sep-Nov and possibly through May (Fig. 541**A**); underwing covs often with white and not uniformly dark brown (Fig. 540**A**-**B**, p. 761); most to all s covs, pp, and ss uniformly brown and relatively worn, contrasting with fresher and slatier scapulars, humerals, and some proximal s covs in Feb-Aug (Fig. 525**A**-**B**, p. 747), the outer pp (and p covs) relatively narrow and pointed (Fig. 526**A**-**B**); outer rects narrow and relatively worn (Fig. 527**A**, p. 748). **Note: Many SYs may also show more extensive white to the underparts in Mar-Aug but study needed (see Marbled Murrelet).**

AHY/ASY (Def. cycle, DB-DA; Sep-Aug): Bill width at gape (Fig. 524) 12.0-14.0 mm; underpart feathers completely white or some with broad dusky fringing in Sep-Feb (Fig. 541**B**); underwing covs completely dark or occasionally with white (Fig. 540**B**-**D**); wing covs, pp, and ss grayish, relatively fresh, and not contrasting with scapulars or humerals, the pp and p covs often showing contrasts among p5-p6 and between s1 and p1 (Fig. 525**E**), and the outer pp relatively broad and blunt (Fig. 526**C**-**D**); outer rects broad and relatively fresh (Fig. 527**B**). **Note: See HY/SY.**

Sex—♀ = ♂ by plumage aspect. Medial BP (Fig. 20**A**, p. 31) developed by both sexes but distended cloaca (Fig. 21, p. 32) indicates ASY ♀ in May-Jul. Measurements unhelpful for sexing (Table 68, p. 764) and no other criteria known.

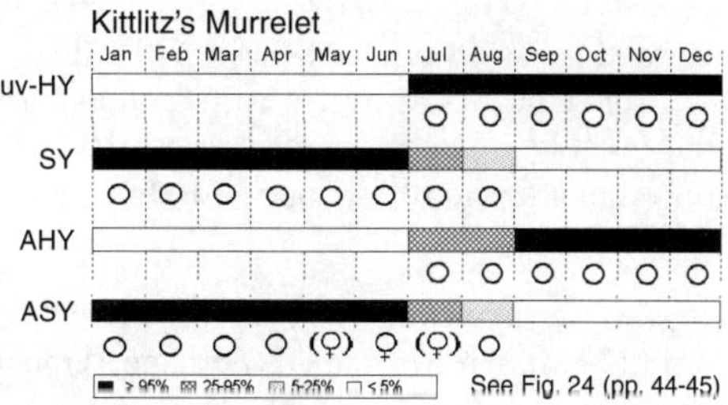

Hybrids reported—None. See Day & Nigro (2004) regarding Marbled Murrelet.

References—Ainley et al. (1994), Bent (1919a), Day et al. (1999), Dement'ev & Gladkov (1951a), Devillers (1972), Kozlova (1957), Pitocchelli et al. (1995), Pyle (unpublished ms.), Ridgway (1919), Sealy (1977), Sealy et al. (1982).

TABLE 68. Measurements (mm) of North American murrelets for identification and sexing. See pp. 4-11 for methods of measurement. Species summaries are in **bold**. Values were derived from 95% confidence intervals as based approximately on the indicated sample sizes (see pp. 4-5). Thus, midpoints of ranges approximate means, and S.D. is approximated by 25% of the range.

Taxon/Sex	*n*	wing chord[1]	tail length	exposed culmen[2]	tarsus
Marbled Murrelet		**121-135**	**27-35**	**13.0-18.3**	**14-19**
♀	100	121-133	27-34	13.0-17.9	14-18
♂	100	123-135	28-35	13.4-18.3	15-19
Kittlitz's Murrelet[3]	**100**	**127-141**	**26-35**	**8.9-12.5**	**13-17**
Xantus' Murrelet[4]		**112-126**	**28-34**	**16.4-21.3**	**23-26**
♀	100	113-126	29-34	16.9-21.3	23-26
♂	100	112-124	28-33	16.4-20.8	23-25
Craveri's Murrelet		**110-124**	**30-37**	**17.9-22.6**	**21-25**
♀	100	111-124	31-37	18.1-22.6	21-25
♂	100	110-122	30-36	17.9-22.3	21-24
Ancient Murrelet		**130-143**	**32-38**	**12.3-14.7**	**24-28**
♀	55	131-143	33-38	12.3-14.3	24-28
♂	65	130-142	32-37	12.8-14.7	25-28

[1] Note that, in most alcids, wing chord of HY/SYs average 10-20% less than that of AHY/ASYs.
[2] See figures and text for bill depth values, which vary substantially by age.
[3] Few data are available on sex-specific differences in morphometrics of Kittlitz's Murrelet, but dimorphism appears to be slight.
[4] Includes both N.Am subspecies, which vary only slightly in bill dimensions (Fig. 543).

XANTUS' MURRELET
Synthliboramphus hypoleucus

XAMU
Species # 0250
Band size: 2

Species—From other murrelets and alcids by small size but proportionally long legs (Table 68); bill proportionately long, thin, with slightly decurved culmen (Fig. 543**A-B**), and black; tail with 12 rects; upperparts and upperwings uniformly blackish; underparts white; legs and feet grayish and yellowish, the tarsus > middle toe without claw (*vs* < middle toe in other alcids). From fledged chicks of murres, which can resemble these species in plumage aspect, by feathering of head and upperparts tightly knit (*vs* loose or downy in murre chicks); legs and feet smaller (tarsus < 27 mm *vs* > 27 mm in murre chicks) and black (*vs* yellowish to brownish in murre chicks). From Marbled and Long-billed murrelets by smaller size but longer tarsus (Table 68); tail with 12 rects (*vs* 14 rects); upperparts blackish (*vs* gray in basic-aspect Long-billed Murrelet); scapulars and nape without white (Fig. 543**A-B**).

From Craveri's Murrelet, with caution, by sides of head whiter and bill averages shorter and thicker (Fig. 543**A-B**); underside of p10 and underwing covs whiter (Fig. 543**A**); upperparts tinged bluish when fresh. See also **Molt** for differences in replacement strategies of pp, p covs, and ss.

Geographic variation—See Carter et al. (2005), Green & Arnold (1939), Jehl & Bond (1975), Keitt (2005), van Rossem (1939a), and Winnett et al. (1979). No other subspecies occur.

S.h. scrippsi (br Channel Is - San Benito Is, disperses to s.BC): Feathers around eye dark and bill slightly shorter but deeper (Fig. 543**A**). The name "*B.h. pontilis*", for populations of San Benito Is, apparently refers to intergrades.

S.h. hypoleucos (br Guadalupe I - San Benito Is, dispersal to s.OR): Feathers around eye white and bill slightly longer but shallower (Fig. 543**B**).

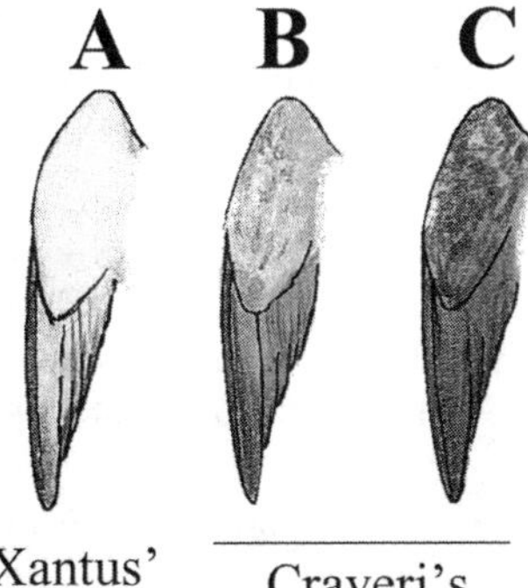

FIGURE 542. Underwing pattern in Xantus' and Craveri's murrelets for identification. Note that Craveri's Murrelet can have whitish underwing s covs (**B**) but the underwing p covs and underside of p10 are much whiter in Xantus' than Craveri's murrelets. The underwing covert coloration in Craveri's Murrelet may or may not correlate with age (*cf.* Fig. 540, p. 761); further study needed.

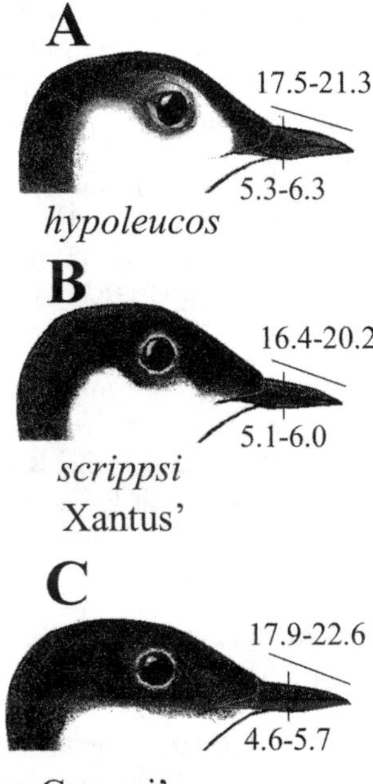

FIGURE 543. Basic-plumage head aspect and bill dimensions in Xantus' and Craveri's murrelets for identification. Measures indicate exposed culmen (Fig. 7**A**, p. 9) and bill depth at distal end of nares (Fig. 8**C**, p. 10). Note that Craveri's Murrelet has a longer but thinner bill; in addition, the distance from the gonydeal angle to the bill tip is longer in Craveri's (~11.5-14.0 mm) than in Xantus' (~10.0-12.5 mm). The extent of dark coloration below the eye also varies by taxon: 0 in *S.h. hypoleucos*, 2-3 mm in *scrippsi*, and 3-5 mm in Craveri's Murrelet, and the area above the tip of the gape is usually white in Xantus' Murrelet and dark in Craveri's Murrelet. Beware of hybrids.

Molt—SAS (CBS or CAS?). PF partial-incomplete (Nov-Feb? in HY/SYs), PA1 absent(?), PB2 complete (Jun?-Sep? in SYs), DPA absent-limited? (Jan?-Mar? in ASYs), DPB complete (Jul-Oct in ASYs). The single inserted first-cycle molt appears to be homologous with a PF rather than a PA1 (Fig. 10**C**, p. 14), although a few head, breast, and/or flank feathers may be replaced twice, indicating the presence of both molts (and CAS; Fig. 10**F**); study needed. All molting occurs at sea, away from breeding grounds, including the PB1 (prejuvenal molt) which occurs in Jun-Sep after fledging. During DPBs, pp and ss are often replaced synchronously but may also be replaced in blocks (see Marbled Murrelet), in May-Jul (SYs) or Jul-Sep (ASYs), followed by body molt. The PF includes most to all body feathers, a few to most s covs, and sometimes the rects(?), but no terts. Occasional ASYs apparently may retain 1-6 outer pp and 2-8 medial ss during the DPB. The DPA appears to include a few crown and back feathers, at least, or it may be absent (indicating CBS; Fig. 10**B**); more study is needed.

Age—Juv (B1; Jul-Dec) resembles basic plumage in aspect but has pp fresh and pointed (Fig. 526**A**, p. 748); Juv ♀=♂. In addition to the following, confirmed breeding individuals can reliably be aged ASY.

Juv-HY/SY (1st cycle, Juv/B1-F1; Jul-Jun): Bill width at gape (Fig. 524, p. 746) ~8.5-10.5 mm; pp, p covs, ss, and usually some gr covs juv and brownish, contrasting with fresher replaced s covs in Nov-Jun (Fig. 525**B-C**, p. 747); some breast feathers sometimes with thin dark fringing in Jul-Oct. **Note: Many intermediates may be difficult to age. Shape of outer pp and**

rects (Figs. 526 & 527, p. 748) may average slightly narrower in HY/SY than AHY/ASY but differences are slight (due to development of these post-fledging; see Molt). Pattern of the underwing coverts (Fig. 532, p. 753) may be too variable to be useful in ageing; study needed. See also AHY/ASY.

AHY/ASY (Def. cycle, DB; Jul-Jun): Bill width at gape (Fig. 524) ~9.5-11 mm; pp, p covs, and ss uniformly basic, not contrasting in aspect or wear with s covs and back feathers (Fig. 525**D**), or occasionally with contrasts among pp (Fig. 525**E**), the outer pp and p covs slightly broader (Fig. 526**C-D**); breast feathers white, without thin dark fringing. **Note: See Juv-HY/SY and ASY/ATY.**

ASY/ATY (Def, cycle, DB; Jul-Jun): Like AHY/ASY but pp and/or ss with two generations, 1-6 outer pp and 1-8 medial ss retained and relatively worn (*cf.* Fig. 16**B**, p. 24). **Note: Only occasional ASY/ATYs can be reliably aged. It is also possible that molt limits in the wing (Fig. 525E) might indicate breeding ASY/ATYs; study needed.**

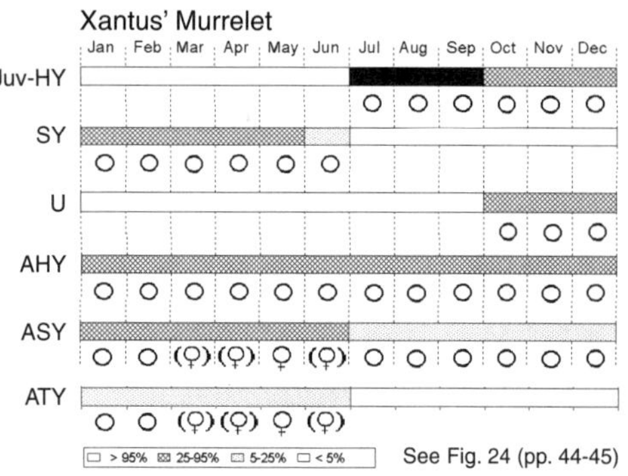

Sex—♀=♂ by plumage aspect. Bilateral BPs (Fig. 20**B**, p. 31) developed by both sexes but distended cloaca (Fig. 21, p. 32) indicates ASY ♀ in Mar-Jun. Measurements unhelpful for sexing (Table 68, p. 764) and no other criteria known.

Hybrids reported—Possibly with Craveri's Murrelet (van Rossem 1939a, Jehl & Bond 1975).

References—Ainley et al. (1994), Beck (1910), Bent (1919a), Brewster (1902b), Carter et al. (2005), Drost & Lewis (1995), Jehl (1975), Jehl & Bond (1975), Pyle (unpublished ms.), Ridgway (1919), Stresemann & Stresemann (1966), van Rossem (1915, 1926b, 1939a).

CRAVERI'S MURRELET

Synthliboramphus craveri

CRMU
Species # 0260
Band size: 2

Species—See Xantus' Murrelet (p. 764) for separation from other alcids. From Xantus' Murrelet, with caution, by sides of head darker and bill averages longer and thinner (Fig. 543**C**, p. 765); underside of p10 and underwing covs darker (Fig. 542**B-C**, p. 765); upperparts blackish, without bluish tinge when fresh. See also **Molt** for differences in replacement strategies of pp, p covs, and ss.

Geographic variation—Monotypic.

Molt—SAS (CBS or CAS?). PF partial-incomplete (Sep-Dec? in HY/SYs), PA1 absent(?), PB2 complete (Feb?-Jul? in SYs), DPA limited (Nov?-Jan? in ASYs), DPB complete (Mar-Aug in ASYs). During DPBs, pp and ss are apparently replaced synchronously or in blocks (see Marbled Murrelet), in Feb-May (SYs) or Mar-Jun (ASYs), possibly followed by suspension of up to three months before body and s cov molt occurs in Jul-Sep. Molts otherwise as in Xantus' Murrelet (p. 764) except note much earlier timing.

Age—Juv (B1; May-Oct) resembles basic plumage in aspect but has pp fresh and pointed (Fig. 526**A**, p. 748); Juv ♀=♂. In addition to the following, confirmed breeding individuals can reliably be aged ASY.

Juv-HY/SY (1st cycle, Juv/B1-F1; May-Apr): Bill width at gape (Fig. 524, p. 746) ~8.0-10.0 mm; pp, p covs ss, and usually some distal gr covs juv and brownish, contrasting with fresher replaced s covs in Oct-Apr (Fig. 525**B-C**); some breast feathers sometimes with thin dark fringing in May-Aug. **Note: Shape of outer pp and rects (Figs. 526 & 527, p. 748) may average slightly narrower in HY/SY than AHY/ASY but differences are slight (due to development of these post-fledging; see Molt). Pattern of the underwing coverts (Fig. 532, p. 753) may be too variable to be useful in ageing; study needed. See also AHY/ASY. Many intermediates may be difficult to age.**

AHY/ASY (Def. cycle, DB; May-Apr): Bill width at gape (Fig. 524) ~9.0-10.5 mm; pp, p covs, and ss relatively fresh, contrasting with more worn s covs in May-Sep, and with fresher s covs and back feathers in Oct-Apr (see **Molt** for derivation of this unique pattern), or occasionally with contrasts among pp (Fig. 525**E**); breast feathers white, without thin dark fringing. **Note: See Juv-HY/SY and ASY/ATY.**

ASY/ATY (Def. cycle, DB; May-Apr): Like AHY/ASY but pp and/or ss with two generations, 1-6 outer pp and 1-8 medial ss retained and relatively worn (*cf.* Fig. 16**B**, p. 24). **Note: Only occasional ASY/ATYs can be aged. It is also possible that molt limits in the wing (Fig. 525E) might indicate breeding ASY/ATYs; study needed.**

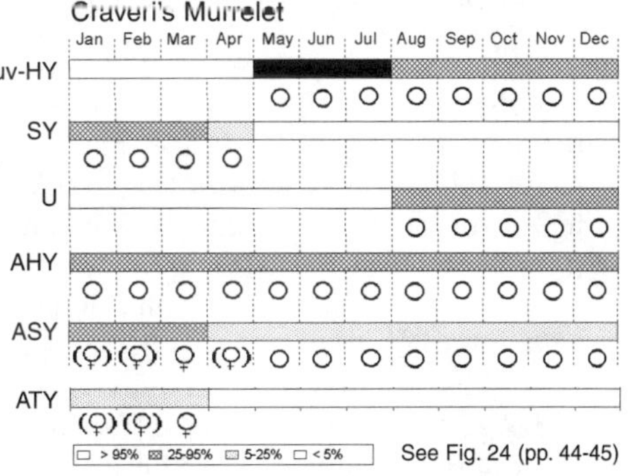

Sex—♀=♂ by plumage aspect. Bilateral BPs (Fig. 20**B**, p. 31) developed by both sexes but distended cloaca (Fig. 21, p. 32) indicates ASY ♀ in Jan-Apr. Measurements unhelpful for sexing (Table 68, p. 764) and no other criteria known.

Hybrids reported—Possibly with Xantus' Murrelet (p. 764).

References—See Xantus' Murrelet (p. 764).

ANCIENT MURRELET
Synthliboramphus antiquus

ANMU
Species # 0210
Band size: 3B-3

Species—From other murrelets and alcids by medium-small size with proportionally short culmen (Table 68, p. 764); bill proportionally deep and primarily whitish to ivory; underparts white except throat usually with dark (Fig. 544, p. 768); back and s covs bluish gray contrasting with duskier or blacker crown, nape, and flight feathers; head of AHYs with postocular plumes extending to nape; underwing covs primarily white; legs and feet whitish to bluish with dusky webs between toes, the outer toe > middle toe (unique among N.Am alcids).

Geographic variation—Considered monotypic here. Populations of the Commander Is, Siberia ("*S.a. microrhynchos*"), may average smaller bills and more black to the sides of the underparts but differences, if present, insufficient and confounded by age-related and molt-related variation. See Flint & Golovkin (1990) and Gaston (1992, 1994) for more information.

Molt—SAS (CAS?). PF/PA1 partial (Dec-May in HY/SYs), PB2 complete (Jun-Aug in SYs), DPA limited (Jan-Apr in AHY/ASYs), DPB complete (Aug-Nov in ASYs). The single inserted first-cycle molt may have resulted from a merging of PF and PA1 molts in ancestral species (Fig. 10**D**, p. 14), although a few head and/or flank feathers may be replaced twice, indicating the presence of both molts (and CAS; Fig. 10**F**); study needed. Most or all molting occurs at sea, away from breeding grounds, including the PB1 (prejuvenal molt) which occurs in Jul-Sep after fledging. The PF/PA1 includes most body feathers (at least some juv scapulars and rump feathers usually retained) but few if any s covs and no terts or rects; head and throat feathers (including postocular plumes) appear to be replaced just once, in Mar-May, following molt of back. During DPBs, pp, p covs, and ss are apparently replaced synchronously (Jun-Aug in SYs; Aug-Sep in ASYs), followed by replacement of body feathers; the postocular plumes appear to be replaced just once per cycle (during the DPB), with protracted development occurring in Oct-Feb. The DPA includes feathers of the head, throat, breast, and flanks. Some SYs over-summer on non-breeding grounds and these may exhibit reduced PA1s and advanced PB2s (see p. 18).

Age—Juv (B1; Jul-Sep) has bill small (depth < 6.0 mm), pp fresh and pointed (Fig. 526**A**, p. 748), crown and nape dark brownish without white postocular plumes, sides of breast often with dusky mottling (*cf.* Fig. 541**A**, p. 762), and throat white or washed indistinctly with dusky (Fig. 544**A**-**B**); Juv ♀ = ♂. In addition to the following, confirmed breeding individuals can reliably be aged ASY.

Juv-HY/SY (1st cycle, Juv/B1-F1/A1; Sep-Aug): Bill averages shallower (depth at distal end of nares 5.8-7.6); bill width at gape (Fig. 524, p. 746) ~8.0-10.0 mm; throat white or indistinctly washed grayish in Sep-Apr (Fig. 544**A**-**B**) or black, usually with indistinct white mottling in Apr-Aug (Fig. 544**C**); scapulars and humerals fresh in Jan-Aug, contrasting with browner pp and wing covs (Fig. 525**A**, p. 747), the scapulars and rump usually with retained juv feathers (*cf.* Fig. 313**A**, p. 418). **Note: Some AHY/ASYs (SY/TYs?) show browner wings and white mottling to the throats in Apr-Aug and can be difficult to separate from HY/SYs. Also. shape of outer pp and rects (Figs. 526 & 527, p. 748) may average slightly narrower in HY/SY than AHY/ASY but differences are slight (due to later acquisition or replacement of these feathers; see Molt).**

AHY/ASY (Def. cycle, DB-DA; Sep-Aug): Bill averages deeper (depth at distal end of nares 6.5-8.5); bill width at gape (Fig. 524) ~9.0-11.0 mm; throat with distinct black patch, usually mot-

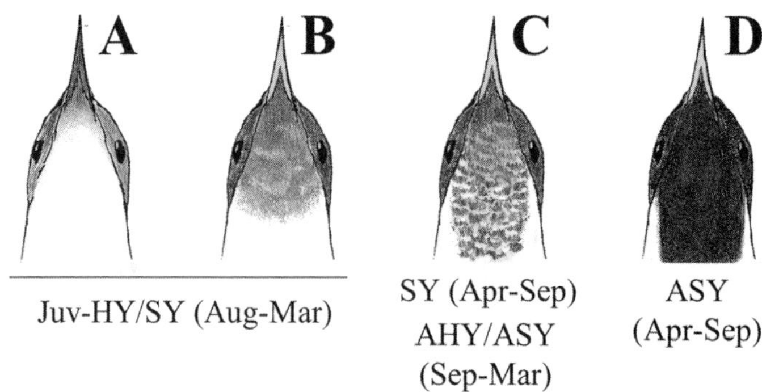

FIGURE 544. Throat pattern by age and season in Ancient Murrelet. Occasional SYs can lack black on the throat (**B**) in Apr-Sep and occasional AHY/ASYs can retain full black throats (**D**) in Oct-Mar.

tled white in Sep-Apr (Fig. 544**C-D**) or black without white mottling in Apr-Aug (Fig. 544**D**); back feathers moderately worn in Jan-Aug, not contrasting markedly with blackish pp and wing covs (Fig. 525**D**), the scapulars and rump without retained feathers (*cf.* Fig. 313**B**). **Note: See HY/SY. Some AHY/ASYs (SY/TYs?) have some white mottling to the throat in Apr-Aug.**

Sex—♀=♂ by plumage aspect. Bilateral BPs (Fig. 20**B**, p. 31) developed by both sexes but distended cloaca (Fig. 21, p. 32) indicates ASY ♀ in Apr-Jul. Measurements largely unhelpful for sexing (Table 68, p. 764); bill depth at distal end of nares averages larger in ♂♂ (7.0-8.5) than ♀♀ (6.5-7.9) in Apr-Aug but there appears to be too much overlap for reliable sexing. Otherwise, no other criteria are known.

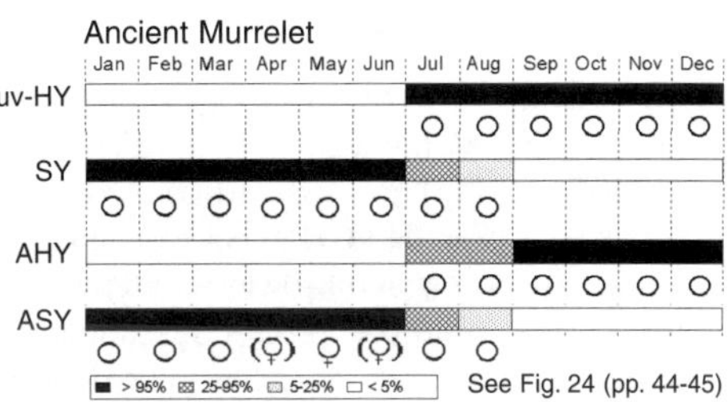

Hybrids reported—None.

References—Ainley et al. (1994), Bent (1919a), Dement'ev & Gladkov (1951a), Gaston (1992, 1994), Kozlova (1957), Pyle (unpublished ms.), Ridgway (1919), Sealy (1976), Sealy et al. (2001).

CASSIN'S AUKLET

Ptychoramphus aleuticus

CAAU
Species # 0160
Band size: 3B-3A

Species—From other auklets and alcids by medium-small size (Table 69, p. 774); bill proportionally large, with relatively straight culmen and mandible distal to gonys, and blackish with distinct pale base to lower mandible (Fig. 547); upperparts and upperwing uniformly dark gray with white feathers above eye (Fig. 547); breast pale gray; abdomen and vent white; underwing covs gray to whitish with distinct black axillars; iris brown (Juv) to white in ATY (Fig. 545, p. 770); legs and feet grayish with dusky webs between toes. From Juv Whiskered Auklet by longer wing, exposed culmen, and tarsus (Table 69); breast distinctly paler than upperparts and white crescent usually present above eye (Fig. 547**A**, p. 771); bill black, without reddish tinge.

Geographic variation—Considered monotypic here. Populations of wc.Baja CA Is ("*P.a. australe*") average smaller but differences slight and consistent with broad population-wide cline in size. See Manuwal & Thoresen (1993) and van Rossem (1939a) for more information.

Molt—CAS. PF absent-limited (Aug-Jan in HY/SYs), PA1 limited-partial (Mar-May in SYs), PB2 complete (Jun-Aug in SYs), DPA partial (Jan-Apr in ASYs), DPB complete (Apr-Oct in ASYs; commencing as early as Jan in breeding populations of Mexico). The PB1 (prejuvenile molt) completes at the natal site and the DPB can commence on breeding grounds (see below); otherwise, all molting occurs at sea on non-breeding grounds. The PF can include scattered body feathers or may be absent in later fledglings. During DPBs, pp and ss are replaced sequentially (non-synchronously), the ss apparently replaced proximally from the terts and distally from s1 and s5 (*cf.* Fig. 12**B**, p. 19), ss among s4-s9 the last replaced. In breeding ASYs the DPB can commence during incubation (inner 3 to 5 pp and some body feathers typically replaced), suspend for chick rearing, and complete at sea after breeding. The PAs include some to most body feathers and often scattered les and med covs (especially in ASYs) but no terts or rects. Some SYs may over-summer on non-breeding grounds and these exhibit reduced PA1s and advanced PB2s (see p. 18).

Age—Juv (B1; May-Dec; Mar-Dec in some Mexican populations) has bill small (depth at distal end of nares < 8.0 mm; Fig. 547**A**, p. 771), pp fresh and pointed (Fig. 526**A**, p. 748), and iris dark brown (Fig. 545**A**); Juv ♀ = ♂. In addition to the following, confirmed breeding individuals can reliably be aged ASY.

HY/SY (1st cycle, F1-A1; Oct-Sep): Bill shallow (Fig. 547**A**); bill width at gape (Fig. 524, p. 746) ~9.5-11.0 mm; iris dark to medium-pale brown (Fig. 545**A-B**); s covs, pp, and ss uniformly juvenal and brownish, often contrasting with grayer replaced scapulars, humerals, and sometimes a few les and med covs in Apr-Sep (Fig. 525**A-B**, p. 747; beware ASYs in Feb-Sep with alternate feathers), the outer pp and p covs relatively narrow, pointed, and worn (Fig. 526**A-B**); outer rects narrow, brownish, and relatively worn (Fig. 527**A**, p. 748); gular pouch extension < 50 mm from bill tip (Fig. 546**A**).

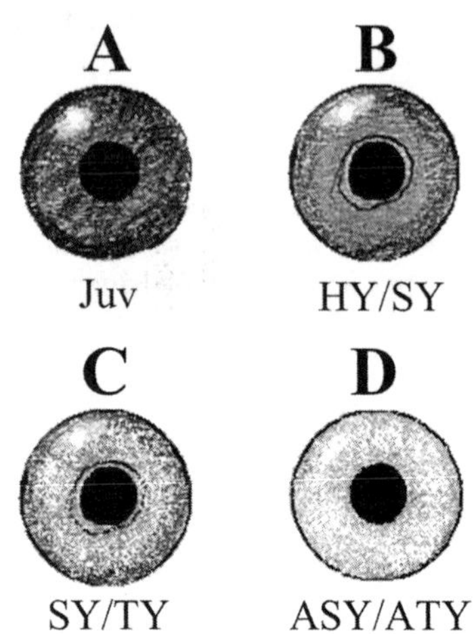

FIGURE 545. Iris color by age in Cassin's Auklet. Occasional ASYs retain darker irises (**B-C**) for life, so caution is warranted.

AHY/ASY (Def. cycle, DB-DA; Oct-Sep): Bill deeper by sex (Fig. 547**B-C**); bill width at gape (Fig. 524) ~10.5-12.0 mm; iris whitish with brown speckling (Fig. 545**C**); wing covs, pp, ss, and back feathers uniformly grayish and fresh, without suspension limits (*cf.* Fig. 525**D**) but often with s1-p1 contrast (*cf.* Fig. 14**B**, p. 21), the outer pp and p covs relatively broad, blunt, and fresh (Fig. 526**C-D**); outer rects broad, blackish, and relatively fresh (Fig. 527**B**); gular pouch extension < 60 mm from bill tip (Fig. 546**A**). **Note: These are primarily SY/TYs but**

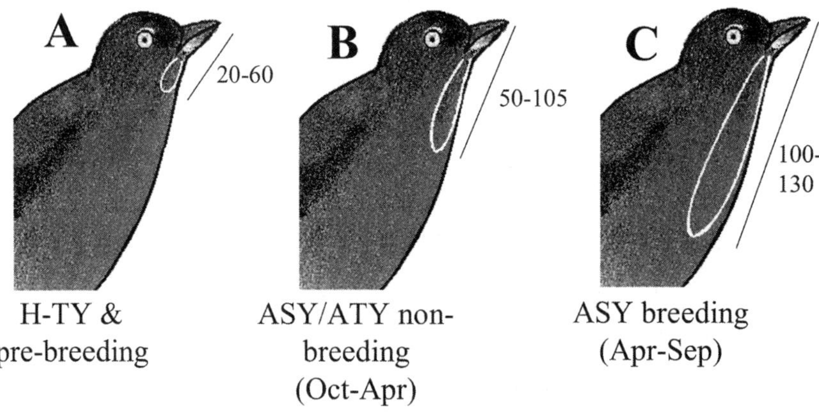

FIGURE 546. Gular pouches in Cassin's Auklet by age, season, and breeding status. Measure indicates the distance from the tip of the bill to the end of the gular pouch, best obtained with a blunt-ended straw or dowel, with head held in position as shown. Prior to breeding the pouch is undeveloped (**A**); all SYs and most TYs have not bred yet and most individuals have bred by 5Y, although occasional individuals as old as 6-8Y have not yet bred. Once breeding, the gular pouch elongates during chick-feeding periods (**C**) and regresses again during the non-breeding season (**B**). Individuals with pouches > 60 mm can be aged ASY/ATY (May-Apr). See Speich & Manuwal (1974) for more information. Dovekie and Crested, Least, Parakeet, and Whiskered auklets also develop gular pouches but lengths as related to age and breeding status need to be determined.

include some non-breeding ASY/ATYs as well. See also SY/TY and ASY/ATY.

SY/TY (2nd cycle, B2-A2; Oct-Sep): Like AHY/ASY but iris medium-pale brown (Fig. 545**B**). **Note: Some ASY/ATYs (5-10%) can retain brown speckling to the outer iris (Fig. 545C) and occasional (< 5%) ASY/ATYs can retain medium-pale brown irises (545C) for life, so only individuals exhibiting even replacement clines in pp and gular pouch < 60 mm (Fig. 546A; a small proportion of TYs breed and can exhibit gular pouch extensions 60-80 mm) should be aged SY/TY. It is possible that bill depth (Fig. 547) and width (Fig. 524) measurements can assist with ageing SY/TYs but more study is needed.**

ASY/ATY (Def. cycle, DB-DA; Oct-Sep): Like AHY/ASY but iris white (Fig. 545**D**); pp often with suspension limit among p1-p5 (Fig. 525**F**); gular pouch extension often > 60 mm from bill tip (Fig. 546**B**-**C**). **Note: See SY/TY. ASY/ATYs with white irises but gular pouch < 50 mm and without suspension limits are likely pre-breeding 4-8Ys.**

Sex—♀=♂ by plumage aspect. Bilateral BPs (Fig. 20**B**, p. 31) developed by both sexes but distended cloaca (Fig. 21, p. 32) indicates ASY ♀ in Apr-Jul. Other than bill depth, measurements unhelpful for sexing (Table 69, p. 774). Bill depth at the distal end of nares can be used to reliably sex AHY ♂♂ and ASY ♀♀ with white irises (Fig. 545**D**); HY/SYs have shallower bills (Fig. 547**A**) and are not reliably sexed.

ASY ♀: Bill depth at distal end of nares < 9.8 (Fig. 547**B**). **Note: Approximately 10% of AHY/ASYs, with bill depth 9.8-10.2, are not reliably sexed.**

AHY ♂: Bill depth at distal end of nares > 10.2 (Fig. 547**C**). **Note: See ASY ♀.**

Hybrids reported—None.

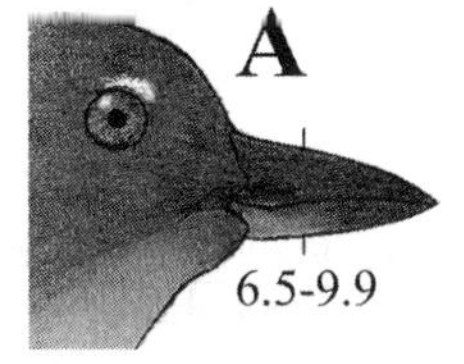

Juv-HY/SY ♀♂

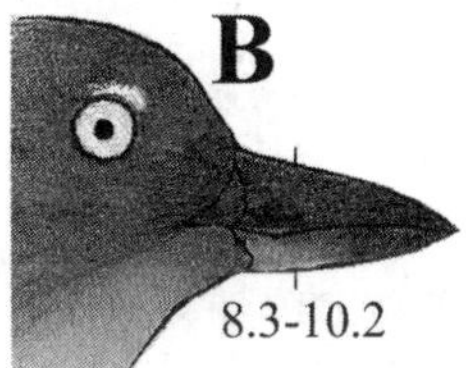

ASY ♀

AHY ♂

FIGURE 547. Bill depth by age and sex in Cassin's Auklet. Measures indicate depth at distal end of nares (Fig. 8**C**, p. 10). ♀♀ and many ♂♂ are not reliably sexed by bill depth until they attain white irises (Fig. 545**D**) as ASYs, whereas some AHY ♂♂ (Jan-Aug) with darker irises (Fig. 546**B**-**C**) and bill depth > 10.2 mm can be sexed. Juv-HY/SYs (**A**) with developing bills generally cannot be sexed, although those with depth < 7.5 may be ♀♀ and those with depth > 9.0 may be ♂♂; study needed.

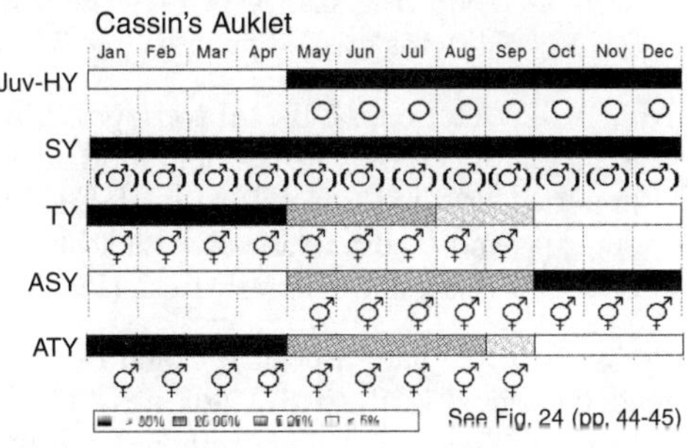

References—Ainley et al. (1994), Bent (1919a), Emslie et al. (1990), Kozlova (1957), Manuwal (1974, 1978), Manuwal & Thoresen (1993), Nelson (1981), Payne (1965, 1966), Pyle (2001, unpublished ms.), Ridgway (1919), Speich & Manuwal (1974), Stresemann & Stresemann (1966).

PARAKEET AUKLET
Aethia psittacula

PAAU
Species # 0170
Band size: 4

Species—From other auklets and alcids by medium size (Table 69, p. 774); bill uniquely shaped, stout, with straight culmen but strongly recurved mandible, dusky-reddish to red with fleshy white swelling at gape (Fig. 548); upperparts and upperwing uniformly blackish with single postocular stripe (AHYs; see **Molt**) and lacking loral crest; underparts white, with variably grayish, black, or mottled black and white throat; underwing covs uniformly blackish-brown; iris pale grayish (Juv) to white in AHYs (Fig. 548); legs and feet grayish with black webs between toes.

Geographic variation—Monotypic.

Molt—SAS (CAS?). PF limited-partial (Oct-Feb? in HY/SYs), PA1 absent(?), PB2 complete (Jul-Oct? in SYs), DPA absent-limited (Mar-May in ASYs), DPB complete (Sep-Oct in ASYs). The single inserted first-cycle molt appears to be homologous with a PF rather than a PA1 (Fig. 10**C**, p. 14), although a few head, breast, and/or flank feathers may be replaced twice, indicating the presence of both molts (and CAS; Fig. 10**F**); study needed. The PB1 (prejuvenile molt) completes at the natal site. Most or all subsequent molting occurs at sea, away from breeding grounds. The PF includes some to most body feathers (some to many rump feathers or uppertail covs usually retained) but few if any s covs and no terts or rects. During DPBs, pp, p covs, and ss are apparently replaced synchronously in Jul-Sep (SYs) or Sep-Nov (ASYs). The ornamental auricular plumes appear to be replaced only once per year in Nov-Dec, during the PF and near the end of the DPB. The DPAs are restricted to feathers of the head, throat, breast, and flanks. Bill plates (upper mandible only?) are apparently shed in Aug-Sep; more study is needed. Some SYs may over-summer on non-breeding grounds and exhibit reduced PA1s and advanced PB2s (see p. 18).

Age—Juv (B1; Jul-Mar) has bill small and dusky, postocular plumes thin or absent, and iris washed grayish (Fig. 548**A**), and outer pp fresh and pointed (Fig. 526**A**, p. 748); Juv ♀ = ♂. In addition to the following, note that confirmed breeders can be reliably aged ATY, and length of gular pouch may be useful for ageing as in Cassin's Auklet (Fig. 546, p. 770); study needed.

Juv-HY/SY (1st cycle, Juv/B1-F1; Oct-Sep): Bill small (Fig. 548**A**-**B**) and dusky-reddish, sometimes orangish-red in Apr-Aug; bill width at gape (Fig. 524, p. 746) ~10.5-12.5 mm; rump and/or uppertail covs usually with retained brown juv feathers in Dec-Sep (*cf.* Fig. 313**A**, p. 418); pp and ss uniformly juvenal, the outer pp and p covs relatively narrow, pointed, brownish, and worn (Fig. 526**A**-**B**), and contrasting with fresher and blacker scapulars and humerals in Dec-Sep (Fig. 525 **A**, p. 747); outer rects narrow, brownish, and relatively worn (Fig. 527**A**, p. 748); iris washed grayish (Fig. 548**A**-**B**) through Feb-Aug.

AHY/ASY (Def. cycle, DB-DA; Oct-Sep): Bill deeper (Fig. 548**C**-**F**) and dusky reddish (Sep-Mar) to bright red (Apr-Aug); bill width at gape (Fig. 524, p. 746) ~12.0-14.5 mm; rump and uppertail covs uniformly blackish (*cf.* Fig. 313**B**); pp and ss uniformly basic (Fig. 525**D**), the outer pp and p covs relatively broad, blunt, blackish, and fresh (Fig. 526**C**-**D**); outer rects broad, blackish, and relatively fresh (Fig. 527**B**); iris bright white (Fig. 548**C**-**F**).

Sex—♀ = ♂ by plumage aspect. Bilateral BPs (Fig. 20**B**, p. 31) developed by both sexes but distended cloaca (Fig. 21, p. 32) indicates ATY ♀ in May-Jul. Measurements generally unhelpful for sexing (Table 69, p. 774), although bill depth can be used to sex many ASYs, (especially mated pairs) in Apr-Aug; Juv-HY/SYs are not reliably sexed.

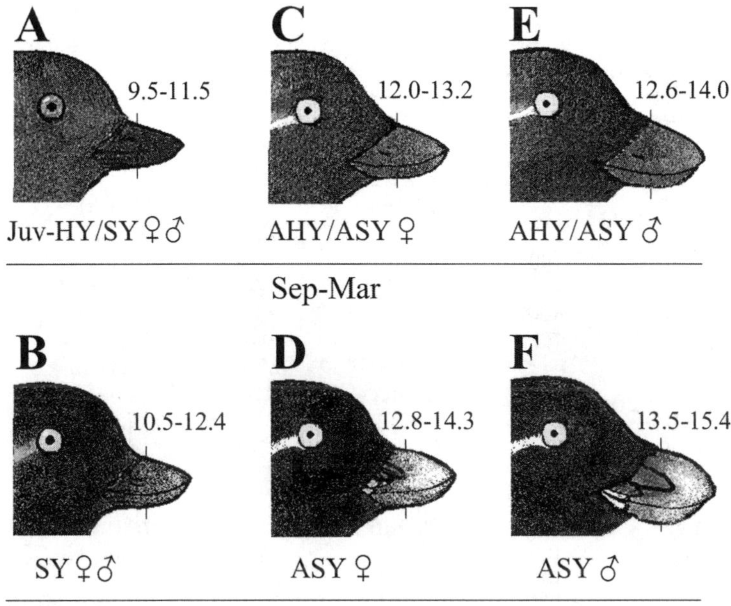

FIGURE 548. Head plumage aspect, eye color, and bill size and color by age and sex in Parakeet Auklet. Measure indicates bill depth at distal end of nares (Fig. 8**C**, p. 10); note that some of the values (e.g. for **B**, **C**, & **E**) are approximate and need to be tested in the field. The post-ocular plumes appear to be replaced just once per year during the PF and DPB, with slow over-winter development, such that plumes are absent in Sep-Oct and gradually become full by Apr-May. Iris is grayish in Juvs (**A**), becomes dull white by May-Aug in SYs (**B**) and is bright white throughout the year in ASYs (**C**-**F**). Reddish bill color begins to be attained during the first cycle (**A**-**B**); after which bright red plates develop in Apr-May, are present in May-Aug (**D**, **F**), and are apparently shed (along with fleshy protuberance at gape) in Aug-Sep, resulting in duskier-reddish bills in Sep-Mar (**C**, **E**). Throat color varies from blackish to whitish, but this seems largely unrelated to age, sex, and/or season.

ASY ♀ (Apr-Aug): Bill depth at distal end of nares < 13.5 mm (Fig. 548**D**). **Note: ASYs with bill depths 13.5-14.3 are not reliably sexed. Bill depth in Sep-Mar is also larger in ♂♂ than ♀♀ (Fig. 548C, E) but there may be too much overlap for reliable sexing; more study needed.**

AHY/ASY ♂ (Sep-Aug): Bill depth at distal end of nares > 14.3 (Fig. 548**F**). **Note: See ASY ♀.**

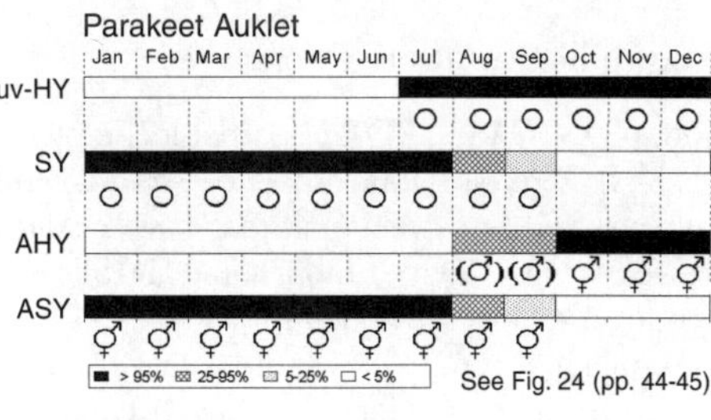

Hybrids reported—None.

References—Ainley et al. (1994), Bédard & Sealy (1984), Bent (1919a), Jones et al. (2001), Kozlova (1957), Pyle (unpublished ms.), Ridgway (1919), Stejneger (1885), Stresemann & Stresemann (1966).

TABLE 69. Measurements (mm) of North American auklets for identification and sexing. See pp. 4-11 for methods of measurement. Species summaries are in **bold**. Values were derived from 95% confidence intervals as based approximately on the indicated sample sizes (see pp. 4-5). Thus, midpoints of ranges approximate means, and S.D. is approximated by 25% of the range.

Taxon/Sex	*n*	wing chord[1]	tail length	exposed culmen[2]	tarsus
Cassin's Auklet		**116-129**	**25-36**	**17.4-21.9**	**22-27**
♀	100	116-128	25-35	17.4-21.6	22-27
♂	100	117-129	25-36	17.7-21.9	22-27
Parakeet Auklet		**139-155**	**37-44**	**13.7-17.4**	**27-32**
♀	65	139-152	37-43	13.7-16.9	27-31
♂	75	141-155	38-44	14.2-17.4	28-32
Least Auklet		**86-102**	**23-28**	**7.4-9.2**	**17-20**
♀	100	87-102	23-28	7.4-9.2	17-20
♂	100	86-101	23-27	7.4-9.2	17-20
Whiskered Auklet[3]		**101-113**	**25-34**	**8.1-10.2**	**19-23**
♀	60	101-112	25-33	8.1-9.9	19-23
♂	100	102-113	25-34	8.3-10.2	19-23
Crested Auklet		**129-146**	**31-42**	**10.0-13.6**	**25-30**
♀	100	129-143	31-40	10.0-12.9	24-29
♂	100	132-146	33-42	10.7-13.6	25-30

[1] Note that, in most alcids, wing chord of HY/SYs average 10-20% less than that of AHY/ASYs.
[2] See figures and text for bill depth values, which vary substantially by age and sex.
[3] Measures from N.Am populations only; see **Geographic variation**.

LEAST AUKLET
Aethia pusilla

LEAU
Species # 0200
Band size: 2-3

Species—From other auklets and alcids by very small size (Table 69); bill small, dusky to reddish and black, with small protuberance above nares in Feb-Jul (Fig. 549), upperparts and upperwing blackish with variable white mottling to scapulars, and whitish loral and (often) postocular plumes in AHYs (Fig. 549**B-C**); medial ss with white tips; chin black, throat white, and rest of underparts variably white to dark gray; most underwing covs white, contrasting with black marginal les covs; iris pale grayish in Juv to white in ASY (Fig. 549); legs and feet grayish with black webs between toes.

Geographic variation—Monotypic.

Molt—SAS (CAS?). PF/PA1 partial-incomplete (Dec?-Jun? in HY/SYs), PB2 complete (Jun-Sep? in SYs), DPA partial-incomplete (Feb-May in ASYs), DPB complete (Jun-Oct in ASYs). The single inserted first-cycle molt may have resulted from a merging of a PF and a PA1 in ancestral species (Fig. 10**D**, p. 14) but some HY/SYs may replace a few body feathers twice within the first cycle, in which case both a PF and a PA1 (and CAS; Fig. 10**F**) would be involved. The PB1 (prejuvenile molt) completes at the natal site and DPBs can commence on the summer grounds (see below); otherwise, most molting occurs at sea, away from breeding grounds. The PF/PA1 includes most to all body feathers, a few to most proximal les and med covs, no to a few proximal gr covs, and no to all rects, but few if any terts. During DPBs, pp and ss are replaced sequentially (non-synchronously), with ss apparently replaced proximally from the terts and distally from s1 (but not s5; *cf.* Fig. 12**B**, p. 19), feathers among s4-s9 the last replaced. In breeding ASYs the DPB can commence during incubation (inner 1-4 pp and some body feathers typically replaced), suspend for chick rearing, and complete at sea after breeding. The ornamental loral and postocular plumes appear to be replaced once per year, in Jan-May (SYs) or Oct-Dec at the end of the

DPB (AHYs). The DPA includes most to all body feathers and often a few proximal s covs but no terts or rects. Bill plates are shed in Jul-Sep. Some SYs may over-summer on non-breeding grounds and these may exhibit reduced PA1s and advanced PB2s (see p. 18).

Age—Juv (B1; Jul-Mar) has pp fresh and pointed (Fig. 526**A**, p. 748) and bill small and blackish, ornamental feathers of head absent or rudimentary, throat and breast white without dark gray mottling, and iris washed grayish (Fig. 549**A**); Juv ♀=♂. In addition to the following, confirmed breeding individuals can reliably be aged ASY, and length of gular pouch might be useful for ageing as in Cassin's Auklet (Fig. 546, p. 770); study needed.

Juv-HY/SY (1st cycle, Juv/B1-F1/A1; Oct-Sep): Bill thinner and blackish, without or with small and developing protuberance (Fig. 549**A-B**); bill width at gape (Fig. 524, p. 746) ~7-8.5 mm; loral and postocular plumes absent to rudimentary in Oct-Jan or reduced in Feb-Sep (Fig. 549**A-B**); most to all s covs, pp, and ss uniformly juv, brown, and relatively worn, contrasting with fresher and grayer scapulars, humerals, and some proximal s covs in Jan-Aug (Fig. 525**B**, p. 747), the outer pp and p covs relatively narrow and pointed (Fig. 526**A-B**, p. 748); outer rects narrow, brownish, and relatively worn in Oct-Jan and often (but not always) in Feb-Sep (Fig. 527**A**, p. 748); iris washed grayish through Dec-Aug (Fig. 549**A-B**). **Note: Underpart aspect in Apr-Sep shows too much individual variation to be reliable in ageing, although SYs likely average more extensive dark grayish than ASYs.**

AHY/ASY (Def. cycle, DB-DA; Oct-Sep): Bill thicker and reddish with enlarged blackish protuberance on culmen in Jan-Aug (Fig. 549**C**); bill width at gape (Fig. 524) ~8-10 mm; loral and postocular plumes developing in Nov-Dec and full in Jan-Sep (Fig. 549**C**); wing covs, pp, and ss uniformly basic (Fig. 525**D**; some s covs can be replaced in Mar-Sep), without suspension limits but often with s1-p1 contrast (*cf.* Fig. 14**B**, p. 21), the outer pp and p covs relatively broad, blunt, and fresh (Fig. 526**C-D**); iris bright white. **Note: See Juv-HY/SY and ASY/ATY.**

ASY/ATY (Def. cycle, DB-DA; Oct-Sep): Like AHY/ASY but pp with suspension limit among p1-p4 (Fig. 525**F**). **Note: Among AHY/ASYs, alternate-plumage aspect averages whiter with age (I.L. Jones 1990), perhaps as related to molt timing (earlier molt producing whiter**

FIGURE 549. Head plumage aspect, eye color, and bill size and color by age in Least Auklet. Note the lack of loral and post-ocular plumes in Juv-HY and reduced plumes in SYs vs. ASYs; these appear to be replaced once per year in Oct-Dec and are thus found in AHY/ASYs year-round. Iris is washed grayish in Juvs (**A**), becomes dull white by May-Aug in SYs (**B**) and is bright white throughout the year in ASYs (**C**). Bill is dusky to blackish in Juvs (**A**), dull orange in SYs (**B**), and black with red tip in ASYs (**C**), often duller in Sep-Mar. Bill plates may or may not be molted, although the small knob above the nares is shed in Jul and re-develops in Feb-Apr. Breast color (below throat) is white in Juvs (**A**) and in Sep-Mar but thereafter becomes variably white to dark gray (as shown); SYs may average more extensive dark gray but this may be related to molt timing and thus appears unreliable for ageing.

feathers; see p. 29). It is thus probable that breeding ASYs with whiter underparts can be aged at least ATY, but confirmation is needed.

Sex—♀=♂ by plumage aspect. Bilateral BPs (Fig. 20**B**, p. 31) developed by both sexes but distended cloaca (Fig. 21, p. 32) indicates ASY ♀ in May-Jul. Measurements generally unhelpful for sexing (Table 69, p. 774). Bill depth at distal end of nares can probably be used to sex a few breeding ASYs (especially mated pairs) in Feb-Aug (♀ 5.7-7.0, ♂ 6.2-7.6). No other criteria known.

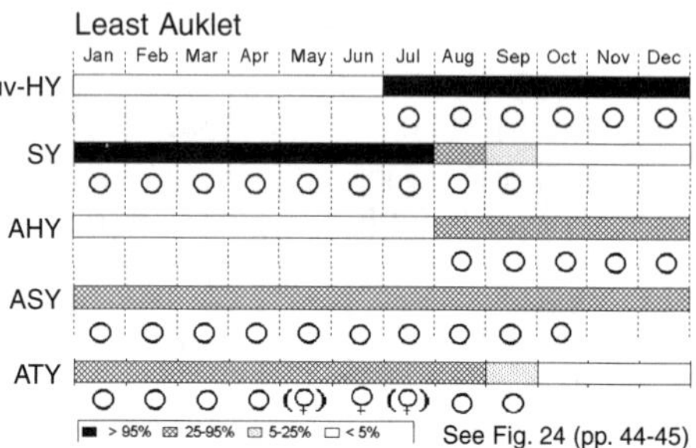

Hybrids reported—None.

References—Ainley et al. (1994), Bédard & Sealy (1984), Bent (1919a), Dement'ev & Gladkov (1951a), I.L. Jones (1990, 1993a), Kozlova (1957), Pyle (unpublished ms.), Ridgway (1919), Stresemann & Stresemann (1966).

WHISKERED AUKLET

Aethia pygmaea

WHAU
Species # 0190
Band size: 3

Species—From other auklets and alcids by small size with proportionally short tarsus (Table 69, p. 774); bill proportionally stout, without protuberance or rictal process, blackish often tinged yellowish (Juv), to deep red (Fig. 550); upperparts and upperwing uniformly dark gray, with white loral and postocular plumes and gray frontal (crest) plumes (Fig. 550); underparts primarily gray with white to whitish vent and undertail covs; underwing covs uniformly or primarily dark gray; iris white; legs and feet bluish gray with black webs between toes. Juv from Juv Cassin's Auklet (p. 769) by shorter wing, exp culmen, and tarsus (Table 69); throat and breast blackish, not distinctly paler than upperparts, and white feathers not present above eye (Fig. 550**A**); bill often tinged yellowish.

Geographic variation—Considered monotypic, in lieu of further study. Populations of the Kurile Is, Siberia ("*A.p. camtschatica*"), average larger and perhaps browner and with more extensive ornamental plumes than those of the Aleutian Is, AK, but differences may be broadly overlapping and/or slight. See Byrd & Williams (1993b) and Feinstein (1959) for more information.

Molt—CBS(?). PF partial (Sep-Jan? in HY/SYs), PB2 complete (Jun-Sep? in SYs), DPB complete (Jun-Oct in ASYs); PA absent? The PB1 (prejuvenile molt) completes at the natal site and the DPB can commence on breeding grounds (see below); otherwise, most molting occurs at sea, away from breeding grounds. The PF includes most to all body feathers and a few to most les and med covs, but few if any gr covs, terts, or rects; more study is needed. During DPBs, pp and ss are replaced sequentially (non-synchronously), with ss apparently replaced proximally from the terts and distally from s1 (but not s5; *cf.* Fig. 12**B**, p. 19), feathers among s4-s8 the last replaced. In breeding ASYs the DPB can commence during incubation (inner 2-5 pp and some body feathers typically replaced), suspend for chick rearing, and complete at sea after breeding. The ornamental frontal (crest), loral, and postocular plumes appear to be replaced once per year, in Jan-May (SYs) or Nov-Mar, developing slowly at the end of the DPB (AHYs). Bill plates are reportedly shed in Jul-Sep but bill depths do not appear to vary substantially by season; more study is needed. Some SYs may over-summer on non-breeding grounds and these may exhibit reduced PA1s and advanced PB2s (see p. 18).

Age—Juv (B1; Jul-Mar) has bill small and black to dusky yellowish (Fig. 550**A**), pp fresh and pointed (Fig. 526**A**, p. 748), and plumage aspect primarily brownish black without ornamental plumes on head (Fig. 550**A**); Juv ♀=♂. In addition to the following, confirmed breeding individuals can reliably be aged ASY, and length of gular pouch might be useful for ageing as in Cassin's Auklet (Fig. 546, p. 770); study needed.

Juv-HY/SY (1st cycle, Juv/B1-F1; Oct-Sep): Bill shallower and dusky yellowish in Oct-Jan to dull orangish in Jan-Sep (Fig. 550**A-B**); bill width at gape (Fig. 524, p. 546) ~6.0-7.5 mm; head without ornamental plumes in Oct-Jan (Fig. 550**A**) and usually with rudimentary or reduced plumes in Feb-Sep (Fig. 550**B**); most to all s covs, pp, and ss uniformly juv, brown, and relatively worn, contrasting with fresher and grayer scapulars, humerals, and sometimes some proximal s covs in Feb-Aug (Fig. 525**A-B**, p. 747), the outer pp and p covs relatively narrow and pointed (Fig. 526**A-B**); outer rects narrow, brownish, and relatively worn (Fig. 527**A**, p. 748). **Note: Look for Juv-HY/SYs to have whiter underwing covs than AHY/ASYs, as in some murrelets (Fig. 540, p. 762).**

AHY/ASY (Def. cycle, DB; Oct-Sep): Bill deeper and dusky red in Oct-Jan to bright red in Jan-Sep (Fig. 550**C-D**); bill width at gape (Fig. 524) ~7.0-8.5 mm; head with developing ornamental plumes in Nov-Feb (Fig. 550**C**) and full ornamental plumes in Feb-Sep (Fig. 550**D**); wing covs, pp, and ss uniformly basic and without suspension limits (*cf.* Fig. 525**D**) but often with s1-p1 contrast (Fig. 14**B**, p. 21), the outer pp and p covs relatively broad, blunt, and fresh (Fig. 526**C-D**); outer rects broad, blackish, and relatively fresh (Fig. 527**B**). **Note: See Juv-HY/SY.**

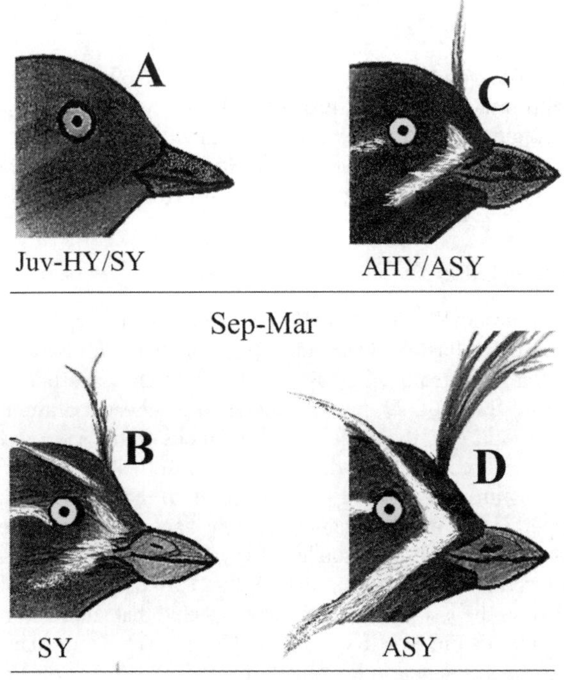

FIGURE 550. Head plumage aspect, eye color, and bill size and color by age in Whiskered Auklet. The loral, post-ocular, and frontal plumes appear to be replaced just once per year during the PF and DPB, with slow over-winter development, such that plumes are absent in Sep-Oct and gradually become full by Apr-May. Iris is slightly tinged grayish in Juvs (**A**) and becomes white by Mar-May in SYs and ASYs (**B-D**). Bill color changes from blackish (sometimes tinged yellowish) in Juv (**A**) to dull orange in SYs (**B**), to bright deep red in ASYs (**D**), becoming dusky reddish during Sep-Mar (**C**). Bill plates may not be molted in this species.

ASY/ATY (Def. cycle, DB; Oct-Sep): Like AHY/ASY but pp with suspension limit among p1-p5 (Fig. 525**F**).

Sex—♀=♂ by plumage aspect. Bilateral BPs (Fig. 20**B**, p. 31) developed by both sexes but distended cloaca (Fig. 21, p. 32) indicates ♀ in May-Jul. Measurements generally unhelpful for sexing (Table 69, p. 774). Bill depth at base can possibly be used to sex a few breeding ASYs (including mated pairs) in Feb-Aug but there may be too much overlap; more study needed. Otherwise, no criteria known for sexing.

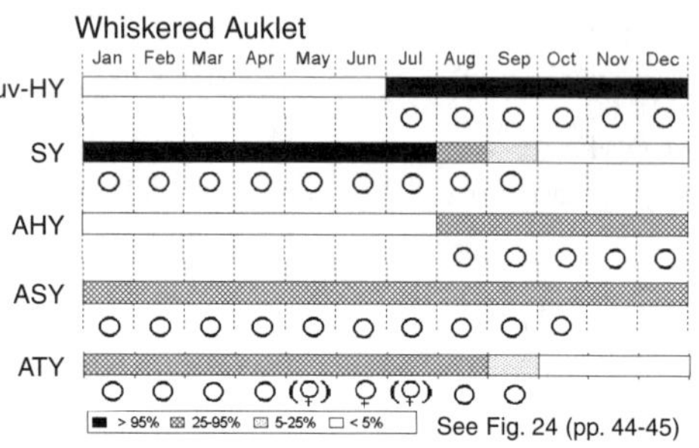

Hybrids reported—None.

References—Ainley et al. (1994), Bent (1919a), Byrd & Williams (1993b), Dement'ev & Gladkov (1951a), Feinstein (1959), Konyukhov (2001), Kozlova (1957), Pitocchelli et al. (2003), Pyle (unpublished ms.), Ridgway (1919), Stejneger (1885), Stresemann & Stresemann (1966).

CRESTED AUKLET

Aethia cristatella

CRAU
Species # 0180
Band size: 4

Species—From other auklets and alcids by medium size (Table 69, p. 774); bill pointed and proportionally stout, with ornamental rictal process in Feb-Aug, dusky orange to bright reddish orange (Fig. 551); upperparts and upperwing uniformly dusky brown, with white postocular and dusky frontal plumes (Fig. 551); underparts (including vent and undertail covs) and underwing covs uniformly grayish to brownish; iris grayish (Juv) to white (ASY); legs and feet grayish with black webs between toes.

Geographic variation—Monotypic.

Molt—SAS (CAS?). PF partial (Nov-Mar? in HY/SYs), PA1 absent(?), PB2 complete (Jun-Sep? in SYs), DPA limited-partial (Mar-May in ASYs), DPB complete (Jul-Nov in ASYs). The single inserted first-cycle molt appears homologous with a PF or may represent merging of a PF and PA1 in ancestral species (Fig. 10**C-D**, p. 14), although a few head, breast, and/or flank feathers may be replaced twice, indicating the presence of both molts (and CAS; Fig. 10**F**); study needed. The PB1 (prejuvenile molt) completes at the natal site; most to all subsequent molting occurs at sea, away from breeding grounds. The PF includes some to most body feathers (some to many rump feathers or uppertail covs usually retained) but few if any s covs and no terts or rects. During DPBs, pp and ss can be replaced sequentially (non-synchronously), with ss apparently replaced proximally from the terts and distally from s1 and s5 (Fig. 12**B**, p. 19; confirmation needed), feathers among s3-4 and s7-s9 the last replaced; it is also possible that some AHYs replace pp and ss synchronously or rapidly in Jun-Sep (SYs) or Aug-Oct (ASYs). The ornamental head plumes appear to be basic feathers, attained in Jul-Aug during the PB1 (prejuvenal molt), possibly again in Nov-Mar during the PF, and once per year in AHY/ASYs (Oct-Nov) at the end of the DPB. The DPA includes some to most feathers of the head, throat, back, breast, and flanks. Many SYs may over-summer on non-breeding grounds and these may exhibit reduced PA1s and advanced PB2s (see p. 18). Bill and rictal plates are molted in Jul-Sep (see Fig. 551).

Age—Juv (B1; Jul-Mar) has pp fresh and pointed (Fig. 526**A**, p. 748) and bill small and dusky, loral and postocular plume rudimentary, and iris grayish (Fig. 551**A**); Juv ♀=♂. In addition to

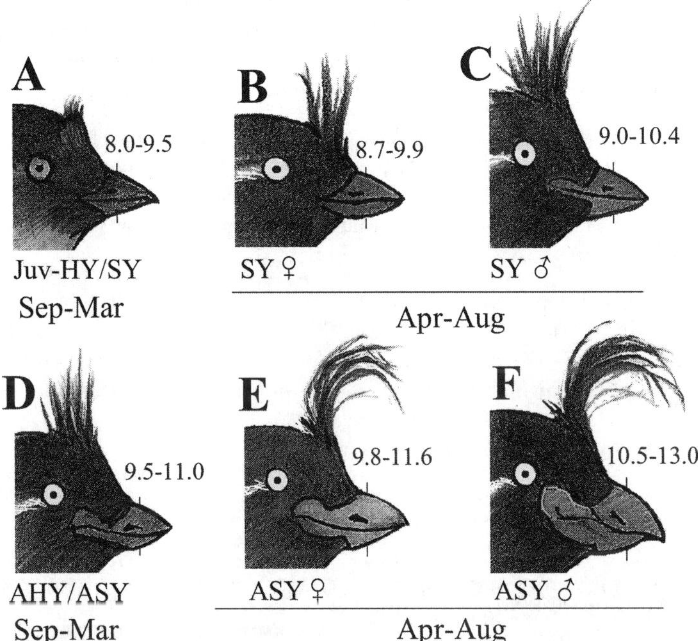

FIGURE 551. Head plumage aspect, eye color, and bill size, shape, and color by age and sex in Crested Auklet. Measure indicates bill depth at distal end of nares (Fig. 8**C**, p. 10); note that some values (e.g., **C** & **D**) are approximate and need to be tested in the field. The frontal plumes appear to be replaced just once per year during the PF and DPB, with slow over-winter development, such that plumes are absent in Sep-Oct and gradually become full by Apr-May. Iris is grayish in Juvs (**A**) and becomes bright white by May-Aug in SYs and year-round thereafter (**B-F**). Bill color is dusky reddish in Juv (**A**), dull orange in SYs (**B-C**), and bright reddish orange in breeding ASYs (**E-F**). Bill plates and ornamental rictal process at gape develop in Feb-Apr, are present in May-Aug, and are shed in Aug-Sep, resulting in duskier-orange bills in Sep-Mar (**D**).

the following, confirmed breeding individuals can reliably be aged ASY and length of gular pouch might be useful for ageing as in Cassin's Auklet (Fig. 546, p. 770); study needed. See Sealy (2006) for information on the occurrence of citrus-like sent in AHY/ASYs but not (or much weaker) in HY/SYs.

Juv-HY/SY (1st cycle, Juv/B1-F1/A1; Oct-Sep): Bill grayish or dusky orange (to dull orange in Mar-Jun) and with reduced or no rictal processes in Mar-Aug (Fig. 551**A-C**); bill width at gape (Fig. 524, p. 746) ~9.0-12.5 mm; frontal plumes reduced (Fig. 551**A-C**); rump and/or uppertail covs usually mixed with grayish formative and brown juv feathers in Dec-Sep (*cf.* Fig. 313**A**, p. 418); pp and ss uniformly juvenal, contrasting with fresher and grayer scapulars and humerals in Dec-Sep (Fig. 525**A**, p. 747), the outer pp and p covs relatively narrow, pointed, brownish, and worn (Fig. 526**A-B**, p. 748); outer rects narrow, brownish, and relatively worn (Fig. 527**A**, p. 748); iris washed grayish through Dec-Apr (Fig. 551**A**).

AHY/ASY (Def. cycle, DB-DA; Oct-Sep): Bill dusky reddish without rictal process (Aug-Jan) to bright orange with large rictal processes by sex in Jan-Aug (Fig. 551**D-F**); bill width at gape (Fig. 524) ~11.0-13.0 mm in Aug-Jan and ~12.0-16.5 mm in Feb-Jul; postocular and frontal plumes fully developed (Fig. 551**D-F**); rump and uppertail covs uniformly grayish (*cf.* Fig. 313**B**); pp and ss uniformly basic (Fig. 525**D**), the outer pp and p covs relatively broad, blunt, blackish, and fresh (Fig. 526**C-D**); outer rects broad, blackish, and relatively fresh (Fig. 527**B**); iris bright white (Fig. 551**D-F**). **Note: Some AHY/ASYs may exhibit suspension limits and/or s1-p1 contrast (Fig. 525F) and can be reliably aged ASY/ATY but these patterns, if present, may be rare and/or difficult to detect in this species.**

Sex—♀=♂ by plumage aspect. Bilateral BPs (Fig. 20**B**, p. 31) developed by both sexes but distended cloaca (Fig. 21, p. 32) indicates ASY ♀ in May-Jul. Measurements generally unhelpful for sexing (Table 69, p. 774) but shape and size of bill and rictal processes can be used for reliable sexing of some SYs and most ASYs in Mar-Aug (or until bill plates have been shed). No reliable means known to sex Juv-HYs or AHYs in Sep-Mar.

AHY ♀ (Apr-Aug): Bill depth at distal end of nares < 9.0 (SY) or < 10.5 (ASY), culmen only slightly decurved, and rictal process absent in SY or reduced in ASY (Fig. 551**B** & **E**). **Note: Many SYs and some (10-20%) ASYs exhibit intermediate bill characters and cannot be reliably sexed; ASYs may include older ♀♀ or non-breeding ♂♂, the latter of which can exhibit smaller rictal processes and duller bill coloration. Combine with ageing criteria for accurate sexing.**

AHY ♂ (Mar-Aug): Bill depth at distal end of nares > 9.9 (SY) or > 11.0 (ASY), culmen strongly decurved, and rictal process reduced in SY or enlarged in ASY) (Fig. 551**C**, **F**). **Note: See AHY ♀.**

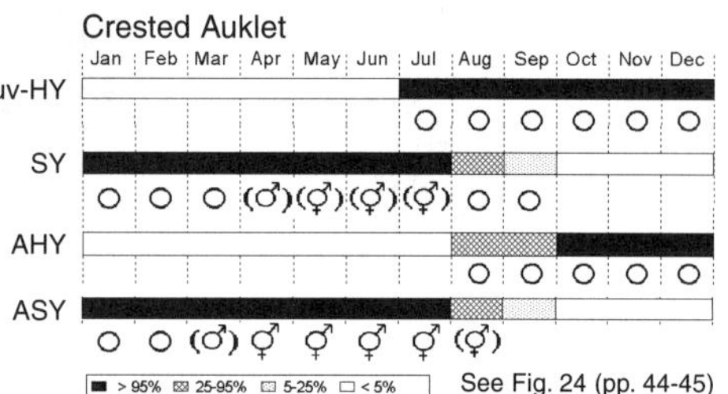

Hybrids reported—None.

References—Ainley et al. (1994), Bédard & Sealy (1984), Bent (1919a), Cramp & Simmons (1985), Dement'ev & Gladkov (1951a), Jones (1993b, 1993c), Jones et al. (2000), Kozlova (1957), Pyle (unpublished ms.), Ridgway (1919), Sealey (2006), Stejneger (1885), Stresemann & Stresemann (1966).

RHINOCEROS AUKLET

Cerorhinca monocerata

RHAU
Species # 0150
Band size: 5-6

Species—From other auklets and alcids by medium-large size (Table 70, p. 783); bill moderately stout, with sheath at base of upper mandible developing keratinous horn during Feb-Aug in ASYs (Figs. 552-553), dusky brownish (Juv) to brownish yellow or orangish (AHYs); tail with 16-18 rects; upperparts and upperwing uniformly dusky brown, with white postocular and malar plumes in AHYs (Fig. 552); underparts brownish with whitish undertail covs; underwing covs dusky brown; iris brown (Juv) to yellowish in AHY (Fig. 552); legs and feet dull yellowish with dusky webs between toes. Juv from Juv Tufted Puffin by shorter average wing length and shorter tail (Table 70); bill base to gonys < gonys to tip and postocular area without pale swath (Fig. 552**A**); underparts whitish or lightly mottled dusky; undertail covs whitish.

Geographic variation—Monotypic.

Molt—SAS (CAS?). PF limited-partial (Nov-Mar in HY/SYs), PA1 absent(?), PB2 complete (Jun-Sep in SYs), DPB complete (Aug-Jan in ASY/ATYs), DPA absent-limited? (Feb-Apr in ASYs). The single inserted first-cycle molt appears to be homologous with a PF rather than a PA1 (Fig. 10**C**, p. 14), although a few head, breast, and/or flank feathers may be replaced twice, indicating the presence of both molts (and CAS; Fig. 10**F**); study needed. The PB1 (prejuvenile molt) completes at the natal site. Subsequent molting occurs at sea, away from breeding grounds. The PF includes some to most upperpart feathers (some to most juv rump feathers usually retained) and no to a few breast and flank feathers; rudimentary ornamental filoplumes develop in some SYs in Jan-Mar (*cf.* Fig. 552**B**). During DPBs, pp, p covs, and ss are replaced synchronously in Jun-Aug (SYs) or Aug-Oct (ASYs), followed by the body feathers. The ornamental head plumes appear to be replaced once per year, in Oct-Nov during the PB2 and in Nov-Jan at the end of the DPB. In ASYs, bill horn and small oval appendage at base of lower mandible (Figs. 552**F** & 553, p. 782) are molted in Jul-Sep. The DPA appears to include a few feathers of the flanks and breast only (perhaps to increase floatation); more study needed. Many SYs over-summer on non-breeding grounds and these may exhibit reduced PA1s and advanced PB2s (see p. 18).

Age—Juv (B1; Jun-Mar) has pp fresh and pointed (Fig. 526**A**, p. 748) and bill small and dusky brownish, postocular and malar plumes absent, and iris brown (Fig. 552**A**); Juv ♀=♂. In addition to the following, confirmed breeding individuals can reliably be aged ATY.

Juv-HY/SY (1st cycle, Juv/B1-F1; Oct-Sep): Bill shallow, dusky brownish to yellowish, without distinct horn, and postocular and malar plumes absent in Oct-Jan, sometimes present but rudimentary in Jan-Jul (Fig. 552**A**-**B**); bill width at gape (Fig. 524, p. 746) ~11.0-14.0 mm; pp, ss, and wing covs uniformly juvenal, contrasting with fresher scapulars and humerals (Fig. 525**A**, p. 747), the outer pp and p covs relatively narrow, pointed, brownish, and worn (Fig. 526**A**-**B**, p. 748), outer rects narrow, brownish, and relatively worn (Fig. 527**A**, p. 748); rump and/or uppertail covs usually mixed with dusky formative and brown juv feathers in Dec-Sep (*cf.* Fig. 313**A**, p. 418); iris brownish yellow (Fig. 552**A**-**B**).

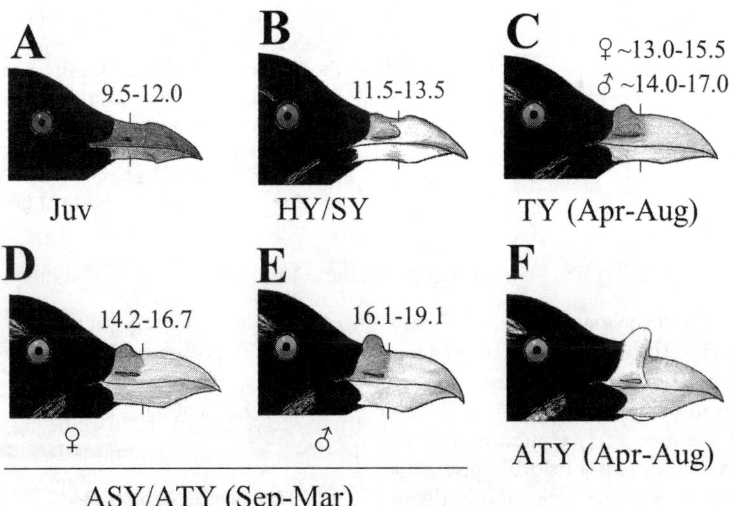

FIGURE 552. Head plumage aspect, eye color, bill characteristics by age and sex in Rhinoceros Auklet. Measure indicates bill depth at distal end of nares (Fig. 8**C**, p. 10); note that some values (e.g., for TY, **C**) are approximate and need to be tested in the field. The post-ocular plumes appear to be replaced just once per year during the PF and DPB, with slow over-winter development, such that plumes are absent in Sep-Oct and gradually become full by Mar-Apr. Iris and bill color varies from dull brownish yellow in Juvs (**A**) to dull yellowish in AHYs (**B**-**F**). Bill plates are not shed (thus bill depth values are reliable for sexing year-round) but the keratinous horn and small oval appendage at base of bill are molted in Aug-Sep and re-develop in Mar-May. See Figure 553 (p. 782) for horn height at maximum development by sex. Juvs (**A**) can be distinguished from Juv Tufted Puffin (Fig. 556, p. 788) by having the distance from bill base to gonydeal angle longer than gonydeal angle to tip.

SY/TY (2nd cycle, B2-A2; Oct-Sep): Bill moderately shallow, yellowish, and with no or small horn in Feb-Aug, and postocular plumes moderately well developed by season (Fig. 552**C**); bill width at gape (Fig. 524) ~13.0-16.0 mm; pp, ss, and wing covs basic, uniform in color and wear with back (Fig. 525**D**), the outer pp and p covs relatively broad, blunt, blackish, and fresh (Fig. 526**C**-**D**); outer rects broad, blackish, and relatively fresh (Fig. 527**B**); rump and uppertail covs uniformly dusky (*cf.* Fig. 313**B**); iris yellowish tinged brown (Fig. 552**C**). **Note: Some intermediates with ASY/ATY occur that are best aged AHY/ASY.**

ASY/ATY (Def. cycle, DB-DA; Oct-Sep): Bill deep, orangish to yellowish, and with substantial horn in Feb-Aug, and postocular and malar plumes full and elongated by season (Fig. 552**D**-**F**); bill width at gape (Fig. 524) ~15.0-18.5 mm; pp, ss, rects, and rump as in SY/TY (flight-feathers may average fresher due to later replacement); iris yellowish with little brown tinge (Fig. 552**D**-**F**). **Note: See SY/TY.**

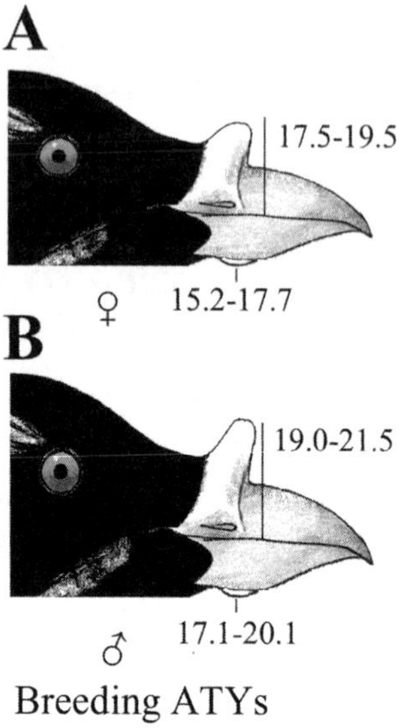

Sex—♀=♂ by plumage aspect. Bilateral BPs (Fig. 20**B**, p. 31) developed by both sexes but distended cloaca (Fig. 21, p. 32) indicates ATY ♀ in Apr-Jul. Measurements generally unhelpful for sexing (Table 70), although bill depth can be used to sex many ASY/ATYs, especially mated pairs. Some TY ♂♂ may also be sexed (Fig. 552**C**, p. 781) but distinguishing these from ATY ♀♀ would be difficult.

A

17.5-19.5

♀ 15.2-17.7

B

19.0-21.5

♂ 17.1-20.1

Breeding ATYs

FIGURE 553. Bill shape and maximum development of keratinous horn in breeding ATY Rhinoceros Auklets by sex. Measures indicate vertical height of horn from cutting edge of upper mandible and bill depth at distal end of nares (Fig. 8**C**, p. 10), the latter similar to depth in Sep-Mar (Fig. 552**D**-**E**), except for the addition of about 1 mm for the oval appendage at the base of the bill, shed in Aug-Sep and redeveloped in Mar-May. Horns should be fully developed by egg-laying and bill depth thus may be most useful for sexing mated pairs. Beware ♂♂ with developing horns in Feb-Apr or May (depending on latitute of breeding).

ASY/ATY ♀: Bill shallower (Figs. 552**D** & 553**A**); horn reduced in May-Jul (Fig. 553**A**). **Note: ASY/ATYs with bill depth of 16.0-16.5 and maximum horn height from cutting edge of upper mandible 19.0-19.5 cannot be reliably sexed but probably represent older ♀♀ or younger ♂♂; compare with eye color. Also, bill (without oval appendage; *cf.* Fig. 553) may average slightly deeper in both sexes in Feb-Aug than in Sep-Jan due to addition of keratinous layer to the upper mandible; more study needed.**

ASY/ATY ♂: Bill deeper (Figs. 552**E**, 553**B**); horn extensive in Apr-Jul (Fig. 553**B**). **Note: See ASY/ATY ♀.**

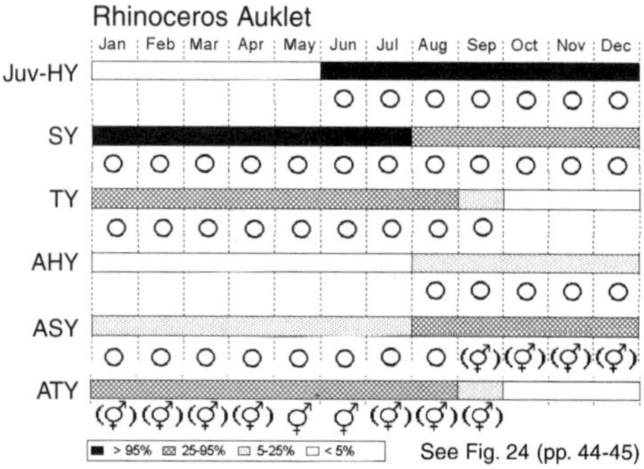

Rhinoceros Auklet

Jan Feb Mar Apr May Jun Jul Aug Sep Oct Nov Dec

Juv-HY

SY

TY

AHY

ASY

ATY

■ > 95% ▨ 25-95% □ 5-25% □ < 5%

See Fig. 24 (pp. 44-45)

Hybrids reported—None.

References—Ainley et al. (1994), Bent (1919a), Dement'ev & Gladkov (1951a), Gaston & Dechesne (1996), Kozlova (1957), Pyle (unpublished ms.), Ridgway (1919).

TABLE 70. Measurements (mm) of Rhinoceros Auklets and North American puffins for identification and sexing. See pp. 4-11 for methods of measurement. Species summaries are in **bold**. Values were derived from 95% confidence intervals as based approximately on the indicated sample sizes (see pp. 4-5). Thus, midpoints of ranges approximate means, and S.D. is approximated by 25% of the range.

Taxon/Sex	*n*	wing chord[1]	tail length	culmen from cere[2]	tarsus
Rhinoceros Auklet		**168-191**	**49-61**	**30.4-37.1**	**26-32**
♀	100	168-186	49-59	30.4-35.6	26-31
♂	100	173-191	51-61	31.8-37.1	27-32
Atlantic Puffin[3]		**155-172**	**43-54**	**43.4-54.9**	**24-30**
♀	100	155-170	43-54	43.4-53.1	24-29
♂	100	156-172	43-53	45.2-54.9	25-30
Horned Puffin		**167-194**	**58-69**	**41.7-55.4**	**25-31**
♀	100	167-190	58-68	41.7-52.9	25-30
♂	100	170-194	59-69	44.1-55.4	26-31
Tufted Puffin		**180-214**	**57-69**	**53.8-64.4**	**27-36**
♀	100	180-211	57-68	53.8-62.2	27-34
♂	100	186-214	58-69	55.7-64.4	28-36

[1] Note that, in most alcids, wing chord of HY/SYs average 10-20% less than that of AHY/ASYs.

[2] Culmen from cere based on ATYs in Apr-Aug with full bill shields; puffins in Sep-Mar, after bill plates are shed but before new ones develop, have shorter exposed culmens (by 10-20%). Also, see figures and text for bill depth values, which vary substantially by age and season.

[3] Measures from N.Am populations only; see **Geographic variation**.

ATLANTIC PUFFIN
Fratercula arctica

ATPU
Species # 0130

HORNED PUFFIN
Fratercula corniculata

HOPU
Species # 0140
Band size: 5

Species—From other alcids by medium-large to large size (Table 70); bill stout (Juv) to very stout and laterally compressed, dusky brownish (Juv), orangish (AHYs) or bright bluish, yellow, and red in alternate-aspect ASYs (Fig. 555, p. 785); upperparts and lower throat blackish, contrasting with grayish or white auriculars (Fig. 555); underparts white; underwing covs grayish (Atlantic Puffin) to dusky (Horned Puffin); legs and feet brownish (Juv) to bright orange (ASYs), the inner toe nail prostrate and angled inward (Fig. 554).

Atlantic Puffin from Horned Puffin by shorter wing and tail (Table 70); bill of ASYs shallower and more angular by age, sex, and season (Fig. 555, p. 785); chin, upper throat, and malar region in all age groups (including Juv) grayish to dusky, contrasting with blackish-brown lower throat band (Fig. 555; *vs* uniformly blackish in Horned Puffin); underwing covs grayish (*vs* duskier in Horned Puffin); bill of AHYs with bluish base. Juv Horned Puffin from Juv Tufted Puffin by shorter wing and tarsus (Table 70); underparts white, contrasting distinctly with blackish throat (see Howell & Pyle 2005).

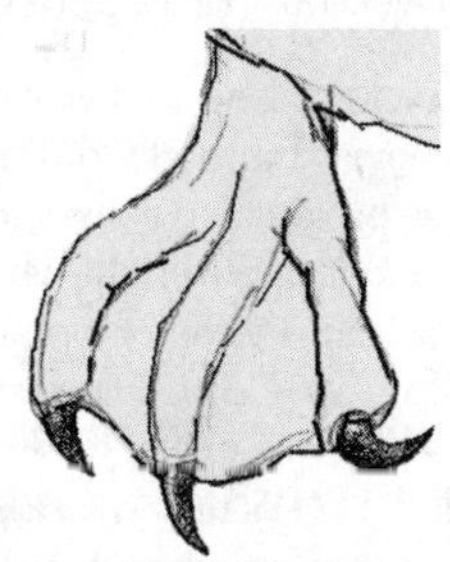

FIGURE 554. Unique, prostrate and inwardly pointing inner toenail of puffins, sometimes useful in identification of Juvs or scavenged carcasses.

Geographic variation—Horned Puffin monotypic, and Atlantic Puffin also considered monotypic following suggestions of Moen (1991); see also Baker (1993), Bédard (1985), Cramp & Simmons (1985), Dement'ev & Gladkov (1951a), Ridgway (1919), and Salomonsen (1944). Atlantic Puffins breeding in w.Europe ("*F.a. grabae*"; vagrant reported from Nfl) average smaller, and populations breeding in n.Greenland and Arctic Europe ("*naumanni*"; vagrant reported from NWT) average larger, but differences are moderately slight, geographically discordant, and broadly clinal.

Molt—SAS. PF absent, PA1 absent-limited? (Apr-Jun? in SYs), PB2 complete (May-Sep in SYs), DPA limited-partial? (Mar-May in AHY/ASYs), PB3 complete (Mar-Aug in non-breeding TYs), DPB complete (Jan-Apr & Aug-Dec in breeding ASYs). The single inserted first-cycle molt, if it occurs, appears to be homologous with a PA1 rather than a PF (Fig. 10**E**, p. 14). The PB1 (prejuvenile molt) completes at the natal site, and most to all subsequent molting occurs at sea, away from breeding grounds. The PA1 includes no to a few body feathers; study needed. During PBs, pp, ss, s covs, and rects are replaced nearly synchronously in May-Jul (SYs; variably to Oct) and Mar-Jun (TYs and possibly older non-breeding ATYs). In ATYs the DPB initiates with flight-feather molt in Jan-Apr, overlapping the DPA, followed by suspension for breeding, and completion with body-feather replacement in Aug-Dec (*cf.* **Molt** under Pacific Loon, p. 218, and Howell & Pyle 2005). Rarely, 1-5 pp (often among p1-p4 and p8-p10) and/or some s covs can be retained during DPBs. The DPAs include feathers of the head, back, and throat, at least, but may be more extensive; more study needed. Most to all SYs and many TYs over-summer on non-breeding grounds and these may exhibit reduced PA1-PA2s (see p. 18). Captive Atlantic Puffins have replaced wing feathers twice during a molt cycle (Swennen 1977) but this is undocumented in the wild (Harris & Yule 1977). Bill plates are molted in Aug-Oct (see Fig. 555).

Age—Juv (B1; Aug-Apr) has bill thin and dusky brownish (Fig. 555**A**), pp fresh and pointed (Fig. 526**A**, p. 748), lore and auricular washed blackish, and legs and feet brownish; Juv ♀ = ♂. See Camphuysen (2003) for information on bursal depth (Fig. 23, p. 34) in freshly dead Atlantic Puffins by age. In addition to the following, confirmed breeding individuals can reliably be aged A4Y (< 1% possibly being 4Ys and most being A5Ys).

Juv-HY/SY (1st cycle, Juv/B1-A1; Oct-Sep): Bill reduced in depth and with little to no grooves (Table 71, p. 786), dusky brownish to dull reddish or orangish, and with straight base proximal to gonydeal angle (Fig. 555**A-B**); bill width at gape (Fig. 524, p. 746) ~10.0-12.5 mm; lores and auricular region variably washed dusky (Fig. 555**A-B**); pp, ss, and wing covs uniformly juv (*cf.* Fig. 525**A**, p. 747), brownish, the outer pp and p covs relatively narrow, pointed, and moderately worn in Oct-Apr (Fig. 526**A-B**), being replaced in May-Aug, and relatively fresh in Aug-Sep; outer rects narrow, brownish, and relatively worn in Oct-Jul (Fig. 527**A**, p. 748); legs and feet dusky-yellow (Oct-Feb) to yellowish (Mar-Sep). **Note: See SY/TY.**

SY/TY (2nd cycle, B2-A2; Oct-Sep): Bill intermediate in depth by season and with an indistinct to distinct groove (Table 71), dull reddish and grayish or yellowish, and with straight or slightly curved base proximal to gonydeal angle (Fig. 555**C-D**); bill width at gape (Fig. 524) ~12.0-16.0 mm; lores moderately bright white in Mar-Aug (Fig. 555**C-D**); pp and ss uniformly basic (Fig. 525**D**), blackish, the outer pp and p covs relatively broad, truncate, and moderately worn in Oct-Apr (Fig. 526**C-D**), being replaced in Mar-Jun, and very fresh in Jul-Sep; outer rects broad, truncate, and relatively fresh (Fig. 527**B**); legs and feet yellowish. **Note: Some advanced SYs or retarded TY/4Ys may overlap SY/TYs in bill development, molt timing, and/or leg color; use caution and age-group codes S-TY or T-4Y (p. 41-42) for intermediates.**

ASY/ATY (Def. cycle, DB-DA; Oct-Sep): Bill full in depth by season and with 1-2 full grooves (Table 71), dull (Oct-Mar) to bright (Apr-Sep) reddish and grayish or yellowish, and with curved or angled base proximal to gonydeal angle (Fig. 555**E**-**F**); bill width at gape (Fig. 524) ~15.0-18.0 mm (Oct-Mar) or ~17.0-19.5 mm (Mar-Sep); lores and auricular region bright white in Mar-Aug; pp and ss as in SY/TY (Figs. 525**D** & 526**C**-**D**) but worn in Oct-Jan, being replaced in Feb-Apr, and relatively fresh in May-Sep; legs and feet yellow-orange (Oct-Jan) to bright orange (Feb-Sep). **Note: See SY/TY. Some TY/4Ys might be identifiable by slimmer bill depth and with 1.0-1.5 grooves (Table 71, *cf.* Fig. 555E-F) but study is needed.**

ATY/A4Y (Def. cycle, DB-DA; Oct-Sep): Like ASY/ATY but bill with 3 grooves (Fig. 555**G**-**H**). **Note: It is possible that individuals with three full bill grooves can be aged A4Y/A5Y but more study is needed.**

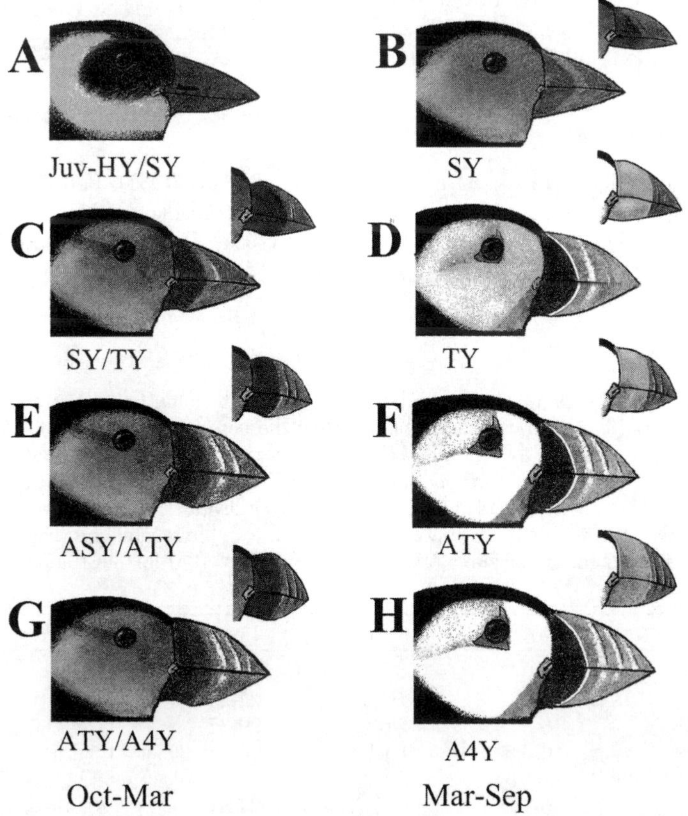

FIGURE 555. Head plumage aspect and bill characteristics by season and age in Atlantic and Horned (insets) puffins. Core bill size develops slowly through the first three cycles (**A**, **C**, **E**, and **G**) and is augmented each spring by ornamental plates (**D**, **F**, & **H**; possibly **B**), which develop in Feb-Apr and shed in Sep. See Table 71 (p. 786) for bill-depth values by species, age, and season. Note the number of grooves in the outer bill plates of both species: 0-0.5 grooves indicate HY/SYs (**A**-**B**), 0.5-1.5 grooves indicate SY/TY (**C**-**D**), 1.5-2.5 grooves indicate ASY/ATY (**E**-**F**), 3 grooves indicates ATY/A4Ys (**G**-**H**), and 4 grooves (not shown) indicates A4Y/A5Y (rare). See Harris (1981) for more information. Note tighter grooves on Horned than on Atlantic puffins. By ATY/A4Y, ♂♂ average slightly deeper bills than ♀♀, possibly represented by **G**-**H** *vs* **D**-**E**, respectively, but reliability and measures for sexing need to be determined. Some TY/4Ys (*cf.* **E**) with 1.0-2.0 grooves might be reliably aged (see also Table 71) but study is needed. Atlantic Puffin is distinguished from Horned Puffin by deeper bill base, more deeply curved upper mandible, and more compressed outer plate (becoming apparent by spring SYs; **B**), and pale throat contrasting with darker chest band (Horned Puffin has a uniformly dark throat).

A4Y/A5Y (Def. cycle, DB; Oct-Mar): Like ASY/ATY but bill with 4 grooves (*cf.* Fig. 555**G-H**). **Note: Individuals exhibiting four grooves are rare.**

Sex—♀=♂ by plumage aspect. Bilateral BPs (Fig. 20**B**, p. 31) developed by both sexes but distended cloaca (Fig. 21, p. 32) indicates A4Y ♀ in May-Jul. Measurements generally unhelpful for sexing (Table 70, p. 783); bill depth may be useful in separating small proportions of breeding A4Y or mated Atlantic Puffins (Fig. 555**F**), averaging 2-4 mm shallower in ♀♀ than in ♂♂, but this criterion unreliable due to individual, age-related, and geographic variation. Otherwise, no criteria known.

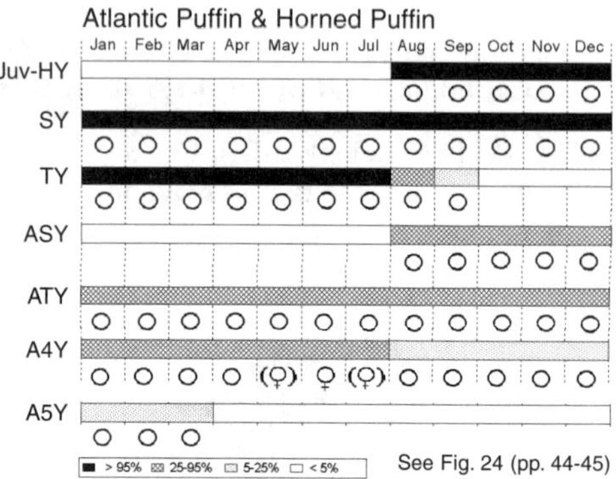

Hybrids reported—None.

References—Ainley et al. (1994), Barrett et al. (1985), Bédard (1985), Bent (1919a), Camphuysen (2003), Cramp & Simmons (1985), Dement'ev & Gladkov (1951a), Harris (1981), Harris & Yule (1977), Howell & Pyle (2005), Kozlova (1957), Lowther et al. (2002), Petersen (1976), Piatt & Kitasky (2002a), Pyle (unpublished ms.), Ridgway (1919), Salomonsen (1944), Stejneger (1885), Swennen (1977).

TABLE 71. Bill depth metrics (mm) and number of grooves on the outer bill plate by age and season in North American puffins. Metrics indicate bill depth at the base (tip of forehead feathers). Values represent 95% confidence intervals (see pp. 4-11); sample sizes were small for predefinitive groups and values may need revision following further study. Although TY/4Y is given below, this age-group may not be reliably identified (see ATY/A4Y); note also that rare individuals with 4 grooves can be aged A4Y/A5Ys. By ATY/A4Y, ♂♂ average slightly deeper bills than ♀♀, but reliability and measures for sexing need to be determined. See Figures 555 (p. 785) & 556 (p. 788) for illustrations representing age/season classes.

	HY/SY	SY/TY	TY/4Y[1]	ASY/ATY	ATY/A4Y[2]
Atlantic Puffin					
Oct-Mar	15-19	19-25	22-28	23-30	23-30
Mar-Sep	18-23	24-32	29-37	32-42	32-42
# Grooves	0.0-0.5	0.5-1.5	1.0-2.0	1.5-2.5	3.0-4.0
Horned Puffin					
Oct-Mar	16-20	21-27	24-31	26-33	26-33
Mar-Sep	19-23	26-34	34-43	37-46	37-46
# Grooves	0	0.5-1.0	1.0-2.0	1.5-2.5	3.0-4.0
Tufted Puffin					
Oct-Mar	16-19	21-28	26-30	26-33	26-33
Mar-Sep	18-23	25-33	33-41	36-44	36-44
# Grooves	0	0.5-1.0	1.0-1.5	1.5-2.5	3.0-4.0

[1] May not be reliably determined; see text.
[2] Individuals with 4 grooves can be aged A4Y/A5Y but these are rare.

TUFTED PUFFIN TUPU
Fratercula cirrhata Species # 0120
Band size: 6-5

Species—From other alcids by large size (Table 70, p. 783); bill proportionately stout (Juv) to very stout and laterally compressed, dusky brownish (Juv) to bright orange in AHYs (Fig. 556, p. 788); upperparts blackish brown; ASYs in Mar-Aug with white faces and yellow ornamental postocular plumes (Fig. 556); underparts whitish with grayer breast and throat (some Juvs) to uniformly blackish brown (ASYs); underwing covs blackish brown; legs and feet brownish (Juv) to bright orange (ASYs in Apr-Jul) with dusky toes in Sep-Feb, the inner toe nail prostrate and angled inward (Fig. 554, p. 783). Juv from Juv Rhinoceros Auklet by longer average wing length and longer tail (Table 70); distance of bill base to gonys > gonys to tip, and postocular area with pale swath (Fig. 556**A**); abdomen whitish to heavily mottled dusky; undertail covs blackish. Juv from Juv Horned Puffin by longer wing and tarsus; underparts variably washed grayish to whitish, not contrasting sharply with throat in color (*cf.* Howell & Pyle 2005).

Geographic variation—Monotypic.

Molt—SAS. PF absent, PA1 absent-limited (Mar?-May? in SYs), PB2 complete (Jun?-Sep? in SYs), DPA limited (Jan-Apr in AHY/ASYs), PB3 complete (Aug-Nov in non-breeding TYs), DPB complete (Aug-Jan in breeding ASY/ATYs). The single inserted first-cycle molt appears to be homologous with a PA1 rather than a PF (Fig. 10**E**, p. 14). The PB1 (prejuvenile molt) completes at the natal site, and most to all subsequent molting occurs at sea, away from breeding grounds. The PA1 includes a few head and other body feathers. During DPBs, pp, p covs, and ss are replaced nearly synchronously (either distally from p1 or distally and proximally from p5-p7 and distally from p1; Thompson & Kitasky 2004) in May-Sep (SYs), Aug-Nov (TYs and possibly non-beeding ATYs), or Nov-Jan (ATY/A4Ys). During DPBs, ornamental postocular plumes are usually the first feathers lost, in Aug-Sep. The DPA is restricted to feathers of the head. SYs and many TYs over-summer on non-breeding grounds and these may exhibit reduced PA1-PA2s and advanced PB2-PB3s (see p. 18). Bill plates are molted in Sep-Oct (see Fig. 556, p. 788).

Age—Juv (B1; Aug-Apr) has bill thin (Fig. 556**A**, p. 788) and dusky brownish, pp fresh and pointed (Fig. 526**A**, p. 748), underparts whitish to pale grayish (darker on breast), iris dark brown, and legs and feet brownish; Juv ♀ = ♂. In addition to the following, confirmed breeding individuals can probably be aged A4Y (see Atlantic Puffin).

Juv-HY/SY (1st cycle, Juv/B1-A1; Oct-Sep): Bill reduced in depth (Table 71), with straight base (out to gonydeal angle), without grooves to outer upper plate, and dusky or with dull orange outer portions (Fig. 556**A-B**); bill width at gape (Fig. 524, p. 746) ~14.0-17.5 mm; face and chin washed blackish, with little to no brownish postocular plumes in Apr-Sep (Fig. 556**A-B**); abdomen whitish or mottled dusky, contrasting with distinctly darker breast and upperparts; pp, ss, and wing covs uniformly juv (*cf.* Fig. 525**A**, p. 747), brownish, the outer pp and p covs relatively narrow, pointed, and moderately worn in Oct-Apr (Fig. 526**A-B**), or often being replaced in May-Sep; outer rects narrow, brownish, and relatively worn (Fig. 527**A**, p. 748); face and chin washed blackish, with little to no brownish postocular plumes in Apr-Aug (Fig. 556**B**); iris dark brown to yellowish brown (Fig. 556**A-B**); legs and feet dusky-yellow (Oct-Feb) to yellowish (Mar-Sep). **Note: See SY/TY.**

SY/TY (2nd cycle, B2-A2; Oct-Sep): Bill intermediate in depth by season (Table 71), with straight or slightly curved base (out to gonydeal angle), usually with one indistinct to distinct groove to upper outer plate, and with bright orange outer portions (Fig. 556**C**-**D**); bill width at gape (Fig. 524) ~17.0-21.5 mm; abdomen often heavily mottled dusky, contrasting slightly with darker breast and upperparts; pp, ss, and wing covs uniformly basic (Fig. 525**D**), blackish, the outer pp and p covs relatively broad and truncate (Fig. 526**C**-**D**), being replaced in Aug-Nov and relatively fresh in Dec-May; outer rects broad, truncate, and relatively fresh (Fig. 527**B**); face and chin variably white and dusky to whitish and with reduced dull yellowish postocular plumes in Apr-Aug (Fig. 556**D**); iris yellowish brown to dull yellow (Fig. 556**C**-**D**); legs and feet dull yellowish (Oct-Mar) to orange (Mar-Sep). **Note: Some advanced SYs or retarded TY/4Ys may overlap SY/TYs in bill development and/or leg or iris color; use caution and age-group codes S-TY or T-4Y (pp. 41-42) for intermediates.**

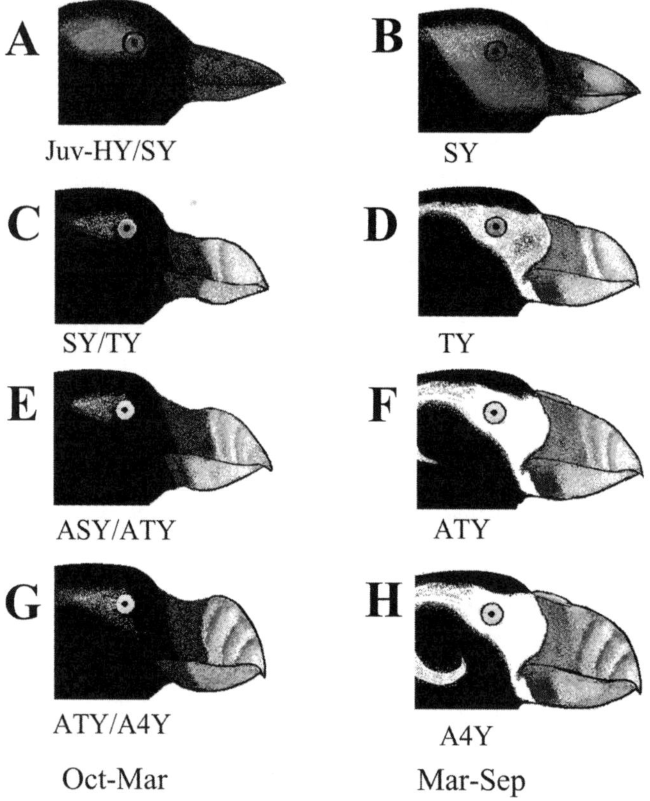

FIGURE 556. Head plumage aspect, bill characteristics, and iris color by age and season in Tufted Puffin. Core bill size develops slowly through the first three cycles (**A**, **C**, **E**, and **G**) and is augmented each spring by ornamental plates (**B**, **D**, **F**, and **H**), which develop in Feb-Apr and shed in Sep. See Table 71 (p. 786) for bill-depth values by age and season. Note the number of grooves in the outer bill plates: 0 grooves indicates HY/SYs (**A**-**B**), 0.5-1.0 groove indicates SY/TYs (**C**-**D**), 1.5-2.5 grooves indicates ASY/ATY (**E**-**F**), 3 full grooves indicates ATY/A4Ys (**G**-**H**), and 4 grooves (not shown) indicates A4Y/A5Y (rare). See Tanaka & Ogi (1986) for more information and note that grooves can be faint in ASYs during Oct-Mar. By ATY/A4Y ♂♂ average slightly deeper bills than ♀♀ but reliability and measures for sexing need to be determined. Some TY/4Ys (*cf.* **E**) with 1.0-1.5 grooves might be reliably aged (see also Table 71) but study is needed.

ASY/ATY (Def. cycle, DB-DA; Oct-Sep): Bill deep by season (Table 71), with 1.5-2.5 distinct grooves to upper outer plate (Fig. 556**E-F**); bill width at gape (Fig. 524) ~19.5-22.5 mm in Oct-Mar, to ~20.5-26.5 mm in Mar-Sep; abdomen brownish black, uniform with or slightly paler than breast and upperparts; pp, ss, wing covs and rects as in SY/TY (Figs. 226**C-D** & 227**B**) except pp and ss replaced in Oct-Jan and relatively fresh in Jan-Sep; face and chin bright white with full yellowish postocular plumes in Apr-Aug (Fig. 556**F**); iris yellowish (Fig. 556**E-F**); legs and feet dull (Oct-Jan) to bright (Feb-Sep) orange. **Note: See SY/TY. Some TY/4Ys might be identifiable by bill slimmer and with 1.0-1.5 grooves (Table 71, *cf.* Fig. 556E-F) but study is needed. See also ATY/A4Y.**

ATY/A4Y (Def. cycle, DB-DA; Oct-Sep): Like ASY/ATY but bill very deep (Table 71) and with 3 grooves to upper outer plate (Fig. 556**G-H**). **Note: The ornamental postocular plume may also average fuller than in TY/4Ys (*cf.* Fig. 356F, H) but study needed.**

A4Y/A5Y (Def. cycle, DB; Oct-Mar): Like ASY/ATY but bill with 4 grooves (*cf.* Fig. 556).

Sex—♀ = ♂ by plumage aspect. Bilateral BPs (Fig. 20**B**, p. 31) developed by both sexes but distended cloaca (Fig. 21, p. 32) indicates A4Y ♀ in May-Jul. Measurements generally unhelpful for sexing (Table 70, p. 783); bill depth may be useful in separating small proportions of breeding A4Ys or mated pairs, averaging 2-4 mm shallower in ♀♀ than in ♂♂ (*cf.* Table 71, p. 786, and Tanaka & Ogi 1986). See also Williams et al. (2007) for a DFA, using wg chord, exp culmen, and "straight tarsus" (Fig. 9**B**, p. 11), that separated 74% of sexes in live individuals from AK. Otherwise, no criteria known.

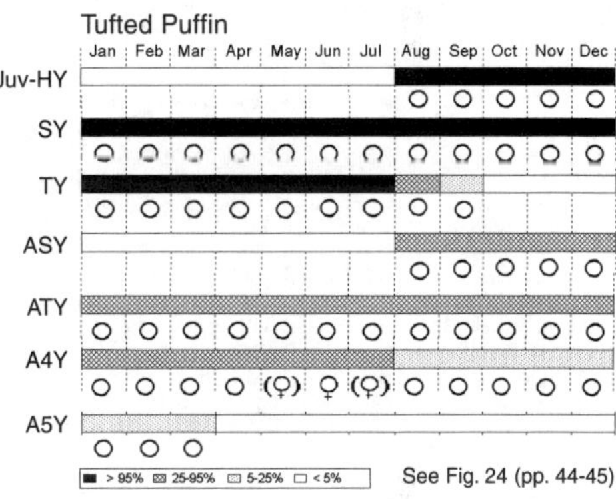

Hybrids reported—None.

References—Ainley et al. (1994), Bent (1919a), Bridge (2004), Dement'ev & Gladkov (1951a), Hamilton (1958), Howell & Pyle (2005), Kozlova (1957), Kuroda (1955), Piatt & Kitasky (2002b), Pyle (unpublished ms.), Ridgway (1919), Shiomi & Ogi (1991), Stejneger (1885), Stresemann & Stresemann (1966), Tanaka & Ogi (1986), Thompson & Kitasky (2004), Williams et al. (2007).

Literature Cited

Abbott, S., S.N.G. Howell, and P. Pyle. 2001. First North American record of Greater Sandplover. N. Am. Birds 55:252-257.

Abraham, K.F. 1980. Moult migration of Lesser Snow Geese. Wildfowl 31:89-93.

____. 2005. Cackling Goose, not new to Ontario. Ontario Field Ornith. News 23:2-6.

____, C.D. Ankney, and H. Boyd. 1983. Assortative mating by Brant. Auk 100:201-203.

____, J.O. Leafloor, and D.H. Rusch. 1999. Molt migrant Canada Geese in northern Ontario and western James Bay. J. Wildl. Manage. 63:649-655.

Acosta Cruz, M., L. Mugica Valdez, and O. Torres Fundora. 1989. Ecomorphology of Dendrocygna bicolor (Viellot; Aves: Anatidae)in Cuba. Biol. Acad. Cienc. Cuba 22:70-78.

Adams, C.T. 1955. Comparative osteology of the night herons. Condor 57:55-60.

Adams, D.A., and T.L. Quay. 1958. Ecology of the Clapper Rail in southeastern North Carolina. J. Wildl. Manage. 22:149-156.

Adams, J., and E.R. Slavid. 1984. Cheek plumage pattern in Columbian Ruddy Duck Oxyura jamaicensis. Ibis 126:405-407.

Adriaens, P. 1999. The American Black Tern in Co. Dublin. Birding World 12:378-379.

____ and B. Mactavish. 2004. Identification of adult American Herring Gull. Dutch Birding 26:151-179.

Aiken, C.E.H. 1930. A Bobwhite X California Quail hybrid. Auk 47:80-81.

Ainley, D.G. 1980. Geographic variation in Leach's Storm-Petrel. Auk 97:837-853.

____. 1983. Further notes on variation in Leach's Storm-Petrel. Auk 100:230-233.

____. 1995. Ashy Storm-Petrel. Birds N. Am. 185:1-12.

____. 2005. The dark storm-petrels of the eastern North Pacific: Speciation, current status, and future prospects. Birding 37:58-65.

____ and W.T. Everett. 2001. Black Storm-Petrel. Birds N. Am. 577:1-16.

____ and B. Manolis. 1979. Occurrence and distribution of the Mottled Petrel. W. Birds 10:113-123.

____, S. Morrell, and T.J. Lewis. 1974. Patterns in the life-histories of storm petrels on the Farallon Islands. Living Bird 13:295-312.

____, T.J. Lewis, and S. Morrell. 1976. Molt in Leach's and Ashy storm-petrels. Wilson Bull. 88:76-95.

____, L.B. Spear, and R.C. Wood. 1985. Sexual color and size variation in the South Polar Skua. Condor 87:427-428.

____, R.E. Jones, R. Stallcup, D.J. Long, G.W. Page, L.T. Jones, L.E. Stenzel, R.E. LeValley, and L. B. Spear. 1994. Beached marine birds and mammals of the North American west coast. Gulf of the Farallones National Marine Sanctuary, San Francisco, CA.

____, T.C. Telfer, and M.H. Reynolds. 1997. Townsend's Shearwater and Newell's Shearwater. Birds N. Am. 297:1-20.

____, D.N. Nettleship, H.R. Carter, and A.E. Storey. 2002. Common Murre. Birds N. Am. 666:1-44.

Alderfer, J. 1992. Immature Black Scoters. Birding World 5:193-194.

____. 1995. The "mystery sandpiper". Birding 27:306-309.

Aldrich, J.W. 1942. New Bobwhite from northeastern Mexico. Proc. Biol. Soc. Washington 55:67-70.

____. 1946a. Speciation in the white-cheeked geese. Wilson Bull. 58:94-103.

____. 1946b. New subspecies of birds from western North America. Proc. Biol Soc. Washington

____. 1946c. The United States races of the Bob-white. Auk 63:493-508.

____. 1948. Additional light on the races of the Dowitcher. Auk 65:285-286.

____. 1963. Geographic orientation of American Tetraonidae. J. Wildl. Manage. 27:528-545.

____. 1967. Taxonomy, distribution, and present status. Pp. 17-44 in O.H. Hewitt, ed., The Wild Turkey and its management. The Wildlife Society, Washington, D.C.

____. 1972. A new subspecies of Sandhill Crane from Mississippi. Proc. Biol Soc. Washington 85:63-70.

____. 1979. Status of the Canadian Sandhill Crane. Proc. N. Am. Crane Workshop 2:139-148.

____ and K.P. Baer. 1970. Status and speciation in the Mexican Duck (Anas diazi). Wilson Bull. 82:63-73.

____ and H. Friedmann. 1943. A revision of the Ruffed Grouse. Condor 45:85-103.

Aldridge, C.L., S.J. Oyler-McCance, and R.M. Brigham. 2001. Occurrence of Greater Sage-Grouse X Sharp-tailed Grouse hybrids in Alberta. Condor 103:657-660.

Alexander, S.A., and C.L. Gratto-Trevor. 1997. Shorebird migration and staging at a large prairie lake and wetland complex: The Quill Lakes, Saskatchewan. Can. Wildl. Serv. Occ. Papers 97:1-45.

Alisauskas, R.T. 1987. Morphometric correlates of age and breeding status in American Coots. Auk 104:640-646.

Alison, R.M. 1975. Breeding biology and behavior of the Oldsquaw (Clangula hyemalis L.). Ornith. Monogr. 18:1-52.

____ and J.P. Prevett. 1976. Occurrences of duck hybrids at James Bay. Auk 93:643-644.

Alkon, P.U. 1982. Estimating the age of juvenile Chukars. J. Wildl. Manage. 46:777-781.

Allaine, D., and J.-D.Lebreton. 1990. The influence of age and sex on wing-tip pattern in adult Black-headed Gulls. Ibis 132:560-567.

Allan, R.G. 1962. The Madeiran Storm-Petrel Oceanodroma castro. Ibis 103b:274-295.

Allen, J.N. 1980. The ecology and behavior of the Long-billed Curlew in southeastern Washington. Wildl. Monographs 73:1-67.

Allen, R.P. 1942. The Roseate Spoonbill. Nat. Audubon Soc. Res. Rep. 2:1-142.

____. 1952. The Whooping Crane. Nat. Audubon Soc. Res. Rep. 3:1-246.

____. 1956. The flamingos: Their life history and survival. Nat. Audubon Soc. Res. Rep. 5:1-285.

Alstrom, P. 1985a. Tertial patterns of Wigeon and American Wigeon. Brit. Birds. 78:397-398.

____. 1985b. Artbestamming av storskav Phalacrocorax carbo och toppskarv Ph. aristotelis. Vår Fågelväld 44:325-350.

____. 1987. The identification of Baird's and White-rumped sandpipers in juvenile plumage. Birding 19(2):10-13.

____. 1989. Identification of marsh terns in juvenile and winter plumage. Brit. Birds. 82:296-319.

____. 1991. Identification of the Double-crested Cormorant. Birding World 4:9-16.

____ and U. Olsson. 1989. The identification of juvenile Red-necked and Long-toed stints. Brit. Birds. 82:360-372.

Amadon, D. 1949. The seventy-five per cent rule for subspecies. Condor 51:250-258.

____. 1960. Notes on the genus Chondrohierax. Noved. Columbianas 1:237-238.

____. 1961. Relationships of the Cinereous Harrier. Auk 78:256-257.

____. 1964. Taxonomic notes on birds of prey. Am. Mus. Novit. 2166:1-24.

____. 1975. Variation in the Everglade Kite. Auk 92:380-382.

____. 1977. Notes on the taxonomy of vultures. Condor 79:413-416.

____. 1982. A review of sub-buteonine hawks (Accipitridae, Aves). Am. Mus. Novit. 2741:1-20.

____. 1983. The Bald Eagle and its relatives. Pp. 1-4 in D.M. Bird, ed., Biology and management of Bald Eagles and Ospreys. Harpell Press, Ste. Anne de Bellevue, QUE.

____ and L.L. Short. 1992. Taxonomy of lower categories - suggested guidelines. Bull. Brit. Ornith. Club Century Suppl. 112A:11-38.

____ and G. Woolfenden. 1952. Notes on the Mathews' collection of Australian birds. The order Ciconiiformes. Am. Mus. Novit. 1564:1-16.

American Ornithologists' Union. 1957. Check-list of North American birds. Fifth edition. Am. Ornith. Union, Baltimore. 691 pp.

____. 1998. Check-list of North American birds. Seventh edition. Am. Ornith. Union, Washington, D.C. 829 pp.

Ammann, G.A. 1944. Determining the age of Pinnated and Sharp-tailed grouses. J. Wild. Manage. 8:170-171.

Anderson, A. 1975. A method of sexing Moorhens. Wildfowl 26:77-82.

Anderson, B.W., and R.L. Timken. 1969. A hybrid Lesser Scaup X Ring-necked Duck. Auk 86:556-557.

____ and ____. 1971. Age and sex characteristics of Common Mergansers. J. Wildl. Manage. 35:388-393.

____ and D.W. Warner. 1969. A morphological analysis of a large sample of Lesser Scaup and Ring-necked Ducks. Bird-Banding 40:85-100.

____, T.E. Ketola, and D.W. Warner. 1969. Spring sex and age ratios of Lesser Scaup and Ring-necked Ducks in Minnesota. J. Wildl. Manage. 33:209-212.

Anderson, D.J. 1993. Masked Booby. Birds N. Am. 73:1-16.

Anderson, J.T., L.M. Smith, and D.A. Haukos. 2000. Food selection and feather molt by non-breeding American Green-winged Teal in Texas playas. J. Wildl. Manage. 64:222-230.

Anderson, S.H., and J.R. Squires. 1997. The Prairie Falcon. University of Texas Press, Austin, TX. 162 pp.

Anderson, W., and A.W. Miller. 1953. Hybridization of Cinnamon and Blue-winged teal in northeastern California. Condor 55:152-153.

Andersson, M. 1999. Hybridization and skua phylogeny. Proc. Royal Soc. London B 266:1579-1585.

Andres, B.A., and G.A. Falxa. 1995. Black Oystercatcher. Birds N. Am. 155:1-20.

Andresen, K., and L. Thomas. 1986. The moult of Glaucous Gull Larus hyperboreus and Iceland Gull Larus glaucoides in Disko, Greenland. Bird Study 33:49-50.

Andrews, R.M., R.J. Higgins, and J.P. Martin. 2006. American Black Tern at Western-soper-Mare: New to Britain. Brit. Birds 99:450-459.

Andrle, R.F. 1972. Another probable hybrid of Larus marinus and L. argentatus. Auk 89:669-671.

Anker-Nilssen, T., P.H. Jones, and O.W. Røstad. 1988. Age, sex and origins of auks (Alcidae) killed in the Skagerrak oiling incident of January 1981. Seabird 11:28-46.

Ankney, C.D. 1984. Nutrient reserve dynamics of breeding and molting Brant. Auk 101:361-370.

____, D.G. Dennis, L.N. Wishand, and J.E. Seeb. 1986. Low genic variation between Black Ducks and Mallards. Auk 103:701-709.

Anthony, A.W. 1898. Two new birds from the Pacific coast of Lower California. Auk 15:36-38.

____. 1899. Hybrid grouse. Auk 16:180-181.

Appleby, R.H., S.C. Madge, and K. Mullarney. 1986. Identification of divers in immature and winter plumages. Brit. Birds. 79:365-391.

Arnold, K.A. 1972a. Banding worksheet for Western Birds. Mountain Quail. Supplement to W. Bird Bander 47(2).

____. 1972b. Recaptures and recoveries of Common Snipe wintering in Texas. W. Bird Bander 47:17-19.

Arroyo, B.E., and J.R. King. 1996. Age and sex differences in molt of the Montagu's Harrier. J. Raptor Res. 30:224-233.

Arterburn, J.W., and J.A. Grzybowski. 2003. Hybridization between Glossy and White-faced ibises. N. Am. Birds 57:136-139.

Arthur, S.C. 1920. A note on the "Southern Teal". Auk 37:126-127.

Artmann, J.W., and L.D. Schroeder. 1976. A technique for sexing woodcock by wing measurement. J. Wildl. Manage. 40:572-574.

Ashley, P., N.A. North, S.A. Petrie, and R.C. Bailey. 2006. Age determination of American Black Ducks in winter and spring. Wildl. Soc. Bull. 34:1401-1410.

____, S.A. Petrie, N.A. North, and R.C. Bailey. 2007. Tertial and upper wing covert molt in young American Black Ducks. Waterbirds 30:433-440.

Ashmole, N.P. 1963a. The biology of the Wideawake or Sooty Tern Sterna fuscata on Ascension Island. Ibis 103b:297-364.

____. 1963b. Molt and breeding in populations of the Sooty Tern Sterna fuscata. Postilla 76:1-18.

____. 1965. Adaptive variation in the breeding regime of a tropical sea bird. Proc. Nat. Acad. Sci. 53:311-318.

____. 1968. Breeding and molt in the White Tern (Gygis alba) on Christmas Island, South Pacific Ocean. Condor 70:35-55.

Astins, D. 1992. Identification of Black Scoter. Birding World 5:58-59.

Atwood, J.L., and B.W. Massey. 1982. The pikei plumage of the Least Tern. J. Field Ornith. 53:47.

Aubry, Y., M. Gosselin, and R. Yank. 1987. Quebec region. Am. Birds 41:404-406.

Austin, J.E. 1987. Activities of postbreeding Lesser Scaup in southwestern Manitoba. Wilson Bull. 99:448-456.

____ and L.H. Fredrickson. 1986. Molt of female Lesser Scaup immediately following breeding. Auk 103:293-298.

____ and M.R. Miller. 1995. Northern Pintail. Birds N. Am. 163:1-32.

____, C.M. Custer, and A.D. Afton. 1998. Greater Scaup. Birds N. Am. 338:1-32.

Austin, J.J., V. Bretagnolle, and E. Pasquet. 2004. A global molecular phylogeny of the small Puffinus shearwaters and implications for systematics of the Little-Audubon's shearwater complex. Auk 121:847-864.

Austin, O.L. Jr. 1929. The races of Cepphus grylle (Linn.). Bull. New England Bird-banding Assoc. 5:1-6.

____. 1952. Notes on some petrels of the North Pacific. Bull. Mus. Comp. Zool. 107:391-407.

Aversa, T. 2001. Nominate Rock Sandpiper at Ocean Shores, Washington. N. Am. Birds 55:242-244.

Azure, D.A., D.E. Naugle, J.E. Toepfer, G. Huschle, and R.D. Crawford. 2000. Sexing American Bitterns, Botaurus lentiginosus, using morphometric characteristics. Can. Field-Nat. 114:307-310.

Bährmann, U. 1974. Der sexualdimorphismus beim Kabicht (Accipiter gentilis). Zool. Abhandlungen Mus. Tierk 33:1-7.

Bailey, A.M. 1928a. Notes on variation in the White-fronted Goose. Condor 30:164-165.

____. 1928b. A study of the Snowy Herons of the United States. Auk 45:430-440.

____. 1942. Siberian Rough-legged Hawk in northwestern Alaska. Auk 59:305.

____. 1943. Birds of Cape Prince of Wales, Alaska. Proc. Colorado Mus. Nat. Hist. 18:1-113.

____. 1949. Hybrid of Snow and Canada goose. Auk 66:197.

Bailey, B.H. 1917. Description of a new subspecies of the Broad-winged Hawk. Auk 34:73-75.

Bailey, E.P., and J.L. Trapp. 1984. A second wild breeding population of the Aleutian Canada Goose. Am. Birds 38:284-286.

Bailey, H.H. 1919. An interesting hybrid of Mareca penelope (Widgeon) and Mareca americana (Balpate). Wilson Bull. 31:25.

____. 1941. An undescribed race of eastern Ruffed Grouse. Bull. Bailey Mus. Library Nat. Hist. 14:1.

Bailey, R.E. 1952. The incubation patch of passerine birds. Condor 54:121-136.

____. 1953. Surgery for sexing and observing gonad condition in birds. Auk 70:497-499.

Bailey, R.W. 1956. Sex determination of adult Wild Turkeys by means of dropping configuration. J. Wildl. Manage. 20:220.

____ and K.T. Rinell. 1967. Events in the Turkey year. Pp. 73-91 in O.H. Hewitt, ed., The Wild Turkey and its management. The Wildlife Society, Washington, D.C.

Bailey, S.F. 1988. Bill characters separating Trumpeter and Tundra swans: A cautionary note. Birding 23:89-91.

____, P. Pyle, and L.B. Spear. 1989a. Dark Pterodroma petrels in the North Pacific: Identification, status, and North American occurrence. Am. Birds 43:400-415.

____, R.A. Erickson, and D.G. Yee. 1989b. Middle Pacific coast region. Am. Birds 43:1362-1366.

Bailey, V. 1928. A hybrid Scaled X Gambel's quail from New Mexico. Auk 45:210.

Bain, M.J. 2006. Ontario. N. Am. Birds 60:61-65.

Bain, M.R., and G.H. Farley. 2002. Display by apparent hybrid prairie-chickens in a zone of geographic overlap. Condor 104:683-687.

Baird, P.H. 1994. Black-legged Kittiwake. Birds N. Am. 92:1-28.

Baker, A.J., et. al. 1996. Red Knots Calidris canutus rufa at their farthest south: An international expedition to Tierra del Fuego, Argentina, in February 1995. Wader Study Group Bull. 79:103-108.

____, T. Piersma, and A.D. Greenslade. 1999. Molecular vs. phenotypic sexing in Red Knots. Condor 101:887-893.

Baker, K. 1993. Identification guide to European non-passerines. BTO Guide 24. British Trust for Ornithology, Thetford, UK. 332 pp.

Baker, M.F. 1953. The prairie chickens of Kansas. Kansas Mus. Nat. Hist. Misc. Publ. 5:1-66.

Balachandran, S., and S.A. Hussain. 1998. Moult, age structure, biometrics and subspecies of Lesser Sand Plover Charadrius mongolus wintering along the south-east coast of India. Stilt 33:3-9.

____, S.A. Hussain, and L.G. Underhill. 2000. Primary moult, biometrics, mass and age composition of Grey Plovers Pluvialis squatarola in southeastern India. Bird Study 47:82-90.

Baldwin, D.H. 1965. Ageing and sexing the Wood Duck. Ontario Bird Banding 1:17-18.

Baldwin, W.P. 1947. Trapping Wild Turkeys in South Carolina. J. Wildl. Manage. 11:24-36.

Balgooyen, T.G. 1976. Behavior and ecology of the American Kestrel (Falco sparverius L.) in the Sierra Nevada of California. Univ. California Pubs. Zool. 103:1-83.

Balkiz, Ö., S. Dano, C. Barbraud, S. Tekin, U. Özesmi, M. Dündar, and A. Béchet. 2007. Sexing Greater Flamingo chicks from feather bulb DNA. Waterbirds 30:450-453.

Ball, S.C. 1934. Hybrid ducks including descriptions of two crosses of Bucephala and Lophodytes. Bull. Peabody Mus. Nat. Hist. 3:1-26.

Balten, B., E.B. Ebels, and W. Hoogendoorn. 1993. Mystery photographs. Dutch Birding 15:267.

Bancroft, C. 1927. Breeding birds of Scammon's Lagoon, Lower California. Condor 29:29-57.

____. 1929. A new Pacific race of Gull-billed Tern. Trans. San Diego Soc. Nat. Hist. 19:283-286.

Bangs, O. 1901. On an apparently unnamed race of Buteo borealis. Proc. New England Zool. Club 2:67-69.

____. 1912. A new subspecies of Ruffed Grouse. Auk 29:378-379.

____. 1913. New birds from Cuba and the Isle of Pines. Proc. New England Zool. Club 4:89-92.

____. 1914. The geographic races of the Scaled Quail. Proc. New England Zool. Club 4:99-100.

____. 1915a. Notes on dichromatic herons and hawks. Auk 32:481-484.

____. 1915b. The American forms of Gallinula chloropus (LINN). Proc. New England Zool. Club 5:93-99.

Bangs, O. 1920. A new Red-shouldered Hawk from the Florida keyes. Proc. New England Zool. Club 7:35.

____ and T.E. Penard. 1918. Notes on a collection of Surinam birds. Bull. Mus. Comp. Zool. 62:25-93.

____ and ____. 1919. Some critical notes on birds. Bull. Mus. Comp. Zool. 63:19-40.

____ and ____. 1920. Two new American hawks. Proc. New England Zool. Club 7:45-47.

Banko, W.E. 1960. The Trumpeter Swan; its history, habits, and population in the United States. N. Am. Fauna 63:1-214.

Banks, R.C. 1975. Plumage variation in the Masked Bobwhite. Condor 77:486-487.

____. 1978. Nomenclature of the Black-bellied Whistling-Duck. Auk 95:348-352.

____. 1986a. Subspecies of the Greater Scaup and their names. Wilson Bull. 98:433-444.

____. 1986b. Subspecies of the Glaucous Gull Larus hyperboreus (Aves: Charadriiformes). Proc. Biol. Soc. Washington 99:149-159.

____ and M.R. Browning. 1999. Questions about Thayer's Gull. Ontario Birds 17:124-130.

____ and R.E. Tomlinson. 1974. Taxonomic status of certain Clapper Rails of southwestern United States and northwestern Mexico. Wilson Bull. 86:325-335.

____ and L.W. Walker. 1964. A hybrid Scaled X Douglas quail. Wilson Bull. 76:378-380.

____, et al. 2007. Forty-eighth supplement to the American Ornithologists' Union Check-list of North American Birds. Auk 124:1109-1115.

Bannerman, D.A. 1915. [Notes on geographic variation in Cory's Shearwater.] Bull. Brit. Ornith. Club 35:118-121.

____. 1927. [On Fregata magnificens lowei, susp. nov.] Bull. Brit. Ornith. Club 48:12-13.

Bannor, B.K., and E. Kiviat. 2002. Common Moorhen. Birds N. Am. 685:1-28.

Barbraud, C., and O. Chastel. 1998. Southern Fulmars molt their primaries while incubating. Condor 100:563-566.

Barnes, G.G. 1989. Determination of Mallard and Black Duck hybrids from wing feathers. J. Wildl. Manage. 53:1061-1064.

Barr, J.F., C. Eberl, and J.W. McIntyre. 2000. Red-throated Loon. Birds N. Am. 513:1-28.

Barrett, R.T., R. Fieler, T. Anker-Nilssen, and F. Rikardsen. 1985. Measurements and weight changes of Norwegian adult Puffins Fratercula arctica and Kittiwakes Rissa tridactyla during the breeding season. Ringing & Migr. 6:102-112.

____, T. Anker-Nilssen, and Y. Krasnov. 1997. Can. Norwegian and Russian Razorbills Alca torda be identified by their measurements? Marine Ornith. 25:5-8.

Barrett, V.A., and E.R. Vyse. 1982. Comparative genetics of three Trumpeter Swan populations. Auk 99:103-108.

Barrowclough, G.F. 1990. The description of geographic variation in bird populations. Acta XX Int. Ornith. Congr. 1:495-503.

____, J.G. Groth, L.A. Mertz, R.J. Gutíerrez. 2004. Phylogeographic structure, gene flow and species status in Blue Grouse (Dendragapus obscurus). Molecular Ecol. 13:1911-1922.

Barter, M.A. 1985. Sex determination by bill length of live adult Curlew Sandpipers Calidris ferruginea. Stilt 7:8-17.

____. 1988. Biometrics and moult of Lesser Golden Plovers Pluvialis dominica fulva in Victoria. Stilt 13:15-19.

____. 1989a. Bar-tailed Godwit Limosa lapponica in Australia. Part 1: Races, breeding areas and migration routes. Stilt 14:43-48.

____. 1989b. Bar-tailed Godwit Limosa lapponica in Australia. Part 2: Weight, moult, and breeding success. Stilt 14:49-53.

____. 1991. Biometrics and moult of Mongolian Plover Charadrius mongolus spending the non-breeding season in Australia. Stilt 18:15-20.

____. 1992. Distribution, abundance, migration, and moult of the Red Knot Calidris canutus rogersi. Wader Study Group Bull. 64(Suppl.):64-70.

____ and S. Davidson. 1990. Ageing Palearctic waders in the hand in Australia. Stilt 16:43-51.

____, A. Jessop, and C. Minton. 1988a. Red Knot (Calidris canutus rogersi) in Australia. Part 1: Subspecies confirmation, distribution and migration. Stilt 12: 29-32.

____, A. Jessop, and C. Minton. 1988b. Red Knot Calidris canutus rogersi in Australia. Part 2: Biometrics and moult in Victoria and North-Western Australia. Stilt 13: 20-27.

Barth, E.K. 1967. Standard body measurements in Larus argentatus, L. fuscus, L. canus, and L. marinus. Nytt Mag. Zool. 14:7-83.

____. 1974. Moult and taxonomy of the Herring Gull Larus argentatus and the Lesser Black-backed Gull L. fuscus in northwestern Europe. Ibis 117:384-387.

Battley, P., D.I. Rogers, and C.J. Hassell. 2005. Prebreeding moult, plumage and evidence for a presupplemental moult in the Great Knot Calidris tenuirostris. Ibis 148:27-38.

Batty, C., and T. Lowe. 2001. Vagrant Canada Geese in Britain and Ireland. Birding World 14:57-61.

____, P. Hackett, and T. Lowe. 2001. Vagrant Canada Geese in Britain: autumn 2001. Birding World 14:515-519.

Bearhop, S., R. Furness, and B. Zonfrillo. 1998. Identification of Catharacta skuas: variability in juvenile Great Skuas. Birding World 11:355-359.

Bechard, M.J. and J.K. Schmutz. 1995. Ferruginous Hawk. Birds N. Am. 172:1-20.

____ and T.R. Swem. 2002. Rough-legged Hawk. Birds N. Am. 641:1-32.

Beck, J.R. 1970. Breeding seasons and moult in some smaller antarctic petrels. Pp. 542-550 in M.W. Holgate, ed., Antarctic ecology. Academic Press, London.

____ and D.W. Brown. 1972. The biology of Wilson's Storm Petrel, Oceanites oceanicus (Kuhl), at Signy Island, South Orkney Islands. Brit. Antarctic Surv. Sci. Reps. 69:1-54.

Beck, R.H. 1910. Water birds in the vicinity of Point Pinos, California. Proc. California Acad. Sci. (4th Ser.) 3:57-72.

Beck, T.D.I., R.B. Gill, and C.E. Braun. 1975. Sex and age determination of Sage Grouse from wing characteristics. Colorado Div. Game Fish and Parks Inf. Leaflet 49:1-4.

Bédard, J. 1969. Feeding of the Least, Crested, and Parakeet auklets around St. Lawrence Island, Alaska. Can. J. Zool. 47:1025-1050.

____. 1985. Evolution and characteristics of the Atlantic alcidae. Pp. 1-51 in D.N. Nettleship and T.R. Birkhead, eds., The Atlantic alcidae. Academic Press, London.

____ and S.G. Sealy. 1984. Moults and feather generations in Least, Crested, and Parakeet auklets. J. Zool. London 202:461-488.

____, A. Nadeau, and M. Lepage. 1995. Double-crested Cormorant morphology and field sexing in the St. Lawrence River Estuary. Colonial Waterbirds 18(Spec. Pub.):86-90

Bednarz, J.C. 1988. Harris' Hawk. Pp. 294-300 in R.L. Glinski, et al., eds., Proceedings of the southwest raptor management symposium and workshop. National Wildlife Federation, Washington, D.C.

____. 1995. Harris' Hawk. Birds N. Am. 146:1-24.

____ and T.J. Hayden. 1991. Skewed sex ratio and sex-biased hatching sequence in Harris's Hawks. Am. Nat 137:116-132.

Beebe, C.W. 1914. Notes on the ontogeny of the White Ibis, Guara alba. Zoologica 1:241-248.

Beebe, F.L. 1960. The marine Peregrines of the Northwest Pacific Coast. Condor 62:145-189.

Behle, W.H. 1958. The bird life of Great Salt Lake. University of Utah Press, Salt Lake City, UT. 203 pp.

____. 1985. Utah birds: Geographic distribution and systematics. Occ. Papers Utah Mus. Nat. Hist. 5:1-147.

____ and R.K. Selander. 1951. A new race of the Dusky Grouse (Dendragapus obscurus) from the Great Basin. Proc. Biol. Soc. Washington 64:125-128.

____ and ____. 1953. The plumage cycle of the California Gull (Larus californicus) with notes on color changes of soft parts. Auk 70:239-260.

Belanger, L., S. Tremblay, and R. Couture. 1988. Bill morphology in American Black Ducks, Anas rubripes, and Mallards, A. platyrhynchos. Can. Field-Nat. 102:720-722.

Belant, J.L., and R.A. Dolbeer. 1996. Age classification of Laughing Gulls based on summer plumage. J. Field Ornith. 67:565-574.

Bell, D.A. 1996. Genetic differentiation, geographic variation, and hybridization in gulls of the Larus glaucescens-occidentalis complex. Condor 98:527-546.

Bellrose, F.C. 1980. Ducks, geese, and swans of North America. Stackpole Books, Harrisburg, PA. 541 pp.

____ and D.J. Holm. 1994. Ecology and management of the Wood Duck. Stackpole Books, Mechanicsburg, PA. 588 pp.

____, T.G. Scott, A.S. Hawkins, and J.B. Low. 1961. Sex ratios and age rations in North American ducks. Illinois Nat, Hist. Survey Bull. 27:391-474.

Bench, J., W.J. Rudersdorf, and J.P. Harley. 1976. A preliminary method to determine sex in Canada Geese by skin transparency. Inland Bird Banding Assoc. News 48:69-70.

Bendell, J.F. 1955. Age, molt and weight characteristics of Blue Grouse. Condor 57:354-361.

____ and F.C. Zwickel. 1984. A survey of the biology, ecology, abundance, and distribution of the Blue Grouse (Genus Dendragapus). Proc. Int. Grouse Symp. 3:163-190.

Bendire, C.E. 1894. T. a. attwateri Bendire. Attwater's or southern Prairie Hen. Auk 11:130-131.

Bengston, S.-A., and D.F. Owen. 1973. Polymorphism in the Arctic Skua Stercorarius parasiticus in Iceland. Ibis 115:264-269.

Bent, A.C. 1912. A new subspecies of ptarmigan from the Aleutian Islands. Smithsonian Misc. Coll. 56(30):1-2.
____. 1919a. Life histories of North American diving birds. U.S. Nat. Mus. Bull. 107:1-243.
____. 1919b. Geographical variation in the Black-throated Loons. Auk 36:238-242.
____. 1921. Life histories of North American gulls and terns. U.S. Nat. Mus. Bull. 113:1-345..
____. 1922. Life histories of North American petrels and pelicans and their allies. U.S. Nat. Mus. Bull. 121:1-335.
____. 1923. Life histories of North American wild fowl. Part 1. U.S. Nat. Mus. Bull. 126:1-244.
____. 1925. Life histories of North American wild fowl. Part 2. U.S. Nat. Mus. Bull. 130:1-314.
____. 1926. Life histories of North American marsh birds. U.S. Nat. Mus. Bull. 135:1-392.
____. 1927. Life histories of North American shore birds. Part 1. U.S. Nat. Mus. Bull. 142:1-420.
____. 1929. Life histories of North American shore birds. Part 2. U.S. Nat. Mus. Bull. 146:1-412.
____. 1932. Life histories of North American gallinaceous birds. U.S. Nat. Mus. Bull. 162:1-490.
____. 1937. Life histories of North American raptors. Part 1. U.S. Nat. Mus. Bull. 167:1-409.
____. 1938. Life histories of North American raptors. Part 2. U.S. Nat. Mus. Bull. 170:1-482.
Bercovitz, A.B., N.M. Czekala, and B.L. Lasley. 1978. A new method of sex determination in monomorphic birds. J. Zoo Animal Med. 9:114-124.
Berger, A.J., and W.A. Lunk. 1954. The pterylosis of nestling Coua ruficeps Wilson Bull. 66:119-126.
Bergerud, A.T., S.S. Peters, and R. MacGrath. 1963. Determining sex and age of Willow Ptarmigan in Newfoundland. J. Wild. Manage. 27:700-711.
Betts, B.J. 1973. A possible hybrid Wattled Jacana X Northern Jacana in Costa Rica. Auk 90:687-689.
Bibles, B.D., R.L. Glinski, and R.R. Johnson. 2002. Gray Hawk. Birds N. Am. 652:1-16.
Bierregaard, R.O. Jr. 1974. Incomplete wing molt and erythrism in Red-tailed Hawks. Auk 91:618-619.
Bildstein, K.L. 1984. Age-related differences in the foraging behavior of White Ibises and the question of deferred maturity. Colonial Waterbirds 7:146-148.
____. 1987. Energetic consequences of sexual size dimorphism in White Ibises. Auk 104:771-775.
____. 1993. White Ibis: Wetland wanderer. Smithsonian Institution Press, Washington DC. 242 pp.
____ and F. Hamerstrom. 1980. Age and sex differences in the size of Northern Harriers. J. Field Ornith. 51:356-360.
____ and K. Meyer. 2000. Sharp-shinned Hawk. Birds N. Am. 482:1-28.
Billard, R.S., and P.S. Humphrey. 1972. Molts and plumages in the Greater Scaup. J. Wildl. Manage. 36:765-774.
Binford, L.C. 1989. A distributional survey of the Mexican state of Oaxaca. Ornith.. Monogr. 43:1-418.
____ and J.V. Remsen. 1974. Identification of the Yellow-billed Loon. W. Birds 5:111-126.
Birch, A., and C.-T. Lee. 1995. Identification of Pacific Diver - a potential vagrant to Europe. Birding World 8:458-466.
____ and ____. 1997. Arctic and Pacific loons. Field identification. Birding 29:106-115.
Birkhead, T.R., and D.N. Nettleship. 1985. Plumage variation in young Razorbills and murres. J. Field Ornith. 56:246-250.
____, S.D. Johnson, and D.N. Nettleship. 1986. Field observation of a possible hybrid murre Uria aalge X Uria lomvia. Can. Field Nat. 100:115-117.
Bishop, L.B. 1910. Two new subspecies of North American birds. Auk 27:59-61.
____. 1912. An apparently unrecognized race of the Red-shouldered Hawk. Auk 29:232-233.
____. 1921. Description of a new loon. Auk 38:364-370.
____. 1927. The status of the Point Barrow Gull. Condor 29:204-205.
Blaauw, F.E. 1897. A monograph of the cranes. Brill & Porter, London. 64 pp.
____. 1904. On the breeding of some waterfowl at Gooilust in the year 1903. Ibis (8th Ser.) 4:67-75.
____. 1905. [On juvenile Ross's Goose]. Ibis (8th Ser.) 5:137-138.
____. 1916. A note on the Emperor Goose (Philacte canagica) and on the Australian Teal (Nettion castaneum). Ibis (10th Ser.) 4:252-254.
Blackburn, D., and G. Gray. 1977. An apparent Ring-necked Pheasant X Blue Grouse hybrid. Murrelet 58:78.
Blake, E.R. 1977. Manual of neotropical birds. University of Chicago Press, Chicago, IL. 674 pp.
Blanco, G., and R. Rodriguez-Estrella. 1999. Reduced sexual plumage dimorphism in Ospreys from Baja California Sur, Mexico. Ibis 141:489-506.
Bland, B. 1998. The Wilson's Snipe on the Isles of Scilly. Birding World 11:382-385.
____. 1999. The Wilson's Snipe on Scilly revisited. Birding World 12:56-61.
Blankenship, L.H. 1957. Investigations of the American Woodcock in Michigan. Michigan Dept. Cons. Rep. 2123:1-217.
Bledsoe, A.H. 1988. Status and hybridization of Clapper and King rails in Connecticut. Connecticut Warbler 8:61-65.
Blokpoel, H., P.J. Blancher, and P.M. Fetterolf. 1985. On the plumages of nesting Ring-billed Gulls of different ages. J. Field Ornith. 56:113-124.
____, D.C. Boersma, R.A. Hughes, and G.D. Tessier. 1989. Field observations of the biology of Common Terns and Elegant Terns wintering in Peru. Col. Waterbirds 12:90-97.
Bloom, P.H. 1973. Seasonal variation in body weight of Sparrow Hawks in California. W. Bird Bander 48:17-19.
____ and W.S. Clark. 2001. Molt and sequence of plumages of Golden Eagles and a technique for in-hand ageing. N. Am. Bird Bander 26:97-116.
Blus, L.J., and J.A. Keahey. 1978. Variation in reproductivity with age in the Brown Pelican. Auk 95:128-134.
Bluso, J.D., J.T. Ackerman, J.Y. Takekawa, and J.L. Lee. 2006. Sexing Forster's Terns using morphometric measurements. Waterbirds 29:512-517.
Bó, N.A. 1956. Observaciones morfologicas y etologicas sobre el bigua. Hornero 10:147-157.
Boag, D.A. 1965. Indicators of sex, age, and breeding phenology in Blue Grouse. J. Wildl. Manage. 29:103-108.
____ and M. Schroeder. 1992. Spruce Grouse. Birds N. Am. 5:1-28.
Bock, W.J. 1956. A generic review of the family Ardidae (Aves). Am. Mus. Novit. 1779:1-49.
____. 1959. The status of the Semipalmated Plover. Auk 76:98-100.
Boekelheide, R.J., and D.G. Ainley. 1989. Age, resource availability, and breeding effort in Brandt's Cormorant. Auk 106:389-401.
Boere, G., K. Roselaar, and M. Engelmoer. 1984. The breeding origins of Purple Sandpipers Calidris maritima present in The Netherlands. Ardea 72:101-109.
Boersma, P.D., and E.M. Davies. 1987. Sexing monomorphic birds by vent measurements. Auk 104:779-783.
____ and M.C. Silva. 2001. Fork-tailed Storm-Petrel. Birds N. Am. 569:1-28.
____, N.T. Wheelwright, M.K. Nerini, and E.S. Wheelwright. 1980. The breeding biology of the Fork-tailed Storm-Petrel (Oceanodroma furcata). Auk 97:268-282.
Boland, C.R.J., M.C. Double, and G.B. Baker. 2004. Assortative mating by tail streamer length in Red-tailed Tropicbirds Phaethon rubricauda breeding in the coral sea. Ibis 146:687-690.
Bolen, E.G. 1964. Weights and linear measurements of Black-bellied Tree-Ducks. Texas J. Sci. 16:257-260.
____, R. Welder, and B. Welder. 1978. Notes on Blue-winged Teal X Cinnamon Teal hybrids. Southwestern Nat. 23:692-696.
Bollinger, K.S., and D.V. Derksen. 1996. Demographic characteristics of molting Black Brant near Teshekpuk Lake, Alaska. J. Field Ornith. 67:141-158.
Bolte, W.J. 1974. Caribbean Coot, Fulica caribbea, in Florida. Am. Birds 28:734-735.
Bolton, M. 2007. Playback experiments indicate absence of vocal recognition among temporally and geographically separated populations of Madeiran Storm-Petrels Oceanodroma castro. Ibis 149:255-263.
Bond, J. 1935. The status of the Great Blue Heron in the West Indies. Auk 56:76-77.
____. 1936. Resident birds of the Bay Islands of Spanish Honduras. Proc. Philadelphia Acad. Nat. Sci. 88:353-364.
____. 1950a. Results of the Catherwood-Chaplin West Indies Expedition 1948. Part II. Birds of the Cayo Largo (Cuba), San Andrés and Providencia. Proc. Philadelphia Acad. Sci. 102:43-68
____. 1950b. Check-list of the birds of the West Indes. 3rd Edition. Academy of Natural Sciences, Philadelphia, PA. 200 pp.
Bond, R.M. 1936. Molting of hawks, with special regard to the Duck Hawk. Condor 38:119-120.
____. 1943. Variation in western Sparrow Hawks. Condor 45:168-185.
____ and R.M. Stabler. 1941. Second-year plumage of the Goshawk. Auk 58:346-349.
Bookhout, T.A. 1995. Yellow Rail. Birds N. Am. 139:1-16.
Bordage, D., and J.-P.L. Savard. 1995. Black Scoter. Birds N. Am. 177:1-20.

Borg, S. 1976. Hybrid Pluvialis apricaria X Pluvialis dominica. Il Merill 17:36.

Bortolotti, G.R. 1984a. Sexual size dimorphism and age-related variation in Bald Eagles. J. Wildl. Manage. 48:72-81.

____. 1984b. Criteria for determining age and sex of nestling Bald Eagles. J. Field Ornith. 55:467-481.

____. 1984c. Notes on plumage changes in the Bald Eagle. Zoologica 37:822-826.

____. 1984d. Age and sex variation in Golden Eagles. J. Field Ornith. 55:54-66.

____ and V. Honeyman. 1983. Flight feather molt of breeding Bald Eagles in Saskatchewan. Pp. 166-178 in J. Gerrard and T Ingram, eds., The Bald Eagle in Canada. White Horse Plains Publ., Headingly, Manitoba.

Bosanquet, S. 2000. The Hudsonian Whimbrel in Gwent. Birding World 13:190-193.

Boss, W.R. 1943. Hormonal determination of adult characters and sex behavior in Herring Gulls (Larus argentatus). J. Experim. Zool. 94:181-209.

Bostwick, K.S., and M.J. Brady. 2002. Phylogenetic analysis of wing feather taxis in birds: Macroevolutionary patterns of genetic drift? Auk 119:943-954.

Bourne, W.R.P. 1955. On the status of the races of Cory's Shearwater Procellaria diomedea. Ibis 97:145-149.

____. 1957. Additional notes on the birds of the Cape Verde Islands, with particular reference to Bulweria mollis and Fregata magnificens. Ibis 99:182-190.

____. 1964. On the occurrence and nomenclature of certain petrels in North America. Bull. Brit. Ornith. Club 84:114-116.

____. 1982. The colour of the tail coverts of the Black-footed Albatross. Sea Swallow 31:61.

____. 1983. The appearance and classification of the Cookilaria petrels. Sea Swallow 32:65-71.

____. 1986. Recent work on the origin and suppression of bird species in the Cape Verde Islands, especially the shearwaters, the herons, the kites, and the sparrows. Bull. Brit. Ornith. Club 106:163-170.

____ and J.R. Jehl Jr. 1982. Variation and nomenclature of Leach's Storm-Petrels. Auk 99:793-797.

____ and K.E.L. Simmons. 1997. A dark-rumped Leach's Storm-Petrel Oceanodroma leucorhoa in the south Atlantic. Sula 11:209-216.

____, P.E.J. Mackrill, A.M. Patterson, and P. Yesou. 1988. The Yelkouan Shearwater Puffinus (puffinus?) yelkouan. Brit. Birds. 81:306-319.

Bouvier, T.M. 1974. Breeding biology of the Hooded Merganser in southwestern Quebec, including interactions with Common Goldeneyes and Wood Ducks. Can. Field-Nat. 88:323-330.

Boyd, H., 1978. Comments on identifying yearling female Atlantic Brant - Joseph M. Penkala. J. Wildl. Manage. 42:697-698.

____ and L.S. Maltby. 1979. The brant of the western Queen Elizabeth Islands, N.W.T. Pp. 5-21 in R.L. Jarvis and J.C. Bartonek, eds., Management and biology of Pacific Flyway geese. The Wildlife Society, Corvallis, OR.

____ and ____. 1980. Weights and growth of Brent Geese Branta bernicla moulting in the Queen Elizabeth Islands, N.W.T., Canada, 1973-1975. Ornis Scand. 11:135-141.

____, H.J. Harrison, and A. Allison. 1975. Duck wings. A study of duck production. WAGBI Conservation Publication, Caxton & Holmesdale Press, Sevenoaks, UK.

____, ____, and A. Reed. 1988. Differences in plumage patterns of Brant breeding in high Arctic Canada. Can. Wildl. Serv. Progr. Notes 174:1-9.

Boyden, E.A. 1922. The development of the cloaca in birds, with special reference to the origin of the bursa of Fabricius, and the function of the urodael sinus, and the regular occurrence of a cloacal fenestra. Am. J. Anat. 30:163-193.

Bradshaw, C. 2005. Identification review - Lesser Scaup. Brit. Birds. 98:89-95.

Braun, C.E. 1971. Determination of Blue Grouse sex and age from wing characteristics. Colorado Game Fish Parks Inform. Leafl. No. 86:1-12.

____ and K. Martin. 2001. Unusual summer plumage of White-tailed Ptarmigan. Wilson Bull. 113:373-377.

____ and C.E. Rogers. 1967. Determination of age and sex of the southern White-tailed Ptarmigan. Colorado Div. Game & Parks Tech Bull. 27:1-80.

____, K. Martin, and L.A. Robb. 1993. White-tailed Ptarmigan. Birds N. Am. 68:1-24.

Braune, B.M. 1987a. Body morphometrics and molt of Bonaparte's Gulls in the Quoddy region, New Brunswick, Canada. Condor 89:150-157.

____. 1987b. Comparison of total mercury levels in relation to diet and molt for nine species of marine birds. Arch. Environmental Toxicology 16:217-224.

Brennan, L.A. 1999. Northern Bobwhite. Birds N. Am. 397:1-28.

Brennan, L.A. and W.M. Block. 1985. Sex determination of Mountain Quail reconsidered. J. Wildl. Manage. 49:475-476.

____, J.B. Buchanan, C.T. Schick, S.G. Herman, and T.M. Johnson. 1984. Sex determination of Dunlins in winter plumage. J. Field Ornith. 55:343-348.

____, ____, ____, and ____. 1991. Estimating sex ratios with discriminant function analysis: The influence of probability cutpoints and sample size. J. Field Ornith. 62:357-366.

Bretagnolle, V., M. Carruthers, M. Cubitt, F. Bioret, and J.-P. Cuillandre. 1991. Six captures of a dark-rumped, fork-tailed storm-petrel in the northeastern Atlantic. Ibis 133:351-356.

____, J.-C. Thibault, and J.-M. Dominici. 1994. Field identification of individual Ospreys using head marking pattern. J. Wildl. Manage. 58:175-178.

____, C. Attié, and F. Mougeot. 2000. Audubon's Shearwaters Puffinus lherminieri on Réunion Island, Indian Ocean: Behaviour, census, distribution, biometrics, and breeding biology. Ibis 142:399-412.

Brewster, W. 1877. An undescribed hybrid between two North American grouse. Bull. Nuttall Ornith. Club 2:66-68.

____. 1885. The Heath Hen of Massachusetts. Auk 2:80-84.

____. 1887. Three new forms of North American birds. Auk 4:145-147.

____. 1888. Descriptions of supposed new birds from Lower California, Sonora, and Chihuahua, Mexico, and the Bahamas. Auk 5:82-95.

____. 1890. A new subspecies of the Solitary Sandpiper. Auk 7:377-379.

____. 1902a. Birds of the cape region of Lower California. Bull. Mus. Comp. Zool. 41:1-241.

____. 1902b. An undescribed form of the Black Duck (Anas obscurus). Auk 19:183-188.

____. 1907. Notes on the Black Rail of California. Auk 24:205-210.

____. 1909a. Something more about Black Ducks. Auk 26:175-179.

____. 1909b. Barrow's Goldeneye in Massachusetts. Auk 26:153-164.

____. 1910. Resurrection of the red-legged Black Duck. Auk 27:323-333.

Bridge, E.S. 2004. The effects of wing molt on diving in alcids and potential influences on the evolution of molt patterns. J. Experim. Biol. 207:3003-3014.

____. 2006. Influences of morphology and behavior on wing-molt strategies in seabirds. Marine Ornith. 34:7-19.

____ and I.C.T. Nisbet. 2004. Wing molt and assortative mating in Common Terns: a test of the molt-signaling hypothesis. Condor 106:336-343.

____, G. Voelker, C.W. Thompson, A.W. Jones, and A.J. Baker. 2007. Effects of size and migratory behavior on the evolution of wing molt in terns (Sternae): A phylogenetic-comparative study. Auk 124:841-856.

Brimley, H.H. 1927. Rare birds in North Carolina. Auk 44:427-428.

Brinkley, E.S., M. Sharp, G.L. Armistead, and B. Patterson. 2001. Gannets, anyone? Birding 33:266-269.

Brisbin, I.L., H.D. Pratt, and T.B. Mowbray. 2002. American Coot and Hawaiian Coot. Birds N. Am. 697:1-44.

Brodkorb, P. 1933. Remarks on the genus Limnodromus Wied. Proc. Biol. Soc. Washington 46:123-128.

____. 1935. A Sparrow Hawk gynadromorph. Auk 52:183-184.

____. 1936. A new subspecies of bittern from western North America. Occ. Papers Mus. Zool. Univ. Michigan 333:1-4.

____. 1942. The chachalaca of interior Chiapas. Proc. Biol. Soc. Washington 55:181-182.

____. 1943a. Birds from the gulf lowlands of southern Mexico. Misc. Pubs. Zool. Univ. Michigan 55:1-88.

____. 1943b. Geographical variation in the Black Vulture. Papers Michigan Acad. Sci. Arts & Letters 29:115-121.

____. 1953. Subspecific status of the Common Loon in Florida. Wilson Bull. 65:41.

Brodskey, L.M., and P.J. Weatherhead. 1984. Behavioural and ecological factors contributing to American Black Duck-Mallard hybridization. J. Wildl. Manage. 48:846-852.

Brooke, M. de L. 1978a. Sexual differences in the voice and individual vocal recognition in the Manx Shearwater Puffinus puffinus. Animal Behav. 26:622-629.

____. 1978b. Weights and measurements of the Manx Shearwater Puffinus puffinus. J. Zool. 186:359-374.

____. 1988. Sexual dimorphism in the voice of the Greater Shearwater. Wilson Bull. 100:319-323.

____. 1996. The Manx Shearwater. T & AD Poyser, London, UK. 246 pp.

____. 2004. Albatrosses and petrels across the world. Oxford University Press, Oxford, U.K. 499 pp.

Brooks, A. 1907. A hybrid grouse, Richardson's X Sharp-tail. Auk 24:167-169.

____. 1914. The races of Branta canadensis. Condor 16:123-124.

____. 1920. Notes on some American ducks. Auk 37:353-367.

____. 1926a. Notes on the geese of the Branta canadensis group. Ibis(12th Ser.) 2: 339--346.

____. 1926b. The display of the Richardson Grouse with some notes on the species and subspecies of the genus Dendragapus. Auk 43:281-287.

Brooks, A. 1926c. Notes on the status of the Peale Falcon. Condor 28:77-79.

____. 1927. Notes on Swarth's report on a collection of birds from the Atlin region. Condor 29:112-114.

____. 1930. The specialized feathers of the Sage Hen. Condor 32:205-207.

____. 1937. Thayer's Gull (Larus argentatus thayeri) on the Pacific coast. Murrelet 18:19-21.

Brooks, W.S. 1915. Notes on birds from east Siberia and Arctic Alaska. Bull. Mus. Comp. Zool. 59:361-406.

Broughton, J.M. 1994. Size of the bursa of Fabricius in relation to gonad size and age in Laysan and Black-footed albatrosses. Condor 96:203-207.

____, D. Rampton, and K. Holanda. 2002. A test of an osteologically based age determination technique in the Double-crested Cormorant Phalacrocorax auritus. Ibis 144:143-146.

Brown, A. 1992. Identification pitfalls and assessment problems: 12. Surf Scoter Melanitta perspicillata. Brit. Birds. 85:437-439.

Brown, D.E. 1989. Arizona game birds. University of Arizona Press, Tucson, AZ. 307 pp.

____, J.C. Hagelin, M. Taylor, and J. Galloway. 1998. Gambel's Quail. Birds N. Am. 321:1-24.

Brown, L., and D. Amadon. 1968. Eagles, hawks, and falcons of the world. Parts 1 & 2. Mcgraw-Hill, New York, NY. 945 pp.

Brown, P.W., and L.H. Fredrickson. 1997. White-winged Scoter. Birds N. Am. 274:1-28.

Brown, R.G.B. 1988. The wing-moult of fulmars and shearwaters (Procellariidae) in Canadian Atlantic waters. Can. Field-Nat. 102:203-208.

____. 1990. The wing-moult Cory's Shearwater, Calonectris diomedea, off Nova Scotia. Can. Field-Nat. 104:306-307.

Browning, M.R. 1974. Taxonomic remarks on recently described subspecies of birds that occur in the northwestern United States. Murrelet 55:32-38.

____. 1977a. The types and type localities of Oreortyx pictus (Douglas) and Ortyx plumiferus Gould. Proc. Biol. Soc. Washington 90:808-812.

____. 1977b. Geographic variation in Dunlins, Calidris alpina, in North America. Can. Field-Nat. 91:391-393.

____. 1978. An evaluation of the new species and subspecies proposed in Oberholser's Bird Life of Texas. Proc. Biol. Soc. Washington 91:85-122.

____. 1979a. Distribution, geographic variation, and taxonomy of Lagopus mutus in Greenland and northern Canada. Dansk Ornith. Forens. Tidsskr. 73:29-40.

____. 1979b. Type specimens of birds collected in Oregon. Northwest Sci. 53:132-140.

____. 1990. Taxa of North American birds described from 1957 to 1987. Proc. Biol. Soc. Washington 103:432-451.

____. 1991. Taxonomic comments on the Dunlin Calidris alpina from northern Alaska and eastern Siberia. Bull. Brit. Ornith. Club 111:140-145.

____. 2002. Taxonomic comments on selected species of birds from the Pacific Northwest. Oregon Birds 28:69-82.

Brua, R.B. 2002. Ruddy Duck. Birds N. Am. 696:1-32.

Bryan, D.C. 2002. Limpkin. Birds N. Am. 627:1-24.

Buchanan, J.B. 2002. Morphology, age, and molt characteristics of some spring migrant Dunlins and Western Sandpipers in coastal Washington. Washington Birds 8:41-50.

Buchanan, F.W., and K.C. Parkes. 1948. A female Bob-white in male plumage Wilson Bull. 60:119-120.

Bucher, J.E. 1978. On sexing American Avocets and Long-billed Curlews. Inland Bind-Banding News 50:15-18.

Buckley, N.J. 1999. Black Vulture. Birds N. Am. 411:1-24.

Buckley, P.A., and F.G. Buckley. 1970. Color variation in the soft parts and down of Royal Tern chicks. Auk 87:1-13.

____ and ____. 2003. Royal Tern. Birds N. Am. 700:1-28.

____ and S.S. Mitra. 2002. The geese resembling "Gray-bellied Brant"/"Lawrence's Brant from Long Island, New York. N. Am. Birds 56:502-507.

____, ____, and E.S. Brinkley. 2004. Multiple occurrences of Dark-bellied Brant (Branta [bernicla] bernicla) in North America. N. Am. Birds 58:180-
185.

Buehler, D.A. 2000. Bald Eagle. Birds N. Am. 506:1-40.

Buehler, D.M., and A.J. Baker. 2005. Population divergence times and historical demography in Red Knots and Dunlins. Condor 107:497-513.

____, ____, and T. Piersma. 2006. Reconstructing paleoflyways of the late Pleistocene and early Holocene Red Knot Calidris canutus. Ardea 94:485-498.

Bull, L.S., B.D. Bell, and S. Pledger. 2005. Patterns of size variation in the shearwater genus Puffinus. Marine Ornith. 33:27-39.

Bump, G., R.W. Darrow, F.C. Edminster, and W.F. Crissey. 1947. The Ruffed Grouse: life history - propagation - management. The Holling Press Inc., Buffalo NY. 915 pp.

Bunnell, S.D., J.A. Rensel, J.F. Kimball Jr., and M.L. Wolfe. 1977. Determination of age and sex of Dusky Blue Grouse. J. Wildl. Manage. 41:662-666.

Burger, J. 1980. Age differences in foraging Black-necked Stilts in Texas. Auk 97:633-636.

____. 1996. Laughing Gull. Birds N. Am. 225:1-28.

____ and M. Gochfeld. 1994. Franklin's Gull. Birds N. Am. 116:1-28.

____ and ____. 2000. Bonaparte's Gull. Birds N. Am. 634:1-24.

____ and C. Beer. 1975. Territoriality in the Laughing Gull (L. atricilla). Behaviour 55:201-220.

____ and M. Howe. 1975. Notes on winter feeding behavior and molt in Wilson's Phalaropes. Auk 92:441-451.

Burleigh, T.D. 1960. Three new subspecies of birds from western North America. Auk 77:210-215.

____ and G.H. Lowery Jr. 1942. An inland race of Sterna albifrons. Occ. Papers Mus. Zool. Louisiana State Univ. 10:173-177.

Burn, D.M., and J.R. Mather. 1974. The White-billed Diver in Britain. Brit. Birds. 67:257-282.

Burness, G.P., K. Lefevre, and C.T. Collins. 1999. Elegant Tern. Birds N. Am. 404:1-28.

Burns, F.L. 1911. A monograph of the Broad-winged Hawk (Buteo platypterus). Wilson Bull. 23:139-320.

Burton, J., and R. McNeil. 1976. Age determination of six species of North American shorebirds. Bird-Banding 47:201-209.

Burton, J.H. 1959. Some population mechanics of the America Coot. J. Wildl. Manage. 23:203-210.

Bush, M. 1986. Laparoscopy and surgery. Pp. 253-260 in M.E. Fowler, ed., Zoo and wild animal medicine. W.B. Saunders Co., Philadelphia, PA.

Buss, I.O., and B.A. Schottelius. 1954. Breeding age of Blue Grouse. J. Wildl. Manage. 18:137-138.

Butler, R.G., and D.E. Buckley. 2002. Black Guillemot. Birds N. Am. 675:1-32.

____ and S. Janes-Butler. 1983. Sexual differences in the behavior of adult Great Black-backed Gulls (Larus marinus) during the pre- and post-hatch periods. Auk 100:63-75.

Butler, R.W. 1992. Great Blue Heron. Birds N. Am. 23:1-20.

____. 1997. The Great Blue Heron: A natural history and ecology of a seashore sentinel. UBC Press, Vancouver, BC. 168 pp.

____, G.W. Kaiser, and G.E.J. Smith. 1987. Migration chronology, length of stay, sex ratio, and weight of Western Sandpipers (Calidris mauri) on the south coast of British Columbia. J. Field Ornith. 58:103-111.

____, A.M. Breault, and T.M. Sullivan. 1990. Measuring animals through a telescope. J. Field Ornith. 61:111-114.

Buzin, V.A. 2002. Descriptive update on gull taxonomy: "West Siberian Gull" (Larus hueglini). Brit. Birds 95:216-232.

Byers, S.M., and J.R. Cary. 1991. Discrimination of Mallard strains on the basis of morphology. J. Wildl. Manage. 55:580-586.

Byrd, G.V., and J.C. Williams. 1993a. Red-legged Kittiwake Birds N. Am. 60:1-12.

____ and ____. 1993b. Whiskered Auklet. Birds N. Am. 76:1-12.

Byrkjedal, I., and D. Thompson. 1998. The Tundra Plovers: The Eurasian, Pacific and American golden plovers and Grey Plover. T & AD Poyser, London, U.K. 422 pp.

Cade, T.J. 1955. Variation of the Common Rough-legged Hawk in North America. Condor 57:313-346.

____. 1960. Ecology of the Peregrine and Gyrfalcon populations in Alaska. Univ. California Publ. Zool. 63: 151-290.

____. 1982. Falcons of the world. Cornell University Press, Ithaca, NY. 192 pp.

____ and S.A. Temple. 1995. Management of threatened bird species: Evaluation of the hands-on approach. Ibis 137(Suppl.):S161-S172.

Cain, B.W. 1970. Growth and plumage development of the Black-bellied Tree-Duck, Dendrocygna autumnalis (Linnaeus). Texas A&I Univ. Stud. 3:25-48.

Cairns, D.K. 1983. Evidence for a hybrid murre reconsidered - a comment. Auk 100:237-238.

____ and B. deYoung. 1981. Back-crossing of a Common Murre (Uria aalge) and a Common Murre - Thick-billed Murre hybrid (U. aalge X U. lomvia). Auk 98:847.

Caithamer, D.F., R.J. Gates, J.D. Hardy, and T.C. Tacha. 1993. Field identification of age and sex of interior Canada Geese. Wildl. Soc. Bull. 21:480-487.

Caldwell, P.J. 1980. Primary shaft measurements in relation to age of Sharp-tailed Grouse. J. Wildl. Manage. 44:202-204.

Calkins, J.D., J.C. Hagelin, and D.F. Lott. 1999. California Quail. Birds N. Am. 473:1-32.

Cameron, E.S. 1908. Changes of plumage in Buteo swainsoni. Auk 25:468-471.

Cameron, E.S. 1913. Notes on Swainson's Hawk (Buteo swainsoni) in Montana. Auk 30:381-394.

Campainolo, P., and J. Pitochelli. 1990. Eastern records of F.c. suckleyi. Kingbird 40:221-225.

Campbell, C. 2000a. Possible anywhere: White-winged Tern. Birding 32:216-230.

____. 2000b. On second-alternate White-winged Terns. Birding 32:540.

Campbell, H. 1972. A population study of Lesser Prairie Chickens in New Mexico. J. Wildl. Manage. 36:689-699.

____ and L. Lee. 1956. Notes on the sex ratio of Gambel's and Scaled quail in New Mexico. J. Wildl. Manage. 20:93-94.

____ and R.E. Tomlinson. 1962. Some observations on the bursa of Fabricius in Chukars. J. Wildl. Manage. 26:324.

Campbell, R.W., and P.T. Gregory. 1976. The Buff-breasted Sandpiper in British Columbia, with notes on its migration in North America. Syesis 9:123-130.

Camphuysen, K. (C.J.) 1989. Biometrics of auks at Jan Mayen. Seabird 12:7-10.

____. 1995. [Ageing guillemots and Razorbills in the hand.] Sula 9:1-22.

____. 2003. Characteristics of Atlantic Puffins Fratercula arctica in The Netherlands, January-February 2003. Atlantic Seabirds 5:21-30.

____ and J. van der Meer. 2001. Pelagic distribution, moult, and (sub-) specific status of Cory's Shearwaters Calonectris [d.] diomedea/borealis wintering off southern Africa. Marine Ornith. 29:89-96.

____, G. Camphuysen-Janker, and J.E. den Ouden. 1995. Colour phase and biometrics of Fulmars Fulmarus glacialis on Svalbard. Sula 9:107-116.

Canadian Wildlife Service (CWS) and U.S. Fish and Wildlife Service (USFWS). 1991. North American Bird Banding. Vols. 1 and 2. Environment Canada, Ottawa, Canada, and Washington, D.C.

Carey, G., and U. Olsson. 1995. Field identification of Common, Wilson's, Pintail and Swinhoe's snipes. Birding World 8:179-190.

Carlson, C.W. 1971. Arctic Loon at Ocean City, Maryland: A field identification problem. Maryland Birdlife 27:68-72.

____. 1979. [On a possible Blue-winged X Green-winged teal hybrid.] American Birds 33:783.

Carlson, G., and C.H. Trost. 1992. Sex determination of the Whooping Crane by analysis of vocalizations. Condor 94:532-536.

Carney, S.M. 1964. Preliminary keys to waterfowl age and sex determination by means of wing plumage. U.S. Fish and Wild. Serv. Spec. Sci. Rep. 82:1-77.

____. 1983. Species, age, and sex identification of Nearctic goldeneyes from wings. J. Wildl. Manage. 47:754-761.

____. 1992. Species, age and sex identification of ducks using wing plumage. U.S. Fish and Wildlife Service. 144 pp.

____ and A.D. Geis. 1960. Mallard age and sex determination from wings. J. Wildl. Manage. 24:372-381.

Carpenter, C.K. 1948. An early Illinois record of "Cory's Least Bittern". Auk 65:80-85.

Carroll, J.P. 1993. Gray Partridge. Birds N. Am. 58:1-20.

Cartar, R.V. 1984. A morphometric comparison of Western and Semipalmated sandpipers. Wilson Bull. 96:277-286.

Carter, H.R., and J.L. Stein. 1995. Molts and plumages in the annual cycle of the Marbled Murrelet. Pp. 99-109 in C.J. Ralph, et al., eds., Ecology and conservation of the Marbled Murrelet. Pacific Southwest Research Station, Albany, CA.

____, S.G. Sealy, E.E. Burkett, and J.F. Piatt. 2005. Biology and conservation of Xantus's Murrelet: Discovery, taxonomy, and distribution. Marine Ornith. 33:81-87.

Castillo-Guerrero, J.A., E. Mellink, E. Penaloza-Padilla, and M. Prado-López. 2005. Anomalously pigmented Brown Boobies in the Gulf of California: Leucism and possible hybridization with the Blue-footed Booby. W. Birds 36:325-328.

Caswell, E.B. 1954. A method for sexing Blue Grouse. J. Wildl. Manage. 18:139.

Causey, D. 2002. Red-faced Cormorant. Birds N. Am. 617:1-16.

Cecile, D.G. 2005. British Columbia. N. Am. Birds 59:311-312.

Chabreck, R.H. 1966. Molting Gadwall (Anas strepera) in Louisiana. Auk 83:664.

Chalmers, M.L. 2002. A review of frigatebird records in Hong Kong. Hong Kong Bird Report 1998:128-142.

Chandler, A.C. 1916. A study of the structure of feathers with reference to their taxonomic significance. Univ. California Pubs. Zool. 13:243-446.

Chandler, R.J. 1987a. Identification and ageing first-winter male King Eider. Brit. Birds. 80:626-627.

____. 1987b. Yellow orbital ring of Semipalmated and Ringed Plover. Brit. Birds 80:241-242.

____. 1989. North Atlantic shorebirds. Facts on File, New York, NY. 208 pp.

____. 1998. Dowitcher identification and ageing: A photographic review. Brit. Birds. 91:93-106.

Chandler, R.J. and J.H. Marchant. 2001. Waders with non-breeding plumage in the breeding season. Brit. Birds. 94:28-34.

____ and C. Wilds. 1994. Little, Least, and Saunder's terns. Brit. Birds 87:60-67.

Chaney, R.C. Jr., K.P. Blemings, J. Bonner, and H. Klandore. 2003. Pentosidine as a measure of chronological age in wild birds. Auk 120:394-399.

Chapman, F.M. 1896a. The standing of Ardetta neoxena. Auk 13:11-19.

____. 1896b. The changes of plumages in the Dunlin and Sanderling. Bull. Am. Mus. Nat. Hist. 8:1-8.

____. 1899. Descriptions of two new subspecies of Colymbus dominicus. Bull. Am. Mus. Nat. Hist. 12:255-256.

____. 1901. A new race of the Great Blue Heron, with remarks on the status and range of Ardea wardi. Bull. Am. Mus. Nat. Hist. 14:87-89.

____. 1902. List of birds collected in Alaska by the Andrew J. Stone Expedition of 1901. Bull. Am. Mus. Nat. Hist. 16:231-247.

____. 1904a. A new grouse from California. Bull. Am. Mus. Nat. Hist. 20:159-160.

____. 1904b. List of birds collected in Alaska by the Andrew J. Stone Expedition of 1903. Bull. Am. Mus. Nat. Hist. 20:399-406.

____. 1905. A contribution to the life history of the American Flamingo (Phoenicopterus ruber) with remarks upon specimens. Bull. Am. Mus. Nat. Hist. 21:53-77.

____. 1914. Diagnoses of apparently new Colombian Birds, II. Bull. Am. Mus. Nat. Hist. 33:167-192.

____. 1915. Descriptions of proposed new birds from Central and South America. Bull. Am. Mus. Nat. Hist. 34:363-388.

____. 1920. Description of a proposed new race of the Killdeer from the coast of Peru. Auk 37:105-108.

____. 1925. Descriptions of one new genus and of species of birds from Peru and Ecuador. Am. Mus. Novit. 205:1-11.

Chapman, J.A. 1970. Weights and measurements of Dusky Canada Geese wintering in Oregon. Murrelet 51:34-37.

Chardine, J.W. 2002. Geographic variation in the wingtip patterns of Black-legged Kittiwakes. Condor 104:687-693.

____ and R.D. Morris. 1989. Sexual size dimorphism and assortative mating in the Brown Noddy. Condor 91:868-874.

____ and ____. 1996. Brown Noddy. Birds N. Am. 220:1-24.

Chase, C.A., III. 1984. Gull hybridization: California X Herring. Colorado Field Ornith. J. 18:62 (abstract).

Chasen, F.N. 1933. Notes on the birds of Christmas Island, Indian Ocean. Bull. Raffles Mus. 8:55-87.

Childress, R.B., and L.A. Bennum. 2002. Sexual character intensity and its relationship to breeding timing, fecundity, and mate choice in the Great Cormorant Phalacrocorax carbo lucidus. J. Avian Biol. 33:23-30.

Childs, H.E. Jr. 1952. Hybrid between a Shoveler and a Blue-winged Teal. Condor 54:67-68.

Chisholm, G., and L.A. Neel. 2002. Birds of the Lahontan Valley. University of Nevada Press. 237 pp.

Christensen, G.C. 1996. Chukar. Birds N. Am. 258:1-20.

Chu, E.W. 1984. Sooty Shearwaters off California: Diet and energy gain. Pp. 64-84 in D.N. Nettleship, et al., eds., Marine birds: Their feeding ecology and commercial fisheries relationships. Can. Wildl. Serv. Spec. Publ., Ottawa, ON.

Chu, P.C. 1994. Historical examination of delayed plumage maturation in the shorebirds (Aves: Charadriiformes). Evolution 48:327-350.

____. 1998. A phylogeny of the gulls (Aves: Larinae) inferred from osteological and integumentary characters. Cladistics 14:1-43.

Ciaranca, M.A., C.C. Allin, and G.S. Jones. 1997. Mute Swan. Birds N. Am. 273:1-28.

Cicero, C., and N.K. Johnson. 2006. Diagnosability of subspecies: lessons from Sage Sparrows (Amphispiza bellii) for analysis of geographic variation in birds. Auk 123:266-274.

Clancey, P.A. 1977. Data from Sooty Terns from Natal and Zululand. Ostrich 48:43-44.

Clapp, R.B. 1989 First record of the Little Tern, Sterna albifrons, from Hawaii. 'Elepaio 49:41-46

Clark, A. 1974. A hybrid Dendrocygna viduata X Dendrocygna bicolor. Ostrich 45:1-4.

Clark, A.H. 1905. Preliminary descriptions of three new birds from St. Vincent, West Indies. Proc. Biol. Soc. Washington 18:61-64.

____. 1907. Eighteen new species and one new genus of birds from eastern Asia and the Aleutian Islands. Proc. U.S. Nat. Mus. 34:467-475.

____. 1910. The birds collected and observed during the cruise of the U.S. Fisheries Steamer "Albatross" in the North Pacific Ocean, and in the Bering, Okhotsk, Japanese, and Eastern seas, from April to December, 1906. Proc. U.S. Nat. Mus. 38:35-74.

Clark, C.T. 1985. Caribbean Coot? Birding 17:84-88.

____. 1992. Identification notes from the coastal bend of Texas. Birding 24:166-167.

Clark, G.A., and J.B. De Cruz. 1989. Functional interpretation of protruding filoplumes in oscines. Condor 91:962-965.

Clark, H.L. 1898. The feather-tracts of North American grouse and quail. Proc. U.S. Nat. Mus. 21:641-653.

Clark, J.M. 1978. Use of toe and shank lengths as sex determinants in woodcock. Proc. S.E. Assoc. Game Fish Wildl. Agencies 32:42-47.

Clark, N.A. 1984. Ageing criteria for Dunlin. Wader Study Group Bull. 42:39.

____ 1987a. A probable hybrid Dunlin X Sanderling. Scottish Birds 14:211-213.

____. 1987b. Ageing criteria for Dunlins in the field. Brit. Birds. 80:242-246.

Clark, W.S. 1983a. The field identification of North American eagles. Am. Birds 37:822-826.

____. 1983b. Migration of the Merlin along the coast of New Jersey. J. Raptor Res. 19:85-88.

____. 1998. First North American record of a melanistic Osprey. Wilson Bull. 110:289-290.

____. 2001a. Aging Bald Eagles. Birding 33:18-28.

____. 2001b. Crested Caracara in basic I plumage. Birding 33:524-527.

____. 2004. Wave moult of the primaries in Accipitrid raptors, and its use in ageing immatures. Pp. 795-804 in R.D. Chancellor and B.-U. Meyersburg, eds., Raptors worldwide. World Working Group on Birds of Prey, Budapest, Hungary.

____ and C.M. Anderson. 1984. First specimen record of the Broad-winged Hawk for Washington. Murrelet 65:93-94.

____ and R.C. Banks. 1992. The taxonomic status of the White-tailed Kite. Wilson Bull. 104:571-579.

____ and P.H. Bloom. 2005. Basic II and basic III plumages of Rough-legged Hawks. J. Field Ornith. 76:83-89.

____ and B.K. Wheeler. 1985. Field identification of Common and Great black-hawks. Birding 17:33-37.

____ and ____. 1987. A field guide to the hawks of North America. Houghton Mifflin Co., Boston, MA. 198 pp.

____ and ____. 1989. Field identification of White-tailed Hawk. Birding 21:190-195.

____ and ____. 1998. 'Dark-morph' Sharp-shinned Hawk reported from California in normal juvenile female of race perobscurus. Bull. Brit. Ornith. Club 118:191-193.

____ and C.C. Witt. 2006. First known specimen of a hybrid Buteo: Swainson's Hawk (Buteo swainsoni) X Rough-legged Hawk (B. lagopus) from Louisiana. Wilson J. Ornith. 118:42-52.

____, M. Reid, and B.K. Wheeler. 2005. Four cases of hybridization in North American Buteos. Birding 37:256-263.

Clarke, T., J.A.L. Gutiérrez, and J. King. 1995. The Lesser Scaup on the Canary Islands: The first female for the western Palearctic. Birding World 8:52-55.

Clegg, M. 1971. Relationships between Tufted Ducks and Mallards. Brit. Birds 64:372-373.

Clench, M.H. 1976. Possible pitfalls in museum specimen data. N. Am. Bird Bander 1:20-21.

Clum, N.J., and T.J. Cade. 1994. Gyrfalcon. Birds N. Am. 114:1-28.

Coale, H.K. 1923. A new subspecies of the Little Black Rail. Auk 40:88-90.

Cobb, D.T. 1994. Morphometric quality of Wild Turkeys harvested from public vs. private lands in Florida. Florida Sci. 57:88-92.

Coker, R.E. 1919. Habits and economic relationships of the guano birds of Peru. Proc. U.S. Nat. Mus. 56:449-511.

Collins, C.T. 1974a. Banding worksheet for Western Birds. Mountain Quail. Supplement to W. Bird Bander 50(1).

____. 1974b. Banding worksheet for Western Birds. Scaled Quail. Supplement to W. Bird Bander 50(1).

____. 1974c. Banding worksheet for Western Birds. California Quail. Supplement to W. Bird Bander 50(1).

____. 1974d. Banding worksheet for Western Birds. Gambel's Quail. Supplement to W. Bird Bander 50(1).

____. 1986. Identification quiz. W. Birds 17:93-94.

____. 1997. Hybridization of a Sandwich Tern and Elegant Tern in California. W. Birds 28:169-173.

____ and P.H. Bloom. 2000. The status of Harlan's Hawk in southern California. W. Birds 31:200-202.

Colwell, M.A., and J.R. Jehl, Jr. 1994. Wilson's Phalarope. Birds N. Am. 83:1-20.

Combs, D.L., and L.H. Fredrickson. 1995. Molt chronology of male Mallards wintering in Missouri. Wilson Bull. 107:359-365.

Compton, L.V. 1932. A probable hybrid between the California Quail and the Texas Bob-white. Condor 34:48.

Connelly, J.W., M.W. Gratson, and K.P. Reese. 1998. Sharp-tailed Grouse. Birds N. Am. 354:1-20.

Connors, P.G. 1983. Taxonomy, distribution, and evolution of golden plovers (Pluvialis dominica and Pluvialis fulva). Auk 100:607-620.

____, B.J. McCaffery, and J.L. Maron. 1993. Speciation in golden-plovers, Pluvialis dominica and P. fulva: Evidence from the breeding grounds. Auk 110:9-20.

Conover, H.B. 1926. Game birds of the Hooper Bay region, Alaska. Auk 43:162-180.

____. 1935. A new race of Ruffed Grouse from Vancouver Island. Condor 37:204-206.

____. 1941. A study of the dowitchers. Auk 58:376-380.

____. 1943. The races of the Knot (Calidris canutus). Condor 45:226-228.

____. 1944a. The races of the Solitary Sandpiper. Auk 61:537-544.

____. 1944b. The North Pacific allies of the Purple Sandpiper. Zool. Ser. Field Mus. Nat. Hist. 29:169-179.

____. 1945a. The breeding Golden Plover of Alaska. Auk 62:568-574.

____. 1945b. Notes on some American shorebirds. Condor 47:211-214.

Conway, C.J. 1995. Virginia Rail. Birds N. Am. 173:1-20.

Cooch, F.G. 1961. Ecological aspects of the Blue Goose complex. Auk 78:72-89.

____ and B. Collins. 1982. A method for rapid identification of the murres (Uria lomvia and Uria aalge) based on tibiotarsus and phalanges. Can. Wildl. Serv. Progr. Notes 134:1-10.

Cooke, F., and F.G. Cooch. 1968. The genetics of polymorphism in the goose Anser caerulescens. Evolution 22:289-300.

____ and P.J. Mirsky. 1972. A genetic analysis of Lesser Snow Goose families. Auk 89:863-871.

____ and J.P. Ryder. 1971. The genetics of polymorphism in the Ross' Goose. Evolution 25:483-490.

____, R.F. Rockwell, and D.B. Lank. 1995. The Snow Geese of La Pérouse Bay. Oxford University Press, Oxford, UK. 297 pp.

____, G.J. Robertson, R.I. Goudie, and W.S. Boyd. 1997. Molt and the basic plumage of male Harlequin Ducks. Condor 99:83-90.

, , and C.M. Smith. 2000. Survival, emigration, and winter population structure of Harlequin Ducks. Condor 102:137-144.

Cooper, J., L.G. Underhill, and G. Avery. 1991. Primary molt and transequatorial migration of the Sooty Shearwater. Condor 93:724-730.

Cooper, J.M. 1994. Least Sandpiper. Birds N. Am. 115:1-28.

____ and D.J. Graham. 1985. Sightings of hybrid 'blue-winged' ducks (Anas) in British Columbia. Contr. Nat. Sci. 1:1-2.

Copelin, F.F. 1963. The Lesser Prairie-Chicken in Oklahoma. Oklahoma Wild. Cons. Dept. Tech. Bull. 6:1-58.

Copestake, P.G., and J.P. Croxall. 1985. Aspects of the breeding biology of Wilson's Storm Petrel Oceanites oceanicus at Bird Island, South Georgia. Brit. Antarctic Surv. Bull. 66:7-17.

____, ____, and P.A. Prince. 1988. Use of cloacal sexing techniques in mark-recapture estimates of breeding population size in Wilson's Stormpetrel Oceanites oceanicus at South Georgia. Polar Biol. 8:271-279.

Corbat, C.A., and P.W. Bergstrom. 2000. Wilson's Plover. Birds N. Am. 516:1-16.

Cormons, G.D. 1976. Roseate Tern bill color change in relation to nesting status and food supply. Wilson Bull. 88: 377-389.

Corso, A., and D. Forsman. 1997. Hybrids between Black Kite and Common Buzzard. Alula 3:44-45.

Cory, C.B. 1886. Description of a new North American species of Ardetta. Auk 3:262.

Cottaar, F. 2004. [Yellow-legged Gulls and hybrids breeding at Ijmuiden.] Dutch Birding 26:36-42.

Cottle, N.W. 1987. Spring moult of Kittiwake. Brit. Birds 80:633-634.

Coulson, J.C. 1959. The plumage and leg color of the Kittiwake and comments on the non-breeding population. Brit. Birds 52:189-196.

____, C.S. Thomas, J.E.L. Butterfield, N. Duncan, P. Monaghan, and C. Shedden. 1983. The use of head and bill length to sex live gulls Laridae. Ibis 125:549-557.

Coulter, M.C. 1986. Assortative mating and sexual dimorphism in the Common Tern. Wilson Bull. 98:93-100.

____, J.A. Rodgers, J.C. Ogden, and F.C. Depkin. 1999. Wood Stork. Birds N. Am. 409:1-28.

Court, E.J. 1908. Treganza Great Blue Heron. Auk 25:291-296.

Cowan, I.M. 1939. The White-tailed Ptarmigan of Vancouver Island. Condor 41:82-83.

Cox, C., and J. Barry. 2005. Identification, molts, and aging of female-type wigeons. Birding 37:156-164.

Cox, J.B. 1990. Notes on affinities of Cooper's and Cox's sandpipers. S. Australian Ornith. 30:169-181.

____. 1990a. Observations of a Hudsonian Godwit in South America. S. Australian Ornith. 31:48-51.

____. 1990b. The measurements of Cooper's Sandpiper and the occurrence of a similar bird in Australia. S. Australian Ornith. 31:38-43.

Cox, J.B. 1990c. The enigmatic Cooper's and Cox's sandpipers. Dutch Birding 12:53-64.
Craik, J.C.A. 1994. Aspects of wing moult in the Common Tern Sterna hirundo. Ringing & Migr. 15:27-32.
____. 1998. Biometric differences between Common Terns Sterna hirundo and Arctic Terns S. paradisaea. Ringing & Migr. 19:75-78.
____. 1999. Sexual dimorphism of Common Terns Sterna hirundo and Arctic Terns S. paradisaea. Ringing & Migr. 19:311-312.
____ and S.M. Harvey. 1984. Biometrics and colour forms of chicks of Common Terns and Arctic Terns. Ringing & Migr. 5:40-48.
Cramp, S., and K.E.L. Simmons, eds. 1977. The birds of the western Palearctic. Vol. I. Oxford University Press, Oxford, UK. 722 pp.
____ and ____, eds. 1980. The birds of the western Palearctic. Vol. II. Oxford University Press, Oxford, UK. 695 pp.
____ and ____, eds. 1983. The birds of the western Palearctic. Vol. III. Oxford University Press, Oxford, UK. 913 pp.
____ and ____, eds. 1985. The birds of the western Palearctic. Vol. IV. Oxford University Press, Oxford, UK. 960 pp.
Crandall, L.S. 1941. Notes on plumage changes in the Bald Eagle. Zoologica 26:7-8.
Craven, S.R., and R.L. Westemeier. 1979. Probable Canada Goose X White-fronted Goose hybrids. Wilson Bull. 91:628-629.
Crawford, J.A. 1978. Morphology and behavior of Greater X Lesser prairie chicken hybrids. Southwest Nat. 23:591-596.
____, P.J. Cole, and K.M. Kilbride. 1987. Atypical plumage of a female California Quail. California Fish and Game 73:246-247.
Crawford, R.D. 1978. Tarsal color of American Coots in relation to age. Wilson Bull. 90:536-543.
Cistidis, L., K. Davies, and M. Westerman. 1996. Molecular assessment of the taxonomic status of Cox's Sandpiper. Condor 98:459-463.
Crochet, P.-A., J.-D. Lebreton, and F. Bonhomme. 2002. Systematics of large white-headed gulls: patterns of mitochondrial DNA variation in western European taxa. Auk 119:603-620.
Crocoll, S.T. 1994. Red-shouldered Hawk. Birds N. Am. 107:1-20.
Cronau, J.P., R.G.M. de Goede, and E. Nieboer. 1986. A new character for age determination in the Bar-tailed Godwit Limosa lapponica. Ringing & Migr. 7:135-138.
Crossin, R.S. 1974. The storm petrels (Hydrobatidae). Pp. 154-205 in W.B. King, ed., Pelagic studies of seabirds in the central and eastern Pacific Ocean. Smithsonian Contributions in Zoology, Washington, D.C.
Crunden, C.W. 1963. Age and sex of Sage Grouse by wings. J. Wildl. Manage. 27:846-850.
Cullen, J.M. 1957. Plumage, age, and mortality in the Arctic Tern. Bird Study 4:197-207.
Cullen, S.A., J.R. Jehl Jr., and G.L. Nuechterlein. 1999. Eared Grebe. Birds N. Am. 433:1-28.
Curtis, W.F., P.A. Lassey, and D.I.M. Wallace. 1985. Identifying the smaller shearwaters. Brit. Birds. 78:123-138.
Custer, T.W., and W.E. Davis Jr. 1982. Nesting by one-year-old Black-crowned Night Herons on Hope Island, Rhode Island. Auk 99:784-786.
Cuthbert, F.J., and L.R. Wires. 1999. Caspian Tern. Birds N. Am. 403:1-32.
Dalgety, C.T., and P. Scott. 1948. A new race of the White-fronted Goose. Bull. Brit. Ornith. Club 68:109-121.
Dalke, P.D., D.B. Pyrah, D.C. Stanton, J.E. Crawford, and E.F. Schlatterer. 1963. Ecology, productivity, and management of Sage Grouse in Idaho. J. Wildl. Manage. 27:811-841.
Dane, C.W. 1968. Age determination of Blue-winged Teal. J. Wildl. Manage. 32:267-274.
____ and D.H. Johnson. 1975. Age determination of female Redhead ducks. J. Wildl. Manage. 39:256-263.
Danforth, S.T., and J.A. Smythe. 1935. The Puerto Rican form of the Broad-winged Hawk. J. Agric. Univ. Puerto Rico 19:485-486.
Daniels, B.E., L. Hays, D. Hays, J. Morlan, and D. Roberson. 1989. First record of the Common Black-Hawk for California. W. Birds 20:11-18.
David, N. 1988. Hybrid duck, perhaps of Blue-winged Teal X Northern Shoveler. Am. Birds 42:411.
Davies, M. 1978. Identification of hybrid leucistic gulls. Brit. Birds. 71:80-82.
Davis, D.E. 1947. Size of bursa of Fabricius compared with ossification of skull and maturity of gonads. J. Wildl. Manage. 11:241-255.
Davis, J.A. 1968. The postjuvenal wing and tail molt in the Ruffed Grouse (Bonasa umbellus monticola) in Ohio. Ohio J. Sci. 68:305-312.
____. 1969. Ageing and sexing criteria for Ohio Ruffed Grouse. J. Wildl. Manage. 33:628-635.
Davis, J. N. 2007. Color abnormalities in birds: A proposed nomenclature for birders. Birding 39:36-46.
Davis, P. 2005. Identification and natural history of the Red-faced Cormorant. Birding 37:638-648.
Davis, R.A., R.N. Jones, C.D. MacInnes, and A.J. Pakulak. 1985. Molt migration of large Canada Geese on the west coast of Hudson Bay. Wilson Bull. 97:296-305.
Davis, W.E. Jr. 1993. Black-crowned Night-Heron. Birds N. Am. 74:1-20.
____. 1999. Black-crowned and Yellow-crowned night-herons. Birding 31:410-415.
____ and J. Kricher. 2000. Glossy Ibis. Birds N. Am. 545:1-20.
____ and J.A. Kushlan. 1994. Green Heron. Birds N. Am. 129:1-24.
Dawson, J. 1994. [On ageing and sexing King Eiders.] Brit. Birds. 87:37-40.
Day, R.H., and D.A. Nigro. 2004. Is the Kittlitz's Murrelet exhibiting reproductive problems in Prince Williams Sound, Alaska? Waterbirds 27:89-95.
____, A.R. DeGange, G.J. Divoky, and D.M. Troy. 1988. Distribution and subspecies of the Dovekie in Alaska. Condor 90:712-714.
____, K.J. Kuletz, and D.A. Nigro. 1999. Kittlitz's Murrelet. Birds N. Am. 435:1-28.
____, I.J. Stenhouse, and H.G. Gilchrist. 2001. Sabine's Gull. Birds N. Am. 593:1-32.
Dean, A.R. 1989. Distinguishing characters of American/East Asian race of Common Scoter. Brit. Birds. 82:615-616.
Deane, R. 1905. Hybridism between Shoveller and Blue-winged Teal. Auk 22:321.
de Knijff, P., F. Denkers, N.D. van Swelm, and M. Kuiper. 2001. Genetic affinities within the Herring Gull Larus argentatus assemblage revealed by AFLP genotyping. J. Molecular Evol. 52:85-93.
____, P., A. Helbig, and D. Liebers. 2005. Speciation in the Herring Gull complex. Birding 37:402-411.
De Korte, J., and T.J. De Vries. 1978. Moult of primaries and rectrices in the Greater Frigatebird, Fregata minor, on Genovesa, Galapagos. Bjdragon tot Dierkunde 48:81-88.
Delacour, J. 1951. Preliminary note on the taxonomy of Canada Geese, Branta canadensis. Am. Mus. Novit. 1537:1-10.
____. 1954. The waterfowl of the world. Vol. I. Country Life Limited, London, UK. 284 pp.
____. 1956. The waterfowl of the world. Vol. II. Country Life Limited, London, UK. 232 pp.
____. 1959. The waterfowl of the world. Vol. III. Country Life Limited, London, UK. 270 pp.
____. 1964. The waterfowl of the world. Vol. III. Country Life Limited, London, UK. 364 pp.
____. 1977. The pheasants of the world. 2nd Ed. Saiga Publishing Company, Surrey, U.K. 395 pp.
____ and D. Amadon. 1973. Currasows and related birds. American Museum of Natural History and Chanticleer Press, Inc., New York, NY. 247 pp.
____ and E. Mayr. 1945. The family Anatidae. Wilson Bull. 57:3-55.
____ and ____. 1946. Supplementary notes on the family Anatidae. Wilson Bull. 58:104-110.
____ and S.D. Ripley. 1975. Description of a new subspecies of the White-fronted Goose Anser albifrons. Am. Mus. Novit. 2565:1-4.
____ and J.T. Zimmer. 1952. The identity of Anser nigricans Lawrence 1846. Auk 69:82-84.
Delehanty, D.J., and N.C. Turek. 2003. Using wing plumage to determine age of Mountain Quail. N. Am. Bird Bander 28:116-120.
____, R.A. Tybie, M.J. Ditsworth, G.A. Hoelzer, L.W. Oring, and J.L. Longmire. 1995. Genetic and morphological methods for gender identification of Mountain Quail. J. Wildl. Manage. 59:785-789.
Delnicki, D. 1974. Ross' Goose-Snow Goose hybrid in south Texas. Auk 91:174.
Dement'ev, G.P., and N.A. Gladkov, eds. 1951a. Birds of the Soviet Union. Vol. II. Gosudarstvennoe Izdatel'stvo "Sovetskaya Nauka", Moscow. [Isreal Program for Scientific Translations, 1968; 704 pp.]
____ and ____, eds. 1951b. Birds of the Soviet Union. Vol. I. Gosudarstvennoe Izdatel'stvo "Sovetskaya Nauka", Moscow. [Isreal Program for Scientific Translations, 1968; 553 pp.]
____ and ____, eds. 1951c. Birds of the Soviet Union. Vol. III. Gosudarstvennoe Izdatel'stvo "Sovetskaya Nauka", Moscow. [Isreal Program for Scientific Translations, 1969; 756 pp.]
____ and ____, eds. 1952. Birds of the Soviet Union. Vol. IV. Gosudarstvennoe Izdatel'stvo "Sovetskaya Nauka", Moscow. [Isreal Program for Scientific Translations, 1969; 683 pp.]
Dennis, R.H. 1973. Possible interbreeding of Slavonian Grebe and Black-necked Grebe. Scottish Birds 7:307-308.
De Santo, T.L., S.G. McDowell, and K.L. Bildstein. 1990. Plumage and behavioral development of nestling White Ibises. Wilson Bull. 102:226-238.
Deuel, B. 2004. Preliminary notes on the identification of Cackling and Canada geese. W. Birds 35:181-183.
Devillers, P. 1972. The juvenal plumage of Kittlitz's Murrelet. California Birds 3:33-38.

Devillers, P. 1977. The skuas of the North American Pacific coast. Auk 94:417-429.
Devlin, C.M., A.W. Diamond, and G.W. Saunders. 2004. Sexing Arctic Terns in the field and laboratory. Waterbirds 27:314-320.
de Wijs, W.J.R. 1985. Reliability of ageing Razorbills. Seabird 8:58.
Diamond, A.W. 1972. Sexual dimorphism in breeding cycles and unequal sex ratio in Magnificent Frigate-birds. Ibis 114:395-398.
____. 1974. The Red-footed Booby on Aldabra Atoll, Indian Ocean. Ardea 62:196-218.
____. 1975. The biology of tropicbirds at Aldabra Atoll, Indian Ocean. Auk 92:16-39.
____. 1976. Subannual breeding and moult cycles in the Bridled Tern Sterna anaethetus in the Seychelles. Ibis 118:414-419.
____ and P.R. Prŷs-Jones. 1986. The biology of terns at Aldabra Atoll, Indian Ocean, with particular reference to breeding seasonality. J. Zool. London 210:527-549.
____ and E.A. Schreiber. 2002. Magnificent Frigatebird. Birds N. Am. 601:1-24.
Dick, W.J.A., M.W. Pienkowski, M. Waltner, and C.D.T. Minton. 1976. Distribution and geographical origins of Knot Calidris canutus breeding in Europe and Africa. Ardea 64:22-47.
Dickson, K.M. 2000. The diversity of Canada Geese. Canadian Wild. Serv. Occ. Papers 103:11-24.
Dickerman, R.W. 1963. The grebe Aechmophorus occidentalis clarkii as a nesting bird of the Mexican Plateau. Condor 65:66-67.
____. 1966. A new subspecies of Virginia Rail from Mexico. Condor 68:215-216.
____. 1971. Notes on various rails in Mexico. Wilson Bull. 83:49-56.
____. 1973a. Further notes on the Western Grebe in Mexico. Condor 75:131-132.
____. 1973b. The Least Bittern in Mexico and Central America. Auk 90:689-691.
____. 1986. Two hitherto unnamed populations of Aechmophorus (Aves: Podicipitidae). Proc. Biol. Soc. Washington 99:435-436.
____. 1989. Identification of Red-tailed Hawks wintering in Kansas. Kansas Ornith. Bull. 40:33-34.
____. 1994. Undescribed subspecies of Red-tailed Hawk from Baja California. Southwestern Nat. 39:375-395.
____. 2004a. A review of the North American subspecies of the Great Blue Heron (Ardea herodias). Proc. Biol. Soc. Washington 117:242-250.
____. 2004b. Characteristics and distribution of Ardea herodias fannini with comments on the effects of washing on the holotype. Northwestern Nat. 85:130-133.
____. 2004c. A review of the literature of Accipiter striatus perobscurus, with a report of specimens from California, Colorado, and New Mexico. W. Birds 35:108-113.
____ and J. Gustafson. 1996. The Prince of Wales Spruce Grouse: A new subspecies from southeastern Alaska. W. Birds 27:41-47.
____ and J.P. Hubbard. 1994. An extinct subspecies of Sharp-tailed Grouse from New Mexico. W. Birds 25:128-136.
____ and K.C. Parkes. 1968. Notes on the plumages and generic status of the Little Blue Heron. Auk 85:437-440.
____ and ____. 1987. Subspecies of the Red-tailed Hawk in the Northeast. Kingbird 37:57-64.
Dickey, D.R. 1923. Description of a new Clapper Rail from the Colorado River Valley. Auk 40:90-94.
____. 1928. A race of Virginia Rail from the Pacific coast.Condor 30:322.
____ and A.J. van Rossem. 1922. The validity of the Catalina Island quail. Condor 24:34.
____ and ____. 1923a. The Fulvous Tree-Ducks of Buena Vista Lake. Condor 25:39-50.
____ and ____. 1923b. Description of a new grouse from southern California. Condor 25:168-169.
____ and ____. 1924a. A new race of the Least Bittern from the Pacific coast. Bull. S. California Acad. Sci. 23:11-12.
____ and ____. 1924b. The status of the Florida Gallinule in North America. Condor 26:93.
____ and ____. 1925. A revisionary study of the Western Gull. Condor 27:162-164.
____ and ____. 1938. The birds of El Salvador. Zool. Ser. Field Mus. Nat. Hist. 23:1-609.
Dickinson, J.C. Jr. 1953. Report on the McCabe collection of British Colombian birds. Bull. Mus. Comp. Zool. 109:123-210.
Dies, J.I., and B. Dies. 1998. Hybridization between Lesser Crested and Sandwich terns in Valencia, Spain, and plumages of offspring. Brit. Birds 91:165-170.
Dieter, M.P. 1973. Sex determination of eagles, owls, and herons by analyzing plasma steroid hormones. U.S. Fish and Wildlife Service Special Report 167:1-13.
Di Labio, B.M., and M. Gosselin. 1994. A probable Wood Duck X Ring-necked Duck hybrid in Ontario. Ontario Birds 12:119-122.
Di Labio, B.M. and R. Pittaway. 1997. Bill color of adult female Barrow's Goldeneye. Birding 19(3):21-22.
____, R. Pittaway, and P. Burke. 1997. Bill colour and identification of female Barrow's Goldeneye. Ontario Birds 15:81-85.
Dimmick, R.W., and M.R. Pelton. 1996. Criteria of sex and age. Pp. 169-214 in T.A. Bookhout, ed., Research and management techniques for wildlife and habitats. The Wildlife Society, Bethesda, MD.
Dinsmore, J.J., and R.W. Schreiber. 1974. Breeding and annual cycle of Laughing Gulls in Tampa Bay, Florida. Wilson Bull. 86:419-427.
Dittberner, H., and W. Dittberner. 1992. Misgelege von Blessralle, Fulica atra, und Rothalstaucher, Podiceps grisegena. Falke 39:392.
Dittman, D.L., and S.W. Cardiff. 1998. Kelp Gull X Herring Gull hybrids: a new saga in gull ID problems. Louisiana Ornith. Soc. News 181:5-7.
____ and ____. 2005. Kelp X Herring gull hybrids: The "Chandeleur" Gull. Birding 37:266-276.
Dixon, J. 1927. The Surf-bird's secret. Condor 29:3-16.
Dolbeer, R.A., and G.E. Bernhardt. 2003. Age-specific reproduction by female Laughing Gulls (Larus atricilla). Auk 120:531-535.
Domm, E.V. 1939. Modifications in sex and secondary sexual characteristics in birds. Pp. 227-327 in E. Allen, ed., Sex and internal secretions: A survey of recent research. Williams and Wilkins, Baltimore, MD.
Donahue, P. 1987. Three subspecies of Merlin. Am. Birds 41:368-369.
Donaldson, G. 1968. Bill color changes in adult Roseate Terns. Auk 85:662-668.
Dorney, R.S. 1966. A new method for sexing Ruffed Grouse in late summer. J. Wildl. Manage. 30:623-625.
____ and F.V. Holzer. 1957. Spring aging methods for Ruffed Grouse cocks. J. Wildl. Manage. 21:268-274.
Dorward, D.F. 1962. Comparative biology of the White Booby and the Brown Booby Sula spp. at Ascension Island. Ibis 103b:174-220.
____ and N.P. Ashmole. 1963. Notes on the biology of the Brown Noddy Anous stolidus on Ascension Island. Ibis 103b:447-457.
Douglas, H., and K. Sowl. 1993. Northeastern extension of the breeding range of the Arctic Loon in northwestern Alaska. W. Birds 24:98-100.
Dove, C.J., and R.C. Banks. 1999. A taxonomic study of Crested Caracaras (Falconidae). Wilson Bull. 111:330-339.
Drewien, R.C., and S.H. Bouffard. 1994. Winter body mass and measurements of Trumpeter Swans Cygnus buccinator. Wildfowl 45:22-32.
Drilling, N., R. Titman, and F. McKinney. 2002. Mallard. Birds N. Am. 658:1-44.
Drost, C.A., and D.B. Lewis. 1995. Xantus' Murrelet. Birds N. Am. 164:1-24.
Drury, W.H. Jr., A.H. Morgan, and R. Stackpole. 1953. Occurrence of an African Cattle Egret (Ardeola ibis ibis) in Massachusetts. Auk 70:364-365.
DuBowy, P.J. 1985. Moults and plumages and testicular regression of post-breeding male Blue-winged Teal (Anas discors) and Northern Shovelers (Anas clypeata). J. Zool. London (A) 207:459-466.
____. 1996. Northern Shoveler. Birds N. Am. 217:1-24.
Dugger, B.D., and K.M. Dugger. 2002. Long-billed Curlew. Birds N. Am. 628:1-28.
____, ____, and L.H. Fredrickson. 1994. Hooded Merganser. Birds N. Am. 98:1-24.
Dumas, J.V. 2000. Roseate Spoonbill. Birds N. Am. 490:1-32.
Du Mont, P.A. 1933. A mensural study of a collection of Grus canadensis from Iowa and Nebraska. Wilson Bull. 45:13-15.
Duncan, D.C. 1985. Differentiating yearling from adult Northern Pintails by wing-feather characteristics. J. Wildl. Manage. 49:576-579.
Dunk, J.R. 1995. White-tailed Kite. Birds N. Am. 178:1-16.
Dunlop, J.N. 1987. Moult and breeding in the Common Noddy Anous stolidus on Christmas Island, Indian Ocean. Corella 11:15-19.
Dunn, E.H., and D.J. Argo. 1995. Black Tern. Birds N. Am. 147:1-24.
Dunn, J. 1988. Tenth report of the California Bird Records Committee. W. Birds 19:129-163.
____. 1993. The identification of Semipalmated and Common Ringed Plovers in alternate plumage. Birding 25:238-243.
____. 1999. Some additional thoughts on dowitchers. Ohio Cardinal 23:30-33.
____ and J. Alderfer. 2007. Wilson's and Common snipes. W. Birds 38:153-156.
____, J. Morlan, and C.P. Wilds. 1987. Field identification of forms of Lesser Golden Plover. Pp 28-33 in Proc. 4th Int. Identification Meeting, Eilat, Isreal.
Dunne, P., D. Sibley, and C. Sutton. 1988. Hawks in flight. Houghton Mifflin Co., Boston, MA. 254 pp.
____, ____, and ____. 2000. Zone-tailed Hawk. Birding 32:234-241.
Dunnet, G.M., and A. Anderson. 1961. A method for sexing live Fulmars in the hand. Bird Study 8:119-126.
Dunning, J.B. Jr. 1993. CRC handbook of avian body masses. CRC Press, Boca Raton, FL. 371 pp.

Duvall, A.J. 1955. The juvenal plumage of the American Woodcock. U.S. Fish Wildl. Serv. Spec. Sci. Rep. 31:43-46.
Dwight, J. Jr. 1900a. The moult of the North American Tetraonidae (quails, partridges and grouse). Auk 17:34-51, 143-166.
____. 1900b. The moult of the North American shore birds (Limicolae). Auk 17:368-385.
____. 1901. The sequence of molts and plumages in the Laridae (gulls and terns). Auk 18:49-63.
____. 1902. Plumage-cycles and the relation between plumages and moults. Auk 19:248-255.
____. 1906. Status and plumages of white-winged gulls of the genus Larus. Auk 23:26-43.
____. 1907. Sequence in molts and plumages with an explanation of plumage cycles. Proc. IV Int. Ornith. Congr. 1905:513-518.
____. 1909. The singular case of the Black Duck of North America. Auk 26:422-423.
____. 1914. The moults and plumages of the scoters,-- genus Oidemia. Auk 31:293-308.
____. 1917. The status of "Larus thayeri, Thayer's Gull." Auk 34:413-414.
____. 1918. A new species of loon (Gavia viridigularis) from northeastern Siberia. Auk 35:196-199.
____. 1919. Reasons for discarding a proposed race of the Glaucous Gull (Larus hyperboreus). Auk 36:242-248.
____. 1925. The gulls (Laridae) of the world: their plumages, moults, variations, relationships, and distribution. Bull. Am. Mus. Nat. Hist. 52:63-402.
____. 1927. The "new" Bermuda shearwater proves to be Puffinus puffinus puffinus. Auk 44:243.
Dwyer, T.J., and J.V. Dobell. 1979. External determination of age of Common Snipe. J. Wildl. Manage. 43:754-756.
Dzubin, A. 1959. Growth and plumage development of wild-trapped juvenile Canvasback (Aythya valisineria). J. Wildl. Manage. 23:279-290.
____. 1964. Two possible wild hybrids of the White-fronted Goose X Snow Goose. Blue Jay 22:106-108.
____. 1965. A study of migrating Ross Geese in western Saskatchewan. Condor 67:511-534.
____ and E. Cooch. 1992. Measurements of geese: General field methods. California Waterfowl Association, Sacramento, CA. 20 pp.
Eadie, J.M., M.L. Mallory, and H.G. Lumsden. 1995. Common Goldeneye. Birds N. Am. 170:1-32.
____, J.-P.L. Savard, and M.L. Mallory. 2000. Barrow's Goldeneye. Birds N. Am. 548:1-32.
Earnheart-Gold, S., and P. Pyle. 2001. Occurrence patterns of Peregrine Falcons on Southeast Farallon Island, California, by subspecies, age, and sex. W. Birds 32:119-126.
Earnst, S.L. 1992. The timing of wing molt in Tundra Swans: Energetic and non-energetic constraints. Condor 94:847-856.
Eaton, S.W. 1970. Primary molt in adult male Meleagris gallopavo silvestris. Auk 87:794.
____. 1992. Wild Turkey. Birds N. Am. 22:1-28.
Ebels, E.B. 1997. Identification of Brent Geese: A new feature? Dutch Birding 19:232-236.
Eckert, K.R. 1970. Winter record of a Canada X White-fronted goose hybrid (?). Loon 42:34-35.
____. 1982. Field identification of the Ferruginous Hawk. Loon 54:161-164.
____. 1989. Identification and status of the Clark's Grebe in Minnesota. Loon 61:99-106.
____. 1993. Identification of Western and Clark's grebes. Birding 25:304-310.
____. 1995. Western and Clark's grebes: Further notes on identification. Birding 27:54-55.
Eddleman, W.R., and C.J. Conway. 1998. Clapper Rail. Birds N. Am. 340:1-32.
____ and F.L. Knopf. 1985. Determining age and sex of American Coots. J. Field Ornith. 56:41-55.
____, R.E. Flores, and M.L. Legare. 1994. Black Rail. Birds N. Am. 123:1-20.
Edelstam, C. 1984. Patterns of moult in large birds of prey. Ann. Zool. Fennici 21:271-276.
Edscorn, J.B. 1974. Florida region. Am. Birds 28:40-44.
Edwards, A.E. 2008. Large-scale variation in flight feather molt as a mechanism enabling biennial breeding in albatrosses. J. Avian Biol. 39:144-151.
____ and S. Rohwer. 2005. Large-scale patterns of molt activation in the flight feathers of two albatross species. Condor 107:835-848.
Edwards, T.C., and M.N. Kochert. 1986. Use of body weight and length of footpad as predictors of sex in Golden Eagles. J. Field Ornith. 57:317-319.
Eichhorst, B.A., and B.D. Parkin. 1991. Clark's Grebes and suspected Western X Clark's grebe hybrids in Manitoba. Blue Jay 49:196-200.
Eifrig, G. 1928. On the status of Harlan's Hawk. Wilson Bull. 40:216-218.
Eigenhuis, K.J. 1984. Presumed hybrids of Great White Egret X Gray Heron in Flevoland in 1981-83. Dutch Birding 6:93-94.
____. 1985. [Scaup Aythya marila, Lesser Scaup Aythya affinis, Scaup type, and Lesser Scaup type.] Wielwaal 51:135-137.
____. 1987. Moult and identification of South Polar Skua. Dutch Birding 9:124-125.
Eisenmann, E. 1963. Mississippi Kite in Argentina; with comments on migration and plumages in the genus Ictinia. Auk 80:74-77.
____ and D.L. Serventy. 1962. An erroneous Panama record of Puffinus tenuirostris and other misidentifications of P. griseus. Emu 62:199-201.
Eitniear, J.C. 1999. Masked Duck. Birds N. Am. 393:1-12.
Elder, W.H. 1946. Age and sex criteria and weights of Canada Geese. J. Wildl. Manage. 10:93-111.
Elgas, B. 1970. Breeding populations of Tule White-fronted Geese in Northwestern Canada. Wilson Bull. 82:420-426.
Ellegren, H., and B. Sheldon. 1997. New tools for sex identification and the study of sex allocation in birds. Trends Ecol. Evol. 12:255-259.
Elliot, D.G. 1892. Hybridism, and a description of a hybrid between Anas boschas and Anas americana. Auk 9:160-166.
Ellis, D.H. 2004. Mottling in the plumage of juvenile Golden Eagles. N. Am. Bird Bander 29:53-58.
____ and M. Kéry. 2004. Variable retention times for rectrices at different loci in a Golden Eagle. J. Raptor Res. 38:270-275.
____ and J.W. Lish. 2006. Thinking about feathers: Adaptations of Golden Eagle rectrices. J. Raptor Res. 40:1-28.
Ellis, P. 1994. Ageing and sexing King Eiders. Brit. Birds. 87:36-37.
Ellison, L.N. 1968. Sexing and aging Alaskan Spruce Grouse by plumage. J. Wildl. Manage. 32:12-16.
Elphick, C.S., and J. Klima. 2002. Hudsonian Godwit. Birds N. Am. 629:1-32.
____ and T.L. Tibbitts. 1998. Greater Yellowlegs. Birds N. Am. 355:1-24.
Ely, C.R., and A.X. Dzubin. 1994. Greater White-fronted Goose. Birds N. Am. 131:1-32.
____, et al. 2005. Circumpolar variation in morphological characteristics of Greater White-fronted Geese Anser albifrons Bird Study 52:104-119.
Emerson, O. 1906. Oceanodroma leucorhoa and its relatives on the Pacific coast. Condor 8:53-55.
Emslie, S.D., R.P. Henderson, and D.G. Ainley. 1990. Annual variation of primary molt with age and sex in Cassin's Auklet. Auk 107:689-695.
Enderson, J.H. 1964. A study of the Prairie Falcon in the central Rocky Mountain region. Auk 81:332-352.
____, S.A. Temple, and L.G. Swartz. 1973. Time-lapse photographic records of nesting Peregrine Falcons. Living Bird 11:113-128.
Endler, J.A. 1990. On the measurement and classification of color in studies of animal color patterns. Biol. J. Linnean Soc. 41:315-352.
Eng, R.L. 1955. A method of obtaining Sage Grouse age and sex ratios from wings. J. Wildl. Manage. 19:267-272.
____. 1971. Two hybrid Sage Grouse X Sharp-tailed Grouse from central Montana. Wilson Bull. 83:491-493.
Engelmoer, M., and C.S. Roselaar. 1998. Geographical variation in waders. Kluwer Academic Publishers, Boston, MA. 331 pp.
____, ____, E. Nieboer, and G.C. Boere. 1987. Biometrics in waders. Wader Study Group Bull. 51:44-47.
Engilis, A., K.J. Uyehara, and J.G. Giffin. 2002. Hawaiian Duck. Birds N. Am. 694:1-20.
England, A.S., M.J. Bechard, and C.S. Houston. 1997. Swainson's Hawk. Birds N. Am. 265:1-28.
Enright, L. 1994. Ecological significance of the white and grey colour morphs of Mute Swan. Ontario Birds 12:19-26.
Erard, C., J.J. Guillou, and N. Mayaud. 1984. Sur l'identité spécifique de certains laridés nicheurs au Sénégal. Alauda 52:184-188.
Erickson, J.G. 1952. A possible hybrid between the Hooded Merganser and the Red-breasted Merganser. Wilson Bull. 64:167.
Erickson, R.A., and R.A. Hamilton. 2001. Report of the California Bird Records Committee: 1998 records. W. Birds 32:13-49.
____, ____, S.N.G. Howell, P. Pyle, and M.A. Patten. 1995. First record of the Marbled Murrelet and third record of the Ancient Murrelet for Mexico. W. Birds 26:39-45.
Erskine, A.J. 1971. Growth and annual cycles in weights, plumages, and reproductive organs of Goosanders in eastern Canada. Ibis 113:42-58.
____. 1972. Buffleheads. Can. Wild. Serv. Monogr. Ser. 4:1-240.
Escalante, R. 1968. Notes on the Royal Tern in Uruguay. Condor 70:243-247.
____. Notes on the Cayenne Tern in Uruguay. Condor 72:89-94.
____. 1985. Taxonomy and conservation of austral-breeding Royal Terns. Ornith. Monogr. 36:935-942.
Eskelin, T., and J. Pursiainen. 1998. The status of 'Lesser Black-backed Gulls' of hueglini, graellsii, and intermedius type in Finland. Alula 42:42-54.
Esler, D., and J.B. Grand. 1994. Comparison of age determination techniques for female Northern Pintail and American Wigeon in spring. Wildl. Soc. Bull. 22:260-264.

Espie, R.H.M., P.C. James, I.G. Warkentin, and L.W. Oliphant. 1996. Ecological correlates of molt in Merlins. Auk 113:363-369.

Etter, S.L., J.E. Warnock, ANd G.B. Joselyn. 1970. Modified wing molt criteria for estimating the ages of wild juvenile Pheasants. J. Wildl. Manage. 34:620-626.

Evanich, J. 1989. Identification and status of fulva and dominica golden plovers. Oregon Birds 15:91-95.

Evans, D.R., E.M. Hopes, and C.R. Griffin. 1993. Discriminating the sex of Laughing Gulls by linear measurements. J. Field Ornith. 64:472-476.

____, P.M. Cavanagh, T.W. French, and B.G. Blodget. 1995. Identifying the sex of Massachusetts Herring Gulls by linear measurements. J. Field Ornith. 66:128-132.

Evans, K. 1966. Observations on a hybrid between the Sharp-tailed Grouse and the Greater Prairie Chicken. Auk 83:128-129.

Evans, M.E., and J. Kear. 1978. Weights and measurements of Bewick's Swan during winter. Wildfowl 29:118-122.

____ and W.J.L. Sladen. 1980. A comparative analysis of the bill markings of Whistling and Bewick's swans and out-of-range occurrences of the two taxa. Auk 97:697-703.

Evans, P.R. 1964. Wader measurements and wader migration. Bird Study 11:23-38.

Evans, R.M., and F.L. Knopf. 1993. American White Pelican. Birds N. Am. 57:1-24.

Evered, D.S. 1985. Pacific (and Arctic) Loon identification. Difficulty, unfamiliarity, and a little bit of confusion. Bird Observer 13:10-14.

Everett, W.T. 1988. Biology of the Black-vented Shearwater. W. Birds 19:89-104.

Ewins, P.J. 1988. The timing of moult in Black Guillemots Cepphus grylle in Shetland. Ringing & Migr. 9:5-10.

____. 1993. Pigeon Guillemot. Birds N. Am. 49:1-24.

____. 1995. Banding, movements and adult biometrics of Ontario Ospreys. Ontario Birds 13:4-10.

____ and Weseloh, D.V. 1999. Little Gull. Birds N. Am. 428:1-20.

Faber, M., J. Betleja, R. Gwiazda, and P. Malczyk. 2001. Mixed colonies of large white-headed gulls in southern Poland. Brit. Birds 94:529-534.

Fall, B.A. 1995. Immature Plegadis ibises at Thielke Lake. Loon 67:123-129.

Falla, R.A. 1933. Notes on New Zealand petrels. Rec. Aukland Inst. Mus. 1:173-180.

____. 1942. Review of the smaller Pacific forms of Pterodroma and Cookilaria. Emu 42:111-118.

Fallon, J.A., R.L. Cochrane, B. Dorr, and H. Kladorf. 2006. Interspecies comparison of pentosidine accumulation and its correlation with age in birds. Auk 123:870-876.

Farquhar, C.C. 1992. White-tailed Hawk. Birds N. Am. 30:1-20.

Farrand, J. Jr. 1990. The red-legged Black Duck. Am. Birds 44:202-203.

Fasola, M., Y. Zhang, D. Zhao, Y. Dong, and H. Wang. 2001. Age-assortative mating related to reproductive success in Black-crowned Night Herons. Waterbirds 4:272-276.

Faulkner, D. 2005. Hybridization and nesting of Glossy Ibis (Plegadis falcinellus) in Wyoming. N. Am. Birds 59:382-384.

Fedynich, A.M. 1995. Mallard-like ducks in the Laya Lakes region. Wilson Bull. 107:548-551.

____ and O.E. Rhodes Jr. 1993. Mallard X American Wigeon hybrid on the southern high plains of Texas. Southwestern Nat. 38:179-181.

Feinstein, B. 1959. Geographic variation in the Whiskered Auklet. Auk 76:60-67.

Fenoglio, S., M. Cucco, and G. Malacarne. 2002. Bill colour and body size in the Moorhen Gallinula chloropus. Bird Study 49:89-92.

Fernández, G., and D.B. Lank. 2006. Sex, age, and body size distributions of Western Sandpipers during the nonbreeding season with respect to local habitat. Condor 108:547-557.

____ and ____. 2007. Variation in the wing morphology of Western Sandpipers (Calidris mauri) in relation to sex, age class, and annual cycle. Auk 124:1037-1046.

____, P.D. O'Hara, and D.B. Lank. 2004. Tropical and subtropical Western Sandpipers (Calidris mauri) differ in life history strategies. Ornit. Neotropical 15(Suppl.):385-394.

Ferns, P.N. 1978a. The onset of prebasic body moult during the breeding season in some high-Arctic waders. Bull. Brit. Ornith. Club. 98:118-122.

____. 1978b. Individual differences in the head and neck plumage of Ruddy Turnstones (Arenaria interpres) during the breeding season. Auk 95:749-755.

Fiala, K.L. 1979. A laparotomy technique for nestling birds. Bird-Banding 50:366-367.

Field, M.H. 1965. Ageing and sexing of Blue-winged Teal in early fall. Ontario Bird Banding 1:31-32.

Figgins, J.D. 1914. The fallacy of the tendency towards ultra-minute distinctions. Auk 31:62-69.

____. 1920. The status of the subspecific races of Branta canadensis. Auk 37:94-102.

Figgins, J.D. 1922. Additional notes on the status of the subspecific races of Branta canadensis. Proc. Colorado Mus. Nat. Hist. 4(3):1-19.

____. 1926. That collection of geese from the San Joaquin Valley, California. Proc. Colorado Mus. Nat. Hist. 6:32-40.

Figuerola, J., and A. Bertolero. 1995. The primary moult of Curlew Sandpiper in the Ebro Delta, north-east Spain. Ringing & Migr. 16:168-171.

Filardi, C.E., and S. Rohwer. 2001. Life history implications of complete and incomplete primary molts in Pelagic Cormorants. Condor 103:555-569.

Finley, W.L. 1910. Life history of the California Condor. Part IV - the young condor in captivity. Condor 12:5-11.

Firsova, L.V., and A.V. Levada. 1982. [Ornithological finds at the south of Koriak Plateau.] Ornithologia 17:112-118.

Fisher, A., and B. Flood. 2004. A Scopoli's Shearwater off the Isles of Scilly. Birding World 17:334-336.

Fisher, A.K., and A. Wetmore. 1931. Report on birds received by the Pinchot Expedition of 1929 to the Caribbean and Pacific. Proc. U.S. Nat. Mus. 79(Art. 10):1-66.

Fisher, H.I. 1972. Sympatry of Laysan and Black-footed albatrosses. Auk 89:381-402.

Fisher, J. 1952. The Fulmar. Collins, London, UK. 496 pp.

Fitch, H.S. 1963. Observations on the Mississippi Kite in southwestern Kansas. Univ. Kansas Mus. Nat. Hist. Publ. 12:503-519.

Fitch, W.T., and J.P. Kelley. 2000. Perception of vocal tract resonances by Whooping Cranes Grus americana. Ethology 106:559-574.

Fitzpatrick, B.M., and J.R. Dunk. 1999. Ecogeographic variation in morphology of Red-tailed Hawks in western North America. J. Raptor Res. 33:305-312.

Fix, D. 1985. Notes on scaup identification. Oregon Birds 11:146-151.

Fjeldså, J. 1973a. Distribution and geographic variation of the Horned Grebe Podiceps auritus (Linnaeus 1758). Ornis Scand. 4:55-86.

____. 1973b. Possible female hybrids between Bucephala islandica and clangula. Bull. Brit. Ornith. Club 93:6-9.

____. 1980. Post-mortem changes in measurements of grebes. Bull. Brit. Ornith. Club 100:151-154.

____. 1982. The adaptive significance of local variations in the bill and jaw anatomy of North European Red-necked Grebes Podiceps grisegena. Ornis Fennica 59:84-98.

____. 1983. Systematic and biological notes on the Colombian Coot Fulica columbiana americana (Aves, Rallidae). Steenstrupia 8:1-21.

____. 1986. Color variation in the Ruddy Duck (Oxyura jamaicensis andina). Wilson Bull. 98:592-594.

____. 1990. Systematic relations of an assembly of allopatric rails from western South America (Aves: Rallidae). Steenstrupia 16:109-116.

____. 2004. The Grebes Podicipedidae. Oxford University Press, Oxford, U.K. 246 pp.

Flann, I, 2003. Gyrfalcon color variation. J. Raptor Res. 37:173-174.

Fleet, R.R. 1974. The Red-tailed Tropicbird on Kure Atoll. Ornith. Monogr. 16:1-64.

Fleming, C.A. 1941. Notes on Neozelanic forms of the subgenus Cookilaria. Emu 41:69-80.

____. 1973. Hybrid oystercatcher reported in Argentina. Notornis 20:382-383.

Fletcher, K.L. 1981. Surgical sexing of birds of prey. Am. Assoc. Zool. Parks Aquariums Reg. Conf. 1981:432-437.

____ and K.C. Hamer. 2003. Sexing terns using biometrics: The advantage of within-pair comparisons. Bird Study 50:78-83.

Flickinger, E.L. 1975. Incubation by a male Fulvous Whistling-Duck. Wilson Bull. 87:106-107.

Flint, V.E., and A.N. Golovkin. 1990. Birds of the U.S.S.R.: Auks murres and puffins. Nauka, Russia. [Translation, Canadian Wildlife Service, Ottawa; 203 pp.]

Flood, R.L., and B. Thomas. 2007. Identification of 'black-and-white' storm-petrels of the North Atlantic. Brit. Birds 100:407-432.

Flores, R.E., and W.R. Eddleman. 1993. Nesting biology of the California Black Rail in southwestern Arizona. W. Birds 24:81-88.

Flower, G. 1983. Hybrid Coot X Moorhen in North Yorkshire. Brit. Birds. 76:409-410.

Folk, M.J., S.A. Nesbitt, J.M. Parker, M.G. Spalding, S.B. Baynes, and K.L. Candelora. In press. Feather molt of non-migratory Whooping Cranes (Grus americana) in Florida. Proc. N. Am. Crane Workshop 10.

Forbes, H.O. 1914. Notes on Molina's Pelican (Pelecanus thagus). Ibis (10th Ser.) 2:403-420.

Forest, B.S. 1982. Ageing the Red-necked Stint in the hand. Stilt 2:29-30.

Forsman, D. 1995. A presumed hybrid Steller's Eider X Common Eider in Norway. Birding World 8:138.

____. 1999. The raptors of Europe and the Middle East. T & AD Poyser, London, UK. 589 pp.

Forsythe, D. 1980. Cory's Shearwater off the South Carolina coast. Wilson Bull. 92:265-266.

Fox, A.D., H. Boyd, and R.G. Bromley. 1995. Mutual benefits of associations between breeding and non-breeding White-fronted Geese, Anser albifrons. Ibis 137:151-156.

____, R. King, and J. Watkin. 1992. Seasonal variation in weight, body measurements and condition of free-living Teal. Bird Study 39:53-62.

____, P. Hartmann, and I.K. Petersen. 2008. Changes in body mass and organ size during remigial moult in Common Scoter Melanitta nigra J. Avian Biol. 39:35-40.

Fox, D.L. 1975. Carotenoids in pigmentation. Pp. 162-182 in J. Kear and N. Duplaix-Hall, eds., Flamingos. T & AD Poyser, Hertfordshire, UK.

Fox, G.A. 1964. Notes on the western race of the Pigeon Hawk. Blue Jay 22:140-147.

____, C.R. Cooper, and J.P. Ryder. 1981. Predicting the sex of Herring Gulls by using external measurements. J. Field Ornith. 52:1-9.

Fox, N.C., and E. Patapov. 2001. Altai Falcon: subspecies, hybrid, or colour morph. P. 6 in Abstracts 4th Eurasian Conference on Raptors, Sevilla, Spain.

Foxhall, R.A. 1979. Presumed hybrids of the Herring Gull and Great Black-backed Gull. Am. Birds 33:838.

Frederick, P.C. 1997. Tricolored Heron. Birds N. Am. 306:1-28.

____ and D. Siegel-Causey. 2000. Anhinga. Birds N. Am. 522:1-24.

Fredrickson, L.H. 1968. Measurements of coots related to sex and age. J. Wildl. Manage. 32:409-411.

____. 2001. Steller's Eider. Birds N. Am. 571:1-24.

Freeman, M.M.R. 1970. Observations on the seasonal behaviour of the Hudson Bay Eider (S.m. sedentarius). Can. Field-Nat. 84:145-153.

Friedmann, H. 1933a. Critical notes on American vultures. Proc. Biol. Soc. Washington 46:187-190.

____. 1933b. The Cuban race of the Snail Kite Rostrhamus sociabilis (Vieillot). Proc. Biol. Soc. Washington 46:199-200.

____. 1934a. The hawks of the genus Chondrohierax. J. Washington Acad. Sci. 24:310-318.

____. 1934b. The Siberian Rough-legged Hawk in Alaska. Condor 36:246.

____. 1943a. A new race of the Sharp-tailed Grouse. J. Washington Acad. Sci. 33:189-191.

____. 1943b. Critical notes on the avian genus Lophortyx. J. Washington Acad. Sci. 33:369-371.

____. 1947. Geographic variation of the Black-bellied, Fulvous, and White-faced tree-ducks. Condor 49:189-195.

____. 1948. The Green-winged Teal of the Aleutian Islands. Proc. Biol. Soc. Washington 61:157-158.

____. 1950. The birds of North and Middle America. Part IX. U.S. Nat. Mus. Bull. 50(11):1-793.

Friesen, V.L., R.T. Barrett, W.A. Montevecchi, and W.S. Davidson. 1993. Molecular evidence of a backcross between a female Common Murre X Thick-billed Murre hybrid and a male Common Murre. Can. J. Zool. 71:1474-1477.

____, J.F. Piatt, and A.J. Baker. 1996. Evidence from cytochrome B sequences and allozymes for a "new" species of alcid: The Long-billed Murrelet (Brachyramphus perdix). Condor 98:681-690.

____, V. Lodha, L.R. Monteiro, and R.W. Furness. 1998. Evidence for sympatric speciation in the Band-rumped Storm-Petrel Oceanodroma castro. [Abstract]. Ostrich 69:400-401.

Frimer, O. 1994. Autumn arrival and moult in King Eiders (Somateria spectabilis) at Disko, West Greenland. Arctic 47:137-141.

Frings, H., and M. Frings. 1961. Some biometric studies on the albatrosses of Midway Atoll. Condor 63:304-312.

Froehlich, D. 2003. Ageing North American landbirds by molt limits and plumage criteria. Slate Creek Press, Bolinas, CA. 51 pp.

Fry, D.M. 1983. Techniques for sexing monomorphic vultures. Pp. 356-375 in S.F. Wilbur and J.A. Jackson, eds., Vulture biology and management. University of California Press, Berkeley, CA.

Furness, R.W. 1987. The Skuas. Poyser, Falton. 363 pp.

Gabrielson, I.N., and F.C. Lincoln. 1949. A new race of ptarmigan in Alaska. Proc. Biol. Soc. Washington 62:175-176.

____ and ____. 1951. A new race of ptarmigan from Alaska. Proc. Biol. Soc. Washington 64:63-64.

____ and ____. 1953a. Status of Lagopus mutus sanfordi Bent. Proc. Biol. Soc. Washington 66:203.

____ and ____. 1953b. Status of the Lesser Common Loon. Condor 55:314-315.

Gaines, G.D., and R.J. Warren. 1984. Genetics and morphology of Sandhill Crane populations in Texas. J. Wildl. Manage. 48:1387-1393.

Galbreath, D.S., and R. Moreland. 1953. The Chukar Partridge in Washington. Washington State Game Dept. Biol. Bull. 11:1-55.

Gammonley, J.H. 1996. Cinnamon Teal. Birds N. Am. 209:1-20.

Gantlett, S. 1989. Hybrid duck resembling Baikal Teal in Norfolk. Birding World 1:426-427.

____. 1993. The status and separation of White-headed Duck and Ruddy Duck. Birding World 6:273-281.

____. 1998. Identification of Great Blue Heron and Grey Heron. Birding World 11:12-20.

Gantlett, S. and R. Millington. 1992. Identification forum: Large falcons. Birding World 5:357-360.

Garbutt, A., and A.L.A. Middleton. 1974. Molt sequence of captive Ruffed grouse. Auk 91:421-423.

Garcelon, D.K., M.S. Martell, P.T. Redig, and L.C. Buøen. 1985. Morphometric, karyotypic, and laparoscopic techniques for determining sex in Bald Eagles. J. Wildl. Manage. 49:595-599.

Garðarsson A. 1997. [First record of the Nearctic White-winged Scoter Melanitta fusca deglandi in Iceland and a note on the identification of the subspecies.] Bliki 18:65-67.

Garner, M. 1989. Common Scoter of nominate race with extensive yellow on bill. Br. Birds 82:616-618.

____. 1991. [On identification of Barrow's Goldeneye.] Br. Birds 84:543-546.

____. 1997. Identification of Yellow-legged Gulls in Britain. Brit. Birds 90:25-62.

____. 1999a. Identification of White-winged and Velvet scoters - males, females and immatures. Birding World 12:319-324.

____. 1999b. Identification of Common Merganser. Birding World 12:31-33.

____. 2002a. Lesser Scaup - the underwing. Birding World 15:506-508.

____. 2002b. Identification and vagrancy of American Merlins in Europe. Birding World 15:468-480.

____. 2005. The Fair Isle sandpiper: A review. Brit. Birds. 98:356-364.

____ and R. Millington. 2001. Gray-bellied Brant and the Dundrum conundrum. Birding World 14:151-155.

____ and D. Quinn. 1997. Identification of yellow-legged Gulls in Britain. Brit. Birds 90:25-62.

____, I. Lewington, and G. Rosenberg. 2004. Stejneger's Scoter in the western Palearctic and North America. Birding World 17:337-347.

Garrett, K.L., and J.C. Wilson. 2003. Report of the California Bird Records Committee: 2001 records. W. Birds 34:15-34.

Gaston, A.J. 1984. How to distinguish first-year murres, Uria spp., from older birds in winter. Can. Field-Nat. 98:52-55.

____. 1992. The Ancient Murrelet. T. and A.D. Poyser, London. 249 pp.

____. 1994. Ancient Murrelet. Birds N. Am. 132:1-20.

____ and S.B.C. Dechesne. 1996. Rhinoceros Auklet. Birds N. Am. 212:1-20.

____ and R. Decker. 1985. Interbreeding of Thayer's Gull, Larus thayeri, and Kumlien's Gull, Larus glaucoides kumlieni, on Southampton Island, Northwest Territories. Canadian Field-Nat. 9:257-259.

____ and J.M. Hipfner. 2000. Thick-billed Murre. Birds N. Am. 497:1-32.

____ and I.L. Jones. 1998. The Auks. Alcidae. Oxford University Press, Oxford, U.K. 349 pp.

____, G. Chapdelaine, and D.G. Noble. 1984. Phenotypic variation among Thick-billed Murres from colonies in Hudson Straight. Arctic 37:284-287.

Gates, J.M. 1966. Validity of spur appearance as an age criterion in the Pheasant. J. Wildl. Manage. 30:81-85.

Gates, R.J., D.F. Caithamer, T.C. Tacha, and C.R. Paine. 1993. The annual molt cycle of Branta canadensis interior in relation to nutrient reserve dynamics. Condor 95:680-693.

Gatti, R.C. 1983. Spring and summer age separation techniques for the Mallard. J. Wildl. Manage. 47:1054-1062.

Gauntlett, S., and P. Grant. 1989. The Salthome sandpiper. Birding World 2:257-260.

Gauthier, G. 1993. Bufflehead. Birds N. Am. 67:1-24.

Gaviño T., G., and R.W. Dickerman. 1972. Nestling development of Green Herons at San Blas, Nayarit, Mexico. Condor 74:72-79.

Gee, J.M. 2004. Gene flow across a climactic barrier between hybridizing avian species, California and Gambel's quail. Evolution 58:1108-1121.

____, J.D. Calkins, and K. Petren. 2003. Isolation and characteristics of microsatellite loci in hybridizing California and Gambel's quail (Callipepla californica and Callipepla gambelii). Mol. Ecol. Notes 3:35-36.

Genelly, R.E. 1955. Annual cycle in a population of California Quail. Condor 57:263-285.

Gerrard, J.M., and G.R. Bartolotti. 1988. The Bald Eagle: Haunts and habits of a wilderness monarch. Smithsonian Institution Press, Washington, D.C. 177 pp.

____, D.W.A. Whitfield, P. Gerrard, P.N. Gerrard, and W.J. Maher. 1978. Migratory movements and plumage of subadult Saskatchewan Bald Eagles. Can. Field-Nat. 92:375-382.

Gibbs, J.P., S. Melvin, and F.A. Reid. 1992a. American Bittern. Birds N. Am. 18:1-12.

Gibbs, J.P., F.A. Reid, and S. Melvin. 1992b. Least Bittern. Birds N. Am. 17:1-12.

Gibson, D.D. 1978. Separation of tattlers and snipe. 'Elepaio 39:8.

____ and B. Kessel. 1989. Geographic variation in the Marbled Godwit and description of an Alaska subspecies. Condor 91:436-443.

____ and ____. 1997. Inventory of the species and subspecies of Alaska. W. Birds 28:45-95.

Gibson, F. 1971. The breeding biology of the American Avocet (Recurvirostra americana) in central Oregon. Condor 73:444-454.

Gibson-Hill, C.A. 1947. Notes on the birds of Christmas Island. Bull. Raffles Mus. 18:87-165.

Giessen, K.M. 1998. Lesser Prairie-Chicken. Birds N. Am. 364:1-20.

Gifford, E.W. 1913. The birds of the Galapagos Islands, with observations on the birds of Cocos and Clipperton islands. Proc. California Acad. Sci. (4th Ser.) 2:1-124.

Gilchrist, H.G. 2001. Glaucous Gull. Birds N. Am. 573:1-32.

Gill, F.B. 1964. The shield color and relationships of certain Andean coots. Condor 66:209-211.

Gill, J.A., J. Clark, N. Clark, and W.J. Sutherland. 1995. Sex differences in the migration, moult, and wintering areas of British-ringed Ruff. Ringing & Migr. 16:159-167.

Gill, R.E., B.J. McCaffery, and P.S. Tomkovich. 2002. Wandering Tattler. Birds N. Am. 642:1-32.

____, P.S. Tomkovich, and B.J. McCaffery. 2002. Rock Sandpiper. Birds N. Am. 686:1-40.

Gillham, E. 1993. Some unusual hybrid ducks. Avicultural Magazine 99:35-42.

____, J.M. Harrison, and J.G. Harrison. 1965. A study of certain Aythya hybrids. Wildfowl 17:49-65.

Gilliland, M. 1984. Western Grebe - One species or two? Blue Jay 42:47-51.

Gilmer, D.S., R.E. Kirby, I.J. Ball, and J.R. Riechmann. 1977. Post-breeding activities in Mallards and Wood Ducks in north-central Minnesota. J. Wildl. Manage. 41:345-359.

Ginn, H.B., and D.S. Melville. 1983. Moult in birds. BTO Guide 19. British Trust for Ornithology, Thetford, UK.

Girard, G.L. 1937. Life history, habits, and food of the Sage Grouse. Univ. Wyoming Publ. Sci. 3:1-56.

Giudice, J.H., and J.T. Ratti. 2001. Ring-necked Pheasant. Birds N. Am. 572:1-32.

Glahn, J.F., and R.B. McCoy. 1995. Measurements of wintering Double-crested Cormorants and discriminant models of sex. J. Field Ornith. 66:299-304.

Glasgow, L.L. 1957. A woodcock sexing tool. J. Wildl. Manage. 21:104.

Glick, B. 1983. Bursa of Fabricius. Avian Biol. 7:443-500.

Gochfeld, M., and J. Burger. 1994. Black Skimmer. Birds N. Am. 108:1-28.

____ and G. Tudor. 1976. An apparent hybrid goldeneye from Maine. Wilson Bull. 88:348-349.

____, J. Burger, and I.C.T. Nisbet. 1998. Roseate Tern. Birds N. Am. 370:1-32.

Godfrey, W.E. 1953. Notes on Ellesmere Island birds. Can. Field-Nat. 67:89-93.

____. 1973. More presumed hybrid gulls: Larus argentatus X L. marinus. Canadian Field-Nat. 87:171-172.

____. 1986. The birds of Canada. Revised edition. National Museums of Canada, Ottawa. 595 pp.

____. 1992. Subspecies of the Red Knot Calidris canutus in the extreme northeastern Canadian Arctic islands. Wader Study Group Bull. 64(Suppl.):24-25.

Goldstein, M.I., P.H. Bloom, J.H. Sarasola, and T.E. Lacher. 1999. Post-migration weight gain of Swainson's Hawks in Argentina. Wilson Bull. 111:428-432.

Golley, M. 1999. The Clay Calidris. Birding World 3:237-238.

____ and A. Stoddart. 1991. Identification of American and Pacific golden plovers. Birding World 4:195-204.

Good, T.P. 1998. Great Black-backed Gull. Birds N. Am. 330:1-32.

Goodrich, L.J. S.C. Crocoll, and S.E. Senner. 1996. Broad-winged Hawk. Birds N. Am. 218:1-28.

Gosbell, K., and C. Minton. 2001. The biometrics and moult of Sanderling Calidris alba in Australia. Stilt 40:7-22.

Gosselin, M. 1979. Notes sur l'observation d'un oiseaux du genre Aythya. Bull. Ornith. (Quebec) 24:40-41.

Goudie, R.I., G.J. Robertson, and A. Reed. 2000. Common Eider. Birds N. Am. 546:1-32.

Gould, P.J., W.B. King, and G.A. Sanger. 1974. Red-tailed Tropicbird (Phaethon rubricauda). Pp. 206-231 in W.B. King, ed., Pelagic studies of seabirds in the central and eastern Pacific Ocean. Smithsonian Contributions in Zoology, Washington, D.C.

____, P. Ostrom, and W. Walker. 1998. Foods of Buller's Shearwaters (Puffinus bulleri) associated with driftnet fisheries in the central North Pacific. Notornis 45:81-93.

Gower, W.C. 1939. The use of the bursa of Fabricius as an indication of age in game birds. Trans. N. Am. Wildl. Conf. 4:426-430.

Grabovsky, V.I., A. Degen, and B. Rupprecht. Unpublished ms. Hybridization of Slaty-backed Gull (Larus schistisagus) and Glaucous-winged Gull (L. glaucescens) in the Commander Islands: Background and effects.

Granadeiro, J.P. 1993. Variation in measurements of Cory's Shearwater between populations and sexing by discriminant analysis. Ringing & Migr. 14:103-112.

Grant, C.H.B. 1914. The moults and plumages of the Common Moorhen (Gallinula chloropus). Ibis 10:298-304.

Grant, C.H.B., and C.W. Mackworth-Praed. 1933. Sula nicolli sp. nov. White-tailed Red-footed Booby. Bull. Brit. Ornith. Club 53:118-119.

Grant, P.J. 1980. Identification of American 'Marsh Hawks'. Brit. Birds. 73:318.

____. 1983. The 'Marsh Hawk' problem. Brit. Birds. 76:373-376.

____. 1986. Gulls: A Guide to Identification, 2nd edition. Academic Press, San Diego. 352 pp.

____, R.A. Hume, B. King, R. Payne, W. Russell, and C.E. Wheeler. 1980. Bare-part colour of Snowy and Little egrets. Brit. Birds. 73:39-40.

Grant, P.R. 1965. A systematic study of the terrestrial birds of the Tres Marias Islands, Mexico. Posilla 60:1-106.

Gratto, C.L., and R.I.G. Morrison. 1981. Partial postjuvenile wing moult of the Semipalmated Sandpiper Calidris pusilla. Wader Study Group Bull. 33:33-37.

Gratto-Trevor, C.L. 1992. Semipalmated Sandpiper. Birds N. Am. 6:1-20.

____. 2000. Marbled Godwit. Birds N. Am. 492:1-24.

____. 2004. The North American bander's manual for banding shorebirds. Can. Wildl. Service, Saskatoon, SK. 45 pp.

Gray, A.P. 1958. Bird hybrids. Commonwealth Bur. Anim. Breed. Genetics Edinburg Tech. Comm. 13:1-390.

Grecian, V.D., A.W. Diamond, and J.W. Chardine. 2003. Sexing Razorbills Alca torda breeding at Machias Seal Island, New Brunswick, Canada, using discriminant function analysis. Atlantic Seabirds 5:73-80.

Greeley, F. 1953. Sex and age studies in fall-shot woodcock (Philohela minor) from southern Wisconsin. J. Wildl. Manage. 17:29-32.

Green, G.H. 1980a. Total head length. Wader Study Group Bull. 29:18.

____. 1980b. Decreased wing length of skins of Ringed Plover and Dunlin. Ringing & Migr. 3:27-28.

Green, J.E., and L.W. Arnold. 1939. An unrecognized race of murrelet on the Pacific Coast of North America. Condor 41:25-29.

Green, J.C. 1967. The identification of Harlan's Hawk. Loon 39:4-7.

Green, R.E. 2004. Age-dependent changes in the shape of the secondary remiges of individual adult Corncrakes Crex crex. Ringing & Migr. 22:83-84.

____, N. Schäffer, and D. Wend. 2001. A method for ageing adult Corncrakes Crex crex. Ringing & Migr. 20:352-357.

Green, P.T., and C.M. Theobald. 1988. Sexing birds by discriminant function analysis: Further considerations. Ibis 131:442-447.

Greenberg, R.E., S.L. Etter, and W.L. Anderson. 1972. Evaluation of proximal primary feather criteria for aging wild Pheasants. J. Wildl. Manage. 36:700-705.

Greenwood, J.G. 1979. Post-mortem shrinkage of Dunlin Calidris alpina skins. Bull. Brit. Ornith. Club 99:143-145.

____. 1983. Post-nuptial primary molt in Dunlin Calidris alpina. Ibis 125:223-228.

____. 1986. Geographical variation and taxonomy of the Dunlin Calidris alpina (L.). Bull. Brit. Ornith. Club 106:43-56.

Greij, E.D. 1973. Effects of hormones on plumages of the Blue-winged Teal. Auk 90:533-551.

Grieb, J.R. 1970. The shortgrass prairie Canada Goose population. Wildl. Monogr. 22:1-49.

Grinnell, J. 1906. The Catalina Island Quail. Auk 23:262-265.

____. 1909. Birds and mammals of the 1907 Alexander expedition to southeastern Alaska. Univ. California Pubs. Zool. 5:171-264.

____. 1910. Birds of the 1908 Alexander Alaska Expedition. Univ. California Pubs. Zool. 12:361-428.

____. 1916. A new Ruffed Grouse from the Yukon Valley. Condor 18:166-167.

____. 1921. Concerning the status of the supposed two races of the Long-billed Curlew. Condor 23:21-27.

____. 1926. Another new race of quail from Lower California. Condor 28:128-129.

____. 1928. The status of the white-rumped storm petrels of the California coast. Condor 20:46.

____ and F.H. Test. 1939. Geographic variation in the Fork-tailed Storm-Petrel. Condor 41:170-172.

____, H.C. Bryant, and T.I. Storer. 1918. The game birds of California. University of California Press, Berkeley, CA. 642 pp.

Griscom, L. 1923. Descriptions of apparently new birds from North America and the West Indes. Am. Mus. Novit. 71:1-8.

____. 1926. The ornithological results of the Mason-Spinden Expedition to Yucatan. Am. Mus. Novit. 235:1-19.

____. 1930. Studies of the Dwight collection of birds II. Am. Mus. Novit. 414:1-8.

____. 1932. The distribution of bird-life in Guatemala. Bull. Am. Mus. Nat. Hist. 44:1-439.

Griscom, L. 1935. Critical notes on Central American birds in the British Museum: Notes on New World skimmers. Ibis (13th Ser.) 5:544-546.
____ and J.C. Greenway Jr. 1941. Birds of lower Amazonia. Bull. Mus. Comp. Zool. 88:83-344.
Gromadzka, J. 1985. Further observations on wing plumage of Dunlins. Wader Study Group Bull. 44:32-33.
____ and B. Przystupa. 1984. Problems with the ageing of Dunlins in autumn. Wader Study Group Bull. 41:19-20.
Gross, A.O. 1923. The Black-crowned Night Heron (Nycticorax nycticorax naevius) of Sandy Neck. Auk 40:1-30, 191-214.
____. 1928. The Heath Hen. Mem. Boston Soc. Nat. Hist. 6:491-588.
____. 1937. Birds of the Bowdoin-MacMillan Arctic Expedition. Auk 54:12-42.
____. 1949. The Antillean Grebe at Central Soledad, Cuba. Auk 66:42-52.
Grubb, T.C. Jr. 1989. Ptilochronology: Feather growth bars as indicators of nutritional status. Auk 106:314-320.
Gruys, R.C., and S.J. Hannon. 1993. Sex determination of hunter-killed and depredated Willow Ptarmigan using a discriminant analysis. J. Field Ornith. 64:11-17.
Gullion, G.W. 1950. Voice differences between sexes in the American Coot. Condor 52:272-273.
____. 1951. The frontal shield of the American Coot. Wilson Bull. 63:157-166.
____. 1952. Sex and age determination in the American Coot. J. Wildl. Manage. 16:191-197.
____. 1953. Observations on molting of the American Coot. Condor 55:102-103.
Gunther, G. 1941. A Mallard-Pintail hybrid. Auk 58:570.
Gurney, J.H. 1880. Notes on a 'Catalogue of the Accipitres in the British Museum' by R. Bowlder Sharpe (1874). Ibis (4th Ser.) 4:312-329.
Gustafson, M.E., and B.G. Peterjohn. 1994. Adult Slaty-backed Gulls: Variability in mantle color and comments on identification. Birding 26:243-249.
Gutiérrez, R. 1998. Field identification of Cory's and Scopoli's shearwaters. Dutch Birding 20:216-225.
Gutiérrez, R.J., and D.J. Delehanty. 1999. Mountain Quail. Birds N. Am. 457:1-28.
Gyldenstolpe, N. 1951. The ornithology of the Rio Purus region in western Brazil. Arkiv Zool. 2:1-120.
Hachisuka, M. 1928. Variations among birds (chiefly game birds). Suppl. Pub. Ornith. Soc. Japan 12:1-85.
Hagelin, J.C. 2003. A field study of ornaments, body size, and mating behavior of the Gambel's Quail. Wilson Bull. 115:246-257.
____ and R.T. Kimball. 1997. A female Gambel's Quail with partial male plumage. Wilson Bull. 109:544-546.
Hahn, S., and H.U. Peter. 2003. Sex and age dependency of wing patch size in Brown Skuas. Emu 103:37-41.
____, ____, and P. Quillfeldt. 1998. Population estimates of the birds of Potter Peninsula. Berichte zur Polarf. 299:174-181.
Haig, S.M. 1992. Piping Plover. Birds N. Am. 2:1-18.
____ and L.W. Oring. 1988a. Genetic differentiation of Piping Plovers across North America. Auk 105:260-267.
____ and ____. 1988b. Distribution and dispersal in the Piping Plover. Auk 105:630-638.
____, C.L. Gratto-Trevor, T.D. Mullins, and M.A. Colwell. 1997. Population identification of Western Hemisphere shorebirds throughout the annual cycle. Molecular. Evol. 6:413-427.
Hale, J.B., R.F. Wendt, and G.C. Halazon. 1954. Sex and age criteria for Wisconsin Ruffed Grouse. Wisconsin Cons. Dep. Tech. Wild. Bull. 9:1-24.
Hamerstrom, F. 1967. On the use of fault bars in ageing birds of prey. Inland Bird-Banding Assoc. News 39:35-41.
____. 1968. Ageing and sexing harriers. Inland Bird-Banding Assoc. News 40:43-46.
____. 1971. Ageing Red-tailed Hawks by tail color in Wisconsin. Inland Bird-Banding Assoc. News 43:9-11.
____. 1986. Harrier: Hawk of the marshes. Smithsonian Institution Press, Washington, D.C. 171 pp.
____ and J.L. Skinner. 1971. Cloacal sexing of raptors. Auk 88:173-174.
____ and J.D. Weaver. 1968. Ageing and sexing Rough-[legged] Hawks in Wisconsin and Illinois. Ontario Bird Banding 4:133-138.
Hamerstrom, F., and F. Hamerstrom. 1978. External sex characters of Harris' Hawks in winter. Raptor Res. 12:1-14.
Hamilton, R.A. 1996. Answers to the June photo quiz. Birding 28:309-311.
____ and N.J. Schmitt. 2000. Identification of Taiga and Black Merlins. W. Birds 31:65-67.
Hamilton, R.B. 1975. Comparative behavior of the American Avocet and the Black-necked Stilt (Recurvirostridae). Ornith. Monogr. 17:1-98.
Hamilton, W.J. III. 1958. Pelagic birds observed on a North Pacific crossing. Condor 60:159-164.
Hancock, J. 1984. Field identification of West Palearctic white herons and egrets. Brit. Birds. 77:451-457.
Hancock, J. and J.A. Kushlan. 1984. The herons handbook. Harper and Row, New York, NY. 288 pp.
____, ____, and M.P. Kahl. 1992. Storks, ibises and spoonbills of the world. Academic Press, San Diego, CA. 385 pp.
Handel, C.M., and R.E. Gill. 2001. Black Turnstone. Birds N. Am. 585:1-28.
Haney, J.C., and S.D. MacDonald. 1995. Ivory Gull. Birds N. Am. 175:1-24.
____, D.S. Lee, and R.D. Morris. 1999. Bridled Tern. Birds N. Am. 468:1-24.
Hanners, L.A., and S.R. Patton. 1985. Sexing Laughing Gulls using external measurements and discriminant analysis. J. Field Ornith. 56:158-164.
Hannon, S.J., and J. Roland. 1983. Morphology and territory acquisition in Willow Ptarmigan. Can. J. Zool. 62:1502-1506.
____, P.K. Eason, and K. Martin. 1998. Willow Ptarmigan. Birds N. Am. 369:1-28.
Hansen, H.A., P.E.K. Shepherd, J.G. King, and W.A. Troyer. 1971. The Trumpeter Swan in Alaska. Wildl. Monogr. 26:1-83.
Hanson, A.R., and C.D. Ankney. 1994. Morphometric similarity of Mallards and American Black Ducks. Can. J. Zool. 72:2248-2251.
Hanson, H.C. 1949. Methods of determining age in Canada Geese and other waterfowl. J. Wildl. Manage. 13:176-183.
____. 1951. A morphometrical study of the Canada Goose, Branta canadensis interior Todd. Auk 68:164-173.
____. 1953. Aids for the exploration of the avian cloaca for characters of age and sex. J. Wildl. Manage. 17:89-90.
____. 1959. The incubation patch of wild geese: Its recognition and significance. Arctic 12:139-150.
____. 1962. Characters of age, sex, and sexual maturity in Canada Geese. Illinois Nat. Hist. Surv. Div. Biol. Notes 49:1-15.
____. 1997. The giant Canada Goose. Revised Ed. Southern Illinois University Press, Carbondale, IL. 320 pp.
____ and R.H. Smith. 1950. Canada Geese of the Mississippi Flyway. Bull. Illinois Nat. Hist. Surv. 25:67-210.
Hantzsch, B. 1929. Contribution to the knowledge of the avifauna of north-eastern Labrador. Can. Field-Nat. 43:11-18.
Haramis, G.M. 1982. Records of Redhead X Canvasback hybrids. Wilson Bull. 94:599-602.
____, E.L. Derleth, and D.A. McAuley. 1982. Techniques for trapping, aging, and banding wintering Canvasbacks. J. Field Ornith. 53:342-351.
Harper, F. 1953. Birds of the Nueltin Lake Expedition, Keewatin, 1947. Am. Mid. Nat. 49:1-116.
Harrington, B.A. 1977. Winter distribution of juvenile and older Red-footed Boobies from the Hawaiian Islands. Condor 79:87-90.
____, F.J. Leeuwenburg, S.L. Resende, R. McNeil, B.T. Thomas, J.S. Grear, and E.F. Martinez. 1991. Migration and mass change of White-rumped Sandpipers in North and South America. Wilson Bull. 103:621-636.
____. 2001. Red Knot. Birds N. Am. 563:1-32.
____ and R.I.G. Morrison. 1979. Semipalmated Sandpiper migration in North America. Studies Avian Biol. 2:83-100.
____ and A.L. Taylor. 1982. Methods for sex identification and estimation of wing area in Semipalmated Sandpipers. J. Field Ornith. 53:174-177.
____, B. Winn, and S.C. Brown. 2007. Molt and body mass of Red Knots in the eastern United States. Wilson J. Ornith. 119:35-42.
Harrington-Tweit, B. 1979. A seabird die-off on the Washington coast in mid-winter 1976. W. Birds 10:49-56.
Harris. H. 1941. The annals of Gymnogyps to 1900. Condor 43:3-55.
Harris, M.P. 1969. The biology of the storm petrels in the Galapagos Islands. Proc. California Acad. Sci. (4th Ser.) 4:95-166.
____. 1981. Age determination and first breeding of British Puffins. Br. Birds 74:246-256.
____ and S. Wanless. 1990. Moult and autumn colony attendance of auks. Brit. Birds. 83:55-66.
____ and R.F. Yule. 1977. The moult of the puffin Fratercula arctica. Ibis 119:535-541.
____, C. Morley, and G.H. Green. 1978. Hybridization of Herring and Lesser Black-backed gulls in Britain. Bird Study 25:161-166.
Harris, S.W. 1974. Status, chronology, and ecology of nesting storm petrels in northwestern California. Condor 76:249-261.
____ and P.E.K. Shepherd. 1965. Age determination and notes on the breeding age of Black Brant. J. Wildl. Manage. 29:643-645.
Harrison, B.A. 1980. Autumn molt and migration of Black-bellied Plovers in eastern North America. Wader Stud. Group Bull. 29:36.
Harrison, J.G. 1957. A review of skull pneumatisation in birds. Bull. Brit. Ornith. Club 77:70-77.
Harrison, J.M. 1965. Some remarks on an anomalous gull. Bull. Brit. Ornith. Club 85:67-70.

Harrison, J.M. and J. Harrison. 1969. The evolutionary position of snow geese as suggested by certain goose hybrids and variants. Bull. Brit. Ornith. Club 89:39-41.
Harrison, P. 1983a. Seabirds: An identification guide. Houghton Mifflin, Boston. 448 pp.
____. 1983b. Identification of white-rumped North Atlantic petrels. Brit. Birds 76:161-174.
____. 1987. Seabirds of the world: A photographic guide. Princeton University Press, Princeton, NJ. 317 pp.
Harrop, A. 1993a. Presumed Red-crested Pochard X Northern Pintail hybrid. Brit. Birds. 86:130-131.
____. 1993b. Identification of Sharp-tailed Sandpiper and Pectoral Sandpiper. Birding World 6:230-238.
____. 1994. Field identification of American Wigeon. Birding World 7:50-56.
____. 1998. Female Aythya hybrid resembling Lesser Scaup. Brit. Birds. 91:195-197.
____. 2004. The 'North American' Peregrine Falcon in Britain. Brit. Birds. 97:130-133.
Hart, C.M., O.S. Lee, and J. Blow. 1950. The Sharp-tailed Grouse in Utah. Utah Dept. Fish Game Publ. 3:1-79.
Harvey, W.F. IV, G.R. Hepp, and R.A. Kennamer. 1989. Age determination of female Wood Ducks during the breeding season. Wildl. Soc. Bull. 17:254-258.
Hasegawa, H., and A.R. DeGange. 1982. The Short-tailed Albatross, Diomedea albatrus, it's status, distribution and natural history. Am. Birds 36:806-814.
Hatch, J.J. 2003. Arctic Tern. Birds N. Am. 707:1-40.
____ and D.V. Weseloh. 1999. Double-crested Cormorant. Birds N. Am. 441:1-36.
____, K.M. Brown, G.G. Hogan, and R.D. Morris. 2000. Great Cormorant. Birds N. Am. 553:1-32.
Hatch, R.M., and A.H. Shortt. 1976. Possible intermediate Ross' Goose and Snow Goose in Manitoba. Auk 93:391-392.
Hatch, S.A. 1991. Evidence for color phase effects on the breeding and life history of Northern Fulmars. Condor 93:409-417.
____. 1995. Changing populations of Double-crested Cormorants. Colonial Waterbirds 18(Spec. Pub.):8-24.
____ and M.A. Hatch. 1983. An isolated population of small Canada Geese on Kaliktagik Island, Alaska. Wildfowl 34:130-136.
____ and D.N. Nettleship. 1998. Northern Fulmar. Birds N. Am. 361:1-32.
Haugen, A.O. 1957. Distinguishing juvenile from adult Bobwhite quail. J. Wildl. Manage. 21:29-32.
Haussmann, M.F., and R.A. Mauck. 2008. Telomeres and longevity: Testing an evolutionary hypothesis. Mol. Biol. Evol. 25:220-228
____ and C.M. Vleck. 2002. Telomere length provides a new technique for aging animals. Oecologia 130:325-328.
____, D.W. Winkler, K.M. O'Reilly, C.E. Huntington, I.C.T. Nisbet, and C.M. Vleck. 2003. Telomeres shorten more slowly in long-lived birds and mammals than in short-lived ones. Proc. Royal Soc. London (Ser. B) 270:1387-1392.
Hawbecker, A.C. 1942. A life history study of the White-tailed Kite. Condor 44:267-276.
Hawfield, E.J. 1986. The number of fault bars in the flight feathers of Red-tailed Hawks, Red-shouldered Hawks, Broad-winged Hawks, and Barred Owls. Chat 50:15-18.
Hayes, F.E. 2002. Geographic variation, hybridization, and taxonomy of New World Butorides herons. N. Am. Birds 56:4-10.
____. 2004. Variability and interbreeding of Sandwich Terns and Cayenne Terns in the Virgin Islands, with comments on their systematic relationship. N. Am. Birds 57:566-572.
____. 2006. Variation and hybridization in the Green Heron (Butorides virescens) and Striated Heron (B. striata) in Trinidad and Tobago, with comments on species limits. J. Caribbean Ornith. 19:12-20.
Hayman, P., T. Marchant, and T. Prater. 1986. Shorebirds: An identification guide. Houghton Mifflin, Boston, MA. 412 pp.
Hays, H. 1972. Polyandry in the Spotted Sandpiper. Living Bird 11:43-73.
____. 1975. Probable Common X Roseate Tern hybrids. Auk 92:219-234.
____ and H.M. Haberman. 1969. Note on bill color of the Ruddy Duck Oxyura jamaicensis rubida. Auk 86:765-766.
____, J. Hudon, G. Cormons, J. Dicostanzo and P. Lima. 2006. The pink feather blush of the Roseate Tern. Waterbirds 29:296-301.
Healy, W.M., and E.S. Nenno. 1980. Growth parameters and sex and age criteria for juvenile Eastern Wild Turkeys. Proc. Nat. Wild Turkey Symp. 4:168-185.
Heather, B.D. 1982. The Cattle Egret in New Zealand, 1978-1980. Notornis 29:241-268.
Hedenström, A., and S. Sunada. 1999. On the aerodynamics of moult gaps in birds. J. Experim. Biol. 202:67-76.
Heindel, M.T. 1999. The status of vagrant Whimbrels in the United States and Canada with notes on identification. N. Am. Birds 53:232-236.
Heitmeyer, M.E. 1987. The prebasic moult and basic plumage of female Mallards (Anas platyrhynchos). Can. J. Zool. 65:2248-2261.
____. 1995. Influences of age, body condition, and structural size on mate selection in dabbling ducks. Can. J. Zool. 73:2251-2258.
Helfenstein F., C. Tirard, E. Danchin, and R.H. Wagner. 2004. Low frequency of extra-pair paternity and high frequency of adoption in Black-legged Kittiwakes. Condor 106:149-155.
Heller, E., and R.E. Snodgrass. 1901. Descriptions of two new species and three new subspecies of birds from the eastern Pacific, collected by the Hopkins-Stanford Expedition to the Galapagos Islands. Condor 3:74-77.
Hellmayr, C.E. 1906. On the birds of the island of Trinidad. Novit. Zool. 13:1-60.
____. 1929. Birds of the James-Simpson-Roosevelts Asiatic Expedition. Field Mus. Nat. Hist. Zool. Ser. 17:27-144.
____ and B. Conover. 1942. Catalogue of birds of the Americas and the adjacent islands. Zool. Ser. Field Mus. Nat. Hist. 13 (Part 1, No. 1):1-636.
____ and ____. 1948a. Catalogue of birds of the Americas and the adjacent islands. Zool. Ser. Field Mus. Nat. Hist. 13 (Part 1, No. 2):1-434.
____ and ____. 1948b. Catalogue of birds of the Americas and the adjacent islands. Zool. Ser. Field Mus. Nat. Hist. 13 (Part 1, No. 3):1-383.
____ and ____. 1949. Catalogue of birds of the Americas and the adjacent islands. Zool. Ser. Field Mus. Nat. Hist. 13 (Part 1, No. 4):1-358.
Helm, R.N. 1994. Purple Gallinule. Pp. 159-165 in T.C. Tacha and C.E. Braun, eds., Migratory shore and upland gamebird management in North America. Allen Press, Lawrence, KS.
Henckel, R.E. 1981. Ageing the Turkey Vulture HY to ASY. N. Am. Bird Bander 6:106-107. [Reprinted Vulture News 6:10-11, 1981]
Henderson, F.R., F.W. Brooks, R.E. Wood, and R.B. Dahlgren. 1967. Sexing of Prairie Grouse by crown feather patterns. J. Wildl. Manage. 31:764-769.
Henny, C.J., and W.S. Clark. 1982. Measurements of fall migrant Peregrine Falcons from Texas and New Jersey. J. Field Ornith. 53:326-332.
____, J.L. Carter, and B.J. Carter. 1981. A review of Bufflehead sex and age criteria with notes on weights. Wildfowl 32:117-122.
____, R.A. Olson, and T.L. Fleming. 1985. Breeding chronology, molt, and measurements of Accipiter hawks in northeastern Oregon. J. Field Ornith. 56:97-112.
____, L.J. Blus, and R.A. Grove. 1990. Western Grebe, Aechmophorus occidentalis, wintering biology and contaminant accumulation in Commencement Bay, Puget Sound, Washington. Can. Field-Nat. 104:460-472.
Henshaw, B. 1992. Ontario round-up. Birders J. 1:167-175.
Henshaw, H.W. 1881. On Podiceps occidentalis and P. clarkii. Bull. Nuttall Ornith. Club 6:214-218.
____. 1885. Hybrid quail (Lophortyx gambelii X L. californicus). Auk 2:247-249.
____. 1910. The migration of the Pacific Plover to and from the Hawaiian Islands. Auk 27:245-262.
Hepp, G.R., and F.C. Bellrose. 1995. Wood Duck. Birds N. Am. 169:1-24.
____, J.M. Novak, K.T. Scribner, and P.W. Stangel. 1988. Genetic distance and hybridization of Black Ducks and Mallards: A morph of a different color? Auk 105:804-807.
Heppleston, P.B. 1973. The distribution and taxonomy of oystercatchers. Notornis 20:102-112.
Herremans, M. 2000. Cases of serial descendent primary moult (Staffelmauser) in the Black-shouldered Kite. Ringing & Migr. 20:15-18.
Hess, P. 1998. Status and field identification problems of the Willet subspecies in Pennsylvania. Pennsylvania Birds 12:42-46.
____. 2005. California X Gambel's quail hybridization. Birding 37:246-247.
Heubeck, M., and D. Suddaby. 1991. Post-mortem examination of Little Auks Alle alle, Shetland, December 1990. Seabird 13:51-53.
____, M.G. Richardson, I.H.J. Lyster, and R.Y. McGowan. 1993. Post-mortem examination of of Great Northern Divers Gavia immer killed by oil pollution in Shetland, 1979. Seabird 15:53-59.
Heusmann, H.W. 1974. Mallard-Black Duck relationships in the Northeast. Wildl. Soc. Bull. 2:171-177.
Hickey, J.J., and R.A. McCabe. 1953. Sex and age classes in the Hungarian Partridge. J. Wildl. Manage. 17:90-91.
Hielman, S. In press. The trouble with tertials. Auk.
Higgins, K.F. 1969. Bursal depths of Lesser Snow and small Canada Geese. J. Wildl. Manage. 33:1006-1008.
____ and L.J. Schoonover. 1969. Aging small Canada Geese by neck plumage. J. Wildl. Manage. 33:212-214.
Higgins, P.J., and S.J.J.F. Davies, eds. 1996. Handbook of Australian, New Zealand, and Antarctic Birds. Vol. 3. Oxford University Press, Oxford, UK. 1028 pp.

Hildebrandt T., C. Pitra, P. Sommer, and M. Pinkowski. 1995. Sex identification in birds of prey by ultrasonography. J. Zoo Wildl. Med. 26:367-376

Hill, G.E., and K.J. McGraw, eds. 2006. Bird Coloration. Vol. 1: Mechanisms and measurements. Harvard University Press, Cambridge, MA. 624 pp.

____ and ____, eds. 2007. Bird Coloration. Vol. 2: Function and evolution. Harvard University Press, Cambridge, MA. 528 pp.

Hill, N.P. 1944. Sexual dimorphism in the Falconiformes. Auk 61:228-234.

Hipes, D.L., and G.R. Hepp. 1995. Nutrient-reserve dynamics of breeding male Wood Ducks. Condor 97:451-460.

Hipfner, J.M., and G. Chapdelaine. 2002. Razorbill. Birds N. Am. 635:1-36.

Hirschfeld, E., C.S. Roselaar, and H. Shirihai. 2000. Identification, taxonomy and distribution of Greater and Lesser Sand Plovers. Brit. Birds 93:162-189.

Hobson, K.A. 1997. Pelagic Cormorant. Birds N. Am. 282:1-28.

____. 1999. Tracing origins and migration of wildlife using stable isotopes: A review. Oecologia 120:314-326.

____. 2000. Incredible journeys. Science 295:981-982.

____, R.B. Brua, W.L. Hohman, and L.I. Wassenaar. 2000. Low frequencies of "double molt" of remiges in Ruddy Ducks revealed by stable isotopes: Implications for tracking migratory waterfowl. Auk 117:129-135.

____, S. Van Wilgenburg, L.I. Wassenaar, H. Hands, W.P. Johnson, M. O'Meilia, and P. Taylor. 2006. Using stable isotope analysis of feathers to delineate origins of harvested Sandhill Cranes in the Central Flyway of North America. Waterbirds 29:137-147.

Hochbaum, H.A. 1942. Sex and age determination of waterfowl by cloacal examination. Trans Seventh N. Am. Wildl. Conf. 1942:299-307.

____. 1944. The Canvasback in a prairie marsh. Monumental Printing Co., Baltimore, MD. 201 pp.

Hoffman, R.W. 1983. Sex classification of juvenile Blue Grouse from wing characteristics. J. Wildl. Manage. 47:1143-1147.

Hoffman, S.W., J.P. Smith, and J.A. Gessaman. 1990. Size of fall-migrant Accipiters from the Goshute Mountains of Nevada. J. Field Ornith. 61:201-211.

Hoffman, W., and G.T. Bancroft. 1984. Molt in Black Scoters wintering in peninsular Florida. Wilson Bull. 96:499-504.

____ and W.P. Elliott. 1974. Occurrence of intergrade Brant in Oregon. W. Birds 5:91-93.

____, J.A. Wiens, and J.M. Scott. 1978. Hybridization between gulls (Larus glaucescens and L. occidentalis) in the Pacific Northwest. Auk 95:441-458.

Höglund, J., and A. Lundberg. 1989. Plumage color correlates with body size in the Ruff (Philomachus pugnax). Auk 106:336-338.

Hohman, W.L. 1993. Body composition dynamics of Ruddy Ducks during wing molt. Can. J. Zool. 71:2224-2228.

____. 1996. Prevalence of double wing molt in free-living Ruddy Ducks. Southwestern Nat. 41:195-197.

____ and R.D. Crawford. 1995. Molt in the annual cycle of Ring-necked Ducks. Condor 97:473-483.

____ and B.L. Cypher. 1986. Age-class determination of Ring-necked Ducks. J. Wildl. Manage. 50:442-445.

____ and T. Eberhardt. 1998. Ring-necked Duck. Birds N. Am. 329:1-32.

____ and S.A. Lee. 2001. Fulvous Whistling-Duck. Birds N. Am. 562:1-24.

____ and D.M. Richard. 1994. Timing of remigial molt in Fulvous Whistling Ducks nesting in Louisiana. Southwestern Nat. 39:190-192

____, C.D. Ankney, and D.H. Gordon. 1992a. Ecology and management of postbreeding waterfowl. Pp. 128-189 in B.D.J. Batt, et al., eds., Ecology and management of breeding waterfowl. University of Minnesota Press, Minneapolis, MN.

____, ____, and D.L. Roster. 1992b. Body condition, food habits, and molt status of late-wintering Ruddy Ducks in California. Southwestern Nat. 37:268-273.

____, J.L. Moore, D.J. Twedt, J.G. Mensik, and E. Logerwell. 1995. Age-class separation of blue-winged ducks. J. Wildl. Manage. 59:727-735.

____, S.W. Manley, and D. Richard. 1997. Relative costs of prebasic and prealternate molts for male Blue-winged Teal. Condor 99:543-548.

Holder, K., and R. Montgomerie. 1993. Rock Ptarmigan. Birds N. Am. 51:1-24.

Holian, J.J., and J.E. Forley. 1992. Lesser Scaup: New to the western Palearctic. Brit. Birds. 85:370-376.

Holmes, R.T. 1966. Molt cycle of the Red-backed Sandpiper (Calidris alpina) in western North America. Auk 83:517-533.

____. 1971. Latitudinal differences in the breeding and molt schedules of Alaskan Red-backed Sandpipers (Calidris alpina). Condor 73:93-99.

____ and F.A. Pitelka. Pectoral Sandpiper. Birds N. Am. 348:1-24.

Holmgren, N., H. Ellegren, and J. Pettersson. 1993. The adaptation of moult pattern in migratory Dunlins Calidris alpina. Ornis Scand. 24:21-27.

Holt, C. 1984. Separating Mandarins and Wood Ducks in late summer. Brit. Birds 77:227-232.

Holt, E.G. 1928. The status of the Great White Heron (Ardea occidentalis Audubon) and the Wurdemann's Heron (Ardea wurdemannii Baird). Sci. Publ. Cleveland Mus. Nat. Hist. 1:1-35.

____ and G.M. Sutton. 1926. Notes on birds observed in southern Florida. Ann. Carnegie Mus. 16:409-439.

Hoogendoorn, W., and E.J. van Ijzendoorn. 1994. Pre-breeding moult in Franklin's Gulls in the Western Palearctic. Dutch Birding 16:61-63.

Hopper, R.M., and H.D. Funk. 1970. Reliability of the Mallard wing age-determination technique for field use. J. Wildl. Manage. 34:333-339.

Höst, P. 1942. Effect of light on the moults and sequences of plumage in the Willow Ptarmigan. Auk 59:388-403.

Houston, C.S., and D.E. Bowen Jr. 2001. Upland Sandpiper. Birds N. Am. 580:1-32.

Howe, R.H. Jr. 1904. A new Bob-white from the United States. Proc. Biol. Soc. Washington 17:168.

Howell, M.D., J.B. Grand, and P.L. Flint. 2003. Body molt of male Long-tailed Ducks in the near-shore waters on the North Slope, Alaska. Wilson Bull. 115:170-175.

Howell, S.N.G. 1994. Magnificent and Great frigatebirds in the eastern Pacific. Birding 26:400-415.

____. 1999. Molt, ageing, and identification of immature Long-tailed Jaegers. W. Birds 30:219-220.

____. 2000. A basic understanding of molt: What, why, when, and how much? Birders J. 8:296-300.

____. 2001a. A new look at moult in gulls. Alula 7:2-11.

____. 2001b. Feather bleaching in gulls. Birders J. 10:198-208.

____. 2001c. Molt of the Ivory Gull. Waterbirds 24:438-442.

____. 2001d. Molt of Heermann's Gull and other gulls. Ontario Birds 19:136-138.

____. 2003a. All you ever wanted to know about molt but were afraid to ask. Part 1. The variety of molt strategies. Birding 35:490-496.

____. 2003b. All you ever wanted to know about molt but were afraid to ask. Part 2. Finding order amid the chaos. Birding 35:640-650.

____. 2003c. Shades of gray: a point of reference for gull identification. Birding 35:32-37.

____. 2004. South Polar Skuas off California. Birding World 17:288-297.

____. 2005. Revisiting an old question: How many species of skua occur in the North Pacific? W. Birds 36:71-73.

____. 2006a. Primary molt in the Black-footed Albatross. W. Birds 37:241-244.

____. 2006b. Identification of "black petrels", Genus Procellaria. Birding 38:52-64.

____. 2006c. Brown Boobies or brown boobies. Birding 38:60-63.

____. 2007a. The short tale of a melanistic Black-vented Shearwater. W. Birds 38:235-237.

____. 2007b. A review of moult and ageing in jaegers (smaller skuas). Alula 13:98-113.

____ and C. Corben. 2000a. A commentary on molt and plumage terminology: Implications from the Western Gull. W. Birds 31:50-56.

____ and ____. 2000b. Molt cycles and sequences in the Western Gull. W. Birds 31:38-49.

____ and ____. 2000c. Retarded wing molt in Black-legged Kittiwakes. W. Birds 31:123-125.

____ and ____. 2000d. Identification of Thayer's-like gulls: the Herring X Glaucous-winged Gull problem. Birders J. 9:25-33.

____ and B.M. de Montes. 1989. Status of the Glossy Ibis in Mexico. Am. Birds 43:43-45.

____ and J.L. Dunn. 2007. A reference guide to gulls of the Americas. Houghton Mifflin Company, Boston, MA. 516 pp.

____ and M.T. Elliott. 2001. Identification and variation of winter adult Thayer's Gulls, with comments on taxonomy. Alula 7:130-144.

____ and B. Mactavish. 2003. Identification and variation of winter adult Kumlien's Gulls. Alula 9:2-15.

____ and B. McKee. 1998. Variation in second-year Mew Gulls. Birders J. 7:210-213.

____ and P. Pyle. 2002. Ageing and molt in nonbreeding Black-bellied Plovers. W. Birds 33:268-270.

____ and ____. 2005. Molt, age determination, and identification of puffins. Birding 37:412-418.

____ and S. Webb. 1995. A guide to the birds of Mexico and northern Central America. Oxford University Press, Oxford, UK. 851 pp.

____ and C. Wood. 2004. First-cycle primary moult in Heermann's Gulls. Birders J. 75:40-43.

____, S. Webb, D.A. Sibley, and L.J. Prairie. 1992. First record of a melanistic Northern Harrier in North America. W. Birds 23:79-80.

____, L.B. Spear, and P. Pyle. 1994. Identification of Manx Shearwaters in the eastern Pacific. W. Birds 25:169-177.

____, S. Webb, and L.B. Spear. 1996. Identification at sea of Cook's, de Filippi's, and Pycroft's petrels. W. Birds 27:57-64.

Howell, S.N.G., J.R. King, and C. Corben. 1999. First prebasic molt in Herring, Thayer's, and Glaucous-winged Gulls. J. Field Ornith. 70:543-554.

____, C. Corben, P. Pyle, and D.I. Rogers. 2003. The first basic problem: A review of molt and plumage homologies. Condor 105:635-653.

____, ____, ____, and ____. 2004. The first basic problem revisited: Reply to commentaries on Howell et al. (2003). Condor 106:206-210.

Howell, T.R. 1959. A hybrid of the Pintail and the Green-winged Teal. Condor 61:226-227.

____. 1965. New subspecies of birds from the lowland pine savannah of northeast Nicaragua. Auk 82:438-462.

Hubbard, J.P. 1966. A possible back-cross hybrid involving Scaled and Gambel's quail. Auk 83:136-137.

____. 1971. Comparison of two presumed European X American Widgeon hybrids. Auk 88:666-668.

____. 1972. Notes on Arizona birds. Nemouria 5:1-22.

____. 1976. Status of the night-herons (Nycticorax) of the Philippines and vicinity. Nemouria 19:1-10.

____. 1977. The biological and taxonomic status of the Mexican Duck. New Mexico Dept. Game Fish Bull. 16:1-56.

____ and R.C. Banks. 1970. The types and taxa of Harold H. Bailey. Proc. Biol Soc. Washington 83:321-332.

Hubbs, C.L. 1960. The marine vertebrates of the outer coast. Syst. Zool. 9:134-147.

Huber, L.N. 1971. Notes on the migration of the Wilson's Storm Petrel Oceanites oceanicus near Eniwetok Atoll, western Pacific Ocean. Notornis 18:38-42.

Huber, W. 1920. Description of a new North American duck. Auk 37:273-274.

Hudon, J., and A.H. Brush. 1990. Carotenoids produce flush in the Elegant Tern plumage. Condor 92:798-801.

Hudson, G.E. 1955. An apparent hybrid between the Ring-necked Pheasant and the Blue Grouse. Condor 57:304.

Huey, L.M. 1927a. A new Louisiana Heron and a new Round-tailed Ground Squirrel from Lower California, Mexico. Trans. San Diego Soc. Nat. Hist. 5:83-86.

____. 1927b. A Pacific coast race of the Yellow-crowned Night Heron. Condor 29:167-168.

____. 1930. Notes on the habits and plumage of young Kaeding Petrels. Condor 32:68-69.

Huey, W.S. 1961. Comparison of female Mallard with female New Mexican Duck. Auk 78:428-431.

Hull, C.L., B.A. Vanderkist, L.W. Lougheed, G.W. Kaiser, and F. Cooke. 2001. Morphometric variation in Marbled Murrelets, Brachyramphus marmoratus, in British Columbia. Northwestern Nat. 82:41-51.

Humphrey, P.S., and G.A. Clark, Jr. 1964. The anatomy of waterfowl. Pp. 167-232 in J. Delacour, ed. The waterfowl of the world. Vol. IV. Country Life Limited, London, UK.

____ and K.C. Parkes. 1959. An approach to the study of molts and plumages. Auk 76:1-31.

____ and ____. 1963. Comments on the study of plumage succession. Auk 80:496-503.

Hunt, G.L. Jr., J.C. Wingfield, A. Newman, and D.S. Farner. 1980. Sex ratio of Western Gulls on Santa Barbara Island, California. Auk 97:473-479.

Hunt, W.G., R.R. Rogers, and D.J. Slowe. 1975. Migratory and foraging behavior of Peregrine Falcons on the Texas coast. Can. Field-Nat. 89:111-123.

Hunter, E.N., and R.H. Dennis. 1972. Hybrid Great Northern X Black-throated diver in Wester Ross. Scottish Birds 7:89-91.

Huntington, C.E., R.G. Butler, and R.A. Mauck. 1996. Leach's Storm-Petrel. Birds N. Am. 233:1-32.

Hupp, J.W., and C.E. Braun. 1991. Geographic variation among Sage Grouse in Colorado. Wilson Bull. 103:255-261.

Hutchinson, C.D., T.C. Kelly, and K. O'Sullivan. 1984. American Coot: New to Britain and Ireland. Brit. Birds. 77:12-16.

Iko, W.M., S.J. Dinsmore, and F.L. Knopf. 2004. On determining the sex of Mountain Plovers (Charadrius montanus) by morphometric measurements. W. N. Am. Nat. 64:492-496.

Iliff, M.J. 2007. Short-tailed Albatrosses in Alaska. N. Am. Birds 61:174-175.

____, B.L. Sullivan, T. Leukering, and B.P. Gibbons. 2004. First record of the Little Stint for Mexico. W. Birds 35:77-87.

____, G. McCaskie, and M.T. Heindel. 2007. The 31st report of the California Bird Records Committee: 2005 records. W. Birds 38:161-205.

Imber, M.J. 1971. Filoplumes of petrels and shearwaters. New Zealand J. Marine and Freshwater Res. 5:396-403.

____ and T.G. Lovegrove. 1982. Leach's Storm Petrels (Oceanodroma l. leucorhoa) prospecting for nest sites on the Chatham Island. Notornis 29:101-108.

Ingolfsson, A. 1970. The moult of remiges and rectrices in Great Black-backed Gulls Larus marinus and Glaucous Gulls Larus hyperboreus in Iceland. Ibis 112:83-92.

____. 1987. Hybridization of Glaucous and Herring gulls in Iceland. Studies Avian Biol. 10:131-140.

Iron, J., and R. Pittaway. 2001. Molts and Plumages of Ontario's Heermann's Gull. Ontario Birds 19:65-78.

Islam, K. 2002. Heermann's Gull. Birds N. Am. 643:1-16.

Iverson, S.A., D. Esler, and W.S. Boyd. 2003. Plumage characteristics as an indicator of age class in the Surf Scoter. Waterbirds 26:56-61.

Jackson, A.C. 1919. Notes on the relation between moult and migration as observed in some waders. Brit. Birds. 11:197-203.

Jackson, B. 2004. Snowy Egret in Argyll & Bute: New to Britain. Brit. Birds 97:270-275.

Jackson, B.J.S., and J.A. Jackson. 2000. Killdeer. Birds N. Am. 517:1-28.

____ and ____. 2006. Vent size as an indicator of sex in nesting Killdeer. N. Am. Bird Bander 31:157-160.

Jackson, G.D. 1991. Field identification of teal in North America. Part 1: Blue-winged, Cinnamon, and Green-winged teal. Birding 23:124-133.

____. 1992. Field identification of teal in North America. Part 2: Female-like plumages. Birding 24:214-223.

Jackson. M.F. 1959. A hybrid between the Barrow's and the Common goldeneyes. Auk 76:92-94.

Jacobsen, E.E., C.M. White, and W.B. Emison. 1983. Molting adaptations of Rock Ptarmigan on Amchitka Island, Alaska. Condor 85:420-426.

Jakubas, D., and K. Wojczulanis. 2007. Predicting the sex of Dovekies by discriminant analysis. Waterbirds 30:92-96.

James, D.J. 2004. Identification of Christmas Island, Great and Lesser frigatebirds. Birding Asia 1:22-38.

James, F.C. 1970. Geographic variation in birds and its relationship to climate. Ecology 51:366-390.

James, J.D., and J.E. Thompson. 2001. Black-bellied Whistling-Duck. Birds N. Am. 578:1-20.

James, P.C. 1986. The filoplumes of the Manx Shearwater Puffinus puffinus. Bird Study 33:117-120.

Jannett, F.J. Jr. 1983. A quantitative method for age determination in adult birds. Am. Midland Nat. 109:145-151.

Janssen, R.B. 1980. A possible Common Goldeneye X Hooded Merganser. Loon 52:37.

Jaramillo, A. 2004. Identification of adult Pacific and American golden plovers in their southbound migration. W. Birds 35:120-123.

____ and B. Henshaw. 1995. Identification of breeding plumaged Long- and Short-billed dowitchers. Birding World 8:221-228.

____, R. Pittaway, and P. Burke. 1991. The identification and migration of breeding-plumaged dowitchers in southern Ontario. Birders J. 1:8-25.

Jehl, D.R., and J.R. Jehl Jr. 1981. A North American record of the Asiatic Marbled Murrelet. Am. Birds 35:911-912.

Jehl, J.R. Jr. 1960. A probable hybrid of Larus argentatus and L. marinus. Auk 77:343-345.

____. 1963. An investigation of fall-migrating dowitchers in New Jersey. Wilson Bull. 75:250-261.

____. 1968a. Relationships in the Charadrii (shorebirds): A taxonomic study based on color patterns of the downy young. Mem. San Diego Soc. Nat. Hist. 3:1-54.

____. 1968b. The systematic position of the Surfbird Aphriza virgata. Condor 70:206-210.

____. 1970. Sexual selection for size differences in two species of sandpipers. Evolution 24:311-319.

____. 1973. Breeding biology and systematic relationships of the Stilt Sandpiper. Wilson Bull. 85:115-147.

____. 1975. A Craveri's Murrelet from Oregon. W. Birds 6:109.

____. 1979. The autumnal migration of the Baird's Sandpiper. Studies Avian Biol. 2:55-68.

____. 1982. The biology and taxonomy of Townsend's Shearwater. Le Gerfaut 72:121-135.

____. 1985. Hybridization and evolution of oystercatchers on the Pacific coast of Baja California. Ornith. Monographs 36:484-504.

____. 1986. Biology of Red-necked Phalaropes (Phalaropus lobatus) at the western edge of the Great Basin in fall migration. Great Basin Nat. 46:185-197.

____. 1987a. Moult and moult migration in a transequatorial migrating shorebird: Wilson's Phalarope. Ornis Scand. 18:173-178.

____. 1987b. Geographic variation and evolution in the California Gull (Larus californicus). Auk 104:421-428.

____. 1987c. A review of "Nelson's Gull Larus nelsoni". Bull. Brit. Ornith. Club 107:86-91.

____. 1988. Biology of the Eared Grebe and Wilson's Phalarope in the nonbreeding season: A study of adaptations to saline lakes. Stud. Avian Biol 12:1-74.

____. 1990. Aspects of molt migration. Pp 102-113 in E. Gwinner, ed., Bird migration. Springer Verlag, Berlin.

Jehl, J.R. Jr., and S.I. Bond. 1975. Morphological variation and species limits in murrelets of the genus Endomychura. Trans. San Diego Nat. Hist. Soc. 18:9-23.

____ and W.T. Everett. 1985. History and status of the avifauna of Isla Guadalupe, Mexico. Trans. San Diego Soc. Nat. Hist. 20:313-336.

____ and E. Johnson. 2004. Wing and tail molts of the Ruddy Duck. Waterbirds 27:54-59.

____, M.A.E. Rumboll, and J.P. Winter. 1973. Winter bird populations of Golfo San Jose, Argentina. Bull. Brit. Ornith. Club 93:56-63.

____, J. Francine, and S.I. Bond. 1990. Growth patterns of two races of the California Gulls raised in a common environment. Condor 92:732-738.

____, A.E. Henry, and S.I. Bond. 1998. Sexing Eared Grebes by bill measurements. Colonial Waterbirds 21:98-100.

____, J. Klima, and R.E. Harris. 2001. Short-billed Dowitcher. Birds N. Am. 564:1-28.

Jenni, D.A., and T.R. Mace. 1999. Northern Jacana. Birds N. Am. 467:1-20.

Jenni, L. and R. Winkler. 1994. Moult and ageing of European passerines. Academic Press, New York, NY. 225 pp.

____ and ____. 2004. The problem of molt and plumage homologies and the first plumage cycle. Condor 106:187-190.

Jett, G.M. 1991. Recycling road- and window-killed birds. Birding 23:28-29.

Jewett, S.G. 1932. An unusual gallinaceous hybrid. Condor 34:191.

____, W.P. Taylor, W.T. Shaw, and J.W. Aldrich. 1953. Birds of Washington State. University of Washington Press, Seattle, WA. 767 pp.

Jiguet, F. 1997. Identification of South Polar Skua: the Brown Skua pitfall. Birding World 10:306-310.

____. 1999. Photo forum: hybrid American Wigeons. Birding World 12:247-252.

____. 2002. Taxonomy of the Kelp Gull Larus dominicanus Lichtenstein inferred from biometrics and wing plumage pattern, including two previously undescribed subspecies. Bull. Brit. Ornith. Club 122:50-71.

____, O. Chastel, and C. Barbraud. 1999. A hybrid South Polar Skua X Brown Skua. Birding World 12:118-122.

Jodice, P.G.R., R.B. Lanctot, V.A. Gill, D.D. Roby, and S.A. Hatch. 2000. Sexing adult Black-legged Kittiwakes by DNA, behavior, and morphology. Waterbirds 23:405-415.

Johansen, H. 1961. Die superspecies Larus canus. Vogelwarte 21:152-156.

Johns, J.E. 1964. Testosterone-induced nuptial feathers in phalaropes. Condor 66:449-455.

____ and E.W. Pfeiffer. 1963. Testosterone-induced incubation patches of phalarope birds. Science 140:1225-1226.

Johnsgard, P.A. 1960a. Hybridization in the Anatidae and its taxonomic implications. Condor 62:25-33.

____. 1960b. A quantitative study of sexual behavior of Mallards and Black Ducks. Wilson Bull. 72:133-135.

____. 1961a. Evolutionary relationships among the North American Mallards. Auk 78:3-43.

____. 1961b. [On the evolutionary relationships of the North American Mallards.] Auk 78:672-674.

____. 1967. Sympatry changes and hybridization incidence in Mallards and Black Ducks. Am. Midland Nat. 77:51-63.

____. 1968. Some putative Mandarin Duck hybrids. Bull. Brit. Ornith. Club. 88:140-148.

____. 1970. A summary of intergeneric New World quail hybrids, and a new intergeneric hybrid combination. Condor 72:85-88.

____. 1973. Grouse and quail of North America. University of Nebraska Press, Lincoln, NE. 553 pp.

____. 1974. The taxonomy and relationships of the northern swans. Wildfowl 25:155-161.

____. 1981a. Etho-ecological aspects of hybridization in the Tetraonidae. J. World Pheasant Assoc. 7:42-57.

____. 1981b. The plovers, sandpipers, and snipes of the world. University of Nebraska Press, Lincoln, NE.

____. 1983a. Hybridization and zoogeographic patterns in pheasants. J. World Pheasant Assoc. 8:89-98.

____. 1983b. Cranes of the world. Indiana University Press, Bloomington, IN. 258 pp.

____. 1990. Hawks, eagles, and falcons of North America. Smithsonian Institution, Washington, D.C. 403 pp.

____. 1993. Cormorants, darters, and pelicans of the world. Smithsonian Institution Press, Washington, D.C. 445 pp.

____. 1999. The pheasants of the world. 2nd edition. Smithsonian Institution Press, Washington, D.C. 398 pp.

____ and M. Carbonell. 1996. Ruddy Ducks and other stifftails. Their ecology and behavior. University of Oklahoma Press, Norman, OK. 291 pp.

____ and R.E. Wood. 1968. Distributional changes and interaction between Prairie Chickens and Sage Grouse in the midwest. Wilson Bull. 80:173-188.

Johnson, A., F. Cezilly, and V. Boy. 1993. Plumage development and maturation in the Greater Flamingo Phoenicopterus ruber roseus. Ardea 81:25-34.

Johnson, D.H., and R.E. Stewart. 1973. Racial composition of migrant populations of Sandhill Cranes in the northern plains states. Wilson Bull. 85:148-162.

____, D.E. Timm, and P.E. Springer. 1979. Morphological characteristics of Canada Geese in the Pacific Flyway. Pp. 56-80 in R.L. Jarvis and J.C. Bartonek, eds., Management and biology of Pacific Flyway geese. The Wildlife Society, Corvallis, OR.

Johnson, D.R. 1989. Body size of Northern Goshawks on coastal islands of British Columbia. Wilson Bull. 101:637-639.

Johnson, E.V., D.L. Aulman, D.A. Clendenen, G. Guliasi, L.M. Morton, P.I. Principe, and G.M. Wegener. 1983. California Condor: Activity patterns and age composition in a foraging area. Am. Birds 37:941-945.

Johnson, K. 1995. Green-winged Teal. Birds N. Am. 193:1-20.

Johnson, N.K., and H.J. Peeters. 1963. The systematic position of certain hawks in the genus Buteo. Auk 80:417-446.

____, J.V. Remsen Jr., and C. Cicero. 1998. Refined colorimetry validates endangered subspecies of the Least Tern. Condor 100:18-26.

Johnson, O.W. 1961. Reproductive cycle of the Mallard duck. Condor 63:351-364.

____. 1973. Reproductive condition and other features of shorebirds resident at Enewetak Atoll during Boreal summer. Condor 75:336-343.

____. 1977. Plumage and molt in shorebirds summering at Enewetak Atoll. Auk 94:222-230.

____. 1979. Biology of shorebirds oversummering on Enewetak Atoll. Studies Avian Biol. 2:193-205.

____. 1985. Timing of primary molt in first-year golden-plovers and some evolutionary implications. Wilson Bull. 97:237-239.

____ and P.G. Connors. 1996. American Golden-Plover and Pacific Golden-Plover. Birds N. Am. 201-202:1-40.

____ and P.M. Johnson. 1983. Plumage-molt-age relationships in "over-summering" and migratory Lesser Golden-Plovers. Condor 85:406-419.

____ and ____. 2004a. Morphometric features of Pacific and American golden-plovers with comments on field identification. Wader Study Group Bull. 103:42-49.

____ and ____. 2004b. Biometrics and field identification of Pacific and American golden-plovers. Brit. Birds. 97:434-443.

Johnson, R.A. 1938. The status of the "white-eyed" murre. Auk 55:56-61.

Johnson, R.R., R.L. Glinski, and S.W. Matteson. 2000. Zone-tailed Hawk. Birds N. Am. 529:1-20.

Johnson, T.W. 1973. The wing molt of the Florida Duck. Wilson Bull. 85:77-78.

Johnston, D.W. 1956. The annual reproductive cycle of the California Gull, I: criteria of age and the testis cycle. Condor 58:134-162.

____. 1958. Sex and age characters and salivary glands of the Chimney Swift. Condor 60:73-84.

____. 1961. Timing of annual molt in the Glaucous Gulls of northern Alaska. Condor 63:474-478.

____ and R.W. McFarlane. 1967. Migration and bioenergetics of flight in the Pacific Golden Plover. Condor 69:156-168.

Jollie, M. 1947. Plumage changes in the Golden Eagle. Auk 64:549-576.

____. 1955. A hybrid between Spruce Grouse and Blue Grouse. Condor 57:213-215.

Jones, I.L., 1990. Plumage variability functions for status signalling in Least Auklets. Animal Behav. 39:967-975.

____. 1993a. Least Auklet. Birds N. Am. 69:1-16.

____. 1993b. Crested Auklet. Birds N. Am. 76:1-12.

____. 1993c. Sexual differences in bill shape and external measurements of Crested Auklet. Wilson Bull. 105:525-529.

____, F.M. Hunter, and G. Fraser. 2000. Patterns of variation in ornaments of Crested Auklets Aethia cristatella. J. Avian Biol. 31:119-127.

____, N.B. Konyukhov, J.C. Williams, and G.V. Byrd. 2001. Parakeet Auklet. Birds N. Am. 594:1-20.

Jones, P.H. 1988.Post-fledging wing and bill development in the Razorbill Alca torda islandica. Ringing & Migr. 9:11-17.

____. 1990. The occurrence of large ('northern') Razorbills in British and Irish waters. Ringing & Migr. 11:105-110.

____ and E.I.S. Rees. 1985. Appearance and behaviour of immature guillemots and Razorbills at sea. Brit. Birds. 78:370-377.

____, C.F. Barrett, G.P. Mudge, and M.P. Harris. 1985. Examination of auks beached on east British coasts in February 1983. Seabird 8:9-14.

Jones, R.E. 1964. The specific distinctness of the Greater and Lesser prairie chickens. Auk 81:65-73.

Jonsson, L. 1984. Identification of juvenile Pomarine and Arctic skuas. Brit. Birds 77:443-446.

____ and P.J. Grant. 1984. Identification of stints and peeps. Brit. Birds. 77:293-315.

____ and B. Mactavish. 2001. American Herring Gulls at Niagara Falls and Newfoundland. Birders J. 10:90-107.

Jordan, M. 1988. Distinguishing Tundra and Trumpeter swans. Oregon Birds 14:37-40 [Reprinted Birding 20:223-226, 1988]

Jorgensen, J.G. 1997. Two hybrid diving ducks at Cunningham Lake, Douglas County. Nebraska Bird Rev. 65:135-136.

Jourdain, F.C.R. 1934. The status of Phalaropus fulicarius jourdaini Iredale. Condor 36:220.

____. 1936. The forms of the Brent Goose Branta bernicla L. Ibis (13th Ser.) 6:829-831.

Joyner, D.E. 1978. Wing molt in female Ruddy Ducks. Condor 80:102-103.

Jukema, J. 1982. Rui en biometrie van de Gouldplevier Pluvialis apricaria. Limosa 55:79-84.

____ and T. Piersma. 1987. Special moult of breast and belly feathers during breeding in Golden Plovers Pluvialis apricaria. Ornis Scand. 18:157-162.

____ and ____. 2000. Contour feather moult of Ruffs Philomachus pugnax during northward migration, with notes on homology and nuptial plumages in scolopacid waders. Ibis 142:289-296.

____ and ____. 2006. Permanent female mimics in a lekking shorebird. Biol. Letters 2:161-164

____, I. Tulp, and L. Bruinzeel. 2003. Differential moult patterns in relation to antipredator behaviour during incubation in four tundra plovers. Ibis 145:270-276.

Julian, P.R. 1967. Harlan's Hawk -- a challenging taxonomic and field problem. Colorado Field Ornith. 1:1-6.

Juola, F.A., M.F. Haussmann, D.C. Dearborn, and C.M. Vleck. 2006. Telomere shortening in a long-lived marine bird: Cross-sectional analysis and test of aging tool. Auk 123:775-783.

Kabat, C., D.R. Thompson, and F.M. Kozklik. 1950. Changes in Pheasant weight and wing molt in relation to reproduction with survival implications. Wisconsin Cons. Dept. Tech. Wildl. Bull. 2:1-26.

Kaczmarek, K., P. Minias, R. Włodarczyk, T. Janiszewski, and A. Kleszcz. 2007. A new insight into the ageing of Common Snipe Gallinago gallinago - the value of contrast within the wing coverts of adults. Ringing & Migr. 23:223-227.

Kaminski, R.M. 1980. Some anatomic characters of southeastern Michigan Canada Geese. Jack-Pine Warbler 58:99-103.

Kania, W. The primary moult of breeding Dunlins Calidris alpina in the central Taymyr in 1989. Wader Study Group Bull. 60:17-19.

Käläs, J.A. 1988. Sexual size dimorphism and plumage of the polyandrous Dotterel (Charadrius morinellus): Sex roles and constraints on sexual selection. Can. J. Zool. 66:1334-1341.

Karlionova, N., P. Pinchuk, W. Meissner, and Y. Verkuil. 2007. Biometrics of Ruffs Philomachus pugnax migrating in spring through southern Balarus with special emphasis on the occurrence of 'faeders'. Ringing & Migr. 23:134-140.

Kaufman, K. 1979a. The double identity of the Western Grebe. Continental Birdlife 1:85-89.

____. 1979b. Answer to snap judgement 3. Continental Birdlife 1:96-97.

____. 1987. The practiced eye: Pectoral Sandpiper and Sharp-tailed Sandpiper. Am. Birds 41:1356-1358.

____. 1988. The practiced eye: Female dabbling ducks. Birding 42:1203-1205.

____. 1989. Buteos of the winter fields. Am. Birds 43:1241-1244.

____. 1990a. Advanced birding. Houghton Mifflin Co., Boston, MA. 299 pp.

____. 1990b. Common Merganser and Red-breasted Merganser. Am. Birds 44:1203-1205.

____. 1990c. Curlew Sandpiper and its I.D. contenders. Am. Birds 44:189-192.

____. 1991. Summertime blues. Am. Birds 45:330-333.

____. 1992. Identifying monochrome grebes in winter. Am. Birds 46:1187-1190.

____. 1994. Over-reported? Birding 26:380-382.

____. 1999. Separating the scaup. Birding World 12:88-89.

____, J. Witzeman, and E. Cook. 1979. Pinning down the blue Ross' Goose. Continental Birdlife 1:112-115.

Kear, J., ed. 2005. Ducks, geese, and swans. Vols. 1 & 2. Oxford University Press, Oxford, U.K. 908 pp.

____ and N. Doplaix-Hall. 1975. Flamingos. T & AD Poyser, Hertfordshire, UK. 246 pp.

Keddy-Hector, D.P. 2000. Aplomado Falcon. Birds N. Am. 549:1-20.

Keeler, C.A. 1893. Evolution of the colors of North American land birds. Occ. Papers California Acad. Sci. 3:1-361.

Kehoe, C. 1992. A possible hybrid Ring-billed Gull (Larus delawarensis) X Common Gull (Larus canus). Birding World 5:312-313.

Keitt, B.S. 2005. Status of Xantus's Murrelet and its nesting habitat in Baja California, Mexico. Marine Ornith. 33:105-114.

____, B.R. Tershy, and D.A. Croll. 2000. Black-vented Shearwater. Birds N. Am. 521:1-16.

Kelly, G. 1975. Indexes for aging eastern Wild Turkeys. Pp. 205-209 in L.K. Halls, ed., Proceedings of the third national Wild Turkey symposium. Texas Parks and Wildlife, Austin, TX.

Kelsall, J.P. 1974. Snow Geese primaries as indicators of age and sex. Netherlands J. Zool. 52:791-794.

Kemp, J.B. 1990. Underwing of Wigeon. Brit. Birds. 83:23.

____. 1999. The "Welney whistler". Birding World 12:125-126.

____. 2000. A Blue-winged Teal X Shoveler hybrid in Norfolk. Birding World 13:460-461.

____. 2001. Identification of Greenland White-fronted Goose. Birding World 14:103-105.

Kennard, F.H. 1919. Notes on a new subspecies of Blue-winged Teal. Auk 36:455-460.

____. 1927. The specific status of the Greater Snow Goose. Proc. New England Zool. Club 9:85-93.

Kennerley, P.R., W. Hoogendoorn, and M.L. Chalmers. 1995. Identification and systematics of large white-headed gulls in Hong Kong. Hong Kong Bird Rep. 1994:127-156.

Kent, D.M. 1986. Flushing lores of a male Least Bittern. Florida Field Nat. 14:49-51.

Kenyon, K.W. 1949. Observations on behavior and populations of oystercatchers in Lower California. Condor 51:193-199.

Kepler, C.B. 1969. Breeding biology of the Blue-faced Booby (Sula dactylatra personata) on Green Island, Kure Atoll. Publ. Nuttall Ornith. Club 8:1-97.

Keppie, D.M., and G.W. Redmond. 1988. A review of possible explanations for reverse size dimorphism of American Woodcock. Can. J. Zool. 66:2390-2397.

____ and R.M. Whiting Jr. 1994. American Woodcock. Birds N. Am. 100:1-28.

Kessel, B. 1989. Birds of the Seward Peninsula, Alaska. University of Alaska Press. 330 pp.

____, D.A. Rocque, and J.S. Barclay. 2002. Greater Scaup. Birds N. Am. 650:1-32.

Kimball, R.T. 2006. Hormonal control of coloration. Pp. 431-468 in G.E. Hill and K.J. McGraw, eds., Bird Coloration. Vol. 1: Mechanisms and measurements. Harvard University Press, Cambridge, MA.

King, J.R. 2000. Field identification of adult californicus and albertaensis California Gulls. Birders J. 9:245-260.

____ and G.J. Carey. 1999. Slaty-backed Gull hybridization and variation in upperpart colour. Birders J. 8:88-93.

King, W.B., and P.J. Gould. 1967. The status of the Newell's race of the Manx Shearwater. Living Bird 6:163-186.

Kinsky, F.C., and J.A. Fowler. 1973. A Manx Shearwater (Puffinus p. puffinus) in New Zealand. Notornis 20:14-20.

____ and J.C. Yaldwyn. 1981. The bird fauna of Niue Island, south-west Pacific, with special notes on the White-tailed Tropicbird and Golden Plover. Nat. Mus. New Zealand Misc. Ser. 2:1-49.

Kirby, R.E., A. Reed, P. Dupuis, H.H. Obrecht III, and W.J. Quist. 2000. Description and identification of American Black Duck, Mallard, and hybrid wing plumage. USGS-BRD Biol. Sci. Rep. 2000-0002:1-26.

Kirk, D.A., and A.G. Gosler. 1994. Body composition varies with migration and competition in migrant and resident South American vultures. Auk 111:933-944.

____ and M.J. Mossman. 1998. Turkey Vulture. Birds N. Am. 339:1-32.

Kirkpatrick, C.M. 1944. The bursa of Fabricius in Ring-necked Pheasants. J. Wild. Manage. 8:118-129.

Klima, J., and J.R. Jehl Jr. 1998. Stilt Sandpiper. Birds N. Am. 341:1-20.

Klint, T. 1982. Wing moult and breeding of female Mallard Anas platyrhynchos. Ibis 124:335-339.

Klomp, N.I., and R.W. Furness. 1992. A technique which may allow accurate determination of the age of adult birds. Ibis 134:245-249.

Knapton, R. 1997. Identification of female Common Eider subspecies in Canada. Birders J. 6:134-136.

____. 2000. Identification of Bewick's Swans. Birders J. 9:130-133.

Knopf, F.L. 1975. Schedule of presupplemental molt of White Pelicans with notes on the bill horn. Condor 77:356-359.

____. 1996. Mountain Plover. Birds N. Am. 211:1-16.

Knox, A. 1994. Claimed occurrences of Red-billed Tropicbird in Britain. Brit. Birds. 87:480-487.

Knudsen, B. 1976. Colony turnover and hybridization in some Canadian Arctic gulls (abstract). Pacific Seabird Group Bull. 3:27.

Kochert, M.N., K. Steenhof, C.L. McIntyre, and E.H. Craig. 2002. Golden Eagle. Birds N. Am. 684:1-44

Koelz, W. 1929. On a collection of Gyrfalcons from Greenland. Wilson Bull. 41:207-219.

Koffijberg, K., and M.R. Van Eerden. 1995. Sexual dimorphism in the Cormorant Phalacrocorax carbo sinensis: Possible implications for differences in structural size. Ardea 83:37-46.

Koford, C.B. 1953. The California Condor. Nat. Audubon Soc. Res. Rep. 4:1-154. [Reprinted, Dover Publications, New York, NY, 1966.]

Kohn, S.C., and G.D. Kobriger. 1986. Occurrence of Sage Grouse/Sharp-tailed Grouse hybrid in North Dakota. Prairie Nat. 18:33-36.
Konyukhov, N.B. 2001. Molting and seasonal bill-plate shedding in the Whiskered Auklet (Aethia pygmaea). Biol Bull. Russian Acad. Sci. 28:266-272.
____ and A.S. Kitaysky. 1995. The Asian race of the Marbled Murrelet. Pp. 23-29 in C.J. Ralph, et al., eds., Ecology and conservation of the Marbled Murrelet. Pacific Southwest Research Station, Albany, CA.
Koopman, K. 1986. Primary moult and weight changes of Ruffs in the Netherlands in relation to migration. Ardea 74:69-77.
____. 1996. The partial pre-breeding primary moult in Common Terns Sterna hirundo. Ringing & Migr. 17:11-14.
Kortright, F.H. 1942. The ducks, geese and swans of North America. Wildlife Management Institute, Washington, D.C. 476 pp.
Koskimies, J. 1956. Determining the age of gallinaceous birds by outer primary method. Viltrevy 2:307-328.
Kozlova, E.V. 1932. The birds of south-west Transbaikalia, Northern Mongolia, and central Gobi, Part III. Ibis 13(2nd Ser.):567-596.
____. 1957. Fauna of the USSR, Birds, Charadriiformes, Suborder Alcae. Academy of Sciences, St. Petersburg, USSR. [Isreal Program for Scientific Translations, 1961; 140 pp.]
Kraft, M., and M. Frede. 1997. Identification of Barrow's and Common goldeneye. Alula 2:56-62.
Kraft, R.H. 1991. Status report of the Lacreek Trumpeter Swan flock. Proc. Papers Trumpeter Swan Society Conf. 12:88-90.
Krapu, G.L., D.H. Johnson, and C.W. Dane. 1979. Age determination of Mallards. J. Wildl. Manage. 43:384-393.
Kratter, A.W., and D.W. Steadman. 2003. First Atlantic Ocean and Gulf of Mexico specimen of Short-tailed Shearwater. N. Am. Birds 57:277-279.
Kristiansen, J.N., A.J. Walsh, A.D. Fox, H. Boyd, and D.A. Stroud. 1999. Variation in the belly barrings of the Greenland White-fronted Goose Anser albifrons flavirostris. Wildfowl 50:21-28.
Krogman, B. 1978. The Tule Goose mystery - a problem in taxonomy. Am. Birds 32:164-166.
____. 1979. A systematic study of Anser albifrons in California. Pp. 29-43 in R.L. Jarvis and J.C. Bartonek, eds., Management and biology of Pacific Flyway geese. The Wildlife Society, Corvallis, OR.
Krohn, W.B., and E.G. Bizeau. 1979. Molt migration of the Rocky Mountain population of the western Canada Goose. Pp. 130-140 in R.L. Jarvis and J.C. Bartonek, eds., Management and biology of Pacific Flyway geese, northwest section. The Wildlife Society, Corvallis, OR.
Kuletz, K.J., and S.J. Kendall. 1998. A productivity index for Marbled Murrelets in Alaska based on surveys at sea. J. Wildl. Manage. 62:446-460.
Kulikova, I.V., et al. Phylogeography of the Mallard (Anas platyrhynchos): Hybridization, dispersal, and lineage sorting contribute to complex geographic structure. Auk 122:949-965.
Kuroda, N. 1929. On the subspecific validity of Anser gambelli Hartlaub. Condor 31:173-180.
____. 1953. A wild hybrid between Branta and Anser obtained in Japan. Condor 55:100-101.
____. 1954. On the classification and phylogeny of the order Tubenares, particularly the shearwaters (Puffinus), with special considerations on their osteology and habit differentiation. Herald Company, Tokyo. 179 pp.
____. 1955. Observations of pelagic birds in the northwest Pacific.Condor 57:290-300.
____. 1960. An assumed hybrid between Mallard and Wigeon. Ann. Zool. Japonenses 33:61-65.
____. 1967. Note on the whitish underparts of Puffinus tenuirostris and a supposed hybrid between P. griseus. Misc. Rep. Yamashina Inst. Ornith. Zool. 5:194-197.
Kus, B.E., P. Ashman, G.W. Page, and L.E. Stenzel. 1984. Age-related mortality in a wintering population of Dunlin. Auk 101:69-73.
Kushlan, J.A. 1977. Sexual dimorphism in the White Ibis. Wilson Bull. 89:92-98.
____ and K.L. Bildstein. 1992. White Ibis. Birds N. Am. 9:1-20.
____ and J. Hancock. 2005. The Herons. Oxford University Press, Oxford, U.K. 433 pp.
Kusters, E. 1991. Ratselvogel und Artbastard Kiebitzregenpfeifer/ Goldregenpfeifer. Ornith. Mitteilungen 43:44-51.
Kuyt, E. 1966. Further observations on large Canada Geese moulting on the Thelon River. Can. Field-Nat. 80:63-69.
Kwater, E. 1992. Identifying a problem yellowlegs. Birding 24:18-20.
Lahrman, F.W. 1970. Possible wild hybrid of the White-fronted Goose × Snow Goose. Blue Jay 28:170.
Lakin, I., and K. Rylands. 1997. The Semipalmated Plover in Devon: The second British record. Brit. Birds. 10:212-216.
Lancaster, D.A. 1970. Breeding behavior of the Cattle Egret in Columbia. Living Bird 9:167-194.
Lanctot, R.B., and C.D. Laredo. 1994. Buff-breasted Sandpiper. Birds N. Am. 91:1-20.
____ , P.J. Weatherhead, B. Kemenaers, and K.T. Scribner. 1998. Male traits, mating tactics and reproductive success in the Buff-breasted Sandpiper, *Tryngites subruficollis*. Animal Behav. 56:419-432.
Lane, B. 1986. The subspecies of Mongolian Plover *Charadrius mongolus* in Australia. Stilt 8:14-15.
Lane, S.G., F.W.C. van Gessel, and C.D.T. Minton. 1981. A hybrid wader? Corella 5:114-115.
Langman, M. 2000. Hybrid Mediterranean × Black-headed Gulls. Birding Scotland 3:56-65.
Langridge, H.P. 1984. Identification of Arctic Loon in winter plumage. Florida Field Nat. 12:61-63.
Langston, N.E., and N. Hillgarth. 1995. Moult varies with parasites in Laysan Albatrosses. Proc. Royal Soc. London (Ser. B) 261:239-243.
____ and S. Rohwer. 1995. Unusual patterns of incomplete primary molt in Laysan and Black-footed albatrosses. Condor 97:1-19.
____ and ____. 1996. Molt -- breeding tradeoffs in albatrosses: Life history implications for big birds. Oikos 76:498-510.
Lansdown, P.G. 2000. Separation of American and Great bitterns. Brit. Birds 93:132-134.
Larkin, P. 2000. Eyelid colour of American Wigeon. Brit. Birds. 93:39-40.
Larson, J.S., and R.D. Taber. 1980. Criteria of sex and age. Pp. 143-202 *in* S.D. Schemnitz, ed., Research and management techniques for wildlife and habitats. The Wildlife Society, Washington, D.C.
Lasley, G.W., and C. Sexton. 1989. Texas region. Am. Birds 43:502-510.
Lassen, R.W., K.E. Doty, and R.D. Saucerman. 1955. Sexing day-old Ring-necked Pheasant chicks by a color characteristic. California Fish Game 41:229-231.
Lauro, A.J., and B.J. Spencer. 1980. A method for separating juvenal and first-winter Ring-billed Gulls (*Larus delawarensis*) and Common Gulls (*Larus canus*). Am. Birds 34:111-117.
Laux, E.V. 1994. Mystery sandpiper. Birding 26:66-68.
Lavers, N. 1975. Status of the Harlan's Hawk in Washington, and notes on its identification in the field. W. Birds 6:55-62.
Lawrence, D. 1993. Spotted Sandpiper displaying to and mating with Common Sandpiper. Brit. Birds. 86:628.
Lawrence, J.S., G.A. Perkins, D.D. Thornburg, R.A. Williamson, and W.D. Klimstra. 1998. Molt migration of giant Canada Geese from west-central Illinois. Pp. 105-111 *in* D.H. Rusch, et al., eds., Biology and management of Canada Geese. Proceedings of the International Canada Goose symposium, Milwaukee, WI.
Layne, J.N. 1981. Observations on wing molt of Florida Sandhill Cranes. Florida Field Nat. 9:60-61.
____. 1986. Plumages and molts of the Crested Caracara. [Abstract]. Annual Meeting of the Raptor Research Fund, Gainesville, FL. p. 22.
____ and D.R. Smith. 1992. Size comparison of resident and wintering American Kestrels in south-central Florida. J. Field Ornith. 63:256-263.
Leader, P. 1999. Identification forum: Common Snipe and Wilson's Snipe. Birding World 12:371-374.
____. 2000. Aleutian Tern. Birding World 13:147-150.
Leafloor, J.O., and D.H. Rusch. 1997. Clinal size variation in Canada Geese affects morphometric discrimination techniques. J. Wildl. Manage. 61:183-190.
____, C.D. Ankney, and K.W. Risi. 1996. Social enhancement of wing molt in female Mallards. Can. J. Zool. 74:1376-1378.
Lebret, T. 1983. Bastarden van Bragens *Branta lecopsis* × Sneeugans *Chen caerulescens*. Limosa 56:18-19.
Le Corre, M., and P. Jouventin. 1999. Geographic variation in the White-tailed Tropicbird *Phaethon lepturus*, with the description of a new subspecies endemic to Europa Island, southern Mozambique Channel. Ibis 141:233-239.
Lee, C.-T., and A. Birch. 2006. Advances in the field identification of North American dowitchers. Birding 38:34-42.
Lee, D.S. 1984. Petrels and storm-petrels in North Carolina's offshore waters: Including species previously unrecorded for North America. Am. Birds 38:151-163.
____. 1992. Specimen records of Aleutian Terns from the Philippines. Condor 94:276-279.
____. 1995. The pelagic ecology of Manx Shearwaters *Puffinus puffinus* off the southeastern United States of America. Marine Ornith. 23:107-115.
____ and M.K. Clark. 1993. Notes on post-breeding American Swallow-tailed Kites, *Elanoides forficatus* (Falconiformes: Accipitridae), in north central Florida. Brimleyana 19:185-203.
____ and J.C. Haney. 1996. Manx Shearwater. Birds N. Am. 257:1-28.
____ and M. Walsh-McGehee. 1998. White-tailed Tropicbird. Birds N. Am. 353:1-24.
____, D.B. Wingate, and H.W. Kale II. 1981. Records of tropicbirds in the North Atlantic and upper Gulf of Mexico, with comments on field identification. Am. Birds 35:887-890.

Lee, P.L.M., and R. Griffiths. 2003. Sexing errors among museum skins of a sexually monomorphic bird, the Moorhen *Gallinula chloropus*. Ibis 145:695-698.

Lehman, P. 1998. Little-known plumages from Alaska. Birders J. 7:105-107.

____. 2000. Two little-known juvenile shorebirds. W. Birds 31:210-212.

____. 2006. Autumn plumages from the Bering Sea region, Alaska. *Birding* 38:26-33.

Lehman, V.W. 1941. Attwater's Prairie Chicken. Its life history and management. N. Am. Fauna 57:1-65.

Lehmann V., F.C. 1946. Two new birds from the Andes of Columbia. Auk 63:218-223.

____. 1960. Notas sobre *Buteo albigula phillippi*. Noved. Colombianas 1:242-255.

Leopold, A.S. 1939. Age determination in quail. J. Wildl. Manage. 3:261-265.

____. 1943. The molts of young wild and domestic Turkeys. Auk 45:133-145.

____. 1944. The nature of heritable wildness in Turkeys. Condor 46:133-197.

____. 1959. Wildlife of Mexico: The game birds and mammals. University of California Press, Berkeley, CA. 608 pp.

____. 1977. The California Quail. University of California Press, Berkeley, CA. 281 pp.

____ and R.A. McCabe. 1957. Natural history of the Montezuma Quail in Mexico. Condor 59:3-26.

Leschack, C.R., S.K. McKnight, and G.R. Hepp. 1997. Gadwall. Birds N. Am. 283:1-28.

Lessells, C.M., and A.C. Mateman. 1998. Sexing birds using random amplified polymorphic DNA(RAPD) markers. Molecular Ecol. 7:187-195.

Lethaby, N. 1995. Undertail-coverts of Solitary Sandpipers. Birding World 8:426-427.

____. 2000. The identification of Long-billed Murrelet in alternate plumage. Birding 32:438-444.

____ and I.A. McLaren. 2002. The identification of Gray Heron. Birding 34:24-33.

LeValley, R., and P. Pyle. 2007. Notes on plumage maturation in the Red-tailed Tropicbird. W. Birds 38:306-310.

Lewin, V. 1963. Reproduction and development of young in a population of California Quail. Condor 65:249-278.

Lewis, H.F. 1929. The natural history of the Double-crested Cormorant (*Phalacrocorax auritus auritus* (Lesson)). Ru-Mi-Lou Books, Ottawa, ON. 94 pp.

Lewis, J.B. 1966. Hybridization between Wild and Domestic turkeys in Missouri. J. Wildl. Manage. 30:431-432.

Lewis, J.C. 1967. Physical characteristics and physiology. Pp. 45-72 *in* O.W. Hewitt, ed., The Wild Turkey and its management. The Wildlife Society, Washington, D.C.

____. 1979a. Molt of the remiges of Grus canadensis. Proc. N. Am. Crane Workshop 2:255-259.

____. 1979b. Field identification of juvenile Sandhill Cranes. J. Wildl. Manage. 43:211-214.

____. 1995. Whooping Crane. Birds N. Am. 153:1-28.

Liebers, D., and A.J. Helbig. 2002. Phylogeography and colonization of Lesser Black-backed Gulls (*Larus fuscus*) as revealed by mtDNA sequences. J. Evol. Biol. 15:1021-1033.

____, A.J. Helbig, and P. de Knijff. 2001. Genetic differentiation and phylogeography of gulls in the *Larus cachinnans-fuscus* group (Aves: Charadriiformes). Molecular Ecol. 10:2447-2462.

____, P. de Knijff, and A.J. Helbig. 2004. The Herring Gull complex is not a ring species. Proc. Royal Soc. London 271:893-901.

Liguori, J. 2001. Pitfalls of classifying light morph Red-tailed Hawks to subspecies. Birding 33:436-446.

____. 2004. How to age Golden Eagles. Birding 36:278-283.

Lillie, F.R. 1931. Bilateral gynandromorphism and lateral hemihypertrophy in birds. Science 74:387-390.

Limpert, R.J., and S.L. Earnst. 1994. Tundra Swan. Birds N. Am. 89:1-20.

____, H.A. Allen Jr., and W.J.L. Sladen. 1987. Weights and measurements of wintering Tundra Swans. Wildfowl 38:108-113.

Lincoln, F.C. 1915. Description of a new Bob-white from Colorado. Proc. Biol Soc. Washington 28:103-104.

____. 1917. A new race of the genus *Pediocetes* in Colorado. Proc. Biol. Soc. Washington 30:83-86.

____. 1918. A strange case of hybridism. Wilson Bull. 30:1-2.

____. 1950. A Ring-necked Pheasant × Prairie Chicken hybrid. Wilson Bull. 62:210-212.

Linder, R.L., R.B. Dahlgren, and C.R. Elliott. 1971. Primary feather pattern as a sex criterion in the Pheasant. J. Wildl. Manage. 35:840-843.

Lindsey, A.A. 1946. The nesting of the New Mexican Duck. Auk 63:483-492.

Lindström, Å., S. Bensch, and P.E. Jönsson. 1998. Low body mass of juvenile Ross's Gull *Rhodostethia rosea* in the Laptev Sea. Arctic 51:280-282.

Linduska, J.P. 1943. A gross study of the bursa of Fabricius and cock spurs as age indicators in the Ring-necked Pheasant. Auk 60:426-437.

____. 1945. Age determination in the Ring-necked Pheasant. J. Wildl. Manage. 9:152-154.

Lingle, G.R., and N.F. Sloan. 1979. Sexing and aging criteria for the White Pelican. Prairie Nat. 11:83-88.

Lippens, L., and G. Burggraeve. 1983. Hibridation de l'Aigrette Garzette (*Egretta garzetta*) et du Heron Cendre (*Ardea cinerea*). Gerfaut 73:303-311.

Lish, J.W. 2007. Comments on the distribution of the Fuertes Red-tailed Hawk on the Great Plains. J. Raptor Res. 41:325-327.

____ and W.G. Voelker. 1986. Field identification aspects of some Red-tailed Hawk subspecies. Am. Birds 40:197-202.

Little, B., and R.W. Furness. 1985. Long-distance migration by British Goosanders *Mergus merganser*. Ringing & Migr. 6:77-82.

Littlefield, C.D. 1970. Flightlessness in Sandhill Cranes. Auk 87:157.

Livezey, B.C. 1991. A phylogenetic analysis and classification of recent dabbling ducks (tribe Anatini) based on comparative morphology. Auk 108:471-507.

Lockwood, W.M., and T.W. Cooper. 1999. A Texas hybrid: Cinnamon × Green-winged teal. Texas Birds 1:38-40.

Loftin, H. 1962. A study of boreal shorebirds summering on Apachee Bay, Florida. Bird-Banding 33:21-41.

Lonergan, P., and K. Mullarney. 2004. Identification of American Herring Gull in a western European context. Dutch Birding 26:1-35.

Long, J. 1981. Introduced birds of the world. Universe Books, New York, NY. 528 pp.

Loncarich, F.L., and D.G. Krementz. 2004. External determination of age and sex in the Common Moorhen. Wildl. Soc. Bull. 32:655-660.

Longcore, J.R., D.C. McAuley, G.R. Hepp, and J.M. Rhymer. 2000. American Black Duck. Birds N. Am. 481:1-36.

Longmire, J.L., M. Maltbie, R.W. Pavelka, L.M. Smith, S.M. Witte, O.A. Ryder, D.L. Ellsworth, and R.J. Baker. 1993. Gender identification in birds using microsatellite DNA fingerprint analysis. Auk 110:378-381.

Loomis, L.M. 1918. A review of the albatrosses, petrels, and diving petrels. Proc. California Acad. Sci. (4th Ser.) 2:1-187.

Løppenthin, B. 1943. Systematic and biological notes on the Long-tailed Skua (Stercorarius longicaudus Viellot). Meddelelser om Grønland 131:1-26.

Lormée, H., P. Jouventin, A. Lacroix, J. Lallemand, and O. Chastel. 2000. Reproductive endocrinology of tropical seabirds: Sex-specific patterns in LH, steroids and prolactin secretion in relation to parental care. Gen. Comp. Endocrinol. 117:413-426.

Lo Valvo, M. 2001. Sexing adult Cory's Shearwaters by discriminant analysis of body measurements on Linosa Island (Sicilian Channel), Italy. Waterbirds 24:169-174.

Loveless, C.M. 1958. The mobility and composition of Bobwhite Quail populations in southern Florida with notes on the post-juvenile and post-nuptial molts. Florida Game Freshw. Fish Comm. Tech. Bull. 4:1-64.

Lovvorn, J.R., and J.A. Barzen. 1988. Molt and the annual cycle of Canvasbacks. Auk 105:543-552.

Low, G.C. 1938. The supposed races of the Grey- or Black-bellied Plover (*Squatarola squatarola*). Ibis (14th Ser.) 2:154-158.

Lowe, P.R. 1924. Some notes on the Fregatidae. Novit. Zool. 31:299-314.

Lowther, P.E., and R.T. Paul. 2002. Reddish Egret. Birds N. Am. 633:1-20.

____, H.D. Douglas III, and C.L. Gratto-Trevor. 2001. Willet. Birds N. Am. 579:1-32.

____, A.W. Diamond, S.W. Kress, G.J. Robertson, and K. Russell. 2002. Atlantic Puffin. Birds N. Am. 709:1-24.

Lumsden, H.G. 1969. A hybrid grouse *Lagopus* × *Canchites* from northern Ontario. Can. Field-Nat. 83:23-30.

____ and R.B. Weeden. 1963. Notes on the harvest of Spruce Grouse. J. Wildl. Manage. 27:586-591.

Lyon, D.L. 1962. Comparative growth and plumage development in *Coturnix* and Bobwhite. Wilson Bull. 74:5-27.

MacDonald, M.A. 1977. The pre-laying exodus of Northern Fulmar *Fulmarus glacialis* (L.). Ornis Scan. 8:33-37.

MacFarlane, R.W. 1973. Florida's Sparrow Hawks. Florida Field Nat. 2:20-22

Machmer, M.M., H. Esselink, C. Steeger, and R.C. Ydenberg. 1992. The occurrence of fault bars in the plumage of nestling Ospreys. Ardea 80:261-272.

MacInnes, C.D. 1966. Population behavior of Arctic Canada Geese. J. Wild. Manage. 30:536-553.

MacKay, G.H. 1892. Habits of the Black-bellied Plover (*Charadrius squatarola*) in Massachusetts. Auk 9:143-152.

MacLean, S.F. Jr., and R.T. Holmes. 1971. Bill lengths, wintering areas, and taxonomy of North American Dunlins, *Calidris alpina*. Auk 88:893-901.

Macnamara, M. 1977. Sexing the Osprey using secondary sexual characteristics. Pp. 43-45 *in* J.C, Odgen, ed., Transactions of the North American Osprey Research Conference. U.S.D.I. National Park Service, Washington, D.C.

Macpherson, A.H. 1961. Observations on Canadian arctic *Larus* gulls and on the taxonomy of *L. thayeri* Brooks. Arctic Inst. N. Am. Tech. Papers 7:1-40.

____ and I.A. McLaren. 1959. Notes on the birds of southern Foxe Peninsula Baffin Island, Northwest Territories. Can. Field-Nat. 73:63-81.

Mactavish, B. 1979. Apparent Mallard × Northern Pintail hybrid. Am. Birds 43:278.

____. 2001. Atlantic Provinces. N. Am. Birds 54:21-23.

____. 2004. Atlantic Provinces & St. Pierre et Miquelon. N. Am. Birds 58:30-32.

____ and K. Knowles. 2004. A hybrid sandpiper in Newfoundland. Birders J. 13:33-34.

MacWhirter, R.B., and K.L. Bildstein. 1996. Northern Harrier. Birds N. Am. 210:1-32.

____, P. Austin-Smith Jr., and D. Kroodsma. 2002. Sanderling. Birds N. Am. 653:1-28.

Maddock, M. 1989. Colour and first age of breeding in Cattle Egrets as determined from wing-tagged birds. Corella 13:1-8.

Mader, W.J. 1976. Banding worksheet for Western Birds. Harris' Hawk. N. Am. Bird Bander 1(Suppl.):1-2.

Madge, S. 1991. Separation of canvasback and redhead from pochard. Birding World 4:365-368.

____ and H. Burn. 1988. Waterfowl: An identification guide to the ducks, geese and swans of the world. Houghton Mifflin Co., Boston MA. 298 pp.

____ and P. McGowan. 2002. Pheasants, partridges, and grouse. Princeton University Press, Princeton, NJ.

Maehr, D.S., and J. Hintermeister. 1982. A possible White Ibis - Scarlet Ibis hybrid in Alachua County, Florida. Florida Field Nat. 10:78.

Maillard, J. 1902. Additions to the list of paicines birds. Condor 4:46.

Malling Olsen, K., and S. Christensen. 1984. Field identification of juvenile skuas. Brit. Birds 77:448-450.

____ and L. Jonsson. 1989. Field identification of the smaller skuas. Brit. Birds 82:143-176.

____ and H. Larsson. 1995. Terns of Europe and North America. A&C Black, London. 176 pp.

____ and ____. 1997. Skuas and Jaegers. Yale University Press. 190 pp.

____ and ____. 2003. Gulls of North America, Europe and Asia. Princeton University Press. [Reprinted with corrections 2004; 608 pp.]

Mallory, M., and K. Metz. 1999. Common Merganser. Birds N. Am. 442:1-28.

Mallory, M.L., and M.R. Forbes. 2005. Sex discrimination and measurement bias in Northern Fulmars *Fulmarus glacialis* from the Canadian Arctic. Ardea 93:25-36.

Malosh, G. 2004. Great Blue Heron × Great Egret in Washington County. Pennsylvania Birds 18:72-73.

Maltby-Prevett, L.S., H. Boyd, and J.D. Heyland. 1975. Observations in Iceland and northwestern Europe of Brant from the Queen Elizabeth Islands, N.W.T., Canada. Bird-Banding 46:155-161.

Manning, T.H. 1942. Blue and Lesser Snow geese on Southampton and Baffin islands. Auk 59:158-179.

____. 1964. Geographical and sexual variation in the Long-tailed Jaeger (Stercorarius longicaudus Viellot). Biol. Papers Univ. Alaska 7:1-16.

____, E.O. Höhn, and A.H. Macpherson. 1956. The birds of Banks Island. Nat. Mus. Can. Bull. 143:1-144.

Manuwal, D.A. 1974. The incubation patches of Cassin's Auklet. Condor 76:481-484.

____. 1978. Criteria for aging Cassin's Auklets. Bird-Banding 49:157-161.

____ and A.C. Thoresen. 1993. Cassin's Auklet. Birds N. Am. 50:1-20.

Manweiler, J. 1939. The combined weight class-rectrix pattern method for determining sex of Sharp-tailed Grouse. J. Wild. Manage. 3:283-287.

Marchant, S., and P.J. Higgins, eds. 1990. Handbook of Australian, New Zealand, and Antarctic Birds. Vol. 1, parts A & B. Oxford University Press, Oxford, UK. 1400 pp.

____ and ____, eds. 1993. Handbook of Australian, New Zealand, and Antarctic Birds. Vol. 2. Oxford University Press, Oxford, UK. 983 pp.

Marcisz, W.J. 1981. A presumed Bufflehead × Hooded Merganser in Illinois. Am. Birds 35:340-341.

Marion, L. 1995. Where two subspecies meet: Origin, habitat choice and niche segregation of Cormorant *Phalacrocorax c. carbo* and *P.c. sinensis* in the common wintering area (France), in relation to breeding isolation in Europe. Ardea 83:103-114.

Marion. W.R. 1977. Growth and development of the Plain Chachalaca in South Texas. Wilson Bull. 89:47-56.

Mariano-Jelicich, R., E. Madrid, and M. Favero. 2007. Sexual dimorphism and diet segregation in the Black Skimmer *Rhynchops niger*. Ardea 95:115-124.

Marks, J.S. 1993. Molt of Bristle-thighed Curlews in the Northwestern Hawaiian Islands. Auk 110:573-587.

____ and L.G, Underhill. 1994. Moult, migration and mass of a handicapped Bristle-thighed Curlew. Ardea 82:153-155.

____, R.L. Redmond, P. Hendricks, R.B. Clapp, and R.E. Gill Jr. 1990. Notes on longevity and flightlessness in Bristle-thighed Curlews. Auk 107:779-781.

____, T.L. Tibbitts, R.E. Gill, and B.J. McCaffery. 2002. Bristle-thighed Curlew. Birds N. Am. 705:1-36.

Maron, J.L., and J.P. Myers. 1984. A description and evaluation of two techniques for sexing wintering Sanderlings. J. Field Ornith. 55:336-342.

Marquardt, R.E. 1962. Identification of age classes of Canada Geese in field flocks. J. Wildl. Manage. 26:96-97.

Marshall, A.J., and D.L. Serventy. 1956. Moult adaptation in relation to long-distance migration in petrels. Nature 177:943.

Martin, F.W. 1964. Woodcock age and sex determination from wings. J. Wildl. Manage. 28:287-293.

Martin, J. 2002. Unusual Brent Geese in Norfolk and Hampshire. Brit. Birds 95:129-136.

Martin, P.R. 1991. Apparent species hybrid Goldeneye × Hooded Merganser. Am. Birds 45:412.

____ and B. Di Labio. 1994a. Natural hybrids between the Common Goldeneye, *Bucephala clangula*, and the Barrow's Goldeneye, *B. islandica*. Can. Field-Nat. 108:195-198.

____ and ____. 1994b. Identification of hybrid Common × Barrow's goldeneye hybrids in the field. Birding 26:104-105.

Massey, B.M. 1976. Vocal differences between American Least Terns and the European Little Tern. Auk 93:760-773.

____. 1998. Species and subspecies limits in Least Terns. Condor 100:180-182.

____ and J.L. Atwood. 1978. Plumages of the Least Tern. Bird-Banding 49:360-371.

Massiah, E. 1996. Identification of Snowy and Little Egret. Birding World 9:434-444.

Mather, D.D., and D. Esler. 1999. Evaluation of bursal depth as an indicator of age class of Harlequin Ducks. J. Field Ornith. 70:200-205.

____. 1914. On the species and subspecies of *Fregata*. Australian Avian. Rec. 2:117-127.

____. 1915. *Phaethon catesbyi* Brandt. Auk 32:195-197.

____. 1934. *Cymochorea castro helena*, subsp. nov. Bull. Brit. Ornith. Club 35:23.

____. 1935. Systematic notes on the Manx Shearwater (*Puffinus puffinus*). Ibis (13th Ser.) 5:577-582.

____. 1937a. *Puffinus diomedea disputans*. Bull. Brit. Ornith. Club 57:123-124.

____. 1937b. *Procellaria* [*Puffinus*] *flavirostris* Gould. Ibis (14th Ser.) 1:869-870.

____. 1938. *Cymochorea castro kumagai*, subs. nov. Bull. Brit. Ornith. Club 38:63-64.

____ and T. Iredale. 1915. On some petrels from the north-east Pacific Ocean. Ibis (10th Ser.) 3:572-609.

____ and ____. 1931. A manual of the birds of Australia. H.F. & G. Witherby, London, UK. 1047 pp.

Mathiasson, S. 1963. [Fulmars (*Fulmarus glacialis*) in Swedish waters, a biometrical-morphological study in order to establish their geographical origin.] Vår Fågelväld 22:271-289.

Matray, P.F. 1974. Broad-winged Hawk nesting and ecology. Auk 91:307-324.

Mattesson, J. 1988. Ross' Goose at Agassiz NWR: Comments on immature plumage and hybrid determination. Loon 60:66-69.

Mattox, W.G. 1969. The White Falcon: Field studies of *Falco rusticolus* L. in Greenland. Polar Notes 9:46-61.

____. 1970. Banding Gyrfalcons (*Falco rusticolus*) in Greenland. Bird-Banding 41:31-37.

Mauer, K. 1980. Barnacle × Red-breasted Goose and White-fronted × Barnacle Goose in 1979/80. Dutch Birding 2:53-54.

Mawhinney, K., and T. Diamond. 1999. Sex determination of Great Black-backed Gulls using morphometric analysis. J. Field Ornith. 70:206-210.

May, J.B. 1930. Simultaneous loss of primaries in prenuptual molt of Loon. Auk 47:412-415.

Mayr, E. 1956. Is the Great White Heron a good species? Auk 73:71-77.

____ and G.W. Cottrell, eds. 1979. Check-list of birds of the world. Vol 1, 2nd Ed. (revision of the work of James L. Peters). Museum of Comparative Zoology, Cambridge, MA.

____ and L.L. Short. 1970. Species taxa of North American birds. Publ. Nuttall Ornith. Club 9:1-127.

McAtee, W.L. 1944. *Anser gambelli*. Auk 61:294-295.

McAuley, D.G., J.R. Longcore, and G.F. Sepik. 1993. Techniques for research into woodcocks: Experiences and recommendations. Proc. 8th Woodcock Symposium, Biological Reports 16:5-11.

McCabe, R.A. 1954. Hybridization between the Bob-white and Scaled Quail. Auk 71:293-297.

____ and A.S. Hawkins. 1946. The Hungarian Partridge in Wisconsin. Am. Midl. Nat. 36:1-75.

McCaffery, B., and R. Gill. 2001. Bar-tailed Godwit. Birds N. Am. 581:1-36.

____, C.M. Harwood, and J.R. Morgart. 1997. First breeding records of Slaty-backed Gull (*Larus schistisagus*) for North America. Pacific Seabirds 24:70.

McCarthy, E.M. 2006. Handbook of avian hybrids of the world. Oxford University Press, New York, NY. 583 pp.

McCaskie, G. 1975. A Rufous-necked Stint in California. W. Birds 6:111-113.

____. 1983. Another look at the Western and Yellow-footed Gulls. W. Birds 14:85-107.

____. J.L. Dunn, C. Roberts, and D.A. Sibley. 1990. Notes on identifying Arctic and Pacific loons in alternate plumage. Birding 22:70-73.

McClelland, B.R., D.S. Shea, and P.T. McClelland. 1998. Size variation of migrant Bald Eagles at Glacier National Park, Montana. J. Raptor Res. 32:120-125.

McCloskey, J.T., and J.E. Thompson. 2000. Aging and sexing Common Snipe using discriminant analysis. J. Wildl. Manage. 64:960-969.

McCollough, M.A. 1989. Molting sequence and aging of Bald Eagles. Wilson Bull. 101:1-10.

McCrimmon, D.A. Jr., J.C. Ogden, and G.T. Bancroft. 2001. Great Egret. Birds N. Am. 570:1-32.

McEneaney, T. 2005. Rare color variants of the Trumpeter Swan. Birding 37:148-154.

McGeehan, A. 2000. Identification of American Black Tern. Birding World 13:37.

McGlauchlin, D.C. 1971. Snow Goose - Canada Goose hybrids. Prairie Nat. 3:115-116.

McGowan, J.D. 1975. Distribution, density and productivity of Goshawks in interior Alaska. Alaska Department of Fish and Game, Juneau, AK. 30 pp.

McGowan, R.Y., and C. Kitchener. 2001. Historical and taxonomic review of the Iceland Gull *Larus glaucoides* complex. Brit. Birds. 94:191-195.

____ and B. Zonfrillo. 1995. Pitfalls in sexing Kittiwakes *Rissa tridactyla* on head + bill length. Ringing & Migr. 16:124-126.

McGuire, H.L. 2002. Taxonomic status of the Great White Heron (*Ardea herodias occidentalis*): An analysis of behavioral, genetic, and morphometric evidence. Florida Fish and Wildlife Conservation Commission, Tallahassee, Florida, USA. 50 pp.

McHenry, E.N., and J.C. Dyes. 1983. First record of juvenal "white-phase" Great Blue Heron in Texas. Am. Birds 37:119.

McIlhenny, E.A. 1937. Results of 1936 bird banding operations at Avery Island, Louisiana, with special references to sex ratios and hybrids. Bird-Banding 8:117-121.

McIntyre, A.E., and J.W. McIntyre. 1974. Spots before the eyes, an aid to identifying wintering loons. Auk 91:413-415.

McIntyre, J.W. 1988. The Common Loon: Spirit of northern lakes. University of Minnesota Press, Minneapolis, MN. 228 pp.

____ and J.F. Barr. 1997. Common Loon. Birds N. Am. 313:1-32.

McKee, T., and R.A. Erickson. 2002. Report of the California Bird records Committee: 2000 records. W. Birds 33:175-201.

____ and P. Pyle. 2002. Plumage variation and hybridization in Black-footed and Laysan albatrosses. N. Am. Birds 56:131-138.

____ and R.S. Terrill. 2004. Dark shearwaters in the North Pacific Ocean. Birding 36:598-607.

McKilligan, N.G. 1985. The breeding success of Cattle Egret *Ardea ibis* in eastern Australia. Ibis 127:530-536.

McKinnon, D.T. 1983. Age separation of yearling and adult Franklin's Spruce Grouse. J. Wildl. Manage. 47:533-535.

McKnight, S.K., and G. Hepp. 1999. Molt chronology of American Coots in winter. Condor 101:893-897.

McLandress, M.R. 1983. Winning with warts? A threat posture suggests a function for carnuncles in Ross's Geese. Wildfowl 34:5-9.

____ and I. McLandress. 1979. Blue-phase Ross' Geese and other blue-phase geese in western North America. Auk 96:544-550.

McLaren, I.A. 1989. Thoughts on North American Little Egrets. Birding 21:284-287.

____ and Z. Lucas. 2004. A possible Brown Skua (*Stercorarius antarcticus*) on Sable Island, Nova Scotia. N. Am. Birds 58:622-626.

McLaughlin, K. 2001. Variation in first year Ring-billed Gull. Ontario Birds 19:114-118.

____ and R. Pittaway. 2003. Early first prebasic molt in Short-billed Dowitcher. Ontario Birds 21:145-146.

____ and A. Wormington. 2000. An apparent Dunlin × White-rumped Sandpiper hybrid. Ontario Birds 18:8-12.

McNeil, R. 1970. Hivernage et estivage d'oiseau aquaticas Nord-Americans dans le nord-est du Venezuela (mue, accumulation de grasse, capacite de vol et routes de migration). Oiseau Rev. Francaise Ornith. 40:185-302.

____ and J. Burton. 1972. Cranial pnematization patterns and bursa of Fabricius in North American shorebirds. Wilson Bull. 84:329-339.

McNicholl, M.K., P.E. Lowther, and J.A. Hall. 2001. Forster's Tern. Birds N. Am. 595:1-24.

McVaugh, W. Jr. 1972. The development of four North American herons. Living Bird 11:155-173.

____. 1975. The development of four North American herons. II Living Bird 14:163-183.

Meanley, B. 1969. Natural history of the King Rail. N. Am. Fauna 67:1-108.

____. 1985. The marsh hen: A natural history of the Clapper Rail of the Atlantic salt marsh. Tidewater Publishers, Centreville, MD. 123 pp.

____. 1988. A King-Clapper rail hybrid from Rappahannock River Marsh. Raven 59:15-16.

____. 1992. King Rail. Birds N. Am. 3:1-12.

____ and A.G. Meanley. 1958. Growth and development of the King Rail. Auk 75:381-386.

____ and D.K. Wetherbee. 1962. Ecological notes on mixed populations of King Rails and Clapper Rails in Delaware Bay marshes. Auk 79:453-457.

Mearns, E.A. 1892. A study of the Sparrowhawk (subgenus *Tinnunculus*) of America, with especial reference to the continental species (*Falco sparverius* Linn.). Auk 9:252-270.

____. 1895. Description of a new heron (*Ardea virescens anthonyi*) from the arid region of the interior of North America. Auk 12:257-259.

____. 1914. Diagnosis of a new subspecies of Gambel's Quail from Colorado. Proc. Biol. Soc. Washington 27:113-114.

____. 1916. Description of a new subspecies of the American Least Tern. Proc. Biol. Soc. Washington 29:71-72.

Meeks, W.A., D.E. Naugle, R.R. Johnson, and K.F. Higgins. 1996. Interbreeding of a Tricolored Heron and a Snowy Egret in South Dakota. Auk 113:955-957.

Meininger, P.L. 1993. Breeding Black-winged Stilts in the Netherlands in 1989-93 including one paired with Black-necked Stilt. Dutch Birding 15:193-197.

Meissner, W. 2005. Sex determination of juvenile Dunlins migrating through the Polish Baltic region. J. Field Ornith. 6:368-372.

____. 2007a. Different timing of autumn migration of two Ringer Plover *Charadrius hiaticula* subspecies through the southern Baltic revealed by biometric analysis. Ringing & Migr. 23:129-133.

____. 2007b. Differences in primary molt and biometrics between adult and second-year Black-headed Gulls in Puck Bay (southern Baltic). Waterbirds 30:144-149.

____ and R. Krupa. 2007. Biometrics and primary moult of Common Tern and Sandwich Tern in autumn in Puck Bay, southern Baltic. Waterbirds 30:158-163.

Melville, D.S. 1981. Spring measurements, weights and plumage status of *Calidris ruficollis* and *C. ferruginea* in Hong Kong. Wader Study Group Bull. 33:18-21.

____. 1985. Long-tailed Skuas Stercorarius longicaudus in New Zealand. Notornis 32:51-73.

Melvin, S.M., and J.P. Gibbs. 1996. Sora. Birds N. Am. 250:1-20.

Mendall, H.L. 1958. The Ring-necked Duck in the Northeast. Univ. Maine Bull. 73:1-317.

____. 1980. Intergradation of eastern American Common Eiders. Can. Field-Nat. 94:286-292.

____. 1986. Identification of eastern races of the Eider. Can. Wildl. Serv. Rep. Ser. 47:82-88.

____ and C.M. Ardous. 1943. The ecology and management of the American Woodcock. Maine Cooperative Fish and Wildlife Research Unit. 201 pp.

Mengel, R.M. 1953. On the name of the Northern Bald Eagle and the identity of Audubon's gigantic "bird of Washington". Wilson Bull. 65:145-151.

Meredino, M.T., C.D. Ankney, D.G. Dennis, and J.O. Leafloor. 1994. Morphometric discrimination of Giant and Akimiski Island Canada Geese. Wildl. Soc. Bull. 22:14-19.

Merrifield, K. 1993. Eurasian × American wigeons in western Oregon. W. Birds 24:105-107.

____ 1998. Two presumed Mallard × Gadwall hybrids (*Anas platyrhynchos* × *A. strepera*) in Lincoln County, Oregon. Northwestern Nat. 79:54-58.

Metz, V.G., and E.A. Schreiber. 2002. Great Frigatebird. Birds N. Am. 681:1-24.

Meyer, K.D. 1995. Swallow-tailed Kite. Birds N. Am. 138:1-24.

Meyerriecks, A.J. 1957. Field observations pertaining to the systematic status of the Great White Heron in the Florida keyes. Auk 74:469-478.

Meyerriecks, A.J. 1960. Comparative breeding behavior of four species of North American herons. Publ. Nuttall Ornith. Club 2:1-158.
Mikami, S. 1989. First Japanese records of crosses between Whistling *Cygnus columbianus columbianus* and Bewick's Swans *C.c. bewicki*. Wildfowl 40:131-133.
Miller, A.H. 1941. The significance of molt centers among secondary remiges in the Falconiformes. Condor 43:113-115.
____ 1946. Endemic birds of the Little San Bernadino Mountains, California. Condor 48:75-79.
____ and H.I. Fisher. 1938. The pterylosis of the California Condor. Condor 40:248-256.
____ and R.C. Stebbins. 1964. The lives of desert animals in Joshua Tree National Monument. University of California Press, Berkeley, CA. 452 pp.
Miller, E.H. 1979. Egg size in the Least Sandpiper *Calidris minutilla* on Sable Island, Nova Scotia. Ornis Scand. lO:lO-16.
Miller, G.C. 1977. Two-year-old White Pelicans at colony sites. Proc. Colonial Waterbird Group 1977:73-77.
____ and W.D. Graul. 1980. Status of the Sharp-tailed Grouse in North America. Pp. 18-28 *in* P.A. Vohls and F.L. Knopf, eds., Proceedings of the prairie grouse symposium. Oklahoma State University, Stillwater, OK.
Miller, K.E., and K.D. Meyer. 2002. Short-tailed Hawk. Birds N. Am. 674:1-16.
____ and J.A. Smallwood. 1997. Juvenal plumage characteristics of male southeastern American Kestrels (*Falco sparverius paulus*). J. Raptor Res. 31:273-274.
Miller, L. 1937. Feather studies in the California Condor. Condor 39:160-162.
____. 1940. Observations on the Black-footed Albatross. Condor 42:229-238.
Miller, M.R. 1986. Molt chronology on Northern Pintails in California. J. Wildl. Manage. 50:57-64.
____, J.P. Fleskes, D.L. Orthmeyer, and D.S. Gilmer. 1992. Survival and other observations of adult female Northern Pintails molting in California. J. Field Ornith. 63:138-144.
Miller, R.S., and J.P. Hatfield. 1974. Age ratios of Sandhill Cranes. J. Wildl. Manage. 38:234-242.
Miller, S.L., M.A. Gregg, A.R. Kuritsubo, S.M. Combs, M.K. Murdock, J.A. Nilsson, B.R. Noon, and R.G. Botzler. 1988. Morphometric variation in Tundra Swans: Relationships among sex and age classes. Condor 90:802-815.
Miller, W. deW. 1915. Notes on ptilosis, with special reference to the feathering of the wing. Bull. Am. Mus. Nat. Hist. 59:129-140.
____. 1925. The secondary remiges and coverts in the Mandarin and Wood Ducks. Auk 42:41-50.
____. 1926. Structural variations in the scoters. Am. Mus. Novit. 243:1-5.
____ and L. Griscom. 1921a. Descriptions of proposed new birds from Central America, with notes on other little-known forms. Am. Mus. Novit. 25:1-5.
____ and ____. 1921b. Notes on *Ortalis vetula* and its allies. Auk 38:44-50.
Millington, R. 1994. A mystery sandpiper at Cley. Birding World 7:61-63. [Reprinted Birding 27:310, 1995]
____. 1997. Separation of Black Brant, dark-bellied Brent Goose and pale-bellied Brent Goose. Birding World 10:11-15.
____. 1998. The Green-winged Teal. Birding World 11:430-434.
____. 2000. An interesting skua in Dorset. Birding World 13:336-339.
____. 2001. Possible Rough-legged Hawk on the Isles of Scilly. Birding World 14:439-440.
Mindell, D.P. 1983. Harlan's Hawk (*Buteo jamaicensis harlani*): A valid subspecies. Auk 100:161-169.
____. 1985. Plumage variation and winter range of Harlan's Hawk (*Buteo jamaicensis harlani*). Am. Birds 39:127-133.
Minton, C.D.T., and L. Serra. 2001. Biometrics and moult of Grey Plovers, *Pluvialis squatarola*, in Australia. Emu 101:13-18.
Mitchell, C.D. 1994. Trumpeter Swan. Birds N. Am. 105:1-24.
Mlodinow, S.G. 1997. The Long-billed Murrelet (*Brachyramphus perdix*) in North America. Birding 29:460-475.
____ and M. Axelson. 2006. Gray-bellied Brant: Identification and vagrancy. Birding 38:48-55.
____, S. Feldstein, and B. Tweit. 1999. The Bristle-thighed Curlew landfall of 1998: Climactic factors and notes on identification. W. Birds 30:133-155.
Moen, S.M. 1991. Morphologic and genetic variation among breeding colonies of the Atlantic Puffin (*Fratercula arctica*). Auk 108:755-763.
Moffitt, J. 1926. Notes on White-fronted and Tule geese in California. Condor 28:241-243.
____. 1937. The White-cheeked Goose in California. Condor 39:149-159.
____. 1938. The downy young of *Dendragapus* Auk 55:589-595.
Monaghan, P., and N. Duncan. 1979. Plumage variation of known-age Herring Gulls. Brit. Birds 72:100-103.
Monroe, B.L. Jr. 1963. Three new subspecies of birds from Honduras. Occ. Papers Louisiana State Univ. 26:1-7.
____. 1968. A distributional survey of the birds of Honduras. Ornith. Monogr. 7:1-458.
____ and M.R. Browning. 1992. A re-analysis of *Butorides*. Bull. Brit. Ornith. Club 112:81-85.
Monson, G., and A.R. Phillips. 1981. Annotated checklist of the birds of Arizona. University of Arizona Press, Tucson, AZ.
Monteiro, L.R., and R.W. Furness. 1996. Molt of Cory's Shearwaters during the breeding season. Condor 98:216-221.
____ and ____. 1998. Speciation through temporal segregation of Madeiran Storm Petrel (*Oceanodroma castro*) populations in the Azores? Phil. Trans. Royal Soc. London (Ser. B) 353:945-953.
____, J.A. Ramos, R.W. Furness, and A.J. del Nevo. 1996. Movements, morphology, breeding, molt, diet and feeding of seabirds in the Azores. Colonial Waterbirds 19:82-97.
Montevecchi, W.A., and I.J. Stenhouse. 2002. Dovekie. Birds N. Am. 701:1-24.
Montgomerie, R., B. Lyon, and K. Holder. 2001. Dirty ptarmigan: Behavioral modification of conspicuous male plumage. Behav. Ecol. 12:429-438.
Monticelli, D., and J.A. Ramos. 2007. Plumage characteristics and return rate of one-year-old tropical Roseate Terns. Waterbirds 30:58-63.
Montoya, A.B., P.J. Zwank, and M. Cardenas. 1997. Breeding biology of Aplomado Falcons in desert grasslands of Chihuahua, Mexico. J. Field Ornith. 68:135-143.
Moore, D.R., and S.H. Pitrowski. 1983. Hybrid Coot × Moorhen resembling American Coot in Suffolk. Brit. Birds. 76:407-409.
Moore, R.T. 1938. A new race of Wild Turkey. Auk 55:112-115.
____ and R.M. Bond. 1946. Notes on *Falco sparverius* in Mexico. Condor 59:230-234.
____ and D.R. Medina. 1957. The status of the chachalacas of western Mexico. Condor 59:230-234.
Moorman, T.E., and P.N. Gray. 1994. Mottled Duck. Birds N. Am. 81:1-20.
____, G.A. Baldassarre, and T.J. Hess. 1993. Carcass mass and nutrient dynamics of Mottled Ducks during molt. J. Wildl. Manage. 57:224-228.
Morgan, R.P. II, D.W. Meritt, S.B. Block, and S.T. Sulkin. 1984. Frequency of Mallard-Black Duck hybrids along the Atlantic coast as determined by electrophoresis and plumage analysis. Biochem. Syst. Ecol. 12:119-123.
Morlan, J. 2004. Apparent hybrids between the American Avocet and Black-necked Stilt in California. W. Birds 35:57-59.
____. 2005. An apparent hybrid between Barrow's Golden and Hooded Merganser at Lake Merritt, Oakland, California. W. Birds 36:279-282.
Morrison, J.L. 1996. Crested Caracara. Birds N. Am. 249:1-28.
____ and M. Maltbie. 1999. Methods for gender determination of Crested Caracaras. J. Raptor Res. 33:128-133.
Morrison, M.L. 1979. The cormorants of Texas. Bull. Texas Ornith. Soc. 12:35-36.
Morrison, R.I.G. 1975. Migration and morphometrics of European Knot and Turnstone on Ellesmere Island, Canada. Bird-Banding 46:290-301.
____. 1976. Moult of the Purple Sandpiper *Calidris maritima* in Iceland. Ibis 118:237-246.
____ and B.A. Harrington. 1992. The migration system of the Red Knot *Calidris canutus rufa* in the New World. Wader Study Group Bull. 64(Suppl.):71-84.
Moser, R.A. 1942. Should the Belted Piping Plover be recognized as a valid race? Nebraska Bird Rev. 10:31-37.
Moser, T.J., and R.E. Rolley. Discrimination of Giant and Interior Canada Geese of the Mississippi Flyway. Wild. Soc. Bull. 18:381-388.
Mosher, J.A., and P.F. Matray. 1974. Size dimorphism: A factor in energy savings for Broad-winged Hawks. Auk 91:325-341.
Moskoff, W. 1995. Solitary Sandpiper. Birds N. Am. 156:1-16.
____ and L. Bevier. Mew Gull. Birds N. Am. 687:1-28.
____ and R. Montgomerie. 2002. Baird's Sandpiper. Birds N. Am. 661:1-20.
Mougin, J.L., B. Despin, and F. Roux. 1986 La détermination du sexe par mensuration du bec chez le Puffin cendré *Calonectris diomedea borealis*. Comp. Rendue Acad. Sci. Paris 302:91-96.
Moulton, D.W., and A.P. Marshall. 1996. Laysan Duck. Birds N. Am. 242:1-20.
Mowbray, T. 1999. American Wigeon. Birds N. Am. 401:1-32.
____. 2002a. Northern Gannet. Birds N. Am. 693:1-28.
____. 2002b. Canvasback. Birds N. Am. 659:1-40.
____, F. Cooke, and B. Ganter. 2000. Snow Goose. Birds N. Am. 514:1-40.
____, C.R. Ely, J.S. Sedinger, and R.E. Trost. 2002. Canada Goose. Birds N. Am. 682:1-44.
Mueller, H.C. 1999. Common Snipe. Birds N. Am. 417:1-20.

Mueller, H.C., and D.D. Berger. 1968. Sex ratios and measurements of migrant Goshawks. Auk 85:431-436.
____, ____, and G. Allez. 1976. Age and sex variation in the size of Goshawks. Bird-Banding 47:310-318.
____, ____, and ____. 1979a. The identification of North American *Accipiters*. Am. Birds 33:236-240.
____, ____, and ____. 1979b. Age and sex differences in size of Sharp-shinned Hawks. J. Field Ornith. 50:34-44.
____, ____, and ____, 1981. Age, sex, and seasonal differences in size of Cooper's Hawks. J. Field Ornith. 52:112-126.
____, ____, N.S. Mueller, W. Robicaud, and J. L. Kasper. 2002. Age and sex differences in wing loading and other aerodynamic characteristics of Merlins. Wilson Bull. 114:272-275.
____, ____, ____, ____, and ____. 2004. Temporal changes in size of Sharp-shinned Hawks during fall migration at Cedar Grove, Wisconsin. J. Field Ornith. 75:386-393.
Mullarney, K. 1980. Another mystery photograph: Great Northern or Black-throated diver? Brit. Birds. 73:419-423.
____. 1988. Identification of Roseate Tern in juvenile plumage. Dutch Birding 10:109-120.
____. 1991. Identification of Semipalmated Plover, a new feature. Birding World 7:254-258.
Muller, M.J., and R.W. Storer. 1999. Pied-billed Grebe. Birds N. Am. 410:1-32.
Munro, J.A. 1939. Studies of waterfowl in British Columbia. Number 9: Barrow's Goldeneye. Trans. Royal Can. Inst. 48:259-318.
____. 1941. Studies of waterfowl in British Columbia: The grebes. Occ. Papers British Columbia Prov. Mus. 3:1-71.
____ and I.M. Cowan. 1947. A review of the bird fauna of British Columbia. Spec. Publ. British Columbia Prov. Mus. 2:1-285.
Murie, O.J. 1944. Two new subspecies of birds from Alaska. Condor 46:121-123.
Murphy, R.C. 1918. A study of the Atlantic *Oceanites*. Bull. Am. Mus. Nat. Hist. 38:117-146.
____. 1922. Notes on the tubinares, including records which affect the A.O.U. check-list. Auk 39:58-65.
____. 1923. Notes on a collection of birds from the Azores. Ibis (11th Ser.) 5:44-49.
____. 1924. The Marine Ornithology of the Cape Verde Islands, with a list of all the birds of the archipelago. Bull. Am. Mus. Nat. Hist. 50:211-278.
____. 1925. Notes on certain species and races of oyster-catchers. Am. Mus. Novit. 194:1-15.
____. 1927. On certain forms of *Puffinus assimilis* and its allies. Am. Mus. Novit. 276:1-15.
____. 1929. Birds collected during the Whitney South Sea Expedition. X. On *Pterodroma cookii* and its allies. Am. Mus. Novit. 370:1-17.
____. 1930. Birds collected during the Whitney South Sea Expedition. XI. Am. Mus. Novit. 419:1-15.
____. 1936. Oceanic birds of South America. Vols. 1 & 2. American Museum of Natural History, New York, NY.
____. 1949. A new species of petrel from the Pacific. Pp. 89-91 *in* E. Mayr and E. Schuz, eds., Ornithologie als Biologische Wissenschaft. Carl Winter, Heidelberg.
____. 1952. The Manx Shearwater, *Puffinus puffinus*, as a species of world-wide distribution. Am. Mus. Novit. 1586:1-21.
____. 1960. Oceanic Birds. Proc. Royal Soc. London 152(Ser. B):642-654.
____ and J.P. Chapin. 1929. On a collection of birds from the Azores. Am. Mus. Novit. 384:1-23.
____ and L.S. Mowbray. 1951. New light on the Cahow, *Pterodroma cahow*. Auk 68:266-280.
____ and J.M. Pennoyer. 1952. Large petrels of the genus *Pterodroma*. Am. Mus. Novit. 1580:1-42.
____ and J.P. Snyder. 1952. The "pealea" phenomenon and other notes on storm-petrels. Am. Mus. Novit. 1596:1-16.
Murphy, W.L. 1992. Notes on the occurrence of the Little Egret (*Egretta garzetta*) in the Americas, with reference to other Palearctic vagrants. Colonial Waterbirds 15:113-123.
Murray, J.B. 1970. Escaped American Red-tailed Hawk nesting with Buzzard in Midlothian. Scottish Birds 6:34-37.
Mussehl, T.W., and T.H. Leik. 1963. Sexing wings of adult Blue Grouse. J. Wildl. Manage. 27:102-106.
Myers, J.P., J.L. Maron, and M. Sallaberry. 1985. Going to extremes: Why do Sanderlings migrate to the Neotropics? Ornith. Monographs 36:520-535.
Naranjo, L.G., R. Franke, and W. Beltran. 1994. Migration and wintering of Western Sandpipers on the Pacific Coast of Columbia. J. Field Ornith. 65:194-200.
Naveen, R. 1981. Storm-petrels of the world: An introductory guide to their identification. Birding 13:216-229.
____. 1982a. Storm-petrels of the world: An introductory guide to their identification. Part IV. Birding 14:140-147.
Naveen, R. 1982b. Storm-petrels of the world: An introductory guide to their identification. Part III. Birding 14:56-62.
____. 1982c. Storm-petrels of the world: An introductory guide to their identification. Part II. Birding 14:10-15.
Nechaev, V.A., and P.S. Tomkovich. 1987. [A new subspecies of Dunlin *Calidris alpina litoralis* ssp.n. (Charadriidae, Aves) from Sakalin Island.] Zool. Zhurnal 66:1110-1113.
Negro, J.J., K.L. Bildstein, and D.M. Bird. 1994. Effects of food deprivation and handling stress on fault-bar formation in nestling American Kestrels *Falco sparverius*. Ardea 82:263-267.
Nelson, C.H. 1983. Eye-color changes in Barrow's Goldeneye and Common Goldeneye ducklings. Wilson Bull. 95:482-487.
____. 1993a. The downy waterfowl of North America. Delta Station Press, Deerfield, IL. 302 pp.
____. 1993b. The identification of Barrow's Goldeneye *Bucephala islandica* and Common Goldeneye *Bucephala clangula americana* ducklings. Wildfowl 44:178-183.
____. 1996. Identification of Greater Scaup, *Aythya marila*, and Lesser Scaup, *A. affinis*, ducklings. Can. Field-Nat. 110:288-293.
____. 1997. Eye-colour changes in flightless ducklings of Lesser and Greater scaup *Aythya affinis* and *Aythya marila*. Wildfowl 47:194-197.
Nelson, D.A. 1981. Sexual differences in measurements of Cassin's Auklets. J. Field Ornith. 52:.233-234
Nelson, E.W. 1899. Descriptions of new birds from Mexico. Auk 16:25-31.
____. 1902. The nomenclature and validity of certain North American gallinae. Auk 19:386-391.
____. 1904. Descriptions of four new birds from Mexico. Proc. Biol. Soc. Washington 17:151-152.
____ and E.A. Goldman. 1933. A new subspecies of the Snail Kite, *Rostrhamus sociabilis* (Vieillot). Proc. Biol. Soc. Washington 46:193-194.
Nelson, J.B. 1975. The breeding biology of frigatebirds: A comparative review. Living Bird 14:113-156.
____. 1978a. The Sulidae. Oxford University Press, Oxford, UK. 1012 pp.
____. 1978b. The Gannet. T & AD Poyser, Hertfordshire, UK. 336 pp.
____. 2005. Pelicans, cormorants, and their relatives. The Pelecaniformes. Oxford University Press, Oxford, U.K. 661 pp.
Nelson, H.K. 1952. Hybridization of Canada Geese with Blue Geese in the wild. Auk 69:425-428.
Nelson, R.C., and T.A. Bookhout. 1980. Counts of periosteal layers invalid for ageing Canada Geese. J. Wildl. Manage. 44:518-521.
Nelson, S.K. 1997. Marbled Murrelet. Birds N. Am. 276:1-32.
Nesbitt, S.A. 1987. A technique for aging Sandhill Cranes using wing molt: preliminary finding. Proc. N. Am. Crane Workshop 3:224-229.
____ and S.T. Schwikert. 1998. Maturation and variation of head characteristics in Sandhill Cranes. Wilson Bull. 110:285-288.
____ and ____. 2005. Wing-molt patterns - a key to aging Sandhill Cranes. Wildl. Soc. Bull. 33:326-331.
____ and ____. In press. Timing of molt in Florida Sandhill Cranes. Proc. N. Am. Crane Workshop 10.
Nettleship, D.N. 2000. Ruddy Turnstone. Birds N. Am. 537:1-32.
____ and T.R. Birkhead, eds. 1985. The Atlantic alcidae. Academic Press, London, U.K.
Nevins, H.M., and H.R. Carter. 2003. Age and sex of Common Murres *Uria aalge* recovered during the 1997-98 Point Reyes tarball incidents in Central California. Marine Ornith. 31:51-58.
Newell, J.G., and G.M. Sutton. 1982. The Olivaceous Cormorant in Oklahoma. Bull. Oklahoma Ornith. Soc. 15:1-5.
Newlon, M.C., and T.H. Kent. 1980. Speciation of dowitchers in Iowa. Iowa Birdlife 50:59-68.
Newson, S.E., B. Hughes, I.C. Russell, G.R. Ekins, and R.M. Sellers. 2004. Sub-specific differentiation and distribution of Great Cormorants *Phalacrocorax carbo* in Europe. Ardea 92:3-10.
Newton, I., and M. Marquiss. 1982. Moult in the Sparrowhawk. Ardea 70:163-172.
Nichols, J.T. 1914. An undescribed Galapagos race of *Oceanodroma castro*. Auk 31:388-390.
Nicoletti, F., and D. Benson. 2000. The Gyrfalcon. Birding 32:22-29.
Nicoll, M., and P. Kemp. 1983. Partial primary moult in first spring/summer Common Sandpipers *Actitis hypoleucos*. Wader Study Group Bull. 37:37-38.
Nicoll, M.J. 1904. On a collection of birds made during the cruise of the 'Valhalla', R.Y.S., in the West Indies (1903-4). Ibis (8th Ser.) 4:555-591.
Nieboer, F., J. Cronau, R. de Goede, J. Lotsohort, and T. van der Have. 1985. Axillary feather colour patterns as indicators of the breeding origin of Bar-tailed Godwits. Wader Study Group Bull. 45:34.
Nietfeld, M.T., and F.C. Zwickel. 1983. Classification of sex in young Blue Grouse. J. Wildl. Manage. 47:1147-1151.
Niewoonder, J.A., H.H. Prince, and D.R. Luukkonen. 1998. Survival and reproduction of female Sichuan, Ring-necked, and F1 hybrid pheasants. J. Wildl. Manage. 62:933-938.

Nisbet, I.C.T. 2002. Common Tern. Birds N. Am. 618:1-40.

____, E.S. Bridge, P. Szcys, and B.J. Heidinger. 2007. Sexual dimorphism, female-female pairs, and tests for assortative mating in Common Terns. Waterbirds 30:169-179.

Nixon, C.M. 1962. Wild Turkey aging. Ohio Dept. Nat. Res. Game Res. 1:107-117.

Noble, G.K. 1916. The resident birds of Guadeloupe. Bull. Mus. Comp. Zool. 60:359-396.

____, M. Wurm, and A. Schmidt. 1938. Social behavior of the Black-crowned Night Heron. Auk 55:7-40.

Nol. E., and M.S. Blanken. 1999. Semipalmated Plover. Birds N. Am. 444:1-24.

____ and R.C. Humphrey. 1994. American Oystercatcher. Birds N. Am. 92:1-24.

Norris-Caneda, K.H., and J.D. Elliott Jr. 1998. Sex identification in raptors using PCR. J. Raptor Res. 32:278-280.

North, M.R. 1994. Yellow-billed Loon. Birds N. Am. 121:1-24.

____. 1997. Aleutian Tern. Birds N. Am. 291:1-20.

Norton, D.W. 1965. Notes on some non-passerine birds from eastern Ecuador. Breviora 230:1-11.

Nota, Y., and O. Takenaka. 1999. DNA extraction from urine and sex identification of birds. Molecular Ecol. 8:1237-1238.

Nuechterlein, G.L. 1981. Courtship behavior and reproductive isolation between Western Grebe color morphs. Auk 98:335-349.

Oberholser, H.C. 1906a. Description of a new *Querquedula*. Proc. Biol. Soc. Washington 19:93-94.

____. 1906b. The North American eagles and their economic relations. U.S. Biol Surv. Bull. 27:1-31.

____. 1912a. A revision of the forms of the Great Blue Heron (*Ardea herodias* Linnaeus). Proc. U.S. Nat Mus. 43:531-559.

____. 1912b. A revision of the subspecies of the Green Heron (*Butorides virescens* [Linnaeus]). Proc. U.S. Nat. Mus. 42:529-577.

____. 1912c. The status of *Butorides brunescens*. Proc. Biol. Soc. Washington 25:53-56.

____. 1917a. A review of the subspecies of the Leach Petrel, *Oceanodroma leucorhoa* (Viellot). Proc. U.S. Nat. Mus. 54(2230):165-172.

____. 1917b. Notes on North American birds. I. Auk 34:191-196.

____. 1918a. Notes on North American birds. IV. Auk 35:62-65.

____. 1918b. Notes on North American birds. V. Auk 35:185-187.

____. 1918c. Notes on the subspecies of *Numenius americanus* Bechstein. Auk 35:188-195.

____. 1918d. The subspecies of *Larus hyperboreus* Gunnerus. Auk 35:467-474.

____. 1919a. Notes on North American birds. IX. Auk 36:556-559.

____. 1919b. Notes on North American birds. VII. Auk 36:81-85.

____. 1919c. The status of *Larus hyperboreus barrovianus* Ridgway. Proc. Biol. Soc. Washington 32:173-176.

____. 1921. Notes on North American birds. X. Auk 38:79-82.

____. 1923. Notes on the forms of the genus *Oreortyx*. Auk 40:80-84.

____. 1932. Descriptions of new birds from Oregon, chiefly from the Warner Valley region. Sci. Publ. Cleveland Mus. Nat. Hist. 4:1-12.

____. 1937. A revision of the Clapper Rails (Rallus longirostris Boddaert). Proc. U.S. Nat. Mus. 84:313-354.

____. 1938. The birdlife of Louisiana. Louisiana Dep. Conserv. Bull. 28:1-834.

____. 1974. The bird life of Texas. Vols. 1 & 2. University of Texas Press, Austin, TX. 1069 pp.

O'Brien, M. 2006. Subspecific identification of the Willet *Catoptrophorus semipalmatus*. Birding 38:40-47.

____, R. Crossley, and K. Karlson. 2006. The shorebird guide. Houghton Mifflin Company, Boston MA. 477 pp.

O'Brien, R.M., and J. Davies. 1990. A new subspecies of Masked Booby *Sula dactylatra* from Lord Howe, Norfolk, and Kermadec Islands. Marine Ornith. 18:1-7.

O'Neill, P., C. Minton, K. Ozaki, and R. White. 2005. Three populations of Roseate Tern (*Sterna dougallii*) in the Swain Reefs, southern Great Barrier Reef, Australia. Emu 105:57-66.

Oddie, B. 1994. Possible Common Gull × Mediterranean Gull hybrid. Dutch Birding 16:72.

Ogden, J.C. 1973. Field identification of difficult birds: I. Short-tailed Hawk. Florida Field Nat. 1:30-33.

Ogi, H., K. Schimazaki, and K. Nakamura. 1981. Sooty Shearwaters in the subarctic North Pacific: Seasonal changes in body weight and molt. Res. Inst. North Pacific Fish. 207(special issue):207-215.

Ogilvie, M.A. 1978. Wild Geese. Buteo Books, Vermillion, SD. 350 pp

O'Hara, P.D., B.D. Lank, and F.S. Delgado. 2002. Is the timing of moult altered by migration? Evidence from a comparison of age and residency classes of Western Sandpipers *Calidris mauri* in Panama. Ardea 90:61-70.

O'Hara, P.D., G. Fernández, B. Haase, H. de la Cueva, and D.B. Lank. 2006. Differential migration in Western Sandpipers with respect to body size and wing length. Condor 108:225-232.

O'Leary, B.E. 1994. Sexing of Red-tailed Hawk by hallux toe depth. J. Raptor Res. 28:70. [Abstract]

Ohmart, R.D. 1967. Comparative molt and pterylography in the quail genera *Callipepla* and *Lophortyx*. Condor 69:535-548.

Okill, J.D., D.D. French, and S. Wanless. 1989. Sexing Red-throated Divers in Shetland. Ringing & Migr. 10:26-30.

Oliphant, L.W. 1991. Hybridization between a Peregrine Falcon and a Prairie Falcon in the wild. J. Raptor Res. 25:36-39.

Oliver, P.J. 1989. Early wing moult of Eiders. Brit. Birds. 82:71.

Olson, S.L. 1974. A melanistic White-tailed Tropicbird. Condor 76:217-218.

____. 1997. Towards a less imperfect understanding of the systematics and biogeography of the Clapper and King rail complex (*Rallus longirostris* and *R. elegans*). Pp. 93-111 *in* R.W. Dickerman, comp., The era of Allan R. Phillips: A Festshrift. R.W. Dickerman, Albuquerque, NM.

Onley, D., and P. Scofield. 2007. Albatross, petrels, and shearwaters of the world. Princeton University Press, Princeton, NJ. 256 pp.

Oreel, G.J. 1979. Field identification of Snowy Egret. Brit. Birds. 72:128-129.

Oring, L.W. 1964. Behavior and ecology of certain ducks during the post-breeding period. J. Wildl. Manage. 28:223-233.

____. 1968. Growth, molts, and plumages of the Gadwall. Auk 85:335-380.

____, E.M. Gray, and J.M. Reed. 1997. Spotted Sandpiper. Birds N. Am. 289:1-32.

Orr, R.T. 1938. An unusually early molt in the Ruddy Duck. Condor 40:87.

____. 1940. An analysis of the subspecific status of dowitchers in California. Condor 39:61-63.

Orthmeyer, D.L., J.Y. Takekawa, C.R. Ely, M.L. Wege, and W.E. Newton. 1995. Morphological differences in Pacific coast populations of Greater White-fronted Geese. Condor 97:123-132.

Osborne. T.O. 1985. Fork-tailed Storm-Petrel records from inland Alaska. Condor 87:432-434.

Osgood, W.H. 1901. New subspecies of North American birds. Auk 18:179-181.

Otto, J.E., and D.L. Strohmeyer. 1985. Wing molt by a nesting Pied-billed Grebe. Wilson Bull. 97:239-240.

Ottomeyer, A.A., and J.A. Crawford. 1996. Revised measurements for classification of age of Sage Grouse from wings. California Fish and Game 82:61-65.

Ouellet, H. 1974. An intergeneric grouse hybrid (*Bonasa* × *Canchites*). Can. Field-Nat. 88:183-186.

____. 1990. A new Ruffed Grouse, Aves: Phasianidae: *Bonasa umbellus*, from Labrador, Canada. Can. Field-Nat. 104:445-449.

____, R. McNeil, and J. Burton. 1973. The Western Sandpiper in Quebec and the Maritime Provinces, Canada. Can. Field-Nat. 87:291-300.

Owen, M., and W.A. Cook. 1977. Variations in body weight, wing length and condition of Mallard *Anas platyrhynchos platyrhynchos* and their relationship to environmental changes. J. Zool. (London) 183:377-395.

Owen, R.B. Jr. and W.B. Krohn. 1973. Molt patterns and weight changes of the American Woodcock. Wilson Bull. 85:31-40.

Owens, I.P.F., and R.V. Short. 1995. Hormonal basis of sexual dimorphism in birds: implications for new theories of sexual selection. Trends in Ecology and Evolution 10:44-47.

Owre, O.T. 1967. Adaptations for locomotion and feeding in the Anhinga and the Double-crested Cormorant. Ornith. Monogr. 6:1-138.

Paclt, J. 1983. A chronology of color charts and color terminology for naturalists Taxon 32:393-405.

Page, G.W. 1974a. Age, sex, molt, and migration of Dunlins at Bolinas Lagoon. W. Birds 5:1-12.

____. 1974b. Molt of wintering Least Sandpipers. Bird-Banding 45:93-105.

____ and M. Bradstreet. 1968. Size and composition of a fall population of Least and Semipalmated sandpipers at Long Point, Ontario. Ontario Bird-Banding 4:82-88.

____ and B. Fearis. 1971. Sexing Western Sandpipers by bill length. Bird-Banding 42:297-298.

____, B. Fearis, and R.M. Jurek. 1972. Age and sex composition of Western Sandpipers on Bolinas Lagoon. California Birds 3:79-86.

____, J.S. Warriner, J.C. Warriner, and P.W.C. Paton. 1995. Snowy Plover. Birds N. Am. 154:1-24.

Palacios, E., and E. Mellink. 1996. Status of the Least Tern in the Gulf of California. J. Field Ornith.. 67:48-58

Palmer, R.S. 1941. "White-faced" terns. Auk 58:164-178.

____. 1962. Handbook of North American birds. Vol. 1. Loons through flamingos. Yale University Press, New Haven, CT. 567 pp.

____. 1967a. Plumage descriptions. Pp 139-141 *in* G.D. Stout, ed., The shorebirds of North America. Viking Press, New York, NY.

____. 1967b. Species accounts. Pp 143-167 *in* G.D. Stout, ed., The shorebirds of North America. Viking Press, New York, NY.

Palmer, R.S. 1972. Patterns of molting. Avian Biol. 2:65-102.
____. 1973. Icelandic eiders - a few observations. Wildfowl 24:154-157.
____. 1976a. Handbook of North American birds. Vol. 2. Waterfowl (part 1). Yale University Press, New Haven, CT. 521 pp.
____. 1976b. Handbook of North American birds. Vol. 3. Waterfowl (part 2). Yale University Press, New Haven, CT. 560 pp.
____. 1977. King Eider studies. Brit. Birds. 70:107-113.
____. 1988a. Handbook of North American birds. Vol. 4. Diurnal raptors (part 1). Yale University Press, New Haven, CT. 433 pp.
____. 1988b. Handbook of North American birds. Vol. 5. Diurnal raptors (part 2). Yale University Press, New Haven, CT. 465 pp.
Palmer, W. 1899. The avifauna of the Pribilof Islands. Pp. 343-355 *in* D.S. Jordan, ed., The fur seals and fur-seal islands of the North Pacific. Vol. 3. U.S. Treasury Dept., Washington, D.C.
Palmer, W.L. 1959. Sexing live-trapped juvenile Ruffed Grouse. J. Wild. Manage. 23:111-112.
Palomares, L.E., B.E. Arroyo, J. Marchamalo, J.J. Sainz, and B. Voslamber. 1997. Sex- and age-related biometric variation of Black-headed Gulls *Larus ridibundus* in western European populations. Bird Study 44:310-317.
Papeschi, A., F. Brigante, and F. Dessí-Fulgheri. 2000. Winter androgen levels and wattle size in male Common Pheasants. Condor 102:193-197.
____, J.P. Carroll, and F. Dessí-Fulgheri. 2003. Wattle size correlated with male territorial rank in juvenile Ring-necked Pheasants. Condor 105:362-366.
Parker, J.S., T.R. Birkhead, S.K. Joshua, S. Taylor, and M.S. Clark. 1991. Sex ratio in a population of Guillemots *Uria aalge* determined from chromosome analysis.
Parker, J.W. 1981. Comments on the first recorded occurrence of Mississippi Kites in New York. Kingbird 31:7-8.
____. 1999. Mississippi Kite. Birds N. Am. 402:1-28.
____, E. Byers, and F. Bonaccorso. 1987. Aspects of the population biology of *Fregata magnificens* in Belize. Am. Birds 41:11-19.
Parkes, K.C. 1952a. Geographic variation in the Horned Grebe. Condor 54:314-315.
____. 1952b. Taxonomic notes on the Laughing Gull. Proc. Biol. Soc. Washington 65:193-196.
____. 1954. Notes on some birds of the Aidirondack and Catskill mountains, New York. Ann. Carnegie Mus. 33:149-178.
____. 1955a. Systematic notes on North American birds. 1. The herons and ibises (Ciconiiformes). Ann. Carnegie Mus. 33:287-293.
____. 1955b. Notes on the molts and plumages of the Sparrow Hawk. Wilson Bull. 67:194-199.
____. 1958a. Systematic notes on North American Birds. 2. The Waterfowl (Anatidae). Ann. Carnegie Mus. 35:117-125.
____. 1958b. Specific relations in the genus *Elanus*. Condor 60:139-140.
____. 1986. Notes on Philippine Birds, 9. Reidentification of a unique stint specimen. Bull. Brit. Ornith. Club 106:133-136.
____. 1989. Sex ratios based on museum specimens - a caution. Colonial Waterbirds 12:130-131.
____. 1995. Moult and ageing terminology. Brit. Birds 88:604-605.
____. 1996. Subspecies and intergrade Red-tailed Hawks in western Pennsylvania. Pennsylvania Birds 10:203-205.
Parmelee, D.F. 1988. The hybrid skua: a Southern Ocean enigma. Wilson Bull. 100:345-356.
____. 1992. White-rumped Sandpiper. Birds N. Am. 29:1-16.
____ and S.D. MacDonald. 1960. The birds of west-central Ellesmere Island and adjacent areas. Nat. Mus. Canada Bull. 169(Ser. 63):1-103.
____, H.A. Stephens, and R.H. Schmidt. 1967. The birds of southeastern Victoria Island and adjacent small islands. Nat. Mus. Canada Bull. 222(Ser. 78):1-229.
____, D.W. Greiner, and W.D. Graul. 1968. Summer schedule and breeding biology of the White-rumped Sandpiper in the central Canadian Arctic. Wilson Bull. 80:5-29.
Parnell, J.F., R.M. Erwin, and K.C. Molina. 1995. Gull-billed Tern. Birds N. Am. 140:1-20.
Parrish, J.R., J. Stoddard, and C.M. White. 1987. Sexually mosaic plumage in a female American Kestrel. Condor 89:911-913.
Parsons, K.C., and T.L. Master. 2000. Snowy Egret. Birds N. Am. 489:1-24.
Paterson, A.M. 1993. Development of head moult of Black-headed Gull *Larus ridibundus* in southern Spain. Seabird 15:68-71.
Paton, D.C. and B.J. Wykes. 1978. Re appraisal of moult of Red necked Stints in southern Australia. Emu 78:54-60.
____, ____, and P. Dann. 1982. Moult of juvenile Curlew Sandpipers in southern Australia. Emu 82:54-56.
Pattee, O.H., and S.L. Beasom. 1977. Rio Grande Turkey hens with leg spurs. Auk 94:159.
Patten, M.A. 1993a. A probable bilateral gynandromophic Black-throated Blue Warbler. Wilson Bull. 105:695-698.
Patten, M.A. 1993b. First record of the Common Pochard in California. W. Birds 24:235-240.
____. 1993c. Notes on immature Double-crested and Neotropic cormorants. Birding 25:343-345.
____. 1996. Yellow-footed Gull. Birds N. Am. 243:1-20.
____. 1997. Systematics of the Marbled Murrelets. Birding 29:473-474.
____ and B.E. Daniels. 1991. First record of the Long-toed Stint in California. W. Birds 22:131-138.
____ and R.A. Erickson. 1996. Subspecies of the Least Tern in Mexico. Condor 98:888-890.
____ and M.T. Heindel. 1994. Identifying Trumpeter and Tundra swans. Birding 26:306-318.
____ and G.W. Lasley. 2000. Range expansion of the Glossy Ibis in North America. N. Am. Birds 54:241-247.
____ and P. Unitt. 2002. Diagnosability versus mean differences of Sage Sparrow subspecies. Auk 119:26-35.
____ and J.C. Wilson. 1996. A dark-morph Sharp-shinned Hawk in California, with comments on dichromatism in raptors. Bull. Brit. Ornith. Club 116:266-267.
____, G. McCaskie, and P. Unitt. 2003. Birds of the Salton Sea: status biogeography, and ecology. University of California Press, Berkeley, CA. 363 pp.
Patterson, J.B., and G.L. Armistead. 2004. First record of Cape Verde Shearwater (*Calonectris edwardsii*) for North America. N. Am. Birds 58:468-473.
Patterson, R.L. 1952. The Sage Grouse in Wyoming. Sage Books, Inc., Denver, CO. 341 pp.
Patterson, M. 1998. The great curlew fallout of 1998. Field Notes 52:150-155.
Paul, R.T., and A.F. Schnapf. 1998. Florida region. N. Am. Birds 52:448-450.
____, A.F. Paul, B. Pranty, A.B. Hodgson, and D.J. Powell. 2003. Probable hybridization between Elegant Tern and Sandwich Tern in west-central Florida. N. Am. Birds 57:280-282.
Paulson, D.R. 1986. Identification of juvenile tattlers, and a Gray-tailed Tattler record from Washington. W. Birds 17:33-36.
____. 1993. Shorebirds of the Pacific Northwest. University of Washington Press, Seattle, WA. 406 pp.
____. 1995. Black-bellied Plover. Birds N. Am. 186:1-28.
____. 2005. Shorebirds of North America: The photographic guide. Princeton University Press, Princeton, NJ. 361 pp.
____ and D.S. Lee. 1992. Wintering Lesser Golden-Plovers in eastern North America. J. Field Ornith. 63:121-128.
Paulus, S.L. 1984. Molts and plumages of Gadwalls in winter. Auk 101:887-889.
Payne, L.X., and E.P. Pierce. 2002. Purple Sandpiper. Birds N. Am. 706:1-36.
Payne, R.B. 1965. The molt of breeding Cassin's Auklets. Condor 67:220-228.
____. 1966. Absence of a brood patch in Cassin Auklets. Condor 68:209-210.
____. 1972. Mechanisms and control of molt. Avian Biology 2:103-155.
____. 1974. Species limits and variation of the New World Green Herons *Butorides virescens* and Striated Herons *B. striatus*. Bull. Brit. Ornith. Club 94:81-88.
____ and L.L. Master. 1983. Breeding of a mixed pair of white-shielded and red-shielded American Coots in Michigan. Wilson Bull. 95:467-469.
____ and C.J. Risley. 1976. Systematic and evolutionary relationships among herons (Ardeidae). Misc. Pubs. Mus. Zool. Univ. Michigan 150:1-115.
Paynter, R.A. Jr. 1955. Ornithogeography of the Yucatán Peninsula. Peabody Mus. Nat. Hist. Bull. 9:1-347.
Pearce, J.M., and K.S. Bollinger. 2003. Morphological traits of Pacific Flyway Canada Geese as an aid to subspecies identification and management. J. Field Ornith. 74:357-369.
____, B.J. Pierson, S.L. Talbot, D.V. Derksen, D. Kraege, and K.T. Scribner. 2000. A genetic evaluation of morphology used to identify harvested Canada Geese. J. Wildl. Manage. 64:863-874.
Pearlstine, E.V., and D.B. Thompson. 2004. Geographic variation in morphology of four species of migratory raptors. J. Raptor Res. 38:334-342.
Pearson, D.J. 1984. The moult of the Little Stint *Calidris minuta* in the Kenyan rift valley. Ibis 126:1-15.
____ and L. Serra. 2002. Biometrics, moult, and migration of Grey Plovers, *Pluvialis squatarola*, at Mida Creek, Kenya. Ostrich 73:143-146.
Peck, M.E. 1911. Hybrid quail. Condor 13:149-151.
Pehrsson, O. 1987. Effects of body condition on molting Mallards. Condor 89:329-339.

Pelham, P.H., and J.G. Dickson. 1992. Physical characteristics. Pp. 32-45 *in* J.D. Dickson, ed., The Wild Turkey: Biology and management. Stackpole Books, Mechanicsburg, PA.

Penkala, J.M. 1977. A technique for identifying yearling female Atlantic Brant. J. Wildl. Manage. 41:585-587.

Pennington, M.G., I.P. Bainbridge, and P. Fearon. 1994. Biometrics and primary moult of non-breeding Kittiwakes *Rissa tridactyla* in Liverpool Bay, England. Ringing & Migr. 15:33-39.

Pérez, G., and K.A. Hobson. 2006. Isotopic evaluation of interrupted molt in northern breeding populations of the Loggerhead Shrike. Condor 108:877-886.

Perkins, S. 1995. New England region. Field Notes 49:227-230.

Perrins, C.M. 1961. The "Lesser Scaup" problem. Brit. Birds. 54:49-54.

____ and R.H. McCleery. 1995. The disadvantage of late-moulting by Mute Swans *Cygnus olor*. Wildfowl 48:147-155.

Perry, H.R. Jr., J.D. Newsome, and P.E. Schilling. 1972. Efforts to develop an external aging and sexing technique for Common Snipe in Louisiana. Proc. Ann. Conf. Southeastern Assoc. Game & Fish Comm. 25:338-346.

Peterle, T.J. 1951. Intergeneric galliform hybrids: A review. Wilson Bull. 65:219-224.

Peters, J.L. 1913. List of birds collected in the interior of Quintana Roo, Mexico, in the winter and spring of 1912. Auk 30:367-380.

____, 1925a. A review of the limpkins (*Aramus*, Veillot). Occ. Papers Boston Soc. Nat. Hist. 5:141-145.

____. 1925b. Notes on the taxonomy of *Ardea canadensis* Linne. Auk 42:120-122.

____. 1927. The North American races of *Falco columbarius*. Bull. Essex County Ornith. Club 8:20-24.

____. 1929. An ornithological survey in the Caribbean lowlands of Honduras. Bull. Mus. Comp. Zool. 69:397-478.

____. 1930a. Two undescribed races of *Phaethon aethereus*. Occ. Papers Boston Soc. Nat. Hist. 5:261-262.

____. 1930b. Notes on some night herons. Proc. Boston Soc. Nat. Hist. 39:263-277.

____. 1931a. Check-list of birds of the world. Vol. 1: Ostrich-ducks. Harvard University Press, Cambridge, MA. 345 pp.

____. 1931b. Additional notes on the birds of the Almirante Bay region of Panama. Bull. Mus. Comp. Zool. 71:291-345.

____. 1934a. Check-list of birds of the world. Vol. 2: New World vultures-guineafowl. Harvard University Press, Cambridge, MA. 401 pp.

____. 1934b. The supposed races of *Squatarola squatarola* (Linn.) and comments on the nomenclature. Condor 36:27-29.

____. 1934c. The status of *Phalaropus fulicarius jourdaini* Iredale. Condor 36:85.

____. 1937. Check-list of birds of the world. Vol. 3: Hoatzins-auks. Harvard University Press, Cambridge, MA. 311 pp.

Petersen, A. 1976. Size variables of Puffin *Fratercula arctica* from Iceland, and bill features as criteria of age. Ornis Scand. 7:185-192.

Petersen, M.R. 1980. Observations of wing-feather moult and summer feeding ecology of Steller's Eiders at Nelson Lagoon, Alaska. Wildfowl 31:99-106.

____. 1981. Populations, feeding ecology, and molt of Steller's Eiders. Condor 83:256-262.

____, J.A. Schmutz, and R.F. Rockwell. 1994. Emperor Goose. Birds N. Am. 97:1-20.

____, W.W. Larned, and D.C. Douglas. 1999. At-sea distribution of Spectacled Eiders: A 120-year-old mystery resolved. Auk 116:1009-1020.

____, J.B. Grand, and C.P. Dau. 2000. Spectacled Eider. Birds N. Am. 547:1-24.

Peterson, M.J. 2000. Plain Chachalaca. Birds N. Am. 550:1-24.

Peterson, S.R., and R.S. Ellarson. 1978. Bursae, reproductive structures, and scapular color in wintering female oldsquaws. Auk 95:115-121.

Petrides, G.A. 1942. Age determination in American gallinaceous game birds. Trans. N. Am. Wild. Conf. 7:308-328.

____. 1945. First-winter plumages in the Galliformes. Auk 62:223-227.

____. 1950. Notes on determination of sex and age in the Woodcock and Mourning Dove. Auk 67:357-360.

____. 1951. Notes on age determination in juvenal European quail. J. Wildl. Manage. 15:116-117.

____ and R.B. Nestler. 1943. Age determination in juvenile Bob-white quail. Am. Midland Nat. 30:774-782.

____ and ____. 1952. Further notes on age determination of juvenile Bobwhite quail. J. Wildl. Manage. 16:109-110.

Petrie, S.A. 1998. Molt patterns of nonbreeding White-faced Whistling-Ducks in South Africa. Auk 115:774-780.

Pettingill, O.S. Jr. 1936. The American Woodcock *Philohela minor* (Gmelin). Mem. Boston Soc. Nat. Hist. 9:169-391.

____. 1959. King Eiders mated with Common Eiders in Iceland. Wilson Bull. 71:205-207.

Pettingill, O.S. Jr. 1962. A hybrid between a King Eider and Common Eider observed in Iceland. Wilson Bull. 74:100-101.

Pezzo, F., and A.G. Gosler. 2005. Evidence of prenuptial moult in the Little Bittern *Ixobrychus minutus*). Ringing & Migr. 22:129-132.

Phillips, A.R. 1958. Las subspecies de la Codorniz de Gambel y el problema de los cambios climaticos en Sonora. Ann. Inst. Biol. Mexico 29:361-374.

____. 1959. The nature of avian species. J. Arizona Acad. Sci. 1:22-30.

____. 1961. [On the evolutionary relationships of the North American Mallards.] Auk 78:670-672.

____. 1962. Notas sistematicas sobre aves Mexicanas. II. Anales Inst. Biol Univ. Mexico 33:331-372.

____. 1966. Further systematic notes on Mexican birds. Bull. Brit. Ornith. Club. 86:86-94.

____. 1975. Semipalmated Sandpiper: Identification, migrations, summer and winter ranges. Am. Birds 29:799-806.

____. 1990. Identification and southward limits, in America, of *Gavia adamsii*, the Yellow-billed Loon. W. Birds 21:17-24.

____. J. Marshall, and G. Monson. 1964. The birds of Arizona. University of Arizona Press, Tucson. 220 pp.

____, C. Chase III, D. Casey, and B. Webb. 1983. Fourth annual CFO/DMNH taxonomy clinic. Parts 1 & 2. Colorado Field Ornith. J. 17:22-34.

Phillips, J.C. 1912. A reconsideration of the American Black Ducks with special reference to certain variations. Auk 29:295-306.

____. 1915a. Experimental studies of hybridization among ducks and pheasants. J. Experim. Zool. 18:69-144.

____. 1915b. The old New England Bob-white. Auk 32:204-207.

____. 1920. Habits of the two Black Ducks *Anas rubripes rubripes* and *Anas rubripes tristis*. Auk 37:289-291.

____. 1921. A further report on species crosses in birds. Genetics 6:366-383.

____. 1922. A natural history of the ducks. Vol. 1. Houghton Mifflin Company, Boston, MA. 264 pp.

____. 1923. A natural history of the ducks. Vol. 2. Houghton Mifflin Company, Boston, MA. 409 pp.

____. 1925. A natural history of the ducks. Vol. 3. Houghton Mifflin Company, Boston, MA. 383 pp.

____. 1926. A natural history of the ducks. Vol. 4. Houghton Mifflin Company, Boston, MA. 489 pp.

Phillips, L.M., and A.N. Powell. 2006. Evidence for wing molt and breeding site fidelity in King Eiders. Waterbirds 29:148-153.

Phillips, R.A., and R.W. Furness. 1997. Predicting the sex of Parasitic Jaegers by discriminant analysis. Col. Waterbirds 20:14-23.

____, D.A. Dawson, and D.J. Ross. 2002. Mating patterns and reversed size dimorphism in Southern Skuas (*Stercorarius skua lonnbergi*). Auk 119:858-863.

Picozzi, N. 1981. Weight, wing-length and iris colour of Hen Harriers in Orkney. Bird Study 28:159-161.

Piatt, J.F., and A.S. Kitasky. 2002a. Horned Puffin. Birds N. Am. 603:1-28.

____ and ____. 2002b. Tufted Puffin. Birds N. Am. 708:1-32.

Pierotti, R. 1981. Male and female parental roles in the Western Gull under different environmental conditions. Auk 98:532-549.

____ and C.A. Annett. 1995. Western Gull. Birds N. Am. 174:1-24.

____ and T.P. Good. 1994. Herring Gull. Birds N. Am. 124:1-28.

Piersma, T. 1988. The annual molt cycle of Great Crested Grebes. Ardea 76:82-95.

____. 1994. Close to the edge: Energetic bottlenecks and the evolution of migratory pathways in Knots. Uitgeverij Het Open Boek, Netherlands. 366 pp.

____. 2004. Understanding evolution of plumages and other cyclic avian life-history phenomena: Role for an improved molt terminology. Condor 106:196-198.

____ and N. Davidson. 1992. The migrations and annual cycle of five subspecies of knots in perspective. Wader Study Group Bull. 64(Suppl.):187-197.

____ and J. Jukema. 1993. Red breasts as honest signals of migratory quality in long-distance migrant, the Bar-tailed Godwit. Condor 95:163-177.

Pierson, B.J., J.M. Pearce, and S.L. Talbot. 2000. Molecular genetic status of Aleutian Canada Geese from Buldir and the Semidi Islands, Alaska. Condor 102:172-180.

Pine, D.S. 1981. Identifying sex of Mountain Quail by length of crest plume. J. Wildl. Manage. 45:1056-1057.

Pitelka, F.A. 1948. Notes on the distribution and taxonomy of Mexican game birds. Condor 50:113-123.

____. 1950. Geographic variation and the species problem in the shorebird genus *Limnodromus*. Univ. California Pubs. Zoology 50:1-86.

____. 1959. Numbers, breeding schedule, and territoriality in Pectoral Sandpipers of northern Alaska. Condor 61:233-264.

Pitman, J.C., C.A. Hagen, R.J. Robel, T.M. Loughin, and R.D. Applegate. 2005. Gender identification and growth of juvenile Lesser Prairie-Chickens. Condor 107:87-96.

Pitman, R.L., and J.R. Jehl Jr. 1998. Geographic variation and reassessment of species limits in the "Masked" Boobies of the eastern Pacific Ocean. Wilson Bull. 110:155-170.

Pitocchelli, J., J. Piatt, and M. Cronin. 1995. Morphological and genetic divergence among Alaskan populations of *Brachyramphus* murrelets. Wilson Bulletin 107:235-250.

____, J.F. Piatt, and H.R. Carter. 2003. Variation in plumage, molt, and morphology of the Whiskered Auklet (*Aethia pygmaea*) in Alaska. J. Field Ornith. 74:90-98.

Pittaway, R. 1992a. Recognizable forms: Subspecies and morphs of the Snow Goose. Ontario Birds 10:72-76.

____. 1992b. Short-billed Dowitcher subspecies. Birding 24:309-311.

____. 1992c. Recognizable forms: Subspecies of the Iceland Gull. Birding 10:24-26.

____. 1993a. Recognizable forms: Subspecies and morphs of the Red-tailed Hawk. Ontario Birds 11:23-29.

____. 1993b. Leg and bill colour of Purple Sandpipers. Ontario Birds 11:107-109.

____. 1994. Recognizable forms: Merlin. Ontario Birds 12:74-80

____. 1997. Recognizable bird forms of Canada. Birders J. 6:76-89.

____. 1999. Taxonomic history of Thayer's Gull. Ontario Birds 17:2-13.

____. 2000. Plumage and molt terminology. Ontario Birds 18:27-43.

____ and P. Burke. 1996a. Recognizable forms: Black-crested and white-crested Double-crested Cormorants. Ontario Birds 14:124-128.

____ and ____. 1996b. Recognizable forms: Cory's Least Bittern. Ontario Birds 14:26-40.

Plant, A.R. 1989. Occurrence of filoplumes in storm-petrels. Seabird 12:32-34.

Plath, K. 1914. With the tropicbirds in Bermuda. Ibis (10th Ser.) 2:552-559

Pons, J.-M., A. Hassanin, and P.-A. Crochet. 2005. Phylogenetic relationships within the Laridae (Charadriiformes: Aves) inferred from mitochondrial markers. Mol. Phylogenetics and Evol. 37:686-699.

Poole, A.F. 1989. Ospreys: A natural and unnatural history. Cambridge University Press, Cambridge, UK. 246 pp.

____ and F. Gill. 1993-2002. The birds of North America. Nos. 41-716. Birds of North America, Inc. Philadelphia, PA.

____, P. Stettenheim, and F. Gill. 1992-1993. The birds of North America. Nos. 1-40. Birds of North America, Academy of Natural Sciences, Philadelphia, PA, and American Ornithologists's Union, Washington, D.C.

____, R.O. Bierregaard, and M.S. Martell. 2002. Osprey. Birds N. Am. 683:1-44.

Poor, H.H. 1946. Plumage and soft-part variations in the Herring Gull. Auk 63:135-151.

Portenko, L.A. 1936. The Bar-tailed Godwit and its races. Auk 53:194-197.

____. 1939. On some new forms of arctic gulls. Ibis 14(3rd Ser.):264-269.

____. 1952. [Age and seasonal changes in plumage among eiders.] Trans. Zool. Inst. Acad. Nauk., USSR 9:1100-1132.

____. 1963. The ornithogeography of the Koryak Highlands (U.S.S.R.). Proc. Int. Ornith. Congr. 13:1140-1146.

____. 1972. Birds of the Chukchi Peninsula and Wrangel Island. Vol. 1. Nauka Publishers, Leningrad. (Smithsonian Institution and National Science Foundation Translation, 1981; 445 pp.).

____. 1973. Birds of the Chukchi Peninsula and Wrangel Island. Vol. 2. Nauka Publishers, Leningrad. (Smithsonian Institution and National Science Foundation Translation, 1989; 379 pp.).

Porter, R., D. Newell, T. Marr, and R. Jolliffe. 1997. Identification of Cape Verde Shearwater. Birding World 10:222-228.

Porter, R.F. 1981. Ageing and sexing of Rough-legged Buzzards. Dutch Birding 3:78-79.

Pospichal, L.B., and W.H. Marshall. 1954. A field study of Sora Rail and Virginia Rail in central Minnesota. Flicker 26:2-32.

Post, P.W., and R.H. Lewis. 1995a. The Lesser Black-backed Gull in the Americas: Occurrence and subspecific identity. Part I: Taxonomy, distribution, and migration. Birding 27:282-290.

____ and ____. 1995b. The Lesser Black-backed Gull in the Americas: Occurrence and subspecific identity. Part II: Field identification. Birding 27:370-381.

Potts, G.R. 1971. Moult in the Shag *Phalacrocorax aristotelis*, and the ontogeny of the "Staffelmauser". Ibis 113:298-305.

Power, D.M. 1980. Evolution of land birds on the California islands. Pp. 613-642 *in* D.M. Power, ed., The California Islands: Proceedings of a multidisciplinary symposium. Santa Barbara Museum of Natural History, Santa Barbara, CA.

____ and D.G. Ainley. 1986. Seabird geographic variation: Similarity among populations of Leach's Storm-Petrel. Auk 103:575-585.

Powers, W.L. 1905. Journal of the ninth annual meeting of the Maine Ornithological Society. J. Maine Ornith. Soc. 7:1-7.

Prater, A.J. 1981. A review of the patterns of primary moult in Palearctic waders (Charadrii). Pp. 393-409 *in* Cooper, J., ed., Proceedings of the symposium on birds of the sea and shore. African Seabird Group, Capetown, South Africa.

____ and J.H. Marchant. 1975. Primary moult of *Tringa brevipes* and *T. incana*. Bull. Brit. Ornith. Club 95:120-122.

____, J.H. Marchant, and J. Vuorinen. 1977. Guide to the identification and ageing of Holarctic waders. BTO Guide 17, British Trust for Ornithology, Tring, U.K. 168 pp.

Pratt, H.D. 1976. Field identification of White-faced and Glossy ibises. Birding 8:1-5.

____. 1980. The White-faced Ibis in Hawaii. 'Elepaio 41:45-46.

Pratt, H.M. 1973. Breeding attempts by juvenile Great Blue Herons. Auk 90:897-899.

Preston, C.R., and R.D. Beane. 1993. Red-tailed Hawk. Birds N. Am. 52:1-24.

Prevett, J.P., and C.D. MacInnes. 1973. Observations of wild hybrids between Canada and Blue geese. Condor 75:124-125.

Prevost, Y. 1983a. Osprey distribution and subspecies taxonomy. Pp. 157-174 *in* D.M. Bird, ed., Biology and management of Bald Eagles and Ospreys. Harpell Press, Ste. Anne de Bellevue, Quebec.

____. 1983b. The moult of the Osprey *Pandion haliaetus*. Ardea 71:199-209.

Prince, H.H., P. Squibb, and G.Y. Belyea. 1988. Sichuans, pheasants of the future? - Learning from past release programs. Pp 291-305 *in* D.L. Hallett, W.R. Edwards, and G.V. Burger, eds, Pheasants: symptoms of wildlife problems on agricultural lands. The Wildlife Society, Bloomington, IN.

Prince, P.A., S. Rodwell, M. Jones, and P. Rothery. 1993. Moult in Black-browed and Gray-headed albatrosses *Diomedea melanophris* and *D. chrysostoma*. Ibis 135:121-131.

____, H. Weimerskirch, N. Huin, and S. Rodwell. Molt, maturation of plumage and ageing in the Wandering Albatross. Condor 99:58-72.

Principe, W.L. Jr. 1977. A hybrid American Avocet × Black-necked Stilt. Condor 79:128-129.

Proctor, B. 1997. Identification of Velvet and White-winged scoters. Birding World 10:56-61.

Prowse, A.D. 2006. Identification of the Fair Isle sandpiper-- a statistical analysis. Br. Birds 99:149-151.

Prum, R.O., and S. Williamson. 2001. Theory of the growth and evolution of feather shape. J. Experim. Zool. 291:30-57.

Pulich, W. Jr. 1982. Documentation and status of Cory's Shearwater in the western Gulf of Mexico. Wilson Bull. 94:381-385.

Pullan, G., and J. Martin. 2004. Presumed hybrid gull resembling adult Franklin's Gull. Brit. Birds 97:264-269.

Putnam, C. 2005. Fall molts of adult dowitchers. Birding 37:380-390.

Pyle, P. 1997. Identification guide to North American Birds. Part 1. Slate Creek Press, Bolinas, CA. 731 pp.

____. 1999. Molts by age in the Bristle-thighed Curlew and other shorebirds. W. Birds 30:181-183.

____. 2001. Age at first breeding and natal dispersal distance in a declining population of Cassin's Auklet. Auk 118:996-1007.

____. 2005a. Molts and plumages of ducks. Waterbirds 28:208-219.

____. 2005b. Preformative molts in North American Falconiformes. Raptor Res. 39:378-385.

____. 2005c. Remigial molt patterns in North American Falconiformes as related to age, sex, breeding status, and life-history strategies. Condor 107:823-834.

____. 2006a. Staffelmauser and other adaptive wing-molt strategies in larger birds. W. Birds 37:179-185.

____. 2006b. Handbook of avian hybrids of the world (book review). W. Birds 37:237-239.

____. 2007. Revision of molt and plumage terminology in Ptarmigan (Phasianidae: *Lagopus* spp.) based on evolutionary considerations. Auk 124:508-514.

____. Unpublished ms. Age determination and molt strategies in alcids.

____ and D.F. DeSante 2003. Four-letter and six-letter alpha codes for birds recorded in the American Ornithologists' Union check-list area. N. Am. Bird Bander 28:64-79

____ and ____. 2005. Updates to four-letter and six-letter alpha codes based on revisions by the American Ornithologists' Union. N. Am. Bird Bander 30:70-72

____ and ____. 2006. Updates to four-letter and six-letter alpha codes based on revisions by the American Ornithologists' Union in 2005-2006. N. Am. Bird Bander 31:194-196.

____ and S.N.G. Howell. 2004. Ornamental plume development and the "prealternate molts" of herons and egrets. Wilson Bull. 116:287-297.

____, ____, R.P. Yunick, and D.F. DeSante. 1987. Identification guide to North American passerines. Slate Creek Press, Bolinas, CA. 278 pp.

____, N. Hoffman, B. Casler, and T. McKee. 2001. Little and Least terns breeding on Midway Atoll: Identification, range extensions, and assortative breeding behavior. N. Am. Birds 55:3-6.

Pyle, P., A. Engilis Jr., and T.G. Moore. 2004. A specimen of the nominate subspecies of Red-shouldered Hawk from California. W. Birds 35:100-104.

Quinn, J.P., and W.H. Burrows. 1936. Artificial insemination in fowl. J. Heredity 27:31-37.

Quinn, J.S. 1990. Sexual size dimorphism and parental care in a monomorphic and a dimorphic larid. Auk 107:260-274.

Raitt, R.J. Jr. 1961. Plumage development and molts of California Quail. Condor 63:294-303.

____ and R.D. Ohmart. 1966. Annual cycle of reproduction and molt in Gambel Quail of the Rio Grande Valley, southern New Mexico. Condor 68:541-561.

Ramo, C., and B. Busto. 1987. Hybridization between the Scarlet Ibis (*Eudocimus ruber*) and the White Ibis (*E. albus*) in Venezuela. Colonial Waterbirds 10:111-114.

Ramos, R. T. Militño, J. Gonzáles-Solis, and X. Ruiz. Unpublished ms. Moulting strategies of a long-distance migratory seabird: The Mediterranean Cory's Shearwater.

Rand, A.L. 1942. *Larus kumlieni* and its allies. Can. Field-Nat. 56:123-126.

____. 1946. List of Yukon birds and those of the Canol Road. Nat. Mus. Can. Bull. 105:1-76.

____. 1947a. Geographical variation in the Loon *Gavia Immer* (Brünnich). Can. Field-Nat. 61:193-195.

____. 1947b. Notes on some Greenland birds. Auk 64:281-284.

____. 1948a. Glaciation, a factor in speciation. Evolution 2:314-321.

____. 1948b. Variation in the Spruce Grouse in Canada. Auk 65:33-40.

____. 1960. Races of the Short-tailed Hawk, *Buteo brachyurus*. Auk 77:448-459.

Randi, E., F. Spina, and B. Massa. 1989. Genetic variability in Cory's Shearwater (*Calonectris diomedea*). Auk 106:411-417.

Randler, C. 2001a. Field identification of hybrid wildfowl - geese. Alula 7:42-48.

____. 2001b. Field identification of hybrid wildfowl - dabbling ducks. Alula 7:82-91.

Ransom, W.H. 1927. Rare hybrid goose taken in Washington state. Condor 29:170.

Rasch, E.M., and P.J. Kurtin. 1976. Sex identification of Sandhill Cranes by karyotype analysis. Proc. N. Am. Crane Workshop 1:309-316.

Rasmussen, P.C. 1987. Molts of the Rock Shag and new interpretations of the plumage sequence. Condor 89:760-766.

____. 1988. Stepwise molt of remiges in Blue-eyed and King shags. Condor 90:220-227.

Rasmussen, P.W., W.E. Wheeler, T.J. Moser, L.E. Vine, B.D. Sullivan, and D.H. Rusch. 2001. Measurements of Canada Goose morphology - sources of error and effects of classification of subspecies. J. Wildl. Manage. 65:716-725.

Ratti, J.T. 1979. Reproductive separation and isolating mechanisms between sympatric dark- and light-phase Western Grebes. Auk 96:573-586.

____. 1981. Identification and distribution of Clark's Grebe. W. Birds 12:41-46. [Reprinted, Loon 58:112-116, 1986]

____, D.E. Timm, and F.C. Robards. 1977. Weights and measurements of Vancouver Canada Geese. Bird-Banding 48:354-357.

____, T.R. McCabe, and L.M. Smith. 1983. Morphological divergence between Western Grebe color morphs. J. Field Ornith. 54:424-426.

Rauzon, M.J. 2006. Occurrence of Bridled and Gray-backed terns in American Samoa. W. Birds 37:169-174.

Raveling, D.G. 1977. Canada Geese of the Churchill River Basin in north-central Manitoba. J. Wildl. Manage 41:35-47.

____. 1978. Morphology of the Cackling Canada Goose. J. Wildl. Manage. 42:897-900.

____ and D.S. Zezulak. 1991. Autumn diet of Cackling Canada Geese in relation to age and nutrient demand. California Fish and Game 77:1-9.

Rea, A.M. 1973. The Scaled Quail (*Callipepla squamata*) of the southwest: Systematic and historical consideration. Condor 75:322-329.

____. 1983a. Once a river: Bird life and habitat changes on the Middle Gila. University of Arizona Press, Tucson, AZ. 285 pp.

____. 1983b. Cathartid affinities: A review. Pp. 26-54 *in* W.R. Sanford and J.A. Jackson, eds., Vulture biology and management. University of California Press, Berkeley, CA.

____. 1998. Black Vulture and Turkey Vulture. Pp. 24-31 *in* R.L. Glinski, ed., The raptors of Arizona. University of Arizona Press, Tucson, AZ.

Reading, C.J. 1990. Molt pattern and duration in a female Northern Goshawk (*Accipiter gentilis*). J. Raptor Res. 24:91-97.

Redman, K.K., S. Lewis, R. Griffiths, S. Wanless, and K.C. Hamer. 2002. Sexing Northern Gannets from DNA, morphology and behavior. Waterbirds 25:230-234.

Reed, A., and H. Boyd. 1972. A revised key for sex and age determination of Black Duck wings. Can. Wildlife Service. 15 pp.

Reed, A., M.A. Davison, and D.K. Kraege. 1989a. Segregation of Brent Geese *Branta bernicla* wintering in the Puget Sound and the Straits of Georgia. Wildfowl 40:22-31.

____, R. Stehn, and D. Ward. 1989b. Autumn use of Izembek Lagoon, Alaska, by Brant from different breeding areas. J. Wildl. Manage. 53:720-725.

____, D.H. Ward, D.V. Derksen, and J.S. Sedinger. 1998. Brant. Birds N. Am. 337:1-28.

Reimchen, T.E., and S. Douglas. 1985. Differential contribution of the sexes to prefledged young in Red-throated Loons. Auk 102:198-201.

Reinhardt, K., K. Blechschmidt, H.-U. Peter, and D. Montalti. 1997. A hitherto unknown hybridization between Chilean and South Polar skua. Polar Biol. 17:114-118.

Reinking, D.L., and S.N.G. Howell. 1993. An Arctic Loon in California. W. Birds 24:189-196.

Renner, M., and P.D. Linegar. 2007. The first specimen record of Gray Heron (*Ardea cinerea*) for North America. Wilson J. Ornith. 119:134-136.

Rensel, J.A., and C.M. White. 1988. First description of a hybrid Blue × Sage Grouse. Condor 90:716-717.

Resende, S.L., F. Leeuwenburg, and B.A. Harrington. 1989. Biometrics of Semipalmated Sandpipers *Calidris pusilla* in southern Brazil. Wader Study Group Bull. 55:25-26.

Reynolds, J.D. 1987. Mating system and nesting biology of the Red-necked Phalarope *Phalaropus lobatus*: what constrains polyandry? Ibis 129:225-242.

Reynolds, R.T. 1972. Sexual dimorphism in *Accipiter* hawks: A new hypothesis. Condor 74:191-197.

Reynolds, S.J., G.R. Martin, L.L. Wallace, C.P. Wearn, and B.J. Hughes. 2008. Sexing Sooty Terns on Ascension Island from morphometric measurements. J. Zoology 274:2-8.

Rice, D.W., and K.W. Kenyon. 1962. Breeding cycles and behavior of Laysan and Black-footed albatrosses. Auk 79:517-567.

Richardson, D.M., and R.M. Kaminski. 1992. Diet restriction, diet quality, and prebasic molt in female Mallards. J. Wildl. Manage. 56:531-539.

Richdale, L.E. 1963. Biology of the Sooty Shearwater *Puffinus griseus*. Proc. Zool. Soc. London 141:1-117.

____. 1964. Notes on the Mottled Petrel *Pterodroma inexpectata* and other petrels. Ibis 106:110-114.

Richner, H. 1989. Avian laparoscopy as a field technique for sexing birds and an assessment of its effects on wild birds. J. Field Ornith. 60:137-142.

Richter, N.A., and G.R. Bourne. 1990. Sexing greater flamingos by weight and linear measurements. Zoo Biol. 9:317-323.

____, ____, and E.N. Diebold. 1991. Gender determination by body weight and linear measurements in American and Chilean flamingos, previously surgically sexed: Within-sex comparison to Greater Flamingo measurements. Zoo Biol. 10:425-431.

Riddington, R. 1994. The Red-necked Stint on Fair Isle-- the first juvenile in Europe. Birding World 7:355-357.

Ridgway, R. 1882. On an apparently new heron from Florida. Bull. Nuttall Ornith. Club 7:1-6.

____. 1886a. A nomenclature of color for naturalists, and compendium of useful knowledge for ornithologists. Little, Brown and Co., Boston. 130 pp.

____. 1886b. On the Glaucous Gull of the Barent's Sea and contiguous waters. Auk 3:330-331.

____. 1890. Observations on the Farallon Rail (*Porzana jamaicensis coturniculus*). Proc. U.S. Nat. Mus. 13:309-311.

____. 1894. Geographical versus sexual variation in *Oreortyx pictus*. Auk 11:193-197.

____. 1897. Birds of the Galapagos Archipelago. Proc. U.S. Nat Mus. 19:459-670.

____. 1912. Color standards and color nomenclature. R. Ridgway, Washington D.C. 43 pp.

____. 1919. The Birds of North and Middle America. Part XIII. U.S. Nat. Mus. Bull. 50(8):1-852.

____ and H. Friedmann. 1941. The birds of North and Middle America. Part IX. U.S. Nat. Mus. Bull. 50(9):1-254.

____ and ____. 1946. The birds of North and Middle America. Part X. U.S. Nat. Mus. Bull. 50(10):1-484.

Riley, J.H. 1908. Notes on the Broad-winged Hawks of the West Indies, with description of a new form. Auk 25:268-276.

____. 1911. Descriptions of three new birds from Canada. Proc. Biol. Soc. Washington 24:233-236.

____. 1913. The King Rail of Cuba. Proc. Biol. Soc. Washington 26:83-86.

____. 1916. Two new ralliformes from tropical America. Proc. Biol. Soc. Washington 29:103-104.

Ripley, S.D. 1977. Rails of the world. David R. Godine, Boston MA. 406 pp.

Ripley, T.H. 1960. Weights of Massachusetts quail and comparisons with other geographic samples for taxonomic significance. Auk 77:445-447.

Risser, A.C. Jr. 1971. A technique for performing laparotomy on small birds. Condor 73:376-379.

Ristow, D., and M. Wink. 1980. Sexual dimorphism of Cory's Shearwater. Il-Merril 21:9-12.

Robbins, M.B. 2000. "Mystery sandpiper" revisited. Birding 32:535-539.

Roberson, D. 1989. More on Pacific versus Arctic loons. Birding 21:154-157.

____. 1993. A note on hybrid white geese. Birding 25:50-53.

____. 1996. Identifying Manx Shearwaters in the northeastern Pacific. Birding 28:18-33.

____. 1998. Sulids unmasked: Which large booby reaches California? Field Notes 52:276-287.

____ and S.F. Bailey. 1991. *Cookilaria* petrels in the eastern Pacific Ocean. Am. Birds 45:1067-1081.

____ and L.F. Baptista. 1988. White-shielded coots in North America: A critical evaluation. Am. Birds 42:1241-1246.

Robert, M., B. Réjean, and J.-P.L. Savard. 2002. Relationship among breeding, molting, and wintering areas of male Barrow's Goldeneyes (*Bucephala islandica*) in eastern North America. Auk 119:676-684.

Roberts, J.O.L. 1967. Iris colour and age of Sharp-shinned Hawks. Ontario Bird Banding 3:95-106.

Roberts, P.J. 1984. Identification and ageing of a Sora Rail. Brit. Birds. 77:108-112.

Roberts, R.P. 1940. The life cycle of Wilson's Storm-Petrel *Oceanites oceanicus* (Kuhl). Sci. Reps. Brit. Graham Land Exp. 1:141-194.

Roberts, T.S. 1955. A manual for the identification of the birds of Minnesota and neighboring states. University of Minnesota Press, Minneapolis. 738 pp.

Robertson, C.J. 1970. Wing measurements of *Accipiters*. Eastern Bird-Banding Assoc. News 33:79-80.

Roberston, G.J., and R.I. Goudie. 1999. Harlequin Duck. Birds N. Am. 466:1-32.

____ and J.-P.L. Savard. 2002. Long-tailed Duck. Birds N. Am. 651:1-28.

____, F. Cooke, R.I. Goudie, and W.S. Boyde. 1997. The timing of arrival and moult chronology of Harlequin Ducks *Histrionicus histrionicus*. Wildfowl 48:147-155.

Robertson, H.A., and P.C. James. 1988. Morphology and egg measurements of seabirds breeding on Great Salvage Island, North Atlantic. Bull. Brit. Ornith. Club 108:79-87.

Robertson, I., and M. Fraker. 1974. Apparent hybridization between a Common Loon and an Arctic Loon. Can. Field-Nat. 88:367.

Robinson, J.A. 1999. Migration and morphometrics of the Red-breasted Merganser *Mergus serrator* in northern Eurasia and the implications for conservation of this species in Britain and Ireland. Wildfowl 50:139-148.

Robinson, J.A., L.W. Oring, J.P. Skorupa, and R. Boettcher. 1997. American Avocet. Birds N. Am. 275:1-32.

____, J.M. Reed, J.P. Skorupa, and L.W. Oring. 1999. Black-necked Stilt. Birds N. Am. 449:1-32.

Robinson, W.L. 1980. Fool Hen: The Spruce Grouse on the Yellow Dog Plains. 221 pp.

Roby, D.D., K.L. Brink, and D.N. Nettleship. 1981. Measurements, chick meals, and breeding distribution of Dovekies (*Alle alle*) in northwest Greenland. Arctic 34:241-248.

Rodgers, J.A. 1978a. Display characteristics and frequency of breeding by subadult Little Blue Herons. Pp. 35-39 *in* A. Sprunt IV, et al., eds., Wading birds. National Audubon Society, New York, NY.

____. 1978b. Breeding behavior of the Louisiana Heron. Wilson Bull. 90:45-59.

____. 1980. Little Blue Heron breeding bare-part coloration and plumage characteristics. Florida Field Nat. 8:46-47.

____ and H.T. Smith. 1995. Little Blue Heron. Birds N. Am. 145:1-32.

Rodgers, R.D. 1979. Ratios of primary calamus diameters for determining age of Ruffed Grouse. Wildl. Soc. Bull. 7:125-127.

Rodriguez, E.F., B.H. Pugesk, and K.L. Diem. 1996. A sexing technique for California Gulls breeding at Bamforth Lake, Wyoming. J. Field Ornith. 67:519-524.

Roest, A.I. 1957. Notes on the American Sparrow Hawk. Auk 74:1-19.

Rogers, C.M. 1991. An evaluation of the method of estimating body fat in birds by quantifying visible subcutaneous fat. J. Field Ornith. 62:349-356.

Rogers, D.I. 1990. The use of feather abrasion in molt studies. Corella 14:141-147.

____, P. Collins, R.E. Jessop, C.D.T. Minton, and C.J. Hassell. 2005. Gull-billed Terns in northwestern Australia: Subspecies identification, moults, and behavioural notes. Emu 105:145-158.

Rogers, M.J., and the Rarities Committee. 1998. Report on rare birds in Great Britain in 1997. Brit. Birds 91:455-517.

Rogers, J.P. 1967. Flightless Green-winged Teal in southeast Missouri. Wilson Bull. 79:339.

Rogers, K.G. 1995. Bivariate sexing criteria for Sharp-tailed Sandpiper and Eastern Curlew. Stilt 27:48-51.

Rohwer, F.C., W.P. Johnson, and E.R. Loos. 2002. Blue-winged Teal. Birds N. Am. 625:1-36.

Rohwer, S. 1999. Time constraints and moult-breeding tradeoffs in large birds. Proc. Int. Ornith. Congr. 22:568-581.

____ and A.E. Edwards. 2006. Reply to Howell on primary molt in albatross. W. Birds 37:245-248.

____, S.D. Fretwell, and D.M. Niles. 1980. Delayed maturation in passerine plumages and the deceptive acquisition of resources. Am. Nat. 115:400-437.

____, C.W. Thompson, and B.E. Young. 1992. Clarifying the Humphrey-Parkes molt and plumage terminology. Condor 94:297-300.

____, C.E. Filardi, K.S. Bostwick, and A.T. Peterson. 2000. A critical evaluation of Kenyon's Shag (*Phalacrocorax* [*Sitocarbo*] *kenyoni*). Auk 117:308-320.

Rooth, J. 1965. The flamingos on Bonaire (Netherlands Antilles): Habitat, diet, and reproduction of *Phoenicopterus ruber ruber*. Uitg. Natuurwet. Studiekring Suriname 41:1-151.

Rosair, D., and D. Cottridge. 1995. Photographic guide to the shorebirds of the world. Facts on File, New York, NY. 175 pp.

Roseberry, J.L., and B.J. Verts. 1963. Relationships between lens-weight, sex, and age in Bobwhites. Trans. Illinois State Acad. Sci. 56:208-212.

Roselaar, C.S. 1983. Subspecies recognition in Knot *Calidris canutus* and occurrence of races in western Europe. Beaufortia 33:97-109.

____. 1985. Primary moult strategies in terns Sternidae. Proc. Int. Ornith. Congr. 18:1054-1055.

____. 1990. Identification and occurrence of American and Pacific golden plover in the Netherlands. Dutch Birding 12:221-232.

Rosene, W. 1969. The Bobwhite quail: Its Life and management. The Sun Press, Hartwell, GA. 418 pp.

____ and F.W. Fitch Jr. 1956. A comparative test of the investigator as a variable in aging quail. J. Wildl. Manage. 20:205-207.

Rosenfield, R.N., and J. Bielefeldt. 1993. Cooper's Hawk. Birds N. Am. 75:1-24.

____ and ____. 1997. Reanalysis of relationships among eye color, age, and sex in the Cooper's Hawk. J. Raptor Res. 31:313-316.

____ and J. Wilde. 1982. Male Cooper's Hawk breeds in juvenal plumage. Wilson Bull. 94:213.

____, J. Bielefeldt, and K.N. Nolte. 1992. Eye color in Cooper's Hawks breeding in Wisconsin. J. Raptor Res. 26:189-191.

____, ____, L.J. Rosenfeld, A.C. Stewart, R.K. Murphy, D.A. Grosshuesch, and M.A. Bozek. 2003. Comparative relationships among eye color, age, and sex in three North American populations of Cooper's Hawks. Wilson Bull. 115:225-230.

Rothschild, W. 1915a. [Notes on the genus *Sula*.] Bull. Brit. Ornith. Club 35:41-45.

____. 1915b. On the genus *Fregata*. Novit. Zool. 22:145-146.

Roussel, Y.E., and R. Ouellet. 1975. A new criterion for sexing Quebec Ruffed Grouse. J. Wild. Manage. 39:443-445.

Rowan, W. 1926. Comments on two hybrid grouse and on the occurrence of *Tympanuchus americanus americanus* in the province of Alberta. Auk 43:333-336.

____. 1932. The status of the dowitchers with a description of a new subspecies from Alberta and Manitoba. Auk 49:14-35.

Rubega, M.A. 1996. Sexual size dimorphism in Red-necked Phalaropes and functional significance of nonsexual bill structure variation for feeding performance. J. Morphology 228:45-60.

____, D. Schamel, and D.M. Tracy. 2000. Red-necked Phalarope. Birds N. Am. 538:1-28.

Rumble, M.A., T.R. Mills, B.F. Wakeling, and R.W. Hoffman. 1996. Age and gender classification of Merriam's Turkeys from foot measurements. Proc. Nat. Wild Turkey Symp. 7:129-134.

Runkles, R.R. 1989. Molting. Pp 33-40 *in* S. Atwater and J. Schnell, eds., Ruffed Grouse. Stackpole Books, Harrisburg, PA.

Rusch, D.H., S. Detefano, M.C. Reynolds, and D. Lauten. 2000. Ruffed Grouse. Birds N. Am. 515:1-28.

Russell, R.P. Jr. 1978. First record of a Hooded Merganser-Wood Duck hybrid in the wild. Loon 50:208-209.

Russell, R.W. 2002. Pacific Loon and Arctic Loon. Birds N. Am. 657:1-40.

Russell, S.M. 1966. Status of the Black Rail and the Gray-breasted Crake in British Honduras. Condor 68:105-107.

Rust, R., and W. Kechele. 1996. Alterbestimmung von Habichten *Accipiter gentilis*: Langfristige Vergleiche gemausterter Handschwingen. Orn. Anzeiger 35:75-83.

Ruusila, V., H. Pöysä, and P. Runko. 2001. Female wing plumage reflects reproductive success in Common Goldeneye *Bucephala clangula*. J. Avian Biol. 32:1-5.

Ryder, J.P. 1978. Sexing Ring-billed Gulls externally. Bird Banding 49:218-222.

____. 1993. Ring-billed Gull. Birds N. Am. 33:1-28.

____ and R.T. Alisauskas. 1995. Ross' Goose. Birds N. Am. 162:1-28.

Ryder, R.R., and D.E. Manry. 1994. White-faced Ibis. Birds N. Am. 130:1-24.

Rylander, M.K., E.G. Bolen, and R.E. McCamant. 1980. Evidence of incubation patches in whistling ducks. Southwestern Nat. 25:126-128.

Sabo, T.J., R. Kesseli, J.L. Halverson, I.C.T. Nisbet, and J.J. Hatch. 1994. PCR-based method for sexing Roseate Terns (*Sterna dougallii*). Auk 111:1023-1027.

Salomonsen, F. 1932. Description of three new guillemots (*Uria aalge*). Ibis (13th Ser.) 2:128-132.

____. 1933. The status of the Greenland Snow Goose, *Anser caerulescens atlantica* (Kenn.). Medd. Gronl. 92:3-11.

____. 1938. Notes on moults of the Rock Ptarmigan (*Lagopus mutus*). Proc. Int. Ornith. Congr. 9:205-310.

____. 1939. Moults and sequence of plumage in the Rock Ptarmigan [*Lagopus mutus* (Montin)]. Vidensk. Medd. Dansk Nat. Forening 103:1-491.

____. 1941. Mauser und Gefiederfolge der Eisente (*Clangula hyemalis* (L.)). J. fur Ornith.. 89:282-337.

____. 1944. The Atlantic alcidae: The seasonal and geographic variation of auks inhabiting the Atlantic Ocean and the adjacent waters. Göteborgs Kung. Vet. Vitt.-Sam. Handl. 3(Ser. B, 5):1-138.

____. 1948. Blisgassen (*Anser albifrons* (Scop.)) og dens Slaetninge. Dansk Ornith. Forenings Tidskrift 42:102-108.

____. 1949. Some notes on the moult of the Long-tailed Duck. Avicultural Mag. 55:59-62.

____. 1950. Rediscovery of *Fulmarus glacialis minor* (Kjaerbølling). Dansk Ornith. Foren. Tidsskr. 44:100-105 (English summary).

____. 1965. The geographic variation of the Fulmar (*Fulmarus glacialis*) and the zones of marine environment in the North Atlantic. Auk 82:327-355.

____. 1968. The moult migration. Wildfowl 19:5-24.

Sandercock, B.K. 1998. Assortative mating and sexual size dimorphism in Western and Semipalmated sandpipers. Auk 115:786-791.

Sangster, G. 2000. Taxonomic status of *bernicla* and *nigricans* Brent Geese. Brit. Birds. 93:94-96.

____, M. Collinson, A.J. Helbig, A.G. Knox, D.T. Parkin, and T. Prater. 2001. The taxonomic status of Green-winged Teal *Anas carolinensis*. Brit. Birds. 94:218-226.

Sauer, E.G.F. 1962. Ethology and ecology of Golden Plovers on St. Lawrence Island, Bering Sea. Psychol. Forsch. 26:399-470.

Saunders, M.B., and G.L. Hansen. 1989. A method for estimating the ages of nestling Northern Harriers (*Circus cyaneus*). Can. J. Zool. 67:1824-1827.

Savard, J.-P.L., D. Bordage, and A. Reed. 1998. Surf Scoter. Birds N. Am. 363:1-28.

Sayler, R.D. 1995. Multivariate assessments of Redheads in spring. J. Wildl. Manage. 59:506-515.

Schamel, D., and D.M. Tracy. 1988. Are yearlings distinguishable from older Red-necked Phalaropes? J. Field Ornith. 59:235-238.

Scharf, W.C., and F. Hamerstrom. 1975. A morphological comparison of two harrier populations. Raptor Res. 9:27-32.

Scheider, F.G. 1966. Hooded Merganser × Common Goldeneye hybrid in Fulton, Oswego County. Kingbird 16:149-150.

Schemnitz, S.D. 1961. Ecology of the Scaled Quail in the Oklahoma panhandle. Wildl. Monogr. 8:1-47.

____. 1994. Scaled Quail. Birds N. Am. 106:1-16.

Schew, W.A., and C.T. Collins. Age and sex determination in Black Skimmer chicks. J. Field Ornith. 61:174-179.

Schmutz, J.A., and R.W. Hoffman. 1991. Variable first prebasic molt in Rio Grande and Merriam's Wild Turkeys. Wilson Bull. 103:295-300.

Schmutz, J.K. 1992. Molt of flight feathers in Ferruginous and Swainson's hawks. J. Raptor Res. 26:124-135.

____ and R.W. Fyfe. 1987. Migration and mortality of Alberta Ferruginous Hawks. Condor 89:169-174.

____ and S.M. Schmutz. 1975. Primary molt in *Circus cyaneus* in relation to nest brood events. Auk 92:105-110.

____ and ____. 1981. Inheritance of color phases of Ferruginous Hawks. Condor 89:187-189.

Schnell, G.D., G.L. Worthern, and M.E. Douglas. 1985. Morphometric assessment of sexual dimorphism in skeletal elements of California Gulls. Condor 87:484-493.

Schnell, J.H. 1994. Common Black-Hawk. Birds N. Am. 122:1-20.

Schorger, A.W. 1957. The beard of the Wild Turkey. Auk 74:441-446.

____. 1961. An ancient Pueblo Turkey. Auk 78:138-144.

____. 1966. The Wild Turkey. Its history and domestication. University of Oklahoma Press, Norman, OK. 625 pp.

____. 1970. A new subspecies of *Meleagris gallopavo*. Auk 87:168-170.

Schreiber, E.A., and R.L. Norton. 2002. Brown Booby. Birds N. Am. 649:1-28.

____ and R.W. Schreiber. 1988. Great Frigatebird size dimorphism on two central Pacific atolls. Condor 90:90-94.

____ and ____. 1993. Red-tailed Tropicbird. Birds N. Am. 43:1-24.

Schreiber, E.A., R.W. Schreiber. and G.A. Schenk. 1996. Red-footed Booby. Birds N. Am. 241:1-24.

____. D.J. Feare, B.A. Harrington, B.G. Murray Jr., W.B. Robertson Jr., M.J. Robertson, and G.E. Woolfenden. 2002. Sooty Tern. Birds N. Am. 665:1-32.

Schreiber, R.W. 1976. Growth and development of nestling Brown Pelicans. Bird-Banding 47:19-39.

____. 1980. Nesting chronology of the Eastern Brown Pelican. Auk 97:491-508.

____ and N.P. Ashmole. 1970. Sea-bird breeding seasons on Christmas Island, Pacific Ocean. Ibis 112:363-394.

____ and E.A. Schreiber. 1979. Notes on Measurements, mortality, molt, and gonad condition in Florida west coast Laughing Gulls. Florida Field Nat. 7:19-23.

____ and ____. 1983. Use of age-classes in monitoring population stability of Brown Pelicans. J. Wildl. Manage. 47:105-111.

____, ____, D.W. Anderson, and D.W. Bradley. 1989. Plumages and molts of Brown Pelicans. Nat. Hist. Mus. Los Angeles Co. Contr. Sci. 402:1-43.

Schroeder, M.A., and L.A. Robb. 1993. Greater Prairie-Chicken Birds N. Am. 36:1-24.

____, J.R. Young, and C.E. Braun. 1999. Sage Grouse. Birds N. Am. 425:1-28.

Schulenberg, T. 1989. More on Pacific versus Arctic loons. Birding 21:157-158.

Schultz, Z.M. 1951. Growth of the Glaucous-winged Gull, Part 1. Murrelet 32:35-42.

Scott, D.K. 1981. Geographical variation in the bill patterns of Bewick's Swans. Wildfowl 32:123-128.

Scott, J.M. 1971. Interbreeding of the Glaucous-winged Gull and Western Gull in the Pacific Northwest. California Birds 2:129-133.

____, R. Pyle, and R. Coleman. 1983. Records of small white egrets in Hawaii and Samoa with notes on identification. 'Elepaio 43:79-82.

Scott, M. 1995. The status and identification of Snow Goose and Ross's Goose. Birding World 8:56-63.

____. 1999. Identification of female Green-winged Teal. Birding World 12:81.

Scott, M.D. 1984. A White-tailed Ptarmigan with black rectrices. Condor 86:94-95.

Scott, N.J. Jr., and R.P. Reynolds. 1984. Phenotypic variation in the Mexican Duck (*Anas platyrhynchos diazi*) in Mexico. Condor 86:266-274.

Scott, P., and The Wildfowl Trust. 1972. The swans. Houghton Mifflin Company, Boston, MA.

Scott, W.E.D. 1890. Description of a new subspecies of Wild Turkey. Auk 7:376-377.

____. 1892. A description of the adult male of *Botaurus neoxenus* (Cory), with additional notes on subspecies. Auk 9:141.

Scribner, K.T., S.L. Talbot, J.M. Pearce, B.J. Pierson, K.S. Bollinger, and D.V. Derksen. 2003. Phylogeography of Canada Geese (*Branta canadensis*) in western North America. Auk 120:889-907.

Scrosati, M. 1990. Hybrid Duck at Saint-Zacharie, Quebec. Am. Birds 44:393.

Sealy, S.G. 1975. Aspects of the breeding biology of the Marbled Murrelet in British Columbia. Bird-Banding 46:141-154.

____. 1976. Biology of nesting Ancient Murrelets. Condor 78:294-306.

____. 1977. Wing molt of the Kittlitz's Murrelet. Wilson Bull. 89:467-469.

____. 2006. A historical perspective on the citrus-like scent of the Crested Auklet. W. Birds 37:139-148.

____, H.R. Carter, and D. Alison. 1982. Occurrences of the Asiatic Marbled Murrelet [*Brachyramphus marmoratus perdix* (Pallas)] in North America. Auk 99:778-781.

____, ____, W.D. Shuford, K.D. Powers, and C.A. Chase III. 1991. Long-distance vagrancy of the Asiatic Marbled Murrelet in North America, 1979-1989. W. Birds 22:145-155.

____, ____, and J. Hudon. 2001. Specimen records and sightings of Ancient Murrelets from the Canadian Prairie Provinces. Blue Jay 59:175-182.

Sedinger, J.S., M.P. Herzog, and D.H. Ward. 2004. Early environment and recruitment of Black Brant (*Branta bernicla nigricans*) into the breeding population. Auk 121:68-73.

Sellers, R.M. 1993. Racial identity of Cormorants *Phalacrocorax carbo* breeding at the Abberton Reservoir colony, Essex. Seabird 15:45-52.

Senner, S.E., and B.J. McCaffery. 1997. Surfbird. Birds N. Am. 266:1-20.

____, G.C. West, and D.W. Norton. 1981. The spring migration of Western Sandpipers and Dunlins in southcentral Alaska: Numbers, timing, and sex ratios. J. Field Ornith. 52:271-284.

Sennett, G.B. 1889. A new species of duck from Texas. Auk 6:263-265.

____. 1892. Description of a new Turkey. Auk 9:167-169.

Serie, J.R., D.L. Trauger, H.A. Doty, and D.E. Sharp. 1982. Age-class determination of Canvasbacks. J. Wildl. Manage. 46:894-904.

Serra, L. 2001. Duration of primary molt affects primary quality in Grey Plovers *Pluvialis squatarola*. J. Avian Biol. 32:377-380.

____ and R. Rusticali. 1998. Biometrics and moult of Grey Plover (*Pluvialis squatarola*) in northeastern Italy. Die Vogelwarte 39:281-292.

____, N. Baccetti, G. Cherubini, and M. Zenatello. 1998. Migration and moult in Dunlin *Calidris alpina* wintering in the central Mediterranean. Bird Study 45:205-218.

____, D.A. Whitelaw, A.J. Tree, and L.G. Underhill. 1999. Moult, mass and migration of Grey Plovers *Pluvialis squatarola* wintering in South Africa. Ardea 87:71-81.

Servello, F.A., and R.L. Kirkpatrick. 1986. Sexing Ruffed Grouse in the Southeast using feather criteria. Wild. Soc. Bull. 14:280-282.

Serventy, D.L. 1944. Notes on some rarer shorebirds. Emu 44:274-280.

____. 1956. A method of sexing petrels in field observations. Emu 56:213-215.

Shaller, G.B. 1964. Breeding behavior of the White Pelican at Yellowstone Lake, Wyoming. Condor 66:3-23.

Shanahan, D. 2001. The Gray Heron: Vagrant among us?. Birders J. 9:294-301.

Shannon, P.W. 2000. Plumages and molt patterns in captive Caribbean Flamingos. Waterbirds 23(Spec. Pub. 1):160-172.

Sharpe, R.S., and P.A. Johnsgard. 1966. Inheritance of behavioural characters in F2 Mallard × Pintail (*Anas platyrhynchos* × *Anas acuta*) hybrids. Behaviour 27:259-272.

Shaughnessy, P.D. 1993. Commentary on statistical oversight used to describe a Masked Booby subspecies. Marine Ornith. 21:69-70.

Shawkey, M.D., M.L. Beck, and G.E. Hill. 2003. Use of a gel documentation system to measure feather growth bars. J. Field Ornith. 74:125-128.

Shealer, D.A., and C.M. Cleary. 2007. Sex determination of adult Black Terns by DNA and morphometrics: Tests of sample size, temporal stability and geographic specificity in the classification accuracy of discriminant function models. Waterbirds 30:180-188.

Sheldon, W.G. 1967. The book of American Woodcock. University of Massachusetts Press, Amherst, MA. 227 pp.

____, F. Greeley, and J. Kupa. 1958. Aging fall-shot American Woodcocks by primary wear. J. Wildl. Manage. 22:310-312.

Shepard, K.B., and S.C. Votier. 1993. Common Gull showing Characteristics apparently consistent with North American race. Brit. Birds. 86:220-223.

Sheppard, J.M., and M.K. Klimkiewicz. 1976. An update to Wood's Bird Bander's Guide. N. Am. Bird Bander 1:25-27. [Reprinted, Inland Bird-Banding Assoc. News 48:88-91, 1976]

Sherony, D.F. 2006. Another look at goldeneyes: Variation in females and immatures. Birding 38:44-51.

Sherrod, S.K., C.M. White, and F.S.L. Williamson. 1976. Biology of the Bald Eagle on Amchitka Island, Alaska. Living Bird 15:143-182.

Shields, G.F., and A.C. Wilson. 1987. Subspecies of the Canada Goose (*Branta canadensis*) have distinct mitochondrial DNA's. Evolution 41:662-666.

Shields, M. 2002. Brown Pelican. Birds N. Am. 609:1-36.

Shiomi, K., and H. Ogi. 1991. Sexual morphological differences based on functional aspects of skeletal and muscular characters in breeding Tufted Puffins. J. Yamashina Inst. Ornith. 23:85-106.

Short, L.L. Jr. 1967. A review of the genera of grouse (Aves, Tetraoninae). Am. Mus. Novit. 2289:1-39.

Shortt, T.M. 1943. Correlation of bill and foot coloring with age and season in the Black Duck. Wilson Bull. 55:3-7.

Shugart, G.W. 1977. A method for externally sexing Ring-billed Gulls. Bird Banding 48:118-121.

____ and S. Rohwer. 1996. Serial descendant primary molt or staffelmauser in Black-crowned Night Herons. Condor 98:222-233.

Shupe, T.E. 1990. Frequency of Northern Bobwhite × Scaled Quail hybridization. Wilson Bull. 102:352-353.

Shurtleff, L.L., and C. Savage. 1996. The Wood Duck and the Mandarin. University of California Press, Berkeley, CA. 232 pp.

Shuskin, P.P. 1927. Notes on *Alectoris chukar*. Bull. Brit. Ornith. Club 48:22-27.

Sibley, C.L. 1938. Hybrids of and within North American Anatidae. Proc. Int. Ornith. Congr. 9:327-335.

Sibley, D.A. 1993. An Asiatic Marbled Murrelet in Ontario. Birders J. 2:276-277.

____. 1994. A guide to finding and identifying hybrid birds. Birding 26:162-177.

____. 2000. The Sibley guide to birds. Alfred A. Knopf, New York, NY. 544 pp.

____. 2001. What is the malar? Brit. Birds 94:80-84.

____. 2002. Sibley's birding basics. Alfred A. Knopf, New York, NY. 154 pp.

Sibley, F.C. 1970. Winter wing molt in the Western Grebe. Condor 72:373.

Siegel-Causey, D. 1989. Cranial pneumatization in the Phalacrocoracidae. Wilson Bull. 101:108-112.

____. 1990. On use of the bursa of Fabricius as an index of age and development. J. Field Ornith. 61:441-444.

____. 1991. Systematics and biogeography of North Pacific shags, with a description of a new species. Occ. Papers Univ. Kansas Mus. Nat. Hist. 140:1-17.

Siegfried, W.R. 1971. Plumage and moult of the Cattle Egret. Ostrich 9(Suppl.):153-164.

____. 1973. Wing moult of Ruddy Ducks in Manitoba. Bull. Brit. Ornith. Club. 93:98-99.

____. 1976. Social organization in Ruddy and Maccoa ducks. Auk 93:560-570.

____, A.E. Burger, and P.J. Caldwell. 1976. Incubation behavior of Ruddy and Maccoa ducks. Condor 78:512-517.

Simmons, R.E. 2000. Harriers of the world. Oxford University Press, Oxford, U.K. 368 pp.

____, P. Barnard, B. MacWhirter, and G.L. Hansen. 1986. The influence of microtines on polygyny, productivity, age, and provisioning of breeding northern Harriers: a 5-year study. Can. J. Zool. 64:2447-2456.

Simon, D. 1978. Identification of Snow and Ross' geese. Birding 10:289-291.

Simpson, K., and J.P. Kelsall. 1978. Capture and banding of adult Great Blue Herons at Pender Harbour, British Columbia. Proc. Colonial Waterbird Group 1978:71-78.

Siopes, T.D., and W.O. Wilson. 1973. Determination of the sex of Chukar Partridge at hatching. J. Wildl. Manage. 37:239-240.

Skeel, M.A. 1982. Sex determination of adult Whimbrels. J. Field Ornith. 53:414-416.

____ and E.P. Mallory. 1996. Whimbrel. Birds N. Am. 219:1-28.

Skewes, J., C. Minton, and K. Rogers. 2004. Primary moult of the Ruddy Turnstone *Arenaria interpres* in Australia. Stilt 45:20-32.

Sloan, N.F. 1967. An external sexual character of the Common Snipe. Publ. Michigan Tech. Univ. 16:11-12.

Slotterback, J.W. 2002. Band-rumped Storm-Petrel and Tristram's Storm-Petrel. Birds N. Am. 673:1-28.

Slud, P. 1979. First record of Leach's Storm-Petrel in Costa Rica: A correction. Condor 81;102-103.

Sluys, R. 1982. Geographic variation in the Kittiwake, *Rissa tridactyla*. Gerfaut 72:221-230.

____. 1983. Evidence for a hybrid murre reconsidered. Auk 100:236-237.

Smallwood, J.A. 1989. Age determination of American Kestrels: A revised key. J. Field Ornith. 60:510-519.

____ and D.M. Bird. 2002. American Kestrel. Birds N. Am. 602:1-32.

____, et al. 1999. Clinal variation in the juvenal plumage of American Kestrels. J. Field. Ornith. 70:425-435.

Smith, C., F. Cooke, and R.I. Goudie. 1998. Ageing Harlequin Duck *Histrionicus histrionicus* drakes using plumage characteristics. Wildfowl 49:245-248.

Smith, D.S., and J.R. Cain. 1984. Criteria for age classification of juvenile Scaled Quail. J. Wildl. Manage. 48:187-191.

Smith, F.W. 1977. Records of molting in the Pintail (*Anas acuta*) and Northern Shoveler (*Anas clypeata*) on the Texas Gulf Coast. Southwestern Nat. 4:558.

Smith, J.P., S.W. Hoffman, and J.A. Gessaman. 1990. Regional size differences among fall-migrant *Accipiters* in North America. J. Field Ornith. 61:192-200.

Smith, L.M., and D.S. Sheeley. 1993. Molt patterns of wintering Northern Pintails in the southern High Plains. J. Wildl. Manage. 57:229-238.

Smith, N.D., and I.O. Buss. 1963. Age determination and plumage observations of Blue Grouse. J. Wildl. Manage. 27:566-578.

Smith, N.G. 1966. Evolution of some arctic gulls (*Larus*): An experimental study in isolating mechanisms. Ornith. Monographs 4:1-99.

____. Polymorphism in Ringed Plovers. Ibis 111:177-188.

Smith, R.D. 1988. Age and sex-related differences in biometrics and moult of Kittiwakes. Ringing & Migr. 9:44-48.

Smith, R.H. 1961. Age classification of the Chukar Partridge. J. Wildl. Manage. 25:84-86.

Smith. T.B., and S.A. Temple. 1982. Feeding habits and bill polymorphism in Hook-billed Kites. Auk 99:197-207.

Smithe, F.B. 1975. Naturalist's color guide. Part 1. American Museum of Natural History, New York. 8 pp plus 16 color plates.

____. 1981. Supplement to Naturalist's Color Guide. Part 2. American Museum of Natural History, New York. 229 pp.

Snell, R.R. 1989. Status of *Larus* gulls at Home Bay, Baffin Island. Col. Waterbirds 12:12-23.

____. 1991a. Variably plumaged Icelandic Herring Gulls reflect founders not hybrids. Auk 108:329-341.

____. 1991b. Interspecific allozyme differentiation among North Atlantic white-headed Larid gulls. Auk 108:319-328.

Snell, R.R. 1991c. Conflation of the observed and the hypothesized: Smith's 1961 research in Home Bay, Baffin Island. Colonial Waterbirds 14:196-202.

____. 1993. Variably plumaged Icelandic Herring Gulls: High intraspecific variation in a founded population. Auk 110:410-413.

____. 2003. Iceland Gull and Thayer's Gull. Birds N. Am. 699:1-36.

Snyder, L.L. 1935. A study of Sharp-tailed Grouse. Univ. Toronto Stud. Biol Ser. 40:1-66.

____. 1938. The Northwest Coast Sharp-shinned Hawk. Royal Ontario Mus. Zool. Occ. Papers 4:1-6.

____. 1941. On the Hudson Bay Eider. Occ. Papers Royal Ontario Mus. Zool. 6:1-7.

____. 1953. An apparently natural hybrid golden-eye. Wilson Bull. 65:199.

____ and H.G. Lumsden. 1951. Variation in *Anas cyanoptera*. Occ. Papers Royal Ontario Mus. Zool. 10:1-18.

____ and T.M. Shortt. 1946. Variation in *Bonasa umbellus*, with particular reference to the species in Canada east of the Rockies. Can. J. Res. 24:118-133.

Snyder, N.F.R., and E.V. Johnson. 1985. Photographic censusing of the 1982-1983 California Condor population. Condor 87:1-13.

____ and N.J. Schmitt. 2002. California Condor. Birds N. Am. 610:1-36.

____ and H.A. Snyder. 1974. Function of eye coloration in North American *Accipiters*. Condor 76:219-222.

____ and ____. 1991. Birds of Prey: Natural history and conservation of North American raptors. Voyager Press, Stillwater, MN. 224 pp.

____ and ____. 2000. The California Condor, a saga of natural history and conservation. Academic Press, London, UK. 410 pp.

____ and J.W. Wiley. 1976. Sexual size dimorphism in hawks and owls of North America. Ornith. Monogr. 20:1-96.

____, E.V. Johnson, and D.A. Clendenen. 1987. Primary molt of California Condors. Condor 89:468-485.

Sodhi, N.S., L.W. Oliphant, P.C. James, and I.G. Warkentin. 1993. Merlin. Birds N. Am. 44:1-20.

Sordhal, T.A. 1988. The American Avocet (*Recurvirostra americana*) as a paradigm for adult automimicry. Evol. Ecol. 2:189-196.

Sorenson, L.G., and S.R. Derrickson. 1994. Sexual selection in Northern Pintail (*Anas acuta*): The importance of female choice versus male-male competition in the evolution of sexually-selected traits. Behav. Ecol. and Sociobiol. 35:389-400.

Southern, H.N. 1941. Quantitative studies in the geographic variations in birds -- the Common Guillemot (*Uria aalge* Pont.). Proc Zool. Soc. London 111(Ser. A):255-276.

____. 1943. The two phases of *Stercorarius parasiticus* (Linnaeus). Ibis 85:443-485.

Southern, L.K. 1981. Sex-related differences in territorial aggression by Ring-billed Gulls. Auk 98:179-181.

Southern, W.E. 1964. Additional observations on winter Bald Eagle populations: Including remarks on biotelemetry techniques and immature plumages. Wilson Bull. 76:121-137.

____. 1967. Further comments on subadult Bald Eagle plumages. Jack-Pine Warbler 45:70-80.

Spaans, A.L. 1976. Molt of flight and tail feathers of the Least Sandpiper in Surinam, South America. Bird-Banding 47:359-364.

____. 1979. Wader studies in Surinam, South America. Wader Study Group Bull. 25:32-37.

____. 1980. Biometrics and moult of Sanderling *Calidris alba* during the autumn in Suriname. Wader Study Group Bull. 28:33-35.

Sparling, D.W. Jr. 1980. Hybrids and taxonomic status of Greater Prairie-Chickens and Sage Grouse. Prairie Nat. 12:92-101.

Spear, L.B. 1987. Hybridization of Glaucous and Herring Gulls at the Mackenzie Delta, Canada. Auk 104:123-125.

____. 1988. Dispersal patterns of Western Gulls from Southeast Farallon Island. Auk 105:128-141.

____ and D.G. Ainley. 1998. Morphological differences relative to ecological segregation in petrels (family: procellariidae) of the southern ocean and tropical Pacific. Auk 115:1017-1033.

____ and ____. 2005. At-sea behaviour and habitat use by tropicbirds in the eastern Pacific. Ibis 147:391-407.

____ and ____. 2007. Storm-petrels of the eastern Pacific Ocean: species assembly and diversity along marine habitat gradients. Ornith. Monogr. 62:1-77.

____, S.N.G. Howell, and D.G. Ainley. 1992. Notes on the at-sea identification of some Pacific gadfly petrels (genus: *Pterodroma*). Colonial Waterbirds 15:202-218.

Speich, S., and D.A. Manuwal. 1974. Gular pouch development and population structure of Cassin's Auklet. Auk 91:291-306.

Spellerberg, I.F. 1970. Body measurements and color phases of the McCormick Skua. Notornis 17:280-285.

Spitzkeit, J.W., and T.C. Tacha. 1986. Subspecific composition of Canada Geese wintering in southern Illinois. Trans. Illinois State Acad. Sci 79:171-173.

Spofford, W.R. 1946. Observations on two Golden Eagles. Auk 63:85-87.

Spring, L. 1971. A comparison of functional and morphological adaptations in the Common Murre (*Uria aalge*) and Thick-billed Murre (*Uria lomvia*). Condor 73:1-27.

Sprunt, A. 1954. A hybrid between the Little Blue Heron and the Snowy Egret. Auk 71:314-315.

Squires, J.R., and R.T. Reynolds. 1997. Northern Goshawk. Birds N. Am. 298:1-32.

Stager, K.E. 1964. The birds of Clipperton Island, Eastern Pacific. Condor 66:357-371.

Stalheim, P.S. 1975. Breeding and behaviour of captive Yellow Rails. Avicultural Mag. 81:133-144.

Stalmaster, M.V. 1987. The Bald Eagle. Universe Books, New York, NY. 227 pp.

Stangel, P.W., J.A. Rodgers Jr., and A.L. Bryan. 1991. Low genetic differentiation between two disjunct White Ibis colonies. Colonial Waterbirds 14:13-16.

____, P.L. Leberg, and J.I. Smith. 1992. Systematics and population genetics. Pp. 18-28 *in* J.D. Dickson, ed., The Wild Turkey: Biology and management. Stackpole Books, Mechanicsburg, PA.

Stavy, M., D. Gilbert, and R.D. Martin. 1979. Routine determination of sex in monomorphic bird species using faecal steroid analysis. Int. Zoo Yearbook 19:209-214.

Stedman, S.J. 2000. Horned Grebe. Birds N. Am. 505:1-28.

Steenhof, K. 1998. Prairie Falcon. Birds N. Am. 346:1-28.

____ and J.O. McKinley. 2006. Size dimorphism, molt status, and body mass of Prairie Falcons nesting in the Snake River Birds of Prey National Conservation Area. J. Raptor. Res. 40:71-75.

Steffen, D.E., C.E. Couvillion, and G.A. Hurst. 1990. Age determination of eastern Wild Turkey gobblers. Wildl. Soc. Bull. 18:119-124.

Stejneger, L. 1882. Outlines of a monograph of the Cygninae. Proc. U.S. Nat. Mus. 5:174-221.

____. 1884. On the shedding of claws in the ptarmigan and allied birds. Am. Nat. 18:774-776.

____. 1885. Results of ornithological explorations in the Commander Islands and Kamtcshatka. U.S. Nat. Mus. Bull. 29:1-382.

____. 1889. Contributions to the history of Pallas' Cormorant. Proc. U.S. Nat. Mus. 12:83-88.

Stempniewicz, L. 1989. Dovekie juvenile plumage dimorphism. Colonial Waterbirds 12:123-125.

____, M. Skakuj, and L. Iliszko. 1996. The Little Auk (*Alle* alle *polaris*) on Franz Joseph Land: A comparison with Svalbard (*Alle a. alle*) populations. Polar Research 15:1-10.

Stenhouse, J.H. 1930. The Little Auk (*Alle alle polaris* Sub-Sp. Nov.) of Franz Josef Land. Scottish Nat. 182:47-49.

Stepanyan, L.S. 1990. A new hypothesis on the origin of *Calidris paramelanotos* (Scolopacidae, Aves). Zool. Zhurnal 69:148-151.

Sterling, T., and A. Dzubin. 1967. Canada Goose molt migrations to the Northwest Territories. Trans. N. Am. Wildl. Nat. Res. Conf. 32:355-373.

Stern, M.A., and R.L. Jarvis. 1991. Sexual dimorphism and assortative mating in Black Terns. Wilson Bull. 103:266-271.

Stevenson, H.M. 1975. Identification of difficult birds. III. Semipalmated and Western sandpipers. Florida Field Nat. 3:39-44. [Reprinted Birding 11:84-89, 1989]

____. and B.H. Anderson. 1994. The birdlife of Florida. University of Florida Press, Gainseville, FL. 892 pp.

Stevenson, J.O., and R.E. Griffith. 1946. Winter life of the Whooping Crane. Condor 48:160-178.

Stewart, D.T. 1993. Sexual dimorphism in Thick-billed Murres, *Uria lomvia*. Can. J. Zool. 71:346-351.

Stewart, R.E., and J.W. Aldrich. 1956. Distinction of maritime and prairie populations of Blue-winged Teal. Proc. Biol. Soc. Washington 69:29-36.

Stoddard, H.L. 1931. The Bobwhite quail: Its habits preservation and increase. C. Scribner's Sons, New York, NY. 559 pp.

Stokes, A.W. 1957. Validity of spur length as an age criterion in Pheasants. J. Wildl. Manage. 21:248-250.

Stokes, T. 1990. The post-juvenal plumages of the Red-tailed Tropicbird *Phaethon rubricauda*. Australian Bird Watcher 13:259-260.

Stokoe, R. 1958. The spring plumage of the Cormorant. Brit. Birds. 51:165-179.

Stone, W. 1897. On the annual molt of the Sanderling. Proc. Acad. Nat. Sci. Philadelphia 49:368-372.

____. 1900. Report on the birds and mammals collected by the McIlhenny Expedition to Pt. Barrow, Alaska. Proc. Acad. Nat. Sci. Philadelphia 52:4-49.

____. 1903. A hybrid duck *Anas boschas* × *Nettion carolinensis*. Auk 20:209-210.

Stone, W.B., and K. Morris. 1981. Aging male Ring-necked Pheasants by bone histology. New York Fish & Game J. 28:223-229.

Stonehouse, B. 1962. The tropicbirds (genus *Phaethon*) of Ascension Island. Ibis 103b:124-161.

Storer, R.W. 1950. Geographic variation in the Pigeon Guillemot in North America. Condor 52:28-31.

____. 1952a. Variation in the resident Sharp-shinned Hawks of Mexico. Condor 54:283-289.

____. 1952b. A comparison of variation, behavior and evolution in the sea bird genera *Uria* and *Cepphus*. Univ. California Pubs. Zool. 52:121-222.

____. 1955. Weight, wing area, and skeletal proportions in three *Accipiters*. Acta IX Int. Ornit. Congr. 1954:287-290.

____. 1962. Variation in Red-tailed Hawks of southern Mexico and Central America. Condor 64:77-78.

____. 1965. The color phases of the Western Grebe. Living Bird 4:59-63.

____. 1966. Sexual dimorphism and food habits in three North American *Accipiters*. Auk 83:423-436.

____. 1967. The patterns of downy grebes. Condor 69:469-478.

____. 1969. The behavior of the Horned Grebe in spring. Condor 71:180-205.

____. 1978. Systematic notes on the loons (Gaviidae, Aves). Breviora 448:1-8.

____. 1988. Variation in the Common Loon (*Gavia immer*). Pp. 54-65 *in* P.I.V. Strong, ed., Papers for the 1987 conference on loon research and management. North American Loon Fund, Meredith, NH.

____. 1992. Least Grebe. Birds N. Am. 24:1-12.

____. 1996. [Review of Bochenski (1994)]. Auk 113:974-975.

____ and T. Getty. 1985. Geographic variation in the Least Grebe (*Tachybaptus dominicus*). Ornith. Monogr. 36:31-39.

____ and J. Jehl Jr. 1985. Moult patterns and moult migration in the Black-necked Grebe *Podiceps nigricollis*. Ornis Scand. 16:253-260.

____ and G.L. Nuechterlein. 1985. An analysis of plumage and morphological characters of the two color forms of the Western Grebe (*Aechmophorus*). Auk 102:102-119.

____ and ____. 1992. Western Grebe and Clark's Grebe. Birds N. Am. 26:1-24.

Stout, B.E., and F. Cooke. 2003. Timing and location of wing molt in Horned, Red-necked, and Western grebes in North America. Waterbirds 26:88-93.

____ and G.L. Nuechterlein. 1999. Red-necked Grebe. Birds N. Am. 465:1-32.

Strang, C.A. 1977. Variation and distribution of Glaucous Gulls in western Alaska. Condor 79:170-175.

Streets, T.H. 1876. Description of a new duck from Washington Island. Bull. Nuttall Ornith. Club 1:46-47.

____. 1877. Contributions ot the natural history of the Hawaiian and Fanning islands and Lower California, made in connection with the United States North Pacific Surveying Expedition. U.S. Nat. Mus. Bull. 7:1-172.

Stresemann, E. 1925. Raubvogelstudien. J. fur Ornith. 73:295-323.

____. 1963a. Variations in the number of primaries. Condor 65:449-459.

____. 1963b. The nomenclature of plumages and molts. Auk 80:1-8.

____ and V. Stresemann. 1966. Die Mauser der Vögel. J. fur Ornith. 107:1-448.

____ and ____. 1970. Über Mauser und Zug von *Puffinus gravis*. J. fur Ornith. 111:378-393.

Stresemann, V. 1948. Eclipse plumage and nuptial plumage in the Old Squaw, or Long-tailed Duck (*Clangula hyemalis*). Avicultural Mag. 54:188-194.

____ and E. Stresemann. 1960. Die Handschwingenmauser der Tagraubvögel. J. fur Ornith. 101:373-403.

Stromberg, L. 1977. Sexing all fowl, baby chicks, game birds, cage birds. Stromberg Publ. Co., Pine River, MN. 96 pp.

Stromberg, M.R. 2000. Montezuma Quail. Birds N. Am. 524:1-20.

Strong, C.S. 1998. Techniques for Marbled Murrelet age determination in the field. Pacific Seabirds 25:6-8.

Stutzenbaker, C.D. 1988. The Mottled Duck, its life history, ecology and management. Texas Parks and Wildlife Department, Austin, TX. 209 pp.

Suddaby, D., K.D. Shaw, P.M. Ellis, and K. Brockie. 1998. King Eiders in Britain and Ireland in 1958-90: Occurrences and ageing. Brit. Birds. 91:418-427.

Sugimora, F., N. Oka, and Y. Ishibashi. 1985. The degree of skull ossification as a means of aging Short-tailed Shearwaters. J. Yamashina Inst. Ornith. 17:159-165.

Summers, R.W. 1976. The value of bill lengths in museum specimens and biometric studies. Wader Study Group Bull. 17:10-11.

____ and M.M. Smith. 1990. An age-related difference in the size of the nasal glands of Brent Geese *Branta bernicla*. Wildfowl 41:35-37.

____, L.G. Underhill, C.F. Clinning, and M. Nicoll. 1989. Populations, migrations, biometrics and moult of the Turnstone *Arenaria i. interpres* on the East Atlantic coastline, with special reference to the Siberian population. Ardea 77:145-167.

Summers, R.W. , L.G. Underhill, M. Nicoll, K.-B. Strann, and S.Ø. Nilson. 2004. Timing and duratiojn of moult in three populations of Purple Sandpipers *Calidris maritima* with different moult/migration patterns. Ibis 146:394-403.

Sumner, E.L. Jr. 1935. A life history study of the California Quail, with recommendations for conservation and management. California Fish and Game 21:167-256, 277-342.

Sutton, G.M. 1932a. The exploration of Southampton Island, Hudson Bay. The birds of Southampton Island. Carnegie Mus. Mem. 12(part 2, sect. 2):1-267.

____. 1932b. Notes on the molts and sequence of plumages in the Old-squaw. Auk 49:42-51.

____. 1939. The Mississippi Kite in spring. Condor 41:41-53.

____. 1943. The wing molts of adult loons: A review of the evidence. Wilson Bull. 55:145-150.

____. 1944. The kites of the genus *Ictinia*. Wilson Bull. 56:3-8.

____. 1963. Interbreeding in the wild of Bobwhite (*Colinus virginianus*) and Scaled Quail (*Callipepla squamata*) in Stonewall County, northwestern Texas. Southwestern Nat. 8:108-111.

____. 1964. On plumages of the young Lesser Prairie Chicken. Southwestern Nat. 9:1-5.

____. 1968a. Sexual dimorphism in the Hudsonian Godwit. Wilson Bull. 80:251-252.

____. 1968b. Evolution of some arctic gulls (*Larus*): An experimental study of isolating mechanisms. [Review of Smith (1966)] Auk 85:142-145.

____. 1977. The Lesser Prairie Chicken's inflatable neck sacs. Wilson Bull. 89:521-522.

____ and T.D. Burleigh. 1941. Some birds recorded in Nuevo Leon, Mexico. Condor 43:158-160.

____ and D.F. Parmelee. 1978. On maturation of Thayer's Gull. Wilson Bull. 90:479-491.

____ and J. Van Tyne. 1935. A new Red-tailed Hawk from Texas. Occ. Papers Mus. Zool. Univ. Michigan 321:1-6.

Suydam, R.S. 2000. King Eider. Birds N. Am. 491:1-28.

Svensson, L. 1992. Identification guide to European Passerines. 4th Ed. L. Svensson, Stockholm.

Swann, H.K. 1922a. A synopsis of the Accipitres (diurnal birds of prey). 2nd Ed. Wheldon & Wesley, London, UK. 233 pp.

____. 1922b. [On observations at the American Museum of Natural History]. Bull. Brit. Ornith. Club 42:65-68.

____. 1925. A monograph of the birds of prey (order Accipitres). Part II. Wheldon & Wesley, London, UK. 52 pp.

Swarth, H.S. 1912. Report on a collection of birds and mammals from Vancouver Island. Univ. California Pubs. Zool. 10:1-124.

____. 1913. A study of a collection of geese of the *Branta canadensis* group from The San Joaquin Valley, California. Univ. California Pubs. Zool. 12:1-24.

____. 1915. An apparent hybrid between species of the genera *Spatula* and *Querquedula*. Condor 17:115-118.

____. 1920. The subspecies of *Branta canadensis* (Linnaeus). Auk 37:268-272.

____. 1921. The Sitkan race of the Dusky Grouse. Condor 23:59-60.

____. 1922. Birds and mammals of the Sitkine River Region of northern British Columbia and southeastern Alaska. Univ. California Pubs. Zool. 24:125-314.

____. 1924. Birds and mammals of the Skeena River region of northern British Columbia. Univ. California Pubs. Zool. 24:315-388.

____. 1926. Report on a collection of birds and mammals from the Atlin region, northern British Columbia. Univ. California Pubs. Zool. 30:51-162.

____. 1928. Taverner's study of Red-tailed Hawks. Condor 30:197-199.

____. 1931a. The avifauna of the Galapagos Islands. California Acad. Sci. Occ. Papers 18:1-299.

____. 1931b. Geographic variation in the Richardson's Grouse. Proc. California Acad Sci. (4th Series) 20:1-7.

____. 1933a. Frigate-birds of the west American coast. Condor 35:148-150.

____. 1933b. Peale Falcon in California. Condor 35:233-234.

____. 1934. Birds of Nunivak Island, Alaska. Pacific Coast Avif. 22:1-64.

____. 1935. Systematic status of some northwestern birds. Condor 37:199-204

____ and H.C. Bryant. 1917. A study of the races of the White-fronted Goose (*Anser albifrons*) occurring in California. Univ. California Pubs. Zool. 17:209-222.

Swennen, C. 1977. Laboratory research in sea-birds. Netherlands Institute for Sea Research, Texel. 44 pp.

____, P. Duiven, and G.J.M. Wintermans. 1989. Abnormal plumage in possibly senile female Eiders *Somateria mollissima*. Wildfowl 40:127-130.

Sykes, P.W. Jr. 1979. Status of the Everglade Kite in Florida - 1968-1978. Wilson Bull. 91:495-511.

Sykes, P.W. Jr. , J.A. Rodgers Jr., and R.E. Bennetts. 1995. Snail Kite. Birds N. Am. 171:1-32.

Syroechkovski, E.E. Jr, C. Zöckler, and E. Lappo. 1998. Status of Brent Goose in northwest Yakutia, East Siberia. Brit. Birds. 91:565-572.

Szantyr, M.S. 1997. Semipalmated Sandpiper or Little Stint? A matter of degrees. Birding 29:132-134.

Szuba, K.J., J.F. Bendell, and B.J. Naylor. 1987. Age determination of Hudsonian Spruce Grouse using primary feathers. Wild. Soc. Bull. 15:539-543.

Taber, R.D. 1969. Criteria for age and sex. Pp. 325-401 *in* R.H. Giles, ed., Wildlife management techniques. 3rd edition. The Wildlife Society, Washington, D.C.

Tacha, T.C., and P.A. Vohs. 1984. Some population parameters of Sandhill Cranes from mid-continental North America. J. Wildl. Manage. 48:89-98.

____, P.A. Vohs, and W.D. Warde. 1985. Morphometric variation of Sandhill Cranes from mid-continental North America. J. Wild. Manage. 49:246-250.

____, D.D. Thornburg, and R.A. Williamson. 1989. Use of wing-tips to estimate age ratios of Canada Geese. Wild. Soc. Bull. 17:146-148.

____, S.A. Nesbitt, and P.A. Vohs. 1992. Sandhill Crane. Birds N. Am. 31:1-24.

Takekawa, J., and D. Orthmeyer. 1993. A simple morphometric method to distinguish Tule and Pacific subspecies of Greater White-fronted Geese. U.S. Dept. Interior Inform. Bull. 84:1-2.

____ and N. Warnock. 2000. Long-billed Dowitcher. Birds N. Am. 493:1-20.

Tallman, D., and A. Hanson. 1997. Clark's Grebe-Western Grebe pair at Sand Lake. South Dakota Bird Notes 49:17.

Tanaka, H., and H. Ogi. 1986. Evaluation of bill furrows as age indicator in the Tufted Puffin *Lunda cirrhata*. Mem. Nat. Inst. Polar Res. 44(Spec. Issue):160-166.

Tarburton, M.K. 1989. Subspeciation in the Red-tailed Tropicbird. Notornis 36:39-49.

Taverner, J.H. 1970. A presumed hybrid Mediterranean × Black-headed gull in Hampshire. Brit. Birds. 63:380-382.

Taverner, P.A. 1914. A new subspecies of *Dendragapus* (*Dendragapus obscurus flemingi*) from southern Yukon Territory. Auk 31:385-388.

____. 1927. A study of *Buteo borealis*, the Red-tailed Hawk, and its varieties in Canada. Victoria Mem. Mus. Bull. 48:1-20.

____. 1928. A study of the Canadian races of Rock Ptarmigan (*Lagopus rupestris*). Nat. Mus. Can. Ann. Rep. 1928:28-39.

____. 1929a. The red plumage coloration of the Little Brown and Sandhill cranes. Auk 46:228-230.

____. 1929b. Bird notes from the Canadian Labrador, 1928. Can. Field-Nat. 3:74-79.

____. 1929c. The summer molt of the Razor-billed Auk (*Alca torda*). Auk 46:223-224.

____. 1930a. A new hybrid grouse *Lagopus lagopus* (Linnaeus) × *Canchites canadensis* (Linnaeus). Nat. Mus. Can. Ann. Rep. 1930:89-91.

____. 1930b. A new subspecies of Willow Ptarmigan. Nat. Mus. Can. Ann. Rep. 1930:87-88.

____. 1931. A study of *Branta canadensis* (Linnaeus), the Canada Goose. Ann, Rep. Nat. Hist. Mus. Can. 1929:30-40.

____. 1933. A study of Kumlien's Gull. Can. Field-Nat. 47:88-90.

____. 1936. Taxonomic comments on Red-tailed Hawks. Condor 38:66-71.

____. 1940. Variation in the American Goshawk. Condor 42:157-160.

____ and G.M. Sutton. 1934. The birds of Churchill, Manitoba. Ann. Carnegie Mus. 23:1-83.

Taylor, A.L. Jr. 1981. Adventitious molt in Red Knot possibly caused by *Actornithophilus* (Mallophaga: Menoponidae). J. Field Ornith. 52:241.

Taylor, B. 1998. Rails: A guide to the rails, crakes, gallinules, and coots of the world. Yale University Press, New Haven, CT. 600 pp.

Taylor, E.J. 1995. Molt of Black Brant (*Branta bernicla nigricans*) on the Arctic coastal Plain, Alaska. Auk 112:904-919.

Taylor, J.R.E. 1994. Changes in body mass and body reserves of breeding Little Auks (*Alle alle* L.). Polish Polar Res. 15:147-161.

Taylor, P.B. 1982. Field identification of sand plovers in East Africa. Dutch Birding 4:113-130.

Taylor, W.P. 1920. A new ptarmigan from Mount Rainier. Condor 22:146-152.

Teather, K.L., and E. Nol. 1997. Mixed sexual dimorphism in Semipalmated Plovers. Condor 99:803-806.

Teixeira, D.M., and H.M.F. Alvarenga. 1985. The first record of Cory's Bittern (*Ixobrychus "neoxenus"*) from South America. Auk 102:413.

Telfair, R.C. II. 1994. Cattle Egret. Birds N. Am. 113:1-32.

____ and M.L. Morrison. 1995. Neotropic Cormorant. Birds N. Am. 137:1-24.

Temeles, E.J. 1986. Reversed sexual size dimorphism: Effect on resource defense and foraging behaviors of nonbreeding Northern Harriers. Auk 103:70-78.

Temple, S.A. 1972a. Systematics and evolution of the North American Merlins. Auk 89:325-338.

____. 1972b. Sex and age characteristics of North American Merlins. Bird-Banding 43:191-196.

Tenovuo, O., and R. Tenovuo. 1983. A hybrid of an Eider *Somateria mollissima* and a merganser species (*Mergus* sp.) found in Finland. Ornis Fennica 60:63-64.

Termaat, B.M. and J.P. Ryder. 1984. Differences in skeletal characters between the disjunct eastern and western populations of ring-billed gulls (*Larus delawarensis*). Can. J. Zool. 62:1067-1074.

Terrill, S.B., D.S. Singer, S.A. Glover, and D. Roberson. 2000. Middle Pacific Coast region. N. Am. Birds 54:322-325.

Thalmann, S., G.B. Baker, M. Hindall, M.C. Double, and R. Gales. 2007. Using biometrics measurements to determine gender of Flesh-footed Shearwaters, and their application as a tool in long-line by-catch management and ecological field studies. Emu 107:231-238.

Thayer, J.E., and O. Bangs. 1905. Aves. Pp. 91-98 *in* O. Bangs, ed., The vertebrata of Gorgona Island, Columbia. Bull. Mus. Comp. Zool. 46:87-102.

____ and ____. 1909. A new subspecies of the Snowy Heron. Proc. New England Zool. Club 4:39-41.

____ and ____. 1912. A new race of Great Blue Heron from Espiritu Santo Island, Lower California. Proc. New England Zool. Club 4:83-84.

____ and ____. 1914. Notes on the birds and mammals of the arctic coast of East Siberia. Proc. New England Zool. Club 5:1-66.

Thibault, J.-C., and V. Bretagnolle. 1998. A Mediterranean breeding colony of Cory's Shearwater *Calonectris diomedea* in which individuals show behavioural and biometric characters of the Atlantic subspecies. Ibis 140:523-528.

Thomas, K.P. 1969. Sex determination of Bobwhites by wing criteria. J. Wildl. Manage. 33:215-216.

Thompson, B.C., and R.D. Slack. 1983. Molt-breeding overlap and timing of pre-basic molt in Texas Least Terns. J. Field Ornith. 54:187-190.

____, M.E. Schmidt, S.W. Calhoun, D.C. Morizot, and R.D. Slack. 1992. Subspecific status of Least Tern populations in Texas: North American implications. Wilson Bull. 104:244-262.

____, J.A. Jackson, J. Burger, L.A. Hill, E.M. Kirsch, and J.L. Atwood. 1997. Least Tern. Birds N. Am. 290:1-32.

Thompson, C.W. 2004. Determining evolutionary homologies of molts and plumages: A commentary on Howell et al. (2003). Condor 106:199-206.

____ and A.S. Kitasky. 2004. Polymorphic flight-feather molt sequence in Tufted Puffins (*Fratercula cirrhata*): A rare phenomenon in birds. Auk 121:35-45.

____ and M. Leu. 1994. Determining homology of molts and plumages to address evolutionary questions: A rejoinder regarding Emberizid finches. Condor 96:769-782.

____, M.L. Wilson, E.F. Melvin, and J.D. Pierce. 1998a. An unusual sequence of flight-feather molt in Common Murres and its evolutionary implications. Auk 115:653-669.

____, M.L. Wilson, D.J. Pierce, and D. DeGhetto. 1998b. Population characteristics of Common Murres and Rhinoceros Auklets entangled in gillnets in Puget Sound, Washington, from 1993 to 1994. Northwestern Nat. 79:77-91.

____, S.A. Hatch, M. Leu, K. Brennan, B. Roca, and B. Krausse. 2000. Novel sequences of flight feather molt in Sooty Shearwaters and Northern Fulmars. Abstracts of the 27th Annual Meeting of the Pacific Seabird Group, Napa, CA. p. 53.

____, K.J. Pullen, R.E. Johnson, and E.B. Cummins. 2003. Specimen record of a Long-billed Murrelet from eastern Washington, with notes on plumage and morphometric differences between Long-billed and Marbled murrelets. W. Birds 34:157-168.

Thompson, D.R., and C. Kabat. 1950. The wing molt of the Bob-white. Wilson Bull. 62:20-31.

____ and R.D. Taber. 1948. Reference tables for dating events in nesting Ring-necked Pheasant, Bobwhite Quail, and Hungarian Partridge by ageing of broods. J. Wildl. Manage. 12:14-19.

Thompson, J.E., and R.D. Drobney. 1995. Intensity and chronology of postreproductive molts in male Canvasbacks. Wilson Bull. 107:338-358.

____, M.R.J. Hill, M.T. Meredino, and C.D. Ankney. 1999. Improving use of morphometric discrimination to identify Canada Goose subspecies. Wildl. Soc. Bull. 27:274-280.

Thompson, M.P., and R.J. Robel. 1968. Skeletal measurements and maceration techniques for aging Bobwhite quail. J. Wildl. Manage. 32:247-255.

Thorpe, J.P. 1988. Juvenile Hen Harriers showing 'Marsh Hawk' characters. Brit. Birds. 81:377-382.

Thorpe, R.I. 1995. Grey-tailed Tattler in Wales: New to Britain and Ireland. Brit. Birds. 88:255-262.

Threlfall, W., and D.D. Jewer. 1978. Notes on standard body measurements of two populations of Herring Gull. *Auk* 95:749-753.
____ and S.P. Mahoney. 1980. The use of measurements in sexing Common Murres from Newfoundland. Wilson Bull. 92:266-268.
Tibbitts, T.L., and W. Moskoff. 1999. Lesser Yellowlegs. Birds N. Am. 427:1-28.
Tickell, W.L.N. 2000. Albatrosses. Pica Press, Sussex, UK. 448 pp.
Timm, D.E., and D. Sellers. 1981. Progress report of the Alaska Department of Fish and Game for 1982. Trans. Nat. Wildl. Nat. Res. Conf. 47:453.
Titman, R.D. 1999. Red-breasted Merganser. Birds N. Am. 443:1-24.
Tjernberg, M. 1988. Age determination of Golden Eagles *Aquila chrysaetos*. Vår Fågelväld 47:321-334.
Tobish, T. 1986. Separation of Barrow's and Common goldeneyes in all plumages. Birding 18:17-27.
____. 1991. Notes on immature swans in spring. Birding 23:88-89.
Todd, F.S. 1974. Maturation and behaviour of the California Condor (*Gymnogyps californianus*) at the Los Angeles zoo. Int. Zoo Yearbook 14:145-147
____ and N.B. Gale. 1970. Further notes on the California Condor at the Los Angeles Zoo. Int. Zoo Yearbook 10:15-17.
Todd, W.E.C. 1916a. The birds of the Isle of Pines. Ann. Carnegie Mus. 10:146-296.
____. 1916b. Preliminary diagnosis of fifteen apparently new neotropical birds. Proc. Biol. Soc. Washington 29:95-98.
____. 1938. A new eastern race of the Canada Goose. Auk 55:661-662.
____. 1940. Eastern races of the Ruffed Grouse. Auk 57:390-397.
____. 1947. A new name for *Bonasa umbellus canescens*. Auk 64:326.
____. 1948. A new booby and new ibis from South America. Proc. Biol. Soc. Washington 61:49-50.
____. 1950a. Nomenclature of the White-fronted Goose. Condor 52:63-68.
____. 1950b. Northern race of the Red-tailed Hawk. Ann. Carnegie Mus. 31:289-295.
____. 1953. A taxonomic study of the American Dunlin (*Erolia alpina* subspp.). J. Washington Acad. Sci. 43:85-88.
____. 1963. Birds of Labrador Peninsula and adjacent areas. A distributional list. University of Toronto Press, Toronto, Ontario. 819 pp.
____ and H. Friedmann. 1947. A study of the Gyrfalcons with particular reference to North America. Wilson Bull. 59:139-150.
____ and W.W. Worthington. 1911. A contribution to the ornithology of the Bahama Islands. Ann Carnegie Mus. 7:388-464.
Tomasulo, A.M., S.N. Del Lama, and C.D. Rocha 2002. Molecular Method of Sexing Waterbirds without DNA Extraction. Waterbirds 25:245-248.
Tomkins, I.R. 1948. More notes on the two races of Sparrow Hawk inhabiting Georgia. Oriole 13:23-24.
Tomkovich, P.S. 1986. [Geographical variability of the Dunlin in the Far East.] Bull. Moscow Soc. Nat. Biol. 91:3-15.
____. 1990. Analysis of geographic variation in the Knot *Calidris canutus*. Bull. Moscow Nat. Biol. Div. 95:59-72.
____. 1992. An analysis of the geographic variability in Knots *Calidris canutus* based on museum skins. Wader Study Group Bull. 64(Suppl.):17-23.
____. 1998. Breeding schedule and primary moult in Dunlins *Calidris alpina* of the Far East. Wader Study Group Bull. 85:29-34.
____. 2004. A new subspecies of Red Knot *Calidris canutus* from New Siberian islands. Bull. Brit. Ornith. Club 121:257-263.
____ and L. Serra. 1999. Morphometrics and prediction of breeding origin in some Holarctic waders. Ardea 87:289-300.
Tomlinson, R.E. 1975. Weights and lengths of wild Sonoran Masked Bobwhites during fall and winter. Wilson Bull. 87:180-186.
Toochin, M. 1998. Possible anywhere: Tufted Duck. Birding 30:370-383.
Tordoff, H.B. 1962. Age and plumage of the Black Tern. Kansas Ornith. Soc. Bull. 13:7-8.
____ and P.T. Redig. 2001. The role of genetic background in reintroduced Peregrine Falcons. Conserv. Biol. 15:528-532.
Tove, M.H. 1993. Field separation of Ring-billed, Mew, Common, and Kamchatka gulls. Birding 25:386-401.
Townsend, C.H. 1890. Scientific results of expeditions by the U.S. Fish Commission Steamer Albatross. Proc. U.S. Nat. Mus. 13:131-142.
Townsend, C.W. 1912. The validity of the red-legged subspecies of Black Duck. Auk 29:176-179.
Tracy, D.M., D. Schamel, and J. Dale. 2002. Red Phalarope. Birds N. Am. 698:1-32.
Trainer, J.E. 1947. The pterylography of the Ruffed Grouse. Pp 741-748 *in* G. Bump, et al., eds., The Ruffed Grouse: life history - propagation - management. The Holling Press Inc., Buffalo NY.
Tranquilla, L.A.M., R.W. Bradley, D.B. Lank, T.D. Williams, L.W. Lougheed, and F. Cooke. 2003. The reliability of brood patches in assessing reproductive status in the Marbled Murrelet: Words of caution. Waterbirds 26:108-118.
Trauger, D.L. 1974. Eye color of female Lesser Scaup in relation to age. Auk 91:243-254.
____, A. Dzubin, and J.P. Ryder. 1971. White geese intermediate between Ross' Geese and Lesser Snow Geese. Auk 88:856-875.
Trautman, M.B., and S.L. Glines. 1964. A nesting of the Purple Gallinule in Ohio. Auk 81:224-226.
____ and M.A. Trautman. 1968. Annotated list of the birds of Ohio. Ohio J. Science 68:253-332.
Tree, A.J., and N.T.W. Klages. 2003. Status, biometrics, moult and possible relationships of the South African population of Roseate Tern. Ostrich 74:74-80.
Trefry, S.A., D.L. Dickson, and A.K. Hoover. 2007. A Common Eider × King Eider hybrid captured on Kent Peninsula, Nunavut. Arctic 60:251-254.
Tsuji, L.J.S., D.R. Kozlovic, M.B. Sokolowski, and R.I.C. Hansell. 1994. Relationship of body size of male Sharp-tailed Grouse to location of individual territories on leks. Wilson Bull. 106:329-337.
Tuck, L.M. 1960. The murres: Their distribution, population, and biology. Can. Wildl. Series 1:1-260.
____. 1972. The snipes: A study of the genus *Capella*. Can. Wildl. Serv. Monogr. Series 5:1-429.
Tucker, A.O., M.J. Maciarello, and S.S. Tucker. 1991. A survey of color charts for biological descriptions. Taxon 40:201-214
Tucker, L.A. 1985. Racial identification of Cattle Egret. Brit. Birds. 78:659-661.
Tufts, R.W. 1940. Some studies in bill measurements and body weights of American Woodcock (*Philohela minor*). Can. Field-Nat. 54:132-134.
____. 1975. Intergeneric hybrid (*Bonasa* × *Canchites*). Can. Field-Nat. 89:72.
Turner, L.B. 1953. A rapid method of sexing Canada Geese. J. Wildl. Manage. 17:542-543.
Twomey, A.C. 1956. A new race of Black Hawk of the species *Buteogallus anthracinus* from the Republic of Honduras. Ann. Carnegie Mus. 33:387-389.
Tyler, W.B., and K. Burton. 1986. A Cook's Petrel specimen from California. W. Birds 17:79-84.
Udvardy, M.D.F. 1963. Zoogeographical study of the Pacific alcidae. Pp. 85-111 *in* J.L. Gressitt, ed., Pacific Basin biogeography, a symposium. B.P. Bishop Museum Press, Honolulu, HI.
Ullman, M. 1984. Field identification of juvenile Pomarine Skua. Brit. Birds 77:446-448.
____. 1989. Wing patterns of Common and Arctic Terns. Brit. Birds. 82:414-416.
Underhill, L.G. 1986. A graphical method to determine the ordering of moult, illustrated with data from the Blackshouldered Kite *Elanus caeruleus*. Bird Study 33:140-143.
____. 1989. Estimating the parameters for primary moult - A new statistical model. Wader Study Group Bull. 44:27-29.
Unitt, P. 2004. San Diego County Bird Atlas. Proc. San Diego Nat. Hist. Mus. 39:1-644.
Uttal, L.J. 1939. Subspecies of the Spruce Grouse. Auk 56:460-464.
____. 1941. Tarsal feathering of Ruffed Grouse. Auk 58:74-79.
Uyehara, K.J. 2004. First record of the Sora in the state of Hawaii. W. Birds 35:47-49.
Valle, C.A., T. de Vries, and C. Hernández. 2006. Plumage and sexual maturation in Great Frigatebird *Fregata minor* in the Galapagos Islands. Marine Ornith. 34:51-59.
Vanderkist, B.A., X.-H. Xue, R. Griffiths, K. Martin, W. Beauchamp, and T.D. Williams. 1999. Evidence of male-bias in capture samples on Marbled Murrelets from genetic studies in British Columbia. Condor 101:398-402.
van de Wetering, D., and F. Cooke. 2000. Body weight and feather growth of male Barrow's Goldeneye during wing molt. Condor 102:228-231.
Van der Winden, J. 2002. The odyssey of the Black Tern *Chlidonias niger*: migration ecology in Europe and Africa. Ardea 90: 421-434.
Van Eerden, M.R., and M.J. Munsterman. 1995. Sex and age dependent distribution in wintering Cormorants *Phalacrocorax carbo sinensis* in western Europe. Ardea 83:285-297.
van Franeker, J.A. 1986. Arctic and Antarctic seabird studies: Fulmarine petrels. Circumpolar J. 1:3-12.
____. 1995. Kleurfasen van de Noordse Stormvogel *Fulmarus glacialis* in de Noordatlantische Oceaan. Sula 9:93-105.
____ and C.J.F. ter Braak. 1993. A generalized discriminant for sexing fulmarine petrels from external measurements. Auk 110:492-502.
____ and J. Wattel. 1982. Geographic variation of the Fulmar *Fulmarus glacialis* in the North Atlantic. Ardea 70:31-44.
van Ijzendoorn, E.J. 1982. On plumage variation in Baird's Sandpiper. Dutch Birding 4:28.
van Kreuningen, J. 1981. Hen Harriers *Circus cyaneus* with features of American Hen Harrier *C.c. hudsonius*. Dutch Birding 2:10.

van Rossem, A.J. 1915. Notes on murrelets and petrels. Condor 17:74-78.
____. 1923. A study on some plumages of the Black Tern. Condor 25:208-213.
____. 1925. Flight feathers as age indicators in *Dendragapus*. Ibis (12th Ser.) 1:417-422.
____. 1926a. The Lower California Reddish Egret. Condor 28:246.
____. 1926b. The Craveri Murrelet in California. Condor 28:80-83.
____. 1929. The status of some Pacific Coast Clapper Rails. Condor 31:213-215.
____. 1930a. A new Least Bittern from Sonora. Trans. San Diego Soc. Nat. Hist. 6:227-228.
____. 1930b. A northwestern race of the Mexican Goshawk. Condor 32:303-304.
____. 1931. Report on a collection of landbirds from Sonora, Mexico. Trans. San Diego Soc. Nat. Hist. 6:237-304.
____. 1932. The avifauna of Tiburon Island, Sonora, Mexico, with descriptions of four new races. Trans. San Diego Soc. Nat. Hist. 7:119-150.
____. 1934. Critical notes on Middle American birds. Bull. Mus. Comp. Zool. 77:387-490.
____. 1936. Notes on birds in relation to the faunal areas of south-eastern Arizona. Trans. San Diego Soc. Nat. Hist. 8:121-148.
____. 1937. A review of the races of the Mountain Quail. Condor 39:20-24.
____. 1938a. Descriptions of three new birds from western Mexico. Trans. San Diego Soc. Nat. Hist. 9:9-12.
____. 1938b. A Mexican race of the Goshawk (*Accipiter gentilis* [Linnaeus]). Proc. Biol. Soc. Washington 51:99-100.
____. 1939a. Some new races of birds from Mexico. Ann. Mag. Nat. Hist. (11th Ser.) 4:439-443.
____. 1939b. A new race of Sharp-shinned Hawk from Mexico. Auk 56:127-128.
____. 1939c. An overlooked race of the California Quail. Auk 56:68-69.
____. 1942a. Preliminary comment on some Pacific coast petrels. Proc. Biol Soc. Washington 55:9-12.
____. 1942b. Notes on some Mexican and Californian birds, with descriptions of six undescribed races. Trans. San Diego Mus. Nat Hist. 33:377-384.
____. 1943. The Yellow-crowned Night Heron of Socorro Island, Mexico. Occ. Papers Mus. Zool. Louisiana State Univ. 15:265-269.
____. 1945. A distributional survey of the birds of Sonora, Mexico. Occ. Papers Mus. Zool. Louisiana State Univ. 21:1-379.
____. 1946. The California Quail of central Baja California. Condor 48:265-267.
____ and the M. Hachisuka. 1937a. A further report on birds from Sonora, Mexico, with descriptions of two new races. Trans. San Diego Soc. Nat. Hist. 8:321-336.
____ and ____. 1937b. A northwestern race of the Mexican Black Hawk. Trans. San Diego Soc. Nat. Hist. 8:361-362.
____ and ____. 1939. A northwestern race of the Mexican Cormorant. Proc. Biol Soc. Washington 52:9-10.
Van Soest, R.W.M., and W.L. Van Utrecht. 1971. The layered structure of bones of birds as possible indication of age. Bjdragen tot Dierkunde 41:61-66.
Van Tyne, J., and G.M. Sutton. 1937. The birds of Brewster County, Texas. Misc. Pubs. Mus. Zool. Univ. Michigan 37:1-119.
Van Wagner, C.E., and A.J. Baker. 1986. Genetic differentiation in populations of Canada Geese (*Branta canadensis*). Can. J. Zool. 64:940-947.
van Wieringen, M., and K. Brouwer. 1990. Morphology and ecology of Scarlet (Eudocimus ruber) and White Ibis (E. albus): A comparative review. Pp. 7-15 in P.C. Frederick, et al., eds., The Scarlet Ibis (Eudocimus ruber): status, conservation and recent research. International Waterfowl and Wetlands Research Bureau, Slimbridge, U.K.
Vaurie, C. 1964. Systematic notes on Palearctic birds. No. 53. Charadriidae: The genera *Charadrius* and *Pluvialis*. Am. Mus. Novit. 2177:1-22.
____. 1965. Systematic notes on the bird family Cracidae. No. 2. Relationships and geographical variation in *Ortalis vetula*, *Ortalis poliocephala*, and *Ortalis leucogastra*. Am. Mus. Novit. 2222:1-36.
____. 1968. Taxonomy of the Cracidae (Aves). Bull. AM. Mus. Nat. Hist. 138:133-259.
Veit, A.C., and I.L. Jones. 2003. Function of tail streamers of Red-tailed Tropicbirds (*Phaethon rubricauda*) as inferred from patterns of variation. Auk 120:1033-1043.
____ and ____. 2004. Timing and patterns of growth of Red-tailed Tropicbird *Phaethon rubricauda* tail streamer ornaments. Ibis 146:355-359.
Veit, R.R. 1988. Identification of the Salton Sea Rufous-necked Sandpiper. W. Birds 19:165-169.
____ and L. Jonsson. 1984. Field-identification of smaller sandpipers within the genus *Calidris*. Am. Birds 38:853-876. [Reprinted Am. Birds 41:213-236, 1987]
Verbeek, M.A.M. 1977. Timing of primary moult in adult Herring Gulls and Lesser Black-backed Gulls. J. Ornith. 118:87-92.
____. 1979. Timing of primary molt and egg-laying in Glaucous-winged Gulls. Wilson Bull. 91:420-425.
____. 1993. Glaucous-winged Gull. Birds N. Am. 59:1-20.
Vickery, P.D., D.W. Finch, and P.K. Donahue. 1987. Juvenile Cox's Sandpiper (*Calidris paramelanotos*) in Massachusetts, a first New World occurrence and a hitherto undescribed plumage. Am. Birds 41:1366-1369.
Vinicombe, K. 1982. Identification of female, eclipse male, and first-winter Ring-necked Ducks. Brit. Birds. 75:327-328.
____. 1985. Identification of first-winter Sora. Brit. Birds. 78:145-146.
____. 1994. Common Teals showing mixed characters of Eurasian and North American races. Brit. Birds. 87:88-89.
____. 2003. The identification of hybrid Canvasback × Common Pochard. Brit. Birds. 96:112-118.
Voelker, G. 1996. A hypothesis for seasonal color change in the genus *Sterna*. J. Avian Biol. 27:257-259.
____. 1997. The molt cycle of the Arctic Tern, with comments on aging criteria. J. Field Ornith. 68:400-412.
Voisin, C. 1991. The herons of Europe. T. & A.D. Poser, London, U.K. 364 pp.
Voitkevich, A.A. 1966. The feathers and plumage of birds. English translation. October House Inc., New York, NY. 335 pp.
von Berlepsch, H.G. 1906. On a new form of *Oceanodroma* inhabiting San Benito Island, off the coast of Lower California. Auk 23:185-186.
Voous, K.H. 1949. The morphological, anatomical, and distributional relationship of the Arctic and Antarctic fulmars (Aves, Procellariidae). Ardea 37:113-122.
____ 1968. Distribution and geographical variation of the White-tailed Hawk (*Buteo albicaudatus*). Beaufortia 15:195-208.
____. 1986. Striated or Green herons in the South Caribbean islands? Ann. Naturh. Mus. Wien 89:101-106.
____ and J. Wattel. 1967. Probable wild hybrid White-fronted × Lesser White-fronted Goose. Limosa 40:9-11.
Votier, S.C., A.H.J. Harrop, and M. Denny. 2003. A review of the status and identification of American Wigeon in Britain and Ireland. Brit. Birds 96:2-22.
____, S. Bearhop, R.G. Newell, K. Orr, R.W. Furness, and M. Kennedy. 2004. The first record of Brown Skua *Catharacta antarctica* in Europe. Ibis 146:95-102.
Vrtiska, M.P., R.M. Kaminski, H.H. Prince, and J.D. Thompson. 1997. Geographical displacement and timing of molt of the remiges in male Wood Ducks. Can. J. Zool. 75:1545-1548.
Vuilleumier, F. 1965. Relationships and evolution within the Cracidae (Aves, Galliformes). Bull. Mus. Comp. Zool. 134:1-27.
____. 1970. Generic relations and speciation patterns in the caracaras (Aves: Falconidae). Breviora 355:1-29.
Wahl, T.R. 1982. Identification of Sooty and Short-tailed shearwaters in the North Pacific Ocean. Sea Swallow 31:42-44.
Wakeling, B.F., F.E. Phillips, and R. Engel-Wilson. 1997. Age and gender differences in Merriam's Turkey tarsometatarsus measurements. Wild. Soc. Bull. 25:706-708.
Wakernagel, H. 1972. Shelduck *Tadorna tadorna* Eider *Somateria mollissima* cross: A new hybrid among ducks. Ornith. Beobachter 69:253-254.
Walbridge, G., B. Small, and R.Y. McGowan. 2003. Ascension Frigatebird on Tiree - new to the Western Palearctic. Brit. Birds. 96:58-73.
Walkinshaw, L.H. 1939. The Yellow Rail in Michigan. Auk 56:227-237.
____. 1949. The Sandhill Cranes. Bull. Cranbrook Inst. Sci. 29:1-202.
____. 1965. A new Sandhill Crane from central Canada. Can. Field-Nat. 79:181-184.
____. 1973. Cranes of the world. Winchester Press, New York, NY. 370 pp.
Wallace, D.I.M. 1971. American Marsh Hawk in Norfolk. Brit. Birds. 64:537-542.
____. 1974. Field identification of small species in the genus *Calidris*. Brit. Birds. 67:1-17.
____. 1979. Review of British records of Semipalmated Sandpipers and claimed Red-necked Stints. Brit. Birds. 72:264-274.
____. 1980. Dowitcher identification: A brief review. Pp. 78-88 *in* J.T.R. Sharrock, ed., The frontiers of bird identification. British Birds Ltd., Biggelswade, UK.
____. 1983. Tertial patterns of Wigeon and American Wigeon. Brit. Birds. 76:218-219.
____. 1986. Four problem stints. Brit. Birds. 79:609-621.
____. 1998. Identification forum: Marsh Hawk. Birding World 7:454-457.
____ and M.A. Ogilvie. 1977. Distinguishing Blue-winged and Cinnamon teals. Brit. Birds. 70:290-291.
____ and ____. 1985. Distinguishing Blue-winged and Cinnamon teals. Pp. 267-271 *in* J.T.R. Sharrock, ed., The frontiers of bird identification. British Birds Ltd., Biggelswade, UK.

Wallace, E.A.H., and G.E. Wallace. 1998. Brandt's Cormorant. Birds N. Am. 362:1-28.

Wallin, J.A. 1982. Sex determination of Vermont fall-harvested juvenile Wild Turkeys by the 10th primary. Wild. Soc. Bull. 10:40-43.

Wallmo, O.C. 1956. Determination of sex and age of Scaled Quail. J. Wildl. Manage. 20:154-158.

Walser, B., and P.H. Barthel. 1994. [The plumages of the Red-necked Grebe *Podiceps grisegena*.] Limicola 8:101-120.

Walsh, C.J., S.I. Wilhelm, I.J. Stenhouse, and A.E. Storey. 2001. Social interactions of breeding Common Murres and a Razorbill. Wilson Bull. 113:449-452.

Walsh, T. 1984. The field identification of Arctic Loon. Bird Observer 12:309-314.

____. 1985. Yellow orbital ring of Semipalmated Plover. Brit. Birds. 78:661.

____. 1988. Identifying Pacific Loons. Some old and new problems. Birding 20:12-28.

Walters, J. 1978. The primary moult in four gull species near Amsterdam. Ardea 66:32-47.

____. 1982. Completion of primary moult in the Black-headed Gull *Larus ridibundus*. Bird Study 29:217-220.

____. 1985. On the primary moult in adult Common Tern. Gerfaut 75:323-326.

____. 1987. Primary moult in Black Terns and Common Terns. Ringing & Migr. 8:83-90.

Ward, J.G., and A.L.A. Middleton. 1971. Weight and histological studies of growth and regression in the bursa of Fabricius in the Mallard, *Anas platyrhynchos*. Can. J. Zool. 49:11-14.

Ward, R.M. 2000. Migration patterns and moult of Common Terns *Sterna hirundo* and Sandwich Terns *Sterna sandvicensis* using Teesmouth in late summer. Ringing & Migr. 20:19-28.

____. 2002. Ageing and moult in Common Terns. Brit. Birds 95:313-316.

____, E. Wood, and G. Myers. 2004. Some observations on the occurrence of three generations of primaries in Common Terns Sterna hirundo. Ringing & Migr. 22:63-64.

Warham, J. 1990. The petrels. Academic Press, New York, NY. 440 pp.

____. 1996. The behaviour, population biology, and physiology of the petrels. Academic Press, New York, NY. 613 pp.

____. B.R. Keeley, and G.J. Wilson. 1977. Breeding of the Mottled Petrel. Auk 94:1-17.

Waring, D. 1993. Female Black Scoter. Birding World 6:78-79.

Warkentin, I.G., P.C. James, and L.W. Oliphant. 1990. Body morphometrics, age structure, and partial migration of urban Merlins. Auk 107:25-34.

____, ____, and ____. 1992. Use of plumage criterion for aging female Merlins. J. Field Ornith. 63:473-475.

Warner, D.W., and R.W. Dickerman. 1959. The status of *Rallus elegans tenuirostris* in Mexico. Condor 61:49-51.

Warnock, N.D., and R.E. Gill. 1996. Dunlin. Birds N. Am. 203:1-24.

Warren, D.C., and C.D. Gordon. 1935. The sequence and appearance, molt, and replacement of the juvenile remiges of some domestic birds. J. Agric. Res. 51:459-470.

Watson, A. 1957. Birds of Cumberland Peninsula, Baffin Island. Can. Field-Nat. 71:87-109.

Watson, G.E. 1962a. Three sibling species of *Alectoris* partridge. Ibis 104:353-367.

____. 1962b. Molt, age determination, and the annual cycle in the Cuban Bobwhite. Wilson Bull. 74:28-42.

____. 1963a. The mechanism of feather replacement during natural molt. Auk 80:486-495.

____. 1963b. Incomplete first prebasic molt in the Chukar Partridge. Auk 80:80-81.

____. 1970a. A shearwater mortality on the Atlantic coast. Atlantic Nat. 25:75-81.

____. 1970b. A presumed wild hybrid Balpate × Eurasian Wigeon Auk 87:353-357.

____. 1971. Molting Greater Shearwaters (*Puffinus gravis*) off Tierra del Fuego. Auk 88:440-442.

____. 1975. Birds of the Antarctic and sub-Antarctic. The William Byrd Press, Richmond, VA. 350 pp.

____, S.L. Olson, and J.R. Miller. 1991. A new subspecies of Double-crested Cormorant, *Phalacrocorax auritus*, from San Salvador, Bahama Islands. Proc. Biol. Soc. Washington 104:356-369.

Watson, J. 1997. The Golden Eagle. T & AD Poyser, London, UK. 374 pp.

Wattel, J. 1973. Geographical differentiation in the genus Accipiter. Publ. Nuttall Ornith. Club 13:1-23.

Watts, B.D. 1995. Yellow-crowned Night-Heron. Birds N. Am. 161:1-24.

Wayne, A.T. 1923. Subdivisions of the Little Black Rail (*Cresiscus jamaicensis jamaicensis*). Auk 40:319.

Weaver, H.R., and W.L. Haskell. 1986. Age and sex determination of the Chukar Partridge. J. Wildl. Manage. 32:46-50.

Webb, B.E., and J.A. Conry. 1979. A Sharp-tailed Sandpiper in Colorado, with notes on plumage and behavior. W. Birds 10:86-91.

Webb, W.D., and J.D. Tyler. 1988. Hybridization of Northern Bobwhites and Scaled Quails in Oklahoma and Texas. Bull. Oklahoma Ornith. Soc. 21:3-5.

Weber, J.W. 1981a. The *Larus* gulls of the Pacific Northwest's interior, with taxonomic comments on several forms. Part 1. Continental Birdlife 2:1-10.

____. 1981b. The *Larus* gulls of the Pacific Northwest's interior, with taxonomic comments on several forms. Part 2. Continental Birdlife 2:74-91.

Webster, J.D. 1942. Notes on the growth and plumages of the Black Oyster-catcher. Condor 44:205-211.

____. 1973. Richardson's Zacatecas Collection, I. Condor 75:239-241.

____. 1988. Some bird specimens from Sitka, Alaska. Murrelet 69:46-48.

Weeden, R.B. 1961. Outer primaries as indicators of age among Rock Ptarmigan. J. Wild. Manage. 25:337-339.

____. 1966. Molt of the primaries of adult Rock Ptarmigan in central Alaska. Auk 83:587-596.

____ and A. Watson. 1967. Determining the age of Rock Ptarmigan in Alaska and Scotland. J. Wild. Manage. 31:825-826.

Wehtje, W. 2005. Identifying hybrid oystercatchers in southern California. W. Birds 36:336-337.

Weir, D.N., R.Y. McGowan, A.C. Kitchener, S. McOrist, B. Zonfrillo, and M. Heubeck. 1995. Iceland Gulls from the Braer disaster, Shetland, 1993. Brit. Birds 88:15-25.

____, A.C. Kitchener, and R.Y. McGowan. 1996. Biometrics of Kittiwakes *Rissa tridactyla* wrecked in Shetland. Seabird 18:5-9.

____, ____, and ____. 2000. Hybridization and changes in distribution of Iceland Gulls (*Larus glaucoides/kumlieni/thayeri*). J. Zool. 252:517-530.

Weller, M.W. 1957. Growth, weights, and plumages of the Redhead, *Aythya americana*. Wilson Bull. 69:5-38.

____. 1970. Additional notes on the plumages of the Redhead (*Aythya americana*). Wilson Bull. 82:320-323.

____. 1980. The island waterfowl. Iowa State University Press, Ames, IA. 121 pp.

Wenstrom, W.P., P.V. Vandershaegen, and G.W. Gullion. 1972. Ruffed Grouse primary molt chronology. Auk 89:671-672.

Wentworth, B.C., E.M. Pollack, and J.R. Smyth Jr. 1967. Sexing day-old pheasants by sex-linked down color. J. Wild. Manage. 31:741-745.

Weseloh, D.V. 1981. A probable Franklin's × Ring-billed Gull pair nesting in Alberta. Canadian Field-Nat. 95:474-476.

____ and P. Mineau. 1986. Apparent hybrid Common Black-headed Gull nesting in Lake Ontario. Am. Birds 40:18-20.

West, G.C., S. Savage, L. Irving, and L.J. Peyton. 1968. Morphological homogeneity of a population of Alaska Willow Ptarmigan. Condor 70:340-347.

____, R.B. Weeden, L. Irving, and L.J. Peyton. 1970. Geographic variation in body size and weight of Willow Ptarmigan. Arctic 23:240-253.

West, R.L., and G.K. Hess. 2002. Purple Gallinule. Birds N. Am. 626:1-28.

Westerskov, K. 1956. Age determination and dating nesting events in the Willow Ptarmigan. J. Wildl. Manage. 20:274-279.

Wetmore, A. 1914. A new *Accipiter* from Porto Rico with notes on the allied forms of Cuba and San Domingo. Proc. Biol. Soc. Washington 27:119-121.

____. 1920. Color of soft parts in *Anhinga anhinga*. Proc. Biol. Soc. Washington 33:182-183.

____. 1926. Observations on the birds of Argentina, Paraguay, Uruguay, and Chile. U.S. Nat. Mus. Bull. 133:1-448.

____. 1939. Birds from Clipperton Island collected on the Presidential cruise of 1938. Smithsonian Misc. Coll. 98(22):1-6.

____. 1943. The birds of southern Veracruz, Mexico. Proc. U.S. Nat. Mus. 93:215-340.

____. 1945. A review of the forms of the Brown Pelican. Auk 62:577-586.

____. 1946a. The birds of San José and Pedro González islands, Republic of Panamá. Smithsonian Misc. Coll. 106(1):1-60.

____. 1946b. New forms of birds from Panama and Columbia. Proc. Biol. Soc. Washington 59:49-54.

____. 1959. Description of a race of the shearwater *Puffinus lherminieri* from Panama. Proc. Biol. Soc. Washington 72:19-22.

____. 1964. A revision of the American vultures of the genus *Cathartes*. Smithsonian Misc. Coll. 146(6):1-18.

____. 1965. The birds of the Republic of Panama. Part 1. Smithsonian Misc. Coll. 150:1-483.

____ and J.L. Peters. 1922. A new genus and four new subspecies of American birds. Proc. Biol. Soc. Washington 35:41-46.

Whaley, W.H., and C.M. White. 1994. Trends in geographic variation of Cooper's Hawk and Northern Goshawk in North America: A multivariate analysis. Proc. W. Found. Vert. Zool. 5:161-209.

Wheeler, B.K. 2000. Gyr ID. Birding 32:206.

____. 2003a. Raptors of western North America. Princeton University Press, Princeton, NJ. 544 pp.

____. 2003b. Raptors of eastern North America. Princeton University Press, Princeton, NJ. 439 pp.

____. 2004. Age- and sex-based plumage variation in the Mississippi Kite. Birding 36:508-519.

____ and W.S. Clark. 1995. A photographic guide to North American raptors. Academic Press, San Diego, CA. 198 pp.

White, C.M. 1968. Diagnosis and relationships of the North American tundra-inhabiting Peregrine Falcons. Auk 85:179-191.

____. 1972. *Falco peregrinus pealei* in Ohio an error. Ohio J. Sci. 72:153-155.

____ and D.A. Boyce Jr. 1988. An overview of Peregrine Falcon subspecies. Pp. 789-810 *in* T.J. Cade, et al., eds., Peregrine Falcon populations: Their management and recovery. The Peregrine Fund Inc., Boise, ID.

____, N.J. Clum, T.J. Cade, and W.G. Hunt. 2002. Peregrine Falcon. Birds N. Am. 660:1-48.

White, G.J., and T.P. Andrews. 1985. Identification pitfalls of a juvenile Cinnamon Teal. Brit. Birds. 78:398-399.

White, S.J., and C.V. Kehoe. 2001. Difficulties in determining the age of Common Terns in the field. Brit. Birds 94:268-277.

Whitfield, D.P. 1986. Plumage variability and territoriality in breeding Turnstone *Arenaria interpres*: Status signalling or individual recognition? Animal Behav. 34:1471-1482.

____. 1999. Methods for ageing Dotterel *Charadrius morinellus*. Ringing & Migr. 19:200-204.

Whittam, R.M. 1998. Interbreeding of Roseate and Arctic terns. Wilson Bull. 110:65-70.

Whittier, J.B., D.M. Leslie Jr., and R.A. Van Den Bussche. 2006. Genetic variation among subspecies of Least Tern (*Sterna antillarum*): Implications for conservation. Waterbirds 29:176-184.

Whittow, G.C. 1993a. Laysan Albatross. Birds N. Am. 66:1-20.

____. 1993b. Black-footed Albatross. Birds N. Am. 65:1-16.

Wiklund, C.G. 1996. Body length and wing length provide univariate estimates of overall body size in the Merlin. Condor 98:581-588.

Wilbur, S.R. 1975. California Condor plumage and molt as field study aids. California Fish and Game 61:144-148.

Wilcox, L. 1959. A twenty year banding study of the Piping Plover. Auk 76:129-152.

____. 1980. Observations on the life history of Willets on Long Island, New York. Wilson Bull. 92:253-258.

Wilds, C. 1982. Separating the yellowlegs. Birding 14:172-178.

____. 1989. The terminology of plumage and molt. Birding 21:148-154.

____. 1990. The dowitchers. Pp. 68-75 *in* Kaufman, K., ed., Advanced birding. Houghton Mifflin Co., Boston, MA.

____. 1993. The identification and aging of Forster's and Common terns. Birding 25:94-108.

____ and M. Newlon. 1983. The identification of dowitchers. Birding 15:151-165.

Wiley, J.W., and O.H. Garrido. 2005. Taxonomic status and biology of the Cuban Black-Hawk, *Buteogallus anthracinus gundlachi* (Aves: Accipitridae). J. Raptor Res. 39:351-364.

Wiley, R.H., and D.S. Lee. 1998. Long-tailed Jaeger. Birds N. Am. 365:1-24.

____ and ____. 1999. Parasitic Jaeger. Birds N. Am. 445:1-28.

____ and ____. 2000. Pomarine Jaeger. Birds N. Am. 483:1-24.

Wilhelm, S.I., C.J. Walsh, I.J. Stenhouse, and A.E. Storey. 2001. A possible Common Guillemot *Uria aalge* × Razorbill *Alca torda* hybrid. Atlantic Seabirds 3:85-88.

____, S.G. Gilliland, G.J. Robertson, P.C. Ryan, and R.D. Elliot. 2008. Development and validation of a wing key to improve harvest management of alcids in the northwest Atlantic. J. Wildl. Manage. 72:1026-1034.

Willett, G. 1912. Report of G. Willett, agent and warden, stationed on St. Lazaria Bird Reservation, Alaska. Bird Lore 14:419-426.

____. 1913. Bird notes from the coast of Lower California. Condor 15:19-24.

____. 1915. Summer birds of Forrester Island, Alaska. Auk 32:295-331.

____ and H. Howard. 1934. Characters differentiating certain species of *Stercorarius*. Condor 36:158-160.

Williams, C.T., S.D. Kildaw, and C.L. Buck. 2007. Sex-specific differences in body condition indices and seasonal mass loss in Tufted Puffins. J. Field Ornith. 78:369-378.

Williams, G.R. 1959. Aging, growth rate and breeding season phenology of wild populations of California Quail in New Zealand. Bird-Banding 30:203-216.

Williams, J.E., and S.C. Kendeigh. 1982. Energetics of the Canada Goose. J. Wildl. Manage. 46:588-600.

Williams, L. 1942. Display and sexual behavior of the Brandt Cormorant. Condor 44:85-104.

Williams, L.E. Jr. 1961. Notes on wing molt in the yearling Wild Turkey. J. Wildl. Manage. 25:439-440.

____. 1971. Tarsometatarsus color in Wild Turkeys. J. Wildl. Manage. 35:550-553.

____. and D.H. Austin. 1970. Complete post-juvenal (pre-basic) molt in Florida Turkeys. J. Wildl. Manage. 34:231-233.

____ and ____. 1988. Studies of the Wild Turkey in Florida. University Press Florida Game Fish Comm. Tech. Bull. 10:1-232.

____ and T. Joanen. 1974. Age of first nesting in the Brown Pelican. Wilson Bull. 86:279-280.

____ and R.D. McGuire. 1971. On prenuptial molt in the Wild Turkey. J. Wildl. Manage. 35:394-395.

Williams, T.J. 1996. Double-crested Cormorant in Cleveland: New to the Western Palearctic. Brit. Birds. 89:263-170.

Williamson, F.S.L., and L.J. Peyton. 1963. Interbreeding of Glaucous-winged and Herring gulls in the Cook Inlet region, Alaska. Condor 65:24-28.

Williamson, M.H. 1957. Polymorphism in Ross's Goose (*Anser rossii*) and the detection of genetic dominance from field data. Ibis 99:516-518.

Willoughby, E.J. 1966. Wing and tail molt in the Sparrow Hawk. Auk 83:201-206.

____. 1992. Incorrect use of the Humphrey-Parkes molt and plumage terminology for buntings of the genus *Passerina*. Condor 94:295-297.

____. 2004. Molt and plumage terminology of Howell et al. (2003)still may not reflect homologies. Condor106:191-196.

____. 2007. Geographic variation in color, measurements, and molt of the Lesser Goldfinch in North America does not support subspecific designation. Condor 109:419-436.

____ and T.J. Cade. 1964. Breeding behavior of the American Kestrel (Sparrow Hawk). Living Bird 3:75-96.

Wilmore, S.B. 1979. Swans of the world. Taplinger, New York, NY. 229 pp.

Wilson, A. 2005. The Red-necked Stint in North America: Status and identification. Birding 37:628-637.

____ and A. Guthrie. 1999. Black Brant in New York state. Kingbird 49:98-105.

____, ____, and P. Pyle. 2002. White-faced Ibis - Europe next? Birding World 15:343-345.

Wilson, J.R., S. Nebel, and C.D.T. Minton. 2007. Migration ecology and morphometrics of two Bar-tailed Godwit populations in Australia. Emu 107:262-274.

Wilson, N.H. 1951. Hybrid Glaucous × Great Black-backed Gull at Limerick. Brit. Birds 44:286-287.

Wilson, S.F., and C.D. Ankney. 1987. Variation in structural size and wing stripe of Lesser and Greater scaup. Can. J. Zool. 66:2045-2048.

Wilson, V.T., and J.B. Van den Akker. 1948. A hybrid Cinnamon Teal × Blue-winged Teal at the Bear River Migratory Bird Refuge, Utah. Auk 65:316.

Wilson, W.S. 1994. Western Sandpiper. Birds N. Am. 90:1-20.

Wingate, D.B. 1964. Discovery of breeding Black-capped Petrels on Hispaniola. Auk 81:147-159.

____. 1982. Successful reintroduction of the Yellow-crowned Night-Heron as a nesting resident on Bermuda. Colonial Waterbirds 5:104-115.

Winger, B. 2003. Molt strategies in adult dowitchers: Criteria for field identification in fall migration in Ohio. Ohio Cardinal 26:125-136.

Wingfield, J.C. and D.S. Farner. 1976. Avian endocrinology - field investigations and methods. Condor 78:570-573.

Winkler, D.W. 1996. California Gull. Birds N. Am. 259:1-28.

____ and S.D. Cooper. 1986. Ecology of Black-necked Grebes *Podiceps nigricollis* at Mono Lake, California. Ibis 128:483-491.

Winkler, R. 1979. Zur Pneumatisation des Schädeldachs der Vögel. Ornith. Beobach. 76:49-l 18.

____. 1987. Zur Grossgefiedermauser junger Kormorane *Phalacrocorax carbo sinensis*. Der Ornith. Beobachter 84:317-323.

Winnett, K.A., K.G. Murray, and J.C. Wingfield. 1979. Southern race of Xantus' Murrelet breeding on Santa Barbara Island, California. W. Birds 10:81-82.

Winters, R. 2006. Moult and plumage variation in immature Lesser Black-backed Gulls in the Netherlands. Dutch Birding 28:140-157.

Wishart, R.A. 1981. Wing-feather criteria for age separation of American Wigeon. J. Wildl. Manage. 45:230-235.

____. 1985. Moult chronology of American Wigeon, *Anas americana*, in relation to reproduction. Can. Field-Nat. 99:172-178.

Wishart, W. 1969. Age determination of Pheasants by measurement of proximal primaries. J. Wildl. Manage. 33:714-717.

Woehler, E.E., and J.M. Gates. 1970. An improved method of sexing Ring-necked Pheasant chicks. J. Wildl. Manage. 34:228-231.

Wollard, L.L., R.D. Sparrowe, and G.D. Chambers. 1977. Evaluation of a Korean Pheasant introduction in Missouri. J. Wildl. Manage. 41:616-623.

Wood, A.G. 1987. Discriminating the sex of Sanderling *Calidris alba*: Some results and their implications. Bird Study 34:200-204.

Wood, D.S. 1986. On iris color in *Botaurus* bittern. Colonial Waterbirds 9:108-109.
Wood, M. 1969. A bird-bander's guide to determination of age and sex of selected species. Pennsylvania State University, University Park, PA. 181 pp.
Wood, N.A. 1932. Harlan's Hawk. Wilson Bull. 44:78-87.
Woodard, A.E., J.C. Hermes, and L. Fuqua. 1986. Shank length for determining sex in Chukars. Poultry Sci. 65:627-630.
Woodin, M.C., and T.C. Michot. 2002. Redhead. Birds N. Am. 695:1-40.
Woodward, P.W. 1972. The natural history of Kure Atoll, North-western Hawaiian Islands. Atoll Res. Bull. 164:1-318.
Woolfenden, G.E. 1967. Selection for delayed simultaneous wing molt in loons (Gaviidae). Wilson Bull. 79:416-420.
____, L.R. Monteiro, and R.A. Duncan. 2001. Recovery from the north-eastern Gulf of Mexico of a Band-rumped Storm-Petrel banded in the Azores. J. Field Ornith. 72:62-65.
Wright, P.L., and R.W. Hiatt. 1943. Outer primaries as age determiners in gallinaceous birds. Auk 60:265-266.
Wymenga, E., M. Engelmoer, C.J. Smit, and T.M. van Spanje. 1990. Geographical breeding origin and migration of waders wintering in West Africa. Ardea 78:83-112.
Wynn, R.B. 2003. Further developments in 'Black Brant' identification, including the effects of body moult on the wintering grounds. Brit. Birds 96:297-301.
Wynne-Edwards, V.C. 1935. On the habits and distribution of birds on the North Atlantic. Proc. Boston Soc. Nat. Hist. 40:233-346.
____. 1939. Intermittent Breeding in the Fulmar (*Fulmarus glacialis* (L)), with some general observations on non-breeding in seabirds. Proc. Zool. Soc. London 109(Ser. A):127-132.
____. 1952a. Geographic variation in the bill of the Fulmar (*Fulmarus glacialis*). Scottish Nat. 64:84-101.
____. 1952b. Zoology of the Baird Expedition (1950) I. The birds observed in central and south-east Baffin Island. Auk 69:353-391.
Yank, R., and Y. Aubrey. 1985. Quebec region. Am. Birds 39:889-890.
Yarris, G.S., M.R. McLandress, and A.E.H. Perkins. 1994. Molt migration of postbreeding female Mallards from Suisun Marsh, California. Condor 96:34-45.
Yésou, P. 1991. The sympatric breeding of *Larus fuscus, L. cachinnans,* and *L. argentatus* in western France. Ibis 133:256-263.
____. 1994. Contribution a l'etude avifaunistique de la peninsule du Taimyr. Alauda 62:247-252.
____. 1997. Déterminer l'âge des mouettes de sabine *Larus sabini*. Ornithos 4:116-121.
____. 2002. Systematics of *Larus argentatus-cachinnans-fuscus* complex revisited. Dutch Birding 24:271-298.
____, A.M. Paterson, E.J. Mackrill, and W.R.P. Bourne. 1990. Plumage variation and identification of 'Yelkouan Shearwater.' Brit. Birds. 83:299-319.
Yocom, C.F. 1972. Weights and measurements of Taverner's and Great Basin Canada Geese. Murrelet 53:33-34.
Young, D.A., and D.A. Boag. 1981. A description of moult in male Mallards. Can. J. Zool. 59:252-259.
Young, J.R., J.W. Hupp, J.W. Bradbury, and C.E. Braun. 1994. Phenotypic divergence of secondary sexual traits among Sage Grouse populations. Animal Behav. 47:1353-1362.
____, C.E. Braun, S.J. Oyler-McCance, J.W. Hupp, and T.W. Quinn. 2000. A new species of sage-grouse (Phasianidae, *Centrocercus*) from south-western Colorado. Wilson Bull. 112:445-453.
Yunick, R.P. 1986. Carpal compression as a variable in taking wing chord measurements. N. Am. Bird Bander 11:78-83.
Zenatello, M., L. Serra, and N. Baccetti. 2002. Trade-offs among body mass and primary moult patterns in migrating Black Terns (*Chlidonias niger*). Ardea 90:411-420.
Zicus, M.C. 1981. Molt migration of Canada Geese from Crex Meadows, Wisconsin. J. Wildl. Manage. 45:54-63.
____. 1982. Age determination of female Wood Ducks in spring. Minnesota Wildl. Res. Quart. 42:12-23.
Zimmer, K.J. 1991. Plumage variation in "Kumlien's" Iceland Gull. Birding 23:254-269.
____. 1992. Murphy's Petrels on Ducie Atoll: Another piece of the puzzle. Am. Birds 46:1100-1105.
Zink, R.M., and J.V. Remsen Jr. 1986. Evolutionary processes and patterns of geographic variation in birds. Current Ornith. 4:1-69.
____ and D.W. Winkler. 1983. Genetic and morphological similarity of two California Gull populations with different life history traits. Biochem. and Syst. Ecol. 11:397-403.
____, D.F. Lott, and D.W. Anderson. 1987. Genetic variation, population structure, and evolution of California Quail. Condor 89:395-405.
Zöckler, C., E.E. Syroechkovski Jr., and E. Lappo. 2000. [Response to Sangster (2000)] Brit. Birds. 93:96-97.
Zusi, R.L., and R.W. Storer. 1969. Osteology and myology of the head and neck of the Pied-billed Grebes (*Podilymbus*). Misc. Pubs. Mus. Zool. Univ. Michigan 139:1-49.
Zwarts, L., B.J. Ens, M. Kersten, and T. Piersma. 1990. Moult, mass and flight range of waders ready to take off for long-distance migrations. Ardea 78:339-364.
Zwickel, F.C. 1992. Blue Grouse. Birds N. Am. 15:1-28.
____ and J.A. Dake. 1977. Primary molt of Blue Grouse (*Dendragapus obscurus*) and its relation to reproduction, activity, and migration. Can. J. Zool. 55:1782-1787.
____ and C.F. Martinsen. 1967. Determining age and sex of Franklin Spruce Grouse. J. Wildl. Manage. 31:760-763.
____, M.A. Degner, D.T. McKinnon, and D.A. Boag. 1991. Sexual and subspecific variation in the number of rectrices of Blue Grouse. Can. J. Zool. 69:134-140.

Index

Notes